ue alerts students
ajor headings.

The Accounting Period

The only way to know for certain how successfully a business has operated is to close its doors, sell all its assets, pay the liabilities, and return any leftover cash to the owner. This process, called liquidation, is the same as going out of business. Obviously, it is not practical for accountants to measure business income in this

Real-World Example: The Yale Express case, settled in the early 1970s, is a famous case involving accrual accounting. In 1963, Yale Express, a trucking firm, acquired Republic Carloading and Distributing Co. Before the merger, Republic failed to accrue freight costs at the end of each year. The error was substantial enough to reduce the reported 1963 net income of $1,140,000 to a $1,880,000 net loss.

9. Real-World Examples- make lectures lively by illustrating abstract concepts with facts and anecdotes about actual business situations.

General Journal				Page 9
Date	Accounts	Post Ref.	Debit	Credit
Nov. 6	Sales Returns and Allowances	43	198	
	Accounts Receivable—Stephanie Baker	12/✓		198
	Credit memo no. 27			

Typical Student Misconception: Students find credit memo and debit memo confusing terms. Have them remember this: If the seller is going to credit a customer's account (to reduce the balance owing) then she issues a credit memo. Likewise, if the buyer is going to debit a supplier's account (to reduce the balance due) then he issues a debit memo.

10. Typical Student Misconceptons-alert you to topics students are likely to misunderstand so you can correct their thinking before proceeding.

Ethical Issue

Community Chest, a charitable organization in Mojave, New Mexico, has a standing agreement with Encino State Bank. The agreement allows Community Chest to overdraw its cash balance at the bank when donations are running low. In the past, Community Chest managed funds wisely and rarely used this privilege. Greg Osborn has recently become the president of Community Chest. To expand operations, Osborn is acquiring office equipment

11. Writing Icons- Indicate assignment material-exercises, problems, or ethical issues-that require essay answers.

Problem 1-5A *Transaction analysis for an actual company* (L.O. 4,5)

A recent balance sheet of Xerox Corporation, the manufacturer of copiers and other office equipment, is summarized as follows, with amounts in thousands. For example, Cash of $266,600,000 is presented as $266,600.

Total assets $9,817,793

12. Check Figures- appear next to every end-of-chapter exercise and problem for your convenience.

Xerox Corporation
Balance Sheet
December 31, 19X4
(thousands)

Assets		Liabilities	
Cash	$ 266,600	Notes payable	$1,985,500
Accounts receivable . . .	1,466,900	Accounts payable	390,300

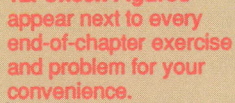

13. Black computer disks-designate exercises and problems that can be solved using the Lotus templates.

Problem 8-4A *Using the percent of sales and aging approaches for uncollectibles* (L.O. 2, 6)

The December 31, 19X4, balance sheet of Brazos Rubber Products reports the following:

Accounts Receivable	$141,000
Allowance for Doubtful Accounts (credit balance)	3,200

Allow. for Doubtful Accts. $3,709

14. White computer disks-designate exercises and problems that can be solved using the Prentice Hall Integrated Accounting Software.

Accounting The Business World's
Measure of Success

Accounting · The Business World's Measure of Success

Accounting, 2/E by Horngren and Harrison illustrates the role of accounting in the business world. In particular, your students will learn how accounting information is used to measure business success according to today's standards. This preview highlights the numerous features of Horngren/Harrison that will facilitate this understanding. Your students will soon discover that **Accounting**, 2/E will mean success for them too.

HORNGREN & HARRISON
ACCOUNTING

SECOND EDITION

Student Pedagogy

Prentice Hall announces the publication of **Accounting,** Second Edition, by Charles T. Horngren and Walter T. Harrison, Jr. We listened to instructors and students who used our highly successful first edition, and to hundreds of accounting instructors who reviewed our efforts to make the second edition even better. This Preview highlights the important features you'll find in **Accounting,** 2/E. The authors' accent on the context of the business world once again helps students learn accounting.

Photos illustrate the chapter-opening vignettes and make the business context of accounting come alive.

Chapter-opening vignettes use actual business situations to introduce students to the chapter topics. These vignettes will foster student interest and help build the framework for understanding the chapter's accounting procedures and concepts.

Chapter 5

Merchandising and the Accounting Cycle

With department stores falling into Chapter 11 [bankruptcy] like dominoes, the rag trade [garment industry] should be the last place to find a superb growth company. But look at Donna Karan Co., the women's clothing concern, which projects net sales of $132 million this year, thanks mainly to the year-old DKNY line. That's up from $107 million last year and $7.4 million in 1985, Karan's first year in business. . . .

Karan clothing sells well, and wholesale buyers know it. . . . How does Karan do it? Says Neiman Marcus President and Chief Executive Terry Lundgren: "She cares about what is selling to the customer, not just what the store buyers are buying." Famous customers help, too. Candice Bergen and Diane Sawyer regularly wear Karan's wool jersey and crepe designs on television.

What's next? International expansion. Karan already sells 20 percent of her merchandise abroad, half of that to Japan. A Donna Karan shop opened in August in Hong Kong. . . . Next spring Karan debuts in France.

Karan says she will remain private for now. But with stellar growth and no long-term debt, Donna Karan, the company, would be even more welcome on Wall Street than it is in America's department and specialty stores.

Source: Katherine Weisman, "Designing Woman," Forbes, October 1, 1990, p. 261.

LEARNING OBJECTIVES

After studying this chapter, you should be able to

1 Explain the operating cycle of a merchandising business

2 Account for the purchase and sale of inventory

3 Compute cost of goods sold and gross margin

4 Prepare a merchandiser's financial statements

5 Adjust and close the accounts of a merchandising business

6 Recognize different formats of the income statement

Learning objectives outline the chapter's most important topics and indicate what the student should understand after studying the chapter.

The chapter narrative refers to the vignette to emphasize the connection of accounting with the business world.

How do the operations of Donna Karan Co. differ from the businesses we have studied so far? In the first four chapters Gary Lyon, CPA, provided an illustration of a business that earns revenue by selling its services. Service enterprises include Holiday Inns, American Airlines, physicians, lawyers, CPAs, the Atlanta Braves baseball team, and the twelve-year-old who cuts lawns in your neighborhood. A *merchandising entity* earns its revenue by selling products, called *merchandise inventory* or simply *inventory*. Donna Karan Co., a Goodyear tire store, a Safeway grocery, a Macy's department store, and an ice-cream shop are merchandising entities. Exhibit 5-1 shows the income statement for a merchandising business. You will notice that this income statement differs from those shown earlier.

The amount that a merchandiser earns from selling its inventory is called **net sales revenue,** often abbreviated as **net sales.** The income statement in Exhibit 5-1 reports net sales revenue of $680,000. The major revenue of a merchandising entity, sales revenue, represents the increase in owner's equity from delivering inventory to customers. The major expense of a merchandiser is *Cost of Goods Sold.* This expense's title is well chosen, because this account represents the entity's cost of the goods (inventory) it has sold to customers. As long as inventory is held, it is an asset. When the inventory is sold to the customer, the inventory's cost becomes an expense. The excess of Sales Revenue over Cost of Goods Sold is called **gross margin** or **gross profit.** This important business statistic is often mentioned in the business press because it helps measure a business's success. A sufficiently high gross margin is often vital to success.

The following illustration will clarify the nature of gross margin. Consider a concession stand at a football game. Assume the business sells a soft drink for $1.00 and the vendor's cost is $.20. Gross margin per unit is $.80 ($1.00 − $.20), and the overall gross margin is $.80 multiplied by the number of drinks sold. If the concession stand sells 400 drinks on a Saturday afternoon, its gross margin on drink sales is $320 (400 × $.80). The gross margin on all sales, including hot dogs, popcorn, and candy, is the sum of the gross margins on all the items sold. Sears's gross margin—and that of a Safeway store, a neighborhood drug store, and every other merchandiser—is computed in exactly the same way: Sales Revenue − Cost of Goods Sold = Gross Margin.

Margin in gross margin refers to the excess of revenue over expense. *Gross* indicates that the operating expenses (rent, depreciation, advertising, and so on) have not yet been subtracted. After subtracting all the expenses we have *net income.* Gross margin and net income are *not* accounts in the ledger, so we cannot make journal entries to them. Instead, we compute these amounts by

Instructor Materials

The **Annotated Instructor's Edition (AIE)** is the complete student text with additional material designed to enrich classroom presentation. The following types of notes appear throughout the AIE: Discussion Questions, Points to Stress, Real-World Examples, Teaching Tips, Class Exercises, and Typical Student Misconceptions. The AIE also includes check figures next to the end-of-chapter exercises and problems.

LEARNING OBJECTIVES

After studying this chapter, you should be able to

1 Explain the operating cycle of a merchandising business

2 Account for the purchase and sale of inventory

3 Compute cost of goods sold and gross margin

4 Prepare a merchandiser's financial statements

5 Adjust and close the accounts of a merchandising business

6 Recognize different formats of the income statement

How do the operations of Donna Karan Co. differ from the businesses we have studied so far? In the first four chapters Gary Lyon, CPA, provided an illustration of a business that earns revenue by selling its services. Service enterprises include Holiday Inns, American Airlines, physicians, lawyers, CPAs, the Atlanta Braves baseball team, and the twelve-year-old who cuts lawns in your neighborhood. A *merchandising entity* earns its revenue by selling products, called *merchandise inventory* or simply *inventory*. Donna Karan Co., a Goodyear tire store, a Safeway grocery, a Macy's department store, and an ice-cream shop are merchandising entities. Exhibit 5-1 shows the income statement for a merchandising business. You will notice that this income statement differs from those shown earlier.

The amount that a merchandiser earns from selling its inventory is called **net sales revenue,** often abbreviated as **net sales.** The income statement in Exhibit 5-1 reports net sales revenue of $680,000. The major revenue of a merchandising entity, sales revenue, represents the increase in owner's equity from delivering inventory to customers. The major expense of a merchandiser is *Cost of Goods Sold*. This expense's title is well chosen, because this account represents the entity's cost of the goods (inventory) it has sold to customers. As long as inventory is held, it is an asset. When the inventory is sold to the customer, the inventory's cost becomes an expense. The excess of Sales Revenue over Cost of Goods Sold is called **gross margin** or **gross profit.** This important business statistic is often mentioned in the business press because it helps measure a business's success. A sufficiently high gross margin is often vital to success.

The following illustration will clarify the nature of gross margin. Consider a concession stand at a football game. Assume the business sells a soft drink for $1.00 and the vendor's cost is $.20. Gross margin per unit is $.80 ($1.00 − $.20), and the overall gross margin is $.80 multiplied by the number of drinks sold. If the concession stand sells 400 drinks on a Saturday afternoon, its gross margin on drink sales is $320 (400 × $.80). The gross margin on all sales, including hot dogs, popcorn, and candy, is the sum of the gross margins on all the items sold. Sears's gross margin—and that of a Safeway store, a neighborhood drug store, and every other merchandiser—is computed in exactly the same way: Sales Revenue − Cost of Goods Sold = Gross Margin.

Margin in gross margin refers to the excess of revenue over expense. *Gross* indicates that the operating expenses (rent, depreciation, advertising, and so

Typical Student Misconception: Students often think the Sales Revenue Account is used to record all sales of assets. Explain that Sales Revenue is used only for sales of merchandise. Donna Karan uses this account to record only the sales of clothing.

Point to Stress: If a car dealer buys a car for $10,000 from the manufacturer and sells it for $15,000, then $10,000 is the cost of the good sold. The dealer had to buy the car before he could sell it; therefore we classify cost of goods sold as an expense. It is usually a merchandising company's largest expense.

Use of Accounting Information in Decision Making

The purpose of accounting is to provide information for decision making. Chief users of accounting information include managers, investors, and creditors. A creditor considering lending money must predict whether the borrower can repay the loan. If the borrower already has lots of debt, the probability of repayment is lower than if the borrower has a small amount of liabilities. To assess financial position, decision makers use ratios on various items drawn from a company's financial statements.

One of the most common financial ratios is the **current ratio**, which is the ratio of an entity's current assets to its current liabilities. The current ratio measures the ability to pay current liabilities with current assets. It is computed as follows:

$$\text{Current ratio} = \frac{\text{Total current assets}}{\text{Total current liabilities}}$$

A company prefers a high current ratio, which means that the business has plenty of current assets to pay current liabilities. An increasing current ratio from period to period indicates improvement in financial position.

A rule of thumb: A strong current ratio is 2.00, which indicates that the company has $2.00 in current assets for every $1.00 in current liabilities. A company with a current ratio of $2.00 would probably have little trouble paying its current liabilities. Most successful businesses operate with current ratios in the range between 1.50 to 2.00.

Hawaiian Airlines, the company in Exhibit 4-11, has a current ratio of .950 (.950 = $40,348/$42,492). What does this ratio value indicate about Hawaiian Airlines? A current ratio of 1.00 is considered quite low, so a value of .95 is dangerously low. Hawaiian Airlines has insufficient current assets to pay all its current liabilities—a risky position.

How would a decision maker use the current ratio? A low current ratio would worry top managers of the company because it indicates difficulty in paying debts. As a matter of fact, Hawaiian Airlines has experienced financial trouble in recent years, as signalled by its low current ratio. Suppose the company needs to borrow money. If the bank agreed to loan money to Hawaiian Airlines—which it might not—the bank would place some restrictions on Hawaiian Airlines because of the company's risky financial position. For example, the lender might charge a high rate of interest and prohibit withdrawals by the owners of the company. A decision maker considering investing in Hawaiian Airlines would recognize the company's risky position and might prefer to invest in another company instead. Lenders and investors would view a company with a current ratio of 2.00 as substantially less risky. Such a company would probably borrow money on better terms and also attract more investors.

A second aid to decision making is the **debt ratio**, which is the ratio of total liabilities to total assets. The debt ratio indicates the proportion of a company's assets that are financed with debt. This ratio measures a business's ability to pay both current and long-term debts. It is computed as follows:

$$\text{Debt ratio} = \frac{\text{Total liabilities}}{\text{Total assets}}$$

Discussion Question: Why does a company need a current ratio of more than 1:1? ANSWER: The answer is twofold. (1) Some companies don't need a larger current ratio. It is typical in some industries, such as the oil industry, to have a current ratio of about 1:1. Different industries have different liquidity requirements. (2) Included in the current assets are assets that are not considered very liquid, such as inventory and prepaids. If these assets are excluded, then the ratio of 1:1 of the remaining current assets to current liabilities may be considered safe.

Discussion Questions encourage critical thinking as students are challenged to apply concepts and procedures to new situations.

Real-World Example: According to Robert Morris Associates, the median current ratio among manufacturers of electronic computers is 1.9:1. The current ratio for those companies in the top 25% of electronic manufacturers is 3.2:1.

Real-World Examples strengthen the connection between accounting and actual business.

Integration of Real Companies

The **time-period concept** ensures that accounting information is reported at regular intervals. It interacts with the revenue principle and the matching principle to underly the use of accruals. To measure income accurately, companies update the revenue and expense accounts immediately prior to the end of the period. Tootsie Roll Industries, Inc., the candy maker, provides an actual example of an expense accrual. At December 31, 1989, Tootsie Roll recorded employee compensation of $3.4 million that the company owed its workers for unpaid services performed before year end. Tootsie Roll's accrual entry was

```
1989
Dec. 31   Salary (or Wage) Expense . . . . . . . . . . . . . .   3,400,00
               Salary (or Wage) Payable . . . . . . . . . . . . .              3,400,000
```

This entry serves two purporses. It assigns the expense to the proper period. Without the accrual entry at December 31, total expenses of 1989 would be understated and as a result net income would be overstated. Incorrectly, the expense would fall in 1990 when Tootsie Roll makes the next payroll disbursement. The accrual entry also records the liability for reporting on the balance sheet at December 31, 1989. Without the accrual entry, total liabilities would be understated.

Credit Card Sales

Credit card sales are common in retailing. American Express, Diners Club, Carte Blanche, VISA, and MasterCard are popular.

The customer presents the credit card as payment for a purchase. The seller prepares a sales invoice in triplicate. The customer and the seller keep copies as receipts. The third copy goes to the credit card company, which then pays the seller the transaction amount and bills the customer.

Credit cards offer consumers the convenience of buying without having to pay the cash immediately. Also, consumers receive a monthly statement from the credit card company, detailing each credit card transaction. They can write a single check to cover the entire month's credit card purchases.

Retailers also benefit from credit card sales. They do not have to check a customer's credit rating. The company that issues the card has already done so. Retailers do not have to keep an accounts receivable subsidiary ledger account for each customer, and they do not have to collect cash from customers. The copy of the sale invoice that retailers send to the credit card company signals the card issuer to pursue payment. Further, retailers receive cash more quickly from the credit card companies than they would from the customers themselves. Of course, these services to the seller do not come free.

The seller receives less than 100 percent of the face value of the invoice. The credit card company takes a 5 percent[1] discount on the sale to cover its services. The seller's entry to record a $100 Diners Club sale is

```
Accounts Receivable—Diners Club . . . . . . . . . . . . . . . . . . . . . . .   100
    Sales Revenue . . . . . . . . . . . . . . . . . . . . . . . . . . . . . . . . . . . .              100
```

On collection of the discounted value, the seller records:

```
Cash . . . . . . . . . . . . . . . . . . . . . . . . . . . . . . . . . . . . . . . . . . . . .   95
Credit Card Discount Expense . . . . . . . . . . . . . . . . . . . . . . . . . .    5
    Accounts Receivable—Diners Club . . . . . . . . . . . . . . . . . . .              100
```

---

[1]The rate varies among companies and over time.

Summary Problem for Your Review

Suppose Exxon, Inc., engaged in the following transactions:

19X4

Apr. 1   Loaned $8,000 to Bland Co., a service station. Received a one-year, 10 percent note.

June 1   Discounted the Bland note at the bank at a discount rate of 12 percent.

Nov. 30   Loaned $6,000 to Flores, Inc., a regional distributor of Exxon products, on a three-month, 11 percent note.

19X5

Feb. 28   Collected the Flores note at maturity.

Exxon's accounting period ends on December 31.

Required

Explanations are not needed.

1. Record the 19X4 transactions on April 1, June 1, and November 30 on Exxon's books.
2. Make any adjusting entries needed on December 31, 19X4.
3. Record the February 28, 19X5, collection of the Flores note.
4. Which transaction creates a contingent liability for Exxon? When does the contingency begin? When does it end?
5. Write a footnote that Exxon could use in its 19X4 financial statements to report the contingent liability.

Accounting, 2/E offers mid-chapter and end-of-chapter Summary Problems for Your Review. These problems—and the fully worked-out solutions, which immediately follow each Summary Problem—reinforce students' understanding in half-chapter segments.

SOLUTION TO REVIEW PROBLEM

19X4

1. Apr. 1   Note Receivable—Bland Co   8,000

   Cash   8,000

   June 1   Cash....................................   7,920*

   Interest Expense   80

   Note Receivable—Bland Co   8,000

   *Computation of proceeds:

Principal	$8,000
+ Interest ($8,000 × .10 × 12/12)	800
= Maturity value...........................	8,800
− Discount ($8,800 × .12 × 10/12)	880
= Proceeds	$7,920

   Nov. 30   Note Receivable—Flores, Inc   6,000

   Cash   6,000

2. **Adjusting Entries**

   19X4

   Dec. 31   Interest Receivable ($6,000 × .11 × 1/12) .   55

   Interest Revenue   55

Writing Problems

To emphasize the importance of effective, clear business communication, **Accounting, 2/E** integrates writing problems throughout the text. These problems ask the student to go beyond their calculations and to evaluate the situation behind the numbers. An icon in the Annotated Instructor's Edition identifies these writing problems.

Required

1. Prepare the income statement of Technical Consultants for the year ended December 31, 19X3. Not all amounts are used. Recall that only revenues and expenses appear on the income statement.
2. What was the amount of the proprietor's withdrawals during the year?

Problems (Group A)

No check figure

Problem 1-1A *Analyzing a loan request* **(L.O. 1,2,3)**

As an analyst for Midlantic Bank, it is your job to write recommendations to the bank's loan committee. Sigma Enterprises has submitted these summary data to support the company's request for a $300,000 loan:

Income Statement Data:	19X5	19X4	19X3
Total revenues	$790,000	$730,000	$720,000
Total expenses	640,000	570,000	540,000
Net income	$150,000	$160,000	$180,000

Statement of Owner's Equity Data:	19X5	19X4	19X3
Beginning capital	$280,000	$300,000	$290,000
Add: Net income	150,000	160,000	180,000
	430,000	460,000	470,000
Less: Withdrawals	190,000	180,000	170,000
Ending capital	$240,000	$280,000	$300,000

Balance Sheet Data:	19X5	19X4	19X3
Total assets	$630,000	$600,000	$560,000
Total liabilities	$390,000	$320,000	$260,000
Total owner's equity	240,000	280,000	300,000
Total liabilities and owner's equity	$630,000	$600,000	$560,000

Required

Should the bank lend $300,000 to Sigma Enterprises? Write a one-paragraph recommendation to the loan committee.

Owner's equity $126,700

Problem 1-2A *Entity concept, transaction analysis, accounting equation* **(L.O. 3,5)**

Kathy Wood practiced law with a large firm, a partnership, for ten years after graduating from law school. Recently she resigned her position to open her own law office, which she operates as a proprietorship. The name of the new entity is Kathy Wood, Attorney and Counselor.

Wood recorded the following events during the organizing phase of her new business and its first month of operations. Some of the events were personal and did not affect the law practice. Others were business transactions and should be accounted for by the business.

July 1   Wood sold 1,000 shares of Eastman Kodak stock, which she had owned for several years, receiving $88,000 cash from her stockbroker.

    2   Wood deposited the $88,000 cash from sale of the Eastman Kodak stock in her personal bank account.

    3   Wood received $135,000 cash from her former partners in the law firm from which she resigned.

Extending Your Knowledge

Decision Problems

1. Recording Transactions Directly in the Ledger, Preparing a Trial Balance, and Measuring Net Income or Loss (L.O. 2,5,6)

Net income $3,850

You have been requested by a friend named Charles Sligh to give advice on the effects that certain business transactions will have on the entity he plans to start. Time is short, so you will not be able to do all the detailed procedures of journalizing and posting. Instead, you must analyze the transactions without the use of a journal. Sligh will continue the business only if he can expect to earn monthly net income of $3,500. Assume the following transactions have occurred:

a. Sligh deposited $6,000 cash in a business bank account.
b. Borrowed $4,000 cash from the bank and signed a note payable due within one year.
c. Paid $300 cash for supplies.
d. Purchased advertising in the local newspaper for cash, $800.

Ethical Issue

No check figure

Community Chest, a charitable organization in Mojave, New Mexico, has a standing agreement with Encino State Bank. The agreement allows Community Chest to overdraw its cash balance at the bank when donations are running low. In the past, Community Chest managed funds wisely and rarely used this privilege. Greg Osborn has recently become the president of Community Chest. To expand operations, Osborn is acquiring office equipment and spending large amounts for fund-raising. During his presidency, Community Chest has maintained a negative bank balance of approximately $1,000.

Required

What is the ethical issue in this situation? State why you approve or disapprove of Osborn's management of Community Chest funds.

Financial Statement Problems

1. Journalizing Transactions (L.O. 2,3)

No check figure

This problem helps to develop skill in recording transactions by using an actual company's account titles. Refer to the Goodyear Tire & Rubber Company financial statements in Appendix C. Assume Goodyear completed the following selected transactions during November 1990:

Nov. 5 Earned sales revenue on account, $55,000.
   9 Borrowed $500,000 by signing a note payable (long-term debt).
  12 Purchased equipment on account, $70,000.
  17 Paid $110,000, which represents payment of $100,000 long-term debt due within one year plus interest expense of $10,000.
  19 Earned sales revenue and immediately received cash of $16,000.
  22 Collected the cash on account that was earned on November 5.

Extending Your Knowledge sections conclude each chapter. These sections present Decision Problems, an Ethical Issue, and Financial Statement Problems.

Decision Problems ask students to take a manager's perspective in analyzing a business situation and recommending a course of action.

The Ethical Issue presents a business scenario that challenges the ethical conduct of an accountant and asks students to resolve the dilemma.

Financial Statement Problems link the chapter subject matter directly to actual financial statements. The first one directs students to the Goodyear annual report, which is Appendix C. The second one refers students to Disclosure, a computerized database of financial information on 100 actual companies. By using this disk, students can solve the requirements of the financial statement problems for any company of their choice.

Invaluable Supplements

We offer an exceptional pool of supplements. Here are just a few you can look forward to:

- **The ABC News/ PH Video Library.**
For two years, Prentice Hall and ABC have worked in unison to bring you high-quality feature and documentary-style videos from the following award-winning programs: *Nightline, World News Tonight/American Agenda, Business World, On Business, 20/20,* and *This Week With David Brinkley.* Carefully researched selections from this line-up enhance material in **Accounting, 2/E.**

- **The Prentice Hall Contemporary View Program.**
Together with the **New York Times,** we offer students a complimentary "mini-newspaper" supplement that consists of recent articles pertaining to the field of accounting. This supplement is updated yearly for timeliness.

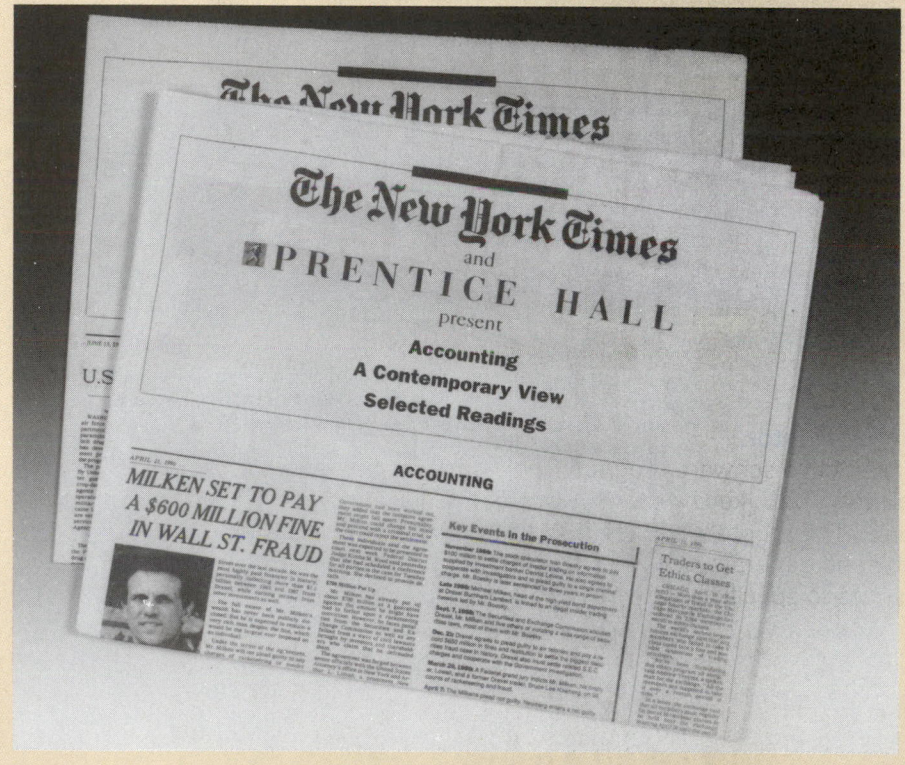

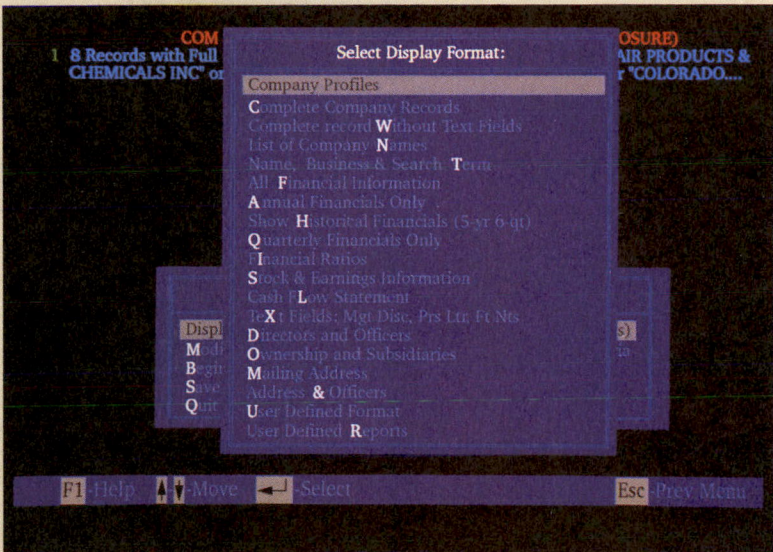

● **Disclosure's Compact d Database Software.**

This disk contains detailed profiles and financial data for 100 publicly traded companies. The assignment material provides suggestions for getting students involved in using this information throughout the course.

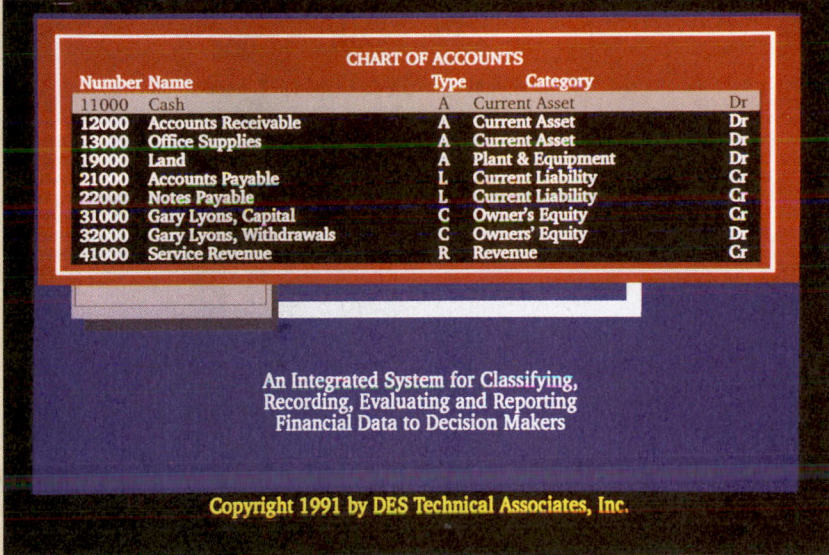

An Integrated System for Classifying,
Recording, Evaluating and Reporting
Financial Data to Decision Makers

Copyright 1991 by DES Technical Associates, Inc.

● **Prentice Hall Integrated Accounting Software.**

With a software package that contains *general ledger, accounts payable, accounts receivable,* and *payroll modules,* your students can solve problems from the text and gain hands-on practical experience.

That's not all of the enormously helpful ancillaries we offer. To find out more about our invaluable package, please contact your local Prentice Hall representative.

● **The Integrator.**

This interactive software program indexes all supplements to **Accounting, 2/E,** keying them by chapter, topic, and page in the textbook. The program allows instructors to select any topic or chapter and generate a printed lecture outline that includes references to specific supplements.

Charles T. Horngren is the Edmund W. Littlefield Professor of Accounting at Stanford University. A graduate of Marquette University, he received his MBA from Harvard University and his Ph.D. from the University of Chicago. He is also the recipient of honorary doctorates from Marquette University and DePaul University. Horngren, himself, has taught a wide variety of accounting courses at many different educational institutions, including two years at a vocational business college.

A Certified Public Accountant, Horngren served on the Accounting Principles Board for six years, the Financial Accounting Standards Board Advisory Council for five years, and the Council of the American Institute of Certified Public Accountants for three years. For six years, he served as a trustee of the Financial Accounting Foundation, which oversees the Financial Accounting Standards Board and the Government Accounting Standards Board.

In 1990, Horngren was elected to the Accounting Hall of Fame.

A member of the American Accounting Association, Horngren has been its President and its Director of Research. He received the Outstanding Accounting Educator Award in 1973, when the association initiated an annual series of such awards.

The California Certified Public Accountants Foundation gave Horngren its Faculty Excellence Award in 1975 and its Distinguished Professor Award in 1983. He is the first person to have received both awards.

In 1985, the American Institute of Certified Public Accountants presented its first Outstanding Educator Award to Horngren. Professor Horngren is also a member of the National Association of Accountants, where he was on its research planning committee for three years. He was a member of the Board of Regents, Institute of Management Accounting, which administers the Certified Management Accountant examinations.

Horngren is the coauthor of four other books published by Prentice Hall: *Cost Accounting: A Managerial Emphasis, Seventh Edition, 1991* (with George Foster); *Accounting, Second Edition, 1992* (with Walter T. Harrison, Jr.); *Introduction to Financial Accounting, Fourth Edition, 1990* (with Gary L. Sundem); and *Introduction to Management Accounting, Eighth Edition, 1990* (with Gary L. Sundem).

Walter T. Harrison, Jr. is Professor of Accounting and holds the KPMG Peat Marwick-Thomas L. Holton Chair in Accounting at the Hankamer School of Business, Baylor University. He received his B.B.A. degree from Baylor University, his M.S. from Oklahoma State University, and his Ph.D. from Michigan State University.

Professor Harrison, recipient of numerous teaching awards from student groups as well as from university administrators, has also taught at Cleveland State Community College, Michigan State University, the University of Texas, and Stanford University.

A member of the American Accounting Association and the American Institute of Certified Public Accountants, Professor Harrison has served as Chairman of the Financial Accounting Standards Committee of the American Accounting Association, on the Teaching/Curriculum Development Award Committee, and on the Program Advisory Committee for Accounting Education and Teaching.

Professor Harrison has published articles in numerous journals, including *The Accounting Review, Journal of Accounting Research, Journal of Accountancy, Journal of Accounting and Public Policy, Consequences of Financial Accounting Standards, Accounting Horizons, Issues in Accountancy Education,* and *Journal of Commerce and Business.* He is coauthor of *Accounting, Second Edition, 1992* (with Charles T. Horngren) published by Prentice Hall. Professor Harrison has received scholarships, fellowships, or research grants from Price Waterhouse & Co., Deloitte & Touche, and the Ernst & Young Tax Research Program.

ACCOUNTING

PRENTICE HALL SERIES IN ACCOUNTING
Charles T. Horngren, Consulting Editor

AUDITING: AN INTEGRATED APPROACH 5/E
Arens/Loebbecke

KOHLER'S DICTIONARY FOR ACCOUNTANTS, 6/E
Cooper/Ijiri

FINANCIAL STATEMENT ANALYSIS, 2/E
Foster

FINANCIAL ACCOUNTING: PRINCIPLES AND ISSUES, 4/E
Granof/Bell

FINANCIAL ACCOUNTING
Harrison/Horngren

COST ACCOUNTING: A MANAGERIAL EMPHASIS, 7/E
Horngren/Foster

ACCOUNTING, 2/E
Horngren/Harrison

INTRODUCTION TO FINANCIAL ACCOUNTING, 4/E
Horngren/Sundem

INTRODUCTION TO MANAGEMENT ACCOUNTING, 8/E
Horngren/Sundem

ADVANCED MANAGEMENT ACCOUNTING, 2/E
Kaplan/Atkinson

GOVERNMENT AND NONPROFIT ACCOUNTING THEORY & PRACTICE, 3/E
Freeman/Shoulders/Lynn

INTRODUCTORY FINANCIAL ACCOUNTING, 3/E
Mueller/Kelly

AUDITING PRINCIPLES, 5/E
Stettler

BUDGETING, 5/E
Welsch/Hilton/Gordon

Second Edition

ACCOUNTING

Charles T. Horngren
Stanford University

Walter T. Harrison, Jr.
Baylor University

Annotations by
Betsy Willis and Becky Jones
Baylor University

PRENTICE HALL Englewood Cliffs, New Jersey 07632

Editor-in Chief: JOSEPH HEIDER
Acquisition Editor: TERRI DALY
Development Editor: STEPHEN DEITMER
Production Editor: ESTHER S. KOEHN
Interior Design: MAUREEN EIDE
Cover Design: BRUCE KENSALAAR
Cover Art: *Magna I*, 1990, Bronze, height: 20″, © JOSEPH A. MCDONNELL, 1992
Copy Editor: MARIE LINES
Photo Research: TERI STRATFORD
Prepress Buyer: TRUDY PISCIOTTI
Manufacturing Buyer: ROBERT ANDERSON
Marketing Manager: ROBERT F. MCCARRY
Editorial Assistants: CHRISTINE CIANCIA and RENEÉ PELLETIER

For our wives, Joan and Nancy

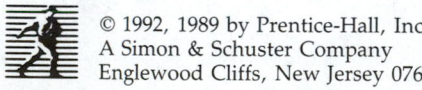
© 1992, 1989 by Prentice-Hall, Inc.
A Simon & Schuster Company
Englewood Cliffs, New Jersey 07632

Printed in the United States of America

10 9 8 7 6 5 4 3 2 1

ISBN 0-13-007329-6

Prentice-Hall International (UK) Limited, *London*
Prentice-Hall of Australia Pty. Limited, *Sydney*
Prentice-Hall Canada Inc., *Toronto*
Prentice-Hall Hispanoamericana, S.A., *Mexico City*
Prentice-Hall of India Private Limited, *New Delhi*
Prentice-Hall of Japan, Inc., *Tokyo*
Simon & Schuster Asia Pte. Ltd., *Singapore*
Editora Prentice-Hall do Brasil, Ltda., *Rio de Janeiro*

Brief Contents

Part One
The Basic Structure of Accounting

1 Accounting and Its
Environment   1
2 Recording Business
Transactions   45
3 Measuring Business Income:
The Adjusting Process   98
4 Completing the Accounting
Cycle   144
5 Merchandising and
the Accounting Cycle   208

Part Two
Introduction to Accounting Systems

6 Accounting Information
Systems   268
7 Internal Control and Cash
Transactions   316

Part Three
**Accounting for Noncash Assets
and Liabilities**

8 Accounts and Notes
Receivable   368
9 Merchandise Inventory   412

10 Plant Assets, Intangible Assets,
and Related Expenses   455
11 Current Liabilities and Payroll
Accounting   500

Part Four
**Generally Accepted Accounting
Principles**

12 The Foundation for Generally
Accepted Accounting
Principles   545

Part Five
**Accounting for Partnerships
and Corporations**

13 Accounting for Partnerships   583
14 Corporations: Organization,
Paid-in Capital, and
the Balance Sheet   625
15 Corporations: Retained
Earnings, Dividends,
Treasury Stock,
and the Income Statement   669
16 Corporations: Long-Term
Liabilities   713
17 Corporations: Investments
and Accounting for
International Operations   761

v

Part Six
Using External Accounting Information

| 18 | Statement of Cash Flows | *807* |
| 19 | Using Accounting Information to Make Business Decisions | *867* |

Part Seven
Management Accounting and Internal Decision Making

20	Introduction to Management Accounting: The Master Budget	*918*
21	Cost-Volume-Profit Relationships and the Contribution Margin Approach to Decision Making	*959*
22	Manufacturing Accounting and Job Order Costing	*998*
23	Process Costing, Activity-Based Costing, and Joint Products	*1044*
24	Flexible Budgets and Standard Costs	*1090*

| 25 | Responsibility Accounting: Departments and Branches | *1129* |
| 26 | Special Decisions and Capital Budgeting | *1164* |

Part Eight
Special Topics

| 27 | Income Taxes and Their Effects on Business Decisions | *1204* |
| 28 | Accounting with Computers | *1241* |

Appendixes

A	Accounting for the Effects of Changing Prices (Inflation)	*1289*
B	Present-Value Tables and Future-Value Tables	*1304*
C	Published Financial Statements	*1310*

Glossary | *G-1* |

Indexes | *I-1* |

| | Company | |
| | Subject | |

Contents

Part One
The Basic Structure of Accounting

1 Accounting and Its Environment *1*

Accounting and Decisions *2*
What Is Accounting? *2*
Users of Accounting Information: The Decision Makers *3*
The Development of Accounting Thought *4*
The Accounting Profession *5*
Accounting Organizations and Designations *6*
Ethical Considerations in Accounting and Business *7*
Specialized Accounting Services *8*
Types of Business Organizations *10*
Accounting Concepts and Principles *11*
The Accounting Equation *13*
Accounting for Business Transactions *14*
Evaluating Business Transactions *19*
Financial Statements *21*
Summary Problem for Your Review *23*
Summary *25*
Self-Study Questions *25*
Accounting Vocabulary *26*
Assignment Material* *28*
Extending Your Knowledge** *42*

2 Recording Business Transactions *45*

The Account *46*
Double-Entry Bookkeeping *49*
The T-Account *49*

Increases and Decreases in Accounts *50*
The Debit-Credit Language of Accounting *52*
Recording Transactions in Journals *52*
Posting from the Journal to the Ledger *54*
Flow of Accounting Data *54*
Illustrative Problem *54*
Summary Problem for Your Review *59*
Details of Journals and Ledgers *61*
Posting *61*
Four-Column Account Format *63*
Chart of Accounts *64*
Normal Balances of Accounts *65*
Additional Owner's Equity Accounts: Revenues and Expenses *65*
Typical Account Titles *67*
Illustrative Problem *68*
Analytical Use of Accounting Information *72*
Computers and Accounting *73*
Summary Problem for Your Review *74*
Summary *77*
Self-Study Questions *78*
Accounting Vocabulary *79*
Assignment Material *79*
Extending Your Knowledge *95*

The following practice set may be started after Chapter 2 and completed after Chapter 4:
A-1 Photography—Sole Proprietorship, Service,
D. Ductions and Company—Sole
Proprietorship, Service to Merchandising

3 Measuring Business Income: The Adjusting Process *98*

Accrual-Basis Accounting versus Cash-Basis Accounting *99*
The Accounting Period *100*

---

*In each chapter, Assignment Material includes Questions, Exercises, and Problems (Group A and Group B).
**Extending Your Knowledge includes Decision Problems, an Ethical Issue, and Financial Statement Problems.

Revenue Principle *101*

Matching Principle *102*

Time-Period Concept *102*

Adjustments to the Accounts *103*

Posting the Adjusting Entries *112*

Adjusted Trial Balance *114*

Preparing the Financial Statements
from the Adjusted Trial Balance *114*

Relationships among the Three Financial
Statements *116*

Computers and the Accounting Process *116*

Summary Problem for Your Review 118

Summary *123*

Self-Study Questions 123

Accounting Vocabulary 124

Assignment Material 125

Extending Your Knowledge 142

**4 Completing the Accounting
Cycle**   *144*

Overview of the Accounting Cycle *145*

The Accountant's Work Sheet *146*

Microcomputer Spreadsheets *154*

Summary Problem for Your Review 155

Using the Worksheet *157*

Reversing Entries *163*

Classification of Assets and Liabilities *167*

Formats of Balance Sheets *168*

Detecting and Correcting Accounting Errors *171*

Summary Problem for Your Review 172

Summary *176*

Self-Study Questions 176

Accounting Vocabulary 177

Assignment Material 179

Extending Your Knowledge 195

**Appendix: Prepaid Expenses,
Unearned Revenues,
and Reversing Entries**   *198*

Prepaid Expenses *198*

Unearned (Deferred) Revenues *201*

Summary *204*

Appendix Assignment Material 204

**5 Merchandising
and the Accounting Cycle**   *208*

The Operation Cycle for a Merchandising
Business *210*

Purchase of Merchandise Inventory *210*

Sale of Inventory *215*

Cost of Goods Sold *217*

Summary Problem for Your Review 220

The Adjusting and Closing Process
for a Merchandising Business *221*

Financial Statements of a Merchandising
Business *224*

Income Statement Format *229*

Use of Accounting Information in Decision
Making *230*

Computers and Inventory *231*

Summary Problem for Your Review 231

Summary *237*

Self-Study Questions 237

Accounting Vocabulary 238

Assignment Material 239

Extending Your Knowledge 254

**Appendix: The Adjusting
and Closing Process
for a Merchandising Business:
Adjusting Entry Method**   *258*

The Adjusting and Closing Process *258*

Alternate Solution to Review Problem *263*

Comprehensive Problem for Part One 266

*The following practice sets may be started after
Chapter 5:*
 *Furniture Forest—Sole Proprietorship,
 Merchandising–and completed after Chapter 6;
 The Luggage Merchant—Sole Proprietorship,
 Merchandising with Payroll—and completed
 after Chapter 11*

Part Two

Introduction to Accounting Systems

**6 Accounting Information
Systems**   *268*

Accounting System Design and Installation *269*

Basic Model of Information Processing *270*

An Effective Information System *270*

Computer Data Processing 272
Overview of an Accounting Information System 274
Special Accounting Journals 274
Summary Problem for Your Review 281
The Credit Memorandum—A Basic Business Document 287
The Debit Memorandum—A Basic Business Document 289
Sales Tax 289
Balancing the Ledgers 290
Documents as Journals 291
Computers and Special Journals 291
Summary Problem for Your Review 292
Summary 292
Self-Study Questions 293
Accounting Vocabulary 294
Assignment Material 295
Extending Your Knowledge 314

7 Internal Control and Cash Transactions   *316*

Effective Systems of Control 318
Limitations of Internal Control 322
The Bank Account as a Control Device 322
Summary Problem for Your Review 330
Reporting of Cash 331
Internal Control over Cash Receipts 332
Internal Control over Cash Disbursements 333
Computers, Internal Control, and Cash 341
Summary Problem for Your Review 342
Summary 344
Self-Study Questions 344
Accounting Vocabulary 345
Assignment Material 346
Extending Your Knowledge 362
Comprehensive Problem for Part Two 364

Part Three
Accounting for Noncash Assets and Liabilities

8 Accounts and Notes Receivable   *368*

Different Types of Receivables 369
The Credit Department 370
Uncollectible Accounts (Bad Debts) 371

Credit Balances in Accounts Receivable 378
Credit Card Sales 379
Internal Control over Collections of Accounts Receivable 379
Summary Problem for Your Review 380
Notes Receivable 381
Reporting Receivables and Allowances: Actual Reports 388
Use of Accounting Information in Decision Making 389
Computers and Accounts Receivable 390
Summary Problem for Your Review 391
Summary 392
Self-Study Questions 392
Accounting Vocabulary 393
Assignment Material 395
Extending Your Knowledge 409

9 Merchandise Inventory   *412*

Figuring Cost of Inventory 413
Inventory Costing Methods 415
Income Effects of FIFO, LIFO, and Weighted-Average Cost 417
The Income Tax Advantage of LIFO 418
Generally Accepted Accounting Principles: A Comparison of the Inventory Methods 420
Consistency Principle 421
Summary Problem for Your Review 421
Accounting Conservation 423
Effect of Inventory Errors 425
Methods of Estimating Inventory 426
Periodic and Perpetual Inventory Systems 428
Internal Control over Inventory 431
Computerized Inventory Records 432
Summary Problems for Your Review 433
Summary 434
Self-Study Questions 435
Accounting Vocabulary 436
Assignment Material 437
Extending Your Knowledge 452

10 Plant Assets, Intangible Assets, and Related Expenses   *455*

The Cost of a Plant Asset 457
Depreciation of Plant Assets 458
Determining the Useful Life of a Plant Asset 459

Measuring Depreciation *459*

Depreciation Methods *460*

Comparison of the Depreciation
Methods *463*

Summary Problem for Your Review 465

Depreciation and Income Taxes *466*

Special Issues in Depreciation
Accounting *468*

Using Fully Depreciated Assets *470*

Disposal of Plant Assets *470*

Accounting for Intangible Assets
and Amortization *475*

Capital Expenditures versus Revenue
Expenditures (Expenses) *478*

Summary Problems for Your Review 479

Summary *480*

Self-Study Questions 481

Accounting Vocabulary 482

Assignment Material 483

Extending Your Knowledge 498

**11 Current Liabilities
and Payroll Accounting   500**

Current Liabilities of Known Amount *501*

Current Liabilities That Must Be Estimated *506*

Contingent Liabilities *508*

Summary Problem for Your Review 509

Accounting for Payroll *510*

Gross Pay and Net Pay *511*

Payroll Entries *513*

The Payroll System *515*

Recording Cash Disbursements for Payroll *518*

Internal Control over Payroll *519*

Reporting Payroll Expense and Liabilities *522*

Computer Accounting Systems for Current
Liabilities *522*

Summary Problem for Your Review 524

Summary *525*

Self-Study Questions 525

Accounting Vocabulary 526

Assignment Material 527

Extending Your Knowledge 541

Comprehensive Problem for Part Three 543

Part Four
Generally Accepted Accounting
Principles

**12 The Foundation for Generally
Accepted Accounting
Principles   545**

The Conceptual Framework *547*

Objective of Financial Reporting *548*

Underlying Concepts *549*

Accounting Principles *551*

Constraints on Accounting *559*

Financial Statements and Their Elements *560*

Accounting Standards Throughout the World *562*

Summary Problem for Your Review 562

Summary *564*

Self-Study Questions 565

Accounting Vocabulary 566

Assignment Material 567

Extending Your Knowledge 581

Part Five
Accounting for Partnerships
and Corporations

13 Accounting for Partnerships   583

Characteristics of a Partnership *584*

Initial Investments by Partners *586*

Sharing Partnership Profits and Losses *588*

Partner Drawings *592*

Dissolution of a Partnership *593*

Summary Problem for Your Review 597

Withdrawal of a Partner *598*

Death of a Partner *601*

Liquidation of a Partnership *601*

Partnership Financial Statements *606*

Summary Problem for Your Review 608

Summary *610*

Self-Study Questions 611

Accounting Vocabulary 612

Assignment Material 613

Extending Your Knowledge 623

14 Corporations: Organization, Paid-In Capital, and the Balance Sheet *625*

Characteristics of a Corporation *626*
Organization of a Corporation *628*
Capital Stock *628*
Stockholders' Equity *630*
Stockholder Rights *631*
Classes of Stock *632*
Issuing Stock *632*
Summary Problems for Your Review 637
Donated Capital *639*
Incorporation of a Going Business *640*
Organization Cost *640*
Dividend Dates *641*
Dividends on Preferred and Common Stock *641*
Convertible Preferred Stock *644*
Rate of Return on Total Assets and Rate of Return on Stockholders' Equity *644*
Different Values of Stock *646*
Summary Problems for Your Review 648
Summary *650*
Self-Study Questions 650
Accounting Vocabulary 652
Assignment Material 654
Extending Your Knowledge 666

The following practice set may be started after Chapter 14 and completed after Chapter 19: Runners Corporation—Merchandising

15 Corporations: Retained Earnings, Dividends, Treasury Stock, and the Income Statement *669*

Retained Earnings and Dividends *670*
Stock Dividends *672*
Stock Splits *675*
Treasury Stock *677*
Summary Problem for Your Review 679
Retirement of Stock *681*
Restrictions on Retained Earnings *682*
Variations in Reporting Stockholders' Equity *683*
Corporation Income Statement *683*
Statement of Retained Earnings *689*
Summary Problem for Your Review 692
Summary *693*
Self-Study Questions 693

Accounting Vocabulary 695
Assignment Material 695
Extending Your Knowledge 710

16 Corporations: Long-Term Liabilities *713*

The Nature of Bonds *714*
Types of Bonds *715*
Bond Prices *716*
Issuing Bonds Payable *718*
Adjusting Entries for Interest Expense *722*
Summary Problem for Your Review 723
Effective-Interest Method of Amortization *725*
Bond Sinking Fund *729*
Retirement of Bonds Payable *730*
Convertible Bonds and Notes *731*
Current Portion of Long-Term Debt *731*
Mortgage Notes Payable *732*
Advantage of Financing Operations with Debt versus Stock *732*
Lease Liabilities *734*
Off-Balance-Sheet Financing *736*
Pension Liabilities *736*
Computers and Corporate Financial Planning *737*
Summary Problem for Your Review 737
Summary *739*
Self-Study Questions 740
Accounting Vocabulary 741
Assignment Material 742
Extending Your Knowledge 753

Appendix: Present Value *755*

Present Value Tables *756*
Present Value of an Annuity *757*
Present Value of Bonds Payable *758*
Capital Leases *759*

17 Corporations: Investments and Accounting for International Operations *761*

ACCOUNTING FOR INVESTMENTS *762*
Stock Prices *762*
Investments in Stock *763*
Classifying Stock Investments *764*
Accounting for Stock Investments *764*
Investments in Bonds and Notes *774*
Summary Problem for Your Review 777

ACCOUNTING FOR INTERNATIONAL
OPERATIONS *779*

Economic Structures and Their Impact
on International Accounting *780*

Foreign Currencies and Foreign-Currency
Exchange Rates *780*

Accounting for International Transactions *781*

Hedging—A Strategy to Avoid Foreign-Currency
Transaction Losses *783*

Consolidation of Foreign Subsidiaries *784*

International Accounting Standards *785*

Computers and Consolidation *786*

Summary Problem for Your Review 786

Summary *788*

Self-Study Questions 788

Accounting Vocabulary 790

Assignment Material 791

Extending Your Knowledge 802

Comprehensive Problem for Part Five 805

Part Six
Using External Accounting Information

18   Statement of Cash Flows   *807*

Purpose of the Statement of Cash Flows *808*

Basic Concept of the Statement of Cash Flows *809*

Operating, Investing, and Financing Activities *809*

Cash and Cash Equivalents *812*

Interest and Dividends *812*

Preparing the Statement of Cash Flows:
The Direct Method *812*

Focus of the Statement of Cash Flows *816*

Summary Problem for Your Review 817

Computing Individual Amounts for the Statement
of Cash Flows *819*

Noncash Investing and Financing Activities *826*

Preparing the Statement of Cash Flows:
The Indirect Method *827*

Supplementary Disclosures *830*

Computers and the Statement of Cash Flows *831*

Summary Problem for Your Review 832

Summary *833*

Self-Study Questions 834

Accounting Vocabulary 835

Assignment Material 836

Extending Your Knowledge 854

**Appendix: The Work-Sheet
Approach to Preparing
the Statement of Cash Flows   857**

Preparing the Work Sheet—Direct Method
for Operating Activities *858*

Preparing the Work Sheet—Indirect Method
for Operating Activities *861*

Assignment Material 864

19   Using Accounting Information
to Make Business Decisions   *867*

Financial Statement Analysis *868*

Horizontal Analysis *869*

Vertical Analysis *872*

Common-Size Statements *874*

Industry Comparisons *875*

The Statement of Cash Flows in Decision Making *876*

Summary Problem for Your Review 877

Using Ratios to Make Business Decisions *879*

Measuring the Ability to Pay Current Liabilities *879*

Measuring the Ability to Sell Inventory and Collect
Receivables *881*

Measuring the Ability to Pay Long-Term Debt *884*

Measuring Profitability *886*

Analyzing Stock as an Investment *888*

The Complexity of Business Decisions *890*

Efficient Markets, Management Action, and
Investor Decisions *891*

Computers and Financial Statement Analysis *891*

Summary Problem for Your Review 892

Summary *894*

Self-Study Questions 896

Accounting Vocabulary 897

Assignment Material 898

Extending Your Knowledge 914

Comprehensive Problem for Part Six 916

Part Seven
Management Accounting
and Internal Decision Making

20   Introduction to Management
Accounting: The Master
Budget   *918*

Two Themes in Management Accounting *919*

The Role of Management *920*

The Budgeting System *921*

Benefits of a Budget *922*

The Performance Report *923*

Components of the Master Budget *924*

Preparing the Master Budget *926*

Importance of Sales Forecasting *933*

Budgeting and Short-Term Financing *934*

Continuous (Rolling) Budgets *935*

Budget Models, What-If Questions, and
  Microcomputer Applications *935*

Summary Problem for Your Review 936

Summary *940*

Self-Study Questions 940

Accounting Vocabulary 941

Assignment Material 942

Extending Your Knowledge 957

21 Cost-Volume-Profit Relationships and the Contribution Margin Approach to Decision Making *959*

Types of Costs *960*

Contribution Margin Approach to Decision
  Making *963*

Relevant Range *964*

Cost-Volume-Profit Analysis *965*

Summary Problem for Your Review 972

Margin of Safety *973*

Assumptions Underlying CVP Analysis *974*

Sales Mix *974*

Separating a Mixed Cost into Its Variable
  and Fixed Components *976*

Computer Spreadsheet Analysis of CVP
  Relationships *978*

Summary Problem for Your Review 979

Summary *982*

Self-Study Questions 982

Accounting Vocabulary 983

Assignment Material 984

Extending Your Knowledge 995

22 Manufacturing Accounting and Job Order Costing *998*

Manufacturing and the Value Chain *999*

Objectives of a Cost System *1000*

Manufacturing Accounts *1001*

Inventoriable Costs and Period Costs *1005*

Perpetual and Periodic Inventory Systems *1007*

Summary Questions for Your Review 1007

Job Order Costing *1008*

Computers and Manufacturing Accounting *1022*

Summary Problem for Your Review 1022

Summary *1024*

Self-Study Questions 1025

Accounting Vocabulary 1026

Assignment Material 1027

Extending Your Knowledge 1042

*The following practice set may be started after
Chapter 22:*
  Four Seasons Furniture Manufacturers, Inc.

23 Process Costing, Activity-Based Costing, and Joint Products *1044*

Process Costing: An Overview *1045*

Recording Costs *1048*

Tracing the Flow of Costs *1049*

Equivalent Units of Production *1050*

Steps in Process Cost Accounting *1050*

Summary Problem for Your Review 1053

Process Costing Extended to a Second
  Department *1055*

Production Cost Report *1059*

Activity-Based Costing *1061*

Product Costing in an Activity-Based System *1063*

Activity-Based Costing and Management Decisions *1064*

Joint Product Cost *1066*

Byproduct Cost *1067*

Just-in-Time (JIT) Production Systems *1067*

Summary Problem for Your Review 1069

Summary *1070*

Self-Study Questions 1071

Accounting Vocabulary 1072

Assignment Material 1073

Extending Your Knowledge 1087

24 Flexible Budgets and Standard Costs *1090*

Cost Behavior Patterns *1091*

Relevant Range *1092*

Flexible Budgets *1093*

Graphing the Budget Expense Formula *1094*

Analyzing the Results *1096*

Summary Problem for Your Review 1097

Standard Costing *1099*

Relationship between Standard Costs and Flexible Budgets *1099*

Illustration of Standard Costing *1100*

Computers and Standard Costs *1110*

Summary Problem for Your Review 1110

Summary *1114*

Self-Study Questions 1114

Accounting Vocabulary 1115

Assignment Material 1116

Extending Your Knowledge 1127

25 Responsibility Accounting: Departments and Branches   1129

Responsibility Accounting *1130*

Performance Report Format *1133*

Design of a Responsibility Accounting System *1133*

Departmental Accounting *1134*

Summary Problem for Your Review 1139

Branch Accounting *1139*

Computers, Responsibility Accounting, and Remote Processing *1144*

Summary Problem for Your Review 1144

Summary *1145*

Self-Study Questions 1145

Accounting Vocabulary 1147

Assignment Material 1147

Extending Your Knowledge 1162

26 Special Decisions and Capital Budgeting   1164

Relevant Information for Decision Making *1165*

Special Sales Order *1166*

Deletion of Products, Departments, Territories—Fixed Costs Unchanged *1169*

Deletion of Products, Departments, Territories—Fixed Costs Changed *1170*

Which Product to Emphasize *1171*

Make or Buy *1172*

Best Use of Facilities *1173*

Sell As-Is or Process Further *1174*

Opportunity Cost *1175*

Summary Problems for Your Review 1176

Capital Budgeting *1177*

Discounted Cash Flow Models *1181*

Computers in Business Decision Analysis *1187*

Summary Problem for Your Review 1188

Summary *1189*

Self-Study Questions 1190

Accounting Vocabulary 1191

Assignment Material 1192

Extending Your Knowledge 1202

Part Eight
Special Topics

27 Income Taxes and Their Effects on Business Decisions   1204

History and Operation of the Income Tax *1205*

Classes and Filing Status of Taxpayers *1206*

Income Taxation of Individuals *1207*

Paying Income Tax through Withholding and Quarterly Payments *1213*

Summary Problem for Your Review 1214

Income Taxation of Corporations *1215*

Tax Factors in Business Decisions *1219*

Summary Problem for Your Review 1225

Summary *1226*

Self-Study Questions 1226

Accounting Vocabulary 1227

Assignment Material 1228

Extending Your Knowledge 1239

28 Accounting with Computers   1241

Advantages of Computer Systems *1242*

Computer Basics *1243*

Spreadsheets *1255*

Summary Problem for Your Review 1269

Summary *1271*

Self-Study Questions 1271

Accounting Vocabulary 1272

Assignment Material 1273

Extending Your Knowledge 1287

Appendixes

A Accounting for the Effects of Changing Prices (Inflation) 1289

B Present-Value Tables and Future-Value Tables   1304

C Published Financial Statements   1310

Glossary   G-1
Indexes   I-1

Preface

Accounting provides full introductory coverage of both financial and management accounting. We have written the book for use throughout a two-semester or three-quarter sequence of accounting courses.

In content and emphasis, instructors will find that **Accounting** is in the mainstream for courses in introductory accounting. This book focuses on the most widely used accounting theory and practice. This text and its supplements supply the most effective tools available for learning fundamental accounting concepts and procedures.

Clarity and Accuracy

Two themes have directed our writing of this text—*clarity* and *accuracy*. We believe that we have produced the clearest prose, learning objectives, exhibits, definitions, and assignment material for courses in principles of accounting. Students will find this book easy to study. We have assumed that students have no previous education in accounting or business.

The contributions of users of the first edition and their students and reviewers of this Second Edition have guided us in writing an accurate text. We and the publishers have sought input on our work from an unprecedented number of accounting educators and students in order to publish a book that meets your strict demands for accuracy.

This demand for accuracy did not stop with the text. The authors and publisher have taken extraordinary care and incurred extraordinary cost to ensure that the supplements are accurate. The *Solutions Manual*, in particular, went through a rigorous review process. The authors' solutions were checked by two independent reviewers, reconciled by the supplements coordinator, and then checked again through a Lotus program. The final typeset solutions were reworked one last time by a third independent reviewer.

The Business Context of Accounting

To enhance our presentation of accounting, we set out in the First Edition to create a business context for the student. As often as possible, we have integrated actual companies and their business data into our text narrative and assignment material. Students reading about companies familiar to them find the material interesting and also develop a deeper appreciation for accounting's importance in today's business world. When information drawn from real companies would be too advanced for introductory students, we illustrated the accounting point at hand by using realistic examples, building a framework of relevance that makes learning the topic more inviting to the students.

We have expanded on this approach in the Second Edition. Each chapter now opens with a description of an actual business situation. We call these *vignettes,* and most are drawn from the business press. We also bring students inside the world of business through three of our supplements: ABC News videos, *New York Times* articles, and Disclosure software (which presents financial data from publicly traded companies).

Distinctive Features of the Second Edition

Increased Assignment Material

Accounting, Second Edition, has increased assignment material. We have added more exercises and problems, which are now referenced to chapter learning objectives. In addition, chapters now conclude with a special feature called Extending Your Knowledge. This section includes two Decision Problems (doubled from the First Edition), an Ethical Issue case (new this edition), and two Financial Statement Problems (doubled from the First Edition). Parts 1, 2, 3, 5, and 6 end with a Comprehensive Problem—also new this edition.

Chapter-Opening Vignettes

Each chapter opens with an actual business situation. We found in the First Edition that emphasis on the real-world environment of business promotes student interest and learning. Our new Second-Edition chapter-opening vignettes build on what we learned from the First Edition.

Recommendations of the Accounting Education Change Commission

The recommendations of this important group have inspired us in several ways.

* Chapter 1 includes a discussion of ethics in business, and, as we mentioned, all chapters include an Ethical Issue case for student analysis.
* To sharpen students' decision-making skills, financial ratios are interspersed throughout the text. For example, Chapter 4 introduces the current ratio and the debt ratio, Chapter 5 covers the gross margin percentage and inventory turnover, and Chapter 8 discusses the acid-test ratio and days' sales in receivables. Other ratios appear throughout the book as appropriate. (Chapter 19, Using Accounting Information to Make Business Decisions, presents all important financial ratios, including those discussed elsewhere in the text.)
* International accounting receives more emphasis and now appears as the second half of Chapter 17.
* To meet the challenge of improving students' communications skills, we include in all chapters new assignment material that requires essay answers (identified by a special icon in the Annotated Instructor's Edition).

Four-Color Design

The four-color design enlivens and eases learning. A strong program of visual features—exhibits and tables—helps reinforce the text. Note that the two-tone beige tint in exhibits denotes financial statements. The green tint in exhibits identifies ledgers, journals, work sheets, and the like. The learning objectives appear in a textured tint panel at the chapter's opening and in the text margin. Key headings appear in blue. And full-color photos tied to the chapter-opening vignettes begin every chapter.

Two-tone beige denotes financial statements	Green identifies ledgers, journals, work sheets, and so on	Pale texture highlights learning objectives

Computers in Accounting

A separate chapter, Chapter 28, provides a thorough introduction to computers as they apply to accounting. We discuss both general ledger software and spreadsheets. The chapter offers students hands-on instruction in the preparation of accounting documents by requiring them to write a spreadsheet template to solve the assignment materials. In addition, all exercises and problems in the Chapter 28 assignment material are referenced in earlier chapters as appropriate. For example, Exercise 28-1 deals with inventory, the principal topic in Chapter 9. In the assignment material to Chapter 9 we cite Exercise 28-1. Instructors who wish to, then, can use the Chapter 28 computer assignment materials throughout the course. Also, we have strengthened our discussions of the impact and benefits of computers in accounting through special sections within many chapters.

Management Accounting

Management accounting chapters follow a logical order. Chapter 20 begins our study of management accounting by demonstrating how budgets are prepared. Chapter 21 introduces a model of cost-volume-profit relationships, an important planning tool of managers. Our first two chapters on management accounting are confined to nonmanufacturing organizations. In this way, we can explore two major tools (budgets and the cost-volume-profit model) without contending with the many new terms associated with manufacturing organizations.

Chapters 22 and 23 describe manufacturing accounting systems. We discuss the value chain, cost drivers, and activity-based costing. Chapters 24, 25, and 26 pursue management accounting tools in more depth. We want students to recognize that management accounting applies to all kinds of organizations, not just to manufacturing companies.

End-of-Chapter Appendixes

For maximum flexibility, several chapters have their own appendixes, enabling instructors to give expanded coverage to certain topics. The Chapter 4 appendix is Prepaid Expenses, Unearned Revenues, and Reversing Entries.

The Chapter 5 appendix is The Adjusting and Closing Process for a Merchandising Business: Adjusting-Entry Method. The Chapter 16 appendix is Present Value. The Chapter 18 appendix is The Work-Sheet Approach to Preparing the Statement of Cash Flows.

End-of-Book Appendixes

Three appendixes are presented at the end of the book:

Appendix A: Accounting for the Effects of Changing Prices (Inflation)

Appendix B: Present-Value and Future-Value Tables. This appendix complements the present-value coverage in Chapter 16 and 26.

Appendix C: The Financial Statements of The Goodyear Tire & Rubber Company.

Chapter Organization

1. Each chapter begins with a vignette, as we have described. Learning objectives also appear at the start of every chapter. These objectives are keyed to the relevant chapter material and are also referenced to the exercises and problems.

2. Most chapters offer two *Summary Problems for Your Review*. Each *Summary Problem* includes its fully worked-out solution. These features, which generally appear at the halfway point and at the end of each chapter, provide students with immediate feedback and serve as key review aids.

3. Each chapter presents three important tools for student review. A text *Summary* recaps the chapter discussion. *Self-Study Questions* allow students to test their understanding of the chapter. The text that supports the answer is referenced by page number, and the answers appear before the Assignment Material. *Accounting Vocabulary* presents the key terms introduced in the chapter, complete with their Glossary definitions. A full Glossary, keyed by page number, appears at the end of the book.

4. *Assignment Material* is more varied and plentiful than in competing texts. *Questions* (covering the major definitions, concepts, and procedures) may be assigned as homework or used to promote discussion in class. *Exercises*, identified by topic area and learning objectives, cover the full spectrum of the chapter text. *Problems*, also identified by topic area and learning objectives, come in A and B sets. The two sets allow instructors to vary assignments from term to term and to solve the A or B problem in class and assign the related problem for homework. Those exercises and problems that can be solved using the Lotus R 1-2-3® templates are designated by a black computer disk. Those exercises and problems that can be solved using the Prentice Hall Integrated Accounting System are designated by a white computer disk.

5. Each chapter ends with an *Extending Your Knowledge* section. Under this heading are presented:

   * two *Decision Problems*, which help students to develop critical thinking skills. Analysis, interpretation, and determining a course of action are ordinarily required.

   * an *Ethical Issue* case, which presents a business scenario that challenges

the ethical conduct of the accountant and asks the student to resolve the dilemma. Many of these cases also challenge students' accounting skills.

* two *Financial Statement Problems* (for most chapters). The first problem links the chapter's subject matter directly to the actual financial statements in the annual report of The Goodyear Tire & Rubber Company, which appears in Appendix C. Students answer the second financial statement problem using data taken from the annual report of another company. Instructors may refer students to annual reports kept in the library or contained in Disclosure's Compact d/SEC Academic Edition.

The Supplements Package

We have a far-reaching, package of teaching and learning tools to supplement the text. A team of contributors devoted hundreds of hours to perfecting the supplements. Our supplements coordinator, who is a professional accounting teacher, together with a full-time development editor worked with the contributors to ensure maximum instructional value, accuracy, and consistency with the text and within the supplements package.

Resources for the Instructor

Annotated Instructor's Edition
Prentice Hall Course Manager (Chapters 1-13, Chapters 14-28)
Instructor's Manual and Supplements Guide
Solutions Manual (Chapters 1-13, Chapters 12-28)
Solutions Transparencies (Chapters 1-13, Chapters 14-28)
Teaching Transparencies
Test Item File
Achievement Tests
Instructor's Manuals to the Practice Sets
ABC News/PH Video Library

Resources for the Student

Study Guide with Demonstration Problems (Chapters 1-13, Chapters 12-28)
Working Papers (Chapters 1-13, Chapters 12-28)
Blank Working Papers
How to Study Accounting Booklet
PHACTS Tutorial Videos
New York Times Dodger

Practice Sets:

   A-1 Photography (Manual & Computerized)
   D. Ductions and Company (Manual)
   Furniture Forest (Manual)
   The Luggage Merchant (Manual & Computerized)
   Runners Corporation (Manual & Computerized)
   Four Seasons Furniture Manufacturers (Manual)

Software

"The Integrator" Lecture and Supplements Manager
ParTest Computerized Testing Package
Instructor's Manual on Disk
Electronic Transparencies
Compact d/SEC Academic Edition from Disclosure
"On Account" Student Tutorial
Microguide Computerized Study Guide
Prentice Hall Integrated Accounting System
PH Integrated Accounting Templates
Lotus Templates: Spreadsheet Working Papers

Resources from the Business World

The three supplements we describe here—unique to **Accounting** and Prentice Hall—show students how the accounting they are learning in the classroom works in the context of actual business.

ABC News/PH Video Library for **Accounting**

Video is the most dynamic of all the supplements you can use to enhance your class. The quality of the video material and how well it relates to your course can make all the difference. For these reasons, Prentice Hall and ABC News have decided to work together to bring you the best and most comprehensive video ancillaries available in the college market.

Through its wide variety of award-winning programs—*Nightline, Business World, On Business, This Week with David Brinkley, World News Tonight,* and *The Health Show*—ABC offers a resource for feature and documentary-style videos related to text concepts and applications. The programs have extremely high production quality, present substantial content, and are hosted by well-versed, well-known anchors. Prentice Hall, its authors, and its editors provide the benefit of having selected videos on topics that will work well with this course and text and give the instructor teaching notes on how to use them in the classroom. "The ABC News/PH Video Library for **Accounting**" offers video material for selected topics in the text. A video guide is provided to integrate the videos into your lecture.

The New York Times

The New York Times and Prentice Hall are sponsoring "A Contemporary View," a program designed to enhance student access to current information of relevance in the classroom. Through this program, the core subject matter provided in the text is supplemented by a collection of time-sensitive articles from one of the world's most distinguished newspapers, *The New York Times.* These articles demonstrate the connection between what is learned in the classroom and what is happening in the world around us. To enjoy the wealth of information of *The New York Times* daily, a reduced subscription rate is available. For information, call toll-free: 1-800-631-1222.

Prentice Hall and *The New York Times* are proud to co-sponsor "A Contemporary View." We hope it will make the reading of both textbooks and newspapers a dynamic learning process.

Compact d/SEC Academic Edition

DISCLOSURE

Through an exclusive arrangement with Disclosure, Prentice Hall is providing adopters of **Accounting** with a software disk containing detailed profiles and financial data for 100 publicly traded companies. By combining this wealth of data with computer-search capabilities, students can analyze companies of their choosing. Financial statement problems written specifically for use with the Compact d/SEC Academic Edition are included in most chapters.

Acknowledgments

The authors and publisher wish to thank our many reviewers, class-testers, and focus group participants, whose contributions have meant so much to this project.

Reviewers

Lucille Berry, Webster U.
John Blahnik, Lorain County Community C.
Nancy Boyd, Middle Tennessee State U.
Ken Boze, U. of Alaska at Anchorage
Wayne Bremser, Villanova U.
Eric Carlsen, Kean C. of New Jersey
Donna Chadwick, Sinclair Community C.
Karen Collins, Lehigh U.
Billie Cunningham, Collin County Community C.
Marilyn Fuller, Paris Junior C.
Michael Garms, Henry Ford Community C.
Sue Garr, Wayne State U.
Lucille Genduso, Nova U.
Selwyn Glincher, Quincy Junior C.
Gloria Grayless, Sam Houston State U.
Rex Hauser, U. of Southern Louisiana
Linda Herrington, Community C. of Allegheny County
Kenneth Hiltebeitel, Villanova U.
Anita Hope, Tarrant County Junior C.
Jean Marie Hudson, Lamar U.
Betty Johns, Dundalk Community C.
Lawrence Killough, Virginia Polytechnic Inst.
Joseph Milligan, C. of DuPage
George Neiswanger, North Seattle Community C.
Lee Nicholas, U. of Northern Iowa
Lawrence Roman, Cuyahoga Community C.
Lynn Saubert, Radford U.
David Skougstad, Metropolitan State C.
William Stahlin, Drexel U.
Maureen Stefanini, Worcester State C.
Robert Sweeny, Memphis State U.
Vicki Vorell, Cuyahoga Community C.
Bea Wallace, St. Philip's C.
Jane Ward, U. of Northern Iowa
Denise Wooten, Erie Community C.

D. Lamar Creager, Hagerstown Junior C.
James Emig, Villanova U.
Bill Francisco, Georgia Southern U.
J. Stanley Fuhrman, U. of Texas–San Antonio
Mohamed Gaber, SUNY–Plattsburgh
Mike Glasscock, Amarillo C.
Inam Hussain, Indiana U. Northwest
Betty Johns, Dundalk Community C.
George Johnson, Norfolk State U.
Mark Kaiser, SUNY–Plattsburgh
Dan Lux, U. of Wisconsin Center–Rock County
Yaw Mensah, Rutgers U.
Frank Molitor, Middlesex County C.
Lowell Mooney, Georgia Southern C.
Paula Mooney, Georgia Southern U.
Vinita Rogers, Fisk U.
Donald Rogoff, California State U.–Northridge
David Schmedel, Amarillo C.
David Smith, Houston Baptist U.
Rodger Trigg, Columbus C.
George Ulseth, Rensselaer Polytechnic Inst.
Barbara Vidulich, Metropolitan State C.
Bea Wallace, St. Philip's C.
Michael Welker, Drexel U.
Richard White, Asheville–Buncombe Technical Community C.
Albert Wolfson, Florida Community C.–Jacksonville

Focus Group Participants

Terry Aime, Delgado Community C.
Pam Anglin, Nararro C.
Don Babbitt, Lindenwood C.
Mohamed Bayou, U. of Michigan–Dearborn
Audrey Beck, American U.
Madeline Carlin, SUNY–Buffalo
Eric Carlsen, Kean C. of New Jersey
Robert Carpenter, Eastfield C.
Janet Cassagio, Nassau Community C.
Donna Chadwick, Sinclair Community C.
Paul Concillio, McLennan Community C.
Judy Cook, Grossmont C.
Dana DiPaolo, Drexel U.
Ravi Dutta, Raritan Valley Community C.
Dave Evans, Johnson County Community C.

Questionnaire Respondents

Lucille Berry, Webster U.
Ken Boze, U. of Alaska at Anchorage
Wayne Bremser, Villanova U.
Jack Cassidy, DeVry Inst. of Technology–Los Angeles
Anthony Cioffi, Lorain County Community C.
Karen Collins, Lehigh U.

Joe Fairchild, Nicholls State U.
Larry Falcetto, Emporia State U.
John Fleming, Drexel U.
Ed Fratantaro, Orange Coast C.
Marilyn Fuller, Paris Junior C.
Sue Garr, Wayne State U.
Roger Gee, San Diego Mesa C.
Rich Geglein, Indiana Vo-Tech–Madison
Shirley Glass, Macomb Community C.–South
Gloria Grayless, Sam Houston State U.
Ann Gregory, South Plains C.
Duane Harper, Johnson County Community C.
Jean Insinga, Middlesex Community C.
Fred Jex, Macomb Community C.–South
Kenneth Johnson, Mississippi State U.
Vern Jorgensen, Southwestern C.
Nancy Kelly, Middlesex Community C.
Christy Kloezeman, Glendale Community C.
Joseph Krebs, U. of the District of Columbia
Cathy Larson, Middlesex Community C.
Lola Locke, Tarrant County Junior C.–Northeast
Dan Luna, Raritan Valley Community C.
Jay Mackie, Towson State U.
Richard Nelson, SUNY–Buffalo
Alfonso Oddo, Niagara U.
Pat Packard, Sanford Brown C.
Lynn Paluska, Nassau Community C.
Sandy Penn, Wayne State U.
Wayne Pfingsten, Belleville Area C.
Jim Ponder, Nicholls State U.
LaVonda Ramey, Schoolcraft C.

Donald Ramsey, U. of the District of Columbia
Tony Riley, South Plains C.
Ramona Seifert, Glendale Community C.
Carolyn Shankel, Johnson County Community C.
Dennis Shannon, Belleville Area C.
William Stahlin, Drexel U.
J.B. Stroud, Nicholls State U.
Gracelyn Stuart, Palm Beach Junior C.–South
John Varga, Orange Coast C.
Vicki Vorell, Cuyahoga Community C.–Western
Martin Ward, DeVry Inst. of Technology–Kansas City
Mike Welker, Drexel U.
Anne Wessley, St. Louis Community C.–Meramec
Stan Wieckert, C. of the Canyons
Denise Wooten, Erie Community C.

Class-Testers

Emmanuel Amobi, Virginia State U.
James Dean, Nova U.
Fred Dial, Stephen F. Austin State U.
Charles Ericksen, Kearney State C.
Lucille Genduso, Nova U.
Vincent Guide, Clemson U.
George Johnson, Norfolk State U.
Don Lucy, Millersville U. of Pennsylvania
A. Qastin, Lakeland C.
DuWayne Wacker, U. of North Dakota
James Weglin, North Seattle Community C.
F. Christian Widmer, Tidewater Community C.–Virginia Beach

The authors also wish to thank Eric Carlsen for his assistance with the computer sections of this text and W. Morley Lemon for his contributions to the Decision Problems.

Among the many people at Prentice Hall who helped to publish this book are: Linda Albelli, Robert Anderson, Lisamarie Brassini, Kris Ann Cappelluti, Bobbie Christenberry, Christine Ciancia, Carol Crowell, Terri Daly, Patti Dant, Stephen Deitmer, Anne DiBisceglie, Maureen Eide, Connie Ghent, David Gillespie, Joseph Heider, Jeanne Hoeting, Esther Koehn, Robert McCarry, Trudy Pisciotti, Elizabeth Robertson, Asha Rohra, Frances Russello, Susan Seuling, Janet Schmid, Joyce Turner, Christine Wolf, and Doreen Yates.

Charles T. Horngren
Walter T. Harrison, Jr.

Our Commitment to Quality

When we asked focus group participants how we could validate this book's strengths, they surprised us. More important than the rubber-stamped name of an accounting firm, they explained, would be the names of the people who made the book what it is. So we have signed our work. Our signatures and the signatures of those people who made the most significant contributions to this book are our pledge to you that this book warrants your highest confidence.

Charles T. Horngren
Stanford University

Walter T. Harrison, Jr.
Baylor University

Betsy Willis
Baylor University

Becky Jones
Baylor University

Carolyn B. Harris
University of Texas-San Antonio

Cathy Xanthaky Larson
Middlesex Community College

Fred R. Jex
Macomb Community College

Joseph Heider
Editor-in-Chief for Accounting
and Information Systems

Bea Wallace
St. Philip's College

Terri Daly
Senior Accounting Editor

Esther Koehn
Editorial and Production Supervisor

Stephen Deitmer
Managing Editor, College Book
Editorial Development

Susan Seuling
Development Editor in Accounting

Photo Credits

1 Stacky Pick/Stock, Boston; **45** David Lawrence/The Stock Market; **85** Westenberger/Sygma; **144** Butch Martin/The Image Bank; **208** Courtesy of Nordstrom; **268** Courtesy of Citibank, Diners Club, Inc.; **316** Shostal/Superstock; **368** Gabe Palmer/The Stock Market; **412** Charles Gupton/Stock, Boston; **455** Superstock; **500** Courtesy of American Airlines; **545** N. Tully/Sygma; **583** Lol, Inc. FPG International **625** Teri Stratford; **670** Courtesy of Texas Instruments; **713** Jon Feingersh/The Stock Market; **761** Reggie C. Parker/FPG International; **807** Alan Carey/The Image Works; **867** Superstock; **918** Joel Gordon; **959** Chrysler Corporation; **998** Chuck O'Rear/Westlight **1044** Alvis Upitis/The Image Bank; **1090** Brian Drake/West Stock; **1129** Tardos Camesi/The Stock Market; **1164** Superstock; **1204** Jim Pikerell/FPG International; **1241** Jon Feingersh/Stock, Boston.

Chapter 1

Accounting and Its Environment

Melissa Roberts is making college plans for next year. She must choose between two alternatives. She can stay at home and attend the Community College of Denver or live on campus and attend the University of Colorado. By staying at home she can save on room and board expense. Also, she can keep her job at Kinko's, the photocopying store, where she earns money for her car payments. If she instead chooses to attend the University of Colorado, she cannot stay at home. Her family can help her with tuition and fees, but Melissa will be on her own to cover room, board, and personal expenses. Would she be able to find a job at the university to pay these personal expenses? Would she have to sell her car?

Of course, Melissa must determine which school offers the better education. The university is more expensive, but will she be able to land a job paying her a higher salary if she chooses the university over the community college? Each year millions of students face similar decisions. They weigh the costs and the benefits of the various educational choices. They must estimate how much their education will be worth and how much it will cost. Financing the education includes determining what the family can afford, what the student may earn while in school, and what amount, if any, must be borrowed. These financial considerations are accounting matters. As you read Chapter 1, consider how Melissa might use accounting information in deciding which school to attend. Also think over how people in nearly every walk of life can apply accounting information in making decisions in their daily lives.

Accounting and Decisions

Point to Stress: In today's business environment, it is impossible to be successful without accounting. Every organization must make decisions about how to use its resources. Accounting provides the information needed for those decisions.

Point to Stress: Accounting provides information. Executives in many areas of a business—such as management, marketing, and personnel—use this information in making business decisions.

Accounting has been called "the language of business." Perhaps a better term is "the language of financial decisions." The better you understand the language, the better you can manage the financial aspects of living. Personal financial planning, education expenses, investments, loans, car payments, income taxes, and many other aspects of daily life are based on accounting. Melissa Roberts is facing some of these decisions.

A recent survey indicates that business managers believe it is more important for college students to learn accounting than any other business subject. Other surveys show that persons trained in accounting and finance make it to the top of their organizations in greater numbers than persons trained in any other field. Indeed, accounting is an important subject.

Regardless of your roles in life—student, head of household, investor, manager, politician—you will find a knowledge of accounting helpful. The major purpose of this book is to help you learn to use accounting information to make informed decisions. Individuals who can do so have a great advantage over those who cannot.

OBJECTIVE 1

Develop a working vocabulary for decision making

What Is Accounting?

Point to Stress: By law, all businesses must keep accounting records. Corporations must send annual reports to the IRS to report the year's operating results.

Accounting is the system that measures business activities, processes that information into reports, and communicates these findings to decision makers. **Financial statements** are the documents that report on an individual's or an organization's business in monetary amounts.

Is our business making a profit? Should we start up a new line of women's clothing? Are sales strong enough to warrant opening a new branch outlet? The most intelligent answers to business questions like these are based on accounting information. Decision makers use the information to develop sound business plans. As new programs affect the business's activities, accounting takes the company's financial pulse rate. The cycle continues as the accounting system measures the results of activities and reports the results to decision makers.

Bookkeeping is a procedural element of accounting as arithmetic is a procedural element of mathematics. Increasingly, people are using computers to do much of the detailed bookkeeping work at all levels—in households, businesses, and organizations of all types. Exhibit 1-1 illustrates the role of accounting in business.

Users of Accounting Information: The Decision Makers

Decision makers beg for information. The more important the decision, the greater the need for relevant information. Virtually all businesses and most individuals keep accounting records to aid decision making. Most of the material in this book describes business situations, but the principles of accounting apply to the financial considerations of individuals as well. The following sections discuss the range of people and groups who use accounting information and the decisions they make.

Individuals. People such as Melissa Roberts use accounting information in day-to-day affairs to manage their bank accounts, to evaluate job prospects, to make investments, and to decide whether to rent or to buy a house.

Businesses. Managers of businesses use accounting information to set goals for their organizations, to evaluate their progress toward those goals, and to take corrective action if necessary. Decisions based on accounting information may include which building and equipment to purchase, how much merchandise inventory to keep on hand, and how much cash to borrow.

Investors and Creditors. Investors provide the money that businesses need to begin operations. To decide whether to help start a new venture,

EXHIBIT 1-1 *The Accounting System: The Flow of Information*

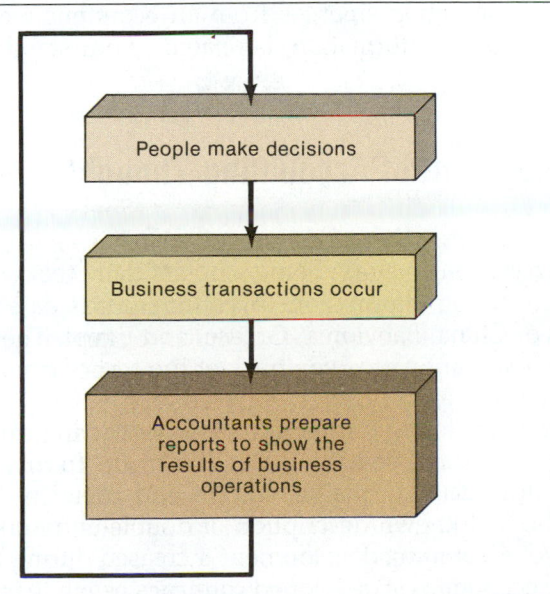

potential investors evaluate what return they can reasonably expect on their investment. This means analyzing the financial statements of the new business. Those people who do invest monitor the progress of the business by analyzing the company's financial statements and by keeping up with its developments in the business press—for example, *The Wall Street Journal*, *Business Week*, *Forbes*, and *Fortune*. Accounting reports are a major source of information for the business press.

Before making a loan, potential lenders determine the borrower's ability to meet scheduled payments. This evaluation includes a projection of future operations, which is based on accounting information.

Government Regulatory Agencies. Most organizations face government regulation. For example, the Securities and Exchange Commission (SEC), a federal agency, requires businesses to disclose certain financial information to the investing public. The SEC, like many government agencies, bases its regulatory activity in part on the accounting information it receives from firms.

Real-World Example: State agencies, such as public utility commissions, use accounting information in setting utility rates.

Taxing Authorities. Local, state, and federal governments levy taxes on individuals and businesses. The amount of the tax is figured using accounting information. Businesses determine their sales tax based on their accounting records that show how much they have sold. Individuals and businesses compute their income tax based on their recorded earnings.

Nonprofit Organizations. Nonprofit organizations—such as churches, most hospitals, government agencies, and colleges, which operate for purposes other than to earn a profit—use accounting information in much the same way that profit-oriented businesses do. Both profit organizations and nonprofit organizations deal with budgets, payrolls, rent payments, and the like—all from the accounting system.

Other users. Employees and labor unions may make wage demands based on the accounting information that shows their employer's reported income. Consumer groups and the general public are also interested in the amount of income that businesses earn. For example, during times of fuel shortages consumer groups have charged that oil companies have earned "obscene profits." On a more positive note, newspapers report "improved profit pictures" of companies as the nation emerges from an economic recession. Such news, based on accounting information, is related to our standard of living.

The Development of Accounting Thought

Real-World Example: The Industrial Revolution, which began in England in the mid 1800's, created the need for large amounts of capital. This need gave rise to the corporation and a new class of owners who did not participate in management but did want assurance of proper business management. English law required corporations to publish financial statements to show stockholders how the business was doing.

Accounting has a long history. Some scholars claim that writing arose in order to record accounting information. Account records date back to the ancient civilizations of China, Babylonia, Greece, and Egypt. The rulers of these civilizations used accounting to keep track of the cost of labor and materials used in building structures like the great pyramids.

Accounting developed further as a result of the information needs of merchants in the city-states of Italy during the 1400s. In that commercial climate the monk Luca Pacioli, a mathematician and friend of Leonardo da Vinci, published the first known description of double-entry bookkeeping in 1494.

The pace of accounting development increased during the Industrial Revolution as the economies of developed countries began to mass-produce goods.

Until that time, merchandise had been priced based on managers' hunches about cost, but increased competition required merchants to adopt more sophisticated accounting systems.

In the nineteenth century, the growth of corporations, especially those in the railroad and steel industries, spurred the development of accounting. Corporation owners—the stockholders—were no longer necessarily the managers of their business. Managers had to create accounting systems to report to the owners how well their businesses were doing.

The role of government has led to still more accounting developments. When the federal government started the income tax, accounting supplied the concept of "income." Also, government at all levels has assumed expanded roles in health, education, labor, and economic planning. To ensure that the information that it uses to make decisions is reliable, the government has required strict accountability in the business community.

The Accounting Profession

OBJECTIVE 2
Identify different aspects of the accounting profession

Positions in the field of accounting may be divided into several areas. Two general classifications are *private accounting* and *public accounting*.

Private accountants work for a single business, such as a local department store, the McDonald's restaurant chain, or the Eastman Kodak Company. Charitable organizations, educational institutions, and government agencies also employ private accountants. The chief accounting officer usually has the title of controller, treasurer, or chief financial officer. Whatever the title, this person usually carries the status of vice-president.

Public accountants are those who serve the general public and collect professional fees for their work, much as doctors and lawyers do. Their work includes auditing, income tax planning and preparation, and management consulting. These specialized accounting services are discussed in the next section. Public accountants are a small fraction (about 10 percent) of all accountants. Those public accountants who have met certain professional requirements are designated as **Certified Public Accountants (CPAs)**.

Some public accountants pool their talents and work together within a single firm. Most public accounting firms are called *CPA firms* because most of their professional employees are CPAs. CPA firms vary greatly in size. Some are small businesses, and others are large partnerships. The largest CPA firms are worldwide partnerships with over 2,000 partners. The six largest American accounting firms, often called the Big Six, are, in alphabetical order,

Arthur Andersen & Co	Ernst & Young
Coopers & Lybrand	Peat Marwick Main & Co.
Deloitte & Touche	Price Waterhouse & Co.

Although these firms employ only about 12 percent of the 350,000 CPAs in the United States, they audit the financial statements of approximately 85 percent of the 2,600 largest corporations. The top partners in large accounting firms earn about the same amount as the top managers of other large businesses.

Exhibit 1-2 shows the accounting positions within public accounting firms and other organizations. Of special interest in the exhibit is the upward movement of accounting personnel, as the arrows show. In particular, note how

Real-World Example: A recent survey by *Forbes* revealed that 30% of the chief executive officers of the 850 largest corporations in the United States had accounting backgrounds—more than from any other business field.

EXHIBIT 1-2 *Accounting Positions within Organizations*

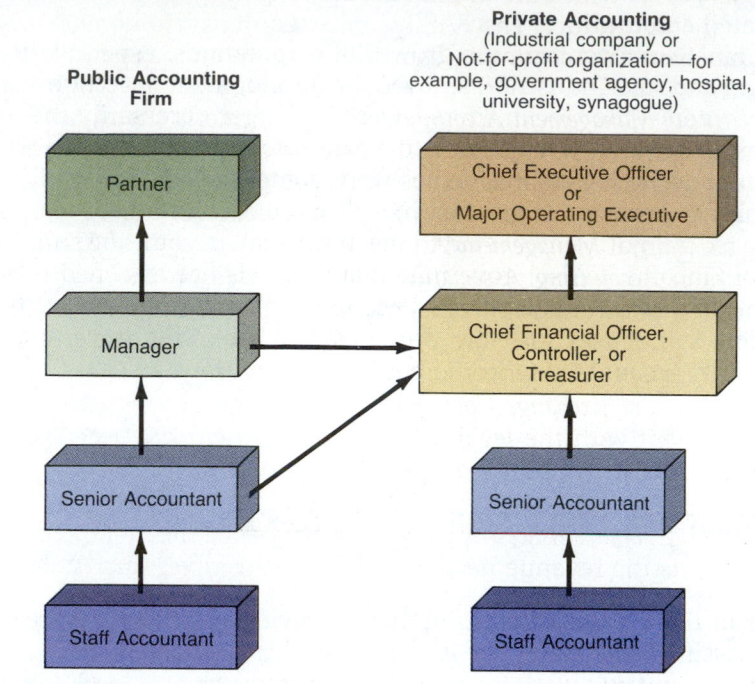

accountants may move from positions in public accounting firms to similar or higher positions in industry and government. This is a frequently traveled career path. Because accounting deals with all facets of an organization—such as purchasing, manufacturing, marketing, and distribution—it provides an excellent basis for gaining broad business experience.

Accounting Organizations and Designations

Real-World Example: The requirements for becoming a CPA vary from state to state. Most states require that the applicant have a bachelor's degree, work experience with a licensed CPA, and passage of a rigorous 2½ day exam. Some states require 150 hours of college credit. The amount of work experience and when an applicant can take the CPA exam vary from state to state.

The position of accounting in today's business world has created the need for control over the professional, educational, and ethical standards for accountants.

The *American Institute of Certified Public Accountants (AICPA)* is the national professional organization of CPAs. A CPA is a professional accountant who earns this title through a combination of education, qualifying experience, and an acceptable score on a written national examination that takes approximately three days. The AICPA prepares and grades the examination and gives the results to the individual states, which then issue licenses that enable qualifying people to practice accounting as CPAs. CPAs must also be of high moral character and must conduct their professional practices according to a code of professional conduct.

The AICPA also develops accounting and auditing principles. The Auditing Standards Board of the AICPA formulates generally accepted auditing standards, which govern the way CPAs perform audits. The AICPA publishes a monthly professional journal, the *Journal of Accountancy.*

The *Financial Accounting Standards Board (FASB)* formulates **generally accepted accounting principles (GAAP)**. These principles are the most important accounting guidelines. The FASB issues documents called *financial accounting standards*, which are to financial accounting what government laws are to our general conduct. The FASB, composed of seven members, is governed by the Financial Accounting Foundation and is an independent organization.

The *Institute of Management Accountants (IMA)*, formerly the *National Association of Accountants (NAA)*, focuses on the practice of management accounting, which is designed to help manage a business. A *CMA*—Certified Management Accountant—earns this designation under the direction of the IMA. The IMA publishes the journal *Management Accounting*.

The *American Accounting Association (AAA)* focuses on the academic and research aspects of accounting. A high percentage of its members are professors. The AAA publishes quarterly journals, *The Accounting Review, Accounting Horizons,* and *Issues in Accounting Education*.

The *Securities and Exchange Commission (SEC)* is an agency of the United States government with the legal power to set and enforce accounting and auditing standards. The SEC has delegated much of this authority to the FASB and the AICPA.

The *Internal Revenue Service (IRS)*, another federal agency, enforces the tax laws and collects the revenue needed to finance the government.

Real-World Example: The predecessor of the FASB was a group called the APB. A major criticism of the APB was that its members were only part-time, and were paid by the businesses for which they worked. This was considered a conflict of interest because the APB members were responsible for making rules that affected the businesses that paid their salaries. The Keating 5, a group of 5 U.S. senators, have been accused of having a conflict of interest in regard to savings and loan organizations. The senators are accused of accepting gifts from S & Ls while being responsible for legislation that would affect the S & Ls.

Ethical Considerations in Accounting and Business

Ethical considerations pervade all areas of accounting and business. Consider a situation that challenges the ethical conduct of the accountant.

Texaco Corporation was recently the defendant in a lawsuit that threatened to put the company out of business. The managers and accountants of Texaco had reason to downplay this lawsuit for fear that customers would stop buying the company's products, that Texaco's stock price would fall, and that banks would stop loaning money to the company. Should Texaco have disclosed this sensitive information? Generally accepted accounting principles required Texaco to describe this situation in its financial statements, and the company's auditor was required to state whether the Texaco disclosure was adequate.

By what criteria do accountants address questions that challenge their ethical conduct? The American Institute of Certified Public Accountants (AICPA), the Institute of Management Accountants (IMA), and most large companies have codes of ethics that bind their members and employees to high levels of ethical conduct.

Real-World Example: During the 1920s, many corporations abused the corporate form of business by reporting things to stockholders that were not true. These abuses contributed to the stock market crash in 1929. In 1933 and 1934, Congress passed the Securities Acts, which created the Securities and Exchange Commission to regulate corporations.

AICPA Code of Professional Conduct

The Code of Professional Conduct was adopted by the members of the AICPA to provide guidance in performing their professional duties. The Preamble to the Code of Conduct states: "[A] certified public accountant assumes an obligation of self-discipline above and beyond the requirements of laws and regulations . . . an unswerving commitment to honorable behavior, even at the sacrifice of personal advantage." Key terms in the Code include *self-discipline, honorable behavior, moral judgments, the public interest, professionalism, integrity,* and *technical and ethical standards.*

Real-World Example: The public is demanding high ethical standards not only for accountants but also for other public figures. At the same time, ethics violations are becoming more common. In a recent survey done by the IMA (formerly the NAA), 87% of managers responded that they were willing to commit fraud. More than 50% would intentionally misstate assets, and 38% would intentionally pad a government contract. This survey alone indicates the need for increased emphasis on ethics.

IMA Standards of Ethical Behavior

The opening paragraph of the IMA Standards of Ethical Conduct states: "Management accountants have an obligation to the organizations they serve, their profession, the public, and themselves to maintain the highest standards of ethical conduct." The Ethical Standards include sections on competence, confidentiality, integrity, objectivity, and resolution of ethical conflict. The requirements for a high level of professional conduct are similar to those in the AICPA code.

The Boeing Company's Business Conduct Guidelines

Most corporations impose standards of ethical conduct on their employees. The Boeing Company, a leading manufacturer of aircraft, has a highly developed set of business conduct guidelines. In the introduction, the chairperson of the board and chief executive officer state: "We owe our success as much to our reputation for integrity as we do to the quality and dependability of our products and services. This reputation is fragile and can easily be lost." For example, Boeing could be ruined if shoddy work led to plane crashes.

Specialized Accounting Services

Because accounting affects people in many different fields, public accounting and private accounting include specialized services.

Public Accounting

Auditing is the accounting profession's most significant service to the public. An audit is the independent examination that ensures the reliability of the accounting reports that management prepares and submits to investors, creditors, and others outside the business. In carrying out an audit, CPAs from outside a business examine the business's financial statements. If the CPAs believe that these documents are a fair presentation of the business's operations, the CPAs give a professional opinion stating that the firm's financial statements are in accordance with generally accepted accounting principles, which is the standard. Why is the audit so important? Creditors considering loans want assurance that the facts and figures the borrower submits are reliable. Stockholders, who have invested in the company, need to know that the financial picture management shows them is complete. Government agencies need accurate information from businesses.

Tax accounting has two aims: complying with the tax laws and minimizing the taxes to be paid. Because federal income tax rates range as high as 31 percent for individuals and 34 percent for corporations, reducing income tax is an important management consideration. Tax work by accountants consists of preparing tax returns and planning business transactions in order to minimize taxes. CPAs advise individuals on what types of investments to make and on how to structure their transactions.

Management consulting is the catchall term that describes the wide scope of advice CPAs provide to help managers run a business. As CPAs conduct audits, they look deep into a business's operations. With the insight they gain,

Discussion Question: As an investor looking at the financial statements of a company, how would you know if the company really had the amount of cash on hand that it had reported? What keeps the company from overstating its profits? ANSWER: An auditor will have examined every item listed on the financial statements and have given written certification of their reliability.

Real-World Example: The tax laws that determine what is reported on the tax return do not also determine what information is reported in the financial statements.

The tax laws change in some way almost every year. The Tax Reform Act of 1986 made sweeping changes in the tax law. The changes made in the 1990 tax law were minor. Among other things, the 1990 changes reduced the deductions for personal interest expense and for charitable contributions by high-income taxpayers, and diminished the tax advantages of employee stock ownership plans.

they often make suggestions for improvements in the business's management structure and accounting systems. (We discuss these areas of accounting in the next section.) Management consulting is the fastest-growing service provided by accountants.

Private Accounting

Cost accounting analyzes a business's costs to help managers control expenses. Good cost accounting records guide managers in pricing their products and services to achieve greater profits. Also, cost accounting information shows management when a product is not profitable and should be dropped.

Budgeting sets sales and profit goals and develops detailed plans—called budgets—for achieving those goals. Some of the most successful companies in the United States have been pioneers in the field of budgeting—Procter & Gamble and General Electric, for example.

Information systems design identifies the organization's information needs, both internal and external. Using flow charts and manuals, designers develop and implement the system to meet those needs.

Internal auditing is performed by a business's own accountants. Large organizations—Motorola, Bank of America, and 3M among them—maintain a staff of internal auditors. These accountants evaluate the firm's own accounting and management systems to improve operating efficiency and ensure that employees follow management's policies.

Exhibit 1-3 summarizes these accounting specializations. They may also

Point to Stress: Even a small local bank will have at least one person identified as an internal auditor.

Discussion Question: For what decisions might outsiders need accounting information? *ANSWER:* Whether to lend money; whether to invest or to sell one's investments.

EXHIBIT 1-3 *Public and Private Accounting*   Transparency T1-1

Public Accounting

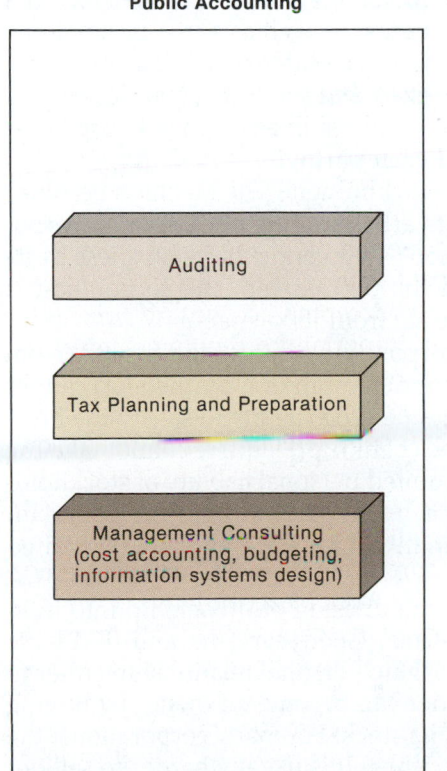

Private Accounting

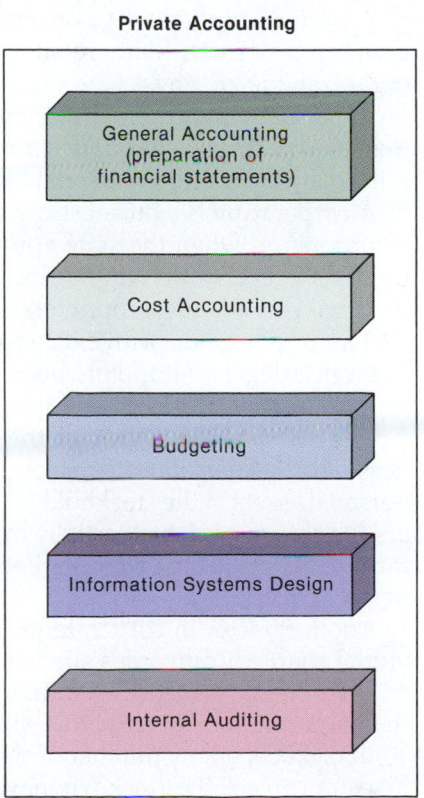

be grouped under the headings financial accounting and management accounting.

Financial accounting provides information to people outside the firm. Creditors and stockholders, for example, are not part of the day-to-day management of the company. Likewise, government agencies, such as the SEC, and the general public are external users of a firm's accounting information. Chapters 2 through 19 of this book deal primarily with financial accounting.

Management accounting generates confidential information for internal decision makers, such as top executives, department heads, college deans, and hospital administrators. Chapters 20 through 26 cover management accounting.

Types of Business Organizations

Businesses take one of three forms of organization, and in some cases the accounting procedures depend on the organization form. Therefore, you should understand the differences between a proprietorship, a partnership, and a corporation.

A **proprietorship** has a single owner, called the proprietor, who is usually also the manager. Proprietorships tend to be small retail establishments and individual professional businesses, such as those of physicians, attorneys, and accountants. From the accounting viewpoint each proprietorship is distinct from its proprietor. Thus the accounting records of the proprietorship do *not* include records of the proprietor's personal affairs.

A **partnership** joins two or more individuals together as co-owners. Each owner is a partner. Many retail establishments, as well as some professional organizations of physicians, attorneys, and accountants, are partnerships. Most partnerships are small and medium-sized, but some are gigantic, exceeding 2,000 partners. Accounting treats the partnership as a separate organization, distinct from the personal affairs of each partner.

A **corporation** is a business owned by **stockholders.** The business becomes a corporation when the state approves its articles of incorporation. A corporation is a legal entity, an "artificial person" that conducts its business in its own name. Like the proprietorship and the partnership, the corporation is also an organization with existence separate from its owners.

From a legal standpoint, however, corporations differ significantly from proprietorships and partnerships. If a proprietorship or a partnership cannot pay its debts, lenders can take the owner's personal assets to satisfy the business's obligations. But if a corporation goes bankrupt, lenders cannot take the personal assets of the stockholders. This limited personal liability of stockholders for corporate debts partially explains why corporations are the dominant form of business organization: People can invest in corporations with limited personal risk.

Another factor in corporate growth is the division of ownership into individual shares. Companies such as Coca-Cola, Goodyear Tire, and IBM have millions of shares of stock. An investor with no personal relationship either to the corporation or to any other stockholder can become an owner by buying 30, 100, 5,000, or any number of shares of its stock. For many corporations, the investor can sell the stock whenever he wishes. It is usually harder to sell out of a proprietorship or a partnership.

Accounting for corporations includes some unique complexities. For this reason, we initially focus on proprietorships. Partnerships are covered in Chapter 13, and corporations begin in Chapter 14.

Accounting Concepts and Principles

OBJECTIVE 3
Apply accounting concepts and principles to business situations

Accounting practices rest on certain guidelines. The rules that govern how accountants measure, process, and communicate financial information fall under the heading GAAP, which stands for generally accepted accounting principles.

The term *accounting principles* is broader than you might at first think. Generally accepted accounting principles include not only principles but also concepts and methods that identify the proper way to produce accounting information. Generally accepted accounting principles are very much like the law—a set of rules for conducting behavior in a way acceptable to the majority of people. GAAP rests on a conceptual framework written by the Financial Accounting Standards Board. The primary objective of financial reporting is to provide information useful for making investment and lending decisions. To be useful, information must be relevant, reliable, and comparable. Accountants strive to meet these goals in the information they produce. Your study of this course will expose you to the generally accepted methods of accounting. First, however, you need to understand the *entity concept*, the *reliability principle*, the *cost principle*, the *going-concern concept*, and the *stable-monetary-unit concept*. These are basic to your first exposure to accounting.

Point to Stress: Think of GAAP as the rules or guidelines or standards that accountants must abide by when preparing financial statements.

The Entity Concept

The most basic concept in accounting is that of the **entity**. An accounting entity is an organization or a section of an organization that stands apart from other organizations and individuals as a separate economic unit. From an accounting perspective, sharp boundaries are drawn around each entity so as not to confuse its affairs with those of other entities.

Consider Mazzio, a pizzeria owner whose bank account shows a $20,000 balance at the end of the year. Only half of that amount—$10,000—grew from the business's operations. The other $10,000 arose from the sale of the family motorboat. If Mazzio follows the entity concept, he will account for the money generated by the business—one economic unit—separately from the money generated by the sale of an item belonging not to the business but to himself— a second economic unit. This separation makes it possible to view the business's financial position clearly.

Suppose Mazzio disregards the entity concept and treats the full $20,000 amount as resulting from the pizzeria's operations. He will be misled into believing that the business has produced twice as much cash as it has. The steps needed to improve the business will likely not be taken.

Consider GM, a huge organization made up of its Chevrolet, Buick, Oldsmobile, Cadillac, and Pontiac divisions. GM management considers each division as a separate accounting entity, and the following example shows why. Suppose sales in the Oldsmobile division are dropping drastically. GM would do well to come up with an immediate solution to the problem. But if sales figures from all five divisions are treated as a single amount, then management will not even know the company is not selling enough Oldsmobiles.

Discussion Question: Suppose that John Doe owns two businesses, a car dealership and a car rental agency. John does not maintain separate records for the two businesses, which have combined income of $50,000. What type of problem could be overlooked in this situation? *ANSWER:* If one of the two businesses is unprofitable, then John would not know which it was unless he kept separate books for each.

If the car rental agency is losing $10,000 a year, how much would John's profits increase if he discontinued operating the car rental agency? *ANSWER:* His profits would increase by $10,000.

In summary, business transactions should not be confused with personal transactions. Similarly, the transactions of different entities should not be accounted for together. Each entity should be evaluated separately.

The Reliability (or Objectivity) Principle

Accounting records and statements are based on the most reliable data available so that they will be as accurate and as useful as possible. This is the *reliability principle*. Reliable data are verifiable. They may be confirmed by any independent observer. Ideally, then, accounting records are based on information that flows from activities that are documented by objective evidence. Without the reliability principle, also called the *objectivity principle*, accounting records would be based on whims and opinions and would be subject to dispute.

Suppose that you start a stereo shop, and to have a place for operations, you transfer a small building to the business. You believe the building is worth $155,000. To confirm its value, you hire two real estate professionals, who appraise the building at $147,000. Is $155,000 or $147,000 the more reliable estimate of the building's value? The real estate appraisal of $147,000 is, because it is supported by external, independent, objective observation.

The Cost Principle

The *cost principle* states that assets and services that are acquired should be recorded at their actual cost (also called historical cost). Even though the purchaser may believe the price paid is a bargain, the item is recorded at the price paid in the transaction.

Suppose your stereo shop purchases some stereo equipment from a supplier who is going out of business. Assume you get a good deal on this purchase and pay only $2,000 for merchandise that would have cost you $3,000 elsewhere. The cost principle requires you to record this merchandise at its actual cost of $2,000, not the $3,000 that you believe the equipment to be worth.

The cost principle also holds that the accounting records should maintain the historical cost of an asset for as long as the business holds the asset. Why? Because cost is a reliable measure. Suppose your store holds the stereo equipment for six months. During that time, stereo prices increase, and the equipment can be sold for $3,500. Should its accounting value—the figure "on the books"—be the actual cost of $2,000 or the current market value of $3,500? According to the cost principle, the accounting value of the equipment remains at actual cost, $2,000.

The Going-Concern Concept

Another reason for measuring assets at historical cost is the *going-concern concept*, which holds that the entity will remain in operation for the foreseeable future. Most assets, such as supplies, land, buildings, and equipment, are acquired to use rather than to sell. Under the going-concern concept, accountants assume that the business will remain in operation long enough to use existing assets for their intended purpose. The market value of an asset—the price for which the asset can be sold—may change many times during the asset's life. Therefore, an asset's current market value may not be relevant for decision making. Moreover, historical cost is a more reliable accounting measure for assets.

To better understand the going-concern concept, consider the alternative, which is to *go out of business.* You have probably seen stores advertise a Going Out of Business Sale. The entity is trying to sell all its assets. In that case, the relevant measure of the assets is their current market value. However, going out of business is the exception rather than the rule, and for this reason accounting records list assets at their historical cost.

The Stable-Monetary-Unit Concept

We think of a loaf of bread, a suit of clothes, and a month's apartment rent in terms of its dollar value. In the United States accountants record transactions in dollars because the dollar is the medium of exchange. British accountants record transactions in terms of the pound sterling, and in Japan transactions are recorded in yen.

Unlike a liter, a mile, or an acre, the value of a dollar changes over time. A rise in prices is called inflation, and during inflation a dollar will purchase less milk, less toothpaste, and less of other necessities. When prices are relatively stable—when there is little inflation—a dollar's purchasing power is also stable. Most periods of American history have experienced low rates of inflation.

Accountants assume that the dollar's purchasing power is relatively stable. The *stable-monetary-unit concept* is the basis for ignoring the effect of inflation in the accounting records. It allows accountants to add and subtract dollar amounts as though each dollar had the same purchasing power.

Accountants have devised ways to take inflation into account. When inflation accelerates, the FASB can require companies to show inflation-adjusted amounts in reports. As we continue to explore accounting, we will discuss other principles that guide accountants.

The Accounting Equation

Financial statements tell us how a business is performing and where it stands. We will see several financial statements in this course of study. But how do accountants arrive at the items and amounts that make up the financial statements?

The most basic tool of the accountant is the accounting equation. This equation presents the assets of the business and the claims to those assets. **Assets** are the economic resources of a business that are expected to be of benefit in the future. Cash, office supplies, merchandise, furniture, land, and buildings are examples. Claims to those assets come from two sources.

Liabilities are "outsider claims," which are economic obligations—debts—payable to outsiders. These outside parties are called *creditors.* For example, a creditor who has loaned money to a business has a claim—a legal right—to a part of the assets until the business pays the debt. "Insider claims" are called **owners' equity** or **capital.** These are the claims held by the owners of the business. An owner has a claim to the entity's assets because he or she has invested in the buiness. Owners' equity is measured by subtracting liabilities from assets.

Discussion Question: (To illustrate the concept of the accounting equation, try asking these questions.) What kind of assets do I as an individual own? *ANSWER:* Car, home, stereo, furniture, stock, etc. How do I acquire these assets? *ANSWER:* (1) Salaries and income from investments that I own and (2) borrowing. The accounting equation illustrates this. Assets=the things that an entity has to use. Liabilities=the amount of money owed. Owner's Equity=the portion of entity assets that the owner owns free and clear of debt.

OBJECTIVE 4

Use the accounting
equation to describe
an organization's financial
position

The accounting equation shows the relationship among assets, liabilities, and owner's equity. Assets appear on the left-hand side of the equation. The legal and economic claims against the assets—the liabilities and owner's equity—appear on the right-hand side of the equation:

$$\text{ASSETS} = \text{LIABILITIES} + \text{OWNER'S EQUITY}$$

Let's take a closer look at the elements that make up the accounting equation. Suppose you run a business that supplies meat to fast-food restaurants. Some customers may pay you in cash when you deliver the meat. Cash is an asset. Other customers may buy on credit and promise to pay you within a certain time after delivery. This promise is also an asset because it is an economic resource that will benefit you in the future when you receive cash from the customer. The meat supplier calls this promise an **account receivable.** If the promise that entitles you to receive cash in the future is formally written out, it is called a **note receivable**. All receivables are assets.

The fast-food restaurant's promise to pay you for the meat it purchases on credit creates a debt for the restaurant. This liability is an **account payable** of the restaurant, which means that the debt is not formally written out. Instead it is backed up by the reputation and the credit standing of the restaurant and its owner. A written promise of future payment is called a **note payable**. All payables are liabilities.

Owner's equity is the amount of the assets that remains after subtracting liabilities. We often write the accounting equation to show that the owner's claim to business assets is a residual:

$$\text{ASSETS} - \text{LIABILITIES} = \text{OWNER'S EQUITY}$$

Class Exercises: If the assets of a business are $174,300 and the liabilities are $82,000, how much is the owner's equity? *ANSWER:* $92,300

If the owner's equity in a business is $22,000 and the liabilities are $36,000, how much are the assets of the business? *ANSWER:* $58,000

Accounting for Business Transactions

In accounting terms, a **transaction** is any event that *both* affects the financial position of the business entity *and* may be reliably recorded. Many events may affect a company, including (1) elections, (2) economic booms and recessions, (3) purchases and sales of merchandise inventory, (4) payment of rent, (5) collection of cash from customers, and so on. However, the accountant records only events with effects that can be measured reliably as transactions.

Which of the above five events would the accountant record? The answer is events (3), (4), and (5) because their dollar amounts can be measured reliably. Dollar effects of elections and economic trends cannot be measured reliably, so they would not be recorded even though they might affect the business more than events (3), (4), and (5).

To illustrate accounting for business transactions, let's assume that Gary Lyon has recently become a CPA and opens his own accounting practice. Because the business has a single owner, it is called a proprietorship.

We now consider eleven events and analyze each in terms of its effect on the accounting equation of Gary Lyon's accounting practice. Transaction analysis is the essence of accounting.

Discussion Question: A transaction is an event that affects the business and can be measured in dollars. Would a Jack in the Box restaurant record as a transaction the opening of a new Whataburger restaurant down the street? *ANSWER:* No. Although it is an event that could affect the business, it cannot be measured in dollars.

OBJECTIVE 5

Use the accounting
equation to analyze
business transactions

Transaction 1. Gary Lyon invests $50,000 of his money to begin the business. Specifically, he deposits $50,000 in a bank account entitled Gary Lyon, CPA. The effect of this transaction on the accounting equation of the business entity is

Assets		Liabilities +	Owner's Equity	Type of Owner's Equity Transaction
Cash	=		Gary Lyon, Capital	
(1) +50,000			+50,000	Owner investment

The first transaction increases both the assets, in this case Cash, and the owner's equity of the business, Gary Lyon, Capital. The transaction involves no liabilities of the business because it creates no obligation for Lyon to pay an outside party. To the right of the transaction we write "Owner investment" to keep track of the reason for the effect on owner's equity.

Note that the amount on the left side of the equation equals the amount on the right side. This equality must hold for every transaction.

Transaction 2.   Lyon purchases land for a future office location, paying cash of $40,000. The effect of this transaction on the accounting equation is

Assets			Liabilities + Owner's Equity	Type of Owner's Equity Transaction
Cash +	Land	=	Gary Lyon, Capital	
(1) 50,000			50,000	Owner investment
(2) −40,000 +	40,000			
Bal. 10,000	40,000		50,000	
50,000			50,000	

Point to Stress: Accounting can be summarized using the accounting equation. After each transaction, make sure that the accounting equation is in balance.

The cash purchase of land increases one asset, Land, and decreases another asset, Cash, by the same amount. After the transaction is completed, Lyon's business has cash of $10,000, land of $40,000, no liabilities, and owner's equity of $50,000. Note that the sums of the balances (which we abbreviate Bal.) on each side of the equation are equal. This equality must always exist.

Transaction 3.   Lyon buys stationery and other office supplies, agreeing to pay $500 within thirty days. This transaction increases the assets and the liabilities of the business. Its effect on the accounting equation is

Assets				Liabilities + Owner's Equity	
Cash +	Office Supplies +	Land	=	Accounts Payable +	Gary Lyon, Capital
Bal. 10,000		40,000			50,000
(3)	+500			+500	
Bal. 10,000	500	40,000		500	50,000
50,500				50,500	

The asset affected is Office Supplies, and the liability is called an account payable. The term *payable* signifies a liability. Since Lyon is obligated to pay $500 in the future but signs no formal promissory note, we record the liability as an Account Payable, not as a Note Payable. We say that purchases supported by the general credit standing of the buyer are made on *open account.*

Point to Stress: Revenue is not the same as cash. Borrowing money and receiving cash for services rendered both involve the receipt of cash, but the borrowing transaction does not produce revenue. Revenue results from delivering goods or performing a service, whether or not cash is received.

Transaction 4. The purpose of business is to increase assets and owner's equity through **revenues,** which are amounts earned by delivering goods or services to customers. Revenues increase owner's equity because they increase the business's assets but not its liabilities. As a result, the owner's interest in the assets of the business increases.

Exhibit 1-4 shows that owner investments and revenues increase the owner's equity of the business.

The exhibit also indicates the types of transactions that decrease owner's equity. Owner withdrawals are those amounts removed from the business by the owner. Withdrawals are the opposite of owner investments. Expenses are the cost of doing business and are the opposite of revenues. Our illustration will also show how to account for expenses and withdrawals. Gary Lyon earns service revenue by providing professional accounting services for his clients. Assume he earns $5,500 and collects this amount in cash. The effect on the accounting equation is an increase in the asset Cash and an increase in Gary Lyon, Capital, as follows:

		Assets				Liabilities +	Owner's Equity	Type of Owner's Equity Transaction
	Cash	+ Office Supplies +	Land			Accounts Payable +	Gary Lyon, Capital	
Bal.	10,000	500	40,000		=	500	50,000	
(4)	+ 5,500						+ 5,500	Service revenue
Bal.	15,500	500	40,000			500	55,500	
		56,000					56,000	

This revenue transaction caused the business to grow, as shown by the increase in total assets and total liabilities plus owner's equity.

Transaction 5. Lyon performs services for a client who does not pay immediately. In return for his accounting services, Lyon receives the client's promise to pay the $3,000 amount within one month. This promise is an asset to Lyon, an account receivable because he expects to collect the cash in the future. In accounting, we say that Lyon performed this service *on account.* When the business performs service for a client or a customer, the business earns revenue regardless of whether it receives cash immediately or expects to

EXHIBIT 1-4 *Transactions That Increase and Decrease Owner's Equity*

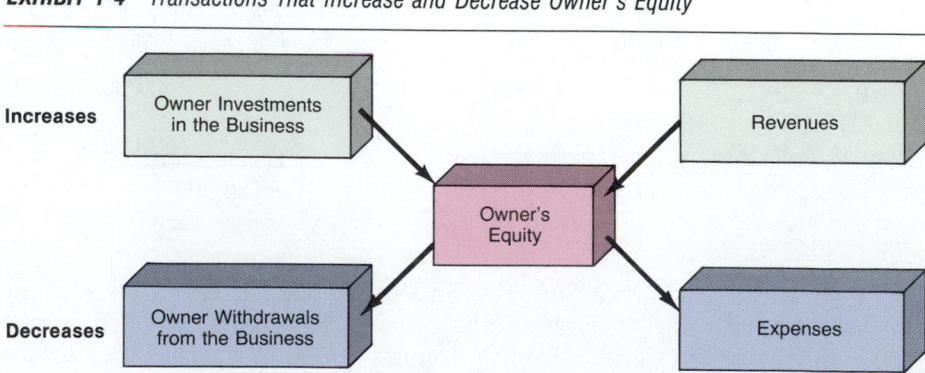

collect cash later. This $3,000 of service revenue is as real to Lyon's business as the $5,500 of revenue that he collected immediately in the preceding transaction. Lyon records an increase in the asset accounts receivable and an increase in owner's equity as follows:

	Assets						Liabilities +	Owner's Equity	Type of Owner's Equity Transaction
	Cash	+	Accounts Receivable	+	Office Supplies	+	Land	Accounts Payable +	Gary Lyon, Capital	
Bal.	15,500				500		40,000	500	55,500	
(5)			+3,000						+ 3,000	Service revenue
Bal.	15,500		3,000		500		40,000	500	58,500	
			59,000						59,000	

Again, this revenue transaction caused the business to grow.

Transaction 6. In earning revenue a business incurs expenses. **Expenses** are decreases in owner's equity that occur in the course of business operations. Expenses decrease owner's equity because they use up the business's assets. Expenses include office rent, salaries paid to employees, newspaper advertisements, and utility payments for light, electricity, gas, and so forth. During the month, Lyon pays $2,700 in cash expenses: office rent, $1,100; employee salary, $1,200 (for a part-time assistant); and total utilities, $400. The effect on the accounting equation is

Point to Stress: Expenses are not the same as cash payments. Purchase of land and payment of salaries both involve cash payments, but the land purchase is not an expense because the land is an asset. Expenses result from using goods or services necessary to the business, not from purchasing assets.

	Assets						Liabilities +	Owner's Equity	Type of Owner's Equity Transaction
	Cash	+	Accounts Receivable	+	Office Supplies	+	Land	Accounts Payable +	Gary Lyon, Capital	
Bal.	15,500		3,000		500		40,000	500	58,500	
(6)	− 2,700								− 1,100	Rent expense
									− 1,200	Salary expense
									− 400	Utilities expense
Bal.	12,800		3,000		500		40,000	500	55,800	
			56,300						56,300	

Because expenses have the opposite effect of revenues, they cause the business to shrink, as shown by the smaller amounts of total assets and total owners' equity.

Each expense should be recorded in a separate transaction. Here, for simplicity, they are recorded together. Note that even though the figure $2,700 does not appear on the right-hand side of the equation, the three individual expenses add up to a $2,700 total. As a result, the "balance" of the equation holds, as we know it must.

Businesspeople, Gary Lyon included, run their businesses with the objective of having more revenues than expenses. An excess of total revenues over total expenses is called **net income, net earnings,** or **net profit**. If total expenses exceed total revenues, the result is called a **net loss**.

Class Exercise: Suppose a company reported monthly revenues of $77,600 and expenses of $81,300. What is the company's net income or net loss for the month? ANSWER: Net loss of $3,700, because expenses are greater than revenues. ($81,300 − $77,600)

Transaction 7. Lyon pays $400 to the store from which he purchased $500 worth of office supplies in Transaction 3. In accounting, we say that he pays $400 *on account*. The effect on the accounting equation is a decrease in the asset Cash and a decrease in the liability Accounts Payable as follows:

	Cash	Accounts + Receivable	Office + Supplies	+ Land		Accounts Payable	Gary Lyon, + Capital
		Assets				**Liabilities +**	**Owner's Equity**
Bal.	12,800	3,000	500	40,000	=	500	55,800
(7)	− 400					−400	
Bal.	12,400	3,000	500	40,000		100	55,800
		55,900				55,900	

The payment of cash on account has no effect on the asset Office Supplies because the payment does not increase or decrease the supplies available to the business.

Transaction 8. Lyon remodels his home at a cost of $30,000, paying cash from his personal funds. This event is a *nonbusiness* transaction. It has no effect on Lyon's accounting practice and therefore is not recorded by the business. It is a transaction of the Gary Lyon *personal* entity, not the Gary Lyon, CPA, *business* entity. We are focusing now solely on the business entity, and this event does not affect it. This transaction illustrates an application of the *entity concept*.

Point to Stress: Transaction 9 does not affect both sides of the accounting equation. Instead, an asset (Cash) increases and another asset (Accounts Receivable) decreases, leaving the accounting equation in balance. The entire business activity shows on one side of the accounting equation.

Transaction 9. In Transaction 5, Gary Lyon performed service for a client on account. Lyon now collects $1,000 from the client. We say that Lyon collects the cash *on account*. Lyon will record an increase in the asset Cash. Should he also record an increase in service revenue? No, because Lyon already recorded the revenue when he earned it in Transaction 5. The phrase "collect cash on account" means to record an increase in Cash and a decrease in the asset Accounts Receivable. The effect on the accounting equation is

	Cash	Accounts + Receivable	Office + Supplies	+ Land		Accounts Payable	Gary Lyon, + Capital
		Assets				**Liabilities +**	**Owner's Equity**
Bal.	12,400	3,000	500	40,000	=	100	55,800
(9)	+ 1,000	−1,000					
Bal.	13,400	2,000	500	40,000		100	55,800
		55,900				55,900	

Total assets are unchanged from the preceding transaction's total. Why? Because Lyon merely exchanged one asset for another. Also, total liabilities and owner's equity are unchanged.

Transaction 10. An individual approaches Lyon about selling a parcel of the land owned by the Gary Lyon, CPA, entity. Lyon and the other person agree to a sale price of $22,000, which is equal to Lyon's cost of the land. Lyon's business sells the land and receives $22,000 cash, and the effect on the accounting equation is

Point to Stress: Revenue did not result from the sale of the land. Why not? The land was not intended for sale to customers; it was intended for use in Gary Lyon's business.

	Assets						Liabilities +	Owner's Equity
	Cash	+ Accounts Receivable	+ Office Supplies	+ Land			Accounts Payable +	Gary Lyon, Capital
Bal.	13,400	2,000	500	40,000		=	100	55,800
(10)	+22,000			−22,000				
Bal.	35,400	2,000	500	18,000			100	55,800
		55,900						55,900

Transaction 11. Lyon withdraws $2,100 cash from the business for personal use. The effect on the accounting equation is

	Assets						Liabilities +	Owner's Equity	Type of Owner's Equity Transaction
	Cash	+ Accounts Receivable	+ Office Supplies	+ Land			Accounts Payable +	Gary Lyon, Capital	
Bal.	35,400	2,000	500	18,000		=	100	55,800	
(11)	− 2,100							− 2,100	Owner withdrawals
Bal.	33,300	2,000	500	18,000			100	53,700	
		53,800						53,800	

Lyon's withdrawal of $2,100 in cash decreases the asset Cash and also the owner's equity of the business.

Does this withdrawal decrease the business entity's holdings? The answer is yes because the cash withdrawn is no longer available for business use after Lyon spends it on food, clothing, home mortgage payments, and so on. The withdrawal does *not* represent a business expense, however, because the cash is used for personal affairs unrelated to the business. We record this decrease in owner's equity as Withdrawals. Another acceptable title is Drawing.

Typical Student Misconception: Point out that when the owner makes a withdrawal from the business, it is generally in the form of cash. It is a reduction in the owner's investment or equity in the business, but it is never considered a business expense.

Evaluating Business Transactions

Exhibit 1-5 summarizes the 11 preceding transactions. Panel A of the exhibit lists the details of the transactions, and Panel B presents the analysis. As you study the exhibit, note that every transaction maintains the equality:

ASSETS = LIABILITIES + OWNER'S EQUITY

Panel A—Details of transactions

1. Lyon invested $50,000 cash in the business.
2. Paid $40,000 cash for land.
3. Purchased $500 of office supplies on account.
4. Received $5,500 cash from clients for accounting service revenue earned.
5. Performed accounting service for a client on account, $3,000.
6. Paid cash expenses: rent, $1,100; employee salary, $1,200; utilities, $400.
7. Paid $400 on the account payable created in Transaction 3.
8. Remodeled his personal residence. This is not a business transaction.
9. Received $1,000 on the account receivable created in Transaction 5.
10. Sold land for cash equal to its cost of $22,000.
11. Withdrew $2,100 cash for personal living expenses.

Panel B—Analysis of transactions

	Assets					Liabilities +	Owner's Equity	Type of Owner's Equity Transaction
	Cash	+ Accounts Receivable +	Office Supplies +	Land		Accounts Payable +	Gary Lyon, Capital	
(1)	+50,000						+50,000	Owner investment
Bal.	50,000						50,000	
(2)	−40,000			+40,000				
Bal.	10,000			40,000			50,000	
(3)			+500			+500		
Bal.	10,000		500	40,000		500	50,000	
(4)	+ 5,500						+ 5,500	Service revenue
Bal.	15,500		500	40,000		500	55,500	
(5)		+3,000					+ 3,000	Service revenue
Bal.	15,500	3,000	500	40,000		500	58,500	
(6)	− 2,700				=		− 1,100	Rent expense
							− 1,200	Salary expense
							− 400	Utilities expense
Bal.	12,800	3,000	500	40,000		500	55,800	
(7)	− 400					−400		
Bal.	12,400	3,000	500	40,000		100	55,800	
(8)	Not a business transaction							
(9)	+ 1,000	−1,000						
Bal.	13,400	2,000	500	40,000		100	55,800	
(10)	+22,000			−22,000				
Bal.	35,400	2,000	500	18,000		100	55,800	
(11)	− 2,100						− 2,100	Owner withdrawal
Bal.	33,300	2,000	500	18,000		100	53,700	
	53,800					53,800		

Financial Statements

The analysis of the transactions complete, what is the next step in the accounting process? How does an accountant present the results of the analysis? We now look at the *financial statements*, which are formal reports of financial information about the entity. The primary financial statements are the (1) balance sheet, (2) income statement, (3) statement of owner's equity, and (4) statement of cash flows. In this chapter, we discuss and illustrate the first three statements. We cover the statement of cash flows in Chapter 18.

The **balance sheet** lists all the *assets, liabilities,* and *owner's equity* of an entity as of a specific date, usually the end of a month or a year. The balance sheet is like a snapshot of the entity. For this reason, it is also called the **statement of financial position**.

The **income statement** presents a summary of the *revenues* and *expenses* of an entity for a specific period of time, such as a month or a year. The income statement, also called the **statement of earnings** or **statement of operations**, is like a moving picture of the entity's operations during the period. The income statement holds perhaps the most important single piece of information about a business—its net income, which is revenues minus expenses. If expenses exceed revenues, the result is a net loss for the period.

The **statement of owner's equity** presents a summary of the changes that occurred in the owner's equity of the entity during a specific time period, such as a month or a year. Increases in owner's equity arise from investments by the owner and from net income earned during the period. Decreases result from withdrawals by the owner and from a net loss for the period. Net income or net loss comes directly from the income statement. Investments and withdrawals by the owner are capital transactions between the business and its owner, so they do not affect the income statement.

Each financial statement has a heading, which gives the name of the business (in our discussion, Gary Lyon, CPA), the name of the particular statement, and the date or time period covered by the statement. A balance sheet taken at the end of year 19X4 would be dated December 31, 19X4. A balance sheet prepared at the end of March 19X7 is dated March 31, 19X7.

An income statement or a statement of owner's equity covering an annual period ending in December 19X5 is dated For the Year Ended December 31, 19X5. A monthly income statement or statement of owner's equity for September 19X9 has in its heading For the Month Ended September 30, 19X9, Month Ended September 30, 19X9, or For the Month of September 19X9. Income is meaningless unless identified with a particular time period.

Exhibit 1-6 illustrates all three statements. Their data come from the transaction analysis in Exhibit 1-5. We are assuming the transactions occurred during the month of April 19X1. Study the exhibit carefully, because it shows the relationships among the three financial statements.

Observe the following in Exhibit 1-6:

1. The *income statement* for the month ended April 30, 19X1
    a. Reports all *revenues* and all *expenses* during the period. Revenues and expenses are reported only on the income statement.
    b. Reports *net income* of the period if total revenues exceed total expenses, as in the case of Gary Lyon's accounting practice for April. If total expenses exceed total revenues, the result is a *net loss.*
2. The *statement of owner's equity* for the month ended April 30, 19X1
    a. Opens with the owner's capital balance at the beginning of the period.

EXHIBIT 1-6 *Financial Statements of Gary Lyon, CPA*

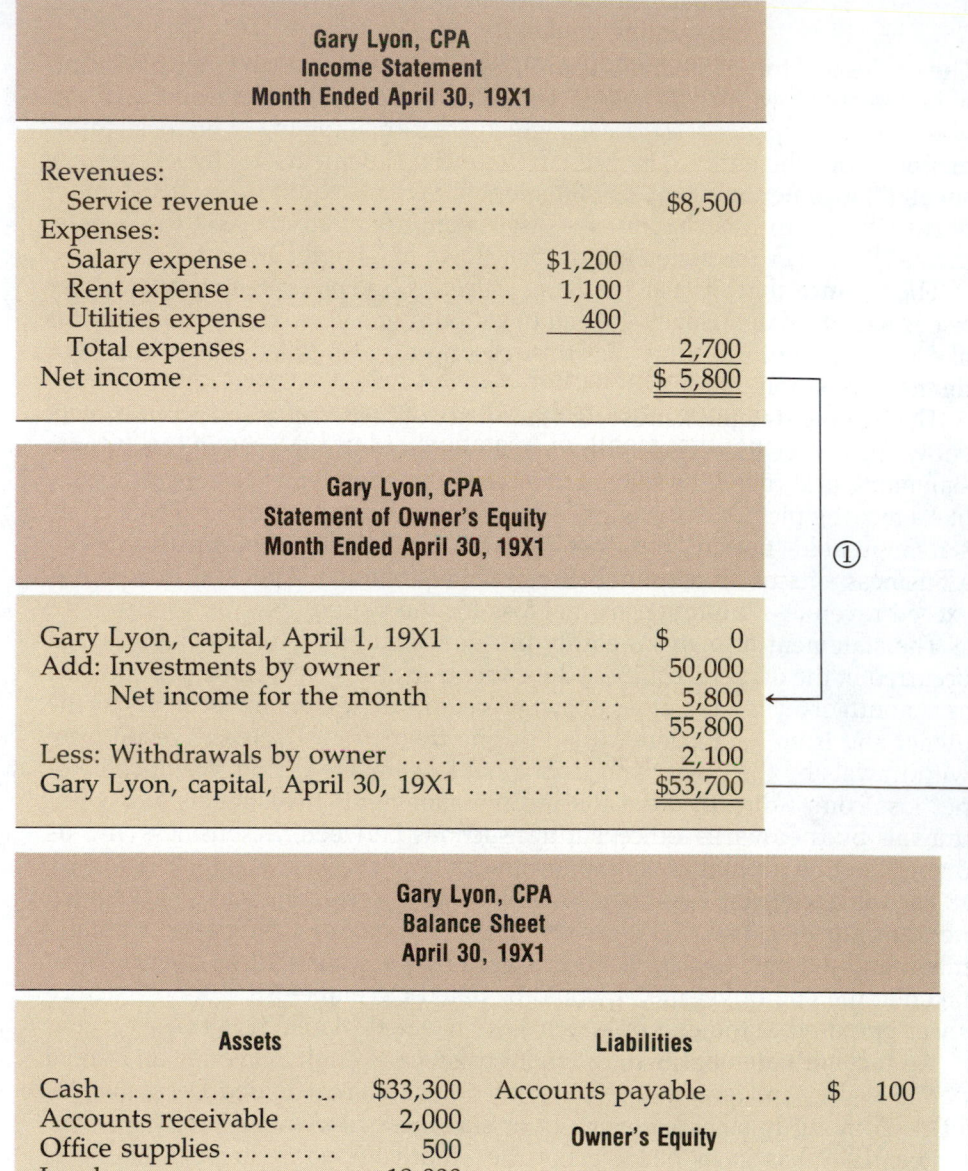

Gary Lyon, CPA Income Statement Month Ended April 30, 19X1		
Revenues:		
Service revenue...................		$8,500
Expenses:		
Salary expense...................	$1,200	
Rent expense....................	1,100	
Utilities expense	400	
Total expenses....................		2,700
Net income.......................		$ 5,800

Gary Lyon, CPA Statement of Owner's Equity Month Ended April 30, 19X1	
Gary Lyon, capital, April 1, 19X1	$ 0
Add: Investments by owner	50,000
Net income for the month	5,800
	55,800
Less: Withdrawals by owner	2,100
Gary Lyon, capital, April 30, 19X1	$53,700

①

Gary Lyon, CPA Balance Sheet April 30, 19X1			
Assets		**Liabilities**	
Cash...................	$33,300	Accounts payable	$ 100
Accounts receivable	2,000	**Owner's Equity**	
Office supplies.........	500		
Land..................	18,000	Gary Lyon, capital	53,700
		Total liabilities and	
Total assets...........	$53,800	owner's equity.......	$53,800

②

Point to Stress: If a company has $53,800 in assets, and no liabilities, then the claims to those assets (owner's equity) must total $53,800. It makes no sense to have unclaimed assets or claims to assets that do not exist.

Typical Student Misconception: Many students don't understand why the balance sheet must balance. Try holding up a coin. The coin's two sides are the same size but look completely different from each other. Similarly, the two sides of the balance sheet show the same amount but look completely different from each other.

   b. Adds *investments by the owner* of the business and also adds *net income* (or subtracts *net loss,* as the case may be). Net income (or net loss) comes directly from the income statement, which includes the effect of all the revenues and all the expenses for the period (see the first arrow in the exhibit).

   c. Subtracts *withdrawals by the owner.*

   d. Ends with the owner's capital balance at the end of the period.

3. The *balance sheet* at April 30, 19X1, the end of the period

   a. Reports all *assets,* all *liabilities,* and *owner's equity* of the business at the end of the period. No other statement reports assets and liabilities.

b. Reports that total assets equal the sum of total liabilities plus total owner's equity. This balancing feature gives the balance sheet its name. It is based on the accounting equation.
c. Reports the owner's ending capital balance, taken directly from the statement of owner's equity (see the second arrow).

Summary Problem for Your Review

Jill Smith opens an apartment-locator business near a college campus. She is the sole owner of the proprietorship, which she names Campus Apartment Locators. During the first month of operations, May 19X1, Smith engages in the following transactions:

a. Smith invests $35,000 of personal funds to start the business.
b. She purchases on account office supplies costing $350.
c. Smith pays cash of $30,000 to acquire a lot next to the campus. She intends to use the land as a future building site for her business office.
d. Smith locates apartments for clients and receives cash of $1,900.
e. She pays $100 on the account payable she created in transaction b.
f. She pays $2,000 of personal funds for a vacation for her family.
g. She pays cash expenses for office rent, $400, and utilities, $100.
h. The business sells office supplies to another business for its cost of $150.
i. Smith withdraws cash of $1,200 for personal use.

Required

1. Analyze the preceding transactions in terms of their effects on the accounting equation of Campus Apartment Locators. Use Exhibit 1-5 as a guide, but show balances only after the last transaction.
2. Prepare the income statement, statement of owner's equity, and balance sheet of the business after recording the transactions. Use Exhibit 1-6 as a guide.

SOLUTION TO REVIEW PROBLEM

Panel A. Details of transactions

a. Smith invested $35,000 cash to start the business.
b. Purchased $350 of office supplies on account.
c. Paid $30,000 to acquire land as a future building site.
d. Earned service revenue and received cash of $1,900.
e. Paid $100 on account.
f. Paid for a personal vacation, which is not a business transaction.
g. Paid cash expenses for rent, $400, and utilities, $100.
h. Sold office supplies for cost of $150.
i. Withdrew $1,200 cash for personal use.

Panel B.   Analysis of transactions

	Assets				Liabilities +	Owner's Equity	Type of Owner's Equity Transaction
	Cash	+ Office Supplies +	Land		Accounts Payable +	Jill Smith, Capital	
(a)	+35,000					+35,000	Owner investment
(b)		+350			+350		
(c)	−30,000		+30,000				
(d)	+ 1,900					+ 1,900	Service revenue
(e)	− 100			=	−100		
(f)	Not a business transaction						
(g)	− 500					− 400	Rent expense
						− 100	Utilities expense
(h)	+ 150	−150					
(i)	− 1,200					− 1,200	Owner withdrawal
Bal.	5,250	200	30,000		250	35,200	
		35,450				35,450	

Financial Statements of Campus Apartment Locators

Campus Apartment Locators
Income Statement
Month Ended May 31, 19X1

Revenues:		
Service revenue		$1,900
Expenses:		
Rent expense..	$400	
Utilities expense	100	
Total expenses		500
Net income		$1,400

Campus Apartment Locators
Statement of Owner's Equity
Month Ended May 31, 19X1

Jill Smith, capital, May 1, 19X1......................	$ 0
Add: Investments by owner	35,000
Net income for the month.........................	1,400
	36,400
Less: Withdrawals by owner...........................	1,200
Jill Smith, capital, May 31, 19X1.....................	$35,200

Campus Apartment Locators
Balance Sheet
May 31, 19X1

Assets		Liabilities	
Cash......................	$ 5,250	Accounts payable	$ 250
Office supplies	200	**Owner's Equity**	
Land	30,000		
		Jill Smith, capital..........	35,200
		Total liabilities and	
Total assets...............	$35,450	owner's equity...........	$35,450

Summary

Accounting is a system for measuring, processing, and communicating financial information. As the "language of business," accounting helps a wide range of decision makers.

Accounting dates back to ancient civilizations, but its importance to society has been greatest since the Industrial Revolution. Today, accountants serve as CPAs, CMAs, or CIAs in all types of organizations. They offer many specialized services for industrial companies, including general accounting, cost accounting, budgeting, system design, and internal auditing. CPAs in public practice deal with auditing, tax planning and preparation, and management consulting.

The three basic forms of business organization are the proprietorship, the partnership, and the corporation. Whatever the form, accountants use the entity concept to keep the business's records separate from the personal records of the people who run it. Accountants at all levels must be ethical to serve their intended purpose.

Generally accepted accounting principles (GAAP) guide accountants in their work. Among these guidelines are the *entity concept*, the *reliability principle*, the *cost principle*, the *going-concern concept*, and the *stable-monetary-unit concept*.

In its most common form, the accounting equation is

$$\text{ASSETS} = \text{LIABILITIES} + \text{OWNER'S EQUITY}$$

Transactions affect a business's assets, liabilities, and owner's equity. Therefore, transactions are analyzed in terms of their effect on the accounting equation.

The *financial statements* communicate information for decision making by the entity's managers, owners, and creditors and by government agencies. The *income statement* presents a moving picture of the entity's operations in terms of revenues earned and expenses incurred during a specific period. Total revenues minus total expenses equal net income. Net income or net loss answers the question, How much income did the entity earn, or how much loss did it incur during the period? The *statement of owner's equity* reports the changes in owner's equity during the period. The *balance sheet* provides a photograph of the entity's financial standing in terms of its assets, liabilities, and owner's equity at a specific time. It answers the question, What is the entity's financial position?

Self-Study Questions

Test your understanding of the chapter by marking the best answer for each of the following questions:

1. To become a CPA, a person must *(p. 6)*
   a. Graduate from college with a master's degree
   b. Obtain four years of accounting experience
   ✓ c. Pass a national examination
   d. Pass an accounting examination that differs from state to state
2. The organization that formulates generally accepted accounting principles is *(p. 6)*
   a. American Institute of Certified Public Accountants (CPAs)
   b. Internal Revenue Service
   ✓ c. Financial Accounting Standards Board
   d. Institute of Management Accountants

3. Which of the following forms of business organization is an "artificial person" and must obtain legal approval from a state to conduct business? *(p. 10)*
   - a. Law firm
   - b. Proprietorship
   - c. Partnership
   - ✓ d. Corporation

4. The economic resources of a business are called *(p. 13)*
   - ✓ a. Assets
   - b. Liabilities
   - c. Owner's equity
   - d. Receivables

5. A business has assets of $140,000 and liabilities of $60,000. How much is its owner's equity? *(p. 14)*
   - a. $0
   - ✓ b. $80,000
   - c. $140,000
   - d. $200,000

6. The purchase of office supplies (or any other asset) on account will *(p. 15)*
   - ✓ a. Increase an asset and increase a liability
   - b. Increase an asset and increase owner's equity
   - c. Increase one asset and decrease another asset
   - d. Increase an asset and decrease a liability

7. The performance of service for a customer or client and immediate receipt of cash will *(p. 16)*
   - a. Increase one asset and decrease another asset
   - ✓ b. Increase an asset and increase owner's equity
   - c. Decrease an asset and decrease a liability
   - d. Increase an asset and increase a liability

8. The payment of an account payable (or any other liability) will *(p. 18)*
   - a. Increase one asset and decrease another asset
   - b. Decrease an asset and decrease owner's equity
   - ✓ c. Decrease an asset and decrease a liability
   - d. Increase an asset and increase a liability

9. The report of assets, liabilities, and owner's equity is called the *(p. 21)*
   - a. Financial statement
   - ✓ b. Balance sheet
   - c. Income statement
   - d. Statement of owner's equity

10. The financial statements that are dated for a time period (rather than a specific time) are the *(p. 21)*
    - a. Balance sheet and income statement
    - b. Balance sheet and statement of owner's equity
    - ✓ c. Income statement and statement of owner's equity
    - d. All financial statements are dated for a time period.

Answers to the Self-Study Questions follow the Accounting Vocabulary.

Accounting Vocabulary

Accounting, like many other subjects, has a special vocabulary. It is important that you understand the following terms. They are explained in the chapter and also in the glossary at the end of the book.

Accounting. The system that measures business activities, processes that information into reports and financial statements, and communicates the findings to decision makers *(p. 2)*.

Account payable. A liability backed by the general reputation and credit standing of the debtor *(p. 14)*.

Account receivable. An asset, a promise to receive cash from customers to whom the business has sold goods or for whom the business has performed services *(p. 14)*.

Asset. An economic resource that is expected to be of benefit in the future *(p. 13)*.

Auditing. The examination of financial statements by outside accountants, the most significant service that CPAs perform. The conclusion of an audit is the accountant's professional opinion about the financial statements (p. 8).

Balance sheet. List of an entity's assets, liabilities, and owner equity as of a specific date. Also called the statement of financial position (p. 21).

Budgeting. Setting of goals for a business, such as its sales and profits, for a future period (p. 9).

Capital. Another name for the owner equity of a business (p. 13).

Certified Public Accountant (CPA). A professional accountant who earns this title through a combination of education, experience, and an acceptable score on a written national examination (p. 5).

Corporation. A business owned by stockholders that begins when the state approves its articles of incorporation. A corporation is a legal entity, an "artificial person," in the eyes of the law (p. 10).

Cost accounting. The branch of accounting that determines and controls a business's costs (p. 9).

Entity. An organization or a section of an organization that, for accounting purposes, stands apart from other organizations and individuals as a separate economic unit. This is the most basic concept in accounting (p. 11).

Expense. Decrease in owner equity that occurs in the course of delivering goods or services to customers or clients (p. 17).

Financial accounting. The branch of accounting that provides information to people outside the business (p. 10).

Financial statements. Business documents that report financial information about an entity to persons and organizations outside the business (p. 2).

Generally accepted accounting principles (GAAP). Accounting guidelines, formulated by the Financial Accounting Standards Board, that govern how businesses report their financial statements to the public (p. 6).

Income statement. List of an entity's revenues, expenses, and net income or net loss for a specific period. Also

called the Statement of operations and the Statement of earnings (p. 21).

Information systems design. Identification of an organization's information needs, and development and implementation of the system to meet those needs (p. 9).

Internal auditing. Auditing that is performed by a business's own accountants to evaluate the firm's accounting and management systems. The aim is to improve operating efficiency and to ensure that employees follow management's procedures and plans (p. 9).

Liability. An economic obligation (a debt) payable to an individual or an organization outside the business (p. 13).

Management accounting. The branch of accounting that generates information for internal decision makers of a business, such as top executives (p. 10).

Net earnings. Another name for Net income or Net profit (p. 17).

Net income. Excess of total revenues over total expenses. Also called Net earnings or Net profit (p. 17).

Net loss. Excess of total expenses over total revenues (p. 17).

Net profit. Another name for Net income or Net earnings (p. 17).

Note payable. A liability evidenced by a written promise to make a future payment (p. 14).

Note receivable. An asset evidenced by another party's written promise that entitles you to receive cash in the future (p. 14).

Owner's equity. The claim of an owner of a business to the assets of the business. Also called Capital (p. 13).

Partnership. A business with two or more owners (p. 10).

Private accountant. Accountant who works for a single business, such as a department store or General Motors (p. 5).

Proprietorship. A business with a single owner (p. 10).

Public accountant. Accountant who serves the general public and collects fees for work, which includes auditing, income tax planning and preparation, and management consulting (p. 5).

Revenue. Increase in owner equity that is earned by delivering goods or services to customers or clients (p. 16).

Statement of earnings. Another name for the Income statement (p. 21).

Statement of financial position. Another name for the Balance sheet (p. 21).

Statement of operations. Another name for the Income statement (p. 21).

Statement of owner's equity. Summary of the changes in the owner equity of an entity during a specific period (p. 21).

Stockholder. A person who owns the stock of a corporation (p. 10).

Transaction. An event that affects the financial position of a particular entity and may be reliably recorded (p. 14).

Answers to Self-Study Questions

1. c	3. d	5. b	7. b	9. b
2. c	4. a	6. a	8. c	10. c

ASSIGNMENT MATERIAL

Questions

1. Distinguish between accounting and bookkeeping.
2. Identify five users of accounting information and explain how they use it.
3. Where did accounting have its beginning? Who wrote the first known description of bookkeeping? In what year?
4. Name two important reasons for the development of accounting thought.
5. Name three professional titles of accountants. Also give their abbreviations.
6. What organization formulates generally accepted accounting principles? Is this organization a government agency?
7. Name the three principal types of services provided by public accounting firms.
8. How do financial accounting and management accounting differ?
9. Give the name(s) of the owner(s) of a proprietorship, a partnership, and a corporation.
10. Why do ethical standards exist in accounting? Which organization directs its standards toward independent auditors? Which organization directs its standards more toward management accountants?
11. Why is the entity concept so important to accounting?
12. Give four examples of accounting entities.
13. Briefly describe the reliability principle.
14. What role does the cost principle play in accounting?
15. If *assets = liabilities + owner's equity*, then how can liabilities be expressed?
16. Explain the difference between an account receivable and an account payable.
17. What role do transactions play in accounting?
18. What is a more descriptive title for the balance sheet?

19. What feature of the balance sheet gives this financial statement its name?
20. What is another title of the income statement?
21. Which financial statement is like a snapshot of the entity at a specific time? Which financial statement is like a moving picture of the entity's operations during a period of time?
22. What information does the statement of owner's equity report?
23. Give two synonyms for the owner's equity of a proprietorship.
24. What piece of information flows from the income statement to the statement of owner's equity? What information flows from the statement of owner's equity to the balance sheet?

Exercises

Exercise 1-1   *Explaining the income statement and the balance sheet*   **(L.O. 1,2)**

No check figure

Felix and Charlotte Jiminez want to open a Mexican restaurant in Oklahoma City. In need of cash, they ask City Bank & Trust for a loan. The bank's procedures require borrowers to submit financial statements to show likely results of operations for the first year and likely financial position at the end of the first year. With little knowledge of accounting, Felix and Charlotte don't know how to proceed. Explain to them the information provided by the statement of operations (the income statement) and the statement of financial position (the balance sheet). Indicate why a lender would require this information.

Exercise 1-2   *Business transactions*   **(L.O. 3)**

No check figure

For each of the following items, give an example of a business transaction that has the described effect on the accounting equation:

a. Increase one asset and decrease another asset.
b. Decrease an asset and decrease owner's equity.
c. Decrease an asset and decrease a liability.
d. Increase an asset and increase owner's equity.
e. Increase an asset and increase a liability.

Exercise 1-3   *Transaction analysis*   **(L.O. 3)**

No check figure

Kreitze Contractors, a proprietorship, or Darren Kreitze, the owner, experienced the following events. State whether each event (1) increased, (2) decreased, or (3) had no effect on the total assets of the business. Identify any specific asset affected.

a. Borrowed money from the bank.
b. Cash purchase of land for a future building site.
c. Kreitze increased his cash investment in the business.
d. Paid cash on accounts payable.
e. Purchased machinery and equipment for a manufacturing plant; signed a promissory note in payment.
f. Performed service for a customer on account.
g. Kreitze, the owner, withdrew cash from the business for personal use.
h. Received cash from a customer on account receivable.
i. Kreitze used personal funds to purchase a swimming pool for his home.
j. Sold land for a price equal to the cost of the land; received cash.

Exercise 1-4 *Accounting equation* **(L.O. 4)**

Compute the missing amount in the accounting equation of each of the following three entities:

	Assets	Liabilities	Owner's Equity
Entity A	$?	$41,800	$34,400
Entity B	65,900	?	34,000
Entity C	61,700	29,800	?

Exercise 1-5 *Accounting equation* **(L.O. 3,4)**

Oriole Travel Agency balance sheet data, at May 31, 19X2, and June 30, 19X2, were as follows:

	May 31, 19X2	**June 30, 19X2**
Total assets	$150,000	$195,000
Total liabilities	109,000	131,000

Required

Below are three assumptions about investments and withdrawals by the owner of the business during June. For each assumption, compute the amount of net income or net loss of the business during June 19X2.

a. The owner invested $30,000 in the business and made no withdrawals.
b. The owner made no additional investments in the business but withdrew $6,000 for personal use.
c. The owner invested $8,000 in the business and withdrew $6,000 for personal use.

Exercise 1-6 *Transaction analysis* **(L.O. 5)**

Indicate the effects of the following business transactions on the accounting equation. Transaction *a* is answered as a guide.

a. Invested cash of $1,800 in the business.
   Answer: Increase asset (Cash)
               Increase owner's equity (Capital)
b. Performed legal service for a client on account, $650.
c. Purchased on account office furniture at a cost of $500.
d. Received cash on account, $400.
e. Paid cash on account, $250.
f. Sold land for $12,000, which was our cost of the land.
g. Paid $90 cash to purchase office supplies.
h. Performed legal service for a client and received cash of $2,000.
i. Paid monthly office rent of $700.

Exercise 1-7 *Transaction analysis; accounting equation* **(L.O. 3,5)**

Allison LaChappelle opens a medical practice to specialize in child care. During her first month of operation, January, her practice, entitled Allison LaChappelle, M.D., experienced the following events:

Jan. 6   LaChappelle invested $120,000 in the business by opening a bank account in the name of Allison LaChappelle, M.D.

9   LaChappelle paid cash for land costing $90,000. She plans to build an office building on the land.

12   She purchased medical supplies for $2,000 on account.

15   On January 15, LaChappelle officially opened for business.

15–31   During the rest of the month she treated patients and earned service revenue of $6,000, receiving cash.

15–31   She paid cash expenses: employee salaries, $1,400; office rent, $1,000; utilities, $300.

28   She sold supplies to another physician for cost of $500.

31   She paid $1,500 on account.

Required

Analyze the effects of these events on the accounting equation of the medical practice of Allison LaChappelle, M.D. Use a format similar to that of Exhibit 1-5 in the chapter, with headings for Cash; Medical Supplies; Land; Accounts Payable; and Allison LaChappelle, Capital.

Exercise 1-8   *Business organization, transactions, and net income* **(L.O. 3,4,5)**

Net income $950

The analysis of the transactions that Allied Leasing engaged in during its first month of operations follows. The company buys equipment that it leases out to earn revenue. The owners of the business made only one investment to start the business and no withdrawals.

	Cash	+	Accounts Receivable	+	Lease Equipment	=	Accounts Payable	+	Partners' Capital
a.	+ 46,000								+ 46,000
b.					+ 80,000		+ 80,000		
c.	+ 1,600								+ 1,600
d.			+ 500						+ 500
e.	− 10,000						− 10,000		
f.			+ 850						+ 850
g.	+ 150		− 150						
h.	− 2,000								− 2,000

Required

1.   What type of business organization is Allied Leasing? How can you tell?
2.   Describe each transaction.
3.   If these transactions fully describe the operations of Allied Leasing during the month, what was the amount of net income or net loss?

Exercise 1-9   *Business organization, balance sheet* **(L.O. 3,6)**

Capital $8,900;
Total assets $17,650

Presented below are the balances of the assets and liabilities of Long-Gone Delivery Service as of September 30, 19X2. Also included are the revenue and expense figures of the business for September.

Delivery service revenue	....$4,100	Delivery equipment	.........$15,500
Accounts receivable	 900	Supplies	 600
Accounts payable	 750	Note payable	 8,000
L. Gone, capital	.... ?	Rent expense	 500
Salary expense	 2,000	Cash	 650

Required

1. What type of business organization is Long-Gone Delivery Service? How can you tell?
2. Prepare the balance sheet of Long-Gone Delivery Service as of September 30, 19X2. Not all amounts are used.

Exercise 1-10   *Income statement* *(L.O. 3,6)*

Presented below are the balances of the assets, liabilities, owner's equity, revenues, and expenses of Technical Consultants at December 31, 19X3, the end of its first year of business. During the year K. Toshi, the owner, invested $15,000 in the business.

Note payable	$ 30,000	Office furniture	$45,000
Utilities expense	5,800	Rent expense	21,000
Accounts payable	3,300	Cash	3,600
K. Toshi, capital	27,100	Office supplies	4,800
Service revenue	131,000	Salary expense	39,000
Accounts receivable	9,000	Salaries payable	2,000
Supplies expense	4,000	Property tax expense	1,200

Required

1. Prepare the income statement of Technical Consultants for the year ended December 31, 19X3. Not all amounts are used.
2. What was the amount of the proprietor's withdrawals during the year?

Problems   (Group A)

Problem 1-1A   *Analyzing a loan request* *(L.O. 1,2,3)*

As an analyst for Midlantic Bank, it is your job to write recommendations to the bank's loan committee. Sigma Enterprises has submitted these summary data to support the company's request for a $300,000 loan:

Income Statement Data:	19X5	19X4	19X3
Total revenues	$790,000	$730,000	$720,000
Total expenses	640,000	570,000	540,000
Net income	$150,000	$160,000	$180,000

Statement of Owner's Equity Data:	19X5	19X4	19X3
Beginning capital	$280,000	$300,000	$290,000
Add: Net income	150,000	160,000	180,000
	430,000	460,000	470,000
Less: Withdrawals	190,000	180,000	170,000
Ending capital	$240,000	$280,000	$300,000

Balance Sheet Data:	19X5	19X4	19X3
Total assets	$630,000	$600,000	$560,000
Total liabilities	$390,000	$320,000	$260,000
Total owner's equity	240,000	280,000	300,000
Total liabilities and owner's equity	$630,000	$600,000	$560,000

Required

Should the bank lend $300,000 to Sigma Enterprises? Write a one-paragraph recommendation to the loan committee.

Problem 1-2A   *Entity concept, transaction analysis, accounting equation*   **(L.O. 3,5)**

Owner's equity $126,700

Kathy Wood practiced law with a large firm, a partnership, for ten years after graduating from law school. Recently she resigned her position to open her own law office, which she operates as a proprietorship. The name of the new entity is Kathy Wood, Attorney and Counselor.

Wood recorded the following events during the organizing phase of her new business and its first month of operations. Some of the events were personal and did not affect the law practice. Others were business transactions and should be accounted for by the business.

July 1   Wood sold 1,000 shares of Eastman Kodak stock, which she had owned for several years, receiving $88,000 cash from her stockbroker.

2   Wood deposited the $88,000 cash from sale of the Eastman Kodak stock in her personal bank account.

3   Wood received $135,000 cash from her former partners in the law firm from which she resigned.

5   Wood deposited $130,000 cash in a new business bank account entitled Kathy Wood, Attorney and Counselor.

6   A representative of a large company telephoned Wood and told her of the company's intention to transfer its legal business to the new entity of Kathy Wood, Attorney and Counselor.

7   Wood paid $550 cash for letterhead stationery for her new law office.

9   Wood purchased office furniture for the law office, agreeing to pay the account payable, $11,500, within three months.

23   Wood finished court hearings on behalf of a client and submitted her bill for legal services, $2,100. She expected to collect from this client within one month.

30   Wood paid office rent expense, $1,900.

31   Wood withdrew $3,500 cash from the business for personal living expenses.

Required

1.   Classify each of the preceding events as one of the following:
   a. Business transaction to be accounted for by the proprietorship of Kathy Wood, Attorney and Counselor.
   b. Business-related event but not a transaction to be accounted for by the proprietorship of Kathy Wood, Attorney and Counselor.
   c. Personal transaction not to be accounted for by the proprietorship of Kathy Wood, Attorney and Counselor.
2.   Analyze the effects of the above events on the accounting equation of the proprietorship of Kathy Wood, Attorney and Counselor. Use a format similar to Exhibit 1–5.

Problem 1-3A   *Balance sheet*   **(L.O. 3,6)**

Total assets $50,000

The bookkeeper of Glass Travel Agency prepared the balance sheet of the company while the accountant was ill. The balance sheet contains numerous errors. In particular, the bookkeeper knew that the balance sheet should balance, so he plugged in the owner's equity amount needed to achieve this balance. However, the owner's equity amount is not correct. All other amounts are accurate.

Glass Travel Agency
Balance Sheet
Month Ended October 31, 19X7

Assets		Liabilities	
Cash...................	$ 1,400	Notes receivable	$11,000
Advertising expense	300	Interest expense	2,000
Land	30,500	Office supplies	800
Salary expense...........	3,300	Accounts receivable	1,600
Office furniture	4,700	Note payable	20,000
Accounts payable	3,000	**Owner's Equity**	
Utilities expense	1,100		
		Owner's equity	8,900
Total assets..............	$44,300	Total liabilities	$44,300

Required

1. Prepare the correct balance sheet as of October 31, 19X7. Compute total assets and total liabilities. Then take the difference to determine correct owner's equity.
2. Identify the accounts listed above that should *not* be presented on the balance sheet and state why you excluded them from the correct balance sheet you prepared for Requirement 1.

Total assets $127,000

Problem 1-4A   *Balance sheet, entity concept*   **(L.O. 3,4,6)**

Matt Thomas is a realtor. He buys and sells properties on his own, and he also earns commission as a real estate agent for buyers and sellers. He organized his business as a proprietorship on March 10, 19X2. Consider the following facts as of March 31, 19X2:

a. Thomas had $5,000 in his personal bank account and $9,000 in his business bank account.
b. Office supplies on hand at the real estate office totaled $1,000.
c. Thomas's business had spent $15,000 for an Electronic Realty Associates (ERA) franchise, which entitled him to represent himself as an ERA agent. ERA is a national affiliation of independent real estate agents. This franchise is a business asset.
d. Thomas owed $48,000 on a note payable for some undeveloped land that had been acquired by his business for a total price of $90,000.
e. Thomas owed $65,000 on a personal mortgage on his personal residence, which he acquired in 19X1 for a total price of $90,000.
f. Thomas owed $950 on a personal charge account with Sears, Roebuck and Co.
g. He had acquired business furniture for $12,000 on March 26. Of this amount, Thomas's business owed $6,000 on open account at March 31.

Required

1. Prepare the balance sheet of the real estate business of Matt Thomas, Realtor, at March 31, 19X2.
2. Identify the personal items given in the preceding facts that would not be reported on the balance sheet of the business.

Problem 1-5A *Transaction analysis for an actual company* (L.O. 4,5)

A recent balance sheet of Xerox Corporation, the manufacturer of copiers and other office equipment, is summarized as follows, with amounts in thousands. For example, Cash of $266,600,000 is presented as $266,600.

Xerox Corporation
Balance Sheet
December 31, 19X4
(thousands)

Assets		Liabilities	
Cash	$ 266,600	Notes payable	$1,985,500
Accounts receivable . . .	1,466,900	Accounts payable	390,300
Merchandise		Other liabilities	2,107,600
inventories	1,469,800	Total liabilities	4,483,400
Land, buildings, and		**Owner Equity**	
equipment	2,659,700		
Other assets	3,953,700	Owner equity	5,333,300
		Total liabilities	
Total assets	$9,816,700	and owner equity . . .	$9,816,700

Suppose the company had the following transactions and events (amounts in thousands) during January:

a. Received cash investment from owners, $160.
b. Purchased inventories on account, $400.
c. Paid cash on account (to reduce accounts payable), $136.
d. Sold equipment to another company on account, $670. The equipment had cost $670.
e. Learned that a national television news program would show members of Congress using Xerox copy machines as part of a Senate investigation. The value of this advertisement to the company is estimated to be $1,000.
f. Borrowed cash, signing a note payable, $550.
g. Purchased equipment for cash, $380.
h. Collected cash on account from customers, $289.
i. Received special equipment from an owner as an investment in the company. The value of the equipment was $119.

Required

1. Showing all amounts in thousands, analyze the January 19X5 transactions of Xerox. Use a format similar to Exhibit 1-5.
2. Prove that assets = liabilities + owner equity after analyzing the transactions.

Problem 1-6A *Business transactions and analysis* (L.O. 5)

No check figure

Amalfi Company was recently formed. The balance of each item in the company's accounting equation is shown below for February 8 and for each of nine following business days.

Chapter 1 Accounting and Its Environment **35**

		Cash	Accounts Receivable	Supplies	Land	Accounts Payable	Owner's Equity
Feb.	8	$3,000	$7,000	$ 800	$11,000	$3,800	$18,000
	12	2,000	7,000	800	11,000	2,800	18,000
	14	6,000	3,000	800	11,000	2,800	18,000
	17	6,000	3,000	1,100	11,000	3,100	18,000
	19	3,000	3,000	1,100	11,000	3,100	15,000
	20	1,900	3,000	1,100	11,000	2,000	15,000
	22	7,900	3,000	1,100	5,000	2,000	15,000
	25	7,900	3,200	900	5,000	2,000	15,000
	26	7,700	3,200	1,100	5,000	2,000	15,000
	28	2,600	3,200	1,100	10,100	2,000	15,000

Required

Assuming a single transaction took place on each day, describe briefly the transaction that was most likely to have occurred, beginning with February 12. Indicate which accounts were affected and by what amount. No revenue or expense transactions occurred on these dates.

Owner's equity, end of year $19,000

Problem 1-7A *Income statement, statement of owner's equity, balance sheet* **(L.O. 6)**

Presented below are the amounts of (a) the assets and liabilities of Coleman Delivery Service as of December 31 and (b) the revenues and expenses of the company for the year ended on that date. The items are listed in alphabetical order.

Accounts payable	$14,000	Note payable	$ 31,000
Accounts receivable	6,000	Property tax expense	2,000
Building	13,000	Rent expense	14,000
Cash	4,000	Salary expense	38,000
Equipment	21,000	Service revenue	100,000
Interest expense	4,000	Supplies	13,000
Interest payable	1,000	Utilities expense	3,000
Land	8,000		

The beginning amount of Jake Coleman, Capital, was $12,000, and during the year Coleman withdrew $32,000 for personal use.

Required

1. Prepare the income statement of Coleman Delivery Service for the year ended December 31 of the current year.
2. Prepare the statement of owner's equity of the company for the year ended December 31.
3. Prepare the balance sheet of the company at December 31.

Owner's equity $37,000

Problem 1-8A *Transaction analysis, accounting equation, financial statements* **(L.O. 5,6)**

Kathy Starr owns and operates an interior design studio called Starr Designers. The following amounts summarize the financial position of her business on April 30, 19X5:

	Assets				=	Liabilities	+	Owner's Equity
	Cash +	Accounts Receivable +	Supplies +	Land	=	Accounts Payable	+	Kathy Starr, Capital
Bal.	720	2,240		23,100		4,400		21,660

36 Part One The Basic Structure of Accounting

During May 19X5 the following events occurred:

a. Starr received $12,000 as a gift and deposited the cash in the business bank account.
b. Paid off the beginning balance of accounts payable.
c. Performed services for a client and received cash of $1,100.
d. Collected cash from a customer on account, $750.
e. Purchased supplies on account, $120.
f. Consulted on the interior design of a major office building and billed the client for services rendered, $5,000.
g. Invested personal cash of $1,700 in the business.
h. Recorded the following business expenses for the month:
   (1) Paid office rent—$1,200
   (2) Paid advertising—$860.
i. Sold supplies to another interior designer for $80 cash, which was the cost of the supplies.
j. Withdrew cash of $2,400 for personal use.

Required

1. Analyze the effects of the above transactions on the accounting equation of Starr Designers. Adapt the format of Exhibit 1-5.
2. Prepare the income statement of Starr Designers for the month ended May 31, 19X5. List expenses in decreasing order by amount.
3. Prepare the statement of owner's equity of Starr Designers for the month ended May 31, 19X5.
4. Prepare the balance sheet of Starr Designers at May 31.

(Group B)

Problem 1-1B *Analyzing a loan request* (L.O. 1,2,3)

No check figure

As an analyst for Salt Lake Bank, it is your job to write recommendations to the bank's loan committee. Lomoni Company has submitted these summary data to support its request for a $100,000 loan:

Income Statement Data:	19X5	19X4	19X3
Total revenues	$850,000	$760,000	$720,000
Total expenses	640,000	570,000	540,000
Net income	$210,000	$190,000	$180,000

Statement of Owner's Equity Data:	19X5	19X4	19X3
Beginning capital	$440,000	$390,000	$330,000
Add: Net income	210,000	190,000	180,000
	650,000	580,000	510,000
Less: Withdrawals	160,000	140,000	120,000
Ending capital	$490,000	$440,000	$390,000

Balance Sheet Data:	19X5	19X4	19X3
Total assets	$730,000	$660,000	$590,000
Total liabilities	$240,000	$220,000	$200,000
Total owner's equity	490,000	440,000	390,000
Total liabilities and owner's equity	$730,000	$660,000	$590,000

Required

Should the bank lend $100,000 to Lomoni Company? Write a one-paragraph recommendation to the loan committee.

Owner's equity $51,000

Problem 1-2B   *Entity concept, transaction analysis, accounting equation*   **(L.O. 3,5)**

Melvin Dexter practiced law with a large firm, a partnership, for five years after graduating from law school. Recently he resigned his position to open his own law office, which he operates as a proprietorship. The name of the new entity is Melvin Dexter, Attorney.

Dexter recorded the following events during the organizing phase of his new business and its first month of operations. Some of the events were personal and did not affect his law practice. Others were business transactions and should be accounted for by the business.

May   4   Dexter received $50,000 cash from his former partners in the law firm from which he resigned.

       5   Dexter deposited $50,000 cash in a new business bank account entitled Melvin Dexter, Attorney.

       6   Dexter paid $300 cash for letterhead stationery for his new law office.

       7   Dexter purchased office furniture for his law office. He agreed to pay the account payable, $5,000, within six months.

      10   Dexter sold 500 shares of IBM stock, which he and his wife had owned for several years, receiving $75,000 cash from his stockbroker.

      11   Dexter deposited the $75,000 cash from sale of the IBM stock in his personal bank account.

      12   A representative of a large company telephoned Dexter and told him of the company's intention to transfer its legal business to the new entity of Melvin Dexter, Attorney.

      29   Dexter finished court hearings on behalf of a client and submitted his bill for legal services, $4,000. Dexter expected to collect from this client within two weeks.

      30   Dexter paid office rent expense, $1,000.

      31   Dexter withdrew $2,000 cash from the business for personal living expenses.

Required

1. Classify each of the preceding events as one of the following:
    a. Business transaction to be accounted for by the proprietorship of Melvin Dexter, Attorney.
    b. Business-related event but not a transaction to be accounted for by the proprietorship of Melvin Dexter, Attorney.
    c. Personal transaction not to be accounted for by the proprietorship of Melvin Dexter, Attorney.
2. Analyze the effects of the above events on the accounting equation of the proprietorship of Melvin Dexter, Attorney. Use a format similar to Exhibit 1-5.

Total assets $36,000

Problem 1-3B   *Balance sheet*   **(L.O. 3,6)**

The bookkeeper of Getz Auction Co. prepared the balance sheet of the company while the accountant was ill. The balance sheet contains numerous errors. In particular, the bookkeeper knew that the balance sheet should balance, so he plugged in the owner's equity amount needed to achieve this balance. However, the owner's equity amount is not correct. All other amounts are accurate.

Getz Auction Co.
Balance Sheet
Month Ended July 31, 19X3

Assets		Liabilities	
Cash....................	$ 2,000	Accounts receivable	$ 3,000
Office supplies	1,000	Service revenue..........	35,000
Land	20,000	Property tax expense	800
Advertising expense	2,500	Accounts payable	8,000
Office furniture	10,000	**Owner's Equity**	
Note payable	16,000		
Rent expense	4,000	Owner's equity	8,700
Total assets..............	$55,500	Total liabilities	$55,500

Required

1. Prepare the correct balance sheet as of July 31, 19X3. Compute total assets and total liabilities. Then take the difference to determine correct owner's equity.
2. Identify the accounts listed above that should *not* be presented on the balance sheet and state why you excluded them from the correct balance sheet you prepared for Requirement 1.

Problem 1-4B   *Balance sheet, entity concept*   **(L.O. 3,4,6)**

Total assets $185,000

Sue Kerault is a realtor. She buys and sells properties on her own, and she also earns commission as a real estate agent for buyers and sellers. She organized her business as a proprietorship on November 24, 19X4. Consider the following facts as of November 30, 19X4:

a. Kerault owed $80,000 on a note payable for some undeveloped land that had been acquired by her business for a total price of $140,000.
b. Kerault's business had spent $15,000 for a Century 21 real estate franchise, which entitled her to represent herself as a Century 21 agent. Century 21 is a national affiliation of independent real estate agents. This franchise is a business asset.
c. Kerault owed $120,000 on a personal mortgage on her personal residence, which she acquired in 19X1 for a total price of $170,000.
d. Kerault had $10,000 in her personal bank account and $12,000 in her business bank account.
e. Kerault owed $1,800 on a personal charge account with Neiman-Marcus Specialty Department Store.
f. Kerault acquired business furniture for $17,000 on November 25. Of this amount, her business owed $6,000 on open account at November 30.
g. Office supplies on hand at the real estate office totaled $1,000.

Required

1. Prepare the balance sheet of the real estate business of Sue Kerault, Realtor, at November 30, 19X4.
2. Identify the personal items given in the preceding facts that would not be reported on the balance sheet of the business.

Problem 1-5B   *Transaction analysis for an actual company*   **(L.O. 4,5)**

Total assets $1,421,346

A recent balance sheet of Levi Strauss & Company, the world's largest seller of jeans and casual pants, is summarized as follows, with amounts in thousands. For example, Cash of $263,389,000 is presented as $263,389.

Levi Strauss & Company
Balance Sheet
November 25, 19X2
(thousands)

Assets		Liabilities	
Cash	$ 263,389	Notes payable	$ 83,361
Accounts receivable ...	339,798	Accounts payable	229,453
Merchandise		Other liabilities	300,847
inventories	387,660	Total liabilities	613,661
Property, plant, and			
equipment..........	330,455	**Owner Equity**	
Other assets	99,800	Owner equity.........	807,441
		Total liabilities	
Total assets	$1,421,102	and owner equity ...	$1,421,102

Suppose that the company had the following transactions and events (amounts in thousands) during December:

a. Received cash investments from owners, $18.
b. Received special equipment from an owner as an investment in the company. The value of the equipment was $90.
c. Borrowed cash, signing a note payable, $100.
d. Purchased equipment for cash, $125.
e. Purchased inventories on account, $90.
f. Paid cash on account (to reduce accounts payable), $54.
g. Sold equipment to another company on account, $14. The equipment had cost $14.
h. Discovered that the president of the United States was going to wear Levi blue jeans while giving his State of the Union address next January.
i. Collected cash on account from customers, $84.

Required:

1. Showing all amounts in thousands, analyze the December transactions of Levi Strauss. Use a format similar to Exhibit 1-5.
2. Prove that assets = liabilities + owner equity after analyzing the transactions.

No check figure

Problem 1-6B   *Business transactions and analysis* (L.O. 5)

Cardinale Company was recently formed. The balance of each item in the company's accounting equation is shown below for May 10 and for each of nine following business days.

	Cash	Accounts Receivable	Supplies	Land	Accounts Payable	Owner's Equity
May 10	$ 8,000	$4,000	$1,000	$ 8,000	$4,000	$17,000
11	11,000	4,000	1,000	8,000	4,000	20,000
12	6,000	4,000	1,000	13,000	4,000	20,000
15	6,000	4,000	3,000	13,000	6,000	20,000
16	5,000	4,000	3,000	13,000	5,000	20,000
17	7,000	2,000	3,000	13,000	5,000	20,000
18	16,000	2,000	3,000	13,000	5,000	29,000
19	13,000	2,000	3,000	13,000	2,000	29,000
22	12,000	2,000	4,000	13,000	2,000	29,000
23	8,000	2,000	4,000	13,000	2,000	25,000

Required

Assuming a single transaction took place on each day, describe briefly the transaction that was most likely to have occurred, beginning with May 11. Indicate which accounts were affected and by what amount. No revenue or expense transactions occurred on these dates.

Problem 1-7B *Income statement, statement of owner's equity, balance sheet* **(L.O. 6)**

Owner's equity, end of year
$175,000

Presented below are the amounts of (a) the assets and liabilities of Petoski Theater as of December 31 and (b) the revenues and expenses of the company for the year ended on that date. The items are listed in alphabetical order.

Accounts payable	$ 19,000	Note payable	$ 85,000
Accounts receivable	12,000	Property tax expense	4,000
Advertising expense	11,000	Rent expense	23,000
Building	170,000	Salary expense	63,000
Cash	10,000	Salary payable	1,000
Furniture	20,000	Service revenue	200,000
Interest expense	9,000	Supplies	3,000
Land	65,000		

The beginning amount of Jean Petoski, Capital, was $150,000, and during the year Petoski withdrew $65,000 for personal use.

Required

1. Prepare the income statement of Petoski Theater for the year ended December 31 of the current year.
2. Prepare the statement of owner's equity of the company for the year ended December 31.
3. Prepare the balance sheet of the company at December 31.

Problem 1-8B *Transaction analysis, accounting equation, financial statements* **(L.O. 5,6)**

Owner's equity $23,050

Lisa Reed owns and operates an interior design studio called Reed Interiors. The following amounts summarize the financial position of her business on August 31, 19X2:

	Assets			=	Liabilities	+	Owner's Equity
Cash +	Accounts Receivable +	Supplies +	Land	=	Accounts Payable	+	Lisa Reed, Capital
Bal. 1,250	1,500		12,000		8,000		6,750

During September 19X2 the following events occurred:

a. Reed inherited $15,000 and deposited the cash in the business bank account.
b. Performed services for a client and received cash of $700.
c. Paid off the beginning balance of accounts payable.
d. Purchased supplies on account, $500.
e. Collected cash from a customer on account, $1,000.
f. Invested personal cash of $1,000 in the business.
g. Consulted on the interior design of a major office building and billed the client for services rendered, $2,400.
h. Recorded the following business expenses for the month:
   (1) Paid office rent—$900.
   (2) Paid advertising—$100.
i. Sold supplies to another business for $150 cash, which was the cost of the supplies.
j. Withdrew cash of $1,800 for personal use.

Required

1. Analyze the effects of the above transactions on the accounting equation of Reed Interiors. Adapt the format of Exhibit 1-5.
2. Prepare the income statement of Reed Interiors for the month ended September 30, 19X2. List expenses in decreasing order by amount.
3. Prepare the statement of owner's equity of Reed Interiors for the month ended September 30, 19X2.
4. Prepare the balance sheet of Reed Interiors at September 30, 19X2.

Extending Your Knowledge

Decision Problems

No check figure

1. Using Financial Statements to Evaluate a Request for a Loan (L.O. 1,3)

The proprietors of two businesses, Dillard's Hardware Store and Leslie Falco Home Decorators, have sought business loans from you. To decide whether to make the loans, you have requested their balance sheets.

Dillard's Hardware Store
Balance Sheet
August 31, 19X4

Assets		Liabilities	
Cash	$ 1,000	Accounts payable	$ 12,000
Accounts receivable	14,000	Note payable	18,000
Merchandise inventory	85,000	Total liabilities	30,000
Store supplies	500		
Furniture and fixtures	9,000	**Owner's Equity**	
Building	90,000	Jack Dillard, capital	183,500
Land	14,000	Total liabilities	
Total assets	$213,500	and owner's equity	$213,500

Leslie Falco Home Decorators
Balance Sheet
August 31, 19X4

Assets		Liabilities	
Cash	$11,000	Accounts payable	$ 3,000
Accounts receivable	4,000	Note payable	18,000
Office supplies	1,000	Total liabilities	21,000
Office furniture	6,000		
Land	19,000	**Owner's Equity**	
		Leslie Falco, capital	20,000
		Total liabilities	
Total assets	$41,000	and owner's equity	$41,000

Required

1. Based solely on these balance sheets, which entity would you be more comfortable loaning money to? Explain fully, citing specific items and amounts from the balance sheets.
2. In addition to the balance sheet data, what other financial statement information would you require? Be specific.

2. Using Accounting Information (L.O. 1,3,4,5,6)

No check figure

A friend learns that you are taking an accounting course. Knowing that you do not plan a career in accounting, the friend asks why you are "wasting your time." Explain to the friend:

1. Why you are taking the course.
2. How accounting information is used or will be used:
   a. In your personal life.
   b. In the business life of your friend, who plans to be a farmer.
   c. In the business life of another friend who plans a career in sales.

Ethical Issue

An ethical issue of current importance centers on the nature of work that accounting firms perform. CPA firms audit the financial statements of companies in order to express a professional opinion on the reliability of those statements. For this audit opinion to be objective and unbiased, it is critical that the auditors be entirely independent of their clients. CPA firms also perform management advisory (consulting) services for clients. This work often includes designing accounting systems. In many cases the same CPA firm audits the financial statements of a company for which it has designed the accounting system.

Required

Discuss the ethical issue in this situation. Propose a solution.

Financial Statement Problems

1. Identifying Items from a Company's Financial Statements (L.O. 4)

No check figure

This and similar problems in succeeding chapters focus on the financial statements of an actual company: The Goodyear Tire & Rubber Company. As you study each problem, you will gradually build the confidence that you can understand and use actual financial statements.

Refer to the Goodyear financial statements in Appendix C, and answer the following questions:

1. How much in cash (including cash equivalents) did Goodyear have on December 31, 1990?
2. What were total assets at December 31, 1990? At December 31, 1989?
3. Write the company's accounting equation at December 31, 1990, by filling in the dollar amounts:

ASSETS = LIABILITIES + OWNER EQUITY

4. Identify net sales (revenue) for the year ended December 31, 1990. (Net sales means sales revenue after certain subtractions.)

5. How much net income or net loss did Goodyear experience for the year ended December 31, 1990? Was 1990 a good year or a bad year compared to 1989?

2. Identifying Items from an Actual Company's Financial Statements *(L. O. 4)*

Obtain the annual report of an actual company of your choosing. Annual reports are available in various forms including the original document in hard copy, microfiche, and computerized data bases such as that provided by Disclosure, Inc.

Answer these questions about the company. Concentrate on the current year in the annual report you select, except as directed for particular questions.

1. How much in cash (which may include cash equivalents) did the company have at the end of the current year? At the end of the preceding year? Did cash increase or decrease during the current year? By how much?
2. What were total assets at the end of the current year? At the end of the preceding year?
3. Write the company's accounting equation at the end of the current year by filling in the dollar amounts:

ASSETS = LIABILITIES + OWNER EQUITY

4. Identify net sales revenue for the current year. The company may label this as *Net sales, Sales, Net revenue,* or other title. How much was the corresponding revenue amount for the preceding year?
5. How much net income or net loss did the company experience for the current year? For the preceding year?

44 Part One   The Basic Structure of Accounting

Chapter 2

Recording Business Transactions

Grant Reynolds was the typical college graduate—bursting with energy and ideas. After finishing his studies at the University of Northern Iowa with a degree in marketing, he took a job with Marshall Field, a department store in Chicago. There he made the contacts in the marketing world needed to launch his own business for exporting lap-top computers to Eastern Europe. In its infancy, the business made only a few sales, but each sale was for a large amount. Grant's payroll consisted only of his personal withdrawals and the salary of an assistant. With only a few sales and a one-person staff, Grant simply kept informal accounting records in a notebook.

At the end of the first year of operations Grant noted that sales totaled $4.3 million. Grant was anxious to expand his business and needed a bank loan. However, he could not produce the financial statements the bank required. Grant's informal records did not give the bank the information it needed to evaluate his business and so make a decision on the loan. Grant had to hire a CPA to reconstruct the accounting records and create the financial statements to show how the business had performed and where it stood financially. As you read Chapter 2, consider the importance of keeping accurate business records and how accounting meets that need.

Discussion Question: What is wrong with using the type of analysis in Chapter 1 for a business like IBM? *ANSWER:* Too time-consuming, inefficient.

Chapter 1 illustrates how to account for business transactions by analyzing their effects on the accounting equation. That approach emphasizes accounting analysis, but it becomes unwieldy in day-to-day business if many transactions occur. In practice, accountants use a different approach to record accounting information. This chapter focuses on processing accounting information as it is actually done in practice.

The Account

OBJECTIVE 1

Define and use new terms introduced in the chapter

The basic summary device of accounting is the **account.** This is the detailed record of the changes that have occurred in a particular asset, liability, or owner's equity during a period of time. Each account appears on its own page. For convenient access to the information in the accounts the pages are grouped together in a single book called the **ledger.** When you hear reference to "keeping the books" or "auditing the books," the word *books* refers to the ledger. The ledger may be a bound book, a loose-leaf set of pages, or a computer record.

In the ledger, the accounts are grouped in three broad categories, based on the accounting equation:

$$\text{ASSETS} = \text{LIABILITIES} + \text{OWNER'S EQUITY}$$

Assets

Those economic resources that will benefit the business in the future are assets. The following asset accounts are common to many firms.

Cash. The Cash account shows the cash effects of a business's transactions. Cash means money and any medium of exchange that a bank accepts at face value. Cash includes currency, coins, money orders, certificates of deposit, and checks. The Cash account includes all cash items whether they are kept on hand, in a safe, in a cash register, or in a bank.

Point to Stress: A receivable is always an asset. A payable is a liability, a debt.

Notes Receivable. A business may sell its goods or services in exchange for a promissory note, which is a written pledge that the customer will pay the business a fixed amount of money by a certain date. The Notes Receivable account is a record of the promissory notes that the business expects to collect in cash.

Accounts Receivable. A business may sell its goods or services in exchange for an oral or implied promise for future cash receipt. Such sales are made on credit (on account). The Accounts Receivable account contains these amounts.

Prepaid Expenses. A business often pays certain expenses in advance. A prepaid expense is an asset because the business avoids having to pay cash in the future for the specified expense. The ledger holds a separate asset account for each prepaid expense. Prepaid Rent and Prepaid Insurance are prepaid expenses that occur often in business. Office Supplies are also accounted for as prepaid expenses.

Land. The Land account is a record of the land that a business owns and uses in its operations.

Building. The cost of a business's buildings—office, warehouse, garage, and the like—appear in the Building account.

Discussion Question: List some assets not categorized as Cash, Receivables, or Prepaid Expenses. ANSWER: Property, Equipment, Investments, Inventory.

Equipment, Furniture, and Fixtures. A business has a separate asset account for each type of equipment—Office Equipment and Store Equipment, for example. The Furniture and Fixtures account shows the cost of this asset.

Other asset categories and accounts will be discussed as needed. For example, many businesses have an Investments account for their investments in other companies.

Liabilities

Recall that a *liability* is a debt. A business generally has fewer liability accounts than asset accounts because a business's liabilities can be summarized under relatively few categories.

Notes Payable. This account is the opposite of the Notes Receivable account. Notes Payable represents the amounts that the business must pay because it signed a promissory note to purchase goods or services.

Accounts Payable. This account is the opposite of the Accounts Receivable account. The oral or implied promise to pay off debts arising from credit purchases of goods appears in the Accounts Payable account. Such a purchase is said to be made on account. Other liability categories and accounts are added as needed. Taxes Payable, Wages Payable, and Salary Payable are accounts that appear in many ledgers.

Owner's Equity

The owner's claim to the assets of the business is called *owner's equity*. In a proprietorship or a partnership, owner's equity is often split into separate accounts for the owner's capital balance and the owner's withdrawals.

Capital. This account shows the owner's claim to the assets of the business. After total liabilities are subtracted from total assets, the remainder is the owner's capital. The owner's investments in the business are recorded directly in the Capital account. The balance of the capital account equals the owner's investments in the business plus its net income and minus net losses and owner withdrawals. In addition to the capital account, the following accounts also appear in the owner's equity section of the ledger.

Point to Stress: Two things increase owner's equity:
1 investments by owner, and
2 net income (revenue greater than expenses).
Two things decrease owner's equity:
1 withdrawals by owner, and
2 net loss (expenses greater than revenue).

Withdrawals. When the owner withdraws cash or other assets from the business for personal use, its assets and its owner's equity both decrease. The amounts taken out of the business appear in a separate account entitled Withdrawals, or Drawing. If withdrawals were recorded directly in the capital account, the amount of owner withdrawals would not be highlighted. To separate these two amounts for decision making, businesses use a separate account for Withdrawals. This account shows a *decrease* in owner's equity.

Revenues. The increase in owner's equity from delivering goods or services to customers or clients is called *revenue*. The ledger contains as many revenue accounts as needed. Gary Lyon's accounting practice would have a Service Revenue account for amounts earned by providing accounting service for clients. If the business loans money to an outsider, it will also need an

EXHIBIT 2-1 *The Ledger (Asset, Liability, and Owner's Equity Accounts)*

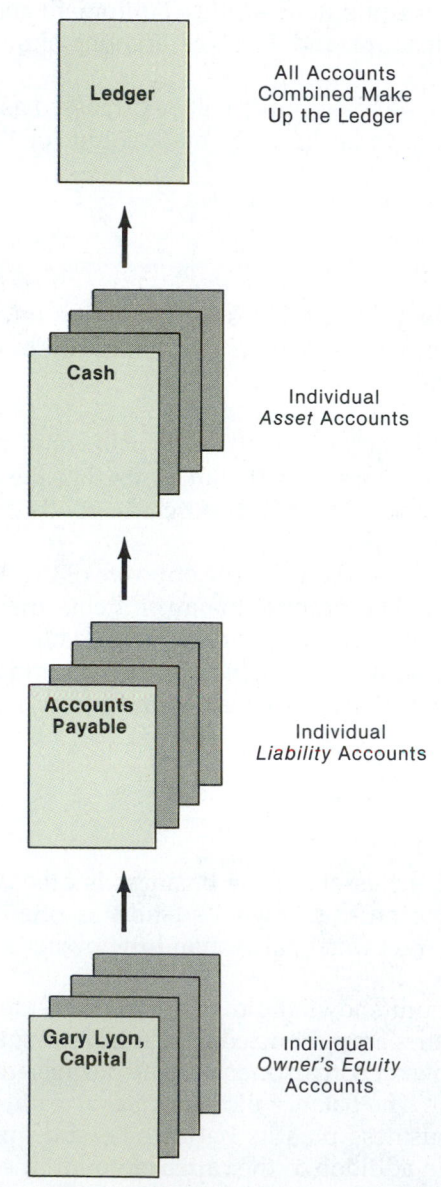

Interest Revenue account for the interest earned on the loan. If the business rents a building to a tenant, it will need a Rent Revenue account. Increases in revenue accounts are *increases* in owner's equity.

Expenses.   The cost of operating a business is called *expense*. Expenses have the opposite effect of revenues, so they decrease owner's equity. A business needs a separate account for each category of its expenses, such as Salary Expense, Rent Expense, Advertising Expense, and Utilities Expense. Expense accounts are decreases in owner's equity.

Exhibit 2-1 shows how asset, liability, and owner's equity accounts can be grouped into the ledger. Typically, each account occupies a separate sheet or record.

Double-Entry Bookkeeping

Accounting is based on double-entry bookkeeping, which means that accountants record the *dual effects* of a business transaction. We know that each transaction affects two accounts. For example, Gary Lyon's $50,000 cash investment in his accounting practice increased both the Cash account and the Capital account of the business. It would be incomplete to record only the increase in the entity's cash without recording the increase in its owner's equity.

Consider a *cash purchase of supplies*. What are the dual effects of this transaction? The purchase (1) decreases cash and (2) increases supplies. A *purchase of supplies on credit* (1) increases supplies and (2) increases accounts payable. A *cash payment on account* (1) decreases cash and (2) decreases accounts payable. All transactions have at least two effects on the entity.

Discussion Question: Refer to the chapter-opening vignette. Grant Reynolds recorded all his business's transactions informally in a notebook. What is the problem with that? *ANSWER:* Recording transactions in a notebook is essentially a single-entry bookkeeping system in which the balance in the notebook cannot be verified. If Grant had used a double-entry system, then certain errors would be revealed if the accounts did not balance.

The T-Account

How do accountants record transactions in the accounts? The account format used for most illustrations in this book is called the T-account. It takes the form of the capital letter "T." The vertical line in the letter divides the account into its left and right sides. The account title rests on the horizontal line. For example, the Cash account of a business appears in the following T-account format:

Teaching Tip: A T-account is a quick way to show the effect of several transactions on a particular account. It is one of the most useful shortcuts in accounting.

Cash	
Left side	Right side
Debit	*Credit*

The left side of the account is called the **debit** side, and the right side is called the **credit** side. Often beginners in the study of accounting are confused by the words *debit* and *credit*. To become comfortable using them, simply remember this:

Typical Student Misconception: Tell the students right now to forget anything they might be thinking about *debits* and *credits*, such as terminology used on a bank statement. They must memorize this rule:

Debit = left side of an account
Credit = right side of an account

The students should think of debit and credit as being directions, with debit meaning left and credit meaning right.

Debit = Left Side
Credit = Right Side

Even though *left side* and *right side* are more descriptive, *debit* and *credit* are too deeply entrenched in accounting to avoid using.[1]

Increases and Decreases in the Accounts

The type of an account determines how increases and decreases in it are recorded. For any given account, all increases are recorded on one side, and all decreases are recorded on the other side. Increases in *assets* are recorded in the left (the debit) side of the account. Decreases in assets are recorded in the right (the credit) side of the account. Conversely, increases in *liabilities* and *owner's equity* are recorded by *credits*. Decreases are recorded by *debits*.

This pattern of recording debits and credits is based on the accounting equation:

$$ASSETS = LIABILITIES + OWNER'S\ EQUITY$$

Notice that assets are on the opposite side of the equation from liabilities and owner's equity. This explains why increases and decreases in assets are recorded in the opposite manner from liabilities and owner's equity. It also explains why liabilities and owner's equity are treated the same way: they are on the same side of the equal sign. Exhibit 2-2 shows the relationship between the accounting equation and the rules of debit and credit.

To illustrate the ideas diagrammed in Exhibit 2-2, reconsider the first transaction from the preceding chapter. Gary Lyon invested $50,000 in cash to begin his accounting practice. Which accounts of the business are affected? By what amounts? On what side (debit or credit)? The answer is that Assets and Capital would increase by $50,000, as the following T-accounts show.

Point to Stress: Emphasize that the accounting equation must balance after every transaction. However, verifying that total assets equal the sum of total liabilities and owner's equity is no longer necessary after every transaction. The accounting equation will balance as long as the debits in each transaction equal the credits in the transaction.

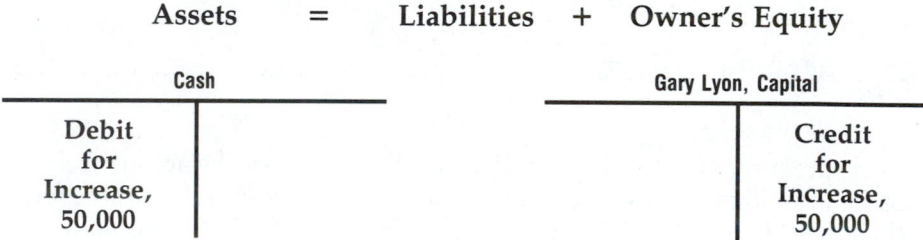

Assets	=	Liabilities	+	Owner's Equity

Cash			Gary Lyon, Capital
Debit for Increase, 50,000			Credit for Increase, 50,000

Notice that Assets = Liabilities + Owner's Equity, *and* that total debits = total credits.

Transparency T2-1

EXHIBIT 2-2 *Accounting Equation and the Rules of Debit and Credit*

Accounting Equation:	Assets		=	Liabilities		+	Owner's Equity	
Rules of Debit and Credit:	Debit for Increase	Credit for Decrease		Debit for Decrease	Credit for Increase		Debit for Decrease	Credit for Increase

---

[1] The words *debit* and *credit* have a Latin origin (*debitum* and *creditum*). Pacioli, the Italian monk who wrote about accounting in the fifteenth century, used these terms.

The amount remaining in an account is called its *balance*. This initial transaction gives Cash a $50,000 debit balance and Gary Lyon, Capital a $50,000 credit balance.

The second transaction is a $40,000 cash purchase of land. This transaction affects two assets: Cash and Land. It decreases (credits) Cash and increases (debits) Land, as shown in the T-accounts:

OBJECTIVE 2

Apply the rules of debit and credit

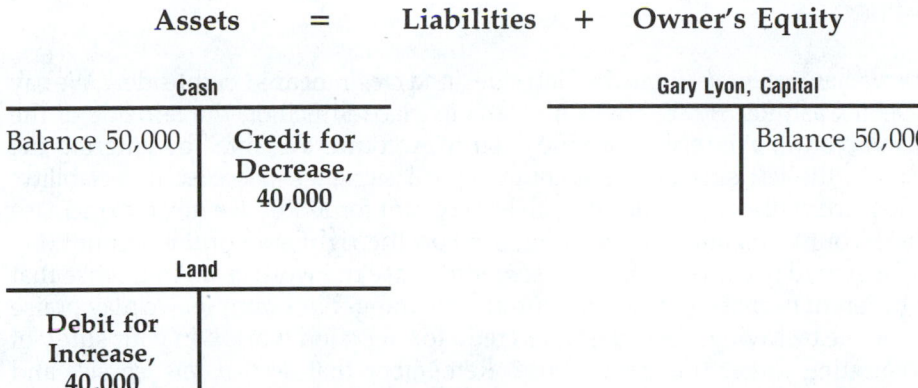

After this transaction, Cash has a $10,000 debit balance ($50,000 debit balance −$40,000 credit amount), Land's debit balance is $40,000, and the Capital account has a $50,000 credit balance

Transaction 3 is a $500 purchase of office supplies on account. This transaction increases the asset Office Supplies and the liability Accounts Payable, as shown in the following accounts:

Assets   =   Liabilities   +   Owner's Equity

Cash	Accounts Payable	Gary Lyon, Capital
Balance 10,000	Credit for Increase, 500	Balance 50,000

Office Supplies
Debit for Increase, 500

Land
Balance 40,000

Teaching Tip: Every account balance derives from four components:

1.   **Beginning balance**
2.   **+ Increases**
3.   **− Decreases**
4.   **= Ending Balance**

For example, if the cash on hand at the beginning of the period was $2,000, cash receipts during the period totalled $26,000, and cash payments were $25,000, how much cash was on hand at the end of the period? *ANSWER:* $3,000. If you know any three of the four components you can always figure out the fourth. Increases in some accounts are recorded on the debit side and some are recorded on the credit side. Likewise, decreases in some accounts are recorded on the debit side and some are recorded on the credit side.

Accountants create accounts as needed. The process of writing a new T-account in preparation for recording a transaction is called *opening the account*. For Transaction 1, we opened the Cash account and the Gary Lyon, Capital account. For Transaction 2, we opened the Land account, and for Transaction 3, Office Supplies and Accounts Payable.

Accountants could record all transactions directly in the accounts, as we have shown for the first three transactions. However, that way of accounting is not practical because it does not leave a clear record of each transaction. Suppose you need to know what account was debited and what account was credited in a particular transaction. Looking at each account in the ledger does not answer this question. Why? Because double-entry accounting always affects at least two accounts. Therefore, you may have to search through all the accounts in the ledger to find both sides of a particular transaction. To avoid this waste of time, accountants keep a record of each transaction in a journal and then transfer this information into the accounts.

The Debit-Credit Language of Accounting

As we have seen, *debit* means "left side" and *credit* means "right side." We say "Debit Cash for $1,000," which means to place $1,000 on the left side of the cash account. We record "a $500 debit to Accounts Payable" by entering the $500 in the left side of this account, which signals a decrease in a liability. When we speak of "crediting a liability account for $750," we mean to increase the account's balance by recording $750 on the right side of the account.

In everyday conversation, we sometimes use the word *credit* in a sense that is different from its technical accounting meaning. For example, we may praise someone by saying, "She deserves credit for her good work." In your study of accounting forget this general use. Remember that *debit means left side* and *credit means right side*. Whether an account is increased or decreased by a debit or credit depends on the type of account (see Exhibit 2-2).

Recording Transactions in Journals

In actual practice, accountants record transactions first in a book called the **journal.** A journal is a chronological record of the entity's transactions. In this section, we describe the recording process and illustrate how to use the journal and the ledger.

The recording process follows these five steps:

1. Identify the transaction from source documents, such as bank deposit slips, sales receipts, and check stubs.
2. Specify each account affected by the transaction and classify it by type (asset, liability, or owner's equity).
3. Determine whether each account is increased or decreased by the transaction.
4. Using the rules of debit and credit, determine whether to debit or credit the account.
5. Enter the transaction in the journal, including a brief explanation for the journal entry. Accountants write the debit side of the entry first and the credit side next.

We have discussed steps 1, 2, 3, and 4. Step 5, "Enter the transaction in the journal," means to write the transaction in the journal. This step is also called "making the journal entry," "preparing the journal entry," or "journalizing the transaction." A major part of learning accounting is understanding how to prepare journal entries.

Let's apply the five steps to journalize the first transaction of the accounting practice of Gary Lyon, CPA—the $50,000 cash investment in the business.

OBJECTIVE 3
Record transactions in the journal

Step 1. The source documents are the bank deposit slip and Lyon's $50,000 check, which is drawn on his personal bank account.

Step 2. *Cash* and *Gary Lyon, Capital* are the accounts affected by the transaction. Cash is an asset account, and Gary Lyon, Capital is an owner's equity account.

Step 3. Both accounts increase by $50,000. Therefore, debit Cash: it is the asset account that is increased. Also, credit Gary Lyon, Capital: it is the owner's equity account that is increased.

Step 4. Debit Cash to record an increase in this asset account. Credit Gary Lyon, Capital to record an increase in this owner's equity account.

Step 5. The journal entry is

Date	Accounts and Explanation	Debit	Credit
Apr. 2	Cash	50,000	
	Gary Lyon, Capital		50,000
	Initial investment by owner.		

Discussion Question: Why do we use two records, the journal and the ledger? Why can't we get by with just one or the other? ANSWER: Businesses need a chronological record of transactions (the journal) and a record of each account's activity and its balance (the ledger). Both are necessary to make sure that all the information is reported accurately.

Note that the journal entry includes (a) the date of the transaction, (b) the title of the account debited (placed flush left) and the title of the account credited (indented slightly), (c) the dollar amounts of the debit (left) and credit (right)—dollar signs are omitted in the money columns, and (d) a short explanation of the transaction.

A helpful hint: To get off to the best start when analyzing a transaction, you should first pinpoint its effects (if any) on cash. Did cash increase or decrease? Then find its effect on other accounts. Typically, it is easier to identify the effect of a transaction on cash than to identify the effect on other accounts.

The journal offers information that the ledger accounts do not provide. Each journal entry shows the complete effect of a business transaction. Let's examine Gary Lyon's initial investment. The Cash account shows a single figure, the $50,000 debit. We know that every transaction has a credit, so in what account will we find the corresponding $50,000 credit? In this simple illustration, we know that the Capital account holds this figure. But imagine the difficulties an accountant would face trying to link debits and credits for hundreds of daily transactions—without a separate record of each transaction. The journal answers this problem and presents the full story for each transaction.

The journal can be a loose-leaf notebook, a bound book, or a computer listing. Exhibit 2-3 shows how a journal page might look with the first transaction entered.

Class Exercise: Prepare the journal entry to record a $1,600 payment on an account payable.

1 Identify the accounts.
  Cash
  Accounts Payable
2 Are they increased or decreased?
  Both are decreased.
3 Debit or credit?
  Debit Accounts Payable; reductions in liabilities are debits.
  Credit Cash; reductions in assets are credits.
4 Enter transaction, debit first.

Accounts Payable   1,600
  Cash   1,600

EXHIBIT 2-3 *The Journal*

			Page 6
	Journal		
Date	Accounts and Explanation	Debit	Credit
Apr. 2	Cash	50,000	
	Gary Lyon, Capital		50,000
	Initial investment by owner.		

Teaching Tip: Refer to Exhibit 2-3. In a journal entry, the account debited is always written first (to the left), the account credited is indented (to the right), and the explanation is flush with the account debited. Although many procedures in accounting vary, journal entries should always be recorded in this format.

EXHIBIT 2-4 *Journal Entry and Posting to the Ledger*

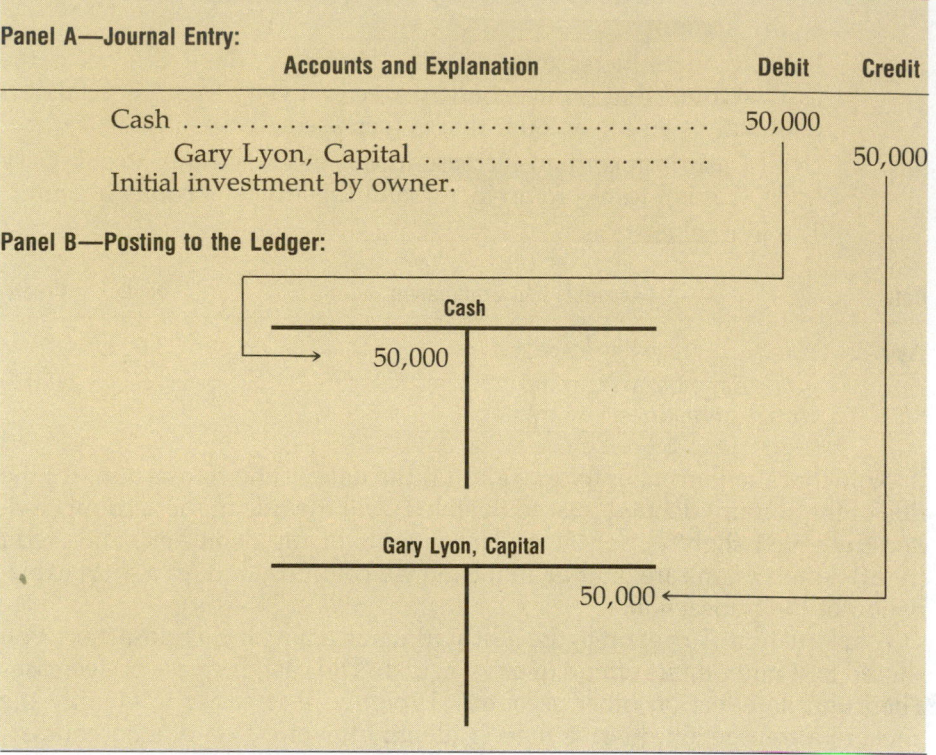

Panel A—Journal Entry:

Accounts and Explanation	Debit	Credit
Cash	50,000	
Gary Lyon, Capital		50,000
Initial investment by owner.		

Panel B—Posting to the Ledger:

Cash

50,000

Gary Lyon, Capital

50,000

In these introductory discussions we temporarily ignore the date of each transaction in order to focus on the accounts and their dollar amounts.

Posting from the Journal to the Ledger

Point to Stress: Posting is merely a process of copying information *from* the journal *to* the ledger. Each part of the journal entry must be copied accurately. Computers perform this part of the recording process automatically in many accounting software packages.

Posting means transferring the amounts from the journal to the appropriate accounts in the ledger. Debits in the journal are posted as debits in the ledger, and credits in the journal as credits in the ledger. The initial investment transaction of Gary Lyon is posted to the ledger as shown in Exhibit 2-4.

Flow of Accounting Data

Teaching Tip: Emphasize again the steps in analyzing a transaction. Students often like to skip the first steps and go right to the debits and credits without first thinking about what is happening in the transaction. Remind them to ask: (1) Which accounts are affected? (2) Are those accounts increased or decreased? (3) Do you debit or credit each account?

Exhibit 2-5 summarizes the flow of accounting data from the business transaction to the ledger.

Illustrative Problem

In this section, we illustrate transaction analysis, journalizing, and posting. We continue the example of Gary Lyon, CPA, and account for six of his early transactions. Transactions that affect cash are the easiest to analyze. Therefore, when a transaction affects cash, we account for the cash effect first.

EXHIBIT 2-5   *Flow of Accounting Data*

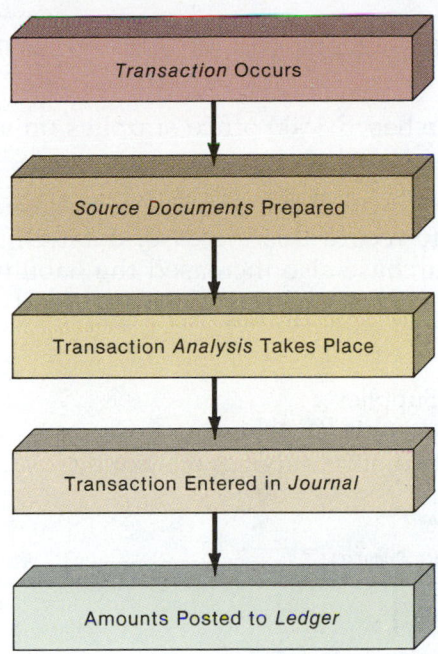

Transaction Analysis, Journalizing, and Posting

1. *Transaction:* Lyon invested $50,000 to begin his accounting practice.

   Analysis: Lyon's investment in the business increased its asset cash; to record this increase, debit Cash.
   His investment also increased the owner's equity of the entity; to record this increase, credit Gary Lyon, Capital.

   Journal Entry:

   Cash 50,000
         Gary Lyon, Capital   50,000
   Initial investment by owner.

   Ledger Accounts:

Cash	Gary Lyon, Capital
(1) 50,000	(1) 50,000

2. *Transaction:* He paid $40,000 cash for land as a future office location.

   Analysis: The purchase decreased cash; therefore, credit Cash. The purchase increased the entity's asset land; to record this increase, debit Land.

   Journal Entry:

   Land 40,000
         Cash   40,000
   Paid cash for land.

Teaching Tip: Notice that each debit (or credit) that is recorded in a T-account will be keyed in some form to its corresponding credit (or debit). Note, for example, the (1) alongside the $50,000 debit in the Cash account and the (1) alongside the $50,000 credit to Gary Lyon, Capital. To save time in tracing both sides of a transaction, never omit these marks.

Cash		Land	
(1) 50,000	(2) 40,000	(2) 40,000	

3. *Transaction:* He purchased $500 office supplies on account payable.

Analysis: The credit purchase of office supplies increased this asset; to record this increase, debit Office Supplies. The purchase also increased the liability, accounts payable; to record this increase, credit Accounts Payable.

Teaching Tip: Point out that Accounts Payable was decreased with a *debit,* while Cash was decreased with a *credit.* Emphasize again that the words debit and credit do not mean increase or decrease.

Journal Entry:
Office Supplies 500
    Accounts Payable 500
Purchased office supplies on account.

Ledger Accounts:

Office Supplies		Accounts Payable	
(3) 500			(3) 500

Discussion Question: What would happen in this transaction if debit meant increase and credit meant decrease? ANSWER: Because both Accounts Payable and Cash are being decreased, both would be credited. That would give us no way to verify that the accounting equation was in balance because debits would not equal credits.

4. *Transaction:* He paid $400 on the account payable created in the preceding transaction.

Analysis: The payment decreased the asset cash; therefore, credit Cash. The payment also decreased the liability, accounts payable; to record this decrease, debit Accounts Payable.

Journal Entry:
Accounts Payable 400
    Cash 400
Paid cash on account.

Ledger Accounts:

Cash		Accounts Payable	
(1) 50,000	(2) 40,000	(4) 400	(3) 500
	(4) 400		

5. *Transaction:* He remodeled his personal residence. This is not a transaction of the accounting practice, so no journal entry is made.

6. *Transaction:* Lyon withdrew $2,100 cash for personal living expenses.

Analysis: The withdrawal decreased the entity's cash; therefore, credit Cash.
The transaction also decreased the owner's equity of the entity and must be recorded by a debit to an owner's equity account. Decreases in the owner's equity of a proprietorship that result from owner withdrawals are debited to a separate owner's

equity account entitled Withdrawals. Therefore, debit Gary Lyon, Withdrawals.

Journal Entry:	Gary Lyon, Withdrawals	2,100	
	Cash		2,100
	Withdrawal of cash by owner.		

Ledger Accounts:

Cash			Gary Lyon, Withdrawals	
(1) 50,000	(2) 40,000		(6) **2,100**	
	(4) 400			
	(6) **2,100**			

As each journal entry is posted to the ledger, it is keyed by date or by transaction number. In this way, a trail is provided through the accounting records so that any transaction can be traced from the journal to the ledger and, if need be, back to the journal. This linking allows the accountant to locate efficiently any information needed.

Discussion Question: Ask the students if they have noticed anything in common among all the transactions. *ANSWER:* Each transaction has a debit and a credit.

Ledger Accounts after Posting

We next illustrate how the accounts look when the amounts of the preceding transactions have been posted. The accounts are grouped under the accounting equation's headings.

Note that each account has a balance figure. This amount is the difference between the account's total debits and its total credits. For example, the balance in the Cash account is the difference between the debits, $50,000, and the credits, $42,500 ($40,000 + $400 + $2,100). Thus the balance figure is $7,500. The balance amounts are not journal entries posted to the accounts, so we set an account balance apart by horizontal lines.

If the sum of an account's debits is greater than the sum of its credits, that account has a debit balance, as the Cash account does here. If the sum of its credits is greater, that account has a credit balance, as Accounts Payable does.

Assets	=	Liabilties	+	Owner's Equity

Cash			Accounts Payable			Gary Lyon, Capital	
(1) 50,000	(2) 40,000	(4) 400	(3) 500			(1) 50,000	
	(4) 400		Bal. 100			Bal. 50,000	
	(6) 2,100						
Bal. 7,500							

Office Supplies			Gary Lyon, Withdrawals	
(3) 500			(6) 2,100	
Bal. 500			Bal. 2,100	

Land	
(2) 40,000	
Bal. 40,000	

Transparency T2-2

Trial Balance

Point to Stress: A trial balance is always prepared in this order: assets, liabilities, capital, and withdrawals. Revenues and expenses follow.

A **trial balance** is a list of all accounts with their balances. It provides a check on accuracy by showing whether the total debits equal the total credits. A trial balance may be taken at any time the postings are up to date. Exhibit 2-6 is the trial balance of the general ledger of Gary Lyon's accounting practice after the first six transactions have been journalized and posted.

The word *trial* is well chosen. The list is prepared as a *test* of the accounts' balances. The trial balance shows the accountant whether the total debits and total credits are equal. In this way it may signal accounting errors. For example, if only the debit (or only the credit) side of a transaction is posted, the total debits will not equal the total credits. If a debit is posted as a credit or vice versa, debits and credits will be out of balance. For example, if the $500 debit in Office Supplies is incorrectly posted as a credit, total debits will be $49,600 and total credits will be $50,600. The trial balance alerts the accountant to such errors in posting.

Some errors may not be revealed by the trial balance. For example, a $1,000 cash payment for supplies may be credited to Accounts Payable instead of to Cash. This error would cause both Cash and Accounts Payable to be overstated, each by $1,000. However, because an asset and a liability are overstated by the same amount, the trial balance would still show total debits equal to total credits. Also, if an accountant erroneously recorded a $5,000 transaction at only $500, the trial balance would show no error. However, total debits and total credits would both be understated by $4,500 (that is, $5,000 − $500).

Transparency T2-2

Do not confuse the trial balance with the balance sheet. Accountants prepare a trial balance for their internal records. The company reports its financial position—both inside and outside the business—on the balance sheet, a formal financial statement.

OBJECTIVE 5
Prepare a trial balance

Discussion Question: Refer to Exhibit 2-6. Assume that Gary Lyon, Withdrawals, $2,100, is erroneously listed in the credit column on the trial balance. Recompute the trial balance totals. ANSWER: Debit = $48,000; Credit = $52,200.

To find the mistake, calculate the difference between the column totals. ANSWER: $52,200 − $48,000 = $4,200.

Then divide the difference by two. ANSWER: $4,200 ÷ 2 = $2,100.

If you find that amount somewhere on the trial balance, you may have entered it in the wrong column.

This is one easy way to find an error if your trial balance does not balance. What other types of errors might you look for?

EXHIBIT 2-6 *Trial Balance*

Gary Lyon, CPA
Trial Balance
April 30, 19X1

Account Titles	Balance	
	Debit	**Credit**
Cash............................	$ 7,500	
Office supplies	500	
Land	40,000	
Accounts payable		$ 100
Gary Lyon, capital		50,000
Gary Lyon, withdrawals	2,100	
Total.........................	$50,100	$50,100

Summary Problem for Your Review

On August 1, 19X5, Liz Shea opens a business that she names Shea's Research Service. She will be the sole owner of the business, so it will be a proprietorship. During the entity's first ten days of operations, the following transactions take place:

a. To begin operations, Shea deposits $50,000 of personal funds in a bank account entitled Shea's Research Service.
b. Shea pays $40,000 cash for a small house to be used as an office.
c. Shea purchases $250 in office supplies on credit (that is, on account).
d. Shea pays cash of $6,000 for office furniture.
e. Shea pays $150 on the account payable she created in transaction c.
f. Shea withdraws $1,000 cash for personal use.

Required

1. Prepare the journal entries to record these transactions. Key the journal entries by letter.
2. Post the entries to the ledger.
3. Prepare the trial balance of Shea's Research Service at August 10, 19X5.

SOLUTION TO REVIEW PROBLEM

Requirement 1

Accounts and Explanation	Debit	Credit
a. Cash	50,000	
Liz Shea, Capital		50,000
Initial investment by owner.		
b. Building	40,000	
Cash		40,000
Purchased building for an office.		
c. Office Supplies	250	
Accounts Payable		250
Purchased office supplies on account.		
d. Office Furniture	6,000	
Cash		6,000
Purchased office furniture.		
e. Accounts Payable	150	
Cash		150
Paid cash on account.		
f. Liz Shea, Withdrawals	1,000	
Cash		1,000
Withdrew cash for personal use.		

Requirement 2

Assets

Cash			Office Supplies	
(a) 50,000	(b) 40,000		(c) 250	
	(d) 6,000			
	(e) 150		Bal. 250	
	(f) 1,000			
Bal. 2,850				

Office Furniture		Building	
(d) 6,000		(b) 40,000	
Bal. 6,000		Bal. 40,000	

Liabilities   Owner's Equity

Accounts Payable		Liz Shea, Capital		Liz Shea, Withdrawals	
(e) 150	(c) 250		(a) 50,000	(f) 1,000	
	Bal. 100		Bal. 50,000	Bal. 1,000	

Requirement 3

Shea's Research Service
Trial Balance
August 10, 19X5

Account Title	Balance	
	Debit	Credit
Cash	$ 2,850	
Office supplies	250	
Office furniture	6,000	
Building	40,000	
Accounts payable		$ 100
Liz Shea, capital		50,000
Liz Shea, withdrawals	1,000	
Total	$50,100	$50,100

Details of Journals and Ledgers

To focus on the main points of journalizing and posting, we purposely omitted certain essential data. In actual practice, the journal and the ledger provide additional details that create a "trail" through the accounting records for future reference. For example, an accountant may need to verify the date of a transaction or to determine whether a journal entry has been posted to the ledger. Let's take a closer look at the journal and the ledger.

Journal. Exhibit 2-7, Panel B, presents the journal format most often used by accountants. Note that the journal page number appears in the upper-right corner.

As the column headings indicate, the *journal* displays the following information:

1. The *date,* which is very important because it indicates when the transaction occurred. The year appears first. It is not necessary to repeat it for each journal entry. The year appears only when the journal is started or when the year has changed. Note that the year appears with an *X* in the third column. We present the year in this way because the dates we choose are for illustration only. Thus 19X1 is followed by 19X2, and so on. We will use this format throughout the book. Like the year, the month is entered only once. The second date column shows the day of the transaction. This column is filled in for every transaction.

2. The *account title* and explanation of the transaction. You are already familiar with this presentation from Exhibit 2-3.

3. The *posting reference,* abbreviated Post. Ref. How this column helps the accountant becomes clear when we discuss the details of posting.

4. The *debit* column, which shows the amount debited.

5. The *credit* column, which shows the amount credited.

Ledger. Exhibit 2-7, Panel C, presents the *ledger* in T-account format. Each account has its own page in the illustrative ledger. Our example shows Gary Lyon's Cash account. This account maintains the basic format of the T-account but offers more information.

The account title appears at the top of the ledger page. Note also the account number at the upper-right column. Each account has its own identification number. We will look later at how accountants assign account numbers.

The column headings identify the ledger account's features.

1. The date.
2. The item column. This space is used for any special notation.
3. The journal reference column, abbreviated Jrnl. Ref. The importance of this column becomes clear when we discuss the mechanics of posting.
4. The debit column, with the amount debited.
5. The credit column, with the amount credited.

> *Discussion Question:* What would happen if the entry were recorded in the journal without an explanation? *ANSWER:* It might be difficult to remember what the entry was several months later. You might have to look up the source document, which would be more time-consuming than recording an explanation in the journal.

Posting

We know that posting means moving information from the journal to the ledger accounts. But how do we handle the additional details that appear in

EXHIBIT 2–7 *Details of Journalizing and Posting*

Panel A—Illustrative Transactions

Date	Transaction
April 2, 19X1	Gary Lyon invested $50,000 in his accounting practice.
3	Paid $500 cash for office supplies.

Panel B—Journal

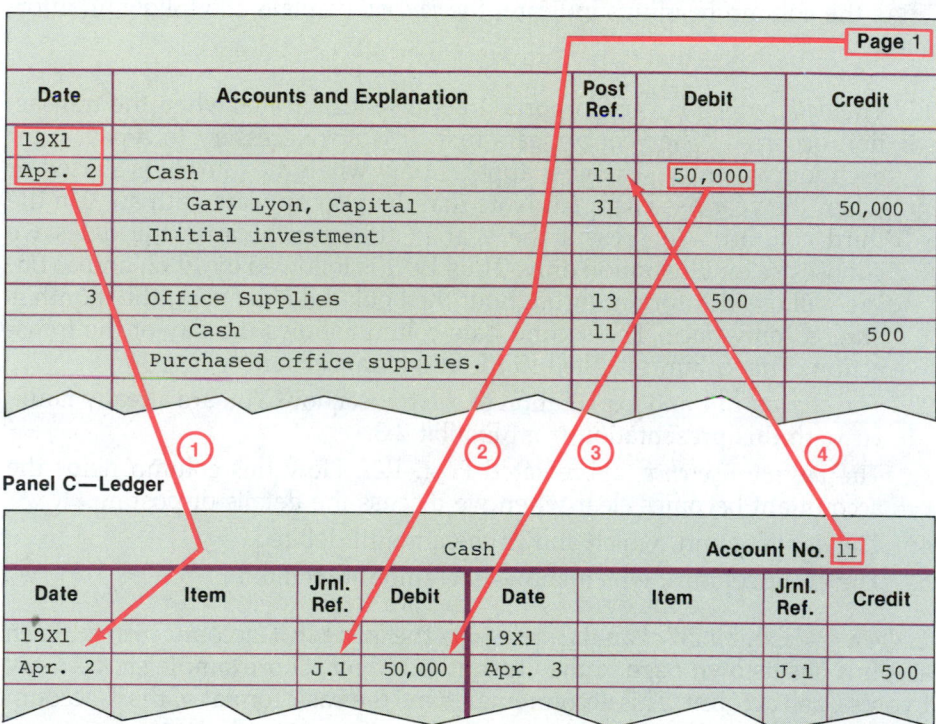

Page 1

Date	Accounts and Explanation	Post Ref.	Debit	Credit
19X1				
Apr. 2	Cash	11	50,000	
	Gary Lyon, Capital	31		50,000
	Initial investment			
3	Office Supplies	13	500	
	Cash	11		500
	Purchased office supplies.			

Point to Stress: Each debit and credit in the journal must be posted accurately to the ledger, and posted only once. The very detailed system of posting reference abbreviations indicates which entries have been posted and to which accounts. An accountant who needs to examine the activity in an account can immediately find the journal where each posted amount was initially recorded.

Panel C—Ledger

Cash   Account No. 11

Date	Item	Jrnl. Ref.	Debit	Date	Item	Jrnl. Ref.	Credit
19X1				19X1			
Apr. 2		J.1	50,000	Apr. 3		J.1	500

Office Supplies   Account No. 13

Date	Item	Jrnl. Ref.	Debit	Date	Item	Jrnl. Ref.	Credit
19X1							
Apr. 3		J.1	500				

Gary Lyon, Capital   Account No. 31

Date	Item	Jrnl. Ref.	Debit	Date	Item	Jrnl. Ref.	Credit
				19X1			
				Apr. 2		J.1	50,000

the journal and the ledger formats that we have just seen? Exhibit 2-7 illustrates the steps in full detail. Panel A lists the first two transactions of Gary Lyon, CPA; Panel B presents the journal; and Panel C shows the ledger.

Since the flow of accounting data moves from the journal to the ledger, the accountant first records the journal entry, as shown in Panel B. The transaction data are given in Panel A, except for the Post. Ref. number. Let's trace the arrows to follow the details of posting.

Arrow 1 traces the date, Apr. 2, 19X1, from the journal to the ledger account Cash.

Arrow 2 begins at the journal's page number, Page 1, and ends in the journal reference column, Jrnl. Ref., of the ledger. The J. 1 entry in that column stands for "Journal (page) 1." Why bother with this detail? If an accountant is using the Cash account and needs to locate the original journal entry, the journal page number tells where to look.

Arrow 3 indicates that the accountant posts the debit figure—$50,000 in this journal entry—as a debit figure in the account.

Arrow 4 points to a posting detail. Once the accountant has posted a dollar figure to the appropriate account, that account's number is entered in the journal's Post. Ref. column. This step indicates that the information for that account has been posted from the journal to the ledger. A blank Post Ref. column for a journal entry means that the entry has not yet been posted to the ledger account.

Having performed these steps for the debit entry, the accountant then posts the credit entry to the ledger. After posting, the accountant draws up the trial balance, as we discussed earlier.

Discussion Question: Suppose a bookkeeper recorded a transaction in the general journal, posted the debit, and was about to post the credit when he became severely ill. How does his replacement know where to begin posting? *ANSWER:* He looks for the last posting reference in the journal.

Four-Column Account Format

The ledger accounts illustrated in Exhibit 2-7 are in two-column T-account format, with the debit column placed left and the credit column placed right. The T-account clearly distinguishes debits from credits and is often used for illustrative purposes that do not require much detail.

Another standard format has four amount columns, as illustrated for the Cash account in Exhibit 2-8. The first pair of amount columns are for the debit and credit amounts, and the second pair of amount columns are for the

EXHIBIT 2-8   *Account in Four-Column Format*

Account Cash						Account No. 11	
						Balance	
Date	**Item**	**Jrnl. Ref.**	**Debit**	**Credit**	**Debit**	**Credit**
19X1						
Apr. 2		J.1	50000		50000	
3		J.1		500	49500	

account's balance. This four-column format keeps a running balance in the account and for this reason is used more often in actual practice.

In the exhibit, Cash has a debit balance of $50,000 after the first transaction is posted and a debit balance of $49,500 after the second transaction.

Chart of Accounts

As you know, the general ledger contains the business's accounts grouped under the headings Assets, Liabilities, Owner's Equity, Revenues, and Expenses. To keep track of their accounts, organizations have a **chart of accounts,** which lists all the accounts and their account numbers. These account numbers are used as posting references, as illustrated by arrow 4 in Exhibit 2–7. It is easier to write the account number, 11, in the posting reference column of the journal than to write the account title, Cash. Also, this numbering system makes it easy to locate individual accounts in the ledger.

Assets are often numbered beginning with 1, liabilities with 2, owner's equity with 3, revenues with 4, and expenses with 5. The second digit in an account number indicates the position of the individual account within the category. For example, Cash may be account number 11, which is the first asset account. Accounts Receivable may be account number 12, the second asset account. Accounts Payable may be account number 21, the first liability account. All accounts are numbered using this system.

Many organizations have so many accounts that they use three- or four-digit account numbers. For example, account number 101 may be Cash on Hand, account number 102 may be Cash on Deposit in First National Bank, and account number 103 may be Cash on Deposit in Lakewood Bank. In the assignment material we use various numbering schemes to correspond to the variety found in practice.

The chart of accounts for Gary Lyon, CPA, appears in Exhibit 2–9. Notice that the account numbers jump from 13 to 17. Gary Lyon realizes that later he may need to add other supplies accounts—for example, Tax Forms Supplies.

EXHIBIT 2-9 *Chart of Accounts—Accounting Practice of Gary Lyon, CPA*

Balance Sheet Accounts:

Assets	Liabilities	Owner's Equity
11 Cash	21 Accounts Payable	31 Gary Lyon, Capital
12 Accounts Receivable	22 Notes Payable	32 Gary Lyon, Withdrawals
13 Office Supplies		
17 Office Furniture		
19 Land		

Income Statement Accounts:

Revenues	Expenses
41 Service Revenue	51 Rent Expense
	52 Salary Expense
	53 Utilities Expense

EXHIBIT 2-10 *Normal Balances of Balance Sheet Accounts*

Assets	=	Liabilities	+	Owner's Equity
Normal Bal. Debit		Normal Bal. Credit		Normal Bal. Credit

Any additional supplies account would logically appear after Office Supplies, and Tax Forms Supplies might be account number 14.

Normal Balances of Accounts

Accountants speak of an account's *normal balance*, which refers to the side of the account—debit or credit—where *increases* are recorded. This term also refers to the usual balance—debit or credit—in the account. For example, Cash and all other assets usually have a debit balance, so assets are *debit-balance* accounts. On the other hand, liabilities and owner's equity usually have a credit balance, so they are *credit-balance* accounts. Exhibit 2-10 illustrates the normal balances of assets, liabilities, and owner's equity.

An account that normally has a debit balance may occasionally have a credit balance. This indicates a negative amount of the item. For example, Cash will have a temporary credit balance if the entity overdraws its bank account. Similarly, the liability Accounts Payable—normally a credit balance account—will have a debit balance if the entity overpays its account. In other instances, the shift of a balance amount away from its normal column indicates an accounting error. For example, a credit balance in Office Supplies, Office Furniture, or Buildings indicates an error because negative amounts of these assets cannot exist.

As we have explained, owner's equity usually contains several accounts. In total, these accounts show a normal credit balance for the owner's equity of the business. Each individual owner's equity account has a normal credit balance if it represents an *increase* in owner's equity (for example, the Capital account in Exhibit 2-11). However, if the individual owner's equity account represents a *decrease* in owner's equity, the account will have a normal debit balance (for example, the Withdrawals account in Exhibit 2-11).

Additional Owner's Equity Accounts: Revenues and Expenses

The owner's equity category includes two additional types of accounts: revenues and expenses. As we have discussed, *revenues* are increases in owner's equity that result from delivering goods or services to customers. *Expenses* are decreases in owner's equity due to the cost of operating the business. Therefore, the accounting equation may be expanded as follows:

Capital

22,000	Bal. ?
	56,000
	15,000
	Bal. 73,000

ANSWER: $24,000

Cash

Bal. 10,000	
20,000	13,000
Bal. ?	

ANSWER: $17,000

Accounts Payable

?	Bal. 12,800
	45,600
	Bal. 23,500

ANSWER: $34,900

ASSETS = LIABILITIES + OWNER'S EQUITY

(CAPITAL − WITHDRAWALS) + (REVENUES − EXPENSES)

Revenues and expenses appear in parentheses because their impact on the accounting equation arises from their effect on owner's equity. If revenues exceed expenses, the net effect—revenues minus expenses—is net income, which increases owner's equity. If expenses are greater, the net effect is a net loss, which decreases owner's equity.

We can now express the rules of debit and credit in final form as shown in Exhibit 2-11, Panel A. Panel B shows the *normal* balances of the five types of accounts: *Assets; Liabilities; Owner's Equity*, and its subparts, *Revenues* and *Expenses*.

All of accounting is based on these five types of accounts. You should become very familiar with the related rules of debit and credit and the normal balances of accounts.

Transparency T2-4

Point to Stress: Students must memorize these rules. Soon they will become second-nature.

EXHIBIT 2-11 *Rules of Debit and Credit and Normal Balances of Accounts*

Panel A—Rules of Debit and Credit:

Assets		=	Liabilities		+	Capital	
Debit for Increase	Credit for Decrease		Debit for Decrease	Credit for Increase		Debit for Decrease	Credit for Increase

Withdrawals

Debit for Increase	Credit for Decrease

Revenues

Debit for Decrease	Credit for Increase

Expenses

Debit for Increase	Credit for Decrease

Panel—Normal Balances:

Assets	Debit	
Liabilities		Credit
Owner's equity-overall		Credit
Capital		Credit
Withdrawals	Debit	
Revenue		Credit
Expenses	Debit	

Teaching Tip: Notice that both withdrawals and expenses represent a reduction in owner's equity, so increases and decreases are recorded opposite from the way they would be recorded for capital. Withdrawals and expenses have normal balances (debit) that are the opposite of the capital normal balance (credit). Revenue transactions *increase* capital, so increases in revenues are recorded in the same way as increases in capital.

Typical Account Titles

Thus far we have dealt with a limited number of transactions and accounts to introduce key concepts. Actual businesses engage in more transactions, requiring more accounts. Additional transactions are recorded in the same manner, with accounts added to the ledger as needed. The following summary describes some of the more common accounts grouped by financial statement and account category. As you work exercises and problems in this and future chapters, you will find these descriptions useful.

Balance Sheet—Assets, Liabilities, and Owner's Equity

Assets

Cash: Money on hand and in the bank.

Accounts receivable: Claim on open account against the cash of a client or a customer. (Open account means that no promissory note exists to support the receivable.)

Note receivable: Claim against the cash of another party, supported by a promissory note signed by the other party. (All receivables are assets, and any account with *receivable* in its title is an asset.)

Merchandise inventory: Merchandise that an entity sells in its business (such as clothing by a department store or stereos by a stereo shop).

Office supplies: Stationery, stamps, paper clips, staples, and so forth.

Office furniture: Desks, chairs, file cabinets, and so forth.

Office equipment: Typewriters, calculators, and other equipment used in a business office. A business may have other types of equipment, such as delivery equipment or store equipment.

Building: Building used in a business.

Land: Land on which a business building stands.

Liabilities

Accounts payable: Liability to pay cash to another party on open account.

Note payable: Liability to pay cash to another party, supported by a signed promissory note.

Salary or wage payable: Liability to pay an employee for work. (Most liabilities have the word *payable* in the account title, and any account with *payable* in its title is a liability.)

Owner's Equity

Gary Lyon, Capital: The interest of the owner of the business in its assets. (This account title bears the name of the owner.)

Gary Lyon, Withdrawals: The owner's withdrawals of assets from the business for personal use.

Teaching Tip: Because withdrawals reduce capital, the Withdrawals account is sometimes referred to as a *contra equity* account, meaning that it has the opposite balance of capital.

Income Statement—Revenues and Expenses

Revenues

Service revenue: Revenue earned by performing a service (accounting service by a CPA firm, laundry service by a laundry, and so forth).

Sales revenue: Revenue earned by selling a product (sales of hardware by a hardware store, food by a grocery store, and so forth).

Expenses

Rent expense: Expense for office rent and the rental of office equipment or the rental of any other business asset.

Salary or wage expense: Expense of having employees work for the business.

Utilities expense: Expense of using electricity, water, gas, and other items provided by utility companies.

Supplies expense: Expense of using supplies such as stationery, stamps, paper clips, and staples.

Advertising expense: Expense of advertising the business.

Interest expense: Expense of using borrowed money.

Property tax expense: Expense for property tax on business land, buildings, and equipment.

Illustrative Problem

Let's account for the revenues and expenses of the accounting practice of Sara Nichols, Attorney, for the month of July 19X1. We follow the same steps illustrated earlier: analyze the transaction, journalize, post to the ledger, and prepare the trial balance. Revenue accounts and expense accounts work just like asset, liability, and owner's equity accounts. Each revenue and each expense account has its own page in the ledger and its own identifying account number.

Transaction Analysis, Journalizing, and Posting

1. *Transaction:* Sara Nichols invested $10,000 cash in a business bank account to open her law practice.

   Analysis: The asset cash is increased; therefore, debit Cash. The owner's equity of the business increased; therefore, credit Sara Nichols, Capital.

Teaching Tip: Point out that there is a logical sequence of steps that must always be followed when recording a journal entry: analyze; apply rules of debit and credit; write the journal entry, with an explanation.

   Journal Entry:

   Cash 10,000
       Sara Nichols, Capital 10,000
   Invested cash in the business.

   Ledger Accounts:

Cash	Sara Nichols, Capital
(1) 10,000	(1) 10,000

2. *Transaction:* Nichols performed service for a client and collected $3,000 cash.

   Analysis: The asset cash is increased; therefore, debit Cash.

   The revenue account Service Revenue is increased; credit Service Revenue.

   Journal Entry:

   Cash 3,000
       Service Revenue.................. 3,000
   Performed service and received cash.

Ledger	Cash		Service Revenue	
Accounts:	(1) 10,000			(2) 3,000
	(2) 3,000			

3. *Transaction:* Nichols performed service for a client and billed the client for $500 on account receivable. This means the client owes the business $500 even though the client signed no formal promissory note.

    Analysis: The asset accounts receivable is increased; therefore, debit Accounts Receivable.

               The revenue service revenue is increased; credit Service Revenue.

    Journal Entry:

```
Accounts Receivable....................    500
    Service Revenue....................            500
Performed service on account.
```

Ledger	Accounts Receivable		Service Revenue	
Accounts:	(3) 500			(2) 3,000
				(3) 500

4. *Transaction:* Nichols performed accounting service of $700 for a client, who paid $300 cash immediately. Nichols billed the remaining $400 to the client on account receivable.

    Analysis: The assets cash and accounts receivable are increased; therefore, debit both of these asset accounts.

               The revenue service revenue is increased; credit Service Revenue for the sum of the two debit amounts.

    Journal Entry:

```
Cash ..................................    300
Accounts Receivable ...................    400
    Service Revenue....................            700
Performed service for cash and on account.
```

    Note: Because this transaction affects more than two accounts at the same time, the entry is called a *compound entry*. No matter how many accounts a compound entry affects—there may be any number—total debits must equal total credits.

Ledger	Cash		Accounts Receivable	
Accounts:	(1) 10,000		(3) 500	
	(2) 3,000		(4) 400	
	(4) 300			

	Service Revenue	
		(2) 3,000
		(3) 500
		(4) 700

5. *Transaction:* Nichols paid the following cash expenses: office rent, $900; employee salary, $1,500; and utilities, $500.

Analysis: The asset cash is decreased; therefore, credit Cash for the sum of the three expense amounts.

The following expenses are increased: Rent Expense, Salary Expense, and Utilities Expense. They should each be debited.

Journal Entry:

Rent Expense......................	900	
Salary Expense	1,500	
Utilities Expense	500	
Cash...........................		2,900

Paid cash expenses.

Ledger Accounts:

Cash		Rent Expense	
(1) 10,000	(5) 2,900	(5) 900	
(2) 3,000			
(4) 300			

Salary Expense		Utilities Expense	
(5) 1,500		(5) 500	

Point to Stress: Recording an expense does not necessarily involve a credit to cash. In Transaction 6 the expense is recorded now but the cash will be paid later. Likewise, a debit to cash does not always reflect revenue. Transaction 7 records cash collected on a receivable (the revenue was recorded in Transaction 3).

6. *Transaction:* Nichols received a telephone bill for $120 and will pay this expense next week.

Analysis: Utilities expense is increased; therefore, debit this expense.

The liability accounts payable is increased; credit this account.

Journal Entry:

Utilities Expense	120	
Accounts Payable		120

Received utility bill.

Ledger Accounts:

Accounts Payable		Utilities Expense	
	(6) 120	(5) 500	
		(6) 120	

7. *Transaction:* Nichols collected $200 cash from the client established in Transaction 3.

Analysis: The asset cash is increased; therefore, debit Cash.

The asset accounts receivable is decreased; therefore, credit Accounts Receivable.

Journal Entry:

Cash	200	
Accounts Receivable		200

Received cash on account.

Note: This transaction has no effect on revenue; the related revenue is accounted for in Transaction 3.

Cash				Accounts Receivable			
(1)	10,000	(5)	2,900	(3)	500	(7)	200
(2)	3,000			(4)	400		
(4)	300						
(7)	**200**						

8. *Transaction:* Nichols paid the telephone bill that was received and recorded in Transaction 6.

   Analysis: The asset cash is decreased; credit Cash.

   The liability accounts payable is decreased; therefore, debit Accounts Payable.

   Journal Entry:
   Accounts Payable..................... 120
       Cash 120
   Paid cash on account.

   Note: This transaction has no effect on expense because the related expense was recorded in Transaction 6.

Typical Student Misconception: Students may need this reminder: You are recording the transactions on the books of the company with which you are working. For example, if supplies are purchased on credit, your company purchased the supplies and will eventually *pay* for them. Therefore an account *payable* (*not* an account receivable) should be recorded.

Ledger Accounts:

Cash				Accounts Payable			
(1)	10,000	(5)	2,900	**(8)**	**120**	(6)	120
(2)	3,000	**(8)**	**120**				
(4)	300						
(7)	200						

9. *Transaction:* Nichols withdrew $1,100 cash for personal use.

   Analysis: The asset cash decreased; credit Cash. The withdrawal decreased owner's equity; therefore, debit Sara Nichols, Withdrawals.

   Journal Entry:
   Sara Nichols, Withdrawals 1,100
       Cash 1,100
   Withdrew for personal use.

Ledger Accounts:

Cash				Sara Nichols, Withdrawals	
(1)	10,000	(5)	2,900	**(9)**	**1,100**
(2)	3,000	(8)	120		
(4)	300	**(9)**	**1,100**		
(7)	200				

Ledger Accounts After Posting

	Assets						Liabilities			Owner's Equity			
	Cash			**Accounts Receivable**			**Accounts Payable**			**Sara Nichols, Capital**		**Sara Nichols, Withdrawals**	
(1)	10,000	(5) 2,900	(3)	500	(7) 200	(8)	120	(6) 120		(1) 10,000	(9)	1,100	
(2)	3,000	(8) 120	(4)	400				Bal. 0		Bal. 10,000	Bal.	1,100	
(4)	300	(9) 1,100	Bal.	700									
(7)	200												
Bal.	9,380												

		Owner's Equity		
Revenue		Expenses		

Service Revenue

	(2)	3,000
	(3)	500
	(4)	700
	Bal.	4,200

Rent Expense

(5)	900	
Bal.	900	

Salary Expense

(5)	1,500	
Bal.	1,500	

Utilities Expense

(5)	500	
(6)	120	
Bal.	620	

Trial Balance

Typical Student Misconception: Which side of the trial balance is affected by a debit to accounts payable? ANSWER: credit side. (Students will want to say debit.) Illustration:

Accounts Payable

	Bal.	6,000

A debit to accounts payable reduces the *credit* balance of accounts payable.

Accounts Payable

	Bal.	6,000
1,000		
	Bal.	5,000

Sara Nichols, Attorney
Trial Balance
July 31, 19X1

Account Title	Balance Debit	Balance Credit
Cash......................................	$ 9,380	
Accounts receivalbe	700	
Accounts payable		$ 0
Sara Nichols, capital		10,000
Sara Nichols, withdrawals	1,100	
Service revenue............................		4,200
Rent expense	900	
Salary expense.............................	1,500	
Utilities expense	620	
Total.....................................	$14,200	$14,200

OBJECTIVE 6

Analyze transactions without a journal

Analytical Use of Accounting Information _____

What dominates the accountant's analysis of transactions: the accounting equation, the journal, or the ledger? The accounting equation is most fundamental. In turn, the ledger is more useful than the journal in providing an overall model of the organization. Accountants and managers must often make quick decisions without the benefit of a complete accounting system: journal, ledger, accounts, and trial balance. For example, the owner of a company may be negotiating the purchase price of another business. For a quick analysis of the effects of transactions, accountants often skip the journal and go directly to the ledger. They compress transaction analysis, journalizing, and posting into one step. This type of analysis saves time that may be the difference between a good business decision and a lost opportunity.

Let's take an example to see how it works. For instance, the first revenue transaction—Sara Nichols performed accounting service for a client and collected cash of $3,000—may be analyzed by debiting the Cash account and crediting the Service Revenue account directly in the ledger as follows:

Cash		Service Revenue	
3,000			3,000

With this shortcut, the accountant can immediately see the effect of the transaction on both the entity's cash and its service revenue. Or you can take the quick analysis a step further—go straight to the financial statements. This transaction increased Cash on the balance sheet by $3,000. It also increased Service Revenue on the income statement—and owner's capital on the balance sheet—by $3,000. Modern computer-assisted accounting systems often have this "journal-less" feature.

Computers and Accounting

Computers have revolutionized accounting. Decades ago, big and expensive computers were available only to the large companies that could afford them. Today, prices for increasingly powerful microcomputers continue to drop, enabling smaller businesses to take advantage of accounting with computers. Microcomputers—also known as personal computers, like Apple, IBM, PC, TRS, and Compaq—electronically handle much of the work done by hand in the past.

Just what benefits does a computer offer? An accountant must analyze every business transaction, whether the accounting system is manual—as we are presenting in these opening chapters—or computerized. Once the transaction has been analyzed, a computerized accounting package performs much the same actions as accountants do in a manual system. The computer automatically makes a journal entry, capturing the necessary information in a consistent format. A computer's ability to perform routine tasks and mathematical operations fast and without error frees accountants for decision making. On the market today is a wide variety of specialized computer programs—known as *software*—that require almost no computer programming expertise. Chapter 28 in this book offers more detailed instruction on how a computer package actually handles transactions.

You may be wondering about the role of debits and credits in a computerized accounting system. The computer interprets debits and credits as increases or decreases by account type. For example, a computer reads a debit to Cash as an increase to that account. Debits and credits actually need not be used in a computerized system. They were originally designed to ensure accuracy in manual accounting systems. Still, debit and credit are so deeply ingrained in the vocabulary of accounting that we use them even when dealing with computerized accounting systems.

In addition to helping with accounting itself, microcomputers assist with many financial applications of accounting information and in business correspondence. Also, thanks to telecommunications, micros can tap into the information stored in larger computers across the globe. As we progress through the study of accounting, we will consider computer applications that fit the topics under discussion.

Point to Stress: Students may use computers, and never record business transactions manually. Nevertheless, they must learn the flow of accounting data in order to understand the accounting process.

Summary Problem for Your Review

The trial balance of Tomassini Computer Service Center on March 1, 19X2, lists the entity's assets, liabilities, and owner's equity on that date.

	Balance	
Account Title	Debit	Credit
Cash	$26,000	
Accounts receivable	4,500	
Accounts payable		$ 2,000
L. Tomassini, capital		28,500
Total	$30,500	$30,500

During March the business engaged in the following transactions:

1. Tomassini borrowed $45,000 from the bank. He signed a note payable in the name of the business.
2. Paid cash of $40,000 to a real estate company to acquire land.
3. Performed service for a customer and received cash of $5,000.
4. Purchased supplies on credit, $300.
5. Performed customer service and earned revenue on account, $2,600.
6. Paid $1,200 on account.
7. Paid the following cash expenses: salaries, $3,000; rent, $1,500; and interest, $400.
8. Received $3,100 on account.
9. Received a $200 utility bill that will be paid next week.
10. Tomassini withdrew $1,800 for personal use.

Required

1. Open the following accounts, with the balances indicated, in the ledger of Tomassini Computer Service Center. Use the T-account format.
   Assets—Cash, $26,000; Accounts Receivable, $4,500; Supplies, no balance; Land, no balance
   Liabilities—Accounts Payable, $2,000; Note Payable, no balance
   Owner's Equity—Larry Tomassini, Capital, $28,500; Larry Tomassini, Withdrawals, no balance
   Revenues—Service Revenue, no balance
   Expenses—(none have balances) Salary Expense, Rent Expense, Utilities Expense, Interest Expense
2. Journalize the preceding transactions. Key journal entries by transaction number.
3. Post to the ledger.
4. Prepare the trial balance of Tomassini Computer Service Center at March 31, 19X2.
5. Compute the net income or net loss of the entity during the month of March. List expenses in order from the largest to the smallest.

Requirement 1

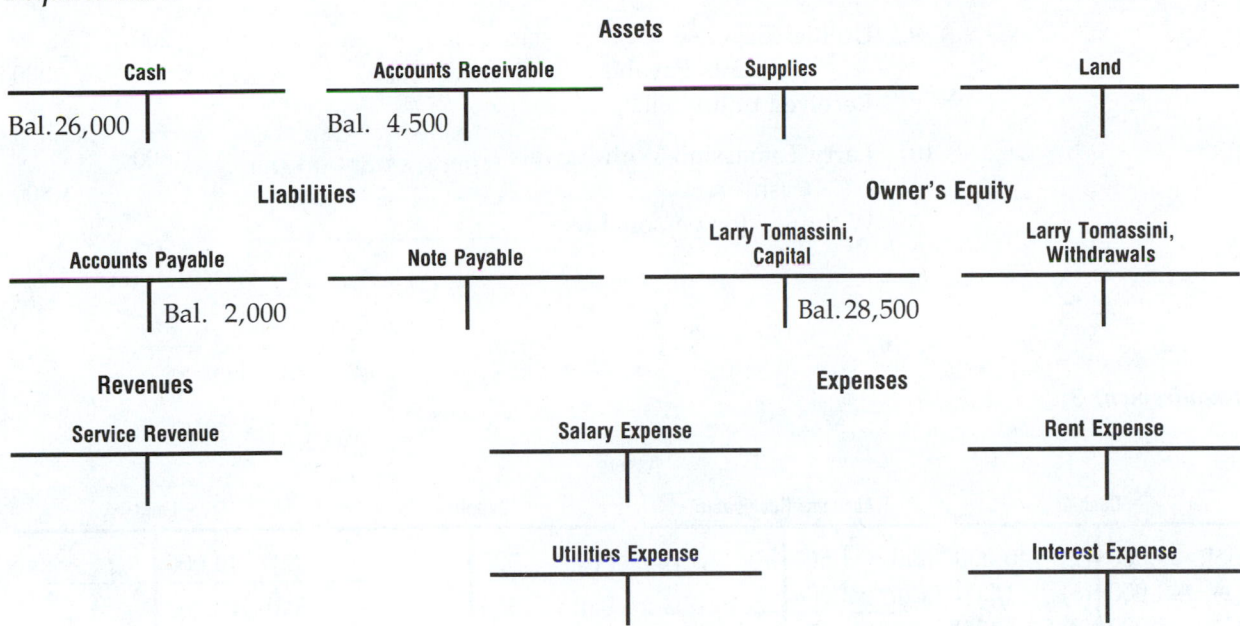

Assets

Cash	Accounts Receivable	Supplies	Land
Bal. 26,000	Bal. 4,500		

Liabilities

Owner's Equity

Accounts Payable	Note Payable	Larry Tomassini, Capital	Larry Tomassini, Withdrawals
Bal. 2,000		Bal. 28,500	

Revenues

Expenses

Service Revenue	Salary Expense	Rent Expense

	Utilities Expense	Interest Expense

Requirement 2

Accounts and Explanation	Debit	Credit
1. Cash	45,000	
Note Payable...............................		45,000
Borrowed cash on note payable.		
2. Land	40,000	
Cash		40,000
Purchased land for cash.		
3. Cash	5,000	
Service Revenue		5,000
Performed service and received cash.		
4. Supplies	300	
Accounts Payable..........................		300
Purchased supplies on account.		
5. Accounts Receivable	2,600	
Service Revenue		2,600
Performed service on account.		
6. Accounts Payable	1,200	
Cash		1,200
Paid on account.		
7. Salary Expense	3,000	
Rent Expense	1,500	
Interest Expense	400	
Cash		4,900
Paid cash expenses.		

8.	Cash	3,100	
	Accounts Receivable		3,100
	Received on account.		
9.	Utilities Expense	200	
	Accounts Payable.........................		200
	Received utility bill.		
10.	Larry Tomassini, Withdrawals	1,800	
	Cash		1,800
	Withdrew for personal use.		

Requirement 3

Assets

	Cash					Accounts Receivable					Supplies				Land	
Bal.	26,000	(2)	40,000		Bal.	4,500	(8)	3,100		(4)	300			(2)	40,000
(1)	45,000	(6)	1,200		(5)	2,600				Bal.	300			Bal.	40,000
(3)	5,000	(7)	4,900		Bal.	4,000									
(8)	3,100	(10)	1,800												
Bal.	31,200														

Liabilities

	Accounts Payable					Note Payable	
(6)	1,200	Bal.	2,000		(1)	45,000
		(4)	300		Bal.	45,000
		(9)	200			
		Bal.	1,300			

Owner's Equity

	Larry Tomassini, Capital			Larry Tomassini, Withdrawals	
	Bal.	28,500	(10)	1,800	
			Bal.	1,800	

Revenues

	Service Revenue	
	(3)	5,000
	(5)	2,600
	Bal.	7,600

Expenses

	Salary Expense			Rent Expense	
(7)	3,000		(7)	1,500	
Bal.	3,000		Bal.	1,500	

	Utilities Expense			Interest Expense	
(9)	200		(7)	400	
Bal.	200		Bal.	400	

Requirement 4

Tomassini Computer Service Center
Trial Balance
March 31, 19X2

Account Title	Balance Debit	Balance Credit
Cash..............................	$31,200	
Accounts receivable	4,000	
Supplies	300	
Land..............................	40,000	
Accounts payable		$ 1,300
Note payable		45,000
Larry Tomassini, capital		28,500
Larry Tomassini, withdrawals	1,800	
Service revenue...................		7,600
Salary expense....................	3,000	
Rent expense	1,500	
Utilities expense	200	
Interest expense	400	
Total.............................	$82,400	$82,400

Requirement 5

Net income for the month of March

Revenues:		
Service revenue		$7,600
Expenses:		
Salary expense....................	$3,000	
Rent expense	1,500	
Interest expense	400	
Utilities expense	200	
Total expenses		5,100
Net income........................		$2,500

Summary

The *account* can be viewed in the form of the letter "T." The left side of each account is its *debit* side. The right side is its *credit* side. The *ledger*, which contains a record for each account, groups and numbers accounts by category in the following order: assets, liabilities, owner's equity, and its subparts: revenues and expenses.

    Assets and *expenses* are increased by debits and decreased by credits. *Liabilities, owner's equity,* and *revenues* are increased by credits and decreased by debits. The side—debit or credit—of the account in which increases are recorded is that account's normal balance. Thus the normal balance of assets and expenses is a debit, and the normal balance of liabilities, owner's equity, and revenues is a credit. The Withdrawals account, which decreases owner's equity, normally has a debit balance. *Revenues,* which are increases in owner's equity, have a normal credit balance. *Expenses,* which are decreases in owner's equity, have a normal debit balance.

The accountant begins the recording process by entering the transaction's information in the *journal,* a chronological list of all the business's transactions. The information is then posted—transferred—to the *ledger* accounts. Posting references are used to trace amounts back and forth between the journal and the ledger. Businesses list their account titles and numbers in a chart of accounts.

The *trial balance* is a summary of all the account balances in the ledger. When *double-entry accounting* has been done correctly, the total debits and the total credits in the trial balance are equal.

We can now trace the flow of accounting information through these steps:

Business Transaction → Source Documents → Journal Entry → Posting to Ledger → Trial Balance

Self-Study Questions

Test your understanding of the chapter by marking the best answer for each of the following questions.

1. An account has two sides called the *(p. 49)*
   a. Debit and credit
   b. Asset and liability
   c. Revenue and expense
   d. Journal and ledger
2. Increases in liabilities are recorded by *(p. 50)*
   a. Debits
   b. Credits
3. Why do accountants record transactions in the journal? *(p. 52)*
   a. To ensure that all transactions are posted to the ledger
   b. To ensure that total debits equal total credits
   c. To have a chronological record of all transactions
   d. To help prepare the financial statements
4. Posting is the process of transferring information from the *(p. 54)*
   a. Journal to the trial balance
   b. Ledger to the trial balance
   c. Ledger to the financial statements
   d. Journal to the ledger
5. The purchase of land for cash is recorded by a *(p. 55)*
   a. Debit to Cash and a credit to Land
   b. Debit to Cash and a debit to Land
   c. Debit to Land and a credit to Cash
   d. Credit to Cash and a credit to Land
6. The purpose of the trial balance is to *(p. 58)*
   a. Indicate whether total debits equal total credits
   b. Ensure that all transactions have been recorded
   c. Speed the collection of cash receipts from customers
   d. Increase assets and owner's equity
7. What is the normal balance of the Accounts Receivable, Office Supplies, and Rent Expense accounts? *(p. 66)*
   a. Debit
   b. Credit
8. A business has Cash of $3,000, Notes Payable of $2,500, Accounts Payable of $4,300, Service Revenue of $7,000, and Rent Expense of $1,800. Based on these data, how much are its total liabilities? *(p. 67)*
   a. $5,500
   b. $6,800
   c. $9,800
   d. $13,800
9. Farber Company earned revenue on account. The journal entry to record this transaction is a *(pp. 68, 69)*

a. Debit to Cash and a credit to Revenue
b. Debit to Accounts Receivable and a credit to Revenue
c. Debit to Accounts Payable and a credit to Revenue
d. Debit to Revenue and a credit to Accounts Receivable

10. The account credited for a receipt of cash on account is *(p. 70)*
   a. Cash   c. Service Revenue
   b. Accounts Payable   d. Accounts Receivable

Answers to the Self-Study Questions follow the Accounting Vocabulary.

Accounting Vocabulary

Account. The detailed record of the changes that have occurred in a particular asset, liability, or owner equity during a period *(p. 46)*.

Chart of accounts. List of all the accounts and their account numbers in the ledger *(p. 64)*.

Credit. The right side of an account *(p. 49)*.

Debit. The left side of an account *(p. 49)*.

Journal. The chronological accounting record of an entity's transactions *(p. 52)*.

Ledger. The book of accounts *(p. 46)*.

Posting. Transferring of amounts from the journal to the ledger *(p. 54)*.

Trial balance. A list of all the ledger accounts with their balances *(p. 58)*.

Answers to Self-Study Questions

1. a   5. c   8. b ($6,800 = $2,500 + $4,300)
2. b   6. a   9. b
3. c   7. a   10. d
4. d

ASSIGNMENT MATERIAL

Questions

1. Name the basic summary device of accounting. What letter of the alphabet does it resemble, and what are its two sides called?

2. Is the following statement true or false? Debit means decrease and credit means increase. Explain your answer.

3. Write two sentences that use the term *debit* in different ways.

4. What are the three *basic* types of accounts? Name two additional types of accounts. To which one of the three *basic* types are these two additional types of accounts most closely related?

5. Suppose you are the accountant for Smith Courier Service. Keeping in mind double-entry bookkeeping, identify the *dual effects* of Mary Smith's investment of $10,000 cash in her business.

6. Briefly describe the flow of accounting information.

7. To what does the *normal balance* of an account refer?

8. Complete the table by indicating the normal balance of the five types of accounts.

Account Type	Normal Balance
Assets	_____
Liabilities	_____
Capital	_____
Revenues	_____
Expenses	_____

9. What does posting accomplish? Why is it important? Does it come before or after journalizing?

10. Label each of the following transactions as increasing owner's equity (+), decreasing owner's equity (-), or as having no effect on owner's equity (0). Write the appropriate symbol in the space provided.

____ a. Investment by owner

____ b. Revenue transaction

____ c. Purchase of supplies on credit

____ d. Expense transaction

____ e. Cash payment on account

____ f. Withdrawal by owner

____ g. Borrowing money on a note payable

____ h. Sale of services on account

11. What four steps does posting include? Which step is the fundamental purpose of posting?

12. Rearrange the following accounts in their logical sequence in the ledger:

Notes Payable
Accounts Receivable
Sales Revenue

Cash
Jane East, Capital
Salary Expense

13. What is the meaning of the statement, Accounts Payable has a credit balance of $1,700?

14. Jack Brown Campus Cleaners launders the shirts of customer Bobby Baylor, who has a charge account at the cleaners. When Bobby picks up his clothes and is short of cash, he charges it. Later, when he receives his monthly statement from the cleaners, Bobby writes a check on Dear Old Dad's bank account and mails the check to Jack Brown. Identify the two business transactions described here. Which transaction increases Jack Brown's owner's equity? Which transaction increases Jack Brown's cash?

15. Explain the difference between the ledger and the chart of accounts.

16. Why do accountants prepare a trial balance?

17. What is a compound journal entry?

18. The accountant for Bower Construction Company mistakenly recorded a $500 purchase of supplies on account as a $5,000 purchase. He debited Supplies and credited Accounts Payable for $5,000. Does this error cause the trial balance to be out of balance? Explain your answer.

19. What is the effect on total assets of collecting cash on account from customers?

20. What is the advantage of analyzing and recording transactions without the use of a journal? Describe how this "journal-less" analysis works.

Exercises

No check figure

Exercise 2-1   *Using accounting vocabulary* *(L.O. 1)*

The trial balance of Auditron, Inc., lists Cash of $62,100. Write a short memo to explain the accounting process that produced this listing on the trial balance. Mention *debits, credits, journals, ledgers, posting,* and so on.

Exercise 2-2 *Analyzing and journalizing transactions* **(L.O. 2,3)**

No check figure

Analyze the following transactions in the manner shown for the December 1 transaction. Also record each transaction in the journal.

Dec. 1 Paid monthly rent expense of $1,000. (Analysis: The expense rent expense is increased; therefore, debit Rent Expense. The asset cash is decreased; therefore, credit Cash.)

  1 Rent Expense 1,000
         Cash   1,000

  4 Received $600 cash on account from a customer.
  8 Performed service on account for a customer, $1,100.
 12 Purchased office furniture on account, $810.
 19 Sold for $69,000 land that had cost this same amount.
 24 Purchased building for $140,000; signed a note payable.
 27 Paid the liability created on December 12.

Exercise 2-3 *Journalizing transactions* **(L.O. 3)**

No check figure

Vines Consulting Service engaged in the following transactions during March 19X3, its first month of operations:

Mar. 1 John Vines invested $65,000 of cash to start the business.
   2 He purchased office supplies of $200 on account.
   4 He paid $25,000 cash for land to use as a future building site.
   6 He performed service for customers and received cash, $2,000.
   9 He paid $100 on accounts payable.
  17 He performed service for customers on account, $1,600.
  23 He received $1,200 cash from a customer on account.
  31 He paid the following expenses: salary, $1,200; rent, $500.

Required

Record the preceding transactions in the journal of Vines Consulting Service. Key transactions by date and include an explanation for each entry, as illustrated in the chapter. Use the following accounts: Cash; Accounts Receivable; Office Supplies; Land; Accounts Payable; John Vines, Capital; Service Revenue; Salary Expense; Rent Expense.

Exercise 2-4 *Posting to the ledger and preparing a trial balance* **(L.O. 4,5)**

Trial balance $68,700

1. After journalizing the transactions of Exercise 2-3, post the entries to the ledger, using T-account format. Key transactions by date as in the following example. Date the ending balance of each account Mar. 31.

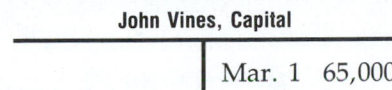

John Vines, Capital	
	Mar. 1 65,000

2. Prepare the trial balance of Vines Consulting Service at March 31, 19X3.

Exercise 2-5 *Describing transactions and posting* **(L.O. 3,4)**

Cash balance $110

The journal of Scholes Company as follows.

Date	Accounts and Explanation	Post Ref.	Debit	Credit
Aug. 5	Cash		530	
	Sales Revenue			530
9	Supplies		270	
	Accounts Payable			270
11	Accounts Receivable		2,100	
	Sales Revenue			2,100
14	Rent Expense		1,200	
	Cash...........................			1,200
22	Cash		1,400	
	Accounts Receivable			1,400
25	Advertising Expense		350	
	Cash...........................			350
27	Accounts Payable....................		270	
	Cash...........................			270
31	Utilities Expense.....................		220	
	Accounts Payable			220

Required

1. Describe each transaction. Example: Aug. 5—Cash sale.
2. Post the transactions to the ledger using the following account numbers: Cash, 11; Accounts Receivable, 12; Supplies, 13; Accounts Payable, 21; Sales Revenue, 41; Rent Expense, 51; Advertising Expense, 52; Utilities Expense, 53. Use dates, journal references, and posting references as illustrated in Exhibit 2-7. You may write the account numbers as posting references directly in your book unless directed otherwise by your instructor.
3. Compute the balance in each account after posting. The first debit amount of $530 is posted to Cash as an example:

Cash
Aug. 5 J.5 530 |

No check figure

Exercise 2-6 *Journalizing transactions* (L.O. 3)

The first five transactions of Rosenthal Security Company have been posted to the company's accounts as follows:

Cash				Supplies		Equipment	
(1) 45,000	(3) 42,000			(2) 400		(5) 6,000	
(4) 7,000	(5) 6,000						

Land		Accounts Payable		Note Payable	
(3) 42,000			(2) 400		(4) 7,000

Stu Rosenthal, Capital	
	(1) 45,000

Required

Prepare the journal entries that served as the sources for the five transactions. Include an explanation for each entry as illustrated in the chapter.

Exercise 2-7 *Preparing a trial balance* **(L.O. 5)**

Trial balance $52,400

Prepare the trial balance of Rosenthal Security Company at September 30, 19X4, using the account data from the preceding exercise.

Exercise 2-8 *Preparing a trial balance* **(L.O. 5)**

Trial balance $94,100

The accounts of Japaridze Realty Company are listed below with their normal balances at September 30, 19X4. The accounts are listed in no particular order.

Account	Balance
Lia Japaridze, capital	$48,800
Advertising expense	650
Accounts payable	4,300
Sales commission revenue	16,000
Land	23,000
Note payable	25,000
Cash	7,000
Salary expense	6,000
Building	45,000
Rent expense	2,000
Lia Japaridze, withdrawals	4,000
Utilities expense	400
Accounts receivable	5,500
Supplies expense	300
Supplies	250

Required

Prepare the company's trial balance at September 30, 19X4, listing accounts in proper sequence, as illustrated in the chapter. Supplies comes before Building and Land. List the expense with the largest balance first, the expense with the next largest balance second, and so on.

Exercise 2-9 *Correcting errors in a trial balance* **(L.O. 5)**

Trial balance $56,200

The trial balance of Thai Enterprises at November 30, 19X9, does not balance:

Cash	$ 4,200	
Accounts receivable	2,000	
Supplies	600	
Land	46,000	
Accounts payable		$ 3,000
Emily Thai, capital		42,000
Service revenue		4,700
Salary expense	1,700	
Rent expense	800	
Utilities expense	300	
Total	$55,600	$49,700

Investigation of the accounting records reveals that the bookkeeper:

1. Recorded a cash revenue transaction by debiting Cash for the correct amount of $5,000 but failed to record the credit to Service Revenue.
2. Posted a $1,000 credit to Accounts Payable as $100.
3. Did not record utilities expense or the related account payable in the amount of $200.
4. Understated Cash and Emily Thai, Capital, by $400 each.

Required

Prepare the correct trial balance at November 30, complete with a heading. Journal entries are not required.

Cash balance $3,100

Exercise 2-10   *Recording transactions without a journal*   *(L.O. 6)*

Open the following T-accounts: Cash; Accounts Receivable; Office Supplies; Office Furniture; Accounts Payable; Albert Peña, Capital; Albert Peña, Withdrawals; Service Revenue; Salary Expense; Rent Expense.
    Record the following transactions directly in the T-accounts without using a journal. Use the letters to identify the transactions.

a. Albert Peña opened an accounting firm by investing $8,800 cash and office furniture valued at $7,400.
b. Paid monthly rent of $1,500.
c. Purchased office supplies on account, $800.
d. Paid employee salary, $1,800.
e. Paid $400 of the account payable created in *c*.
f. Performed accounting service on account, $1,700.
g. Withdrew $2,000 for personal use.

Trial balance $18,300

Exercise 2-11   *Preparing a trial balance*   *(L.O. 5)*

After recording the transactions in Exercise 2-10, prepare the trial balance of Albert Peña, CPA, at May 31, 19X7.

No check figure

Problems   (Group A)

Problem 2-1A   *Analyzing a trial balance*   *(L.O.1)*

The owner of McBee Service Company is selling the business. She offers the trial balance shown at the top of the next page to prospective buyers.
    Your best friend is considering buying McBee Service Company. He seeks your advice in interpreting this information. Specifically, he asks whether this trial balance is the same as a balance sheet and an income statement. He also wonders whether McBee must be a sound company. After all, the accounts are in balance.

Required

Write a short note to answer your friend's questions. To aid his decision, state how he can use the information on the trial balance to determine whether McBee has earned a net income or experienced a net loss for the current period.

McBee Service Company
Trial Balance
December 31, 19XX

Cash	$ 4,000	
Accounts receivable	11,000	
Prepaid expenses	4,000	
Land	31,000	
Accounts payable		$ 31,000
Note payable		20,000
Laura McBee, capital		30,000
Laura McBee, withdrawals	21,000	
Sales revenue		47,000
Rent expense	14,000	
Advertising expense	3,000	
Wage expense	33,000	
Supplies expense	7,000	
	$128,000	$128,000

Problem 2-2A *Analyzing and journalizing transactions* **(L.O. 2,3)**   No check figure

Lee Quinius practices medicine under the business title Lee Quinius, M.D. During April his medical practice engaged in the following transactions:

Apr. 1   Quinius deposited $75,000 cash in the business bank account.
     5   Paid monthly rent on medical equipment, $700.
     9   Paid $42,000 cash to purchase land for an office site.
    10   Purchased supplies on account, $1,200.
    19   Paid $1,000 on account.
    30   Revenues earned during the month included $6,000 cash and $5,000 on account.
    30   Paid employee salaries ($2,400), office rent ($1,500), and utilities ($400).
    30   Borrowed $20,000 from the bank for business use. Quinius signed a note payable to the bank in the name of the business.
    30   Withdrew $4,000 from the business to take his family on a trip.

Quinius's business uses the following accounts: Cash; Accounts Receivable; Supplies; Land; Accounts Payable; Notes Payable; Lee Quinius, Capital; Lee Quinius, Withdrawals; Service Revenue; Salary Expense; Rent Expense; Utilities Expense.

Required

1. Prepare an analysis of each business transaction of Lee Quinius, M.D., as shown for the April 1 transaction:

    Apr. 1   The asset Cash is increased. Increases in assets are recorded by debits; therefore, debit Cash.

           The owner's equity is increased. Increases in owner's equity are recorded by credits; therefore, credit Lee Quinius, Capital.

2. Prepare the journal entry for each transaction. Explanations are not required.

Trial balance $45,200

Problem 2-3A *Journalizing transactions, posting to T-accounts, and preparing a trial balance* **(L.O. 2,3,4,5)**

Marie Haley opened a law office on January 2 of the current year. During the first month of operations the business completed the following transactions:

Jan. 2 Haley deposited $40,000 cash in a business bank account entitled Marie Haley, Attorney.

3 Purchased supplies, $500, and furniture, $2,600, on account.

4 Performed legal services for a client and received cash, $1,500.

7 Paid cash to acquire land for a future office site, $22,000.

11 Defended a client in court, billed the client, and received his promise to pay the $800 within one week.

15 Paid secretary salary, $650.

16 Paid for the furniture purchased January 3 on account.

17 Paid the telephone bill, $110.

18 Received partial payment from client on account, $400.

19 Prepared legal documents for a client on account, $600.

22 Paid the water and electricity bills, $130.

29 Received $1,800 cash for helping a client sell real estate.

31 Paid secretary salary, $650.

31 Paid rent expense, $700.

31 Withdrew $2,200 for personal use.

Required

Open the following T-accounts: Cash; Accounts Receivable; Supplies; Furniture; Land; Accounts Payable; Marie Haley, Capital; Marie Haley, Withdrawals; Service Revenue; Salary Expense; Rent Expense; Utilities Expense.

1. Record each transaction in the journal, using the account titles given. Key each transaction by date. Explanations are not required.
2. Post the transactions to the ledger, using transaction dates as posting references in the ledger. Label the balance of each account *Bal.*, as shown in the chapter.
3. Prepare the trial balance of Marie Haley, Attorney, at January 31 of the current year.

Trial balance $54,700

Problem 2-4A *Journalizing transactions, posting to accounts in four-column format, and preparing a trial balance* **(L.O. 2,3,4,5)**

The trial balance of the accounting practice of William Pittenger, CPA, at November 15, 19X3, is shown on the next page.

During the remainder of November, Pittenger completed the following transactions:

Nov. 16 Collected $4,000 cash from a client on account.

17 Performed tax services for a client on account, $1,700.

19 Paid utilities, $200.

21 Paid on account, $2,600.

22 Purchased supplies on account, $200.

23 Withdrew $2,100 for personal use.

23 Paid for the renovation of private residence, $55,000.

24 Received $1,900 cash for audit work just completed.

30 Paid rent, $700.

30 Paid employees' salaries, $1,800.

William Pittenger, CPA
Trial Balance
November 15, 19X3

Account Number	Account	Debit	Credit
11	Cash	$ 5,000	
12	Accounts receivable	8,000	
13	Supplies	600	
14	Land........................	35,000	
21	Accounts payable		$ 4,400
31	William Pittenger, capital		42,000
32	William Pittenger, withdrawals	2,100	
41	Service revenue		7,100
51	Salary expense	1,800	
52	Rent expense	700	
53	Utilities expense	300	
	Total.....................	$53,500	$53,500

Required

1. Record the transactions that occurred during November 16 through 30 in *page 6* of the journal. Include an explanation for each entry.

2. Post the transactions to the ledger, using dates, account numbers, journal references, and posting references. Open the ledger accounts listed in the trial balance together with their balances at November 15. Use the four-column account format illustrated below. Enter *Bal.* (for previous balance) in the Item column, and place a check mark (✓) in the journal reference column for the November 15 balance, as illustrated for Cash:

Account	Cash				Account No. 11	
		Jrnl. Ref.			Balance	
Date	Item		Debit	Credit	Debit	Credit
Nov. 15	Bal.	✓			5,000	

3. Prepare the trial balance of William Pittenger, CPA, at November 30, 19X3.

Problem 2-5A   *Journalizing, posting to T-accounts, and preparing a trial balance* (L.O. 2,3,4,5)

Trial balance $17,010

Steakley Delivery Service began operations during May of the current year. During a short period thereafter, the entity engaged in the following transactions:

a. Lou Steakley, the owner, deposited $3,500 cash in a bank account entitled Steakley Delivery Service and also invested in the business a delivery truck valued at $8,000.

b. Purchased $40 fuel for the delivery truck, using a business credit card.

c. Paid $100 cash for supplies.

d. Completed a delivery job and received cash, $700.

e. Performed delivery services on account, $3,200.
f. Purchased advertising leaflets for cash, $200.
g. Paid the office manager salary, $950.
h. Received $1,000 cash for performing delivery services.
i. Received cash from customer on account, $1,800.
j. Purchased used office furniture on account, $600.
k. Paid office utility bills, $120.
l. Purchased $70 fuel on account for the truck.
m. Completed a delivery job and received the customer's promise to pay the amount due, $100, within ten days.
n. Paid cash to creditor on account, $200.
o. Paid $250 for repairs to the delivery truck.
p. Paid office manager the salary of $950 and office rent of $250.
q. Withdrew $1,900 for personal use.

Required

1. Record each transaction in the journal, using the account titles given. Key each transaction by letter. Explanations are not required.
2. Open the following T-accounts: Cash; Accounts Receivable; Supplies; Delivery Truck; Office Furniture; Accounts Payable; Lou Steakley, Capital; Lou Steakley, Withdrawals; Delivery Service Revenue; Salary Expense; Rent Expense; Repair Expense; Advertising Expense; Utilities Expense; Fuel Expense. Post the transactions to the ledger, keying transactions by letter. Label the balance of each account *Bal.*, as shown in the chapter.
3. Prepare the trial balance of Steakley Delivery Service, using the current date.

Trial balance $62,500

Problem 2-6A   *Correcting errors in a trial balance.*   *(L.O. 2,5)*

The trial balance in this problem shown on page 89, does not balance. The following errors were detected:

a. The cash balance is understated by $400.
b. Office maintenance expense of $200 is omitted from the trial balance.
c. Rent expense of $200 was posted as a credit rather than a debit.
d. The balance of Advertising Expense is $300, but it is listed as $400 on the trial balance.
e. A $600 debit to Accounts Receivable was posted as $60.
f. The balance of Utilities Expense is understated by $60.
g. A $500 debit to the withdrawal account was posted as a credit to Laura Hewitt, Capital.
h. A $100 purchase of supplies on account was neither journalized nor posted.
i. A $5,600 credit to Service Revenue was not posted.
j. Office furniture should be listed in the amount of $1,300.

Required

Prepare the correct trial balance at October 31. Journal entries are not required.

Hewitt Speed & Marine
Trial Balance
October 31, 19X1

Cash	$ 3,800	
Accounts receivable	2,000	
Supplies	500	
Office furniture	2,300	
Land	46,800	
Accounts payable		$ 2,000
Note payable		18,300
Laura Hewitt, capital		32,100
Laura Hewitt, withdrawals	3,700	
Service revenue		4,900
Salary expense	1,000	
Rent expense	600	
Advertising expense	400	
Utilities expense	200	
Property tax	100	
Total	$61,400	$57,300

Problem 2-7A *Recording transactions directly in the ledger, preparing a trial balance*   Trail balance $108,700
(L.O. 2,5,6)

Ken Mazanec started a cable television service and during the first month of operations completed the following selected transactions:

a. Mazanec began the business with an investment of $30,000 cash and a building valued at $50,000.
b. Borrowed $25,000 from the bank; signed a note payable.
c. Paid $32,000 for transmitting equipment.
d. Purchased office supplies on account, $400.
e. Paid employee salary, $1,300.
f. Received $500 for cable TV service performed for customers.
g. Sold cable service to customers on account, $2,300.
h. Paid $100 of the account payable created in *d*.
i. Received a $600 bill for utility expense that will be paid in the near future.
j. Received cash on account, $1,100.
k. Paid the following cash expenses:
    (1) Rent on land, $1,000
    (2) Advertising, $800.
l. Withdrew $2,600 for personal use.

Required

1. Open the following T-accounts: Cash; Accounts Receivable; Office Supplies; Transmitting Equipment; Building; Accounts Payable; Note Payable; Ken Mazanec, Capital; Ken Mazanec, Withdrawals; Service Revenue; Salary Expense; Rent Expense; Advertising Expense; Utilities Expense.
2. Record the following transactions directly in the T-accounts without using a journal. Use the letters to identify the transactions.
3. Prepare the trial balance of Mazanec Cable TV Service at January 31, 19X7.

No check figure

Problem 2-1B *Analyzing a trial balance* **(L.O. 1)**

The owner of Wang Service Company is selling the business. She offers the following trial balance to prospective buyers:

Wang Service Company Trial Balance December 31, 19XX		
Cash	$ 18,000	
Accounts receivable	27,000	
Prepaid expenses..................	4,000	
Land	81,000	
Accounts payable		$41,000
Note payable		32,000
Li-Ping Wang, capital..............		30,000
Li-Ping Wang, withdrawals	18,000	
Sales revenue		104,000
Rent expense	26,000	
Advertising expense	3,000	
Wage expense	23,000	
Supplies expense..................	7,000	
	$207,000	$207,000

Your best friend is considering buying Wang Service Company. He seeks your advice in interpreting this information. Specifically, he asks whether this trial balance is the same as a balance sheet and an income statement. He also wonders whether Wang must be a sound company. After all, the accounts are in balance.

Required

Write a short note to answer your friend's questions. To aid his decision, state how he can use the information on the trial balance to determine whether Wang has earned a net income or experienced a net loss for the current period.

No check figure

Problem 2-2B *Analyzing and journalizing transactions* **(L.O. 2,3)**

Good Times Theater Company owns movie theaters in the shopping centers of a major metropolitan area. Its owner, Jill Mead, engaged in the following business transactions:

Dec. 1 Mead invested $75,000 personal cash in the business by depositing this amount in a bank account entitled Good Times Theater Company.

2 Paid $55,000 cash to purchase land for a theater site.

5 Borrowed $250,000 from the bank to finance the construction of the new theater. Mead signed a note payable to the bank in the name of Good Times Theater Company.

7 Received $20,000 cash from ticket sales and deposited this amount in the bank. (Label the revenue as Sales Revenue.)

10 Purchased supplies for the older theaters on account, $1,700.

15 Paid theater employee salaries, $2,800, and rent on a theater building, $1,800.

15 Paid property tax expense on theater building, $1,200.

16 Paid $800 on account.

17 Withdrew $3,000 from the business to take her family to a nearby resort.

Good Times uses the following accounts: Cash; Supplies; Land; Accounts Payable; Notes Payable; Jill Mead, Capital; Jill Mead, Withdrawals; Sales Revenue; Salary Expense; Rent Expense; Property Tax Expense.

Required

1. Prepare an analysis of each business transaction of Good Times Theater Company, as shown for the December 1 transaction:

    Dec. 1 The asset Cash is increased. Increases in assets are recorded by debits; therefore, debit Cash.

    The owner's equity of the entity is increased. Increases in owner's equity are recorded by credits; therefore, credit Jill Mead, Capital.

2. Prepare the journal entry for each transaction. Explanations are not required.

Problem 2-3B *Journalizing transactions, posting to T-accounts, and preparing a trial balance* **(L.O. 2,3,4,5)**

Trial balance $24,400

Oliver Goldsmith opened a law office on September 3 of the current year. During the first month of operations, the business completed the following transactions:

Sep. 3 Goldsmith transferred $20,000 cash from his personal bank account to a business account entitled Oliver Goldsmith, Attorney.
      4 Purchased supplies, $200, and furniture, $1,800, on account.
      6 Performed legal services for a client and received $1,000 cash.
      7 Paid $15,000 cash to acquire land for a future office site.
      10 Defended a client in court, billed the client, and received her promise to pay the $900 within one week.
      14 Paid for the furniture purchased September 4 on account.
      15 Paid secretary salary, $600.
      16 Paid the telephone bill, $120.
      17 Received partial payment from client on account, $700.
      20 Prepared legal documents for a client on account, $800.
      24 Paid the water and electricity bills, $110.
      28 Received $1,500 cash for helping a client sell real estate.
      30 Paid secretary salary, $600.
      30 Paid rent expense, $500.
      30 Withdrew $2,000 for personal use.

Required

Open the following T-accounts: Cash; Accounts Receivable; Supplies; Furniture; Land; Accounts Payable; Oliver Goldsmith, Capital; Oliver Goldsmith, Withdrawals; Service Revenue; Salary Expense; Rent Expense; Utilities Expense.

1. Record each transaction in the journal, using the account titles given. Key each transaction by date. Explanations are not required.
2. Post the transactions to the ledger, using transaction dates as posting references in the ledger. Label the balance of each account *Bal.*, as shown in the chapter.
3. Prepare the trial balance of Oliver Goldsmith, Attorney, at September 30 of the current year.

Problem 2-4B *Journalizing transactions, posting to accounts in four-column format, and preparing a trial balance* **(L.O. 2,3,4,5)**

The trial balance of the accounting practice of Elizabeth Staar, CPA, is dated February 14, 19X3.

During the remainder of February, Staar completed the following transactions:

Feb. 15 Staar collected $2,000 cash from a client on account.
   16 Performed tax services for a client on account, $900.
   18 Paid utilities, $300.
   20 Paid on account, $1,000.
   21 Purchased supplies on account, $100.
   21 Withdrew $1,200 for personal use.
   21 Paid for a swimming pool for private residence, using personal funds, $13,000.
   22 Received cash of $2,100 for audit work just completed.
   28 Paid rent, $800.
   28 Paid employees' salaries, $1,600.

Elizabeth Staar, CPA
Trial Balance
February 14, 19X3

Account Number	Account	Debit	Credit
11	Cash...............................	$ 4,000	
12	Accounts receivable	11,000	
13	Supplies	800	
14	Land	18,600	
21	Accounts payable		$ 3,000
31	Elizabeth Staar, capital		30,000
32	Elizabeth Staar, withdrawals	1,200	
41	Service revenue.......................		7,200
51	Salary expense........................	3,600	
52	Rent expense	800	
53	Utilities expense	200	
	Total...............................	$40,200	$40,200

Required

1. Record the transactions that occurred during February 15 through 28 in *page 3* of the journal. Include an explanation for each entry.
2. Open the ledger accounts listed in the trial balance, together with their balances at February 14. Use the four-column account format illustrated below. Enter *Bal.* (for previous balance) in the Item column, and place a check mark (✓) in the journal reference column for the February 14 balance, as illustrated for Cash:

Account	Cash					Account No. 11	
						Balance	
Date	Item	Jrnl. Ref.	Debit	Credit		Debit	Credit
Feb. 14	Bal.	✓				4,000	

Post the transactions to the ledger, using dates, account numbers, journal references, and posting references.

3. Prepare the trial balance of Elizabeth Staar, CPA, at February 28, 19X3.

Problem 2-5B *Journalizing, posting to T-accounts, and preparing a trial balance*
(L.O. 2,3,4,5)

Trial balance $19,300

Dwyer Delivery Service completed the following transactions during its first month of operations:

a. Paul Dwyer, the proprietor of the business, began operations by investing in the business $5,000 cash and a truck valued at $10,000.
b. Paid $200 cash for supplies.
c. Used a company credit card to purchase $50 fuel for the delivery truck. (Credit Accounts Payable.)
d. Performed delivery services for a customer and received $600 cash.
e. Completed a large delivery job, billed the customer $2,000, and received a promise to be paid the $2,000 within one week.
f. Paid employee salary, $800.
g. Received $900 cash for performing delivery services.
h. Purchased fuel for the truck on account, $40.
i. Received $2,000 cash from a customer on account.
j. Paid for advertising in the local newspaper, $170.
k. Paid utility bills, $100.
l. Purchased fuel for the truck, paying $30 with a company credit card.
m. Performed delivery services on account, $800.
n. Paid for repairs to the delivery truck, $110.
o. Paid employee salary, $800, and office rent, $200.
p. Paid $120 on account.
q. Withdrew $1,900 for personal use.

Required

1. Record each transaction in the journal, using the account titles given. Key each transaction by letter. Explanations are not required.
2. Open the following T-accounts: Cash; Accounts Receivable; Supplies; Delivery Truck; Accounts Payable; Paul Dwyer, Capital; Paul Dwyer, Withdrawals; Delivery Service Revenue; Salary Expense; Rent Expense; Advertising Expense; Fuel Expense; Repair Expense; Utilities Expense. Post the transactions to the ledger, keying transactions by letter. Label the balance of each account *Bal.*, as shown in the chapter.
3. Prepare the trial balance of Dwyer Delivery Service, using the current date.

Problem 2-6B *Correcting errors in a trial balance* *(L.O. 2,5)*

Trial balance $48,600

The following trial balance on page 94 does not balance.

The following errors were detected:

a. The cash balance is understated by $300.
b. A property tax payment of $500 was not recorded.
c. Land should be listed in the amount of $24,000.
d. A $200 purchase of supplies on account was neither journalized nor posted.
e. A $2,800 credit to Counseling Service Revenue was not posted.
f. Rent expense of $200 was posted as a credit rather than a debit.

Samaritan Counseling Center
Trial Balance
June 30, 19X2

Cash	$ 2,000	
Accounts receivable.................	10,000	
Supplies	900	
Office furniture	3,600	
Land	26,000	
Accounts payable....................		$ 4,000
Note payable........................		14,000
Carmen Cathay, capital		22,000
Carmen Cathay, withdrawals	2,000	
Counseling service revenue		6,500
Salary expense	1,600	
Rent expense	1,000	
Advertising expense	500	
Utilities expense....................	300	
Property tax expense	100	
Total	$48,000	$46,500

g. The balance of Advertising Expense is $600, but it was listed as $500 on the trial balance.
h. A $300 debit to Accounts Receivable was posted as $30.
i. The balance of Utilities Expense is overstated by $70.
j. A $900 debit to the Withdrawal account was posted as a credit to Carmen Cathay, Capital.

Required

Prepare the correct trial balance at June 30. Journal entries are not required.

Trial balance $110,100

Problem 2-7B *Recording transactions directly in the ledger, preparing a trial balance (L.O. 2,5,6)*

Diana Flori started a consulting service and during the first month of operations completed the following selected transactions:

a. Flori began the business with an investment of $15,000 cash and a building valued at $60,000.
b. Borrowed $30,000 from the bank; signed a note payable.
c. Purchased office supplies on account, $1,300.
d. Paid $18,000 for office furniture.
e. Paid employee salary, $2,200.
f. Performed consulting service on account for client, $2,100.
g. Paid $800 of the account payable created in *c.*
h. Received a $900 bill for advertising expense that will be paid in the near future.
i. Performed consulting service for customers and received cash, $1,600.
j. Received cash on account, $1,200.
k. Paid the following cash expenses:
   (1) Rent on land, $700.
   (2) Utilities, $400.
l. Withdrew $3,500 for personal use.

Required

1. Open the following T-accounts: Cash; Accounts Receivable; Office Supplies; Office Furniture; Building; Accounts Payable; Note Payable; Diana Flori, Capital; Diana Flori, Withdrawals; Service Revenue; Salary Expense; Advertising Expense; Rent Expense; Utilities Expense.
2. Record each transaction directly in the T-accounts without using a journal. Use the letters to identify the transactions.
3. Prepare the trial balance of Flori Consulting Service at June 30, 19X3.

Extending Your Knowledge

Decision Problems

1. Recording Transactions Directly in the Ledger, Preparing a Trial Balance, and Measuring Net Income or Loss (L.O. 2,5,6)

Net income $3,850

You have been requested by a friend named Charles Sligh to give advice on the effects that certain business transactions will have on the entity he plans to start. Time is short, so you will not be able to do all the detailed procedures of journalizing and posting. Instead, you must analyze the transactions without the use of a journal. Sligh will continue the business only if he can expect to earn monthly net income of $3,500. Assume the following transactions have occurred:

a. Sligh deposited $6,000 cash in a business bank account.
b. Borrowed $4,000 cash from the bank and signed a note payable due within one year.
c. Paid $300 cash for supplies.
d. Purchased advertising in the local newspaper for cash, $800.
e. Purchased office furniture on account, $1,500.
f. Paid the following cash expenses for one month: secretary salary, $1,400; office rent, $400; utilities, $300; interest, $50.
g. Earned revenue on account $4,300.
h. Earned revenue and received $2,500 cash.
i. Collected cash from customers on account, $1,200.
j. Paid on account, $1,000.
k. Withdrew $900 for personal use.

Required

1. Open the following T-accounts: Cash; Accounts Receivable; Supplies; Furniture; Accounts Payable; Notes Payable; Charles Sligh, Capital; Charles Sligh, Withdrawals; Service Revenue; Salary Expense; Advertising Expense; Rent Expense; Utilities Expense; Interest Expense.
2. Record the transactions directly in the accounts without using a journal. Key each transaction by letter.
3. Prepare a trial balance at the current date. List expenses with the largest amount first, the next largest amount second, and so on. The business name will be Sligh Apartment Locators.

4. Compute the amount of net income or net loss for this first month of operations. Would you recommend that Sligh continue in business?

No check figure

2. *Using the accounting equation* (L.O. 2)

Although all the following questions deal with the accounting equation, they are not related:

1. Explain the advantages of double-entry bookkeeping over single-entry bookkeeping to a friend who is opening a used book store.
2. When you deposit money in your bank account, the bank credits your account. Is the bank misusing the word *credit* in this context? Why does the bank use the term *credit* to refer to your deposit, and not *debit?*
3. Your friend asks, "When revenues increase assets and expenses decrease assets, why are revenues credits and expenses debits and not the other way around?" Explain to your friend why revenues are credits and expenses are debits.

Ethical Issue

Community Chest, a charitable organization in Mojave, New Mexico, has a standing agreement with Encino State Bank. The agreement allows Community Chest to overdraw its cash balance at the bank when donations are running low. In the past, Community Chest managed funds wisely and rarely used this privilege. Greg Osborn has recently become the president of Community Chest. To expand operations, Osborn is acquiring office equipment and spending large amounts for fund-raising. During his presidency, Community Chest has maintained a negative bank balance of approximately $1,000.

Required

What is the ethical issue in this situation? State why you approve or disapprove of Osborn's management of Community Chest funds.

Financial Statement Problems

No check figure

1. *Journalizing Transactions* (L.O. 2,3)

This problem helps to develop skill in recording transactions by using an actual company's account titles. Refer to The Goodyear Tire & Rubber Company financial statements in Appendix C. Assume Goodyear completed the following selected transactions during November 1990:

Nov. 5 Earned sales revenue on account, $55,000.
9 Borrowed $500,000 by signing a note payable (long-term debt).
12 Purchased equipment on account, $70,000.
17 Paid $110,000, which represents payment of $100,000 long-term debt due within one year plus interest expense of $10,000.
19 Earned sales revenue and immediately received cash of $16,000.
22 Collected the cash on account that was earned on November 5.
24 Paid rent of $14,000 for three months in advance.
28 Received a home-office electricity bill for $1,000, which will be paid in December (this is an administrative and general expense).
30 Paid off half the account payable created on November 12.

Required

Journalize these transactions using the following account titles taken from the financial statements of Goodyear: Cash; Accounts Receivable; Prepaid Expenses; Equipment; Long-term Debt Due Within One Year; Trade Accounts Payable; Long-Term Debt; Sales Revenue; Selling, Administrative, and General Expense; Interest Expense. Explanations are not required.

2. Journalizing Transactions   (L.O. 2,3)

No check figure

Obtain the annual report of an actual company of your choosing. Assume the company completed the following selected transactions during May of the current year:

May 3   Borrowed $350,000 by signing a short-term note payable (may be called *short-term debt* or other account title).

   5   Paid rent for six months in advance, $4,600.

   9   Earned revenue on account, $74,000.

   12   Purchased equipment on account, $33,000.

   17   Paid a telephone bill, $300 (this is Selling Expense).

   19   Paid $90,000 of the money borrowed on May 3.

   26   Collected one half of the cash on account from May 9.

   30   Paid the account payable from May 12.

Chapter 3

Measuring Business Income: The Adjusting Process

A few years ago, a group of executives at Hasbro Inc., the big toy maker, leafed through a comic book about a bunch of tough-talking turtles and thought about marketing them. "Too bizarre," they decided, quickly rejecting the idea. So instead, little Playmate Toys Inc. has made millions selling Teenage Mutant Ninja Turtles dolls, swords, robots. . . .

Anyone can miss an opportunity, of course. But for Hasbro, the bad decision was one in a series that brought the company down from highflier of the 1980s to a company that could use some new batteries.

Hasbro's earnings peaked in 1986, and with sales essentially flat for four years and possibly dropping this year, the company may lose its No. 1 spot to a resurgent Mattel. Last week, citing a need to cut costs, Hasbro laid off 90 people from its 1,600-member corporate staff, including some toy designers.

Hasbro executives concede that times have been tough, but point out that Hasbro still has many strengths. "Sure, we've made mistakes. . . . But Hasbro is on its way back. At the end of the year when you add up the totals we'll be on top—still."

Source: Joseph Pereira, "A Highflier in the 80s, Hasbro Has Lost Its Touch for Picking Hot Toys," *The Wall Street Journal*, October 17, 1990, p. A1.

The primary goal of business is to earn a profit. Many companies such as Hasbro expect to earn increasing amounts of profit each year. When they do, they expand the business, hire more employees, and make their owners happy. When profits fail to meet goals, the result can be layoffs, idle facilities, and unhappy owners, as in the case of Hasbro.

Gary Lyon, the CPA whose accounting practice we discussed in the earlier chapters, earns business income by providing accounting services for clients. Regardless of the type of activity, the profit motive increases the owner's drive to carry on the business. As you read Chapter 3, consider how important income is to a business and how important accounting procedures are in measuring income.

At the end of each accounting period, the accountant prepares the entity's financial statements. The period may be a month, three months, six months, or a full year. Whatever the length of the period, the end accounting product is the same, the financial statements. And the most important single amount in these statements is the net income or net loss—the profit or loss—for the period. A double-entry accounting system produces not only the income statement but the other financial statements as well.

An important step in financial statement preparation is the trial balance that we discussed in Chapter 2. The trial balance includes the effects of the transactions that occurred during the period—the cash collections, purchases of assets, payments of bills, sales of assets, and so on. To measure its income properly, however, a business must do some additional accounting at the end of the period to bring the records up to date before preparing the financial statements. This process is called *adjusting the books,* and it consists of making special entries called *adjusting entries.* This chapter focuses primarily on these adjusting entries to help you better understand the nature of business income.

Accountants have devised concepts and principles to guide the measurement of business income. Chief among these are the concepts of accrual accounting, the accounting period, the revenue principle, and the matching principle. In this chapter, we apply these concepts and principles to measure the income and prepare the financial statements of Gary Lyon's business for the month of April.

Point to Stress: While all the parts of the financial statements are important in describing the financial condition of a business, the income statement is particularly important because it reports how profitable or unprofitable a company is.

Accrual-Basis Accounting versus Cash-Basis Accounting

OBJECTIVE 1
Distinguish accrual-basis accounting from cash-basis accounting

There are two widely used bases of accounting: the accrual basis and the cash basis. In **accrual-basis accounting**, an accountant recognizes the impact of a business event as it occurs. When the business performs a service, makes a sale, or incurs an expense, the accountant enters the transaction into the books, whether or not cash has been received or paid. In **cash-basis accounting,** however, the accountant does not record a transaction until cash is received or paid. Cash receipts are treated as revenues, and cash payments are handled as expenses.

GAAP requires that a business use the accrual basis. This means that the accountant records revenues as they are earned and expenses as they are *incurred*—not necessarily when cash changes hands.

Using accrual-basis accounting, Gary Lyon records revenue when he performs services for a client on account. Lyon has earned the revenue at that time because his efforts have generated an account receivable, a legal claim against the client for whom he did the work. By contrast, if Gary Lyon used cash-basis accounting, he would not record revenue at the time he performed the service. He would wait until he received cash.

Why does GAAP require that businesses use the accrual basis? What advantage does accrual-basis accounting offer? Suppose Gary Lyon's accounting period ends after he has earned the revenue but before he has collected the money due him. If he used the cash-basis method, his financial statements would not include this revenue or the related account receivable. As a result, the financial statements would be misleading. Revenue and the asset Accounts Receivable would be understated, and thus his business would look less successful than it actually is. If he wants to get a bank loan to expand his practice, the understated revenue and asset figures might hurt his chances.

Gary Lyon, using accrual-basis accounting, treats expenses in a like manner. For instance, salary expense includes amounts paid to employees plus any amount owed to employees but not yet paid. Lyon's use of the employee's service, not the payment of cash to the employee, brings about the expense. Under cash-basis accounting, Lyon would record the expense only when he actually paid the employee.

Suppose Gary Lyon owes his secretary a salary and the financial statements are drawn up before Lyon pays. Expenses and liabilities would be understated, so the business would look more successful than it really is. This incomplete information would not provide an accurate accounting to potential creditors.

As these examples show, accrual accounting provides more complete information than does cash-basis accounting. This is important because the more complete the data, the better equipped decision makers are to reach intelligent conclusions about the firm's financial health and future prospects. Three concepts used in accrual accounting are the accounting period, the revenue principle, and the matching principle.

The Accounting Period

The only way to know for certain how successfully a business has operated is to close its doors, sell all its assets, pay the liabilities, and return any leftover cash to the owner. This process, called liquidation, is the same as going out of business. Obviously, it is not practical for accountants to measure business income in this manner. Instead, businesses need periodic reports on their progress. Accountants slice time into small segments and prepare financial statements for specific periods. Until a business liquidates, the amounts reported in its financial statements must be regarded as estimates.

The most basic accounting period is one year, and virtually all businesses

Point to Stress: Students can remember the difference between cash and accrual accounting this way:

Cash basis: Record revenue when the cash comes to you, regardless of when the service was performed or the sale made. Record expenses when the cash is paid out, regardless of when the expense was incurred or the item purchased.

Accrual basis: Forget cash flow. Record revenue when the sale is made or the service is performed. Record expenses when incurred (when the business uses goods or services). Revenues and expenses will not necessarily coincide with cash flows.

Point to Stress: Salary expense and salary payable are not recorded just to create additional work for accountants. Salary payable is an obligation. If Gary Lyon were to go out of business, he would still have to pay the secretary for the work she had already done.

Real-World Example: The Yale Express case, settled in the early 1970s, is a famous case involving accrual accounting. In 1963, Yale Express, a trucking firm, acquired Republic Carloading and Distributing Co. Before the merger, Republic failed to accrue freight costs at the end of each year. The error was substantial enough to reduce the reported 1963 net income of $1,140,000 to a $1,880,000 net loss.

prepare annual financial statements. For about 60 percent of large companies in a recent survey, the annual accounting period runs the calendar year from January 1 through December 31. Other companies use what is called a *fiscal year*, which ends on some date other than December 31. The year-end date is usually the low point in business activity for the year. Depending on the type of business, the fiscal year may end on April 30, July 31, or some other date. Retailers are a notable example. For example, J. C. Penney Company uses a fiscal year ending on January 31 because the low point in Penney's business activity has followed the after-Christmas sales during January.

Companies cannot wait until the end of the year to gauge their progress. The manager of a business wants to know how well the business is doing each month, each quarter, and each half year. Outsiders such as lenders also demand current information about the business. So companies also prepare financial statements for *interim* periods, which are less than a year. Monthly financial statements are common, and a series of monthly statements can be combined for quarterly and semiannual periods. Most of the discussions in this book are based on an annual accounting period. However, the procedures and statements can also be applied to interim periods as well.

Real-World Example: American Airlines has the capability to prepare an income statement daily so it can maximize its profits by either adding or dropping routes. In this way, it gets immediate feedback and does not have to wait until the end of the month, when the need for a route change might no longer be an issue.

Revenue Principle

The **revenue principle** tells accountants (1) *when* to record revenue by making a journal entry and (2) the *amount* of revenue to record. When we speak of "recording" something in accounting, the act of recording the item naturally leads to posting to the ledger accounts and preparing the trial balance and the financial statements. Although the financial statements are the end product of accounting and what accountants are most concerned about, our discussions often focus on recording the entry in the journal because that is where the accounting process starts.

The general principle guiding *when* to record revenue says to record revenue as it has been earned—but not before. In most cases, revenue is earned when the business has delivered a completed good or service to the customer. The business has done everything required by the agreement, including transferring the item to the customer. Two situations that provide guidance on when to record revenue follow. The first situation illustrates when *not* to record revenue. Situation 2 illustrates when revenue should be recorded.

Point to Stress: Revenue is recorded when Gary Lyon has done virtually everything needed to complete his part of the transaction, and the customer has accepted his work.

Situation 1—Do not record revenue.   A client of another CPA expresses her intention to transfer her tax work to Gary Lyon. Should Lyon record any revenue based on this intention? The answer is no because no transaction has occurred.

Situation 2—Record revenue.   Next month Gary Lyon consults with this client and tailors a business plan to her goals. After transferring the business plan to the client, Lyon should record revenue. If the client pays for this service immediately, Lyon will debit Cash. If the service is performed on account, Lyon will debit Accounts Receivable. In either case, Lyon should record revenue by crediting the Service Revenue account.

OBJECTIVE 2
Apply the revenue and matching principles

The general principle guiding the *amount* of revenue says to record revenue equal to the cash value of the goods or the service transferred to the customer. Suppose that in order to obtain a new client, Gary Lyon performs accounting

Discussion Question: On March 15, a client pays Lyon $900 to cover April 1–June 30. Has Lyon earned revenue on March 15? ANSWER: No. He has received the cash but the service will not be performed until later. Under the accrual method, on March 15 Gary Lyon will record Unearned Service Revenue (a liability). It is a liability because Lyon has an obligation to perform a service in the future.

Point to Stress: Refer to the chapter-opening vignette. Although an increase in revenue usually causes an increase in expenses, many companies try to cut expenses without reducing revenue.

service for the price of $500. Ordinarily, Lyon would have charged $600 for this service. How much revenue should Lyon record? The answer is $500 because that was the cash value of the transaction. Lyon will not receive the full value of $600, so that is not the amount of revenue to record. He will receive only $500 cash, and that pinpoints the amount of revenue earned.

Matching Principle

The **matching principle** is the basis for recording expenses. Recall that expenses, such as rent, utilities, and advertising, are the costs of operating a business. Expenses are the costs of assets that are used up in the earning of revenue. The matching principle directs accountants (1) to identify all expenses incurred during the accounting period, (2) to measure the expenses, and (3) to "match" the expenses against the revenues earned during that same span of time. To "match" expenses against revenues means to subtract the expenses from the revenues in order to compute net income or net loss.

There is a natural link between revenues and some types of expenses. Accountants follow the matching principle by first identifying the revenues of a period and the expenses that can be linked to particular revenues. For example, a business that pays sales commissions to its sales personnel will have commission expense if the employees make sales. If they make no sales, the business has no commission expense. Cost of goods sold is another example. When merchandise is sold, there must also be a cost—the cost incurred by the seller— assigned to the goods sold. If there are no sales, there can be no cost of goods sold.

Other expenses are not so easy to link with particular sales. Monthly rent expense occurs, for example, regardless of the revenues earned during the period. The matching principle directs accountants to identify these types of expenses with a particular time period, such as a month or a year. If Gary Lyon employs a secretary at a monthly salary of $1,900, the business will record salary expense of $1,900 each month. Because financial statements appear at definite intervals, there must be some cutoff date for the necessary information. Most entities engage in so many transactions that some are bound to spill over into more than a single accounting period. Gary Lyon prepares monthly statements for his business at April 30. How does he handle a transaction that begins in April but ends in May? How does he bring the accounts up to date for preparing the financial statements? To answer these questions, accountants use the time-period concept.

Time-Period Concept

Managers, investors, and creditors are making decisions daily and need periodic readings on the business's progress. To meet this need for information, accountants prepare financial statements at regular intervals. Virtually all companies report net income for an annual period and their assets, liabilities, and owner's equity at the end of the year. Most companies also prepare monthly and quarterly financial statements.

The **time-period concept** ensures that accounting information is reported at regular intervals. It interacts with the revenue principle and the matching principle to underlie the use of accruals. To measure income accurately, companies update the revenue and expense accounts immediately prior to the end of the period. Tootsie Roll Industries, Inc., the candy maker, provides an actual example of an expense accrual. At December 31, 1989, Tootsie Roll recorded employee compensation of $3.4 million that the company owed its workers for unpaid services performed before year end. Tootsie Roll's accrual entry was

```
1989
Dec. 31   Salary (or Wage) Expense ...............   3,400,000
                 Salary (or Wage) Payable ...........               3,400,000
```

This entry serves two purporses. It assigns the expense to the proper period. Without the accrual entry at December 31, total expenses of 1989 would be understated and as a result net income would be overstated. Incorrectly, the expense would fall in 1990 when Tootsie Roll makes the next payroll disbursement. The accrual entry also records the liability for reporting on the balance sheet at December 31, 1989. Without the accrual entry, total liabilities would be understated.

At the end of the accounting period, companies also accrue revenues that have been earned but not collected. The remainder of the chapter discusses how to make the necessary adjustments to the accounts.

Adjustments to the Accounts

At the end of the period, the accountant prepares the financial statements. This end-of-the-period process begins with the trial balance that lists the accounts and their balances after the period's transactions have been recorded in the journal and posted to the accounts in the ledger. Exhibit 3-1 is the trial balance of Gary Lyon's accounting practice at April 30, 19X1.

Point to Stress: Adjusting entries are necessary under the accrual basis of accounting in order to carry through the revenue and matching principles.

EXHIBIT 3-1 *Unadjusted Trial Balance*

Gary Lyon, CPA Unadjusted Trial Balance April 30, 19X1		
Cash	$24,800	
Accounts receivable	2,250	
Supplies.......................................	700	
Prepaid rent	3,000	
Furniture	16,500	
Accounts payable		$13,100
Unearned service revenue.....................		450
Gary Lyon, capital		31,250
Gary Lyon, withdrawals	3,200	
Service revenue		7,000
Salary expense................................	950	
Utilities expense	400	
Total...	$51,800	$51,800

Point to Stress: The amounts recorded for daily transactions are usually taken from source documents (such as bills and receipts). Preparing adjusting entries usually requires a calculation, and generally requires more accounting knowledge than the recording of daily transactions. In many businesses, an accountant would be responsible for the adjusting entries whereas a bookkeeper could account for daily transactions. Many small businesses use the cash method of accounting.

This *unadjusted* trial balance includes some new accounts that will be explained in this section. It lists most, but not all, of the revenue and the expenses of Lyon's accounting practice for the month of April. These trial balance amounts are incomplete because they omit certain revenue and expense transactions that affect more than one accounting period. That is why it is called an *unadjusted* trial balance. In most cases, however, we refer to it simply as the trial balance, without the "unadjusted" label.

Under the cash basis of accounting, there would be no need for adjustments to the accounts because all April cash transactions would have been recorded. The accrual basis requires adjusting entries at the end of the period in order to produce correct balances for the financial statements. To see why, consider the Supplies account in Exhibit 3-1.

Lyon's accounting practice uses supplies in providing accounting services for clients during the month. This reduces the quantity of supplies on hand and thus constitutes an expense, just like salary expense or rent expense. Gary Lyon does not bother to record his daily expense, and it is not worth his while to record supplies expense more than once a month. It is time-consuming to make hourly, daily, or even weekly journal entries to record the expense for the use of supplies. So how does he account for supplies expense?

By the end of the month, the Supplies balance is not correct. The balance represents the amount of supplies on hand at the start of the month plus any supplies purchased during the month. This balance fails to take into account the supplies used (supplies expense) during the accounting period. It is necessary, then, to subtract the month's expenses from the amount of supplies listed on the trial balance. The resulting new adjusted balance measures the cost of supplies that are still on hand at April 30. This is the correct amount of supplies to report on the balance sheet. Adjusting entries in this way will bring the accounts up to date.

Adjusting entries assign revenues to the period in which they are earned and expenses to the period in which they are incurred. They are needed (a) to measure properly the period's income and (b) to bring related asset and liability accounts to correct balances for the financial statements. For example, an adjusting entry is needed to transfer the amount of supplies used during the period from the asset account Supplies to the expense account Supplies Expense. The adjusting entry updates both the Supplies asset account and the Supplies Expense account. This achieves accurate measures of assets and expenses. Adjusting entries, which are the key to the accrual basis of accounting, are made before preparing the financial statements.

The end-of-period process of updating the accounts is called *adjusting the accounts, making the adjusting entries,* or *adjusting the books.* Adjusting entries can be divided into five categories:

1. Prepaid expenses
2. Depreciation
3. Accrued expenses
4. Accrued revenues
5. Unearned revenues

Prepaid Expenses

Prepaid expenses is a category of miscellaneous assets that typically expire or are used up in the near future. Prepaid rent and prepaid insurance are examples of prepaid expenses. They are called prepaid expenses because they are expenses that are paid in advance. Salary expense and utilities expense, among others, are typically *not* prepaid expenses because they are not paid in advance.

Prepaid Rent.   Landlords usually require tenants to pay rent in advance. This prepayment creates an asset for the renter because that person has purchased the future benefit of using the rented item. Suppose Gary Lyon prepays three months' rent on April 1, 19X1, after negotiating a lease for his business office. If the lease specifies monthly rental amounts of $1,000 each, the entry to record the payment for three months is a debit to the asset account, Prepaid Rent, as follows:

Apr. 1   Prepaid Rent ($1,000 × 3)   3,000
                    Cash   3,000
             Paid three months' rent in advance.

After posting, Prepaid Rent appears as follows:

Prepaid Rent	
Apr. 1 3,000	

The trial balance at April 30, 19X1, lists Prepaid Rent as an asset with a debit balance of $3,000. Throughout April, the Prepaid Rent account maintains this beginning balance as shown in Exhibit 3-1.

At April 30 Prepaid Rent should be adjusted to remove from its balance the amount of the asset that has expired, which is one month's worth of the prepayment. By definition, the amount of an asset that has expired is *expense*. The adjusting entry transfers one-third, or $1,000 ($3,000 × 1/3), of the debit balance from Prepaid Rent to Rent Expense. The debit side of the entry records an increase in Rent Expense, and the credit records a decrease in the asset Prepaid Rent.

Apr. 30   Rent Expense ($3,000 × 1/3)   1,000
                    Prepaid Rent   1,000
             To record rent expense.

After posting, Prepaid Rent and Rent Expense appear as follows:

Prepaid Rent			Rent Expense	
Apr. 1 3,000	Apr. 30 1,000	⟷	Apr. 30 1,000	
Bal. 2,000			Bal. 1,000	

Correct asset amount, $2,000 → | **Total accounted for, $3,000** | ← **Correct expense amount, $1,000**

The full $3,000 has been accounted for: two-thirds measures the asset, and one-third measures the expense. This is correct because two-thirds of the asset remains for future use, and one-third of the prepayment has expired. Recording this expense illustrates the matching principle. The same analysis applies to a prepayment of three months' insurance premiums. The only difference is in the account titles, which would be Prepaid Insurance and Insurance

Teaching Tip: Some students tend to memorize the adjusting entries rather than understand their impact on the financial statements. Suggest that students ask themselves these questions: What is the balance of the account (such as Prepaid Rent)? *ANSWER:* $3,000. What do we need the balance to be? *ANSWER:* $2,000, because only two months' rent is now prepaid. How do we achieve the $2,000 balance? *ANSWER:* By reducing Prepaid Rent $1,000.

Discussion Question: Assume that Gary Lyon pays his rent at the beginning of each month. Would the $1,000 monthly payment be a prepaid expense? *ANSWER:* Technically, yes. However, accountants would record rent expense because the benefit from the paid rent expires at the end of the month.

OBJECTIVE 3
Make the typical adjusting entries at the end of the accounting period

Point to Stress: The adjusting entry is important only in that it affects the account balance that will be reported in the statements. Therefore, the result of the adjusting entry should be emphasized and not just the entry itself. The entry is a means to an end, an accurate financial statement.

Class Exercise: Suppose instead that the three months' rent was recorded as Rent Expense when paid on April 1:

Rent Expense

April 1	3,000	

To adjust the accounts to their current balances, the following adjusting entry is required:

4/30	Prepaid Rent . . .	2,000	
	Rent Exp.		2,000

Rent Expense now has a $1,000 debit balance, and Prepaid Rent has a $2,000 debit balance.

Class Exercise: This supplies example gives the amount of the supplies on hand at the end of April. Therefore, the amount used, or expended, is computed by subtracting the amount of supplies on hand from the amount available ($700 − $400 = $300). The resulting adjusting entry is:

4/30	Supplies Exp. . . .	300	
	Supplies		300

Let's take a different approach to this adjusting entry. Assume instead that the amount of the supplies used is $300. This amount would appear in the adjusting entry because the adjusting entry records the amount of supplies used.

4/30	Supplies Exp. . . .	300	
	Supplies		300

Expense instead of Prepaid Rent and Rent Expense. This adjusting entry illustrates the matching principle.

Supplies. Supplies are accounted for in the same way as prepaid expenses. On April 2 Gary Lyon paid cash of $700 for office supplies:

Apr. 2	Supplies	700	
	Cash		700
	Paid cash for supplies.		

Assume that Lyon purchased no additional supplies during April. The April 30 trial balance, therefore, lists Supplies with a $700 debit balance, as shown in Exhibit 3-1.

During April, Lyon used supplies in performing services for clients. The cost of the supplies used is the measure of *supplies expense* for the month.

Lyon does not keep a continuous record of supplies used each day or each week during April. To keep these detailed records would be impractical. Instead, to measure his firm's supplies expense during April, Gary Lyon counts the supplies on hand at the end of the month. This is the amount of the asset still available to the business. Assume the count indicates that supplies costing $400 remain. Subtracting the entity's $400 supplies on hand at the end of April from the cost of supplies available during April ($700) measures supplies expense during the month ($300).

Cost of asset available during the period	−	Cost of asset on hand at the end of the period	=	Cost of asset used (expense) during the period
$700	**−**	**$400**	**=**	**$300**

The April 30 adjusting entry to update the Supplies account and to record the supplies expense for the month debits the expense and credits the asset as follows:

Apr. 30	Supplies Expense ($700 − $400)	300	
	Supplies		300
	To record supplies expense.		

After posting, the Supplies and Supplies Expense accounts appear as follows:

Supplies					**Supplies Expense**			
Apr. 2	700	Apr. 30	300		Apr. 30	300		
Bal.	400				Bal.	300		

Correct asset amount, $400	→	**Total accounted for, $700**	←	Correct expense amount, $300

The Supplies account then enters the month of May with a $400 balance, and the adjustment process is repeated each month.

Transparency T 3-2

Depreciation and Plant Assets

The logic of the accrual basis is probably best illustrated by how businesses account for plant assets. **Plant assets** are long-lived assets, such as land, buildings, furniture, machinery, and equipment used in the operations of the business. As one accountant said, "All assets but land are on a march to the junkyard." That is, all plant assets but land decline in usefulness as they age. This decline is an *expense* to the business. Accountants systematically spread the cost of each plant asset, except land, over the years of its useful life. This process is called the recording of **depreciation.** The concept underlying accounting for plant assets and depreciation expense is the same as for prepaid expenses. In both cases the business purchases an asset that wears out or is used up. As the asset is used, more and more of its cost is transferred from the asset account to the expense account. The major difference between prepaid expenses and plant assets is the length of time it takes for the asset to lose its usefulness. Prepaid expenses usually expire within a year. Most plant assets remain useful for a number of years.

Consider Gary Lyon's accounting practice. Suppose that on April 3 Lyon purchased furniture on account for $16,500:

Apr. 3	Furniture	16,500	
	Accounts Payable		16,500
	Purchased office furniture on account.		

After posting, the Furniture account appears as follows:

Furniture	
Apr. 3 16,500	

Using cash-basis accounting, Gary Lyon would enter in the ledger the entire $16,500 as an expense for April. As a result, his financial statements for that month would be extremely misleading. Income would be significantly understated. Also, the cash-basis approach fails to take into consideration that the asset will be of benefit to Lyon's business in future accounting periods.

In accrual-basis accounting, an asset is recorded when the furniture is acquired. Then, a portion of the asset's cost is transferred from the asset account to Depreciation Expense each period that the asset is used. This method matches the asset's expense to the revenue of the period, which is an application of the matching principle.

Lyon believes the furniture will remain useful for five years and be virtually worthless at the end of its life. One way to compute the amount of depreciation for each year is to divide the cost of the asset ($16,500 in our example) by its expected useful life (5 years). This procedure gives annual depreciation of $3,300 ($16,500/5 years = $3,300 per year). Depreciation for the month of April is $275 ($3,300/12 months = $275 per month). Chapter 10 covers depreciation in more detail.

Depreciation expense for April is recorded by the following entry:

Apr. 30	Depreciation Expense—Furniture	275	
	Accumulated Depreciation—Furniture		275
	To record depreciation on furniture.		

You may be wondering why Accumulated Depreciation is credited instead of Furniture. The reason is that the original cost of the plant asset is an objective measurement, and that figure remains in the original asset account as long as the business uses the asset. Accountants may refer to that account if they need to know how much the asset cost. This information may be useful in a decision about whether to replace the furniture and the amount to pay. The amount of depreciation, however, is an *estimate*. Accountants use the **Accumulated Depreciation** account to show the cumulative sum of all depreciation expense from the date of acquiring the asset. Therefore, the balance in this account increases over the life of the asset.

Accumulated Depreciation is a **contra asset** account, which means an asset account with a normal credit balance. A **contra account** has two distinguishing characteristics: (1) it always has a companion account, and (2) its normal balance is opposite that of the companion account. In this case, Accumulated Depreciation accompanies Furniture. It appears in the ledger directly after Furniture. Furniture has a debit balance, and therefore Accumulated Depreciation, a contra asset, has a credit balance. All contra asset accounts have credit balances.

Teaching Tip: Consider the Furniture and Accumulated Depreciation accounts to be one account split into two different accounts; this is why the two accounts always appear together.

A business carries an accumulated depreciation account for each depreciable asset. If a business has a building and a machine, for example, it will carry the accounts Accumulated Depreciation—Building, and Accumulated Depreciation—Machine.

After posting the depreciation entry, the Furniture, Accumulated Depreciation, and Depreciation Expense accounts are

Furniture		Accumulated Depreciation—Furniture		Depreciation Expense	
Apr. 3 16,500			Apr. 30 275	Apr. 30 275	
Bal. 16,500			Bal. 275	Bal. 275	

The balance sheet shows the relationship between Furniture and Accumulated Depreciation. The balance of Accumulated Depreciation is subtracted from the balance of Furniture. The net amount of a plant asset (cost minus accumulated depreciation) is called its **book value,** as shown below for Furniture.

Point to Stress: Even though the Accumulated Depreciation account is sometimes referred to as a valuation account, remember that the balance of Accumulated Depreciation does not reflect the decrease in market value of the asset. Remember that depreciation is only a way to expense the cost of an asset, not a method of determining its market value.

Plant Assets:

Furniture	$16,500
Less Accumulated depreciation	275
Book value.	$16,225

Because Accumulated Depreciation is subtracted from its companion account to determine the asset's book value, Accumulated Depreciation is also called a *valuation* account.

Suppose Lyon's accounting practice owns a building that cost $48,000 and on which annual depreciation is $2,400. The amount of depreciation for one month would be $200 ($2,400/12), and the entry to record depreciation for April is

Class Exercise: What is the asset's book value at the end of May? $15,950 ($16,500—$275—$275). At the end of its life? $0.

Apr. 30	Depreciation Expense—Building 200	
	Accumulated Depreciation—Building	200
	To record depreciation on building.	

The balance sheet at April 30 would report Lyon's plant assets as shown in Exhibit 3-2. Now, however, let's return to Gary Lyon's actual situation.

EXHIBIT 3-2 *Plant Assets on the Balance Sheet (April 30)*

Plant assets:

Furniture	$16,500	
Less Accumulated depreciation ..	275	$16,225
Building	48,000	
Less Accumulated depreciation ..	200	47,800
Book value of plant assets		$64,025

Accrued Expenses

Businesses often incur expenses before they pay cash. Payment is not due until later. Consider an employee's salary. The employer's salary expense and salary payable grow as the employee works, so the liability is said to *accrue*. Another example is interest expense on a note payable. Interest accrues as the clock ticks. The term **accrued expense** refers to an asset that arises from an expense that the business has incurred but has not yet paid.

It is time-consuming to make hourly, daily, or even weekly journal entries to accrue expenses. Consequently, the accountant waits until the end of the period. Then an adjusting entry brings each expense (and related liability) up to date just before the financial statements are prepared.

Salary Expense. Most companies pay their employees at set times. Suppose Gary Lyon pays his employee a monthly salary of $1,900, half on the 15th and half on the last day of the month. Here is a calendar for April that has paydays circled:

APRIL

Sun.	Mon.	Tue.	Wed.	Thur.	Fri.	Sat.
					1	2
3	4	5	6	7	8	9
10	11	12	13	14	(15)	16
17	18	19	20	21	22	23
24	25	26	27	28	29	(30)

Assume that if either payday falls on a weekend, Lyon pays the employee on the following Monday. During April Lyon paid his employee's first half-month salary of $950 on Friday, April 15, and recorded the following entry:

Apr. 15	Salary Expense	950	
	Cash		950
	To pay salary.		

After posting, the Salary Expense account is

Salary Expense	
Apr. 15 950	

The trial balance at April 30 (Exhibit 3-1) includes Salary Expense, with its debit balance of $950. Because April 30, the second payday of the month, falls on a Saturday, the second half-month amount of $950 will be paid on Monday, May 2. Without an adjusting entry, this second $950 amount is not included in the April 30 trial balance amount for Salary Expense. Therefore, at April 30 Lyon adjusts for additional *salary expense* and *salary payable* of $950 by recording an increase in each of these accounts as follows:

Apr. 30   Salary Expense   950
                Salary Payable............................   950
            To accrue salary expense.

After posting, the Salary Expense and Salary Payable accounts appear as follows:

Class Exercise: What would the adjusting entry be in this situation: Weekly salaries for a five-day week total $3,500, payable on Friday. April 30 is on a Tuesday.
ANSWER:

$\dfrac{\$3,500}{5 \text{ days}} =$

$700/day
× 2 days (Monday and Tuesday)
$1,400   Salary Payable

Adjusting entry is:

Salary Expense 1,400
   Salary Payable 1,400

Transparency T3-4

Salary Expense		
Apr. 15	950	
Apr. 30	950	
Bal.	1,900	

Salary Payable		
		Apr. 30 950
		Bal. 950

The accounts at April 30 now contain the complete salary information for the month. The expense account has a full month's salary, and the liability account shows the portion that the business still owes.

Lyon will record the payment of this liability on May 2 by debiting Salary Payable and crediting Cash for $950. This payment entry does not affect April or May expenses because the April expense was recorded on April 15 and April 30. May expense will be recorded in a like manner. All accrued expenses are recorded with similar entries—a debit to the appropriate expense account and a credit to the related liability account.

Accrued Revenues

Businesses often earn revenue before they receive the cash because payment is not due until later. A revenue that has been earned but not yet received in cash creates an asset called an **accrued revenue.** Assume Gary Lyon is hired on April 15 by Guerrero Construction Company to perform services on a monthly basis. Under this agreement, Guerrero will pay Lyon $500 monthly, with the first payment on May 15. During April, Lyon will earn half a month's fee, $250. On April 30 he makes the following adjusting entry to record an increase in Accounts Receivable and Service Revenue:

Apr. 30   Accounts Receivable ($500 × 1/2)   250
               Service Revenue   250
            To accrue service revenue.

Typical Student Misconception: Students often find the terminology confusing here.
Accrued Revenue: Revenue has been earned, but the cash has not been received.
Unearned Revenue: Cash is received before the work is performed.

Recall that Accounts Receivable has an unadjusted balance of $2,250, and the Service Revenue unadjusted balance is $7,000 (Exhibit 3-1). Posting this adjusting entry has the following effects on these two accounts:

Accounts Receivable		
	2,250	
Apr. 30	250	
Bal.	2,500	

Service Revenue		
		7,000
		Apr. 30 250
		Bal. 7,250

This adjusting entry illustrates accrual accounting and the revenue principle in action. Without the adjustment, Lyon's financial statements would be misleading. All accrued revenues are accounted for similarly—by debiting a receivable and crediting a revenue.

Unearned Revenues

Transparency T3-5

Some businesses collect cash from customers in advance of doing work for the customer. This creates a liability called **unearned revenue,** which is an obligation arising from receiving cash in advance of providing a product or a service. Only when the job is completed will the business have earned the revenue. Suppose Baldwin Computing Service Center engages Lyon's services, agreeing to pay him $450 monthly, beginning immediately. If Baldwin makes the first payment on April 20, Lyon records this increase in the business's liabilities by recording:

Apr. 20   Cash   450
           Unearned Service Revenue   450
           Received revenue in advance.

After posting, the liability account appears as follows:

Unearned Service Revenue		
	Apr. 20	450

Unearned Service Revenue is a liability because it represents Lyon's obligation to perform service for the client. The April 30 unadjusted trial balance (Exhibit 3-1) lists this account with a $450 credit balance prior to the adjusting entries. During the last 10 days of the month, Lyon will have earned one-third (10 days divided by April's total 30 days) of the $450, or $150. Therefore, he makes the following adjustment to decrease the liability, Unearned Service Revenue, and to record an increase in Service Revenue:

Apr. 30   Unearned Service Revenue ($450 × 1/3)   150
           Service Revenue   150
           To record unearned service revenue that has been
           earned.

Discussion Question: What would happen if Lyon failed to make this adjusting entry? ANSWER: His liabilities would be overstated and revenue understated. Even though the cash was received earlier, the service has now been performed and the revenue has been earned.

This adjusting entry shifts $150 of the total amount from the liability account to the revenue account. After posting, the balance of Service Revenue is increased by $150 and the balance of Unearned Service Revenue has been reduced to $300:

Unearned Service Revenue					Service Revenue		
Apr. 30	**150**	Apr. 20	450				7,000
						Apr. 30	250
		Bal.	300			**Apr. 30**	**150**
						Bal.	7,400

Typical Student Misconception: Students often report unearned revenue as a revenue on the income statement rather than a liability on the balance sheet.

Correct liability amount, $300 → | Total accounted for, $450 | ← Correct revenue amount, $150

EXHIBIT 3-3 *Summary of Adjusting Entries*

Adjusting Entry	Type of Account Debited	Type of Account Credited
Prepaid expense, supplies	Expense	Prepaid expense, supplies (Asset)
Depreciation	Expense	Accumulated depreciation (Contra asset)
Accrued expenses	Expense	Payable (Liability)
Accrued revenues	Receivable (Asset)	Revenue
Unearned revenues	Unearned revenue (Liability)	Revenue

Adapted from Beverly Terry.

Accounting for all types of revenues that are collected in advance follows the same pattern.

Summary of the Adjusting Process

Class Exercise: In which, if any, of the five categories of adjusting entries would the following transactions fall?

1   Paid one year's insurance in advance *ANSWER:* Prepaid expense

2   Recorded a portion of the cost of a building as an expense for the current period *ANSWER:* Depreciation

3   Recorded the revenue from renting a portion of the building before receiving cash *ANSWER:* Accrued revenue

4   Received and paid a bill for maintenance on company automobiles *ANSWER:* No adjusting entry necessary

Because one purpose of the adjusting process is to measure business income properly, each adjusting entry affects at least one income statement account— a revenue or an expense. The other side of the entry—a debit or a credit, as the case may be—is to a balance sheet account—an asset or a liability. This step updates the accounts for preparation of the balance sheet, which is the second purpose of the adjustments. No adjusting entry debits or credits Cash because the cash transactions are recorded earlier in the period. The end-of-period adjustment process is reserved for the noncash transactions that are required by accrual accounting. Exhibit 3-3 summarizes the adjusting entries.

Posting the Adjusting Entries

Exhibit 3-4 summarizes the adjusting entries of Lyon's business at April 30. Panel A of the exhibit briefly describes the data for each adjustment, Panel B gives the adjusting entries, and Panel C shows the accounts. The adjustments are keyed by letter.

EXHIBIT 3-4 *Journalizing and Posting the Adjusting Entries*

Panel A—Information for Adjustments at April 30, 19X1

a. Accrued service revenue, $250.
b. Supplies on hand, $400.
c. Prepaid rent expired, $1,000.
d. Depreciation on furniture, $275.
e. Accrued salary expense, $950.
f. Amount of unearned service revenue that has been earned, $150.

Panel B—Adjusting Entries

a. Accounts Receivable 250
     Service Revenue   250
   To accrue service revenue

b. Supplies Expense 300
     Supplies   300
   To record supplies used.

c. Rent Expense 1,000
     Prepaid Rent   1,000
   To record rent expense.

d. Depreciation Expense 275
     Accumulated Depreciation   275
   To record depreciation on furniture.

e. Salary Expense 950
     Salary Payable   950
   To accrue salary expense.

f. Unearned Service Revenue 150
     Service Revenue   150
   To record unearned revenue that has been earned.

Panel C—Ledger Accounts

Assets

Cash

| Bal. | 24,800 | | |

Accounts Receivable

	2,250		
(a)	250		
Bal.	2,500		

Supplies

| | 700 | (b) | 300 |
| Bal. | 400 | | |

Prepaid Rent

| | 3,000 | (c) | 1,000 |
| Bal. | 2,000 | | |

Furniture

| Bal. | 16,500 | | |

Accumulated Depreciation

| | | (d) | 275 |
| | | Bal. | 275 |

Liabilities

Accounts Payable

| | | Bal. | 13,100 |

Salary Payable

| | | (e) | 950 |
| | | Bal. | 950 |

Unearned Service Revenue

| (f) | 150 | | 450 |
| | | Bal. | 300 |

Owner's Equity

Gary Lyon, Capital

| | | Bal. | 31,250 |

Gary Lyon, Withdrawals

| Bal. | 3,200 | | |

Revenues

Service Revenue

			7,000
		(a)	250
		(f)	150
		Bal.	7,400

Expenses

Rent Expense

| (c) | 1,000 | | |
| Bal. | 1,000 | | |

Salary Expense

	950		
(e)	950		
Bal.	1,900		

Supplies Expense

| (b) | 300 | | |
| Bal. | 300 | | |

Depreciation Expense

| (d) | 275 | | |
| Bal. | 275 | | |

Utilities Expense

| Bal. | 400 | | |

This chapter began with the trial balance before any adjusting entries—the unadjusted trial balance (Exhibit 3-1). After the adjustments are journalized and posted, the accounts appear as shown in Exhibit 3-4, Panel C. A useful step in preparing the financial statements is to list the accounts, along with their adjusted balances, on an **adjusted trial balance.** This document has the advantage of listing all the accounts and their adjusted balances in a single place. Exhibit 3-5 shows the preparation of the adjusted trial balance.

The format of Exhibit 3-5 is called a work sheet. We will take a long look at the accounting work sheet in the next chapter. For now simply note how clearly this format presents the data. The information in the Account Title column and in the Trial Balance columns is drawn directly from the trial balance. The two Adjustments columns list the debit and credit adjustments directly across from the appropriate account title. Each adjusting debit is identified by a letter in parentheses that refers back to the adjusting entry. For example, the debit labeled *a* on the worksheet refers back to the debit adjusting entry of $250 to Accounts Receivable in Panel B of Exhibit 3-4. Likewise for adjusting credits, the corresponding credit—labeled *a*—refers back to the $250 credit to Service Revenue.

The Adjusted Trial Balance columns give the adjusted account balances. Each amount on the adjusted trial balance of Exhibit 3-5 is computed by combining the amounts from the unadjusted trial balance plus or minus the adjustments. For example, Accounts Receivable starts with a debit balance of $2,250. Adding the $250 debit amount from adjusting entry *a* gives Accounts Receivable an adjusted balance of $2,500. Supplies begins with a debit balance of $700. After the $300 credit adjustment, its adjusted balance is $400. More than one entry may affect a single account, as is the case for Service Revenue. If accounts are unaffected by the adjustments, they show the same amount on both trial balances. This is true for Cash, Furniture, Accounts Payable, and the Owner's Equity accounts.

OBJECTIVE 4
Prepare an adjusted trial balance

Preparing the Financial Statements from the Adjusted Trial Balance

The April financial statements of Gary Lyon, CPA, can be prepared from the information on the adjusted trial balance. Exhibit 3-6 shows how the accounts are distributed from the adjusted trial balance to these three financial statements. The income statement (Exhibit 3-7) comes from the revenue and expense accounts. The statement of owner's equity (Exhibit 3-8) shows the reasons for the change in the owner's capital during the period. The balance sheet (Exhibit 3-9) reports the assets, liabilities, and owner's equity.

Financial Statements

The accounts and the amounts for the income statement and the balance sheet are taken from the adjusted trial balance. The adjusted trial balance also provides the data for the statement of owner's equity. Exhibits 3-7, 3-8, and 3-9 illustrate these three financial statements, best prepared in the order shown:

EXHIBIT 3-5 *Preparation of Adjusted Trial Balance*

Gary Lyon, CPA
Preparation of Adjusted Trial Balance
April 30, 19X1

Account Title	Trial Balance Debit	Trial Balance Credit	Adjustments Debit		Adjustments Credit		Adjusted Trial Balance Debit	Adjusted Trial Balance Credit
Cash	24,800						24,800	
Accounts receivable	2,250		(a)	250			2,500	
Supplies	700				(b)	300	400	
Prepaid rent	3,000				(c)	1,000	2,000	
Furniture	16,500						16,500	
Accumulated depreciation					(d)	275		275
Accounts payable		13,100						13,100
Salary payable					(e)	950		950
Unearned service revenue		450	(f)	150				300
Gary Lyon, capital		31,250						31,250
Gary Lyon, withdrawals	3,200						3,200	
Service revenue		7,000			(a)	250		7,400
					(f)	150		
Rent expense			(c)	1,000			1,000	
Salary expense	950		(e)	950			1,900	
Supplies expense			(b)	300			300	
Depreciation expense			(d)	275			275	
Utilities expense	400						400	
	51,800	51,800		2,925		2,925	53,275	53,275

EXHIBIT 3-6 *Preparing the Financial Statements from the Adjusted Trial Balance*

Account Title	Adjusted Trial Balance Debit	Adjusted Trial Balance Credit	
Cash	24,800		
Accounts receivable	2,500		
Supplies	400		
Prepaid rent	2,000		
Furniture	16,500		
Accumulated depreciation		275	**Balance Sheet**
Accounts payable		13,100	
Salary payable		950	
Unearned service revenue		300	
Gary Lyon, capital		31,250	**Statement of**
Gary Lyon, withdrawals	3,200		**Owner's Equity**
Service revenue		7,400	
Rent expense	1,000		
Salary expense	1,900		
Supplies expense	300		**Income Statement**
Depreciation expense	275		
Utilities expense	400		
	53,275	53,275	

Point to Stress: Point out to students that everything is added in the columns in Exhibit 3-5, even the contra asset Accumulated Depreciation. This process of adding the columns is called footing.

Teaching Tip: Look at Exhibit 3-5. The differences between the amounts in the trial balance and the amounts in the adjusted trial balance are due to the adjusting entries. If the adjusting entries were not given, they could be reconstructed by computing the differences between the adjusted and the unadjusted amounts.

the income statement first, followed by the statement of owner's equity, and last, the balance sheet. The essential features of all financial statements are (1) the name of the entity, (2) the title of the statement, (3) the date or the period covered by the statement, and (4) the body of the statement.

It is customary to list expenses in descending order by amount, as shown in Exhibit 3-7. However, Miscellaneous Expense, a catchall account for expenses that do not fit another category, is usually reported last regardless of its amount.

Transparency T3-6

Relationships among the Three Financial Statements

The arrows in Exhibits 3-7, 3-8, and 3-9 illustrate the relationships among the income statement, the statement of owner's equity, and the balance sheet.

1. The income statement reports net income or net loss, figured by subtracting expenses from revenues. Because revenues and expenses are owner's equity accounts, their net figure is then transferred to the statement of owner's equity. Note that net income in Exhibit 3-7, $3,525, increases owner's equity in Exhibit 3-8. A net loss would decrease owner's equity.

2. Capital is a balance sheet account, so the ending balance in the statement of owner's equity is transferred to the balance sheet. This amount is the final balancing element of the balance sheet. To solidify your understanding of this relationship, trace the $31,575 figure from Exhibit 3-8 to Exhibit 3-9.

You may be wondering why the total assets on the balance sheet ($45,925 in Exhibit 3-9) do not equal the total debits on the adjusted trial balance ($53,275 in Exhibit 3-6). Likewise, the total liabilities and owner's equity do not equal the total credits on the adjusted trial balance. The reason for these differences is that Accumulated Depreciation and Owner Withdrawals are *subtracted* from their related accounts on the balance sheet but *added* in their respective columns on the adjusted trial balance.

Computers and the Accounting Process

How would adjusting entries be handled in a computerized system that a large company like Occidental Petroleum might use? A company's general ledger accounting software package would print out a trial balance. The accountants would then analyze the account balances on the trial balance, testing them for reasonableness and tracing the balances back to the general ledger, and, if necessary, back to the individual transactions and the supporting documents that first generated the transactions. This analysis results in the adjusting entries.

Once the adjusting entries are posted—that is, entered into the computer—the general ledger accounts are changed. The trial balance has now become the adjusted trial balance. We discuss computerized accounting packages in more detail in Chapter 28.

Computerized accounting packages also print out financial statements. These statements include the income statement, statement of owner's equity, and balance sheet. Also, the computer package may give the company the

EXHIBIT 3-7   *Income Statement*

Gary Lyon, CPA Income Statement For the Month Ended April 30, 19X1		
Revenue		
Service revenue		$7,400
Expenses:		
Salary expense	$1,900	
Rent expense	1,000	
Utilities expense	400	
Supplies expense	300	
Depreciation expense	275	
Total expenses		3,875
Net income		$3,525

OBJECTIVE 5

Prepare the financial statements from the adjusted trial balance

Teaching Tip: Emphasize the relationship among the three statements by following the arrows from net income to the statement of owner's equity to the balance sheet.

EXHIBIT 3-8   *Statement of Owner's Equity*

Gary Lyon, CPA Statement of Owner's Equity For the Month Ended April 30, 19X1	
Gary Lyon, capital, April 1, 19X1	$31,250
Add: Net income	3,525
	34,775
Less: Withdrawals	3,200
Gary Lyon, capital, April 30, 19X1	$31,575

EXHIBIT 3-9   *Balance Sheet*

Gary Lyon, CPA Balance Sheet April 30, 19X1				
Assets			**Liabilities**	
Cash		$24,800	Accounts payable ..	$13,100
Accounts receivable		2,500	Salary payable	950
Supplies		400	Unearned service	
Prepaid rent		2,000	revenue	300
Furniture	$16,500		Total liabilities	14,350
Less Accumulated				
depreciation ...	275	16,225	**Owner's Equity**	
			Gary Lyon, capital .	31,575
			Total liabilities and	
Total assets		$45,925	owner's equity ...	$45,925

Point to Stress: Why should accountants be so impressed with a machine that saves so much time? Because as the accountant spends less time doing bookkeeping chores, she has more time to analyze results of operations, evaluate the company's performance, and perform other tasks that require professional judgment. With the computer, the accountant spends less time doing the bookkeeping.

flexibility to print out selected data in a specialized presentation to meet a particular company's information needs.

For example, an owner may want a forecast of the year's net income. The accountant can make several sets of estimates for the ending quantities of supplies, accrued salaries, unearned revenues, and all the other items that will be adjusted. The computer can produce several different sets of financial statements—one for each set of estimated data. Using these data the owner may identify a lagging division in the business immediately, rather than at the end of the period, when the routine financial statements are issued. The owner would then be able to take steps quickly to help the lagging division before its operations grew worse. Alternately, the company's bank may require forecasted financial statements before making a loan. Without a computer these forecasts may be very expensive to obtain.

Summary Problem for Your Review

The trial balance of State Service Company pertains to December 31, 19X1, which is the end of its yearlong accounting period.

Data needed for the adjusting entries include:

a. Supplies on hand at year end, $2,000.
b. Depreciation on furniture and fixtures, $20,000.
c. Depreciation on building, $10,000.
d. Salaries owed but not yet paid, $5,000.
e. Accrued service revenue, $12,000.
f. Of the $45,000 balance of unearned service revenue, $32,000 was earned during the year.

Required

1. Open the ledger accounts with their unadjusted balances. Show dollar amounts in thousands, as shown for Accounts Receivable:

Accounts Receivable
370

2. Journalize State Service Company's adjusting entries at December 31, 19X1. Key entries by letter as in Exhibit 3-4.
3. Post the adjusting entries.
4. Write the trial balance on a sheet of paper, enter the adjusting entries, and prepare an adjusted trial balance, as shown in Exhibit 3-5.
5. Prepare the income statement, the statement of owner's equity, and the balance sheet. Draw the arrows linking the three statements.

State Service Company
Trial Balance
December 31, 19X1

Cash	$ 198,000	
Accounts receivable	370,000	
Supplies	6,000	
Furniture and fixtures	100,000	
Accumulated depreciation—furniture and fixtures		$ 40,000
Building	250,000	
Accumulated depreciation—building		130,000
Accounts payable		380,000
Salary payable		
Unearned service revenue		45,000
Capital		293,000
Owner's withdrawals	65,000	
Service revenue		286,000
Salary expense	172,000	
Supplies expense		
Depreciation expense—furniture and fixtures		
Depreciation expense—building		
Miscellaneous expense	13,000	
Total	$1,174,000	$1,174,000

SOLUTION TO REVIEW PROBLEM

Requirements 1 and 3

Assets

Cash

Bal. 198	

Accounts Receivable

370	
(e) 12	
Bal. 382	

Supplies

6	(a) 4
Bal. 2	

Furniture and Fixtures

Bal. 100	

Accumulated Depreciation—Furniture and Fixtures

	40
	(b) 20
	Bal. 60

Building

Bal. 250	

Accumulated Depreciation—Building

	130
	(c) 10
	Bal. 140

Liabilities

Accounts Payable

	Bal. 380

Salary Payable

	(d) 5
	Bal. 5

Unearned Service Revenue

(f) 32	45
	Bal. 13

Owner's Equity

Capital			Owner's Withdrawals	
	Bal. 293		Bal. 65	

Revenues

Service Revenue

	286
(e)	12
(f)	32
Bal.	330

Expenses

Salary Expense

	172
(d)	5
Bal. 177	

Supplies Expense

(a)	4
Bal.	4

Depreciation Expense—Furniture and Fixtures

(b)	20
Bal.	20

Depreciation Expense—Building

(c)	10
Bal.	10

Miscellaneous Expense

Bal. 13	

Requirement 2

19X1

a. Dec. 31   Supplies Expense ($6,000 − $2,000) 4,000
         Supplies 4,000
         To record supplies used.

b.   31   Depreciation Expense—
         Furniture and Fixtures 20,000
         Accumulated Depreciation—
         Furniture and Fixtures 20,000
         To record depreciation expense on furniture and fixtures.

c.   31   Depreciation Expense—Building 10,000
         Accumulated Depreciation—
         Building 10,000
         To record depreciation expense on building.

d.   31   Salary Expense 5,000
         Salary Payable 5,000
         To accrue salary expense.

e.   31   Accounts Receivable 12,000
         Service Revenue 12,000
         To accrue service revenue.

f.   31   Unearned Service Revenue 32,000
         Service Revenue 32,000
         To record unearned service revenue that has been earned.

Requirement 4

State Service Company
Preparation of Adjusted Trial Balance
December 31, 19X1
(amounts in thousands)

	Trial Balance		Adjustments		Adjusted Trial Balance	
	Debit	**Credit**	**Debit**	**Credit**	**Debit**	**Credit**
Cash	198				198	
Accounts receivable	370		(e) 12		382	
Supplies	6			(a) 4	2	
Furniture and fixtures	100				100	
Accumulated depreciation— furniture and fixtures		40		(b) 20		60
Building	250				250	
Accumulated depreciation—building		130		(c) 10		140
Accounts payable		380				380
Salary payable				(d) 5		5
Unearned service revenue		45	(f) 32			13
Capital		293				293
Owner's withdrawals	65				65	
Service revenue		286		(e) 12 (f) 32		330
Salary expense	172		(d) 5		177	
Supplies expense			(a) 4		4	
Depreciation expense— furniture and fixtures			(b) 20		20	
Depreciation expense— building			(c) 10		10	
Miscellaneous expense	13				13	
	1,174	1,174	83	83	1,221	1,221

Requirement 5

State Service Company
Income Statement
For the Year Ended December 31, 19X1
(amounts in thousands)

Revenues:		
Service revenue		$330
Expenses:		
Salary expense	$177	
Depreciation expense—furniture & fixtures	20	
Depreciation expense—building	10	
Supplies expense	4	
Miscellaneous expense	13	
Total expenses		224
Net income		$106

State Service Company
Statement of Owner's Equity
For the Year Ended December 31, 19X1
(amounts in thousands)

Capital, January 1, 19X1	$293
Add: Net income	106
	399
Less: Withdrawals	65
Capital, December 31, 19X1	$334

State Service Company
Balance Sheet
December 31, 19X1
(amounts in thousands)

Assets			Liabilities		
Cash		$198	Accounts payable		$380
Accounts receivable		382	Salary payable		5
Supplies		2	Unearned service revenue		13
Furniture and fixtures	$100		Total liabilities		398
Less Accumulated depreciation............	60	40			
Building	250		**Owner's Equity**		
Less Accumulated depreciation............	140	110	Capital		334
Total assets		$732	Total liabilities and owner's equity		$732

Summary

In *accrual-basis accounting*, business events are recorded as they affect the entity. In *cash-basis accounting*, only those events that affect cash are recorded. The cash basis omits important events such as purchases and sales of assets on account. It also distorts the financial statements by labeling as expenses those cash payments that have long-term effects, like the purchases of buildings and equipment. Some small organizations use cash-basis accounting, but the generally accepted method is the accrual basis.

Accountants divide time into definite periods—such as a month, a quarter, and a year—to report the entity's financial statements. The year is the basic *accounting period*, but companies prepare financial statements as often as they need the information. Accountants have developed the *revenue principle* to determine when to record revenue and the amount of revenue to record. The *matching principle* guides the accounting for expenses. *Adjusting entries* are a result of the accrual basis of accounting. These entries, made at the end of the accounting period, update the accounts for preparation of the financial statements. One of the most important pieces of accounting information is net income or net loss, and the adjusting entries help to measure the *net income* of the period.

Adjusting entries can be divided into five categories: *prepaid expenses, depreciation, accrued expenses, accrued revenues,* and *unearned revenues*. To prepare the *adjusted trial balance*, enter the adjusting entries next to the *unadjusted trial balance*. This document can be used to prepare the income statement, the statement of owner's equity, and the balance sheet.

These three financial statements are related as follows: Income, shown on the *income statement*, increases owner's equity, which also appears on the *statement of owner's equity*. The ending balance of capital is the last amount reported on the *balance sheet*.

Computers can aid the accounting process in a number of ways, chiefly by performing routine operations. Many adjusting entries, however, require analysis that is best done manually, without the computer.

Self-Study Questions

Test your understanding of the chapter by marking the best answer for each of the following questions.

1. Accrual-basis accounting *(p. 100)*
   a. Results in higher income than cash-basis accounting
   b. Leads to the reporting of more complete information than does cash-basis accounting
   c. Is not acceptable under GAAP
   d. Omits adjusting entries at the end of the period
2. Under the revenue principle, revenue is recorded *(p. 101)*
   a. At the earliest acceptable time
   b. At the latest acceptable time
   c. After it has been earned, but not before
   d. At the end of the accounting period
3. The matching principle provides guidance in accounting for *(p. 102)*
   a. Expenses   c. Assets
   b. Owner's equity   d. Liabilities
4. Adjusting entries *(p. 104)*
   a. Assign revenues to the period in which they are earned
   b. Help to properly measure the period's net income or net loss
   c. Bring asset and liability accounts to correct balances
   d. All of the above

5. A law firm began November with office supplies of $160. During the month, the firm purchased supplies of $290. At November 30 supplies on hand total $210. Supplies expense for the period is (p. 106)
   a. $210
   c. $290
   b. $240
   d. $450

6. A building that cost $120,000 has accumulated depreciation of $50,000. The book value of the building is (p. 108)
   a. $50,000
   c. $120,000
   b. $70,000
   d. $170,000

7. The adjusting entry to accrue salary expense (p. 110)
   a. Debits Salary Expense and credits Cash
   b. Debits Salary Payable and credits Salary Expense
   c. Debits Salary Payable and credits Cash
   d. Debits Salary Expense and credits Salary Payable

8. A business received cash of $3,000 in advance for service that will be provided later. The cash receipt entry debited Cash and credited Unearned Revenue for $3,000. At the end of the period, $1,100 is still unearned. The adjusting entry for this situation will (p. 111)
   a. Debit Unearned Revenue and credit Revenue for $1,900
   b. Debit Unearned Revenue and credit Revenue for $1,100
   c. Debit Revenue and credit Unearned Revenue for $1,900
   d. Debit Revenue and credit Unearned Revenue for $1,100

9. The links between the financial statements are (p. 117)
   a. Net income from the income statement to the statement of owner's equity
   b. Ending capital from the statement of owner's equity to the balance sheet
   c. Both of the above
   d. None of the above

10. Accumulated Depreciation is reported on the (p. 116)
    a. Balance sheet
    c. Statement of owner's equity
    b. Income statement
    d. Both a and b

Answers to the Self-Study Questions follow the Accounting Vocabulary.

Accounting Vocabulary

Accrual-basis accounting. Accounting that recognizes (records) the impact of a business event as it occurs, regardless of whether the transaction affected cash (p. 99).

Accrued expense. An expense that has been incurred but not yet paid in cash (p. 109).

Accrued revenue. A revenue that has been earned but not yet received in cash (p. 110).

Accumulated depreciation. The cumulative sum of all depreciation expense from the date of acquiring a plant asset (p. 108).

Adjusted trial balance. A list of all the ledger accounts with their adjusted balances (p. 114).

Adjusting entry. Entry made at the end of the period to assign revenues to the period in which they are earned and expenses to the period in which they are incurred. Adjusting entries help measure the period's income and bring the related asset and liability accounts to correct balances for the financial statements (p. 104).

Book value of a plant asset. The asset's cost less accumulated depreciation (p. 108).

Cash-basis accounting. Accounting that records only transactions in which cash is received or paid (p. 100).

Contra account. An account with two distinguishing characteristics: (1) it always has a companion account, and (2) its normal balance is opposite that of the companion account (p. 108).

Contra asset. An asset account with a normal credit balance. A contra account always has a companion account and its balance is opposite that of the companion account (p. 108).

Depreciation. Expense associated with spreading (allocating) the cost of a plant asset over its useful life (p. 107).

Matching principle. The basis for recording expenses. Directs accountants to identify all expenses incurred during the period, to measure the expenses, and to match them against the revenues earned during that same span of time (p. 102).

Plant asset. Long-lived assets, like land, buildings, and equipment, used in the operation of the business (p. 107).

Prepaid expense. A category of miscellaneous assets that typically expire or get used up in the near future. Examples include prepaid rent, prepaid insurance, and supplies (p. 104).

Revenue principle. The basis for recording revenues, tells accountants when to record revenue and the amount of revenue to record (p. 101).

Time-period concept. Ensures that accounting information is reported at regular intervals. (p. 102).

Unearned revenue. A liability created when a business collects cash from customers in advance of doing work for the customer. The obligation is to provide a product or a service in the future. Also called Deferred revenue (p. 111).

Answers to Self-Study Questions

1. b
2. c
3. a

4. d
5. b ($160 + $290 − $210 = $240)

6. b ($120,000 − $50,000 = $70,000)
7. d
8. a ($3,000 received − $1,100 unearned = $1,900 earned)
9. c
10. a

ASSIGNMENT MATERIAL

Questions

1. Distinguish the accrual basis of accounting from the cash basis.
2. How long is the basic accounting period? What is a fiscal year? What is an interim period?
3. What two questions does the revenue principle help answer?
4. Briefly explain the matching principle.
5. What is the purpose of making adjusting entries?
6. Why are adjusting entries made at the end of the accounting period, not during the period?
7. Name five categories of adjusting entries and give an example of each.
8. Do all adjusting entries affect the net income or net loss of the period? Include in your answer the definition of an adjusting entry.
9. Why does the balance of Supplies need to be adjusted at the end of the period?
10. Manning Supply Company pays $1,800 for an insurance policy that covers three years. At the end of the first year, the balance of its Prepaid Insurance account contains two elements. What are the two elements, and what is the correct amount of each?

11. The title Prepaid Expense suggests that this type of account is an expense. If so, explain why. If not, what type of account is it?

12. What is a contra account? Identify the contra account introduced in this chapter, along with the account's normal balance.

13. The manager of a Quickie-Pickie convenience store presents his entity's balance sheet to a banker to obtain a loan. The balance sheet reports that the entity's plant assets have a book value of $135,000 and accumulated depreciation of $65,000. What does *book value* of a plant asset mean? What was the cost of the plant assets?

14. Give the entry to record accrued interest revenue of $800.

15. Why is an unearned revenue a liability? Use an example in your answer.

16. Identify the types of accounts (assets, liabilities, and so on) debited and credited for the five types of adjusting entries.

17. What purposes does the adjusted trial balance serve?

18. Explain the relationship among the income statement, the statement of owner's equity, and the balance sheet.

19. Bellevue Company failed to record the following adjusting entries at December 31, the end of its fiscal year: (a) accrued expenses, $500; (b) accrued revenues, $850; and (c) depreciation, $1,000. Did these omissions cause net income for the year to be understated or overstated and by what overall amount?

20. Identify several accounting tasks for which it is efficient to use a microcomputer. What is the basic limitation on the use of a computer?

Exercises

No check figure

Exercise 3-1   *Cash basis versus accrual basis*   (L.O. 1)

The Oak Lodge had the following selected transactions during August:

Aug. 1 Prepaid damage and liability insurance for the year, $6,000.
      5 Paid electricity expenses, $700.
      9 Received cash for the day's room rentals, $1,400.
    31 Purchased six television sets, $3,000.
    31 Served a banquet, receiving a note receivable, $1,200.
    31 Made an adjusting entry for insurance expense (from Aug. 1).

Show how each transaction would be handled using the cash basis and the accrual basis. Under each column give the amount of revenue or expense for August. Journal entries are not required. Use the following format for your answer, and show your computations:

	Amount of Revenue or Expense for August	
Date	Cash Basis	Accrual Basis

No check figure

Exercise 3-2   *Applying accounting concepts and principles*   (L.O. 2)

Identify the accounting concept or principle that gives the most direction on how to account for each of the following situations:

a. Expenses of $2,600 must be accrued at the end of the period to properly measure income.

b. A customer states her intention to shift her business to a travel agency. Should the travel agency record revenue based on this intention?

c. The owner of a business desires monthly financial statements to measure the progress of the entity on an ongoing basis.

d. Expenses of the period total $6,100. This amount should be subtracted from revenue to compute the period's income.

Exercise 3-3 *Applying accounting concepts (L.O. 2)*

No check figure

Write a short paragraph to explain in your own words the concept of depreciation as it is used in accounting.

Exercise 3-4 *Allocating prepaid expense to the asset and the expense (L.O. 2)*

1. Total to account for, $1,200; Rent expense, $1,000

Compute the amounts indicated by question marks for each of the following Prepaid Rent situations. Consider each situation separately.

	Situation			
	1	**2**	**3**	**4**
Beginning Prepaid Rent	$ 300	$ 500	$ 600	$ 900
Payments for Prepaid Rent during the year	900	?	?	1,100
Total amount to account for	?	?	1,500	2,000
Ending Prepaid Rent	200	600	500	?
Rent Expense	$?	$ 300	$1,000	$1,600

Exercise 3-5 *Journalizing adjusting entries (L.O. 3)*

No check figure

Journalize the entries for the following adjustments at December 31, the end of the accounting period.

a. Interest revenue accrued, $4,100.

b. Unearned service revenue earned, $800.

c. Depreciation, $6,200.

d. Employee salaries owed for two days of a five-day workweek; weekly payroll, $9,000.

e. Prepaid insurance expired, $450.

Exercise 3-6 *Analyzing the effects of adjustments on net income. (L.O. 3)*

Overall effect—net income overstated by $5,350

Suppose the adjustments required in Exercise 3-5 were not made. Compute the overall overstatement or understatement of net income as a result of the omission of these adjustments.

Exercise 3-7 *Recording adjustments in T-accounts (L.O. 3)*

Service Revenue balance, $5,700

The accounting records of Lucca Galvez, Artist, include the following unadjusted balances at May 31: Accounts Receivable, $1,200; Supplies, $600; Salary Payable, $0; Unearned Service Revenue, $400; Service Revenue, $5,100; Salary Expense, $1,200; Supplies Expense, $0.

Galvez's accountant develops the following data for the May 31 adjusting entries:

a. Supplies on hand, $100.

b. Salary owed to employee, $400.

c. Service revenue accrued, $350.

d. Unearned service revenue that has been earned, $250.

Open the foregoing T-accounts and record the adjustments directly in the accounts, keying each adjustment amount by letter. Show each account's adjusted balance. Journal entries are not required.

Adjusted trial balance, $41,590

Exercise 3-8 *Adjusting the accounts* (L.O. 3, 4)

Preparation of the Pack-n-Mail Service adjusted trial balance is incomplete. Enter the adjustment amounts directly in the adjustment columns of the text. Service Revenue is the only account affected by more than one adjustment.

Pack-n-Mail Service
Preparation of Adjusted Trial Balance
October 31, 19X2

Account Title	Trial Balance Debit	Trial Balance Credit	Adjustments Debit	Adjustments Credit	Adjusted Trial Balance Debit	Adjusted Trial Balance Credit
Cash	3,000				3,000	
Accounts receivable	6,500				7,100	
Supplies	1,040				800	
Office furniture	19,300				19,300	
Accumulated depreciation		11,060				11,320
Salary payable						600
Unearned revenue		900				690
Capital		16,340				16,340
Owner's withdrawals	6,200				6,200	
Service revenue		11,830				12,640
Salary expense	2,690				3,290	
Rent expense	1,400				1,400	
Depreciation expense					260	
Supplies expense					240	
	40,130	40,130			41,590	41,590

No check figure

Exercise 3-9 *Journalizing adjustments* (L.O. 3, 4)

Make journal entries for the adjustments that would complete the preparation of the adjusted trial balance in Exercise 3-8. Include explanations.

Total assets, $18,880

Exercise 3-10 *Preparing the financial statements* (L.O. 5)

Refer to the adjusted trial balance in Exercise 3-8. Prepare Pack-n-Mail Service's income statement and statement of owner's equity for the three months ended October 31, 19X2, and its balance sheet on that date. Draw the arrows linking the three statements.

Net income, $101,000

Exercise 3-11 *Preparing the financial statements* (L.O. 5)

The accountant for Artie Sudan, M.D., has posted adjusting entries *a* through *e* to the accounts at September 30, 19X2. Selected balance sheet accounts and all the revenues and expenses of the entity are listed at the top of the next page in T-account form.

Required

Prepare the income statement of Artie Sudan, M.D., for the year ended September 30, 19X2. List expenses in order from the largest to the smallest.

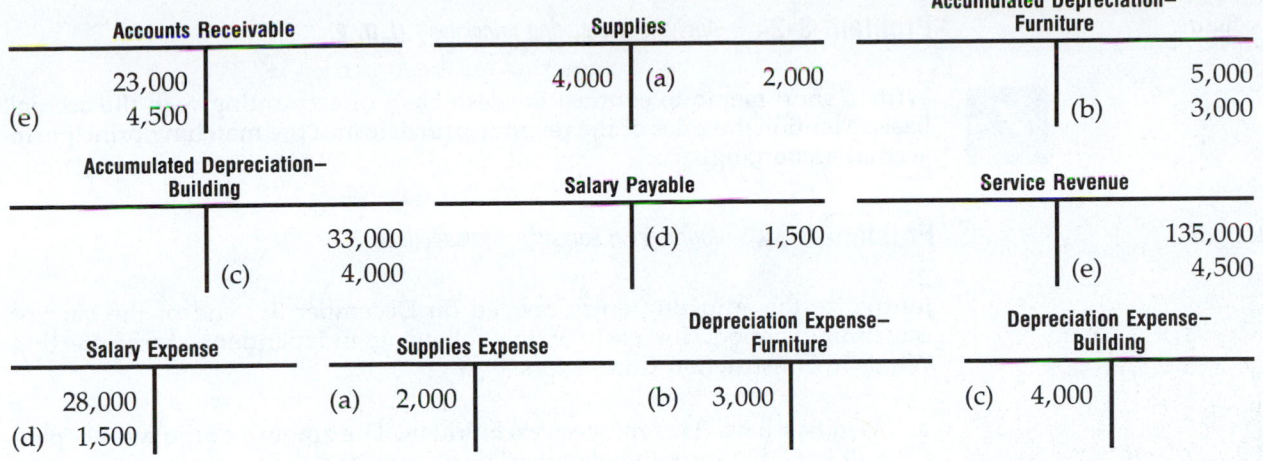

Accounts Receivable		Supplies		Accumulated Depreciation–Furniture	
23,000		4,000	(a) 2,000		5,000
(e) 4,500				(b) 3,000	

Accumulated Depreciation–Building		Salary Payable		Service Revenue	
	33,000	(d) 1,500			135,000
(c)	4,000			(e) 4,500	

Salary Expense	Supplies Expense	Depreciation Expense–Furniture	Depreciation Expense–Building
28,000	(a) 2,000	(b) 3,000	(c) 4,000
(d) 1,500			

Exercise 3-12 *Preparing the statement of owner's equity* (L.O. 5)

Ending capital, $121,000

J. C. Norris Company began the year with capital of $85,000. On July 9 the owner invested $12,000 cash in the business. On September 26 he transferred to the company land valued at $70,000. The income statement for the year ended September 30, 19X5, reported a net loss of $28,000. During this fiscal year, the owner withdrew $1,500 monthly for personal use. Prepare the company's statement of owner's equity for the year ended September 30, 19X5.

Problems

(Group A)

Problem 3-1A *Cash basis versus accrual basis* (L.O. 1, 2)

Cash net loss, $2,300; accrual net income, $300

Temporary Manpower Services experienced the following selected transactions during January:

Jan. 1 Prepaid insurance for January through March, $600.
 4 Purchased office equipment for cash, $1,400.
 5 Received cash for services performed, $900.
 8 Paid gas bill, $300.
 12 Performed services on account, $1,000.
 14 Purchased office equipment on account, $300.
 28 Collected $500 on account from January 12.
 31 Paid salary expense, $1,100.
 31 Paid account payable from January 14.
 31 Recorded adjusting entry for January insurance expense (see Jan. 1).

Required

1. Show how each transaction would be handled using the cash basis and the accrual basis. Under each column give the amount of revenue or expense for January. Journal entries are not required. Use the following format for your answer, and show your computations:

Amount of Revenue or Expense for January

Date	Cash Basis	Accrual Basis

2. Compute January net income or net loss under each method.
3. Indicate which measure of net income or net loss is preferable. Give your reason.

No check figure

Problem 3-2A *Applying accounting principles (L.O. 2)*

Write a short memo to contrast the cash basis of accounting with the accrual basis. Mention the roles of the revenue principle and the matching principle in accrual accounting.

No check figure

Problem 3-3A *Journalizing adjusting entries (L.O. 3)*

Journalize the adjusting entry needed on December 31, end of the current accounting period, for each of the following independent cases affecting Windsor Construction Contractors.

a. Windsor pays its employees each Friday. The amount of the weekly payroll is $2,100 for a five-day workweek, and the daily salary amounts are equal. The current accounting period ends on Monday.

b. Windsor has loaned money, receiving notes receivable. During the current year the entity has earned accrued interest revenue of $737 that it will receive next year.

c. The beginning balance of Supplies was $2,680. During the year the entity purchased supplies costing $6,180, and at December 31 the inventory of supplies on hand is $2,150.

d. Windsor is servicing the air-conditioning system in a large building, and the owner of the building paid Windsor $12,900 as the annual service fee. Windsor recorded this amount as Unearned Service Revenue. Ralph Windsor, the owner, estimates that the company has earned one-fourth of the total fee during the current year.

e. Depreciation for the current year includes: Office Furniture, $650; Equipment, $3,850; Trucks, $10,320. Make a compound entry.

f. Details of Prepaid Rent are shown in the account:

Prepaid Rent		
Jan. 1 Bal.	600	
Mar. 31	1,200	
Sep. 30	1,200	

Windsor pays office rent semiannually on March 31 and September 30. At December 31, $600 of the last payment is still an asset.

No check figure

Problem 3-4A *Analyzing and journalizing adjustments (L.O. 3)*

Patricia Wood Court Reporting Company's unadjusted and adjusted trial balances at April 30, 19X1, are shown at the top of the next page.

Required

Journalize the adjusting entries that account for the differences between the two trial balances.

Patricia Wood Court Reporting Company
Adjusted Trial Balance
April 30, 19X1

Account Title	Trial Balance Debit	Trial Balance Credit	Adjusted Trial Balance Debit	Adjusted Trial Balance Credit
Cash	8,180		8,180	
Accounts receivable	6,360		6,540	
Interest receivable			300	
Note receivable	4,100		4,100	
Supplies	980		290	
Prepaid rent	1,440		720	
Building	66,450		66,450	
Accumulated depreciation		14,970		16,070
Accounts payable		6,920		6,920
Wages payable				320
Unearned service revenue		670		110
Patricia Wood, capital		60,770		60,770
Patricia Wood, withdrawals	3,600		3,600	
Service revenue		9,940		10,680
Interest revenue				300
Wage expense	1,600		1,920	
Rent expense			720	
Depreciation expense			1,100	
Insurance expense	370		370	
Supplies expense			690	
Utilities expense	190		190	
	93,270	93,270	95,170	95,170

Problem 3-5A *Journalizing and posting adjustments to T-accounts; preparing the adjusted trial balance* **(L.O. 3, 4)**

Adjusted trial balance, $49,790

The trial balance of Insurors of Texas at October 31, 19X2, and the data needed for the month-end adjustments are on page 132.

Adjustment data:

a. Prepaid rent still in force at October 31, $400.
b. Supplies used during the month, $440.
c. Depreciation for the month, $700.
d. Accrued advertising expense at October 31, $320. (Credit Accounts Payable.)
e. Accrued salary expense at October 31, $180.
f. Unearned commission revenue still unearned at October 31, $2,000.

Required

1. Open T-accounts for the accounts listed in the trial balance, inserting their October 31 unadjusted balances.

Insurors of Texas
Trial Balance
October 31, 19X2

Cash	$1,460	
Accounts receivable	14,750	
Prepaid rent	3,100	
Supplies...........................	780	
Furniture..........................	22,370	
Accumulated depreciation		$11,640
Accounts payable		1,940
Salary payable		
Unearned commission revenue		2,290
Peggy Bailes, capital................		24,140
Peggy Bailes, withdrawals	2,900	
Commission revenue		8,580
Salary expense......................	2,160	
Rent expense		
Utilities expense	340	
Depreciation expense		
Advertising expense.................	730	
Supplies expense....................		
Total	$48,590	$48,590

2. Journalize the adjusting entries and post them to the T-accounts. Key the journal entries and the posted amounts by letter.
3. Prepare the adjusted trial balance.

Total assets, $47,780

Problem 3-6A   *Preparing the financial statements from an adjusted trial balance* (L.O. 5)

The adjusted trial balance of Tradewinds Travel Designers at December 31, 19X6, follows:

Tradewinds Travel Designers
Adjusted Trial Balance
December 31, 19X6

Cash	$ 3,320	
Accounts receivable	11,920	
Supplies...........................	2,300	
Prepaid rent	600	
Office equipment	21,180	
Accumulated depreciation—office equipment		$ 4,350
Office furniture	17,680	
Accumulated depreciation—office furniture		4,870
Accounts payable		3,640
Property tax payable		1,100
Interest payable		830
Unearned service revenue		620
Note payable		27,500
Monica Gillen, capital		6,090
Monica Gillen, withdrawals	44,000	
Service revenue		127,880
Depreciation expense—office equipment	6,680	
Depreciation expense—office furniture .		
	2,370	
Salary expense.....................	39,900	
Rent expense	14,400	
Interest expense	3,100	
Utilities expense	2,670	
Insurance expense	3,810	
Supplies expense...................	2,950	
Total	$176,880	$176,880

132

Required

Prepare Tradewinds' 19X6 income statement, statement of owner's equity, and balance sheet. List expenses in decreasing order on the income statement and show total liabilities on the balance sheet. Draw the arrows linking the three financial statements.

Problem 3-7A *Preparing an adjusted trial balance and the financial statements* **(L.O. 3, 4, 5)**

The unadjusted trial balance of Joe Heider, Attorney, at July 31, 19X2, and the related month-end adjustment data are as follows:

	Joe Heider, Attorney Trial Balance July 31, 19X2	
Cash	$14,600	
Accounts receivable	11,600	
Prepaid rent	3,600	
Supplies	800	
Furniture	16,800	
Accumulated depreciation		$ 3,500
Accounts payable		3,450
Salary payable		
Joe Heider, capital		38,650
Joe Heider, withdrawals	4,000	
Legal service revenue		8,750
Salary expense	2,400	
Rent expense		
Utilities expense	550	
Depreciation expense		
Supplies expense		
Total	$54,350	$54,350

Adjustment data:

a. Prepaid rent expired during the month. The unadjusted prepaid balance of $3,600 relates to the period July through October.
b. Supplies on hand at July 31, $500.
c. Depreciation on furniture for the month. The estimated useful life of the furniture is four years.
d. Accrued salary expense at July 31 for one day only. The five-day weekly payroll is $1,000.
e. Accrued legal service revenue at July 31, $700.

Required

1. Write the trial balance on a sheet of paper similar to Exhibit 3-5 and prepare the adjusted trial balance of Joe Heider, Attorney, at July 31, 19X2. Key each adjusting entry by letter.
2. Prepare the income statement, the statement of owner's equity, and the balance sheet. Draw the arrows linking the three financial statements.

Problem 3-8A *Journalizing and posting adjustments to four-column accounts; preparing the adjusted trial balance and the financial statements* **(L.O. 3, 4, 5)**

The trial balance of Foster Cleaning Service at July 31, 19X3, and the data needed to make the year-end adjustments are as follows:

Adjustment data:

a. At July 31 the business has earned $1,420 of service revenue that has not yet been recorded.
b. Supplies used during the year totaled $3,060.
c. Prepaid rent still in force at July 31 is $1,040.
d. Depreciation for the year is based on cleaning equipment costing $37,300 and an estimated useful life of 10 years.
e. The entity cleans the carpets of a large apartment complex that pays in advance. At July 31 the entity has earned $2,210 of the unadjusted balance of Unearned Service Revenue.
f. At July 31 the business owes its employees accrued salaries for two-thirds of a four-week payroll. Total payroll for the four weeks is $2,670.

Required

1. Open the accounts listed in the trial balance, inserting their July 31 unadjusted balances. Use four-column accounts. The following accounts have experienced no activity during the month, so their balances should be dated July 1: Supplies, Prepaid Rent, Accumulated Depreciation, and Unearned Service Revenue.

Foster Cleaning Service
Trial Balance
July 31, 19X3

Account No.			
101	Cash	$ 1,010	
121	Accounts receivable	6,200	
131	Supplies	3,400	
133	Prepaid rent	1,890	
141	Cleaning equipment	37,300	
151	Accumulated depreciation		$ 14,360
201	Accounts payable		6,410
211	Salary payable		
221	Unearned service revenue		3,110
301	J. B. Foster, capital		14,310
302	J. B. Foster, withdrawals	40,100	
401	Service revenue		91,060
501	Salary expense	32,150	
504	Depreciation expense		
506	Supplies expense		
509	Rent expense	6,000	
511	Utilities expense	1,200	
	Total	$129,250	$129,250

2. Journalize the adjusting entries, using page 4 of the journal.
3. Post the adjusting entries to the ledger accounts, using all posting references.
4. Prepare the adjusted trial balance at July 31.
5. Prepare the income statement, the statement of owner's equity, and the balance sheet. Draw the arrows linking the three financial statements.

Problem 3-1B *Cash basis versus accrual basis* (L.O. 1, 2)

Samaritan Counseling Service had the following selected transactions during October:

Oct. 1 Prepaid insurance for October through December, $450.
    4 Purchased office equipment for cash, $800.
    5 Performed counseling services and received cash, $700.
    8 Paid advertising expense, $100.
  11 Performed counseling service on account, $1,200.
  19 Purchased office furniture on account, $150.
  24 Collected $400 on account for the October 11 service.
  31 Paid account payable from October 19.
  31 Paid salary expense, $600.
  31 Recorded adjusting entry for October insurance expense (see Oct. 1).

Required

1. Show how each transaction would be handled using the cash basis and the accrual basis. Under each column give the amount of revenue or expense for October. Journal entries are not required. Use the following format for your answer, and show your computations:

	Amount of Revenue or Expense for October	
Date	**Cash Basis**	**Accrual Basis**

2. Compute October net income or net loss under each method.
3. Indicate which measure of net income or net loss is preferable. Give your reason.

Problem 3-2B *Applying accounting principles* (L.O. 2)

As the controller of Hillsborough Auto Glass Company, you have hired a new bookkeeper, whom you must train. Write a memo to explain why adjusting entries are needed to measure net income properly. Mention the accounting principles underlying the use of adjusting entries.

Problem 3-3B *Journalizing adjusting entries* (L.O. 3)

Journalize the adjusting entry needed on December 31, end of the current accounting period, for each of the following independent cases affecting Randolph Engineering Consulting Company.

a. Each Friday Randolph pays its employees for the current week's work. The amount of the payroll is $2,500 for a five-day work week. The current accounting period ends on Thursday.
b. Randolph has received notes receivable from some clients for professional services. During the current year, Randolph has earned accrued interest revenue of $8,575, which will be received next year.
c. The beginning balance of Engineering Supplies was $3,800. During the year the entity purchased supplies costing $12,530, and at December 31 the inventory of supplies on hand is $2,970.
d. Randolph is conducting tests of the strength of the steel to be used in a

large building, and the client paid Randolph $27,000 at the start of the project. Randolph recorded this amount as Unearned Engineering Revenue. The tests will take several months to complete. Randolph executives estimate that the company has earned two-thirds of the total fee during the current year.

e. Depreciation for the current year includes: Office Furniture, $4,500; Engineering Equipment, $6,360; Building, $3,790. Make a compound entry.

f. Details of Prepaid Insurance are shown in the account:

Prepaid Insurance		
Jan. 1 Bal.	2,400	
Apr. 30	3,600	
Oct. 31	3,600	

Randolph pays semiannual insurance premiums (the payment for insurance coverage is called a *premium*) on April 30 and October 31. At December 31, $2,400 of the last payment is still in force.

No check figure

Problem 3-4B *Analyzing and journalizing adjustments* **(L.O. 3)**

Ahmed Rashad Commission Company's unadjusted and adjusted trial balances at December 31, 19X0, are shown below.

Required

Journalize the adjusting entries that account for the differences between the two trial balances.

Ahmed Rashad Commission Company
Adjusted Trial Balance
December 31, 19X0

Account Title	Trial Balance Debit	Trial Balance Credit	Adjusted Trial Balance Debit	Adjusted Trial Balance Credit
Cash	3,620		3,620	
Accounts receivable	11,260		14,090	
Supplies	1,090		780	
Prepaid insurance	2,200		1,330	
Office furniture	21,630		21,630	
Accumulated depreciation		8,220		10,500
Accounts payable		6,310		6,310
Salary payable				960
Interest payable				280
Note payable		12,000		12,000
Unearned commission revenue		1,440		960
Ahmed Rashad, capital		13,010		13,010
Ahmed Rashad, withdrawals	29,370		29,370	
Commission revenue		72,890		76,200
Depreciation expense			2,280	
Supplies expense			310	
Utilities expense	4,960		4,960	
Salary expense	26,660		27,620	
Rent expense	12,200		12,200	
Interest expense	880		1,160	
Insurance expense			870	
	113,870	113,870	120,220	120,220

Problem 3-5B

Journalizing and posting adjustments to T-accounts; preparing the adjusted trial balance (L.O. 3, 4)

Adjusted trial balance, $61,100

The trial balance of Griffin Realty at August 31 of the current year and the data needed for the month-end adjustments follow.

Adjustment data:

a. Prepaid rent still in force at August 31, $620.
b. Supplies used during the month, $300.
c. Depreciation for the month, $400.
d. Accrued advertising expense at August 31, $110. (Credit Accounts Payable.)
e. Accrued salary expense at August 31, $550.
f. Unearned commission revenue still unearned at August 31, $1,670.

Griffin Realty
Trial Balance
August 31, 19X6

Cash.	$ 2,200	
Accounts receivable	23,780	
Prepaid rent	2,420	
Supplies	1,180	
Furniture.	19,740	
Accumulated depreciation		$ 3,630
Accounts payable		2,410
Salary payable		
Unearned commission revenue		2,790
Tom Griffin, capital		39,510
Tom Griffin, withdrawals	4,800	
Commission revenue		11,700
Salary expense.	3,800	
Rent expense		
Utilities expense	550	
Depreciation expense.		
Advertising expense	1,570	
Supplies expense		
Total.	$60,040	$60,040

Required

1. Open T-accounts for the accounts listed in the trial balance, inserting their August 31 unadjusted balances.
2. Journalize the adjusting entries and post them to the T-accounts. Key the journal entries and the posted amounts by letter.
3. Prepare the adjusted trial balance.

Problem 3-6B

Preparing the financial statements from an adjusted trial balance (L.O. 5)

Total assets, $106,030

The adjusted trial balance of Blaine Delivery Services at December 31, 19X8 follows:

Blaine Delivery Services
Adjusted Trial Balance
December 31, 19X8

Cash	$ 8,340	
Accounts receivable	41,490	
Prepaid rent	1,350	
Supplies	970	
Equipment	70,690	
Accumulated depreciation—equipment		$ 22,240
Office furniture	24,100	
Accumulated depreciation—office furniture		18,670
Accounts payable		13,600
Unearned service revenue		4,520
Interest payable		2,130
Salary payable		930
Note payable		40,000
Ray Blaine, capital		32,380
Ray Blaine, withdrawals	48,000	
Service revenue		201,790
Depreciation expense—equipment	11,300	
Depreciation expense—office furniture	2,410	
Salary expense	102,800	
Rent expense	12,000	
Interest expense	4,200	
Utilities expense	3,770	
Insurance expense	3,150	
Supplies expense	1,690	
Total	$336,260	$336,260

Required

Prepare Blaine's 19X8 income statement, statement of owner's equity, and balance sheet. List expenses in decreasing order on the income statement and show total liabilities on the balance sheet. Draw the arrows linking the three financial statements.

Total assets, $40,450

Problem 3-7B *Preparing an adjusted trial balance and the financial statements (L.O. 3, 4, 5)*

Consider the unadjusted trial balance of Terri Peterson, Audio Therapist, at October 31, 19X2, and the related month-end adjustment data.

Adjustment data:

a. Prepaid rent expired during the month. The unadjusted prepaid balance of $4,000 relates to the period October through January.
b. Supplies on hand at October 31, $400.
c. Depreciation on furniture for the month. The furniture's expected useful life is five years.
d. Accrued salary expense at October 31 for one day only. The five-day weekly payroll is $1,500.
e. Accrued consulting service revenue at October 31, $1,000.

Terri Peterson, Audio Therapist
Trial Balance
October 31, 19X2

Cash	$16,300	
Accounts receivable	8,000	
Prepaid rent	4,000	
Supplies	600	
Furniture	15,000	
Accumulated depreciation		$ 3,000
Accounts payable		2,800
Salary payable		
Terri Peterson, capital		36,000
Terri Peterson, withdrawals	3,600	
Consulting service revenue		7,400
Salary expense	1,400	
Rent expense		
Utilities expense	300	
Depreciation expense		
Supplies expense		
Total	$49,200	$49,200

Required

1. Write the trial balance on a sheet of paper, using as an example Exhibit 3-5, and prepare the adjusted trial balance of Terri Peterson, Audio Therapist, at October 31, 19X2. Key each adjusting entry by letter.

2. Prepare the income statement, the statement of owner's equity, and the balance sheet. Draw the arrows linking the three financial statements.

Problem 3-8B *Journalizing and posting adjustments to four-column accounts; preparing the adjusted trial balance and the financial statements* **(L.O. 3, 4, 5)**

Net income, $43,960

The trial balance of Air-Tite Security Service at May 31, 19X3 is on page 140. The data needed to make the year-end adjustments follow.

Adjustment data:

a. At May 31 the business has earned $1,000 service revenue that has not yet been recorded.
b. Supplies used during the year totaled $5,650.
c. Prepaid rent still in force at May 31 is $330.
d. Depreciation for the year is based on tools and installation equipment costing $27,900 and having an estimated useful life of 9 years.
e. Air-Tite installs locks in a large apartment complex that pays in advance. At May 31 the entity has earned $3,600 of the unadjusted balance of Unearned Service Revenue.
f. At May 31 the business owes its employees accrued salaries for half a four-week payroll. Total payroll for the four weeks is $2,600.

Air-Tite Security Service
Trial Balance
May 31, 19X3

Account No.			
101	Cash	$ 3,260	
112	Accounts receivable	4,700	
127	Supplies	7,700	
129	Prepaid rent	1,430	
143	Equipment	27,900	
154	Accumulated depreciation		$ 12,150
211	Accounts payable		4,240
221	Salary payable		
243	Unearned service revenue		5,810
301	Thomas King, capital		7,080
311	Thomas King, withdrawals	34,800	
401	Service revenue		80,610
511	Salary expense	28,800	
513	Depreciation expense		
515	Supplies expense		
519	Rent expense		
521	Utilities expense	1,300	
	Total	$109,890	$109,890

Required

1. Open the accounts listed in the trial balance, inserting their May 31 unadjusted balances. Use four-column accounts. The following accounts have experienced no activity during the month, so their balances should be dated May 1: Supplies, Prepaid Rent, Accumulated Depreciation, and Unearned Service Revenue.
2. Journalize the adjusting entries, using page 7 of the journal.
3. Post the adjusting entries to the ledger accounts, using all posting references.
4. Prepare the adjusted trial balance at May 31.
5. Prepare the income statement, the statement of owner's equity, and the balance sheet. Draw the arrows linking the three financial statements.

Extending Your Knowledge

Decision Problems

Ending adjusted owner's
equity, $135,400

1. Valuing a Business Based on its Net Income (L.O. 4, 5)
Ace Black has owned and operated Black Biomedical Systems, a management consulting firm for physicians, since its beginning ten years ago. From all appearances the business has prospered. Black lives in the fast lane—flashy car, home located in an expensive suburb, frequent trips abroad, and other

signs of wealth. In the past few years, you have become friends with him and his wife through weekly rounds of golf at the country club. Recently, he mentioned that he has lost his zest for the business and would consider selling it for the right price. He claims that his clientele is firmly established and that the business "runs on its own." According to Black, the consulting procedures are fairly simple and anyone could perform the work.

Assume you are interested in buying this business. You obtain its most recent monthly trial balance, which follows. Assume that revenues and expenses vary little from month to month and April is a typical month.

Your investigation reveals that the trial balance does not include the effects of monthly revenues of $1,100 and expenses totaling $2,100. If you were to buy Black Biomedical Systems, you would hire a manager so you could devote your time to other duties. Assume that this person would require a monthly salary of $2,000.

Black Biomedical Systems
Trial Balance
April 30, 19XX

Cash	$ 7,700	
Accounts receivable	4,900	
Prepaid expenses	2,600	
Plant assets	241,300	
Accumulated depreciation		$189,600
Land	138,000	
Accounts payable		11,800
Salary payable.................		
Unearned consulting revenue		56,700
Ace Black, capital		137,400
Ace Black, withdrawals	9,000	
Consulting revenue		12,300
Salary expense	3,400	
Rent expense..................		
Utilities expense	900	
Depreciation expense		
Supplies expense		
Total	$407,800	$407,800

Required

1. Is this an unadjusted or an adjusted trial balance? How can you tell?
2. Assume that the most you would pay for the business is thirty times the monthly net income you could expect to earn from it. Compute this possible price.
3. Black states that the least he will take for the business is his ending capital. Compute this amount.
4. Under these conditions, how much should you offer Black? Give your reason.

2. Understanding the Concepts Underlying the Accrual Basis of Accounting   No check figure
   (L.O. 1, 2)

The following independent questions relate to the accrual basis of accounting:

1. It has been said that the only time a company's financial position is known for certain is when the company is ended and its only asset is cash. Why is this statement true?
2. A friend suggests that the purpose of adjusting entries is to correct errors in the accounts. Is your friend's statement true? What is the purpose of adjusting entries if the statement is wrong?
3. The text suggested that furniture (and each other plant asset that is depreciated) is a form of prepaid expense. Do you agree? Why do you think some accountants view plant assets this way?

Ethical Issue

The net income of Christopher's, a department store, decreased sharply during 1991. Matthew Christopher, owner of the store, anticipates the need for a bank loan in 1992. Late in 1991 he instructed the accountant to record a $4,500 sale of furniture to the Christopher family, even though the goods will not be shipped from the manufacturer until January 1992. Christopher also told the accountant not to make the following December 31, 1991, adjusting entries:

Salaries owed to employees.................	$1,800
Prepaid insurance that has expired	670

Required

1. Compute the overall effect of these transactions on the store's reported income for 1991.
2. Why did Christopher take this action? Is this action ethical? Give your reason, identifying the parties helped and the parties harmed by Christopher's action.
3. As a personal friend, what advice would you give the accountant?

Financial Statement Problems

No check figure

1. Journalizing and Posting Transactions, and Tracing Account Balances to the Financial Statements (L.O. 3, 4, 5)

Goodyear Tire & Rubber Company—like all other businesses—makes adjusting entries prior to year end in order to measure assets, liabilities, revenues, and expenses properly. Examine Goodyear's balance sheet, paying particular attention to Prepaid expenses, Accrued payrolls and other compensation (similar to Salary payable), and Other current liabilities. The amount reported for Other current liabilities is the sum of several accounts combined under this heading. Assume the Other current liabilities of $278.9 million at December 31, 1989, include two accounts with the following balances: Interest Payable, $110.0 million, and Unearned Sales Revenue, $168.9 million.

Required

1. Open T-accounts for these four accounts. Insert Goodyear's balances (in millions) at December 31, 1989. (Examples: Prepaid Expenses, $170.7; Interest Payable, $110.0.)
2. Journalize the following for 1990. Key entries by letter. Explanations are not required.

Cash transactions (amounts in millions):
a. Paid prepaid expenses, $184.6.
b. Paid the December 31, 1989, accrued payrolls and other compensation.
c. Paid the December 31, 1989, interest payable.
d. Received $54.3 cash for unearned sales revenue.

Adjustments at December 31, 1990 (amounts in millions):
e. Prepaid expenses expired, $149.0. (Debit Administrative and General Expense.)
f. Accrued payrolls and other compensation, $442.7. (Debit Selling Expense.)
g. Accrued interest payable, $123.1.
h. Earned sales revenue for which cash had been collected in advance, $63.8.

3. After these entries are posted, show that the balances in the four accounts opened in Requirement 1 agree with the corresponding amounts reported in the December 31, 1990, balance sheet.

2. Adjusting the Accounts of an Actual Company (L.O. 2)

No check figure

Obtain the annual report of an actual company of your choosing. Assume the company accountants *failed* to make four adjustments at the end of the current year. For illustrative purposes, we shall assume that the amounts reported for the related assets and liabilities are *incorrect*.

Adjustments omitted:
a. Depreciation of equipment, $800,000
b. Salaries owed to employees but not yet paid, $230,000
c. Prepaid rent used up during the year, $100,000
d. Accrued sales (or service) revenue, $140,000

Required

1. Compute the correct amounts for the following balance sheet items:
    a. Book value of plant assets
    b. Total liabilities
    c. Prepaid expenses
    d. Accounts receivable
2. Compute the amount of net income or net loss that the company would have reported if the accountants had recorded these transactions properly. Ignore income tax.

Chapter 4

Completing the Accounting Cycle

"Homer, if you don't get those invoices and check stubs to the office in Baton Rouge this week, you can just hang it up."

Ed Simpson, the owner of a Baton Rouge, Louisiana, construction company, was talking to his construction superintendent, Homer Huntley. . . . By the time Simpson left the small construction shack, Homer was furious. Muttering under his breath, "Book-keepers! Don't they have anything better to do than ruin my day?" he started yanking invoices, check stubs, handwritten notes, and other papers off the nails he had driven into the shack's walls as a haphazard filing system for job records.

Homer stuffed the papers into a brown grocery bag he'd been using as a trash container, folded the bag's top, and fastened it with a nail pulled from the wall. . . . On his way home later that night, Homer stuffed the bag into a mail box outside the local post office.

Homer was understandably surprised when the company's bookkeeper called a few days later to say that he had received the bag. For years after that, the bag hung on the wall in the accounting office at Simpson Construction Company.

Source: Arthur Sharplin, "Brown Bag Bookkeeping," *Journal of Accountancy* (July 1986), p. 122.

Our humorous actual example illustrates how some small businesses keep their accounting records. As you study Chapter 4, consider the advantages that a more formal way of keeping records and completing the accounting cycle offers a business.

You have studied how accountants journalize transactions, post to the ledger accounts, prepare the trial balance and the adjusting entries, and draw up the financial statements. One major step remains to complete the accounting cycle—closing the books. This chapter illustrates the closing process for Gary Lyon's accounting practice at April 30, 19X1. It also shows how to use three additional accounting tools that are optional. One of these optional tools is the accountant's work sheet. Building upon the adjusted trial balance, the work sheet leads directly to the financial statements, which are the focal point of financial accounting. The chapter also presents an example of an actual balance sheet to show how companies classify assets and liabilities to provide meaningful information for decision making.

Point to Stress: Setting up an adequate accounting system takes time, but the time is well spent. The more organized an information system is, the less time will be spent retrieving information or looking for lost information. In Chapter 4 we will be looking at an organizational tool to help the accountant—the work sheet.

Overview of the Accounting Cycle

The **accounting cycle** is the process by which accountants produce an entity's financial statements for a specific period of time. For a new business, the cycle begins with setting up (opening) the ledger accounts. Gary Lyon started his accounting practice from scratch on April 1, 19X1, so the first step in the cycle was to open the accounts. After a business has operated for one period, however, the account balances carry over from period to period. Therefore, the accounting cycle usually starts with the account balances at the beginning of the period, as shown in Exhibit 4-1. The exhibit highlights the new steps that we will be discussing in this chapter.

The accounting cycle is divided into work performed during the period—journalizing transactions and posting to the ledger—and work performed at the end of the period to prepare the financial statements. A secondary purpose of the end-of-period work is to get the accounts ready for recording the transactions of the next period. The greater number of individual steps at the end of the period may imply that most of the work is done at the end. Nevertheless, the recording and posting during the period takes far more time than the end-of-period work. Some of the terms in Exhibit 4-1 may be unfamiliar, but they will become clear by the end of the chapter.

Point to Stress: The entire accounting cycle is repeated with each new accounting period. The goal of the completed cycle is the financial statements.

EXHIBIT 4-1 *The Accounting Cycle*

During the period	1.	Start with the account balances in the ledger at the beginning of the period.
	2.	Analyze and journalize transactions as they occur.
	3.	Post journal entries to the ledger accounts.
End of the period	4.	Compute the unadjusted balance in each account at the end of the period.
	5.	**Enter the trial balance on the work sheet, and complete the work sheet.***
	6.	Using the work sheet as a guide, a. Prepare the financial statements. b. Journalize and post the adjusting entries. **c. Journalize and post the closing entries.**
	7.	**Prepare the postclosing, or afterclosing, trial balance. This trial balance becomes step 1 for the next period.**

*Optional

The Accountant's Work Sheet

Accountants often use a **work sheet,** a columnar document that is designed to help move data from the trial balance to the finished financial statements. The work sheet provides an orderly way to compute net income and arrange the data for the financial statements. By listing all the accounts and their unadjusted balances, it helps the accountant identify the accounts needing adjustment. Although it is not essential, the work sheet is helpful because it brings together in one place the effects of all the transactions of a particular period. The work sheet aids the closing process by listing the adjusted balances of all the accounts. It also helps the accountant discover potential errors.

Point to Stress: The work sheet is a tool to help the accountant. It is never presented along with the period's financial statements.

The work sheet is not part of the ledger or the journal, nor is it a financial statement. Therefore, it is not part of the formal accounting system. Instead, it is a summary device that exists for the accountant's convenience.

Exhibits 4-2 through 4-6 illustrate the development of a typical work sheet for the business of Gary Lyon, CPA. The heading at the top names the business, identifies the document, and states the accounting period. A step-by-step description of its preparation follows. Observe that steps 1 through 3 use the adjusted trial balance that was introduced in Chapter 3. Only steps 4 and 5 are entirely new.

Steps introduced in Chapter 3 to prepare the adjusted trial balance:

1. Write the account titles and their unadjusted ending balances in the Trial Balance columns of the work sheet and total the amounts.
2. Enter the adjustments in the Adjustments columns and total the amounts.
3. Compute each account's adjusted balance by combining the trial balance and adjustment figures. Enter the adjusted amounts in the Adjusted Trial Balance columns.

New steps introduced in this chapter:

4. Extend the asset, liability, and owner's equity amounts from the Adjusted Trial Balance to the Balance Sheet columns. Extend the revenue and expense amounts to the Income Statement columns. Total the statement columns.

5. Compute net income or net loss as the difference between total revenues and total expenses on the income statement. Enter net income or net loss as a balancing amount on the income statement and on the balance sheet and compute the adjusted column totals. After completion, total debits equal total credits in the income statement columns and in the balance sheet columns.

1. Write the account titles and their unadjusted ending balances in the Trial Balance columns of the work sheet and total the amounts. Of course, total debits should equal total credits as shown in Exhibit 4-2. The account titles and balances come directly from the ledger accounts before preparing the adjusting entries. If the business uses a work sheet, there is no need for a separate trial balance. It is written directly onto the work sheet, as shown in the exhibit. Accounts are grouped on the work sheet by category and are usually listed in the order they appear in the ledger. By contrast, their order on the financial statements follows a different pattern. For example, the expenses on the work sheet in Exhibit 4-2 indicate no particular order. But on the income statement, expenses are ordered by amount with the largest first (see Exhibit 4-7).

Accounts may have zero balances (for example, Depreciation Expense). All accounts are listed on the trial balance because they appear in the ledger. Electronically prepared work sheets list all the accounts, not just those with a balance.

2. Enter the adjusting entries in the Adjustments columns and total the amounts. Exhibit 4-3 includes the April adjusting entries. These are the same adjustments that were illustrated in Chapter 3 to prepare the adjusted trial balance.

How does the accountant identify the accounts that need to be adjusted? By scanning the trial balance. Cash needs no adjustment because all cash transactions are recorded as they occur during the period. Consequently, Cash's balance is up to date.

Accounts Receivable is listed next. Has Gary Lyon earned revenue that he has not yet recorded? The answer is yes. Lyon provides professional service for a client who pays a $500 fee on the 15th of each month. At April 30 Lyon has earned half of this amount, $250, which must be accrued. To accrue this service revenue, Lyon debits Accounts Receivable and credits Service Revenue on the work sheet in Exhibit 4-3. A letter is used to link the debit and the credit of each adjusting entry. By moving down the trial balance, Lyon identifies the remaining accounts needing adjustment. Supplies is next. The business has used supplies during April, so Lyon debits Supplies Expense and credits Supplies. The other adjustments are analyzed and entered on the work sheet as shown in the exhibit.

The process of identifying accounts that need to be adjusted is aided by listing the accounts in their proper sequence. However, suppose one or more accounts is omitted from the trial balance. It can always be written below the first column totals—$51,800. Assume that Supplies Expense was accidentally omitted and thus did not appear on the trial balance. When the accountant identifies the need to update the Supplies account, he or she knows that the debit in the adjusting entry is to Supplies Expense. In this case, the accountant

EXHIBIT 4-2

Gary Lyon, CPA
Work Sheet
For the Month Ended April 30, 19X1

Account Title	Trial Balance		Adjustments		Adjusted Trial Balance		Income Statement		Balance Sheet	
	Debit	Credit	Debit	Credit	Debit	Credit	Debit	Credit	Debit	Credit
Cash	24,800									
Accounts receivable	2,250									
Supplies	700									
Prepaid rent	3,000									
Furniture	16,500									
Accumulated depreciation										
Accounts payable		13,100								
Salary payable										
Unearned service revenue		450								
Gary Lyon, capital		31,250								
Gary Lyon, withdrawals	3,200									
Service revenue		7,000								
Rent expense										
Salary expense	950									
Supplies expense										
Depreciation expense										
Utilities expense	400									
	51,800	51,800								

Write the account titles and their unadjusted ending balances in the Trial Balance columns of the work sheet, and total the amounts.

EXHIBIT 4-3

Gary Lyon, CPA
Work Sheet
For the Month Ended April 30, 19X1

Account Title	Trial Balance Debit	Trial Balance Credit	Adjustments Debit	Adjustments Credit	Adjusted Trial Balance Debit	Adjusted Trial Balance Credit	Income Statement Debit	Income Statement Credit	Balance Sheet Debit	Balance Sheet Credit
Cash	24,800									
Accounts receivable	2,250		(a) 250							
Supplies	700			(b) 300						
Prepaid rent	3,000			(c) 1,000						
Furniture	16,500									
Accumulated depreciation		13,100		(d) 275						
Accounts payable										
Salary payable		450		(e) 950						
Unearned service revenue		31,250	(f) 150							
Gary Lyon, capital										
Gary Lyon, withdrawals	3,200									
Service revenue		7,000		(a) 250						
				(f) 150						
Rent expense			(c) 1,000							
Salary expense	950		(e) 950							
Supplies expense			(b) 300							
Depreciation expense			(d) 275							
Utilities expense	400									
	51,800	51,800	2,925	2,925						

Enter the adjusting entries in the Adjustments columns, and total the amounts.

can write Supplies Expense on the line beneath the amount totals and enter the debit adjustment—$300—on the Supplies Expense line. Keep in mind that the work sheet is not the finished version of the financial statements, so the order of the accounts on the work sheet is not critical. When the accountant prepares the income statement, Supplies Expense can be listed in its proper sequence.

After the adjustments are entered on the work sheet, the amount columns should be totaled to see that total debits equal total credits. This provides some assurance that each debit adjustment is accompanied by an equal credit. Exhibit 4-4 shows the work sheet with the adjusted trial balance added.

This step is performed as it was in Chapter 3. For example, the Cash balance is up to date, so it receives no adjustment. Accounts Receivable's adjusted balance of $2,500 is computed by adding the trial balance amount of $2,250 to the $250 debit adjustment. Supplies' adjusted balance of $400 is determined by subtracting the $300 credit adjustment from the unadjusted debit balance of $700. An account may receive more than one adjustment, as does Service Revenue. The column totals should maintain the equality of debits and credits.

4. Extend the asset, liability, and owner's equity amounts from the Adjusted Trial Balance to the Balance Sheet columns. Extend the revenue and expense amounts to the Income Statement columns. Total the statement columns. Every account is either a balance sheet account or an income statement account. The asset, liability, and owner's equity accounts go to the balance sheet, and the revenues and expenses go to the income statement. Debits on the adjusted trial balance remain debits in the statement columns, and likewise for credits. Each account's adjusted balance should appear in only one statement column, as shown in Exhibit 4-5.

The income statement indicates total expenses in the debit column ($3,875) and total revenues ($7,400) in the credit column. The balance sheet shows total debits of $49,400 and total credits of $45,875. At this stage, the column totals should not necessarily be equal.

5. Compute net income or net loss as the difference between total revenues and total expenses on the income statement. Enter net income or net loss as a balancing amount on the income statement and on the balance sheet and compute the adjusted column totals. Exhibit 4-6 presents the completed work sheet, which shows net income of $3,525, computed as follows:

Revenue (total credits on the income statement .	$7,400
Expenses (total debits on the income statement).	3,875
Net income	$3,525

Net income of $3,525 is entered in the debit column of the income statement, and the income statement columns are totaled at $7,400. The net income amount is then extended to the credit column of the balance sheet. This is because an excess of revenues over expenses increases capital, and increases in capital are recorded by a credit. In the closing process, which we discuss later, net income will find its way into the capital account.

If expenses exceed revenue, the result is a net loss. In that event, the accountant writes the words Net loss on the work sheet. The loss amount should be entered in the credit column of the income statement and in the debit column of the balance sheet. This is because an excess of expenses over revenue decreases capital, and decreases in capital are recorded by a debit.

The balance sheet columns are totaled at $49,400. An out-of-balance condition indicates an error in preparing the work sheet. Common mistakes include

---

Point to Stress: When the adjusting entries on the work sheet are prepared, any additional asset, liability, revenue or expense account needed may be added in the account title column of the work sheet.

Teaching Tip: Tell the students to stop if any of the first three sets of columns do not balance. Proceed with the income statement and balance sheet columns only after getting the first three in balance.

Point to Stress: Net income is the difference between the debit and credit Income Statement columns.

Point to Stress: Accounts from the adjusted trial balance will go on either the income statement or the balance sheet, but not both.

Point to Stress: When you are all through with the work sheet, each of the five sets of columns must balance. Sometimes the work sheet does not balance in this last step. If you added accounts during the adjustment process, double check that they have been properly extended. Look for Unearned Revenue and make sure it is extended to the Balance Sheet credit column; be sure all "payables" are on the Balance Sheet, in the credit column. Look at Withdrawals and be sure it is in the debit column of the Balance Sheet. (Those are three frequent mistakes.) Check for any item omitted or for transposed numbers.

EXHIBIT 4-4

Transparency T4-1

Gary Lyon, CPA
Work Sheet
For the Month Ended April 30, 19X1

Account Title	Trial Balance Debit	Trial Balance Credit	Adjustments Debit	Adjustments Credit	Adjusted Trial Balance Debit	Adjusted Trial Balance Credit	Income Statement Debit	Income Statement Credit	Balance Sheet Debit	Balance Sheet Credit
Cash	24,800				24,800					
Accounts receivable	2,250		(a) 250		2,500					
Supplies	700			(b) 300	400					
Prepaid rent	3,000			(c) 1,000	2,000					
Furniture	16,500				16,500					
Accumulated depreciation				(d) 275		275				
Accounts payable		13,100				13,100				
Salary payable				(e) 950		950				
Unearned service revenue		450	(f) 150			300				
Gary Lyon, capital		31,250				31,250				
Gary Lyon, withdrawals	3,200				3,200					
Service revenue		7,000		(a) 250 (f) 150		7,400				
Rent expense			(c) 1,000		1,000					
Salary expense	950		(e) 950		1,900					
Supplies expense			(b) 300		300					
Depreciation expense			(d) 275		275					
Utilities expense	400				400					
	51,800	51,800	2,925	2,925	53,275	53,275				

Compute each account's adjusted balance by combining the trial balance and adjustment figures. Enter the adjusted amounts in the Adjusted Trial balance columns.

EXHIBIT 4-5

Gary Lyon, CPA
Work Sheet
For the Month Ended April 30, 19X1

Account Title	Trial Balance Debit	Trial Balance Credit	Adjustments Debit	Adjustments Credit	Adjusted Trial Balance Debit	Adjusted Trial Balance Credit	Income Statement Debit	Income Statement Credit	Balance Sheet Debit	Balance Sheet Credit
Cash	24,800				24,800				24,800	
Accounts receivable	2,250		(a) 250		2,500				2,500	
Supplies	700			(b) 300	400				400	
Prepaid rent	3,000			(c) 1,000	2,000				2,000	
Furniture	16,500				16,500				16,500	
Accumulated depreciation				(d) 275		275				275
Accounts payable		13,100				13,100				13,100
Salary payable				(e) 950		950				950
Unearned service revenue		450	(f) 150			300				300
Gary Lyon, capital		31,250				31,250				31,250
Gary Lyon, withdrawals	3,200				3,200				3,200	
Service revenue		7,000		(a) 250 (f) 150		7,400		7,400		
Rent expense			(c) 1,000		1,000		1,000			
Salary expense	950		(e) 950		1,900		1,900			
Supplies expense			(b) 300		300		300			
Depreciation expense			(d) 275		275		275			
Utilities expense	400				400		400			
	51,800	51,800	2,925	2,925	53,275	53,275	3,875	7,400	49,400	45,875

Extend the asset, liability, and owner's equity amounts from the Adjusted Trial Balance to the Balance Sheet columns. Extend the revenue and expense amounts to the Income Statement columns. Total the statement columns.

152

EXHIBIT 4-6

Gary Lyon, CPA
Work Sheet
For the Month Ended April 30, 19X1

Account Title	Trial Balance Debit	Trial Balance Credit	Adjustments Debit	Adjustments Credit	Adjusted Trial Balance Debit	Adjusted Trial Balance Credit	Income Statement Debit	Income Statement Credit	Balance Sheet Debit	Balance Sheet Credit
Cash	24,800				24,800				24,800	
Accounts receivable	2,250		(a) 250		2,500				2,500	
Supplies	700			(b) 300	400				400	
Prepaid rent	3,000			(c) 1,000	2,000				2,000	
Furniture	16,500				16,500				16,500	
Accumulated depreciation				(d) 275		275				275
Accounts payable		13,100				13,100				13,100
Salary payable				(e) 950		950				950
Unearned service revenue		450	(f) 150			300				300
Gary Lyon, capital		31,250				31,250				31,250
Gary Lyon, withdrawals	3,200				3,200				3,200	
Service revenue		7,000		(a) 250 (f) 150		7,400		7,400		
Rent expense			(c) 1,000		1,000		1,000			
Salary expense	950		(e) 950		1,900		1,900			
Supplies expense			(b) 300		300		300			
Depreciation expense			(d) 275		275		275			
Utilities expense	400				400		400			
	51,800	51,800	2,925	2,925	53,275	53,275	3,875	7,400	49,400	45,875
Net income							3,525			3,525
							7,400	7,400	49,400	49,400

Compute net income or net loss as the difference between total revenues and total expenses on the income statement. Enter net income or net loss as a balancing amount on the income statement and on the balance sheet, and compute the adjusted column totals.

arithmetic errors and carrying an amount to the wrong column, to the incorrect statement column, or extending a debit as a credit or vice versa. Columns that balance offer some, but not complete, assurance that the work sheet is correct. For example, it is possible to have offsetting errors. Fortunately, that is unlikely.

The watchwords are: Work deliberately, and do not rush. By avoiding errors, you can save time and reduce frustration.

Microcomputer Spreadsheets

Computerized general ledger packages, which we discussed in the last chapter, have a disadvantage. With most general ledger packages, the trial balance, adjustments, and adjusted trial balance cannot appear on the computer screen at the same time. To counter this disadvantage, some software programs create an electronically prepared work sheet, also called a **spreadsheet** or an **electronic spreadsheet.** Lotus 1-2-3® is a popular electronic spreadsheet. Chapter 28 tells you how to work with Lotus 1-2-3®.

An electronic spreadsheet is a grid of information *cells* named by row and column. Columns are designated alphabetically from left to right, rows numerically from top to bottom. For example, the cell in the third row from the top and the fourth column from the left is labeled D3. Spreadsheets typically can have thousands of rows and hundreds of columns. Accountants skilled in using electronic spreadsheets can use them for work sheet analysis.

An electronic spreadsheet has three types of information: numbers, labels, and formulas. For example, the title of an account on an electronic spreadsheet formatted as a worksheet would be entered in, say cells A3 and A4 as a label: Accounts Receivable. The unadjusted debit balance of $2,250 debit (see the work sheet in Exhibits 4-4 through 4-6) would be entered as a number in the next column, B4. A credit balance for an account would appear in Column C. Column D would hold an adjustment if a debit ($250 in our example), and column E would hold an adjustment if a credit. Column F would hold the adjusted trial balance for this account if a debit, and Column G would hold the adjusted trial balance if a credit.

How does the accountant get the correct amount displayed in Column F or Column G? Let's use a simplified example to illustrate. A formula is entered in cell F4 as follows: @ SUM(B4+D4)−E4. The formula itself would not appear in the cell. It would appear in the upper-left corner of the spreadsheet when the cursor (the electronic marker) is in that cell. Notice this formula on the sample screen on the next page. What would appear is the numerical result of that formula, which is 2,500 (2,250 + 250 − 0).

The spreadsheet can be programmed to complete the entire work sheet after the accountant has entered the trial balance and the adjustment amounts. This is a big time saver because once the spreadsheet program is set up, it can be saved as a spreadsheet template. This can be used over and over again without the user having to rewrite the account titles or the cell formulas and do the arithmetic by hand. The spreadsheet can also be programmed to journalize and post the adjusting and closing entries and prepare the financial statements directly from the data on the work sheet.

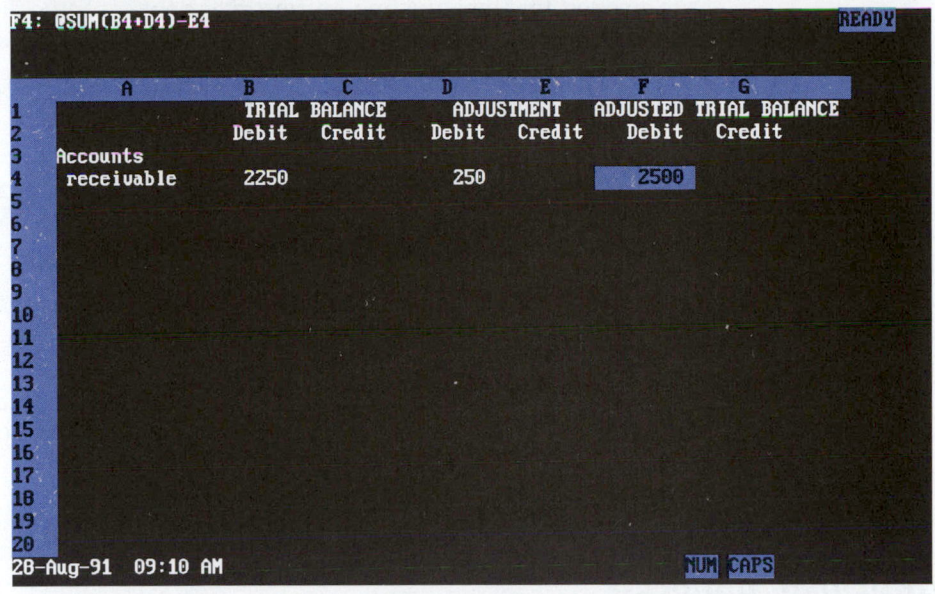

Summary Problem for Your Review

The trial balance of State Service Company at December 31, 19XI, the end of its year, is presented below:

State Service Company		
Trial Balance		
December 31, 19XI		
Cash	$ 198,000	
Accounts receivable	370,000	
Supplies	6,000	
Furniture and fixtures	100,000	
Accumulated depreciation—furniture and fixtures		$ 40,000
Building	250,000	
Accumulated depreciation—building		130,000
Accounts payable		380,000
Salary payable		
Unearned service revenue		45,000
Capital		293,000
Withdrawals	65,000	
Service revenues		286,000
Salary expense	172,000	
Supplies expense		
Depreciation expense—furniture and fixtures		
Depreciation expense—building		
Miscellaneous expense	13,000	
Total	$1,174,000	$1,174,000

Data needed for the adjusting entries include:

a. Supplies on hand at year end, $2,000.
b. Depreciation on furniture and fixtures, $20,000.
c. Depreciation on building, $10,000.
d. Salaries owed but not yet paid, $5,000.
e. Accrued service revenue, $12,000.
f. Of the $45,000 balance of Unearned Service Revenue, $32,000 was earned during 19Xl.

Required

Prepare the work sheet of State Service Company for the year ended December 31, 19X1. Key each adjusting entry by the letter corresponding to the data given.

SOLUTION TO REVIEW PROBLEM

State Service Company
Work Sheet
For the Year Ended December 31, 19X1

Account Title	Trial Balance Debit	Trial Balance Credit	Adjustments Debit	Adjustments Credit	Adjusted Trial Balance Debit	Adjusted Trial Balance Credit	Income Statement Debit	Income Statement Credit	Balance Sheet Debit	Balance Sheet Credit
Cash	198,000				198,000				198,000	
Accounts receivable	370,000		(e) 12,000		382,000				382,000	
Supplies	6,000			(a) 4,000	2,000				2,000	
Furniture and fixtures	100,000				100,000				100,000	
Accumulated depreciation— furniture and fixtures		40,000		(b) 20,000		60,000				60,000
Building	250,000				250,000				250,000	
Accumulated depreciation— building		130,000		(c) 10,000		140,000				140,000
Accounts payable		380,000				380,000				380,000
Salary payable				(d) 5,000		5,000				5,000
Unearned service revenue		45,000	(f) 32,000			13,000				13,000
Capital		293,000				293,000				293,000
Withdrawals	65,000				65,000				65,000	
Service revenue		286,000		(e) 12,000 (f) 32,000		330,000		330,000		
Salary expense	172,000		(d) 5,000		177,000		177,000			
Supplies expense			(a) 4,000		4,000		4,000			
Depreciation expense— furniture and fixtures			(b) 20,000		20,000		20,000			
Depreciation expense— building			(c) 10,000		10,000		10,000			
Miscellaneous expense	13,000				13,000		13,000			
	1,174,000	1,174,000	83,000	83,000	1,221,000	1,221,000	224,000	330,000	997,000	891,000
Net Income							106,000			106,000
							330,000	330,000	997,000	997,000

Using the Work Sheet

As illustrated thus far, the work sheet helps to organize accounting data and to compute the net income or net loss for the period. It also aids in preparing the financial statements, recording the adjusting entries, and closing the accounts.

Preparing the Financial Statements

Even though the work sheet shows the amount of net income or net loss for the period, it is still necessary to prepare the financial statements. The sorting of accounts to the balance sheet and the income statement eases the preparation of the statements. The work sheet also provides the data for the statement of owner's equity. Exhibit 4-7 presents the April financial statements for the accounting practice of Gary Lyon, CPA (based on data from the work sheet in Exhibit 4-6).

The financial statements can be prepared directly from the adjusted trial balance as shown in Chapter 3. That is why completion of the work sheet is optional.

Recording the Adjusting Entries

The adjusting entries are a key element of accrual-basis accounting. The work sheet helps identify the accounts that need adjustments, which may be conveniently entered directly on the work sheet as shown in Exhibits 4-2 through 4-6. However, these work sheet procedures do not adjust the accounts in the ledger itself. Recall that the work sheet is neither a journal nor a ledger. Actual adjustment of the accounts requires journal entries that are posted to the ledger accounts. Therefore, the adjusting entries must be recorded in the journal as shown in Panel A of Exhibit 4-8. Panel B of the exhibit shows the postings to the accounts, with "Adj." denoting an amount posted from an adjusting entry. Only the revenue and expense accounts are presented here in order to focus on the closing process, which is discussed in the next section.

The adjusting entries could have been recorded in the journal when they were entered on the work sheet. However, it is not necessary to journalize them at that time. Most accountants prepare the financial statements immediately after completing the work sheet. They can wait to journalize and post the adjusting entries just before they make the closing entries.

Delaying the journalizing and posting of the adjusting entries illustrates another use of the work sheet. Many companies journalize and post the adjusting entries—as in Exhibit 4-8—only once annually, at the end of the year. The need for monthly and quarterly financial statements, however, requires a tool like the work sheet. The entity can use the work sheet to aid in preparing interim statements without entering the adjusting entries in the journal and posting them to the ledger.

Closing the Accounts

Accountants use the term **closing the accounts** to refer to the step at the end of the period that prepares the accounts for recording the transactions of the next period. Closing the accounts consists of journalizing and posting the closing

Discussion Question: To review, where are each of these accounts extended? The possible answers are: Income Statement, debit column; Income Statement, credit column; Balance Sheet, debit column; or Balance Sheet, credit column:

1 Cash *ANSWER:* Balance Sheet, debit
2 Supplies *ANSWER:* Balance Sheet, debit
3 Supplies Expense *ANSWER:* Income Statement, debit
4 Unearned Revenue *ANSWER:* Balance Sheet, credit
5 Service Revenue *ANSWER:* Income Statement, credit
6 Capital *ANSWER:* Balance Sheet, credit
7 Withdrawals *ANSWER:* Balance Sheet, debit*
8 Accumulated Depreciation *ANSWER:* Balance Sheet, credit
9 Depreciation Expense *ANSWER:* Income Statement, debit
10 Salary Payable *ANSWER:* Balance Sheet, credit

*Repeat that Withdrawals is not an expense and does not belong in the Income Statement column as a debit. Students must remember that Withdrawals is a reduction in the owner's capital.

Discussion Question: Why are the revenue and expense account balances reset to zero at the end of the year? *ANSWER:* So that the information accumulated in those accounts relates only to the current accounting period. Information for the current period is still relevant and must be available. Information relating to past periods has already been used, either on financial statements or tax returns, and therefore is not needed.

EXHIBIT 4-7 *April Financial Statements of Gary Lyon, CPA*

Transparency T4-2

Gary Lyon, CPA
Income Statement
For the Month Ended April 30, 19X1

Revenues:		
Service revenue		$7,400
Expenses:		
Salary expense	$1,900	
Rent expense	1,000	
Utilities expense	400	
Supplies expense..................	300	
Depreciation expense	275	
Total expenses		3,875
Net income		$3,525

Gary Lyon, CPA
Statement of Owner's Equity
For the Month Ended April 30, 19X1

Gary Lyon, capital, April 1, 19X1	$31,250
Add: Net income	3,525
	34,775
Less: Withdrawals....................................	3,200
Gary Lyon, capital, April 30, 19X1	$31,575

Discussion Question: Refer to Exhibit 4-7. What is the balance in Capital after the financial statements have been prepared? ANSWER: $31,250. Students may want to say $31,575 because that amount appears on the financial statements. However, closing entries have not yet been posted to the ledger. Therefore, the balance in Capital is still the beginning balance.

Discussion Question: Refer to Exhibit 4-6. Why doesn't the total of the debit column of the Balance Sheet equal total assets on Gary Lyon's Balance Sheet here in Exhibit 4-7? ANSWER: First, included in the debit column is Withdrawals, which is not an asset but which does have a debit balance. Withdrawals is not reported individually on the balance sheet, but will be on the statement of owner's equity. Second, included on the balance sheet as a deduction in the asset section is Accumulated Depreciation, a contra asset account. It appears in the credit column on the work sheet.

Gary Lyon, CPA
Balance Sheet
April 30, 19X1

Assets			Liabilities		
Cash		$24,800	Accounts payable ..		$13,100
Accounts receivable		2,500	Salary payable		950
Supplies		400	Unearned service		
Prepaid rent		2,000	revenue		300
Furniture	$16,500		Total liabilities		14,350
Less Accumulated					
depreciation ...	275	16,225	**Owner's Equity**		
			Gary Lyon, capital .		31,575
			Total liabilities and		
Total assets		$45,925	owner's equity ...		$45,925

entries. Closing sets the balances of the revenue and expense accounts back to zero in order to measure the net income of the next period. Closing is a clerical procedure devoid of any new accounting theory. Recall that the income statement reports only one period's income. For example, net income for McDonald's, Inc., for 1993 relates exclusively to 1993. At December 31, 1993, McDonald's accountants close the company's revenue and expense accounts for that year. Because these accounts' balances relate to a particular accounting period and are therefore closed at the end of the period, the revenue and expense

EXHIBIT 4-8 *Journalizing and Posting the Adjusting Entries*

Panel A—Journalizing: **Page 4**

Adjusting Entries

Apr. 30	Accounts Receivable	250	
	Service Revenue		250
30	Supplies Expense	300	
	Supplies		300
30	Rent Expense	1,000	
	Prepaid Rent		1,000
30	Depreciation Expense	275	
	Accumulated Depreciation		275
30	Salary Expense	950	
	Salary Payable		950
30	Unearned Service Revenue	150	
	Service Revenue		150

Panel B—Posting the Adjustments to the Revenue and Expense Accounts:

    Revenue   **Expenses**

Service Revenue

	7,000
Adj.	250
Adj.	150
Bal.	**7,400**

Rent Expense

Adj. 1,000	
Bal. 1,000	

Salary Expense

950	
Adj. 950	
Bal. 1,900	

Depreciation Expense

Adj. 275	
Bal. 275	

Utilities Expense

400	
Bal. 400	

Supplies Expense

Adj. 300	
Bal. 300	

Adj. = Amount posted from an adjusting entry
Bal. = Balance

accounts are called **temporary (nominal) accounts.** The owner's withdrawal account—although not a revenue or an expense—is also a temporary account because it is important to measure withdrawals for a specific period. The closing process applies only to temporary accounts.

To understand better the closing process, contrast the nature of the temporary accounts with the nature of the **permanent (real) accounts**—the assets, liabilities, and capital. The permanent accounts are *not* closed at the end of the period because their balances are not used to measure income. Consider Cash, Accounts Receivable, Supplies, Buildings, Accounts Payable, Notes Payable, and Gary Lyon, Capital. These accounts do not represent increases and decreases for a single period as do the revenues and expenses, which relate exclusively to only one accounting period. Instead, the permanent accounts represent assets, liabilities, and capital that are on hand at a specific time. This is why their balances at the end of one accounting period carry over to become the beginning balances of the next period. For example, the Cash balance at December 31, 19Xl, is also the beginning balance for 19X2.

Briefly, **closing entries** transfer the revenue, expense, and owner withdrawal balances from their respective accounts to the capital account. As you know, revenues increase owner's equity, and expenses and owner withdrawals decrease it. It is when we post the closing entries that the capital account absorbs the impact of the balances in the temporary accounts. As an intermediate step, however, the revenues and the expenses are transferred first to an account entitled **Income Summary,** which collects in one place the total debit for the sum of all expenses and the total credit for the sum of all revenues of the period. The Income Summary account is like a temporary "holding tank" that is used only in the closing process. Then the balance of Income Summary is transferred to capital. The steps in closing the accounts of a proprietorship like Gary Lyon, CPA, are as follows:

1. Debit each revenue account for the amount of its credit balance. Credit Income Summary for the sum of the revenues. This entry transfers the sum of the revenues to the credit side of Income Summary.

2. Credit each expense account for the amount of its debit balance. Debit Income Summary for the sum of the expenses. This entry transfers the sum of the expenses to the debit side of Income Summary.

3. Debit Income Summary for the amount of its credit balance (revenues minus expenses) and credit the Capital account. If Income Summary has a debit balance, then credit Income Summary for this amount, and debit Capital. This entry transfers the net income or loss from Income Summary to the Capital account.

EXHIBIT 4-9 *Journalizing and Posting the Closing Entries*

Panel A-Journalizing:

		Closing Entries		Page 5
1.	Apr. 30	Service Revenue	7,400	
		Income Summary		7,400
2.	30	Income Summary	3,875	
		Rent Expense		1,000
		Salary Expense		1,900
		Supplies Expense		300
		Depreciation Expense		275
		Utilities Expense		400
3.	30	Income Summary ($7,400–$3,875)	3,525	
		Gary Lyon, Capital		3,525
4.	30	Gary Lyon, Capital	3,200	
		Gary Lyon, Withdrawals		3,200

Exhibit 4-9 continues on the following page.

Panel B—Posting:

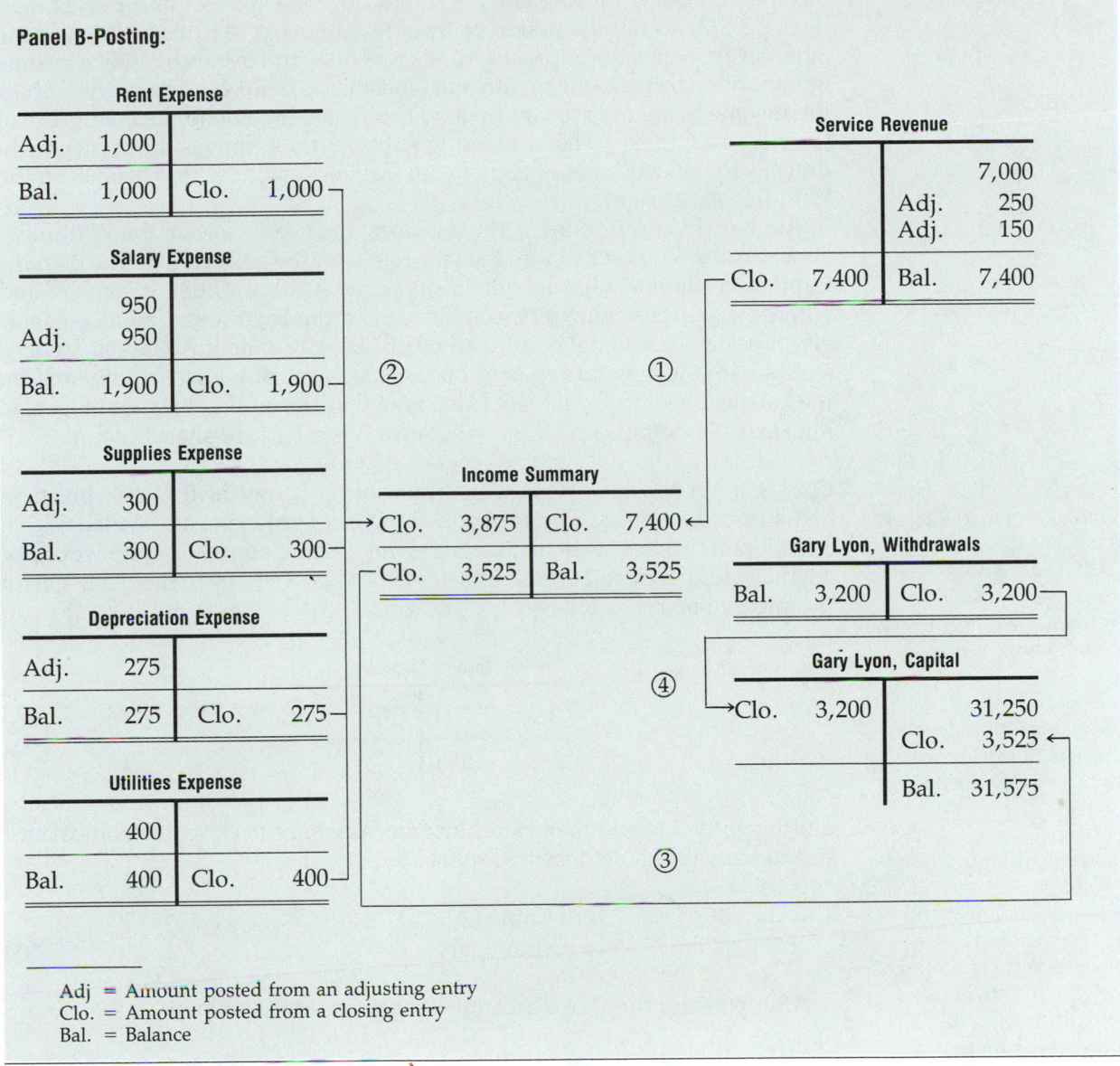

Adj = Amount posted from an adjusting entry
Clo. = Amount posted from a closing entry
Bal. = Balance

4. Credit the Withdrawals account for the amount of its debit balance. Debit the Capital account of the proprietor. Withdrawals are not expenses and do not affect net income or net loss. Therefore, this account is *not* closed to the Income Summary. This entry transfers the withdrawal amount to the debit side of the Capital account.

To illustrate, suppose Gary Lyon closes the books at the end of April. Exhibit 4-9 presents the complete closing process for Lyon's business. Panel A gives the closing journal entries, and Panel B shows the accounts after the closing entries have been posted.

The amount in the debit side of each expense account is its adjusted balance. For example, Rent Expense has a $1,000 debit balance. Also note that Service Revenue has a credit balance of $7,400 before closing. These amounts come directly from the adjusted balances in Exhibit 4-8, Panel B.

Closing entry 1, denoted in the Service Revenue account by *Clo.*, transfers Service Revenue's balance to the Income Summary account. This entry zeroes out Service Revenue for April and places the revenue on the credit side of

Income Summary. Closing entry 2 zeroes out the expenses and moves their total ($3,875) to the debit side of Income Summary. At this point, Income Summary contains the impact of April's revenues and expenses; hence Income Summary's balance is the month's net income ($3,525). Closing entry 3 closes the Income Summary account by transferring net income to the credit side of Gary Lyon, Capital.[1] The last closing entry (entry 4) moves the owner withdrawals to the debit side of Gary Lyon, Capital, leaving a zero balance in the Withdrawals account.

After all the closing entries, the revenues, the expenses, and the Withdrawals account are set back to zero to make ready for the next period. The owner's Capital account includes the full effects of the April revenues, expenses, and withdrawals. These amounts, combined with the beginning Capital balance, give Capital an ending balance of $31,575. Note that this Capital balance agrees with the amount reported on the statement of owner's equity and on the balance sheet in Exhibit 4-7. Also note that the ending balance of Capital remains. We do not close it out—because it is a balance sheet account.

Discussion Question: Would the Income Summary have a debit or a credit balance if the company suffers a net loss? ANSWER: Expenses would exceed revenues, and Income Summary would have a debit balance.

In the event of a loss, how is Income Summary closed? ANSWER: Income Summary is credited and Capital is debited.

Closing a Net Loss. What would the closing entries be if Lyon's business had suffered a net *loss* during April? Suppose April expenses totaled $7,700 and all other factors were unchanged. Only closing entries 2 and 3 would be altered. Closing entry 2 would transfer expenses of $7,700 to the debit side of Income Summary, as follows:

Income Summary			
Clo.	7,700	Clo.	7,400
Bal.	300		

Closing entry 3 would then credit Income Summary to close its debit balance and to transfer the net loss to Capital:

3. Apr. 30   Gary Lyon, Capital 300
                  Income Summary 300

After posting, these two accounts would appear as follows:

Teaching Tip: The double line in each of the revenue and expense, income summary, and withdrawals T-accounts means that the account has a zero balance and nothing more will be posted to it in the current period. The double line is drawn immediately after the closing entry is posted. In the general ledger, the account would show a zero balance.

Income Summary					Gary Lyon, Capital		
Clo.	7,700	Clo.	7,400	→ Clo.	300		31,250
Bal.	300	Clo.	300				

Finally, the Withdrawals balance would be closed to Capital, as before.

Postclosing Trial Balance

The accounting cycle ends with the **postclosing trial balance** (see Exhibit 4-10). The postclosing trial balance is the final check on the accuracy of journalizing

Point to Stress: Only real accounts should appear on the postclosing trial balance. Remind students that the postclosing trial balance is prepared from the ledger (rather than from the work sheet) because the purpose of the postclosing trial balance is to verify that all adjusting and closing entries have been correctly posted.

---

[1]The Income Summary account is a convenience for combining the effects of the revenues and expenses prior to transferring their income effect to Capital. It is not necessary to use the Income Summary account in the closing process. Another way of closing the revenues and expenses makes no use of this account. In this alternative procedure, the revenues and expenses are closed directly to Capital.

EXHIBIT 4-10 *Postclosing Trial Balance*

Gary Lyon, CPA
Postclosing Trial Balance
April 30, 19X1

Cash	$24,800	
Accounts receivable	2,500	
Supplies	400	
Prepaid rent	2,000	
Furniture	16,500	
Accumulated depreciation		$ 275
Accounts payable		13,100
Salary payable		950
Unearned service revenue		300
Gary Lyon, capital		31,575
Total	$46,200	$46,200

Discussion Questions: (1) What is the difference between a permanent account and a temporary account? ANSWER: Permanent accounts (assets, liabilities and capital) are never closed. Their balances carry over from period to period. Temporary accounts must be closed each period so that revenue and expenses are accumulated for one period only, then closed to Capital. (2) What one account that appears on the Balance Sheet column of the work sheet must be closed because it is a temporary account? ANSWER: Withdrawals

and posting the adjusting and closing entries. Like the trial balance that begins the work sheet, the postclosing trial balance is a list of the ledger's accounts and balances. This step ensures that the ledger is in balance for the start of the next accounting period. The postclosing trial balance is dated as of the end of the accounting period for which the statements have been prepared.

Note that the postclosing trial balance resembles the balance sheet. It contains the ending balances of the permanent accounts—the balance sheet accounts: the assets, liabilities, and capital. No temporary accounts—revenues, expenses, or withdrawal accounts—are included because their balances have been closed. The ledger is up-to-date and ready for the next period's transactions.

Discussion Question: (1) Name three types of accounts that will appear on the postclosing trial balance. ANSWER: assets, liabilities, owner's equity (2) Name four account types that must never appear on a postclosing trial balance. ANSWER: all revenues, all expenses, withdrawals and income summary

Reversing Entries

Reversing entries are special types of entries that ease the burden of accounting after adjusting and closing entries have been made at the end of a period. Reversing entries are used most often in conjunction with accrual-type adjustments such as accrued salary expense and accrued service revenue. GAAP does not require reversing entries. They are used only for convenience and to save time.

OBJECTIVE 5
Use reversing entries to save time

Reversing Entries for Accrued Expense. Accrued expenses accumulate with the passage of time and are paid at a later date. At the end of the period the business makes an adjusting entry to record the expense that has accumulated up to that time.

To see how reversing entries work, return to the adjusting entries (Exhibit 4-8) that Gary Lyon used to update his accounting records for the April financial statements. At April 30—prior to the adjusting entries—Salary Expense has a debit balance of $950 from salaries paid during April. At April 30 the business owes employees an additional $950 for their service during the last part of the month. Assume for the purpose of this illustration that on May 5, the next payroll date, Lyon will pay the $950 of accrued salaries plus $100 in salaries that employees have earned in the first few days of May. The next payroll payment will be $1,050 ($950 + $100). However, to present the correct financial picture, the $950 in salaries incurred in April must be included in the April statements, not in the May statements. Accordingly, Lyon makes the following adjusting entry on April 30:

Adjusting Entries

Apr. 30   Salary Expense   950
                 Salary Payable   950

After posting, the Salary Payable and Salary Expense accounts appear as follows:

Salary Payable

	Apr. 30 Adj.* 950
	Apr. 30 Bal. 950

Salary Expense

Paid during	
April CP 950	
Apr. 30 Adj. 950	
Apr. 30 Bal. 1,900	

After the adjusting entry, the April income statement reports salary expense of $1,900, and the balance sheet at April 30 reports Salary Payable, a liability, of $950. The $1,900 debit balance of Salary Expense is eliminated by a closing entry at December 31, 19X1, as follows:

Closing Entries

April 30   Income Summary   1,900
                 Salary Expense   1,900

After posting, Salary Expense appears as follows:

Salary Expense

Paid during	
April CP 950	
Apr. 30 Adj. 950	
Apr. 30 Bal. 1,900	Apr. 30 Clo. 1,900

---

*Entry explanations used throughout this discussion are
Adj. = Adjusting entry   CP   = Cash payment entry
Bal. = Balance   CR   = Cash receipt entry
Clo. = Closing entry   Rev. = Reversing entry

In the normal course of recording salary payments during the year, Gary Lyon makes the standard entry, as follows:

       Salary Expense XXX
            Cash   XXX

Class Exercise: Suppose a company pays its employees $1,500 every Friday, the end of a 5-day work week. What journal entry is made each Friday?

Salary Expense .   1,500
   Cash   1,500

Suppose now that December 31 falls on a Tuesday. What would be the adjusting entry?

Salary Expense . . .   600
   Salary Payable .   600

What would be the reversing entry on January 1?

Salary Payable . .   600
   Salary Expense   600

What would be the entry to record the payroll on the next Friday?

Salary Expense .   1,500
   Cash   1,500

In our example, however, payday does not land on the day the accounting period ends, and Lyon has made an adjusting entry to accrue salary payable of $950, as we have just seen. On May 5, the next payday, assume the total payroll is $1,050. Lyon credits Cash for $1,050, but what account—or accounts—should he debit? The cash payment entry is

May 5	Salary Payable	950	
	Salary Expense	100	
	Cash		1,050

This method of recording the cash payment is correct but inefficient because Lyon must refer back to the adjusting entries of April 30. Otherwise, he does not know the amount of the required debit to Salary Payable (in this example, $950). Searching the preceding period's adjusting entries takes time, and in business, time is money. To avoid having to separate the debit of a later cash payment entry into two accounts, accountants have devised a technique called reversing entries.

Making a Reversing Entry. A **reversing entry** switches the debit and the credit of a previous adjusting entry. A reversing entry, then, is the exact opposite of an adjusting entry. The reversing entry is dated the first day of the period following the adjusting entry.

Let's continue with our example of the May 5 cash payment of $1,050 for salaries. On April 30, Lyon made the following adjusting entry to accrue Salary Payable:

Adjusting Entries

Apr. 30	Salary Expense	950	
	Salary Payable		950

The reversing entry simply reverses the position of the debit and the credit:

Reversing Entries

May 1	Salary Payable	950	
	Salary Expense		950

Notice that the reversing entry is dated the first day of the new period. It is the exact opposite of the April 30 adjusting entry. Ordinarily, the accountant who makes the adjusting entry also prepares the reversing entry at the same time. Lyon postdates the reversing entry to the first day of the next period, however, so that it affects only the new period. Note how the accounts appear after Lyon posts the reversing entry:

Salary Payable

May 1	Rev.	950	Apr. 30	Bal.	950

Zero balance

Salary Expense

Apr. 30	Bal.	1,900	Apr. 30	Clo.	1,900

Zero balance

			May 1	**Rev.**	**950**

Discussion Question: Refer to the Class Exercise above. What are some of the advantages of using reversing entries?

ANSWER: During the year, the bookkeeper made 51 identical weekly entries for salaries. The bookkeeper does not usually make the adjusting entries and so might not be aware of the adjusting entry. Without the reversing entry, the bookkeeper would be expected to know that the adjusting entry had been made by the accountant, be aware of the amount involved in that adjusting entry, and then record the last payment in a way that is different than the way it was recorded 51 other times. The chances of errors are greatly increased, which increases the likelihood that the financial statements might be in error.

The arrow shows the transfer of the $950 credit balance from Salary Payable to Salary Expense. This credit balance in Salary Expense does not mean that the entity has negative salary expense, as might be suggested by a credit balance in an expense account. Instead, the odd credit balance is merely a temporary result of the reversing entry. The credit balance is eliminated on May 5, when the $1,050 cash payment for salaries is debited to Salary Expense in the customary manner:

May 5 Salary Expense   1,050
     Cash   1,050

Then this cash payment entry is posted:

Salary Expense

May 5	CP	1,050	May 1	Rev.	950
May 5	Bal.	100			

Now Salary Expense has its correct debit balance of $100, which is the amount of salary expense incurred thus far in May. The $1,050 cash disbursement also pays the liability for Salary Payable. Thus the Salary Payable account has a zero balance, which is correct, as shown on the previous page.

The adjusting and reversing process is repeated period after period. Cash payments for salaries are debited to Salary Expense, and these amounts accumulate in that account. At the end of the period, the accountant makes an adjusting entry to accrue salary expense incurred but not yet paid. At the same time, the accountant also makes a reversing entry, which allows her to record all payroll entries in the customary manner—by routinely debiting Salary Expense. Even in computerized systems, making reversing entries is more efficient than writing a program to locate the amount accrued from the preceding period and making the more complicated journal entry. Reversing entries may be made for all types of accrued expenses.

Reversing Entries for Accrued Revenues. Certain revenues, such as services performed on a continuous basis and interest earned on notes receivable, accrue with the passage of time, just as expenses do. However, a business usually does not record accrued revenues daily, weekly, or even monthly. Thus at the end of the accounting period, the business may have to accrue revenue that will be collected later. Then, when cash is received, a second entry is needed.

To illustrate reversing entries for accrued revenue, recall that Gary Lyon performs services for clients on a monthly basis. At April 30, Lyon has earned $250 of service revenue that he will collect on May 15, along with an additional $250 for services performed in the first half of May. On April 30, Lyon made this adjusting entry:

Adjusting Entries

Apr. 30 Accounts Receivable   250
      Service Revenue   250

At the same time, Lyon can make the following reversing entry, postdated to May 1:

Reversing Entries

May 1	Service Revenue.........................	250	
	Accounts Receivable		250

The net effect of the reversing entry is that Lyon need not refer back to the April 30 adjusting entry when recording the May cash transaction. On May 15, when he receives $500 from the client, Lyon can record the cash receipt as follows:

May 15	Cash	500	
	Service Revenue		500

After this entry is posted, the accounts have their correct balances.

The appendix at the end of this chapter discusses the use of reversing entries for prepaid expenses and unearned revenues.

Classification of Assets and Liabilities

On the balance sheet, assets and liabilities are classified as either *current* or *long-term* to indicate their relative *liquidity*. **Liquidity** is a measure of how quickly an item may be converted to cash. Therefore, cash is the most liquid asset. Accounts receivable is a relatively liquid asset because the business expects to collect the amount in cash in the near future. Supplies are less liquid than accounts receivable, and furniture and buildings are even less so.

Users of financial statements are interested in liquidity because business difficulties often arise owing to a shortage of cash. How quickly can the business convert an asset to cash and pay a debt? How soon must a liability be paid? These are questions of liquidity. Balance sheets list assets and liabilities in the order of their relative liquidity.

Current Assets. **Current assets** are assets that are expected to be converted to cash, sold, or consumed during the next 12 months or within the business's normal operating cycle if longer than a year. The **operating cycle** is the time span during which (1) cash is used to acquire goods and services, and (2) these goods and services are sold to customers, who in turn pay for their purchases with cash. For most businesses, the operating cycle is a few months. A few types of business have operating cycles longer than a year. Cash, Accounts Receivable, Notes Receivable due within a year or less, and Prepaid Expenses are current assets. Merchandising entities such as Sears, Penney's and K Mart have an additional current asset, Inventory. This account shows the cost of goods that are held for sale to customers.

Long-Term Assets. **Long-term assets** are all assets other than current assets. They are not held for sale, but rather they are used to operate the business. One category of long-term assets is plant assets, or fixed assets. Land, Buildings, Furniture and Fixtures, and Equipment are examples of plant assets.

Financial statement users such as creditors are interested in the due dates of an entity's liabilities. The sooner a liability must be paid, the more current it is. Liabilities that must be paid on the earliest future date create the greatest strain

OBJECTIVE 6
Classify assets and liabilities as current or long-term

Real-World Example: Creditors of a business, such as bankers, are particularly interested in the liquidity of the firm's assets. A banker will not look favorably upon lending money to a business that does not have adequate liquid assets (cash and receivables) to meet both principal and interest payments as they come due.

Point to Stress: There are five categories of current assets. In order of their liquidity, they are: Cash, Short-term Investments, Receivables, Inventory, and Prepaid Expenses.

on cash. Therefore, the balance sheet lists liabilities in the order in which they are due. Knowing how many of a business's liabilities are current and how many are long-term helps creditors assess the likelihood of collecting from the entity. Balance sheets usually have at least two liability classifications, *current liabilities* and *long-term liabilities*.

Current Liabilities. **Current liabilities** are debts that are due to be paid within one year or within the entity's operating cycle if the cycle is longer than a year. Accounts Payable, Notes Payable due within one year, Salary Payable, Unearned Revenue, and Interest Payable owed on notes payable are current liabilities.

Discussion Question: Which of the five categories of current assets is the least liquid? Why? ANSWER: Prepaid Expenses, because although they will be used within one year, it is not anticipated that they will be converted to cash.

Long-Term Liabilities. All liabilities that are not current are classified as **long-term liabilities.** Many notes payable are long-term. Other notes payable are paid in installments, with the first installment due within one year, the second installment due the second year, and so on. In this case, the first installment would be a current liability and the remainder a long-term liability.

An Actual Classified Balance Sheet

Exhibit 4-11 is a classified balance sheet of Hawaiian Airlines, Inc. Hawaiian Airlines labels its plant assets Property and Equipment. (Another common title is Property, Plant, and Equipment.) It is also common to report the *book value,* or *net* amount, of property and equipment ($121,532,000), along with the amount of accumulated depreciation ($32,398,000). The original cost of the assets included in the property and equipment category is the sum of the two amounts, $153,930,000 ($121,532,000 + $32,398,000).

As you study the balance sheet, you will be delighted at how much of it you already understand. So far, you have been exposed to every type of asset and liability reported by this actual company. Other Assets and Other Liabilities are catchall categories for items that are difficult to classify. Stockholders' equity is the owners' equity of a corporation.

For your understanding, we have added bracketed explanations for several accounts. The bracketed items do not appear on the actual balance sheet.

Formats of Balance Sheets

The balance sheet of Hawaiian Airlines shown in Exhibit 4-11 lists the assets at the top, with the liabilities and the owners' equity below. This is the **report format.** The balance sheet of Gary Lyon, CPA, presented in Exhibit 4-7 lists the assets at the left, with the liabilities and the owner's equity at the right. That is the **account format.**

Teaching Tip: Students can find this survey in Accounting Trends and Techniques (AICPA, 1991, p. 109).

Either format is acceptable. A recent survey of 600 companies indicated that 56 percent use the account format and that 44 percent use the report format.

Use of Accounting Information in Decision Making

The purpose of accounting is to provide information for decision making. Chief users of accounting information include managers, investors, and cred-

EXHIBIT 4-11 *Classified Balance Sheet*

Hawaiian Airlines, Inc. Balance Sheet March 31, 19XX	
Assets	(dollar amounts in thousands)
Current assets:	
Cash	$ 25,116
Accounts receivable	10,061
Inventories	2,307
Prepaid expenses and other current assets (such as	
supplies)	2,864
Total current assets.........................	40,348
Property and equipment	
Less Accumulated depreciation of $32,398	121,532
Other assets	5,285
Total	$167,165
Liabilities	
Current liabilities:	
Current portion of long-term debt	$ 6,258
Notes payable	3,103
Accounts payable	12,243
Accrued liabilities (such as salary and wage	
payable, interest payable)	19,192
Other current liabilities (such as unearned	
revenue, current)	1,696
Total current liabilities	42,492
Long-term debt (such as notes payable, long-term)	111,156
Other liabilities and deferred credits (such as	
unearned revenues, long-term)	4,622
Owners' Equity	
Stockholders' equity (Capital for a proprietorship)......	8,895
Total	$167,165

Teaching Tip: Remember that when we studied plant assets and accumulated depreciation in Chapter 3, you learned that:

Cost
− Accumulated depreciation
Book value

Therefore, if you know book value and accumulated depreciation, you merely add the two numbers to get original cost of the assets.

itors. A creditor considering lending money must predict whether the borrower can repay the loan. If the borrower already has lots of debt, the probability of repayment is lower than if the borrower has a small amount of liabilities. To assess financial position, decision makers use ratios on various items drawn from a company's financial statements.

One of the most common financial ratios is the **current ratio**, which is the ratio of an entity's current assets to its current liabilities. The current ratio measures the ability to pay current liabilities with current assets. It is computed as follows:

$$\text{Current ratio} = \frac{\text{Total current assets}}{\text{Total current liabilities}}$$

A company prefers a high current ratio, which means that the business has plenty of current assets to pay current liabilities. An increasing current ratio from period to period indicates improvement in financial position.

Discussion Question: Why does a company need a current ratio of more than 1? ANSWER: The answer is twofold. (1) Some companies don't need a larger current ratio. It is typical in some industries, such as the oil industry, to have a current ratio of about 1. Different industries have different liquidity requirements. (2) Included in the current assets are assets that are not considered very liquid, such as inventory and prepaids. If these assets are excluded, then the ratio of 1 of the remaining current assets to current liabilities may be considered safe.

Real-World Example: According to Robert Morris and Associates, the median current ratio among manufacturers of electronic computers is 1.9. The current ratio for those companies in the top 25% of electronic manufacturers is 3.2.

Real-World Example: The debt ratio of General Dynamics is 68%. The debt ratio of another aerospace/defense contractor, Boeing, is 52%.

Real-World Example: A high debt ratio can also mean that a company does not have financial flexibility. 7-Eleven, the convenience store company, filed for bankruptcy because of its inability to make its debt payments. Companies often borrow large amounts of money in good times, but become unable to make their debt payments in the event of a recession or a downturn in their business.

Point to Stress: A high current ratio may mean that a company has too much in current assets (such as uncollectible receivables or unsalable inventory) and is not managing assets as profitably as it could.

A rule of thumb: A strong current ratio is 2.00, which indicates that the company has $2.00 in current assets for every $1.00 in current liabilities. A company with a current ratio of 2.00 would probably have little trouble paying its current liabilities. Most successful businesses operate with current ratios in the range between 1.50 and 2.00.

Hawaiian Airlines, the company in Exhibit 4-11, has a current ratio of .950 (.950 = $40,348/$42,492). What does this ratio value indicate about Hawaiian Airlines? A current ratio of 1.00 is considered quite low, so a value of .95 is dangerously low. Hawaiian Airlines has insufficient current assets to pay all its current liabilities—a risky position.

How would a decision maker use the current ratio? A low current ratio would worry top managers of the company because it indicates difficulty in paying debts. As a matter of fact, Hawaiian Airlines has experienced financial trouble in recent years, as signalled by its low current ratio. Suppose the company needs to borrow money. If the bank agreed to loan money to Hawaiian Airlines—which it might not—the bank would place some restrictions on Hawaiian Airlines because of the company's risky financial position. For example, the lender might charge a high rate of interest and prohibit withdrawals by the owners of the company. A decision maker considering investing in Hawaiian Airlines would recognize the company's risky position and might prefer to invest in another company instead. Lenders and investors would view a company with a current ratio of 2.00 as substantially less risky. Such a company would probably borrow money on better terms and also attract more investors.

A second aid to decision making is the **debt ratio**, which is the ratio of total liabilities to total assets. The debt ratio indicates the proportion of a company's assets that are financed with debt. This ratio measures a business's ability to pay both current and long-term debts—total liabilities. It is computed as follows:

$$\text{Debt ratio} = \frac{\text{Total liabilities}}{\text{Total assets}}$$

A low debt ratio is safer than a high debt ratio. Why? Because a company with a small amount of liabilities has low required payments. Such a company is unlikely to get into financial difficulty. By contrast, a business with a high debt ratio may have trouble paying its liabilities, especially when sales are low and cash is scarce. When a company fails to pay its debts, the creditors can take the business away from its owner.

Hawaiian Airlines (Exhibit 4-11) has a debt ratio of .947 [.947 = ($42,492 + $111,156 + $4,622)/$167,165]. A debt ratio of .947 is extremely high in comparison to the norm of around .50. Lenders would place severe restrictions on a borrower with liabilities of this magnitude. Many people would be reluctant to invest in the company, and the managers of Hawaiian Airlines would feel pressure to reduce the company's debt.

In general, a high current ratio is preferred over a low current ratio. Increases in the current ratio indicate improving financial position. By contrast, a low debt ratio is preferred over a high debt ratio. Improvement is indicated by a decrease in the debt ratio.

Financial ratios are an important aid to decisions. However, it is unwise to place too much confidence in a single ratio or any group of ratios. For example, a company may have a high current ratio, which indicates financial strength. It may also have a high debt ratio, which suggests weakness. Which ratio gives the more reliable signal about the company? Experienced managers, lenders, and investors evaluate a company by examining a large number of ratios over several years to spot trends and turning points. These people also consider other facts, such the company's cash position and its trend in net income. No single ratio gives the whole picture about a company.

As you progress through the study of accounting, we will introduce key ratios used for decision making. Chapter 19, Using Accounting Information to Make Business Decisions, summarizes all the ratios discussed throughout this book. This chapter provides a good overview of ratios used in decision making.

Detecting and Correcting Accounting Errors _____

You have now learned all the steps that an accountant takes from opening the books and recording a transaction in the journal through closing the books and the postclosing trial balance. Along the way, errors may occur. Accounting errors include incorrect journal entries, mistakes in posting, and transpositions and slides. This section discusses their detection and correction.

Incorrect Journal Entries.   When a journal entry contains an error, the entry can be erased and corrected—if the error is caught immediately. Other accountants prefer to draw a line through the incorrect entry to maintain a record of all entries to the journal. After the incorrect entry is crossed out, the accountant can make the correct entry.

If the error is detected after posting, the accountant makes a *correcting entry*. Suppose Gary Lyon paid $5,000 cash for furniture and erroneously debited Supplies as follows:

OBJECTIVE 7
Correct typical accounting errors

Incorrect Entry

May 13	Supplies	5,000	
	Cash		5,000
	Bought supplies.		

The debit to Supplies is incorrect, so it is necessary to make a correcting entry as follows:

Correcting Entry

May 15	Furniture	5,000	
	Supplies		5,000
	To correct May 13 entry.		

The credit to Supplies in the second entry offsets the incorrect debit of the first entry. The debit to Furniture in the correcting entry places the purchase amount in the correct account.

Incorrect posting.   Sometimes an accountant posts a debit as a credit or a credit as a debit. Such an error shows up in the trial balance—total debits do not equal total credits.

Suppose a $100 debit to Cash is posted as a $100 credit. The trial balance's total debits are $200 too low. Total credits are correct. The difference is $200. Whenever a debit or credit has been misplaced, the resulting difference is evenly divisible by 2, as is the $200 figure in our example. Dividing that difference by 2 yields the amount of the incorrect posting, which in this case we

Class Exercise: John Doe recorded the collection of a $1,000 receivable as a debit to Cash and a credit to Service Revenue for $1,000. Prepare the correcting entry.
ANSWER:

Service Revenue 1,000
　　Accounts　　　　　　1,000

　There is no entry to Cash because the original debit to Cash was recorded correctly. If John Doe's net income before the correction was $26,000, how much is the corrected net income? *ANSWER:* $25,000 ($26,000 − $1,000)

know is $100. The accountant may then search the journal for the $100 entry and make the corrections.

Transpositions and slides. A **transposition** occurs when digits are reversed—for example, $85 is a transposition of $58. Transpositions cause errors that are evenly divisible by 9. In this particular case, the transposition causes a $27 error ($85 − $58), which is evenly divisible by 9 ($27/9 = $3).

A **slide** results from adding one or more zeroes to a number or from dropping off a zero, for example, writing $500 as $5,000 or vice versa. The difference of $4,500 ($5,000 − $500) is evenly divisible by 9 ($4,500/9 = $500). Transpositions and slides occur in the transfer of numbers, for example, from the journal to the ledger or from the ledger to the trial balance.

Incorrect postings, transpositions, and slides can be corrected by crossing out the incorrect amount and then inserting the correct amount in its appropriate place.

Summary Problem for Your Review

Refer to the data in the earlier Summary Problem for Your Review, presented on pages 155–56.

Required

1. Journalize and post the adjusting entries. (Before posting to the accounts, enter their balances as shown in the trial balance. For example, enter the $370,000 balance in the Accounts Receivable account before posting its adjusting entry.) Key adjusting entries by *letter,* as shown in the work sheet solution to the first review problem. You can take the adjusting entries straight from the work sheet on page 156.

2. Journalize and post the closing entries. (Each account should carry its balance as shown in the adjusted trial balance.) To distinguish closing entries from adjusting entries, key the closing entries by *number.* Draw the arrows to illustrate the flow of data, as shown in Exhibit 4-9, page 161. Indicate the balance of the Capital account after the closing entries are posted.

3. Prepare the income statement for the year ended December 31, 19X1. List Miscellaneous Expense last among the expenses, a common practice.

4. Prepare the statement of owner's equity for the year ended December 31, 19Xl. Draw the arrow that links the income statement to the statement of owner's equity.

5. Prepare the classified balance sheet at December 31, 19X1. Use the report form. All liabilities are current. Draw the arrow that links the statement of owner's equity to the balance sheet.

Requirement 1

				Dr	Cr
a.	Dec. 31	Supplies Expense		4,000	
		Supplies			4,000
b.	31	Depreciation Expense—Furniture and Fixtures		20,000	
		Accumulated Depreciation—Furniture and Fixtures			20,000
c.	31	Depreciation Expense—Building		10,000	
		Accumulated Depreciation—Building			10,000
d.	31	Salary Expense		5,000	
		Salary Payable			5,000
e.	31	Accounts Receivable		12,000	
		Service Revenue			12,000
f.	31	Unearned Service Revenue		32,000	
		Service Revenue			32,000

Accounts Receivable

	370,000		
(e)	12,000		

Supplies

	6,000	(a)	4,000

Accumulated Depreciation—Furniture and Fixtures

			40,000
		(b)	20,000

Accumulated Depreciation—Building

			130,000
		(c)	10,000

Salary Payable

		(d)	5,000

Unearned Service Revenue

(f)	32,000		45,000

Service Revenue

			286,000
		(e)	12,000
		(f)	32,000
		Bal.	330,000

Salary Expense

	172,000		
(d)	5,000		
Bal.	177,000		

Supplies Expense

(a)	4,000		
Bal.	4,000		

Depreciation Expense—Furniture and Fixtures

(b)	20,000		
Bal.	20,000		

Depreciation Expense—Building

(c)	10,000		
Bal.	10,000		

Requirement 2

1.	Dec. 31	Service Revenue....................	330,000	
		Income Summary		330,000
2.	31	Income Summary....................	224,000	
		Salary Expense		177,000
		Supplies Expense		4,000
		Depreciation Expense— Furniture and Fixtures		20,000
		Depreciation Expense—Building .		10,000
		Miscellaneous Expense		13,000
3.	31	Income Summary ($330,000 − $224,000)	106,000	
		Capital		106,000
4.	31	Capital	65,000	
		Withdrawals		65,000

Salary Expense

	172,000		
(d)	5,000		
Bal.	177,000	(2)	177,000

Supplies Expense

(a)	4,000		
Bal.	4,000	(2)	4,000

**Depreciation Expense–
Furniture & Fixtures**

(b)	20,000		
Bal.	20,000	(2)	20,000

**Depreciation Expense–
Building**

(c)	10,000		
Bal.	10,000	(2)	10,000

Miscellaneous Expense

	13,000		
Bal.	13,000	(2)	13,000

Income Summary

(2)	224,000	(1)	330,000
(3)	106,000	Bal.	106,000

Service Revenue

			286,000
		(e)	12,000
		(f)	32,000
(1)	330,000	Bal.	330,000

Withdrawals

Bal.	65,000	(4)	65,000

Capital

(4)	65,000		293,000
		(3)	106,000
		Bal.	334,000

Requirement 3

State Service Company
Income Statement
For the Year Ended December 31, 19X1

Revenues:		
Service revenue		$330,000
Expenses:		
Salary expense	$177,000	
Depreciation expense–furniture and fixtures	20,000	
Depreciation expense–building	10,000	
Supplies expense	4,000	
Miscellaneous expense	13,000	
Total expenses		224,000
Net income		$106,000

Requirement 4

State Service Company
Statement of Owner's Equity
For the Year Ended December 31, 19X1

Capital, January 1, 19X1	$293,000
Add: Net income	106,000
	399,000
Less: Withdrawals	65,000
Capital, December 31, 19X1	$334,000

Requirement 5

State Service Company
Balance Sheet
December 31, 19X1

Assets

Current assets:		
Cash		$198,000
Accounts receivable		382,000
Supplies		2,000
Total current assets		582,000
Plant assets:		
Furniture and fixtures	$100,000	
Less Accumulated depreciation	60,000	40,000
Building	250,000	
Less Accumulated depreciation	140,000	110,000
Total assets		$732,000

Liabilities

Current liabilities:	
Accounts payable	$380,000
Salary payable	5,000
Unearned service revenue	13,000
Total current liabilities	398,000

Owner's Equity

Capital	334,000
Total liabilities and owner's equity	$732,000

Summary

The *accounting cycle* is the process by which accountants produce the financial statements for a specific period of time. The cycle starts with the beginning account balances. During the period, the business journalizes transactions and posts them to the ledger accounts. At the end of the period, the trial balance is prepared, and the accounts are adjusted in order to measure the period's net income or net loss.

Completion of the accounting cycle is aided by use of a *work sheet*. This columnar document summarizes the effects of all the activity of the period. It is neither a journal nor a ledger but merely a convenient device for completing the accounting cycle.

The work sheet has columns for the trial balance, the adjustments, the adjusted trial balance, the income statement, and the balance sheet. It aids the adjusting process, and it is the place where the period's net income or net loss is first computed. The work sheet also provides the data for the financial statements and the *closing entries*. However, it is not necessary. The accounting cycle can be completed from the less elaborate adjusted trial balance.

Microcomputer *spreadsheets* are extremely useful for tasks such as completing the accounting cycle. Their main advantage is that they can be programmed to print documents such as the work sheet and perform repetitious calculations without errors.

Revenues, expenses, and withdrawals represent increases and decreases in owner's equity for a specific period. At the end of the period, their balances are closed out to zero, and, for this reason, they are called *temporary accounts*. Assets, liabilities, and owner's equity are not closed because they are the *permanent accounts*. Their balances at the end of one period become the beginning balances of the next period. The final accuracy check of the period is the *postclosing trial balance*. *Reversing entries*, the opposite of prior-period adjusting entries, ease the accountant's work.

Four common accounting errors are incorrect journal entries, incorrect postings, *transpositions*, and *slides*. Techniques exist for detecting and correcting these errors.

The balance sheet reports *current* and *long-term assets, current* and *long-term liabilities*, and can be presented in report or *account format*. Two decision aids are the *current ratio*—total current assets divided by total current liabilities—and the *debt ratio*—total liabilities divided by total assets.

Self-Study Questions

Test your understanding of the chapter by marking the best answer to each of the following questions.

1. The focal point of the accounting cycle is the *(p. 145)*
   ✓ a. Financial statements   c. Adjusted trial balance
   b. Trial balance   d. Work sheet

2. Arrange the following accounting cycle steps in their proper order *(p. 146):*
   a. Complete the work sheet
   b. Journalize and post adjusting entries
   c. Prepare the postclosing trial balance
   d. Journalize and post cash transactions
   e. Prepare the financial statements
   f. Journalize and post closing entries

3. The work sheet is a *(p. 146)*
   a. Journal   c. Financial statement
   b. Ledger   ✓ d. Convenient device for completing the accounting cycle

4. The usefulness of the work sheet is *(p. 146)*
   a. Identifying the accounts that need to be adjusted
   b. Summarizing the effects of all the transactions of the period
   c. Aiding the preparation of the financial statements
   ✓ d. All of the above
5. Which of the following accounts is not closed? *(pp. 158, 159)*
   a. Supplies Expense   c. Interest Revenue
   ✓ b. Prepaid Insurance   d. Owner Withdrawals
6. The closing entry for Salary Expense, with a balance of $322,000, is *(p. 160)*

   a. Salary Expense   322,000
         Income Summary   322,000
   b. Salary Expense   322,000
         Salary Payable   322,000
   ✓ c. Income Summary   322,000
         Salary Expense   322,000
   d. Salary Payable   322,000
         Salary Expense   322,000

7. The purpose of the postclosing trial balance is to *(p. 162)*
   a. Provide the account balances for preparation of the balance sheet
   ✓ b. Ensure that the ledger is in balance for the start of the next period
   c. Aid the journalizing and posting of the closing entries
   d. Ensure that the ledger is in balance for completion of the work sheet
8. Reversing entries are used to *(pp. 163, 165)*
   ✓ a. Avoid having to refer back to a preceding period's adjusting entry when recording a cash transaction of a later period
   b. Prepare the financial statements
   c. Close the accounts
   d. Bring accounts to their correct balances at the beginning of a new period
9. The classification of assets and liabilities as current or long-term depends on *(p. 167)*
   a. Their order of listing in the general ledger
   ✓ b. Whether they appear on the balance sheet or the income statement
   c. The relative liquidity of the item
   d. The format of the balance sheet—account format or report format
10. Posting a $300 debit as a credit causes an error *(p. 171)*
   a. That is evenly divisible by 9
   b. That is evenly divisible by 2
   ✓ c. In the journal
   d. Known as a transposition

Answers to the self-study questions follow the Accounting Vocabulary.

Accounting Vocabulary

Account format of the balance sheet. Format that lists the assets at the left, with liabilities and owner equity at the right *(p. 168)*.

Accounting cycle. Process by which accountants produce an entity's financial statements for a specific period *(p. 145)*.

Closing entries. Entries that transfer the revenue, expense, and owner withdrawal balances from these respective accounts to the capital account *(p. 160)*.

Closing the accounts. Step in the accounting cycle at the end of the period that prepares the accounts for recording the transactions of the next period. Closing the accounts consists of journalizing and posting the closing entries to set the balances of the revenue, expense, and owner withdrawal accounts to zero (p. 157).

Current asset. An asset that is expected to be converted to cash, sold, or consumed during the next twelve months, or within the business's normal operating cycle if longer than a year (p. 167).

Current liability. A debt due to be paid within one year or one of the entity's operating cycles if the cycle is longer than a year (p. 168).

Current ratio. Current assets divided by current liabilities. Measures the ability to pay current liabilities from current assets (p. 169).

Debt ratio. Ratio of total liabilities to total assets. Tells the proportion of a company's assets that it has financed with debt (p. 170).

Income summary. A temporary "holding tank" account into which the revenues and expenses are transferred prior to their final transfer to the capital account (p. 160).

Liquidity. Measure of how quickly an item may be converted to cash (p. 167).

Long-term asset. An asset other than a current asset (p. 167).

Long-term liability. A liability other than a current liability (p. 168).

Nominal account. Another name for a Temporary account—revenues and expenses—that are closed at the end of the period. In a proprietorship the owner withdrawal account is also nominal (p. 159).

Operating cycle. Time span during which cash is paid for goods and services that are sold to customers who then pay the business in cash (p. 167).

Permanent accounts. Another name for a Real account—the assets, liabilities, and capital accounts. These accounts are not closed at the end of the period because their balances are not used to measure income (p. 159).

Postclosing trial balance. List of the ledger accounts and their balances at the end of the period after the journalizing and posting of the closing entries. The last step of the accounting cycle, the postclosing trial balance ensures that the ledger is in balance for the start of the next accounting period (p. 162).

Real account. Another name for a Permanent account—asset, liability, and capital—that are *not* closed at the end of the period (p. 159).

Report format of the balance sheet. Format that lists the assets at the top, with the liabilities and owner equity below (p 168).

Reversing entry. An entry that switches the debit and the credit of a previous adjusting entry. The reversing entry is dated the first day of the period following the adjusting entry (p. 165).

Slide. An accounting error that results from adding one or more zeros to a number, or from dropping a zero. For example, writing $500 as $5,000 or as $50 is a slide. A slide is evenly divisible by 9. (p. 172).

Spreadsheet. Integrated software program that can be used to solve many different kinds of problems. An electronically prepared work sheet (p. 154).

Temporary account. Another name for a Nominal account. The revenue and expense accounts that relate to a particular accounting period and are closed at the end of the period are temporary accounts. For a proprietorship, the owner withdrawal account is also temporary (p. 159).

Transposition. An accounting error that occurs when digits are flip-flopped. For example, $85 is a transposition of $58. A transposition is evenly divisible by 9 (p. 172).

Work sheet. A columnar document designed to help move data from the trial balance to the financial statements (p. 146).

Answers to Self-Study Questions

1. a	3. d	5. b	7. b	9. c
2. d, a, e, b, f, c	4. d	6. c	8. a	10. b

ASSIGNMENT MATERIAL

Questions

1. Identify the steps in the accounting cycle, distinguishing those that occur during the period from those that are performed at the end.

2. Why is the work sheet a valuable accounting tool?

3. Name two advantages the work sheet has over the adjusted trial balance.

4. Briefly explain how a microcomputer spreadsheet can be programmed to complete the work sheet.

5. Why must the adjusting entries be journalized and posted if they have already been entered on the work sheet?

6. Why should the adjusting entries be journalized and posted before making the closing entries?

7. Which types of accounts are closed?

8. What purpose is served by closing the accounts?

9. State how the work sheet helps with recording the closing entries.

10. Distinguish between permanent accounts and temporary accounts, indicating which type is closed at the end of the period. Give five examples of each type of account.

11. Is Income Summary a permanent account or a temporary account? When and how is it used?

12. Give the closing entries for the following accounts (balances in parentheses): Service Revenue ($4,700), Salary Expense ($1,100), Income Summary (credit balance of $2,000), Rhonda McGill, Withdrawals ($2,300).

13. Briefly describe a reversing entry by stating what it is, when it is dated, and what it accomplishes.

14. Why are assets classified as current or long-term? On what basis are they classified? Where do the classified amounts appear?

15. Indicate which of the following accounts are current assets and which are long-term assets: Prepaid Rent, Building, Furniture, Accounts Receivable, Merchandise Inventory, Cash, Note Receivable (due within one year), Note Receivable (due after one year).

16. In what order are assets and liabilities listed on the balance sheet?

17. Name an outside party that is interested in whether a liability is current or long-term. Why is this party interested in this information?

18. A friend tells you that the difference between a current liability and a long-term liability is that they are payable to different types of creditors. Is your friend correct? Include in your answer the definitions of these two categories of liabilities.

19. Show how to compute the current ratio and the debt ratio. Indicate what ability each ratio measures, and state whether a high value or a low value is safer.

20. Give the name of the following accounting errors:
    a. Posted a $300 debit from the journal as a $300 credit in the ledger.
    b. Posted a $300 debit from the journal as a $3,000 debit in the ledger.
    c. Recorded a transaction by debiting one account for $3,100 and crediting the other account for $1,300.

21. How would you detect each of the errors in the preceding question?

22. Capp Company purchased supplies of $120 on account. The accountant debited Supplies and credited Cash for $120. A week later, after this

entry has been posted to the ledger, the accountant discovers the error. How should he correct the error?

Exercises

Net income, $1,540

Exercise 4-1 *Preparing a work sheet* **(L.O. 1)**

The trial balance of Makovic Pest Control Service follows.

Additional information at September 30, 19X6:

a. Accrued salary expense, $200.
b. Prepaid rent expired, $900.
c. Supplies used, $2,250.
d. Accrued service revenue, $210.
e. Depreciation, $40.

Required

Complete Makovic's work sheet for September 19X6.

Makovic Pest Control Service
Trial Balance
September 30, 19X6

Cash............................	$ 1,560	
Accounts receivable	2,840	
Prepaid rent.....................	1,200	
Supplies	3,390	
Equipment	12,600	
Accumulated depreciation		$ 2,240
Accounts payable		1,600
Salary payable....................		
Lee Makovic, capital		16,030
Lee Makovic, withdrawals	3,000	
Service revenue...................		7,300
Depreciation expense...............		
Salary expense....................	1,800	
Rent expense		
Utilities expense	780	
Supplies expense		
Total.............................	$27,170	$27,170

No check figure

Exercise 4-2 *Journalizing adjusting and closing entries* **(L.O. 3)**

Journalize the adjusting and closing entries in Exercise 4-1.

No check figure

Exercise 4-3 *Posting adjusting and closing entries* **(L.O. 3)**

Set up T-accounts for those accounts affected by the adjusting and closing entries in Exercise 4-1. Post the adjusting and closing entries to the accounts, denoting adjustment amounts by Adj., closing amounts by Clo., and balances by Bal. Double rule the accounts with zero balances after closing and show the ending balance in each account.

Postclosing trial balance, $18,650

Exercise 4-4 *Preparing a postclosing trial balance* **(L.O. 3)**

Prepare the postclosing trial balance in Exercise 4-1.

Exercise 4-5 *Identifying and journalizing closing entries* **(L.O. 4)**

No check figure

From the following selected accounts that Langefeld Catering Service reported in its June 30, 19X4, annual financial statements, prepare the entity's closing entries.

P. Langefeld, capital	$45,600	Interest expense	$ 2,200
Service revenue	92,100	Accounts receivable	26,000
Unearned revenues	1,350	Salary payable	850
Salary expense	12,500	Depreciation expense	10,200
Accumulated depreciation	35,000	Rent expense	5,900
Supplies expense	1,400	P. Langefeld, withdrawals	40,000
Interest revenue	700	Supplies	1,100

Exercise 4-6 *Identifying and journalizing closing entries* **(L.O. 4)**

No check figure

The accountant for Damon Reed, Attorney, has posted adjusting entries *a* through *e* to the accounts at December 31, 19X2. All the revenue, expense, and owner's equity accounts of the entity are listed here in T-account form.

Accounts Receivable
23,000	
(e) 3,500	

Supplies
4,000	(a) 2,000

Accumulated Depreciation— Furniture
	5,000
	(b) 1,100

Accumulated Depreciation— Building
	33,000
	(c) 6,000

Salary Payable
	(d) 700

Damon Reed, Capital
	49,400

Damon Reed, Withdrawals
52,400	

Service Revenue
	103,000
	(e) 3,500

Salary Expense
28,000	
(d) 700	

Supplies Expense
(a) 2,000	

Depreciation Expense— Furniture
(b) 1,100	

Depreciation Expense— Building
(c) 6,000	

Required

Journalize Reed's closing entries at December 31, 19X2.

Exercise 4-7 *Preparing a statement of owner's equity* **(L.O. 4)**

Ending owner's equity, $82,000

From the following accounts of Overhead Door Company, prepare the entity's statement of owner's equity for the year ended December 31, 19X5:

Debra Ringle, Capital
Dec. 31	41,000	Jan. 1	52,000
		Mar. 9	28,000
		Dec. 31	43,000

Debra Ringle, Withdrawals
Mar. 31	8,000	Dec. 31	41,000
Jun. 30	8,000		
Sep. 30	8,000		
Dec. 31	17,000		

Income Summary
Dec. 31	85,000	Dec. 31	128,000
Dec. 31	43,000		

Exercise 4-8 *Identifying and recording adjusting and closing entries* (L.O. 3, 4)

The trial balance and income statement amounts from the March work sheet of Bigelow Bonding Company are presented below.

Required

Journalize the adjusting and closing entries of Bigelow Bonding Company at March 31.

Account Title	Trial Balance		Income Statement	
Cash	$ 3,100			
Supplies	2,400			
Prepaid rent	1,100			
Office equipment	30,800			
Accumulated depreciation		$ 6,900		
Accounts payable.................		4,600		
Salary payable...................				
Unearned service revenue		4,400		
Bernard Bigelow, capital		4,800		
Bernard Bigelow, withdrawals	1,000			
Service revenue		12,700		$16,000
Salary expense	3,000		$ 3,800	
Rent expense...................	1,200		1,400	
Depreciation expense			400	
Supplies expense			500	
Utilities expense.................	800		800	
	$43,400	$43,400	6,900	16,000
Net income			9,100	
			$16,000	$16,000

Exercise 4-9 *Journalizing reversing entries* (L.O. 5)

Return to Exercise 4-6. Identify the two adjustments for which reversing entries would be most useful. Journalize those reversing entries.

Exercise 4-10 *Journalizing and posting an accrued expense and the related reversing entry* (L.O. 5)

During 19X2 London Sales Company pays wages of $44,200 to its employees. At December 31, 19X2, the company owes accrued wages of $900 that will be included in the $1,200 weekly payroll payment on January 4, 19X3.

Required

1. Open T-accounts for Wage Expense and Wage Payable.
2. Journalize all wage transactions for 19X2 and 19X3, including adjusting, closing, and reversing entries. Record the $44,200 amount by a single debit to Wage Expense.
3. Post amounts to the two T-accounts, showing their balances at January 4, 19X3. Denote cash payment entries by *CP*, adjusting entries by *Adj.*, closing entries by *Clo.*, reversing entries by *Rev.*, and balances by *Bal.*

Exercise 4-11 *Preparing a classified balance sheet* (L.O. 6)

1. Use the data in Exercise 4-8 to prepare Bigelow Bonding Company's classified balance sheet at March 31 of the current year. Use the report format.
2. Compute Bigelow's current ratio and debt ratio at March 31. One year ago the current ratio was 1.20 and the debt ratio was .30. Indicate whether Bigelow's ability to pay its debts has improved or deteriorated during the current year.

Exercise 4-12 *Correcting accounting errors* **(L.O. 7)**

Prepare a correcting entry for each of the following accounting errors:

a. Adjusted prepaid rent by debiting Prepaid Rent and crediting Rent Expense for $700. This adjusting entry should have debited Rent Expense and credited Prepaid Rent for $700.
b. Debited Salary Expense and credited Cash to accrue salary expense of $500.
c. Recorded the earning of $3,200 service revenue collected in advance by debiting Accounts Receivable and crediting Service Revenue.
d. Accrued interest revenue of $800 by a debit to Accounts Receivable and a credit to Interest Revenue.
e. Recorded a $600 cash purchase of supplies by debiting Supplies and crediting Accounts Payable.
f. Debited Supplies and credited Accounts Payable for a $2,300 credit purchase of office equipment.

Problems   (Group A)

Problem 4-1A   *Preparing a work sheet* **(L.O. 1)**

Net income, $8,220

The trial balance of Agape Counseling Center at May 31, 19X2, follows:

Agape Counseling Center
Trial Balance
May 31, 19X2

Cash	$ 1,670	
Notes receivable	10,340	
Interest receivable		
Supplies	560	
Prepaid insurance	1,790	
Furniture	27,410	
Accumulated depreciation—furniture		$ 1,480
Building	55,900	
Accumulated depreciation—building		33,560
Land	13,700	
Accounts payable		14,730
Interest payable		
Salary payable		
Unearned service revenue		6,800
Note payable, long-term		18,700
Rex Jennings, capital		34,290
Rex Jennings, withdrawals	3,800	
Service revenue		9,970
Interest revenue		
Depreciation expense—furniture		
Depreciation expense—building		
Salary expense	2,170	
Insurance expense		
Interest expense		
Utilities expense	490	
Property tax expense	640	
Advertising expense	1,060	
Supplies expense		
Total	$119,530	$119,530

Chapter 4   Completing the Accounting Cycle   **183**

Additional data at May 31, 19X2:

a. Accrued salary expense, $600.
b. Supplies on hand, $410.
c. Prepaid insurance expired during May, $390.
d. Accrued interest expense, $220.
e. Unearned service revenue earned during May, $4,400.
f. Accrued advertising expense, $60 (credit Accounts Payable).
g. Accrued interest revenue, $170.
h. Depreciation: furniture, $380; building, $160.

Required

Complete Agape's work sheet for May.

Ending owner's equity, $29,440; current ratio 19X2, 1.30

Problem 4-2A *Preparing financial statements from an adjusted trial balance; journalizing the adjusting and closing entries (L.O. 3, 6)*

The adjusted trial balance of Lopez Tailoring Service at April 30, 19X2, the end of the company's fiscal year, follows:

Lopez Tailoring Service **Adjusted Trial Balance** **April 30, 19X2**		
Cash	$ 2,370	
Accounts receivable	25,740	
Supplies	3,690	
Prepaid insurance	2,290	
Equipment	63,930	
Accumulated depreciation—equipment		$ 28,430
Building	74,330	
Accumulated depreciation—building		18,260
Accounts payable		19,550
Interest payable		2,280
Wage payable		830
Unearned service revenue		3,660
Note payable, long-term		69,900
Maria Lopez, capital		46,200
Maria Lopez, withdrawals	47,500	
Service revenue		99,550
Depreciation expense—equipment	6,700	
Depreciation expense—building	3,210	
Wage expense	29,800	
Insurance expense	5,370	
Interest expense	8,170	
Utilities expense	5,670	
Property tax expense	3,010	
Supplies expense	6,880	
Total	$288,660	$288,660

Additional data at April 30, 19X2:

a. Supplies used during the year, $6,880.
b. Prepaid insurance expired during the year, $5,370.
c. Accrued interest expense, $2,280.

d. Accrued service revenue, $2,200.
e. Depreciation for the year: equipment, $6,700; building, $3,210.
f. Accrued wage expense, $830.
g. Unearned service revenue earned during the year, $5,180.

Required

1. Journalize the adjusting and closing entries.
2. Prepare Lopez's income statement and statement of owner's equity for the year ended April 30, 19X2, and the classified balance sheet on that date. Use the account format for the balance sheet.
3. Compute Lopez's current ratio and debt ratio at April 30, 19X2. One year ago the current ratio stood at 1.21, and the debt ratio was .82. Did Lopez's ability to pay debts improve or deteriorate during 19X2?

Problem 4-3A *Taking the accounting cycle through the closing entries* **(L.O. 3, 4)**   Ending owner's equity, $50,000

The unadjusted T-accounts of Dave Laufenberg, M.D., at December 31, 19X2, and the related year-end adjustment data follow:

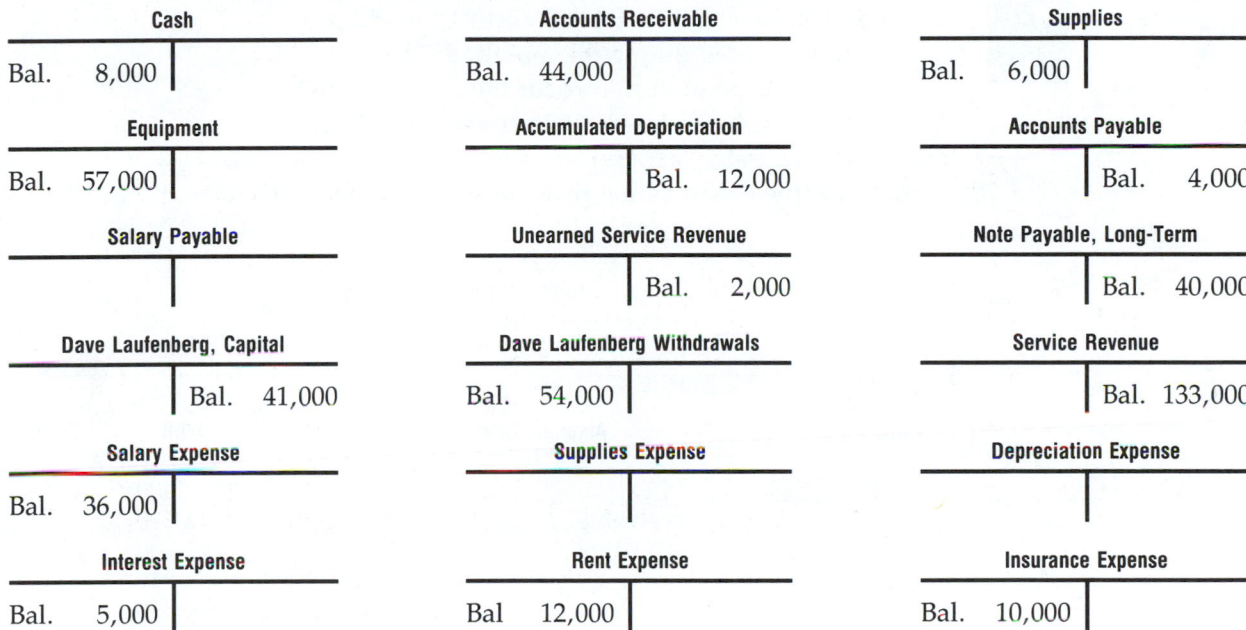

Cash		Accounts Receivable		Supplies	
Bal. 8,000		Bal. 44,000		Bal. 6,000	

Equipment		Accumulated Depreciation		Accounts Payable	
Bal. 57,000			Bal. 12,000		Bal. 4,000

Salary Payable		Unearned Service Revenue		Note Payable, Long-Term	
			Bal. 2,000		Bal. 40,000

Dave Laufenberg, Capital		Dave Laufenberg Withdrawals		Service Revenue	
	Bal. 41,000	Bal. 54,000			Bal. 133,000

Salary Expense		Supplies Expense		Depreciation Expense	
Bal. 36,000					

Interest Expense		Rent Expense		Insurance Expense	
Bal. 5,000		Bal 12,000		Bal. 10,000	

Adjustment data at December 31, 19X2, include:

a. Supplies on hand, $2,000.
b. Depreciation for the year, $6,000.
c. Accrued salary expense, $3,000.
d. Accrued service revenue, $4,000.
e. Unearned service revenue earned during the year, $2,000.

Required

1. Write the trial balance on a work sheet and complete the work sheet. Key each adjusting entry by the letter corresponding to the data given.
2. Prepare the income statement, the statement of owner's equity, and the classified balance sheet in account format.
3. Journalize the adjusting and closing entries.

Postclosing trial balance, $115,000

Problem 4-4A   *Completing the accounting cycle*   (L.O. 3, 4)

This problem should be used only in conjunction with Problem 4-3A. It completes the accounting cycle by posting to T-accounts and preparing the postclosing trial balance.

Required

1. Using the Problem 4-3A data, post the adjusting and closing entries to the T-accounts, denoting adjusting amounts by *Adj.*, closing amounts by *Clo.*, and account balances by *Bal.*, as shown in Exhibit 4-9. Double underline all accounts with a zero ending balance.
2. Prepare the postclosing trial balance.

Net income, $5,690

Problem 4-5A   *Completing the accounting cycle*   (L.O. 3, 4, 6)

The trial balance of Hubby Insurance Agency at October 31, 19X0, and the data needed for the month-end adjustments are as follows:

Adjustment data:

a. Prepaid rent still in force at October 31, $2,000.
b. Supplies used during the month, $570.
c. Depreciation on furniture for the month, $250.
d. Depreciation on building for the month, $280.
e. Accrued salary expense at October 31, $310.
f. Unearned commission revenue still unearned at October 31, $4,700.

Hubby Insurance Agency
Trial Balance
October 31, 19X0

Account Number	Account Title	Debit	Credit
11	Cash	$ 2,900	
12	Accounts receivable	12,310	
13	Prepaid rent	2,200	
14	Supplies	840	
15	Furniture	26,830	
16	Accumulated depreciation—furniture		$ 3,400
17	Building	68,300	
18	Accumulated depreciation—building		9,100
21	Accounts payable		7,290
22	Salary payable		
23	Unearned commission revenue		5,300
31	Erin Hubby, capital		85,490
32	Erin Hubby, withdrawals	3,900	
41	Commission revenue		9,560
51	Salary expense	1,840	
52	Rent expense		
53	Utilities expense	530	
54	Depreciation expense—furniture		
55	Depreciation expense—building		
56	Advertising expense	490	
57	Supplies expense		
	Total	$120,140	$120,140

Required

1. Open the accounts listed in the trial balance, inserting their October 31 unadjusted balances. Also open the Income Summary account, number 33. Use four-column accounts. Date the balances of the following accounts October 1: Prepaid Rent, Supplies, Building, Accumulated Depreciation—Building, Furniture, Accumulated Depreciation—Furniture, Unearned Commission Revenue, and Erin Hubby, Capital.

2. Write the trial balance on a work sheet and complete the work sheet of Hubby Insurance Agency for the month ended October 31, 19X0.

3. Prepare the income statement, the statement of owner's equity, and the classified balance sheet in report format.

4. Using the work sheet data, journalize and post the adjusting and closing entries. Use dates and posting references. Use 12 as the number of the journal page.

5. Prepare a postclosing trial balance.

Problem 4-6A *Using reversing entries* *(L.O. 5)*

Salary Expense balance, Nov. 3, $160

Refer to the data in Problem 4-5A.

Required

1. Open accounts for Salary Payable and Salary Expense. Insert their unadjusted balances at October 31, 19X0.

2. Journalize adjusting entry *e* and the closing entry for Salary Expense at October 31. Post to the ledger accounts.

3. On November 3, Hubby Insurance Agency paid the next payroll amount of $470. Journalize this cash payment, and post to the accounts. Show the balance in each account.

4. Repeat requirements 1-3 using a reversing entry. Compare the balances of Salary Payable and Salary Expense computed using a reversing entry, with those balances computed without using a reversing entry (as appear in your answer to requirement 3).

Problem 4-7A *Journalizing adjusting and reversing entries* *(L.O. 5)*

No check figure

The accounting records of Conner Company reveal the following information before adjustments at December 31, 19X6, the end of the accounting period.

a. On July 31 Conner deposited $25,000 in a savings account. The bank will pay Conner interest of $1,200 on January 31, 19X7. Of this amount, five sixths is earned in 19X6.

b. On November 29 Conner Company received a property tax bill from the city. The total amount, due on January 15, 19X7, is $3,900. Three fourths of this amount is property tax expense of 19X6.

c. Commissions owed to sales employees at December 31 are $2,565, and salaries owed to home office employees are $1,870.

Required

1. Journalize the adjusting entry needed for each situation at December 31, 19X6, identifying each entry by its corresponding letter.

2. Journalize reversing entries as needed. Use the corresponding letters for references. Date the entries.

3. Use the first situation that calls for a reversing entry to explain the practical value of the reversal.

Ending owner's equity $56,900;
current ratio 19X3, 1.41

Problem 4-8A *Preparing a classified balance sheet in report format* **(L.O. 6)**

The accounts of Louise Pinkoff, CPA, at March 31, 19X3, are listed in alphabetical order.

Accounts payable	$12,700	Louise Pinkoff, capital,	
Accounts receivable	11,500	March 31, 19X2	$42,800
Accumulated deprecia-		Louise Pinkoff,	
tion—building	47,300	withdrawals	31,200
Accumulated deprecia-		Note payable, long-term	3,200
tion—furniture	7,700	Note receivable, long-term	6,900
Advertising expense	900	Other assets	1,300
Building	55,900	Other current assets	900
Cash	1,400	Other current liabilities	1,100
Current portion of note		Prepaid insurance	600
payable	800	Prepaid rent	4,700
Current portion of note		Salary expense	17,800
receivable	3,100	Salary payable	1,400
Depreciation expense	1,900	Service revenue	71,100
Furniture	43,200	Supplies	3,800
Insurance expense	600	Supplies expense	4,600
Interest payable	200	Unearned service revenue	2,800
Interest receivable	800		

Required

1. All adjustments have been journalized and posted, but the closing entries have not yet been made. Prepare the company's classified balance sheet in report format at March 31, 19X3. Use captions for total assets, total liabilities, and total liabilities and owner's equity.
2. Compute Pinkoff's current ratio and debt ratio at March 31, 19X3. At March 31, 19X2, the current ratio was 1.28, and debt ratio was .32. Did Pinkoff's ability to pay debts improve or deteriorate during 19X3?

d. Overall effect—net income
overstated, $880

Problem 4-9A *Analyzing and journalizing corrections, adjustments, and closing entries* **(L.O. 4, 7)**

The accountants of Polanski Catering Service, a proprietorship, encountered the following situations while adjusting and closing the books at February 28. Consider each situation independently.

a. The company bookkeeper made the following entry to record a $950 credit purchase of supplies:

Feb. 26	Equipment	950	
	Accounts Payable		950

Prepare the correcting entry, dated February 28.
b. A $390 credit to Accounts Receivable was posted as $930.
   (1) At what stage of the accounting cycle will this error be detected?
   (2) Describe the technique for identifying the amount of the error.
c. The $1,620 balance of Utilities Expense was entered as $16,200 on the trial balance.
   (1) What is the name of this type of error?
   (2) Assume this is the only error in the trial balance. Which will be greater, the total debits or the total credits, and by how much?
   (3) How can this type of error be identified?

d.   The accountant failed to make the following adjusting entries at February 28:
     (1) Accrued service revenue, $700
     (2) Insurance expense, $460
     (3) Accrued interest expense on a note payable, $520
     (4) Depreciation of equipment, $3,300
     (5) Earned service revenue that had been collected in advance, $2,700
     Compute the overall net income effect of these omissions.
e.   Record each of the adjusting entries identified in item *d.*
f.   The revenue and expense accounts after the adjusting entries had been posted were Service Revenue, $95,330; Wage Expense, $29,340; Depreciation Expense, $6,180; Interest Expense, $4,590; Utilities Expense, $1,620; and Insurance Expense, $740. Two balances prior to closing were Eva Polanski, Capital, $75,150; and Eva Polanski, Drawing, $48,000. Journalize the closing entries.

(Group B)

Problem 4-1B   *Preparing a work sheet*   **(L.O. 1)**

Net income, $10,570

The trial balance of Ross Family Painting Contractors at July 31, 19X3 appears below.

Ross Family Painting Contractors Trial Balance July 31, 19X3		
Cash	$ 4,200	
Accounts receivable	37,820	
Supplies	17,660	
Prepaid insurance....................	2,300	
Equipment	32,690	
Accumulated depreciation—equipment .		$ 26,240
Building	36,890	
Accumulated depreciation—building ...		10,500
Land	28,300	
Accounts payable		22,690
Interest payable		
Wage payable		
Unearned service revenue		10,560
Note payable, long-term..............		22,400
Peter Ross, capital		62,130
Peter Ross, withdrawals	4,200	
Service revenue......................		17,190
Depreciation expense—equipment		
Depreciation expense—building........		
Wage expense.......................	6,200	
Insurance expense		
Interest expense		
Utilities expense	270	
Property tax expense.................	840	
Advertising expense	340	
Supplies expense		
Total	$171,710	$171,710

Additional data at July 31, 19X3:

a. Accrued wage expense, $440.
b. Supplies on hand, $14,740.
c. Prepaid insurance expired during July, $500.
d. Accrued interest expense, $180.
e. Unearned service revenue earned during July, $4,770.
f. Accrued advertising expense, $100 (credit Accounts Payable).
g. Accrued service revenue, $1,100.
h. Depreciation: equipment, $430; building, $270.

Required

Complete Ross's work sheet for July.

Ending owner's equity, $76,720; current ratio 19X1, 1.15

Problem 4-2B *Preparing financial statements from an adjusted trial balance; journalizing the adjusting and closing entries* **(L.O. 3, 6)**

The adjusted trial balance of Federal Security Couriers at June 30, 19X1, the end of the company's fiscal year, follows:

Federal Security Couriers
Adjusted Trial Balance
June 30, 19X1

Cash	$ 18,350	
Accounts receivable	26,470	
Supplies	1,290	
Prepaid insurance	1,700	
Equipment	55,800	
Accumulated depreciation—equipment		$ 16,480
Building	144,900	
Accumulated depreciation—building		16,850
Accounts payable		36,900
Interest payable		1,490
Wage payable		770
Unearned service revenue		2,300
Note payable, long-term		97,000
Ramon DeSoto, capital		67,390
Ramon DeSoto, withdrawals	45,300	
Service revenue		108,360
Depreciation expense—equipment	6,300	
Depreciation expense—building	3,470	
Wage expense	18,800	
Insurance expense	3,100	
Interest expense	11,510	
Utilities expense	4,300	
Property tax expense	2,670	
Supplies expense	3,580	
Total	$347,540	$347,540

Additional data at June 30, 19X1:

a. Supplies used during the year, $3,580.
b. Prepaid insurance expired during the year, $3,100.
c. Accrued interest expense, $680.
d. Accrued service revenue, $940.
e. Depreciation for the year: equipment, $6,300; building, $3,470.

f. Accrued wage expense, $770.

g. Unearned service revenue earned during the year, $6,790.

Required

1. Journalize the adjusting and closing entries.

2. Prepare Federal's income statement and statement of owner's equity for the year ended June 30, 19X1, and the classified balance sheet on that date. Use the account format for the balance sheet.

3. Compute Federal's current ratio and debt ratio at June 30, 19X1. One year ago the current ratio stood at 1.01, and the debt ratio was .71. Did Federal's ability to pay debts improve or deteriorate during 19X1?

Problem 4-3B *Taking the accounting cycle through the closing entries* **(L.O. 3, 4)**   Ending owner's equity, $27,000

The unadjusted T-accounts of Christine Ciancia, Psychologist, at December 31, 19X2, and the related year-end adjustment data follow:

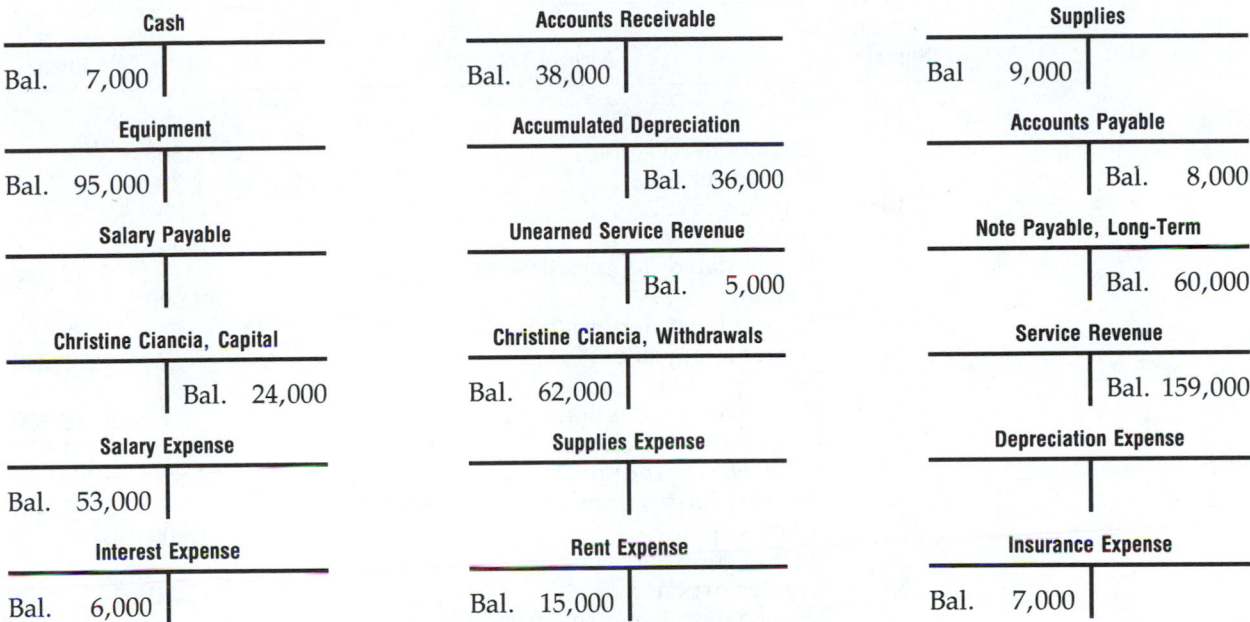

Adjustment data at December 31, 19X2, include:

a. Supplies on hand, $1,000.

b. Depreciation for the year, $9,000.

c. Accrued salary expense, $2,000.

d. Accrued service revenue, $1,000.

e. Unearned service revenue earned during the year, $5,000.

Required

1. Write the trial balance on a work sheet, and complete the work sheet. Key each adjusting entry by the letter corresponding to the data given.

2. Prepare the income statement, the statement of owner's equity, and the classified balance sheet in account format.

3. Journalize the adjusting and closing entries.

Problem 4-4B *Completing the accounting cycle* **(L.O. 3, 4)**   Postclosing trial balance, $142,000

This problem should be used only in conjunction with Problem 4-3B. It completes the accounting cycle by posting to T-accounts and preparing the postclosing trial balance.

Required

1. Using the Problem 4-3B data, post the adjusting and closing entries to the T-accounts, denoting adjusting amounts by *Adj.*, closing amounts by *Clo.*, and account balances by *Bal.*, as shown in Exhibit 4-9. Double underline all accounts with a zero ending balance.
2. Prepare the postclosing trial balance.

Net income, $4,950

Problem 4-5B *Completing the accounting cycle* **(L.O. 3, 4, 6)**

The trial balance of Nix Insurance Agency at August 31, 19X9, and the data needed for the month-end adjustments follow.

Nix Insurance Agency
Trial Balance
August 31, 19X9

Account Number	Account Title	Debit	Credit
11	Cash	$ 6,800	
12	Accounts receivable	17,560	
13	Prepaid rent	1,290	
14	Supplies	900	
15	Furniture	15,350	
16	Accumulated depreciation—furniture		$ 12,800
17	Building	89,900	
18	Accumulated depreciation—building		28,600
21	Accounts payable		6,240
22	Salary payable		
23	Unearned commission revenue		8,900
31	L. M. Nix, capital		74,920
32	L. M. Nix, withdrawals	4,800	
41	Commission revenue		7,800
51	Salary expense	1,600	
52	Rent expense		
53	Utilities expense	410	
54	Depreciation expense—furniture		
55	Depreciation expense—building		
56	Advertising expense	650	
57	Supplies expense		
	Total	$139,260	$139,260

a. Prepaid rent still in force at August 31, $1,050.
b. Supplies used during the month, $140.
c. Depreciation on furniture for the month, $370.
d. Depreciation on building for the month, $130.
e. Accrued salary expense at August 31, $460.
f. Unearned commission revenue still unearned at August 31, $7,750.

Required

1. Open the accounts listed in the trial balance, inserting their August 31 unadjusted balances. Also open the Income Summary account, number 33. Use four column accounts. Date the balances of the following accounts as of August 1: Prepaid Rent, Supplies, Furniture, Accumulated Depreci-

ation—Furniture, Building, Accumulated Depreciation—Building, Unearned Commission Revenue, and L. M. Nix, Capital.

2. Write the trial balance on a work sheet and complete the work sheet of Nix Insurance Agency for the month ended August 31, 19X9.
3. Prepare the income statement, the statement of owner's equity, and the classified balance sheet in report format.
4. Using the work sheet data, journalize and post the adjusting and closing entries. Use dates and posting references. Use page 7 as the number of the journal page.
5. Prepare a postclosing trial balance.

Problem 4-6B *Using reversing entries* *(L.O. 5)*

Salary Expense balance, Sep. 5, $120

Refer to the data in Problem 4-5B.

Required

1. Open accounts for Salary Payable and Salary Expense. Insert their unadjusted balances at August 31, 19X9.
2. Journalize adjusting entry *e* and the closing entry for Salary Expense at August 31. Post to the accounts.
3. On September 5, Nix Insurance Agency paid the next payroll amount of $580. Journalize this cash payment, and post to the accounts. Show the balance in each account.
4. Repeat requirements 1-3 using a reversing entry. Compare the balances of Salary Payable and Salary Expense computed using a reversing entry, with those balances computed without using a reversing entry (as appear in your answer to requirement 3).

Problem 4-7B *Journalizing adjusting and reversing entries* *(L.O. 5)*

No check figure

Vidmar Company's accounting records reveal the following information before adjustments at December 31, 19X3, the end of the accounting period:

a. Wages owed to hourly employees total $3,400. Total salaries owed to salaried employees are $2,790. These amounts will be paid on the next scheduled payday in January 19X4.
b. On October 31 Vidmar loaned $40,000 to another business. The loan agreement requires the borrower to pay Vidmar interest of $2,400 on April 30, 19X4. One third of this interest is earned in 19X3.
c. On December 23 Vidmar Company received a property tax bill from the city. The total amount, due on February 1, 19X4, is $4,600. Half of this amount is property tax expense for 19X3.

Required

1. Journalize the adjusting entry needed for each situation at December 31, 19X3, identifying each entry by its corresponding letter.
2. Journalize reversing entries as needed. Use the corresponding letters for references. Date the entries appropriately.
3. Use the first situation that calls for a reversing entry to explain the practical value of the reversal.

Problem 4-8B *Preparing a classified balance sheet in report format* *(L.O. 6)*

Ending owner's equity, $63,800; current ratio 19X6, 1.40

The accounts of Hankins Travel Agency at December 31, 19X6, are listed in alphabetical order.

Accounts payable	$ 3,100	Barry Hankins, capital,	
Accounts receivable	4,600	December 31, 19X5.....	$50,300
Accumulated deprecia-		Barry Hankins,	
tion—building........	37,800	withdrawals	47,400
Accumulated deprecia-		Note payable, long-term .	27,800
tion—furniture	11,600	Note receivable,	
Advertising expense	2,200	long-term	4,000
Building	104,400	Other assets	3,600
Cash	4,500	Other current assets	1,700
Commission revenue....	93,500	Other current liabilities ..	4,700
Current portion of note		Prepaid insurance.......	1,100
payable	2,200	Prepaid rent............	6,600
Current portion of note		Salary expense	22,600
receivable	1,000	Salary payable	1,900
Depreciation expense ...	1,300	Supplies	2,500
Furniture	22,700	Supplies expense	5,700
Insurance expense	800	Unearned commission	
Interest payable	600	revenue..............	3,400
Interest receivable	200		

Required

1. All adjustments have been journalized and posted, but the closing entries have not yet been made. Prepare the company's classified balance sheet in report format at December 31, 19X6. Use captions for total assets, total liabilities, and total liabilities and owner's equity.

2. Compute Hankins's current ratio and debt ratio at December 31, 19X6. At December 31, 19X5, the current ratio was 1.52, and the debt ratio was .37. Did Hankins's ability to pay debts improve or deteriorate during 19X6?

d. Overall effect—net income understated, $660

Problem 4-9B *Analyzing and journalizing corrections, adjustments, and closing entries (L.O. 4, 7)*

Accountants for Osaka Catering Service, a proprietorship, encountered the following situations while adjusting and closing the books at December 31. Consider each situation independently.

a. The company bookkeeper made the following entry to record a $400 credit purchase of office equipment:

Nov. 12	Office Supplies	400	
	Accounts Payable		400

Prepare the correcting entry, dated December 31.

b. A $750 debit to Cash was posted as a credit.
   (1) At what stage of the accounting cycle will this error be detected?
   (2) Describe the technique for identifying the amount of the error.

c. The $35,000 balance of Equipment was entered as $3,500 on the trial balance.
   (1) What is the name of this type of error?
   (2) Assume this is the only error in the trial balance. Which will be greater, the total debits or the total credits, and by how much?
   (3) How can this type of error be identified?

d. The accountant failed to make the following adjusting entries at December 31:
   (1) Accrued property tax expense, $200

(2) Supplies expense, $1,390
(3) Accrued interest revenue on a note receivable, $950
(4) Depreciation of equipment, $4,000
(5) Earned service revenue that had been collected in advance, $5,300.
   Compute the overall net income effect of these omissions.

e. Record each of the adjusting entries identified in item *d*.

f. The revenue and expense accounts, after the adjusting entries had been posted, were Service Revenue, $55,800; Interest Revenue, $2,000; Salary Expense, $13,200; Rent Expense, $5,100; Depreciation Expense, $5,550; Supplies Expense, $1,530; and Property Tax Expense, $1,190. Two balances prior to closing were Mitsuo Osaka, Capital, $58,600; and Mitsuo Osaka, Withdrawals, $30,000. Journalize the closing entries.

Extending Your Knowledge

Decision Problems

1. *Completing the Accounting Cycle to Develop the Information for a Bank Loan* *(L.O. 4, 6)*

Net income, $34,130

One year ago, your friend Grant Thornton founded Thornton Computing Service. The business has prospered. Thornton, who remembers that you took an accounting course while in college, comes to you for advice. He wishes to know how much net income his business earned during the past year. He also wants to know what the entity's total assets, liabilities, and capital are. His accounting records consist of the T-accounts of his ledger, which were prepared by an accountant who moved to another city. The ledger at December 31

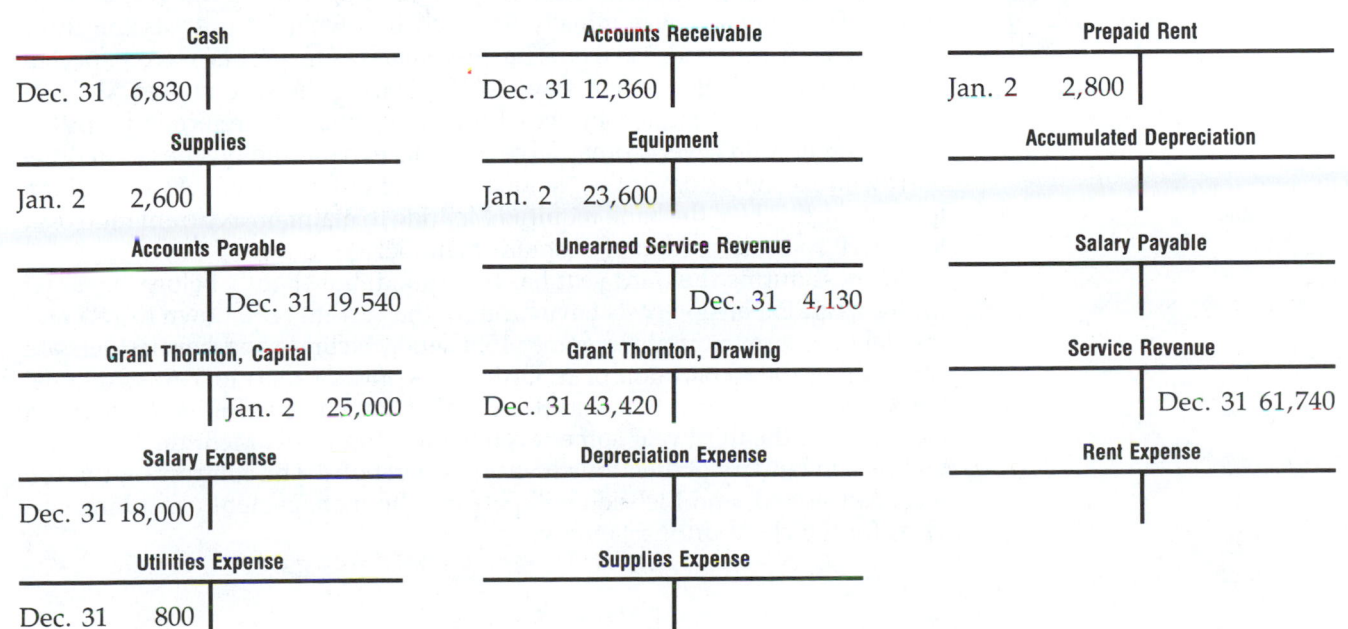

Cash		Accounts Receivable		Prepaid Rent	
Dec. 31 6,830		Dec. 31 12,360		Jan. 2 2,800	

Supplies		Equipment		Accumulated Depreciation	
Jan. 2 2,600		Jan. 2 23,600			

Accounts Payable		Unearned Service Revenue		Salary Payable	
	Dec. 31 19,540		Dec. 31 4,130		

Grant Thornton, Capital		Grant Thornton, Drawing		Service Revenue	
	Jan. 2 25,000	Dec. 31 43,420			Dec. 31 61,740

Salary Expense		Depreciation Expense		Rent Expense	
Dec. 31 18,000					

Utilities Expense		Supplies Expense	
Dec. 31 800			

Thornton indicates that at the year's end customers owe him $1,600 accrued service revenue, which he expects to collect early next year. These revenues have not been recorded. During the year he collected $4,130 service revenue in advance from customers, but he earned only $1,190 of that amount. Rent expense for the year was $2,400, and he used up $2,100 in supplies. Thornton estimates that depreciation on his equipment was $5,900 for the year. At December 31 he owes his employee $1,200 accrued salary.

At the conclusion of your meeting, Thornton expresses concern that his withdrawals during the year might have exceeded his net income. To get a loan to expand the business, Thornton must show the bank that his capital account has grown from its original $25,000 balance. Has it? You and Thornton agree that you will meet again in one week. You perform the analysis and prepare the financial statements to answer his questions.

No check figure

2. Finding an Error in the Work Sheets   (L.O. 1, 7)

You are preparing the financial statements for the year ended October 31, 19X5 for Woodside Publishing Company, a weekly newspaper. You began with the trial balance of the ledger, which balanced, and then made the required adjusting entries. To save time, you omitted preparing an adjusted trial balance. After making the adjustments on the work sheet, you extended the balances from the trial balance, adjusted for the adjusting entries, and computed amounts for the income statement and balance sheet columns.

a.   You added the debits and credits on the income statement and found that the credits exceeded the debits by $X. Did Woodside Publishing have a profit or a loss based on your finding?

b.   You entered the balancing amount from the income statement columns in the balance sheet columns and found the total debits exceeded total credits in the balance sheet. The difference between the debits and credits is twice the amount ($2X) you calculated in question a. What is the likely cause of the difference? What assumption have you made in your answer?

Ethical Issue

McBride Associates, a management consulting firm, is in its third year of operations. The company was initially financed by owner's equity as the three partners each invested $30,000. The first year's slim profits were expected because new businesses often start slowly. During the second year McBride Associates landed a large contract with a paper mill, and referrals from that project brought in several other large jobs. To expand the business, McBride borrowed $100,000 from Texas National Bank of Lufkin, Texas. As a condition for making this loan the bank required McBride to maintain a current ratio of at least 1.50 and a debt ratio of no more than .50.

Business during the third year has been good, but slightly below the target for the year. Expansion costs have brought the current ratio down to 1.47 and the debt ratio up to .51 at December 15. Glenda McBride and her partners are considering the implication of reporting this current ratio to Texas National Bank. One course of action that the partners are considering is to record in December of the third year some revenue on account that McBride Associates will earn in January of their fourth year of operations. The contract for this job has been signed, and McBride will perform the management consulting services for the client during January.

Required

1. Journalize the revenue transaction, and indicate how recording this revenue in December would affect the current ratio and the debt ratio.
2. State whether it is ethical to record the revenue transaction in December. Identify the accounting principle relevant to this situation.
3. Propose for McBride Associates a course of action that is ethical.

Financial Statement Problems

1. Using An Actual Balance Sheet   (L.O. 6)

Debt ratio 1990, .77

This problem, based on The Goodyear Tire & Rubber Company's balance sheet in Appendix C, will familiarize you with some of the assets and liabilities of this actual company. Answer these questions, using Goodyear's balance sheet.

1. Which balance sheet format does Goodyear use?
2. Name the company's largest current asset and largest current liability at December 31, 1990.
3. Compute Goodyear's current ratios at December 31, 1990, and December 31, 1989. Also compute the debt ratios at these dates. Did the ratio values improve or deteriorate during 1990? Refer to the income statement to explain why the ratio values improved or deteriorated.
4. Under what category does Goodyear report land, buildings, machinery and equipment?
5. What was the cost of the company's plant assets at December 31, 1990? What was the book value of the plant assets? To answer this question, refer to the Properties and Plants note.

2. Using An Actual Balance Sheet   (L.O. 6)

No check figure

Obtain the annual report of an actual company of your choosing. Answer these questions about the company:

1. Which balance sheet format does the company use?
2. Name the company's largest asset and largest liability at the end of the current year and at the end of the preceding year. Name the largest *current* asset and the largest *current* liability at the end of the current year and at the end of the preceding year.
3. Compute the company's current ratio at the end of the current year and the current ratio at the end of the preceding year. Also compute the debt ratio at the end of the current year and at the end of the preceding year. Did these ratio values improve or deteriorate during the current year? Does the income statement help to explain why the ratios improved or deteriorated? Give your reason.

Appendix

Prepaid Expenses, Unearned Revenues, and Reversing Entries

Chapters 1 through 4 illustrate the most popular way to account for prepaid expenses and unearned revenues. This appendix expands that coverage by illustrating an alternate approach to handling prepaid expenses and unearned revenues—equally appropriate—that calls for reversing entries.

Prepaid Expenses

Prepaid expenses are advance payments of expenses. Prepaid Insurance, Prepaid Rent, Prepaid Advertising, and Prepaid Legal Cost are prepaid expenses. Supplies that will be used up in the current period or within one year are also accounted for as prepaid expenses.

When a business prepays an expense—rent, for example—it can debit an *asset* account (Prepaid Rent) as follows:

Prepaid Rent	XXX	
Cash..................................		XXX

Alternatively, the accountant can debit an *expense* account in the entry to record this cash payment, as follows:

Rent Expense	XXX	
Cash..................................		XXX

Regardless of the account debited, the business must adjust the accounts at the end of the period. Making the adjustment allows the business to report the correct amount of expense for the period and the correct amount of asset at the period's end.

Prepaid Expense Recorded Initially as an Asset

Prepayments of expenses provide a future benefit to the business, so it is logical to record the prepayment by debiting an *asset* account. Suppose on August 1, 19X6, the business prepays one year's rent of $6,000 ($500 per month). The cash payment is recorded:

19X6				
Aug. 1	Prepaid Rent	6,000		
	Cash		6,000	

On December 31, the end of the accounting period, five months' prepayment has expired and must be accounted for as *expense*. The adjusting entry is

Adjusting Entries

19X6				
Dec. 31	Rent Expense ($6,000 × 5/12)	2,500		
	Prepaid Rent		2,500	

The adjusting entry transfers $2,500 of the original $6,000 prepayment from Prepaid Rent to Rent Expense. This leaves a $3,500 debit balance in Prepaid Rent, which is seven months' rent still prepaid. After posting, the accounts appear as follows:

Prepaid Rent

19X6			19X6		
Aug. 1	CP	6,000	Dec. 31	Adj.	2,500
Dec. 31	Bal.	3,500			

Rent Expense

19X6				
Dec. 31	Adj.	2,500		
Dec. 31	Bal.	2,500		

CP = Cash payments; Adj. = Adjusting entry; Bal. = Balance

The $2,500 balance of Rent Expense is closed to Income Summary, along with all other expenses and revenues, at the end of the accounting period.

No reversing entry is used under this approach. The asset account Prepaid Rent has a debit balance to start the new period. This is consistent with recording prepaid expenses initially as assets.

The balance sheet at December 31, 19X6, reports Prepaid Rent of $3,500 as an asset. The 19X6 income statement reports Rent Expense of $2,500 as an expense, which is the expired portion of the initial $6,000 rent prepayment. Keep this reporting result in mind as you study the next section.

Prepaid Expense Recorded Initially as an Expense

Prepaying an expense creates an asset. However, the asset may be so short-lived that it will expire in the current accounting period—within one year or less. Thus the accountant may decide to debit the prepayment to an expense account at the time of payment. Continuing with the rent example, the $6,000 cash payment on August 1 may be debited to Rent Expense:

```
19X6
Aug. 1   Rent Expense . . . . . . . . . . . . . . . . . . . . .   6,000
              Cash . . . . . . . . . . . . . . . . . . . . . . . .            6,000
```

At December 31 only five months' prepayment has expired, leaving seven months' rent still prepaid. In this case, the accountant must transfer $7/12$ of the original prepayment of $6,000, or $3,500, to Prepaid Rent. The adjusting entry decreases the balance of Rent Expense to $5/12$ of the original $6,000, or $2,500. The December 31 adjusting entry is

Adjusting Entries

```
19X6
Dec. 31   Prepaid Rent ($6,000 × 7/12) . . . . . . . .   3,500
               Rent Expense . . . . . . . . . . . . . . .              3,500
```

After posting, the two accounts appear as follows:

Teaching Tip: Ask this question to help your students understand why to record the prepayment in the expense account: If a business pays its rent monthly, what journal entry is made?

Rent Expense xx
    Cash   xx

If a business pays utilities, what entry is made?

Utilities Expense xx
    Cash   xx

If salaries are paid, then Salary Expense is debited. Then what entry would the bookkeeper be inclined to make for the prepayment of three months' rent in advance?

Rent Expense xx
    Cash   xx

The bookkeeper will find it easier to record the payment as an expense than as an asset because most other payments are recorded as expenses. Students find this difficult because it is not how they learned it originally.

Prepaid Rent

19X6			
Dec. 31	Adj.	3,500	
Dec. 31	Bal.	3,500	

Teaching Tip: Point out to students that if they ask these questions, then the adjusting entries will not be that difficult to make: What is the balance of the expense account? What should it be? What must be done to the expense account to ensure that balance? Students should ask these questions regardless of how the initial payment is recorded.

Rent Expense

19X6				19X6		
Aug. 1	CP	6,000		Dec. 31	Adj.	3,500
Dec. 31	Bal.	2,500				

The balance sheet for 19X6 reports Prepaid Rent of $3,500, and the income statement for 19X6 reports Rent Expense of $2,500. Whether the business initially debits the prepayment to an asset account or to an expense account, the financial statements report the same amounts for prepaid rent and rent expense. The Rent Expense's balance is closed at the end of the period.

During the next accounting period, the $3,500 balance in Prepaid Rent will expire and become expense. It is efficient on the beginning date of the new year to make a *reversing entry* that transfers the ending balance of Prepaid Rent back to Rent Expense:

Reversing Entries

19X7
Jan. 1   Rent Expense   3,500
              Prepaid Rent   3,500

This reversing entry avoids later worry about which prepayments become expenses. The arrow shows the transfer of the debit balance from Prepaid Rent to Rent Expense after posting:

Prepaid Rent

19X6				19X7		
Dec. 31	Bal.	3,500		Jan. 1	**Rev.**	**3,500**

Zero balance

Rent Expense

19X6				19X6		
Aug. 1	CP	6,000		Dec. 31	Adj.	3,500
Dec. 31	Bal.	2,500		Dec. 31	Clo.	2,500
19X7						
Jan. 1	**Rev.**	**3,500**				

Clo. = Closing entry

After the reversing entry, the $3,500 amount is lodged in the expense account. This is consistent with recording prepaid expenses initially as expenses. Because this $3,500 amount will become expense during 19X7, no additional adjustment is needed. Subsequent expense prepayments are debited to Rent Expense and then adjusted at the end of the period as outlined here. Reversing entries ease the work of the accounting process for all types of prepaid expenses that are recorded initially as expenses. Reversing entries are not used for prepaid expenses that are recorded initially as assets.

Transparency T 4-5

Comparing the Two Approaches to Recording Prepaid Expenses

In summary, the two approaches to recording prepaid expenses are similar in that the asset amount reported on the balance sheet and the expense amount reported on the income statement are the same. They differ, however, in the prepayment entries and the adjusting entries. When a prepaid expense is recorded initially as an asset, (1) the adjusting entry transfers the *used* portion of the asset to the expense account and (2) no reversing entry is used. When a prepaid expense is recorded initially as an expense, (1) the adjusting entry transfers the *unused* portion of the expense to the asset account and (2) a *reversing entry* transfers the amount of the asset account back to the expense account to start the new accounting period.

Class Exercise: Suppose that a business purchased supplies for $2,000, and originally recorded the purchase in the asset account, Supplies. If $200 of supplies are on hand at the end of the year, what would the adjusting entry be?
ANSWER:

Supplies Expense 1,800
    Supplies   1,800

Unearned (Deferred) Revenues

If the supplies had been recorded in the expense account, what would the adjusting entry be?

Supplies 200
    Supplies Expense . .   200

Unearned (deferred) revenues arise when a business collects cash in advance of earning the revenue. The recognition of revenue is *deferred* until later when it is earned. Unearned revenues are liabilities because the business that receives cash owes the other party goods or services to be delivered later.

The balance in Supplies Expense was $2,000 prior to adjustment. Only $1,800 of supplies were used up, so the expense account had to be reduced (credited) for $200.

Recall the prepaid expense examples listed on p. 198—insurance, rent, advertising, and so on. Prepaid expenses create assets for the business that pays the cash. The business that receives the cash in advance, however, faces a liability. For example, the landlord who receives a tenant's rent in advance must provide future service to the tenant. This is a liability, and the cash the landlord receives is unearned rent revenue. Similarly, unearned revenue arises as magazine publishers sell subscriptions, colleges collect tuition, airlines sell tickets, and attorneys accept advance fees.

When a business receives cash before earning the related revenue, the business debits Cash. It can credit either a *liability* account or a *revenue* account. In either case, the business must make adjusting entries at the end of the period to report the correct amounts of liability and revenue on the financial statements.

Unearned (Deferred) Revenue Recorded Initially as a Liability

Receipt of cash in advance of earning revenue creates a liability, so it is logical to debit Cash and credit a liability account. Assume an attorney receives a $7,200 fee in advance from a client on October 1, 19X2. The attorney will earn this amount at the rate of $800 per month during the nine-month period ending June 30, 19X3. The attorney's cash receipt entry is

19X2
Oct. 1   Cash   7,200
            Unearned Legal Revenue   7,200

On December 31, 19X2, the end of the law firm's accounting period, three months of the fee agreement have elapsed. The attorney has earned ⅜ of the $7,200, or $2,400. The adjusting entry to transfer $2,400 to the revenue account is

19X2
Dec. 31   Unearned Legal Revenue ($7,200 × ⅓)   2,400
                    Legal Revenue.   2,400

After posting, the liability and revenue accounts are

Unearned Legal Revenue

19X2				19X2		
Dec. 31	Adj.	2,400		Oct. 1	CR	7,200
				Dec. 31	Bal.	4,800

Legal Revenue

	19X2		
	Dec. 31	Adj.	2,400
	Dec. 31	Bal.	2,400

CR = Cash receipt

The law firm's 19X2 income statement reports legal revenue of $2,400, while its balance sheet reports unearned legal revenue of $4,800 as a liability. During 19X3 the attorney will earn the remaining $4,800 and will then make an adjusting entry to transfer $4,800 to the Legal Revenue account. No reversing entry is used. The balance in the liability account is consistent with recording the unearned revenue initially as a liability.

Unearned (Deferred) Revenue Recorded Initially as a Revenue

Receipt of cash in advance of earning the revenue can be credited initially to a *revenue* account. If the business has earned all the revenue within the period during which it received the cash, no adjusting entry is necessary. However, if the business earns only a part of the revenue at the end of the period, it must make adjusting entries.

Suppose on October 1, 19X2, the law firm records the nine-month advance fee of $7,200 as revenue. The cash receipt entry is

19X2
Oct. 1   Cash.   7,200
                    Legal Revenue   7,200

At December 31 the attorney has earned only ⅓ of the $7,200, or $2,400. Accordingly, the firm makes an adjusting entry to transfer the unearned portion (⅔ of $7,200, or $4,800) from the revenue account to a liability account.

Adjusting Entries

19X2
Dec. 31   Legal Revenue ($7,200 × ⅔)   4,800
                    Unearned Legal Revenue   4,800

The adjusting entry leaves the earned portion (⅓, or $2,400) of the original amount in the revenue account. After posting, the total amount ($7,200) is

Typical Student Misconception: Students often use the wrong adjusting entry because they do not realize that the adjusting entry depends on the way the transaction was originally recorded. If the receipt of cash before it is earned is recorded as a liability, then the adjusting entry has to be:

Unearned Revenue xx
    Revenue.   xx

If the receipt is originally recorded as revenue, then the adjusting entry must be:

Revenue. xx
    Unearned Revenue . . .   xx

These entries are not interchangeable.

properly divided between the liability account ($4,800) and the revenue account ($2,400), as follows:

Unearned Legal Revenue

	19X2		
	Dec. 31	Adj.	4,800
	Dec. 31	Bal.	4,800

Legal Revenue

19X2			19X2		
Dec. 31 Adj.	4,800		Oct. 1	CR	7,200
			Dec. 31	Bal.	2,400

The attorney's 19X2 income statement reports legal revenue of $2,400, and the balance sheet at December 31, 19X2, reports as a liability the unearned legal revenue of $4,800. Whether the business initially credits a liability account or a revenue account, the financial statements report the same amounts for unearned legal revenue and legal revenue.

The law firm will earn the $4,800 during 19X3. On January 1, 19X3, it is efficient to make a reversing entry in order to transfer the liability balance back to the revenue account. By making the reversing entry, the accountant avoids having to reconsider the situation one year later, when the 19X3 adjusting entries will be made. The reversing entry is

Reversing Entries

19X3
Jan. 1 Unearned Legal Revenue   4,800
                Legal Revenue   4,800

After posting, the liability account has a zero balance. The $4,800 credit is now lodged in the revenue account because it will be earned during 19X3. The arrow in the following example shows the transfer from the liability account to the revenue account.

Unearned Legal Revenue

			19X2		
			Dec. 31	Adj.	4,800
19X3			19X2		
Jan. 1	**Rev.**	**4,800**	Dec. 31	Bal.	4,800

Zero balance

Legal Revenue

19X2			19X2		
Dec. 31	Adj.	4,800	Oct. 1	CR	7,200
Dec. 31	Clo.	2,400	Dec. 31	Bal.	2,400
			19X3		
			Jan. 1	**Rev.**	**4,800** ⟵

Subsequent advance receipts of revenue are credited to the Legal Revenue account. The year-end adjusting process is the same for every period.

Comparing the Two Approaches to Recording Unearned (Deferred) Revenues

The two approaches to recording unearned revenue are similar in that the liability amount reported on the balance sheet and the revenue amount reported on the income statement are the same. The approaches differ, though, in how adjustments are handled. When unearned revenues are recorded initially as liabilities, (1) the adjusting entry transfers to the revenue account the amount of the advance collection that has been *earned* during the period, and (2) *no* reversing entry is used. When unearned revenues are recorded initially as revenue, (1) the adjustment transfers to the liability account the amount of the advance collection that is still *unearned*, and (2) a *reversing entry* transfers the balance of the liability account to the revenue account to begin the next accounting period.

Class Exercise: Suppose that a company receives $3,000 for magazine subscriptions in advance, and records that as a liability. If $1,600 of the subscriptions are still unearned at the end of the year, what is the adjusting entry?
ANSWER:

Unearned Revenue 1,400
   Revenue   1,400

If the subscriptions were originally recorded as revenue, what would the adjusting entry be?
ANSWER:

Revenue 1,600
   Unearned Revenue . .   1,600

The revenue account had a balance of $3,000 prior to adjustment. Since $1,600 was still unearned, only $1,400 had been earned. The revenue account needs a $1,400 balance and to ensure that, the revenue account must be reduced (debited) for $1,600.

Summary

Prepaid expenses may be recorded initially in an *asset* account or an *expense* account. When prepaid expenses are recorded initially as an asset, no need exists for a reversing entry because the asset account balance will be adjusted at the end of the next period. However, when prepaid expenses are recorded initially as an expense, a reversing entry eases accounting for the expense of the new period. Regardless of the approach taken, the financial statements should report the same amount of asset and expense.

Unearned (deferred) revenues may be recorded initially as a *liability* or a *revenue*. Recording unearned revenues initially as liabilities causes no need for a reversing entry. However, when recording them initially as revenues, a reversing entry eases accounting. Either recording approach is acceptable as long as the *financial statements* report the *correct* amounts.

Appendix Assignment Material

Exercises

Acct. bals. should be the same

Exercise 4A-1   *Recording supplies transactions two ways*

At the beginning of the year supplies of $1,490 were on hand. During the year the business paid $3,300 cash for supplies. At the end of the year the count of supplies indicates the ending balance is $1,260.

Required

1. Assume the business records supplies by initially debiting an *asset* account. Therefore, place the beginning balance in the Supplies T-account and record the above entries directly in the accounts without using a journal.
2. Assume the business records supplies by initially debiting an *expense* account. Therefore, place the beginning balance in the Supplies Expense

T-account and record the above entries directly in the accounts without using a journal.

3. Compare the ending account balances under the two approaches. Are they the same or different? Why?

Exercise 4A-2 *Recording unearned revenues two ways*

Acct. bals. should be the same

At the beginning of the year the company owed customers $6,450 for unearned sales collected in advance. During the year the business received advance cash receipts of $10,000. At year end the unearned revenue liability is $3,900.

Required

1. Assume the company records unearned revenues by initially crediting a liability account. Open T-accounts for Unearned Sales Revenue and Sales Revenue and place the beginning balance in Unearned Sales Revenue. Journalize the cash collection and adjusting entries and post their dollar amounts. As references in the T-accounts, denote a balance by Bal., a cash receipt by CR, and an adjustment by Adj.

2. Assume the company records unearned revenues by initially crediting a revenue account. Open T-accounts for Unearned Sales Revenue and Sales Revenue and place the beginning balance in Sales Revenue. Journalize the cash collection and adjusting entries and post their dollar amounts. As references in the T-accounts, denote a balance by Bal., a cash receipt by CR, and an adjustment by Adj.

3. Compare the ending balances in the two accounts. Explain why they are the same or different.

Exercise 4A-3 *Using reversing entries to account for unearned revenues*

Final bals.:
Unearned Sales Rev. $0
Sales Rev. $3,900

One approach to recording unearned revenue in Exercise 4A-2 calls for a reversing entry. Identify that approach. Journalize and post the entries required in Exercise 4A-2 and also the closing and reversing entries. The end of the current period is December 31, 19X1. Use dates for all entries and postings except the cash collection, which is a summary of the year's transactions. As references in the ledger accounts, denote a balance by Bal., cash receipts by CR, adjusting entries by Adj., closing entries by Clo., and reversing entries by Rev.

Exercise 4A-4 *Identifying transactions from a ledger account*

No check figure

McGraw Company makes its annual insurance payment on June 30. Identify each of the entries (a) through (e) to the Insurance Expense account as a cash payment, an adjusting entry, a closing entry, or a reversing entry, Also give the other account debited or credited in each entry,

Insurance Expense

Date	Item	Debit	Credit	Balance Debit	Balance Credit
19X4					
Jan. 1	(a)	800		800	
June 30	(b)	1,240		2,040	
Dec. 31	(c)		410	1,630	
Dec. 31	(d)		1,630	—	
19X5					
Jan. 1	(e)	410			410

Problem 4A-1 *Recording prepaid rent and rent revenue collected in advance two ways*

DeGroot Sales and Service completed the following transactions during 19X4:

Aug. 31 Paid $9,000 store rent covering the six-month period ending February 28, 19X5.

Dec. 1 Collected $2,200 cash in advance from customers. The service revenue will be earned $550 monthly over the period ending March 30, 19X5.

Required

1. Journalize these entries by debiting an asset account for Prepaid Rent and by crediting a liability account for Unearned Service Revenue. Explanations are unnecessary.
2. Journalize the related adjustments at December 31, 19X4.
3. Post the entries to the ledger accounts and show their balances at December 31, 19X4. Posting references are unnecessary.
4. Repeat Requirements 1 through 3. This time debit Rent Expense for the rent payment and credit Service Revenue for the collection of revenue in advance.
5. Compare the account balances in Requirements 3 and 4. They should be equal.

Problem 4A-2 *Journalizing adjusting and reversing entries*

The accounting records of Friedman, Inc., reveal the following information before adjustments at December 31, 19X7, end of the accounting period:

a. Friedman routinely debits Sales Supplies when it purchases supplies. At the beginning of 19X7 supplies of $800 were on hand, and during the year the company purchased supplies of $6,700. At year end the count of sales supplies on hand indicates the ending amount is $950.

b. Friedman collects revenue in advance from customers and credits such amounts to Sales Revenue because the revenue is usually earned within a short time. At December 31, 19X7, however, the company has a liability of $6,840 to customers for goods they paid for in advance.

c. Rentals cost the company $1,000 per month. The company prepays rent of $6,000 each May 1 and November 1 and debits Rent Expense for such payments.

d. The company prepaid $3,500 for television advertising that will run daily for two weeks—December 27, 19X7 through January 9, 19X8. Freidman debited Prepaid Advertising for the full amount on December 1.

Required

1. Journalize the adjusting entry needed for each situation at December 31, 19X7, identifying each entry by its corresponding letter.
2. Journalize reversing entries as needed. Use the corresponding letters for references. Date the entries appropriately.

Problem 4A-3 *Recording supplies and unearned revenue transactions two ways*

The accounting records of Stone Company reveal the following information about sales supplies and unearned sales revenue for 19X5:

Sales Supplies

19X5

Jan. 1	Beginning amount on hand..................	$ 420
Mar. 16	Cash purchase of supplies.................	3,740
Dec. 31	Ending amount on hand	290

Unearned Sales Revenue

19X5

Jan. 1	Beginning amount on advance collections.....	6,590
July 22	Advance cash collection from customer.......	16,480
Nov. 4	Advance cash collection from customer.......	38,400
Dec. 31	Advance collections earned during the year ...	52,160

Required

1. Assume Stone Company records (a) supplies by initially debiting an asset account and (b) advance collections from customers by initially crediting a liability account.
   a. Open T-accounts for Sales Supplies, Sales Supplies Expense, Unearned Sales Revenue, and Sales Revenue. Insert the beginning balances in the appropriate accounts.
   b. Record the cash transactions during 19X5 directly in the accounts.
   c. Record the adjusting and closing entries at December 31, 19X5, directly in the accounts.
   d. If appropriate, record the reversing entries at January 1, 19X6, directly in the accounts.
2. Assume Stone Company records (a) supplies by initially debiting an expense account and (b) advance collections by initially crediting a revenue account. Perform steps a through d as in Requirement 1.
3. Using the following format, compare the amounts that would be reported for the above accounts in the 19X5 balance sheet and income statement under the two recording approaches of Requirements 1 and 2. Explain any similarity or difference.

	Requirement 1	Requirement 2
Balance sheet at December 31, 19X5 reports:	$	$
Sales supplies...........................		
Unearned sales revenue		
Income statement for year ended December 31, 19X5, reports:		
Sales revenue...........................		
Sales supplies expense..................		

Chapter 5

Merchandising
and the Accounting Cycle

With department stores falling into Chapter 11 [bankruptcy] like dominoes, the rag trade [garment industry] should be the last place to find a superb growth company. But look at Donna Karan Co., the women's clothing concern, which projects net sales of $132 million this year, thanks mainly to the year-old DKNY line. That's up from $107 million last year and $7.4 million in 1985, Karan's first year in business. . . .

Karan clothing sells well, and wholesale buyers know it. . . . How does Karan do it? Says Neiman Marcus President and Chief Executive Terry Lundgren: "She cares about what is selling to the customer, not just what the store buyers are buying." Famous customers help, too. Candice Bergen and Diane Sawyer regular-ly wear Karan's wool jersey and crepe designs on tele-vision.

What's next? International expansion. Karan already sells 20 percent of her merchandise abroad, half of that to Japan. A Donna Karan shop opened in August in Hong Kong. . . . Next spring Karan debuts in France.

Karan says she will remain private for now. But with stellar growth and no long-term debt, Donna Karan, the company, would be even more welcome on Wall Street than it is in America's department and specialty stores.

Source: Katherine Weisman, "Designing Woman," *Forbes*, October 1, 1990, p. 261.

How do the operations of Donna Karan Co. differ from the businesses we have studied so far? In the first four chapters Gary Lyon, CPA, provided an illustration of a business that earns revenue by selling its services. Service enterprises include Holiday Inns, American Airlines, physicians, lawyers, CPAs, the Atlanta Braves baseball team, and the twelve-year-old who cuts lawns in your neighborhood. A *merchandising entity* earns its revenue by selling products, called *merchandise inventory* or simply *inventory*. Donna Karan Co., a Goodyear tire store, a Safeway grocery, a Macy's department store, and an ice-cream shop are merchandising entities. Exhibit 5-1 shows the income statement for a merchandising business. You will notice that this income statement differs from those shown earlier.

The amount that a merchandiser earns from selling its inventory is called **net sales revenue,** often abbreviated as **sales revenue.** The income Statement in Exhibit 5-1 reports net sales revenue of $680,000. The major revenue of a merchandising entity, sales revenue, represents the increase in owner's equity from delivering inventory to customers. The major expense of a merchandiser is *Cost of Goods Sold.* This expense's title is well chosen, because its amount represents the entity's cost of the goods (inventory) it has sold to customers. As long as inventory is held, it is an asset. When the inventory is sold to the customer, the inventory's cost becomes an expense. The excess of Sales Revenue over Cost of Goods Sold is called **gross margin** or **gross profit.** This important business statistic is often mentioned in the business press because it helps measure a business's success. A sufficiently high gross margin is often vital to success.

The following illustration will clarify the nature of gross margin. Consider a concession stand at a football game. Assume the business sells a soft drink for $1.00 and the vendor's cost is $.20. Gross margin per unit is $.80 ($1.00 − $.20), and the overall gross margin is $.80 multiplied by the number of drinks sold. If the concession stand sells 400 drinks on a Saturday afternoon, its gross margin on drink sales is $320 (400 × $.80). The gross margin on all sales, including hot dogs, popcorn, and candy, is the sum of the gross margins on all the items sold. Sears's gross margin—and that of a Safeway store, a neighborhood drug store, and every other merchandiser—is computed in exactly the same way: Sales Revenue − Cost of Goods Sold = Gross Margin.

Margin in gross margin refers to the excess of revenue over expense. *Gross* indicates that the operating expenses (rent, depreciation, advertising, and so on) have not yet been subtracted. After subtracting all the expenses we have *net income.* Gross margin and net income are *not* accounts in the ledger, so we cannot make journal entries to them. Instead, we compute these amounts by subtracting one amount from another: Gross Margin − Operating Expenses = Net Income. Study Exhibit 5-1, focusing on the sales revenue, cost of goods sold, and gross margin. Note the separate category for operating expenses.

Typical Student Misconception: Students often think the Sales Revenue account is used to record all sales of assets. Explain that Sales Revenue is used only for sales of merchandise. Donna Karan uses this account to record only the sales of clothing.

Point to Stress: If a car dealer buys a car for $10,000 from the manufacturer and sells it for $15,000, then $10,000 is the cost of the good sold. The dealer had to buy the car before he could sell it; therefore we classify cost of goods sold as an expense. It is usually a merchandising company's largest expense.

Real-World Example: The gross profit or gross margin is often expressed by management as a percentage of sales. It is referred to as the gross profit percentage or the average mark-up percentage on sales. Managers monitor this percentage very closely.

EXHIBIT 5-1   A Merchandiser's Income Statement

Discussion Question: Calculate the gross margin percentage in Exhibit 5-1. ANSWER: $310,000 / $680,000 = 46%. Now calculate the cost of goods sold as a percentage of sales. ANSWER: $370,000 / $680,000 = 54%.

What do these percentages tell management? ANSWER: For every dollar in sales, Austin Sound spends 54¢ to acquire the merchandise; the company makes a gross margin of 46¢ on each dollar of sales revenue.

Midwest Supply Company
Income Statement
For the Year Ended December 31, 19X6

Net sales revenue		$680,000
Cost of goods sold		370,000
Gross margin		310,000
Operating expenses:		
Salary expense	$130,000	
Rent expense	60,000	
Insurance expense	18,000	
Depreciation expense	14,000	
Supplies expense	8,000	230,000
Net income		$ 80,000

The Operating Cycle for a Merchandising Business

OBJECTIVE 1
Explain the operating cycle of a merchandising business

A merchandising entity buys inventory, sells the inventory to its customers, and uses the cash to purchase more inventory to repeat the cycle. Exhibit 5-2 diagrams the operating cycle for *cash sales* and for *sales on account*. For a cash sale—item *a* in the exhibit—the cycle is from cash to inventory, which is purchased for resale, and back to cash. For a sale on account—item *b*—the cycle is from cash to inventory to accounts receivable and back to cash.

Purchase of Merchandise Inventory

Typical Student Misconception: The account called Purchases should be used only for purchases of merchandise for resale. Purchases of any other assets are recorded in the corresponding asset account. For example, the purchase of land is debited to the Land account, not to Purchases.

The cycle of a merchandising entity begins with cash, which is used to purchase inventory, as Exhibit 5-2 shows. **Purchases,** in the accounting sense, are only those items of merchandise inventory that a firm buys to resell to customers in the normal course of business. For example, a stereo center records in the Purchases account the price it pays for tape decks, turntables, and other items of inventory acquired for resale. A bicycle shop debits Purchases when it buys ten-speeds for its inventory. A grocery store debits Purchases when it buys canned goods, meat, frozen food, and other inventory. A $500 purchase on account is recorded as follows:

June 14 Purchases	500	
Accounts Payable		500
Purchased inventory on account.		

The Purchase Invoice: A Basic Business Document

Point to Stress: Although the purchase order is a business document, it is not the one that signals a journal entry. The invoice (bill) is the document upon which the journal entry is based. The journal entry is not made until the invoice is received.

Business documents are the tangible evidence of transactions. As we trace the steps that Austin Sound Stereo Center, an actual business, takes in ordering, receiving, and paying for inventory, we point out the roles that documents play in carrying on business.

1. Suppose Austin Sound wants to stock JVC brand turntables, cassette decks, and speakers. Austin Sound prepares a *purchase order* and mails it to JVC.

EXHIBIT 5-2 *Operating Cycle of a Merchandiser*

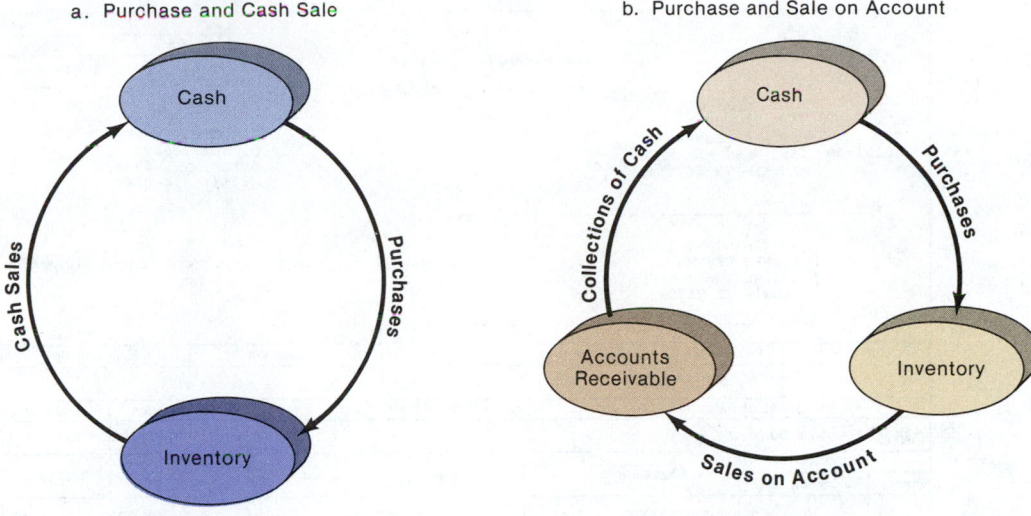

a. Purchase and Cash Sale

b. Purchase and Sale on Account

2. On receipt of the purchase order, JVC scans its warehouse for the inventory that Austin Sound ordered. JVC ships the equipment and mails the invoice to Austin on the same day. The **invoice** is the seller's request for payment from the purchaser. It is also called the *bill*.

3. Often the purchaser receives the invoice before the inventory arrives. Austin Sound does not pay immediately. Instead, Austin waits until the inventory arrives in order to ensure that it is (1) the correct type, (2) the quantity ordered, and (3) in good condition. After the inventory is inspected and approved, Austin Sound pays JVC the invoice amount.

Exhibit 5-3 is a copy of an actual invoice from JVC to Austin Sound Stereo Center. From Austin Sound's perspective, this document is a *purchase invoice*, whereas to JVC it is a *sales invoice*. The circled numbers that appear on the exhibit correspond to the following numbered explanations:

1. The seller is JVC Southwest Branch.

2. The invoice date is 05/27/92. The date is needed for determining whether the purchaser gets a discount for prompt payment (see item 5 below).

3. The purchaser is Austin Sound Stereo Center. The inventory is invoiced (billed) and shipped to the same address, 305 West Martin Luther King Blvd., Austin, Texas.

4. Austin Sound's purchase order (P.O.) date was 05/25/92.

5. Credit terms of the transaction are 3% 15, NET 30 DAYS. This means that Austin Sound may deduct 3 percent of the total amount due if Austin pays within 15 days of the invoice date. Otherwise, the full amount—net—is due in 30 days. (A full discussion of discounts appears in the next section.)

6. Austin Sound ordered six turntables, three cassette decks, and two speakers.

7. JVC shipped five turntables, no cassette decks, and no speakers.

8. Total invoice amount is $707.

9. Austin Sound paid on 6-10-92. How much did Austin pay? (See item 10.)

Teaching Tip: Ask your students these questions to help them understand the concept of the operating cycle: Approximately how long does it take for a department store to sell its merchandise? ANSWER: Students might guess two or three months. Since most merchandise is seasonal, two or three months would probably be a good guess.

Then ask another question: About how long does it take a department store to collect the cash from the sale of its merchandise? ANSWER: Students will probably answer 30 days. Some of the sales will be collected immediately and some collections will be overdue. The operating cycle would then be the 2-3 months it takes to sell the inventory + the 30 days it takes to collect the cash from the sale. The cash can then be used to buy merchandise and begin the cycle all over again.

Real-World Example: The merchandise and invoice are sent separately. If the two were sent together and if the merchandise did not arrive, then the purchaser would not know of the shipment. If the merchandise is sent separately, and if the merchandise does not arrive, then the receipt of the invoice will alert the buyer that something has happened to the merchandise.

Discussion Question: What is meant by the terms (a) 1/10 n/60; (b) 2/10 n/eom; and (c) n/30? ANSWER: (a) 1% discount if paid within 10 days, gross amount of invoice due in 60 days; (b) 2% discount within 10 days or gross due at end of month; (c) no discount, gross due in 30 days.

EXHIBIT 5-3 *Business Invoice*

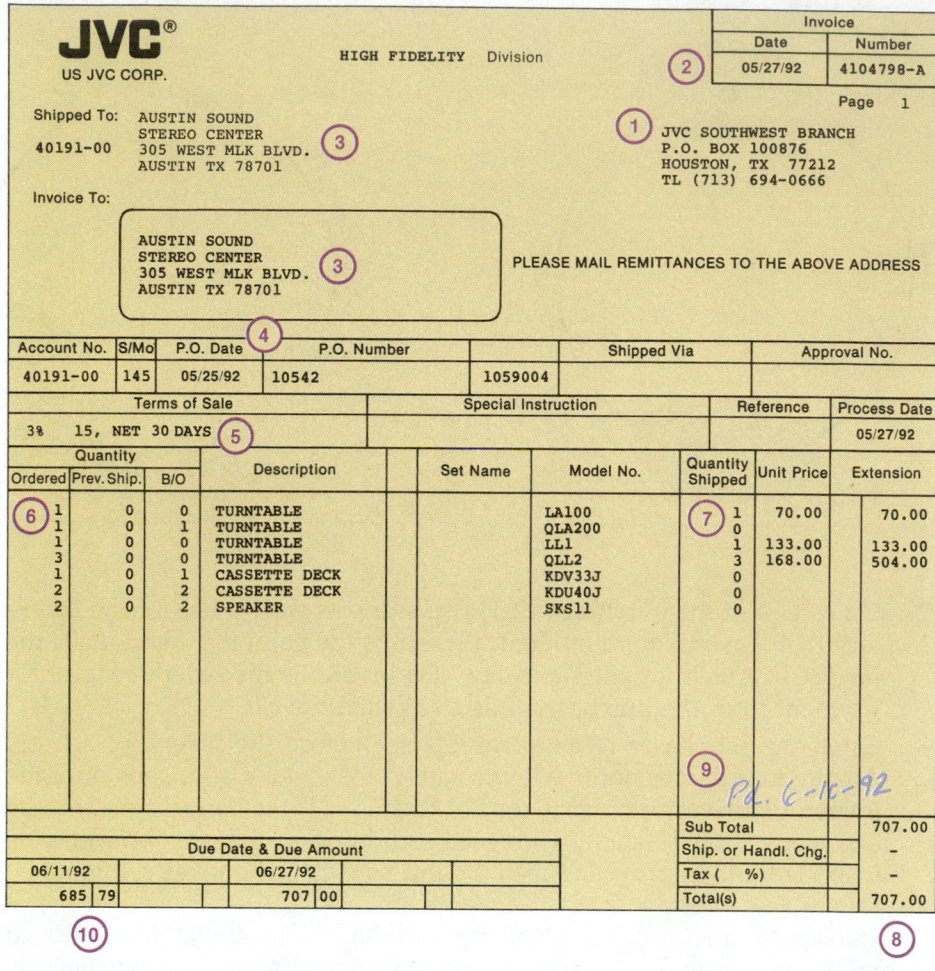

10. Payment occurred 14 days after the invoice date—within the discount period. Therefore, Austin Sound paid $685.79 ($707 minus the 3 percent discount).

Discounts from Purchase Prices

There are two major types of discounts from purchase prices: quantity discounts and cash discounts (called purchase discounts).

Quantity Discounts. A **quantity discount** works this way: the larger the quantity purchased, the lower the price per item. For example, JVC may offer no discount for the purchase of only one or two cassette decks and charge the list price—the full price—of $200 per unit. However, JVC may offer the following quantity discount terms in order to persuade customers to buy a larger number of cassette decks:

Teaching Tip: In their catalogs, many manufacturers print the retail price rather than wholesale cost so that retail customers will not see the wholesale cost. The manufacturer then gives the wholesale purchaser a quantity discount. If catalog retail price is $100 and quantity discount is 40%, then wholesale cost is $60.

Quantity	Quantity Discount	Net Price Per Unit
Buy minimum quantity, 3 cassette decks....	5%	$190[$200 − .05($200)]
Buy 4–9 decks	10%	$180[$200 − .10($200)]
Buy more than 9 decks...................	20%	$160[$200 − .20($200)]

Suppose Austin Sound purchases five cassette decks from this manufacturer. The cost of each cassette deck is, therefore, $180. Purchase of five units on account would be recorded by debiting Purchases and crediting Accounts Payable for the total price of $900 ($180 X 5).

There is no quantity discount account, and there is no special accounting entry for a quantity discount. Instead, all accounting entries are based on the net price of a purchase after subtracting the quantity discount. If a quantity discount is also offered, the purchase discount is computed on the net purchase amount after subtracting the quantity discount.

Purchase Discounts. Many businesses also offer purchase discounts to their customers. A **purchase discount** is a reward for prompt payment. If a quantity discount is also offered, the purchase discount is computed on the net purchase amount after subtracting the quantity discount.

JVC's credit terms of 3% 15 NET 30 DAYS can also be expressed as 3/15 n/30. Terms of simply n/30 indicate that no discount is offered and that payment is due 30 days after the invoice date. Terms of *eom* usually mean that payment is due at the end of the current month. However, a purchase after the twenty-fifth of the current month on terms of *eom* can be paid at the end of the next month.

Let's use the Exhibit 5-3 transaction to illustrate accounting for a purchase discount. Austin Sound records this purchase on account as follows:

May 27   Purchases 707.00
             Accounts Payable 707.00
         Purchased inventory on account.

Since Austin Sound paid within the discount period, its cash payment entry is

June 10   Accounts Payable 707.00
             Cash ($707.00 × .97) 685.79
             Purchase Discounts ($707.00 × .03) 21.21
         Paid on account within discount period.

Purchase Discounts, which has a credit balance, is a contra account to Purchases. We show how to report Purchase Discounts on the income statement later in the chapter.

Alternatively, if Austin Sound pays this invoice after the discount period, it must pay the full invoice amount. In this case, the payment entry is

June 29   Accounts Payable 707.00
             Cash 707.00
         Paid on account after discount period.

Purchase Returns and Allowances

Most businesses allow their customers to *return* merchandise that is defective, damaged in shipment, or otherwise unsuitable. Or if the buyer chooses to keep damaged goods, the seller may deduct an *allowance* from the amount the buyer owes. Because returns and allowances are closely related, they are usually recorded in a single account, **Purchase Returns and Allowances.** This account, a contra account to Purchases, gives a record of the amount of returns and allowances for the period. Later in the chapter, we show how to report this account on the income statement.

Teaching Tip: It is usually a good idea for a company to take a discount when offered. For example, a 2% discount for paying twenty days early is equivalent to approximately 36% interest for a year (360/20 = 18 twenty-day periods in a year X 2% = 36%).

Discussion Question: Why do suppliers offer purchase discounts to their customers? *ANSWER:* The discount is an incentive for the purchaser to pay sooner. The sooner the supplier gets paid, the sooner he can put that money to work. Students might mention the time value of money.

Discussion Question: Why is accounts payable debited for $707 when only $685.79 has been paid? *ANSWER:* Because of the discount, $685.79 represents payment in full. Preparation of a T-account may help.

OBJECTIVE 2
Account for the purchase and sale of inventory

Suppose the $70 turntable purchased by Austin Sound (in Exhibit 5-3) was not the turntable ordered. Austin returns the merchandise to the seller and records the purchase return as follows:

June 3	Accounts Payable	70.00	
	Purchase Returns and Allowances		70.00
	Returned inventory to seller.		

Now assume that one of the JVC turntables is damaged in shipment to Austin Sound. The damage is minor, and Austin decides to keep the turntable in exchange for a $10 allowance from JVC. To record this purchase allowance, Austin Sound makes this entry:

June 4	Accounts Payable	10.00	
	Purchase Returns and Allowances		10.00
	Received a purchase allowance.		

Observe that the return and the allowance had two effects. (1) They decreased Austin Sound's liability, which is why we debit Accounts Payable. (2) They decreased the net cost of the purchase, which is why we credit Purchase Returns and Allowances. It would be incorrect to credit Purchases because Austin Sound did in fact make the purchase. Changes because of returns and allowances are recorded in the contra account.

During the period, the business records the cost of all inventory bought in the Purchases account. The balance of Purchases is a *gross* amount because it does not include subtractions for purchase discounts, returns, or allowances. **Net purchases** is the remainder that is computed by subtracting the contra accounts as follows:

> **Purchases** (*debit* balance account)
> − **Purchase Discounts** (*credit* balance account)
> − **Purchase Returns and Allowances** (*credit* balance account)
> _____
> = **Net purchases** (a *debit* subtotal, not a separate account)

Transportation Costs

The transportation cost of moving inventory from seller to buyer can be significant. The purchase agreement specifies FOB terms to indicate who pays the shipping charges. The term *FOB* stands for *free on board* and governs when the legal title to the goods passes from seller to buyer. Under FOB *shipping point* terms, title passes when the inventory leaves the seller's place of business—the shipping point. The buyer owns the goods while they are in transit and therefore pays the transportation cost. Under FOB *destination* terms, title passes when the goods reach the destination, so the seller pays transportation cost.

	FOB Shipping Point	FOB Destination
When does title pass to buyer?	Shipping point	Destination
Who pays transportation cost?	Buyer	Seller

FOB shipping point terms are most common, so generally, the buyer bears the shipping cost. The buyer debits Freight In (sometimes called Transportation In) and credits Cash or Accounts Payable for the amount. Suppose the buyer receives a shipping bill directly from the freight company. The buyer's entry to record payment of the freight charge is:

March 3   Freight In   190
                Cash   190
           Paid a freight bill.

Under FOB shipping point terms, the seller sometimes prepays the transportation cost as a convenience and lists this cost on the invoice. The buyer would *not* debit Purchases for the combined cost of the inventory and the shipping cost. Rather, the buyer would debit Purchases for the cost of the goods and Freight In separately. A $5,000 purchase of goods, coupled with a related freight charge of $400, would be recorded as follows:

March 12   Purchases................................   5,000
            Freight In   400
                Accounts Payable   5,400
            Purchased inventory on account plus freight.

Purchase discounts and quantity discounts are computed only on the cost of the inventory, *not* on the freight charges. Suppose the $5,000 credit purchase allows a $100 discount for early payment. The cash payment within the discount period would be $5,300 [net payment of $4,900 on the inventory ($5,000, less the $100 purchase discount), plus the freight charge of $400].

Real-World Example: Freight costs are cheaper if paid in advance by the seller than if paid COD by the buyer. For that reason, most freight is prepaid by the seller if the terms are FOB shipping point. The buyer will be billed by the seller for the merchandise and the freight.

Sale of Inventory _____

The sale of inventory may be for cash or on account, as Exhibit 5-2 shows.

Cash Sale.   Sales of retailers like department stores, drug stores, gift shops, and restaurants are often for cash. A $3,000 cash sale is recorded by debiting Cash and crediting the revenue account, Sales Revenue, as follows:

Jan. 9   Cash   3,000
              Sales Revenue   3,000
          Cash sale.

Sale on Account.   Most sales by wholesalers, manufacturers, and retailers are made on account (on credit). A $5,000 sale on account is recorded by a debit to Accounts Receivable and a credit to Sales Revenue, as follows:

Jan. 11   Accounts Receivable   5,000
               Sales Revenue   5,000
           Sale on account.

The related cash receipt on account is journalized as follows:

Jan. 19   Cash   5,000
               Accounts Receivable....................   5,000
           Collection on account.

Sales Discounts, Sales Returns and Allowances

Sales Discounts and **Sales Returns and Allowances** are contra accounts to Sales Revenue, just as Purchase Discounts and Purchase Returns and Allowances are contra accounts to Purchases. Let's examine a sequence of the sale transactions of JVC.

On July 7, JVC sells stereo components for $7,200 on credit terms of 2/10 n/30. JVC's entry to record this credit sale follows:

July 7   Accounts Receivable   7,200
                Sales Revenue   7,200
            Sale on account.

Assume the buyer returns goods that cost $600. JVC records the sales return and the related decrease in Accounts Receivable as follows:

July 12   Sales Returns and Allowances   600
                Accounts Receivable.....................   600
            Received returned goods.

JVC grants a $100 sales allowance for damaged goods. JVC journalizes this transaction by debiting Sales Returns and Allowances and crediting Accounts Receivable as follows:

July 15   Sales Returns and Allowances   100
                Accounts Receivable.....................   100
            Granted a sales allowance for damaged goods.

After the preceding entries are posted, Accounts Receivable has a $6,500 debit balance, as follows:

Accounts Receivable			
July 7	7,200	July 12	600
		15	100
Bal.	6,500		

On July 17, the last day of the discount period, JVC collects half ($3,250) of this receivable ($6,500 X 1/2 = $3,250). The cash receipt is $3,185 [$3,250 − ($3,250 X .02)], and the collection entry is

July 17   Cash   3,185
                Sales Discounts ($3,250 X .02)   65
                    Accounts Receivable   3,250
            Cash collection within the discount period.

Suppose JVC collects the remainder on July 28—after the discount period—so there is no sales discount. To record this collection on account, JVC debits Cash and credits Accounts Receivable for the same amount, as follows:

July 28   Cash   3,250
                Accounts Receivable   3,250
            Cash collection after the discount period.

Net sales is computed in a manner similar to net purchases. We subtract the contra accounts as follows:

> **Sales Revenue** (*credit* balance account)
> **− Sales Discounts** (*debit* balance account)
> **− Sales Returns and Allowances** (*debit* balance account)
> ────────────────────────────────
> **= Net sales** (a *credit* subtotal, not a separate account)

Cost of Goods Sold

Cost of goods sold is the largest single expense of most merchandising businesses. It is the cost of the inventory that the business has sold to customers. Another name for cost of goods sold is **cost of sales**. How is it computed?

Recall from Chapter 3 that supplies expense is computed as follows:

> **Beginning supplies**
> **+ Supplies purchased during the period**
> ────────────────────────────────
> **= Supplies available for use during the period**
> **− Supplies on hand at the end of the period**
> ────────────────────────────────
> **= Supplies expense**

Cost of goods sold is computed this same way, as shown in Exhibit 5-4.

EXHIBIT 5-4 *Measurement of Cost of Goods Sold* Transparency T5-1

Computation:

> **Beginning inventory**
> **+Net purchases**
> **+Freight in**
> ────────────────────────────────
> **=Cost of goods available for sale**
> **−Ending inventory**
> ────────────────────────────────
> **=Cost of goods sold**

Diagram:

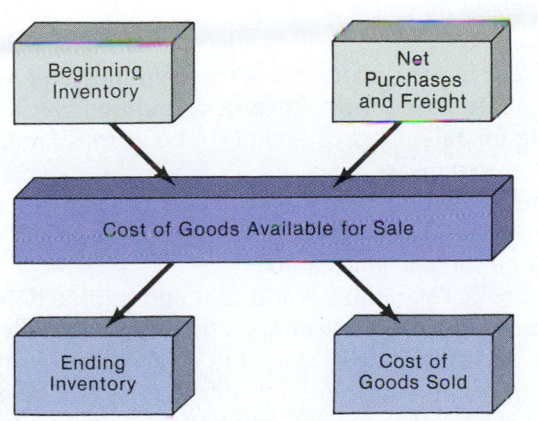

Teaching Tip: Put this summarized formula on the board as you discuss Exhibit 5-4:

> BI
> + Pur
> ────
> GA
> − EI
> ────
> COGS

Students must learn this formula.

By studying the exhibit, you will see that the computation and the diagram tell the same story. That is, a company's goods available for sale during a period come from beginning inventory plus the period's net purchases and freight costs. Either the merchandise is sold during the period, or it remains on hand at the end. The merchandise that remains is an asset, Inventory. The cost of the inventory that has been sold is an expense, Cost of Goods Sold.

Two main types of inventory accounting systems exist: the periodic system and the perpetual system. The periodic method is used by businesses that sell relatively inexpensive goods. A grocery store without an optical-scanning cash register does not keep a daily running record of every loaf of bread and every can of pineapple that it buys and sells. The cost of the record keeping would be overwhelming. Instead, grocers count their inventory periodically—at least once a year—to determine the quantities on hand. The inventory amounts are used to prepare the annual financial statements. Other businesses such as office supply outlets, restaurants, and department stores also use the periodic inventory system. The key idea is that detailed inventory records are not necessary in the ledger for controlling merchandise and managing day-to-day operations. In small businesses, the owner can visually inspect the goods on hand for control purposes.

Under the perpetual inventory system, the business maintains a running record of inventory on hand. This system achieves control over expensive goods such as automobiles, jewelry, and furniture. The loss of one item would be significant, and this justifies the cost of a perpetual system. More and more businesses are using the perpetual system as computers become more flexible and less expensive. Even under a perpetual system the business counts the inventory on hand annually. The physical count establishes the correct amount of ending inventory and serves as a check on the perpetual records.

In this chapter, we illustrate the periodic inventory system because it highlights the relationship between inventory and cost of goods sold, as shown in Exhibit 5-4. This model for computing expense is used throughout accounting and is extremely useful for analytical purposes. Furthermore, the periodic system is used by many small businesses, such as the proprietorships we illustrate in the early chapters of this book. Chapter 9 discusses the perpetual system.

Under the periodic system, as we have noted, the business does not keep a running record of the cost of its inventory on hand. Instead, it counts the goods on hand at the end of each year to determine the inventory to be reported on the balance sheet. This ending inventory amount becomes the beginning inventory of the next period and is used to compute cost of goods sold for the income statement. *In the periodic inventory system, entries to the Inventory account are made only at the end of the period.*

In this inventory system, cost of goods sold is *not* a ledger account like Salary Expense, Rent Expense, and the other operating expenses. Instead, it is the cost left over when we subtract the cost of ending inventory from the cost of goods available for sale. Cost of goods sold is computationally more complex than the other expenses.

Exhibit 5-5 summarizes the first half of the chapter by showing Austin Sound's net sales revenue, cost of goods sold—including net purchases—and gross margin on the income statement.

Note that arithmetic operations—addition and subtraction—move across the columns from left to right. For example, the figures for Sales Discounts and for Sales Returns and Allowances appear in a separate column. Their sum—$3,400—appears to the right, where it is subtracted from Sales Revenue. The net sales amount of $135,900 appears in the right-most column.

EXHIBIT 5-5   *Partial Income Statement*

Austin Sound
Income Statement
For the Year Ended December 31, 19X6

Sales revenue.................			$139,300
Less: Sales discounts		$ 1,400	
Sales returns and			
allowances		2,000	3,400
Net sales			$135,900
Cost of goods sold:			
Beginning inventory			$ 40,500
Purchases		$89,300	
Less: Purchase discounts .	$3,000		
Purchase returns			
and allowances ...	1,200	4,200	
Net purchases			85,100
Freight in			5,200
Cost of goods available for			
sale...................			130,800
Less: Ending inventory ...			42,000
Cost of goods sold			88,800
Gross margin			$ 47,100

Transparency T5-2

Teaching Tip: Refer to Exhibit 5-5 and discuss the form of the income statement through gross margin. Students often spend too much time on setting up an income statement and not enough time on content. Make sure your students understand the formula for cost of goods sold (Ex. 5-4) and do not just memorize it.

Teaching Tip: Have students turn back to the journal entry for May 27 (p. 213) and show that the Inventory account was not used in the journal entry. Explain that this is because we are using the periodic inventory system, which means all inventory purchased during the period is recorded by a debit to Purchases.

Contra accounts—discounts, returns and allowances, and the like—are frequently netted against their related accounts parenthetically. Thus many accountants would report sales in our example as follows:

Net sales revenue (net of sales discounts, $1,400,
and returns and allowances, $2,000) $135,900

Purchases can also be reported at its net amount in the following manner:

Cost of goods sold:
Beginning inventory ....$ 40,500
Net purchases (net of purchase discounts, $3,000,
and returns and allowances, $1,200) 85,100
Freight in 5,200
Cost of goods available for sale 130,800
Less: Ending inventory 42,000
Cost of goods sold ....$ 88,800

Class Exercise: Assume the following facts:

Purchases	$265,000
Sales..............	463,000
Gross Margin.......	200,000
Purchase Returns	
and Allowances...	2,600
Beginning Inventory	12,000
Sales Returns and	
Allowances.......	4,500
Purchase Discounts .	2,400
Ending Inventory ...	?
Sales Discounts	8,500

How much is Ending Inventory? ANSWER: $22,000

Show the student that the easiest way to work this is to set up the income statement through gross margin because many of the unknowns will be easier to compute.

These presentations of *net sales* and *net* purchases underscore an important fact: published financial statements usually report only *net* amounts for these items because discounts and returns and allowances are relatively small in amount. For most businesses, these contra items are details of primary interest only to managers and therefore are not highlighted in the financial statements. For example, Colgate-Palmolive Company recently reported:

	19X9	19X8
Net sales...............	$5,038,813	$4,734,325
Cost of sales	2,843,050	2,725,218
Gross profit	$2,195,763	$2,009,107

Summary Problem for your Review

Brun Sales Company engaged in the following transactions during June of the current year:

June 3 Purchased inventory on credit terms of 1/10 net eom (end of month), $1,610.

9 Returned 40 percent of the inventory purchased on June 3. It was defective.

9 Sold goods for cash, $920.

15 Purchased merchandise of $5,100, less a $100 quantity discount. Credit terms were 3/15 net 30.

16 Paid a $260 freight bill on goods purchased.

18 Sold inventory on credit terms of 2/10 n/30, $2,000.

22 Received damaged merchandise from the customer to whom the June 18 sale was made, $800.

24 Borrowed money from the bank to take advantage of the discount offered on the June 15 purchase. Signed a note payable to the bank for the net amount.

24 Paid supplier for goods purchased on June 15, less all discounts.

28 Received cash in full settlement of the account from the customer who purchased inventory on June 18.

29 Paid the amount owed on account from the purchase of June 3.

30 Purchased inventory for cash, $900, less a quantity discount of $35.

Required

1. Journalize the above transactions. Explanations are not required.
2. Assume the note payable signed on June 24 requires the payment of $95 interest expense. Was the decision wise or unwise to borrow funds to take advantage of the cash discount?

SOLUTION TO REVIEW PROBLEM

Requirement 1

June 3	Purchases......................................	1,610	
	Accounts Payable.........................		1,610
9	Accounts Payable ($1,610 X .40)...............	644	
	Purchase Returns and Allowances........		644
9	Cash	920	
	Sales Revenue...........................		920
15	Purchases ($5,100 − $100)	5,000	
	Accounts Payable........................		5,000
16	Freight In....................................	260	
	Cash		260

June 18	Accounts Receivable	2,000	
	Sales Revenue		2,000
22	Sales Returns and Allowances	800	
	Accounts Receivable		800
24	Cash [$5,000 − .03($5,000)]	4,850	
	Note Payable		4,850
24	Accounts Payable	5,000	
	Purchase Discounts ($5,000 X. 03)		150
	Cash ($5,000 X .97)		4,850
28	Cash [($2,000 − $800) X .98]	1,176	
	Sales Discounts [($2,000 − $800) X .02]	24	
	Accounts Receivable ($2,000 − $800)		1,200
29	Accounts Payable ($1,610 − $644)	966	
	Cash		966
30	Purchases ($900–$35)	865	
	Cash		865

Requirement 2.   The decision to borrow funds was wise because the discount ($150) exceeded the interest paid on the amount borrowed ($95). Thus the entity was $55 better off as a result of its decision.

The Adjusting and Closing Process for a Merchandising Business

A merchandising business adjusts and closes the accounts much as a service entity does. The steps of this end-of-period process are the same: If a work sheet is used, enter the trial balance, and complete the work sheet to determine net income or net loss. The work sheet provides the data for preparing the financial statements and for journalizing the adjusting and closing entries. After these entries are posted to the ledger, a postclosing trial balance can be prepared.

The Inventory account affects the adjusting and closing entries of a merchandiser. At the end of the period, before any adjusting or closing entries, the Inventory account balance is still the cost of the inventory that was on hand at the beginning date. It is necessary to remove this beginning balance and replace it with the cost of the ending inventory. Various acceptable bookkeeping techniques might be used to bring the inventory records up to date. In this chapter we illustrate the closing-entry method. In the chapter appendix we present an alternative approach, the adjusting-entry method.

To illustrate a merchandiser's adjusting and closing process, let's use Austin Sound's December 31, 19X6, trial balance in Exhibit 5-6. All the new accounts—Inventory, Freight In, and the contra accounts—are highlighted for emphasis. However, Inventory is the only account that is affected by the new closing procedures. Note that additional-data item *g* gives the ending inventory of $42,000.

EXHIBIT 5-6 *Trial Balance*

Austin Sound
Trial Balance
December 31, 19X6

Cash	$ 2,850	
Accounts receivable	4,600	
Note receivable, current	8,000	
Interest receivable		
Inventory	**40,500**	
Supplies	650	
Prepaid insurance	1,200	
Furniture and fixtures	33,200	
Accumulated depreciation		$ 2,400
Accounts payable		47,000
Unearned sales revenue		2,000
Interest payable		
Note payable, long-term		12,600
C. Ernest, capital		25,900
C. Ernest, withdrawals	34,100	
Sales revenue		**138,000**
Sales discounts	**1,400**	
Sales returns and allowances	**2,000**	
Interest revenue		600
Purchases	**89,300**	
Purchase discounts		**3,000**
Purchase returns and allowances		**1,200**
Freight in	**5,200**	
Rent expense	8,400	
Depreciation expense		
Insurance expense		
Supplies expense		
Interest expense	1,300	
Total	$232,700	$232,700

Additional data at December 31, 19X6:

a. Interest revenue earned but not yet collected, $400.
b. Supplies on hand, $100.
c. Prepaid insurance expired during the year, $1,000.
d. Depreciation, $600.
e. Unearned sales revenue earned during the year, $1,300.
f. Interest expense incurred but not yet paid, $200.
g. Inventory on hand, $42,000.

Point to Stress: If you were preparing a manual work sheet, you could also omit the adjusted trial balance columns. Once you understand the mechanics of preparing a work sheet, it is fairly easy to take a trial balance amount, add or subtract the adjustments, and extend the new amount to either the income statement or balance sheet columns.

Work Sheet of a Merchandising Business

The Exhibit 5-7 work sheet is similar to the work sheets we have seen so far, but a few differences appear. Note that this work sheet does not include adjusted trial balance columns. In most accounting systems, a single operation combines trial balance amounts with the adjustments and extends the adjusted balances directly to the income statement and balance sheet columns. Therefore, to reduce clutter, the adjusted trial balance columns are omitted. A

EXHIBIT 5-7 *Work Sheet*

Austin Sound
Work Sheet
For the Year Ended December 31, 19X6

Account Title	Trial Balance Debit	Trial Balance Credit	Adjustments Debit	Adjustments Credit	Income Statement Debit	Income Statement Credit	Balance Sheet Debit	Balance Sheet Credit
Cash	2,850						2,850	
Accounts receivable	4,600						4,600	
Note receivable, current	8,000						8,000	
Interest receivable			(a) 400				400	
Inventory	40,500				40,500	42,000	42,000	
Supplies	650			(b) 550			100	
Prepaid insurance	1,200			(c) 1,000			200	
Furniture and fixtures	33,200						33,200	
Accumulated depreciation		2,400		(d) 600				3,000
Accounts payable		47,000						47,000
Unearned sales revenue		2,000	(e) 1,300					700
Interest payable				(f) 200				200
Note payable, long-term		12,600						12,600
C. Ernest, capital		25,900						25,900
C. Ernest, withdrawals	34,100						34,100	
Sales revenue		138,000		(e) 1,300		139,300		
Sales discounts	1,400				1,400			
Sales returns and allowances	2,000				2,000			
Interest revenue		600		(a) 400		1,000		
Purchases	89,300				89,300			
Purchase discounts		3,000				3,000		
Purchase returns and allowances		1,200				1,200		
Freight in	5,200				5,200			
Rent expense	8,400				8,400			
Depreciation expense			(d) 600		600			
Insurance expense			(c) 1,000		1,000			
Supplies expense			(b) 550		550			
Interest expense	1,300		(f) 200		1,500			
	232,700	232,700	4,050	4,050	150,450	186,500	125,450	89,400
Net income					36,050			36,050
					186,500	186,500	125,450	125,450

second difference is that the merchandiser's work sheet includes inventory and purchase amounts (which are highlighted here). Let's examine the entire work sheet.

Account Title Columns.   The trial balance lists a number of accounts without balances. Ordinarily, these accounts are affected by the adjusting process. Examples include Interest Receivable, Interest Payable, and Depreciation Expense. The accounts are listed in the order they appear in the ledger. This eases the preparation of the work sheet. If additional accounts are needed, they can be written in at the bottom of the work sheet before net income is determined. Simply move net income down to make room for the additional accounts.

Trial Balance columns.   Examine the Inventory account, $40,500 in the trial balance. This $40,500 is the cost of the beginning inventory. The work sheet is designed to replace this outdated amount with the new ending balance, which

Point to Stress: The Inventory account is not changed when inventory is bought or sold. Beginning Inventory remains on the books and on the trial balance until Ending Inventory replaces it during the closing process.

in our example is $42,000 (additional-data item *g* in Exhibit 5-6). As we shall see, this task is accomplished later in the columns for the income statement and the balance sheet.

Adjustments Columns. The adjustments are similar to those discussed in Chapters 3 and 4. They may be entered in any order desired. The debit amount of each entry should equal the credit amount, and total debits should equal total credits.

Discussion Question: Refer to Exhibit 5-7. Ask: Are all the accounts in the debit column of the Income Statement expenses? *ANSWER:* No. Beginning Inventory, Sales Discounts, and Sales Returns and Allowances are not expenses. What accounts in the credit column are not revenue accounts? *ANSWER:* Ending Inventory, Purchase Discounts, and Purchase Returns and Allowances.

Point to Stress: No longer is the debit column of the Income Statement solely for expenses and the credit column solely for revenues.

Point to Stress: Notice that net income is still the difference between the debit and credit columns, as discussed in Chapter 4.

Income Statement Columns. The income statement columns contain adjusted amounts for the revenues and the expenses. Sales Revenue, for example, is $139,300, which includes the $1,300 adjustment.

You may be wondering why the two inventory amounts appear in the income statement columns. The reason is that both beginning inventory and ending inventory enter the computation of cost of goods sold. Recall that beginning inventory is added to purchases and ending inventory is subtracted. Even though the resulting cost-of-goods-sold amount does not appear on the work sheet, all the components of cost of goods sold are evident there. *Placement of beginning inventory ($40,500) in the work sheet's income statement debit column has the effect of adding beginning inventory in computing cost of goods sold. Placing ending inventory ($42,000) in the credit column has the opposite effect.*

Purchases and Freight In appear in the debit column because they are added in computing cost of goods sold. Purchase Discounts and Purchase Returns and Allowances appear as credits because they are subtracted. Together, all these items are used to compute cost of goods sold—$88,800 on the income statement in Exhibit 5-5.

The income statement column subtotals on the work sheet indicate whether the business earned net income or incurred a net loss. If total credits are greater, the result is net income, as shown in the exhibit. Inserting the net income amount in the debit column brings total debits into agreement with total credits. If total debits are greater, a net loss has occurred. Inserting a net loss amount in the credit column would equalize total debits and total credits. Net income or net loss is then extended to the opposite column of the balance sheet.

Balance Sheet Columns. The only new item on the balance sheet is inventory. The balance listed is the ending amount of $42,000, which is determined by a physical count of inventory on hand at the end of the period.

Financial Statements of a Merchandising Business _____

OBJECTIVE 4

Prepare a merchandiser's financial statements

Exhibit 5-8 presents Austin Sound's financial statements. The *income statement* through gross margin repeats Exhibit 5-5. This information is followed by the **operating expenses,** which are those expenses other than cost of goods sold that are incurred in the entity's major line of business—merchandising. Rent is the cost of obtaining store space for Austin Sound's operations. Insurance is necessary to protect the inventory. The business's store furniture and fixtures wear out, and that expense is depreciation. Supplies expense is the cost of stationery, mailing, packages, and the like, used in operations.

Many companies report their operating expenses in two categories. *Selling expenses* are those expenses related to marketing the company's products— sales salaries; sales commissions; advertising; depreciation, rent, utilities, and property taxes on store buildings; depreciation on store furniture; delivery expense, and the like. *General expenses* include office expenses, such as the

EXHIBIT 5-8 *Financial Statements of Austin Sound*

Austin Sound
Income Statement
For the Year Ended December 31, 19X6

Sales revenue			$139,300
Less: Sales discounts		$ 1,400	
Sales returns and allowances		2,000	3,400
Net sales revenue			$135,900
Cost of goods sold:			
Beginning inventory		$ 40,500	
Purchases		$89,300	
Less: Purchase discounts	$3,000		
Purchase returns and allowances	1,200	4,200	
Net purchases		85,100	
Freight in		5,200	
Cost of goods available for sale		130,800	
Less: Ending inventory		42,000	
Cost of goods sold			88,800
Gross margin			47,100
Operating expenses:			
Rent expense		8,400	
Insurance expense		1,000	
Depreciation expense		600	
Supplies expense		550	10,550
Income from operations			36,550
Other revenue and (expense):			
Interest revenue		1,000	
Interest expense		(1,500)	(500)
Net income			$ 36,050

Austin Sound
Statement of Owner's Equity
For the Year Ended December 31, 19X6

C. Ernest, capital, December 31, 19X5	$25,900
Add: Net income	36,050
	61,950
Less: Withdrawals	34,100
C. Ernest, capital, December 31, 19X6	$27,850

Austin Sound
Balance Sheet
December 31, 19X6

Assets

Current:		
Cash		$ 2,850
Accounts receivable		4,600
Note receivable		8,000
Interest receivable		400
Inventory		42,000
Prepaid insurance		200
Supplies		100
Total current assets		58,150
Plant:		
Furniture and fixtures	$33,200	
Less: Accumulated depreciation	3,000	30,200
Total assets		$88,350

Liabilities

Current:	
Accounts payable	$47,000
Unearned sales revenue	700
Interest payable	200
Total current liabilities	47,900
Long-term:	
Note payable	12,600
Total liabilities	60,500

Owner's Equity

C. Ernest, capital	27,850
Total liabilities and owner's equity	$88,350

salaries of the company president and office employees, depreciation, rent, utilities, property taxes on the home office building, and office supplies.

Gross margin minus operating expenses equals **income from operations,** or **operating income,** as it is also called. Many businesspeople view operating income as the most reliable indicator of a business's success because it measures the entity's major ongoing activities.

The last section of Austin Sound's income statement is **other revenue and expense.** This category reports revenues and expenses that are outside the main operations of the business. Examples include gains and losses on the sale of plant assets (not inventory) and gains and losses on lawsuits. Accountants have traditionally viewed Interest Revenue and Interest Expense as "other" items because they arise from loaning money and borrowing money—financing activities that are outside the operating scope of selling merchandise or, for a service entity, rendering services.

The bottom line of the income statement is net income, which includes the effects of all the revenues and gains less all the expenses and losses. We often hear the term *bottom line* used to refer to a final result. The term originated in the position of net income on the income statement.

A merchandiser's *statement of owner's equity* looks exactly like that of a service business. In fact, you cannot determine whether the entity is merchandising or service oriented from looking at the statement of owner's equity.

If the business is a merchandiser, the *balance sheet* shows inventory as a major current asset. In contrast, service businesses usually have minor amounts of inventory.

Adjusting and Closing Entries for a Merchandising Business

Exhibit 5-9 presents Austin Sound's adjusting entries, which are similar to those you have seen previously.

The closing entries in the exhibit include two new effects. The first closing entry debits Inventory for the ending balance of $42,000 and also debits the revenue and expense accounts that have credit balances. For Austin Sound these accounts are Sales Revenue, Interest Revenue, Purchase Discounts, and Purchase Returns and Allowances. The offsetting credit of $186,500 transfers their sum to Income Summary. This amount comes directly from the credit column of the income statement on the work sheet (Exhibit 5-7).

The second closing entry includes a credit to Inventory for its beginning balance, and credits to the revenue and expense accounts with debit balances. These are Sales Discounts, Sales Returns and Allowances, Purchases, Freight In, and the expense accounts. The offsetting $150,450 debit to Income Summary comes from the debit column of the income statement on the work sheet.

The last two closing entries close net income from Income Summary and also close owner Withdrawals into the Capital account.

The entries to the Inventory account deserve additional explanation. Recall that before the closing process Inventory still has the period's beginning balance. At the end of the period, this balance is one year old and must be replaced with the ending balance in order to prepare the financial statements at December 31, 19X6. The closing entries give Inventory its correct ending balance of $42,000, as shown here:

Inventory			
Jan. 1 Bal.	40,500	Dec. 31 Clo.	40,500
Dec. 31 Clo.	42,000		
Dec. 31 Bal.	42,000		

The inventory amounts for these closing entries are taken directly from the income statement columns of the work sheet. The offsetting debits and credits to Income Summary in these closing entries also serve to record the dollar amount of cost of goods sold in the accounts. Income Summary contains the cost of goods sold amount after Purchases and its related contra accounts and Freight In are closed.

Study Exhibits 5-7, 5-8, and 5-9 carefully because they illustrate the entire end-of-period process that leads to the financial statements. As you progress through this book, you may want to refer to these exhibits to refresh your understanding of the adjusting and closing process for a merchandising business.

Cost of Goods Sold	XX
Purchase Discounts	XX
Purchase Returns and Allowances	XX
Inventory (ending bal.) . .	XX
Inventory (beginning bal.)	XX
Purchases	XX
Freight In	XX

The Cost of Goods Sold account is then closed into Income Summary:

Income Summary	XX
Cost of Goods Sold	XX

EXHIBIT 5-9A *Journalizing and Posting the Adjusting and Closing Entries*

Journal

Adjusting Entries

a. Dec. 31	Interest Receivable	400	
	Interest Revenue		400
b. 31	Supplies Expense ($650 − $100)	550	
	Supplies		550
c. 31	Insurance Expense	1,000	
	Prepaid Insurance		1,000
d. 31	Depreciation Expense	600	
	Accumulated Depreciation		600
e. 31	Unearned Sales Revenue	1,300	
	Sales Revenue		1,300
f. 31	Interest Expense	200	
	Interest Payable		200

Closing Entries

Dec. 31	Inventory (ending balance)	42,000	
	Sales Revenue	139,300	
	Interest Revenue	1,000	
	Purchase Discounts	3,000	
	Purchase Returns and Allowances	1,200	
	Income Summary		186,500
31	Income Summary	150,450	
	Inventory (beginning balance)		40,500
	Sales Discounts		1,400
	Sales Returns and Allowances		2,000
	Purchases		89,300
	Freight In		5,200
	Rent Expense		8,400
	Depreciation Expense		600
	Insurance Expense		1,000
	Supplies Expense		550
	Interest Expense		1,500
31	Income Summary ($186,500 − $150,450)	36,050	
	C. Ernest, Capital		36,050
31	C. Ernest, Capital	34,100	
	C. Ernest, Withdrawals		34,100

Point to Stress: Closing entries of a merchandising business accomplish the same tasks they did in Ch. 4 together with a new function. The beginning inventory is replaced with the ending inventory during the closing process.

Teaching Tip: Refer to the work sheet at Exhibit 5-7. Notice that the Income Statement debit column total ($150,450) equals the debit to Income Summary in the closing entries, and the Income Statement credit column total ($186,500) equals the credit to Income Summary in the closing entries.

Point to Stress: In the first closing entry we still debit every account that appears in the credit column of the income statement on the work sheet, even though some of those accounts are not revenues (for example, Ending Inventory and Purchase Discounts). In the second closing entry we still credit every account that appears in the debit column of the income statement on the work sheet, even though some of those accounts are not expenses (for example, Sales Discounts and Beginning Inventory).

EXHIBIT 5-9B   Ledger Accounts of Austin Sound

Teaching Tip: Follow the closing entries for inventory from journal to ledger to show how the ending inventory value replaces the beginning inventory value.

Assets

Cash

2,850	

Accounts Receivable

4,600	

Note Receivable

8,000	

Interest Receivable

(A) 400	

Inventory

40,500	(C) 40,500
(C) 42,000	

Supplies

650	(A) 550
100	

Prepaid Insurance

1,200	(A) 1,000
200	

Furniture and Fixtures

33,200	

Accumulated Depreciation

	2,400
	(A) 600
	3,000

Liabilities

Accounts Payable

	47,000

Unearned Sales Revenue

(A) 1,300	2,000
	700

Interest Payable

	(A) 200

Note Payable

	12,600

Owner's Equity

C. Ernest, Capital

(C) 34,100	25,900
	(C) 36,050
	27,850

C. Ernest, Withdrawals

34,100	(C) 34,100

Income Summary

(C)150,450	(C)186,500
(C) 36,050	

Revenues

Sales Revenue

	138,000
	(A) 1,300
(C)139,300	139,300

Sales Discounts

1,400	(C) 1,400

Sales Returns and Allowances

2,000	(C) 2,000

Interest Revenue

	600
	(A) 400
(C) 1,000	1,000

Expenses

Purchases

89,300	(C) 89,300

Purchase Discounts

(C) 3,000	3,000

Purchase Returns and Allowances

(C) 1,200	1,200

Freight In

5,200	(C) 5,200

Rent Expense

8,400	(C) 8,400

Depreciation Expense

(A) 600	(C) 600

Insurance Expense

(A) 1,000	(C) 1,000

Supplies Expense

(A) 550	(C) 550

Interest Expense

1,300	
(A) 200	
1,500	(C) 1,500

A = Adjusting entry; C = Closing entry

Income Statement Format

We have seen that the balance sheet appears in two formats: the account format and the report format. There are also two basic formats for the income statement: *multiple-step* and *single-step*.

OBJECTIVE 6

Recognize different formats of the income statement

Multiple-Step Income Statement

The income statements presented thus far in this chapter have been multiple-step income statements. Austin Sound's multiple-step income statement for the year ended December 31, 19X6, appears in Exhibit 5-8. The **multiple-step format** contains subtotals to highlight significant relationships. In addition to net income, it also presents gross margin and income from operations. This format communicates a merchandiser's results of operations especially well because gross margin and income from operations are two key measures of operating performance.

Single-Step Income Statement

The **single-step format** groups all revenues together and then lists and deducts all expenses together without drawing any subtotals. The single-step format has the advantage of listing all revenues together and all expenses together, as shown in Exhibit 5-10. Thus it clearly distinguishes revenues from expenses. The income statements in Chapters 1 through 4 were single-step. This format works well for service entities because they have no gross margin to report. A recent survey of 600 companies indicated that 56 percent use the single-step format and 44 percent use the multiple-step format.

Most published financial statements are highly condensed. Appendix C, page 1310, at the end of the book gives the income statement of The Goodyear Tire & Rubber Company. Notice that only seven categories of expenses are reported. Of course, condensed statements can be supplemented with desired

Real-World Example: According to Accounting Trends and Techniques, a little over half of the companies surveyed used the single-step format, and the rest used the multiple-step.

EXHIBIT 5-10 *Single-Step Income Statement*

Austin Sound Income Statement For the Year Ended December 31, 19X6	
Revenues:	
Net sales (net of sales discounts, $1,400, and returns and allowances, $2,000) ...	$135,900
Interest revenue....................	1,000
Total revenues	136,900
Expenses:	
Cost of goods sold	$ 88,800
Rent expense	8,400
Interest expense...................	1,500
Insurance expense..................	1,000
Depreciation expense	600
Supplies expense...................	550
Total expenses	100,850
Net income	$ 36,050

details. For example, in Exhibit 5-10, the single-step income statement could be accompanied by a supporting schedule that gives the detailed computation of cost of goods sold.

Use of Accounting Information in Decision Making _____

Real-World Example: According to Robert Morris Associates, the average gross margin percentage for companies in the electronic computer industry is 41%. That figure has remained within 2 percentage points for the past five years.

Merchandise inventory is the most important asset to a merchandising business because it captures the essence of the entity. To manage the firm, owners and managers focus their energies on the best way to sell the inventory. They use several ratios to evaluate operations.

A key decision tool for a merchandiser relates to gross margin, which is net sales minus cost of goods sold. Merchandisers strive to increase the *gross margin percentage,* which is computed as follows:

Class Exercise: Given below is the income statement of a company. Compute the gross margin percentage.

Net Sales	$400,000
COGS	225,000
Gross Margin	$175,000

ANSWER:

$$\frac{\text{Gross Margin}}{\text{Net Sales}} = 43.75\%$$

**For Austin Sound
(Exhibit 5-8)**

$$\text{Gross margin percentage} = \frac{\text{Gross margin}}{\text{Net sales revenue}} = \frac{\$47,100}{\$135,900} = .347$$

The gross margin (or gross profit) percentage is one of the most carefully watched measures of profitability because it is fundamental to a merchandiser. For most firms, the gross margin percentage changes little from year to year, and a small downturn may signal an important drop in income. A small increase in the gross margin percentage usually indicates an increase in profitability.

Austin Sound's gross margin percentage of 34.7 percent compares favorably with the industry average for electronic retailers, which is 34.9 percent. By contrast, the average gross margin percentage is 14.1 percent for automobile dealers, 22.8 percent for grocery stores, and 55.7 percent for restaurants.

Real-World Example: The average inventory turnover in the electronic computer industry is about 3.8 times per year, or about every 96 days. The top 25% of the firms had an inventory turnover of about 8.8 times, or every 41 days. The higher the turnover, the more quickly a company can turn its inventory into cash.

Owners and managers strive to sell inventory as quickly as possible because unsold merchandise drains profits. The faster the sales occur, the higher the income. The slower the sales, the lower the income. Ideally a business could operate with zero inventory. Most businesses, however, including retailers such as Austin Sound, must keep goods on hand for customers. Successful merchandisers purchase carefully to keep the goods moving through the business at a rapid pace. **Inventory turnover,** the ratio of cost of goods sold to average inventory, indicates how rapidly inventory is sold. Its computation follows:

**For Austin Sound
(Exhibit 5-8)**

$$\frac{\text{Inventory}}{\text{turnover}} = \frac{\text{Cost of goods sold}}{\text{Average inventory}} = \frac{\text{Cost of goods sold}}{(\text{Beginning inventory} + \text{ending inventory})/2} = \frac{\$88,800}{(\$40,500 + \$42,000)/2}$$

$$= 2.2 \text{ times per year}$$

Point to Stress: Many accountants consider the replacement of the beginning inventory with the ending inventory an adjustment of the inventory balance rather than as a closing entry.

Inventory turnover is usually computed for an annual period, and the relevant cost-of-goods sold figure is the amount for the entire year. Average inventory is computed from the beginning and ending amounts. The resulting inventory turnover statistic shows how many times inventory was sold during the year. A high rate of turnover is preferred over a low turnover. An increase in the rate of turnover usually means higher profits.

Inventory turnover varies from industry to industry. Grocery stores, for example, turn their goods over faster than automobile dealers do. Drug stores have higher turnover than furniture stores do. Retailers of electronic products, such as Austin Sound, have an average turnover of 3.6 times per year. What does Austin Sound's turnover rate of 2.2 times per year indicate about its ability to sell inventory? It suggests that Austin Sound is not very successful. The lower one-fourth of electronics retailers average a turnover rate of 2.7, so Austin Sound's turnover of 2.2 looks rather bad.

Financial analysis is complex. For Austin Sound we see an acceptable gross margin percentage but a poor rate of inventory turnover. These two ratios do not provide enough information to yield an overall conclusion about the firm, but the illustration shows how owners and managers may apply ratios to evaluate a company.

Class Exercise: Give the adjusting entries for Inventory if the beginning inventory is $23,400 and the ending inventory is $27,800.

ANSWER:

Income Summary ...	23,400	
Inventory		23,400
Inventory	27,800	
Income Summary .		27,800

Computers and Inventory

Inventory record keeping is a demanding manual accounting task, from the paperwork required in purchasing and selling inventory to the job of periodically counting it. Computers have dramatically reduced the time required to manage inventory and have greatly increased a company's ability to control its inventory.

A computerized system enhances accounting control over inventory because the computer can keep accurate and up-to-the-minute records of the number of units purchased, the number of units sold, and the quantities on hand. The computer can also issue purchase-order forms automatically when inventory on hand falls below the minimum amount.

Computerized inventory systems are now often integrated with accounts receivable and sales. For example, once a prospective customer's order is entered into the computer, the computer checks warehouse records to see if the requested units are in stock. If so, details of the shipment are entered into the computer, which then multiplies the number of units shipped by the unit price. The computer then prints an invoice for the customer and calculates the debit to Accounts Receivable (for that specific customer), the credit to Sales, and the reduction in inventory units.

The computer can keep up-to-the-minute records, so managers can call up current inventory information at any time. This type of inventory system is explored in more detail in Chapter 9.

Summary Problem for Your Review

The accompanying trial balance relates to Jan King Distributing Company.

Required:

1. Make a single summary journal entry to record King's
   a. Unadjusted sales for the year, assuming all sales were made on credit.
   b. Sales returns and allowances for the year.

c. Sales discounts for the year, assuming the cash collected on account was $329,000.

d. Purchases of inventory for the year, assuming all purchases were made on credit.

e. Purchase returns and allowances for the year.

f. Purchase discounts for the year, $6,000. Cash paid on account was $188,400.

g. Transportation costs for the year, assuming a cash payment in a separate entry.

2. Enter the trial balance on a work sheet and complete the work sheet.

3. Journalize the adjusting and closing entries at December 31. Post to the Income Summary account as an accuracy check on the entries affecting that account. The credit balance closed out of Income Summary should equal net income computed on the work sheet.

4. Prepare the company's multiple-step income statement, statement of owner's equity, and balance sheet in account format.

5. Compute the inventory turnover for 19X3. Turnover for 19X2 was 2.1. Would you expect Jan King Distributing Company to be more profitable or less profitable in 19X3 than in 19X2? Give your reason.

Jan King Distributing Company
Trial Balance
December 31, 19X3

Cash	$ 5,670	
Accounts receivable	37,100	
Inventory	60,500	
Supplies	3,930	
Prepaid rent	6,000	
Furniture and fixtures	26,500	
Accumulated depreciation		$ 21,200
Accounts payable		46,340
Salary payable		
Interest payable		
Unearned sales revenue		3,500
Note payable, long-term		35,000
Jan King, capital		23,680
Jan King, withdrawals	48,000	
Sales revenue		346,700
Sales discounts	10,300	
Sales returns and allowances	8,200	
Purchases	175,900	
Purchases discounts		6,000
Purchase returns and allowances		7,430
Freight in	9,300	
Salary expense	82,750	
Rent expense	7,000	
Depreciation expense		
Utilities expense	5,800	
Supplies expense		
Interest expense	2,900	
Total	$489,850	$489,850

Additional data at December 31, 19X3:

a. Supplies used during the year, $2,580.
b. Prepaid rent in force, $1,000.
c. Unearned sales revenue still not earned, $2,400. The company expects to earn this amount during the next few months.
d. Depreciation. The furniture and fixtures' estimated useful life is 10 years, and they are expected to be worthless when they are retired from service.
e. Accrued salaries, $1,300.
f. Accrued interest expense, $600.
g. Inventory on hand, $65,800.

Note: If your instructor assigned the appendix to this chapter, which illustrates the adjusting-entry method, turn to page 263 for the Alternate Solution to Review Problem. If you were not assigned this appendix, then study the Solution to Review Problem that follows.

SOLUTION TO REVIEW PROBLEM

Requirement 1
Sales, purchases, and related discount and return and allowance entries:

	19X3		
a.	Accounts Receivable	346,700	
	Sales Revenue		346,700
b.	Sales Returns and Allowances	8,200	
	Accounts Receivable		8,200
c.	Cash	329,000	
	Sales Discounts	10,300	
	Accounts Receivable		339,300
d.	Purchases	175,900	
	Accounts Payable		175,900
e.	Accounts Payable	7,430	
	Purchase Returns and Allowances		7,430
f.	Accounts Payable	194,400	
	Purchase Discounts		6,000
	Cash		188,400
g.	Freight In	9,300	
	Cash		9,300

Requirement 2

Jan King Distributing Company
Work Sheet
For the Year Ended December 31, 19X3

Account Title	Trial Balance Debit	Trial Balance Credit	Adjustments Debit		Adjustments Credit		Income Statement Debit	Income Statement Credit	Balance Sheet Debit	Balance Sheet Credit
Cash	5,670								5,670	
Accounts receivable	37,100								37,100	
Inventory	60,500						60,500	65,800	65,800	
Supplies	3,930				(a)	2,580			1,350	
Prepaid rent	6,000				(b)	5,000			1,000	
Furniture and fixtures	26,500								26,500	
Accumulated depreciation		21,200			(d)	2,650				23,850
Accounts payable		46,340								46,340
Salary payable					(e)	1,300				1,300
Interest payable					(f)	600				600
Unearned sales revenue		3,500	(c)	1,100						2,400
Note payable, long-term		35,000								35,000
Jan King, capital		23,680								23,680
Jan King, withdrawals	48,000								48,000	
Sales revenue		346,700			(c)	1,100		347,800		
Sales discounts	10,300						10,300			
Sales returns and allowances	8,200						8,200			
Purchases	175,900						175,900			
Purchase discounts		6,000						6,000		
Purchase returns and allowances		7,430						7,430		
Freight in	9,300						9,300			
Salary expense	82,750		(e)	1,300			84,050			
Rent expense	7,000		(b)	5,000			12,000			
Depreciation expense			(d)	2,650			2,650			
Utilities expense	5,800						5,800			
Supplies expense			(a)	2,580			2,580			
Interest expense	2,900		(f)	600			3,500			
	489,850	489,850	13,230		13,230		374,780	427,030	185,420	133,170
Net income							52,250			52,250
							427,030	427,030	185,420	185,420

Requirement 3

Adjusting entries

19X3

Dec. 31	Supplies Expense	2,580	
	Supplies		2,580
31	Rent Expense	5,000	
	Prepaid Rent		5,000
31	Unearned Sales Revenue	1,100	
	Sales Revenue		1,100
31	Depreciation Expense ($26,500/10)	2,650	
	Accumulated Depreciation		2,650
31	Salary Expense	1,300	
	Salary Payable		1,300
31	Interest Expense	600	
	Interest Payable		600

Closing entries

19X3

Dec. 31	Inventory (ending balance)	65,800	
	Sales Revenue	347,800	
	Purchase Discounts	6,000	
	Purchase Returns and Allowances	7,430	
	Income Summary		427,030
31	Income Summary	374,780	
	Inventory (beginning balance)		60,500
	Sales Discounts		10,300
	Sales Returns and Allowances		8,200
	Purchases		175,900
	Freight In		9,300
	Salary Expense		84,050
	Rent Expense		12,000
	Depreciation Expense		2,650
	Utilities Expense		5,800
	Supplies Expense		2,580
	Interest Expense		3,500
31	Income Summary ($427,030 − $374,780)	52,250	
	Jan King, Capital		52,250
31	Jan King, Capital	48,000	
	Jan King, Withdrawals		48,000

Income Summary

Clo.	374,780	Clo.	427,030
Clo.	52,250	Bal.	52,250

Requirement 4

Jan King Distributing Company
Income Statement
For the Year Ended December 31, 19X3

Sales revenue			$347,800
Less: Sales discounts		$ 10,300	
Sales returns and allowances		8,200	18,500
Net sales revenue			$329,300
Cost of goods sold:			
Beginning inventory			$60,500
Purchases		$175,900	
Less: Purchase discounts	$6,000		
Purchase returns and allowances	7,430	13,430	
Net purchases			162,470
Freight in			9,300
Cost of goods available for sale			232,270
Less: Ending inventory			65,800
Cost of goods sold			166,470
Gross margin			162,830
Operating expenses:			
Salary expense			84,050
Rent expense			12,000
Utilities expense			5,800
Depreciation expense			2,650
Supplies expense			2,580	107,080
Income from operations			55,750
Other expense:			
Interest expense			3,500
Net income			$ 52,250

Jan King Distributing Company
Statement of Owner's Equity
For the Year Ended December 31, 19X3

Jan King, capital, December 31, 19X2	$23,680
Add: Net income	52,250
	75,930
Less: Withdrawals	48,000
Jan King, capital, December 31, 19X3	$27,930

Jan King Distributing Company
Balance Sheet
December 31, 19X3

Assets

Current:		
Cash		$ 5,670
Accounts receivable		37,100
Inventory		65,800
Supplies		1,350
Prepaid rent		1,000
Total current assets		110,920
Plant:		
Furniture and fixtures	$26,500	
Less: Accumulated depreciation	23,850	2,650
Total assets		$113,570

Liabilities

Current:	
Accounts payable	$ 46,340
Salary payable	1,300
Interest payable	600
Unearned sales revenue	2,400
Total current liabilities	50,640
Long-term:	
Note payable	35,000
Total liabilities	85,640

Owner's Equity

Jan King, capital	27,930
Total liabilities and owner's equity	$113,570

Requirement 5

$$\text{Inventory turnover} = \frac{\text{Cost of goods sold}}{\text{Average inventory}} = \frac{\$166,470}{(\$60,500 + \$65,800)/2} = 2.6$$

The increase in the rate of inventory turnover from 2.1 to 2.6 suggests higher profits in 19X3 than in 19X2.

Summary

The major revenue of a merchandising business is *sales revenue,* or *sales.* The major expense is *cost of goods sold.* Net sales minus cost of goods sold is called *gross margin,* or *gross profit.* This amount measures the business's success or failure in selling its products at a higher price than it paid for them.

The merchandiser's major asset is *inventory.* In a merchandising entity the accounting cycle is from cash to inventory as the inventory is purchased for resale, and back to cash as the inventory is sold.

Cost of goods sold is unlike the other expenses in that it is not an account in the ledger. Instead, cost of goods sold is the remainder when beginning inventory and net purchases and freight in are added and ending inventory is subtracted from that sum.

The *invoice* is the business document generated by a purchase/sale transaction. Most merchandising entities offer *discounts* to their customers and allow them to *return* unsuitable merchandise. They also grant *allowances* for damaged goods that the buyer chooses to keep. Discounts and Returns and Allowances are *contra* accounts to both Purchases and Sales.

The end-of-period adjusting and closing process of a merchandising business is similar to that of a service business. In addition, a merchandiser makes inventory entries at the end of the period. These closing entries replace the period's beginning balance with the cost of inventory on hand at the end. A by-product of these closing entries is the computation of cost of goods sold for the income statement.

The income statement may appear in the *single-step format* or the *multiple-step format.* A single-step income statement has only two sections—one for revenues and the other for expenses—and a single income amount for net income. A multiple-step income statement has subtotals for gross margin and income from operations. Both formats are widely used in practice.

Two key decision aids for a merchandiser are the *gross margin percentage* and the *rate of inventory turnover.* Increases in these measures usually signal an increase in profits.

Self-Study Questions

Test your understanding of the chapter by marking the best answer for each of the following questions.

1. The major expense of a merchandising business is *(p. 209)*
   - ✓ a. Cost of goods sold
   - b. Depreciation
   - c. Rent
   - d. Interest

2. Sales total $440,000, cost of goods sold is $210,000, and operating expenses are $160,000. How much is gross margin? *(p. 209)*
   - a. $440,000
   - ✓ b. $230,000
   - c. $210,000
   - d. $70,000

3. A purchase discount results from *(p. 213)*
   a. Returning goods to the seller
   b. Receiving a purchase allowance from the seller
   c. Buying a large enough quantity of merchandise to get the discount
   √ d. Paying within the discount period

4. Which one of the following pairs includes items that are the most similar? *(p. 217)*
   a. Purchase discounts and purchase returns
   b. Cost of goods sold and inventory
   c. Net sales and sales discounts
   √ d. Sales returns and sales allowances

5. Which of the following is *not* an account? *(p. 218)*
   a. Sales revenue   c. Inventory
   √ b. Net sales   d. Supplies expense

6. Cost of goods sold is computed by adding beginning inventory and net purchases and subtracting X. What is X? *(p. 217)*
   a. Net sales   √ c. Ending inventory
   b. Sales discounts   d. Net purchases

7. Which account causes the main difference between a merchandiser's adjusting and closing process and that of a service business? *(p. 221)*
   a. Advertising Expense   √ c. Inventory
   b. Interest Revenue   d. Accounts Receivable

8. The major item on a merchandiser's income statement that a service business does not have is *(p. 225)*
   √ a. Cost of goods sold   c. Salary expense
   b. Inventory   d. Total revenue

9. The closing entry for Sales Discounts is *(p. 226)*
   a. Sales Discounts   √ c. Income Summary
      Income Summary   Sales Discounts
   b. Sales Discounts   d. Not used because Sales Dis-
      Sales Revenue   counts is a permanent account,
                                        which is not closed.

10. Which income statement format reports income from operations? *(p. 229)*
   a. Account format   c. Single-step format
   b. Report format   √ d. Multiple-step format

Answers to the Self-Study Questions follow the Accounting Vocabulary.

Accounting Vocabulary

Cost of goods sold. The cost of the inventory that the business has sold to customers, the largest single expense of most merchandising businesses. Also called Cost of sales *(p. 217)*.

Cost of sales. Another name for Cost of goods sold *(p. 217)*.

Gross margin. Excess of sales revenue over cost of goods sold. Also called Gross profit *(p. 209)*.

Gross profit. Excess of sales revenue over cost of goods sold. Also called Gross margin *(p. 209)*.

Income from operations. Gross margin (sales revenue minus cost of goods sold) minus operating expenses. Also called Operating income *(p. 226)*.

Inventory turnover. Ratio of cost of goods sold to average inventory. Measures the number of times a company sells its average level of inventory during a year *(p. 230)*.

Invoice. Seller's request for payment from a purchaser. Also called a bill *(p. 211)*.

Multiple-step income statement. Format that contains subtotals to highlight significant relationships. In addition to net income, it also presents gross margin and income from operations *(p. 229)*.

Net purchases. Purchases less purchase discounts and purchase returns and allowances (p. 214).

Net sales revenue. Sales revenue less sales discounts and sales returns and allowances (p. 209).

Operating expenses. Expenses, other than cost of goods sold, that are incurred in the entity's major line of business. Examples include rent, depreciation, salaries, wages, utilities, property tax, and supplies expense (p. 224).

Operating income. Another name for Income from operations (p. 226).

Other expense. Expense that is outside the main operations of a business, such as a loss on the sale of plant assets (p. 226).

Other revenue. Revenue that is outside the main operations of a business, such as a gain on the sale of plant assets (p. 226).

Purchases. The cost of inventory that a firm buys to resell to customers in the normal course of business (p. 210).

Purchase discount. Reduction in the cost of inventory that is offered by a seller as an incentive for the customer to pay promptly. A contra account to Purchases (p. 213).

Purchase returns and allowances. Decrease in a buyer's debt from returning merchandise to the seller or from receiving from the seller a reduction in the amount owed. A contra account to Purchases (p. 213).

Quantity discount. A purchase discount that provides a lower price per item the larger the quantity purchased (p. 212).

Sales discount. Reduction in the amount receivable from a customer, offered by the seller as an incentive for the customer to pay promptly. A contra account to Sales Revenue (p. 216).

Sales returns and allowances. Decrease in the seller's receivable from a customer's return of merchandise or from granting the customer an allowance from the amount the customer owes the seller. A contra account to Sales Revenue (p. 216).

Sales revenue. Amount that a merchandiser earns from selling inventory before subtracting expenses (p. 209).

Single-step income statement. Format that groups all revenues together and then lists and deducts all expenses together without drawing any subtotals (p. 229).

Answers to Self-Study Questions

1. a
2. b ($440,000 − $210,000 = $230,000)
3. d
4. d
5. b
6. c
7. c
8. a
9. c
10. d

ASSIGNMENT MATERIAL

Questions

1. Gross margin is often mentioned in the business press as an important measure of success. What does gross margin measure, and why is this important?

2. Describe the operating cycle for (a) the purchase and cash sale of inventory and (b) the purchase and sale of inventory on account.

3. Identify 10 items of information on an invoice.

4. What is the similarity and what is the difference between purchase discounts and quantity discounts?

5. Indicate which accounts are debited and credited for (a) a credit purchase of inventory and the subsequent cash payment and (b) a credit sale of

inventory and the subsequent cash collection. Assume no discounts, returns, allowances, or freight.

6. Inventory costing $1,000 is purchased and invoiced on July 28 under terms of 3/10 n/30. Compute the payment amount on August 6. How much would the payment be on August 8? What explains the difference? What is the latest acceptable payment date under the terms of sale?

7. Inventory listed at $35,000 is sold subject to a quantity discount of $3,000 and underpayment terms of 2/15 n/45. What is the net sales revenue on this sale if the customer pays within 15 days?

8. Name four contra accounts introduced in this chapter.

9. Briefly discuss the similarity in computing supplies expense and computing cost of goods sold.

10. Why is the title of cost of goods sold especially descriptive? What type of item is cost of goods sold?

11. Beginning inventory is $5,000, net purchases total $30,000, and freight in is $1,000. If ending inventory is $8,000, what is cost of goods sold?

12. Identify two ways that cost of goods sold differs from operating expenses such as Salary Expense and Depreciation Expense.

13. Suppose you are evaluating two companies as possible investments. One entity sells its services, and the other entity is a merchandiser. How can you identify the merchandiser by examining the two entities' balance sheets and their income statements?

14. You are beginning the adjusting and closing process at the end of your company's fiscal year. Does the trial balance carry the beginning or the ending amount of inventory? Will the balance sheet that you prepare report the beginning or the ending inventory?

15. Give the two closing entries for inventory (using no specific amount).

16. During the closing process, what accounts contain the amount of cost of goods sold for the period? Where is the final resting place of cost of goods sold?

17. What is the identifying characteristic of the "other" category of revenues and expenses? Give an example of each.

18. Name and describe the two income statement formats and identify the type of business to which each format best applies.

19. List eight different operating expenses.

20. Which financial statement reports sales discounts, sales returns and allowances, purchase discounts, and purchase returns and allowances? Show how they are reported, using any reasonable amounts in your illustration.

21. Does a merchandiser prefer a high or a low rate of inventory turnover? Give your reason.

Exercises

No check figure

Exercise 5-1 *Journalizing purchase and sale transactions* **(L.O. 2)**

Journalize, without explanations, the following transactions of Gonzaga, Inc., during July:

July 3 Purchased $2,000 of inventory under terms of 2/10 n/eom (end of month) and FOB shipping point.
      7 Returned $300 of defective merchandise purchased on July 3.
      9 Paid freight bill of $110 on July 3 purchase.
     10 Sold inventory for $2,200, collecting cash of $400. Payment terms on the remainder were 2/15 n/30.
     12 Paid amount owed on credit purchase of July 3, less the discount and the return.

16 Granted a sales allowance of $800 on the July 10 sale.

23 Received cash from July 10 customer in full settlement of her debt, less the allowance and the discount.

Exercise 5-2 *Journalizing transactions from a purchase invoice* **(L.O. 2)** No check figure

As the proprietor of Kendrick Tire Company, you receive the accompanying invoice from a supplier.

ABC TIRE WHOLESALE DISTRIBUTORS, INC.
2600 Commonwealth Avenue
Boston, Massachusetts 02215

Invoice date: May 14, 19X3   **Payment terms:** 2/10 n/30

Sold to: Kendrick Tire Co,
4219 Crestwood Parkway
Lexington, Mass. 02173

Quantity Ordered	Description	Quantity Shipped	Price	Amount
6	P135-X4 Radials.........	6	$37.14	$ 222.84
8	L912 Belted-bias........	8	41.32	330.56
14	R39 Truck tires	10	50.02	500.20
	Total...			$1,053.60

Due date: **Amount:**
May 24, 19X3 $1,032.53
May 25 through June 13, 19X3 $1,053.60

Paid:

Required

1. Record the May 15 purchase on account.
2. The R39 truck tires were ordered by mistake and therefore were returned to ABC. Journalize the return on May 19.
3. Record the May 22 payment of the amount owed.

Exercise 5-3 *Journalizing purchase transactions* **(L.O. 2)** No check figure

On April 30 Feldman Jewelers purchased inventory of $4,300 on account from a wholesale jewelry supplier. Terms were 3/15 net 45. On receiving the goods, Feldman checked the order and found $800 of items that were not ordered. Therefore, Feldman returned this amount of merchandise to the supplier on May 4.

To pay the remaining amount owed, Feldman had to borrow from the bank because of a temporary cash shortage. On May 14 Feldman signed a short-term note payable to the bank and immediately paid the borrowed funds to the wholesale jewelry supplier. On May 31 Feldman paid the bank the net amount of the invoice, which was borrowed, plus $30 interest.

Required

Record the indicated transactions in the journal of Feldman Jewelers. Explanations are not required.

Exercise 5-4 *Journalizing sale transactions* (L.O. 2)

Refer to the business situation in Exercise 5-3. Journalize the transactions of the wholesale jewelry supplier. Explanations are not required.

Exercise 5-5 *Computing the elements of a merchandiser's income statement* (L.O. 3)

Supply the missing income statement amounts in each of the following situations:

Sales	Sales Discounts	Net Sales	Beginning Inventory	Net Purchases	Ending Inventory	Cost of Goods Sold	Gross Margin
$98,300	(a)	$92,800	$32,500	$66,700	$39,400	(b)	$33,000
82,400	$2,100	(c)	27,450	43,000	(d)	$44,100	36,200
91,500	1,800	89,700	(e)	54,900	22,600	59,400	(f)
(g)	3,000	(h)	40,700	(i)	48,230	62,500	36,600

Exercise 5-6 *Computing cost of goods sold for an actual company* (L.O. 3)

For the year ended December 31, 19X9, House of Fabrics, a retailer of home-related products, reported net sales of $338 million and cost of goods sold of $154 million. The company's balance sheet at December 31, 19X8 and 19X9 reported inventories of $133 million and $129 million, respectively. What were House of Fabrics's net purchases during 19X9?

Exercise 5-7 *Preparing a merchandiser's multiple-step income statement* (L.O. 3, 4, 6)

Selected accounts of Payless Cashways Company are listed in alphabetical order.

Accounts receivable	$ 48,300	Purchases	$ 71,300
Accumulated depreciation	18,700	Purchase discounts	3,000
		Purchase returns	2,000
Freight in	2,200	Sales discounts	9,000
General expenses	23,800	Sales returns	4,600
Interest revenue	1,500	Sales revenue	201,000
Inventory, June 30	21,870	Selling expenses	37,840
Inventory, May 31	19,450	Unearned sales revenue	6,500
Owner's equity, May 31	126,070		

Required

Prepare the business's multiple-step income statement for June of the current year. Compute the rate of inventory turnover. Last year the turnover was 2.8 times. Does this two-year trend suggest improvement or deterioration in profitability?

Exercise 5-8 *Preparing a single-step income statement for a merchandising business* (L.O. 3, 4, 6)

Prepare Payless Cashways' single-step income statement for June, using the data from the preceding exercise. In a separate schedule, show the computation of cost of goods sold.

Exercise 5-9 *Using work sheet data to prepare a merchandiser's income statement* (L.O. 5, 6)

The trial balance and adjustments columns of the work sheet of Midway Auto Supply include the following accounts and balances at March 31, 19X2.

Account Title	Trial Balance Debit	Trial Balance Credit	Adjustments Debit	Adjustments Credit
Cash	2,000			
Accounts receivable	8,500		(a) 2,100	
Inventory	36,070			
Supplies	13,000			(b) 8,600
Store fixtures	22,500			
Accumulated depreciation		11,250		(c) 2,250
Accounts payable		9,300		
Salary payable..................				(d) 1,200
Note payable, long-term.........		7,500		
K. Brownlee, Capital		33,920		
K. Brownlee, Withdrawals.......	45,000			
Sales revenue		213,000		(a) 2,100
Sales discounts	2,000			
Purchases......................	114,200			
Purchase returns		2,600		
Selling expense..................	21,050		(b) 5,200	
			(d) 1,200	
General expense................	10,500		(b) 3,400	
			(c) 2,250	
Interest expense	2,750			
Total	277,570	277,570	14,150	14,150

Ending inventory at March 31, 19X2, is $34,500.

Prepare the company's multiple-step income statement for the year ended March 31, 19X2. Compute the gross margin percentage and the inventory turnover for the year. Compare these figures with the gross margin percentage of .43 and the inventory turnover of 3.16 for 19X1. Does the two-year trend suggest improvement or deterioration in profitability?

Exercise 5-10 *Use work sheet data to prepare the closing entries of a merchandising business* **(L.O. 5)**

No check figure

Use the data from Exercise 5-9 to journalize Midway Auto Supply's closing entries at March 31, 19X2.

Problems

(Group A)

Problem 5-1A *Explaining the operating cycle of a retailer* **(L.O. 1)**

No check figure

Macy's Department Store is one of the most famous retailers in the world. The women's sportswear department of Macy's purchases clothing from manufacturers such as Ruff Hewn, Jones New York, and Prophecy. Macy's advertising department is promoting end-of-year sales.

Required

You are the manager of the Macy's store in Dallas. Write a memo to a new employee in the women's sportswear department explaining how the company's operating cycle works.

Problem 5-2A *Accounting for the purchase and sale of inventory* **(L.O. 2)**

No check figure

The following transactions occurred between American Hospital Supply and Prucare Medical Clinic during June of the current year.

June 8 American Hospital Supply sold $3,900 worth of merchandise to Prucare Medical Clinic on terms of 2/10 n/30, FOB shipping point. American prepaid freight charges of $200 and included this amount in the invoice total. (American's entry to record the freight payment debits Accounts Receivable and credits Cash.)

11 Prucare returned $600 of the merchandise purchased on June 8. American issued a credit memo for this amount.

17 Prucare paid $2,000 of the invoice amount owed to American for the June 8 purchase. This payment included none of the freight charge.

26 Prucare paid the remaining amount owed to American for the June 8 purchase.

Required

Journalize these transactions, first on the books of Prucare Medical Clinic and second on the books of American Hospital Supply.

Receivable, $1,600

Problem 5-3A *Journalizing purchase and sale transactions* (L.O. 2)

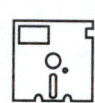

Davis Book Store engaged in the following transactions during July of the current year:

July 2 Purchased inventory for cash, $800, less a quantity discount of $150.

3 Purchased store supplies on credit terms of net eom (end of month), $2,300.

8 Purchased inventory of $3,000 less a quantity discount of 10 percent, plus freight charges of $230. Credit terms are 3/15 n/30.

9 Sold goods for cash, $1,200.

11 Returned $200 (net amount after the quantity discount) of the inventory purchased on July 8. It was damaged in shipment.

12 Purchased inventory on credit terms of 3/10 n/30, $3,330.

14 Sold inventory on credit terms of 2/10 n/30, $9,600, less a $600 quantity discount.

16 Paid the electricity and water bills, $275.

20 Received returned inventory from July 14 sale, $400 (net amount after the quantity discount). Davis shipped the wrong goods by mistake.

21 Borrowed the amount owed on the July 8 purchase. Signed a note payable to the bank for $2,655, which takes into account the return of inventory on July 11.

21 Paid supplier for goods purchased on July 8 less the discount and the return.

23 Received $6,860 cash in partial settlement of his account from the customer who purchased inventory on July 14. Granted the customer a 2 percent discount and credited his account receivable for $7,000.

30 Paid for the store supplies purchased on July 3.

Required

1. Journalize the above transactions.
2. Compute the amount of the receivable at July 31 from the customer to whom Davis sold inventory on July 14. What amount of cash discount applies to this receivable at July 31?

Problem 5-4A *Computing cost of goods sold and gross margin* (L.O. 3)

Cost of goods sold, $101,000

Selected accounts of Montpelier Supply Company had these balances at June 30, 19X9.

Purchases	$ 98,100
Selling expenses	29,800
Equipment	44,700
Purchase discounts	1,300
Accumulated depreciation—equipment.....	6,900
Note payable	30,000
Sales discounts......................	3,400
General expenses	16,300
Accounts receivable	22,600
Accounts payable	23,800
Cash	13,600
Freight in...........................	4,300
Sales revenue	173,100
Purchases returns and allowances	1,400
Salary payable	1,800
John Wilfong, capital	36,000
Sales returns and allowances	12,100
Inventory: May 31......................	33,800
June 30.......................	32,500

Required

1. Show the computation of Montpelier Supply's net sales, cost of goods sold, and gross margin for the year ended June 30, 19X9.
2. John Wilfong, owner of Montpelier Supply, strives to earn a gross margin percentage of 40 percent. Did he achieve this goal?
3. Did the rate of inventory turnover reach the industry average of 2.8?

Problem 5-5A *Preparing a merchandiser's financial statements* **(L.O. 3, 4, 6)**   Net income, $76,790

The accounts of Curtis Mathes Home Entertainment Center are listed in alphabetical order.

Accounts payable	$27,380	Purchases		$273,100
Accounts receivable	31,200	Purchase discounts		4,670
Accumulated depreciation		Purchase returns and		
—office equipment	9,500	allowances.............		10,190
Accumulated depreciation		Salary payable		6,120
—store equipment	6,880	Sales discounts..........		8,350
Capital, June 30	73,720	Sales returns and		
Cash	12,320	allowances.............		17,900
General expenses.........	75,830	Sales revenue		531,580
Interest expense..........	7,200	Selling expenses..........		84,600
Interest payable	3,000	Store equipment		47,500
Inventory: June 30........	190,060	Supplies		4,350
July 31	187,390	Unearned sales revenue...		9,370
Note payable, long-term ..	160,000	Withdrawals		11,000
Office equipment.........	79,000			

Required

1. Prepare the entity's multiple-step income statement for July of the current year.
2. Prepare the income statement in single-step format.
3. Prepare the balance sheet in report format at July 31 of the current year. Show your computation of the July 31 balance of Capital.

Problem 5-6A *Using work sheet data to prepare financial statements* (L.O. 3, 4, 6)

The trial balance and adjustments columns of the work sheet of Lawson Coffee Company include the following accounts and balances at September 30, 19X5:

Account Title	Trial Balance Debit	Trial Balance Credit	Adjustments Debit	Adjustments Credit
Cash....................	7,300			
Accounts receivable	4,360		(a) 1,800	
Inventory	31,530			
Supplies	10,700			(b) 7,640
Equipment	79,450			
Accumulated depreciation ..		29,800		(c) 9,900
Accounts payable		13,800		
Salary payable				(e) 200
Unearned sales revenue		3,780	(d) 2,600	
Note payable, long-term		10,000		
Leslie Lawson, capital		58,360		
Leslie Lawson, drawing	35,000			
Sales revenue.............		242,000		(a) 1,800
				(d) 2,600
Sales returns	3,100			
Purchases	127,400			
Purchase discounts.........		3,700		
Selling expense	40,600		(b) 7,640	
			(e) 200	
General expense	21,000		(c) 9,900	
Interest expense	1,000			
Total..................	361,440	361,440	22,140	22,140

Required

1. Inventory on hand at September 30, 19X5, is $32,580. Without entering the preceding data on a formal work sheet, prepare the company's multiple-step income statement for the year ended September 30, 19X5, and its September 30, 19X5, balance sheet. Show your computation of the ending balance of Leslie Lawson, Capital.

2. Compute the gross margin percentage and the inventory turnover for 19X5. For 19X4, Lawson's gross margin percentage was .57 and the rate of inventory turnover was 4.2. Does the two-year trend in these ratios suggest improvement or deterioration in profitability?

Problem 5-7A *Preparing a merchandiser's work sheet* (L.O. 5)

Paschall Paint Company's trial balance relates to December 31 of the current year.

Additional data at December 31, 19XX:

a. Insurance expense for the year, $6,090.
b. Store fixtures have an estimated useful life of 10 years and are expected to be worthless when they are retired from service.
c. Accrued salaries at December 31, $1,260.
d. Accrued interest expense at December 31, $870.
e. Store supplies on hand at December 31, $760.
f. Inventory on hand at December 31, $99,350.

Paschall Paint Company
Trial Balance
December 31, 19XX

Cash	$ 2,910	
Accounts receivable	6,560	
Inventory	101,760	
Store supplies	1,990	
Prepaid insurance	3,200	
Store fixtures	63,900	
Accumulated depreciation		$ 37,640
Accounts payable		29,770
Salary payable		
Interest payable		
Note payable, long-term		37,200
Camilo Paschall, capital		63,120
Camilo Paschall, withdrawals	36,300	
Sales revenue		286,370
Purchases	161,090	
Salary expense	46,580	
Rent expense	14,630	
Utilities expense	6,780	
Depreciation expense		
Insurance expense	5,300	
Store supplies expense		
Interest expense	3,100	
Total	$454,100	$454,100

Required

Complete Paschall's work sheet for the year ended December 31 of the current year.

Problem 5-8A *Journalizing the adjusting and closing entries of a merchandising business* **(L.O. 5)**

Ending capital, $62,760

Required

1. Journalize the adjusting and closing entries for the data in Problem 5-7A.
2. Determine the December 31 balance of Camilo Paschall, Capital.

Problem 5-9A *Preparing a merchandiser's work sheet, financial statements, and adjusting and closing entries* **(L.O. 3, 4, 5)**

Total assets, $134,580

The year-end trial balance of Wang Sales Company on the next page relates to July 31 of the current year.

Additional data at July 31, 19XX:

a. Accrued interest revenue, $350.
b. Prepaid insurance still in force, $310.
c. Furniture has an estimated useful life of eight years. Its value is expected to be zero when it is retired from service.
d. Unearned sales revenue still unearned, $1,900.
e. Accrued salaries, $1,640.
f. Accrued sales commissions, $1,430.
g. Inventory on hand, $102,600.

Wang Sales Company
Trial Balance
July 31, 19XX

Cash	$ 3,120	
Notes receivable, current	6,900	
Interest receivable		
Inventory	104,000	
Prepaid insurance	2,810	
Notes receivable, long-term	19,300	
Furniture	16,000	
Accumulated depreciation		$ 12,000
Accounts payable		14,360
Salary payable		
Sales commission payable		
Unearned sales revenue		4,090
Ken-Hsi Wang, capital		102,270
Ken-Hsi Wang, withdrawals	59,000	
Sales revenue		337,940
Sales discounts	3,440	
Sales returns and allowances	8,900	
Interest revenue		1,910
Purchases	163,200	
Purchase discounts		2,100
Purchase returns and allowances		5,760
Freight in	11,100	
Salary expense	39,030	
Sales commission expense	31,500	
Rent expense	10,000	
Utilities expense	2,130	
Insurance expense		
Depreciation expense		
Total	$480,430	$480,430

Required

1. Enter the trial balance on a work sheet, and complete the work sheet for the year ended July 31 of the current year.
2. Prepare the company's multiple-step income statement and statement of owner's equity for the year ended July 31 of the current year. Also prepare its balance sheet at that date. Long-term notes receivable should be reported on the balance sheet between current assets and plant assets in a separate section labeled Investments.
3. Journalize the adjusting and closing entries at July 31.
4. Post to the Ken-Hsi Wang, Capital account and to the Income Summary account as an accuracy check on the adjusting and closing process.

(Group B)

No check figure

Problem 5-1B *Explaining the operating cycle of a retailer* *(L.O. 1)*

EyeMasters is a regional chain of optical shops in the southwestern United States. They specialize in offering a large selection of eyeglass frames, and they provide while-you-wait service. EyeMasters carries frames made by Logo

Paris, Liz Claiborne, Ralph Lauren, and others. EyeMasters has launched a vigorous advertising campaign promoting its two-for-the-price-of-one frame sales.

Required

You are the president of this company. Write a memo to your store manager explaining how the company's operating cycle works.

Problem 5-2B *Accounting for the purchase and sale of inventory* **(L.O. 2)**   No check figure

The following transactions occurred between Allcare Medical Supply and Greenview Clinic during February of the current year.

Feb. 6   Allcare Medical Supply sold $5,300 worth of merchandise to Greenview Clinic on terms of 2/10 n/30, FOB shipping point. Allcare prepaid freight charges of $300 and included this amount in the invoice total. (Allcare's entry to record the freight payment debits Accounts Receivable and credits Cash.)

10   Greenview returned $900 of the merchandise purchased on February 6. Allcare issued a credit memo for this amount.

15   Greenview paid $3,000 of the invoice amount owed to Allcare for the February 6 purchase. This payment included none of the freight charge.

27   Greenview paid the remaining amount owed to Allcare for the February 6 purchase.

Required

Journalize these transactions, first on the books of Greenview Clinic and second on the books of Allcare Medical Supply.

Problem 5-3B *Journalizing purchase and sale transactions* **(L.O. 2)**   Discount earned $80; interest paid, $50

Monarch Paper Company engaged in the following transactions during May of the current year:

May 3   Purchased office supplies for cash, $300.

7   Purchased inventory on credit terms of 2/10 net eom (end of month), $1,100.

8   Returned half the inventory purchased on May 7. It was not the inventory ordered.

10   Sold goods for cash, $450.

13   Sold inventory on credit terms of 2/15 n/45, $3,900, less $600 quantity discount offered to customers who purchased in large quantities.

16   Paid the amount owed on account from the purchase of May 7, less the discount and the return.

17   Received defective inventory returned from May 13 sale, $900, which is the net amount after the quantity discount.

18   Purchased inventory of $4,000 on account. Payment terms were 2/10 net 30.

26   Borrowed $3,920 from the bank to take advantage of the discount offered on May 18 purchase. Signed a note payable to the bank for this amount.

26   Paid supplier for goods purchased on May 18, less the discount.

28 Received cash in full settlement of his account from the customer who purchased inventory on May 13, less the discount and the return.

29 Purchased inventory for cash, $2,000, less a quantity discount of $400, plus freight charges of $160.

Required

1. Journalize the above transactions.
2. Assume the note payable signed on May 26 requires the payment of $30 interest expense. Was the decision wise or unwise to borrow funds to take advantage of the cash discount?

Cost of goods sold, $134,300

Problem 5-4B *Computing cost of goods sold and gross margin* (L.O. 3)

Selected accounts of Cargill Coin Collectors had these balances at November 30 of the current year.

Accumulated depreciation—furniture and fixtures	$ 13,600
Note payable	14,000
Purchase discounts	600
Sales discounts	2,100
General expenses	19,300
Accounts receivable	7,200
Purchases	132,000
Selling expenses	8,800
Furniture and fixtures	37,200
Purchase returns and allowances	900
Salary payable	300
Gretchen Cargill, capital	52,800
Sales revenue	184,600
Sales returns and allowances	3,200
Inventory: October 31	41,700
November 30	39,500
Accounts payable	9,500
Cash	3,700
Freight in	1,600

Required

1. Show the computation of Cargill's net sales, cost of goods sold, and gross margin for the year ended November 30 of the current year.
2. Gretchen Cargill, owner of Cargill Coin Collectors, strives to earn a gross margin percentage of 25 percent. Did she achieve this goal?
3. Did the rate of inventory turnover reach the industry average of 3.4?

Net income, $91,130

Problem 5-5B *Preparing a merchandiser's financial statements* (L.O. 3, 4, 6)

The accounts of Pure Milk Company are listed in alphabetical order at the top of the next page.

Required

1. Prepare the business's multiple-step income statement for May of the current year.
2. Prepare the income statement in single-step format.
3. Prepare the balance sheet in report format at May 31 of the current year. Show your computation of the May 31 balance of Capital.

Accounts payable	$16,950	Purchases $364,000
Accounts receivable	43,700	Purchase discounts 1,990
Accumulated depreciation		Purchase returns
—office equipment	22,450	and allowances......... 3,400
Accumulated depreciation		Salary payable 2,840
—store equipment	16,000	Sales revenue 731,000
Capital, April 30	74,620	Sales discounts.......... 10,400
Cash	7,890	Sales returns and
General expenses........	116,700	allowances............. 18,030
Interest expense..........	5,400	Selling expenses.......... 132,900
Interest payable	1,100	Store equipment 88,000
Inventory: April 30	69,350	Supplies................ 5,100
May 31........	71,520	Unearned sales revenue... 13,800
Note payable, long-term ..	45,000	Withdrawals 9,000
Office equipment.........	58,680	

Problem 5-6B *Using work sheet data to prepare financial statements* (L.O. 3, 4, 6)

Net income, $56,020; gross margin percentage 19X4, .61

The trial balance and adjustments columns of the work sheet of Scarlatti Development Company include the following accounts and balances at November 30, 19X4:

Account Title	Trial Balance Debit	Trial Balance Credit	Adjustments Debit	Adjustments Credit
Cash	4,000			
Accounts receivable	14,500		(a) 6,000	
Inventory	47,340			
Supplies....................	2,800			(b) 2,400
Furniture	39,600			
Accumulated depreciation		4,900		(c) 2,450
Accounts payable		12,600		
Salary payable				(e) 1,000
Unearned sales revenue		13,570	(d) 6,700	
Note payable, long-term		15,000		
C. Scarlatti, capital		60,310		
C. Scarlatti, drawing	42,000			
Sales revenue		164,000		(a) 6,000
				(d) 6,700
Sales returns.................	6,300			
Purchases	73,200			
Purchase discounts		2,040		
Selling expense	28,080		(e) 1,000	
General expense	13,100		(b) 2,400	
			(c) 2,450	
Interest expense	1,500			
Total	272,420	272,420	18,550	18,550

Required

1. Inventory on hand at November 30, 19X4, is $52,650. Without entering the preceding data on a formal work sheet, prepare the company's multiple-step income statement for the year ended November 30, 19X4, and its November 30, 19X4, balance sheet. Show your computation of the ending balance of C. Scarlatti, Capital.

2. Compute the gross margin percentage and the rate of inventory turnover for 19X4. For 19X3, Scarlatti's gross margin percentage was .58, and inventory turnover was 1.1. Does the two-year trend in these ratios suggest improvement or deterioration in profitability?

Net income, $57,390

Problem 5-7B *Preparing a merchandiser's work sheet* **(L.O. 5)**

Randall Apparel's trial balance relates to December 31 of the current year.

Additional data at December 31, 19XX:

a. Rent expense for the year, $10,200.
b. Store fixtures have an estimated useful life of 10 years and are expected to be worthless when they are retired from service.
c. Accrued salaries at December 31, $900.
d. Accrued interest expense at December 31, $360.
e. Inventory on hand at December 31, $80,200.

Required

Complete Randall's work sheet for the year ended December 31 of the current year.

Randall Apparel
Trial Balance
December 31, 19XX

Cash	$ 1,270	
Accounts receivable	4,430	
Inventory	73,900	
Prepaid rent	4,400	
Store fixtures	22,100	
Accumulated depreciation		$ 8,380
Accounts payable		6,290
Salary payable		
Interest payable		
Note payable, long-term		18,000
Roberta Randall, capital		55,920
Roberta Randall, withdrawals	39,550	
Sales revenue....................		170,150
Purchases	67,870	
Salary expense...................	24,700	
Rent expense	7,700	
Advertising expense..............	4,510	
Utilities expense	3,880	
Depreciation expense.............		
Insurance expense	2,770	
Interest expense	1,660	
Total...........................	$258,740	$258,740

Ending capital, $73,760

Problem 5-8B *Journalizing the adjusting and closing entries of a merchandising business* **(L.O. 5)**

Required

1. Journalize the adjusting and closing entries for the data in Problem 5-7B.
2. Determine the December 31 balance of Roberta Randall, Capital.

Problem 5-9B
Preparing a merchandiser's work sheet, financial statements, and adjusting and closing entries **(L.O. 3, 4, 5)**

The year-end trial balance of Weisner Sales Company pertains to March 31 of the current year.

Additional data at March 31, 19XX:

a. Accrued interest revenue, $1,030.
b. Insurance expense for the year, $3,000.
c. Furniture has an estimated useful life of 6 years. Its value is expected to be zero when it is retired from service.
d. Unearned sales revenue still unearned, $8,200.
e. Accrued salaries, $1,200.
f. Accrued sales commissions, $1,700.
g. Inventory on hand, $133,200.

Weisner Sales Company
Trial Balance
March 31, 19XX

Cash	$ 7,880	
Notes receivable, current	12,400	
Interest receivable		
Inventory	130,050	
Prepaid insurance	3,600	
Notes receivable, long-term	62,000	
Furniture	6,000	
Accumulated depreciation		$ 4,000
Accounts payable........................		12,220
Sales commission payable		
Salary payable		
Unearned sales revenue...................		9,610
Ed Weisner, capital		172,780
Ed Weisner, withdrawals..................	66,040	
Sales revenue		440,000
Sales discounts	4,800	
Sales returns and allowances	11,300	
Interest revenue		8,600
Purchases...............................	233,000	
Purchase discounts		3,100
Purchase returns and allowances..........		7,600
Freight in	10,000	
Sales commission expense.................	78,300	
Salary expense	24,700	
Rent expense	6,000	
Utilities expense	1,840	
Depreciation expense		
Insurance expense		
Total	$657,910	$657,910

Required

1. Enter the trial balance on a work sheet, and complete the work sheet for the year ended March 31 of the current year.
2. Prepare the company's multiple-step income statement and statement of

owner's equity for the year ended March 31 of the current year. Also prepare its balance sheet at that date. Long-term notes receivable should be reported on the balance sheet between current assets and plant assets in a separate section labeled Investments.

3. Journalize the adjusting and closing entries at March 31.
4. Post to the Ed Weisner, Capital account and to the Income Summary account as an accuracy check on the adjusting and closing process.

Extending Your Knowledge

Decision Problems

Corrected owner's equity,
$53,380

1. Using the Financial Statements to Decide on a Business Expansion (L.O. 4, 6)

David Wheelis owns Heights Pharmacy, which has prospered during its second year of operation. In deciding whether to open another pharmacy in the area, David has prepared the current financial statements of the business.

Heights Pharmacy
Income Statement
For the Year Ended December 31, 19X1

Sales revenue		$175,000
Interest revenue		24,600
Total revenue		199,600
Cost of goods sold:		
Beginning inventory	$ 27,800	
Net purchases	87,500	
Cost of goods available for sale	115,300	
Less: Ending inventory	30,100	
Cost of goods sold		85,200
Gross margin		114,400
Operating expenses:		
Salary expense	18,690	
Rent expense	12,000	
Interest expense	6,000	
Depreciation expense	4,900	
Utilities expense	2,330	
Supplies expense	1,400	
Total operating expense		45,320
Income from operations		69,080
Other expense:		
Sales discounts ($3,600) and returns ($7,100)		10,700
Net income		$ 58,380

Heights Pharmacy
Statement of Owner's Equity
For the Year Ended December 31, 19X1

D. Wheelis, capital, January 1, 19X1 . . .	$40,000
Add increases in owner's equity:	
Net income	58,380
D. Wheelis, capital, December 31, 19X1	$98,380

Heights Pharmacy
Balance Sheet
December 31, 19X1

Assets

Current:	
Cash	$ 5,320
Accounts receivable	9,710
Inventory	30,100
Supplies	2,760
Store fixtures	63,000
Total current assets	110,890
Other:	
Withdrawals	45,000
Total assets	$155,890

Liabilities

Current:	
Accumulated depreciation—store	
fixtures	$ 6,300
Accounts payable	10,310
Salary payable	900
Total current liabilities	17,510
Other:	
Note payable due in 90 days	40,000
Total liabilities	57,510

Owner's Equity

D. Wheelis, capital	98,380
Total liabilities and owner's equity	$155,890

David recently read in an industry trade journal that a successful pharmacy meets all of these criteria:

(a) Gross margin is at least one half of net sales

(b) Current assets are at least two times current liabilities

(c) Owner's equity is at least as great as total liabilities

Basing his opinion on the entity's financial statement data, David believes the business meets all three criteria. He plans to go ahead with his expansion plan and asks your advice on preparing the pharmacy's financial statements in accordance with generally accepted accounting principles. He assures you that all amounts are correct.

Required

1. Prepare a correct multiple-step income statement, a statement of owner's equity, and a balance sheet in report format.
2. Based on the corrected financial statements, compute correct measures of the three criteria listed in the trade journal.
3. Assuming the criteria are valid, make a recommendation about whether to undertake the expansion at this time.

2. Understanding the Operating Cycle of a Merchandiser (L.O. 1, 3)

A. Gayle Yip-Chuk has come to you for advice. Earlier this year she opened a record store in a plaza near the university she had attended. The store sells records, cassettes, and compact discs for cash and on credit cards and, as a special feature, on credit to certain students. Many of the students at the university are co-op students who alternate school and work terms. Gayle allows co-op students to buy on credit while they are on a school term, with the understanding that they will pay their account shortly after starting a work term.

   Business has been very good. Gayle is sure it is because of her competitive prices and the unique credit terms she offers. Her problem is that she is short of cash, and her loan with the bank has grown significantly. The bank manager has indicated that he wishes to reduce Gayle's line of credit because he is worried that Gayle will get into financial difficulties.

Required

1. Explain to Gayle why you think she is in this predicament.
2. Gayle has asked you to explain her problem to the bank manager and to assist in asking for more credit. What might you say to the bank manager to assist Gayle?

B. The employees of Schneider Ltd. made an error when they performed the periodic inventory count at year end, October 31, 19X2. Part of one warehouse was not counted and therefore was not included in inventory.

Required

1. Indicate the effect of the inventory error on cost of goods sold, gross margin, and net income for the year ended October 31, 19X2.
2. Will the error affect cost of goods sold, gross margin, and net income in 19X3? If so, what will the effects be?

Ethical Issue

Kingston & Barnes, a partnership, makes all sales of industrial conveyor belts under terms of FOB shipping point. The company usually receives orders for sales approximately one week before shipping inventory to customers. For orders received late in December, Lisa Kingston and Meg Barnes, the owners, decide when to ship the goods. If profits are already at an acceptable level, they delay shipment until January. If profits are lagging behind expectations, they ship the goods during December.

Required

1. Under Kingston & Barnes's FOB policy, when should the company record a sale?
2. Do you approve or disapprove of Kingston & Barnes's means of deciding when to ship goods to customers? If you approve, give your reason. If you disapprove, identify a better way to decide when to ship goods. (There is no accounting rule against the Kingston & Barnes practice.)

Financial Statement Problems

1. Closing Entries for a Merchandising Corporation; Evaluating Ratio Data (L.O. 5)

Gross margin percentage 1990, .219
Inventory turnover 1990, 5.9

This problem uses both the income statement (statement of income) and the balance sheet of The Goodyear Tire & Rubber Company in Appendix C. It will aid your understanding of the closing process of a business with inventories.

Assume that the inventory and closing procedures outlined in this chapter are appropriate for Goodyear. Further, use the amounts of inventories reported on the balance sheet. Ignore freight in, and assume net purchases for the year ended December 31, 1990, totaled $8,509.1 million.

Required

1. Using Net Purchases and amounts from the income statement, journalize Goodyear's closing entries for the year ended December 31, 1990. You will be unfamiliar with certain costs and expenses, but you should treat them all similarly. Corporations like Goodyear close Income Summary into an account called Retained Earnings (instead of Capital). Also, corporations have no Withdrawals account to close.

2. What amount was closed to Retained Earnings? How is this amount labeled on Goodyear's income statement?

3. Compute Goodyear's gross margin percentages and inventory turnover rates during 1990 and 1989. (In addition to the information in the Goodyear report in Appendix C, you will also need the December 31, 1988, Inventories balance, which was $1,635.5 million.) Did these ratio values of Goodyear improve or deteriorate during 1990? Summarize these results in a sentence.

2. Identifying Items from an Actual Company's Financial Statements (L.O. 5)

No check figure

Obtain the annual report of an actual company of your choosing. *Make sure that the company's balance sheet reports Inventories, Merchandise Inventories, or a similar asset category.* Answer these questions about the company:

1. What was the balance of total inventories reported on the balance sheet at the end of the current year? At the end of the preceding year? (If you selected a manufacturing company, you may observe more than one category of inventories. If so, name these categories and briefly explain what you think they mean.)

2. Corporations, such as the one you are analyzing, close Income Summary to an account called Retained Earnings (instead of Capital). Give the company's journal entry to close Income Summary to Retained Earnings.

3. Compute the company's gross margin percentage for the current year and for the preceding year. Did the gross margin percentage increase or decrease during the current year? Is this a favorable signal or an unfavorable signal about the company?

4. Compute the rate of inventory turnover for the current year. Would you expect your company's rate of inventory turnover to be higher or lower than that of a grocery chain such as Safeway or Kroger? Higher or lower than that of an aircraft manufacturer such as Boeing or McDonnell Douglas? State your reasoning.

Appendix

The Adjusting and Closing Process for a Merchandising Business: Adjusting-Entry Method

Point to Stress: Many accountants consider the replacement of the beginning inventory with the ending inventory an adjustment of the inventory balance rather than as a closing entry.

This appendix illustrates the adjusting-entry method for completing the accounting cycle of a merchandising business. In this approach we record the end-of-period inventory entries as adjustments rather than as closing entries. Except for this difference in handling inventory entries, the adjusting-entry method and the closing-entry method are identical. *No other adjusting or closing entries are affected by the approach taken, and the financial statements that result from both methods are the same.* Because of the way computers operate, computerized systems use the adjusting-entry method.

The Adjusting and Closing Process

To illustrate a merchandiser's adjusting and closing process, let's use Austin Sound's December 31, 19X6, trial balance in Exhibit 5-6, page 000. All the new accounts—Inventory, Freight In, and the contra accounts—are highlighted for emphasis. Inventory is the only new account that is affected by the adjusting procedures. Note that additional-data item *g* gives the ending inventory of $42,000.

Work Sheet of a Merchandising Business

The Exhibit 5A-1 work sheet is similar to the work sheets we have seen so far, but a few differences appear. Note that this work sheet does not include adjusted trial balance columns. In most accounting systems, a single operation combines trial balance amounts with the adjustments and extends the adjusted balances directly to the income statement and balance sheet columns. Therefore, to reduce clutter, the adjusted trial balance columns are omitted. A second difference is that the merchandiser's work sheet includes inventory and purchase amounts (which are highlighted). Let's examine the entire work sheet.

Account Title Columns. The trial balance lists a number of accounts without balances. Ordinarily, these accounts are affected by the adjusting process. Examples include Interest Receivable, Interest Payable, and Depreciation Expense. The accounts are listed in the order they appear in the ledger. This eases the preparation of the work sheet. Note that Income Summary—used for the inventory adjustments—is listed between the owner withdrawals and sales revenue. If additional accounts are needed, they can be written in at the bottom of the work sheet before net income is determined. Simply move net income down to make room for the additional accounts.

Trial Balance Columns. Examine the Inventory account, $40,500 in the trial balance. This $40,500 is the cost of the beginning inventory. The work sheet is designed to replace this outdated amount with the new ending balance, which in our example is $42,000 (additional-data item *g* in Exhibit 5-6). As we shall see, this task is accomplished through the adjusting process.

**Austin Sound
Work Sheet
For the Year Ended December 31, 19X6**

Account Title	Trial Balance Debit	Trial Balance Credit	Adjustments Debit	Adjustments Credit	Income Statement Debit	Income Statement Credit	Balance Sheet Debit	Balance Sheet Credit
Cash	2,850						2,850	
Accounts receivable	4,600						4,600	
Note receivable, current	8,000						8,000	
Interest receivable			(a) 400				400	
Inventory	40,500		(g2) 42,000	(g1) 40,500			42,000	
Supplies	650			(b) 550			100	
Prepaid insurance	1,200			(c) 1,000			200	
Furniture and fixtures	33,200						33,200	
Accumulated depreciation		2,400		(d) 600				3,000
Accounts payable		47,000						47,000
Unearned sales revenue		2,000	(e) 1,300					700
Interest payable				(f) 200				200
Note payable, long-term		12,600						12,600
C. Ernest, capital		25,900						25,900
C. Ernest, withdrawals	34,100						34,100	
Income summary			(g1) 40,500	(g2) 42,000	40,500	42,000		
Sales revenue		138,000		(e) 1,300		139,300		
Sales discounts	1,400				1,400			
Sales returns and allowances	2,000				2,000			
Interest revenue		600		(a) 400		1,000		
Purchases	89,300				89,300			
Purchase discounts		3,000				3,000		
Purchase returns and allowances		1,200				1,200		
Freight in	5,200				5,200			
Rent expense	8,400				8,400			
Depreciation expense			(d) 600		600			
Insurance expense			(c) 1,000		1,000			
Supplies expense			(b) 550		550			
Interest expense	1,300		(f) 200		1,500			
	232,700	232,700	86,550	86,550	150,450	186,500	125,450	89,400
Net income					36,050			36,050
					186,500	186,500	125,450	125,450

Adjustments Columns. The adjustments are similar to those discussed in Chapters 3 and 4. They may be entered in any order desired. The debit amount of each entry should equal the credit amount, and total debits should equal total credits.

The inventory adjustments are new. At the end of the period, accountants replace the beginning Inventory balance with the ending Inventory balance. Entry *g1* removes the beginning balance ($40,500) by crediting the Inventory account. The debit portion of entry *g1* transfers the beginning inventory amount to the Income Summary. This is done because beginning inventory becomes part of cost of goods sold during the year. Entry *g2* places the ending balance ($42,000) in the Inventory account with a debit. The credit to Income Summary signifies that the ending inventory amount is subtracted in computing cost of goods sold. Therefore, the two inventory adjustments prepare Inventory for the balance sheet and aid in computing cost of goods sold for the income statement.

Income Statement Columns. The income statement columns contain adjusted amounts for the revenues and the expenses. Sales Revenue, for example, is $139,300, which includes the $1,300 adjustment.

The two inventory amounts appear in the income statement columns alongside Income Summary because beginning inventory and ending inventory enter the computation of cost of goods sold. Recall that beginning inventory is added to purchases and ending inventory is subtracted. Even though the resulting cost-of-goods-sold amount does not appear on the work sheet, all the components of cost of goods sold are evident there. Placement of beginning inventory ($40,500) in the work sheet's income statement debit column has the effect of adding beginning inventory in computing cost of goods sold. Placing ending inventory ($42,000) in the credit column has the opposite effect.

Purchases and Freight In appear in the debit column because they are added in computing cost of goods sold. Purchase Discounts and Purchase Returns and Allowances appear as credits because they are subtracted. Together, all these items are used to compute cost of goods sold—$88,800 on the income statement in Exhibit 5-5, on page 219.

The income statement column subtotals on the work sheet indicate whether the business earned net income or incurred a net loss. If total credits are greater, the result is net income, as shown in the exhibit. Inserting the net income amount in the debit column brings total debits into agreement with total credits. If total debits are greater, a net loss has occurred. Inserting a net loss amount in the credit column would equalize total debits and total credits. Net income or net loss is then extended to the opposite column of the balance sheet.

Balance Sheet Columns. The only new item on the balance sheet is inventory. The balance listed is the ending amount of $42,000, which is determined by a physical count of inventory on hand at the end of the period. On the work sheet this amount comes from the $42,000 amount in the Adjustments Debit column.

Recall that the financial statements for a company are the same whether the adjusting-entry method or the closing-entry method is used. Exhibit 5-8, on page 225, presents Austin Sound's financial statements, which are based on the information in the work sheet. The text on page 224 discusses these financial statements in detail.

<table>
<tr><td>

OBJECTIVE 5

Adjust and close the accounts of a merchandising business

</td></tr>
</table>

Adjusting and Closing Entries for a Merchandising Business

Exhibit 5A-2 presents Austin Sound's adjusting entries, which are similar to those you have seen previously. Adjustment *g1* transfers the beginning Inventory balance to Income Summary. Entry *g2* sets up the ending Inventory balance.

The first closing entry debits the revenue and expense accounts that have credit balances. For Austin Sound these accounts are Sales Revenue, Interest Revenue, Purchase Discounts, and Purchase Returns and Allowances. The offsetting credit of $144,500 transfers their sum to Income Summary.

The second closing entry credits the revenue and expense accounts with debit balances. These are Sales Discounts, Sales Returns and Allowances, Purchases, Freight In, and the expense accounts.

		Journal		
		Adjusting Entries		
a.	Dec. 31	Interest Receivable	400	
		Interest Revenue		400
b.	31	Supplies Expense ($650–$100)	550	
		Supplies		550
c.	31	Insurance Expense	1,000	
		Prepaid Insurance		1,000
d.	31	Depreciation Expense	600	
		Accumulated Depreciation		600
e.	31	Unearned Sales Revenue	1,300	
		Sales Revenue		1,300
f.	31	Interest Expense	200	
		Interest Payable		200
g1	31	Income Summary	40,500	
		Inventory		40,500
g2	31	Inventory	42,000	
		Income Summary		42,000
		Closing Entries		
	Dec. 31	Sales Revenue	139,300	
		Interest Revenue	1,000	
		Purchase Discounts	3,000	
		Purchase Returns and Allowances	1,200	
		Income Summary		144,500
	31	Income Summary	109,950	
		Sales Discounts		1,400
		Sales Returns and Allowances		2,000
		Purchases		89,300
		Freight In		5,200
		Rent Expense		8,400
		Depreciation Expense		600
		Insurance Expense		1,000
		Supplies Expense		550
		Interest Expense		1,500
	31	Income Summary ($186,500–$150,450)*	36,050	
		C. Ernest, Capital		36,050
	31	C. Ernest, Capital	34,100	
		C. Ernest, Withdrawals		34,100

* The $186,500 amount is the sum of the $144,500 credit in the closing entry and the $42,000 credit in the g2 adjusting entry. The $150,450 amount is the sum of the $109,950 debit in the closing entry and the $40,500 debit in the g1 adjusting entry.

The last two closing entries close net income from Income Summary and also close owner Withdrawals into the Capital account.

The entries to the Inventory account deserve additional explanation. Recall that before the adjusting process Inventory still has the period's beginning balance. At the end of the period, this balance is one year old and must be replaced with the ending balance in order to prepare the financial statements at December 31, 19X6. The adjusting entries give Inventory its correct ending balance of $42,000, as shown at the top of page 263.

Class Exercise: Give the adjusting entries for Inventory if the beginning inventory is $23,400 and the ending inventory is $27,800.

ANSWER:

Income Summary . . .	23,400	
Inventory		23,400
Inventory	27,800	
Income Summary .		27,800

Assets

Cash		Accounts Receivable		Note Receivable		Interest Receivable	
2,850		4,600		8,000		(A) 400	

Inventory		Supplies		Prepaid Insurance		Furniture and Fixtures	
40,500	(A) 40,500	650	(A) 550	1,200	(A) 1,000	33,200	
(A) 42,000		100		200			

Accumulated Depreciation	
	2,400
	(A) 600
	3,000

Liabilities

Accounts Payable		Unearned Sales Revenue		Interest Payable		Note Payable	
	47,000	(A) 1,300	2,000		(A) 200		12,600
			700				

Owner's Equity

C. Ernest, Capital		C. Ernest, Withdrawals		Income Summary	
34,100	25,900	34,100	(C) 34,100	(A) 40,500	(A) 42,000
	(C) 36,050			(C)109,950	(C)144,500
	27,850			(C) 36,050	

Revenues

Sales Revenue		Sales Discounts		Sales Returns and Allowances		Interest Revenue	
	138,000	1,400	(C) 1,400	2,000	(C) 2,000		600
	(A) 1,300						(A) 400
(C)139,300	139,300					(C) 1,000	1,000

Expenses

Purchases		Purchase Discounts		Purchase Returns and Allowances		Freight In	
89,300	(C) 89,300	(C) 3,000	3,000	(C) 1,200	1,200	5,200	(C) 5,200

Rent Expense		Depreciation Expense		Insurance Expense		Supplies Expense	
8,400	(C) 8,400	(A) 600	(C) 600	(A) 1,000	(C) 1,000	(A) 550	(C) 550

Interest Expense	
1,300	
(A) 200	
1,500	(C) 1,500

(A) = Adjusting entry; (C) = Closing entry

Inventory

Jan. 1 Bal.	40,500	Dec. 31 Adj.	40,500
Dec. 31 Adj.	42,000		
Dec. 31 Bal.	42,000		

The inventory amounts for these adjusting entries are taken directly from the Adjustments columns of the work sheet. The offsetting debits and credits to Income Summary in these adjusting entries also serve to record the dollar amount of cost of goods sold in the accounts. Income Summary contains the cost-of-goods-sold amount after Purchases and its related contra accounts and Freight In are closed.

Study Exhibits 5A-1, 5A-2, and 5-8 carefully because they illustrate the entire end-of-period process that leads to the financial statements. As you progress through this book, you may want to refer to these exhibits to refresh your understanding of the adjusting and closing process for a merchandising business.

Return to the heading Income Statement Format on page 229.

Alternate Solution to Review Problem

Requirement 1

Sales, purchases, and related discount and return and allowance entries:

	19X3		
a.	Accounts Receivable	346,700	
	Sales Revenue		346,700
b.	Sales Returns and Allowances	8,200	
	Accounts Receivable		8,200
c.	Cash	329,000	
	Sales Discounts	10,300	
	Accounts Receivable		339,300
d.	Purchases	175,900	
	Accounts Payable		175,900
e.	Accounts Payable	7,430	
	Purchase Returns and Allowances		7,430
f.	Accounts Payable	194,400	
	Purchase Discounts		6,000
	Cash		188,400
g.	Freight In	9,300	
	Cash		9,300

Requirement 2

Jan King Distributing Company
Work Sheet
For the Year Ended December 31, 19X3

Account Title	Trial Balance Debit	Trial Balance Credit	Adjustments Debit	Adjustments Credit	Income Statement Debit	Income Statement Credit	Balance Sheet Debit	Balance Sheet Credit
Cash	5,670						5,670	
Accounts receivable	37,100						37,100	
Inventory	60,500		(g2) 65,800	(g1) 60,500			65,800	
Supplies	3,930			(a) 2,580			1,350	
Prepaid rent	6,000			(b) 5,000			1,000	
Furniture and fixtures	26,500						26,500	
Accumulated depreciation		21,200		(d) 2,650				23,850
Accounts payable		46,340						46,340
Salary payable				(e) 1,300				1,300
Interest payable				(f) 600				600
Unearned sales revenue		3,500	(c) 1,100					2,400
Note payable, long-term		35,000						35,000
Jan King, capital		23,680						23,680
Jan King, withdrawals	48,000						48,000	
Income summary			(g1) 60,500	(g2) 65,800	60,500	65,800		
Sales revenue		346,700		(c) 1,100		347,800		
Sales discounts	10,300				10,300			
Sales returns and allowances	8,200				8,200			
Purchases	175,900				175,900			
Purchase discounts		6,000				6,000		
Purchase returns and allowances		7,430				7,430		
Freight in	9,300				9,300			
Salary expense	82,750		(e) 1,300		84,050			
Rent expense	7,000		(b) 5,000		12,000			
Depreciation expense			(d) 2,650		2,650			
Utilities expense	5,800				5,800			
Supplies expense			(a) 2,580		2,580			
Interest expense	2,900		(f) 600		3,500			
	489,850	489,850	139,530	139,530	374,780	427,030	185,420	133,170
Net income					52,250			52,250
					427,030	427,030	185,420	185,420

Requirement 3

Adjusting entries

19X3				
Dec. 31	Supplies Expense	2,580		
	Supplies		2,580	
31	Rent Expense	5,000		
	Prepaid Rent......................		5,000	
31	Unearned Sales Revenue................	1,100		
	Sales Revenue		1,100	
31	Depreciation Expense ($26,500/10)	2,650		
	Accumulated Depreciation		2,650	
31	Salary Expense........................	1,300		
	Salary Payable		1,300	

31	Interest Expense		600	
	Interest Payable			600
31	Income Summary		60,500	
	Inventory			60,500
31	Inventory		65,800	
	Income Summary			65,800

Closing entries:

19X3

Dec. 31	Sales Revenue		347,800	
	Purchase Discounts		6,000	
	Purchase Returns and Allowances		7,430	
	Income Summary			361,230
31	Income Summary		314,280	
	Sales Discounts			10,300
	Sales Returns and Allowances			8,200
	Purchases			175,900
	Freight In			9,300
	Salary Expense			84,050
	Rent Expense			12,000
	Depreciation Expense			2,650
	Utilities Expense			5,800
	Supplies Expense			2,580
	Interest Expense			3,500
31	Income Summary ($65,800 + $361,230 − $60,500 − $314,280)		52,250	
	Jan King, Capital			52,250
31	Jan King, Capital		48,000	
	Jan King, Withdrawals			48,000

Income Summary

Adj.	60,500	Adj.	65,800
Clo.	314,280	Clo.	361,230
Clo.	52,250	Bal.	52,250

Turn back to page 236 for the solution to requirement 4, which shows the financial statements for Jan King Distributing Company.

Comprehensive Problem for Part One

Net income, $23,230; current ratio, 2.8 gross margin percentage 19XX, .40

Completing a merchandiser's accounting cycle

The end-of-month trial balance of Lansing Building Materials at January 31 of the current year follows:

Lansing Building Materials
Trial Balance
January 31, 19XX

Account Number	Account	Balance Debit	Balance Credit
11	Cash	$ 6,430	
12	Accounts receivable	19,090	
13	Inventory	65,400	
14	Supplies	2,700	
15	Building	195,000	
16	Accumulated depreciation—building		$ 36,000
17	Fixtures	45,600	
18	Accumulated depreciation—fixtures		5,800
21	Accounts payable		28,300
22	Salary payable		
23	Interest payable		
24	Unearned sales revenue		6,560
25	Note payable, long-term		87,000
31	Ed Lansing, capital		144,980
32	Ed Lansing, withdrawals	9,200	
41	Sales revenue		177,970
42	Sales discounts	7,300	
43	Sales returns and allowances	8,140	
51	Purchases	103,000	
52	Purchase discounts		4,230
53	Purchase returns and allowances		2,600
54	Selling expense	21,520	
55	General expense	10,060	
56	Interest expense		
	Total	$493,440	$493,440

Additional data at January 31, 19XX:

a. Supplies consumed during the month, $1,500. One-half is selling expense, and the other half is general expense.

b. Depreciation for the month: building, $4,000; fixtures, $4,800. One-fourth of depreciation is selling expense, and three-fourths is general expense.

c. Unearned sales revenue still unearned, $1,200.

d. Accrued salaries, a general expense, $1,150.

e. Accrued interest expense, $780.

f. Inventory on hand, $60,720.

Required

1. Using four-column accounts, open the accounts listed on the trial balance, inserting their unadjusted balances. Date the balances of the following accounts January 1: Inventory; Supplies; Building; Accumulated Depreciation—Building; Fixtures; Accumulated Depreciation—Fixtures; Unearned Sales Revenue; and Ed Lansing, Capital. Date the balance of Ed Lansing, Withdrawals, January 31.

2. Enter the trial balance on a work sheet, and complete the work sheet for the month ended January 31 of the current year. Lansing groups all operating expenses under two accounts, Selling Expense and General Expense. Leave two blank lines under Selling Expense and three blank lines under General Expense.

3. Prepare the company's multiple-step income statement and statement of owner's equity for the month ended January 31 of the current year. Also prepare the balance sheet at that date in report form.

4. Journalize the adjusting and closing entries at January 31, using page 3 of the journal.

5. Post the adjusting and closing entries, using dates and posting references.

6. Compute Lansing's current ratio and debt ratio at January 31, and compare these values with the industry averages of 1.9 for the current ratio and .57 for the debt ratio. Compute the gross margin percentage and the rate of inventory turnover for the month, and compare these ratio values with the industry averages of .26 for the gross margin percentage and .5 for inventory turnover. Does Lansing Building Materials appear to be stronger or weaker than the average company in the building materials industry?

Chapter 6

Accounting Information Systems

Diners Club was the first credit card company. It was started in 1952 as a club for frequent diners by a man who ran out of money at a restaurant. . . .

Before 1984, [Diners Club service] representatives had to start a file for each card holder inquiry, keep track of the accumulating paperwork until it had all been received, make a decision, and then contact the card holder. All the files were kept on paper. The personal card group handles about 10,000 pieces of correspondence a month, so there was a lot of clerical effort maintaining the paper files.

With the image processing system [which can convert pictures, drawings, and written characters to machine-readable form], all correspondence to the personal card group is scanned at the mail room to digitize it. Each digitized image is stored on an optical storage system and given four indices for retrieval purposes—date received, date of credit card charge, account number, and amount. From there, only the electronic images are used; the paper is discarded.

Source: *I/S Analyzer* (formerly *EDP Analyzer*), May 1989, Vol. 27, No. 5, p. 1

LEARNING OBJECTIVES

After studying this chapter, you should be able to

1 Describe the features of an effective information system

2 Use the sales journal

3 Use control accounts and subsidiary ledgers

4 Use the cash receipts journal

5 Use the purchases journal

6 Use the cash disbursements journal

7 Journalize return and allowance transactions

An **accounting information system**—often called simply an *information system*—is the combination of personnel, records, and procedures that a business uses to meet its routine needs for financial data. Because each business has different information demands, each uses a different accounting information system. For example, a jewelry store earns revenue by selling inventory, so the store's management usually wants an up-to-the-minute, accurate level of goods on hand for sale. A physician, however, earns revenue by providing service, and there is little or no inventory to control. The physician needs to keep track of the time spent on each patient. The jewelry store and the physician, then, need different information systems to answer the special sorts of questions that arise as they conduct their business. For maximum effectiveness, the information system is tailored to the business's specific needs.

A basic understanding of accounting systems is important for managing and evaluating a business. As a manager, you may be tempted to reply, "I can always hire an accountant to design the information system and do the accounting." Perhaps, but you will be better able to communicate with the members of your organization if you understand how the accounting system operates. The accounting system is the glue that holds the various parts of an organization together. It helps managers stay on top of their responsibilities. Indeed, a potential buyer of a business examines its accounting system to understand how the organization works.

Also, you do not want your employees to take advantage of you by manipulating your accounting system to cover theft. Business owners who are unfamiliar with accounting systems are victims of this practice to an alarming degree.

This chapter describes accounting information system designs and how they are implemented. It also provides a basic model of information processing and discusses what makes an information system effective. The chapter then discusses computer data processing and illustrates special journals and ledgers that accountants use to streamline information systems.

Accounting System Design and Installation

System Design. An accounting information system begins with a design. The manager and the designer study the business's goals and organizational structure. They also identify management's information needs, breaking down the required information-processing tasks. The designer must consider the personnel who will operate the system, the documents and reports to be

Teaching Tip: Refer to the chapter-opening vignette. Ask the students how they think Diners Club saved money by implementing the image-processing system. Students' answers might include personnel time saved from reading the mail to direct it to the right department, personnel time saved from recording the information, personnel time saved from retrieving the information manually, and storage of the paper formerly retained.

Point to Stress: A well designed accounting system is necessary to produce reliable accounting information for financial statements and decision making.

produced, and the equipment to be used. Almost every information system uses a computer for at least some tasks. Some CPA firms specialize in system design and install accounting systems for their clients.

System Installation. Installation includes selecting and training employees to operate the system, testing the system, and modifying it as needed. For a large system, installation may take months or even years. Often installation is more difficult than planned. Even after careful consideration in the design phase, unforeseen difficulties may emerge. If the system is not debugged, it will not perform its intended tasks.

Basic Model of Information Processing

Processing information means collecting, organizing, and processing data, and communicating the information to statement users. In addition, accounting data are used by managers. For example, accounts receivable might be analyzed to identify the biggest customers, who will receive special privileges. Exhibit 6-1 shows how the *basic model of information processing* relates to an accounting system.

Point to Stress: Most transactions are recorded from source documents.

1. The *source data* for the accounting system are the documents, such as invoices, canceled checks, and Diners Club tickets, that business transactions generate.
2. *Organizing and processing* data require transaction analysis, journalizing, posting, and preparation of the work sheet.
3. The output is *information*—the *financial statements.*

Notice that the system converts data to reports, fulfilling accounting's role of providing information.

An Effective Information System

Each business's accounting information system follows the basic model shown in Exhibit 6-1. Also, a well-designed information system offers control, compatibility, flexibility, and an acceptable cost/benefit relationship.

Control

OBJECTIVE 1

Describe the features of an effective information system

A good accounting system gives management control over operations. *Internal controls* are the methods and procedures used to authorize transactions, safeguard assets, and ensure the accuracy of accounting records. For example, most companies exert tight controls over cash disbursements to avoid theft through unauthorized payments. Also, keeping accurate records of accounts receivable is the only way to ensure that customers are billed and collections are received on time. The accounting system controls assets to different degrees. Usually control over cash is tighter than control over supplies and prepaid expenses because cash is more open to theft. Chapter 7 details internal control procedures.

EXHIBIT 6-1 *Information-Processing Model and the Accounting System*

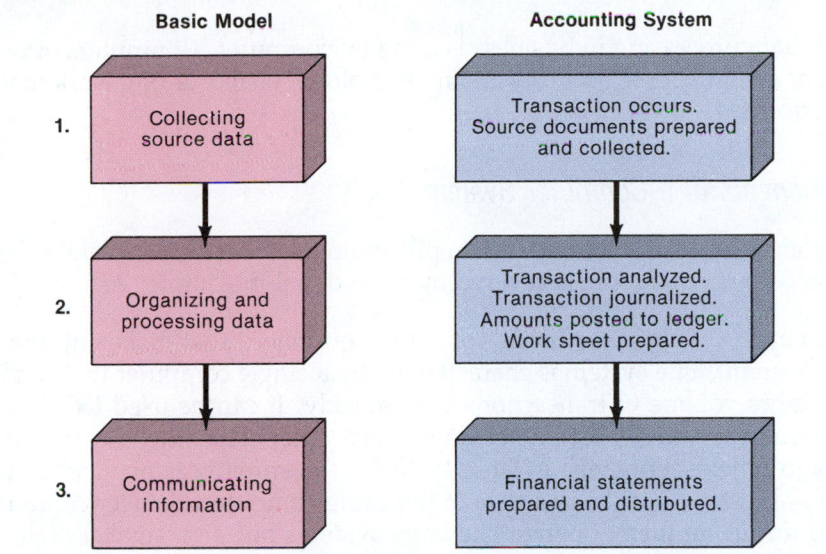

Real-World Example: Computers can make an information system less controllable since many employees have access to a terminal. For example, in a department store, it would be very dangerous for any employee with access to a computer to be able to access a particular customer's account. That employee might be able to change a customer's account or perhaps learn confidential information from that customer's file. To make sure that does not happen, employee access code numbers should be required to access certain information. The computer should not accept changes to other information without a source document number.

Compatibility

An information system meets the compatibility guideline when it works smoothly with the business's particular structure, personnel, and special features. For example, Diners Club designed its system to process inquiries from its card holders. One company may be organized by geographical region, another company by product line. The accounting system for the first company would accumulate revenues and expenses by region. The second company's system would group revenues and expenses by product. Any combination of data accumulation by region and by product is possible—whatever best suits the business. The compatibility guideline means designing the information system with the human factor in mind.

Flexibility

Organizations evolve. They develop new products, sell off unprofitable operations, and adjust employee pay scales. Changes in the business often call for changes in the accounting system. A well-designed system meets the flexibility guideline if it can accommodate such changes without needing a complete overhaul. In most organizations, systems are rarely replaced in their entirety. For example, a system for control of cash might be installed one year and a system for controlling inventories a year later.

Point to Stress: A flexible system should be structured so that as the business grows, new parts may be added without redesigning the whole system.

Acceptable Cost/Benefit Relationship

Control, compatibility, and flexibility can be achieved in an accounting system, but they cost money. At some point, the cost of the system outweighs its benefits. Identifying that point is the job of the accountant as systems analyst and of the manager as user of the information.

Consider the growing number of businesses that have bought computers. For many companies, the computer saves time and money and results in improved decisions. The benefits usually far exceed the cost of a simple computer system. In other cases, the savings are not sufficient to justify the cost of an increasingly elaborate system.

Point to Stress: A business must weigh the benefits of implementing an accounting information system against the benefits obtained from such a system. For example, a grocery store may find it practical as well as economical to use optical price scanners at the checkout counter, while a jewelry store might not.

Computer Data Processing

Much data processing in business is done by computer. Computers offer significant advantages in accuracy and in the volume of accounting work that can be performed.

Components of a Computer System

The components of a computer data processing system are *hardware, software,* and *personnel.* This topic is covered in more detail in Chapter 28.

Hardware.   Computer **hardware** is the equipment that makes up the system. A **mainframe system** is characterized by a single computer that can handle a large volume of transactions very quickly. It can be used locally or by employees at various locations. Employees enter data into the mainframe through remote terminals. In large systems, the employees may be scattered all over the world yet have access to the same computer. Smaller computers, called **minicomputers,** operate like large systems but on a smaller scale.

Exhibit 6-2 shows a microcomputer system, which is based on a different concept. In a **microcomputer** system, each work station has its own computer, often called a personal computer (PC). These small computers can be connected so that employees can work on the same project together. A group of microcomputers connected for common use is called a *network,* which achieves many of the benefits of a mainframe system. Micro systems are popular because they are more flexible and less expensive than large mainframes.

The basic hardware in the Diners Club system includes image-processing equipment and optical storage equipment.

EXHIBIT 6-2   *Microcomputer System*

Software. Computer **software** is the set of programs, or instructions, that cause the computer to perform the work desired. In a computer system, transactions are not entered into the accounting records by writing entries in a journal. They are entered by typing data on a keyboard similar to that of a typewriter. The keyboard is wired to the computer, which converts the typed data into instructions the computer uses to process the data. In some systems, the data are entered into the computer on punched cards.

Mainframe software includes programs written in computer languages such as FORTRAN, COBOL, and PL/1. Microcomputers use software based on computer languages such as BASIC and PASCAL. Other micro software is designed to do specialized tasks. For example, LOTUS® 1-2-3 performs financial analysis, and dBASE III organizes, stores, and retrieves large quantities of data. Peachtree's Insight program processes data and prints the balance sheet, income statement, and subsidiary records of accounts receivable, accounts payable, and payroll, among many other accounting tasks. Microcomputer software is popular because much of it is menu driven. This means that by following instructions—the "menu"—you can do complex tasks with little or no computer training.

Personnel. Computer personnel in a mainframe system include a systems analyst, a programmer, and a machine operator. The *systems analyst* designs the system, based on managers' information needs and the available accounting data. It is the analyst's job to design systems that convert data into useful information—at the lowest cost. The *programmer* writes the programs (instructions) that direct the computer's actions. The computer *operator* runs the machine.

In microcomputer systems, the distinction between the programmer and the operator becomes blurry because an employee may handle both responsibilities. For example, a marketing manager may use a microcomputer to identify the territory needing an advertising campaign. The company treasurer may use a micro to analyze the effects of borrowing money at various interest rates. The controller may prepare the budget on a micro. These people may program the computer to meet their specific needs, and also operate the machine.

Batch versus On-Line Processing

Computers process data in two main ways, in batches and on-line. **Batch processing** handles similar transactions in a group, or batch. Payroll accounting systems use batch processing. Suppose each employee fills out a weekly time sheet showing the number of hours worked. Stored in the computer are the employee's hourly pay and payroll deductions. The machine operator enters the hours worked, and the computer multiplies hours by hourly pay to determine each employee's gross pay. The computer subtracts deductions to compute net pay and prints payroll checks for the net amount. It also prints the weekly payroll report and updates the ledger accounts—all in one batch operation.

On-line processing handles transaction data continuously, often from various locations, rather than in batches at a single location. In retail stores like Sears and Penney's, the cash register does more than make change. It also doubles as a computer terminal. When you charge merchandise at a Penney's store in the United States, the transaction is recorded at Penney's data processing center in Dallas, Texas, directly from the store cash register. For any one transaction the computer in Dallas may perform the following steps:

1. Accounts receivable—
   a. Compares your account number with the list of approved accounts. *Assume your account is approved.*
   b. Adds the amount of this transaction to your previous balance and determines whether the new balance, including this transaction amount, exceeds your credit limit. *Assume it does not exceed your credit limit.*
   c. Debits the Accounts Receivable account and updates your personal account balance to include the effect of this transaction.
2. Sales Revenue—Credits the Sales Revenue account.
3. Inventory—
   a. Updates inventory records for the decrease due to this transaction.
   b. Prepares an order for replacement merchandise if the updated quantity on hand is below the reorder point.

Discussion Question: If a cash register doubles as a computer terminal, could the cashier gain access to other information on the computer? ANSWER: No. In most cases employees have only limited access to computer-based records.

The interactive nature of on-line processing—accounting for accounts receivable, sales, and inventory simultaneously—requires a large share of the computer's capacity. On-line processing, therefore, is used more in mainframe systems than in micro systems.

Overview of an Accounting Information System

The purpose of an accounting information system is to produce the financial statements and other reports used by managers, creditors, and interested people who evaluate the business. Companies use computers to meet specific needs. One company's accounting system may use a computer for accounts receivable and cash receipts and a manual system for the rest of its business. Another business may computerize payroll, accounts payable, and cash disbursements, with the remainder accounted for manually. Many large companies have completely computerized systems, and many small businesses use mostly manual systems. Each entity designs its system to achieve the goals of control, compatibility, flexibility, and an acceptable cost/benefit relationship. Exhibit 6-3 diagrams a typical accounting system for a merchandising business.

Accounting procedures may be manual or computerized, mainframe or microcomputer, batch or on-line. The remainder of the chapter describes some of the more important aspects of the system described in Exhibit 6-3. Later chapters discuss the remaining system topics diagrammed in the exhibit.

Special Accounting Journals

Teaching Tip: In a business of any size, some type of streamlining is necessary for recording hundreds of daily entries. Recording transactions in special journals promotes division of labor among employees.

Point to Stress: The general journal will have the fewest entries. Almost every transaction during the accounting period will fall into one of the four categories listed here: sales on account, cash receipts, purchases on account, or cash disbursements.

The journal entries illustrated so far in this book have been made in the *general journal.* In practice, however, it is inefficient to record all transactions there.

Think of using the general journal to debit Accounts Receivable and credit Sales Revenue for each credit sale made in a department store on a busy Saturday! Assuming you survived that, consider posting each journal entry to the ledger. Not only would the work be tedious, but it would be time consuming and expensive.

In fact, most of a business's transactions fall into one of four categories, so accountants use special journals to record these transactions. This system reduces the time and cost otherwise spent journalizing, as we will see. The

EXHIBIT 6-3 *Overview of an Accounting System*

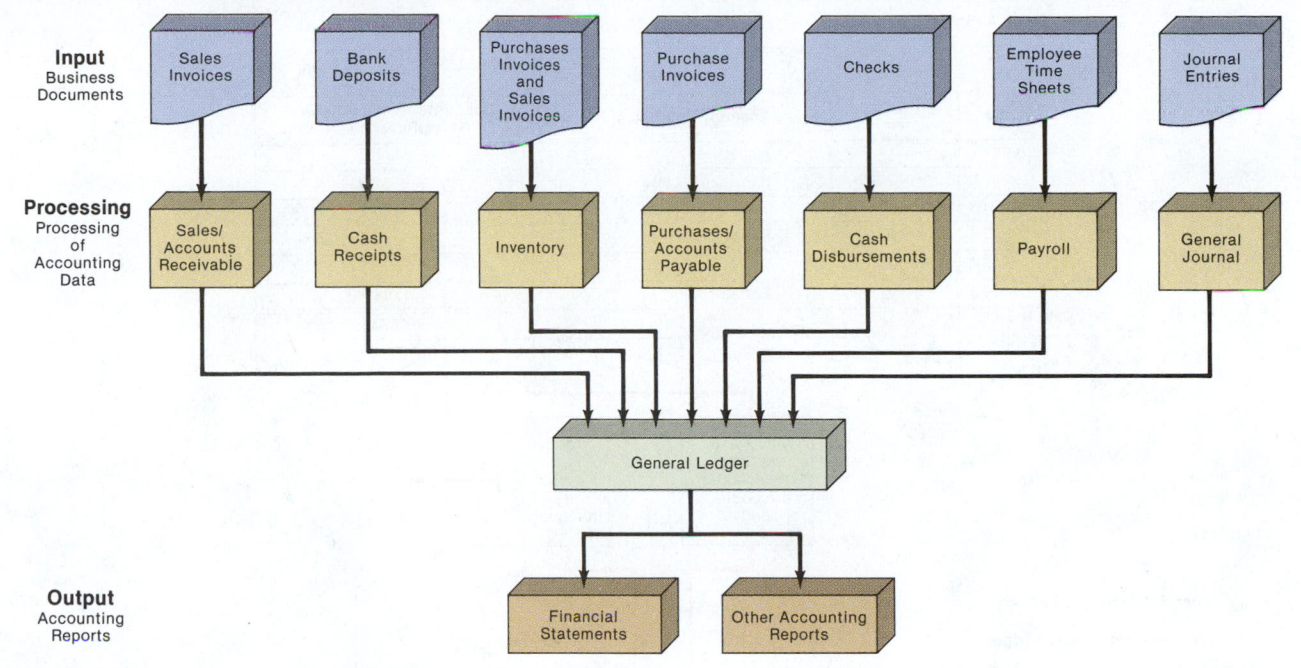

four categories of transactions, the related special journal, and the posting abbreviations follow.

Transaction	Special Journal	Posting Abbreviation
1. Sale on account	Sales journal	S
2. Cash receipt	Cash receipts journal	CR
3. Purchase on account	Purchases journal	P
4. Cash disbursement	Cash disbursements journal	CD

Businesses use the **general journal** for transactions that do not fit one of the special journals. For example, adjusting and closing entries are entered in the general journal. Its posting abbreviation is J.

Sales Journal

Most merchandisers sell at least some of their inventory on account. These *credit sales* are recorded in the **sales journal,** also called the *credit sales journal.* Credit sales of assets other than inventory—for example, buildings—occur infrequently and are recorded in the general journal.

Exhibit 6-4 illustrates a sales journal (Panel A) and the related posting to the ledgers (Panel B) of Austin Sound, the stereo shop introduced in Chapter 5.

The sales journal in Exhibit 6-4 (Panel A) has only one amount column, on the far right. Each entry in this column is a debit (Dr.) to Accounts Receivable and a credit (Cr.) to Sales Revenue, as the heading above this column indicates. For each transaction, the accountant enters the date, invoice number, and customer account along with the transaction amount. This streamlined way of recording sales on account saves a vast amount of time that would be spent writing account titles and dollar amounts in the general journal.

In recording credit sales in previous chapters, we did not keep a record of the names of credit sale customers. In practice the business must know the

Point to Stress: Only credit sales are recorded in the sales journal. Cash sales are recorded in the cash receipts journal.

OBJECTIVE 2

Use the sales journal

Typical Student Misconception: Transactions are recorded in either the general journal or a special journal, but not in both. All special journals are books of original entry.

Point to Stress: The accounts debited and credited in an entry will be the same whether the accounting system uses special journals or not. However, the debits and credits are arranged differently in a special journal system.

EXHIBIT 6-4 *Sales Journal and Posting to Ledgers*   Transparency T6-1

Panel A–Sales Journal:

Sales Journal				Page 3
Date	Invoice No.	Account Debited	Post Ref.	Accounts Receivable Dr. Sales Revenue Cr.
19X6				
Nov. 2	422	Maria Galvez	✓	935
13	423	Brent Harmon	✓	694
18	424	Susan Levy	✓	907
27	425	Clay Schmidt	✓	783
30		Total		3,319
				(12/41)

Individual accounts receivable are posted daily.

Totals are posted at the end of the month.

Panel B–Posting to Ledgers:

Accounts Receivable Ledger

Maria Galvez

Date	Jrnl. Ref.	Debit	Credit	Balance
Nov. 2	S.3	935		935

Brent Harmon

Date	Jrnl. Ref.	Debit	Credit	Balance
Nov. 13	S.3	694		694

Susan Levy

Date	Jrnl. Ref.	Debit	Credit	Balance
Nov. 18	S.3	907		907

Clay Schmidt

Date	Jrnl. Ref.	Debit	Credit	Balance
Nov. 27	S.3	783		783

General Ledger

Accounts Receivable   No. 12

Date	Jrnl. Ref.	Debit	Credit	Balance
Nov. 30	S.3	3,319		3,319

Sales Revenue   No. 41

Date	Jrnl. Ref.	Debit	Credit	Balance
Nov. 30	S.3		3,319	3,319

amount receivable from each customer. How else can the company keep track of who owes it money—and how much?

Consider the first transaction. On November 2 Austin Sound sold stereo equipment on account to Maria Galvez for $935. The invoice number is 422. All this information appears on a single line in the sales journal. Note that no explanation is necessary. The transaction's presence in the sales journal means that it is a credit sale—debited to Accounts Receivable-Maria Galvez and credited to Sales Revenue. To gain any additional information about the transaction, a person looks up the actual invoice.

Posting to the General Ledger.   Note the term *general ledger*. The ledger we have used so far is the **general ledger,** which holds the accounts reported in the financial statements. However, we will soon introduce other ledgers.

Posting from the sales journal to the general ledger is done monthly. First, the amounts in the journal are summed. In Exhibit 6-4, the total credit sales for November are $3,319. Recall that this column has two headings, Accounts Receivable and Sales Revenue. When the $3,319 is posted to these accounts in the general ledger, the accountant enters their account numbers beneath the total in the sales journal. Note in Panel B of Exhibit 6-4 that the account number for Accounts Receivable is 12 and the account number for Sales Revenue is 41. These account numbers are written beneath the credit sales total in the sales journal to signify that the $3,319 has been posted to the two accounts. The $3,319 is a debit to Accounts Receivable and a credit to Sales Revenue, as the heading in the sales journal states. The number of the account debited (12) appears on the left, the number of the account credited (41) on the right.

Posting to the Subsidiary Ledger.   The $3,319 sum of the November debits does not identify the amount receivable from any specific customer. Most businesses would find keeping a separate accounts receivable account in the general ledger for each customer to be unmanageable. A business may have thousands of customers. Imagine how many pages thick the general ledger for Sears would be. Locating a specific customer's account among the other accounts (Cash, Inventory, Salary Expense, and so on) would be frustrating and time consuming. To streamline operations, businesses instead place the accounts of their individual credit customers in a subsidiary ledger, called the Accounts Receivable ledger. A **subsidiary ledger** is a book of accounts that provides supporting details on individual balances, the total of which appears in a general ledger account. The customer accounts are filed alphabetically.

Amounts in the sales journal are posted to the subsidiary ledger daily to keep a current record of the amount receivable from each customer. Note that the amounts are debits. Daily posting allows the business to answer customer inquiries promptly. Suppose Maria Galvez telephones Austin Sound on November 11 to ask how much money she owes. The subsidiary ledger readily provides that information.

When each transaction amount is posted to the subsidiary ledger, a check mark is written in the posting reference column of the sales journal.

Journal References in the Ledgers.   When amounts are posted to the ledgers, the journal page number is written in the account to identify the source of the data. All transaction data in Exhibit 6-4 originated on page 3 of the sales journal so all journal references in the ledger accounts are S.3. The S. indicates sales journal.

Trace all the postings in Exhibit 6-4. The most effective way to learn about accounting systems and special journals is to study the flow of data. The arrows indicate the direction of the information.

The arrows show the links between the individual customer accounts in the subsidiary ledger and the Accounts Receivable account. These links are summarized at the top of page 278.

Accounts Receivable in the general ledger is a **control account,** which is an account whose balance equals the sum of the balances of a group of related accounts in a subsidiary ledger. In this simple illustration, Accounts Receivable's balance is the total amount of credit sales. The individual customer accounts are subsidiary accounts. They are "controlled" by the Accounts Receivable account in the general ledger.

Let's look at the advantages the sales journal offers. Each transaction is

Accounts Receivable debit balance...... $3,319

Customer Accounts Receivable

Customer	Balance
Maria Galvez........................	$ 935
Brent Harmon......................	694
Susan Levy	907
Clay Schmidt.......................	783
Total accounts receivable	$3,319

Point to Stress: The control
account should equal the sum
of all subsidiary accounts after
all the postings have been
made at the end of the period.

entered on a single line, and the account titles do not have to be written. The accountant, then, does not have to write as much in the sales journal as in the general journal. Also, the sales journal streamlines posting. That is, fewer postings to the general ledger are necessary. Suppose Austin Sound had 400 credit sales for the month. How many postings to the general ledger would be made from the sales journal? There are only two, one to Accounts Receivable and one to Sales Revenue. How many postings would there be from the general journal? The total would be 800 (400 debits to Accounts Receivable and 400 credits to Sales Revenue).

Additional data can be recorded in the sales journal. For example, a company may add a column to record sale terms, such as 2/10 n/30. The design of the journal depends on managers' needs for information.

*Teaching Tip: Point out that
special journals are just that;
they can be tailored to meet
any special needs of a business.*

Cash Receipts Journal

OBJECTIVE 4

Use the cash receipts journal

Cash transactions are common in most businesses because cash receipts from customers are the lifeblood of business. To streamline the recording of repetitive cash receipt transactions, accountants use the **cash receipts journal.**

Exhibit 6-5, Panel A, illustrates the cash receipts journal. The related posting to ledgers is shown in Panel B. The exhibit illustrates November transactions for Austin Sound.

Every transaction recorded in this journal is a cash receipt, so the first column is for debits to the Cash account. The next column is for debits to Sales Discounts on collections from customers. In a typical merchandising business, the main sources of cash are collections on account and cash sales. Thus the cash receipts journal has credit columns for Accounts Receivable and Sales Revenue. The journal also has a credit column for Other Accounts, which lists sources of cash other than cash sales and collections on account. This Other Accounts column is also used to record the names of customers from whom cash is received on account.

In Exhibit 6-5, cash sales occurred on November 6, 19, and 28. Observe the debits to Cash and the credits to Sales Revenue ($517, $853, and $1,802).

On November 11 Austin Sound borrowed $1,000 from First Bank. Cash is debited, and Note Payable to First Bank is credited in the Other Accounts column because no specific credit column is set up to account for borrowings. For this transaction, it is necessary to write the account title, Note Payable to First Bank, in the Other Accounts/Account Title column to record the source of cash.

On November 25 Austin Sound collected $762 of interest revenue. The account credited, Interest Revenue, must be written in the Other Accounts column. The November 11 and 25 transactions illustrate an important fact about business. Different entities have different types of transactions, and they design their special journals to meet their particular needs. In this case, the Other Accounts credit column is the catchall that is used to record all nonroutine cash receipt transactions.

*Teaching Tip: Notice that every
entry in the cash receipts
journal must have an amount
in the Cash debit column. Also
notice that cash sales are
recorded in the cash receipts
journal rather than in the sales
journal. Ask: What is the entry
for cash sales? ANSWER: Debit
Cash, credit Sales Revenue.*

*Discussion Question: Ask
students to suggest other
transactions that would entail a
debit to cash (besides
collections on account and cash
sales). ANSWER: Investment by
owner; bank loan; sale of plant
assets; collection of interest
revenue.*

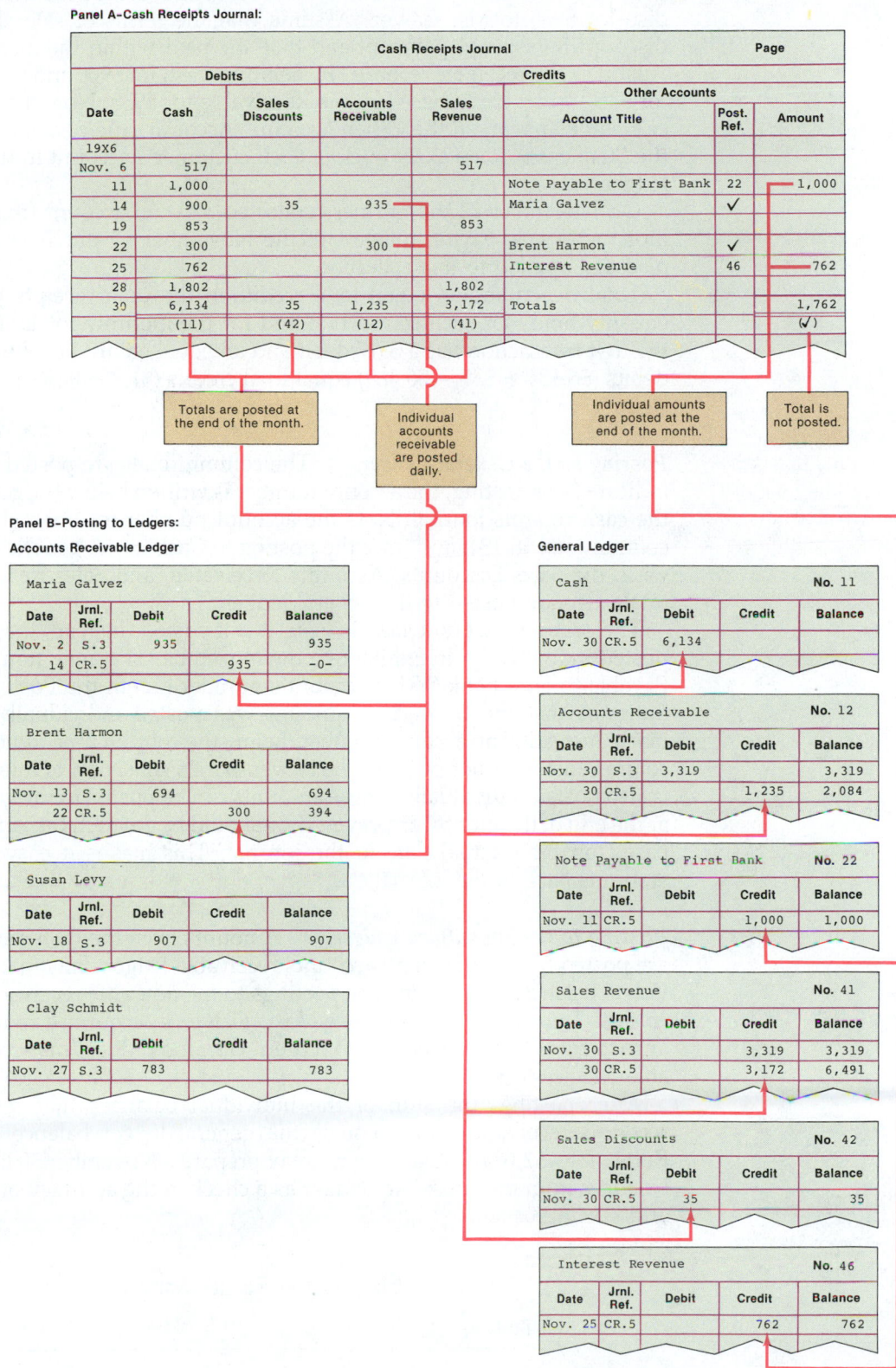

Panel A–Cash Receipts Journal:

Panel B–Posting to Ledgers:

Accounts Receivable Ledger

General Ledger

On November 14 Austin Sound collected $900 from Maria Galvez. Referring back to Exhibit 6-4, we see that on November 2 Austin Sound sold merchandise for $935 to Ms. Galvez. Assume that the terms of sale allowed a $35 discount for prompt payment and that she paid within the discount period. Austin's cash receipt is recorded by debiting Cash for $900 and Sales Discounts for $35 and by crediting Accounts Receivable for $935. Note that the customer's name appears in the Other Accounts/Account Title column. This enables the business to keep exact track of each customer's account in the subsidiary ledger.

On November 22 the business collected $300 on account from Brent Harmon, who was paying for part of the November 13 purchase. Assume no discount applied to this collection.

Total debits should equal total credits in the cash receipts journal. This equality holds for each transaction and for the monthly totals. For example, the first transaction has a $517 debit and an equal credit. For the month, total debits ($6,134 + $35 = $6,169) equal total credits ($1,235 + $3,172 + $1,762 = $6,169).

Posting to the General Ledger.   The column totals are posted monthly. To indicate their posting, the account number is written below the column total in the cash receipts journal. Note the account number for Cash (11) below the column total $6,134, and trace the posting to Cash in the general ledger. Likewise, the Sales Discounts, Accounts Receivable, and Sales Revenue column totals also are posted to the general ledger.

The column total for *Other Accounts* is not posted. Instead, these credits are posted individually. In Exhibit 6-5, the November 11 transaction reads "Note Payable to First Bank." This account's number (22) in the Post. Ref. column indicates that the transaction amount was posted individually. The check mark, instead of an account number, below the column total indicates that the column total was not posted. The November 25 collection of interest revenue is also posted individually. These amounts can be posted to the general ledger at the end of the month. However, they should be dated in the ledger accounts based on their actual date in the journal. This makes it easy to trace the amounts back to the journal.

Posting to the Subsidiary Ledger.   Amounts from the cash receipts journal are posted to the subsidiary accounts receivable ledger daily to keep the individual balances up to date. The postings to the accounts receivable ledger are credits. Trace the $935 posting to Maria Galvez's account. It reduces her balance to zero. The $300 receipt from Brent Harmon reduces his accounts receivable balance to $394.

After posting, the sum of the individual balances that remain in the accounts receivable ledger equals the general ledger balance in Accounts Receivable ($2,084). Austin Sound may prepare a November 30 list of account balances from the subsidiary ledger as a check of the accuracy of journalizing and posting:

Customer Accounts Receivable

Customer	Balance
Brent Harmon	$ 394
Susan Levy	907
Clay Schmidt	783
Total accounts receivable	$2,084

Keeping good accounts receivable records reduces errors and helps customer relations.

The cash receipts journal offers the same advantages as the sales journal: streamlined journalizing of transactions and fewer postings to the ledgers.

Summary Problem for Your Review

A company completed the following selected transactions during March:

Mar. 4 Received $500 from a cash sale to a customer.

6 Received $60 on account from Brady Lee. The full invoice amount was $65, but Lee paid within the discount period to gain the $5 discount.

9 Received $1,080 on a note receivable from Beverly Mann. This amount includes the $1,000 note receivable plus interest revenue.

15 Received $800 from a cash sale to a customer.

24 Borrowed $2,200 by signing a note payable to Interstate Bank.

27 Received $1,200 on account from Lance Albert. Payment was received after the discount period lapsed.

The general ledger showed the following balances at February 28: Cash, debit balance of $1,117; Accounts Receivable, debit balance of $2,790; Note Receivable—Beverly Mann, debit balance of $1,000. The accounts receivable subsidiary ledger at February 28 contained debit balances as follows: Lance Albert, $1,840; Brady Lee, $65; Melinda Fultz, $885.

Required

1. Record the transactions in the cash receipts journal, page 7.
2. Compute column totals at March 31. Show that total debits equal total credits in the cash receipts journal.
3. Post to the general ledger and the accounts receivable subsidiary ledger. Use complete posting references, including the account numbers illustrated: Cash, 11; Accounts Receivable, 12; Note Receivable—Beverly Mann, 13; Note Payable—Interstate Bank, 22; Sales Revenue, 41; Sales Discounts, 42; Interest Revenue, 46. Insert a check mark (✓) in the posting reference column for each February 28 account balance.
4. Prove the accuracy of posting by showing that the total of the balances in the subsidiary ledger equals the general ledger balance in Accounts Receivable.

SOLUTION TO REVIEW PROBLEM

Requirements 1 and 2

Cash Receipts Journal   Page 7

	Debits		Credits				
					Other Accounts		
Date	Cash	Sales Discounts	Accounts Receivable	Sales Revenue	Account Title	Post. Ref.	Amount
Mar. 4	500			500			
6	60	5	65		Brady Lee	✓	
9	1,080				Note Receivable–		
					Beverly Mann	13	1,000
					Interest Revenue	46	80
15	800			800			
24	2,200				Note Payable–		
					Interstate Bank	22	2,200
27	1,200		1,200		Lance Albert	✓	
31	5,840	5	1,265	1,300	Total		3,280
	(11)	(42)	(12)	(41)			(✓)

5,845   5,845

Requirement 3

Accounts Receivable Ledger

Lance Albert

Date	Jrnl. Ref.	Debit	Credit	Balance
Feb. 28	✓			1,840
Mar. 27	CR.7		1,200	640

Melinda Fultz

Date	Jrnl. Ref.	Debit	Credit	Balance
Feb. 28	✓			885

Brady Lee

Date	Jrnl. Ref.	Debit	Credit	Balance
Feb. 28	✓			65
Mar. 6	CR.7		65	—

General Ledger

Cash   No. 11

Date	Jrnl. Ref.	Debit	Credit	Balance
Feb. 28	✓			1,117
Mar. 31	CR.7	5,840		6,957

Accounts Receivable   No. 12

Date	Jrnl. Ref.	Debit	Credit	Balance
Feb. 28	✓			2,790
Mar. 31	CR.7		1,265	1,525

Note Receivable-Beverly Mann   No. 13

Date	Jrnl. Ref.	Debit	Credit	Balance
Feb. 28	✓			1,000
Mar. 9	CR.7		1,000	—

Note Payable-Interstate Bank   No. 22

Date	Jrnl. Ref.	Debit	Credit	Balance
Mar. 24	CR.7		2,200	2,200

Sales Revenue   No. 41

Date	Jrnl. Ref.	Debit	Credit	Balance
Mar. 31	CR.7		1,300	1,300

Sales Discounts   No. 42

Date	Jrnl. Ref.	Debit	Credit	Balance
Mar. 31	CR.7	5		5

Interest Revenue   No. 46

Date	Jrnl. Ref.	Debit	Credit	Balance
Mar. 9	CR.7		80	80

Requirement 4

Lance Albert .... $ 640
Melinda Fultz 885
Total accounts receivable $1,525

This total agrees with the balance in Accounts Receivable.

Purchases Journal

A merchandising business purchases inventory and supplies frequently. Such purchases are usually made on account. The **purchases journal** is designed to account for all purchases of inventory, supplies, and other assets *on account*. It can also be used to record expenses incurred on account. Cash purchases are recorded in the cash disbursements journal.

Exhibit 6-6 illustrates Austin Sound's purchases journal (Panel A) and posting to ledgers (Panel B).[1]

The purchases journal in Exhibit 6-6 has amount columns for credits to Accounts Payable and debits to Purchases, Supplies, and Other Accounts. The Other Accounts columns accommodate purchases of items other than inventory and supplies. These columns make the journal flexible enough to accommodate a wide variety of transactions. Each business designs its purchases journal to meet its own needs for information and efficiency. Accounts Payable is credited for all transactions recorded in the purchases journal. Inventory purchases are debited to Purchases. Purchases of supplies are debited to Supplies.

On November 2 Austin Sound purchased from JVC Corporation stereo inventory costing $700. The creditor's name (JVC Corporation) is entered in the Account Credited column. The purchase terms of 3/15 n/30 are also entered to help identify the due date and the discount available. Accounts Payable is credited and Purchases is debited for the transaction amount. On November 19 a credit purchase of supplies is entered as a debit to Supplies and a credit to Accounts Payable.

Note the November 9 purchase of fixtures from City Office Supply. Since the purchases journal contains no column for fixtures, the Other Accounts debit column is used. Because this was a credit purchase, the accountant enters the creditor name (City Office Supply) in the Account Credited column and writes "Fixtures" in the Other Accounts/Account Title column.

The total credits in the journal ($2,876) are compared with the total debits ($1,706 + $103 + $1,067 = $2,876) to prove the accuracy of the entries in the purchases journal.

To pay debts efficiently, a company must know how much it owes particular creditors. The Accounts Payable account in the general ledger shows only a single total, however, and therefore does not indicate the amount owed to each creditor. Companies keep an accounts payable subsidiary ledger. The accounts payable ledger lists the creditors in alphabetical order, along with the amounts owed to them. Exhibit 6-6, Panel B, shows Austin Sound's accounts payable subsidiary ledger, which includes accounts for Audio Electronics, City Office Supply, and others. After posting at the end of the period, the total of the individual balances in the subsidiary ledger equals the balance in the Accounts Payable control account in the general ledger. This system is like the accounts receivable system discussed earlier in the chapter.

Posting from the Purchases Journal. Posting from the purchases journal is similar to posting from the sales journal and the cash receipts journal. Exhibit 6-6, Panel B, illustrates the posting process.

Individual accounts payable in the *accounts payable subsidiary ledger* are posted daily, and column totals and other amounts are posted to the *general*

---

[1]This is the only special journal that we illustrate with the credit column placed to the left and the debit columns to the right. This arrangement of columns focuses on Accounts Payable, which is credited for each entry to this journal—and on the individual supplier to be paid.

EXHIBIT 6-6 *Purchases Journal and Posting to Ledgers*   Transparency T6-3

Panel A–Purchases Journal:

				Credit	Debits				
							Other Accounts		
Date	Account Credited	Terms	Post. Ref.	Accounts Payable	Purchases	Supplies	Account Title	Post. Ref.	Amount
19X6									
Nov. 2	JVC Corp.	3/15 n/30	✓	700	700				
5	Pioneer Sound	n/30	✓	319	319				
9	City Office Supply	2/10 n/30	✓	440			Fixtures	19	440
12	Audio Electronics, Inc.	n/30	✓	236	236				
13	JVC Corp.	3/15 n/30	✓	451	451				
19	City Office Supply Co.	2/10 n/30	✓	103		103			
23	O'Leary Furniture Co.	n/60	✓	627			Furniture	18	627
30	Totals			2,876	1,706	103			1,067
				(21)	(51)	(16)			(✓)

Purchases Journal — Page 8

Individual accounts payable are posted daily.

Totals are posted at the end of the month.

Total is not posted.

Individual amounts are posted at the end of the month.

Panel B–Posting to Ledgers:

Accounts Payable Ledger

Audio Electronics

Date	Jrnl. Ref.	Debit	Credits	Balance
Nov. 12	P.8		236	236

City Office Supply Co.

Date	Jrnl. Ref.	Debit	Credit	Balance
Nov. 9	P.8		440	440
19	P.8		103	543

JVC Corp.

Date	Jrnl. Ref.	Debit	Credit	Balance
Nov. 2	P.8		700	700
13	P.8		451	1,151

O'Leary Furniture Co.

Date	Jrnl. Ref.	Debit	Credit	Balance
Nov. 23	P.8		627	627

Pioneer Sound

Date	Jrnl. Ref.	Debit	Credit	Balance
Nov. 5	P.8		319	319

General Ledger

Supplies No. 16

Date	Jrnl. Ref.	Debit	Credit	Balance
Nov. 30	P.8	103		103

Furniture No. 18

Date	Jrnl. Ref.	Debit	Credit	Balance
Nov. 23	P.8	627		627

Fixtures No. 19

Date	Jrnl. Ref.	Debit	Credit	Balance
Nov. 9	P.8	440		440

Accounts Payable No. 21

Date	Jrnl. Ref.	Debit	Credit	Balance
Nov. 30	P.8		2,876	2,876

Purchases No. 51

Date	Jrnl. Ref.	Debit	Credit	Balance
Nov. 30	P.8	1,706		1,706

Teaching Tip: Have students look carefully at the Accounts Payable credit column on the purchases journal. Ask: What does every entry in this journal have in common? *ANSWER:* A credit to Accounts Payable. Notice that cash purchases are not included here. Ask: Where will cash purchases be recorded? *ANSWER:* Cash Disbursements journal.

ledger at the end of the month. In the ledger accounts, P.8 indicates the source of the posted amounts—that is, page 8 of the purchases journal.

Use of the special purchases journal offers advantages over the general journal. Each transaction is *journalized* on one line, and the general ledger accounts do not have to be written. A written explanation of each transaction is unnecessary because each transaction is a purchase on account. Posting to the general ledger is streamlined with the special journal because monthly totals can be posted to the general ledger. Contrast the number of postings from the purchases journal in Exhibit 6-6 with the number that would be required if the general journal were used to record the same seven transactions. Use of the purchases journal requires only five general ledger postings—$2,876 to Accounts Payable, $1,706 to Purchases, $103 to Supplies, $440 to Fixtures, and $627 to Furniture. Without the purchases journal, there would have been fourteen postings, two for each of the seven transactions.

Cash Disbursements Journal

Businesses make most cash disbursements by check. All payments by check are recorded in the **cash disbursements journal.** Other titles of this special journal are the *check register* and the *cash payments journal.* Like the other special journals, it has multiple columns for recording cash payments that occur frequently.

Exhibit 6-7, Panel A, illustrates the cash disbursements journal, and Panel B shows the postings to the ledgers of Austin Sound.

The cash disbursements journal in the exhibit has two debit columns—for Accounts Payable and Other Accounts—and two credit columns—for Cash and Purchase Discounts. It also has columns for the date and the check number of each cash payment.

Suppose a business makes numerous cash purchases of inventory. What additional column would its cash disbursements journal need to be most useful? A column for Purchases, which would appear under the Debits heading, would streamline the accounting.

All entries in the cash disbursements journal include a credit to Cash. Payments on account are debits to Accounts Payable. On November 15 Austin Sound paid JVC on account, with credit terms of 3/15 n/30 (for details, see the first transaction in Exhibit 6-6). Therefore, Austin took the 3 percent discount and paid $679 ($700 less the $21 discount).

The Other Accounts column is used to record debits to accounts for which no special column exists. For example, on November 3 Austin Sound paid rent expense of $1,200, and on November 8 the business purchased supplies for $61.

As with all other journals, the total debits ($3,161 + $819 = $3,980) should equal the total credits ($21 + $3,959 = $3,980).

Posting from the Cash Disbursements Journal.

Posting from the cash disbursements journal is similar to posting from the cash receipts journal. Individual creditor amounts are posted daily, and column totals and Other Accounts are posted at the end of the month. Exhibit 6-7, Panel B, illustrates the posting process.

Observe the effect of posting to the Accounts Payable account in the general ledger. The first posted amount in the Accounts Payable account (credit $2,876) originated in the purchases journal, page 8 (P.8). The second posted amount (debit $819) came from the cash disbursements journal, page 6 (CD.6). The resulting credit balance in Accounts Payable is $2,057. Also, see the Cash account. After posting, its debit balance is $2,175.

Real-World Example: The reason businesses make most of their cash disbursements by check is to maintain better control over cash. Imagine the confusion that would ensue if every employee were able to take cash from the register to pay for purchases. (Also consider the likelihood of theft of cash.)

Discussion Question: Can you name some other often-used columns which might appear in the cash disbursements journal? ANSWER: Salary Expense; Purchases; Supplies.

Discussion Question: How many postings would be in the general ledger (a) Cash account? ANSWER: two—one from cash receipts and one from cash disbursements. (b) Sales Revenue account? ANSWER: two—one from the sales journal and one from cash receipts. Of course, there may be various adjustments.

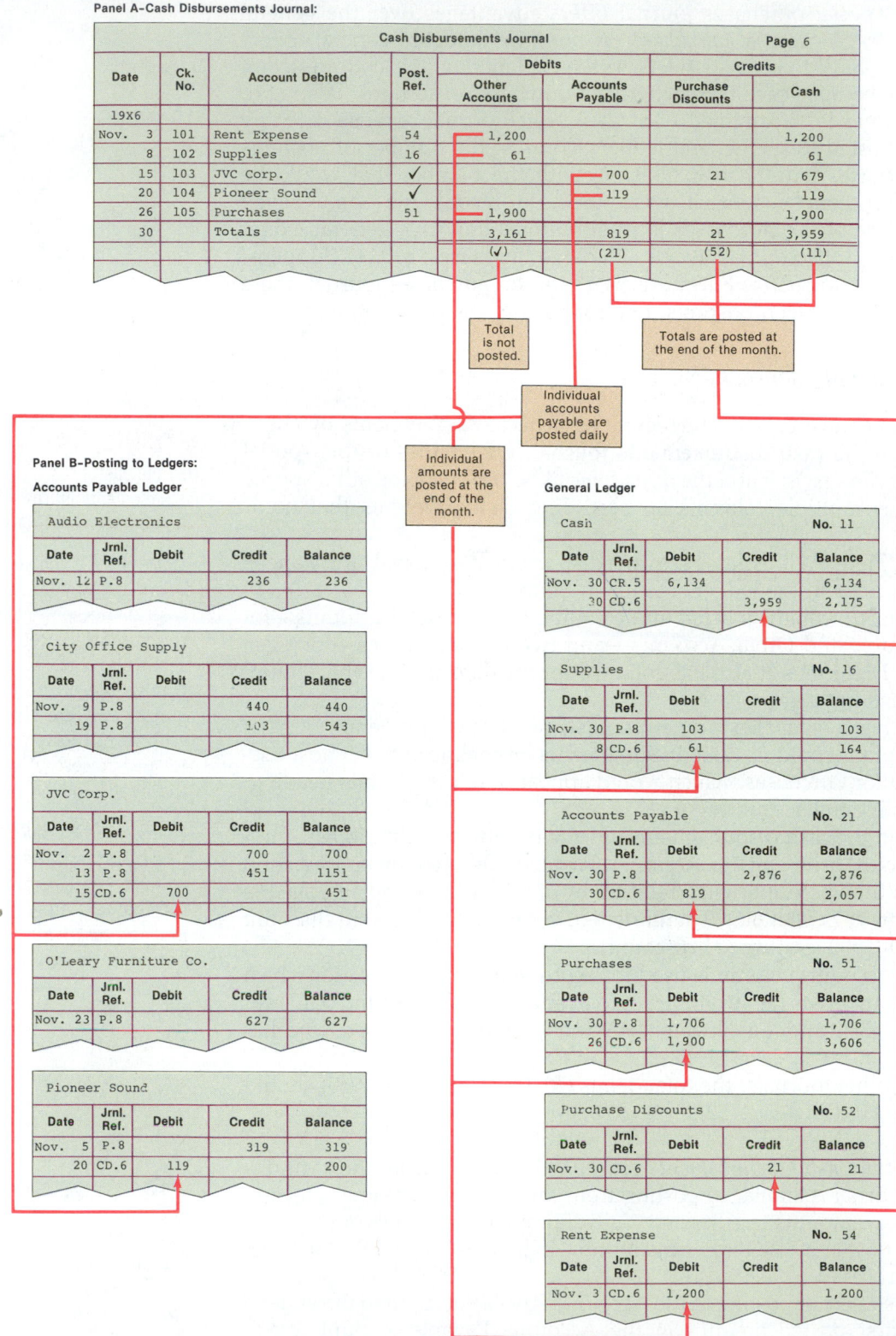

Panel A—Cash Disbursements Journal:

Panel B—Posting to Ledgers:

Accounts Payable Ledger

General Ledger

Amounts in the Other Accounts column are posted individually (for example, Rent Expense—debit $1,200). When each Other Accounts amount is posted to the general ledger, the account number is written in the Post. Ref. column of the journal.

As a proof of accuracy, companies total the individual creditor balances in the accounts payable subsidiary ledger for comparison with the Accounts Payable balance in the general ledger:

Creditor Accounts Payable

Creditor	Balance
Audio Electronics	$ 236
City Office Supply	543
JVC Corp	451
O'Leary Furniture	627
Pioneer Sound	200
Total accounts payable	$2,057

This total, computed at the end of the period, agrees with the Accounts Payable balance in Exhibit 6-7. Agreement of the two amounts indicates that journalizing and posting have been performed correctly and that the resulting account balances are correct.

Use of the cash disbursements journal streamlines journalizing and posting in the same way as for the other special journals.

The Credit Memorandum—
A Basic Business Document

Customers sometimes bring merchandise back to the seller, and sellers grant sales allowances to customers because of product defects and for other reasons. The effect of sales returns and sales allowances is the same—both decrease net sales in the same way a sales discount does. The document issued by the seller to indicate having credited the customer's Account Receivable is called a **credit memorandum,** or **credit memo,** because the company gives the customer credit for the returned merchandise. When a company issues a credit memo, it records the transaction by debiting Sales Returns and Allowances and crediting Accounts Receivable.

Suppose Austin Sound sold two stereo speakers for $198 on account to Stephanie Baker. Later she discovered a defect and returned the speakers. Austin Sound would issue to Ms. Baker a credit memo like the one in Exhibit 6-8.

To record the *sales return,* Austin Sound would make the following entry in the general journal:

General Journal   Page 9

Date	Accounts	Post Ref.	Debit	Credit
Nov. 6	Sales Returns and Allowances	43	198	
	Accounts Receivable—Stephanie Baker	12/✓		198
	Credit memo no. 27			

Discussion Question: In which journal would each of these transactions be recorded?

1. Owner withdraws cash *ANSWER:* cash disbursements journal
2. Sale of unused business auto to customer J. Brown *ANSWER:* cash receipts journal
3. Owner invests additional cash *ANSWER:* cash receipts journal
4. Owner invests his personal computer *ANSWER:* general journal
5. Purchase of supplies on credit *ANSWER:* purchases journal
6. Accrue salary payable *ANSWER:* general journal

OBJECTIVE 7
Journalize return and allowance transactions

EXHIBIT 6-8   *Credit Memorandum*

Typical Student Misconception: Students find credit memo and debit memo confusing terms. Have them remember this: If the seller is going to credit a customer's account (to reduce the balance owing) then she issues a credit memo. Likewise, if the buyer is going to debit a supplier's account (to reduce the balance due) then he issues a debit memo.

Credit Memorandum		No. 27
Austin Sound 305 West Martin Luther King Blvd. Austin, Texas 78701		**Date** November 6, 19X6

Customer Name   Stephanie Baker

538 Rio Grande, Apt. 236

Austin, Texas 78703

Reason for Credit   Defective merchandise returned

	Description	Amount
2	Trailblazer JU170456 Speakers	$198

Discussion Question: When do you suppose the general journal entry to record the credit memo in Exhibit 6-8 should be posted, daily or monthly? ANSWER: The credit to Accounts Receivable— Stephanie Baker must be posted on the date that appears on the credit memo. Otherwise, her subsidiary ledger balance will not reflect the actual amount she owes. Any journal entry that involves a subsidiary ledger must be posted daily.

The debit side of the entry is posted to Sales Returns and Allowances. Its account number (43) is written in the posting reference column when $198 is posted. The credit side of the entry requires two $198 postings, one to Accounts Receivable, the control account in the general ledger (account number 12), and the other to Stephanie Baker's account in the accounts receivable subsidiary ledger. These credit postings explain why the document is called a *credit memo*.

Observe that the posting references of the credit include two notations. The account number (12) denotes the posting to Accounts Receivable in the general ledger. The check mark (✓) denotes the posting to Ms. Baker's account in the subsidiary ledger. Why are two postings needed? Because this is the general journal. Without specially designed columns, it is necessary to write both posting references on the same line. Posting to the general ledger usually occurs monthly; and posting to the subsidiary ledger, daily.

Suppose Ms. Baker had paid cash. Austin Sound would either give her a credit memo or refund her cash. Austin Sound would record the cash refund in the *cash disbursements journal* as follows:

Cash Disbursements Journal   **Page 8**

				Debits		Credits	
Date	Ck. No.	Account Debited	Post Ref.	Other Accounts	Accounts Payable	Purchase Discounts	Cash
Nov. 6	106	Sales Returns and Allowances	43	198			198

A business with a high volume of sales returns, such as a department store chain, may find it efficient to use a special journal for sales returns and allowances.

The Debit Memorandum—
A Basic Business Document

Purchase Returns occur when a business returns goods to the seller. The procedures for handling purchase returns are similar to those dealing with sales returns. The purchaser gives the merchandise back to the seller and receives either a cash refund or replacement goods.

When a business returns merchandise to the seller, it may also send a business document known as a **debit memorandum,** or **debit memo.** This document states that the buyer no longer owes the seller for the amount of the returned purchase. The buyer debits the Account Payable to the seller and credits Purchase Returns and Allowances. If the volume of purchase returns is high enough, the business may use a special journal for purchase returns.

Many businesses record their purchase returns in the general journal. Austin Sound would record its return of defective speakers to JVC as follows:

	General Journal			Page 9
Date	**Accounts**	**Post Ref.**	**Debit**	**Credit**
Nov. 6	Accounts Payable—JVC Corp	21/✓	244	
	Purchase Returns and Allowances	53		244
	Debit memo no. 16			

Sales Tax

Most states and many cities levy tax on sales (sales tax). Sellers must add the tax to the sale amount, then pay the tax to the government. In most jurisdictions, sales tax is levied only on final consumers, so retail businesses usually do not pay sales tax on the goods they purchase for resale. For example, Austin Sound would not pay tax on a purchase of equipment from JVC, a wholesaler. However, when retailers like Austin Sound make sales, they must collect sales tax from the consumer. In effect, retailers serve as collecting agents for the taxing authorities. The amount of tax depends on the total sales.

Retailers set up procedures to collect the tax, account for it, and pay it on time. Invoices may be preprinted with a place for entering the sales tax amount, and the general ledger has an account entitled Sales Tax Payable. The sales journal may include a special column for sales tax, such as the one illustrated in Exhibit 6-9.

Note that the amount debited to Accounts Receivable ($3,484.95) is the sum of the credits to Sales Tax Payable ($165.95) and Sales Revenue ($3,319.00). This is so because the customers' payments—the Accounts Receivable figures—are partly for the purchase of merchandise (Sales Revenue) and partly for tax created by the sale. Individual customer accounts are posted daily to the accounts receivable subsidiary ledger, and each column total is posted at the end of the month. The check marks in the Posting Reference column show that individual amounts have been posted to the customer accounts. The absence of account numbers under the column totals means that the total amounts have not yet been posted.

Real-World Example: A customer's checking account on the books of a bank is considered a liability of the bank, and therefore has a credit balance. When a customer has an overdraft, the bank has to reduce the customer's account by debiting it for the service charge. The bank will send a debit memorandum to show that the customer's account has been reduced (debited).

Class Exercise: What is the entry to record the return of $100 of merchandise purchased on credit? Account numbers for various accounts are:

Inventory	105
Accounts Payable	201
Purchases	501
Purchase Returns and Allowances	502

	Post. Ref.	
Accounts Payable	201/✓	100
Purchase Returns and Allowances	502	100

Will two references in the posting reference column for Accounts Payable cause the trial balance to be out of balance? ANSWER: No. The check mark indicates that the $100 is posted to the subsidiary ledger.

Would we send a debit memo or credit memo? ANSWER: Debit memo, to inform the creditor that we have debited Accounts Payable on our books. Notice that anytime there is a general journal entry involving Accounts Receivable or Accounts Payable, three items will be posted—one to the subsidiary ledger and two to the general ledger.

EXHIBIT 6-9 *Sales Journal Designed to Account for Sales Tax*

		Sales Journal				Page 4
Date	Invoice No.	Account Debited	Post. Ref.	Accounts Receivable Dr.	Sales Tax Payable Cr.	Sales Revenue Cr.
19X6						
Nov. 2	422	Maria Galvez	✓	981.75	46.75	935.00
13	423	Brent Harmon	✓	728.70	34.70	694.00
18	424	Susan Levy	✓	952.35	45.35	907.00
27	425	Clay Schmidt	✓	822.15	39.15	783.00
30		Totals		3,484.95	165.95	3,319.00

Point to Stress: The tax that is collected by the seller does not belong to the seller but to the city or state government. The seller has an obligation to send that tax money to the government and, therefore, sales taxes are considered a liability. Because the tax comes out of the customer's pocket rather than the seller's, the seller does not incur an expense.

Class Exercise: Assume a 7½% sales tax rate and credit sales as follows:

  $100 to F. Smith
   250 to M. Blackmon
    75 to J. Adams
   320 to B. Taylor

Compute the following amounts:

1. Credit to Sales Revenue
ANSWER: $100 + $250 + $75 + $320 = $745
2. Total sales tax to be collected ANSWER: $745 × 7½% = $56
3. Total to be received ANSWER: $745 + $56 = $801
4. If a credit of $801 is recorded to Sales, how do we separate out sales revenue? ANSWER: $801 / 1.075 = $745. Therefore, Sales Tax Payable is $56 ($801 − $745).

Another way to account for sales tax is to enter a single amount—which is the sum of sales revenue and sales tax—in the Sales Revenue account. This amount is what the customer pays the retailer. At the end of the period, the business computes the tax collected and transfers that amount from Sales Revenue to Sales Tax Payable through a general journal entry. This procedure eliminates the need for a special multicolumn journal.

Suppose a retailer's Sales Revenue account shows a $10,500 balance at the end of the period. This retailer chooses to enter the full amount of each sale—the actual sales revenue and the sales tax—as Sales Revenue. How does the retailer divide the total amount into its two parts?

To compute the actual sales revenue, the Sales Revenue balance is divided by 1 plus the tax rate. Assume that sales tax is 5 percent. Thus the retailer divides $10,500 by 1.05 (1 + .05), which yields $10,000. Subtracting the actual sales revenue—the $10,000—from the $10,500 total yields $500, the sales tax. The retailer records sales tax with the following entry in the general journal:

	General Journal			Page 9
Date	Accounts	Post. Ref.	Debit	Credit
July 31	Sales Revenue	41	500	
	Sales Tax Payable	28		500
	To transfer sales tax to the liability account			

Balancing the Ledgers

At the end of the period, after all postings, equality should exist between:

1. Total debits and total credits of the account balances in the general ledger. These amounts are used to prepare the trial balance that has been used throughout Chapters 3 through 5.
2. The balance of the Accounts Receivable control account in the general ledger and the sum of individual customer accounts in the accounts receivable subsidiary ledger.

3. The balance of the Accounts Payable control account in the general ledger and the sum of individual creditor accounts in the accounts payable subsidiary ledger.

This process is called **balancing the ledgers,** or proving the ledgers. It is an important control procedure because it helps ensure the accuracy of the accounting records. Equality between Accounts Receivable control and the accounts receivable subsidiary ledger was proved as shown on page 280. A simpler and less costly procedure is to total the individual customer balances on a calculator tape for comparison with Accounts Receivable control. Balancing the accounts payable ledger follows the same pattern as illustrated on page 280.

Transparency T6-5

Documents as Journals _____

Many small businesses streamline their accounting systems to save money by using the actual business documents as the journals. For example, Austin Sound could let its sales invoices serve as its sales journal and keep all invoices for credit sales in a loose-leaf binder. At the end of the period, the accountant simply totals the sales on account and posts that amount to Accounts Receivable and Sales Revenue. Also, the accountant can post directly from invoices to customer accounts in the accounts receivable ledger. This "journal-less" system reduces accounting cost because the accountant does not have to write in journals the information already in the business documents.

Point to Stress: Special journals are used as labor saving devices. A business does not have to use any special journals.

Computers and Special Journals _____

The manual accounting system we discuss in this chapter should help you understand the importance of computers for companies with large numbers of customers and suppliers and a high volume of transactions. Imagine entering manually the few transactions shown in this chapter—multiplied by a thousand or even ten thousand!

Computerizing special journals requires no drastic change in the accounting system's design. Systems designers create a special screen for each accounting application—credit sales, cash collections, credit purchases, and cash payments. The special screen for credit sales would ask the person at the computer keyboard to type in the following information: date, customer number, customer name, invoice number, and the dollar amount of the sale. These data can generate debits and credits to the subsidiary accounts receivable, debits to Cash, and monthly customer statements that show account activity and ending balance. Also, additional computer files keep information on individual customers and vendors.

Ensuring that the general ledger Accounts Receivable balance or the Accounts Payable balance equals the sum of the balances in the subsidiary ledger is routine with a computerized system. Posting to subsidiary accounts is automatic. With daily sales amounts stored electronically, computerized posting to the general ledger may occur daily.

Summary Problem for Your Review

Identify the journal in which each of the following transactions would be recorded. Use journal abbreviations: sales journal = S; cash receipts journal = CR; purchases journal = P; cash disbursements journal = CD; general journal = J.

Cash sale_____
Sale on account_____
Loaned cash on note receivable_____
Received cash on account_____
Purchase of building on long-term note payable_
Paid cash on account_____
Cash purchase of inventory_____
Owner investment of cash in the business_____
Owner withdrawal of cash_____
Purchase of supplies on account_____

Receipt of cash on account_____
Adjusting entry for accrued salaries_____
Cash purchase of land_____
Credit purchase of inventory_____
Collection of interest revenue_____
Paid interest expense_____
Cash sale of equipment_____
Closing entries_____
Owner investment of land in the business_____

SOLUTION TO REVIEW PROBLEM

Cash sale	CR
Sale on account	S
Loaned cash on note receivable	CD
Received cash on account	CR
Purchase of building on long-term note payable	J
Paid cash on account	CD
Cash purchase of inventory	CD
Owner investment of cash in the business	CR
Owner withdrawal of cash	CD
Purchase of supplies on account	P

Receipt of cash on account	CR
Adjusting entry for accrued salaries	J
Cash purchase of land	CD
Credit purchase of inventory	P
Collection of interest revenue	CR
Paid interest expense	CD
Cash sale of equipment	CR
Closing entries	J
Owner investment of land in the business	J

Summary

An efficient accounting system combines *personnel, records,* and *procedures* to meet a business's information needs. Processing accounting information means collecting data from source documents, organizing and recording the data, and communicating the information through the financial statements. Each business designs its accounting system to satisfy its particular information needs.

To be effective, the system must provide management with the information needed to *control* the organization. Also, the system must be *compatible* with the business's operations. As businesses change, the system must be *flexible* enough to handle new needs. Finally, the system must be *cost-beneficial*.

Computer data processing systems include *hardware, software,* and *personnel*. Hardware may consist of a mainframe computer or microcomputers. Computer operators use software to process data *on-line* or in *batches*.

Many businesses use special journals to account for repetitive transactions such as credit sales, cash receipts, credit purchases, and cash disbursements.

Special journals reduce the amount of writing and posting required. Some businesses find it efficient to use source documents as journals.

Computer systems can be programmed to possess all the special journal features described in this chapter. The major goal of system design is efficient, routine handling of high volumes of transactions. Special journals were originally created to meet that objective. Similarly, computer systems can store records of sales, cash receipts, purchases, and cash disbursements and print special journals as desired.

Businesses use a subsidiary ledger to account for individual customer accounts receivable. The subsidiary ledger gives information on each customer's account. The total of the subsidiary ledger's individual account balances must match the balance in the Accounts Receivable control account in the general ledger. Companies may also keep a subsidiary ledger for accounts payable.

Self-Study Questions

Test your understanding of the chapter by marking the best answer for each of the following questions.

1. Why does a jewelry store need a different kind of accounting system than a physician uses? *(p. 269)*
   a. They have different kinds of employees.
   b. They have different kinds of journals and ledgers.
   ✓ c. They have different kinds of business transactions.
   d. They work different hours.

2. Which feature of an effective information system is most concerned with safeguarding assets? *(p. 270)*
   ✓ a. Control   c. Flexibility
   b. Compatibility   d. Acceptable cost/benefit relationship

3. Which of the following components of a computerized accounting system is more likely to be developed in-house rather than by outsiders? Why? *(pp. 272 through 274)*
   a. Hardware, because of the desire for control
   ✓ b. Hardware, because of the desire for compatibility
   c. Software, because of the desire for control
   d. Software, because of the desire for compatibility

4. Special journals help most by *(p. 274)*
   a. Limiting the number of transactions that have to be recorded
   b. Reducing the cost of operating the accounting system
   c. Improving accuracy in posting to subsidiary ledgers
   ✓ d. Easing the preparation of the financial statements

5. Galvan Company recorded 523 credit sale transactions in the sales journal. How many postings would be required if these transactions were recorded in the general journal? *(p. 278)*
   a. 523   ✓ c. 1,569
   b. 1,046   d. 2,092

6. Which two dollar-amount columns in the cash receipts journal will be used the most by a department store that makes half of its sales for cash and half on credit? *(p. 279)*
   a. Cash Debit and Sales Discounts Debit
   ✓ b. Cash Debit and Accounts Receivable Credit
   c. Cash Debit and Other Accounts Credit
   d. Accounts Receivable Debit and Sales Revenue Credit

7. Entries in the purchases journal are posted to the *(p. 284)*
   a. General ledger only
   ✓ b. General ledger and the accounts payable ledger
   c. General ledger and the accounts receivable ledger
   d. Accounts receivable ledger and the Accounts payable ledger

8. Every entry in the cash disbursements journal includes a *(p. 286)*
   a. Debit to Accounts Payable
   b. Debit to an Other Account
   c. Credit to Purchase Discounts
   ✓ d. Credit to Cash

9. Mazarotti Company has issued a debit memo. The related journal entry is *(p. 289)*

   ✓ a. Accounts Payable XXX
       Purchase Returns and Allowances   XXX

   b. Purchase Returns and Allowances XXX
       Accounts Payable   XXX

   c. Accounts Receivable........................... XXX
       Sales Returns and Allowances   XXX

   d. Sales Returns and Allowances XXX
       Accounts Receivable   XXX

10. Balancing the ledgers at the end of the period is most closely related to *(p. 291)*
    ✓ a. Control
    b. Compatibility
    c. Flexibility
    d. Acceptable cost/benefit relationship

Answers to the Self-Study Questions follow the Accounting Vocabulary.

Accounting Vocabulary

Accounting information system. The combination of personnel, records, and procedures that a business uses to meet its need for financial data *(p. 269)*.

Balancing the ledgers. Establishing the equality of (a) total debits and total credits in the general ledger or (b) the balance of a control account in the general ledger and the sum of individual accounts in the related subsidiary ledger *(p. 291)*.

Batch processing. Computerized accounting for similar transactions in a group or batch *(p. 273)*.

Cash disbursements journal. Special journal used to record cash disbursements by check *(p. 285)*.

Cash receipts journal. Special journal used to record cash receipts *(p. 278)*.

Control account. An account whose balance equals the sum of the balances in a group of related accounts in a subsidiary ledger *(p. 277)*.

Credit memorandum. Document issued by a seller to indicate having credited a customer's account receivable account *(p. 287)*.

Debit memorandum. Business document issued by a buyer to state that the buyer no longer owes the seller for the amount of returned purchases *(p. 289)*.

General journal. Journal used to record all transactions that do not fit one of the special journals *(p. 275)*.

General ledger. Ledger of accounts that are reported in the financial statements *(p. 277)*.

Hardware. Equipment that makes up a computer system *(p. 272)*.

Mainframe. Computer system characterized by a single computer *(p. 272)*.

Microcomputer. A computer small enough for each employee (work station) to have its own *(p. 272)*.

Minicomputer. Small computer that operates like a large system but on a smaller scale *(p. 272)*.

On-line processing. Computerized accounting for transaction data on a continuous basis, often from various locations, rather than in batches at a single location *(p. 273)*.

Purchases journal. Special journal used to record all purchases of inventory, supplies, and other assets on account *(p. 283)*.

Sales journal. Special journal used to record credit sales *(p. 275)*.

Software. Set of programs or instructions that cause the computer to perform the work desired (p. 273).

Subsidiary ledger. Book of accounts that provides supporting details on individual balances, the total of which appears in a general ledger account (p. 277).

Answers to Self-Study Questions

1. c
2. a
3. d
4. b

5. c [523 × 3 (one debit, one credit, and one to the accounts receivable ledger) = 1,569]
6. b

7. b
8. d
9. a
10. a

ASSIGNMENT MATERIAL

Questions

1. Briefly describe the two phases of implementing an accounting system.
2. Describe the basic information processing model of an accounting system.
3. What are the attributes of an effective information system? Briefly describe each attribute.
4. How does a mainframe computer system differ from a microcomputer system?
5. Identify three computer languages used with mainframes. Identify four software programs used with microcomputers.
6. Distinguish batch computer processing from on-line processing.
7. Describe an on-line computer processing operation for accounts receivable, sales, and inventory by a large retailer, such as Sears or Penney's.
8. Name four special journals used in accounting systems. For what type of transaction is each designed?
9. Describe the two advantages that special journals have over recording all transactions in the general journal.
10. What is a control account, and how is it related to a subsidiary ledger? Name two common control accounts.
11. Graff Company's sales journal has one amount column headed Accounts Receivable Dr. and Sales Revenue Cr. In this journal, 86 transactions are recorded. How many posting references appear in the journal? State what each posting reference represents.
12. Use S = Sales; CR = Cash Receipts; P = Purchases; CD = Cash Disbursements; and SRA = Sales Returns and Allowances to identify the special journal in which the following column headings appear. Some headings may appear in more than one journal.

    Sales Revenue Cr._____   Invoice No._____
    Accounts Payable Dr._____   Sales Discounts Dr._____
    Cash Dr._____   Other Accounts Cr._____
    Purchase Discounts Cr._____   Purchases Dr._____
    Accounts Receivable Cr._____   Cash Cr._____
    Check No._____   Credit Memo No._____
    Other Accounts Dr._____   Accounts Payable Cr._____
    Post. Ref._____   Accounts Receivable Dr._____

13. Identify two ways a check mark (✓) is used as a posting reference in the cash receipts journal.

14. The accountant for Bannister Company posted all amounts correctly from the cash receipts journal to the general ledger. However, she failed to post three credits to customer accounts in the accounts receivable subsidiary ledger. How would this error be detected?

15. In posting from the cash receipts journal of Enfield Homebuilders, the accountant failed to post the amount of the sales revenue credit column. Identify two ways this error can be detected.

16. At what two times is posting done from a special journal? What items are posted at each time?

17. For what purposes are a credit memo and a debit memo issued? Who issues each document, the seller or the purchaser?

18. The following entry appears in the general journal:

Nov. 25   Sales Returns and Allowances ....?   539
           Accounts Receivable—B.Goodwin....?   539

Prepare likely posting references.

19. Describe two ways to account for sales tax collected from customers.

20. What is the purpose of balancing the ledgers?

21. Posting from the journals of McKedrick Realty is complete. However, the total of the individual balances in the accounts payable subsidiary ledger does not equal the balance in the Accounts Payable control account in the general ledger. Does this necessarily indicate that the trial balance is out of balance? Give your reason.

22. Assume that posting is completed. The trial balance shows no errors, but the sum of the individual accounts payable does not equal the Accounts Payable control balance in the general ledger. What two errors could cause this problem?

23. Describe how some businesses use their documents as journals.

Exercises

Total cash, $4,101.60

Exercise 6-1   *Using the sales and cash receipts journals*   (L.O. 2, 4)

The sales and cash receipts journals of CompuGraphics Company include the following entries:

Sales Journal

Date	Account Debited	Post Ref.	Amount
Oct. 7	C. Carlson	✓	730
10	T. Muecke	✓	3,100
10	E. Lovell..	✓	190
12	B. Goebel	✓	5,470
31	Total		9,490

Cash Receipts Journal

	Debits		Credits				
					Other Accounts		
Date	Cash	Sales Discounts	Accounts Receivable	Sales Revenue	Account Title	Post Ref.	Amount
Oct. 16					C. Carlson	✓	
19					E. Lovell	✓	
24	100			100			
30					T. Muecke	✓	

CompuGraphics makes all sales on credit terms of 2/10 n/30. Complete the cash receipts journal for those transactions indicated. Also, total the journal and show that total debits equal total credits. Assume that each cash receipt was for the full amount of the receivable.

Exercise 6-2 *Classifying postings from the cash receipts journal* **(L.O. 3, 4)**   No check figure

The cash receipts journal of Schwarzkopf, Inc., follows.

Cash Receipts Journal   **Page 7**

| | Debits | | | Credits | | | | |
| | | | | | | Other Accounts | | |
Date	Cash	Sales Discounts	Accounts Receivable	Sales Revenue	Account Title	Post. Ref.	Amount
Dec. 2	794	16	810		Swingline Co.	(a)	
9	1,291		1,291		Kamm, Inc.	(b)	
14	3,904			3,904		(c)	
19	4,480				Note Receivable	(d)	4,000
					Interest Revenue	(e)	480
30	314	7	321		L. M. Roose	(f)	
31	4,235			4,235		(g)	
31	15,018	23	2,422	8,139	Totals		4,480
	(h)	(i)	(j)	(k)			(l)

Required

Identify each posting reference (a) through (l) as (1) a posting to the general ledger as a column total, (2) a posting to the general ledger as an individual amount, (3) a posting to a subsidiary ledger account, or (4) an amount not posted.

Exercise 6-3 *Identifying transactions from postings to the accounts receivable ledger*   No check figure
(L.O. 3)

An account in the accounts receivable ledger of Tyler Pipe Company follows.

John Babcock

| | | | | | Balance | |
Date		Jrnl. Ref.	Dr.	Cr.	Dr.	Cr.
May 1	....				703	
10	....	S.5	1,180		1,883	
15	....	J.8		191	1,692	
21	....	CR.9		703	989	

Required

Describe the three posted transactions.

Exercise 6-4 *Posting directly from sales invoices; balancing the ledgers* **(L.O. 3)**   Total of balances in A/R ledger, $8,457

Emery Printing Company uses its sales invoices as the sales journal and posts directly from them to the accounts receivable subsidiary ledger. During June the company made the following sales on account:

Date	Invoice No.	Customer Name	Amount
June 6	256	Emily Jacques	$ 716
9	257	Forrest Ashworth ...	798
13	258	Paul Scott	550
16	259	Jan Childres	3,678
22	260	Emily Jacques	1,915
30	261	Jan Childres	800
		Total	$8,457

Required

1. Open general ledger accounts for Accounts Receivable and Sales Revenue and post to those accounts. Use dates and use June Sales as the journal reference in the ledger accounts.

2. Open customer accounts in the accounts receivable subsidiary ledger and post to those accounts. Use dates and use invoice numbers as journal references.

3. Balance the ledgers.

Total Accounts Payable, $5,824

Exercise 6-5 *Recording purchase transactions in the general journal and in the purchases journal* **(L.O. 5)**

During April, Ippolito, Inc., completed the following credit purchase transactions:

April 4 Purchased inventory, $1,604, from Textan Co.
7 Purchased supplies, $107, from JJ Maine Corp.
19 Purchased equipment, $1,903, from Liston-Fry Co.
27 Purchased inventory, $2,210, from Milan, Inc.

Record these transactions first in the general journal—with explanations—and then in the purchases journal. Omit credit terms and posting references. Which procedure for recording transactions is quicker?

Total of balances in A/P ledger, $2,538

Exercise 6-6 *Posting from the purchases journal, balancing the ledgers* **(L.O. 3,5)**

The purchases journal of Odegaard Company follows.

Purchases Journal   Page 7

							Other Accounts Dr.		
Date	Account Credited	Terms	Post. Ref.	Account Payable Cr.	Purchases Dr.	Supplies Dr.	Acct. Title	Post. Ref.	Amt. Dr.
Sep. 2	Schaeffer Company	n/30		1,100	1,100				
5	Rolf Office Supply	n/30		175		175			
13	Schaeffer Company	2/10 n/30		347	347				
26	Marks Equipment Company	n/30		916			Equipment		916
30	Totals			2,538	1,447	175			916

Required

1. Open ledger accounts for Supplies, Equipment, Accounts Payable, and Purchases. Post to these accounts from the purchases journal. Use dates and posting references in the ledger accounts.

2. Open accounts in the accounts payable subsidiary ledger for Schaeffer Company, Rolf Office Supply, and Marks Equipment Company. Post from the purchases journal. Use dates and journal references in the ledger accounts.

3. Balance the Accounts Payable control account in the general ledger with the total of the balances in the accounts payable subsidiary ledger.

Exercise 6-7 *Using the cash disbursements journal* **(L.O. 6)**

Total cash, $15,716

During July Scott Products had the following transactions:

July 3 Paid $792 on account to Hellenic Corp. net of an $8 discount.
6 Purchased inventory for cash, $817.
11 Paid $375 for supplies.
15 Purchased inventory on credit from Monroe Corporation, $774.
16 Paid $8,062 on account to LaGrange Associates; there was no discount.
21 Purchased furniture for cash, $960.
26 Paid $3,910 on account to Graff Software. The discount was $90.
31 Made a semiannual interest payment of $800 on a long-term note payable. The entire payment was for interest.

Required

1. Draw a cash disbursements journal similar to the one illustrated in this chapter. Omit the check number (Ck. No.) and posting reference (Post. Ref.) columns.

2. Record the transactions in the journal. Which transaction should not be recorded in the cash disbursements journal. In what journal does it belong?

3. Total the amount columns of the journal. Determine that the total debits equal the total credits.

Exercise 6-8 *Using business documents to record transactions* **(L.O. 6)**

Cash paid/received, $627

The following documents describe two business transactions:

Invoice		
Date:	August 14, 19X0	
Sold to:	Zephyr Bicycle Shop	
Sold by:	Schwinn Company	
Terms:	2/10 n/30	

Items Purchased	Bicycles	
Quantity	Price	Total
4	$90	$360
2	70	140
5	60	300
Total		$800

Debit Memo		
Date:	August 20, 19X0	
Issued to:	Schwinn Company	
Issued by:	Zephyr Bicycle Shop	

Items Returned	Bicycles	
Quantity	Price	Total
1	$90	$ 90
1	$70	70
Total		$160
Reason:	Wrong sizes	

Use the general journal to record these transactions and Zephyr's cash payment on August 21. Record the transactions first on the books of Zephyr Bicycle Shop and, second, on the books of Schwinn Company, which makes and sells bicycles. Round to the nearest dollar. Explanations are not required. Set up your answer in the following format:

Date	Zephyr Journal Entries	Schwinn Journal Entries

No check figure

Exercise 6-9   *Journalizing return and allowance transactions*   (*L.O. 7*)

Medoff Company records returns and allowances in its general journal. During June the company had the following transactions:

June	4	Issued credit memo to Fidelity, Inc., for inventory that Fidelity returned to us	$1,043
	10	Received debit memo from B. R. Inman, who purchased merchandise from us on June 6. We shipped the wrong items, and Inman returned them to us.................	1,238
	14	Issued debit memo for merchandise we purchased from Wyle Supply Company that was damaged in shipment. We returned the damaged inventory to Wyle...........	4,600
	22	Received credit memo from Dietrich Distributing Co., from whom we purchased inventory on June 15. Dietrich discovered that they overcharged us	300

Required

Journalize the transactions in the general journal. Explanations are not required.

No check figure

Exercise 6-10   *Detecting errors in the special journals*   (*L.O. 2, 3, 4, 6*)

Financial MicroSystems uses special journals for credit sales, cash receipts, credit purchases, and cash disbursements, and the subsidiary ledgers illustrated in this chapter. During March the accountant made four errors. State the procedure that will detect each error described in the following:

(a) Posted a $260 debit to Raoul Gortari's account in the accounts receivable subsidiary ledger as a $260 credit.

(b) Added the Cash Credit column of the cash disbursements journal as $4,176 and posted this incorrect amount to the Cash account. The correct total was $4,026.

(c) Recorded receipt of $500 on account from Eichler, Inc., as a credit to Accounts Receivable in the cash receipts journal. Failed to record "Eichler, Inc."

(d) Failed to post the total of the Accounts Receivable Dr./Sales Revenue Cr. column of the sales journal.

Problems   (Group A)

No check figure

Problem 6-1A   *Features of an effective information system*   (*L.O. 1*)

Discuss the features of an effective information system. Write at least two sentences on each feature. Indicate which feature you believe is most important, and defend your position.

Total cash, $58,748

Problem 6-2A   *Using the sales, cash receipts, and general journals*   (*L.O. 2, 4, 7*)

The general ledger of Monterrey Telecommunications Company includes the following accounts:

Cash	111	Sales Revenue	411
Accounts Receivable	112	Sales Discounts	412
Notes Receivable	115	Sales Returns and Allowances	413
Equipment	141	Interest Revenue	417
Land	142	Gain on Sale of Land	418

All credit sales are on the company's standard terms of 2/10 n/30. Transactions in February that affected sales and cash receipts were as follows:

Feb. 1 Sold inventory on credit to G. M. Titcher, $900.
   5 As an accommodation to another company, sold new equipment for its cost of $770, receiving cash in this amount.
   6 Cash sales for the week totaled $2,107.
   8 Sold merchandise on account to McNair Co., $2,830.
   9 Sold land that cost $22,000 for cash of $40,000.
  11 Sold goods on account to Nickerson Builders, $6,099.
  11 Received cash from G. M. Titcher in full settlement of her account receivable from February 1.
  13 Cash sales for the week were $1,995.
  15 Sold inventory on credit to Montez and Montez, a partnership, $800.
  18 Issued credit memo to McNair Co. for $120 of merchandise returned to us by McNair. The goods we shipped were unsatisfactory.
  19 Sold merchandise on account to Nickerson Builders, $3,900.
  20 Cash sales for the week were $2,330.
  21 Received $1,200 cash from McNair Co. in partial settlement of its account receivable. There was no discount.
  22 Received cash from Montez and Montez for its account receivable from February 15.
  22 Sold goods on account to Diamond Co., $2,022.
  25 Collected $4,200 on a note receivable, of which $200 was interest.
  27 Cash sales for the week totaled $2,970.
  27 Sold inventory on account to Littleton Corporation, $2,290.
  28 Issued credit memo to Diamond Co. for $680 for damaged goods it returned to us.
  28 Received $1,510 cash on account from McNair Co. There was no discount.

Required

1. Use the appropriate journal to record the above transactions in a single-column sales journal (omit the Invoice No. column), a cash receipts journal, and a general journal. Monterrey records sales returns and allowances in the general journal.
2. Total each column of the cash receipts journal. Determine that the total debits equal the total credits.
3. Show how postings would be made from the journals by writing the account numbers and check marks in the appropriate places in the journals.

Problem 6-3A *Correcting errors in the cash receipts journal* *(L.O. 4)*

Total cash, $10,090

The cash receipts journal below contains five entries. All five entries are for legitimate cash receipt transactions, but the journal contains some errors in recording the transactions. In fact, only one entry is correct, and each of the other four entries contains one error.

| Date | Debits | | Credits | | | | |
| | Cash | Sales Discounts | Accounts Receivable | Sales Revenue | Other Accounts | | |
					Account Title	P.R.	Amount
7/5	611	34	645		Meg Davis	✓	
9			346	346	Carl Ryther	✓	
10	8000			8000	Land	19	
19	73						
31	1060			1133			
	9744	34	991	9479	Totals		
	(11)	(42)	(12)	(41)			(✓)

Total Dr. = $9,778   Total Cr. = $10,470

Required

1. Identify the correct entry.
2. Identify the error in each of the other four entries.
3. Using the following format, prepare a corrected cash receipts journal.

| Date | Debits | | Credits | | | | |
| | Cash | Sales Discounts | Accounts Receivable | Sales Revenue | Other Accounts | | |
					Account Title	P.R.	Amount
7/5					Meg Davis	✓	
9					Carl Ryther	✓	
10					Land	19	
19							
31							
	10090	34	991	1133	Totals		8000
	(11)	(42)	(12)	(41)			(✓)

Total Dr. = $10,124   Total Cr. = $10,124

Total cash, $14,963

Problem 6-4A   *Using the purchases, cash disbursements, and general journals* **(L.O. 5,6,7)**

The general ledger of Greensboro Custom Frames includes the following accounts:

Cash	111	Purchases	511
Prepaid Insurance	116	Purchase Discounts	512
Supplies	117	Purchase Returns and	
Equipment	149	Allowances	513
Accounts Payable	211	Rent Expense	562
		Utilities Expense	565

Transactions in March that affected purchases and cash disbursements were as follows:

Mar. 1 Paid monthly rent, debiting Rent Expense for $1,150.

3 Purchased inventory on credit from Broussard Co., $4,600. Terms were 2/15 n/45.

6 Purchased supplies on credit terms of 2/10 n/30 from Harmon Sales, $800.

7 Paid gas and water bills, $406.

10 Purchased equipment on account from Lancer Co., $1,050. Payment terms were 2/10 n/30.

11 Returned the equipment to Lancer Co. It was defective. We issued a debit memo for $1,050 and mailed a copy to Lancer.

12 Paid Broussard Co. the amount owed on the purchase of March 3.

12 Purchased inventory on account from Lancer Co., $1,100. Terms were 2/10 n/30.

14 Purchased inventory for cash, $1,585.

15 Paid an insurance premium, debiting Prepaid Insurance, $2,416.

16 Paid our account payable to Harmon Sales, less the discount, from March 6.

17 Paid electricity bill, $165.

20 Paid account payable to Lancer Co., less the discount, from March 12.

21 Purchased supplies on account from Master Supply, $754. Terms were net 30.

22 Purchased inventory on credit terms of 1/10 n/30 from Linz Brothers, $3,400.

26 Returned inventory purchased on March 22, to Linz Brothers, issuing a debit memo for $500.

31 Paid Linz Brothers the net amount owed from March 22, less the return on March 26.

Required

1. Use the appropriate journal to record the above transactions in a purchases journal, a cash disbursements journal (omit the Check No. column), and a general journal. Greensboro records purchase returns in the general journal.

2. Total each column of the special journals. Show that the total debits equal the total credits in each special journal.

3. Show how postings would be made from the journals by writing the account numbers and check marks in the appropriate places in the journals.

Ending cash, $29,365

Problem 6-5A *Using the sales, cash receipts, and general journals, posting, and balancing the ledgers. (L.O. 2,3,4,7)*

During June, Boatright Custom Floors engaged in the following transactions:

June 1 Issued invoice no. 113 for credit sale to Aspen Co., $4,750. All credit sales are on the company's standard terms of 2/10 n/30.

3 Collected cash of $882 from Leah Burnet in payment of her account receivable within the discount period.

6 Cash sales for the week totaled $1,748.

7 Collected note receivable, $3,500, plus 10 percent interest.

9 Issued invoice no. 114 for sale on account to Wilder Co., $4,300.

11 Received cash from Aspen Co. in full settlement of its account receivable from the sale on June 1.

13 Cash sales for the week were $2,964.

14 Sold inventory on account to Goss Corp., issuing invoice no. 115 for $858.

15 Issued credit memo to Goss Corp. for $154 of merchandise returned to us by Goss. Part of the goods we shipped were defective.

19 Received cash from Wilder Co. in full settlement of its account receivable from June 9.

20 Cash sales for the week were $2,175.

22 Received cash of $2,904 from Goss Corp. on account from June 1.

24 Sold supplies to an employee for cash of $106, which was Boatright's cost.

27 Cash sales for the week totaled $1,650.

28 Issued invoice no. 116 to Thompson Co. for credit sale of inventory, $5,194.

29 Sold goods on credit to Leah Burnet, issuing invoice no. 117 for $3,819.

29 Issued credit memo to Leah Burnet for $1,397 of inventory she returned to us because it was unsatisfactory.

The general ledger of Boatright Custom Floors includes the following accounts and balances at June 1:

Account Number	Account Title	Balance	Account Number	Account Title	Balance
111	Cash	$4,217	411	Sales Revenue	
112	Accounts Receivable	3,804	412	Sales Discounts	
116	Supplies	1,290	413	Sales Returns	
141	Notes Receivable . . .	7,100		and Allowances . .	
			418	Interest Revenue . . .	

Boatright's accounts receivable subsidiary ledger includes the following accounts and balances at June 1: Aspen Company, -0-; Leah Burnet, $900; Goss Corp., $2,904; Thompson Company, -0-; and Wilder Co., -0-.

Required

1. Open the general ledger and the accounts receivable subsidiary ledger accounts given, inserting their balances at June 1.

2. Record the above transactions on page 6 of a single-column sales journal, page 9 of a cash receipts journal, and page 5 of a general journal, as appropriate. Boatright records sales returns and allowances in the general journal.

3. Post daily to the accounts receivable subsidiary ledger. On June 30 post to the general ledger.

4. Total each column of the special journals. Show that the total debits equal the total credits in each special journal.

5. Balance the total of the customer account balances in the accounts receivable subsidiary ledger against the Accounts Receivable balance in the general ledger.

Problem 6-6A *Using the purchases, cash disbursements, and general journals; posting and balancing the ledgers* **(L.O. 3, 5, 6, 7)**

Ending cash, $1,558

De Gortari Company's September transactions affecting purchases and cash disbursements were as follows:

Sep. 1 Issued check no. 406 to pay AmeriCorp. in full on account. De Gortari received a 2 percent discount for prompt payment.

1 Issued check no. 407 to pay quarterly rent, debiting Prepaid Rent for $2,100.

2 Issued check no. 408 to pay net amount owed to Lynn Co. De Gortari took a 3 percent discount.

5 Purchased supplies on credit terms of 2/10 n/30 from Westside Supply, $121.

7 Paid delivery expense, issuing check no. 409 for $739.

10 Purchased inventory on account from Hayden, Inc., $2,008. Payment terms were net 30.

11 Returned the inventory to Hayden, Inc., because it was defective. We issued a debit memo and mailed a copy to Hayden.

15 Issued check no. 410 for a cash purchase of inventory, $2,332.

15 Paid semimonthly payroll with check no. 411 for $1,224.

19 Issued check no. 412 to pay our account payable to Westside Supply from September 5.

21 Purchased inventory on credit terms of 2/10 n/30 from Lynn Co., $4,150.

24 Purchased machinery on credit terms of 2/10 n/30 from AmeriCorp., $3,195.

26 Purchased supplies on account from Hayden, Inc., $467. Terms were net 30.

29 Issued check no. 413 to Lynn Co., paying the net amount owed from September 21.

30 Paid semimonthly payroll with check no. 414 for $1,224.

The general ledger of De Gortari Company includes the following accounts and balances at September 1:

Account Number	Account Title	Balance	Account Number	Account Title	Balance
111	Cash	$15,996	511	Purchases	
115	Prepaid Rent		512	Purchase Discounts	
116	Supplies...........	703	513	Purchase Returns	
151	Machinery.........	21,800		and Allowances ..	
211	Accounts Payable ..	2,700	521	Salary Expense.....	
			551	Delivery Expense ..	

De Gortari's accounts payable subsidiary ledger includes the following balances at September 1: AmeriCorp., $1,200; Hayden, Inc., -0-; Lynn Company, $1,500; and Westside Supply, -0-.

Required

1. Open the general ledger and the accounts payable subsidiary ledger accounts, inserting their balances at September 1.

2. Record the above transactions on page 10 of a purchases journal, page 5 of a cash disbursements journal, and page 8 of a general journal, as appropriate. De Gortari records purchase returns in the general journal.

3. Post daily to the accounts payable subsidiary ledger. On September 30 post to the general ledger.

4. Total each column of the special journals. Determine that the total debits equal the total credits in each special journal.

5. Balance the total of the creditor account balances in the accounts payable subsidiary ledger against the balance of the Accounts Payable control account in the general ledger.

Cash rec. journal—Cash, $12,720; cash disburse.: journal—Cash, $11,234

Problem 6-7A *Using all the journals, posting, and balancing the ledgers (L.0. 2, 3, 4, 5, 6, 7)*

Talbert Company completed the following transactions during July:

July 2 Issued invoice no. 913 for sale on account to N. J. Seiko, $4,100.

3 Purchased inventory on credit terms of 3/10 n/60 from Chicosky Co., $2,467.

5 Sold inventory for cash, $1,077.

5 Issued check no. 532 to purchase furniture for cash, $2,185.

8 Collected interest revenue of $1,775.

9 Issued invoice no. 914 for sale on account to Bell Co., $5,550.

10 Purchased inventory for cash, $1,143, issuing check no. 533.

12 Received cash from N. J. Seiko in full settlement of her account receivable, net of a 2 percent discount, from the sale on July 2.

13 Issued check no. 534 to pay Chicosky Co. the net amount owed from July 3.

13 Purchased supplies on account from Manley, Inc., $441. Terms were net end-of-month.

15 Sold inventory on account to M. O. Brown, issuing invoice no. 915 for $665.

17 Issued credit memo to M. O. Brown for $665 for defective merchandise returned to us by Brown.

18 Issued invoice no. 916 for credit sale to N. J. Seiko, $357.

19 Received $5,439 from Bell Co. in full settlement of its account receivable, $5,550, from July 9.

20 Purchased inventory on credit terms of net 30 from Sims Distributing, $2,047.

22 Purchased furniture on credit terms of 3/10 n/60 from Chicosky Co., $645.

22 Issued check no. 535 to pay for insurance coverage, debiting Prepaid Insurance for $1,000.

24 Sold supplies to an employee for cash of $54, which was Talbert's cost.

25 Issued check no. 536 to pay utilities, $453.

28 Purchased inventory on credit terms of 2/10 n/30 from Manley, Inc., $675.

29 Returned damaged inventory to Manley, Inc., issuing a debit memo for $675.

29 Sold goods on account to Bell Co., issuing invoice no. 917 for $496.

30 Issued check no. 537 to pay Manley, Inc., the amount owed from July 13.

31 Received $357 on account from N. J. Seiko on credit sale of January 18.

31 Issued check no. 538 to pay monthly salaries, $3,619.

Required

1. Open the following general ledger accounts using the account numbers given:

Cash	111	Sales Returns	
Accounts Receivable	112	and Allowances	413
Supplies	116	Interest Revenue	419
Prepaid Insurance	117	Purchases..................	511
Furniture	151	Purchase Discounts	512
Accounts Payable............	211	Purchase Returns	
Sales Revenue...............	411	and Allowances	513
Sales Discounts	412	Salary Expense	531
		Utilities Expense	541

2. Open these accounts in the subsidiary ledgers:
   Accounts receivable subsidiary ledger: Bell Co., M. O. Brown, and N. J. Seiko.
   Accounts payable subsidiary ledger: Chicosky Co., Manley, Inc., and Sims Distributing.
3. Enter the transactions in a sales journal (page 7), a cash receipts journal (page 5), a purchases journal (page 10), a cash disbursements journal (page 8), and a general journal (page 6), as appropriate.
4. Post daily to the accounts receivable subsidiary ledger and the accounts payable subsidiary ledger. On July 31 post to the general ledger.
5. Total each column of the special journals. Show that the total debits equal the total credits in each special journal.
6. Balance the total of the customer account balances in the accounts receivable subsidiary ledger against Accounts Receivable in the general ledger. Do the same for the accounts payable subsidiary ledger and Accounts Payable in the general ledger.

(Group B)

Problem 6-1B *Components of a computer information system* **(L.O. 1)**

No check figure

Discuss the interaction among the three components of a computer information system. Indicate which component is the most important in any information system—computer or manual—and defend your position.

Problem 6-2B *Using the sales, cash receipts, and general journals* **(L.O. 2,4,7)**

Total cash, $34,953

The general ledger of Fuselier, Inc., includes the following accounts, among others:

Cash	11	Sales Revenue..............	41
Accounts Receivable	12	Sales Discounts.............	42
Notes Receivable	15	Sales Returns and	
Supplies	16	Allowances	43
Land	18	Interest Revenue	47

All credit sales are on the company's standard terms of 2/10 n/30. Transactions in May that affected sales and cash receipts were as follows:

May 2 Sold inventory on credit to Dockery Co., $700.

May 4   As an accommodation to a competitor, sold supplies at cost, $85, receiving cash.

7   Cash sales for the week totaled $1,890.

9   Sold merchandise on account to A. L. Prince, $7,320.

10   Sold land that cost $10,000 for cash of $10,000.

11   Sold goods on account to Sloan Electric, $5,104.

12   Received cash from Dockery Co. in full settlement of its account receivable from May 2.

14   Cash sales for the week were $2,106.

15   Sold inventory on credit to the partnership of Wilkie & Blinn, $3,650.

18   Issued credit memo to A. L. Prince for $600 of merchandise returned to us by Prince. The goods shipped were unsatisfactory.

20   Sold merchandise on account to Sloan Electric, $629.

21   Cash sales for the week were $990.

22   Received $4,000 cash from A. L. Prince in partial settlement of his account receivable.

25   Received cash from Wilkie & Blinn for its account receivable from May 15.

25   Sold goods on account to Olsen Co., $720.

27   Collected $5,125 on a note receivable, of which $125 was interest.

28   Cash sales for the week totaled $3,774.

29   Sold inventory on account to R. O. Bankston, $242.

30   Issued credit memo to Olsen Co. for $40 for inventory the company returned to us because it was damaged in shipment.

31   Received $2,720 cash on account from A. L. Prince.

Required

1. Fuselier records sales returns and allowances in the general journal. Use the appropriate journal to record the above transactions in a single-column sales journal (omit the Invoice No. column), a cash receipts journal, and a general journal.
2. Total each column of the cash receipts journal. Show that the total debits equal the total credits.
3. Show how postings would be made from the journals by writing the account numbers and check marks in the appropriate places in the journals.

Total cash, $4,189

Problem 6-3B   *Correcting errors in the cash receipts journal*   *(L.O. 4)*

The cash receipts journal on page 309 contains five entries. All five entries are for legitimate cash receipt transactions, but the journal contains some errors in recording the transactions. In fact, only one entry is correct, and each of the other four entries contains one error.

Required

1. Identify the correct entry.
2. Identify the error in each of the other four entries.
3. Using the following format, prepare a corrected cash receipts journal.

	Debits			Credits			
					Other Accounts		
Date	Cash	Sales Discounts	Accounts Receivable	Sales Revenue	Account Title	P.R.	Amount
5/6		500		500			
7	429	22			Mike Harrison	✓	451
12	2160				Note Receivable	13	2000
					Interest Revenue	45	160
18				330			
24	1100		770				
	3689	522	770	830	Totals		2611
	(11)	(42)	(12)	(41)			(✓)

Total Dr. = $4,211   Total Cr. = $4,211

	Debits			Credits			
					Other Accounts		
Date	Cash	Sales Discounts	Accounts Receivable	Sales Revenue	Account Title	P.R.	Amount
5/6							
7					Mike Harrison	✓	
12					Note Receivable	13	
					Interest Revenue	45	
18							
24							
	4189	22	1221	830	Totals		2160
	(11)	(42)	(12)	(41)			(✓)

Total Dr. = $4,211   Total Cr. = $4,211

Problem 6-4B   *Using the purchases, cash disbursements, and general journals (L.O. 5, 6, 7)*

Total cash, $16,640

The general ledger of Schiffman, Inc., includes the following accounts:

Cash	11	Purchases	51
Prepaid Insurance	16	Purchase Discounts	52
Supplies	17	Purchase Returns and	
Furniture	19	Allowances	53
Accounts Payable	21	Rent Expense	56
		Utilities Expense	58

Transactions in August that affected purchases and cash disbursements were as follows:

Aug. 1   Purchased inventory on credit from Wood Co., $3,400. Terms were 2/10 n/30.

      1   Paid monthly rent, debiting Rent Expense for $2,000.

      5   Purchased supplies on credit terms of 2/10 n/30 from Ross Supply, $450.

8   Paid electricity bill, $588.

9   Purchased furniture on account from A-1 Office Supply, $4,100. Payment terms were net 30.

10   Returned the furniture to A-1 Office Supply. It was the wrong color. Issued a debit memo for $4,100, and mailed a copy to A-1 Office Supply.

11   Paid Wood Co. the amount owed on the purchase of August 1.

12   Purchased inventory on account from Wynne, Inc., $4,400. Terms were 3/10 n/30.

13   Purchased inventory for cash, $655.

14   Paid a semiannual insurance premium, debiting Prepaid Insurance, $1,200.

15   Paid our account payable to Ross Supply, from August 5.

18   Paid gas and water bills, $196.

21   Purchased inventory on credit terms of 1/10 n/45 from Software, Inc., $5,200.

21   Paid account payable to Wynne, Inc. from August 12.

22   Purchased supplies on account from Office Sales, Inc., $274. Terms were net 30.

25   Returned part of the inventory purchased on August 21 to Software, Inc., issuing a debit memo for $1,200.

31   Paid Software, Inc., the net amount owed from August 21, less the return, on August 25.

Required

1. Schiffman, Inc., records purchase returns in the general journal. Use the appropriate journal to record the above transactions in a purchases journal, a cash disbursements journal (omit the Check No. column), and a general journal.

2. Total each column of the special journals. Show that the total debits equal the total credits in each special journal.

3. Show how postings would be made from the journals by writing the account numbers and check marks in the appropriate places in the journals.

Ending cash, $32,874

Problem 6-5B   *Using the sales, cash receipts, and general journals, posting, and balancing the ledgers* **(L.O. 2, 3, 4, 7)**

During April, Baldwin Wallace Company had these transactions:

Apr. 2   Issued invoice no. 436 for credit sale to Vail Co., $5,200. All credit sales are made on the company's standard terms of 2/10 n/30.

3   Collected cash from H. M. Burger in payment of his account receivable within the discount period.

5   Cash sales for the week totaled $2,057.

7   Collected note receivable, $2,000, plus interest of $210.

10   Issued invoice no. 437 for sale on account to Van Allen Co., $1,850.

11   Sold supplies to an employee for cash of $54, which was the cost.

12   Received $5,096 cash from Vail Co. in full settlement of its account receivable from the sale of April 2.

12   Cash sales for the week were $1,698.

14   Sold inventory on account to Electro, Inc., issuing invoice no. 438 for $2,000.

16 Issued credit memo to Electro, Inc., for $610 of merchandise returned to us by Electro. Part of the shipped goods were damaged.

19 Cash sales for the week were $3,130.

20 Received $1,813 from Van Allen Co. in full settlement of its account receivable, $1,850, from April 10.

25 Received cash of $7,455 from Electro, Inc., on account.

26 Cash sales for the week totaled $2,744.

27 Issued invoice no. 439 to Clay Co. for credit sales of inventory, $3,640.

28 Sold goods on credit to H. M. Burger, issuing invoice no. 440 for $2,689.

30 Issued credit memo to H. M. Burger for $404 for inventory he returned to us because it was unsatisfactory.

The general ledger of Baldwin Wallace includes the following accounts and balances at April 1:

Account Number	Account Title	Balance	Account Number	Account Title	Balance
111	Cash.............	$ 3,579	411	Sales Revenue	
112	Accounts Receivable	10,555	412	Sales Discounts	
116	Supplies...........	1,756	413	Sales Returns and	
141	Notes Receivable ...	5,000		Allowances	
			418	Interest Revenue ...	

Baldwin Wallace's accounts receivable subsidiary ledger includes the following accounts and balances at April 1: H. M. Burger, $3,100; Clay Company, -0-; Electro, Inc., $7,455; Vail Company, -0-; and Van Allen Co., -0-.

Required

1. Open the general ledger and the accounts receivable subsidiary ledger accounts given, inserting their balances at April 1.
2. Record the transactions on page 4 of a single-column sales journal, page 13 of a cash receipts journal, and page 7 of a general journal, as appropriate. Baldwin Wallace records sales returns and allowances in the general journal.
3. Post daily to the accounts receivable subsidiary ledger, and on April 30 post to the general ledger.
4. Show that the total debits equal the total credits in each special journal.
5. Balance the total of the customer account balances in the accounts receivable subsidiary ledger against the Accounts Receivable balance in the general ledger.

Problem 6-6B *Using the purchases, cash disbursements, and general journals; posting and balancing the ledgers* **(L.O. 3, 5, 6, 7)**

Ending cash, $1,683

Noonan Company's November purchases and cash disbursement transactions are as follows:

Nov. 1 Issued check no. 346 to pay ENTEL Corp. in full on account. Noonan received a 2 percent discount for prompt payment.

1 Issued check no. 347 to pay quarterly rent, debiting Prepaid Rent for $2,400.

2 Issued check no. 348 to pay net amount owed to Arbor Machine Co. Noonan took a 2 percent discount.

5 Purchased supplies on credit terms of 1/10 n/30 from Chin Music Co., $264.

7 Paid delivery expense, issuing check no. 349 for $388.

10 Purchased inventory on account from W. A. Mozart, Inc., $1,681. Payment terms were net 30.

11 Returned the inventory to W. A. Mozart, Inc. It was defective. We issued a debit memo and mailed a copy to Mozart.

15 Issued check no. 350 for a cash purchase of inventory, $2,889.

15 Paid semimonthly payroll with check no. 351 for $1,595.

19 Issued check no. 352 to pay our account payable to Chin Music Co. from November 5.

21 Purchased inventory on credit terms of 2/10 n/30 from Arbor Machine Co., $3,250.

24 Purchased machinery on credit terms of 2/10 n/30 from ENTEL Corp., $1,558.

26 Purchased supplies on account from W. A. Mozart, Inc., $309. Terms were net 30.

29 Issued check no. 353 to Arbor Machine Co., paying the net amount owed from November 21.

30 Paid semimonthly payroll with check no. 354 for $1,595.

The general ledger of Noonan Company includes the following accounts and balances at November 1:

Account Number	Account Title	Balance	Account Number	Account Title	Balance
111	Cash	$17,674	511	Purchases	
115	Prepaid Rent	800	512	Purchase Discounts	
116	Supplies	884	513	Purchase Returns	
151	Machinery	33,600		and Allowances . .	
211	Accounts Payable . .	3,750	521	Salary Expense	
			551	Delivery Expense . .	

Noonan's accounts payable subsidiary ledger includes the following balances at November 1: Arbor Machine Co., $650; Chin Music Co., -0-; ENTEL Corp., $3,100; and W. A. Mozart, Inc., -0-.

Required

1. Open the general ledger and the accounts payable subsidiary ledger accounts given, inserting their balances at November 1.

2. Record the above transactions on page 3 of a purchases journal, page 8 of a cash disbursements journal, and page 12 of a general journal, as appropriate. Noonan records purchase returns in the general journal.

3. Post daily to the accounts payable subsidiary ledger. Post to the general ledger on November 30.

4. Total each column of the special journals. Show that the total debits equal the total credits in each special journal.

5. Balance the total of the creditor account balances in the accounts payable subsidiary ledger against the balance of the Accounts Payable control account in the general ledger.

Cash rec. journal—Cash, $11,587; cash disburse. journal—Cash, $9,328

Problem 6-7B *Using all the journals, posting, and balancing the ledgers (L.O. 2, 3, 4, 5, 6, 7)*

Van Tright Sales Company had these transactions during January:

Jan. 2 Issued invoice no. 191 for sale on account to L. E. Wooten, $2,350.

3 Purchased inventory on credit terms of 3/10 n/60 from Delwood Plaza, $1,900.

4 Sold inventory for cash, $808.

5 Issued check no. 473 to purchase furniture for cash, $1,087.

8 Collected interest revenue of $440.

9 Issued invoice no. 192 for sale on account to Cortez Co., $6,250.

10 Purchased inventory for cash, $776, issuing check no. 474.

12 Received cash from L. E. Wooten in full settlement of her account receivable, net of a 2 percent discount, from the sale of January 2.

13 Issued check no. 475 to pay Delwood Plaza net amount owed from January 3.

13 Purchased supplies on account from Havrilla Corp., $689. Terms were net end-of-month.

15 Sold inventory on account to J. R. Wakeland, issuing invoice no. 193 for $743.

17 Issued credit memo to J. R. Wakeland for $743 for defective merchandise returned to us by Wakeland.

18 Issued invoice no. 194 for credit sale to L. E. Wooten, $1,825.

19 Received cash from Cortez Co. in full settlement of its account receivable from January 9.

20 Purchased inventory on credit terms of net 30 from Jasper Sales, $2,150.

22 Purchased furniture on credit terms of 3/10 n/60 from Delwood Plaza, $775.

22 Issued check no. 476 to pay for insurance coverage, debiting Prepaid Insurance for $1,345.

24 Sold supplies to an employee for cash of $86, which was Van Tright's cost.

25 Issued check no. 477 to pay utilities, $388.

28 Purchased inventory on credit terms of 2/10 n/30 from Havrilla Corp., $421.

29 Returned damaged inventory to Havrilla Corp., issuing a debit memo for $421.

29 Sold goods on account to Cortez Co., issuing invoice no. 195 for $567.

30 Issued check no. 478 to pay Havrilla Corp. on account from January 13.

31 Received cash on account from L. E. Wooten on credit sale of January 18.

31 Issued check no. 479 to pay monthly salaries, $3,200.

Required

1. Open the following general ledger accounts using these account numbers

Cash	111	Sales Returns and Allowances	413
Accounts Receivable	112	Interest Revenue	419
Supplies	116	Purchases	511
Prepaid Insurance	117	Purchase Discounts	512
Furniture	151	Purchase Returns	
Accounts Payable	211	and Allowances	513
Sales Revenue	411	Salary Expense	531
Sales Discounts	412	Utilities Expense	541

2. Open these accounts in the subsidiary ledgers. Accounts receivable subsidiary ledger: Cortez Co., J. R. Wakeland, and L. E. Wooten. Accounts payable subsidiary ledger: Delwood Plaza, Havrilla Corp., and Jasper Sales.

3. Enter the transactions in a sales journal (page 8), a cash receipts journal (page 3), a purchases journal (page 6), a cash disbursements journal (page 9), and a general journal (page 4), as appropriate.

4. Post daily to the accounts receivable subsidiary ledger and to the accounts payable subsidiary ledger. On January 31 post to the general ledger.

5. Total each column of the special journals. Show that the total debits equal the total credits in each special journal.

6. Balance the total of the customer account balances in the accounts receivable subsidiary ledger against Accounts Receivable in the general ledger. Do the same for the accounts payable subsidiary ledger and Accounts Payable in the general ledger.

Extending Your Knowledge

Decision Problems

Total cash receipts on account, $5,578

1. Reconstructing Transactions from Amounts Posted to the Accounts Receivable Ledger (L.O. 2,3,4)

A fire destroyed some accounting records of Roemer Company. The owner, Charles Roemer, asks for your help in reconstructing the records. *He needs to know the beginning and ending balances of Accounts Receivable and the credit sales and cash receipts on account from customers during March.* All Roemer Company's sales are on credit, with payment terms of 2/10 n/30. All cash receipts on account reached Roemer within the 10-day discount period, except as noted. The only accounting record preserved from the fire is the accounts receivable subsidiary ledger, which follows.

Grant Adams

Date	Item	Jrnl. Ref.	Debit	Credit	Balance
Mar. 8		S.6	2,178		2,178
16		S.6	903		3,081
18		CR.8		2,178	903
19		J.5		221	682
27		CR.8		682	-0-

Lou Gross

Date	Item	Jrnl. Ref.	Debit	Credit	Balance
Mar. 1	Balance				1,096
5		CR.8		1,096	-0-
11		S.6	396		396
21		CR.8		396	-0-
24		S.6	1,944		1,944

Norris Associates

Date	Item	Jrnl. Ref.	Debit	Credit	Balance
Mar. 1	Balance				883
15		S.6	2,635		3,518
29		CR.8		883*	2,635

*Cash receipt did not occur within the discount period.

Suzuki, Inc.

Date	Item	Jrnl. Ref.	Debit	Credit	Balance
Mar. 1	Balance				440
3		CR.8		440	-0-
25		S.6	3,655		3,655
29		S.6	1,123		4,778

2. Understanding an Accounting System   (L.O. 1, 3, 6)

No check figure

The external auditor must ensure that the amounts shown on the balance sheet for Accounts Receivable represent actual amounts that customers owe the company. Each customer account in the accounts receivable subsidiary ledger must represent an actual credit sale to the person indicated, and the customer's balance must not have been collected. This auditing concept is called *validity* or *validating the accounts receivable*.

The auditor must also ensure that all amounts that the company owes are included in Accounts Payable and other liability accounts. For example, all credit purchases of inventory made by the company—and not yet paid— should be included in the balance of the Accounts Payable account. This auditing concept is called *completeness*.

Required:

Suggest how an auditor might test a customer's account receivable balance for validity. Indicate how the auditor might test the balance of the Accounts Payable account for completeness.

Ethical Issue

On a recent trip to the Soviet Union, Randolph Buchholz, sales manager of Microelectronic Devices, took his wife at company expense. Melanie Johnson, vice-president of sales and Mr. Buchholz's boss, thought his travel and entertainment expenses seemed excessive. However, Ms. Johnson approved the reimbursement because she owed Mr. Buchholz a favor. Ms. Johnson, well aware that the company president routinely reviewed all expenses recorded in the cash disbursements journal, had the accountant record Mrs. Buchholz's expenses in the general journal as follows:

Sales Promotion Expense	3,500	
Cash		3,500

Required

1. Does recording the transaction in the general journal rather than in the cash disbursements journal affect the amounts of cash and total expenses reported in the financial statements?
2. Why did Ms. Johnson want this transaction recorded in the general journal?
3. What is the ethical issue in this situation? What role does accounting play in the ethical issue?

Chapter 7

Internal Control
and Cash Transactions

The U.S. bowling boom peaked three decades ago. But for Bowl America's Eddie Goldberg and his son, Les, business has never been better.

Bowl America's roots go back to an energetic young man named Edward Goldberg. During the Depression, Goldberg ran a luncheonette in Baltimore. In 1940 he and three backers put up $30,000 to open a bowling alley in Clarendon, Va., a few miles outside Washington.

Having weathered the *cash* crunch of the early Sixties, Bowl America has since chosen to steer clear of leverage [debt]. The company has less than $100,000 in long-term debt, and over $12 million . . . in *cash* and securities. Expansion, says Goldberg, will be paid for out of *cash flow*. This conservative approach has served Bowl America's investors well. [Emphasis added]

Source: Fleming Meeks, "Bowling for Dollars," *Forbes*, March 19, 1990, pp. 112, 114.

Among all the receivables, payables, inventory, and plant assets, it is easy to lose sight of the basics of running a business. Cash is the most scarce asset, and having enough of it to weather hard times and expand is the secret of Bowl America's success and the success of most other companies. How does a business protect its cash and other assets? With a system of internal controls.

You learned in Chapter 6 that a well-designed accounting system helps managers control the business. Chapter 7 looks in more detail at internal control and accounting for cash. **Internal control** is the organizational plan and all the related measures adopted by an entity to

OBJECTIVE 1
Define internal control

1. Safeguard assets
2. Ensure accurate and reliable accounting records
3. Promote operational efficiency
4. Encourage adherence to company policies

Internal controls include *administrative controls* and *accounting controls.*

Administrative controls include the plan of organization, the methods, and the procedures that help managers achieve operational efficiency and adherence to company policies. Moreover, administrative controls help eliminate waste.

Teaching Tip: An example of an administrative control is the credit approval for a customer's charge.

Accounting controls include the methods and procedures that safeguard assets, authorize transactions, and ensure the accuracy of the financial records. Of these elements, safeguarding assets is the most important. This chapter focuses on internal accounting controls, with emphasis on cash transactions.

The need for laws requiring internal control has received increased attention over the past twenty years. During that time many illegal payments, embezzlements, and other criminal business practices came to light. Concerned citizens wanted to know why the companies' internal controls had failed to alert management that these illegalities had occurred. To answer these growing worries, the U.S. Congress passed the Foreign Corrupt Practices Act. This act requires companies under SEC jurisdiction to maintain an appropriate system of internal control whether or not they have foreign operations.[1] Thus its title is a bit misleading.

Real-World Example: Refer to the chapter-opening vignette. When Bowl America was a new company, Eddie Goldberg could personally make sure that the business assets were being protected. The business was small and easy to oversee. As a business grows and the owner is no longer able to oversee every aspect of operations, a system of internal control can help ensure that policies are being followed and assets are not being mishandled.

---

[1]The Foreign Corrupt Practices Act contains specific prohibitions against bribery and other corrupt practices in addition to requiring the maintenance of accounting records in reasonable detail and accuracy.

Real-World Example: One of the CPA's first steps in auditing a business is to evaluate the system of internal control. If a company has a good system of internal controls, then mistakes are minimized, and are usually found and corrected before the financial statements are prepared. If a system of internal controls is weak, then mistakes can be made and go undetected. The auditor determines how extensive the testing of accounting records should be based on the strength or weakness of the company's system of internal control.

Report of Management Responsibilities

The management of General Mills, Inc. includes corporate executives, operating managers, *controllers* and other personnel working full time on company business. These managers are responsible for the fairness and accuracy of our financial statements. . . . The statements have been prepared in accordance with generally accepted accounting principles. . . .

Management has established a system of *internal controls* that provides reasonable assurance that, in all material respects, assets are maintained and accounted for in accordance with management's authorization, and transactions are recorded accurately on our books. Our *internal controls* provide for appropriate separation of duties and responsibilities, and there are documented policies regarding utilization of company assets and proper financial reporting. These . . . policies demand high *ethical conduct* from all employees.

We maintain a strong *audit* program that independently evaluates the adequacy and effectiveness of *internal controls*. The independent *auditors*, internal *auditors*, and *controllers* have full and free access to the *Audit Committee* at any time.

KPMG Peat Marwick, independent certified public accountants, are retained to *audit* the consolidated financial statements. [Emphasis added]

H. B. Atwater, Jr.
Chairman of the Board and Chief Executive Officer

F. C. Blodgett
Vice Chairman of the Board,
Chief Financial and Administrative Officer

Source: General Mills, Inc., *1990 Annual Report*, p. 19.

Wise management has always kept a system of strong internal control, so before the law was enacted many businesses had already met the requirements for internal control policies. However, the Foreign Corrupt Practices Act has affected companies' approaches to internal control. Formerly, internal control was viewed as the accountant's responsibility. The act shifted responsibility for internal control to company managers. Furthermore, boards of directors, to comply with the act and with other SEC requirements, compile written evidence of management's evaluations and ongoing reviews of the internal control system.

Exhibit 7-1 presents excerpts from the General Mills Report of Management Responsibilities, included in its annual report. Note the frequent references to internal controls, audits, and ethical conduct. Observe that the chairman of the board of directors, who heads the entire organization, and the chief financial officer, who is one of the top three officers of the company, sign the statement. Likewise, management teams in other organizations state their responsibility for internal control in their annual reports.

OBJECTIVE 2
Identify the characteristics of an effective system of internal control

Effective Systems of Internal Control

Whether the business is General Mills or a local department store, its system of internal controls, if effective, has the following noteworthy characteristics.

Competent and Reliable Personnel

Employees should be *competent* and *reliable*. Paying top salaries to attract top-quality employees, training them to do their job well, and supervising their work all help to build a competent staff. A business adds flexibility to its staffing by rotating employees through various jobs. If one employee is sick or on vacation, a second employee is already trained to step in and do the job.

Rotating employees through various jobs also promotes reliability. An employee is less likely to handle her job improperly if she knows that her misconduct may come to light when a second employee takes over the job. This same reasoning leads businesses to require that employees take an annual vacation. A second employee, stepping in to handle the position, may uncover any wrongdoing.

Assignment of Responsibilities

In a business with an effective internal control system, no important duty is overlooked. A model of such assignment of responsibilities appears in the corporate organizational chart in Exhibit 7-2.

Notice that the corporation has a vice-president of finance and accounting. Two other officers, the treasurer and the controller, report to the vice-president. The treasurer is responsible for cash management. The controller performs accounting duties.

Within this organization, the controller may be responsible for approving invoices for payment, and the treasurer may actually sign the checks. Working under the controller, one accountant may be responsible for property taxes, another accountant for income taxes. In sum, all duties are clearly defined and assigned to individuals who bear responsibility for carrying them out.

Proper Authorization

An organization generally has a written set of rules that outlines approved procedures. Any deviation from standard policy requires *proper authorization*. For example, managers or assistant managers of retail stores must approve customer checks for amounts above the store's usual limit. Likewise, deans or department chairpersons of colleges and universities must give the authorization for a freshman, sophomore, or junior to enroll in courses otherwise restricted to seniors.

Separation of Duties

Smart management divides the responsibilities for transactions between two or more people or departments. Separation of duties limits the chances for fraud and also promotes the accuracy of the accounting records. This crucial and often neglected component of the internal control system may be subdivided into four parts.

1. *Separation of operations from accounting.* The entire accounting function should be completely separate from operating departments so that objective records may be kept. For example, product inspectors, not machine operators, should count units produced by a manufacturing process. Accountants, not sales persons, should keep inventory records. Observe the separation of accounting from production and marketing in Exhibit 7-2.

Real-World Example: According to a University of Pennsylvania Wharton School study of 443 industrial salespeople, highly supervised employees at bureaucratic firms were more likely to act ethically than employees at less supervised businesses.

Real-World Example: Many banks require employees in certain departments to take an annual two-week vacation, during which time another employee performs the vacationing employee's duties. An employee who is engaged in fraudulent activity may refuse to take a vacation for fear of discovery.

Teaching Tip: In management, this is called having the authority commensurate with the responsibility. The person who is held responsible for a task also has the authority to make the decisions concerning that task.

Real-World Example: In most banks and retail businesses, such as Home Depot or A&P, it is common practice to assign each cashier his own money tray and hold him responsible if that fund is short at the end of his shift. This is an internal control device that clearly assigns responsibility to each employee. Any shortages or discrepancies may easily be traced to the person responsible.

EXHIBIT 7-2 *Organization Chart of a Corporation*

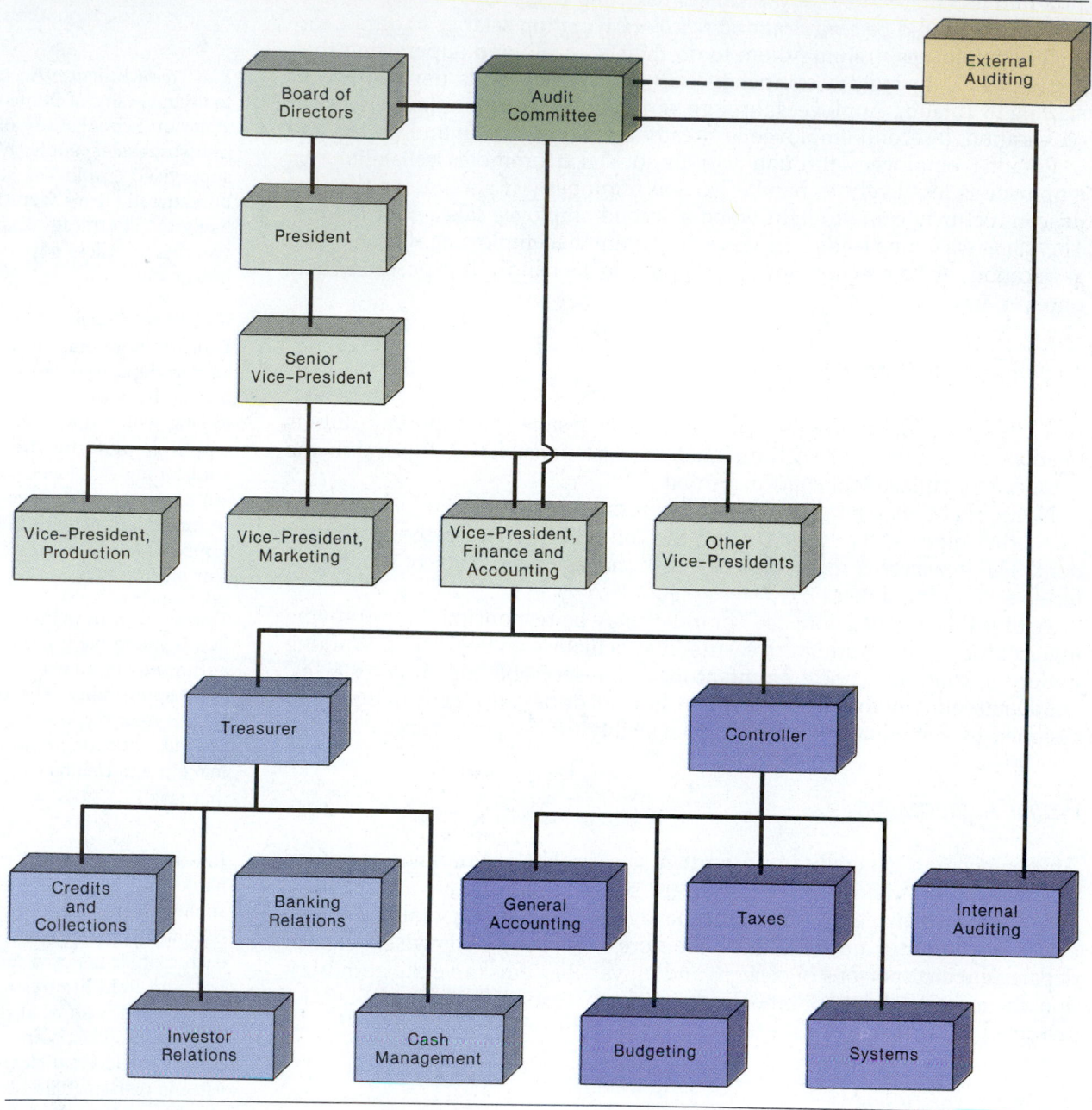

Discussion Question: Assume that a sales clerk is also responsible for granting credit approval and recording the sale. What are some of the problems that could result? *ANSWER:* The clerk could (1) grant credit approval to friends who do not meet the credit standards; or (2) steal merchandise and hide the theft in the accounting records; or (3)

2. *Separation of the custody of assets from accounting.* To reduce temptation and fraud, the accountant should not handle cash, and the cashier should not have access to the accounting records. If one employee had both cash-handling and accounting duties, this person could steal cash and conceal the theft by making a bogus entry on the books. We see this component of internal control in the organization chart in Exhibit 7-2. Note that the treasurer has custody of the cash and the controller accounts for the cash. Neither person has both responsibilities.

Warehouse employees with no accounting duties should handle inventory. If they were allowed to account for the inventory, they could steal it and write it off as obsolete. In a computerized accounting system, a person with custody of assets should not have access to the computer programs. Similarly, the programmer should not have access to tempting assets like cash.

3. *Separation of the authorization of transactions from the custody of related assets.* If possible, persons who authorize transactions should not handle the related asset. For example, the same individual should not authorize the payment of a supplier's invoice and also sign the check to pay the bill. With both duties, the person can authorize payments to himself and then sign the checks. By separating these duties, only legitimate bills are paid.

For another example, an individual who handles cash receipts should not have the authority to write off accounts receivable. (Businesses that sell on credit declare certain of their accounts receivable as uncollectible, realizing that these receivables will never be collected. Chapter 8 looks at uncollectible accounts receivable in detail.) Suppose the company shown in Exhibit 7-2 employs V. Saucier. He works in Credits and Collections (under the treasurer) and handles cash receipts from customers.

Among the business's accounts receivable in the subsidiary ledger is Gina Kowalski's $500 balance. Saucier could label Kowalski's account as uncollectible, and the business might cease trying to collect from her. When Kowalski mails a $500 check to pay off her balance, Saucier forges the endorsement and pockets the money. Kowalski, of course, has no reason to notify anyone else at the business that she has mailed a check, so Saucier's crime goes undetected. This theft would have been avoided by denying Saucier either the access to cash receipts or the authority to declare accounts uncollectible.

4. *Separation of duties within the accounting function.* Independent performance of various phases of accounting helps to minimize errors and the opportunities for fraud. For example, different accountants in a manual system keep the cash receipts journal and the cash disbursements journal. In a computer system, the employees who enter data into the computer do not also operate the machines.

fail to do all three jobs well and make mistakes; or (4) forget to do one of the tasks when the sales floor is busy.

Point to Stress: Even a small business should have internal controls and some degree of separation of responsibilities. For example, if the bookkeeper writes all checks and keeps the general ledger records, the owner should sign the checks and reconcile the monthly bank statement.

Internal and External Audits

It is not economically feasible for auditors to examine all the transactions during a period, so they must rely to some degree on the accounting system to produce accurate accounting records. To gauge the reliability of the company's accounting system, auditors evaluate its system of internal controls. Auditors also spot the weaknesses in the system and recommend corrections. Auditors offer *objectivity* in their reports, while managers immersed in operations may overlook weaknesses.

Audits are internal or external. Exhibit 7-2 shows *internal auditors* as employees of the business reporting directly to the audit committee. Some organizations have the internal auditors report directly to the vice-president. Throughout the year, they audit various segments of the organization. *External auditors* are entirely independent of the business. These people, employed by an accounting firm, are hired by an entity as outsiders to audit the entity as a whole. Both groups of auditors are independent of the operations they examine, and their reviews of internal controls often are similar.

An auditor may find that an employee has both cash-handling and cash-accounting duties or may learn that a cash shortage has resulted from lax efforts to collect accounts receivable. In such cases, the auditor suggests improvements. Auditors' recommendations assist the business in running smoothly and economically.

Point to Stress: External auditors are concerned primarily with the presentation of the financial statements and the factors affecting them, while internal auditors also want to ensure that the employees adhere to all administrative and accounting controls.

Real-World Example: When a CPA firm or a bank examiner audits a bank, often the first day of the audit work is on a surprise entry basis so that employees will not have the opportunity to cover up any weaknesses in the system or any fraud being perpetrated. This is true only for audits of financial institutions.

Documents and Records

Real-World Example: In a retail business, if a clerk makes a mistake on the sales ticket, the ticket is not destroyed, but is marked VOID. Since most companies use prenumbered sales receipts, a missing receipt would be noted.

Business *documents and records* vary considerably, from source documents like sales invoices and purchase orders to special journals and subsidiary ledgers. Specially designed records—for example, the special journals discussed in the last chapter—speed the flow of paper work and enhance efficiency.

Documents should be prenumbered. A gap in the numbered sequence calls attention to a missing document.

Prenumbering cash sale receipts discourages theft by the cashier because the copy retained by the cashier, which lists the amount of the sale, can be checked against the actual amount of cash received. If the receipts are not prenumbered, the cashier can destroy the copy and pocket the cash sale amount. However, if the receipts are prenumbered, the missing copy can easily be identified.

In the bowling-alley example of the chapter-opening vignette, a key document is the score sheet. The manager can check on cashiers by comparing the number of games scored to the amount of cash received. By multiplying the number of games by the price of a game and comparing the result to each day's cash receipts, the manager can see whether all the bowling revenue is being collected by the business. If cash on hand is low, this may indicate that the cashier is stealing.

Real-World Example: Some companies are losing so much money from theft by employees that they are trying a variety of deterrents. Some retail stores give rewards to those employees who uncover another employee's theft.

Real-World Example: It is not unheard of for employees of a firm to engage in collusion to defraud other firms. One of the most notorious fraud cases dealing with collusion is the Equity Funding Case (*United States v. Wiener*, 1973.) Equity Funding of America, a mutual fund and insurance company, experienced tremendous growth during the 1960s. When earnings began to falter, top management created bogus insurance policies to be sold to reinsurance companies, and a fictitious bank to perpetuate the fraud. The reinsurance companies advanced cash for the bogus companies, and of course lost most of it. The fraud was so well known in the company that employees joked about it. Eventually a disgruntled employee blew the whistle and the Equity Funding scandal was revealed as one of the largest and most brazen ever on Wall Street. As a result, the AICPA issued auditing standards for detecting fraud.

Limitations of Internal Control

Most internal control measures can be overcome. Systems designed to thwart an *individual* employee's fraud can be beaten by two or more employees working as a team—colluding—to defraud the firm. Consider a movie theater. The ticket seller takes in the cash, and the ticket taker tears the tickets in half so they cannot be reused, retaining the torn ticket stub. But suppose they put a scheme together in which the ticket seller pockets the cash from ten customers and the ticket taker admits the customers without tickets. Who would catch them? The manager could take the additional control measure of counting the people in the theater and matching that figure against the number of ticket stubs retained. But that takes time away from other duties. As you see, the stricter the internal control system, the more expensive it becomes.

A system of internal control that is too complex may strangle people in red tape. Efficiency and control are hurt rather than helped. The more complicated the system, the more time and money it takes to maintain. Just how tight should an internal control system be? Managers must make sensible judgments. Investments in internal control must be judged in the light of the costs and benefits.

The Bank Account as a Control Device

Keeping cash in a *bank account* is part of internal control because banks have established practices for safeguarding cash. Banks also provide depositors with detailed records of cash transactions. To take full advantage of these control features, the business should deposit all cash receipts in the bank account and make all cash payments through it (except petty cash disbursements, which we look at later). We now discuss banking records and documents.

For many businesses, cash is the most important asset. After all, cash is the most common means of exchange, and most transactions ultimately affect cash.

Cash is the most tempting asset for theft. Consequently, internal controls for cash are more elaborate than for most other assets. The rest of this chapter describes internal control over cash. We consider cash to be not just paper money and coins but also checks, money orders, and money kept in bank accounts. Cash includes neither stamps, because they are supplies, nor IOUs payable to the business, because they are receivables.

The documents used to control a bank account include the signature card, the deposit ticket, the check, the bank statement, and the bank reconciliation.

Signature Card. Banks require each person authorized to transact business through an account in that bank to sign a *signature card*. The bank compares the signatures on documents against the signature card to protect the bank and the depositor against forgery.

Deposit Ticket. Banks supply standard forms as *deposit tickets*. The customer fills in the dollar amount and the date of deposit. The customer retains either (1) a duplicate copy of the deposit ticket or (2) a deposit receipt, depending on the bank's practice, as proof of the transaction.

Check. To draw money from an account, the depositor writes a **check**, which is the document that instructs the bank to pay the designated person or business the specified amount of money. There are three parties to a check: the *maker*, who signs the check; the *payee*, to whose order the check is drawn; and the *bank* on which the check is drawn.

Most checks are serially numbered and preprinted with the name and address of the depositor and the bank. The checks have places for the date, the name of the payee, the signature of the maker, and the amount. The bank name and bank identification number and the depositor account number are usually imprinted in magnetic ink for machine processing.

Exhibit 7-3 shows a check drawn on the bank account of Business Research, Inc. The check has two parts, the check itself and the remittance advice. The *remittance advice*, an optional attachment, tells the payee the reason for the payment. The maker (Business Research) retains a carbon copy of the check for its recording in the check register (cash disbursements journal). Note that internal controls at Business Research require two signatures on checks.

Bank Statement. Most banks send monthly **bank statements** to their depositors. The statement shows the account's beginning and ending balance for the period and lists the month's transactions. Included with the statement are the maker's *canceled checks,* those checks that have been paid by the bank on behalf of the depositor. The bank statement also lists any other deposits and changes in the account. Deposits appear in chronological order, checks in a logical order, along with the date each check cleared the bank.

Exhibit 7-4 on page 325 is the bank statement of Business Research, Inc., for the month ended January 31, 19X6. At many banks, some depositors receive their statements on the first of the month, some on the second, and so on. This spacing eliminates the clerical burden of supplying all the statements at one time. Most businesses—like Business Research—receive their bank statement for the calendar month.

Bank Reconciliation. There are two records of the business's cash: its Cash account in its own general ledger and the bank statement, which tells the

Teaching Tip: A small business might not use checks with a carbon copy. Instead, it will include all the information about the check on the check stub and then use the stub as a source document for making entries to the cash disbursements journal.

Discussion Question: When do you receive your monthly bank statement? (Probably not on the last day of the month.) Why is it more important for a business than for an individual to receive a month-end statement? ANSWER: The business must reconcile or balance its statement with the cash balance in the general ledger at the end of the accounting period. An individual needs merely to compare his bank statement against his check register.

EXHIBIT 7-3 *Check with Remittance Advice*

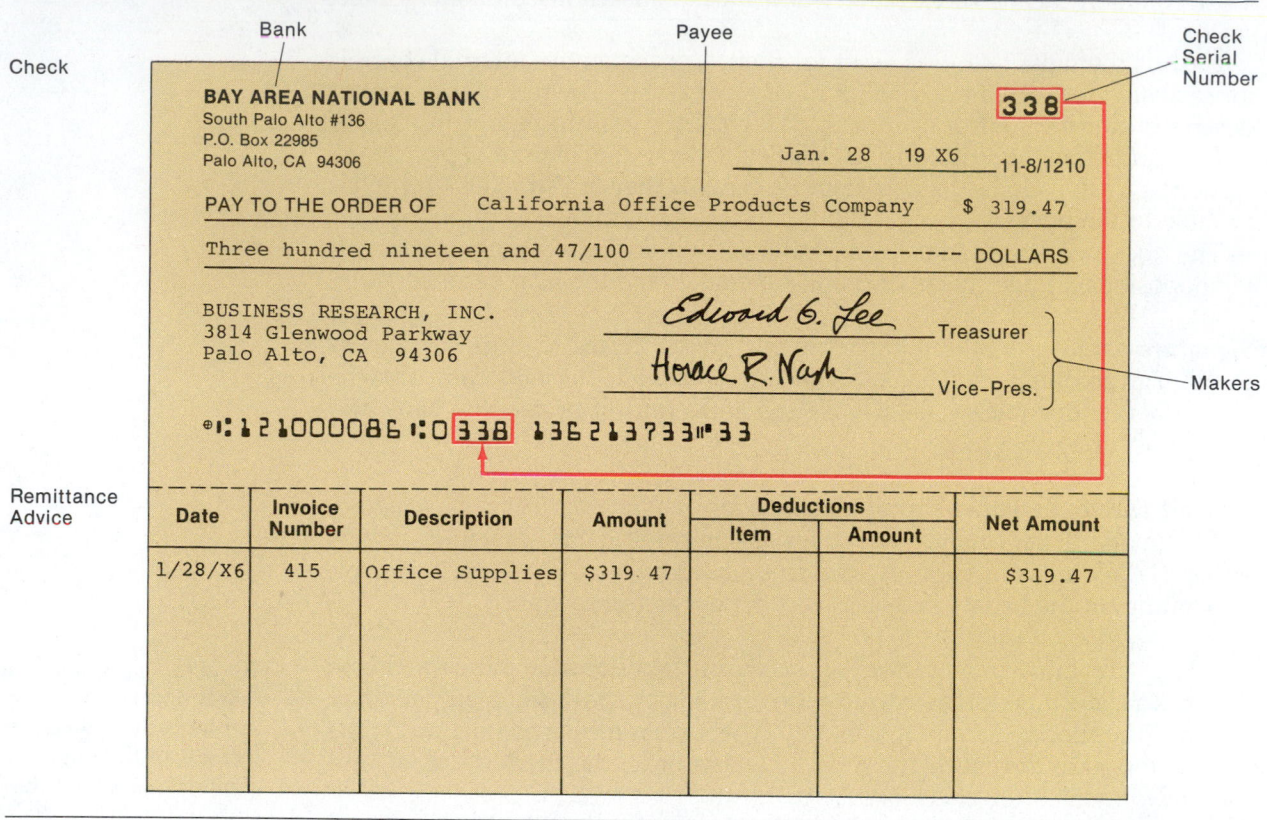

Check / Bank / Payee / Check Serial Number / Makers

BAY AREA NATIONAL BANK
South Palo Alto #136
P.O. Box 22985
Palo Alto, CA 94306

338

Jan. 28   19 X6   11-8/1210

PAY TO THE ORDER OF   California Office Products Company $ 319.47

Three hundred nineteen and 47/100 ------------------------ DOLLARS

BUSINESS RESEARCH, INC.
3814 Glenwood Parkway
Palo Alto, CA 94306

Edward G. Lee ___ Treasurer
Horace R. Nash ___ Vice-Pres.

⑆1210000086⑈0338 136213733⑈33

Remittance Advice

Date	Invoice Number	Description	Amount	Deductions		Net Amount
				Item	Amount	
1/28/X6	415	Office Supplies	$319.47			$319.47

Point to Stress: A business must keep a separate cash account in the general ledger for each of its bank accounts. If a business had three bank accounts, and posted all the cash receipts and disbursements to one general ledger account, it would be impossible to reconcile the three bank statements. Therefore, a general ledger cash account is set up for each bank account.

actual amount of cash the business has in the bank. The balance in the business's Cash account rarely equals the balance shown on the bank statement.

The books and the bank statement may show different amounts but both are correct. The difference arises because of a time lag in recording certain transactions. When a firm writes a check, it immediately credits its Cash account. The bank, however, will not subtract the amount of the check until the check reaches it for payment. This may take days, even weeks if the payee waits to cash the check. Likewise, the business debits Cash for all cash receipts, and it may take a day or so for the bank to add this amount to the business's bank balance.

Good internal control means knowing where a company's money comes from, how it is spent, and the current cash balance. How else can the accountant keep the accurate records management needs to make informed decisions? The accountant must report the correct cash amount on the balance sheet. To ensure accuracy the accountant explains the reasons for the difference between the firm's records and the bank statement figures on a certain date. This process is called the **bank reconciliation.** Properly done, the bank reconciliation ensures that all cash transactions have been accounted for and that the bank and book records of cash are correct.

Common items that cause differences between the bank balance and the book balance are

1. Items recorded by the company but not yet recorded by the *bank:*
    a. **Deposits in transit** (outstanding deposits). The company has recorded these deposits but the bank has not.

EXHIBIT 7-4 *Bank Statement*

BAY AREA NATIONAL BANK   **ACCOUNT STATEMENT**
South Palo Alto #136
P.O. Box 22985
Palo Alto, CA   94306

```
Business Research, Inc.                      CHECKING ACCOUNT 136-213733
3814 Glenwood Parkway
Palo Alto, CA    94306
```

CHECKING ACCOUNT SUMMARY AS OF 01-31-X6

BEGINNING BALANCE	TOTAL DEPOSITS	TOTAL WITHDRAWALS	SERVICE CHARGES	ENDING BALANCE
6556.12	3448.61	4602.00	14.25	5388.48

──────── CHECKING ACCOUNT TRANSACTIONS ────────

DEPOSITS

DEPOSIT	01-04	1000.00
DEPOSIT	01-04	112.00
DEPOSIT	01-08	194.60
BANK COLLECTION	01-26	2114.00
INTEREST	01-31	28.01

CHARGES

SERVICE CHARGE	01-31	14.25

CHECKS:

CHECKS			CHECKS			BALANCES	
NUMBER	DATE	AMOUNT	NUMBER	DATE	AMOUNT	DATE	BALANCE
332	01-12	3000.00	334	01-10	100.00	12-31	6556.12
656	01-06	100.00	335	01-06	100.00	01-04	7616.12
333	01-12	150.00	336	01-31	1100.00	01-06	7416.12
						01-08	7610.72
						01-12	4360.72
						01-26	6474.12
						01-31	5388.48

OTHER CHARGES		DATE	AMOUNT
NSF		01-04	52.00

MONTHLY SUMMARY

7 WITHDRAWALS	4360 MINIMUM BALANCE	5812 AVERAGE BALANCE

b. **Outstanding checks.** These checks have been issued by the company and recorded on its books but have not yet been paid by its bank.

2. Items recorded by the bank but not yet recorded by the *company:*

a. **Bank collections.** The bank sometimes collects money on behalf of depositors. Many businesses have their customers pay directly to the company bank account. This practice, called a lock-box system, reduces the possibility of theft and also places the business's cash in circulation faster than if the cash had to be collected and deposited by company personnel. An example is a bank's collecting cash on a note receivable and the related interest revenue for the depositor. The bank may notify the depositor of these bank collections on the bank statement.

b. **Service charge.** This amount is the bank's fee for processing the depositor's transactions. Banks commonly base the service charge on the balance in the account. The depositor learns the amount of the service charge from the bank statement.

c. *Interest revenue on checking account.* Many banks pay interest to depositors who keep a large enough balance of cash in the account. This is generally the case with business checking accounts. The bank notifies the depositor of this interest on the bank statement.

d. **NSF (nonsufficient funds) checks** received from customers. To understand how to handle NSF checks, also called hot checks, you first need to know the route a check takes. The maker writes the check, credits Cash to record the payment on the books, and gives the check to the payee. On receiving the check, the payee debits Cash on his or her books and deposits the check in the bank. The payee's bank immediately adds the receipt amount to the payee's bank balance on the assumption that the check is good. The check is returned to the maker's bank, which then deducts the check amount from the maker's bank balance. If the maker's bank balance is insufficient to pay the check, the maker's bank refuses to pay the check, reverses this deduction, and sends an NSF notice back to the payee's bank. The payee bank subtracts the receipt amount from the payee's bank balance and notifies the payee of this action. This process may take from three to seven days. The company may learn of NSF checks through the bank statement, which lists the NSF check as a charge (subtraction), as shown near the bottom of Exhibit 7-4.

e. *Checks collected, deposited, and returned to payee by the bank for reasons other than NSF.* Banks return checks to the payee if (1) the maker's account has closed, (2) the date is stale (some checks state "void after 30 days"), (3) the signature is not authorized, (4) the check has been altered, or (5) the check form is improper. Accounting for all returned checks is the same as for NSF checks.

f. *The cost of printed checks.* This charge against the company's bank account balance is handled like a service charge.

3. Errors by either the company or the bank. For example, a bank may improperly charge (decrease) the bank balance of Business Research, Inc., for a check drawn by another company, perhaps Business Research Associates. Or a company may miscompute its bank balance on its own books. Computational errors are becoming less frequent with widespread use of computers. Nevertheless, all errors must be corrected, and the corrections will be a part of the bank reconciliation.

Steps in Preparing the Bank Reconciliation

The steps in preparing the bank reconciliation are

1. Start with two figures, the balance shown on the bank statement (*balance per bank*) and the balance in the company's Cash account (*balance per books*) as in Exhibit 7-5, Panel B. These two amounts will probably disagree because of the timing differences discussed earlier.

2. Add to, or subtract from, the *bank* balance those items that appear on the books but not on the bank statement:
   a. Add *deposits in transit* to the bank balance. Deposits in transit are identified by comparing the deposits listed on the bank statement to the company list of cash receipts. They show up as cash receipts on the

books but not as deposits on the bank statement. As a control measure, the accountant should also ensure that deposits in transit from the preceding month appear on the current month's bank statement. If they do not, the deposits may be lost.

b. Subtract *outstanding checks* from the bank balance. Outstanding checks are identified by comparing the canceled checks returned with the bank statement to the company list of checks in the cash disbursements journal. They show up as cash payments on the books but not as paid checks on the bank statement. This comparison also verifies that all checks paid by the bank were valid company checks and were correctly recorded by the bank and by the company. Outstanding checks are usually the most numerous items on a bank reconciliation.

3. Add to, or subtract from, the *book* balance those items that appear on the bank statement but not on the company books:

a. Add to the book balance (a) *bank collections* and (b) any *interest revenue* earned on the money in the bank. These items are identified by comparing the deposits listed on the bank statement to the company list of cash receipts. They show up as cash receipts on the bank statement but not on the books.

b. Subtract from the book balance (a) *service charges*, (b) *cost of printed checks*, and (c) *other bank charges* (for example, charges for NSF or stale date checks). These items are identified by comparing the other charges listed on the bank statement to the cash disbursements recorded on the company books. They show up as subtractions on the bank statement but not as cash payments on the books.

4. Compute the *adjusted bank balance* and the *adjusted book balance*. The two adjusted balances should be equal.

5. Journalize each item in 3, that is, each item listed on the book portion of the bank reconciliation. These items must be recorded on the company books because they affect cash.

6. Correct all book errors and notify the bank of any errors it has made.

Bank Reconciliation Illustrated

The bank statement in Exhibit 7-4 indicates that the January 31 bank balance of Business Research, Inc., is $5,388.48. However, the company's Cash account has a balance of $3,294.21. In following the steps outlined above, the accountant finds these reconciling items:

1. The January 30 deposit of $1,591.63 does not appear on the bank statement.

2. The bank erroneously charged a $100 check—number 656—written by Business Research Associates against the Business Research, Inc., account.

3. Five company checks issued late in January and recorded in the cash disbursements journal have not been paid by the bank:

Check No.	Date	Amount
337	Jan. 27	$286.00
338	28	319.47
339	28	83.00
340	29	203.14
341	30	458.53

Here is a summary:
Bank balance
    Always *add* deposits in transit
    Always *subtract* outstanding checks
Book balance
    Always *add* bank collection items and interest revenue
    Always *subtract* service charges, NSF checks, and other charges
Errors—adjusted to the side where the error was made
Entries—made only for those items adjusted to the book balance

Point to Stress: Preparing the bank reconciliation does not change the balance of cash on the books; it just shows what the balance should be. Journal entries must be made and posted for every reconciling item on the *book side* in order to bring the book balance of cash to its correct current amount.

OBJECTIVE 3

Prepare a bank reconciliation and related journal entries

4. The bank collected on behalf of the company a note receivable, $2,114 (including interest revenue of $214). This cash receipt has not been recorded in the cash receipts journal.
5. The bank statement shows interest revenue of $28.01 that the bank has paid the company on its cash balance.
6. Check number 333 for $150 paid to Brown Company on account was recorded in the cash disbursements journal as a $510 amount, creating a $360 understatement of the Cash balance per books.
7. The bank service charge for the month was $14.25.
8. The bank statement shows an NSF check for $52, which was received from customer L. Ross.

Exhibit 7-5 is the bank reconciliation based on the above data. Panel A lists the reconciling items, which are keyed by number to the actual reconciliation in Panel B. Note that after the reconciliation, the adjusted bank balance equals the adjusted book balance. This equality is the accuracy check for the reconciliation.

Recording Entries from the Reconciliation

Point to Stress: Remember that journal entries must be made for every reconciling item that appears on the book side of the reconciliation, but *not* for the items that appear on the bank side.

The bank reconciliation does not directly affect the journals or the ledgers. Like the work sheet, the reconciliation is an accountant's tool, separate from the company's books.

The bank reconciliation acts as a control device by signaling the company to record the transactions listed as reconciling items in the Books section because the company has not yet done so. For example, the bank collected the note receivable on behalf of the company, but the company has not yet recorded this cash receipt. In fact, the company learned of the cash receipt only when it received the bank statement.

Why does the company *not* need to record the reconciling items on the Bank side of the reconciliation? Those items have already been recorded on the company books.

Transparency T 7-1

Based on the reconciliation in Exhibit 7-5, Business Research, Inc., makes these entries. They are dated January 31 to bring the Cash account to the correct balance on that date:

Jan. 31	Cash	2,114.00	
	Notes Receivable		1,900.00
	Interest Revenue		214.00
	Note receivable collected by bank.		
31	Cash	28.01	
	Interest Revenue		28.01
	Interest earned on bank balance.		
31	Cash	360.00	
	Accounts Payable—Brown Co.		360.00
	Correction of check register, check no. 333.		
31	Miscellaneous Expense	14.25	
	Cash		14.25
	Bank service charge.		
31	Accounts Receivable—L. Ross	52.00	
	Cash		52.00
	NSF check returned by bank.		

EXHIBIT 7-5 *Bank Reconciliation*

Panel A—Reconciling Items:

1. Deposit in transit, $1,591.63.
2. Bank error; add $100 to bank balance.
3. Outstanding checks: no. 337, $286; no. 338, $319.47; no. 339, $83; no. 340, $203.14; no. 341, $458.53.

4. Bank collection, $2,114, including interest revenue of $214.
5. Interest earned on bank balance, $28.01.
6. Book error; add $360 to book balance.
7. Bank service charge, $14.25.
8. NSF check from L. Ross, $52.

Panel B—Bank Reconciliation:

Business Research, Inc.
Bank Reconciliation
January 31, 19X6

Bank:			Books:		
Balance, January 31		$5,388.48	Balance, January 31		$3,294.21
Add:			Add:		
1. Deposit of January 30 in transit .		1,591.63	4. Bank collection of note receivable, including interest revenue of $214		2,114.00
2. Correction of bank error-Business Research Associates check erroneously charged against company account		100.00	5. Interest revenue earned on bank balance		28.01
		7,080.11	6. Correction of book error— Overstated amount of check no. 333		360.00
					5,796.22
3. Less outstanding checks:			Less:		
No. 337	$286.00		7. Service charge	$14.25	
No. 338	319.47		8. NSF check	52.00	(66.25)
No. 339	83.00				
No. 340	203.14				
No. 341	458.53	(1,350.14)			
Adjusted bank balance		$5,729.97	Adjusted book balance		$5,729.97

Note: Miscellaneous Expense is debited for the bank service charge because the service charge pertains to no particular expense category.

These entries bring the business's books up to date.

The entry for the NSF check needs explanation. Upon learning that L. Ross's $52 check was not good, Business Research credits Cash to bring the Cash account up to date. Since Business Research still has a receivable from Ross, it debits Accounts Receivable—L. Ross and pursues collection from him.

Summary Problem for Your Review

1. The Cash account of Bain Company at February 28, 19X3, follows.

<table>
<tr><th colspan="4">Cash</th></tr>
<tr><td>Feb. 1</td><td>Balance 4,195</td><td>Feb. 3</td><td>400</td></tr>
<tr><td>6</td><td>800</td><td>12</td><td>3,100</td></tr>
<tr><td>15</td><td>1,800</td><td>19</td><td>1,100</td></tr>
<tr><td>23</td><td>1,100</td><td>25</td><td>500</td></tr>
<tr><td>28</td><td>2,400</td><td>27</td><td>900</td></tr>
<tr><td>Feb. 28</td><td>Balance 4,095</td><td></td><td></td></tr>
</table>

2. Bain Company receives this bank statement on February 28, 19X3 (negative amounts appear in parentheses):

Bank Statement for February 19X3

Beginning balance		$4,195
Deposits:		
Feb. 7	$ 800	
15	1,800	
24	1,100	3,500
Checks (total per day):		
Feb. 8	$ 400	
16	3,100	
23	1,100	(4,600)
Other items:		
Service charge		(10)
NSF check from M. E. Crown		(700)
Bank collection of note receivable for the company		1,000*
Interest on account balance		15
Ending balance		$3,400

*Includes interest of $119.

Additional data:
Bain Company deposits all cash receipts in the bank and makes all cash disbursements by check.

Required:

1. Prepare the bank reconciliation of Bain Company at February 28, 19X3.
2. Record the entries based on the bank reconciliation.

Requirement 1

Bain Company
Bank Reconciliation
February 28, 19X3

Bank:

Balance, February 28, 19X3	$3,400
Add: Deposit of February 28 in transit........	2,400
	5,800
Less: Outstanding checks issued on Feb. 25 ($500) and Feb. 27 ($900)	(1,400)
Adjusted bank balance, February 28, 19X3	$4,400

Books:

Balance, February 28, 19X3		$4,095
Add: Bank collection of note receivable, including interest of $119............		1,000
Interest earned on bank balance		15
		5,110
Less: Service charge	$ 10	
NSF check...........................	700	(710)
Adjusted book balance, February 28, 19X3		$4,400

Requirement 2

Feb. 28	Cash	1,000	
	Note Receivable ($1,000 − $119)		881
	Interest Revenue		119
	Note receivable collected by bank.		
28	Cash	15	
	Interest Revenue		15
	Interest earned on bank balance.		
28	Miscellaneous Expense............................	10	
	Cash..		10
	Bank service charge.		
28	Accounts receivable—M. E. Crown	700	
	Cash..		700
	NSF check returned by bank.		

Reporting of Cash

Cash is the first current asset listed on the balance sheet of most companies. Even small businesses have several bank accounts and one or more petty cash funds that are kept on hand for making small disbursements. However, companies usually combine all cash amounts into a single total for reporting on the balance sheet. They also include liquid assets like time deposits and certificates of deposit. These are interest-bearing accounts that can be withdrawn with no penalty after a short period of time. Although they are slightly less liquid than cash, they are sufficiently similar to be reported along with cash. For example, the balance sheet of Kraft, Inc., maker of Miracle Whip, Philadelphia Cream Cheese, Duracell batteries, and other well-known products, recently reported (in millions of dollars):

Assets:

Cash, time deposits, and certificates of deposit	**$ 194.1**
Temporary investments......................	127.6
Accounts and notes receivable	941.7
Inventories	1,211.3
Total current assets	$2,474.7

It is important to perform the bank reconciliation on the balance sheet date in order to be assured of reporting the correct amount of cash.

Internal Control over Cash Receipts

OBJECTIVE 4

Apply internal controls to cash receipts

Real-World Example: Stores often give customers a bonus, such as a loaf of bread or gallon of ice cream, if the clerk fails to give them a receipt.

Discussion Question: Why is it important for each customer to receive a receipt? *ANSWER:* To make sure each sale is recorded in the register.

Internal control over cash receipts ensures that all cash receipts are deposited in the bank and the company's accounting record is correct. Many businesses receive cash over the counter and through the mail. Each source of cash receipts calls for *security measures.*

The cash register offers management control over cash received in a store. First, the machine should be positioned so that customers can see the amounts the cashier enters into the register. No person willingly pays more than the marked price for an item, so the customer helps prevent the sales clerk from overcharging and pocketing the excess over actual prices. Also, company policy should require issuance of a receipt to make sure each sale is recorded in the register.

Second, the register's cash drawer opens only when the sales clerk enters an amount on the keys, and a roll of tape locked inside the machine records each amount. At the end of the day, a manager proves the cash by comparing the total amount in the cash drawer against the tape's total. This step helps prevent outright theft by the clerk. For security reasons, the clerk should not have access to the tape.

Third, pricing merchandise at "uneven" amounts—say, $3.95 instead of $4.00—means that the clerk generally must make change, which in turn means having to get into the cash drawer. This requires entering the amount of the sale on the keys and so onto the register tape.

At the end of the day, the cashier or other employee with cash-handling duties deposits the cash in the bank. The tape goes to the accounting department as the basis for an entry in the cash receipts journal. These security measures, coupled with periodic on-site inspection by a manager, discourage fraud.

All incoming mail should be opened by a mail-room employee. This person should compare the actual enclosed amount of cash or check with the attached remittance advice. If no advice was sent, the mail-room employee should prepare one and enter the amount of each receipt on a control tape. At the end of the day, this control tape is given to a responsible official, such as the controller, for verification. Cash receipts should be given to the cashier, who combines them with any cash received over the counter and prepares the bank deposit.

Having a mail-room employee be the first to handle postal cash receipts is just another application of a good internal control procedure—in this case, separation of duties. If the accountants opened postal cash receipts, they could easily hide a theft.

The mail-room employee forwards the remittance advices to the accounting department. They provide the data for entries in the cash receipts journal and postings to customers' accounts in the accounts receivable ledger. As a final step, the controller compares the three records of the day's cash receipts: (1) the control tape total from the mail room, (2) the bank deposit amount from the cashier, and (3) the debit to Cash from the accounting department.

An added measure used to control cash receipts is a *fidelity bond*, which is an insurance policy that the business buys to guard against theft. The fidelity bond helps in two ways. First, the insurance company that issues the policy investigates the backgrounds of the workers whose activities will be covered, such as the mail-room employees who handle incoming cash and the employees who handle inventory. Second, if the company suffers a loss due to the misconduct of a covered employee, the insurance company reimburses the business.

Discussion Question: If a mail room employee decided to steal some cash receipts from the mail room, how would this theft be discovered? *ANSWER:* The customers whose cash was stolen would notice that their accounts had not been settled when they received their next bill.

Cash Short and Over.   A difference often exists between actual cash receipts and the day's record of cash received. Usually the difference is small and results from honest errors. Suppose the cash register tapes of a large department store indicate sales revenue of $25,000, but the cash received is $24,980. To record the day's sales, the store would make this entry:

Cash	24,980	
Cash Short and Over	20	
Sales Revenue		25,000
Daily cash sales.		

As the entry shows, Cash Short and Over is debited when sales revenue exceeds cash receipts. This account is credited when cash receipts exceed sales. A debit balance in Cash Short and Over appears on the income statement as Miscellaneous Expense, a credit balance as Other Revenue.

This account's balance should be small. The debits and credits for cash short and over collected over an accounting period tend to cancel each other out. A large balance signals the accountant to investigate. For example, too large a debit balance may mean an employee is stealing. Cash Short and Over, then, acts as an internal control device.

Internal Control Over Cash Disbursements

OBJECTIVE 5
Apply internal controls to cash disbursements

Payment by *check* is an important control over cash disbursements. First, the check acts as a source document. Second, to be valid the check must be signed by an authorized official, so each payment by check draws the attention of management. Before signing the check, the manager should study the invoice, the receiving report, the purchase order, and other supporting documents. (A discussion of these documents follows.) As further security and control over cash disbursements, many firms require two signatures on a check, as we saw in Exhibit 7-3. To avoid document alteration, some firms also use machines that indelibly stamp the amount on the check.

In very small businesses, the proprietor or partners may control cash disbursements by reviewing the supporting documents themselves and personally writing all checks. However, in larger businesses this is impractical, so the duties of approving invoices for payment and writing checks are performed by authorized employees. Strong internal control is achieved through clear-cut assignment of responsibility, proper authorization, and separation of duties.

Controlling the Cost of Inventory

Cost of goods sold is the major expense of most merchandising businesses. Therefore, it is important to control the cost of inventory purchases. Overall control is achieved by the same measures used to control all other cash disbursements—assignment of responsibility, authorization for payment, separation of duties, and so on.

A measure that is designed specifically to control the cost of inventory concerns the manner of recording purchases. There are two ways to record purchases: (1) at the *gross* cost, as illustrated thus far; and (2) at the *net* cost, which takes into account any discount on the purchase. For example, a $2,000 invoice subject to credit terms of 2/10 n/30 could be recorded at gross ($2,000) or net ($1,960). The discount terms of 2/10 n/30 (that is, a 2 percent discount for payment within 10 days, or the full $2,000 within 30 days) indicate a very high rate of interest when expressed as an annual rate. Paying after the discount period costs 2 percent for the extra 20 days of credit, an annual rate of 36 percent (.02 X 360 days/20 days = .36). For this reason, companies adopt the policy of taking all such discounts.

Recording the purchase at its net amount has a control advantage because it highlights the inefficiency of paying late. Recorded at net cost, the purchase entry is

Purchases ($2,000 − $40)	1,960	
Accounts Payable		1,960
Purchase on account.		

The actual cost of the inventory is $1,960 because this is the cash cost of the goods if they are paid for immediately. The gross cost of $2,000 includes a $40 charge for payment beyond the discount period. Therefore, the net cost method is helpful. To see the control advantage of the net cost approach, suppose the invoice is *not* paid within the discount period. This inefficiency costs an extra $40, debited to Purchase Discounts Lost as follows:

Accounts Payable	1,960	
Purchase Discounts Lost	40	
Cash in Bank		2,000
Payment after discount period.		

Purchase Discounts Lost is an expense account reported as Other Expense on the income statement as shown at the top of the next page.

Reporting Purchase Discounts Lost on the income statement draws attention to the inefficiency of losing the discounts. The net method thus captures the information needed to evaluate employee performance. Managers can then correct those actions that led to payment of the full amount. Contrast this accounting treatment with recording the purchases at gross cost. If the invoice is paid late, there is no record of the discount because the purchase and the related payment are both recorded at $2,000. Managers lose the notification provided by the Purchase Discounts Lost account.

Teaching Tip: The Purchase Discounts Lost account records the discounts that have *not* been taken. The Purchase Discounts account records the discounts that *have* been taken. The Purchase Discounts account is deducted from Purchases in determining the Cost of Goods Sold. Purchase Discounts Lost is considered an operating expense, and is *not* figured into Cost of Goods Sold.

Typical Student Misconception: A lost discount is an error made by the accounts payable clerk and should not be charged to the purchasing department.

Grant Company Income Statement Year Ended December 31, 19X8	
Sales revenue..................	$700,000
Cost of goods sold	380,000
Gross margin.................	320,000
Operating expenses	230,000
Income from operations	90,000
Other revenue (expense):	
Purchase discounts lost	**(2,000)**
Net income...................	$ 88,000

Petty Cash Disbursements

It would be uneconomical for a business to write a separate check for an executive's taxi fare, a box of pencils needed right away, or the delivery of a special message across town. Therefore, companies keep a small amount of cash on hand to pay for such minor amounts. This fund is called **petty cash.**

Even though the individual amounts paid through the petty cash fund may be small, such expenses occur so often that the total amount over an accounting period may grow quite large. Thus the business needs to set up these controls over petty cash: (1) designate an employee to administer the fund as its custodian, (2) keep a specific amount of cash on hand, (3) support all fund disbursements with a petty cash ticket, and (4) replenish the fund through normal cash disbursement procedures.

To open the petty cash fund, a payment is approved for a predetermined amount and a check for this amount is issued to Petty Cash. Assume that on February 28 the business decides to establish a petty cash fund of $200. The custodian cashes the check and places the currency and coin in the fund, which may be a cash box, safe, or other device. The petty cash custodian is assigned the responsibility for controlling the fund. Starting the fund is recorded as follows:

Feb. 28	Petty Cash.........................	200	
	Cash in Bank...................		200
	To open the petty cash fund.		

For each petty cash disbursement, the custodian prepares a *petty cash ticket* like the one illustrated in Exhibit 7-6.

EXHIBIT 7-6 *Petty Cash Ticket*

Petty Cash Ticket

PETTY CASH TICKET

Date Mar. 25, 19X4   **No.** 45

Amount $23.00

For Box of floppy diskettes

Debit Office Supplies, Acct. No. 145

Received by *Lewis Wright*   **Fund Custodian** WAR

Class Exercise: Your company has purchased $1,650 of merchandise subject to terms of 3/10 n/30. Three days later, you receive the goods and find that $150 of the merchandise is defective. You return the items for credit to your account. Due to an employee sickness, you fail to pay within the discount period. Record the payment *after* the discount period, assuming you use the net method. ANSWER:

Accts. Payable....... 1,455*

Purch. Disct. Lost 45**

  Cash ($1,650 − $150) ... 1,500

*[($1,650 − $150) x .97]
**[($1,650 − $150) x .03]

Note that the Purchase Return would be recorded at its net amount of $145.50 ($150 x .97)

Point to Stress: Access to the petty cash fund should be permitted only to the petty cash custodian.

OBJECTIVE 6
Account for petty cash transactions

Point to Stress: The sum of the cash remaining in the fund plus petty cash tickets should always equal the predetermined petty cash amount.

Point to Stress: No journal entries are made for petty cash disbursements until the fund is replenished. At that time, all petty cash payments will be recorded in a summary entry. This procedure avoids the need to journalize large numbers of payments for very small amounts.

Typical Student Misconception: Students want to debit Petty Cash for the $82 reimbursement. Draw a T-account and enter the balance before the replenishment:

Petty Cash

2/28 200	

If the $82 is posted to Petty Cash in error, the account will have a $282 balance when there is actually only $200 in the fund:

Petty Cash

2/28 200	
3/31 82	
Bal. 282	
(Incorrect)	

Therefore, the entry must show the debits to the various expense accounts, not to the Petty Cash account.

OBJECTIVE 7

Use the voucher system

Observe the signatures (or initials, for the custodian) that identify the recipient of petty cash and the fund custodian. Requiring both signatures reduces unauthorized cash disbursements. The custodian keeps all the petty cash tickets in the fund. The sum of the cash plus the total of the ticket amounts should equal the opening balance at all times—in this case, $200. Also, the Petty Cash account keeps its prescribed $200 balance at all times. Maintaining the Petty Cash account at this balance, supported by the fund (cash plus tickets totaling the same amount), is a characteristic of an imprest system. The control feature of an **imprest system** is that it clearly identifies the amount that the custodian is responsible for.

Disbursements reduce the amount of cash in the fund, so periodically the fund must be replenished. Suppose that on March 31 the fund has $118 in cash and $82 in tickets. A check for $82 is issued, made payable to Petty Cash. The fund custodian cashes this check for currency and coins and puts the money in the fund to return its actual cash to $200. The petty cash tickets identify the accounts to be debited: Office Supplies for $23, Delivery Expense for $17, and Miscellaneous Selling Expense for $42. The entry to record replenishment of the fund is

Mar. 31	Office Supplies	23	
	Delivery Expense	17	
	Miscellaneous Selling Expense	42	
	Cash in Bank...................		82
	To replenish the petty cash fund.		

If this cash payment exceeds the sum of the tickets—that is, if the fund comes up short, Cash Short and Over is debited for the missing amount. If the sum of the tickets exceeds the payment, Cash Short and Over is credited. Note that replenishing the fund does *not* affect the Petty Cash account. Petty Cash keeps its $200 balance at all times.

Whenever petty cash runs low, the fund is replenished. It *must* be replenished on the balance sheet date. Otherwise, the reported balance for Petty Cash will be overstated by the amount of the tickets in the fund. The income statement will understate the expenses listed on these tickets.

Petty Cash is debited only when starting the fund (see the February 28 entry) or changing its amount. In our illustration, suppose the business decides to raise the fund amount from $200 to $250 because of increased demand for petty cash. This step would require a $50 debit to Petty Cash.

The Voucher System

As we saw in Chapter 6, some businesses use the purchases journal and the cash disbursements journal to record cash payments. Other businesses use a voucher system. The **voucher system** for recording cash payments offers the business greater internal control by formalizing the process of approving and recording invoices for payment. We will examine the voucher system as it is used by a merchandising business.

The voucher system uses (1) vouchers, (2) a voucher register, (3) an unpaid voucher file, (4) a check register, and (5) a paid voucher file. The merchandising business we discuss has separate departments for purchasing goods, receiving goods, disbursing cash, and accounting.

Vouchers. A **voucher** is a document authorizing a cash disbursement. The accounting department prepares vouchers. Exhibit 7-7 illustrates the voucher of Bliss Wholesale Company. In addition to places for writing in the *payee, due*

EXHIBIT 7-7 *Voucher*

Front of
Voucher

Voucher No. 326
BLISS WHOLESALE COMPANY

Payee   Van Heusen, Inc.
Address   4619 Shotwell Avenue
          Brooklyn, NY 10564

Due Date   March 7
Terms   2/10, n/30

Date	Invoice No.	Description	Amount
Mar. 1	6380	144 men's shirts stock no. X14	$1,800

Approved *Jane Trent*   Approved *Bob Kraft*
     Controller   **Treasurer**

Back of
Voucher

Voucher No. 326
Payee Van Heusen, Inc.

Invoice Amount $1,800

Discount   36

Net Amount $1,764

Due Date   Mar. 7

Date Paid   Mar. 6

Check No.   694

Account Distribution

Account Debited	Acct. No.	Amount
Purchases	501	1,800
Store Supplies	145	
Salary Expense	538	
Advertising Expense	542	
Utilities Expense	548	
Delivery Expense	544	
Total		**$1,800**

Point to Stress: In a voucher system, all expenditures must be approved before payment can be made. This approval takes the form of a voucher. The larger the business, the more likely it is to need strict control over disbursements. The voucher system helps to supply this control.

Point to Stress: The voucher system illustrates good internal control procedures, especially separation of duties. The accounting department is the only department to have copies of the purchase order, the invoice, and the receiving report. The accounting department compares these documents before approving the payment. However, the accounting department does not prepare the check, and thus has no access to cash. Also, the accounting department never has access to the inventory that has been purchased. There would have to be collusion between someone in the accounting department and someone in another department for an accounting department employee to benefit from some unauthorized activity.

date, terms, description, and *invoice amount,* the voucher includes a section for designated officers to sign their *approval* for payment. The back of the voucher has places for recording the *account debited, date paid,* and *check number.* You should locate these nine items in Exhibit 7-7.

To better understand the voucher system, let's take an in-depth look at the purchasing process. Exhibit 7-8 lists the various business documents used to ensure that the company receives the goods it ordered and pays only for the goods it has actually received.

The purchasing process starts when the sales department identifies the need for merchandise and prepares a *purchase request* (or requisition). A separate purchasing department specializes in locating the best buys and mails a *purchase order* to the supplier, the outside company that sells the needed goods. When the supplier ships the goods to the requesting business, the supplier also mails the *invoice* (or bill), which is a notification of the need to pay. As the goods arrive, the receiving department checks them for any damage and lists the merchandise received on a document called the *receiving*

EXHIBIT 7-8 Purchasing Process

Business Document	Prepared by	Sent to
Purchase request	Sales department	Purchasing department
Purchase order	Purchasing department	Outside company that sells the needed merchandise (supplier, or vendor)
Invoice	Outside company that sells the needed merchandise (supplier, or vendor)	Accounting department
Receiving report	Receiving department	Accounting department
Voucher	Accounting department	Officer who signs the check

report. The accounting department prepares a *voucher* and attaches all the foregoing documents, checks them for accuracy and agreement, and forwards this voucher packet to designated officers for approval and payment. The voucher packet includes the voucher, invoice, receiving report, purchase order, and purchase request, as shown in Exhibit 7-9.

Before approving the voucher, the controller and the treasurer should examine a sample of vouchers to determine that the following control steps have been performed by the accounting department:

1. The invoice is compared with a copy of the purchase order and purchase request to ensure that the business pays cash only for the goods that it ordered.
2. The invoice is compared with the receiving report to ensure that cash is paid only for the goods that are actually received.
3. The mathematical accuracy of the invoice is proved.

Voucher Register.   After approval by the designated officers, the voucher goes to the accounting department where it is recorded in the **voucher register.** This journal is similar to the purchases journal (discussed in Chapter 6), but the voucher register is more comprehensive. In a voucher system, *all* expenditures are recorded first in the voucher register. This is a fundamental control feature of the voucher system because it centralizes the initial recording of all expenditures in this one journal. That is, all cash payments must be

EXHIBIT 7-9 Voucher Packet

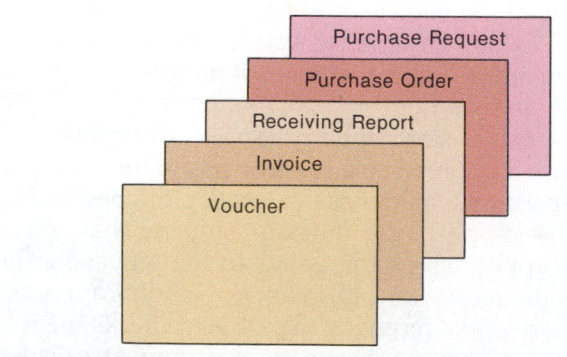

vouchered and approved prior to payment. For each transaction, the debit is to the account for which payment is being made, and the credit is to Vouchers Payable, the account that replaces Accounts Payable if a voucher system is used. Exhibit 7-10 illustrates the voucher register of Bliss Wholesale Company.

The voucher register has columns to record payment date and check number, which are entered when the voucher is paid. The absence of a payment date and check number means that the voucher is unpaid. In Exhibit 7-10, for example, Bliss Wholesale has a $2,202 liability at March 31 for vouchers 330 ($369 payable to the *Daily Journal*), 348 ($1,638 payable to Carr Products), and 350 ($195 payable to Consumers Gas Company). If these were the company's only unpaid vouchers at March 31, the balance sheet would report:

> Current liabilities:
>   Vouchers payable* $2,202
> *Usually reported as Accounts Payable, even by companies
> that use a voucher system.

Unpaid Voucher File.   After recording a voucher in the voucher register, the accountant places the voucher packet in the unpaid voucher file, where it stays until the voucher is paid. The unpaid voucher file acts as the accounts payable subsidiary ledger because each voucher serves as an individual account payable. There is no need for a separate accounts payable ledger.

The unpaid voucher file has 31 slots, one for each day of the month. Each voucher is filed according to its due date. For example, voucher no. 326, in Exhibit 7-7, was due March 7, so it was filed in the slot marked 7.

Point to Stress: The Voucher Register eliminates the need for an Accounts Payable subsidiary ledger. The Payment column and the Unpaid Voucher File indicate which vouchers have not yet been paid.

Check Register.   The **check register** is the journal in which are recorded all checks issued in a voucher system. It replaces the cash disbursements journal. All entries in the check register debit Vouchers Payable and credit Cash (and Purchase Discounts, as appropriate).

Exhibit 7-11 shows a check register. Notice that all the transactions include a credit to the Cash in Bank account.

On or before the due date, the accountant removes the voucher packet from the unpaid voucher file and sends it to the officers for signing. After the checks are signed, the check number and payment date are entered on the back of the voucher, in the check register, and in the voucher register.

Paid Voucher File.   After payment, the voucher packet is canceled to avoid paying the bill twice. Typically, a hole is punched through the voucher packet. It is then filed alphabetically by payee name. Most businesses also file a copy in numerical sequence by voucher number as a cross reference. With this dual filing system, a voucher can be located using either classification scheme.

In summary, the voucher system works as follows:

1. The accounting department prepares a *voucher* for each invoice to be paid.
2. Supporting documents (invoice, receiving report, purchase order, and purchase request) are compared in the accounting department for accuracy and attached to the voucher. These documents make up the *voucher packet.*
3. Designated officials examine the supporting documents and approve the voucher for payment.
4. The accounting department enters the voucher payable in the *voucher register.* The entry is a debit to the account of the item purchased (for example, Purchases) and a credit to Vouchers Payable. The voucher remains in the *unpaid voucher file* until payment.

EXHIBIT 7-10 *Voucher Register*

Voucher Register

Page 16

Date	Voucher No.	Payee	Payment Date	Check No.	Credit Vouchers Payable	Debit Purchases	Store Supplies	Salary Expense	Advertising Expense	Utilities Expense	Delivery Expense	Other Accounts Title	No.	Amount
Mar. 1	326	Van Heusen, Inc.	3/6	694	1,800	1,800								
1	327	Howell Properties	3/2	693	1,500							Rent Expense	547	1,500
4	328	Bell Telephone	3/10	696	128					128				
5	329	Schick Supplies	3/11	697	85		85							
8	330	Daily Journal			369				369					
9	331	Ace Delivery Service	3/9	695	37						37			
26	348	Carr Products			1,638	1,638								
28	349	Petty Cash	3/31	717	82		23				17	Miscellaneous Selling Expense	563	42
29	350	Consumers Gas Co.			195					195				
30	351	City National Bank	3/31	718	360							Interest Expense	546	360
31	352	Ralph Grant	3/31	719	864			864						
31		Totals			12,580	6,209	137	1,781	753	602	185			2,913
					(201)	(501)	(145)	(538)	(542)	(548)	(544)			(✓)

Account numbers in parentheses indicate the accounts to which these amounts have been posted.

340

EXHIBIT 7-11   Check Register

				Debit	Credit	
Date	Check No.	Payee	Voucher No.	Vouchers Payable	Purchase Discounts	Cash in Bank
Mar. 1	692	Trent Co.	322	600	18	582
2	693	Howell Properties	327	1,500		1,500
6	694	Van Heusen, Inc.	326	1,800	36	1,764
9	695	Ace Delivery Service	331	37		37
10	696	Bell Telephone	328	128		128
11	697	Schick Supplies	329	85		85
31	717	Petty Cash	349	82		82
31	718	City National Bank	351	360		360
31	719	Ralph Grant	352	864		864
31	720	Krasner Supply Co.	336	92		92
31		Totals		11,406	317	11,089
				(201)	(503)	(103)

Check Register — *Page 9*

Account numbers in parentheses indicate the accounts to which these amounts have been posted.

5. Prior to the invoice due date, a check is issued to pay the voucher. The official reviews the supporting documents and signs the check.
6. The accounting department enters the check in the *check register* and updates the voucher and the voucher register to record payment. All checks are debits to Vouchers Payable and credits to Cash.
7. Paid vouchers are canceled and filed by payee name and by voucher number.

To gain a complete understanding of the voucher system, trace voucher no. 326 from Exhibit 7-7 through the voucher register in Exhibit 7-10 to the check register in Exhibit 7-11. Also, trace the check register entries from Exhibit 7-11 back to Exhibit 7-10.

Computers, Internal Control, and Cash

Within a single company, each department may take steps to maintain control over its assets and accounting records. Consider a large company like Raytheon, a manufacturer of sophisticated defense-related equipment. Computerized record keeping means that the raw data provided by one department leads to a whole array of *accurate* output—from journals to ledgers to checks and so on—all consistent with the original information. Manually copying information—a time-consuming, error-prone process—is reduced or eliminated.

If Raytheon's system is well designed, each department can ensure that its transactions are processed correctly. The user department needs to maintain record counts or dollar control totals. For example, the accounts receivable department submits daily credit sales totals for processing by the computing department. The accounts receivable department expects a printout showing a total sales amount agreeing with the control total that was calculated *before* its documents went to the computer department. This amount is the control figure.

The accounts receivable department—and every other department—relies on the computing department to post correctly to the thousands of customer accounts. To assure proper posting, customer account numbers may be devised so that the last digit is a mathematical function of the previous digits (for example, 1359, where $1 + 3 + 5 = 9$). Any miskeying of a customer account number would trigger an error message to the keyboarder, and the computer would not accept that number.

Real-World Example: The Social Security Administration uses EFT to make payments to millions of Americans each month.

Also, the computer has brought about an important development in cash payments. **Electronic funds transfer (EFT)** is a system that relies on electronic impulses—not paper documents—to account for cash transactions. To manage payroll, an employer enters the employee's name, pay rate, and any other needed data on a magnetic tape, which is transferred to a bank. The bank runs the tape, which automatically decreases the business's cash account and increases the employee's cash account. Some retailers use EFT to handle sales. Customers pay with a card that activates a computer. The computer automatically decreases the customer's bank account balance and increases the store's account balance.

EFT systems reduce the cost of processing cash transactions. However, this savings is achieved by reducing the documentary evidence of transactions. Traditional approaches to internal control have relied on documents, so EFT and other computer systems pose a significant challenge to managers and accountants who design and enforce internal control systems. Computer systems also create problems in protecting private information. For example, a group of students in Milwaukee gained access to highly confidential national defense data by computer! Such situations point to the need for computer security measures.

Summary Problem for Your Review

Grudnitski Company established a $300 petty cash fund. James C. Brown is the fund custodian. At the end of the first week, the petty cash fund contains the following:

1. Cash: $171
2. Petty cash tickets:

No.	Amount	Issued to	Signed by	Account Debited
44	$14	B. Jarvis	B. Jarvis and JCB	Office Supplies
45	9	S. Bell	S. Bell	Miscellaneous Expense
47	43	R. Tate	R. Tate and JCB	—
48	33	L. Blair	L. Blair and JCB	Travel Expense

Required

1. Identify the four internal control weaknesses revealed in the above data.
2. Prepare the general journal entries to record:
   a. Establishment of the petty cash fund.
   b. Replenishment of the fund. Assume petty cash ticket no. 47 was issued for the purchase of office supplies.
3. What is the balance in the Petty Cash account immediately before replenishment? Immediately after replenishment?

SOLUTION TO REVIEW PROBLEM

Requirement 1.   The four internal control weaknesses are

a. Petty cash ticket no. 46 is missing. Coupled with weakness *b*, this omission raises questions about the administration of the petty cash fund and about how the petty cash funds were used.

b. The $171 cash balance means that $129 has been disbursed ($300 − $171 = $129). However, the total amount of the petty cash tickets is only $99 ($14 + $9 + $43 + $33). The fund, then, is $30 short of cash ($129 − $99 = $30). Was petty cash ticket no. 46 issued for $30? The data in the problem offer no hint that helps answer this question. In a real-world setting, management would investigate the problem.

c. The petty cash custodian (JCB) did not sign petty cash ticket no. 45. This omission may have been an oversight on his part. However, it raises the question of whether he authorized the disbursement. Both the fund custodian and the recipient of cash should sign the ticket.

d. Petty cash ticket no. 47 does not indicate which account to debit. What did Tate do with the money, and what account should be debited? At worst, the funds have been stolen. At best, reconstructing the transaction from memory is haphazard. With no better choice available, debit Miscellaneous Expense.

Requirement 2.   Petty cash journal entries:

a. Entry to establish the petty cash fund:

Petty Cash	300	
Cash in Bank		300

b. Entry to replenish the fund:

Office Supplies	14	
Miscellaneous Expense ($9 + $43)	52	
Travel Expense	33	
Cash Short and Over	30	
Cash in Bank		129

Requirement 3.   The balance in Petty Cash is *always* its specified balance, in this case $300, as shown by posting the above entries to the account:

Petty Cash

(a) 300	

Note that the entry to establish the fund (entry *a*) debits Petty Cash. The entry to replenish the fund (entry *b*) neither debits nor credits Petty Cash.

Summary

Internal controls should safeguard assets, ensure accurate accounting records, promote operational efficiency, and encourage adherence to company policies. An effective internal control system includes these features: *reliable personnel, clear-cut assignment of responsibility, proper authorization, and separation of duties,* which is the primary element of internal control. Many businesses use security devices, audits, and specially designed documents and records in their internal control systems.

The *bank account* helps to control and safeguard cash. Businesses use the *bank statement* and the *bank reconciliation* to account for banking transactions. An *imprest system* is used to control petty cash disbursements. Many companies record purchases at *net cost* in order to highlight the inefficiency of paying invoices late and thus losing purchase discounts.

Businesses often control cash disbursements by using a *voucher system,* which features the voucher, the unpaid voucher file, the voucher register, and the check register.

Businesses may handle their payroll by computer and through *electronic funds transfers.* Effective computerized internal control systems must meet the same basic standards that good manual systems do.

Self-Study Questions

Test your understanding of the chapter by marking the best answer for each of the following questions.

1. Which of the following is an element of internal control? *(p. 317)*
    a. Safeguarding assets
    b. Ensuring accurate and reliable accounting records
    c. Promoting operational efficiency
    d. Encouraging adherence to company policies
    e. All the above are elements of internal control

2. Which of the characteristics of an effective system of internal control is violated by allowing the employee who handles inventory to also account for inventory? *(p. 319)*
    a. Competent and reliable personnel   c. Proper authorization
    b. Assignment of responsibilities   d. Separation of duties

3. What control function is performed by auditors? *(p. 321)*
    a. Objective opinion of the effectiveness of the internal control system
    b. Assurance that all transactions are accounted for correctly
    c. Communication of the results of the audit to regulatory agencies
    d. Guarantee that a proper separation of duties exists within the business

4. The bank account serves as a control device over *(pp. 322, 332, 333, 334)*
    a. Cash receipts   c. Both of the above
    b. Cash disbursements   d. None of the above

5. Which of the following items appears on the bank side of a bank reconciliation? *(p. 329)*
    a. Book error   c. NSF check
    b. Outstanding check   d. Interest revenue earned on bank balance

6. Which of the following reconciling items requires a journal entry on the books of the company? *(pp. 328, 329)*
    a. Book error   d. Interest revenue earned on
    b. Outstanding check   bank balance
    c. NSF check   e. All of the above but b
                                  f. None of the above

7. What is the major internal control measure over the cash receipts of a K Mart store? *(p. 332)*
   a. Reporting the day's cash receipts to the controller
   b. Preparing a petty cash ticket for all disbursements from the fund
   c. Pricing merchandise at uneven amounts, coupled with use of a cash register
   d. Channeling all cash receipts through the mail room, whose employees have no cash-accounting responsibilities

8. What is the control advantage of the net method of accounting for inventory purchases? *(pp. 333, 334)*
   a. It highlights the inefficiency of losing purchase discounts.
   b. It guarantees that all purchase discounts will be taken.
   c. It automatically increases the business's cash balance.
   d. It results in a higher quality of inventory on hand for customers.

9. The internal control feature that is specific to petty cash is *(p. 336)*
   a. Separation of duties   c. Proper authorization
   b. Assignment of responsibility   d. The imprest system

10. The most fundamental control feature provided by a voucher system is *(p. 339)*
    a. Assuring that only approved invoices are paid
    b. Centralizing the recording of all expenditures in one place—the voucher register
    c. Using the check register along with the voucher register
    d. Placing all incoming invoices in the unpaid voucher file

Answers to the Self-Study questions follow the Accounting Vocabulary.

Accounting Vocabulary

Accounting controls. Methods and procedures that safeguard assets, authorize transactions, and ensure the accuracy of the financial records *(p. 317)*.

Administrative controls. Plan of organization, methods, and procedures that help managers achieve operational efficiency and adherence to company policies *(p. 317)*.

Bank collection. Collection of money by the bank on behalf of a depositor *(p. 325)*.

Bank reconciliation. Process of explaining the reasons for the difference between a depositor's records and the bank's records about the depositor's bank account *(p. 324)*.

Bank statement. Document for a particular bank account showing its beginning and ending balances and listing the month's transactions that affected the account *(p. 323)*.

Check. Document that instructs the bank to pay the designated person or business the specified amount of money *(p. 323)*.

Check register. Special journal used to record all checks issued in a voucher system *(p. 339)*.

Deposit in transit. A deposit recorded by the company but not yet by its bank *(p. 324)*.

Electronic funds transfer. System that accounts for cash transactions by electronic impulses rather than paper documents *(p. 342)*.

Imprest system. A way to account for petty cash by maintaining a constant balance in the petty cash account, supported by the fund (cash plus disbursement tickets) totaling the same amount *(p. 336)*.

Internal control. Organizational plan and all the related measures adopted by an entity to safeguard assets, ensure accurate and reliable accounting records, promote operational efficiency, and encourage adherence to company policies *(p. 317)*.

Nonsufficient funds (NSF) check. A "hot" check, one for which the payer's bank account has insufficient money to pay the check *(p. 326)*.

Outstanding check. A check issued by the company and recorded on its books but not yet paid by its bank (p. 325).

Petty cash. Fund containing a small amount of cash that is used to pay minor expenditures (p. 335).

Service charge. Bank's fee for processing a depositor's transactions (p. 326).

Voucher. Document authorizing a cash disbursement (p. 336).

Voucher register. Special journal used to record all expenditures in a voucher system, similar to but more comprehensive than the purchases journal (p. 338).

Voucher system. A way to record cash payments that enhances internal control by formalizing the process of approving and recording invoices for payment (p. 336).

Answers to Self-Study Questions

1. e	3. a	5. b	7. c	9. d
2. d	4. c	6. e	8. a	10. b

ASSIGNMENT MATERIAL _____

Questions

1. Which of the features of effective internal control is the most fundamental? Why?

2. What is the title of the federal act that affects internal control? What requirement does it place on management?

3. Which company employees bear primary responsibility for a company's financial statements and for maintaining the company's system of internal control? How do these persons carry out this responsibility?

4. Identify features of an effective system of internal control.

5. Separation of duties may be divided into four parts. What are they?

6. How can internal control systems be circumvented?

7. Are internal control systems designed to be foolproof and perfect? What is a fundamental constraint in planning and maintaining systems?

8. Briefly state how each of the following serves as an internal control measure over cash: bank account, signature card, deposit ticket, and bank statement.

9. What is the remittance advice of a check? What use does it serve?

10. Each of the items in the following list must be accounted for in the bank reconciliation. Next to each item, enter the appropriate letter from the following possible treatments: (a) bank side of reconciliation—add the item; (b) bank side of reconciliation—subtract the item; (c) book side of reconciliation—add the item; (d) book side of reconciliation—subtract the item.
    - _____ Outstanding check
    - _____ NSF check
    - _____ Bank service charge
    - _____ Cost of printed checks
    - _____ Bank error that decreased bank balance
    - _____ Deposit in transit
    - _____ Bank collection
    - _____ Customer check returned because of unauthorized signature
    - _____ Book error that increased balance of Cash account

11. What purpose does a bank reconciliation serve?

12. Suppose a company has six bank accounts, two petty cash funds, and three certificates of deposit that can be withdrawn on demand. How many cash amounts would this company likely report on its balance sheet?

13. What role does a cash register play in an internal control system?

14. Describe internal control procedures for cash received by mail.

15. Large businesses often have elaborate internal control systems that may be uneconomical for small businesses. Where does the internal control rest in small proprietorships, and how do they control cash disbursements?

16. What is the internal control advantage of recording purchases at net cost?

17. What balance does the Petty Cash account have at all times? Does this balance always equal the amount of cash in the fund? When are the two amounts equal? When are they unequal?

18. List the five elements of a voucher system, and briefly describe the purpose of each.

19. Describe how a voucher system works.

20. What documents make up the voucher packet? Describe three procedures that use the voucher packet to ensure that each payment is appropriate.

21. Why should the same employee not write the computer programs for cash disbursements, sign checks, and mail the checks to payees?

Exercises

Exercise 7-1   *Identifying internal control strengths and weaknesses*   **(L.O. 2)**   No check figure

The following situations suggest either a strength or weakness in internal control. Identify each as *strength* or *weakness*, and give the reason for your answer.

a. The vice-president who signs checks assumes the accounting department has matched the invoice with other supporting documents and therefore does not examine the voucher packet.

b. Purchase invoices are recorded at net amount to highlight purchase discounts lost because of late payment.

c. The accounting department orders merchandise and approves vouchers for payment.

d. The operator of the computer has no other accounting or cash-handling duties.

e. Cash received over the counter is controlled by the sales clerk, who rings up the sale and places the cash in the register. The sales clerk has access to the control tape stored in the register.

f. Cash received by mail goes straight to the accountant, who debits Cash and credits Accounts Receivable from the customer.

Exercise 7-2   *Identifying internal controls*   **(L.O. 2)**   No check figure

Identify the missing internal control characteristic in the following situations:

1. Business is slow at Malibu Theme Park on Tuesday, Wednesday, and Thursday nights. To reduce expenses the owner decides not to use a ticket taker on those nights. The ticket seller (cashier) is told to keep the tickets as a record of the number sold.

2. The manager of a discount store wants to speed the flow of customers through check-out. She decides to reduce the time spent by cashiers making change, so she prices merchandise at round dollar amounts—such as $8.00 and $15.00—instead of the customary amounts—$7.95 and $14.95.

3. Grocery stores such as Kroger and Winn Dixie purchase large quantities of their merchandise from a few suppliers. At another grocery store the manager decides to reduce paper work. He eliminates the requirement that a

receiving department employee prepare a receiving report, which lists the quantities of items received from the supplier.

4. When business is brisk, Seven-Eleven and many other retail stores deposit cash in the bank several times during the day. The manager at another convenience store wants to reduce the time spent by employees delivering cash to the bank, so he starts a new policy. Cash will build up over Saturdays and Sundays, and the total two-day amount will be deposited on Sunday evening.

5. In the course of auditing the records of a company, you find that the same employee orders merchandise and approves invoices for payment.

No check figure

Exercise 7-3   *Classifying bank reconciliation items*   **(L.O. 3)**

The following seven items may appear on a bank reconciliation:

1. Outstanding checks.
2. Bank error: the bank charged our account for a check written by another customer.
3. Service charge.
4. Deposits in transit.
5. NSF check.
6. Bank collection of a note receivable on our behalf.
7. Book error: We debited Cash for $1,000. The correct debit was $100.

Classify each item as (a) an addition to the bank balance, (b) a subtraction from the bank balance, (c) an addition to the book balance, or (d) a subtraction from the book balance.

Adj. book bal. $1,141

Exercise 7-4   *Bank reconciliation*   **(L.O. 3)**

Betsy Willis's checkbook lists the following:

Date	Check No.	Item	Check	Deposit	Balance
9/1					$ 525
4	622	Apple Tree Gift Shop	$ 19		506
9		Dividends		$ 116	622
13	623	Bell Telephone Co.	43		579
14	624	Gulf Oil Co.	58		521
18	625	Cash	50		471
26	626	St. Alban's Episcopal Church	25		446
28	627	Bent Tree Apartments	275		171
30		Paycheck		1,000	1,171

The September bank statement shows:

Balance		$525
Add: Deposits		116
Deduct checks: No.	Amount	
622	$19	
623	43	
624	68*	
625	50	(180)
Other charges:		
Printed checks	$ 8	
Service charge	12	(20)
Balance		$441

*This is the correct amount of check number 624.

Required:

Prepare Betsy's bank reconciliation at September 30.

Exercise 7-5 *Bank reconciliation* **(L.O. 3)**

Adj. book bal. $4,261

Mike Gilliam operates four EXXON stations. He has just received the monthly bank statement at October 31 from First National Bank, and the statement shows an ending balance of $3,940. Listed on the statement are a service charge of $12, two NSF checks totaling $74, and a $9 charge for printed checks. In reviewing his cash records, Gilliam identifies outstanding checks totaling $467 and an October 31 deposit of $788, which does not appear on the bank statement. During October he recorded a $190 check for the salary of a part-time employee by debiting Salary Expense and crediting Cash for $19. Gilliam's cash account shows an October 31 cash balance of $4,527. Prepare the bank reconciliation at October 31.

Exercise 7-6 *Journal entries from a bank reconciliation* **(L.O. 3)**

No check figure

Using the data from Exercise 7-5, record the entries that Gilliam should make in the general journal on October 31. Include an explanation for each of the entries.

Exercise 7-7 *Internal control over cash receipts* **(L.O. 4)**

No check figure

A cash register is located in each department of Kestner's Payless Discount Store. The register shows the amount of each sale, the cash received from the customer, and any change returned to the customer. The machine also produces a customer receipt but keeps no record of transactions. At the end of the day, the clerk counts the cash in the register and gives it to the cashier for deposit in the company bank account.

Required:

Write a memo to convince the store manager that there is an internal control weakness over cash receipts. Identify the weakness that gives an employee the best opportunity to steal cash, and state how to prevent this theft.

Exercise 7-8 *Income statements with purchases at gross and at net* **(L.O. 5)**

Net income $264,000; Pur. disc. lost, net method, $2,000

Assume Bulova Company, the watch manufacturer, began July with inventory of $570,000 and ended the month with inventory of $510,000. During July the company purchased $800,000 of inventory and took the 2 percent discount on $700,000 of the purchases. The remaining $100,000 in inventory cost was paid after the discount period. Sales during July were $1,600,000, and operating expenses (including income tax) were $490,000.

Required:

1. Prepare the company's income statement for July assuming Bulova records inventory purchases at gross cost.
2. Prepare the company's income statement for July assuming the company records inventory purchases at net cost.
3. Which method provides the internal control advantage? Describe how this internal control feature works.

Exercise 7-9 *Purchases at gross and at net* **(L.O. 5)**

No check figure

Rolfe Office Supplies uses a voucher system. Prepare its general journal entries for the following transactions under two assumptions (explanations are not required):

Assumption 1—Inventory purchases recorded at gross cost
Assumption 2—Inventory purchases recorded at net cost

May 3 Purchased inventory costing $5,100 on account, subject to terms of 2/10 n/30.
     11 Paid the liability created on May 3.
     14 Purchased inventory costing $2,200 on account, subject to terms of 2/10 n/30.
     27 Paid the liability created on May 14.

Which method provides Rolfe Office Supplies with a measure of discounts lost? Describe how this internal control feature works.

Exercise 7-10 *Accounting for petty cash* **(L.O. 5, 6)**

Community Charities of Gatlinburg, Tennessee, created a $100 imprest petty cash fund. During the first month of use, the fund custodian authorized and signed petty cash tickets as follows:

Ticket No.	Item	Account Debited	Amount
1	Delivery of pledge cards to donors	Delivery Expense	$22.19
2	Mail package	Postage Expense	2.80
3	Newsletter	Supplies Expense	4.14
4	Key to closet	Miscellaneous Expense	.85
5	Waste basket	Miscellaneous Expense	3.78
6	Staples	Supplies Expense	5.37

Required:

1. Make general journal entries for creation of the petty cash fund and its replenishment. Include explanations.
2. Immediately prior to replenishment, describe the items in the fund.
3. Immediately after replenishment, describe the items in the fund.

Exercise 7-11 *Petty cash; cash short and over* **(L.O. 4, 5, 6)**

Record the following selected transactions in general journal format (explanations are not required):

April 1 Issued voucher no. 637 to establish a petty cash fund with a $300 balance.
       1 Issued check no. 344 to pay voucher no. 637.
       2 Journalized the day's cash sales. Cash register tapes show a $2,859 total, but the cash in the register is only $2,853.
      10 The petty cash fund has $169 in cash and $131 in petty cash tickets issued to pay for Office Supplies ($61), Delivery Expense ($23), and Entertainment Expense ($47). Issued voucher no. 669 to replenish the fund.
      10 Issued check no. 402 to pay voucher no. 669.

Problems   *(Group A)*

Problem 7-1A *Identifying the characteristics of an effective internal control system* **(L.O. 1)**

Nassar Real Estate Development Company prospered during the lengthy economic expansion of the 1980s. Business was so good that the company bothered with few internal controls. The recent decline in the local real estate

No check figure

No check figure

No check figure

market, however, has caused Nassar to experience a shortage of cash. Abraham Nassar, the company owner, is looking for ways to save money.

Required

As controller of the company, write a memorandum to convince Mr. Nassar of the company's need for a system of internal control. Be specific in telling him how an internal control system could possibly lead to saving money. Include the definition of internal control, and briefly discuss each characteristic beginning with competent and reliable personnel.

Problem 7-2A   *Identifying internal control weaknesses*   *(L.O. 2, 4, 5)*

No check figure

Each of the following situations has an internal control weakness.

a. Jack Kiger owns a firm that performs engineering services. His staff consists of twelve professional engineers, and he manages the office. Often his work requires him to travel to meet with clients. During the past six months he has observed that when he returns from a business trip, the engineering jobs in the office have not progressed satisfactorily. He learns that when he is away several of his senior employees take over office management and neglect their engineering duties. One employee could manage the office.

b. Marta Frazier has been an employee of Griffith's Shoe Store for many years. Because the business is relatively small, Marta performs all accounting duties, including opening the mail, preparing the bank deposit, and preparing the bank reconciliation.

c. Most large companies have internal audit staffs that continuously evaluate the business's internal control. Part of the auditor's job is to evaluate how efficiently the company is running. For example, is the company purchasing inventory from the least expensive wholesaler? After a particularly bad year, Mason Tile Company eliminates its internal audit department to reduce expenses.

d. CPA firms, law firms, and other professional organizations use paraprofessional employees to do some of their routine tasks. For example, an accounting paraprofessional might examine documents to assist a CPA in conducting an audit. In the CPA firm of Grosso & Howe, Lou Grosso, the senior partner, turns over a significant portion of his high-level audit work to his paraprofessional staff.

e. In evaluating the internal control over cash disbursements, an auditor learns that the purchasing agent is responsible for purchasing diamonds for use in the company's manufacturing process, approving the invoices for payment, and signing the checks. No supervisor reviews the purchasing agent's work.

Required

1. Identify the missing internal control characteristic in each situation.
2. Identify the business's possible problem.
3. Propose a solution to the problem.

Problem 7-3A   *Identifying internal control weakness*   *(L.O. 2)*

No check figure

Rocky Mountain Supply Co. makes all sales on credit. Cash receipts arrive by mail, usually within 30 days of the sale. Jan Sharp opens envelopes and separates the checks from the accompanying remittance advices. Sharp forwards the checks to another employee who makes the daily bank deposit but has no access to the accounting records. Sharp sends the remittance advices, which show the amount of cash received, to the accounting department for entry in the accounts. Sharp's only other duty is to grant sales allowances to customers. When she receives a customer check for less than the full amount of the invoice, she records the sales allowance and forwards the document to the accounting department.

Required

You are the outside auditor of Rocky Mountain Supply Co. Write a memo to the company president to identify the internal control weakness in this situation. State how to correct the weakness.

Adj. book bal. $6,293.33

Problem 7-4A *Bank reconciliation and related journal entries* (L.O. 3)

The August 31 bank statement of Master Control Company has just arrived from United Bank. To prepare the Master Control bank reconciliation, you gather the following data:

1. Master Control's Cash account shows a balance of $5,616.14 on August 31.
2. The bank statement includes two charges for returned checks from customers. One is a $395.00 check received from Shoreline Express and deposited on August 20, returned by Shoreline's bank with the imprint "Unauthorized Signature." The other is an NSF check in the amount of $146.67 received from Lipsey, Inc. This check had been deposited on August 17.
3. The following Master Control checks are outstanding at August 31:

Check No.	Amount
237	$ 46.10
288	141.00
291	578.05
293	11.87
294	609.51
295	8.88
296	101.63

4. The bank statement includes a deposit of $1,191.17, collected by the bank on behalf of Master Control. Of the total, $1,011.81 is collection of a note receivable, and the remainder is interest revenue.
5. The bank statement shows that Master Control earned $38.19 of interest on its bank balance during August. This amount was added to Master Control's account by the bank.
6. The bank statement lists a $10.50 subtraction for the bank service charge.
7. On August 31 the Master Control treasurer deposited $306.15, but this deposit does not appear on the bank statement.
8. The bank statement includes a $300.00 deposit that Master Control did not make. The bank had erroneously credited the Master Control account for another bank customer's deposit.
9. The August 31 bank balance is $7,784.22.

Required

1. Prepare the bank reconciliation for Master Control Company at August 31.
2. Record in general journal form the entries necessary to bring the book balance of Cash into agreement with the adjusted book balance on the reconciliation. Include an explanation for each entry.

Assume selected columns of the cash receipts journal and the check register of Hard Rock Cafe appear as follows at April 30, 19X4:

Cash Receipts Journal (Posting reference is CR)		Check Register (Posting reference is CD)	
Date	Cash Debit	Check No.	Cash Credit
Apr. 2	$ 4,174	3113	$ 991
8	407	3114	147
10	559	3115	1,930
16	2,187	3116	664
22	1,854	3117	1,472
29	1,060	3118	1,000
30	37	3119	632
Total	$10,578	3120	1,675
		3121	100
		3122	2,413
		Total	$11,024

Assume the Cash account of Hard Rock Cafe shows the following information at April 30, 19X4.

Cash

Date	Item	Jrnl. Ref.	Debit	Credit	Balance
Apr. 1	Balance				7,911
30		CR.6	10,578		18,489
30		CD.11		11,024	7,465

Hard Rock Cafe received the following bank statement on April 30, 19X4.

Bank Statement for April 19X4

Beginning balance		$ 7,911
Deposits and other Credits:		
Apr. 4..........................	$4,174	
9..........................	407	
12..........................	559	
17..........................	2,187	
22..........................	1,368 BC	
23..........................	1,854	10,549
Checks and other Debits:		
Apr. 7..........................	$ 991	
13..........................	1,390	
14..........................	903 US	
15..........................	147	
18..........................	664	
26..........................	1,472	
30..........................	1,000	
30..........................	20 SC	6,587
Ending Balance..........................		$11,873

Explanation: BC—Bank Collection   US—Unauthorized Signature
SC—Service Charge

Additional data for the bank reconciliation include:

1. The unauthorized signature check was received from S. M. Holt.
2. The $1,368 bank collection of a note receivable on April 22 included $185 interest revenue.
3. The correct amount of check number 3115, a payment on account, is $1,390. (The Hard Rock Cafe accountant mistakenly recorded the check for $1,930.)

Required

1. Prepare the bank reconciliation of Hard Rock Cafe at April 30, 19X4.
2. Record the entries based on the bank reconciliation. Include explanations.

Net income, $39,500; Pur. disc. lost, net method, $946

Problem 7-6A *Recording and reporting purchases at gross and at net* *(L.O. 5)*

Dickens & Briscoe, a partnership, does not use a voucher system. On June 1 of the current year, the company had inventory of $71,300. On June 30 the company had inventory of $74,100. Net sales for June were $263,700, and operating expenses were $106,200. During June, Dickens & Briscoe completed the following transactions:

June 2 Purchased inventory costing $41,800 under terms of 2/10 n/30.
      8 Returned $5,800 of the inventory purchased on June 2.
   11 Purchased inventory costing $39,000 on credit terms of 2/10 n/45.
   11 Paid the amount owed from the June 2 invoice, net of the return on June 8.
   17 Purchased inventory costing $47,300 on credit terms of 2/10 n/30.
   20 Paid for the inventory purchased on June 11.
   30 Paid for the purchase on June 17.

Required

1. Assuming Dickens & Briscoe records inventory purchases at gross cost:
    a. Record the transactions in a general journal. Explanations are not required.
    b. Prepare the company's income statement for June of the current year.
2. Assuming Dickens & Briscoe records inventory purchases at net cost:
    a. Record the transactions in a general journal. Explanations are not required.
    b. Prepare the company's income statement for June of the current year.
3. Which method of recording purchases offers the internal control advantage? Give your reason.

No check figure

Problem 7-7A *Accounting for petty cash transactions* *(L.O. 5,6)*

Suppose that on June 1 Hitachi Electronics opens a district office in Little Rock and creates a petty cash fund with an imprest balance of $350. During June, Sharon Dietz, the fund custodian, signs the following petty cash tickets:

Ticket Number	Item	Amount
1	Postage for package received	$ 8.40
2	Decorations and refreshments for office party	13.19
3	Two boxes of floppy disks	16.82
4	Typewriter ribbons	27.13
5	Dinner money for sales manager entertaining a customer	50.00
6	Plane ticket for executive business trip to Memphis	69.00
7	Delivery of package across town	6.30

On June 30, prior to replenishment, the fund contains these tickets plus $173.51. The accounts affected by petty cash disbursements are Office Supplies Expense, Travel Expense, Delivery Expense, Entertainment Expense, and Postage Expense.

Required

1. Explain the characteristics and the internal control features of an imprest fund.
2. Make the general journal entries to create the fund and to replenish it. Include explanations. Also, briefly describe what the custodian does on these dates.
3. Make the entry on July 1 to increase the fund balance to $500. Include an explanation, and briefly describe what the custodian does.

Problem 7-8A *Voucher system entries* (L.O. 7)

Assume a ComputerGraphics store in Dallas, Texas, uses a voucher system and records purchases at *gross* cost. Assume further that the store completed the following transactions during January:

Vouchers Payable, Jan. 31, $17,425

Jan. 3 Issued voucher no. 135 payable to Bell Telephone for telephone service of $1,007.

5 Issued voucher no. 136 payable to IBM for the purchase of inventory costing $15,500, with payment terms of 3/10 n/30.

6 Issued voucher no. 137 payable to City Supply Company for inventory costing $250, with payment terms of 2/10 n/45.

7 Issued check no. 404 to pay voucher no. 136.

10 Issued check no. 405 to pay voucher no. 135.

14 Issued check no. 406 to pay voucher no. 137.

15 Issued voucher no. 138 payable to the *Dallas Morning News* for advertising of $1,990.

17 Issued voucher no. 139 payable to replenish the petty cash fund. The payee is Petty Cash, and the petty cash tickets list Store Supplies ($16), Delivery Expense ($96), and Miscellaneous Expense ($64). Also issued check no. 407 to pay the voucher.

18 Issued voucher no. 140 payable to Apple Computer Company for inventory costing $27,600, with payment terms of 2/10 n/30.

24 Issued voucher no. 141 payable to city of Dallas for property tax of $4,235.

27 Issued voucher no. 142 payable to First State Bank for payment of a note payable ($10,000) and interest expense ($1,200).

30 Issued check no. 408 to pay voucher no. 140.

31 Issued voucher no. 143 to pay salesperson salary of $2,309 to Lester Gibbs. Also issued check no. 409 to pay the voucher.

Vouchers Payable, Jan. 31, $17,425

Required

1. Record ComputerGraphics' transactions in a voucher register and a check register like those illustrated in the chapter. Posting references are unnecessary.
2. Open the Vouchers Payable account and post amounts to that account.
3. Prepare the list of unpaid vouchers at January 31 and show that the total matches the balance of Vouchers Payable.

Problem 7-9A *Voucher system; purchases at net* **(L.O. 7)**

Assume that the ComputerGraphics store in Problem 7-8A records its purchases of inventory at *net* cost.

Required

1. Record the transactions of Problem 7-8A in a voucher register and a check register. To account for purchase discounts lost, it is necessary to use a check register designed as follows:

				Check Register		Page 4
				Debit		Credit
Date	Check No.	Payee	Voucher No.	Vouchers Payable	Purchase Discounts Lost	Cash in Bank

2. Post to the Vouchers Payable account.
3. Prepare the list of unpaid vouchers at January 31, and show that the total matches the balance of Vouchers Payable.

(Group B)

No check figure

Problem 7-1B *Identifying the characteristics of an effective internal control system* **(L.O. 1)**

An employee of McNemar Aircraft Service Company recently stole thousands of dollars of the company's cash. The company has decided to install a new system of internal controls.

Required

As controller of McNemar Aircraft Service Company, write a memo to the president explaining how a separation of duties helps to safeguard assets.

No check figure

Problem 7-2B *Identifying internal control weaknesses* **(L.O. 2,4,5)**

Each of the following situations has an internal control weakness:

a. Discount stores such as Walmart and Meier's receive a large portion of their sales revenue in cash, with the remainder in credit-card sales. To reduce expenses, a store manager ceases purchasing fidelity bonds on the cashiers.

b. The office supply company from which Toland Sporting Goods purchases cash receipt forms recently notified Toland that the last shipped receipts were not prenumbered. Dick Toland, the owner, replied that he did not use the receipt numbers, so the omission is not important.

c. Lancer Computer Programs is a software company that specializes in computer programs with accounting applications. The company's most popular program prepares the general journal, cash receipts journal, voucher register, check register, accounts receivable subsidiary ledger, and general ledger. In the company's early days, the owner and eight employees wrote the computer programs, lined up manufacturers to produce the diskettes, sold the products to stores such as ComputerLand and ComputerCraft, and performed the general management and accounting of the company. As the company has grown, the number of employees has increased dramatically. Recently, the development of a new software program stopped while the programmers redesigned Lancer's accounting system. Lancer's own accountants could have performed this task.

d. Myra Jones, a widow with no known sources of outside income, has been a trusted employee of Stone Products Company for 15 years. She performs all cash-handling and accounting duties, including opening the mail, preparing the bank deposit, accounting for all aspects of cash and accounts receivable, and preparing the bank reconciliation. She has just purchased a new Cadillac and a new home in an expensive suburb. Lou Stone, the owner of the company, wonders how she can afford these luxuries on her salary.

e. Linda Cyert employs three professional interior designers in her design studio. She is located in an area with a lot of new construction, and her business is booming. Ordinarily, Linda does all the purchasing of furniture, draperies, carpets, fabrics, sewing services, and other materials and labor needed to complete jobs. During the summer she takes a long vacation, and in her absence she allows each designer to purchase materials and labor. At her return, Cyert reviews operations and notes that expenses are much higher and net income much lower than in the past.

Required

1. Identify the missing internal control characteristic in each situation.
2. Identify the business's possible problem.
3. Propose a solution to the problem.

Problem 7-3B *Identifying internal control weakness* **(L.O. 2)**

No check figure

Appalachian Dental Supply makes all sales on credit. Cash receipts arrive by mail, usually within 30 days of the sale. Brad Stokes opens envelopes and separates the checks from the accompanying remittance advices. Stokes forwards the checks to another employee who makes the daily bank deposit but has no access to the accounting records. Stokes sends the remittance advices, which show the amount of cash received, to the accounting department for entry in the accounts. Stokes's only other duty is to grant sales allowances to customers. When he receives a customer check for less than the full amount of the invoice, he records the sales allowance and forwards the document to the accounting department.

Required

You are the outside auditor of Appalachian Dental Supply. Write a memo to the company president to identify the internal control weakness in this situation. State how to correct the weakness.

Problem 7-4B *Bank reconciliation and related journal entries* **(L.O. 3)**

Adj. book bal. $4,168.77

The May 31 bank statement of Pressler Institute has just arrived from Central Bank. To prepare the Pressler bank reconciliation, you gather the following data:

1. The May 31 bank balance is $4,330.82.
2. The bank statement includes two charges for returned checks from customers. One is an NSF check in the amount of $67.50 received from Harley Doherty, a customer, recorded on the books by a debit to Cash, and deposited on May 19. The other is a $195.03 check received from Maria Gucci and deposited on May 21. It was returned by Ms. Gucci's bank with the imprint "Unauthorized Signature."
3. The following Pressler checks are outstanding at May 31:

Check No.	Amount
616	$403.00
802	74.25
806	36.60
809	161.38
810	229.05
811	48.91

4. The bank statement includes two special deposits: $899.14, which is the amount of dividend revenue the bank collected from General Electric Company on behalf of Pressler; and $16.86, the interest revenue Pressler earned on its bank balance during May.
5. The bank statement lists a $6.25 subtraction for the bank service charge.
6. On May 31 the Pressler treasurer deposited $381.14, but this deposit does not appear on the bank statement.
7. The bank statement includes a $410.00 deduction for a check drawn by Marimont Freight Company. Pressler promptly notified the bank of its error.
8. Pressler's Cash account shows a balance of $3,521.55 on May 31.

Required

1. Prepare the bank reconciliation for Pressler Institute at May 31.
2. Record in general journal form the entries necessary to bring the book balance of Cash into agreement with the adjusted book balance on the reconciliation. Include an explanation for each entry.

Adj. book bal. $12,425

Problem 7-5B *Bank reconciliation and related journal entries* **(L.O. 3)**

Selected columns of the cash receipts journal and the check register of Gulf Resources appear as follows at March 31, 19X5:

Cash Receipts Journal (Posting reference is CR)		Check Register (Posting reference is CD)	
Date	Cash Debit	Check No.	Cash Credit
Mar. 4	$2,716	1413	$ 1,465
9	544	1414	1,004
11	1,655	1415	450
14	896	1416	8
17	367	1417	775
25	890	1418	88
31	2,038	1419	4,126
Total	$9,106	1420	930
		1421	200
		1422	2,267
		Total	$11,313

Assume the Cash account of Gulf Resources shows the following information on March 31, 19X5.

Cash

Date	Item	Jrnl. Ref.	Debit	Credit	Balance
Mar. 1	Balance				14,188
31		CR. 10	9,106		23,294
31		CD. 16		11,313	11,981

Gulf Resources received the following bank statement on March 31, 19X5.

Bank Statement for March 19X5

Beginning balance		$14,188
Deposits and other Credits:		
Mar. 5	$2,716	
10	544	
11	1,655	
15	896	
18	367	
25	890	
31	1,000 BC	8,068
Checks and other Debits:		
Mar. 8	$ 441 NSF	
9	1,465	
13	1,004	
14	450	
15	8	
22	775	
29	88	
31	4,216	
31	25 SC	8,472
Ending balance		$13,784

Explanation: BC—Bank Collection   NSF—Nonsufficient Fund Check
SC—Service Charge

Additional data for the bank reconciliation include:

1. The NSF check was received late in February from L. M. Arnett.
2. The $1,000 bank collection of a note receivable on March 31 included $122 interest revenue.
3. The correct amount of check number 1419, a payment on account, is $4,216. (The Gulf Resources accountant mistakenly recorded the check for $4,126.)

Required

1. Prepare the bank reconciliation of Gulf Resources at March 31, 19X5.
2. Record the entries based on the bank reconciliation. Include explanations.

Problem 7-6B *Recording and reporting purchases at gross and at net* **(L.O. 5)**

Advanced Design, Inc., does not use a voucher system. On May 1 of the current year the company had inventory of $58,000. On May 31 the company had inventory of $53,700. Net sales for May were $212,800, and operating expenses were $65,100. During May Advanced Design completed the following transactions:

May 3 Purchased inventory costing $38,500 under terms of 2/10 n/30.
     7 Returned $2,000 of the inventory purchased on May 3.
    10 Purchased inventory costing $28,500 on credit terms of 2/10 n/45.
    12 Paid the amount owed from the May 3 invoice, net of the return on May 7.
    18 Purchased inventory costing $34,000 on credit terms of 2/10 n/30.
    19 Paid for the inventory purchased on May 10.
    29 Paid for the purchase on May 18.

Required

1. Assuming Advanced Design records inventory purchases at gross cost:
   a. Record the transactions in a general journal. Explanations are not required.
   b. Prepare the company's income statement for May of the current year.
2. Assuming Advanced Design records inventory purchases at net cost:
   a. Record the transactions in a general journal. Explanations are not required.
   b. Prepare the company's income statement for May of the current year.
3. Which method of recording purchases offers the internal control advantage? Give your reason.

Problem 7-7B *Accounting for petty cash transactions* **(L.O. 5, 6)**

Suppose that on April 1 IBM opens a regional office in Omaha and creates a petty cash fund with an imprest balance of $200. During April, Eleanor McGillicuddy, the fund custodian, signs the following petty cash tickets:

Ticket Number	Item	Amount
101	Pencils	$ 6.89
102	Cab fare for executive	25.00
103	Delivery of package across town	7.75
104	Dinner money for executives entertaining a customer	80.00
105	Postage for package received	10.00
106	Christmas decorations for office party	18.22
107	Two boxes of floppy disks	14.37

On April 30, prior to replenishment, the fund contains these tickets plus $34.77. The accounts affected by petty cash disbursements are Office Supplies Expense, Travel Expense, Delivery Expense, Entertainment Expense, and Postage Expense.

Required

1. Explain the characteristics and the internal control features of an imprest fund.
2. Make the general journal entries to create the fund and to replenish it. Include explanations. Also, briefly describe what the custodian does on these dates.

3. Make the entry on May 1 to increase the fund balance to $300. Include an explanation, and briefly describe what the custodian does.

Problem 7-8B   *Voucher system entries*   *(L.O. 7)*

Vouchers Payable, July 31, $18,965

Assume Federated Stores, the department-store chain, uses a voucher system and records purchases at *gross cost*. Assume further that a Federated store completed the following transactions during July:

July 2 Issued voucher no. 614 payable to Hathaway Shirt Company for the purchase of inventory costing $21,000, with payment terms of 2/10 n/30.

3 Issued voucher no. 615 payable to Edison Electric for electricity usage of $2,589.

5 Issued check no. 344 to pay voucher no. 614.

6 Issued voucher no. 616 payable to Baylor Supply Company for inventory costing $850, with payment terms of 2/10 n/45.

7 Issued check no. 345 to pay voucher no. 615.

13 Issued voucher no. 617 payable to replenish the petty cash fund. The payee is Petty Cash, and the petty cash tickets list store supplies ($119), delivery expense ($48), and miscellaneous expense ($36). Also issued check no. 346 to pay the voucher.

14 Issued check no. 347 to pay voucher no. 616.

18 Issued voucher no. 618 payable to the *New York Times* for advertising, $2,800.

19 Issued voucher no. 619 payable to Levi Strauss & Company for inventory costing $65,800, with payment terms of 3/10 n/30.

28 Issued voucher no. 620 payable to city of New York for property tax of $9,165.

30 Issued check no. 348 to pay voucher no. 619.

31 Issued voucher no. 621 payable to Maine Bank for interest expense of $7,000.

31 Issued voucher no. 622 to pay executive salary of $4,644 to Sharon Kratzman. Also issued check no. 349 to pay the voucher.

Required

1. Record Federated's transactions in a voucher register and a check register like those illustrated in the chapter. Posting references are unnecessary.
2. Open the Vouchers Payable account with a zero beginning balance, and post amounts to that account.
3. Prepare the list of unpaid vouchers at July 31 and show that the total matches the balance of Vouchers Payable.

Problem 7-9B   *Voucher system; purchases at net*   *(L.O. 7)*

Vouchers Payable, July 31, $18,965

Assume that the Federated store in Problem 7-8B records its purchases of inventory at *net* cost.

Required

1. Record the transactions of Problem 7-8B in a voucher register and a check register. To account for purchase discounts lost, it is necessary to use a check register designed as follows:

Check Register

				Debit		Credit
					Purchase	
	Check		Voucher	Vouchers	Discounts	Cash in
Date	No.	Payee	No.	Payable	Lost	Bank

2. Post to the Vouchers Payable account.
3. Prepare the list of unpaid vouchers at July 31 and show that the total matches the balance of Vouchers Payable.

Extending Your Knowledge

Decision Problems

Adj. bank bal., $19,158;
Adj. book bal., $19,658

1. Using the Bank Reconciliation to Detect a Theft (L.O. 3)

Agricultural Equipment Company has poor internal control over its cash transactions. Recently Grace Goodrich, the owner, has suspected the cashier of stealing. Details of the business's cash position at September 30 follow.

1. The Cash account shows a balance of $19,502. This amount includes a September 30 deposit of $3,794 that does not appear on the September 30 bank statement.
2. The September 30 bank statement shows a balance of $16,424. The bank statement lists a $200 credit for a bank collection, an $8 debit for the service charge, and a $36 debit for an NSF check. The Agricultural Equipment accountant has not recorded any of these items on the books.
3. At September 30 the following checks are outstanding:

Check No.	Amount
154	$116
256	150
278	253
291	190
292	206
293	145

4. The cashier handles all incoming cash and makes bank deposits. He also reconciles the monthly bank statement. His September 30 reconciliation follows.

Balance per books, September 30		$19,502
Add: Outstanding checks		560
Bank collection		200
		20,262
Less: Deposits in transit	$3,794	
Service charge	8	
NSF check	36	3,838
Balance per bank, September 30		$16,424

Goodrich has requested that you determine whether the cashier has stolen cash from the business and, if so, how much. Goodrich also asks you to identify how the cashier has attempted to conceal the theft. To make this determination, you perform your own bank reconciliation using the format illustrated in the chapter. There are no bank or book errors. Goodrich also asks you to evaluate the internal controls and to recommend any changes needed to improve them.

2. The role of Internal Control (L.O. 2)

The following questions are unrelated except that they all pertain to internal control.

No check figure

1. Separation of duties is an important consideration if a system of internal control is to be effective. Why is this so?
2. Cash may be a relatively small item on the financial statements. Nevertheless, internal control over cash is very important. Why do you think this is true?
3. Archer Ltd. requires that all documents supporting a check be canceled by the person who signs the check. Why do you think this practice is required? What might happen if it were not required?
4. Many managers think that safeguarding assets is the most important objective of internal control systems. Auditors, on the other hand, emphasize reliable accounting data. Explain why auditors are more concerned about the quality of the accounting records.

Ethical Issue

Phil Esposito owns apartment buildings in California, Nevada, and Utah. Each property has a manager who collects rent, arranges for repairs, and runs advertisements in the local newspaper. The property managers transfer cash to Esposito monthly and prepare their own bank reconciliations. The manager in Las Vegas has been stealing large sums of money. To cover the theft, he understates the amount of the outstanding checks on the monthly bank reconciliation. As a result, each monthly bank reconciliation appears to balance. However, the balance sheet reports more cash than Esposito actually has in the bank. In negotiating the sale of the Las Vegas property, Esposito is showing the balance sheet to prospective investors.

Required:

1. Identify two parties other than Esposito who can be harmed by this theft. In what ways can they be harmed?
2. Discuss the role accounting plays in this situation.

Financial Statement Problems

1. Internal Controls and Cash (L.O. 1)

No check figure

Study the Goodyear responsibility statement and the audit opinion of The Goodyear Tire & Rubber Company's financial statement, given at the end of Appendix C. Answer the following questions about Goodyear's internal controls and cash position.

1. What is the name of Goodyear's outside auditing firm? What office of this firm signed the audit report? How long after Goodyear's year end did the auditors issue their opinion?

2. Who bears primary responsibility for the financial statements? How can you tell?
3. Does it appear that the Goodyear's internal controls are adequate? How can you tell?
4. What standard of auditing did the outside auditors use in examining the Goodyear financial statements? By what accounting standards were the statements evaluated?
5. By how much did Goodyear's cash position change during 1990? The statement of cash flows (discussed in detail in a later chapter) tells why this increase occurred. Which type of activity—operating, investing, or financing—contributed most to this increase?

No check figure

2. *Audit Opinion, Management Responsibility, Internal Controls, and Cash* (L.O. 1)

Obtain the annual report of an actual company of your choosing. Study the audit opinion and the management statement of responsibility (if present) in conjunction with the financial statements. Answer these questions about the company.

1. What is the name of the company's outside auditing firm? What office of this firm signed the audit report? How long after the company's year end did the auditors issue their opinion?
2. Who bears primary responsibility for the financial statements? How can you tell?
3. Does it appear that the company's internal controls are adequate? Give your reason.
4. What standard of auditing did the outside auditors use in examining the company's financial statements? By what accounting standards were the statements evaluated?
5. By how much did the company's cash position (including cash equivalents) change during the current year? The statement of cash flows (discussed in a later chapter) tells why this increase occurred. Which type of activity—operating, investing, or financing—contributed most to the change in the cash balance?
6. Where is the balance of petty cash reported? Name the financial statement and the account, and identify the specific amount that includes petty cash.

Comprehensive Problem for Part Two

Total assetes, $117,727

Complete Accounting Cycle for a Merchandising Entity; Special Journals

J. T. McCord Company closes its books and prepares financial statements at the end of each month. The company completed the following transactions during August:

Aug. 1 Issued check no. 682 for August office rent of $2,000. (Debit Rent Expense.)

Aug. 2 Issued check no. 683 to pay salaries of $1,240, which includes salary payable of $930 from July 31. McCord does *not* use reversing entries.

2 Issued invoice no. 503 for sale on account to R. T. Loeb, $600.

3 Purchased inventory on credit terms of 1/15 n/60 from Grant Publishers, $1,400.

4 Received net amount of cash on account from Fullam Company, $2,156, within the discount period.

4 Sold inventory for cash, $330.

5 Issued credit memo no. 267 to Park-Hee, Inc., for merchandise returned to McCord, $550.

5 Issued check no. 684 to purchase supplies for cash, $780.

6 Collected interest revenue of $1,100.

7 Issued invoice no. 504 for sale on account to K. D. Skipper, $2,400.

8 Issued check no. 685 to pay Federal Company $2,600 of the amount owed at July 31. This payment occurred after the end of the discount period.

11 Issued check no. 686 to pay Grant Publishers the net amount owed from August 3.

12 Received cash from R. T. Loeb in full settlement of her account receivable from August 2.

16 Issued check no. 687 to pay salary expense of $1,240.

19 Purchased inventory for cash, $850, issuing check no. 688.

22 Purchased furniture on credit terms of 3/15 n/60 from Beaver Corporation, $510.

23 Sold inventory on account to Fullam Company, issuing invoice no. 505 for $9,966.

24 Received half the July 31 amount receivable from K. D. Skipper— after the end of the discount period.

25 Issued check no. 689 to pay utilities, $432.

26 Purchased supplies on credit terms of 2/10 n/30 from Federal Company, $180.

30 Returned damaged inventory to company from whom McCord made the cash purchase on August 19, receiving cash of $850.

30 Granted a sales allowance of $175 to K. D. Skipper, issuing credit memo no. 268.

31 Purchased inventory on credit terms of 1/10 n/30 from Suncrest Supply, $8,330.

31 Issued check no. 690 to J. T. McCord, owner of the business, for personal withdrawal, $1,700.

Required:

1. Open these accounts with their account numbers and July 31 balances in the various ledgers.

General Ledger:

101	Cash	$ 4,490
102	Accounts Receivable	22,560
104	Interest Receivable	
105	Inventory	41,800
109	Supplies	1,340
117	Prepaid Insurance	2,200

140	Note Receivable, Long-term	11,000
160	Furniture	37,270
161	Accumulated Depreciation	10,550
201	Accounts Payable	12,600
204	Salary Payable	930
207	Interest Payable	320
208	Unearned Sales Revenue	
220	Note Payable, Long-term	42,000
301	J. T. McCord, Capital	54,260
302	J. T. McCord, Withdrawals	
400	Income Summary	
401	Sales Revenue	
402	Sales Discounts	
403	Sales Returns and Allowances	
410	Interest Revenue	
501	Purchases	
502	Purchase Discounts	
503	Purchase Returns and Allowances	
510	Salary Expense	
513	Rent Expense	
514	Depreciation Expense	
516	Insurance Expense	
517	Utilities Expense	
519	Supplies Expense	
523	Interest Expense	

Accounts Receivable Subsidiary Ledger: Fullam Company, $2,200; R. T. Loeb; Park-Hee, Inc., $11,590; K. D. Skipper, $8,770.

Accounts Payable Subsidiary Ledger: Beaver Corporation; Federal Company, $12,600; Grant Publishers; Suncrest Supply.

2. Journalize the August transactions in a sales journal (page 4), a cash receipts journal (page 11), a purchases journal (page 8), a cash disbursements journal (page 5), and a general journal (page 9). Use the journals as illustrated in Chapter 6. McCord makes all credit sales on terms of 2/10 n/30.

3. Post daily to the accounts receivable subsidiary ledger and the accounts payable subsidiary ledger. On August 31, post to the general ledger.

4. Prepare a trial balance in the Trial Balance columns of a work sheet, and use the following information to complete the work sheet for the month ended August 31:

a. Accrued interest revenue, $100.

b. Supplies on hand, $990.

c. Prepaid insurance expired, $550.

d. Depreciation expense, $230.

e. Accrued salary expense, $1,030.

f. Accrued interest expense, $320.

g. Unearned sales revenue, $450.*

h. Inventory on hand, $47,700.

*Sales revenue was credited when collected in advance. At August 31, $450 of unearned sales revenue needs to be recorded.

5. Prepare J. T. McCord Company's bank reconciliation at August 31. The bank statement shows a cash balance of $2,863 and lists all cash receipts for the month except the amount received on the 30th. Checks 689 and 690 did not clear the bank during August. The bank statement also reveals a bank error. The bank mistakenly deducted $870 for check number 684. J. T. McCord Company keeps just enough money on deposit to avoid service charges but earns no interest on the bank balance.

6. Prepare McCord's multiple-step income statement and statement of owner's equity for August. Prepare the balance sheet at August 31.

7. Journalize and post the adjusting and closing entries.

8. Prepare a postclosing trial balance at August 31. Also, balance the total of the customer accounts in the accounts receivable subsidiary ledger against the Accounts Receivable balance in the general ledger. Do the same for the accounts payable subsidiary ledger and Accounts Payable in the general ledger.

Chapter 8

Accounts and Notes Receivable

An executive writes:

Most of us try not to run nonprofit businesses. Yet, by failing to collect money that is due us we allow our firms to be robbed of many dollars.

The National Association of Credit Management estimates that collection costs and inflation reduce the value of a current-account-receivable dollar to 67 cents when it is overdue six months, to 45 cents when it is overdue one year, and to 4 cents when it is overdue five years.

I used to be nervous about discussing payment terms with customers and rarely did it. The resulting abuse of my good nature and my pocketbook cured my shyness. Customers rarely hesitate to say what they expect from the services or goods they are considering. Neither should you hesitate to discuss the terms under which you will meet their needs.

Source: Scott Witmer, "Those Pesky Overdue Accounts," *Nation's Business*, February 1984, pp. 38–39.

From automobiles to houses to bicycles to dinners, people buy on credit every day. As high as annual credit sales for retailers are, credit sales are even higher for manufacturers and wholesalers. Clearly, credit sales lie at the heart of the United States economy, as they do in other developed countries.

Each credit transaction involves at least two parties—the **creditor,** who sells a service or merchandise and obtains a receivable, and the **debtor,** who makes the purchase and creates a payable. This chapter focuses on the creditor's accounting. The accounts that generally appear on a creditor's balance sheet are highlighted in Exhibit 8-1. We will discuss these accounts in our study of receivables.

Class Discussion: What is the major advantage of selling on credit? *ANSWER:* A company usually will have more sales because it is easier for customers to buy.

What is the major disadvantage of selling on credit? *ANSWER:* Some customers will pay late or not at all.

Different Types of Receivables

A receivable arises when a business (or person) sells goods or services to a second business (or person) on credit. A receivable is the seller's claim against the buyer for the amount of the transaction.

Receivables are monetary claims against businesses and individuals. They are acquired mainly by selling goods and services and by lending money.

The two major types of receivables are accounts receivable and notes receivable. A business's *accounts receivable* are the amounts that its customers owe it. These accounts receivable are sometimes called *trade receivables.* They are *current assets.*

Accounts receivable should be distinguished from accruals, notes, and other assets not arising from everyday sales because accounts receivable pertain to the main thrust of the business's operations. Moreover, amounts included as accounts receivable should be collectible according to the business's normal receivables terms (such as net 30, or 2/10 n/30).

Notes receivable are more formal than accounts receivable. The debtor in a note receivable arrangement promises in writing to pay the creditor a definite sum at a definite future date. The terms of these notes usually extend for at least 60 days. A written document known as a *promissory note* serves as evidence of the receivable. A note may require the debtor to pledge *security* for the loan. This means that the borrower promises that the lender may claim certain assets if the borrower fails to pay the amount due at maturity.

Notes receivable due within one year or less are *current assets.* Those notes due beyond one year are *long-term receivables.* Some notes receivable are collected in periodic installments. The portion due within one year is a current asset, with the remaining amount a long-term asset. GM may hold a $6,000

Point to Stress: Trade Accounts Receivable do not include amounts due from employees or officers (Receivables from Employees). Trade Accounts Receivable are amounts due from customers that arise only from selling goods or services.

EXHIBIT 8-1 *Balance Sheet*

Example Company
Balance Sheet
Date

Assets

Current:

Cash	$X,XXX
Accounts receivable .... **$X,XXX**	
Less Allowance for	
uncollectible accounts **(XXX)**	X,XXX
Notes receivable, short-term	X,XXX
Inventories	X,XXX
Prepaid expenses	X,XXX
Total	X,XXX

Investments and long-term receivables:

Investments in other companies	X,XXX
Notes receivable, long-term	X,XXX
Other receivables	X,XXX
Total	X,XXX

Plant assets:

Property, plant, and equipment	X,XXX
Total assets	$X,XXX

Liabilities

Current:

Accounts payable	$X,XXX
Notes payable, short-term ...	X,XXX
Accrued current liabilities ...	X,XXX
Total current liabilities	X,XXX

Long-term:

Notes payable, long-term	X,XXX
Total liabilities..............	X,XXX

Owner's Equity

Capital	X,XXX
Total liabilities and owner's equity	$X,XXX

note receivable from you, but only the $1,500 you owe on it this year is a current asset to GM.

Other receivables is a miscellaneous category that includes loans to employees and branch companies. Usually these are long-term assets, but they are current if receivable within one year or less. Long-term notes receivable, and other receivables, are often reported on the balance sheet after current assets and before plant assets as shown in Exhibit 8-1 and by The Goodyear Tire & Rubber Company in Appendix C.

Each type of receivable is a separate account in the general ledger and may be supported by a subsidiary ledger if needed.

The Credit Department

A customer who buys goods using a credit card is buying on account. This transaction creates a receivable for the store. Most companies with a high proportion of sales on account have a separate credit department. This department evaluates customers who apply for credit cards by using standard formulas—which include the applicant's income and credit history, among other factors—for deciding which customers the store will sell to on account. After approving a customer, the credit department monitors customer payment records. Customers with a history of paying on time may receive higher credit limits. Those who fail to pay on time have their limits reduced or eliminated.

The goal is to cut losses from noncollection of receivables, as indicated in the chapter-opening vignette. The credit department also assists the accounting department in measuring collection losses on customers who do not pay.

Uncollectible Accounts (Bad Debts)

Selling on credit creates both a benefit and a cost. Customers may be unwilling or unable to pay cash immediately and may make a purchase on credit. Revenue and profit rise as sales increase. The cost to the seller of extending credit arises from the failure to collect from some credit customers. Accountants label this cost **uncollectible account expense, doubtful account expense,** or **bad debt expense.**

The extent of uncollectible account expense varies from company to company. In the opening vignette, a six-month-old receivable of $1 is worth only 67 cents. A five-year-old receivable of $1 is worth only 4 cents. Uncollectible account expense depends on the credit risks that managers are willing to accept. Many small retail businesses accept a higher level of risk than do large stores like Sears. Why? Small businesses often have personal ties to customers, which increases the likelihood that customers will pay their accounts.

Measuring Uncollectible Accounts

For a firm that sells on credit, uncollectible account expense is as much a part of doing business as salary expense and depreciation expense. Uncollectible Account Expense—an operating expense—must be measured, recorded, and reported. To do so, accountants use the allowance method or the direct write-off method.

Allowance Method.   To present the most accurate financial statements possible, accountants in firms with large credit sales use the **allowance method** of measuring bad debts. This method records collection losses based on estimates instead of waiting to see which customers the business will not collect from.

Smart managers know that not every customer will pay in full. But at the time of sale, managers do not know which customers will not pay. Managers do not simply credit Accounts Receivable to write off a customer's account until the business has exhausted its collection effort.

Rather than try to guess which accounts will go bad, managers, based on collection experience, estimate the total bad debt expense for the period. The business debits Uncollectible Account Expense (or Doubtful Account Expense) for the estimated amount and credits **Allowance for Uncollectible Accounts** (or **Allowance for Doubtful Accounts**), a contra account related to Accounts Receivable. This account shows the estimated amount of collection losses.

To properly match expense against revenue, the uncollectible account expense is estimated—based on past collection experience—and recorded as an adjusting entry during the same period that the sales are made. This expense entry has two effects: (1) it decreases net income by debiting an expense account, and (2) it decreases *net* accounts receivable by crediting the allowance account. (Allowance for Uncollectible Accounts, the contra account, is subtracted from Accounts Receivable to measure *net* accounts receivable.)

Assume the company's sales for 19X1 are $240,000 and that past collection experience suggests estimated bad debt expense of $3,100 for the year. The

19X1 journal entries are as follows, with accounts receivable from customers Rolf and Anderson separated for emphasis:

19X1	Accounts Receivable—Rolf	1,300	
	Accounts Receivable—Anderson	1,700	
	Accounts Receivable—Various Customers....	237,000	
	Sales Revenue		240,000
	To record credit sales.		

19X1	Uncollectible Account Expense	3,100	
	Allowance for Uncollectible Accounts....		3,100
	To record estimated bad debt expense, based on past collection experience.		

The account balances at December 31, 19X1, are as follows:

Accounts Receivable	Allowance for Uncollectible Accounts	Sales Revenue	Uncollectible Account Expense
240,000	3,100	240,000	3,100

Net accounts receivable
= $236,900

The 19X1 financial statements will report:

Income Statement:	**19X1**
Revenue:	
Sales revenue	$240,000
Expense:	
Uncollectible account expense	3,100

Balance Sheet:	**December 31, 19X1**
Current assets:	
Accounts receivable	$240,000
Less: Allowance for uncollectible accounts	3,100
Net accounts receivable	$236,900

Point to Stress: Allowance for Uncollectible Accounts is a valuation account. The net realizable value of accounts receivable is an estimate of what management expects to collect on the total of accounts receivable.

Accounts Receivable
− Allowance for Uncollectible
   Accounts
_____
Net Realizable Value (NRV)
   (or Net Accounts Receivable)

Class Exercise: Write on the board:

Accounts Receivable.... $90,000
− Allowance for
   Uncollectible Accounts −3,500
Net Realizable Value ... $86,500

Assume a $700 account receivable for Kathy Brown is written off. What is the net realizable value now? The journal entry to write off the account is:

Allowance for
   Uncollectible Accounts 700
Accounts
   Receivable—K. Brown   700

Writing off Uncollectible Accounts

During 19X2 the company collects on most of the accounts receivable. However, the credit department determines that customers Rolf and Anderson cannot pay the amounts they owe. The accountant writes off their receivables and makes the following entries:

19X2	Cash	235,000	
	Accounts Receivable—Various Customers		235,000
	To record collections on account.		

19X2 Allowance for Uncollectible Accounts........ 3,000

  Accounts Receivable—Rolf 1,300

  Accounts Receivable—Anderson 1,700

  To write off uncollectible accounts.

The write-off entry has no effect on net income because it includes no debit to an expense account. The entry also has no effect on *net* accounts receivable because both the Allowance account debited and the Accounts Receivable account credited are part of *net* accounts receivable. The account balances at December 31, 19X2, are as follows:

Accounts Receivable		Allowance for Uncollectible Accounts	
240,000	235,000	3,000	3,100
	1,300		
	1,700		100
2,000			

The financial statements for 19X1 and 19X2 will report the following. To highlight the matching of expense and revenue, we are assuming no sales are made in 19X2.

Income Statement:	19X1	19X2
Revenue:		
Sales revenue................................	$240,000	$ 0
Expense:		
Uncollectible account expense.................	3,100	0

	December 31,	
Balance Sheet:	19X1	19X2
Current assets:		
Accounts receivable	$240,000	$ 2,000
Less: Allowance for uncollectible accounts......	3,100	100
Net accounts receivable......................	$236,900	$ 1,900

Bad Debt Write-Offs Rarely Equal the Allowance for Uncollectibles

Bad debt write-offs of customer accounts are actual amounts due from customers, but the allowance amount is based on estimates. Write-offs equal the allowance only if the estimate of bad debts is perfect—a rare occurrence. Usually the difference between write-offs and the allowance is small, as shown in the preceding example. If the allowance is too large for one period, the estimate of bad debts for the next period can be cut back. If the allowance is too low, an adjusting entry debiting Uncollectible Account Expense and crediting Allowance for Uncollectible Accounts can be made at the end of the period. This credit brings the Allowance account to a realistic balance. Estimating uncollectibles will be discussed shortly.

Accounts Receivable	
90,000	700
89,300	

Allowance for Uncollectible Accounts	
700	3,500
	2,800

The NRV is the same $86,500:

Accounts Receivable ...	$89,300
− Allowance for Uncollectible Accounts	−2,800
NRV	$86,500

NRV does not change as a result of writing off a specific customer's account because the same amount is taken out of both Accounts Receivable and the contra account, Allowance for Uncollectible Accounts.

Point to Stress: Refer to the chapter-opening vignette. There is a cost associated with collecting an account late even if it is collected in full. As Scott Witmer indicates, the longer an account is outstanding the less likely the chance of collection. Also, when an account is past due, the seller does not have the cash to use in the business. This increases the seller's cost of doing business.

Typical Student Misconception: Students often try to record the collection of an account previously written off in one entry instead of the two that are illustrated here. If one entry were used, it would look like this:

Cash xx

  Allow. for Uncoll. Accts.   xx

The problem with recording the recovery in this way is that the customer's account in the subsidiary ledger would not reflect the recovery. It would appear as though the customer had never paid this particular account. With the two-entry method, the customer's account will show that the account receivable was recovered.

Recoveries of Uncollectible Accounts

When an account receivable is written off as uncollectible, the customer still has an obligation to pay. However, the likelihood of receiving cash is so low that the company ceases its collection effort and writes off the account. Such accounts are filed for use in future credit decisions. Some companies turn them over to an attorney for collection in the hope of recovering part of the receivable. To record a recovery, the accountant reverses the write-off and records the collection in the regular manner. The reversal of the write-off is needed to give the customer account receivable a debit balance.

Assume that the write-off of Rolf's account ($1,300) occurs in February 19X2. In August Rolf pays the account in full. The journal entries for this situation follow:

Teaching Tip: Follow through the entries to Rolf's subsidiary ledger account: first the credit sale, then the write-off, then the reversal of the write-off, and finally the credit to the account when Rolf pays in full. Notice that the customer's subsidiary account contains a complete credit history—an important feature of the subsidiary ledger system.

Feb. 19X2	To write off Rolf's account as uncollectible (same as above):		
	Allowance for Uncollectible Accounts	1,300	
	Accounts Receivable—Rolf		1,300
Aug. 19X2	To reinstate Rolf's account:		
	Accounts Receivable—Rolf	1,300	
	Allowance for Uncollectible Accounts		1,300
	To record collection from Rolf:		
	Cash	1,300	
	Accounts Receivable—Rolf		1,300

Transparency T8-1

Estimating Uncollectibles

The more accurate the estimate, the more reliable the information in the financial statements. How are bad debt estimates made? The most logical way to estimate bad debts is to look at the business's past records. Both the *percentage of sales* method and the *aging of accounts receivable* method use the company's collection experience.

Percentage of Sales. A popular method of estimating uncollectibles computes the expense as a percentage of total credit sales (or total sales). Uncollectible account expense is recorded as an adjusting entry at the end of the period.

OBJECTIVE 2
Estimate uncollectibles by the percentages of sales and the aging approaches

Basing its decision on figures from the last four periods, a business estimates that bad debt expense will be 2.5 percent of credit sales. If credit sales for 19X3 total $500,000, the adjusting entry to record bad debt expense for the year is

Adjusting Entries

Dec. 31	Uncollectible Account Expense ($500,000 × .025)	12,500	
	Allowance for Uncollectible Accounts . .		12,500

Point to Stress: The percentage-of-sales method is often referred to as the income statement approach to estimating bad debt expense because the entry is based on credit sales for the period (an income statement figure).

Under the percentage of sales method, the amount of this entry ignores the prior balance in Allowance for Uncollectible Accounts.

A business may change the percentage rate from year to year, depending on its collection experience. Suppose collections of accounts receivable in 19X4 are greater, and write-offs are less, than expected. The credit balance in Allowance for Uncollectible Accounts would be too large in relation to the debit balance of Accounts Receivable. How would the business change its bad debt percentage rate in this case? *Decreasing* the percentage rate would reduce the credit entry to the allowance account, and the allowance account balance would not grow too large.

New businesses, with no credit history on which to base their rates, may obtain estimated bad debt percentages from industry trade journals, government publications, and other sources of collection data.

Aging the Accounts. The second popular method of estimating bad debts is called **aging the accounts.** In this approach, individual accounts receivable are analyzed according to the length of time that they have been receivable from the customer. Performed manually, this is time-consuming. Computers greatly ease the burden. Schmidt Home Builders groups its accounts receivable into 30-day periods, as the accompanying table shows.

Transparency T8-2

Point to Stress: The aging-of-accounts method is often referred to as the balance sheet approach because the computation focuses on Accounts Receivable (a balance sheet figure).

| | Age of Account | | | | |
Customer Name	1–30 Days	31–60 Days	61–90 Days	Over 90 Days	Total Balance
Oxwall Tools Co. ...	$20,000				$ 20,000
Chicago Pneumatic Parts.............	10,000				10,000
Sarasota Pipe Corp. .		$13,000	$10,000		23,000
Seal Coatings, Inc. ...			3,000	$1,000	4,000
Other accounts*	39,000	12,000	2,000	2,000	55,000
Totals.............	$69,000	$25,000	$15,000	$3,000	$112,000
Estimated percentage uncollectible	0.1%	1%	5%	90%	
Allowance for Uncollectible Accounts.........	$69	$250	$750	$2,700	$3,769

* Each of the "Other accounts" would appear individually.

Schmidt bases the percentage figures on the company's collection experience. In the past, the business has collected all but 0.1 percent of accounts aged from 1 to 30 days, all but 1 percent of accounts aged 31 to 60 days, and so on.

The total amount receivable in each age group is multiplied by the appropriate percentage figure. For example, the $69,000 in accounts aged 1 to 30 days is multiplied by 0.1 percent (.001), which comes to $69. The total balance needed in the Allowance for Uncollectible Accounts—$3,769—is the sum of the amounts computed for the various groups ($69 + $250 + $750 + $2,700).

Suppose the Allowance account has a $2,100 *credit* balance from the previous period—that is, before any current-period adjustment:

Allowance for Uncollectible Accounts

	Unadjusted balance 2,100

Teaching Tip: Ask the students to look at this T-account. What does the balance of $2,100 represent? *ANSWER:* Accounts Receivable that were recorded as Uncollectible Account Expense in a previous period but have not yet been written off.

Under the aging method, the adjusting entry is designed to adjust this account balance from $2,100 to $3,769, the needed amount determined by the aging schedule. To bring the Allowance balance up to date, Schmidt makes this entry:

Adjusting Entries

Dec. 31   Uncollectible Account Expense   1,669
           Allowance for Uncollectible Accounts
             ($3,769 − $2,100)   1,669

Observe that under the aging method, the adjusting entry takes into account the prior balance in Allowance for Uncollectibles. Now the Allowance account has the correct balance:

Allowance for Uncollectible Accounts		
	Unadjusted balance	2,100
	Adjustment amount	1,669
	Adjusted balance	3,769

It is possible that the allowance account might have a *debit* balance at year end prior to the adjusting entry. How can this occur? Bad debt write-offs during the year could have exceeded the allowance amount. Suppose the unadjusted balance in Allowance for Uncollectible Accounts is a *debit* amount of $1,500:

Allowance for Uncollectible Accounts	
Unadjusted balance 1,500	

In this situation, the adjusting entry is

Adjusting Entries

Dec. 31   Uncollectible Account Expense
         ($3,769 + $1,500)   5,269
           Allowance for Uncollectible Accounts   5,269

After posting, the allowance account is up to date:

Allowance for Uncollectible Accounts			
Unadjusted balance 1,500	Adjustment amount	5,269	
	Adjusted balance	3,769	

On the balance sheet, the $3,769 is subtracted from the Accounts Receivable figure—which the table on page 000 shows is $112,000—to report the expected realizable value of the accounts receivable—$108,231 ($112,000 − $3,769).

In addition to supplying the information needed for accurate financial reporting, the aging method directs management's attention to the accounts that should be pursued for payment.

Comparing the Percentage-of-Sales and the Aging Methods.   In practice, many companies use both the percentage-of-sales and the aging-of-accounts methods. For interim statements (monthly or quarterly), companies use the percent of sales method because it is easier to apply. At the end of the year,

Typical Student Misconception: Students often calculate bad debt expense under the aging method without taking the unadjusted balance in the Allowance account into consideration. Remind them that the unadjusted balance of the Allowance account represents current accounts receivable that have been expensed as bad debts in a previous period but have not yet been written off. These doubtful accounts should not be included in bad debt expense again.

Discussion Question: Why is the $1,500 debit balance in the Allowance account added to the $3,769 to arrive at the Uncollectible Account Expense? ANSWER: The debit balance indicates that $1,500 of accounts have been written off but the bad debt expense has not yet been recorded. The total expense then includes the $1,500 of accounts already written off and $3,769 of the Accounts Receivable that are considered uncollectible but have not yet been written off.

Point to Stress: The sales occurred in 19X1; therefore, the expenses related to the sales (doubtful account expense) should be recorded in that same period. (Remember the matching principle.) If the amount of uncollectible accounts is small (immaterial), then recording the amount as bad debt expense in the period when the accounts are written off is acceptable. However, if the amount of uncollectible accounts is large (material), then it is misleading to record the amount in a period different from the period in which the sales were made.

these companies use the aging method to ensure that Accounts Receivable is reported at expected realizable value. For this reason, auditors usually require an aging of the accounts on the year-end date. The two methods work well together because the percent-of-sales approach focuses on measuring bad debt expense on the income statement, whereas the aging approach is designed to measure net accounts receivable on the balance sheet.

Direct Write-off Method. Under the **direct write-off method** of accounting for bad debts, the company waits until the credit department decides that a customer's account receivable is uncollectible. Then the accountant debits Uncollectible Account Expense and credits the customer's account receivable to write off the account.

Assume it is 19X2 and most credit customers have paid for their 19X1 purchases. At this point, the credit department believes that two customers—Garcia and Smith—will never pay. The department directs the accountant to write off Garcia and Smith as bad debts.

The following entries show the business's accounting for 19X1 credit sales and 19X2 collections and uncollectible accounts.

19X1	Accounts Receivable—Garcia	800	
	Accounts Receivable—Smith	1,200	
	Accounts Receivable—Various Customers	98,000	
	Sales Revenue		100,000
	To record credit sales of $100,000.		
19X2	Cash	97,000	
	Accounts Receivable—Various Customers		97,000
	To record cash collections of $97,000.		
19X2	Uncollectible Account Expense	2,000	
	Accounts Receivable—Garcia		800
	Accounts Receivable—Smith		1,200
	To write off uncollectible accounts and record bad debt expense of $2,000.		

Of course, this company would continue making credit sales as an important part of doing business. But what we want to know right now is how the direct write-off method affects financial statements. To see its impact most clearly, let's assume that the company stopped making credit sales altogether in 19X2. Consider the following partial financial statements for 19X1 and 19X2, based on the above journal entries.

Income Statement:	19X1	19X2
Revenue:		
Sales revenue	$100,000	$ 0
Expense:		
Uncollectible account expense	0	2,000

	December 31,	
Balance Sheet:	19X1	19X2
Accounts receivable	$100,000	$1,000

Let's ask two important questions about this approach to accounting for bad debts:

1. How accurately does the direct write-off method measure income? As we have seen, following generally accepted accounting principles means matching an accounting period's expenses against its revenues. This provides the most accurate picture of operating income, which measures how well a business's operations are performing. But the direct write-off method does not match a period's bad debt expense against the same period's sales revenue. In our example, the full amount of sales revenue appears for 19Xl, but the expenses incurred to generate this revenue—the bad debts—appear in 19X2. This gives misleading income figures for both years, as would failing to report any other expense—salary, depreciation, and so on—in the correct period. The $2,000 bad debt expense should be matched against the $100,000 sales revenue.

2. How accurately does the direct write-off method value accounts receivable? The 19Xl balance sheet shows accounts receivable at the full $100,000 figure. But any businessperson knows that bad debts are unavoidable when selling on credit. No intelligent manager expects to collect the entire amount. Is the $100,000 figure, then, the expected realizable value of the accounts? No, showing the full $100,000 in the balance sheet falsely implies that these accounts receivable are worth their face value.

The direct write-off method is simple to use, and it causes no great error if collection losses are insignificant in amount. However, you see that the resulting accounting records are not as accurate as they could be. The allowance method is a better way to account for uncollectible account expense.

Credit Balances in Accounts Receivable

Point to Stress: A credit balance in Accounts Receivable is a result of a customer's overpayment on his account. This means that a customer has advanced cash to the business but has not received anything in return. The business then owes the customer the cash. Most customers will apply an overpayment to their next order.

Occasionally, customers overpay their accounts or return merchandise for which they have already paid. The result is a credit balance in the customer's account receivable. Assume the company's subsidiary ledger contains 213 accounts, with balances as shown:

210 accounts with *debit* balances totaling	$185,000
3 accounts with *credit* balances totaling	2,800
Net total of all balances	$182,200

The company should *not* report the asset Accounts Receivable at the net amount—$182,200. Why not? The credit balance—the $2,800—is a liability. Like any other liability, customer credit balances are debts of the business. A balance sheet that did not indicate to management or to other financial statement users that the company had this liability amount would be misleading if the $2,800 is material in relation to net income or total current assets. Therefore, the company would report on its balance sheet:

Assets	Liabilities
Current:	Current:
Accounts receivable ... $185,000	Credit balances in customer accounts ..$2,800

Credit-Card Sales

Credit-card sales are common in retailing. American Express, Diners Club, Carte Blanche, VISA, and MasterCard are popular.

The customer presents the credit card as payment for a purchase. The seller prepares a sales invoice in triplicate. The customer and the seller keep copies as receipts. The third copy goes to the credit-card company, which then pays the seller the transaction amount and bills the customer.

Credit-cards offer consumers the convenience of buying without having to pay the cash immediately. Also, consumers receive a monthly statement from the credit-card company, detailing each credit-card transaction. They can write a single check to cover the entire month's credit-card purchases.

Retailers also benefit from credit-card sales. They do not have to check a customer's credit rating. The company that issues the card has already done so. Retailers do not have to keep an accounts receivable subsidiary ledger account for each customer, and they do not have to collect cash from customers. The copy of the sale invoice that retailers send to the credit-card company signals the card issuer to pursue payment. Further, retailers receive cash more quickly from the credit-card companies than they would from the customers themselves. Of course, these services to the seller do not come free.

The seller receives less than 100 percent of the face value of the invoice. The credit-card company takes a 5 percent[1] discount on the sale to cover its services. The seller's entry to record a $100 Diners Club sale is

Point to Stress: Credit-card sales are essentially a sale of the receivable to the credit-card company. A sale of receivables is called factoring receivables.

Accounts Receivable—Diners Club	100	
Sales Revenue		100

On collection of the discounted value, the seller records:

Cash	95	
Credit-Card Discount Expense	5	
Accounts Receivable—Diners Club		100

Internal Control over Collections of Accounts Receivable

Businesses that sell on credit receive most of their cash receipts by mail. Internal control over collections on account is an important part of the overall internal control system. Chapter 7 detailed control procedures over cash receipts, but a critical element of internal control deserves emphasis here: the separation of cash-handling and cash-accounting duties. Consider the following case.

OBJECTIVE 4
Identify internal control weaknesses in accounts receivable

Butler Supply Co. is a small, family-owned business that takes pride in the loyalty of its workers. Most company employees have been with the Butlers for at least five years. The company makes 90 percent of its sales on account.

The office staff consists of a bookkeeper and a supervisor. The bookkeeper maintains the general ledger and the accounts receivable subsidiary ledger. He

---

[1]The rate varies among companies and over time.

also makes the daily bank deposit. The supervisor prepares monthly financial statements and any special reports the Butlers require. She also takes sales orders from customers and serves as office manager.

Can you identify the internal control weakness? The bookkeeper has access to the general ledger, the accounts receivable subsidiary ledger, and the cash. The bookkeeper could take a customer check and write off the customer's account as uncollectible.[2] Unless the supervisor or some other manager reviews the bookkeeper's work regularly, the theft may go undetected. In small businesses like Butler Supply Co., such a review may not be routinely performed.

How can this control weakness be corrected? The supervisor could open incoming mail and make the daily bank deposit. The bookkeeper should not be allowed to handle cash. Only the remittance slips would be forwarded to the bookkeeper to indicate which customer accounts to credit. Removing cash-handling duties from the bookkeeper, and keeping the accounts receivable subsidiary ledger away from the supervisor, separates duties and strengthens internal control. It reduces an employee's opportunity to steal cash and then cover it up with a false credit to a customer account.

Another step should be taken. The bookkeeper should total the amount posted as credits to customer accounts receivable each day. The owner should then compare this total with the day's bank deposit slip. Agreement of the two records gives some assurance that customer accounts were posted correctly and helps avoid accounting errors. Also, the owner should prepare the bank reconciliation.

---

[2]The bookkeeper would need to forge the endorsements of the checks and deposit them in a bank account he controls. This is easier to do than you might imagine.

Summary Problem for Your Review

CPC International, Inc., is the food-products company that produces Skippy peanut butter, Hellmann's mayonnaise, and Mazola corn oil. The company balance sheet at December 31, 19X7, reported:

	Millions
Notes and accounts receivable [total]	$549.9
Allowances for doubtful accounts	(12.5)

Required

a. How much of the December 31, 19X7, balance of notes and accounts receivable did CPC expect to collect? Stated differently, what was the expected realizable value of these receivables?

b. Journalize, without explanations, 19X8 entries for CPC International, assuming:
   1) Estimated Doubtful Account Expense of $19.2 million, based on the percentage of sales method.
   2) Write-offs of accounts receivable totaling $23.6 million.
   3) December 31, 19X8, aging of receivables, which indicates that $15.3 million of the total receivables of $582.7 million is uncollectible.

c. Show how CPC International's receivables and related allowance will appear on the December 31, 19X8, balance sheet.

d. What is the expected realizable value of receivables at December 31, 19X8? How much is doubtful account expense for 19X8?

SOLUTION TO REVIEW PROBLEM

			Millions
a.	Expected realizable value of receivables ($549.9 − $12.5)		$537.4

			Millions	
b.	1) Doubtful Account Expense	19.2		
	Allowance for Doubtful Accounts		19.2	
	2) Allowance for Doubtful Accounts	23.6		
	Accounts Receivable		23.6	

Allowance for Doubtful Accounts

19X8 Write offs	23.6	Dec. 31, 19X7	12.5
		19X8 Expense	19.2
		19X8 balance prior to December 31, 19X8	8.1

		Millions
3) Doubtful Account Expense ($15.3 − $8.1)	7.2	
Allowance for Doubtful Accounts		7.2

		Millions
c.	Notes and accounts receivable	$582.7
	Allowance for doubtful accounts	(15.3)

		Millions
d.	Expected realizable value of receivables at December 31, 19X8 ($582.7 − $15.3)	$567.4
	Doubtful account expense for 19X8 ($19.2 + $7.2)	26.4

Notes Receivable

As we pointed out earlier in this chapter, notes receivable are more formal arrangements than accounts receivable. Often the debtor signs a promissory note, which serves as evidence of the debt. Let's take a moment to define the special terms used to discuss notes receivable.

Promissory note. A written promise to pay a specified amount of money at a particular future date.

Maker of a note. The person or business that signs the note and promises to pay the amount required by the note agreement. The maker is the debtor.

Payee of the note. The person or business to whom the maker promises future payment. The payee is the creditor.

Principal amount, or **principal.** The amount loaned out by the payee and borrowed by the maker of the note.

1 Refer to Exhibit 8-2 and discuss the note-related terms.

2 Compute the interest that will be due on the maturity date. *ANSWER:* $1,000 × 9% × 1 = $90 (yr).

3 Compute the maturity value. *ANSWER:* $1,000 + $90 = $1,090.

4 Review the number of days in each month. It is amazing how many students do not know which months have 30 days and which have 31.

Class Exercise: Have students calculate the maturity dates of these notes:

1 A 90-day note dated January 4, 19X3. *ANSWER:* April 4,19X3

2 A 150-day note dated September 30, 19X1. *ANSWER:* February 27, 19X2

3 A 45-day note dated May 15, 19X2. *ANSWER:* June 29,19X2

Point out that you begin counting on the day following the date of the note, so that the due date on a 90-day note is day number 90.

Interest. The revenue to the payee for loaning out the principal and the expense to the maker for borrowing the principal.

Interest period. The period of time during which interest is to be computed. It extends from the original date of the note to the maturity date. Also called the *note period* or *note term*.

Interest rate. The percentage rate that is multiplied by the principal amount to compute the amount of interest on the note.

Maturity date, or *due date.* The date on which final payment of the note is due.

Maturity value. The sum of principal and interest due at the maturity date of a note.

Exhibit 8-2 illustrates a promissory note. Study it carefully, and identify each of the above items for the note agreement.

Identifying the Maturity Date of a Note

Some notes specify the maturity date of a note, as shown in Exhibit 8-2. Other notes state the period of the note, in days or months. When the period is given in months, the note's maturity date falls on the same day of the month as the date the note was issued. For example, a 6-month note dated February 16 matures on August 16.

When the period is given in days, the maturity date is determined by counting the days from date of issue. A 120-day note dated September 14, 19X2, matures on January 12, 19X3, as shown below:

Month	Number of Days	Cumulative Total
Sep. 19X2	16*	16
Oct. 19X2	31	47
Nov. 19X2	30	77
Dec. 19X2	31	108
Jan. 19X3	12	120

*30 − 14 = 16.

EXHIBIT 8-2 *A Promissory Note*

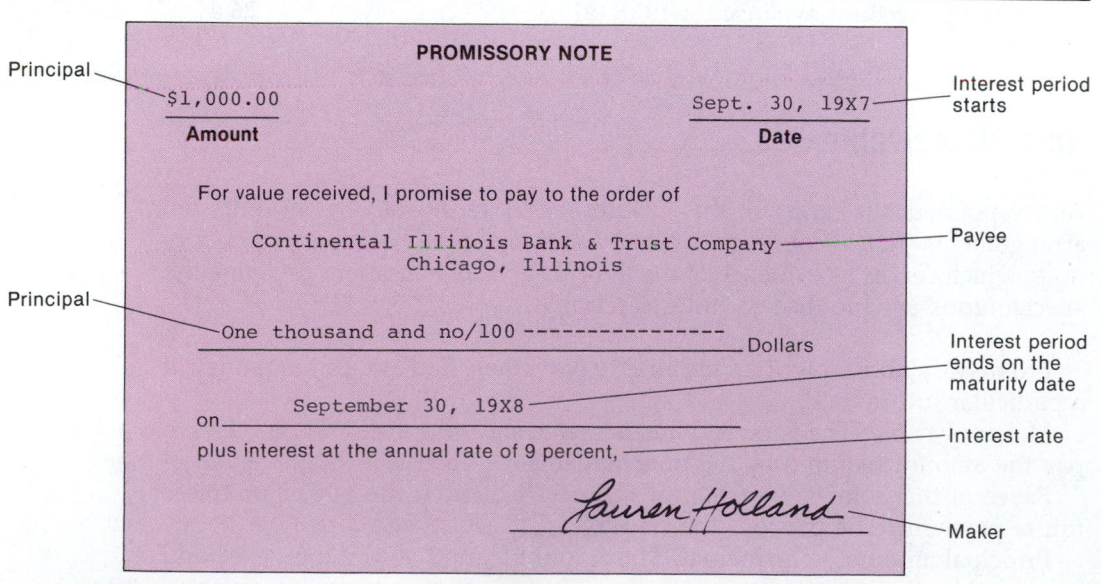

Computing Interest on a Note

The formula for computing interest is

Principal × Rate × Time = Amount of Interest

Using the data in Exhibit 8-2, Continental Bank computes its interest revenue for one year on its note receivable as:

Teaching Tip: Interest rates are usually stated as an annual rate. Therefore, the time in the formula should also be expressed in terms of a year.

Principal	Rate	Time	Interest
$1,000	× .09 ×	1 yr. =	$90

The *maturity value* of the note is $1,090 ($1,000 principal + $90 interest). Note that the time element is one (1) because interest is computed over a 1-year period.

When the interest period of a note is stated in months, we compute the interest based on the 12-month year. Interest on a $2,000 note at 15 percent for 3 months is computed as:

Class Exercise: Have students practice calculating interest:

$30,000, 12½%, 180 day note ($30,000 × .125 × 180/360) = $1,875

$8,500, 9%, 6 month note ($8,500 × .09 × 6/12) = $383

Principal	Rate	Time	Interest
$2,000	× .15 ×	3/12 =	$75

When the interest period of a note is stated in days, we sometimes compute interest based on a 360-day year rather than a 365-day year. The interest on a $5,000 note at 12 percent for 60 days is computed as:

Principal	Rate	Time	Interest
$5,000	× .12 ×	60/360 =	$100

Recording Notes Receivable

Consider the loan agreement shown in Exhibit 8-2. After Holland signs the note and presents it to the bank, Continental Bank gives her $1,000 cash. At maturity, Holland pays the bank $1,090 ($1,000 principal plus $90 interest). The bank's entries are

OBJECTIVE 5
Account for notes receivable

Sep. 30, 19X7	Note Receivable—L. Holland	1,000	
	Cash		1,000
	To record the loan.		

Sep. 30, 19X8	Cash	1,090	
	Note Receivable—L. Holland		1,000
	Interest Revenue ($1,000 × .09 × 1).		90
	To record collection at maturity.		

Some companies sell merchandise in exchange for notes receivable. This arrangement occurs often when the payment term extends beyond the customary accounts receivable period, which generally ranges from 30 to 60 days.

Suppose that on October 20, 19X3, General Electric sells equipment for $15,000 to Dorman Builders. Dorman signs a 90-day promissory note at 10 percent annual interest. General Electric's entries to record the sale and collection from Dorman are

Teaching Tip: Look at the
journal entries on October 20
and January 18. Do they look
similar to general journal
entries that affect Accounts
Receivable control and
subsidiary ledger? ANSWER:
Yes, they do. Very often a
company will set up a
subsidiary ledger for Notes
Receivable that operates in just
the same manner as the
Accounts Receivable subsidiary
ledger.. The subsidiary ledger is
especially helpful if the
business has a large number of
notes receivable.

Oct. 20, 19X3	Note Receivable—Dorman Builders ...	15,000	
	Sales Revenue		15,000
	To record sale.		
Jan. 18, 19X4	Cash	15,375	
	Note Receivable—Dorman Builders......................		15,000
	Interest Revenue ($15,000 × .10 × 90/360)		375
	To record collection at maturity.		

A company may accept a note receivable from a trade customer who fails to pay an account receivable within the customary 30 to 60 days. The customer signs a promissory note—that is, becomes the maker of the note—and gives it to the creditor, who becomes the payee.

Suppose Casa de Sanchez, Inc., sees that it will not be able to pay off its account payable to Hoffman Supply that is due in 15 days. Hoffman may accept a note receivable from Casa de Sanchez. Hoffman's entry is

May 3	Note Receivable—Casa de Sanchez, Inc.	2,400	
	Accounts Receivable—Casa de Sanchez, Inc		2,400
	To receive a note on account from a customer.		

Hoffman later records interest and collection as illustrated in the preceding examples.

Why does a company accept a note receivable instead of pressing its demand for payment of the account receivable? The company may pursue receipt but learn that its customer does not have the money. A note receivable gives the company written evidence of the maker's debt, which may aid any legal action for collection. Also, the note receivable may carry a pledge by the maker that gives the payee certain assets if cash is not received by the due date. The company's reward for its patience is the interest revenue that it earns on the note receivable.

Transparency T8-3

Teaching Tip: Summarize the
discounting procedure into
these five steps:

1. Compute the maturity
   value (principal + interest).
2. Compute the bank's
   discount period (length of
   note − days held prior to
   discounting).
3. Compute the bank's
   discount (maturity value ×
   discount rate × discount
   period).

Discounting a Note Receivable

A note receivable is a *negotiable instrument*, which means it is readily transferable from one business or person to another and may be sold for cash. To get cash quickly, payees sometimes sell a note receivable to another party before the note matures. The payee endorses the note and hands it over to the note purchaser—often a bank—who collects the maturity value of the note at the maturity date.

Selling a note receivable before maturity is called **discounting a note receivable** because the payee of the note receives less than its maturity value. This lower price decreases the amount of interest revenue the payee earns on the note. Giving up some of this interest is the price the payee is willing to pay for the convenience of receiving cash early.

Return to the preceding example with General Electric and Dorman Builders. Recall that the maturity date of the Dorman note is January 18, 19X4. Let's assume General Electric discounts the Dorman note at First City National Bank on December 9, 19X3. The discount period—which is the number of days from the date of discounting to the date of maturity (this is the period the bank will hold the note)—is 40 days; 22 days in December, and 18 days in January. Assume the bank applies a 12 percent annual interest rate in computing the discounted value of the note. The bank will want to use a discount rate that is higher than the interest rate on the note in order to increase its earnings. GE may be willing to accept this higher rate in order to get cash quickly. The discounted value, called the *proceeds,* is the amount that GE receives from the bank. The proceeds are computed as follows:

4. Compute the proceeds (maturity value − discount).
5. Prepare the general journal entry:

Principal amount	$15,000
+ Interest ($15,000 × .10 × 90/360)	375
= Maturity value	15,375 $170 $170
− Discount ($15,375 × .12 × 40/360)	(205)
= Proceeds	$15,170

Cash (as calc. in Step 4) . . . XXX
   Interest Revenue (or
     expense) XXX
   Note Receivable
     (principal) XXX

At maturity the bank collects $15,375 from the maker of the note, earning $205 of interest revenue.

Observe two points in the above computation: (1) The discount is computed on the *maturity value* of the note (principal plus interest) rather than on the original principal amount, and (2) the discount period extends *backward* from the maturity date (January 18, 19X4) to the date of discounting (December 9, 19X3). Follow this diagram:

Teaching Tip: Students have trouble calculating the discount period. Try this: If a 60-day note dated April 16 is discounted on May 2, what is the discount period? *ANSWER:* 44 days. Method: Compute how many days the note was held (April 16 to May 2 is 16 days). Subtract the days held from the length of the note (60 − 16 = 44).

Oct. 20, 19X3   90 Days   Jan. 18, 19X4

Principal   +   Interest   =   Maturity
$15,000 $375 $15,375

Dec. 9, 19X3   40 Days   Jan. 18, 19X4

Proceeds   =   Discount   −   Maturity
$15,170 $205 $15,375

General Electric's entry to record discounting the note is

Dec. 9, 19X3	Cash	15,170	
	Note Receivable—Dorman Builders		15,000
	Interest Revenue ($15,170 −		
	$15,000)		170
	To record discounting a note receivable.		

When the proceeds from discounting a note receivable are less than the principal amount of the note, the payee records a debit to Interest Expense for the amount of the difference. For example, General Electric could discount the note receivable for cash proceeds of $14,980. The entry to record this transaction is

Class Exercise: January 5, received a $5,000, 90-day, 10% note from Barney Fife. Sold the Fife note on January 25 by discounting it to a bank at 12%. Prepare the journal entry to record the discounted note on January 25. *ANSWER:*

1 Maturity value = $5,000 + ($5,000 × 10% × 90/360) = $5,125
2 Discount period = 90 − 20 70 days
3 Discount = $5,125 × 12% × 70/360 = $120
4 Proceeds = $5,125 − $120 = $5,005
5 Journal entry:

Cash 5,005
  Interest Revenue   5
  Note Receivable—
   Barney Fife 5,000

Dec. 9, 19X3	Cash	14,980	
	Interest Expense	20	
	Note Receivable—Dorman Builders		15,000

The term *discount* has been used here to distinguish the interest earned by the payee of the note from the interest to be earned by the purchaser of the note. Fundamentally, the discount is interest.

Contingent Liabilities on Discounted Notes Receivable

Teaching Tip: Refer to the financial statements in the appendix. Ask students to look for any contingencies mentioned in the footnotes.

Discounting a note receivable creates a **contingent**—that is, a potential—**liability** for the endorser. The contingent liability is this: If the maker of the note (Dorman, in our example) fails to pay the maturity value to the new payee (the bank), then the original payee (General Electric, the note's endorser) legally must pay the bank the amount due.[3] Now we see why the liability is "potential." If Dorman pays the bank, then General Electric can forget the note. But if Dorman dishonors the note—fails to pay it—General Electric has an actual liability.

This contingent liability of General Electric exists from the time of endorsement to the maturity date of the note. In our example, the contingent liability exists from December 9, 19X3—when General Electric endorsed the note—to the January 18, 19X4, maturity date.

Contingent liabilities are not reported with actual liabilities on the balance sheet. After all, they are not real debts. However, financial-statement users should be alerted that the business has *potential* debts. Many businesses report contingent liabilities in a footnote to the financial statements. General Electric's end-of-period balance sheet might carry this note:

> As of December 31, 19X3, the Company is contingently liable on notes receivable discounted in the amount of $15,000.

Dishonored Notes Receivable

Class Exercise: Refer to the previous Class Exercise. Assume that the note is dishonored by Barney Fife on its due date. What entry would the payee make? *ANSWER:*

Accounts Receivable—
　Barney Fife......5,125
　　Cash ....　　5,125

Ask students why the maturity value was charged back to Fife's subsidiary account receivable? *ANSWER:* We want to maintain a complete credit history of each customer in the subsidiary ledger. This entry shows the dishonored note on his account.

If the maker of a note does not pay a note receivable at maturity, the maker is said to **dishonor,** or **default on,** the note. Because the term of the note has expired, the note agreement is no longer in force, nor is it negotiable. However, the payee still has a claim against the maker of the note and usually transfers the claim from the note receivable account to Accounts Receivable. The payee records interest revenue earned on the note and debits Accounts Receivable for the full maturity value of the note.

Suppose Rubinstein Jewelers has a six-month, 10 percent note receivable for $1,200 from D. Hatachi. On the February 3 maturity date, Hatachi defaults. Rubinstein Jewelers would record the default as follows:

Feb. 3	Accounts Receivable—D. Hatachi		
	[$1,200 + ($1,200 × .10 × 6/12)]	1,260	
	Note Receivable—D. Hatachi		1,200
	Interest Revenue ($1,200 × .10 × 6/12)		60
	To record dishonor of note receivable.		

Rubinstein would pursue collection from Hatachi as a promissory note default. The company may treat accounts receivable such as this as a special category to highlight them for added collection efforts. If the account receivable later proves uncollectible, the account is written off against Allowance for Uncollectible Accounts in the manner previously discussed.

The maker may dishonor a note after it has been discounted by the original payee. For example, suppose Dorman Builders dishonors its note (maturity value, $15,375) to General Electric (GE) after GE has discounted the note to the

---

[3]The discounting agreement between the endorser and the purchaser may specify that the endorser has no liability if the note is dishonored at maturity.

bank. On dishonor, the bank adds a *protest fee* to cover the cost of a statement about the facts of the dishonor and requests payment from General Electric, which then becomes the holder of the dishonored note. Assume GE pays the maturity value of the note, plus the $25 protest fee, to the bank. This creates an obligation for Dorman to pay GE. GE then presents the statement to Dorman and makes the following entry on the maturity date of the note:

Jan. 18, 19X4	Accounts Receivable—Dorman Builders ($15,375 + $25)	15,400	
	Cash		15,400
	To record payment of dishonored note receivable that has been discounted, plus a protest fee.		

GE's collection of cash, or write off of the uncollectible account receivable, would be recorded in the normal manner, depending on the ultimate outcome. If GE charges Dorman additional interest, GE's collection entry debits Cash and credits Accounts Receivable and Interest Revenue.

Accruing Interest Revenue

Notes receivable may be outstanding at the end of the accounting period. The interest revenue that was accrued on the note up to that point should be recorded as part of that period's earnings. Recall that interest revenue is earned over time, not just when cash is received.

Suppose First City Bank receives a one-year $1,000 note receivable, with 9 percent interest, on October 1, 19X7. The bank's accounting period ends December 31. How much of the total interest revenue does First City Bank earn in 19X7? How much in 19X8?

The bank will earn three months' interest in 19X7—for October, November, and December. In 19X8, the bank will earn nine months' interest—for January through September. Therefore, at December 31, 19X7, First City will make the following adjusting entry to accrue interest revenue:

Dec. 31, 19X7	Interest Receivable ($1,000 × .09 × 3/12)...........................	22.50	
	Interest Revenue............		22.50
	To accrue interest revenue earned in 19X7 but not yet received.		

Then, on the maturity date First City Bank may record collection of principal and interest as follows:

Point to Stress: If reversing entries are used, then Interest Revenue will be credited for $90 on Sept. 30.

Sept. 30, 19X8	Cash [$1,000 + ($1,000 × .09)]	1,090.00	
	Note Receivable		1,000.00
	Interest Receivable ($1,000 × .09 × 3/12)		22.50
	Interest Revenue ($1,000 × .09 × 9/12)		67.50
	To record collection of note receivable on which interest has been previously accrued.		

The entries to accrue interest revenue earned in 19X7 and to record collection in 19X8 assign the correct amount of interest to each year.

Reporting Receivables and Allowances: Actual Reports

OBJECTIVE 6

Report receivables on the balance sheet

Let's take a look at how some well-known companies report their receivables and related allowances for uncollectibles on the balance sheet. The terminology and setup vary, but you can understand these actual presentations based on what you have learned in this chapter.

Bobbie Brooks, a manufacturer of women's clothing, reported under Current Assets (in thousands):

Accounts receivable, less allowance
  for doubtful accounts of $602 . . . . . . $35,873

To figure the total accounts receivable amount, add the allowance to the net accounts receivable amount: $602 + $35,873 = $36,475.

Premark International, Inc., which makes Tupperware plastic food-storage containers, combines accounts and notes receivable (amounts in millions):

Accounts and notes receivable, less
  allowances of $19.5 . . . . $309.9

General Electric Company reports a single amount for its current receivables in the body of the balance sheet and supplements it with a detailed note (amounts in millions):

Current receivables (note 8) $4,872

Note 8: Current Receivables

Customers' accounts and notes.	$3,989
Associated companies	49
Nonconsolidated affiliates	21
Other	927
	4,986
Less allowance for losses	(114)
	$4,872

Deere & Company, maker of farm machinery, lists more detail in the body of the balance sheet (amounts in thousands of dollars):

Trade receivables:

Dealer accounts and notes	$2,373,018
Retail notes	40,558
Total	2,413,576
Less allowances	39,183
Trade receivables, net	$2,374,393

Nashua Corporation, manufacturer of copying machines and paper products, reported approximately $70,000,000 in net accounts and notes receivable. In addition, the company disclosed a contingent liability for discounted accounts and notes receivable in its Notes to Financial Statements:

ACCOUNTS RECEIVABLE:

At December 31, 19X1 and 19X0, the company was contingently liable to third parties as a result of the sale of certain accounts and notes receivable of approximately $19,000,000 and $16,000,000, respectively.

The companies we have featured so far list receivables as *current assets*. National Can Corporation, however, had some long-term receivables that it reported as other assets (amounts in thousands of dollars).

OTHER ASSETS:

Notes and accounts receivable, less allowances $36,970

National Can also disclosed in a note entitled Notes and Accounts Receivable that:

Notes and accounts receivable included in other assets are net of allowances for doubtful accounts of $16,772.

Use of Accounting Information in Decision Making

The balance sheet lists assets in the order of relative liquidity. Cash, of course, comes first because it is the medium of exchange and can be used to purchase any item or pay any bill. Current receivables are less liquid than cash because receivables must be collected. Merchandise inventory is less liquid than receivables because the goods must first be sold, which creates a receivable that can be collected. Exhibit 8-1 provides an example of a balance sheet showing these accounts.

In making decisions, owners and managers use some ratios based on the relative liquidity of assets. In Chapter 4, for example, we discussed the current ratio, which indicates the ability to pay current liabilities with current assets. A more stringent measure of the ability to pay current liabilities is the **acid-test** (or **quick**) ratio. The acid-test ratio assumes that all current liabilities are payable immediately and that the debtor will convert the most liquid assets to cash. The three most liquid asset categories are cash, short-term investments, and current receivables. Short-term investments (covered in Chapter 17) are the second most liquid assets because they are readily convertible to cash at the will of the owner. All the owner must do to generate cash is sell these investments. The acid-test ratio is computed as follows:

$$\text{Acid-test ratio} = \frac{\text{Cash + Short-term investments + Net current receivables}}{\text{Total current liabilities}}$$

The higher the acid-test ratio, the better able is the business to pay its current liabilities. An increasing acid-test ratio over time usually indicates improving business operations.

Inventory is excluded from the acid-test ratio because it may not be easy to sell the goods. A company may have an acceptable current ratio and a poor acid-test ratio because of a large amount of inventory. Note that inventory is included in the computation of the current ratio but not of the acid-test ratio.

What is an acceptable acid-test ratio value? It depends on the industry. Automobile dealers can operate smoothly with an acid-test ratio of .20. The average acid-test ratio for women's dress manufacturers is .90. Most department stores' ratio values cluster about .80, and travel agencies average 1.10. In general, an acid-test ratio of 1.00 is considered safe.

After a business makes a credit sale, the next critical event in the business cycle is collection of the receivable. Several financial ratios center on receivables. **Days' sales in receivables**, also called the *collection period*, indicates how

Point to Stress: Inventory and prepaid assets are current assets, but are excluded from the acid-test ratio because they are not readily convertible into cash.

Class Exercise: Given below are selected accounts and their balances at 12/31. Compute the current and acid-test ratios.

Equipment	$4,000
Supplies	500
Interest Payable	600
Accounts Receivable	2,600
Accounts Payable . .	3,400
Accumulated Deprec.	1,200
Inventory	1,600
Cash	1,300

ANSWER: Current ratio = 1.5 ($6,000*/$4,000†)

*($500 + $2,600 + $1,600 + $1,300 = $6,000)
†($600 + $3,400 = $4,000)
Acid-test ratio = .975
($3,900/$4,000)
($2,600 + $1,300 = $3,900)

Real-World Example: The average acid-test ratio in the electronic computer industry is 1.1. For auto dealers, the average is .2, and for restaurants, .4.

Class Exercise: Assume the following information:

Net Sales $48,000
Accts. Rec. (1/1) . .   10,000
Accts. Rec. (12/31)   14,000

What is the average collection period?
ANSWER:
One day's sales = $132 ($48,000/365). Days' sales in average accounts receivable = 91 days ($12,000/$132)

Real-World Example: The average collection period in the electronic computer industry is 62 days. The companies in the top 25% of the electronic computer industry took only 49 days to collect their accounts receivable. Comparable figures for department stores are 31 days for the industry average and 3 days for the top 25%.

many days it takes to collect the average level of receivables. The shorter the collection period, the more quickly the organization can use cash for operations. The longer the collection period, the less cash is available to pay bills and expand. Days' sales in receivables can be computed in two steps, as follows:

$$1. \quad \text{One day's sales} = \frac{\text{Net sales}}{365 \text{ days}}$$

$$2. \quad \begin{array}{c} \text{Days' sales in} \\ \text{average accounts} \\ \text{receivable} \end{array} = \frac{\text{Average net accounts receivable}}{\text{One day's sales}} = \frac{(\text{Beginning net receivables} + \text{Ending net receivables})/2}{\text{One day's sales}}$$

The length of the collection period depends on the credit terms of the company's sales. For example, sales on net 30 terms should be collected within approximately 30 days. When there is a discount, such as 2/10 net 30, the collection period may be shorter. Terms of net 45 or net 60 will result in longer collection periods. Companies watch their collection period closely. Whenever the collection period lengthens, the business must find other sources of financing, such as borrowing. During recessions, customers pay more slowly, and a longer collection period may be unavoidable.

Computers and Accounts Receivable

Accounting for receivables by a company like M & M Mars requires tens of thousands of postings to customer accounts each month for credit sales and cash collections. Manual accounting methods cannot keep up.

As Chapter 28 explains in more detail, Accounts Receivable can be set up on a computer as a menu-driven module (a module is a part of a software program). The menu—so called because it presents the user with a number of choices, as a diner would have at a restaurant—allows the person using the computer to choose the appropriate action. See Exhibit 28-8, on p. 1250. The person at the keyboard could choose to set up the accounts receivable ledger, to modify the ledger, or to take whatever action is appropriate. The screen would then ask for information from the computer operator: customer number, product number of the items ordered, number of items ordered, discount terms, shipment terms, and so on.

The computer then creates a sales invoice. At the same time, the computer generates records that lead to the sales journal printout. The printout is checked and approved. Finally, computerized posting to the general ledger and the accounts receivable subledger occurs.

Computerized accounting packages prepare a report for aging accounts receivable. The computer accesses files of customer data and sorts accounts by customer number and date of invoice.

Computers also discount notes. If the company deals with relatively few discounted notes, a spreadsheet may handle the accounting (if the accounting software package does not include a special function for discounting). The column heads would be date of note, principal amount, interest rate, maturity date, maturity value, date of discounting, and so on. (Chapter 28 offers instructions on how to use a popular spreadsheet.) Big-league spreadsheets calculate interest based on their internal calendar. The accountant need not even enter the number of days the note is outstanding.

Summary Problem for Your Review

Suppose Exxon, Inc., engaged in the following transactions:

19X4

Apr. 1   Loaned $8,000 to Bland Co., a service station. Received a one-year, 10 percent note.

June 1   Discounted the Bland note at the bank at a discount rate of 12 percent.

Nov. 30   Loaned $6,000 to Flores, Inc., a regional distributor of Exxon products, on a three-month, 11 percent note.

19X5

Feb. 28   Collected the Flores note at maturity.

Exxon's accounting period ends on December 31.

Required

Explanations are not needed.

1. Record the 19X4 transactions on April 1, June 1, and November 30 on Exxon's books.
2. Make any adjusting entries needed on December 31, 19X4.
3. Record the February 28, 19X5, collection of the Flores note.
4. Which transaction creates a contingent liability for Exxon? When does the contingency begin? When does it end?
5. Write a footnote that Exxon could use in its 19X4 financial statements to report the contingent liability.

SOLUTION TO REVIEW PROBLEM

19X4

1.

Apr. 1	Note Receivable—Bland Co	8,000	
	Cash		8,000
June 1	Cash	7,920*	
	Interest Expense	80	
	Note Receivable—Bland Co		8,000

*Computation of proceeds:

Principal	$8,000
+ Interest ($8,000 × .10 × 12/12)	800
= Maturity value	8,800
− Discount ($8,800 × .12 × 10/12)	880
= Proceeds	$7,920

Nov. 30	Note Receivable—Flores, Inc.	6,000	
	Cash		6,000

2.

Adjusting Entries

19X4

Dec. 31	Interest Receivable ($6,000 × .11 × 1/12) .	55	
	Interest Revenue		55

19X5

3. Feb. 28 Cash [$6,000 + ($6,000 × .11 × 3/12)] 6,165
                Note Receivable—Flores, Inc.   6,000
                Interest Receivable   55
                Interest Revenue ($6,000 × . 11 × 2/12)   110

4. Discounting the Bland note receivable creates a contingent liability for Exxon. The contingency exists from the date of discounting the note receivable (June 1) to the maturity date of the note (April 1, 19X5).

5. Note XX—Contingent liabilities: At December 31, 19X4, the Company is contingently liable on notes receivable discounted in the amount of $8,000.

Summary

Credit sales create receivables. Accounts receivable are usually current assets, and notes receivable may be current or long-term.

Uncollectible receivables are accounted for by the allowance method or the direct write-off method. The *allowance method* matches expenses to sales revenue and also results in a more realistic measure of net accounts receivable. The *percent-of-sales method* and the *aging-of-accounts receivable method* are the two main approaches to estimating bad debts under the allowance method. The *direct write-off method* is easy to apply, but it fails to match the uncollectible account expense to the corresponding sales revenue. Also, Accounts Receivable are reported at their full amount, which misleadingly suggests that the company expects to collect all its accounts receivable.

In *credit-card* sales, the seller receives cash from the credit-card company (American Express, for example), which bills the customer. For the convenience of receiving cash immediately, the seller pays a fee, which is a percentage of the sale.

Companies that sell on credit receive most customer collections in the mail. Good *internal control* over mailed-in cash receipts means separating cash-handling duties from cash-accounting duties.

Notes receivable are formal credit agreements. Interest earned by the creditor is computed by multiplying the note's principal amount by the interest rate times the length of the interest period.

Because notes receivable are negotiable, they may be sold. Selling a note receivable—called *discounting a note*—creates a *contingent (possible) liability* for the note's payee.

All accounts receivable, notes receivable, and allowance accounts appear in the balance sheet. However, companies use various formats and terms to report these assets.

The *acid-test ratio* measures ability to pay current liabilities from the most liquid current assets. *Days' sales in receivables* indicates how long it takes to collect the average level of receivables.

Self-Study Questions

Test your understanding of the chapter by marking the best answer for each of the following questions.

1. The party that holds a receivable is called the *(p. 369)*
   √ a. Creditor   c. Maker
     b. Debtor   d. Security holder

2. The function of the credit department is to *(p. 370)*
   a. Collect accounts receivable from customers
   b. Report bad credit risks to other companies
   √ c. Evaluate customers who apply for credit
   d. Write off uncollectible accounts receivable

3. Longview, Inc., made the following entry related to uncollectibles:

   Uncollectible Account Expense.................... 1,900
       Allowance for Uncollectible Accounts.........   1,900

   The purpose of this entry is to *(p. 372)*
   a. Write off uncollectibles   c. Age the accounts receivable
   b. Close the expense account   √d. Record bad debt expense

4. Longview, Inc., also made this entry:

   Allowance for Uncollectible Accounts 2,110
       Accounts Receivable (detailed)   2,110

   The purpose of this entry is to *(p. 373)*
   √ a. Write off uncollectibles   c. Age the accounts receivable
   b. Close the expense account   d. Record bad debt expense

5. The credit balance in Allowance for Uncollectibles is $14,300 prior to the adjusting entries at the end of the period. The aging of accounts indicates that an allowance of $78,900 is needed. The amount of expense to record is *(p. 376)*
   a. $14,300   c. $78,900
   √ b. $64,600   d. $93,200

6. The most important internal control over cash receipts is *(p. 379)*
   a. Assigning an honest employee the responsibility for handling cash
   √ b. Separating the cash-handling and cash-accounting duties
   c. Ensuring that cash is deposited in the bank daily
   d. Centralizing the opening of incoming mail in a single location

7. A six-month, $30,000 note specifies interest of 9 percent. The full amount of interest on this note will be *(p. 383)*
   a. $450   √ c. $1,350
   b. $900   d. $2,700

8. The note in the preceding question was issued on August 31, and the company's accounting year ends on December 31. The year-end balance sheet will report interest receivable of *(p. 387)*
   a. $450   c. $1,350
   √ b. $900   d. $2,700

9. Discounting a note receivable is a way to *(p. 384)*
   √ a. Collect on a note   c. Both of the above
   b. Increase interest revenue   d. None of the above

10. Discounting a note receivable creates a (an) *(p. 385)*
   a. Cash disbursement   c. Protest fee
   b. Interest expense   √ d. Contingent liability

Answers to the Self-Study Questions follow the Accounting Vocabulary.

Accounting Vocabulary

Acid-test ratio. Ratio of the sum of cash plus short-term investments plus net current receivables to current liabilities. Tells whether the entity could pay all its current liabilities if they came due immediately. Also called the Quick ratio *(p. 389)*.

Aging of accounts receivable. A way to estimate bad debts by analyzing individual accounts receivable according to the length of time they have been due *(p. 375)*.

Allowance for doubtful accounts. A contra account, related to accounts receivable, that holds the estimated amount of collection losses. Also called Allowance for uncollectible accounts *(p. 371)*.

Allowance for uncollectible accounts. Another name for Allowance for doubtful accounts *(p. 371)*.

Allowance method. A method of recording collection losses based on estimates prior to determining that the business will not collect from specific customers *(p. 371)*.

Bad debt expense. Another name for Uncollectible account expense *(p. 371)*.

Contingent liability. A potential liability *(p. 386)*.

Creditor. The party to a credit transaction who sells a service or merchandise and obtains a receivable *(p. 369)*.

Days' sales in receivables. Ratio of average net accounts receivable to one day's sales. Tells how many days' sales remain in Accounts Receivable awaiting collection *(p. 389)*.

Debtor. The party to a credit transaction who makes a purchase and creates a payable *(p. 369)*.

Default on a note. Failure of the maker of a note to pay at maturity. Also called Dishonor of a note *(p. 386)*.

Direct write-off method. A method of accounting for bad debts by which the company waits until the credit department decides that a customer's account receivable is uncollectible and then records uncollectible account expense and credits the customer's account receivable *(p. 377)*.

Discounting a note receivable. Selling a note receivable before its maturity *(p. 384)*.

Dishonor of a note. Another name for Default on a note *(p. 386)*.

Doubtful account expense. Another name for Uncollectible account expense *(p. 371)*.

Interest. The revenue to the payee for loaning out the principal, and the expense to the maker for borrowing the principal *(p. 382)*.

Interest period. The period of time during which interest is to be computed, extending from the original date of the note to the maturity date *(p. 382)*.

Interest rate. The percentage rate that is multiplied by the principal amount to compute the amount of interest on a note *(p. 382)*.

Maker of a note. The person or business that signs the note and promises to pay the amount required by the note agreement. The maker is the debtor *(p. 381)*.

Maturity date. The date on which the final payment of a note is due. Also called the Due date *(p. 382)*.

Maturity value. The sum of the principal and interest due at the maturity date of a note *(p. 382)*.

Other receivables. A miscellaneous category that includes loans to employees and branch companies— usually long-term assets reported on the balance sheet after current assets and before plant assets. *(p. 370)*.

Payee of a note. The person or business to whom the maker of a note promises future payment. The payee is the creditor *(p. 381)*.

Principal amount. The amount loaned out by the payee and borrowed by the maker of a note *(p. 381)*.

Promissory note. A written promise to pay a specified amount of money at a particular future date *(p. 381)*.

Quick ratio. Another name for the Acid-test ratio *(p. 389)*.

Receivable. A monetary claim against a business or an individual, acquired mainly by selling goods and services and by lending money *(p. 369)*.

Uncollectible account expense. Cost to the seller of extending credit. Arises from the failure to collect from credit customers *(p. 371)*.

Answers to Self-Study Questions

1. a
2. c
3. d
4. a
5. b ($78,900 − $14,300 = $64,600)

6. b
7. c ($30,000 × .09 × 6/12 = $1,350)
8. b ($30,000 × .09 × 4/12 = $900)
9. a
10. d

ASSIGNMENT MATERIAL

Questions

1. Name the two parties to a receivable/payable transaction. Which party has the receivable? Which party has the payable? Which party has the asset? Which party has the liability?

2. List three categories of receivables. State how each category is classified for reporting on the balance sheet.

3. Name the two methods of accounting for uncollectible receivables. Which method is easier to apply? Which method is consistent with generally accepted accounting principles?

4. Which of the two methods of accounting for uncollectible accounts is preferable? Why?

5. Identify the accounts debited and credited to account for uncollectibles under (a) the allowance method and (b) the direct write-off method.

6. What is another term for Allowance for Uncollectible Accounts? What are two other terms for Uncollectible Account Expense?

7. Which entry decreases net income under the allowance method of accounting for uncollectibles: the entry to record uncollectible account expense or the entry to write off an uncollectible account receivable?

8. May a customer pay his or her account receivable after it has been written off? If not, why not? If so, what entries are made to account for reinstating the customer's account and for collecting cash from the customer?

9. Identify and briefly describe the two ways to estimate bad debt expense and uncollectible accounts.

10. Briefly describe how a company may use both the percentage-of-sales method and the aging method to account for uncollectibles.

11. How does a credit balance arise in a customer's account receivable? How does the company report this credit balance on its balance sheet?

12. Many businesses receive most of their cash on credit sales through the mail. Suppose you own a business so large that you must hire employees to handle cash receipts and perform the related accounting duties. What internal control feature should you use to ensure that the cash received from customers is not taken by a dishonest employee?

13. Use the terms *maker, payee, principal amount, maturity date, promissory note,* and *interest* in an appropriate sentence or two.

14. For each of the following notes receivable, compute the amount of interest revenue earned during 19X6:

	Principal	Interest Rate	Interest Period	Maturity Date
a. Note 1	$ 10,000	9%	90 days	11/30/19X6
b. Note 2	50,000	10%	6 months	9/30/19X6
c. Note 3	100,000	8%	5 years	12/31/19X7
d. Note 4	15,000	12%	60 days	1/15/19X7

15. Name three situations in which a company might receive a note receivable. For each situation, show the account debited and the account credited to record receipt of the note.

16. Suppose you hold a 180-day, $5,000 note receivable that specifies 10 percent interest. After 60 days you discount the note at 12 percent. How much cash do you receive?

17. How does a contingent liability differ from an ordinary liability? How does discounting a note receivable create a contingent liability? When does the contingency cease to exist?

18. When the maker of a note dishonors the note at maturity, what accounts does the payee debit and credit?

19. Why does the payee of a note receivable usually need to make adjusting entries for interest at the end of the accounting period?

20. Recall the real-world disclosures of receivables the chapter presents. Show three ways to report Accounts Receivable of $100,000 and Allowance for Uncollectible Accounts of $2,800 on the balance sheet or in the related notes.

21. Why is the acid-test ratio a more stringent measure of the ability to pay current liabilities than is the current ratio?

22. Which measure of days' sales in receivables is preferable, 30 or 40? Give your reason.

Exercises

Net accounts receivable $19,140

Exercise 8-1 *Using the allowance method for bad debts* **(L.O. 1)**

On September 30, Trinity Fruit Supply had a $26,000 debit balance in Accounts Receivable. During October the company had sales of $135,000, which included $88,000 in credit sales. October collections were $91,000 and write-offs of uncollectible receivables totaled $1,070. Other data include:

September 30 credit balance in Allowance for Uncollectible Accounts, $2,100
Uncollectible account expense, estimated as 2 percent of credit sales

Required

1. Prepare journal entries to record sales, collections, uncollectible account expense by the allowance method, and write-offs of uncollectibles during October.
2. Show the ending balances in Accounts Receivable, Allowance for Uncollectible Accounts, and *net* accounts receivable at October 31. Does Trinity expect to collect the net amount of the receivable?

No check figure

Exercise 8-2 *Recording bad debts by the allowance method* **(L.O. 1)**

Prepare general journal entries to record the following transactions under the allowance method of accounting for uncollectibles:

Apr. 2 Sold merchandise for $3,700 on credit terms of 2/10 n/30 to McBee Sales Company.
May 28 Received legal notification that McBee Sales Company was bankrupt. Wrote off McBee's accounts receivable balance.
Aug. 11 Received $2,000 from McBee Sales Company, together with a letter indicating that the company intended to pay its account within the next month.
      30 Received the remaining amount due from McBee.

Exercise 8-3 *Using the aging approach to estimate bad debts* **(L.O. 1, 2)**

Allow. for Doubtful Accts. $12,888

At December 31, 19X7, the accounts receivable balance of Wang, Limited is $266,000. The allowance for doubtful accounts has a $3,910 credit balance. Accountants for Wang, Limited prepare the following aging schedule for its accounts receivable:

Total Balance	Age of Accounts			
	1–30 Days	31–60 Days	61–90 Days	Over 90 Days
$266,000	$104,000	$78,000	$69,000	$15,000
Estimated percentage uncollectible	0.3%	1.2%	6.0%	50%

Journalize the adjusting entry for doubtful accounts based on the aging schedule. Show the T-account for the allowance.

Exercise 8-4 *Using the direct write-off method for bad debts* **(L.O. 3)**

Net accounts receivable $21,930

Refer to the situation of Exercise 8–1.

Required

1. Record uncollectible account expense for October by the direct write-off method.
2. What amount of *net* accounts receivable would Trinity report on its October 31 balance sheet under the direct write-off method? Does Trinity expect to collect this much of the receivable? Give your reason.

Exercise 8-5 *Controlling cash receipts from customers* **(L.O. 4)**

No check figure

As a recent college graduate, you land your first job in the customer collections department of Coffey & Schwayze, a partnership. Lela Coffey, the president, has asked you to propose a system to ensure that cash received by mail from customers is properly handled. Draft a short memorandum identifying the essential element in your proposed plan, and state why this element is important. Refer to Chapter 7 if necessary.

Exercise 8-6 *Recording a note receivable and accruing interest revenue* **(L.O. 5)**

Accrued interest revenue $495

Record the following transactions in the general journal.

Nov. 1 Loaned $30,000 cash to R. Milpas on a 1-year, 9 percent note.
Dec. 3 Sold goods to Lofland, Inc., receiving a 90-day, 12 percent note for $3,750.
    16 Received a $2,000, 6-month, 12 percent note on account from J. Baker.
    31 Accrued interest revenue on all notes receivable.

Exercise 8-7 *Recording a note receivable and accruing interest revenue* **(L.O. 5)**

No check figure

Record the following transactions in the general journal:

Apr. 1, 19X2 Loaned $6,000 to Bing Bingham on a 1-year, 9 percent note.
Dec. 31, 19X2 Accrued interest revenue on the Bingham note.
Dec. 31, 19X2 Closed the interest revenue account.
Apr. 1, 19X3 Received the maturity value of the note from Bing Bingham.

No check figure

Exercise 8-8 *Accounting for a dishonored note receivable* **(L.O. 5)**

Record the following transactions in the general journal, assuming the company uses the allowance method to account for uncollectibles:

May 18 Sold goods to Joliff Cartographers, receiving a 120-day, 12 percent note for $2,700.

Sep. 15 The note is dishonored.

Nov. 30 After pursuing collection from Joliff Cartographers, wrote off their account as uncollectible.

Proceeds from discounting $2,852

Exercise 8-9 *Recording notes receivable, discounting a note, and reporting the contingent liability in a note* **(L.O. 5, 6)**

Prepare general journal entries to record the following transactions:

Aug. 14 Sold goods on account to E. Pucci, $2,900.

Dec. 2 Received a $2,900, 180-day, 10 percent note from E. Pucci in satisfaction of his past-due account receivable.

30 Sold the Pucci note by discounting it to a bank at 15 percent. (Use a 360-day year, and round amounts to the nearest dollar.)

Write the note to disclose the contingent liability at December 31.

Doubtful acct. expense:
(a) $3,000
(b) $5,700

Exercise 8-10 *Recording bad debts by the allowance method* **(L.O. 1, 2, 6)**

At December 31, 19X5, Glanville Contractors has an accounts receivable balance of $129,000. Sales revenue for 19X5 is $950,000, including credit sales of $600,000. For each of the following situations, prepare the year-end adjusting entry to record doubtful account expense. Show how the accounts receivable and the allowance for doubtful accounts are reported on the balance sheet.

a. Allowance for Doubtful Accounts has a credit balance before adjustment of $1,600. Glanville Contractors estimates that doubtful account expense for the year is 1/2 of 1 percent of credit sales.

b. Allowance for Doubtful Accounts has a debit balance before adjustment of $1,100. Glanville Contractors estimates that $4,600 of the accounts receivable will prove uncollectible.

No check figure

Exercise 8-11 *Reporting receivables with credit balances* **(L.O. 6)**

The accounts receivable subsidiary ledger includes the following summarized data:

83 accounts with debit balances totaling	$113,650
9 accounts with credit balances totaling	3,980
Net total of balances........................	$109,670

The company accountant proposes to report only the net total of $109,670. Show how these data should be reported on the balance sheet.

19X8 acid-test ratio .86; days' sales in receivables 32 days

Exercise 8-12 *Evaluating ratio data* **(L.O. 7)**

McKaig & Laughlin, a department store, reported the following amounts in its 19X8 financial statements. The 19X7 figures are given for comparison.

		19X8		19X7
Current assets:				
Cash		$ 12,000		$ 8,000
Short-term investments		13,000		11,000
Accounts receivable	$80,000		$74,000	
less Allowance for				
uncollectibles	7,000	73,000	6,000	68,000
Inventory		191,000		187,000
Prepaid insurance		2,000		2,000
Total current assets		291,000		276,000
Total current liabilities		114,000		107,000
Net sales		813,000		762,000

Required

1. Determine whether the acid-test ratio improved or deteriorated from 19X7 to 19X8. How does McKaig & Laughlin's acid-test ratio compare with the industry average of .80?
2. Compare the days' sales in receivables measure for 19X8 with the company's credit terms of net 30.

Problems   (Group A)

Problem 8-1A   *Accounting for uncollectibles by the direct write-off and allowance methods* **(L.O. 1, 2, 3, 6)**

Uncollect. acct. expense, direct method, $8,700; allow. method, $12,800

On May 31, Sironia, Inc., had a $216,000 debit balance in Accounts Receivable. During June the company had sales revenue of $788,000, which included $640,000 in credit sales. Other data for June include:

Collections on accounts receivable, $599,400
Write-offs of uncollectible receivables, $8,700

Required

1. Record uncollectible account expense for June by the *direct write-off* method. Show all June activity in Accounts Receivable and Uncollectible Account Expense.
2. Record uncollectible account expense and write-offs of customer accounts for June by the *allowance* method. Show all June activity in Accounts Receivable, Allowance for Uncollectible Accounts, and Uncollectible Account Expense. The May 31 unadjusted balance in Allowance for Uncollectible Accounts was $2,200 (credit). Uncollectible Account Expense was estimated at 2 percent of credit sales.
3. What amount of uncollectible account expense would Sironia, Inc., report on its June income statement under the two methods? Which amount better matches expense with revenue? Give your reason.
4. What amount of net accounts receivable would Sironia, Inc., report on its June 30 balance sheet under the two methods? Which amount is more realistic? Give your reason.

Chapter 8   Accounts and Notes Receivable   **399**

Problem 8-2A   *Uncollectibles, notes receivable, discounting notes, dishonored notes, and accrued interest revenue* **(L.O. 2, 5)**

Assume Ralston Purina, manufacturer of pet foods, completed the following selected transactions:

19X5

Nov. 1   Sold goods to Safeway, Inc., receiving a $22,000, 3-month, 12 percent note.

Dec. 31   Made an adjusting entry to accrue interest on the Safeway note.

     31   Made an adjusting entry to record doubtful account expense based on an aging of accounts receivable. The aging analysis indicates that $197,400 of accounts receivable will not be collected. Prior to this adjustment, the credit balance in Allowance for Doubtful Accounts is $189,900.

19X6

Feb. 1   Collected the maturity value of the Safeway note.

     23   Received a 90-day, 15 percent, $4,000 note from Bliss Company on account. (This year February has 28 days.)

Mar. 31   Discounted the Bliss Co. note to Lakewood Bank at 20 percent.

Apr. 23   Sold merchandise to Lear Corporation, receiving a 60-day, 10 percent note for $6,000.

June 22   Lear Corp. dishonored its note at maturity; converted the maturity value of the note to an account receivable.

July 15   Loaned $8,500 cash to McNeil, Inc., receiving a 30-day, 12 percent note.

     17   Sold merchandise to Grant Corp., receiving a 3-month, 10 percent, $8,000 note.

Aug. 5   Collected $6,100 on account from Lear Corporation.

     14   Collected the maturity value of the McNeil, Inc., note.

     17   Discounted the Grant Corp. note to Lakewood Bank at 15 percent.

Oct. 17   Grant Corp. dishonored its note at maturity; paid Lakewood Bank the maturity value of the note plus a protest fee of $50 and debited an account receivable from Grant Corp.

Dec. 15   Wrote off as uncollectible the account receivable from Grant Corp.

Required

Record the transactions in the general journal. Explanations are not required.

Problem 8-3A   *Using the percent of sales and aging approaches for uncollectibles* **(L.O. 2, 6)**

Kaleidoscope Jewelry completed the following selected transactions during 19X1 and 19X2:

19X1

Dec. 31   Estimated that uncollectible account expense for the year was 1/2 of 1 percent on credit sales of $450,000 and recorded that amount as expense.

     31   Made the appropriate closing entry.

19X2

Feb. 4   Sold inventory to Gary Carter, $1,521, on credit terms of 2/10 n/30.

July 1 Wrote off Gary Carter's account as uncollectible after repeated efforts to collect from him.

Oct. 19 Received $521 from Gary Carter, along with a letter stating his intention to pay his debt in full within 30 days. Reinstated his account in full.

Nov. 15 Received the balance due from Gary Carter.

Dec. 31 Made a compound entry to write off the following accounts as uncollectible: Kris Moore, $899; Marie Mandue, $530; and Grant Frycer, $672.

   31 Estimated that uncollectible account expense for the year was 1/2 of 1 percent on credit sales of $540,000 and recorded the expense.

   31 Made the appropriate closing entry.

Required

1. Open general ledger accounts for Allowance for Uncollectible Accounts and Uncollectible Account Expense. Keep running balances.

2. Record the transactions in the general journal, and post to the two ledger accounts.

3. The December 31, 19X2, balance of Accounts Receivable is $158,300. Show how Accounts Receivable would be reported at that date.

4. Assume that Kaleidoscope Jewelry Company begins aging its accounts receivable on December 31, 19X2. The balance in Accounts Receivable is $158,300, the credit balance in Allowance for Uncollectible Accounts is $149, and the company estimates that $3,245 of its accounts receivable will prove uncollectible.
   a. Make the adjusting entry for uncollectibles.
   b. Show how Accounts Receivable will be reported on the December 31, 19X2, balance sheet.

Problem 8-4A *Using the percent of sales and aging approaches for uncollectibles (L.O. 2, 6)*

Allow. for Doubtful Accts. $3,709

The December 31, 19X4, balance sheet of Brazos Rubber Products reports the following:

Accounts Receivable $141,000
Allowance for Doubtful Accounts (credit balance) 3,200

At the end of each quarter, Brazos estimates doubtful account expense to be 1½ percent of credit sales. At the end of the year, the company ages its accounts receivable and adjusts the balance in Allowance for Doubtful Accounts to correspond to the aging schedule. During 19X5 Brazos completes the following selected transactions:

Jan. 16 Wrote off as uncollectible the $403 account receivable from DePaul, Inc., and the $1,719 account receivable from Frank Shoe Company.

Mar. 31 Recorded doubtful account expense based on credit sales of $100,000.

Apr. 15 Received $300 from Frank Shoe Company after prolonged negotiations with Frank Shoe Company's attorney. Brazos has no hope of collecting the remainder.

May 13 Wrote off as uncollectible the $2,980 account receivable from M. E. Cate.

June 30 Recorded doubtful account expense based on credit sales of $114,000.

Aug. 9 Made a compound entry to write off the following uncollectible accounts: Clifford, Inc., $235; Matz Co., $188; and Lew Norris, $1,006.

Sep. 30 Recorded doubtful account expense based on credit sales of $130,000.

Oct. 18 Wrote off as uncollectible the $767 account receivable from Bliss Co. and the $430 account receivable from Micro Data.

Dec. 31 Recorded doubtful account expense based on the following summary of the aging of accounts receivable.

Total Balance	Age of Accounts			
	1–30 Days	31–60 Days	61–90 Days	Over 90 Days
$127,400	$74,600	$31,100	$12,000	$9,700
Estimated percentage uncollectible	0.1%	0.4%	5.0%	30.0%

Dec. 31 Made the closing entry for Doubtful Account Expense for the entire year.

Required

1. Record the transactions in the general journal.
2. Open the Allowance for Doubtful Accounts and post entries affecting that account. Keep a running balance.
3. Most companies report two-year comparative financial statements. If Brazos's Accounts Receivable balance is $127,400 at December 31, 19X5, show how the company would report its accounts receivable on a comparative balance sheet for 19X5 and 19X4, as follows:

	19X5	19X4
Accounts receivable	_____	_____
Less: Allowance for doubtful accounts	_____	_____
Net accounts receivable	_____	_____

No check figure

Problem 8-5A *Controlling cash receipts from customers (L.O. 4)*

Medical Laboratory Service provides laboratory testing for samples that physicians send in. All work is performed on account, with regular monthly billing to participating doctors. Agnes Bisset, accountant for Medical Laboratory Service, receives and opens the mail. Company procedure requires her to separate customer checks from the remittance slips, which list the amounts she posts as credits to customer accounts receivable. Bisset deposits the checks in the bank. She computes each day's total amount posted to customer accounts and agrees this total to the bank deposit slip. This is intended to ensure that all receipts are deposited in the bank.

Required

As the auditor of Medical Laboratory Service, write a memo to management to evaluate the company's internal controls over cash receipts from customers. If the system is effective, identify its strong features. If the system has flaws, propose a way to strengthen the controls.

Accrued interest revenue $405

Problem 8-6A *Accounting for notes receivable, including discounting notes and accruing interest revenue (L.O. 5)*

A company received the following notes during 19X5. Notes (1), (2), and (3) were discounted on the dates and at the rates indicated.

Note	Date	Principal Amount	Interest Rate	Term	Date Discounted	Discount Rate
(1)	July 15	$ 6,000	8%	6 months	Oct. 15	12%
(2)	Aug. 19	11,000	12%	90 days	Aug. 30	15%
(3)	Sep. 1	16,000	15%	120 days	Nov. 2	20%
(4)	Oct. 30	7,000	12%	3 months	—	—
(5)	Nov. 19	15,000	10%	60 days	—	—
(6)	Dec. 1	12,000	9%	1 year	—	—

Required

As necessary in requirements 1 through 5, identify each note by number, compute interest using a 360-day year for those notes with terms specified in days or years, round all interest amounts to the nearest dollar, and present entries in general journal form. Explanations are not required.

1. Determine the due date and maturity value of each note.
2. For each discounted note, determine the discount and proceeds from sale of the note.
3. Journalize the discounting of notes (1) and (2).
4. Journalize a single adjusting entry at December 31, 19X5, to record accrued interest revenue on notes (4), (5), and (6).
5. Journalize the collection of principal and interest on note (4).

Problem 8-7A *Notes receivable, discounted notes, dishonored notes, and accrued interest revenue* **(L.O. 2, 5)**

No check figure

Record the following selected transactions in the general journal. Explanations are not required.

19X2

Dec. 21 Received a $10,800, 30-day, 10 percent note on account from Zettler Gas Service.

31 Made an adjusting entry to accrue interest on the Zettler note.

31 Made an adjusting entry to record doubtful account expense in the amount of 2/3 of 1 percent on credit sales of $604,800.

31 Made a compound closing entry for the appropriate accounts.

19X3

Jan. 20 Collected the maturity value of the Zettler note.

Apr. 19 Sold merchandise to city of Denver, receiving $500 cash and a 120-day, 12 percent note for $5,000.

May 1 Discounted the city of Denver note to First National Bank at 15 percent.

Sep. 14 Loaned $6,000 cash to Allstate Investors, receiving a 3-month, 13 percent note.

30 Received a $1,675, 60-day, 16 percent note from Matt Kurtz on his past-due account receivable.

Nov. 29 Matt Kurtz dishonored his note at maturity; accrued no interest revenue and wrote off the note as uncollectible, debiting Allowance for Doubtful Accounts.

Dec. 14 Collected the maturity value of the Allstate Investors note.

31 Wrote off as uncollectible the accounts receivable of Ty Larson, $330, and Terry Gee, $460.

Problem 8-8A *Using ratio data to evaluate a company's position* **(L.O. 7)**

The comparative financial statements of Associated Mills Corp. for 19X6, 19X5, and 19X4 included the following selected data:

	Millions		
Balance sheet:	19X6	19X5	19X4
Current assets:			
Cash	$ 49	$ 66	$ 51
Short-term investments	131	174	122
Receivables, net of allowance for doubtful accounts of $6, $6, and $5	237	265	218
Inventories	389	341	302
Prepaid expenses	61	27	46
Total current assets	867	873	739
Total current liabilities	482	528	403
Income statement:			
Sales revenue	$5,189	$4,995	$4,206
Cost of sales	2,834	2,636	2,418

Required

1. For 19X6 and 19X5 compute these ratios:
    a. Current ratio
    b. Acid-test ratio
    c. Inventory turnover
    d. Days' sales in average receivables
2. Explain for top management which ratio values showed improvement from 19X5 to 19X6 and which ratio values showed deterioration. Which item in the financial statements caused some ratio values to improve and others to deteriorate?

(Group B)

Uncollect. acct. expense, direct
method, $3,300; allow. method
$8,860

Problem 8-1B *Accounting for uncollectibles by the direct write-off and allowance methods* **(L.O. 1, 2, 3, 6)**

On February 28 Centex Warehouse Co. had a $72,000 debit balance in Accounts Receivable. During March the company had sales revenue of $509,000, which included $443,000 in credit sales. Other data for March include:

Collections on accounts receivable, $451,600
Write-offs of uncollectible receivables, $3,300

Required

1. Record uncollectible account expense for March by the *direct write-off* method. Show all March activity in Accounts Receivable and Uncollectible Account Expense.
2. Record uncollectible account expense and write-offs of customer accounts for March by the *allowance* method. Show all March activity in Accounts Receivable, Allowance for Uncollectible Accounts, and Uncollectible Account Expense. The February 28 unadjusted balance in Allowance for Uncollectible Accounts was $800 (debit). Uncollectible Account Expense was estimated at 2 percent of credit sales.

3. What amount of uncollectible account expense would Centex Warehouse Co. report on its March income statement under the two methods? Which amount better matches expense with revenue? Give your reason.

4. What amount of *net* accounts receivable would Centex Warehouse Co. report on its March 31 balance sheet under the two methods? Which amount is more realistic? Give your reason.

Problem 8-2B   *Uncollectibles, notes receivable, discounting notes, dishonored notes, and accrued interest revenue (L.O. 2, 5)*

No check figure

Assume the Sherwin-Williams Company, a major paint manufacturer, completed the following selected transactions:

19X4

Dec. 1   Sold goods to Central Paint Supply, receiving a $15,000, 3-month, 10 percent note.

   31   Made an adjusting entry to accrue interest on the Central Paint Supply note.

   31   Made an adjusting entry to record doubtful account expense based on an aging of accounts receivable. The aging analysis indicates that $355,800 of accounts receivable will not be collected. Prior to this adjustment, the credit balance in Allowance for Doubtful Accounts is $346,100.

19X5

Feb. 18   Received a 90-day, 10 percent, $5,000 note from Dilley, Inc., on account. (This year February has 28 days.)

Mar. 1   Collected the maturity value of the Central Paint Supply note.

   8   Discounted the Dilley note to First State Bank at 16 percent.

Apr. 21   Sold merchandise to Brown Group, receiving a 60-day, 9 percent note for $4,000.

June 20   Brown Group dishonored its note at maturity and converted the maturity value of the note to an account receivable.

July 12   Loaned $60,000 cash to Consolidated Investments, receiving a 90-day, 13 percent note.

   13   Sold merchandise to Pearson Paint Shop, receiving a 4-month, 12 percent, $2,500 note.

Aug. 2   Collected $4,060 on account from Brown Group.

Sep. 13   Discounted the Pearson Paint Shop note to First State Bank at 18 percent.

Oct. 10   Collected the maturity value of the Consolidated Investments note.

Nov. 13   Pearson Paint Shop dishonored its note at maturity; paid First State Bank the maturity value of the note plus a protest fee of $35 and debited an account receivable from Pearson Paint Shop.

Dec. 31   Wrote off as uncollectible the account receivable from Pearson Paint Shop.

Required

Record the transactions in the general journal. Explanations are not required.

Problem 8-3B   *Using the percent of sales and aging approaches for uncollectibles (L.O. 2, 6)*

Allow. for Uncollect. Accts.
$3,343

Shuster, Inc., completed the following transactions during 19X1 and 19X2:

19X1

Dec. 31 Estimated that uncollectible account expense for the year was 3/4 of 1 percent on credit sales of $300,000, and recorded that amount as expense.

31 Made the appropriate closing entry.

19X2

Jan. 17 Sold inventory to Mary Lee, $652, on credit terms of 2/10 n/30.

June 29 Wrote off the Mary Lee account as uncollectible after repeated efforts to collect from her.

Aug. 6 Received $250 from Mary Lee, along with a letter stating her intention to pay her debt in full within 30 days. Reinstated her account in full.

Sep. 4 Received the balance due from Mary Lee.

Dec. 31 Made a compound entry to write off the following accounts as uncollectible: Bernard Klaus, $737; Louis Mann, $348; and Millie Burnett, $622.

31 Estimated that uncollectible account expense for the year was 2/3 of 1 percent on credit sales of $420,000, and recorded that amount as expense.

31 Made the appropriate closing entry.

Required

1. Open general ledger accounts for Allowance for Uncollectible Accounts and Uncollectible Account Expense. Keep running balances.
2. Record the transactions in the general journal, and post to the two ledger accounts.
3. The December 31, 19X2, balance of Accounts Receivable is $123,000. Show how Accounts Receivable would be reported at that date.
4. Assume that Shuster, Inc., begins aging accounts receivable on December 31, 19X2. The balance in Accounts Receivable is $123,000, the credit balance in Allowance for Uncollectible Accounts is $543, and the company estimates that $2,600 of its accounts receivable will prove uncollectible.
   a. Make the adjusting entry for uncollectibles.
   b. Show how Accounts Receivable will be reported on the December 31, 19X2, balance sheet.

Allow. for Doubtful Accts.
$9,583

Problem 8-4B *Using the percent-of-sales and aging approaches for uncollectibles (L.O. 2, 6)*

The December 31, 19X6, balance sheet of Safelite Auto Glass reports the following:

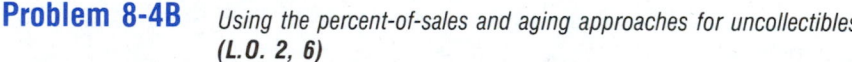

Accounts Receivable $256,000
Allowance for Doubtful Accounts (credit balance).... 7,100

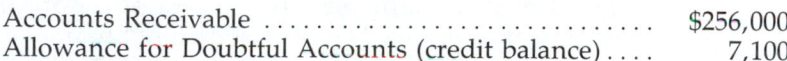

At the end of each quarter, Safelite Auto Glass estimates doubtful account expense to be 2 percent of credit sales. At the end of the year, the company ages its accounts receivable and adjusts the balance in Allowance for Doubtful Accounts to correspond to the aging schedule. During 19X7 Safelite completes the following selected transactions:

Jan. 31 Wrote off as uncollectible the $855 account receivable from Spinelli Company and the $3,287 account receivable from Leo Maltsberger.

Mar. 31 Recorded doubtful account expense based on credit sales of $120,000.

May 2 Received $1,000 from Leo Maltsberger after prolonged negotiations with Maltsberger's attorney. Safelite has no hope of collecting the remainder.

June 15 Wrote off as uncollectible the $1,120 account receivable from Lisa Brown.

June 30 Recorded doubtful account expense based on credit sales of $166,000.

July 14 Made a compound entry to write off the following uncollectible accounts: C. H. Harris, $766; Graphics Unlimited, $2,413; and Ben McQueen, $134.

Sep. 30 Recorded doubtful account expense based on credit sales of $141,400.

Nov. 22 Wrote off the following accounts receivable as uncollectible: Monet Corp., $1,345; Blocker, Inc., $2,109; and Main Street Plaza, $755.

Dec. 31 Recorded doubtful account expense based on the following summary of the aging of accounts receivable:

Total Balance	Age of Accounts			
	1–30 Days	31–60 Days	61–90 Days	Over 90 Days
$294,600	$161,500	$86,000	$32,000	$15,100
Estimated percentage uncollectible	0.2%	0.5%	4.0%	50.0%

Dec. 31 Made the closing entry for Doubtful Account Expense for the entire year.

Required

1. Record the transactions in the general journal.
2. Open the Allowance for Doubtful Accounts, and post entries affecting that account. Keep a running balance.
3. Most companies report two-year comparative financial statements. If Safelite's Accounts Receivable balance is $294,600 at December 31, 19X7, show how the company would report its accounts receivable in a comparative balance sheet for 19X7 and 19X6, as follows:

	19X7	19X6
Accounts receivable		
Less: Allowance for doubtful accounts		
Net accounts receivable		

Problem 8-5B *Controlling cash receipts from customers* **(L.O. 4)**   No check figure

Chavanne Sporting Goods distributes merchandise to sporting goods stores. All sales are on credit, so virtually all cash receipts arrive in the mail. Evelyn Hupp, the company president, has just returned from a trade association meeting with new ideas for the business. Among other things, Hupp plans to institute stronger internal controls over cash receipts from customers.

Required

Outline a set of procedures to ensure that all cash receipts are deposited in the bank and that the total amounts of each day's cash receipts are posted as credits to customer accounts receivable.

Problem 8-6B
Accounting for notes receivable, including discounting notes and accruing interest revenue (L.O. 5)

A company received the following notes during 19X3. Notes (1), (2), and (3) were discounted on the dates and at the rates indicated.

Note	Date	Principal Amount	Interest Rate	Term	Date Discounted	Discount Rate
(1)	July 12	$12,000	10%	3 months	Aug. 12	15%
(2)	Sep. 4	6,000	11%	90 days	Sep. 30	13%
(3)	Oct. 21	5,000	15%	60 days	Nov. 3	18%
(4)	Nov. 30	12,000	12%	6 months	—	—
(5)	Dec. 7	9,000	10%	30 days	—	—
(6)	Dec. 23	15,000	9%	1 year	—	—

Required

As necessary in requirements 1 through 5, identify each note by number, compute interest using a 360-day year for those notes with terms specified in days or years, round all interest amounts to the nearest dollar, and present entries in general journal form. Explanations are not required.

1. Determine the due date and maturity value of each note.
2. For each discounted note, determine the discount and proceeds from sale of the note.
3. Journalize the discounting of notes (1) and (2).
4. Journalize a single adjusting entry at December 31, 19X3, to record accrued interest revenue on notes (4), (5), and (6).
5. Journalize the collection of principal and interest on note (5).

Problem 8-7B
Notes receivable, discounted notes, dishonored notes, and accrued interest revenue (L.O. 2, 5)

Record the following selected transactions in the general journal. Explanations are not required.

19X6

Dec. 19 Received a $5,000, 60-day, 12 percent note on account from City Cablevision.

31 Made an adjusting entry to accrue interest on the City Cablevision note.

31 Made an adjusting entry to record doubtful account expense in the amount of 8/10 of 1 percent of credit sales of $474,500.

31 Made a compound closing entry for the appropriate accounts.

19X7

Feb. 17 Collected the maturity value of the City Cablevision note.

Mar. 22 Sold merchandise to Idaho Power Co., receiving $1,400 cash and a 90-day, 10 percent note for $6,000.

May 3 Discounted the Idaho Power Co. note to First National Bank at 15 percent.

June 1 Loaned $10,000 cash to Linz Brothers, receiving a 6-month, 11 percent note.

Oct. 31 Received a $1,500, 60-day, 12 percent note from Ned Pierce on his past-due account receivable.

Dec. 1 Collected the maturity value of the Linz Brothers note.

30 Ned Pierce dishonored his note at maturity; accrued no interest revenue and wrote off the note receivable as uncollectible.

31 Wrote off as uncollectible the accounts receivable of Al Bynum, $435; and Ray Sharp, $276.

Problem 8-8B   *Using ratio data to evaluate a company's position*   *(L.O. 7)*

19X4 Inventory turnover 2.9 times

The comparative financial statements of Domingo Catalog Merchants for 19X4, 19X3, and 19X2 included the following selected data:

	Millions		
Balance sheet:	19X4	19X3	19X2
Current assets:			
Cash	$ 17	$ 28	$ 22
Short-term investments	73	101	69
Receivables, net of allowance for doubtful accounts of $7, $6, and $4	136	154	127
Inventories	428	373	341
Prepaid expenses.................................	42	31	25
Total current assets	696	687	584
Total current liabilities	430	446	388
Income statement:			
Sales revenue	$2,671	$2,505	$1,944
Cost of sales	1,180	1,160	963

Required

1. For 19X4 and 19X3 compute these ratios:
   a. Current ratio
   b. Acid-test ratio
   c. Inventory turnover
   d. Days' sales in average receivables

2. Explain for top management which ratio values showed improvement from 19X3 to 19X4 and which ratio values showed deterioration. Which item in the financial statements caused some ratio values to improve and others to deteriorate?

Extending Your Knowledge

Decision Problems

1. Uncollectible Accounts and Evaluating a Business (L.O. 1, 2, 3, 5, 6)

Data Control sells its products either for cash or on notes receivable that earn interest. The business uses the direct write-off method to account for bad debts. David Messier, the owner, has prepared Data Control's financial statements. The most recent comparative income statements, for 19X3 and 19X2, are as follows:

Net income, 19X3, $52,000

	19X3	19X2
Total revenue	$210,000	$195,000
Total expenses	157,000	153,000
Net income	$ 53,000	$ 42,000

Based on the increase in net income, Messier seeks to expand his operations. He asks you to invest $50,000 in the business. You and Messier have several meetings, at which you learn that notes receivable from customers were $200,000 at the end of 19X1 and $400,000 at the end of 19X2. Also, total revenues for 19X3 and 19X2 include interest at 15 percent on the year's beginning notes receivable balance. Total expenses include doubtful account expense of $2,000 each year, based on the direct write-off basis. Messier estimates that doubtful account expense would be 2 percent of sales revenue if the allowance method were used.

Required

1. Prepare for Data Control a comparative single-step income statement that identifies sales revenue, interest revenue, doubtful account expense, and other expenses, all computed in accordance with generally accepted accounting principles.

2. Is Data Control's future as promising as Messier's income statement makes it appear? Give the reason for your answer.

No check figure

2. Estimating the Collectibility of Accounts Receivable   (L.O. 1, 6, 7)

Assume you work in the corporate loan department of Brunswick Bank. Maria Presti, owner of MP Manufacturing Inc., a manufacturer of wooden furniture, has come to you seeking a loan for $350,000 to buy new manufacturing equipment to expand her operations. She proposes to use her accounts receivable as collateral for the loan and has provided you with the following information from her most recent audited financial statements:

	19X9	19X8	19X7
Sales	$1,475	$1,589	$1,502
Cost of goods sold	876	947	905
Gross profit	599	642	597
Other expenses	518	487	453
Net profit or (loss) before taxes	$ 81	$ 155	$ 144
Accounts receivable	$ 458	$ 387	$ 374
Allowance for doubtful accounts	23	31	29

Required

1. What analysis would you perform on the information Ms. Presti has provided? Would you grant the loan based on this information? Give your reason.

2. What additional information would you request from Ms. Presti? Give your reason.

3. Assume Ms. Presti provided you with the information requested in question 2. What would make you change the decision you made in question 1?

Ethical Issue

Goodwill Finance Company is in the consumer loan business. It borrows from banks and loans out the money at higher interest rates. Goodwill's bank requires Goodwill to submit quarterly financial statements in order to keep its line of credit. Goodwill's main asset is Notes Receivable. Therefore, Uncollectible Account Expense and Allowance for Uncollectible Accounts are important accounts.

Goodwill's owner, Jacob Marleybone, likes net income to increase in a smooth pattern rather than to increase in some periods and decrease in other periods. To report smoothly increasing net income, Marleybone underestimates Uncollectible Account Expense in some periods. In other periods, Marleybone overestimates the expense. He reasons that the income overstatements roughly offset the income understatements over time.

Required

Is Goodwill's practice of smoothing income ethical? Give your reasons.

Financial Statement Problems

1. Accounts Receivable and Related Uncollectibles **(L.O. 1)**

No check figure

Use data from the Goodyear Tire & Rubber Company balance sheet and the related note titled Accounts and Notes Receivable, in Appendix C, to answer these questions. Show all amounts in millions, rounded to the nearest $100,000. For example, show $8,600,000 as $8.6 million.

1. How much did Goodyear's customers owe the company at December 31, 1989? Of this amount, how much did Goodyear expect to collect?
2. Journalize the following for the year ended December 31, 1990, using Goodyear's actual account titles. Explanations are not required.
   a. Net sales revenue of $11,272.5 million. Give one entry for the year's total, assuming all net sales revenue is earned on account.
   b. Doubtful account expense, estimated to equal 1 percent of net sales.
   c. Cash collections on account, $10,909.2 million.
   d. Write-offs of uncollectibles totaling $112.4 million.
3. Post to Accounts and Notes Receivable and Allowance for Doubtful Accounts, inserting these accounts' December 31, 1989 balances.
4. After posting, compare your account balances to those at December 31, 1990, in the Accounts and Notes Receivable note. Your figures should agree with the Goodyear actual amounts.
5. How much did Goodyear's customers owe the company at December 31, 1990? How much of this total did Goodyear expect to collect? Describe in words the amount reported for Accounts and Notes Receivable on Goodyear's December 31, 1990, balance sheet.

2. Accounts Receivable, Uncollectibles, and Notes Receivable **(L.O. 1, 5)**

No check figure

Obtain the annual report of an actual company of your choosing.

Required

1. How much did customers owe the company at the end of the current year? Of this amount how much did the company expect to collect? How much did the company expect *not* to collect?
2. Assume during the current year that the company recorded doubtful account expense equal to 1 percent of net sales. Starting with the beginning balance, analyze the Allowance for Doubtful Accounts to determine the amount of the receivable write-offs during the current year.
3. If the company does not have notes receivable, you may skip this requirement. If notes receivable are present at the end of the current year, assume their interest rate is 9 percent. Also assume that no new notes receivable arose during the following year. Journalize these transactions that took place during the following year:
   a. Received cash for 75 percent of the interest revenue earned during the year.
   b. Accrued the remaining portion of the interest revenue earned during the year.
   c. At year end collected one half of the notes receivable.
4. Suppose the company discounted a $500,000 note receivable. Under what heading in the annual report would the company report the discounting of a note receivable? Show how the company would disclose this fact.

Chapter 9

Merchandise Inventory

Whittaker Corporation, a manufacturer of precision tools, announced yesterday that it was slashing inventories in anticipation of slower sales during the third and fourth quarters of 1991. Analysts were caught off guard by the Whittaker announcement. As recently as June 30, Whittaker was expanding rapidly to take advantage of the new markets arising from the European business unification scheduled for 1992. Company plans called for opening an assembly plant in Belgium and also increasing the sales force by 30 percent. What caused operations to sour so suddenly?

Rafael Montalban, senior analyst at Piper & Jeffries in New York City, argues that Whittaker's slide began late last year. Mr. Montalban issued a blistering attack on Whittaker management in March, noting that the company's inventory was becoming obsolete. Unlike competitors, who were using electrically controlled robots in their manufacturing processes, Whittaker stuck to the hydraulic robots developed during the 1980s. The obsolete machinery produced inferior products that ceased to sell. Whittaker has a warehouse full of unsaleable inventory, which will pose a challenge for the company and its accountants.

Among other topics, this chapter discusses how to account for inventory that has lost some of its value.

Merchandise inventory is the largest *current asset* on the balance sheet of most businesses that manufacture or buy inventory for resale. Polaroid Corporation reported inventories of $412.7 million, compared with receivables of $289.5 million and cash of $187.0 million. Inventories are important to merchandisers of all sizes. Buying and selling inventory is the heart of wholesaling and retailing, whether the business is Sears, Safeway, or the corner hardware store.

Inventory is the major current asset of most merchandisers. What is their major expense? It is *cost of sales,* or *cost of goods sold.* For example, Westinghouse Electric Corporation reported its cost of sales at $7.1 billion compared with distribution, administrative, and general expenses of $1.5 billion. For Westinghouse and many other companies, cost of goods sold is greater than all other expenses combined.

Exhibit 9-1 traces the flow of inventory costs during the accounting period. The model presented in Exhibit 9-1 is fundamental to accounting for inventory.

The business starts each period with **beginning inventory,** the goods that are left over from the preceding period. During the period, the business purchases additional goods for resale. Together, beginning inventory and net purchases make up **goods available for sale.** Over the course of the period, the business sells some of the available goods. The cost of the inventory sold to customers is called the **cost of goods sold.** This cost is an expense because the inventory is no longer of use to the company. The goods still on hand at the end of the period are called **ending inventory.** Its cost is an asset because these goods are still available for sale.

Exhibit 9-2 uses data from the financial statements of Revco D.S., Inc., a chain of discount drug stores concentrated in Ohio, Texas, and the Southeast, to present the flow of inventory costs in a format different from that shown in Exhibit 9-1. Notice that ending inventory is subtracted from cost of goods available for sale to figure the cost of goods sold. Throughout this chapter we ignore freight-in to avoid clutter.

The rest of this chapter fills in the details of our inventory cost flow model.

Figuring the Cost of Inventory

A necessary step in accounting for inventory is determining the cost of *ending inventory.* At the end of each period the *quantity* of inventory is multiplied by the *unit cost* of inventory to compute the cost of ending inventory.

Real-World Example: Inventory averages about 29% of total assets in the electronic computer industry, and cash represents about 11%. Inventory makes up 62% of total assets for auto dealers, and cash, 7%. Comparable figures for grocery stores are inventory, 32%, and cash, 10%.

Real-World Example: Typically, a business selects its year end to coincide with the time of year when inventory is at the lowest level, so that counting the inventory ("taking inventory") will be as simple as possible. For example, Wal-Mart Stores, Inc. has a January 31 year end.

Point to Stress: Remember the derivation of the balance of every account, including Inventory:

   Beg. Bal.
+ Increases (purchases)
− Decreases (COGS)
= End. Bal.

Cost of Goods Sold is computed the same way. The unknown is COGS. Rearranging, we can solve for COGS:

   Beg. Inventory
+ Purchases
− Ending Inventory
= COGS

EXHIBIT 9-1 *Flow of Inventory Costs*

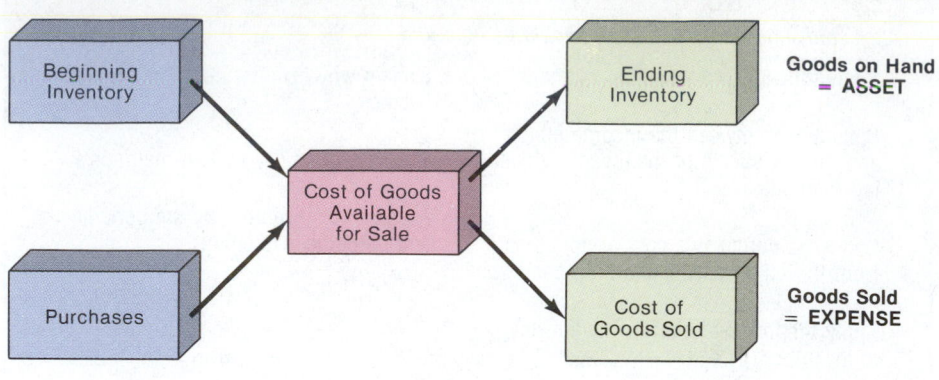

Determining the Quantity of Inventory. Most businesses physically count their inventory at least once each year, often on the last day of the fiscal year. Inventory, an asset, must be reported accurately on the balance sheet.

You may have worked at a grocery store or some other type of retail business. If so, you will recall the process of "taking the inventory." Some entities shut the business down to get a good count of inventory on hand. Others count the goods on a weekend. Still others inventory the merchandise while business is being conducted. How is it done in a large organization?

Assume Revco Drug takes a complete physical inventory on its year-end date. Teams of counters in the company's approximately 1,700 stores record the quantities of each inventory item on hand. Each store forwards its total count to corporate headquarters, where home office employees determine the inventory grand total.

Complications may arise in determining the inventory quantity. Suppose the business has purchased some goods that are in transit when the inventory is counted. Even though these items are not physically present, they should be included in the inventory count if title to the goods has passed to the purchaser. When title passes from seller to purchaser, the purchaser becomes the legal owner of the goods.

The FOB—free on board—terms of the transaction govern when title passes from the seller to the purchaser. **FOB shipping point** indicates that title passes when the goods leave the seller's place of business. **FOB destination** means that title passes when the goods arrive at the purchaser's location. Therefore, goods in transit that are purchased FOB shipping point should be included in the purchaser's inventory. Goods in transit that are bought FOB destination should not be included.

EXHIBIT 9-2 *Inventory and Cost of Goods Sold for Revco D.S., Inc.*

	(amounts in millions)
Beginning inventory.............................	$ 276
+ Net purchases	1,348
= Cost of goods available for sale..................	1,624
− Ending inventory	317
= Cost of goods sold	$1,307

Usually, the business has a purchase invoice, which lists the quantity of goods in transit and shows the FOB terms. Similarly, the business may have sold inventory that has not yet been shipped to the customer. If title has passed, these goods should be excluded from the seller's inventory, even though they may still be at the seller's place of business.

Another complication in counting inventory arises from consigned goods. In a **consignment** arrangement, the owner of the inventory (the consignor) transfers the goods to another business (the consignee). For a fee, the consignee sells the inventory on the owner's behalf. The consignee does *not* take title to the consigned goods and, therefore, should not include them in its own inventory. Consignments are common in retailing. Suppose Revco Drug is the consignee for some L'Eggs hosiery in its stores. Should Revco include this consigned merchandise in its inventory count? No, because Revco does not own the goods. Instead, the L'Eggs wholesaler—the consignor—includes the consigned goods in his or her inventory. A rule of thumb is to include in inventory only what the business owns.

Determining the Unit Cost of Inventory. Inventories are normally accounted for at historical cost, as the *cost principle* requires. **Inventory cost** is the price the business pays to acquire the inventory—not the selling price of the goods. Suppose a business purchases inventory for $10 and offers it for sale at $15. The inventory cost is reported at $10, not $15. Inventory cost includes its invoice price, less any purchase discount, plus sales tax, tariffs, transportation charges, insurance while in transit, and all other costs incurred to make the goods ready for sale.

The inventory quantity multiplied by the unit cost equals the cost of inventory. Thirty tape recorders at a cost of $100 each results in an inventory cost of $3,000.

Inventory Costing Methods

Determining the unit cost of inventory is easy when the unit cost remains constant during the period. However, the unit cost often changes. For example, during times of inflation, prices rise. The tape recorder model that cost the retailer $100 in January may cost $115 in June and $122 in October. Suppose the retailer sells 15 tape recorders in November. How many of them cost $100, how many cost $115, and how many cost $122? To compute the cost of goods sold and ending inventory amounts, the accountant must have some means of assigning the business's cost to each item sold. The four costing methods that GAAP allows are

OBJECTIVE 1
Apply four inventory costing methods

1. Specific unit cost
2. Weighted-average cost
3. First-in, first-out (FIFO) cost
4. Last-in, first-out (LIFO) cost

A company can use any of these methods. Many companies use several methods—different methods for different categories of inventory.

Point to Stress: These four methods are methods of recording the cost of ending inventory (and therefore, cost of goods sold). Stress that the method used for accounting does not have to match the physical flow of goods.

Specific Unit Cost

Some businesses deal in inventory items that may be identified individually, like automobiles, jewels, and real estate. These businesses usually cost their inventory at the **specific cost** of the particular unit. For instance, a Chevrolet dealer may have two vehicles in the showroom—a "stripped-down" model

Teaching Tip: It is easy to determine the actual cost of the inventory of a car dealership because the invoice price of

each car can be easily
identified.

What if you own a hardware store and are trying to determine the cost of your inventory of nails? Some nails were purchased for $.01 each and others for $.015 each. You cannot tell by looking which is which. Therefore, you must assume either that:

1 the ending inventory represents the latest purchases (FIFO), or
2 the ending inventory represents the earliest purchases (LIFO), or
3 the ending inventory represents a mix of all the purchases (Weighted-average cost)

Transparency T9-1

Teaching Tip: To illustrate the weighted-average cost method, assume that an oil tank is 1/3 full of oil, and new oil is pumped in to fill the tank. The new oil mixes with the old, and it is impossible to separate them. We assume that the oil remaining in the tank at year end will consist of 1/3 old oil and 2/3 new.

Transparency T9-2

Discussion Question: How does inventory usually flow in and out of a business? *ANSWER:* The first goods purchased are the first sold. This is essentially the first-in, first-out method.

Which items would be in ending inventory? *ANSWER:* The most recently purchased goods. Stress, however, that cost flow need not coincide with the physical flow of goods.

Transparency T9-3

that cost $14,000 and a "loaded" model that cost $17,000. If the dealer sells the loaded model for $19,700, cost of goods sold is $17,000, the cost of the specific unit. The gross margin on this sale is $2,700 ($19,700 − $17,000). If the stripped-down auto is the only unit left in inventory at the end of the period, ending inventory is $14,000, the cost to the retailer of the specific unit on hand.

The specific unit cost method is also called the *specific identification* method. This method is not practical for inventory items that have common characteristics, such as bushels of wheat, gallons of paint, or boxes of laundry detergent.

Weighted-Average Cost, FIFO Cost, and LIFO Cost

The weighted-average cost, first-in, first-out (FIFO), and last-in, first-out (LIFO) methods are fundamentally different from the specific unit cost method. These methods do not assign to inventory the specific cost of particular units. Instead, they assume different flows of costs into and out of inventory.

Weighted-Average Cost. The **weighted-average cost method,** often called the **average cost method,** is based on the weighted-average cost of inventory during the period. Average cost is determined by dividing the cost of goods available for sale (beginning inventory plus purchases) by the number of units available. Ending inventory and cost of goods sold are computed by multiplying the number of units by weighted-average cost per unit. Assume that cost of goods available for sale is $90, and 60 units are available. Weighted-average cost is $1.50 per unit ($90/60 = $1.50). Ending inventory of 20 units has an average cost of $30 (20 × $1.50 = $30). Cost of goods sold (40 units) is $60 (40 × $1.50). Panel A of Exhibit 9-3 gives the data in more detail. Panel B of the exhibit shows the weighted-average cost computations.

First-in, First-out (FIFO) Cost. Under the **first-in, first-out (FIFO) method,** the company must keep a record of the cost of each inventory unit purchased. The unit costs used in computing the ending inventory may be different from the unit costs used in computing the cost of goods sold. Under FIFO, the first costs into inventory are the first costs out to cost of goods sold—hence the name *first-in, first-out.* Ending inventory is based on the costs of the most recent purchases. In our example, the FIFO cost of ending inventory is $36. Cost of goods sold is $54. Panel A of Exhibit 9-3 gives the data, and Panel B shows the FIFO computations.

Last-in, First-out (LIFO) Cost. The **last-in, first-out (LIFO) method** also depends on the costs of particular inventory purchases. LIFO is the opposite of FIFO. Under LIFO, the last costs into inventory are the first costs out to cost of goods sold. This leaves the oldest costs—those of beginning inventory and the earliest purchases of the period—in ending inventory. In our example, the LIFO cost of ending inventory is $24. Cost of goods sold is $66. Panel A of Exhibit 9-3 gives the data, and Panel B shows the LIFO computations.

Income Effects of FIFO, LIFO, and Weighted-Average Cost

In our discussion and examples, the cost of inventory rose during the accounting period. When prices change, different costing methods produce different

EXHIBIT 9-3 *Inventory and Cost of Goods Sold under Weighted-Average, FIFO, and LIFO Inventory Costing Methods*

Panel A—Illustrative Data:

Beginning inventory (10 units @ $1 per unit).........		$ 10
Purchases:		
No. 1 (25 units @ $1.40 per unit)	$ 35	
No. 2 (25 units @ $1.80 per unit)	45	
Total		80
Cost of goods available for sale (60 units)		90
Ending inventory (20 units @ $? per unit)		?
Cost of goods sold (40 units @ $? per unit		$?

Panel B—Ending Inventory and Cost of Goods Sold:

Weighted-Average Cost Method:

Cost of goods available for sale—see Panel A (60 units @ average cost of $1.50* per unit).........................	$ 90
Ending inventory (20 units @ $1.50 per unit)	30
Cost of goods sold (40 units @ $1.50 per unit)	$ 60

*Cost of goods available for sale	$ 90
Number of units available for sale	÷60
Average cost per unit....................	$1.50

FIFO Cost Method:

Cost of goods available for sale (60 units—see Panel A)		$ 90
Ending inventory (cost of the *last* 20 units available:		
20 units @ $1.80 per unit (from purchase no. 2)		36
Cost of goods sold (cost of the *first* 40 units available):		
10 units @ $1.00 per unit (all of beginning inventory)	$ 10	
25 units @ $1.40 per unit (all of purchase no. 1)	35	
5 units @ $1.80 per unit (from purchase no. 2)	9	
Total		$ 54

LIFO Cost Method:

Cost of goods available for sale (60 units—see Panel A)		$ 90
Ending inventory (cost of the *first* 20 units available):		
10 units @ $1.00 per unit (all of beginning inventory)	$ 10	
10 units @ $1.40 per unit (from purchase no. 1)	14	
Total		24
Cost of goods sold (cost of the *last* 40 units available):		
25 units @ $1.80 per unit (all of purchase no. 2)	45	
15 units @ $1.40 per unit (from purchase no. 1)	21	
Total		$ 66

Teaching Tip: A sand company illustrates the concept of LIFO. When a sand company dumps new sand on a pile, the new sand is on the top. When the company needs sand, it takes the new sand off the top. Therefore, the last sand on the pile (the new sand) is the first sand off the pile.

Point to Stress: A company can choose any of the four inventory methods that it prefers. When costs are increasing, FIFO shows the highest inventory, lowest COGS, and highest net income. LIFO reports the lowest inventory, highest COGS, and lowest net income. Weighted-average cost reports amounts somewhere between those reported by FIFO and LIFO.

Typical Student Misconception: Students often are confused by LIFO and FIFO and get the two methods reversed. The terms FIFO and LIFO describe not which goods are left, but which goods are sold.

FIFO—Assumes that goods in first are sold first; therefore the last goods in are left in ending inventory.

LIFO—Assumes that the last goods in are sold first; therefore the first goods in are left in ending inventory.

Discussion Question: In a period of rising prices, which inventory costing method forces the highest inventory costs into Cost of Goods Sold? *ANSWER:* LIFO assigns the most recent unit costs to COGS. Since COGS is highest using LIFO, net income will be lowest.

cost of goods sold and ending inventory figures, as Exhibit 9-3 shows. When inventory costs are increasing, FIFO ending inventory is *highest* because it is priced at the most recent costs, which are the highest. LIFO ending inventory is *lowest* because it is priced at the oldest costs, which are the lowest. *Weighted-average* cost avoids the extremes of FIFO and LIFO. When inventory costs are decreasing, FIFO ending inventory is lowest, and LIFO is highest.

EXHIBIT 9-4 *Income Effects of FIFO, LIFO, and Weighted-Average Cost Inventory Methods*

	FIFO	LIFO	Weighted-Average
Sales revenue (assumed)	$100,000	$100,000	$100,000
Costs of goods sold:			
Goods available for sale (assumed)	$ 90,000	$ 90,000	$ 90,000
Ending inventory	36,000	24,000	30,000
Cost of goods sold.................	54,000	66,000	60,000
Gross margin	$ 46,000	$ 34,000	$ 40,000

Summary of Income Effects—When Inventory Costs Are Increasing:

FIFO—Highest ending inventory
    Lowest cost of goods sold
    Highest gross margin

LIFO—Lowest ending inventory
    Highest cost of goods sold
    Lowest gross margin

Weighted-average—Results fall between the extremes of FIFO and LIFO

Exhibit 9-4 summarizes the income effects of the three inventory methods based on the data from Exhibit 9-3. Study the exhibit carefully, focusing on ending inventory, cost of goods sold, and gross margin.

The Income Tax Advantage of LIFO

When prices are rising, applying the LIFO method results in the *lowest taxable income* and thus the *lowest income taxes*. Let's use the gross margin data of Exhibit 9-4.

	FIFO	LIFO	Weighted-Average
Gross margin	$46,000	$34,000	$40,000
Operating expenses (assumed)	26,000	26,000	26,000
Income before income tax	$20,000	$ 8,000	$14,000
Income tax expense (40%)	$ 8,000	$ 3,200	$ 5,600

Income tax expense is lowest under LIFO ($3,200) and highest under FIFO ($8,000). The most attractive feature of LIFO is reduced income tax payments.

The Internal Revenue Service allows companies to use LIFO for tax purposes only if they use LIFO for financial reporting purposes. However, they may also report an alternative inventory amount in the notes to their financial statements. Federal-Mogul Corporation, a maker of industrial products, reported inventories at LIFO cost but also disclosed the FIFO cost of inventory in Note D, as follows. Observe that FIFO cost is higher than LIFO cost (amounts in millions):

	19X6	19X5
Inventories—Note D	$189	$148

Note D: *Inventories*
Inventories are stated at . . . last-in, first-out (LIFO) cost. . . . Use of the first-in, first-out (FIFO) cost method would have increased inventories by $95 million in 19X6 and $89 million in 19X5. . . .

Teaching Tip: In an inflationary period, with FIFO, the income statement might overstate profits because replacement costs keep rising, but the income statement does not reflect that. As a counteractive measure, companies use the inventory method that yields the highest cost of goods sold—LIFO.

Point to Stress: The IRS makes no stipulations for inventory reporting for methods other than LIFO. For example, you can use FIFO for income tax reporting and weighted-average cost for financial reporting.

Of what use is Federal-Mogul's disclosure of the alternative amounts under FIFO? An investor may be comparing Federal-Mogul with a company that uses FIFO. Federal-Mogul's inventory and cost of goods sold amounts under LIFO are not comparable with the other company's FIFO figures. To compare the two companies, the investor can convert Federal-Mogul's LIFO amounts to the FIFO basis. Simply substitute the FIFO amounts in place of those reported under LIFO. Here are the cost of goods sold figures (amounts in millions):

	LIFO Amounts as Reported in the Income Statement			FIFO Amounts Based on Information in the Notes
Beginning inventory	$ 148	+ $89	=	$ 237
Net purchases	765			765
Cost of goods available for sale	913			1,002
Less: Ending inventory . . .	189	+ $95	=	284
Cost of goods sold	$ 724			$ 718

OBJECTIVE 3

Convert a company's cost of goods sold from the LIFO basis to the FIFO basis

Cost of goods sold under FIFO ($718 million) can now be used to compare the two companies. In the computation, notice that purchases is the same under FIFO and LIFO. Beginning FIFO inventory is the LIFO amount ($148 million) plus the increase to FIFO ($89 million), a total of $237 million. Ending FIFO inventory is the LIFO amount ($189 million) plus the increase ($95 million), a total of $284 million. These changes cause FIFO cost of goods sold to be less than the LIFO amount, which would cause income to be higher under FIFO. This is valuable information for an investor.

The 1970s and early 1980s were marked by high inflation, so many companies changed to LIFO for its tax advantage. Exhibit 9-5, based on an American Institute of Certified Public Accountants (AICPA) survey of 600 companies, indicates that LIFO and FIFO are the most popular inventory costing methods.

Exhibit 9-5 *Use of the Various Inventory Methods*

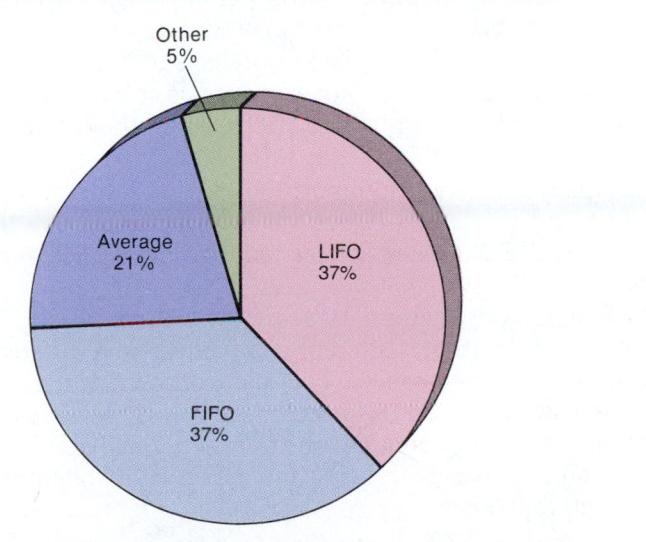

Generally Accepted Accounting Principles: A Comparison of the Inventory Methods

We may ask three questions to judge the three major inventory costing methods. (1) How well does each method match inventory expense—the cost of goods sold—to sales revenue on the income statement? (2) Which method reports the most up-to-date inventory amount on the balance sheet? (3) What effect do the methods have on income taxes? The weighted-average cost method produces amounts between the extremes of LIFO and FIFO.

LIFO better matches the current value of cost of goods sold with current revenue by assigning to this expense the most recent inventory costs. By contrast, FIFO matches the oldest inventory costs against the period's revenue—a poor matching of current expense with current revenue.

FIFO reports the most current inventory costs on the balance sheet. LIFO can result in absurd balance sheet valuations of inventories because the oldest prices are left in ending inventory.

As shown in the preceding section, LIFO results in the lowest income tax payments when prices are rising. Tax payments are highest under FIFO. When inventory prices are decreasing, tax payments are highest under LIFO and lowest under FIFO.

FIFO is criticized because it overstates income by so-called inventory profit during periods of inflation. Briefly, **inventory profit** is the difference between gross margin figured on the FIFO basis and gross margin figured on the LIFO basis. Exhibit 9-4 illustrates inventory profit. The $12,000 difference between FIFO and LIFO gross margins ($46,000 − $34,000 = $12,000) results from the difference in cost of goods sold. This $12,000 amount is called *FIFO inventory profit, phantom profit,* or *illusory profit.* Why? Because to stay in business the company must replace the inventory it has sold. The replacement cost of the merchandise is more closely approximated by the cost of goods sold under LIFO ($66,000) than the FIFO amount ($54,000).

LIFO is criticized because it allows managers to manipulate net income. Assume inventory prices are rising rapidly, and a company wants to show less income for the year (in order to pay less taxes). Managers can buy a large amount of inventory near the end of the year. Under LIFO these high inventory costs immediately become expense—as cost of goods sold. As a result, the income statement reports a lower net income. Conversely, if the business is having a bad year, management may wish to increase reported income. To do so, managers can delay a large purchase of high-cost inventory until the next period. This inventory is not expensed as cost of goods sold in the current year. Thus management avoids decreasing the current year's reported income.

A company may want to report the highest income, and FIFO meets this need when prices are rising. But the company must pay the highest income taxes under FIFO. When prices are falling, LIFO reports the highest income.

Which inventory method is better—LIFO or FIFO? There is no single answer to this question. Different companies have different motives for the inventory method they choose. Polaroid Corporation uses FIFO, J. C. Penney Company uses LIFO, and Motorola, Inc., uses weighted-average cost. Still other companies use more than one method. The Black and Decker Manufacturing Company uses both LIFO and FIFO, as it stated in an annual report (amounts in millions):

Inventories $390

NOTES TO CONSOLIDATED FINANCIAL STATEMENTS
Note 1: Summary of Accounting Policies
Inventories: The cost of United States inventories is based on the last-in, first-out (LIFO) method; all other inventories are based on the first-in, first-out (FIFO) method. The cost of . . . inventories stated under the LIFO method represents approximately 40% of the value of total inventories.

Consistency Principle

The **consistency principle** states that businesses should use the same accounting methods and procedures from period to period. Consistency makes it possible to compare a company's financial statements from one period to the next.

Suppose you are analyzing a company's net income pattern. The company has switched from LIFO to FIFO. Its net income has increased dramatically but only as a result of the change in inventory method. If you did not know of the change, you might believe that the company's increased income arose from improved operations, which is not the case.

The consistency principle does not require that all companies within an industry use the same accounting method. Nor does it mean that a company may *never* change its own accounting method. However, a company making an accounting change must disclose the effect of the change on net income, as shown below for Midland-Ross Corporation, a large company that makes electrical products, mechanical controls, foundry products, and thermal systems:

Point to Stress: Companies cannot switch inventory methods without violating the consistency principle. If a company does change methods, the change and the effect of the change must be disclosed.

Real-World Example: On July 1, 1988, the beginning of its fiscal year, the Quaker Oats Company changed from FIFO to LIFO. This change decreased net income for fiscal 1989 by $16 million.

EXCERPT FROM NOTE A OF THE MIDLAND-ROSS FINANCIAL STATEMENTS
Inventories: The LIFO method of valuing inventories was extended to substantially all of the electrical and mechanical controls inventories. . . . The effect of the change was to reduce net income . . . by $4,638,000. . . .

Summary Problem for Your Review

Suppose an IBM division that handles computer components has these inventory records for January 19X6:

Date	Item	Quantity	Unit Cost	Sale Price
Jan. 1	Beginning inventory	100 units	$ 8	
6	Purchase	60 units	9	
13	Sale	70 units		$20
21	Purchase	150 units	9	
24	Sale	210 units		22
27	Purchase	90 units	10	
30	Sale	30 units		25

Company accounting records reveal that related operating expense for January was $1,900.

Required

1. Prepare the January income statement, showing amounts for LIFO, FIFO, and weighted-average cost. Label the bottom line "Operating income." (Round figures to whole dollar amounts.)

2. Suppose you are the financial vice-president of IBM Corporation. Which inventory method would you use if your motive is to
   a. Minimize income taxes?
   b. Report the highest operating income?
   c. Report operating income between the extremes of FIFO and LIFO?
   d. Report inventory at the most current cost?
   e. Attain the best matching of current expense with current revenue?

State the reason for each of your answers.

SOLUTION TO REVIEW PROBLEM

Requirement 1

IBM Corporation
Income Statement for Component
Month Ended January 31, 19X6

	LIFO		FIFO		Weighted-Average
Sales revenue		$6,770		$6,770	$6,770
Cost of goods sold:					
Beginning inventory	$ 800		$ 800		$ 800
Net purchases	2,790		2,790		2,790
Cost of goods					
available for sale .	3,590		3,590		3,590
Ending inventory. . .	720		900		808
Cost of goods sold .		2,870		2,690	2,782
Gross margin		3,900		4,080	3,988
Operating expenses . .		1,900		1,900	1,900
Operating income		$2,000		$2,180	$2,088

Computations:

Sales revenue: $(70 \times \$20)$ $+ (210 \times \$22) + (30 \times \$25) = \$6,770$
Beginning inventory: $100 \times \$8$ $= \$800$
Purchases: $(60 \times \$9)$ $+ (150 \times \$9) - (90 \times \$10) = \$2,790$
Ending inventory–LIFO: $90* \times \$8$ $= \$720$
            FIFO: $90 \times \$10$ $= \$900$
   Weighted-average: $90 \times \$8.975** = \$808$ (rounded from \$807.75)

---

* Number of units in ending inventory $= 100 + 60 - 70 + 150 - 210 + 90 - 30 = 90$
**$\$3,590/400$ units $= \$8.975$ per unit
Number of units available $= 100 + 60 + 150 + 90 = 400$

Requirement 2

a. Use LIFO to minimize income taxes. Operating income under LIFO is lowest when inventory unit costs are increasing, as they are in this case (from $8 to $10). (If inventory costs were decreasing, income under FIFO would be lowest.)

b. Use FIFO to report the highest operating income. Income under FIFO is highest when inventory unit costs are increasing, as in this situation.

c. Use weighted-average cost to report an operating income amount between the FIFO and LIFO extremes. This is true in this problem situation and in others whether inventory unit costs are increasing or decreasing.

d. Use FIFO to report inventory at the most current cost. The oldest inventory costs are expensed as cost of goods sold, leaving in ending inventory the most recent (most current) costs of the period.

e. Use LIFO to attain the best matching of current expense with current revenue. The most recent (most current) inventory costs are expensed as cost of goods sold.

Accounting Conservatism

Conservatism in accounting means to report items in the financial statements at amounts that lead to the gloomiest immediate financial results. Conservatism comes into play when there are alternative ways to account for the item. What advantage does conservatism give a business? Management often looks on the brighter side of operations and may overstate a company's income and asset values. Many accountants regard conservatism as a counterbalance to management's optimistic tendencies. The goal is for financial statements to present realistic figures.

Conservatism appears in accounting guidelines like "anticipate no gains, but provide for all probable losses" and "if in doubt, record an asset at the lowest reasonable amount and a liability at the highest reasonable amount."

Accountants generally regard the historical cost of acquiring an asset as its maximum value. Even if the current market value of the asset increases above its cost, businesses do not write up (that is, increase) the asset's accounting value. Assume that a company purchased land for $100,000, and its value increased to $300,000. Accounting conservatism dictates that the historical cost $100,000 be maintained as the accounting value of the land.

Conservatism also directs accountants to decrease the accounting value of an asset if it appears unrealistically high—even if no transaction occurs. Assume that a company paid $35,000 for inventory that has become obsolete, and its current value is only $12,000. Conservatism dictates that the inventory be written down (that is, decreased) to $12,000.

Lower-of-Cost-or-Market Rule

The **lower-of-cost-or-market rule** (abbreviated as LCM) shows accounting conservatism in action. LCM requires that an asset be reported in the financial statements at the lower of its historical cost or its market value. Applied to inventories, *market value* generally means *current replacement cost* (that is, how much the business would have to pay in the market on that day to purchase

Point to Stress: Assets are recorded at historical cost because that is an objective, verifiable amount. It would be subjective and *not* verifiable to record an asset at what the business "thinks" or estimates that asset to be worth.

Discussion Question: In an inflationary period, most companies do not experience declining inventory prices. However, in some cases inventory replacement cost is lower than historical cost. Give examples and reasons. *ANSWER:* Video recorders and computers, because technology improves, decrease in costs; fuel and some food products may decrease in cost because of changes in global politics, supply, and patterns of consumption.

Point to Stress: Refer to the chapter-opening vignette. Inventory that is obsolete, as in the Whittaker Corporation case, should be written down to market value, if market is lower than cost.

the same amount of inventory that it has on hand). If the replacement cost of inventory falls below its historical cost, the business must write down the value of its goods. The business reports ending inventory at its LCM value on the balance sheet. In the chapter-opening vignette, Whittaker Corporation has a warehouse full of obsolete inventory. This inventory must be written down to market value. How is the write-down accomplished?

Suppose a business paid $3,000 for inventory on September 26. By December 31, its value has fallen. The inventory can now be replaced for $2,200. Market value is below cost, and the December 31 balance sheet reports this inventory at its LCM value of $2,200. Usually, the market value of inventory is higher than historical cost, so inventory's accounting value is cost for most companies. Exhibit 9-6 presents the effects of LCM on the income statement and the balance sheet. The point of the exhibit is to show that the lower of (a) cost or (b) market value—replacement cost—is the relevant amount for valuing inventory on the income statement and the balance sheet. Companies are not required to show both cost and market value amounts. However, they may report the higher amount in parentheses, as shown on the balance sheet in the exhibit.

LCM states that of the $3,000 cost of ending inventory in Exhibit 9-6, $800 is considered to have expired even though the inventory was not sold during the period. Its replacement cost is only $2,200, and that amount is carried forward to the next period as the cost of beginning inventory. Suppose during the next period the replacement cost of this inventory increases to $2,500. Accounting conservatism states that it would not be appropriate to write up the book value of inventory. The market value of inventory ($2,200 in this case) is used as its cost in future LCM determinations.

Examine the following income statement effect of LCM summarized from Exhibit 9-6. What expense absorbs the impact of the $800 inventory write

EXHIBIT 9-6 *Lower-of-Cost-or-Market (LCM) Effects*

Income Statement:

Sales revenue		$20,000
Cost of goods sold:		
Beginning inventory (LCM = Cost)	$ 2,800	
Net purchases	11,000	
Cost of goods available for sale	13,800	
Ending inventory—		
Cost = $3,000		
Replacement cost (market value) = $2,200		
LCM = Market	2,200	
Cost of goods sold		11,600
Gross margin		$ 8,400

OBJECTIVE 4
Apply the lower-of-cost-or-market rule to inventory

Balance Sheet:

Current assets:		
Cash	$	XXX
Short-term investments		XXX
Accounts receivable		XXX
Inventories, at market (which is lower than $3,000 cost)		2,200
Prepaid expenses		XXX
Total current assets		$ X,XXX

Point to Stress: Refer to "Ending inventory" in Exhibit 9-6. The matching principle is applied here. The reduction in the value of the inventory is shown in the year the inventory declined in value, not in the year the inventory is sold.

down? Cost of goods sold is increased by $800 because ending inventory is $800 less at market ($2,200) than it would have been at cost ($3,000).

	Ending Inventory at	
	Cost	LCM
Cost of goods available for sale	$13,800	$13,800
Ending inventory:		
Cost............................	3,000	} $800 Lower
Replacement cost (market value)		2,200 } at LCM
Cost of goods sold.................	$10,800	$11,600} $800 Higher
		at LCM

Exhibit 9-6 also reports the application of LCM for inventories in the body of the balance sheet. Companies often disclose LCM in notes to their financial statements, as shown below for CBS, Inc.:

> NOTE 1: STATEMENT OF SIGNIFICANT ACCOUNTING POLICIES
>
> Inventories. Inventories are stated at the *lower of cost* (principally based on average cost) *or market value.* [emphasis added]

Effect of Inventory Errors

Businesses determine inventory amounts at the end of the period. In the process of counting the items, applying unit costs, and computing amounts, errors may arise. As the period 1 segment of Exhibit 9-7 shows, an error in the ending inventory amount creates errors in the cost of goods sold and gross margin amounts. Compare period 1, when ending inventory is overstated, and cost of goods sold is understated, each by $5,000, with period 3, which is correct. Period 1 should look exactly like period 3.

Recall that one period's ending inventory is the next period's beginning inventory. Thus the error in ending inventory carries over into the next period: note the highlighted amounts in Exhibit 9-7.

OBJECTIVE 5

Explain why inventory errors counterbalance

EXHIBIT 9-7 *Effects of Inventory Errors*

	Period 1 Ending Inventory Overstated By $5,000		Period 2 Beginning Inventory Overstated By $5,000		Period 3 Correct	
Sales revenue		$100,000		$100,000		$100,000
Cost of goods sold:						
Beginning inventory	$10,000		$15,000		$10,000	
Net purchases..................	50,000		50,000		50,000	
Cost of goods available for sale ...	60,000		65,000		60,000	
Ending inventory	15,000		10,000		10,000	
Cost of goods sold..............		45,000		55,000		50,000
Gross margin		$ 55,000		$ 45,000		$ 50,000
			$100,000			

The authors thank Carl High for this example.

Because the same ending inventory figure that is *subtracted* in computing cost of goods sold in one period is *added* as beginning inventory to compute cost of goods sold in the next period, the error's effect cancels out at the end of the second period. The overstatement of cost of goods sold in period 2 counterbalances the understatement in cost of goods sold in period 1. Thus the total gross margin amount for the two periods is the correct $100,000 figure whether or not an error entered into the computation.

However, inventory errors cannot be ignored simply because they counterbalance. Suppose you are analyzing trends in the business's operations. Exhibit 9-7 shows a drop in gross margin from period 1 to period 2, followed by an increase in period 3. But that picture of operations is untrue because of the accounting error. Correct gross margin is $50,000 each period. To provide accurate information for decision making, all inventory errors should be corrected.

Methods of Estimating Inventory

Often a business must *estimate* the value of its inventory. Because of cost and inconvenience, few companies physically count their inventories at the end of each month, yet they may need monthly financial statements. A fire or a flood may destroy inventory, and to file an insurance claim, the business must estimate the value of its loss. In both cases, the business needs to know the value of ending inventory without being able to count it. Two methods for estimating ending inventory are the *gross margin method* (or *gross profit method*) and the *retail method*. These methods are widely used in actual practice.

Gross Margin (Gross Profit) Method

The **gross margin method** is a way of estimating inventory based on the familiar cost-of-goods-sold model:

> Beginning inventory
> + Net purchases
> ―――――――――――――
> = Cost of goods available for sale
> − Ending inventory
> ―――――――――――――
> = Cost of goods sold

Rearranging *ending inventory* and *cost of goods sold,* the model becomes useful for estimating ending inventory:

> Beginning inventory
> + Net purchases
> ―――――――――――――
> = Cost of goods available for sale
> − Cost of goods sold
> ―――――――――――――
> = Ending inventory

Suppose a fire destroys your business's inventory. To collect insurance, you must estimate the cost of the ending inventory. If the fire did not also destroy your accounting records, beginning inventory and net purchases amounts may be taken directly from the accounting records. The Sales Revenue, Sales

EXHIBIT 9-8 *Gross Margin Method of Estimating Inventory (amounts assumed)*

Beginning inventory		$14,000
Net purchases		66,000
Cost of goods available for sale		80,000
Cost of goods sold:		
Net sales revenue	$100,000	
Less estimated gross margin of 40%	40,000	
Estimated cost of goods sold		60,000
Estimated cost of *ending inventory*		$20,000

Returns, and Sales Discounts accounts indicate net sales up to the date of the fire. Using the entity's normal *gross margin rate* (that is, gross margin divided by net sales revenue), you can estimate cost of goods sold. The last step is to subtract cost of goods sold from goods available to estimate ending inventory. Exhibit 9-8 illustrates the gross margin method.

Accountants, managers, and auditors use the gross margin method to test the overall reasonableness of an ending inventory amount that has been determined by a physical count for all types of businesses. This method helps to detect large errors.

Retail Method

Retail establishments (department stores, drug stores, hardware stores, and so on) use the **retail method** to estimate their inventory cost. The retail method, like the gross margin method, is based on the cost-of-goods-sold model. However, the retail method requires that the business record inventory purchases both at *cost*—as shown in the purchase records—and at *retail* (selling) price—as shown on the price tags. This is not a burden because price tags show the retail price of inventory, and most retailers set their retail prices by adding standard markups to their cost. For example, a department store may pay $6 for a man's belt, mark it up $4, and price the belt at $10 retail. In the retail method, the seller's inventory cost is determined by working backward from its retail value. Exhibit 9-9 illustrates the process.

In Exhibit 9-9 the accounting records show the goods available for sale at cost ($168,000) and at retail ($280,000). The cost ratio is .60 ($168,000/$280,000). For simplicity, we round all such percentages to two decimal places in this chapter. Subtracting *net sales revenue* (a retail amount) from *goods available for*

EXHIBIT 9-9 *Retail Method of Estimating Inventory (amounts assumed)*

	Cost	Retail
Beginning inventory	$ 24,000	$ 40,000
Net purchases	144,000	240,000
Goods available for sale	$168,000	280,000
Cost ratio: $168,000/$280,000 = .60		
Less: Net sales revenue (which is stated at retail)		(230,000)
Ending inventory, at retail		$ 50,000
Ending inventory, at cost ($50,000 × .60)	$ 30,000	

sales total $480,000. With a normal gross margin rate of 40%, how much is the ending inventory? ANSWER: $74,000 ($70,000 + $295,000 − $3,000 − $288,000)

Point to Stress: The gross profit method is also used for estimating inventory for interim periods when taking a physical inventory is too expensive and impractical.

Discussion Question: Suppose that you are in charge of making a count of the physical inventory of a department store like Macy's. Would it be easier to take inventory at the retail prices or at the cost? ANSWER: The retail prices are marked on each item but the cost would have to be looked up in the records or taken from invoices. It is, therefore, easier to take inventory using retail prices. Can the retail value of inventory be reported on the balance sheet? ANSWER: No. The historical cost must be used on the balance sheet. How do we compute the historical cost of the inventory from the retail value? ANSWER: By establishing a relationship between cost and retail value (cost ratio) and multiplying the retail value by this ratio.

Typical Student Misconception: Students often confuse the *gross margin ratio* used in the gross profit method with the *cost ratio* used in the retail inventory method. Explain that both ratios are used to express cost as a percentage of the retail price. The gross margin ratio is calculated as follows:

$$\text{Gross margin ratio} = \frac{\text{Gross Margin}}{\text{Net Sales}}$$

The cost ratio is calculated as follows:

$$\text{Cost ratio} = \frac{\text{Goods Available at Cost}}{\text{Goods Available at Retail}}$$

Transparency T9-5

sale at retail yields *ending inventory at retail* ($50,000). The business multiplies *ending inventory at retail* by the cost ratio to figure *ending inventory at cost* ($30,000).

Suppose the retailer has four categories of inventory, each with a different cost ratio. How would the business use the retail method to estimate the overall cost of the ending inventory? Apply the retail method separately to each category of inventory, using its specific cost ratio, then add the costs of the four categories to determine the overall cost of inventory.

Even though the retail method is an estimation technique, some retailers use it to compute the inventory value for their financial statements. They make physical counts of inventory throughout the year to validate the retail-method amounts. For example, Marshall Field & Company, a department store chain headquartered in Chicago, uses the retail method, as disclosed in its annual report:

Merchandise inventories (note 1C) $179,007,250
_____

Note 1C: Inventory Pricing
    Substantially all merchandise inventories are valued by use of the *retail method*. [emphasis added]

Periodic and Perpetual Inventory Systems

OBJECTIVE 7

Account for inventory by the periodic and perpetual systems

Different businesses have different inventory information needs. We now look at the two main inventory systems: the *periodic system* and the *perpetual system*.

Periodic Inventory System

Point to Stress: Remember that under the periodic system the inventory account balance does not change during the year.

In the **periodic inventory system,** the business does not keep a continuous record of the inventory on hand. Instead, at the end of the period, the business makes a physical count of the inventory on hand and applies the appropriate unit costs to determine the cost of ending inventory. The business makes the standard end-of-period inventory entries, as discussed in Chapter 5 and shown in the example that follows. This system is also called the *physical system* because it relies on the actual physical count of inventory. The periodic system is used to account for inventory items that have a low unit cost. Low-cost items may not be valuable enough to warrant the cost of keeping a running record of the inventory on hand.

Entries under the Periodic System. In the periodic system, the business records purchases of inventory in the Purchases account (an expense account). At the end of the period, the business removes the beginning balance from the Inventory account and enters the ending balance, as determined by the physical count. Assume the following data for a K Mart store's April transactions.

Beginning inventory	$ 80,000
Ending inventory	102,000
Credit purchases (net of discounts and returns)	600,000
Credit sales (net of discounts and returns)	900,000

Summary entries for April:

To record credit purchases:

Purchases..................................	600,000	
Accounts Payable..........................		600,000

To record credit sales:

Accounts Receivable	900,000	
Sales Revenue............................		900,000

Inventory entries at the end of the period:

Income Summary...........................	80,000	
Inventory (beginning balance)		80,000
Inventory (ending balance)	102,000	
Income Summary..........................		102,000

Reporting on the financial statements:

Balance sheet at April 30:

Inventory	$102,000

Income statement for April:

Sales revenue.................................		$900,000
Cost of goods sold:		
Beginning inventory	$ 80,000	
Net purchases	600,000	
Cost of goods available	680,000	
Ending inventory	102,000	
Cost of goods sold		578,000
Gross margin		$322,000

Perpetual Inventory System

In the **perpetual inventory system,** the business keeps a continuous record for each inventory item. The records thus show the inventory on hand at all times. Perpetual records are useful in preparing monthly, quarterly, or other interim financial statements. The business can determine the cost of ending inventory and the cost of goods sold directly from the accounts without having to physically count the merchandise.

Typical Student Misconception: Using the perpetual inventory system is not a substitute for making a physical count of inventory.

The perpetual system offers a higher degree of control than the periodic system because the inventory information is always up to date. Consequently businesses use the perpetual system for high-unit-cost inventories, such as gemstones and automobiles. Nevertheless, companies physically count their inventory at least once each year to check the accuracy of their perpetual records.

Perpetual inventory records can be computer listings of inventory items or inventory cards like the Computerworld record shown in Exhibit 9-10. The accountant adds information to the computer list or the card on a daily basis. A running balance conveniently shows the latest inventory value. The perpetual record serves as a subsidiary record to the inventory account in the general ledger.

The perpetual inventory record indicates that the business uses the FIFO basis, as shown by the November 30 sale. The cost of the first unit sold is the oldest unit cost on hand. Perpetual records may also be kept on the average cost basis. However, most companies that use the weighted-average cost method, and virtually all companies that use the LIFO method, keep their perpetual records either on the FIFO basis or stated in units only (not dollars).

Teaching Tip: Refer to Exhibit 9-10. The total in the Received column represents total purchases. The total in the Sold column represents cost of goods sold. The total in the Balance column represents the cost of the inventory on hand. Remind students to use cost, not sale price, in the Sold column.

Discussion Question: Why is it necessary to make a physical count of the inventory if the perpetual system is used? *ANSWER:* The perpetual system will tell you how much inventory should be on hand. Breakage, spoilage, and theft all can reduce the physical count without being noted in the records.

Class Exercise: Let's review the differences and similarities in the periodic and perpetual systems by answering the following questions:

EXHIBIT 9-10 *Perpetual Inventory Record—FIFO Basis*

Item   Home Computer Model RK-42

Date	Received Qty.	Received Unit Cost	Received Total	Sold Qty.	Sold Unit Cost	Sold Total	Balance Qty.	Balance Unit Cost	Balance Total
Nov. 1							14	$300	$4,200
5				4	$300	$1,200	10	300	3,000
7				9	300	2,700	1	300	300
12	5	$320	$1,600				1	300	300
							5	320	1,600
26	7	330	2,310				1	300	300
							5	320	1,600
							7	330	2,310
30				1	300	300	1	320	320
				4	320	1,280	7	330	2,310
Totals	12	—	$3,910	18	—	$5,480	8	—	$2,630

	Periodic	Perpetual
1 Which method uses the Purchases account?	X	
2 Which method uses the general ledger account Cost of Goods Sold?		X
3 Which method has the same balance in Inventory all year until closing?	X	
4 Which method is preferred for high-unit-cost inventory items?		X
5 Which method requires an actual physical count at least once a year?	X	X
6 Which method debits Inventory for goods purchased?		X

This is much easier computationally and minimizes bookkeeping costs. At the end of the period these companies convert ending inventory and cost of goods sold to the LIFO or weighted-average cost basis for the financial statements. Perpetual inventory records provide information such as the following:

1. When customers inquire about how soon they can get a home computer, the salesperson can answer the question after referring to the perpetual inventory record. On November 7 the salesperson would reply that the company's stock is low, and the customer may have to wait a few days. On November 26 the salesperson could offer immediate delivery.

2. The perpetual records alert the business to reorder when inventory becomes low. On November 7 the company would be wise to purchase inventory. Sales may be lost if the business cannot promise immediate delivery.

3. At November 30 the company prepares monthly financial statements. The perpetual inventory records show the company's ending inventory of home computers at $2,630, and its cost of goods sold for this product at $5,480. No physical count is necessary at this time. However, a physical inventory is needed once a year to verify the accuracy of the records.

Perpetual inventory systems are becoming increasingly sophisticated. *The Wall Street Journal* (June 11, 1990) carried a story about Frito-Lay's Decision Support System. It can tell the company president (and other managers) the weekly sales of Ruffles Light potato chips by each route salesman. In one case, Frito-Lay identified a drop in sales of tortilla chips by a particular chain of stores. Within two weeks, the company revised its marketing strategy and turned sales up again. Without the perpetual system, this would have taken three months.

Entries under the Perpetual System.   In the perpetual system, the business records purchases of inventory by debiting the Inventory account. When the business makes a sale, two entries are necessary. The company records the sale in the usual manner—debits Cash or Accounts Receivable and credits Sales Revenue for the sale price of the goods. The company also debits Cost of Goods Sold and credits Inventory for cost. The debit to Inventory (for purchases) and the credit to Inventory (for sales) serve to keep an up-to-date record of inventory on hand. Therefore, no end-of-period adjusting entries are needed. The Inventory account already carries the correct ending balance.

In the perpetual system, Cost of Goods Sold is an account in the general ledger. By contrast, in the periodic system, cost of goods sold is simply a total on the income statement.

To illustrate the entries under the perpetual system, let's use the same data we used in discussing the periodic system, which follow.

Ending inventory	$102,000
Credit purchases (net of discounts and returns) ...	600,000
Credit sales (net of discounts and returns)........	900,000
Cost of goods sold	578,000

Summary entries for April:

To record credit purchases:		
Inventory	600,000	
Accounts Payable		600,000
To record credit sales:		
Accounts Receivable	900,000	
Sales Revenue		900,000
Cost of Goods Sold	578,000	
Inventory		578,000

Reporting on the financial statements:

Balance sheet at April 30:	
Inventory	$102,000
Income statement for April:	
Sales revenue...................................	$900,000
Cost of goods sold	578,000
Gross margin	$322,000

You should compare the entries and financial statement presentations under the *periodic* and the *perpetual* systems. Note that the entries to record purchases and sales differ under the two systems but that the financial statement amounts are the same.

Internal Control over Inventory

Internal control over inventory is important because inventory is the lifeblood of a merchandiser. Successful companies take great care to protect their inventory. Elements of good internal control over inventory include:

1. Physically counting inventory at least once each year no matter which system is used
2. Maintaining efficient purchasing, receiving, and shipping procedures
3. Storing inventory to protect it against theft, damage, and decay
4. Limiting access to inventory to personnel who do *not* have access to the accounting records

5. Keeping perpetual inventory records for high-unit-cost merchandise
6. Purchasing inventory in economical quantities
7. Keeping enough inventory on hand to prevent shortage situations, which lead to lost sales
8. Not keeping too large an inventory stockpiled, thus avoiding the expense of tying up money in unneeded items

The annual physical count of inventory (item 1) is necessary because the only way to be certain of the amount of inventory on hand is to count it. Errors arise in the best accounting systems, and the count is needed to establish the correct value of the inventory. When an error is detected, the records are brought into agreement with the physical count.

Keeping inventory handlers away from the accounting records (item 4) is an essential separation of duties, discussed in Chapter 7. An employee with access to inventory and the accounting records can steal the goods and make an entry to conceal the theft. For example, he could increase the amount of an inventory write-down to make it appear that goods decreased in value when in fact they were stolen.

Computerized Inventory Records

Computer systems have revolutionized accounting for inventory. Perpetual inventory systems are rapidly replacing periodic methods. Computerized systems can provide up-to-the-minute inventory data useful for managing the business. They help cut accounting cost by processing large numbers of transactions without computational error. Computer systems also enhance internal control. They increase efficiency because managers always know the quantity and cost of inventory on hand. Managers can make better decisions about quantities to buy, prices to pay for the inventory, prices to charge customers, and sale terms to offer. Knowing the quantity on hand helps to safeguard the inventory.

Computer inventory systems vary considerably. At one extreme are complex systems used by huge retailers like Sears, J. C. Penney, and K Mart. Purchases of inventory are recorded in perpetual records stored in a central computer. The inventory tags are coded electronically for updating the perpetual records when a sale is recorded on the cash register. Have you noticed sales clerks passing the inventory ticket over a particular area of the checkout counter? A sensing device in the counter reads the stock number, quantity, cost, and sale price of the item sold. In other systems, the sales clerk passes an electronic device over the inventory tag. The computer records the sale and updates the inventory records. In effect, a journal entry is recorded for each sale, a procedure that is not economical without a computer.

Small companies also use minicomputers and microcomputers to keep perpetual inventory records. These systems may be similar to the systems used by large companies. In less-sophisticated operations, a company may have sales clerks write inventory stock numbers on sales slips. The stock number identifies the particular item of inventory, such as men's shirts or children's shoes. The business may accumulate all sales slips for the week. If the company has its own computer system, an employee may type the sales information into the computer and store the perpetual records on a magnetic disk. To learn the quantity, cost, or other characteristic of a particular item of inventory, a manager can view the inventory record on the computer monitor. For broader-based decisions affecting the entire inventory, managers use printouts of all

Point to Stress: Computers that can electronically scan coded items perform several importance tasks:

1 The item that is being sold can be taken out of inventory and the cost of goods sold can be recorded.

2 The scanner can ring up the sale more quickly than a sales clerk can.

3 The scanner is less likely than the sales clerk to make errors.

items in stock. Many small businesses hire outside computer service centers to do much of the accounting for inventory. Regardless of the arrangement, managers get periodic printouts showing inventory data needed for managing the business. Manual reporting of this information is more time consuming and expensive.

Summary Problems for Your Review

Problem 1

Centronics Data Computer Corporation reported a net loss for the year. In its financial statements, the company noted:

Balance Sheet:

Current assets:
 Inventories (notes 1C and 2) $48,051,000

> Note 1C: Inventories are stated at the lower of cost or market. Cost is determined on a first-in, first-out (FIFO) basis.
>
> Note 2: Declining . . . market conditions during [the] fiscal [year] adversely affected anticipated sales of the Company's older printer products; . . . Accordingly, the statement of loss . . . includes a [debit) of $9,600,000.

Required

1. At which amount did Centronics report its inventory, cost or market value? How can you tell?
2. If the reported inventory of $48,051,000 represents market value, what was the cost of the inventory?

Problem 2

American Hospital Supply Corporation reported using the LIFO inventory method. Its inventory amount was $490.5 million.

Required

1. Suppose that during the period covered by this report, the company made an error that understated its ending inventory by $15 million. What effect would this error have on *cost of goods sold* and *gross margin* of the period? On *cost of goods sold* and *gross margin* of the following period? On *total gross margin* of both periods combined?
2. When American Hospital Supply reported the above amount for inventory, prices were rising. Would FIFO or LIFO have shown a higher gross margin? Why?

SOLUTIONS TO REVIEW PROBLEMS

Problem 1

1. Centronics reported its inventory at *market value,* as indicated by (a) their valuing inventories at LCM and (b) the declining market conditions that caused the company to "include a [debit] of $9,600,000" in "the statement

of loss." The company debited the $9,600,000 to a loss account or to cost of goods sold. The credit side of the entry was to Inventory—for a write-down to market value.

2. The cost of inventory before the write-down was $57,651,000 ($48,051,000 + $9,600,000). The $48,051,000 market value is what is left of the original cost. Thus the amount to be carried forward to future periods is $48,051,000.

Problem 2

1. Understating ending inventory by $15 million has the following effects on *cost of goods sold* and *gross margin:*

	Cost of Goods Sold	Gross Margin
Period during which error was made	OVERSTATED by $15 million	UNDERSTATED by $15 million
Following period	UNDERSTATED by $15 million	OVERSTATED by $15 million
Combined total	CORRECTLY STATED	CORRECTLY STATED

2. When prices are rising, FIFO results in higher gross margin than LIFO. FIFO matches against sales revenue the lower inventory costs of beginning inventory and purchases made during the early part of the period.

Summary

Accounting for inventory plays an important part in merchandisers' accounting systems because selling inventory is the heart of their business. Inventory is generally the largest current asset on their balance sheet, and inventory expense—called cost of goods sold—is usually the largest expense on the income statement.

Businesses multiply the quantity of inventory items by their unit cost to determine inventory cost. Inventory costing methods are *specific unit cost; weighted-average cost; first-in, first-out (FIFO) cost; and last-in, first-out* (LIFO) cost. Only businesses that sell unique items, like automobiles and jewels, use the specific identification method. Most other companies use the other methods.

FIFO reports ending inventory at the most current cost. LIFO reports cost of goods sold at the most current cost. When inventory costs increase, LIFO produces the highest cost of goods sold and the lowest income, thus minimizing income taxes. FIFO results in the highest income. The weighted-average cost method avoids the extremes of FIFO and LIFO.

The *consistency principle* demands that a business stick with the inventory method it chooses. If a change in inventory method is warranted, the company must report the effect of the change on income. The *lower-of-cost-or-market rule*—an example of accounting *conservatism*—requires that businesses report inventory on the balance sheet at the lower of its cost or current replacement value.

The *gross profit method* and the *retail method* are two techniques for estimating the cost of inventory. These methods come in handy for preparing interim financial statements and for estimating the cost of inventory destroyed by fire and other casualties.

Merchandisers with high-price-tag items generally use the *perpetual inventory system,* which features a running inventory balance. In the past most merchandisers handling low-price-tag items used the *periodic system.* Recent advances in information technology have led to replacement of periodic inventory systems with perpetual systems. A physical count of inventory is needed in both systems for control purposes.

Self-Study Questions

Test your understanding of the chapter by marking the best answer to each of the following questions.

1. Which of the following items is the greatest in dollar amount? *(p. 414)*
    a. Beginning inventory
    b. Purchases
    √ c. Cost of goods available for sale
    d. Ending inventory
    e. Cost of goods sold

2. Sound Warehouse counts 15,000 compact disks, including 1,000 CDs held on consignment, in its Waco, Texas, store. The business has purchased an additional 2,000 units on FOB destination terms. These goods are still in transit. Each CD cost $3.40. The cost of the inventory to report on the balance sheet is *(p. 415)*
    √ a. $47,600
    b. $51,000
    c. $54,400
    d. $57,800

3. The inventory costing method that best matches current expense with current revenue is *(p. 420)*
    a. Specific unit cost
    b. Weighted-average cost
    c. FIFO
    √ d. LIFO
    e. FIFO or LIFO, depending on whether inventory costs are increasing or decreasing

4. The consistency principle has the most direct impact on *(p. 421)*
    a. Whether to include or exclude an item in inventory
    √ b. Whether to change from one inventory method to another
    c. Whether to write inventory down to a market value below cost
    d. Whether to use the periodic or the perpetual inventory system

5. Application of the lower-of-cost-or-market rule often results in *(p. 424)*
    a. Higher ending inventory
    √ b. Lower ending inventory
    c. A counterbalancing error
    d. A change from one inventory method to another

6. An error understated ending inventory of 19X7. This error will *(p. 425)*
    a. Overstate 19X7 cost of sales
    b. Understate 19X8 cost of sales
    c. Not affect owner's equity at the end of 19X8
    √ d. All of the above

7. Beginning inventory was $35,000, purchases were $146,000, and sales totaled $240,000. With a normal gross margin rate of 35 percent, how much is ending inventory? *(p. 426)*
    √ a. $25,000
    b. $35,000
    c. $97,000
    d. $181,000

8. Beginning inventory was $20,000 at cost and $40,000 at retail. Purchases were $120,000 at cost and $210,000 at retail. Sales were $200,000. How much is ending inventory at cost? *(p. 427)*
    a. $22,000
    b. $26,000
    √ c. $28,000
    d. $50,000

9. The year-end entry to close beginning inventory in a perpetual inventory system is *(p. 431)*
    a. Income Summary XXX
       Inventory XXX

b. Inventory XXX

Income Summary XXX

c. Either of the above, depending on whether inventory increased or decreased during the period

√d. Not needed

10. Which of the following statements is true? *(pp. 431, 432)*

a. Separation of duties is not an important element of internal control for inventories.

b. The perpetual system is used primarily for low-unit-cost inventory.

√c. An annual physical count of inventory is needed regardless of the type of inventory system used.

d. All the above are true.

Answers to the Self-Study Questions follow the Accounting Vocabulary.

Accounting Vocabulary

Average cost method. Inventory costing method based on the weighted-average cost of inventory during the period. Weighted-average cost is determined by dividing the cost of goods available for sale by the number of units available *(p. 416)*.

Beginning inventory. Goods left over from the preceding period *(p. 413)*.

Conservatism. Concept that underlies presenting the gloomiest possible figures in the financial statements *(p. 423)*.

Consignment. Transfer of goods by the owner (consignor) to another business (consignee) who, for a fee, sells the inventory on the owner's behalf. The consignee does not take title to the consigned goods *(p. 415)*.

Consistency principle. A business must use the same accounting methods and procedures from period to period *(p. 421)*.

Ending inventory. Goods still on hand at the end of the period *(p. 413)*.

First-in, first-out (FIFO) method. Inventory costing method by which the first costs into inventory are the first costs out to cost of goods sold. Ending inventory is based on the costs of the most recent purchases *(p. 416)*.

FOB destination. Terms of a transaction that govern when the title to the inventory passes from the seller to the purchaser—when the goods arrive at the purchaser's location *(p. 414)*.

FOB shipping point. Terms of a transaction that govern when the title to the inventory passes from the seller to the purchaser—when the goods leave the seller's place of business *(p. 414)*.

Goods available for sale. Beginning inventory plus net purchases *(p. 413)*.

Gross margin method. A way to estimate inventory based on a rearrangement of the cost of goods sold model: Beginning inventory + Net purchases = Cost of goods available for sale. Cost of goods available for sale − Cost of goods sold = Ending inventory. Also called the Gross profit method *(p. 426)*.

Inventory cost. Price paid to acquire inventory—not the selling price of the goods. Inventory cost includes its invoice price, less all discounts, plus sales tax, tariffs, transportation fees, insurance while in transit, and all other costs incurred to make the goods ready for sale *(p. 415)*.

Inventory profit. Difference between gross margin figured on the FIFO basis and gross margin figured on the LIFO basis *(p. 420)*.

Last-in, first-out (LIFO) method. Inventory costing method by which the last costs into inventory are the first costs out to cost of goods sold. This leaves the oldest costs—those of beginning inventory and the earliest purchases of the period—in ending inventory *(p. 416)*.

Lower-of-cost-or-market (LCM) rule. Requires that an asset be reported in the financial statements at the lower of its historical cost or its market value (current replacement cost) *(p. 423)*.

Periodic inventory system. The business does not keep a continuous record of the inventory on hand. Instead, at the end of the period the business makes a physical count of the on-hand inventory and applies the appropriate unit costs to determine the cost of the ending inventory *(p. 428)*.

Perpetual inventory system. The business keeps a continuous record for each inventory item to show the inventory on hand at all times *(p. 429)*.

Retail method. A way to estimate inventory cost based on the cost-of-goods-sold model. The retail method requires that the business record inventory purchases both at cost and at retail. Multiply ending inventory at retail by the cost ratio to estimate the ending inventory's cost *(p. 427)*.

Specific unit cost method. Inventory cost method based on the specific cost of particular units of inventory *(p. 416)*.

Weighted-average cost method. Inventory costing method based on the weighted average cost of inventory during the period. Weighted-average cost is determined by dividing the cost of goods available for sale by the number of units available. Also called the Average cost method *(p. 416)*.

Answers to Self-Study Questions

1. c
2. a $(15,000 - 1,000) \times \$3.40 = \$47,600$
3. d
4. b
5. b
6. d
7. a $\$35,000 + \$146,000 = \$181,000$
   $\$240,000 - (.35 \times \$240,000) = \$156,000$
   $\$181,000 - \$156,000 = \$25,000$

		Cost	Retail	
8.	c Beginning inventory	$ 20,000	$ 40,000	
	Purchases	120,000	210,000	**Cost Ratio**
	Goods available	140,000 ÷	250,000 =	.56
	Sales		200,000	
	Ending inventory—at retail		$ 50,000	
	at cost ($50,000 × .56)	$ 28,000		

9. d
10. c

ASSIGNMENT MATERIAL

Questions

1. Why is merchandise inventory so important to a retailer or whole-saler?
2. If beginning inventory is $10,000, purchases total $85,000, and ending inventory is $12,700, how much is cost of goods sold?
3. If beginning inventory is $32,000, purchases total $119,000, and cost of goods sold is $127,000, how much is ending inventory?
4. What role does the cost principle play in accounting for inventory?
5. What two items determine the cost of ending inventory?
6. Briefly describe the four generally accepted inventory cost methods. During a period of rising prices, which method produces the highest reported income? Which produces the lowest reported income?

7. Which inventory costing method produces the ending inventory valued at the most current cost? Which method produces the cost-of-goods-sold amount valued at the most current cost?

8. What is the most attractive feature of LIFO? Does LIFO have this advantage during periods of increasing prices or during periods of decreasing prices? Why has LIFO had this advantage recently?

9. Which inventory costing methods are used the most in practice?

10. What is inventory profit? Which method produces it?

11. Identify the chief criticism of LIFO.

12. How does the consistency principle affect accounting for inventory?

13. Briefly describe the influence that the concept of conservatism has on accounting for inventory.

14. Manley Company's inventory has a cost of $48,000 at the end of the year, and the current replacement cost of the inventory is $51,000. At which amount should the company report the inventory on its balance sheet? Suppose the current replacement cost of the inventory is $45,000 instead of $51,000. At which amount should Manley report the inventory? What rule governs your answers to these questions?

15. Gabriel Company accidentally overstated its ending inventory by $10,000 at the end of period 1. Is gross margin of period 1 overstated or understated? Is gross margin of period 2 overstated, understated, or unaffected by the period 1 error? Is total gross margin for the two periods overstated, understated, or correct? Give the reason for your answer.

16. Identify two methods of estimating inventory amounts. What familiar model underlies both estimation methods?

17. A fire destroyed the inventory of Olivera Company, but the accounting records were saved. The beginning inventory was $22,000, purchases for the period were $71,000, and sales were $140,000. Olivera's customary gross margin is 45 percent of sales. Use the gross margin method to estimate the cost of the inventory destroyed by the fire.

18. Suppose your company deals in expensive jewelry. Which inventory system should you use to achieve good internal control over the inventory? If your business is a hardware store that sells low-cost goods, which inventory system would you be likely to use? Why would you choose this system?

19. Identify the accounts debited and credited in the standard purchase and sale entries under (a) the periodic inventory system and (b) the perpetual inventory system.

20. What is the role of the physical count of inventory in (a) the periodic inventory system and (b) the perpetual inventory system?

21. True or false? A company that sells inventory of low unit cost needs no internal controls over the goods. Any inventory loss would probably be small.

Exercises

Additional computer-related exercise: Exercise 28-1

Exercise 9-1 *Computing ending inventory by four methods* **(L.O. 1)**

COGS:
Specific unit $3,150
Wtd.-avg. $3,146
FIFO $3,060
LIFO $3,250

Malzone Precision Instruments' inventory records for industrial switches indicate the following at October 31:

Oct.	1	Beginning inventory	10 units @ $130
	8	Purchase	4 units @ 140
	15	Purchase	11 units @ 150
	26	Purchase	5 units @ 156

The physical count of inventory at October 31 indicates that eight units are on hand, and the company owns them. Compute ending inventory and cost of goods sold using each of the following methods:

1. Specific unit cost, assuming five $150 units and three $130 units are on hand
2. Weighted-average cost
3. First in, first out
4. Last in, first out

Exercise 9-2 *Recording periodic inventory transactions* *(L.O. 1)*

No check figure

Use the data in Exercise 9-1 and the periodic inventory system to journalize:

1. Total October purchases in one summary entry. All purchases were on credit.
2. Total October sales in one summary entry. Assume the selling price was $300 per unit, and all sales were on credit.
3. October 31 entries for inventory. Malzone Precision Instruments uses LIFO.

Exercise 9-3 *Computing the tax advantage of LIFO over FIFO* *(L.O. 2)*

LIFO advantage $57

Use the data in Exercise 9-1 to illustrate the income tax advantage of LIFO over FIFO, assuming sales revenue is $7,000, operating expenses are $1,100, and the income tax rate is 30 percent.

Exercise 9-4 *Converting LIFO financial statements to the FIFO basis* *(L.O. 1,2)*

FIFO reports higher income by $1,700

Hennig Nursery reported:

Balance sheet:	19X5	19X4
Inventories—note 4	$ 65,800	$ 59,300
Income statement:		
Net purchases	404,100	372,700
Cost of goods sold	397,600	381,400

Note 4. The company determines inventory cost by the last-in, first-out method. If the first-in, first-out method were used, inventories would be $5,200 higher at year end 19X5 and $3,500 higher at year end 19X4.

Required

Show the cost-of-goods-sold computations for 19X5 under LIFO and FIFO. Which method would result in higher reported income? Show the amount of the difference.

Exercise 9-5 *Note disclosure of a change in inventory method* *(L.O. 2, 3)*

No check figure

CPC International, Inc., maker of Hellmann's mayonnaise, Mazola corn oil, and other foods, included the following in its annual report:

> *Inventories* are stated at the lower of cost or market. . . . Outside the United States, inventories generally are valued at average cost. In the United States, vegetable oils and corn are valued at cost on the last-in, first-out method. Other United States inventories are valued at cost on the first-in, first-out method. Had the first-in, first-out method been used for all United States inventories, the carrying value of these inventories would have increased by $20.3 million.

Suppose CPC International were to change to the FIFO method for all its inventories. Write the note to disclose this accounting change in the company's financial statements. Indicate the effect of the change on income before income tax.

Gross margin $86,141

Exercise 9-6 *The effect of lower-of-cost-or-market on the income statement* **(L.O. 4)**

From the following inventory records of DeGaulle Corporation for 19X7, prepare the company's income statement through gross margin. Apply the lower-of-cost-or-market rule.

Beginning inventory (average cost)	300 @ $41.33 =	$ 12,399
(replacement cost)	300 @ 41.91 =	12,573
Purchases during the year	2,600 @ 45.50 =	118,300
Ending inventory (average cost)	400 @ 45.07 =	18,028
(replacement cost)	400 @ 42.10 =	16,840
Sales during the year......................	2,500 @ 80.00*=	200,000

*Selling price per unit.

Gross margin $39,500

Exercise 9-7 *Applying the lower-of-cost-or-market rule* **(L.O. 4)**

Imhoff Company's income statement for March reported the following data:

Income Statement:

Sales revenue		$88,000
Cost of goods sold:		
Beginning inventory	$17,200	
Net purchases...................	51,700	
Cost of goods available for sale ...	68,900	
Ending inventory	22,800	
Cost of goods sold...............		46,100
Gross margin		$41,900

Prior to releasing the financial statements, it was discovered that the current replacement cost of ending inventory was $20,400. Correct the above data to include the lower-of-cost-or-market value of ending inventory. Also, show how inventory would be reported on the balance sheet.

Net income:
19X4 $32,300
19X5 $31,100

Exercise 9-8 *Correcting an inventory error* **(L.O. 5)**

Robinette Auto Supply reported the following comparative income statement for the years ended September 30, 19X5 and 19X4:

Robinette Auto Supply
Income Statements
For the Year Ended September 30,

	19X5		19X4	
Sales revenue		$132,300		$121,700
Cost of goods sold:				
Beginning inventory	$14,000		$12,800	
Net purchases..............	72,000		66,000	
Cost of goods available......	86,000		78,800	
Ending inventory	16,600		14,000	
Cost of goods sold.........		69,400		64,800
Gross margin		62,900		56,900
Operating expenses............		30,300		26,100
Net income		$ 32,600		$ 30,800

During 19X5 accountants for the company discovered that ending 19X4 inventory was understated by $1,500. Prepare the corrected comparative income statement for the two-year period. What was the effect of the error on net income for the two years combined? Explain your answer.

Exercise 9-9 *Estimating inventory by the gross margin method* **(L.O. 6)**

Jansen Unpainted Furniture began April with inventory of $41,000. The business made net purchases of $37,600 and had net sales of $55,000 before a fire destroyed the company's inventory. For the past several years, Jansen's gross margin on sales has been 40 percent. Estimate the cost of the inventory destroyed by the fire.

Exercise 9-10 *Estimating inventory by the retail method* **(L.O. 6)**

Assume the inventory records of Brewster's, a regional chain of stereo shops, revealed the following:

	At Cost	At Retail
Beginning inventory..............	$ 30,400	$ 48,000
Net purchases	113,000	191,000
Net sales		201,000

Use the retail inventory method to estimate the ending inventory of the business.

Exercise 9-11 *Recording perpetual inventory transactions* **(L.O. 7)**

Jerrel Bolton Chevrolet Company keeps perpetual inventory records for its automobile inventory. During May the company made credit purchases of inventory costing $93,300. Cash sales came to $63,100, credit sales on notes receivable totaled $85,400, and cost of goods sold reached $119,550. Record these summary transactions in the general journal.

Exercise 9-12 *Computing the ending amount of a perpetual inventory* **(L.O. 7)**

Piazza String World Music Center carries a large inventory of guitars, keyboards, and other musical instruments. Because each item is expensive, Piazza uses a perpetual inventory system. Company records indicate the following for a particular line of Casio keyboards:

Date	Item	Quantity	Unit Cost
May 1	Balance	5	$80
6	Sale	3	
8	Purchase	11	85
17	Sale	4	
30	Sale	3	

Compute ending inventory and cost of goods sold for keyboards by the FIFO method. Also show the computation of cost of goods sold by the standard formula: Beginning inventory + Purchases − Ending inventory = Cost of goods sold.

Problems   (Group A)

Problem 9-1A *Computing inventory by three methods* **(L.O. 1)**

Emerson Electric Co. began the year with 73 units of inventory that cost $26 each. During the year Emerson made the following purchases:

Mar. 11	113 @ $27
May 2	81 @ 29
July 19	167 @ 32
Nov. 18	44 @ 36

The company uses the periodic inventory system, and the physical count at December 31 indicates that ending inventory consists of 91 units.

Required

Compute the ending inventory and cost of goods sold amounts under (1) weighted-average cost, (2) FIFO cost, and (3) LIFO cost. Round weighted-average cost per unit to the nearest cent, and round all other amounts to the nearest dollar.

FIFO inventory profit $255

Problem 9-2A   *Computing inventory, cost of goods sold, and FIFO inventory profit (L.O. 1, 2)*

Lincoln Beverage Distributors specializes in soft drinks. The business began operations on January 1, 19X1, with an inventory of 500 cases of drinks that cost $2.01 each. During the first month of operations the store purchased inventory as follows:

Purchase no. 1	60 @ $2.10
Purchase no. 2	120 @ 2.35
Purchase no. 3	600 @ 2.50
Purchase no. 4	40 @ 2.75

The ending inventory consists of 500 cases of drinks.

Required

1. Complete the following tabulation, rounding weighted-average cost to the nearest cent and all other amounts to the nearest dollar:

	Ending Inventory	Cost of Goods Sold
a. Weighted-average cost		
b. FIFO cost		
c. LIFO cost		

2. Compute the amount of inventory profit under FIFO.
3. Which method produces the most current ending inventory cost? Which method produces the most current cost-of-goods-sold amount? Give the reason for your answers.

Gross margin:
 Weighted-average $62,320
 FIFO $62,970
 LIFO $61,880

Problem 9-3A   *Preparing an income statement directly from the accounts (L.O. 1, 2)*

The records of Upjohn Healthcare Products include the following accounts for one of its products at December 31 of the current year:

Inventory		
Jan. 1 Balance	{700 units @ $7.00}	4,900

Purchases		
Jan. 6	300 units @ $7.05	2,115
Mar. 19	1,100 units @ 7.35	8,085
June 22	8,400 units @ 7.50	63,000
Oct. 4	500 units @ 8.80	4,400
Dec. 31 Balance		77,600

Sales Revenue		
Feb. 5	1,000 units @ $12.00	12,000
Apr. 10	700 units @ 12.10	8,470
July 31	1,800 units @ 13.25	23,850
Sep. 4	3,500 units @ 13.50	47,250
Nov. 27	3,100 units @ 15.00	46,500
Dec. 31	Balance	138,070

Required

1. Compute the quantities of goods in (a) ending inventory and (b) cost of goods sold during the year.
2. Prepare a partial income statement through gross margin under the weighted-average cost, FIFO cost, and LIFO cost methods.

Problem 9-4A *Converting an actual company's reported income from the LIFO basis to the FIFO basis* **(L.O. 3)**

FIFO gross margin $2,200

Colgate-Palmolive Company uses the LIFO method for inventories. In a recent annual report, Colgate-Palmolive reported these amounts on the balance sheet (in millions):

	December 31,	
	19X9	**19X8**
Inventories	$591	$630

A note to the financial statements indicated that if current cost (assume FIFO) had been used, inventories would have been higher by $25 million at the end of 19X9 and higher by $21 million at the end of 19X8. The income statement reported sales revenue of $5,039 million and cost of goods sold of $2,843 million for 19X9.

Required

1. Show the computation of Colgate-Palmolive's cost of goods sold and gross margin for 19X9 by the LIFO method as actually reported.
2. Compute Colgate-Palmolive's cost of goods sold and gross margin for 19X9 by the FIFO method.
3. Which method makes the company look better in 19X9? Give your reason. What is the amount of inventory profit for 19X9?

Problem 9-5A *Applying the lower-of-cost-or-market rule* **(L.O. 4)**

Gross margin $147,000

The financial statements of Dubrovnik Business Systems were prepared on the cost basis without considering whether the replacement value of ending inventory was less than cost. Following are selected data from those statements:

From the income statement:

Sales revenue		$278,000
Cost of goods sold:		
Beginning inventory	$ 60,000	
Net purchases	122,000	
Cost of goods available for sale . . .	182,000	
Ending inventory	53,000	
Cost of goods sold		129,000
Gross margin		$149,000

From the balance sheet:

Current assets:
Inventory . . . . $ 53,000

The replacement costs were $68,000 for beginning inventory and $51,000 for ending inventory.

Required

1. Revise the data to include the appropriate lower-of-cost-or-market value of inventory.
2. How is the lower-of-cost-or-market rule conservative? How is conservatism shown in Dubrovnik's situation?

Problem 9-6A   *Correcting inventory errors over a three-year period*   **(L.O. 5)**

Net income:
  19X4 $7 million
  19X5 $58 million
  19X6 $55 million

The Elm Mott Custom Window Frames books show these data (in millions):

	19X6	19X5	19X4
Net sales revenue	$350	$280	$240
Cost of goods sold:			
Beginning inventory	$ 65	$ 55	$ 70
Net purchases	195	135	130
Cost of goods available	260	190	200
Less Ending inventory	70	65	55
Cost of goods sold	190	125	145
Gross margin	160	155	95
Operating expenses	113	109	76
Net income	$ 47	$ 46	$ 19

In early 19X7, a team of internal auditors discovered that the ending inventory of 19X4 had been overstated by $12 million. Also, the ending inventory for 19X6 had been understated by $8 million. The ending inventory at December 31, 19X5, was correct.

Required

1. Prepare corrected income statements for the three years.
2. State whether each year's net income and owner's equity amounts are understated or overstated. For each incorrect figure, indicate the amount of the understatement or overstatement.

Est. cost of end. inventory
$193,200

Problem 9-7A   *Estimating inventory by the gross margin method; preparing a multiple-step income statement*   **(L.O. 6)**

Assume Baldwin Piano Company estimates its inventory by the gross margin method when preparing monthly financial statements. For the past two years, the gross margin has averaged 40 percent of net sales. Assume further that the company's inventory records for stores in the southwestern region reveal the following data:

Inventory, July 1	$ 267,000
Transactions during July:	
Purchases	3,689,000
Purchase discounts	26,000
Purchase returns	12,000
Sales	6,230,000
Sales returns	22,000

Required

1. Estimate the July 31 inventory using the gross margin method.
2. Prepare the July income statement through gross margin for the Baldwin Piano Company stores in the southwestern region. Use the multiple-step format.

Problem 9-8A *Estimating inventory by the retail method; recording periodic inventory transactions* **(L.O. 6)**

End. inventory at cost $28,963

The fiscal year of Dayton Hudson Corporation ends on January 31. Assume the following inventory data for the jewelry department of a Dayton Hudson Store:

	Cost	Retail
Inventory, Jan. 31, 19X3	$ 31,200	$ 63,300
Transactions during the year ended January 31, 19X4:		
Purchases	154,732	301,190
Purchase returns................................	5,800	11,290
Sales..		314,600
Sales returns		18,190

Required

1. Use the retail method to estimate the cost of the store's ending inventory of jewelry at January 31, 19X4.
2. Assuming Dayton Hudson uses the periodic inventory system, prepare general journal entries to record:
   a. Inventory purchases and sales during fiscal year 19X4. Assume all purchases and one-half of company sales were on credit. All other sales were for cash.
   b. Inventory entries at January 31, 19X4. Closing entries for Purchases and Purchase Returns are not required.

Problem 9-9A *Using the perpetual inventory system; applying the lower-of-cost-or-market rule* **(L.O. 4, 7)**

FIFO end. inventory $720

Midas is a popular brand of automobile mufflers. Assume the following data for a Midas Muffler store:

	Purchased	Sold	Balance
Dec. 31, 19X3			120 @ $6 = $720
Mar. 15, 19X4	50 @ $7 = $350		
Apr. 10		80	
May 29	100 @ 8 = 800		
Aug. 3		130	
Nov. 16	90 @ 9 = 810		
Dec. 12		70	

Required

1. Prepare a perpetual inventory card for Midas, using the FIFO method.
2. Assume Midas sold the 130 units on August 3 on account for $22 each. Record the sale and related cost of goods sold in the general journal under the FIFO method.
3. Suppose the current replacement cost of the ending inventory of this Midas store is $750 at December 31, 19X4. Use the answer to requirement 1 to compute the lower-of-cost-or-market (LCM) value of the ending inventory.

End. inventory $8,900

Problem 9-10A *Recording periodic and perpetual inventory transactions* **(L.O. 7)**

Yankee Sales Company records reveal the following at December 31 of the current year.

Inventory

Jan. 1 Balance	
900 units @ $7.00 6,300	

Purchases

Feb. 4 300 units @ $7.05 2,115	
Apr. 11 1,100 units @ 7.35 8,085	
June 22 8,400 units @ 7.50 63,000	
Aug. 19 500 units @ 8.80 4,400	
Dec. 31 Balance 77,600	

Sales Revenue

	Mar. 8 1,000 units @ $12.00 12,000
	May 24 700 units @ 12.10 8,470
	Aug. 19 1,800 units @ 13.25 23,850
	Oct. 4 3,500 units @ 13.50 47,250
	Nov. 14 3,100 units @ 15.00 46,500
	Dec. 31 Balance 138,070

Required

Make summary journal entries to record:

1. Purchases, sales, and end-of-period inventory entries, assuming Yankee Sales Company uses the periodic inventory system and the FIFO cost method. All purchases are on credit. Cash sales are $20,000, with the remaining sales on account.
2. Purchases, sales, and cost of goods sold, assuming Yankee Sales Company uses the perpetual inventory system and the FIFO cost method. All purchases are on credit. Cash sales are $20,000, with the remaining sales on account.

(Group B)

LIFO end. inventory $18,409

Problem 9-1B *Computing inventory by three methods* **(L.O. 1)**

Pearle Vision Center began the year with 140 units of inventory that cost $80 each. During the year Pearle made the following purchases:

Feb. 3	217 @ $81
Apr. 12	95 @ 82
Aug. 8	210 @ 84
Oct. 24	248 @ 88

The company uses the periodic inventory system, and the physical count at December 31 indicates that ending inventory consists of 229 units.

Required

Compute the ending inventory and cost of goods sold amounts under (1) weighted-average cost, (2) FIFO cost, and (3) LIFO cost. Round weighted-average cost per unit to the nearest cent, and round all other amounts to the nearest dollar.

Problem 9-2B *Computing inventory, cost of goods sold, and FIFO inventory profits* *(L.O. 1, 2)*

FIFO inventory profit $600

Shellenberger's specializes in men's shirts. The store began operations on January 1, 19X1, with an inventory of 200 shirts that cost $13 each. During the year the store purchased inventory as follows:

Purchase no. 1	110 @ $14
Purchase no. 2	80 @ 15
Purchase no. 3	320 @ 15
Purchase no. 4	100 @ 18

The ending inventory consists of 150 shirts.

Required

1. Complete the following tabulation, rounding average cost to the nearest cent and all other amounts to the nearest dollar:

	Ending Inventory	Cost of Goods Sold
a. Weighted-average cost	_____	_____
b. FIFO cost	_____	_____
c. LIFO cost	_____	_____

2. Compute the amount of inventory profit under FIFO.
3. Which method produces the most current ending inventory cost? Which method produces the most current cost-of-goods-sold amount? Give the reason for your answers.

Problem 9-3B *Preparing an income statement directly from the accounts* *(L.O. 1, 2)*

Gross margin:
Weighted-average $2,350
FIFO $2,520
LIFO $2,194

The records of The Kitchen Cupboard include the following accounts for one of its products at December 31 of the current year:

Inventory

Jan.	1	Balance	300 units @ $3.00	1,210	
			100 units @ 3.10		

Purchases

Feb.	6	800 units @ $3.15	2,520	
May	19	600 units @ 3.35	2,010	
Aug.	12	460 units @ 3.50	1,610	
Oct.	4	800 units @ 3.75	3,000	
Dec.	31	Balance	9,140	

Sales Revenue		
Mar. 12	500 units @ $4.00	2,000
June 9	1,100 units @ 4.20	4,620
Aug. 21	300 units @ 4.50	1,350
Nov. 2	600 units @ 4.50	2,700
Dec. 18	100 units @ 4.75	475
Dec. 31 Balance		11,145

Required

1. Compute the quantities of goods in (a) ending inventory and (b) cost of goods sold during the year.
2. Prepare a partial income statement through gross margin under the weighted-average cost, FIFO cost, and LIFO cost methods. Round weighted-average cost to the nearest cent and all other amounts to the nearest dollar.

FIFO gross margin $4,948

Problem 9-4B *Converting an actual company's reported income from the LIFO basis to the FIFO basis* **(L.O. 3)**

J. C. Penney, Inc., uses the LIFO method for inventories. In a recent annual report, Penney reported these amounts on the balance sheet (in millions):

	End of Fiscal Year	
	19X6	19X5
Merchandise inventories	$2,168	$2,298

A note to the financial statements indicated that if another method (assume FIFO) had been used, inventories would have been higher by $10 million at the end of fiscal year 19X6 and higher by $16 million at the end of 19X5. The income statement reported sales revenue of $14,740 million and cost of goods sold of $9,786 million for 19X6.

Required

1. Show the computation of Penney's cost of goods sold and gross margin for fiscal year 19X6 by the LIFO method as actually reported.
2. Compute Penney's cost of goods sold and gross margin for 19X6 by the FIFO method.
3. Which method makes the company look better in 19X6? Give your reason. Were inventory costs increasing or decreasing during 19X6? How can you tell?

Gross margin $370,000

Problem 9-5B *Applying the lower-of-cost-or-market rule* **(L.O. 4)**

Assume that accountants prepared the financial statements of Takamoto TV and Appliance on the cost basis without considering whether the replacement value of ending inventory was less than cost. Following are selected data from those statements:

From the income statement:

Sales revenue		$832,000
Cost of goods sold:		
Beginning inventory	$104,000	
Net purchases	493,000	
Cost of goods available for sale	597,000	
Ending inventory	143,000	
Cost of goods sold		454,000
Gross margin		$378,000

From the balance sheet:

Current assets:
    Inventory $143,000

The replacement costs were $107,000 for beginning inventory and $135,000 for ending inventory.

Required

1. Revise the data to include the appropriate lower-of-cost-or-market value of inventory.
2. How is the lower-of-cost-or-market rule conservative? How is conservatism shown in Takamoto's situation?

Problem 9-6B   *Correcting inventory errors over a three-year period* **(L.O. 5)**

Net income
19X1 $32 million
19X2 $4 million
19X3 $1 million

The accounting records of the Tanglewood Farms Restaurant chain show these data (in millions):

	19X3		19X2		19X1	
Net sales revenue		$200		$160		$175
Cost of goods sold:						
Beginning inventory	$ 15		$ 25		$ 40	
Net purchases	135		100		90	
Cost of goods available	150		125		130	
Less Ending inventory	30		15		25	
Cost of goods sold		120		110		105
Gross margin		80		50		70
Operating expenses		74		38		46
Net income		$ 6		$ 12		$ 24

In early 19X4, a team of internal auditors discovered that the ending inventory of 19X1 had been understated by $8 million. Also, the ending inventory for 19X3 had been overstated by $5 million. The ending inventory at December 31, 19X2, was correct.

Required

1. Prepare corrected income statements for the three years.
2. State whether each year's net income as reported here and the related owner's equity amounts are understated or overstated. For each incorrect figure, indicate the amount of the understatement or overstatement.

Est. cost of end. inventory
$338,500

Problem 9-7B   *Estimating inventory by the gross margin method; preparing a multiple-step income statement* **(L.O. 6)**

Assume Taco Bell estimates its inventory by the gross margin method when preparing monthly financial statements. For the past two years, gross margin has averaged 25 percent of net sales. Assume further that the company's inventory records for stores in the southeastern region reveal the following data:

Inventory, March 1	$ 398,000
Transactions during March:	
Purchases	6,585,000
Purchase discounts	149,000
Purchase returns	8,000
Sales	8,667,000
Sales returns	17,000

Required

1. Estimate the March 31 inventory using the gross margin method.
2. Prepare the March income statement through gross margin for the Taco Bell stores in the southeastern region. Use the multiple-step format.

End. inventory at cost $114,292

Problem 9-8B *Estimating inventory by the retail method; recording periodic inventory transactions* **(L.O. 6)**

The fiscal year of F. W. Woolworth Co. (and many other retailers) ends on January 31. Assume the following inventory data for the housewares department of a Woolworth store:

	Cost	Retail
Inventory, Jan. 31, 19X5	$ 84,500	$153,636
Transactions during the year ended January 31, 19X6:		
Purchases	419,220	762,500
Purchase returns...............................	18,090	33,172
Sales...		690,300
Sales returns		15,140

Required

1. Use the retail method to estimate the cost of the store's ending inventory of housewares at January 31, 19X6. Round off the ratio to two decimal places.
2. Assuming Woolworth uses the periodic inventory system, prepare general journal entries to record:
   a. Inventory purchases and sales during fiscal year 19X6. Assume all purchases and 10 percent of company sales were on credit. All other sales were for cash.
   b. Inventory entries at January 31, 19X6. Closing entries for Purchases and Purchase Returns are not required.

FIFO end. inventory $320

Problem 9-9B *Using the perpetual inventory system; applying the lower-of-cost-or-market rule* **(L.O. 4, 7)**

United Technologies manufactures high-technology products used in the aviation and other industries. Perhaps its most famous product is the Pratt & Whitney aircraft engine. Assume the following data for United Technologies' product SR450:

	Purchased	Sold	Balance
Dec. 31, 19X1			110 @ $5 = $550
Feb. 10, 19X2	80 @ $6 = $480		
Apr. 7		160	
May 29	110 @ 7 = 770		
July 13		120	
Oct. 4	100 @ 8 = 800		
Nov. 22		80	

Required

1. Prepare a perpetual inventory record for product SR450, using the FIFO method.

2. Assume United Technologies sold the 160 units on April 7 on account for $13 each. Record the sale and related cost of goods sold in the general journal under the FIFO method.

3. Suppose the current replacement cost of the ending inventory of product SR450 is $305 at December 31, 19X2. Use the answer to Requirement 1 to compute the lower-of-cost-or-market (LCM) value of the ending inventory.

Problem 9-10B *Recording periodic and perpetual inventory transactions* **(L.O. 7)**   End. inventory $2,100

Diego Associates records reveal the following at December 31 of the current year:

Inventory

Jan. 1	Balance $\begin{cases}400 \text{ units @ } \$3.00 \\ 100 \text{ units @ } 3.10\end{cases}$	1,510	

Purchases

Jan. 22	800 units @ $3.15	2,520	
Apr. 8	600 units @ 3.35	2,010	
July 12	460 units @ 3.50	1,610	
Sep. 11	800 units @ 3.75	3,000	
Dec. 31	Balance	9,140	

Sales Revenue

		Feb. 8	500 units @ $4.00	2,000
		Apr. 22	1,100 units @ 4.20	4,620
		July 21	300 units @ 4.50	1,350
		Oct. 14	600 units @ 4.50	2,700
		Nov. 27	100 units @ 4.75	475
		Dec. 31	Balance	11,145

Required

Make summary journal entries to record:

1. Purchases, sales, and end-of-period inventory entries, assuming Diego Associates uses the periodic inventory system and the FIFO cost method. All purchases are on credit. Cash sales are $4,000, with the remaining sales on account.

2. Purchases, sales, and cost of goods sold, assuming Diego Associates uses the perpetual inventory system and the FIFO cost method. All purchases are on credit. Cash sales total $4,000, with the remainder on account.

Extending Your Knowledge

Decision Problems

Net income without purchase:
    FIFO $252,000
    LIFO $222,000
Net income with purchase:
    FIFO $252,000
    LIFO $150,000

1. Assessing the Impact of a Year-End Purchase of Inventory (L.O. 2)

Tailwind Cycling Center is nearing the end of its first year of operations. The company made the following inventory purchases:

January	1,000	$100	$100,000
March	1,000	100	100,000
May	1,000	110	110,000
July	1,000	130	130,000
September	1,000	140	140,000
November	1,000	150	150,000
Totals	6,000		$730,000

Sales for the year will be 5,000 units for $1,200,000 revenue. Expenses other than cost of goods sold and income taxes will be $200,000. The president of the company is undecided about whether to adopt FIFO or LIFO.

The company has storage capacity for 5,000 additional units of inventory. Inventory prices are expected to stay at $150 per unit for the next few months. The president is considering purchasing 4,000 additional units of inventory at $150 each before the end of the year. He wishes to know how the purchase would affect net income under both FIFO and LIFO. The income tax rate is 40 percent, and income tax is an expense.

Required

1. To aid company decision making, prepare income statements under FIFO and under LIFO, both without and with the year-end purchase of 4,000 units of inventory at $150 per unit.
2. Compare net income under FIFO without and with the year-end purchase. Make the same comparison under LIFO. Under which method does the year-end purchase have the greater effect on net income?
3. Under which method can a year-end purchase be made in order to manipulate net income?

No check figure

2. Assessing the Impact of the Inventory Costing Method on the Financial Statements (L.O. 2,3,4)

The inventory costing method chosen by a company can affect the financial statements and thus the decisions of the users of those statements.

Required

1. A leading accounting researcher stated that one inventory costing method reports the most recent costs in the income statement, while another method reports the most recent costs in the balance sheet. In this person's opinion, this results in one or the other of the statements being "inaccurate" when prices are rising. What did the researcher mean?
2. Conservatism is an accepted accounting concept. Would you want management to be conservative in accounting for inventory if you were (a) a shareholder and (b) a prospective shareholder? Give your reason.

3. Beechwood Ltd. follows conservative accounting and writes the value of its inventory of bicycles down to market, which has declined below cost. The following year, an unexpected cycling craze results in a demand for bicycles that far exceeds supply, and the market price increases above the previous cost. What effect will conservatism have on the income of Beechwood over the two years?

Ethical Issue

During 19X6, Crocker-Hinds Company changed to the LIFO method of accounting for inventory. Suppose that during 19X7 Crocker-Hinds changes back to the FIFO method, and the following year switches back to LIFO again.

Required

1. What would you think of a company's ethics if it changed accounting methods every year?
2. What accounting principle would changing methods every year violate?
3. Who can be harmed when a company changes its accounting methods too often? How?

Financial Statement Problems

1. Inventories   (L.O. 1, 2)

Gross margin, FIFO $2,472.2 million

The notes are an important part of a company's financial statements, giving valuable details that would clutter the tabular data presented in the statements. This problem will help you learn to use a company's inventory notes. Refer to the Goodyear Tire & Rubber Company statements and related notes in Appendix C. Answer the following questions.

1. How much were Goodyear's total inventories at December 31, 1990? The Inventories note lists three categories of inventories that are classified as current assets. Name these, and briefly explain what you think each category means.
2. How does Goodyear value its inventories? Which cost methods does the company use?
3. By rearranging the cost-of-goods-sold formula, you can solve for net purchases, which are not disclosed in Goodyear's statements. Show how to compute Goodyear's net purchases during 1990. For this computation you should use the beginning and ending balances of Finished product inventories.
4. Compute the amounts of cost of goods sold and gross margin that Goodyear would have reported for 1990 if the company had used the FIFO method for inventories. The Inventories note gives relevant information on the difference between LIFO and FIFO costs of beginning and ending inventories (the approximate current cost of inventories is the FIFO cost). Assume this difference applies exclusively to Finished product inventories. As a top manager of Goodyear, which inventory method would you select if your motive were to report the maximum acceptable gross margin? Which method would you select to minimize income tax.

2. Inventories   (L.O. 1, 2)

No check figure

Obtain the annual report of an actual company *that includes Inventories among its current assets.* Answer these questions about the company.

1. How much were the company's total inventories at the end of the current year? At the end of the preceding year?

2. How does the company value its inventories? Which cost method or methods does the company use?

3. Depending on the nature of the company's business, would you expect the company to use a periodic inventory system or a perpetual system? Give your reason.

4. By rearranging the cost-of-goods-sold formula, you can solve for net purchases, which are not disclosed. Show how to compute the company's net purchases during the current year. You should examine the company's note titled *Inventories, Merchandise inventories,* or a similar term. If the company discloses several categories of inventories, including a title similar to Finished Goods, use the beginning and ending balances of Finished Goods for the computation of net purchases. If only one category of Inventories is disclosed, use these beginning and ending balances.

5. If the company does not use the LIFO method for inventories, you can omit this requirement. If the company uses LIFO, convert gross margin from the LIFO basis, as reported, to the FIFO basis, which approximates current cost. For this computation, assume the entire amount of the excess of FIFO (or current) cost over LIFO cost applies to Finished Goods inventories. If your motive were to maximize reported income, would you prefer LIFO or FIFO? If your goal were to minimize income tax, which method is preferable?

Chapter 10

Plant Assets, Intangible Assets, and Related Expenses

Business assets are separated into current assets—those typically useful for one year or less and long-lived assets—those useful for longer than a year. Count the references to long-lived assets in this excerpt from *The Wall Street Journal*, August 16, 1990, p. A1:

Iraq has just invaded Kuwait, and Larry Brady is thumbing through documents to gauge the effect on his company, a far-flung conglomerate called FMC Corp. Halfway through, he stops and looks up in horror. Five new FMC street-sweepers, worth $400,000, are on a *freighter* bound for Kuwait City—and they're just hours from their destination.

"Get that *ship* turned around!" Mr. Brady, the executive vice president, barks to Joe Murdock, international business manager at FMC's sweeper division in Pomona, Calif. "Saddam Hussein isn't getting his hands on those *sweepers*."

Mr. Murdock is already phoning the *freighter*'s captain when Mr. Brady calls. Take a quick turn into Abu Dhabi, Mr. Murdock orders the captain, just in time.

It's crisis management time at FMC Corp., as at hundreds of businesses across the U.S. and the world. For the past two weeks, FMC executives have been meeting and moving nearly nonstop to prevent damage—for instance, by planning Middle East evacuation routes for employees—and to take advantage of opportunities, such as gearing up *factories* in Malaysia to speed production of *oil-field equipment*. [Emphasis added]

Point to Stress: For some businesses, plant assets represent a significant portion of total assets. FMC Corporation is a company with very expensive assets—freighters, street sweepers, factories, and equipment.

Point to Stress: Long-lived assets are often called long-term assets. Another term often associated with property, plant, and equipment is fixed assets.

Point to Stress: Land is not depreciated because it does not wear out as do buildings and equipment.

Long-lived assets used in the operation of the business and not held for sale as investments are further divided into plant assets and intangible assets. **Plant assets** are those long-lived assets that are tangible. Their physical form provides their usefulness, for instance, land, buildings, equipment, and coal and other minerals. Of the plant assets, land is unique. Its cost is *not* depreciated—expensed over time—because its usefulness does not decrease like that of other assets. Most companies report plant assets under the heading Property, Plant, and Equipment.

Intangible assets are useful not because of their physical characteristics but because of the special rights they carry. Patents, copyrights, and trademarks are intangible assets. Examples of famous patents are the recipe for Coca-Cola and the Dolby noise-reduction process. Accounting for intangibles is similar to accounting for plant assets.

This area has its own terminology. Different names apply to the expense for the cost of the various assets, as shown in Exhibit 10-1.

The first half of the chapter discusses and illustrates how to identify the cost of a plant asset and how to expense its cost. The second half considers disposing of plant assets and how to account for natural resources and intangible assets. Unless stated otherwise, we describe accounting in accordance with generally accepted accounting principles, as distinguished from reporting to the IRS for income tax purposes.

The Cost of a Plant Asset

Point to Stress: The cost of an asset includes all costs necessary to ready the asset for its intended use.

The cost principle directs a business to carry an asset on the balance sheet at the amount paid for it. The **cost of a plant asset** is the purchase price, applicable taxes, purchase commissions, and all other amounts paid to acquire the

EXHIBIT 10-1 *Terminology Used in Accounting for Plant Assets and Intangible Assets*

Asset Account on the Balance Sheet	Related Expense Account on the Income Statement
Land	None
Buildings, Machinery and Equipment, Furniture and Fixtures, and Land Improvements	Depreciation
Natural Resources	Depletion
Intangibles	Amortization

asset and to ready it for its intended use. Because the types of costs differ for various categories of plant assets, we discuss the major groups individually.

Land

The cost of land includes its purchase price (cash plus any note payable given), brokerage commission, survey fees, legal fees, and any back property taxes that the purchaser pays. Land cost also includes any expenditures for grading and clearing the land and for demolishing or removing any unwanted buildings.

OBJECTIVE 1

Identify the elements of a plant asset's cost

The cost of land does *not* include the cost of fencing, paving, sprinkler systems, and lighting. These separate plant assets—called land improvements—are subject to depreciation.

Suppose you are a real estate developer, and you sign a $300,000 note payable to purchase 100 acres of land for subdivision into 5-acre lots. You also pay $10,000 in back property tax, $8,000 in transfer taxes, $5,000 for removal of an old building, a $1,000 survey fee, and $260,000 for the construction of fences, all in cash. What is the cost of this land?

Purchase price of land		$300,000
Add related costs:		
Back property tax	$10,000	
Transfer taxes	8,000	
Removal of building	5,000	
Survey fee	1,000	
Total incidental costs		24,000
Total cost of land		$324,000

The entry to record purchase of the land is

Land	324,000	
Note Payable		300,000
Cash		24,000

Teaching Tip: Encourage students to tell you which costs they think should be included in the cost of land. If they have difficulty thinking of some answers, ask them what kinds of costs would be considered permanent improvements to the land. Students answers should include the cost of the land, legal fees, broker's fees, clearing costs, drainage costs, leveling costs, back property taxes, sewers, the cost of removing an old building, and landscaping.

Buildings

The cost of constructing a building includes architectural fees, building permits, contractors' charges, and payments for materials, labor, and overhead. When an existing building (new or old) is purchased, its cost includes the purchase price, brokerage commission, sales and other taxes, and cash or credit expenditures for repairing and renovating the building for its intended purpose. The factories mentioned in the chapter-opening vignette would be classified as buildings.

Machinery and Equipment

The cost of machinery and equipment, such as the oil-field equipment mentioned in the vignette, includes its purchase price (less any discounts), transportation charges, insurance while in transit, sales and other taxes, purchase commission, installation costs, and any expenditures to test the asset before placing it in service. The freighters mentioned in the vignette are also equipment. Companies may carry a Ships account for ocean-going vessels.

Discussion Question: Which of these items would you include as part of the cost of a piece of machinery used in your factory?

1 Installation charges
2 Testing of the machine
3 Repair to machinery because of installer's error
4 First-year maintenance costs

ANSWER: Include 1 and 2, not 3 and 4.

Land Improvements

Class Exercise: How would a business divide a $120,000 lump-sum purchase price for land, building, and equipment? The estimated market values come from property tax reports.

Estimated Market Value

Land	$40,000
Building	95,000
Equipment	15,000

ANSWER:

	Estimated Market Value	% of Total
Land	$ 40,000	27
Building . .	95,000	63
Equipment	15,000	10
	$150,000	100

Allocation of Purchase Price

$ 32,400
75,600
12,000
$120,000

In the land example, the cost of the fences ($260,000) is not part of the cost of the land. Instead, the $260,000 would be recorded in a separate account entitled Land Improvements. This account includes costs for such other items as driveways, parking lots, and sprinkler systems. Although these assets are located on the land, they are subject to decay, and therefore their cost should be depreciated, as we discuss later in this chapter. Also, the cost of a new building constructed on the land is a debit to the asset account Building.

Group (or Basket) Purchases of Assets

Businesses often purchase several assets (as a group, or in a "basket") for a single amount. For example, a company may pay one price for land and an office building. The company must identify the cost of each asset. The total cost is divided between the assets according to their relative sales (or market) values. This allocation technique is called the **relative-sales-value method.**

Suppose Xerox Corporation purchases land and a building in Kansas City for a midwestern sales office. The building sits on two acres of land, and the combined purchase price of land and building is $2,800,000. An appraisal indicates that the land's market (sales) value is $300,000 and the building's market (sales) value is $2,700,000.

An accountant first figures the ratio of each asset's market price to the total market price. Total appraised value is $3,000,000. Thus land, valued at $300,000, is 10 percent of the total market value. Building's appraised value is 90 percent of the total.

Asset	Market (Sales) Value		Total Market Value		Percentage
Land	$ 300,000	÷	$3,000,000	=	10%
Building	2,700,000	÷	$3,000,000	=	90%
Total	$3,000,000				100%

The percentage for each asset is multiplied by the total purchase price to give its cost in the purchase.

Asset	Total Purchase Price		Percentage		Allocated Cost
Land	$2,800,000	×	.10	=	$ 280,000
Building	$2,800,000	×	.90	=	2,520,000
Total			1.00		$2,800,000

Assuming Xerox pays cash, the entry to record the purchase of the land and building is

Land	280,000	
Building	2,520,000	
Cash		2,800,000

Point to Stress: Sometimes the amount to be depreciated is referred to as a "quantity of usefulness" to be divided over the asset's useful life. The asset's useful life is the length of time it will be used, not its physical life. A delivery service would probably choose a short estimated useful life for a delivery truck (perhaps three years), even though physically the truck could be driven for several years more.

OBJECTIVE 2

Explain the concept of depreciation

Depreciation of Plant Assets

The process of allocating a plant asset's cost to expense over the period the asset is used is called *depreciation.* This process is designed to match the asset's expense against the revenue generated over the asset's life, as the matching principle directs. The primary purpose of depreciation accounting is therefore to measure income. Of less importance is the need to account for the asset's decline in usefulness.

Suppose a bank buys a computer. The business believes the computer offers four years of service after which obsolescence will make it worthless. Using straight-line depreciation (which we discuss later in this chapter), the bank expenses one quarter of the asset's cost in each of its four years of use.

Let's contrast what depreciation accounting is with what it is *not*. (1) *Depreciation is not a process of valuation.* Businesses do not record depreciation based on appraisals of their plant assets made at the end of each period. Instead, businesses allocate the asset's cost to the periods of its useful life based on a specific depreciation method. (We discuss these methods in this chapter.) (2) *Depreciation does not mean that the business sets aside cash to replace assets as they become fully depreciated.* Establishing such a cash fund is a decision entirely separate from depreciation. *Accumulated depreciation* is that portion of the plant asset's cost that has already been recorded as expense. Accumulated depreciation does not represent a growing amount of cash.

Determining the Useful Life of a Plant Asset

No asset (other than land) offers an unlimited useful life. For some plant assets physical *wear and tear* from operations and the elements may be the important cause of depreciation. For example, physical deterioration takes its toll on the usefulness of trucks and furniture.

Assets like computers, other electronic equipment, and airplanes may become *obsolete* before they physically deteriorate. An asset is obsolete when another asset can do the job better or more efficiently. Thus an asset's useful life may be much shorter than its physical life. Accountants usually depreciate computers over a short period of time—perhaps four years—even though they know the computers will remain in working condition much longer. Whether wear and tear or obsolescence causes depreciation, the asset's cost is depreciated over its expected useful life.

Measuring Depreciation

To measure depreciation for a plant asset, we must know its *cost*, its *estimated useful life*, and its *estimated residual value*.

Cost is the purchase price of the asset. We discussed cost under the heading The Cost of a Plant Asset, beginning on page 456.

Estimated useful life is the length of the service the business expects to get from the asset. Useful life may be expressed in years (as we have seen so far), units of output, miles, or other measures. For example, the useful life of a building is stated in years. The useful life of a bookbinding machine may be stated as the number of books the machine is expected to bind—that is, its expected units of output. A reasonable measure of a delivery truck's useful life is the total number of miles the truck is expected to travel. Companies base such estimates on past experience and information from industry trade magazines and government publications.

Estimated residual value—also called *scrap value* and *salvage value*—is the expected cash value of the asset at the end of its useful life. For example, a

Point to Stress: Accumulated depreciation is a contra asset account with a credit balance. Because we want to maintain the historical cost in the Plant Asset accounts, all depreciation over the asset's useful life is recorded in the Accumulated Depreciation account.

Review this:
Cost
− Accumulated depreciation
Book value
Accumulated Depreciation is a balance sheet account, a permanent account; its balance is not closed out. However, at the end of each period the Depreciation Expense account, a temporary account, is closed.

Point to Stress: It is impossible to quantify the exact amount that an asset has depreciated during the period, but there is no doubt that a portion of the asset has been consumed. Since the exact amount of depreciation cannot be determined, an estimate of the amount must be made using one of the depreciation methods.

Point to Stress: The residual value of an asset is the part of the asset's cost that the company expects will be returned at the end of the asset's useful life. The residual value is the portion of the asset's cost that will not be consumed; therefore it should not be depreciated.

Point to Stress: The maximum amount of depreciation that a business may record for an asset is equal to that asset's depreciable cost. Even if the asset is used longer in the business's operations, no additional depreciation may be recorded once the depreciable cost amount has been recorded as an expense. In fact, businesses often continue to use an asset after it has been fully depreciated.

business may believe that a machine's useful life will be seven years. After that time, the company expects to sell the machine as scrap metal. The amount the business believes it can get for the machine is the estimated residual value. In computing depreciation, estimated residual value is *not* depreciated because the business expects to receive this amount from disposing of the asset. The full cost of a plant asset is depreciated if the asset is expected to have no residual value. The plant asset's cost minus its estimated residual value is called the **depreciable cost**.

Of the factors entering the computation of depreciation, only one factor is known—cost. The other two factors—residual value and useful life—must be estimated. Depreciation, then, is an estimated amount.

OBJECTIVE 3

Account for depreciation by four methods

Depreciation Methods

Four basic methods exist for computing depreciation: straight-line, units-of-production, declining-balance, and sum-of-years-digits. These four methods allocate different amounts of depreciation expense to different periods. However, they all result in the same total amount of depreciation, the asset's depreciable cost over the life of the asset. Exhibit 10-2 presents the data used to illustrate depreciation computations by the four methods.

Point to Stress: The use of the straight-line method will result in equal amounts of depreciation expense every year. This method might be appropriate for an asset that depreciates in value at about the same rate every year. For example, a building does not wear out much faster if 100 people use the building or 500 people use the building. Time and weather cause a fairly uniform deterioration under normal conditions.

Straight-Line (SL) Method

In the **straight-line (SL)** method, an equal amount of depreciation expense is assigned to each year (or period) of asset use. Depreciable cost is divided by useful life in years to determine the annual depreciation expense. The equation for SL depreciation, applied to the limo data from Exhibit 10-2, is

$$\text{Straight-line depreciation per year} = \frac{\text{Cost} - \text{Residual value}}{\text{Useful life in years}}$$

$$= \frac{\$41,000 - \$1,000}{5}$$

$$= \$8,000$$

Transparency T10-1

The entry to record this depreciation is

Depreciation Expense   8,000
  Accumulated Depreciation   8,000

Class Exercise: The following facts will be used in the next several Class Exercises:

An asset with an original cost of $10,000, a useful life of 5 years or 16,000 units, and a residual value of $2,000, was purchased on 1/1. What was straight-line depreciation for the first year? ANSWER: $1,600 ($10,000-$2,000/5)

EXHIBIT 10-2 *Data for Depreciation Computations*

Data Item	Amount
Cost of limousine.	$41,000
Estimated residual value	1,000
Depreciable cost	$40,000
Estimated useful life:	
Years	5 years
Units of production	400,000 units

EXHIBIT 10-3 *Straight-Line Depreciation Schedule*

Date	Asset Cost	Depreciation for the Year				Accumulated Depreciation	Asset Book Value
		Depreciation Rate		Depreciable Cost			
		Depreciation Rate		Depreciable Cost	Depreciation Amount	Accumulated Depreciation	Asset Book Value
1- 1-X1	$41,000						$41,000
12-31-X1		.20	×	$40,000	= $8,000	$ 8,000	33,000
12-31-X2		.20	×	40,000	= 8,000	16,000	25,000
12-31-X3		.20	×	40,000	= 8,000	24,000	17,000
12-31-X4		.20	×	40,000	= 8,000	32,000	9,000
12-31-X5		.20	×	40,000	= 8,000	40,000	1,000

Assume that the limo was purchased on January 1, 19X1, and the business's fiscal year ends on December 31. A *straight-line depreciation schedule* is presented in Exhibit 10-3.

The final column of Exhibit 10-3 shows the asset's *book value*, which is its cost less accumulated depreciation. Book value is also called carrying amount.

As an asset is used, accumulated depreciation increases, and the book value decreases. (Note the Accumulated Depreciation column and the Book Value column.) An asset's final book value is its *residual value* ($1,000 in the exhibit). At the end of its useful life, the asset is said to be fully depreciated.

Units-of-Production (UOP) Method

In the **units-of-production (UOP)** method, a fixed amount of depreciation is assigned to each unit of output produced by the plant asset. Depreciable cost is divided by useful life in units to determine this amount. This per-unit depreciation expense is multiplied by the number of units produced each period to compute depreciation for the period. The UOP depreciation equation for the limo data in Exhibit 10-2 is

$$\text{Units-of-production depreciation per unit of output} = \frac{\text{Cost} - \text{Residual value}}{\text{Useful life in units}}$$

$$= \frac{\$41,000 - \$1,000}{400,000 \text{ miles}}$$

$$= \$.10$$

Teaching Tip: Refer to Exhibit 10-3. Notice that an equal amount of depreciation is recorded each year with the straight-line method. This method assumes that each year X1 through X5 the company receives equal benefit from the use of the limo; thus, an equal amount of expense is recorded each year.

Teaching Tip: Refer to Exhibit 10-4. Notice that with the units-of-production method depreciation is a different amount each year, based on the number of miles driven each of those years. This method best matches depreciation expense with the benefit derived from the use of the asset each year.

Transparency T10-1

EXHIBIT 10-4 *Units-of-Production Depreciation Schedule*

Date	Asset Cost	Depreciation for the Year				Accumulated Depreciation	Asset Book Value
		Depreciation Per Unit		Number of Units	Depreciation Amount		
1- 1-19X1	$41,000						$41,000
12-31-19X1		$.10	×	$ 90,000	= $ 9,000	$ 9,000	32,000
12-31-19X2		.10	×	120,000	= 12,000	21,000	20,000
12-31-19X3		.10	×	100,000	= 10,000	31,000	10,000
12-31-19X4		.10	×	60,000	= 6,000	37,000	4,000
12-31-19X5		.10	×	30,000	= 3,000	40,000	1,000

Class Exercise: Refer to the preceding class exercise. The asset produced 3,000 units in the first year; 4,000 in the second; 4,500 in the third; 2,500 in the fourth; and 2,000 units in the last year. What was units-of-production depreciation for each year?

ANSWER: Depreciation per unit ($10,000 − $2,000) /16,000=$.50 =
Yr. 1—$1,500 (3,000 × $.50)
Yr. 2—$2,000 (4,000 × $.50)
Yr. 3—$2,250 (4,500 × $.50)
Yr. 4—$1,250 (2,500 × $.50)
Yr. 5—$1,000 (2,000 × $.50)

Class Exercise: Refer to the preceding class exercise. What would DDB depreciation expense be for each year?

ANSWER:
Yr. 1—$4,000 ($10,000 × 40%)
Yr. 2—$2,400 ($6,000 × 40%)
Yr. 3—$1,440 ($3,600 × 40%)
Yr. 4—$160 ($2,160 − $2,000)*

*The asset is never depreciated below residual value.

Point to Stress: Rarely will the asset book value equal the residual value in the final year of the asset's life. Depreciation expense in the final year will have to equal the amount of depreciation that will reduce the asset's book value to the residual value.

Transparency T10-2

Assume the limo is expected to be driven 90,000 miles (*miles* are the *units* in our example) during the first year, 120,000 during the second, 100,000 during the third, 60,000 during the fourth, and 30,000 during the fifth. The UOP depreciation schedule for this asset is shown in Exhibit 10-4.

The amount of UOP depreciation per period varies with the number of units the asset produces. Note that the total number of units produced is 400,000, the measure of this asset's useful life. Therefore, UOP depreciation does not depend directly on time as the other methods do.

Double-Declining-Balance (DDB) Method

Double-declining-balance (DDB) is one of the accelerated-depreciation methods. An **accelerated-depreciation** method writes off a relatively larger amount of the asset's cost nearer the start of its useful life than does straight-line. **DDB depreciation** computes annual depreciation by multiplying the asset's book value by a constant percentage, which is two times the straight-line depreciation rate. DDB amounts are computed as follows:

First, the straight-line depreciation rate per year is computed. For example, a 5-year limousine has a straight-line depreciation rate of 1/5, or 20 percent. A 10-year asset has a straight-line rate of 1/10, or 10 percent, and so on.

Second, the straight-line rate is multiplied by 2 to compute the DDB rate. The DDB rate for a 5-year asset is 40 percent (20% × 2 = 40%). For a 10-year asset the DDB rate is 20 percent (10% × 2 = 20%).

Third, The DDB rate is multiplied by the period's beginning asset book value (cost less accumulated depreciation). Residual value of the asset is ignored in computing depreciation by the DDB method, except during the last year.

The DDB rate for the limousine in Exhibit 10-2 is

$$\text{DDB rate per year} = \left(\frac{1}{\text{Useful life in years}} \times 2\right) = \left(\frac{1}{5 \text{ years}} \times 2\right)$$

$$= (20\% \times 2) = 40\%$$

Fourth, the final year's depreciation amount is the amount needed to reduce the asset's book value to its residual value. In the DDB depreciation schedule in Exhibit 10-5, the fifth and final year's depreciation is $4,314—the $5,314

EXHIBIT 10-5 Double-Declining-Balance Depreciation Schedule

| | | | Depreciation for the Year | | | | Asset |
Date	Asset Cost	DDB Rate	Asset Book Value	Depreciation Amount	Accumulated Depreciation	Book Value
1- 1-19X1	$41,000					$41,000
12-31-19X1		.40 ×	$41,000 =	$16,400	$16,400	24,600
12-31-19X2		.40 ×	24,600 =	9,840	26,240	14,760
12-31-19X3		.40 ×	14,760 =	5,904	32,144	8,856
12-31-19X4		.40 ×	8,856 =	3,542	35,686	5,314
12-31-19X5				4,314*	40,000	1,000

*Last-year depreciation is the amount needed to reduce asset book value to the residual value ($5,314 − $1,000 = $4,314).

book value less the $1,000 residual value. The residual value should not be depreciated but should remain on the books until the asset's disposal.

Many companies change to the straight-line method during the next-to-last year of the asset's life. Under this plan, annual depreciation for 19X4 and 19X5 is $3,928. Depreciable cost at the end of 19X3 is $7,856 (book value of $8,856 less residual value of $1,000). Depreciable cost can be spread evenly over the last two years of the asset's life ($7,856 ÷ 2 remaining years = $3,928 per year).

The DDB method differs from the other methods in two ways. (1) The asset's residual value is ignored initially. In the first year, depreciation is computed on the asset's full cost. (2) The final year's calculation is changed in order to bring the asset's book value to the residual value.

Sum-of-Years-Digits (SYD) Method

In the **sum-of-years-digits (SYD)** method—another accelerated method—depreciation is figured by multiplying the depreciable cost of the asset by a fraction. The *denominator* of the SYD fraction is the sum of the years' digits. For a 5-year asset, the years' digits are 1, 2, 3, 4, and 5, and their sum is 15 (1 + 2 + 3 + 4 + 5 = 15). For a 10-year asset, the denominator is 55. Adding the years for a very long-lived asset is tedious. Chances arise for error in the mathematics. Thus we have an easy formula for computing the sum of the years' digits:

$$\text{Sum of the years' digits} = N(N + 1)/2$$

where N is the useful life of the asset expressed in years. For example, when N equals 5, we have:

$$\frac{5(5 + 1)}{2} = \frac{30}{2} = 15$$

The *numerator* of the SYD fraction for the first year of a 5-year asset is 5. The numerator is 4 for the second year, 3 for the third year, 2 for the fourth year, and 1 for the fifth year.

The SYD depreciation equation for the limo in Exhibit 10-2 is

$$\begin{aligned}
\text{SYD depreciation per year} &= (\text{Cost} - \text{Residual value}) \times \frac{\text{Years' digits, largest first}}{\text{Sum of years' digits}} \\
&= (\$41,000 - \$1,000) \times \frac{5^*}{1 + 2 + 3 + 4 + 5} \\
&= \$40,000 \times \frac{5}{15} = \$13,333
\end{aligned}$$

_____

*5 for first year; 4 for second year; 3 for third year; 2 for fourth year; 1 for fifth year.

Exhibit 10-6 is the SYD depreciation schedule based on our example data. Note that each year's fraction is multiplied by the depreciable cost ($40,000).

Typical Student Misconception: Students often compute the depreciation for the first year by multiplying the depreciable cost (cost − salvage) by DDB rate rather than multiplying the cost by the DDB rate. Remind them that it is the three other methods that use the depreciable cost in their formulas.

Point to Stress: The double-declining-balance and sum-of-years-digits methods are accelerated depreciation methods. Accelerated depreciation methods write off more of the asset's cost in the earlier years of an asset's life than in its later years. These methods assume that an asset is more useful (productive) in its earlier years and therefore should be depreciated more in the earlier years of its life.

Class Exercise: Refer to the preceding class exercises. What would SYD depreciation expense be for each year?

ANSWER:
Yr. 1—$8,000 × 5/15 = $2,667
Yr. 2—$8,000 × 4/15 = $2,133
Yr. 3—$8,000 × 3/15 = $1,600
Yr. 4—$8,000 × 2/15 = $1,067
Yr. 5—$8,000 × 1/15 = $ 533

Typical Student Misconception: Students are inclined to use the fractions in this order: 1/15, 2/15, 3/15, etc. This is wrong. Point out that SYD is an accelerated method, which means higher depreciation in the earlier years; therefore the fractions must be 5/15, 4/15, 3/15, 2/15, and 1/15, in order to give highest depreciation in year one, slightly less in year two, and so on.

Transparency T10-2

EXHIBIT 10-6 *Sum-of-Years-Digits Depreciation Schedule*

Date	Asset Cost	Depreciation for the Year				Accumulated Depreciation	Asset Book Value
		SYD Fraction	Depreciable Cost		Depreciation Amount		
1- 1-19X1	$41,000						$41,000
12-31-19X1		5/15	× $40,000	=	$13,333	$13,333	27,667
12-31-19X2		4/15	× 40,000	=	10,667	24,000	17,000
12-31-19X3		3/15	× 40,000	=	8,000	32,000	9,000
12-31-19X4		2/15	× 40,000	=	5,333	37,333	3,667
12-31-19X5		1/15	× 40,000	=	2,667	40,000	1,000

Comparison of the Depreciation Methods

Compare the four methods in terms of the yearly amount of depreciation:

Amount of Depreciation Per Year

Year	Straight-Line	Units-of-Production	Accelerated Methods	
			Double-Declining-Balance	Sum-of-Years-Digits
1	$ 8,000	$ 9,000	$16,400	$13,333
2	8,000	12,000	9,840	10,667
3	8,000	10,000	5,904	8,000
4	8,000	6,000	3,542	5,333
5	8,000	3,000	4,314	2,667
Total	$40,000	$40,000	$40,000	$40,000

The yearly amount of depreciation varies by method, but the total $40,000 depreciable cost systematically becomes expense under all four methods.

Generally accepted accounting principles (GAAP) direct a business to match the expense of an asset against the revenue that the asset produces. For a plant asset that generates revenue evenly over time, the straight-line method best meets the matching principle. During each period the asset is used, an equal amount of depreciation is recorded.

The units-of-production method best fits those assets that wear out because of physical use, not obsolescence. Depreciation is recorded only when the asset is used, and the more units the asset generates in a given year, the greater the depreciation expense.

The accelerated methods (DDB and SYD) apply best to those assets that generate greater revenue earlier in their useful lives. The greater expense recorded under the accelerated methods in the early periods is matched against those periods' greater revenue.

Exhibit 10-7 graphs the relationship between annual depreciation amounts for straight-line, units-of-production, and the accelerated depreciation methods.

The graph of straight-line depreciation is flat because annual depreciation is the same amount in each period. Units-of-production depreciation follows no particular pattern because annual depreciation depends on the use of the asset. The greater the use, the greater is the amount of depreciation. Accelerated depreciation is greatest in the asset's first year and less in the later years.

EXHIBIT 10-7   *Depreciation Patterns*

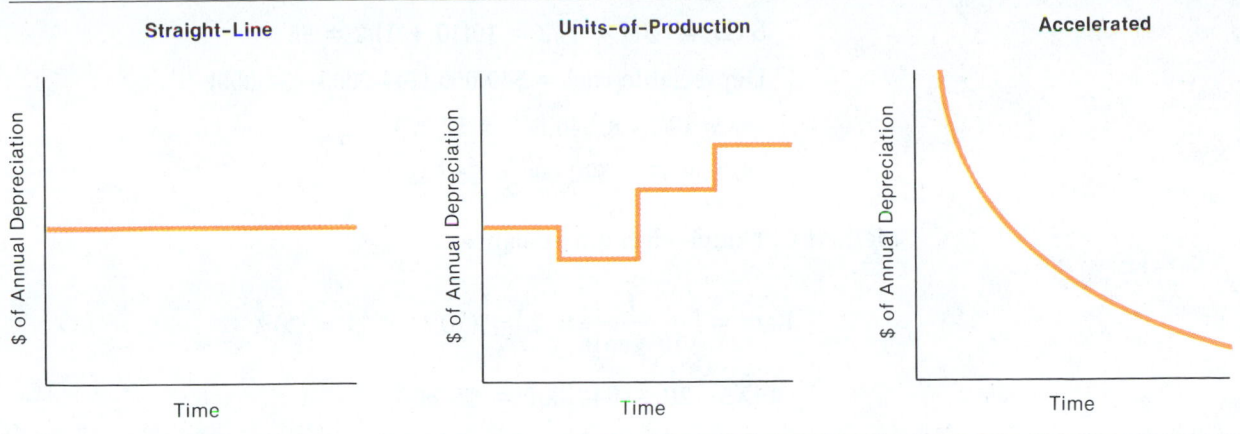

A recent survey indicated that over 70 percent of companies use the straight-line method, approximately 20 percent use an accelerated method, and the remainder use the units-of-production method. For example, Sears uses straight-line, Motorola uses double-declining-balance, Eastman Kodak uses sum-of-years-digits, and Gulf Oil uses units-of-production.

Summary Problem for Your Review

Hubbard Company purchased equipment on January 1, 19X5, for $44,000. The expected life of the equipment is 10 years, and its residual value is $4,000. Under three depreciation methods, the annual depreciation expense and the balance of accumulated depreciation at the end of 19X5 and 19X6 are

	Method A		Method B		Method C	
Year	**Annual Depreciation Expense**	**Accumulated Depreciation**	**Annual Depreciation Expense**	**Accumulated Depreciation**	**Annual Depreciation Expense**	**Accumulated Depreciation**
19X5	$4,000	$4,000	$7,273	$ 7,273	$8,800	$ 8,800
19X6	4,000	8,000	6,545	13,818	7,040	15,840

Required

1. Identify the depreciation method used in each instance, and show the equation and computation for each. (Round off to the nearest dollar.)
2. Assume continued use of the same method through year 19X7. Determine the annual depreciation expense, accumulated depreciation, and book value of the equipment for 19X5 through 19X7 under each method.

SOLUTION TO REVIEW PROBLEM

Requirement 1

   Method A: Straight-line

   Depreciable cost = $40,000 ($44,000 − $4,000)

   Each year: $40,000/10 years = $4,000

Method B: Sum-of-years-digits

$$SYD = N(N + 1)/2 = 10(10 + 1)/2 = 55$$

$$\text{Depreciable cost} = \$40,000 \ (\$44,000 - \$4,000)$$

$$19X5: 10/55 \times \$40,000 = \$7,273$$

$$19X6: 9/55 \times \$40,000 = \$6,545$$

Method C: Double-declining-balance

$$\text{Rate} = \left(\frac{1}{10 \text{ years}} \times 2\right) = (10\% \times 2) = 20\%$$

$$19X5: .20 \times \$44,000 = \$8,800$$

$$19X6: .20 \times (\$44,000 - \$8,800) = \$7,040$$

Requirement 2

	Method A Straight-Line			Method B Sum-of-Years-Digits			Method C Double-Declining-Balance		
Year	Annual Depreciation Expense	Accumulated Depreciation	Book Value	Annual Depreciation Expense	Accumulated Depreciation	Book Value	Annual Depreciation Expense	Accumulated Depreciation	Book Value
Start			$44,000			$44,000			$44,000
19X5	$4,000	$ 4,000	40,000	$7,273	$ 7,273	36,727	$8,800	$ 8,800	35,200
19X6	4,000	8,000	36,000	6,545	13,818	30,182	7,040	15,840	28,160
19X7	4,000	12,000	32,000	5,818	19,636	24,364	5,632	21,472	22,528

Computations for 19X7:

Straight-line: $40,000/10 years = $4,000

Sum-of-years-digits: 8/55 × $40,000 = $5,818

Double-declining-balance: .20 × $28,160 = $5,632

Depreciation and Income Taxes

The majority of companies use the straight-line depreciation method for reporting to their stockholders and creditors on their financial statements. Companies keep a separate set of depreciation records for computing their income taxes. For income tax purposes, most companies use an accelerated depreciation method.

Suppose you are a business manager. The IRS allows an accelerated depreciation method, which most managers choose in preference to straight-line depreciation. Why? Because it provides the most depreciation expense as quickly as possible, thus decreasing your immediate tax payments. The cash you save may be applied to best fit your business needs. This is the strategy most businesses follow.

To understand the relationships among cash flow (cash provided by operations), depreciation, and income tax, recall our earlier depreciation example:

First-year depreciation under straight-line is $8,000, and under double-declining-balance it is $16,400. For illustrative purposes here, assume that DDB is permitted for reporting to the income tax authorities. Assume that the business has $400,000 in cash sales and $300,000 in cash operating expenses during the asset's first year, and the income tax rate is 30 percent. The cash flow analysis appears in Exhibit 10-8.

Exhibit 10-8 highlights several important business relationships. Compare the amount of cash provided by operations before income tax. Both columns show $100,000. If there were no income taxes, the total cash provided by operations would be the same regardless of the depreciation method used. Depreciation is a noncash expense and so does not affect cash from operations.

However, depreciation is a tax-deductible expense. The higher the depreciation expense, the lower the income before tax and thus the lower the income tax payment. Therefore, accelerated depreciation helps conserve cash for use in the business. Exhibit 10-8 indicates that the business will have $2,520 more cash at the end of the first year if it uses accelerated depreciation instead of SL ($74,920 against $72,400). Suppose the company invests this money to earn a return of 10 percent during the second year. Then the company will be better off by $252 ($2,520 × 10% = $252). The cash advantage of using the accelerated method is the $252 of additional revenue.

The Tax Reform Act of 1986 created a special depreciation method—used only for income tax purposes—called the Modified Accelerated Cost Recovery System (MACRS). Under this method, assets are grouped into one of eight classes, as shown in Exhibit 10-9. Depreciation for the first four classes is computed by the double-declining-balance method. Depreciation for 15-year assets and 20-year assets is computed by the 150-percent-declining-balance method. Under this method, the annual depreciation rate is computed by multiplying the straight-line rate by 1.50. For a 20-year asset, the straight-line

OBJECTIVE 4
Identify the best depreciation method for income tax purposes

Point to Stress: A shortcut to figuring the DDB rate is to divide 200% by the years of useful life. For example, the DDB rate for an asset that is to be used for 7 years is 28.57% (200%/7 = 28.57%) A shortcut to figuring the 150% declining-balance rate is to divide 150% by the years of useful life. For example, an asset that has a 15-year life has a 150%-declining-balance rate of 10% (150%/15 = 10%).

Class Exercise: Have students practice applying the rules for calculating depreciation, as follows:

1   $12,000 truck purchased 3/14/X3; $1,500 salvage value, 6-year life; straight-line depreciation. Calculate depreciation expense for 19X3.

   ANSWER: $\dfrac{\$12,000 - \$1,500}{6} = \dfrac{\$10,500}{6}$

   $= \$1,750 \times {}^{10}\!/_{12} = \underline{\$1,458}$

2   $27,500 equipment purchased 10/19/X4; $1,600 salvage value, 6-year life; SYD depreciation. Figure depreciation for the first two years.

   ANSWER:
   SYD = 21(6 + 5 + 4 + 3 + 2 + 1)

   ($27,500 − $1,600) × $^6\!/_{21}$
   $= \$25,900 \times {}^6\!/_{21} = \$7,400 \times {}^2\!/_{12}$
   $= \underline{\$1,233}$ year 1
   (($25,900 × $^6\!/_{21}$) × $^{10}\!/_{12}$)
   $6,166.67
   + (($25,900 × $^5\!/_{21}$) × $^2\!/_{12}$)
   $1,027.78
   $= \underline{\$7,194.45}$ year 2

3   $38,650 computer purchased 6/30/X1; $850 salvage value, 4-year life; DDB depreciation. Figure depreciation for the first two years.

EXHIBIT 10-8   *Cash Flow Advantage of Accelerated Depreciation over Straight-Line (SL) Depreciation for income Tax Purposes*

	Income Tax Rate 30 percent	
	SL	**Accelerated**
Revenues	$400,000	$400,000
Cash operating expenses	300,000	300,000
Cash provided by operations before income tax .	100,000	100,000
Depreciation expense (a noncash expense)	8,000	16,400
Income before income tax.....................	92,000	83,600
Income tax expense (30%)	27,600	25,080
Net income.................................	$ 64,400	$ 58,520
Supplementary cash flow analysis:		
Cash provided by operations before income tax	$100,000	$100,000
Income tax expense	27,600	25,080
Cash provided by operations................	$ 72,400	$ 74,920
Extra cash available for investment if DDB is used ($74,920 − $72,400)		$ 2,520
Assumed earnings rate on investment of extra cash		×.10
Cash advantage of using DDB over SL		$ 252

ANSWER: $\$38,650 \times \dfrac{200\%}{4}$

$= \$19,325 \times \dfrac{6}{12} = \underline{\$9,663}$ Year 1

$(\$38,650 - \$9,663) \times \dfrac{200\%}{4} = \dfrac{\$14,494}{\text{Year 2}}$

Transparency T10-3

EXHIBIT 10-9 *Details of the Modified Accelerated Cost Recovery System (MACRS) Depreciation Method*

Class Identified by Years of Asset Life	Representative Assets	Depreciation Method
3 years	Race horses	DDB
5 years	Automobiles, light trucks	DDB
7 years	Equipment	DDB
10 years	Equipment	DDB
15 years	Sewage treatment plants	150% DDB
20 years	Certain real estate	150% DDB
27 1/2 years	Residential rental property	Straight-line
31 1/2 years	Nonresidential rental property	Straight-line

rate is .05 (1/20 = .05), so the annual MACRS depreciation rate is .075 (.05 × 1.50 = .075). Most real estate is depreciated by the straight-line method.

Special Issues in Depreciation Accounting

Two special issues in depreciation accounting are (1) depreciation for partial years and (2) change in the useful life of a depreciable asset.

Depreciation for Partial Years

Companies purchase plant assets as needed. They do not wait until the beginning of a year or a month. Therefore, companies must develop policies to compute *depreciation for partial years.* Suppose a company purchases a building on April 1 for $500,000. The building's estimated life is 20 years, and its estimated residual value is $80,000. The company's fiscal year ends on December 31. Consider how the company computes depreciation for the year ended December 31.

Many companies compute partial-year depreciation by first computing a full year's depreciation. They then multiply this amount by the fraction of the year they held the asset. Assuming the straight-line method, the year's depreciation is $15,750, computed as follows:

$$\dfrac{(\$500,000 - \$80,000)}{20} = \$21,000 \text{ per year} \times \dfrac{9}{12} = \$15,750$$

What if the company bought the asset on April 18? A widely used policy directs businesses to record no depreciation on assets purchased after the fifteenth of the month and to record a full month's depreciation on an asset bought on or before the fifteenth. Thus the company would record no depreciation for April on an April 18 purchase. In this case, the year's depreciation would be $14,000 ($21,000 × 8/12).

How is partial-year depreciation computed under the other depreciation methods? Suppose this building is acquired on October 4 and the company uses the double-declining-balance method. For a 20-year asset, the DDB rate is 10 percent (1/20 = 5% × 2 = 10%). The annual depreciation computations for 19X1, 19X2, and 19X3 are as follows:

			Depreciation for the Year				
Date	Asset Cost	DDB Rate	Asset Book value	Fraction of the year	Depreciation Amount	Accumulated Depreciation	Asset Book Value
10- 4-19X1	$500,000						$500,000
12-31-19X1		1/20 × 2 = .10 ×	$500,000 ×	3/12 =	$12,500	$ 12,500	487,500
12-31-19X2		.10 ×	487,500 ×	12/12 =	48,750	61,250	438,750
12-31-19X3		.10 ×	438,750 ×	12/12 =	43,875	105,125	394,875

Partial-year depreciation under the sum-of-years-digits method is computed similarly, by taking the appropriate fraction of a full year's amount. Assuming the building is acquired on September 28, 19X1, depreciation for the remainder of 19X1 will cover three months. With a 20-year life, the sum of the years' digits is 210 [(20 × 21)/2], and the first-year fraction is 20/210. SYD depreciation, which is based on depreciable cost of $420,000 (cost of $500,000 less residual value of $80,000), is computed as follows for the remainder of 19X1, for 19X2, and for 19X3:

Period	SYD Depreciation Computations
April-December 19X1	($420,000 × 20/210 × 3/12) = $10,000
Calendar year 19X2	($420,000 × 20/210 × 9/12) + ($420,000 × 19/210 × 3/12) = $39,500
Calendar year 19X3	($420,000 × 19/210 × 9/12) + ($420,000 × 18/210 × 3/12) = $37,500

No special computation is needed for partial-year depreciation under the units-of-production method. Simply use the number of units produced, regardless of the time period the asset is held.

Change in the Useful Life of a Depreciable Asset

As previously discussed, a business must estimate the useful life of a plant asset to compute depreciation. This prediction is the most difficult part of accounting for depreciation. After the asset is put into use, the business is able to refine its estimate based on experience and new information. Such a change is called a *change in accounting estimate*. In an actual example, Walt Disney Productions included the following note in its financial statements:

Note 5
    . . . [T]he Company extended the estimated useful lives of certain theme park ride and attraction assets based upon historical data and engineering studies. The effect of this change was to decrease depreciation by approximately $8 million (an increase in net income of approximately $4.2 million …).

Such accounting changes are common because no business has perfect foresight. Generally accepted accounting principles require the business to report

Point to Stress: Remember that depreciation is an estimate. Sometimes something occurs in the business that enables management to make a more accurate estimate. Any depreciation expense recorded in previous years is *not* changed or corrected.

the nature, reason, and effect of the change on net income, as the Disney example shows. To *record* a change in accounting estimate, the remaining book value of the asset is spread over its adjusted remaining useful life. The adjusted useful life may be longer or shorter than the original useful life.

Assume that a Disney hot dog stand cost $40,000 and the company originally believed the asset had an 8-year useful life with no residual value. Using the straight-line method, the company would record $5,000 depreciation each year ($40,000/8 years = $5,000). Suppose Disney used the asset for 2 years. Accumulated depreciation reached $10,000, leaving a remaining depreciable book value (cost *less* accumulated depreciation *less* residual value) of $30,000 ($40,000 − $10,000). From its experience with the asset during the first 2 years, management believes the asset will remain useful for an additional 10 years. The company would compute a revised annual depreciation amount and record it as follows:

Asset's Remaining Depreciable Book Value	÷	(New) Estimated Useful Life Remaining	=	(New) Annual Depreciation Amount
$30,000	÷	10 years	=	$3,000

Yearly depreciation entry based on new estimated useful life:

Depreciation Expense-Hot Dog Stand	3,000	
Accumulated Depreciation-Hot Dog Stand		3,000

Using Fully Depreciated Assets

A fully depreciated asset is one that has reached the end of its *estimated* useful life. No more depreciation is recorded for the asset. If the asset is no longer suitable for its purpose, the asset is disposed of, as discussed in the next section. However, the company may be in a cash bind and unable to replace the asset. Or the asset's useful life may have been underestimated at the outset. Foresight is not perfect. In any event, companies sometimes continue using fully depreciated assets. The asset account and its related accumulated depreciation account remain in the ledger even though no additional depreciation is recorded for the asset.

Disposal of Plant Assets

OBJECTIVE 5

Account for disposal of plant assets

Eventually, a plant asset ceases to serve a company's needs. The asset may have become worn out, obsolete, or for some other reason no longer useful to the business. Generally, a company disposes of a plant asset by selling or exchanging it. If the asset cannot be sold or exchanged, then disposal takes the form of junking the asset. Whatever the method of disposal, the business should bring depreciation up to date to measure the asset's final book value properly.

To account for disposal, credit the asset account and debit its related accumulated depreciation account. Suppose the final year's depreciation expense has just been recorded for a machine that cost $6,000 and was estimated to have zero residual value. The machine's accumulated depreciation thus totals $6,000. Assuming this asset cannot be sold or exchanged, the entry to record its disposal is

Teaching Tip: Remind students that there can never be a gain on the *disposal* (or *junking*) of a plant asset unless the asset is sold. The asset will either have a zero book value, or there will be a loss equal to the remaining book value.

Accumulated Depreciation—Machinery	6,000	
Machinery		6,000

To dispose of fully depreciated machine.

If assets are junked prior to being fully depreciated, the company records a loss equal to the asset's book value. Suppose store fixtures that cost $4,000 are disposed of in this manner. Accumulated depreciation is $3,000, and book value is therefore $1,000. Disposal of these store fixtures is recorded as follows:

Accumulated Depreciation-Store Fixtures ...	3,000	
Loss on Disposal of Store Fixtures	1,000	
Store Fixtures		4,000

To dispose of store fixtures.

Loss accounts such as Loss on Disposal of Store Fixtures decrease net income. Losses are reported on the income statement and closed to Income Summary along with expenses.

Selling a Plant Asset

Transparency T10-5

Suppose the business sells furniture on September 30, 19X4, for $5,000 cash. The furniture cost $10,000 when purchased on January 1, 19X1, and has been depreciated on a straight-line basis. Managers estimated a 10-year useful life and no residual value. Prior to recording the sale of the furniture, accountants must update depreciation. Since the business uses the calendar year as its accounting period, partial depreciation must be recorded for the asset's expense from January 1, 19X4, to the sale date. The straight-line depreciation entry at September 30, 19X4, is

Sep. 30	Depreciation Expense ($10,000/10 years $\times$ 9/12)	750	
	Accumulated Depreciation—Furniture		750
	To update depreciation.		

After this entry is posted, the Furniture account and the Accumulated Depreciation—Furniture account appear as follows. The furniture book value is $6,250 ($10,000 − $3,750).

Furniture		Accumulated Depreciation—Furniture		
Jan. 1, 19X1 10,000			Dec. 31, 19X1	1,000
			Dec. 31, 19X2	1,000
			Dec. 31, 19X3	1,000
			Sep. 30, 19X4	750
			Balance	3,750

Point to Stress: When an asset is sold, a gain or loss on the sale is determined by comparing the proceeds from the sale to the book value of the asset. To summarize:

Proceeds > BV: gain

Proceeds < BV: loss

The entry to record sale of the furniture for $5,000 cash is

Sep. 30	Cash	5,000	
	Accumulated Depreciation—Furniture........	3,750	
	Loss on Sale of Furniture	1,250	
	Furniture		10,000
	To sell furniture.		

Class Exercise: Equipment with original cost of $10,000, residual value of $2,000, and 5-year life was sold on 3/31/X3 for $6,400. Accumulated depreciation (SL method) on the asset was $2,500 as of 12/31/X2. Record the sale.

ANSWER: First, calculate depreciation from 12/31/X2 to 3/31/X3: ($10,000 − $2,000)/5 × 3/12.= $400. Adding this figure to the $2,500 as of 12/31/X2 brings accumulated depreciation as of 3/31 to $2,900. Now, make the entry:

Cash 6,400
Acc. Depr. 2,900
Loss on Sale 700
    Equipment .. 10,000

When recording the sale of a plant asset, the business must remove the balances in the asset account (Furniture, in this case) and its related accumulated depreciation account and also record a gain or a loss if the amount of cash received differs from the asset's book value. In our example, cash of $5,000 is less than the book value of the furniture, $6,250. The result is a loss of $1,250.

Suppose the sale price had been $7,000. The business would have had a gain of $750 (Cash, $7,000 − asset book value, $6,250).

The entry to record this transaction would be

Sep. 30	Cash	7,000	
	Accumulated Depreciation—Furniture........	3,750	
	Furniture		10,000
	Gain on Sale of Furniture		750
	To sell furniture.		

A gain is recorded when an asset is sold for a price greater than the asset's book value. A loss is recorded when the sale price is less than book value. Gains increase net income. Gains are reported on the income statement and closed to Income Summary along with the revenues.

Exchanging Plant Assets

Point to Stress: Trade-in allowance will not always be the fair market value.

Businesses often exchange (trade in) their old plant assets for similar assets that are newer and more efficient. For example, a pizzeria may decide to trade in its five-year-old Nissan delivery car for a newer model. To record the exchange, the business must remove from the books the balances for the asset being exchanged and its related accumulated depreciation account.

Assume that the pizzeria's old delivery car cost $7,000 and has accumulated depreciation totaling $6,000. The book value, then, is $1,000. The cash price for a new delivery car is $9,000, and the auto dealer offers a $1,000 trade-in allowance. The pizzeria pays cash for the remaining $8,000. The trade-in is recorded with this entry:

Delivery Auto (new)	9,000	
Accumulated Depreciation (old)	6,000	
Delivery Auto (old).............................		7,000
Cash ($9,000 − $1,000)		8,000

In this example, the book value and the trade-in allowance are both $1,000, and so no gain or loss occurs on the exchange. Usually, however, an exchange results in a gain or a loss. If the trade-in allowance received is greater than the book value of the asset being given, the business has a gain. If the trade-in allowance received is less than the book value of the asset given, the business has a loss. Generally accepted accounting principles require that losses (but not gains) be recognized on the exchange of similar assets. We now turn to the entries for gains and losses on exchanges, continuing our delivery-car example and its data.[1]

Situation 1.   Loss recognized on asset exchange:

Assume that the new Nissan has a cash price of $9,000 and the dealer gives a trade-in allowance of $600 on the old vehicle. The pizzeria pays the balance, $8,400, in cash. The loss on the exchange is $400 (book value of old asset given, $1,000, minus trade-in allowance received, $600). The account Loss on Exchange of Delivery Auto is debited for $400. The entry to record this exchange is

Delivery Auto (new)	9,000	
Accumulated Depreciation—Delivery Auto (old)	6,000	
Loss on Exchange of Delivery Auto	400	
Delivery Auto (old)...............................		7,000
Cash ($9,000 − $600)		8,400

Situation 2.   Gain *not* recognized on asset exchange:

Assume that the new Nissan's cash price is $9,000 and the seller gives a $1,300 trade-in allowance. The pizzeria pays the balance, $7,700, in cash. The gain is $300 (trade-in allowance received, $1,300, minus book value of old asset given, $1,000). However, the pizzeria does not recognize the gain. Instead, it reduces the cost of the new asset by the amount of the unrecognized gain.

Delivery Auto (new) ($9,000—gain of $300)	8,700	
Accumulated Depreciation—Delivery Auto (old)	6,000	
Delivery Auto (old)...............................		7,000
Cash ($9,000 − $1,300)		7,700

Why are losses, and not gains, recognized? The Accounting Principles Board reasoned a company should not record a gain merely because it has substituted one plant asset for a similar plant asset. However, losses are recorded because conservatism favors the recognition of losses rather than gains.

Control of Plant Assets

Control of plant assets includes safeguarding them and having an adequate accounting system. To see the need for controlling plant assets, consider the following actual situation. The home office and top managers of the company are in New Jersey. The company manufactures gas pumps in Canada, which are sold in Europe. Top managers and owners of the company rarely see the manufacturing plant and therefore cannot control plant assets by on-the-spot management. What features does their internal control system need?

Safeguarding plant assets includes:

1. Assigning responsibility for custody of the assets.
2. Separating custody of assets from accounting for the assets. (This is a cornerstone of internal control in almost every area.)
3. Setting up security measures, for instance, armed guards and restricted access to plant assets, to prevent theft.

---

[1]GAAP rules for exchanges may differ from income tax rules. In this discussion, we are concerned with the accounting rules.

Point to Stress: Summarize the steps in calculating gain or loss on a trade-in:

1   Calculate partial year's depreciation up to the date of the trade-in.

2   Calculate remaining book value:

>   Cost
> − Accumulated depreciation
>   Remaining BV

3   Calculate cash paid:

>   Cash price (cost of asset)
> − Trade-in allowance
>   Cash paid

4   Calculate gain or loss: *Gain* if BV is < trade-in.

>   Trade-in allowance
> − Remaining BV
>   Gain on trade-in (is not recorded)

>   *Loss* if BV is > trade-in.

>   Remaining BV
> − Trade-in allowance
>   Loss on trade-in (is recorded)

5   Calculate cost basis of new asset:
If gain is not recognized (recorded),

>   Remaining BV (old)
> + Cash paid
>   Cost basis (new)

or,

>   Cash price (new)
> − Gain not recorded
>   Cost basis (new)

Either of these calculations gives the same answer. Depreciation on the new asset is based on this "cost basis" figure. If a loss is recognized, the cost basis of the new asset will equal the cash price.

Point to Stress: In addition, plant assets may be numbered or marked with some type of serial number or identification.

4. Protecting assets from the elements (rain, snow, and so on).
5. Having adequate insurance against fire, storm, and other casualty losses.
6. Training operating personnel in the proper use of the asset.
7. Keeping a regular maintenance schedule.

Plant assets are controlled in much the same way that high-priced inventory is controlled—with the help of subsidiary records. For plant assets, companies use a plant asset ledger. Each plant asset is represented by a record describing the asset and listing its location and the employee responsible for it. These details aid in safeguarding the asset. The ledger record also shows the asset's cost, useful life, and other accounting data. Exhibit 10-10 is an example.

The ledger record provides the data for computing depreciation on the asset. It serves as a subsidiary record of accumulated depreciation. The asset balance ($190,000) and accumulated depreciation amount ($45,000) agree with the balances in the respective general ledger accounts (Store Fixtures and Accumulated Depreciation—Store Fixtures).

Accounting for Natural Resources and Depletion

OBJECTIVE 6

Account for natural resource assets and depletion

Point to Stress: The formula for depletion of a natural resource is:

Cost − Residual value*
÷ Estimated total units of resource

= Depletion per unit

*Residual value is similar to salvage value on plant assets.

Natural resources such as iron ore, coal, oil, gas, and timber are plant assets of a special type. An investment in natural resources could be described as an investment in inventories in the ground (coal) or on top of the ground (timber). As plant assets (such as machines) are expensed through depreciation, so natural resource assets are expensed through depletion. **Depletion expense** is that portion of the cost of natural resources that is used up in a particular period. Depletion expense is computed in the same way as *units-of-production* depreciation.

An oil well may cost $100,000 and contain an estimated 10,000 barrels of oil. The depletion rate would be $10 per barrel ($100,000/10,000 barrels). If 3,000 barrels are extracted during the year, depletion expense is $30,000 (3,000 barrels × $10 per barrel). The depletion entry for the year is

Depletion Expense (3,000 barrels × $10).............	30,000	
Accumulated Depletion—Oil...................		30,000

EXHIBIT 10-10 *Plant Asset Ledger Record*

Asset	Clothing racks			Location	Ladies better dresses			
Employee responsible for the asset	Department manager							

Cost $190,000   Purchased From Boone Supply Co.
Depreciation Method SL
Useful Life 10 years   Residual Value $10,000
General Ledger Account Store fixtures

Date	Explanation	Asset			Accumulated Depreciation		
		Dr	Cr	Bal	Dr	Cr	Bal
Jul. 3, 19X4	Purchase	190,000		190,000			
Dec. 31, 19X4	Deprec.					9,000	9,000
Dec. 31, 19X5	Deprec.					18,000	27,000
Dec. 31, 19X6	Deprec.					18,000	45,000

If 4,500 barrels are removed the next year, that period's depletion is $45,000 (4,500 barrels X $10 per barrel). Accumulated Depletion is a contra account similar to Accumulated Depreciation.

Point to Stress: Cost depletion is calculated in the same way as UOP depreciation.

Natural resource assets can be reported as follows:

Property, Plant, and Equipment:

Land		$120,000
Buildings	$800,000	
Equipment	160,000	
	960,000	
Less: Accumulated depreciation	410,000	550,000
Oil	**$340,000**	
Less: Accumulated depletion	**90,000***	**250,000**
Total property, plant, and equipment		$920,000

*Includes the $30,000 recorded above.

Computers and Depreciation

A computer is invaluable in helping a company keep track of all plant asset transactions, from acquisition to depreciation to disposal. The general ledger account Machinery may have hundreds of subsidiary machine accounts, each with its own Accumulated Depreciation account.

Complications in tax law have resulted in complex depreciation calculations. The tax reforms of 1981 and on have brought about a material difference in depreciation amounts calculated using generally accepted accounting principles and those calculated under tax laws. Also, depreciation allowable under federal tax law can differ from depreciation permitted by state law. A company may, then, have to deal with three different depreciation systems at the same time. And suppose an asset is disposed of before it is fully depreciated. The calculations grow in complexity. Computers greatly ease the accounting burden.

Companies of all sizes may use depreciation modules included with their computerized accounting packages. The computer performs its functions accurately, but an accountant with solid knowledge of tax law and depreciation must ensure that the calculations are reasonable. Auditors use spreadsheets to perform independent recalculations of depreciation.

Accounting for Intangible Assets and Amortization

Intangible assets are a class of long-lived assets that are not physical in nature. Instead, these assets are special rights to current and expected future benefits from patents, copyrights, trademarks, franchises, leaseholds, and goodwill.

The acquisition cost of an intangible asset is debited to an asset account. The intangible is expensed through **amortization,** the systematic reduction of a lump-sum amount. Amortization applies to intangible assets in the same way depreciation applies to plant assets and depletion applies to natural resources. All three methods of expensing assets are conceptually the same.

Amortization is generally computed on a straight-line basis over the asset's estimated useful life—up to a maximum of 40 years, according to GAAP. However, obsolescence often cuts an intangible asset's useful life shorter than its legal life. Amortization expense is written off directly against the asset

OBJECTIVE 7

Account for intangible assets and amortization

Point to Stress: Amortization of intangibles is similar to depreciation of plant assets and depletion of natural resources.

Point to Stress: Unlike depreciation and depletion, amortization of intangibles is credited directly to the asset account instead of a contra account.

account rather than held in an accumulated amortization account. The residual value of most intangible assets is zero.

Assume that a business purchases a patent on a special manufacturing process. Legally, the patent may run for 17 years. However, the business realizes that new technologies will limit the patented process's life to 4 years. If the patent cost $80,000, each year's amortization expense is $20,000 ($80,000/4). The balance sheet reports the patent at its acquisition cost less amortization expense to date. After 1 year, the patent has a $60,000 balance ($80,000 − $20,000), after 2 years a $40,000 balance, and so on.

Real-World Example: A patent must be registered at the U.S. Patent and Trademark Office by a patent attorney. The applicant may apply for the patent himself, or may hire a patent attorney. Patent attorneys must be certified by the U.S. Patent and Trademark Office and have an undergraduate degree in an applied field, such as engineering.

Patents are federal government grants giving a holder the exclusive right for 17 years to produce and sell an invention. Patented products include IBM computers and the recipe for Coca-Cola. Like any other asset, a patent may be purchased. Suppose a company pays $170,000 to acquire a patent and the business believes the expected useful life of the patent is only 5 years. Amortization expense is $34,000 per year ($170,000/5 years). The company's acquisition and amortization entries for this patent are

Jan. 1	Patents	170,000	
	Cash		170,000
	To acquire a patent.		
Dec. 31	Amortization Expense—Patents ($170,000/5)	34,000	
	Patents		34,000
	To amortize the cost of a patent.		

Real-World Example: Companies protect their exclusive rights to an invention. Polaroid Corporation filed suit in 1976 against Eastman Kodak Company charging an infringement of certain Polaroid patents for instant cameras and instant film. Polaroid sought an injunction and treble damages. An injunction was finally issued in 1986 that prohibited Kodak from manufacturing and selling such products in the U.S. Eastman Kodak Company appealed the injunction but the appeal was denied.

Copyrights are exclusive rights to reproduce and sell a book, musical composition, film, or other work of art. Issued by the federal government, copyrights extend 50 years beyond the author's (composer's, artist's) life. The cost of obtaining a copyright from the government is low, but a company may pay a large sum to purchase an existing copyright from the owner. For example, a publisher may pay the author of a popular novel $1 million or more for the book's copyright. The useful life of a copyright is usually no longer than 2 or 3 years, so each period's amortization amount is a high proportion of the copyright's cost.

Trademarks and **trade names** are distinctive identifications of products or services. The "eye" symbol that flashes across the television screen is a trademark that identifies the CBS television network. NBC uses the peacock as its trademark. Seven-Up, Pepsi, Egg McMuffin, and Rice-a-Roni are everyday trade names. Advertising slogans that are legally protected include United Airlines' "Fly the friendly skies" and Avis Rental Car's "We try harder."

Real-World Example: A trademark can be registered with the U.S. Patent and Trademark Office, but federal registration does not mean that someone already using that trademark has to cease. The nonregistered company has exclusive rights to use the trademark in the area in which it is operating, but cannot use it anywhere else. The

The cost of a trademark or trade name is amortized over its useful life, not to exceed 40 years. The cost of advertising and promotions that use the trademark or trade name is not a part of the asset's cost but a debit to the advertising expense account.

Franchises and **licenses** are privileges granted by a private business or a government to sell a product or service in accordance with specified conditions. The Dallas Cowboys football organization is a franchise granted to its owner by the National Football League. McDonald's restaurants and Holiday Inns are popular franchises. Consolidated Edison Company (ConEd) holds a New York City franchise right to provide electricity to residents. The acquisition costs of franchises and licenses are amortized over their useful lives rather than over legal lives, subject to the 40-year maximum.

A **leasehold** is a prepayment that a lessee (renter) makes to secure the use of an asset from a lessor (landlord). Often leases require the lessee to make this prepayment in addition to monthly rental payments. The lessee debits the monthly lease payments to the Rent Expense account. The prepayment, however, is a debit to an intangible asset account entitled Leaseholds. This amount is amortized over the life of the lease by debiting Rent Expense and crediting Leaseholds. Some leases stipulate that the last year's rent must be paid in advance when the lease is signed. This prepayment is debited to Leaseholds and transferred to Rent Expense during the last year of the lease.

Sometimes lessees modify or improve the leased asset. For example, a lessee may construct a fence on leased land. The lessee debits the cost of the fence to a separate intangible asset account, Leasehold Improvements, and amortizes its cost over the term of the lease or the life of the asset, if shorter.

Goodwill in accounting is a more limited term than in everyday use, as in "goodwill among men." In accounting, **goodwill** is defined as the excess of the cost of an acquired company over the sum of the market values of its net assets (assets minus liabilities). Suppose Company A acquires Company B at a cost of $10 million. The sum of the market values of Company B's assets is $9 million, and its liabilities total $1 million. In this case, Company A paid $2 million for goodwill, computed as follows:

Purchase price paid for Company B.............		$10 million
Sum of the market values of Company B's assets.	$9 million	
Less: Company B's liabilities	1 million	
Market value of Company B's net assets.........		8 million
Excess is called *goodwill*		$ 2 million

Company A's entry to record the acquisition of Company B, including its goodwill, would be

Assets (Cash, Receivables, Inventories, Plant		
Assets, all at market value)	9,000,000	
Goodwill	2,000,000	
Liabilities		1,000,000
Cash		10,000,000

Goodwill has special features, which include the following points:

1. Goodwill is recorded, at its cost, only when it is purchased in the acquisition of another company. Even though a favorable location, a superior product, or an outstanding reputation may create goodwill for a company, it is never recorded by that entity. Instead, goodwill is recorded only by an acquiring company. A purchase transaction provides objective evidence of the value of the goodwill.

2. According to generally accepted accounting principles, goodwill is amortized over a period not to exceed 40 years. In reality, the goodwill of many entities increases in value. Nevertheless, the Accounting Principles Board specified in *Opinion No. 17* that the cost of all intangible assets must be amortized as expense. Some foreign countries do not require their companies to amortize goodwill. American companies complain of a competitive disadvantage because foreign companies omit this expense and, as a result, report higher net income. The *Opinion* prohibits a lump-sum write-off of the cost of goodwill upon acquisition.

registered company can use the trademark in any geographical region except the one in which the nonregistered company is operating.

A trademark has a life of twenty years and must be renewed every five years.

Discussion Questions: What are some reasons that a business might have goodwill? Why could a business earn more than a normal rate of return on its assets? Why might an acquiring company be willing to pay an amount greater than the market value of net assets acquired when purchasing a going business? (If students have difficulty answering these questions, ask them what athletic franchise would be valuable, and what aspects would make it so.) ANSWERS: Good customer relations; good location of the business; especially efficient operations; monopoly in the marketplace; strong sources of financing; good personnel relations; and so on.

Capital Expenditures versus Revenue Expenditures (Expenses)

OBJECTIVE 8

Distinguish capital expenditures from revenue expenditures

When a company makes a plant asset expenditure, it must decide whether to debit an asset account or an expense account. In this context, **expenditure** refers to either a cash or credit purchase of goods or services related to the asset. Examples of these expenditures range from replacing the windshield wipers on an automobile to adding a wing to a building.

Expenditures that increase the capacity or efficiency of the asset or extend its useful life are called **capital expenditures.** For example, the cost of a major overhaul that extends a taxi's useful life is a capital expenditure. Repair work that generates a capital expenditure is called an **extraordinary repair.** The amount of the capital expenditure, said to be capitalized, is a debit to an asset account. For an extraordinary repair on a taxi, we would debit the asset account Automobile.

Point to Stress: The cost of painting a taxi immediately after purchase is recorded as part of the purchase price and is therefore a capital expenditure. Repainting a taxi is a maintenance cost and is considered a revenue expenditure.

Other expenditures do not extend the asset's capacity or efficiency. Expenditures that merely maintain the asset in its existing condition or restore the asset to good working order are called **revenue expenditures** because these costs are matched against revenue. Examples include the costs of repainting a taxi, repairing a dented fender, and replacing tires. The work that creates the revenue expenditure, said to be expensed, is a debit to an expense account. For the **ordinary repairs** on the taxi, we would debit Repair Expense.

Point to Stress: A capital expenditure causes the asset's cost to increase, which necessitates a revision of depreciation.

Costs associated with intangible assets and natural resource assets also must be identified as either a capital expenditure or a revenue expenditure. For example, a license fee paid to the state of Arkansas to mine bauxite is a capital expenditure. This cost should be debited to the Bauxite Mineral Asset account. The cost of selling the ore—sales commissions paid to a broker, for example—is a revenue expenditure and should be debited to an expense account.

The distinction between capital and revenue expenditures is often a matter of opinion. Does the work extend the life of the asset, or does it only maintain the asset in good order? When doubt exists as to whether to debit an asset or an expense, companies tend to debit an expense for two reasons. First, many expenditures are minor in amount, and most companies have a policy of debiting expense for all expenditures below a specified minimum, such as $1,000. Second, the income tax motive favors debiting all borderline expenditures to expense in order to create an immediate tax deduction. Capital expenditures are not immediate tax deductions.

Exhibit 10-11 illustrates the distinction between capital expenditures and revenue expenditures (expense) for several delivery truck expenditures. Note also the difference between extraordinary and ordinary repairs.

Would additional costs for shipping, security, fuel, and communications that FMC incurred due to the Persian Gulf crisis be capital expenditures or operating expense? Operating expense, because those costs do not add to the lives or the usefulness of FMC's assets.

Treating a capital expenditure as a revenue expenditure, or vice versa, creates errors in the financial statements. Suppose a company makes an extraordinary repair to equipment and erroneously expenses this cost. It is a capital expenditure that should have been debited to an asset account. This accounting error overstates expenses and understates net income on the income statement. On the balance sheet, the equipment account is understated, and so is owner's equity. Capitalizing the cost of an ordinary repair creates the opposite error. Expenses are understated and net income is overstated on the income statement. The balance sheet reports overstated amounts for assets and owner's equity.

EXHIBIT 10-11   *Delivery Truck Expenditures*

Debit an Asset Account for Capital Expenditures	Debit Repair and Maintenance Expense for Revenue Expenditures

Extraordinary repairs:
  Major engine overhaul
  Modification of body for new
    use of truck
  Addition to storage capacity of
    truck
	Ordinary repairs:
	  Repair of transmission or other
	    mechanism
	  Oil change, lubrication, and so
	    on
	  Replacement tires, windshield,
	    and the like
	  Paint job

Summary Problems for Your Review

Problem 1

The figures that follow appear in the Solution to the Summary Problem, Requirement 2, on page 466.

	Method A Straight-Line			Method C Double-Declining-Balance		
Year	Annual Depreciation Expense	Accumulated Depreciation	Book Value	Annual Depreciation Expense	Accumulated Depreciation	Book Value
Start			$44,000			$44,000
19X5	$4,000	$ 4,000	40,000	$8,800	$ 8,800	35,200
19X6	4,000	8,000	36,000	7,040	15,840	28,160
19X7	4,000	12,000	32,000	5,632	21,472	22,528

Required

Suppose the income tax authorities permitted a choice between these two depreciation methods. Which method would you select for income tax purposes? Why?

Problem 2

A corporation purchased a building at a cost of $500,000 on January 1, 19X3. Management has depreciated the building by using the straight-line method, a 35-year life, and a residual value of $150,000. On July 1, 19X7, the company sold the building for $575,000 cash. The fiscal year of the corporation ends on December 31.

Required

Record depreciation for 19X7 and record the sale of the building on July 1, 19X7.

SOLUTIONS TO REVIEW PROBLEMS

Problem 1

For tax purposes, most companies select the accelerated method because it results in the most depreciation in the earliest years of the equipment's life. Accelerated depreciation minimizes taxable income and income tax payments in the early years of the asset's life, thereby maximizing the business's cash at the earliest possible time.

Problem 2

To record depreciation to date of sale and related sale of building:

19X7			
July 1	Depreciation Expense—Building [($500,000 − $150,000)/35 years × ½ year]	5,000	
	Accumulated Depreciation— Building		5,000
	To update depreciation.		
July 1	Cash	575,000	
	Accumulated Depreciation—Building [($500,000 − $150,000)/35 years × 4 ½ years]	45,000	
	Building		500,000
	Gain on Sale of Building		120,000
	To record sale of building.		

Summary

Plant assets are long-lived assets that the business uses in its operation. These assets are not held for sale as inventory. The cost of all plant assets but land is expensed through *depreciation*. The cost of natural resources, a special category of long-lived assets, is expensed through *depletion*. Long-lived assets called *intangibles* are rights that have no physical form. The cost of intangibles is expensed through *amortization*. Depreciation, depletion, and amortization are identical in concept.

Businesses may compute the depreciation of plant assets by four methods: *straight-line, units-of-production,* and the *accelerated* methods: *double-declining-balance* and *sum-of-years-digits*. To measure depreciation, the accountant subtracts the asset's estimated residual value from its cost and divides that amount by the asset's estimated useful life. Most companies use the straight-line method for financial reporting purposes, and almost all companies use an accelerated method for income tax purposes. Accelerated depreciation results in greater tax deductions early in the asset's life. These deductions decrease income tax payments and conserve cash that the company can use in its business.

Before disposing of a plant asset, the business updates the asset's depreciation. Disposal is recorded by removing the book balances from both the asset account and its related accumulated depreciation account. Disposal often results in recognition of a gain or a loss.

Depletion of natural resources is computed on a units-of-production basis. *Amortization* of intangibles is computed on a straight-line basis over a maximum of 40 years. However, the useful lives of most intangibles are shorter than their legal lives.

Capital expenditures increase the capacity or the efficiency of an asset or extend its useful life. Accordingly, they are debited to an asset account. *Revenue expenditures*, on the other hand, merely maintain the asset's usefulness and are debited to an expense account.

Self-Study Questions

Test your understanding of the chapter by marking the best answer for each of the following questions.

1. Which of the following payments is *not* included in the cost of land? *(p. 457)*
    a. Removal of old building
    b. Legal fees
    c. Back property taxes paid at acquisition
    ✓ d. Cost of fencing and lighting

2. A business paid $120,000 for two machines valued at $90,000 and $60,000. The business will record these machines at *(p. 458)*
    a. $90,000 and $60,000
    b. $60,000 each
    ✓ c. $72,000 and $48,000
    d. $70,000 and $50,000

3. Which of the following definitions fits depreciation? *(pp. 458, 459)*
    a. Allocation of the asset's market value to expense over its useful life
    ✓ b. Allocation of the asset's cost to expense over its useful life
    c. Decreases in the asset's market value over its useful life
    d. Increases in the fund set aside to replace the asset when it is worn out

4. Which depreciation method's amounts are not computed based on time? *(p. 462)*
    a. Straight-line
    ✓ b. Units-of-production
    c. Double-declining-balance
    d. Sum-of-years-digits

5. Which depreciation method gives the largest amount of expense in the early years of using the asset and therefore is best for income tax purposes? *(p. 466)*
    a. Straight-line
    b. Units-of-production
    ✓ c. Accelerated
    d. All are equal.

6. A company paid $450,000 for a building and was depreciating it by the straight-line method over a 40-year life with estimated residual value of $50,000. After 10 years, it became evident that the building's remaining useful life would be 40 years. Depreciation for the eleventh year is *(p. 470)*
    ✓ a. $7,500
    b. $8,750
    c. $10,000
    d. $12,500

7. Labrador, Inc., scrapped an automobile that cost $14,000 and had book value of $1,100. The entry to record this disposal is *(p. 470)*
    a. Loss on Disposal of Automobile 1,100
        Automobile 1,100
    b. Accumulated Depreciation 14,000
        Automobile 14,000
    c. Accumulated Depreciation 12,900
        Automobile 12,900
    ✓ d. Accumulated Depreciation 12,900
        Loss of Disposal of Automobile 1,100
        Automobile 14,000

8. Depletion is computed in the same manner as which depreciation method? *(p. 474)*
    a. Straight-line
    ✓ b. Units-of-production
    c. Double-declining-balance
    d. Sum-of-years-digits

9. Lacy Corporation paid $550,000 to acquire Gentsch, Inc. Gentsch's assets had a market value of $900,000, and its liabilities were $400,000. In recording the acquisition, Lacy will record goodwill of *(p. 477)*
   ✓ a. $50,000   c. $550,000
     b. $100,000   d. $0
10. Which of the following items is a revenue expenditure? *(p. 478)*
   ✓ a. Property tax paid on land one year after it is acquired
     b. Survey fee paid during the acquisition of land
     c. Legal fee paid to acquire land
     d. Building permit paid to construct a warehouse on the land

Answers to the Self-Study Questions follow the Accounting Vocabulary.

Accounting Vocabulary

Accelerated depreciation. A type of depreciation method that writes off a relatively larger amount of the asset's cost nearer the start of its useful life than does the straight-line method *(p. 462)*.

Amortization. The systematic reduction of a lump-sum amount. Expense that applies to intangible assets in the same way depreciation applies to plant assets and depletion applies to natural resources *(p. 475)*.

Capital expenditure. Expenditure that increases the capacity or efficiency of an asset or extends its useful life. Capital expenditures are debited to an asset account *(p. 478)*.

Copyright. Exclusive right to reproduce and sell a book, musical composition, film, or other work of art. Issued by the federal government, copyrights extend 50 years beyond the author's life *(p. 476)*.

Cost of a plant asset. Purchase price, sales tax, purchase commission, and all other amounts paid to acquire the asset and to ready it for its intended use *(p. 456)*.

Depletion expense. That portion of a natural resource's cost that is used up in a particular period. Depletion expense is computed in the same way as units of production depreciation *(p. 474)*.

Depreciable cost. The cost of a plant asset minus its estimated residual value *(p. 460)*.

Double-declining-balance (DDB) method. An accelerated depreciation method that computes annual depreciation by multiplying the asset's decreasing book value by a constant percentage, which is two times the straight-line rate *(p. 462)*.

Estimated residual value. Expected cash value of an asset at the end of its useful life. Also called Residual value, Scrap value and Salvage value *(p. 459)*.

Estimated useful life. Length of the service that a business expects to get from an asset, may be expressed in years, units of output, miles, or other measures *(p. 459)*.

Expenditure. Either a cash or credit purchase of goods or services related to an asset *(p. 478)*.

Extraordinary repair. Repair work that generates a capital expenditure *(p. 478)*.

Franchises and licenses. Privileges granted by a private business or a government to sell a product or service in accordance with specified conditions *(p. 476)*.

Goodwill. Excess of the cost of an acquired company over the sum of the market values of its net assets (assets minus liabilities) *(p. 477)*.

Intangible asset. An asset with no physical form, a special right to current and expected future benefits *(p. 456)*.

Leasehold. Prepayment that a lessee (renter) makes to secure the use of an asset from a lessor (landlord) *(p. 477)*.

Ordinary repair. Repair work that creates a revenue expenditure, which is debited to an expense account *(p. 478)*.

Patent. A federal government grant giving the holder the exclusive right for 17 years to produce and sell an invention *(p. 476)*.

Plant asset. Long-lived assets, like land, buildings, and equipment, used in the operation of the business (p. 456).

Relative sales value method. Allocation technique for identifying the cost of each asset purchased in a group for a single amount (p. 458).

Revenue expenditure. Expenditure that merely maintains an asset in its existing condition or restores the asset to good working order. Revenue expenditures are expensed (matched against revenue) (p. 478).

Straight-line method. Depreciation method in which an equal amount of depreciation expense is assigned to each year (or period) of asset use (p. 460).

Sum-of-years-digits (SYD) method. An accelerated depreciation method by which depreciation is figured by multiplying the depreciable cost of the asset by a fraction. The denominator of the SYD fraction is the sum of the years' digits of the asset's life. The numerator of the SYD fraction starts with the asset life in years and decreases by one each year thereafter (p. 462).

Trademarks and trade names. Distinctive identifications of a product or service (p. 476).

Units-of-production (UOP) method. Depreciation method by which a fixed amount of depreciation is assigned to each unit of output produced by the plant asset (p. 461).

Answers to Self-Study Questions

1. d
2. c $90,000/($90,000 + $60,000) × $120,000 = $72,000;
   $60,000/($90,000 + $60,000) × $120,000 = $48,000
3. b
4. b
5. c
6. a Depreciable cost = $450,000 − $50,000 = $400,000
   $400,000/40 years = $10,000 per year
   $400,000 − ($10,000 × 10 years) = $300,000/40 years = $7,500 per year
7. d
8. b
9. a $550,000 − ($900,000 − $400,000) = $50,000
10. a

ASSIGNMENT MATERIAL _____

Questions

1. To what types of long-lived assets do the following expenses apply: depreciation, depletion, and amortization?
2. Describe how to measure the cost of a plant asset. Would an ordinary cost of repairing the asset after it is placed in service be included in the asset's cost?
3. Suppose land is purchased for $100,000. How do you account for the $8,000 cost of removing an unwanted building?
4. When assets are purchased as a group for a single price and no individual asset cost is given, how is each asset's cost determined?
5. Define depreciation. Present the common misconceptions about depreciation.
6. Which depreciation method does each of the graphs on the next page characterize—straight-line, units-of-production, or accelerated?

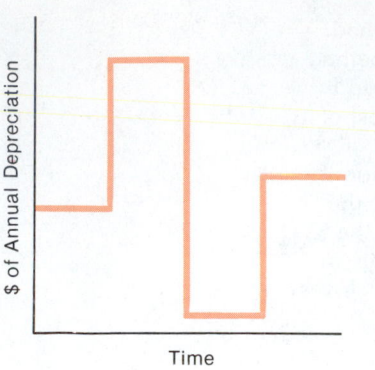

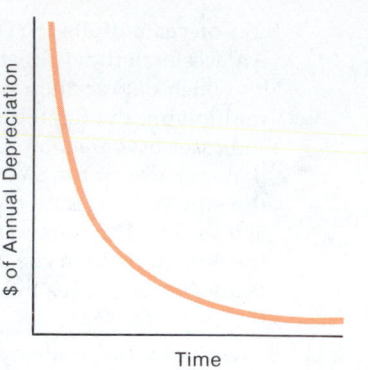

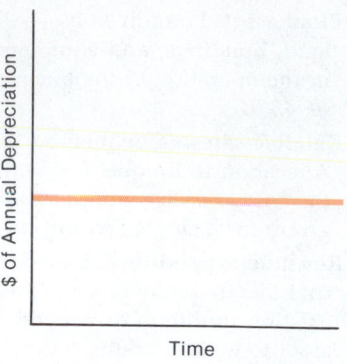

7. Which of the four depreciation methods results in the most depreciation in the first year of the asset's life?

8. Explain the concept of accelerated depreciation. Which other depreciation method is used in the definition of declining-balance depreciation?

9. The level of business activity fluctuates widely for Harwood Delivery Service, reaching its peak around Christmas each year. At other times, business is slow. What depreciation method is most appropriate for the company's fleet of Chevy Luv trucks?

10. Oswalt Computer Service Center uses the most advanced computers available to keep a competitive edge over other service centers. To maintain this advantage, Oswalt usually replaces its computers before they are worn out. Describe the major factors affecting the useful life of a plant asset and indicate which seems more relevant to Oswalt's computers.

11. Estimated residual value is not considered in computing depreciation during the early years of the asset's life by one of the methods. Which method is it?

12. Which type of depreciation method is best from an income tax standpoint? Why?

13. How does depreciation affect income taxes? How does depreciation affect cash provided by operations?

14. Describe how to compute depreciation for less than a full year and how to account for depreciation for less than a full month.

15. Ragland Company paid $10,000 for office furniture. The company expected it to remain in service for 6 years and to have a $ 1,000 residual value. After 2 years' use, company accountants believe the furniture will last an additional 6 years. How much depreciation will Ragland record for each of these 6 years, assuming straight-line depreciation and no change in the estimated residual value?

16. When a company sells a plant asset before the year's end, what must it record before accounting for the sale?

17. Describe how to determine whether a company experiences a gain or a loss when an old plant asset is exchanged for a new one. Does generally accepted accounting favor the recognition of gains or losses? Which accounting concept underlies your answer?

18. Identify seven elements of internal control designed to safeguard plant assets.

19. What expense applies to natural resources? By which depreciation method is this expense computed?

20. How do intangible assets differ from most other assets? Why are they assets at all? What expense applies to intangible assets?

21. Why is the cost of patents and other intangible assets often expensed over a shorter period than the legal life of the asset?

22. Your company has just purchased another company for $400,000. The market value of the other company's net assets is $325,000. What is the $75,000 excess called? What type of asset is it? What is the maximum period over which its cost is amortized under generally accepted accounting principles?

23. IBM Corporation is recognized as a world leader in the manufacture and sale of computers. The company's success has created vast amounts of business goodwill. Would you expect to see *this* goodwill reported on IBM's financial statements? Why or why not?

24. Distinguish a capital expenditure from a revenue expenditure. The title "revenue expenditure" is curious in that a revenue expenditure is a debit to an expense account. Explain why revenue expenditures are so named.

25. Are ordinary repairs capital expenditures or revenue expenditures? Which type of expenditures are extraordinary repairs?

Exercises

Additional computer-related exercise: Exercise 28-2

Exercise 10-1 *Identifying the elements of a plant asset's cost* (L.O. 1)

Land $181,900

A company purchased land, paying $56,000 cash as a down payment and signing a $120,000 note payable for the balance. In addition, the company paid delinquent property tax of $2,000, a title fee of $500, and a $3,400 charge for leveling the land and removing an unwanted building. The company constructed an office building on the land at a cost of $410,000. It also paid $12,000 for a fence around the boundary of the property, $2,400 for the company sign near the entrance to the property, and $6,000 for special lighting of the grounds. Determine the cost of the company's land, land improvements, and building.

Exercise 10-2 *Allocating cost to assets acquired in a basket purchase* (L.O. 1)

Machine #2, $10,000

Faber Castell Company bought three used machines in a $20,000 purchase. An independent appraisal of the machines produced the following figures:

Machine No.	Appraised Value
1	$ 4,000
2	12,000
3	8,000

Assuming Faber Castell paid cash for the machines, record the purchase in the general journal, identifying each machine's individual cost in a separate Machine account.

Exercise 10-3 *Explaining the concept of depreciation* (L.O. 2)

No check figure

Greg Davenport has just slept through the class in which Professor Spyros explained the concept of depreciation. Because the next test is scheduled for Wednesday, Greg telephones Leah Gerbing to get her notes from the lecture. Leah's notes are concise: "Depreciation—Sounds like Greek to me." Greg next tries Ray Mellichamp, who says he thinks depreciation is what happens when an asset wears out. Peggy Bower is confident that depreciation is the process of building up a cash fund to replace an asset at the end of its useful life. Explain the concept of depreciation for Greg. Evaluate the explanations of Ray and Peggy. Be specific.

SL $2,750/yr.
UOP $.125/mile
DDB $6,000, 19X1
SYD $4,400, 19X1

Exercise 10-4   *Computing depreciation by four methods* (L.O. 3)

A company delivery truck was acquired on January 2, 19X1, for $12,000. The truck was expected to remain in service for 4 years and last 88,000 miles. At the end of its useful life, company officials estimated that the truck's residual value would be $1,000. The truck traveled 24,000 miles in the first year, 28,000 in the second year, 21,000 in the third year, and 15,000 in the fourth year. Prepare a schedule of *depreciation expense* per year for the truck under the four depreciation methods. Show your computations.

Situation 1: $175
Situation 2: $1,500

Exercise 10-5   *Recording partial-year depreciation computed by two methods* (L.O. 3)

Situation 1.   Baylor Corporation purchased office furniture on June 3, 19X4, for $2,600 cash. Anne Baylor expects it to remain useful for 8 years and to have a residual value of $200. Baylor uses the straight-line depreciation method. Record Baylor's depreciation on the furniture for the year ended December 31, 19X4.

Situation 2.   Spain Company purchased equipment on October 19, 19X2, for $19,500, signing a note payable for that amount. Spain estimated that this equipment will be useful for 3 years and have a residual value of $1,500. Assuming Spain uses sum-of-years-digits depreciation, record Spain's depreciation on the machine for the year ended December 31, 19X2.

Year 15, $20,000
Year 16, $60,000

Exercise 10-6   *Journalizing a change in a plant asset's useful life* (L.O. 3)

A company purchased a building for $680,000 and depreciated it on a straight-line basis over a 30-year period. The estimated residual value was $80,000. After using the building for 15 years, the company realized that wear and tear on the building would force the company to replace it before 30 years. Starting with the 16th year, the company began depreciating the building over a revised total life of 20 years, retaining the $80,000 estimate of residual value. Record depreciation expense on the building for years 15 and 16.

Accum. Depr. 12/31/X4, $43,688

Exercise 10-7   *Preparing a plant ledger card; units-of-production depreciation* (L.O. 3)

Citizens Wholesale Grocers uses a plant ledger card to account for its delivery vehicles, which are located at the company's service garage. The fleet of vehicles cost $96,000 when purchased from Ericksen Ford Company on September 1, 19X2. This cost is the debit balance in the Delivery Vehicles account in the general ledger. Citizens uses the units-of-production depreciation method and estimates a useful life of 480,000 miles and a $6,000 residual value for the trucks. The garage foreman is responsible for the vehicles. The company's fiscal year ends on December 31. Miles traveled were 30,000 in 19X2; 105,000 in 19X3; and 98,000 in 19X4. Complete a plant ledger card for these vehicles through December 31, 19X4, using a format similar to Exhibit 10-10.

Tax, DDB
Financial statements, SL

Exercise 10-8   *Identifying depreciation methods for income tax and financial reporting purposes* (L.O. 4)

Using the data in Exercise 10-4, identify the depreciation method that would be most advantageous from an income tax perspective. Which depreciation method do most companies use for reporting to their stockholders and creditors on their financial statements?

Gain on sale $360

Exercise 10-9   *Recording the sale of a plant asset* (L.O. 5)

On January 2, 19X1, Ribbon Paper Products purchased store fixtures for $7,700 cash, expecting the fixtures to remain in service for 10 years. Ribbon has depreciated the fixtures on a sum-of-years-digits basis, assuming no estimated residual value. On October 30, 19X8, Ribbon sold the fixtures for $850 cash. Record depreciation expense on the fixtures for the 10 months ended October 30, 19X8, and also record the sale of the fixtures.

Exercise 10-10 *Exchanging plant assets* **(L.O. 5)**

Situation 1: Cost of new machine $12,400
Situation 2: Cost of new machine $12,600

A machine cost $10,000. At the end of 4 years, its accumulated depreciation was $4,500. For each of the following situations, record the trade-in of this old machine for a new, similar machine.

Situation 1.   The new machine had a cash price of $12,400; the dealer allowed a trade-in allowance of $4,000 on the old machine, and you paid the $8,400 balance in cash.

Situation 2.   The new machine had a cash price of $13,000; the dealer allowed a trade-in allowance of $5,900 on the old machine; and you signed a note payable for the $7,100 balance.

Exercise 10-11 *Recording natural resource assets and depletion* **(L.O. 6)**

Depletion $35,000

Yellowstone Mines paid $198,500 for the right to extract ore from a 200,000-ton mineral deposit. In addition to the purchase price, Yellowstone also paid a $500 filing fee and a $1,000 license fee to the state of Wyoming. Because Yellowstone purchased the rights to the minerals only, the company expected the asset to have zero residual value when fully depleted. During the first year of production, Yellowstone removed 35,000 tons of ore. Make general journal entries to record (a) purchase of the mineral rights (debit Mineral Asset), (b) payment of fees, and (c) depletion for first-year production.

Exercise 10-12 *Recording intangibles, amortization, and a change in the asset's useful life* **(L.O. 7)**

Part 1: Amortiz. $440,000
Part 2: Amortiz. $880,000

Part 1.   Ryther Corporation manufactures high-speed printers and has recently purchased for $3.52 million a patent for the design for a new laser printer. Although it gives legal protection for 17 years, the patent is expected to provide Ryther with a competitive advantage for only 8 years. Assuming the straight-line method of amortization, use general journal entries to record (a) the purchase of the patent and (b) amortization for 1 year.

Part 2.   After using the patent for 4 years, Ryther learns at an industry trade show that another company is designing a more efficient printer. Based on this new information, Ryther decides, starting with year 5, to amortize the remaining cost of the patent over 2 additional years, giving the patent a total useful life of 6 years. Record amortization for year 5.

Exercise 10-13 *Computing and recording goodwill* **(L.O. 7)**

Amortiz. $40,000

Company P purchased Company S, paying $1 million cash. The market value of Company S assets was $1.7 million, and Company S had liabilities of $1.1 million.

(a) Compute the cost of the goodwill purchased by Company P.
(b) Record the purchase by Company P.
(c) Record amortization of goodwill for year 1, assuming the straight-line method and a useful life of 10 years.

Exercise 10-14 *Distinguishing capital expenditures from revenue expenditures* **(L.O. 8)**

No check figure

Classify each of the following expenditures as a capital expenditure or a revenue expenditure (expense) related to machinery: (a) purchase price, (b) sales tax paid on the purchase price, (c) transportation and insurance while machinery is in transport from seller to buyer, (d) installation, (e) training of personnel for initial operation of the machinery, (f) special reinforcement to the machinery platform, (g) income tax paid on income earned from the sale of products manufactured by the machinery, (h) major overhaul to extend useful life by three years, (i) ordinary recurring repairs to keep the machinery in good working order, (j) lubrication of the machinery before it is placed in service, (k) periodic lubrication after the machinery is placed in service.

Problems

(Group A)

Additional computer-related problems: Problems 28-1A and 28-1B

Depr.–Land improve. $1,883
Office bldg. $12,953
Storage bldg. $1,037
Furniture $9,017

Problem 10-1A   *Identifying the elements of a plant asset's cost*   **(L.O. 1)**

United America Insurance Company incurred the following costs in acquiring land, making land improvements, and constructing and furnishing an office building.

(a)	Purchase price of four acres of land, including an old building that will be used for storage (land market value is $380,000; building market value is $20,000)	$316,000
(b)	Landscaping (additional dirt and earth moving)	8,100
(c)	Fence around the boundary of the land	17,650
(d)	Attorney fee for title search on the land	600
(e)	Delinquent real estate taxes on the land to be paid by United America	5,900
(f)	Company signs at front of the company property	1,800
(g)	Building permit for the office building	350
(h)	Architect fee for the design of the office building	19,800
(i)	Masonry, carpentry, roofing, and other labor to construct office building	509,000
(j)	Concrete, wood, steel girders, and other materials used in the construction of the office building	214,000
(k)	Renovation of the storage building	41,800
(l)	Repair of storm damage to storage building during construction	2,200
(m)	Landscaping (trees and shrubs)	6,400
(n)	Parking lot and concrete walks on the property	19,750
(o)	Lights for the parking lot, walkways, and company signs	7,300
(p)	Supervisory salary of construction supervisor (85 percent to office building, 9 percent to fencing, parking lot, and concrete walks, and 6 percent to storage building renovation)	40,000
(q)	Office furniture for the office building	107,100
(r)	Transportation and installation of furniture	1,100

United America depreciates buildings over 40 years, land improvements over 20 years, and furniture over 8 years, all on a straight-line basis with zero residual value.

Required

1. Using the following format, account for each cost by listing it as a debit to Land, Land Improvements, Office Building, Storage Building, or Furniture:

Item	Land	Land Improvements	Office Building	Storage Building	Furniture
(a)	$	$	$	$	$
⋮					
(r)					
Totals	$	$	$	$	$

2. Assuming that all construction was complete and the assets were placed in service on May 4, record depreciation for the year ended December 31. Round off figures to the nearest dollar.

Problem 10-2A *Explaining the concept of depreciation* **(L.O. 2)**

No check figure

The board of directors of Fort Worth Parking Lot Company is reviewing the 19X8 annual report. A new board member—a consulting psychologist with little business experience—questions the company accountant about the depreciation amounts. The psychologist wonders why depreciation expense has decreased from $20,000 in 19X6 to $18,400 in 19X7 to $17,200 in 19X8. She states that she could understand the decreasing annual amounts if the company had been disposing of properties each year, but that has not occurred. Further, she notes that growth in the city is increasing the values of company properties. Why is the company recording depreciation when the property values are increasing?

Required

Write a paragraph or two to explain the concept of depreciation to the psychologist and to answer that person's questions.

Problem 10-3A *Computing depreciation by four methods and the cash flow advantage of accelerated depreciation for tax purposes* **(L.O. 3, 4)**

Depr. 19X5
SL $18,000
UDP $13,500
DDB $2,960
SYD $6,000

On January 9, 19X1, Ross, Inc., paid $92,000 for equipment used in manufacturing automotive supplies. In addition to the basic purchase price, the company paid $700 transportation charges, $100 insurance for the goods in transit, $4,100 sales tax, and $3,100 for a special platform on which to place the equipment in the plant. Ross management estimates that the equipment will remain in service for 5 years and have a residual value of $10,000. The equipment will produce 50,000 units in the first year, with annual production decreasing by 5,000 units during each of the next 4 years (that is, 45,000 units in year 2, 40,000 units in year 3, and so on). In trying to decide which depreciation method to use, Diane Ross has requested a depreciation schedule for each of the four generally accepted depreciation methods (straight-line, units-of-production, double-declining-balance, and sum-of-years-digits).

Required

1. For each of the four generally accepted depreciation methods, prepare a depreciation schedule showing asset cost, depreciation expense, accumulated depreciation, and asset book value. Use the format of Exhibits 10-3 through 10-6.
2. Ross reports to stockholders and creditors in the financial statements using the depreciation method that maximizes reported income in the early years of asset use. For income tax purposes, however, the company uses the depreciation method that minimizes income tax payments in those early years. Consider the first year Ross uses the equipment. Identify the depreciation methods that meet Ross's objectives, assuming the income tax authorities would permit the use of any of the methods.

3. Assume cash provided by operations before income tax is $120,000 for the equipment's first year. The income tax rate is 30 percent. For the two depreciation methods identified in Requirement 2, compare the net income and cash provided by operations (cash flow). Use the format of Exhibit 10-8 for your answer. Show which method gives the net-income advantage and which method gives the cash-flow advantage. Ignore the earnings rate in the cash-flow analysis.

Depr. Exp. 19X3, before closing, $3,867

Problem 10-4A   *Journalizing and posting plant asset transactions; capital expenditures versus revenue expenditures* **(L.O. 1, 3, 5, 8)**

Assume that an Eckerd drugstore completed the following transactions:

19X2
Jan.   6   Paid $9,000 cash for a used delivery truck.
        7   Paid $800 to have the truck engine overhauled.
        8   Paid $200 to have the truck modified for business use.
Aug. 21   Paid $156 for a minor tuneup.
Dec. 31   Recorded depreciation on the truck by the sum-of-years-digits method (assume a 4-year life and a $2,000 residual value).
        31   Closed the appropriate accounts.

19X3
Feb.   8   Traded in the delivery truck for a new truck costing $13,000. The dealer granted a $4,000 allowance on the old truck, and the store paid the balance in cash. Recorded 19X3 depreciation for the year to date and then recorded the exchange of trucks.
July   8   Repaired the new truck's damaged fender for $625 cash.
Dec. 31   Recorded depreciation on the new truck by the sum-of-years-digits method. (Assume a 4-year life and a residual value of $3,000.)
        31   Closed the appropriate accounts.

Required

1. Open the following accounts in the general ledger: Delivery Trucks; Accumulated Depreciation—Delivery Trucks; Truck Repair Expense; Depreciation Expense—Delivery Trucks; and Loss on Exchange of Delivery Trucks.
2. Record the transactions in the general journal, and post to the ledger accounts opened.

No check figure

Problem 10-5A   *Recording plant asset transactions; exchanges; changes in useful life* **(L.O. 1, 3, 5, 8)**

Consolidated Freightways, Inc., provides nationwide general freight service. The company's balance sheet includes the following assets under Property, Plant, and Equipment: Land, Buildings, Motor Carrier Equipment, and Leasehold Improvements. Assume the company has a separate accumulated depreciation account for each of these assets except land and leasehold improvements. Amortization on leasehold improvements is credited directly to the Leasehold Improvements account rather than to Accumulated Amortization—Leasehold Improvements.

Assume that Consolidated Freightways completed the following transactions:

Jan.   5   Traded in motor-carrier equipment with book value of $47,000 (cost of $130,000) for similar new equipment with a cash cost of $176,000. Consolidated received a trade-in allowance of $50,000 on the old equipment and paid the remainder in cash.

Feb. 22   Purchased motor-carrier equipment for $136,000 plus 5 percent sales tax and $200 title fee. The company gave a 60-day, 12 percent note in payment.

Apr. 23   Paid the equipment note and related interest.

July 9   Sold a building that had cost $550,000 and had accumulated depreciation of $247,500 through December 31 of the preceding year. Depreciation is computed on a straight-line basis. The building has a 30-year useful life and a residual value of $55,000. Consolidated received $100,000 cash and a $600,000 note receivable.

Aug. 16   Paid cash to improve leased assets at a cost of $10,200.

Oct. 26   Purchased land and a building for a single price of $300,000. An independent appraisal valued the land at $115,000 and the building at $230,000.

Dec. 31   Recorded depreciation as follows:
          Motor-carrier equipment has an expected useful life of 5 years and an estimated residual value of 5 percent of cost. Depreciation is computed on the sum-of-years-digits method. Make separate depreciation entries for equipment acquired on January 5 and February 22.
          Amortization on leasehold improvements is computed on a straight-line basis over the life of the lease, which is 10 years, with zero residual value.
          Depreciation on buildings is computed by the straight-line method. The company had assigned to its older buildings, which cost $200,000,000, an estimated useful life of 30 years with a residual value equal to 10 percent of the asset cost. However, management has come to believe that the buildings will remain useful for a total of 40 years. Residual value remains unchanged. The company has used all its buildings, except for the one purchased on October 26, for 10 years. The new building carries a 40-year useful life and a residual value equal to 10 percent of its cost. Make separate entries for depreciation on the building acquired on October 26 and the other buildings purchased in earlier years.

Required

Record the transactions in the general journal.

Problem 10-6A   *Distinguishing capital expenditures from revenue expenditures; preparing a plant ledger record* **(L.O. 3, 5, 8)**

Cost of new truck $17,867

Suppose Consolidated Edison Co. uses plant ledger cards to control its service trucks, purchased from Bird-Kultgen Ford. The supervisor is responsible for the trucks, which are located at the company's service garage. The following transactions were completed during 19X3 and 19X4:

19X3
Jan. 6   Paid $10,420 cash for a used service truck (truck no. 501).
      7   Paid $2,500 to have the truck engine overhauled.
      8   Paid $180 to have the truck modified for business use.

Nov. 5   Paid $107 for replacement of one tire.

Dec. 31   Recorded depreciation on the truck by the double-declining-balance method, based on a 4-year useful life and a $1,100 residual value.

19X4
July 16   Repaired a damaged fender on truck no. 501 at a cash cost of $877.

Sep. 6   Traded in service truck no. 501 for a new one (truck no. 633) with a cash cost of $18,000. The dealer granted a $4,500 allowance on the old truck, and Consolidated Edison paid the balance in cash. Recorded 19X4 depreciation for year to date and then recorded exchange of the trucks.

Dec. 31 Recorded depreciation on truck no. 633 by the double-declining-balance method, on a 4-year life and a $1,500 residual value.

Required

1. Identify the capital expenditures and the revenue expenditures in the transactions. Which expenditures are debited to an asset account? Which expenditures are debited to an expense account?
2. Prepare a separate plant ledger record for each of the trucks.

Depletion $441,000

Problem 10-7A *Recording intangibles, natural resources, and the related expenses (L.O. 6, 7)*

Part 1.   Georgia-Pacific Corporation is one of the world's largest forest products companies. The company's balance sheet includes the assets Natural Gas, Oil, and Coal.

Suppose Georgia-Pacific paid $1.5 million cash for a lease giving the firm the right to work a mine that contained an estimated 125,000 tons of coal. Assume that the company paid $10,000 to remove unwanted buildings from the land and $45,000 to prepare the surface for mining. Further assume that Georgia-Pacific signed a $20,000 note payable to a landscaping company to return the land surface to its original condition after the lease ends. During the first year, Georgia-Pacific removed 35,000 tons of coal, which it sold on account for $17 per ton.

Required

Make general journal entries to record all transactions related to the coal, including depletion and sale of the first-year production.

Part 2.   Collins Foods International, Inc., is the largest of the companies that operate Kentucky Fried Chicken franchised restaurants and is also the majority owner of Sizzler Restaurants. The company's balance sheet reports the asset Cost in Excess of Net Assets of Purchased Businesses. Assume that Collins purchased this asset as part of the acquisition of another company, which carried these figures:

Book value of assets...............	$2.4 million
Market value of assets.............	3.1 million
Liabilities........................	2.2 million

Required

1. What is another title for the asset Cost in Excess of Net Assets of Purchased Businesses?
2. Make the general journal entry to record Collins's purchase of the other company for $1.3 million cash.
3. Assuming Collins amortizes Cost in Excess of Net Assets of Purchased Businesses over 20 years, record the straight-line amortization for one year.

Part 3.   Suppose Collins purchased a Kentucky Fried Chicken franchise license for $240,000. In addition to the basic purchase price, Collins also paid a lawyer $8,000 for assistance with the negotiations. Collins management believes the appropriate amortization period for its cost of the franchise license is 8 years.

Required

Make general journal entries to record the franchise transactions, including straight-line amortization for one year.

(Group B)

Problem 10-1B   *Identifying the elements of a plant asset's cost*   **(L.O. 1)**

Depr.–Land improv. $2,865
Home office bldg. $24,878
Garage $1,425
Furniture $11,644

Song Kim Company incurred the following costs in acquiring land and a garage, making land improvements, and constructing and furnishing a home office building.

(a)   Purchase price of 3 1/2 acres of land, including an old building that will be used as a garage for company vehicles (land market value is $600,000; building market value is $60,000) $550,000

(b)   Delinquent real estate taxes on the land to be paid by Song Kim 3, 700

(c)   Landscaping (additional dirt and earth moving)   3,550

(d)   Title insurance on the land acquisition   1,000

(e)   Fence around the boundary of the land   14,100

(f)   Building permit for the home office building   200

(g)   Architect fee for the design of the home office building   25,000

(h)   Company signs near front and rear approaches to the company property   23,550

(i)   Renovation of the garage   23,800

(j)   Concrete, wood, steel girders, and other materials used in the construction of the home office building   514,000

(k)   Masonry, carpentry, roofing, and other labor to construct home office building   734,000

(l)   Repair of vandalism damage to home office building during construction   4,100

(m)   Parking lots and concrete walks on the property   17,450

(n)   Lights for the parking lot, walkways, and company signs   8,900

(o)   Supervisory salary of construction supervisor (90 percent to home office building, 6 percent to fencing, parking lot, and concrete walks, and 4 percent to garage renovation)   55,000

(p)   Office furniture for the home office building   123,500

(q)   Transportation of furniture from seller to the home office building   700

(r)   Landscaping (trees and shrubs)   9,100

Song Kim depreciates buildings over 40 years, land improvements over 20 years, and furniture over 8 years, all on a straight-line basis with zero residual value.

Required

1.   Using the following format, account for each cost by listing it as a debit to Land, Land Improvements, Home Office Building, Garage, or Furniture:

Item	Land	Land Improvements	Home Office Building	Garage	Furniture
(a)	$	$	$	$	$
⋮					
(r)					
Totals	$_____	$_____	$_____	$_____	$_____

2. Assuming that all construction was complete and the assets were placed in service on March 19, record depreciation for the year ended December 31. Round figures to the nearest dollar.

Problem 10-2B *Explaining the concept of depreciation* (L.O. 2)

The board of directors of Sacramento Construction Company is having its regular quarterly meeting. Accounting policies are on the agenda, and depreciation is being discussed. A new board member, a physician, has some strong opinions about two aspects of depreciation policy. Dr. Johansson argues that depreciation must be coupled with a fund to replace company assets. Otherwise, there is no substance to depreciation, he argues. He also challenges the 5-year estimated life over which Sacramento is depreciating company computers. He notes that the computers will last much longer and should be depreciated over at least 10 years.

Required

Write a paragraph or two to explain the concept of depreciation to Dr. Johansson and to answer his arguments.

Depr. 19X6
  SL $9,000
  UOP $9,720
  DDP $1,901
  SYD $2,571

Problem 10-3B *Computing depreciation by four methods and the cash flow advantage of accelerated depreciation for tax purposes* (L.O. 3,4)

On January 2, 19X1, Industrial Products, Inc., purchased 3 used delivery trucks at a total cost of $53,000. Before placing the trucks in service, the company spent $1,200 painting them, $1,800 replacing their tires, and $4,000 overhauling their engines and reconditioning their bodies. Industrial Products management estimates that the trucks will remain in service for 6 years and have a residual value of $6,000. The trucks' combined annual mileage is expected to be 16,000 miles in each of the first 4 years and 18,000 miles in each of the next 2 years. In trying to decide which depreciation method to use, Ralph Winter, the general manager, requests a depreciation schedule for each of the four generally accepted depreciation methods (straight-line, units-of-production, double-declining-balance, and sum-of-years-digits).

Required

1. Assuming Industrial Products depreciates its delivery trucks as a unit, prepare a depreciation schedule for each of the four generally accepted depreciation methods, showing asset cost, depreciation expense, accumulated depreciation, and asset book value. Use the formats of Exhibits 10-3 through 10-6.
2. Industrial Products reports to stockholders and creditors in the financial statements using the depreciation method that maximizes reported income in the early years of asset use. For income tax purposes, however, the company uses the depreciation method that minimizes income tax payments in those early years. Consider the first year that Industrial Products uses the delivery trucks. Identify the depreciation methods that meet the general manager's objectives, assuming the income tax authorities would permit the use of any of the methods.
3. Assume cash provided by operations before income tax is $80,000 for the delivery trucks' first year. The income tax rate is 30 percent. For the two depreciation methods identified in Requirement 2, compare the net income and cash provided by operations (cash flow). Use the format of Exhibit 10-8 for your answer. Show which method gives the net-income advantage and which method gives the cash-flow advantage. Ignore the earnings rate in the cash-flow analysis.

Problem 10-4B *Journalizing and posting plant asset transactions; capital expenditures versus revenue expenditures* **(L.O. 1, 3, 5, 8)**

Depr. Exp. 19X5, before closing $9,688

Consumers Power Company provides electrical power to part of Michigan. Assume that the company completed the following transactions:

19X4

Jan. 3 Paid $22,000 cash for a used service truck.

5 Paid $1,200 to have the truck engine overhauled.

7 Paid $300 to have the truck modified for business use.

Oct. 3 Paid $930 for transmission repair and oil change.

Dec. 31 Used the double-declining-balance method to record depreciation on the truck. (Assume a 4-year life.)

31 Closed the appropriate accounts.

19X5

Mar. 13 Replaced the truck's broken windshield for $275 cash.

June 26 Traded in the service truck for a new truck costing $27,000. The dealer granted an $8,000 allowance on the old truck, and Consumers Power paid the balance in cash. Recorded 19X5 depreciation for the year to date and then recorded the exchange of trucks.

Dec. 31 Used the double-declining-balance method to record depreciation on the new truck. (Assume a 4-year life.)

31 Closed the appropriate accounts.

Required

1. Open the following accounts in the general ledger: Service Trucks; Accumulated Depreciation—Service Trucks; Truck Repair Expense; Depreciation Expense—Service Trucks; and Loss on Exchange of Service Trucks.

2. Record the transactions in the general journal and post to the ledger accounts opened.

Problem 10-5B *Recording plant asset transactions; exchanges; changes in useful life* **(L.O. 1, 3, 5, 8)**

No check figure

A. C. Nielsen Company surveys American viewing trends. Nielsen's balance sheet reports the following assets under Property and Equipment: Land, Buildings, Office Furniture, Communication Equipment, Televideo Equipment, and Leasehold Improvements. The company has a separate accumulated depreciation account for each of these assets except land and leasehold improvements. Amortization on leasehold improvements is credited directly to the Leasehold Improvements account rather than to Accumulated Depreciation—Leasehold Improvements.

Assume that Nielsen completed the following transactions:

Jan. 4 Traded in communication equipment with book value of $31,000 (cost of $66,000) for similar new equipment with a cash cost of $78,000. The seller gave Nielsen a trade-in allowance of $20,000 on the old equipment, and Nielsen paid the remainder in cash.

19 Purchased office furniture for $45,000 plus 6 percent sales tax and $300 shipping charge. The company gave a 90-day, 10 percent note in payment.

Apr. 19 Paid the furniture note and related interest.

Aug. 29 Sold a building that had cost $475,000 and had accumulated depreciation of $353,500 through December 31 of the preceding year. Depreciation is computed on a straight-line basis. The building has a 30-year useful life and a residual value of $47,500. Nielsen received $250,000 cash and a $750,000 note receivable.

Sep. 6   Paid cash to improve leased assets at a cost of $26,000.

Nov. 10   Purchased used communication and televideo equipment from the Gallup polling organization. Total cost was $90,000 paid in cash. An independent appraisal valued the communication equipment at $65,000 and the televideo equipment at $35,000.

Dec. 31   Recorded depreciation as follows:

   Equipment is depreciated by the double-declining-balance method over a 5-year life with zero residual value. Record depreciation on the equipment purchased on January 4 and on November 10 separately.

   Office furniture has an expected useful life of 8 years with an estimated residual value of $5,000. Depreciation is computed by the sum-of-years-digits method.

   Amortization on leasehold improvements is computed on a straight-line basis over the life of the lease, which is 6 years, with zero residual value.

   Depreciation on buildings is computed by the straight-line method. The company had assigned buildings an estimated useful life of 30 years and a residual value that is 10 percent of cost. After using the buildings for 20 years, the company has come to believe that their total useful life will be 35 years. Residual value remains unchanged. The buildings cost $96,000,000.

Required

Record the transactions in the general journal.

Cost of new truck $22,690

Problem 10-6B *Distinguishing capital expenditures from revenue expenditures; preparing a plant ledger card* **(L.O. 3, 5, 8)**

Suppose Kraft, Inc., uses plant ledger cards to control its service trucks, purchased from Rountree Motors. The supervisor is responsible for the trucks, which are located at the company's service garage. The following transactions were completed during 19X6 and 19X7:

19X6

Jan. 10   Paid $14,000 cash for a used service truck (truck no. 214).

    11   Paid $1,500 to have the truck engine overhauled.

    12   Paid $250 to have the truck modified for business use.

Aug. 3   Paid $603 for transmission repair and oil change.

Dec. 31   Recorded depreciation on the truck by the double-declining-balance method, based on a 5-year life and a $1,500 residual value.

19X7

Mar. 13   Replaced a damaged bumper on truck no. 214 at a cash cost of $295.

May 12   Traded in service truck no. 214 for a new one (truck no. 267) with a cash cost of $23,500. The dealer granted a $9,000 allowance on the old truck, and Kraft paid the balance in cash. Recorded 19X7 depreciation for year to date and then recorded exchange of the trucks.

Dec. 31   Recorded depreciation on truck no. 267 by the double-declining-balance method, based on a 5-year life and a $2,000 residual value.

Required

1. Identify the capital expenditures and the revenue expenditures in the transactions. Which expenditures are debited to an asset account? Which expenditures are debited to an expense account?

2. Prepare a separate plant ledger record for each of the trucks.

Problem 10-7B

Recording intangibles, natural resources, and the related expenses
(L.O. 6, 7)

Part 1.   Transco Energy Company operates a pipeline that provides natural gas to Atlanta; Washington, D.C.; Philadelphia; and New York City. The company's balance sheet includes the asset Oil Properties.

Suppose Transco paid $6 million cash for an oil lease that contained an estimated reserve of 725,000 barrels of oil. Assume that the company paid $350,000 for additional geological tests of the property and $110,000 to prepare the surface for drilling. Prior to production, the company signed a $65,000 note payable to have a building constructed on the property. Because the building provides on-site headquarters for the drilling effort and will be abandoned when the oil is depleted, its cost is debited to the Oil Properties account and included in depletion charges. During the first year of production, Transco removed 82,000 barrels of oil, which it sold on credit for $19 per barrel.

Required

Make general journal entries to record all transactions related to the oil and gas property, including depletion and sale of the first-year production.

Part 2.   United Telecommunications, Inc., (United Telecom) provides communication services in Florida, North Carolina, New Jersey, Texas, and other states. The company's balance sheet reports the asset Cost of Acquisitions in Excess of the Fair Market Value of the Net Assets of Subsidiaries. Assume that United Telecom purchased this asset as part of the acquisition of another company, which carried these figures:

Book value of assets	$640,000
Market value of assets	920,000
Liabilities	405,000

Required

1. What is another title for the asset Cost of Acquisitions in Excess of the Fair Market Value of the Net Assets of Subsidiaries?
2. Make the general journal entry to record United Telecom's purchase of the other company for $600,000 cash.
3. Assuming United Telecom amortizes Cost of Acquisitions in Excess of the Fair Market Value of the Net Assets of Subsidiaries over 20 years, record the straight-line amortization for one year.

Part 3.   Suppose United Telecom purchased a patent for $190,000. Before using the patent, United incurred an additional cost of $25,000 for a lawsuit to defend the company's right to purchase it. Even though the patent gives United legal protection for 17 years, company management has decided to amortize its cost over a 5-year period because of the industry's fast-changing technologies.

Required

Make general journal entries to record the patent transactions, including straight-line amortization for one year.

Extending Your Knowledge

Decision Problems

Net income:
  PanAm $80,000
  Lucerne $31,000

1. Measuring Profitability Based on Different Inventory and Depreciation Methods (L.O. 3)

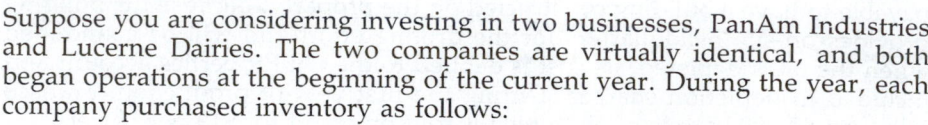

Suppose you are considering investing in two businesses, PanAm Industries and Lucerne Dairies. The two companies are virtually identical, and both began operations at the beginning of the current year. During the year, each company purchased inventory as follows:

Jan. 4	12,000 units at $4 =	$ 48,000
Apr. 6	5,000 units at 5 =	25,000
Aug. 9	7,000 units at 6 =	42,000
Nov. 27	10,000 units at 7 =	70,000
Totals	34,000	$185,000

Over the first year, both companies sold 25,000 units of inventory.

In early January both companies purchased equipment costing $200,000 that had a 10-year estimated useful life and a $20,000 residual value. PanAm uses the first-in, first-out (FIFO) method for its inventory and straight-line depreciation for its equipment. Lucerne uses last-in, first-out (LIFO) and double-declining-balance depreciation. Both companies' trial balances at December 31 included the following:

Sales revenue	$300,000
Purchases	185,000
Operating expenses	80,000

Required

1. Prepare both companies' income statements.
2. Prepare a schedule that shows why one company appears to be more profitable than the other. Explain the schedule and amounts in your own words. What accounts for the different amounts?
3. Is one company more profitable than the other? Give your reason.

No check figure

2. Plant Assets and Intangible Assets (L.O. 7, 8)

The following questions are unrelated except that they apply to fixed assets and intangible assets:

1. The Manager of Meadowlake, Inc., regularly buys plant assets and debits the cost to Repairs and Maintenance Expense. Why would he do that, since he knows this action violates GAAP?
2. The manager of Spruce Lake Company regularly debits the cost of repairs and maintenance of plant assets to Plant and Equipment. Why would she do that, since she knows she is violating GAAP?
3. It has been suggested that, since many intangible assets have no value except to the company that owns them, they should be valued at $1.00 or zero on the balance sheet. Many accountants disagree with this view. Which view do you support? Why?

Ethical Issue

Champion Air Filters purchased land and a building for the lump sum of $3 million. To get the maximum tax deduction, Champion managers allocated 90 percent of the purchase price to the building and only 10 percent to the land. A

498 Part Three   Accounting for Noncash Assets and Liabilities

more realistic allocation would have been 75 percent to the building and 25 percent to the land.

Required

1. Explain the tax advantage of allocating too much to the building and too little to the land.
2. Was Champion's allocation ethical? If so, state why. If not, why not? Identify who was harmed.

Financial Statement Problems

1. Plant Assets and Intangible Assets   (L.O. 4, 5, 8)

Gain on sale of properties $6.5 million

Refer to the Goodyear Tire & Rubber Company financial statements in Appendix C, and answer the following questions.

1. Which depreciation method does Goodyear use for the purpose of reporting to stockholders and creditors in the financial statements? What type of depreciation method does the company use for income tax purposes? Why is this method preferable for income tax purposes?
2. Depreciation expense is embedded in the expense amounts listed on the income statement. The statement of cash flows gives the amount of depreciation. What was depreciation for 1990? Record depreciation expense for 1990.
3. The statement of cash flows also reports purchases of plant assets and the proceeds (sale prices) received on disposal of plant assets. How much were Goodyear's plant asset acquisitions during 1990? Journalize Goodyear's acquisition of plant assets.
4. How much did Goodyear receive on the sale of plant assets during 1990? Assume the plant assets that were sold had a cost of $55.0 million and accumulated depreciation of $43.1 million. Record the sale of these plant assets.
5. In what category on the income statement are revenue expenditures most likely included?

2. Plant Assets and Intangible Assets   (L.O. 3, 5, 7)

No check figure

Obtain the annual report of an actual company of your choosing. Annual reports are available in various forms including the original document in hard copy, microfiche, and computerized data bases such as that provided by Disclosure, Inc.

Answer these questions about the company. Concentrate on the current year in the annual report you select. .

1. Which depreciation method or methods does the company use for reporting to stockholders and creditors in the financial statements? Does the company disclose the estimated useful lives of plant assets for depreciation purposes? If so, identify the useful lives.
2. Depreciation and amortization expenses are often combined since they are similar. Many income statements embed depreciation and amortization in other expense amounts. To learn the amounts of these expenses, it often becomes necessary to examine the statement of cash flows. Where does your company report depreciation and amortization? What were these expenses for the current year? (Note: The company you selected may have only depreciation—no amortization.)
3. How much did the company spend to acquire plant assets during the current year? Journalize the acquisitions in a single entry.
4. How much did the company receive on the sale of plant assets? Assume a particular cost and accumulated depreciation of the plant assets sold. Journalize the sale of the plant assets, assuming the sale resulted in a $700,000 loss.
5. What categories of intangible assets does the company report? What is their reported amount?

Chapter 11

Current Liabilities
and Payroll Accounting

In the annals of marketing devices run amok, few can compare to the airlines' wildly popular frequent flier plans. Early this year, when most carriers tripled the free mileage a suitcase-happy passenger can win, even they knew things had gone too far. "In the back of our minds," says Michael Gunn, head of marketing at American Airlines, "we were trying to figure out how to get out of this mess." With every day that passes, the airlines have fresh reasons to worry about what the giveaways are costing—and they are out to clip the programs' wings.

Up to now most airlines have not bothered to account for frequent flier liabilities on their balance sheets in any significant way. The reasoning has been that most free flights filled airline seats that otherwise would have been empty and that the programs were a minor addition to the cost of doing business. American, for instance, puts the cost of free tickets issued in 1987 at about 10% of their full value, or some $20 million.

Source: Thomas Moore, "Cutting Back on Fliers' Freebies," *Fortune,* June 6, 1988, pp. 149–50.

This actual example illustrates the challenge of accounting for current liabilities. In this case the airlines have a liability for the cost of providing customers with free trips.

A *liability* is an obligation to transfer assets or to provide services in the future. The obligation may arise from a transaction with an outside party. For example, a business incurs a liability when it issues a note payable to buy equipment or to borrow money. Also, the obligation may arise in the absence of individual transactions. For example, interest expense accrues with the passage of time. Until this interest is paid it is a liability. Income tax, a liability of corporations, accrues as income is earned. Proper accounting for liabilities is as important as proper accounting for assets. The failure to record an accrued liability causes the balance sheet to understate the related expense and thus overstates owner's equity. An overly positive view of the business is the result.

Current liabilities are obligations due within one year or within the company's operating cycle if it is longer than one year. Obligations due beyond this period of time are classified as long-term liabilities. We discuss long-term liabilities in Chapter 16. We now turn to accounting for current liabilities, including those arising from payroll expenses.

Point to Stress: Refer to the chapter-opening vignette. A liability is an obligation that results from past transactions. The obligation requires the business to either pay money or provide goods or services in the future. The past transaction that creates a frequent flier liability occurs when the customer earns the mileage.

Current Liabilities of Known Amount

Current liabilities fall into one of two categories: those of a known amount and those whose amount must be estimated. We look first at current liabilities of known amount.

OBJECTIVE 1
Account for current liabilities

Trade Accounts Payable

Amounts owed to suppliers for products or services that are purchased on open account are accounts payable. We have seen many accounts payable examples in previous chapters. For example, a business may purchase inventories and office supplies on an account payable.

Short-Term Notes Payable

Short-term notes payable, a common form of financing, are notes payable that are due within one year. Companies often issue short-term notes payable to borrow cash or to purchase inventory or plant assets. In addition to recording the note payable and its eventual payment, the business must also accrue

Teaching Tip: Note that the liability, Interest Payable, must have a zero balance after the September 30, 19X2, note payment is recorded. When the interest is paid, it is no longer a liability; therefore the previous amount accrued must be written off as a debit to Interest Payable.

interest expense and interest payable at the end of the period. The following entries are typical of this liability:

19X1
Sep. 30 Purchases 8,000
            Note Payable, Short-Term   8,000
         Purchase of inventory by issuing a one-year 10 percent note payable.

Dec. 31 Interest Expense ($8,000 × .10 × 3/12)   200
            Interest Payable   200
         Adjusting entry to accrue interest expense at year end.

The balance sheet at December 31, 19X1, will report the Note Payable of $8,000 and the related Interest Payable of $200 as current liabilities. The 19X1 income statement will report interest expense of $200.

The following entry records the note's payment:

19X2
Sep. 30 Note Payable, Short-Term 8,000
         Interest Payable   200
         Interest Expense ($8,000 × .10 × 9/12)   600
            Cash [$8,000 + ($8,000 × .10)]   8,800
         Payment of a note payable and interest at maturity.

The cash payment entry must split the total interest on the note between the portion accrued at the end of the previous period ($200) and the current period's expense ($600).

Short-Term Notes Payable Issued at a Discount

In another common borrowing arrangement, a company may **discount a note payable** at the bank. Discounting means that the bank subtracts the interest amount from the note's face value. The borrower receives the net amount. In effect, the borrower prepays the interest, which is computed on the principal of the note.

Suppose Procter & Gamble discounts a $100,000, 60-day note payable to its bank at 12 percent. The company will receive $98,000—that is, the $100,000 face value less interest of $2,000 ($100,000 × .12 × 60/360). Assume this transaction occurs on November 25, 19X1. Procter & Gamble's entries to record discounting the note would be

19X1
Nov. 25 Cash ($100,000 − $2,000)   98,000
         Discount on Note Payable ($100,000 x .12 × 60/360)   2,000
            Note Payable, Short-Term   100,000
         Discounted a $100,000, 60-day, 12 percent note payable to borrow cash.

Discount on Note Payable is a contra account to the liability Note Payable, Short-Term. A balance sheet prepared immediately after this transaction would report the note payable at its net amount of $98,000, as follows:

Current liabilities:		
Note payable, short-term		$100,000
Less: Discount on note payable .		(2,000)
Note payable, short-term, net		$ 98,000

The accrued interest at year end must still be recorded, as it would for any note payable. The adjusting entry at December 31 records interest for 36 days as follows:

19X1
Dec. 31   Interest Expense ($100,000 × .12 × 36/360)..... 1,200
        Discount on Note Payable 1,200
        Adjusting entry to accrue interest expense at year end.

This entry credits the Discount account instead of Interest Payable. Why? Because the Discount balance represents future interest expense, and the accrual of interest records the current-period portion of the expense. Furthermore, crediting the Discount reduces this contra account's balance and increases the net amount of the Note Payable. After the adjusting entry, only $800 of the Discount remains, and the carrying value of the Note Payable increases to $99,200, as follows:

Current liabilities:
    Note payable, short-term $100,000
      Less: Discount on note payable
        ($2,000 − $1,200) .... (800)
    Note payable, short-term, net .... $ 99,200

Finally, the business records the note's payment:

19X2
Jan. 24   Interest Expense ($100,000 × .12 × 24/360). 800
        Discount on Note Payable 800
        To record interest expense.

        Note Payable, Short-Term 100,000
           Cash 100,000
        To pay note payable at maturity.

After these entries, the balances in the note payable account and the discount account are zero. Each period's income statement reports the appropriate amount of interest expense.

Sales Tax Payable

Most states levy a sales tax on retail sales. Retailers charge their customers the sales tax in addition to the price of the item sold. Because the retailers owe the state the sales tax collected, the account Sales Tax Payable is a current liability. For example, Pizza Time Theatre, Inc. (home of Chuck E. Cheese) reported sales tax payable of $737,712 as a current liability. States do not levy sales tax on the sales of manufacturers like Procter & Gamble and General Motors. Such companies sell their products to wholesalers and retailers rather than to final consumers. Therefore, they have no sales tax liability.

Suppose one Saturday's sales at a Pizza Time Theatre totaled $2,000. The business would have collected an additional 5 percent in sales tax, which would equal $100 ($2,000 × .05). The business would record that day's sales as follows:

Cash ($2,000 × 1.05) 2,100
    Sales Revenue.................... 2,000
    Sales Tax Payable ($2,000 × .05) 100
To record cash sales of $2,000 subject to 5 percent sales tax.

Discussion Question: What is the difference between how interest is paid on a loan and how it is paid on a discounted note? ANSWER: When you borrow on a loan—or note payable—the interest is generally paid at maturity or over the life of the note. When you borrow on a discounted note, the bank takes the interest out before you receive the proceeds of the note. In either case the amount of interest expense is the same.

Typical Student Misconception: Students often confuse discounted notes receivable with Discount on Notes Payable. Remind them that one is a receivable, an asset, and the other is a contra account to a liability.

Class Exercise: How might Harry's Hardware record the month's sales of $35,650 and the related 7½% sales tax liability? Give two methods.
ANSWER:

Method 1

Cash	38,324
Sales Revenue .	35,650
Sales Tax Payable . .	2,674
(Only one entry required)	

Method 2

Cash	38,324
Sales Revenue .	38,324
Sales Revenue . . 2,674	
Sales Tax Payable . .	2,674

$\left(\$2{,}674 = \$38{,}324 - \dfrac{\$38{,}324}{1.075}\right)$

(Two entries required)

Point to Stress: A current liability is a liability due within the year. The portion of a long-term debt that will be paid within the year should be classified as a current liability. Remember that the interest due within the year is classified separately from the principal.

Companies forward the collected sales tax to the taxing authority at regular intervals, at which time they debit Sales Tax Payable and credit Cash. Observe that Sales Tax Payable does *not* correspond to any sales tax expense that the business is incurring. Nor does this liability arise from the purchase of any asset. Rather, the obligation arises because the business is collecting for the government.

Many companies consider it inefficient to credit Sales Tax Payable when recording sales. They record the sale in an amount that includes the tax. Then prior to paying tax to the state, they make a single entry for the entire period's transactions to bring Sales Revenue and Sales Tax Payable to their correct balances.

Suppose a company made July sales of $100,000, subject to a tax of 6 percent. Its summary entry to record the month's sales could be

July 31	Cash ($100,000 × 1.06)	106,000
	Sales Revenue	106,000
	To record sales for the month.	

The entry to adjust Sales Revenue and Sales Tax Payable to their correct balances is

July 31	Sales Revenue [$106,000 − ($106,000 ÷ 1.06)] . . .	6,000
	Sales Tax Payable	6,000
	To record sales tax.	

Companies that follow this procedure need to make an adjusting entry at the end of the period in order to report the correct amounts of revenue and sales tax liability on their financial statements.

Current Portion of Long-Term Debt

Some long-term notes payable and long-term bonds payable must be paid in installments. The **current portion of long-term debt,** or *current maturity*, is the amount of the principal that is payable within one year. This amount does not include the interest due. Of course, any liability for accrued interest payable must also be reported, but a separate account, Interest Payable, is used for that purpose.

H. J. Heinz Company, probably best known for its ketchup, owed almost $200 million on long-term debt at April 30, the end of its fiscal year. Nearly $14 million was a current liability because it was due within one year. The remaining $186 million was a long-term liability. Suppose the interest rate on the debt was 6 percent and that interest was last paid the preceding November 30. Heinz Company's April 30 balance sheet would report:

Current Liabilities (in part)	Millions
Portion of long-term debt due within one year	$ 14
Interest payable ($200 × .06 × 5/12)	5
Long-Term Debt and Other Liabilities (in part)	
Long-term debt	$186

Accrued Expenses

As shown in the Heinz Company presentation, *accrued expenses,* such as interest on the note, create current liabilities because the interest is due within the year. Therefore, the interest payable (accrued interest) is reported as a current liability. Other important liabilities for accrued expenses are payroll and the related payroll taxes, which we discuss in the second part of this chapter.

Unearned Revenues

Unearned revenues are also called *deferred revenues, revenues collected in advance,* and *customer prepayments.* Each account title indicates that the business has received cash from its customers before earning the revenue. The company has an obligation to provide goods or services to the customer.

The Dun & Bradstreet (D&B) Corporation provides credit evaluation services on a subscription basis. When finance companies pay in advance to have D&B investigate the credit histories of potential customers, D&B incurs a liability to provide future service. The liability account is called Unearned Subscription Revenue (which could also be titled Unearned Subscription Income).

Assume that Dun & Bradstreet charges $150 for a finance company's three-year subscription. Dun & Bradstreet's entries would be

Typical Student Misconception: Students often confuse the Unearned Revenue account and the Revenue account. Unearned Revenue is a liability arising from revenue received in advance of being earned; it is a liability. When it has been earned, it becomes revenue and is no longer a liability.

19X1

Jan. 1	Cash	150	
	Unearned Subscription Revenue		150
	To record receipt of cash at start of the three-year subscription agreement.		

19X1, 19X2, 19X3

Dec. 31	Unearned Subscription Revenue.................	50	
	Subscription Revenue ($150/3)		50
	To record subscription revenue earned at the end of each of three years.		

Dun & Bradstreet's financial statements would report this sequence:

| | December 31 | | |
Balance Sheet	Year 1	Year 2	Year 3
Current liabilities			
Unearned subscription revenue ..	$100	$50	$-0-

Income Statement	Year 1	Year 2	Year 3
Revenues			
Subscription revenue	$ 50	$50	$50

Customer Deposits Payable

Some companies require cash deposits from customers as security on borrowed assets. These amounts are called Customer Deposits Payable because the company must refund the cash to the customer under certain conditions.

For example, telephone companies demand a cash deposit from a customer before installing a telephone. Utility companies and businesses that lend tools and appliances commonly demand a deposit as protection against damage and theft. When the customer ends service or returns the borrowed asset, the company refunds the cash deposit—if the customer has paid all the bills and has not damaged the company's property. Because the company generally

Real-World Example: Accounting Trends and Techniques (AICPA, 1990) reports that of 600 surveyed companies, 53 listed customer deposits as a current liability in 1989. For example, Josten's Inc., the manufacturer of class rings and publisher of school annuals, reported customer deposits of $32,221,000 out of total current liabilities of $153,534,000.

must return the deposit, that obligation is a liability. The uncertainty of when the deposits will be refunded and their relatively small amounts cause many companies to classify Customer Deposits Payable as current liabilities. This is consistent with the concept of conservatism.

Certain manufacturers demand security deposits from the merchandisers who sell their products. Stanley Home Products, Inc., for example, demands a deposit from its dealers. The security deposits, called Dealers' Security Deposits, recently came to $4 million on Stanley's balance sheet, a small amount compared with its total current liabilities of over $62 million.

Current Liabilities That Must Be Estimated

A business may know that a liability exists but not know the exact amount. The liability may not simply be ignored. The unknown amount of a liability must be estimated for reporting on the balance sheet.

Estimated current liabilities vary among companies. As an example, let's look at Estimated Warranty Payable, a liability account common among merchandisers.

Estimated Warranty Payable

Many merchandising companies guarantee their products against defects under *warranty* agreements. The warranty period may extend for any length of time. Ninety-day warranties and one-year warranties are common.

Whatever the warranty's lifetime, the matching principle demands that the company record the *warranty expense* in the same period that the business recognizes sales revenue. After all, offering the warranty—and incurring any possible expense through the warranty agreement—is a part of generating revenue through sales. At the time of the sale, however, the company does not know which products are defective. The exact amount of warranty expense cannot be known with certainty, so the business must estimate its warranty expense and open the related liability account—Estimated Warranty Payable (also called Accrued Warranty Costs and Product Warranty Liability). Even though the warranty liability is a contingency, it is accounted for as an actual liability because the obligation for the warranty expense has occurred and its amount can be estimated.

Companies may make a reliable estimate of their warranty expense based on their experience. Assume a company made sales of $200,000, subject to product warranties. Company management, noting that in past years between 2 percent and 4 percent of products proved defective, estimates that 3 percent of the products will require repair or replacement during the one-year warranty period. The company records warranty expense of $6,000 ($200,000 × .03) for the period:

Warranty Expense	6,000	
Estimated Warranty Payable		6,000

To accrue warranty expense.

Assume that defective merchandise totals $5,800. The company may either repair or replace it. Corresponding entries follow.

Estimated Warranty Payable	5,800	
Cash		5,800

To repair defective products sold under warranty.

Real-World Example: According to the FASB, 40% of all electronic and appliance products are sold with extended warranties, but only 20% of these products are repaired under those warranties.

Point to Stress: Most companies that sell merchandise recognize that some of their products may require repair or replacement during the warranty period. The merchandise may be sold in one year and the warranty period may extend into the next year or beyond. To properly *match* revenue with expenses, the warranty expense is deducted from sales revenue in the period of sale. Warranty expense must therefore be estimated.

Class Exercise: A company made sales of $400,000, and estimated warranty repairs at 5% of the sales. Actual warranty costs were $19,000. Prepare the journal entries to record the sales, the warranty expense estimate, and the actual warranty costs.

ANSWER:

Accounts Rec.	400,000
Sales Revenue	400,000

```
Estimated Warranty Payable...................  5,800
      Inventory ...............................           5,800
   To replace defective products sold under warranty.
```

```
Warranty Expense
(400,000 × 5%) .....   20,000
   Est. Warranty Pay.       20,000
Est. Warranty Pay...   19,000
   Cash, Inventory,
      etc..............           19,000
```

Note that the expense is $6,000 on the income statement no matter what the cash payment or the cost of the replacement inventory. In future periods, the company may come to debit the liability Estimated Warranty Payable for the remaining $200. However, *when* the company repairs or replaces defective merchandise has no bearing on when the company records warranty expense. The business records warranty expense in the same period as the sale.

Other Estimated Current Liabilities

Estimated Vacation Pay Liability.   Most companies grant paid vacations to their employees. The employees receive this benefit during the time they take their vacation, but they earn the compensation by working the other days of the year. Two-week vacations are common. To match expense with revenue properly, the company accrues the vacation pay expense and liability for each of the 50 workweeks of the year. Then, the company records payment during the two-week vacation period. Employee turnover, terminations, and ineligibility force companies to estimate the vacation pay liability.

Suppose a company's January payroll is $100,000 and vacation pay adds 4 percent (2 weeks of annual vacation divided by 50 workweeks each year). Experience indicates that only 80 percent of the vacations will be taken in any one month, so the January vacation pay estimate is $3,200 ($100,000 × .04 × .80). In January the company records vacation pay as follows:

```
Jan. 31   Vacation Pay Expense .......................  3,200
                Estimated Vacation Pay Liability ..........           3,200
```

Each month thereafter, the company makes a similar entry for 4 percent of the payroll.

If an employee takes a vacation in August, his $2,000 monthly salary is recorded as follows:

```
Aug. 31   Estimated Vacation Pay Liability ..............  2,000
                Cash ...................................           2,000
```

Estimated Frequent Flier Liability of an Airline Company.   The chapter-opening vignette describes airlines' frequent flier plans. In a typical arrangement, a passenger who travels a certain number of miles can take a free trip or upgrade her ticket from coach class to first class. The operating expense of providing this free service creates a liability for the airline. When should the expense and estimated frequent flier liability be recorded? As the airline earns revenue from its paying customers. Under the matching principle, a company should record expense when it earns the related revenue. Because the ultimate cost of providing the free transportation is uncertain, the airline must estimate this expense and the related liability. Suppose American Airlines records revenue of $1 million in February. Further, assume American estimates that this revenue-producing travel will give customers free trips that are estimated to cost American 3 percent of the revenue. American could record frequent flier expense and liability as follows:

```
Feb. 28   Frequent Flier Expense ($1,000,000 × .03) ....   30,000
                Estimated Frequent Flier Liability .......           30,000
```

In July, when a frequent flier takes a free trip costing the airline $150, American could record the transaction as follows:

July 8 Estimated Frequent Flier Liability 150
        Cash, Wages Payable, and other
         accounts 150

The credit side of this entry would depend on the airline's particular situation. Cash is credited for expenses paid currently, Wages Payable for the cost of ticketing passengers and baggage handling, and so on.

Contingent Liabilities

OBJECTIVE 2

Account for contingent liabilities

A *contingent liability* is not an actual liability. Instead, it is a potential liability that depends on a *future* event arising out of a past transaction. For example, a town government may sue the company that installed new street lights, claiming that the electrical wiring is faulty. The past transaction is the street-light installation. The future event is the court case that will decide the suit. The lighting company thus faces a contingent liability, which may or may not become an actual obligation.

It would be unethical for the company to withhold knowledge of the lawsuit from its creditors and from anyone considering investing in the business. A person or business could be misled into thinking the company is stronger financially than it really is. The disclosure principle of accounting requires a company to report any information deemed relevant to outsiders of the business. The goal is to arm people with relevant, reliable information for decision making.

Sometimes the contingent liability has a definite amount. From Chapter 8 recall that the payee of a discounted note has a contingent liability. If the maker of the note pays at maturity, the contingent liability ceases to exist. However, if the maker defaults, the payee, who sold the note, must pay its maturity value to the purchaser. In this case, the payee knows the note's maturity value, which is the amount of the contingent liability.

Another contingent liability of known amount arises from guaranteeing that another company will pay a note payable that the other company owes to a third party. This practice, called cosigning a note, obligates the guarantor to pay the note and interest if, and only if, the primary debtor fails to pay. Thus the guarantor has a contingent liability until the note becomes due. If the primary debtor pays off, the contingent liability ceases to exist. If the primary debtor fails to pay, the guarantor's liability becomes actual.

The amount of a contingent liability may be hard to determine. For example, companies face lawsuits, which may cause possible obligations of amounts to be determined by the courts.

Contingent liabilities may be reported in two ways. In what is called a **short presentation,** the contingent liability appears in the body of the balance sheet, after total liabilities, but with no amount given. Generally an explanatory note accompanies a short presentation. Sears, Roebuck and Company reported contingent liabilities this way:

	Millions
Total liabilities	$27,830.7
Contingent liabilities (note 10)	—

Note 10: Various legal actions and governmental proceedings are pending against Sears, Roebuck and Co. and its subsidiaries. . . . The consequences of these matters are not presently determinable but, in the opinion of management, the ultimate liability resulting, if any, will not have a material effect on the company.

Discussion Question: You are president of a utility company which has just completed a nuclear power plant. Nuclear leaks in other plants resulted in millions of dollars in legal damages. Should your company report a contingent liability? ANSWER: No. A contingent liability results from a past transaction. No nuclear leak has yet occurred in your plant.

Real-World Example: According to *Accounting Trends and Techniques* (AICPA, 1990), many companies report contingencies. Of 600 companies surveyed, 379 reported loss contingencies from litigation, and 128 reported loss contingencies from environmental regulation. 220 of the surveyed companies used the short form for reporting contingencies. The rest reported their contingencies in the footnotes.

Real-World Example: The Manville Corporation filed for bankruptcy in 1982 and shocked the financial community. An asbestos manufacturer, the corporation was a target of numerous lawsuits. The lawsuits were first disclosed in financial

Contingent liabilities do not have to be mentioned in the body of the balance sheet. Many companies use a second method of reporting, presenting the footnote only. International Business Machines Corporation (IBM) mentions its contingent liabilities in a half-page supplementary note labeled *litigation*.

The line between a contingent liability and a real liability may be hard to draw. As a practical guide, the FASB says to record an actual liability if (1) it is probable that the business has suffered a loss and (2) its amount can be reasonably estimated. If both of these conditions are met, the FASB reasons that the obligation has passed from contingent to real, even if its amount must be estimated. Suppose that at the balance sheet date, a hospital has lost a court case for uninsured malpractice but the amount of damages is uncertain. The hospital estimates that the liability will fall between $1.0 and $2.5 million. In this case, the hospital must record a loss or expense and a liability for $1.0 million. The income statement will report the loss and the balance sheet the liability. Also, the hospital must disclose in a note the possibility of an additional $1.5 million loss.

statement footnotes in 1979. By 1982, the claims that had accumulated exceeded the corporation's assets and caused it to file for bankruptcy.

Point to Stress: Contingent liabilities should be reported on the balance sheet if it is probable that the business has suffered a loss and the loss can be reasonably estimated. The possibility of contingent liability loss is disclosed in a footnote.

Summary Problem for Your Review

This problem consists of three independent parts.

1. A Wendy's hamburger restaurant made cash sales of $4,000 subject to a 5 percent sales tax. Record the sales and the related sales tax. Also record Wendy's payment of the tax to the state government.

2. At April 30, 19X2, H. J. Heinz Company reported its 6 percent long-term debt:

    Current Liabilities (in part)

Portion of long-term debt due within one year	$ 14,000,000
Interest payable ($200 × .06 × 5/12)	5,000,000

    Long-Term Debt and Other Liabilities (in part)

Long-term debt	$186,000,000

    The company pays interest on its long-term debt on November 30 each year.

    Show how Heinz Company would report its liabilities on the year-end balance sheet at April 30, 19X3. Assume the current maturity of its long-term debt is $16 million.

3. What distinguishes a contingent liability from an actual liability?

SOLUTION TO REVIEW PROBLEM

1. | | | |
    |---|---:|---:|
    | Cash ($4,000 × 1.05) .... | 4,200 | |
    | Sales Revenue .... | | 4,000 |
    | Sales Tax Payable ($4,000 × .05) .... | | 200 |
    | To record cash sales and related sales tax. | | |

Sales Tax Payable.............................	200	
Cash		200
To pay sales tax to the state government.		

2. H. J. Heinz Company balance sheet at April 30, 19X3:

Current Liabilities (in part)

Portion of long-term debt due within one year	$ 16,000,000
Interest payable ($186 × .06 × 5/12)	4,650,000

Long-Term Debt and Other Liabilities (in part)

Long-term debt	$170,000,000

3. A contingent liability is a *potential* liability, which may or may not become an actual liability.

Accounting for Payroll

Objective 3
Compute payroll amounts

Payroll, also called *employee compensation,* is a major expense of many businesses. For service organizations, such as CPA firms, real estate brokers, and travel agents, payroll is *the* major expense of conducting business. Service organizations sell their personnel's services, so employee compensation is their primary cost of doing business, just as cost of goods sold is the largest expense in merchandising.

Employee compensation takes different forms. Some employees collect a **salary,** which is income stated at a yearly, monthly, or weekly rate. Other employees work for **wages,** which is employee pay stated at an hourly figure. Sales employees often receive a **commission,** which is a percentage of the sales the employee has made. Some companies reward excellent performance with a **bonus,** an amount over and above regular compensation.

Businesses often pay employees at a base rate for a set number of hours—called straight time. For working any additional hours—called overtime—the employee receives a higher rate.

Assume that Lucy Childres is an accountant for an electronics company. Lucy earns $600 per week straight time. The company workweek runs 40 hours, so Lucy's hourly straight-time pay is $15 ($600/40). Her company pays her **time and a half** for overtime. That rate is 150 percent (1.5 times) the straight-time rate. Thus Lucy earns $22.50 for each hour of overtime she works ($15.00 × 1.5 = $22.50). For working 42 hours during a week, she earns $645, computed as follows:

Straight-time pay for 40 hours	$600
Overtime pay for 2 overtime hours:	
2 × $22.50	45
Total pay	$645

Gross Pay and Net Pay

Many years ago, employees brought home all that they had earned. For example, Lucy Childres would have taken home the full $645 total that she made. Payroll accounting was straightforward. Those days are long past.

The federal government, most state governments, and even some city governments demand that employers act as collection agents for employee taxes, which are deducted from employee checks. Insurance companies, labor unions, and other organizations may also receive pieces of employees' pay. Amounts withheld from an employee's check are called deductions.

Gross pay is the total amount of salary, wages, commissions, or any other employee compensation before taxes and other deductions are taken out. **Net pay**—the gross pay minus all deductions—is the amount that the employee actually takes home.

Many companies also pay employee **fringe benefits,** which are a form of employee compensation. Examples include health and life insurance paid directly to the insurance companies. Another example is retirement pay, which the employee does not receive immediately in cash. Payroll accounting has become quite complex. Let's turn now to a discussion of payroll deductions.

Payroll Deductions

Payroll deductions that are *withheld* from employees' pay fall into two categories: (1) *required deductions,* which include employee income tax and social security tax; and (2) *optional deductions,* which include union dues, insurance premiums, charitable contributions, and other amounts that are withheld at the employee's request. After they are withheld, payroll deductions become the liability of the employer, who assumes responsibility for paying the outside party. For example, the employer pays the government the employee income tax withheld and pays the union the employee union dues withheld.

Required Payroll Deductions

Employee Income Tax. The law requires most employers to withhold income tax from their employees' salaries and wages. The amount of income tax deducted from gross pay is called **withheld income tax.** For many employees, this deduction is the largest. The amount withheld depends on the employee's gross pay and on the number of withholding allowances the employee claims.

Each employee may claim himself or herself, his or her spouse, and each dependent as a withholding allowance. An unmarried taxpayer has one allowance, a married couple two allowances, a married couple with one child three allowances, and so on. Each allowance lowers the amount of tax withheld from the employee's paycheck. The employee files a Form W-4 with the employer to indicate the number of allowances claimed for withholding purposes. Exhibit 11-1 shows a W-4 for R. C. Dean, who claims four.

The employer sends its employees' withheld income tax to the government. The amount of the income tax withheld determines how often the employer submits tax payments. The employer must remit the taxes to the government

Point to Stress: Even though your tax return is not due until April 15, most of the taxes owed should have been deducted from your paycheck by the end of the previous year.

EXHIBIT 11-1 W-4 Form

- - - - - - - Cut here and give the certificate to your employer. Keep the top portion for your records. - - - - - - -

| Form **W-4** Department of the Treasury Internal Revenue Service | **Employee's Withholding Allowance Certificate** ▶ For Privacy Act and Paperwork Reduction Act Notice, see reverse. | OMB No. 1545-0010 19**91** |

1 Type or print your first name and middle initial R.C.   Last name Dean   **2** Your social security number 344-86-4529

Home address (number and street or rural route) 4376 Palm Drive

City or town, state, and ZIP code Fort Lauderdale, FL 33317

3 Marital status ☐ Single ☒ Married ☐ Married, but withhold at higher Single rate. **Note:** If married, but legally separated, or spouse is a nonresident alien, check the Single box.

4 Total number of allowances you are claiming (from line G above or from the Worksheets on back if they apply) . . . **4**

5 Additional amount, if any, you want deducted from each pay . . . . **5** $

6 I claim exemption from withholding and I certify that I meet **ALL** of the following conditions for exemption:
- Last year I had a right to a refund of **ALL** Federal income tax withheld because I had **NO** tax liability; **AND**
- This year I expect a refund of **ALL** Federal income tax withheld because I expect to have **NO** tax liability; **AND**
- This year if my income exceeds $550 and includes nonwage income, another person cannot claim me as a dependent.

If you meet all of the above conditions, enter the year effective and "EXEMPT" here . . . ▶ **6** 19

7 Are you a full-time student? (**Note:** *Full-time students are not automatically exempt.*) . . . . **7** ☐ Yes ☒ No

Under penalties of perjury, I certify that I am entitled to the number of withholding allowances claimed on this certificate or entitled to claim exempt status.

Employee's signature ▶ *R.C. Dean*   Date ▶ 7-22 , 19 92

8 Employer's name and address (**Employer:** Complete 8 and 10 **only if** sending to IRS) Blumenthal's Crescent Square Shopping Center Fort Lauderdale, FL 33310   **9** Office code (optional) 14   **10** Employer identification number 83-19475

at least quarterly. Every business must account for payroll taxes on a calendar-year basis regardless of its fiscal year.

The employer accumulates taxes in the Employee Income Tax Payable account. The word *payable* indicates that the account is the employer's liability to the government, even though the employees are the people taxed.

Employee Social Security (FICA) Tax.   The *Federal Insurance Contributions Act (FICA),* also known as the Social Security Act, created the Social Security Tax. The Social Security program provides retirement, disability, and medical benefits. The law requires employers to withhold **Social Security (FICA) tax** from employees' pay. The amount of tax withheld from employees' pay varies from year to year. Congress adjusts tax rates and the level of employee pay subject to the tax as shown in Exhibit 11-2 for the retirement benefit portion of the tax. The Medicare portion of the Social Security tax—also included in the 7.65 percent tax rate—applies to higher levels of employee earnings.

Because the FICA tax rate is approximately 8 percent of the first $50,000 that the employee earns in a year, we use these figures in our examples and in the assignment materials at the end of the chapter. For each employee who earns

EXHIBIT 11-2 Social Security Taxes

Year	Employee Earnings Subject to the Tax	Social Security (FICA) Tax Rate	Maximum Amount of Social Security (FICA) Tax Withheld from Employee Pay During the Year
1991	$53,400	.0765	$4,085
1992	*	.0765	*
⋮	⋮	⋮	⋮
1996	69,000†	.0765	5,279†

*Not set by Congress at the time of this writing.
†Estimated

$50,000 or more, the employer withholds $4,000 ($50,000 X .08) from the employee's pay and sends that amount to the federal government. The employer records this employee tax in the account FICA Tax Payable.

Assume that Rex Jennings, an employee, earned $48,500 prior to December. Jennings's salary for December is $3,500. How much FICA tax will be withheld from his December paycheck? The computation follows.

Employee earnings subject to the tax in one year	$50,000
Employee earnings prior to the current pay period	48,500
Current pay subject to FICA tax	$ 1,500
FICA tax rate	× .08
FICA tax to be withheld from current pay	$ 120

Optional Payroll Deductions

As a convenience to its employees, many companies make payroll deductions and disburse cash according to employee instructions. Union dues, insurance payments, payroll savings plans, and gifts to charities are examples. The account Employees' Union Dues Payable holds employee deductions for union membership.

Employer Payroll Taxes

Employers must bear the expense of at least three payroll taxes: (1) Social Security (FICA) tax, (2) state **unemployment compensation tax,** and (3) federal unemployment compensation tax.

Employer FICA Tax. In addition to the responsibility for handling the employee contribution to Social Security, the employer also must pay into the program. The employer's Social Security tax is the same as the amount withheld from employee pay. Thus the Social Security system is funded by equal contributions from employees and employers. Using our 8 percent and $50,000 annual pay figures, the maximum annual employer tax on each employee is $4,000 ($50,000 X .08). The liability account the employer uses for this payroll tax is the same FICA Tax Payable account used for the amount withheld from employee pay. The tax rate and the amount of earnings subject to the tax both change as Congress passes new legislation.

State and Federal Unemployment Compensation Taxes. These two payroll taxes are products of the Federal Unemployment Tax Act (FUTA). In recent years, employers have paid a combined tax of 6.2 percent on the first $7,000 of each employee's annual earnings. The proportion paid to the state is 5.4 percent, and 0.8 percent is paid to the federal government. The state government then uses the money to pay unemployment benefits to people who are out of work. The employer uses the accounts Federal Unemployment Tax Payable and State Unemployment Tax Payable. Exhibit 11-3 shows a typical disbursement of payroll costs by an employer company.

Payroll Entries

Exhibit 11-4 summarizes an employer's entries to record a monthly payroll of $10,000 (all amounts are assumed for illustration only).

Gross pay	$190,000
FICA rate	8%
Empl. fed. inc. tax withheld	$ 35,800
State unemployment tax rate	5.4%
Fed. unemployment tax rate	.8%
Life insurance paid by employees . . .	2,000

ANSWER:

Payroll entry:

Salary Expense . . .	190,000	
FICA Tax Pay . . .		15,200
Life Insurance Premiums Pay. . .		2,000
Empl. Inc. Tax Pay.		35,800
Salary Payable . . .		137,000

Payment of payroll taxes:

Payroll Tax Exp. . .	26,980	
FICA Tax Pay. . . .		15,200
Fed. Unempl. Tax Pay.		10,260
State Unempl. Tax Pay.		1,520

Objective 4
Make basic payroll entries

EXHIBIT 11-3 Typical Disbursement of Payroll Costs by an Employer Company

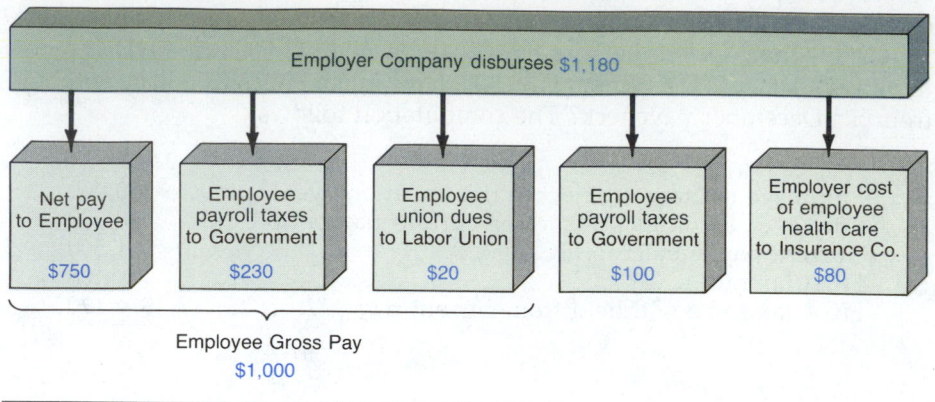

Entry A in Exhibit 11-4 records the employer's *salary expense*. The *gross salary* of all employees, $10,000, is their monthly pay before any deductions. The federal government imposes the two taxes. Most states and some cities also levy income taxes, which are accounted for in like manner. The union dues are optional. Employees' take-home (net) pay is $7,860. One important point about this payroll transaction is that the employees pay their own income and FICA taxes and union dues. The employer serves merely as a collecting agent and sends these amounts to the government and the union.

Entry B records the employer's *payroll taxes*. In addition to the employees' FICA tax ($800 in entry A), the employer must also pay the $800 FICA tax shown in entry B. The other two employer payroll taxes are state and federal unemployment taxes. Employees make no payments for unemployment taxes.

Entry C records employee *fringe benefits* paid by the employer. The company in the exhibit pays health and life insurance for its employees, a common

EXHIBIT 11-4 Payroll Accounting by the Employer

A.	Salary Expense (or Wage Expense or Commission Expense)	10,000	
	Employee Income Tax Payable		1,200
	FICA Tax Payable ($10,000 × .08)		800
	Employee Union Dues Payable		140
	Salary Payable to Employees (take-home pay)		7,860
	To record *salary expense*.		
B.	Payroll Tax Expense	1,420	
	FICA Tax Payable ($10,000 × .08)		800
	State Unemployement Tax Payable ($10,000 × .054)		540
	Federal Unemployment Tax Payable ($10,000 × .008)		80
	To record employer's *payroll taxes*.		
C.	Health Insurance Expense for Employees	800	
	Life Insurance Expense for Employees	200	
	Pension Expense	500	
	Employee Benefits Payable		1,500
	To record employee *fringe benefits* payable by employer.		

practice. Also, the employer funds pensions (that is, pays cash into a pension plan) for the benefit of employees when they retire. In the exhibit, the employer's pension expense for the month is $500, and the total employer expense for fringe benefits is $1,500. The total payroll expense of the employer in Exhibit 11-4 is $12,920 (gross salary of $10,000 + employer payroll taxes of $1,420 + fringe benefits of $1,500).

A company's payments to people who are not employees—outsiders called independent contractors—are *not* company payroll expenses. Consider two CPAs, Fermi and Scott. Fermi is a corporation's chief financial officer. Scott is the corporation's outside auditor. Fermi is an employee of the corporation and his compensation is a debit to Salary Expense. Scott, on the other hand, performs auditing service for many clients, and the corporation debits Auditing Expense when it pays her. Any payment for services performed by a person outside the company is a debit to an expense account other than payroll.

Point to Stress: The fringe benefits are expenses of the employer. These do not represent amounts withheld from the employee's check.

The Payroll System

Good business means paying employees accurately and paying them on time. Also, companies face the legal responsibility for handling employees' and their own payroll taxes, as we have seen. These demands require companies to process a great deal of payroll data. Efficient accounting is important. To make payroll accounting accurate and timely, accountants have developed the payroll system.

The components of the payroll system are a *payroll register*, a special *payroll bank account*, *payroll checks*, and an *earnings record* for each employee.

Real-World Example: In 1938, Congress passed the Fair Labor Standards Act, which imposed strict recordkeeping and reporting requirements on employers. A payroll journal or record had to be kept by pay period to report each employee's gross pay, all deductions, and net pay.

Payroll Register

Each pay period, the company organizes the payroll data in a special journal called the *payroll register*, or *payroll journal*. This register lists each employee and the figures the business needs to record payroll amounts. The payroll register, which resembles the cash disbursements journal, or check register, also serves as a check register by providing a column for recording each payroll check number.

The payroll register in Exhibit 11-5 includes sections for recording Gross Pay, Deductions, Net Pay, and Account Debited. *Gross Pay* has columns for straight-time pay, overtime pay, and total gross pay for each employee. Columns under the *Deductions* heading vary from company to company. Of course the employer must deduct federal income tax and FICA tax. (State income tax is left out for convenience.) Additional column headings depend on which optional deductions the business handles. In the exhibit, the employer deducts employee payroll taxes, union dues, and gifts to United Way and then sends the amounts to the proper parties. The business may add deduction columns as needed. The *Net Pay* section lists each employee's net (take-home) pay and the number of the check issued to him or her. The last two columns indicate the *Account Debited* for the employee's gross pay. (The company has office workers and salespeople.)

In the exhibit, W. L. Chen earned gross pay of $500. His net pay was $381.45, paid with check number 1621. Chen is an office worker, so his salary is debited to Office Salary Expense.

OBJECTIVE 5
Use a payroll-accounting system

Teaching Tip: Look at the Gross Pay column in Exhibit 11-5. Straight-time pay for R. C. Dean is 40 hours × $10 = $400. His overtime pay is the overtime hours multiplied by 1½ times the regular pay rate (6 hours × $15 = $90). Overtime pay must be computed before gross pay is computed.

Discussion Question: Companies should monitor overtime to see when it is more economical to hire another employee than to pay overtime. Should the company in Exhibit 11-5 hire another employee? *ANSWER:* No. Straight time × 3/2 = overtime, so straight time = overtime ÷ 3/2:

$$\text{Straight time} = \$714 \div \tfrac{3}{2}$$
$$= \$714 \times \tfrac{2}{3}$$
$$= \$476$$

The company is paying $238 more for the overtime, just over half of the minimum $400 it would have to pay a new employee.

EXHIBIT 11-5 Payroll Register

Week ended December 27, 19X3

		a	b	c	d	e	f	g	h	i	j	k	l
		Gross Pay			Deductions					Net Pay		Account Debited	
Employee Name	Hours	Straight-time	Overtime	Total	Federal Income Tax	FICA Tax	Union Dues	United Way Charities	Total	(c–h) Amount	Check No.	Office Salary Expense	Sales Salary Expense
Chen, W. L.	40	500.00		500.00	71.05	40.00	5.00	2.50	118.55	381.45	1621	500.00	
Dean, R. C.	46	400.00	90.00	490.00	59.94	39.20		2.00	101.14	388.86	1622		490.00
Ellis, M.	41	560.00	21.00	581.00	86.14	46.48	5.00		137.62	443.38	1623	581.00	
Trimble, E. A.	40	1,360.00		1,360.00	463.22			15.00	478.22	881.78	1641		1,360.00
Total		12,940.00	714.00	13,654.00	3,167.76	861.94	85.00	155.00	4,269.70	9,384.30		4,464.00	9,190.00

Note that the business deducted no FICA tax from E. A. Trimble. She has already earned more than $50,000. Any employee whose earnings exceed this annual maximum pays no additional FICA tax during that year.[1]

The payroll register in Exhibit 11-5 gives the employer the information needed to record salary expense for the pay period. Using the total amounts for columns d through l, the employer records total salary expense as follows:

Dec. 27	Office Salary Expense	4,464.00	
	Sales Salary Expense	9,190.00	
	Employee Income Tax Payable		3,167.76
	FICA Tax Payable		861.94
	Employee Union Dues Payable		85.00
	Employee United Way Payable		155.00
	Salary Payable to Employees		9,384.30

Payroll Bank Account

After recording the payroll, the company books include a credit balance in Salary Payable to Employees for net pay of $9,384.30. (See column i in Exhibit 11-5.) How the business pays this liability depends on its payroll system. Many companies disburse paychecks to employees from a special payroll bank account. The employer draws a check for net pay ($9,384.30 in our illustration) on its regular bank account and deposits this check in the special payroll bank account. Then the company writes paychecks to employees out of the payroll account. When the paychecks clear the bank, the payroll account has a zero balance, ready for the activity of the next pay period. Disbursing paychecks from a separate bank account isolates net pay for analysis and control, as discussed later in the chapter.

Other payroll disbursements—for withheld taxes, union dues, and so on—are neither as numerous nor as frequent as weekly or monthly paychecks. The employer pays taxes, union dues, and charities from its regular bank account.

Point to Stress: Even a small business that uses a manual bookkeeping system may find a computer to be a great time-saving device for payroll recordkeeping. Very often a payroll report printed each pay period serves as the detailed payroll documentation required by law.

Payroll Checks

Most companies pay employees by check. A *payroll check* is like any other check except that its perforated attachment lists the employee's gross pay, payroll deductions, and net pay. These amounts are taken from the payroll register. Exhibit 11-6 shows payroll check number 1622, issued to R. C. Dean for net pay of $388.86 earned during the week ended December 27, 19X3. To enhance your ability to use payroll data, trace all amounts on the check attachment to the payroll register in Exhibit 11-5.

Increasingly, companies are paying employees by automatic deposits to the employee's personal bank account. By a prearranged agreement, the employee can authorize the company to make the deposit directly to the bank. With no check to write and deliver to the employee, the company saves time and money. The employee avoids the trouble of receiving, endorsing, and depositing the paycheck.

Point to Stress: A payable is credited when recording salary or wage expense. Often, a company needs time to assemble all the information for the payroll. There is sometimes a few days' lag from the end of the pay period to the actual payment date.

---

[1]For clarity we ignore the additional tax for Medicare benefits.

Recording Cash Disbursements for Payroll

Most employers must make at least three entries to record payroll cash disbursements: net pay to employees, payroll taxes to the government and payroll deductions, and employee fringe benefits.

Net Pay to Employees. When the employer issues payroll checks to employees, the company debits Salary Payable to Employees and credits Cash.

Using the data in Exhibit 11-5, the company would make the following entry to record the cash payment (column i) for the December 27 weekly payroll:

Point to Stress: Even though there are two sets of payroll taxes due (for taxes withheld from the employees and those paid by the employer), in reality the business sends only one check for federal taxes withheld and total social security taxes due.

Dec. 27	Salary Payable to Employees	9,384.30	
	Cash		9,384.30

Payroll Taxes to the Government and Payroll Deductions. The employer must send to the government two sets of payroll taxes: those withheld from employees' pay and those paid by the employer. Based on Exhibit 11-5, columns d through g, the business would record a series of cash payment entries summarized as follows (employer tax amounts are assumed):

Teaching Tip: According to this journal entry, what is the total amount that the business will pay to the government on December 27 for taxes withheld and social security taxes due? *ANSWER:* $3,167.76 + $1,723.88 = $4,891.64

Dec. 27	Employee Income Tax Payable	3,167.76	
	FICA Tax Payable ($861.94 × 2)	1,723.88	
	Employee Union Dues Payable	85.00	
	Employee United Way Payable	155.00	
	State Unemployment Tax Payable	104.62	
	Federal Unemployment Tax Payable	15.50	
	Cash		5,251.76

EXHIBIT 11-6 *Payroll Check*

Blumenthal's
Payroll Account
Fort Lauderdale, FL

1622

12-27 19 X3

Pay to the Order of _____ R.C. Dean _____ $ 388.86

Three hundred eighty-eight & 86/100 . . . . Dollars

Republic Bank
Fort Lauderdale,
Florida 33310

Anna Figaro

Treasurer

⑈ ⑆111900031⑆ 078 7⑈ 500004 54⑈

Pay			Deductions					Net Pay	Check No.
Straight-time	Over-time	Gross	Income Tax	FICA	Union Dues	United Way	Total		
400.00	90.00	490.00	59.94	39.20		2.00	101.14	388.86	1622

Fringe Benefits. The employer might pay for employees' insurance coverage and pension plan. Assuming the total cash payment for these benefits is $1,927.14, this entry for payments to third parties would be

Dec. 27	Employee Benefits Payable...............	1,927.14	
	Cash		1,927.14

Earnings Record

The employer must file payroll tax returns with the federal and state governments and must provide the employee with a wage and tax statement, Form W-2, at the end of the year. Therefore, employers maintain an earnings record for each employee. Exhibit 11-7 is a five-week excerpt from the earnings record of employee R. C. Dean.

The employee earnings record is not a journal or a ledger, and it is not required by law. It is an accounting tool—like the work sheet—that the employer uses to prepare payroll tax reports. Year-to-date earnings also indicate when an employee has earned $50,000, the point at which the employer can stop deducting FICA tax.

Exhibit 11-8 is the Wage and Tax Statement, Form W-2, for employee R. C. Dean. The employer prepares this statement and gives copies to the employee and to the Internal Revenue Service (IRS). Dean uses the W-2 to prepare his personal income tax return. The IRS uses the W-2 to ensure that Dean is paying income tax on all his income from that job. The IRS matches Dean's income as reported on his tax return with his earnings as reported on the W-2.

Internal Control over Payrolls

The internal controls over cash disbursements discussed in Chapter 7 apply to payroll. In addition, companies adopt special controls in payroll accounting. The large number of transactions and the many different parties involved increase the risk of a control failure. Accounting systems feature two types of special controls over payroll: controls for efficiency and controls for safeguarding cash.

Controls for Efficiency

For companies with many employees, reconciling the bank account can be time consuming because of the large number of outstanding payroll checks. For example, a March 30 payroll check would probably not have time to clear the bank before a bank statement on March 31. This check and others in a March 30 payroll would be outstanding. Identifying a large number of outstanding checks for the bank reconciliation increases accounting expense. To limit the number of outstanding checks, many companies use two payroll bank accounts. They make payroll disbursements from one payroll account one month and from the other payroll account the next month. By reconciling each account every other month, a March 30 paycheck has until April 30 to clear the bank before the account is reconciled. This essentially eliminates outstanding checks, cuts down the time it takes to prepare the bank reconciliation, and decreases accounting expense. Also, many companies' checks become void if not cashed within a certain period of time. This too limits the number of outstanding checks.

Teaching Tip: The To Date column in Exhibit 11-7 shows how much gross pay R. C. Dean has accumulated during the year. Gross pay must go on the W-2 form. It also shows which employees have exceeded the base for FICA and unemployment taxes. R. C. Dean is not near the maximum salary established for FICA, but has exceeded the base established for unemployment taxes.

EXHIBIT 11-7 *Employee Earnings Record for 19X3*

Employee Name and Address:

Dean, R. C.
4376 Palm Drive
Fort Lauderdale, FL 33317

Social Security No.: 344-86-4529
Marital Status: Married
Withholding Exemptions: 4
Pay Rate: $400 per week
Job Title: Salesperson

Week Ended	Hours	Gross Pay				Deductions					Net Pay	
		Straight-time	Overtime	Total	To Date	Federal Income Tax	FICA Tax	Union Dues	United Way Charities	Total	Amount	Check No.
Nov. 29	40	400.00		400.00	21,340.00	42.19	32.00		2.00	76.19	323.81	1525
Dec. 6	40	400.00		400.00	21,740.00	42.19	32.00		2.00	76.19	323.81	1548
Dec. 13	44	400.00	60.00	460.00	22,200.00	54.76	36.80		2.00	93.56	366.44	1574
Dec. 20	48	400.00	120.00	520.00	22,720.00	66.75	41.60		2.00	110.35	409.65	1598
Dec. 27	46	400.00	90.00	490.00	23,210.00	59.94	39.20		2.00	101.14	388.86	1622
Total		20,800.00	2,410.00	23,210.00		2,346.72	1,856.80		104.00	4,307.52	18,902.48	

EXHIBIT 11-8 *Employee Wage and Tax Statement, Form W-2*

1 Control number	2222	For Paperwork Reduction Act Notice, see separate instructions OMB No. 1545-0008	**For Official Use only ▶**			
2 Employer's name, address, and ZIP code			6 Statutory employee ⊠ Deceased ☐ Pension plan ☐ Legal rep. ☐ 942 emp. ☐ Subtotal ☐ Deferred compensation ☐ Void ☐			

2 Employer's name, address, and ZIP code

Blumenthal's
Crescent Square Shopping Center
Fort Lauderdale, FL 33310

7 Allocated tips | 8 Advance EIC payment

9 Federal income tax withheld 2,346.72 | 10 Wages, tips, other compensation 23,210.00

3 Employer's identification number 83-19475 | 4 Employer's state I.D. number
11 Social security tax withheld 1,856.80 | 12 Social security wages 23,210.00

5 Employee's social security number 344-86-4529
13 Social security tips | 14 Nonqualified plans

19a Employee's name, address and ZIP code
R.C. Dean
15 Dependent care benefits | 16 Fringe benefits incl. in Box 10

4376 Palm Drive
Fort Lauderdale, FL 33310
17 See instr. for Forms W-2/W-2P | 18 Other

19b Employee's address and ZIP code

20 | 21 | 22 | 23

24 State income tax | 25 State wages, tips, etc. | 26 Name of state | 27 Local income tax | 28 Local wages, tips, etc. | 29 Name of locality

Copy A For Social Security Administration   Dept. of the Treasury—Internal Revenue Service

Form **W-2 Wage and Tax Statement 1990**

Do NOT CUT or Separate Forms on This Page

---

1 Control number	2222	For Paperwork Reduction Act Notice, see separate instructions OMB No. 1545-0008	**For Official Use only ▶**

2 Employer's name, address, and ZIP code

6 Statutory employee ⊠ Deceased Pension plan Legal rep. 942 emp. Subtotal Deferred compensation Void

Blumenthal's
Crescent Square Shopping Center
Fort Lauderdale, FL 33310

7 Allocated tips | 8 Advance EIC payment

9 Federal income tax withheld 2,346.72 | 10 Wages, tips, other compensation 23,210.00

3 Employer's identification number 83-19475 | 4 Employer's state I.D. number
11 Social security tax withheld 1,856.80 | 12 Social security wages 23,210.00

5 Employee's social security number 344-86-4529
13 Social security tips | 14 Nonqualified plans

19a Employee's name, address and ZIP code
R.C. Dean
15 Dependent care benefits | 16 Fringe benefits incl. in Box 10

4376 Palm Drive
Fort Lauderdale, FL 33310
17 See instr. for Forms W-2/W-2P | 18 Other

19b Employee's address and ZIP code

20 | 21 | 22 | 23

24 State income tax | 25 State wages, tips, etc. | 26 Name of state | 27 Local income tax | 28 Local wages, tips, etc. | 29 Name of locality

Copy A For Social Security Administration   Dept. of the Treasury—Internal Revenue Service

Form **W-2 Wage and Tax Statement 1990**

Other payroll controls for efficiency include following established policies for hiring and firing employees and complying with government regulations. Hiring and firing policies provide guidelines for keeping a qualified, diligent work force dedicated to achieving the business's goals. Complying with government regulations avoids paying fines and penalties.

Controls for Safeguarding Cash

Owners and managers of small businesses can monitor their payroll disbursements by personal contact with their employees. Large corporations cannot do so. These businesses must establish controls to ensure that payroll disbursements are made only to legitimate employees and for the correct amounts. A particular danger is that payroll checks may be written to a fictitious employee and cashed by a dishonest employee. To guard against this crime and other possible breakdowns in internal control, large businesses adopt strict internal control policies.

The duties of hiring and firing employees should be separated from the duties of distributing paychecks. Otherwise, a dishonest supervisor, for example, could add a fictitious employee to the payroll. When paychecks are issued, the supervisor could simply pocket the nonexistent person's paycheck for his or her own use.

Requiring an identification badge bearing an employee's photograph helps internal control. Issuing paychecks only to employees with badges ensures that only actual employees receive pay.

Point to Stress: Another internal control feature is direct depositing of paychecks into employees' bank accounts. This eliminates the possibility of lost or stolen checks and makes it more difficult to deposit checks to a fictitious employee. It is also advantageous to compare the list of current employees to a list of employees who have recently left the company in order to ensure that terminated employees are not receiving paychecks.

On occasion management should instruct an employee from the home office, perhaps an internal auditor, to distribute checks in the branch office personally rather than have the payroll department mail the checks. No one will claim a paycheck that has been issued to a fictitious employee. Any check left over after the distribution signals that payroll fraud has been attempted. Management would pursue an investigation.

A time-keeping system helps ensure that employees have actually worked the number of hours claimed. Having employees punch time cards at the start and end of the workday proves their attendance—as long as management makes sure that no employee punches in and out for others too. Some companies have their workers fill in weekly or monthly time sheets.

Again we see that the key to good internal control is separation of duties. The responsibilities of the personnel department, the payroll department, the accounting department, time-card management, and paycheck distribution should be kept separate.

Reporting Payroll Expense and Liabilities

OBJECTIVE 6
Report current liabilities

Point to Stress: Employers have mountains of paperwork to file and maintain for payrolls. Let's review these:

Form 941— Employer's Quarterly Federal Tax Return. Reports FICA and income tax withheld. Must be filed quarterly and sometimes requires deposits of taxes up to eight times a quarter.

Form 940— Federal Unemployment Tax Return. Must be filed annually. May require

At the end of its fiscal year, the company reports the amount of *payroll liability* owed to all parties—employees, state and federal governments, unions, and so forth. Payroll liability is *not* the payroll expense for the year. The liability at year end is the amount of the expense that is still unpaid. Payroll expense appears on the income statement, payroll liability on the balance sheet.

Unisys Corporation reported accrued payrolls and commissions of approximately $164 million as a current liability on its year-end balance sheet (see Exhibit 11-9). However, Unisys's payroll expense for the year far exceeded $164 million. (Exhibit 11-9 also presents the other current liabilities that we have discussed in this chapter.)

Exhibit 11-10 summarizes all the current liabilities that we have discussed in this chapter.

Computer Accounting Systems for Current Liabilities

Current liabilities arising from a high volume of similar transactions are well suited for computerized accounting. One of the most common transactions of a merchandiser is the credit purchase of inventory. It is efficient to integrate the accounts payable and perpetual inventory systems. When merchandise

EXHIBIT 11-9 *Partial Unisys Corporation Balance Sheet*

Current Liabilities	Millions
Notes payable within one year	$ 397
Current maturities of long-term debt	31
Accounts payable	397
Accrued payrolls and commissions	**164**
Accrued taxes other than income taxes	69
Customers' deposits and prepayments	155
Dividends payable to shareholders..........	28
Estimated income taxes	111
Total current liabilities	$1,352

deposits of unemployment taxes during the year.

State Unemployment Tax Returns— Filed quarterly in most states.

Form W-2—Must be sent to every employee by January 31 detailing salary or wages, FICA taxes withheld, income taxes withheld, and various other data.

dips below a predetermined level, the system automatically prepares a purchase request. After the order is placed and the goods are received, inventory and accounts payable data are entered on magnetic tape. The computer reads the tape, then debits Inventory and credits Accounts Payable to account for the purchase. For payments, the computer debits Accounts Payable and credits Cash. The program may also update account balances and print journals, ledger accounts, and the financial statements.

The face amount of notes payable and their interest rates and payment dates can be stored for electronic data processing. Computer programs calculate interest, print the interest checks, journalize the transactions, and update account balances.

Payroll transactions are also ideally suited for computer processing. Employee pay rates and withholding data are stored on magnetic tape. Each payroll period, computer operators enter the number of hours worked by each employee. The machine performs the calculations, prints the payroll register and paychecks, and updates the employee earnings records. The program also computes payroll taxes and prepares quarterly reports to government agencies. Expense and liability accounts are automatically updated for the payroll transactions.

Transparency T11-3

EXHIBIT 11-10 *Categories of Current Liabilities*

Amount of Liability Known When Recorded	Amount of Liability Must Be Estimated When Recorded
Trade accounts payable	Warranty payable
Short-term notes payable	Income tax payable
Sales tax payable	Vacation pay liability
Current portion of long-term debt	
Accrued expenses payable:	
Interest payable	
Payroll liabilities (salary payable, wages payable, and commissions payable)	
Payroll taxes payable (employee and employer)	
Unearned revenues (revenues collected in advance of being earned)	
Customer deposits payable	

Summary Problem for Your Review

Beth Denius, Limited, a clothing store, employs one salesperson, Alan Kingsley. His straight-time pay is $360 per week. He earns time and a half for hours worked in excess of 40 per week. Denius withholds income tax (11.0 percent) and FICA tax (8.0 percent) from Kingsley's pay. She also pays the following employer payroll taxes: FICA (8.0 percent) and state and federal unemployment (5.4 percent and 0.8 percent, respectively). In addition, Denius contributes to a pension plan an amount equal to 10 percent of Kingsley's gross pay.

During the week ended December 26, 19X4, Kingsley worked 48 hours. Prior to this week Kingsley has earned $5,470.

Required

1. Compute Kingsley's gross pay and net pay for the week.
2. Record the following payroll entries that Denius would make:
   a. Expense for Kingsley's salary, including overtime pay
   b. Employer payroll taxes
   c. Expense for fringe benefits
   d. Payment of cash to Kingsley
   e. Payment of all payroll taxes
   f. Payment for fringe benefits
3. How much total payroll expense did Denius incur for the week? How much cash did the business spend on its payroll?

SOLUTION TO REVIEW PROBLEM

Requirement 1

Gross Pay:	Straight-time pay for 40 hours		$360.00
	Overtime pay:		
	Rate per hour ($360/40 × 1.5) ..	$ 13.50	
	Hours (48 − 40)	× 8	108.00
	Total gross pay		$468.00
Net Pay:	Gross pay		$468.00
	Less: Withheld income tax ($468 × .11) ...	$ 51.48	
	Withheld FICA tax ($468 × .08)	37.44	88.92
	Net pay		$379.08

Requirement 2

a.	Sales Salary Expense	468.00	
	Employee Income Tax Payable		51.48
	FICA Tax Payable		37.44
	Salary Payable to Employee		379.08
b.	Payroll Tax Expense	66.45	
	FICA Tax Payable ($468 × .08)		37.44
	State Unemployment Tax Payable ($468 × .054)..		25.27
	Federal Unemployment Tax Payable ($468 × .008)		3.74
c.	Pension Expense ($468 × .10)	46.80	
	Employee Benefits Payable....................		46.80
d.	Salary Payable to Employee	379.08	
	Cash...		379.08

e.	Employee Income Tax Payable	51.48	
	FICA Tax Payable ($37.44 × 2)	74.88	
	State Unemployment Tax Payable	25.27	
	Federal Unemployment Tax Payable	3.74	
	Cash...		155.37
f.	Employee Benefits Payable....................	46.80	
	Cash...		46.80

Requirement 3

Denius incurred *total payroll expense* of $581.25 (gross salary of $468.00 + payroll taxes of $66.45 + fringe benefits of $46.80). See entries a–c.

Denius *paid cash* of $581.25 on payroll (Kingsley's net pay of $379.08 + payroll taxes of $155.37 + fringe benefits of $46.80). See entries d–f.

Summary

Current liabilities may be divided into those of *known amount* and those that must be *estimated*. Trade accounts payable, short-term notes payable, and the related liability for accrued expenses are among current liabilities of known amount. Current liabilities that must be estimated are warranties payable and corporations' income tax payable.

Contingent liabilities are not actual liabilities but potential liabilities that may arise in the future. Contingent liabilities, like current liabilities, may be of known amount or an indefinite amount. A business that faces a lawsuit not yet decided in court has a contingent liability of indefinite amount.

Payroll accounting handles the expenses and liabilities arising from compensating employees. Employers must withhold income and FICA taxes from employees' pay and send these *employee payroll taxes* to the government. In addition, many employers allow their employees to pay for insurance and union dues and to make gifts to charities through payroll deductions. An employee's net pay is the gross pay less all payroll taxes and optional deductions.

An *employer's* payroll expenses include FICA and unemployment taxes, which are separate from the payroll taxes borne by the employees. Also, most employers provide their employees with fringe benefits, like insurance coverage and retirement pensions.

A *payroll system* consists of a payroll register, a payroll bank account, payroll checks, and an earnings record for each employee. Good *internal controls* over payroll disbursements help the business to conduct payroll accounting efficiently and to safeguard the company's cash. The cornerstone of internal controls is the separation of duties.

Current liabilities arising from a high volume of repetitive transactions are well suited for computer processing. Trade accounts payable, notes payable and the related interest, and payrolls are three examples.

Self-Study Questions

Test your understanding of the chapter by marking the best answer for each of the following questions.

1. A $10,000, 9 percent, one-year note payable was issued on July 31. The balance sheet at December 31 will report interest payable of (p. 502)
   a. $0 because the interest is not due yet
   b. $300
   √c. $375
   d. $900

2. If the note payable in the preceding question had been discounted, the cash proceeds from issuance would have been *(p. 502)*
   - ✓ a. $9,100
   - b. $9,625
   - c. $9,700
   - d. $10,000

3. Which of the following liabilities creates *no* expense for the company? *(p. 503)*
   - a. Interest
   - ✓ b. Sales tax
   - c. FICA tax
   - d. Warranty

4. Suppose Unitex Tire Company estimates that warranty costs will equal 1 percent of tire sales. Assume that November sales totaled $900,000, and the company's outlay in tires and cash to satisfy warranty claims was $7,400. How much warranty expense should the November income statement report? *(p. 506, 507)*
   - a. $1,600
   - b. $7,400
   - ✓ c. $9,000
   - d. $16,400

5. Apex Sporting Company is a defendant in a lawsuit that claims damages of $55,000. On the balance sheet date, it appears likely that the court will render a judgment against Apex. How should Apex report this event in its financial statements? *(pp. 508, 509)*
   - a. Omit mention because no judgment has been rendered
   - b. Disclose the contingent liability in a note
   - c. Use a short presentation only
   - ✓ d. Report the loss on the income statement and the liability on the balance sheet

6. Emilie Frontenac's weekly pay is $320, plus time and a half for overtime. The tax rates applicable to her earnings are 8 percent for income tax and 8 percent for FICA. What is Emilie's take-home pay for a week in which she works 50 hours? *(pp. 510, 513)*
   - ✓ a. $369.60
   - b. $392.00
   - c. $404.80
   - d. $440.00

7. Which payroll tax applies (or taxes apply) mainly to the employer? *(p. 513)*
   - a. Withheld income tax
   - b. FICA tax
   - ✓ c. Unemployment compensation tax
   - d. Both b and c

8. The main reason for using a separate payroll bank account is to *(p. 517)*
   - a. Safeguard cash by avoiding writing payroll checks to fictitious employees
   - b. Safeguard cash by limiting paychecks to amounts based on time cards
   - ✓ c. Increase efficiency by isolating payroll disbursements for analysis and control
   - d. All of the above

9. The key to good internal controls in the payroll area is *(p. 519)*
   - a. Using a payroll bank account
   - ✓ b. Separating payroll duties
   - c. Using a payroll register
   - d. Using time cards

10. Which of the following items is reported as a current liability on the balance sheet? *(p. 523)*
    - a. Short-term notes payable
    - b. Estimated warranties
    - c. Accrued payroll taxes
    - ✓ d. All of the above

Answers to the Self-Study Questions follow the Accounting Vocabulary.

Accounting Vocabulary

Bonus. Amount over and above regular compensation *(p. 510)*.

Commission. Employee compensation computed as a percentage of the sales that the employee has made *(p. 510)*.

Current portion of long-term debt. Amount of the principal that is payable within one year *(p. 504)*.

Discounting a note payable. A borrowing arrangement in which the bank subtracts the interest amount from the note's face value. The borrower receives the net amount *(p. 502)*.

FICA tax. Federal Insurance Contributions Act (FICA), or Social Security tax, which is withheld from employees' pay *(p. 512)*.

Fringe benefits. Employee compensation, like health and life insurance and retirement pay, which the employee does not receive immediately in cash *(p. 511)*.

Gross pay. Total amount of salary, wages, commissions, or any other employee compensation before taxes and other deductions are taken out *(p. 511)*.

Net pay. Gross pay minus all deductions, the amount of employee compensation that the employee actually takes home *(p. 511)*.

Payroll. Employee compensation, a major expense of many businesses *(p. 510)*.

Salary. Employee compensation stated at a yearly, monthly, or weekly rate *(p. 510)*.

Short presentation. A way to report contingent liabilities in the body of the balance sheet, after total liabilities but with no amount given *(p. 508)*.

Short-term note payable. Note payable due within one year, a common form of financing *(p. 501)*.

Social Security tax. Another name for FICA tax *(p. 512)*.

Time and a half. Overtime pay computed as 150 percent (1.5 times) the straight-time rate *(p. 510)*.

Unemployment compensation tax. Payroll tax paid by employers to the government, which uses the money to pay unemployment benefits to people who are out of work *(p. 513)*.

Wages. Employee pay stated at an hourly figure *(p. 510)*.

Withheld income tax. Income tax deducted from employees' gross pay *(p. 511)*.

Answers to Self-Study Questions

1. c $10,000 \times .09 \times 5/12 = \$375$
2. a $\$10,000 - (\$10,000 \times .09) = \$9,100$
3. b
4. c $\$900,000 \times .01 = \$9,000$
5. d
6. a Overtime pay: $\$320/40 = \$8 \times 1.5 = \$12$ per hour $\times 10$ hours $= \$120$
   Gross pay $= \$320 + \$120 = \$440$
   Deductions $= \$440 \times (.08 + .08) = \$70.40$
   Take-home pay $= \$440 - \$70.40 = \$369.60$
7. c
8. c
9. b
10. d

ASSIGNMENT MATERIAL

Questions

1. Give a more descriptive account title for each of the following current liabilities: Accrued Interest, Accrued Salaries, Accrued Income Tax.

2. What distinguishes a current liability from a long-term liability? What distinguishes a contingent liability from an actual liability?

3. A company purchases a machine by signing a $21,000, 10 percent, one-year note payable on July 31. Interest is to be paid at maturity. What two current liabilities related to this purchase does the company report on its December 31 balance sheet? What is the amount of each liability?

4. A company borrowed cash by discounting a $15,000, 8 percent, six-month note payable to the bank, receiving cash of $14,400. (a) Show how the amount of cash was computed. Also, identify (b) the total amount of interest expense to be recognized on this note and (c) the amount of the borrower's cash payment at maturity.

5. Explain how sales tax that is paid by consumers is a liability of the store that sold the merchandise.

6. What is meant by the term *current portion of long-term debt*, and how is this item reported in the financial statements?

7. At the beginning of the school term, what type of account is the tuition that your college or university collects from students? What type of account is the tuition at the end of the school term?

8. Why is a customer deposit a liability? Give an example.

9. Patton Company warrants its products against defects for three years from date of sale. During the current year, the company made sales of $300,000. Store management estimates warranty costs on those sales will total $18,000 over the three-year warranty period. Ultimately, the company paid $22,000 cash on warranties. What is the company's warranty expense for the year? What accounting principle governs this answer?

10. Identify two contingent liabilities of a definite amount and two contingent liabilities of an indefinite amount.

11. Describe two ways to report contingent liabilities.

12. Why is payroll expense relatively more important to a service business such as a CPA firm than it is to a merchandising company?

13. Two persons are studying Allen Company's manufacturing process. One person is Allen's factory supervisor, and the other person is an outside consultant who is an expert in the industry. Which person's salary is the payroll expense of Allen Company? Identify the expense account that Allen would debit to record the pay of each person.

14. What are two elements of an employer's payroll expense in addition to salaries, wages, commissions, and overtime pay?

15. What determines the amount of income tax that is withheld from employee paychecks?

16. What are FICA taxes? Who pays them? What are the funds used for?

17. Identify two required deductions and four optional deductions from employee paychecks.

18. Identify three employer payroll taxes.

19. Who pays state and federal unemployment taxes? What are these funds used for?

20. Briefly describe a payroll accounting system's components and their functions.

21. How much Social Security tax has been withheld from the pay of an employee who has earned $52,288 during the current year? How much Social Security tax must the employer pay for this employee?

22. Briefly describe the two principal categories of internal controls over payroll.

23. Why do some companies use two special payroll bank accounts?

24. Identify three internal controls designed to safeguard payroll cash.

Exercises

Sales tax payable $5,852

Exercise 11-1 *Recording sales tax two ways* **(L.O. 1)**

Make general journal entries to record the following transactions of Meridian Golf Company for a two-month period. Explanations are not required.

March 31 Recorded cash sales of $83,600 for the month, plus sales tax of 7 percent collected on behalf of the state of Idaho. Record sales tax in a separate account.

April 6 Sent March sales tax to the state.

Journalize these transactions a second time. Record the sales tax initially in the Sales Revenue account.

Exercise 11-2 *Accounting for warranty expense and the related liability* (*L.O. 1*)

Est. Warranty Pay. bal. $4,540

The accounting records of Nathan Cook, Inc., included the following balances at the end of the period:

Estimated Warranty Payable	Sales Revenue	Warranty Expense
Beg. bal. 4,100	141,000	

In the past, Cook's warranty expense has been 7 percent of sales. During the current period, Cook paid $9,430 to satisfy the warranty claims of customers.

Required

1. Record Cook's warranty expense for the period and the company's cash payments during the period to satisfy warranty claims. Explanations are not required.
2. What ending balance of Estimated Warranty Payable will Cook report on its balance sheet?

Exercise 11-3 *Recording note payable transactions* (*L.O. 1*)

Dec. 31 interest payable $400

Record the following note payable transactions of Toronto Development, Inc., in the company's general journal. Explanations are not required.

19X2

May 1 Purchased equipment costing $6,000 by issuing a one-year, 10 percent note payable.

Dec. 31 Accrued interest on the note payable.

19X3

May 1 Paid the note payable at maturity.

Exercise 11-4 *Discounting a note payable* (*L.O. 1*)

Note pay. short-term, net $11,520

On November 1, 19X4, Budget Counseling Center discounted a six-month, $12,000 note payable to the bank at 12 percent.

Required

1. Prepare general journal entries to record (a) issuance of the note, (b) accrual of interest at December 31, and (c) payment of the note at maturity in 19X5. Explanations are not required.
2. Show how the Budget Counseling Center would report the note on the December 31, 19X4, balance sheet.

Exercise 11-5 *Reporting a contingent liability* (*L.O. 2*)

No check figure

National Instrument Control is a defendant in lawsuits brought against the marketing and distribution of its products. Damages of $1.8 million are claimed against National, but the company denies the charges and is vigorously defending itself. In a recent talk-show interview, the president of the company stated that he could not predict the outcome of the lawsuits. Nevertheless, he said, management does not believe that any actual liabilities resulting from the lawsuits will significantly affect the company's financial position.

Required

Prepare a partial balance sheet to show how National Instrument Control would report this contingent liability in a short presentation. Total actual liabilities are $4.7 million. Also, write the disclosure note to describe the contingency.

No check figure

Exercise 11-6 *Accruing a contingency* (L.O. 2)

Refer to the National Instrument Control situation in the preceding exercise. Suppose National's attorneys believe it is probable that a judgment of $500,000 will be rendered against the company.

Required

Describe how to report this situation in the National Instrument Control financial statements. Journalize any entry required under GAAP. Explanations are not required.

Gross pay $5,454
Net pay $4,716.84

Exercise 11-7 *Computing net pay* (L.O. 3)

Hatch Bailey is a salesman in the men's department of Rich's Department Store in Atlanta. He earns a base monthly salary of $550 plus an 8 percent commission on his sales. Through payroll deductions, Hatch donates $5 per month to a charitable organization, and he authorizes Rich's to deduct $12.50 monthly for health insurance on his family. Tax rates on Hatch's earnings are 9 percent for income tax and 8 percent for FICA, subject to the maximum. During the first 11 months of the year, he earned $47,140. Compute Hatch's gross pay and net pay for December, assuming his sales for the month are $61,300.

Wage payable $213.94

Exercise 11-8 *Computing and recording gross pay and net pay* (L.O. 3, 4)

Sandy Jastremsky works for a Seven-Eleven store for straight-time earnings of $6 per hour, with time-and-a-half compensation for hours in excess of 40 per week. Sandy's payroll deductions include withheld income tax of 10 percent of total earnings, FICA tax of 8 percent of total earnings, and a weekly deduction of $5 for a charitable contribution to United Fund. Assuming Sandy worked 43 hours during the week, (a) compute her gross pay and net pay for the week, and (b) make a general journal entry to record the store's wage expense for Sandy's work, including her payroll deductions. Explanations are not required. Round all amounts to the nearest cent.

Payroll tax exp. $3,636.20

Exercise 11-9 *Recording a payroll* (L.O. 3, 4)

Famous & Barr Department Store incurred salary expense of $42,000 for December. The store's payroll expense includes employer FICA tax of 8 percent in addition to state unemployment tax of 5.4 percent and federal unemployment tax of 0.8 percent. Of the total salaries, $38,400 is subject to FICA tax, and $9,100 is subject to unemployment tax. Also, the store provides the following fringe benefits for employees: health insurance (cost to the store, $1,062.15); life insurance (cost to the store, $351.07); and pension benefits (cost to the store, $707.60). Record Famous & Barr's payroll taxes and its expenses for employee fringe benefits. Explanations are not required.

Exercise 11-10 *Reporting current and long-term liabilities* **(L.O. 6)**

Interest payable:
19X1, $45,000
19X5, $9,000

Suppose Jack in the Box borrowed $500,000 on December 31, 19X0, by issuing 9 percent long-term debt that must be paid in annual installments of $100,000 plus interest each January 2. By inserting appropriate amounts in the following excerpts from the company's partial balance sheet, show how Jack in the Box would report its long-term debt.

| | December 31, | | | | |
	19X1	19X2	19X3	19X4	19X5
Current liabilities:					
Current portion of long-term debt .	$___	$___	$___	$___	$___
Interest payable	___	___	___	___	___
Long-term liabilities:					
Long-term debt	___	___	___	___	___

Exercise 11-11 *Reporting current and long-term liabilities* **(L.O. 6)**

No check figure

Assume Wilson Sporting Goods completed these selected transactions during December 19X6:

1. Sport Spectrum, a chain of sporting goods stores, ordered $60,000 of baseball and golf equipment. With its order, Sport Spectrum sent a check for $60,000. Wilson will ship the goods on January 3, 19X7.
2. The December payroll of $295,000 is subject to employee withheld income tax of 9 percent, FICA tax of 8 percent (employee and employer), state unemployment tax of 5.4 percent, and federal unemployment tax of 0.8 percent. On December 31, Wilson pays employees but accrues all tax amounts.
3. Sales of $2,000,000 are subject to estimated warranty cost of 1.4 percent.
4. On December 2, Wilson signed a $100,000 note payable that requires annual payments of $20,000 plus 9 percent interest on the unpaid balance each December 2.

Required

Report these items on Wilson's balance sheet at December 31, 19X6.

Problems   *(Group A)*

Additional Computer-Related Problems: Problems 28-2A and 28-2B

Problem 11-1A *Journalizing liability-related transactions* **(L.O. 1)**

No check figure

The following transactions of University Cooperative occurred during 19X2 and 19X3. Record the transactions in the company's general journal. Explanations are not required.

19X2
Feb. 3 Purchased a machine for $4,200, signing a six-month, 11 percent note payable.
     28 Recorded the week's sales of $27,000, one-third for cash, and two-thirds on credit. All sales amounts are subject to a 5 percent state sales tax.

Mar. 7 Sent the last week's sales tax to the state.

Apr. 30 Borrowed $100,000 on a 9 percent note payable that calls for annual installment payments of $25,000 principal plus interest.

May 10 Received $1,125 in security deposits from customers. University Cooperative refunds most deposits within three months.

Aug. 3 Paid the six-month, 11 percent note at maturity.

10 Refunded security deposits of $1,125 to customers.

Sep. 14 Discounted a $6,000, 12 percent, 60-day note payable to the bank, receiving cash for the net amount after interest was deducted from the note's maturity value.

Nov. 13 Recognized interest on the 12 percent discounted note and paid off the note at maturity.

30 Purchased inventory at a cost of $7,200, signing a 10 percent, three-month note payable for that amount.

Dec. 31 Accrued warranty expense, which is estimated at 3 percent of sales of $145,000.

31 Accrued interest on all outstanding notes payable. Make a separate interest accrual entry for each note payable.

19X3

Feb. 28 Paid off the 10 percent inventory note, plus interest, at maturity.

Apr. 30 Paid the first installment and interest for one year on the long-term note payable.

No check figure

Problem 11-2A   *Identifying contingent liabilities*   **(L.O. 2)**

Hunting Horn Farm provides riding lessons for girls ages 8 through 15. Most students are beginners, and none of the girls owns her own horse. Janet Christie, the owner of Hunting Horn, uses horses stabled at her farm and owned by the Averys. Most of the horses are for sale, but the economy has been bad for several years and horse sales have been slow. The Averys are happy that Janet uses their horses in exchange for rooming and boarding them. Because of a recent financial setback, Janet cannot afford insurance. She seeks your advice about her business exposure to liabilities.

Required

Write a memorandum to inform Janet of specific contingent liabilities arising from the business. It will be necessary to define a contingent liability because she is a professional horse trainer, not a businessperson. Propose a way for Janet to limit her exposure to these liabilities.

Wage exp. $19,207

Problem 11-3A   *Computing and recording payroll amounts*   **(L.O. 3, 4)**

The partial monthly records of Yokohama Company show the following figures.

Employee Earnings:

(1) Straight-time earnings	$?	(7)	Medical insurance	$ 1,373
(2) Overtime pay	5,109	(8)	Total deductions	?
(3) Total employee earnings	?	(9)	Net pay	58,813

Deductions and Net Pay: **Accounts Debited:**

(4) Withheld income tax ..	9,293	(10)	Salary Expense	31,278
(5) FICA tax.............	8,052	(11)	Wage Expense	?
(6) Charitable contributions	885	(12)	Sales Commission Expense	27,931

Required

1. Determine the missing amounts on lines (1), (3), (8), and (11).
2. Prepare the general journal entry to record Yokohama's payroll for the month. Credit Payrolls Payable for net pay. No explanation is required.

Problem 11-4A   *Computing and recording payroll amounts*   **(L.O. 3, 4)**

Total annual cost of employee $69,474

Assume that Margo Benson is a commercial lender in Chase Manhattan Bank's mortgage banking department in New York City. During 19X2 she worked for the bank all year at a $4,195 monthly salary. She also earned a year-end bonus equal to 12 percent of her salary

Benson's federal income tax withheld during 19X2 was $822 per month. Also, there was a one-time withholding of $2,487 on her bonus check. State income tax withheld came to $61 per month, and the city of New York withheld income tax of $21 per month. In addition, Benson paid one-time withholdings of $64 (state) and $19 (city) on the bonus. The FICA tax withheld was 8 percent of the first $50,000 in annual earnings. Benson authorized the following payroll deductions: United Fund contribution of 1 percent of total earnings, and life insurance of $17 per month

Chase Manhattan Bank incurred payroll tax expense on Benson for FICA tax of 8 percent of the first $50,000 in annual earnings. The bank also paid state unemployment tax of 5.4 percent, and federal unemployment tax of 0.8 percent on the first $7,000 in annual earnings. The bank also provided Benson with the following fringe benefits: health insurance at a cost of $48 per month, and pension benefits to be paid to Benson during her retirement. During 19X2 Chase Manhattan's cost of Benson's pension program was $8,083.

Required

1. Compute Benson's gross pay, payroll deductions, and net pay for the full year of 19X2. Round all amounts to the nearest dollar.
2. Compute Chase Manhattan Bank's total 19X2 payroll cost for Benson.
3. Prepare Chase Manhattan Bank's summary general journal entries to record its expense for
   a. Benson's total earnings for the year, her payroll deductions, and her net pay. Debit Salary Expense and Executive Bonus Compensation as appropriate. Credit liability accounts for the payroll deductions and Cash for net pay.
   b. Employer payroll taxes for Benson. Credit liability accounts.
   c. Fringe benefits provided to Benson. Credit a liability account.

   Explanations are not required.

Problem 11-5A   *Selecting the correct data to record a payroll*   **(L.O. 4)**

3. Cash payment $54,292
4. Cash payment $36,311

Assume the payroll information at the top of page 534 appeared in the records of a small plant operated by Sharp Electronics.

Required

1. Prepare the general journal entry to record the payroll for the week ended July 31, including payroll taxes and fringe benefits.
2. Prepare the general journal entry to record the payment of the week's salaries to employees on July 31.
3. Assume that Sharp pays all its liabilities to the federal government in a single monthly amount. Prepare the general journal entry to record the July 31, 19X4, payment of federal taxes. (Liabilities to the federal government include FICA taxes and those items with *federal* and *U.S.* in the account title.)

4. Assume that Sharp pays all other payroll liabilities shortly after the end of the month. Prepare a single general journal entry to record the August 3 payment for these July liabilities.

Explanations are not required for journal entries.

	Payroll for Week Ended Friday July 31, 19X4	Payroll for Month of July 19X4
Salaries:		
Supervisor salaries	$42,375	$162,639
Office salaries	9,088	37,261
Deductions:		
Employee federal income tax	5,960	23,182
FICA tax	3,266	13,392
Employee health insurance	922	3,780
Employee union dues	708	2,903
Employee U.S. savings bonds	665	2,727
Net pay	39,942	153,916
Employer payroll taxes:		
FICA tax	3,266	13,392
State unemployment tax	2,119	10,793
Federal unemployment tax	314	1,599
Employer cost of fringe benefits for employees:		
Health insurance	2,034	7,904
Life insurance	1,053	4,096
Pension	1,667	6,835

Note: One challenge of this problem is to use only the relevant data. Not all the information given is necessary for making the required journal entries.

Total liab. $363,532

Problem 11-6A *Journalizing, posting, and reporting liabilities* **(L.O. 1, 2, 4, 6)**

The TU Electric Company general ledger at September 30, 19X7, the end of the company's fiscal year, includes the following account balances before adjusting entries. Parentheses indicate a debit balance.

Notes Payable, Short-Term	$29,000	Employer Payroll Taxes Payable	$ _____
Discount on Notes Payable	(2,100)	Employee Benefits Payable	_____
Accounts Payable	88,240	Estimated Vacation Pay Liability	2,105
Current Portion of Long-Term Debt Payable	_____	Sales Tax Payable	372
Interest Payable	_____	Property Tax Payable	1,433
Salary Payable	_____	Unearned Rent Revenue . .	3,900
Employee Payroll Taxes Payable	_____	Long-Term Debt Payable . .	220,000
		Contingent Liabilities	_____

The additional data needed to develop the adjusting entries at September 30 are as follows:

a. The $29,000 balance in Notes Payable, Short-Term consists of two notes. The first note, with a principal amount of $21,000, was issued on August 31, matures one year from date of issuance, and was discounted at 10 percent. The second note, with a principal amount of $8,000, was issued on September 2 for a term of 90 days and bears interest at 9 percent. It was not discounted.

b. The long-term debt is payable in annual installments of $55,000, with the next installment due on January 31, 19X8. On that date, TU Electric will also pay one year's interest at 10.5 percent. Interest was last paid on January 31. To shift the current installment of the long-term debt to a current liability, debit Long-Term Debt Payable and credit Current Portion of Long-Term Debt Payable.

c. Gross salaries for the last payroll of the fiscal year were $4,319. Of this amount, employee payroll taxes payable were $958, and salary payable was $3,361.

d. Employer payroll taxes payable were $755, and TU Electric's liability for employee life insurance was $1,004.

e. TU Electric estimates that vacation pay is 4 percent of gross salaries.

f. On August 1 the company collected six months' rent of $3,900 in advance.

g. At June 30 TU Electric is the defendant in a $200,000 lawsuit, which the company expects to win. However, the outcome is uncertain. TU Electric reports contingent liabilities "short," with an explanatory note.

Required

1. Open the listed accounts, inserting their unadjusted September 30 balances.

2. Journalize and post the September 30 adjusting entries to the accounts opened. Key adjusting entries by letter.

3. Prepare the liability section of TU Electric's balance sheet at September 30.

Problem 11-7A *Using a payroll register; recording a payroll* **(L.O. 5)**

Net pay $1,617

Assume that payroll records of a district sales office of General Mills, Inc., provided the following information for the weekly pay period ended December 18, 19X3:

Employee	Hours Worked	Weekly Earnings Rate	Federal Income Tax	Health Insurance	United Way Contribution	Earnings through Previous Week
Ginny Akin	43	$400	$ 94	$9	$7	$17,060
Leroy Dixon	46	480	121	5	5	22,365
Karol Stastny	47	800	219	6	—	49,247
David Trent	40	240	32	4	2	3,413

Ginny Akin and David Trent work in the office, and Leroy Dixon and Karol Stastny work in sales. All employees are paid time and a half for hours worked in excess of 40 per week. For convenience, round all amounts to the nearest dollar. Show computations. Explanations are not required for journal entries.

Required

1. Enter the appropriate information in a payroll register similar to Exhibit 11-5. In addition to the deductions listed, the employer also takes out FICA tax: 8 percent of the first $50,000 of each employee's annual earnings.

2. Record the payroll information in the general journal.

3. Assume that the first payroll check is number 178, paid to Ginny Akin. Record the check numbers in the payroll register. Also, prepare the general journal entry to record payment of net pay to the employees.

4. The employer's payroll taxes include FICA of 8 percent of the first $50,000 of each employee's annual earnings. The employer also pays unemployment taxes of 6.2 percent (5.4 percent for the state and 0.8 percent for the federal government) on the first $7,000 of each employee's annual earnings. Record the employer's payroll taxes in the general journal.

No check figure

Problem 11-8A   *Reporting current liabilities*   **(L.O. 6)**

Following are six pertinent facts about events during the current year at Alliance Rubber Company.

1. On August 31, Alliance signed a six-month, 12 percent note payable to purchase a machine costing $31,000. The note requires payment of principal and interest at maturity.
2. On October 31, Alliance received rent of $2,000 in advance for a lease on a building. This rent will be earned evenly over four months.
3. On November 30, Alliance discounted a $10,000 note payable to InterBank Savings. The interest rate on the one-year note is 12 percent.
4. December sales totaled $104,000 and Alliance collected sales tax of 9 percent. This amount will be sent to the state of Tennessee early in January.
5. Alliance owes $75,000 on a long-term note payable. At December 31, $25,000 of this principal plus $900 of accrued interest are payable within one year.
6. Sales of $909,000 were covered by Alliance's product warranty. At January 1 estimated warranty payable was $11,300. During the year Alliance recorded warranty expense of $27,900 and paid warranty claims of $30,100.

Required

For each item, indicate the account and the related amount to be reported as a current liability on Alliance's December 31 balance sheet.

(Group B)

No check figure

Problem 11-1B   *Journalizing liability-related transactions*   **(L.O. 1)**

The following transactions of Munoz, Inc., occurred during 19X4 and 19X5. Record the transactions in the company's general journal. Explanations are not required.

19X4

Jan. 9 Purchased a machine at a cost of $5,000, signing a 12 percent, six-month note payable for that amount.

29 Recorded the week's sales of $22,200, three-fourths on credit, and one-fourth for cash. Sales amounts are subject to an additional 6 percent state sales tax.

Feb. 5 Sent the last week's sales tax to the state.

28 Borrowed $300,000 on a 10 percent note payable that calls for annual installment payments of $50,000 principal plus interest.

Apr. 8 Received $778 in deposits from distributors of company products. Munoz refunds the deposits after six months.

July 9 Paid the six-month, 12 percent note at maturity.

Oct. 8 Refunded security deposits of $778 to distributors.

22 Discounted a $5,000, 10 percent, 90-day note payable to the bank, receiving cash for the net amount after interest was deducted from the note's maturity value.

Nov. 30 Purchased inventory for $3,100, signing a six-month, 8 percent note payable.

Dec. 31 Accrued warranty expense, which is estimated at 2 1/2 percent of sales of $650,000.

 31 Accrued interest on all outstanding notes payable. Make a separate interest accrual entry for each note payable.

19X5

Jan. 20 Paid off the 10 percent discounted note payable. Made a separate entry for the interest.

Feb. 28 Paid the first installment and interest for one year on the long-term note payable.

May 31 Paid off the 8 percent note plus interest at maturity.

Problem 11-2B *Identifying contingent liabilities* **(L.O. 2)**

No check figure

Covert Buick Company is the only Buick dealer in Austin, Texas, and one of the largest Buick dealers in the southwestern United States. The dealership sells new and used cars and operates a body shop and a service department. Duke Covert, the general manager, is considering changing insurance companies because of a disagreement with Doug Stillwell, Austin agent for the Travelers Insurance Company. Travelers is doubling Covert's liability insurance cost for the next year. In discussing insurance coverage with you, a trusted business associate, Stillwell brings up the subject of contingent liabilities.

Required

Write a memorandum to inform Covert Buick Company of specific contingent liabilities arising from the business. In your discussion, define a contingent liability.

Problem 11-3B *Computing and recording payroll amounts* **(L.O. 3,4)**

Salary exp. $9,695

The partial monthly records of The Art Center show the following figures:

Employee Earnings:

(1) Straight-time employee earnings .	$16,431		(7) Medical insurance	$ 668	
(2) Overtime pay	?		(8) Total deductions	3,409	
(3) Total employee earnings	?		(9) Net pay	15,936	

Deductions and Net Pay:

Accounts Debited:

(4) Withheld income tax .	1,403	(10) Salary Expense	?
(5) FICA tax	?	(11) Wage Expense	4,573
(6) Charitable contributions	340	(12) Sales Commission Expense	5,077

Required

1. Determine the missing amounts on lines (2), (3), (5), and (10).
2. Prepare the general journal entry to record The Art Center's payroll for the month. Credit Payrolls Payable for net pay. No explanation is required.

Problem 11-4B *Computing and recording payroll amounts* **(L.O. 3, 4)**

Total annual cost of employee $59,710

Assume that Seth Reichlin is a vice-president of Bank of America's leasing operations in San Francisco. During 19X6 he worked for the company all year at a $3,625 monthly salary. He also earned a year-end bonus equal to 10 percent of his salary.

Reichlin's federal income tax withheld during 19X6 was $537 per month. Also, there was a one-time federal withholding tax of $1,007 on his bonus check. State income tax withheld came to $43 per month, and there was a one-time state withholding tax of $27 on the bonus. The FICA tax withheld was 8.0 percent of the first $50,000 in annual earnings. Reichlin authorized the following payroll deductions: United Fund contribution of 1 percent of total earnings, and life insurance of $19 per month.

Bank of America incurred payroll tax expense on Reichlin for FICA tax of 8 percent of the first $50,000 in annual earnings. The bank also paid state unemployment tax of 5.4 percent and federal unemployment tax of 0.8 percent on the first $7,000 in annual earnings. In addition, the bank provides Reichlin with health insurance at a cost of $35 per month and pension benefits. During 19X6 Bank of America paid $7,178 into Reichlin's pension program.

Required

1. Compute Reichlin's gross pay, payroll deductions, and net pay for the full year 19X6. Round all amounts to the nearest dollar.
2. Compute Bank of America's total 19X6 payroll cost for Reichlin.
3. Prepare Bank of America's summary general journal entries to record its expense for
   a. Reichlin's total earnings for the year, his payroll deductions, and his net pay. Debit Salary Expense and Executive Bonus Compensation as appropriate. Credit liability accounts for the payroll deductions and Cash for net pay.
   b. Employer payroll taxes on Reichlin. Credit liability accounts.
   c. Fringe benefit provided to Reichlin. Credit a liability account.
   Explanations are not required.

3. Cash payment $12,543
4. Cash payment $11,455

Problem 11-5B *Selecting the correct data to record a payroll* *(L.O. 4)*

Assume these payroll data are in the records of *Car and Driver* magazine.

	Payroll for Week Ended Friday March 31, 19X9	Payroll for Month of March 19X9
Salaries:		
Editorial salaries	$6,203	$27,178
Warehousing salaries	3,118	13,128
Deductions:		
Employee federal income tax	1,115	5,612
FICA tax	641	2,699
Employee health insurance	481	2,025
Employee contributions to United Fund	367	1,545
Employee U.S. savings bonds	288	1,213
Net pay	6,429	27,212
Employer payroll taxes:		
FICA tax	641	2,699
State unemployment tax	520	2,160
Federal unemployment tax	77	320
Employer cost of fringe benefits for employees:		
Health insurance	663	2,458
Life insurance	324	1,368
Pensions	451	1,899

Note: One challenge of this problem is to use only the relevant data. Not all the information given is necessary for making the required journal entries.

Required

1. Prepare the general journal entries to record the payroll for the week ended March 31, including payroll taxes and fringe benefits.
2. Prepare the general journal entry to record the payment of the week's salaries to employees on March 31.
3. Assume that *Car and Driver* pays all its liabilities to the federal government in a single monthly amount. Prepare the general journal entry to record the April 1, 19X9, payment of federal taxes. (Liabilities to the federal government include FICA taxes and those items with *federal* and *U.S.* in the account title.)
4. Assume that *Car and Driver* pays all other payroll liabilities shortly after the end of the month. Prepare a single general journal entry to record the April 4 payment for these March liabilities.

Explanations are not required for journal entries.

Problem 11-6B   *Journalizing, posting, and reporting liabilities*   (L.O. 1, 2, 4, 6)

Total liab. $285,738

The general ledger of Tea Rose, Inc., at June 30, 19X3, end of the company's fiscal year, includes the following account balances before adjusting entries. Parentheses indicate a debit balance.

Notes Payable, Short-Term	$ 25,000	Employee Benefits Payable	$ _____
Discount on Notes Payable	(900)	Estimated Vacation Pay	
Accounts Payable........	105,520	Liability	7,620
Current Portion of Long-		Sales Tax Payable	738
Term Debt Payable	_____	Customer Deposits	
Interest Payable	_____	Payable	6,950
Salary Payable...........	_____	Unearned Rent Revenue ..	4,800
Employee Payroll		Long-Term Debt Payable..	120,000
Taxes Payable	_____	Contingent Liabilities	_____
Employer Payroll			
Taxes Payable	_____		

The additional data needed to develop the adjusting entries at June 30 are as follows:

a. The $25,000 balance in Notes Payable, Short-Term consists of two notes. The first note, with a principal amount of $15,000, was issued on January 31. It matures six months from date of issuance and was discounted at 12 percent. The second note, with a principal amount of $10,000, was issued on April 22 for a term of 90 days. It bears interest at 10 percent. It was not discounted. Interest on this note will be paid at maturity.
b. The long-term debt is payable in annual installments of $40,000 with the next installment due on July 31. On that date, Tea Rose will also pay one year's interest at 9 percent. Interest was last paid on July 31 of the preceding year. To shift the current installment of the long-term debt to a current liability, debit Long-Term Debt Payable and credit Current Portion of Long-Term Debt Payable.
c. Gross salaries for the last payroll of the fiscal year were $5,044. Of this amount, employee payroll taxes payable were $1,088, and salary payable was $3,956.
d. Employer payroll taxes payable were $876, and Tea Rose's liability for employee health insurance was $1,046.
e. Tea Rose estimates that vacation pay expense is 4 percent of gross salaries.

f. On February 1 the company collected one year's rent of $4,800 in advance.

g. At June 30 Tea Rose is the defendant in a $500,000 lawsuit, which the company expects to win. However, the outcome is uncertain. Tea Rose reports contingent liabilities short, with an explanatory note.

Required

1. Open the listed accounts, inserting their unadjusted June 30 balances.
2. Journalize and post the June 30 adjusting entries to the accounts opened. Key adjusting entries by letter.
3. Prepare the liability section of the balance sheet at June 30.

Net pay $1,926

Problem 11-7B   *Using payroll register; recording a payroll*   **(L.O. 5)**

Assume that the payroll records of a district sales office of Liquid Paper Corporation provided the following information for the weekly pay period ended December 21, 19X5:

Employee	Hours Worked	Hourly Earnings Rate	Federal Income Tax	Union Dues	United Way Contributions	Earnings Through Previous Week
Lance Blanks	42	$18	$153	$6	$5	$52,474
James English	47	8	56	4	4	23,154
Louise French	40	11	72	—	4	4,880
Roberto Garza	41	22	188	6	8	49,600

James English and Louise French work in the office, and Lance Blanks and Roberto Garza work in sales. All employees are paid time and a half for hours worked in excess of 40 per week. For convenience, round all amounts to the nearest dollar. Show computations. Explanations are not required for journal entries.

Required

1. Enter the appropriate information in a payroll register similar to Exhibit 11-5. In addition to the deductions listed, the employer also takes out FICA tax: 8 percent of the first $50,000 of each employee's annual earnings.
2. Record the payroll information in the general journal.
3. Assume that the first payroll check is number 319, paid to Lance Blanks. Record the check numbers in the payroll register. Also, prepare the general journal entry to record payment of net pay to the employees.
4. The employer's payroll taxes include FICA tax of 8 percent of the first $50,000 of each employee's earnings. The employer also pays unemployment taxes of 6.2 percent (5.4 percent for the state and 0.8 percent for the federal government on the first $7,000 of each employee's annual earnings). Record the employer's payroll taxes in the general journal.

No check figure

Problem 11-8B   *Reporting current liabilities*   **(L.O. 6)**

Following are six pertinent facts about events during the current year at Herbissimo Fragrances.

1. On September 30, Herbissimo signed a six-month, 9 percent note payable to purchase inventory costing $30,000. The note requires payment of principal and interest at maturity.
2. On October 31, Herbissimo discounted a $50,000 note payable to Lake Air National Bank. The interest rate on the one-year note is 10 percent.

3. On November 30, Herbissimo received rent of $4,200 in advance for a lease on a building. This rent will be earned evenly over three months.

4. December sales totaled $38,000 and Herbissimo collected an additional state sales tax of 7 percent. This amount will be sent to the state of Arizona early in January.

5. Herbissimo owes $100,000 on a long-term note payable. At December 31, $20,000 of this principal plus $2,100 of accrued interest are payable within one year.

6. Sales of $430,000 were covered by Herbissimo's product warranty. At January 1, estimated warranty payable was $8,100. During the year Herbissimo recorded warranty expense of $22,300 and paid warranty claims of $23,600.

Required

For each item, indicate the account and the related amount to be reported as a current liability on Herbissimo's December 31 balance sheet.

Extending Your Knowledge

Decision Problems

1. Identifying Internal Control Weaknesses and their Solution   (L.O. 5)

No check figure

Hall Custom Homes is a large home-building business in Phoenix, Arizona. The owner and manager is Lawrence Hall, who oversees all company operations. He employs 15 work crews, each made up of 6 to 10 members. Construction supervisors, who report directly to Hall, lead the crews. Most supervisors are longtime employees, so Hall trusts them greatly. Hall's office staff consists of an accountant and an office manager.

Because employee turnover is rapid in the construction industry, supervisors hire and terminate their own crew members. Supervisors notify the office of all personnel changes. Also, supervisors forward to the office the employee W-4 forms, which the crew members fill out to claim tax-withholding exemptions. Each Thursday the supervisors submit weekly time sheets for their crews, and the accountant prepares the payroll. At noon on Friday the supervisors come to the office to get paychecks for distribution to the workers at 5 P.M.

Hall's accountant prepares the payroll, including the payroll checks, which are written on a single payroll bank account. Hall signs all payroll checks after matching the employee name to the time sheets submitted by the foremen. Often the construction workers wait several days to cash their paychecks. To verify that each construction worker is a bona-fide employee, the accountant matches the employee's endorsement signature on the back of the canceled payroll check with the signature on that employee's W-4 form.

Required

1. List one *efficiency* weakness in Hall's payroll accounting system. How can Hall correct this weakness?

2. Identify one way that a supervisor can defraud Hall under the present system.

3. Discuss a control feature Hall can use to *safeguard* against the fraud you identified in Requirement 2.

2. Questions About Liabilities (L.O. 1, 2)

The following questions are not related.

a. A friend comments that he thought liabilities represented amounts owed by a company and asks why unearned revenues are shown as a current liability. How would you respond?

b. A warranty is like a contingent liability in that the amount to be paid is not known at year end. Why are warranties payable shown as a current liability while contingent liabilities are reported in the notes to the financial statements?

c. Auditors have procedures for determining whether they have discovered all of a company's contingent liabilities. These procedures differ from the procedures used for determining that accounts payable are correctly stated. If you were an auditor, how would you go about identifying a client's contingent liabilities?

Ethical Issue

IBM is the defendant in numerous lawsuits claiming unfair trade practices. IBM has strong incentives not to disclose these contingent liabilities. However, generally accepted accounting principles require companies to report their contingent liabilities.

Required

1. State why a company would prefer not to disclose its contingent liabilities.

2. Describe how a bank could be harmed if a company seeking a loan did not disclose its contingent liabilities.

3. What is the ethical tightrope that a company must walk in reporting its contingent liabilities?

Financial Statement Problems

1. Current and Contingent Liabilities and Payroll (L.O. 1, 2, 6)

Details about a company's current and contingent liabilities and payroll costs appear in a number of places in the annual report. Use the Goodyear Tire & Rubber Company financial statements to answer these questions.

1. Give the breakdown of Goodyear's current liabilities at December 31, 1990. Give the 1991 entry to record the payment of December 31, 1990, accounts payable.

2. How much of Goodyear's long-term debt at December 31, 1990, was due within one year? In the Credit Arrangements note, which liabilities were obviously included in the portion due within one year?

3. Does Goodyear use a short presentation for contingent liabilities? Where does the company report contingencies? What is the Goodyear management opinion as to the ultimate effect of lawsuits pending against the company?

4. The balance sheet lists a $442.7 million liability for "Accrued payrolls and other compensation." Was compensation expense for the year equal to, less than, or greater than this amount? Give your reason.

2. Current and Contingent Liabilities and Payroll (L.O. 1, 2, 6)

Obtain the annual report of an actual company of your choosing. Details about the company's current and contingent liabilities and payroll costs may appear in a number of places in the annual report. Use the statements of the company you select to answer these questions. Concentrate on the current year in the annual report.

1. Give the breakdown of the company's current liabilities at the end of the current year. Journalize the payment in the following year of Accounts Payable reported on the balance sheet.
2. How much of the company's long-term debt at the end of the current year was reported as a current liability? Do the notes to the financial statements identify the specific items of long-term debt coming due within the next year? If so, identify the specific liabilities.
3. Identify the payroll-related current liability at the end of the current year. Give its amount, and record its payment in the next year.
4. Does the company report any unearned revenue? If so, identify the item and give its amount.
5. Where does the company report contingent liabilities—on the face of the balance sheet or in a note? Give important details about the company's contingent liabilities at the end of the current year.

Comprehensive Problem for Part Three

Comparing Two Businesses

Lakeway total assets, revised $1,914,000
Lakeway net income, revised $241,600

At age 25, you invented a mechanical pencil that is now being sold worldwide. After laboring diligently for several years, you have recently sold the business to a large company. Now you are ready to invest in a small resort property located where the golf is great and your family and friends will enjoy visiting. Several locations fit this description: Jekyll Island, Georgia; Lakeway, Texas; and La Jolla, California. Each place has its appeal, but Lakeway finally wins out. The main allure is that prices there are low, so a dollar will stretch further. Two small resorts are available, both with access to a golf course designed by Jack Nicklaus. The property owners provide the following data:

	Lakeway Resort	Texas Hideaway
Cash	$ 44,100	$ 63,800
Accounts receivable	20,500	18,300
Inventory	74,200	68,400
Land	270,600	269,200
Buildings	1,880,000	1,960,000
Accumulated depreciation	(350,000)	(822,600)
Furniture and fixtures	740,000	933,000
Accumulated depreciation	(207,000)	416,300)
Total assets	$2,472,400	$2,073,800
Total liabilities	$1,124,300	$1,008,500
Owner equity	1,348,100	1,065,300
Total liabilities and owner equity	$2,472,400	$2,073,800

Income statements for the last three years report total net income of $441,000 for Lakeway Resorts and $283,000 for Texas Hideaway.

Inventories. Lakeway Resorts uses the FIFO inventory method, and Texas Hideaway uses the LIFO method. If Lakeway had used LIFO, its reported inventory would have been $7,000 lower. If Texas Hideaway had used FIFO, its reported inventory would have been $6,000 higher. Three years ago there was little difference between LIFO and FIFO amounts for either company.

Plant Assets. Lakeway uses the straight-line depreciation method and an estimated useful life of 40 years for buildings and 10 years for furniture and fixtures. Estimated residual values are $480,000 for buildings and $50,000 for furniture and fixtures. Lakeway's buildings are 10 years old, and the furniture and fixtures have been used for 3 years.

Texas Hideaway uses the sum-of-years-digits method and depreciates buildings over 30 years with an estimated residual value of $460,000. The furniture and fixtures, now 3 years old, are being depreciated over 10 years with an estimated residual value of $85,000.

Accounts Receivable. Lakeway Resort uses the direct write-off method for uncollectibles. Texas Hideaway uses the allowance method. The Lakeway owner estimates that $2,000 of Lakeway's receivables are doubtful. Prior to the current year, uncollectibles were insignificant. Texas Hideaway's receivables are already reported at net realizable value.

Required

1. Puzzled at first by how to compare the two resorts, you decide to convert Lakeway Resort's balance sheet to the accounting methods and the estimated useful lives used by Texas Hideaway. Round all depreciation amounts to the nearest $100. The necessary revisions will not affect Lakeway's total liabilities.

2. Convert Lakeway's total net income for the last three years to reflect the accounting methods used by Texas Hideaway. Round all depreciation amounts to the nearest $100.

3. Compare the pictures of the two resorts after revising Lakeway's figures with the pictures of the two resorts beforehand. Which resort looked better at the outset? Which resort looks better when they are placed on equal footing?

The Foundation for Generally Accepted Accounting Principles

enerally accepted accounting principles (GAAP) are important not only to accountants. People who rely on financial statements require that the information correspond to GAAP. When the statements are in doubt, then investors, creditors, and regulators may file lawsuits against the outside auditor. Arthur Young & Co., now part of Ernst & Young, CPAs, is the subject of this dispute over the audit of Lincoln Savings Association.

In terms of challenges to its judgment on complex accounting, Arthur Young did not face a problem until May 1987. That month, the Federal Home Loan Bank of San Francisco, Lincoln's primary [government] regulator, completed its 1986 examination of Lincoln.

In a report that would eventually become the basis for two years of fighting between [government] regulators in San Francisco and those in Washington, the San Francisco examiners recommended that Lincoln take a $130 million write-off to account for overstated profits and unrecognized losses. Since Lincoln's net worth—its assets minus its liabilities—was only $210 million at the time, carrying out the examiners' recommendations would have meant wiping out nearly two-thirds of that net worth.

In this case a prominent savings and loan association is alleged to have abused generally accepted accounting principles by reporting income that it never earned.

Source: Eric N. Berg, ''The Lapses by Lincoln's Auditors,'' *The New York Times*, December 28, 1989, p. C3.

Real-World Example: The FASB is not responsible for policing the accounting profession. When violations occur, as with Lincoln Savings, a lawsuit is often brought against the company by stockholders, creditors, or even the SEC. Any penalty is assessed by the courts not by the FASB.

Every technical area seems to have professional associations and regulatory bodies that govern the practice of the profession. Accounting is no exception. During the 1970s and 1980s generally accepted accounting principles in the United States have been influenced most by the Financial Accounting Standards Board (FASB) and its predecessor, the Accounting Principles Board (APB). The FASB consists of seven full-time members. A large staff and an annual budget of $14 million support the FASB. Its financial support comes from various professional associations, such as the American Institute of Certified Public Accountants.

From 1962 to 1973 the APB issued accounting pronouncements called *Opinions*, many of which are still part of generally accepted accounting principles (GAAP). In 1973 the FASB was established to replace the APB. The FASB is an independent organization with no government or professional affiliation. The FASB's pronouncements, called *Statements of Financial Accounting Standards*, currently specify how to account for certain business transactions. Each new *Standard* becomes part of GAAP, the "accounting law of the land." In the same way that our laws draw authority from their acceptance by the people, GAAP depends upon the general acceptance by the business community. Throughout this book, we refer to GAAP as the proper way to do financial accounting.

The United States Congress has given the Securities and Exchange Commission (SEC) ultimate responsibility for establishing accounting rules for companies that are owned by the general investing public. However, the SEC has delegated much of its rule-making power to the FASB. Exhibit 12-1 outlines the flow of authority for developing GAAP.

Setting accounting standards is a complex process involving the FASB, the SEC, and occasionally Congress. Also, individuals and companies often exert pressure on all three bodies in their efforts to shape accounting decisions to their advantage. Accountants also try to influence accounting decisions. Although any overruling is rare, the SEC has the authority to override an FASB decision, and Congress itself can override an SEC or an FASB decision, as the authority structure in Exhibit 12-1 shows. In most cases, however, the FASB plays the key role.

We have seen that GAAP guides companies in their financial statement preparation. Independent auditing firms of certified public accountants (CPAs) hold the responsibility for making sure companies do indeed follow GAAP.

EXHIBIT 12-1   *Flow of Authority for Developing GAAP*

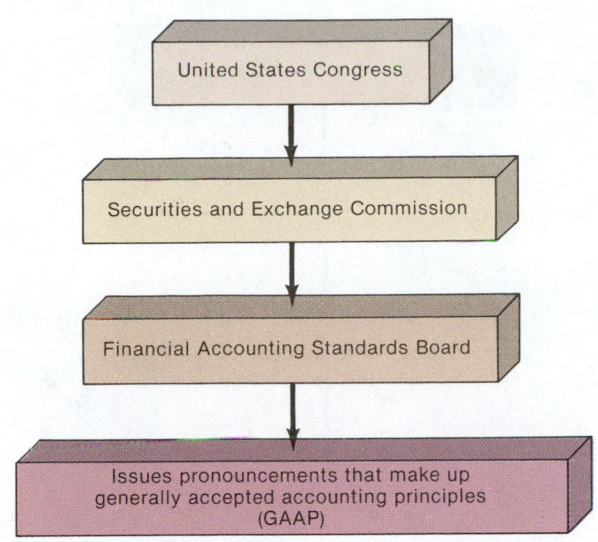

The Conceptual Framework

Throughout the first 11 chapters, we have introduced key concepts and principles as they have applied to the topics under discussion. For example, Chapter 1 introduced the entity concept so that we could account for the transactions of a particular business. In Chapter 2, we discussed the revenue and matching principles as the guidelines for measuring income. Now that you have an overview of the accounting process, we consider the full range of accounting concepts and principles. Collectively, they form the foundation for accounting practice—GAAP.

Shortly after its formation in 1973, the Financial Accounting Standards Board (FASB) began the Conceptual Framework Project. The FASB's goal is to develop a constitution that will define the nature and function of financial accounting. This project provides a framework for the various accounting concepts and principles that are used to prepare the financial statements.

Accounting principles differ from natural laws like the law of gravity. Accounting principles draw their authority from their acceptance in the business community rather than from their ability to explain physical phenomena. Thus they really are *generally accepted* by those people and organizations who need guidelines in accounting for their financial undertakings. Exhibit 12-2 diagrams how we move from the conceptual framework to the financial statements.

We now look at the objective of financial reporting. This objective tells what financial accounting is intended to accomplish. Thus it provides the goal for accounting information. Next, we examine particular accounting concepts and principles used to implement the objective. What is the difference between a concept and a principle? The concepts are broader in their application, and the principles are more specific. Last, we discuss the financial statements—the end product of financial accounting—and their elements—assets, liabilities, owner's equity, revenues, expenses, and so on.

Point to Stress: Because the writing of the Conceptual Framework is such a complex project, it may take many years to complete.

Typical Student Misconception: Students often think that financial reporting is the same as tax-return preparation or that the statements are prepared for management. The objective of financial reporting is to provide information that is useful in making investment and lending decisions. The investment decisions are made by potential owners (usually people interested in purchasing stock), and lending decisions are made by banks and other financial institutions.

EXHIBIT 12-2 *Overview of Generally Accepted Accounting Principles*

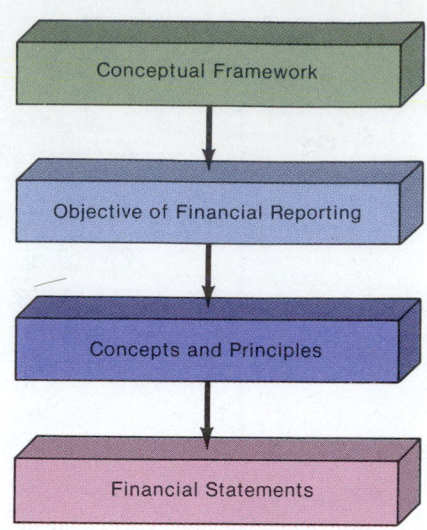

Objective of Financial Reporting

OBJECTIVE 1
Identify the basic objective of financial reporting

The basic *objective of financial reporting* is to provide information that is useful in making investment and lending decisions. To be useful in decision making, the FASB believes accounting information should be *relevant, reliable,* and *comparable.*

Relevant information is useful for making predictions and for evaluating past performance—that is, the information has feedback value. To be relevant, information must be timely. *Reliable* information is free from significant error—that is, it has validity. Also, it is free from the bias of a particular viewpoint—that is, it is verifiable and neutral. *Comparable* information can be compared from period to period to help investors and creditors track the entity's progress through time. These characteristics combine to shape the concepts and principles that make up GAAP. Exhibit 12-3 summarizes the qualities that increase the value of accounting information.

Transparency T12-1

Underlying Concepts

OBJECTIVE 2
Identify and apply the underlying concepts of accounting

Entity Concept

The **entity concept** is the most basic concept in accounting because it draws a boundary around the organization being accounted for. That is, the transactions of each entity are accounted for separately from transactions of all other organizations and persons, including the owners of the entity. This separation allows us to measure the performance and the financial position of each entity independent of all other entities.

A business entity may be a sole proprietorship (owned and operated by a single individual), a partnership of two or more persons, or a large corporation like Exxon. The entity concept applies with equal force to all types and sizes of organizations. The proprietor of a travel agency, for example, accounts for her personal transactions separately from those of her business. This division

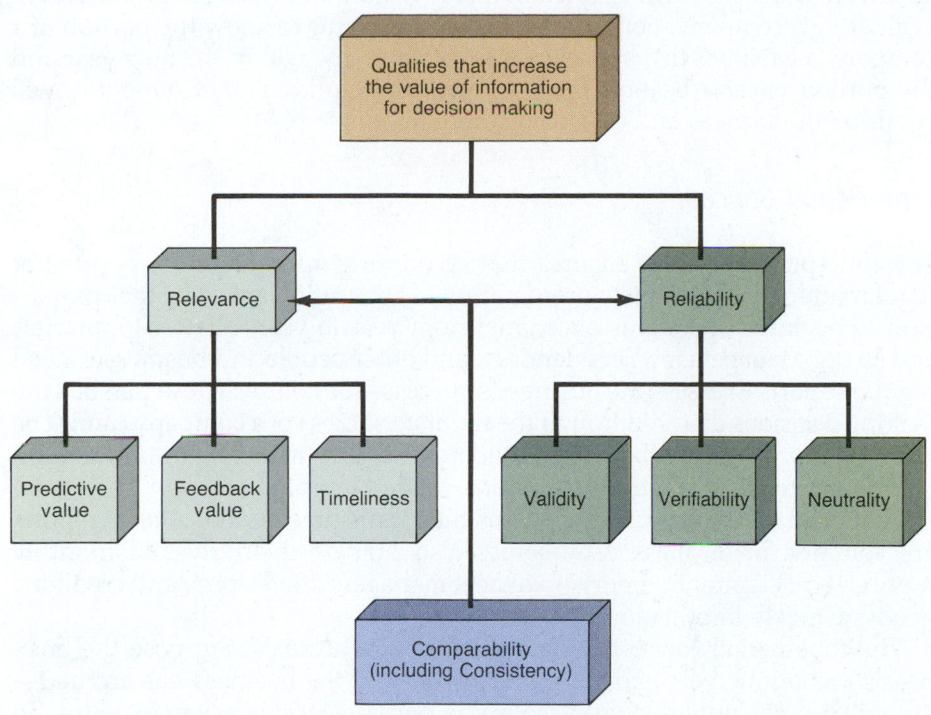

allows her to evaluate the success or failure of the travel agency. If she were to mix her personal and business accounting records, she would lose sight of the information needed to evaluate the business alone.

At the other end of the spectrum, Exxon is a giant company with oil-refining, retail gasoline sales, and chemical operations. Exxon accounts for each of these divisions separately in order to know which part of the business is earning a profit, which needs to borrow money, and so on. The entity concept also provides the basis for consolidating subentities into a single set of financial statements. Exxon reports a single set of consolidated financial statements to the public.

Point to Stress: The entity concept requires that the transactions of each entity are accounted for separately from the transactions of all other organizations and persons.

Going-Concern Concept

Under the **going-concern** (or **continuity) concept,** accountants assume the business will continue operating for the foreseeable future. The logic behind the going-concern concept is best illustrated by considering the alternative assumption: going out of business.

When a business stops, it sells its assets, converting them to cash. This process is called liquidation. With the cash, the business pays off its liabilities, and the owners keep any remaining cash. In liquidation, the amount of cash for which the assets are sold measures their current value. Likewise, the liabilities are paid off at their current value. However, if the business does not halt operations—if it remains a going concern—how are its assets and liabilities reported on the balance sheet?

For a going concern, the balance sheet reports assets and liabilities based on historical cost. To consider what the asset may be worth on the current market requires making an estimate. This may or may not be objective. Under the going-concern concept, it is assumed that the entity will continue long enough to recover the cost of its assets.

Point to Stress: The going-concern concept assumes that a business will continue to operate long enough for it to recover the cost of its assets.

The going-concern concept allows for the reporting of assets and liabilities as current or long-term, a distinction that investors and creditors find useful in evaluating a company. For example, a creditor wants to know the portion of a company's liabilities that are scheduled to come due within the next year and the portion payable beyond the year. The assumption is that the entity will continue in business and honor its commitments.

Time-Period Concept

The **time-period concept** ensures that accounting information is reported at regular intervals. This timely presentation of accounting data aids the comparison of business operations over time; from year to year, quarter to quarter, and so on. Managers, owners, lenders, and other people and businesses need regular reports to assess the business's success—or failure. These persons are making decisions daily. Although the ultimate success of a company cannot be known for sure until the business liquidates, decision makers cannot wait until liquidation to learn whether operations yielded a profit.

Nearly all companies use the year as their basic time period. *Annual* reports are common in business. Companies also prepare quarterly and monthly reports—called interim reports—to meet managers', investors', and creditors' need for timely information.

The time-period concept underlies the use of accruals. Suppose the business's accounting year ends at December 31 and the business has accrued—but will not pay until the next accounting period—$900 in salary expense. To tie this expense to the appropriate period, the accountant enters this adjusting entry, as we have seen:

```
Dec. 31   Salary Expense  ...............................    900
                Salary Payable  ...........................              900
```

Accrual entries assign revenue and expense amounts to the correct accounting period and thus help produce meaningful financial statements.

Stable-Monetary-Unit Concept

Accounting information is expressed primarily in monetary terms. The monetary unit is the prime means of measuring assets. This measure is not surprising given that money is the common denominator in business transactions. In the United States, the monetary unit is the dollar; in Great Britain, the pound sterling; in Japan, the yen. The stable-monetary-unit concept provides an orderly basis for handling account balances to produce the financial statements.

Unlike a liter, a foot, and many other measurements, the value of the monetary unit may change over time. Most of us are familiar with inflation. Groceries that cost $50 three years ago may cost $60 today. The value of the dollar changes. In view of the fact that the dollar does not maintain a constant value, how does a business measure the worth of assets and liabilities acquired over a long span of time? The business records all assets and liabilities at cost. Each asset and each liability on the balance sheet is the sum of all the individual dollar amounts added over time. For example, if a company bought 100 acres of land in 1975 for $60,000 and another 100 acres of land in 1992 for $300,000, the asset Land on the balance sheet carries a $360,000 balance, and the change in the purchasing power of the dollar is ignored. The **stable-monetary-unit concept** is the accountant's basis for ignoring the effect of inflation and making

Point to Stress: In order for accounting information to be useful, it must be made available at regular intervals. The time-period concept ensures that accounting information is reported at regular intervals.

Teaching Tip: Students often have difficulty grasping the concept of the changing value of the dollar. Try the following illustration:

Assume that there are two identical desks. One desk was purchased five years ago for $100 and the other was purchased this year for $120. Why has the price changed? Has the value of the desk changed or has the value of the dollar changed? ANSWER: The desk is about as valuable today as it was five years ago. The dollar does not buy as much today as it did five years ago, so it takes more dollars to buy a new desk.

no restatements for the changing value of the dollar. Let's look at the short-comings of this concept.

Suppose another company paid $600,000 for the same 200 acres of land in 1992. Its land would be the same as the preceding company's land, but its balance sheet would show a much higher amount for the land. How do we compare the two companies' balance sheets? The comparison based on the stable-monetary-unit concept may not be valid because mixing dollar values at different times is like mixing apples and oranges.

Many businesspeople believe that accounting information must be restated for changes in the dollar's purchasing power. The FASB encourages large companies to present supplementary inflation-adjusted information in their financial reports, a topic we examine in Appendix A, page 1291. Generally, however, accounting is based on historical costs.

Accounting Principles

Reliability (Objectivity) Principle

The **reliability principle** requires that accounting information be dependable—free from significant error and bias. Users of accounting information rely on its truthfulness. To be reliable, information must be verifiable by people outside the business. Financial statement users may consider information reliable if independent experts would agree that the information is based on objective and honest measurement.

Consider the error in a company's failure to accrue interest revenue at the end of an accounting period. This error results in understated interest revenue and understated net income. Clearly, this company's accounting information is unreliable.

Biased information—data prepared from a particular viewpoint and not based on objective facts—is also unreliable. Suppose a company purchased inventory for $25,000. At the end of the accounting period, the inventory has declined in value and can be replaced for $20,000. Under the lower-of-cost-or-market rule, the company must record a $5,000 loss for the decrease in the inventory's value. Company management may believe that the appropriate value for the inventory is $22,000, but that amount is only an opinion. If management reports the $22,000 figure, total assets and owner's equity will be overstated on the balance sheet. Income will be overstated on the income statement.

To establish a *reliable* figure for the inventory's value, management could get a current price list from the inventory supplier or call in an outside professional appraiser to revalue the inventory. Evidence obtained from outside the company leads to reliable, verifiable information. The reliability principle applies to all financial accounting information—from assets to owner's equity on the balance sheet and from revenue to net income on the income statement.

Comparability Principle

The **comparability principle** has two requirements. First, accounting information must be comparable from business to business. Second, a single business's financial statements must be comparable from one period to the next. The FASB encourages comparability in order to make possible useful analysis from business to business, from period to period.

Discussion Question: What makes accounting information reliable? ANSWER: Verifiability, and freedom from error and bias.

Teaching Tip: Ask students to look at the auditor's opinion of the financial statements in the appendix to the text. Point out the statement that the accounting principles were applied on a consistent basis.

Point to Stress: It is difficult to compare the performance of a company from one period to another if the company does not consistently use the same accounting practices. Over time, regardless of which depreciation or inventory method is used, a profitable company will appear profitable and an unprofitable company will appear unprofitable. However, changes in accounting methods would make it difficult to detect profitable and unprofitable trends.

Discussion Question: What is one way that businesses report their accounting methods selected so that the users can compare statements? ANSWER: By footnotes. Financial statements must include footnotes describing methods used, such as for inventory and depreciation, so that profit or loss may be compared with that of previous periods or other companies.

Class Exercise: Which of the following is a violation of the principle of comparability or consistency?

1 Firms in the same industry use different accounting methods for a given type of transaction.
2 A company changes from FIFO to LIFO for inventory.
3 A company fails to write down its inventory to the lower of cost or market.
4 A firm fails to adjust its financial statements for changes in the purchasing power of the dollar.

ANSWER: #2

Standard formats for financial statements promote comparability among different companies. Using the same terms to describe the statement elements—assets, liabilities, revenues, and so on—aids the comparison process.

Even among companies that adhere to standard formats and standard terms, comparability may be less than perfect. Comparisons of companies that use different inventory methods—LIFO and FIFO, for example—are difficult. When GAAP allows a choice among acceptable accounting methods—in inventory, depreciation, and other areas—comparability may be hard to achieve.

Recall that the comparability principle directs each individual company to produce accounting information that is comparable over time. To achieve this quality—which accountants call *consistency*—companies must follow the same accounting practices from period to period. The business that uses FIFO for inventory and straight-line for depreciation in one period ought to use those same methods in the next period. Otherwise, a financial statement user could not tell whether changes in income and asset values result from operations or from the way the business accounts for operations.

Companies may change accounting methods in response to a change in business operations. A company may add a new product line that calls for a different inventory method. GAAP allows the company to make a change in accounting method, but the business must disclose the change, the reason for making the change, and the effect of the change on net income. This disclosure is made in a note to the financial statements.

Cost Principle

The **cost principle** states that assets and services are recorded at their purchase cost and that the accounting record of the asset continues to be based on cost rather than current market value. By specifying that assets be recorded at cost, this principle also governs the recording of liabilities and owner's equity. Suppose a land developer purchased 20 acres of land for $50,000. Additional costs included fees paid to the county ($1,500), removal of an unwanted building ($10,000), and landscaping ($20,000), a total cost of $81,500. The Land account carries this balance because it is the cost of bringing the land to its intended use. Assume that the developer holds the land for one year, then offers it for sale at a price of $200,000. The cost principle requires the accounting value of the land to remain at $81,500.

The developer may wish to lure buyers by showing them a balance sheet that reports the land at $200,000. However, this would be inappropriate under GAAP because $200,000 is merely the developer's opinion of what the land is worth.

The underlying basis for the cost principle is the reliability principle. Cost is a reliable value for assets and services because cost is supported by completed transactions between parties with opposing interests. Buyers try to pay the lowest price possible, and sellers try to sell for the highest price. The actual cost of an asset or service is objective evidence of its value.

Revenue Principle

The **revenue principle** provides guidance on the *timing* of the recording of revenue and the *amount* of revenue to record. The general rule is that revenue should be recorded when it is earned and not before.

Some revenues, such as interest and rent, accrue with the passage of time. Their timing and amount are easy to figure. The accountant records the amount of revenue earned over each period of time.

Other revenues are earned by selling goods or rendering services. Identifying *when* these revenues are earned depends on more factors than the passage of time. Under the revenue principle, three conditions must be met before revenue is recorded: (1) the seller has done everything necessary to expect to collect from the buyer; (2) the amount of revenue can be objectively measured; and (3) collectibility is reasonably assured. In most cases, these conditions are met at the point of sale or when services are performed.

The *amount* of revenue to record is the value of the assets received—usually cash or a receivable. However, situations may arise in which the amount of revenue or the timing of earning the revenue is not easily determined. We turn now to four methods that guide the accountant in applying the revenue principle in different circumstances.

Sales Method.   Under the **sales method,** revenue is recorded at the point of sale. Consider a retail sale in a hardware store. When a sale occurs, the customer pays the store and takes the merchandise. The store records the sale by debiting Cash and crediting Sales Revenue. In other situations, the point of sale occurs when the seller ships the goods to the buyer. Suppose a mining company sells iron ore to Bethlehem Steel Corporation. By shipping the ore to Bethlehem Steel, the mining company has completed its duty and may expect to collect cash for the revenue earned. If the amount of revenue can be objectively measured and collection is reasonably certain, the mining company can then record revenue. The sale entry is a debit to Accounts Receivable and a credit to Sales Revenue. The sales method is used for most sales of goods and services.

Collection Method.   The **collection method** is used only if the receipt of cash is uncertain. Under this method, the seller waits until cash is received to record the sale. Professionals such as physicians and attorneys use the collection method because they often find it difficult to collect their receivables. They may not reasonably assume that they can collect the revenue, so they wait until actual receipt of the cash before recording it. The collection method is conservative in that revenue is not recorded in advance of its receipt.

Installment Method.   The **installment method** is a type of collection method that is used for installment sales. In a typical installment sale, the buyer makes a down payment when the contract is signed and pays the remainder in installments. Real estate companies sell on the installment plan. Under the installment method, gross profit (sales revenue minus cost of goods sold) is recorded as cash is collected.

Suppose a real estate developer sells land for a down payment of $80,000 plus three annual installments of $120,000, $140,000, and $160,000 (a total of $500,000). The developer's cost of the land is $300,000, so the gross profit is $200,000, computed as follows:

Installment sale	$500,000
Cost of the land sold	300,000
Gross profit	$200,000

To determine the gross profit associated with each collection under the installment method, we must compute the gross profit percentage, as follows:

$$\text{Gross profit percentage} = \frac{\text{Gross profit}}{\text{Installment sale}} = \frac{\$200,000}{\$500,000} = 40\%$$

Point to Stress: Under the revenue principle, three conditions must be met before revenue is recorded: (1) the seller has done everything necessary to expect to collect from the buyer; (2) the amount of revenue can be objectively determined; and (3) collectibility is reasonably assured.

OBJECTIVE 4
Allocate revenue to the appropriate period by four methods

Discussion Question: The installment method can only be used for financial reporting if there is no reasonable basis for estimating collections, that is, if collectibility is not reasonably assured. Would a company like Sears, which sells on the installment basis, sell a refrigerator to a customer from whom it did not expect payment? *ANSWER:* Of course not. Sears will sell merchandise on the installment basis only to customers whose credit the company has approved.

What type of company might use the installment method with a customer whose credit is not satisfactory? *ANSWER:* A real estate developer could afford to sell land to a person or company that did not have good credit. If the buyer defaulted on the payments, the developer could repossess the land. Another common use for the installment method is for sales of franchises. Sears, however, is not going to sell a refrigerator on the installment basis to someone who does not have approved credit because Sears could not sell a repossessed refrigerator for the same price or more.

Class Exercise: A business makes sales on the installment basis: 19X3 sales are $27,500, downpayments are $2,750, and collections on installments total $8,000. Beginning inventory is $4,000, ending inventory is $3,500, and purchases are $16,000. What are cost of goods sold, total gross profit, and the gross profit percentage for the year?

ANSWER:

COGS = BI + Pur − EI
$16,500 = $4,000 + $16,000 − $3,500

GP = Sales − COGS
$11,000 = $27,500 − $16,500

GP = 40% ($11,000/$27,500)

Now, what gross profit will the business report if it uses the installment method?

ANSWER:

Downpayment	$ 2,750
Collections ...	8,000
Total rec'd ...	10,750
	× 40%
Inst. method	
GP	$ 4,300

We next apply the gross profit percentage to each collection. The result is the amount of gross profit recorded as revenue at the time of cash receipt.

Year	Collections	×	Gross Profit Percentage	=	Gross Profit
1	$ 80,000	×	40%	=	$ 32,000
2	120,000	×	40%	=	48,000
3	140,000	×	40%	=	56,000
4	160,000	×	40%	=	64,000
Total	$500,000	×	40%	=	$200,000

Accountants would record gross profit of $32,000 in year 1, $48,000 in year 2, and so on. The total gross profit ($200,000) is the same as under the sales method. However, under the sales method, the full $200,000 of gross profit would be recorded at the beginning of the contract.

Of course, companies make installment sales year after year. Each year's sales may have a different gross profit percentage. In the preceding example, year 1 installment sales earned gross profit of 40 percent. Suppose year 2 sales earn gross profit of 45 percent, year 3 sales earn 42 percent, and year 4 sales earn 35 percent. The total gross profit for a year is the sum of all the gross profit amounts recorded on cash collections made that year.

Using assumed cash receipts on installment sales made in years 2, 3, and 4, the gross profit computations for years 1 through 4 follow. All year 1 amounts are taken from our computations above.

	Year 1 Sales	Year 2 Sales	Year 3 Sales	Year 4 Sales
Gross profit percentage	40%	45%	42%	35%

Gross profit by year

	Year 1	Year 2	Year 3	Year 4
Year 1 sales:	$80,000 × .40 = $32,000	$120,000 × .40 = $48,000	$140,000 × .40 = $56,000	$160,000 × .40 = $64,000
Year 2 sales:		90,000 × .45 = 40,500	100,000 × .45 = 45,000	20,000 × .45 = 9,000
Year 3 sales:			75,000 × .42 = 31,500	65,000 × .42 = 27,300
Year 4 sales:				30,000 × .35 = 10,500
Total gross profit	$32,000	$88,500	$132,500	$110,800

The installment method is attractive for income tax purposes because it postpones the recording of revenue and thus the payment of taxes. However, it can be used under limited circumstances—for example, the sale of real estate. Under generally accepted accounting principles, this method is permissible only when no reasonable basis exists for estimating collections.

Discussion Question: For a construction company, what is the major drawback of the completed-contract method?

Percentage-of-Completion Method. Construction of office buildings, bridges, dams, and other large assets often extends over several years. The accounting issue for the construction company is *when* to record the revenue. The most conservative approach is to record all the revenue earned on the project in the period when the project is completed. This procedure, called the **completed-contract method,** is acceptable under limited circumstances.

Under the preferred method, called the **percentage-of-completion method,** the construction company recognizes revenue as work is performed. Each year the company estimates the percentage of project completion as construction progresses. One way to make this estimate is to compare the cost incurred for the year with the total estimated project cost. This percentage is then multiplied by the total project revenue to compute the construction revenue for the year. Construction income for the year is revenue minus cost.

Assume Combustion Engineering Company receives a contract to build a power plant for a price of $42 million. Combustion estimates total costs of $36 million over the three-year construction period: $6 million in year 1, $18 million in year 2, and $12 million in year 3. Construction revenue and income during the three years are as follows (amounts in millions):

ANSWER: Under the completed-contract method, all of the profit is reported when the project is complete. In the years during construction, no profit is reported. The company may appear to be unstable because it may show no profit one year and a large profit the next.

Year	Cost for Year	Total Project Cost	Percentage of Project Completion for Year	Total Project Revenue	Construction Revenue for Year	Construction Income for year
1	$ 6	$36	$ 6/$36 = $1/6$	$42	$42 \times 1/6$ = $ 7	$ 7 − $ 6 = $1
2	18	36	18/ 36 = $1/2$	42	42 \times 1/2 = 21	21 − 18 = 3
3	12	36	12/ 36 = $1/3$	42	42 \times 1/3 = 14	14 − 12 = 2
	$36				$42	$42 $36 $6

The percentage-of-completion method is appropriate when the company can estimate the degree of completion during the construction period, which most construction companies can do. When estimates are not possible, the completed-contract method is required. If Combustion Engineering had used the completed-contract method, its income statement for year 3 would report total project revenue of $42 million, total project expenses of $36 million, and income of $6 million. The income statements of years 1 and 2 would report nothing concerning this project. Most accountants believe the results under the percentage-of-completion method are more realistic.

Class Discussion: Percentage-of-completion is appropriate when the company can estimate fairly accurately the total costs of a project so that the degree of completion can be computed. What types of companies would find it difficult to estimate total costs? ANSWER: Defense contractors; utility companies that build nuclear power plants.

Matching Principle

The **matching principle** governs the recording and reporting of expenses. This principle goes hand in hand with the revenue principle to govern income recognition in accounting. Recall that income is revenue minus expense. During any period, the company first measures its revenues by the revenue principle. The company then identifies and measures all the expenses it incurred during the period to earn the revenues. To *match* the expenses against the revenues means to subtract the expenses from the revenues. The result is the income for the period.

Some expenses are easy to match against particular revenues. For example, cost of goods sold relates directly to sales revenue, because without the sales, there would be no cost of goods sold. Commissions and fees paid for selling the goods, delivery expense, and sales supplies expense relate to sales revenue for the same reason.

Other expenses are not so easily linked to particular sales because they occur whether or not any revenues arise. Depreciation, salaries, and all types of home-office expense are in this category. Accountants usually match these expenses against revenue on a time basis. For example, the company's home-office building may be used for general management, manufacturing, and marketing. Straight-line depreciation of a 40-year building assigns one-fortieth of the building's cost to expense each year, whatever the level of revenue. The annual salary expense for an employee is the person's total salary for the year, regardless of revenue.

Losses, like expenses, are matched against revenue on a time basis. For example, if an asset like inventory loses value, the loss is recorded when it occurs, without regard for the revenues earned during the period.

Disclosure Principle

Teaching Tip: Ask the students to look at the notes to the financial statements in Appendix C. Point out where the inventory and depreciation methods are disclosed.

OBJECTIVE 5

Report information that satisfies the disclosure principle

The **disclosure principle** holds that a company's financial statements should report enough information for outsiders to make knowledgeable decisions about the company. In short, the company should report *relevant, reliable,* and *comparable* information about its economic affairs. This section of the chapter discusses and illustrates different types of disclosures.

Summary of Significant Accounting Policies. To evaluate a company, investors and creditors need to know how its financial statements were prepared. This consideration is especially important when the company can choose from several acceptable methods. Companies summarize their accounting policies in the first note to their financial statements. The note may include both monetary amounts and written descriptions. Companies commonly disclose revenue-recognition method, inventory method, and depreciation method.

Dresser Industries, Inc., a manufacturer of oilfield and other industrial equipment, reported the following:

NOTE A—SUMMARY OF SIGNIFICANT ACCOUNTING POLICIES [IN PART]

Long-Term Contracts

Revenues and earnings related to products requiring long-term construction periods, principally draglines and electrostatic precipitators, are recognized for financial reporting purposes on the percentage of completion basis.

Inventories

Substantially all the U.S. inventories of the Company are recorded on a last-in, first-out (LIFO) cost basis. Inventories not on LIFO cost valuation, principally foreign inventories, are recorded at the "lower of cost (principally average cost) or market."

Fixed Assets

Fixed assets are depreciated over the estimated service life. Accelerated depreciation methods are used for financial statement purposes, except for U.S. fixed assets with a service life of 10 years or less which are depreciated on a straight-line basis. Accelerated depreciation methods are also used for tax purposes wherever permitted.

Probable Losses. The disclosure principle directs a business to record and report a probable loss *before* it occurs if the loss is likely and its amount can be estimated. Phillips Petroleum Company reported such a loss in a recent financial statement. Observe that the disposal of assets has not occurred yet, but the company does *expect* the disposal to result in a loss.

NOTE 1—DISCONTINUED OPERATION [IN PART]

[T]he company announced plans to discontinue its minerals operation. Assets associated with these operations were sold, abandoned, or written down . . . in anticipation of their future sale or abandonment, resulting in an estimated net loss on disposal . . . of $171 million, net of income tax. . . .

The $171 million loss on disposal appeared on Phillips's income statement as follows:

	Millions
Income from Continuing Operations	$ 596
Discontinued operations (net of income taxes)	
Loss from operations	(7)
Loss on disposal	**(171)**
Net Income	$ 418

Accounting Changes. Consistent use of accounting methods and procedures is important, as we saw in discussing comparability. When a company does change from one accounting method or procedure to another, it must disclose the change, the reason for making the change, and the effect of the change on net income. Two common accounting changes are *changes in accounting principles* and *changes in accounting estimates.*

A **change in accounting principle** is a change in accounting method. A switch from the LIFO method to the FIFO method for inventories and a switch from the double-declining-balance depreciation method to the straight-line method are examples of accounting changes. Special rules that apply to changes in accounting principles are discussed in later accounting courses. Whatever the change in principle, the notes to the financial statements must inform the reader of the change and its effect on income.

A **change in accounting estimate** occurs in the normal course of business as the company alters earlier expectations. A company may record uncollectible account expense based on the estimate that bad debts will equal 2 percent of sales. If actual collections exceed this estimate, the company may lower its estimated expense to 1½ percent of sales in the future.

An airline company such as American or Delta may originally estimate that a new Boeing 767 airplane will provide fifteen years' service. After ten years of using the plane, the company sees that the plane's full useful life will stretch to eighteen years. The company must recompute depreciation based on this new information at the start of the plane's eleventh year of service. Assume that this plane cost $30 million, has an estimated residual value of $6 million, and is depreciated by the straight-line method.

Annual depreciation for each of the first ten years of the asset's life is $1.6 million, computed as follows:

$$\text{Depreciation per year} = \frac{\$30 \text{ million} - \$6 \text{ million}}{15 \text{ years}} = \$1.6 \text{ million}$$

Changes in estimate are accounted for by spreading the asset's remaining depreciable book value over its remaining life. Annual depreciation after the accounting change is $1 million, computed in the following manner:

$$\frac{\text{Depreciation}}{\text{per year}} = \frac{\text{Remaining depreciable book value}}{\text{Remaining life}} = \frac{\$30 \text{ million} - \$6 \text{ million} - (\$1.6 \text{ million} \times 10)}{18 \text{ total years} - 10 \text{ years used}}$$

$$= \frac{\$8 \text{ million}}{8 \text{ years}} = \$1 \text{ million}$$

This revised amount of depreciation is recorded in the usual manner.

Point to Stress: A change in estimate is not a correction of an error. Previous years' financial statements are not changed to reflect a change in estimate. Changes in estimates are routine for most companies.

Discussion Question: Have students recall other recorded expenses that are estimated. ANSWER: Product Warranties, Amortization, Depletion, and Uncollectible Accounts.

Subsequent Events. A company usually takes several weeks after the end of the year to close its books and to publish its financial statements. Occasionally, events occur during this period that affect the interpretation of the information in those financial statements. Such an occurrence is called a **subsequent event** and should be disclosed in the prior period's statements. The most common examples of subsequent events are borrowing money, paying debts, making investments, selling assets, and becoming a defendant in a lawsuit.

United Merchants and Manufacturers, Inc., operates principally in the apparel, textiles, and home furnishings industries. The company reported the following subsequent event in its financial statements for the year ended June 30, 19X6:

NOTE 17—SUBSEQUENT EVENTS

On September 11, 19X6, the Company sold 17 percent of [its investment in] Victoria Creations, Inc., which is in the costume jewelry business. The sale resulted in cash proceeds to the Company of $13,910,000, which has been used to reduce indebtedness. The sale also resulted in a gain . . . of approximately $6,400,000, which will be reflected in the Company's results of operations for . . . 19X7.

Point to Stress: A business does not have to report the results of every segment regardless of its size. A segment is defined as a reportable segment if it satisfies one of the three following tests:

1 Revenue Test. Its revenues are 10% or more of the combined revenues of all segments.
2 Operating Profit Test. Its operating profit (loss) is 10% or more of the combined operating profits of all segments that did not incur an operating loss.
3 Asset Test. Its identifiable assets are 10% or more of the combined identifiable assets of all industry segments.

Business Segments. Most large companies operate in more than one product line or industry. Each area is called a *business segment.* Sears, Roebuck, and Company, best known for its retail stores, also has real estate, investment banking, and other financial service operations. Union Pacific Corporation, the railroad company, is also active in the oil and gas business. Diversification like this is not limited to large international companies. A realtor may also own a restaurant. A farmer may sell farm implements. An automobile dealer may also own a furniture store.

Suppose you are considering investing in a company that is active in the steel industry but also owns a meat packer and several leisure resorts. Assume the American steel industry is in retreat because of intense foreign competition. With income and asset data broken down by business segments, you can determine how much of the company's assets are committed to each segment and which lines of business are most (and least) profitable. Companies disclose segment data in notes to their financial statements.

The Scott Paper Company data in the accompanying table meet the GAAP requirement for adequate disclosure of business segments.

Year 19X6	(Millions)	Sales	Income before Taxes	Identifiable Assets	Capital Expenditures	Depreciation and Cost of Timber Harvested
Business Segment	Personal Care and Cleaning	$2,349.5	$252.7	$2,105.4	$220.0	$124.1
	Printing and Publishing Papers	921.2	149.2	1,217.4	178.3	62.4
	Pulp, Forest Products and Minerals	166.3	17.6	188.4	16.7	11.6
	Total business segments	$3,437.0	$419.5	$3,511.2	$415.0	$198.1

Disclosure Techniques. Companies use parenthetical notes in the financial statements. An example is the allowance for uncollectibles, reported as follows by RJR Nabisco, Inc. (in millions):

	December 31,	
	19X7	19X6

Accounts and notes receivable
(less allowances of $61 and $67, respectively) $1,745 $1,675

Other companies, including CPC International, Inc., list the allowance on a separate line of the balance sheet, as follows (in millions):

	December 31,	
	19X7	19X6
Notes and accounts receivable [summarized]	$549.9	$592.5
Allowances for doubtful accounts	(12.5)	(14.2)

Both disclosure techniques provide adequate information on the total amount receivable and the net amount expected to be collected.

Constraints on Accounting

Do financial statements report every detail, no matter how small, to meet the need for relevant, reliable, and comparable information? The result would be an avalanche of data. To address this problem, accountants use the *materiality concept*. Also, a company's top managers are responsible for its financial statements. To add balance to managers' optimism—which could bias the statements and present too favorable a picture of company operations—accountants follow the *conservatism concept*. This section discusses these constraints on accounting information.

Materiality Concept

The **materiality concept** states that a company must perform strictly proper accounting only for items and transactions that are significant to the business's financial statements. Information is significant—accountants call it *material*—when its inclusion and correct presentation in the financial statement would cause a statement user to change a decision because of that information. Immaterial—insignificant—items justify less than perfect accounting. The inclusion and proper presentation of *immaterial* items would not affect a statement user's decision. The materiality concept frees accountants from having to compute and report every last item in strict accordance with GAAP. Thus the materiality concept reduces the cost of accounting.

How does a business decide where to draw the line between what is material and what is immaterial? This decision rests to a great degree on how large the business is. Wendy's, for example, has close to $500 million in assets. Management would likely treat as immaterial a $100 purchase of wastebaskets. These wastebaskets may well remain useful for ten years, and strictly speaking, Wendy's should capitalize their cost and depreciate the wastebaskets. However, this treatment is not practical. The accounting costs of computing, recording, and properly reporting this asset outweighs the benefits of any information provided. No statement user—a potential investor or lender, for example—would change a decision based on so insignificant (immaterial) an amount. The cost of accounting in this case outweighs the benefit of the resulting information.

Large companies may draw the materiality line at as high a figure as $10,000 and expense any smaller amount. Smaller firms may choose to expense only

Typical Student Misconception: Students often want to know an amount or a percentage to use in judging materiality and immateriality. Stress that it is a case-by-case decision—what is immaterial in one instance (or for one business) may be material in another instance (or for another business). There is no rule-of-thumb, customary measurement as to what is material.

Also, the type of account must be considered in determining whether an amount is material or immaterial. A difference of $700 in cost of goods sold would not be material to many businesses; however, a discrepancy of $700 in Cash would certainly call for some action.

OBJECTIVE 6
Apply two constraints to accounting

Class Exercise: Which of the following principles or concepts directs a business to record as an expense all items that cost $50 or less, even if the item will be used for more than one accounting period.

1 Disclosure
2 Matching
3 Objectivity
4 Materiality
5 Going-concern

ANSWER: #4

those items less than $50. Materiality varies from company to company. An amount that is material to the local service station may not be material to General Motors.

The materiality concept does not free a business from having to account for every item. Wendy's, for example, must still account for the wastebaskets. Wendy's would credit Cash (or Accounts Payable) to record their purchase, of course, but what account would the company debit? Because the amount is immaterial, management may decide to debit Supplies Expense. No matter what account receives the debit, no statement user's decision would be changed by the information.

Conservatism Concept

Class Exercise: Which of the following accounting principles or concepts is best described by this statement: "Recognize that some accounting measurements take place in a context of significant uncertainty and that possible errors in measurement could occur. Statements should tend to understate rather than overstate net assets and income."

1 Materiality
2 Disclosure
3 Entity
4 Reliability
5 Conservatism

ANSWER: #5

Business managers are often optimists. Asked how well the company is doing, its president will likely answer, "Great, we're having our best year ever." Without constraints this optimism could find its way into the company's reported assets and profits. Managers may try to present too favorable a view of the company. For example, they may pressure accountants to capitalize costs associated with fixed assets that should be expensed. This would result in less immediate expense and higher current income on the income statement. The balance sheet would report unduly high fixed asset values and owner's equity. The overall result would be that the managers' performance would appear to be better than it actually was. Traditionally, accountants have been conservative, to counter management's optimism.

Conservatism has been interpreted as "Anticipate no profits, but anticipate all losses." A clear-cut example is the lower-of-cost-or-market (LCM) method for inventories. Under LCM, inventory is reported at the *lower* of its cost or market value, which results in higher cost of goods sold and lower net income. Thus profits and assets are reported at their lowest reasonable amount. Other conservative accounting practices include the LIFO method for inventories when inventory costs are increasing, accelerated depreciation, and the completed-contract method for construction revenues. These methods result in earlier recording of expenses or later recording of revenues. Both effects postpone the reporting of net income and therefore are conservative.

In recent years, conservatism's effect on accounting has decreased. The FASB has stated that conservatism should not mean deliberate understatement of assets, profits, and owner's equity. However, if two different values can be used for an asset or a liability, the concept suggests using the less optimistic value. Conservatism is a secondary consideration in accounting. Relevant, reliable, and comparable information is the goal, and conservatism is a factor only after these primary goals are met.

Financial Statements and Their Elements _____

We have examined the concepts and principles that shape accounting practice. The FASB aims for financial statements that best meet user needs for business information.

This accounting information appears in four statements: the balance sheet, the income statement, the statement of owner's equity, and the statement of cash flows (which we cover in Chapter 18). The FASB provides definitions for the elements that make up these statements. Financial information presentation, to be most useful to the greatest number of statements users, must be presented in a standard format with well-defined terms, as we learned in our discussion of the comparability concept.

FASB Concepts Statement No. 3 provides authoritative definitions of the elements of financial statements.[1]

Balance Sheet Elements

Assets are future economic benefits obtained or controlled by a particular entity as a result of past transactions.

Liabilities are the obligations of an entity to transfer assets or provide services to other entities as a result of past transactions.

Equity (Owner's Equity) is the interest in the assets of an entity that remains after subtracting its liabilities. It is the ownership interest in the entity.

Income Statement Elements

Revenues are inflows of assets that arise from delivering or producing goods, rendering services, or performing other activities that constitute the entity's ongoing central operations.

Expenses are outflows of assets or the incurrences of liabilities that arise from delivering or producing goods, rendering services, or carrying out activities that constitute the entity's ongoing central operations.

Gains are increases in owner's equity that do not result from revenues or investments by owners.

Losses are decreases in owner's equity that do not result from expenses or distributions to owners.

Note that *revenues* and *expenses* arise from the business's ongoing central operations, but *gains* and *losses* do not. Sales and interest earned are revenues because most companies make sales and earn interest as part of their central operations. Selling cars and trucks lies at the heart of an automobile dealership. To this business, a gain on the sale of a truck is revenue, and a loss on the sale is expense. However, a gain on the sale of a truck is not revenue for a trucking company because that entity buys trucks for use rather than for sale. Selling a truck is not a part of central operations. Exhibit 12-4 shows how to report revenues, expenses, gains, and losses on a multiple-step and a single-step income statement.

---

[1] The definitions here are paraphrased from *FASB Concepts Statement No. 3,* "Elements of Financial Statements of Business Enterprises" (Stamford, CT: December 1980), Highlights.

Point to Stress: Revenues and expenses arise from the business's ongoing central operations. Gains and losses arise from peripheral transactions that contribute to a business's overall profitability.

Class Exercise: Classify the following as either revenue, expense, gain, or loss for a grocery store chain.

1 Loss from the sale of all stores on the West Coast.
2 Rent for one year on the chain's main office complex.
3 Sale of a computer no longer used in the business below book value.
4 Sale of groceries to Mary Westlake.

ANSWER:

1 loss
2 expense
3 loss
4 revenue

EXHIBIT 12-4 *Reporting Revenues, Expenses, Gains, and Losses*

Multiple-Step Income Statement			Single-Step Income Statement		
Sales revenue		$XXX	Revenues and gains:		
Cost of goods sold		XXX	Sales revenue		$XXX
Gross profit		XXX	Gain on sale of land		XXX
Operating expenses		XXX	Total revenues and gains		XXX
Income from operations		XXX	Expenses and losses:		
Other items:			Cost of goods sold	$XXX	
Gain on sale of land	$XXX		Operating expenses	XXX	
Loss due to fire	XXX	XXX	Loss due to fire	XXX	
			Total expenses and losses		XXX
Net income		$XXX	Net income		$XXX

Statement of Owner's Equity Elements

Investments by owners are increases in owner's equity that result from the owner's transferring to the entity something of value. The most common investment is cash, but owners sometimes invest land, buildings, legal services, or other assets. In some cases, an owner's investment in the business may consist of paying off its liabilities. **Distributions to owners** are decreases in owner's equity that result from the owner's transferring assets or services from the business to himself or herself, or from the business taking on the owner's liabilities. When the business is a corporation, owner withdrawals are called dividends. The most commonly distributed asset is cash, but businesses sometimes distribute other assets, such as stock investments they hold in other companies, to their owners.

Exhibit 12-5 summarizes the main points of the foundation for generally accepted accounting principles.

Accounting Standards Throughout the World

Real-World Example: The International Accounting Standards Committee (IASC) is engaged in a project to increase the comparability of international financial standards. The IASC has already issued an exposure draft (E32) that explores amending 13 standards and eliminating 23 accounting treatments that are currently allowed. For example, the proposed standards specify FIFO as the preferable method but they do allow LIFO, effectively reducing the inventory options to two. Also, a 5 to 20 year period could be used for amortizing goodwill instead of the maximum of 40 years now allowed by GAAP in the United States.

We have focused on the principles of accounting that are generally accepted in the United States. Most of the methods of accounting are consistent throughout the world. Double-entry bookkeeping, the accrual accounting system, and the basic financial statements are used worldwide. Differences, however, do exist among countries.

In discussing depreciation—Chapter 11—we emphasized that in the United States the methods used for reporting to tax authorities differ from the methods used for reporting to shareholders. In contrast, tax reporting and shareholder reporting are identical in many countries. For example, France has a "Plan Compatible" that specifies a National Uniform Chart of Accounts used for both tax returns and reporting to shareholders. German financial reporting is also determined primarily by tax laws. If accounting records are not kept according to strict tax laws, the tax authorities can reject the records as a basis for taxation.

In some countries, tax laws have a major influence on shareholder reporting even if tax and shareholder reports are not required to be identical. In Japan, for example, certain principles are allowed for tax purposes only if they are also used for shareholder reporting.

A significant difference among countries is the extent to which financial statements account for inflation. In the 1980s, the FASB experimented with requiring supplementary disclosure of inflation-adjusted numbers, but there is no requirement for such supplementary disclosure in the United States. In contrast, some countries have full or partial adjustments for inflation as part of their reporting to both investors and tax authorities. For example, Argentina and Brazil, which have experienced very high inflation rates, require all statements to be adjusted for changes in the general price level.

The globalization of business enterprises and capital markets is creating much interest in establishing common, worldwide accounting standards. There are probably too many cultural, social, and political differences to expect complete worldwide standardization of financial reporting in the near future. However, the number of differences is decreasing. Cooperation among accountants has been fostered by the International Federation of Accountants (IFAC), an organization of accountancy bodies from more than seventy-five countries. International standards are being formulated and published by the International Accounting Standards Committee (IASC).

EXHIBIT 12-5 *Statements of Financial Accounting Concepts (SFAC)*

Statement	Highlights
SFAC No. 1, Objectives of Financial Reporting by Business Enterprises	• Accounting should provide information useful for making economic decisions • Focuses on external users, mainly creditors and investors • Information should aid the prediction of cash flows • Earnings based on accrual accounting provide a better measure of performance than do cash receipts and disbursements
SFAC No. 2, Qualitative Characteristics of Accounting Information	• Both relevance and reliability are necessary for information to be useful • Relevance requires timeliness and either predictive or feedback value • Reliable information must have representational faithfulness and be verifiable and neutral • Comparability and consistency aid usefulness • To be useful, information must be material, that is, reported amounts must be large enough to make a difference in decisions • Benefits from using information should exceed its cost
SFAC No. 3, Elements of Financial Statements of Business Enterprises	• Defines the building blocks that comprise financial statements: (1) assets, (2) liabilities, (3) equity, (4) investments by owners, (5) distributions to owners, (6) revenues, (7) expenses, (8) gains, and (9) losses
SFAC No. 5, Recognition and Measurement in Financial Statements of Business Enterprises	• All components of financial statements are important, not just a single "bottom-line" number • A statement of financial position provides information about assets, liabilities, and equity; it does not show the market value of the entity • Earnings measures periodic performance • Revenue is recorded when it is earned, it can be measured objectively, and its collectibility is reasonably assured • Information based on current prices, if reliable and more relevant than alternative information, should be reported if costs involved are not too high

Summary Problem for Your Review

This chapter has discussed the following principles and concepts:

Entity concept
Going-concern concept
Time-period concept
Reliability principle
Comparability principle

Cost principle
Revenue principle
Matching principle
Disclosure principle
Materiality concept

Indicate which of these concepts is being violated in each of the following situations:

1. A construction company signs a two-year contract to build a bridge for the state of Montana. The president of the company immediately records the full contract price as revenue.
2. Competition has taken away much of the business of a small airline. The airline is unwilling to report its plans to sell half its fleet of planes.
3. After starting the business in February 19X2, a coal-mining company keeps no accounting records for 19X2, 19X3, and 19X4. The owner is waiting until the mine is exhausted to determine the success or failure of the business.
4. Assets recorded at cost by a drug store chain are written up to their fair market value at the end of each year.
5. The accountant for a manufacturing company keeps detailed depreciation records on every asset no matter how small its value.
6. A physician mixes her personal accounting records with those of the medical practice.
7. Expenses are reported whenever the bookkeeper records them rather than when related revenues are earned.
8. The damaged inventory of a discount store is being written down. The store manager bases the write-down entry on his own subjective opinion in order to minimize income taxes.
9. A quick-copy center changes accounting methods every year in order to report the maximum amount of net income possible under generally accepted accounting principles.
10. The owners of a private hospital base its accounting records on the assumption that the hospital might have to close at any time. The hospital has a long record of service to the community.

SOLUTION TO REVIEW PROBLEM

1. Revenue principle
2. Disclosure principle
3. Time-period concept
4. Cost principle
5. Materiality concept
6. Entity concept
7. Matching principle
8. Reliability principle
9. Comparability principle
10. Going-concern concept

Summary

The Financial Accounting Standards Board (FASB) formulates generally accepted accounting principles (GAAP) to provide relevant, reliable, and comparable accounting information. *Relevant* information allows users to make business predictions and to evaluate past decisions. *Reliable* data are free from material error and bias. Accounting information is also intended to be *comparable* from company to company and from period to period.

Four concepts underlie accounting. The most basic, the *entity concept*, draws clear boundaries around the accounting entity. The entity, based on the *going-concern concept*, is assumed to remain in business for the foreseeable future.

The *time-period concept* is the basis for reporting accounting information for particular time periods such as months, quarters, and years. Under the *stable-monetary-unit concept,* no adjustment is made for the changing value of the dollar.

Accounting principles provide detailed guidelines for recording transactions and preparing the financial statements. The *reliability* and *comparability principles* require that accounting information be based on objective data and be useful for comparing companies across different time periods. The *cost principle* governs accounting for assets and liabilities, and the *revenue principle* governs accounting for revenues. *Matching* is the basis for recording expenses. The *disclosure* principle requires companies to report their accounting policies, probable future losses, accounting changes, subsequent events, and business-segment data. They use different disclosure techniques.

Two constraints on accounting are materiality and conservatism. The *materiality concept* allows companies to avoid excessive cost in accounting for immaterial items. *Conservatism* constrains the optimism of managers by anticipating no profits, but anticipating all losses.

Financial statements and their elements include:
Balance sheet: assets, liabilities, and *equity (owner's equity)*
Income statement: revenues, expenses, gains, and *losses*
Statement of owner's equity: investments by owners and *distributions to owners.*

Self-Study Questions

Test your understanding of the chapter by marking the best answer for each of the following questions.

1. The organization that issues accounting pronouncements that make up GAAP is the *(p. 546, 547)*
    a. U.S. Congress
    b. Accounting Principles Board
    ✓ c. Financial Accounting Standards Board
    d. Securities and Exchange Commission

2. Which of the following characteristics of accounting information does the objective of financial reporting omit? *(p. 548)*
    ✓ a. Timeliness
    b. Relevance
    c. Reliability
    d. Comparability

3. A new business is starting. The president wishes to wait until significant contracts have been fulfilled before reporting the results of the business's operations. Which underlying concept serves as the basis for preparing financial statements at regular intervals? *(p. 550)*
    a. Entity
    b. Going concern
    ✓ c. Time period
    d. Stable monetary unit

4. Which of these revenue methods is the most conservative? *(pp. 553, 560)*
    a. Sales method
    ✓ b. Collection method
    c. Percentage-of-completion method
    d. All the above are equally conservative

5. Suppose a Montgomery Ward store sells $10,000 worth of kitchen appliances on the installment plan and collects a down payment of $1,500. Ward's cost of the appliances is $7,000. How much gross profit will the company report this period under the installment revenue method? *(pp. 553, 554)*
    ✓ a. $450
    b. $1,500
    c. $3,000
    d. $10,000

6. A construction company spent $180,000 during the current year on a building with a contract price of $900,000. The company estimated total

construction cost at $720,000. How much construction *income* will the company report under the percentage-of-completion method? *(p. 555)*

√ a. $45,000   c. $180,000
b. $144,000   d. $225,000

7. Which of the following items should be reported to satisfy the disclosure principle? *(pp. 556, 557, 558)*
   a. Business segment data   c. Accounting changes
   b. Probable losses   d. All of the above

8. Important subsequent events should be disclosed because they *(p. 558)*
   a. Occur immediately after the current period
   b. Describe changes in accounting methods
   c. Reveal losses that have a high probability of occurring in the future
   √ d. May affect the interpretation of the current-period financial statements

9. Which of the following statements is most in keeping with the materiality concept? *(p. 559)*
   a. Accountants record material losses but are reluctant to record material gains
   √ b. Different companies have different materiality limits, depending on their size
   c. Business-segment data are disclosed to fulfill the materiality concept
   d. Companies report all the information needed to communicate a material view of the entity

10. Gains and losses are most similar to *(pp. 561, 562)*
    a. Assets and liabilities   c. Investments by owners and dis-
    √ b. Revenues and expenses   tributions to owners

Answers to the Self-Study Questions follow the Accounting Vocabulary.

Accounting Vocabulary

Change in accounting estimate. A change that occurs in the normal course of business as a company alters earlier expectations. *(p. 557)*.

Change in accounting principle. A change in accounting method, such as from the LIFO method to the FIFO method for inventories and a switch from an accelerated depreciation method to the straight-line method *(p. 557)*.

Collection method. Method of applying the revenue principle by which the seller waits until cash is received to record the sale. This method is used only if the receipt of cash is uncertain *(p. 553)*.

Comparability principle. Specifies that accounting information must be comparable from business to business and that a single business's financial statements must be comparable from one period to the next *(p. 551)*.

Completed-contract method. Method of applying the revenue principle by

a construction company by which all revenue earned on the project is recorded in the period when the project is completed *(p. 555)*.

Cost principle. States that assets and services are recorded at their purchase cost and that the accounting record of the asset continues to be based on cost rather than current market value *(p. 552)*.

Disclosure principle. Holds that a company's financial statements should report enough information for outsiders to make knowledgeable decisions about the company *(p. 556)*.

Gain. An increase in owner equity that does not result from a revenue or an investment by an owner in the business *(p. 561)*.

Going-concern concept. Accountants' assumption that the business will continue operating in the foreseeable future *(p. 549)*.

Installment method. Method of applying the revenue principle in which gross profit (sales revenue minus cost of goods sold) is recorded as cash is collected *(p. 553)*.

Loss. A decrease in owner equity that does not result from an expense or a distribution to an owner of the business *(p. 561)*.

Materiality concept. States that a company must perform strictly proper accounting only for items and transactions that are significant to the business's financial statements *(p. 559)*.

Percentage-of-completion method. Method of applying the revenue principle by a construction company, by which revenue is recorded as the work is performed *(p. 555)*.

Reliability principle. Requires that accounting information be dependable (free from error and

bias). Also called the Objectivity principle *(p. 551)*.

Sales method. Method of applying the revenue principle in which revenue is recorded at the point of sale. This method is used for most sales of goods and services *(p. 553)*.

Stable-monetary-unit concept. Accountants' basis for ignoring the effect of inflation and making no adjustments for the changing value of the dollar *(p. 550)*.

Subsequent event. An event that occurs after the end of a company's accounting period but before publication of its financial statements and which may affect the interpretation of the information in those statements *(p. 558)*.

Time-period concept. Ensures that accounting information is reported at regular intervals *(p. 550)*.

Answers to Self-Study Questions

1. c
2. a
3. c
4. b
5. a ($10,000 − $7,000)/$10,000 = .30 × $1,500 = $450
6. a $180,000/$720,000 =.25 × $900,000 = $225,000;
   $225,000 − $180,000 = $45,000

7. d
8. d
9. b
10. b

ASSIGNMENT MATERIAL

Questions

1. How do accounting principles differ from natural laws?
2. State the basic objective of financial reporting.
3. What three characteristics make accounting information useful for decision making? Briefly discuss each characteristic.
4. What is the entity concept?
5. How does the going-concern concept affect accounting? What is liquidation?
6. Identify two practical results of the time-period concept.
7. What is the shortcoming of the stable-monetary-unit concept?
8. What are the two requirements of the comparability principle?
9. Why is consistency important in accounting?
10. Discuss the relationship between the cost principle and the reliability principle.
11. What three conditions must be met before revenue is recorded? What determines the amount of the revenue?
12. Which revenue recognition method is more conservative, the sales method or the collection method? Give your reason.

13. Suppose Century Realty sold land for $200,000 on an installment basis, receiving a down payment of $50,000 to be followed by 12 installments of $12,500 each. If Century's cost of the land was $120,000, how much gross profit would Century record under the installment method (a) when the down payment is received and (b) when each installment is received?

14. Briefly discuss two methods of recognizing revenue on long-term construction contracts.

15. Give two examples of expenses that are easy to relate to sales revenue and two examples of expenses that are not so easy to relate to particular sales. On what basis are the latter expenses matched against revenue?

16. Phoenix Company agreed on November 22, 19X7, to sell an unprofitable manufacturing plant. Phoenix estimates on December 31 that the company is likely to incur a $4 million loss on the sale when it is finalized in 19X8. In which year should Phoenix report the loss? What accounting principle governs this situation?

17. Identify three items commonly disclosed in a company's summary of significant accounting policies.

18. What is a subsequent event? Why should companies disclose important subsequent events in their financial statements?

19. How does information on business segments help an investor?

20. Classify each of the following as a change in accounting principle or a change in accounting estimate:
    a. Change from straight-line to double-declining-balance depreciation
    b. Change in the uncollectibility of accounts receivable
    c. Change from LIFO to FIFO for inventory
    d. Change from the percentage-of-completion method to the completed-contract method for revenue on long-term construction contracts
    e. Change from an 8-year life to a 10-year life for a machine
    f. Change in estimated warranty expense rate stated as a percent of sales

21. Sloan Sales Company expenses the cost of plant assets below $500 at the time of purchase. What accounting concept allows this departure from strictly proper accounting? Why would Sloan Sales follow such a policy?

22. Give three examples of conservative accounting methods, stating why the methods are conservative.

23. Identify two balance sheet elements that are defined independently and give the definition of the third balance sheet element.

24. The four income statement elements may be divided into two pairs of similar elements. What elements make up these two pairs?

Exercises

Exercise 12-1 *Identifying the objective of financial reporting* **(L.O. 1)**

As a financial analyst with Merrill Lynch, your job is to follow the aerospace industry. Specifically, you compare companies in this industry to recommend to Merrill Lynch clients which companies to invest in. What is the basic objective of financial reporting? Briefly discuss some of the predictions and related evaluations of past performance that an investment analyst would make. Also state why the analyst feels more comfortable using information that has been audited by an independent CPA.

No check figure

Exercise 12-2 *Applying accounting concepts* **(L.O. 2)**

The Merrimac Insider is a magazine devoted to cultural affairs in the Tidewater region of Virginia, North Carolina, and South Carolina. Its owner, Marla Griffis, is better attuned to cultural affairs than to the business aspects of running a magazine. Readership is at an all-time high, but the financial position of the business has suffered. For each of the following items indicate the accounting action needed at December 31, the end of the accounting year. Also identify the underlying accounting concept most directly applicable to your answer.

a. On March 31, *The Merrimac Insider* had to borrow $200,000 to pay bills. The interest rate of this one-year loan is 11 percent, payable March 31.

b. Ms. Griffis intermingles her personal assets with those of the business. In applying for the $200,000 loan, she wanted to include on the company books her Lincoln automobile, which was worth $24,000. Her reasoning was that the business is a proprietorship and that her personal assets are available to the magazine if needed.

c. Its financial position is so dismal that *The Merrimac Insider* is in danger of failure. Assets measured at historical cost total $1.3 million, but their current market value is only $900,000, which barely exceeds liabilities of $850,000. For now it appears that the magazine will remain in business.

Exercise 12-3 *Reporting assets as a going concern and as a liquidating entity*
(L.O. 2, 3)

Ferris-Browning Company has the following assets:

Cash, $9,000

Accounts receivable, $25,600; allowance for uncollectible accounts, $4,300

Office supplies, cost $280; scrap value $70

Office machinery, cost $72,000; accumulated depreciation, $14,000; current sales value, $47,400

Land, cost $85,000; current sales value, $135,000

Required

1. Assume Ferris-Browning continues as a going concern. Compute the amount of its assets for reporting on the balance sheet.
2. Assume Ferris-Browning is going out of business by liquidating its assets. Compute the amount of its assets at liquidation value.

Total assets:
Going concern $173,580
Liquidation $212,770

Exercise 12-4 *Reporting assets under GAAP* **(L.O. 3)**

Identify the amount at which each of the following assets should be reported in the financial statements of Charter Corporation. Cite the concept, principle, or constraint that is most applicable to each answer.

a. Charter purchased a machine for $25,000 less a $1,300 cash discount. To ship the machine to the office, Charter paid transportation charges of $500 and insurance of $200 while in transit. After using the machine for one month, Charter purchases lubricating oil costing $150 for use in operating the machine.

b. Inventory has a cost of $72,000, but its current market value is $69,400.

c. Charter purchased land for $175,000 and paid $2,500 to have the land surveyed, $15,400 to have old buildings removed, and $40,300 for grading land. Charter is offering the land for sale at $225,000 and has received a $200,000 offer.

a. Cost of machine $24,400

Exercise 12-5 *Reporting income under GAAP* **(L.O. 3)**

Mayfair Building Materials Company failed to record the following items at December 31, 19X4, the end of its fiscal year:

Accrued salary expense, $1,300
Prepaid insurance, $700
Accrued interest expense, $600
Depreciation expense, $500

Correct net inc.:
19X4, $8,300
19X5, $8,600

Instead of recording the accrued expenses at December 31, 19X4, Mayfair recorded the expenses when it paid them in 19X5. The company recorded the insurance as expense when it was prepaid for one year, late in 19X4. Depreciation expense for 19X5 was correctly recorded.

Mayfair incorrectly reported net income of $10,000 in 19X4 and $7,400 in 19X5 because of the above errors.

Required

Compute Mayfair's correct net income for 19X4 and 19X5. Compare the trend in net income, as corrected, with the reported trend.

b. Current-year revenue $3,150

Exercise 12-6 *Reporting revenues under GAAP* (L.O. 4)

For each of the following situations, indicate the amount of revenue to report for the current year ended December 31 and for the following year:

a. Sold merchandise for $4,400, receiving a down payment of $1,100 and the customer's receivable for the balance. The company accounts for these sales by the sales method.

b. On April 1 loaned $35,000 at 12 percent on a three-year note.

c. Performed $900 of services for a high-risk customer on August 18, accounting for the revenue by the collection method. At December 31 the company had received $200 of the total; $550 was received the following year.

d. On September 1 collected one year's rent of $12,000 in advance on a building leased to another company.

e. Sold gift certificates, collecting $4,000 in advance. At December 31, $2,200 of the gifts have been claimed. The remainder were claimed during the next year.

Gross profit $156,000

Exercise 12-7 *Computing gross profit under the sales method and the installment method* (L.O. 4)

Hometown Pawn Shop sells on the installment plan. The store's installment sales figures for 19X7 follow.

Sales	$390,000
Down payments received on the sales	80,000
Collections on installments	170,000
Inventory at beginning of 19X7.......	60,000
Inventory at end of 19X7	42,000
Purchases	216,000

Required

Compute the store's gross profit if it uses (a) the sales method of revenue recognition and (b) the installment method.

Percentage-completion revenue $500,000

Exercise 12-8 *Computing construction revenue under the completed-contract method and the percentage-of-completion method* (L.O. 4)

Ecclesia Construction Company builds bridges for the state of Florida. The construction period typically extends for several years. During 19X5 Ecclesia completed a small bridge with a contract price of $500,000. Ecclesia's $320,000 cost of the bridge was incurred as follows: $20,000 in 19X3, $180,000 in 19X4, and $120,000 in 19X5. Compute Ecclesia's revenue for each year 19X3 through 19X5 if the company uses (a) the completed-contract method and (b) the percentage-of-completion method. Which method better matches expense with revenue?

Exercise 12-9   *Changing the useful life of a depreciable asset*   **(L.O. 5)**

Depr. 19X5, $30,000

Ecclesia Construction Company uses a crane on its construction projects. The company purchased the crane early in January 19X3 for $400,000. For 19X3 and 19X4 depreciation was taken by the straight-line method based on an eight-year life and an estimated residual value of $80,000. In early 19X5 it became evident that the crane would be useful beyond the original life of eight years. Therefore, beginning in 19X5, Ecclesia changed the depreciable life of the crane to a total life of ten years. The company retained the straight-line method and did not alter the residual value.

Required

Prepare Ecclesia's depreciation entries for 19X4 and 19X5. Identify the accounting principles most important in this situation.

Exercise 12-10   *Identifying subsequent events for the financial statements*   **(L.O. 5)**

No check figure

Bavarian Merchants experienced the following events after May 31, 19X8, the end of the company's fiscal year, but before publication of its financial statements on July 12:

a. Increased demand for Bavarian products suggests that the next fiscal year will be the best in the company's history.

b. On July 6 Bavarian is sued for $3 million. Loss of the lawsuit could lead to Bavarian's bankruptcy.

c. Bavarian collected $126,000 of the $480,000 accounts receivable reported on the May 31 balance sheet. Bavarian expects to collect the remainder in the course of business during the next fiscal year.

d. A major customer, who owed Bavarian $220,000 at May 31, declared bankruptcy on June 21.

e. Bavarian sales personnel received a contract to supply Bronson Company with laser equipment.

Required

Identify the subsequent events that Bavarian should disclose in its May 31, 19X8, financial statements.

Exercise 12-11   *Using accounting concepts and principles*   **(L.O. 2, 6)**

No check figure

Identify the accounting concept or principle, if any, that is violated in each of the following situations. You may choose among *disclosure, conservatism, cost, entity,* and *matching.*

a. The inventory of a clothing store has a current market value of $62,000. The store reports the inventory at its cost of $106,000.

b. The owner of a court reporting service used the business bank account to pay her family's household expenses, making no note that the expenses were personal.

c. A manufacturing company changed from the FIFO inventory method to the LIFO method and failed to report the accounting change in the financial statements.

d. A paper company that purchased 1,000 acres of timberland at $300 per acre in 1973 reports the land at its current market value of $3,000 per acre.

e. A railroad records depreciation during years when net income is high but fails to record depreciation when net income is low. Revenues are relatively constant.

Exercise 12-12 *Using accounting concepts and principles* (L.O. 2, 6)

Indicate the accounting concept or principle that applies to the following situations. Choose among *comparability, materiality, reliability, revenue,* and *time period*.

a. Bert's Barbecue was recently sued for $200,000, but the plaintiff has indicated a willingness to settle for less than that amount. Bert's hopes to settle for $50,000, but its attorneys believe the settlement will be between $90,000 and $100,000. Bert's auditor reports the settlement as a real liability on the balance sheet. The only remaining issue is whether to report the liability at $50,000 or at $95,000.

b. Southern Kraft Company is considering publishing quarterly financial statements to provide more current information about its affairs.

c. POA, Inc., is negotiating the sale of $500,000 of inventory. POA has been in financial difficulty and desperately needs to report this sale on its income statement of the current year. At December 31, the end of the company's accounting year, the sale has not been closed.

d. New Wave Distributors expenses the cost of plant assets that cost less than $300.

e. Although Bracken Company could increase its reported income by changing depreciation methods, Bracken management has decided not to make the change.

Problems   (Group A)

Problem 12-1A *Disclosing a change in accounting method* (L.O. 1, 5)

Your company's board of directors is debating a change from the FIFO inventory method to the LIFO method. The main points of contention are the effects of the accounting change on net income and cash flow. Two members of the board favor keeping the FIFO method because of its effect on net income during periods of rising prices. Recently, however, prices have risen so fast that other members of the board think the company is wasting money by paying too high taxes. These board members are willing to have the company report lower income in order to save precious cash. All members of the board agree that if the company changes inventory methods, it would be best *not* to disclose the change in the annual report.

Required

Assume the board of directors has decided to change accounting methods. Draft a memorandum to convince the board members of the need to disclose the relevant aspects of the accounting change. Explain to the board in your memorandum the basic objective of financial reporting. Also draft the disclosure note to report the accounting change in the financial statements, using your own made-up figures to disclose relevant information about the change. Discuss how the information in your proposed disclosure note meets the objective of financial reporting. Refer to two accounting principles directly applicable to this situation.

Problem 12-2A *Identifying the basis for good accounting practices* (L.O. 2, 3, 6)

The following accounting practices are in accord with generally accepted accounting principles. Identify all the accounting concepts and principles that form the basis for each accounting practice. More than one concept or principle may apply.

a. A theater company accrues employee salaries at year end even though the salaries will be paid during the first few days of the new year.

b. Assets are reported at liquidation value on the financial statements of a company that is going out of business.

c. The cost of machinery is being depreciated over a 5-year life because independent engineers believe the machinery will become obsolete after that time. (The company had hoped to depreciate the machinery over 10 years to report lower depreciation and higher net income in the early years of the asset's life.)

d. A manufacturing firm built some specialized equipment for its own use. The equipment would have cost $110,000 if purchased from an outside company, but the cost of constructing the equipment was only $89,000. The firm recorded the equipment at cost of $89,000.

e. Depreciation of the home-office building is difficult to relate to particular sales. Therefore, the company records depreciation expense on a time basis.

f. A company wishes to change its method of accounting for revenue. However, the company does not switch because it wants to use the same accounting method that other companies in the industry use.

g. Because it is often difficult to collect installment receivables, a realtor uses the installment method of revenue recognition rather than the sales method.

h. The cost of office equipment such as staplers and wastebaskets is not capitalized and depreciated because of their relative insignificance.

i. A fire destroyed the company garage after December 31, 19X7, and before the financial statements were published in early February 19X8. Although the fire loss is insured, reconstruction of the garage will disrupt the company's operations. This subsequent event will be reported in the 19X7 financial statements.

j. A paint company accounts for its operations by dividing the business into four separate units. This division enables the company to evaluate each unit apart from the others.

Problem 12-3A *Identifying the concepts and principles violated by bad accounting practices* **(L.O. 2, 3, 6)**   No check figure

The following accounting practices are *not* in accord with generally accepted accounting principles. A few of the practices violate more than one concept or principle. Identify all the accounting concepts and principles not followed in each situation.

a. All amounts on the balance sheet and income statement of Cleveland Consulting Company have been adjusted for changes in the value of the dollar during the period.

b. Waterloo Wheat Processor records one-half of the depreciation of its grain silos when it purchases them and the other half over their estimated useful lives.

c. Linda's Threads sells high-fashion clothing to customers on credit. Thus far, collection losses on receivables have been very small. Nevertheless, Linda Vela, the owner, uses the collection method to recognize revenue. The entity's revenue is understated because credit sales are not accounted for properly.

d. Canton Importers changed from the FIFO method to the LIFO method for inventory but did not report the accounting change in the financial statements.

e. Quebec Fisheries, Inc., applied the lower-of-cost-or-market method to account for its inventory. Quebec used an estimate of the inventory value developed by its management. This estimate differed widely from estimates supplied by two independent appraisers. The estimates of the two appraisers were close together.

f. Butler Manufacturing does not report a lawsuit in which it is the defendant. Alvin Butler, the president, argues that the outcome of the case is uncertain and that to report the lawsuit would introduce subjective data into the financial statements.

g. Todd Department Store records cost of goods sold in a predetermined amount each month regardless of the level of sales.

h. Tim Ihnacek is having difficulty evaluating the success of his advertising firm because he fails to separate business assets from personal assets.

i. Tapes Unlimited is continuing in business, but its owner accounts for assets as though the store were liquidating.

j. Major Construction Company recognizes all revenue on long-term construction projects at the start of construction.

Problem 12-4A *Using the installment-revenue method* **(L.O. 4)**

Net inc. year 2, $23,450

Indianapolis Realty Company makes all sales on the installment basis but uses the sales method to record revenue. The company's income statements for the most recent three years are as follows:

	Year 1	Year 2	Year 3
Sales	$380,000	$404,000	$370,000
Cost of goods sold	190,000	181,800	199,800
Gross profit	190,000	222,200	170,200
Operating expenses	110,600	130,700	125,100
Net income (net loss)	$ 79,400	$ 91,500	$ 45,100
Collections from sales of year 1	$140,000	$151,000	$ 72,000
Collections from sales of year 2		143,000	209,000
Collections from sales of year 3			163,000

Required

Compute the amount of net income Indianapolis would have reported if the company had used the installment method for revenue. Ignore the effect of uncollectible accounts and present your answer in the following format:

Installment-method net income:	Year 1	Year 2	Year 3
Gross profit	$	$	$
Operating expenses	110,600	130,700	125,100
Net income	$	$	$

Problem 12-5A *Using the installment-revenue method* **(L.O. 4)**

Gross profit, installment method, $583,600

Harbor Springs Land Company sells land on the installment plan. Collections of installment receivables have deteriorated. The company's accountants are considering the different methods of recording revenues. Revenue, expense, and collection data for the current year are as follows:

	19X3
Installment sales	$2,400,000
Cost of land sold	1,320,000
Collections of installment receivables from sales of 19X2	760,000
19X3	520,000

The gross profit percentage on 19X2 installment sales was 46 percent.

Required

1. Which method should be used to account for revenues if collections are extremely doubtful? If collections are reasonably assured? Which method is more advantageous for income tax purposes? Why?

2. Compute gross profit for 19X3 under the sales method, the collection method, and the installment method.

Problem 12-6A *Accounting for construction income (L.O. 4)*

Income, percentage-completion method 19X5, $898,000

Brooklyn Bridge Company constructs bridges under long-term contracts. During 19X5, Brooklyn began three projects that progressed according to the following schedule during 19X5, 19X6, and 19X7:

Project	Contract Price	Total Project Cost	19X5 Cost for Year	19X5 % Completed During Year	19X6 Cost for Year	19X6 % Completed During Year	19X7 Cost for Year	19X7 % Completed During Year
1	$2,400,000	$1,800,000	$1,800,000	100%	—	—	—	—
2	3,100,000	2,200,000	484,000	22	$1,716,000	78%	—	—
3	1,900,000	1,400,000	280,000	20	840,000	60	$280,000	20%

Required

1. Assume Brooklyn uses the completed-contract method for construction revenue. Compute the company's construction revenue and income to be reported in 19X5, 19X6, and 19X7.
2. Compute Brooklyn's construction revenue and income to be reported in the three years if the company uses the percentage-of-completion method.

Problem 12-7A *Accounting for revenues and expenses according to GAAP (L.O. 2, 3, 4)*

Correct net inc. 19X7, $51,650

Kate Krupp established Krupp Home Furnishings in January 19X7. During 19X7, 19X8, and most of 19X9 Krupp kept the company's books and prepared its financial statements, although she had no training or experience in accounting. As a result, the accounts and statements contain numerous errors. For example, Krupp recorded only cash receipts from customers as revenue. The sales method is appropriate for the business. She recorded inventory purchases as the cost of goods sold. When the current market value of her company's equipment increased by $6,200 in 19X7 and by $1,700 in 19X9, Krupp debited the Equipment account and credited Revenue. She recorded no depreciation during 19X7, 19X8, and 19X9.

Late in 19X9 Krupp employed an accountant, who determined that depreciable assets of the firm cost $150,000 on June 30, 19X7, had an expected residual value of $10,000, and a total useful life of eight years. The accountant believes the straight-line depreciation method is appropriate for Krupp's plant assets. The company's fiscal year ends December 31. At the end of 19X9 the company's records reveal the amounts in the accompanying table.

Required

Apply the concepts and principles of GAAP to compute the correct net income of Krupp Home Furnishings for 19X7, 19X8, and 19X9.

	19X7	19X8	19X9
Reported net income (net loss)	$ 24,300	$ (6,200)	$ 62,900
Sales	131,800	164,700	226,100
Cash collections from customers	106,500	151,300	239,600
Purchases of inventory	100,600	136,000	191,700
Ending inventory	20,800	47,400	83,700
Accrued expenses not recorded at year end; these expenses were recorded during the next year, when paid	3,800	2,700	6,800
Depreciation expense recorded	-0-	-0-	-0-
Revenue recorded for increase in the value of equipment	6,200		1,700

Chapter 12   The Foundation for Generally Accepted Accounting Principles   **575**

No check figure

Problem 12-8A *Recording and reporting transactions according to GAAP (L.O. 2, 3, 4, 5, 6)*

The accounting records of Treadway Publishing Company reveal the following information prior to closing the books at April 30, the end of the current fiscal year:

a. Accounts receivable include $12,600 from Miller Bookstore, which has declared bankruptcy. Treadway, which uses the allowance method to account for bad debts, expects to receive only one-fourth of the amount receivable from Miller.

b. No interest has been accrued on a $35,000, 12 percent, 90-day note payable issued on March 31.

c. The merchandise inventory, with a cost of $54,000, has a current market value of only $51,700. Treadway uses a periodic inventory system and has not made the April 30 entry to record ending inventory.

d. Property tax is due each April 30, and Treadway has received the city/county property tax bill of $4,960. However, the company has not recorded property tax at April 30 because Treadway plans to record the tax when it is paid in May.

e. The company's office building was recently valued by independent appraisers at $750,000. This valuation is $150,000 more than Treadway paid for the building and is $410,000 more than its cost less accumulated depreciation.

f. Three years ago on May 1, Treadway paid $440,000 for its printing equipment. The company has depreciated the equipment by the straight-line method over an expected useful life of 10 years using a residual value of $40,000. Having used the equipment for 2 years, Treadway determined at the beginning of the current year that it will remain in service for a total of only 8 years. The company will continue to use the straight-line method and $40,000 residual value for accounting purposes.

g. On May 13, before Treadway issued its financial statements for the year ended April 30, the company's principal customer, Mears, Rareback and Co., declared its intention to cease doing business with Treadway. This event is significant because for the past 10 years Mears has accounted for approximately 65 percent of Treadway's sales. Consequently, Treadway's ability to sustain its recent level of sales in future years is seriously in doubt.

Required

Make all journal entries needed at April 30 to record this information. Explanations are not required. Identify those items not requiring a journal entry, giving the reason why an entry is not needed. If a note to the financial statements is needed, write the note.

(Group B)

No check figure

Problem 12-1B *Disclosing significant accounting policies (L.O. 1, 5)*

BPI Systems, a company that constructs large office buildings, is approaching the end of its first year of operations. Three projects are under way and scheduled for completion during the next year. The board of directors is considering the adoption of certain accounting policies. After a lengthy discussion, the board decides to use the revenue method most preferred for long-term construction contracts. The board further decides to use the inventory method that best matches the cost of inventory sold with current revenue and to apply the most widely used depreciation method for plant assets. Estimated useful lives of plant assets range from 5 years for tools to 10 years for equipment and to 20 years for buildings. Disclosure of the accounting policies used by BPI

Systems is a point of contention because two influential board members believe that it will enable competitors to gain an undue advantage.

Required

Draft a memorandum to convince the board members of the need to disclose significant accounting policies. In this memo, explain the basic objective of financial reporting. Also draft the note to disclose the company's accounting methods. Relate the information in your proposed disclosure note to the objective of financial accounting.

Problem 12-2B   *Identifying the basis for good accounting practices   (L.O. 2, 3, 6)*   No check figure

The following accounting practices are in accord with generally accepted accounting principles. Identify all the accounting concepts and principles that form the basis for each accounting practice. More than one concept or principle may apply.

a.   TGI Friday's, a restaurant, makes such small payments for fire insurance that TGI expenses them and makes no year-end adjustment for prepaid insurance.

b.   The inventory of a personal computer store declined substantially in value because of changing technology, and the store wrote its computer inventory down to the lower of cost or market.

c.   A construction company changed from the completed-contract method to the percentage-of-completion method of recording revenue on its long-term construction contracts. The company disclosed this accounting change in the notes to its financial statements.

d.   A mining company recorded an intangible asset at the cost of the mineral lease and all other costs necessary to bring the mine to the point of production. After the mine was in operation, the company amortized the asset's cost as expense in proportion to the revenues from sale of the minerals.

e.   Because of a downturn in the economy, a jeweler increased his business's allowance for doubtful accounts.

f.   The personal residence of the owner of a freight company is not disclosed in the financial statements of the business.

g.   A manufacturing company's plant assets are carried on the books at cost under the assumption that the company will remain in operation for the foreseeable future.

h.   A clothing store discloses in notes to its financial statements that it uses the FIFO inventory method.

i.   A real estate developer paid $1.3 million for land and held it for three years before selling it for $2 million. There was significant inflation during this period, but the developer reports the $.7 million gain on sale with no adjustment for the change in the value of the dollar.

j.   Liabilities are reported in two categories, current and long-term.

Problem 12-3B   *Identifying the concepts and principles violated by bad accounting practices   (L.O. 2, 3, 6)*   No check figure

The following accounting practices are *not* in accord with generally accepted accounting principles. Identify the single accounting concept or principle that is most clearly violated by each accounting practice.

a.   The balance sheet of Jean-Paul Pascal's medical practice includes significant receivables that he will probably never collect. Nevertheless, Pascal's accountant refuses to use the collection method to account for revenue.

b. The current market value of Miska Electronics' inventory is $119,000, but the company reports its inventory at cost of $134,000. The decline in value is permanent.

c. The liabilities of Waco Jet Company exceed the company's assets. To get a loan from the bank, Waco Jet's owner, Slade McQueen, includes his personal investments as assets on the balance sheet of the business.

d. Lancer Corporation increases the carrying value of its land based on recent sales of adjacent property.

e. Mission Ford Sales records expenses on an irregular basis without regard to the pattern of the company's revenues.

f. Frisco Software Company omits the significant accounting policies note from its financial statements because the company uses the same accounting methods that its competitors use.

g. National Seed Supply regularly changes accounting methods in order to report a target amount of net income each year.

h. Texas Land Company reports land at its market value of $820,000, which is greater than the cost of $400,000.

i. A flood on July 2 caused $150,000 in damage to Tyler Construction property. The company did not report the flood as a subsequent event in the June 30 financial statements.

j. Hernandez, Inc., overstates depreciation expense in order to report low amounts of net income.

Net inc. year 2, $9,260

Problem 12-4B *Using the installment-revenue method* **(L.O. 4)**

Springfield Office Furniture makes all sales on the installment basis but uses the sales method to record revenue. The company's income statements for the most recent three years follow.

	Year 1	Year 2	Year 3
Sales	$240,000	$210,000	$290,000
Cost of goods sold	144,000	121,800	179,800
Gross profit	96,000	88,200	110,200
Operating expenses	51,400	49,300	61,300
Net income	$ 44,600	$ 38,900	$ 48,900
Collections from sales of year 1	$100,000	$ 75,000	$ 60,000
Collections from sales of year 2		68,000	120,000
Collections from sales of year 3			145,000

Required

Compute the amount of net income Springfield would have reported if the company had used the installment method for revenue. Ignore the effect of uncollectible accounts and present your answer in the following format:

Installment-method net income:	Year 1	Year 2	Year 3
Gross profit	$	$	$
Operating expenses	51,400	49,300	61,300
Net income (net loss)	$	$	$

Gross profit, installment method, $26,400

Problem 12-5B *Using the installment-revenue method* **(L.O. 4)**

Payless Cashways sells on the installment plan. Collections of installment receivables have deteriorated. The store's accountants are considering the different methods of recording revenues. Revenue, expense, and collection data for the current year are as follows:

	19X6
Installment sales	$120,000
Cost of goods sold	72,000
Collections of installment receivables from sales of 19X5	40,000
19X6	24,000

The gross profit percentage on 19X5 installment sales was 42 percent.

Required

1. Which method should be used to account for revenues if collections are reasonably assured? If collections are extremely doubtful? Which method is more advantageous for income tax purposes? Why?
2. Compute gross profit for 19X6 under the sales method, the collection method, and the installment method.

Problem 12-6B *Accounting for construction income* **(L.O. 4)**

Income percentage-completion method, 19X8, $985,000

U.S. Construction Company participates in the construction of small ships under long-term contracts. During 19X7 U.S. Construction began three projects that progressed according to the following schedule during 19X7, 19X8, and 19X9:

			19X7		19X8		19X9	
Project	Contract Price	Total Project Cost	Cost for Year	% Completed During Year	Cost for Year	% Completed During Year	Cost for Year	% Completed During Year
1	$2,100,000	$1,200,000	$ 400,000	33⅓%	$ 800,000	66⅔%	—	
2	1,200,000	880,000	880,000	100	—	—	—	
3	7,400,000	6,300,000	1,260,000	20	2,205,000	35	$2,835,000	45%

Required

1. Assume U.S. Construction uses the completed-contract method for construction revenue. Compute the company's construction revenue and income to be reported in 19X7, 19X8, and 19X9.
2. Compute U.S. Construction's construction revenue and income to be reported in the three years if the company uses the percentage-of-completion method.

Problem 12-7B *Accounting for revenues and expenses according to GAAP* **(L.O. 2, 3, 4)**

Correct net inc. 19X4, $50,700

Molly McGillicuddy established McGillicuddy's Boutique in January 19X4 to import woolens from Scotland. During 19X4 and 19X5 McGillicuddy kept the company's books and prepared the financial statements, although she had no training or experience in accounting. As a result, the accounts contain numerous errors. McGillicuddy recorded revenue from sales on the collection method, which is not appropriate for the company. McGillicuddy should have been using the sales method for revenues. She also recorded inventory purchases as the cost of goods sold.

When the value of the store building increased by $50,000 in 19X6, McGillicuddy recorded an increase in the Building account and credited Revenue. On January 2, 19X4, she borrowed $30,000 on a 9 percent, three-year note. She intended to wait until 19X7, when the note was due, to record the full amount of interest expense for three years. The company's records reveal the following amounts:

	19X4	19X5	19X6
Reported net income (net loss)	$ (15,200)	$ 31,600	$ 64,100
Sales	256,700	303,500	366,800
Cash collections from customers	210,400	309,000	317,800
Purchases of inventory.................	141,000	187,400	202,300
Ending inventory.......................	35,800	59,900	73,400
Accrued expenses not recorded at year end; these expenses were recorded during the next year, when paid	13,500	22,600	30,100
Interest expense recorded	-0-	-0-	-0-
Revenue recorded for increase in the value of the store building			50,000

Required

In early 19X7 McGillicuddy employed you as an accountant. Apply the concepts and principles of GAAP to compute the correct net income of McGillicuddy's Boutique for 19X4, 19X5, and 19X6.

No check figure

Problem 12-8B *Recording and reporting transactions according to GAAP (L.O. 2, 3, 4, 5, 6)*

The accounting records of Jefferson City Carbonic reveal the following information prior to closing the books at September 30, the end of the current fiscal year:

a. Accounts receivable include $63,000 from Glenwood Drug Company, which has declared bankruptcy. Jefferson City, which uses the allowance method to account for bad debts, expects to receive one-third of the amount receivable from Glenwood.

b. No interest has been accrued on a $25,000, 12 percent, six-month note receivable that was received on May 31.

c. The merchandise inventory, with a cost of $69,000, has a current market value of only $58,000. Jefferson City uses a periodic inventory system and has not made the September 30 entry to record ending inventory.

d. Accrued salaries of $12,100 have been earned by Jefferson City employees but have not been recorded at September 30 because the company plans to record the salaries when it pays them in October.

e. The company's office building has been valued recently by independent appraisers at $400,000. This valuation is $180,000 more than Jefferson City paid for the building and is $270,000 more than its cost less accumulated depreciation.

f. Two years ago on October 1, Jefferson City paid $120,000 for its delivery trucks. During the prior year the company depreciated the trucks by the straight-line method over an expected useful life of 4 years, using a residual value of $10,000. After using the trucks for the first year, Jefferson City decided at the beginning of the current year that the trucks will remain in service for a total of 5 years. The company will continue to use the straight-line method and the $10,000 residual value for accounting purposes.

g. On October 19, before Jefferson City issued its financial statements for the year ended September 30, a competitor sued the company for damages of $500,000. Attorneys for Jefferson City believe Jefferson City will win the case. However, a $500,000 loss would make it difficult for the company to continue in business.

Required

Make all journal entries needed at September 30 to record this information. Explanations are not required. Identify those items not requiring a journal entry, giving the reason why an entry is not needed. If a note to the financial statements is needed, write the note.

Extending Your Knowledge

Decision Problems

1. Measuring Income According to GAAP (L.O. 2, 3, 4)

Net inc. $37,800

Valley View Camera Shop was founded in January 19X5 by Steve and Alice Beard, who share the management of the business. Alice does the purchasing and manages the sales staff. Steve keeps the books and handles financial matters. The Beards believe the store has prospered, but they are uncertain about precisely how well it has done. It is now December 31, 19X5, and they are trying to decide whether to borrow a substantial sum in order to expand the business.

They have asked for your help because of your accounting knowledge. You learn that the Beards opened the store with an initial investment of $51,000 cash and a building valued at $100,000. The cash receipts totaled $180,000, which included collections, $15,000 invested by the Beards, $50,000 borrowed from the bank in the name of the camera shop, and $7,500 of earnings from a family inheritance. The store made credit sales of $105,000 that have not been collected at December 31. The Beards purchased camera and film inventory on credit for $160,000, and inventory at December 31, 19X5, was $75,000. The store paid $90,000 on account.

The 19X5 cash expenses were $92,000. Additional miscellaneous expenses totaled $2,700 at year's end. These expenses included the Beards' household costs of $10,000 and interest on the business debt. The $5,000 of depreciation on the store building was omitted.

Steve and Alice have decided to proceed with the expansion plan only if net income for the first year was $40,000 or more. Steve's analysis of the cash account leads him to believe that net income was $49,000, so he is ready to expand. You are less certain than Steve of the wisdom of this decision primarily because the Beards have mixed personal and business assets.

Required

1. Use a Cash T-account to show how Steve arrived at the $49,000 amount for net income.
2. Prepare the income statement of the camera shop for 19X5.
3. Should the Beards borrow to expand their business?
4. Which accounting concept or principle is most fundamental to this problem situation?

2. Examining the Disclosure Principle (L.O. 3, 5)

No check figure

1. It has been suggested that the disclosure principle is perhaps one of the most important concepts and principles underlying financial reporting. Why is it so important?
2. Accounting researchers are studying the understandability of financial statements. Why are they doing this? What contribution might their research make?
3. The text suggests that *subsequent events* and *long-term commitments* should be disclosed in the notes to the financial statements. What about these two items makes their disclosure so important to users?

Ethical Issue

Some real estate companies sell land under terms that permit low down payments by purchasers and stretch payments over many years. In many cases, the land had not yet been subdivided into the individual lots that would be sold. Also, the land often had not been landscaped. Estimating the cost of preparing the land for eventual use was difficult. Under accounting practices widespread in the 1960s and 1970s, real estate companies could record the full amount of the revenue in the year of the sale. These companies were thus able to report unusually high net incomes even though their cash collections were quite low.

Required

1. What three conditions must a company meet in order to record revenue on a sale? Which conditions did the real estate companies meet? Which conditions did they not meet?
2. Which revenue method were companies using during the 1960s and 1970s? In your opinion, was it ethical for these companies to use this method? Give your reason.
3. Which collection method is well suited for this situation? Give your reason.

Financial Statement Problems

No check figure

1. Disclosure in Action   (L.O. 5)

The tabular portion of a company's financial statements—the balance sheet, income statement, cash flow statement, and so on—can display limited verbal descriptions. Companies disclose a great deal of important information in notes. Use the Goodyear Tire & Rubber Company statements in Appendix C to answer these questions.

1. The income statement lists "Unusual items." Identify Goodyear's unusual items for 1990, and give their individual amounts.
2. Of Goodyear's Other Income for 1990, how much was interest income (the same as interest revenue)? Where was most of the interest income earned? How much of the Other Income came from sources other than interest?
3. Identify Goodyear's long-term debt with the lowest interest rate. For these liabilities compute interest expense for 1991.
4. How much research and development cost did Goodyear incur during 1990? Identify the income statement item that includes research and development cost.

No check figure

2. Disclosure in Action   (L.O. 5)

Obtain the annual report of an actual company of your choosing. Use the company's financial statements and related notes to answer these questions illustrating the disclosure principle. Concentrate on the current year in the annual report you select.

1. Identify any unusual items, discontinued operations, effects of accounting changes, or extraordinary items reported on the income statements. Examine any notes that give additional details about these special items of income or loss. Identify their individual amounts and state whether each item increased or decreased net income.
2. What are the company's business segments? These may be reported by geographical area, by product line, or in both ways. Identify each segment's revenues and operating income or net income for the current year.
3. Examine the company's multi-year financial summary. Compute the percentage increase or decrease in total revenues over this entire period. Compute the percentage increase or decrease in net income over the same period. Which increased faster, total revenues or net income?

Chapter **13**

Accounting for Partnerships

"That rotten [so-and-so]! After all I've done for him over the last 20 years, and that's the way he treats me? Well, he ought to think again. My lawyer's got a nice little surprise waiting for him!"

Sound familiar? The cries of an angry wife railing against her husband during a stormy divorce? A good guess, but wrong. This was a man we recently overheard in a Boston restaurant. He was talking about his business partner.

It reminded us of how much the business partnerships we've seen over the years look like marriages.

They begin with heady dreams. They bristle with excitement through a start-up period that's much like a honeymoon. They settle into a "reality" phase when the bloom leaves the rose. Then, sadly, many of them sink into a prolonged period of disenchantment. Cracks widen into crevasses between the partners. Then one day a partner wakes up and says, "I can't take this any longer." And a painful separation and divorce unfold.

Source: Peter Wylie and Mardy Grothe, "Breaking Up Is Hard to Do," *Nation's Business*, July 1988, p. 24.

Point to Stress: A partnership is really a "multiple proprietorship." We will see that most of the features of a proprietorship also apply to a partnership, in particular the characteristics of limited life and unlimited liability.

Discussion Question: Why do people form partnerships? ANSWER: Raise larger sums of capital; use the talents and skills of several different people; and so on.

Forming a partnership is easy. It requires no permission from government authorities and involves no legal procedures. When two persons decide to go into business together, a partnership is automatically formed.

A **partnership** is an association of two or more persons who co-own a business for profit. This definition stems from the Uniform Partnership Act, which nearly every state has adopted to regulate partnership practice.

A partnership brings together the capital, talents, and experience of the partners. Business opportunities closed to an individual may open up to a partnership. Suppose neither Pedigo nor Lee has enough capital individually to buy a $300,000 parcel of land. They may be able to afford it together in a partnership. Or VanAllen, a tax accountant, and Kahn, an investment counselor, may pool their talents and know-how. Their partnership may offer a fuller range of money management services than either person could offer alone. Combining their experience may increase income for each of them.

Partnerships come in all sizes. Many partnerships have fewer than 10 partners. Some medical and law firms may have 20 or more partners. The largest CPA firms have almost 2,000 partners.

Characteristics of a Partnership

OBJECTIVE 1

Identify the characteristics, including advantages and disadvantages, of a partnership

Starting a partnership is voluntary. A person cannot be forced to join a partnership, and partners cannot be forced to accept another person as a partner. Although the partnership agreement may be oral, a written agreement between the partners reduces the chance of a misunderstanding. Several features are unique to the partnership form of business. The following characteristics distinguish partnerships from sole proprietorships and corporations, which we examine in later chapters.

The Written Partnership Agreement

Real-World Example: According to the Department of Commerce, the number of partnerships increased 40% during the 1970's. One reason for this increase was the use of

A business partnership is like a marriage, as the beginning of this chapter suggests. To be successful, the partners must cooperate. However, business partners do not vow to remain together for life. Business partnerships come and go. To make certain that each partner fully understands how a particular partnership operates, and to lower the chances that any partner might misunderstand how the business is run, partners may draw up a **partnership**

agreement, also called the **articles of partnership.** This agreement is a contract between the partners, so transactions involving the agreement are governed by contract law. The articles of partnership should make the following points clear:

1. Name, location, and nature of the business
2. Name, capital investment, and duties of each partner
3. Method of sharing profits and losses by the partners
4. Withdrawals of assets allowed to the partners
5. Procedures for settling disputes between the partners
6. Procedures for admitting new partners
7. Procedures for settling up with a partner who withdraws from the business
8. Procedures for liquidating the partnership—selling the assets, paying the liabilities, and disbursing any remaining cash to the partners

As partners enter and leave the business, the old partnership is dissolved and a new partnership is formed. Preparing a separate agreement for each new partnership may be expensive and time consuming.

Limited Life

A partnership has a life limited by the length of time that all partners continue to own the business. When a partner withdraws from the business, that partnership ceases to exist. A new partnership may emerge to continue the same business, but the old partnership has been *dissolved.* **Dissolution** is the ending of a partnership. Likewise, the addition of a new partner dissolves the old partnership and creates a new partnership. Partnerships are sometimes formed for a particular business venture, like a mining operation or a real estate investment. When the mine is depleted or the real estate is sold, the partnership may be dissolved.

Mutual Agency

Mutual agency in a partnership means that every partner can bind the business to a contract within the scope of the partnership's regular business operations. If an individual partner in a CPA firm enters into a contract with a person or another business to provide accounting service, then the firm—not the individual who signs the contract—is bound to provide that service. However, if that same CPA signs a contract to purchase home lawn services for the summer months, the partnership would not be bound to pay. Contracting for personal lawn services does not fall within the partnership's regular business operations.

Unlimited Liability

Each partner has an **unlimited personal liability** for the debts of the partnership. When a partnership cannot pay its debts with business assets, the partners must use their personal assets to meet the debt.

Avilla and Davis are the two partners in AD Company. The business has had an unsuccessful year, and the partnership's liabilities exceed its assets by $120,000. Davis and Avilla must pay this amount with their personal assets.

the limited partnership, designed to serve as a tax shelter. A limited partnership must have at least one general partner who manages the business and who incurs unlimited liability. As long as the other partners are not active in managing the partnership, they may enjoy a limited liability.

The Omnibus Budget Reconciliation Act of 1987 imposed some restrictions on limited partnerships. Those that are publicly traded are taxed now as corporations and the income is treated as dividends. Other limited partnerships are not affected.

Point to Stress: Refer to the chapter-opening vignette. A partnership is not required to have a formal written agreement. However, a written agreement prevents confusion as to the way profits and losses will be split, partners' responsibilities, admission of new partners, how the partnership will be liquidated, and so on. The existence of a written agreement does not preclude discord, however. As the vignette indicates, partnerships are prone to bitter splits.

Point to Stress: When a partner leaves the partnership, it dissolves and its books are closed. If the remaining partners want to continue as partners, they become a new partnership and must have a new set of books. Dissolution does not require liquidation; when a partnership dissolves, its assets do not have to be sold.

Real-World Example: If a partner leaves a partnership, then he is no longer an agent and no longer has the authority to bind the business to contracts. Third parties with whom the partnership has dealt must be notified that the partner no longer is an agent of the partnership. For all other third parties, constructive notice, such as an advertisement in the newspaper, is sufficient.

Point to Stress: All partners become personally liable for any debt incurred by any partner on behalf of the business. It is therefore extremely important to choose your partners carefully.

Point to Stress: A personal asset invested in the partnership becomes the joint property of all the partners.

Discussion Question: Under what circumstances would a partner make an initial contribution of a liability? ANSWER: A partner could contribute an asset with a liability attached to it. For example, let's say a partner contributes to the partnership a building that has a mortgage (note payable) on it. In transferring the building to the partnership, the partner would also be transferring the note payable—a liability.

Recall that each partner has *unlimited* liability. If a partner is unable to pay his or her part of the debt, the other partner (or partners) must make payment. If Davis can pay only $50,000 of the liability, Avilla must pay $70,000.

Unlimited liability and mutual agency are closely related. A dishonest partner or a partner with poor judgment may commit the partnership to a contract under which the business loses money. In turn, creditors may force *all* the partners to pay the debt from their personal assets. Hence, a business partner should be chosen with great care.

Partners can avoid unlimited personal liability for partnership obligations by forming a limited partnership. In this form of business organization, one or more general partners assume the unlimited liability for business debts. In addition there is another class of owners—limited partners. The limited partners can lose only as much as their investment in the business. In this sense limited partners have limited liability that is similar to the limited liability that stockholders of a corporation have.

Co-Ownership of Property

Any asset—cash, inventory, machinery, and so on—that a partner invests in the partnership becomes the joint property of all the partners. Also, each partner has a claim to the business's profits.

No Partnership Income Taxes

A partnership pays no income tax on its business income. Instead, the net income of the partnership is divided and becomes the taxable income of the partners. Suppose AD Company earned net income of $80,000, shared equally by partners Avilla and Davis. AD Company would pay no income tax *as a business entity*. However, Avilla and Davis would pay income tax as individuals on their $40,000 shares of partnership income.

Accounting for a partnership is much like accounting for a proprietorship. We record buying and selling, collecting and paying in a partnership just as we do for a business with only one owner. However, because a partnership has more than one owner, the partnership must have more than one owner's equity account. Every partner in the business—whether the firm has two or two thousand partners—has an individual owner's equity account. Often these accounts carry the name of the particular partner and the word *capital*. For example, the owner's equity account for Larry Insdorf would read "Insdorf, Capital." Similarly, each partner has a withdrawal account. If the number of partners is large, the general ledger may contain the single account Partners' Capital, or Owners' Equity. A subsidiary ledger can be used for individual partner accounts.

Let's see how to account for the multiple owner's equity accounts—and learn how they appear on the balance sheet—by looking at how to account for starting up a partnership.

Initial Investments by Partners

Partners in a new partnership may invest assets and liabilities in the business. These contributions are entered in the books in the same way that a proprietor's assets and liabilities are recorded. Subtracting each person's liabilities from his or her assets yields the amount to be credited to the capital account for that person. Often the partners hire an independent firm to appraise their assets and liabilities at current market value at the time a partnership is formed. This outside evaluation assures an objective accounting for what each partner brings into the business.

Assume Benz and Hanna form a partnership to manufacture and sell computer software. Benz brings to the partnership cash of $10,000, accounts receivable of $30,000, inventory of $70,000, computer equipment with a cost of $600,000 and accumulated depreciation of $120,000, and accounts payable of $85,000. Hanna contributes cash of $5,000 and a software program. The development of this program cost Hanna $18,000, but its current market value is much greater. Suppose the partners agree on the following values based on an independent appraisal:

OBJECTIVE 2

Account for partners' initial investments in a partnership

Benz's contributions:

Cash, $10,000; inventory, $70,000; and accounts payable, $85,000 (the appraiser believes the current market values for these items equal Benz's values)
Accounts receivable, $30,000, less allowance for doubtful accounts of $5,000
Computer equipment, $450,000

Hanna's contributions:

Cash, $5,000
Computer software, $100,000

Note that current market value differs only slightly from book value for Benz's computer equipment. However, the appraiser valued Hanna's $18,000 computer software at the much higher $100,000 figure. The partners record their initial investments at the current market values. The title of each owner's equity account includes the owner's name and *Capital*—exactly as for a proprietorship.

Benz's investment:

June 1	Cash	10,000	
	Accounts Receivable	30,000	
	Inventory	70,000	
	Computer Equipment	450,000	
	Allowance for Doubtful Accounts		5,000
	Accounts Payable		85,000
	Benz, Capital		470,000
	To record Benz's investment in the partnership.		

Hanna's investment:

June 1	Cash	5,000	
	Computer Software	100,000	
	Hanna, Capital		105,000
	To record Hanna's investment in the partnership.		

The initial partnership balance sheet reports these amounts as follows:

Discussion Question: How could a partner allow the partnership to use a personal asset, such as a car or money, without losing his claim to the asset? ANSWER: The partner could lease the car to the partnership. If the partnership were liquidated, the car would have to be returned to its owner. The partner could also lend money to the partnership instead of investing it. In the event of liquidation, the loan would have to be returned to the lending partner before any distribution of capital was made.

Point to Stress: The major difference in accounting for a proprietorship and a partnership is the number of capital and drawing accounts. In a partnership, there will be a capital account and a drawing account for each partner.

Discussion Question: Notice the credits to Capital in the two journal entries on June 1. Must the partners contribute equal amounts? ANSWER: No. They can agree on any split of ownership interests they desire, regardless of the amounts of capital invested.

Benz and Hanna			
Balance Sheet			
June 1, 19X5			
Assets		**Liabilities**	
Cash	$ 15,000	Accounts payable	$ 85,000
Accounts receivable . . $30,000			
Less Allowance for		**Capital**	
doubtful accounts . 5,000	25,000		
Inventory	70,000	Benz, capital	470,000
Computer equipment	450,000	Hanna, capital	105,000
Computer software . .	100,000	Total liabilities	
Total assets	$660,000	and capital	$660,000

Each owner's capital account appears under the heading Capital. Having more than one capital account distinguishes a partnership balance sheet from a proprietorship balance sheet.

Sharing Partnership Profits and Losses

How to allocate profits and losses among partners is one of the most challenging aspects of managing a partnership. If the partners have not drawn up an agreement, or if the agreement does not state how the partners will divide profits and losses, then, according to law, the partners must share profits and losses equally. If the agreement specifies a method for sharing profits but not losses, then losses are shared in the same proportion as profits. For example, a partner allocated 75 percent of the profits would likewise absorb 75 percent of any losses.

In some cases, an equal division is not fair. One partner may perform more work for the business than the other partner, or one partner may make a larger capital contribution. In the preceding example, Hanna might agree to work longer hours for the partnership than Benz in order to earn a greater share of profits. Benz could argue that he should share in more of the profits because he contributed more net assets ($470,000) than Hanna did ($105,000). Hanna might contend that her computer software program is the partnership's most important asset and that her share of the profits should be greater than Benz's share. Agreeing on a fair sharing of profits and losses in a partnership may be difficult. We now discuss options available in determining partners' shares.

Sharing Based on a Stated Fraction

Partners may agree to any profit-and-loss-sharing method they desire. Suppose the partnership agreement of Cagle and Dean allocates two-thirds of the business profits and losses to Cagle and one-third to Dean. If net income for the year is $90,000 and all revenue and expense accounts have been closed, the Income Summary account has a credit balance of $90,000, as follows:

Income Summary	
	Bal. 90,000

The entry to close this account and allocate the profit to the partners' capital accounts is

Dec. 31	Income Summary	90,000	
	Cagle, Capital ($90,000 × ⅔)		60,000
	Dean, Capital ($90,000 × ⅓)		30,000
	To allocate net income to partners.		

Consider the effect of this entry. Does Cagle get cash of $60,000 and Dean cash of $30,000? No. The increase in the capital accounts of the partners cannot be linked to any particular asset, including cash. Instead, the entry indicates that Cagle's ownership in *all* the assets of the business increased by $60,000 and Dean's by $30,000.

If the year's operations resulted in a net loss of $66,000, the Income Summary account would have a debit balance of $66,000. In that case, the closing entry to allocate the loss to the partners' capital accounts would be

Dec. 31	Cagle, Capital ($66,000 × ⅔)	44,000	
	Dean, Capital ($66,000 × ⅓)	22,000	
	Income Summary		66,000
	To allocate net loss to partners.		

Sharing Based on Partners' Capital Contributions

Profits and losses are often allocated in proportion to the partners' capital contributions in the business. Suppose Antoine, Barber, and Cabañas are partners in ABC Company. Their capital accounts have the following balances at the end of the year, before the closing entries:

Antoine, Capital	$ 40,000
Barber, Capital	60,000
Cabañas, Capital	50,000
Total capital balances	$150,000

Assume that the partnership earned a profit of $120,000 for the year. To allocate this amount based on capital contributions, compute each partner's percentage share of the partnership's total capital balance. Simply divide each partner's contribution by the total capital amount. These figures, multiplied by the $120,000 profit amount, yield each partner's share of the year's profits:

Antoine:	$40,000/$150,000 × $120,000	= $ 32,000
Barber:	$60,000/$150,000 × $120,000	= 48,000
Cabañas:	$50,000/$150,000 × $120,000	= 40,000
	Net income allocated to partners	= $120,000

The closing entry to allocate the profit to the partners' capital accounts is

Dec. 31	Income Summary	120,000	
	Antoine, Capital		32,000
	Barber, Capital		48,000
	Cabañas, Capital		40,000
	To allocate net income to partners.		

After this closing entry, the partners' capital balances are

Antoine, Capital ($40,000 + $32,000)	$ 72,000
Barber, Capital ($60,000 + $48,000)	108,000
Cabañas, Capital ($50,000 + $40,000)	90,000
Total capital balances after allocation of net income .	$270,000

Sharing Based on Capital Contributions and Service to the Partnership

Class Exercise: Ash, Black, and Cole have capital balances of $10,000, $20,000, and $70,000, respectively. The partners share profits and losses as follows:

1 The first $25,000 of partnership profits is allocated based on partners' capital balances.

2 The next $19,000 is allocated based on service, with Ash, Black, and Cole receiving $5,000, $6,000, and $8,000, respectively.

3 The remainder is divided equally.

Compute each partner's share of net income if the partnership earns $50,000. *ANSWER:*

Ash: ($10,000/$100,000 × $25,000) + $5,000 + $2,000*
= $9,500

Black: ($20,000/$100,000 × $25,000) + $6,000 + $2,000*
= $13,000

Cole: ($70,000/$100,000 × $25,000) + $8,000 + $2,000*
= $27,500

---

*Remainder shared equally: ($50,000 − $25,000 − $19,000 = $6,000)

One partner, regardless of his or her capital contribution, may put more work into the business than the other partners. Even among partners who log equal service time, one person's superior experience and knowledge may command a greater share of income. To reward the harder-working or more valuable person, the profit-and-loss-sharing method may be based on a combination of contributed capital *and* service to the business.

Assume Randolph and Scott formed a partnership in which Randolph invested $60,000 and Scott invested $40,000, a total of $100,000. Scott devotes more time to the partnership and earns the larger salary. Accordingly, the two partners have agreed to share profits as follows:

1. The first $50,000 of partnership profits is to be allocated based on partners' capital contributions to the business.

2. The next $60,000 of profits is to be allocated based on service, with Randolph receiving $24,000 and Scott receiving $36,000.

3. Any remaining amount is allocated equally.

If net income for the first year is $125,000, the partners' shares of this profit are computed as follows:

	Randolph	Scott	Total
Total net income.			$125,000
Sharing of first $50,000 of net income, based on capital contributions:			
Randolph ($60,000/$100,000 × $50,000) . .	$30,000		
Scott ($40,000/$100,000 × $50,000)		$20,000	
Total			50,000
Net income remaining for allocation			75,000
Sharing of next $60,000, based on service:			
Randolph	24,000		
Scott		36,000	
Total			60,000
Net income remaining for allocation			15,000
Remainder shared equally:			
Randolph ($15,000 × ½)	7,500		
Scott ($15,000 × ½)		7,500	
Total			15,000
Net income remaining for allocation			$ -0-
Net income allocated to the partners	$61,500	$63,500	$125,000

Based on this allocation, the closing entry is

Dec. 31	Income Summary	125,000		
	Randolph, Capital		61,500	
	Scott, Capital		63,500	
	To allocate net income to partners.			

Sharing Based on Salaries and Interest

Partners may be rewarded for their service and their capital contributions to the business in other ways. In one sharing plan, the partners are allocated salaries plus interest on their capital balances. Assume Lewis and Clark form an oil-exploration partnership. At the beginning of the year, their capital balances are $80,000 and $100,000, respectively. The partnership agreement allocates annual salary of $43,000 to Lewis and $35,000 to Clark. After salaries are allocated, each partner earns 8 percent interest on his beginning capital balance. Any remaining net income is divided equally. Partnership profit of $96,000 would be allocated as follows:

Point to Stress: The amount of profits allocated based on service may appear to be a salary. Remember that salaries paid to owners/partners are considered not salary expense but rather a distribution of profit.

	Lewis	Clark	Total
Total net income................................			$96,000
First, salaries:			
Lewis....................................	$43,000		
Clark		$35,000	
Total			78,000
Net income remaining for allocation			18,000
Second, interest on beginning capital balances:			
Lewis ($80,000 × .08)	6,400		
Clark ($100,000 × .08).....................		8,000	
Total			14,400
Net income remaining for allocation			3,600
Third, remainder shared equally:			
Lewis ($3,600 × ½)	1,800		
Clark ($3,600 × ½)......................		1,800	
Total			3,600
Net income remaining for allocation			$ -0-
Net income allocated to the partners	$51,200	$44,800	$96,000

Class Exercise: Ash, Black, and Cole have capital balances of $10,000, $20,000, and $70,000, respectively. The partners share profits and losses as follows:

1 Ash and Cole receive salaries of $6,000 and $7,000, respectively.

2 Interest of 10% is paid on the capital balances.

3 The remainder is divided equally.

Compute each partner's share of net income if the partnership earns $50,000. ANSWER:

Ash: $6,000 + (10% × $10,000) + $9,000* = $16,000
Black: (10% × $20,000) + $9,000* = $11,000
Cole: $7,000 + (10% × $70,000) + $9,000* = $23,000

*Remainder = ($50,000 − $6,000 − $7,000 − $10,000 = $27,000)

Based on this allocation, the closing entry is

Dec. 31	Income Summary	96,000	
	Lewis, Capital........................		51,200
	Clark, Capital		44,800
	To allocate net income to partners.		

These salaries and interest amounts are *not* business expenses in the usual sense. Partners do not work for their own business to earn a salary, as an employee does. They do not loan money to their own business to earn interest. Their goal is for the partnership to earn a profit. Therefore, salaries and interest in partnership agreements are simply ways of expressing the allocation of profits and losses to the partners. For example, the salary component of partner income rewards service to the partnership. The interest component rewards a partner's investment of cash or other assets in the business.

In the preceding illustration, net income exceeded the sum of salary and interest. If the partnership profit is less than the allocated sum of salary and interest, a negative remainder will occur at some stage in the allocation process. Even so, the partners use the same method for allocation purposes. For example, assume that Lewis and Clark Partnership earned only $82,000.

	Lewis	Clark	Total
Total net income............................			$ 82,000
First, salaries:			
Lewis...................................	$43,000		
Clark...................................		$35,000	
Total................................			78,000
Net income remaining for allocation.......			4,000
Second, interest on beginning capital balances:			
Lewis ($80,000 × .08).................	6,400		
Clark ($100,000 × .08)................		8,000	
Total................................			14,400
Net income remaining for allocation.......			(10,400)
Third, remainder shared equally:			
Lewis ($10,400 × ½)..................	(5,200)		
Clark ($10,400 × ½)..................		(5,200)	
Total................................			(10,400)
Net income remaining for allocation.......			$ -0-
Net income allocated to the partners.......	$44,200	$37,800	$ 82,000

A net loss would be allocated to Lewis and Clark in the same manner outlined for net income. The sharing procedure would begin with the net loss and then allocate salary, interest, and any other specified amounts to the partners.

We see that partners may allocate profits and losses based on a stated fraction, contributed capital, service, interest on capital, or any combination of these factors. Each partnership shapes its profit-and-loss-sharing ratio to fit its own needs.

Partner Drawings

Point to Stress: Each partner's withdrawals (Drawing) must be closed into his capital account, just as for a proprietorship. The amount of the drawings is not dependent on income or loss of the partnership for the year.

Partners, like anyone else, need cash for personal living expenses. Partnership agreements usually allow partners to withdraw cash or other assets from the business. Drawings from a partnership are recorded exactly as illustrated in previous chapters for drawings from a proprietorship. Assume Lewis and Clark are each allowed a monthly withdrawal of $3,500. The partnership records the March withdrawal with this entry:

Mar. 31	Lewis, Drawing............................	3,500	
	Clark, Drawing...........................	3,500	
	Cash.................................		7,000
	Monthly partner withdrawals.		

During the year, each partner drawing account accumulates 12 such amounts, a total of $42,000 ($3,500 × 12). At the end of the period, the general ledger shows the following account balances immediately after net income has been closed to the partners' capital accounts. Assume these beginning balances for Lewis and Clark at the start of the year and that $82,000 of profit has been allocated based on the preceding illustration.

Lewis, Capital	
	Jan. 1 Bal. 80,000
	Dec. 31 Net inc. 44,200

Clark, Capital	
	Jan. 1 Bal. 100,000
	Dec. 31 Net inc. 37,800

Lewis, Drawing			Clark, Drawing	
Dec. 31 Bal.	42,000		Dec. 31 Bal.	42,000

The withdrawal accounts must be closed at the end of the period. The final closing entries transfer their balances to the partner's capital account as follows:

Dec. 31	Lewis, Capital............................	42,000	
	Lewis, Drawing		42,000
	Clark, Capital............................	42,000	
	Clark, Drawing		42,000
	To close partner drawing accounts.		

After closing, the accounts appear as follows:

Lewis, Capital				
→ Dec. 31 Clo.	42,000	Jan. 1 Bal.	80,000	
		Dec. 31 Net inc.	44,200	
		Dec. 31 Bal.	82,200	

Clark, Capital				
→ Dec. 31 Clo.	42,000	Jan. 1 Bal.	100,000	
		Dec. 31 Net inc.	37,800	
		Dec. 31 Bal.	95,800	

Lewis, Drawing				
Dec. 31 Bal.	42,000	Dec. 31 Clo.	42,000	

Clark, Drawing				
Dec. 31 Bal.	42,000	Dec. 31 Clo.	42,000	

In this case, Lewis withdrew less than his share of the partnership net income. Consequently, his capital account grew during the period. Clark, however, withdrew more than his share of net income. His capital account decreased.

Partnerships, as we have mentioned, do not last forever. We turn now to a discussion of how partnerships dissolve—and how new partnerships arise.

Dissolution of a Partnership

A partnership lasts only as long as its partners remain in the business. The addition of a new member or the withdrawal of an existing member dissolves the partnership.

Often a new partnership is formed to carry on the former partnership's business. In fact, the new partnership may choose to retain the dissolved partnership's name. Price Waterhouse & Company, for example, is an accounting firm that retires and hires partners during the year. Thus the former partnership dissolves and a new partnership begins many times. The business, however, retains the name and continues operations. Other partnerships may dissolve and then reform under a new name. Let's look now at the ways that a new member may gain admission into an existing partnership.

Admission by Purchasing a Partner's Interest

A person may become a member of a partnership by gaining the approval of the other partner (or partners) for entrance into the firm *and* by purchasing a present partner's interest in the business. Let's assume that Fisher and Garcia have a partnership that carries these figures:

Cash	$ 40,000	Total liabilities	$120,000
Other assets	360,000	Fisher, capital	110,000
		Garcia, capital	170,000
		Total liabilities and	
Total assets	$400,000	capital	$400,000

Business is going so well that Fisher receives an offer from Dynak, an outside party, to buy her $110,000 interest in the business for $150,000. Fisher agrees to sell out to Dynak, and Garcia approves Dynak as a new partner. The firm records the transfer of capital interest in the business with this entry:

Apr. 16	Fisher, Capital	110,000	
	Dynak, Capital		110,000
	To transfer Fisher's equity in the business to Dynak.		

The debit side of the entry closes Fisher's capital account because she is no longer a partner in the firm. The credit side opens Dynak's capital account because Fisher's equity has been transferred to Dynak. Notice that the entry amount is Fisher's capital balance ($110,000) and not the $150,000 price that Dynak paid Fisher to buy into the business. The full $150,000 goes to Fisher, including the $40,000 difference between her capital balance and the price received from Dynak. In this example, the partnership receives no cash because the transaction was between Dynak and Fisher, not between Dynak and the partnership. Suppose Dynak pays Fisher less than Fisher's capital balance. That does not affect the entry on the partnership books. Fisher's equity is transferred to Dynak at book value ($110,000).

Class Exercise: Ted and Fred are partners with capital balances of $16,000 and $24,000, respectively. Profits and losses are shared based on capital balances. Joe offers Fred $60,000 for his interest in the business. What is the entry to record the transfer of capital?

ANSWER:

Fred, Capital	24,000	
Joe, Capital		24,000

The old partnership has dissolved. Garcia and Dynak draw up a new partnership agreement, with a new profit-and-loss-sharing ratio, and continue business operations. If Garcia does not accept Dynak as a partner, Dynak gets no voice in management of the firm. However, under the Uniform Partnership Act, the purchaser shares in the profits and losses of the firm and in its assets at liquidation.

Admission by Investing in the Partnership

A person may also be admitted as a partner by investing directly in the partnership rather than by purchasing an existing partner's interest. The new partner contributes assets—for example, cash, inventory, or equipment—to the business. Assume that the partnership of Ingel and Jay has the following assets, liabilities, and capital:

Cash	$ 20,000	Total liabilities	$100,000
Other assets	240,000	Ingel, capital	70,000
		Jay, capital	90,000
		Total liabilities and	
Total assets	$260,000	capital	$260,000

Kahn offers to invest equipment and land (Other assets) with a market value of $80,000 to persuade the existing partners to take her into the business. Ingel and Jay agree to dissolve the existing partnership and to start up a new business, giving Kahn one-third interest in exchange for the contributed assets. The entry to record Kahn's investment is

```
July 18   Other Assets. . . . . . . . . . . . . . . . . . . . . . . . . . .    80,000
              Kahn, Capital . . . . . . . . . . . . . . . . . . . . . .                80,000
          To admit L. Kahn as a partner with a one-third
          interest in the business.
```

After this entry, the partnership books show:

Cash	$ 20,000	Total liabilities	$100,000
Other assets ($240,000 +		Ingel, capital	70,000
$80,000).	320,000	Jay, capital	90,000
		Kahn, capital	80,000
		Total liabilities and	
Total assets	$340,000	capital	$340,000

Kahn's one-third interest in the partnership [$80,000/($70,000 + $90,000 + $80,000) = ⅓] does not necessarily entitle her to one-third of the profits. The sharing of profits and losses is a separate element in the partnership agreement.

In the previous example, Dynak paid an individual member (Fisher), not the partnership. Note that Kahn's payment (the other assets) goes into the partnership.

Admission by Investing in the Partnership—Bonus to the Old Partners.

The more successful a partnership, the higher the payment the partners may demand from a person entering the business. Partners in a business that is doing quite well might require an incoming person to pay them a bonus. The bonus increases the current partners' capital accounts.

Suppose that Nagasawa and Osburn's partnership has earned above-average profits for 10 years. The two partners share profits and losses equally. The balance sheet carries these figures:

Cash	$ 40,000	Total liabilities	$100,000
Other assets	210,000	Nagasawa, capital	70,000
		Osburn, capital	80,000
		Total liabilities and	
Total assets	$250,000	capital	$250,000

The partners agree to admit Parker to a one-fourth interest with his cash investment of $90,000. Parker's capital balance on the partnership books is $60,000, computed as follows:

Partnership capital before Parker is admitted ($70,000 + $80,000)	$150,000
Parker's investment in the partnership.	90,000
Partnership capital after Parker is admitted	$240,000
Parker's capital in the partnership ($240,000 × ¼)	$ 60,000

The entry on the partnership books to record Parker's investment is

```
Mar. 1   Cash . . . . . . . . . . . . . . . . . . . . . . . . . . . . . . . . . . . . .    90,000
              Parker, Capital . . . . . . . . . . . . . . . . . . . . . . .                60,000
              Nagasawa, Capital ($30,000 × ½) . . . . . .                15,000
              Osburn, Capital ($30,000 × ½) . . . . . . . .                15,000
          To admit G. Parker as a partner with a one-
          fourth interest in the business.
```

Parker's capital account is credited for his one-fourth interest in the partnership. The other partners share the $30,000 difference between Parker's investment ($90,000) and his equity in the business ($60,000). This difference is

Class Exercise: Ted and Fred are partners with capital balances of $16,000 and $24,000, respectively. Profits and losses are shared based on capital balances. Ted and Fred admit Jill to a 20% interest with a $12,000 investment. What is the entry to record Jill's admission to the partnership?
ANSWER:

Cash	12,000	
Jill, Capital		10,400
Ted, Capital . . .		640
Fred, Capital . .		960

Jill: $10,400 = ($16,000 + $24,000 + $12,000) × .2
Ted: $640 = $16,000/$40,000 × ($12,000 − $10,400)
Fred: $960 = $24,000/$40,000 × ($12,000 − $10,400)

Teaching Tip: Look at the March 1 journal entry. Notice that although both Nagasawa's and Osburn's capital accounts increased because of Parker's investment, they have not received cash. The cash all went into the partnership. Their increased capital accounts include the bonus amount that was contributed by Parker.

Point to Stress: The bonus in this example is shared equally because the partners share profits equally. A bonus is normally shared by the existing partners in the profit-sharing ratio.

called a bonus and is accounted for as income to the old partners and is, therefore, allocated to them based on their profit-and-loss ratio.

The new partnership's balance sheet reports these amounts:

Cash ($40,000 + $90,000)	$130,000	Total liabilities	$100,000
Other assets	210,000	Nagasawa, capital	
		($70,000 + $15,000) ...	85,000
		Osburn, capital	
		($80,000 + $15,000) ...	95,000
		Parker, capital	60,000
		Total liabilities and	
Total assets	$340,000	capital	$340,000

Class Exercise: Ted and Fred are partners with capital balances of $16,000 and $24,000, respectively. They share profits and losses in a 4:6 ratio. Ted and Fred admit Lana to a 20% interest with an $8,000 investment. What is the entry to record Lana's admission as a new partner?

ANSWER:

Cash	8,000	
Ted, Capital ...	640	
Fred, Capital ..	960	
Lana, Capital		9,600

L: $9,600 = ($16,000 + $24,000 + $8,000) × .2
T: $640 = ($9,600 − $8,000) × .4
F: $960 = ($9,600 − $8,000) × .6

Admission by Investing in the Partnership—Bonus to the New Partner. A potential new partner may be so important that the existing partners offer him or her a partnership share that includes a bonus. A law firm may strongly desire a former governor or other official as a partner because of the person's reputation. A restaurant owner may want to go into partnership with a famous sports personality like Jack Nicklaus or Magic Johnson.

Suppose Page and Osuka is a law partnership. The firm's balance sheet appears as follows:

Cash	$140,000	Total liabilities	$120,000
Other assets	360,000	Page, capital	230,000
		Osuka, capital	150,000
		Total liabilities and	
Total assets	$500,000	capital	$500,000

The partners admit Schiller, a former attorney general, as a partner with a one-third interest in exchange for his cash investment of $100,000. At the time of Schiller's admission, the firm's capital is $380,000—Page, $230,000, and Osuka, $150,000. Page and Osuka share profits and losses in the ratio of two-thirds to Page and one-third to Osuka. The computation of Schiller's equity in the partnership is

Partnership capital before Schiller is admitted ($230,000 + $150,000)..	$380,000
Schiller's investment in the partnership	100,000
Partnership capital after Schiller is admitted	$480,000
Schiller's capital in the partnership ($480,000 × ⅓)	$160,000

The capital accounts of Page and Osuka are debited for the $60,000 difference between the new partner's equity ($160,000) and his investment ($100,000). The existing partners share this decrease in capital, which is accounted for as though it were a loss, based on their profit-and-loss ratio.

The entry to record Schiller's investment is

Aug. 24	Cash	100,000	
	Page, Capital ($60,000 × ⅔)	40,000	
	Osuka, Capital ($60,000 × ⅓)	20,000	
	Schiller, Capital		160,000
	To admit M. Schiller as a partner with a one-third interest in the business.		

The new partnership's balance sheet reports these amounts:

Cash		Total liabilities	$120,000
($140,000 + $100,000) .	$240,000	Page, capital	
Other assets	360,000	($230,000 − $40,000) ..	190,000
		Osuka, capital	
		($150,000 − $20,000) ..	130,000
		Schiller, capital	160,000
		Total liabilities and	
Total assets	$600,000	capital	$600,000

Summary Problem for Your Review

The partnership of Taylor and Uvalde is considering admitting Vaughn as a partner on January 1, 19X8. The partnership general ledger includes the following balances on that date:

Cash	$ 9,000	Total liabilities	$ 50,000
Other assets	110,000	Taylor, capital	45,000
		Uvalde, capital............	24,000
Total assets	$119,000	Total liabilities and capital ..	$119,000

Taylor's share of profits and losses is 60 percent, and Uvalde's share is 40 percent.

Required (Items 1 and 2 are independent)

1. Suppose Vaughn pays Uvalde $31,000 to acquire Uvalde's interest in the business. Taylor approves Vaughn as a partner.
   a. Record the transfer of owner's equity on the partnership books.
   b. Prepare the partnership balance sheet immediately after Vaughn is admitted as a partner.
2. Suppose Vaughn becomes a partner by investing $31,000 cash to acquire a one-fourth interest in the business.
   a. Compute Vaughn's capital balance, and record Vaughn's investment in the business.
   b. Prepare the partnership balance sheet immediately after Vaughn is admitted as a partner. Include the heading.
3. Which way of admitting Vaughn to the partnership increases its total assets? Give your reason.

SOLUTION TO REVIEW PROBLEM

Requirement 1

a. Jan. 1 Uvalde, Capital 24,000
              Vaughn, Capital   24,000
           To transfer Uvalde's equity in the partnership to Vaughn.

b. The balance sheet for the partnership of Taylor and Vaughn is identical to the balance sheet given for Taylor and Uvalde in the problem, except that Vaughn's name replaces Uvalde's name in the title and in the listing of capital accounts.

Requirement 2

a. Computation of Vaughn's capital balance:

Partnership capital before Vaughn is admitted ($45,000 + $24,000)	$ 69,000
Vaughn's investment in the partnership	31,000
Partnership capital after Vaughn is admitted	$100,000
Vaughn's capital in the partnership ($100,000 × ¼)	$ 25,000

Jan. 1	Cash.	31,000	
	Vaughn, Capital		25,000
	Taylor, Capital [($31,000 − $25,000) × .60]		3,600
	Uvalde, Capital [($31,000 − $25,000) × .40]		2,400
	To admit Vaughn as a partner with a one-fourth interest in the business.		

b.

Taylor, Uvalde, and Vaughn
Balance Sheet
January 1, 19X8

Cash			Total liabilities	$ 50,000
($9,000 + $31,000).	$ 40,000		Taylor, capital	
Other assets	110,000		($45,000 + $3,600).	48,600
			Uvalde, capital	
			($24,000 + $2,400).	26,400
			Vaughn, capital	25,000
Total assets	$150,000		Total liabilities and capital.	$150,000

Requirement 3

Vaughn's investment in the partnership increases its total assets by the amount of his contribution. Total assets of the business are $150,000 after his investment, compared to $119,000 before. By contrast, Vaughn's purchase of Uvalde's interest in the business is a personal transaction between the two individuals. It does not affect the assets of the partnership regardless of the amount Vaughn pays Uvalde.

Withdrawal of a Partner

OBJECTIVE 5

Account for the withdrawal of a partner from the business

A partner may withdraw from the business for many reasons, including retirement or a dispute with the other partners. The withdrawal of a partner dissolves the old partnership. The partnership agreement should contain a provision to govern how to settle with a withdrawing partner. In the simplest case, as illustrated on page 594, a partner may withdraw and sell his or her interest to another partner in a personal transaction. The only entry needed to record this transfer of equity debits the withdrawing partner's capital account and credits the purchaser's capital account. The dollar amount of the entry is the capital balance of the withdrawing partner, regardless of the price paid by the purchaser. The accounting when one current partner buys a second partner's interest is the same as when an outside party buys a current partner's interest.

If the partner withdraws in the middle of the accounting period, the partnership books should be updated to determine the withdrawing partner's capital balance. The business must measure net income or net loss for the fraction of the year up to the withdrawal date and allocate profit or loss according to the existing ratio. After closing the books, the business then accounts for the change in partnership capital.

The withdrawing partner may receive his or her share of the business in partnership assets other than cash. The question arises as to what value to assign the partnership assets: book value or current market value. The settlement procedure may specify an independent appraisal of assets to determine their current market value. If market values have changed, the appraisal will result in revaluing the partnership assets. Thus the partners share in any market value changes that their efforts caused.

Suppose Isaac is retiring in midyear from the partnership of Green, Henry, and Isaac. After the books have been adjusted for partial-period income but before the asset appraisal, revaluation, and closing entries, the balance sheet reports:

Cash	$ 39,000	Total liabilities	$ 80,000
Inventory	44,000	Green, capital	54,000
Land	55,000	Henry, capital	43,000
Building $95,000		Issac, capital	21,000
Less accum.			
depr 35,000	60,000	Total liabilities and	
Total assets	$198,000	capital	$198,000

Assume an independent appraiser revalues the inventory at $38,000 (down from $44,000) and the land at $101,000 (up from $55,000). The partners share the differences between these assets' market values and their prior book values based on their profit-and-loss ratio. The partnership agreement has allocated one-fourth of the profits to Green, one-half to Henry, and one-fourth to Isaac. (This ratio may be written 1 : 2 : 1 for one part to Green, two parts to Henry, and one part to Isaac.) For each share that Green or Isaac has, Henry has two. The entries to record the revaluation of the inventory and land are

July 31	Green, Capital ($6,000 × ¼)	1,500	
	Henry, Capital ($6,000 × ½)	3,000	
	Isaac, Capital ($6,000 × ¼)	1,500	
	Inventory ($44,000 − $38,000)		6,000
	To revalue the inventory and allocate the loss in value to the partners.		
31	Land ($101,000 − $55,000)	46,000	
	Green, Capital ($46,000 × ¼)		11,500
	Henry, Capital ($46,000 × ½)		23,000
	Isaac, Capital ($46,000 × ¼)		11,500
	To revalue the land and allocate the gain in value to the partners.		

After the revaluations, the partnership balance sheet reports:

Class Exercise: Jane, Wayne, and Shane are partners whose capital account balances are $20,000, $30,000, and $50,000, respectively. They share profits in a 2:3:5 ratio. Wayne is retiring and wants to withdraw from the business. The partners therefore have the assets appraised. The building's market value is $4,000 more than its book value. The inventory's market value is $6,000 less than its cost. What are the journal entries to revalue these assets?

ANSWER:

Building	4,000	
Jane, Capital		800
Wayne, Capital		1,200
Shane, Capital		2,000
Jane, Capital	1,200	
Wayne, Capital	1,800	
Shane, Capital	3,000	
Inventory		6,000

What are the partner's capital account balances after these revaluations?

ANSWER:

Jane: ($20,000 + $800 − $1,200) = $19,600
Wayne: ($30,000 + $1,200 − $1,800) = $29,400
Shane: ($50,000 + $2,000 − $3,000) = $49,000

Transparency T13-2

Point to Stress: These two journal entries are restating assets from historical cost to current market value. Does this violate an accounting principle we discussed in Chapter 12?

ANSWER: Yes, the going concern and historical cost concepts. However, the partnership is no longer a going concern; one partner's interest is being liquidated. That means the old partnership ends and another one begins. Therefore, departure from cost is acceptable.

Cash.................	$ 39,000		Total liabilities	$ 80,000
Inventory	38,000		Green, capital	
Land	101,000		($54,000 − $1,500 +	
Building $95,000			$11,500)	64,000
Less accum.			Henry, capital	
depr 35,000	60,000		($43,000 − $3,000 +	
			$23,000)	63,000
			Isaac, capital ($21,000 −	
			$1,500 + $11,500)	31,000
			Total liabilities and	
Total assets............	$238,000		capital	$238,000

The books now carry the assets at current market value, which becomes the new book value, and the capital accounts have been adjusted accordingly. Isaac has a claim to $31,000 in partnership assets. How is his withdrawal from the business accounted for?

Withdrawal at Book Value

If Isaac withdraws by receiving cash equal to the book value of his owner's equity, the entry would be

July 31	Isaac, Capital	31,000	
	Cash...............................		31,000
	To record withdrawal of K. Isaac from the partnership.		

This entry records the payment of partnership cash to Isaac and the closing of his capital account upon withdrawal from the business.

Withdrawal at Less Than Book Value

The withdrawing partner may be so eager to leave the business that he is willing to take less than his equity. This situation has occurred in real estate and oil-drilling partnerships. Assume Isaac withdraws from the business and agrees to receive partnership cash of $10,000 and the new partnership's note for $15,000. This $25,000 settlement is $6,000 less than Isaac's $31,000 equity in the business. The remaining partners share this $6,000 difference—which is a gain to them—according to their profit-and-loss ratio. However, since Isaac has withdrawn from the partnership, a new agreement—and a new profit-and-loss ratio—must be drawn up. Henry and Green, in forming a new partnership, may decide on any ratio that they see fit. Let's assume they agree that Henry will earn two-thirds of partnership profits and losses and Green one-third. The entry to record Isaac's withdrawal at less than book value is

July 31	Isaac, Capital	31,000	
	Cash		10,000
	Note Payable to K. Isaac		15,000
	Green, Capital ($6,000 × ⅓)		2,000
	Henry, Capital ($6,000 × ⅔)		4,000
	To record withdrawal of K. Isaac from the partnership.		

Isaac's account is closed, and Henry and Green may or may not continue the business.

Withdrawal at More Than Book Value

The settlement with a withdrawing partner may allow him to take assets of greater value than the book value of his capital. Also, the remaining partners may be so eager for the withdrawing partner to leave the firm that they pay him a bonus to withdraw from the business. In either case, the partner's withdrawal causes a decrease in the book equity of the remaining partners. This decrease is allocated to the partners based on their profit-and-loss ratio.

Assume Chang, Daley, and Evans share profits in a ratio of 3:2:1. Their partnership accounts include the following balances:

Cash...............	$ 50,000	Total liabilities	$110,000
Other assets	220,000	Chang, capital	80,000
		Daley, capital...........	50,000
		Evans, capital	30,000
		Total liabilities and	
Total assets............	$270,000	capital	$270,000

Assume Evans withdraws, accepting cash of $15,000 and the new partnership's note for $25,000. This $40,000 settlement exceeds Evans's capital balance by $10,000. Chang and Daley share this loss in equity based on their profit-and-loss ratio (3:2). The withdrawal entry is

Nov. 30	Evans, Capital...........................	30,000	
	Chang, Capital ($10,000 × ⅗)..............	6,000	
	Daley, Capital ($10,000 × ⅖)..............	4,000	
	Cash................................		15,000
	Note Payable to R. Evans		25,000
	To record withdrawal of R. Evans from the partnership.		

The withdrawal entry closes Evans's capital account and updates those of Chang and Daley.

Death of a Partner

Death of a partner, like any other form of partnership withdrawal, dissolves a partnership. The partnership accounts are adjusted to measure net income or loss for the fraction of the year up to the date of death, then closed to determine the partners' capital balances on that date. Settlement with the deceased partner's estate is based on the partnership agreement. The estate commonly receives partnership assets equal to the partner's capital balance. The partnership closes the deceased partner's capital account with a debit. This entry credits a payable to the estate.

Alternatively, a remaining partner may purchase the deceased partner's equity. The deceased partner's equity is debited and the purchaser's equity is credited. The amount of this entry is the ending credit balance in the deceased partner's capital account.

Liquidation of a Partnership

Admission of a new partner or withdrawal or death of an existing partner dissolves the partnership. However, the business may continue operating with no apparent change to outsiders such as customers and creditors.

Class Exercise: Refer to the preceding class exercise. Assume that Jane and Shane agree to pay Wayne $40,000 for his partnership interest. What is the journal entry to record Wayne's retirement?
ANSWER:

Jane, Capital ..	3,029*	
Wayne, Capital	29,400	
Shane, Capital.	7,571*	
Cash		40,000

*$10,600 × 2/7
**$10,600 × 5/7

OBJECTIVE 6
Account for the liquidation of a partnership

Point to Stress: As you discuss the three steps in a business liquidation, remind students that both the profit-and-loss ratio and the partners' capital balances are used in determining how to divide gains, losses, and remaining cash.

Occasionally when a business liquidates, not enough cash remains to pay off all liabilities. In that case, the partners (who are personally liable for partnership debts) must contribute cash based on their profit-and-loss ratio to cover any unpaid debts.

Point to Stress: The partners' profit-and-loss sharing ratios do not have to match their capital account balances. Here, for instance, Aviron has a 60% sharing ratio but he owns 4/7 (or 57%) of the capital.

Transparency T13-4

Point to Stress: Note that the gain is shared in the profit-and-loss sharing ratio, while the cash distributed is based on capital account balances.

Business **liquidation**, however, is the process of going out of business by selling the entity's assets and paying its liabilities. The final step in liquidation of a business is the *distribution of the remaining cash to the owners*. Before liquidating the business, the books should be adjusted and closed. After closing, only asset, liability, and partners' capital accounts remain open.

Liquidation of a partnership includes three basic steps:

1. Sell the assets. Allocate the gain or loss to the partners' capital accounts based on the profit-and-loss ratio.
2. Pay the partnership liabilities.
3. Disburse the remaining cash to the partners based on their capital balances.

In actual practice, the liquidation of a business can stretch over weeks or months. Selling every asset and paying every liability of the entity takes time. To avoid excessive detail in our illustrations, we include only two asset categories—Cash and Noncash Assets—and a single liability category—Liabilities. Our examples also assume that the business sells the noncash assets in a single transaction and pays the liabilities in a single transaction.

Assume that Aviron, Bloch, and Crane have shared profits and losses in the ratio of 3:1:1. (This ratio is equal to ⅗, ⅕, ⅕, or a 60-percent, 20-percent, 20-percent sharing ratio.) They decide to liquidate their partnership. After the books are adjusted and closed, the general ledger contains the following balances:

Cash..................	$ 10,000	Liabilities	$ 30,000
Noncash assets	90,000	Aviron, capital..........	40,000
		Bloch, capital	20,000
		Crane, capital	10,000
		Total liabilities and	
Total assets.............	$100,000	capital	$100,000

We will use the Aviron, Bloch, and Crane partnership data to illustrate accounting for liquidation in three different situations.

Sale of Noncash Assets at a Gain

Assume the partnership sells its noncash assets (shown on the balance sheet at $90,000) for cash of $150,000. The partnership realizes a gain of $60,000, which is allocated to the partners based on their profit-and-loss-sharing ratio. The entry to record this sale and allocation of the gain is

Oct. 31	Cash	150,000	
	Noncash Assets		90,000
	Aviron, Capital ($60,000 × .60)		36,000
	Bloch, Capital ($60,000 × .20)		12,000
	Crane, Capital ($60,000 × .20)		12,000
	To sell noncash assets in liquidation and allocate gain to partners.		

The partnership must next pay off its liabilities:

Oct. 31	Liabilities	30,000	
	Cash		30,000
	To pay liabilities in liquidation.		

In the final liquidation transaction, the remaining cash is disbursed to the partners. *The partners share in the cash according to their capital balances.* (By contrast, *gains and losses* on the sale of assets are shared by the partners based on their profit-and-loss-sharing ratio.) The amount of cash left in the partnership is $130,000—the $10,000 beginning balance plus the $150,000 cash sale of assets minus the $30,000 cash payment of liabilities. The partners divide the remaining cash according to their capital balances:

Oct. 31	Aviron, Capital ($40,000 + $36,000)	76,000	
	Bloch, Capital ($20,000 + $12,000)........	32,000	
	Crane, Capital ($10,000 + $12,000)	22,000	
	Cash		130,000
	To disburse cash to partners in liquidation.		

A convenient way to summarize the transactions in a partnership liquidation is given in Exhibit 13-1.

After the disbursement of cash to the partners, the business has no assets, liabilities, or owners' equity. The balances are all zero. At all times, partnership assets must equal partnership liabilities plus partnership capital, by the accounting equation.

Sale of Noncash Assets at a Loss

Assume that Aviron, Bloch, and Crane sell the noncash assets for $75,000, realizing a loss of $15,000. The summary of transactions appears in Exhibit 13-2. The journal entries to record the liquidation transactions are

Oct. 31	Cash	75,000	
	Aviron, Capital ($15,000 × .60)	9,000	
	Bloch, Capital ($15,000 × .20)	3,000	
	Crane, Capital ($15,000 × .20)	3,000	
	Noncash Assets		90,000
	To sell noncash assets in liquidation and allocate loss to partners.		

Typical Student Misconception: The amount of cash distributed is based on the capital account balances and not on the profit-and-loss sharing ratio.

Class Exercise: Kyle and Keith are partners in a partnership that has cash of $10,000 and non-cash assets of $50,000. All liabilities have been paid. The capital balances of Kyle and Keith are $40,000 and $20,000, respectively. Kyle and Keith share profits and losses in a 60:40 ratio. The non-cash assets are sold for $26,000. What are the journal entries to sell the assets and distribute the remaining cash to the partners?
ANSWER:

Cash.........	26,000	
Kyle, Capital .	14,400*	
Keith, Capital	9,600*	
Non-cash assets		50,000

*$24,000 loss × 60%
**$24,000 × 40%

Kyle, Capital ($40,000 − $14,400).....	25,600	
Keith, Capital ($20,000 − $9,600)......	10,400	
Cash		36,000

EXHIBIT 13-1 *Partnership Liquidation—Sale of Assets at a Gain*

	Cash	+ Noncash Assets =	Liabilities +	Aviron (60%) +	Bloch (20%) +	Crane (20%)
					Capital	
Balances before sale of assets	$ 10,000	$ 90,000	$ 30,000	$ 40,000	$ 20,000	$ 10,000
Sale of assets and sharing of gain	150,000	(90,000)		36,000	12,000	12,000
Balances	160,000	-0-	30,000	76,000	32,000	22,000
Payment of liabilities .	(30,000)		(30,000)			
Balances	130,000	-0-	-0-	76,000	32,000	22,000
Disbursement of cash to partners	(130,000)			(76,000)	(32,000)	(22,000)
Balances	$ -0-	$ -0-	$ -0-	$ -0-	$ -0-	$ -0-

EXHIBIT 13-2 *Partnership Liquidation—Sale of Assets at a Loss*

	Cash	+ Noncash Assets	= Liabilities +	Aviron (60%)	+ Bloch (20%)	+ Crane (20%)
					Capital	
Balance before sale of assets .	$ 10,000	$ 90,000	$ 30,000	$ 40,000	$ 20,000	$ 10,000
Sale of assets and sharing of loss	75,000	(90,000)		(9,000)	(3,000)	(3,000)
Balances	85,000	-0-	30,000	31,000	17,000	7,000
Payment of liabilities	(30,000)		(30,000)			
Balances	55,000	-0-	-0-	31,000	17,000	7,000
Disbursement of cash to partners	(55,000)			(31,000)	(17,000)	(7,000)
Balances	$ -0-	$ -0-	$ -0-	$ -0-	$ -0-	$ -0-

Discussion Question: How is the loss of $15,000 on the sale of noncash assets divided in the first journal entry? ANSWER: In the profit and loss sharing ratios. Have students calculate the amounts. ANSWER:

Aviron 60% × $15,000 = $ 9,000
Bloch 20% × 15,000 =   3,000
Crane 20% × 15,000 =   3,000
                        $15,000

Have students compare their answers to Exhibit 13-2.

Oct. 31	Liabilities	30,000	
	Cash		30,000
	To pay liabilities in liquidation.		

31	Aviron, Capital ($40,000 − $9,000)	31,000	
	Bloch, Capital ($20,000 − $3,000)	17,000	
	Crane, Capital ($10,000 − $3,000)	7,000	
	Cash		55,000
	To disburse cash to partners in liquidation.		

Sale of Noncash Assets at a Loss—Deficiency in a Partner's Capital Account. The sale of noncash assets at a loss may result in a debit balance in a partner's capital account. This situation is called a **capital deficiency** because the partner's capital balance is insufficient to cover his share of the partnership's loss. The unlimited liability of partners forces the other partners to absorb this deficiency through debits to their own capital accounts if the deficient partner does not erase his deficiency. The deficiency is a loss to the other partners, and they share it based on their profit-and-loss ratio.

DEFICIENT PARTNER UNABLE TO ERASE DEFICIENCY.   Assume that Aviron, Bloch, and Crane's partnership has had losses for several years. The market value of the noncash assets of the business is far less than book value ($90,000). In liquidation, the partnership sells these assets for $30,000, realizing a loss of $60,000. Crane's 20 percent share of this loss is $12,000. Because the loss exceeds his $10,000 capital balance, Crane's account has a $2,000 deficit. Crane is obligated to contribute personal funds to the business in order to meet this debt. Assume that Crane cannot erase the deficiency by contributing personal assets. Because of mutual agency, the other partners must absorb the deficiency before the final distribution of cash.

Point to Stress: Because a partner has unlimited liability, Aviron and Bloch must absorb Crane's deficiency.

Because Aviron and Bloch share losses in the ratio of 3:1, Aviron absorbs three-fourths of the deficiency [3/(3 + 1) = ¾] and Bloch absorbs one-fourth [1/(3 + 1) = ¼]. Aviron's share of Crane's $2,000 deficiency is $1,500 ($2,000 × ¾), and Bloch's share is $500 ($2,000 × ¼).

The journal entries to record the foregoing liquidation transactions are

Oct. 31	Cash	30,000	
	Aviron, Capital ($60,000 × .60)	36,000	
	Bloch, Capital ($60,000 × .20)	12,000	
	Crane, Capital ($60,000 × .20)	12,000	
	Noncash Assets		90,000
	To sell noncash assets in liquidation and allocate loss to partners.		
31	Liabilities	30,000	
	Cash		30,000
	To pay liabilities in liquidation.		
31	Aviron, Capital ($2,000 × ¾)	1,500	
	Bloch, Capital ($2,000 × ¼)	500	
	Crane, Capital.......................		2,000
	To allocate Crane's capital deficiency to the other partners.		
31	Aviron, Capital ($40,000 − $36,000 − $1,500)	2,500	
	Bloch, Capital ($20,000 − $12,000 − $500) ...	7,500	
	Cash		10,000
	To disburse cash to partners in liquidation.		

Teaching Tip: Show students how the remaining partners, Aviron and Bloch, share the $2,000 deficiency:

Aviron: 60% interest = 6/8
Bloch: 20% interest = 2/8
        80%

Aviron: 6/8 or 3/4 × $2,000 = $1,500
Bloch: 2/8 or 1/4 × 2,000 =   500
                              $2,000

The summary of transactions in Exhibit 13-3 includes a separate transaction (highlighted) to allocate Crane's deficiency to Aviron and Bloch.

DEFICIENT PARTNER ERASES DEFICIENCY.   A partner may erase his or her deficiency by contributing cash or other assets to the partnership. Such contributions are credited to the deficient partner's account and then distributed to the other partners. Suppose Crane erases his deficiency by investing $2,000 cash in the partnership.

The journal entries to record Crane's contribution and the disbursement of cash to the partners are on the following page.

EXHIBIT 13-3   *Partnership Liquidation—Deficient Partner Unable to Erase a Capital Deficiency*

| | | | | Capital | | |
| | | | | Aviron | Bloch | Crane |
	Cash	+ Noncash Assets =	Liabilities +	(60%) +	(20%) +	(20%)
Balance before sale of assets .	$ 10,000	$ 90,000	$ 30,000	$ 40,000	$ 20,000	$ 10,000
Sale of assets and sharing of loss	30,000	(90,000)		(36,000)	(12,000)	(12,000)
Balances	40,000	-0-	30,000	4,000	8,000	(2,000)
Payment of liabilities	(30,000)		(30,000)			
Balances	10,000	-0-	-0-	4,000	8,000	(2,000)
Sharing of Crane's deficiency by Aviron and Bloch				**(1,500)**	**(500)**	**2,000**
Balances	10,000	-0-	-0-	2,500	7,500	-0-
Disbursement of cash to partners	(10,000)			(2,500)	(7,500)	
Balances	$ -0-	$ -0-	$ -0-	$ -0-	$ -0-	$ -0-

			Oct. 31	Cash	2,000	

Oct. 31   Cash 2,000
               Crane, Capital 2,000
          Crane's contribution to erase his capital
          deficiency in liquidation.

     31   Aviron, Capital 4,000
          Bloch, Capital 8,000
               Cash 12,000
          To disburse cash to partners in liquidation.

In this case, the summary of transactions, beginning with the balances after payment of the liabilities, appears in Exhibit 13-4.

EXHIBIT 13-4   *Partnership Liquidation—Partner Erases Capital Deficiency*

	Cash	+ Noncash Assets	= Liabilities	+ Aviron (60%)	+ Bloch (20%)	+ Crane (20%)
				Capital		
Balances after payment of liabilities	$ 10,000	$ -0-	$ -0-	$ 4,000	$ 8,000	$(2,000)
Crane's contribution to erase his deficiency	2,000	-0-	-0-			2,000
Balances	12,000	-0-	-0-	4,000	8,000	-0-
Disbursement of cash to partners	(12,000)			(4,000)	(8,000)	
Balances	$ -0-	$ -0-	$ -0-	$ -0-	$ -0-	$ -0-

Partnership Financial Statements

Objective 7
Prepare partnership financial statements

Partnership financial statements are much like those of a proprietorship. However, a partnership income statement includes a section showing the division of net income to the partners. For example, the partnership of Gray and Hayward might report its income statement for the year ended June 30, 19X6, as follows:

Gray and Hayward
Income Statement
For the Year Ended June 30, 19X6

Sales revenue	$381,000
Net income	$ 79,000
Allocation of net income:	
M. Gray	$ 36,600
L. Hayward	42,400
Total	$ 79,000

Large partnerships may not find it feasible to report the net income of every partner. Instead, the firm may report the allocation of net income to active and retired partners and average earnings per partner. For example, the CPA firm of Main Price & Anders reported the following:

Main Price & Anders
Combined Statement of Earnings
For the Year Ended August 31, 19X0

Dollar amounts in thousands	
Fees for Professional Services	$914,492
Earnings for the year	$297,880
Allocation of earnings:	
To partners active during the year—	
Resigned, retired, and deceased partners	$ 19,901
Partners active at year end	253,270
To retired and deceased partners—retirement and death benefits	8,310
Not allocated to partners—retained for specific partnership purposes	16,399
	$297,880
Average earnings per partner active at year end (1,336 partners)	$223

Exhibit 13-5 summarizes the financial statements of a proprietorship and a partnership.

EXHIBIT 13-5   *Financial Statements of a Proprietorship and a Partnership*

Income Statements
For the Year Ended December 31, 19X1

Proprietorship		Partnership		
Revenues	$460	Revenues		$460
Expenses	(270)	Expenses		(270)
Net income	$190	Net income		$190
		Allocation of net income:		
		To Smith	$114	
		To Jones	76	$190

Statements of Owner Equity
For the Year Ended December 31, 19X1

Proprietorship		Partnership	Smith	Jones
Capital, December 31, 19X0	$ 90	Capital, December 31, 19X0	$ 50	$ 40
Additional investments	10	Additional investments	10	—
Net income	190	Net income	114	76
Subtotal	290	Subtotal	174	116
Drawings	(120)	Drawings	(72)	(48)
Capital, December 31, 19X1	$170	Capital, December 31, 19X1	$102	$ 68

	Balance Sheets December 31, 19X1		
Proprietorship		**Partnership**	
Assets		**Assets**	
Cash and other assets	$170	Cash and other assets	$170
Owners' Equity		**Owners' Equity**	
		Smith, capital	$102
		Jones, capital	68
Smith, capital	$170	Total capital	$170

Summary Problem for Your Review

The partnership of Prolux, Roberts, and Satulsky is liquidating. Its accounts have the following balances after closing:

Cash	$ 22,000	Liabilities	$ 77,000
Noncash assets	104,000	Prolux, capital	23,000
		Roberts, capital	10,000
		Satulsky, capital	16,000
Total assets	$126,000	Total liabilities and capital .	$126,000

The partnership agreement allocates profits to Prolux, Roberts, and Satulsky in the ratio of 3:4:3. In liquidation, the noncash assets were sold in a single transaction for $64,000 on May 31, 19X7. The partnership paid the liabilities the same day.

Required

1. Journalize the liquidation transactions. The partnership books remain open until June 7 to allow Roberts to make an additional $4,000 contribution to the business in view of her capital deficiency. This cash is immediately disbursed to the other partners. Use T-accounts if necessary.
2. Prepare a summary of the liquidation transactions, as illustrated in the chapter. Roberts invests cash of $4,000 in the partnership in partial settlement of her capital deficiency. The other partners absorb the remainder of Roberts's capital deficiency.

SOLUTION TO REVIEW PROBLEM

Requirement 1 (Liquidation journal entries)

May 31	Cash	64,000	
	Prolux, Capital [($104,000 − $64,000) × .30] .	12,000	
	Roberts, Capital [($104,000 − $64,000) × .40]	16,000	
	Satulsky, Capital [($104,000 − $64,000) × .30]	12,000	
	Noncash Assets		104,000
	To sell noncash assets in liquidation and distribute loss to partners.		

May 31   Liabilities   77,000

           Cash   77,000

        To pay liabilities in liquidation.

June 7   Cash   4,000

           Roberts, Capital   4,000

        Roberts's contribution to erase part of her
capital deficiency in liquidation.

After posting the entries, Roberts's capital account still has a $2,000 deficiency, indicated by its debit balance:

Roberts, Capital

Loss on sale	16,000	Bal.	10,000
		Investment	4,000
Bal.	2,000		

Prolux and Satulsky must make up Roberts's remaining $2,000 deficiency. Since Prolux and Satulsky had equal shares in the partnership profit-and-loss ratio (30 percent each), they divide Roberts's deficiency equally.

June 7   Prolux, Capital ($2,000 × ½)   1,000

        Satulsky, Capital ($2,000 × ½)   1,000

           Roberts, Capital   2,000

        To allocate Roberts's capital deficiency to the
other partners.

At this point, the capital accounts of Prolux and Satulsky appear as follows:

Prolux, Capital

Loss on sale	12,000	Bal.	23,000
Loss on Roberts	1,000		
		Bal.	10,000

Satulsky, Capital

Loss on sale	12,000	Bal.	16,000
Loss on Roberts	1,000		
		Bal.	3,000

The final disbursement entry is

June 7   Prolux, Capital   10,000

        Satulsky, Capital   3,000

           Cash   13,000

        To disburse cash to partners in liquidation.

Activity in the Cash account appears as follows:

Cash

Bal.	22,000	Payment of liabilities	77,000
Sale of assets	64,000		
Roberts's contribution	4,000		
Bal.	13,000	Final distribution	13,000

Requirement 2.   (Summary of liquidation transactions)

	Cash	+	Noncash Assets	=	Liabilities	+	Capital Prolux (30%)	+	Roberts (40%)	+	Satulsky (30%)
Balances before sale of assets	$ 2,000		$ 104,000		$ 77,000		$ 23,000		$ 10,000		$ 16,000
Sale of assets and sharing of loss .	64,000		(104,000)				(12,000)		(16,000)		(12,000)
Balances	86,000		-0-		77,000		11,000		(6,000)		4,000
Payment of liabilities	(77,000)				(77,000)						
Balances	9,000		-0-		-0-		11,000		(6,000)		4,000
Roberts's investment of cash to erase part of her deficiency	4,000								4,000		
Balances	13,000		-0-		-0-		11,000		(2,000)		4,000
Sharing of Roberts's deficiency by Prolux and Satulsky							(1,000)		2,000		(1,000)
Balances	13,000		-0-		-0-		10,000		-0-		3,000
Disbursement of cash to partners .	(13,000)						(10,000)				(3,000)
Balances	$ -0-		$ -0-		$ -0-		$ -0-		$ -0-		$ -0-

Summary

A *partnership* is a business co-owned by two or more persons for profit. The characteristics of this form of business organization are its *ease of formation, limited life, mutual agency, unlimited liability,* and *no partnership income taxes.*

A written *partnership agreement,* or *articles of partnership,* establishes procedures for admission of a new partner, withdrawals of a partner, and the sharing of profits and losses among the partners.

When a new partner is admitted to the firm or an existing partner withdraws, the old partnership is *dissolved,* or ceases to exist. A new partnership may or may not emerge to continue the business.

Accounting for a partnership is similar to accounting for a proprietorship. However, a partnership has more than one owner. Each partner has an individual capital account and a withdrawal account.

Partners share net income or loss in any manner they choose. Common sharing agreements base the *profit-and-loss ratio* on a stated fraction, partners' capital contributions, and/or their service to the partnership. Some partnerships call the cash drawings of partners *salaries* and *interest,* but these amounts are not expenses of the business. Instead, they are merely ways of allocating partnership net income to the partners.

An outside person may become a partner by purchasing a current partner's interest or by investing in the partnership. In some cases the new partner must pay the current partners a bonus to join. In other situations the new partner may receive a bonus to join.

When a partner withdraws, partnership assets may be reappraised. Partners share any gain or loss on the asset revaluation based on their profit-and-loss ratio. The withdrawing partner may receive payment equal to, greater than, or less than, his or her capital book value, depending on the agreement with the other partners.

In *liquidation,* a partnership goes out of business by selling the assets, paying the liabilities, and disbursing any remaining cash to the partners. Any partner's capital deficiency, which may result from sale of assets at a loss, must be absorbed before remaining cash is distributed.

Partnership *financial statements* are similar to those of a proprietorship. However, the partnership income statement commonly reports the allocation of net income to the partners.

Self-Study Questions

Test your understanding of the chapter by marking the best answer for each of the following questions.

1. Which of these characteristics does *not* apply to a partnership? *(p. 585)*
   - ✓ a. Unlimited life
   - b. Mutual agency
   - c. Unlimited liability
   - d. No business income tax

2. A partnership records a partner's investment of assets in the business at *(p. 587)*
   - a. The partner's book value of the assets invested
   - ✓ b. The market value of the assets invested
   - c. A special value set by the partners
   - d. Any of the above, depending upon the partnership agreement

3. The partnership of Lane, Murdock, and Nu divides profits in the ratio of 4:5:3. During 19X6 the business earned $40,000. Nu's share of this income is *(p. 588)*
   - ✓ a. $10,000
   - b. $13,333
   - c. $16,000
   - d. $16,667

4. Suppose the partnership of Lane, Murdock, and Nu in the preceding question lost $40,000 during 19X6. Murdock's share of this loss is *(p. 588)*
   - a. Not determinable because the ratio applies only to profits
   - b. $13,333
   - c. $16,000
   - ✓ d. $16,667

5. Placido, Quinn, and Rolfe share profits and losses $1/5$, $1/6$, and $19/30$. During 19X3, the first year of their partnership, the business earned $120,000, and each partner had drawings of $50,000 for personal use. What is the balance in Rolfe's capital account after all closing entries? *(p. 592)*
   - ✓ a. Not determinable because Rolfe's investment in the business is not given
   - b. Minus $10,000
   - c. $26,000
   - d. $70,000

6. Fuller buys into the partnership of Graff and Harrell by purchasing a one-third interest for $55,000. Prior to Fuller's entry, Graff's capital balance was $46,000, and Harrell's balance was $52,000. The entry to record Fuller's buying into the business is *(pp. 594, 595)*

   a. Cash............55,000
       Fuller, Capital 55,000

   b. Graff, Capital.... 27,500
       Harrell, Capital .. 27,500
         Fuller, Capital 55,000

   ✓ c. Cash............55,000
       Fuller, Capital 51,000
       Graff, Capital........ 2,000
       Harrell, Capital 2,000

   d. Cash............51,000
       Graff, Capital.... 2,000
       Harrell, Capital .. 2,000
         Fuller, Capital 55,000

7. Thomas, Valik, and Wollenberg share profits and losses equally. Their capital balances are $40,000, $50,000, and $60,000, respectively, when Wollenberg sells her interest in the partnership to Valik for $90,000. Thomas and Valik continue the business. Immediately after Wollenberg's retirement, the total assets of the partnership are *(p. 598)*
   - a. Increased by $30,000
   - b. Increased by $90,000

    c. Decreased by $60,000

✓ d. The same as before Wollenberg sold her interest to Valik

8. Prior to Hogg's withdrawal from the partnership of Hogg, Hamm, and Bacon, the partners' capital balances were $140,000, $110,000, and $250,000, respectively. The partners share profits and losses ⅓, ¼, and ⁵⁄₁₂. The appraisal indicates that assets should be written down by $36,000. Hamm's share of the write-down is *(p. 600)*

    a. $7,920   ✓ b. $9,000   c. $12,000   d. $18,000

9. Closing the business, selling the assets, paying the liabilities, and disbursing remaining cash to the owners is called *(p. 602)*

    a. Dissolution   c. Withdrawal

    b. Forming a new partnership   ✓ d. Liquidation

10. Huber and Hudson have shared profits and losses equally. Immediately prior to the final cash disbursement in a liquidation of their partnership, the books show:

Cash	= Liabilities	+ Huber, Capital	+ Hudson, Capital
$100,000	$ -0-	$60,000	$40,000

How much cash should Huber receive? *(p. 603)*

    a. $40,000   c. $60,000

    b. $50,000   ✓ d. None of the above

Answers to the Self-Study Questions follow the Accounting Vocabulary.

Accounting Vocabulary

Articles of partnership. Agreement that is the contract between partners specifying such items as the name, location, and nature of the business; the name, capital investment, and duties of each partner; and the method of sharing profits and losses by the partners. Also called the partnership agreement *(p. 585)*.

Capital deficiency. Debit balance in a partner's capital account *(p. 604)*.

Dissolution. Ending of a partnership *(p. 585)*.

Liquidation. The process of going out of business by selling the entity's assets and paying its liabilities. The final step in liquidation of a business is the distribution of any remaining cash to the owners *(p. 602)*.

Mutual agency. Every partner can bind the business to a contract within the scope of the partnership's regular business operations *(p. 585)*.

Partnership agreement. Another name for the articles of partnership *(p. 584)*.

Unlimited personal liability. When a partnership (or a proprietorship) cannot pay its debts with business assets, the partners (or the proprietor) must use personal assets to meet the debt *(p. 585)*.

Answers to Self-Study Questions

1. a

2. b

3. a   ($40,000 × ³⁄₁₂ = $10,000)

4. d   ($40,000 × ⁵⁄₁₂ = $16,667)

5. a

6. c   [($46,000 + $52,000 + $55,000) × ⅓ = $51,000; $55,000 − $51,000 = $4,000; $4,000 ÷ 2 = $2,000 each to Graff and Harrell]

7. d

8. b   ($36,000 × ¼ = $9,000)

9. d

10. c

ASSIGNMENT MATERIAL

Questions

1. What is another name for a partnership agreement? List eight items that the agreement should specify.

2. Montgomery, who is a partner in M&N Associates, commits the firm to a contract for a job within the scope of its regular business operations. What term describes Montgomery's ability to obligate the partnership?

3. If a partnership cannot pay a debt, who must make payment? What term describes this obligation of the partners?

4. How is partnership income taxed?

5. Identify the advantages and disadvantages of the partnership form of business organization.

6. Randall and Smith's partnership agreement states that Randall gets 60 percent of profits and Smith gets 40 percent. If the agreement does not discuss the treatment of losses, how are losses shared? How do the partners share profits and losses if the agreement specifies no profit-and-loss-sharing ratio?

7. Are salary and interest allocated to partners expenses of the business? Why or why not?

8. What determines the amount of the credit to a partner's capital account when the partner contributes assets other than cash to the business?

9. Do partner withdrawals of cash for personal use affect the sharing of profits and losses by the partner? If so, explain how. If not, explain why not.

10. Name two events that can cause the dissolution of a partnership.

11. Briefly describe how to account for the purchase of an existing partner's interest in the business.

12. Malcolm purchases Brown's interest in the Brown & Kareem partnership. What right does Malcolm obtain from the purchase? What is required for Malcolm to become Kareem's partner?

13. Assissi and Carter each have capital of $75,000 in their business and share profits in the ratio of 55:45. Denman acquires a one-fifth share in the partnership by investing cash of $50,000. What are the capital balances of the three partners immediately after Denman is admitted?

14. When a partner resigns from the partnership and receives assets greater than her capital balance, how is the excess shared by the other partners?

15. Why are the assets of a partnership often revalued when a partner is about to withdraw from the firm?

16. Distinguish between dissolution and liquidation of a partnership.

17. Name the three steps in liquidating a partnership.

18. Why does the cash of a partnership equal the sum of its partner capital balances after the business sells its noncash assets and pays its liabilities?

19. The partnership of Ralls and Sauls is in the process of liquidation. How do the partners share (a) gains and losses on the sale of noncash assets and (b) the final cash disbursement?

20. Fernandez, Garcia, and Estrada are partners, sharing profits and losses in the ratio of 3:2:1. In liquidation, Estrada's share of losses on the sale of assets exceeds his capital balance. What becomes of Estrada's capital deficiency if Estrada cannot make it up?

21. Compare and contrast the financial statements of a proprietorship and a partnership.

22. Summarize the situations in which partnership allocations are based on (a) the profit-and-loss ratio and (b) the partners' capital balances.

Exercises

Additional computer-related exercise: Exercise 28-3.

Additional computer-related exercise: Exercise 28-3.

No check figure

Exercise 13-1 *Organizing a business as a partnership* (L. O. 1)

Alan Bowden, a friend from college, approaches you about forming a partnership to export software. Since graduation, Alan has worked for the Export-Import Bank, developing important contacts among government officials and business leaders in Czechoslovakia and Hungary. Eager to upgrade their data-processing capabilities, Eastern Europeans are looking for ways to obtain American computers. Alan believes he is in a unique position to capitalize on this opportunity. With expertise in finance, you would have responsibility for accounting and finance in the partnership.

Required

Discuss the advantages and disadvantages of organizing the export business as a partnership rather than a proprietorship. Comment on how partnership income is taxed.

Caballero, Capital $33,500

Exercise 13-2 *Recording a partner's investment* (L. O. 2)

Celeste Caballero has operated an apartment-locater service as a proprietorship. She and Julia Wiethorn have decided to reorganize the business as a partnership. Celeste's investment in the partnership consists of cash, $3,700; accounts receivable, $10,600 less allowance for uncollectibles, $800; office furniture, $2,700 less accumulated depreciation, $1,100; a small building, $55,000 less accumulated depreciation, $27,500; accounts payable, $3,300; and a note payable to the bank, $10,000.

To determine Celeste's equity in the partnership, she and Julia hire an independent appraiser. This outside party provides the following market values of the assets and liabilities that Celeste is contributing to the business: cash, accounts receivable, office furniture, accounts payable, and note payable—the same as Celeste's book value; allowance for uncollectible accounts, $2,900; building, $35,000; and accrued expenses payable (including interest on the note payable), $1,200.

Required

Make the entry on the partnership books to record Celeste's investment.

d. Mitten net inc. $43,500

Exercise 13-3 *Computing partners' shares of net income and net loss* (L. O. 3)

Alice Mitten and Martha Gibney form a partnership, investing $30,000 and $60,000, respectively. Determine their shares of net income or net loss for each of the following situations:

a. Net loss is $31,000, and the partners have no written partnership agreement.

b. Net income is $102,000, and the partnership agreement states that the partners share profits and losses based on their capital contributions.

c. Net loss is $78,000, and the partnership agreement states that the partners share profits based on their capital contributions.

d. Net income is $125,000. The first $60,000 is shared based on the partner capital contributions. The next $45,000 is based on partner service, with

Mitten receiving 30 percent and Gibney receiving 70 percent. The remainder is shared equally.

Exercise 13-4 *Computing partners' capital balances* (L. O. 3)

Gibney's capital increased by $31,500

Alice Mitten withdrew cash of $62,000 for personal use, and Martha Gibney withdrew cash of $50,000 during the year. Using the data from situation d in Exercise 13-3, journalize the entries to close the (a) income summary account and (b) the partners' drawing accounts. Explanations are not required.

Indicate the amount of increase or decrease in each partner's capital balance. What was the overall effect on partnership capital?

Exercise 13-5 *Admitting a new partner* (L. O. 4)

c. Battistoni, Capital $107,500

Bob Lemley is admitted to a partnership. Prior to the admission of Lemley, the partnership books show Richard Battistoni's capital balance at $100,000 and Carol Terry's capital balance at $50,000. Compute the amount of each partner's equity on the books of the new partnership under each of the following plans:

a. Lemley pays $50,000 for Terry's equity. Lemley's payment is not an investment in the partnership but instead goes directly to Terry.
b. Lemley invests $50,000 to acquire a one-fourth interest in the partnership.
c. Lemley invests $70,000 to acquire a one-fourth interest in the partnership.

Exercise 13-6 *Recording the admission of a new partner* (L.O. 4)

No check figure

Make the partnership journal entry to record the admission of Lemley under plans a, b, and c in Exercise 13-5. Explanations are not required.

Exercise 13-7 *Withdrawal of a partner* (L. O. 5)

Brooks receives $36,667

After closing the books, Brooks & Linam's partnership balance sheet reports capital of $50,000 for Brooks and $70,000 for Linam. Brooks is withdrawing from the firm. The partners agree to write down partnership assets by $40,000. They have shared profits and losses in the ratio of one third to Brooks and two thirds to Linam. If the partnership agreement states that a withdrawing partner will receive assets equal to the book value of his owner's equity, how much will Brooks receive?

Linam will continue to operate the business as a proprietorship. What is Linam's beginning capital on the proprietorship books?

Exercise 13-8 *Withdrawal of a partner* (L. O. 5)

b. Debit Backus, Capital $52,000

Derek Backus is retiring from the partnership of Backus, Cantu, and Gill on May 31. After the books are closed on that date, the partner capital balances are Backus, $36,000; Cantu, $51,000; and Gill, $22,000. The partners agree to have the partnership assets revalued to current market values. The independent appraiser reports that the book value of the inventory should be decreased by $3,000, and the book value of the building should be increased by $35,000. The partners agree to these revaluations. The profit-and-loss ratio has been 5:3:2 for Backus, Cantu, and Gill, respectively. In retiring from the firm, Backus receives $30,000 cash and a $25,000 note from the partnership. Journalize (a) the asset revaluations and (b) Backus's withdrawal from the firm.

Exercise 13-9 *Liquidation of a partnership* (L. O. 6)

b. Dooney receives $20,000

Dooney, Casini, and Oleg are liquidating their partnership. Before selling the noncash assets and paying the liabilities, the capital balances are Dooney,

$23,000; Casini, $14,000; and Oleg, $11,000. The partnership agreement divides profits and losses equally.

a. After selling the noncash assets and paying the liabilities, the partnership has cash of $48,000. How much cash will each partner receive in final liquidation?
b. After selling the noncash assets and paying the liabilities, the partnership has cash of $39,000. How much cash will each partner receive in final liquidation?

Cash to Sims $22,400

Exercise 13-10   *Liquidation of a partnership* **(L. O. 6)**

Prior to liquidation, the accounting records of Sims, Trent, and Udall included the following balances and profit-and-loss-sharing percentages:

				Capital		
	Cash +	Noncash Assets =	Liabilities +	Sims (40%)	Trent (30%)	Udall (30%)
Balances before sale of assets	$8,000	$57,000	$19,000	$20,000	$15,000	$11,000

The partnership sold the noncash assets for $63,000, paid the liabilities, and disbursed the remaining cash to the partners. Complete the summary of transactions in the liquidation of the partnership. Use the format illustrated in the chapter.

Black, Capital $96,300
White, Capital $92,600

Exercise 13-11   *Preparing a partnership balance sheet* **(L.O 7)**

On October 31, 19X9, Black and White agree to combine their proprietorships as a partnership. Their balance sheets on October 31 are as follows:

	Black's Business		White's Business	
Assets	Book Value	Current Market Value	Book Value	Current Market Value
Cash.....................	$ 8,000	$ 8,000	$ 3,700	$ 3,700
Accounts receivable (net) .	8,000	6,300	22,000	20,200
Inventory	34,000	35,100	51,000	46,000
Plant assets (net).........	53,500	57,400	121,800	123,500
Total assets	$103,500	$106,800	$198,500	$193,400

Liabilities and Capital

Accounts payable	$ 9,100	$ 9,100	$ 23,600	$ 23,600
Accrued expenses payable	1,400	1,400	2,200	2,200
Notes payable	—	—	75,000	75,000
Black, capital	93,000	96,300		
White, capital............			97,700	92,600
Total liabilities and capital	$103,500	$106,800	$198,500	$193,400

Required

Prepare the partnership balance sheet at October 31, 19X9.

Problems

Problem 13-1A   *Writing a partnership agreement*   (L. O. 1)

No check figure

John Haggai and Jody Magliolo are discussing the formation of a partnership to manufacture trapper-keeper ring binders used by schoolchildren. John is especially artistic, and he is convinced that his designs will draw large sales volumes. Jody is a super salesperson and has already lined up several large stores to sell the merchandise.

Required

Write a partnership agreement to cover all elements essential for the business to operate smoothly. Make up names, amounts, profit-and-loss sharing percentages, and so on as needed.

Problem 13-2A   *Investments by partners*   (L. O. 2, 7)

2. Dukakis, Capital $49,550
   Pilot, Capital $49,550

On June 30 Dukakis and Pilot formed a partnership. The partners agreed to invest equal amounts of capital. Dukakis invested his proprietorship's assets and liabilities (credit balances in parentheses).

On June 30 Pilot invested cash in an amount equal to the current market value of Dukakis's partnership capital. The partners decided that Dukakis would earn two thirds of partnership profits because he would manage the business. Pilot agreed to accept one third of the profits. During the remainder of the year, the partnership earned $60,000. Dukakis's drawings were $35,200, and Pilot's drawings were $23,000.

	Dukakis's Book Value	Current Market Value
Accounts receivable	$ 16,300	$ 16,300
Allowance for doubtful accounts	(-0-)	(1,050)
Inventory	22,340	24,100
Prepaid expenses	1,700	1,700
Office equipment	45,900	27,600
Accumulated depreciation	(15,300)	-0-
Accounts payable	(19,100)	(19,100)

Required

1. Journalize the partners' initial investments.
2. Prepare the partnership balance sheet immediately after its formation on June 30.
3. Journalize the December 31 entries to close the Income Summary account and the partner drawing accounts.

Problem 13-3A   *Computing partners' shares of net income and net loss*   (L. O. 3, 7)

2. Net income:
   Conway $63,750
   Stroube $47,500
   Henke $50,750

L. Conway, S. Stroube, and E. Henke have formed a partnership. Conway invested $15,000, Stroube $18,000, and Henke $27,000. Conway will manage the store, Stroube will work in the store half time, and Henke will not work in the business.

Required

1. Compute the partners' shares of profits and losses under each of the following plans.

   a. Net loss is $63,900, and the articles of partnership do not specify how profits and losses are shared.

b. Net loss is $70,000, and the partnership agreement allocates 40 percent of profits to Conway, 25 percent to Stroube, and 35 percent to Henke. The agreement does not discuss the sharing of losses.

c. Net income is $92,000. The first $40,000 is allocated based on salaries, with Conway receiving $28,000 and Stroube receiving $12,000. The remainder is allocated based on partner capital contributions.

d. Net income for the year ended January 31, 19X8, is $162,000. The first $75,000 is allocated based on partner capital contributions, and the next $36,000 is based on service, with Conway receiving $28,000 and Stroube receiving $8,000. Any remainder is shared equally.

2. Revenues for the year ended January 31, 19X8, were $872,000, and expenses were $710,000. Under plan d, prepare the partnership income statement for the year.

4. Benson, Capital $90,000

Problem 13-4A *Recording changes in partnership capital* (L. O. 4, 5)

Leading Edge Optics is a partnership, and its owners are considering admitting Curt Benson as a new partner. On March 31 of the current year the capital accounts of the three existing partners and their shares of profits and losses are as follows:

	Capital	Profit-and-Loss Percent
Lee Gingiss	$ 50,000	15%
Diedre Hauk	125,000	30
Paul Kaiser	200,000	55

Required

Journalize the admission of Benson as a partner on March 31 for each of the following independent situations:

1. Hauk gives her partnership share to C. Benson, who is her son.
2. Benson pays Kaiser $145,000 cash to purchase half of Kaiser's interest in the partnership.
3. Benson invests $75,000 in the partnership, acquiring a one-sixth interest in the business.
4. Benson invests $75,000 in the partnership, acquiring a one-fifth interest in the business.
5. Benson invests $50,000 in the partnership, acquiring a 10 percent interest in the business.

4. Debit:
  Uzzel, Capital $49,000
  Speed, Capital $15,500
  Ross, Capital $15,500

Problem 13-5A *Recording changes in partnership capital* (L.O. 4, 5)

Advantage Investors is a partnership owned by three individuals. The partners share profits and losses in the ratio of 31 percent to Speed, 38 percent to Uzzel, and 31 percent to Ross. At December 31, 19X7, the firm has the following balance sheet.

Cash		$ 31,000	Total liabilities	$ 94,000
Accounts receivable .	$ 22,000			
Less Allowance for				
uncollectibles	4,000	18,000	Speed, capital	84,000
Building	$310,000		Uzzel, capital.....	49,000
Less Accumulated			Ross, capital......	62,000
depreciation	70,000	240,000	Total liabilities and	
Total assets		$289,000	capital	$289,000

Uzzel withdraws from the partnership on December 31, 19X7, to establish his own consulting practice.

Required

Record Uzzel's withdrawal from the partnership under the following plans:

1. Uzzel gives his interest in the business to Zagat, his niece.
2. In personal transactions, Uzzel sells his equity in the partnership to Grimes and Hirsh, who each pay Uzzel $50,000 for one-half of his interest. Speed and Ross agree to accept Grimes and Hirsh as partners.
3. The partnership pays Uzzel cash of $15,000 and gives him a note payable for the remainder of his book equity in settlement of his partnership interest.
4. Uzzel receives cash of $10,000 and a note for $70,000 from the partnership.
5. The partners agree that the building is worth only $280,000 and that its accumulated depreciation should remain at $70,000. After the revaluation, the partnership settles with Uzzel by giving him cash of $10,600 and a note payable for the remainder of his book equity.

Problem 13-6A *Liquidation of a partnership* **(L. O. 6)**

Cash to Renoir $2,000
Cash to Dixon $6,000

The partnership of Renoir, Dixon, and Palma has experienced operating losses for three consecutive years. The partners, who have shared profits and losses in the ratio of Renoir 10 percent, Dixon 30 percent, and Palma 60 percent, are considering the liquidation of the business. They ask you to analyze the effects of liquidation under various possibilities about the sale of the noncash assets. They present the following condensed partnership balance sheet at December 31, end of the current year:

Cash..................	$ 27,000	Liabilities	$131,000
Noncash assets	202,000	Renoir, capital	13,000
		Dixon, capital	39,000
		Palma, capital	46,000
Total assets............	$229,000	Total liabilities and capital	$229,000

Required

1. Prepare a summary of liquidation transactions (as illustrated in the chapter) for each of the following situations:
   a. The noncash assets are sold for $212,000.
   b. The noncash assets are sold for $182,000.
   c. The noncash assets are sold for $122,000, and the partner with a capital deficiency pays cash to the partnership to erase the deficiency.
   d. The noncash assets are sold for $112,000, and the partner with a capital deficiency is personally bankrupt.
2. Make the journal entries to record the liquidation transactions in Requirement 1d.

Problem 13-7A *Liquidation of a partnership* **(L.O. 6)**

Cash to Sen $6,375
Cash to Sundem $12,625

Clover Associates is a partnership owned by Sen, Sundem, and Dopuch, who share profits and losses in the ratio of 5:3:2. The adjusted trial balance of the partnership (in condensed form) at September 30, end of the current fiscal year, follows.

Clover Associates
Adjusted Trial Balance
September 30, 19XX

Cash	$ 15,000	
Noncash assets	177,000	
Liabilities		$138,000
Sen, capital		57,000
Sundem, capital		53,000
Dopuch, capital		14,000
Sen, drawing....................	45,000	
Sundem, drawing	37,000	
Dopuch, drawing...............	18,000	
Revenues		211,000
Expenses	181,000	
Totals	$473,000	$473,000

Required

1. Prepare the September 30 entries to close the revenue, expense, income summary, and drawing accounts.

2. Insert the opening capital balances in the partner capital accounts, post the closing entries to the capital accounts, and determine each partner's ending capital balance.

3. The partnership liquidates on September 30 by selling the noncash assets for $142,000. Using the ending balances of the partner capital accounts, prepare a summary of liquidation transactions (as illustrated in the chapter). Any partner with a capital deficiency is unable to contribute assets to erase the deficiency.

(Group B)

No check figure

Problem 13-1B   *Writing a partnership agreement*   **(L.O. 1)**

Cindy Marable and Sara Gish are discussing the formation of a partnership to import dresses from Guatemala. Cindy is especially artistic, so she will travel to Central America to buy merchandise. Sara is a super salesperson and has already lined up several large stores to sell the dresses.

Required

Write a partnership agreement to cover all elements essential for the business to operate smoothly. Make up names, amounts, profit-and-loss sharing percentages, and so on as needed.

2. Alton, Capital $68,560
   Bouchard, Capital $68,560

Problem 13-2B   *Investments by partners*   **(L.O. 2, 7)**

Alton and Bouchard formed a partnership on March 15. The partners agreed to invest equal amounts of capital. Bouchard invested his proprietorship's assets and liabilities (credit balances in parentheses):

	Bouchard's Book Value	Current Market Value
Accounts receivable...................	$ 12,000	$ 12,000
Allowance for doubtful accounts	(740)	(1,360)
Inventory	43,850	51,220
Prepaid expenses	2,400	2,400
Store equipment.....................	36,700	26,600
Accumulated depreciation	(9,200)	(-0-)
Accounts payable....................	(22,300)	(22,300)

On March 15 Alton invested cash in an amount equal to the current market value of Bouchard's partnership capital. The partners decided that Bouchard would earn 70 percent of partnership profits because he would manage the business. Alton agreed to accept 30 percent of profits. During the period ended December 31, the partnership earned $70,000. Alton's drawings were $32,000, and Bouchard's drawings were $36,000.

Required

1. Journalize the partners' initial investments.
2. Prepare the partnership balance sheet immediately after its formation on March 15.
3. Journalize the December 31 entries to close the Income Summary account and the partner drawing accounts.

Problem 13-3B   *Computing partners' shares of net income and net loss*   **(L.O. 3, 7)**

T. Daly, J. Heider, and N. Coons have formed a partnership. Daly invested $20,000, Heider $40,000, and Coons $60,000. Daly will manage the store, Heider will work in the store three-quarters of the time, and Coons will not work in the business.

2. Net income:
Daly $35,333
Heider $30,333
Coons $25,334

Required

1. Compute the partners' shares of profits and losses under each of the following plans.
   a. Net income is $36,000, and the articles of partnership do not specify how profits and losses are shared.
   b. Net loss is $47,000, and the partnership agreement allocates 45 percent of profits to Daly, 35 percent to Heider, and 20 percent to Coons. The agreement does not discuss the sharing of losses.
   c. Net income is $104,000. The first $50,000 is allocated based on salaries of $34,000 for Daly and $16,000 for Heider. The remainder is allocated based on partner capital contributions.
   d. Net income for the year ended September 30, 19X4, is $91,000. The first $30,000 is allocated based on partner capital contributions. The next $30,000 is based on service, with $20,000 going to Daly and $10,000 going to Heider. Any remainder is shared equally.
2. Revenues for the year ended September 30, 19X4, were $572,000, and expenses were $481,000. Under plan d, prepare the partnership income statement for the year.

Problem 13-4B   *Recording changes in partnership capital*   **(L.O. 4, 5)**

Angel Fire Properties is a New Mexico partnership, and its owners are considering admitting V. Posner as a new partner. On July 31 of the current year the capital accounts of the three existing partners and their shares of profits and losses are as follows:

4. Posner, Capital $37,500

	Capital	Profit-and-Loss Ratio
R. Blue	$44,000	⅙
M. Leath	70,000	⅓
P. Houston	86,000	½

Required

Journalize the admission of Posner as a partner on July 31 for each of the following independent situations:

1. Blue gives her partnership share to Posner, who is her nephew.
2. Posner pays Houston $50,000 cash to purchase one-half of Houston's interest.

3. Posner invests $50,000 in the partnership, acquiring a one-fifth interest in the business.
4. Posner invests $50,000 in the partnership, acquiring a 15 percent interest in the business.
5. Posner invests $25,000 in the partnership, acquiring a 15 percent interest in the business.

4. Debit:
Buckalew, Capital $34,000
Moore, Capital $3,429
Concepcion, Capital $2,571

Problem 13-5B *Recording changes in partnership capital* (L.O. 4, 5)

Nuestra Oil Exploration is a partnership owned by three individuals. The partners share profits and losses in the ratio of 30 percent to Buckalew, 40 percent to Moore, and 30 percent to Concepcion. At December 31, 19X6, the firm has the following balance sheet:

Cash		$ 25,000	Total liabilities	$103,000
Accounts receivable .	$ 16,000		
Less Allowance for uncollectibles ...	1,000	15,000	
Inventory		92,000	Buckalew, capital..	34,000
Equipment	130,000		Moore, capital	53,000
Less Accumulated depreciation	30,000	100,000	Concepcion, capital	42,000
			Total liabilities and
Total assets		$232,000	capital.........	$232,000

Buckalew withdraws from the partnership on this date.

Required

Record Buckalew's withdrawal from the partnership under the following plans:

1. Buckalew gives his interest in the business to Pavcek, his son-in-law.
2. In personal transactions, Buckalew sells his equity in the partnership to Lincoln and Saxe, who each pay Buckalew $15,000 for one-half of his interest. Moore and Concepcion agree to accept Lincoln and Saxe as partners.
3. The partnership pays Buckalew cash of $5,000 and gives him a note payable for the remainder of his book equity in settlement of his partnership interest.
4. Buckalew receives cash of $20,000 and a note for $20,000 from the partnership.
5. The partners agree that the equipment is worth $150,000 and that accumulated depreciation should remain at $30,000. After the revaluation, the partnership settles with Buckalew by giving him cash of $10,000 and inventory for the remainder of his book equity.

Cash to Canton $2,600
Cash to Mears $400

Problem 13-6B *Liquidation of a partnership* (L.O. 6)

The partnership of Canton, Mears, and Tsang has experienced operating losses for three consecutive years. The partners, who have shared profits and losses in the ratio of Canton 15 percent, Mears 60 percent, and Tsang 25 percent, are considering the liquidation of the business. They ask you to analyze the effects of liquidation under various possibilities about the sale of the noncash assets. They present the following condensed partnership balance sheet at December 31, end of the current year:

Cash..................	$ 7,000	Liabilities	$ 63,000
Noncash assets	163,000	Canton, capital	19,000
		Mears, capital	66,000
		Tsang, capital	22,000
		Total liabilities and
Total assets............	$170,000	capital	$170,000

Required

1. Prepare a summary of liquidation transactions (as illustrated in the chapter) for each of the following situations:
   a. The noncash assets are sold for $175,000.
   b. The noncash assets are sold for $141,000.
   c. The noncash assets are sold for $63,000, and the partner with a capital deficiency is personally bankrupt.
   d. The noncash assets are sold for $56,000, and the partner with a capital deficiency pays cash of $3,000 to the partnership to erase part of the deficiency.
2. Make the journal entries to record the liquidation transactions in Requirement *1d*.

Problem 13-7B *Liquidation of a partnership* (L.O. 6)

Cash to Fisk $6,857
Cash to Metz $9,143

Daniel, Fisk, and Metz is a partnership owned by B. Daniel, A. Fisk, and M. Metz, who share profits and losses in the ratio of 1:3:4. The adjusted trial balance of the partnership (in condensed form) at June 30, end of the current fiscal year, follows.

	Daniel, Fisk, and Metz Adjusted Trial Balance June 30, 19XX	
Cash	$ 21,000	
Noncash assets	126,000	
Liabilities		$107,000
Daniel, capital		22,000
Fisk, capital...........		41,000
Metz, capital..........		62,000
Daniel, drawing.......	24,000	
Fisk, drawing	35,000	
Metz, drawing	54,000	
Revenues.............		118,000
Expenses	90,000	
Totals	$350,000	$350,000

Required

1. Prepare the June 30 entries to close the revenue, expense, income summary, and drawing accounts.
2. Insert the opening capital balances in the partner capital accounts, post the closing entries to the capital accounts, and determine each partner's ending capital balance.
3. The partnership liquidates on June 30 by selling the noncash assets for $102,000. Using the ending balances of the partner capital accounts, prepare a summary of liquidation transactions (as illustrated in the chapter). Any partner with a capital deficiency is unable to contribute assets to erase the deficiency.

Extending Your Knowledge

Decision Problems

1. *Disagreements Among Partners* (L.O. 3)

No check figure

Larry Pepper invested $30,000 and Debra Frakes invested $10,000 in a public relations firm that has operated for 10 years. Neither partner has made an additional investment. They have shared profits and losses in the ratio of 3:1, which is the ratio of their investments in the business. Pepper manages the office, supervises the 16 employees, and does the accounting. Frakes, the moderator of a television talk show, is responsible for marketing. Her high profile generates important revenue for the business. During the year ended December 19X4 the partnership earned net income of $87,000, shared in the 3:1 ratio. On December 31, 19X4, Pepper's capital balance was $150,000, and Frakes's capital balance was $100,000.

Required

Respond to each of the following situations:

1. What explains the difference between the ratio of partner capital balances at December 31, 19X4, and the 3:1 ratio of partner investments and profit sharing?
2. Frakes believes the profit-and-loss-sharing ratio is unfair. She proposes a change, but Pepper insists on keeping the 3:1 ratio. What two factors may underlie Frakes's unhappiness?
3. During January 19X5 Pepper learned that revenues of $16,000 were omitted from the reported 19X4 income. He brings this to Frakes's attention, pointing out that his share of this added income is three fourths, or $12,000, and Frakes's share is one fourth, or $4,000. Frakes believes they should share this added income based on their capital balances—60 percent, or $9,600, to Pepper and 40 percent, or $6,400, to Frakes. Which partner is correct? Why?
4. Assume the 19X4 $16,000 omission was an account payable for an operating expense. How would the partners share this amount?

No check figure

2. Questions About Partnerships (L.O. 1, 5)

1. The text suggests that a written partnership agreement should be drawn up between the partners in a partnership. One benefit of an agreement is that it provides a mechanism for resolving disputes between the partners. List five areas of dispute that might be resolved by a partnership agreement.
2. The statement has been made that "If you must take on a partner, make sure the partner is richer than you are." Why is this statement valid?
3. Zalinski, Waller, and Gunz is a partnership of CPAs. Gunz is planning to move to Australia. What options are available to Gunz to enable her to convert her share of the partnership assets to cash?

Ethical Issue

Paula Fitz and Rosemary Campbell operate Noteworthy, a gift shop in The Grand Hotel on Mackinac Island, Michigan. The partners split profits and losses equally, and each takes an annual salary of $30,000. To even out the work load, Rosemary does the buying and Paula serves as the accountant. From time to time they use small amounts of store merchandise for personal use. In preparing for a large private party, Paula took engraved invitations, napkins, place mats, and other goods that cost $800. She recorded the transaction as follows:

Cost of Goods Sold	800	
Inventory		800

Required

1. How should Paula have recorded this transaction?
2. Discuss the ethical dimension of Paula's action.

Chapter 14

Corporations: Organization, Paid-In Capital, and the Balance Sheet

Data General Corporation
1990 Annual Report

What highflying computer stock has risen 300 percent since January 1? Apple Computer? Sun Microsystems? Or maybe Microsoft?

Wrong. It's Data General, the aging maker of minicomputers for corporate and industrial use. This stock was almost given up for dead by traders who watched its relentless slide from . . . 38 in 1987 to 4½ as this year began. But Data General *shares* have since quadrupled. Now analysts who practically ignored the *stock* are looking at it again and, in some cases, boosting their earnings forecasts.

Yesterday, the Westborough, Mass., computer maker continued its startling comeback, reporting its second consecutive profitable quarter on a narrow 1.8 percent revenue increase from a year earlier. The stock jumped 1½ to 18 on the New York *Stock* Exchange. . . . [emphasis added]

Source: William M. Bulkalay, "Data General's Stock Rises from Ashes," *The Wall Street Journal* (April 26, 1991), p. C1.

The period surrounding the date of this article's publication would be a good time for Data General to raise money by issuing new stock. Profits are up, the outlook for the company is bright, and Data General's stock price is higher than it has been in the recent past. Issuing stock, as we will see in this chapter, is an important way for a corporation to finance its operations.

LEARNING OBJECTIVES

After studying this chapter, you should be able to

1 Identify the characteristics of a corporation

2 Record the issuance of stock

3 Prepare the stockholders' equity section of a corporation balance sheet

4 Account for the incorporation of a going business

5 Allocate dividends to preferred and common stock

6 Compute two standard profitability measures

7 Distinguish among various stock "values"

OBJECTIVE 1

Identify the characteristics of a corporation

The corporation is the dominant form of business organization in the United States. Data General is a prime example, with operations around the world. Although proprietorships and partnerships are more numerous, corporations transact more business and are larger in terms of total assets, sales revenue, and number of employees. Most well-known companies, such as PepsiCo, CBS, General Motors, IBM, and Boeing, are corporations. Their full names include *Corporation* or *Incorporated* (abbreviated *Corp.* and *Inc.*) to indicate that they are corporations—for example, CBS, Inc. and General Motors Corporation. This chapter and the next three chapters discuss corporations.

Characteristics of a Corporation

Why is the corporation form of business so attractive? We now look at the features that distinguish corporations from proprietorships and partnerships.

Separate Legal Entity

A **corporation** is a business entity formed under state law. The state grants a **charter,** which is the document that gives the state's permission to form a corporation.

A corporation is a distinct entity from a legal perspective. We may consider the corporation as an artificial person that exists apart from its owners, who are called **stockholders** or **shareholders.** The corporation has many of the rights that a person has. For example, a corporation may buy, own, and sell property. Assets and liabilities in the business belong to the corporation. The corporation may enter into contracts, sue, and be sued.

The owners' equity of a corporation is divided into shares of **stock.** A person becomes a stockholder by purchasing the stock of the corporation. The corporate charter specifies how much stock the corporation can issue (sell) and lists the other details of its relationship with the state.

Continuous Life and Transferability of Ownership

Most corporations have continuous lives regardless of changes in the ownership of their stock. Stockholders may transfer stock as they wish. They may sell or trade the stock to another person, give it away, bequeath it in a will, or dispose of it in any other way they desire. The transfer of the stock does not affect the continuity of the corporation. Proprietorships and partnerships, on the other hand, terminate when their ownership changes.

No Mutual Agency

Mutual agency of the owners is *not* present in a corporation. The stockholder of a corporation cannot commit the corporation to a contract (unless he or she is also an officer in the business). For this reason, a stockholder need not exercise the care that partners must in selecting co-owners of the business.

Limited Liability of Stockholders

A stockholder has **limited liability** for corporation debts. He or she has no personal obligation for corporation liabilities. The most that a stockholder can lose on an investment in a corporation's stock is the cost of the investment. Recall that proprietors and partners are personally liable for the debts of their businesses.

The combination of limited liability and no mutual agency means that persons can invest limited amounts in a corporation without fear of losing all their personal wealth because of a business failure. This feature enables a corporation to raise more capital from a wider group of investors than proprietorships and partnerships.

Real-World Example: Because of limited stockholder liability, commercial lenders will seldom lend money to a small corporation unless a third party (usually a corporate officer) signs a personal guaranty to repay the loan in the event of default by the corporation.

Separation of Ownership and Management

Stockholders own the business, but a board of directors—elected by the stockholders—appoints corporate officers to manage the business. Thus stockholders may invest $1,000 or $1 million in the corporation without having to manage the business or disrupt their personal affairs.

However, this separation between owners—stockholders—and management may create problems. Corporate officers may decide to run the business for their own benefit and not to the stockholders' advantage. Stockholders may find it difficult to lodge an effective protest against management policy because of the distance between them and management.

Corporate Taxation

Corporations are separate taxable entities. They pay a variety of taxes not borne by proprietorships or partnerships. These taxes include an annual franchise tax levied by the state. The franchise tax is paid to keep the corporation charter in force and enables the corporation to continue in business. Corporations also pay federal and state income taxes. Corporate earnings are subject to **double taxation.** First, corporations pay their own income taxes on corporate income. Then, the stockholders pay personal income tax on the cash dividends that they receive from corporations. This is different from proprietorships and partnerships, which pay no business income tax. Instead, the tax falls solely on the owners.

Discussion Question: How does taxation of a corporation differ from taxation of a proprietorship or a partnership? ANSWER: A corporation pays tax each year on its taxable income. Dividends are paid from the after-tax income. Shareholders pay tax on their income from the dividends. Proprietorships and partnerships are not tax-paying entities; the owners pay the tax on all earned income regardless of how much they draw for personal use.

Point to Stress: Large corporations are required to have an audit and file certain reports with the SEC. These requirements add to a corporation's expenses without increasing its income.

Government Regulation

Strong government regulation is an important disadvantage to the corporation. Because stockholders have only limited liability for corporation debts, outsiders doing business with the corporation can look no further than the corporation itself for any claims that may arise against the business. To protect persons who loan money to a corporation or who invest in its stock, states monitor the affairs of corporations. This government regulation consists mainly of ensuring that corporations disclose the business information that investors and creditors need to make informed decisions. For many corporations, this government regulation is expensive.

Organization of a Corporation

Creation of a corporation begins when its organizers, called the **incorporators,** obtain a charter from the state. The **charter** includes the authorization for the corporation to issue a certain number of shares of stock, which are shares of ownership in the corporation. The incorporators pay fees, sign the charter, and file the required documents with the state. Then the corporation comes into existence. The incorporators agree to a set of **bylaws,** which act as the constitution for governing the corporation.

The ultimate control of the corporation rests with the stockholders, who receive one vote for each share of stock they own. The stockholders elect the members of the **board of directors**, which sets policy for the corporation and appoints the officers. The board elects a **chairperson,** who usually is the most powerful person in the corporation. The board also designates the **president**, who is the chief operating officer in charge of managing day-to-day operations. Most corporations also have vice-presidents in charge of sales, manufacturing, accounting and finance, and other key areas. Often the president and one or more vice-presidents are also elected to the board of directors. Exhibit 14-1 shows the authority structure in a corporation.

EXHIBIT 14-1 *Authority Structure in a Corporation*

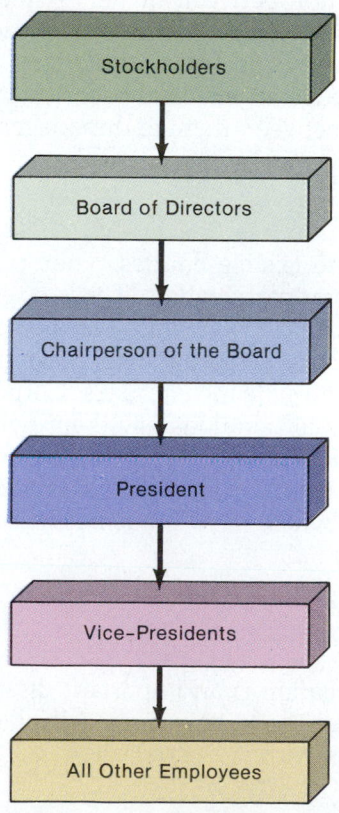

Most corporations have an annual meeting at which the stockholders elect directors and make other stockholder decisions. Stockholders unable to attend this annual meeting may vote on corporation matters by use of a **proxy**, which is a legal document that expresses the stockholder's preference and appoints another person to cast the vote.

The structure of proprietorships, partnerships, and corporations is similar in that all three types of business have owners, managers, and employees. In proprietorships and partnerships, policy decisions are usually made by the owners—the proprietor or the partners. In a corporation, however, the managers who set policy—the board of directors—may or may not be owners (stockholders).

A corporation keeps a subsidiary record of its stockholders. The business must notify the stockholders of the annual stockholder meeting and mail them dividend payments (which we discuss later in this chapter). Large companies use a registrar to maintain the stockholder list and a transfer agent to issue stock certificates. Banks provide these registration and transfer services. The transfer agent handles the change in stock ownership from one shareholder to another.

Capital Stock

A corporation issues stock certificates to its owners in exchange for their investments in the business. The basic unit of capital stock is called a *share*. A corporation may issue a stock certificate for any number of shares it wishes—one share, one hundred shares, or any other number. Exhibit 14-2 depicts an

EXHIBIT 14-2 *Stock Certificate*

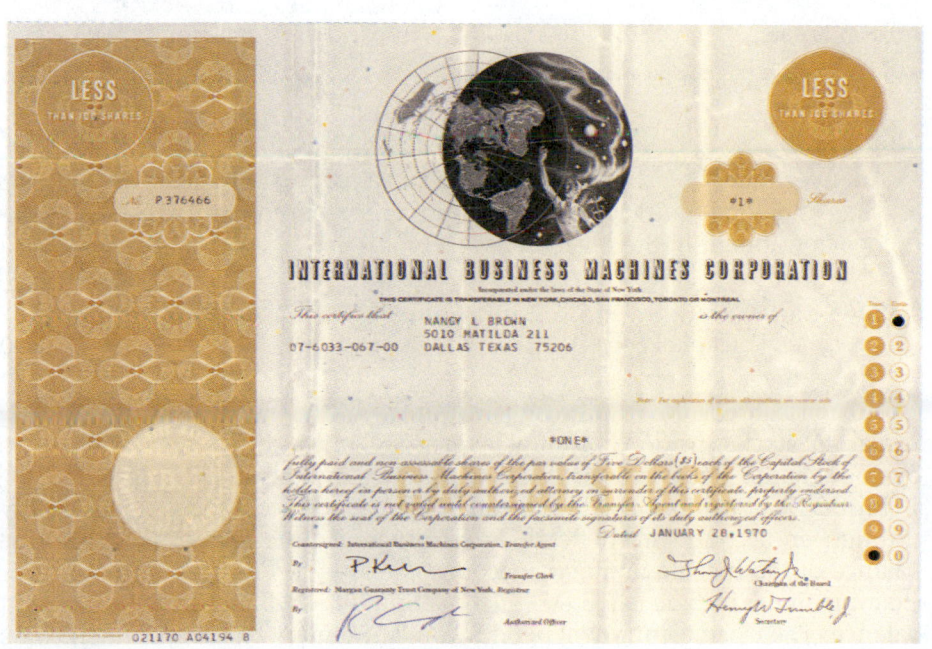

Teaching Tip: Emphasize the difference between the following terms:

1   Authorized stock—The number of shares the corporation is permitted to issue. This number is specified in the charter, but can be increased if necessary.

2   Issued stock—Stock that has been sold to a stockholder. A stock certificate has been granted. No more shares than the state has authorized may be issued.

3   Outstanding stock—Stock that is in the hands of a stockholder. Not all issued stock is outstanding. Corporations may buy their stock back (treasury stock). Treasury stock has been issued but is not outstanding. No more shares than have been issued may be outstanding.

Transparency T14-1

Teaching Tip: Ask students how a corporation aquires the capital to purchase assets. Students will say borrowed funds, issuance of stock, and corporate income. Point out that they have just expressed the accounting equation: **A = L + OE**

In a proprietorship, income and investments are both recorded in the Capital account. A corporation is required to separate invested capital, called paid-in capital, from earned capital, called retained earnings. Chapter 14 discusses paid-in capital and Chapter 15 discusses retained earnings.

actual stock certificate for one share of IBM stock. The certificate shows the company name, the stockholder name, the number of shares, and the par value of the stock (which we discuss later).

Stock in the hands of a stockholder is said to be **outstanding.** The total number of shares of stock outstanding at any time represents 100 percent ownership of the corporation. Because stock represents the corporation's capital, it is often called capital stock.

Stockholders' Equity

The balance sheet of a corporation reports assets and liabilities in the same way as a proprietorship or a partnership. However, owners' equity of a corporation—called **stockholders' equity**—is reported differently. State laws require corporations to report the sources of their capital. The two most basic sources of capital are investments by the stockholders, called **paid-in capital** or **contributed capital,** and capital earned through profitable operation of the business, called **retained earnings.** Exhibit 14-3 outlines a simplified corporation balance sheet to show how to report these categories of stockholders' equity.

EXHIBIT 14-3 *Simplified Corporation Balance Sheet*

Assets	$600,000	Liabilities	$240,000
		Stockholders' Equity	
		Paid-in capital:	
		Capital stock	**200,000**
		Retained earnings	**160,000**
		Total stockholders'	
		equity	**360,000**
		Total liabilities and	
Total assets	$600,000	stockholders' equity	$600,000

An investment of cash or any other asset in a corporation increases its assets and stockholders' equity. The corporation's entry for receipt of a $20,000 stockholder investment in the business is

Oct. 20	Cash	20,000	
	Capital Stock		20,000
	Investment by stockholders.		

Capital stock is paid-in capital. It is regarded as the permanent capital of the business because it is *not* subject to withdrawal by the stockholders.

Profitable operations produce income, which increases stockholders' equity through an account called Retained Earnings. At the end of the year, the balance of the Income Summary account is closed to Retained Earnings. For example, if net income is $95,000, Income Summary will have a $95,000 credit balance. The closing entry will debit Income Summary to transfer net income to Retained Earnings as follows:

Point to Stress: Recall that proprietorship and partnership balance sheets show a capital account that reflects the previous capital balance, plus net income or minus net loss, and minus withdrawals. A corporation's equity section is slightly different. Not one, but two types of capital accounts must be reported, in this order:

1 Contributed (paid-in) capital
2 Earned capital

Teaching Tip: Compare this entry to the one that records an investment of $20,000 into a proprietorship.

Cash 20,000
    J. Doe, Capital   20,000
Investment by owner.

In both entries, assets and owner's equity increase.

Point to Stress: The permanent capital is sometimes referred to as the "legal capital" of the business. In effect, it is an amount for the protection of creditors because it cannot be paid out to shareholders even upon liquidation until all creditors have been paid.

```
Dec. 31   Income Summary ........................   95,000
              Retained Earnings ...................            95,000
          To close Income Summary by transferring net
          income to Retained Earnings.
```

If operations produce a net *loss* rather than net income, the Income Summary account will have a debit balance. Income Summary must be credited to close it. With a $60,000 loss, the closing entry is:

```
Dec. 31   Retained Earnings.......................   60,000
              Income Summary ....................            60,000
          To close Income Summary by transferring net
          loss to Retained Earnings.
```

A large loss may cause a debit balance in the Retained Earnings account. This condition—called a Retained Earnings **deficit**, or accumulated deficit—is reported on the balance sheet as a negative amount in stockholders' equity. Assume a $50,000 deficit:

Stockholders' Equity

Paid-in capital:	
Capital stock	$200,000
Deficit	(50,000)
Total stockholders' equity	$150,000

If the corporation has been profitable and has sufficient cash, a distribution of cash may be made to the stockholders. Such distributions—called **dividends**—decrease both the assets and the retained earnings of the business. The balance of the Retained Earnings account at any time is the sum of earnings accumulated since incorporation, minus any losses, and minus all dividends distributed to stockholders. Retained Earnings is entirely separate from the paid-in capital invested in the business by the stockholders.

Some people think of Retained Earnings as a fund of cash. It is not, because Retained Earnings is an element of stockholders' equity, representing a claim against all assets resulting from cumulative earnings minus cumulative dividends since the corporation's beginning.

Stockholder Rights

The ownership of stock entitles stockholders to four basic rights, unless specific rights are withheld by agreement with the stockholders.

1. The right to participate in management by voting on matters that come before the stockholders. This is the stockholder's sole right to a voice in the management of the corporation. Each share of stock entitles the owner to one vote.
2. The right to receive a proportionate part of any dividend. Each share of stock in a particular class receives an equal dividend.
3. The right to receive a proportionate share (based on number of shares held) of any assets remaining after the corporation pays its liabilities in liquidation.
4. The right to maintain one's proportionate ownership in the corporation. Suppose you own 5 percent of a corporation's stock. If the corporation

Teaching Tip: How are these two entries different from closing entries for a proprietorship? ANSWER: The income or loss is closed into Retained Earnings rather than into Capital. Retained Earnings includes all previous earnings minus all losses and minus amounts declared as dividends. There may be a debit balance (deficit) in Retained Earnings.

Typical Student Misconception: Students often believe that Retained Earnings is an asset, like cash. Emphasize that Retained Earnings is part of stockholders' equity.

   Students often think that Retained Earnings has a debit balance. Reviewing the accounting equation should help them remember that equity accounts (including all paid-in-capital accounts and Retained Earnings) always have a credit as their normal balance.

Point to Stress: The right to receive a proportionate share of assets means that in the event of liquidation, creditors are paid first, preferred shareholders are paid next, and then, if anything remains, common shareholders get their proportionate share of what is left. Thus, common shareholders are said to have a residual ownership interest in the corporation.

Discussion Question: Why do some corporations withhold the preemptive right? ANSWER: 1) It is much more complicated to issue new stock if all of the current stockholders must be notified first; and 2) In large corporations, very few stockholders could afford enough stock to gain a voting influence, so the preemptive right is moot.

issues 100,000 new shares of stock, it must offer you the opportunity to buy 5 percent (5,000) of the new shares. This right, called the **preemptive right,** is usually withheld from the stockholders.

Classes of Stock

Corporations issue different types of stock to appeal to a wide variety of investors. The stock of a corporation may be either common or preferred and either par or no-par.

Common and Preferred Stock

Every corporation issues **common stock,** the most basic form of capital stock. Unless designated otherwise, the word *stock* is understood to mean "common stock." Common stockholders have the four basic rights of stock ownership, unless a right is specifically withheld. For example, some companies issue Class A common stock, which usually carries the right to vote, and Class B common stock, which may be nonvoting. (Classes of common stock may also be designated Series A, Series B, and so on.) The general ledger has a separate account for each class of common stock. In describing a corporation, we would say the common stockholders are the owners of the business.

Owners of **preferred stock** also have the four basic stockholder rights, unless a right is specifically denied. Often the right to vote is withheld from preferred stockholders. Preferred stock gives its owners certain advantages over common stockholders. These benefits include the priority to receive dividends before the common stockholders and the priority to receive assets before the common stockholders if the corporation liquidates. Because of the preferred stockholders' priorities, we see that common stock represents the residual ownership in the corporation's assets after subtracting the liabilities and the claims of preferred stockholders. Companies may issue different classes of preferred stock. (Class A and Class B or Series A and Series B, for example). Each class is recorded in a separate account.

Par Value and No-Par Stock

Stock may be par value stock or no-par stock. **Par value** is an arbitrary amount assigned to a share of stock. Most companies set the par value of their common stock quite low. J. C. Penney's common stock par value is 50¢ per share, Bethlehem Steel's common stock par value is $8 per share, and Ralston Purina's common stock par value is 41 $\frac{2}{3}$¢ per share. Par value of preferred stock is often higher; $100 per share is typical, but some preferred stocks have par value of $25 and $10. Par value is used to compute dividends on preferred stock, as we shall see. **No-par** stock does not have par value, but some no-par stock has a *stated value,* which makes it similar to par value stock. The stated value is also an arbitrary amount that accountants treat as though it were par value.

Issuing Stock

Large corporations such as PepsiCo, Xerox, and British Petroleum need huge quantities of money to operate. They cannot expect to finance all their operations through borrowing. They need capital that they raise by issuing stock.

Teaching Tip: Students are often confused about the nature of par value. Explain that many years ago stocks were issued at par. Stock was difficult to sell because, while company value changed, its stock prices were constrained to par value. To remedy this situation, stock prices were allowed to fluctuate with the market. However, the par value was required to be accounted for separately from other paid-in capital.

Today par value has little relationship to market value. Because the Securities Act of 1933 still requires par value to be accounted for separately from other paid-in capital, par value is recorded separately in the Common Stock account, and the excess over par is recorded in another account.

The charter that the incorporators receive from the state includes an **authorization** for the business to issue—that is, to sell—a certain number of shares of stock. Corporations may sell the stock directly to the stockholders or they may use the service of an *underwriter*, such as the brokerage firms Merrill Lynch and Dean Witter. An underwriter agrees to buy all the stock it cannot sell to its clients.

Point to Stress: Owners invest in a corporation by buying stock. Issuance of stock increases the corporation's assets and stockholders' equity.

The corporation need not issue all the stock that the state allows. Management may hold some stock back and issue it later if the need for additional capital arises. The stock that the corporation does issue to stockholders is called issued stock. Only by issuing stock—not by receiving authorization—does the corporation increase the asset and stockholders' equity amounts on its balance sheet.

The price that the stockholder pays to acquire stock from the corporation is called the *issue price*. Often the issue price far exceeds the stock's par value because the par value was intentionally set quite low. A combination of market factors, including the company's comparative earnings record, financial position, prospects for success, and general business conditions, determines issue price. Investors will not pay more than market value for the stock. The following sections show how to account for the issuance of stock.

Issuing Common Stock

Issuing Common Stock at Par.   Suppose Medina Corporation issues 500 shares of its $10 par common stock for cash equal to its par value. The stock issuance entry is

Jan. 8	Cash (500 × $10)	5,000	
	Common Stock		5,000
	To issue common stock at par.		

OBJECTIVE 2
Record the issuance of stock

The amount invested in the corporation, $5,000 in this case, is called paid-in capital or contributed capital. The credit to Common Stock records an increase in the paid-in capital of the corporation.

Typical Student Misconception: Students often think of paid-in capital on common stock as a gain, or as an income statement item. It is not. A corporation makes a profit by selling its goods or services, not by selling its own stock. An amount received in excess of par value is part of stockholder's equity but not part of income.

Issuing Common Stock at a Premium.   A corporation usually issues its common stock for a price above par value. The excess amount above par is called a **premium.** Assume Medina issues $10 par common stock for a price of $25. The $15 difference is a premium. This sale of stock increases the corporation's paid-in capital by $25, the total issue price of the stock. Both the par value of the stock and the premium are part of paid-in capital. A premium on the sale of stock is not gain, income, or profit to the corporation, because the entity is dealing with its own stockholders. This illustrates one of the fundamentals of accounting: a company cannot earn a profit, nor can it incur a loss, when it sells its stock to, or buys its stock from, its own stockholders.

Suppose Medina Corporation issues 4,000 shares of its $10 par common stock for $25 per share—a total of $100,000 (4,000 × $25). The premium per share is $15 ($25 − $10), and the entry to record the issuance of the stock is

Jan. 23	Cash (4,000 × $25).......................	100,000	
	Common Stock (4,000 × $10)		40,000
	Paid-in Capital in Excess of Par—		
	Common (4,000 × $15)		60,000
	To issue common stock at a premium.		

Class Exercise: Assume that stock was issued at $23 per share. This is the journal entry:

Cash...............276,000
  Common Stock 180,000
  Paid-in Capital in
    Excess of Par
    Common........ 96,000

Ask students

1 How many shares of stock were sold? *ANSWER:* $276,000 / $23 = 12,000 shares

2 What is the par value? *ANSWER:* $180,000 / 12,000 shares = $15

3 What is the excess over par value (the premium) per share? *ANSWER:* $23 − $15 = $8 per share

Account titles that could be used in place of Paid-in Capital in Excess of Par—Common are Additional Paid-in Capital—Common, and Premium on Common Stock. Since both par value and premium amounts increase the corporation's capital, they appear in the stockholders' equity section of the balance sheet.

At the end of the first year, Medina Corporation would report stockholders' equity on its balance sheet as follows, assuming the corporate charter authorizes 20,000 shares of common stock and retained earnings is $85,000:

Stockholders' Equity

Paid-in capital:	
Common stock, $10 par, 20,000 shares authorized, 4,500 shares issued	$ 45,000
Paid-in capital in excess of par	60,000
Total paid-in capital	105,000
Retained earnings	85,000
Total stockholders' equity	$190,000

We determine the dollar amount reported for common stock by multiplying the total number of shares *issued* (500 + 4,000) by the par value per share. The *authorization* reports the maximum number of shares the company may issue under its charter.

Issuing Common Stock at a Discount. Stock issued at a price below par is said to be issued at a **discount.** For example, the issuance of $5 par common stock for $3 creates a $2 discount per share. The entry to record 1,000 shares of $5 par common stock issued for $3 per share is

Feb. 18	Cash (1,000 × $3)	3,000	
	Discount on Common Stock (1,000 × $2)	2,000	
	Common Stock (1,000 × $5)		5,000
	To issue common stock at a discount.		

What is the paid-in capital in this case? It is $3,000, the amount invested by the stockholders. The discount is reported in the stockholders' equity section of the balance sheet immediately after the stock account (as just shown for reporting a premium). However, the discount account—because it has a debit balance—is subtracted from the credit-balance par value of the stock issued to figure the capital amount.

The issuance of stock at a discount is rare. In fact, it is illegal in most states. When stock is sold at a discount, the stockholder has a *contingent liability* for the discount amount. If the corporation later liquidates, its creditors can require the original stockholder to pay the discount amount. Many companies set the par value of their common stock very low to avoid this contingent liability. A company is not likely to issue its stock at a price below an already low par value.

Issuing No-Par Common Stock. The contingent liability on common stock issued at a discount may explain why some state laws allow companies to issue no-par stock. If the stock has no par value, there can be no discount and thus no contingent liability. A recent survey of 600 companies revealed that they had 108 issues of no-par stock.

When no-par stock is issued, the asset received is debited and the stock account is credited. Glenwood Corporation issues 300 shares of no-par common stock for $20 per share. The stock issuance entry is

Aug. 14	Cash (300 × $20)	6,000	
	Common Stock		6,000
	To issue no-par common stock.		

Regardless of the stock's price, Cash is debited and Common Stock is credited for the amount of cash received. There is no Paid-in Capital in Excess of Par for true no-par stock.

Assume that the charter authorizes Glenwood to issue 5,000 shares of no-par stock and the company has $3,000 in retained earnings. The corporation would report stockholders' equity as follows:

Stockholders' Equity

Paid-in capital:	
Common stock, no-par, 5,000 shares	
authorized, 300 shares issued	$6,000
Retained earnings....................	3,000
Total stockholders' equity...........	$9,000

Issuing No-Par Common Stock with a Stated Value. Accounting for no-par stock with a stated value is identical to accounting for par value stock. The premium account for no-par common is entitled Paid-in Capital in Excess of Stated Value—Common.

Issuing Common Stock for Assets Other Than Cash. When a corporation issues stock in exchange for assets other than cash, it debits the assets received for their current market value and credits the capital accounts accordingly. The assets' prior book value does not matter because the stockholder will demand stock equal to the market value of the asset given. Assume Kahn Corporation issues 15,000 shares of its $1 par common stock for equipment worth $4,000 and a building worth $120,000. The entry is

Nov. 12	Equipment	4,000	
	Building	120,000	
	Common Stock (15,000 × $1)		15,000
	Paid-in Capital in Excess of Par—		
	Common ($124,000 − $15,000)		109,000
	To issue common stock in exchange for		
	equipment and a building.		

Paid-in capital increases by the amount of the assets' current market value, $124,000 in this case.

Issuing Common Stock through Subscriptions. Established companies usually issue stock and receive the full price in a single transaction. New corporations, to gauge their ability to raise capital, often take subscriptions for their stock. A **stock subscription** is a contract that obligates an investor to purchase the corporation's stock at a later date. Because a contract exists between the two parties, the corporation acquires an asset, Subscription Receivable, when it receives the subscription. The investor gains an equity in the corporation by promising to pay the subscription amount. Depending on the subscription agreement, the subscriber may pay the subscription in a lump sum or in installments.

ANSWER:
Cash
(50,000 × $15).... 750,000
  Common Stock
  (50,000 × $10).. 500,000
  Paid-in Capital in
  Excess of Par—
  Common
  (50,000 × $5) ... 250,000

3 A company issues 160,000 shares of $1 par value common stock in exchange for land valued at $55,000, a small office building valued at $125,000, and a computer valued at $5,000.
ANSWER:
Equipment 5,000
Building 125,000
Land 55,000
  Common Stock . 160,000
  Paid-in Capital in
  Excess of
  Par-Common ... 25,000

4 A company issues 20,000 shares of no-par common stock with a $2 stated value for $3.50 per share.
ANSWER:
Cash (20,000 ×
$3.50) 70,000
  Common Stock
  (20,000 × $2) ... 40,000
  Paid-in Capital in
  Excess of Stated
  Value—Common
  (20,000 × $1.50) 30,000

Teaching Tip: Compare issuing stock on a subscription basis to buying clothes on layaway. The clothes are earmarked for you, but you don't have the rights and privileges of an owner—to possess and wear the clothes—until you have made full payment.

Buying stock on a subscription is essentially the

Assume Medina Corporation receives a subscription on May 31 for 1,000 shares of $10 par common stock. The subscription price is $22 per share. The subscriber makes a down payment of $6,000 and agrees to pay the $16,000 balance in two monthly installments of $8,000 each. Medina Corporation will issue the stock when the subscriber pays in full. The entry to record receipt of the subscription is

May 31	Cash	6,000	
	Subscription Receivable—Common ($22,000 − $6,000)	16,000	
	Common Stock Subscribed (1,000 × $10)		10,000
	Paid-in Capital in Excess of Par— Common (1,000 × $12)		12,000

To receive common stock subscription at $22 per share.

Subscription Receivable—Common is a current asset if collection is expected within one year. Otherwise it is long-term and is reported in the Other Assets category on the balance sheet. Common Stock Subscribed is an element of stockholders' equity, reported immediately beneath Common Stock (and above Paid-in Capital in Excess of Par—Common) on the balance sheet. The "Subscribed" label will be dropped when the subscription is paid off and the stock is issued. Paid-in Capital in Excess of Par—Common is the same premium account that is credited when stock is sold for cash at a price in excess of par. The entries to record receipt of the two installments and issuance of the stock are

June 30	Cash ($16,000 × ½)	8,000	
	Subscription Receivable—Common		8,000
	To collect first installment on common stock subscription.		
July 31	Cash ($16,000 × ½)	8,000	
	Subscription Receivable—Common		8,000
	To collect second installment on common stock subscription.		
31	Common Stock Subscribed.................	10,000	
	Common Stock		10,000
	To issue common stock under subscription agreement.		

The last entry is needed to transfer the par value of the stock from the Subscribed account to Common Stock.

Because the subscription is a legally binding contract, subscribers must pay their subscriptions in full. If they fail to do so, state laws govern the settlement between the corporation and the defaulting subscriber.

Issuing Preferred Stock

Not all corporations issue preferred stock. A recent survey of 600 companies indicated that only 213 had preferred stock outstanding. Accounting for preferred stock follows the pattern illustrated for common stock. Assume the Medina Corporation charter authorizes issuance of 5,000 shares of 5 percent, $100 par preferred stock. On July 31 the company issues 400 shares at a price of

$110. (Preferred stock usually sells at its par value or at a premium.) The issuance entry is

July 31	Cash (400 × $110)	44,000	
	Preferred Stock (400 × $100)		40,000
	Paid-in Capital in Excess of Par—Preferred		
	(400 × $10)		4,000
	To issue preferred stock at a premium.		

Observe that the Paid-in Capital in Excess of Par account title includes the word Preferred. A corporation lists separate accounts for Paid-in Capital in Excess of Par on Preferred Stock and on Common Stock to differentiate the two classes of equity.

Accounting for *no-par preferred stock* follows the pattern illustrated for no-par common stock.

Let's review the first half of this chapter by showing the stockholders' equity section of Medina Corporation's balance sheet. (Assume that all figures, which are arbitrary, are correct.) Note the two sections of stockholders' equity: paid-in capital and retained earnings. Also observe the order of the equity accounts: preferred stock at par value, paid-in capital in excess of par on preferred stock, common stock at par value, common stock subscribed, and paid-in capital in excess of par on common stock. If Medina had a Preferred Stock Subscribed account, it would appear after Preferred Stock and before Paid-in Capital in Excess of Par—Preferred (corresponding to the order illustrated for the common stock accounts).

Stockholders' Equity

Paid-in capital:	
Preferred stock, 5%, $100 par, 5,000 shares authorized,	
400 shares issued	$ 40,000
Paid-in capital in excess of par—preferred	4,000
Common stock, $10 par, 20,000 shares authorized,	
4,500 shares issued	45,000
Common stock subscribed, 1,000 shares	10,000
Paid-in capital in excess of par—common	72,000
Total paid-in capital	171,000
Retained earnings	85,000
Total stockholders' equity	$256,000

How does it differ from the descriptions of common stock we have studied? ANSWER: The description contains a dividend rate (5 percent). Preferred stock always has a stated rate or amount of dividend. Common stock never has a stated rate or amount of dividend.

Class Exercise: From the following list, calculate total paid-in capital and total stockholders' equity. Select only equity items for your calculation!

Common Stock	$12,500
Preferred Stock	6,000
Common Stock	
Subscribed	500
Common Stock	
Subscriptions	
Receivable	780
Paid-in Capital in	
Excess of Stated	
Value—Common ..	3,255
Paid-in Capital—	
Preferred..........	836
Retained Earnings ...	18,934

ANSWER: Total paid-in capital = $23,091 ($12,500 + 6,000 + 500 + 3,255 + 836)

Total stockholder's equity = $42,025 ($23,091 + $18,934)

OBJECTIVE 3

Prepare the stockholders' equity section of a corporation balance sheet

Summary Problems for Your Review

1. Test your understanding of the first half of this chapter by answering whether each of the following statements is true or false.

   _____ a. A stockholder may bind the corporation to a contract.

   _____ b. The policy-making body in a corporation is called the board of directors.

   _____ c. The owner of 100 shares of preferred stock has greater voting rights than the owner of 100 shares of common stock.

_____ d. Par value stock is worth more than no-par stock.

_____ e. Issuance of 1,000 shares of $5 par value stock at $12 increases contributed capital by $12,000.

_____ f. The issuance of stock at a discount occurs less frequently than issuance of stock at a premium.

_____ g. The issuance of no-par stock with a stated value is fundamentally different from issuing par value stock.

_____ h. A corporation issues its preferred stock in exchange for land and a building with a combined market value of $200,000. This transaction increases the corporation's owner equity by $200,000 regardless of the assets' prior book value.

_____ i. Receipt of a subscription contract does not increase the stockholders' equity of the corporation unless the subscriber makes a down payment.

_____ j. Common Stock Subscribed is a part of stockholders' equity.

2. Adolph Coors Company is a leading brewery. The company has two classes of common stock. Note that only the Class A common stockholders are entitled to vote. The company's balance sheet included the following presentation:

Shareholders' Equity

Capital stock	
Class A common stock, voting, $1 par value, authorized and issued 1,260,000 shares	$ 1,260,000
Class B common stock, non-voting, no-par value, authorized and issued 46,200,000 shares	11,000,000
	12,260,000
Additional paid-in capital.............................	2,011,000
Retained earnings	872,403,000
	$886,674,000

Required

a. Record the issuance of the Class A common stock. Assume the additional paid-in capital amount relates to the Class A common stock. Use the Coors account titles.

b. Record the issuance of the Class B common stock. Use the Coors account titles.

c. Rearrange the Coors stockholders' equity section to correspond to the following format:

Shareholders' Equity

Paid-in Capital:	
Class A common stock	$
Paid-in capital in excess of par—Class A common stock	
Class B common stock	
Total paid-in capital	
Retained earnings................................	
Total shareholders' equity	$

d. What is the total paid-in capital of the company?

e. How did Coors withhold the voting privilege from their Class B common stockholders?

SOLUTIONS TO SUMMARY PROBLEMS

1. Answers to true-false statements:

a. False   b. True   c. False   d. False   e. True

f. True   g. False   h. True   i. False   j. True

2. a.

Cash	3,271,000	
Class A Common Stock		1,260,000
Additional Paid-in Capital		2,011,000

To record issuance of Class A common stock at a premium.

b.

Cash	11,000,000	
Class B Common Stock		11,000,000

To record issuance of Class B common stock.

c. Shareholders' Equity

Paid-in Capital:

Class A common stock, voting, $1 par value, authorized and issued 1,260,000 shares	$ 1,260,000
Paid-in capital in excess of par—Class A common stock	2,011,000
Class B common stock, non-voting, no par value, authorized and issued 46,200,000 shares	11,000,000
Total paid-in capital	14,271,000
Retained earnings	872,403,000
Total shareholders' equity	$886,674,000

d. Total paid-in capital is $14,271,000, as shown in the answer to c.

e. The voting privilege was withheld from stockholders by specific agreement with them.

Donated Capital

Corporations occasionally receive gifts, or donations. For example, city council members may offer a company free land to encourage it to locate in their city. Cities in the southern United States have lured some companies away from the North using this offer. The free land is called a donation. Also, a stockholder may make a donation to the corporation in the form of cash, land, or other assets or stock that the corporation can resell.

A donation is a gift that increases the assets of the corporation. However, the donor (giver) receives no ownership interest in the company in return. A transaction to receive a donation does not increase the corporation's revenue, and thus it does not affect income. Instead, the donation creates a special category of stockholders' equity called **donated capital.** The corporation records a donation by debiting the asset received at its current market value, and by crediting Donated Capital, a stockholders' equity account.

Point to Stress: Occasionally, a shareholder may give some or all of his shares of stock back to the corporation (similar to Treasury Stock, which we will discuss in Chapter 15). When the stock is received, there is no journal entry made, but rather a memorandum entry noting that the shares were received. When the corporation later sells the shares, then the entry is made. Assume John Smith gives 400 shares of $20 par common stock back to Smith Manufacturing Company. A memo entry is made that records receipt of 400 shares of common stock. The stock is subsequently sold for $25 per share. Journal entry for the sale:

Cash 10,000
    Donated Capital 10,000

Suppose Burlington Industries receives 100 acres of land as a donation from the city of Raleigh, North Carolina. The current market value of the land is $150,000. Burlington records receipt of the donation as follows:

Apr. 18   Land.................................. 150,000
             Donated Capital.....................   150,000
        To receive land as a donation from the city.

Donated capital is reported on the balance sheet after the stock accounts in the paid-in capital section of stockholders' equity.

Incorporation of a Going Business

OBJECTIVE 4
Account for the incorporation of a going business

You may dream of having your own business someday, or you may currently be a business proprietor or partner. Businesses that begin as a proprietorship or a partnership often incorporate at a later date. By incorporating a going business, the proprietor or partners avoid the unlimited liability for business debts. And as we discussed earlier, incorporating also makes it easier to raise capital.

To account for the incorporation of a going business, we close the owner equity accounts of the prior entity and set up the stockholder equity accounts of the corporation. Suppose Santa Fe Travel Associates is a partnership owned by Joe Brown and Monica Lee. The partnership balance sheet, after all adjustments and closing entries, reports Joe Brown, Capital, of $50,000, and Monica Lee, Capital, of $70,000. They incorporate the travel agency as Santa Fe Travel Company, Inc., with an authorization to issue 200,000 shares of $1 par common stock. Joe and Monica agree to receive common stock equal in par value to their partnership owner equity balances. The entry to record the incorporation of the business is

Feb. 1   Joe Brown, Capital 50,000
       Monica Lee, Capital 70,000
           Common Stock   120,000
       To incorporate the business, close the capital accounts of the partnership, and issue common stock to the incorporators.

Organization Cost

Typical Student Misconception: Students often assume that organization costs are an expense. Organization costs benefit the entire life of the corporation and are therefore considered an asset—not an expense.

The costs of organizing a corporation include legal fees, taxes and fees paid to the state, and charges by promoters for selling the stock. These costs are grouped in an account titled Organization Cost, which is an asset because these costs contribute to a business's start-up. Suppose Mary Kay Cosmetics, Inc., pays legal fees of $15,000 and the state of Texas incorporation fee of $500 to organize the corporation. In addition, a promoter charges a fee of $24,000 for selling the stock and receives the corporation's no-par stock as payment. Mary Kay's journal entries to record these organization costs are

Mar. 31   Organization Cost ($15,000 + $500) 15,500
          Cash   15,500
       Legal fees and state incorporation fee to organize the corporation.

```
Apr.  3   Organization Cost.......................   24,000
              Common Stock ......................              24,000
          Promoter fee for selling stock in organization.
```

Organization Cost is an *intangible asset,* reported on the balance sheet along with patents, trademarks, goodwill, and any other intangibles. We know that an intangible asset should be amortized over its useful life, and organization costs will benefit the corporation for as long as the corporation operates. But how long will that be? We cannot know in advance, but we still must expense these costs over some period of time. The Internal Revenue Service tax laws allow corporations to use a minimum 5-year useful life for amortization. GAAP allows a maximum 40-year useful life. Companies therefore amortize organization costs over a period between 5 and 40 years. Assume a 10-year life, and the preceding organization cost of $39,500 ($15,500 + $24,000) would be amortized by a debit to Amortization Expense and a credit to Organization Cost for $3,950 ($39,500/10) each year.

Dividend Dates

A corporation must declare a dividend before paying it. The board of directors alone has the authority to declare a dividend. The corporation has no obligation to pay a dividend until the board declares one, but once declared, the dividend becomes a legal liability of the corporation. Three relevant dates for dividends are

1. **Declaration date.** On the declaration date, the board of directors announces the intention to pay the dividend. The declaration creates a liability for the corporation. Declaration is recorded by debiting Retained Earnings and crediting Dividends Payable.
2. **Date of record.** The people who own the stock on the date of record receive the dividend. The corporation announces the record date, which follows the declaration date by a few weeks, as part of the declaration. The corporation makes no journal entry on the date of record because no transaction occurs. Nevertheless, much work takes place behind the scenes to properly identify the stockholders of record on this date because the stock is being traded continuously.
3. **Payment date.** Payment of the dividend usually follows the record date by two to four weeks. Payment is recorded by debiting Dividends Payable and crediting Cash.

Point to Stress: A stock will sell "ex-dividend" (without the dividend) three business days before the date of record. This three-day period gives the registrar time to record all previous stock transactions.

Dividends on Preferred and Common Stock

Declaration of a cash dividend is recorded by debiting Retained Earnings and crediting Dividends Payable as follows:

```
June 19   Retained Earnings ..........................   XXX
              Dividends Payable .....................            XXX
          To declare a cash dividend.
```

Typical Student Misconception: Students tend to equate dividends with expenses of a corporation. Dividends are a distribution of earnings of the corporation, not an expense. They never appear as an expense on the Income Statement.
Transparency T14-2

Payment of the dividend, which usually follows declaration by a few weeks, is recorded by debiting Dividends Payable and crediting Cash:

July 2	Dividends Payable	XXX	
	Cash		XXX
	To pay a cash dividend.		

Dividends Payable is a current liability. When a company has issued both preferred and common stock, the preferred stockholders receive their dividends first. The common stockholders receive dividends only if the total declared dividend is large enough to pay the preferred shareholders first.

Pine Industries, Inc., in addition to its common stock, has 9,000 shares of preferred stock outstanding. Preferred dividends are paid at the annual rate of $1.75 per share. Assume Pine declares an annual dividend of $150,000. The allocation to preferred and common stockholders is

	Total Dividend of $150,000
Preferred dividend (9,000 shares × $1.75 per share)	$ 15,750
Common dividend (remainder: $150,000 − $15,750)	134,250
Total dividend	$150,000

If Pine declares only a $20,000 dividend, preferred stockholders receive $15,750, and the common stockholders receive $4,250 ($20,000 − $15,750).

This example illustrates an important relationship between preferred stock and common stock. To an investor, the preferred stock is safer because it receives dividends first. For example, if Pine Industries earns only enough net income to pay the preferred stockholders' dividends, the owners of common stock receive no dividends at all. However, the earnings potential from an investment in common stock is much greater than from an investment in preferred stock. Preferred dividends are usually limited to the specified amount, but there is no upper limit on the amount of common dividends.

We noted that preferred stockholders enjoy the advantage of priority over common stockholders in receiving dividends. The dividend preference is stated as a percentage rate or a dollar amount. For example, preferred stock may be "6 percent preferred," which means that owners of the preferred stock receive an annual dividend of 6 percent of the par value of the stock. If par value is $100 per share, preferred stockholders receive an annual cash dividend of $6 per share (6 percent of $100). The preferred stock may be "$3 preferred," which means that stockholders receive an annual dividend of $3 per share regardless of the preferred stock's par value. The dividend rate on no-par preferred stock is stated in a dollar amount per share.

Cumulative and Noncumulative Preferred Stock

The allocation of dividends may be complex if the preferred stock is cumulative. Corporations sometimes fail to pay a dividend to their preferred stockholders. This occurrence is called passing the dividend, and the passed dividends are said to be in arrears. The owners of cumulative preferred stock must receive all dividends in arrears before the corporation pays dividends to the common stockholders.

The preferred stock of Pine Industries is cumulative. Suppose the company passed the 19X4 preferred dividend of $15,750. Before paying dividends to its common stockholders in 19X5, the company must first pay preferred dividends of $15,750 for both 19X4 and 19X5, a total of $31,500. *Preferred stock is cumulative in the eyes of the law unless it is specifically labeled as noncumulative.*

Assume that Pine Industries passes its 19X4 preferred dividend. In 19X5 the company declares a $50,000 dividend. The entry to record the declaration is

Sep. 6	Retained Earnings 50,000		
	Dividends Payable, Preferred ($15,750 × 2).		31,500
	Dividends Payable, Common		
	($50,000 − $31,500)		18,500
	To declare a cash dividend.		

If the preferred stock is **noncumulative**, the corporation is not obligated to pay dividends in arrears. Suppose that the Pine Industries preferred stock was noncumulative, and the company passed the 19X4 preferred dividend of $15,750. The preferred stockholders would lose the 19X4 dividend forever. Of course, the common stockholders would not receive a 19X4 dividend either. Before paying any common dividends in 19X5, the company would have to pay the 19X5 preferred dividend of $15,750.

Having dividends in arrears on cumulative preferred stock is *not* a liability to the corporation. (A liability for dividends arises only after the board of directors declares the dividend.) Nevertheless, a corporation must report cumulative preferred dividends in arrears. This information alerts common stockholders as to how much in cumulative preferred dividends must be paid before any dividends will be paid on the common stock. This gives the common stockholders an idea about the likelihood of receiving dividends and satisfies the disclosure principle.

Dividends in arrears are often disclosed in notes, as follows (all dates and amounts assumed). Observe the two references to Note 3 in this section of the balance sheet. The "6 percent" after "Preferred stock" is the dividend rate.

Preferred stock, 6 percent, par $50, 2,000 shares issued (Note 3).	$100,000
Retained earnings (Note 3).................................	414,000

Note 3—Cumulative preferred dividends in arrears. At December 31, 19X2, dividends on the company's 6 percent preferred stock were in arrears for 19X1 and 19X2, in the amount of $12,000 (6% × $100,000 × 2 years).

Participating and Nonparticipating Preferred Stock

The owners of **participating preferred stock** may receive—that is, *participate in*—dividends beyond the stated amount or stated percentage. Assume that the corporation declares a dividend. First, the preferred stockholders receive their dividends. If the corporation has declared a large enough dividend, then the common stockholders receive their dividends. If an additional dividend amount remains to be distributed, common stockholders and participating preferred stockholders share it. For example, the owners of a $4 preferred stock must receive the specified annual dividend of $4 per share before the common stockholders receive any dividends. Then a $4 dividend is paid on each common share. The participation feature takes effect only after the preferred and common stockholders have received the specified $4 rate. Payment of an extra *common* dividend of, say, $1.50 is accompanied by a $1.50 dividend on each preferred share.

Participating preferred stock is rare. In fact, preferred stock is nonparticipating unless it is specifically described as participating on the stock certificate and in the financial statements. Therefore, if the preferred stock in our example is nonparticipating (the usual case), the largest annual dividend that a preferred stockholder will receive is $4.

Convertible Preferred Stock

Point to Stress: Convertible preferred stock may be exchanged for common stock at the shareholder's option.

Class Exercise: Prepare the journal entry to record the conversion of 100 shares of $100 par value, 9% convertible preferred stock, which was originally issued at par. The preferred stock has a conversion rate of 4 shares of $10 par value common stock for each share of preferred.

ANSWER:
Preferred Stock (100 × $100) 10,000

    Common Stock
    (400 × $10) 4,000

    Paid-in Capital in
    Excess of Par—
    Common 6,000

Convertible preferred stock may be exchanged by the preferred stockholders, if they choose, for another class of stock in the corporation. For example, the Pine Industries preferred stock may be converted into the company's common stock. A note to Pine's balance sheet describes the conversion terms as follows:

> The . . . preferred stock is convertible at the rate of 6.51 shares of common stock for each share of preferred stock outstanding.

If you owned 100 shares of Pine's convertible preferred stock, you could convert it into 651 (100 × 6.51) shares of Pine common stock. Under what condition would you exercise the conversion privilege? You would do so if the market value of the common stock that you could receive from conversion exceeded the market value of the preferred stock that you presently held. This way, you as an investor could increase your personal wealth.

Pine Industries preferred stock has par value of $100 per share, and the par value of the common stock is $1. The company would record conversion of 100 shares of preferred stock, issued previously at par, into 651 shares of common stock as follows:

Mar. 7	Preferred Stock (100 × $100)	10,000	
	Common Stock (651 × $1)		651
	Paid-in Capital in Excess of Par—		
	Common		9,349
	Conversion of preferred stock into common.		

If the preferred stock was issued at a premium, Paid-in Capital in Excess of Par—Preferred must also be debited to remove its balance from the books.

Preferred stock, we see, offers alternative features not available to common stock. Preferred stock is cumulative or noncumulative, participating or nonparticipating, and convertible or not convertible.

Rate of Return on Total Assets and Rate of Return on Stockholders' Equity

Investors and creditors are constantly evaluating the ability of managers to earn profits. Investors search for companies whose stocks are likely to increase in value. Creditors are interested in profitable companies that can pay their debts. Investment and credit decisions often include a comparison of companies. But a comparison of IBM's net income to the net income of a new company in the computer industry simply is not meaningful. IBM's profits may run into the billions of dollars, which far exceed a new company's net income. Does that automatically make IBM a better investment? Not necessarily. To make relevant comparisons between companies different in size, scope of operations, or any other measure, investors, creditors, and managers use some standard profitability measures, including rate of return on total assets and rate of return on stockholders' equity.

The **rate of return on total assets,** or simply **return on assets,** measures a company's success in using its assets to earn income for the persons who are financing the business. Creditors have loaned money to the corporation and earn interest. Stockholders have invested in the corporation's stock and expect the company to earn net income. The sum of interest expense and net income is the return to the two groups that have financed the corporation's activities, and this is the numerator of the return on assets ratio. The denominator is average total assets. Return on assets is computed as follows, using actual data from the 1990 annual report of Birmingham Steel Corporation (amounts in thousands of dollars):

Point to Stress: Investors and managers can compute ratios any way that is meaningful to their decisions. For example, it is also common to compute return on assets as Income from operations divided by average total assets—where interest is treated as a nonoperating expense.

$$\begin{array}{l}\text{Rate of} \\ \text{return} \\ \text{on total} \\ \text{assets}\end{array} = \dfrac{\begin{array}{c}\text{Net income} + \\ \text{interest expense}\end{array}}{\begin{array}{c}\text{Average total} \\ \text{assets}\end{array}} = \dfrac{\$16,306 + \$8,376}{(\$300,752 + \$314,405)/2} = \dfrac{\$24,682}{\$307,579} = .080$$

OBJECTIVE 6
Compute two standard profitability measures

Net income and interest expense are taken from the income statement. Average total assets is computed from the beginning and ending balance sheets. How is this profitability measure used in decision making? To compare companies. By relating the sum of net income and interest expense to average total assets, we have a standard measure that describes the profitability of all types of companies. Brokerage companies such as Merrill Lynch and Kidder Peabody often single out particular industries as good investments. For example, brokerage analysts may believe that the steel industry is in a growth phase. These analysts would identify specific steel companies whose profitabilities are likely to lead the industry and so be sound investments. Return on assets is one measure of profitability.

What is a good rate of return on total assets? There is no single answer to this question because rates of return vary widely by industry. For example, high-technology companies earn much higher returns than do utility companies, groceries, and manufacturers of consumer goods such as toothpaste.

Rate of return on stockholders' equity, often called **return on equity,** shows the relationship between net income and average common stockholders' equity. The numerator is net income minus preferred dividends, information taken from the income statement. The denominator is average common stockholders' equity—total stockholders' equity minus preferred equity. Birmingham Steel Corporation's rate of return on common stockholders' equity for 1990 is computed as follows (amounts in thousands of dollars):

$$\begin{array}{l}\text{Rate of} \\ \text{return} \\ \text{on common} \\ \text{stock-} \\ \text{holders'} \\ \text{equity}\end{array} = \dfrac{\begin{array}{c}\text{Net income} - \\ \text{preferred} \\ \text{dividends}\end{array}}{\begin{array}{c}\text{Average} \\ \text{common} \\ \text{stockholders'} \\ \text{equity}\end{array}} = \dfrac{\$16,306 - \$0}{(\$145,044 + \$150,782)/2} = \dfrac{\$16,306}{\$147,913} = .110$$

Birmingham Steel has no preferred stock, so preferred dividends are zero. With no preferred stock outstanding, average *common* stockholders' equity is the same as average *total* equity—the average of the beginning and ending amounts.

Observe that return on equity (11 percent) is higher than return on assets (8 percent). This difference results from the interest expense component of return on assets. Companies such as Birmingham Steel borrow at one rate, say 7 percent, and invest the funds to earn a higher rate, say 10 percent. The company's creditors are guaranteed a fixed rate of return on their loans. The stockholders, conversely, have no guarantee that the corporation will earn net income, so their investments are more risky. Consequently, stockholders demand a higher rate of return than do creditors, and this explains why return on equity should exceed return on assets. If return on assets is higher, the company is in trouble.

Investors and creditors use return on common stockholders' equity in much the same way as they use return on total assets—to compare companies. The higher the rate of return, the more successful the company. A 15-percent return on common stockholders' equity is considered quite good in most industries. Investors also compare a company's return on stockholders' equity to interest rates available in the market. If interest rates are almost as high as return on equity, many investors will lend their money to earn interest. They choose to forgo the extra risk of investing in stock when the rate of return on equity is too low.

Different Values of Stock

The business community refers to several different *stock values* in addition to par value. These values include market value, redemption value, liquidation value, and book value.

Market Value

A stock's **market value** is the price for which a person could buy or sell a share of the stock. The issuing corporation's net income, financial position, its future prospects, and the general economic conditions determine market value (also called market price). Daily newspapers report the market price of many stocks. Corporate financial statements report the high and the low market values of the company's common stock for each quarter of the year. *In almost all cases, stockholders are more concerned about the market value of a stock than any of the other values discussed below.* A stock listed at (an alternative term is *quoted at*) 29¼ sells for, or may be bought for, $29.25 per share. The purchase of 100 shares of this stock would cost $2,925 ($29.25 × 100), plus a commission. If you were selling 100 shares of this stock, you would receive cash of $2,925 less a commission. The commission is the fee an investor pays to a stockbroker for buying or selling the stock.

Redemption Value

Preferred stock's fixed dividend rate makes it somewhat like debt. However, companies do not get a tax deduction for preferred dividend payments. Thus they may wish to buy back, or redeem, their preferred stock to avoid paying the dividends. Preferred stock that provides for redemption at a set price is called redeemable preferred stock. In some cases, the company has the *option* of redeeming its preferred stock at a set price. In other cases, the company is *obligated* to redeem the preferred stock. The price the corporation agrees to pay for the stock, which is set when the stock is issued, is called **redemption value.**

The preferred stock of Pine Industries, Inc., is "redeemable at the option of the Company at $25 per share." Beginning in 1992, Pine is "required to redeem annually 6,765 shares of the preferred stock ($169,125 annually)." Pine's annual redemption payment to the preferred stockholders will include this redemption value plus any dividends in arrears.

Liquidation Value

Liquidation value, which applies only to preferred stock, is the amount the corporation agrees to pay the preferred stockholder per share if the company liquidates. Great Northern Nekoosa Corporation, a large paper company, has preferred stock with "a preference of $50 in liquidation." Dividends in arrears are added to liquidation value in determining the payment to the preferred stockholders if the company liquidates.

Book Value

The **book value** of a stock is the amount of owners' equity on the company's books for each share of its stock. Corporations often report this amount in their annual reports. If the company has only common stock outstanding, its book value is computed by dividing total stockholders' equity by the number of shares outstanding. A company with stockholders' equity of $180,000 and 5,000 shares of common stock outstanding has book value of $36 per share ($180,000/5,000 shares).

If the company has both preferred and common stock outstanding, the preferred stockholders have the first claim to owners' equity. Ordinarily, preferred stock has a specified liquidation or redemption value. The book value of preferred is its redemption value plus any cumulative dividends in arrears on the stock. Its book value *per share* equals the sum of redemption value and any cumulative dividends in arrears divided by the number of preferred shares outstanding. After the corporation figures the preferred shares' book value, it computes the common stock book value per share. The corporation divides the common equity (total stockholders' equity minus preferred equity) by the number of common shares outstanding.

Assume that the company balance sheet reports the following amounts:

Stockholders' Equity

Paid-in capital:	
Preferred stock, 6%, $100 par, 5,000 shares authorized,	
400 shares issued	$ 40,000
Paid-in capital in excess of par—preferred	4,000
Common stock, $10 par, 20,000 shares authorized,	
4,500 shares issued	45,000
Common stock subscribed, 1,000 shares	10,000
Paid-in capital in excess of par—common	72,000
Total paid-in capital	171,000
Retained earnings	85,000
Total stockholders' equity	$256,000

Suppose that four years (including the current year) of cumulative preferred dividends are in arrears and preferred stock has a redemption value of $130 per share.

Book value computations treat subscribed stock as though it were issued stock. The book-value-per-share computations for this corporation follow.

Point to Stress: Review the accounting equation:

Assets = Liabilities + Owner Equity
or,
Assets − Liabilities = Owner Equity

"Assets − Liabilities" is often referred to as "net assets."

Therefore, Net Assets = Owner Equity

Book value could be described as a measure of the net assets owned by each share of stock. This is the same as saying book value is the amount of owners' equity per share of stock.

Teaching Tip: Use this formula to compute book value of common stock:

$$BV = \frac{TSE - PRV - DIA}{SCSO}$$

Book Value = (Total Stockholders' Equity − Preferred Redemption Value − Dividends in Arrears) / Shares of Common Stock Outstanding

Preferred:

Redemption value (400 shares × $130)	$ 52,000
Cumulative dividends ($40,000 × .06 × 4).................	9,600
Stockholders' equity allocated to preferred	$ 61,600
Book value per share ($61,600/400 shares)	$ 154.00

Common:

Total stockholders' equity.....................................	$256,000
Less stockholders' equity allocated to preferred	61,600
Stockholders' equity allocated to common	$194,400
Book value per share [$194,400/(4,500 shares + 1,000 shares)] .	$35.35

Transparency T14-4

How is book value per share used in decision making? Companies negotiating the purchase of a corporation may wish to know the book value of its stock. The book value of stockholders' equity may figure into the negotiated purchase price. Corporations—especially those whose stock is not publicly traded—may buy out a retiring executive, agreeing to pay the book value of the person's stock in the company. In general, however, book value is virtually meaningless to an outside investor when book value is not directly related to the market value of stock.

Summary Problems for Your Review

1. Use the following accounts and related balances to prepare the classified balance sheet of Whitehall, Inc., at September 30, 19X4. Use the account format of the balance sheet.

Common stock, $1 par, 50,000 shares authorized, 20,000 shares issued	$ 20,000	Long-term note payable .	$ 74,000
		Inventory	85,000
		Property, plant, and equipment, net	225,000
Dividends payable	4,000	Donated capital	18,000
Cash	9,000	Accounts receivable, net .	23,000
Accounts payable	28,000	Preferred stock, $3.75, no-par, 10,000 shares, authorized, 2,000 shares issued	24,000
Stock subscription receivable—common ..	2,000		
Retained earnings.......	56,000		
Paid-in capital in excess of par—common	115,000	Common stock subscribed 3,000 shares ...	3,000
Organization cost, net ...	1,000	Accrued liabilities	3,000

2. The balance sheet of Trendline Corporation reported the following at March 31, 19X6, end of its fiscal year. Note that Trendline reports paid-in capital in excess of par or stated value after the stock accounts.

Stockholders' Equity

Preferred stock, 4%, $10 par, 10,000 shares authorized (redemption value, $110,000)	$100,000
Common stock, no-par, $5 stated value, 100,000 shares authorized	250,000
Common stock subscribed	17,500
Paid-in capital in excess of par or stated value:	
Common stock	214,000
Donated capital	55,000
Retained earnings	330,000
Total stockholders' equity.....................................	$966,500

Required

a. Is the preferred stock cumulative or noncumulative? Is it participating or nonparticipating? How can you tell?

b. What is the total amount of the annual preferred dividend?

c. How many shares of preferred stock and common stock has the company issued?

d. How many shares of common stock are subscribed?

e. What was the market value of the assets donated to the corporation?

f. Compute the book value per share of the preferred stock and the common stock. No prior year preferred dividends are in arrears, but Trendline has not declared the current-year dividend.

SOLUTIONS TO REVIEW PROBLEMS

1.

Whitehall, Inc.
Balance Sheet
September 30, 19X4

Assets		Liabilities	
Current:		Current:	
Cash	$ 9,000	Accounts payable	$ 28,000
Accounts receivable, net	23,000	Dividends payable	4,000
Stock subscription receivable—		Accrued liabilities	3,000
common	2,000	Total current liabilities	35,000
Inventory	85,000	Long-term note payable	74,000
Total current assets	119,000	Total liabilities	109,000
Property, plant, and equipment, net	225,000		
Intangible assets:		**Stockholders' Equity**	
Organization cost, net . . . :	1,000	Paid-in capital:	
		Preferred stock, $3.75, no-par,	
		10,000 shares authorized,	
		2,000 shares issued	$ 24,000
		Common stock, $1 par, 50,000	
		shares authorized, 20,000	
		shares issued	20,000
		Common stock subscribed, 3,000	
		shares	3,000
		Paid-in capital in excess of	
		par—common	115,000
		Donated capital	18,000
		Total paid-in capital	180,000
		Retained earnings	56,000
		Total stockholders' equity	236,000
		Total liabilities and	
Total assets	$345,000	stockholders' equity	$345,000

2. Answers to Trendline Corporation questions:

a. The preferred stock is *cumulative* and *nonparticipating* because it is not specifically labeled otherwise.

b. Total annual preferred dividend: $4,000 ($100,000 × .04)

c. Preferred stock issued: 10,000 shares Common stock issued: 50,000 shares ($250,000/$5 stated value)
d. Common stock subscribed: 3,500 shares ($17,500/$5 stated value)
e. Market value of donated assets: $55,000
f. Book values per share of preferred and common stock:

Preferred:
Redemption value	$110,000
Cumulative dividend for current year ($100,000 × .04)	4,000
Stockholders' equity allocated to preferred	$114,000
Book value per share ($114,000/10,000 shares)	$11.40

Common:
Total stockholders' equity.................................	$976,500
Less stockholders' equity allocated to preferred	114,000
Stockholders' equity allocated to common	$862,500
Book value per share [$862,500/(53,500 shares = 50,000 shares issued + 3,500 shares subscribed)].........................	$16.12

Summary

A corporation is a separate legal and business entity. *Continuous life,* the *ease of raising large amounts of capital* and *transferring ownership,* and *limited liability* are among the advantages of the corporate form of organization. An important disadvantage is *double taxation.* Corporations pay *income taxes,* and stockholders pay tax on dividends. *Stockholders* are the owners of corporations. They elect a *board of directors,* which elects a chairperson and appoints the officers to manage the business.

Corporations may issue different classes of stock: *par value, no-par value, common,* and *preferred.* Stock is usually issued at a *premium*—an amount above par value. Also, corporations may issue stock under a *subscription* agreement. The balance sheet carries the capital raised through stock issuance under the heading Paid-in Capital or Contributed Capital in the stockholders' equity section.

Corporations may receive *donations* from outsiders or from stockholders. Donated Capital is a stockholders' equity account.

Only when the board of directors declares a *dividend* does the corporation incur the liability to pay dividends. Preferred stock has priority over common stock as to dividends, which may be stated as a percentage of par value or as a dollar amount per share. In addition, preferred stock has a claim to dividends in arrears if it is *cumulative* and a claim to further dividends if it is *participating.* *Convertible* preferred stock may be exchanged for the corporation's common stock.

Return on assets and *return on stockholders' equity* are two standard measures of profitability. A healthy company's return on equity should exceed its return on assets.

A stock's *market value* is the price for which a share may be bought or sold. *Redemption value, liquidation value,* and *book value*—the amount of owners' equity per share of company stock—are other values that may apply to stock.

Self-Study Questions

Test your understanding of the chapter by marking the best answer for each of the following questions.

1. Which of the following is a *disadvantage* of the corporate form of business organization? *(p. 627)*
   a. Limited liability of stockholders
   c. No mutual agency
   ✓ b. Government regulation
   d. Transferability of ownership

2. The person with the most power in a corporation is the *(p. 628)*
   a. Incorporator
   c. President
   ✓ b. Chairman of the board
   d. Vice-president

3. The dollar amount of the stockholder investments in a corporation is called *(p. 539)*
   a. Outstanding stock
   ✓ c. Paid-in capital
   b. Total stockholders' equity
   d. Retained earnings

4. The arbitrary value assigned to a share of stock is called *(p. 632)*
   a. Market value
   c. Book value
   b. Liquidation value
   ✓ d. Par value

5. Which is the most widely held class of stock? *(p. 632)*
   ✓ a. Par value common stock
   c. Par value preferred stock
   b. No-par common stock
   d. No-par preferred stock

6. Mangum Corporation receives a subscription for 1,000 shares of $100 par preferred stock at $104 per share. This transaction increases Mangum's paid-in capital by *(pp. 636, 637)*
   a. $0 because the corporation received no cash
   c. $100,000
   ✓ d. $104,000
   b. $4,000

7. Organization cost is classified as a (an) *(p. 641)*
   a. Operating expense
   c. Contra item in stockholders' equity
   b. Current asset
   ✓ d. None of the above *intangible asset*

8. Trade Days, Inc., has 10,000 shares of $3.50, $50 par preferred stock, and 100,000 of $4 par common stock outstanding. Two years' preferred dividends are in arrears. Trade Days declares a cash dividend large enough to pay the preferred dividends in arrears, the preferred dividend for the current period, and a $1.50 dividend to common. What is the total amount of the dividend? *(p. 642)*
   ✓ a. $255,000
   c. $150,000
   b. $220,000
   d. $105,000

9. The preferred stock of Trade Days, Inc., in the preceding question was issued at $55 per share. Each preferred share can be converted into 10 common shares. The entry to record the conversion of this preferred stock into common is *(p. 644)*

a. Cash	550,000	
Preferred Stock		500,000
Paid-in Capital in Excess of Par— Preferred Stock		50,000
b. Preferred Stock	500,000	
Paid-in Capital in Excess of Par— Preferred Stock	50,000	
Common Stock		550,000
✓ c. Preferred Stock	500,000	
Paid-in Capital in Excess of Par— Preferred Stock	50,000	
Common Stock		400,000
Paid-in Capital in Excess of Par— Common Stock		150,000

d. Preferred Stock 550,000
   Common Stock 400,000
   Paid-in Capital in Excess of Par—
      Common Stock 150,000

10. When an investor is buying stock as an investment, the value of most direct concern is *(p. 646)*
    a. Par value   c. Liquidation value
    ✓b. Market value   d. Book value

Answers to the Self-Study Questions follow the Accounting Vocabulary.

Accounting Vocabulary

Additional paid-in capital. Another name for Paid-in capital in excess of par *(p. 634)*.

Authorization of stock. Provision in a corporate charter that gives the state's permission for the corporation to issue—that is, to sell—a certain number of shares of stock *(p. 633)*.

Board of directors. Group elected by the stockholders to set policy for a corporation and to appoint its officers *(p. 628)*.

Book value of stock. Amount of owners' equity on the company's books for each share of its stock *(p. 647)*.

Bylaws. Constitution for governing a corporation *(p. 628)*.

Chairperson of the board. Elected by a corporation's board of directors, usually the most powerful person in the corporation *(p. 628)*.

Charter. Document that gives the state's permission to form a corporation *(pp. 626, 628)*.

Common stock. The most basic form of capital stock. In describing a corporation, the common stockholders are the owners of the business *(p. 632)*.

Contributed capital. Another name for Paid-in capital *(p. 630)*.

Convertible preferred stock. Preferred stock that may be exchanged by the preferred stockholders, if they choose, for another class of stock in the corporation *(p. 644)*.

Cumulative preferred stock. Preferred stock whose owners must receive all dividends in arrears before the

corporation pays dividends to the common stockholders *(p. 642)*.

Date of record. Date on which the owners of stock to receive a dividend are identified *(p. 641)*.

Declaration date. Date on which the board of directors announce the intention to pay a dividend. The declaration creates a liability for the corporation *(p. 641)*.

Deficit. Debit balance in the retained earnings account *(p. 631)*.

Discount on stock. Excess of the par value of stock over its issue price *(p. 634)*.

Dividends. Distributions by a corporation to its stockholders *(p. 631)*.

Dividends in arrears. Cumulative preferred dividends that the corporation has failed to pay *(p. 642)*.

Donated capital. Special category of stockholders' equity created when a corporation receives a donation (gift) from a donor who receives no ownership interest in the company *(p. 639)*.

Double taxation. Corporations pay their own income taxes on corporate income. Then, the stockholders pay personal income tax on the cash dividends that they receive from corporations *(p. 627)*.

Incorporators. Persons who organize a corporation *(p. 628)*.

Limited liability. No personal obligation of a stockholder for corporation debts. The most that a stockholder can lose on an investment in a corporation's stock is the cost of the investment (p. 627).

Liquidation value of stock. Amount a corporation agrees to pay a preferred stockholder per share if the company liquidates (p. 647).

Market value of stock. Price for which a person could buy or sell a share of stock (p. 646).

Organization cost. The costs of organizing a corporation, including legal fees, taxes and fees paid to the state, and charges by promoters for selling the stock. Organization cost is an intangible asset (p. 641).

Outstanding stock. Stock in the hands of stockholders. (p. 630).

Paid-in capital. A corporation's capital from investments by the stockholders. Also called Contributed capital (p. 630).

Par value. Arbitrary amount assigned to a share of stock (p. 632).

Participating preferred stock. Preferred stock whose owners may receive—that is, participate in—dividends beyond the stated amount or stated percentage (p. 643).

Payment date. Payment of the dividend usually follows the record date by two to four weeks. (p. 641).

Preemptive right. A stockholder's right to maintain a proportionate ownership in a corporation (p. 632).

Preferred stock. Stock that gives its owners certain advantages over common stockholders, such as the priority to receive dividends before the common stockholders and the priority to receive assets before the common stockholders if the corporation liquidates (p. 632).

Premium on stock. Excess of the issue price of stock over its par value (p. 633)

President. Chief operating officer in charge of managing the day-to-day

operations of a corporation (p. 628).

Proxy. Legal document that expresses a stockholder's preference and appoints another person to cast the vote (p. 628).

Rate of return on total assets. The sum of net income plus interest expense divided by average total assets. This ratio measures the success a company has in using its assets to earn income for the persons who finance the business. Also called Return on assets (p. 645).

Rate of return on common stockholders' equity. Net income minus preferred dividends, divided by average common stockholders' equity. A measure of profitability. Also called Return on common stockholders' equity (p. 645).

Redemption value of stock. Price a corporation agrees to pay for stock, which is set when the stock is issued (p. 646).

Retained earnings. A corporation's capital that is earned through profitable operation of the business (p. 630).

Return on assets. Another name for Rate of return on total assets (p. 645).

Return on common stockholders' equity. Another name for Rate of return on common stockholders' equity (p. 645).

Shareholder. Another name for Stockholder (p. 626).

Stock. Shares into which the owners' equity of a corporation is divided (p. 626).

Stockholders' equity. Owners' equity of a corporation (p. 630).

Stock subscription. Contract that obligates an investor to purchase the corporation's stock at a later date (p. 635).

Answers to Self-Study Questions

1. b
2. b
3. c
4. d
5. a

6. d (1,000 shares × $104 = $104,000)
7. d Intangible asset
8. a [(10,000 × $3.50 × 3 = $105,000) + (100,000 × $1.50 = $150,000) = $255,000]
9. c
10. b

ASSIGNMENT MATERIAL _____

1. Why is a corporation called a creature of the state?
2. Identify the characteristics of a corporation.
3. Explain why corporations face a tax disadvantage.
4. Briefly outline the steps in the organization of a corporation.
5. How are the structures of a partnership and a corporation similar and different?
6. Name the four rights of a stockholder. Is preferred stock automatically nonvoting? Explain how a right may be withheld from a stockholder.
7. Dividends on preferred stock may be stated as a percentage rate or a dollar amount. What is the annual dividend on these preferred stocks: 4 percent, $100 par; $3.50, $20 par; and 6 percent, no-par with $50 stated value?
8. Which event increases the assets of the corporation: authorization of stock or issuance of stock? Explain.
9. Suppose H. J. Heinz Company issued 1,000 shares of its 3.65 percent, $100 par preferred stock for $120. How much would this transaction increase the company's paid-in capital? How much would it increase Heinz's retained earnings? How much would it increase Heinz's annual cash dividend payments?
10. Give two alternative account titles for Paid-in Capital in Excess of Par—Common Stock.
11. Explain the contingent liability created by issuance of stock at a discount.
12. How does issuance of 1,000 shares of no-par stock for land and a building, together worth $150,000, affect paid-in capital?
13. Why does receipt of a stock subscription increase the corporation's assets and owners' equity?
14. Give an example of a transaction that creates donated capital for a corporation.
15. Journalize the incorporation of the Barnes & Connally partnership. The partners' capital account balances exceed the par value of the new corporation's common stock. (Omit amounts.)
16. Rank the following accounts in the order they would appear on the balance sheet: Common Stock, Organization Cost, Donated Capital, Preferred Stock, Common Stock Subscribed, Stock Subscription Receivable (due within six months), Retained Earnings, Dividends Payable. Also, give each account's balance sheet classification.
17. What type of account is Organization Cost? Briefly describe how to account for organization cost.
18. Briefly discuss the three important dates for a dividend.
19. Mancini Inc. has 3,000 shares of its $2.50, $10 par preferred stock outstanding. Dividends for 19X1 and 19X2 are in arrears, and the company has declared no dividends on preferred stock for the current year, 19X3. Assume that Mancini declares total dividends of $35,000 at the end of 19X3. Show how to allocate the dividends to preferred and common (a) if preferred is cumulative and (b) if preferred is noncumulative.
20. As a preferred stockholder, would you rather own cumulative or noncumulative preferred? If all other factors are the same, would the corporation rather the preferred stock be cumulative or noncumulative? Give your reason.

21. How are cumulative preferred dividends in arrears reported in the financial statements? When do dividends become a liability of the corporation?

22. Distinguish between the market value of stock and the book value of stock. Which is more important to investors?

23. How is book value per share of common stock computed when the company has both preferred stock and common stock outstanding?

24. Why should a healthy company's rate of return on stockholders' equity exceed its rate of return on total assets?

Exercises

Exercise 14-1 *Organizing a corporation* *(L.O. 1)*

No check figure

Matt Hershfeld and Chip Heinze are opening a limousine service to be named H&H Transportation Enterprises. They need outside capital, so they plan to organize the business as a corporation. Because your office is in the same building, they come to you for advice. Write a memorandum informing them of the steps in forming a corporation. Identify specific documents used in this process, and name the different parties involved in the ownership and management of a corporation.

Exercise 14-2 *Issuing Stock* *(L.O. 2)*

No check figure

Journalize the following stock issuance transactions of Adams Corporation. Explanations are not required.

Feb. 19 Issued 1,000 shares of $1.50 par common stock for cash of $12.50 per share

Mar. 3 Sold 300 shares of $4.50, no-par Class A preferred stock for $12,000 cash.

  11 Received inventory valued at $25,000 and equipment with market value of $16,000 for 3,300 shares of the $1.50 par common stock.

  15 Issued 1,000 shares of 5 percent, no-par Class B preferred stock with stated value of $50 per share. The issue price was cash of $60 per share.

Exercise 14-3 *Stock subscriptions* *(L.O. 2)*

Paid-in-cap. in excess of par—com. $9,500

Betsy Ross Corporation has just been organized and is selling its stock through stock subscriptions. Record the following selected transactions that occurred during June 19X6.

June 3 Received a subscription to 500 shares of $1 par common stock at the subscription price of $20 per share. The subscriber paid one-fourth of the subscription amount as a down payment. The corporation will issue the stock when it is fully paid.

  18 Collected one-half of the amount receivable from the subscriber.

July 3 Collected the remainder from the subscriber and issued the stock.

Exercise 14-4 *Recording issuance of stock* *(L.O. 2)*

Cap. in excess of par—com. $68,282

The actual balance sheet of Gulf Resources & Chemical Corporation, as adapted, reported the following stockholders' equity. Note that Gulf has two separate classes of preferred stock, labeled as Series A and Series B. All dollar amounts, except for per-share amounts, are given in thousands.

Stockholders' Investment
(same as stockholders' equity)

Preferred stock, $1 par, authorized 4,000,000 shares (Note 7)

Series A . . . . $ 58

Series B   376

Common stock, $.10 par, authorized 20,000,000, [issued and]

outstanding 9,130,000 shares   913

Capital in excess of par   75,542

Note 7. Preferred Stock:	Shares [Issued and] Outstanding
Series A	58,000
Series B	376,000

Required

Assume that the Series A preferred stock was issued for $3 cash per share, the Series B preferred was issued for $20 cash per share, and the common was issued for cash of $69,195. Make the summary journal entries to record issuance of all the Gulf Resources stock. Explanations are not required.

(b) Paid-in-cap. in excess of stated value—com. $450,000

Exercise 14-5   *Recording issuance of no-par stock*   (*L.O. 2*)

Alexanians, located in Lansing, Michigan, is an importer of European furniture and Oriental rugs. The corporation issues 10,000 shares of no-par common stock for $50 per share. Record issuance of the stock (a) if the stock is true no-par stock and (b) if the stock has stated value of $5 per share.

Total stock. equity $196,500

Exercise 14-6   *Stockholders' equity section of a balance sheet*   (*L.O. 3*)

The charter of Majorex Corporation authorizes the issuance of 5,000 shares of Class A preferred stock, 1,000 shares of Class B preferred stock, and 10,000 shares of common stock. During a two-month period, Majorex completed these stock-issuance transactions:

June 23   Issued 1,000 shares of $1 par common stock for cash of $12.50 per share.

July   2   Sold 300 shares of $4.50, no-par Class A preferred stock for $20,000 cash.

     12   Received inventory valued at $25,000 and equipment with market value of $16,000 for 3,300 shares of the $1 par common stock.

     17   Issued 1,000 shares of 5 percent, no-par Class B preferred stock with stated value of $50 per share. The issue price was cash of $60 per share.

Prepare the stockholders' equity section of the Majorex balance sheet for the transactions given in this exercise. Retained Earnings has a balance of $63,000.

Total paid-in cap. $956,200

Exercise 14-7   *Paid-in capital for a corporation*   (*L.O. 2*)

Flavan Corp. has recently organized. The company issued common stock to an attorney who gave Flavan legal services of $6,200 to help her in organizing the corporation. It issued common stock to another person in exchange for his patent with a market value of $40,000. In addition, Flavan received cash both for 2,000 shares of its preferred stock at $110 per share and for 26,000 shares of its common stock at $15 per share. The city of Fond du Lac donated 50 acres of land to the company as a plant site. The market value of the land was $300,000,

Without making journal entries, determine the total paid-in capital created by these transactions.

Exercise 14-8   *Stockholders' equity section of a balance sheet* **(L.O. 3)**

Total stock. equity $1,130,000

Mexico Lindo, Inc., has the following selected account balances at June 30, 19X7. Prepare the stockholders' equity section of the company's balance sheet.

Common stock, no-par with $5 stated value, 500,000 shares authorized, 120,000 shares issued	$600,000	Preferred stock subscribed, 1,000 shares	$ 20,000
		Inventory	112,000
Donated capital	103,000	Machinery and equipment............	109,000
Accumulated depreciation— machinery and equipment............	62,000	Preferred stock subscription receivable..	8,000
		Preferred stock, 5%, $20 par, 20,000 shares authorized, 10,000 shares issued	200,000
Retained earnings	119,000		
Paid-in capital in excess of par—preferred stock.................	88,000	Organization cost, net	3,000

Exercise 14-9   *Incorporating a partnership* **(L.O. 4)**

Paid-in cap. in excess of par com. $10,500

The Podunk Jaybirds are a semiprofessional baseball team that has been operated as a partnership by D. Robertson and G. Childres. In addition to their management responsibilities, Robertson also plays second base and Childres sells hot dogs. Journalize the following transactions in the first month of operation as a corporation:

May 14   The incorporators paid legal fees of $990 and state taxes and fees of $500 to obtain a corporate charter.

14   Issued 2,500 shares of $5 par common stock to Robertson and 1,000 shares to Childres. Robertson's capital balance on the partnership books was $20,000, and Childres's capital balance was $8,000.

18   The city of Podunk donated 20 acres of land to the corporation for a stadium site. The land's market value was $40,000.

Exercise 14-10   *Computing dividends on preferred and common stock* **(L.O. 5)**

19X6:
  Series A Pfd. $23,200
  Series B Pfd. $977,600
  Common $199,200

The following elements of stockholders' equity are adapted from the balance sheet of Gulf Resources & Chemical Corporation. All dollar amounts, except the dividends per share, are given in thousands.

Stockholders' Equity

Preferred stock, cumulative and nonparticipating, $1 par (Note 7)	
Series A, 58,000 shares issued	$ 58
Series B, 376,000 shares issued	376
Common stock, $.10 par, 9,130,000 shares issued	913

Note 7. Preferred Stock:	Designated Annual Cash Dividend Per Share
Series A	$ .20
Series B	1.30

Assume that the Series A preferred has preference over the Series B preferred and the company has paid all preferred dividends through 19X4.

Exercise 14-11   *Book value per share of preferred and common stock* **(L.O. 6)**

The balance sheet of International Graphics Corporation reported the following, with all amounts, including shares, in thousands:

Redeemable preferred stock; redemption value $5,103	$ 4,860
Common stockholders' equity 8,120 shares issued	
and outstanding	216,788
Total stockholders' equity	$221,648

Assume that International has paid preferred dividends for the current year and all prior years (no dividends in arrears), and the company has 100 shares of preferred stock outstanding. Compute the book value per share of the preferred stock and the common stock.

Exercise 14-12   *Book value per share of preferred and common stock; preferred dividends in arrears* **(L.O. 5, 6)**

Refer to Exercise 14-11. Compute the book value per share of the preferred stock and the common stock, assuming that three years' preferred dividends (including dividends for the current year) are in arrears. Assume the preferred stock is cumulative and its dividend rate is 6 percent.

Exercise 14-13   *Evaluating profitability* **(L.O. 7)**

Kelly Services, Inc., reported these figures for 19X7 and 19X6:

	19X7	19X6
Income statement:		
Interest expense	$ 7,400,000	7,100,000
Net income	24,000,000	21,700,000
Balance sheet:		
Total assets	351,000,000	317,000,000
Preferred stock, $1.30, no-par, 100,000		
shares issued and outstanding	2,500,000	2,500,000
Common stockholders' equity	164,000,000	151,000,000
Total stockholders' equity	166,500,000	153,500,000

Compute rate of return on total assets and rate of return on common stockholders' equity for 19X7. Do these rates of return suggest strength or weakness? Give your reason.

Problems *(Group A)*

Problem 14-1A   *Organizing a corporation* **(L.O. 1)**

Marla Fredricks and Allison LaChapelle are opening a Sav-On office supply store in a shopping center in Hagerstown, Maryland. The area is growing, and no competitors are located in the immediate vicinity. Their most fundamental decision is how to organize the business. Marla thinks the partnership form is best. Allison favors the corporate form of organization. They seek your advice.

Required

Discuss the advantages and the disadvantages of organizing the business as a corporation.

Problem 14-2A *Journalizing corporation transactions and preparing the stockholders' equity section of the balance sheet* **(L.O. 2, 3)**

Total stock. equity $240,000

Lanz Corporation received a charter from the state of New Jersey. The company is authorized to issue 20,000 shares of 5 percent, $50 par preferred stock and 300,000 shares of no-par common stock. During its start-up phase, the company completed the following transactions:

Oct. 2 Paid fees of $4,000 and incorporation taxes of $3,000 to the state of New Jersey to obtain the charter and file the required documents for incorporation.

4 Issued 900 shares of common stock to the promoters who organized the corporation. Their fee was $45,000.

5 Accepted subscriptions for 1,000 shares of common stock at $50 per share and received a down payment of one-fourth of the subscription amount.

9 Issued 2,000 shares of common stock in exchange for equipment valued at $100,000.

14 Issued 600 shares of preferred stock for cash of $54 per share.

30 Collected one-third of the stock subscription receivable.

31 Earned a small profit for October and closed the $12,600 credit balance of Income Summary into Retained Earnings.

Required

1. Record the transactions in the general journal.
2. Prepare the stockholders' equity section of the Lanz balance sheet at October 31.

Problem 14-3A *Journalizing corporation transactions and preparing the stockholders' equity section of the balance sheet* **(L.O. 2, 3)**

Total stock. equity $446,800

The partners who owned Horner & Roads wished to avoid the unlimited personal liability of the partnership form of business, so they incorporated the partnership as Penrod Drilling, Inc. The charter from the state of Texas authorizes the corporation to issue 10,000 shares of 6 percent, $100 par preferred stock and 250,000 shares of no-par common stock with a stated value of $5 per share. In its first month, Penrod Drilling completed the following transactions:

Dec. 1 Paid incorporation taxes of $1,500 and a charter fee of $2,000 to the state of Texas and paid legal fees of $1,900 to organize as a corporation.

3 Issued 750 shares of common stock to the promoter for assistance with issuance of the common stock. The promotion fee was $7,500.

3 Issued 5,100 shares of common stock to Horner and 3,800 shares to Roads in return for the net assets of the partnership. Horner's capital balance on the partnership books was $51,000, and Roads's capital balance was $38,000.

5 Accepted subscriptions for 5,000 shares of common stock at $10 per share and received a down payment of 25 percent of the subscription amount.

7 Received a small parcel of land valued at $84,000 as a donation from the city of Midland.

Dec. 12 Issued 1,000 shares of preferred stock to acquire a patent with a market value of $110,000.

   22 Issued 1,500 shares of common stock for $10 cash per share.

   28 Collected 20 percent of the stock subscription receivable.

Required

1. Record the transactions in the general journal.
2. Prepare the stockholders' equity section of the Penrod Drilling balance sheet at December 31. Retained Earnings balance is $91,300.

Total stock. equity:
   Advantage $578,000
   Vanguard $567,000

Problem 14-4A   *Stockholders' equity section of the balance sheet* **(L.O. 3)**

Stockholders' equity information is given for Advantage Consultants, Inc., and Vanguard Corporation. The two companies are independent.

Advantage Consultants, Inc.   Advantage Consultants, Inc., is authorized to issue 50,000 shares of $5 par common stock. All the stock was issued at $8 per share. The company incurred a net loss of $12,000 in 19X1. It earned net income of $60,000 in 19X2 and $130,000 in 19X3. The company declared no dividends during the three-year period.

Vanguard Corporation.   Vanguard's charter authorizes the company to issue 10,000 shares of $2.50 preferred stock with par value of $100 and 120,000 shares of no-par common stock. Vanguard issued 1,000 shares of the preferred stock at $110 per share. It issued 40,000 shares of the common stock for a total of $320,000. The company's retained earnings balance at the beginning of 19X3 was $72,000, and net income for the year was $90,000. During 19X3 the company declared the specified dividend on preferred and a $.50 per share dividend on common. Preferred dividends for 19X2 were in arrears.

Required

For each company, prepare the stockholders' equity section of its balance sheet at December 31, 19X3. Show the computation of all amounts. Entries are not required.

6. Pfd. div. $212,080

Problem 14-5A   *Analyzing the stockholders' equity of an actual corporation* **(L.O. 3, 5)**

The purpose of this problem is to familiarize you with the financial statement information of a real company, U and I Group. U and I, which makes food products and livestock feeds, included the following stockholders' equity on its year-end balance sheet at February 28:

Stockholders' Equity	($ Thousands)
Voting Preferred Stock, 5.5% cumulative—par value $23 per share; authorized 100,000 shares in each class:	
Class A—issued 75,473 shares	$ 1,736
Class B—issued 92,172 shares	2,120
Common stock—par value $5 per share; authorized 5,000,000 shares; issued 2,870,950 shares	14,355
[Additional] Paid-in Capital	5,548
Retained earnings	8,336
	$32,095

Required

1. Identify the different issues of stock U and I has outstanding.
2. Is the preferred stock participating or nonparticipating? How can you tell?

3. Give the summary entries to record issuance of all the U and I stock. Assume that all the stock was issued for cash and that the additional paid-in capital applies to the common stock. Explanations are not required.

4. Rearrange the U and I stockholders' equity section to correspond, as appropriate, to the format and terminology illustrated on page 000. Assume the total stockholders' equity of $32,095,000 is correct.

5. Suppose U and I passed its preferred dividends for one year. Would the company have to pay these dividends in arrears before paying dividends to the common stockholders? Give your reason.

6. What amount of preferred dividends must U and I declare and pay each year to avoid having preferred dividends in arrears?

7. Assume preferred dividends are in arrears for 19X8.
   a. Write Note 5 of the February 28, 19X8, financial statements to disclose the dividends in arrears.
   b. Record the declaration of a $500,000 dividend in the year ended February 28, 19X9. An explanation is not required.

Problem 14-6A *Preparing a corporation balance sheet* (L.O. 3, 7)

Total assets $513,000
Return on common .087

The following accounts and related balances of Gillen Art Associates, Inc., are arranged in no particular order. Use them to prepare the company's classified balance sheet in the account format at June 30, 19X2. Also compute rate of return on total assets and rate of return on common stockholders' equity for the year ended June 30, 19X2. Do these rates of return suggest strength or weakness? Give your reason.

Trademark, net	$ 9,000	Common stockholders'	
Organization cost, net ...	14,000	equity, June 30, 19X1..	$322,000
Preferred stock, $.20,		Net income	31,000
no-par, 10,000 shares		Total assets, June 30,	
authorized and issued .	27,000	19X1.................	504,000
Stock subscription		Interest expense	6,100
receivable—common ..	12,000	Property, plant, and	
Cash	19,000	equipment, net	267,000
Accounts receivable, net .	34,000	Common stock, $1 par,	
Paid-in capital in excess		500,000 shares	
of par—common	19,000	authorized, 214,000	
Accrued liabilities	26,000	shares issued	214,000
Long-term note payable .	72,000	Prepaid expenses	10,000
Inventory	148,000	Common stock	
Dividends payable	9,000	subscribed, 22,000	
Retained earnings.......	?	shares	22,000
Accounts payable	31,000	Donated capital.........	6,000

Problem 14-7A *Computing dividends on preferred and common stock* (L.O. 5)

2. 19X3 Div. Pay.:
   Pfd. $35,000
   Com. $230,000

Whitehead Institute, Inc., has 10,000 shares of $3.50, no-par preferred stock and 50,000 shares of no-par common stock outstanding. Whitehead declared and paid the following dividends during a three-year period: 19X1, $20,000; 19X2, $90,000; and 19X3, $265,000.

Required

1. Compute the total dividends to preferred stock and common stock for each of the three years if
   a. Preferred is noncumulative and nonparticipating.
   b. Preferred is cumulative and nonparticipating.

2. For case 1b, record the declaration of the 19X3 dividends on December 28, 19X3, and the payment of the dividends on January 17, 19X4.

Problem 14-8A *Analyzing the stockholders' equity of an actual corporation* **(L.O. 5, 6)**

The balance sheet of Elsimate, Inc., reported the following:

Shareholders' Investment
(same as stockholders' equity)

Redeemable non-voting preferred stock, no-par (Redemption value $358,000)	$320,000
Common stock, $1.50 par value, authorized 75,000 shares; issued 36,000 shares	54,000
[Additional] paid-in capital	231,000
Retained earnings	119,000
Total shareholders' investment	$724,000

Notes to the financial statements indicate that 8,000 shares of $2.60 preferred stock with a stated value of $40 per share were issued and outstanding. Preferred dividends are in arrears for three years, including the current year. The additional paid-in capital was contributed by the common stockholders. On the balance sheet date, the market value of the Elsimate common stock was $7.50 per share.

Required

1. Is the preferred stock cumulative or noncumulative, participating or nonparticipating? How can you tell?
2. What is the amount of the annual preferred dividend?
3. Which class of stockholders controls the company? Give your reason.
4. What is the total paid-in capital of the company?
5. What was the total market value of the common stock?
6. Compute the book value per share of the preferred stock and the common stock.

(Group B)

Problem 14-1B *Organizing a corporation* **(L.O. 1)**

Patrick Ledoux and Michael Suttle are opening a Big Boy Restaurant in a growing section of Seattle. There are no competing family restaurants in the immediate vicinity. Their most fundamental decision is how to organize the business. Patrick thinks the partnership form is best for their business. Michael favors the corporate form of organization. They seek your advice.

Required

Discuss the advantages and the disadvantages of organizing the business as a corporation.

Problem 14-2B *Journalizing corporation transactions and preparing the stockholders' equity section of the balance sheet* **(L.O. 2, 3)**

Metzger Brothers Corporation was organized under the laws of the state of Vermont. The charter authorizes Metzger to issue 100,000 shares of $3, no-par preferred stock and 500,000 shares of common stock with $1 par value. During its start-up phase, the company completed the following transactions:

July 5 Paid fees and incorporation taxes of $12,000 to the state of Vermont to obtain the charter and file the required documents for incorporation.

July 6 Issued 500 shares of common stock to the promoters who organized the corporation. Their fee was $20,000.

7 Accepted subscriptions for 1,000 shares of common stock at $30 per share and received a down payment of one-third of the subscription amount.

12 Issued 300 shares of preferred stock for cash of $20,000.

14 Issued 800 shares of common stock in exchange for land valued at $24,000.

31 Collected one-half of the stock subscription receivable.

31 Earned a small profit for July and closed the $21,000 credit balance of Income Summary into the Retained Earnings account.

Required

1. Record the transactions in the general journal.
2. Prepare the stockholders' equity section of the Metzger balance sheet at July 31.

Problem 14-3B *Journalizing corporation transactions and preparing the stockholders' equity section of the balance sheet* **(L.O. 2, 3)**

Total stock. equity $327,500

The partnership of Endicott and Barbisch needed additional capital to expand into new markets, so the business incorporated as Salinas, Inc. The charter from the state of Arizona authorizes Salinas to issue 50,000 shares of 6 percent, $100 par preferred stock and 100,000 shares of no-par common stock with a stated value of $5 per share. In its first month, Salinas completed the following transactions:

Dec. 1 Paid a charter fee of $500 and incorporation taxes of $2,100 to the state of Arizona and paid legal fees of $1,000 to organize as a corporation.

2 Issued 300 shares of common stock to the promoter for assistance with issuance of the common stock. The promotional fee was $1,800.

2 Issued 9,000 shares of common stock to Endicott and 12,000 shares to Barbisch in return for the net assets of the partnership. Endicott's capital balance on the partnership books was $54,000, and Barbisch's capital balance was $72,000.

4 Accepted subscriptions for 4,000 shares of common stock at $6 per share and received a down payment of 20 percent of the subscription amount.

8 Received a small parcel of land valued at $80,000 as a donation from the city of Phoenix.

10 Issued 400 shares of preferred stock to acquire a patent with a market value of $50,000.

16 Issued 600 shares of common stock for cash of $3,600.

30 Collected one-third of the stock subscription receivable.

Required

1. Record the transactions in the general journal.
2. Prepare the stockholders' equity section of the Salinas, Inc., balance sheet at December 31. Retained Earnings' balance is $42,100.

Problem 14-4B *Stockholders' equity section of the balance sheet* **(L.O. 3)**

Total stock. equity:
Navarro $331,000
Action $445,000

The following summaries for Navarro Corp. and Action Manpower, Inc., provide the information needed to prepare the stockholders' equity section of the company balance sheet. The two companies are independent.

Navarro Corp.   Navarro Corp. is authorized to issue 50,000 shares of $1 par common stock. All the stock was issued at $6 per share. The company incurred net losses of $30,000 in 19X1 and $14,000 in 19X2. It earned net incomes of $23,000 in 19X3 and $52,000 in 19X4. The company declared no dividends during the four-year period.

Action Manpower, Inc.   Action's charter authorizes the company to issue 5,000 shares of 5 percent, $100 par preferred stock and 500,000 shares of no-par common stock. Action issued 1,000 shares of the preferred stock at $105 per share. It issued 100,000 shares of the common stock for $150,000. The company's retained earnings balance at the beginning of 19X4 was $120,000. Net income for 19X4 was $80,000, and the company declared a 5 percent preferred dividend for 19X4. Preferred dividends for 19X3 were in arrears.

Required

For each company, prepare the stockholders' equity section of its balance sheet at December 31, 19X4. Show the computation of all amounts. Entries are not required.

6. Pfd. div. $22,500,000

Problem 14-5B   *Analyzing the stockholders' equity of an actual corporation* **(L.O. 3, 5)**

The purpose of this problem is to familiarize you with the financial statement information of a real company. Bethlehem Steel Corporation is one of the nation's largest steel companies. Bethlehem included the following stockholders' equity on its balance sheet:

Stockholders' Equity	($ Millions)
Preferred stock—	
Authorized 20,000,000 shares in each class; issued:	
$5.00 Cumulative Convertible Preferred Stock, at $50.00	
stated value, 2,500,000 shares	$ 125
$2.50 Cumulative Convertible Preferred Stock, at $25.00	
stated value, 4,000,000 shares	100
Common stock—$8 par value—	
Authorized 80,000,000 shares; issued 48,308,516 shares	621
Retained earnings	529
	$1,375

Observe that Bethlehem reports no Paid-in Capital in Excess of Par or Stated Value. Instead, the company reports these items in the stock accounts.

Required

1. Identify the different issues of stock Bethlehem has outstanding.
2. Is the preferred stock participating or nonparticipating? How can you tell?
3. Which class of stock did Bethlehem issue at par or stated value, and which class did it issue above par or stated value?
4. Rearrange the Bethlehem Steel stockholders' equity section to correspond, as appropriate, to the terminology and format illustrated on page 647. Assume Bethlehem is authorized to issue 20,000,000 shares of the $5 preferred stock and an additional 20,000,000 shares of the $2.50 preferred. Assume the total stockholders' equity of $1,375 million is correct. Report dollar amounts in millions, as Bethlehem does.
5. Suppose Bethlehem passed its preferred dividends for one year. Would the company have to pay these dividends in arrears before paying dividends to the common stockholders? Give your reason.

6. What amount of preferred dividends must Bethlehem declare and pay each year to avoid having preferred dividends in arrears?

7. Assume preferred dividends are in arrears for 19X5.
   a. Write Note 6 of the December 31, 19X5, financial statements to disclose the dividends in arrears.
   b. Journalize the declaration of a $60 million dividend for 19X6. An explanation is not required.

Problem 14-6B *Preparing a corporation balance sheet; measuring profitability*
(L.O. 3, 7)

Total assets $797,000
Return on common $.064

The following accounts and related balances of McIntosh Products, Inc., are arranged in no particular order. Use them to prepare the company's classified balance sheet in the account format at November 30, 19X7. Also compute rate of return on total assets and rate of return on common stockholders' equity for the year ended November 30, 19X7. Do these rates of return suggest strength or weakness? Give your reason.

Accounts payable	$ 31,000	Accrued liabilities	$ 17,000
Stock subscription		Long-term note payable .	104,000
receivable, preferred . .	1,000	Accounts receivable, net .	101,000
Retained earnings	?	Preferred stock, 4%, $10	
Common stock, $5 par,		par, 25,000 shares	
100,000 shares		authorized, 3,000	
authorized, 42,000		shares issued	30,000
shares issued	210,000	Cash	41,000
Dividends payable	3,000	Inventory	226,000
Total assets, November		Property, plant, and	
30, 19X6	781,000	equipment, net	378,000
Net income	36,200	Organization cost, net . . .	6,000
Common stockholders'		Prepaid expenses	13,000
equity, November 30,		Preferred stock	
19X6	483,000	subscribed 700 shares .	7,000
Interest expense	12,800	Patent, net	31,000
Donated capital	109,000		
Additional paid-in			
capital—common	85,000		

Problem 14-7B *Computing dividends on preferred and common stock* *(L.O. 5)*

2. 19X3 Div. pay.:
Pfd. $2,500
Com. $24,500

Hankamer Corporation has 5,000 shares of 5 percent, $10 par value preferred stock and 100,000 shares of $1.50 par common stock outstanding. During a three-year period Hankamer declared and paid cash dividends as follows: 19X1, $0; 19X2, $10,000; and 19X3, $27,000.

Required

1. Compute the total dividends to preferred stock and common stock for each of the three years if
   a. Preferred is noncumulative and nonparticipating.
   b. Preferred is cumulative and nonparticipating.
2. For case *1b*, record the declaration of the 19X3 dividends on December 22, 19X3, and the payment of the dividends on January 14, 19X4.

Problem 14-8B *Analyzing the stockholders' equity of an actual corporation* *(L.O. 5, 6)*

BV per share:
Pfd. $28.20
Com. $ 7.16

The balance sheet of Oak Manufacturing, Inc., reported the following:

Stockholders' Investment (same as stockholders' equity)	($ Thousands)
Cumulative convertible preferred stock	$ 45
Common stock, $1 par value, authorized 40,000,000 shares; issued 16,000,000 shares	16,000
[Additional] paid-in capital	176,000
Retained earnings	(77,165)
Total stockholders' investment	$114,880

Notes to the financial statements indicate that 9,000 shares of $1.60 preferred stock with a stated value of $5 per share were issued and outstanding. The preferred stock has a redemption value of $25 per share, and preferred dividends are in arrears for two years, including the current year. The additional paid-in capital was contributed by the common stockholders. On the balance sheet date, the market value of the Oak Manufacturing common stock was $7.50 per share.

Required

1. Is the preferred stock cumulative or noncumulative, participating or non-participating? How can you tell?
2. What is the amount of the annual preferred dividend?
3. What is the total paid-in capital of the company?
4. What was the total market value of the common stock?
5. Compute the book value per share of the preferred stock and the common stock.

Extending Your Knowledge

Decision Problems

Total stock. equity:
 Plan 1, $515,200
 Plan 2, $500,200

1. Evaluating Alternative Ways Of Raising Capital   (L.O. 2, 3)

R. Atari and G. Stacey have written a computer program for a video game that they believe will rival Nintendo. They need additional capital to market the product, and they plan to incorporate their partnership. They are considering alternative capital structures for the corporation. Their primary goal is to raise as much capital as possible without giving up control of the business. The partners plan to receive 170,000 shares of the corporation's common stock in return for the net assets of the partnership. After the partnership books are closed and the assets adjusted to current market value, Atari's capital balance is $90,000 and Stacey's balance is $80,000.

The corporation's plans for a charter include an authorization to issue 5,000 shares of preferred stock and 500,000 shares of $1 par common stock. Atari and Stacey are uncertain about the most desirable features for the preferred stock. Prior to incorporating, the partners have discussed their plans with two investment groups. The corporation can obtain capital from outside investors under either of the following plans:

Plan 1.   Group 1 will invest $105,000 to acquire 1,000 shares of $5, no-par preferred stock and $130,000 to acquire 130,000 shares of common stock. Each preferred share receives 50 votes on matters that come before the stockholders. The investors in Group 1 would attempt to control the corporation if they have the majority of the corporate votes.

Plan 2. Group 2 will invest $220,000 to acquire 2,000 shares of 6 percent, $100 par nonvoting, noncumulative, participating preferred stock.

Required

Assume the corporation is chartered.

1. Journalize the issuance of common stock to Atari and Stacey.
2. Journalize the issuance of stock to the outsiders under both plans.
3. Assume net income for the first year is $130,000 and total dividends of $19,800 are properly subtracted from retained earnings. Prepare the stockholders' equity section of the corporation balance sheet under both plans.
4. Recommend one of the plans to Atari and Stacey. Give your reasons.

2. Questions about Corporations (L.O. 2, 6)

No check figure

1. Why do you think capital stock and retained earnings are shown separately in the shareholders' equity section?
2. Mary Reznick, major shareholder of M-R Inc., proposes to sell some land she owns to the company for common shares in M-R. What problem does M-R, Inc. face in recording the transaction?

3. Preferred shares generally are preferred with respect to dividends and on liquidation. Why would investors buy common stock when preferred stock is available?
4. What does it mean if the liquidation value of a company's preferred stock is greater than its market value.
5. If you owned 100 shares of stock in Magna Corporation and someone offered to buy the stock for its book value, would you accept their offer? Why or why not?

Ethical Issue

George Campbell paid $50,000 for a franchise that entitled him to market Success Associates software programs in the countries of the European Common Market. Campbell intended to sell individual franchises for the major language groups of western Europe—German, French, English, Spanish, and Italian. Naturally, investors considering buying a franchise from Campbell asked to see the financial statements of his business.

Believing the value of the franchise to be greater than $50,000, Campbell sought to capitalize his own franchise at $500,000. The law firm of McDonald & LaDue helped Campbell form a corporation chartered to issue 500,000 shares of common stock with par value of $1 per share. Attorneys suggested the following chain of transactions:

1. A third party borrows $500,000 and purchases the franchise from Campbell.
2. Campbell pays the corporation $500,000 to acquire all its stock.
3. The corporation buys the franchise from the third party, who repays the loan.

In the final analysis, the third party is debt-free and out of the picture. Campbell owns all the corporation's stock, and the corporation owns the franchise. The corporation balance sheet lists a franchise acquired at a cost of $500,000. This balance sheet is Campbell's most valuable marketing tool.

Required

1. What is unethical about this situation?
2. Who can be harmed? How can they be harmed? What role does accounting play?

Financial Statement Problems

2. Avg. issue price of common $2.11

1. Stockholders' Equity   (L.O. 2)

The Goodyear Tire & Rubber Company financial statements appear in Appendix C. Answer these questions about the company's common stock.

1. What classes of stock does the balance sheet report? What is the par value? How many shares are authorized? How many shares were outstanding at December 31, 1990?
2. For issuances of stock, Goodyear obviously credited the Common Stock account for a specific amount per share. What was the amount? What was the average issue price per share?
3. The Quarterly Data and Market Price Information note, near the end of Goodyear's annual report, indicates that during 1990, the company's common stock was priced in the $12–$46 range. Based on this fact, does Goodyear's balance sheet suggest that the company issued its common stock recently or in the distant past? How can you tell?
4. Like most other corporations, Goodyear allows its stockholders and employees to purchase the company's stock through dividend reinvestment and stock purchase plans. These are mentioned in the statement of stockholders' equity. Record Goodyear's issuance of stock under these plans during 1990, assuming the company received cash.

No check figure

2. Stockholders' Equity   (L.O. 2, 6)

Obtain the annual report of an actual company of your choosing. Annual reports are available in various forms including the original document in hard copy, microfiche, and computerized data bases such as that provided by Disclosure, Inc.

Answer these questions about the company. Concentrate on the current year in the annual report you select.

1. What classes of stock does the company have outstanding? What is its par value? How many shares are authorized? How many shares were outstanding on the most current balance sheet date?
2. Under what title does the company report additional paid-in capital?
3. How much is total stockholders' equity? If the total is not labeled, compute total stockholders' equity.
4. Using the company's terminology, journalize the issuance of 100,000 shares of the company's common stock at $55 per share. Recompute all account balances to include the effect of this transaction.
5. Compute the average amount paid in per share of the company's common stock. Then examine the recent market prices of the company's stock in the multiyear summary of financial data. Compare the average amount paid in per share with recent market prices to determine whether the bulk of the company's stock was issued within the recent past. Give the reason for your answer.

Chapter 15

Corporations:
Retained Earnings, Dividends,
Treasury Stock, and
the Income Statement

In the 1991 annual report, the following footnote appeared:

Unusual Losses and Events

In February 1991, it came to the attention of Magid Corp. directors that certain officers of its Milwaukee-based mail order operations had engaged in unauthorized accounting procedures and computer manipulations in the areas of accounts receivable and accounts payable. The adjustments necessary to restate accounts receivable and related accounts resulted in losses of approximately $8.6 million, and the adjustments to correct accounts payable resulted in losses of approximately $3.1 million.

Company executives believe that the overstatement of accounts receivable and the understatement of liabilities occurred prior to 1991. However, mainly because of the absence of the related accounting records and other data, accountants have been unable to identify the periods in which the unauthorized procedures and manipulations occurred.

Clearly the losses resulting from the computer manipulations fall outside the major ongoing operations of the corporation. It would be inappropriate to report the losses as though they resulted from the sale of inventory or from any other ongoing operation. The section of this chapter on the corporation income statement discusses how to report special gains and losses.

Chapter 14 introduced the corporate form of business. Chapter 15 continues our discussion of corporation retained earnings and cash dividends and also considers stock dividends, treasury stock, and the corporate income statement.

Retained Earnings and Dividends

Point to Stress: Retained Earnings is the owners' equity account in which net income and dividends are recorded. In a proprietorship, all investments, net income and withdrawals are recorded in the capital account, but for a corporation the stockholders' equity is divided into two distinct sections—Paid-in Capital and Retained Earnings. The Paid-in Capital section is used to record investments of capital, and Retained Earnings is used to record net income, losses, and dividends.

We have seen that the equity section on the corporation balance sheet is called stockholders' equity or shareholders' equity. The paid-in capital accounts and retained earnings make up the stockholders' equity section.

Retained Earnings is the corporation account that carries the balance of the business's net income less its net losses from operations and less any declared dividends accumulated over the corporation's lifetime. *Retained* means "held on to." Retained Earnings is accumulated income to cover dividends and any future losses. Because Retained Earnings is an owners' equity account, it normally has a credit balance. Corporations may use other labels for Retained Earnings, among them Earnings Reinvested in the Business and Retained Income.

A debit balance in Retained Earnings, which arises when a corporation's expenses exceed its revenues, is called a *deficit*. This amount is subtracted from the sum of the credit balances in the other equity accounts on the balance sheet to determine total stockholders' equity. In a recent survey, 37 of 600 companies (6.2 percent) had a retained earnings deficit.

At the end of each accounting period, the Income Summary account—which carries the balance of net income for the period—is closed to the Retained Earnings account. Assume the following amounts are drawn from a corporation's temporary accounts.

Income Summary					
Dec. 31, 19X1	Expenses	750,000	Dec. 31, 19X1	Revenues	850,000
			Dec. 31, 19X1	Bal.	100,000

This final closing entry transfers net income from Income Summary to Retained Earnings:

19X1

Dec. 31	Income Summary	100,000	
	Retained Earnings		100,000
	To close net income to Retained Earnings.		

If 19X1 was the corporation's first year of operations, the Retained Earnings account now has an ending balance of $100,000:

Retained Earnings

	Jan. 1, 19X1	Bal.	-0-
	Dec. 31, 19X1	Net inc.	100,000
	Dec. 31, 19X1	Bal.	100,000

Teaching Tip: Remind students of this relationship:

Beg. Retained Earnings
+ Net Income
− Dividends or Net Loss

= End. Retained Earnings

A $60,000 net loss for the year would produce this debit balance in Income Summary:

Income Summary

Dec. 31, 19X3	Expenses	470,000	Dec. 31, 19X3	Revenues	410,000
Dec. 31, 19X3	Bal.	60,000			

To close a $60,000 loss, we would credit Income Summary and debit Retained Earnings, as follows:

Dec. 31	Retained Earnings	60,000	
	Income Summary		60,000
	To close net loss to Retained Earnings.		

After posting, Income Summary's balance is zero, and the Retained Earnings balance is decreased by $60,000.

Remember that the account title includes the word *earnings. Credits to the Retained Earnings account arise only from net income.* When we examine a corporation's financial statements and want to learn how much net income the corporation has earned and retained in the business, we turn to Retained Earnings.

After the corporation has earned net income, its board of directors may declare and pay a cash dividend to the stockholders. The entry on January 15, 19X2, to record the declaration of a $35,000 dividend is

Jan. 15	Retained Earnings	35,000	
	Dividends Payable		35,000
	To declare a cash dividend.		

After the dividend declaration is posted, the Retained Earnings account has a $65,000 credit balance:

Retained Earnings

Jan. 15, 19X2	Dividend	35,000	Jan. 1, 19X2		Bal.	100,000
			Jan. 15, 19X2		Bal.	65,000

Discussion Question: Dividends are a distribution of assets or stock by a corporation to its owners. Why does a corporation usually not pay its entire amount of income as dividends? ANSWER: 1. The corporation may not have the cash to pay out the entire amount. 2. Income increases capital and assets. If no income and assets are retained for reinvestment in the business, the company will have to use other means to expand.

Discussion Question: Does the declaration or the payment of dividends represent an expense of the corporation? ANSWER: No. Neither involves an expense or an income statement account. Dividends are never an expense.

The Retained Earnings account is not a reservoir of cash waiting for the board of directors to pay dividends to the stockholders. Instead, Retained Earnings is an owners' equity account representing a claim on all assets in general and not on any asset in particular. Its balance is the cumulative, lifetime earnings of the company less its cumulative losses and dividends. In fact, the corporation may have a large balance in Retained Earnings but not have the cash to pay a dividend. Why? Because the company purchased a building. The company may have abundant cash from borrowing but very little retained earnings. To *declare* a dividend, the company must have an adequate balance in Retained Earnings. To *pay* the dividend, it must have the cash. Cash and Retained Earnings are two entirely separate accounts having no necessary relationship.

Stock Dividends

A **stock dividend** is a proportional distribution by a corporation of its own stock to its stockholders. Stock dividends are fundamentally different from cash dividends because stock dividends do not transfer the assets of the corporation to the stockholders. Cash dividends are distributions of the asset cash, but stock dividends cause changes *only* in the stockholders' equity of the corporation. The effect of a stock dividend is an increase in the stock account and a decrease in Retained Earnings. Because both of these accounts are elements of stockholders' equity, total stockholders' equity is unchanged. There is merely a transfer from one stockholders' equity account to another, and no asset or liability is affected by a stock dividend.

The corporation distributes stock dividends to stockholders in proportion to the number of shares they already own. For example, suppose you owned 300 shares of Xerox Corporation common stock. If Xerox distributed a 10 percent common stock dividend, you would receive 30 (300 × .10) additional shares. You would now own 330 shares of the stock. All other Xerox stockholders would receive additional shares equal to 10 percent of their prior holdings. You would all be in the same relative position after the dividend as you were before.

In distributing a stock dividend, the corporation gives up no assets. Why, then, do companies issue stock dividends?

Reasons for Stock Dividends

A corporation may choose to distribute stock dividends for these reasons:

1. To continue dividends but conserve cash. A company may want to keep cash in the business in order to expand, buy inventory, pay off debts, and so on. Yet the company may wish to continue dividends in some form. To do so, the corporation may distribute a stock dividend. The debit to Retained Earnings indirectly conserves cash by decreasing the Retained Earnings available for the declaration of future cash dividends. Stockholders pay tax on cash dividends but not on stock dividends.

2. To reduce the market price per share of its stock. Many companies pay low cash dividends and grow by reinvesting their earnings in operations. As they grow, the company's stock price increases. If the price gets high enough, eventually some potential investors may be prevented from purchasing the stock. Distribution of a stock dividend may cause the market price of a share of the company's stock to decrease because of the increased supply of the stock.

Suppose the market price of a share of stock is $50. If the corporation doubles the number of shares of its stock outstanding by issuing a stock dividend, the market price of the stock would drop by approximately one-half, to $25 per share. The objective is to make the stock less expensive and thus attractive to a wider range of investors.

Entries for Stock Dividends

The board of directors announces stock dividends on the declaration date. The date of record and the distribution date follow. (This is the same sequence of dates used for a cash dividend.) The declaration of a stock dividend does *not* create a liability because the corporation is not obligated to pay assets. (Recall that a liability is a claim on *assets*.) Instead, the corporation has declared its intention to distribute its stock. Assume General Lumber Corporation has the following stockholders' equity prior to the dividend:

Stockholders' Equity

Paid-in capital:
Common stock, $10 par, 50,000 shares authorized,	
20,000 shares issued	$200,000
Paid-in capital in excess of par—common	70,000
Total paid-in capital	270,000
Retained earnings	85,000
Total stockholders' equity	$355,000

The entry to record a stock dividend depends on the size of the dividend. Generally accepted accounting principles (GAAP) distinguish between **small stock dividends** (less than 25 percent of the corporation's issued stock) and **large stock dividends** (25 percent or more of issued stock). Stock dividends between 20 percent and 25 percent are rare.

Assume General Lumber Corporation declares a 10 percent (small) common stock dividend on November 17. The company will distribute 2,000 (20,000 × .10) shares in the dividend. On November 17 the market value of its common stock is $16 per share. GAAP requires small stock dividends to be accounted for at market value. Therefore, Retained Earnings is debited for the market value of the 2,000 dividend shares. Common Stock Dividend Distributable is credited for par value, and Paid-in Capital in Excess of Par is credited for the remainder. General Lumber makes the following entry on the declaration date:[1]

Nov. 17	Retained Earnings (20,000 × .10 × $16)	32,000	
	Common Stock Dividend Distributable		
	(20,000 × .10 × $10)		20,000
	Paid-in Capital in Excess of Par—		
	Common		12,000
	To declare a 10 percent common stock dividend.		

---

[1]Committee on Accounting Procedure, "Accounting Research Bulletin No. 43," *Restatement and Revision of Accounting Research Bulletins* (New York: AICPA, 1961), Chap. 7, Sec. B, pars. 10–14.

On the distribution (payment) date, the company records issuance of the dividend shares as follows:

Dec. 12	Common Stock Dividend Distributable...... 20,000	
	Common Stock	20,000
	To issue common stock in a stock dividend.	

Common Stock Dividend Distributable is an owner's equity account. (It is *not* a liability because the corporation has no obligation to pay assets.) If the company prepares financial statements after the declaration of the stock dividend but before issuing it, Common Stock Dividend Distributable is reported in the stockholders' equity section of the balance sheet immediately after Common Stock and Common Stock Subscribed and before Paid-in Capital in Excess of Par—Common. However, this account holds the par value of the dividend shares only from the declaration date to the date of distribution.

The following tabulation shows the changes in stockholders' equity caused by the stock dividend:

Stockholders' Equity	Before the Dividend	After the Dividend	Change
Paid-in capital:			
Common stock, $10 par,			
50,000 shares authorized,			
20,000 shares issued	$200,000		
22,000 shares issued		$220,000	**Up by $20,000**
Paid-in capital in excess of			
par—common	70,000	82,000	**Up by $12,000**
Total paid-in capital	270,000	302,000	**Up by $32,000**
Retained earnings	85,000	53,000	**Down by $32,000**
Total stockholders' equity .	$355,000	$355,000	**Unchanged**

Compare stockholders' equity before and after the stock dividend. Observe the increase in the balances of Common Stock and Paid-in Capital in Excess of Par—Common and the decrease in Retained Earnings. Also observe that total stockholders' equity is unchanged from $355,000.

Amount of Retained Earnings Transferred in a Stock Dividend.   Stock dividends are said to be *capitalized retained earnings* because they transfer an amount from retained earnings to paid-in capital. The paid-in capital accounts are more permanent than retained earnings because they are not subject to dividends. As we saw in the preceding illustration, the amount transferred from Retained Earnings in a *small* stock dividend is the market value of the dividend shares because the effect on the market price of each share of the company's stock is likely to be small. Therefore, many stockholders view small stock dividends as distributions little different from cash dividends.

A *large* stock dividend, though, significantly increases the number of shares available in the market and so is likely to decrease the stock price significantly. Because of the drop in market price per share, a large stock dividend is not likely to be perceived as a dividend. GAAP does not require that large stock dividends be accounted for at a specific amount. A common practice is to use the par value of the dividend shares.

Suppose General Lumber declared a 50 percent common stock dividend. The declaration entry is

Dec. 7   Retained Earnings (20,000 × .50 × $10 par) .   100,000
                 Common Stock Dividend Distributable.   100,000
              To declare a 50 percent common stock dividend.

Issuance of the dividend shares on the payment date is recorded by this entry:

Dec. 22   Common Stock Dividend Distributable   100,000
                 Common Stock   100,000
              To issue common stock in a stock dividend.

Once again, total stockholders' equity is unchanged. For a large stock dividend, the increase in Common Stock is exactly offset by the decrease in Retained Earnings.

Stock Splits

Real-World Example: Some corporations have split their stock several times. Oneida, the silverware manufacturer, has declared one 5-for-1 split and three 5-for-4 stock splits. In addition, Oneida declared a 10% stock dividend in 1989.

Transparency T15-1

A large stock *dividend* may decrease the market price of the stock. The stock then becomes attractive to more people. A stock *split* also decreases the market price of stock—with the intention of making the stock more attractive. A **stock split** is an increase in the number of authorized, issued, and outstanding shares of stock coupled with a proportionate reduction in the par value of the stock. For example, if the company splits its stock 2 for 1, the number of outstanding shares is doubled and each share's par value is halved. Most leading companies in the United States—IBM, Ford Motor Company, Borg-Warner Corporation, Giant Food, Inc., and others—have split their stock.

Assume that the market price of a share of IBM common stock is $120 and that the company wishes to decrease the market price to approximately $30. IBM decides to split the common stock 4 for 1 in order to reduce the stock's market price from $120 to $30. A 4-for-1 stock split means that the company would have four times as many shares of stock outstanding after the split as it had before and that each share's par value would be quartered. Assume IBM had 150 million shares of $5 par common stock issued and outstanding before the split.

Teaching Tip: Students can often grasp a 2-for-1 stock split, but have trouble with more complicated ratios. Try this example: A company with 20,000 shares of $10 par common stock issued and outstanding declares a 5-for-4 stock split. The new number of shares issued would be 25,000 (20,000 × 5/4), and the new par value would be $8 ($10 × 4/5). Total par value outstanding remains the same:

20,000 shares × $10 par = $200,000

25,000 shares × $8 par = $200,000

Discussion Question: Why would a company want to decrease the price of its stock? ANSWER: Reducing the stock price increases the pool of potential investors. If the stock price is too high, some people may not be able or willing to buy it.

Stockholders' Equity	($ Millions)
Paid-in capital:	
Common stock, **$5 par**, 900 million shares authorized, **150 million shares issued**	$ 750
Paid-in capital in excess of par—common	5,200
Total paid-in capital	5,950
Retained earnings	20,000
Total stockholders' equity	$25,950

After the 4-for-1 stock split, IBM would have 3,600 million shares authorized and 600 million shares (150 million shares × 4) of $1.25 par ($5/4) common stock issued and outstanding. Total stockholders' equity would be exactly as before the stock split. Indeed, the balance in the Common Stock account does not even change. Only the par value of the stock and the number of shares authorized and issued change. Compare the highlighted figures in the two stockholders' equity presentations.

Paid-in capital:		
Common stock, **$1.25 par, 3,600 million shares authorized,**		
600 million shares issued	$	750
Paid-in capital in excess of par—common		5,200
Total paid-in capital		5,950
Retained earnings		20,000
Total stockholders' equity		$25,950

Because the stock split affects no account balances, no formal journal entry is necessary. Instead, the split is recorded in a memorandum entry such as the following:

Aug. 19   Called in the outstanding $5 par common stock and distributed four shares of $1.25 par common stock for each old share previously outstanding.

A company may engage in a reverse split to decrease the number of shares of stock outstanding. For example, IBM could split its stock 1 for 4. After the split, par value would be $20 ($5 × 4), shares authorized would be 225 million (900 million/4), and shares issued and outstanding would be 37.5 million (150 million/4). Reverse splits are rare.

Stock Dividends and Stock Splits

A stock dividend and a stock split both increase the number of shares of stock owned per stockholder. Also, neither a stock dividend nor a stock split changes the investor's total cost of the stock owned. For example, assume you paid $3,000 to acquire 150 shares of Avon Products common stock. If Avon distributes a 100 percent stock dividend, your 150 shares increase to 300, but your total cost is still $3,000. Likewise, if Avon distributes a 2-for-1 stock split, your shares increase in number to 300, but your total cost is unchanged. Neither type of stock action is taxable income to the investor.

Both a stock dividend and a stock split increase the corporation's number of shares outstanding. For example, a 100 percent stock dividend and a 2-for-1 stock split both double the outstanding shares and cut the stock's market price per share in half. They differ in that a stock *dividend* shifts an amount from retained earnings to paid-in capital, leaving par value per share unchanged. A stock *split* affects no account balances whatsoever but instead changes the par value of the stock. It also increases the number of shares authorized.

Exhibit 15-1 summarizes the effects of dividends and stock splits on total stockholders' equity.

EXHIBIT 15-1   *Effects of Dividends and Stock Splits on Total Stockholders' Equity*

	Declaration	Payment of Cash or Distribution of Stock
Cash dividend	Decrease	None
Stock dividend	None	None
Stock split	None	None

Source: Adapted from Beverly Terry.

Teaching Tip: Use these questions to review stock and cash dividends:

1 How is a stock dividend similar to a cash dividend? ANSWER: Both are a distribution to shareholders; both reduce Retained Earnings.

2 What happens to total paid-in capital as a result of cash and stock dividends? ANSWER: No change with a cash dividend; increase with a stock dividend (by the same amount that Retained Earnings decreases).

3 What happens to total stockholders' equity as a result of cash and stock dividends? ANSWER: Decrease with cash dividend; no change with stock dividend.

4 Which type of dividend gives taxable income to the shareholder? ANSWER: Cash dividend only.

OBJECTIVE 2
Distinguish stock splits from stock dividends

Teaching Tip: Use this chart to help compare a stock split and a large stock dividend.

Stock Split
Changes the number of shares authorized, issued, outstanding, and in the treasury.
Decreases par value and market value.
Does *not* change the balance of Common Stock.
Does *not* change total stockholders' equity.

Large Stock Dividend
Does *not* change the number of authorized shares. Increases the number of shares issued and outstanding.
Does *not* change the par value.
Decreases the market value.
Increases the balance of Common Stock.
Does *not* change total stockholders' equity.

Treasury Stock

Corporations may purchase their own stock from their shareholders for several reasons. (1) The company may have issued all its authorized stock and need the stock for distributions to officers and employees under bonus plans or stock purchase plans. (2) The purchase may help support the stock's current market price by decreasing the supply of stock available to the public. (3) The business may be trying to increase net assets by buying its shares low and hoping to sell them for a higher price later. (4) Management may gather in the stock to avoid a takeover by an outside party.

A corporation's own stock that it has issued and later reacquired is called **treasury stock.**[2] (In effect, the corporation holds the stock in its treasury.) For practical purposes, treasury stock is like unissued stock: neither category of stock is outstanding in the hands of shareholders. The company does not receive cash dividends on its treasury stock, and treasury stock does not entitle the company to vote or to receive assets in liquidation. The difference between unissued stock and treasury stock is that treasury stock has been issued and bought back.

The purchase of treasury stock decreases the company's assets and its stockholders' equity. The size of the company literally decreases, as shown on the balance sheet. The Treasury Stock account has a debit balance, which is the opposite of the other owners' equity accounts. Therefore, Treasury Stock is a contra stockholders' equity account.

Purchase of Treasury Stock

We record the purchase of treasury stock by debiting Treasury Stock and crediting the asset given in exchange—usually Cash. Suppose that Southwest Drilling Company had the following stockholders' equity before purchasing treasury stock:

Stockholders' Equity

Paid-in capital:
Common stock, $1 par, 10,000 shares authorized,
  8,000 shares issued . . . . $ 8,000
Paid-in capital in excess of par—common 12,000
  Total paid-in capital 20,000
Retained earnings 14,600
  Total stockholders' equity $34,600

On November 22 Southwest purchases 1,000 shares of its $1 par common as treasury stock, paying cash of $7.50 per share. Southwest records the purchase as follows:

Nov. 22 Treasury Stock, Common (1,000 × $7.50) 7,500
             Cash   7,500
             Purchased 1,000 shares of treasury stock at
             $7.50 per share.

Treasury stock is recorded at cost, without reference to the par value of the stock. The Treasury Stock account appears beneath retained earnings on the

---

[2]In this book we illustrate the *cost* method of accounting for treasury stock because it is used most widely. Alternative methods are presented in intermediate accounting courses.

balance sheet, and its balance is subtracted from the sum of total paid-in capital and retained earnings, as follows:

Stockholders' Equity

Paid-in capital:
Common stock, $1 par, 10,000 shares authorized,	
8,000 shares issued	$ 8,000
Paid-in capital in excess of par—common	12,000
Total paid-in capital	20,000
Retained earnings	14,600
Subtotal	34,600
Less Treasury stock (1,000 shares at cost)	(7,500)
Total stockholders' equity	$27,100

Observe that the purchase of treasury stock does not decrease the number of shares issued. The Common Stock, Paid-in Capital in Excess of Par, and Retained Earnings accounts remain unchanged. However, total stockholders' equity decreases by the cost of the treasury stock. Also, shares of stock *outstanding* decrease from 8,000 to 7,000. To compute the number of outstanding shares, subtract the treasury shares (1,000) from the shares issued (8,000). Although the number of outstanding shares is not required to be reported on the balance sheet, this figure is important. Only outstanding shares have a vote, receive cash dividends, and share in assets if the corporation liquidates.

Sale of Treasury Stock

Sale of Treasury Stock at Cost. Treasury stock may be sold at any price agreeable to the corporation and the purchaser. If the stock is sold for the same price that the corporation paid to reacquire it, the entry is a debit to Cash and a credit to Treasury Stock for the same amount.

Sale of Treasury Stock above Cost. If the sale price is greater than reacquisition cost, the difference is credited to the account Paid-in Capital from Treasury Stock Transactions. Suppose Southwest Drilling Company resold 200 of its treasury shares for $9 per share. The entry is

Dec. 7	Cash (200 × $9)	1,800	
	Treasury Stock, Common (200 × $7.50—		
	the purchase cost per share)		1,500
	Paid-in Capital from Treasury Stock		
	Transactions		300
	To sell 200 shares of treasury stock at $9 per share.		

Paid-in Capital from Treasury Stock Transactions is reported with the other paid-in capital accounts on the balance sheet, beneath the Common Stock and Capital in Excess of Par accounts.

Sale of Treasury Stock below Cost. At times the resale price is less than cost. The difference between these two amounts is debited to Paid-in Capital from Treasury Stock Transactions if this account has a credit balance, as in our example. If the difference between resale price and cost is greater than the credit balance in Paid-in Capital from Treasury Stock Transactions, or if Paid-in Capital from Treasury Stock Transactions has a zero balance, then the company debits Retained Earnings for the remaining amount. For example, South-

---

Point to Stress: Par value is irrelevant in treasury stock transactions. Treasury Stock is debited for the *cost* of the shares bought. When the shares are sold, the account is credited for the cost. Treasury stock transactions are different from other stock transactions that are based on par value.

Typical Student Misconception: Purchase of treasury stock does not decrease the Common Stock account. The Common Stock account is not used in treasury stock transactions, so its account balance will not change. Illustrate this point by asking students to answer the following question:

Jackson Products, Inc., issued 100,000 shares of $10 par value common stock. Later, when the market price was $15 per share, they distributed a 10% stock dividend. Then they purchased 500 shares of stock to hold in the treasury, at a cost of $20 a share. What is the balance in Common Stock? *ANSWER:* $1,100,000

100,000 shares × $10 = $1,000,000
plus 10% × 100,000 × $10 = 100,000
$1,100,000

Notice that the treasury stock was not used in the calculation because it does not affect the Common Stock account.

Point to Stress: The owners of callable preferred stock are required to sell their stock back to the issuing corporation at the call price stated on the stock certificate and registered with the SEC. Common stockholders are not required to sell their stock back to the corporation.

---

west Drilling records the sale of 400 shares of treasury stock at $5 per share in the following entry:

Dec. 23	Cash (400 × $5)	2,000	
	Paid-in Capital from Treasury Stock Transactions	300	
	Retained Earnings	700	
	Treasury Stock, Common (400 × $7.50— the purchase cost per share)		3,000
	To sell 400 shares of treasury stock at $5 per share.		

Paid-in Capital from Treasury Stock Transactions receives only a $300 debit because that is the extent of this account's credit balance. (See the preceding example illustrating the sale of treasury stock above cost.) The remaining $700 is debited to Retained Earnings.

No Gain or Loss from Treasury Stock Transactions

The purchase and sale of treasury stock do not affect net income. Sale of treasury stock above cost is an increase in paid-in capital, not income. Likewise, sale of treasury stock below cost is a decrease in paid-in capital or Retained Earnings, not a loss. Treasury stock transactions take place between the business and its owners, the stockholders. Because a company cannot earn a profit in dealing in its own stock with its owners, we credit Paid-in Capital from Treasury Stock Transactions for sale above cost and debit that account (and, if necessary, Retained Earnings) for a sale below cost. These accounts appear on the balance sheet, not on the income statement.

Does this mean that a company cannot increase its net assets by buying treasury stock low and selling it high? Not at all. Management often buys treasury stock because it believes the market price of its stock is too low. For example, a company may buy 500 shares of its stock at $10 per share. Suppose it holds the stock as the market price rises and resells the stock at $14 per share. Net assets of the company increase by $2,000 [500 shares × ($14 − $10 = $4 difference per share)]. This increase is reported as paid-in capital not as income.

Class Exercise: Record the purchase of 1,500 shares of $5 par common as treasury stock for $15 per share.
ANSWER:

Treasury Stock, Com.
  (1,500 × $15) 22,500
    Cash   22,500

Record the sale of treasury stock, 500 shares for $20 per share.
ANSWER:

Cash (500 × $20) ...10,000
  Treasury Stock,
    Common (500 ×
    $15)   7,500
  Paid-in Capital from
    Treasury Stock
    Transactions ...   2,500

Record the sale of the remaining 1,000 shares for $12 per share.
ANSWER:

Cash (1,000 × $12) .12,000
Paid-in Capital from
  Treasury Stock
  Transactions 2,500
Retained Earnings ..   500
  Treasury Stock,
    Common   15,000

Summary Problem for Your Review

Simplicity Pattern Co., Inc., reported the following stockholders' equity:

Shareholders' Equity	($ Thousands)
Preferred stock, $1.00 par value	
Authorized − 10,000,000 shares	
Issued None	$ —
Common stock, 8 ⅓ cents par value	
Authorized, 30,000,000 shares	
Issued 13,733,229 shares	1,144
Capital in excess of par value	48,122
Earnings retained in business	89,320
	138,586
Less treasury stock, at cost (1,919,000 common shares)	14,742
	$123,844

Required

1. What was the average issue price per share of the common stock?
2. Journalize the issuance of 1,200 shares of common stock at $4 per share. Use Simplicity's account titles.
3. How many shares of Simplicity's common stock are outstanding?
4. How many shares of common stock would be outstanding after Simplicity split its common stock 3 for 1?
5. Using Simplicity account titles, journalize the declaration of a stock dividend when the market price of Simplicity common stock is $3 per share. Consider each of the following stock dividends independently:
   a. Simplicity declares a 10 percent common stock dividend on the shares outstanding, computed in 3.
   b. Simplicity declares a 100 percent common stock dividend on the shares outstanding, computed in 3.
6. Journalize the following treasury stock transactions, assuming they occur in the order given:
   a. Simplicity purchases 500 shares of treasury stock at $8 per share.
   b. Simplicity sells 100 shares of treasury stock for $9 per share.
   c. Simplicity sells 100 shares of treasury stock for $5 per share.

SOLUTION TO SUMMARY PROBLEM

1. Average issue price of the common stock was $3.59 per share [($1,144,000 + $48,122,000)/13,733,229 shares = $3.59].

2.
Cash (1,200 × $4)	4,800	
Common Stock (1,200 × $.08 1/3)		100
Capital in Excess of Par Value		4,700

To issue common stock at a premium.

3. Shares outstanding = 11,814,229 (13,733,229 shares issued minus 1,919,000 shares of treasury stock)

4. Shares outstanding after a 3-for-1 stock split = 35,442,687 (11,814,229 shares outstanding × 3)

5a.
Earnings Retained in Business (11,814,229 × .10 × $3)	3,544,269	
Common Stock Dividend Distributable (11,814,229 × .10 × $.08 1/3)		98,452
Capital in Excess of Par Value		3,445,817

To declare a 10 percent common stock dividend.

b.
Earnings Retained in Business (11,814,229 × $.08 1/3)	984,519	
Common Stock Dividend Distributable		984,519

To declare a 100 percent common stock dividend.

6a.
Treasury Stock (500 × $8)	4,000	
Cash		4,000

To purchase 500 shares of treasury stock at $8 per share.

b.
Cash (100 × $9)	900	
Treasury Stock (100 × $8)		800
Paid-in Capital from Treasury Stock Transactions		100

To sell 100 shares of treasury stock at $9 per share.

c. Cash (100 × $5)   500
   Paid-in Capital from Treasury Stock   100
     Transactions (balance from answer 6b) ...
   Earnings Retained in Business   200
     Treasury Stock (100 × $8)   800
   To sell 100 shares of treasury stock at $5 per share.

Retirement of Stock

A corporation may purchase its own common stock or preferred stock and retire it by canceling the stock certificates. The retired stock cannot be reissued. Companies usually retire their stock in order to replace it with another issue of stock or to liquidate shares when they go out of business. Retiring stock, like purchasing treasury stock, decreases the outstanding stock of the corporation. Unlike a treasury stock purchase, stock retirement decreases the number of shares issued. Assets are decreased by the amount paid to buy the shares being retired. In retiring stock, the corporation removes the balances from all paid-in capital amounts related to the retired shares, like Capital in Excess of Par.

A corporation may repurchase shares for retirement for a price that is below the stock's issue price (par value plus any capital in excess of par). This difference between purchase price and issue price is a credit to Paid-in Capital from Retirement of Common Stock (or Preferred Stock).

Assume that a corporation issued its $10 par common stock for $14, a $4 premium per share. If the company later purchases 500 shares of the stock for retirement at $13 per share, the retirement entry is

May 22 Common Stock (500 × $10)..................   5,000
     Paid-in Capital in Excess of Par—Common
       (500 × $4)   2,000
       Cash (500 × $13)   6,500
       Paid-in Capital from Retirement of
        Common Stock   500
    To purchase and retire common stock.

Paid-in Capital from Retirement of Common Stock is reported after Capital in Excess of Par—Common, along with any other paid-in capital accounts related to the common.

If the corporation must pay more for the stock than its issue price, the excess is debited to Retained Earnings. Assume the corporation paid $16 per share to purchase the stock for retirement. The entry is

May 22 Common Stock (500 × $10)..................   5,000
     Paid-in Capital in Excess of Par—Common
       (500 × $4)   2,000
     Retained Earnings   1,000
       Cash (500 × $16)   8,000
    To purchase and retire common stock.

Retiring stock, like purchasing stock, is a transaction that does not affect net income. No gain or loss arises from stock retirement because the company is doing business with its owners. The entries we presented in illustrating stock retirement affect *balance sheet accounts*, not income statement accounts.

Point to Stress: When a company retires stock, it purchases its own outstanding stock and cancels the stock certificates. The numbers of shares issued and outstanding both decrease.

Class Exercise: Suppose a company retires 1,000 shares of its $1 par common stock that was originally issued for $18 a share. Record the retirement of the stock at $12 per share.
ANSWER:
Common Stock
  (1,000 × $1) 1,000
Paid-in Capital in Excess
  of Par—Common
  (1,000 × $17) 17,000
    Cash (1,000 × 12)... 12,000
    Paid-in Capital from
    Retirement of
    Common Stock 6,000

Record the retirement of the stock at $20 per share.
ANSWER:
Common Stock
  (1,000 × $1) 1,000
Paid-in Capital in Excess
  of Par—Common
  (1,000 × $17) 17,000
Retained Earnings .. 2,000
    Cash (1,000 × $20).... 20,000

Point to Stress: Net income (or net loss) and dividends are the main items that affect Retained Earnings. However, other transactions can *reduce* Retained Earnings. Treasury stock transactions and the retirement of stock are two examples. The only other type of transaction that can increase Retained Earnings is a prior period adjustment (discussed at the end of this chapter).

Restrictions on Retained Earnings

Dividends, purchases of treasury stock, and retirements of stock require payments by the corporation to its stockholders. In fact, treasury stock purchases and stock retirements are returns of paid-in capital to the stockholders. These outlays decrease the corporation's assets, so fewer assets are available to pay liabilities. Therefore, its creditors seek to restrict a corporation's dividend payments and treasury stock purchases. For example, a bank may agree to loan $500,000 only if the borrowing corporation limits dividend payments and purchases of its stock.

To ensure that corporations maintain a minimum level of stockholders' equity for the protection of creditors, state laws restrict the amount of its own stock that a corporation may purchase. The maximum amount a corporation can pay its stockholders without decreasing paid-in capital is its balance of retained earnings. Therefore, restrictions on dividends and stock purchases focus on the balance of retained earnings.

Companies usually report their retained earnings restrictions in notes to the financial statements. The following actual disclosure by RTE Corporation, a manufacturer of electronic transformers, is typical:

> **NOTES TO CONSOLIDATED FINANCIAL STATEMENTS**
> **NOTE F—LONG-TERM DEBT**
>
> The . . . loan agreements . . . restrict cash dividends and similar payments to shareholders. Under the most restrictive of these provisions, retained earnings of $4,300,000 were unrestricted as of December 31, 19X3.

In another actual example, Chromalloy American Corporation could not declare dividends, purchase treasury stock, or purchase stock for retirement, as indicated by its Note 8:

> **NOTES TO CONSOLIDATED FINANCIAL STATEMENTS**
> **8: LONG-TERM DEBT**
>
> The Company's loan agreements contain covenants which restrict the declaration or payment of cash dividends and the purchase . . . or retirement of capital stock. At December 31, 19X3, . . . all of the Company's [retained] earnings were restricted due to these covenants.

Appropriations of Retained Earnings

Appropriations are restrictions of Retained Earnings that are recorded by formal journal entries. A corporation may appropriate—segregate in a separate account—a portion of Retained Earnings for a specific use. For example, the board of directors may appropriate part of Retained Earnings for building a new manufacturing plant, for meeting possible future liabilities, or for other reasons. A debit to Retained Earnings and a credit to a separate account—Retained Earnings Appropriated for Plant Expansion—records the appropriation. This appropriated retained earnings account appears directly above the regular Retained Earnings account on the balance sheet.

An appropriation does *not* decrease total retained earnings. Any appropriated amount is simply a portion of retained earnings that is earmarked for a particular purpose. When the need for the appropriation no longer exists, an entry debits the Retained Earnings Appropriated account and credits Retained

Earnings. This entry closes the Appropriation account and returns its amount back to the regular Retained Earnings account.

Retained earnings appropriations are rare. Corporations generally disclose any retained earnings restrictions in the notes to the financial statements as illustrated in the preceding section. The notes give the corporation more room to describe the nature and amounts of any restrictions. Thus corporations satisfy the requirement for adequate disclosure.

Disclosing any restriction on retained earnings is important to stockholders and possible investors because the restricted amounts may not be used for dividends. A corporation with a $100,000 balance in Retained Earnings and a $60,000 restriction may declare a maximum dividend of $40,000—if the cash is available and the board of directors so decides.

Real-World Example: Of the 600 companies surveyed in *Accounting Trends and Techniques,* 434 companies reported dividend restrictions, primarily to protect creditors.

Variations in Reporting Stockholders' Equity

Real-world accounting and business practices may use terminology and formats in reporting stockholders' equity that differ from our general examples. We use a more detailed format in this book to help you learn the components of the stockholders' equity section. Companies assume that readers of their statements already understand the omitted details.

One of the most important skills you will learn in this course is the ability to understand the financial statements of actual companies. Thus we present in Exhibit 15-2 a side-by-side comparison of our general teaching format and the format that you are more likely to encounter in real-world balance sheets. Note the following points in the real-world format:

1. The heading Paid-in Capital does not appear. It is commonly understood that Preferred Stock, Common Stock, and Additional Paid-in Capital are elements of paid-in capital.
2. Preferred stock is often reported in a single amount that combines its par value and premium.
3. For presentation in the financial statements, all additional paid-in capital—from capital in excess of par on common stock, treasury stock transactions, stock retirement, and donated capital—appears as a single amount labeled Additional Paid-in Capital. Additional Paid-in Capital belongs to the common stockholders, and so it follows Common Stock in the real-world format.
4. Often, total stockholders' equity ($4,053,000 in the exhibit) is not specifically labeled.

Teaching Tip: Send students to the library to read an annual report and note how many shares of common stock are issued, the par value, the number of treasury shares, and any other fact that you consider important. Stress that each annual report will be differently presented. Students must understand the stockholders' equity section. They must be able to apply the principles taught in this text in order to understand the financial position of real-life companies.

Corporation Income Statement

A corporation's net income receives more attention than any other item in the financial statements. Net income measures the business's ability to earn a profit and answers the question of how successfully the company has managed its operations. To stockholders, the larger the corporation's profit, the greater the likelihood of dividends. To creditors, the larger the corporation's profit, the better able it is to pay its debts. Net income builds up a company's assets and owners' equity. It also helps to attract capital from new investors who hope to receive dividends from future successful operations.

Suppose you are considering investing in the stock of two manufacturing companies. In reading their annual reports and examining their past records,

Point to Stress: Businesses operate to generate profits; without profits a business will not exist for long. The main source of income for a business must be from regular, continuing operations, not from miscellaneous sources such as selling off a segment of the business.

Transparency T15-3

EXHIBIT 15-2 *Formats for Reporting Stockholders' Equity*

General Teaching Format		Real-World Format	

Stockholders' equity

Paid-in capital:

Preferred stock, 8%, $10 par, 30,000 shares authorized and issued ..	$300,000		
Paid-in capital in excess of par—preferred	10,000		

Common stock, $1 par, 100,000 shares authorized, 60,000 shares issued	60,000

Paid-in capital in excess of par—common	1,940,000
Paid-in capital from treasury stock transactions, common	9,000
Paid-in capital from retirement of preferred stock	11,000
Donated capital-plant site	200,000

Total paid-in capital	2,530,000
Retained earnings appropriated for contingencies	400,000
Retained earnings-unappropriated .	1,165,000
Total retained earnings	1,565,000
Subtotal	4,095,000
Less treasury stock, common (1,400 shares at cost)............	(42,000)
Total stockholders' equity	$4,053,000

Real-World Format

Stockholders' equity

Preferred stock, 8%, $10 par, 30,000 shares authorized and issued ...	$ 310,000
Common stock, $1 par, 100,000 shares authorized, 60,000 shares issued	60,000
Additional paid-in capital.........	2,160,000
Retained earnings (Note 7)	1,565,000
Less treasury stock, common (1,400 shares at cost)	(42,000)
	$4,053,000

Note 7—Restriction on retained earnings.
At December 31, 19XX, $400,000 of retained earnings is restricted by the company's board of directors to absorb the effect of any contingencies that may arise. Accordingly, possible dividend declarations are restricted to a maximum of $1,165,000 ($1,565,000 − $400,000).

Point to Stress: The income tax expense item listed separately on the income statement relates solely to income from continuing operations. Therefore, the tax effect of the discontinued segment's operating income or loss is not included in income tax expense; rather, it is deducted in the discontinued operations part of the income statement.

Point to Stress: Refer to the chapter-opening vignette. The losses of this company were not a part of their continuing operations, and therefore should be separated from ongoing operations such as sales and salaries.

you learn that the companies showed the same net income figure for last year and that each company has increased its net income by 15 percent annually over the last five years. You observe, however, that the two companies have generated income in different ways.

Company A's income has resulted from the successful management of its central operations (manufacturing). Company B's manufacturing operations have been flat for two years. Its growth in net income has resulted from selling off segments of its business at a profit. Which company would you invest in?

Company A holds the promise of better future earnings. This corporation earns profits from continuing operations. We may reasonably expect the business to match its past earnings in the future. Company B shows no growth from operations. Its net income results from one-time transactions, the selling off of its operating assets. Sooner or later, Company B will have sold off the last of its assets used in operations. When that occurs, the business will have no means of generating income. Based on this reasoning, your decision is to invest in the stock of Company A.

This example points to two important investment considerations: the *trend* of a company's earnings and the *makeup* of its net income. More intelligent investment decisions are likely if the income statement separates the results of central, continuing operations from special, one-time gains and losses. We now discuss the components of the corporation income statement. We will see how the income statement reports the results of operations in a manner that allows statement users to get a good look at the business's operations. Exhibit 15-3 will be used throughout these discussions. The items of primary interest are highlighted for emphasis.

Continuing Operations

We have seen that income from a business's continuing operations helps financial statement users make predictions about the business's future earnings. In the income statement of Exhibit 15-3, the topmost section reports income from continuing operations. This part of the business is expected to continue from period to period. We may use this information to predict that Electronics Corporation will earn income of approximately $54,000 next year.

EXHIBIT 15-3 *Corporation Income Statement*

Electronics Corporation Income Statement For the Year Ended December 31, 19X5		
Sales revenue		$500,000
Cost of goods sold		240,000
Gross margin		260,000
Operating expenses (detailed)		181,000
Operating income		79,000
Other gains (losses)		
Gain on sale of machinery		11,000
Income from continuing operations before income tax		90,000
Income tax expense		36,000
Income from continuing operations		54,000
Discontinued operations:		
Operating income, $30,000,		
less income tax of $12,000	$18,000	
Gain on disposal, $5,000,		
less income tax of $2,000	3,000	21,000
Income before extraordinary item and cumulative		
effect of change in depreciation method		75,000
Extraordinary flood loss, $20,000,		
less income tax saving of $8,000		(12,000)
Cumulative effect of change in depreciation		
method, $10,000, less income tax of $4,000		6,000
Net income		$ 69,000
Earnings per share of common stock (20,000 shares outstanding):		
Income from continuing operations		$2.70
Income from discontinued operations		1.05
Income before extraordinary item and cumulative		
effect of change in depreciation method		3.75
Extraordinary loss		(.60)
Cumulative effect of change in depreciation method		.30
Net income		$3.45

Operating loss,
   $480,000, less
   income tax savings,
   $144,000 ....$(336,000)
Gain on disposal,
   $850,000, less
   income tax,
   $255,000   595,000
                        $259,000

Discussion Question: Would an earthquake be extraordinary? ANSWER: Yes, except in California. Would a tornado be extraordinary? ANSWER: Yes, except in those states with frequent tornadoes. Would a fire loss be extraordinary? ANSWER: Not unless it results from an extraordinary event. Most businesses are insured against loss by fire.

Real-World Example: Russ Togs, Inc., reported an agreement to postpone commencement of its new chief executive's employment for 60 days in exchange for $2,500,000 from the executive's former employer. Russ Togs recorded the $2,500,000 compensation payment as an extraordinary gain.

Point to Stress: Three criteria must be met before an item is considered extraordinary and will be shown separately below discontinued operations on the income statement. The gain or loss must be (1) infrequent, (2) unusual, and (3) material.

Note that income tax expense has been deducted in arriving at income from continuing operations. The tax that corporations pay on their income is a significant expense. The federal income tax rate for corporations varies from time to time, and the current maximum rate is 34 percent. For computational ease, let's use an income tax rate of 40 percent in our illustrations. This is a reasonable estimate of combined federal and state income taxes. The $36,000 income tax expense in Exhibit 15-3 equals the pretax income from continuing operations multiplied by the tax rate ($90,000 × .40 = $36,000).

Discontinued Operations

Most large corporations engage in several lines of business. For example, General Mills, Inc., best known for its food products, also has retailing and restaurant operations. Sears, Roebuck & Co., in addition to its retail stores, has a real estate subsidiary, an insurance company, and a savings and loan enterprise. We call each significant part of a company a **segment of the business.**

A company may sell a segment of its business. Such a sale is not a regular source of income because a company cannot keep on selling its segments indefinitely. The sale of a business segment is viewed as a one-time transaction. The income statement carries information on the segment that has been disposed of under the heading Discontinued Operations. This section of the income statement is divided into two components: (1) operating income or (loss) on the segment that is disposed of and (2) any gain (or loss) on the disposal. Income and gain are taxed at the 40 percent rate and reported as follows:

Discontinued operations:
Operating income, $30,000, less income tax,
   $12,000..................................... $18,000
Gain on disposal, $5,000, less income tax, $2,000 .   3,000
                                                  $21,000

Trace this presentation to Exhibit 15-3.

It is necessary to separate discontinued operations into these two components because the company may operate the discontinued segment for part of the year. This is the operating income (or loss) component. Then, usually a gain (or loss) on the disposal of the segment occurs.

Discontinued operations are common in business. The Black and Decker Manufacturing Company disposed of its gasoline chain saw business. Purolator, Inc., sold its armored-car segment, and RJR Nabisco disposed of its fast-food business, including Kentucky Fried Chicken. Each of these items was disclosed as discontinued operations in the company's income statement.

Extraordinary Gains and Losses

Extraordinary gains and losses, also called extraordinary items, are both unusual for the company and infrequent. Losses from natural disasters (like earthquakes, floods, and tornadoes), and the taking of company assets by a foreign government (expropriation), are extraordinary.

Extraordinary items are reported along with their income tax effect. Assume Electronics Corporation lost $20,000 of inventory in a flood. This flood loss, which reduces income, also reduces the company's income tax. The tax effect of the loss is computed by multiplying the amount of the loss by the tax rate. The tax effect decreases the net amount of the loss in the same way that the tax effect of income reduces the amount of net income. An extraordinary loss can be reported along with its tax effect as follows:

Extraordinary flood loss	$(20,000)	
Less income tax saving	8,000	$(12,000)

Trace this item to the income statement in Exhibit 15-3. An extraordinary gain is reported the same way, net of the income tax on the gain.

Gains and losses due to employee strikes, the settlement of lawsuits, discontinued operations, and the sale of plant assets are *not* extraordinary items. They are considered normal business occurrences. However, because they are outside the business's central operations, they are reported on the income statement as other gains and losses. An example is the gain on sale of machinery in Exhibit 15-3.

Cumulative Effect of a Change in Accounting Principle

Companies sometimes change from one accounting method to another, such as from double-declining-balance (DDB) to straight-line depreciation, or from FIFO to weighted-average cost for inventory. An accounting change makes it difficult to compare one period's financial statements with the statements of preceding periods. Without detailed information, investors and creditors can be led to believe the current year is better or worse than the preceding year when in fact the only difference is a change in accounting method. To help investors separate the effects of business operations from those effects generated by a change in accounting method, companies report the effect of the accounting change in a special section of the income statement. The section usually appears after extraordinary items.

A relevant aspect of the accounting change is the cumulative effect on net income of prior years. GAAP requires companies that change accounting methods to disclose the difference between net income actually reported under the old method being discontinued and the net income that the company would have experienced if it had used the new method all along.

Suppose Electronics Corporation changed from DDB to straight-line depreciation at the beginning of 19X5. How will this affect the 19X5 financial statements? The change in depreciation method will have two consequences. The first consequence affects income from continuing operations, which will include the effect of 19X5 depreciation expense by the new method, straight-sine. The second consequence affects cumulative amounts from previous years. If the company had been using straight-line depreciation every year, net income would have been $6,000 higher ($10,000 less the additional income tax of $4,000). In this case the cumulative effect of the change increases net income. A change from straight-line to double-declining-balance would usually produce a negative cumulative effect.

Changes in inventory methods and changes in revenue methods are also generally reported in this manner. Numerous exceptions make changes in accounting principle—usually a change in accounting method—a complicated area. Details are covered in later accounting courses.

Earnings Per Share (EPS)

The final segment of a corporation income statement presents the company's earnings per share, abbreviated as EPS. In fact, GAAP requires that corporations disclose EPS figures on the income statement.

Earnings per share is the amount of a company's net income per share of its outstanding common stock. EPS is a key measure of a business's success. Consider a corporation with net income of $200,000 and 100,000 shares of common stock outstanding. Its EPS is $2 ($200,000/100,000). A second corporation may also have net income of $200,000 but only 50,000 shares of common stock outstanding. Its EPS is $4 ($200,000/50,000).

Just as the corporation lists separately its different sources of income—from continuing operations, discontinued operations, and so on—it lists separately the EPS figure based on different income sources. Consider that Electronics Corporation had $54,000 in income from continuing operations, $21,000 in income from discontinued operations, an extraordinary loss of $12,000, and a $6,000 cumulative effect of an accounting change. Net income was $69,000 ($54,000 + $21,000 − $12,000 + $6,000). Electronics had 20,000 common shares outstanding for the entire accounting period. The company's EPS is reported on the income statement as follows:

Earnings per share of common stock (20,000 shares outstanding):	
Income from continuing operations ($54,000/20,000)	$2.70
Income from discontinued operations ($21,000/20,000)	1.05
Income before extraordinary item and cumulative effect of	
change in depreciation method ($75,000/20,000)	3.75
Extraordinary loss ($12,000/20,000)	(.60)
Cumulative effect of change in depreciation method	
($6,000/20,000)	.30
Net income ($69,000/20,000)	$3.45

The income statement user can understand the nature of the business's EPS amounts when presented in this detail.

Exhibit 15-3 presents the detailed income statement of Electronics Corporation for the year ended December 31, 19X5. The income statement is in multiple-step format.

Weighted Average Number of Shares of Common Stock Outstanding. Computing EPS is straightforward if the number of common shares outstanding does not change over the entire accounting period. For many corporations, however, this figure varies over the course of the year. Consider a corporation that had 100,000 shares outstanding from January through November, then purchased 60,000 shares as treasury stock. This company's EPS would be misleadingly high if computed using 40,000 (100,000 − 60,000) shares. To make EPS as meaningful as possible, corporations use the weighted average number of common shares outstanding during the period.

Let's assume the following figures for Diskette Demo Corporation. From January through May the company had 240,000 shares of common stock outstanding; from June through August, 200,000 shares; and from September through December, 210,000 shares. We compute the weighted average by considering the outstanding shares per month as a fraction of the year:

Number of Common Shares Outstanding		Fraction of Year		Weighted Average Number of Common Shares Outstanding
240,000	×	5/12	(January through May)	= 100,000
200,000	×	3/12	(June through August)	= 50,000
210,000	×	4/12	(September through December)	= 70,000
			Weighted average number of common shares outstanding during the year	220,000

Point to Stress: A share outstanding for only half of the year will be equal to half of one share. A share outstanding for only three months will be equal to one-fourth of one share. Shares are weighted because a share outstanding for only a part of the year represents capital that could be used for only a part of the year to help generate income.

Class Exercise: Suppose that the net income of Multi Media, Inc., amounted to $3,750,000. Multi Media had 200,000 shares of 9%, $100 par preferred stock and 310,000 shares of common stock at the end of the year. At the beginning of the year, Multi Media had 270,000 shares outstanding and issued 40,000 shares on April 1. Calculate EPS. ANSWER:

Weighted average:
270,000 × 3/12 = 67,500
310,000 × 9/12 = 232,500
300,000 shares

$$EPS = \frac{\$3,750,000 - (200,000 \times \$100 \times 9\%)}{300,000 \text{ shares}}$$

$$= \frac{\$3,750,000 - \$1,800,000}{300,000}$$

$$= \$6.50$$

The 220,000 weighted average would be divided into net income to compute the corporation's EPS.

Preferred Dividends.   Throughout the EPS discussion we have used only the number of shares of common stock outstanding. Holders of preferred stock have no claim to the business's income beyond the stated preferred dividend. However, preferred dividends do affect the EPS figure. Recall that EPS is earnings per share of *common* stock. Also recall that dividends on preferred stock are paid first. Therefore, preferred dividends must be subtracted from income subtotals (income from continuing operations, income before extraordinary items, and net income) in the computation of EPS. Preferred dividends are not subtracted from income or loss from discontinued operations, and they are not subtracted from extraordinary gains and losses.

If Electronics Corporation had 10,000 shares of preferred stock outstanding, each with a $1.50 dividend, the annual preferred dividend would be $15,000 (10,000 × $1.50). The $15,000 would be subtracted from each of the different income subtotals, resulting in the following EPS computations for the company:

Earnings per share of common stock (20,000 shares outstanding):

Income from continuing operations ($54,000 − $15,000)/20,000	$1.95
Income from discontinued operations ($21,000/20,000)	1.05
Income before extraordinary item and cumulative effect of change in depreciation method ($75,000 − $15,000)/20,000	3.00
Extraordinary loss ($12,000/20,000)	(.60)
Cumulative effect of change in depreciation method ($6,000/20,000)	.30
Net income ($69,000 − $15,000)/20,000	$2.70

Dilution.   Some corporations make their preferred stock more attractive to investors by offering convertible preferred stock. Holders of convertible preferred may exchange the preferred stock for common stock. If in fact the preferred stock is converted to common stock, then the EPS will be *diluted—* reduced—because more common stock shares are divided into net income. Because convertible preferred can be traded in for common stock, the common stockholders want to know the amount of the decrease in EPS if the preferred stock is converted into common. To provide this information, corporations present two sets of EPS amounts: EPS based on outstanding common shares (primary EPS), and EPS based on outstanding common shares plus the number of additional common shares that would arise from conversion of the preferred stock into common (diluted EPS).

EPS is the most widely used accounting figure. Many income statement users place top priority on EPS. Also, a stock's market price is related to the company's EPS. By dividing the market price of a company's stock by its EPS, we compute a statistic called the price-to-earnings ratio. *The Wall Street Journal* reports the price-to-earnings ratios (listed as P/E) daily for more than 3,000 companies.

Real-World Example: Of the 600 companies surveyed by *Accounting Trends and Techniques,* only 34 reported no EPS dilution. Most corporations have potentially dilutive securities such as convertible preferred stock or stock options.

Statement of Retained Earnings _____

Retained earnings may be a significant portion of a corporation's owners' equity. The year's income increases the retained earnings balance, and dividends decrease it. Retained earnings are so important that corporations prepare a

Transparency T15-5

Point to Stress: Retained Earnings is also decreased by net losses. Both cash dividends and stock dividends decrease Retained Earnings.

financial statement to report the major changes in this equity account, much as the statement of owner's equity presents information on changes in the equity of a proprietorship. The statement of retained earnings for Electronics Corporation appears in Exhibit 15-4.

Some companies report income and retained earnings on a single statement. Exhibit 15-5 illustrates how Electronics would combine its income statement and its statement of retained earnings.

OBJECTIVE 6
Account for prior period adjustments

Prior Period Adjustments

What happens when a company makes an error in recording revenues or expenses? Detecting the error in the period in which it occurs allows the company to make a correction before preparing that period's financial statements.

EXHIBIT 15-4 *Statement of Retained Earnings*

Electronics Corporation Statement of Retained Earnings For the Year Ended December 31, 19X5	
Retained earnings balance, December 31, 19X4	$130,000
Net income for 19X5	69,000
	199,000
Dividends for 19X5	(21,000)
Retained earnings balance, December 31, 19X5	$178,000

EXHIBIT 15-5 *Statement of Income and Retained Earnings*

Electronics Corporation Statement of Income and Retained Earnings For the Year Ended December 31, 19X5	
Sales revenue	$500,000
Cost of goods sold	240,000
Net income for 19X5	69,000
Retained earnings, December 31, 19X4	130,000
	199,000
Dividends for 19X5	(21,000)
Retained earnings, December 31, 19X5	$178,000
Earnings per share of common stock (20,000 shares outstanding):	
Income from continuing operations	$2.70
Income from discontinued operations	1.05
Income before extraordinary item and cumulative effect of change in depreciation method . . .	3.75
Extraordinary loss	(.60)
Cumulative effect of change in depreciation method	.30
Net income	$3.45

But failure to detect the error until a later period means that the business will have reported an incorrect amount of income on its income statement. After closing the revenue and expense accounts, the Retained Earnings account will absorb the effect of the error, and its balance will be wrong until the error is corrected.

Corrections to the beginning balance of Retained Earnings for errors of an earlier period are called **prior period adjustments.** The correcting entry includes a debit or credit to Retained Earnings for the error amount and a debit or credit to the asset or liability account that was misstated. The prior period adjustment appears on the corporation's statement of retained earnings to indicate to readers the amount and the nature of the change in the Retained Earnings balance.

Assume that De Graff Corporation recorded income tax expense for 19X4 as $30,000. The correct amount was $40,000. This error resulted in understating 19X4 expenses by $10,000 and overstating net income by $10,000. A bill from the government in 19X5 for the additional $10,000 in taxes alerts the De Graff management to the mistake. The entry to record this prior period adjustment in 19X5 is

19X5			
June 19	Retained Earnings	10,000	
	Income Tax Payable...................		10,000
	Prior period adjustment to correct error in recording income tax expense of 19X4.		

The debit to Retained Earnings keeps the error correction from being reported on the income statement of 19X5. Recall the matching principle. If Income Tax Expense is debited when the prior period adjustment is recorded in 19X5, then this $10,000 in taxes would appear on the 19X5 income statement. This would not be proper, since the expense arose from 19X4 operations.

This prior period adjustment would appear on the statement of retained earnings, as follows:

Discussion Question: Suppose you overstated Depreciation Expense last year. Is the Depreciation Expense account this year affected? ANSWER: No, because last year's Depreciation Expense was closed. If the error is not in the Depreciation Expense account, where is it? ANSWER: In Retained Earnings; the incorrect Depreciation Expense was closed into Retained Earnings. What would you have to do to Retained Earnings to correct it? ANSWER: If Depreciation Expense was overstated, then net income and Retained Earnings were understated. Therefore, the amount in retained earnings would have to be increased by the amount of its understatement. What is the prior period adjusting entry required? ANSWER:

Accumulated
   Depreciation XX
     Retained Earnings XX

De Graff Corporation Statement of Retained Earnings For the Year Ended December 31, 19X5	
Retained earnings balance, December 31, 19X4, **as originally reported**	$390,000
Prior period adjustment—debit to correct error in recording income tax expense of 19X4	(10,000)
Retained earnings balance, December 31, 19X4, **as adjusted**	380,000
Net income for 19X5	114,000
	494,000
Dividends for 19X5.................................	(41,000)
Retained earnings balance, December 31, 19X5............	$453,000

Our example shows a prior period adjustment for additional expense. To make a prior period adjustment for additional income, Retained Earnings is credited and the misstated asset or liability is debited.

Summary Problem for Your Review

The following information was taken from the ledger of Kraft Corporation:

Loss on sale of discontinued operations	$ 5,000	Selling expenses	$ 78,000
Prior period adjustment—credit to Retained Earnings	5,000	Common stock, no-par, 45,000 shares issued	180,000
Gain on sale of plant assets	21,000	Sales revenue	620,000
Cost of goods sold	380,000	Interest expense	30,000
Income tax expense (saving):		Extraordinary gain	26,000
Continuing operations	32,000	Operating income, discontinued operations	25,000
Discontinued operations:		Loss due to lawsuit	11,000
Operating income	10,000	General expenses	62,000
Loss on sale	(2,000)	Preferred stock, 8%, $100 par, 500 shares issued	50,000
Extraordinary gain	10,000	Paid-in capital in excess of par—preferred	7,000
Cumulative effect of change in inventory method	(4,000)	Retained earnings, beginning, as originally reported	103,000
Treasury stock, common (5,000 shares at cost)	25,000	Cumulative effect of change in inventory method	(10,000)
Dividends	16,000		

Required

Prepare a single-step income statement and a statement of retained earnings for Kraft Corporation for the current year ended December 31. Include the earnings per share presentation and show computations. Assume no changes in the stock accounts during the year.

SOLUTION TO SUMMARY PROBLEM

Kraft Corporation
Income Statement
For the Year Ended December 31, 19XX

Revenue and gains:		
Sales revenue		$620,000
Gain on sale of plant assets		21,000
Total revenues and gains		641,000
Expenses and losses:		
Cost of goods sold	$380,000	
Selling expenses	78,000	
General expenses	62,000	
Interest expense	30,000	
Loss due to lawsuit	11,000	
Income tax expense	32,000	
Total expenses and losses		593,000
Income from continuing operations		48,000
Discontinued operations:		
Operating income, $25,000, less income tax, $10,000	15,000	
Loss on sale of discontinued operations, $5,000, less income tax saving, $2,000	(3,000)	12,000
Income before extraordinary item and cumulative effect of change in inventory method		60,000
Extraordinary gain, $26,000, less income tax, $10,000		16,000
Cumulative effect of change in inventory method, $10,000, less income tax saving, $4,000		(6,000)
Net income		$ 70,000

Earnings per share:
Income from continuing operations
[($48,000 − $4,000)/40,000 shares] $1.10
Income from discontinued operations ($12,000/40,000 shares) 30
Income before extraordinary item and cumulative effect of
change in inventory method
($60,000 − $4,000)/40,000 shares] 1.40
Extraordinary gain ($16,000/40,000 shares) 40
Cumulative effect of change in inventory method ($6,000/40,000) . . . . (.15)
Net income [($70,000 − $4,000)/40,000 shares] $1.65

Computations:

$$EPS = \frac{Income - Preferred\ dividends}{Common\ shares\ outstanding}$$

Preferred dividends: $50,000 × .08 = $4,000
Common shares outstanding: 45,000 shares issued − 5,000 treasury shares = 40,000
shares outstanding

Kraft Corporation
Statement of Retained Earnings
For the Year Ended December 31, 19XX

Retained earnings balance, beginning, as originally reported	$103,000
Prior period adjustment—credit	5,000
Retained earnings balance, beginning, as adjusted	108,000
Net income for current year	70,000
	178,000
Dividends for current year	(16,000)
Retained earnings balance, ending	$162,000

Summary

Retained Earnings carries the balance of the business's net income accumulated over its lifetime, less its declared dividends and any net losses. *Cash dividends* are distributions of corporate assets made possible by earnings. *Stock dividends* are distributions of the corporation's own stock to its stockholders. Stock dividends and *stock splits* increase the number of shares outstanding and lower the market price per share of stock.

Treasury stock is the corporation's own stock that has been issued and reacquired and is currently held by the company. The corporation may sell treasury stock for its cost or for more or less than cost. *Retirement* of stock cancels the designated shares, which cannot then be reissued.

Retained earnings may be *restricted* by law or contract or by the corporation itself. An *appropriation* is a restriction of retained earnings that is recorded by formal journal entries.

The corporate *income statement* lists separately the various sources of income—*continuing operations*, which include other gains and losses, *discontinued operations*, and *extraordinary gains and losses*. The bottom line of the income statement reports *net income* or *net loss* for the period. *Income tax expense* and *earnings-per-share* figures also appear on the income statement, likewise divided into different categories based on the nature of income. The *statement of retained earnings* reports the causes for changes in the Retained Earnings account. This statement may be combined with the income statement.

Self-Study Questions

Test your understanding of the chapter by marking the best answer for each of the following questions.

1. A corporation has total stockholders' equity of $100,000, including retained earnings of $19,000. The cash balance is $35,000. The maximum cash dividend the company can declare and pay is (p. 672)
   ✓ a. $19,000   c. $65,000
   b. $35,000   d. $100,000

2. A stock dividend (p. 672)
   a. Decreases stockholders' equity   ✓c. Leaves total stockholders'
   b. Decreases assets   equity unchanged
                                       ✓ d. None of the above

3. Meyer's Thrifty Acres has 100,000 shares of $20 par common stock outstanding. The stock's market value is $37 per share. Meyer's board of directors declares and distributes a 1 percent common stock dividend. Which of the following entries shows the full effect of declaring and distributing the dividend? (p. 673)

   a. Retained Earnings 37,000
          Common Stock Dividend Distributable   20,000
          Paid-in Capital in Excess of Par—Common   17,000

   b. Retained Earnings 20,000
          Common Stock   20,000

   ✓ c. Retained Earnings 17,000
          Paid-in Capital in Excess of Par—Common   17,000

   ✓ d. Retained Earnings 37,000
          Common Stock   20,000
          Paid-in Capital in Excess of Par—Common   17,000

4. Lang Real Estate Investment Corporation declared and distributed a 50 percent stock dividend. Which of the following stock splits would have the same effect on the number of Lang shares outstanding? (p. 676)
   a. 2 for 1   c. 4 for 3
   ✓b. 3 for 2   d. 5 for 4

5. A company purchased 10,000 of its $1.50 par common stock as treasury stock, paying $6 per share. This transaction (p. 678)
   a. Has no effect on company   c. Decreases owners' equity by
      assets $15,000
   b. Has no effect on owners' equity   ✓ d. Decreases owners' equity by
                                          $60,000

6. A restriction of retained earnings (p. 682)
   a. Has no effect on total retained earnings
   b. Reduces retained earnings available for the declaration of dividends
   c. Can be reported by a note or by appropriation of retained earnings, or both
   ✓d. All of the above

7. Which of the following items is not reported on the income statement? (p. 685)
   ✓a. Premium on stock   c. Income tax expense
   b. Extraordinary gains and losses   d. Earnings per share

8. The income statement item that is likely to be most useful for predicting income from year to year is (p. 685)
   a. Extraordinary items   ✓c. Income from continuing
   b. Discontinued operations   operations
                                      d. Net income

9. In computing earnings per share (EPS), dividends on preferred stock are (p. 689)
   a. Added because they represent earnings to the preferred stockholders
   ✓ b. Subtracted because they represent earnings to the preferred stockholders

c. Ignored because they do not pertain to the common stock

d. Reported separately on the income statement

10. A corporation accidentally overlooked an accrual of property tax expense at December 31, 19X4. Accountants for the company detect the error early in 19X5 before the expense is paid. The entry to record this prior period adjustment is *(p. 691)*

a. Retained Earnings .   XXX
    Property Tax
    Expense   XXX

b. Property Tax
    Expense   XXX
    Property Tax
    Payable   XXX

✓c. Retained Earnings .   XXX
    Property Tax
    Payable   XXX

d. Property Tax
    Payable   XXX
    Property Tax
    Expense   XXX

Answers to the Self-Study Questions follow the Accounting Vocabulary.

Accounting Vocabulary

Appropriation of retained earnings. Restriction of retained earnings that is recorded by a formal journal entry *(p. 682)*.

Earnings per share (EPS). Amount of a company's net income per share of its outstanding common stock *(p. 688)*.

Extraordinary item. A gain or loss that is both unusual for the company and infrequent *(p. 686)*.

Large stock dividend. A stock dividend of 25 percent or more of the corporation's issued stock *(p. 673)*.

Prior period adjustment. Correction to retained earnings for an error of an earlier period is a prior period adjustment *(p. 691)*.

Segment of a business. A significant part of a company *(p. 686)*.

Small stock dividend. A stock dividend of less than 25 percent of the corporation's issued stock *(p. 673)*.

Stock dividend. A proportional distribution by a corporation of its own stock to its stockholders *(p. 672)*.

Stock split. An increase in the number of outstanding shares of stock coupled with a proportionate reduction in the par value of the stock *(p. 675)*.

Treasury stock. A corporation's own stock that it has issued and later reacquired *(p. 677)*.

Answers to Self-Study Questions

1. a	2. c	3. d	4. b	5. d
6. d	7. a	8. c	9. b	10. c

ASSIGNMENT MATERIAL _____

Questions

1. Identify the two main parts of stockholders' equity.

2. Identify the account debited and the account credited from the last closing entry a corporation makes each year. What is the purpose of this entry?

3. Ametek, Inc., reported a cash balance of $73 million and a retained earnings balance of $162.5 million. Explain how Ametek can have so much

more retained earnings than cash. In your answer, identify the nature of retained earnings and state how it ties to cash.

4. A friend of yours receives a stock dividend on an investment. He believes stock dividends are the same as cash dividends. Explain why this is not true.

5. Give two reasons for a corporation to distribute a stock dividend.

6. A corporation declares a stock dividend on December 21 and reports Stock Dividend Payable as a liability on the December 31 balance sheet. Is this correct? Give your reason.

7. What percentage distinguishes a small stock dividend from a large stock dividend? What is the main difference in accounting for small and large stock dividends?

8. To an investor, a stock split and a stock dividend have essentially the same effect. Explain the similarity and difference to the corporation between a 100 percent stock dividend and a 2-for-1 stock split.

9. Give four reasons why a corporation may purchase treasury stock.

10. What effect does the purchase of treasury stock have on the (a) assets, (b) issued stock, and (c) outstanding stock of the corporation?

11. What is the normal balance of the Treasury Stock account? What type of account is Treasury Stock? Where is Treasury Stock reported on the balance sheet?

12. Revell Inc. purchased treasury stock for $25,000. If Revell sells half the treasury stock for $15,000, what account should it credit for the $2,500 difference? If Revell later sells the remaining half of the treasury stock for $9,000, what accounts should be debited for the $3,500 difference?

13. What effect does the purchase and retirement of common stock have on the (a) assets, (b) issued stock, and (c) outstanding stock of the corporation?

14. Why do creditors wish to restrict a corporation's payment of cash dividends and purchases of treasury stock?

15. What are two ways to report a retained earnings restriction? Which way is more common?

16. Identify three items on the income statement that generate income tax expense. What is an income tax saving, and how does it arise?

17. Why is it important for a corporation to report income from continuing operations separately from discontinued operations and extraordinary items?

18. Give two examples of extraordinary gains and losses and four examples of gains and losses that are *not* extraordinary.

19. What is the most widely used of all accounting statistics? What is the price-to-earnings ratio? Compute the price-to-earnings ratio for a company with EPS of $2 and market price of $12 per share of common stock.

20. What is the earnings per share of a company with net income of $5,500, issued common stock of 12,000 shares, and treasury common stock of 1,000 shares.

21. What account do all prior period adjustments affect? On what financial statement are prior period adjustments reported?

Exercises

Total stock. equity $585,000

Exercise 15-1 *Journalizing dividends and reporting stockholders' equity* **(L.O. 1)**

Bremond, Inc., is authorized to issue 100,000 shares of $1 par common stock. The company issued 50,000 shares at $6 per share, and all 50,000 shares are outstanding. When the retained earnings balance was $300,000, Bremond declared and distributed a 50 percent stock dividend. Later, Bremond declared and paid a $.20 per share cash dividend.

Required

1. Journalize the declaration and distribution of the stock dividend.
2. Journalize the declaration and payment of the cash dividend.
3. Prepare the stockholders' equity section of the balance sheet after both dividends.

Exercise 15-2 *Journalizing a stock dividend and reporting stockholders' equity* **(L.O. 1)**

Total stock. equity $830,000

The stockholders' equity for Taps Jewelry Corporation on September 30, 19X4—end of the company's fiscal year—follows.

Stockholders' Equity

Common stock, $10 par, 100,000 shares authorized, 50,000 shares issued	$500,000
Paid-in capital in excess of par—common	50,000
Retained earnings	280,000
Total stockholders' equity	$830,000

On November 16 the market price of Taps's common stock was $12 per share and the company declared a 10 percent stock dividend. Taps issued the dividend shares on November 30.

Required

1. Journalize the declaration and distribution of the stock dividend.
2. Prepare the stockholders' equity section of the balance sheet after the stock dividend.

Exercise 15-3 *Reporting stockholders' equity after a stock split* **(L.O. 2)**

Total stock. equity $890,000

McMillan Enterprises had the following stockholders' equity at May 31:

Common stock, $10 par, 200,000 shares authorized, 50,000 shares issued	$500,000
Paid-in capital in excess of par	180,000
Retained earnings	210,000
Total stockholders' equity	$890,000

On June 7, McMillan split its $10 par common stock 4 for 1. Make the memorandum entry to record the stock split, and prepare the stockholders' equity section of the balance sheet immediately after the split.

Exercise 15-4 *Journalizing treasury stock transactions* **(L.O. 3)**

No check figure

Journalize the following transactions of The Cobbler, Inc., a national chain of shoe repair shops:

May 19   Issued 10,000 shares of no-par common stock at $12 per share.
Aug. 22   Purchased 900 shares of treasury stock at $14 per share.
Nov. 11   Sold 200 shares of treasury stock at $15 per share.
Dec. 28   Sold 100 shares of treasury stock at $11 per share.

Total stock. equity $606,000

Exercise 15-5 *Journalizing treasury stock transactions and reporting stockholders' equity* **(L.O. 3)**

Varsity Guild, Inc., had the following stockholders' equity on November 30:

Stockholders' Equity

Common stock, $5 par, 500,000 shares authorized, 50,000 shares issued	$250,000
Paid-in capital in excess of par	150,000
Retained earnings	220,000
Total stockholders' equity	$620,000

On December 19 the company purchased 2,000 shares of treasury stock at $7 per share. Journalize the purchase of the treasury stock and prepare the stockholders' equity section of the balance sheet at December 31.

Total stock. equity $1,290,000

Exercise 15-6 *Reporting a retained earnings restriction* **(L.O. 4)**

The agreement under which Reicher Corporation issued its long-term debt requires the restriction of $250,000 of the company's retained earnings balance. Total retained earnings is $470,000, and total paid-in capital is $820,000.

Required

Show how to report stockholders' equity (including retained earnings) on Reicher's balance sheet, assuming:

a. Reicher discloses the restriction in a note. Write the note.
b. Reicher appropriates retained earnings in the amount of the restriction and includes no note in its statements.

Net inc. $6,200

Exercise 15-7 *Preparing a multiple-step income statement* **(L.O. 5)**

The ledger of Innsbruck Corporation contains the following information for 19X7 operations:

Cost of goods sold	$45,000	Income tax saving—loss on discontinued operations	$ 20,000
Loss on discontinued operations	50,000		
Income tax expense— extraordinary gain	4,800	Extraordinary gain	12,000
		Sales revenue	130,000
Income tax expense— cumulative effect of change in depreciation method	2,000	Operating expenses (including income tax) . .	60,000
		Cumulative effect of change in depreciation method	6,000

Required

Prepare a multiple-step income statement for 19X7. Omit earnings per share. Was 19X7 a good year or a bad year for Innsbruck Corporation? Explain your answer in terms of the outlook for 19X8.

EPS = $1.38

Exercise 15-8 *Computing earnings per share* **(L.O. 5)**

Fenner Corporation earned net income of $56,000 for the second quarter of 19X6. The ledger reveals the following figures:

Preferred stock, $1.75 per year, no-par, 1,600 shares issued and
outstanding .... $ 70,000
Common stock, $10 par, 42,000 shares issued................. 420,000
Treasury stock, common, 2,000 shares at cost................. 36,000

Required

Compute EPS for the quarter, assuming no changes in the stock accounts during the quarter.

Exercise 15-9 *Computing earnings per share* **(L.O. 5)**

EPS = $3.42

Massachusetts Supply had 40,000 shares of common stock and 10,000 shares of $10 par, 5 percent preferred stock outstanding on December 31, 19X8. On April 30, 19X9, the company issued 9,000 additional common shares and ended 19X9 with 49,000 shares of common stock outstanding. Income from continuing operations of 19X9 was $115,400, and loss on discontinued operations (net of income tax) was $8,280. The company had an extraordinary gain (net of tax) of $55,200.

Required

Compute Massachusetts Supply's EPS amounts for 19X9, starting with income from continuing operations.

Exercise 15-10 *Preparing a statement of retained earnings with a prior period adjustment* **(L.O. 6)**

End. RE $451.4 million

Big Red, Inc., a soft-drink company, reported a prior period adjustment in 19X9. An accounting error caused net income of prior years to be understated by $3.8 million. Retained earnings at January 1, 19X9, as previously reported, stood at $395.3 million. Net income for 19X9 was $92.1 million, and dividends were $39.8 million. Prepare the company's statement of retained earnings for the year ended December 31, 19X9.

Exercise 15-11 *Preparing a combined statement of income and retained earnings* **(L.O. 5, 6)**

End. RE $820.9 million

The Kroger Company, a large grocery company, had retained earnings of $792.6 million at the beginning of 19X7. The company showed these figures at December 31, 19X7:

	($ Millions)
Increases in retained earnings:	
Net income	$127.1
Decreases in retained earnings:	
Cash dividends—preferred	2.3
common	85.2
Debit to retained earnings due to purchase of preferred stock.	11.3

Required

Beginning with net income, prepare a combined statement of income and retained earnings for The Kroger Company for 19X7. The debit to Retained Earnings was caused by Kroger's paying $11.3 more to retire its preferred stock than the original issue price of the stock.

Problems (Group A)

Problem 15-1A *Journalizing stockholders' equity transactions* **(L.O. 1, 3)**

No check figure

Feather, Inc., completed the following selected transactions during 19X6:

Jan. 13   Discovered that income tax expense of 19X5 was overstated by $9,000. Recorded a prior period adjustment to correct the error.

21   Split common stock 3 for 1 by calling in the 10,000 shares of $15 par common and issuing 30,000 shares of $5 par common.

Feb. 6   Declared a cash dividend on the 4,000 shares of $2.25, no-par preferred stock. Declared a $.20 per share dividend on the common stock outstanding. The date of record was February 27, and the payment date was March 20.

Mar. 20   Paid the cash dividends.

Apr. 18   Declared a 50 percent stock dividend on the common stock to holders of record April 30, with distribution set for May 30. The market value of the common stock was $8 per share.

May 30   Issued the stock dividend shares.

June 18   Purchased 2,000 shares of the company's own common stock at $12 per share.

Nov. 14   Sold 800 shares of treasury common stock for $10 per share.

Dec. 22   Sold 700 shares of treasury common stock for $16 per share.

Required

Record the transactions in the general journal.

Total stock. equity:
Dec. 31, 19X8, $438,000
Dec. 31, 19X9, $525,000

Problem 15-2A   *Journalizing dividend and treasury stock transactions and reporting stockholders' equity* **(L.O. 1, 2, 3)**

The balance sheet of Best of New Mexico, Inc., at December 31, 19X7, reported 10,000 shares of $.50, no-par preferred stock authorized and outstanding. The preferred was issued in 19X1 at $8 per share. Best of New Mexico also had 500,000 shares of $1 par common stock authorized with 100,000 shares issued. Paid-in Capital in Excess of Par—Common had a balance of $300,000. Retained Earnings had a balance of $18,000, and the preferred dividend for 19X7 was in arrears. During the two-year period ended December 31, 19X9, the company completed the following selected transactions:

19X8

Feb. 15   Purchased 5,000 shares of the company's own common stock for the treasury at $6 per share.

Apr. 2   Declared the cash dividend on the preferred stock in arrears for 19X7 and the current cash dividend on preferred. The date of record was April 16, and the payment date was May 1.

May 1   Paid the cash dividends.

May 2   Purchased and retired all the preferred stock at $7.50 per share.

Dec. 31   Earned net income of $55,000 for the year.

19X9

Mar. 8   Sold 2,000 shares of treasury common stock for $7 per share.

Sep. 28   Declared a 10 percent stock dividend on the *outstanding* common stock to holders of record October 15, with distribution set for October 31. The market value of Best of New Mexico common stock was $5 per share.

Oct. 31   Issued the stock dividend shares.

Nov. 5   Split the common stock 2 for 1 by calling in the 109,700 shares of old $1 par common stock and issuing twice as many shares of $.50 par common. (Stock splits affect all issued stock, including treasury stock and stock that is outstanding.)

Dec. 31   Earned net income of $73,000 during the year.

Required

1. Record the transactions in the general journal. Explanations are not required.
2. Prepare the stockholders' equity section of the balance sheet at two dates: December 31, 19X8, and December 31, 19X9.

Problem 15-3A   *Using actual-company data to record transactions and report earnings per share*   *(L.O. 1, 3, 5)*

2. Debit to RE $1.3 million
4. End. bal. T/Stock $213.5 million
7. EPS = $4.46

The following four items were taken from actual financial statements that reported amounts in millions, rounded to the nearest $100,000.

Hampton Industries, Inc., declared and paid cash dividends of $.1 million to preferred stockholders and also declared and issued a 10 percent stock dividend on its 2.0 million common shares outstanding. The par value of Hampton's common stock was $1.00 per share, and the market value of the stock at the time of the stock dividend was $6.50 per share.

Required

1. Journalize the declaration and payment of the cash dividend.
2. Journalize the declaration and issuance of the stock dividend.

At the beginning of the period, the Louisiana Land and Exploration Company had a treasury stock balance of $1.2 million. During the period, Louisiana paid $212.8 million to purchase treasury stock, and the company also sold treasury stock for $.6 million. The cost of the treasury stock was $.5 million.

Required

3. Journalize the purchase and the sale of treasury stock.
4. Compute the ending balance of the Treasury Stock account.

Crown Cork & Seal Company, Inc., purchased and retired 800,000 shares of its common stock at a cost of $40 per share. Assume that par value was $1 per share and that the common stock was issued for $9 per share.

Required

5. Journalize the purchase and retirement of the common stock.

G. C. Murphy Company reported a $1.3 million extraordinary gain on the issuance of treasury stock, which cost $3.4 million, to pay off long-term debt of $4.7 million. Murphy's income before extraordinary item was $17.0 million, and the company had 4.1 million shares of common stock outstanding.

Note: An extraordinary gain or loss is recorded exactly as any other gain or loss, but with "Extraordinary" in its account title.

Required

6. Journalize the transaction.
7. Show how Murphy reported earnings per share for the year.

Problem 15-4A   *Purchasing treasury stock to fight off a takeover of the corporation*   *(L.O. 3)*

No check figure

Cinquante Corporation is positioned ideally in its industry. Located in Nogales, Arizona, Cinquante is the only company between Texas and California with reliable sources for its imported gifts. The company does a brisk business with specialty stores such as Pier 1 Imports. Cinquante's recent success has made the company a prime target for a takeover. An investment group from Minneapolis is attempting to buy 51 percent of Cinquante's outstanding stock against the wishes of Cinquante's board of directors. Board members are convinced that the Minneapolis investors would sell off the most desirable pieces of the business and leave little of value.

At the most recent board meeting, several suggestions were advanced to fight off the hostile takeover bid. The suggestion with the most promise is to purchase a huge quantity of treasury stock. Cinquante has the cash to carry out this plan.

Required

1. As a significant stockholder of Cinquante, write a memorandum to explain for the board how the purchase of treasury stock would make it more difficult for the Minneapolis group to take over Cinquante. Include in your memo a discussion of the effect that purchasing treasury stock would have on stock outstanding and on the size of the corporation.

2. Suppose Cinquante management is successful in fighting off the takeover bid and later sells the treasury stock at prices greater than the purchase price. Explain what effect these sales will have on assets, stockholders' equity, and net income.

Total stock. equity $546,080

Problem 15-5A *Journalizing prior period adjustments and dividend and treasury stock transactions; reporting retained earnings and stockholders' equity (L.O. 1, 3, 6)*

The balance sheet of Topeka Corporation at December 31, 19X3, presented the following stockholders' equity:

Paid-in capital:	
Common stock, $1 par, 250,000 shares authorized,	
50,000 shares issued	$ 50,000
Paid-in capital in excess of par—common	350,000
Total paid-in capital	400,000
Retained earnings	110,000
Total stockholders' equity	$510,000

During 19X4, Topeka completed the following selected transactions:

Jan.   7   Discovered that income tax expense of 19X3 was understated by $4,000. Recorded a prior period adjustment to correct the error.

Mar. 29   Declared a 50 percent stock dividend on the common stock. The market value of Topeka common stock was $7 per share. The record date was April 19, with distribution set for May 19.

May 19   Issued the stock dividend shares.

July 13   Purchased 2,000 shares of the company's own common stock at $6 per share.

Oct.   4   Sold 600 shares of treasury common stock for $8 per share.

Dec. 27   Declared a $.20 per share dividend on the common stock outstanding. The date of record was January 17, 19X5, and the payment date was January 31.

      31   Closed the $62,000 credit balance of Income Summary to Retained Earnings.

Required

1. Record the transactions in the general journal.
2. Prepare the retained earnings statement at December 31, 19X4.

3. Prepare the stockholders' equity section of the balance sheet at December 31, 19X4.

Problem 15-6A *Preparing a single-step income statement and a statement of retained earnings and reporting stockholders' equity on the balance sheet* **(L.O. 5, 6)**

Total stock. equity $531,000

The following information was taken from the ledger and other records of California Sales Corporation at June 30, 19X5:

Interest expense	$ 23,000	Dividends on common	
Gain on settlement of		stock	$ 12,000
lawsuit	8,000	Sales revenue	589,000
Sales returns	15,000	Retained earnings,	
Paid-in capital from		beginning, as	
retirement of preferred		originally reported	63,000
stock	16,000	Selling expenses	87,000
Interest revenue	5,000	Common stock, no-par,	
Treasury stock, common		22,000 shares autho-	
(2,000 shares at cost) ..	28,000	rized and issued	350,000
General expenses	71,000	Sales discounts	7,000
Loss on sale of		Extraordinary gain	27,000
discontinued segment .	8,000	Operating loss, discon-	
Prior period		tinued segment	9,000
adjustment-debit to		Loss on sale of plant	
Retained Earnings	4,000	assets	10,000
Cost of goods sold	319,000	Dividends on preferred	
Income tax expense (saving):		stock	?
Continuing operations	28,000	Preferred stock, 6%, $25	
Discontinued segment:		par, 20,000 shares au-	
Operating loss	(3,600)	thorized, 4,000 shares	
Loss on sale........	(3,200)	issued	100,000
Extraordinary gain	10,800	Cumulative effect of	
Cumulative effect of		change in depreciation	
change in depreci-		method	7,000
ation method	3,000		

Required

1. Prepare a single-step income statement, including earnings per share, for California Sales Corporation for the fiscal year ended June 30, 19X5. Evaluate income for the year ended June 30, 19X5, in terms of the outlook for 19X6. Assume 19X5 was a typical year and that California Sales managers hoped to earn income from continuing operations equal to 8 percent of net sales.

2. Prepare the statement of retained earnings for the year ended June 30, 19X5.

3. Prepare the stockholders' equity section of the balance sheet at that date.

Problem 15-7A *Preparing a corrected combined statement of income and retained earnings* **(L.O. 5, 6)**

RE, June 30, 19X4, $112,000
EPS = $3.40

Susan Clay, accountant for Verbatim, Inc., was injured in a sailing accident. Another employee prepared the following income statement for the fiscal year ended June 30, 19X4:

Verbatim, Inc.
Income Statement
June 30, 19X4

Revenues and gains:		
Sales		$533,000
Gain on retirement of preferred stock (issued for		
$70,000; purchased for $59,000)		11,000
Paid-in capital in excess of par—common		100,000
Total revenues and gains		644,000
Expenses and losses:		
Cost of goods sold............................	$233,000	
Selling expenses	103,000	
General expenses	74,000	
Sales returns	22,000	
Prior period adjustment—debit	4,000	
Dividends	15,000	
Sales discounts	10,000	
Income tax expense	32,000	
Total expenses and losses		493,000
Income from operations		151,000
Other gains and losses:		
Extraordinary gain...........................	30,000	
Operating income on discontinued segment......	25,000	
Loss on sale of discontinued operations	(40,000)	
Total other gains		15,000
Net income		$166,000
Earnings per share..............................		$7.30

The individual amounts listed on the income statement are correct. However, some accounts are reported incorrectly, and others do not belong on the income statement at all. Also, income tax (40 percent) has not been applied to all appropriate figures. Verbatim issued 24,000 shares of common stock in 19X1 and held 4,000 shares as treasury stock during the fiscal year 19X4. The retained earnings balance, as originally reported at June 30, 19X3, was $63,000.

Required

Prepare a corrected combined statement of income and retained earnings for fiscal year 19X4. Prepare the income statement in single-step format.

Problem 15-8A *Computing earnings per share and reporting a retained earnings restriction* **(L.O. 4,5,6)**

EPS = $3.07
Stock. equity $1,778,945

Augustine Construction's capital structure at December 31, 19X2, included 5,000 shares of $2.50 preferred stock and 130,000 shares of common stock. Common shares outstanding during 19X3 were 130,000 January through February; 119,000 during March; 121,000 April through October; and 128,000 during November and December. Income from continuing operations during 19X3 was $371,885. The company discontinued a segment of the business at a gain of $69,160, and an extraordinary item generated a loss of $49,510. The board of directors of Augustine has restricted $440,000 of retained earnings for expansion of the company's office facilities.

Required

1. Compute Augustine's earnings per share. Start with income from continuing operations. Income and loss amounts are net of income tax.

2. Show two ways of reporting Augustine's retained earnings restriction. Retained earnings at December 31, 19X2, was $439,800, and total paid-in capital at December 31, 19X3, is $947,610. Augustine declared no dividends during 19X3.

(Group B)

Problem 15-1B *Journalizing stockholders' equity transactions* **(L.O. 1, 3)**

No check figure

Littlepage, Inc., completed the following selected transactions during the current year:

Jan. 9 Discovered that income tax expense of the preceding year was understated by $5,000. Recorded a prior period adjustment to correct the error.

Feb. 10 Split common stock 2 for 1 by calling in the 20,000 shares of $10 par common and issuing 40,000 shares of $5 par common.

Mar. 18 Declared a cash dividend on the 5 percent, $100 par preferred stock (1,000 shares outstanding). Declared a $.20 per share dividend on the common stock outstanding. The date of record was April 2, and the payment date was April 23.

Apr. 23 Paid the cash dividends.

July 30 Declared a 10 percent stock dividend on the common stock to holders of record August 21, with distribution set for September 11. The market value of the common stock was $15 per share.

Sep. 11 Issued the stock dividend shares.

    26 Purchased 2,000 shares of the company's own common stock at $16 per share.

Nov. 8 Sold 1,000 shares of treasury common stock for $20 per share.

Dec. 13 Sold 500 shares of treasury common stock for $14 per share.

Required

Record the transactions in the general journal.

Problem 15-2B *Journalizing dividend and treasury stock transactions and reporting stockholders' equity* **(L.O. 1, 2, 3)**

Total stock. equity:
Dec. 31, 19X6, $374,250
Dec. 31, 19X7, $391,850

The balance sheet of Benton Harbor Manufacturing Company at December 31, 19X5, reported 100,000 shares of no-par common stock authorized, with 30,000 shares issued and a Common Stock balance of $180,000. Benton Harbor Manufacturing also had 5,000 shares of 6 percent, $10 par preferred stock authorized and outstanding. The preferred stock was issued in 19X1 at par. Retained Earnings had a credit balance of $104,000. During the two-year period ended December 31, 19X7, the company completed the following selected transactions:

19X6
Mar. 15 Purchased 1,000 shares of the company's own common stock for the treasury at $5 per share.

July 2 Declared the annual 6 percent cash dividend on the preferred stock and a $.75-per-share cash dividend on the common stock. The date of record was July 16, and the payment date was July 31.

July 31 Paid the cash dividends.

Nov. 30 Declared a 20 percent stock dividend on the *outstanding* common stock to holders of record December 21, with distribution set for January 11, 19X7. The market value of Benton Harbor common stock was $10 per share.

Dec. 31   Earned net income of $70,000 for the year.
19X7

Jan. 11   Issued the stock dividend shares.

June 30   Declared the annual 6 percent cash dividend on the preferred stock. The date of record was July 14, and the payment date was July 29.

July 29   Paid the cash dividends.

Aug. 2   Purchased and retired all the preferred stock at $14 per share.

Oct. 8   Sold 800 shares of treasury common stock for $12 per share.

Dec. 19   Split the no-par common stock 2 for 1 by issuing two new no-par shares for each old no-par share previously issued. Prior to the split, the corporation had issued 35,800 shares. Stock splits affect all issued stock, including treasury stock as well as stock that is outstanding.

31   Earned net income of $81,000 during the year.

Required

1. Record the transactions in the general journal. Explanations are not required.
2. Prepare the stockholders' equity section of the balance sheet at two dates: December 31, 19X6, and December 31, 19X7.

Problem 15-3B   *Using actual-company data to record transactions and report earnings per share* **(L.O. 1, 3, 5)**

The following three items were taken from the financial statements of actual companies that showed amounts in millions and rounded to the nearest $100,000.

The General Tire & Rubber Company declared and paid cash dividends of $35.2 million to its common stockholders and also declared and issued a 2 percent stock dividend on its 23.6 million common shares outstanding. The par value of General's common stock was $.30 per share, and the market value of the stock at the time of the stock dividend was $60 per share.

Required

1. Journalize the declaration and payment of the cash dividend.
2. Journalize the declaration and issuance of the stock dividend.

At the beginning of the year, IU International Corporation had a treasury stock balance of $288.3 million. During the year, IU paid $2.2 million to purchase treasury stock. The company also sold treasury stock for $79.9 million. The cost of the treasury stock sold was $68.3 million. In addition, IU paid $19.6 million to purchase and retire preferred stock with par value of $18.8 million. The preferred stock had been issued at par in previous years.

Required

3. Journalize the purchase and the sale of treasury stock.
4. Compute the ending balance of the Treasury Stock account.
5. Journalize the purchase and retirement of preferred stock.

Chesapeake Corporation of Virginia, a paper company, reported a $4.0 million extraordinary gain that resulted from issuing 200,000 shares of its $5 par common stock and giving $4.5 million in cash to pay off long-term debt of $16.5 million. Chesapeake's income before the extraordinary item was $8.5 million, and the company had 6.4 million shares of common stock outstanding.

2. Debit to RE $28.3 million
4. End. bal. T/Stock $222.2 million
7. EPS = $1.95

Note: An extraordinary gain or loss is recorded exactly as any other gain or loss, but with "Extraordinary" in its account title.

Required

6. Journalize the transaction.
7. Show how Chesapeake reported earnings per share for the year.

Problem 15-4B *Increasing dividends to fight off a takeover of the corporation* *(L.O. 1)*   No check figure

Simon Corporation is positioned ideally in the clothing business. Located in Syracuse, New York, Simon is the only company with a distribution network for its imported goods. The company does a brisk business with specialty stores such as Bloomingdale's, I. Magnin, and Bonwit Teller. Simon's recent success has made the company a prime target for a takeover. Against the wishes of Simon's board of directors, an investment group from Kansas City is attempting to buy 51 percent of Simon's outstanding stock. Board members are convinced that the Kansas City investors would sell off the most desirable pieces of the business and leave little of value.

At the most recent board meeting, several suggestions were advanced to fight off the hostile takeover bid. One suggestion is to increase the stock outstanding by distributing a 100 percent stock dividend.

Required

As a significant stockholder of Simon Corporation, write a short memo to explain to the board whether distributing the stock dividend would make it more difficult for the investor group to take over Simon Corporation. Include in your memo a discussion of the effect that the stock dividend would have on assets, liabilities, and total stockholders' equity—that is, the dividend's effect on the size of the corporation.

Problem 15-5B *Journalizing prior period adjustments and dividend and treasury stock*   Total stock. equity $762,700
transactions; reporting retained earnings and stockholders' equity
(L.O. 1, 3, 6)

The balance sheet of Mendoza Corporation at December 31, 19X1, reported the following stockholders' equity:

Paid-in capital:
Common stock, $10 par, 100,000 shares
   authorized, 20,000 shares issued $200,000
Paid-in capital in excess of par-common 300,000
   Total paid-in capital 500,000
Retained earnings 190,000
   Total stockholders' equity $690,000

During 19X2 Mendoza completed the following selected transactions:

Jan. 11 Discovered that income tax expense of 19X1 was overstated by $19,000. Recorded a prior period adjustment to correct the error.

Apr. 30 Declared a 10 percent stock dividend on the common stock. The market value of Mendoza common stock was $24 per share. The record date was May 21, with distribution set for June 5.

June 5 Issued the stock dividend shares.

July 29 Purchased 2,000 shares of the company's own common stock at $21 per share.

Nov. 13 Sold 1,000 shares of treasury common stock for $22 per share.

27 Declared a $.30 per share dividend on the common stock outstanding. The date of record was December 17, and the payment date was January 7, 19X3.

Dec. 31 Closed the $80,000 credit balance of Income Summary to Retained Earnings.

Required

1. Record the transactions in the general journal.
2. Prepare a retained earnings statement at December 31, 19X2.
3. Prepare the stockholders' equity section of the balance sheet at December 31, 19X2.

Total stock. equity $629,000

Problem 15-6B *Preparing a single-step income statement and a statement of retained earnings; reporting stockholders' equity on the balance sheet* **(L.O. 5,6)**

The following information was taken from the ledger and other records of Yoshima, Inc., at September 30, 19X6.

Gain on sale of discontinued segment	$ 20,000	Sales revenue	$860,000
Prior period adjustment—credit to Retained Earnings	6,000	Treasury stock, common (1,000 shares at cost) .	11,000
		Dividends	35,000
		Interest revenue	4,000
Contributed capital from treasury stock transactions	7,000	Extraordinary loss	30,000
		Operating loss, discontinued segment	15,000
Sales discounts	18,000	Loss on insurance settlement	12,000
Interest expense	11,000		
Cost of goods sold	364,000	General expenses	113,000
Cumulative effect of change in depreciation method	(3,000)	Preferred stock, $3, no-par 10,000 shares authorized, 5,000 shares issued	200,000
Loss on sale of plant assets	8,000	Paid-in capital in excess of par-common	20,000
Sales returns	9,000		
Income tax expense (saving):		Retained earnings, beginning, as originally reported . . .	88,000
Continuing operations	72,000		
Discontinued segment:		Selling expenses	136,000
Operating loss	(6,000)	Common stock, $10 par, 25,000 shares authorized and issued	250,000
Gain on sale	8,000		
Extraordinary loss	(12,000)		
Cumulative effect of change in depreciation method	(1,000)		

Required

1. Prepare a single-step income statement, including earnings per share, for Yoshima, Inc., for the fiscal year ended September 30, 19X6. Evaluate income for the year ended September 30, 19X6, in terms of the outlook for 19X7. Assume 19X6 was a typical year and that Yoshima managers hoped to earn income from continuing operations equal to 14 percent of net sales.
2. Prepare the statement of retained earnings for the year ended September 30, 19X6.
3. Prepare the stockholders' equity section of the balance sheet at that date.

Problem 15-7B
Preparing a corrected combined statement of income and retained earnings **(L.O. 5, 6)**

RE, Dec. 31, 19X3, $146,000
EPS = $.56

Andie Beck, accountant for Cambridge Book Distributors, was injured in a skiing accident. Another employee prepared the accompanying income statement for the fiscal year ended December 31, 19X3.

The individual amounts listed on the income statement are correct. However, some accounts are reported incorrectly, and others do not belong on the income statement at all. Also, income tax (40 percent) has not been applied to all appropriate figures. Cambridge issued 52,000 shares of common stock in 19X1 and held 2,000 shares as treasury stock during 19X3. The retained earnings balance, as originally reported at December 31, 19X2, was $111,000.

Required

Prepare a corrected combined statement of income and retained earnings for 19X3. Prepare the income statement in single-step format.

Cambridge Book Distributors
Income Statement
19X3

Revenue and gains:		
Sales		$362,000
Prior period adjustment—credit		14,000
Gain on retirement of preferred stock (issued for $81,000; purchased for $71,000)		10,000
Paid-in capital in excess of par—common		80,000
Total revenues and gains		466,000
Expenses and losses:		
Cost of goods sold	$145,000	
Selling expenses	76,000	
General expenses	61,000	
Sales returns	11,000	
Dividends	7,000	
Sales discounts	6,000	
Income tax expense	20,000	
Total expenses and losses		326,000
Income from operations		140,000
Other gains and losses:		
Gain on sale of discontinued operations	10,000	
Extraordinary flood loss	(20,000)	
Operating loss on discontinued segment	(15,000)	
Total other losses		(25,000)
Net income		$115,000
Earnings per share		$2.30

Problem 15-8B
Computing earnings per share and reporting a retained earnings restriction **(L.O. 4, 5, 6)**

EPS = $1.63
Stock. equity $528,130

The capital structure of Magna Entertainment Center, Inc., at December 31, 19X6, included 20,000 shares of $1.25 preferred stock and 44,000 shares of common stock. Common shares outstanding during 19X7 were 44,000 January through May, 50,000 June through August, and 60,500 September through December. Income from continuing operations during 19X7 was $81,100. The company discontinued a segment of the business at a loss of $6,630, and an extraordinary item generated a gain of $33,660. Magna's board of directors restricts $135,000 of retained earnings for contingencies.

Required

1. Compute Magna's earnings per share. Start with income from continuing operations. Income and loss amounts are net of income tax.
2. Show two ways of reporting Magna's retained earnings restriction. Retained earnings at December 31, 19X6, was $190,000, and total paid-in capital at December 31, 19X7, is $230,000. Magna declared no dividends during 19X7.

Extending Your Knowledge

Decision Problems

No check figure

1. Analyzing Cash Dividends and Stock Dividends   (L.O. 1)

Pacific Union Corporation had the following stockholders' equity on June 30 of the current year:

Common stock, no-par, 100,000 shares issued	$ 750,000
Retained earnings	830,000
Total stockholders' equity	$1,580,000

In the past, Pacific Union has paid an annual cash dividend of $1.50 per share. Despite the large retained earnings balance, the board of directors wished to conserve cash for expansion. The board delayed the payment of cash dividends by one month and in the meantime distributed a 20 percent stock dividend. During the following year, the company's cash position improved. The board declared and paid a cash dividend of $1.25 per share.

Suppose you own 4,000 shares of Pacific Union common stock, acquired three years ago. The market price of the stock was $30 per share before any of the above dividends.

Required

1. How does the stock dividend affect your proportionate ownership in the company? Explain.
2. What amount of cash dividends did you receive last year? What amount of cash dividends will you receive after the above dividend action?
3. Immediately after the stock dividend was distributed, the market value of Pacific Union stock decreased from $30 per share to $25 per share. Does this represent a loss to you? Explain.
4. Suppose Pacific Union announces at the time of the stock dividend that the company will continue to pay the annual $1.50 cash dividend per share, even after the stock dividend. Would you expect the market price of the stock to decrease to $25 per share as in 3 above? Explain.

No check figure

2. Earnings and Dividends   (L.O. 1, 3, 5)

a. An investor noted that the market price of stocks seemed to decline after the date of record. Why do you think that would be the case?
b. The treasurer of Miske Brewing Corp. wanted to disclose a large loss as an extraordinary item because Miske produced too much product just prior

to a very cool summer. Why do you think the treasurer wanted to use that particular disclosure? Would such disclosure be acceptable?

c. Corporations sometimes purchase their own stock. When asked why they do so, management often respond that they feel the stock is undervalued. What advantage would the company gain by buying and selling its own stock under these circumstances?

d. Carter Inc. earned a significant profit in the year ended November 30, 19X2 because land it held was expropriated for a new highway. The company proposes to treat the sale of land to the government as other revenue. Why do you think Carter is proposing such treatment? Is this disclosure appropriate?

Ethical Issue

Oklatex Corporation is an independent oil producer in Odessa, Texas. In February, company geologists discovered a pool of oil that tripled the company's proven reserves. Prior to disclosing the new oil to the public, top managers of the company quietly bought most of Oklatex stock for themselves personally. After the discovery announcement, Oklatex stock price increased from $13 to $40.

Required

1. Did Oklatex managers behave ethically? Explain your answer.
2. Identify the accounting principle relevant to this situation.
3. Who was helped and who was harmed by management's action?

Financial Statement Problems

1. Treasury Stock, Retained Earnings, and Earnings per Share (L.O. 3, 5)

No check figure

Use the Goodyear Tire & Rubber Company financial statements in Appendix C to answer these questions.

1. Goodyear reports stock *outstanding* on the balance sheet and gives details in the statement of shareholders' equity. At December 31, 1990, how many shares of Goodyear common stock were outstanding? How many shares were in the treasury? How many shares had Goodyear issued through December 31, 1990?

2. Goodyear uses a method of accounting for treasury stock that is different from the method discussed in this chapter. You can determine from the Statement of Changes in Shareholders' Equity the number of shares of treasury stock purchased during 1990. What was this amount?

3. Prepare a T-account for Retained Earnings to show the beginning and ending balances and all activity in the account during 1990.

4. Show how to compute net loss *per share* for 1990 and all three earnings *per share* amounts for 1989.

2. Treasury Stock, Retained Earnings, and Earnings Per Share (L.O. 3, 5)

No check figure

Obtain the annual report of an actual company of your choosing. Answer these questions about the company. Concentrate on the current year in the annual report you select.

1. How many shares of common stock did the company have outstanding at the end of the current year? How many shares were in the treasury? How

many shares had the company issued through the date of the current balance sheet?

2. Compute average cost per share of treasury stock (common). Compare this figure to book value per share of common stock. Does it appear that the company was able to purchase treasury stock at book value?

   Note: This question can be answered only if the company reports the cost of treasury stock.

3. Prepare a T-account for Retained Earnings to show the beginning and ending balances and all activity in the account during the current year.

4. Did the company have any prior period adjustments during any year reported in the annual report? How can you tell?

5. Show how to compute all earnings (losses) *per share* amounts for the current year.

Chapter 16

Corporations: Long-Term Liabilities

The tension was easily felt . . . when the top financial executives from IBM met with investment advisers from the brokerage firms of Merrill Lynch and Salomon Brothers. The purpose of their meeting was to price the largest public debt offering in U.S. corporate history.

Those attending the meeting were well aware of the numerous economic shocks that had recently hit the financial world: rapidly rising interest rates, falling stock and bond prices, gold and silver selling at record high prices, and the U.S. dollar sinking in value in foreign exchange markets. In the midst of this, the world's largest computer and business equipment company was going to the public debt market for the first time in its corporate history in an effort to borrow $1 billion. The public offering by IBM was to consist of $500 million in 7-year notes and $500 million in 25-year debentures. Because of the rapidly changing economic environment, the small group of executives and investment bankers felt a need to act quickly on the deal.

Source: Kenneth R. Ferris, *Financial Accounting and Corporate Reporting: A Casebook*, 2nd ed. (Homewood, IL: BPI, 1989), p. 184.

LEARNING OBJECTIVES

After studying this chapter, you should be able to

1 Account for basic bonds payable transactions using the straight-line amortization method

2 Amortize bond discount and premium by the effective-interest method

3 Account for retirement of bonds payable

4 Account for conversion of bonds payable

5 Explain the advantages and disadvantages of borrowing

6 Account for lease transactions and pension liabilities

Corporations may finance—that is, raise money for—their operations in different ways. They may issue stock to their owners, and they may reinvest assets earned by profitable operations, as we have seen. This chapter discusses the third way of financing operations, **long-term liabilities.**

Two common long-term liabilities are notes payable and bonds payable. A note payable, which we studied in Chapter 11, is a promissory note issued by the company to borrow money from a single lender, like a bank or an insurance company. **Bonds payable** are groups of notes payable issued to multiple lenders, called bondholders. This chapter also discusses accounting for lease liabilities and pension liabilities.

The Nature of Bonds

A company needing millions of dollars may be unable to borrow so large an amount from a single lender. To gain access to more investors, the company may issue bonds. Each bond is, in effect, a long-term note payable that bears interest. Bonds are debts of the company for the amounts borrowed from the investors.

Purchasers of bonds receive a bond certificate, which carries the issuing company's name. The certificate also states the *principal,* which is the amount that the company has borrowed from the bondholder. This figure, typically stated in units of $1,000, is also called the bond's face value, maturity value, or par value. The bond obligates the issuing company to pay the holder the principal amount at a specific future date, called the maturity date, which also appears on the certificate.

Bondholders loan their money to companies for a price: interest on the principal. The bond certificate states the interest rate that the issuer will pay the holder and the dates that the interest payments are due (generally twice a year). Some bond certificates name the bondholder (the investor). When the company pays back the principal, the holder returns the certificate, which the company retires (or cancels). Exhibit 16-1 shows an actual bond certificate, with the various features highlighted.

The board of directors may authorize a bond issue. In some companies the stockholders—as owners—may also have to vote their approval.

Issuing bonds usually requires the services of a securities firm, like Merrill Lynch, to act as the *underwriter* of the bond issue. The **underwriter** purchases the bonds from the issuing company and resells them to its clients, or it may sell the bonds for a commission from the issuer, agreeing to buy all unsold bonds.

EXHIBIT 16-1 *Bond (Note) Certificate*

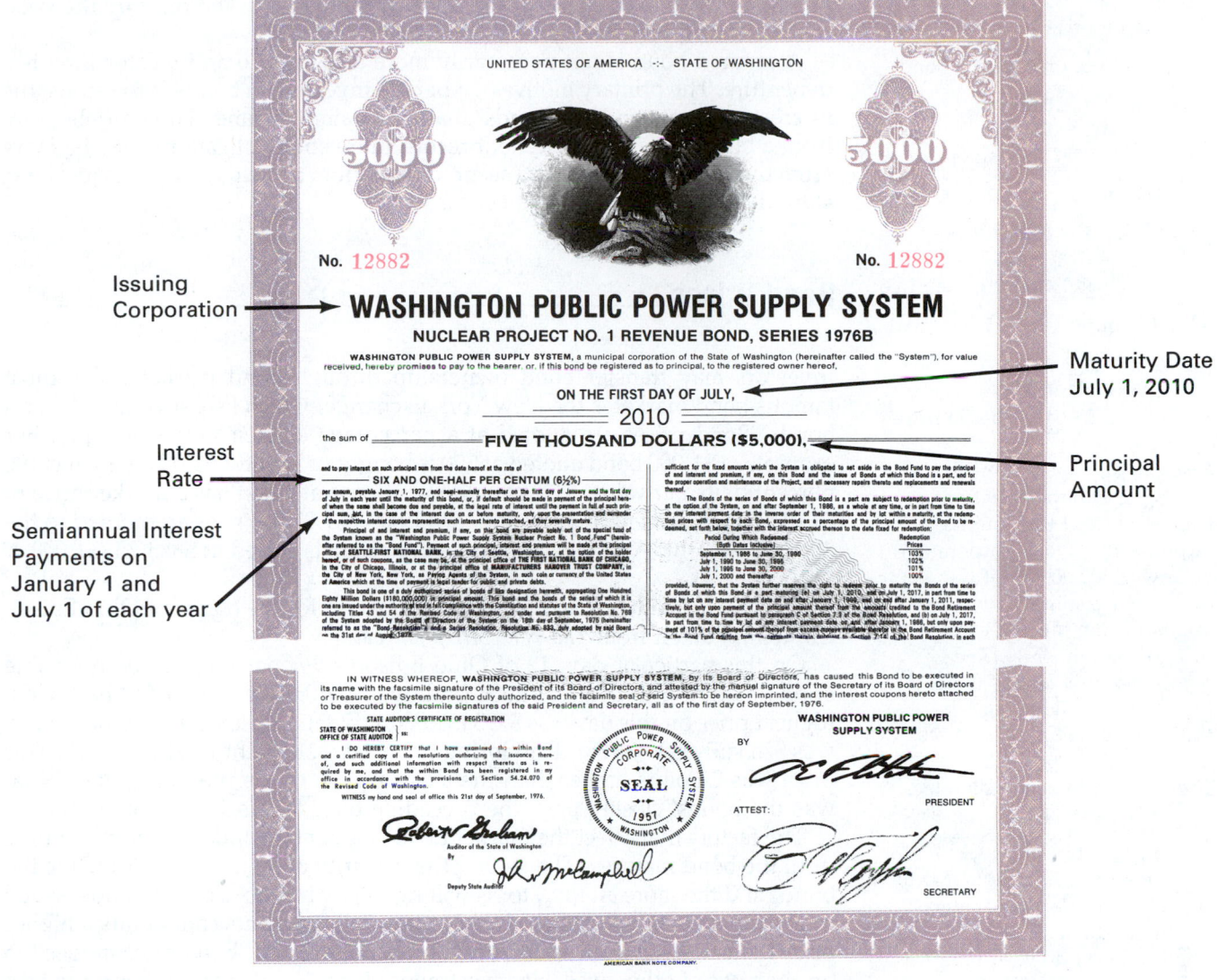

Issuing Corporation → **WASHINGTON PUBLIC POWER SUPPLY SYSTEM**

Maturity Date July 1, 2010

Principal Amount

Interest Rate → SIX AND ONE-HALF PER CENTUM (6½%)

Semiannual Interest Payments on January 1 and July 1 of each year

Types of Bonds

Bonds may be *registered* bonds or *coupon* bonds. The owner of a **registered bond** receives interest checks from the issuing company, which keeps a listing of the names and addresses of the bondholders. Owners of **coupon bonds** receive interest by detaching a perforated coupon—which states the interest due and the date of payment—from the bond and depositing it in a bank for collection. A company with coupon bonds needs no registry of bondholders. The responsibility for cashing coupons rests with the bondholders. Most bonds issued today are registered.

All the bonds in a particular issue may mature at the same time **(term bonds),** or they may mature in installments over a period of time **(serial bonds).** By issuing serial bonds, the company spreads its principal payments over time and avoids paying the entire principal at one time. Serial bonds are like installment notes payable.

5 Interest is a tax-deductible expense of the corporation.
6 Bonds have a fixed cost (to the corporation) and a fixed return (to the bondholder).
7 Corporation must repay bond payable at maturity.

Point to Stress: Generally, a debenture bond carries a higher rate of interest than a mortgage bond because the debenture bond is unsecured. With a secured or mortgage bond, which is backed by some asset (the collateral), the risk to the investor is lower and so is the rate of interest.

Secured, or *mortgage*, bonds give the bondholder the right to take specified assets of the issuer if the company *defaults*, that is, fails to pay interest or principal. Unsecured bonds, called **debentures,** are backed only by the good faith of the borrower.

A secured bond is not necessarily more attractive to an investor than is a debenture. The primary motive of a person investing in bonds is to receive the interest amounts and the bonds' maturity value on time. Thus a debenture from a business with an excellent record in meeting obligations may be more attractive to an investor than a secured bond from a business that has just been started or that has a bad credit record.

Bond Prices

Investors may transfer bond ownership through bond markets. The most famous bond market is the New York Exchange, which lists several thousand bonds. Bond prices are quoted at a percentage of their maturity value. For example, a $1,000 bond quoted at 100 is bought or sold for $1,000, which is 100 percent of its par value. The same bond quoted at 101½ has a market price of $1,015 (101.5 percent of par value, or $1,000 × 1.015). Prices are quoted to the 8th of 1 percent. A $1,000 bond quoted at 88⅜ is priced at $883.75 ($1,000 × .88375).

Exhibit 16-2 contains actual price information for the bonds of Ohio Edison Company, taken from *The Wall Street Journal.*

On this particular day, 12 of Ohio Edison's 9½ percent, $1,000 par value bonds maturing in the year 2006 (indicated by 06) were traded. The bonds' highest price on this day was $795 ($1,000 × .795). The lowest price of the day was $785 ($1,000 × .785). The closing price (last sale of the day) was $795. This price was 2 points higher than the closing price of the preceding day. What was the bonds' closing price the preceding day? It was 77½ (79½ − 2).

The factors that affect the market price of a bond include the length of time until the bond matures. The sooner the maturity date, the more attractive the bond, and the more an investor is willing to pay for it. Also, the bonds issued by a company with a proven ability to meet all payments commands a higher price than an issue from a company with a poor record. Bond price hinges too on the rates of other available investment plans. Is a 12 percent bond the best way to invest $1,000, or does another investment strategy pay a higher rate? Of course, the higher the percentage rate, the higher the market price. Buying a 13 percent bond will cost you more than buying an 8 percent bond, given that both issues have the same maturity date and have been issued by equally sound businesses.

A bond issued at a price above its maturity (par) value is said to be issued at a **premium,** and a bond issued at a price below maturity (par) value has a **discount.** As a bond nears maturity, its market price moves toward par value. On the maturity date the market value of a bond exactly equals its par value because the company that issued the bond pays that amount to retire the bond.

EXHIBIT 16-2   *Bond Price Information*

Bonds	Volume	High	Low	Close	Net Change
OhEd 9½ 06	12	79½	78½	79½	+2

Present Value[1]

A dollar received today is worth more than a dollar received in the future. You may invest today's dollar and earn income from it. Likewise, deferring any payment gives your money a longer period to grow. Money earns income over time, a fact called the *time value of money*. Let's examine how the time value of money affects the pricing of bonds.

Assume a bond with a face value of $1,000 reaches maturity three years from today and carries no interest. Would you pay $1,000 to purchase the bond? No, because the payment of $1,000 today to receive the same amount in the future provides you with no income on the investment. You would not be taking advantage of the time value of money. Just how much would you pay today in order to receive $1,000 at the end of three years? The answer is some amount *less* than $1,000. Let's suppose that you feel $750 is a good price. By investing $750 now to receive $1,000 later, you earn $250 interest revenue over the three years. The issuing company sees the transaction this way: It pays you $250 interest for the use of your $750 for three years.

The amount that a person would invest *at the present time* to receive a greater amount at a future date is called the **present value** of a future amount. In our example, $750 is the present value of the $1,000 amount to be received three years later.

Our $750 bond price is a reasonable estimate. The exact present value of any future amount depends on (1) the amount of the future payment (or receipt), (2) the length of time from the investment to the date when the future amount is to be received (or paid), and (3) the interest rate during the period. Present value is always less than the future amount. We discuss the method of computing present value in the appendix that follows this chapter. We need to be aware of the present-value concept, however, in the discussion of bond prices that follows. Therefore, please study the appendix now.

Bond Interest Rates

Bonds are sold at market price, which is the amount that investors are willing to pay at any given time. Market price is the bond's present value, which equals the present value of the principal payment plus the present value of the cash interest payments (which are made semiannually, annually, or quarterly over the term of the bond).

Two interest rates work to set the price of a bond. The **contract interest rate,** or **stated rate,** is the interest rate that determines the amount of cash interest the borrower pays—and the investor receives—each year. For example, Chrysler's 8 percent bonds have a contract interest rate of 8 percent. Thus Chrysler pays $8,000 of interest annually on each $100,000 bond. Each semiannual interest payment is $4,000 ($100,000 × .08 × ½).

The **market interest rate,** or **effective rate,** is the rate that investors demand for loaning their money. The market rate varies, sometimes daily. A company may issue bonds with a contract interest rate that differs from the prevailing market interest rate. Chrysler may issue its 8 percent bonds when the market rate has risen to 9 percent. Will the Chrysler bonds attract investors in this market? No, because investors can earn 9 percent on other bonds of similar risk. Therefore, investors will purchase Chrysler bonds only at a price less than par value. The

Discussion Question: Would you rather receive $1,000 today or $1,000 in ten years? Why? *ANSWER:* $1,000 today, because it can be invested today and start earning interest. Students might say that inflation is a factor. Point out that interest rates usually reflect the expected rate of inflation. The *time value of money* is the amount of interest that can be earned over time:

Present Value + Interest Earned = Future Value; or

Future Value − Interest Earned = Present Value

Changes in interest rates will change the present value. Think of a see-saw. As interest rates rise, present value decreases. As interest rates fall, present value increases.

Point to Stress: Notice that present value is always less than future value. You should always be able to invest today's money (present value) so that it will increase (future value). The difference between present value and future value is interest.

Real-World Example: Market rates fluctuate with interest rates on Treasury instruments (notes, bill, and bonds) and are usually ½ to 2 points higher than the Treasuries. The spread depends in part on whether the bond is highly rated or not. For instance, Standard and Poor's Index rates bonds as "AAA," "AA," "A," or "A-B." "AAA" bonds are considered least risky and thus carry a lower interest rate than "AA" bonds.

Point to Stress: Because market interest rates fluctuate daily, the contract interest rate will seldom equal the market interest rate on the date the bonds are sold. Bonds sell at a premium if the market rate drops below the contract rate, and at a discount if the market rate rises above the contract rate.

---

[1] The chapter appendix covers present value in more detail.

difference between the lower price and face value is a *discount*. Conversely, if the market interest rate is 7 percent, Chrysler's 8 percent bonds will be so attractive that investors will pay more than face value for them. The difference between the higher price and face value is a *premium*.

Issuing Bonds Payable

Suppose Chrysler Corporation has $50 million in 8 percent bonds that mature in 10 years. Assume that Chrysler issues these bonds at par on January 1, 1992. The issuance entry is

```
1992
Jan.  1   Cash .............................   50,000,000
               Bonds Payable .................                 50,000,000
          To issue 8%, 10-year bonds at par.
```

The corporation that is borrowing money makes a one-time entry similar to this to record the receipt of cash and the issuance of bonds. Afterward, investors buy and sell the bonds through the bond markets. The buy-and-sell transactions between investors do not involve the corporation that issued the bonds. It keeps no records of these transactions, except for the names and addresses of the bondholders. This information is needed for mailing the interest and principal payments.

Interest payments occur each January 1 and July 1. Chrysler's entry to record the first semiannual interest payment is

```
1992
July  1   Interest Expense ($50,000,000 × .08 ×       2,000,000
                ⁶⁄₁₂) ...............................
               Cash ...........................                 2,000,000
          To pay semiannual interest on bonds payable.
```

At maturity, Chrysler will record payment of the bonds as follows:

```
2002
Jan.  1   Bonds Payable.......................   50,000,000
               Cash ...........................                 50,000,000
          To pay bonds payable at maturity.
```

Issuing Bonds Payable between Interest Dates

The foregoing entries to record Chrysler's bond transactions are straightforward because the company issued the bonds on an interest payment date (January 1). However, corporations often issue bonds between interest dates.

Suppose Cincinnati Milacron, Inc., issues $75 million of 12 percent debentures due June 15, 2012. These bonds are dated June 15, 1992, and carry the price "100 plus accrued interest from date of original issue." An investor purchasing the bonds after the bond date must pay market value *plus accrued interest*. The issuing company will pay the full semiannual interest amount to the bondholder at the next interest payment date. Companies do not split semiannual interest payments among two or more investors who happen to hold the bonds during a particular six-month interest period.

Class Exercise: The following information will be used to illustrate various points covered in the next several Class Exercises:

Assume Quill Corporation issues, at par, $300,000 in 9%, 10-year bonds on May 31, 1992. The bonds pay interest each May 31 and November 30.

What are the entries to record issuance, first semiannual interest payment, and retirement at maturity?

Stock
ANSWER:
1 Issuance:
   5/31/92 Cash 300,000
              Bonds Pay.   300,000
2 First interest payment:
   11/30/92 Interest Exp. 13,500
               Cash   13,500
3 Maturity:
   5/31/02 Bonds Pay. .. 300,000
              Cash   300,000

Discussion Question: Refer to the Chrysler illustration. What happens to interest expense and the cash payment if the market interest rate later increases to 10%? ANSWER: Nothing. Interest expense and the interest paid to investors ($2,000,000) would not change. Also, the amount paid to investors at maturity would not change.

Point to Stress: Bonds are generally sold on some date other than their original date and therefore are sold "plus accrued interest." This is done so that the issuing corporation can make a single semiannual interest payment on each bond and not have to keep up with the number of days each successive buyer held the bond. The current bondholder receives a full semiannual interest payment.

Assume that Cincinnati Milacron sells $100,000 of its bonds on July 15, 1992, one month after the date of original issue on June 15. Also assume that the market price of the bonds on July 15 is the face value. The company receives one month's accrued interest in addition to the bond's face value. Cincinnati's entry to record issuance of the bonds payable is

1992			
July 15	Cash	101,000	
	Bonds Payable		100,000
	Interest Payable ($100,000 × .12 × 1/12) .		1,000
	To issue 12%, 20-year bonds at par, one month after the original issue date.		

Cincinnati's entry to record the first semiannual interest payment is

1992			
Dec. 15	Interest Expense ($100,000 × .12 × 5/12)	5,000	
	Interest Payable	1,000	
	Cash ($100,000 × .12 × 6/12)..........		6,000
	To pay semiannual interest on bonds payable.		

The debit to Interest Payable eliminates the credit balance in that account (from July 15). Cincinnati has now paid off that liability.

Note that Cincinnati Milacron pays a full six months' interest on December 15. After subtracting the one month's accrued interest received at the time of issuing the bond, Cincinnati has recorded interest expense for five months ($5,000). This interest expense is the correct amount for the five months that the bonds have been outstanding.

Selling bonds between interest dates at market value plus accrued interest simplifies the borrower's bookkeeping. The business pays the same amount of interest on each bond regardless of the length of time the person has held the bond. The business need not compute each bondholder's interest payment on an individual basis. Imagine the paperwork necessary to keep track of the interest due hundreds of bondholders who each bought bonds on a different date.

When an investor sells bonds to another investor, the price is always "plus accrued interest." Suppose you hold bonds as an investment for two months of a semiannual interest period and sell the bonds to another investor before receiving your interest. The person who buys the bonds will receive your two months of interest on the next specified interest date. Business practice dictates that you must collect your share of the interest from the buyer when you sell the bonds. For this reason, all bond transactions are "plus accrued interest."

Issuing Bonds Payable at a Discount

We know that market conditions may force the issuing corporation to accept a discount price for its bonds. Suppose Chrysler issues $100,000 of its 8 percent, 10-year bonds when the market interest rate is slightly above 8 percent. The market price of the bonds drops to 98, which means 98 percent of par value. Chrysler receives $98,000 ($100,000 × .98) at issuance. The entry is

1992			
Jan. 1	Cash ($100,000 × .98)	98,000	
	Discount on Bonds Payable	2,000	
	Bonds Payable		100,000
	To issue 8%, 10-year bonds at a discount.		

Class Exercise: Assume Quill Corporation issues its $300,000 of 9%, 10-year bonds at par on September 30,1992 (four months after the interest date, May 31). What are the entries for the original issuance and the first interest payment?

ANSWER:
Issuance:

9/30/92	Cash	309,000	
	Bonds Pay.		300,000
	Interest Pay.		9,000

($300,000 × 9% × 4/12 = $9,000)

Note that four months of interest is received in advance, in addition to the par value.

First interest payment:

11/30/92	Interest Exp.	4,500	
	Interest Pay.	9,000	
	Cash.....		13,500

Note that six months of interest has been paid in cash but only two months of interest expense has been incurred by the corporation. This is correct because the bonds have been outstanding only two months.

How much interest has been paid to the bondholders on November 30? *ANSWER:* 6 months, or $13,500. How much interest has been earned by the bondholders? *ANSWER:* 2 months, or $4,500.

Class Exercise: Assume Quill Corporation issues its $300,000, 9% bonds on May 31, 1992, when the market rate of interest is just under 10%. The bonds are issued at 97½. What is the entry to record the issuance?

ANSWER:

5/31/92	Cash	292,500	
	Discount on Bonds Pay.	7,500	
	Bonds Pay.		300,000

($300,000 × .975 = $292,500)

Note that the carrying amount on the balance sheet on 5/31/92 is:

Bonds payable	$300,000
Less: Discount on bonds pay.	7,500
Carrying Amount	$292,500

After posting, the bond accounts have the following balances:

Bonds Payable	Discount on Bonds Payable
100,000	2,000

Chrysler's balance sheet immediately after issuance of the bonds reports:

Long-term liabilities:
Bonds payable, 8%, due 2002 . . . . $100,000
Less: Discount on bonds payable 2,000 $98,000

Discount on Bonds Payable is a contra account to Bonds Payable. Subtracting its balance from Bonds Payable yields the book value, or carrying amount, of the bonds. The relationship between Bonds Payable and the Discount account is similar to the relationships between Equipment and Accumulated Depreciation and between Accounts Receivable and Allowance for Uncollectible Accounts. Thus Chrysler's liability is $98,000, which is the amount the company borrowed. If Chrysler were to pay off the bonds immediately (an unlikely occurrence), Chrysler's required outlay would be $98,000 because the market price of the bonds is $98,000.

Interest Expense on Bonds Issued at a Discount. We earlier discussed the difference between the contract interest rate and the market interest rate. Suppose the market rate is 8¼ percent when Chrysler issues its 8 percent bonds. The ¼ percent interest rate difference creates the $2,000 discount on the bonds. Chrysler borrows $98,000 cash but must pay $100,000 cash when the bonds mature, 10 years later. What happens to the $2,000 balance of the discount account over the life of the bond issue?

The $2,000 discount is really an additional interest expense to the issuing company. That amount is a cost—beyond the stated interest rate—that the business pays for borrowing the investors' money.

The discount amount is an interest expense not paid until the bond matures. However, the borrower—the bond issuer—benefits from the use of the investors' money each accounting period over the full term of the bond issue. The matching principle directs the business to match expense against its revenues on a period-by-period basis. The discount is allocated to interest expense through amortization each accounting period over the life of the bonds.

STRAIGHT-LINE AMORTIZATION OF DISCOUNT. We may amortize bond discount by dividing it into equal amounts for each interest period. This method is called straight-line amortization. In our example, the beginning discount is $2,000, and there are 20 semiannual interest periods during the bonds' 10-year life. Therefore, ¹⁄₂₀ of the $2,000 ($100) of bond discount is amortized each interest period. Chrysler's semiannual interest entry on July 1, 1992, is

1992
July 1   Interest Expense   4,100
                 Cash ($100,000 × .08 × 6⁄12)   4,000
                 Discount on Bonds Payable ($2,000/20)   100
         To pay semiannual interest and amortize
         discount on bonds payable.

Interest expense of $4,100 is the sum of the contract interest ($4,000, which is paid in cash) plus the amount of discount amortized ($100). Discount on Bonds Payable is credited to amortize (reduce) the account's debit balance.

OBJECTIVE 1

Account for basic bonds payable transactions using the straight-line amortization method

Because Discount on Bonds Payable is a contra account, each reduction in its balance increases the book value of Bonds Payable. Twenty amortization entries will decrease the discount balance to zero, which means that the carrying amount of Bonds Payable will have increased by $2,000 up to its face value of $100,000. The entry to pay off the bonds at maturity is

2002
Jan. 1	Bonds Payable.........................	100,000	
	Cash...............................		100,000
	To pay bonds payable at maturity.		

Issuing Bonds Payable at a Premium

To illustrate issuing bonds at a premium, let's change the Chrysler example. Assume that the market interest rate is 7½ percent when the company issues its 8 percent, 10-year bonds. Because 8 percent bonds are attractive in this market, investors pay a premium price to acquire them. If the bonds are priced at 103½ (103.5 percent of par value), Chrysler receives $103,500 cash upon issuance. The entry is

1992
Jan. 1	Cash ($100,000 × 1.035)	103,500	
	Bonds Payable		100,000
	Premium on Bonds Payable		3,500
	To issue 8%, 10-year bonds at a premium.		

After posting, the bond accounts have the following balances:

Bonds Payable	Premium on Bonds Payable
100,000	3,500

Chrysler's balance sheet immediately after issuance of the bonds reports:

Long-term liabilities:
Bonds payable, 8%, due 2002........	$100,000	
Premium on bonds payable	3,500	$103,500

Premium on Bonds Payable is added to Bonds Payable to show the book value, or carrying amount, of the bonds. Chrysler's liability is $103,500, which is the amount that the company borrowed. Immediate payment of the bonds would require an outlay of $103,500 because the market price of the bonds at issuance is $103,500. The investors would be unwilling to give up the bonds for less than their market value.

Interest Expense on Bonds Issued at a Premium. The ½ percent difference between the 8 percent contract rate on the bonds and the 7½ percent market interest rate creates the $3,500 premium. Chrysler borrows $103,500 cash but must pay only $100,000 cash at maturity. We treat the premium as a savings of interest expense to Chrysler. The premium cuts Chrysler's cost of borrowing the money. We account for the premium much as we handled the discount. We amortize the bond premium as a decrease in interest expense over the life of the bonds.

11/30/92 Interest Exp. . . . 13,200

    Premium on

      Bonds Pay   300

      Cash   13,500

($300,000 × .09 × 6/12 = $13,500 interest paid in cash; $6,000 ÷ 20 = $300 amortization)

Note that the Premium on Bonds Payable account is reduced equally in each of the 20 periods, until the balance has been fully amortized. The effect of recording the premium amortization is to *decrease* Interest Expense each period. In other words, Interest Expense is less than the cash paid for interest.

Typical Student Misconception: Interest Expense is always the amount of expense incurred during the period (since the last interest date). Therefore, the discount or premium amortized at year-end reflects the discount or premium amortized since the last interest payment date. Students often get confused because the time period used in the calculations can be different from the accounting period.

Class Exercise: Use the data in the previous Class Exercise. What year-end adjusting entry is required on December 31, 1992, and what entry will follow on May 31,1993?

ANSWER:

12/31/92 Interest Exp. . . . 2,200

    Premium on

      Bonds Pay. . . .   50

      Interest Pay. .   2,250

($13,500 × 1/6 = $2,250 for one month; $300 × 1/6 = $50 for one month)

STRAIGHT-LINE AMORTIZATION OF PREMIUM. In our example, the beginning premium is $3,500, and there are 20 semiannual interest periods during the bonds' 10-year life. Therefore, 1/20 of the $3,500 ($175) of bond premium is amortized each interest period. Chrysler's semiannual interest entry on July 1, 1992, is

1992

July 1	Interest Expense	3,825	
	Premium on Bonds Payable ($3,500/20)	175	
	Cash ($100,000 × .08 × 6/12)		4,000
	To pay semiannual interest and amortize premium on bonds payable.		

Interest expense of $3,825 is the remainder of the contract cash interest ($4,000) less the amount of premium amortized ($175). The debit to Premium on Bonds Payable reduces its credit balance.

Reporting Bonds Payable

Bonds payable are reported on the balance sheet at their maturity amount plus any unamortized premium or minus any unamortized discount. For example, at December 31, Chrysler in the preceding example would have amortized Premium on Bonds Payable for two semiannual periods ($175 × 2 = $350). The Chrysler balance sheet would show these bonds payable as follows:

Long-term liabilities:

Bonds payable, 8%, due 2002	$100,000	
Premium on bonds payable [$3,500 − (2 × $175)] . .	3,150	$103,150

Over the life of the bonds, twenty amortization entries will decrease the premium balance to zero. The payment at maturity will debit Bonds Payable and credit cash for $100,000.

Adjusting Entries for Interest Expense ———————————

Companies issue bonds when they need cash. The interest payments seldom occur on December 31 (or the end of the fiscal year). Nevertheless, interest expense must be accrued at the end of the period to measure income accurately. The accrual entry may often be complicated by the need to amortize a discount or a premium for only a partial interest period.

Suppose Xenon issues $100,000 of its 8 percent, 10-year bonds at a $2,000 discount on October 1, 1992. Assume that interest payments occur on March 31 and September 30 each year. On December 31 Xenon records interest for the three-month period (October, November, and December) as follows:

1992

Dec. 31	Interest Expense	2,050	
	Interest Payable ($100,000 × .08 × 3/12) . . .		2,000
	Discount on Bonds Payable ($2,000/10 × 3/12)		50
	To accrue three months' interest and amortize discount on bonds payable for three months.		

Interest Payable is credited for the three months of cash interest that have accrued since September 30. Discount on Bonds Payable is credited for three months of amortization.

The balance sheet at December 31, 1992, reports Interest Payable of $2,000 as a current liability. Bonds Payable appears as a long-term liability, presented as follows:

Long-term liabilities:
Bonds payable, 8%, due 2002 . . . . $100,000
Less: Discount on bonds payable ($2,000 − $50) . .   <u>1,950</u> $98,050

Observe that the balance of Discount on Bonds Payable decreases by $50. The bonds' carrying amount also increases by $50. The bonds' carrying amount continues to increase over its 10-year life, reaching $100,000 at maturity, when the discount will be fully amortized.

The next semiannual interest payment occurs on March 31, 1993:

1993
Mar. 31   Interest Expense   2,050
          Interest Payable   2,000
               Cash ($100,000 × .08 × 6/12)   4,000
               Discount on Bonds Payable ($2,000/10 × 3/12)   50
          To pay semiannual interest, part of which was
          accrued, and amortize three months' discount
          on bonds payable.

Amortization of a premium over a partial interest period is similar except that Premium on Bonds Payable is debited.

Summary Problem for Your Review

Assume that Alabama Power Company has outstanding an issue of 9 percent bonds that mature on May 1, 2013. Further, assume that the bonds are dated May 1, 1993, and Alabama Power pays interest each April 30 and October 31.

Required

1. Will the bonds be issued at par, at a premium, or at a discount if the market interest rate is 8 percent at date of issuance? if the market interest rate is 10 percent?

2. Assume Alabama Power issued $1,000,000 of the bonds at 104 on May 1, 1993.
   a. Record issuance of the bonds.
   b. Record the interest payment and amortization of premium or discount on October 31, 1993.
   c. Accrue interest and amortize premium or discount on December 31, 1993.
   d. Show how the company would report the bonds on the balance sheet at December 31, 1993.
   e. Record the interest payment on April 30, 1994.

SOLUTION TO REVIEW PROBLEM

Requirement 1. If the market interest rate is 8 percent, 9 percent bonds will be issued at a *premium*. If the market rate is 10 percent, the 9 percent bonds will be issued at a *discount*.

Requirement 2

1993

a. May 1	Cash ($1,000,000 × 1.04)	1,040,000	
	Bonds Payable		1,000,000
	Premium on Bonds Payable		40,000
	To issue 9%, 20-year bonds at a premium.		

b. Oct. 31	Interest Expense........................	44,000	
	Premium on Bonds Payable ($40,000/40) .	1,000	
	Cash ($1,000,000 × .09 × 6/12)		45,000
	To pay semiannual interest and amortize premium on bonds payable.		

c. Dec. 31	Interest Expense........................	14,667	
	Premium on Bonds Payable		
	($40,000/40 × 2/6)	333	
	Interest Payable ($1,000,000		
	× .09 × 2/12)		15,000
	To accrue interest and amortize bond premium for two months.		

d. Long-term liabilities:

Bonds payable, 9%, due 2013 ...	$1,000,000	
Premium on bonds payable		
($40,000 − $1,000 − $333)	38,667	$1,038,667

1994

e. Apr. 30	Interest Expense........................	29,333	
	Interest Payable	15,000	
	Premium on Bonds Payable		
	($40,000/40 × 4/6)	667	
	Cash ($1,000,000 × .09 × 6/12)		45,000
	To pay semiannual interest, part of which was accrued, and amortize four months' premium on bonds payable.		

SUPPLEMENT TO SUMMARY PROBLEM SOLUTION

Bond problems include many details. You may find it helpful to check your work. We verify the answers to the Summary Problem in this supplement.

On April 30, 1994, the bonds have been outstanding for one year. After the entries have been recorded, the account balances should show the results of one year's cash interest payments and one year's bond premium amortization.

Fact 1:   Cash interest payments should be $90,000 ($1,000,000 × .09).

Accuracy check: Two credits to Cash of $45,000 each = $90,000. Cash payments are correct.

Fact 2:	Premium amortization should be $2,000 ($40,000/40 semiannual periods × 2 semiannual periods in 1 year).
Accuracy check:	Three debits to Premium on Bonds Payable ($1,000 + $333 + $667) = $2,000. Premium amortization is correct.
Fact 3:	Also we can check the accuracy of interest expense recorded during the year ended December 31, 1993.
	The bonds in this problem will be outstanding for a total of 20 years, or 240 (that is, 20 × 12) months. During 1993 the bonds are outstanding for 8 months (May through December).
	Interest expense for 8 months *equals* payment of cash interest for 8 months minus premium amortization for 8 months. Interest expense should therefore be ($1,000,000 × .09 × $8/12$ = $60,000) minus [($40,000/240) × 8 = $1,333] or ($60,000 − $1,333 = $58,667).
Accuracy check:	Two debits to Interest Expense ($44,000 + $14,667) = $58,667. Interest expense for 1993 is correct.

Effective-Interest Method of Amortization _____

The straight-line amortization method has a theoretical weakness. Each period's amortization amount for a premium or discount is the same dollar amount over the life of the bonds. However, over that time the bonds' carrying amount continues to increase (with a discount) or decrease (with a premium). Thus the fixed dollar amount of amortization changes as a percentage of the bonds' carrying amount, making it appear that the bond issuer's interest rate changes over time. This appearance misleads because in fact the issuer locked in a fixed interest rate when the bonds were issued. The interest rate on the bonds does not change.

GAAP *(Accounting Principles Board Opinion No. 21)* specifies that discounts and premiums be amortized using the effective-interest method unless the difference between the straight-line method and the effective-interest method is immaterial. In that case, either method is permitted. We will see how the effective-interest method keeps each interest expense amount at the same percentage of the bonds' carrying amount for every interest payment over the bonds' life. The total amount amortized over the life of the bonds is the same under both methods.

Effective-Interest Method of Amortizing Discount

OBJECTIVE 2
Amortize bond discount and premium by the effective-interest method

Assume that Bethlehem Steel Corporation issues $100,000 of its 9 percent bonds at a time when the market rate of interest is 10 percent. Also assume that these bonds mature in five years and pay interest semiannually, so there are 10 semiannual interest payments. The issue price of the bonds is $96,149.[2] The discount on these bonds is $3,851 ($100,000 − $96,149).

Exhibit 16-3 illustrates amortization of the discount by the effective-interest method.

_____

[2] We compute this present value using the tables that appear in the appendix to this chapter.

EXHIBIT 16-3 *Effective-Interest Method of Amortizing Bond Discount*

Teaching Tip: In Exhibit 16-3, look at column A, Interest Payment. This number never changes over the life of the bonds because it is always based on par value times the contract rate.

Teaching Tip: Ask students to recite the formula for computing interest expense every time you illustrate a problem in class. That formula is:

Interest expense = Preceding carrying amount × Market interest rate

Teaching Tip: Remind students that the amortization of the discount is the difference between the interest expense and the cash interest paid. Interest expense will be larger than the cash paid because the discount is being amortized.

Point to Stress: The entry to record the issuance of the bonds is unaffected by the method used to amortize the premium or discount.

Panel A—Bond Data

Maturity value—$100,000

Contract interest rate—9%

Interest paid—4½% semiannually, $4,500 ($100,000 × .045)

Market interest rate at time of issue—10% annually, 5% semiannually

Issue price—$96,149

Panel B—Amortization Table

	A	B	C	D	E
Semiannual Interest Period	Interest Payment (4½% of Maturity Value)	Interest Expense (5% of Preceding Bond Carrying Amount)	Discount Amortization (B − A)	Discount Account Balance (D − C)	Bond Carrying Amount ($100,000 − D)
Issue Date				$3,851	$ 96,149
1	$4,500	$4,807	$307	3,544	96,456
2	4,500	4,823	323	3,221	96,779
3	4,500	4,839	339	2,882	97,118
4	4,500	4,856	356	2,526	97,474
5	4,500	4,874	374	2,152	97,848
6	4,500	4,892	392	1,760	98,240
7	4,500	4,912	412	1,348	98,652
8	4,500	4,933	433	915	99,085
9	4,500	4,954	454	461	99,539
10	4,500	4,961*	461	-0-	100,000

* Adjusted for effect of rounding.

The exhibit reveals the following important facts about effective interest method amortization of bond discount:

Point to Stress: With the straight-line method, the interest expense for any six-month period is the same throughout the life of the bond. With the interest method, the interest expense changes each period as the carrying value of the bond changes.

Typical Student Misconception: Students often forget which interest rate to use when. Remind them that the contract or stated rate is used only to figure the semiannual interest payment, which never changes over the life of the bonds. The market (effective) rate is used to figure the interest expense.

Column A. The semiannual interest payments are constant because they are governed by the contract interest rate and the bonds' maturity value.

Column B. The interest expense each period is computed by multiplying the preceding bond carrying amount by the market interest rate (5 percent semiannually). This rate is the *effective interest rate* because its effect determines the interest expense each period. The amount of interest each period increases as the effective interest rate, a constant, is applied to the increasing bond carrying amount (column E).

Column C. The excess of each interest expense amount (column B) over each interest payment amount (column A) is the discount amortization for the period.

Column D. The discount balance decreases by the amount of amortization for the period (column C). The discount decreases from $3,851 at the bonds' issue date to zero at their maturity. The balance of the discount plus the bonds' carrying amount equal the bonds' maturity value.

Column E. The bonds' carrying amount increases from $96,149 at issuance to $100,000 at maturity.

Recall that we want to present interest expense amounts over the full life of the bonds at a fixed percentage of the bonds' carrying amount. The 5 percent rate—the effective-interest rate—*is* that percentage. We have figured the cost of the money borrowed by the bond issuer—the interest expense—as a constant percentage of the carrying amount of the bonds. The dollar *amount* of interest expense varies from period to period but not the interest percentage *rate.*

The accounts debited and credited under the effective interest amortization method and the straight-line method are the same. Only the amounts differ. We may take the amortization amounts directly from the table in the exhibit. We assume that the first interest payment occurs on July 1 and use the appropriate amounts from Exhibit 16-3, reading across the line for the first interest payment date:

July 1	Interest Expense (column B)	4,807	
	Discount on Bonds Payable (column C)		307
	Cash (column A).........................		4,500
	To pay semiannual interest and amortize discount on bonds payable.		

Effective-Interest Method of Amortizing Premium

Let's modify the Bethlehem Steel example to illustrate the interest method of amortizing bond premium. Assume that Bethlehem Steel issues $100,000 of five-year, 9 percent bonds that pay interest semiannually. If the bonds are issued when the market interest rate is 8 percent, their issue price is $104,100.[3] The premium on these bonds is $4,100, and Exhibit 16-4 illustrates amortization of the premium by the interest method.

Exhibit 16-4 reveals the following important facts about the effective-interest method of amortizing bond premium:

Column A. The semiannual interest payments are a constant amount fixed by the contract interest rate and the bonds' maturity value.

Column B. The interest expense each period is computed by multiplying the preceding bond carrying amount by the effective interest rate (4 percent semiannually). Observe that the amount of interest decreases each period as the bond carrying amount decreases.

Column C. The excess of each interest payment (column A) over the period's interest expense (column B) is the premium amortization for the period.

Column D. The premium balance decreases by the amount of amortization for the period (column C) from $4,100 at issuance to zero at maturity. The bonds' carrying amount minus the premium balance equals the bonds' maturity value.

Column E. The bonds' carrying amount decreases from $104,100 at issuance to $100,000 at maturity.

Assuming that the first interest payment occurs on October 31, we read across the line for the first interest payment date and pick up the appropriate amounts.

---

[3]Again, we compute the present value of the bonds using the tables in this chapter's appendix.

That market rate is used each period to calculate the expense; it is a constant percentage, multiplied by a bond carrying value that increases (discount) or decreases (premium). Thus, the amount of interest expense changes each period, although the interest rate remains the same.

Class Exercise: Back to Quill Corporation, and the $300,000, 9%, 10-year bonds dated 5/31/92. Assume the bonds are sold on 5/31/92, for $281,337, to yield an effective rate of 10%. Using the effective interest method of amortization, what is the entry required on 11/30/92, the first interest payment date?

ANSWER:

11/30/92 Interest Exp ..	14,067	
Discount on Bonds Pay. .		567
Cash		13,500

Beg. carrying value	$281,337
× Market rate.........	5%
Interest Exp.	14,067
Interest paid in cash ...	13,500
Discount amortized	$ 567

Note that the Discount account has been reduced by $567. A T-account may help students follow this:

Discount on Bonds Payable

18,663	567
18,096	

Beginning Discount = $300,000 − $281,337 = $18,663
The bond carrying amount is now $281,904 ($300,000 − $18,096).

EXHIBIT 16-4 *Effective-Interest Method of Amortizing Bond Premium*

Teaching Tip: Refer to Exhibit 16-4. The amortization table indicates that the carrying amount is the principal *plus* the premium. The carrying amount changes each period by the amortization of the premium. The new carrying amount each period can be calculated by subtracting the amortization of the premium from the previous bond carrying amount. Look at the carrying amount at the end of the third period—$103,052. The carrying amount at the end of the fourth period will be:

$103,052
−   378
= $102,674

Panel A—Bond Data

Maturity value—$100,000

Contract interest rate—9%

Interest paid—4½% semiannually, $4,500 ($100,000 × .045)

Market interest rate at time of issue—8% annually, 4% semiannually

Issue price—$104,100

Panel B—Amortization Table

	A	B	C	D	E
Semiannual Interest Period	Interest *Payment* (4½% of Maturity Value)	Interest *Expense* (4% of Preceding Bond Carrying Amount)	Premium Amortization (A − B)	Premium Account Balance (D − C)	Bond Carrying Amount ($100,000 + D)
Issue Date				$4,100	$104,100
1	$4,500	$4,164	$336	3,764	103,764
2	4,500	4,151	349	3,415	103,415
3	4,500	4,137	363	3,052	103,052
4	4,500	4,122	378	2,674	102,674
5	4,500	4,107	393	2,281	102,281
6	4,500	4,091	409	1,872	101,872
7	4,500	4,075	425	1,447	101,447
8	4,500	4,058	442	1,005	101,005
9	4,500	4,040	460	545	100,545
10	4,500	3,955*	545	-0-	100,000

* Adjusted for effect of rounding.

Oct. 31   Interest Expense (column B)   4,164
           Premium on Bonds Payable (column C)   336
               Cash (column A)   4,500
           To pay semiannual interest and amortize
           premium on bonds payable.

At year end it is necessary to make an adjusting entry for accrued interest and amortization of the bond premium for a partial period. In our example, the last interest payment occurred on October 31. The adjustment for November and December must cover two months, or one-third of a semiannual period. The entry, with amounts drawn from Exhibit 16-4, line 2, is

Dec. 31   Interest Expense ($4,151 × ⅓)   1,384
           Premium on Bonds Payable ($349 × ⅓)   116
               Interest Payable ($4,500 × ⅓)   1,500
           To accrue two months' interest and amortize
           premium on bonds payable for two months.

The second interest payment occurs on April 30 of the following year. The payment of $4,500 includes interest expense for four months (January through April), the interest payable at December 31, and premium amortization for four months. The payment entry is

```
Apr. 30   Interest Expense ($4,151 × ⅔) ...............   2,767
          Interest Payable ...........................   1,500
          Premium on Bonds Payable ($349 × ⅔) .......     233
              Cash .............................                4,500
          To pay semiannual interest, some of which
          was accrued, and amortize premium on bonds
          payable for four months.
```

If these bonds had been issued at a discount, procedures for these interest entries would be the same, except that Discount on Bonds Payable would be credited.

Bond Sinking Fund

Bond indentures—the contracts under which bonds are issued—often require the borrower to make regular periodic payments to a *bond sinking fund*. A fund is a group of assets that are segregated for a particular purpose. A **bond sinking fund** is used to retire bonds payable at maturity. A trustee manages this fund for the issuer, investing the company's payments in income-earning assets. The company's payments into the fund and the interest revenue—which the trustee reinvests in the fund—accumulate. The target amount of the sinking fund is the face value of the bond issue at maturity. When the bonds come due, the trustee sells the sinking-fund assets and uses the cash proceeds to pay off the bonds. The bond sinking fund provides security of payment to investors in unsecured bonds.

Most companies report sinking funds under the heading Investments, a separate asset category between current assets and plant assets on the balance sheet. A bond sinking fund is not a current asset because it may not be used to pay current liabilities. Accounting for the interest, dividends, and other earnings on the bond sinking fund requires use of the accounts Sinking Fund and Sinking-Fund Revenue.

Sperry Corporation has outstanding $40 million of 8.2 percent sinking-fund debentures. The company must make annual sinking-fund payments. The entry to deposit $2 million with the trustee is

Point to Stress: The purpose of the bond sinking fund is to accumulate enough cash to retire the bonds at maturity, not to accumulate cash to make the periodic interest payments.

```
Jan. 5    Sinking Fund .....................   2,000,000
              Cash .........................                2,000,000
          To make annual sinking-fund deposit.
```

If the trustee invests the cash and reports annual sinking-fund revenue of $150,000, the fund grows by this amount, and Sperry makes the following entry at year end:

```
Dec. 31   Sinking Fund .....................     150,000
              Sinking-Fund Revenue .........                  150,000
          To record sinking-fund earnings.
```

Assume that Sperry has made the required sinking-fund payments over a period of years and that these payments plus the fund earnings have accumulated a cash balance of $40.2 million at maturity. The trustee pays off the bonds and returns the excess cash to Sperry, which makes the following entry:

Point to Stress: It is difficult for many corporations to generate the cash required to retire bonds. Some corporations use sinking funds, some corporations issue new bonds to retire the maturing bonds, and some corporations issue bonds with staggered maturity dates (serial bonds).

OBJECTIVE 3

Account for retirement of bonds payable

Point to Stress: Any time bonds are retired before their maturity date, these steps must be followed:

1 Record partial period amortization of premium or discount, if it is some date other than an interest payment date.

2 Write off the portion of Premium or Discount that relates to the portion of bonds being retired.

3 Calculate extraordinary gain or loss on retirement.

Point to Stress: Gains or losses on early retirement of debt do not fit the definition of an extraordinary item (infrequent and unusual). However, GAAP requires these gains or losses to be reported as extraordinary.

Class Exercise: Quill Corporation has sold $300,000 of 10-year bonds at a discount. Interest has just been paid and the remaining carrying value of the bonds is $299,000. Half the bonds are retired when the market price is 96½. What entry is required?

Jan. 4	Cash	200,000	
	Bonds Payable....................	40,000,000	
	Sinking Fund		40,200,000

To record payment of bonds payable and receipt of excess sinking-fund cash at maturity.

If the fund balance is less than the bonds' maturity value, the entry is similar to the foregoing entry. However, the company pays the extra amount and credits Cash.

Retirement of Bonds Payable

Normally companies wait until maturity to pay off, or retire, their bonds payable. All bond discount or premium has been amortized, and the retirement entry debits Bonds Payable and credits Cash for the bonds' maturity value.

Companies sometimes retire their bonds payable prior to maturity. The main reason for retiring bonds early is to relieve the pressure of making interest payments. Interest rates fluctuate. The company may be able to borrow at a lower interest rate and use the proceeds from new bonds to pay off the old bonds, which bear a higher rate.

Some bonds are **callable,** which means that the issuer may *call,* or pay off, the bonds at a specified price whenever the issuer wants. The call price is usually a few percent above par, perhaps 104 or 105. Callable bonds give the issuer the benefit of being able to take advantage of low interest rates by paying off the bonds at the most favorable time. An alternative to calling the bonds is to purchase them in the open market at their current market price. Whether the bonds are called or purchased in the open market, the journal entry is the same.

Air Products and Chemicals, Inc., has $70,000,000 of debentures outstanding with unamortized discount of $350,000. Lower interest rates in the market may convince management to pay off these bonds now. Assume that the bonds are callable at 103. If the market price of the bonds is 99¼ will Air Products call the bonds or purchase them in the open market? The market price is lower than the call price, so market price is the better choice. Retiring the bonds at 99¼ results in a gain of $175,000, computed as follows:

Par value of bonds being retired	$70,000,000
Unamortized discount	350,000
Book value........................	69,650,000
Market price ($70,000,000 × .9925)	69,475,000
Gain on retirement	$ 175,000

The entry to record retirement of the bonds, immediately after an interest date, is

June 30	Bonds Payable	70,000,000	
	Discount on Bonds Payable		350,000
	Cash ($70,000,000 × .9925).....		69,475,000
	Extraordinary Gain on		
	Retirement of Bonds Payable .		175,000

To retire bonds payable before maturity.

The entry removes the bonds payable and the related discount from the accounts and records a gain on retirement. Of course, any existing premium would be removed with a debit. If Air Products and Chemicals had retired only half of these bonds, the accountant would remove half of the discount or premium. Likewise, if the price paid to retire the bonds exceeds their carrying amount, the retirement entry would record a loss with a debit to the account Extraordinary Loss on Retirement of Bonds. GAAP identifies gains and losses on early retirement of debt as *extraordinary*, and they are reported separately on the income statement, net of tax.

Convertible Bonds and Notes

Many corporate bonds and notes payable may be converted into the common stock of the issuing company at the option of the investor. These bonds and notes, called **convertible bonds** (or **notes**), combine the safety of assured interest receipts and receipt of principal on the bonds with the opportunity for large gains on the stock. The conversion feature is so attractive that investors usually accept a lower contract, or stated, interest rate than they would on non-convertible bonds. The lower cash interest payments benefit the issuer. Convertible bonds are recorded like any other debt at issuance.

If the market price of the issuing company's stock gets high enough, the bondholders will convert the bonds into stock. The corporation records conversion by debiting the bond accounts and crediting the stockholders' equity accounts. The carrying amount of the bonds becomes the book value of the newly issued stock. No gain or loss is recorded.

Prime Western, Inc., had convertible *notes* outstanding carried on the books at $12.5 million. Assume that the maturity value of the notes was $13 million. Also assume that Prime Western's stock rose significantly so that noteholders converted the notes into 400,000 shares of the company's $1 par common stock. Prime Western's entry to record conversion is

May 14	Notes Payable	13,000,000	
	Discount on Notes Payable		500,000
	Common Stock (400,000 × $1) . .		400,000
	Paid-in Capital in Excess of Par—Common		12,100,000
	To record conversion of notes payable.		

Observe that the carrying amount of the notes ($13,000,000 − $500,000) becomes the amount of increase in stockholders' equity ($400,000 + $12,100,000). The entry closes the notes (or bonds) payable account and its related discount or premium account.

Current Portion of Long-Term Debt

Serial bonds and serial notes are payable in serials, or installments. The portion payable within one year is a current liability, and the remaining debt is long-term. At June 30, 1990, Birmingham Steel Corporation, had $30,961,000 of long-term debt maturing in various annual amounts from 1994 through 2001. The portion payable in 1991 was $3,809,000. Therefore, $3,809,000 was a current liability at June 30, 1990, and $27,152,000 was a long-term liability. Bir-

---

ANSWER:

Bonds Pay	150,000	
Discount on Bond Pay.		500
Cash		144,750
EO Gain on Retirement of Bonds Pay		4,750

($300,000 Bonds payable × ½ =	$150,000	
− 1,000 Unamortized discount × ½ =	500	
$299,000 Carrying amount × ½ =	$149,500	

$150,000 × .965 = $144,750 market price;
$149,500 − $144,750 = $4,750 gain)

OBJECTIVE 4
Account for conversion of bonds payable

Class Exercise: Quill Corporation has issued $300,000 of 10-year bonds at a premium. Assume that the bonds are convertible into common stock at the rate of 25 shares of $20 par value stock for each $1,000 bond. The market price rises and bondholders convert the bonds into stock after an interest payment, when the remaining carrying amount is $301,550. What journal entry records the conversion?

ANSWER:

Bonds Pay.	300,000	
Premium on Bonds Pay.	1,550	
Com. Stock . . .		150,000
Paid in Cap.in Excess of Par— Com.		151,550

$$\frac{\$300,000}{\$1,000} = 300 \text{ bonds converted}$$

×	25 shares per bond
	7,500 shares to be issued
×	$20 par value
	$150,000 Com. Stock issued)

Note that the premium on common stock is a "plug" figure; there is no gain or loss recorded on a bond conversion. The remaining carrying amount of the bonds ($301,550) merely becomes the amount of paid-in capital.

mingham Steel reported the following among its liabilities at June 30, 1990:

	$ Millions
Current liabilities:	
Current portion of long-term debt	$ 3,809
Long-term debt less current portion	27,152

Mortgage Notes Payable

You have probably heard of mortgage payments. Many notes payable are mortgage notes, which actually contain two agreements. The *note* is the borrower's promise to pay the lender the amount of the debt. The **mortgage**—a security agreement related to the note—is the borrower's promise to transfer the legal title to certain assets to the lender if the debt is not paid on schedule. The borrower is said to pledge these assets as security for the note. Often the asset that is pledged was acquired with the borrowed money. For example, most homeowners sign mortgage notes to purchase their residence, pledging that property as security for the loan. Businesses sign mortgage notes to acquire buildings, equipment, and other long-term assets. Mortgage notes are usually serial notes that require monthly or quarterly payments.

Advantage of Financing Operations with Debt versus Stock

OBJECTIVE 5

Explain the advantages and disadvantages of borrowing

Teaching Tip: Advantages of issuing stock:

1 Raise capital without increasing debt
2 No obligation exists to pay dividends
3 There is no debt to repay

Advantages of borrowing:

1 EPS is greater
2 Interest is tax deductible
3 Investing the borrowed funds (trading on the equity, or leverage) results in a return on investment that exceeds the cost of borrowing.

Businesses have different ways to acquire assets. Management may decide to purchase or to lease equipment. The money to finance the asset may come from the business's retained earnings, a note payable, a stock issue, or a bond issue. Each financing strategy has its advantages and disadvantages. Let's examine how issuing stock compares with issuing bonds.

Bonds differ from stocks in important ways. Stock shares give the holder part ownership of the corporation and a voice in management. Bonds merely give the holder a creditor's claim to the debtor's assets. Bond certificates carry dates for maturity and interest payments, unlike stock, which does not come due at any specific time. Companies are not obligated to declare dividends on stock.

Issuing stock raises capital without incurring the liabilities and interest expense that accompany bonds. However, by issuing stock the business spreads the ownership, control, and income of the corporation among more shares. Management may wish to avoid this dilution of its ownership. Borrowing money through bonds raises liabilities and interest expense, which the corporation must pay whether or not it earns a profit. But borrowing does not affect stockholder control: bondholders are creditors with no voice in management. Borrowing also provides a tax advantage in that interest expense is tax-deductible. Dividends paid to stockholders are not tax-deductible because they are not an expense.

Exhibit 16-5 illustrates the earnings-per-share (EPS) advantage of borrowing. Suppose a corporation with 100,000 shares of common stock outstanding needs $500,000 for expansion. Management is considering two financing plans. Plan 1 is to issue $500,000 of 10 percent bonds payable, and plan 2 is to issue 50,000 shares of common stock for $500,000. Management believes the

	Plan 1 Borrow $500,000 at 10%	Plan 2 Issue $500,000 of Common Stock
Income before interest and income tax....	$200,000	$200,000
Less interest expense ($500,000 × .10)	50,000	-0-
Income before income tax	150,000	200,000
Less income tax expense (40%)	60,000	80,000
Net income	$ 90,000	$120,000
Earnings per share on new project:		
Plan 1 ($90,000/100,000 shares).........	$ .90	
Plan 2 ($120,000/150,000 shares)........		$ .80

new cash can be invested in operations to earn income of $200,000 before interest and taxes.

The earnings-per-share amount is higher if the company borrows. The business earns more on the investment ($90,000) than the interest it pays on the bonds ($50,000). Earning more income on borrowed money than the related interest expense increases the earnings for common stockholders and is called **trading on the equity.** It is widely used in business to increase earnings per share of common stock.

Dividend payments to the new stockholders under plan 2 would also make borrowing more attractive than issuing stock. Assume that net income generates an increase in cash of the same amount. If under plan 2 the company were to pay dividends of $50,000—the same as the interest expense under plan 1— its net cash inflow would be $70,000 ($120,000 − $50,000), compared with $90,000 under plan 1.

Borrowing has its disadvantages. Interest expense may be high enough to eliminate net income and lead to a cash crisis and even bankruptcy. Also, borrowing creates liabilities that accrue during bad years as well as during good years. In contrast, a company that issues stock can omit its dividends during a bad year.

The following quotation from *Business Week* (July 2, 1990, p. 38) describes how a major company overextended its financial capabilities. A *leveraged buyout* is a debt-financed acquisition of another company, often with so-called junk bonds. These bonds bear high interest rates because their probability of repayment is relatively low.

> Was it only last year that financier Henry Kravis and his partners borrowed a whopping $28 billion to buy RJR Nabisco in the biggest leveraged buyout in history? It seems like an age—namely, the age of excessive debt. Now, only 17 months later, the landscape is littered with casualties of overborrowing—Robert Campeau, Merv Griffin, Donald Trump. Kravis, whose name became synonymous with leveraged buyouts in the go-go 1980s, seems determined to avoid the same fate. Adapting to the pay-as-you-go 1990s, Kohlberg Kravis Roberts is planning to put RJR on a sounder financial footing. The firm indicated that it would plow $1.7 billion of new equity into the food and tobacco giant and retire some $4 billion of high-yield junk bonds. Said a Shearson Lehman Hutton trader, "It's the official end of the junk-bond era."

Point to Stress: Trading on the equity is also referred to as *leverage.*

Discussion Question: If trading on the equity improved EPS (as in Exhibit 16-5), can you think of how it might be to the corporation's disadvantage to finance with debt? ANSWER: The corporation would suffer if the interest rate on its debt is greater than the rate of earnings from that money. Harm would also result if the company borrows so much (too much leverage) that they cannot meet interest and principal payments as they come due.

Lease Liabilities

A **lease** is a rental agreement in which the tenant (**lessee**) agrees to make rent payments to the property owner (**lessor**) in exchange for the use of the asset. Leasing allows the lessee to acquire the use of a needed asset without having to make the large initial cash down payment that purchase agreements require. Accountants divide leases into two types: operating and capital.

Operating Leases

Point to Stress: For an operating lease; the lessor, not the lessee, records depreciation expense on the asset leased.

You are already familiar with **operating leases**, which are usually short-term or cancelable. Many apartment leases and most car-rental agreements are for a year or less. These operating leases give the lessee the right to use the asset but provide the lessee with no continuing rights to the asset. The lessor retains the usual risks and rewards of owning the leased asset. To account for an operating lease, the lessee debits Rent Expense (or Lease Expense) and credits Cash for the amount of the lease payment. The lessee's books do not report the leased asset or any lease liability (except perhaps a prepaid rent amount or a rent accrual at the end of the period).

Capital Leases

Point to Stress: A capital lease is different from an operating lease in that the capital lease transfers substantially all the risks and rewards of ownership to the lessee. The lessor remains the owner of record and continues to hold the deed, but the lessee functions as the owner of the leased asset and will record the lease as a purchase.

More and more businesses nationwide are turning to capital leasing to finance the acquisition of assets. A *capital lease* is long-term and noncancelable. Accounting for a capital lease is much like accounting for a purchase. The lessor removes the asset from her books. The lessee enters the asset into his accounts and records a lease liability at the beginning of the lease term.

Most companies lease some of their plant assets rather than buy them. *A recent survey of 600 companies indicates that they have more leases than any other type of long-term debt.*

Southland Corporation owns 7-Eleven convenience stores. Suppose the company leases a building, agreeing to pay $10,000 annually for a 20-year period, with the first payment due immediately. This arrangement is similar to purchasing the building on an installment plan. In an installment purchase, Southland would debit Building and credit Cash and Installment Note Payable. The company would then pay interest and principal on the note payable and record depreciation on the building. Accounting for a capital lease follows this pattern.

Real-World Example: Leases are very popular. Only 69 of 600 companies surveyed by *Accounting Trends and Techniques* reported no use of leases.

Southland records the building at cost, which is the sum of the $10,000 initial payment plus the present value of the 19 future lease payments of $10,000 each. The company credits Cash for the initial payment and credits Lease Liability for the present value of the future lease payments. Assume the interest rate on Southland's lease is 10 percent and the present value (PV) of the future lease payments is $83,650.[4] At the beginning of the lease term, Southland makes the following entry:

19X1			
Jan. 2	Building ($10,000 + $83,650)	93,650	
	Cash		10,000
	Lease Liability (PV of future lease payments)		83,650
	To acquire a building and make the first annual lease payment on a capital lease.		

---

[4] This computation appears in the chapter appendix.

Because Southland has capitalized the building, the company records depreciation. Assume the building has an expected life of 25 years. It is depreciated over the lease term of 20 years because the lessee has the use of the building only for that period. No residual value enters into the depreciation computation because the lessee will have no residual asset when the building is returned to the lessor at the expiration of the lease. Therefore, the annual depreciation entry is

19X1			
Dec. 31	Depreciation Expense ($93,650/20)	4,683	
	Accumulated Depreciation—Building . . .		4,683
	To record depreciation on leased building.		

At year end Southland must also accrue interest on the lease liability. Interest expense is computed by multiplying the lease liability by the interest rate on the lease. The following entry credits Lease Liability (not Interest Payable) for this interest accrual:

19X1			
Dec. 31	Interest Expense ($83,650 × .10)	8,365	
	Lease Liability		8,365
	To accrue interest on the lease liability.		

The balance sheet at December 31, 19X1 reports:

Assets

Plant assets:		
Building	$93,650	
Less Accumulated depreciation	4,683	$88,967

Liabilities

Current liabilities:	
Lease liability (next payment due on Jan. 2, 19X2)	$10,000
Long-term liabilities:	
Lease liability [beginning balance ($83,650) + interest accrual	
($8,365) − current portion ($10,000)]	82,015

The lease liability is split into current and long-term portions because the next payment ($10,000) is a current liability and the remainder is long-term.

The January 2, 19X2, lease payment is recorded as follows:

19X2			
Jan. 2	Lease Liability	10,000	
	Cash		10,000
	To make second annual lease payment on building.		

Distinguishing a Capital Lease from an Operating Lease. How would you distinguish a capital lease from an operating lease? *FASB Statement No. 13* provides the guidelines. To be classified as a **capital lease,** a particular lease agreement must meet any *one* of the following criteria:

1. The lease transfers title of the leased asset to the lessee at the end of the lease term. Thus the lessee becomes the legal owner of the leased asset.

Point to Stress: FASB 13 requires that a lease that meets any one of these must be accounted for as a capital lease.

2. The lease contains a *bargain purchase option*. The lessee can be expected to purchase the leased asset and become its legal owner.

3. The lease term is 75 percent or more of the estimated useful life of the leased asset. The lessee uses up most of the leased asset's service potential.

4. The present value of the lease payments is 90 percent or more of the market value of the leased asset. In effect, the lease payments operate as installment payments for the leased asset.

Only those leases that fail to meet *all* of these criteria may be accounted for as operating leases.

Point to Stress: A bargain purchase option is an option for the lessee to purchase the leased asset at a price well below its market value.

Off-Balance-Sheet Financing

An important part of business is obtaining the funds needed to acquire assets. To finance operations a company may issue stock, borrow money, or retain earnings in the business. Notice that all three of these financing plans affect the right-hand side of the balance sheet. Issuing stock affects preferred or common stock. Borrowing creates notes or bonds payable. Internal funds come from retained earnings.

Off-balance-sheet financing is the acquisition of assets or services with debt that is not reported on the balance sheet. A prime example is an operating lease. The lessee has the use of the leased asset, but neither the asset nor any lease liability is reported on the balance sheet. In the past, most leases were accounted for by the operating method. However, *FASB Statement No. 13* has required businesses to account for an increasing number of leases by the capital lease method. Also, *FASB Statement No. 13* has brought about detailed reporting of operating lease payments in the notes to the financial statements. The inclusion of more lease information—be they capital or operating leases—makes the accounting information for decision making more complete.

Pension Liabilities

Point to Stress: A pension plan is a contract between a business and its employees. The terms of the contract outline the retirement benefits that the company will pay to the employees who qualify.

Most companies have a pension plan for their employees. A **pension** is employee compensation that will be received during retirement. Employees earn the pensions by their service, so the company records pension expense as employees work for the company. *FASB Statement No. 87* gives the rules for measuring pension expense. To record the company's payment into a pension plan, the company debits Pension Expense and credits Cash. Insurance companies and pension trusts manage pension plans. They receive the employer payments and any employee contributions, then invest these amounts for the future benefit of the employees. The goal is to have the funds available to meet any obligations to retirees, much as a bond sinking fund is designed to retire bonds payable at maturity.

Point to Stress: There are two types of pension plans:

1 Defined Contribution Plan—The employee, employer, or both, must contribute a certain amount each period to the pension fund. The retirement benefits depend on how much is in the fund.

Pensions are perhaps the most complex area of accounting. As employees earn their pensions and the company pays into the pension plan, the assets of the plan grow. The obligation for future pension payments to employees also accumulates. At the end of each period, the company compares the fair market value of the assets in the pension plan—cash and investments—with the accumulated benefit obligation of the pension plan. The *accumulated benefit obligation* is the present value of promised future pension payments to retirees. If the plan assets exceed the accumulated benefit obligation, the plan is said to be overfunded. In this case, the asset and obligation amounts need be reported only in the notes to the financial statements. However, if the accumulated benefit obligation exceeds plan assets, the company must report the excess liability amount as a long-term pension liability in the balance sheet.

The pension plan of Mainstream Manufacturing & Sales, Inc., has assets with a fair market value of $3 million on December 31, 19X0. On this date the accumulated pension benefit obligation to employees is $4 million. Mainstream's balance sheet will report Long-Term Pension Liability of $1 million. This liability will be listed, in no particular order, along with Bonds Payable, Long-Term Notes Payable, Lease Liabilities, and other long-term liabilities.

FASB Statement No. 87 started requiring companies to report pension liabilities in this manner in 1987. Before that date, pensions were another example of off-balance-sheet financing. Companies received the benefit of their employees' service but could avoid reporting pension liabilities on the balance sheet.

2 Defined Benefit Plan—The amount of the retirement benefit is defined by an uncertain quantity, for example, 80% of salary in the year of retirement. The amount to be contributed to this type of pension fund requires a very complex calculation and usually involves the services of an actuary.

Computers and Corporate Financial Planning

Corporations, large and small, deal with complex financial planning issues. A large corporation such as Tenneco, a major manufacturer of petrochemicals, might consider how to finance a new project. Suppose Tenneco wants to build a new refinery and expects total costs of $75,000,000. How does Tenneco find the best way to raise the needed funds? Financial-modelling techniques on microcomputers can help answer these questions thanks to spreadsheet capabilities.

The company may consider the financing alternatives: issue common stock, preferred stock, bonds, or different combinations of stocks and bonds. This assessment is often called "what if" analysis—that is, "what if" we finance with common stock, "what if" we finance with new bonds, and so on.

The answers to these "what if" questions appear on a spreadsheet template that projects the company's financial statements for, say, the next five years. A preferred stock issue would probably mean higher annual dividend payments than would a common stock issue. The financial statements would show this higher payment. Likewise, long-term borrowing would involve interest expense, but these charges are tax-deductible, unlike dividend payments to stockholders. The spreadsheet could show the consequences of financing through stock and through bonds, with a summary such as Exhibit 16-5. By studying the projected financial statements, management can select the most favorable path.

Nonmonetary considerations cannot be modelled so easily on a spreadsheet. For example, is the company willing to dilute the control of the shareholders by issuing more stock? If the company borrows the needed funds, will the rating of its existing bonds suffer? Computers are not as well suited to answering qualitative questions such as these.

Summary Problem for Your Review

The Cessna Aircraft Company has outstanding an issue of 8 percent convertible bonds that mature in 2012. Suppose the bonds were dated October 1, 1992, and pay interest each April 1 and October 1.

Required

1. Complete the following effective interest amortization table through October 1, 1994.

Bond Data:

Maturity value—$100,000
Contract interest rate—8%
Interest paid—4% semiannually, $4,000 ($100,000 × .04)

Market interest rate at time of issue—9% annually, 4½% semiannually
Issue price—90¾

Amortization Table:

Semiannual Interest Date	A Interest Payment (4% of Maturity Amount)	B Interest Expense (4½% of Preceding Bond Carrying Amount)	C Discount Amortization (B − A)	D Discount Account Balance (D − C)	E Bond Carrying Amount ($100,000 − D)
10-1-92					
4-1-93					
10-1-93					
4-1-94					
10-1-94					

2. Using the amortization table, record the following transactions:
   a. Issuance of the bonds on October 1, 1992.
   b. Accrual of interest and amortization of discount on December 31, 1992.
   c. Payment of interest and amortization of discount on April 1, 1993.
   d. Conversion of one-third of the bonds payable into no-par stock on October 2, 1994.
   e. Retirement of two-thirds of the bonds payable on October 2, 1994. Purchase price of the bonds was 102.

SOLUTION TO REVIEW PROBLEM

Requirement 1   (Amortization Table)

Semiannual Interest Date	A Interest Payment (4% of Maturity Amount)	B Interest Expense (4½% of Preceding Bond Carrying Amount)	C Discount Amortization (B − A)	D Discount Account Balance (D − C)	E Bond Carrying Amount ($100,000 − D)
10-1-92				$9,250	$ 90,750
4-1-93	$4,000	$4,084	$84	9,166	90,834
10-1-93	4,000	4,088	88	9,078	90,922
4-1-94	4,000	4,091	91	8,987	91,013
10-1-94	4,000	4,096	96	8,891	91,109

Requirement 2

a. Oct. 1 Cash ($100,000 × .9075) 90,750
            Discount on Bonds Payable 9,250
                Bonds Payable   100,000
            To issue 8%, 20-year bonds at a discount.

b. Dec. 31 Interest Expense ($4,084 × 3/6) 2,042
             Discount on Bonds Payable
                ($84 × 3/6)   42
             Interest Payable ($4,000 × 3/6)   2,000
             To accrue interest and amortize bond
             discount for three months.

1993

c. Apr. 1 Interest Expense 2,042
             Interest Payable 2,000
                Discount on Bonds Payable ($84 × 3/6)   42
                Cash   4,000
             To pay semiannual interest, part of which was
             accrued, and amortize three months' discount
             on bonds payable.

1994

d. Oct. 2 Bonds Payable ($100,000 × 1/3) 33,333
                Discount on Bonds Payable ($8,891 × 1/3)   2,964
                Common Stock ($91,109 × 1/3)   30,369
             To record conversion of bonds payable.

e. Oct. 2 Bonds Payable ($100,000 × 2/3) 66,667
             Extraordinary Loss on Retirement of Bonds 7,260
                Discount on Bonds Payable ($8,891 × 2/3)   5,927
                Cash ($100,000 × 2/3 × 1.02)   68,000
             To retire bonds payable before maturity.

Summary

A corporation may borrow money by issuing bonds and long-term notes payable. A bond contract, called an *indenture*, specifies the maturity value of the bonds, the contract interest rate, and the dates for paying interest and principal. The owner of *registered* bonds receives an interest check from the company. The owner of *coupon* bonds deposits an interest coupon in the bank. Bonds may be secured (*mortgage* bonds) or unsecured (*debenture* bonds).

Bonds are traded through organized markets, like the New York Exchange. Bonds are typically divided into $1,000 units. Their prices are quoted at a percentage of face value.

Market interest rates fluctuate and may differ from the contract rate on a bond. If a bond's contract rate exceeds the market rate, the bond sells at a *premium*. A bond with a contract rate below the market rate sells at a *discount*.

Money earns income over time, a fact that gives rise to the *present-value concept*. An investor will pay a price for a bond equal to the present value of the bond principal plus the present value of the bond interest.

Straight-line amortization allocates an equal amount of premium or discount to each interest period. In the *effective-interest method* of amortization, the market rate at the time of issuance is multiplied by the bonds' carrying amount to determine the interest expense each period and to compute the amount of discount or premium amortization.

A *bond sinking fund* accumulates the money to pay the bonds' face value at maturity. Companies may retire their bonds payable before maturity. *Callable* bonds give the borrower the right to pay off the bonds at a specified call price, or the company may purchase the bonds in the open market. Any gain or loss on early extinguishment of debt is classified as *extraordinary*.

Convertible bonds and notes give the investor the privilege of trading the bonds in for stock of the issuing corporation. The carrying amount of the bonds becomes the book value of the newly issued stock.

A lease is a rental agreement between the *lessee* and the *lessor*. In an *operating lease* the lessor retains the usual risks and rights of owning the asset. The lessee debits Rent Expense and credits Cash when making lease payments. A *capital lease* is long-term, noncancelable, and similar to an installment purchase of the leased asset. In a capital lease, the lessee capitalizes the leased asset and reports a lease liability.

Companies also report a *pension liability* on the balance sheet if the accumulated benefit obligation exceeds the market value of pension plan assets.

Self-Study Questions

Test your understanding of the chapter by marking the best answer for each of the following questions.

1. An unsecured bond is called a *(p. 716)*
   a. Serial bond
   b. Registered bond
   c. Debenture bond
   d. Mortgage bond

2. How much will an investor pay for a $100,000 bond priced at 101⅞, plus a brokerage commission of $1,100? *(p. 716)*
   a. $100,000
   b. $101,100
   c. $101,875
   d. $102,975

3. A bond with a stated interest rate of 9½ percent is issued when the market interest rate is 9¾ percent. This bond will sell at *(p. 717)*
   a. Par value
   b. A discount
   c. A premium
   d. A price minus accrued interest

4. Ten-year, 11 percent bonds payable of $500,000 were issued for $532,000. Assume the straight-line amortization method is appropriate. The total annual interest expense on these bonds is *(pp. 722, 724)*
   a. $51,800
   b. $55,000
   c. $58,200
   d. A different amount each year because the bonds' book value decreases as the premium is amortized

5. Use the facts in the preceding question but assume the effective-interest method of amortization is used. Total annual interest expense on the bonds is *(p. 725)*
   a. $51,800
   b. $55,000
   c. $58,200
   d. A decreasing amount each year because the bonds' book value decreases as the premium is amortized

6. Bonds payable with face value of $300,000 and carrying amount of $288,000 are retired before their scheduled maturity with a cash outlay of $292,000. Which of the following entries correctly records this bond retirement? *(p. 730)*

a. Bonds Payable 300,000
   Discount on Bonds Payable 12,000
      Cash 292,000
      Extraordinary Gain 20,000

✓ b. Bonds Payable 300,000
   Extraordinary Loss 4,000
      Discount on Bonds Payable 12,000
      Cash 292,000

c. Bonds Payable 300,000
      Discount on Bonds Payable 6,000
      Cash 292,000
      Extraordinary Gain 2,000

d. Bonds Payable 288,000
   Discount on Bonds Payable 12,000
      Extraordinary Gain 8,000
      Cash 292,000

7. An advantage of financing operations with debt versus stock is *(pp. 732– 733)*
   ✓ a. The tax-deductibility of interest expense on debt
   b. The legal requirement to pay interest and principal
   c. Lower interest payments compared with dividend payments
   d. All of the above

8. In a capital lease, the lessee records *(pp. 734–736)*
   a. A leased asset and a lease liability   c. Interest on the lease liability
   b. Depreciation on the leased asset   ✓ d. All of the above

9. Which of the following is an example of off-balance-sheet financing? *(p. 736)*
   ✓ a. Operating lease   c. Debenture bonds
   b. Current portion of long-term debt   d. Convertible bonds

10. A corporation's pension plan has accumulated benefit obligations of $830,000 and assets that are worth $790,000. What will this company report for its pension plan? *(p. 737)*
   a. Accumulated benefit obligation of $830,000
   b. Note disclosure of the $40,000 excess of accumulated benefit obligation over plan assets
   ✓ c. Long-term pension liability of $40,000
   d. Nothing

Answers to the Self-Study Questions follow the Accounting Vocabulary.

Accounting Vocabulary

Bond discount. Excess of a bond's maturity (par) value over its issue price *(p. 716)*.

Bond indenture. Contract under which bonds are issued *(p. 729)*.

Bond premium. Excess of a bond's issue price over its maturity (par) value *(p. 716)*.

Bond sinking fund. Group of assets segregated for the purpose of retiring bonds payable at maturity *(p. 729)*.

Bonds payable. Groups of notes payable (bonds) issued to multiple lenders called bondholders *(p. 714)*.

Callable bonds. Bonds that the issuer may call or pay off at a specified price whenever the issuer wants *(p. 730)*.

Capital lease. Lease agreement that meets any one of four criteria: (1) The lease transfers title of the leased asset to the lessee. (2) The lease contains a bargain purchase option. (3) The lease term is 75 percent or more of the estimated useful life of the leased asset. (4) The present value of the lease payments is 90 percent or more of the market value of the leased asset (p. 735).

Contract interest rate. Interest rate that determines the amount of cash interest the borrower pays and the investor receives each year. Also called the Stated interest rate (p. 717).

Convertible bonds. Bonds that may be converted into the common stock of the issuing company at the option of the investor (p. 731).

Coupon bonds. Bonds for which the owners receive interest by detaching a perforated coupon (which states the interest due and the date of payment) from the bond and depositing it in a bank for collection (p. 715).

Debentures. Unsecured bonds, backed only by the good faith of the borrower (p. 716).

Effective interest rate. Another name for Market interest rate (p. 717).

Lease. Rental agreement in which the tenant (lessee) agrees to make rent payments to the property owner (lessor) in exchange for the use of the asset (p. 734).

Lessee. Tenant in a lease agreement (p. 734).

Lessor. Property owner in a lease agreement (p. 734).

Market interest rate. Interest rate that investors demand in order to loan their money. Also called the Effective interest rate (p. 717).

Mortgage. Borrower's promise to transfer the legal title to certain assets to the lender if the debt is not paid on schedule (p. 732).

Off-balance-sheet financing. Acquisition of assets or services with debt that is not reported on the balance sheet (p. 736).

Operating lease. Usually a short-term or cancelable rental agreement (p. 734).

Pension. Employee compensation that will be received during retirement (p. 736).

Present value. Amount a person would invest now to receive a greater amount at a future date (p. 717).

Registered bonds. Bonds for which the owners receive interest checks from the issuing company (p. 715).

Serial bonds. Bonds that mature in installments over a period of time (p. 715).

Stated interest rate. Another name for the Contract interest rate (p. 717).

Term bonds. Bonds that all mature at the same time for a particular issue (p. 715).

Trading on the equity. Earning more income on borrowed money than the related interest expense, which increases the earnings for the owners of the business. (p. 733),

Underwriter. Organization that purchases the bonds from an issuing company and resells them to its clients, or sells the bonds for a commission, agreeing to buy all unsold bonds (p. 714).

Answers to Self-Study Questions

1. c
2. d [($100,000 × 1.01875) + $1,100 = $102,975]
3. b
4. a [($500,000 × .11) − ($32,000/10) = $51,800]
5. d
6. b
7. a
8. d
9. a
10. c

ASSIGNMENT MATERIAL

Questions

1. Identify three ways to finance the operations of a corporation.
2. How do bonds payable differ from a note payable?
3. How does an underwriter assist with the issuance of bonds?
4. Why would an investor require the borrower to set up a sinking fund?

5. Compute the price to the nearest dollar for the following bonds with a face value of $10,000:

   a. 93   b. 88¾   c. 101⅜   d. 122½   e. 100

6. In which of the following situations will bonds sell at par? at a premium? at a discount?

   a. 9% bonds sold when the market rate is 9%

   b. 9% bonds sold when the market rate is 10%

   c. 9% bonds sold when the market rate is 8%

7. Identify the accounts to debit and credit for transactions (a) to issue bonds at *par*, (b) to pay interest, (c) to accrue interest at year end, and (d) to pay off bonds at maturity.

8. Identify the account to debit and credit for transactions (a) to issue bonds at a *discount*, (b) to pay interest, (c) to accrue interest at year end, and (d) to pay off bonds at maturity.

9. Identify the accounts to debit and credit for transactions (a) to issue bonds at a *premium*, (b) to pay interest, (c) to accrue interest at year end, and (d) to pay off bonds at maturity.

10. Why are bonds sold for a price "plus accrued interest"? What happens to accrued interest when bonds are sold by an individual?

11. How does the straight-line method of amortizing bond discount (or premium) differ from the effective-interest method?

12. A company retires ten-year bonds payable of $100,000 after five years. The business issued the bonds at 104 and called them at 103. Compute the amount of gain or loss on retirement. How is this gain or loss reported on the income statement?

13. Bonds payable with a maturity value of $100,000 are callable at 102½. Their market price is 101¼. If you are the issuer of these bonds, how much will you pay to retire them before maturity?

14. Why are convertible bonds attractive to investors? Why are they popular with borrowers?

15. Describe how to report serial bonds payable on the balance sheet.

16. Contrast the effects on a company of issuing bonds versus issuing stock.

17. Identify the accounts a lessee debits and credits when making operating lease payments.

18. What characteristics distinguish a capital lease from an operating lease?

19. A business signs a capital lease for the use of a building. What accounts are debited and credited (a) to begin the lease term and make the first lease payment, (b) to record depreciation, (c) to accrue interest on the lease liability, and (d) to make the second lease payment?

20. Show how a lessee reports on the balance sheet any leased equipment and the related lease liability under a capital lease.

21. What is off-balance-sheet financing? Give two examples.

22. Distinguish an overfunded pension plan from an underfunded plan. Which situation requires the company to report a pension liability on the balance sheet? How is this liability computed?

Exercises

Additional computer-related exercise: Exercise 28-4

Exercise 16-1   *Issuing bonds payable and paying interest*   *(L.O. 1)*

Interest exp. $12,500

Malachite, Inc., issues $300,000 of 10 percent, 20-year bonds payable that are dated April 30. Record (a) issuance of bonds at par on May 31 and (b) the next semiannual interest payment on October 31.

Interest exp. Dec. 31, $42,084

Exercise 16-2 *Issuing bonds payable, paying and accruing interest, and amortizing discount by the straight-line method* **(L.O. 1)**

On February 1 Truly Fine Corp. issues 20-year, 10 percent bonds payable with a face value of $1,000,000. The bonds sell at 98 and pay interest on January 31 and July 31. Truly Fine amortizes bond discount by the straight-line method. Record (a) issuance of the bonds on February 1, (b) the semiannual interest payment on July 31, and (c) the interest accrual on December 31.

Interest exp. Dec. 31, $99,375

Exercise 16-3 *Issuing bonds payable, paying and accruing interest, and amortizing premium by the straight-line method* **(L.O. 1)**

A. V. Cross Corporation issues 30-year, 8 percent bonds payable with a face value of $5,000,000 on March 31. The bonds sell at 101½ and pay interest on March 31 and September 30. Assume Cross amortizes bond premium by the straight-line method. Record (a) issuance of the bonds on March 31, (b) payment of interest on September 30, and (c) accrual of interest on December 31.

Interest exp. Dec. 31, $22,661

Exercise 16-4 *Preparing an effective-interest amortization table; recording interest payments and the related discount amortization* **(L.O. 2)**

Southwest Mortgage Co. is authorized to issue $500,000 of 11 percent, 10-year bonds payable. On January 2, when the market interest rate is 12 percent, the company issues $400,000 of the bonds and receives cash of $377,060. Southwest amortizes bond discount by the effective-interest method.

Required

1. Prepare an amortization table for the first four semiannual interest periods. Follow the format of Exhibit 16-3, Panel B.
2. Record the first semiannual interest payment on June 30 and the second payment on December 31.

Interest exp. Mar. 31, $8,910

Exercise 16-5 *Preparing an effective-interest amortization table; recording interest accrual and payment and the related premium amortization* **(L.O. 2)**

On September 30, 1992, the market interest rate is 11 percent. Auto Power, Inc., issues $300,000 of 12 percent, 20-year sinking-fund bonds payable at 108. The bonds pay interest on March 31 and September 30. Auto Power amortizes bond premium by the effective-interest method.

Required

1. Prepare an amortization table for the first four semiannual interest periods. Follow the format of Exhibit 16-4, Panel B.
2. Record issuance of the bonds on September 30, 1992, the accrual of interest at December 31, 1992, and the semiannual interest payment on March 31, 1993.

No check figure

Exercise 16-6 *Journalizing sinking fund transactions* **(L.O. 2)**

Auto Power established a sinking fund for the bond issue in Exercise 16-5. Record payment of $8,000 into the sinking fund on March 31, 1993. Also record sinking-fund revenue of $900 on December 31, 1993, and the payment of the bonds at maturity on September 30, 2012. At maturity date the sinking-fund balance was $296,000.

Extraordinary loss $10,625

Exercise 16-7 *Recording retirement of bonds payable* **(L.O. 3)**

Alliance Corp. issued $500,000 of 9 percent bonds payable at 97 on October 1, 19X0. These bonds mature on October 1, 19X8, and are callable at 101. Allied pays interest each April 1 and October 1. On October 1, 19X5, when the bonds' market price is 104, Allied retires the bonds in the most economical way available. Record the payment of interest and amortization of bond discount at October 1, 19X5, and the retirement of the bonds on that date. Alliance uses the straight-line amortization method.

Exercise 16-8   *Recording conversion of bonds payable*   (L.O. 4)

Paid-cap. in x/s of par $83,800

Mending Tape Company issued $400,000 of 8½ percent bonds payable on July 1, 19X4, at a price of 101½. After 5 years the bonds may be converted into the company's common stock. Each $1,000 face amount of bonds is convertible into 40 shares of $20 par stock. The bonds' term to maturity is 15 years. On December 31, 19X9, bondholders exercised their right to convert the bonds into common stock.

Required

1. What would cause the bondholders to convert their bonds into common stock?
2. Without making journal entries, compute the carrying amount of the bonds payable at December 31, 19X9. Mending Tape Company uses the straight-line method to amortize bond premium and discount.
3. All amortization has been recorded properly. Journalize the conversion transaction at December 31, 19X9.

Exercise 16-9   *Recording early retirement and conversion of bonds payable*   (L.O. 3, 4)

Paid-in cap. in x/s of par $28,500

Monolithic Industries reported the following at September 30:

Long-term liabilities:
  Convertible bonds payable, 9%, 8 years to maturity $200,000
  Discount on bonds payable 6,000 $194,000

Required

1. Record retirement of one half of the bonds on October 1 at the call price of 101.
2. Record conversion of one fourth of the bonds into 4,000 shares of Monolithic's $5 par common stock on October 1.

No check figure

Exercise 16-10   *Reporting long-term debt and pension liability on the balance sheet*   (L.O. 5)

a. A note to the financial statements of Mapco, Inc., reported (in thousands):

Note 5: Long-Term Debt
   Total $537,888
   Less—Current portion   22,085
      Unamortized discount   1,391
   Long-term debt $514,412

Assume that none of the unamortized discount relates to the current portion of long-term debt. Show how Mapco's balance sheet would report these liabilities.

b. El Campo Incorporated's pension plan has assets with a market value of $720,000. The plan's accumulated benefit obligation is $840,000. What amount of long-term pension liability, if any, will El Campo report on its balance sheet?

Exercise 16-11   *Analyzing alternative plans for raising money*   (L.O. 5)

EPS Plan A $.96
EPS Plan B $.63

Link Inc. is considering two plans for raising $1,000,000 to expand operations. Plan A is to borrow at 10 percent, and plan B is to issue 200,000 shares of common stock. Before any new financing, Link has 200,000 shares of common stock outstanding. Management believes the company can use the new funds to earn income of $420,000 before interest and taxes. The income tax rate is 40 percent.

Required

Prepare an analysis like Exhibit 16-5 to determine which plan will result in higher earnings per share.

Interest exp. Dec. 31, $5,115

Exercise 16-12 *Journalizing capital lease and operating lease transactions* **(L.O. 6)**

A capital lease agreement for equipment requires 10 annual payments of $8,000, with the first payment due on January 2, 19X5. The present value of the 9 future lease payments at 12 percent is $42,624.

a. Journalize the following lessee transactions:

   19X5
   Jan. 2 Beginning of lease term and first annual payment.
   Dec. 31 Depreciation of equipment.
        31 Interest expense on lease liability.
   19X6
   Jan. 2 Second annual lease payment.

b. Journalize the January 1, 19X5, lease payment if this is an operating lease.

Problems   *(Group A)*

19X7 Interest exp. $106,667

Problem 16-1A *Journalizing bond transactions (at par) and reporting bonds payable on the balance sheet* **(L.O. 1)**

The board of directors of Sabatini Carbonic Company authorizes the issue of $2 million of 8 percent, 20-year bonds payable. The semiannual interest dates are February 28 and August 31. The bonds are issued through an underwriter on April 30, 19X7, at par plus accrued interest.

Required

1. Journalize the following transactions:
    a. Issuance of the bonds on April 30, 19X7.
    b. Payment of interest on August 31, 19X7.
    c. Accrual of interest on December 31, 19X7.
    d. Payment of interest on February 28, 19X8.
2. Check your recorded interest expense for 19X7, using as a model the supplement to the summary problem on pages 724 and 725.
3. Report interest payable and bonds payable as they would appear on the Sabatini Carbonic Company balance sheet at December 31, 19X7.

4. Interest exp. $26,850

Problem 16-2A *Issuing notes at a premium, amortizing by the straight-line method, and reporting notes payable on the balance sheet* **(L.O. 1,2)**

On March 1, 19X6, Leviton Laboratories issues 9¼ percent, 10-year notes payable with a face value of $300,000. The notes pay interest on February 28 and August 31, and Leviton amortizes premium and discount by the straight-line method.

Required

1. If the market interest rate is 10½ percent when Leviton issues its notes, will the notes be priced at par, at a premium, or at a discount? Explain.

2. If the market interest rate is 8⅝ percent when Leviton issues its notes, will the notes be priced at par, at a premium, or at a discount? Explain.

3. Assume the issue price of the notes is 103. Journalize the following note payable transactions:
   a. Issuance of the notes on March 1, 19X6.
   b. Payment of interest and amortization of premium on August 31, 19X6.
   c. Accrual of interest and amortization of premium on December 31, 19X6.
   d. Payment of interest and amortization of premium on February 28, 19X7.

4. Check your recorded interest expense for the year ended February 28, 19X7, using as a model the supplement to the summary problem on pages 724 and 725.

5. Report interest payable and notes payable as they would appear on the Leviton balance sheet at December 31, 19X6.

Problem 16-3A *Analyzing a company's long-term debt, journalizing its transactions, and reporting the long-term debt on the balance sheet* **(L.O. 2)**

9/30/X4 Bond carrying amount
$164,464

Assume that the notes to Popeye's Fried Chicken's financial statements reported the following data on September 30, Year 1 (the end of the fiscal year):

NOTE E—LONG-TERM DEBT

7% debentures due Year 20, net of unamortized discount
   of $71,645,000 (effective interest rate of 11%) $159,855,000
Notes payable, interest of 8.67%, due in annual amounts
   of $22,840,000 in Years 5 through 16   274,080,000

Assume Popeye's amortizes discount by the effective-interest method.

Required

1. Answer the following questions about Popeye's long-term liabilities:
   a. What is the maturity value of the 7% debenture bonds?
   b. What are Popeye's annual cash interest payments on the 7% debenture bonds?
   c. What is the carrying amount of the 7% debenture bonds at September 30, Year 1?

2. Prepare an amortization table through September 30, Year 4, for the 7% debenture bonds. Round all amounts to the nearest thousand dollars and assume Popeye's pays interest annually on September 30. Use the following format for the amortization table:

End of Annual Interest Period	A Interest Payment (7% of Maturity Value)	B Interest Expense (11% of Preceding Bond Carrying Amount)	C Discount Amortization (B − A)	D Discount Balance (D − C)	E Bond Carrying Amount ($231,500 − D)
Sep. 30, Yr. 1					
Sep. 30, Yr. 2					
Sep. 30, Yr. 3					
Sep. 30, Yr. 4					

3. Record the September 30, Year 3 and Year 4, interest payments on the 7% debenture bonds.

4. There is no premium or discount on the notes payable. Assuming annual interest is paid on September 30 each year, record Popeye's September 30, Year 2, interest payment on the notes payable. Round interest to the nearest thousand dollars.

5. Show how Popeye's would report the debenture bonds payable and notes payable at September 30, Year 4.

12/31/X3 Bond carrying amount $451,280

Problem 16-4A *Issuing convertible bonds at a discount, amortizing by the effective-interest method, retiring bonds early, converting bonds, and reporting the bonds payable on the balance sheet* **(L.O. 2, 3, 4)**

On December 31, 19X1, Herrera, Inc., issues 11 percent, 10-year convertible bonds with a maturity value of $500,000. The semiannual interest dates are June 30 and December 31. The market interest rate is 13 percent, and the issue price of the bonds is 89. Herrera amortizes bond premium and discount by the effective-interest method.

Required

1. Prepare an effective-interest method amortization table like Exhibit 16-3 for the first four semiannual interest periods.
2. Journalize the following transactions:
   a. Issuance of the bonds on December 31, 19X1. Credit Convertible Bonds Payable.
   b. Payment of interest on June 30, 19X2.
   c. Payment of interest on December 31, 19X2.
   d. Retirement of bonds with face value of $100,000 on July 1, 19X3. Herrera purchases the bonds at 94 in the open market.
   e. Conversion by the bondholders on July 1, 19X3, of bonds with face value of $200,000 into 50,000 shares of Herrera $1 par common stock.
3. Prepare the balance sheet presentation of the bonds payable that are outstanding at December 31, 19X3.

12/31 Interest exp. (bonds) $93,000

Problem 16-5A *Journalizing bonds payable and capital lease transactions* **(L.O. 1, 6)**

Journalize the following transactions of Republic Iron Works:

19X11

Jan. 1 Issued $2,000,000 of 9 percent, 10-year bonds payable at 97.

    1 Signed a 5-year capital lease on machinery. The agreement requires annual lease payments of $16,000, with the first payment due immediately. At 12 percent, the present value of the four future lease payments is $48,590.

July 1 Paid semiannual interest and amortized discount by the straight-line method on our 9 percent bonds payable.

    1 Made the $100,000 sinking-fund payment required by the indenture on our 9 percent bonds payable.

Dec. 31 Accrued semiannual interest expense and amortized discount by the straight-line method on our 9 percent bonds payable.

    31 Recorded depreciation on leased machinery.

    31 Accrued interest expense on the lease liability.

    31 Recorded bond sinking-fund earnings of $5,500.

19X1

Jan. 1 Paid the 9 percent bonds at maturity from the sinking fund ($1,993,000) and the remainder from company cash.

No check figure

Problem 16-6A *Financing operations with debt or with stock* **(L.O. 5)**

Marketing studies have shown that consumers prefer upscale stores, and recent trends in industry sales have supported the research. To capitalize on this trend, Modern Views, Inc., is embarking on a massive expansion. Plans call for opening 100 new stores within the next 18 months. Each store is scheduled to be 50 percent larger than the company's existing stores, furnished more elaborately, and stocked with more expensive merchandise. Management estimates that company operations will provide $8 million of the cash needed for expansion. Modern Views must raise the remaining $5.5 million from outsiders. The board of directors is considering obtaining the $5.5 million either through borrowing or by issuing common stock.

Required

Discuss for company management the advantages and the disadvantages of borrowing and of issuing common stock to raise the needed cash. Which method of raising the funds would you recommend?

Problem 16-7A *Reporting liabilities on the balance sheet* **(L.O. 6)**   No check figure

The Naval Salvage Supply Corp. accounting records include these items:

Bonds payable, current portion	$ 75,000	Mortgage note payable, long-term	$ 82,000
Capital lease liability, long-term	81,000	Accumulated depreciation, equipment	46,000
Discount on bonds payable	7,000	Bond sinking fund	119,000
Interest revenue	5,000	Capital lease liability, current	18,000
Equipment acquired under capital lease	113,000	Mortgage note payable, current	23,000
Pension plan assets (market value)	116,000	Accumulated pension benefit obligation	124,000
Interest payable	13,000	Bonds payable, long-term	400,000
Interest expense	57,000		

Required

Show how these items would be reported on the Naval Salvage Supply balance sheet, including headings for current liabilities, long-term liabilities, and so on. Note disclosures are not required.

(Group B)

Problem 16-1B *Journalizing bond transactions (at par) and reporting bonds payable on the balance sheet* **(L.O. 1)**   19X5 Interest exp. $135,000

The board of directors of Hunt Boston Corp. authorizes the issue of $3 million of 9 percent, 10-year bonds payable. The semiannual interest dates are May 31 and November 30. The bonds are issued through an underwriter on June 30, 19X5, at par plus accrued interest.

Required

1. Journalize the following transactions:
    a. Issuance of the bonds on June 30, 19X5.
    b. Payment of interest on November 30, 19X5.
    c. Accrual of interest on December 31, 19X5.
    d. Payment of interest on May 31, 19X6.
2. Check your recorded interest expense for 19X5, using as a model the supplement to the summary problem on pages 724 and 725.
3. Report interest payable and bonds payable as they would appear on the Hunt Boston Corp. balance sheet at December 31, 19X5.

4. Interest exp. $53,500

Problem 16-2B *Issuing bonds at a discount, amortizing by the straight-line method, and reporting bonds payable on the balance sheet* **(L.O. 1, 2)**

On March 1, 19X4, Garth Corp. issues 10½ percent, 20-year bonds payable with a face value of $500,000. The bonds pay interest on February 28 and August 31. Garth amortizes premium and discount by the straight-line method.

Required

1. If the market interest rate is 9⅜ percent when Garth issues its bonds, will the bonds be priced at par, at a premium, or at a discount? Explain.
2. If the market interest rate is 10⅞ percent when Garth issues its bonds, will the bonds be priced at par, at a premium, or at a discount? Explain.
3. Assume the issue price of the bonds is 96. Journalize the following bond transactions:
   a. Issuance of the bonds on March 1, 19X4.
   b. Payment of interest and amortization of discount on August 31, 19X4.
   c. Accrual of interest and amortization of discount on December 31, 19X4.
   d. Payment of interest and amortization of discount on February 28, 19X5.
4. Check your recorded interest expense for the year ended February 28, 19X5, using as a model the supplement to the summary problem on pages 724 and 725.
5. Report interest payable and bonds payable as they would appear on the Garth balance sheet at December 31, 19X4.

9/30/X4 Bond carrying amount $106,801

Problem 16-3B *Analyzing an actual company's long-term debt, journalizing its transactions, and reporting the long-term debt on the balance sheet* **(L.O. 2)**

The notes to Baker International's financial statements recently reported the following data on September 30, Year 1 (the end of the fiscal year):

NOTE 4. INDEBTEDNESS

Long-Term debt at September 30, Year 1, included the following:

6.00% debentures due Year 20 with an effective-interest rate of 14.66%, net of unamortized discount of $123,152,000	$101,848,000
Other indebtedness with an interest rate of 10.30%, due $12,108,000 in Year 5 and $19,257,000 in Year 6	31,365,000

Assume Baker amortizes discount by the effective-interest method.

Required

1. Answer the following questions about Baker's long-term liabilities:
   a. What is the maturity value of the 6.00% debenture bonds?
   b. What are Baker's annual cash interest payments on the 6.00% debenture bonds?
   c. What is the carrying amount of the 6.00% debenture bonds at September 30, Year 1?
2. Prepare an amortization table through September 30, Year 4, for the 6.00% debenture bonds. Round all amounts to the nearest thousand dollars, and assume Baker pays interest annually on September 30. Use the following format for the amortization table:

End of Annual Interest Period	A Interest Payment (6% of Maturity Value)	B Interest Expense (14.66% of Preceding Bond Carrying Amount)	C Discount Amortization (B − A)	D Discount Balance (D − C)	E Bond Carrying Amount ($225,000 − D)
Sep. 30, Yr. 1					
Sep. 30, Yr. 2					
Sep. 30, Yr. 3					
Sep. 30, Yr. 4					

3. Record the September 30, Year 3 and Year 4, interest payments on the 6.00% debenture bonds.

4. There is no premium or discount on the other indebtedness. Assuming annual interest is paid on September 30 each year, record Baker's September 30, Year 2, interest payment on the other indebtedness. Round interest to the nearest thousand dollars.

5. Show how Baker would report the debenture bonds payable and other indebtedness of September 30, Year 4.

Problem 16-4B *Issuing convertible bonds at a premium, amortizing by the effective-interest method, retiring bonds early, converting bonds, and reporting the bonds payable on the balance sheet* **(L.O. 2, 3, 4)**

12/31/X3 Bond carrying amount $315,785

On December 31, 19X1, Ernst, Inc., issues 12 percent, 10-year convertible bonds with a maturity value of $300,000. The semiannual interest dates are June 30 and December 31. The market interest rate is 11 percent, and the issue price of the bonds is 106. Ernst amortizes bond premium and discount by the effective-interest method.

Required

1. Prepare an effective-interest method amortization table like Exhibit 16-4 for the first four semiannual interest periods.

2. Journalize the following transactions:
   a. Issuance of the bonds on December 31, 19X1. Credit Convertible Bonds Payable.
   b. Payment of interest on June 30, 19X2.
   c. Payment of interest on December 31, 19X2.
   d. Retirement of bonds with face value of $100,000 on July 1, 19X3. Ernst pays the call price of 102.
   e. Conversion by the bondholders on July 1, 19X3, of bonds with face value of $150,000 into 10,000 shares of Ernst's $10 par common stock.

3. Prepare the balance sheet presentation of the bonds payable that are outstanding at December 31, 19X3.

Problem 16-5B *Journalizing bonds payable and capital lease transactions* **(L.O. 1, 6)**

12/31 Interest exp. (bonds) $21,750

Journalize the following transactions of Evergreen Products, Inc.:

19X1
Jan. 1 Issued $500,000 of 8 percent, 10-year bonds payable at 93.
     1 Signed a 5-year capital lease on equipment. The agreement requires annual lease payments of $20,000, with the first payment due immediately. At 12 percent, the present value of the four future lease payments is $60,750.

July	1	Paid semiannual interest and amortized discount by the straight-line method on our 8 percent bonds payable.
	1	Made the $25,000 sinking-fund payment required by the indenture on our 8 percent bonds payable.
Dec.	31	Accrued semiannual interest expense, and amortized discount by the straight-line method on our 8 percent bonds payable.
	31	Recorded depreciation on leased equipment.
	31	Accrued interest expense on the lease liability.
	31	Recorded bond sinking-fund earnings of $1,000.
19X11		
Jan.	1	Paid the 8 percent bonds at maturity from the sinking fund and received excess cash of $7,800.

No check figure

Problem 16-6B *Financing operations with debt instead of with stock* **(L.O. 5)**

Two businesses must consider how to raise $10 million.

Minneapolis Corporation is in the midst of its most successful period since it began operations in 1960. For each of the past 10 years, net income and earnings per share have increased by 15 percent. The outlook for the future is equally bright, with new markets opening up and competitors unable to manufacture products of Minneapolis's quality. Minneapolis Corporation is planning a large-scale expansion.

St. Paul Company has fallen on hard times. Net income has remained flat for five of the last six years, even falling by 10 percent from last year's level of profits. Top management has experienced unusual turnover, and the company lacks strong leadership. To become competitive again, St. Paul Company desperately needs $10 million for expansion.

Required

Propose a plan for each company to raise the needed cash. Which company should borrow? Which company should issue stock? Consider the advantages and the disadvantages of raising money by borrowing and by issuing stock, and discuss them in your answer.

No check figure

Problem 16-7B *Reporting liabilities on the balance sheet* **(L.O. 6)**

The accounting records of Pantel Corp. include the following items:

Bond sinking fund	$ 80,000	Mortgage note payable, long-term	$ 67,000
Accumulated pension benefit obligation	210,000	Building acquired under capital lease	190,000
Bonds payable, long-term	180,000	Interest expense	47,000
Premium on bonds payable	13,000	Pension plan assets (market value)	190,000
Interest payable	9,200	Bonds payable, current portion	60,000
Interest revenue	5,300	Accumulated depreciation, building	108,000
Capital lease liability, long-term	73,000		

Required

Show how these items would be reported on the Pantel balance sheet, including headings for current liabilities, long-term liabilities, and so on. Note disclosures are not required.

Extending Your Knowledge

Decision Problems

1. Analyzing Alternative Ways of Raising $5 Million (L.O. 6)

EPS Plan A $1.86

Business is going well for MicroCraft of Vermont, Inc. The board of directors of this family-owned company believes that MicroCraft could earn an additional $2,000,000 in income before interest and taxes by expanding into new markets. However, the $5,000,000 that the business needs for growth cannot be raised within the family. The directors, who strongly wish to retain family control of MicroCraft, must consider issuing securities to outsiders. They are considering three financing plans.

Plan A is to borrow at 9 percent. Plan B is to issue 200,000 shares of common stock. Plan C is to issue 100,000 shares of nonvoting, $3.75 preferred stock. MicroCraft presently has 500,000 shares of common stock outstanding. The income tax rate is 40 percent.

Required

1. Prepare an analysis similar to Exhibit 16-5 to determine which plan will result in the highest earnings per share of common stock.
2. Recommend one plan to the board of directors. Give your reasons.

2. Questions about Long-Term Debt (L.O. 6 and Appendix)

No check figure

The following questions are not related.

a. Why do you think corporations prefer operating leases over capital leases? How do you think a wise shareholder would view an operating lease?

b. Companies like to borrow for longer terms when interest rates are low and for shorter terms when interest rates are high? Why is this statement true?

c. If you were to win $2,000,000 from a Canadian lottery, you would receive the $2,000,000, whereas if you win $2,000,000 in one of the big U.S. lotteries, you would receive 20 annual payments of $100,000. Are the prizes equivalent? If not, why not?

Ethical Issue

Ling-Temco-Vought, Inc. (LTV), manufacturer of aircraft and related electronic devices, borrowed heavily during the 1960s to exploit the advantage of financing operations with debt. At first, LTV was able to earn operating income much higher than its interest expense and was therefore quite profitable. However, when the business cycle turned down, LTV's debt burden pushed the company to the brink of bankruptcy. Operating income was less than interest expense.

Required

Is it unethical for managers to saddle a company with a high level of debt? Or is it just risky? Who could be hurt by a company's taking on too much debt? Discuss.

Financial Statement Problems

No check figure

1. Long-Term Debt (L.O. 2, 3)

The Goodyear Tire & Rubber Company's balance sheet, statement of cash flow, and note titled "Credit Arrangements"—all given in Appendix C—provide details about the company's long-term debt. Use those data to answer the following questions.

1. How much long-term debt did Goodyear pay off during 1990? How much new long-term debt did the company incur during 1990? Journalize these transactions using Goodyear's actual account titles.
2. Prepare a T-account for Long-Term Debt and Capital Leases to show the beginning and ending balances and all activity in the account during 1990. Note: There is a $1.8 million inconsistency in the account that the authors are unable to explain! Insert the $1.8 million inconsistency in the appropriate place.
3. Journalize, in a single entry, Goodyear's interest expense for 1990, assuming amortization of Discount on Long-Term Debt was $7.3 million for the year.
4. In what foreign currencies is some of Goodyear's long-term debt stated?
5. Study the Credit Arrangements Note. At December 31, 1990, how much additional long-term debt had Goodyear already lined up for use as needed?

No check figure

2. Long-Term Debt (L.O. 2, 3)

Obtain the annual report of an actual company of your choosing. Answer these questions about the company. Concentrate on the current year in the annual report you select.

1. Examine the statement of cash flows. How much long-term debt did the company pay off during the current year? How much new long-term debt did the company incur during the year? Journalize these transactions using the company's actual account balances.
2. Prepare a T-account for the Long-Term Debt account to show the beginning and ending balances and all activity in the account during the year. If there is a discrepancy, insert this amount in the appropriate place. Note: Even the authors cannot explain details in actual financial statements!
3. Study the notes to the financial statements. Is any of the company's retained earnings balance restricted as a result of borrowings? If so, indicate the amount of the retained earnings balance that is restricted and the amount that is unrestricted. How will the restriction affect the company's dividend payments in the future?
4. Journalize the company's interest expense for the current year in a single entry. If the company discloses the amount of amortization of premium or discount on long-term debt, use the actual figures. If not, assume the amortization of discount totaled $700,000 for the year.

Appendix

Present Value

After studying this appendix, you should be able to

1. Compute the market value of a note or a bond.
2. Determine the cost of an asset acquired through a capital lease.

Present value (PV) has many applications in accounting. For example, a company may issue 10 percent bonds payable when the market interest rate is 11 percent. The company needs to know how much cash it will receive from issuing the bonds. The investors must determine how much to pay for the bonds. Both parties must compute the present value of the bonds. Another example is the acquisition of an asset through a capital lease. The lessee (tenant) must know the cost of the asset. The time value of money leads us to evaluate bonds, leases, and investments in terms of present value.

Suppose an investment promises to pay you $5,000 at the *end* of one year. How much would you pay *now* to acquire this investment? You would be willing to pay the present value of the $5,000 future amount.

Present value depends on three factors: (1) the amount of payment (or receipt), (2) the length of time between investment and future receipt (or payment), and (3) the interest rate. The process of computing a present value is called *discounting* because the present value is *less* than the future value.

In our investment example, the future receipt is $5,000. The investment period is one year. Assume that you demand an annual interest rate of 10 percent on your investment. With all three factors specified, you can compute the present value of $5,000 at 10 percent for one year. The computation is

$$\frac{\text{Future value}}{(1 + \text{Interest rate})} = \frac{\$5,000}{1.10} = \$4,545$$

(Throughout this discussion we round off to the nearest dollar.) By turning the problem around, we verify the present-value computation:

Amount invested (present value)	$4,545
Expected earnings ($4,545 × .10)	455
Amount to be received one year from now (future value)	$5,000

The $455 income amount is interest revenue, also called the return on the investment.

If the $5,000 is to be received two years from now, you would pay only $4,132 for the investment, computed as follows:

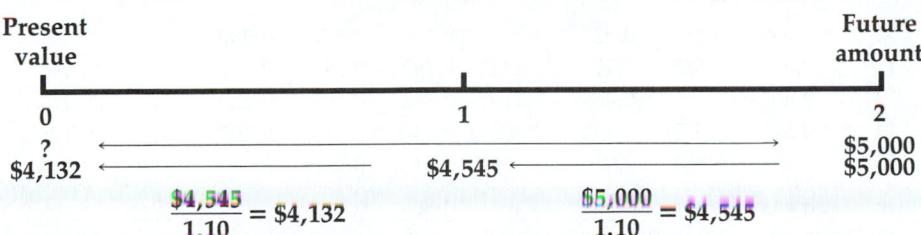

$$\frac{\$4,545}{1.10} = \$4,132 \qquad \frac{\$5,000}{1.10} = \$4,545$$

By turning the problem around, we verify that $4,132 accumulates to $5,000 at 10 percent for two years.

Amount invested (present value)	$4,132
Expected earnings for first year ($4,132 × .10)	413
Amount invested after one year	4,545
Expected earnings for second year ($4,545 × .10)	455
Amount to be received two years from now (future value)	$5,000

Teaching Tip: Draw a time diagram on the board. Ask students which they would rather receive—$1,000 today or $1,000 in 5 years.

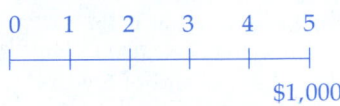

What is the difference? Students should answer that the difference is the amount of interest that they could have earned on the $1,000, and reinvested. The difference between a future amount and its present value is *interest.*

You would pay $4,132—the present value of $5,000—to receive the $5,000 future amount at the end of two years at 10 percent per year. The $868 difference between the amount invested ($4,132) and the amount to be received ($5,000) is the return on the investment, the sum of the two interest receipts: $413 + $455 = $868.

Present-Value Tables

We can compute present value by using the formula

$$\text{Present value} = \frac{\text{Future value}}{(1 + \text{Interest rate})}$$

Class Exercise: What is the present value of $1,000 to be received at the end of 5 years at 10%? ANSWER: Look in the PV of $1 table at the factor for 5 periods and 10%. The factor is .621. The present value is: $1,000 × .621 = $621. The amount of interest that could be earned over 5 years with an initial investment of $621 is $379 ($1,000 − $621).

as we have shown. However, figuring present value "by hand" for investments spanning many years becomes drawn out. The "number crunching" presents too many opportunities for arithmetical errors. Present-value tables ease our work. Let's reexamine our examples of present value by using Table 16-1: Present Value of $1.[1]

For the 10 percent investment for one year, we find the junction under the 10% column and across from 1 in the period column. The table figure of 0.909 is computed as follows: $1/1.10 = .909$. This work has been done for us, and only the present values are given in the table. Note that the table heading states $1. To figure present value for $5,000, we multiply 0.909 by $5,000. The result is $4,545, which matches the result we obtained by hand.

Table 16-1   *Present Value of $1*

					Present Value				
Periods	4%	5%	6%	7%	8%	10%	12%	14%	16%
1	0.962	0.952	0.943	0.935	0.926	0.909	0.893	0.877	0.862
2	0.925	0.907	0.890	0.873	0.857	0.826	0.797	0.769	0.743
3	0.889	0.864	0.840	0.816	0.794	0.751	0.712	0.675	0.641
4	0.855	0.823	0.792	0.763	0.735	0.683	0.636	0.592	0.552
5	0.822	0.784	0.747	0.713	0.681	0.621	0.567	0.519	0.476
6	0.790	0.746	0.705	0.666	0.630	0.564	0.507	0.456	0.410
7	0.760	0.711	0.665	0.623	0.583	0.513	0.452	0.400	0.354
8	0.731	0.677	0.627	0.582	0.540	0.467	0.404	0.351	0.305
9	0.703	0.645	0.592	0.544	0.500	0.424	0.361	0.308	0.263
10	0.676	0.614	0.558	0.508	0.463	0.386	0.322	0.270	0.227
11	0.650	0.585	0.527	0.475	0.429	0.350	0.287	0.237	0.195
12	0.625	0.557	0.497	0.444	0.397	0.319	0.257	0.208	0.168
13	0.601	0.530	0.469	0.415	0.368	0.290	0.229	0.182	0.145
14	0.577	0.505	0.442	0.388	0.340	0.263	0.205	0.160	0.125
15	0.555	0.481	0.417	0.362	0.315	0.239	0.183	0.140	0.108
16	0.534	0.458	0.394	0.339	0.292	0.218	0.163	0.123	0.093
17	0.513	0.436	0.371	0.317	0.270	0.198	0.146	0.108	0.080
18	0.494	0.416	0.350	0.296	0.250	0.180	0.130	0.095	0.069
19	0.475	0.396	0.331	0.277	0.232	0.164	0.116	0.083	0.060
20	0.456	0.377	0.312	0.258	0.215	0.149	0.104	0.073	0.051

[1] Appendix B provides a fuller table for the present value of $1. It also gives the amounts for the future value of $1. (The future-value amounts are presented for completeness and are not needed for the present-value analysis.)

For the two-year investment, we read down from the 10% column and across from the period 2 row. We multiply 0.826 (which is computed as follows: .909/1.10 = .826) by $5,000 and get $4,130, which confirms our earlier computation of $4,132 (the difference is due to rounding in the present-value table). We can compute the present value of any single future amount using the table.

Present Value of an Annuity

The investment in the preceding example provided the investor with only a single future receipt ($5,000 at the end of two years). Some investments, called annuities, provide multiple receipts of an equal amount at fixed intervals over the investment's duration.

Consider an investment that promises *annual* cash receipts of $10,000 to be received at the end of each of three years. Assume that you demand a 12 percent return on your investment. What is the investment's present value? What would you pay today to acquire the investment? The investment spans three periods, and you would pay the sum of three present values. The computation is

Year	Annual Cash Receipt	Present Value of $1 at 12% (Table 1)	Present Value of Annual Cash Receipt
1	$10,000	.893	$ 8,930
2	10,000	.797	7,970
3	10,000	.712	7,120
Total present value of investment			$24,020

Point to Stress: The PV of an annuity table (Table 16-2) adds all the factors together from the PV of $1 table (Table 16-1). For example, the factor for 20 periods at 5% in the annuity table is the sum of all 20 factors from the PV of $1 table in the 5% column.

Class Exercise: What is the present value of $1,000 to be received at the end of each of the next five years at 10%? *ANSWER:* Look at the PV of an annuity table at 5 periods and 10%. The factor is 3.791. The present value of *all five* $1,000 receipts is $1,000 × 3.791 = $3,791.

The present value of this annuity is $24,020. By paying this amount today, you would receive $10,000 at the end of each of three years while earning 12 percent on your investment.

The example illustrates repetitive computations of the three future amounts, a time-consuming process. One way to ease the computational burden is to add the three present values of $1 (.893 + .797 + .712) and multiply their sum (2.402) by the annual cash receipt ($10,000) to obtain the present value of the annuity ($10,000 × 2.402 = $24,020).

An easier approach is to use a present value of an annuity table. Table 16-2 shows the present value of $1 to be received periodically for a given number of periods.[2] The present value of a three-period annuity at 12 percent is 2.402. Thus $10,000 received annually at the end of each of three years, discounted at 12 percent, is $24,020 ($10,000 × 2.402), which is the present value.

Present Value of Bonds Payable

The present value of a bond—its market price—is the present value of the future principal amount at maturity plus the present value of the future contract interest payments. The principal is a single amount to be paid at maturity. The interest is an annuity because it occurs periodically.

---

[2] Appendix B provides a fuller table for the present value of an annuity of $1. It also gives the amounts for the future value of an annuity of $1. (The future-value amounts are presented for completeness and are not needed for the present-value analysis.)

TABLE 16-2 *Present Value of Annuity of $1*

Periods	4%	5%	6%	7%	8%	10%	12%	14%	16%
				Present Value					
1	0.962	0.952	0.943	0.935	0.926	0.909	0.893	0.877	0.862
2	1.886	1.859	1.833	1.808	1.783	1.736	1.690	1.647	1.605
3	2.775	2.723	2.673	2.624	2.577	2.487	2.402	2.322	2.246
4	3.630	3.546	3.465	3.387	3.312	3.170	3.037	2.914	2.798
5	4.452	4.329	4.212	4.100	3.993	3.791	3.605	3.433	3.274
6	5.242	5.076	4.917	4.767	4.623	4.355	4.111	3.889	3.685
7	6.002	5.786	5.582	5.389	5.206	4.868	4.564	4.288	4.039
8	6.733	6.463	6.210	5.971	5.747	5.335	4.968	4.639	4.344
9	7.435	7.108	6.802	6.515	6.247	5.759	5.328	4.946	4.607
10	8.111	7.722	7.360	7.024	6.710	6.145	5.650	5.216	4.833
11	8.760	8.306	7.887	7.499	7.139	6.495	5.938	5.453	5.029
12	9.385	8.863	8.384	7.943	7.536	6.814	6.194	5.660	5.197
13	9.986	9.394	8.853	8.358	7.904	7.103	6.424	5.842	5.342
14	10.563	9.899	9.295	8.745	8.244	7.367	6.628	6.002	5.468
15	11.118	10.380	9.712	9.108	8.559	7.606	6.811	6.142	5.575
16	11.652	10.838	10.106	9.447	8.851	7.824	6.974	6.265	5.669
17	12.166	11.274	10.477	9.763	9.122	8.022	7.120	6.373	5.749
18	12.659	11.690	10.828	10.059	9.372	8.201	7.250	6.467	5.818
19	13.134	12.085	11.158	10.336	9.604	8.365	7.366	6.550	5.877
20	13.590	12.462	11.470	10.594	9.818	8.514	7.469	6.623	5.929

Point to Stress: An investor buying a bond is in effect buying two future cash receipts:

1 The right to receive principal at maturity (calculate the present value of this future cash receipt by using Table 16-1).

2 The right to receive semiannual interest amounts over the life of the bond (calculate the present value of these future cash receipts by using Table 16-2).

Class Exercise: What is the present value of a $100,000, 12%, ten-year bond priced to yield 14% interest? Interest is paid semiannually.

ANSWER:

PV of principal:
$100,000 × .258 = $25,800
PV of interest:
$6,000 × 10.594 = 63,564
PV of bond $89,364

Note that the factors are for 20 interest periods, since the 10-year bond pays interest semiannually. The interest rate used to compute the semiannual receipts of cash interest is the bond's stated rate (12%). The interest rate used in the present value table is the effective rate (14%). How would the issue price of this bond be quoted? *ANSWER:* $89,364/$100,000 = 89⅜ approx.

Let's compute the present value of the 9 percent, five-year bonds of Bethlehem Steel. The face value of the bonds is $100,000, and they pay 4 ½ percent contract (cash) interest semiannually. At issuance the market interest rate is expressed as 10 percent, but it is computed at 5 percent semiannually. Therefore, the effective interest rate for each of the 10 semiannual periods is 5 percent. We use 5 percent in computing the present value of the maturity and of the interest. The market price of these bonds is $96,149, as follows:

	Effective annual interest rate ÷ 2	Number of semiannual interest payments	

PV of principal:
$100,000 × PV of single amount at 5%   for   10 periods
($100,000 × .614—Table 16-1) $61,400

PV of interest:
($100,000 × .045) × PV of annuity at 5%   for   10 periods
($4,500 × 7.722—Table 16-2) 34,749
PV (market price) of bonds $96,149

The market price of the Bethlehem Steel bonds shows a discount because the contract interest rate on the bonds (9 percent) is less than the market interest rate (10 percent). We discuss these bonds in more detail on pages 725–726.

Let's consider a premium price for the Bethlehem Steel bonds. Assume that the market interest rate is 8 percent at issuance. The effective interest rate is 4 percent for each of the 10 semiannual periods.

	Effective annual interest rate ÷ 2	Number of semiannual interest payments	

PV of principal:
   $100,000 × PV of single amount at 4%   for   10 periods
   ($100,000 × .676—Table 16-1) ......\...........|........... $ 67,600

PV of interest:
   ($100,000 × .045) × PV of annuity at 4%   for   10 periods
   ($4,500 × 8.111—Table 16-2)   36,500
   PV (market price) of bonds $104,100

We discuss accounting for these bonds on pages 727 and 729.

Capital Leases

How does a lessee compute the cost of an asset acquired through a capital lease? Consider that the lessee gets the use of the asset but does *not* pay for the leased asset in full at the beginning of the lease. Therefore, the lessee must record the leased asset at the present value of the lease liability. The time value of money must be weighed.

The cost of the asset to the lessee is the sum of any payment made at the beginning of the lease period plus the present value of the future lease payments. The lease payments are equal amounts occurring at regular intervals—that is, they are annuity payments.

Consider the 20-year building lease of the Southland Corporation, which owns 7-Eleven stores. The lease requires 20 annual payments of $10,000 each, with the first payment due immediately. The interest rate in the lease is 10 percent, and the present value of the 19 future payments is $83,650 ($10,000 × PV of annuity at 10 percent for 19 periods, or 8.365 from Table 16-2). Southland's cost of the building is $93,650 (the sum of the initial payment, $10,000, plus the present value of the future payments, $83,650). The entries for a capital lease are illustrated on pages 734 and 735.

Appendix Assignment Material

Problem 16A-1   *Computing the present values of notes and bonds*

2. $112,472
3. $127,140

Determine the present value of the following notes and bonds:

1. $40,000, five-year note payable with contract interest rate of 11 percent, paid annually. The market interest rate at issuance is 12 percent.
2. Ten-year bonds payable with maturity value of $100,000 and contract interest rate of 12 percent, paid semiannually. The market rate of interest is 10 percent at issuance.
3. Same bonds payable as in 2, but the market interest rate is 8 percent.
4. Same bonds payable as in 2, but the market interest rate is 12 percent.

Problem 16A-2   *Computing a bond's present value; recording its issuance at a discount and interest payments*

12/31/X2 Bond carrying
amount $285,629

On December 31, 19X1, when the market interest rate is 8 percent, Interstate Express Co. issues $300,000 of 10-year, 7.25 percent bonds payable. The bonds pay interest semiannually.

Required

1. Determine the present value of the bonds at issuance.
2. Assume that the bonds are issued at the price computed in 1. Prepare an effective-interest method amortization table for the first two semiannual interest periods.
3. Using the amortization table prepared in 2, journalize issuance of the bonds and the first two interest payments.

12/31/X2 Bond carrying amount $2,292,455

Problem 16A-3 *Computing a bond's present value; recording its issuance at a premium and interest payments*

On December 31, 19X1, when the market interest rate is 10 percent, JAX Gold Corporation issues $2,000,000 of 10-year, 12.5 percent bonds payable. The bonds pay interest semiannually.

Required

1. Determine the present value of the bonds at issuance.
2. Assuming the bonds were issued at the price computed in 1, prepare an effective-interest method amortization table for the first two semiannual interest periods.
3. Using the amortization table in 2, journalize issuance of the bonds on December 31, 19X1, and the first two interest payments on June 30 and December 31, 19X2.

Depr. exp. $7,123
Interest exp. $5,238

Problem 16A-4 *Computing the cost of equipment acquired under a capital lease and recording the lease transactions*

Goldblatt Institute acquired equipment under a capital lease that requires six annual lease payments of $10,000. The first payment is due when the lease begins, on January 1, 19X6. Future payments are due on January 1 of each year of the lease term. The interest rate in the lease is 16 percent.

Required

1. Compute Goldblatt's cost of the equipment.
2. Journalize the (a) acquisition of the equipment, (b) depreciation for 19X6, (c) accrued interest at December 31, 19X6, and (d) second lease payment on January 1, 19X7.

Chapter 17

Corporations: Investments and Accounting for International Operations

Corporations do not always greet FASB statements with enthusiasm. Consider this complaint about an FASB rule.

Did you know that General Electric's assets have ballooned to $110 billion as of Dec. 31, up from $40 billion at the end of 1987? Or that General Motors' debt is now 47 percent of [stockholders' equity], up from 10 percent at the end of 1987?

No, these blue chips have not turned into [high-risk investments]. What's going on is just the sort of nonsense that the critics predicted from the Financial Accounting Standards Board rule on consolidation. Under this rule . . . all majority-owned subsidiaries must be [included in] the parent [company]'s financial statements, no matter what business the [subsidiary companies] are in. Before the rule took effect with 1988 annual reports, companies with subsidiaries outside their core business . . . were not forced to fold the subs' assets and liabilities into the parent's consolidated balance sheet. . . .

Justification for the [new] rule was that [formerly] companies could bury liabilities in their subsidiaries. But the cure is worse than the disease. ''Now GM looks like a finance company with a car division,'' quips Norman Strauss, a partner at [CPA firm] Ernst & Young.

Source: Dana Wechsler, ''Mishmash Accounting,'' *Forbes*, November 27, 1989, p. 192.

LEARNING OBJECTIVES

After studying this chapter, you should be able to

1 Account for investments in stock by the cost (LCM) method

2 Use the equity method for stock investments

3 Consolidate parent and subsidiary balance sheets

4 Eliminate intercompany items from a consolidated balance sheet

5 Account for investments in bonds

6 Account for transactions stated in a foreign currency

7 Compute a foreign-currency translation adjustment

Real-World Example: Refer to the chapter-opening vignette. One of the main reasons that GM created GMAC as a separate corporation was to take advantage of the nonconsolidation rule. This finance subsidiary arrangement was a great example of off-balance-sheet financing. GM would sell an asset on credit, then sell the receivable to GMAC for cash. GMAC would have to borrow the cash to pay GM for the receivable. Essentially, GM was borrowing money through GMAC but did not have to report any liability on its own balance sheet. The FASB changed all that when it required the two companies to consolidate (combine) their financial statements.

Prior to the new accounting rule, General Motors Corporation reported its financing company, GMAC, separately. A major impact of the new rule is that parent companies such as General Motors and Sears must now include the financial statements of subsidiaries such as GMAC and Allstate in the parent's consolidated financial statements. This gives the parent company's balance sheet and income statement a new look that some accountants find strange. In this chapter, we discuss how to account for investments in stocks—including consolidation accounting—and bonds. We also consider the challenging area of accounting for international operations.

Accounting for Investments

Stock Prices

Investors buy more stocks in transactions among themselves than in purchases directly from the issuing company. Each share of stock is issued only once, but it may be traded among investors many times thereafter. People and businesses buy and sell stocks from each other in markets, such as the New York Stock Exchange and the American Stock Exchange. Recall that stock ownership is transferable. Investors trade millions of stock shares each day. Brokers like Merrill Lynch and Prudential Bache handle stock transactions for a commission.

A broker may "quote you a stock price," which means to state the current market price per share. The financial community quotes stock prices in dollars and one-eighth fractions. A stock selling at 32⅛ costs $32.125 per share. A stock listed at 55¾ sells at $55.75. Financial publications and many newspapers carry daily information on the stock issues of thousands of corporations. These one-line summaries carry information as of the close of trading the previous day.

Teaching Tip: Illustrate the reporting of stock prices from the financial section of a local paper. Look for a company that has made an announcement—either good (such as an earnings increase) or bad (such as a decrease in cash dividends)—to illustrate how news of that nature can effect a stock's price.

Exhibit 17-1 presents information for the common stock of the Boeing Company, a large aircraft manufacturer, just as this information appears in the newspaper listings.

During the previous 52 weeks, Boeing common stock reached a high of $64.875 and a low of $43.75. The annual cash dividend is $1.40 per share. During the previous day 678,800 (6,788 X 100) shares of Boeing common stock were traded. The prices of these transactions ranged from a high of $46.50 to a

EXHIBIT 17-1 *Stock Price Information*

| 52 Weeks | | | | | | | | |
High	Low	Stock	Dividend	Sales 100s	High	Low	Close	Net Change
64⅞	43¾	Boeing	1.40	6788	46½	45½	46⅛	+⅝

low of $45.50 per share. The day's closing price of $46.125 was $.625 (⅝ of one dollar) higher than the closing price of the preceding day.

What causes a change in a stock's price? The company's net income trend, the development of new products, court rulings, new legislation, business success, and upward market trends drive a stock's price up, and business failures and bad economic news pull it down. The market sets the price at which a stock changes hands.

Investments in Stock

To begin the discussion of investments in stock, we need to define two key terms. The person or company that owns stock in a corporation is the *investor*. The corporation that issued the stock is the *investee*. If you own shares of Boeing common stock, you are an investor and Boeing is the investee.

A business may purchase another corporation's stock simply to put extra cash to work in the hope of earning dividends and gains on the sale of the stock. Alternatively, the business may make the investment to gain a degree of control over the investee's operation. After all, stock is ownership. An investor holding 25 percent of the outstanding stock of the investee owns one-fourth of the business. This one-quarter voice in electing the directors of the corporation is likely to give the investor a lot of say in how the investee conducts its business. An investor holding more than 50 percent of the outstanding shares controls the investee.

Let's consider why one corporation might want to gain a say in another corporation's business. The investor may want to exert some control over the level of dividends paid by the investee. Or perhaps the investee has a line of products closely linked to the investor's own sales items. By influencing the investee's business, the investor may be able to exert some control on product distribution, product-line improvements, pricing strategies, and other important business considerations. A swimming-pool manufacturer might want to purchase stock in a diving-board company, a swimsuit maker, or some other corporation with related business.

Why doesn't the investor simply diversify its own operations, expanding into diving boards, swimsuits, and other related products? The cost may be too great. Also, the investor may not have experience with these other products. Why challenge a successful business in the marketplace when the investor can "buy into" a successful corporation's existing operations? The reasons for investing in a corporation in order to affect its operations to some degree make corporate investments attractive to many businesses.

Investments are not without risk. To offset the ill effects of a sudden downturn in the operations of any one investee, smart investors hold a portfolio of stocks. The portfolio holds investments in different companies. By diversifying its holdings, the investor gains protection from losing too much if any one investee runs into problems and its stock price plummets.

Real-World Example: The P/E (price/earnings) ratio is also quoted in the information concerning stocks. The P/E ratio equals market price of the stock divided by EPS. It shows the price the market is willing to pay for $1 of the company's net income.

Real-World Example: After rumors that CBS and Disney were going to merge, the stock prices of both companies increased. Both companies denied the rumors, but CBS stock increased $8 a share and Disney stock increased $3 a share. Reebok International Ltd.'s announcement that it would buy back about two-thirds of its largest shareholder's stake silenced rumors of a hostile takeover. The announcement caused the stock of Reebok to increase 25 cents, up to $18.50 per share.

EXHIBIT 17-2 *Reporting Investments on the Balance Sheet*

Current Assets
Cash.. $X
Short-term investments X
Accounts receivable X
Inventories X
Prepaid expenses X
    Total current assets .... $X
Long-term investments (or simply Investments) X
Property, plant, and equipment X
Intangible assets X
Other assets X

Classifying Stock Investments

Investments in stock are assets to the investor. The investments may be short-term or long-term. **Short-term investments** are current assets. To be listed on the balance sheet as short-term, investments must be liquid (readily convertible to cash). Also, the investor must intend either to convert the investments to cash within one year or to use them to pay a current liability. Some companies report short-term investments under the heading **marketable securities**. Investments not meeting these two requirements are classified on the balance sheet as **long-term investments.**

Short-term investments include certificates of deposit, and stocks and bonds of other companies. *Long-term investments* include bond sinking funds and stocks and bonds that the investor expects to hold longer than one year or that are not readily marketable, for instance, real estate not used in the operations of the business. Exhibit 17-2 shows the positions of short-term and long-term investments on the balance sheet.

Observe that we report assets in the order of their liquidity. Cash is the most liquid asset, followed by Short-Term Investments, Accounts Receivable, and so on. Long-Term Investments are less liquid than Current Assets but more liquid than Property, Plant, and Equipment.

Accounting for Stock Investments

Accounting for stock investments varies with the nature and extent of the investment. The specific accounting method that GAAP directs us to follow depends first on whether the investment is short-term or long-term and second on the percentage of the investee's voting stock that the investor holds.

Short-Term Investments—The Cost Method (with LCM)

The **cost method** (with lower of cost or market) is used to account for short-term investments in stock. *Cost* is used as the initial amount for recording investments and as the basis for measuring gains and losses on their sale. These investments are reported on the balance sheet at the *lower of their cost or market* value. Therefore, we refer to the overall method as cost (with lower of cost or market).

All investments, including short-term investments, are recorded initially at cost. Cost is the price paid for the stock plus the brokerage commission. Accountants use no separate account for the brokerage commission paid. At purchase, the commission increases the cost of the investment. When the investment is sold, the sale commission decreases the amount of cash received. Suppose that Dade, Inc., purchases 1,000 shares of Hewlett-Packard Company common stock at the market price of 35¾ and pays a $550 commission. Dade intends to sell this investment within one year or less and, therefore, classifies it as short-term. Dade's entry to record the investment is

July 23	Short-Term Investment in Hewlett-Packard		
	Common Stock [(1,000 × $35.75) + $550]	36,300	
	Cash		36,300
	Purchased 1,000 shares of Hewlett-Packard		
	common stock at $35.75 plus commission of $550.		

OBJECTIVE 1

Account for investments in stock by the cost (LCM) method

Assume Dade receives a $.22 per share cash dividend on the Hewlett-Packard stock. Dade's entry to record receipt of the dividends is

Oct. 14	Cash (1,000 × $.22)	220	
	Dividend Revenue...........................		220
	Received $.22 per share cash dividend on Hewlett-		
	Packard common stock.		

Dividends do not accrue with the passage of time (as interest does). The investee has no liability for dividends until the dividends are declared. An investor makes no accrual entry for dividend revenue at year end in anticipation of a dividend declaration.

However, if a dividend declaration *does* occur before year end—say, on December 28—the investor debits Dividend Receivable and credits Dividend Revenue on that date. The investor reports this receivable and the revenue in the December 31 financial statements. Receipt of the cash dividend in January is recorded by a debit to Cash and a credit to Dividend Receivable.

Receipt of a *stock* dividend is *not* income to the investor, and no formal journal entry is needed. As we have seen, a stock dividend increases the number of shares held by the investor but does not affect the total cost of the investment. The *cost per share* of the stock investment therefore decreases. The investor usually makes a memorandum entry of the number of dividend shares received and the new cost per share. Assume that Dade, Inc., receives a 10 percent stock dividend on its 1,000-share investment in Hewlett-Packard Company, which cost $36,300. Dade would make a memorandum entry along this line:

Nov. 22 Received 100 shares of Hewlett-Packard common stock in 10 percent stock dividend. New cost per share is $33.00 ($36,300/1,100 shares).

Any gain or loss on the sale of the investment is the difference between the sale proceeds and the cost of the investment. Assume that Dade sells 400 shares of Hewlett-Packard stock for $35 per share, less a $280 commission. The entry to record the sale is

Dec. 18	Cash [(400 × $35) − $280]	13,720	
	Short-Term Investment in Hewlett-		
	Packard Common Stock (400 × $33.00) .		13,200
	Gain on Sale of Investment		520
	Sold 400 shares of investment in Hewlett-		
	Packard common stock.		

Observe that the cost per share of the investment ($33.00) is based on the total number of shares held, including those received as a dividend.

Reporting Short-Term Investments at Lower of Cost or Market (LCM)

Because of accounting conservatism, short-term investments in stock are reported at the lower of their cost or market (LCM) value. LCM is based on the view that losses, but not gains, should be recorded prior to the sale of the asset. LCM is applied to the *entire* short-term investment portfolio, not to individual stocks in the portfolio. On the balance sheet date, the investor computes the total cost and the total market value of the short-term investment portfolio and reports the investments at the lower amount. Assume Dade, Inc., owns three short-term investments—including the Hewlett-Packard common stock from the preceding example—with the following costs and market values. Also assume Dade purchased all the investments during the current year.

Short-term Investment Portfolio

Stock	Cost	Current Market Value
Ford Motor Co	$122,000	$128,000
Hewlett-Packard Company (cost: $36,300 − $13,200)	23,100	22,000
Kellogg	160,000	142,000
Total	$305,100	$292,000

Because the total market value of the investment portfolio ($292,000) is less than cost ($305,100), the investor's balance sheet will report short-term investments at market value of $292,000. However, the Short-Term Investments account carries a balance equal to the investments' cost, $305,100. The following entry is needed to bring the investments to the LCM value of $292,000:

Dec. 31   Unrealized Loss on Short-Term Investments
            ($305,100 − $292,000)   13,100
         Allowance to Reduce Short-Term
            Investments to Market Value   13,100
   Wrote short-term investments down to market value.

Unrealized Loss on Short-Term Investments is reported on the income statement among the Other Expenses and Losses. The Allowance account is reported contra to Short-Term Investments on the balance sheet as follows:

Current Assets

Cash.		$ XXX
Short-term investments, at cost	$305,100	
Less: Allowance to reduce short-term investments to market value	13,100	
Short-term investments, at market value.		292,000
Accounts receivable, net of allowance of $XXX.		XXX

An alternative and more-often-used way to report these investments is to show the LCM value on the balance sheet and the higher amount in a note, as follows:

Current Assets

Cash . . . . $ XXX
Short-term investments, at market value (Note 4)   292,000
Accounts receivable, net of allowance of $XXX   XXX

> NOTE 4—SHORT-TERM INVESTMENTS:
>
> Short-term investments are reported at the lower of their cost or market value. At December 31, 19XX, cost was $305,100.

If the portfolio cost is lower than market value, the investor reports short-term investments at cost and discloses market value in the note.

Long-Term Investments Accounted for by the Cost Method (with LCM)

An investor may own numerous investments, some short-term and others long-term. For accounting purposes, the two investment portfolios are *not* mixed. They are reported separately on the balance sheet, as shown in Exhibit 17-2. *Long-term* is seldom used in the account title. An investment is understood to be long-term unless specifically labeled as short-term.

Accounting for long-term investments in which the investor holds less than 20 percent of the investee's voting stock follows the procedures outlined for short-term investments. The beginning accounting value is cost, which is debited to an Investments account at the date of purchase. Gains and losses are recorded on sales. Long-term investments are reported on the balance sheet at the lower of total portfolio cost or market value. The main difference in accounting for long-term investments is that the debit balance of Unrealized Loss on Long-Term Investments is reported as a contra item in the stockholders' equity section of the balance sheet. As a practical matter, long-term investments accounted for by the cost method are rare. Most companies that purchase long-term investments in stock are seeking some measure of control. Thus, they use either the equity method or the consolidation method.

Long-Term Investments Accounted for by the Equity Method

The *cost* method (with LCM) of accounting for long-term investments applies when an investor holds less than 20 percent of the investee's voting stock. Such an investor usually plays no important role in the investee's operations. However, an investor with a larger stock holding—between 20 percent and 50 percent of the investee's voting stock—may *significantly influence* how the investee operates the business. Such an investor can likely affect the investee's decisions on dividend policy, product lines, sources of supply, and other important matters. For example, General Motors owns 34 percent of Isuzu, and Toyota owns part of 23 key suppliers. Because the investor has a voice in shaping business policy and operations, accountants believe that some measure of the investee's success and failure should be included in accounting for the investment. We use the **equity method** to account for investments in which the investor can significantly influence the decisions of the investee.

Investments accounted for by the equity method are recorded initially at cost. Suppose Phillips Petroleum Company pays $400,000 for 30 percent of the common stock of White Rock Corporation. Phillips's entry to record the purchase of this investment is

Jan. 6   Investment in White Rock Common Stock . .   400,000
                Cash   400,000
           To purchase 30% investment in White Rock
           common stock.

Discussion Question: Assume the market price has risen to $316,400, while the cost is $305,100 as illustrated. Will the balance sheet report Short-Term Investments of $316,400? *ANSWER:* No; the LCM rule says you will never write up the investment to market if it has risen above cost (conservatism concept). Never report the investments at an amount greater than cost.

OBJECTIVE 2
Use the equity method for stock investments

Point to Stress: An investor who holds 20% of the stock of a company can usually elect one or more hand-picked representatives to the board of directors. This investor may be able to control the board of directors.

Point to Stress: When an investor owns 20% or more of the outstanding stock, the investor has influence over that company and some degree of responsibility for its profits. Therefore, that investor's income statement should include the investor's proportionate share of investee's profits.

Under the equity method, Phillips, as the investor, applies its percentage of ownership—30 percent, in our example—in recording its share of the investee's net income and dividends. If White Rock reports net income of $250,000 for the year, Phillips records 30 percent of this amount as an increase in the investment account and as equity-method investment revenue, as follows:

Dec. 31	Investment in White Rock Common Stock	
	($250,000 × .30)	75,000
	Equity-Method Investment Revenue ..	75,000
	To record 30% of White Rock net income.	

The Investment Revenue account carries the Equity-Method label to identify its source. This labeling is similar to distinguishing Sales Revenue from Service Revenue.

The investor increases the Investment account and records Investment Revenue when the investee reports income because of the close relationship between the two companies. As the investee's owner equity increases, so does the Investment account on the books of the investor.

Phillips records its proportionate part of cash dividends received from White Rock. Assuming White Rock declares and pays a cash dividend of $100,000, Phillips receives 30 percent of this dividend, recording it as follows:

Jan. 17	Cash ($100,000 × .30)	30,000
	Investment in White Rock	
	Common Stock....................	30,000
	To record receipt of 30% of White Rock cash dividend.	

Observe that the Investment account is credited for the receipt of a dividend on an equity-method investment. Why? Because the dividend decreases the investee's owner equity and so it also reduces the investor's investment. The investor received cash for this portion of the investment and reduced the investor's claim against the investee.

After the above entries are posted, Phillips's Investment account reflects its equity in the net assets of White Rock:

Investment in White Rock Common Stock

19X1				19X2		
Jan. 6	Purchase	400,000		Jan. 17	Dividends	30,000
Dec. 31	Net income	75,000				
19X2						
Jan. 17	Balance	445,000				

Gain or loss on the sale of an equity-method investment is measured as the difference between the sale proceeds and the carrying amount of the investment. For example, sale of one-tenth of the White Rock common stock for $41,000 would be recorded as follows:

Feb. 13	Cash	41,000
	Loss on Sale of Investment	3,500
	Investment in White Rock Common Stock	
	($445,000 × ¹⁄₁₀)	44,500
	Sold one-tenth of investment in White Rock common stock.	

Companies with investments accounted for by the equity method often refer to the investee as an *affiliated company*. The account title Investments in Affiliated Companies refers to investments that are accounted for by the equity method.

Consolidation Method

Most large corporations own controlling interests in other corporations. A **controlling** (or **majority**) **interest** is the ownership of more than 50 percent of the investee's voting stock. Such an investment enables the investor to elect a majority of the investee's board of directors and so control the investee. The investor is called the **parent company,** and the investee company is called the **subsidiary.** For example, Libbey-Owens-Ford, a glass manufacturer, is a subsidiary of General Motors Corporation, the parent. The stockholders of General Motors control GM, and because GM owns Libbey-Owens-Ford, the stockholders also control Libbey-Owens-Ford.

Why have subsidiaries? Why not have the corporation take the form of a single legal entity? Subsidiaries may enable the parent to save on income taxes, may limit the parent's liabilities in a risky venture, and may ease expansion into foreign countries. For example, IBM may find it more feasible to operate in France through a French-based subsidiary company than through the American parent company.

Consolidation accounting is a method of combining the financial statements of two or more companies that are controlled by the same owners. This method implements the entity concept by reporting a single set of financial statements for the consolidated entity, which carries the name of the parent company.

Consolidated statements combine the balance sheets, income statements, and other financial statements of the parent company with those of majority-owned subsidiaries into an overall set as if the parents and its subsidiaries were a single entity. The goal is to provide a better perspective on total operations than could be obtained by examining the separate reports of each of the individual companies. The assets, liabilities, revenues, and expenses of each subsidiary are added to the parent's accounts. The consolidated financial statements present the combined account balances. For example, the balance in the Cash account of Libbey-Owens-Ford is added to the balance in the GM Cash account, and the sum of the two amounts is presented as a single amount in the consolidated balance sheet of General Motors. Each account balance of a subsidiary loses its identity in the consolidated statements. GM's financial statements are entitled "General Motors Corporation and Consolidated Subsidiaries." Libbey-Owens-Ford and the names of all other GM subsidiaries do not appear in the statement titles. But the names of the subsidiary companies are listed in the parent company's annual report. A reader of corporate annual reports cannot hope to understand them without knowing how consolidated statements are prepared. Exhibit 17-3 diagrams a corporate structure whose parent corporation owns controlling interests in five subsidiary companies and an equity-method investment in another investee company.

Consolidated Balance Sheet—Parent Corporation Owns All of Subsidiary's Stock.   Suppose that Parent Corporation has purchased all the outstanding common stock of Subsidiary Corporation at its book value of $150,000. In addition, Parent Corporation loaned Subsidiary Corporation $80,000. Note that the $150,000 is paid to the *former owners* of Subsidiary Corporation as private investors. The $150,000 is *not* an addition to the existing assets and stockholders' equity of Subsidiary Corporation. *That is, the books of Subsidiary*

Point to Stress: GM might not own all of the stock of Libbey-Owens-Ford. There might be minority shareholders. Minority shareholders can look only to Libbey-Owens-Ford for dividends or earnings, not to GM. A creditor of Libbey-Owens-Ford cannot look to GM to pay off a debt. Therefore Libbey-Owens-Ford must maintain its own set of books.

OBJECTIVE 3
Consolidate parent and subsidiary balance sheets

Entities that are consolidated are enclosed by these dashed lines.

Parent, such as General Motors

Sub Sub Sub Sub Sub

Consolidated subsidiaries

Investment in affiliated company (20%–50% owned), such as 34% in a Japanese company like Isuzu would be accounted for by the equity method.

Point to Stress: The parent and subsidiary companies are treated as one economic unit when they are consolidated. For this reason, intercompany receivables and payables must be eliminated. The consolidated company should not report a liability of $80,000 because only liabilities that are payable to those outside the economic unit should be recorded. Likewise, the consolidated company cannot report an $80,000 receivable as an asset because the consolidated company cannot collect money from itself.

Point to Stress: Only investments in companies outside the consolidated business should be reported as assets. The consolidated company should not record an investment in itself as an asset. Therefore, the investment account must be eliminated from the consolidated balance sheet.

Discussion Question: Who owns the stock of the subsidiary? *ANSWER:* The parent company. Do the stockholders' equity accounts of the subsidiary represent outside equity? *ANSWER:* No. The only common stock owned by parties outside the consolidated firm is the stock issued by the parent company.

Corporation are completely unaffected by Parent Corporation's initial investment and Parent's subsequent accounting for that investment. Subsidiary Corporation is not dissolved. It lives on as a separate legal entity but with a new owner, Parent Corporation.

Parent Books[1]		Subsidiary Books	
Investment in Subsidiary			
Corporation	150,000	No entry	
Cash		150,000 Cash	80,000
Note Receivable from		Note Payable	
Subsidiary	80,000	to Parent ...	80,000
Cash	80,000		

Each legal entity has its individual set of books. The consolidated entity does not keep a separate set of books. Instead, a work sheet is used to prepare the consolidated statements. A major concern in consolidation accounting is this: Do not double-count.

Companies may prepare a consolidated balance sheet immediately after the acquisition. The consolidated balance sheet shows all the assets and liabilities of both the parent and the subsidiary. The Investment in Subsidiary account on the parent's books represents all the assets and liabilities of Subsidiary. The consolidated statements cannot show both the investment amount *plus* the amounts for the subsidiary's assets and liabilities. That would count the same resources twice. In fact, intercompany accounts—those that appear in both the parent's books and the subsidiary's books—should not be included in the consolidated statements at all. To avoid this double-counting we eliminate (a) the $150,000 Investment in Subsidiary on the parent's books and (b) the $150,000 stockholders' equity on the subsidiary's books ($100,000 Common Stock and $50,000 Retained Earnings).

---

[1]The parent company may use either the cost method or the equity method for work sheet entries to the Investment account. Regardless of the method used, the consolidated statements are the same. Advanced accounting courses deal with this topic.

Explanation of Elimination—Entry (a). Exhibit 17-4 shows the work sheet for consolidating the balance sheet. Consider the elimination entry for the parent-subsidiary ownership accounts, which are intercompany accounts. Entry (a) credits the parent Investment account to eliminate its debt balance. It also eliminates the subsidiary stockholders' equity accounts by debiting Common Stock for $100,000 and Retained Earnings for $50,000. The resulting consolidated balance sheet reports no Investment in Subsidiary account, and the Common Stock and Retained Earnings are those of Parent Corporation only. The consolidated balance sheet amounts are in the final column of the consolidation work sheet.

In summary, if the intercompany accounts were not eliminated, there would be a double-counting in the consolidated statement. The following chart summarizes the parent-subsidiary relationship:

Point to Stress: The elimination entries are a part of the consolidation process. The consolidation process is recorded on working papers as a supplement to the existing accounting records. Elimination entries do not appear on the accounting records of either firm.

Entity	Types of Records
Parent Corporation	Parent books
+ Subsidiary Corporation	Subsidiary books
= Preliminary consolidated balance sheet	No separate books, but periodically Parent and Subsidiary assets and liabilities are added together in a work sheet
− Eliminating entries	Intercompany accounts offset against each other to eliminate double-counting
= Consolidated balance sheet to outside investors	The report of the overall economic entity

Explanation of Elimination—Entry (b). Parent Corporation loaned $80,000 to Subsidiary Corporation, and Subsidiary signed a note payable to Parent. Therefore, Parent's balance sheet includes an $80,000 note receivable and Subsidiary's balance sheet reports a note payable for this amount. This loan was entirely within the consolidated entity and so must be eliminated. Entry (b) accomplishes this. The $80,000 credit in the elimination column of the work sheet offsets Parent's debit balance in Notes Receivable from Subsidiary.

EXHIBIT 17-4 *Work Sheet for Consolidated Balance Sheet—Parent Corporation Owns All of Subsidiary's Stock*

Transparency T17-1

Assets	Parent Corporation	Subsidiary Corporation	Eliminations Debit	Eliminations Credit	Consolidated Amounts
Cash	12,000	18,000			30,000
Notes receivable from Subsidiary	80,000	—		(b) 80,000	—
Inventory	104,000	91,000			195,000
Investment in Subsidiary	150,000	—		(a) 150,000	—
Other assets	218,000	138,000			356,000
Total	564,000	247,000			581,000
Liabilities and Stockholders' Equity					
Accounts payable	43,000	17,000			60,000
Notes payable	190,000	80,000	(b) 80,000		190,000
Common stock	176,000	100,000	(a) 100,000		176,000
Retained earnings	155,000	50,000	(a) 50,000		155,000
Total	564,000	247,000	230,000	230,000	581,000

Assets

	P	S
Cash	$ 200,000	$ 50,000
Accounts rec.	275,000	60,000
Inventory	300,000	80,000
Investment in S	280,000	
Plant & equip.	500,000	170,000
	$1,555,000	$360,000

Liabilities and Stockholders' Equity

Accounts payable	$ 350,000	$ 60,000
Common stock	500,000	120,000
Retained earnings	705,000	180,000
	$1,555,000	$360,000

After this work sheet entry, the consolidated amount for notes receivable is zero. The $80,000 debit in the elimination column offsets the credit balance of Subsidiary's notes payable, and the resulting consolidated amount for notes payable is the amount owed to those outside the consolidated entity.

Parent Corporation Buys Subsidiary's Stock at a Price above Book Value.[2] A company may acquire a controlling interest in a subsidiary by paying a price above the book value of the subsidiary's owner equity. The excess of the price paid by the parent over the market value of the subsidiary's net assets (assets minus liabilities) is *goodwill.* What drives a company's market value up? The company may create goodwill through its superior products, service, or location. Goodwill is discussed in Chapter 10.

The subsidiary does not record goodwill. Doing so would violate the reliability principle. Goodwill is recorded only when a company purchases it as part of the acquisition of another company, that is, when a parent company purchases a subsidiary. The goodwill is recorded in the process of consolidating the parent and subsidiary financial statements.

Suppose Parent Corporation paid $450,000 to acquire 100 percent of the common stock of Subsidiary Corporation, which had Common Stock of $200,000 and Retained Earnings of $180,000. Parent's payment included $70,000 for goodwill ($450,000 − $200,000 − $180,000 = $70,000). The entry to eliminate Parent's Investment account against Subsidiary's equity accounts is

Dec. 31	Common Stock, Subsidiary	200,000	
	Retained Earnings, Subsidiary	180,000	
	Goodwill	70,000	
	Investment in Subsidiary		450,000
	To eliminate cost of investment in subsidiary against Subsidiary's equity balances and to recognize Subsidiary's unrecorded goodwill.		

In actual practice, this entry would be made only on the consolidation work sheet. Here we show it in general journal form for instructional purposes.

The asset goodwill is reported on the consolidated balance sheet among the intangible assets, after plant assets. Goodwill is amortized to expense over its useful life.

Consolidated Balance Sheet—Parent Company Owns Less Than 100 Percent of Subsidiary's Stock. When a parent company owns more than 50 percent (a majority) of the subsidiary's stock but less than 100 percent of it, a new category of owners' equity, called *minority interest,* must appear on the balance sheet. Suppose Parent buys 75 percent of Subsidiary's common stock. The minority interest is the remaining 25 percent of Subsidiary's equity. Thus **minority interest** is the subsidiary's equity that is held by stockholders other than the parent company. Most companies report minority interest as a liability, while a few show it as a separate element of stockholders' equity. In this book, we list minority interest as a liability to be consistent with actual practice. Exhibit 17-5 is the consolidation work sheet. Again, focus on the Eliminations columns and the Consolidated Amounts.

---

[2]For simplicity, we are assuming that the fair market value of the subsidiary's net assets (assets minus liabilities) equals the book value of the company's owner equity. Advanced courses consider other situations.

Assets	P Company	S Company	Eliminations Debit	Eliminations Credit	Consolidated Amounts
Cash	33,000	18,000			51,000
Note receivable from P............	—	50,000		(b) 50,000	—
Accounts receivable, net	54,000	39,000			93,000
Inventory	92,000	66,000			158,000
Investment in S	120,000	—		(a) 120,000	—
Plant and equipment, net	230,000	123,000			353,000
Total	529,000	296,000			655,000
Liabilities and Stockholders' Equity					
Accounts payable.................	141,000	94,000			235,000
Notes payable...................	50,000	42,000	(b) 50,000		42,000
Minority interest	—	—		(a) 40,000	40,000
Common stock	170,000	100,000	(a) 100,000		170,000
Retained earnings	168,000	60,000	(a) 60,000		168,000
Total	529,000	296,000	210,000	210,000	655,000

Entry (a) eliminates P Company's Investment balance of $120,000 against the $160,000 owners' equity of S Company. Observe that all of S's equity is eliminated even though P holds only 75 percent of S's stock. The outside 25 percent interest in S's equity is credited to Minority Interest ($160,000 × .25 = $40,000). Thus entry *(a)* reclassifies 25 percent of S Company's equity as minority interest.

Entry (b) in Exhibit 17-5 eliminates S Company's $50,000 note receivable against P's note payable of the same amount. The consolidated amount of notes payable ($42,000) is the amount that S Company owes to outsiders.

The consolidated balance sheet of P Company, below, is based on the work sheet of Exhibit 17-5.

**P Company and Consolidated Subsidiary
Consolidated Balance Sheet
December 31, 19XX**

Assets

Cash....................................	$ 51,000
Accounts receivable, net.................	93,000
Inventory	158,000
Plant and equipment, net.................	353,000
Total assets.............................	$655,000

Liabilities and Stockholders' Equity

Accounts payable	$235,000
Notes payable	42,000
Minority interest.......................	40,000
Common stock	170,000
Retained earnings.......................	168,000
Total liabilities and stockholders' equity	$655,000

Assuming that P Company owes S Company $10,000 on account, prepare the elimination entry in general journal form and the consolidated balance sheet.

ANSWER:

Accounts Payable .	10,000	
Common Stock ...	120,000	
Retained Earnings .	180,000	
Goodwill	40,000	
[$280,000 − ($300,000 × 80%)]		
Investment in S		280,000
Minority Interest ($300,000 × 20%).....		60,000
Accounts Receivable....		10,000

Assets

Cash	$ 250,000
Accounts rec.	325,000
Inventory	380,000
Plant & equip.	670,000
Goodwill	40,000
Total	$1,665,000

Liabilities & Stockholders' Equity

Accounts pay......	$ 400,000
Minority int.	60,000
Common stock	500,000
Retained earn.	705,000
Total	$1,665,000

The consolidated balance sheet reveals that ownership of P Company and its consolidated subsidiary is divided between P's stockholders (common stock and retained earnings totaling $338,000) and the minority interest of S Company ($40,000).

Income of a Consolidated Entity.   The income of a consolidated entity is the net income of the parent plus the parent's proportion of the subsidiaries' net income. Suppose Parent Company owns all the stock of Subsidiary S-1 and 60 percent of the stock of Subsidiary S-2. During the year just ended, Parent earned net income of $330,000, S-1 earned $150,000, and S-2 had a net loss of $100,000. Parent Company would report net income of $420,000, computed as follows:

	Net Income (Net Loss)	Parent Stockholders' Ownership	Parent Net Income (Net Loss)
Parent Company	$330,000	100%	$330,000
Subsidiary S-1	150,000	100	150,000
Subsidiary S-2	(100,000)	60	(60,000)
Consolidated net income			$420,000

The parent's net income is the same amount that would be recorded under the equity method. However, the equity method stops short of reporting the investees' assets and liabilities on the parent balance sheet because with an investment in the range of 20–50 percent, the investor owns less than a controlling interest in the investee company.

The procedures for preparation of a consolidated income statement parallel those outlined above for the balance sheet. The consolidated income statement is discussed in an advanced course.

Investments in Bonds and Notes

Industrial and commercial companies invest far more in stock than they invest in bonds. The major investors in bonds are financial institutions, such as pension plans, bank trust departments, and insurance companies. For every issuer of bonds payable, at least one investor owns the bonds. The relationship between the issuer and the investor may be diagrammed as follows:

OBJECTIVE 5
Account for investments in bonds

Issuing Corporation		Investor (Bondholder)
Bonds payable	⟷	Investment in bonds
Interest expense	⟷	Interest revenue

The dollar amount of a bond transaction is the same for issuer and investor, but the accounts debited and credited differ. However, the accounts are parallel. For example, the issuer's interest expense is the investor's interest revenue.

An investment in bonds is classified either as short-term (a current asset) or as long-term. An investment is a current asset if (1) the investment is liquid (can readily be sold for cash) and (2) the owner intends to convert it to cash within one year or to use it to pay a current liability. An investment that is intended to be held longer than a year is classified as long-term.

Bond investments are recorded at cost, which includes the purchase price and any brokerage fees. Amortization of bond premium or discount is *not* recorded on short-term investments because the investor plans to hold the bonds for so short a period that any amortization would be immaterial. Investors hold long-term investments for a significant period and therefore amortize any premium or discount on the bonds.

Let's look at accounting for a *short-term* bond investment. Suppose that an investor purchases $10,000 of bonds on August 1, 19X2, paying 93 plus accrued interest and a brokerage commission of $250. The annual contract interest rate is 12 percent, paid semiannually on April 1 and October 1. The cost of the bonds is $9,550 [($10,000 × .93) + $250]. In addition, the investor pays accrued interest for the four months (April through July) since the last interest payment. The investor records the purchase on August 1 as follows:

Aug. 1 Short-Term Investment in Bonds
       [($10,000 × .93) + $250] 9,550
      Interest Receivable ($10,000 × .12 × 4/12) 400
        Cash 9,950
      To purchase short-term bond investment.

Accrued interest is *not* included in the cost of the investment but is debited to Interest Receivable.

The investor's entry for receipt of the first semiannual interest amount on October 1 is

Oct. 1 Cash ($10,000 × .12 × 6/12) 600
        Interest Receivable 400
        Interest Revenue ($10,000 × .12 × 2/12) 200
      To receive semiannual interest, part of which was accrued.

At October 1 the investor has held the bonds for two months. The entry correctly credits Interest Revenue for two months' interest. This entry does not include discount amortization on the bonds because the investment is short-term.

At December 31 the investor accrues interest revenue for three months (October, November, and December), debiting Interest Receivable and crediting Interest Revenue for $300 ($10,000 × .12 × 3/12). The investor's December 31 balance sheet reports the following information (we assume that the market price of the bonds is 96):

Current assets:
    Short-term investment in bonds (Note 4) $9,550
    Interest receivable 300

Note 4: Short-term investments:
At December 31 the current market value of short-term investments in bonds was $9,600.

Observe that the investment is reported at cost, with the current market value disclosed in a note. The market value may also be reported parenthetically.

Current assets:
  Short-term investment in bonds (Current market value, $9,600) . $9,550
  Interest receivable 300

The investor measures any gain or loss on sale as the difference between the sale price (less any broker's commission) and the cost of the investment. For example, sale of the bonds for $9,700 will result in a gain of $150. This gain is reported as Other Revenue on a multiple-step income statement or beneath

Class Exercise: Assume the Quill Corporation is buying bonds as a short-term investment. If Quill buys $300,000, 9%, 10-year bonds at 104, and pays a $400 commission, what are the entries to record (1) the purchase on August 1, 1992, (2) the first semiannual interest received, and (3) the year-end accrual? (The bonds were dated 5/31/92 and pay interest 5/31 and 11/30.) ANSWER:

(1)
8/1/92 Short-Term
    Investment in
     Bonds 312,400
    Interest
     Rec. 4,500
      Cash 316,900
($300,000 × .09 × 2/12 = $4,500 "plus accrued interest"; $300,000 × 1.04 = $312,000 + $400 = $312,400 cost)

Note that there is *not* an account called "Premium on Investment in Bonds"; any premium or discount is included in the Investment account.

(2)
11/30/92 Cash 13,500
    Interest
     Rec. 4,500
    Interest
     Rev. 9,000

Note that Quill Corporation has held the bonds four months and four months of interest has been earned and recorded.

(3)
12/31/92 Interest
     Rec. 2,250
    Interest
     Rev. 2,250

Note that there has been no amortization of the premium amount because this is a short-term investment.

Class Exercise: Now assume Quill Corporation sells these bonds on May 31, 1993, when the market price is 103½. What journal entry is required?

ANSWER:

5/31/93 Cash   310,500
     Loss on Sale of
       Investments. .   1,900
     Short-Term
     Investment
     in Bonds.   312,400
($300,000 × 1.035 = $310,500 Sales price
$312,400 − $310,500 = $1,900 loss)

Class Exercise: Assume Quill
Corporation bought the bonds
in the previous class exercise as
a long-term investment. What
would be the journal entries to
record (1) the purchase of the
bonds on August 1, 1992, (2)
receipt of the first semiannual
interest, and (3) the December
31, 1992, interest accrual?

ANSWER:

(1)
    The entry to record the
    purchase of the bonds
    would be the same except
    for the account title,
    Long-Term Investment in
    Bonds.

(2)
    Cash. 13,500
      Interest Rec. .   4,500
      Interest Rev.   9,000
      Interest
        Rev. 525*
      Long-Term
      Investment
      in Bonds . .   525
    *[($312,400 − $300,000)/118 × 5]
    = $525

(3)
    Interest Rec. . . . 2,250
      Interest Rev.   2,250
      Interest Rev. . .   105*
      Long-Term
      Investment
      in Bonds . .   105
    *[($312,400 − $300,000)/118]
    = $105

Sales Revenue among the revenues and gains on a single-step statement. A loss would be reported as Other Expense on a multiple-step statement or among the expenses on a single-step statement.

Accounting for *long-term* investments in bonds follows the general pattern illustrated for short-term investments. For long-term investments, however, discount or premium is amortized to account more precisely for interest revenue. This additional step is needed because the bond investment will be held for longer than a year and, therefore, the amortization amount is likely to be material. The amortization of discount or premium on a bond investment affects Interest Revenue in the same way that the amortization affects Interest Expense for the company that issued the bonds.

The accountant records amortization on the cash interest dates and at year end, along with the accrual of interest receivable. Accountants rarely use separate discount and premium accounts for investments. Amortization of a discount is recorded by directly debiting the Long-Term Investment in Bonds account and crediting Interest Revenue. Amortization of a premium is credited directly to the Long-Term Investment account. This entry debits Interest Revenue. These entries bring the investment balance to the bonds' face value on the maturity date and record the correct amount of interest revenue each period.

Suppose the $10,000 of 12 percent bonds in the preceding illustration were purchased on August 1, 19X2, as a long-term investment. Interest dates are April 1 and October 1. These bonds mature on October 1, 19X6, so they will be outstanding for 50 months. Assume amortization of the discount by the straight-line method. The following entries for a long-term investment highlight the differences between accounting for a short-term bond investment and for a long-term bond investment:

Aug. 1	**Long-Term Investment in Bonds**			
	[($10,000 × .93) + $250].	9,550	
	Interest Receivable ($10,000 × .12 × $\frac{4}{12}$)	400	
	Cash		9,950
	To purchase long-term bond investment.		
Oct. 1	Cash ($10,000 × .12 × $\frac{6}{12}$)	600	
	Interest Receivable		400
	Interest Revenue ($10,000 × .12 × $\frac{2}{12}$)		200
	To receive semiannual interest, part of which was accrued.		
Oct. 1	**Long-Term Investment in Bonds**			
	[($10,000 − $9,550)/50 × 2]	**18**	
	Interest Revenue		**18**
	To amortize discount on bond investment for two months.		
Dec. 31	Interest Receivable ($10,000 × .12 × $\frac{3}{12}$)	300	
	Interest Revenue		300
	To accrue interest revenue for three months.		
Dec. 31	**Long-Term Investment in Bonds**			
	[($10,000 − $9,550)/50 × 3]	**27**	
	Interest Revenue		**27**
	To amortize discount on bond investment for three months.		

The financial statements at December 31, 19X2, report the following effects of this long-term investment in bonds (assume the bonds' market price is 102):

Balance sheet at December 31, 19X2:
Current assets:

Interest receivable	....	$ 300
Total current assets	....	X,XXX
Long-term investments in bonds ($9,550 + $18 + $27)—Note 6		9,595
Property, plant, and equipment	....	X,XXX

Note 6: Long-term investments:
At December 31, 19X2, the market value of long-term investments in bonds was $10,200.

Income statement (multiple-step) for the year ended December 31, 19X2:
Other revenues:

Interest revenue ($200 + $18 + $300 + $27)	....	$ 545

In particular, note that the long-term investments in bonds are reported by the *amortized cost* method.

The amortization entry for a premium debits Interest Revenue and credits Long-Term Investment in Bonds. Where discount or premium is amortized by the effective-interest method, accounting for long-term investments follows the pattern illustrated here. Effective-interest amortization amounts are computed as shown for bonds payable in Chapter 16.

Exhibit 17-6 summarizes the accounting methods for investments.

EXHIBIT 17-6 *Accounting Methods for Investments*

Type of Investments	Accounting Method
Short-term investment in stock	Cost (lower of cost or market)
Long-term investment in stock:	
Investor owns less than 20 percent of investee stock	Cost (lower of cost or market)
Investor owns between 20 and 50 percent of investee stock	Equity
Investor owns greater than 50 percent of investee stock	Consolidation
Short-term investment in bonds	Cost
Long-term investment in bonds	Amortized cost

Summary Problem for Your Review

This problem consists of four independent items.

1. Identify the appropriate accounting method for each of the following situations:
    (a) Investment in 25 percent of investee's stock
    (b) Short-term investment in stock
    (c) Investment in more than 50 percent of investee's stock

2. At what amount should the following long-term investment portfolio be reported on the December 31 balance sheet? All the investments are less than 5 percent of the investee's stock and were purchased during the current year.

Stock	Investment Cost	Current Market Value
Eastman Kodak	$ 5,000	$ 5,500
Exxon	61,200	53,000
General Motors	3,680	6,230

Journalize any adjusting entry required by these data.

3. Investor paid $67,900 to acquire a 40 percent equity-method investment in the common stock of Investee. At the end of the first year, Investee's net income was $80,000, and Investee declared and paid cash dividends of $55,000. Journalize Investor's (a) purchase of the investment, (b) share of Investee's net income, (c) receipt of dividends from Investee, and (d) sale of Investee stock for $80,100.

4. Parent Company paid $100,000 for all the common stock of Subsidiary Company, and Parent owes Subsidiary $20,000 on a note payable. Complete the following consolidation work sheet:

Assets	Parent Company	Subsidiary Company	Eliminations Debit	Eliminations Credit	Consolidated Amounts
Cash	7,000	4,000			
Note receivable from Parent	—	20,000			
Investment in Subsidiary	100,000	—			
Goodwill	—	—			
Other assets	108,000	99,000			
Total	215,000	123,000			

Liabilities and Stockholders' Equity					
Accounts payable	15,000	8,000			
Notes payable	20,000	30,000			
Common stock	135,000	60,000			
Retained earnings	45,000	25,000			
Total	215,000	123,000			

SOLUTION TO SUMMARY PROBLEM

1. (a) Equity   (b) Cost (LCM)   (c) Consolidation
2. Report the investments at market value, $64,730, because market value is less than cost.

Stock	Investment Cost	Current Market Value
Eastman Kodak	$ 5,000	$ 5,500
Exxon	61,200	53,000
General Motors	3,680	6,230
Totals	$69,880	$64,730

Adjusting entry:
    Unrealized Loss on Long-Term Investments
        ($69,880 − $64,730)   5,150
        Allowance to Reduce Long-Term Investments
            to Market Value   5,150
    To write investments down to market value.

3. a. Investment in Investee Common Stock 67,900
      Cash   67,900
    To purchase 40% investment in Investee common stock.
   b. Investment in Investee Common Stock
       ($80,000 × .40) 32,000
         Equity-Method Investment Revenue   32,000
    To record 40% of Investee net income.
   c. Cash ($55,000 × .40) 22,000
        Investment in Investee Common Stock ...   22,000
    To record receipt of 40% of Investee cash dividend.
   d. Cash 80,100
        Investment in Investee Common Stock
         ($67,900 + $32,000 − $22,000)   77,900
        Gain on Sale of Investment   2,200
    Sold investment in Investee common stock.

4. Consolidation work sheet: Transparency T17-3

Assets	Parent Company	Subsidiary Company	Eliminations Debit	Eliminations Credit	Consolidated Amounts
Cash	7,000	4,000			11,000
Note receivable from Parent	—	20,000		(a) 20,000	—
Investment in Subsidiary	100,000	—		(b) 100,000	—
Goodwill.............................	—	—	(b) 15,000		15,000
Other assets	108,000	99,000			207,000
Total	215,000	123,000			233,000
Liabilities and Stockholders' Equity					
Accounts payable	15,000	8,000			23,000
Notes payable	20,000	30,000	(a) 20,000		30,000
Common stock	135,000	60,000	(b) 60,000		135,000
Retained earnings...................	45,000	25,000	(b) 25,000		45,000
Total	215,000	123,000	120,000	120,000	233,000

Accounting for International Operations

Did you know that Exxon and Bank of America earn most of their revenue outside the United States? It is common for American companies to do a large part of their business abroad. IBM, Ford, Coca-Cola, Boeing, and Kraft (Foods), among many others, are very active in other countries.

    Accounting for business activities across national boundaries makes up the field of *international accounting*. As communications and transportation improve and trade barriers fall, global integration makes international accounting more important.

Economic Structures and Their Impact on International Accounting

The business environment varies widely across the globe. New York reflects the diversity of the market-driven economy of the United States. Japan's economy is similar to ours, although Japanese business activity focuses more on imports and exports. The central government has controlled the economy of Czechoslovakia and other Eastern-bloc countries, so private business decisions are only beginning to take root there. In Brazil, extremely high rates of inflation have made historical-cost amounts meaningless. Accountants must continually adjust the price levels because of the rapid change in the value of the cruzeiro, Brazil's monetary unit. International accounting deals with these and other differences in economic structures.

Foreign Currencies and Foreign-Currency Exchange Rates

Each country uses its own national currency. Assume Boeing, a United States company, sells a 747 jet to Air France. Will Boeing receive United States dollars or French francs? If the transaction takes place in dollars, Air France must exchange its francs for dollars in order to pay Boeing in U.S. currency. If the transaction takes place in francs, Boeing will receive francs, which it must exchange for dollars. In either case, a step has been added to the transaction: one company must convert domestic currency into foreign currency, or the other company must convert foreign currency into domestic currency.

The price of one nation's currency may be stated in terms of another country's monetary unit. This measure of one currency against another currency is called the **foreign-currency exchange rate**. In Exhibit 17-7, the dollar value of a French franc is $.20. This means that one French franc could be bought for twenty cents. Other currencies, such as the pound and the yen (also listed in Exhibit 17-7), are similarly bought and sold.

We use the exchange rate to convert the cost of an item given in one currency to its cost in a second currency. We call this conversion a *translation*. Suppose an item costs two hundred French francs. To compute its cost in dollars, we multiply the amount in francs by the conversion rate: 200 French francs × $.20 = $40.

To aid the flow of international business, a market exists for foreign currencies. Traders buy and sell U.S. dollars, French francs, and other currencies

Real-World Example: Two exchange rates are usually quoted—the buying spot rate and the selling spot rate. The buying spot rate is generally more than the selling spot rate. The difference (the *agio* or *spread*) represents gross profit to the trader.

EXHIBIT 17-7 *Foreign-Currency Exchange Rates*

Country	Monetary Unit	Dollar Value	Country	Monetary Unit	Dollar Value
Canada	Dollar	$ .87	Great Britain	Pound	$1.95
European Common Market	European Currency Unit	1.37	Italy	Lira	.0009
France	Franc	.20	Japan	Yen	.0075
Germany	Mark	.67	Mexico	Peso	.0003

Source: *The Wall Street Journal,* January 4, 1991, p. C10.

in the same way that they buy and sell other commodities like beef, cotton, and automobiles. And just as supply and demand cause the prices of these other commodities to shift, so supply and demand for a particular currency cause exchange rates to fluctuate daily. When the demand for a nation's currency exceeds the supply of that currency, its exchange rate rises. When supply exceeds demand, the currency's exchange rate falls.

Two main factors determine the supply and demand for a particular currency: (1) the ratio of a country's imports to its exports, and (2) the rate of return available in the country's capital markets.

The Import/Export Ratio. Japanese exports far surpass Japan's imports. Customers of Japanese companies must buy yen (the Japanese unit of currency) in the international currency market to pay for their purchases. This strong demand drives up the price—the foreign exchange rate—of the yen. France, on the other hand, imports more goods than it exports. French businesses must sell francs in order to buy the foreign currencies needed to acquire the foreign goods. This increases the supply of the French franc and so decreases its price.

The Rate of Return. The rate of return available in a country's capital markets affects the amount of investment funds flowing into the country. When rates of return are high in a politically stable country such as the United States, international investors buy stocks, bonds, and real estate in that country. This increases the demand for the nation's currency and drives up its exchange rate.

Currencies are often described in the financial press as "strong" or "weak." What do these terms mean? The exchange rate of a **strong currency** is rising relative to other nations' currencies. The exchange rate of a **weak currency** is falling relative to other currencies.

Suppose on January 5 *The Wall Street Journal* listed the exchange rate for the British pound as $1.95. On January 6 that rate has changed to $1.93. We would say that the dollar has risen against the British pound—the dollar is stronger than the pound—because the pound has become less expensive, and so the dollar now buys more pounds. A stronger dollar would make travel to England more attractive to Americans.

Assume that *The Wall Street Journal* reports a rise in the exchange rate of the Japanese yen from $.0075 to $.0076. This indicates that the yen is stronger than the dollar. Japanese automobiles, cameras, and electronic products are more expensive because each dollar buys fewer yen.

In our example situation—in which the pound has dropped relative to the dollar and the yen has risen relative to the dollar—we would describe the yen as the strongest currency, the pound as the weakest currency, and the dollar as somewhere between the other two currencies.

Accounting for International Transactions

When an American company transacts business with a foreign company, the transaction price can be stated either in dollars or in the national currency of the other company. If the price is stated in dollars, the American company has no special accounting difficulties. The transaction is recorded and reported in dollars exactly as though the other company were also American.

OBJECTIVE 6
Account for transactions stated in a foreign currency

Purchases on Account

If the transaction price is stated in units of the foreign currency, the American company encounters two accounting steps. First, the transaction price must be translated into dollars for recording in the accounting records. Second, credit transactions (the most common international transaction) usually cause the American company to experience a **foreign-currency transaction gain** or **loss.** This type of gain or loss occurs when the exchange rate changes between the date of the purchase on account and the date of the subsequent payment of cash.

The credit purchase creates an Account Payable that is recorded at the prevailing exchange rate. Later, when the buyer pays cash, the exchange rate has almost certainly changed. Accounts Payable is debited for the amount recorded earlier, and Cash is credited for the amount paid at the current exchange rate. A debit difference is a loss, and a credit difference is a gain.

Suppose on April 1, Macy's Department Store imports Shalimar perfume from a French supplier at a price of 200,000 francs. The exchange rate is $.19 per French franc. Macy's records this credit purchase as follows:

Apr.1	Purchases	38,000	
	Accounts Payable (200,000 × $.19)		38,000

Macy's translates the French franc price of the merchandise (200,000 Fr) into dollars ($38,000) for recording the purchase and the related account payable.

If Macy's were to pay this account immediately—which is unlikely in international commerce—Macy's would debit Accounts Payable and credit Cash for $38,000. Suppose, however, that the credit terms specify payment within 60 days. On May 20, when Macy's pays this debt, the exchange rate has fallen to $.18 per French franc. Macy's payment entry is

May 20	Accounts Payable	38,000	
	Cash (200,000 × $.18)		36,000
	Foreign-Currency Transaction Gain		2,000

Macy's has a gain because the company has settled the debt with fewer dollars than the amount of the original account payable. If on the payment date the exchange rate of the French franc had exceeded $.19, Macy's would have paid more dollars than the original $38,000. The company would have recorded a loss on the transaction as a debit to Foreign-Currency Transaction Loss.

Sales on Account

International sales on account also may be measured in foreign currency. Suppose IBM sells a small computer to the German government on December 9. The price of the computer is 140,000 German marks, and the exchange rate is $.64 per German mark. IBM's sale entry is

Dec. 9	Accounts Receivable (140,000 × $.64)	89,600	
	Sales Revenue		89,600

Assume IBM collects from Germany on December 30, when the exchange rate has fallen to $.63 per German mark. IBM receives fewer dollars than the recorded amount of the receivable and so experiences a foreign-currency transaction loss. The collection entry is

Class Exercise: Assume that on April 18 the exchange rate for German marks was DM = $.45. International Corp. (a U.S. company) purchased merchandise from a West German company at a cost of 50,000 DM. Record the purchase in dollars.

ANSWER:

Purchases 22,500
  Accts. Pay. ...   22,500
50,000 DM × $.45 = $22,500

Suppose that the exchange rate on April 30, the payment date, is DM = $.44. Record the payment.

ANSWER:

Accts. Pay 22,500
  Foreign-Currency
    Transaction Gain....   500
  Cash................22,000
(50,000 DM × $.44 = $22,000)

```
Dec. 30    Cash (140,000 × $.63) . . . . . . . . . . . . . . . . . . . .    88,200
             Foreign-Currency Transaction Loss . . . . . . . . .     1,400
                 Accounts Receivable . . . . . . . . . . . . . . . . .              89,600
```

Foreign-Currency Transaction Gains and Losses are combined for each accounting period. The net amount of gain or loss can be reported as Other Revenue and Expense on the income statement.

Unrealized Foreign-Currency Transaction Gains and Losses.   Foreign-currency transaction gains and losses are *realized* when cash is paid or received. In the illustrations thus far, cash receipts and cash payments occurred in the same period as the related sale or purchase. This will not always be the case. For example, in the preceding example, suppose IBM collects from the German government during January. At December 31, the German mark is worth only $.63. This is $.01 less than the exchange rate at which IBM recorded the receivable. In this case IBM will record a foreign-currency transaction loss for the decrease in the dollar value of the account receivable. The adjusting entry is

```
Dec. 31    Foreign-Currency Transaction Loss
             [140,000 × ($.64 − $.63)] . . . . . . . . . . . . . . . . .     1,400
                 Accounts Receivable . . . . . . . . . . . . . . . . .              1,400
```

This loss is *unrealized* in the sense that IBM has not yet received cash from the customer. Suppose IBM collects on January 9, when the exchange rate is $.62 per mark. The cash receipt entry records a further loss as follows:

```
Jan.  9    Cash (140,000 × $.62) . . . . . . . . . . . . . . . . . . . .    86,800
             Foreign-Currency Transaction Loss
             [140,000 × ($.63 − $.62)] . . . . . . . . . . . . . . . . .     1,400
                 Accounts Receivable ($89,600 − $1,400) .              88,200
```

IBM would have recorded a foreign-currency transaction gain on January 9 if the exchange rate had exceeded $.63 per mark. In that case the cash collection would have been greater than the carrying amount of Accounts Receivable.

Hedging—A Strategy to Avoid Foreign-Currency Transaction Losses

One approach to avoiding foreign-currency transaction losses is to insist that international transactions be settled in dollars, which puts the burden of currency translation on the foreign party. However, that strategy may alienate customers and result in lost sales, or it may cause suppliers to demand unreasonable credit terms. Another way for a company to insulate itself from the effects of fluctuating foreign-currency exchange rates is called hedging.

Hedging means to protect oneself from losing by engaging in a counterbalancing transaction. An American company selling goods measured in Mexican pesos expects to receive a fixed number of pesos in the future. If the peso is weak, the American company would expect the pesos to be worth fewer dollars than the amount of the receivable—an expected loss situation.

The American company may have accumulated payables stated in Mexican pesos in the normal course of its business. Losses on the receipt of pesos

Real-World Example: Chiquita is an international company that ships over a billion dollars' worth of bananas annually. A small change in currency rates can make a big change in Chiquita's profits. Therefore, Chiquita purchases currency options to hedge the foreign currency exchange risk. The purchase of currency options offsets any change in the foreign exchange rate.

Point to Stress: A forward exchange (futures) contract is an agreement to buy or sell currencies of different countries at the current exchange rate for delivery on a specified future date. It locks in the current exchange rate.

Real-World Example: When a U.S. firm buys goods on credit from a foreign company, the U.S. firm is exposed to the risk that the exchange rate will change unfavorably before the payable is settled. To eliminate or reduce this risk, the U.S. company may enter into a forward contract to buy or sell a foreign currency. For example, if International Corp. purchases inventory on account for 50,000 DM, payable in 30 days, then the company would expect to owe $22,500 on the payment date if the exchange rate is DM = $.45. To hedge the foreign currency exchange risk, International Corp. could acquire 50,000 DM for $22,500. Then if the exchange rate rises to DM = $.46 on the payment date, International Corp. is protected against the need to buy 50,000 DM for $23,000 (50,000 DM × $.46). Another way to hedge this loss is to buy a forward exchange contract for 50,000 DM to be delivered in 30 days.

Points to Stress: When a subsidiary prepares financial statements in a currency other than dollars, the subsidiary must translate the financial statements into dollars for the consolidated financial statements in the United States.

Point to Stress: For assets and liabilities, the current exchange rate at the balance sheet date is used for translation. For revenues and expenses, the exchange rate in effect on the date of the transaction is used. In practice, for ease of calculation, companies use the average exchange rate of the period for revenues and expenses.

would be approximately offset by gains on the payment of pesos to Mexican suppliers. Most companies do not have equal amounts of receivables and payables in the same foreign currency. However, buying futures contracts in the foreign currency effectively creates a payable to offset a receivable and vice versa. Many companies that do business internationally use hedging techniques.

Consolidation of Foreign Subsidiaries

An American company with a foreign subsidiary must consolidate the subsidiary's financial statements into its own statements for reporting to the public. The consolidation of a foreign subsidiary poses two special challenges. Many countries outside the United States specify accounting treatments that differ from American accounting principles. For the purpose of reporting to the American public, accountants for the parent company must first bring the subsidiary's statements into conformity with American GAAP.

The second accounting challenge arises when the subsidiary statements are expressed in a foreign currency. A preliminary step in the consolidation process is to translate the subsidiary statements into dollars. Then the dollar-value statements of the subsidiary can be combined with the parent statements in the usual manner, as illustrated in the first half of this chapter.

The process of translating a foreign subsidiary's financial statements into dollars may create a *foreign-currency translation adjustment*. This item appears in the financial statements of most multinational companies and is reported as part of stockholders' equity on the consolidated balance sheet.

A translation adjustment arises because of changes in the foreign exchange rate over time. In general, *assets* and *liabilities* in the foreign subsidiaries' financial statements are translated into dollars at the exchange rate in effect on the date of the statements. However, *stockholders' equity* is translated into dollars at older, historical exchange rates. This difference in exchange rates creates an out-of-balance condition on the balance sheet. The translation adjustment amount brings the balance sheet back into balance.

Suppose U.S. Express Corporation owns Mexican Imports, Inc., whose financial statements are expressed in pesos. U.S. Express wants to consolidate the Mexican subsidiary's financial statements into its own financial statements. When U.S. Express acquired Mexican Imports in 19X1, a peso was worth $.00040. When Mexican Imports earned its retained income during 19X1 through 19X6, the average exchange rate was $.00037. On the balance sheet

EXHIBIT 17-8 *Translation of a Foreign-Currency Balance Sheet into Dollars*

Mexican Imports Amounts	Pesos	Exchange Rate	Dollars
Assets	80,000,000	$.00030	$240,000
Liabilities	50,000,000	.00030	$150,000
Stockholders' equity:			
Common stock	10,000,000	.00040	40,000
Retained earnings	20,000,000	.00037	74,000
Translation adjustment	—		(24,000)
	80,000,000		$240,000

date in 19X6, a peso is worth only $.00030. Exhibit 17-8 shows how to translate Mexican Imports' balance sheet into dollars and illustrates how the translation adjustment arises.

The **foreign-currency translation adjustment** is the balancing amount that brings the dollar amount of the total liabilities and stockholders' equity of a foreign subsidiary into agreement with the dollar amount of its total assets ($240,000). Only after the translation adjustment do total liabilities and stockholders' equity equal total assets stated in dollars. In this case the translation adjustment is negative, and total stockholders' equity becomes $90,000 ($40,000 + $74,000 − $24,000).

What in the economic environment caused the negative translation adjustment? A weakening of the peso since the acquisition of Mexican Imports brought about the need for this adjustment. When U.S. Express acquired the foreign subsidiary in 19X1, a peso was worth $.00040. When Mexican Imports earned its retained income during 19X1 through 19X6, the average exchange rate was $.00037. On the balance sheet date in 19X6, a peso is worth only $.00030, so Mexican Imports' net assets (assets minus liabilities) are translated into only $90,000 ($240,000 − $150,000).

To bring stockholders' equity to $90,000 requires a $24,000 negative amount. In a sense, a negative translation adjustment is like a loss. But it is reported as a contra item in the stockholders' equity section of the balance sheet, not on the income statement. The Mexican Imports dollar figures in Exhibit 17-8 are the amounts that U.S. Express Corporation would include in its consolidated balance sheet.

The translation adjustment can be positive—a gain—as well as negative, depending on the movement of foreign currency exchange rates. The following excerpt from IBM's actual balance sheet shows a positive translation adjustment:

Class Exercise: Assume that a subsidiary of a U.S. enterprise uses the French franc as its currency. During the year, the franc weakened against the dollar. (It takes more francs to make up one dollar). Will there be a positive or a negative translation adjustment?
ANSWER: The subsidiary's assets are recorded in francs. The weakening of the franc means that when translated into U.S. dollars, the assets' value is reduced. This creates a negative translation adjustment.

Stockholders' Equity:	Dollars in millions
Capital stock, par value $1.25 per share	$ 6,442
Shares authorized: 750,000,000	
Issued: 1988—590,037,328	
Retained earnings	31,186
Translation adjustments	**1,917**
	39,545
Less: Treasury stock, at cost (Shares: 19X8—296,820)	36
	$39,509

International Accounting Standards

For the most part, accounting principles are similar from country to country. However, some important differences exist. For example, some countries, such as Italy, require financial statements to conform closely to income tax laws. In other countries, such as Brazil and Argentina, high inflation rates dictate that companies make price-level adjustments to report amounts in units of common purchasing power. Neither practice is followed as closely in the United States.

Several organizations are working to achieve worldwide harmony of accounting standards. Chief among these is the International Accounting Standards Committee (IASC). Headquartered in London, the IASC operates much as the Financial Accounting Standards Board in the United States. It has the support of the accounting professions in the United States, most of the British Commonwealth countries, Japan, France, Germany, the Netherlands, and Mexico. However, the IASC has no authority to require compliance with its accounting standards. It must rely on cooperation by the various national accounting professions. Since its creation in 1973, the IASC has succeeded in narrowing some differences in international accounting standards.

Computers and Consolidations

Consider a large consolidated entity like W. R. Grace & Co., a company with widely diversified operations and perhaps 40 subsidiary firms included in its consolidated financial statements. Accountants performing Grace's consolidations face several problems. One, the 40 firms may not all use the same accounting system and classifications. Two, finding intercompany receivables and payables may be difficult. A computer search for each of the 40 companies may be necessary to bring to light all intercompany items (there are 40×39, which comes to 1,560 different possibilities!).

Large consolidated firms may custom design their own software to prepare consolidated financial statements. Alternatively, or in connection with custom-designed software, these businesses may use linked electronic spreadsheets (also called linked spreadsheets). With a linked spreadsheet, a value entered on one company's spreadsheet is automatically transmitted to other companies' spreadsheets as appropriate, a decision the computer makes based on account classification. Eliminations too can be entered on the consolidating spreadsheet. The amounts for the consolidated financial statements are drawn from this spreadsheet.

Windows offer computer users access to multiple spreadsheets, or parts of spreadsheets, on screen at the same time. Consider the benefit of entering a change in the spreadsheet of a subsidiary and seeing immediately on screen its effect on the parent company.

Summary Problems for Your Review

1. Journalize the following transactions of American Corp.:

19X5

Nov. 16   Purchased equipment on account for 40,000 Swiss francs when the exchange rate was $.63 per Swiss franc.

27   Sold merchandise on account to a Belgian company for 700,000 Belgian francs. Each franc is worth $.0305.

Dec. 22   Paid the Swiss company when the franc's exchange rate was $.625.

31   Adjusted for the change in the exchange rate of the Belgian franc. Its current exchange rate is $.0301.

19X6

Jan.   4   Collected from the Belgian company. The exchange rate is $.0307.

2. Translate the balance sheet of the Spanish subsidiary of American Corp. into dollars. When American acquired this subsidiary, the exchange rate of the peseta was $.0101. The average exchange rate applicable to retained earnings is $.0108. The peseta's current exchange rate is $.0111.

Before performing the translation, predict whether the translation adjustment will be positive or negative. Does this situation generate a translation gain or a translation loss? Give your reasons.

	Pesetas
Assets	200,000,000
Liabilities	110,000,000
Stockholders' equity:	
Common stock	20,000,000
Retained earnings	70,000,000
	200,000,000

SOLUTION TO REVIEW PROBLEMS

1. Entries for transactions stated in foreign currencies:

19X5

Nov. 16	Equipment (40,000 × $.63)	25,200	
	Accounts Payable		25,200
27	Accounts Receivable (700,000 × $.0305)	21,350	
	Sales Revenue		21,350
Dec. 22	Accounts Payable	25,200	
	Cash (40,000 × $.625)		25,000
	Foreign-Currency Transaction Gain		200
31	Foreign-Currency Transaction Loss		
	[700,000 × ($.0305 − $.0301)	280	
	Accounts Receivable		280

19X6

Jan. 4	Cash (700,000 × $.0307)	21,490	
	Accounts Receivable		
	($21,350 − $280)		21,070
	Foreign-Currency Transaction Gain		420

2. Translation of foreign-currency balance sheet:

This situation will generate a *positive* translation adjustment, which is like a gain. The gain occurs because the peseta's current exchange rate, which is used to translate net assets (assets minus liabilities), exceeds the historical exchange rates used for stockholders' equity.

	Pesetas	Exchange Rate	Dollars
Assets	200,000,000	$.0111	$2,220,000
Liabilities	110,000,000	.0111	$1,221,000
Stockholders' equity:			
Common stock	20,000,000	.0101	202,000
Retained earnings	70,000,000	.0108	756,000
Translation adjustment	—		41,000
	200,000,000		$2,220,000

Summary

Investments are classified as short-term or long-term. *Short-term investments* are liquid, and the investor intends to convert them to cash within one year or less or to use them to pay a current liability. All other investments are *long-term*.

Different methods are used to account for stock investments, depending on the investor's degree of influence over the investee. All investments are recorded initially at *cost*. Short-term investments and long-term investments of less than 20 percent of the investee's stock are accounted for by the cost method (with lower-of-cost-or-market). These investments are reported on the balance sheet at the lower of their cost or current market (LCM) value. Separate LCM determinations apply to the short-term investment portfolio and the long-term portfolio.

The *equity* method is used to account for investments of between 20 and 50 percent of the investee company's stock. Such an investment enables the investor to significantly influence the investee's activities. Investee income is recorded by the investor by debiting the Investment account and crediting an account entitled Equity-Method Investment Revenue. The investor records receipt of dividends from the investee by crediting the Investment account.

Ownership of more than 50 percent of the voting stock creates a parent-subsidiary relationship, and the *consolidation* method must be used. Because the parent has control over the subsidiary, the subsidiary's financial statements are included in the consolidated statements of the parent company. Two features of consolidation accounting are (1) addition of the parent and subsidiary accounts to prepare the parent's consolidated statements and (2) elimination of intercompany items. When a parent owns less than 100 percent of the subsidiary's stock, the portion owned by outside investors is called *minority interest*. Purchase of a controlling interest at a cost greater than the market value of the subsidiary creates an intangible asset called *goodwill*. A consolidation work sheet is used to prepare the consolidated financial statements.

International accounting deals with accounting for business activities across national boundaries. A key issue is the translation of foreign-currency amounts into dollars, accomplished through a *foreign-currency exchange rate*. Changes in exchange rates cause companies to experience *foreign-currency transaction gains and losses* on credit transactions.

Consolidation of a foreign subsidiary's financial statements into the parent-company statements requires adjusting the subsidiary statements to American accounting principles and then translating the foreign-company statements into dollars. The translation process creates a *translation adjustment* that is reported in stockholders' equity. The International Accounting Standards Committee is working to harmonize accounting principles worldwide.

Self-Study Questions

Test your understanding of the chapter by marking the best answer for each of the following questions.

1. Short-term investments are reported on the balance sheet *(p. 764)*
   - ✓ a. Immediately after cash
   - b. Immediately after accounts receivable
   - c. Immediately after inventory
   - d. Immediately after current assets

2. Byforth, Inc., distributes a 10 percent stock dividend. An investor who owns Byforth stock should *(p. 765)*
   - a. Debit Investment and credit Dividend Revenue for the par value of the stock received in the dividend distribution

b. Debit Investment and credit Dividend Revenue for the market value of the stock received in the dividend distribution

c. Debit Cash and credit Investment for the market value of the stock received in the dividend distribution

✓d. Make a memorandum entry to record the new cost per share of Byforth stock held

3. Short-term investments are reported at the *(p. 766)*
   a. Total cost of the portfolio
   b. Total market value of the portfolio
   ✓c. Lower of total cost or total market value of the portfolio
   d. Total equity value of the portfolio

4. Putsch Corporation owns 30 percent of the voting stock of Mazelli, Inc. Mazelli reports net income of $100,000 and declares and pays cash dividends of $40,000. Which method should Putsch use to account for this investment? *(p. 767)*

a. Cost (with LCM)	✓ c. Equity
b. Market value	d. Consolidation

5. Refer to the facts of the preceding question. What effect do Mazelli's income and dividends have on Putsch's net income? *(pp. 767, 768)*

a. Increase of $12,000	✓ c. Increase of $30,000
b. Increase of $18,000	d. Increase of $42,000

6. In applying the consolidation method, elimination entries are *(p. 770)*
   ✓ a. Necessary
   b. Required only when the parent has a receivable from, or a payable to, the subsidiary
   c. Required only when there is a minority interest
   d. Required only for the preparation of the consolidated balance sheet

7. Parent Company has separate net income of $155,000. Subsidiary A, of which Parent owns 90 percent, reports net income of $60,000, and Subsidiary B, of which Parent owns 60 percent, reports net income of $80,000. What is Parent Company's consolidated net income? *(p. 774)*

a. $155,000	c. $263,000
✓ b. $257,000	d. $295,000

8. On May 16, the exchange rate of a German mark was $.58. On May 20, the exchange rate is $.57. Which of the following statements is true? *(p. 781)*
   ✓ a. The dollar has risen against the mark.
   b. The dollar has fallen against the mark.
   c. The dollar is weaker than the mark.
   d. The dollar and the mark are equally strong.

9. A strong dollar encourages *(p. 782)*
   a. Travel to the United States by foreigners
   b. Purchase of American goods by foreigners
   ✓c. Americans to travel abroad
   d. Americans to save dollars

10. Ford Motor Company purchased auto accessories from an English supplier at a price of 500,000 British pounds. On the date of the credit purchase the exchange rate of the British pound was $1.80. On the payment date the exchange rate of the pound is $1.82. If payment is in pounds, Ford experiences *(p. 782)*
    a. A foreign-currency transaction gain of $10,000
    ✓ b. A foreign-currency transaction loss of $10,000
    c. Neither a transaction gain nor a loss because the debt is paid in dollars
    d. A translation adjustment to stockholders' equity

Answers to the Self-Study Questions follow the Accounting Vocabulary.

Accounting Vocabulary

Consolidated statements. Financial statements of the parent company plus those of majority-owned subsidiaries as if the combination were a single legal entity *(p. 769)*.

Consolidation accounting. A way to combine the financial statements of two or more companies that are controlled by the same owners *(p. 769)*.

Controlling (majority) interest. Ownership of more than 50 percent of an investee company's voting stock *(p. 769)*.

Cost method for investments. The method used to account for short-term investments in stock and for long-term investments when the investor holds less than 20 percent of the investee's voting stock. Under the cost method, investments are recorded at cost and reported at the lower of their cost or market value *(p. 764)*.

Equity method for investments. The method used to account for investments in which the investor can significantly influence the decisions of the investee. Under the equity method, investments are recorded initially at cost. The investment account is debited (increased) for ownership in the investee's net income and credited (decreased) for ownership in the investee's dividends *(p. 767)*.

Foreign-currency exchange rate. The measure of one currency against another currency *(p. 780)*.

Foreign-currency transaction gain or loss. A gain or loss that occurs when the exchange rate changes between the date of a purchase or sale on account and the subsequent payment or receipt of cash *(p. 782)*.

Foreign-currency translation adjustment. The balancing figure that brings the dollar amount of the total liabilities and stockholders' equity of a foreign subsidiary into agreement with the dollar amount of its total assets *(p. 785)*.

Hedging. Protecting oneself from losing money in one transaction by engaging in a counterbalancing transaction *(p. 783)*.

Long-term investment. Separate asset category reported on the balance sheet between current assets and plant assets *(p. 764)*.

Marketable security. Another name for Short-term investment, one that may be sold any time the investor wishes *(p. 764)*.

Minority interest. A subsidiary company's equity that is held by stockholders other than the parent company *(p. 772)*.

Parent company. An investor company that owns more than 50 percent of the voting stock of a subsidiary company *(p. 769)*.

Short-term investment. Investment that is readily convertible to cash and that the investor intends either to convert to cash within one year or to use to pay a current liability. Also called a Marketable security, a current asset *(p. 764)*.

Strong currency. A currency that is rising relative to other nations' currencies *(p. 781)*.

Subsidiary company. An investee company in which a parent company owns more than 50 percent of the voting stock *(p. 769)*.

Weak currency. A currency that is falling relative to other nations' currencies *(p. 781)*.

Answers to Self-Study Questions

1. a
2. d
3. c
4. c
5. c ($100,000 × .30 = $30,000; dividends have *no* effect on investor net income under the equity method)
6. a

7. b [$155,000 + ($60,000 × .90) + ($80,000 × .60) = $257,000]
8. a
9. c
10. b [500,000 × ($1.82 − $1.80)]

ASSIGNMENT MATERIAL _____

Questions

1. How are stock prices quoted in the securities market? What is the investor's cost of 1,000 shares of Ford Motor Company stock at 55¾, with a brokerage commission of $1,350?

2. What distinguishes a short-term investment from a long-term investment?

3. Show the positions of short-term investments and long-term investments on the balance sheet.

4. Outline the accounting methods for the different types of investment.

5. How does an investor record the receipt of a cash dividend on an investment accounted for by the cost method? How does this investor record receipt of a stock dividend?

6. An investor paid $11,000 for 1,000 shares of stock and later received a 10 percent stock dividend. Compute the gain or loss on sale of 300 shares of the stock for $2,600.

7. At what amount are short-term investments reported on the balance sheet? Are the short-term and long-term investment portfolios mixed, or are they kept separate?

8. When is an investment accounted for by the equity method? Outline how to apply the equity method. Include in your answer how to record the purchase of the investment, the investor's proportion of the investee's net income, and receipt of a cash dividend from the investee. Describe how to measure gain or loss on sale of this investment.

9. Identify three transactions that cause debits or credits to an equity-method investment account.

10. What are two special features of the consolidation method for investments?

11. Why are intercompany items eliminated from consolidated financial statements? Name two intercompany items that are eliminated.

12. Name the account that expresses the excess of cost of an investment over the market value of the subsidiary's owner equity. What type of account is this, and where in the financial statements is it reported?

13. When a parent company buys less than 100 percent of a subsidiary's stock, a certain account is created. What is it called and how do most companies report it?

14. How would you measure the net income of a parent company with three subsidiaries? Assume that two subsidiaries are wholly (100 percent) owned and that the parent owns 60 percent of the third subsidiary.

15. What is the difference between accounting for a short-term bond investment and a long-term bond investment?

16. Explain the difference between a foreign-currency transaction gain or loss and a translation adjustment. Indicate the specific location in the financial statements where each item is reported.

17. Which situation results in a foreign-currency transaction gain for an American business? Which situation results in a loss?
   a. Credit purchase denominated in pesos, followed by weakness in the peso

b. Credit purchase denominated in pesos, followed by weakness in the dollar

c. Credit sale denominated in pesos, followed by weakness in the peso

d. Credit sale denominated in pesos, followed by weakness in the dollar

18. Explain the concept of hedging against foreign-currency transaction losses.

19. What is the difference between a realized foreign-currency transaction gain and an unrealized foreign-currency transaction gain?

20. McVey, Inc., acquired a foreign subsidiary when the foreign-currency's exchange rate was $.32. Over the years the foreign currency has steadily risen against the dollar. Will McVey's balance sheet report a positive or a negative translation adjustment?

21. Describe the computation of a foreign-currency translation adjustment.

Exercises

Exercises 17-1 *Journalizing transactions under the cost method* *(L.O. 1)*

Loss on sale of investments $436

Journalize the following investment transactions of August Bush, Inc.:

1. Purchased 400 shares (8 percent) of Advanced Corporation common stock at $44 per share, with brokerage commission of $300.

2. Received cash dividend of $1 per share on the Advanced Corporation investment.

3. Received 200 shares of Advanced Corporation common stock in a 50 percent stock dividend.

4. Sold 200 shares of Advanced Corporation stock for $29 per share, less brokerage commission of $270.

Exercise 17-2 *Reporting investments at the lower of cost or market* *(L.O. 1)*

Unrealized loss $4 million

Colgate-Palmolive Company recently reported the following information (not including the question mark) on its balance sheet:

Current Assets	(Dollars in millions)
Cash and cash equivalents	$ 398
Marketable securities [short-term investments], at lower of cost or market	?

Assume that the cost of Colgate-Palmolive's short-term investments is $130 million and that current market value is $126 million.

Required

Apply the lower-of-cost-or-market method to Colgate-Palmolive's short-term investments by inserting the appropriate amount in place of the question mark. Write a note to identify the method used to report short-term investments and to disclose cost and market value. Journalize any needed adjustment, assuming the marketable securities were purchased during the current year.

Exercise 17-3 *Journalizing transactions under the equity method* *(L.O. 2)*

No check figure

Sears, Roebuck and Co. owns equity-method investments in several companies. Suppose Sears paid $200,000 to acquire a 25 percent investment in All-Star Company. Further, assume All-Star Company reported net income of $140,000 for the first year and declared and paid cash dividends of $70,000.

Record the following in Sears's general journal: (a) purchase of the investment, (b) Sears's proportion of All-Star's net income, and (c) receipt of the cash dividends.

Exercise 17-4 *Recording equity-method transactions directly in the accounts* **(L.O. 2)**

Gain on sale of investments
$22,500

Without making journal entries, record the transactions of Exercise 17-3 directly in the Investment in All-Star Company Common Stock account. Assume that after all the above transactions took place, Sears sold its entire investment in All-Star common stock for cash of $240,000. Journalize the sale of the investment.

Exercise 17-5 *Comparing the cost and equity methods* **(L.O. 1, 2)**

3. Investment acct. bal.
$177,000

Electrix Corporation paid $160,000 for a 25 percent investment in the common stock of Bluebonnet, Inc. For the first year, Bluebonnet reported net income of $84,000 and at year end declared and paid cash dividends of $16,000. On the balance sheet date the market value of Electrix's investment in Bluebonnet stock was $153,000.

Required

1. On Electrix's books, journalize the purchase of the investment, recognition of Electrix's portion of Bluebonnet's net income, and receipt of dividends from Bluebonnet under the equity method, which is appropriate for these circumstances.
2. Repeat Requirement 1 but follow the cost method for comparison purposes only.
3. Show the amount that Electrix would report for the investment on its year-end balance sheet under the two methods.

Exercise 17-6 *Completing a consolidation work sheet with minority interest* **(L.O. 3, 4)**

Consol. total assets $704,000

Liquid Gas Corp. owns an 80 percent interest in Nino, Inc. Complete the following consolidation work sheet.

Assets	Liquid Gas Corp.	Nino, Inc.
Cash	$ 19,000	$ 14,000
Accounts receivable, net	82,000	53,000
Note receivable from Liquid Gas	—	12,000
Inventory	114,000	77,000
Investment in Nino	80,000	—
Plant assets, net	186,000	129,000
Other assets	22,000	8,000
Total	$503,000	$293,000

Liabilities and Stockholders' Equity		
Accounts payable	$ 44,000	$ 26,000
Notes payable	47,000	36,000
Other liabilities	52,000	131,000
Minority interest	—	—
Common stock	200,000	80,000
Retained earnings	160,000	20,000
Total	$503,000	$293,000

Exercise 17-7 *Elimination entries under the consolidation method* **(L.O. 4)**

No check figure

Assume on December 31 that Shearson Financial Consultants, a 100 percent-owned subsidiary of American Express Company, had the following owners' equity:

Common Stock	$200,000
Retained Earnings	160,000

Assume further that American Express's cost of its investment in Shearson was $360,000 and that Shearson owed American Express $45,000 on a note.

Required

Give the work sheet entry in general journal form to eliminate (a) the investment of American Express and the stockholders' equity of Shearson and (b) the note receivable of American Express and note payable of Shearson.

Exercise 17-8 *Recording short-term bond investment transactions* **(L.O. 5)**

On June 30 Statistical Research, Inc., paid 92¼ for 8 percent bonds of Erdman Company as a short-term investment. The maturity value of the bonds is $20,000, and they pay interest on March 31 and September 30. Record Statistical Research's purchase of the bond investment, the receipt of semiannual interest on September 30, and the accrual of interest revenue on December 31.

Exercise 17-9 *Recording long-term bond investment transactions* **(L.O. 5)**

Assume the Erdman Company bonds in the preceding exercise are purchased as a long-term investment on June 30, 19X3. The bonds mature on September 30, 19X7.

Required

a. Using the straight-line method of amortizing the discount, journalize all transactions on the bonds for 19X3.
b. How much more interest revenue would the investor record in 19X3 for a long-term investment than for a short-term investment in these bonds? What accounts for this difference?

Exercise 17-10 *Journalizing foreign-currency transactions* **(L.O. 6)**

Journalize the following foreign-currency transactions:

Nov. 17 Purchased goods on account from a Japanese company. The price was 200,000 yen, and the exchange rate of the yen was $.0080.
Dec. 16 Paid the Japanese supplier when the exchange rate was $.0081.
19 Sold merchandise on account to a French company at a price of 60,000 French francs. The exchange rate was $.16.
31 Adjusted for the decrease in the value of the franc, which had an exchange rate of $.155.
Jan. 14 Collected from the French company. The exchange rate was $.17.

Exercise 17-11 *Translating a foreign-currency balance sheet into dollars* **(L.O. 7)**

Translate the balance sheet of Munson, Inc.'s Italian subsidiary into dollars. When Munson acquired the foreign subsidiary, an Italian lira was worth $.00090. The current exchange rate is $.00085. During the period when retained earnings were earned, the average exchange rate was $.00088.

Before performing the translation operation, predict whether the translation adjustment will be positive (a gain) or negative (a loss). Explain your answer.

	Lire
Assets	500,000,000
Liabilities	300,000,000
Stockholders' equity:	
Common stock	100,000,000
Retained earnings	100,000,000
	500,000,000

Problems   *(Group A)*

Problem 17-1A   *Journalizing transactions under the cost and equity methods*   **(L.O. 1, 2)**

Iowa Beef Packers owns numerous investments in the stock of other companies. Assume Iowa Beef Packers completed the following investment transactions:

Loss on sale of inv., Jan. 14, $13,400

19X6

Jan.   2   Purchased 24,000 shares, which exceeds 20 percent, of the common stock of Agribusiness, Inc., at total cost of $810,000.

Mar. 16   Purchased 800 shares of Apex Company common stock as a short-term investment, paying 41½ per share plus brokerage commission of $800.

July   1   Purchased 8,000 additional shares of Agribusiness common stock at cost of $300,000.

Aug.   9   Received annual cash dividend of $.90 per share (total of $28,800) on the Agribusiness investment.

     30   Received semiannual cash dividend of $.60 per share on the Apex investment.

Sep. 14   Received 200 shares of Apex common stock in a 25 percent stock dividend.

Oct. 22   Sold 400 shares of Apex stock for 30¼ per share less brokerage commission of $450.

Dec. 31   Received annual report from Agribusiness, Inc. Net income for the year was $440,000. Of this amount, Iowa Beef Packers' proportion is 35 percent.

19X7

Jan. 14   Sold 4,000 shares of Agribusiness stock for net cash of $141,000.

Required

Record the transactions in the general journal of Iowa Beef Packers.

Problem 17-2A   *Applying the cost method (with LCM) and the equity method*   **(L.O. 1, 2)**

Inv. in affiliates, Dec. 31, $11,549,000

The beginning balance sheet of Ranco Incorporated recently included:

     Investments in Affiliates $10,984,000

Investments in Affiliates refers to investments accounted for by the equity method. Ranco included its short-term investments among the current assets. Assume the company completed the following investment transactions during the year:

Jan.   2   Purchased 2,000 shares of common stock as a short-term investment, paying 12¼ per share plus brokerage commission of $1,000.

     5   Purchased new long-term investment in affiliate at cost of $540,000. Debit Investments in Affiliates.

Apr. 21   Received semiannual cash dividend of $.75 per share on the short-term investment purchased January 2.

May 17   Received cash dividend of $47,000 from affiliated company.

July 16   Sold 1,600 shares of the short-term investment (purchased on January 2) for 10⅛ per share less brokerage commission of $720.

Sep. 8   Sold other short-term investments for $136,000 less brokerage commission of $5,100. Cost of these investments was $120,600.

Nov. 17   Received cash dividend of $49,000 from affiliated company.

Dec. 31   Received annual reports from affiliated companies. Their total net income for the year was $550,000. Of this amount, Ranco's proportion is 22 percent.

Required

1. Record the transactions in the general journal of Ranco Incorporated.
2. Post entries to the Investments in Affiliates T-account and determine its balance at December 31.
3. Assume the beginning balance of Short-Term Investments was cost of $293,600. Post entries to the Short-Term Investments T-account and determine its balance at December 31.
4. Assuming the market value of the short-term investment portfolio is $190,300 at December 31, show how Ranco would report short-term investments and investments in affiliates on the ending balance sheet. Use the following format:

Cash	$XXX
Short-term investments, at lower of cost or market (___?___, $___)..	
Accounts receivable	XXX
≷	≷
Total current assets	XXX
Investments in affiliates	

Consol. total assets $830,000

Problem 17-3A   *Preparing a consolidated balance sheet; no minority interest* **(L.O. 3, 4)**

Bethlehem Corp. paid $166,000 to acquire all the common stock of Massada, Inc., and Massada owes Bethlehem $81,000 on a note payable. Immediately after the purchase on June 30, 19X3, the two companies' balance sheets were as follows:

Assets	Bethlehem Corp.	Massada, Inc.
Cash	$ 21,000	$ 20,000
Accounts receivable, net	91,000	42,000
Note receivable from Massada	81,000	—
Inventory	145,000	114,000
Investment in Massada	166,000	—
Plant assets, net	178,000	219,000
Total	$682,000	$395,000

Liabilities and Stockholders' Equity		
Accounts payable	$ 54,000	$ 49,000
Notes payable	177,000	149,000
Other liabilities	29,000	31,000
Common stock	274,000	118,000
Retained earnings................	148,000	48,000
Total	$682,000	$395,000

Required

1. Prepare a consolidation work sheet.
2. Prepare the consolidated balance sheet on June 30, 19X3. Show total assets, total liabilities, and total stockholders' equity. It is not necessary to classify assets and liabilities as current and long-term.

Problem 17-4A *Preparing a consolidated balance sheet with minority interest* **(L.O. 3, 4)**

Consol. total assets $899,000

On March 22, 19X4, Titanium Corporation paid $180,000 to purchase 80 percent of the common stock of Millbank Company, and Millbank owes Titanium $67,000 on a note payable. Immediately after the purchase, the two companies' balance sheets were as follows:

Assets	Titanium Corporation	Millbank Company
Cash	$ 41,000	$ 43,000
Accounts receivable, net	86,000	75,000
Note receivable from Millbank	67,000	—
Inventory	128,000	81,000
Investment in Millbank...........	180,000	—
Plant assets, net	277,000	168,000
Total	$779,000	$367,000

Liabilities and Stockholders' Equity		
Accounts payable	$ 72,000	$ 65,000
Notes payable	301,000	67,000
Other liabilities	11,000	10,000
Minority interest.................	—	—
Common stock	141,000	160,000
Retained earnings................	254,000	65,000
Total	$779,000	$367,000

Required

1. Prepare a consolidation work sheet.
2. Prepare the consolidated balance sheet on March 22, 19X4. Show total assets, total liabilities, and total stockholders' equity. It is not necessary to classify assets and liabilities as current and long-term.

Problem 17-5A *Accounting for a long-term bond investment purchased at a premium* **(L.O. 5)**

2. Long-term investments $605,550

Financial institutions such as insurance companies and pension plans hold large quantities of bond investments. Suppose Southwestern Mutual Life purchases $600,000 of 9 percent bonds of Texell Corporation for 101 on July 1, 19X1. These bonds pay interest on March 1 and September 1 each year. They mature on March 1, 19X8.

Required

1. Journalize Southwestern Mutual's purchase of the bonds as a long-term investment on July 1, 19X1, receipt of cash interest and amortization of premium on September 1, 19X1, and accrual of interest revenue and amortization of premium at December 31, 19X1. Assume the amortization amounts are immaterial, so the straight-line method is appropriate for amortizing premium.

2. Show all financial statement effects of this long-term bond investment at December 31, 19X1. Assume a multiple-step income statement.

3. Repeat Requirement 2 under the assumption that Southwestern Mutual purchased these bonds as a short-term investment.

Note: Problem 17-6A is based on the present-value appendix in Chapter 16.

Cost of bond $487,444

Problem 17-6A *Computing the cost of a bond investment and journalizing its transactions* **(L.O. 5)**

On December 31, 19X1, when the market interest rate is 12 percent, an investor purchases $500,000 of Advanced Systems 6-year, 11.4 percent bonds at issuance. Determine the cost (present value) of this long-term bond investment. Journalize the purchase on December 31, 19X1, the first semiannual interest receipt on June 30, 19X2, and the year-end interest receipt on December 31, 19X2. The investor uses the effective-interest amortization method. Prepare a schedule for amortizing the discount on bond investment through December 31, 19X2. If necessary, refer to Chapter 16 and its appendix.

A. Loss $100
B. Adj. $98,000

Problem 17-7A *Journalizing foreign-currency transactions and reporting the transaction gain or loss; translating a foreign currency balance sheet* **(L.O. 6, 7)**

Part A. Suppose Coca-Cola Company completed the following transactions.

Dec. 4 Sold soft-drink syrup on account to a Mexican company for $36,000. The exchange rate of the Mexican peso is $.0004, and the customer agrees to pay in dollars.

13 Purchased inventory on account from a Canadian company at a price of Canadian $100,000. The exchange rate of the Canadian dollar is $.80, and payment will be in Canadian dollars.

20 Sold goods on account to an English firm for 70,000 British pounds. Payment will be in pounds, and the exchange rate of the pound is $1.80.

27 Collected from the Mexican company.

31 Adjusted the accounts for changes in foreign-currency exchange rates. Current rates: Canadian dollar, $.81; English pound, $1.79.

Jan. 21 Paid the Canadian company. The exchange rate of the Canadian dollar is $.78.

Feb. 17 Collected from the English firm. The exchange rate of the British pound is $1.77.

Record these transactions in Coca-Cola's general journal, and show how to report the transaction gain or loss on the income statement.

Part B. Translate the foreign-currency balance sheet of the Japanese subsidiary of Rotan Mosby, Inc., into dollars. When Rotan Mosby acquired this subsidiary, the Japanese yen was worth $.0064. The current exchange rate is $.0073. During the period when the subsidiary earned its income, the average exchange rate was $.0069 per yen.

Before performing the translation calculations, indicate whether Rotan Mosby has experienced a positive or a negative translation adjustment. State whether the adjustment is a gain or a loss, and show where it is reported in the financial statements.

	Yen
Assets	300,000,000
Liabilities	80,000,000
Stockholders' equity:	
Common stock	20,000,000
Retained earnings	200,000,000
	300,000,000

Problem 17-1B *Journalizing transactions under the cost and equity methods* **(L.O. 1, 2)**

Gain on sale of inv., Feb. 6, $5,513

Ford Motor Company owns numerous investments in the stock of other companies. Assume Ford completed the following investment transactions:

19X4

Mar. 19 Purchased 1,000 shares of ROX Corporation common stock as a short-term investment, paying 22½ per share plus brokerage commission of $700.

Apr. 1 Purchased 8,000 shares, which exceeds 20 percent, of the common stock of MIC Company at total cost of $720,000.

July 1 Purchased 1,600 additional shares of MIC Company common stock at cost of $140,000.

Aug. 14 Received semiannual cash dividend of $.75 per share on the ROX investment.

Sep. 15 Received semiannual cash dividend of $1.40 per share on the MIC investment.

Oct. 12 Received ROX common stock in a 10 percent stock dividend. Round the new cost per share to the nearest cent.

Nov. 9 Sold 200 shares of ROX stock for 28¼ per share, less brokerage commission of $175.

Dec. 31 Received annual report from MIC Company. Net income for the year was $350,000. Of this amount, Ford's proportion is 21.25 percent

19X5

Feb. 6 Sold 1,920 shares of MIC stock for net cash of $189,700.

Required

Record the transactions in the general journal of Ford Motor Company.

Problem 17-2B *Applying the cost method (with LCM) and the equity method* **(L.O. 1, 2)**

Inv. in affiliates, Dec. 31, $84,595,000

The beginning balance sheet of Fairchild Industries, Inc., recently included:

Investments in Affiliates $84,057,000

Investments in Affiliates refers to investments accounted for by the equity method. Fairchild included its short-term investments among the current assets. Assume the company completed the following investment transactions during the year:

Jan. 3 Purchased 5,000 shares of common stock as a short-term investment, paying 9¼ per share plus brokerage commission of $1,350.

4 Purchased new long-term investment in affiliate at cost of $408,000. Debit Investments in Affiliates.

May 14 Received semiannual cash dividend of $.82 per share on the short-term investment purchased January 3.

June 15 Received cash dividend of $27,000 from affiliated company.

Aug. 28 Sold 1,000 shares of the short-term investment (purchased on January 3) for 10½ per share, less brokerage commission of $750.

Oct. 24 Sold other short-term investments for $226,000, less brokerage commission of $11,400. Cost of these investments was $243,100.

Dec. 15 Received cash dividend of $29,000 from affiliated company.

31 Received annual reports from affiliated companies. Their total net income for the year was $620,000. Of this amount, Fairchild's proportion is 30 percent.

Required

1. Record the transactions in the general journal of Fairchild Industries.
2. Post entries to the Investments in Affiliates T-account, and determine its balance at December 31.
3. Assume the beginning balance of Short-Term Investments was cost of $356,400. Post entries to the Short-Term Investments T-account and determine its balance at December 31.
4. Assuming the market value of the short-term investment portfolio is $142,600 at December 31, show how Fairchild Industries would report short-term investments and investments in affiliates on the ending balance sheet. Use the following format:

Cash	$XXX
Short-term investments, at lower of cost or market (? ,$___)	
Accounts receivable	XXX
Total current assets	XXX
Investments in affiliates	

Consol. total assets $824,000

Problem 17-3B   *Preparing a consolidated balance sheet; no minority interest* **(L.O. 3, 4)**

Polski Corporation paid $179,000 to acquire all the common stock of Smackover, Inc., and Smackover owes Polski $55,000 on a note payable. Immediately after the purchase on May 31, 19X7, the two companies' balance sheets were as follows:

Assets	Polski Corporation	Smackover, Inc.
Cash	$ 18,000	$ 32,000
Accounts receivable, net	64,000	43,000
Note receivable from Smackover ..	55,000	—
Inventory	171,000	153,000
Investment in Smackover	179,000	—
Plant assets, net	205,000	138,000
Total	$692,000	$366,000

Liabilities and Stockholders' Equity		
Accounts payable	$ 76,000	$ 37,000
Notes payable	196,000	123,000
Other liabilities	44,000	27,000
Common stock	282,000	90,000
Retained earnings................	94,000	89,000
Total	$692,000	$366,000

Required

1. Prepare a consolidation work sheet.
2. Prepare the consolidated balance sheet on May 31, 19X7. Show total assets, total liabilities, and total stockholders' equity. It is not necessary to classify assets and liabilities as current and long-term.

Consol. total assets $1,002,000

Problem 17-4B   *Preparing a consolidated balance sheet with goodwill* **(L.O. 3, 4)**

On August 17, 19X8, Concrete Products Corp. paid $229,000 to purchase all the common stock of Travelers, Inc., and Travelers owes Concrete Products $42,000 on a note payable. Immediately after the purchase, the two companies' balance sheets were as follows:

Assets	Concrete Products Corp.	Travelers, Inc.
Cash	$ 23,000	$ 37,000
Accounts receivable, net	104,000	54,000
Note receivable from Travelers	42,000	—
Inventory	213,C00	170,000
Investment in Travelers	229,000	—
Plant assets, net	197,000	175,000
Goodwill	—	—
Total	$808,000	$436,000

Liabilities and Stockholders' Equity		
Accounts payable	$119,000	$ 77,000
Notes payable	223,000	71,000
Other liabilities	33,000	88,000
Common stock	219,000	113,000
Retained earnings................	214,000	87,000
Total	$808,000	$436,000

Required

1. Prepare a consolidation work sheet.
2. Prepare the consolidated balance sheet on August 17, 19X8. Show total assets, total liabilities, and total stockholders' equity. It is not necessary to classify assets and liabilities as current and long-term.

Problem 17-5B *Accounting for a long-term bond investment purchased at a discount* **(L.O. 5)**

2. Long-term investments $486,350

Financial institutions such as insurance companies and pension plans hold large quantities of bond investments. Suppose Aetna Life Insurance Company of New York purchases $500,000 of 8 percent bonds of General Motors Corporation for 97 on March 31, 19X0. These bonds pay interest on January 31 and July 31 each year. They mature on July 31, 19X8.

Required

1. Journalize Aetna's purchase of the bonds as a long-term investment on March 31, 19X0, receipt of cash interest and amortization of discount on July 31, 19X0, and accrual of interest revenue and amortization of discount at December 31, 19X0. Assume the amortization amounts are immaterial, so the straight-line method is appropriate for amortizing discount.
2. Show all financial statement effects of this long-term bond investment at December 31, 19X0. Assume a multiple-step income statement.
3. Repeat Requirement 2 under the assumption that Aetna purchased these bonds as a short-term investment.

Note: Problem 17-6B is based on the present-value appendix in Chapter 16.

Problem 17-6B *Computing the cost of a bond investment and journalizing its transactions* **(L.O. 5)**

Cost of bond $462,350

On December 31, 19X1, when the market interest rate is 10 percent, an investor purchases $400,000 of Jax Gold 10-year, 12.5 percent bonds at issuance. Determine the cost (present value) of the bond investment. Assume that the investment is long-term. Journalize the purchase on December 31, 19X1, the first seminannual interest receipt on June 30, 19X2, and the year-end interest receipt on December 31, 19X2. The investor uses the effective-interest amortization method. Prepare a schedule for amortizing the premium on the bond investment through December 31, 19X2. If necessary, refer to Chapter 16 and its appendix.

A. Gain $500
B. Adj. ($30,000)

Problem 17-7B *Journalizing foreign-currency transactions and reporting the transaction gain or loss; translating a foreign-currency balance sheet (L.O. 6, 7)*

Part A. Suppose Xerox Corporation completed the following transactions.

Dec. 1 Sold a photocopy machine on account to Pirelli Tire Company for $70,000. The exchange rate of the Italian lira is $.0007, and Pirelli agrees to pay in dollars.

     10 Purchased supplies on account from a Canadian company at a price of Canadian $50,000. The exchange rate of the Canadian dollar is $.80, and payment will be in Canadian dollars.

     17 Sold a photocopy machine on account to an English firm for 100,000 British pounds. Payment will be in pounds, and the exchange rate of the pound is $1.80.

     22 Collected from Pirelli.

     31 Adjusted the accounts for changes in foreign-currency exchange rates. Current rates: Canadian dollar, $.82; English pound, $1.78.

Jan. 18 Paid the Canadian company. The exchange rate of the Canadian dollar is $.77.

     24 Collected from the English firm. The exchange rate of the British pound is $1.79.

Record these transactions in Xerox's general journal, and show how to report the transaction gain or loss on the income statement.

Part B. Translate the foreign-currency balance sheet of the Danish subsidiary of Millbank, Inc., into dollars. When Millbank acquired this subsidiary, the Danish krone was worth $.17. The current exchange rate is $.16. During the period when the subsidiary earned its income, the average exchange rate was $.18 per krone.

Before performing the translation calculations, indicate whether Millbank has experienced a positive or a negative translation adjustment. State whether the adjustment is a gain or a loss. Explain your answer.

	Krone
Assets	3,000,000
Liabilities	1,000,000
Stockholders' equity:	
Common stock	1,000,000
Retained earnings	1,000,000
	3,000,000

Extending Your Knowledge

Decision Problems

No check figure

1. Understanding the Cost and Equity Methods of Accounting for Investments (L.O. 1, 2)

Bruce Joyce is the accountant for Dunrobin Inc. whose year end is December 31. The company made two investments during the first week of January

19X7. Both investments are to be held for at least five years. Information about the investments follows:

a. Dunrobin purchased forty percent of the common stock of Lonesome Dove, Inc., for its book value of $200,000. During the year ended December 31, 19X7, Lonesome Dove earned $85,000 and paid a total dividend of $30,000.

b. Ten percent of the common stock of M-J Western Music Inc. was purchased for its book value of $50,000. During the year ended December 31, 19X7, M-J paid Dunrobin a dividend of $3,000. M-J earned a profit of $85,000 for that period.

Bruce has come to you as his auditor to ask how to account for the investments. Dunrobin has never had such investments before. You attempt to explain the proper accounting to him by indicating that different accounting methods apply to different situations.

Required

Help Bruce understand by:

1. Describing the methods of accounting applicable to these investments.
2. Identifying which method should be used to account for the investments in Lonesome Dove and M-J Western Music.

2. Understanding the Consolidation Method for Investments and for International Accounting   (L.O. 3, 4, 7)

No check figure

Srikant Datar inherited some investments, and he has received the annual reports of the companies in which the funds are invested. The financial statements of the companies are puzzling to Srikant, and he asks you the following questions:

1. The companies label their financial statements as *consolidated* balance sheet, *consolidated* income statement, and so on. What are consolidated financial statements?
2. Notes to the statements indicate that "certain intercompany transactions, loans, and other accounts have been eliminated in preparing the consolidated financial statements." Why does a company eliminate transactions, loans, and accounts? Srikant states that he thought a transaction was a transaction and that a loan obligated a company to pay real money. He wonders if the company is juggling the books to defraud the IRS.
3. The balance sheet lists the asset Goodwill. What is Goodwill? Does this mean that the company's stock has increased in value?
4. The stockholders' equity section of the balance sheet reports Translation Adjustments. Srikant asks what is being translated and why this item is negative.

Required

Respond to each of Srikant's questions.

Ethical Issue

Montpelier Company owns 18 percent of the voting stock of Nashua Corporation. The remainder of the Nashua stock is held by numerous investors with small holdings. Ralph Knox, president of Montpelier and a member of Nashua's board of directors, heavily influences Nashua's policies.

Under the cost method of accounting for investments, Montpelier's net income increases as it receives dividends from Nashua. Montpelier pays President Knox a bonus computed as a percentage of Montpelier's net income. Therefore, Knox can control his personal bonus to a certain extent by influencing Nashua's dividends.

A recession occurs in 19X0, and corporate income is low. Knox uses his power to have Nashua Corporation pay a large cash dividend. This action requires Nashua to borrow so heavily that it may lead to financial difficulty.

Required

1. In getting Nashua to pay the large cash dividend, is Knox acting within his authority as a member of the Nashua board of directors? Are Knox's actions ethical? Whom can his actions harm?
2. Discuss how using the equity method of accounting for investments would decrease Knox's potential for manipulating his bonus.

Financial Statement Problems

1. Investments in Stock (L.O. 1, 2, 3)

The Goodyear Tire & Rubber Company financial statements and related notes in Appendix C describe some of the company's investment activity. The balance sheet reveals that Goodyear's equity-method investment account is titled Investment in Affiliates, at Equity. The equity-method investment revenue could be included as part of Other Income.

Required

1. Journalize the following assumed transactions of 1990. Use Goodyear account titles, and show amounts in millions rounded to the nearest $100,000 (for example, $101.4 million).
   a. Equity-method investment revenue of $41.4 million. Label this account Equity in Earnings of Affiliates.
   b. Receipt of cash dividends of $39.7 million from affiliated companies. Insert the December 31, 1989, balance in Investment in Affiliates, and post the entries to this account. Compare its balance to the amount shown on the balance sheet at December 31, 1990.
2. What were Goodyear's balances of short-term investments (short-term securities) at December 31, 1989, and December 31, 1990? What method is used to account for these investments? Make a single journal entry for 1990 to account for the change in this account's balance from the beginning to the end of the year.
3. What is the only word appearing in the title of all the Goodyear financial statements? What does this word indicate?
4. Goodyear's financial statements indicate whether the company owns 100 percent or less of its consolidated subsidiaries. Which is it, and what is the evidence supporting your answer?

2. Investments in Stock (L.O. 1, 2, 3)

Obtain the annual report of an actual company of your choosing. Answer these questions about the company. Concentrate on the current year in the annual report you select.

1. Many companies refer to other companies in which they own equity-method investments as *affiliated companies*. This signifies the close relation-

ship between the two entities even though the investor does not own a controlling interest.

Does the company have equity-method investments? Cite the evidence. If present, what were the balances in the investment account at the beginning and the end of the current year? If the company had no equity-method investments, skip the next question, and go to number 3.

2. Scan the income statement. If equity-method investments are present, what amount of revenue (or income) did the company earn on the investments during the current year? Scan the statement of cash flows. What amount of dividends did the company receive during the current year from companies in which it held equity-method investments? Note: The amount of dividends received may not be disclosed. If not, you can still compute the amount of dividends received—from the following T-account.

Investments, at Equity

Beg. bal. (from balance sheet)	W	
Equity-method revenue (from income statement)	X	Dividends received (unknown; must compute) Y
End. bal. (from balance sheet)	Z	

3. The company probably owns some consolidated subsidiaries. You can tell whether the parent company owns 100 percent or less of the subsidiaries. Examine the income statement and the balance sheet to determine whether there are any minority interests. If so, what does that fact indicate?

4. The stockholders' equity section of most balance sheets lists Foreign Currency Translation Adjustment or a similar account title. A positive amount signifies a gain, and a negative amount indicates a loss. The change in this account balance from the beginning of the year to the end of the year signals whether the U.S. dollar was strong or weak during the year in comparison to the foreign currencies. For the company you are analyzing, was the dollar strong or weak during the current year?

Comprehensive Problem For Part Seven

Accounting for Corporate Transactions

North American Industries' corporate charter authorizes the company to issue 500,000 shares of $1 par value common stock and 100,000 shares of 5 percent, $10 par value preferred stock. During the first quarter of operations, North American completed the following selected transactions:

3. Total liab.:
   Current $71,250
   Long-term $289,536
   Total S/E: $675,874

Oct. 1 Issued 75,000 shares of common stock for cash of $6 per share.

2 Signed a capital lease for equipment. The lease requires a down payment of $50,000, plus 20 quarterly lease payments of $10,000. Present value of the future lease payments is $135,900 at an annual interest rate of 16 percent.

5 Issued 2,000 shares of preferred stock to attorneys who helped organize the corporation. Their bill listed legal services of $22,000.

22 Received land from the county as an incentive for locating in Nashville. Fair market value of the land was $150,000.

30 Purchased 5,000 shares (20 percent) of the outstanding common stock of Newbold Corp. as a long-term investment, $85,000.

Nov. 1 Issued $200,000 of 9 percent, 10-year bonds payable at 94.

14 Purchased short-term investments in the common stocks of Coca-Cola, $22,000, and Goodyear Tire, $31,000.

19 Experienced an extraordinary flood loss of inventory that cost $21,000. Cash received from the insurance company was $8,000.

20 Purchased 2,000 shares of the company's common stock for the treasury. Cost was $5 per share.

Dec. 1 Received cash dividends of $1,100 on the Coca-Cola investment.

16 Sold 1,000 shares of the treasury stock for cash of $6.25 per share.

29 Received a report from Newbold Corp. indicating that net income for November and December was $70,000.

30 Sold merchandise on account, $716,000. Cost of the goods was $439,000. Operating expenses totaled $174,000, with $166,000 of this amount paid in cash. North American uses a perpetual inventory system.

31 Accrued interest and amortized discount (straight-line method) on the bonds payable.

31 Accrued interest on the capital lease liability.

31 Depreciated the equipment acquired by the capital lease. The company uses the double-declining-balance method.

31 Market values of short-term investments: Coca-Cola stock, $24,000, and the Goodyear stock, $30,000.

31 Accrued income tax expense of $20,000.

31 Closed all revenues, expenses, and losses to Retained Earnings in a single closing entry.

31 Declared a quarterly cash dividend of $.125 per share on the preferred stock. Record date is January 11, with payment scheduled for January 19.

Required

1. Record these transactions in the general journal. Explanations are not required.

2. Prepare a single-step income statement for the quarter ended December 31, including earnings per share. Income tax expense of $20,000 should be reported as follows: Income tax expense of $24,000 is used in arriving at income before extraordinary items. The tax effect of the extraordinary loss is an income tax saving of $4,000.

3. Report the liabilities and the stockholders' equity as they would appear on the balance sheet at December 31.

Chapter 18

Statement of Cash Flows

For decades we've made the most fundamental and far-reaching economic decisions on the basis of that supposedly magic number, the bottom line.

As investors, we buy and sell stocks depending on whether a company's earnings are growing or shrinking. As managers, we decide what investments to make based largely on what earnings the projects will yield.

We're making a big mistake. Reported earnings have become virtually worthless in terms of their ability to tell us what's really going on at a company.

Take Prime Motor Inns, until a few months ago the world's second-largest hotel operator. Last year Prime reported a healthy net income of $77 million—18 percent of revenues—up nearly 15 percent from the year before. In September Prime filed for Chapter 11 bankruptcy.

What happened? Could the bankruptcy filing have been foreseen? Prime's problem was that it didn't have enough cash coming in. . . . According to banking consultants Financial Proformas, Inc., Prime had a $15 million cash *outflow* from operations in 1989—the year it reported a $77 million profit—compared with a positive cash flow of $58 million the year before.

Source: Dana Wechsler Linden, *Forbes*, November 12, 1990, p. 106.

Discussion Question: Have you
ever known people who lived
way beyond their means? What
are some characteristics of that
kind of person? *ANSWER:* They
may 1) have a lot of debt; 2)
spend unwisely; 3) not be
concerned about repaying the
debt; 4) spend more money
than they make, and 5) be
unable to save.

What are some
characteristics of people who
manage their finances well?
ANSWER: They probably 1)
spend less than they make, 2)
invest for the future, 3) do not
have a lot of debt, 4) consider
carefully before making a
purchase.

Businesses, too, can spend
beyond their means or manage
their finances well. Where
could you look to find out if a
company was borrowing
money to buy its assets or
using its earnings to acquire
assets? *ANSWER:* The cash flow
statement shows where a
business gets its cash and what
it is using the cash for. It
shows how a company is
financing its operations and
what the cash is invested in. It
provides information about
cash receipts and cash
disbursements.

LEARNING OBJECTIVES
After studying this chapter, you should be able to

1 Identify the purposes of the statement
of cash flows

2 Distinguish among operating, investing,
and financing activities

3 Prepare a statement of cash flows using
the direct method

4 Use the financial statements to compute
the cash effects of a wide variety of
business transactions

5 Prepare a statement of cash flows using
the indirect method

Income statements and balance sheets are anchored to the accrual basis of
accounting for measuring performance and financial position. Another major
statement, the statement of cash flows, is required by GAAP to complete the
picture of performance and position.

Consider some common questions asked by managers, investors, and creditors. What were the company's sources of cash during the period? Did operations—buying and selling the company's major products—generate the bulk
of its cash receipts, or did the business have to sell off plant assets to keep the
cash balance at an acceptable level? Did the company have to borrow heavily
during the period? How did the entity spend its cash? Was it busy paying off
debts, or were cash disbursements devoted to expanding the business? This
chapter discusses the statement of cash flows. As its title implies, the statement of cash flows helps explain a company's performance in generating
cash.

Cash flows are cash receipts and cash payments (disbursements). The **statement of cash flows** reports cash receipts and cash disbursements classified
according to the entity's major activities: operating, investing, and financing.
The statement reports a net cash inflow or a net cash outflow for each activity
and for the overall business.

OBJECTIVE 1
Identify the purposes of
the statement of cash
flows

Purposes of the Statement of Cash Flows

The statement of cash flows is designed to fulfill the following purposes:

1. To predict future cash flows. Cash, not reported accounting income, pays
the bills. In many cases, a business's sources and uses of cash do not change
dramatically from year to year. If so, past cash receipts and disbursements are
a reasonably good predictor of future cash receipts and disbursements.

2. To evaluate management decisions. If managers make wise investment decisions, their businesses prosper. If they make unwise decisions, the businesses
suffer. The statement of cash flows reports the company's investment in plant
and equipment and thus gives investors and creditors cash-flow information
for evaluating managers' decisions. A classic example is Montgomery Ward's
decision shortly after World War II *not* to expand the business. Ward's top
management expected a recession and decided to play it safe until the United
States economy settled down after the war. Sears, Roebuck, on the other
hand, predicted a strong economy and went full speed ahead. Sears's decision
proved better, and Montgomery Ward fell significantly behind Sears.

Point to Stress: A business
operates in order to earn a
profit; it must operate
profitably and remain solvent if
it is to continue in business
over the long run. The balance
sheet and income statement tell
us in part if the business has
earned a profit plus remained
solvent. But more information
can be obtained by evaluating
these two statements along
with the cash flow statement.

3. *To determine the ability to pay dividends to stockholders and interest and principal to creditors.* Stockholders are interested in receiving dividends on their investments in the company's stock. Creditors want to receive their interest and principal amounts on time. The statement of cash flows helps investors and creditors predict whether the business can make these payments.

4. *To show the relationship of net income to changes in the business's cash.* Usually, cash and net income move together. High levels of income tend to lead to increases in cash, and vice versa. However, a company's cash balance can decrease when net income is high, and cash can increase when income is low. The failures of companies such as Prime Motor Inns, which was earning net income but had insufficient cash, have pointed to the need for cash flow information.

Basic Concept of the Statement of Cash Flows _____

The balance sheet reports the cash balance at the end of the period. By examining two consecutive balance sheets, you can tell whether cash increased or decreased during the period. However, the balance sheet does not indicate *why* the cash balance changed. The income statement reports revenues, expenses, and net income—clues about the sources and uses of cash—but it still does not tell *why* cash increased or decreased.

The statement of cash flows reports the entity's cash receipts and cash payments during the period—where cash came from and how it was spent. It explains the *causes* for the change in the cash balance. This information cannot be learned solely from the other financial statements.

The balance sheet is the only financial statement that is dated as of the end of the period. The income statement and the statement of retained earnings cover the period from beginning to end. The statement of cash flows also covers the entire period and therefore is dated "For the Year Ended XXX" or "For the Month Ended XXX." Its timing and its position among the statements is shown in this diagram:

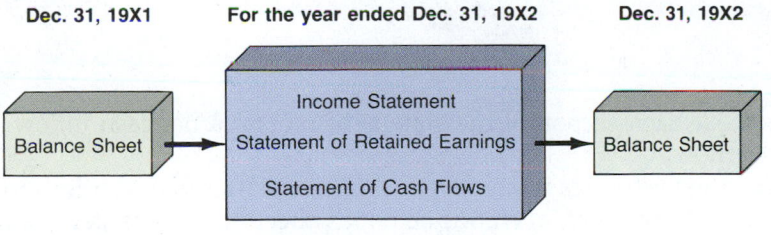

Dec. 31, 19X1	For the year ended Dec. 31, 19X2	Dec. 31, 19X2
Balance Sheet	Income Statement / Statement of Retained Earnings / Statement of Cash Flows	Balance Sheet

Operating, Investing, and Financing Activities _____

A good way to evaluate a business is based on three types of business activities. After the business is up and running, operations are the most important activity, followed by investing activities and financing activities. The statement of cash flows in Exhibit 18-1 shows how cash receipts and disbursements are divided into operating activities, investing activities, and financing activities. As Exhibit 18-1 illustrates, each set of activities (operating, investing, and financing) includes both cash inflows—receipts—and cash outflows—payments. Outflows are shown in parentheses to indicate that payments must be

Teaching Tip: Before explaining
the complicated calculations
that are required to prepare a
cash flow statement, explain
the statement itself in Exhibit
18-1.

Discussion Question: Analyze the
statement in Exhibit 18-1.
ANSWER: The cash from
operations is positive, meaning
the cash inflows exceeded the
cash outflows. Cash was used
for investing activities, perhaps
for the acquisition of plant
assets. There was a need to
finance this acquisition and
therefore common stock and
some long-term debt were
issued. Overall, there was a net
decrease in cash during the
year. You can see this further
by comparing beginning cash
($42) with ending cash ($22).

Teaching Tip: Here's a hint to
help students see where they
are headed when preparing the
statement of cash flows: Start
by comparing beginning cash
and ending cash. Has it
increased or decreased during
the year? An increase means
the statement will show a "net
increase in cash."

EXHIBIT 18-1   *Statement of Cash Flows*

Anchor Corporation
Statement of Cash Flows
For the Year Ended December 31, 19X2
Increase (Decrease) in Cash and Cash Equivalents
(amounts in thousands)

Cash flows from operating activities:
  Receipts:
    Collections from customers .... $ 271
    Interest received on notes receivable 10
    Dividends received on investments in stock 9
      Total cash receipts .... $ 290
  Payments:
    To suppliers .... $(133)
    To employees .... (58)
    For interest................................. (16)
    For income tax .... (15)
      Total cash payments .... (222)
      Net cash inflow from operating activities....... 68

Cash flows from investing activities:
  Acquisition of plant assets .... $(306)
  Loan to another company .... (11)
  Proceeds from sale of plant assets 62
    Net cash outflow from investing activities ...... (255)

Cash flows from financing activities:
  Proceeds from issuance of common stock .... $ 101
  Proceeds from issuance of long-term debt 94
  Payment of long-term debt .... (11)
  Payment of dividends .... (17)
    Net cash inflow from financing activities 167
Net decrease in cash .... **$ (20)**
Cash balance, December 31, 19X1 42
Cash balance, December 31, 19X2 .... $ 22

OBJECTIVE 2

Distinguish among
operating, investing,
and financing activities

subtracted. Each section of the statement reports a net cash inflow or a net
cash outflow.

Operating activities create revenues and expenses in the entity's major line
of business. Therefore, operating activities affect the income statement, which
reports the accrual-basis effects of operating activities. The statement of cash
flows reports their impact on cash. The largest cash inflow from operations is
the collection of cash from customers. Less important inflows are receipts of
interest on loans and dividends on stock investments. The operating cash
outflows include payments to suppliers and to employees and payments for
interest and taxes. Anchor's net cash inflow from operating activities is
$68,000. A large positive operating cash flow is a good sign about a company.
In the long run operations must be the main source of a business's cash.

Investing activities increase and decrease the assets that the business has to
work with. A purchase or sale of a plant asset like land, a building, or equipment is an investing activity, as is the purchase or sale of an investment in
stock or bonds of another company. On the statement of cash flows, investing
activities include more than the buying and selling of assets that are classified

as investments on the balance sheet. Making a loan—an investing activity because the loan creates a receivable for the lender—and collecting on the loan are also reported as investing activities on the statement of cash flows. The acquisition of plant assets dominates the company's investing activities, which produce a net cash outflow of $255,000.

Investments in plant assets lay the foundation for future operations. A company that invests in plant and equipment appears stronger than one that is selling off its plant assets. Why? The latter company may have to sell income-producing assets in order to pay the bills. Its outlook is bleak.

Financing activities obtain the cash from investors and creditors needed to launch and sustain the business. Financing activities include issuing stock, borrowing money by issuing notes and bonds payable, selling treasury stock, and making payments to the stockholders—dividends and purchases of treasury stock. Payments to the creditors include principal payments only. The payment of interest is an operating activity. Financing activities brought in net cash of $167,000. One thing to watch among financing activities is whether the business is borrowing heavily. Excessive borrowing has been the downfall of many companies.

Overall, cash decreased by $20,000 during 19X2. The company began the year with cash of $42,000 and ended with $22,000.

Each of these categories of activities includes both cash receipts and cash disbursements, as shown in Exhibit 18-2. The exhibit lists the more common cash receipts and cash disbursements that appear on the statement of cash flows.

EXHIBIT 18-2 *Cash Receipts and Disbursements Reported on the Statement of Cash Flows*

Operating Activities	
Cash Receipts	**Cash Disbursements**
Collections from customers	Payments to suppliers
Receipts of interest and dividends on investments	Payments to employees
	Payments of interest and income tax
Other operating receipts	Other operating disbursements

Investing Activities	
Cash Receipts	**Cash Disbursements**
Sale of plant assets	Acquisition of plant assets
Sale of investments that are not cash equivalents	Acquisition of investments that are not cash equivalents
Cash receipts on loans receivable	Making loans

Financing Activities	
Cash Receipts	**Cash Disbursements**
Issuing stock	Purchase of treasury stock
Selling treasury stock	Payment of dividends
Borrowing money	Paying principal amounts of debts

Teaching Tip: Under Investing Activities—Cash Disbursements, remind students that the last item, Making loans, means loaning money.

Teaching Tip: For a proprietorship or partnership, under Financing Activities—Cash Receipts, another possible item is capital investments by owners, and under Cash Disbursements, another possible item is cash payments to owners (withdrawals).

Cash and Cash Equivalents

On a statement of cash flows, *Cash* has a broader meaning than just cash on hand and cash in the bank. It includes **cash equivalents,** which are highly liquid short-term investments that can be converted into cash with little delay. Because one reason for holding these investments is their liquidity, they are treated as cash. Examples include money market investments and investments in U.S. Government Treasury bills. Businesses invest their extra cash in these types of liquid assets rather than let it remain idle. Throughout this chapter, the term *cash* refers to cash and cash equivalents.

Interest and Dividends

You may be puzzled by the listing of receipts of interest and dividends as operating activities. After all, these cash receipts result from investing activities. Interest comes from investments in loans, and dividends come from investments in stock. Equally puzzling is listing the payment of interest as part of operations. Interest expense results from borrowing money—a financing activity. After much debate, the FASB decided to include these items as part of operations. Why? Mainly because they affect the computation of net income. Interest revenue and dividend revenue increase net income, and interest expense decreases income. Therefore, cash receipts of interest and dividends and cash payments of interest are reported as operating activities on the cash flow statement.

In contrast, notice that dividend payments are not listed among the operating activities of Exhibit 18-2. Why? Because they do not enter the computation of income. Dividend payments are reported in the financing activities section of the cash flow statement because they go to the entity's owners, who finance the business by holding its stock.

Preparing the Statement of Cash Flows: The Direct Method

OBJECTIVE 3

Prepare a statement of cash flows using the direct method

There are two basic ways to present the statement of cash flows. Both methods arrive at the same subtotals for operating activities, investing activities, financing activities, and the net change in cash for the period. They differ only in the manner of showing the cash flows from operating activities. The **direct method**, which the FASB prefers, lists the major categories of operating cash receipts and cash disbursements as shown in Exhibit 18-1. We discuss the indirect method later in the chapter.

Illustrative Problem

Let's see how to prepare the statement of cash flows by the direct method in Exhibit 18-1. Suppose Anchor Corporation accountants have assembled the following summary of 19X2 transactions. Those transactions with cash effects are denoted by an asterisk.

Summary of 19X2 Transactions

Operating Activities:

1. Sales on credit, $284,000
*2. Collections from customers, $271,000
3. Interest revenue on notes receivable, $12,000
*4. Collection of interest receivable, $10,000
*5. Cash receipt of dividend revenue on investments in stock, $9,000
6. Cost of goods sold, $150,000
7. Purchases of inventory on credit, $147,000
*8. Payments to suppliers, $133,000
9. Salary and wage expense, $56,000
*10. Payments of salaries and wages, $58,000
11. Depreciation expense, $18,000
12. Other operating expense, $17,000
*13. Interest expense and payments, $16,000
*14. Income tax expense and payments, $15,000

Investing Activities:

*15. Cash payments to acquire plant assets, $306,000
*16. Loan to another company, $11,000
*17. Proceeds from sale of plant assets, $62,000, including $8,000 gain

Financing Activities:

*18. Proceeds from issuance of common stock, $101,000
*19. Proceeds from issuance of long-term debt, $94,000
*20. Payment of long-term debt, $11,000
*21. Declaration and payment of cash dividends, $17,000

These summary transactions give the data for both the income statement and the statement of cash flows. Some transactions affect one statement, some the other. Sales, for example, are reported on the income statement, but cash collections appear on the cash flow statement. Other transactions, such as the cash receipt of dividend revenue, affect both statements. *The statement of cash flows reports only those transactions with cash effects.*

Preparation of the statement of cash flows follows these steps: (1) identify the activities that increased cash and decreased cash—those items with asterisks in the Summary of 19X2 Transactions above; (2) classify each cash increase and each cash decrease as an operating activity, an investing activity, or a financing activity; and (3) identify the cash effect of each transaction. Preparing the statement is discussed in the next section.

Cash Flows from Operating Activities. Operating cash flows are listed first because they are the largest and most important source of cash for most businesses. The failure of a company's operations to generate the bulk of its cash inflows for an extended period may signal trouble. This is not true of Anchor Corporation in Exhibit 18-1. Its operating activities were the largest source of cash receipts, $290,000.

CASH COLLECTIONS FROM CUSTOMERS. Cash sales bring in cash immediately. Credit sales, however, increase Accounts Receivable but not Cash. Receipts of cash on account are a separate transaction, and only cash receipts are reported on the statement of cash flows. "Collections from customers" on the statement include both cash sales and collections of accounts receivable from credit sales.

Teaching Tip: Refer to Exhibit 18-1 (use Teaching Transparency 18-1). Start with collections from customers, and identify (1) the *income statement account*, and (2) the *balance sheet account(s)* that are used to compute each item on the cash flow statement. Example: For collections from customers, use

(1) Sales from the income statement, and

(2) Accounts Receivable from the balance sheet.

Point to Stress: Cash collections from customers is not the same as Sales. Cash collections from customers includes collections from sales that were made last year and does not include credit sales from the current year that have not yet been collected.

Collections from customers are Anchor's major operating source of cash—$271,000—in Exhibit 18-1.

CASH RECEIPTS OF INTEREST.   Interest revenue is earned on notes receivable. The income statement reports interest revenue. As the clock ticks, interest accrues, but cash interest is received only on specified dates. Only the cash receipts of interest appear on the statement of cash flows—$10,000 in Exhibit 18-1.

CASH RECEIPTS OF DIVIDENDS.   Dividends are earned on investments in stock. Dividend revenue is ordinarily recorded as an income statement item when cash is received. This cash receipt is reported on the statement of cash flows—$9,000 in Exhibit 18-1. (Note that dividends *received* are part of operating activities, but dividends *paid* are a financing activity.)

PAYMENTS TO SUPPLIERS.   Payments to suppliers include all cash disbursements for inventory and operating expenses except employee compensation, interest, and income taxes. Suppliers are those entities that provide the business with its inventory and essential services. For example, a clothing store's payments to Levi Strauss, Liz Claiborne, and Reebok are listed as payments to suppliers. A grocery store makes payments to suppliers like Nabisco, Campbell's, and Coca-Cola. Other suppliers provide advertising, utility, and other services that are classified as operating expenses. This category *excludes* payments to employees, payments for interest, and payments for income taxes because these are separate categories of operating cash payments. In Exhibit 18-1, Anchor Corporation reports payments to suppliers of $133,000.

PAYMENTS TO EMPLOYEES.   This category includes disbursements for salaries, wages, commissions, and other forms of employee compensation. Accrued amounts are excluded because they have not yet been paid. The income statement reports the expense, including accrued amounts. The statement of cash flows reports only the payments ($58,000) in Exhibit 18-1.

PAYMENTS FOR INTEREST EXPENSE AND INCOME TAX EXPENSE.   These cash payments are reported separately from the other expenses. Interest payments show the cash cost of borrowing money. Excessive borrowing can lead to a large amount of interest payments resulting in financial trouble. Donald Trump's casinos and Macy's are examples of businesses that have faced problems because of too much borrowing. Income tax payments also deserve emphasis because of their significant amount. In the Anchor Corporation illustration, these expenses equal the cash payments. Therefore, the same amount appears on the income statement and the statement of cash flows. In actual practice, this is rarely the case. Year-end accruals and other transactions usually cause the expense and cash payment amounts to differ. The cash flow statement reports the cash payments for interest ($16,000) and income tax ($15,000).

DEPRECIATION, DEPLETION, AND AMORTIZATION EXPENSES.   These expenses are *not* listed on the statement of cash flows in Exhibit 18-1 because they do not affect cash. For example, depreciation is recorded by debiting the expense and crediting Accumulated Depreciation. No debit or credit to the Cash account occurs.

Cash Flows from Investing Activities.   Many analysts regard investing as a critical activity because a company's investments determine its future course. Large purchases of plant assets signal expansion, which is usually a good sign about the company. Low levels of investing activities over a lengthy period

Discussion Question: Cash payments to suppliers is not the same as operating expenses on the income statement. What are some differences between the two? *ANSWER:* Depreciation, amortization of intangibles, and depletion are all operating expenses that do not result in a cash payment. A prepaid expense is paid in one period but recorded as an expense in a later period. An accrued expense is recorded as an expense in one period and paid in a later period. Recording expenses and making cash payments do not always occur simultaneously.

Teaching Tip: Amortization of bond premium causes cash payment of interest to be greater than interest expense. Amortization of bond discount causes payment of interest to be less than interest expense. Remind students to watch for Premium (or Discount) on Bonds Payable. It will signal that an adjustment is required to calculate cash paid for interest.

Point to Stress: After you have listed all the accounts used in converting the income statement items to the cash basis, point out that changes in the remaining asset accounts will signal an *investing* activity. Changes in the remaining liability and stockholders' equity accounts will signal *financing* activities.

mean the business is not replenishing its capital assets. Knowing these cash flows helps investors and creditors evaluate the direction that managers are charting for the business.

CASH PAYMENTS TO ACQUIRE PLANT ASSETS AND INVESTMENTS, AND LOANS TO OTHER COMPANIES. These cash payments are similar because they acquire a noncash asset. The first transaction purchases plant assets, such as land, buildings, and equipment ($306,000) in Exhibit 18-1. In the second transaction, Anchor Corporation makes an $11,000 loan and obtains a note receivable. These are investing activities because the company is investing in assets for use in the business rather than for resale. These transactions have no effect on revenues or expenses and thus are not reported on the income statement. Another transaction in this category—not shown in Exhibit 18-1—is a purchase of an investment in the stocks or bonds of another company.

PROCEEDS FROM THE SALES OF PLANT ASSETS AND INVESTMENTS, AND COLLECTIONS OF LOANS. These transactions are the opposites of acquisitions of plant assets and investments, and making loans. They are cash receipts from investment transactions.

The sale of the plant assets needs explanation. The statement of cash flows reports that Anchor Corporation received $62,000 cash on the sale of plant assets. The income statement shows an $8,000 gain on this transaction. What is the appropriate amount to show on the cash flow statement? It is $62,000, the cash proceeds from the sale. Assuming Anchor sold equipment that cost $64,000 and had accumulated depreciation of $10,000, the journal entry to record this sale is

Cash	62,000	
Accumulated Depreciation	10,000	
Equipment		64,000
Gain on Sale of Plant Assets (from income statement)		8,000

The analysis indicates that the book value of the equipment was $54,000 ($64,000 − $10,000). However, the book value of the asset sold is not reported on the statement of cash flows. Only the cash proceeds of $62,000 are reported on the statement. For the income statement, only the gain is reported. Since a gain occurred, you may wonder why this cash receipt is not reported as part of operations. Operations consist of buying and selling merchandise or rendering services to earn revenue. Investing activities are the acquisition and disposition of assets used in operations. Therefore, the FASB views the sale of plant assets and the sale of investments as cash inflows from investing activities.

Investors and creditors are often critical of a company that sells large amounts of its plant assets. Such sales may signal an emergency. In other situations, selling off fixed assets may be good news about the company if it is getting rid of an unprofitable division. Whether sales of plant assets are good news or bad news should be evaluated in light of a company's operating and financing characteristics.

Cash Flows from Financing Activities. Cash flows from financing activities include the following:

PROCEEDS FROM ISSUANCE OF STOCK AND DEBT. Readers of the financial statements want to know how the entity obtains its financing. Issuing stock (preferred and common) and debt are two common ways to finance operations. In Exhibit 18-1, Anchor Corporation issued common stock of $101,000 and long-term debt of $94,000.

PAYMENT OF DEBT AND PURCHASES OF THE COMPANY'S OWN STOCK. The payment of debt decreases Cash, which is the opposite of borrowing money. Anchor Corporation reports debt payments of $11,000. Other transactions in this category are purchases of treasury stock and payments to retire the company's stock.

PAYMENT OF CASH DIVIDENDS. The payment of cash dividends decreases Cash and is therefore reported as a cash payment, as illustrated by Anchor's $17,000 payment in Exhibit 18-1. A dividend in another form—a stock dividend, for example—has no effect on Cash and is *not* reported on the cash flow statement.

Point to Stress: It is the payment of dividends, not the declaration, that appears on the cash flow statement. Why? Because the credit to Cash was made on the date of payment, not the date of declaration.

Focus of the Statement of Cash Flows

The statement of cash flows focuses on the increase or decrease in cash during the period (highlighted in Exhibit 18-1 for emphasis). This check figure is taken from the comparative balance sheet that shows the beginning and ending balances. The cash flow statement, which adds up to the change in cash, shows the reasons why cash changed.

Exhibit 18-1 illustrates how the cash-balance information may be shown at the bottom of a statement of cash flows, a common format. Another practice places the beginning cash balance at the top of the statement and the ending balance at the bottom. However, the FASB does not require that the beginning and ending cash balances appear on the statement. Because the balance sheet reports these amounts, it is sufficient to show on the statement of cash flows only the change that occurred during the period.

EXHIBIT 18-3 *Income Statement*

Anchor Corporation Income Statement For the Year Ended December 31, 19X2 (amounts in thousands)		
Revenues and gains:		
Sales revenue	$284	
Interest revenue	12	
Dividend revenue	9	
Gain on sale of plant assets	8	
Total revenues and gains		$313
Expenses:		
Cost of goods sold	$150	
Salary and wage expense	56	
Depreciation expense	18	
Other operating expense	17	
Interest expense	16	
Income tax expense	15	
Total expenses		272
Net income		$ 41

In our example, cash decreased by $20,000. Readers of the annual report might wonder why cash decreased during a good year. After all, Exhibit 18-3, Anchor's income statement, reports net income of $41,000. When a business is expanding, its cash often declines. Why? Because cash is invested in plant assets, such as land, buildings, and equipment, as reported in the cash flow statement. Conversely, cash may increase in a year when income is low—if the company borrows heavily. The statement of cash flows gives its readers a direct picture of where cash came from (cash inflows) and how cash was spent (cash outflows).

Summary Problem for Your Review

Drexel Corporation accounting records include the following information for the year ended June 30, 19X8:

1. Salary expense, $104,000
2. Interest revenue, $8,000
3. Proceeds from issuance of common stock, $31,000
4. Declaration and payment of cash dividends, $22,000
5. Collection of interest receivable, $7,000
6. Payments of salaries, $110,000
7. Credit sales, $358,000
8. Loan to another company, $42,000
9. Proceeds from sale of plant assets, $18,000, including $1,000 loss
10. Collections from customers, $369,000
11. Cash receipt of dividend revenue on stock investments, $3,000
12. Payments to suppliers, $319,000
13. Cash sales, $92,000
14. Depreciation expense, $32,000
15. Proceeds from issuance of short-term debt, $38,000
16. Payments of long-term debt, $57,000
17. Interest expense and payments, $11,000
18. Loan collections, $51,000
19. Proceeds from sale of investments, $22,000, including $13,000 gain
20. Amortization expense, $5,000
21. Purchases of inventory on credit, $297,000
22. Income tax expense and payments, $16,000
23. Cash payments to acquire plant assets, $83,000
24. Cost of goods sold, $284,000
25. Cash balance: June 30, 19X7—$83,000
              June 30, 19X8—$54,000

Required

Prepare Drexel Corporation's statement of cash flows and income statement for the year ended June 30, 19X8. Follow the formats of Exhibits 18-1 and 18-3.

SOLUTION TO REVIEW PROBLEM

Drexel Corporation
Statement of Cash Flows
For the Year Ended June 30, 19X8
Increase (Decrease) in Cash and Cash Equivalents
(amounts in thousands)

Item No. (Reference Only)			
	Cash flows from operating activities:		
	Receipts:		
10, 13	Collections from customers ($369 + $92)		$ 461
5	Interest received on notes receivable		7
11	Dividends received on investments in stock		3
	Total cash receipts		471
	Payments:		
12	To suppliers	$(319)	
6	To employees	(110)	
17	For interest	(11)	
22	For income tax	(16)	
	Total cash payments		(456)
	Net cash inflow from operating activities		15
	Cash flows from investing activities:		
23	Acquisition of plant assets	$ (83)	
8	Loan to another company	(42)	
19	Proceeds from sale of investments	22	
9	Proceeds from sale of plant assets	18	
18	Collection of loans	51	
	Net cash outflow from investing activities		(34)
	Cash flows from financing activities:		
15	Proceeds from issuance of short-term debt	$ 38	
3	Proceeds from issuance of common stock	31	
16	Payments of long-term debt	(57)	
4	Dividends declared and paid	(22)	
	Net cash outflow from financing activities		(10)
	Net decrease in cash		$ (29)
25	Cash balance, June 30, 19X7		83
25	Cash balance, June 30, 19X8		$ 54

Transparency T18-3

Drexel Corporation
Income Statement
For the Year Ended June 30, 19X8
(amounts in thousands)

Revenue and gains:		
Sales revenue ($358 + $92)	$450	
Gain on sale of investments	13	
Interest revenue	8	
Dividend revenue	3	
Total revenues and gains		$474
Expenses and losses:		
Cost of goods sold	$284	
Salary expense	104	
Depreciation expense	32	
Income tax expense	16	
Interest expense	11	
Amortization expense	5	
Loss on sale of plant assets	1	
Total expenses		453
Net income		$ 21

Computing Individual Amounts for the Statement of Cash Flows

How do accountants compute the amounts for the statement of cash flows? Many accountants prepare the statement of cash flows using the income statement amounts and *changes* in the related balance sheet accounts. Accountants label this the T-account approach.[1] Learning to analyze T-accounts in this manner is one of the most useful skills you will acquire from accounting. It will enable you to identify the cash effects of a wide variety of transactions. The following discussions use Anchor Corporation's comparative balance sheet in Exhibit 18-4 and income statement in Exhibit 18-3. For continuity, trace the $22,000 and $42,000 cash amounts on the balance sheet in Exhibit 18-4 to the bottom part of the cash flow statement in Exhibit 18-1, page 810.

Computing the Cash Amounts of Operating Activities

Computing Cash Collections from Customers. Collections can be computed by converting sales revenue (an accrual-basis amount) to the cash basis. A decrease in the balance of Accounts Receivable during the period indicates

EXHIBIT 18-4 *Comparative Balance Sheet*

				Increase
Anchor Corporation				
Comparative Balance Sheet				
December 31, 19X2 and 19X1				
(amounts in thousands)				
Assets		**19X2**	**19X1**	**(Decrease)**
Current:				
Cash...............................		$ 22	$ 42	$(20)
Accounts receivable		93	80	13
Interest receivable		3	1	2
Inventory		135	138	(3)
Prepaid expenses		8	7	1
Long-term receivable from another company .		11	—	11
Plant assets, net		453	219	234
Total..........................		$725	$487	$238
Liabilities				
Current:				
Accounts payable		$ 91	$ 57	$ 34
Salary and wage payable		4	6	(2)
Accrued liabilities		1	3	(2)
Long-term debt		160	77	83
Stockholders' Equity				
Common stock		359	258	101
Retained earnings.................		110	86	24
Total..........................		$725	$487	$238

OBJECTIVE 4

Use the financial statements to compute the cash effects of a wide variety of business transactions

Teaching Tip: It is very easy for students to memorize the formulas in this section without understanding them. Writing the formula on the board with an explanation of what the increase or decrease in an account means may be helpful.

Teaching Tip:
  Decrease in Accounts Receivable—Indicates that cash collections were greater than sales. The decrease is added to Sales.
  Increase in Accounts Receivable—Indicates that sales were greater than cash collections. The increase is deducted from Sales.

Class Exercise: Refer to Exhibit 18-4. Ask these questions: If Accounts Receivable increased $13,000, were sales more or less than collections? *ANSWER:* Write this on the board:

Sales	**$284**
Increase in A/R	**13**
= Collections	**$?**

An increase in Accounts Receivable indicates that the increase was *not* collected in cash. The increase in Accounts Receivable therefore must be *subtracted* from Sales to compute the cash collections from customers.

Sales	**$284**
Increase in A/R	**−13**
= Collections	**$271**

[1]The chapter appendix covers the work sheet approach to preparation of the statement of cash flows.

that cash collections exceeded sales revenue. Therefore, we add the decrease to sales revenue to compute collections. An increase in Accounts Receivable means that sales exceeded cash receipts. This amount is subtracted from sales to compute collections. These relationships suggest the following computation for collections from customers:

$$\begin{array}{l} \text{Collections} \\ \text{from} \\ \text{customers} \end{array} = \text{Sales Revenue} \left\{ \begin{array}{c} + \text{ Decrease in Accounts Receivable} \\ \text{or} \\ - \text{ Increase in Accounts Receivable} \end{array} \right.$$

Anchor Corporation's income statement (Exhibit 18-3 page 816) reports sales of $284,000. Exhibit 18-4 shows that Accounts Receivable increased from $80,000 at the beginning of the year to $93,000 at year end, a $13,000 increase. Based on these amounts, Collections equal $271,000: Sales Revenue, $284,000 minus the $13,000 increase in Accounts Receivable. Posting these amounts directly to Accounts Receivable highlights the Collections amount, $271,000.

Accounts Receivable

Beginning balance	80,000		
Sales	284,000	Collections	271,000
Ending balance	93,000		

We see that this computation required the income statement amount of Sales Revenue and the *change* in the related balance sheet account, Accounts Receivable. The amount of cash collections from customers is derived from these accounts. Cash collections—and the other amounts reported on the cash flow statement—are *not* the balances of separate ledger accounts. Instead, the cash flow amounts must be computed by analysis of related income statement and balance sheet accounts, as illustrated in this section.

All collections of receivables can be computed in the same way. For example, the illustrative problem indicates that Anchor Corporation received cash interest. To compute this operating cash receipt, note that the income statement, Exhibit 18-3, page 816, reports interest revenue of $12,000. Interest Receivable's balance in Exhibit 18-4 increased by $2,000. Cash receipts of interest must be $10,000 (Interest Revenue of $12,000 minus the $2,000 increase in Accounts Receivable).

Computing Payments to Suppliers. This computation includes two parts, payments for inventory and payments for expenses other than interest and income tax.

Payments for inventory are computed by converting cost of goods sold to the cash basis. We accomplish this by analyzing Cost of Goods Sold and Accounts Payable. Many companies also purchase inventory on short-term notes payable. In that case, we would analyze Short-Term Notes Payable in the same manner as Accounts Payable. The computation of cash payments for inventory is

$$\begin{array}{l} \text{Payments} \\ \text{for} \\ \text{inventory} \end{array} = \text{Cost of goods sold} \left\{ \begin{array}{c} + \text{ Increase in} \\ \text{Inventory} \\ \text{or} \\ - \text{ Decrease in} \\ \text{Inventory} \end{array} \right. \text{and} \left\{ \begin{array}{c} + \text{ Decrease in} \\ \text{Accounts Payable*} \\ \text{or} \\ - \text{ Increase in} \\ \text{Accounts Payable*} \end{array} \right.$$

*+ Decrease (or − Increase) in Short-Term Notes Payable for inventory purchases

The logic behind this computation is that an increase in inventory leads to

---

Teaching Tip: Remind students that each account contains these 4 basic elements:

Beg. bal.
+Increase
−Decrease
=End bal.

Increases in Accounts Receivable are caused by sales, and decreases are caused by collections. The beginning and ending balances are found on the balance sheet, and Sales is on the income statement. Try using this equation to compute collections for the company discussed here in the text:

Beg. A/R	$ 80,000
+Sales	284,000
−Collections	?
=End. A/R	$ 93,000

Compute collections by solving for the unknown.

ANSWER:
Collections = $271,000

Teaching Tip:
Increase in Inventory—Indicates more inventory has been purchased than sold. An increase in inventory is added to cost of goods sold.
Decrease in Inventory—Indicates that less merchandise has been purchased than sold. The decrease is deducted from cost of goods sold.
Decrease in Accounts Payable—Indicates that the cash payments for merchandise were greater than what was purchased. The decrease is added to cost of goods sold.
Increase in Accounts Payable—Indicates that more merchandise was purchased than was paid for. The increase is deducted from cost of goods sold.

an increase in accounts payable that finds its way into a cash payment. A decrease in accounts payable can occur only if cash was paid. By contrast, an increase in accounts payable indicates that cash was *not* paid. A detailed analysis will show the validity of this computation.

Anchor Corporation reports cost of goods sold of $150,000. The balance sheet shows that Inventory decreased by $3,000. Accounts Payable increased by $34,000. These amounts combine to compute payments for inventory of $113,000: Cost of Goods Sold, $150,000, minus the decrease in Inventory, $3,000, minus the increase in Accounts Payable, $34,000—a total of $113,000.

The T-account analysis also indicates payments of $113,000 (with Purchases inserted for completeness):

Cost of Goods Sold

Beginning inventory	138,000	Ending inventory	135,000
Purchases	147,000		
Cost of goods sold	150,000		

Accounts Payable

		Beginning balance	57,000
Payments for inventory ..	113,000	Purchases	147,000
		Ending balance	91,000

Payments to suppliers ($133,000 in Exhibit 18-1) equal the sum of payments for inventory ($113,000) plus payments for operating expenses ($20,000), as explained next.

Computing Payments for Operating Expenses. Payments for operating expenses other than interest and income tax can be computed by analyzing Prepaid Expenses and Other Accrued Liabilities, as follows:

$$
\begin{array}{c}
\text{Payments} \\
\text{for operating} \\
\text{expenses}
\end{array}
=
\begin{array}{c}
\text{Operating} \\
\text{expenses other} \\
\text{than salaries,} \\
\text{wages, and} \\
\text{depreciation}
\end{array}
\left\{
\begin{array}{c}
\text{+ Increase in} \\
\text{Prepaid Expenses} \\
\text{or} \\
\text{– Decrease in} \\
\text{Prepaid Expenses}
\end{array}
\right.
\text{and}
\left\{
\begin{array}{c}
\text{+ Decrease in} \\
\text{Accrued Liabilities} \\
\text{or} \\
\text{– Increase in} \\
\text{Accrued Liabilities}
\end{array}
\right.
$$

Increases in prepaid expenses require cash payments, and decreases indicate that payments were less than expenses. Decreases in accrued liabilities can occur only from cash payments, and increases mean that cash was *not* paid.

Anchor's income statement reports operating expenses—other than salaries, wages, and depreciation—of $17,000. The balance sheet shows that prepaid expenses increased by $1,000, and accrued liabilities decreased by $2,000. Based on these data, payments for operating expenses total $20,000 ($17,000 + $1,000 + $2,000).

This result is confirmed by the T-account analysis, at the top of page 822.

Computing Payments to Employees. The company may have separate accounts for salaries, wages, and other forms of cash compensation to employees. To compute payments to employees, it is convenient to combine them into one account. Anchor's calculation begins with Salary and Wage Expense (an income statement account) and adjusts for the change in Salary and Wage

Prepaid Expenses

Beginning balance	7,000	Expiration of prepaid		
Payments	**8,000**	expense	7,000	←
Ending balance	8,000			

Accrued Liabilities

Payment of beginning		Beginning balance.........	3,000
balance **3,000**		Accrual of expense at year	
		end	1,000 ←
		Ending balance	1,000

Operating Expenses (other than Salaries, Wages, and Depreciation)

→ Expiration of prepaid	
expense	7,000
→ Accrual of expense at year	
end	1,000
Payments	**9,000**
Ending balance	17,000

Total payments = $20,000 ($8,000 + $3,000 + $9,000)

Teaching Tip: Indicate that increases and decreases in Salary Payable are treated in the same way as increases and decreases in Accounts Payable and Accrued Liabilities.

Decrease in Salary Payable— Indicates that salaries paid exceeded salary expense. The decrease is added to Salary Expense.

Increase in Salary Payable— Indicates that salary expense exceeded salaries paid. The increase is deducted from Salary Expense.

Teaching Tip:

Decrease in Interest Payable or Income Tax Payable— Indicates that interest or income taxes paid exceeded interest expense or income tax expense. The decrease is added to Interest Expense or Income Tax Expense.

Increase in Interest Payable or Income Taxes Payable— Indicates that interest expense or income tax expense exceeded interest or income taxes paid. The increase is deducted from Interest Expense or Income Tax Expense.

Payable (a balance sheet account). The computation follows:

$$\begin{matrix} \text{Payments} \\ \text{to} \\ \text{employees} \end{matrix} = \begin{matrix} \text{Salary} \\ \text{and Wage} \\ \text{Expense} \end{matrix} \begin{cases} + \textbf{ Decrease in Salary and Wage Payable} \\ \text{or} \\ - \textbf{ Increase in Salary and Wage Payable} \end{cases}$$

A decrease in the liability is added because it requires a cash payment. An increase in the liability indicates that the expense exceeds cash payments, so the increase is subtracted. Anchor's salary and wage expense is $56,000. The balance sheet in Exhibit 18-4 reports a $2,000 decrease in the liability. Thus cash payments to employees are $58,000 ($56,000 + $2,000). This is confirmed by analysis of the Salary and Wage Payable account:

Salary and Wage Payable

		Beginning balance........	6,000
Payments	**58,000**	Salary and wage expense ..	56,000
		Ending balance	4,000

Computing Payments of Interest and Income Taxes. In our illustrative problem, the expense and payment amount is the same for each of these expenses. Therefore, no analysis is required to determine the payment amount. If the expense and the payment differ, the payment can be computed by analyzing the related liability account. The payment computation follows the pattern illustrated for payments to employees.

Computing the Cash Amounts of Investing Activities

Investing activities affect asset accounts, such as Plant Assets, Investments, and Notes Receivable. The cash amounts of investing activities can be identified by analyzing these accounts. Most data for the computations are taken directly from the income statement and the beginning and ending balance sheets. Other amounts come from analysis of accounts in the ledger.

Computing Acquisitions and Sales of Plant Assets.   Most companies have separate accounts for Land, Buildings, Equipment, and other plant assets. It is helpful to combine these accounts into a single summary for computing the cash flows from acquisitions and sales of these assets. Also, we subtract accumulated depreciation from the assets' cost and work with a net figure for plant assets. This allows us to work with a single plant asset account as opposed to a large number of plant asset and related accumulated depreciation accounts.

To illustrate, observe that Anchor Corporation's balance sheet (Exhibit 18-4) reports beginning plant assets, net of depreciation, of $219,000 and an ending net amount of $453,000. The income statement shows depreciation of $18,000 and an $8,000 gain on sale of plant assets. Further, the acquisitions total $306,000. How much are the proceeds from the sale of plant assets? First, we must determine their book value, computed as follows:

Point to Stress: Changes in asset accounts, other than those used to compute cash flow from operating activities, are investing activities. An increase in an asset represents a cash outflow, and a decrease in an asset represents a cash inflow.

Beginning Plant Asset balance (net)	+ Acquisitions	− Depreciation	− Book value of plant assets sold	= Ending Plant Asset balance (net)
$219,000	+ $306,000	− $18,000	− Book value sold	= $453,000

Typical Student Misconception: Students often forget that when an asset is sold, the asset account is decreased by the asset's original cost, not its selling price.

Isolating book value sold on the left-hand side rearranges the equation as follows:

− Book value sold = $453,000 − $219,000 − $306,000 + $18,000

Book value sold = $54,000

Now we can compute the sale proceeds as follows:

Sale proceeds = Book value sold, $54,000 + Gain, $8,000 − Loss, $0

= $62,000

Trace the sale proceeds of $62,000 to the statement of cash flows in Exhibit 18-1. If the sale resulted in a loss of $3,000, the sale proceeds would be $51,000 ($54,000 − $3,000), and the statement would report $51,000 as a cash receipt from this investing activity.

The book value of plant assets sold can also be computed by analysis of the Plant Assets T-account:

Point to Stress: Proceeds from the sale of an asset do not necessarily equal the asset's book value. Remember:

Book Value + Gain = Proceeds
Book Value − Loss = Proceeds

The book value information comes from the balance sheet, the gain or loss from the income statement.

Plant Assets (net)

Beginning balance	219,000	Depreciation	18,000
Acquisitions	306,000	Book value of assets sold .	54,000
Ending balance...........	453,000		

Computing Acquisitions and Sales of Assets Classified as Investments, and Loans and Their Collections.   Accountants use a separate category of assets for investments in stocks, bonds, and other types of assets. The cash amounts of transactions involving these assets can be computed in the manner illustrated for plant assets. Investments are easier to analyze, however, because there is no depreciation to account for, as shown in the following T-account:

Investments			
Beginning balance	XXX		
Purchases	**XXX**	Cost of investments sold	XXX
Ending balance	XXX		

Loan transactions follow the pattern illustrated on pages 819 and 820 for collections from customers. New loans cause a debit to a receivable and an outflow of cash. Collections increase cash and cause a credit to the receivable, as this T-account illustrates:

Loans and Notes Receivable			
Beginning balance	XXX		
New loans made	**XXX**	Collections	XXX
Ending balance	XXX		

Computing the Cash Amounts of Financing Activities

Point to Stress: Changes in
liability and stockholders'
equity accounts, other than
those used to compute cash
flow from operating activities,
are financing activities.

Financing activities affect liability and stockholders' equity accounts, such as Notes Payable, Bonds Payable, Long-term Debt, Common Stock, Paid-in Capital in Excess of Par, and Retained Earnings. The cash amounts of financing activities can be computed by analyzing these accounts.

Computing Issuances and Payments of Long-term Debt. The beginning and ending balances of Long-term Debt, Notes Payable, or Bonds Payable are taken from the balance sheet. If either the amount of new issuances or the amount of the payments is known, the other amount can be computed. New debt issuances total $94,000. The computation of debt payments follows, using balances from Exhibit 18-4:

Teaching Tip: Write the
accounting equation on the
board in this order:
1) A = L + S/E
2) A = Cash + Noncash
Assets
3) Cash + Noncash Assets =
L + S/E
4) Cash = L + S/E − Noncash
Assets
Two conclusions can be drawn:
1. The changes in all noncash
accounts *must* equal the
changes in the Cash
balance.
2. A change in liabilities or
stockholders' equity usually
signals a change in Cash.

Beginning					**Ending**
Long-term Debt + Issuance of new debt − Payments = Long-term Debt					
balance					**balance**
$77,000	+	$94,000	− Payments =		$160,000

Rearranging this equation results in the following:

$$- \text{Payments} = \$160,000 - \$77,000 - \$94,000$$

$$\text{Payments} = \$11,000$$

This computation arises from analysis of the Long-term Debt account:

Long-term Debt			
		Beginning balance	77,000
Payments	11,000	Issuance of new debt	94,000
		Ending balance	160,000

Computing Issuances and Retirements of Stock and Purchases and Sales of Treasury Stock. The cash effects of these financing activities can be determined by analyzing the various stock accounts. For example, the amount of a new issuance of common stock is determined by combining the Common Stock and any related Capital in Excess of Par account. It is convenient to work with a single summary account for stock as we do for plant assets. Using Exhibit 18-4 data, we have:

$$\begin{array}{ccccccc} \text{Beginning} & & & & & & \text{Ending} \\ \text{Stock} & + & \text{Issuance of new stock} & - & \text{Retirements} & = & \text{Stock} \\ \text{balance} & & & & & & \text{balance} \\ \$258{,}000 & + & \text{New Stock} & - & \$0 & = & \$359{,}000 \end{array}$$

Isolating new stock gives the final equation:

$$\text{Issuance of new stock} = \$359{,}000 - \$258{,}000 = \$101{,}000$$

The Common Stock T-account shows these amounts:

Common Stock

		Beginning balance	258,000
Retirements of stock	0	**Issuance of new stock**	**101,000**
		Ending balance	359,000

Cash flows affecting Treasury Stock, a debit balance account, can be analyzed using the following equation:

$$\begin{array}{ccc} \text{Beginning} & & \text{Ending} \\ \text{Treasury Stock} + \text{Purchases} - \text{Cost of treasury stock sold} = & \text{Treasury Stock} \\ \text{balance} & & \text{balance} \end{array}$$

Transaction amounts can also be computed by analyzing the Treasury Stock T-account:

Treasury Stock

Beginning balance	XXX		
Purchases of treasury stock .	**XXX**	Cost of treasury stock sold . .	XXX
Ending balance	XXX		

If either the purchase amount or the cost of treasury stock sold is known, the other amount can be computed. For a sale of treasury stock, the amount to report on the cash flow statement is the sale proceeds. Suppose a sale brought in cash that was $2,000 less than the $14,000 cost of the treasury stock sold. In this case, the statement of cash flows would report a cash receipt of $12,000 ($14,000 − $2,000).

Computing Dividend Payments. If the amount of the dividends is not given elsewhere (for example, in a statement of retained earnings), it can be computed by analyzing the Retained Earnings account. Beginning and ending amounts come from the balance sheet, and the income statement reports net income. Dividend declarations can be computed as shown here, using net

Discussion Question: How would a financial statement reader know by looking at the balance sheet if all the dividends that had been declared had also been paid? ANSWER: If there is no Dividend Payable account, then all the dividends declared have been paid.

income from Exhibit 18-3 and Retained Earnings balances from Exhibit 18-4. We assume Anchor Corporation had no stock dividends or other transactions that affected Retained Earnings during the year. If, for example, a stock dividend and a cash dividend occurred during the year, total dividends must be separated into stock dividends and cash dividends because stock dividends do not affect cash.

$$\begin{array}{ccccccc} \text{Beginning} \\ \text{Retained Earnings} & + & \text{Net income} & - & \text{Dividend} & = & \text{Ending} \\ \text{balance} & & & & \text{declarations} & & \text{Retained Earnings} \\ & & & & & & \text{balance} \\ \$86{,}000 & + & \$41{,}000 & - & \text{Dividends} & = & \$110{,}000 \end{array}$$

Keeping dividends on the left-hand side produces the following equation:

$$- \text{Dividends} = \$110{,}000 - \$86{,}000 - \$41{,}000$$

$$\text{Dividends} = -\$110{,}000 + \$86{,}000 + \$41{,}000$$

$$\text{Dividends} = \$17{,}000$$

Analysis of the Retained Earnings T-account illustrates the equation approach:

Retained Earnings

	Beginning balance	86,000
Dividend declarations 17,000	Net income	41,000
	Ending balance	110,000

A change in the Dividends Payable account means that dividend payments differ from the amount declared. In this case, dividend payments are determined by first computing dividends declared as shown here. Then add the amount of any decrease in the balance of Dividends Payable or subtract the amount of any increase in that account balance. The result is the dividend payments figure. The Dividends Payable account illustrates the analysis:

Dividends Payable

	Beginning balance	XXX
Dividend payments XXX	Dividend declarations	XXX
	Ending balance	XXX

Noncash Investing and Financing Activities

Typical Student Misconception: Students often fail to report noncash investing and financing activities in a supplemental schedule, and erroneously include them on the statement.

Companies make investments that do not require cash. They also obtain financing other than cash. Our illustrative problem included none of these transactions.

Suppose Anchor Corporation issued no-par common stock valued at $320,000 to acquire a warehouse. Anchor would journalize this transaction as follows:

Warehouse Building	320,000	
Common Stock		320,000

Acquisition of building by issuing common stock	$320
Acquisition of land by issuing note payable	72
Payment of long-term debt by transferring investment assets to the creditor	104
Acquisition of equipment by issuing short-term note payable . . .	37
Total noncash investing and financing activities	$533

Discussion Question: Look at the balance sheet in Exhibit 18-4. Have we fully explained the change in every account on the balance sheet? *ANSWER:* Yes. All the changes in the accounts have been accounted for and used in one of the three categories on the statement of cash flows or in the schedule of noncash investing and financing activities. Until the change in *every* account has been explained, the statement is not complete.

Teaching Tip: Put a check mark by each account on the balance sheet after you have used it in preparing the statement of cash flows. The checks will help you make sure that you have considered each balance sheet account change.

This transaction would not be reported on the cash flow statement because Anchor paid no cash. But the importance of the investment in the warehouse and the financing aspect of issuing stock require that the transaction be reported. Noncash investing and financing activities like this transaction are reported in a separate schedule that accompanies the statement of cash flows. Exhibit 18-5 illustrates how to report noncash investing and financing activities (all amounts are assumed). This information can be included in a schedule immediately following the cash flow statement or in a note.

Preparing the Statement of Cash Flows: The Indirect Method

OBJECTIVE 5
Prepare a statement of cash flows using the indirect method

An alternative way to compute cash flows from *operating* activities is the **indirect method.** This method, also called the **reconciliation method,** starts with net income and shows the reconciliation from net income to operating cash flows. It shows the link between net income and cash flow from operations better than the direct method. The main drawback of the indirect method is that it does not report the detailed operating cash flows—collections from customers and other cash receipts, payments to suppliers, payments to employees, and payments for interest and taxes.

Point to Stress: Currently, more companies are using the indirect method than the direct method. Students should understand both.

The indirect method and the direct method are both permitted by the FASB. *These methods of preparing the cash flow statement affect only the operating activities section of the statement.* No difference exists in the reporting of investing activities or financing activities.

Point to Stress: The financing and investing activities are the same under both the direct method and the indirect method.

Exhibit 18-6 is Anchor Corporation's statement prepared by the indirect method. You will see that only the operating section of the statement differs from the direct method format in Exhibit 18-1.

Logic Behind the Indirect Method

The operating section of the statement begins with net income, taken directly from the income statement. A series of additions and subtractions follows. These are labeled "Add (subtract) items that affect net income and cash flow differently." In this section, we discuss those items.

Point to Stress: Uncollectible Account Expense and Amortization of Bond Premium or Discount are other examples of items which will affect net income and cash flow differently.

Depreciation, Depletion, and Amortization Expenses. These expenses are added back in going from net income to cash flow from operations. Let's see why.

EXHIBIT 18-6 *Statement of Cash Flows*

Anchor Corporation
Statement of Cash Flows—Indirect Method for Operating Activities
For the Year Ended December 31, 19X2
Increase (Decrease) in Cash and Cash Equivalents
(amounts in thousands)

Cash flows from operating activities:		
Net income		$ 41
Add (subtract) items that affect net income and cash flow differently:		
Depreciation	$ 18	
Gain on sale of plant assets	(8)	
Increase in accounts receivable	(13)	
Increase in interest receivable	(2)	
Decrease in inventory	3	
Increase in prepaid expenses	(1)	
Increase in accounts payable	34	
Decrease in salary and wage payable	(2)	
Decrease in accrued liabilities	(2)	27
Net cash inflow from operating activities		68
Cash flows from investing activities:		
Acquisition of plant assets	$(306)	
Loan to another company	(11)	
Proceeds from sale of plant assets	62	
Net cash outflow from investing activities		(255)
Cash flows from financing activities:		
Proceeds from issuance of common stock	$ 101	
Proceeds from issuance of long-term debt	94	
Payment of long-term debt	(11)	
Payment of dividends	(17)	
Net cash inflow from financing activities		167
Net decrease in cash		$ (20)
Cash balance, December 31, 19X1		42
Cash balance, December 31, 19X2		$ 22

Depreciation is recorded as follows:

Depreciation Expense	18,000	
Accumulated Depreciation		18,000

This entry contains no debit or credit to Cash, so depreciation expense has no cash effect. However, depreciation is deducted from revenues in the computation of income. Therefore, in going from net income to cash flow from operations, we add depreciation back to net income. The addback simply cancels the earlier deduction. The following example should help: Suppose a company had only two transactions during the period, a $1,000 cash sale and depreciation expense of $300. Net income is $700 ($1,000 − $300). Cash flow from operations is $1,000. To show how net income ($700) relates to cash flow ($1,000), we must add the depreciation amount of $300.

All expenses with no cash effects are added back to net income on the cash flow statement. Depletion and amortization are two other examples. Likewise, revenues that do not provide cash are subtracted from net income. An example is equity-method investment revenue.

Gains and Losses on the Sale of Assets. Sales of plant assets are investing activities on the cash flow statement. A gain or loss on the sale is an adjustment to income. Exhibit 18-6 includes an adjustment for a gain. Recall that equipment with a book value of $54,000 was sold for $62,000, producing a gain of $8,000. The way to learn how to treat an item on the cash flow statement is to examine the journal entry that recorded it, as shown on page 815.

The $8,000 gain is reported on the income statement and, therefore, is included in net income. However, the cash receipt from the sale is $62,000, which includes the gain. To avoid counting the gain twice, we need to remove its effect from income and report the cash receipt of $62,000 in the investing-activities section of the statement. Starting with net income, we subtract the gain. This deduction removes the gain's earlier effect on income. The sale of plant assets is reported as a $62,000 cash receipt from an investing activity, as shown in Exhibits 18-1 and 18-6.

A loss on the sale of plant assets is also an adjustment to net income on the statement of cash flows. However, a loss is added back to income to compute cash flow from operations. The proceeds from selling the plant assets are reported under investing activities.

Changes in the Current Asset and Current Liability Accounts. Most current assets and current liabilities result from operating activities. Accounts receivable result from sales, inventory generates revenues, and prepaid expenses are used up in operations. On the liability side, accounts payable and short-term notes payable are ordinarily incurred to buy inventory, and accrued liabilities relate to salaries, utilities, and other expenses. Changes in these current accounts are reported as adjustments to net income on the cash flow statement. The following rules apply:

1. An *increase* in a current asset other than cash is subtracted from net income to compute cash flow from operations. Suppose a company makes a sale. Income is increased by the sale amount. However, collection of less than the full amount leaves Accounts Receivable with an increase. To compute the impact of revenue on the cash flow amount, it is necessary to subtract the $13,000 increase in Accounts Receivable from net income in Exhibit 18-6. The same logic applies to the other current assets. If they increase during the period, subtract the increase from net income.

2. A *decrease* in a current asset other than cash is added to net income. For example, suppose Accounts Receivable's balance decreased by $4,000 during the period. Cash receipts cause the Accounts Receivable balance to decrease, so decreases in Accounts Receivable and the other current assets are added to net income.

3. A *decrease* in a current liability is subtracted from net income. The payment of a current liability causes it to decrease, so decreases in current liabilities are subtracted from net income. For example, in Exhibit 18-6, the $2,000 decrease in Accrued Liabilities is subtracted from net income to compute net cash inflow from operating activities.

4. An *increase* in a current liability is added to net income. Suppose Accrued Liabilities increased during the year. This can occur only if cash is not spent to pay this liability, which means that cash payments are less than the related expense. Thus increases in current liabilities are added to net income.

Exhibit 18-7 summarizes these adjustments to convert net income to net cash inflow (or net cash outflow) from operating activities.

The computation of net cash inflow or net cash outflow from *operating* activities by the indirect method takes a path that is very different from the com-

Teaching Tip: Here are some rules that may help your students with the indirect method:

1 An increase in a current asset is deducted from net income.
2 A decrease in a current asset is added to net income.
3 An increase in a current liability is added to net income.
4 A decrease in a current liability is deducted from net income.

Exhibit 18-7 *Relationship Between Net Income and Net Cash Flow from Operating Activities— Indirect Method*

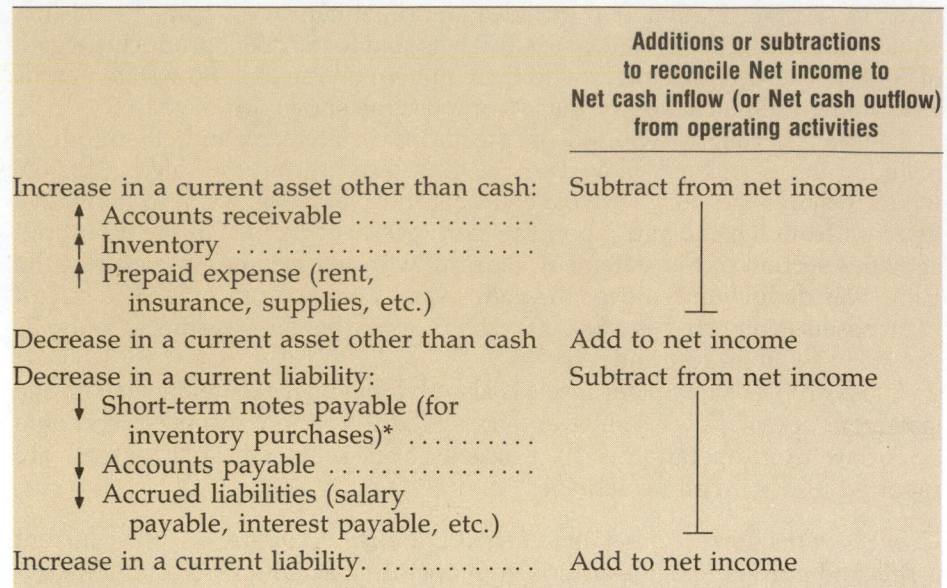

	Additions or subtractions to reconcile Net income to Net cash inflow (or Net cash outflow) from operating activities
Increase in a current asset other than cash:	Subtract from net income
↑ Accounts receivable	
↑ Inventory	
↑ Prepaid expense (rent, insurance, supplies, etc.)	
Decrease in a current asset other than cash	Add to net income
Decrease in a current liability:	Subtract from net income
↓ Short-term notes payable (for inventory purchases)*	
↓ Accounts payable	
↓ Accrued liabilities (salary payable, interest payable, etc.)	
Increase in a current liability.	Add to net income

*Short-term notes payable for general borrowing relate to financing, not operating, activities.

Authors' note: We thank Jean Marie Hudson for suggesting this exhibit.

putation by the direct method. However, the two methods arrive at the same amount of net cash flow. This is shown in Exhibits 18-1 and 18-6, which report a net cash inflow of $68,000.

Supplementary Disclosures

The company that uses the direct method for reporting operating activities on the cash flow statement must, according to *FASB Statement No. 95,* also report the reconciliation of net income to cash flow from operations. A format similar to the operating section under the indirect method (Exhibit 18-6) is suitable. The company that uses the indirect method may report the components of operating cash flows in a way similar to that used in the direct method. These supplementary disclosures can appear in notes to the statement or immediately beneath the statement near the noncash investing and financing activities. The goal is to give readers of the financial statements the information they need to make informed decisions about the company.

Exhibit 18-8 is the cash flow statement of Nike, Inc., maker of athletic shoes and clothing. Notice that Nike uses the indirect method to report cash flows from operating activities. Most companies use this format. Most of the items in Exhibit 18-8 have been discussed earlier, but three are new. First, deferred income taxes are added back to net income in the operating section. These taxes do not require current cash payments and are, therefore, similar to accrued liabilities. Second, financing activities include proceeds from exercise of options. This is the amount of cash received from issuance of stock to executives. Third, changes in exchange rates show the cash effect of fluctuations in foreign currencies, a topic that is beyond the scope of this course. Nike's reporting of this item agrees with GAAP.

Nike, Inc.
Statement of Cash Flows
For the Year Ended May 31, 19X7
(in thousands)

Cash provided (used) by operations:	
Net income	$ 35,879
Income charges (credits) not affecting cash:	
Depreciation	12,078
Deferred income taxes	8,486
Other...	2,494
Changes in certain working capital components:	
Decrease in inventory	59,542
Decrease in accounts receivable	1,174
Decrease in other current assets..................	4,331
Increase in accounts payable, accrued liabilities,	
and income taxes payable	8,462
Cash provided by operations	132,446
Cash provided (used) by investing activities:	
Additions to property, plant and equipment	(11,874)
Disposals of property, plant and equipment..............	1,728
Additions to other assets	(930)
Cash used by investing activities	(11,076)
Cash provided (used) by financing activities:	
Additions to long-term debt	30,332
Reductions in long-term debt including current portion ..	(10,678)
Decrease in notes payable to banks....................	(18,489)
Proceeds from exercise of options	1,911
Dividends—common and preferred	(15,188)
Cash used by financing activities	(12,112)
Effect of exchange rate changes on cash	(529)
Net increase (decrease) in cash........................	108,729
Cash and equivalents, beginning of year.................	18,138
Cash and equivalents, end of year	$126,867

Computers and the Statement of Cash Flows

When the statement of cash flows became a required financial statement, computerized accounting systems were changed so that they could generate this statement as easily as they do the balance sheet and the income statement. Consider the direct method for preparing the statement of cash flows (see Exhibit 18-2). To get the amounts for the operating section, cash inflows and outflows (grouped by the related revenue and expense category) can be drawn from the posted files generated from cash receipts and cash payment records. Specifically, the cash receipts postings to Accounts Receivable provide the information necessary to show Cash Receipts from Customers. The computer adds the monthly postings to reach the yearly total. All other cash flows for operating activities, as well as cash flows for financing and investing activities, are handled similarly.

The computer can generate the statement of cash flows using the indirect method with equal ease. The only additional information needed, noncash income statement flows and changes in noncash current assets and current liabilities, comes from the computer general ledger files.

Do not be misled into believing that the statement of cash flows created from a computer's general ledger files is automatically correct from a generally accepted accounting principles point of view. For example, noncash financing and investing activities of a large corporation, such as Abbott Laboratories, a manufacturer of pharmaceuticals, might be incorrectly combined with the company's cash flows. The computerized system must be sophisticated enough to distinguish among the various categories of cash activities. Most important, accountants must analyze the information fed into the computer and check that its output adheres to generally accepted accounting principles. Revisions to a company's computer accounting system are common.

Summary Problem for Your Review

Prepare the 19X3 statement of cash flows for Robins Corporation, using the indirect method to report cash flows from operating activities. In a separate schedule, report Robins's noncash investing and financing activities.

	December 31,	
	19X3	19X2
Current assets:		
Cash and cash equivalents	$19,000	$ 3,000
Accounts receivable	22,000	23,000
Inventories	34,000	31,000
Prepaid expenses	1,000	3,000
Current liabilities:		
Notes payable (for inventory purchases)	$11,000	$ 7,000
Accounts payable	24,000	19,000
Accrued liabilities	7,000	9,000
Income tax payable	10,000	10,000

Transaction data for 19X3:

Purchase of equipment	$98,000	Depreciation expense	$ 7,000
Payment of cash dividends	18,000	Issuance of long-term note payable to borrow cash	7,000
Net income	26,000	Issuance of common stock for cash	19,000
Issuance of common stock to retire bonds payable	13,000	Sale of building	74,000
Purchase of long-term investment	8,000	Amortization expense	3,000
		Purchase of treasury stock	5,000
Issuance of long-term note payable to purchase patent	37,000	Loss on sale of building	2,000

Robins Corporation
Statement of Cash Flows
Year Ended December 31, 19X3
increase (Decrease) in Cash and Cash Equivalents

Cash flows from operating activities:		
Net income		$26,000
Add (subtract) items that affect net income and cash flow differently:		
Depreciation	$ 7,000	
Amortization	3,000	
Loss on sale of building	2,000	
Decrease in accounts receivable	1,000	
Increase in inventories	(3,000)	
Decrease in prepaid expenses	2,000	
Increase in notes payable, short-term	4,000	
Increase in accounts payable	5,000	
Decrease in accrued liabilities	(2,000)	19,000
Net cash inflow from operating activities		45,000
Cash flows from investing activities:		
Purchase of equipment	$(98,000)	
Sale of building	74,000	
Purchase of long-term investment	(8,000)	
Net cash outflow from investing activities		(32,000)
Cash flows from financing activities:		
Issuance of common stock	$ 19,000	
Payment of cash dividends	(18,000)	
Issuance of long-term note payable	7,000	
Purchase of treasury stock	(5,000)	
Net cash inflow from financing activities		3,000
Net increase in cash and cash equivalents		$16,000
Noncash investing and financing activities:		
Issuance of long-term note payable to purchase patent		$37,000
Issuance of common stock to retire bonds payable		13,000
Total noncash investing and financing activities		$50,000

Summary

The *statement of cash flows* reports a business's cash receipts, cash disbursements, and net change in cash for the accounting period. It shows *why* cash increased or decreased during the period. A required financial statement, it gives a different view of the business from the accrual-basis statements. The cash flow statement helps financial statement users predict the future cash flows of the entity. Cash includes cash on hand, cash in bank, and *cash equivalents* such as liquid, short-term investments.

The statement is divided into *operating activities, investing activities,* and *financing activities.* Operating activities create revenues and expenses; investing activities affect long-term assets; and financing activities obtain the cash needed to launch and sustain the business. Each section of the statement includes cash receipts and cash payments and concludes with a net cash increase or decrease. In addition, *noncash investing and financing activities* are reported in an accompanying schedule.

Two formats are used to report operating activities. The *direct method* lists the major sources of cash receipts and disbursements—for example, cash collections from customers and cash payments to suppliers and to employees. The *indirect method* shows the reconciliation from net income to cash flow from operations. The FASB permits both methods but prefers the direct method. However, the indirect method is more widely used in practice.

Self-Study Questions

Test your understanding of the chapter by marking the best answer for each of the following questions.

1. The income statement and the balance sheet *(p. 808)*
    a. Report the cash effects of transactions
    ✓ b. Fail to report why cash changed during the period
    c. Report the sources and uses of cash during the period
    d. Are divided into operating, investing, and financing activities
2. The purpose of the statement of cash flows is to *(pp. 808, 809)*
    a. Predict future cash flows
    b. Evaluate management decisions
    c. Determine the ability to pay dividends and interest
    ✓ d. All of the above
3. A successful company's major source of cash should be *(pp. 809-812)*
    ✓ a. Operating activities   c. Financing activities
    b. Investing activities   d. A combination of the above
4. Dividends paid to stockholders are reported on the statement of cash flows as a (an) *(pp. 813, 816)*
    a. Operating activity   ✓ c. Financing activity
    b. Investing activity   d. Combination of the above
5. Which of the following items appears on a cash flow statement prepared by the direct method? *(p. 810)*
    a. Depreciation expense   c. Loss on sale of plant assets
    b. Decrease in accounts receivable   ✓ d. Cash payments to suppliers
6. Interest Receivable's beginning balance is $18,000, and its ending amount is $14,000. Interest revenue earned during the year is $43,000. How much cash interest was received? *(pp. 819, 820, 821)*
    a. $39,000   c. $45,000
    b. $43,000   ✓ d. $47,000
7. McGrath Company sold an investment at a gain of $22,000. The Investment account reports a beginning balance of $104,000 and an ending balance of $91,000. During the year, McGrath purchased new investments costing $31,000. What were the proceeds from the sale of investments? *(pp. 823, 824)*.
    a. $22,000   ✓ c. $66,000
    b. $44,000   d. $186,000
8. Noncash investing and financing activities *(p. 827)*
    a. Are reported in the main body of the cash flow statement
    ✓ b. Are reported in a separate schedule that accompanies the cash flow statement
    c. Are reported on the income statement
    d. Are not reported in the financial statements
9. The indirect method does a better job than the direct method at *(p. 827)*

a. Reporting the cash effects of financing activities
b. Reporting why the cash balance changed
√c. Showing the link between net income and cash flow from operations
d. Reporting the separate components of operating cash flows such as collections from customers and payments to suppliers and employees

10. Net income is $17,000, depreciation is $9,000, and amortization is $3,000. In addition, the sale of a plant asset generated a $4,000 gain. Current assets other than cash increased by $6,000, and current liabilities increased by $8,000. What was the amount of cash flow from operations? *(p. 828)*

a. $23,000   c. $31,000
√b. $27,000   d. $35,000

Answers to the Self-Study Questions follow the Accounting Vocabulary.

Accounting Vocabulary

Cash equivalents. Highly liquid short-term investments that can be converted into cash with little delay *(p. 812)*.

Cash flows. Cash receipts and cash payments (disbursements) *(p. 808)*.

Direct method. Format of the operating activities section of the statement of cash flows that lists the major categories of operating cash receipts (collections from customers and receipts of interest and dividends) and cash disbursements (payments to suppliers, to employees, for interest and income taxes) *(p. 812)*.

Financing activity. Activity that obtains the funds from investors and creditors needed to launch and sustain the business. A section of the statement of cash flows *(p. 811)*.

Indirect method. Format of the operating activities section of the statement of cash flows that starts with net income and shows the reconciliation from net income to operating cash flows. Also called the Reconciliation method *(p. 827)*.

Investing activity. Activity that increases and decreases the assets that the business has to work with. A section of the statement of cash flows *(p. 810)*.

Operating activity. Activity that creates revenue or expense in the entity's major line of business. Operating activities affect the income statement. A section of the statement of cash flows *(p. 810)*.

Reconciliation method. Another name for the Indirect method of formatting the operating activities section of the statement of cash flows *(p. 827)*.

Statement of cash flows. Reports cash receipts and cash disbursements classified according to the entity's major activities: operating, investing, and financing *(p. 808)*.

Answer to Self-Study Questions

1. b
2. d
3. a
4. c
5. d
6. d ($43,000 + $4,000 decrease in Interest Receivable = $47,000)
7. c ($104,000 + $31,000 − Cost of investment sold = $91,000; Cost = $44,000; Proceeds = Cost, $44,000 + Gain, $22,000 = $66,000)
8. b
9. c
10. b ($17,000 + $9,000 + $3,000 − $4,000 − $6,000 + $8,000 = $27,000)

ASSIGNMENT MATERIAL

Questions

1. What information does the statement of cash flows report that is not shown on the balance sheet, the income statement, or the statement of retained earnings?
2. Identify four purposes of the statement of cash flows.
3. Identify and briefly describe the three types of activities that are reported on the statement of cash flows.
4. How is the statement of cash flows dated and why?
5. What is the check figure for the statement of cash flows, where is it obtained, and how is it used?
6. What is the most important source of cash for most successful companies?
7. How can cash decrease during a year when income is high? How can cash increase during a year when income is low? How can investors and creditors learn these facts about the company?
8. DeBerg, Inc., prepares its statement of cash flows using the *direct* method for operating activities. Identify the section of DeBerg's statement of cash flows where each of the following transactions will appear. If the transaction does not appear on the cash flow statement, give the reason.

a.	Cash	14,000	
	Note Payable, Long-Term		14,000
b.	Salary Expense	7,300	
	Cash		7,300
c.	Cash	28,400	
	Sales Revenue		28,400
d.	Amortization Expense	6,500	
	Goodwill		6,500
e.	Accounts Payable	1,400	
	Cash		1,400

9. Why are depreciation, depletion, and amortization expenses *not* reported on a cash flow statement that reports operating activities by the direct method? Why and how are these expenses reported on a statement prepared by the indirect method?
10. Mainline Distributing Company collected cash of $92,000 from customers and $6,000 interest on notes receivable. Cash payments included $24,000 to employees, $13,000 to suppliers, $6,000 as dividends to stockholders, and $5,000 as a loan to another company. How much was Mainline's net cash inflow from operating activities?
11. Summarize the major cash receipts and cash disbursements in the three categories of activities that appear on the cash flow statement.
12. Kirchner, Inc., recorded salary expense of $51,000 during a year when the balance of Salary Payable decreased from $10,000 to $2,000. How much cash did Kirchner pay to employees during the year? Where on the statement of cash flows should Kirchner report this item?
13. Marshall Corporation's beginning plant asset balance, net of accumulated depreciation, was $193,000, and the ending amount was $176,000. Marshall recorded depreciation of $37,000 and sold plant assets with a book value of $9,000. How much cash did Marshall pay to purchase plant assets during the period? Where on the statement of cash flows should Marshall report this item?

14. How should issuance of a note payable to purchase land be reported in the financial statements? Identify three other transactions that fall in this same category.

15. Which format of the cash flow statement gives a clearer description of the individual cash flows from operating activities? Which format better shows the relationship between net income and operating cash flow?

16. An investment that cost $65,000 was sold for $80,000, resulting in a $15,000 gain. Show how to report this transaction on a statement of cash flows prepared by the indirect method.

17. Identify the cash effects of increases and decreases in current assets other than cash. What are the cash effects of increases and decreases in current liabilities?

18. Milano Corporation earned net income of $38,000 and had depreciation expense of $22,000. Also, noncash current assets decreased $13,000, and current liabilities decreased $9,000. What was Milano's net cash flow from operating activities?

19. What is the difference between the direct method and the indirect method of reporting investing activities and financing activities?

20. Milgrom Company reports operating activities by the direct method. Does this method show the relationship between net income and cash flow from operations? If so, state how. If not, how can Milgrom satisfy this purpose of the cash flow statement?

Exercises

Exercise 18-1   *Identifying the purposes of the statement of cash flows*   **(L.O. 1)**

No check figure

Monterrey Western, a real estate partnership, has experienced an unbroken string of 10 years of growth in net income. Nevertheless, the business is facing bankruptcy! Creditors are calling all of Monterrey Western's outstanding loans for immediate payment, and the cash is simply not available. In trying to explain where Monterrey Western went wrong, it becomes clear that managers placed undue emphasis on net income and gave too little attention to cash flows.

Required

Write a brief memo, in your own words, to explain for Monterrey Western managers the purposes of the statement of cash flows.

Exercise 18-2   *Identifying activities for the statement of cash flows*   **(L.O. 2)**

No check figure

Identify each of the following transactions as an operating activity (O), an investing activity (I), a financing activity (F), a noncash investing and financing activity (NIF), or a transaction that is not reported on the statement of cash flows (N). Assume the direct method is used to report cash flows from operating activities.

_____ a.   Purchase of long-term investment
_____ b.   Payment of wages to employees
_____ c.   Collection of cash interest
_____ d.   Cash sale of land
_____ e.   Distribution of stock dividend
_____ f.   Acquisition of equipment by issuance of note payable
_____ g.   Payment of long-term debt
_____ h.   Acquisition of building by issuance of common stock
_____ i.   Accrual of salary expense

Chapter 18   Statement of Cash Flows   837

_____ j. Payment of account payable

_____ k. Issuance of preferred stock for cash

_____ l. Payment of cash dividend

_____ m. Sale of long-term investment

_____ n. Amortization of bond discount

_____ o. Collection of account receivable

_____ p. Issuance of long-term note payable to borrow cash

_____ q. Depreciation of equipment

_____ r. Purchase of treasury stock

_____ s. Issuance of common stock for cash

No check figure

Exercise 18-3 *Classifying transactions for the statement of cash flows* **(L.0. 2)**

Indicate where, if at all, each of the following transactions would be reported on a statement of cash flows prepared by the *direct* method and the accompanying schedule of noncash investing and financing activities.

a.	Accounts Payable		8,300	
	Cash			8,300
b.	Cash		81,000	
	Common Stock			12,000
	Paid-in Capital in Excess of Par—Common			69,000
c.	Treasury Stock		13,000	
	Cash			13,000
d.	Retained Earnings		36,000	
	Common Stock			36,000
e.	Cash		2,000	
	Interest Revenue			2,000
f.	Land		87,700	
	Cash			87,700
g.	Salary Expense		4,300	
	Cash			4,300
h.	Equipment		18,000	
	Cash			18,000
i.	Cash		7,200	
	Long-Term Investment			7,200
j.	Bonds Payable		45,000	
	Cash			45,000
k.	Building		164,000	
	Note Payable, Long-Term			164,000
l.	Cash		1,400	
	Accounts Receivable			1,400
m.	Dividends Payable		16,500	
	Cash			16,500
n.	Furniture and Fixtures		22,100	
	Note Payable, Short-Term			22,100

Net cash inflow from operations $4,000

Exercise 18-4 *Computing cash flows from operating activities—direct method* **(L.0. 3)**

Analysis of the accounting records of Manufacturers Coop reveals:

Collection of dividend revenue	$ 7,000	Depreciation		$12,000
Payment of interest	16,000	Decrease in current liabilities		20,000

Cash sales	12,000	Increase in current assets other than cash	17,000
Loss on sale of land	5,000	Payment of dividends	7,000
Acquisition of land	37,000	Collection of accounts receivable	93,000
Payment of accounts payable	45,000		
Net income	24,000	Payment of salaries and wages	34,000
Payment of income tax	13,000		

Compute cash flows from operating activities by the direct method. Use the format of the operating section of Exhibit 18-1.

Exercise 18-5 *Identifying items for the statement of cash flows—direct method* **(L.O. 3)** No check figure

Selected accounts of Quartz Products Corporation show:

Interest Receivable

Beginning balance	16,000	Cash receipts of interest	40,000
Interest revenue	40,000		
Ending balance	16,000		

Investments in Stock

Beginning balance	0	Cost of investments sold	9,000
Acquisitions	27,000		
Ending balance	18,000		

Long-Term Debt

Payments	69,000	Beginning balance	134,000
		Issuance of debt for cash	83,000
		Ending balance	148,000

For each account, identify the item or items that should appear on a statement of cash flows prepared by the direct method. State where to report the item.

Exercise 18-6 *Preparing the statement of cash flows—direct method* **(L.O. 3)** Increase in cash $16,000

The income statement and additional data of Illini Paper Company follow.

Illini Paper Company
Income Statement
Year Ended September 30, 19X2

Revenues:		
Sales revenue	$339,000	
Dividend revenue	8,000	$347,000
Expenses:		
Cost of goods sold	163,000	
Salary expense	85,000	
Depreciation expense	29,000	
Advertising expense	19,000	
Interest expense	2,000	
Income tax expense	9,000	307,000
Net income		$ 40,000

Additional data:

a. Collections from customers are $7,000 more than sales.
b. Payments to suppliers are $9,000 less than the sum of cost of goods sold plus advertising expense.
c. Payments to employees are $1,000 more than salary expense.
d. Dividend revenue, interest expense, and income tax expense equal their cash amounts.
e. Acquisition of plant assets is $116,000. Of this amount, $91,000 is paid in cash, $25,000 by signing a note payable.
f. Proceeds from sale of land, $19,000.
g. Proceeds from issuance of common stock, $30,000.
h. Payment of long-term note payable, $15,000.
i. Payment of dividends, $11,000.
j. Increase in cash balance, $?

Prepare Illini Paper Company's statement of cash flows and accompanying schedule of noncash investing and financing activities. Report operating activities by the *direct* method.

b. Payments for inventory $70,000

Exercise 18-7   *Computing amounts for the statement of cash flows*   (L.O. 4)

Compute the following items for the statement of cash flows:

a. Beginning and ending Accounts Receivable are $26,000 and $22,000, respectively. Credit sales for the period total $81,000. How much are cash collections?
b. Cost of goods sold is $71,000. Beginning Inventory balance is $25,000, and ending Inventory balance is $21,000. Beginning and ending Accounts Payable are $11,000 and $8,000, respectively. How much are cash payments for inventory?

a. Cash proceeds of sale $6,000

Exercise 18-8   *Computing amounts for the statement of cash flows*   (L.O. 4)

Compute the following items for the statement of cash flows:

a. Beginning and ending Plant Assets, net, are $103,000 and $107,000, respectively. Depreciation for the period is $16,000, and acquisitions of new plant assets are $27,000. Plant assets were sold at a $1,000 loss. What were the cash proceeds of the sale?
b. Beginning and ending Retained Earnings are $45,000 and $73,000, respectively. Net income for the period is $62,000, and stock dividends are $12,000. How much are cash dividend payments?

Net cash inflow from operations $4,000

Exercise 18-9   *Computing cash flows from operating activities—indirect method*
(L.O. 5)

The accounting records of Manufacturers Coop reveal the following:

Collection of dividend revenue	$ 7,000	Depreciation	$12,000
Payment of interest	16,000	Decrease in current liabilities	20,000
Cash sales	12,000	Increase in current assets other than cash	17,000
Loss on sale of land	5,000		
Acquisition of land	37,000	Payment of dividends	7,000
Payment of accounts payable	45,000	Collection of accounts receivable	93,000
Net income	24,000	Payment of salaries and wages	34,000
Payment of income tax	13,000		

Compute cash flows from operating activities by the indirect method. Use the format of the operating section of Exhibit 18-6.

Exercise 18-10   *Classifying transactions for the statement of cash flows*   **(L.O. 3, 5)**   No check figure

Two transactions of Hoffman Banana Co. are recorded as follows:

a.	Cash	9,000	
	Accumulated Depreciation	83,000	
	Loss on Sale of Equipment	43,000	
	Equipment		135,000
b.	Land	230,000	
	Cash		130,000
	Note Payable		100,000

Required

1. Indicate where, how, and in what amount to report these transactions on the statement of cash flows and accompanying schedule of noncash investing and financing activities. Hoffman reports cash flows from operating activities by the *direct* method.
2. Repeat Requirement 1, assuming Hoffman reports cash flows from operating activities by the *indirect* method.

Exercise 18-11   *Preparing the statement of cash flows by the indirect method*   **(L.O. 5)**   Increase in cash $16,000

Use the income statement of Illini Paper Company in Exercise 18-6, plus these additional data:

a. Collections from customers are $7,000 more than sales.
b. Payments to suppliers are $9,000 less than the sum of cost of goods sold plus advertising expense.
c. Payments to employees are $1,000 more than salary expense.
d. Dividend revenue, interest expense, and income tax expense equal their cash amounts.
e. Acquisition of plant assets is $116,000. Of this amount, $91,000 is paid in cash, $25,000 by signing a note payable.
f. Proceeds from sale of land, $19,000.
g. Proceeds from issuance of common stock, $30,000.
h. Payment of long-term note payable, $15,000.
i. Payment of dividends, $11,000.
j. Increase in cash balance, $?
k. From the balance sheet:

	September 30,	
	19X2	**19X1**
Current Assets:		
Accounts receivable	$51,000	$58,000
Inventory	83,000	77,000
Prepaid expenses	9,000	8,000
Current Liabilities:		
Notes payable (for inventory purchases)	$20,000	$20,000
Accounts payable	35,000	22,000
Accrued liabilities	23,000	21,000

Prepare Illini Paper Company's statement of cash flows for the year ended September 30, 19X2, using the indirect method.

No check figure

Problem 18-1A *Using cash-flow information to evaluate performance* **(L.O. 1)**

Top managers of Quest Programs, Inc., are reviewing company performance for 19X7. The income statement reports a 20 percent increase in net income over 19X6. However, most of the increase resulted from an extraordinary gain on insurance proceeds covering fire damage to the manufacturing plant. The balance sheet shows large increases in receivables and inventory. The cash flow statement, in summarized form, reports the following:

Net cash outflow from operating activities	$(80,000)
Net cash inflow from investing activities	40,000
Net cash inflow from financing activities	50,000
Increase in cash during 19X7	$ 10,000

Required

Write a memo to give Quest managers your assessment of 19X7 operations and your outlook for the future. Focus on the information content of the cash flow data.

Increase in cash $21,300

Problem 18-2A *Preparing the statement of cash flows—direct method* **(L.O. 2, 3)**

Texana Corporation accountants have developed the following data from the company's accounting records for the year ended April 30, 19X5:

1. Cash payments to acquire plant assets, $59,400
2. Cost of goods sold, $382,600
3. Proceeds from issuance of common stock, $8,000
4. Payment of cash dividends, $48,400
5. Collection of interest, $4,400
6. Acquisition of equipment by issuing short-term note payable, $16,400
7. Payments of salaries, $93,600
8. Credit sales, $583,900
9. Loan to another company, $12,500
10. Proceeds from sale of plant assets, $22,400, including $6,800 loss
11. Collections on accounts receivable, $562,600
12. Interest revenue, $3,800
13. Cash receipt of dividend revenue on stock investments, $4,100
14. Payments to suppliers, $478,500
15. Cash sales, $171,900
16. Depreciation expense, $59,900
17. Proceeds from issuance of short-term debt, $19,600
18. Payments of long-term debt, $50,000
19. Interest expense and payments, $13,300
20. Salary expense, $95,300
21. Loan collections, $12,800
22. Proceeds from sale of investments, $9,100, including $2,000 gain
23. Payment of short-term note payable by issuing common stock, $31,000
24. Amortization expense, $2,900
25. Income tax expense and payments, $37,900
26. Cash balance: April 30, 19X4—$39,300
 April 30, 19X5—$?

Required

Prepare Texana Corporation's statement of cash flows for the year ended April 30, 19X5. Follow the format of Exhibit 18–1, but do *not* show amounts in thousands. Include an accompanying schedule of noncash investing and financing activities. Evaluate 19X5 from a cash-flow standpoint. Give your reasons.

Problem 18-3A *Preparing the statement of cash flows—direct method* **(L.O. 2, 3, 4)**

Net cash inflow from operations $77,800

The 19X5 comparative balance sheet and income statement of Palo Duro Corp. follow.

Comparative Balance Sheet

	19X5	19X4	Increase (Decrease)
Current assets:			
Cash and cash equivalents	$ 15,400	$ 5,300	$10,100
Accounts receivable	28,600	26,900	1,700
Interest receivable	1,900	700	1,200
Inventories	83,600	87,200	(3,600)
Prepaid expenses.	2,500	1,900	600
Plant assets:			
Land	89,000	60,000	29,000
Equipment, net	53,500	49,400	4,100
Total assets	$274,500	$231,400	$43,100
Current liabilities:			
Accounts payable	$ 31,400	$ 28,800	$ 2,600
Interest payable	4,400	4,900	(500)
Salary payable	3,100	6,600	(3,500)
Other accrued liabilities	13,700	16,000	(2,300)
Income tax payable	8,900	7,700	1,200
Long-term liabilities:			
Notes payable	75,000	100,000	(25,000)
Stockholders' equity:			
Common stock, no-par	88,300	64,700	23,600
Retained earnings	49,700	2,700	47,000
Total liabilities and stockholders' equity . .	$274,500	$231,400	$43,100

Income Statement for 19X5

Revenues:		
Sales revenue		$243,000
Interest revenue		8,600
Total revenues		251,600
Expenses:		
Cost of goods sold	$92,400	
Salary expense	27,800	
Depreciation expense	4,000	
Other operating expense	10,500	
Interest expense	11,600	
Income tax expense	29,100	
Total expenses		175,400
Net income		$ 76,200

Palo Duro had no noncash investing and financing transactions during 19X5. During the year there were no sales of land or equipment, no issuances of notes payable, no retirements of stock, and no treasury stock transactions.

Prepare the 19X5 statement of cash flows, formatting operating activities by the direct method.

Problem 18-4A *Preparing the statement of cash flows—indirect method* **(L.O. 2, 3, 5)**

Required

Using the Palo Duro Corp. data from the preceding problem, prepare the 19X5 statement of cash flows by the indirect method. If your instructor also assigned Problem 18-3A, prepare only the operating activities section of the statement.

Problem 18-5A *Preparing the statement of cash flows—indirect method* **(L.O. 2, 5)**

Plywood Products Corporation of America accountants have assembled the following data for the year ended December 31, 19X7:

	December 31,	
	19X7	**19X6**
Current accounts (all result from operations):		
Current assets:		
Cash and cash equivalents..............	$85,700	$22,700
Accounts receivable	59,700	64,200
Inventories...........................	88,600	83,000
Prepaid expenses	5,300	4,100
Current liabilities:		
Notes payable (for inventory purchases)	$22,600	$18,300
Accounts payable	52,900	55,800
Income tax payable	18,600	16,700
Accrued liabilities....................	25,500	27,200

Transaction data for 19X7:

Acquisition of long-term		Sale of equipment	$58,000
investment............	$ 31,600	Amortization expense....	5,300
Acquisition of land by		Purchase of treasury stock	14,300
issuing long-term note		Loss on sale of equipment	11,700
payable...............	113,000	Payment of cash	
Stock dividends	31,800	dividends.............	18,300
Collection of loan........	8,700	Issuance of long-term	
Depreciation expense	26,800	note payable to borrow	
Acquisition of building...	125,300	cash.................	34,400
Retirement of bonds		Net income	67,100
payable by issuing		Issuance of common stock	
common stock	65,000	for cash	41,200

Required

Prepare Plywood Products' statement of cash flows, using the *indirect* method to report operating activities. Include an accompanying schedule of noncash investing and financing activities.

Problem 18-6A *Preparing the statement of cash flows—indirect method* **(L.O. 2, 5)**

The comparative balance sheet of Oefinger, Inc., at March 31, 19X7, reported the following:

	March 31,	
	19X7	19X6
Current assets:		
Cash and cash equivalents	$ 9,100	$ 4,000
Accounts receivable	19,400	21,700
Inventories	63,200	60,600
Prepaid expenses	1,900	1,700
Current liabilities:		
Notes payable (for inventory		
purchases)	$ 4,000	$ 4,000
Accounts payable	30,300	27,600
Accrued liabilities	10,700	11,100
Income tax payable.............	8,000	4,700

Oefinger's transactions during the year ended March 31, 19X7, included the following:

Payment of cash dividend..	$30,000	Cash acquisition of building	$47,000
Cash acquisition of		Net income	70,000
equipment..............	78,700	Issuance of common stock	
Issuance of long-term note		for cash	11,000
payable to borrow cash ..	50,000	Stock dividend	18,000
Acquisition of land by		Sale of long-term	
issuing note payable.....	62,000	investment	13,700
Amortization expense	2,000	Depreciation expense	9,000

Required

Prepare Oefinger's statement of cash flows for the year ended March 31, 19X7, using the *indirect* method to report cash flows from operating activities. Report noncash investing and financing activities in an accompanying schedule. All current account balances resulted from operating transactions.

Problem 18-7A *Preparing the statement of cash flows—direct and indirect methods (L.O. 3, 5)*

Net cash inflow from operations $100,800

To prepare the statement of cash flows, accountants for The Inn of Charleston, Inc., have summarized 19X3 activity in two accounts as follows:

Cash

Beginning balance	53,600	Payments on accounts	
Collection of loan	13,000	payable	399,100
Sale of investment	8,200	Payments of dividends ...	27,200
Receipts of interest.......	12,600	Payments of salaries	
Collections from		and wages	143,800
customers	706,700	Payments of interest	26,900
Issuance of common stock	19,300	Purchase of equipment ...	31,400
Receipts of dividends	4,500	Payments of operating	
		expenses	34,300
		Payment of long-term	
		debt	41,300
		Purchase of treasury stock	26,400
		Payment of income tax ...	18,900
Ending balance	68,600		

Common Stock

Beginning balance	84,400
Issuance for cash	19,300
Issuance to acquire land ..	80,100
Issuance to retire long-term debt	19,000
Ending balance	202,800

Required

1. Prepare The Inn of Charleston's statement of cash flows for the year ended December 31, 19X3, using the *direct* method to report operating activities. Also prepare the accompanying schedule of noncash investing and financing activities.

The Inn of Charleston's 19X3 income statement and selected balance sheet data follow.

The Inn of Charleston, Inc.
Income Statement
For the Year Ended December 31, 19X3

Revenues:		
Sales revenue....................		$734,300
Interest revenue		12,600
Dividend revenue		4,500
Total revenues		751,400
Expenses and losses:		
Cost of goods sold	$402,600	
Salary and wage expense	150,800	
Depreciation expense	24,300	
Other operating expense.........	44,100	
Interest expense	28,800	
Income tax expense	16,200	
Loss on sale of investments	1,100	
Total expenses		667,900
Net income......................		$ 83,500

The Inn of Charleston, Inc. Balance Sheet Data	Increase (Decrease)
Current assets:	
Cash and cash equivalents................	$?
Accounts receivable	27,600
Inventories..............................	(11,800)
Prepaid expenses	600
Current liabilities:	
Accounts payable	$ (8,300)
Interest payable	1,900
Salary payable..........................	7,000
Other accrued liabilities	10,400
Income tax payable	(2,700)

Required

2. Use these data to prepare a supplementary schedule showing cash flows from operating activities by the *indirect* method. All activity in the current accounts results from operations.

Problem 18-8A *Preparing the statement of cash flows—indirect and direct methods* (L.O. 3, 4, 5)

Net cash inflow from operations $65,900

The comparative balance sheet of Paper Clips, Inc., at June 30, 19X7, included the following balances:

Paper Clips, Inc.
Partial Balance Sheet
June 30, 19X7 and 19X6

	19X7	19X6	Increase (Decrease)
Current assets:			
Cash	$21,300	$ 8,600	$12,700
Accounts receivable	45,900	48,300	(2,400)
Interest receivable	2,900	3,600	(700)
Inventories	68,600	60,200	8,400
Prepaid expenses......................	3,700	2,800	900
Current liabilities:			
Notes payable, short-term			
(for general borrowing)	$13,400	$18,100	$(4,700)
Accounts payable	42,400	40,300	2,100
Income tax payable....................	13,800	14,500	(700)
Accrued liabilities	8,200	9,700	(1,500)
Interest payable	3,700	2,900	800
Salary payable	900	2,600	(1,700)

Transaction data for the year ended June 30, 19X7:

a. Net income, $56,200.
b. Depreciation expense on equipment, $10,200.
c. Purchased long-term investment, $4,900.
d. Sold land for $46,900, including $6,700 loss.
e. Acquired equipment by issuing long-term note payable, $14,300.
f. Paid long-term note payable, $61,000.
g. Received cash for issuance of common stock, $3,900.
h. Paid cash dividends, $38,100.
i. Paid short-term note payable by issuing common stock, $4,700.

Required

1. Prepare the statement of cash flows of Paper Clips, Inc., for the year ended June 30, 19X7, using the *indirect* method to report operating activities. Also prepare the accompanying schedule of noncash investing and financing activities. All current accounts except short-term notes payable result from operating transactions.
2. Prepare a supplementary schedule showing cash flows from operations by the *direct* method. The income statement reports the following: sales, $237,300; interest revenue, $10,600; cost of goods sold, $82,800; salary

expense, $38,800; other operating expenses, $37,200; depreciation expense, $10,200; income tax expense, $9,900; loss on sale of land, $6,700; interest expense, $6,100.

(Group B)

Problem 18-1B *Using cash-flow information to evaluate performance* *(L.O. 1)*

Top managers of Leadership Dynamics, Inc., are reviewing company performance for 19X4. The income statement reports a 12 percent increase in net income, the fifth consecutive year with an income increase above 10 percent. The income statement includes a nonrecurring loss without which net income would have increased by 16 percent. The balance sheet shows modest increases in assets, liabilities, and stockholders' equity. The assets posting the largest increases are plant and equipment because the company is halfway through a five-year expansion program. No other assets and no liabilities are increasing dramatically. A summarized version of the cash flow statement reports the following:

Net cash inflow from operating activities	$120,000
Net cash outflow from investing activities . . .	(90,000)
Net cash inflow from financing activities	10,000
Increase in cash during 19X4	$ 40,000

Required

Write a memo to give top managers of Leadership Dynamics your assessment of 19X4 and your outlook for the future. Focus on the information content of the cash flow data.

Problem 18-2B *Preparing the statement of cash flows—direct method* *(L.O. 1, 3)*

Oakland Bay Corporation accountants have developed the following data from the company's accounting records for the year ended July 31, 19X9:

1. Proceeds from issuance of short-term debt, $44,100
2. Payments of long-term debt, $18,800
3. Proceeds from sale of plant assets, $49,700, including $10,600 gain
4. Interest revenue, $12,100
5. Cash receipt of dividend revenue on stock investments, $5,700
6. Payments to suppliers, $683,300
7. Interest expense and payments, $37,800
8. Salary expense, $105,300
9. Cash payments to purchase plant assets, $181,000
10. Cost of goods sold, $481,100
11. Collection of interest revenue, $11,700
12. Acquisition of equipment by issuing short-term note payable, $35,500
13. Payments of salaries, $104,000
14. Credit sales, $608,100
15. Loan to another company, $35,000
16. Income tax expense and payments, $56,400
17. Depreciation expense, $27,700
18. Collections on accounts receivable, $673,100
19. Loan collections, $74,400
20. Proceeds from sale of investments, $34,700, including $3,800 loss
21. Payment of long-term debt by issuing preferred stock, $107,300
22. Amortization expense, $23,900
23. Cash sales, $146,000

24. Proceeds from issuance of common stock, $116,900
25. Payment of cash dividends, $50,500
26. Cash balance: July 31, 19X8—$53,800
                     July 31, 19X9—$?

Required

Prepare Oakland Bay Corporation's statement of cash flows for the year ended July 31, 19X9. Follow the format of Exhibit 18-1, but do *not* show amounts in thousands. Include an accompanying schedule of noncash investing and financing activities. Evaluate 19X9 from a cash-flow standpoint. Give your reasons.

Problem 18-3B *Preparing the statement of cash flows—direct method* **(L.O. 2, 3, 4)**

Net cash inflow from operations $99,400

The 19X3 comparative balance sheet and income statement of Gold Imari, Inc., follow:

Comparative Balance Sheet

	19X3	19X2	Increase (Decrease)
Current assets:			
Cash and cash equivalents	$ 37,500	$ 15,600	$ 21,900
Accounts receivable	41,500	43,100	(1,600)
Interest receivable	600	900	(300)
Inventories	94,300	89,900	4,400
Prepaid expenses	1,700	2,200	(500)
Plant assets:			
Land	35,100	10,000	25,100
Equipment, net	100,900	93,700	7,200
Total assets	$311,600	$255,400	$ 56,200
Current liabilities:			
Accounts payable	$ 16,400	$ 17,900	$ (1,500)
Interest payable	6,300	6,700	(400)
Salary payable	2,100	1,400	700
Other accrued liabilities	18,100	18,700	(600)
Income tax payable	6,300	3,800	2,500
Long-term liabilities:			
Notes payable	55,000	65,000	(10,000)
Stockholders' equity:			
Common stock, no-par	131,100	122,300	8,800
Retained earnings	76,300	19,600	56,700
Total liabilities and stockholders' equity	$311,600	$255,400	$ 56,200

Income Statement for 19X3

Revenues:		
Sales revenue		$461,800
Interest revenue		11,700
Total revenues		473,500
Expenses:		
Cost of goods sold	$205,200	
Salary expense	76,400	
Depreciation expense	15,300	
Other operating expense	49,700	
Interest expense	24,600	
Income tax expense	16,900	
Total expenses		388,100
Net income		$ 85,400

Gold Imari had no noncash investing and financing transactions during 19X3. During the year there were no sales of land or equipment, no issuances of notes payable, no retirements of stock, and no treasury stock transactions.

Required

Prepare the 19X3 statement of cash flows, formatting operating activities by the direct method.

Net cash inflow from operations $99,400

Problem 18-4B   *Preparing the statement of cash flows—indirect method* (L.O. 2,3,5)

Required

Using the Gold Imari data from the preceding problem, prepare the 19X3 statement of cash flows by the indirect method. If your instructor also assigned Problem 18-3B, prepare only the operating activities section.

Net cash inflow from operations $126,000

Problem 18-5B   *Preparing the statement of cash flows—indirect method* (L.O. 2,5)

Accountants for Creve Coeur Manufacturing have assembled the following data for the year ended December 31, 19X4:

	December 31,	
	19X4	**19X3**
Current accounts (all result from operations):		
Current assets:		
Cash and cash equivalents	$30,600	$34,800
Accounts receivable	70,100	73,700
Inventories	90,600	96,500
Prepaid expenses	3,200	2,100
Current liabilities:		
Notes payable (for inventory purchases)	$36,300	$36,800
Accounts payable	72,100	67,500
Income tax payable............	5,900	6,800
Accrued liabilities	28,300	23,200

Transaction data for 19X4:

Acquisition of long-term investment	$ 44,800	Sale of long-term investment	$12,200
Acquisition of building by issuing long-term note payable	162,000	Amortization expense	1,100
		Payment of long-term debt	47,800
		Gain on sale of investment	3,500
Stock dividends	12,600	Payment of cash dividends	48,300
Collection of loan	10,300	Issuance of long-term debt to borrow cash	21,000
Depreciation expense	19,200		
Acquisition of equipment .	69,000	Net income	92,500
Payment of long-term debt by issuing common stock	89,400	Issuance of preferred stock for cash	36,200

Required

Prepare Creve Coeur Manufacturing's statement of cash flows, using the *indirect* method to report operating activities. Include an accompanying schedule of noncash investing and financing activities.

Problem 18-6B *Preparing the statement of cash flows—indirect method* (L.0. 2, 5)

Net cash inflow from operations $40,500

The comparative balance sheet of Gold's Gym, Inc., at December 31, 19X5, reported the following:

	December 31,	
	19X5	**19X4**
Current assets:		
Cash and cash equivalents	$10,600	$ 2,500
Accounts receivable	28,600	29,300
Inventories	51,600	53,000
Prepaid expenses	4,200	3,700
Current liabilities:		
Notes payable		
(for inventory purchases)	$ 9,200	$ -0-
Accounts payable	21,900	28,000
Accrued liabilities	14,300	16,800
Income tax payable............	11,000	14,300

Gold's transactions during 19X5 included the following:

Retirement of bonds payable by issuing common stock	$40,000	Sale of long-term investment	$ 6,000
		Depreciation expense	15,000
Amortization expense	5,000	Cash acquisition of	
Payment of cash dividends	17,000	building	104,000
Cash acquisition of		Net income	21,600
equipment.............	55,000	Issuance of common stock	
Issuance of long-term note		for cash	105,600
payable to borrow cash .	32,000	Stock dividend	13,000

Required

Prepare Gold's Gym's statement of cash flows for the year ended December 31, 19X5. Use the *indirect* method to report cash flows from operating activities. Report noncash investing and financing activities in an accompanying schedule. All current account balances result from operating transactions.

Problem 18-7B *Preparing the statement of cash flows—direct and indirect methods* (L.0. 3, 5)

Net cash inflow from operations $37,200

To prepare the statement of cash flows, accountants for Republic Publishing Company have summarized 19X8 activity in two accounts as follows:

Cash

Beginning balance	. 87,100	Payments of operating expenses	46,100
Issuance of common stock	34,600	Payment of long-term	
Receipts of dividends	1,900	debt.................................	78,900
Collection of loan	18,500	Purchase of treasury stock	10,400
Sale of investments	9,900	Payment of income tax	8,000
Receipts of interest....................	12,200	Payments on accounts	
Collections from		payable............................	101,600
customers	268,100	Payments of dividends	1,800
Sale of treasury stock	26,200	Payments of salaries	
		and wages	67,500
		Payments of interest	21,800
		Purchase of equipment	79,900
Ending balance	42,500		

Common Stock

Beginning balance	103,500
Issuance for cash	34,600
Issuance to acquire land	62,100
Issuance to retire long-term debt	21,100
Ending balance	221,300

Required

1. Prepare Republic's statement of cash flows for the year ended December 31, 19X8, using the *direct* method to report operating activities. Also prepare the accompanying schedule of noncash investing and financing activities.

Republic's 19X8 income statement and selected balance sheet data follow.

Republic Publishing Company
Income Statement
For the Year Ended December 31, 19X8

Revenues and gains:		
Sales revenue....................		$251,800
Interest revenue		12,200
Dividend revenue................		1,900
Gain on sale of investments......		700
Total revenues and gains		266,600
Expenses:		
Cost of goods sold	$103,600	
Salary and wage expense	66,800	
Depreciation expense............	10,900	
Other operating expense.........	44,700	
Interest expense	24,100	
Income tax expense	2,600	
Total expenses		252,700
Net income........................		$ 13,900

Republic Publishing Company
Balance Sheet Data

	Increase (Decrease)
Current assets:	
Cash and cash equivalents.................	$?
Accounts receivable.....................	(16,300)
Inventories.............................	5,700
Prepaid expenses	(1,900)
Current liabilities:	
Accounts payable........................	$ 7,700
Interest payable	2,300
Salary payable..........................	(700)
Other accrued liabilities	(3,300)
Income tax payable	(5,400)

Required

2. Use these data to prepare a supplementary schedule showing cash flows from operating activities by the *indirect* method. All activity in the current accounts results from operations.

Problem 18-8B *Preparing the statement of cash flows—indirect and direct methods* (L.O. 3, 4, 5)

Net cash inflow from operations $88,400

Longenecker-Scott Corporation's comparative balance sheet at September 30, 19X4, included the following balances:

Longenecker-Scott Corporation
Partial Balance Sheet
September 30, 19X4 and 19X3

	19X4	19X3	Increase (Decrease)
Current assets:			
Cash..................................	$ 69,700	$ 17,600	$ 52,100
Accounts receivable	41,900	44,000	(2,100)
Interest receivable	4,100	2,800	1,300
Inventories	121,700	116,900	4,800
Prepaid expenses	8,600	9,300	(700)
Current liabilities:			
Notes payable, short-term	$ 22,000	$ -0-	$ 22,000
Accounts payable	61,800	70,300	(8,500)
Income tax payable....................	21,800	24,600	(2,800)
Accrued liabilities	17,900	29,100	(11,200)
Interest payable......................	4,500	3,200	1,300
Salary payable	1,500	1,100	400

Transaction data for the year ended September 30, 19X4:

a. Net income, $114,900.
b. Depreciation expense on equipment, $8,500.
c. Acquired long-term investments, $37,300.
d. Sold land for $38,100, including $10,900 gain.
e. Acquired equipment by issuing long-term note payable,$26,300.
f. Paid long-term note payable, $24,700.
g. Received cash of $51,900 for issuance of common stock.
h. Paid cash dividends, $64,300.
i. Acquired equipment by issuing short-term note payable, $22,000.

Required

1. Prepare Longenecker-Scott's statement of cash flows for the year ended September 30, 19X4, using the *indirect* method to report operating activities. Also prepare the accompanying schedule of noncash investing and financing activities. All current accounts except short-term notes payable result from operating transactions.

2. Prepare a supplementary schedule showing cash flows from operations by the *direct* method. The income statement reports the following: sales, $391,600; gain on sale of land, $10,900; interest revenue, $7,300; cost of goods sold, $161,500; salary expense, $63,400; other operating expenses, $29,600; income tax expense, $18,400; interest expense, $13,500; depreciation expense, $8,500.

Extending Your Knowledge

Decision Problems

1. Using the Statement of Cash Flows to Evaluate a Company's Operations (L.O. 1)

The statement of changes in financial position, forerunner of the statement of cash flows, included information in only two categories: sources of funds and uses of funds. *Funds* were usually defined as working capital (current assets minus current liabilities). The earlier statement permitted the information to report changes in working capital while today's statement of cash flows reports information about flows in cash and cash equivalents.

Required

a. Explain why you think the present day statement of cash flows, with its disclosure of the three different kinds of activities, is or is not an improvement over the earlier statement format that showed only sources and uses of funds.
b. Is information about cash flows more informative to users than information about working capital flows?
c. Briefly explain why comparative balance sheets and a statement of cash flows are more informative than just comparative balance sheets.

2. Preparing and Using the Statement of Cash Flows to Evaluate Operations (L.O. 4, 5)

The 19X6 comparative income statement and the 19X6 comparative balance sheet of Towers & Foster, Inc., have just been distributed at a meeting of the company's board of directors.

Towers & Foster, Inc. Comparative Income Statement Years Ended December 31, 19X6 and 19X5 (amounts in thousands)		
	19X6	**19X5**
Revenues and gains:		
Sales revenue	$484	$310
Gain on sale of equipment (sale price, $33)	—	18
Totals	$484	$328
Expenses and losses:		
Cost of goods sold	$221	$162
Salary expense	48	28
Depreciation expense	46	22
Interest expense	13	20
Amortization expense on patent	11	11
Loss on sale of land (sale price, $61)	—	35
Totals	339	278
Net income	$145	$ 50

Towers & Foster, Inc.
Comparative Balance Sheet
December 31, 19X6 and 19X5
(amounts in thousands)

Assets	19X6	19X5
Cash	$ 23	$ 63
Accounts receivable, net	72	61
Inventories	194	181
Long-term investments	31	-0-
Property, plant, and equipment	401	259
Accumulated depreciation	(244)	(198)
Patents	177	188
Totals	$654	$554

Liabilities and Owners' Equity	19X6	19X5
Notes payable, short-term (for general borrowing)	$ 32	$101
Accounts payable	63	56
Accrued liabilities	12	17
Notes payable, long-term	147	163
Common stock, no-par	139	61
Retained earnings	261	156
Totals	$654	$554

In discussing the company's results of operations and year-end financial position, the members of the board of directors raise a fundamental question: Why is the cash balance so low? This question is especially troublesome to the board members because 19X6 showed record profits. As the controller of the company, you must answer the question.

Required

1. Prepare a statement of cash flows for 19X6 in the format that best shows the relationship between net income and operating cash flow. The company sold no plant assets or long-term investments and issued no notes payable during 19X6. The changes in all current accounts except short-term notes payable arose from operations. There were *no* noncash investing and financing transactions during the year. Show all amounts in thousands.

2. Answer the board members' question: Why is the cash balance so low? In explaining the business's cash flows, identify two significant cash receipts that occurred during 19X5 but not in 19X6. Also point out the two largest cash disbursements during 19X6.

3. Considering net income and the company's cash flows during 19X6, was it a good year or a bad year? Give your reasons.

Ethical Issue

FASB Statement No. 95 requires companies to report the statement of cash flows. Prior to 1988, companies disclosed similar information in the statement of changes in financial position (SCFP). The SCFP started with net income and made certain adjustments similar to the indirect method for reporting cash flows from operating activities.

Statement No. 95 states the FASB's preference for the direct method of reporting cash flows from operating activities. In public hearings, however, companies have argued that it would be expensive to assemble the data required by the direct method. Therefore, *FASB Statement No. 95* permits the indirect method. Most companies follow the indirect-method format.

Required

1. Which method of reporting cash flows from operating activities is easier for you to understand—the direct method (page 812) or the indirect method (page 827)? Give your reason.
2. Consider the computations of operating cash flows outlined on pages 819–822. Do the direct-method computations require many new data? Do the computations appear to be as expensive as companies have claimed?
3. Why do you think companies have resisted reporting operating cash flows by the direct method? Is this resistance in any way unethical? Give your reasons.

Financial Statement Problems

2. a. Collections $11,021.9 million

   b. Payments to employees $802.9 million

1. Using the Statement of Cash Flows   (L.O. 1, 2, 3, 4, 5)

The Goodyear Tire & Rubber Company statement of cash flows appears in Appendix C. Use this statement along with the company's other financial statements to answer the following questions.

1. By which method does Goodyear report net cash flows from *operating* activities? How can you tell?
2. Suppose Goodyear reported net cash flows from operating activities by the direct method. Compute these amounts for 1990:
   a. Collections from customers.
   b. Payments to employees. Assume Salary Expense, Wage Expense, and other payroll expenses totaled $850.0 million for the year.
   c. Payments for income tax.
3. Evaluate 1990 in terms of net income, cash flows, balance sheet position, and overall results. Be specific.

No check figure

2. Computing Cash Flow Amounts and Using Cash Flow Data for Analysis (L.O. 1, 2, 3, 4, 5)

Obtain the annual report of an actual company of your choosing. Annual reports are available in various forms including the original document in hard copy, microfiche, and computerized data bases such as that provided by Disclosure, Inc.

Answer these questions about the company. Concentrate on the current year in the annual report you select.

1. By which method does the company report net cash flows from *operating activities?* How can you tell?
2. Suppose the company reported net cash flows from operating activities by the direct method. Compute these amounts for the current year:
   a. Collections from customers.
   b. Payments to employees. Assume that the sum of Salary Expense, Wage Expense, and other payroll expenses for the current year make up 60 percent of Selling, General, and Administrative Expenses (or expense of similar title).
   c. Payments for income tax.
3. Evaluate the current year in terms of net income (or net loss), cash flows, balance sheet position, and overall results. Be specific.

Appendix:

The Work-Sheet Approach to Preparing the Statement of Cash Flows

The main body of the chapter discusses the use of the statement of cash flows in decision making and shows how to prepare the statement using T-accounts. The T-account approach works well as a learning device, especially for simple situations. In actual practice, however, most companies face complex situations. In these cases, a work sheet can help accountants prepare the statement of cash flows. This appendix shows how to prepare the statement of cash flows using a specially designed work sheet.

The basic task in preparing the statement of cash flows is to account for all the cash effects of transactions that took the business from its beginning financial position to its ending financial position. Like the T-account approach, the work sheet approach helps the accountant identify the cash effects of all transactions of the period. The work sheet starts with the beginning balance sheet and concludes with the ending balance sheet. Two middle columns— one for debit amounts and the other for credit amounts—complete the work sheet. These columns, labeled Transaction Analysis, contain the data for the statement of cash flows. Exhibit 18A-1 presents the basic framework of the work sheet. Accountants can prepare the statement directly from the lower part of the work sheet (Panel B in Exhibit 18A-1). The advantage of the work sheet approach is that it organizes in one place all relevant data for the statement's preparation. Exhibit 18A-1 and the other exhibits in this appendix are based on the Anchor Coporation data in the chapter.

The work sheet can be used with either the direct method or the indirect method for operating activities. As with the T-account approach, cash flows from investing activities and cash flows from financing activities are unaffected by the method used for operating activities.

EXHIBIT 18A-1

Anchor Corporation
Work Sheet for Statement of Cash Flows
For the Year Ended December 31, 19X2

	Balances Dec. 31, 19X1	Transaction Debit	Analysis Credit	Balances Dec. 31, 19X2
Panel A—Account Titles				
Cash				
Accounts receivable ..				
Retained earnings				
Panel B—Statement of Cash Flows				
Cash flows from operating activities: ...				
Cash flows from investing activities: ...				
Cash flows from financing activities: ...				
Net increase (decrease) in cash				

Preparing the Work Sheet—Direct Method for Operating Activities

The direct method separates operating activities into cash receipts and cash payments. Exhibit 18A-2 is the work sheet for preparing the statement of cash flows by the direct method. The work sheet can be prepared by following these steps:

Step 1. In Panel A, insert the beginning and ending balances for Cash, Accounts Receivable, and all other balance sheet accounts through Retained Earnings. The amounts are taken directly from the beginning and ending balance sheets in Exhibit 18-4, page 819.

Step 2. In Panel B, lay out the framework of the statement of cash flows as shown in Exhibit 18A-1—that is, enter the headings for cash flows from operating activities, investing activities, and financing activities. Exhibit 18A-2 is based on the direct method and splits operating activities into Receipts and Payments.

Step 3. At the bottom of the work sheet, write Net Increase in Cash or Net Decrease in Cash, as the case may be. This final amount on the work sheet is the difference between ending cash and beginning cash, as reported on the balance sheet. Fundamentally, the statement of cash flows is designed to explain *why* this change in cash occurred during the period.

Step 4. Analyze the period's transactions in the middle columns of the work sheet. Transaction analysis is the most challenging part of preparing the work sheet. The remainder of this appendix explains this crucial step.

Step 5. Prepare the statement of cash flows directly from Panel B of the work sheet.

Transaction Analysis on the Work Sheet

For your convenience, we repeat the Anchor Corporation transaction data from page 813 of the text. Transactions with cash effects are denoted by an asterisk.

Operating Activities:

- a. Sales on credit, $284,000
- * b. Collections from customers, $271,000
- c. Interest revenue earned, $12,000
- * d. Collection of interest receivable, $10,000
- * e. Cash receipt of dividend revenue, $9,000
- f. Cost of goods sold, $150,000
- g. Purchases of inventory on credit, $147,000
- * h. Payments to suppliers, $133,000
- i. Salary and wage expense, $56,000
- * j. Payments of salaries and wages, $58,000
- k. Depreciation expense, $18,000
- l. Other operating expense, $17,000
- * m. Interest expense and payments, $16,000
- * n. Income tax expense and payments, $15,000

Investing Activities:

* o. Cash payments to acquire plant assets, $306,000

* p. Loan to another company, $11,000

* q. Proceeds from sale of plant assets, $62,000, including $8,000 gain

Financing Activities:

* r. Proceeds from issuance of common stock, $101,000

* s. Proceeds from issuance of long-term debt, $94,000

* t. Payments of long-term debt, $11,000

* u. Declaration and payment of cash dividends, $17,000

Operating Activities. The transaction analysis on the work sheet appears in the form of journal entries. Observe that only balance sheet accounts appear on the work sheet. There are no income statement accounts. Therefore, revenue transactions are entered on the work sheet as credits to Retained Earnings. For example, in transaction *a*, sales on account are entered on the work sheet by debiting Accounts Receivable and crediting Retained Earnings. Cash is neither debited nor credited because credit sales do not affect cash. Nevertheless, this transaction and all other transactions should be entered on the work sheet in order to identify all the cash effects of the period's transactions. In transaction *c*, the earning of interest revenue is entered by debiting Interest Receivable and crediting Retained Earnings.

The revenue transactions that generate cash are also recorded by crediting Retained Earnings. For example, transaction *e* is a cash receipt of dividend revenue. The work sheet entry credits Retained Earnings and debits Dividends Received as a cash receipt from operating activities. Transaction *d* is a collection of interest receivable. The work sheet entry debits Interest Received—a cash receipt from operating activities—and credits Interest Receivable.

Expense transactions are entered on the work sheet as debits to Retained Earnings. In transaction *f*, cost of goods sold is entered by debiting Retained Earnings and crediting Inventory. Transaction *i* for salary and wage expense is entered by debiting Retained Earnings and crediting Salary and Wage Payable. In transaction *k*, depreciation is entered by debiting Retained Earnings and crediting Plant Assets, Net (this work sheet uses no Accumulated Depreciation account). In transaction *l*, other operating expense is entered by debiting Retained Earnings and crediting Accrued Liabilities. These transactions should be entered on the work sheet even though they have no direct effect on cash.

Transaction *m* is a cash payment of interest expense. The work sheet entry debits Retained Earnings and credits Payments for Interest under operating activities. Transaction *n* is a cash payment for income tax.

Transaction *h* deserves special emphasis. The Payment to Suppliers of $133,000 includes three individual amounts: payments of accounts payable, $113,000; payments of accrued liabilities, $19,000; and payments of prepaid expenses, $1,000. How were these three amounts computed? These amounts are the differences needed to reconcile each account's beginning balance to its ending balance. For example, Prepaid Expenses increased from a beginning balance of $7,000 to an ending amount of $8,000. This increase must occur through a cash payment of $1,000 (transaction *h3*). Payments of prepaid expenses are labeled as Payments to Suppliers on the statement of cash flows when operating activities are reported by the direct method. The $113,000 debit to Accounts Payable (transaction *h1*) is computed as the amount needed to complete the reconciliation from the beginning balance ($57,000) to the ending amount ($91,000), taking into consideration the $147,000 credit purchase of inventory in transaction *g* ($57,000 + $147,000 − $91,000 = $113,000). The

Anchor Corporation
Work Sheet for Statement of Cash Flows (Direct Method)
For the Year Ended December 31, 19X2

Panel A—Account Titles	Balances Dec. 31, 19X1	(Amounts in thousands) Transaction Analysis Debit	(Amounts in thousands) Transaction Analysis Credit	Balances Dec. 31, 19X2
Cash	42		(v) 20	22
Accounts receivable	80	(a) 284	(b) 271	93
Interest receivable	1	(c) 12	(d) 10	3
Inventory	138	(g) 147	(f) 150	135
Prepaid expenses	7	(h3) 1		8
Long-term receivable from another company	—	(p) 11		11
Plant assets, net	219	(o) 306	(k) 18	
			(q) 54	453
Totals	487			725
Accounts payable	57	(h1) 113	(g) 147	91
Salary and wage payable	6	(j) 58	(i) 56	4
Accrued liabilities	3	(h2) 19	(l) 17	1
Long-term debt	77	(t) 11	(s) 94	160
Common stock	258		(r) 101	359
Retained earnings	86	(f) 150	(a) 284	110
		(l) 17	(c) 12	
		(i) 56	(e) 9	
		(k) 18	(q) 8	
		(m) 16		
		(n) 15		
		(u) 17		
Totals	487	1,251	1,251	725

Panel B—Statement of Cash Flows		Debit	Credit	
Cash flows from operating activites:				
Receipts:				
Collections from customers		(b) 271		
Interest received		(d) 10		
Dividends received		(e) 9		
Payments:				
To suppliers			(h1) 113	
			(h2) 19	
			(h3) 1	
To employees			(j) 58	
For interest			(m) 16	
For income tax			(n) 15	
Cash flows from investing activities:				
Acquisition of plant assets			(o) 306	
Proceeds from sale of plant assets		(q) 62		
Loan to another company			(p) 11	
Cash flows from financing activities:				
Proceeds from issuance of common stock		(r) 101		
Proceeds from issuance of long-term debt		(s) 94		
Payment of long-term debt			(t) 11	
Payment of dividends			(u) 17	
		547	567	
Net decrease in cash		(v) 20		
Totals		567	567	

$19,000 debit to Accrued Liabilities (transaction *h2*) is the amount needed to reconcile the beginning balance to the ending balance after considering the $17,000 credit amount in transaction *l*.

Investing Activities.   The first investing activity listed in Panel B of the work sheet is transaction *o*, the $306,000 cash payment to acquire plant assets. This transaction is entered on the work sheet by debiting Plant Assets, Net and crediting Acquisition of Plant Assets under cash flows from operating activities. Transaction *q* is a cash receipt from an investing activity. The cash proceeds of $62,000 from sale of plant assets are entered as a cash receipt under investing activities. The $8,000 gain is credited to Retained Earnings, with the remaining $54,000—the asset's book value—credited to Plant Assets, Net. The last investing transaction (transaction *p*) is a loan to another company, entered on the work sheet by debiting Long-term Receivable from Another Company and crediting Loan to Another Company under investing activities.

Financing Activities.   The issuance of common stock for $101,000 cash (transaction *r*) is entered on the work sheet by debiting Proceeds from Issuance of Common Stock under financing activities and crediting Common Stock. The $94,000 issuance of long-term debt (transaction *s*) is entered in a similar manner but with a credit to Long-term Debt. The payment of long-term debt (transaction *t*) debits Long-term Debt and credits Payment of Long-term Debt under financing activities. The payment of dividends (transaction *u*) debits Retained Earnings and credits Payment of Dividends as a financing cash payment.

Net Increase (Decrease) in Cash.   The net increase or net decrease in cash for the period is the balancing amount needed to equate the total debits and total credits ($567,000) on the statement of cash flows. In Exhibit 18A-2, Anchor Corporation experienced a $20,000 decrease in cash. This amount is entered as a credit to Cash (transaction *v*) at the top of the work sheet and a debit to Net Decrease in Cash at the bottom. Totaling the columns completes the work sheet.

Preparing the Statement of Cash Flows from the Work Sheet

To prepare the statement of cash flows, which appears as Exhibit 18-1, page 810 of the text, the accountant has only to rewrite Panel B of the work sheet and add subtotals for the three categories of activities. In Exhibit 18A-2, net cash *inflows* from operating activities total $68,000 [receipts of $290,000 ($271,000 + $10,000 + $9,000) minus payments of $222,000 ($113,000 + $19,000 + $1,000 + $58,000 + $16,000 + $15,000)]. Net cash *outflows* from investing activities are $255,000 ($306,000 + $11,000 − $62,000). Net cash *inflows* from financing activities equal $167,000 ($101,000 + $94,000 − $11,000 − $17,000). Altogether, these three subtotals explain why cash decreased by $20,000 ($68,000 − $255,000 + $167,000 = −$20,000).

Preparing the Work Sheet—Indirect Method for Operating Activities

The indirect method shows the reconciliation from net income to net cash inflow (or net cash outflow) from operating activities. Exhibit 18A-3 is the work sheet for preparing the statement of cash flows by the indirect method.

Anchor Corporation
Work Sheet for Statement of Cash Flows (Indirect Method)
For the Year Ended December 31, 19X2

Panel A—Account Titles	Balances Dec. 31, 19X1	(Amounts in thousands) Transaction Analysis Debit		Credit		Balances Dec. 31, 19X2
Cash	42			(q)	20	22
Accounts receivable	80	(d)	13			93
Interest receivable	1	(e)	2			3
Inventory	138			(f)	3	135
Prepaid expenses	7	(g)	1			8
Long-term receivable from another company	—	(l)	11			11
Plant assets, net	219	(k)	306	(b)	18	
				(c)	54	453
Totals	487					725
Accounts payable	57			(h)	34	91
Salary and wage payable	6	(i)	2			4
Accrued liabilities	3	(j)	2			1
Long-term debt	77	(o)	11	(n)	94	160
Common stock	258			(m)	101	359
Retained earnings	86	(p)	17	(a)	41	110
Totals	487		365		365	725

Panel B—Statement of Cash Flows

		Debit		Credit		
Cash flows from operating activities:						
Net income		(a)	41			
Add (subtract) items that affect net income and cash flow differently:						
Depreciation		(b)	18			
Gain on sale of plant assets				(c)	8	
Increase in accounts receivable				(d)	13	
Increase in interest receivable				(e)	2	
Decrease in inventory		(f)	3			
Increase in prepaid expenses				(g)	1	
Increase in accounts payable		(h)	34			
Decrease in salary and wage payable				(i)	2	
Decrease in accrued liabilities				(j)	2	
Cash flows from investing activities:						
Acquisition of plant assets				(k)	306	
Proceeds from sale of plant assets		(c)	62			
Loan to another company				(l)	11	
Cash flows from financing activities:						
Proceeds from issuance of common stock		(m)	101			
Proceeds from issuance of long-term debt		(n)	94			
Payment of long-term debt				(o)	11	
Payment of dividends				(p)	17	
			353		373	
Net decrease in cash		(q)	20			
Totals			373		373	

The steps in completing the work sheet using the indirect method are the same as those taken using the direct method. However, the data for the operating cash flows come from different sources. Net income, depreciation, depletion and amortization, and gains and losses on disposals of plant assets come from the income statement. The changes in noncash current asset accounts (Receivables, Inventory, and Prepaid Expenses for Anchor Corporation) and the current liability accounts (Accounts Payable, Salary and Wage Payable, and Accrued Liabilities) are taken directly from the comparative balance sheet.

The analysis of investing activities and financing activities uses the information presented on page 813 and given on page 859 of this appendix. As mentioned previously, there is no difference for investing activities or financing activities between the direct-method work sheet and the indirect-method work sheet. Therefore, the analysis that follows focuses on cash flows from operating activities. The Anchor Corporation data come from the income statement (Exhibit 18-3, page 816) and the comparative balance sheet (Exhibit 18-4, page 819).

Transaction Analysis Under the Indirect Method

Net income (transaction *a*) is the first operating cash inflow. Net income is entered on the work sheet as a debit to Net Income under cash flows from operating activities and a credit to Retained Earnings. Next come the additions to, and subtractions from, net income, starting with depreciation (transaction *b*), which is debited to Depreciation on the work sheet and credited to Plant Assets, Net. Transaction *c* is the sale of plant assets. The $8,000 gain on the sale is entered as a credit to Gain on Sale of Plant Assets under operating cash flows—a subtraction from net income. This credit removes the $8,000 amount of the gain from cash flow from operations because the cash proceeds from the sale were not $8,000. The cash proceeds were $62,000, so this amount is entered on the work sheet as a debit under investing activities. To complete entry *c*, the plant assets' book value of $54,000 ($62,000 − $8,000) is credited to the Plant Assets, Net account.

Entries *d* through *j* reconcile net income to cash flows from operations for increases and decreases in the current assets other than Cash and for increases and decreases in the current liabilities. Entry *d* debits Accounts Receivable for its $13,000 increase during the year. This decrease in cash flows is credited to Increase in Accounts Receivable under operating cash flows. Entries *e* and *g* are similar for Interest Receivable and Prepaid Expenses.

During the year, Inventory decreased by $3,000. This increase in cash is credited to Inventory in work sheet entry *f*, with the debit to Decrease in Inventory under operating activities.

Entry *h* records the $34,000 increase in Accounts Payable by crediting this account. The resulting increase in cash is debited to Increase in Accounts Payable under operating cash flows. Entry *i* debits Salary and Wage Payable for its $2,000 decrease, with the offsetting credit to Decrease in Salary and Wage Payable. Entry *j* for Accrued Liabilities is similar.

Do not be confused by the different keying of investing transactions and financing transactions in Exhibits 18A-2 and 18A-3. Except for the letters used to key transactions, the entries are identical. For example, the $306,000 acquisition of plant assets is transaction *o* in Exhibit 18A-2 and transaction *k* in Exhibit 18A-3. In each exhibit, we maintain a continuous listing of transactions starting with the letter *a*. The two exhibits simply have different keyed letters because of the number of transactions.

The final item in Exhibit 18A-3 is the Net Decrease in Cash—transaction *q* on the work sheet—a credit to Cash and a debit to Net Decrease in Cash, exactly as in Exhibit 18A-2.

To prepare the statement of cash flows from the work sheet, the accountant merely rewrites Panel B of the statement, adding subtotals for the three categories of activities. In Exhibit 18A-3, net cash inflow from operating activities is $68,000 ($41,000 + $18,000 + $3,000 + $34,000 − $8,000 − $13,000 − $2,000 − $1,000 − $2,000 − $2,000). Of course, this is the same amount of net cash inflow from operating activities computed under the direct method from Exhibit 18A-2. The indirect-method statement of cash flows appears in Exhibit 18-6, page 828 of the text.

Noncash Investing and Financing Activities on the Work Sheet. Noncash investing and financing activities can also be analyzed on the work sheet. Because this type of transaction includes both an investing activity and a financing activity, it requires two work sheet entries. For example, suppose Anchor Corporation purchased a building by issuing common stock of $320,000. Exhibit 18A-4 illustrates the transaction analysis of this noncash investing and financing activity. Observe that Cash is unaffected.

Work sheet entry *t1* records the purchase of the building, and entry *t2* records the issuance of the stock. The order of these entries is unimportant.

EXHIBIT 18A-4 *Noncash Investing and Financing Activities on the Work Sheet*

Anchor Corporation
Work Sheet for Statement of Cash Flows
For the Year Ended December 31, 19X2

	Balances Dec. 31, 19X1	Transaction Debit	Analysis Credit	Balances Dec. 31, 19X2
Panel A—Account Titles				
Cash				
Accounts receivable				
Building	650,000	(t1) 320,000		970,000
Common Stock...............	890,000		(t2) 320,000	1,210,000
Retained earnings				
Panel B—Statement of Cash Flows				
Cash flows from operating activities:				
Net increase (decrease) in cash ..				
Noncash investing and financing transactions				
Purchase of building by issuance of common stock		(t2) 320,000	(t1) 320,000	

ASSIGNMENT MATERIAL

Transaction analysis total debits, Panel A $1,555,900

Problem 18A-1 *Preparing the work sheet for the statement of cash flows—direct method*

The 19X3 comparative balance sheet and income statement of Gold Imari, Inc., follow:

Comparative Balance Sheet

	19X3	19X2	Increase (Decrease)
Current assets:			
Cash and cash equivalents	$ 37,500	$ 15,600	$21,900
Accounts receivable	41,500	43,100	(1,600)
Interest receivable	600	900	(300)
Inventories	94,300	89,900	4,400
Prepaid expenses	1,700	2,200	(500)
Plant assets:			
Land	35,100	10,000	25,100
Equipment, net	100,900	93,700	7,200
Total assets	$311,600	$255,400	$56,200
Current liabilities:			
Accounts payable	$ 16,400	$ 17,900	$ (1,500)
Interest payable	6,300	6,700	(400)
Salary payable	2,100	1,400	700
Other accrued liabilities	18,100	18,700	(600)
Income tax payable	6,300	3,800	2,500
Long-term liabilities:			
Notes payable	55,000	65,000	(10,000)
Stockholders' equity:			
Common stock, no-par	131,100	122,300	8,800
Retained earnings	76,300	19,600	56,700
Total liabilities and stockholders' equity	$311,600	$255,400	$56,200

Income Statement for 19X3

Revenues:		
Sales revenue		$461,800
Interest revenue		11,700
Total revenues		473,500
Expenses:		
Cost of goods sold	$205,200	
Salary expense	76,400	
Depreciation expense	15,300	
Other operating expense	49,700	
Interest expense	24,600	
Income tax expense	16,900	
Total expenses		388,100
Net income		$ 85,400

Gold Imari had no noncash investing and financing transactions during 19X3.

Required

Prepare the work sheet for the 19X3 statement of cash flows. Format cash flows from operating activities by the *direct* method.

Problem 18A-2 *Preparing the work sheet for the statement of cash flows—indirect method*

Transaction analysis total debits, Panel A $115,100

Using the Gold Imari, Inc., data from the preceding problem, prepare the work sheet for the 19X3 statement of cash flows. Format cash flows from operating activities by the *indirect* method.

Problem 18A-3 *Preparing the work sheet for the statement of cash flows—indirect method*

Transaction analysis total debits, Panel A $225,300

Longenecker-Scott Corporation's comparative balance sheet at September 30, 19X4, follows.

	19X4	19X3	Increase (Decrease)
Current assets:			
Cash	$ 69,700	$ 17,600	$ 52,100
Accounts receivable	41,900	44,000	(2,100)
Interest receivable	4,100	2,800	1,300
Inventories......................	121,700	116,900	4,800
Prepaid expenses	8,600	9,300	(700)
Long-term investments	55,400	18,100	37,300
Plant assets:			
Land	65,800	93,000	(27,200)
Equipment, net....................	89,500	49,700	39,800
Total assets	$456,700	$351,400	$105,300
Current liabilities:			
Notes payable, short-term	$ 22,000	$ -0-	$ 22,000
Accounts payable	61,800	70,300	(8,500)
Income tax payable	21,800	24,600	(2,800)
Accrued liabilities.................	17,900	29,100	(11,200)
Interest payable	4,500	3,200	1,300
Salary payable....................	1,500	1,100	400
Note payable, long-term..............	62,900	61,300	1,600
Stockholders' equity:			
Common stock	142,100	90,200	51,900
Retained earnings	122,200	71,600	50,600
Total liabilities and stockholders' equity	$456,700	$351,400	$105,300

Transaction data for the year ended September 30, 19X4:

a. Net income, $114,900.

b. Depreciation expense on equipment, $8,500.

c. Acquired long-term investments, $37,300.

d. Sold land for $38,100, including $10,900 gain.

e. Acquired equipment by issuing long-term note payable, $26,300.

f. Paid long-term note payable, $24,700.

g. Received cash of $51,900 for issuance of common stock.

h. Paid cash dividends, $64,300.

i. Acquired equipment by issuing short-term note payable, $22,000.

Required

Prepare Longenecker-Scott's work sheet for the statement of cash flows for the year ended September 30, 19X4, using the *indirect* method to report operating activities. Include on the work sheet the noncash investing and financing activities.

Problem 18A-4 *Preparing the work sheet for the statement of cash flows—direct method*

Transaction analysis total debits, Panel A $1,398,800

Refer to the data of Problem 18A-3.

Required

Prepare Longenecker-Scott's work sheet for the statement of cash flows for the year ended September 30, 19X4, using the *direct* method for operating activities. The income statement reports the following: sales, $391,600; gain on sale of land, $10,900; interest revenue, $7,300; cost of goods sold, $161,500; salary expense, $63,400; other operating expenses, $29,600; income tax expense, $18,400; interest expense, $13,500; depreciation expense, $8,500. Include on the work sheet the noncash investing and financing activities.

Chapter 19

Using Accounting Information to Make Business Decisions

Eugene Lerner is a rumpled, pipe-smoking professor of finance at Northwestern University in Evanston, Ill. He lectures in Thailand, quotes Moses, writes books on investing, and is "closest to heaven" when he hooks a big fish.

Lerner, 58, also fishes for hot stocks, using some mechanical quantitative rules he and fellow professor William Breen, 49, developed at Northwestern. Both men, still full-time professors, are putting their academic research to work. Their company, Disciplined Investment Advisors Inc. [DIA] of Evanston, manages $462 million for 68 clients.

It took DIA a lot of wading through financial databases to develop its system for buying stocks. But now the . . . partners are sitting pretty. The buy signals are generated on a computer, and little human intervention is called for. . . . The basic rule, elicited from a study of stock price behavior over a 15-year period, is as simple as looking for earnings gains. DIA buys . . . stocks whose earnings for the past four quarters are above those of the year-earlier period.

Among the other criteria: a [dividend] yield of at least 1 percent, a return on equity between 5 percent and 50 percent, and a price/earnings [P/E] multiple between 2 and 60. Companies with unusually high returns or low P/Es may look like bargains but are excluded as likely freak situations. . . . Companies that meet these criteria are ranked according to the ratio of price to book value, with the cheapest stocks topping the shopping list. The firm also has a simple sell strategy. When per-share earnings in the most recent four quarters drop 5 percent from the year-earlier period, DIA dumps the stock.

Source: Charles Siler, "Strictly by the Numbers," *Forbes*, November 2, 1987, p. 187.

Point to Stress: Refer to the chapter-opening vignette. How does an investor know which securities to buy? The use of certain key ratios can help make that assessment.

Point to Stress: After mastering this chapter, students should be able to pick up financial statements for a company with which they are not familiar and, by calculating these ratios and performing other analyses, be able to learn many facts about that company.

As this vignette illustrates, sophisticated investors such as Disciplined Investment Advisors rely on accounting information to make business decisions. Creditors and individual investors do, too. Should the bank loan officer lend money to the Joneses? Should the investor buy more stock in Xerox or sell those shares presently owned? People need information to make these decisions. The balance sheet, the income statement, and the statement of cash flows provide a large part of the information that is used for making decisions such as these. In Chapters 1 through 18, we have described the process of accounting and the preparation of the financial statements. We have tried to relate each topic to the real world of business by showing the relevance of the accounting data. In this chapter, we discuss in more detail how to use the information that appears in these statements. (Appendix C features the financial statements of The Goodyear Tire & Rubber Company. You may apply the analytical skills you learn in this chapter to those real-world data.)

Financial Statement Analysis

Financial statement analysis focuses on techniques used by analysts external to the organization, although managers use many of the same methods. These analysts rely on publicly available information. A major source of such information is the annual report. In addition to the financial statements (income statement, balance sheet, and statement of cash flows), annual reports usually contain

Discussion Question: Who is interested in financial statement analysis? ANSWER: Investors, management, creditors, bankers, owners, governmental agencies, etc.

What are some things that they want to learn from financial statements? ANSWER: Solvency, profitability, liquidity, trends over time, and so on.

Where can information be found to use in analyzing a company? ANSWER: Financial statements, tax returns, *Wall Street Journal,* business publications, Dun and Bradstreet reports, SEC reports, and so on.

1. Footnotes to the financial statements
2. A summary of the accounting methods used
3. Management's discussion and analysis of the financial results
4. The auditor's report
5. Comparative financial data for a series of years

Management's discussion and analysis of financial results is especially important. For example, the 1990 annual report of The Boeing Company includes eight pages of top management discussion ranging from company revenues and earnings to the market environment and the company's backlog of unfilled sales orders. Under Market Environment, Boeing managers reveal that in 1990, world airline passenger traffic increased by 7.4 percent. The greatest growth came from routes linked to the Pacific Rim. Management predicted that airline traffic would grow by approximately 5.2 percent annually from 1991 to 2005. The discussion covered bargain air fares, the effects of jet fuel prices on airline profits, and the expectation that one major airline will cease operations. What have these facts and predictions to do with the use of accounting information to make decisions about Boeing? Everything, because they help investors and creditors interpret the financial statements. The balance sheet, income statement, and statement of cash flows are based on historical data. The management discussion offers top management's glimpses into the company's future. Investors and creditors are primarily interested in where the business is headed.

Objective of Financial Statement Analysis

Investors purchase capital stock expecting to receive dividends and an increase in the value of the stock. Creditors make loans with the expectation of receiving interest and principal. Both groups bear the risk that they will not receive their expected returns. They use financial statement analysis to (1) predict the amount of expected returns and (2) assess the risks associated with those returns.

Because creditors generally expect to receive specific fixed amounts and have the first claim on assets, they are most concerned with assessing short-term liquidity and long-term solvency. **Short-term liquidity** is an organization's ability to meet current payments as they become due. **Long-term solvency** is the ability to generate enough cash to pay long-term debts as they mature.

In contrast, investors are more concerned with profitability, dividends, and future security prices. Why? Because dividend payments depend on profitable operations, and stock price appreciation depends on the market's assessment of the company's prospects. Creditors also assess profitability because profitable operations are the prime source of cash to repay loans.

We divide the tools and techniques that the business community uses in evaluating financial statement information into three broad categories: horizontal analysis, vertical analysis, and ratio analysis.

Horizontal Analysis

Many business decisions hinge on whether the numbers—in sales, income, expenses, and so on—are increasing or decreasing over time. Has the sales figure risen from last year? From two years ago? By how many dollars? We may find that the net sales figure has risen by $20,000. This may be interesting, but considered alone it is not very useful for decision making. An analysis of the *percentage change* in the net sales figure over time improves our ability to use the dollar amounts. It is more useful to know that sales have increased by 20 percent than to know that the increase in sales is $20,000.

The study of percentage changes in comparative statements is called **horizontal analysis.** Computing a percentage change in comparative statements requires two steps: (1) Compute the dollar amount of the change from the earlier (base) period to the later period, and (2) divide the dollar amount of change by the base period amount. Horizontal analysis is illustrated as follows:

Teaching Tip: Horizontal analysis often involves a percentage calculated as:

$$\frac{\$ \text{ change}}{\text{base year } \$} = \% \text{ change}$$

It is important to look at both dollar changes and percentage changes together when using horizontal analysis. It is not necessarily bad if a company's earnings are growing at a declining rate. The dollar increase may be the same as or more than the base year. The percentage change may be less because the base is greater each year.

Transparency T19-1

	Year 3	Year 2	Year 1	Increase (Decrease) During Year 3 Amount	%	Increase (Decrease) During Year 2 Amount	%
Sales	$120,000	$100,000	$80,000	$20,000	20%	$20,000	25%
Net income	12,000	8,000	10,000	4,000	50%	(2,000)	(20%)

The increase in sales is $20,000 in both year 3 and year 2. However, the percentage increase in sales differs from year to year because of the change in the base amount. To compute the percentage change for year 2, we divide the amount of increase ($20,000) by the base period amount ($80,000), an increase of 25 percent. For year 3 the dollar amount increases again by $20,000. However, the base period amount for figuring this percentage change is $100,000. Dividing $20,000 by $100,000 computes a percentage increase of only 20 percent during year 3. Observe that net income *decreases* by 20 percent during year 2 and increases by 50 percent during year 3.

Detailed horizontal analyses of a comparative income statement and a comparative balance sheet are shown in the two right-hand columns of Exhibits 19-1 and 19-2. McColpin, Inc., is a small retailer of office furniture.

The comparative income statement in Exhibit 19-1 reveals that net sales increased by 6.8 percent during 19X7 and that the cost of goods sold grew by much less. As a result, gross profit rose by 17.3 percent. Note that general expenses actually decreased, and so the company significantly increased income from operations and net income during 19X7. Our analysis shows that 19X7 was a much better year than 19X6. We see that the growth in income resulted more from slowing the increase in expenses than from boosting sales revenue.

Point to Stress: Arithmetically, you cannot calculate a percentage change if the base year is zero.

No percentage increase is computed for interest revenue because dividing the $4,000 increase by a zero amount would produce a meaningless percentage. Also, we compute no percentage change when a base-year amount is negative. For example, when a company goes from a net loss one year to a profit the next year, we would be dividing a positive number by a negative amount.

(Throughout this chapter, we discuss only some of the elements of the various statements that we present. For example, we mention McColpin's cost of goods sold but not its selling expenses. Understand, however, that the manager of the sales staff—and likely top management also—would examine

OBJECTIVE 1

Perform a horizontal analysis of comparative financial statements

EXHIBIT 19-1   *Comparative Income Statement—Horizontal Analysis*

McColpin, Inc. Comparative Income Statement Years Ended December 31, 19X7 and 19X6				
			Increase (Decrease)	
	19X7	19X6	Amount	Percent
Net sales	$858,000	$803,000	$55,000	6.8%
Cost of goods sold	513,000	509,000	4,000	0.8
Gross profit.................	345,000	294,000	51,000	17.3
Operating expenses:				
Selling expenses	126,000	114,000	12,000	10.5
General expenses	118,000	123,000	(5,000)	(4.1)
Total operating expenses ...	244,000	237,000	7,000	3.0
Income from operations......	101,000	57,000	44,000	77.2
Interest revenue.............	4,000	—	4,000	—
Interest expense.............	24,000	14,000	10,000	71.4
Income before income taxes ..	81,000	43,000	38,000	88.4
Income tax expense	33,000	17,000	16,000	94.1
Net income	$ 48,000	$ 26,000	$22,000	84.6

EXHIBIT 19-2 *Comparative Balance Sheet—Horizontal Analysis*

McColpin, Inc.
Comparative Balance Sheet
December 31, 19X7 and 19X6

			Increase (Decrease)	
Assets	**19X7**	**19X6**	**Amount**	**Percent**
Current assets:				
Cash	$ 29,000	$ 32,000	$ (3,000)	(9.4%)
Accounts receivable, net	114,000	85,000	29,000	34.1
Inventories	113,000	111,000	2,000	1.8
Prepaid expenses...........	6,000	8,000	(2,000)	(25.0)
Total current assets.......	262,000	236,000	26,000	11.0
Long-term investments	18,000	9,000	9,000	100.0
Property, plant, and				
equipment, net	507,000	399,000	108,000	27.1
Total assets	$787,000	$644,000	$143,000	22.2
Liabilities				
Current liabilities:				
Notes payable	$ 42,000	$ 27,000	$ 15,000	55.6
Accounts payable	73,000	68,000	5,000	7.4
Accrued liabilities	27,000	31,000	(4,000)	(12.9)
Total current liabilities	142,000	126,000	16,000	12.7
Long-term debt	289,000	198,000	91,000	46.0
Total liabilities	431,000	324,000	107,000	33.0
Stockholders' Equity				
Common stock, no-par	186,000	186,000	—	0.0
Retained earnings	170,000	134,000	36,000	26.9
Total stockholders' equity .	356,000	320,000	36,000	11.3
Total liabilities and				
stockholders' equity	$787,000	$644,000	$143,000	22.2

the selling expenses in conducting a full analysis of the company's operations.)

The comparative balance sheet in Exhibit 19-2 shows that 19X7 was a year of expansion for the company. Property, plant, and equipment increased from $399,000 to $507,000, a growth rate of 27.1 percent. Total assets increased by 22.2 percent. To help finance this expansion, McColpin borrowed heavily, increasing short-term notes payable by 55.6 percent and long-term debt by 46 percent. The increase in assets was also financed in part by profitable operations, as shown by the 26.9 percent increase in retained earnings.

The sharpest percentage increase on the balance sheet is in long-term investments (100 percent). However, the dollar amounts are small compared with the other balance sheet figures. Note this key point of financial analysis: percentage changes must be evaluated in terms of the item's relative importance to the company as a whole. In this instance, the large percentage increase in long-term investments means little because the company holds such a small amount. The 27.1 percent increase in property, plant, and equipment is more important because their cost represents the largest asset and their use is intended to generate profits for years to come.

Trend Percentages

Point to Stress: Trend percentages indicate the change between a base year and any later year. The percentage is calculated:

$$\frac{\text{Any year \$}}{\text{Base year \$}}$$

Trend percentages are a form of horizontal analysis. Trends are important indicators of the direction a business is taking. How have sales changed over a five-year period? What trend does gross profit show? These questions can be answered by an analysis of trend percentages over a representative period, such as the most recent five or ten years. To gain a realistic view of the company, it is often necessary to examine more than just a two- or three-year period.

Trend percentages are computed by selecting a base year, with each amount during that year set equal to 100 percent. The amounts of each following year are expressed as a percent of the base amount. To compute trend percentages, divide each item for years after the base year by the corresponding amount during the base year. Suppose McColpin, Inc., showed sales, cost of goods sold, and gross profit for the past six years as follows:

Real-World Example: Although most companies present only two and sometimes three years' financial statements, they also report selected financial data such as net income, sales, and certain key ratios for the last five to ten years so that trend percentages can be computed. For example, Coca Cola's 1989 financial statement included information about all income statement accounts and selected balance sheet accounts for the previous ten years. Revenues in 1979 were $3,895,000,000 and in 1989 were $8,966,000,000.

	(amounts in thousands)					
	19X7	19X6	19X5	19X4	19X3	19X2
Net sales	$858	$803	$781	$744	$719	$737
Cost of goods sold	513	509	490	464	450	471
Gross profit	$345	$294	$291	$280	$269	$266

Assume we want trend percentages for a five-year period starting with 19X3. We use 19X2 as the base year. Trend percentages for net sales are computed by dividing each net sales amount by the 19X2 amount of $737,000. Likewise, dividing each year's cost-of-goods-sold amount by the base-year amount ($471,000) yields the trend percentages for cost of goods sold. Gross-profit trend percentages are computed similarly. The resulting trend percentages follow (19X2, the base year = 100%):

	19X7	19X6	19X5	19X4	19X3	19X2
Net sales	116%	109%	106%	101%	98%	100%
Cost of goods sold	109	108	104	99	96	100
Gross profit	130	111	109	105	101	100

Point to Stress: While horizontal analysis shows the relationship between several years, vertical analysis shows the relationship between numbers for one year.

Teaching Tip: Vertical analysis presents everything on the income statement as a percentage of net sales in order to show the relative importance of each item on the income statement. The formula is:

$$\text{Vertical analysis \%} = \frac{\text{Each income statement item}}{\text{Net sales}}$$

McColpin's sales and cost of goods sold have trended upward since a downturn in 19X3. Gross profit has increased steadily, with the most dramatic growth coming during 19X7. What signal about the company does this information provide? It suggests that operations are becoming increasingly more successful. A similar analysis can be performed for any related set of items in the financial statements. For example, an increase in inventory and accounts receivable, coupled with a decrease in sales, may reveal difficulty in making sales and collecting receivables.

Vertical Analysis

Horizontal analysis highlights changes in an item over time. However, no single technique provides a complete picture of a business. Another way to analyze a company is called vertical analysis.

Vertical analysis of a financial statement reveals the relationship of each statement item to a specified base, which is the 100 percent figure. For example, when an income statement is subjected to vertical analysis, net sales is

Transparency T19-1

usually the base. Suppose under normal conditions a company's gross profit is 50 percent of net sales. A drop in gross profit to 40 percent may cause the company to report a net loss on the income statement. Management, investors, and creditors view a large decline in gross profit with alarm. Exhibit 19-3 shows the vertical analysis of McColpin, Inc.'s income statement as a percentage of net sales. Exhibit 19-4 shows the vertical analysis of the balance sheet amounts as a percentage of total assets.

The 19X7 comparative income statement (Exhibit 19-3) reports that cost of goods sold dropped to 59.8 percent of net sales from 63.4 percent in 19X6. This explains why the gross profit percentage rose in 19X7. The gross profit percentage is one of the most important items of information in financial analysis because it shows the relationship between net sales and cost of goods sold. All other things equal, a company that can steadily increase its gross profit percentage over a long period is more likely to succeed than a business whose gross profit percentage is steadily declining. The net income percentage almost doubled in 19X7, mostly because of the decrease in the cost-of-goods-sold percentage.

Vertical analysis gives a view of the income statement that differs from the view provided by horizontal analysis. Decision makers use these two forms of analysis together. For example, Exhibit 19-1 reports that gross profit increased by 17.3 percent, and net income increased by 84.6 percent from 19X6 to 19X7. Exhibit 19-3 indicates that gross profit grew from 36.6 percent of sales in 19X6 to 40.2 percent of sales in 19X7 and that net income increased from 3.2 percent of sales to 5.6 percent of sales. Together, vertical analysis and horizontal analysis paint a favorable picture of McColpin's operations.

We can apply trend analysis to the balance sheet of McColpin, Inc., as Exhibit 19-4 shows. For example, among the changes during 19X7, we note that current assets have become a smaller percentage of total assets. A decrease in current assets may signal difficulty paying bills. However, this does not present a problem for McColpin, Inc., because current liabilities also decreased as a percentage of total assets during 19X7.

Teaching Tip: Look at Exhibit 19-3. Think of vertical analysis in this way: every item on the Income Statement is expressed as a percentage of net sales; or, consider the percentage of net sales to be $1.00 and each subsequent percentage becomes a dollar amount. In other words, in Exhibit 19-3, Net Sales for 19X7, which is 100%, may be expressed as $1.00. Cost of Goods Sold represents 59.8¢ ($.598) out of every sales dollar; out of each dollar of sales the company makes $.402 (40.2¢) of gross profit. After tax, the company earns 5.6¢ from each dollar of sales.

Teaching Tip: Notice that each year is calculated separately; for 19X6, the denominator is always $803,000 (19X6 Net Sales).

General expenses =

$$\frac{\$123,000}{\$803,000}, \text{ or } 15.3\%$$

In 19X7, each number is expressed as a percent of $858,000 (19X7 Net Sales). Remember that the Percent column could not be added in horizontal analysis. In vertical analysis, the percentages must be totaled correctly to equal the net income percentage. In other words, for 19X7, 5.6% represents both the sum of the Percent column and Net Income ($48,000) divided by Net Sales ($858,000).

EXHIBIT 19-3 *Comparative Income Statement—Vertical Analysis*

McColpin, Inc.
Comparative Income Statement
Years Ended December 31, 19X7 and 19X6

	19X7		19X6	
	Amount	Percent	Amount	Percent
Net sales	$858,000	100.0%	$803,000	100.0%
Cost of goods sold	513,000	59.8	509,000	63.4
Gross profit	345,000	40.2	294,000	36.6
Selling expenses	126,000	14.7	114,000	14.2
General expenses	118,000	13.7	123,000	15.3
Total operating expenses	244,000	28.4	237,000	29.5
Income from operations	101,000	11.8	57,000	7.1
Interest revenue	4,000	0.4	—	—
Interest expense	24,000	2.8	14,000	1.8
Income before income tax	81,000	9.4	43,000	5.3
Income tax expense	33,000	3.8	17,000	2.1
Net income	$ 48,000	5.6%	$ 26,000	3.2%

OBJECTIVE 2

Perform a vertical analysis of financial statements

Class Discussion: Look at Exhibit 19-3. What information about McColpin can we derive from this analysis? ANSWER:

1 The company is more profitable than the previous year.

2 Net income increased. One reason that the income increased is because the cost of goods as a percentage of sales was less in 19X7. This increased gross profit.

3 Operating expenses declined as a percentage of sales.

4 Income before tax was 4.3 percent higher in 19X7.

5 Income tax took a larger bite out of income in 19X7. Taxes represented 3.8 percent of revenue in 19X7 compared to only 2.1 percent in 19X6.

Class Exercise: Calculate common size percentages for the following income statement.

Net sales	$150,000
COGS	60,000
Gross margin	90,000
Operating expenses	40,000
Operating income	50,000
Income tax expense	15,000
Net income	$ 35,000

ANSWER:

Net sales	100%
COGS	40
Gross margin	60
Operating expenses	27
Operating income	33
Income tax expense	10
Net income	23%

EXHIBIT 19-4 *Comparative Balance Sheet—Vertical Analysis*

McColpin, Inc.
Comparative Balance Sheet
December 31, 19X7 and 19X6

	19X7		19X6	
Assets	**Amount**	**Percent**	**Amount**	**Percent**
Current assets:				
Cash	$ 29,000	3.7%	$ 32,000	5.0%
Accounts receivable, net ...	114,000	14.5	85,000	13.2
Inventories	113,000	14.3	111,000	17.2
Prepaid expenses..........	6,000	.8	8,000	1.2
Total current assets	262,000	33.3	236,000	36.6
Long-term investments	18,000	2.3	9,000	1.4
Property, plant, and equipment, net............	507,000	64.4	399,000	62.0
Total assets	$787,000	100.0%	$644,000	100.0%
Liabilities				
Current liabilities:				
Notes payable.............	$ 42,000	5.3%	$ 27,000	4.2%
Accounts payable	73,000	9.3	68,000	10.6
Accrued liabilities	27,000	3.4	31,000	4.8
Total current liabilities ...	142,000	18.0	126,000	19.6
Long-term debt	289,000	36.7	198,000	30.7
Total liabilities	431,000	54.7	324,000	50.3
Stockholders' Equity				
Common stock, no-par	186,000	23.7	186,000	28.9
Retained earnings	170,000	21.6	134,000	20.8
Total stockholders' equity	356,000	45.3	320,000	49.7
Total liabilities and stockholders' equity ...	$787,000	100.0%	$644,000	100.0%

Common-Size Statements

The percentages in Exhibits 19-3 and 19-4 can be presented as a separate statement that reports only percentages (no dollar amounts). Such a statement, called a **common-size statement,** is a type of vertical analysis.

On a common-size income statement, each item is expressed as a percentage of the net sales amount. Net sales is the "common size" to which we relate the statement's other amounts. In the balance sheet, the "common size" is the total on each side of the accounting equation (total assets *or* the sum of total liabilities and stockholders' equity). A common-size statement eases the comparison of different companies because their amounts are stated in percentages.

Common-size statements may identify the need for corrective action. Exhibit 19-5 is the common-size analysis of current assets taken from Exhibit 19-4.

EXHIBIT 19-5 *Common-Size Analysis of Current Assets*

McColpin, Inc. Common-Size Analysis of Current Assets December 31, 19X7 and 19X6		
	Percent of Total Assets	
	19X7	19X6
Current assets:		
Cash	3.7%	5.0%
Accounts receivable, net	14.5	13.2
Inventories	14.3	17.2
Prepaid expenses	.8	1.2
Total current assets	33.3%	36.6%

Exhibit 19-5 shows cash as a smaller percentage of total assets at December 31, 19X7, than at the previous year end. Accounts receivable, on the other hand, is a larger percentage of total assets. What could cause a decrease in cash and an increase in accounts receivable as percentages of total assets? McColpin may have been lax in collecting accounts receivable, which may explain a cash shortage and reveal that the company needs to pursue collection more vigorously. Or the company may have sold to less-creditworthy customers. In any event, the company should monitor its cash position and collection of accounts receivable to avoid a cash shortage. Common-size statements provide information useful for this purpose.

Industry Comparisons

We study the records of a company in order to understand past results and predict future performance. Still, the knowledge that we can develop from a single company's records is limited to that one company. We may learn that gross profit has decreased and net income has increased steadily for the last ten years. While this information is helpful, it does not consider how businesses in the same industry have fared over this time. Have other companies in the same line of business increased their sales? Is there an industrywide decline in gross profit? Has cost of goods sold risen steeply for other businesses that sell the same products? Managers, investors, creditors, and other interested parties need to know how one company compares with other companies in the same line of business.

Exhibit 19-6 gives the common-size income statement of McColpin, Inc., compared with the average for the retail furniture industry. This analysis compares McColpin with all other companies in its line of business. The industry averages were adapted from Robert Morris Associates' *Annual Statement Studies*. Analysts specialize in a particular industry and make such comparisons in deciding which companies' stocks to buy or sell. For example, financial-service companies like Merrill Lynch have airline-industry specialists, health-care-industry specialists, and so on. Boards of directors evaluate top managers based on how well the company compares with other companies in the industry. Exhibit 19-6 shows that McColpin compares favorably with competing

Real-World Example: Interested parties can gain insight into a company by comparing it to similar companies. Suppose that you wanted to invest in Public Service Electric & Gas, but its financial statements revealed a high percentage of debt. Comparing PSE&G's financial statements with those of other utility companies would show you that such capital-intensive companies normally have a high percentage of debt. It would not be as helpful to compare PSE&G's financial statements with those of a non-capital-intensive company such as the Kelly Services temporary job placement agency.

EXHIBIT 19-6 *Common-Size Income Statement Compared with the Industry Average*

	McColpin, Inc.	Industry Average
McColpin, Inc. Common-Size Income Statement for Comparison with Industry Average Year Ended December 31, 19X7		
Net sales	100.0%	100.0%
Cost of goods sold	59.8	59.7
Gross profit	**40.2**	**40.3**
Operating expenses:		
Selling expenses	14.7	23.6
General expenses	13.7	13.4
Total operating expenses	28.4	37.0
Income from operations	**11.8**	**3.3**
Other revenue (expense)	(2.4)	(0.4)
Income before income tax	9.4	2.9
Income tax expense	3.8	0.9
Net income	**5.6%**	**2.0%**

OBJECTIVE 3

Prepare common-size
financial statements

Teaching Tip: Prepare a list of
several companies that provide
annual reports for use in your
school's library. Have students
use one of these and practice
performing horizontal and
vertical analysis and calculating
some of the ratios covered later
in this chapter. Then have the
students compare their findings
with industry averages from
Robert Morris or Dun and
Bradstreet.

furniture retailers. Its gross profit percentage is virtually identical to the industry average. The company does a good job of controlling operating expenses, and as a result, its percentage of income from operations and net income percentage are significantly higher than the industry average.

Another use of common-size statements is to aid the comparison of different-sized companies. Suppose you are considering an investment in the stock of an automobile manufacturer, and you are choosing between General Motors (GM) and Chrysler. GM is so much larger than Chrysler that a direct comparison of their financial statements in dollar amounts is not meaningful. However, you can convert the two companies' income statements to common size and compare the percentages. You may find that one company has a higher percentage of its assets in inventory and the other company has a higher percentage of its liabilities in long-term debt.

The Statement of Cash Flows in Decision Making

OBJECTIVE 4

Use the statement of cash
flows in decision making

The chapter so far has centered on the income statement and balance sheet. We may also perform horizontal and vertical analysis on the statement of cash flows. In the preceding chapter, we discussed how to prepare the statement. To discuss its role in decision making, let's use Exhibit 19-7.

Some analysts use cash flow analysis to identify danger signals about a company's financial situation. For example, the statement in Exhibit 19-7 reveals what may be a weakness in DeMaris Corporation.

First, operations provided a net cash inflow of $52,000, which is much less than the $91,000 generated by the sale of fixed assets. An important question arises: Can the company remain in business by generating the majority of its cash by selling its property, plant, and equipment? No, because these assets will be needed to manufacture the company's products in the future. Note also that borrowing by issuing bonds payable brought in $72,000. No company can long survive living on borrowed funds. DeMaris must eventually pay off the bonds. Indeed, the company paid $170,000 on older debt. Also, interest

EXHIBIT 19-7 *Statement of Cash Flows*

DeMaris Corporation Statement of Cash Flows For the Current Year		
Operating activities:		
Income from operations		$ 35,000
Add (subtract) noncash items:		
Depreciation	$ 14,000	
Net increase in current assets other than		
cash	(5,000)	
Net increase in current liabilities	8,000	17,000
Net cash inflow from operating activities .		52,000
Investing activities:		
Sale of property, plant, and equipment	$ 91,000	
Net cash inflow from investing activities . .		91,000
Financing activities:		
Issuance of bonds payable	$ 72,000	
Payment of long-term debt	(170,000)	
Payment of interest expense	(9,000)	
Payment of dividends	(33,000)	
Net cash outflow from financing activities		(140,000)
Increase in cash		$ 3,000

Point to Stress: The statement of cash flows informs the financial statement reader of where a company gets its cash and how the company uses its cash. If a company must sell off part of its plant and equipment to obtain the cash needed for operations, then its future operations may be seriously impaired.

expense must be incurred as the price of borrowing. Successful companies like IBM, Coca-Cola, and Procter & Gamble generate the greatest percentage of their cash from operations, not from selling their fixed assets or from borrowing money. These conditions may be only temporary for DeMaris Corporation, but they are worth investigating.

The most important information that the statement of cash flows provides is a summary of the company's use of cash. How a company spends its cash today determines its sources of cash in the future. The company may wisely use its cash to purchase assets that will generate income in the years ahead. However, if a company invests unwisely, cash will eventually run short. DeMaris's statement of cash flows reveals problems. The exhibit information indicates that DeMaris invested in no fixed assets to replace those that it sold. The company may in fact be going out of business. Also, DeMaris paid dividends of $33,000, an amount that is very close to its net income. Is the company retaining enough cash to finance future operations without excessive borrowing? Analysts seek answers to questions such as this. They analyze the information from the statement of cash flows along with the information from the balance sheet and the income statement to form a well-rounded picture of the business.

Summary Problem for Your Review

Perform a horizontal analysis and a vertical analysis of the comparative income statement of TRE Corporation. State whether 19X3 was a good year or a bad year and give your reasons.

TRE Corporation
Comparative Income Statement
Years Ended December 31, 19X3 and 19X2

	19X3	19X2
Total revenues	$275,000	$225,000
Expenses:		
Cost of products sold	$194,000	$165,000
Engineering, selling, and administrative expenses .	54,000	48,000
Interest expense................................	5,000	5,000
Income tax expense	9,000	3,000
Other expense (income).........................	1,000	(1,000)
Total expenses	263,000	220,000
Net earnings...................................	$ 12,000	$ 5,000

SOLUTION TO REVIEW PROBLEM

TRE Corporation
Horizontal Analysis of Comparative Income Statement
Years Ended December 31, 19X3 and 19X2

	19X3	19X2	Increase (Decrease) Amount	Increase (Decrease) Percent
Total revenues	$275,000	$225,000	$50,000	22.2%
Expenses:				
Cost of products sold	$194,000	$165,000	$29,000	17.6
Engineering, selling, and administrative expenses	54,000	48,000	6,000	12.5
Interest expense	5,000	5,000	—	—
Income tax expense	9,000	3,000	6,000	200.0
Other expense (income)	1,000	(1,000)	2,000	—
Total expenses	263,000	220,000	43,000	19.5
Net earnings...................	$ 12,000	$ 5,000	$ 7,000	140.0

TRE Corporation
Vertical Analysis of Comparative Income Statement
Years Ended December 31, 19X3 and 19X2

	19X3 Amount	19X3 Percent	19X2 Amount	19X2 Percent
Total revenue	$275,000	100.0%	$225,000	100.0%
Expenses:				
Cost of products sold	$194,000	70.5	$165,000	73.3
Engineering, selling, and administrative expenses.....	54,000	19.6	48,000	21.3
Interest expense..............	5,000	1.8	5,000	2.2
Income tax expense...........	9,000	3.3	3,000	1.4
Other expense (income).......	1,000	0.4	(1,000)	(0.4)
Total expenses	263,000	95.6	220,000	97.8
Net earnings	$ 12,000	4.4%	$ 5,000)	2.2%

The horizontal analysis shows that total revenues increased 22.2 percent. This percentage increase was greater than the 19.5 percent increase in total expenses, resulting in a 140 percent increase in net earnings.

The vertical analysis shows decreases in the percentages of net sales consumed by the cost of products sold (from 73.3 percent to 70.5 percent) and the engineering, selling, and administrative expenses (from 21.3 percent to 19.6 percent). These two items are TRE's largest dollar expenses, so their percentage decreases are quite important. The relative reduction in expenses raised 19X3 net earnings to 4.4 percent of sales, compared with 2.2 percent the preceding year. The overall analysis indicates that 19X3 was significantly better than 19X2.

Using Ratios to Make Business Decisions

The preceding analyses were based on each financial statement considered alone. Another set of decision tools develops relationships among items taken from throughout the statements.

Ratios are important tools for financial analysis. A ratio expresses the relationship of one number to another number. For example, if the balance sheet shows current assets of $100,000 and current liabilities of $25,000, the ratio of current assets to current liabilities is $100,000 to $25,000. We simplify this numerical expression to the ratio of 4 to 1, which may also be written 4:1 and $\frac{4}{1}$. Other acceptable ways of expressing this ratio include (1) "current assets are 400 percent of current liabilities" and (2) "the business has four dollars in current assets for every one dollar in current liabilities."

We often reduce the ratio fraction by writing the ratio as one figure over the other, for example, $\frac{4}{1}$, and then dividing the numerator by the denominator. In this way, the ratio $\frac{4}{1}$ may be expressed simply as 4. The 1 that represents the denominator of the fraction is understood, not written. Consider the ratio $175,000:$165,000. After dividing the first figure by the second, we come to 1.06:1, which we state as 1.06. The second part of the ratio, the 1, again is understood. Ratios provide a convenient and useful way of expressing a relationship between numbers. For example, the ratio of current assets to current liabilities gives information about a company's ability to pay its current debts with existing current assets.

A manager, lender, or financial analyst may use any ratio that is relevant to a particular decision. We discuss the more important ratios used in credit and investment analysis and in managing a business. Many companies include these ratios in a special section of their annual financial reports. Investment services—Moody's, Standard & Poor's, Robert Morris Associates, and others—report these ratios for companies and industries. They are widely used in all aspects of business—finance, management, and marketing as well as accounting.

Measuring the Ability to Pay Current Liabilities

Working capital is defined as current assets minus current liabilities. Working capital is widely used to measure a business's ability to meet its short-term obligations with its current assets. In general, the larger the working capital, the better able the business is to pay its debts. Recall that capital, or owners' equity, is total assets minus total liabilities. Working capital is like a "current" version of total capital. The working capital amount considered alone does not give a complete picture of the entity's working capital position, however. Consider two companies with equal working capital:

	Company A	Company B
Current assets	$100,000	$200,000
Current liabilities	50,000	150,000
Working capital	$ 50,000	$ 50,000

Discussion Question: Is a high current ratio always good? ANSWER: A high current ratio may indicate that too much of the company's assets are tied up in current assets, which typically do not produce a return. A receivable is not productive, nor is inventory if it is sitting on a shelf.

Transparency T19-2

Both companies have working capital of $50,000, but Company A's working capital is as large as its current liabilities. Company B's working capital, on the other hand, is only one-third as large as its current liabilities. Which business has a better working capital position? Company A, because its working capital is a higher percentage of current assets and current liabilities. To use working capital data in decision making, it is helpful to develop ratios. Two decision tools based on working capital data are the *current ratio* and the *acid-test ratio*.

Current Ratio

OBJECTIVE 5

Compute the standard financial ratios used for decision making

Discussion Question: What types of businesses can operate at very high and very low current ratios? ANSWER: A utilities company, with very little capital tied up in inventory, could easily operate with a low current ratio. A department store, with a large investment in inventory, requires a much higher current ratio.

When considering the current ratio, it is important to look at the industry norms, the ratio itself, and the make-up of the items included in that ratio.

The most common ratio using current asset and current liability data is the *current ratio*, which is current assets divided by current liabilities. Recall the makeup of current assets and current liabilities. Inventory is converted to receivables through sales, the receivables are collected in cash, and the cash is used to buy inventory and pay current liabilities. A company's current assets and current liabilities represent the core of its day-to-day operations.

The current ratios of McColpin, Inc. at December 31, 19X7 and 19X6, follow (data from Exhibit 19-2).

Current Ratio of McColpin, Inc.

Formula	19X7	19X6
Current ratio = $\dfrac{\text{Current assets}}{\text{Current liabilities}}$	$\dfrac{\$262,000}{\$142,000} = 1.85$	$\dfrac{\$236,000}{\$126,000} = 1.87$

The current ratio decreased slightly during 19X7. The average current ratio for furniture retailers is 1.80. Lenders, stockholders, and managers closely monitor changes in a company's current ratio. In general, a higher current ratio indicates a stronger financial position. A high current ratio suggests that the business has sufficient liquid assets to maintain normal business operations. Compare McColpin's current ratio of 1.85 with the current ratios of some actual companies:

Class Exercise: Company A has current assets of $100,000 and current liabilities of $50,000. Company B has current assets of $200,000 and current liabilities of $150,000. Both have

Company	Current Ratio
Chesebrough-Pond's, Inc.	2.50
International Business Machines Corporation (IBM)	1.52
General Mills, Inc.	1.05
The Superior Oil Company	1.46

What is an acceptable current ratio? The answer to this question depends on the nature of the industry. The norm for companies in most industries is between 1.60 and 1.90, as reported by Robert Morris Associates. McColpin's current ratio of 1.85 is within the range of these actual values. In most industries a current ratio of 2.0 is considered good.

Acid-Test Ratio

The **acid-test** (or **quick**) **ratio** tells us whether the entity could pay all its current liabilities if they came due immediately. That is, could the company pass this *acid test?* The company would convert its most liquid assets to cash. To compute the acid-test ratio, we add cash, short-term investments, and net current receivables (accounts and notes receivable, net of allowances) and divide by current liabilities. Inventory and prepaid expenses are the two current assets not included in the acid-test computations. These accounts are omitted because they are the least liquid of the current assets. A business may not be able to convert them to cash immediately to pay current liabilities. The acid-test ratio measures liquidity using a narrower asset base than the current ratio does.

McColpin's acid-test ratios for 19X7 and 19X6 follow (data from Exhibit 9-2).

Acid-Test Ratio of McColpin, Inc.

Formula	19X7	19X6
Acid-test ratio = $\dfrac{\text{Cash + short-term investments + net current receivables}}{\text{Current liabilities}}$	$\dfrac{\$29{,}000 + \$0 + \$114{,}000}{\$142{,}000} = 1.01$	$\dfrac{\$32{,}000 + \$0 + \$85{,}000}{\$126{,}000} = .93$

The company's acid-test ratio improved considerably during 19X7. Its ratio of 1.01 is near the top quartile for the retail furniture industry and significantly better than the industry average of .50. McColpin's ratio value is within range of those of Chesebrough-Pond's (1.25), General Motors (.91), and IBM (1.07). The norm ranges from .20 for shoe retailers to 1.00 for manufacturers of paperboard containers and certain other equipment, as reported by Robert Morris Associates. An acid-test ratio of .90 to 1.00 is acceptable in most industries.

Measuring the Ability to Sell Inventory and Collect Receivables

The ability to sell inventory and collect receivables is fundamental to business success. Recall the operating cycle of a merchandiser: cash to inventory to receivables and back to cash. This section discusses three ratios that measure the ability to sell inventory and collect receivables.

Inventory Turnover

Companies generally seek to achieve the quickest possible return on their investments. A return on an investment in inventory—usually a substantial amount—is no exception. The faster inventory sells, the sooner the business creates accounts receivable, and the sooner it collects cash.

working capital of $50,000. Which company is more liquid? ANSWER: Company A is, because it has more current assets compared to current liabilities.

We express the relationship of current assets to current liabilities by computing the current ratio.

$$\text{Co. A: } \frac{\text{CA}}{\text{CL}} = \frac{\$100}{\$50} = 2$$

$$\text{Co B: } \frac{\text{CA}}{\text{CL}} = \frac{\$200}{\$150} = 1.33$$

Company A is in a much stronger current financial position and can more easily meet current obligations as they come due because it has a larger proportion of current assets compared to current liabilities.

Class Exercise: Assume that two companies have the following current assets (amounts in thousands):

	Co. A	Co. B
Cash	$ 31	$ 20
Accounts receivable	45	75
Inventory	21	102
Prepaid expenses	3	3
Current assets	$100	$200
Current liabilities	$ 50	$150

Which current assets are not very liquid? ANSWER: Inventory and Prepaid Expenses. These are excluded when calculating the Acid-Test Ratio. Now calculate the Acid-Test (Quick) Ratios.

ANSWER:

$$\text{Co. A: } \frac{\text{Cash + A/R}}{\text{CL}} = \frac{\$76}{\$50} = 1.5$$

$$\text{Co. B: } \frac{\text{Cash + A/R}}{\text{CL}} = \frac{\$95}{\$150} = .63$$

The make-up of current assets is critical here. Company B has so much tied up in Inventory that it has a lower acid-test ratio. Company A, with most of its current assets

Inventory turnover is a measure of the number of times a company sells its average level of inventory during a year. A high rate of turnover indicates relative ease in selling inventory, whereas a low turnover indicates difficulty in selling. Generally, companies prefer a high inventory turnover. A value of 6 means that the company's average level of inventory has been sold 6 times during the year. In most cases this is better than a turnover of 3 or 4. However, a high value can mean that the business is not keeping enough inventory on hand, and this can result in lost sales if the company cannot fill a customer's order. Therefore, a business strives for the most profitable rate of inventory turnover, not necessarily the highest.

To compute the inventory turnover ratio we divide cost of goods sold by the average inventory for the period. We use the cost of goods sold—not sales—in the computation because both cost of goods sold and inventory are stated *at cost.* Sales is stated at the sales value of inventory and therefore is not comparable with inventory cost.

McColpin's inventory turnover for 19X7 is

Formula	Inventory Turnover of McColpin, Inc.
$\text{Inventory turnover} = \dfrac{\text{Cost of goods sold}}{\text{Average inventory}}$	$\dfrac{\$513,000}{\$112,000} = 4.58$

Cost of goods sold appears in the income statement (Exhibit 19-1). Average inventory is figured by averaging the beginning inventory ($111,000) and ending inventory ($113,000). (See the balance sheet, Exhibit 19-2.) If inventory levels vary greatly from month to month, compute the average by adding the 12 monthly balances and dividing this sum by 12.

Inventory turnover varies widely with the nature of the business. For example, most manufacturers of farm machinery have an inventory turnover close to 3 times a year. By contrast, companies that remove natural gas from the ground hold their inventory for a very short period of time and have an average turnover of 30. McColpin's turnover of 4.58 times a year is high for its industry, which has an average turnover of 2.70. McColpin's high inventory turnover results from its policy of keeping little inventory on hand. The company takes customer orders and has its suppliers ship directly to customers.

To evaluate fully a company's inventory turnover, compare the ratio over time. A sudden sharp decline or a steady decline over a long period suggests the need for corrective action. Analysts also compare a company's inventory turnover with other companies in the same industry and with the industry average.

Accounts Receivable Turnover

Accounts receivable turnover measures a company's ability to collect cash from credit customers. Generally, the higher the ratio, the more successfully the business collects cash, and the better off its operations are. However, too high a receivable turnover may indicate that credit is too tight, causing the loss of sales to good customers. To compute the accounts receivable turnover we divide net credit sales by average net accounts receivable. The resulting ratio indicates how many times during the year the average level of receivables was turned into cash.

McColpin's accounts receivable turnover ratio for 19X7 is computed as follows. (We assume that all sales were on credit.)

Formula	Accounts Receivable Turnover of McColpin, Inc.
$\text{Accounts receivable turnover} = \dfrac{\text{Net credit sales}}{\text{Average net accounts receivable}}$	$\dfrac{\$858,000}{\$99,500} = 8.62$

The sales figure comes from the income statement (Exhibit 19-1). McColpin makes all sales on credit. If the company makes both cash and credit sales, this ratio is best computed using only net credit sales. Average net accounts receivable is figured using the beginning accounts receivable balance ($85,000) and the ending balance ($114,000). (See the balance sheet, Exhibit 19-2.) If accounts receivable balances exhibit a seasonal pattern, compute the average using the 12 monthly balances.

Receivable turnover ratios vary little from company to company. Most companies' ratios range between 7.0 and 10.0. McColpin's receivable turnover of 8.62 falls within this range.

Days' Sales in Receivables

Businesses must convert accounts receivable to cash. All other things equal, the lower the Accounts Receivable balance, the more successful the business has been in converting receivables into cash, and the better off the business.

The **days'-sales-in-receivables** ratio tells us how many days' sales remain in Accounts Receivable. We express the money amount in terms of an average day's sales. This relation becomes clearer as we compute the ratio, a two-step process. First, divide net sales by 365 days to figure the average sales amount for one day. Second, divide this average day's sales amount into the average net accounts receivable.

The data to compute this ratio for McColpin, Inc., for 19X7 are taken from the income statement and the balance sheet.

Formula	Days' Sales in Accounts Receivable of McColpin, Inc.

Days' Sales in AVERAGE Accounts Receivable:

1. One day's sales $= \dfrac{\text{Net sales}}{365 \text{ days}}$	$\dfrac{\$858,000}{365 \text{ days}} = \$2,351$	
2. Days' sales in average accounts receivable $= \dfrac{\text{Average net accounts receivable}}{\text{One day's sales}}$	$\dfrac{\$99,500}{\$2,351} = 42 \text{ days}$	

The computation in two steps is designed to increase your understanding of the meaning of the ratio. We may compute days' sales in average receivables in one step: $\$99,500/(\$858,000/365 \text{ days}) = 42$ days.

McColpin's ratio tell us that 42 average days' sales remain in accounts receivable and need to be collected. The company will increase its cash inflow if it can decrease this ratio. To detect any changes over time in McColpin's ability to collect its receivables, let's compute the days'-sales-in-receivables ratio at the beginning and the end of 19X7.

Point to Stress: The accounts receivable turnover indicates the reasonableness of the balance in accounts receivable. It measures how effective the company's credit collections are. As with inventory turnover, a high ratio is preferable to a low ratio.

Typical Student Misconception: Students often will use total sales rather than net credit sales in the numerator. Explain that cash sales are collected immediately and are not involved in the company's receivables collection efforts. Likewise, cash sales are not figured into days' sales in receivables.

Point to Stress: The days'-sales-in-receivables ratio is also called days' sales uncollected. This ratio gives more useful information than the receivables turn-over ratio because it tells you, on the average, how many days there will be from the date of the credit sale until cash is received.

Teaching Tip: There is another way to calculate days' sales in receivables that is something of a shortcut:

$$\text{Number of days} = \dfrac{365}{\text{Accounts receivable turnover}}$$

Discussion Question: What does the 42 days mean? ANSWER: It takes approximately 42 days to collect a receivable.

Is this good or bad? ANSWER: It depends on the credit period. If the credit period is 60 days, then the ratio is good. If the credit period is 30 days, then perhaps McColpin needs to make a few changes in its credit policies. To a short-term creditor, the important point is that in 42 days the cash from the receivables will be available to pay off a debt.

How could McColpin improve this ratio? ANSWER: Offer discounts for early payment. Tighten credit policies. Use more aggressive collection procedures.

Days' Sales in ENDING 19X6 Accounts Receivable:

$$\text{One day's sales} = \frac{\$803,000}{365 \text{ days}} = \$2,200$$

$$\begin{array}{c}\text{Days' sales in}\\ \text{ending 19X6 accounts}\\ \text{receivable}\end{array} = \frac{\$85,000}{\$2,200} = 39 \text{ days at beginning of 19X7}$$

Days' Sales in ENDING 19X7 Accounts Receivable:

$$\text{One day's sales} = \frac{\$858,000}{365 \text{ days}} = \$2,351$$

$$\begin{array}{c}\text{Days' sales in}\\ \text{ending 19X7 accounts}\\ \text{receivable}\end{array} = \frac{\$114,000}{\$2,351} = 48 \text{ days at end of 19X7}$$

This analysis shows a drop in McColpin's collection of receivables; days' sales in accounts receivable has increased from 39 at the beginning of the year to 48 at year end. The credit and collection department should strengthen its collection efforts. Otherwise, the company may experience a cash shortage in 19X8 and beyond.

Measuring the Ability to Pay Long-Term Debt _____

The ratios discussed so far give us insight into current assets and current liabilities. They help us measure a business's ability to sell inventory, to collect receivables, and to pay current liabilities. Most businesses also have long-term debts. Bondholders and banks that loan money on long-term notes payable and bonds payable take special interest in a business's ability to meet long-term obligations. Two key indicators of a business's ability to pay long-term liabilities are the *debt ratio* and the *times-interest-earned ratio*.

Debt Ratio

Discussion Question: What makes a corporation with a lot of debt a more risky loan prospect than one with a lot of equity? ANSWER: Interest on debt is contractual and not discretionary. Dividends are discretionary and do not have to be paid.

What happens if interest on debt is not paid? ANSWER: The creditors could force the company into bankruptcy.

Suppose you are a loan officer at a bank and you are evaluating loan applications from two companies with equal sales revenue and total assets. Sales and total assets are the two most common measures of firm size. Both companies have asked to borrow $500,000, and each has agreed to repay the loan over a ten-year period. The first customer already owes $600,000 to another bank. The second owes only $250,000. Other things equal, which company is likely to get the loan at the lower interest rate? Why?

Company Two is more likely to get the loan. The bank faces less risk by loaning to Company Two because that company owes less to creditors than Company One owes.

This relationship between total liabilities and total assets—called the *debt ratio*—tells us the proportion of the company's assets that it has financed with debt. If the debt ratio is 1, then debt has been used to finance all the assets. A debt ratio of .50 means that the company has used debt to finance half its assets. The owners of the business have financed the other half. The higher the debt ratio, the higher the strain of paying interest each year and the principal amount at maturity. The lower the ratio, the less the business's future obligations. Creditors view a high debt ratio with caution. If a business seeking financing already has many liabilities, then additional debt payments may be too much for the business to handle. Creditors, to help protect themselves, generally charge higher interest rates on new borrowing to companies with an already high debt ratio.

McColpin's debt ratio at the end of 19X7 and 19X6 follow (data from Exhibit 19-2).

Point to Stress: The debt ratio also shows the amount or extent of leverage that a company has used. If McColpin, Inc. has a debt ratio of 55% in 19X7, then they have a 45% equity ratio (the amount of assets financed by equity). The debt and equity ratios always total 100%. In other words, all assets are financed either by debt or by equity.

Debt Ratio of McColpin, Inc.

Formula	19X7	19X6
Debt ratio $= \dfrac{\text{Total liabilities}}{\text{Total assets}}$	$\dfrac{\$431,000}{\$787,000} = .55$	$\dfrac{\$324,000}{\$644,000} = .50$

Recall from our vertical and horizontal analyses that McColpin, Inc., expanded operations by financing the purchase of property, plant, and equipment through borrowing, which is common.

Even after the increase in 19X7, McColpin's debt is not very high. Robert Morris Associates reports that the average debt ratio for most companies ranges around .57 to .67, with relatively little variation from company to company. McColpin's .55 debt ratio indicates a fairly low-risk debt position in comparison with the retail furniture industry average of .64.

Discussion Question: The formula for the debt ratio is:

Total liabilities

Total assets

Where have we seen this ratio before? *ANSWER:* The debt ratio is a common-size percentage. Remember, all common-size percentages on the balance sheet are expressed as a percentage of total assets.

Times-Interest-Earned Ratio

The debt ratio measures the effect of debt on the company's *financial position* (balance sheet) but says nothing about its ability to pay interest expense. Analysts use a second ratio—the **times-interest-earned ratio**—to relate income to interest expense. To compute this ratio, we divide income from operations by interest expense. This ratio measures the number of times that operating income can *cover* interest expense. For this reason, the ratio is also called the **interest-coverage ratio.** A high ratio indicates ease in paying interest expense; a low value suggests difficulty.

McColpin's times-interest-earned ratios follow (data from Exhibit 19-1).

Times-Interest-Earned Ratio of McColpin, Inc.

Formula	19X7	19X6
Times-interest-earned ratio $= \dfrac{\text{Income from operations}}{\text{Interest expense}}$	$\dfrac{\$101,000}{\$24,000} = 4.21$	$\dfrac{\$57,000}{\$14,000} = 4.07$

McColpin's interest-coverage ratio increased in 19X7. This is a favorable sign about the company, especially since the company's short-term notes payable and long-term debt rose substantially during the year. (See the horizontal analysis in Exhibit 19-2.) McColpin's new plant assets, we conclude, have earned more in operating income than they have cost the business in interest expense. The company's coverage ratio of around 4 is significantly better than the 2.60 average for furniture retailers. The norm for American business, as reported by Robert Morris Associates, falls in the range of 2.0 to 3.0 for most companies.

Typical Student Misconception: Notice that the numerator of the times-interest-earned formula is operating income— not net income. Calculate operating income, if it is not given, by using the following formula:

Operating income = Net income + Interest expense + Income tax expense

Discussion Question: What is the meaning of McColpin's times-interest-earned ratio of 4.21? *ANSWER:* McColpin earned enough to pay its interest 4.2 times. Therefore, McColpin could afford to borrow more money.

Based on its debt ratio and times-interest-earned ratio, McColpin appears to have little difficulty paying its liabilities, also called *servicing its debt*.

Measuring Profitability

The fundamental goal of business is to earn a profit. Ratios that measure profitability play a large role in decision making. These ratios are reported in the business press, by investment services, and in the annual financial reports of companies.

Rate of Return on Net Sales

Discussion Question: The formula for the rate of return on sales is:

Net income
──────────
Net sales

Where have we seen this formula before?
ANSWER: The rate of return on sales is also a common-size percentage. Every common-size percentage on the income statement is expressed as a percentage of net sales.

Discussion Question: McColpin's return on sales for 19X6 is .032. Keeping in mind our discussion of the common-size income statement, describe what this figure means for sales.
ANSWER: In 19X6 McColpin earned 3.2¢ of net income for every sales dollar.

In business, the term *return* is used broadly and loosely as an evaluation of profitability. For example, consider a percentage called the **rate of return on net sales,** or simply **return on sales.** (The word *net* is usually omitted for convenience, even though the net sales figure is used to compute the ratio.) McColpin's rate of return on sales ratios follow:

	Rate of Return on Sales of McColpin, Inc.	
Formula	**19X7**	**19X6**
Rate of return on sales $= \dfrac{\text{Net income}}{\text{Net sales}}$	$\dfrac{\$48{,}000}{\$858{,}000} = .056$	$\dfrac{\$26{,}000}{\$803{,}000} = .032$

You will recognize this ratio from the vertical analysis of the income statement in Exhibit 19-3. The increase in McColpin's return on sales is significant and identifies McColpin as a leader in its industry. Companies strive for a high rate of return. The higher the rate of return, the more net sales dollars are providing income to the business and the fewer net sales dollars are absorbed by expenses. The 5.6 percent rate compares favorably with General Motors (5.4 percent) and Kraft [Foods], Inc. (4.7 percent) but is less than IBM (13.6 percent) and Chesebrough-Pond's (7.6 percent). As these rates of return on sales indicate, this ratio varies widely from industry to industry.

One strategy for increasing the rate of return on sales is to develop a product that commands a premium price, such as Sony products, Maytag appliances, and certain brands of clothing. Another strategy is to control costs. If successful, either strategy converts a higher proportion of sales into net income and increases the rate of return on net sales.

A return measure can be computed on any revenue and sales amount. Return on net sales, as we have seen, is net income divided by net sales. Return on total revenues is net income divided by total revenues. A company can compute a return on other specific portions of revenue as its information needs dictate.

Rate of Return on Total Assets

Teaching Tip: The rate of return on total assets tells those who finance the assets, both creditors and owners, the level of return that was earned from each dollar invested in the assets. A return of 10.1% indicates that each dollar invested in an asset earned $.101.

The **rate of return on total assets,** or simply **return on assets,** measures the success a company has in using its assets to earn a profit. Creditors have loaned money to the company, and the interest they receive is the return on their investment. Shareholders have invested in the company's stock, and net income is their return. The sum of interest expense and net income is the return to the two groups that have financed the company's operations, and this amount is the numerator of the return on assets ratio. Average total assets is the denominator. McColpin's return on assets ratio follows.

Formula	Rate of Return on Total Assets of McColpin, Inc. 19X7
Rate of return on assets $= \dfrac{\text{Net income} + \text{interest expense}}{\text{Average total assets}}$	$\dfrac{\$48{,}000 + \$24{,}000}{\$715{,}500} = .101$

Net income and interest expense are taken from the income statement. To compute average total assets, we use beginning and ending total assets from the comparative balance sheet. McColpin's 10.1 percent return on assets is higher than the 4.9 percent average return on assets in the retail furniture industry and compares favorably with Superior Oil (8.0 percent) and General Motors (10.4 percent). General Mills, Inc. (12.4 percent) and IBM (15.0 percent) earn somewhat higher returns.

Rate of Return on Common Stockholders' Equity

A popular measure of profitability is **rate of return on common stockholders' equity.** This ratio shows the relationship between net income and common stockholders' investment in the company. To compute this ratio, we first subtract preferred dividends from net income. This leaves only net income available to the common stockholders, which is needed to compute the ratio. We then divide net income available to common stockholders by the average stockholders' equity during the year. Common stockholders' equity is total stockholders' equity minus preferred equity. McColpin's rate of return on common stockholders' equity follows. (Data from Exhibits 19-1 and 19-2.)

Formula	Rate of Return on Common Stockholders' Equity of McColpin, Inc. 19X7
Rate of return on common stockholders' equity $= \dfrac{\text{Net income} - \text{preferred dividends}}{\text{Average common stockholders' equity}}$	$\dfrac{\$48{,}000 - \$0}{\$338{,}000} = .142$

We compute average equity using the beginning and ending balances [($356,000 + $320,000)/2 = $338,000]. Observe that common stockholders' equity includes Retained Earnings and any Paid-in Capital in Excess of Par on Common Stock.

McColpin's 14.2 percent return on common equity compares favorably with returns of companies in most industries, which average around 10 percent. However, some leading companies show higher ratios: IBM (22 percent), Chesebrough-Pond's (20 percent), and General Motors (20 percent).

Typical Student Misconception: Students often confuse the numerator for return on assets with numerators for other ratios. The numerator here is net income + interest expense. Contrast this numerator to the numerator for the times-interest-earned ratio, which is operating income.

Point to Stress: In the formula, notice that the denominator is average total assets. Income is earned throughout the year. For the denominator to be stated in the same terms as the numerator, an average of assets for the year is used.

Point to Stress: Return on common stockholders' equity measures the earning power of common stock equity.

Typical Student Misconception: Again we have a different income figure in the numerator for return on common stockholders' equity. The numerator for this ratio is net income less preferred dividends—the same numerator as for EPS.

Point to Stress: The rate of return on common stockholders' equity should be higher than the rate of return on assets.

Observe that return on equity (14.2 percent) is higher than return on assets (10.1 percent). This 4.1 percent difference results from borrowing at one rate, say 8 percent, and investing the funds to earn a higher rate, such as McColpin's 14.2 percent return on stockholders' equity. This practice is called **trading on the equity,** or the use of **leverage.** It is directly related to the debt ratio. The higher the debt ratio, the higher the leverage. Companies that finance operations with debt are said to *lever* their positions. Leverage increases the risk to common stockholders. For McColpin, Inc., and for many other companies leverage increases profitability. That is not always the case, however. Leverage can also have a negative impact on profitability. If revenues drop, debt and interest expense still must be paid. Therefore, leverage is a double-edged sword, increasing profits during good times but compounding losses during bad times.

Earnings per Share of Common Stock

Teaching Tip: For a review of earnings per share, refer to Chapter 15.

Earnings per share of common stock, or simply *earnings per share (EPS),* is perhaps the most widely quoted of all financial statistics. EPS is the only ratio that must appear on the face of the income statement. EPS is the amount of net income per share of the company's *common* stock. Earnings per share is computed by dividing net income available to common stockholders by the number of common shares outstanding during the year. Preferred dividends are subtracted from net income because the preferred stockholders have a prior claim to their dividends. McColpin has no preferred stock outstanding and so has no preferred dividends. McColpin's EPS for 19X7 and 19X6 follow. (Data are from Exhibits 19-1 and 19-2, and the company had 10,000 shares of common stock outstanding throughout 19X6 and 19X7.)

	Formula	Earnings Per Share of McColpin, Inc.	
		19X7	19X6
Earnings per share of common stock (EPS) $=$	$\dfrac{\text{Net income} - \text{preferred dividends}}{\text{Number of shares of common stock outstanding}}$	$\dfrac{\$48,000 - \$0}{10,000} = \$4.80$	$\dfrac{\$26,000 - \$0}{10,000} = \$2.60$

McColpin's EPS rose from $2.60 to $4.80, an increase of 85 percent. McColpin's stockholders should not expect such a significant boost in EPS every year. However, most companies strive to increase EPS by 10 to 15 percent annually, and the more successful companies do so. However, even the most dramatic upward trends include an occasional bad year.

Analyzing Stock as an Investment

Investors purchase stock to earn a return on their investment. This return consists of two parts: (1) gains (or losses) from selling the stock at a price that is different from the investors' purchase price, and (2) dividends, the periodic distributions to stockholders. The ratios we examine in this section help analysts evaluate stock in terms of market price or dividend payments.

Price/Earnings Ratio

The **price/earnings ratio** is the ratio of the market price of a share of common stock to the company's earnings per share. This ratio, abbreviated P/E, appears in *The Wall Street Journal* stock listings. P/E plays an important part in evaluating decisions to buy, hold, and sell stocks.

The price/earnings ratios of McColpin, Inc., follow. The market price of its common stock was $50 at the end of 19X7 and $35 at the end of 19X6. These prices can be obtained from a financial publication, a stockbroker, or some other source outside the accounting records.

Point to Stress: The P/E ratio shows the relationship between the EPS and the market price of the stock. It helps an investor to analyze the price of the stock and decide whether to buy or sell. In the chapter-opening vignette, Eugene Lerner used the P/E ratio to help make investment decisions.

	Formula	Price/Earnings Ratio of McColpin, Inc.	
		19X7	19X6
Price/ earnings = ratio	$\dfrac{\text{Market price per share of common stock}}{\text{Earnings per share}}$	$\dfrac{\$50.00}{\$4.80} = 10.4$	$\dfrac{\$35.00}{\$2.60} = 13.5$

Given McColpin's 19X7 price/earnings ratio of 10.4, we would say that the company's stock is selling at 10.4 times earnings. The decline from the 19X6 P/E ratio of 13.5 is not a cause for alarm because the numerator—market price of the stock—is not under McColpin's control. The denominator—net income—is more controllable, and it increased during 19X7. Like most other ratios, P/E ratios vary from industry to industry, ranging from 8 to 10 for electric utilities (Texas Utilities and Pennsylvania Power and Light, for example) to 50 to 80 for glamour stocks such as Angen, a leader in the biotechnological industry.

Dividend Yield

Dividend yield is the ratio of dividends per share of stock to the stock's market price per share. This ratio measures the percentage of a stock's market value that is returned annually as dividends, an important concern of stockholders. *Preferred* stockholders, who invest primarily to receive dividends, pay special attention to this ratio.

McColpin paid annual cash dividends of $1.20 per share in 19X7 and $1.00 in 19X6 and market prices of the company's common stock were $50 in 19X7 and $35 in 19X6. McColpin's dividend yields follow:

Point to Stress: Dividend yield shows the rate of dividends earned by a specific class of shareholders based on the current market price for a share of that class of stock. It is calculated separately for preferred and common stock.

Discussion Question: What kind of investor would look for stock with a high dividend yield? With a low dividend yield? ANSWER: An investor who is interested mainly in long-term growth of the company would be satisfied with a lower yield. He wants to see earnings reinvested in the company rather than paid out in current dividends. On the other hand, an investor who is looking for high current distributions (dividends) will require a higher dividend yield. She prefers to maximize current dividend payments rather than have those earnings reinvested.

	Formula	Dividend Yield on Common Stock of McColpin, Inc.	
		19X7	19X6
Dividend yield on common stock	$\dfrac{\text{Dividend per share of common stock}}{\text{Market price per share of common stock}}$	$\dfrac{\$1.20}{\$50.00} = .024$	$\dfrac{\$1.00}{\$35.00} = .029$

An investor who buys McColpin common stock for $50 can expect to receive almost 2½ percent of her investment annually in the form of cash dividends. Dividend yields vary widely, from 5 to 8 percent for older established firms (like Procter & Gamble and General Motors) down to the range of 0 to 3 percent for young, growth-oriented companies (like Anacomp, Inc., the world's largest maker of microfiche). McColpin's dividend yield places the company in the second group.

Book Value per Share of Common Stock

Point to Stress: Book value per share is also considered to be a measure of the net assets represented by each share of stock. Although book value may not represent market value, it can help the investor determine whether the stock is a good buy.

Book value per share of common stock is simply common stockholders' equity divided by the number of shares of common stock outstanding. Common shareholders' equity equals total stockholders' equity less preferred equity. McColpin has no preferred stock outstanding. Its book-value-per-share-of-common-stock ratios follow. Recall that 10,000 shares of common stock were outstanding at the ends of years 19X7 and 19X6.

Formula	Book Value per Share of the Common Stock of McColpin, Inc.	
	19X7	19X6
Book value per share of common stock = $\dfrac{\text{Total stockholders' equity} - \text{preferred equity}}{\text{Number of shares of common stock outstanding}}$	$\dfrac{\$356{,}000 - \$0}{10{,}000} = \$35.60$	$\dfrac{\$320{,}000 - \$0}{10{,}000} = \$32.00$

The market price of a successful company's stock usually exceeds its book value. Some investors buy a stock when its market value approaches book value. Suppose you decided to buy McColpin stock at the end of 19X6, when its market price of $35 was close to book value of $32. That investment would have proved wise. The stock's price increased to $50 in 19X7. Of course, when you bought the stock in 19X6, there was no guarantee the stock price would increase.

The chapter-opening vignette shows one use of book value per share in investment analysis—ranking stocks based on the ratio of market price to book value. Observe, however, that DIA, like other investment advisers, bases its decisions on complex formulas that use many of the ratios described in this chapter. This leads to the next topic. •

The Complexity of Business Decisions _____

OBJECTIVE 6

Use ratios in decision making

Business decisions are made in a world of uncertainty. Legislation, international affairs, competition, scandals, and many other factors can turn profits into losses, and vice versa. To be most useful, ratios should be analyzed over a period of years to take into account a representative group of these factors. Any one year, or even any two years, may not be representative of the company's performance over the long term.

For example, a business's acid-test ratio may show a substantial increase over a ten-year period. However, a two-year period during the early part of that decade might show a slight downturn. An evaluation based on the two-year analysis might lead to an unwise decision. To make the best use of ratios, we must consider them within a broad time frame.

As useful as ratios may be, they do have limitations. We may liken their use in decision making to a physician's use of a thermometer. A reading of 101.6 degrees Fahrenheit indicates that something is wrong with the patient, but the temperature alone does not indicate what the problem is or how to cure it.

In financial analysis, a sudden drop in a company's current ratio signals that *something* is wrong, but this change does not identify the problem or show how to correct it. The business manager must analyze the figures that go into the ratio to determine whether current assets have decreased, current liabilities have increased, or both. If current assets have dropped, is the problem a cash shortage? Are accounts receivable down? Are inventories too low? Only by analyzing the individual items that make up the ratio can the manager determine how to solve the problem. The manager must evaluate data on all ratios in the light of other information about the company and about its particular line of business, such as increased competition or a slowdown in the economy.

Efficient Markets, Management Action, and Investor Decisions

Much research in accounting and finance has focused on whether the stock markets are "efficient." An **efficient capital market** is one in which market prices fully reflect all information available to the public. Stocks are priced in full recognition of all publicly accessible data.

That a market is efficient has implications for management action and for investor decisions. It means that managers cannot fool the market with accounting gimmicks. As long as sufficient information is available, the market as a whole can translate accounting data into a "fair" price for the company's stock.

Suppose you are the president of Company A. Reported earnings per share are $4 and the stock price $40—a price/earnings ratio of 10. You believe the corporation's stock is underpriced in comparison with other companies in the same industry. To correct this situation you are considering changing your method of depreciation from accelerated to straight-line. The accounting change will increase earnings per share to $5. Will the stock price then rise to $50? Probably not. The company's stock price will probably remain at $40 because the market can understand the accounting change. After all, the company merely changed its method of computing depreciation. There is no effect on the company's cash flows, and its economic position is unchanged.

In an efficient market the search for "underpriced" stock is fruitless unless the investor has relevant private information. Moreover, it is unlawful to invest based on inside information, which is available only to corporate managers. For outside investors in an efficient market, an appropriate investment strategy seeks to manage risk, to diversify, and to minimize transactions costs. The role of financial statement analysis consists mainly of identifying the risks of various stocks in order to manage the risk of the overall investment portfolio.

Computers and Financial Statement Analysis

How much can a computer help in analyzing financial statements for investment purposes? Time yourself as you perform one of the financial ratio problems in this chapter. Multiply your efforts by, say, 100 companies that you are comparing in terms of this ratio. Now consider ranking these 100 companies on the basis of four or five additional ratios.

Professional investment consultants may bring an impressive array of computer hardware and software into their analysis, but even individuals can take advantage of the computer in determining their investments—rather than merely "playing a hunch." Individual investors may arm themselves with a microcomputer, a spreadsheet, a modem (which transports data from a centralized storage area into your computer across the telephone lines), and a subscription to any one of several on-line financial databases. These on-line services offer quarterly financial figures for thousands of public corporations going back as much as ten years.

Assume you wanted to compare companies' recent earnings histories to perform an analysis similar to that of DIA in the opening vignette. You might have the computer compare hundreds of companies on the basis of price-earnings ratio and rates of return on stockholders' equity and total assets. The computer could then give you the names of the 20 (or however many) companies that appear most favorable in terms of these ratios. Alternatively, you could have the computer download financial statement data to your spreadsheet (that is, place the data in the appropriate cells of your spreadsheet) and crunch the numbers yourself.

Accountants use computerized financial analysis a great deal. CPAs focus on the individual client. They want to know how the client is doing compared to the previous year and compared to other firms in the industry. Auditors also want to detect any emerging trends in the company's ratios and compare the results of actual operations with expected results. To do so, an auditor can download monthly financial statistics on a spreadsheet and compute the financial ratios to gain insight into the client's situation.

Summary Problem for Your Review

This problem is based on the following financial data adapted from the financial statements of Pizza Inn, Inc., which operates approximately 1,000 pizza restaurants.

Pizza Inn, Inc.
Balance sheets
19X3 and 19X2

	19X3	19X2
	(Thousands of Dollars)	
Assets		
Current assets:		
Cash	$ 4,123	$ 6,453
Marketable securities (same as short-term investments)	4,236	—
Receivables, net	6,331	7,739
Inventories	5,840	4,069
Prepaid expenses and others	3,830	2,708
Total current assets	24,360	20,969
Net property, plant, and equipment	35,330	28,821
Net property under capital leases	23,346	20,886
Intangibles and other assets	10,493	11,349
	$93,529	$82,025

Liabilities and Stockholders' Equity

Current liabilities:

Notes payable............................	$ 1,244	$ 785
Current installments of long-term debt and capital lease obligations	5,220	6,654
Accounts payable–trade...........................	8,631	8,791
Accrued liabilities	5,822	5,983
Total current liabilities	20,917	22,213
Long-term debt, less current installments	22,195	15,549
Capital lease obligations, less current portion	24,296	22,350
Deferred income and deferred income taxes	2,211	1,522
Total common stockholders' equity (shares outstanding 3,017,381 at year end 19X3 and 2,729,274 at year end 19X2)..	23,910	20,391
	$93,529	$82,025

Pizza Inn, Inc.
Statements of Earnings
Years 19X3 and 19X2

	19X3	19X2
	(Thousands of Dollars)	
Total revenue	$148,889	$140,539
Costs and expenses:		
Cost of products sold	$114,335	$111,188
Selling, administrative, and general expenses	23,475	20,816
	137,810	132,004
Earnings from operations	11,079	8,535
Interest expense....................................	5,771	5,902
Earnings before income taxes	5,308	2,633
Income taxes.......................................	1,713	932
Net earnings	$ 3,595	$ 1,701

Required

Compute the following ratios for Pizza Inn for 19X3:

a. Current ratio
b. Acid-test ratio
c. Inventory turnover
d. Days' sales (total revenue) in average receivables
e. Debt ratio
f. Times-interest-earned ratio
g. Rate of return on sales (total revenue)

h. Rate of return on total assets
i. Rate of return on common stockholders' equity
j. Price/earnings ratio, assuming the market price of common stock is $15.50 and earnings per share is $1.16.
k. Book value per share of common stock

SOLUTION TO REVIEW PROBLEM

a. $\text{Current Ratio} = \dfrac{\text{Current Assets}}{\text{Current Liabilities}} = \dfrac{\$24,360}{\$20,917} = 1.16$

b. $\text{Acid-Test Ratio} = \dfrac{\text{Cash + Short-Term Investments + Net Current Receivables}}{\text{Current Liabilities}} = \dfrac{\$4{,}123 + \$4{,}236 + \$6{,}331}{\$20{,}917} = .70$

c. $\text{Inventory Turnover} = \dfrac{\text{Cost of Goods sold}}{\text{Average Inventory}} = \dfrac{\$114{,}335}{(\$5{,}840 + \$4{,}069)/2} = 23.08$

d. Days' Sales (Total Revenue) in Average Receivables:

1. $\text{One day's sales} = \dfrac{\text{Net Sales}}{365 \text{ Days}} = \dfrac{\$148{,}889}{365} = \$407.92$

2. $\text{Days' sales in average accounts receivable} = \dfrac{\text{Average Accounts Receivables}}{\text{One Day's Sales}} = \dfrac{(\$6{,}331 + \$7{,}739)/2}{\$407.92} = 17 \text{ days}$

e. $\text{Debt Ratio} = \dfrac{\text{Total Liabilities}}{\text{Total Assets}} = \dfrac{\$20{,}917 + \$22{,}195 + \$24{,}296 + \$2{,}211}{\$93{,}529} = .74$

f. $\text{Times-Interest-Earned Ratio} = \dfrac{\text{Income from Operations}}{\text{Interest Expense}} = \dfrac{\$11{,}079}{\$5{,}771} = 1.92$

g. $\text{Rate of Return on Sales (Total Revenue)} = \dfrac{\text{Net Income}}{\text{Total Revenue}} = \dfrac{\$3{,}595}{\$148{,}889} = .024$

h. $\text{Rate of Return on Total Assets} = \dfrac{\text{Net income + Interest Expense}}{\text{Average Total Assets}} = \dfrac{\$3{,}595 + \$5{,}771}{(\$93{,}529 + \$82{,}025)/2} = .107$

i. $\text{Rate of Return on Common Stockholders' Equity} = \dfrac{\text{Net Income} - \text{Preferred Dividends}}{\text{Average Common Stockholders' Equity}} = \dfrac{\$3{,}595 - \$0}{(\$23{,}910 + \$20{,}391)/2} = .162$

j. $\text{Price/Earnings Ratio} = \dfrac{\text{Market Price per Share of Common Stock}}{\text{Earnings per Share}} = \dfrac{\$15.50^*}{\$1.16^*} = 13.4$

k. $\text{Book Value per Share of Common Stock} = \dfrac{\text{Total Stockholders' Equity} - \text{Preferred Equity}}{\text{Number of Shares of Common Stock Outstanding}} = \dfrac{\$23{,}910{,}000^* - \$0^*}{3{,}017{,}381^*} = \$7.92$

*All dollar amounts are expressed in thousands except those denoted by *

Summary

Accounting provides information for decision making. Banks loan money, investors buy stocks, and managers run businesses based on the analysis of accounting information.

Horizontal analysis shows the dollar amount and the percentage change in each financial statement item from one period to the next. *Vertical analysis* shows the relationship of each item in a financial statement to its total: total assets on the balance sheet and net sales on the income statement.

Common-size statements—a form of vertical analysis—show the component percentages of the items in a statement. Investment advisory services report common-size statements for various industries, and analysts use them to compare a company with its competitors and with the industry averages.

The *statement of cash flows* shows the net cash inflow or outflow caused by a company's operating, investing, and financing activities. By analyzing the inflows and outflows of cash listed on this statement, an analyst can see where a business's cash comes from and how it is being spent.

Ratios play an important part in business decision making because they show relationships between financial statement items. Analysis of ratios over a period of time is an important way to track a company's progress. The accompanying list presents the ratios discussed in this chapter:

Ratio	Computation	Information Provided
Measuring the ability to pay current liabilities:		
1. Current ratio	$\dfrac{\text{Current assets}}{\text{Current liabilities}}$	Measures ability to pay current liabilities from current assets.
2. Acid-test (quick) ratio	$\dfrac{\text{Cash} + \text{short-term investments} + \text{net current receivables}}{\text{Current liabilities}}$	Shows ability to pay current liabilities from the most liquid assets
Measuring the ability to sell inventory and collect receivables:		
3. Inventory turnover	$\dfrac{\text{Cost of goods sold}}{\text{Average inventory}}$	Indicates saleability of inventory.
4. Accounts receivable turnover	$\dfrac{\text{Net credit sales}}{\text{Average net accounts receivable}}$	Measures collectibility of receivables.
5. Days' sales in receivables	$\dfrac{\text{Average net accounts receivable}}{\text{One day's sales}}$	Shows how many days it takes to collect average receivables.
Measuring the ability to pay long-term debts:		
6. Debt ratio	$\dfrac{\text{Total liabilities}}{\text{Total assets}}$	Indicates percentage of assets financed through borrowing.
7. Times-interest-earned ratio	$\dfrac{\text{Income from operations}}{\text{Interest expense}}$	Measures coverage of interest expense by operating income.
Measuring profitability:		
8. Rate of return on net sales	$\dfrac{\text{Net income}}{\text{Net sales}}$	Shows the percentage of each sales dollar earned as net income.
9. Rate of return on total assets	$\dfrac{\text{Net income} + \text{interest expense}}{\text{Average total assets}}$	Gauges how profitably assets are used.
10. Rate of return on common stockholders' equity	$\dfrac{\text{Net income} - \text{preferred dividends}}{\text{Average common stockholders' equity}}$	Gauges how profitabily the assets financed by the common stockholders are used.
11. Earnings per share of common stock	$\dfrac{\text{Net income} - \text{preferred dividends}}{\text{Number of shares of common stock outstanding}}$	Gives the amount of earnings per one share of common stock.

Ratio	Computation	Information Provided
Analyzing stock as an investment:		
12. Price/earnings ratio	$$\frac{\text{Market price per share of common stock}}{\text{Earnings per share}}$$	Indicates the market price of one dollar of earnings.
13. Dividend yield	$$\frac{\text{Dividend per share of common stock}}{\text{Market price per share of common stock}}$$	Shows the proportion of the market price of each share of stock returned as dividends to stockholders each period.
14. Book value per share of common stock	$$\frac{\text{Total stockholders' equity} - \text{preferred equity}}{\text{Number of shares of common stock outstanding}}$$	Indicates the recorded accounting value of each share of common stock outstanding

Self-Study Questions

Test your understanding of the chapter by marking the best answer for each of the following questions.

1. Net income was $240,000 in 19X4, $210,000 in 19X5, and $252,000 in 19X6. The change from 19X5 to 19X6 is a (an) *(p. 869)*
   a. Increase of 5 percent
   √ b. Increase of 20 percent
   c. Decrease of 10 percent
   d. Decrease of 12.5 percent

2. Vertical analysis of a financial statement shows *(p. 872)*
   a. Trend percentages
   b. The percentage change in an item from period to period
   √ c. The relationship of an item to its total on the statement
   d. Net income expressed as a percentage of stockholders' equity

3. Common-size statements are useful for comparing *(pp. 874, 875)*
   a. Changes in the makeup of assets from period to period
   b. Different companies
   c. A company with its industry
   √ d. All of the above

4. The statement of cash flows is used for decision making by *(pp. 876, 877)*
   √ a. Reporting where cash came from and how it was spent
   b. Indicating how net income was earned
   c. Giving the ratio relationships between selected items
   d. Showing a horizontal analysis of cash flows

5. Cash is $10,000, net accounts receivable amount to $22,000, inventory is $55,000, prepaid expenses total $3,000, and current liabilities are $40,000. What is the acid-test ratio? *(p. 881)*
   a. .25
   √ b. .80
   c. 2.18
   d. 2.25

6. Inventory turnover is computed by dividing *(p. 882)*
   a. Sales revenue by average inventory
   √ b. Cost of goods sold by average inventory
   c. Credit sales by average inventory
   d. Average inventory by cost of goods sold

7. Capp Corporation is experiencing a severe cash shortage due to inability to collect accounts receivable. The decision tool most likely to help identify the appropriate corrective action is the *(p. 883)*
   a. Acid-test ratio
   b. Inventory turnover
   c. Times-interest-earned ratio
   √ d. Days' sales in receivables

8. Analysis of the Mendoza Company financial statements over five years reveals that sales are growing steadily, the debt ratio is higher than the industry average and is increasing, interest coverage is decreasing, return on total assets is declining, and earnings per share of common stock is decreasing. Considered together, these ratios suggest that *(pp. 884, 885, 886)*
   a. Mendoza should pursue collections of receivables more vigorously
   b. Competition is taking sales away from Mendoza
   c. Mendoza is in a declining industry
   ✓ d. The company's debt burden is hurting profitability
9. Which of the following is most likely to be true? *(p. 887)*
   ✓ a. Return on common equity exceeds return on total assets.
   b. Return on total assets exceeds return on common equity.
   c. Return on total assets equals return on common equity.
   d. None of the above.
10. How are financial ratios used in decision making? *(p. 890, 891)*
    a. They remove the uncertainty of the business environment.
    b. They give clear signals about the appropriate action to take.
    ✓ c. They can help identify the reasons for success and failure in business, but decision making requires information beyond the ratios.
    d. They aren't useful because decision making is too complex.

Answers to the Self-Study Questions follow the Accounting Vocabulary.

Accounting Vocabulary

Accounts receivable turnover. Ratio of net credit sales to average net accounts receivable. Measures ability to collect cash from credit customers *(p. 882).*

Acid-test ratio. Ratio of the sum of cash plus short-term investments plus net current receivables to current liabilities. Tells whether the entity could pay all its current liabilities if they came due immediately. Also called the Quick ratio *(p. 881).*

Book value per share of common stock. Common stockholders' equity divided by the number of shares of common stock outstanding *(p. 890).*

Common-size statement. A financial statement that reports only percentages (no dollar amounts); a type of vertical analysis *(p. 874).*

Days' sales in receivables. Ratio of average net accounts receivable to one day's sales. Tells how many days' sales remain in Accounts Receivable awaiting collection *(p. 883).*

Dividend yield. Ratio of dividends per share of stock to the stock's market price per share. Tells the percentage of a stock's market value that the company pays to stockholders as dividends *(p. 889).*

Efficient capital market. A capital market in which market prices fully reflect all information available to the public *(p. 891).*

Horizontal analysis. Study of percentage changes in comparative financial statements *(p. 869).*

Interest-coverage ratio. Another name for the Times-interest-earned ratio *(p. 885).*

Leverage. Another name for Trading on the equity *(p. 888).*

Long-term solvency. Ability to generate enough cash to pay long-term debts as they mature *(p. 869).*

Price/earnings ratio. Ratio of the market price of a share of common stock to the company's earnings per share. Measures the value that the stock market places on $1 of a company's earnings *(p. 889).*

Quick ratio. Another name for the Acid-test ratio *(p. 881).*

Rate of return on common stockholders' equity. Net income minus preferred dividends, divided by average common stockholders' equity. A measure of profitability. Also called Return on common stockholders' equity *(p. 887).*

Rate of return on net sales. Ratio of net income to net sales. A measure of profitability. Also called Return on sales *(p. 886)*.

Rate of return on total assets. The sum of net income plus interest expense divided by average total assets. This ratio measures the success a company has in using its assets to earn income for the persons who finance the business. Also called Return on assets *(p. 886)*.

Return on assets. Another name for Rate of return on total assets *(p. 886)*.

Return on common stockholders' equity. Another name for Rate of return on common stockholders' equity *(p. 887)*.

Return on sales. Another name for Rate of return on net sales *(p. 886)*.

Short-term liquidity. Ability to meet current payments as they come due *(p. 869)*.

Times-interest-earned ratio. Ratio of income from operations to interest expense. Measures the number of times that operating income can cover interest expense. Also called the Interest-coverage ratio *(p. 885)*.

Trading on the equity. Earning more income on borrowed money than the related expense, which increases the earnings for the owners of the business. *(p. 888)*.

Vertical analysis. Analysis of a financial statement that reveals the relationship of each statement item to the total, which is the 100 percent figure *(p. 872)*.

Working capital. Current assets minus current liabilities; measures a business's ability to meet its short-term obligations with its current assets *(p. 879)*.

Answers to Self-Study Questions

1. b $252,000 − $210,000 = $42,000; $42,000/$210,000 = .20
2. c
3. d
4. a
5. b   ($10,000 + $22,000)/$40,000 = .80
6. b
7. d
8. d
9. a
10. c

ASSIGNMENT MATERIAL _____

Questions

1. Identify two groups of users of accounting information and the decisions they base on accounting data.
2. What are three analytical tools that are based on accounting information?
3. Briefly describe horizontal analysis. How do decision makers use this tool of analysis?
4. What is vertical analysis, and what is its purpose?
5. What use is made of common-size statements?
6. State how an investor might analyze the statement of cash flows. How might the investor analyze investing activities data?
7. Why are ratios an important tool of financial analysis? Give an example.
8. Identify two ratios used to measure a company's ability to pay current liabilities. Show how they are computed.

9. Why is the acid-test ratio called by this name?

10. What does the inventory-turnover ratio measure?

11. Suppose the days'-sales-in-receivables ratio of Gomez, Inc., increased from 36 at January 1 to 43 at December 31. Is this a good sign or a bad sign about the company? What would Gomez management do in response to this change?

12. Company A's debt ratio has increased from .50 to .70. Identify a decision maker to whom this increase is important, and state how the increase affects this party's decisions about the company.

13. Which ratio measures the *effect of debt* on (a) financial position (the balance sheet) and (b) the company's ability to pay interest expense (the income statement)?

14. Company A is a chain of grocery stores, and Company B is a computer manufacturer. Which company is likely to have the higher (a) current ratio, (b) inventory turnover, and (c) rate of return on sales? Give your reasons.

15. Identify four ratios used to measure a company's profitability. Show how to compute these ratios and state what information each ratio provides.

16. The price/earnings ratio of General Motors was 6, and the price/earnings ratio of American Express was 45. Which company did the stock market favor? Explain.

17. McDonald's Corporation, the hamburger company, paid cash dividends of $.78⅔ (78 and ⅔ cents) per share when the market price of the company's stock was $58. What was the dividend yield on McDonald's stock. What does dividend yield measure?

18. Hold all other factors constant and indicate whether each of the following situations generally signals good or bad news about a company:
    a. Increase in current ratio
    b. Decrease in inventory turnover
    c. Increase in debt ratio
    d. Decrease in interest-coverage ratio
    e. Increase in return on sales
    f. Decrease in earnings per share
    g. Increase in price/earnings ratio
    h. Increase in book value per share

19. Explain how an investor might use book value per share of stock in making an investment decision.

20. Describe how decision makers use ratio data. What are the limitations of ratios?

Exercises

Exercise 19-1   *Computing year-to-year changes in working capital*   **(L.O. 1)**

What was the amount of change, and the percentage change, in Lux Corporation's working capital during 19X4 and 19X5? Is this trend favorable or unfavorable?

Yr. 4.:
Increase of $13,000 and 2.1%

	Year 5	Year 4	Year 3
Total current assets	$312,000	$260,000	$280,000
Total current liabilities	150,000	117,000	140,000

Exercise 19-2   *Horizontal analysis of an income statement*   **(L.O. 1)**

Prepare a horizontal analysis of the following comparative income statement of Milltown Incorporated. Round percentage changes to the nearest one-tenth percent (three decimal places):

Revenue increased 18.0%
Expenses increased 14.6%

Milltown Incorporated
Comparative Income Statement
Years Ended December 31, 19X9 and 19X8

	19X9	19X8
Total revenue	$440,000	$373,000
Expenses:		
Cost of goods sold	$202,000	$188,000
Selling and general expenses	118,000	93,000
Interest expense	7,000	4,000
Income tax expense	42,000	37,000
Total expenses	369,000	322,000
Net income	$ 71,000	$ 51,000

Why did net income increase by a higher percentage than total revenues increased during 19X9?

Yr. 5.:
Net sales 145%
Net income $149%

Exercise 19-3 *Computing trend percentages* **(L.O. 1)**

Compute trend percentages for net sales and net income for the following five-year period, using year 1 as the base year:

	Year 5	Year 4	Year 3	Year 2	Year 1
	(amounts in thousands)				
Net sales	$1,510	$1,287	$1,106	$1,009	$1,043
Net income	127	114	93	71	85

Which grew more during the period, net sales or net income?

Total liabilities 48.1%

Exercise 19-4 *Vertical analysis of a balance sheet* **(L.O. 2)**

Overseas Shipping, Inc., has requested that you perform a vertical analysis of its balance sheet to determine the component percentages of its assets, liabilities, and stockholders' equity.

Overseas Shipping, Inc.
Balance Sheet
December 31, 19X3

Assets

Total current assets	$ 62,000
Long-term investments	35,000
Property, plant, and equipment, net	227,000
Total assets	$324,000

Liabilities

Total current liabilities	$ 38,000
Long-term debt	118,000
Total liabilities	156,000

Stockholders' Equity

Total stockholders' equity	168,000
Total liabilities and stockholders' equity	$324,000

Exercise 19-5 *Preparing a common-size income statement* **(L.O. 3)**

Prepare a comparative common-size income statement for Milltown Incorporated, using the 19X9 and 19X8 data of Exercise 19-2 and rounding percentages to one-tenth percent (three decimal places).

Exercise 19-6 *Analyzing the statement of cash flows* **(L.O. 4)**

Identify any weaknesses revealed by the statement of cash flows of Perini Investment Consultants.

Perini Investment Consultants
Statement of Cash Flows
For the Current Year

Operating activities:		
Income from operations......................		$12,000
Add (subtract) noncash items:		
Depreciation	$ 23,000	
Net increase in current assets other than cash..	(15,000)	
Net increase in current liabilities exclusive of		
short-term debt	11,000	19,000
Net cash inflow from operating activities		31,000
Investing activities:		
Sale of property, plant, and equipment..........		81,000
Financing activities:		
Issuance of bonds payable	$114,000	
Payment of short-term debt	(101,000)	
Payment of long-term debt....................	(79,000)	
Payment of dividends	(12,000)	
Net cash outflow from financing activities		(78,000)
Increase in cash		$ 34,000

Exercise 19-7 *Computing five ratios* **(L.O. 5)**

The financial statements of Union Electric Corp. include the following items:

	Current Year	Preceding Year
Balance sheet:		
Cash	$ 17,000	$ 22,000
Short-term investments	21,000	26,000
Net receivables	64,000	73,000
Inventory	87,000	71,000
Prepaid expenses	6,000	8,000
Total current assets	195,000	200,000
Total current liabilities	121,000	91,000
Income statement:		
Net credit sales..............	$444,000	
Cost of goods sold...........	237,000	

Required

Compute the following ratios for the current year: (a) current ratio, (b) acid-test ratio, (c) inventory turnover, (d) accounts receivable turnover, and (e) days' sales in average receivables.

Exercise 19-8 *Analyzing the ability to pay current liabilities* (L.O. 5, 6)

Premark Associates has requested that you determine whether the company's ability to pay its current liabilities and long-term debts has improved or deteriorated during 19X5. To answer this question, compute the following ratios for 19X5 and 19X4: (a) current ratio, (b) acid-test ratio, (c) debt ratio, and (d) times-interest-earned ratio. Summarize the results of your analysis.

	19X5	19X4
Cash	$ 31,000	$ 37,000
Short-term investments	28,000	—
Net receivables	102,000	116,000
Inventory	226,000	263,000
Prepaid expenses	11,000	9,000
Total assets	553,000	519,000
Total current liabilities	205,000	241,000
Total liabilities	261,000	273,000
Income from operations	165,000	158,000
Interest expense	26,000	31,000

Exercise 19-9 *Analyzing profitability* (L.O. 5, 6)

Compute four ratios that measure ability to earn profits for Lerner Carbide, Inc., whose comparative income statement appears below. Additional data follow:

Lerner Carbide, Inc.
Comparative Income Statement
Years Ended December 31, 19X1 and 19X0

	19X1	19X0
Net sales	$174,000	$158,000
Cost of goods sold	93,000	86,000
Gross profit	81,000	72,000
Selling and general expenses	48,000	41,000
Income from operations	33,000	31,000
Interest expense	9,000	10,000
Income before income tax	24,000	21,000
Income tax expense	6,000	8,000
Net income	$ 18,000	$ 13,000

Additional data:	19X1	19X0
1. Average total assets	$204,000	$191,000
2. Average common stockholders' equity	$ 96,000	$ 89,000
3. Preferred dividends	$ 3,000	$ 3,000
4. Shares of common stock outstanding	18,000	18,000

Did the company's operating performance improve or deteriorate during 19X1?

Exercise 19-10 *Evaluating a stock as an investment* (L.O. 5, 6)

Evaluate the common stock of Fieldcrest Mills, Inc., as an investment. Specifically, use the three stock ratios to determine whether the stock has increased or decreased in attractiveness during the past year.

	Current Year	Preceding Year
Net income.....................................	$ 58,000	$ 55,000
Dividends (half on preferred stock)	28,000	28,000
Common stockholders' equity at year end		
(100,000 shares)..................................	530,000	500,000
Preferred stockholders' equity at year end...........	200,000	200,000
Market price per share of common stock at year end .	$7.25	$5.75

Problems   (Group A)

Problem 19-1A *Trend percentages, return on sales, and comparison with the industry*
(L.O. 1, 5, 6)

19X6:
1. Net sales 136%
2. .070

Net sales, net income, and total assets for Evergreen Fragrances for a six-year period follow.

	19X6	19X5	19X4	19X3	19X2	19X1
	(amounts in thousands)					
Net sales	$327	$303	$266	$271	$245	$241
Net income	23	21	12	17	14	13
Total assets	286	244	209	197	181	166

Required

1. Compute trend percentages for 19X2 through 19X6, using 19X1 as the base year.
2. Compute the rate of return on net sales for 19X2 through 19X6, rounding to three decimal places. In this industry, rates above 5 percent are considered good, and rates above 7 percent are viewed as outstanding.
3. How does Evergreen's return on net sales compare with the industry?

Problem 19-2A *Common-size statements, analysis of profitability, and comparison with the industry (L.O. 2, 3, 5, 6)*

Net income 1.6%; S/E 41.3%

Top managers of Golden Key Company have asked your help in comparing the company's profit performance and financial position with the average for the department-store industry. The accountant has given you the company's income statement and balance sheet and also the following actual data for the department-store industry.

Golden Key Company
Income Statement
Compared with Industry Average
Year Ended December 31, 19X3

	Golden Key	Industry Average
Net sales.........................	$957,000	100.0%
Cost of goods sold	653,000	65.9
Gross profit	304,000	34.1
Operating expenses	287,000	31.1
Operating income	17,000	3.0
Other expenses	2,000	.4
Net income	$ 15,000	2.6%

Golden Key Company
Balance Sheet
Compared with Industry Average
December 31, 19X3

	Golden Key	Industry Average
Current assets	$448,000	74.4%
Fixed assets, net	127,000	20.0
Intangible assets, net.............	42,000	.6
Other assets.....................	13,000	5.0
Total	$630,000	100.0%
Current liabilities	$246,000	35.6
Long-term liabilities	124,000	19.0
Stockholders' equity	260,000	45.4
Total	$630,000	100.0%

Required

1. Prepare a two-column common-size income statement and a two-column common-size balance sheet for Golden Key. The first column of each statement should present Golden Key's common-size statement, and the second column should show the industry averages.

2. For the profitability analysis, compare Golden Key's (a) ratio of gross profit to net sales, (b) ratio of operating income (loss) to net sales, and (c) ratio of net income (loss) to net sales. Compare these figures with the industry averages. Is Golden Key's profit performance better or worse than average for the industry?

3. For the analysis of financial position, compare Golden Key's (a) ratio of current assets to total assets and (b) ratio of stockholders' equity to total assets. Compare these ratios with the industry averages. Is Golden Key's financial position better or worse than the average for the industry?

Invest in Rocky Mountain

Problem 19-3A *Using the statement of cash flows for decision making* **(L.O. 4)**

You are evaluating two companies as possible investments. The two companies, similar in size, are in the commuter airline business. They fly passengers from Denver and Omaha to smaller cities in their area. Assume that all other available information has been analyzed and that the decision on which company's stock to purchase depends on the information given in their statements of cash flows which appear on the facing page.

Required

Discuss the relative strengths and weaknesses of Coreland and Rocky Mountain. Conclude your discussion by recommending one of the company's stocks as an investment.

2. b. Current ratio 2.05
Debt ratio .48
EPS $3.34

Problem 19-4A *Effects of business transactions on selected ratios* **(L.O. 5, 6)**

Financial statement data of Navasota Building Supply include the following items:

Cash	$ 47,000
Short-term investments	21,000
Accounts receivable, net	102,000
Inventories	274,000
Prepaid expenses	15,000
Total assets	933,000
Short-term notes payable	72,000
Accounts payable	96,000
Accrued liabilities	50,000
Long-term notes payable	146,000
Other long-term liabilities	78,000
Net income	119,000
Number of common shares outstanding	32,000

Required

1. Compute Navasota's current ratio, debt ratio, and earnings per share.
2. Compute each of the three ratios after evaluating the effect of each transaction that follows. Consider each transaction *separately*.
   a. Borrowed $56,000 on a long-term note payable.
   b. Sold short-term investments for $34,000 (cost, $46,000); assume no tax effect of the loss.
   c. Issued 14,000 shares of common stock, receiving cash of $168,000.
   d. Received cash on account, $6,000.

Coreland Airways, Inc.
Statements of Cash Flows
For the Years Ended November 30, 19X9 and 19X8

	19X9	19X8
Operating activities:		
Income (loss) from operations	$ (67,000)	$ 154,000
Add (subtract) noncash items:		
Total	84,000	(23,000)
Net cash inflow from operating activities	17,000	131,000
Investing activities:		
Purchase of property, plant, and equipment	$(120,000)	$ (91,000)
Sale of property, plant, and equipment	118,000	39,000
Sale of long-term investments	52,000	4,000
Net cash inflow (outflow) from investing activities	50,000	(48,000)
Financing activities:		
Issuance of short-term notes payable	$ 122,000	$ 143,000
Payment of short-term notes payable	(179,000)	(134,000)
Payment of cash dividends	(45,000)	(64,000)
Net cash outflow from financing activities	(102,000)	(55,000)
Increase (decrease) in cash	$ (35,000)	$ 28,000
Cash summary from balance sheet:		
Cash balance at beginning of year	$ 131,000	$ 103,000
Increase (decrease) in cash during the year	(35,000)	28,000
Cash balance at end of year	$ 96,000	$ 131,000

Rocky Mountain Express
Statements of Cash Flows
For the Years Ended November 30, 19X9 and 19X8

	19X9	19X8
Operating activities:		
Income from operations	$ 184,000	$ 131,000
Add (subtract) noncash items:		
Total	64,000	62,000
Net cash inflow from operating activities	248,000	193,000
Investing activities:		
Purchase of property, plant, and equipment	$(303,000)	$(453,000)
Sale of property, plant, and equipment	46,000	39,000
Sale of long-term investments	—	33,000
Net cash outflow from investing activities	(257,000)	(381,000)
Financing activities:		
Issuance of long-term notes payable	$ 131,000	$ 83,000
Issuance of short-term notes payable	43,000	35,000
Payment of short-term notes payable	(66,000)	(18,000)
Net cash inflow from financing activities	108,000	100,000
Increase (decrease) in cash	$(99,000)	$(88,000)
Cash summary from balance sheet:		
Cash balance at beginning of year	$ 116,000	$ 204,000
Increase (decrease) in cash during the year	99,000	(88,000)
Cash balance at end of year	$ 215,000	$ 116,000

e. Paid short-term notes payable, $51,000.
f. Purchased merchandise of $48,000 on account, debiting Inventory.
g. Paid off long-term liabilities, $78,000.
h. Declared, but did not pay, a $31,000 cash dividend on the common stock.

Use the following format for your answer:

Requirement 1.		Current Ratio	Debt Ratio	Earnings Per Share

Requirement 2.	Transaction (letter)	Current Ratio	Debt Ratio	Earnings Per Share

Problem 19-5A *Using ratios to evaluate a stock investment* **(L.O. 5, 6)**

19X4:
Inven. turnover 1.15
Return on assets .140
EPS $3.35

Comparative financial statement data of Ameron, Inc., are as follows:

Ameron, Inc.
Comparative Income Statement
Years Ended December 31, 19X4 and 19X3

	19X4	19X3
Net sales	$667,000	$599,000
Cost of goods sold	378,000	283,000
Gross profit	289,000	316,000
Operating expenses	129,000	147,000
Income from operations	160,000	169,000
Interest expense	47,000	41,000
Income before income tax	113,000	128,000
Income tax expense	44,000	53,000
Net income	$ 69,000	$ 75,000

Ameron, Inc.
Comparative Balance Sheet
December 31, 19X4 and 19X3
(selected 19X2 amounts given for computation of ratios)

	19X4	19X3	19X2
Current assets:			
Cash	$ 37,000	$ 40,000	
Current receivables, net	188,000	151,000	$138,000
Inventories	372,000	286,000	184,000
Prepaid expenses	5,000	20,000	
Total current assets	602,000	497,000	
Property, plant, and equipment, net	287,000	276,000	
Total assets	$889,000	$773,000	707,000
Total current liabilities	$286,000	$267,000	
Long-term liabilities	245,000	235,000	
Total liabilities	531,000	502,000	
Preferred stockholders' equity, 4%, $20 par	50,000	50,000	
Common stockholders' equity, no-par	308,000	221,000	148,000
Total liabilities and stockholders' equity	$889,000	$773,000	

Other information:

a. Market price of Ameron common stock: $30.75 at December 31, 19X4, and $40.25 at December 31, 19X3.

b. Common shares outstanding: 20,000 during 19X4 and 19,000 during 19X3.

c. All sales on credit.

Required

1. Compute the following ratios for 19X4 and 19X3:
   a. Current ratio
   b. Inventory turnover
   c. Accounts receivable turnover
   d. Times-interest-earned ratio
   e. Return on assets
   f. Return on common stockholders' equity
   g. Earnings per share of common stock
   h. Price/earnings ratio
   i. Book value per share of common stock
2. Decide (a) whether Ameron's financial position improved or deteriorated during 19X4 and (b) whether the investment attractiveness of its common stock appears to have increased or decreased.

Problem 19-6A *Using ratios to decide between two stock investments* **(L.O. 5, 6)**

Buy Health Corp.;
Price/earnings 21.6

Assume you are purchasing stock in a company in the hospital supply industry. Suppose you have narrowed the choice to HealthCorp and Providence, Inc., and have assembled the following data:

Selected income statement data for current year:

	HealthCorp	Providence, Inc.
Net sales (all on credit)	$603,000	$519,000
Cost of goods sold	454,000	387,000
Income from operations	93,000	72,000
Interest expense	—	8,000
Net income	56,000	38,000

Selected balance sheet and market price data at end of current year:

	HealthCorp	Providence, Inc.
Current assets:		
Cash	$ 25,000	$ 39,000
Short-term investments	6,000	13,000
Current receivables, net	189,000	164,000
Inventories	211,000	183,000
Prepaid expenses	19,000	15,000
Total current assets	450,000	414,000
Total assets	974,000	938,000
Total current liabilities	366,000	338,000
Total liabilities	667,000	691,000
Preferred stock, 4%, $100 par		25,000
Common stock, $1 par (150,000 shares)	150,000	
$5 par (20,000 shares)		100,000
Total stockholders' equity	307,000	247,000
Market price per share of common stock	$8	$47.50

Selected balance sheet data at beginning of current year:

	HealthCorp	Providence, Inc.
Current receivables, net	$142,000	$193,000
Inventories	209,000	197,000
Total assets	842,000	909,000
Preferred stockholders' equity, 4%, $100 par ...		25,000
Common stock, $1 par (150,000 shares)	150,000	
$5 par (20,000 shares)		100,000
Total stockholders' equity	263,000	215,000

Your investment strategy is to purchase the stocks of companies that have low price/earnings ratios but appear to be in good shape financially. Assume you have analyzed all other factors, and your decision depends on the results of the ratio analysis to be performed.

Required

Compute the following ratios for both companies for the current year and decide which company's stock better fits your investment strategy.

1. Current ratio
2. Acid-test ratio
3. Inventory turnover
4. Days' sales in average receivables
5. Debt ratio
6. Times-interest-earned ratio
7. Return on net sales

8. Return on total assets
9. Return on common stockholders' equity
10. Earnings per share of common stock
11. Book value per share of common stock
12. Price/earnings ratio

(Group B)

19X9:
1. Net sales 123%
2. .138

Problem 19-1B   *Trend percentages, return on common equity, and comparison with the industry   (L.O. 1, 5, 6)*

Net sales, net income, and common stockholders' equity for ConEd Corporation for a six-year period follow.

	19X9	19X8	19X7	19X6	19X5	19X4
			(amounts in thousands)			
Net sales	$781	$714	$621	$532	$642	$634
Net income	51	45	42	38	41	40
Ending common stockholders' equity	386	354	330	296	272	252

Required

1. Compute trend percentages for 19X5 through 19X9, using 19X4 as the base year.
2. Compute the rate of return on average common stockholders' equity for 19X5 through 19X9, rounding to three decimal places. In this industry, rates of 13 percent are average, rates above 16 percent are considered good, and rates above 20 percent are viewed as outstanding.
3. How does ConEd's return on common stockholders' equity compare with the industry?

Common-size statements, analysis of profitability, and comparison with the industry **(L.O. 2, 3, 5, 6)**   Net income 4.6%; S/E 35.1%

Mears Illuminating has asked your help in comparing the company's profit performance and financial position with the average for the sporting goods retail industry. The proprietor has given you the company's income statement and balance sheet and also the industry average data for retailers of sporting goods.

Mears Illuminating
Income Statement
Compared with Industry Average
Year Ended December 31, 19X6

	Mears	Industry Average
Net sales...............	$781,000	100.0%
Cost of goods sold........	497,000	65.8
Gross profit.............	284,000	34.2
Operating expenses.......	243,000	29.7
Operating income.........	41,000	4.5
Other expenses...........	5,000	.4
Net income.............	$ 36,000	4.1%

Mears Illuminating
Balance Sheet
Compared with Industry Average
December 31, 19X6

	Mears	Industry Average
Current assets............	$350,000	70.9%
Fixed assets, net..........	74,000	23.6
Intangible assets, net......	4,000	.8
Other assets..............	22,000	4.7
Total	$450,000	100.0%
Current liabilities	$230,000	48.1%
Long-term liabilities.......	62,000	16.6
Stockholders' equity	158,000	35.3
Total	$450,000	100.0%

Required

1. Prepare a two-column common-size income statement and a two-column common-size balance sheet for Mears. The first column of each statement should present Mears's common-size statement, and the second column should show the industry averages.

2. For the profitability analysis, compare Mears's (a) ratio of gross profit to net sales, (b) ratio of operating income to net sales, and (c) ratio of net income to net sales. Compare these figures with the industry averages. Is Mears's profit performance better or worse than the industry average?

3. For the analysis of financial position, compute Mears's (a) ratio of current assets to total assets and (b) ratio of stockholders' equity to total assets. Compare these ratios with the industry averages. Is Mears's financial position better or worse than the industry averages?

Problem 19-3B *Using the statement of cash flows for decision making* **(L.O. 4)**   Invest in Southern

You have been asked to evaluate two companies as possible investments. The two companies, similar in size, buy computers, airplanes, and other high-cost assets to lease to other businesses. Assume that all other available information has been analyzed, and the decision on which company's stock to purchase depends on the information given in their statements of cash flows which appear on the next page.

Required

Discuss the relative strengths and weaknesses of each company. Conclude your discussion by recommending one company's stock as an investment.

Southern Leasing Corporation
Statements of Cash Flows
For the Years Ended September 30, 19X5 and 19X4

	19X5	19X4
Operating activities:		
Income from operations..	$ 79,000	$ 71,000
Add (subtract) noncash items:		
Total	19,000	—
Net cash inflow from operating activities	98,000	71,000
Investing activities:		
Purchase of property, plant, and equipment.. $(121,000)		$(91,000)
Sale of long-term investments 13,000		18,000
Net cash outflow from investing activities	(108,000)	(73,000)
Financing activities:		
Issuance of long-term notes payable .... $ 46,000		$ 43,000
Payment of short-term notes payable .... (15,000)		(40,000)
Payment of cash dividends .... (12,000)		(9,000)
Net cash inflow (outflow) from financing activities.........	19,000	(6,000)
Increase (decrease) in cash	$ 9,000	$ (8,000)
Cash summary from balance sheet:		
Cash balance at beginning of year	$ 72,000	$ 80,000
Increase (decrease) in cash during the year ...	9,000	(8,000)
Cash balance at end of year..............	$ 81,000	$ 72,000

Leasehold Assets, Inc.
Statements of Cash Flows
For the Years Ended September 30, 19X5 and 19X4

	19X5	19X4
Operating activities:		
Income from operations..	$ 37,000	$ 74,000
Add (subtract) noncash items:		
Total	14,000	(4,000)
Net cash inflow from operating activities	51,000	70,000
Investing activities:		
Purchase of property, plant, and equipment.. $ (13,000)		$ (3,000)
Sale of property, plant, and equipment......... 86,000		79,000
Sale of long-term investments 13,000		—
Net cash inflow from investing activities......	86,000	76,000
Financing activities:		
Issuance of short-term notes payable .... $ 73,000		$ 19,000
Issuance of long-term notes payable 31,000		42,000
Payment of short-term notes payable .... (181,000)		(148,000)
Payment of long-term notes payable .... (55,000)		(32,000)
Net cash outflow from financing activities	(132,000)	(119,000)
Increase in cash	$ 5,000	$ 27,000
Cash summary from balance sheet:		
Cash balance at beginning of year	$ 31,000	$ 4,000
Increase in cash during the year	5,000	27,000
Cash balance at end of year..............	$ 36,000	$ 31,000

Problem 19-4B *Effects of business transactions on selected ratios* **(L.O. 5, 6)**

2. a. Current ratio 2.07
Debt ratio .49
EPS $1.58

Financial statement data of Ashkenazy, Inc., include the following items.

Cash	$ 22,000
Short-term investments	19,000
Accounts receivable, net	83,000
Inventories	141,000
Prepaid expenses........................	8,000
Total assets	657,000
Short-term notes payable	49,000
Accounts payable	103,000
Accrued liabilities	38,000
Long-term notes payable..................	160,000
Other long-term liabilities	31,000
Net income	71,000
Number of common shares outstanding	40,000

Required

1. Compute Ashkenazy's current ratio, debt ratio, and earnings per share.
2. Compute each of the three ratios after evaluating the effect of each transaction that follows. Consider each transaction *separately*.
   a. Issued 5,000 shares of common stock, receiving cash of $120,000.
   b. Received cash on account, $19,000.
   c. Paid short-term notes payable, $32,000.
   d. Purchased merchandise of $26,000 on account, debiting Inventory.
   e. Paid off long-term liabilities, $31,000.
   f. Declared, but did not pay, a $22,000 cash dividend on common stock.
   g. Borrowed $85,000 on a long-term note payable.
   h. Sold short-term investments for $18,000 (cost, $11,000); assume no income tax on the gain.

Use the following format for your answer:

Requirement 1.		Current Ratio	Debt Ratio	Earnings per Share
		————	————	————
Requirement 2.	Transaction (letter)	Current Ratio	Debt Ratio	Earnings per Share
	————	————	————	————

Problem 19-5B *Using ratios to evaluate a stock investment* **(L.O. 5, 6)**

19X7:
Inven. turnover 1.33
Return on assets .117
EPS $4.00

Comparative financial statement data of Cambridge Development Corp. appear below.

Required

1. Compute the following ratios for 19X7 and 19X6:
   a. Current ratio
   b. Inventory turnover
   c. Accounts receivable turnover
   d. Times-interest-earned ratio
   e. Return on assets
   f. Return on common stockholders' equity
   g. Earnings per share of common stock
   h. Price/earnings ratio
   i. Book value per share of common stock
2. Decide (a) whether Cambridge's financial position improved or deteriorated during 19X7 and (b) whether the investment attractiveness of its common stock appears to have increased or decreased.

Cambridge Development Corp.
Comparative Income Statement
Years Ended December 31, 19X7 and 19X6

	19X7	19X6
Net sales	$462,000	$427,000
Cost of goods sold	229,000	218,000
Gross profit	233,000	209,000
Operating expenses	136,000	134,000
Income from operations	97,000	75,000
Interest expense	21,000	12,000
Income before income tax	76,000	63,000
Income tax expense	30,000	27,000
Net income	$ 46,000	$ 36,000

Cambridge Development Corp.
Comparative Balance Sheet
December 31, 19X7 and 19X6
(selected 19X5 amounts given for computation of ratios)

	19X7	19X6	19X5
Current assets:			
Cash	$ 91,000	$ 97,000	
Current receivables, net	107,000	116,000	$103,000
Inventories	182,000	162,000	207,000
Prepaid expenses	16,000	7,000	
Total current assets	396,000	382,000	
Property, plant, and equipment, net	189,000	178,000	
Total assets	$585,000	$560,000	598,000
Total current liabilities	$206,000	$223,000	
Long-term liabilities	119,000	117,000	
Total liabilities	325,000	340,000	
Preferred stockholders' equity, 6%, $100 par	100,000	100,000	
Common stockholders' equity, no-par	160,000	120,000	90,000
Total liabilities and stockholders' equity	$585,000	$560,000	

Other information:

a. Market price of Cambridge common stock: $39 at December 31, 19X7, and $32.50 at December 31, 19X6.

b. Common shares outstanding: 10,000 during 19X7 and 9,000 during 19X6.

c. All sales on credit.

Buy Advantage;
Price/earnings 8.3

Problem 19-6B   *Using ratios to decide between two stock investments* **(L.O. 5, 6)**

Assume you are purchasing an investment and have decided to invest in a company in the air-conditioning and heating business. Suppose you have narrowed the choice to Odegaard Corp. and Advantage, Inc. You have assembled the following selected data:

Selected income statement data for current year:

	Odegaard Corp.	Advantage, Inc.
Net sales (all on credit)	$371,000	$497,000
Cost of goods sold	209,000	258,000
Income from operations........................	79,000	138,000
Interest expense................................	—	19,000
Net income	48,000	72,000

Selected balance sheet and market price data at end of current year:

	Odegaard Corp.	Advantage, Inc.
Current assets:		
Cash	$ 22,000	$ 19,000
Short-term investments	20,000	18,000
Current receivables, net......................	42,000	46,000
Inventories	87,000	100,000
Prepaid expenses............................	2,000	3,000
Total current assets..........................	173,000	186,000
Total assets	265,000	328,000
Total current liabilities	108,000	98,000
Total liabilities	108,000	131,000
Preferred stock: 5%, $100 par..................		20,000
Common stock, $1 par (10,000 shares)...........	10,000	
$2.50 par (5,000 shares)		12,500
Total stockholders' equity	157,000	197,000
Market price per share of common stock	$51	$118

Selected balance sheet data at beginning of current year:

	Odegaard Corp.	Advantage, Inc.
Current receivables, net..........................	$ 40,000	$ 48,000
Inventories	93,000	88,000
Total assets	259,000	270,000
Preferred stockholders' equity 5%, $100 par.........	—	20,000
Common stock, $1 par (10,000 shares).............	10,000	
$2.50 par (5,000 shares)		12,500
Total stockholders' equity	118,000	126,000

Your investment strategy is to purchase the stocks of companies that have low price/earnings ratios but appear to be in good shape financially. Assume you have analyzed all other factors, and your decision depends on the results of the ratio analysis to be performed.

Required

Compute the following ratios for both companies for the current year and decide which company's stock better fits your investment strategy.

1. Current ratio
2. Acid-test ratio
3. Inventory turnover
4. Days' sales in average receivables
5. Debt ratio
6. Times-interest-earned ratio
7. Return on net sales
8. Return on total assets
9. Return on common stockholders' equity
10. Earnings per share of common stock
11. Book value per share of common stock
12. Price/earnings ratio

Extending Your Knowledge

Decision Problems

No check figure

1. Identifying Action to Cut Losses and Establish Profitability   (L.O. 2, 5, 6)

Suppose you manage Early Bird, Inc., a sporting goods and bicycle shop, which lost money during the past year. Before you can set the business on a successful course, you must first analyze the company and industry data for the current year in an effort to learn what is wrong. The data appear below.

Required

Based on your analysis of these figures, suggest four courses of action Early Bird should take to reduce its losses and establish profitable operations. Give your reasons for each suggestion.

Early Bird Balance Sheet Data

	Early Bird	Industry Average
Cash and short-term investments	2.1%	6.8%
Trade receivables, net	16.1	11.0
Inventory	64.2	60.5
Prepaid expenses	1.0	0.0
Total current assets	83.4	78.3
Fixed assets, net	12.6	15.2
Other assets	4.0	6.5
Total assets	100.0%	100.0%
Notes payable, short-term, 12%	18.1%	14.0%
Accounts payable	20.1	25.1
Accrued liabilities	7.8	7.9
Total current liabilities	46.0	47.0
Long-term debt, 11%	19.7	16.4
Total liabilities	65.7	63.4
Common stockholders' equity	34.3	36.6
Total liabilities and stockholders' equity	100.0%	100.0%

Early Bird Income Statement Data

	Early Bird	Industry Average
Net sales	100.0%	100.0%
Cost of sales	(69.7)	(64.8)
Gross profit	30.3	35.2
Operating expense	(35.6)	(32.3)
Operating income (loss)	(5.3)	2.9
Interest expense	(6.8)	(1.3)
Other revenue	1.1	.3
Income (loss) before income tax	(11.0)	1.9
Income tax (expense) saving	4.4	(.8)
Net income (loss)	(6.6)%	1.1%

2. Understanding the Components of Accounting Ratios *(L.O. 5, 6)*

No check figure

a. Harvey Drago is the controller of Hunan Industries, Inc., whose year end is December 31. He prepares checks for suppliers in December and posts them to the appropriate accounts in that month. However, he holds on to the checks and actually mails them to the suppliers in January. What financial ratio(s) are most affected by the action? What is Drago's purpose in undertaking this activity?

b. Janet Wong has asked you about the stock of a particular company. She finds it attractive because it has a high dividend yield relative to another stock she is also considering. Explain to her the meaning of the ratio and the danger of making a decision based on it alone.

c. Limeridge Ltd.'s owners are concerned because the number of days' sales in receivables has increased over the previous two years. Explain why the ratio might have increased.

Ethical Issue

Krisler Corporation's long-term debt agreements make certain demands on the business. Krisler may not purchase treasury stock in excess of the balance of Retained Earnings. Also, Long-term Debt may not exceed Stockholders' Equity, and the current ratio may not fall below 1.50. If Krisler fails to meet these requirements, the company's lenders have the authority to take over management of the corporation.

Changes in consumer demand have made it hard for Krisler to sell its products. Current liabilities have mounted faster than current assets, causing the current ratio to fall to 1.47. Prior to releasing financial statements, Krisler management is scrambling to improve the current ratio. The controller points out that an investment can be classified as either long-term or short-term, depending on management's intention. By deciding to convert an investment to cash within one year, Krisler can classify the investment as short-term—a current asset. On the controller's recommendation, Krisler's board of directors votes to reclassify long-term investments as short-term.

Required

1. What effect will reclassifying the investment have on the current ratio? Is Krisler Corporation's financial position stronger as a result of reclassifying the investment?

2. Shortly after releasing the financial statements, sales improve and so, then, does the current ratio. As a result, Krisler management decides not to sell the investments it had reclassified as short-term. Accordingly, the company reclassifies the investments as long-term. Has management behaved unethically? Give your reason.

Financial Statement Problems

1. Measuring Profitability and Analyzing Stock as an Investment *(L.O. 5, 6)*

Use the financial statements and the data labeled Comparison with Prior Years that appear at the end of the Goodyear Tire & Rubber Company financial statements (Appendix C) to chart the company's progress during 1987 through 1990. Compute the following ratios that measure profitability and which are used to analyze stock as an investment.

b. Return on common S/E 1990, (.018); 1989, .099
Return on assets 1990, .033; 1989, .054

PROFITABILITY MEASURES
a. Return on net sales
b. Return on common stockholders' equity
c. Return on total assets. Interest expense for 1987 was $282.5 million.

STOCK ANALYSIS MEASURE
d. Price/earnings ratio. (Use the average of the "High" and the "Low" stock prices for each year.)

Is the trend in the profitability measures consistent with the trend in the stock analysis measure? Evaluate Goodyear's overall outlook for the future.

2. Measuring Profitability and Analyzing Stock as an Investment (L.O. 5, 6)

Obtain the annual report of an actual company of your choosing. Annual reports are available in various forms including the original document in hard copy, microfiche, and computerized data bases such as that provided by Disclosure, Inc.

Use the financial statements and the multi-year summary data to chart the company's progress during the three most recent years including the current year. Compute the following ratios that measure profitability and which are used to analyze stock as an investment.

PROFITABILITY MEASURES
a. Return on net sales
b. Return on common stockholders' equity
c. Return on total assets

STOCK ANALYSIS MEASURE
d. Price/earnings ratio (If given, use the average of the "high" and "low" stock prices for each year.)

Is the trend in the profitability measures consistent with the trend in the stock analysis measure? Evaluate the company's overall outlook for the future.

Comprehensive Problem for Part Six

In this problem you are to decide whether to lend $100 million to The Goodyear Tire & Rubber Company, whose financial statements appear in Appendix C. Examine the statements, including the Management Discussion and Analysis, Accounting Policies, Notes to Financial Statements, Comparison With Prior Years, and the Reports of Management and Independent Accountants. In addition to the statements in the appendix, you will also need these data from Goodyear's December 31, 1988, 1987, and 1986 annual reports:

	Millions		
	1988	**1987**	**1986**
Cash and cash equivalents...............	$ 234.1	$ 200.5	$ 130.5
Short term securities	—	—	—
Accounts and notes receivable	1,578.4	1,501.3	1,367.2
Inventories.............................	1,635.5	1,501.4	1,352.2
Prepaid expenses	109.9	101.3	82.7
Net assets held for sale..................	—	—	—
Total current assets	$3,557.9	$3,304.5	—
Total current liabilities	$2,458.5	$2,139.6	$2,142.9
Cost of goods sold	—	$7,374.6	—
Interest expense	—	$ 282.5	—

To aid your lending decision, compute or locate in the Goodyear report the following ratios and other decision-relevant items for each year 1987 through 1990:

1. Current ratio
2. Acid-test ratio
3. Cash collections from customers
4. Inventory turnover
5. Days' sales in average receivables
6. Debt ratio
7. Times-interest-earned ratio (For convenience, use income from continuing operations before extraordinary item, in the Comparison with Prior Years)
8. Gross margin percentage
9. Rate of return on total assets
10. Rate of return on common stockholders' equity
11. Earnings per share of common stock.
12. Book value per share of common stock
13. Price/earnings ratio (Use the average of the "High" and "Low" stock prices for each year.)

Required

Analyze the trends in these ratios, and write a one-page memo to the loan committee of the bank where you work as a credit analyst. Make a recommendation to the loan committee, giving the reasoning behind your conclusion.

Chapter 20

Introduction to Management Accounting: The Master Budget

Cambridge, Mass.—Lotus Development Corp. said it has lowered its growth and profitability *goals*, reflecting what it calls a "maturation" of the software market.

Jim P. Manzi, chairman and president of the software maker, . . . said the company . . . has scaled back its *goal* of 25 percent pretax profit margins. But he noted that the new *target* of a 20 percent to 25 percent range would represent an improvement over the company's actual margins of 15 percent last year and 17 percent in 1988. . . .

He said the lower growth *goal* reflects slower growth in sales of personal computers. However, he said that . . . the revenue will be more *predictable* than it has been.

"This isn't rocket science," he said. "There is a long-term dynamic going on in the entire industry." [Emphasis added]

Source: Adapted from William M. Bulkeley, "Lotus Trims Goals for Growth, Cites Maturity of Market," *The Wall Street Journal*, September 12, 1990, p. B5.

Our study of accounting has focused on gathering, processing, and reporting information for decision makers outside the business. Some of these outside parties are investors, creditors, and government agencies. Thus far we have looked through their eyes at a business's past performance and financial position. The income statement tells users the results of the company's operations. The statement of cash flows reports where cash came from and how it was spent. The balance sheet shows the company's current financial position. Accounting designed to report to parties outside the business is called financial accounting.

We now shift our focus. We turn to a discussion of how accounting information helps shape the business's future, and we do this through the eyes of the people who run the business. The decision makers inside the company are called managers, and accounting designed to meet their information needs is called *management accounting*. The opening vignette illustrates this shift in focus. As you were reading it, did you notice the emphasis on goals, targets, and management predictions? The final two paragraphs of the vignette underscore the difficulty of budgeting. Exhibit 20-1 summarizes the distinctions between management accounting and financial accounting.

Chapter 20 begins our study of management accounting by showing how budgets are prepared. We deal with the familiar financial statements: income statements and balance sheets. However, our statements will compile planned figures, not past figures, and we will evaluate performance by comparing actual results with budgeted amounts.

Chapter 21 introduces a model of cost-volume-profit relationships, a favorite planning tool of managers. Our first two chapters on management accounting are confined to nonmanufacturing organizations. In this way, we can explore two major tools (budgets and the cost-volume-profit model) without contending with the many new terms associated with manufacturing organizations. The latter appear in Chapters 22 and 23, which describe manufacturing accounting systems. Then Chapters 24, 25, and 26 pursue management accounting tools in more depth. Chapter 24 extends the coverage of budgeting to flexible budgets and standard costs. Chapter 25 covers responsibility accounting, and Chapter 26 shows how to use accounting information to make some special decisions. Above all, recognize that management accounting applies to all kinds of organizations, not just manufacturing companies.

Two Themes in Management Accounting

Two themes of management accounting are (1) the cost-benefit criterion and (2) behavioral implications. The *cost-benefit criterion* is a means for choosing among alternative accounting systems or methods—how well they help achieve management goals in relation to their costs. We use this common-

Point to Stress: Financial accounting is used to produce financial statements for use by outsiders in evaluating the performance of the business. Financial statements must thus be prepared according to GAAP.

Management accounting provides managers with information needed to run the business successfully. Because the information is used only by insiders, it does not have to be reported according to GAAP.

Keep in mind that management accounting reports on the same data that is included in financial statements, but the information is presented in a manner and with a degree of detail that is most helpful to management.

Point to Stress: Remember that the financial statements are prepared for investors and creditors. This group does not need the detail that a manager does. For example, an investor does not need to know how much the long-distance telephone rates are. That piece of information is probably irrelevant to an investing decision. But telephone rates are manageable and should be the concern of someone in the organization. Thus, telephone rates would be important to management.

EXHIBIT 20-1 *Distinctions Between Management Accounting and Financial Accounting*

	Management Accounting	Financial Accounting
1. Primary users	Managers of the business	Outside parties (investors and creditors) and managers of the business
2. Decision criterion	Comparison of costs and benefits of proposed action	Comparison of accounts with generally accepted accounting principles (GAAP)
3. Behavioral implications	Concern about how reports will affect employee behavior	Concern about adequacy of disclosure. Behavioral implications are secondary
4. Time focus	Future orientation: Example: 19X3 **budget** versus 19X3 **actual** performance	Past orientation: Example: 19X3 **actual** versus 19X2 **actual** performance
5. Reports	Detailed reports on parts of the entity: products, departments, territories	Summary reports primarily on the entity as a whole

sense technique every day. For example, suppose you are asked whether you want cheese on your hamburger for an extra 25 cents. You weigh the benefit of adding the cheese against the cost. If the benefit exceeds the cost, you order cheese. If the benefit is less than 25 cents, you forgo the cheese.

A business application of the cost-benefit criterion is the installation of a budgeting system. A major benefit is to compel managers to plan and thus make different decisions than would have occurred from using only a historical system. Is an accounting system a good buy? The answer depends on managers' weighing perceived benefits against additional costs.

The *behavioral implications* of a course of action are also critical. Managers consider the effect of the action on people's behavior. Suppose the company in our example tries to increase sales by pressuring its sales staff to meet quotas. If a salesperson fails to meet quota for three consecutive months, he is fired. Depending on the personalities of the people involved, such a policy may lead to increased sales. But it may also create fear and cause a decline in sales. Effective management accounting systems apply the cost-benefit criterion in light of the behavioral implications of proposed action.

The Role of Management

How do managers use accounting information? Managers determine the company's goals and then plan and control its operations to reach those goals. They set long-range targets by asking questions such as: What will the company's total assets be in 5 years? By how much can the business increase sales over the next 10 years? Should the company spend $5 million on research to develop a new product line? Will it be profitable to enter the California-Oregon-Washington market? The most successful executives are able to consider a wide range of possible courses of action for their company. They answer these types of long-range questions by developing concrete plans of action.

Business must operate day by day also. Managers set short-range targets and communicate these goals to subordinates. To increase profits, suppose a business must increase production to 35,000 units next month. Similarly, cash inflow from operations must be $600,000 during December. Short-range goals like these must fit within the company's long-range strategy.

What features must an accounting system have to best meet management's information needs? What data help managers to plan and control business operations? How are decisions made by managers? This chapter and the next several answer these questions. We begin our discussion of management accounting by studying a manager's most valuable accounting tool: the budget.

The Budgeting System

A well-designed budgeting system includes the budget, the budget committee, and the budget period.

The Budget

The **budget** is management's quantitative expression of a plan of action and an aid to coordination and implementation. Budgets include quantities of products to be sold and their expected selling prices, numbers of employees and their pay, and a host of other amounts that are ultimately expressed in dollars. The budget summarizes the planning decisions of the business. A company may use a single budget to control all its operations or a separate budget for each subunit. This choice depends on the plans of the particular company's management. Our discussion will center on a company that uses an overall master budget to guide its operations. The **master budget** is the set of major financial statements and supporting schedules for the entire organization.

Point to Stress: A budget is a financial forecast, in writing, that communicates management's goals to employees. It is far more effective to have a formal plan than to just say, for example, "Okay, let's get sales up this year, you guys!" There should be no misunderstanding if the plan is in writing.

The Budget Committee

In many small businesses, the budgeting process is rather informal, with the owner and the employees deciding on goals for the future. In most medium-size-to-large organizations the **budget committee** oversees the preparation of the master budget. Because the master budget is the overall financial plan for the entire company, the budget committee includes representatives from all departments. Working together, they develop budget estimates "from the bottom up." Employees at the lowest level provide budget estimates to their supervisors, who make adjustments and forward the budget to middle managers, and so on up the line. For example, the vice-president of sales has each salesperson set a goal for the next period. The vice-president considers the goals of each salesperson and prepares an overall budget for the sales department. With sales personnel at all levels participating in the budget process, they are likely to work harder to achieve the budget than if it is handed down

Point to Stress: Extensive participation throughout all levels of the company is critical to formulating a workable budget. Employees cooperate more if they have a part in the budgeting process.

by top management. All other departments likewise collect budget information and forward it to the budget committee.

The committee coordinates the budget for the company as a whole. Without this coordination, the cost-of-goods-sold budget or the operating expense budget may be out of line with the sales budget, and vice versa.

Although top management has the final say in establishing the budget, it is best when many employees contribute to the overall process. An ideal budget results in all employees striving for excellence by trying to meet a clear-cut, coordinated set of goals.

The Budget Period

Point to Stress: Many companies use a continuous budgeting process, which is discussed later in this chapter, so they always have a budget for the next period. As one month passes, another is added to the budget.

Budgets may cover any time period. Many companies use monthly, weekly, and daily cash budgets to ensure that they have enough cash on hand to meet immediate needs. Sales and expense budgets usually cover the accounting period, which may be a month, a quarter, or a year. Aligning the budget period with the accounting period makes the comparison of budgeted amounts and actual amounts easy. Most long-range budgets cover a five-year period. However, spans of 2, 3, or even 10 years are used.

Benefits of a Budget

The budgeting process offers these advantages:

Point to Stress: It is easy for managers to get so involved in daily crises that they fail to see beyond today. Budgeting forces management to plan for the future.

1. *Provides direction.* The budgeting system forces managers to set realistic goals for the future. Without a formal plan, managers lack direction. This lack of planning filters throughout the company. The budget guides managers and department employees toward the achievement of specific goals. We all work better with a goal in mind.

Point to Stress: Most people perform better if they know what is expected of them. The budgeting process communicates goals to employees so that they will be aware of management's expectations.

2. *Motivates employees.* The budget motivates employees at all levels to meet the business's goals. Their work in preparing the budget makes it their personal target. This motivational aspect of budgeting underscores how budgeting affects employee behavior. Budgets can have negative effects on employee morale if used improperly. For example, some top managers simply impose the budget on their employees and hold employees responsible for its achievement. In this case, the budgeting system may demoralize workers and actually result in lower, rather than higher, profits.

Point to Stress: In many large companies, the vice-presidents of different departments may be in different buildings or even different cities. The budgeting process forces communication among all departments.

3. *Coordinates activities.* The budget coordinates the activities of the entire organization. Coordination is crucial because the budget for one department affects other departments. For example, the company may be able to sell 50,000 units to earn its target net income. But the manufacturing plant may be able to produce only 40,000 units. The budget thus helps top managers identify the need to expand the plant by purchasing additional equipment. In turn managers may identify the need for additional sales personnel, office workers, delivery vehicles, and so on.

Point to Stress: Employees are often antagonistic toward the budgeting process because it entails performance evaluation.

4. *Helps performance evaluation.* A budgeting system aids performance evaluation. The comparison of budgeted and actual amounts highlights areas that are performing according to plan and areas that need improvement. Actual cost of goods sold in excess of the budgeted amount may lead the business to start buying from a new supplier, or it may lead top management to fire the purchasing manager responsible for paying too high a price for inventory.

EXHIBIT 20-2 *Management Use of Budgeting and Accounting*

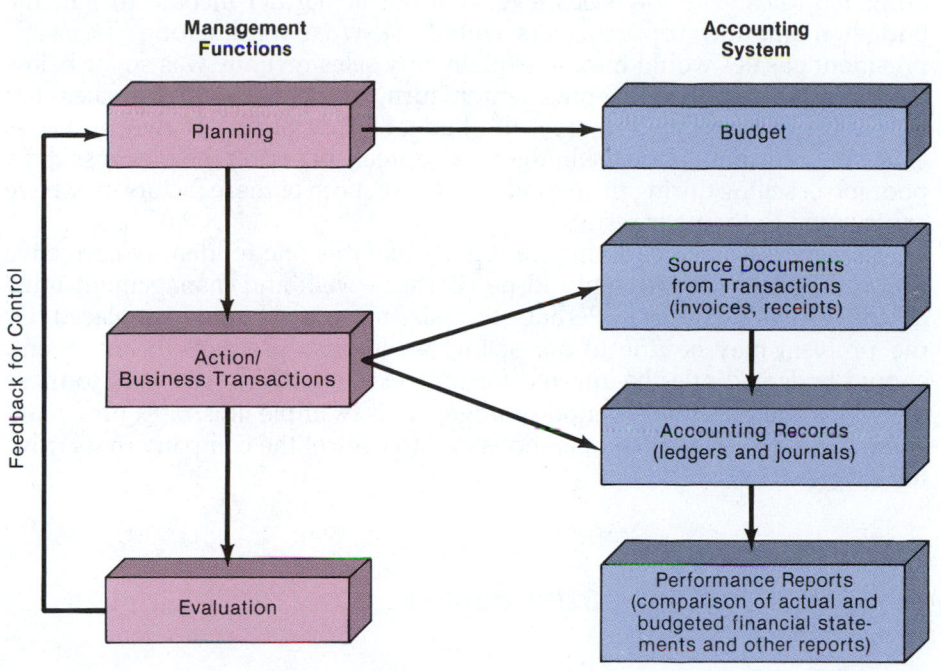

Point to Stress: In the chapter-opening vignette, Lotus redefines its goals. The company can do this, in part, because it had established some goals in the first place. Budgeting helps a company define its goals, and pinpoint when it is not meeting those goals. Budgeting highlights those areas needing change. If Lotus had not budgeted, it would probably have been slower to react to changes in its environment.

Without the budget, the top management may not even know the company is spending too much on inventory.

Exhibit 20-2 diagrams how managers use budgeting. Management planning (see the upper-left corner of the exhibit) leads to the budget. During the period, the business takes action by engaging in transactions—buying and selling. These transactions produce source documents, accounting records, and in turn performance reports. The performance reports are evaluated by managers whose feedback helps to control the organization. Managers then make new plans. Thus begins a new cycle of management planning and control.

The Performance Report

The comparison of budgeted goals with actual results is a key element in evaluating operations, identifying the need for corrective action, and preparing next period's budget. This point deserves a closer look. The performance report in Exhibit 20-3 serves as the basis for our discussion.

Discussion Question: Let's assume the production department of a business decides to produce at 100% of capacity for the next quarter. However, sales are forecast to decline slightly for the next six months due to an economic recession. If no budget has been prepared for this business, what happens? *ANSWER:* Excess inventory will be stockpiled. The business will either keep the inventory that cannot be sold, or will sell it at a discount price just to move it. Either way the business may lose money.

OBJECTIVE 1
Use a performance report

EXHIBIT 20-3 *Summarized Income Statement Performance Report for 19X7— Used for Control by Management*

	Actual	Budget	Actual–Budget
Sales revenue	$550,000	$600,000	($50,000)
Total expenses ...	510,000	520,000	(10,000)
Net income	$ 40,000	$ 80,000	($40,000)

Actual 19X7 sales in Exhibit 20-3 were $550,000, which is $50,000 less than budgeted sales. The low sales level reduced actual net income to half the budgeted amount. Top managers would ask what went wrong. The vice-president of sales would have to explain why sales revenue was so far below the budgeted goal. The vice-president, in turn, would meet with the sales staff to learn why they failed to meet the budget. At least one of two problems exists in this example: (1) the budget was unrealistic, or (2) the business did a poor job of selling during the period. Of course, both of these factors may have contributed to the poor results.

Managers also use performance reports like this one to identify corrective action. The sales department did not perform well, and management must decide what to do about it. Perhaps the sales manager should be replaced. Or the problem may be due to our selling an inferior product. In any event, should budgeted sales be lowered for the next period? The answers to these questions will affect next period's budget. This example illustrates how managers use a budget to plan operations and to control the company in its drive for success.

Components of the Master Budget

Point to Stress: The capital expenditures budget covers a much longer period of time than the operating budget. Because capital expenditures are generally large dollar amounts, they are planned several years in advance. The capital expenditures budget generally covers several (perhaps 5 to 10) years.

Discussion Question: Which budget is prepared first and why? ANSWER: The sales budget, because the number of units to be sold determines the purchases budget, which determines the cost of goods sold budget, and so on.

What factors would influence the estimated sales volume projected in the sales budget? ANSWER: First, all sales managers must have input as to what is happening in their territory or area. Prior years' sales, the general economic conditions, the trend of sales in that particular industry, competition, and the business's expected place in the market all should be considered when budgeting sales volume. Often the sales budget will be in numbers of units and in dollars of revenue.

The master budget includes the operating budget, the capital expenditures budget, and the financial budget. The **operating budget** sets the target revenues and expenses—and thus net income—for the period. The **capital expenditures budget** presents the company's plan for purchases of property, plant, and equipment and other assets that management uses to produce revenues over a long time. The **financial budget** projects the means of raising money from stockholders and creditors and plans cash management. This chapter discusses components of the operating budget and the financial budget. Chapter 26 covers budgeting for capital expenditures.

We summarize the components of the master budget as follows:

A. Operating budget
   1. Sales or revenue budget
   2. Purchases, cost of goods sold, and inventory budget
   3. Operating expense budget
   4. Budgeted income statement
B. Capital expenditures budget
C. Financial budget
   1. Cash budget: Statement of budgeted cash receipts and disbursements
   2. Budgeted balance sheet

The capstone of the operating budget is the budgeted income statement, which shows target revenues, expenses, and net income for the period. The financial budget results in the budgeted balance sheet, which gives budgeted amounts for each asset, liability, and owner equity. The budgeted financial statements look exactly like ordinary statements. The only difference is that they list budgeted rather than actual figures.

Exhibit 20-4 diagrams the various sections of the master budget for a non-manufacturing company, like K Mart, Safeway, or a wholesaler of auto parts. In addition to the components of the master budget in the preceding list, the

EXHIBIT 20-4 *Master Budget for a Nonmanufacturing Company*

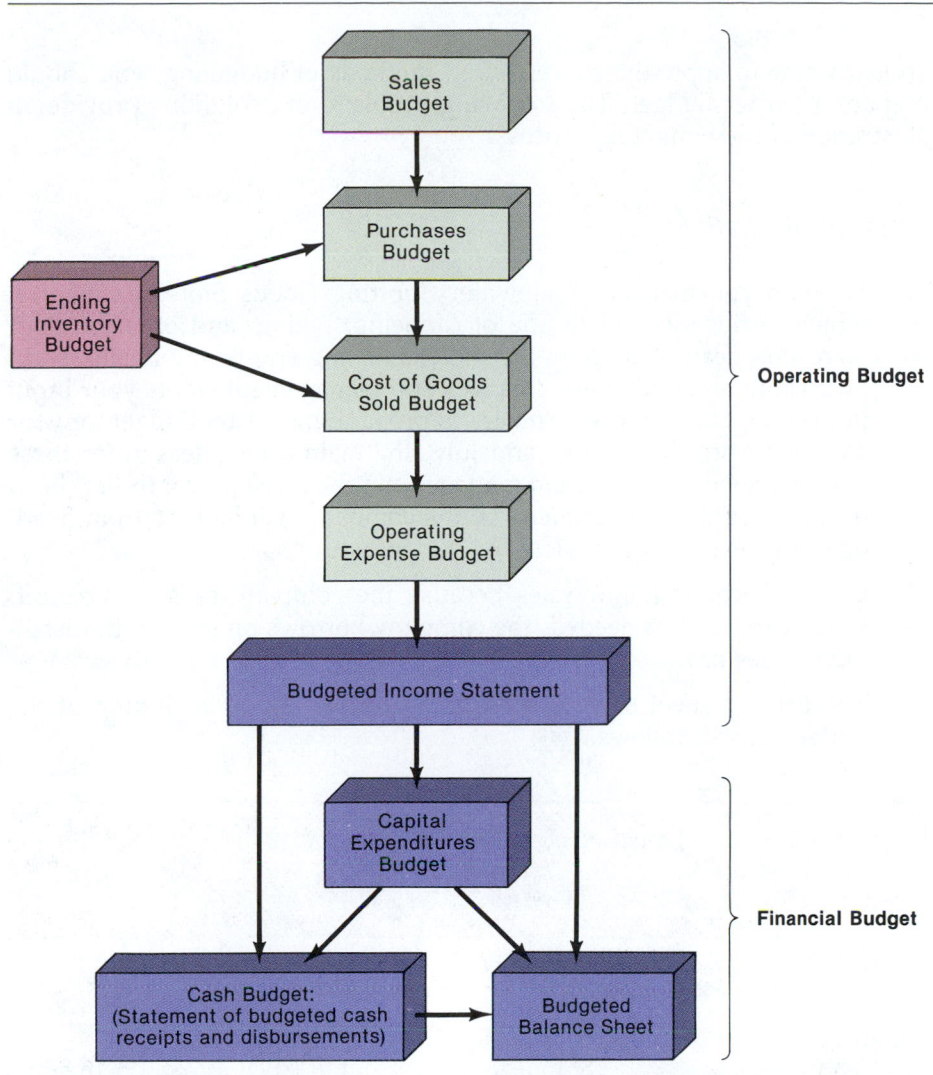

diagram includes ending inventory, which is directly related to sales, purchases, and cost of goods sold. Without a budget for inventory, the company could accidentally end the period with too much or too little inventory, and either event would be unwelcome. Too much inventory is expensive to keep in stock, and too little inventory risks losing a customer who needs the goods immediately.

Sales—the cornerstone of the master budget—is usually budgeted first because inventory levels, purchases, cost of goods sold, and operating expenses depend on sales activity. Sales revenue is the major measure of business activity. After sales and expenses are projected, the budgeted income statement can be prepared.

The capital expenditures budget, the income statement, and the plans for raising cash and paying debts provide information for the cash budget, which feeds into the budgeted balance sheet. Preparing the budgeted balance sheet is usually the last step in the process. We use Exhibit 20-4 as the framework for the remainder of the chapter.

Preparing the Master Budget

Point to Stress: After the sales budget is prepared, the cost of goods sold, purchases, and inventory budget can be prepared. The cost of goods sold will be a part of the budgeted income statement and inventory will appear on the budgeted balance sheet.

Serial Class Exercise No. 1: We are going to prepare parts of a budget for Coleman Corporation for January and February. Unit sales for January are expected to be 3,000 at $13.50 each, and for February, 4,500 at $13.75 each. Prepare the sales budget for Jan. and Feb. ANSWER:

Budgeted Sales

January	February
3,000 units	4,500 units
× $13.50	× $13.75
$40,500	$61,875

Serial Class Exercise No. 2: Now we can prepare the Purchases, Cost of Goods Sold, and Inventory Budget for the Coleman Corporation. Refer to the Sales Budget that we just prepared. Also, assume that Coleman's cost-of-goods-sold percentage is 65% of sales, and sales for March are predicted to be 4,300 units at $13.75, or $59,125 of sales revenue. Coleman desires each month's ending inventory to be $10,000 plus 50% of the next month's cost of goods sold.

ANSWER:

	January	February
COGS (65% × ea. month's sales)	$26,325*	$40,219†
+ Desired End. Inv. ($10,000 + 50% of next month's COGS)	30,110**	29,216††
− Beg. Inv.	−23,163***	−30,110
= Purchases	$33,272	$39,325

To learn how to apply the concepts and methods of budgeting, you should prepare a master budget. The following problem and solutions provide an illustration of the budgeting process.

Facts for Illustration

1. Suppose you manage Whitewater Sporting Goods Store number 18, which carries a complete line of canoeing, hiking, and other outdoor recreation gear. You know the merchandising end of the business but little about accounting and finance. Top management wants your input in the budgeting process. You are to prepare the master budget for your store for April, May, June, and July, the main selling season for these sporting goods. The division manager and the assistant controller (head of the accounting department) of the company will be here from headquarters next week to review the budget with you.

2. Cash collections follow sales because the company sells on account. When extra cash is needed, the company borrows on six-month installment notes payable.

3. The balance sheet of your store at March 31, 19X5, beginning of the budget period, follows.

Whitewater Sporting Goods Store No. 18
Balance Sheet
March 31, 19X5

Assets		Liabilities	
Current assets:		**Current liabilities:**	
Cash	$ 15,000	Accounts payable . . .	$ 16,800
Accounts receivable, net	16,000	Wages and commissions payable	4,250
Inventory	48,000	Total liabilities	21,050
Prepaid insurance . .	1,800		
	80,800	**Owners' Equity**	
Plant assets:		Owners' equity	78,950
Equipment and fixtures	32,000		
Accumulated depreciation	(12,800)		
	19,200	Total liabilities	
Total assets	$100,000	and owners' equity .	$100,000

4. Sales in March were $40,000. Monthly sales are projected by sales personnel as follows:

April	$50,000
May	80,000
June	60,000
July	50,000

Sales are 60 percent cash and 40 percent on credit. All accounts receivable amounts are collected in the month following sale. The $16,000 of accounts receivable at March 31 arose from credit sales made in March (40 percent of $40,000). Uncollectible accounts are insignificant, so you can ignore them.

*$40,500 × 65% = $26,325
†$61,875 × 65% = $40,219
**$40,219 × 50% + $10,000 = $30,110
††($59,125 × 65% × 50%) + $10,000 = $29,216
***$26,325 × 50% + $10,000 = $23,163

5. Whitewater wishes to maintain inventory equal to $20,000 plus 80 percent of the budgeted cost of goods sold for the following month. (All these percentages are drawn from the business's past experience.) Cost of goods sold averages 70 percent of sales. These data explain why the inventory on March 31 is $48,000, computed as follows:

$$\frac{\text{March 31}}{\text{inventory}} = \$20,000 \; +.80 \times (.70 \times \text{April sales of } \$50,000)$$

$$= \$20,000$$
$$= \$20,000 \quad + (.80 \times \$35,000)$$
$$= \$48,000 \quad + \$28,000$$

Whitewater pays for inventory as follows: 50 percent during the month of purchase and 50 percent during the next month. Accounts payable consist of inventory purchases only.

6. Monthly payroll consists of two parts: fixed wages of $2,500 plus sales commissions equal to 15 percent of sales. The company pays half of this amount during the month and half early in the following month. Therefore, at the end of each month Whitewater reports wages and commissions payable equal to half the month's payroll. This is why the $4,250 liability appears on the March 31 balance sheet—half the March payroll of $8,500:

$$\frac{\text{March}}{\text{payroll}} = \frac{\text{Fixed wages}}{\text{of } \$2,500} + \frac{\text{Sales commissions}}{\text{of } \$6,000 \, (.15 \times \$40,000)}$$

$$= \$8,500$$

$$\frac{\text{March 31 wages and}}{\text{commissions payable}} = .50 \times \$8,500$$

$$= \$4,250$$

7. Other monthly expenses are

Rent expense	$2,000, paid as incurred
Depreciation expense, including truck	500
Insurance expense	200 expiration of prepaid amount
Miscellaneous expense	5% of sales, paid as incurred

8. A used delivery truck will be purchased in April for $3,000 cash.

9. The company wishes to maintain a minimum cash balance of $10,000 at the end of each month. If necessary, the business can borrow the money on notes payable of $1,000 each at an annual interest rate of 12 percent. Management borrows no more money than the amount needed to maintain the $10,000 minimum cash balance. Notes payable require six equal monthly payments consisting of principal plus monthly interest on the entire unpaid principal. Borrowing and all principal and interest payments occur at the end of the month.

10. Income taxes are the responsibility of corporate headquarters, so you can ignore tax for budgeting purposes.

Point to Stress: The amount of inventory on hand is usually carefully planned and usually has a relationship to the sales for the next month. Obviously more units will be needed in ending inventory preceding a month with a high volume of sales than in a month with a lower volume of sales. Leaving the amount of inventory to chance may result in levels of inventory that are too high or too low.

Assume you have studied the company guidelines on how to prepare a budget. The directions instruct you to prepare the following detailed schedules:

Schedule

A	Sales budget
B	Purchases, cost of goods sold, and inventory budget
C	Operating expense budget
D	Budgeted cash collections from customers
E	Budgeted cash disbursements for purchases
F	Budgeted cash disbursements for operating expenses

After compiling the schedules, you must prepare the following statements:

Exhibit

20-5	Budgeted income statement for the four months ended July 31, 19X5
20-6	Statement of budgeted cash receipts and disbursements by month for the four months ended July 31, 19X5
20-7	Budgeted balance sheet at July 31, 19X5

OBJECTIVE 2

Budget the components of the income statement

Preparing the Operating Budget

As you work through the preparation of this budget, keep in mind that you are developing the company's operating and financial plan for the next four months. The steps in this process may seem mechanical, but remember that budgeting stimulates thoughts about pricing, product lines, job assignments, needs for additional equipment, and negotiations of loans with banks. Preparation of the budget leads to decisions that affect the future course of the business. The operating budget—consisting of the sales budget, the purchases, cost of goods sold, and inventory budget, and the operating expense budget—results in the budgeted income statement.

Preparing the Budgeted Income Statement. *Step 1.* Sales—Schedule A—is the start of the budget effort. The budgeted sales amount for each product is determined by multiplying its sale price by the predicted unit sales. The overall sales budget is the sum of the budgets for individual products.

Point to Stress: The difficult part of the Sales Budget is estimating the number of units that are going to be sold. That information is usually given as a part of the problem, but in the business world, the expected unit sales would have to be estimated.

Teaching Tip: Look at Exhibit 20-5. Let's assume that the budgeted income statement projects a net loss instead of net income. What can be done? *ANSWER:* Since the sales budget is the starting point, we must first evaluate sales. Perhaps the sale price can be raised. Perhaps we can begin an advertising campaign to boost sales.

Next we evaluate cost of goods sold. Can we buy the units at a lower price from another supplier or save by buying in larger quantities?

Finally we analyze each of the operating expenses. Where can costs be cut?

The budgeted income statement must be revised and reworked, until net income is an acceptable amount.

Schedule A—Sales Budget
    (Fact 4, pages 926–25)

	April	May	June	July	April-July Total
Cash sales, 60%	$30,000	$48,000	$36,000	$30,000	
Credit sales, 40%	20,000	32,000	24,000	20,000	
Total sales, 100%	$50,000	$80,000	$60,000	$50,000	$240,000

Trace the April-July total sales—$240,000—to the budgeted income statement in Exhibit 20-5.

EXHIBIT 20-5 *Budgeted Income Statement*

OBJECTIVE 3

Prepare a budgeted income statement

		Amount		Source
Whitewater Sporting Goods Store No. 18				
Budgeted Income Statement				
Four Months Ending July 31, 19X5				
Sales....................		$240,000		Schedule A
Cost of goods sold		168,000		Schedule B
Gross margin		72,000		
Operating expenses:				
Wages and commissions	$46,000			Schedule C
Rent	8,000			
Depreciation.................	2,000			
Insurance	800			
Miscellaneous	12,000	68,800		—
Income from operations		3,200		
Interest expense		225		Exhibit 20-6
Net income.....................		$ 2,975		

Typical Student Misconception: Students are often confused by the formula for purchases. Try explaining it by using the four basic elements of every account:

Beg. Bal. (units in beg. inv.)
+Increases (Purchases)
−Decreases (units sold)
=End. Bal. (units in end. inv.)

If the formula is rearranged to solve for the units purchased, it looks like this:

Units sold
+End. Inv.
−Beg. Inv.
=Units purchased

Point to Stress: Some operating expenses, such as sales commissions and delivery expenses, are related to the level of sales. The operating expenses will be a part of the budgeted income statement.

Point to Stress: The cash budget may be the most important of the budgets. It can help a manager control cash flows and avoid cash shortages.

Step 2. After budgeting sales, prepare the purchases, cost of goods sold, and inventory budget, which is Schedule B. This schedule determines cost of goods sold for the budgeted income statement, ending inventory for the budgeted balance sheet, and purchases for the cash budget. The relationship among these items is given by the cost-of-goods-sold computation:

Beginning Inventory + Purchases − Ending Inventory = Cost of Goods Sold

Beginning inventory is known, budgeted cost of goods is a fixed percentage of sales, and budgeted ending inventory is a specified amount. Therefore, you must solve for the budgeted purchases figure. By moving beginning inventory and ending inventory to the right side of the equation, isolate Purchases on the left side:

Purchases = Cost of Goods Sold + Ending Inventory − Beginning Inventory

Schedule B—Purchases, Cost of Goods Sold, and Inventory Budget
    (Fact 5, page 927)

	April	May	June	July	April-July Total
Cost of goods sold (.70 × sales, from Schedule A).............	$35,000	$56,000	$42,000	$35,000	$168,000
+ Desired ending inventory ($20,000 + .80 × Cost of goods sold for next month) ...	64,800*	53,600	48,000	42,400‡	
= Total needs	99,800	109,600	90,000	77,400	
− Beginning inventory	(48,000)†	(64,800)	(53,600)	(48,000)	
= Purchases	$51,800	$44,800	$36,400	$29,400	

* 20,000 + (.80 × $56,000) = $64,800   ‡ Assumed for illustrative purposes.
† Balance at March 31 (Fact 3, page 926)

Schedule C—Operating Expenses Budget
(Facts 6 and 7, page 927)

	April	May	June	July	April-July Total
Wages, fixed amount	$ 2,500	$ 2,500	$ 2,500	$ 2,500	
Commission, 15% of sales from Schedule A	7,500	12,000	9,000	7,500	
Total wages and commissions	10,000	14,500	11,500	10,000	$46,000
Rent, fixed amount	2,000	2,000	2,000	2,000	8,000
Depreciation, fixed amount	500	500	500	500	2,000
Insurance, fixed amount	200	200	200	200	800
Miscellaneous, 5% of sales	2,500	4,000	3,000	2,500	12,000
Total operating expenses	$15,200	$21,200	$17,200	$15,200	$68,800

Teaching Tip: Before the cash budget can be prepared, several supplementary schedules must be prepared:

1 Schedule of cash collections from customers

2 Schedule of cash disbursements for purchases

3 Schedule of cash disbursements for operating expenses

In addition, we need a list of capital expenditures in order to determine the cash required for them.

Since Schedule B is a forecast, you cannot know the *actual* ending inventory amount. You must include the desired ending inventory figure in the computation of projected purchases.

To solidify your understanding of how this information fits into the master budget, trace the total budgeted cost of goods sold ($168,000) to the income statement in Exhibit 20-5. We will be using the budgeted inventory and purchases amounts later.

Step 3. Some budgeted operating expenses, like sales commissions and delivery expenses, fluctuate and thus vary with changing sales. Other expenses, like rent, depreciation, and insurance, are the same each month (fixed) and do not vary with sales. Schedule C is the operating expense budget.

Trace the April-July totals (wages and commissions of $46,000, rent of $8,000, and so on) to the budgeted income statement in Exhibit 20-5.

Step 4. Steps 1 through 3 provide the information to determine income from operations on the budgeted income statement in Exhibit 20-5. (We explain computation of the interest expense as part of the cash budget.)

Point to Stress: Not all items on the budgeted income statement will be on the cash budget. Depreciation, depletion, and amortization, for example, as well as uncollectible account expense, are deducted in calculating net income but are not a part of cash receipts and disbursements.

Point to Stress: The cash budget will uncover financing needs before they arise. The financing can be arranged in advance to ensure its availability.

Transparency T20-2

Preparing the Financial Budget

The second major section of the master budget is the financial budget, which consists of the budgeted statement of cash receipts and disbursements (cash budget) and the budgeted balance sheet.

Preparing the Cash Budget (Statement of Budgeted Cash Receipts and Disbursements). The **cash budget,** or **statement of budgeted cash receipts and disbursements,** details how the business intends to go from the beginning cash balance to the desired ending balance. Cash receipts and disbursements depend in part on revenues and expenses, which appear in the budgeted income statement. The cash budget, then, is usually prepared after the budgeted income statement.

The cash budget has the following major parts: cash collections from customers (Schedule D), cash disbursements for purchases (Schedule E), cash disbursements for operating expenses (Schedule F), and capital expenditures.

Schedule D—Budgeted Cash Collections from Customers

	April	May	June	July
Cash sales from Schedule A	$30,000	$48,000	$36,000	$30,000
Collection of last month's credit sales from Schedule A (Fact 4, pages 926–27)	16,000*	20,000	32,000	24,000
Total collections	$46,000	$68,000	$68,000	$54,000

*March 31 accounts receivable

Schedule E—Budgeted Cash Disbursements for Purchases

	April	May	June	July
50% of last month's purchases, from Schedule B	$16,800*	$25,900	$22,400	$18,200
50% of this month's purchases, from Schedule B	25,900	22,400	18,200	14,700
Total disbursements for purchases	$42,700	$48,300	$40,600	$32,900

*.50 × March purchases of $33,600 (amount assumed)

Schedule F—Budgeted Cash Disbursements for Operating Expenses

	April	May	June	July
Expense amounts from Schedule C:				
Wages and commissions:				
50% of last month's expenses from Schedule C (Fact 6, page 927)	$ 4,250*	$ 5,000	$ 7,250	$ 5,750
50% of this month's expenses from Schedule C	5,000	7,250	5,750	5,000
Total wages and commissions	9,250	12,250	13,000	10,750
Rent (Fact 7, page 927)	2,000	2,000	2,000	2,000
Miscellaneous (5% of sales, Schedule A)	2,500	4,000	3,000	2,500
Total disbursements for operating expenses	$13,750	$18,250	$18,000	$15,250

*March 31 wages and commissions payable

The cash receipt and disbursement data in Schedules D, E, and F and the $3,000 capital expenditure to acquire the truck appear in the cash budget, Exhibit 20-6. Acquisitions of long-term assets like the truck are based on a decision process called *capital budgeting*. We cover this management tool in Chapter 26.

In preparing the cash budget (Exhibit 20-6) you must first determine the cash available before financing. (This amount is $61,000 for April.) Add total disbursements ($59,450) to the minimum desired cash balance ($10,000) to find the total cash needed during April—$69,450. If cash available exceeds cash needed, an excess occurs. If cash needed is greater, a deficiency results. During April, you budget an $8,450 deficiency. The company then borrows $9,000 on a six-month note payable. (The loan exceeds the deficiency because White-water borrows in even $1,000 amounts.) Compute the budgeted cash balance

OBJECTIVE 4

Prepare a cash budget

Transparency T 20-3

EXHIBIT 20-6 *Cash Budget*

Transparency T 20-4

Whitewater Sporting Goods Store No. 18
Statement of Budgeted Cash Receipts and Disbursements
Four Months Ending July 31, 19X5

	April	May	June	July
Beginning cash balance	$15,000	$10,550	$10,410	$18,235
Cash receipts, collections from customers (Schedule D)	46,000	68,000	68,000	54,000
Cash available before financing	$61,000	$78,550	$78,410	$72,235
Cash disbursements:				
Purchases of inventory (Schedule E)	$42,700	$48,300	$40,600	$32,900
Operating expenses (Schedule F)	13,750	18,250	18,000	15,250
Purchase of truck (Fact 8, page 927)	3,000	—	—	—
Total disbursements	59,450	66,550	58,600	48,150
(1) Ending cash balance before financing	1,550	12,000	19,810	24,085
Minimum cash balance desired	10,000	10,000	10,000	10,000
Cash excess (deficiency)	$(8,450)	$ 2,000	$ 9,810	$14,085
Financing of cash deficiency (See Notes b–d below):				
Borrowing (at end of month)	$ 9,000			
Principal payments (at end of month)		$(1,500)	$(1,500)	$(1,500)
Interest expense (at 12% annually)		(90)	(75)	(60)
(2) Total effects of financing	9,000	(1,590)	(1,575)	(1,560)
Ending cash balance (1) + (2)	$10,550	$10,410	$18,235	$22,525

Notes: a. Insurance expense is the expiration of prepaid insurance, and depreciation is the expensing of the cost of a plant asset. Therefore, these expenses do not require cash outlays in the current accounting period.

b. Borrowing occurs in multiples of $1,000 and only for the amount needed to maintain a minimum cash balance of $10,000.

c. Monthly principal payments: $9,000/6 = $1,500.

d. Interest expense: May: $9,000 \times (.12 \times \frac{1}{12}) = \$90$.
June: $(\$9,000 - \$1,500) \times (.12 \times \frac{1}{12}) = \$75$.
July: $(\$9,000 - \$1,500 - \$1,500) \times (.12 \times \frac{1}{12}) = \$60$.
Total: $\$90 + \$75 + \$60 = \$225$.

Serial Class Exercise No. 3:
Assume Coleman's sales are 25% cash and 75% on credit. Past collection history indicates that credit sales are collected:

30% in the month of sale
60% in the following month
8% in the 2nd month following sale
2% are never collected

November sales were 2,900 units ($39,150) and December sales were 2,950 units ($39,825). Prepare the Budgeted Cash Collections for January and February.

OBJECTIVE 5
Prepare a budgeted balance sheet

at the end of each month by subtracting total disbursements from the cash available before financing and then adding the total projected effects of financing.[1] Exhibit 20-6 shows that Whitewater expects to end April with $10,550 of cash. The exhibit also shows the budgeted cash balance at the end of May, June, and July.

Interest expense for the four months totals $225 ($90 + $75 + $60). This item is listed on the budgeted income statement in Exhibit 20-5.

Preparing the Budgeted Balance Sheet.   The final step in preparing the master budget is to complete the balance sheet. You project each asset, liability, and owner equity account based on the plans outlined in the previous schedules and exhibits. Exhibit 20-7 presents the budgeted balance sheet. If desired, you can prepare separate schedules to show the computations of accounts receivable, plant assets, and so on.

The *master budget* has now been completed. It consists of the budgeted financial statements and all supporting schedules.

---

[1] In the case of loan payments, you will be adding a negative amount.

EXHIBIT 20-7 *Budgeted Balance Sheet*

Whitewater Sporting Goods Store No. 18
Budgeted Balance Sheet
July 31, 19X5

Assets

Current assets:		
Cash (Exhibit 20-6)	$ 22,525	
Accounts receivable, net (.40 × July sales of $50,000; Schedule A)	20,000	
Inventory (Schedule B)	42,400	
Prepaid insurance (beginning balance of $1,800 − $800 for four months' expiration; fact 7 on page 927)	1,000	$ 85,925
Plant assets:		
Equipment and fixtures (beginning balance of $32,000 + $3,000 truck acquisition; fact 8 on page 927)	35,000	
Accumulated depreciation (beginning balance of $12,800 + $500 depreciation for each of four months; fact 7 on page 927)	(14,800)	20,200
Total assets		$106,125

Liabilities

Current liabilities:		
Short-term note payable ($9,000 − $4,500 paid back; Exhibit 20-6)	$ 4,500	
Accounts payable (.50 × July purchases of $29,400; Schedule B)	14,700	
Wages and commissions payable (.50 × July expense of $10,000; Schedule C)	5,000	
Total liabilities		$ 24,200

Owners' Equity

Owners' equity (beginning balance of $78,950 + $2,975 net income; Exhibit 20-5)		81,925
Total liabilities and owners' equity		$106,125

Summary of Budgeting Procedures

The most important budget documents are the budgeted income statement (Exhibit 20-5), the budgeted statement of cash receipts and disbursements (Exhibit 20-6), and the budgeted balance sheet (Exhibit 20-7). Top management analyzes these statements to ensure that all the budgeted figures are consistent with company goals. As the business strives to reach these goals, management controls operations by comparing actual results with the forecasted performance (as shown in Exhibit 20-3, the performance report).

Importance of Sales Forecasting

The Whitewater Sporting Goods illustration began with the sales budget, which is the foundation of a master budget. Managers—under the direction of the top marketing executive—invest ample resources in accurately forecasting sales. Factors considered in projecting sales include:

1. *Patterns of past sales.* By learning from past sales activity, a company can fine-tune its sales budget. This includes subdividing sales by product line,

ANSWER:

	January	February
Cash Sales (25% of each month's sales) . .	$10,125	$15,469
Collection from current month's credit sales	9,113*	13,922†
Collection from last month's credit sales	17,921**	18,225††
Collection from credit sales two months previous	2,349***	2,390†††
Total	$39,508	$50,006

*$40,500 × .75 × .30 = $9,113
†$61,875 × .75 × .30 = $13,922
**$39,825 × .75 × .60 = $17,921
††$40,500 × .75 × .60 = $18,225
***$39,150 × .75 × .08 = $2,349
†††$39,825 × .75 × .08 = $2,390

geographical region, and salesperson. The more detailed the budget, the more helpful it is likely to be.

2. *Predictions of marketing personnel.* These people are calling on customers on a regular basis and can provide the most reliable, current information for forecasting sales. They conduct market research to learn which customers prefer certain products.

3. *Analysis of general and industry economic conditions.* In an economic recession, consumers usually delay expenditures on leisure-time products like Whitewater's sporting goods. What is the outlook for the economy next year?

4. *Strength of competitors.* A business must stay informed about what competitors are doing. For example, an effective advertising campaign by Chrysler can lure customers away from Ford and General Motors and decrease Ford and GM profits. An effective budget must consider the activity of competitors.

5. *Future changes in prices.* Budgeted sales equal the budgeted quantity multiplied by the expected future selling price. Any changes in prices affect the sales budget.

6. *Development of new product lines and phasing out of old product lines.* The budget must include the sales of new products expected to be introduced and eliminate old products that will be phased out. This ensures that the budget is based on an up-to-date product line.

7. *Plans for advertising and sales promotion.* Advertising stimulates sales, so plans for upcoming promotional efforts will affect the budgeted level of sales.

The importance of the sales forecast is not limited to profit-seeking organizations. For example, the revenue forecast is critical to hospitals, churches and synagogues, universities, cities, and states. Unless these organizations budget revenues accurately, they risk spending too much and running out of money just like profit-seeking businesses. All types of organizations base their budgets on general economic and industry data plus information that is specific to the entity. An entire industry exists to provide economic forecasting data. All types of organizations subscribe to forecasting newsletters, primarily to aid their budgeting efforts.

Budgeting and Short-Term Financing

The cash budget in Exhibit 20-6 illustrates the usual pattern of **short-term, self-liquidating financing.** This term refers to debt incurred to buy inventories that will be sold on credit. Cash collections are used to pay the debt.

The diagram below shows the financing plan budgeted in Exhibit 20-6. Whitewater had a temporary need for $9,000. The company borrowed this amount and paid it back from cash generated by operations.

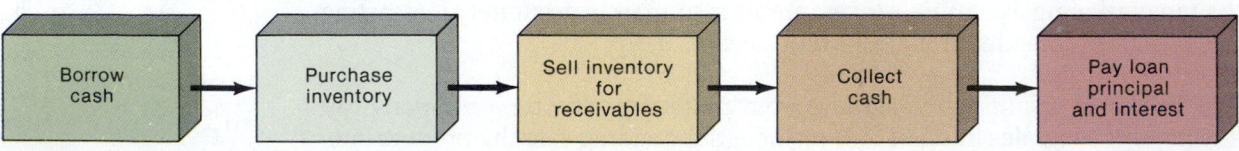

Many companies have seasonal peaks of high sales volume and valleys of low activity. For example, retailers like Sears, J. C. Penney, and K Mart make most of their sales during November, December, and January. June, July, and August are slow months. Companies use the slow months to stock up on inventory for the rush near the end of the year and to remodel stores and make repairs. By increasing a store's attractiveness and efficiency, the company can attract more customers and increase sales.

When monthly sales fluctuate seasonally, companies often borrow on short-term, self-liquidating loans. A cash budget can help managers avoid a cash shortage. By planning ahead, the manager can shop around for the best interest rate on a short-term loan. Then, if a cash shortage looms in some months, the company is prepared. A carefully mapped budget keeps the cash balance well matched to cash needs.

Real-World Example: Many businesses require a specific cash balance on hand at the end of each month so that they have adequate cash to meet their needs. This may mean that they have to borrow at the end of some months if their ending cash balance is too low. The business may have an agreement with its bank for a line of credit against which it may borrow. In months when there is excess cash on hand, the note will be repaid.

Of course, the business must present a realistic budget so that the bank has some evidence as to how the loan will be repaid. This further underscores the need for thorough, realistic budgeting.

Continuous (Rolling) Budgets

A **continuous**, or **rolling, budget** systematically adds a month as the month just ended is deleted. This budget keeps managers thinking ahead, with a steady planning horizon. Suppose Whitewater Sporting Goods prepared the following six-month sales budget:

OBJECTIVE 6
Use a continuous budget

	March	April	May	June	July	August
Budgeted sales ...	$40,000	$50,000	$80,000	$60,000	$50,000	$40,000

The first budget covers March through August. Roll 1 deletes March and adds September; roll 2 then deletes April and adds October; and so on.

Roll 1:	March	April	May	June	July	August	September	October
Budgeted sales ...	—	$50,000	$80,000	$60,000	$50,000	$40,000	$25,000	—

Roll 2:	March	April	May	June	July	August	September	October
Budgeted sales ...	—	—	$80,000	$60,000	$50,000	$40,000	$25,000	$20,000

When managers desire, the sales budgets for individual months can be combined into quarterly or semiannual totals.

Budget Models, What-If Questions, and Microcomputer Applications

The master budget models the entire organization's objectives, inputs, and outputs. When we combine the budget's broad coverage with the speed and ease of microcomputers, we have a powerful tool for management analysis, planning, and control.

Many software programs allow preparation of the master budget on an electronic spreadsheet. The manager or the accountant can then ask "what-if" questions by changing any figure. *What* net income can we expect *if* we increase advertising by 20 percent? *What* will the cash balance be *if* we prepay the full cost of the advertising campaign at the beginning of the next period?

Point to Stress: A continuous, rolling budget means there is some budgeting going on all the year long. This saves the annual "crunch" of trying to get next year's budget prepared, and keeps management actively involved in the budgeting process all the time.

When the accountant changes one amount, the computer prepares a new budget that includes all the effects of that change. Computers make possible this nearly instant analysis of changes in the company's forecast. Managers can then study the answers to these questions.

The spreadsheet that displays these changes to "what-if" questions may be linked to increasingly detailed subsets of information. For example, assume that General Motors (GM) wants to examine "what-if" questions regarding possible car sales for February. The results of this investigation lead to changes in GM's net sales, required purchases, and projected cash receipts, not just for February but also for one or two subsequent months.

The first draft of a budget is seldom the final draft. Answers to what-if questions can provide revenue, expense, and income data on a wide range of possible sales levels. Managers can then respond to changes in the business with information rather than hunches. Suppose the budget—based on the best possible forecast—shows a poor year ahead. Managers can examine various patterns of sales and net income, and cash receipts and disbursements. They can study ways to cut costs and develop marketing strategies to increase demand for the company's products. The master budget may then be revised. Chapter 24 examines flexible budgets—those based on various levels of activity—in greater detail.

The computer's speed also enables managers to react promptly to new and unexpected situations as they arise. For example, an executive of a New Jersey utility, Public Service Electric and Gas Company, has commented on the company's plans if an oil embargo were announced tomorrow. Within 24 hours management would know from the master budget the major financial effects of the embargo. Without having to wait for monthly or quarterly financial statements, they could begin reacting to its effects immediately. Microcomputers and user-friendly software give these capabilities to many employees who are not expert computer programmers. Knowing what to expect is a result of a successful budgeting system. Chapter 28 shows how to prepare a budget with a popular electronic spreadsheet.

Summary Problem for Your Review

Review the Whitewater Sporting Goods illustration in the chapter. Suppose you think that July sales might be $40,000 instead of the projected $50,000 in Schedule A, page 928. You draw up a new budget to learn what effect the change in the sales amount will have on the store.

Required

1. Revise schedules A, B, and C. Prepare a revised budgeted income statement for the four months ended July 31, 19X5.
2. Revise schedules D, E, and F. Prepare a revised cash budget for July and a revised budgeted balance sheet at July 31, 19X5.

   Note: You need not repeat the parts of the revised schedules that do not change.

Note: Although not required, for completeness this solution repeats the budgeted amounts for April, May, and June Revised figures appear in boldface for emphasis.

Requirement 1

Revised Schedule A—Sales Budget

	April	May	June	July	April–July Total
Cash sales, 60%	$30,000	$48,000	$36,000	**$24,000**	
Credit sales, 40%	20,000	32,000	24,000	**16,000**	
Total sales, 100%	$50,000	$80,000	$60,000	**$40,000**	$230,000

Revised Schedule B—Purchases, Cost of Goods Sold, and Inventory Budget

	April	May	June	July	April–July Total
Cost of goods sold (.70 × sales from Revised Schedule A)	$ 35,000	$ 56,000	$ 42,000	**$ 28,000**	$161,000
+ Desired ending inventory ($20,000 + .80 × cost of goods sold for next month) ..	64,800	53,600	**42,400**	**42,400**	
= Total needs............................	99,800	109,600	84,400	**70,400**	
− Beginning inventory	(48,000)	(64,800)	(53,600)	**(42,400)**	
= Purchases	$ 51,800	$ 44,800	$ 30,800	**$ 28,000**	

Revised Schedule C—Operating Expenses Budget

	April	May	June	July	April–July Total
Wages, fixed amount	$ 2,500	$ 2,500	$ 2,500	**$ 2,500**	
Commission, 15% of sales from Revised Schedule A	7,500	12,000	9,000	**6,000**	
Total wages and commissions	10,000	14,500	11,500	**8,500**	$44,500
Rent, fixed amount	2,000	2,000	2,000	**2,000**	8,000
Depreciation, fixed amount	500	500	500	**500**	2,000
Insurance, fixed amount	200	200	200	**200**	800
Miscellaneous, 5% of sales	2,500	4,000	3,000	**2,000**	11,500
Total operating expenses	$15,200	$21,200	$17,200	**$13,200**	$66,800

Whitewater Sporting Goods Store No. 18
Budgeted Income Statement
Four Months Ending July 31, 19X5

	Amount		Source
Sales		$230,000	Revised Schedule A
Cost of goods sold		161,000	Revised Schedule B
Gross margin		69,000	
Operating expenses:			
Wages and commissions	$44,500		Revised Schedule C
Rent	8,000		Revised Schedule C
Depreciation	2,000		Revised Schedule C
Insurance	800		Revised Schedule C
Miscellaneous	11,500	66,800	Revised Schedule C
Income from operations		2,200	
Interest expense		225	Revised Exhibit 20-6
Net income		$ 1,975	

Requirement 2

Revised Schedule D—Budgeted Cash Collections from Customers

	April	May	June	July
Cash sales from Revised Schedule A	$30,000	$48,000	$36,000	$24,000
Collection of last month's credit sales,				
from Revised Schedule A	16,000*	20,000	32,000	24,000
Total collections	$46,000	$68,000	$68,000	$48,000

*March 31 accounts receivable

Revised Schedule E—Budgeted Disbursements for Purchases

	April	May	June	July
50% of last month's purchases, from Revised Schedule B	$16,800*	$25,900	$22,400	$15,400
50% of this month's purchases, from Revised Schedule B	25,900	22,400	15,400	14,000
Total disbursements for purchases	$42,700	$48,300	$37,800	$29,400

*Amount assumed for illustration

Revised Schedule F—Budgeted Disbursements for Operating Expenses

	April	May	June	July
Expense amounts from Revised Schedule C:				
Wages and commissions:				
50% of last month's expenses from Revised Schedule C .	$ 4,250*	$ 5,000	$ 7,250	$ 5,750
50% of this month's expenses from Revised Schedule C .	5,000	7,250	5,750	4,250
Total wages and commissions	9,250	12,250	13,000	10,000
Rent	2,000	2,000	2,000	2,000
Miscellaneous	2,500	4,000	3,000	2,000
Total disbursements for operating expenses	$13,750	$18,250	$18,000	$14,000

*March 31 wages and commissions payable

Whitewater Sporting Goods Store No. 18
Statement of Budgeted Cash Receipts and Disbursements
Four Months Ending July 31, 19X5

	April	May	June	July
Beginning cash balance	$15,000	$10,550	$10,410	**$21,035**
Cash receipts, collections from customers (Revised Schedule D)	46,000	68,000	68,000	**48,000**
Cash available before financing	$61,000	$78,550	$78,410	**$69,035**
Cash disbursements:				
Purchases of inventory (Revised Schedule E)	$42,700	$48,300	**$37,800**	**$29,400**
Operating expenses (Revised Schedule F)	13,750	18,250	18,000	**14,000**
Purchase of truck	3,000	—	—	—
Total disbursements	59,450	66,550	55,800	43,400
(1) Ending cash balance before financing	1,550	12,000	**22,610**	25,635
Minimum cash balance desired	10,000	10,000	10,000	**10,000**
Cash excess (deficiency)	$(8,450)	$ 2,000	**$12,610**	**$15,635**
Financing of cash deficiency:				
Borrowing (at end of month)	$ 9,000			
Principal payments (at end of month)		$(1,500)	$(1,500)	**$(1,500)**
Interest expense (at 12% annually)		(90)*	(75)*	**(60)***
(2) Total effects of financing	9,000	(1,590)	(1,575)	**(1,560)**
Ending cash balance (1) + (2)	$10,550	$10,410	**$21,035**	**$24,075**

*Interest expense: $90 + $75 + $60 = $225

Whitewater Sporting Goods Store No. 18
Budgeted Balance Sheet
July 31, 19X5

Assets

Current assets:
Cash (Revised Exhibit 20-6) .... $ 24,075
Accounts receivable, net (.40 X July sales of $40,000; Revised Schedule A) ... 16,000
Inventory (Revised Schedule B) 42,400
Prepaid insurance .... 1,000 $ 83,475
Plant assets:
Equipment and fixtures 35,000
Accumulated depreciation .... (14,800)   20,200
Total assets $103,675

Liabilities

Current liabilities:
Short-term note payable .... $ 4,500
Accounts payable (.50 X July purchases of **$28,000**; Revised Schedule B) 14,000
Wages and commissions payable (.50 X July expense of $8,500; Revised Schedule C) 4,250
Total liabilities .... $ 22,750

Owners' Equity

Owners' equity (beginning balance of $78,950 + **$1,975** net income; Revised Exhibit 20-5) 80,925
Total liabilities and owners' equity $103,675

SUMMARY

Management accounting helps managers plan and control the operations of their organizations. A major element of the management plan is the *budget*, which expresses the business's goals for earning income and for asset, liability, and owner equity position. The master budget consists of the budgeted financial statements and supporting schedules.

The budget forces managers to set specific goals. Such goals provide direction for the organization and meaning to the work of individual employees. The budget coordinates the various activities of the organization and aids performance evaluation. Comparisons of budgeted and actual amounts reveal areas of the business that need improvement.

Many organizations have a *budget committee*, which includes representatives of all departments, to prepare the budget. The *budget period* usually coincides with the accounting period to ease the comparison of actual and budgeted amounts.

The components of the master budget that cover operations include *sales, purchases, cost of goods sold, inventory,* and *operating expenses.* These budgets are usually prepared in this order and are combined into the *budgeted income statement.* Sales comes first because most expenses, assets, and liabilities depend on sales volume. A second component of the master budget is the *capital expenditures budget,* which includes plans for purchasing long-term capital assets. The third main component is the financial budget, consisting of the *cash budget,* which is a statement of budgeted cash receipts and disbursements, and the *budgeted balance sheet.*

Many companies use *continuous,* or *rolling, budgets* that systematically add a future month as the month just ended is deleted. Continuous budgets keep managers thinking ahead with a steady planning horizon.

Microcomputers and electronic spreadsheets are ideally suited for use in budgeting because they allow managers to answer what-if questions. Analyzing data over a wide range of outcomes enables managers to meet the challenges brought about by changes in the business.

Self-Study Questions

Test your understanding of the chapter by marking the best answer for each of the following questions.

1. The budget is *(p. 921)*
   a. A general, not specific, statement of the business's goals
   b. Not used by most successful businesses
   c. A major tool of financial, rather than management, accounting
   d. None of the above

2. For the budget to be most effective, it should be prepared *(pp. 921, 922)*
   a. From the bottom up, with participation from employees at all levels
   b. From the top down, with managers developing goals based on their own experience
   c. Without reference to results obtained in past periods
   d. None of the above

3. Which of the following is *not* a benefit of a budgeting system? *(pp. 922, 923)*
   a. Coordinates activities
   b. Automatically fires under-achieving employees
   c. Aids performance evaluation
   d. Provides direction to the business

4. Chewning Corporation's actual revenues are $90,000, and expenses are $50,000. Budgeted revenues were $86,000, and budgeted expenses were

$51,000. What is the relationship between actual net income and budgeted net income? *(p. 923)*

a. Actual exceeds budget by
$40,000

b. Budget exceeds actual by
$35,000

c. Actual exceeds budget by
$5,000

d. Budget exceeds actual by
$5,000

5. The master budget starts with *(p. 924)*

a. Cash

b. Owners' equity

c. Sales

d. Inventory

6. The operating budget ends with *(pp. 924, 925)*

a. Budgeted sales

b. The budgeted income statement

c. The cash budget

d. The budgeted balance sheet

7. The most complex single part of the master budget is preparation of *(p. 931)*

a. Budgeted sales

b. The budgeted income statement

c. The cash budget

d. The budgeted balance sheet

8. The master budget usually ends with *(p. 932)*

a. Budgeted sales

b. The budgeted income statement

c. The cash budget

d. The budgeted balance sheet

9. A continuous (rolling) budget *(p. 935)*

a. Adds a month and deletes the month just ended

b. Keeps managers thinking ahead

c. Maintains a steady planning horizon

d. All of the above

10. Managers can use a microcomputer along with a master budget to *(pp. 935, 936)*

a. Develop strategies for dealing with a variety of possible situations

b. Eliminate all the uncertainty of the business environment

c. Prepare the budget correctly on the first attempt

d. Set near-perfect goals for the company

Answers to the Self-Study Questions follow the Accounting Vocabulary.

Accounting Vocabulary

Budget. Management's quantitative expression of a plan of action and an aid to coordination and implementation *(p. 921)*.

Budget committee. Group that prepares the master budget; includes representatives from all departments of the business *(p. 921)*.

Capital expenditures budget. Plan for purchases of property, plant, and equipment and other assets that management uses over a long time *(p. 924)*.

Cash budget. Details the way a business intends to go from the beginning cash balance to the desired ending balance. Also called the Statement of budgeted cash receipts and disbursements *(p. 930)*.

Continuous budget. Systematically adds a month or a quarter as the month or quarter just ended is deleted. Also called a Rolling budget *(p. 935)*.

Financial budget. Projects the means of raising money from stockholders and creditors and plans cash management *(p. 924)*.

Master budget. Budget that includes the major financial statements and supporting schedules. The master budget can be divided into the operating budget, the capital expenditures budget, and the financial budget *(p. 921)*.

Operating budget. Sets the target revenues and expenses, and thus net income, for the period *(p. 924)*.

Rolling budget. Another name for a Continuous budget (*p. 935*).

Short-term, self-liquidating financing. Debt incurred to buy inventories that will be sold and with the related cash collections used to pay the debt (*p. 934*).

Statement of budgeted cash receipts and disbursements. Another name for the Cash budget (*p. 930*)

Answers to Self-Study Questions

1. d
2. a
3. b
4. c   Actual: $90,000 − $50,000 = $40,000
       Budget: 86,000 −   51,000 =   35,000
       Actual over budget: $ 5,000
5. c

6. b
7. c
8. d
9. d

10. a

ASSIGNMENT MATERIAL _____

Questions

1. How does management accounting differ from financial accounting?
2. Identify two types of goals set by managers.
3. Briefly discuss three components of a budgeting system.
4. What are four benefits of using a budgeting system?
5. Draw a diagram that shows how managers use a budgeting system.
6. How does a manager use a performance report?
7. List the components of a master budget.
8. A Ford dealer sets a goal of selling more Ford automobiles than any other dealer in the city. Does this goal represent a budget? Give your reason.
9. Taft Corporation installs a budgeting system in which the president sets all the goals for the company. The vice-president checks up on all 90 employees to ensure that they are meeting top management's budget goals. What is the weakness in this budgeting system? How can the system be improved?
10. In most successful budgeting systems, who or what group in the organization prepares the budget? What makes this approach successful?
11. Why should the capital expenditures budget be prepared before the cash budget and the budgeted balance sheet?
12. How does a company budget inventory purchases? In your answer, show the relationships among purchases, cost of goods sold, and inventories.
13. What is the first step in preparing the master budget? Why does this step come first?
14. Outline the four steps in preparing an operating budget.
15. Identify the last item (prior to net income) to compute for the budgeted income statement. Where is this item computed initially, and why does it come last?
16. What is another name for the cash budget? Identify six subtotals or totals listed on the cash budget.
17. What is the last document to prepare for the master budget? Why does it come last?

18. Is sales forecasting important only to a profit-seeking business, or is it used by nonprofit organizations like hospitals and colleges? Give your reason.

19. Suppose you are the marketing vice-president of a company. What factors would you consider in forecasting the company's sales for the coming year?

20. Describe how short-term, self-liquidating financing works.

21. Tick-Tock Clocks is a chain of specialty shops operating in resort areas. During some periods, the managers of the company's 42 stores budget for the coming quarter, and during other periods they budget for the coming year. What type of budget should top management use to keep store managers looking ahead with a steady planning horizon? How does this budget work?

22. Why are microcomputers and electronic spreadsheets well suited for budgeting?

Exercises

Additional computer-related exercises: Exercises 28-5, 28-6, 28-7, 28-8

Exercise 20-1 *Preparing a performance report* (L.O. 1)

Net. inc. $1,000 below budget

During August Chez Bon, Inc.'s actual revenues were $131,000 compared with budgeted revenues of $142,000. August operating expenses were $122,000, and budgeted operating expenses were $137,000. The company also incurred interest expense, a nonoperating expense, of $5,000, which was not included in the budget because it arose from unexpected borrowing.

Prepare a performance report for Chez Bon to show the differences between actual income and budgeted income for August. What caused August results to turn out as they did? Comment on results as measured by operating income.

Exercise 20-2 *Budgeting sales, cost of goods sold, and gross profit* (L.O. 2)

Quarter gross profit $5,583

Lisa Gatti operates a boutique called The Second Edition. She expects cash sales of $3,000 for October and a $500 monthly increase during November and December. Credit-card sales of $1,000 during October should be followed by 20 percent increases during November and December. Sales returns can be ignored. Credit card-companies like VISA, MasterCard, and American Express charge 5 percent on credit-card sales, so The Second Edition will net 95 percent. Cost of goods sold averages 60 percent of net sales.

Lisa asks you to prepare a schedule of budgeted sales, cost of goods sold, and gross profit for each month of the last quarter of 19X3. Also show totals for the quarter.

Exercise 20-3 *Budgeting purchases, cost of goods sold, and inventory* (L.O. 2)

Sept. purchases $67,925

The sales budget of Whitehouse Corp. for the nine months ended September 30 follows.

| | Quarter Ended | | | Nine-Month |
	March 31	June 30	Sep. 30	Total
Cash sales, 30%	$27,000	$ 42,000	$ 31,500	$100,500
Credit sales, 70%	63,000	98,000	73,500	234,500
Total sales, 100%	$90,000	$140,000	$105,000	$335,000

In the past, cost of goods sold has been 65 percent of total sales. The director of marketing, the production manager, and the financial vice-president agree that ending inventory should not go below $20,000 plus 10 percent of cost of goods sold for the following quarter. Whitehouse expects sales of $100,000 during the fourth quarter. The January 1 inventory was $22,000.

Required

Prepare a purchases, cost of goods sold, and inventory budget for each of the first three quarters of the year. Compute the cost of goods sold for the entire nine-month period. (Use Schedule B, page 929, as a model.)

A Purchases $59,000
E Beginning inventory $14,700

Exercise 20-4 *Identifying amounts of purchases, inventory, and cost of goods sold* **(L.O. 2)**

Compute the missing amount for each of the independent situations below:

	A	B	C	D	E
Beginning inventory ...	$14,000	$?	$ 24,800	$11,100	$?
Purchases.............	?	86,200	?	45,300	77,900
Available	73,000	118,800	103,100	?	?
Ending inventory......	11,000	?	?	13,700	22,600
Cost of goods sold.....	$?	$ 87,700	$ 75,300	$?	$70,000

Full year net inc. $354,046

Exercise 20-5 *Budgeting quarterly income for a year* **(L.O. 3)**

Century 21 is a nationwide real estate firm. Suppose a suburban St. Louis office of the firm projects that year 2 quarterly sales will increase by 3 percent in quarter one, 3 percent in quarter two, 5 percent in quarter three, and 5 percent in quarter four. Management expects total operating expenses to be 85 percent of revenues during each of the first two quarters, 86 percent of revenues during the third quarter, and 81 percent during the fourth. The office manager expects to borrow $100,000 on July 1, with quarterly principal payments of $10,000 beginning on September 30 and interest paid at the annual rate of 12 percent. Year 1 last quarter sales were $520,000.

Required

Prepare a budgeted income statement for each of the four quarters of year 2 and for the entire year. Present the year 2 budget as follows:

Quarter 1	Quarter 2	Quarter 3	Quarter 4	Full Year

Principal payments, June $4,045

Exercise 20-6 *Identifying amounts in a cash budget* **(L.O. 4)**

Cablevision, Inc., has completed its cash budget for May and June. The budget is presented with missing amounts identified by a question mark (?). Cablevision's plan for eliminating any cash deficiency is to borrow the exact amount needed from its bank. The current annual interest rate is 12 percent. Cablevision pays back all borrowed amounts within one month to the extent cash is available without going below the desired minimum balance.

Required

Fill in each amount identified by a question mark.

Cablevision, Inc.
Cash Budget
May and June

	May	June
Beginning cash balance	$10,900	$?
Cash collections from customers	65,700	74,800
Sale of plant assets		900
Cash available before financing	$88,800	$?
Cash disbursements:		
Purchases of inventory	$52,400	$41,100
Operating expenses	31,900	30,500
Total disbursements	84,300	71,600
(1) Ending cash balance before financing	?	?
Minimum cash balance desired	10,000	10,000
Cash excess (deficiency)	$(5,500)	$?
Financing of cash deficiency:		
Borrowing (at end of month)	$?	
Principal payments (at end of month)		$?
Interest expense (at .010 monthly)		?
(2) Total effects of financing	?	?
Ending cash balance (1) + (2)	$?	$?
Interest expense: June: ?		

Exercise 20-7 *Computing cash receipts and disbursements* **(L.O. 4)**

a. $24,920
b. $27,250
c. $10,100
d. $10,960

For each of the items *a* through *d*, compute the amount of cash receipts or disbursements Gulf States Company would budget for December. A solution to one item may depend on the answer to an earlier item.

a. Management expects to sell 4,000 units in November and 4,200 in December. Each unit sells for $6. Cash sales average 30 percent of the total sales, and credit sales make up the rest. Two-thirds of credit sales are collected in the month of sale, with the balance collected the following month.

b. Management has budgeted inventory purchases of $30,000 for November and $25,000 for December. Gulf States Company pays for 50 percent of its inventory at the time of purchase in order to get a 2 percent discount. The business pays the balance the following month, with no further discount.

c. Management expects to sell equipment that cost $14,100 at a gain of $2,000. Accumulated depreciation on this equipment is $6,000.

d. The company pays rent and property taxes of $6,000 each month. Commissions and other selling expenses average 20 percent of sales. Gulf States Company pays two-thirds of these costs in the month incurred, with the balance paid in the following month.

Exercise 20-8 *Preparing a cash budget* **(L.O. 4)**

Ending cash, Nov., $9,195

Waxman's, a family-owned furniture store, began October with $5,400 cash. Management forecasts that collections from credit customers will be $9,000 in October and $12,200 in November. The store is scheduled to receive $5,000 cash on a business note receivable in November. Projected cash disbursements include inventory purchases ($10,200 in October and $12,100 in November) and operating expenses ($3,000 each month).

Waxman's bank requires a $7,500 minimum balance in the store's checking account. At the end of any month when the account balance goes below $7,500, the bank automatically extends credit to the store in multiples of $1,000. Waxman's borrows as little as possible and pays back these loans in monthly installments of $1,000 plus 1.5 percent monthly interest on the entire unpaid principal. The first payment occurs at the end of the month following the loan.

Required

Prepare the store's cash budget for October and November.

Total assets $34,400

Exercise 20-9   *Preparing a budgeted balance sheet*   (L.O. 5)

Use the following information to prepare a budgeted balance sheet for Little Einstein's Book Store at July 31, 19X6. Show computations for cash and owners' equity amounts.

a. July 31 inventory balance, $16,000.
b. July payments for inventory, $5,900.
c. July payments of June 30 accounts payable and accrued liabilities, $6,100.
d. July 31 accounts payable balance, $4,900.
e. June 30 furnitures and fixtures balance, $34,800; accumulated depreciation balance, $27,700.
f. July capital expenditures of $3,200 budgeted for cash purchase of furniture.
g. July operating expenses, including income tax, total $4,200, half of which will be paid during July and half accrued at July 31.
h. July depreciation, $300.
i. Cost of goods sold, 50 percent of sales.
j. June 30 owners' equity, $25,700.
k. June 30 cash balance, $10,300.
l. July budgeted sales, $12,400.
m. July 31 accounts receivable balance, one-fourth of July sales.
n. July cash receipts, $12,300.

Budgeted net inc., quarter ended Dec. $92,000

Exercise 20-10   *Preparing a rolling budget for the income statement*   (L.O. 6)

El Conquistador, Inc., budgets the following total revenues, total expenses, and net income for the last four months of the year:

	September	October	November	December
Budgeted total revenues	$175,000	$160,000	$170,000	$189,000
Budgeted total expenses	93,000	87,000	89,000	97,000
Budgeted net income	$ 82,000	$ 73,000	$ 81,000	$ 92,000

Prepare El Conquistador's rolling monthly income statement budget for the quarters ending on November 30 and December 31.

Additional computer-related problems: Problems 28-3A, 28-3B, 28-4A, 28-4B, 28-5A, 28-5B

Problem 20-1A *Budgeting income and evaluating income with a performance report*
(L.O. 1, 2, 3)

Per. 2—Actual NI exceeds budget $2,000

The Northeastern district office of Impala Fan Company divides its annual budget into semiannual periods. The district manager forecast that sales would increase during the first half of the current year by 8.1 percent over the first half of the preceding year. The manager also believed that second-half sales of the current year would exceed second-half sales of the preceding year by 4.5 percent. Cost of goods sold was budgeted at 43 percent of budgeted sales. Total operating expenses, including income taxes, were expected to be 36 percent of revenues during the first six-month period and 34 percent during the second period.

Actual sales, operating expenses, and net income for the four most recent semiannual periods follow.

	Preceding Year		**Current Year**	
	Semiannual Period		**Semiannual Period**	
	1	**2**	**1**	**2**
Sales	$113,000	$145,000	$124,000	$165,000
Cost of goods sold	40,000	63,000	66,000	81,000
Gross margin	73,000	82,000	58,000	84,000
Operating expenses	52,000	49,000	39,000	47,000
Net income (loss)	$ 21,000	$ 33,000	$ 19,000	$ 37,000

Required

1. Prepare a budgeted income statement for each semiannual period of the current year. Round all amounts to the nearest $1,000.

2. Prepare a summarized income statement performance report for the same period. Present the actual and budgeted income statements side by side. Show the differences between them. Round all amounts to the nearest $1,000.

3. Have operations been more or less successful in the current semiannual period compared with the preceding period? What aspects of operations have improved? What aspects have deteriorated?

Problem 20-2A *Budgeting income for three months* *(L.O. 2, 3)*

June net inc. $4,300

The budget committee of Altenau & Company has assembled the following data. You are the business manager, and you must prepare the budgeted income statements for April, May, and June 19X3.

1. Sales in March were $31,300. You forecast that monthly sales will increase 1.3 percent in April and May and 1.8 percent in June.

2. The company tries to maintain inventory of $8,000 plus 20 percent of sales budgeted for the following month. Monthly purchases average 55 percent of sales. Actual inventory on March 31 is $12,000. Sales budgeted for July are $30,600.

3. Monthly salaries amount to $3,000. Sales commissions equal 5 percent of sales. Combine salaries and commissions as a single figure.

4. Other monthly expenses are
Rent expense	$2,700, paid as incurred
Depreciation expense	500
Insurance expense	100, expiration of prepaid amount
Miscellaneous expense	3% of sales
Income tax	20% of income from operations

Required

Prepare Altenau's budgeted income statements for April, May, and June. Show cost of goods sold computations. Round *all* amounts to the nearest $100. For example, budgeted April sales are $31,700 ($31,300 × 1.013), May sales are $32,100 ($31,700 × 1.013), and June sales are $32,700 ($32,100 × 1.018).

Note: Problem 20-3A is designed to be completed using a computer spreadsheet model, although it can also be solved manually. Chapter 28 includes a tutorial on computer spreadsheets.

Net inc., 6 months $5,192

Problem 20-3A *Preparing a budgeted income statement* **(L.O. 2, 3)**

Hulme TV Appliances is budgeting net income for the six months ended June 30, 19X4. Fred Hulme, the owner, expects January sales of $50,000 for TVs and $10,000 for VCRs. He is hoping for 1 percent monthly sales growth for TVs and 3 percent for VCRs. Cost of goods sold is 70 percent of sales for TVs and 60 percent for VCRs. Hulme budgets monthly expenses as follows:

Salaries	$14,000 per month
Rent.	2,000 per month
Depreciation	1,000 per month
Insurance	500 per month
Travel	750 per quarter (in January and April only)
Utilities	500 per month
Income tax rate	40%

Required

Create a spreadsheet model to prepare Hulme's budgeted income statement for the six months ended June 30, 19X4. Show each expense, total operating expenses, income from operations, income tax expense, and net income. Format the statement as follows:

	A	B	C	D	E	F	G	H
1				Hulme TV Applicances				
2				Budgeted Income Statement				
3				For the Six Months Ended June 30, 19X4				
4								
5		JAN	FEB	MAR	APR	MAY	JUN	TOTAL
6	Sales							
7	TVS							
8	VCRs							
9								
10	Total Sales							
11								
12	COGS							
13	TVs							
14	VCRs							
15								
16	Total COGS							
17								
18	Gross Pft							
19	TVs							
20	VCRs							
21								
22	Total GP							
23								
24	Oper exp							
25								

Problem 20-4A *Preparing a cash budget for three months* **(L.O. 4)**

Ending cash, July $12,350

Genie Products, Inc., is considering opening a sales office in a suburb of Charlotte, North Carolina, during May of the current year. The business estimates the office opening will cost $92,000. To finance start-up, Interstate Bank has agreed to loan Genie, in multiples of $10,000, the amount needed to keep Genie's cash balance above $5,000. The loan begins on the last day of any month in which Genie's cash balance goes below $5,000. The company will repay the loan in monthly installments of $10,000 each, beginning one month after the loan starts. Genie will also pay monthly interest of 1.5 percent on the entire unpaid balance until the loan is fully repaid.

Management expects Genie's operations to generate the following:

	May	June	July
Sales	$63,000	$71,000	$74,000
Cost of goods sold	45,000	51,000	52,000
Cash operating expenses	6,000	9,000	9,000

On May 1 Genie expects to have $9,000 cash and $36,000 of inventory. Inventory is expected to decrease by $4,000 each month. Monthly cash receipts average 95 percent of sales. The company purchases inventory through cash disbursements.

Required

Prepare Genie's cash budgets for the months of May, June, and July.

Problem 20-5A *Preparing a budgeted balance sheet* **(L.O. 5)**

Total assets $119,100
Owners' equity $88,600

Boyd Motor Company has applied for a loan. Alliance Bank has requested a budgeted balance sheet at April 30, 19X8. As the controller (chief accounting officer) of Boyd, you have assembled the following information:

a. March 31 equipment balance, $35,200; accumulated depreciation, $22,800.

b. April capital expenditures of $41,700 budgeted for cash purchase of equipment.

c. April operating expenses, including income tax, total $13,600, 25 percent of which will be paid in cash and the remainder accrued at April 30.

d. April depreciation, $700.

e. Cost of goods sold, 60 percent of sales.

f. March 31 owners' equity, $74,900.

g. March 31 cash balance, $26,200.

h. April budgeted sales, $70,000, 60 percent of which is for cash sales. Of the remaining 40 percent, half will be collected in April and half in May.

i. April cash collections on March sales, $31,200.

j. April cash payments of March 31 liabilities, $17,300.

k. March 31 inventory balance, $22,400.

l. April purchases of inventory, $9,000 for cash and $40,600 on credit. Half of the credit purchases will be paid in April and half in May.

Required

Prepare the budgeted balance sheet of Boyd Motor Company at April 30, 19X8. Show separate computations for cash, inventory, and owners' equity balances.

Dec. 31, 19X3, net inc. $37,000

Problem 20-6A *Preparing a rolling budget for the income statement* **(L.O. 6)**

The budgeted income statements of Buzze Music Company for the six most recent quarters follow.

	Buzze Music Company					
	Budgeted Income Statements					
	For the Quarters Ended September 30, 19X2, through December 31, 19X3					
	19X2		**19X3**			
	Sep. 30	**Dec. 31**	**Mar. 31**	**June 30**	**Sep. 30**	**Dec. 31**
Sales	$20,000	$70,000	$50,000	$60,000	$30,000	$80,000
Cost of goods sold	8,000	30,000	22,000	23,000	11,000	30,000
Gross margin . .	12,000	40,000	28,000	37,000	19,000	50,000
Operating expenses	5,000	16,000	12,000	17,000	10,000	22,000
Net income	$ 7,000	$24,000	$16,000	$20,000	$ 9,000	$28,000

Required

1. Combine the quarterly totals necessary to prepare Buzze's rolling budgeted income statement for the last semiannual period in 19X2 and for the four semiannual periods ending in 19X3. (The first semiannual period in 19X3 ends March 31, the second June 30, and so on.)

2. Based on the comparison of the last half of 19X2 with the last half of 19X3, does Buzze management appear to expect increasing or decreasing sales and net income for 19X3?

Net inc. $42,470
Total assets $222,670

Problem 20-7A *Preparing all the components of a master budget* **(L.O. 2, 3, 4, 5)**

Grant-Pfizer's balance sheet at September 30, 19X4, follows.

	Grant-Pfizer Limited		
	Balance Sheet		
	September 30, 19X4		
Assets		**Liabilities**	
Current assets:		Current liabilities:	
Cash	$ 11,000	Accounts payable	$ 40,000
Accounts receivable, net	45,000	Salaries and commissions payable .	10,000
Inventory	62,000	Total liabilities	50,000
Prepaid insurance	4,000		
	122,000	**Owners' Equity**	
Plant assets:		Owners' equity	140,000
Furniture and fixtures	96,000		
Accumulated depreciation	(28,000)		
	68,000	Total liabilities	
Total assets	$190,000	and owners' equity	$190,000

Additional budget information follows.

a. Sales in September were $90,000. Management projects these monthly sales: October $80,000; November $70,000; December $80,000; January $60,000.

   Sales are half for cash and half on credit. All accounts receivable are collected in the month following sale. Uncollectible accounts are insignificant and can be ignored.

b. For the new budget period management wishes to maintain inventory of $22,000 plus 75 percent of the cost of goods to be sold in the following month. Cost of goods sold averages 60 percent of sales. Grant-Pfizer pays for inventory as follows: 20 percent in the month of purchase and 80 percent in the next month.

c. Payroll is made up of fixed salaries of $1,000 and sales commissions equal to 10 percent of sales. The monthly payroll is accrued at the end of the month and paid early the next month.

d. Other monthly expenses are

Advertising expense	$3,600, paid as incurred
Rent expense	1,300, paid as incurred
Depreciation expense	1,000
Insurance expense	400, expiration of prepaid amount
Miscellaneous expense	2% of sales, paid as incurred

e. Management has budgeted $26,000 cash for the acquisition of furniture in October.

f. The company is required by its bank to maintain a minimum cash balance of $8,000 at the end of each month. Money can be borrowed in multiples of $1,000. Management borrows no more than what is needed to maintain the $8,000 minimum balance and pays back all debts less than $5,000 at the end of the next month. Short-term notes payable greater than $5,000 are paid back in three equal monthly principal payments. The monthly interest rate on all notes payable is 1 percent on the entire unpaid principal. Borrowing and all principal and interest payments occur at the end of the month.

g. In September purchases were $50,000, and salaries and commissions were $10,000.

h. The business is a partnership. The partners, therefore, pay personal income tax on their earnings. The business itself incurs no income tax liability, so income taxes do not enter into the computations.

Required

Prepare Grant-Pfizer's master budget for the fourth quarter of 19X4. Include the following statements and schedules:

Statements:

Budgeted income statement for the quarter ending December 31, 19X4
Statement of budgeted cash receipts and disbursements for the quarter ending December 31, 19X4
Budgeted balance sheet at December 31, 19X4

Schedules:

Sales
Purchases, cost of goods sold, and inventory
Operating expenses
Cash collections from customers
Cash disbursements for purchases
Cash disbursements for operating expenses

Per. 2, Actual NI exceeds
budget $2,000

Problem 20-1B *Budgeting income and evaluating income with a performance report (L.O. 1, 2, 3)*

The Indiana office of Precision Instruments divides its annual budget into semiannual periods. The regional manager forecast that sales would increase during the first half of the current year by 2.5 percent over the first half of the preceding year. The manager also believed that second-half sales of the current year would exceed second-half sales of the preceding year by 8 percent. Cost of goods sold was budgeted at 56 percent of budgeted sales. Total operating expenses, including income taxes, were expected to be 30 percent of revenues during the first six-month period and 32 percent during the second period.

Actual sales, operating expenses, and net income for the four most recent semiannual periods follow.

	Preceding Year		Current Year	
	Semiannual Period		Semiannual Period	
	1	2	1	2
Sales	$32,000	$30,000	$34,000	$36,000
Cost of goods sold	19,000	14,000	16,000	17,000
Gross margin	13,000	16,000	18,000	19,000
Operating expenses	10,000	11,000	11,000	13,000
Net income (loss)	$ 3,000	$ 5,000	$ 7,000	$ 6,000

Required

1. Prepare a budgeted income statement for each semiannual period of the current year. Round all amounts to the nearest $1,000.

2. Prepare a summarized income statement performance report for the same period. Present the actual and the budgeted income statement side by side. Show the differences between them. Round all amounts to the nearest $1,000.

3. Identify the aspects of operations that are performing most successfully and the aspects that are performing least successfully. Comment on the relative success of overall operations.

Sept. net inc. $1,600

Problem 20-2B *Budgeting income for three months (L.O. 2, 3)*

Representatives of the various departments of Tallahassee Construction Co. have assembled the following data. You are the business manager, and you must prepare the budgeted income statements for July, August, and September 19X6.

1. Sales in June were $18,400. You forecast that monthly sales will increase 2 percent in July, 2 percent in August, and 3 percent in September.

2. Tallahassee tries to maintain inventory of $5,000 plus 20 percent of sales budgeted for the following month. Monthly purchases average 65 percent of sales. Actual inventory on June 30 is $8,000. Sales budgeted for October are $20,500.

3. Monthly salaries amount to $1,200. Sales commissions equal 6 percent of sales. Combine salaries and commissions as a single figure on the income statements.

4. Other monthly expenses are
   Rent expense .... $1,200, paid as incurred
   Depreciation expense 300
   Insurance expense.......... 100, expiration of prepaid amount
   Miscellaneous expense...... 5% of sales
   Income tax .... 20% of income from operations

Required

Prepare Tallahassee's budgeted income statements for July, August, and September. Show cost of goods sold computations. Round *all* amounts to the nearest $100. For example, budgeted July sales are $18,800 ($18,400 × 1.02), August sales are $19,200 ($18,800 × 1.02), and September sales are $19,800 ($19,200 × 1.03).

Note: Problem 20-3B is designed to be completed using a computer spreadsheet model, although it can also be solved manually. Chapter 28 includes a tutorial on computer spreadsheets.

Problem 20-3B   *Preparing a budgeted income statement*   **(L.O. 2, 3)**

Net inc., 6 months $32,210

Advanced Information Systems, Inc., is budgeting gross profit (gross margin) for the six months ended June 30, 19X5. Lynn Bradshaw, the owner, expects January sales of $70,000 for computer hardware and $25,000 for software. She is hoping for 2 percent monthly sales growth for hardware and 4 percent for software. Cost of goods sold is 70 percent of sales for hardware and 50 percent for software. The business budgets expenses as follows:

Salaries	$20,000 per month
Rent	2,500 per month
Depreciation	2,000 per month
Insurance	1,500 per month
Travel	900 per quarter (in January and April only)
Utilities	650 per month
Income tax rate	40%

Required

Create a spreadsheet model to prepare the Advanced Information Systems income statement for the six months ended June 30, 19X5. Show each expense, total operating expenses, income from operations, income tax expense, and net income. Format the statement as follows:

	A	B	C	D	E	F	G	H
1			Advanced Information Systems, Inc.					
2			Budgeted Income Statement					
3			For the Six Months Ended June 30, 19X4					
4								
5		JAN	FEB	MAR	APR	MAY	JUN	TOTAL
6	Sales							
7	Hardware							
8	Software							
9								
10	Total Sales							
11								
12	COGS							
13	Hardware							
14	Software							
15								
16	Total COGS							
17								
18	Gross Pft							
19	Hardware							
20	Software							
21								
22	Total GP							
23								
24	Oper exp							

Ending cash, Oct., $10,070

Problem 20-4B *Preparing a cash budget for three months* **(L.O. 4)**

Midlantic Development Company is considering opening an office in a suburb of Chesapeake County, Virginia, during September of the current year. The business estimates that the office opening will cost $17,000. To finance start-up, Guaranty Bank has agreed to loan Midlantic, in multiples of $1,000, the amount needed to keep Midlantic's cash balance above $10,000. The loan begins on the last day of any month in which Midlantic's cash balance goes below $10,000. The company will repay the loan in monthly installments of $1,000 each, beginning two months after the loan starts. Midlantic will also pay monthly interest of 1 percent on the entire unpaid balance until the loan is repaid.

Management expects Midlantic's operations to generate the following:

	August	September	October
Sales	$41,000	$44,000	$52,000
Cost of goods sold	17,000	21,000	26,000
Cash operating expenses	19,000	22,000	24,000
Collection of note receivable		25,000	

On August 1 Midlantic expects to have $7,000 cash and $7,000 of inventory. Inventory is expected to increase by $3,000 each month. Monthly cash receipts average 95 percent of sales. The company purchases inventory through cash disbursements.

Required

Prepare Midlantic's cash budgets for the months of August, September, and October.

Problem 20-5B *Preparing a budgeted balance sheet* **(L.O. 5)**

Total assets $109,100
Owners' equity $85,700

Kluzewski Supply has applied for a loan. The bank, Master Bank, has requested a budgeted balance sheet at June 30, 19X4. As the controller (chief accounting officer) of Kluzewski, you have assembled the following information:

a. May 31 equipment balance, $60,600; accumulated depreciation, $11,700.
b. June capital expenditures of $15,800 budgeted for cash purchase of equipment.
c. June operating expenses, including income tax, total $38,800, 75 percent of which will be paid in cash and the remainder accrued at June 30.
d. June depreciation, $400.
e. Cost of goods sold, 45 percent of sales.
f. May 31 owners' equity, $97,400.
g. May 31 cash balance, $18,900.
h. June budgeted sales, $50,000, 40 percent of which is for cash. Of the remaining 60 percent, half will be collected in June and half in July.
i. June cash collections on May sales, $14,900.
j. June cash payments of May 31 liabilities, $10,700.
k. May 31 inventory balance, $10,400.
l. June purchases of inventory, $11,000 for cash and $27,400 on credit. Half of the credit purchases will be paid in June and half in July.

Required

Prepare the budgeted balance sheet of Kluzewski Supply at June 30, 19X4. Show separate computations for cash, inventory, and owners' equity balances.

Problem 20-6B   *Preparing a rolling budget for the income statement*   **(L.O. 6)**   Dec. 31, 19X6, net inc. $11,000

The budgeted income statements of Niagara Corp. for the six most recent quarters follow.

Niagara Corp.
Budgeted Income Statements
For the Quarters Ended September 30, 19X5, through December 31, 19X6

| | 19X5 | | 19X6 | | | |
	Sep. 30	Dec. 31	Mar. 31	June 30	Sep. 30	Dec. 31
Sales........	$50,000	$90,000	$60,000	$80,000	$ 40,000	$120,000
Cost of goods sold	25,000	50,000	35,000	50,000	25,000	75,000
Gross margin	25,000	40,000	25,000	30,000	15,000	45,000
Operating expenses ..	22,000	20,000	22,000	23,000	25,000	24,000
Net income (loss)	$ 3,000	$20,000	$ 3,000	$ 7,000	$(10,000)	$ 21,000

Required

1. Combine the quarterly totals necessary to prepare Niagara's rolling budgeted income statement for the last semiannual period in 19X5 and for the four semiannual periods ending in 19X6. (The first semiannual period in 19X6 ends March 31, the second June 30, and so on.)
2. Based on the comparison of the last half of 19X6 with the last half of 19X5, does management appear to expect increasing or decreasing sales and net income for 19X6?

Problem 20-7B   *Preparing all the components of a master budget*   **(L.O. 2, 3, 4, 5)**   Net inc. $40,150
Total assets $180,550

Fitness Associates' balance sheet at September 30, 19X4, follows.

Fitness Associates
Balance Sheet
September 30, 19X4

Assets		Liabilities	
Current assets:		Current liabilities:	
Cash	$ 7,000	Accounts payable	$ 32,000
Accounts receivable, net	25,000	Salaries and commissions payable .	8,000
Inventory......................	67,000	Total liabilities	40,000
Prepaid insurance	2,000		
	101,000	**Owners' Equity**	
Plant assets:			
Furniture and fixtures	48,000	Owners' equity	90,000
Accumulated depreciation.........	(19,000)		
	29,000	Total liabilities	
Total assets	$130,000	and owners' equity	$130,000

Chapter 20   Introduction to Management Accounting: The Master Budget   **955**

Additional budget information follows.

a. Sales in September were $50,000. Management projects these monthly sales: October $60,000; November $70,000; December $80,000; January $80,000.

    Sales are half for cash and half on credit. All accounts receivable are collected in the month following sale. Uncollectible accounts are insignificant and can be ignored.

b. Management wishes to maintain inventory of $40,000 plus 75 percent of the cost of goods sold in the following month. Cost of goods sold averages 60 percent of sales. Fitness Associates pays for inventory as follows: 20 percent of each month's purchases in the month of purchase and the remaining 80 percent in the next month.

c. Payroll is made up of fixed salaries of $3,000 and sales commissions equal to 10 percent of sales. The monthly payroll is accrued at the end of the month and paid early the following month.

d. Other monthly expenses are

Advertising expense.........	$1,500, paid as incurred
Rent expense	900, paid as incurred
Depreciation expense........	600
Insurance expense	200, expiration of prepaid amount
Miscellaneous expense	2% of sales, paid as incurred

e. Management has budgeted $8,000 cash for the acquisition of furniture in October.

f. The company keeps a minimum cash balance of $5,000 at the end of each month. The company may borrow on short-term notes payable in multiples of $1,000. Management borrows no more than necessary. The company repays the notes in three equal monthly installments that begin one month after the company borrows. The notes also carry monthly interest of 1 percent on the entire unpaid principal. Borrowing and all principal and interest payments occur at the end of the month.

g. In September purchases were $40,000, and salaries and commissions were $8,000.

h. The business is a partnership. The partners, therefore, pay personal income tax on their earnings. The business itself incurs no income tax liability, so income taxes do not enter into the computations.

Required

Prepare Fitness Associates' master budget for the fourth quarter of 19X4. Include the following statements and schedules:

Statements:
Budgeted income statement for the quarter ending December 31, 19X4
Statement of budgeted cash receipts and disbursements for the quarter ending December 31, 19X4
Budgeted balance sheet at December 31, 19X4

Schedules:
Sales
Purchases, cost of goods sold, and inventory
Operating expenses
Cash collections from customers
Cash disbursements for purchases
Cash disbursements for operating expenses

Extending Your Knowledge

Decision Problems

1. Preparing a Cash Budget to Analyze a Loan Request (L.O. 4)

Cash bal. before financing $1,578

Billy Disch Marine Co., a boat dealer, is requesting a $40,000 loan to finance the remodeling of its store. The bank requires a statement of budgeted cash receipts and disbursements to support the loan application.

The Disch Marine cash balance at February 28 is $5,100. During March the business expects to collect $3,900 from sales made in January and February. Also, in February the store sold an old display case for $700, and the owners expect to receive that amount during March. During March the business will pay off accounts payable of $2,100 and a note payable of $6,000 plus $540 interest.

The business expects monthly sales of $9,500 for March, April, and May. Experience indicates that Disch will collect 60 percent of sales in the month of sale, 30 percent in the month following sale, and 7 percent in the second month after sale. The remaining 3 percent is uncollectible.

The February 28 inventory is $37,800. Purchases average one-half of sales. Billy Disch pays all accounts payable arising from inventory purchases in time to receive a 2 percent discount, 80 percent in the month of purchase and 20 percent the next month.

Budgeted operating expenses for March are rent (8 percent of sales), advertising ($500), utilities ($330), depreciation ($240), and insurance ($120). Depreciation and insurance are recorded as the assets expire. Half of the advertising expense is paid as incurred, and half is accrued at the end of the month. During March Disch Marine will pay advertising of $160 that was accrued at February 28.

In order to make the loan, the bank requires that Disch Marine's cash balance be at least $2,000 before any effects of financing.

Required

Prepare a cash budget (a statement of budgeted cash receipts and disbursements) for Billy Disch Marine Co. for March. As the bank loan officer, decide if the business qualifies for the loan.

2. Projecting Cash Flow and Financial Statements to Analyze Alternatives (L.O. 2,3,4,5)

Ending cash:
Cotton $285
Linen $0

Jacky Carleton is a librarian in the business library of Canada Trust. Each autumn, as a hobby, Jacky weaves cotton placemats for sale through a local craft shop. The shop charges 10% commission and remits the net proceeds to Jacky at the end of December. The mats sell in the shop for $20 per set of four; the cost of the cotton is $7 per set. Jacky has woven and sold 25 sets each year for the past two years. Each December 31st, Jacky has always paid for the cotton and repaid $200 of the principal, along with accrued interest at 9%, on the loan she received on September 1, 19X1 for her four-harness loom. This was also the day the loom was purchased.

Jacky's weaving is very professional. She is considering buying an eight-harness loom immediately so she can weave more intricate placemats in linen. She estimates that each set would sell for $50, and the cost of the linen would be $18 per set. She can weave 15 sets in time for the Christmas rush. Jacky's supplier will sell her linen on credit until December 31. The new loom would cost $1,000. The bank has agreed to lend her the money at 12% per annum, with $200 principal plus accrued interest payable each December 31. Jacky plans to keep her original loom. She could make 25 sets of cotton placemats with her newly-purchased supply of cotton. The old loom is depreciated at $10 per month; monthly depreciation on the new loom would be $20. The balance sheet for Jacky's weaving at August 31, 19X3 follows:

Jacky Carleton, Weaver
Balance Sheet
August 31, 19X3

Current assets:		Current liabilities:	
Cash	$ 15	Bank loan payable	$100
Inventory of cotton	175	Accounts payable	74
	190	Interest payable	6
Fixed assets:			180
Loom	500		
Accumulated		Owner's equity	270
depreciation	(240)		
	260	Total liabilities	
Total assets	$ 450	and owner's equity	$450

Required

Prepare a statement of budgeted cash receipts and disbursements for the four months ended December 31, 19X3 for two alternatives: weaving the placemats in cotton and weaving the placemats in linen. For each alternative, prepare a budgeted income statement for the four months ended December 31, 19X3, and a budgeted balance sheet at December 31, 19X3. Which alternative would you recommend for Jacky? Give your reason.

Ethical Issue

Maxim Gorky, Inc., practices top-down budgeting. Top managers set targets for sales managers, who then develop goals for individual salespersons. Grace Faile, manager for the western district, uses her contacts and interpersonal skills to raise money for the Republican party. Randall Van Houten, president of Maxim Gorky, is a prominent Democrat. He suspects that Ms. Faile is using too much time for fund-raising and shirking her duty to the company. For 1994, Mr. Van Houten sets Ms. Faile's sales goal 40 percent above actual amounts for 1993. The increases expected of other sales managers average 25 percent. Van Houten justifies Faile's sales budget on the grounds that the western district has experienced the greatest growth and that Ms. Faile is extremely talented.

Required

1. What is the preferred model for establishing a budget—top-down or bottom-up? Give your reason.
2. Is Mr. Van Houten's treatment of Ms. Faile ethical? Explain.

Chapter 21

Cost-Volume-Profit Relationships and the Contribution Margin Approach to Decision Making

His big sin, Mr. Iacocca says, was trying to diversify. His decision put the company into the aerospace and defense businesses, but siphoned management attention and money from the crucial task of producing new vehicles. Now Chrysler has sold, or is trying to sell, those businesses. . . .

Along with diversification came a top-heavy . . . company structure that sent Chrysler's costs soaring. The company must now sell 1.9 million cars and trucks a year just to *break even*. That's far above the *break-even point* of 1.1 million vehicles in 1985 and a much bigger increase than can be justified by Chrysler's 1987 purchase of American Motors Corp.

"If I made a mistake, it was following other companies, and maybe those were grandiose schemes," says Mr. Iacocca. "We didn't need a [new] company [structure]. That's what made us top-heavy." [Emphasis added]

Source: Paul Ingrassia and Bradley A. Stertz, "With Chrysler Ailing, Lee Iacocca Concedes Mistakes in Managing," *The Wall Street Journal*, September 17, 1990, p. A1.

Point to Stress: An understanding of cost behavior is the key to many decisions in an organization, in that by understanding how costs behave a manager is better able to predict what costs will be under various operating circumstances.

Discussion Question: Define variable costs, and ask: What are some examples of variable costs? *ANSWER:* Sales commissions, fuel, delivery expense, utilities based on usage, cost of goods sold, depreciation by the units-of-production method.

Typical Student Misconception: Students often fail to realize that total variable costs vary with changes in volume, but the unit variable cost is constant. If T-shirts cost $2 and 1,000 T-shirts are sold, cost of goods sold is $2,000 (1,000 × $2). If 2,000 T-shirts are sold, cost of goods sold is $4,000 (2,000 × $2). The total cost increased, but the unit cost is $2 at any level.

OBJECTIVE 1

Identify different cost behavior patterns

How much additional income does Chrysler Corporation earn when it sells 5,000 more Dodge Caravans? How much in additional expense does the sale of these 5,000 cars cost Chrysler? How many Caravans must the company sell for the Dodge Division to break even—earn zero profit?

Many questions in business—on the number of cars sold, the number of passengers transported by an airline, and so on—boil down to this general question: *What effects does a change in volume have on profits?* To answer these questions, managers study the links among cost, volume, and profit.

Cost-volume-profit (CVP) analysis helps managers to predict the outcome of their decisions by expressing the relationships among a business's costs, volume, and profit or loss. It is an important part of the budgeting system. We begin our discussion of this valuable decision-making tool by looking at costs.

Types of Costs

A **cost driver** is any factor whose change makes a difference in a related total cost. There are many possible cost drivers. The most prominent driver is volume, which is often expressed in physical *units* sold or produced or in total sales *dollars*. For example, the more T-shirts a company produces—that is, the greater the T-shirt volume—the greater the costs the company incurs. Non-volume factors also act as cost drivers. An example is weight, which may affect freight costs. To emphasize basic concepts in this chapter, we focus on volume as the cost driver.

Cost behavior describes how costs change—indeed, if they change—in response to a shift in a cost driver. We examine three basic types of costs: variable, fixed, and mixed. A **variable cost (variable expense)** is a cost that changes in total in direct proportion to a change in volume. For example, sales commissions are variable costs; the higher the sales, the higher the sales commissions. Variable costs also include cost of goods sold and delivery expense. Each of these costs rises or falls directly with any increase or decrease in sales volume.

Exhibit 21-1 shows the graphs of three different variable costs. The first graph presents the cost behavior of a product that costs $2 an item. The sloped line in the first graph indicates the 3,000 T-shirts cost $6,000 (3,000 × $2). We see that 4,500 T-shirts cost $9,000 (4,500 × $2).

The higher the cost of an item, the steeper the graph of its variable cost. For example, the second graph in Exhibit 21-1 is based on each item costing $3. Study this graph to confirm that 2,000 T-shirts cost $6,000 (2,000 × $3) and that

EXHIBIT 21-1 *Variable Cost Pattern*

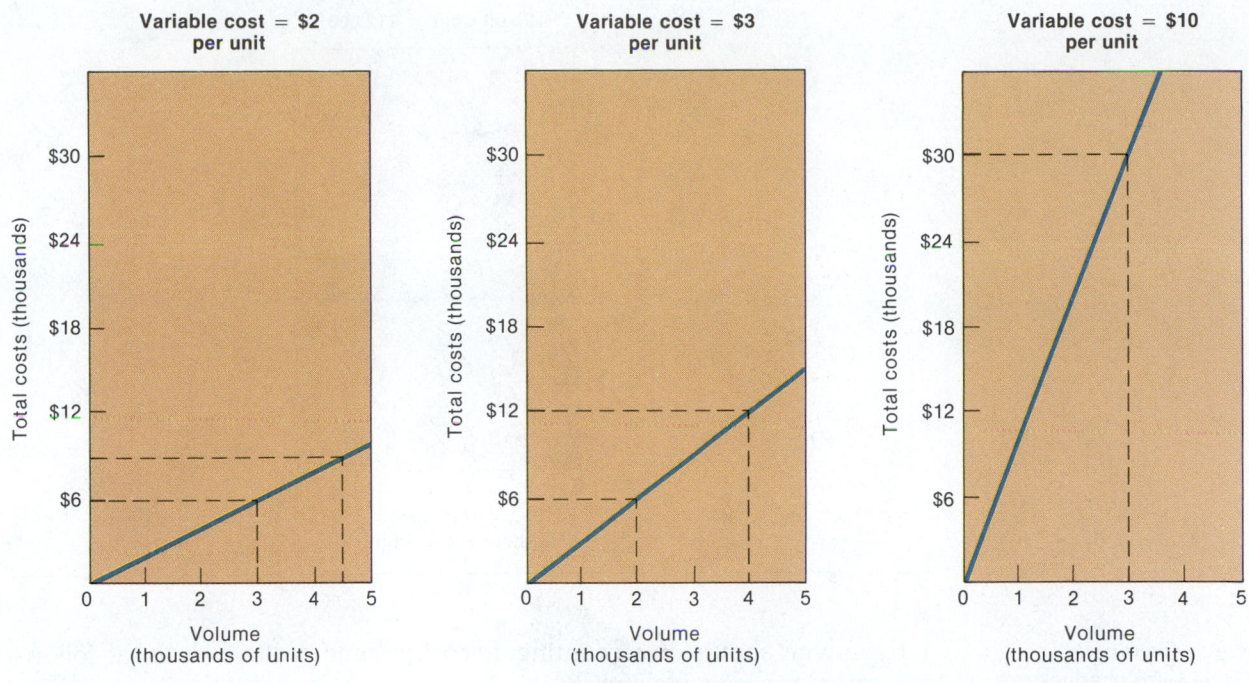

4,000 T-shirts cost $12,000 (4,000 × $3). The third variable cost graph, showing the cost behavior of designer T-shirts that cost $10 each, is steeper yet.

A variable cost graph always passes through the origin (where the cost and volume axes intersect) because at zero volume, the variable cost is zero. As volume increases, variable cost increases in a straight line that leads out from the origin. The steepness of the graph's slope depends on the variable cost per unit. A higher variable unit cost results in a steeper slope. A lower variable unit cost has a lower slope.

A **fixed cost (fixed expense)** is a cost that does not change in total despite changes in volume. For example, office rent does not usually change with the volume of business. A company must still pay its monthly rent regardless of whether sales volume rises, falls, or stays steady. Other examples of fixed costs are depreciation, property taxes, and many executive salaries. These costs occur even if the company makes no sales, for this is the nature of a fixed cost. Exhibit 21-2 graphs a fixed cost, which is always a horizontal line intersecting the cost axis at the level of the fixed cost. In the graph, fixed cost is $12,000, not changing with any shift in the volume.

A **mixed cost (mixed expense)** is part variable and part fixed. It is also called a semivariable cost. Consider a utility expense like electricity, for example. The company must pay a minimum charge regardless of how much electricity it used. In our illustrations, this fixed cost is $6,000. In addition, the company must pay a variable cost of $3 for every product sold. Exhibit 21-3 shows this mixed cost graph.

In a mixed cost graph, total cost is the sum of fixed cost plus the variable cost. At sales volume of 2,000 units, total cost is $12,000 [fixed cost of $6,000 + variable cost of $6,000 (2,000 × $3)]. At volume of 4,000 units, total cost is $18,000 [fixed cost of $6,000 + variable cost of $12,000 (4,000 × $3)]. All graphs of mixed costs show the same pattern. They intersect the cost axis at the fixed cost point, and the slope of the graph is the variable cost per unit.

Discussion Question: Define fixed costs, and ask: What are some examples of fixed costs? *ANSWER:* Rent, depreciation, president's salary, insurance, and so on.

Class Exercise: Have students fill in the blanks:

Variable Costs

1 _____ in total amount

2 _____ per unit

Fixed Costs

3 _____ in total amount

4 _____ per unit

ANSWER:

1 Vary   *3* Fixed

2 Fixed   *4* Vary

Teaching Tip: Although total fixed costs remain constant as volume varies, the unit cost changes. If fixed expenses are $5,000 and 1,000 units are sold, then the fixed expense per unit is $5 ($5,000/1,000). If 2,000 units are sold, the fixed expense per unit is $2.50 ($5,000/2,000).

EXHIBIT 21-2 *Fixed Cost Pattern*

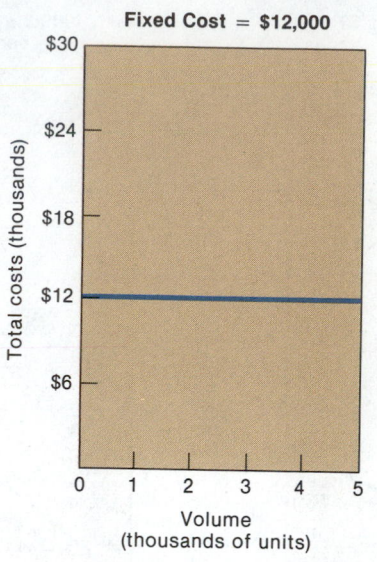

Synonyms abound in accounting. In cost-volume-profit analysis the following synonyms are widely used:

Point to Stress: Mixed costs change in total with changes in volume, but not proportionately.

> *sales* and *revenue*
> *variable cost* and *variable expense*
> *fixed cost* and *fixed expense*
> *income from operations* and *operating income*
> *net income* and *net profit*

Because you will encounter these synonyms in actual practice, we will use them freely in this chapter. To underscore basic relationships, income tax is assumed to be included among the expenses.

EXHIBIT 21-3 *Mixed Cost Pattern*

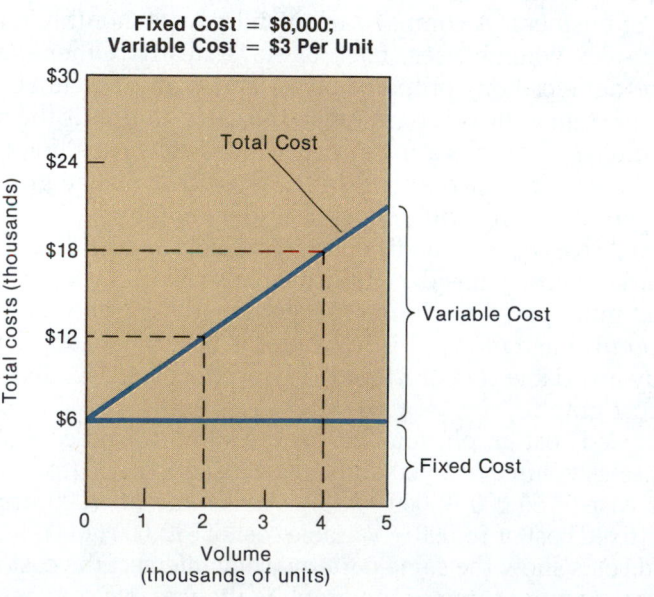

Contribution Margin Approach to Decision Making _____

An income statement can be prepared using two fundamentally different approaches. The early part of this book focused on accounting from the perspective of external users of the financial statements. That emphasis leads to the conventional income statement.

The present focus on management's use of accounting information calls for a different format for the income statement. In the management focus, the nature of an expense is important. Whether a cost is variable or fixed affects management decisions. Managers, then, want an income statement format that identifies the different types of costs. The contribution margin income statement provides this information.

The **contribution margin income statement** separates expenses into variable costs and fixed costs and highlights the **contribution margin**, which is the excess of sales over variable expenses. Exhibit 21-4 presents a contribution margin income statement alongside a conventional income statement for comparison.

Income from operations is the same on both income statements. However, the contribution margin of $9,000 differs from the gross margin of $16,000. The primary categories of expenses on the contribution margin statement are variable expenses and fixed expenses. By contrast, the conventional income statement contains no such distinctions. Instead, its primary categories of expenses are cost of goods sold and operating expenses.

The contribution margin receives its name because the excess of revenues over variable expenses "contributes" to the payment of fixed expenses. The amount of revenues left over "contributes" to profit. Management's goal, of course, is to make the contribution margin as large as possible.

Suppose that Reynolds Company managers are trying to predict the impact on operating income if sales increase by $4,000 (10 percent), from $40,000 to $44,000. Management, in drawing up the company budget, must know the impact of this possible sales increase on income from operations. If sales increase by 10 percent, variable expenses can be expected to increase by the same percentage. Fixed expenses will remain at $3,000.

Real-World Example: The contribution margin income statement is often used by managers to study different departments or product lines. Suppose a department is operating at a loss. By looking at the contribution margin of the department, management can decide whether or not to close that department. A general rule of thumb is that if the department shows a positive contribution margin (or if the variable costs are less than sales revenue), then the company as a whole would be more profitable if the department is kept operating. In other words, that department is covering some fixed costs, and should be kept.

OBJECTIVE 2

Use a contribution margin income statement to make business decisions

EXHIBIT 21-4 *Contribution Margin Income Statement*

Reynolds Company Conventional Income Statement Month Ended December 31, 19XX		
Sales revenue		$40,000
Cost of goods sold		24,000
Gross margin		16,000
Operating expenses:		
Selling	$6,000	
General and administrative	4,000	10,000
Income from operations		$ 6,000

Reynolds Company Contribution Margin Income Statement Month Ended December 31, 19XX		
Sales revenue		$40,000
Variable expenses:		
Cost of goods sold	$24,000	
Selling	4,000	
General and administrative	3,000	31,000
Contribution margin		9,000
Fixed expenses:		
Selling	2,000	
General and administrative	1,000	3,000
Income from operations		$ 6,000

We compute the income from operations resulting from the sales increase as follows:

Increase in sales revenue	$4,000
Increase in expenses:	
Fixed expenses	-0-

Variable expenses:

$$\frac{\text{Increase in sales}}{\text{Current sales}} \times \text{Current variable expenses}$$

$\dfrac{\$4,000}{\$40,000}$	$\times$	$31,000	3,100

Increase in contribution margin	**900**
Income from operations before sales increase	6,000
Income from operations after sales increase	$6,900

Management can use this information to decide whether to expand operations. If the $900 increase in contribution margin is considered adequate, Reynolds will expand the business. If $900 is considered inadequate, then Reynolds will come up with another plan.

Important points about the analysis are that (1) fixed expenses do not change and (2) variable expenses increase proportionately with sales. That is, sales are expected to increase by 10 percent ($4,000/$40,000 = .10), and so variable expenses and the contribution margin also increase by 10 percent.

Similar analysis using the conventional income statement is not possible. Managers cannot use the conventional income statement to accurately predict the change in income from an increase in sales because this statement does not show which expenses are variable and which are fixed.

Relevant Range

A **relevant range** is the band of volume in which a specific relationship between cost and volume is valid. A fixed cost is fixed only in relation to a given relevant range (usually large) and a given time span (usually a particular budget period). Exhibit 21-5 shows a fixed cost level of $50,000 for the volume range of 0 to 10,000 units. Between 10,000 and 20,000 units, fixed expenses may be $80,000, and they may increase to $120,000 for volume above 20,000 units.

Companies use the relevant range concept in budgeting their costs. Suppose the business in Exhibit 21-5 expects sales volume of 12,000 during the year. For this period the relevant range is between 10,000 and 20,000 units, and managers would budget fixed expenses of $80,000. If actual sales for the year exceed 20,000 units, the company will consider hiring additional employees and perhaps open a new store, increasing rent expense. Fixed expenses will increase as the relevant range shifts to a new band of volume.

Fixed costs change from year to year, and so does the relevant range. Expecting sales of only 8,000 units next year, the business would budget fixed expenses in a lower relevant range. The company may have to shut down a sales office, lay off employees, and eliminate other fixed expenses.

The relevant range concept also applies to variable costs. Some variable expenses may behave differently at different levels of volume. For example, utility expenses for water and electricity often cost less per unit as usage increases. Also, a company may pay higher sales commission rates for higher levels of sales to encourage extra selling effort. Therefore, businesses should

Class Exercise: The Allen Co. has fixed expenses of $100,000, variable expenses of $5 per unit, and a selling price of $20 per unit. Prepare a contribution margin income statement at a sales level of 15,000 units. *ANSWER:*

Sales	$300,000
Var. expenses......	75,000
Contribution	
margin	225,000
Fixed expenses.....	100,000
Operating income ..	$125,000

By how much would operating income increase if 25,000 units were sold? *ANSWER:* Operating income would increase by the contribution margin of the additional units sold—$150,000 (10,000 units × $15 CM).

Point to Stress: The relevant range assumes the cost behavior patterns are intact only for a certain range of activity. Any activity above or below the relevant range may show different cost behavior patterns.

EXHIBIT 21-5 *Relevant Range*

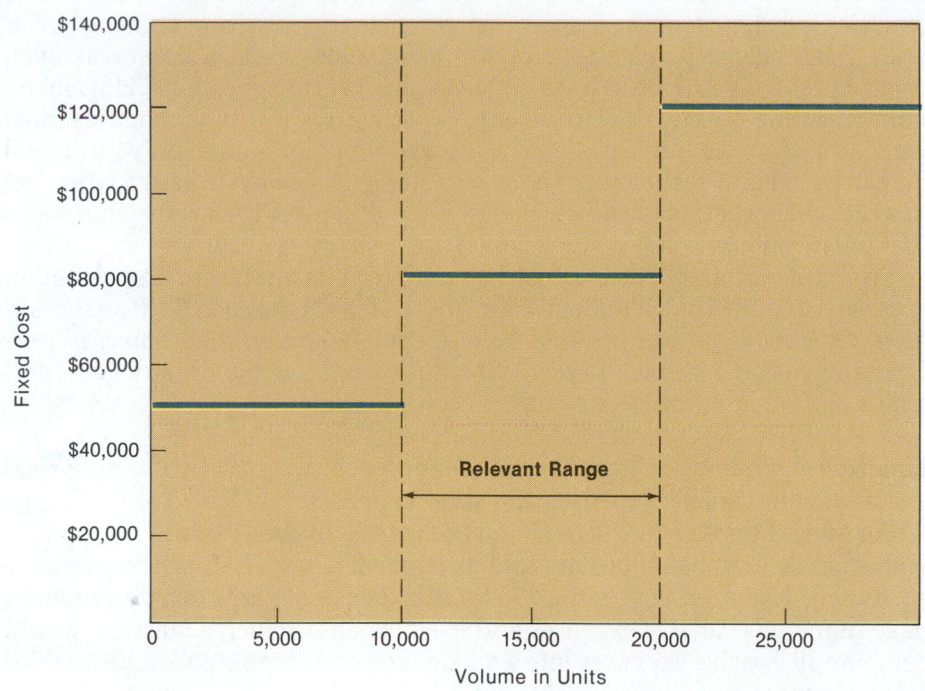

consider cost behavior—how both fixed and variable expenses change—over the full range of sales volumes that are likely to occur during the budget period.

Cost behavior is one of the most challenging aspects of budgeting. After managers set the business's sales goal for the next period, accountants estimate costs. The behavior of various costs affects the expense budget. If budgeted expenses are too high, top managers may revise budgets for sales or expenses before finally setting the profit goal for the period.

In cost-volume-profit analysis, which we discuss next, we begin by classifying each cost as either variable or fixed. Later in this chapter, we show how to separate a mixed cost into its variable and fixed components.

Cost-Volume-Profit Analysis

The easiest way to learn cost-volume-profit analysis is with an example. Suppose Maria Martinez is considering renting a booth at a county fair. Maria plans to sell travel posters for $3.50 each. She can purchase the posters for $2.10 each and can return all unsold items for a full refund. Rent for the booth will cost $700. Using this information, let's answer six questions about Maria's business.

Question 1: What Is Maria's Break-Even Sales Level?

The study of cost-volume-profit analysis is often called **break-even analysis.** Why? CVP analysis allows us to compute an amount in unit sales or dollar

Point to Stress: Not all costs are strictly variable or fixed, but because they must be classified as one or the other in order to use cost-volume-profit analysis, they must be broken down into their fixed and variable components.

Point to Stress: Refer to the chapter-opening vignette. The break-even point is very important. Most businesses know how many units they must sell in order to break even. Chrysler apparently has increased its break-even point, meaning that Chrysler must sell more cars before it can become profitable. The reason cited was the acquisition of other businesses, which added additional costs and made it more difficult for Chrysler to break even.

Point to Stress: The break-even point is the point at which total expenses equal total revenue and the profit is zero.

sales at which revenue equals expenses. This sales level is called the **break-even point.** In other words, we may calculate the sales volume at which the business breaks even. Revenue must reach the break-even point to cover costs. Sales below the break-even point mean a loss. Sales above break-even bring a profit. CVP, or break-even, analysis answers the questions, How many units must the business sell to cover expenses? and How much in sales must we reach before we earn a profit? The break-even point is often only incidental to managers because their focus is on the sales level needed to earn a target net income. However, the break-even point is a useful place to start the analysis of CVP relationships.

Two popular methods in cost-volume-profit analysis are the equation approach and the contribution margin approach. The focus in CVP analysis is often on *operating income* (income from operations) rather than on *net income.* Operating income is easier to predict because it omits extraordinary gains and losses and other special items that affect net income.

Equation Approach. In the equation approach, we start by dividing total expenses into variable expenses and fixed expenses.

For Maria Martinez, the variable cost is her cost of goods sold. This expense will equal the number of posters sold multiplied by her $2.10 cost to purchase each item. Her fixed cost is the $700 rent expense. A large company would have numerous variable expenses and fixed expenses. Such a business would combine all variable expenses into a single total and compute a single total for fixed expenses.

Our next step is to express income in equation form:

$$\text{Sales} - \text{Variable expenses} - \text{Fixed expenses} = \text{Operating income}$$

We find it useful to rearrange the equation to place the variables on the left-hand side and the dollar amounts on the right:

$$\text{Sales} - \text{Variable expenses} = \text{Fixed expenses} + \text{Operating income}$$

At the break-even point, income equals expenses, so net income is zero. Sales equals the unit selling price multiplied by the number of units sold. Variable expenses equals variable cost per unit times the number of units sold. We substitute these terms into the equation and enter the dollar amounts that we have:

Sales –	Variable expenses	= Fixed expenses + Operating income
$\left(\begin{array}{c}\text{Unit}\\ \text{sale} \times \text{Units sold}\\ \text{price}\end{array}\right)$ –	$\left(\begin{array}{c}\text{Unit}\\ \text{variable} \times \text{Units sold}\\ \text{cost}\end{array}\right)$	= Fixed expenses + Operating income
($3.50 × Units sold) –	($2.10 × Units sold)	= $700 + $0
($3.50 –	$2.10) × Units sold	= $700 + $0
	$1.40 × Units sold	= $700
	Units sold	= $700/$1.40
	Break-even sales in units	= **500 units**

Maria must sell 500 units to break even. Her break-even sales in dollars is the 500 units times their selling price of $3.50. Break-even dollar sales are $1,750 (500 units × $3.50).

OBJECTIVE 3
Compute break-even sales

Serial Class Exercise No. 1: Given the following information, compute the break-even point in units.

Unit sale price	$ 250
Unit variable expenses	150
Total fixed expenses .	35,000

ANSWER:
Let x = units sold at break even

$$\$250x - \$150x = \$35{,}000 + \$0$$
$$\$100x = \$35{,}000$$
$$x = \$35{,}000/\$100$$
$$= \mathbf{350\ units}$$

Let's prove this by preparing an income statement.

ANSWER:

Revenue (350 units × $250)	$87,500
Less Expenses:	
Variable expenses (350 units × $150) .	52,500
Fixed expenses	35,000
Net income	$ -0-

The calculated 350 units to break even is correct.

Another form of the equation approach determines dollar sales first and unit sales second. We divide the variable expense per unit $2.10, by the selling price, $3.50, to determine the ratio of the variable expense to the selling price:

$$\frac{\text{Variable expense}}{\text{Selling price}} = \frac{\$2.10}{\$3.50} = .60$$

We use this ratio in the equation, as follows:

Sales − Variable expense	=	Fixed expenses + Operating income
Sales − (.60 × Sales)	=	$700 + $0
Sales − (.60 × Sales)	=	$700
.40 × Sales	=	$700
Sales	=	$700/.40
Break-even sales in dollars	=	$1,750
Break-even sales in units	=	500 ($1,750/$3.50)

Contribution Margin Approach.   A second way to do CVP analysis is the contribution margin approach. Each unit sold has a *contribution margin,* which is the excess of the sale price over variable expenses. The contribution margin can be expressed per unit, as a percentage, or as a ratio. Sales revenue "contributes" this excess, so to speak, to the recovery of fixed costs, with any remaining excess going to operating income, as follows for Maria Martinez's business:

	Per Unit	Percent	Ratio
Sale price	$ 3.50	100%	1.00
Variable expense	−2.10	−60	−.60
Contribution margin	$ 1.40	40%	.40

In percentage terms, sales of 100 percent minus the variable expense percentage equals the **contribution margin percentage.** Likewise, 100 percent minus the contribution margin percentage equals the variable expense percentage. These relationships can be diagrammed:

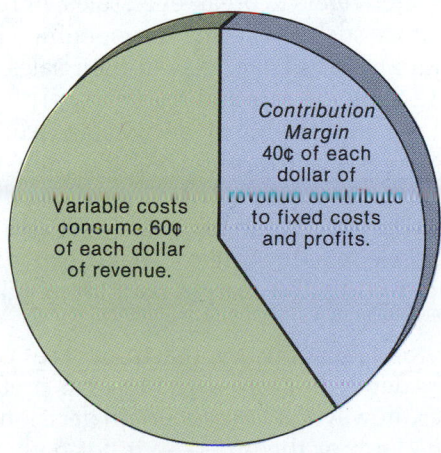

Breakdown of $1 of Revenue

Point to Stress: One purpose of using CVP analysis is to summarize results and relationships without a complicated income statement. You have been asked to prepare income statements to prove that CVP analysis will give you the same information because the income statement is familiar.

Point to Stress: The contribution margin per unit is the amount that each unit contributes to covering fixed expenses and profit. If the contribution margin is $5 per unit, each unit will contribute $5 to cover fixed expenses and profit.

At break even, the total contribution margin equals total fixed expenses.

Serial Class Exercise No. 2: Refer to Serial Class Exercise No. 1. Calculate the contribution margin per unit, contribution margin ratio, and the treak-even point in units.
ANSWER:

	Per Unit	Ratio
Sale price .	$250	1.00
Variable expense	−150	−.60
Contribution margin .	$100	.40

$$= \frac{\$35,000 \quad \text{Fixed expenses}}{\$100 \quad \text{Contribution margin}}$$

= 350 units = Break-even point

Use the solution from Serial Class Exercise No. 1 to illustrate the similarities between the two methods of calculating break even. Note that the contribution margin approach comes from the equation approach.

In our illustration, the contribution margin *per unit* is $1.40 ($3.50 − $2.10). To compute break-even sales in units sold, divide fixed expenses by the contribution margin per unit:

$$\text{Break-even sales in units} = \frac{\text{Fixed expenses}}{\text{Contribution margin per unit}}$$

$$= \frac{\$700}{\$1.40}$$

$$= \ 500 \text{ units}$$

We may use percentages in the contribution margin approach. In our example, the contribution margin percentage is $1.40/$3.50, or 40 percent. Earlier we subtracted the variable cost percentage (60 percent) from sales (100 percent) to compute the 40 percent contribution margin percentage. The contribution margin percentage equals the contribution margin divided by the sale price.

We may use the sale price and variable cost of a single item, or we may use the total sales figure and the total variable cost amount of the entire product line in our computations. For example, consider the figures that arise from Maria's selling 500 items. Total sales equals $1,750 ($3.50 × 500), and the total contribution margin is $700 ($1.40 × 500). We see that $700/$1,750 equals .40, or 40 percent. Break-even sales in dollars can be computed as follows by the contribution margin approach:

$$\text{Break-even sales in dollars} = \frac{\text{Fixed expenses}}{\text{Contribution margin ratio}}$$

$$= \frac{\$700}{.40}$$

$$= \ \$1,750$$

If unit variable costs rise, then the amount needed to reach break-even sales increases. Why? A higher unit variable cost lowers the contribution margin. In contrast, a lower unit variable cost means a higher contribution margin, which leads to lower break-even sales.

If sales increase, so does net income. To find the increase in operating income, we can multiply the increase in sales by the contribution margin ratio. For example, Maria's contribution margin ratio is .40. If sales increase by $1,000, for example, then operating income grows by $400.

The business press often refers to break-even sales, or break-even revenues. For example, a news story such as the chapter-opening vignette might report that "the Big Three auto makers have slashed their sales break-even point in North America from 12.2 million cars and trucks to only 9.1 million this year." The companies could accomplish this by decreasing fixed expenses, which is the numerator of the break-even formula. As the numerator decreases, the break-even amount decreases too. Similarly, increasing the contribution margin per unit—the denominator in the formula—will also decrease the break-even amount. For example, a reduction in variable expenses like tires or radiators will increase the contribution margin per automobile and so reduce the break-even amount.

Should you use the equation approach or the contribution margin approach? Use either, depending on your personal preference. You should know both approaches, however, because certain decision situations may give the information in one form or the other—but not both.

We return to questions about Maria's business.

Question 2. If a Fixed Cost (Such as Rent Expense) Is Changed, What Would Break-Even Sales Be?

Suppose the rental on the booth were $1,050 instead of $700. What is Maria's break-even point in units sold and dollar sales?

Use the formula discussed in the contribution margin approach:

$$\text{Break-even sales in units} = \frac{\text{Fixed expenses}}{\text{Contribution margin per unit}}$$

$$= \frac{\$1,050}{\$1.40}$$

$$= 750 \text{ units}$$

$$\text{Break-even sales in dollars} = \frac{\text{Fixed expenses}}{\text{Contribution margin ratio}}$$

$$= \frac{\$1,050}{.40}$$

$$= \$2,625$$

The $1,050 in fixed expenses is an increase of $350, or 50 percent, in excess of $700. Note that the break-even point also rises by 50 percent, from 500 to 750 units. This match in percentage between the increase in fixed expenses and the increase in the break-even point always exists (if other factors are held constant). Maria must sell more posters to cover the higher fixed costs. Similarly, a decrease in fixed expenses means that she can sell less and still cover these costs.

Question 3. If the Sale Price Is Changed, What Would Break-Even Sales Be?

Suppose the sale price per poster is $3.85 rather than $3.50. Variable expense per unit remains at $2.10, and fixed expenses stay at $700. What are Maria's revised break-even sales in units and in dollars? The unit contribution margin becomes $1.75 ($3.85 − $2.10) and the new contribution margin ratio is .4545 ($1.75/ $3.85).

Compute break-even in units and in dollars as follows:

$$\text{Break-even sales in units} = \frac{\text{Fixed expenses}}{\text{Contribution margin per unit}}$$

$$= \frac{\$700}{\$1.75}$$

$$= 400 \text{ units}$$

$$\text{Break-even sales in dollars} = \frac{\text{Fixed expenses}}{\text{Contribution margin ratio}}$$

$$= \frac{\$700}{.4545}$$

$$= \$1,540$$

Note that an increase in sale price reduces break-even sales, in units and in dollars. This occurs because the contribution margin per unit increases. Con-

$$\frac{\$35,000}{\$140} = \textbf{250 units}$$

The new contribution margin is $140 ($250 − $110).

$$\frac{\$35,000}{.56} = \$62,500$$

The new contribution margin ratio is 56% ($140/$250).

Class Exercise: If fixed expenses increase while variable expenses and sale price remain constant, what happens to the contribution margin and break-even point? *ANSWER:* The contribution margin remains unchanged while the break-even point increases. For instance,

Fixed expenses increase from $10,000 to $15,000.

Sale price	$100
Variable expenses	75
Contribution margin	$ 25

Note that the contribution margin remains the same regardless of the change in fixed expenses.

$$\text{Break-even at } \$10,000 = \frac{\$10,000}{\$25}$$

$$= \textbf{400 units}$$

$$\text{Break-even at } \$15,000 = \frac{\$15,000}{\$25}$$

$$= \textbf{600 units}$$

OBJECTIVE 4

Compute the sales level needed to earn a target operating income

Teaching Tip: Why is operating income added to the numerator when determining target sales in dollars? Look at the original equation for calculating break-even. Remember that operating income was added to fixed expenses on the right hand side, but operating income was zero.

sequently, it takes fewer sales at the higher price to break even. Conversely, a reduction in sale price would decrease the contribution margin and force Maria to increase sales just to break even.

Question 4. If a Variable Cost Is Changed, What Would Break-Even Sales Be?

Suppose variable cost per unit is $2.38 instead of $2.10. The unit sale price remains $3.50, and fixed costs stay at $700. Compute break-even sales in units and in dollars.

The new unit contribution margin is $1.12 ($3.50 − $2.38), and the new contribution margin ratio is .32 ($1.12/$3.50). Break-even sales are

$$\textbf{Break-even sales in units} = \frac{\textbf{Fixed expenses}}{\textbf{Contribution margin per unit}}$$

$$= \frac{\$700}{\$1.12}$$

$$= \textbf{625 units}$$

$$\textbf{Break-even sales in dollars} = \frac{\textbf{Fixed expenses}}{\textbf{Contribution margin ratio}}$$

$$= \frac{\$700}{.32}$$

$$= \textbf{\$2,187.50}$$

An increase in variable cost per unit decreases the contribution margin and means that Maria must increase sales in units and in dollars to break even. A decrease in variable cost per unit would lower the break-even point.

Question 5. How Many Units Must Be Sold to Earn a Target Operating Income?

Suppose Maria would be content with operating income of $490 for a week's work in the booth. Assuming a unit sale price of $3.50, variable expense of $2.10 per unit, and fixed expenses of $700, how many posters must Maria sell to earn a profit of $490?

Until now, we have concentrated on break-even sales, the point where operating income is zero. How should we consider a target operating income greater than zero? The contribution margin must be sufficient to cover the fixed expenses plus the target operating income. Our contribution margin approach is basically unchanged. However, the numerator now contains both fixed expenses and the target operating income.

$$\textbf{Target sales in units} = \frac{\textbf{Fixed expenses + Target operating income}}{\textbf{Contribution margin per unit}}$$

$$= \frac{\$700 + \$490}{\$1.40}$$

$$= \frac{\$1,190}{\$1.40}$$

$$= \textbf{850 units}$$

$$\text{Target sales in dollars} = \frac{\text{Fixed expenses} + \text{Target operating income}}{\text{Contribution margin ratio}}$$

$$= \frac{\$700 + \$490}{.40}$$

$$= \frac{\$1,190}{.40}$$

$$= \$2,975$$

The minimum level needed to earn operating income of $490 is 850 units, or $2,975 (850 × $3.50).

Question 6. What Operating Income Is Expected at Various Sales Levels?

A convenient way to answer this question is to graph the cost-volume-profit relationships, as shown in Exhibit 21-6.

To set up the graph, we place units on the horizontal axis and dollars on the vertical axis. We label each axis appropriately. (We have chosen to place labels every 100 units and every $500. These labels offer enough detail for ease in understanding the graph but do not clutter it. Labels on the graphs depend on the data in the problem. The labels should be helpful but not crowd the information.) We use Maria Martinez's data (as originally given) and follow five steps:

Step 1. Choose a relevant sales volume, such as 1,000 units. Plot the point for sales dollars at that volume: 1,000 units × $3.50 per unit = sales of $3,500. Draw the *sales line* from the origin through the $3,500 point.

EXHIBIT 21-6 *Cost-Volume-Profit Graph*

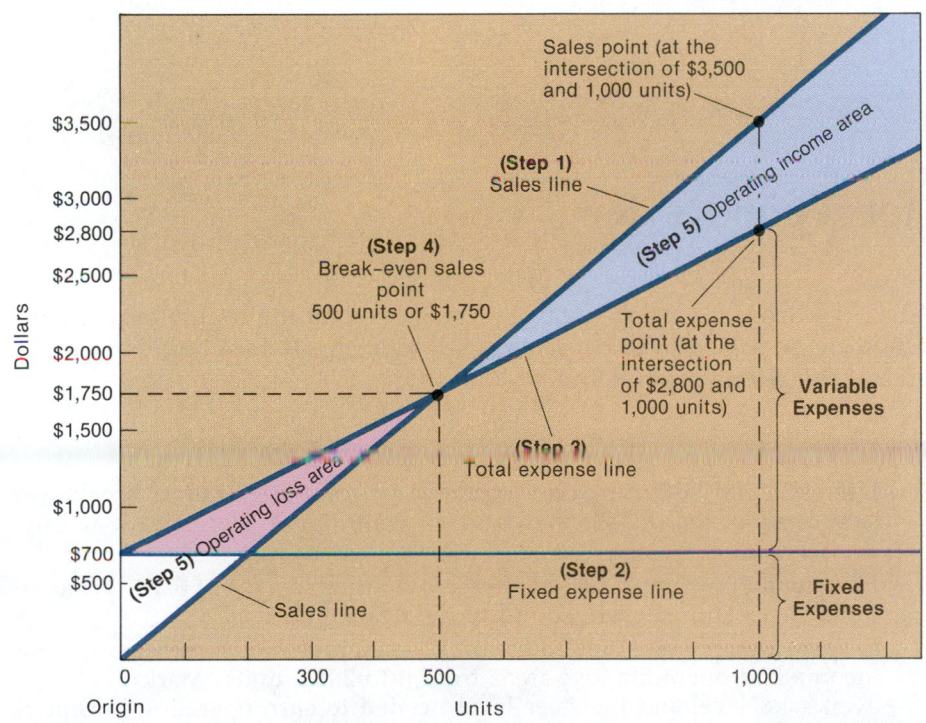

Serial Class Exercise No. 7: (corresponds to Question 5 in the text) Using the data in Serial Class Exercise No. 1, calculate how many units would have to be sold to reach a target operating income of $40,000. What would be the total sales revenue?

ANSWER:

Target unit sales

$$= \frac{\$40,000 + \$35,000}{\$100}$$

$$= 750 \text{ units}$$

Target dollar sales

$$= \frac{\$40,000 + \$35,000}{.40}$$

$$= \$187,500$$

Let's verify this by preparing an income statement:

Revenue (750 × $250) .	$187,500
Less Expenses:	
Variable (750 × $150)	112,500
Fixed	35,000
Oper. income	$ 40,000

The calculation is correct.

Transparency T21-2

OBJECTIVE 5

Graph a set of cost-volume-profit relationships

Point to Stress: Remember these features of a CVP graph:

1 The revenue line always passes through the origin because when no units are sold, there is no revenue.

2 The fixed expense line is parallel to the horizontal axis. The reason is that fixed expenses do not change with changes in units.

3 The total expense line and the fixed expense line will intersect the vertical axis in the same place.

4 The point at which the total expense line intersects the total revenue line is the break-even point.

Step 2. Draw the *fixed expense line,* which intersects the dollar amount axis at $700 and runs across the graph horizontally.

Step 3. Compute variable expense at a relevant sales volume, such as 1,000 units: 1,000 units × $2.10 per unit = variable expense of $2,100. Add variable expense to fixed expense: $2,100 + $700 = $2,800. Plot the total expense point ($2,800) for 1,000 units. Then draw a line through this point from the $700 fixed expenses intercept on the dollar amount axis. This is the *total expense line.*

Step 4. Identify the *break-even point.* The break-even point is the spot where the sales line intersects the total expense line. The equations we used earlier told us that Maria's break-even point was 500 units, or $1,750 in sales. The graph gives us the same information visually.

Step 5. Mark the *operating income* and the *operating loss* areas on the graph. To the left of the break-even point, expenses exceed sales. Consider unit sales of 300, which provide dollar sales of $1,050 (300 × $3.50). Total expenses are $1,330 [(300 × $2.10) + $700]. Therefore, the graph point for sales of 300 units lies in the operating loss area. The vertical distance between the total expense line and the sales line equals the operating loss. For sales of 300 units, the loss is $280 (sales of $1,050 minus total expenses of $1,330).

To the right of the break-even point, Maria earns a profit. The vertical distance between the sales line and the total expense line equals the amount of operating income.

We can tell from the graph whether operating loss, break-even, or operating income results from a given sales figure. We can also see the amount of any operating loss or operating income. By contrast, the equation approach indicates income or loss for a single sales amount. Many computer programs display graphs for CVP analysis. The CVP graph is a valuable budgeting tool because it can show expected operating income or operating loss for all sales levels, from zero units to the company's upper limit.

Summary Problem for Your Review

Grady Nutt is considering opening a small booth at the county fair. Grady's rent expense will be $600. He plans to sell souvenirs, which cost $.95 each, at an average selling price of $1.75.

Required

1. Use the contribution margin approach to compute Grady's break-even sales in units and in dollars. Round the contribution margin ratio to three decimal places.
2. How many units must he sell to earn operating income of $720? What are dollar sales at this level? Round to the nearest dollar.
3. Prepare a graphic solution to the break-even problem, showing operating income and operating loss areas from 0 to 2,000 units. Mark the break-even sales level and the sales level needed to earn operating income of $720.

Requirement 1

The unit contribution margin is $.80 ($1.75 − $.95). The contribution margin ratio is .457 ($.80/$1.75)

$$\textbf{Break-even sales in units} = \frac{\textbf{Fixed expenses}}{\textbf{Contribution margin per unit}} = \frac{\$600}{\$.80} = \textbf{750 units}$$

$$\textbf{Break-even sales in dollars} = \frac{\textbf{Fixed expenses}}{\textbf{Contribution margin ratio}} = \frac{\$600}{.457} = \textbf{\$1,313}$$

Requirement 2

$$\textbf{Target sales in units} = \frac{\textbf{Fixed expenses + Operating income}}{\textbf{Contribution margin per unit}}$$

$$= \frac{\$600 + \$720}{\$.80} = \frac{\$1,320}{\$.80} = \textbf{1,650 units}$$

Target sales in dollars = $2,888 (1,650 units × $1.75)

Requirement 3

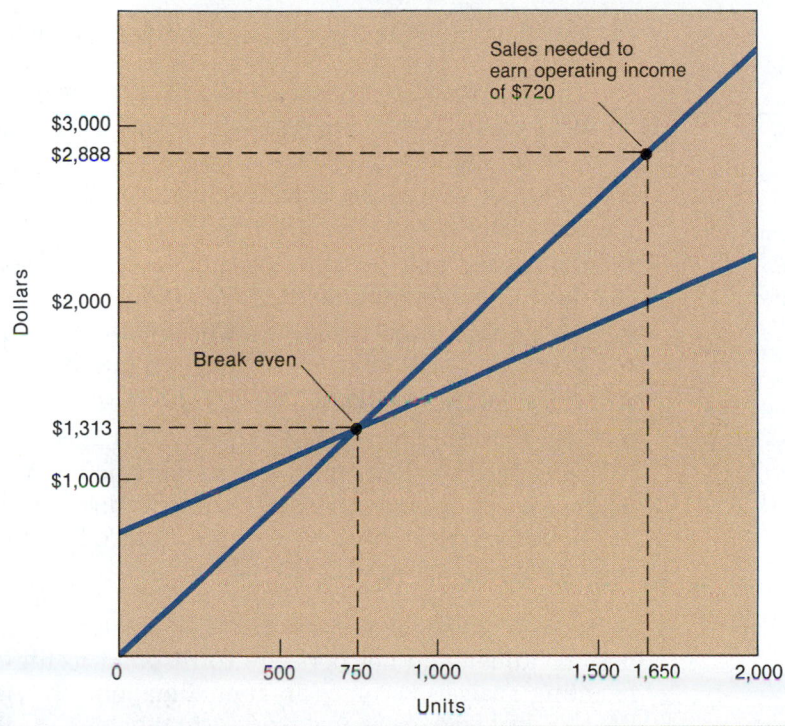

Margin of Safety

Teaching Tip: Margin of Safety (as a percentage) =

$$\frac{\text{Actual sales} - \text{Break-even sales}}{\text{Actual sales}}$$

This ratio tells us by how much sales would have to fall before the company would be unprofitable.

The **margin of safety** is the excess of expected sales over break-even sales. In other words, the margin of safety is the drop in sales dollars that the company can absorb before incurring an operating loss. A high margin of safety serves as a cushion. A low margin of safety is a warning. Managers use the margin of safety to evaluate current operations or to measure the risk of a new business plan. The lower the margin, the higher the risk. The higher the margin, the lower the risk.

Suppose the break-even point is 375 units and the company expects to sell 825 units during the period. Assuming a sale price of $3.50 per unit, we compute the margin of safety as follows:

Margin of safety in units = Expected sales in units − Break-even sales in units

= 825 − 375 = 450

Margin of safety in dollars = Margin of safety in units × Sale price per unit

= 450 units × $3.50 = $1,575

Sales can drop by 450 units, or $1,575, before the company incurs a loss.

For any level of sales, managers can compute the margin of safety as a percentage. We divide the margin of safety in units (450) by sales in units (825), which equals 55 percent. We reach the same percentage by dividing the margin of safety in dollars ($1,575) by sales in dollars (825 units × $3.50 = $2,888).

Assumptions Underlying CVP Analysis

Cost-volume-profit analysis is based on the following assumptions:

1. The cost-volume-profit relationships are linear over a wide range of production and sales. Linear relationships can be graphed as straight lines (like all the lines in Exhibit 21-6).
2. Expenses can be classified as either variable or fixed (we discuss mixed costs later in this chapter).
3. Sale prices, unit variable costs, and total fixed expenses will be unchanged during the period under consideration.
4. Volume is the sole cost driver. The influences of other possible cost drivers (such as weight or size) are held constant or regarded as insignificant.
5. The relevant range of volume is specified.
6. The sales mix of products will be unchanged during the period under consideration. **Sales mix** is the combination of products that make up total sales. For example, the sales mix of a furniture store may be 70 percent household furniture and 30 percent office furniture. We discuss sales mix in the next section.

When these conditions are met, CVP analysis is precise. Most actual business conditions do not perfectly correspond to these assumptions, and the resulting analysis becomes an approximation. The next two sections discuss how to deal with these real-world situations.

Point to Stress: These assumptions do not always hold in practice, but CVP analysis can still be very useful in decision making.

The CVP model, like any model, is based on assumptions and estimates. Another example of a model is the freezing point of water—32°F. Strictly speaking, water freezes at 32°F only under certain conditions—at sea level and with no impurities. Nevertheless, the model still gives a fair estimate of the temperature at which water will freeze even when the conditions are not met strictly.

It is usually better to make some analysis with imperfect information than to make no analysis at all. If the manager is aware of the assumptions underlying CVP analysis, then the manager is often able to evaluate how these assumptions should affect the final decision.

Sales Mix

Our illustrations thus far have focused on a single product, travel posters. Most companies sell more than one product, so sales mix must be considered in figuring CVP relationships. Sales mix has an important effect on profits. For example, the business earns more income selling high-margin products than by selling an equal number of low-margin items.

Management's discussion of income statements often refers to sales mix. For example, an annual report of Deere and Company, a manufacturer of farm equipment, stated that profits decreased because of "a less favorable mix of products sold." What is a "less favorable mix of products"? It is the selling of items with relatively low contribution margins.

We may perform CVP analysis for a company that sells more than one product by using the same equations that we have discussed in analyzing a company selling a single product. *However, we must first express the number of units in terms of a single product.*

Let's return to the Maria Martinez example. Suppose Maria plans to sell two types of posters instead of one. Recall that the basic poster costs $2.10 and sells for $3.50. The second, larger, poster costs $3.92 and will sell for $6.00.

An ongoing business uses its experience to compute its sales mix. Maria, however, is starting a new venture. Suppose she estimates that she will sell 500 large posters and 400 regular posters. To compute break-even sales in units, Maria arranges the data as follows:

	Regular Posters	Large Posters	Total
Sale price per unit	$3.50	$6.00	
Variable expense per unit	2.10	3.92	
Contribution margin per unit	$1.40	$2.08	
Estimated sales in units	×400	×500	900
Estimated contribution margin	$ 560 +	$1,040 =	$1,600
Weighted-average contribution margin per unit ($1,600/900 units)— rounded to three decimal places			$1.778

$$\text{Break-even sales in total units} = \frac{\text{Fixed expenses}}{\text{Weight-average contribution margin per unit}} = \frac{\$700}{\$1.778} = \underline{\underline{394 \text{ units}}}$$

Break-even sales of regular posters $\left(394 \times \frac{400}{900}\right)$ .... $\underline{175 \text{ units}}$

Break-even sales of large posters $\left(394 \times \frac{500}{900}\right)$ .... $\underline{219 \text{ units}}$

The overall break-even point in dollar sales is $1,927: 175 regular posters (175 × $3.50 = $613) plus 219 large posters (219 × $6 = $1,314). At break-even, Maria's net income can be computed:

	Regular	Large	Total
Sales:			
Regular (175 units × $3.50)	$613		
Large (219 units × $6.00)		$1,314	$1,927
Variable expenses:			
Regular (175 units × $2.10)	368		
Large (219 units × $3.92)		859	1,227
Contribution margin	$245	$ 455	$ 700
Fixed expenses			700
Operating income			$ -0-

Let's review our approach. First, we computed the weighted-average contribution margin per unit. This figure expresses both types of posters in terms of a single hypothetical product that has a contribution margin of $1.778. From here on, the contribution margin approach follows the usual pattern. Divide fixed expenses by contribution margin per unit to determine break-even sales in total units. The last step is to separate total units (394) into regular posters (175) and large posters (219).

After performing a CVP analysis, prepare an income statement as a check on your analysis. If the CVP analysis focuses on breaking even, as in the preceding example, the income statement should show operating income of zero. If the CVP analysis shows the sales level needed to earn a target operating income, the income statement should report that income amount.

If Maria's sales mix changes, planned operating income will differ from these estimates. For example, if she sells a higher proportion of large posters, she stands a chance of earning more money because the large posters generate a higher contribution margin.

CVP sales-mix analysis enters the budgeting system. Suppose a company's profits have decreased. Analysis of the sales mix in the past may indicate that this decrease resulted from concentrating on low-margin products. This information can be used to budget a campaign to try to sell products with a higher contribution margin.

Separating a Mixed Cost into its Variable and Fixed Components

OBJECTIVE 7
Separate a mixed cost into its variable and fixed components

An assumption of CVP analysis is that each cost is either variable or fixed. As mentioned previously, some expenses are mixed, combining variable expenses and fixed expenses. We cited utility expense as an example of a mixed cost. Similarly, businesses often pay sales personnel a set monthly salary (a fixed expense) plus a sales commission (a variable expense) based on their sales. The salesperson's overall compensation is a mixed cost to the employer. Mixed expenses, also called semivariable costs, must be separated into their variable and fixed components for CVP analysis.

A number of methods exist for separating mixed expenses into variable and fixed expenses. The more sophisticated methods use statistical computations that are covered in more advanced accounting courses and statistics courses. To introduce you to the concept of separating mixed costs, we present the *high-low* method.

Assume Baylor Appliance Repair keeps few accounting records. The available records show total monthly revenues and expenses only. The manager wants to separate the expense of making home service calls into fixed and variable components. See Exhibit 21-7. To use the **high-low method,** pick the highest and the lowest monthly expense figures. Do the same for revenues. For both expenses and revenues, subtract the lower amount from the higher amount. Baylor Appliance Repair's records show:

Point to Stress: The high-low method requires that the mixed cost be analyzed at high and low volume. The difference in expenses at the two levels is divided by the change in volume to determine the variable expense as a percentage of sales. This percentage is then used to compute fixed expenses.

	Total Expenses	Revenues
High	$18,000	$25,000
Low	15,000	20,000
Change	$ 3,000	$ 5,000

EXHIBIT 21-7 *CVP Graph for High-Low Method*   Transparency T 21-5

$$\begin{array}{l} \text{Variable} \\ \text{expense} \\ \text{percentage} \end{array} = \frac{\text{Change in total expenses}}{\text{Change in revenues}} = \frac{\$18,000 - \$15,000}{\$25,000 - \$20,000} = \frac{\$3,000}{\$5,000} = .60 \text{ of revenues}$$

Fixed expenses	=	Total expenses	−	Variable expenses	
At high point:		$18,000	−	($25,000 × .60)	= $3,000
At low point:		$15,000	−	($20,000 × .60)	= $3,000

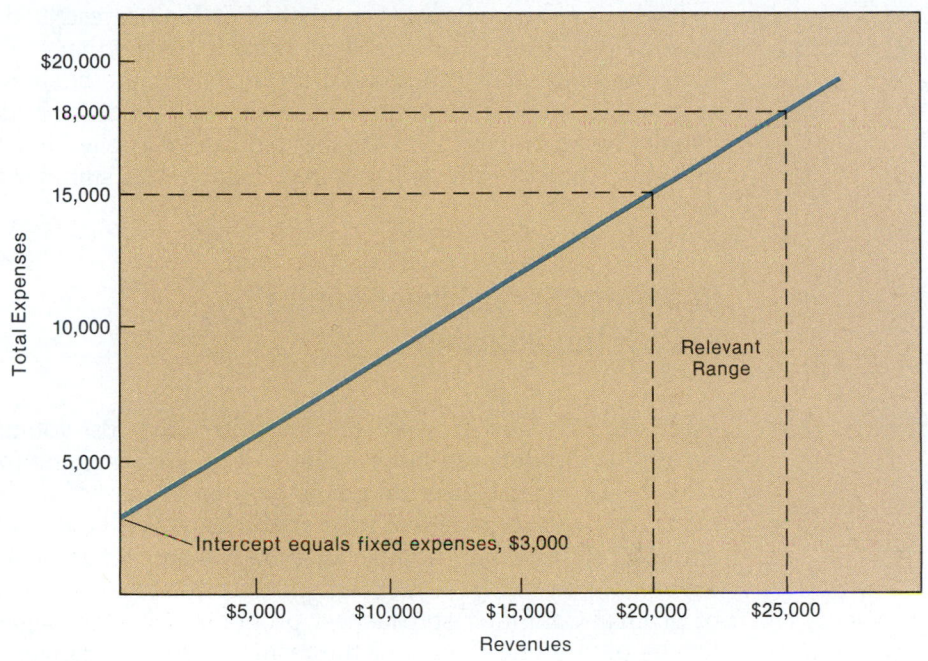

Exhibit 21-7 graphs the CVP relationships for the relevant range, which is between revenues of $20,000 and $25,000.

Divide the difference in total expenses (in our example, $3,000) by the difference in revenues ($5,000). The result is the ratio of variable expenses to revenues. Multiply this ratio ($3,000/$5,000 = .60) by the *high* revenue amount to determine variable expenses:

Variable expenses	=	.60 of revenues
	=	$25,000 × .60
	=	$15,000

By subtracting variable expenses from total expenses at the *high* level of volume, we arrive at fixed expenses:

Fixed expenses	=	Total expenses − Variable expenses	
	=	$18,000 −	$15,000
	=	$3,000	

Class Exercise: Suppose that the high and low maintenance expenses and sales for the year are as follows:

	Maintenance Expense	Sales
High	$2,000	$8,000
Low	1,400	5,000
Change . .	$ 600	$3,000

Using the high-low method, calculate the variable and fixed maintenance expense at the $8,000 sales level.

ANSWER:

Variable expenses
= 20% of sales ($600/$3,000)
= 20% × $8,000
= $1,600
Fixed expenses = $2,000 − $1,600
= $400

Chapter 21   Cost-Volume-Profit Relationships and the Contribution Margin Approach   **977**

Alternatively, we can multiply the .60 ratio by the *low* revenue amount ($20,000) to compute variable expenses ($12,000) at that revenue level. Subtract variable expenses from the corresponding total expense amount ($15,000) to compute fixed expenses:

$$\text{Fixed expenses} = \text{Total expenses} - \text{Variable expenses}$$
$$= \$15,000 - (\$20,000 \times .60)$$
$$= \$15,000 - \$12,000$$
$$= \$3,000$$

Baylor Appliance Repair's cost behavior can be described as fixed monthly expenses of $3,000 plus variable monthly expenses that average 60 percent of revenue. These data can be used for analyzing the business's CVP relationships—for example, to prepare a cost budget. Because budget estimates are usually based on past data, the method can be applied to actual past costs in order to estimate budgeted amounts. Exhibit 21-7 summarizes these computations.

Computer Spreadsheet Analysis of CVP Relationships

Computer spreadsheets are ideally suited for cost-volume-profit analysis because computers can be programmed to show income for any number of sales levels. Spreadsheet programs answer as many "what-if" questions as managers wish to ask: What will variable expenses be if sales rise by a certain amount? By a certain number of units? What if sales fall? If we cut fixed expenses, how many units of each product must we sell to reach a certain level of profits? Computer spreadsheet programs allow managers to analyze the results of any one change or the results of many changes in the business's figures.

Suppose Hyden Company wishes to expand its operations by opening two new stores. The business has received two bids from outside contractors for the construction job. The first bid is $100,000, and the second bid is $140,000. Variable expenses fluctuate between 40 percent and 50 percent of its sales. Fixed costs are expected to be from $280,000 to $420,000. Managers need to know the sales level that the business must reach to earn operating income of $100,000, operating income of $150,000, and operating income of $200,000. A computer spreadsheet program provides the answers to these questions, as shown in Exhibit 21-8, which helps management make an informed decision.

The person who writes the spreadsheet program uses a single formula based on the CVP relationships. The computer places the varying input amounts in the formula and computes the 27 amounts that appear in the exhibit. The computer handles this job in seconds and figures the amounts without computational error.

Managers can insert new figures for fixed expenses, variable expenses, operating income—whatever they wish to change—in order to evaluate the financial results of the various situations. Managers use the computer output—which covers the wide range of cost, volume, and profit patterns—to plan their best course of action. As discussed in the preceding chapter, the spreadsheet is a valuable budgeting tool. Chapter 28 assignment materials include an exercise and problems that will develop your ability to write such a spreadsheet program.

EXHIBIT 21-8   *Spreadsheet Analysis of CVP Relationships*

```
D8: [W13] ^$716,667                                              READY
```

	A	B	C	D	E
1			Sales Required to Earn Annual Operating Income of		
2			----------	----------	----------
3			$100,000	$150,000	$200,000
4	Fixed	Variable	----------	----------	----------
5	Expenses	Expenses			
6		----------			
7					
8	$280,000	40% of Sales	$633,333	$716,667	$800,000
9		45% of Sales	690,909	781,818	872,727
10		50% of Sales	760,000	860,000	960,000
11					
12					
13	$350,000	40% of Sales	750,000	833,333	916,667
14		45% of Sales	818,818	909,091	1,000,000
15		50% of Sales	900,000	1,000,000	1,100,000
16					
17					
18	$420,000	40% of Sales	866,667	950,000	1,033,333
19		45% of Sales	945,455	1,036,364	1,127,273
20		50% of Sales	1,040,000	1,140,000	1,240,000

```
17-Jul-91   11:29 AM                                            NUM
```

Summary Problem for Your Review

Part A.   Chambers Company sells T-shirts for $8. Management expects October sales to be between 12,000 units and 20,000 units. The business will incur expenses of $58,000 in selling 12,000 units and expenses of $90,000 in selling 20,000 units.

Required

1. Use the high-low method to separate total expenses into variable and fixed components.
2. Use both the equation approach and the contribution margin approach to compute the company's break-even monthly sales in units and in dollars.
3. Compute the monthly sales level needed to earn operating income of $14,000. Use either the equation approach or the contribution margin approach.

Part B.   Chambers's sales reach 18,000 units during October. Cost of goods sold makes up 60 percent of variable expenses. Operating expenses are the other 40 percent of variable expenses and all of fixed expenses.

Required

1. Prepare a contribution margin income statement for Chambers for the month of October.
2. Compute income from operations if sales decrease by 10 percent.

SOLUTION TO SUMMARY PROBLEM

Part A—Requirement 1

	Total Expenses	Sales	
High	$90,000	$160,000	(20,000 × $8)
Low	58,000	96,000	(12,000 × $8)
Change	$32,000	$ 64,000	

$$\text{Variable expense percentage} = \frac{\text{Change in total expenses}}{\text{Change in sales}} = \frac{\$32,000}{\$64,000} = .50 \text{ of sales}$$

Fixed expenses = Total expenses − Variable expenses

At high point: $90,000   −   ($160,000 × .50)   = $10,000

At low point: $58,000   −   ($96,000 × .50)   = $10,000

Requirement 2

Equation approach:

Sales   −   Variable expenses   =   Fixed expenses + Operating income

$$\left(\begin{array}{c}\text{Unit} \\ \text{sale} \\ \text{price}\end{array} \times \text{Units sold}\right) - \left(\begin{array}{c}\text{Unit} \\ \text{variable} \times \text{Units sold} \\ \text{cost}\end{array}\right) = \text{Fixed expenses} + \text{Operating income}$$

($8 × Units sold) −   ($8 × .50) × Units sold   = $10,000   + $0

($8 − $4) × Units sold   = $10,000   + $0

$4 × Units sold   = $10,000

Units sold   = $10,000/$4

Break-even sales in units   =   2,500 units

Break-even sales in dollars   =   2,500 units × $8 = $20,000

Contribution margin approach:

$$\text{Break-even sales in units} = \frac{\text{Fixed expenses} + \text{Target operating income}}{\text{Contribution margin per unit}}$$

$$= \frac{(\$10,000 + \$0)}{(\$8 - \$4)}$$

$$= \frac{\$10,000}{\$4}$$

$$= 2,500 \text{ units}$$

Break-even sales in dollars = 2,500 units × $8 = $20,000

Requirement 3

Equation approach:

$$\left(\begin{array}{c} \text{Unit} \\ \text{sale} \\ \text{price} \end{array} \times \text{Units sold} \right) - \left(\begin{array}{c} \text{Unit} \\ \text{variable} \\ \text{cost} \end{array} \times \text{Units sold} \right) = \text{Fixed expenses} + \begin{array}{c} \text{Target} \\ \text{operating income} \end{array}$$

($8 × Units sold) − ($8 × .50) × Units sold	=	$10,000	+	$14,000
($8 − $4) × Units sold	=	$10,000	+	$14,000
$4 × Units sold	=	$24,000		
Units sold	=	$24,000/$4		
Target sales in units	=	6,000 units		
Target sales in dollars	=	6,000 units × $8 = $48,000		

Contribution margin approach:

$$\text{Target sales in units} = \frac{\text{Fixed expenses} + \text{Target operating income}}{\text{Contribution margin per unit}}$$

$$= \frac{(\$10,000 + \$14,000)}{(\$8 - \$4)}$$

$$= \frac{\$24,000}{\$4}$$

$$= 6,000 \text{ units}$$

$$\text{Target sales in dollars} = 6,000 \text{ units} \times \$8 = \$48,000$$

Part B—Requirement 1

Chambers Company
Contribution Margin Income Statement
Month of October 19XX

Sales revenue (18,000 × $8)		$144,000
Variable expenses:		
Cost of goods sold ($144,000 × .50 × .60)	$43,200	
Operating expenses ($144,000 × .50 × .40)	28,800	72,000
Contribution margin		72,000
Fixed expenses:		
Operating expenses		10,000
Income from operations		$ 62,000

Requirement 2

Decrease in sales revenue ($144,000 × .10)		$14,440
Decrease in expenses:		
Fixed expenses		$ -0-
Variable expenses ($72,000 × .10)		7,200
Decrease in contribution margin		(7,200)
Income from operations before sales decrease		62,000
Income from operations after sales decrease		$54,800

Summary

Cost-volume-profit (CVP) analysis examines the relationships among a company's expenses, revenues, and income. These relationships depend on cost behavior. We classify costs as *fixed, variable,* or *mixed.*

Two popular ways to use cost-volume-profit analysis are the *equation approach* and the *contribution margin approach.* The contribution margin is the excess of sale price over total variable expenses. The contribution margin ratio is the contribution margin divided by the sale price.

CVP analysis yields an amount in unit sales or in dollar sales at which operating income equals expenses, which is the *break-even point.* Management can also project target sales using CVP analysis. *Graphic* displays of CVP relationships present information over a wide range of sales levels, not just at the break-even point. CVP analysis is widely used in budgeting.

The *margin of safety* is the excess of actual or expected sales over the sales figure at break-even. The larger the margin, the lower the risk of a given plan.

CVP analysis has certain limitations. For example, we must restrict analysis to the span of volume over which fixed costs remain unchanged, which we call the *relevant range.* Also, mixed costs must be separated into fixed costs and variable costs. We can use the *high-low method* to achieve this separation.

The *contribution margin income statement* reports variable expenses and fixed expenses separately. This format allows management to analyze costs. Computer spreadsheet programs can be programmed to measure CVP relationships across a wide range of conditions.

Self-Study Questions

Test your understanding of the chapter by marking the best answer for each of the following questions.

1. Cost-volume-profit analysis is most directly useful to *(p. 960)*
   a. Managers for predicting the outcome of their decisions
   b. Investors for deciding how much to pay for a company's stock
   c. Lenders for analyzing a loan request
   d. Tax authorities for setting income tax rates

2. The graph of a mixed cost *(p. 962)*
   a. Passes through the origin and slopes upward
   b. Is horizontal from the point marking the level of fixed costs
   c. Has a steeper slope than the graph of a fixed cost or a variable cost
   d. Slopes upward from the point marking the level of fixed costs

3. Refer to Exhibit 21-4, page 963. What will income from operations be if sales increase by 25 percent? *(pp. 963, 964)*
   a. $7,500   c. $10,000
   b. $8,250   d. $12,750

4. Refer to Exhibit 21-5, page 965. If sales are 21,000 units, the business can expect fixed expenses of *(pp. 964, 965)*
   a. $50,000   c. $120,000
   b. $80,000   d. Cannot be determined from the information given

5. At the break-even point *(p. 966)*
   a. Sales equal fixed expenses   c. Sales equal total expenses
   b. Sales equal variable expenses   d. Sales exactly equal operating income

6. Variable expenses consume 70 percent of sales, and fixed expenses total $420,000. The break-even point in dollars is *(p. 967)*
   a. $140,000   c. $1,260,000
   b. $600,000   d. $1,400,000

7. What happens to the break-even point if both variable expenses and fixed expenses increase? *(pp. 969, 970)*
   a. Break-even sales increase
   b. Break-even sales decrease
   c. Break-even sales are unchanged because the two changes offset each other
   d. The effect on break-even cannot be determined from the information given

8. William Thomas Corporation's monthly sales have averaged $480,000 for the past year. The monthly break-even point is $400,000. The company's margin of safety percentage is *(p. 974)*
   a. 16⅔%
   b. 20%
   c. 62½%
   d. 100%

9. Raj Mujadeen sells handmade Oriental rugs for $1,000 each and machine-made rugs for $300 each. Customers buy five times as many machine-made rugs as handmade rugs. Variable expenses consume 80 percent of sales, and monthly fixed expenses total $2,000. How many of each type of rug must Raj sell to earn monthly operating income of $3,000? *(p. 975)*
   a. 8 handmade and 40 machine-made
   b. 10 handmade and 50 machine-made
   c. 12 handmade and 60 machine-made
   d. 20 handmade and 100 machine-made

10. Separating mixed costs into fixed and variable components is useful for *(pp. 976, 977)*
   a. Budgeting costs
   b. Analyzing cost-volume-profit relationships
   c. Computing break-even sales
   d. All of the above

Answers to the Self-Study Questions follow the Accounting Vocabulary.

Accounting Vocabulary

Break-even analysis. Another name for Cost-volume-profit analysis *(p. 965)*.

Break-even point. Amount of unit sales or dollar sales at which revenue equals expenses *(p. 966)*.

Contribution margin. Excess of sale price over total variable expenses *(p. 963)*.

Contribution margin income statement. Separates expenses into variable costs and fixed costs and highlights the contribution margin, which is the excess of sales over total variable expenses *(p. 963)*.

Contribution margin percentage. Sales of 100 percent minus the variable expense percentage *(p. 967)*.

Cost behavior. Description of how costs change in response to a shift in a cost driver *(p. 960)*.

Cost driver. Any factor whose change causes a change in a related total cost *(p. 960)*.

Cost-volume-profit (CVP) analysis. Expresses the relationships among costs, volume, and profit or loss. An important part of a budgeting system that helps managers predict the outcome of their decisions *(p. 960)*.

Fixed cost. Cost that does not change in total as volume changes *(p. 961)*.

Fixed expense. Expense that does not change in total as volume changes *(p. 961)*.

High-low method. Method of separating a mixed cost into its variable and fixed components *(p. 976)*.

Margin of safety. Excess of expected sales over break-even sales *(p. 973)*.

Mixed cost. Cost that is part variable and part fixed *(p. 961)*.

Mixed expense. Expense that is part variable and part fixed *(p. 961)*.

Relevant range. Band of activity or volume in which actual operations are likely to occur. Within this range, a particular relationship exists between revenue and expenses (p. 964).

Sales mix. Combination of products that make up total sales (p. 974).

Variable cost. Cost that changes in total in direct proportion with changes in volume or activity (p. 960).

Variable expense. Expense that changes in total in direct proportion with changes in volume or activity (p. 960)

Answers to Self-Study Questions

1. a
2. d
3. b

Increase in contribution margin ($9,000 × .25)	$2,250
Income from operations before sales increase	6,000
Income from operations after sales increase	$8,250

4. c
5. c
6. d Sales − .70 Sales = $420,000; .30 Sales = $420,000;
Break-even sales = $420,000/.30 = $1,400,000
7. a
8. a Margin of safety in dollars = $80,000 ($480,000 − $400,000)
Margin of safety as a percentage = 16⅔% ($80,000/$480,000)

9. b

	Handmade	Machine-Made	Total
Sale price per unit	$1,000	$300	
Variable expense per unit (80%)	800	240	
Contribution margin per unit	$ 200	$ 60	
Estimated sales in units	× 1	× 5	6
Estimated contribution margin	$ 200 +	$300 =	$ 500
Weighted-average contribution margin per unit ($500/6 units)			$83.333

$$\text{Target sales in total units} = \frac{\text{Fixed expenses + Target operating income}}{\text{Weighted-average contribution margin per unit}} = \frac{\$2,000 + \$3,000}{\$83.333} = \underline{60 \text{ units}}$$

Target sales of handmade rugs (60 units × ⅙)	10 units
Target sales of machine-made rugs (60 units × ⅚)	50 units

10. a or d

ASSIGNMENT MATERIAL

Questions

1. How is cost-volume-profit analysis used in budgeting?
2. Define the three types of cost behavior patterns.
3. Draw graphs of the three types of costs.
4. What are six questions cost-volume-profit analysis can answer?
5. How does a contribution margin income statement differ from a conventional income statement? Which income statement is more useful for predicting the income effect of a change in sales? Why?

6. Why is the concept of the relevant range important to cost-volume-profit analysis?

7. Draw a graph of fixed expenses from 0 to 50,000 units. The relevant range lies between 20,000 and 35,000 units, where fixed expenses are $300,000. Below the relevant range, fixed expenses are $200,000. Above the relevant range, fixed expenses are $400,000.

8. What is the break-even point? What is its significance to a business?

9. Give the contribution margin formulas for break-even sales in units and in dollars.

10. How does an increase in fixed expenses affect the break-even point? How does a decrease in fixed expenses affect break-even sales? Give the reason for each answer.

11. How does an increase in variable expenses affect the break-even point? How does a decrease in variable expenses affect break-even sales? Give the reason for each answer.

12. How does an increase in selling price affect the break-even point? How does a decrease in selling price affect break-even sales? Give the reason for each answer.

13. Briefly outline two ways to compute the target sales in dollars needed to earn a given operating income.

14. Give the contribution margin formula for target sales in units needed to earn a given operating income. Do the same for target sales in dollars.

15. Identify the steps in the preparation of a cost-volume-profit graph.

16. What advantages does a CVP graph have over the equation approach and the contribution margin approach?

17. How does the margin of safety serve as a measure of risk?

18. Give the assumptions underlying cost-volume-profit analysis.

19. Briefly describe how to perform CVP analysis when a company sells more than one product.

20. McMillan Corporation's expenses are mixed. Management wishes to know its break-even point and seeks your advice. How can you separate total expenses into variable and fixed components?

21. Why are computer spreadsheets useful for CVP analysis?

Exercises

Additional computer-related exercise: Exercise 28-9

Exercise 21-1 *Graphing cost behaviors* (L.O. 1)

Graph each of the following cost behavior patterns over a relevant range from 0 to 10,000 units:

a. Fixed expenses of $25,000.

b. Mixed expenses made up of fixed costs of $10,000 and variable costs of $3 per unit.

c. Variable expenses of $5 per unit.

Exercise 21-2 *Preparing a contribution margin income statement* (L.O. 2, 3)

Contrib. margin $110,400

Vela Shirtmakers's April income statement appears on the next page.

Vela accounting records indicate that cost of goods sold is a variable expense and that selling expense is 20 percent fixed and 80 percent variable. General and administrative expense is half fixed and half variable.

Vela Shirtmakers
Income Statement
April 19XX

Sales revenue...............................		$637,000
Cost of goods sold		448,000
Gross margin		189,000
Operating expenses:		
Selling	$72,000	
General and administrative (including income tax) ..	42,000	114,000
Income from operations		$ 75,000

Required

Prepare Vela's contribution margin income statement for April. Compute the expected increase in operating income to the nearest $1,000 if sales increase by $100,000. Round decimals to three places.

B/E sales $326,667

Exercise 21-3   *Using a contribution margin income statement*   **(L.O. 2, 3)**

For its top managers, Sun Refining Corp. formats its income statement as follows:

Sun Refining Corp.
Contribution Margin Income Statement
Three Months Ended March 31, 19X3

Sales revenue........................	$385,000
Variable expenses	154,000
Contribution margin	231,000
Fixed expenses	196,000
Income from operations	$ 35,000

Sun's relevant range is between sales of $310,000 and $430,000. Prepare contribution margin income statements at those volume levels. Also compute break-even sales in dollars.

Contrib. margin ratio .454545
B/E = $110,000

Exercise 21-4   *Computing break-even sales by the contribution margin approach*   **(L.O. 3)**

NMNB of Santa Fe has fixed expenses of $50,000 and variable expenses of $3 per unit of its product, which it sells for $5.50 per unit.

Required

1. Compute the company's contribution margin per unit and its contribution margin ratio to six decimal places.
2. Determine the break-even point in units and in dollars, using the contribution margin approach.

B/E sales:
Before $6,750
After $9,450

Exercise 21-5   *Computing break-even sales under different CVP relationships*   **(L.O. 3)**

For several years, Schlotzsky's Restaurant has offered a lunch special for $4.50. Monthly fixed expenses have been $4,500. The variable cost of a meal has been $1.50. Rudy Valero, the owner, believes that by remodeling the restaurant and upgrading the food services, he can increase the price of the lunch special to $5.25. Monthly fixed expenses would increase to $6,300, and the variable expenses would increase to $1.75 per meal.

Required

Use the equation approach to compute Schlotzsky's monthly break-even sales in dollars before and after remodeling.

Exercise 21-6 *Computing break-even sales and operating income or loss under different conditions (L.O. 3,4)*

Oper. loss at $500,000: $70,000
Oper. inc. at $700,000: $70,000

Red Ball Motor Freight delivers freight through Iowa, Nebraska, and Kansas. The company has monthly fixed expenses of $420,000 and a contribution margin of 70 percent of revenues.

Required

1. Compute Red Ball's monthly break-even sales in dollars. Use the contribution margin approach.
2. Compute Red Ball's monthly operating income or operating loss if revenues are $500,000 and if they are $700,000.

Exercise 21-7 *Computing break-even sales and sales needed to earn a given operating income; sales-mix considerations (L.O. 3,4)*

Target sales:
A. $24,000
B. $16,000

A. Dale's Auto Supply has fixed monthly expenses of $3,900 and a contribution margin ratio of 30 percent. What must monthly sales be for the business to break even? to earn operating income of $3,300?
B. Barb's Boutique sells two product lines, one with a contribution margin ratio of 50 percent, the other with a contribution margin ratio of 60 percent. Each product line makes up one half of sales. If monthly fixed expenses are $3,850, what must monthly sales be for the business to break even? to earn operating income of $4,950?

Exercise 21-8 *Cost-volume-profit analysis with a sales mix (L.O. 3,4)*

Target sales of std. T-shirts 250;
fancy T-shirts 560

Three college friends open an off-campus shop named Wild Eyes T-Shirts. They plan to sell a standard T-shirt for $6 and a fancier version for $7.50. The $6 shirt costs them $3, and the $7.50 shirt costs them $3.50. The friends expect to sell two fancy T-shirts for each standard T-shirt. Their monthly fixed expenses are $1,870. How many of each type of T-shirt must they sell monthly to break even? to earn $1,210? Round decimals to three places.

Exercise 21-9 *Graphing cost-volume-profit relationships (L.O. 5)*

B/E sales $9 million

Suppose that Wrigley Field, the home field for the Chicago Cubs baseball team, earns total revenue that averages $9 for every ticket sold. Assume that annual fixed expenses are $8 million and that variable expenses are $1 per ticket.

Required

Prepare the ballpark's cost-volume-profit graph under these assumptions. Show the break-even point in dollars and in tickets. Label fixed expenses, variable expenses, operating loss area, and operating income area on the graph.

Exercise 21-10 *Analyzing a cost-volume-profit graph (L.O. 5)*

3. 2,500 units
5. $6,700

The top managers of Burdick Hunter, Inc., are planning the budget for 19X6. The accountant who prepared the accompanying cost-volume-profit graph forgot to label the lines.

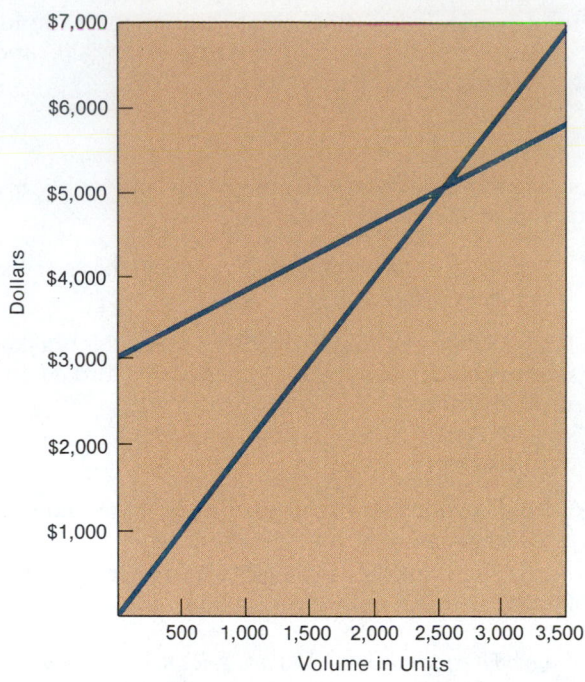

Required

Answer the following questions asked by the managers:

1. What do the lines mean?
2. Where is the operating income area? The operating loss area?
3. What is break-even sales in units and in dollars?
4. What will operating income (or operating loss) be if sales are 1,700 units?
5. What sales level in dollars is needed to earn operating income of $1,000?

Margin of safety, 42% or
$12,500

Exercise 21-11   *Computing a margin of safety   (L.O. 6)*

Pink Panther convenience store has a monthly operating profit goal of $5,000. Variable expenses are 60 percent of sales, and fixed monthly expenses are $7,000. Compute the monthly margin of safety in dollars if the store achieves its profit goal. Express Pink Panther's margin of safety as a percent of target sales.

Variable exp., 60% of revenue
B/E sales $650,000

Exercise 21-12   *Analyzing cost behavior by the high-low method   (L.O. 2, 7)*

Providence Supply is struggling to break even. Its management has decided to install a new accounting system. Management wishes to know the behavior of the hospital's costs. The lowest and highest expected monthly revenues are $450,000 and $900,000. Corresponding total expenses are $530,000 and $800,000.

Required

Separate total expenses into variable and fixed components. Express the company's cost behavior as follows: Total monthly expenses = Fixed expenses + Variable expenses as a percent of revenues. Compute Providence Supply's break-even monthly revenues in dollars. Follow the equation approach.

Problems (Group A)

Additional computer-related problems: Problems 28-6A and 28-6B

Problem 21-1A
Explaining the effects of different cost behavior patterns on the break-even point and on likely profits **(L.O. 1)**

No check figure

Saffron Restaurant Supply is opening early next year. The owner is considering two plans for obtaining the plant assets and employee labor needed for operations. Plan 1 calls for purchasing all equipment outright and paying employees straight salaries. Under plan 2, Saffron would lease equipment month by month and pay employees low salaries but give them a big part of their pay in commissions on sales.

Required

Discuss the effects of the two plans on variable expenses, fixed expenses, break-even sales, and likely profits for a new business in the start-up stage. Indicate which plan you favor for Saffron.

Problem 21-2A
Analyzing cost behavior; computing break-even sales and operating income under different CVP relationships; preparing a contribution margin income statement **(L.O. 1, 2, 3, 7)**

3. B/E sales $750,000
5. Income $90,000

The accounting records of Bergdorf, Inc., summarize the fiscal year ended February 28, 19X3:

Quarter ended	Sales	Total expenses
May 31, 19X2	$230,500	$210,000
Aug. 31, 19X2	185,000	186,500
Nov. 30, 19X2	199,500	187,000
Feb. 28, 19X3	265,000	218,500

Required

1. Categorize total expenses as fixed, variable, or mixed. Give your reasoning.
2. Use the high-low method to separate total quarterly expenses into fixed and variable components. Multiply quarterly fixed expenses by 4 to compute annual fixed expenses.
3. Compute break-even sales in dollars for the year. Use the contribution margin approach.
4. Prepare Bergdorf's contribution margin income statement at the break-even point for the year ended February 28, 19X3. Cost of goods sold is 83 percent of total variable expenses. The remainder of variable expenses is 11 percent selling and 6 percent general. Fixed expenses are 40 percent selling and 60 percent general.
5. Compute income from operations if sales increase by $150,000 above the break-even point.

Problem 21-3A
Contribution margin and break-even analysis **(L.O. 2, 3)**

A. Unit contrib. margin $1.50
B. Contrib. margin ratio .471

The accounting records of four different companies yield the information given at the top of the next page.

Required

Fill in the blanks for each company. Show your work, and round contribution margin ratios to three decimal places. By just looking over the data, which company do you think has the lowest break-even point? Which company actually does have the lowest break-even point? What causes the low break-even point?

	A	B	C	D
Target sales	$560,000	$280,000	$248,000	$
Variable expenses			132,000	130,000
Fixed expenses	312,000	120,000		
Income (loss) from operations	$	$	$ 7,000	$160,000
Units sold	112,000	11,000		8,000
Unit contribution margin		$12		$40
Contribution margin ratio	.30		$4	

2. B/E 30 cruises
4. Income $270,200

Problem 21-4A *Computing break-even revenue and the revenue needed to earn a target operating income; preparing a contribution margin income statement* **(L.O. 2, 3, 4)**

Windjammer Cruises sails a schooner from Miami. The average cruise has 80 tourists on board. Each person pays $75 for a day sail in the Caribbean. The ship sails 100 days each year.

The schooner has a crew of 12. Each member earns an average of $85 per cruise. The crew is paid only when the ship sails. Other variable expenses are for refreshments, which average $14 per passenger per cruise. Fixed annual expenses total $115,800.

Required

1. Compute revenue and variable expenses for each cruise.
2. Use the equation approach to compute the number of cruises needed annually to break even.
3. Use the contribution margin approach to compute the number of cruises needed annually to earn $200,000. Is this profit goal realistic? Give the reason.
4. Prepare Windjammer's contribution margin income statement for 100 cruises each year. Report only two categories of expenses: variable and fixed.

3. Income $60,000
4. B/E $2,150,400

Problem 21-5A *CVP analysis under different conditions* **(L.O. 2, 3, 4)**

Suppose Tynes Advertising Associates imprints calendars with company names. The company has fixed expenses of $480,000 each month plus variable expense of $2 per carton of calendars. For each carton of calendars sold, Tynes earns revenue of $3.20.

Required

1. Use the equation approach to compute the number of cartons of calendars Tynes must sell each month to break even.
2. Use the contribution margin approach to compute the dollar amount of monthly sales Tynes needs in order to earn $60,000 in operating income.
3. Prepare Tynes's contribution margin income statement for June for sales of 450,000 cartons of calendars. Cost of goods sold is 70 percent of variable expenses. Operating expenses make up the rest of variable and all of fixed expenses.
4. The company is considering an expansion that will increase fixed expenses by 40 percent and variable expenses by 10 percent. Compute the new break-even point in units and in dollars. Use either the equation approach or the contribution margin approach. Compute the contribution margin ratio to four decimal places.

Problem 21-6A *Using a contribution margin income statement for break-even analysis; sales mix, margin of safety, and changes in the CVP relationship* **(L.O. 2, 3, 6)**

4. New B/E sales $56,000

The contribution margin income statement of The Right Stuff Men's Store for November 19X5 is as follows:

The Right Stuff Men's Store
Contribution Margin Income Statement
November 19X5

Sales revenue		$60,000
Variable expenses:		
Cost of goods sold	$22,000	
Selling	13,000	
General and administrative	7,000	42,000
Contribution margin		18,000
Fixed expenses:		
Selling	11,000	
General and administrative	1,000	12,000
Income from operations		$ 6,000

The Right Stuff sells two ties for every belt. The ties sell for $7, with variable expense of $4.90 per unit. The belts sell for $6, with variable unit cost of $4.20.

Required

1. Determine The Right Stuff's monthly break-even point in the numbers of ties and belts. Prove the correctness of your computation by preparing a summary contribution income statement at break even. You need show only two categories of expenses: variable and fixed.
2. Compute The Right Stuff's margin of safety in dollars.
3. Suppose The Right Stuff increases monthly sales by 15 percent above $60,000. Compute income from operations.
4. The Right Stuff may expand the store and increase monthly fixed expenses by $4,800. Use the contribution margin approach to determine the new break-even sales in dollars.

Problem 21-7A *Computing break-even sales and sales needed to earn a given operating income; graphing cost-volume-profit relationships* **(L.O. 3, 4, 5)**

2. Target sales $12,375
4. B/E 13 units

Mission Viejo Travel is opening an office in San Diego. Fixed monthly expenses are office rent ($3,400), depreciation of office furniture ($190), utilities ($140), a special telephone line ($390), a connection with the airlines' computerized reservation service ($480), and the salary of a travel agent ($1,800). Variable expenses are utilities (3 percent of sales), incentive compensation of the employee (6 percent of sales), advertising (6 percent of sales), supplies and postage (1 percent of sales), and a usage fee for the telephone line and computerized reservation service (4 percent of sales). The business is a partnership, so it pays no business income tax.

Required

1. Use the contribution margin approach to compute the travel agency's break-even sales in dollars. If the average sale is a $400 plane ticket, how many units does it take to break even?

2. Use the equation approach to compute dollar sales needed to earn monthly operating income of $3,500.

3. Graph the travel agency's cost-volume-profit relationships. Assume an average sale is a $400 plane ticket. Show the break-even point, fixed expenses, variable expenses, operating loss area, operating income area, and the sales in units and dollars where monthly operating income of $3,500 is earned. The graph should range from 0 to 40 units.

4. Assume that the average sale price increases to $600. Use the contribution margin approach to compute the new break-even point in units. What is the effect of the sale price increase on the break-even point?

(Group B)

No check figure

Problem 21-1B *Explaining the contribution margin approach and the margin of safety to decision makers (L.O. 2, 6)*

Huntington Clothiers is managed as traditionally as the button-down shirts that have made it famous. Arch Huntington founded the business in 1952 and has directed operations "by the seat of his pants" ever since. Approaching retirement, he must turn the business over to his son, Ralph. Recently Mr. Huntington and Ralph had this conversation:

Ralph: Dad, I am convinced that we can increase sales by advertising. With our contribution margin, I think we can spend $500 monthly on advertising and increase monthly sales by $6,000. Net income should increase by $3,100.

Mr. Huntington: You know how I feel about advertising. We've never needed it in the past. Why now?

Ralph: Two new shops have opened near us this year, and those guys are getting lots of business. I've noticed our profit margin slipping as the year has unfolded. Our margin of safety is at its lowest point ever.

Mr. Huntington: Profit margin I understand, but what is the contribution margin that you mentioned? And what is this margin of safety?

Required

Explain for Mr. Huntington the contribution margin approach to decision making. Show how Ralph computed the $3,100. (Treat advertising as a fixed cost.) Also, describe what Ralph means by the margin of safety, and explain why the business's situation is critical.

3. B/E sales $315,429
5. Income $16,800

Problem 21-2B *Analyzing cost behavior; computing break-even sales and operating income under different CVP relationships; preparing a contribution margin income statement (L.O. 1, 2, 3, 7)*

Federal Trading Company accounting records summarize the fiscal year ended November 30, 19X2:

Quarter ended	Sales	Total expenses
Feb. 28, 19X2	$161,000	$115,000
May 31, 19X2	138,000	109,000
Aug. 31, 19X2	111,000	93,000
Nov. 30, 19X2	119,000	101,000

Required

1. Categorize total expenses as fixed, variable, or mixed. Give your reasoning.

2. Use the high-low method to separate total quarterly expenses into fixed and variable components. Multiply quarterly fixed expenses by 4 to compute annual fixed expenses.

3. Compute break-even sales in dollars for the year. Use the contribution margin approach.

4. Prepare Federal's contribution margin income statement at the break-even point for the year ended November 30, 19X2. Cost of goods sold is 71 percent of total variable expenses. The remainder of variable expenses is 19 percent selling and 10 percent general. Fixed expenses are evenly divided between selling and general.

5. Compute income from operations if sales increase by $30,000 above the break-even point.

Problem 21-3B   *Contribution margin and break-even analysis*   **(L.O. 2, 3)**

A. Unit contrib. margin $5
B. Contrib. margin ratio .586

The accounting records of four different companies yield the following information:

	A	B	C	D
Target sales	$	$290,000	$	$500,000
Variable expenses	100,000	120,000	104,000	
Fixed expenses	80,000	138,000		
Income (loss) from operations	$	$	$ 35,000	$ 60,000
Units sold	5,000			100,000
Unit contribution margin		$100	$6	$2
Contribution margin ratio	.200		.600	

Required

Fill in the blanks for each company. Show your work, and round contribution margin ratios to three decimal places. By just looking over the data, which company do you think has the lowest break-even point? Which company actually does have the lowest break-even point? What causes the low break-even point?

Problem 21-4B   *Computing break-even revenue and the revenue needed to earn a target operating income; preparing a contribution margin income statement*   **(L.O. 2, 3, 4)**

2. B/E 51 cruises
4. Income $29,000

The Mystic Clipper is a schooner that sails from Annapolis, Maryland, during the spring and fall. During the summer the ship leaves from Mystic, Connecticut. The average cruise has 45 tourists on board, and each person pays $50 for a day sail. The ship sails 80 days each year.

The Clipper has a crew of 8. Each member earns an average of $100 per cruise. The crew is paid only when the ship sails. The other variable expenses are for refreshments, which average $10 per passenger per cruise. Fixed annual expenses total $51,000.

Required

1. Compute revenue and variable expenses for each cruise.
2. Use the equation approach to compute the number of cruises the Clipper must take each year to break even.
3. Use the contribution margin approach to compute the number of cruises needed each year to earn $70,000. Is this profit goal realistic? Give your reason.
4. Prepare the Clipper's contribution margin income statement for 80 cruises for the year. Report only two categories of expenses: variable and fixed.

3. Loss $19,500
4. B/E $1,041,463

Problem 21-5B   *CVP analysis under different conditions* (L.O. 2, 3, 4)

Suppose Toledo Ballpoints imprints ballpoint pens with company logos. The company has fixed expenses of $331,500 each month plus variable expenses of $1.60 per box of pens. For each box of pens sold, the company earns revenue of $2.90.

Required

1. Use the equation approach to compute the number of boxes of pens Toledo must sell each month to break even.
2. Use the contribution margin approach to compute the dollar amount of monthly sales Toledo needs in order to earn $25,500 in operating income. Round the contribution margin ratio to six decimal places.
3. Prepare Toledo's contribution margin income statement for August for sales of 240,000 boxes of pens. Cost of goods sold is 80 percent of variable expenses. Operating expenses make up the rest of variable expenses and all of fixed expenses.
4. The company is considering an expansion that will increase fixed expenses by 30 percent and variable expenses by 10 cents per box of pens. Compute the new break-even point in units and in dollars. Use either the equation approach or the contribution margin approach. (Round the contribution margin ratio to six decimal places.)

4. New B/E sales $41,600

Problem 21-6B   *Using a contribution margin income statement for break-even analysis; sales mix, margin of safety, and changes in the CVP relationship* (L.O. 2, 3, 6)

The contribution margin income statement of Gino's Trattoria for May 19X6 is as follows:

Gino's Trattoria Contribution Margin Income Statement May 19X6		
Sales revenue		$160,000
Variable expenses:		
Cost of goods sold	$32,000	
Selling	25,000	
General and administrative	3,000	60,000
Contribution margin		100,000
Fixed expenses:		
Selling	27,000	
General and administrative	9,000	36,000
Income from operations		$ 64,000

Gino's sells three small pizzas for every large pizza. A small pizza sells for $10, with variable expense of $4.25. A large pizza sells for $20, with variable expense of $6.

Required

1. Determine Gino's monthly break-even point in the numbers of small pizzas and large pizzas. Prove the correctness of your computation by preparing a summary contribution margin income statement at break-even. You need show only two categories of expenses: variable and fixed.
2. Compute Gino's margin of safety in dollars.

3. If Gino's can increase monthly sales by 15 percent above $160,000, what will income from operations be?

4. Gino's hopes to decrease monthly fixed expenses by $10,000 to scale back operations. Use the contribution margin approach to determine the new break-even sales in dollars.

Problem 21-7B *Computing break-even sales and sales needed to earn a given operating income; graphing cost-volume-profit relationships* **(L.O. 3, 4, 5)**

2. Target sales $11,306
4. B/E 15 units

Water Oaks Travel is opening an office in Oklahoma City. Fixed monthly expenses are office rent ($3,000), depreciation of office furniture ($200), utilities ($110), a special telephone line ($520), a connection with the airlines' computerized reservation service ($380), and the salary of a travel agent ($1,400). Variable expenses are utilities (2 percent of sales), incentive compensation for the employee (5 percent of sales), advertising (4 percent of sales), supplies and postage (1 percent of sales), and a usage fee for the telephone line and computerized reservation service (3 percent of sales). The business is a proprietorship, so it pays no business income tax.

Required

1. Use the contribution margin approach to compute Water Oaks' break-even sales in dollars. If the average sale is a $300 plane ticket, how many units does it take to break even?

2. Use the equation approach to compute dollar sales needed to earn monthly operating income of $4,000.

3. Graph the travel agency's cost-volume-profit relationships. Assume an average sale is a $300 plane ticket. Show the break-even point, fixed expenses, variable expenses, operating loss area, operating income area, and the sales in units and dollars where monthly operating income of $4,000 is earned. The graph should range from 0 to 50 units.

4. Assume that the average sale price increases to $440. Use the contribution margin approach to compute the new break-even point in units. What is the effect of the sale price increase on the break-even point?

Extending Your Knowledge

Decision Problems

1. Using Cost-Volume-Profit Analysis to Make Business Decisions **(L.O. 1,3,4)**

B/E $89,143

William and Roberta Higgins live in Calgary, Alberta. Their daughter, Celine, is now six months old, and Roberta is considering going back to work. Roberta's mother lives in Calgary and would be delighted to babysit her new granddaughter.

Two years ago, William and Roberta spent their vacation in Thailand. Both of them enjoyed the Thai food. Roberta is a professional chef and was impressed with the cooking methods and the spices used. Calgary has no Thai restaurant, and the Higgins are contemplating opening one. Roberta would supervise the cooking, and William would leave his current job with an oil company to be the maitre'd. The restaurant would serve dinner Tuesday through Saturday, 6 p.m. to midnight.

Calgary is one of the fastest growing cities in Canada. International companies have established offices in the city, and services, including retailers of high-quality merchandise, have quickly expanded. People eat dinner out two or three nights a week. Business entertaining is also frequent.

William has noticed a restaurant for lease a short drive from the Higgins' home. The seating capacity is seven tables, each of which can seat four. Tables could be moved together for a large party. Roberta is planning two seatings per evening.

William and Roberta have drawn up the following estimates:

Average revenue, including drinks and dessert	$40 per meal
Average cost of the food, including preparation	$12 per meal
Chef and dishwasher's salaries	$50,000 per year
Rent (premises, equipment)	$3,000 per month
Cleaning (linen and premises)	$500 per month
Replacement of dishes, cutlery, glasses	$300 per month
Utilities, advertising, telephone	$1,400 per month

Required

Compute break-even revenue for the restaurant. Also compute the amount of revenue needed to earn net income of $80,000 for the year. Is this target net income realistic? Give your reason.

2. Using a Contribution Margin Income Statement to Make Business Decisions (L.O. 2,3)

Humpty Dumpty Toy Company markets three lines of toys. Each line is manufactured by a different company, and each line has a different set of cost-volume-profit relationships.

	Newborns	Toddlers	Preschoolers
Sales	$320,000	$150,000	$270,000
Variable expenses	64,000	75,000	108,000
Contribution margin	256,000	75,000	162,000
Fixed expenses	188,000	120,000	126,000
Income (loss) from operations	$ 68,000	$(45,000)	$ 36,000

Average sale prices are $2 for toys for newborns, $3 for toys for toddlers, and $5 for preschoolers' toys.

Required

1. Which product line is the least profitable?
2. Compute break-even sales in units for the company as a whole. Carry the weighted average contribution margin per unit to four decimal places.
3. Prepare a contribution margin income statement—for each product line—at the break-even point.
4. Prepare a contribution margin income statement assuming that sales of toddler toys are eliminated altogether.
5. Would it be wise to drop the toddler toy line? What would explain the overall operating loss that would result if the company did drop the toddler toy line?

3. Contrib. margin:
   Newborns $225,366
   Toddlers $66,025
   Preschoolers $142,614

Ethical Issue

In recent years, professional sports teams have shifted from paying stars straight salaries to paying them lower salaries but adding a bonus that depends on team revenues. In this way a star is more motivated to play harder. The more the team wins, the greater the team revenues as more and more fans flock to the stadium and as television companies increase payments for the rights to broadcast the games. If the star has a bad year, the team may lose more and revenue could drop, which would lower the star's compensation. By shifting player compensation from straight salary to a bonus based on team revenues, these player contracts increase the team's percentage of variable costs and decrease its percentage of fixed costs.

Required

1. Why would team owners favor these contracts?
2. Are team owners taking advantage of stars? Are these contracts ethical?

Chapter 22

Manufacturing Accounting and Job Order Costing

When Japanese automobile makers took the momentum for penetrating the U.S. market after the first oil crisis in 1973, American counterparts regarded it as a temporary phenomenon, convinced of their superiority in technology and management practices. Since the beginning of the 1980s, American automobile producers have recognized that their Japanese counterparts have comparative advantages in these areas as well as low labor cost. Meanwhile, Japan has captured a sizable portion of the U.S. automobile market and taken leadership in several additional areas such as consumer electronics, steel, robotics, ship-building, etc. Japan has even been gradually catching up with the United States in such highly technical areas as computers, aerospace, and communication equipment. Wheelwright and Hayes insist:

> What makes this challenge so difficult is that the "secret weapon" of [America's] fiercest competitors is based not so much on better product design, marketing ingenuity, or financial strength as on something much harder to duplicate: superior overall *manufacturing* capability. [Emphasis added]

Source: Jin H. Im, "Lessons from Japanese Production Management," *Production and Inventory Management Journal*, Third Quarter 1989, p. 25.

This chapter shifts gears to focus on an important sector of business: manufacturing. Previous chapters dealt with merchandisers that acquired their inventory through purchases. This chapter and the next show how manufacturers account for the cost of the goods they produce. Consider the distinction between a sporting goods store and the manufacturer of athletic shoes.

The Sportster specializes in athletic shoes. Like all merchandisers, The Sportster buys its inventory ready for resale to customers. Determining the cost of the shoes is relatively easy. Cost is the price that the merchandiser pays for the goods plus the freight and insurance charges incurred in transporting them to the store.

How do we account for the companies—Nike, Reebok, Adidas, and others—that make the shoes The Sportster sells? Manufacturers use their labor force and factory assets to shape raw materials into finished products. Their manufacturing processes begin with materials—cloth, rubber, plastics, and related items. These materials are cut, glued, stitched, and formed into athletic shoes. The process of converting these materials into finished products makes it more difficult to measure a manufacturer's inventory cost than that of a merchandiser.

In this and the next chapter we turn our attention to manufacturers, with emphasis on their cost accounting systems. The first part of this chapter introduces manufacturing accounting. The second part discusses a particular system for controlling and determining a manufacturer's costs—job order costing.

Manufacturing and the Value Chain

Before proceeding, let us regard manufacturing in perspective. Consider a company like Apple Computer. Many people would describe Apple (or IBM or Hewlett-Packard) as a manufacturing company. More accurately, Apple may be described as a company that does manufacturing. Why? Because manufacturing is only one of its major business functions. Indeed, Apple's marketing costs exceed its manufacturing costs. Companies that do manufacturing also do many other things, as illustrated by the value chain shown on page 1000.

In talking about the value chain, managers sometimes use the image of a river to describe the flow of value. Research, development, and product design are "upstream." That is, they occur prior to manufacturing. Similarly, marketing, distribution, and customer service are "downstream" in the sense that they follow manufacturing.

Point to Stress: A manufacturing company manufactures the goods it sells. A merchandising company purchases the goods it sells.

Point to Stress: Accounting for manufacturing operations is more complex than accounting for service and merchandising businesses.

Point to Stress: The only difference between a merchandising and a manufacturing income statement is that merchandising uses net purchases, while manufacturing uses COGM.

Merchandising Company COGS:

Beginning Inventory
+Net Purchases
−Ending Inventory

=COGS

Manufacturing Company COGS:

Beg. Fin. Goods Inv.
+Cost of Goods Manufactured
−End. Fin. Goods Inv.

=COGS

As we will learn, the calculation of COGM is much more complex than the calculation of net purchases.

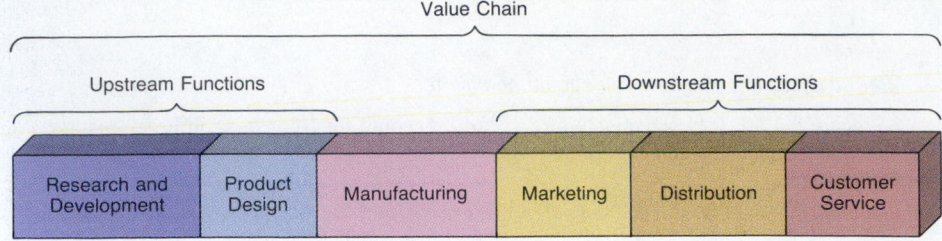

Value Chain

Upstream Functions | Downstream Functions

| Research and Development | Product Design | Manufacturing | Marketing | Distribution | Customer Service |

Considered in relationship to one another, the two upstream functions, manufacturing, and the three downstream functions form a chain. A **value chain** is the sequence of all business functions in which value is added to a firm's products or services.

Modern companies are concerned about the value chain taken as a whole. They aim to control the total costs of the entire chain. For example, companies may willingly spend more in manufacturing to enhance product quality and therefore reduce the customer service costs of honoring product warranties later on. Even though the manufacturing costs are higher then, the total costs of the product—as measured by the entire value chain—may be lower.

Traditionally, cost accounting has been associated with manufacturing. Why? Because manufacturers must determine the costs of the products they make, and accountants can measure these costs. Nevertheless, the basic concepts of how to plan and control costs and how to compute the costs of products and services are applicable to the entire value chain.

Many companies commonly regarded as manufacturers do little if any manufacturing themselves. Instead, they subcontract manufacturing to suppliers. Examples are shoe companies like Nike or Reebok. Almost all their shoes are manufactured by low-wage factories in places like Taiwan and South Korea. Nike and Reebok are intermediaries between the manufacturer and the consumer. Nike's and Reebok's principal functions are product design and marketing.

Objectives of a Cost System

Companies that do manufacturing have developed cost accounting systems to serve more than one purpose simultaneously:

Cost control—to help plan and control the manufacturing function

Product costing—to compute manufacturing product costs for financial statements

Product costing—to compute manufacturing product costs for pricing and product-mix decisions. The full cost of a product extends beyond manufacturing and encompasses all the upstream and downstream business functions in the value chain.

Exhibit 22-1 illustrates the dual objectives of *cost control* and *product costing* for a supplier to a shoe company like Nike, Inc.

An important focus of cost accounting is the control of cost. Businesses achieve cost control through the evaluation of management performance. Managers strive for the maximum output of finished products at the minimum total cost to the company—not only of manufacturing but of all the functions in the value chain. The company's actual manufacturing product cost and

EXHIBIT 22-1   *Dual Objectives of a Manufacturing Cost Accounting System*

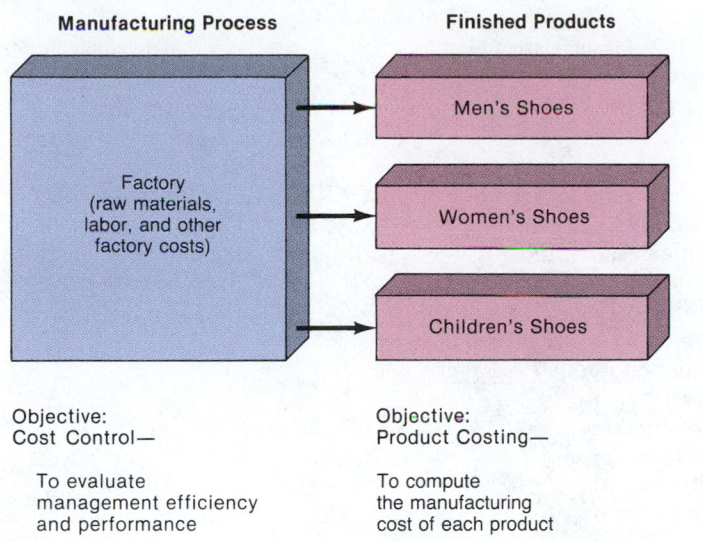

output provide the information the company needs to measure manufacturing performance—how well a manager succeeds in controlling costs while manufacturing goods.

Product costing—determining the cost to the company of each of its products—is a primary objective in manufacturing cost accounting. The company must know its product costs in order to measure inventory values (and so the cost of goods sold) and profitability (revenues minus expenses, which include the cost of goods sold).

Product costs for the entire value chain frequently help managers decide on pricing: How much does the manufacturer charge the merchandiser for its goods? The answer depends in large part on how much it costs to manufacture and market these goods. Also, managers must determine which products to emphasize. For example, Nike managers may learn that the company is losing money on children's shoes, and this information may lead the company to drop that product line. This decision depends on accurate product cost data for each product.

Our discussion in this chapter centers on product costing. Chapter 24 focuses on cost control. We will now take a closer look at manufacturing inventory.

Point to Stress: A goal of manufacturing accounting is product costing, or determining the cost of each product manufactured during the period.

Manufacturing Accounts

Inventory Accounts—Materials, Work in Process, and Finished Goods

Inventory considerations differ between merchandiser and manufacturer. Merchandisers need only one category of inventory for the finished goods they buy and sell. By contrast, manufacturers have three inventory accounts, as we discuss in a moment. Exhibit 22-2 compares the inventory accounts of a manufacturing company and a merchandising company. *Note that the two types of business have identical balance sheets except for the inventory accounts.*

OBJECTIVE 1

Prepare the financial statements of a manufacturing company

EXHIBIT 22-2 *Inventory Accounts of a Manufacturing Firm and a Merchandising Firm*

Manufacturing Firm			Merchandising Firm		
Current assets:			Current assets:		
Cash		$ X,XXX	Cash		$ X,XXX
Short-term			Short-term		
investments ...		X,XXX	investments ...		X,XXX
Receivables......		X,XXX	Receivables......		X,XXX
Inventories:			**Inventories......**		**13,000**
Materials	$1,000		Prepaid expenses		X,XXX
Work in					
process	4,000				
Finished goods	8,000				
Total					
inventories ...		13,000			
Prepaid expenses		X,XXX			
Total current			Total current		
assets		$XX,XXX	assets		$XX,XXX

The **Materials Inventory,** also called **Raw Materials Inventory,** account holds the cost of materials on hand and intended for use in the manufacturing process. A shoe manufacturer's materials include leather, glue, plastics, cloth, and thread. Raw materials for Bethlehem Steel include iron ore, coal, and chemicals. Materials—kept in vats, bins, or other storage areas—are collectively called *stores.*

The **Work in Process Inventory** account gives the cost of the goods that are in the manufacturing process and not yet complete. For a shoe manufacturer, partially completed shoes make up its work in process inventory. For a petroleum refiner, work in process is the crude oil being distilled into gasoline, different grade oils, and other products. Work in process inventory is also called *work in progress* and *goods in process.*

The cost of completed goods that have not yet been sold makes up the **Finished Goods Inventory** account. Manufacturers store finished goods in warehouses, tanks, or whatever storage facility is appropriate to the particular type of inventory. Finished goods are what the manufacturer sells to a merchandising business. For example, Procter & Gamble manufactures Tide soap and Crest toothpaste, which it sells to Safeway, K Mart, and other stores. The Finished Goods account of a manufacturer, then, becomes the Inventory account of a merchandiser.

Materials, work in process, and finished goods are assets to the manufacturer and so are reported as current assets on the balance sheet, as Exhibit 22-2 shows. Our goal is to take the information in these inventory accounts to compute the cost of goods manufactured.

Cost of Goods Manufactured

You know the merchandiser's computation of cost of goods sold: beginning inventory + purchases − ending inventory = cost of goods sold. All of a merchandiser's inventory is finished goods. The merchandiser has no materials or work in process inventory. A manufacturer, however, produces its own inventory. **Cost of goods manufactured** is the manufacturer's counterpart to the merchandiser's Purchases account. Therefore, cost of goods manufactured

EXHIBIT 22-3 *Cost of Goods Manufactured on the Income Statement*

Manufacturing Firm		Merchandising Firm	
Sales revenue	$XX,XXX	Sales revenue	$XX,XXX
Cost of goods sold:		Cost of goods sold:	
Beginning finished		Beginning	
goods inventory .	$ 6,000	inventory	$ 6,000
Cost of goods		**Purchases**	**42,000**
manufactured . . .	**42,000**	Goods available	
Goods available		for sale	48,000
for sale	48,000	Ending inventory . .	(8,000)
Ending finished		Cost of goods sold .	40,000
goods inventory .	(8,000)	Gross margin	X,XXX
Cost of goods sold .	40,000	Operating expenses:	
Gross margin	X,XXX	Marketing	X,XXX
Operating expenses:		General	X,XXX
Marketing	X,XXX	Total operating	
General	X,XXX	expenses	X,XXX
Total operating		Net income	$ X,XXX
expenses	X,XXX		
Net income	$ X,XXX		

Discussion Question: Which inventory in a manufacturing business most closely corresponds to Merchandise Inventory, and why does a merchandising company have only the Merchandise Inventory account? *ANSWER:* Finished Goods Inventory is like the account Merchandise Inventory. The merchandising company will not have raw materials on hand, nor will it have units in process, so it does not need these inventory accounts.

Teaching Tip: Look at Exhibit 22-3. Other than Cost of Goods Manufactured and Purchases, do you see any differences between the two statements? *ANSWER:* No. In all other respects, they are identical. Both companies earn revenue, both incur operating expenses, and both show net income or net loss.

   Would there be any differences on the Balance Sheets of the two firms? *ANSWER:* Only in the current asset section. The manufacturing firm would show

   Materials Inventory

   Work in Process Inventory

   Finished Goods Inventory

while the merchandising firm would list only Merchandise Inventory.

Transparency T 22-1

Discussion Question: What costs are necessary to manufacture leather shoes? *ANSWER:* Most students will answer leather, shoe strings (these are direct materials), labor to put the shoes together (direct labor), etc.

   If we put together all these materials that you have mentioned, and hire someone to assemble the materials, is that all we would need to manufacture shoes? *ANSWER:* Students may mention

represents the cost of *finished* goods that the business has produced. Exhibit 22-3 shows that Cost of Goods Manufactured takes the place of Purchases in computing cost of goods sold. *Otherwise, a manufacturer's income statement is identical to the income statement of a merchandiser.*

   Purchases, for a merchandiser, is simply the total cost of all goods bought for resale during the current period. Cost of goods manufactured is more complex. Before we illustrate how to compute this amount, we must introduce some new terms.

Definitions of Key Manufacturing Terms

Direct Materials.   To be considered **direct materials,** materials must meet two requirements: (1) the materials must become a physical part of the finished product, and (2) the cost of the materials must be separately and conveniently traceable through the manufacturing process to finished goods. Consider again the athletic-shoe manufacturer. The leather uppers, the rubber and plastic soles, and the laces are among the direct materials. We can trace them *directly* to the finished shoe. Also, we can follow their costs from the purchase of raw materials through work in process to finished goods.

Direct Labor.   **Direct labor** is the compensation of the employees who physically convert materials into the company's products. For a shoe manufacturer, direct labor includes the wages of the machine operators and the persons who actually assemble the shoes. For General Motors, direct labor is the pay of employees who work on production lines manufacturing automobiles. The efforts of these persons can be traced *directly* to finished goods.

Factory Overhead.   **Factory overhead** includes all manufacturing costs other than direct materials and direct labor. Examples include indirect materials, machines, buildings, insurance, and utilities as necessary costs of manufacturing. Point out that the costs of using the machines and the buildings are as necessary to the manufacturing process as the direct materials and direct labor. Depreciation of the manufacturing equipment and the plant building, insurance, and utilities are called factory overhead costs.

Point to Stress: Factory Overhead is often referred to as factory burden. It includes all costs involved in the manufacturing operations *except* direct materials and direct labor.

indirect labor, and other costs, such as factory utilities, repairs, maintenance, rent, insurance, and property taxes and depreciation on the factory building and equipment. Factory overhead is also called *manufacturing overhead* and, more accurately, *indirect manufacturing cost*.

Indirect Materials. The glue and the thread used in the athletic shoes are also materials that become physical parts of the finished product. However, compared with the cost of the leather uppers and the rubber soles, the glue and thread costs are minor. Measuring the cost of these low-priced materials is difficult for a single pair of shoes. How would a supervisor figure the cost of a brushful of glue? Of the thread used in a shoe? And how useful would this detailed information be? We call the material whose cost cannot conveniently be traced directly to particular finished products **indirect material.** Indirect materials are accounted for as part of factory overhead cost.

Indirect Labor. Other factory labor costs are classified as **indirect labor.** These costs are difficult to trace to specific products. Examples include the pay of forklift operators, janitors, and plant guards. Forklift operators move a wide variety of materials and finished goods around the factory. Plant guards provide security for the entire building. Indirect labor, like indirect materials, is a part of factory overhead.

Two of the major cost elements are sometimes combined in cost terminology as follows. **Prime costs** consist of direct materials plus direct labor. **Conversion costs** consist of direct labor plus factory overhead.

OBJECTIVE 2

Compute cost of goods manufactured

Class Exercise: Identify these expenses as DM (direct materials), DL (direct labor), FOH (overhead), or X (not a manufacturing cost).

Small tools used in factory— FOH

Labor of factory workers— DL

Salary for maintenance worker—FOH

Property tax on plant—FOH

Salesman's expenses—X

Income tax expense—X

Wood for manufacture of desks—DM

Paint and nails for manufacture of desks— FOH

Factory repairs; maintenance—FOH

Depreciation—office furniture—X

EXHIBIT 22-4 *Statement of Cost of Goods Manufactured*

Shoes Unlimited Statement of Cost of Goods Manufactured Year Ended December 31, 19X3			
Beginning work in process inventory .			$ 5,000
Add: Direct materials used:			
Beginning inventory	$ 9,000		
Purchases of materials	27,000		
Available for use	36,000		
Ending inventory	(22,000)		
Direct materials used		$14,000	
Direct labor		19,000	
Factory overhead:			
Indirect materials	$ 1,500		
Indirect labor	3,500		
Depreciation—factory building	2,000		
Depreciation—factory equipment . . .	1,000		
Utilities	2,500		
Insurance	1,000		
Property tax	500	12,000	
Total manufacturing costs incurred during the year			45,000
Total manufacturing costs to account for			50,000
Less: ending work in process inventory			(4,000)
Cost of goods manufactured			$46,000

Teaching Tip: Students often find it difficult to understand the calculation for Cost of Goods Manufactured. Remind them that the Cost of Goods Manufactured is the cost of all

Prime costs $\left\{\begin{array}{l}\text{Direct materials} \\ \text{Direct labor} \\ \text{Factory overhead}\end{array}\right.$ $\left.\begin{array}{l}\\ \\ \end{array}\right\}$Conversion costs

Exhibit 22-4 shows the computation of cost of goods manufactured. This statement of cost of goods manufactured is an internal statement, prepared by cost accountants for the business's managers.

Computation of cost of goods manufactured starts with the work in process inventory ($5,000) at the beginning of the period. These goods become complete in the manufacturing process during the current period, so their cost becomes part of cost of goods manufactured. To this amount we add the three components of manufacturing cost: direct materials used ($14,000), direct labor ($19,000), and factory overhead cost ($12,000). Exhibit 22-4 looks closely at direct materials used. Direct labor is simply the total direct labor cost incurred during the period. Factory overhead is the sum of various costs. Direct materials used, direct labor, and factory overhead total $45,000, which is the **total manufacturing cost** incurred during the period. We subtract ending work in process inventory—because cost of goods manufactured refers to the cost of *finished goods* manufactured—to get $46,000.

Exhibit 22-5 diagrams the flow of costs through a manufacturing system. It reveals a similar computational format at all three stages—direct materials, work in process, and finished goods. The cost of direct materials used is beginning direct materials plus purchases minus the ending balance. Observe that the final amount at each stage flows into the next stage. Thus, the cost of direct materials used becomes part of cost of goods manufactured, which in turn is included in cost of goods sold. Trace the direct materials and work in process portions of the exhibit in Exhibit 22-4, which gives more details for computing costs of goods manufactured.

EXHIBIT 22-5   *Flow of Costs Through a Manufacturing Company—Three Similar Computations*

Direct Materials	Work in Process	Finished Goods
Beginning inventory + Purchases	Beginning inventory + Direct materials used Direct labor Factory overhead	Beginning inventory + Cost of goods manufactured
= Direct materials available for use − Ending inventory	= Subtotal − Ending inventory	= Goods available for sale − Ending inventory
= Direct materials used	= Cost of goods manufactured	= Cost of goods sold

The authors are indebted to Judith Cassidy for this presentation.

Inventoriable Costs and Period Costs

The rules of financial accounting have a major influence on accounting for manufacturing costs. For example, the manufacturing costs are **inventoriable costs**, which are all costs of a product regarded as an asset for financial reporting under generally accepted accounting principles. Inventoriable costs be-

completed goods, that is, all goods that rolled off the end of the assembly line this period. At the beginning of the period, some incomplete goods (the beginning Work in Process Inventory) were already on the assembly line. These goods were the first to be completed this period, so their cost is a part of the Cost of Goods Manufactured. At the end of the period, some incomplete goods (the ending Work in Process Inventory) remained on the assembly line. Since these goods are not completed, their cost is subtracted from total manufacturing costs to compute Cost of Goods Manufactured.

Point to Stress: Cost of Goods Manufactured is not the same as Manufacturing Costs.

Manufacturing Costs

Direct Materials
+Direct Labor
+Factory Overhead
=Manufacturing Costs*

Cost of Goods Manufactured

Beginning Work in Process Inventory
*+Manufacturing Costs
−Ending Work in Process Inventory
=Cost of Goods Manufactured

The COGM includes costs from the previous period (beginning work in process inventory) and current period manufacturing costs, but does not include costs for goods started but not yet finished (ending work in process inventory). Remind students that Cost of Goods Manufactured refers to finished goods, and that unfinished goods must not be included.

Teaching Tip: Another term used for *inventoriable costs* is *product costs.*

come expenses (in the form of cost of goods sold) only when the units in inventory are sold. Of course, the sales may occur in the same accounting period as manufacture or in a subsequent period. Manufacturing costs are regarded as inventoriable because direct materials, direct labor, and factory overhead costs are necessary to obtain the physical products in inventory.

All costs other than manufacturing costs are regarded as immediate expenses. These costs are often called **period costs** because they are expensed in the period in which they are incurred. They are never traced through the inventory accounts. Examples are research, marketing, and distribution expenses.

The distinction between inventoriable costs and period costs is illustrated as follows:

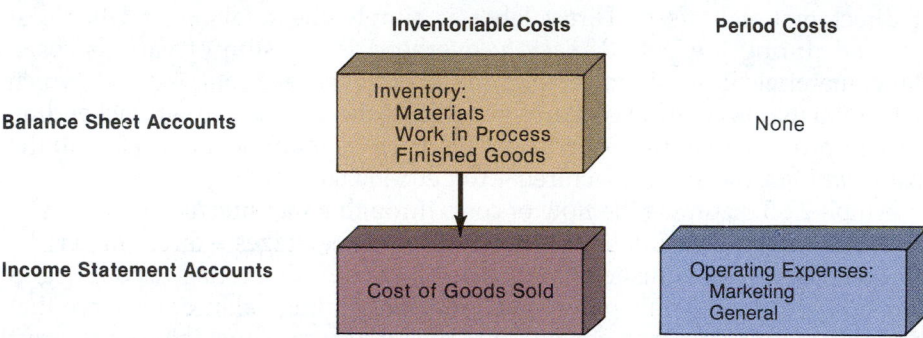

The boxes also help distinguish between companies that do manufacturing and those that do not. For example, a retailer or wholesaler buys goods for resale without changing their basic form. The *only* inventoriable cost is the cost of merchandise. All labor, depreciation, insurance, utilities, and other operating costs are period costs. In contrast, any of these costs that are related to the manufacturing effort are inventoriable for companies that do manufacturing.

Note that a manufacturing company may classify some labor, depreciation, utilities, and other operating costs as inventoriable costs and some as period costs. All such costs identified with the manufacturing function are inventoriable costs. Those costs identified with marketing or other functions in the value chain are period costs.

Various Meanings of Product Costs

Accountants frequently use the term *product costs* to describe those costs allocated to units of product. **Product cost** is a general term that denotes different costs allocated to products for different purposes. As Exhibit 22-6 shows, accountants should use *manufacturing product costs* to denote *inventoriable costs*.

The term *full product costs* denotes a set of complete product costs encompassing the entire value chain. For decisions regarding choices and pricing of products, managers want the cost of products to include all (or nearly all) the costs of the entire business.

Perpetual and Periodic Inventory Systems

Chapter 9 compared the accounting for inventories under the periodic system and the perpetual system. Most manufacturers use the perpetual system because they need a continuous record of materials, work in process, and

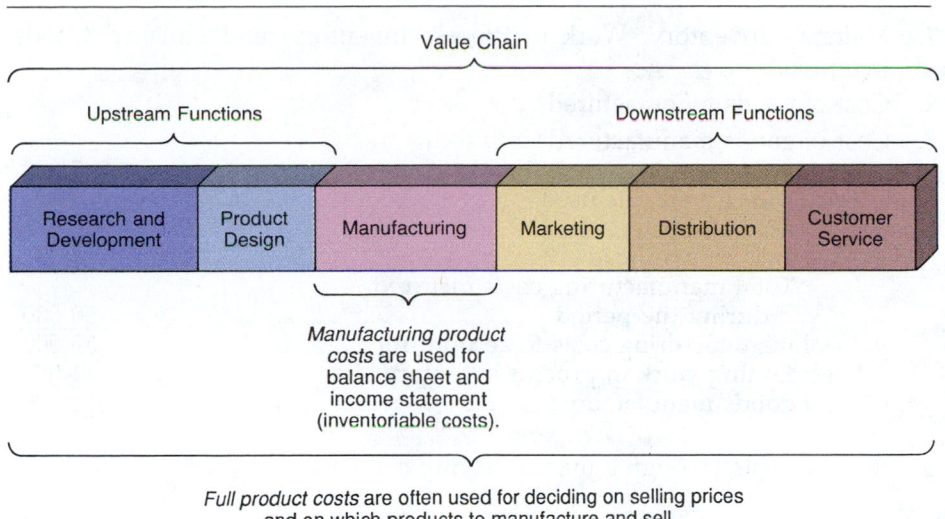

Value Chain

Upstream Functions   Downstream Functions

| Research and Development | Product Design | Manufacturing | Marketing | Distribution | Customer Service |

Manufacturing product costs are used for balance sheet and income statement (inventoriable costs).

Full product costs are often used for deciding on selling prices and on which products to manufacture and sell.

Typical Student Misconception: A perpetual inventory system does not negate the need for an annual physical inventory. Goods on hand still must be counted, verified, and costed whether the inventory system is perpetual or periodic.

An advantage to the perpetual inventory system is that it gives the current cost information needed to determine the cost of the manufactured goods.

finished goods on hand. The perpetual records help managers control operations and also provide the data for interim financial statements. Physical counts of inventories are taken at least annually to check the accuracy of the records.

Manufacturers that use a periodic inventory system follow the general accounting procedures that merchandisers use, as discussed in Chapter 9. In this chapter we concentrate on the perpetual system because it is more commonly used by manufacturers.

Summary Questions for Your Review

1. What inventory accounts does a manufacturer have that a merchandising entity does not need?
2. What is the manufacturer's counterpart to a merchandiser's Purchases account?
3. Show how to compute cost of goods manufactured. Use the following amounts: direct materials used ($24,000), direct labor ($9,000), factory overhead ($17,000), and work in process, beginning ($5,000) and ending ($4,000).
4. Diagram the flow of costs through a manufacturing company.
5. Identify the following as either an inventoriable cost or a period cost:
   a. Depreciation on factory equipment
   b. Depreciation on salespersons' automobiles
   c. Insurance on factory building
   d. Factory manager's salary
   e. Marketing manager's salary

ANSWERS TO REVIEW QUESTIONS

1. Materials Inventory, Work in Process Inventory, and Finished Goods Inventory

2. Cost of goods manufactured

3. Cost of goods manufactured:

Beginning work in process inventory		$ 5,000
Add: Direct materials used	$24,000	
Direct labor	9,000	
Factory overhead	17,000	
Total manufacturing costs incurred during the period		50,000
Total manufacturing costs to account for		55,000
Less: Ending work in process inventory		(4,000)
Cost of goods manufactured		$51,000

4. Flow of costs through a manufacturing company:

Direct Materials	Work in Process	Finished Goods
Beginning inventory + Purchases	Beginning inventory + Direct materials used Direct labor Factory overhead	Beginning inventory + Cost of goods manufactured
= Direct materials available for use − Ending inventory	= Subtotal − Ending inventory	= Goods available for sale − Ending inventory
= Direct materials used	= Cost of goods manufactured	= Cost of goods sold

5. a. Inventoriable cost; b. Period cost; c. Inventoriable cost; d. Inventoriable cost; e. Period cost

Job Order Costing

There are two main types of accounting systems for product costing: *job order costing* and *process costing*. This chapter discusses job order costing, and the next chapter covers process costing. Because these chapters deal primarily with inventory costs, our discussions emphasize inventoriable costs, not period costs. *Manufacturers account for and control period costs the same way that merchandisers do.*

Job order costing is an accounting system used by companies that manufacture products (1) as individual units or (2) in distinct batches that receive varying degrees of attention and skill. Industries using job order costing include aircraft, furniture, construction, and machinery. Their inventory items are unique or few of a kind, differing from the identical products that roll off a production line, such as tubes of toothpaste, boxes of cereal, and rolls of carpet. Mass-produced inventories are accounted for by the process costing system, discussed in the next chapter.

The essential feature of job order costing (often shortened to *job costing*) is the allocation of costs to a specific job. (The job may be a production order, work order, project, or batch.) The job may consist of a single unit, like a bridge built by a construction contractor, or a group of similar units in a distinct batch, like 10 recliner chairs built by a furniture manufacturer. We illustrate job order costing for a manufacturing situation, but the system applies to other types of business, such as an auto-repair shop (the job is one automobile needing repair), a research organization (the job is a research project), and an accounting firm (the job is a tax return).

In a job cost system, the job is the focus, so the manufacturer accumulates materials, labor, and overhead costs by job. Cost control is the key to earning a profit on each job. If cost is too high, profit is reduced or eliminated. Managers monitor each job to help ensure that its cost stays within the budgeted limits.

Job Costing Illustrated

Consider the Ramirez Furniture Company, which has a job order costing system with the following inventories on December 31, 19X4:

Materials inventory (many kinds)	$20,000
Work in process inventory (5 jobs)	29,000
Finished goods inventory (unsold units from 2 jobs)	12,000

OBJECTIVE 3
Use job order costing information

The following is a summary of relevant transactions for the year 19X5:

1.	Materials purchased on account	$320,000
2.	Direct materials requisitioned for manufacturing	285,000
	Indirect materials requisitioned for manufacturing	40,000
3.	Factory wages incurred	335,000
4.	Direct labor on jobs	250,000
	Indirect labor to support factory activities	85,000
5.	Factory overhead (depreciation on plant and equipment)	50,000
6.	Factory overhead (factory utilities)	20,000
7.	Factory overhead (factory insurance)	5,000
8.	Factory overhead (property taxes—factory)	10,000
9.	Factory overhead applied to jobs	200,000
10.	Cost of goods completed and transferred to finished goods inventory	740,000
11.	Sales on account	996,000
	Cost of goods sold	734,000

The accounting for these transactions will now be explained, step by step.

Job Cost Record

The bulk of the work in cost accounting is a detailed recording and summarization of source documents such as requisitions, time tickets, and invoices. The document used to accumulate and control cost in a job order system is a **job cost record.** This cost record lists the materials, labor, and overhead costs charged to the job. It is the basic internal document used by management to control the manufacturing costs of products in this system. Exhibit 22-7 illustrates a job cost record. It includes sections for direct materials, direct labor, and overhead costs.

materials (LIFO or FIFO, for instance) which does not map the physical flow of goods. All these are limitations to varying degrees, but the cost accountant can still give a reasonable approximation of unit costs.

Point to Stress: Job order accounting is used by a business that produces inventory organized by jobs or job lots. The job may be an order from a customer or an order to manufacture goods for inventory. Process cost accounting is used by a business that produces a continuous flow of similar units.

Real-World Example: Valmont/American Lighting Standard Corp., a job-shop steel fabricator in Texas, uses a job order accounting system. In an effort to increase inventory turnover, decrease overtime, and increase profits, they switched from their old method of producing a large inventory of manufactured parts and finished goods, and began to produce only to customer order. Production lead time was greatly reduced, unit costs were reduced, earnings were about 40% greater than had been budgeted, and cash flow was about 60% better than had been forecast.

Point to Stress: The job cost record is the heart of a job order accounting system. On the record is the name of the customer, the job number, and a description of the job. Costs by job (materials, labor, and overhead) are recorded. When the job is complete, the job cost record will show the total cost of the job and the cost per unit.

EXHIBIT 22-7 *Job Cost Record*

Point to Stress: The job cost records are a subsidiary ledger to Work in Process, which means that the job cost records give detailed information about the amount of materials, labor, and overhead in each job. All subsidiary ledgers are updated daily. Corresponding summary entries appear in the Work in Process control account, and are usually posted monthly.

Teaching Tip: Review procedures related to subsidiary and control accounts (Chapter 6).

Teaching Tip: Refer to Transparency T22-1. Draw this diagram on the board to help illustrate the flow of costs in a manufacturing business:

Teaching Tip: Refer to Transparency T22-1 and the preceding teaching tip, but this time draw the diagram in the form of T-accounts:

Discussion Question: What event causes an increase in Materials Inventory? What event causes a decrease in Materials Inventory? ANSWER: The purchase of materials causes Materials Inventory to increase, and the requisition of materials causes Materials Inventory to decrease.

OBJECTIVE 4

Account for materials in a job order costing system

Job Cost Record

Job No.   293

Customer Name and Address   Macy's New York City

Job Description   10 recliner chairs

Date Promised 7–31		Date Started 7–24		Date Completed 7–29		

Date	Direct Materials		Direct Labor		Factory Overhead Costs		
	Requisition Numbers	Amount	Time Ticket Numbers	Amount	Date	Rate	Amount
19X5 7-24 25 28	334 338 347	$ 90 180 230	236,251,258 264,269,273,291 305	$150 200 50	7-29	120% of Direct labor	$480
					Overall Cost Summary		
					Direct materials ..... $ 500 Direct labor .... 400 Factory overhead 480		
Totals		$500		$400	Total Job Cost $1,380		

This cost record shows that for Job 293, the direct materials cost $500, direct labor cost $400, and factory overhead cost $480, for a total of $1,380. Each chair cost the manufacturer $138 ($1,380/10). Managers would use this information by comparing these actual costs with budgeted amounts. Suppose the direct materials budget for this job was $470. The $500 actual cost of direct materials exceeds budget, so managers would determine the reason for the cost overrun and seek to improve future performance. The remainder of the chapter discusses how to account for the direct materials, direct labor, and factory overhead costs.

The job cost record in Exhibit 22-7 is the basic record for product costing. A file of current job cost records is the subsidiary ledger for the general ledger account, Work in Process Inventory. As each job begins, a job cost record is prepared. As units are worked on, costs are applied to the products. When the job is completed, its cost is transferred to Finished Goods Inventory. We now illustrate these accounting procedures.

Accounting for Materials in a Job Cost System

Manufacturing companies that use job order costing tend to have relatively low inventories. Only when they receive an order do they acquire the added materials needed to fill the order, produce the goods, and deliver the merchandise. Suppose Ramirez, our furniture manufacturer, receives an order for 10 recliner chairs. The company may need to buy additional lumber, so Ramirez sends a *purchase order* to a lumber supplier.

In practice, general ledger entries are made monthly. To offer a sweeping overview, however, we use a summary entry for the entire year 19X5. Our first entry is for purchases of materials (data from page 1009):

1. Materials Inventory 320,000
    Accounts Payable 320,000

Point to Stress: The perpetual inventory system is generally used in cost accounting to ensure that the level of materials inventory is sufficient. Unless they can visually supervise the level of materials inventory, managers will need perpetual inventory records to indicate quantities on hand.

Ramirez receives the lumber and stores it. Control over materials in storage is established with a subsidiary materials ledger. This ledger holds perpetual inventory records, which list the quantity and the cost of manufacturing materials received and used. They show the cost of materials on hand at all times. Exhibit 22-8 shows a materials ledger record for the lumber (only) that goes into the manufacture of chairs.

Materials received are logged in by receiving report number (abbreviated as *Rec. Report No.* in Exhibit 22-8). Materials used in the product are recorded by materials requisition number (*Mat. Req. No.*). Management can use these underlying data to follow the flow of materials through the production process and so control operations on a day-to-day basis.

EXHIBIT 22-8 *Materials Ledger Record*

Point to Stress: There will be one subsidiary materials ledger record (card) set up for each item in raw materials inventory. The Materials Inventory account in the general ledger is the control account.

Materials Ledger Record

Item No. B-220   Description   Lumber/Recliner chairs

	Received				Used				Balance		
Date	Rec. Report No.	Units	Price	Total Price	Mat. Req. No.	Units	Price	Total Price	Units	Price	Total Price
19X5											
7-20									30	$9.00	$270
7-23	678	20	$9.00	$180					50	9.00	450
7-24					334	10	$9.00	$90	40	9.00	360

The general ledger has a Materials Inventory account. This account is supported by a subsidiary ledger—the materials ledger—that includes a separate record for each raw material. Exhibit 22-9 illustrates the general ledger account and the materials ledger for Ramirez. The balance of Materials Inventory in the general ledger equals the sum of the balances in the materials ledger.

After materials are purchased and stored, the manufacturing process is set in motion by a document called a **materials requisition,** the formal title for a request prepared by manufacturing personnel. In effect, they ask that the lumber be moved from storage to the factory so work can begin. Exhibit 22-10 illustrates a materials requisition for the lumber needed to manufacture the 10 recliner chairs that make up job 293. (See the job description in Exhibit 22-7 and the "Used" section in Exhibit 22-8.) The details in materials requisitions are posted to job cost records.

Direct and Indirect Materials.   To introduce the main points of manufacturing accounting, the first half of this chapter omitted some of the detailed procedures. One such step is the way to account for *direct* materials separately

EXHIBIT 22-9 *Materials Inventory Accounts*

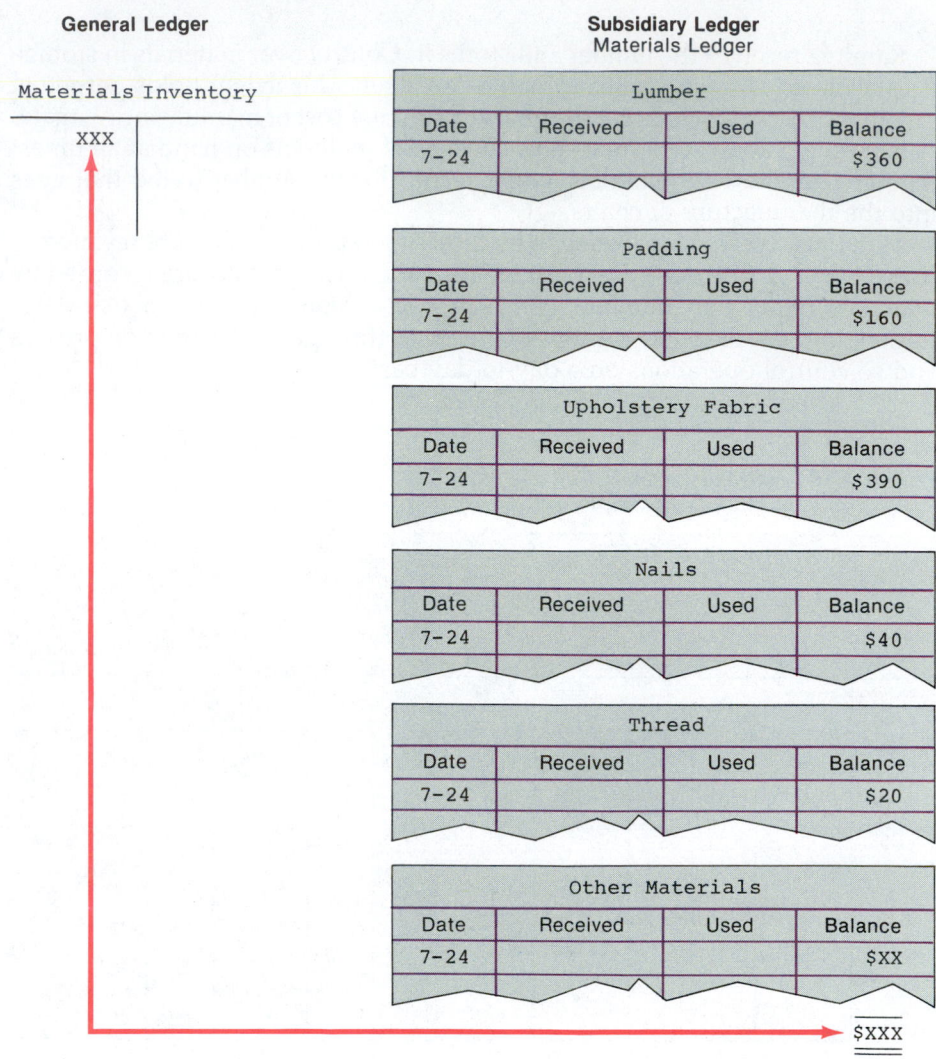

General Ledger

Materials Inventory

XXX

Subsidiary Ledger
Materials Ledger

Lumber

Date	Received	Used	Balance
7-24			$360

Padding

Date	Received	Used	Balance
7-24			$160

Upholstery Fabric

Date	Received	Used	Balance
7-24			$390

Nails

Date	Received	Used	Balance
7-24			$40

Thread

Date	Received	Used	Balance
7-24			$20

Other Materials

Date	Received	Used	Balance
7-24			$XX

$XXX

Total balances equal the balance in the general ledger account.

from *indirect* materials. Recall that the cost of indirect materials is part of Factory Overhead. The flow of materials costs is diagrammed as (data from page 1009):

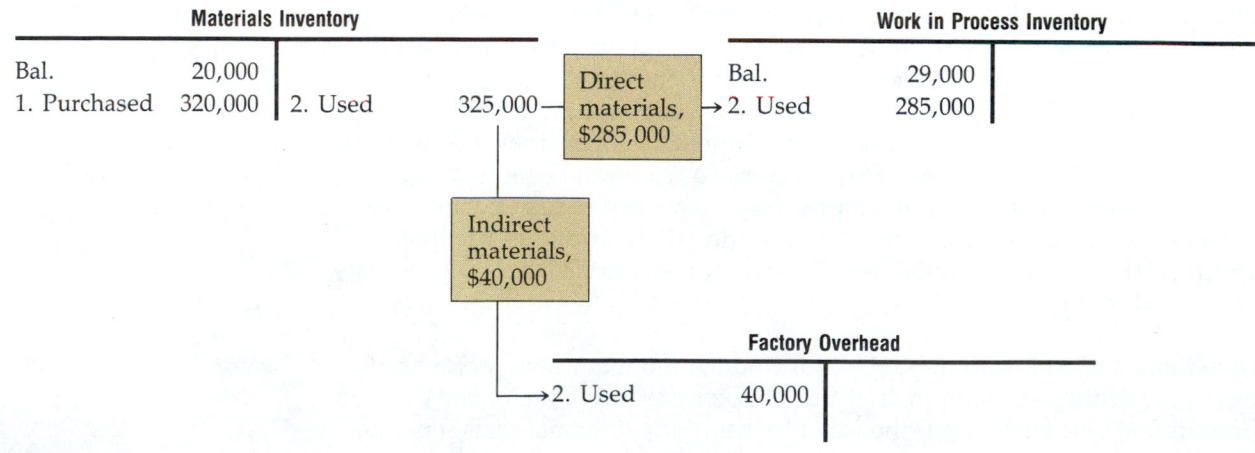

		Materials Inventory		
Bal.	20,000			
1. Purchased	320,000	2. Used	325,000	

Direct materials, $285,000

		Work in Process Inventory	
Bal.	29,000		
2. Used	285,000		

Indirect materials, $40,000

Factory Overhead

2. Used   40,000

EXHIBIT 22-10 *Materials Requisition*

Materials Requisition No. 334				
Date 7-24-X5			Job No. 293	
Item No.	Item	Quantity	Unit Price	Amount
B-220	Lumber/Recliner chairs	10	$9.00	$90

Teaching Tip: Look at the materials requisition (Exhibit 22-10). The job number must be included on the requisition. This source document is used to enter materials used on the job cost record. If the materials are used in the factory as overhead, a notation of that will appear instead of a job number. No inventory should be released to production without proper documentation.

Materials Inventory is debited for the cost of all materials purchased, direct *and* indirect. Observe that the Materials Inventory account in Exhibit 22-9 includes the cost of direct materials—lumber, padding, and upholstery fabric—and the cost of indirect materials—nails and thread. When either type of materials is used in production, Materials Inventory is credited. For direct materials, the debit is made directly to Work in Process Inventory. For indirect materials, the debit is made to Factory Overhead. (Recall that factory overhead includes all manufacturing costs other than direct materials and direct labor.)

Of course, the furniture manufacturer will work on many jobs over the course of the accounting period. At regular intervals (commonly a month but for our illustration a year), accountants collect the data from the materials requisitions to make a single journal entry, like the following 19X5 entry for Ramirez:

Point to Stress: On a regular basis (daily or weekly), materials requisitions are collected and the materials used are recorded on the job cards. Job cost records must be kept current.

2. Work in Process Inventory 285,000
    Factory Overhead............................ 40,000
        Materials Inventory 325,000

As Exhibit 22-10 indicates, $90 of the direct materials relates to job 293. The Ramirez computer would enter the $90 on the job cost record.

Job Cost Record

Job. No. 293

Customer Name and Address   Macy's New York City

Job Description   10 recliner chairs

| Date Promised 7-31 | Date Started 7-24 | Date Completed |

Date	Direct Materials		Direct Labor		Factory Overhead Costs		
	Requisition Numbers	Amount	Time Ticket Numbers	Amount	Date	Rate	Amount
19X5							
7-24	334	$90					

Overall Cost Summary

Direct materials ...... $
Direct labor ....
Factory overhead .....

| Totals | | | | | Total Job Cost .... $ | | |

Accounting for Labor in a Job Cost System

OBJECTIVE 5

Account for labor in a job order costing system

Control over labor cost in a job cost system is established through time tickets and payroll registers, as discussed in Chapter 11. Exhibit 22-11 illustrates a time ticket used in a job cost system. Managers use its data to charge labor cost to a particular job.

The **labor time ticket** identifies the employee, the hours spent on a particular job, and the labor cost charged to the job. Time tickets are accumulated by job to determine the labor cost to be allocated to each job.

The company's entry for 19X5 for all factory wages for all jobs is

Point to Stress: The entry to record factory wages is almost the same as the entry to record salaries. The difference is that factory wages are considered an inventoriable cost and, therefore, not an expense.

```
Factory Wages ...    XX
    Wages Payable .        XX
```

| 3. | Factory Wages............................... | 335,000 | |
| | Wages Payable .... | | 335,000 |

This entry records the actual labor cost incurred. The separation of direct labor and indirect labor is accomplished as shown in the accompanying diagram.

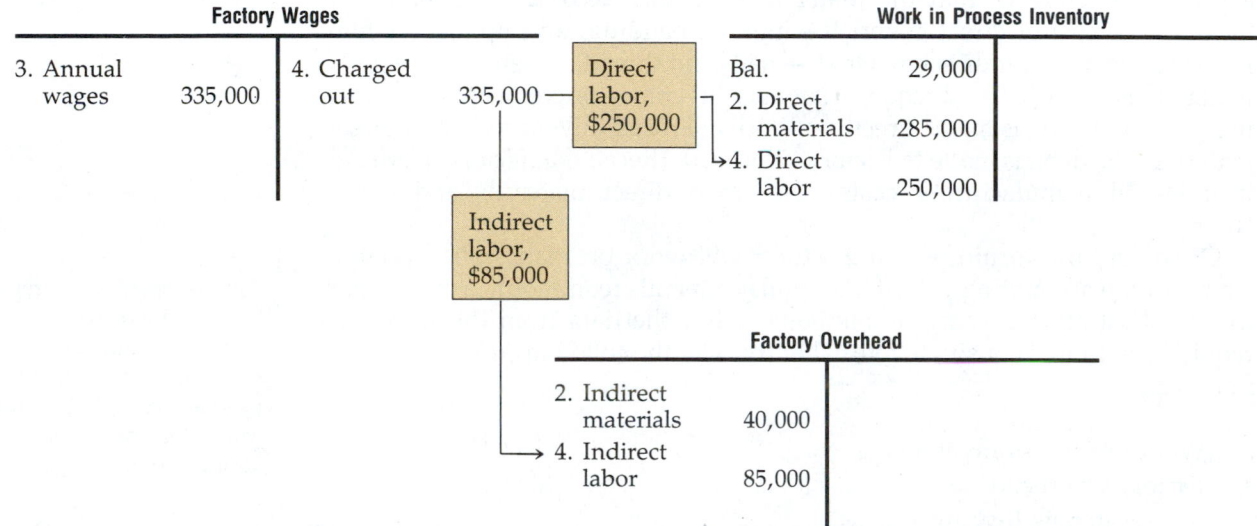

Point to Stress: As with materials requisitions, the labor time tickets are source documents. They are the basis for entering labor used on the job cost sheets. Regularly, they are accumulated and recorded so that the job cost reports are kept current.

Teaching Tip: Look at the labor time ticket (Exhibit 22-11). The job number must be included in order to trace costs to a specific job. This information allows the business to determine whether it had a profit or a loss on each job.

Direct and Indirect Labor. After the factory wages have been recorded, direct labor is debited directly to Work in Process Inventory. Indirect labor

EXHIBIT 22-11 *Labor Time Ticket*

Labor Time Ticket	No. 251
EMPLOYEE Jay Barlow	Date 7-24
JOB 293	

Time:		Rate $8.00
Started	1:00	Cost of labor
Stopped	8:30	charged to job $60.00
Elapsed	7:30	

Employee *Jay Barlow*

Supervisor *G. Dean Childres*

passes through the Factory Overhead account en route to Work in Process Inventory. The transfer of labor cost to production results in a credit to the Factory Wages account. The following entry allocates factory wages to Work in Process Inventory and Factory Overhead:

4.	Work in Process Inventory	250,000	
	Factory Overhead	85,000	
	Factory Wages		335,000

This entry brings the balance in Factory Wages to zero, its transferred balance now allocated between Work in Process Inventory (direct labor) and Factory Overhead (indirect labor).

Assume that $150 of the direct labor cost relates to Job 293. The Ramirez computer would enter Job 293's direct labor on the job cost record. The $150 amount in the accompanying job cost record includes Jay Barlow's wages of $60 (ticket 251, Exhibit 22-11) and the labor costs entered onto time tickets 236 and 258.

Discussion Question: What event(s) cause the Factory Wages account to increase? To decrease? *ANSWER:* Factory Wages is increased when factory wages are incurred and decreased when those wages are charged to jobs (direct labor) or to factory overhead (indirect labor).

Job Cost Record

Job No. _293_

Customer Name and Address _Macy's, New York City_

Job Description _10 recliner chairs_

Date Promised 7-31	Date Started 7-24	Date Completed

Date	Direct Materials		Direct Labor		Factory Overhead Costs		
	Requisition Numbers	Amount	Time Ticket Numbers	Amount	Date	Rate	Amount
19X5 7-24	334	$ 90	236,251,258	$150			

Overall Cost Summary

Direct materials...... $
Direct labor........
Factory overhead....

Total Job Cost...... $

Totals

The Work in Process Inventory account now contains the cost of direct materials and direct labor charged to Job 293—and the costs of many other jobs as well. Work in Process Inventory serves as a control account, with the job cost records giving the supporting details for each job. The balance in Work in Process Inventory should equal the total of the individual job costs, in the same manner illustrated for Materials Inventory in Exhibit 22-9. The job cost records thus serve as a subsidiary ledger for the general ledger balance in Work in Process Inventory.

We summarize the accounting for materials and labor just illustrated:

Work in process inventory	=	**General ledger (usually monthly totals only)**
↑		↑
Job cost records	=	**Subsidiary ledger (perhaps daily summaries)**
↑		↑
Material requisitions and time tickets	=	**Source documents (minute-to-minute, hour-to-hour records)**

Teaching Tip: The balance in the Work in Process Inventory should be the total of the costs of all the incomplete jobs in the job cost records—similar to Exhibit 22-9 for Materials Inventory.

We see that accounting data are most condensed in the general ledger and most detailed in the source documents.

In practice, the daily accounting duties are carried out using source documents and subsidiary ledgers. Copies of the source documents are independently summarized and are usually journalized and posted to the general ledger only once a month.

Accounting for Factory Overhead in a Job Cost System

Materials requisitions and labor time tickets make it easy to identify direct materials and direct labor with a specific job. Factory overhead, on the other hand, includes a variety of costs that cannot be linked to a particular job. How do we allocate overhead cost to jobs?

Overhead costs are recorded as incurred. The following entries—depreciation on plant and equipment, factory utilities, insurance, and property taxes—are typical. Note that all these overhead costs are debited to a single account—Factory Overhead in the general ledger. The account titles in parentheses in the following entries indicate the subsidiary accounts that are debited in an overhead subsidiary ledger. Budgeting these individual items and then keeping track of their actual amounts help managers control overhead costs.

5.	Factory Overhead (Depreciation—Plant and Equipment)	50,000	
	Accumulated Depreciation—Plant and Equipment		50,000
6.	Factory Overhead (Factory Utilities)	20,000	
	Cash....................................		20,000
7.	Factory Overhead (Factory Insurance)	5,000	
	Prepaid Insurance—Factory		5,000
8.	Factory Overhead (Property Taxes—Factory)	10,000	
	Property Tax Payable		10,000

Typical Student Misconception: Actual factory overhead costs are debited to the Factory Overhead account, and the applied overhead is credited to Factory Overhead.

The Factory Overhead account now contains all the overhead costs of the period:

Discussion Question: We know that materials used comes from the requisitions and labor from the time tickets, but how is the amount of overhead determined for each job? *ANSWER:* Overhead must be estimated by using an overhead rate. Remember that total overhead is not known until the end of the accounting period. If the job is completed before the end of the accounting period, overhead on the job has to be estimated.

Teaching Tip: Draw these simple T-accounts on the board to help

Factory Overhead

2.	Indirect materials	40,000	
4.	Indirect labor	85,000	
5.	Depreciation—plant and equipment	50,000	
6.	Factory utilities	20,000	
7.	Factory insurance	5,000	
8.	Property taxes—factory	10,000	
	Total actual overhead cost	210,000	

It would be virtually impossible to say that a specific amount of overhead (for example, the cost of heating the factory) was incurred on any particular job. Yet factory overhead costs certainly add to the costs of producing goods. We now discuss how accountants apply overhead in job costing.

The Budgeted Rate in Applying Overhead

Management wants to tie overhead cost to the costs of manufacturing the business's different products. After all, indirect materials, indirect labor, and all the other individual accounts that make up factory overhead contribute to product costs. And if product costs are to help management in product pricing, income determination, and inventory valuation, they must be timely as well as accurate.

The most accurate application of overhead could be made only at the end of the year, after actual results are determined. However, this timing would be too late. Managers want product-cost information throughout the year, not only at the end of the period. To meet these needs, accountants usually budget overhead application rates—that is, they compute a rate in advance of production. The usual steps in applying factory overhead using an annual averaging process follow.

1. Select a **cost application base,** which is a common denominator linking costs among all products. Ideally, this application base should be the primary cost driver, the best available measure of the cause-and-effect relationship between overhead costs and production volume. In many companies direct labor costs rise and fall proportionately with changes in production volume, and direct labor dollars or direct labor hours are chosen as the cost application base. In companies with highly automated production processes, labor is less important, and the cost allocation base is often machine hours.

2. Prepare a budget for the planning period, ordinarily a year. The two key items are (a) budgeted total overhead and (b) budgeted total volume of the cost application base, which is direct labor cost in our Ramirez illustration.

3. Compute the **budgeted factory overhead rate** by dividing the total budgeted overhead by the cost application base.

4. Obtain the actual application base data (such as direct labor cost or machine hours) as the year unfolds.

5. Apply the budgeted overhead to the jobs by multiplying the budgeted rate times the actual application base data for each job.

6. At the end of the year, account for any differences between the amount of overhead actually incurred and the amount of overhead applied to products.

The Ramirez forecast is based on a volume of activity expressed in direct labor cost. Assume detailed forecasts predict total overhead of $212,000 for the next year at an anticipated $265,000 direct-labor-cost level of activity. The budgeted factory overhead rate is computed as follows:

$$\text{Budgeted factory overhead rate} = \frac{\text{Total budgeted overhead}}{\text{Total budgeted direct labor cost}} = \frac{\$212,000}{\$265,000} = .80 \text{ or } 80\%$$

The 80 percent rate would be used for applying overhead cost to jobs.

To *apply overhead* means to debit Work in Process Inventory for the cost of overhead and to credit the Factory Overhead account. The overhead application rate is used to compute the amount of overhead to apply to a specific job. In our example, for each dollar of direct labor debited to Work in Process Inventory, 80 cents in overhead cost is also debited to that account. If the actual direct labor cost of a job is $800 (see Step 4), 80 percent of that amount, or $640, is debited to Work in Process Inventory as factory overhead (see Step 5 above).

The budgeted factory overhead rate is applied to all jobs uniformly throughout the year. After the direct materials and direct labor costs have been applied to a job, the overhead is applied, as shown in the accompanying record for Job 293. Recall that total direct labor cost for the job is $400. With an overhead application rate of 80 percent of direct labor, the amount of overhead to charge to Job 293 is $320 ($400 × .80).

Teaching Tip: Look at the completed job cost record. It now includes all three components of manufacturing costs:

Direct Material
Direct Labor
Factory Overhead

If the total cost is $1,380, then we can calculate the unit cost of the ten chairs ($138 each). Remember that calculating unit cost is one of the goals of cost accounting.

Class Exercise: Answer the following questions using these T-accounts. Assume no beginning balances. (A transparency may be helpful to work this exercise in class.)

Job Cost Record

Job No. 293

Customer Name and Address   Macy's, New York City

Job Description   10 recliner chairs

| Date Promised | 7-31 | | Date Started | 7-24 | | | Date Completed | 7-29 |

Date	Direct Materials		Direct Labor			Factory Overhead Costs		
	Requisition Numbers	Amount	Time Ticket Numbers	Amount	Date	Rate		Amount
19X5 7-24	334	$ 90	236,251,258	$150	7-29	120% of Direct labor		$480
25	338	180	264,269,273,291	200				
28	347	230	305	50				

Overall Cost Summary

Direct materials...... $ 500
Direct labor........   400
Factory overhead....   480

| Totals | | $500 | | $400 | Total Job Cost...... $ 1,380 |

The job cost record for job 293 is complete. It provides the detailed subsidiary ledger support for the debits to the general ledger account, Work in Process Inventory.

Of course, similar applications of overhead have been made for other jobs in 19X5. The total overhead applied to all jobs worked on during 19X5 was 80 percent of $250,000 direct labor, .80 × $250,000 = $200,000. The journal entry to apply overhead to production is

9.   Work in Process Inventory 200,000
         Factory Overhead 200,000

Trace this application of Factory Overhead to Work in Process Inventory.

Materials

52,000	44,000

WIP

40,000	136,000
60,000	
48,000	

FG

136,000	122,000

Labor

70,000	70,000

FOH

4,000	48,000
10,000	
37,000	

Factory Overhead

2.	40,000	9. Applied	200,000
4.	85,000		
5.	50,000		
6.	20,000		
7.	5,000		
8.	10,000		
Actual costs	210,000		
Bal.	10,000		

Factory Overhead Applied →

Work in Process Inventory

Bal.	29,000
2.	285,000
4.	250,000
9.	200,000

1   What is the cost of the direct materials used? Indirect materials?

An additional detail exists in accounting for overhead cost. First, however, we need to discuss accounting for finished goods and the sale of inventory.

Accounting for Finished Goods, Sales, and Cost of Goods Sold

As each job is completed, its cost is transferred from Work in Process Inventory to Finished Goods Inventory. The completion date is written on the job cost record, which is compared with the budget and filed away. Then, sales of finished goods are recorded as they occur.

A summary entry for goods completed in 19X5 follows:

10. Finished Goods Inventory   740,000
         Work in Process Inventory   740,000

In turn, familiar entries would be made for sales and cost of goods sold.

11. Accounts Receivable   996,000
         Sales Revenue   996,000

     Cost of Goods Sold   734,000
         Finished Goods Inventory   734,000

The second entry is needed to maintain the perpetual inventory record. (Only the first entry is needed as sales are made in a periodic inventory system.)

The key accounts for product costs now show:

Work in Process Inventory				Finished Goods Inventory				Cost of Goods Sold	
Bal.	29,000	10.	740,000	Bal.	12,000	11.	734,000 →11.	734,000	
2.	285,000			10.	740,000				
4.	250,000								
9.	200,000			Bal.	18,000				
Bal.	24,000								

Disposing of Overapplied and Underapplied Overhead

The application of factory overhead cost to production will usually not bring to zero the balance in the Factory Overhead account. This account is debited for *actual cost* and credited for *applied amounts*—equal to the budgeted factory overhead rate multiplied by the actual direct labor cost.

The total debits to Factory Overhead for the year may not equal the total credits to the account. A *debit* balance remaining in the Factory Overhead account is called **underapplied overhead.** In our illustration, actual overhead ($210,000 debited to the account) exceeded the amount applied to jobs ($200,000 credited to the account) during the period, which resulted in $10,000 in underapplied overhead. Conversely, a *credit* balance, called **overapplied overhead,** results when applied overhead exceeds the actual amount. Accountants usually ignore over- and underapplied overhead during the year and dispose of it at year end. The entry to close the Factory Overhead account adjusts the records to account for the actual overhead cost incurred during the year. The more accurate the budgeted overhead rate, the less the difference between actual and applied amounts of factory overhead for the year.

If the amount of over- or underapplied overhead is *significant*, it often is allocated to Work in Process, Finished Goods, and Cost of Goods Sold based on their relative balances before the allocation. For example, suppose 15 percent of the year's production is still in process, 25 percent is finished but

2 What is the cost of direct labor applied to production? Indirect labor?

3 What is the cost of goods manufactured?

4 What is the actual overhead? Applied overhead?

5 What is the cost of goods sold?

6 What is the budgeted overhead rate stated as a percentage of direct labor?

7 Is overhead over- or underapplied? By how much?

ANSWER:

1   $40,000; $4,000
2   $60,000; $10,000
3   $136,000
4   $51,000; $48,000
5   $122,000
6   80% ($48,000/$60,000)
7   Underapplied by $3,000

Discussion Question: Seldom is estimated overhead equal to actual overhead. How do we treat the over- or underapplied overhead? *ANSWER:* First we have to identify the result of under- or overapplying overhead. Look at the Work in Process Inventory account. Notice that it is debited for the applied overhead of $200,000 instead of the $210,000 of actual overhead. This means that the total debits to Work in Process Inventory are understated. The amount credited to Work in Process Inventory and debited to Finished Goods Inventory will also be understated because the cost of the finished goods was determined by using the applied overhead. Also, Cost of Goods Sold will be understated. Therefore, all three accounts—Work in Process Inventory, Finished Goods Inventory, and Cost of Goods Sold—are affected by the underapplied overhead.

Which account is affected the most? *ANSWER:* Cost of Goods Sold, because it has the largest balance. If the over- or underapplied overhead is an insignificant (immaterial) amount, then all of the under- or overapplied overhead will be transferred to Cost of Goods Sold. But if the under- or overapplied overhead is significant (material), then all three accounts must be adjusted.

Teaching Tip: A simple T-account often helps in working with overhead.

Overhead

Actual	Applied

A debit balance at the end of the period means actual was greater than applied and is called underapplied overhead. A credit balance means applied was greater than actual and is called overapplied overhead.

unsold, and the remaining 60 percent has been sold. If *overapplied* overhead at the end of the period is $50,000—a significant amount in relation to total factory overhead, cost of goods sold, or another appropriate benchmark—the Factory Overhead Account will have a $50,000 credit balance. The entry to dispose of this credit balance debits Factory Overhead as follows:

Dec. 31	Factory Overhead	50,000	
	Work in Process Inventory ($50,000 × .15)		7,500
	Finished Goods Inventory ($50,000 × .25)		12,500
	Cost of Goods Sold ($50,000 × .60)		30,000

This entry removes the $50,000 credit balance from Factory Overhead. It also adjusts Work in Process, Finished Goods, and Cost of Goods Sold to actual costs.

If the over- or underapplied amount is *insignificant,* it can be closed to Cost of Goods Sold without seriously affecting the financial statements. This is an application of the *materiality concept.* Suppose actual overhead cost exceeded the amount of overhead applied to jobs. In our illustration the year's production resulted in the following summary activity in the Factory Overhead account:

Factory Overhead

Actual	210,000	Applied	200,000
Balance—Underapplied	10,000		

The $10,000 is minor relative to the $210,000 of actual overhead cost for the year. Moreover, the Cost of Goods Sold balance ($734,000) dwarfs the balances of Work in Process Inventory and Finished Goods Inventory ($24,000 and $18,000, respectively). This means that an allocation of $10,000 to the three accounts would have tiny effects on the balances in ending work in process and finished goods. Therefore, we may close this underapplied overhead to Cost of Goods Sold as follows:

Dec. 31	Cost of Goods Sold	10,000	
(Entry 12)	Factory Overhead		10,000

Posting this entry brings the Factory Overhead account to a zero balance and completes the job order cost accounting example.

Overview of Illustration

Exhibit 22-12 provides an overview of the Ramirez job order costing illustration. The key inventory accounts and Cost of Goods Sold are displayed at the top. Accounts for Factory Wages and Factory Overhead also are shown. The relationships of subsidiary material records to Materials Inventory and of subsidiary job cost records to Work in Process Inventory are also illustrated.

As Exhibit 22-12 makes clear, the ending balance sheet accounts would be

Materials Inventory	$15,000
Work in Process Inventory	24,000
Finished Goods Inventory	18,000

Transparency T 22-4

EXHIBIT 22-12 *Job Order Costing, General Flow of Costs (in thousands)*

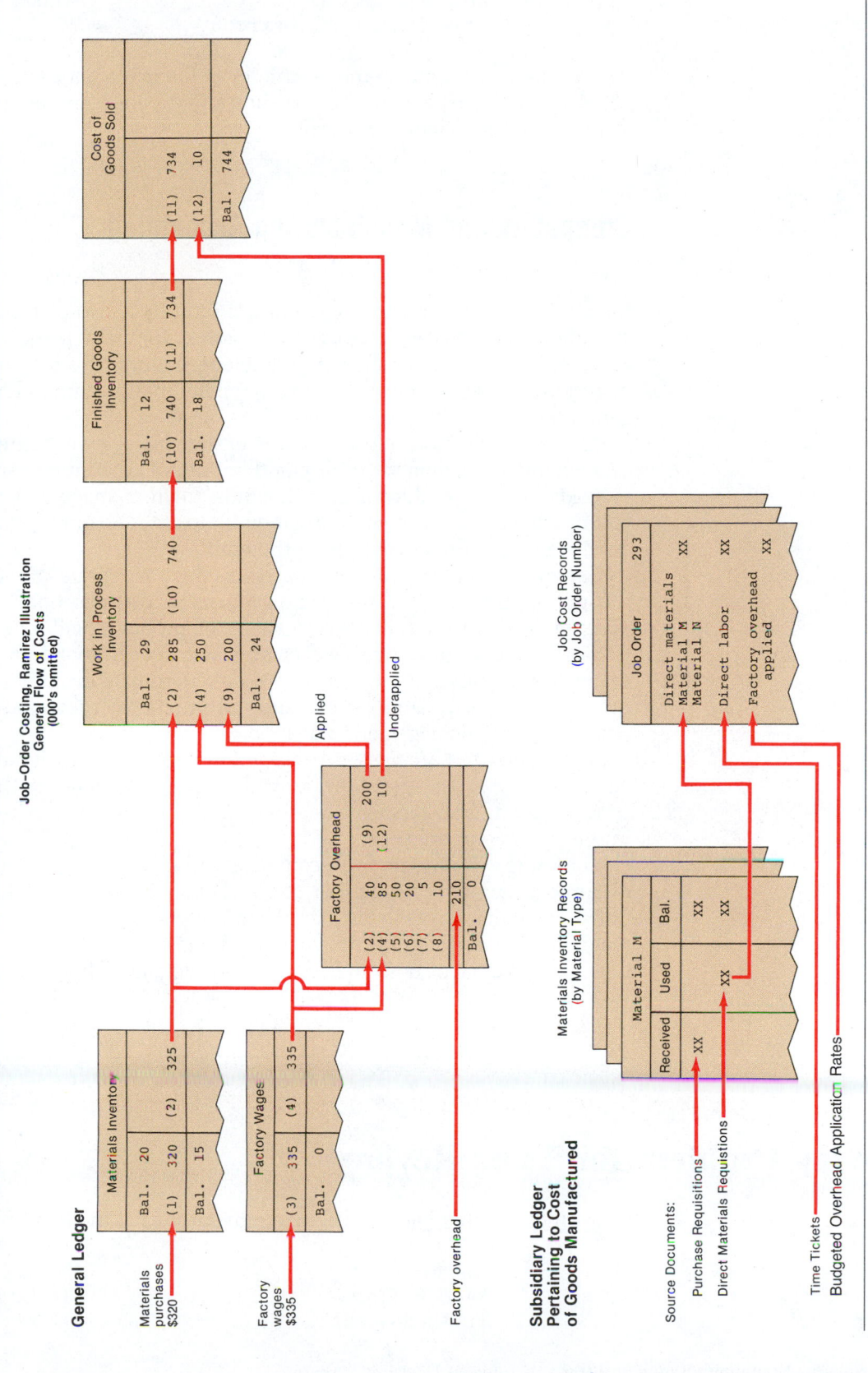

The condensed income statement for 19X5 would report the following through gross margin:

Sales	$996,000
Cost of goods sold	734,000
Gross margin (or gross profit)	$262,000

As mentioned previously, the remainder of the manufacturer's income statement (operating expenses, other revenue and expense, and net income) is the same as for a merchandising entity.

Computers and Manufacturing Accounting

Managers need a tremendous amount of information to plan manufacturing operations and to keep costs under control. A company manufacturing hundreds of items may have a materials subledger running to perhaps thousands of accounts. Little wonder then that so many manufacturers have turned to computerized accounting.

Also, during periods of high customer demand, a manufacturer will focus on meeting production schedules, and important accounting controls may be relaxed. As peak production season winds down, managers may find it difficult to bring the accounting information up to date. A computerized system is easier to keep current throughout the entire year.

Computer software for manufacturers may integrate all facets of cost accounting, from materials purchases to overhead application. Assume management wants to manufacture a range of products within a certain time frame. The computer can access engineering specifications for the product, calculate materials and time requirements, coordinate deadlines with limited production capacity, and issue a series of purchase orders and work orders consistent with management plans.

A computerized accounting package can generate a broad variety of management reports. These reports are available at critical points in the production process, giving management the opportunity to monitor progress and make improvements on the spot.

Collecting certain data for a computerized system is straightforward. For example, a number of computer terminals may be set up on the production floor. At various stages in the manufacturing process, an employee inserts his magnetically imprinted identification card into the terminal. The system thus captures direct labor time and cost without detailed labor records.

Summary Problem for Your Review

Hillis Incorporated had the following inventories at the end of 19X4:

Materials	$20,000
Work in Process	17,000
Finished Goods	11,000

During January 19X5 Hillis completed the following transactions:

1. Purchased materials on account, $31,000.
2. Requisitioned (placed into production) direct materials, $39,000.
3. Factory payroll incurred, $40,000.
4. Allocated factory labor as follows: direct labor, 90 percent; indirect labor, 10 percent.
5. Requisitioned (placed into production) indirect materials, $3,000.
6. Incurred other factory overhead, $13,000 (credit Accounts Payable).
7. Applied factory overhead to production at 50 percent of direct labor.
8. Completed production, $99,000.
9. Sold goods on account, $172,000; cost of goods sold, $91,400.
10. Closed ending balance of Factory Overhead to Cost of Goods Sold.

Required

1. Record the transactions in the general journal.
2. Determine the ending balances in the three inventory accounts and Cost of Goods Sold.

SOLUTION TO REVIEW PROBLEM

Requirement 1 (Journal entries)

1.	Materials Inventory	31,000	
	Accounts Payable		31,000
2.	Work in Process Inventory	39,000	
	Materials Inventory		39,000
3.	Factory Wages	40,000	
	Wages Payable		40,000
4.	Work in Process Inventory ($40,000 × .90)	36,000	
	Factory Overhead ($40,000 × .10)	4,000	
	Factory Wages		40,000
5.	Factory Overhead	3,000	
	Materials Inventory		3,000
6.	Factory Overhead	13,000	
	Accounts Payable		13,000
7.	Work in Process Inventory ($36,000 × .50)	18,000	
	Factory Overhead		18,000
8.	Finished Goods Inventory	99,000	
	Work in Process Inventory		99,000
9.	Accounts Receivable	172,000	
	Sales Revenue		172,000
	Cost of Goods Sold	91,400	
	Finished Goods Inventory		91,400
10.	Cost of Goods Sold	2,000	
	Factory Overhead		2,000

Balance in Factory Overhead for entry 10:

Factory Overhead

(4)	4,000	(7)	18,000
(5)	3,000		
(6)	13,000		
Bal.	2,000		

Requirement 2 (Ending balances)

Materials Inventory

Bal.	20,000	(2)	39,000
(1)	31,000	(5)	3,000
Bal.	9,000		

Work in Process Inventory

Bal.	17,000	(8)	99,000
(2)	39,000		
(4)	36,000		
(7)	18,000		
Bal.	11,000		

Finished Goods Inventory

Bal.	11,000	(9)	91,400
(8)	99,000		
Bal.	18,600		

Cost of Goods Sold

(9)	91,400		
(10)	2,000		
Bal.	93,400		

Summary

Manufacturing companies use cost accounting systems to help plan and control the manufacturing function and to compute manufacturing product costs for the financial statements and for pricing and product mix decisions. They use separate inventory accounts for raw materials, work in process, and finished goods. The *Materials Inventory* account carries the cost of direct and indirect materials that are held for use in production. The *Work in Process Inventory* account shows the cost of goods that are still in the manufacturing process and not yet complete. *Finished Goods Inventory* represents completed goods that have not yet been sold. This account corresponds to the single inventory account of a merchandising business.

A manufacturer obtains inventory for resale by producing the goods. The manufacturer's *cost of goods manufactured* replaces the purchases account of a merchandiser. Otherwise, a manufacturer's income statement resembles the income statement of a merchandiser.

Direct materials include all the important materials used to make the product. *Direct labor* is the cost of employing people who physically produce the company's product. These two costs are traced directly to finished goods. *Factory overhead* includes all other manufacturing costs, including *indirect materials* and *indirect labor*.

Manufacturers keep inventory costs separate from all the other costs of running the business. *Inventoriable costs* are those identified with inventory. *Period costs* are accounted for as operating expenses and are never traced through the inventory accounts.

In a *job order costing system*—designed to account for products manufactured as individual units or in batches—costs are accumulated for specific jobs. A *job cost record* lists the materials, labor, and overhead costs of completing the job. In a job cost system this document is the basic internal management device for accumulating and controlling costs. It serves as the subsidiary record for Work in Process Inventory. The cost of materials is traced via materials ledger cards. Labor costs are traced by time tickets.

The Factory Overhead account, which includes many different costs, is debited for actual costs incurred. Overhead cost is applied to product at a budgeted rate usually stated as a percentage of direct labor cost. At the end of the period, any *underapplied* or *overapplied overhead* is closed.

Self-Study Questions

Test your understanding of the chapter by marking the best answer for each of the following questions.

1. Which of the following is an inventory account of a manufacturer but not of a merchandiser? *(p. 1002)*
   a. Cost of goods manufactured
   b. Merchandise inventory
   c. Work in process
   d. Direct labor

2. Cost of goods manufactured is used to compute *(p. 1003)*
   a. Cost of goods sold
   b. Factory overhead applied
   c. Direct materials used
   d. Finished goods inventory

3. Beginning work in process inventory is $35,000; manufacturing costs for the period total $140,000; and ending work in process inventory is $20,000. What is the cost of goods manufactured? *(pp. 1003-04)*
   a. $125,000
   b. $155,000
   c. $175,000
   d. $195,000

4. Which of the following is a period cost? *(p. 1006)*
   a. Materials inventory
   b. Direct labor
   c. Factory overhead
   d. Selling expense

5. Job order costing would be an appropriate system to account for the manufacture of *(p. 1008)*
   a. Aircraft
   b. Matches
   c. Zippers
   d. Cardboard boxes

6. What purpose does a job cost record serve? *(pp. 1009-10)*
   a. Lists total materials, labor, and overhead costs charged to a job
   b. Is management's basic internal document that helps to control cost in a job cost system
   c. Both of the above
   d. Neither of the above

7. Using direct materials in production and charging direct labor costs to a job result in a debit to *(pp. 1013, 1015)*
   a. Direct materials and direct labor
   b. Work in process inventory
   c. Finished goods inventory
   d. Materials inventory and factory wages

8. Which documents serve as a subsidiary ledger for the general ledger balance of Work in Process Inventory? *(pp. 1009, 1015)*
   a. Job cost records
   b. Materials requisitions
   c. Labor time tickets
   d. Materials ledger accounts

9. Why is direct labor often used as a basis for applying overhead cost to jobs? *(p. 1017)*
   a. Overhead is very similar to direct labor
   b. Overhead includes direct labor
   c. Overhead occurs before direct labor is charged to a job
   d. Overhead occurs in relation to the incurrence of direct labor cost

10. At the end of the period, after overhead has been applied to all jobs, Factory Overhead has a credit balance of $900. We would say that overhead has been *(p. 1019)*
   a. Misstated
   b. Incorrectly applied
   c. Overapplied
   d. Underapplied

Answers to the Self-Study Questions follow the Accounting Vocabulary.

Accounting Vocabulary

Budgeted factory overhead rate. Budgeted total overhead cost divided by the budgeted rate base *(p. 1017)*.

Conversion costs. Direct labor plus overhead *(p. 1004)*.

Cost application base. A common denominator linking costs among all products. Ideally the best available measure of the cause-and-effect relationship between overhead costs and production volume *(p. 1017)*.

Cost of goods manufactured. Manufacturers' counterpart to the Purchases account. Cost of goods manufactured takes the place of purchases in the computation of cost of goods sold *(p. 1002)*.

Direct labor. Cost of salaries and wages for the employees who physically convert materials into the company's products; labor costs that are conveniently traceable to finished goods *(p. 1003)*.

Direct material. Material that becomes a physical part of a finished product and whose cost is separately and conveniently traceable through the manufacturing process to finished goods *(p. 1003)*.

Factory overhead. All manufacturing costs other than direct materials and direct labor *(p. 1003)*.

Finished goods inventory. Completed goods that have not yet been sold *(p. 1002)*.

Indirect labor. Factory labor costs other than direct labor. Indirect labor costs, which are difficult to trace to specific products, include the pay of forklift operators, janitors, and plant guards *(p. 1004)*.

Indirect materials. Manufacturing materials whose cost cannot easily be traced directly to particular finished products *(p. 1004)*.

Inventoriable cost. A cost of a product regarded as an asset under GAAP *(p. 1005)*.

Job cost record. Document used to accumulate and control cost in a job order system *(p. 1009)*.

Job order costing. Accounting system used by companies that manufacture products as individual units or in batches, each of which receives varying degrees of attention and skill *(p. 1008)*.

Labor time ticket. Document that identifies an employee, the amount of time the employee spent on a particular job, and the employee's labor cost charged to the job *(p. 1014)*.

Materials inventory. Materials on hand and intended for use in the manufacturing process. Also called Raw materials inventory *(p. 1002)*.

Materials requisition. Request for materials prepared by manufacturing personnel, the document that sets a manufacturing process in motion *(p. 1011)*.

Overapplied overhead. Credit balance in the Factory Overhead account; results when applied overhead exceeds the actual overhead cost *(p. 1019)*.

Period cost. Operating expenses that are never traced through the inventory accounts *(p. 1006)*.

Prime costs. Direct materials plus direct labor *(p. 1004)*.

Product cost. General term that denotes different costs allocated to products for different purposes *(p. 1007)*.

Raw materials inventory. Another name for Materials inventory *(p. 1002)*.

Total manufacturing cost. Sum of direct materials used, direct labor, and factory overhead. Total manufacturing cost is used to compute cost of goods manufactured, which is part of cost of goods sold *(p. 1005)*.

Underapplied overhead. Debit balance remaining in the Factory Overhead account after overhead is applied; means that actual overhead cost exceeded the amount applied to jobs (p. 1019).

Value chain. Sequence of all business functions in which value is added to a firm's products or services (p. 1000).

Work in process inventory. Cost of the goods that are in the manufacturing process and not yet complete (p. 1002).

Answers to Self-Study Questions

1.	c		5.	a	8. a
2.	a		6.	c	9. d
3.	b	($35,000 + $140,000 − $20,000 = $155,000)	7.	b	10. c
4.	d				

ASSIGNMENT MATERIAL _____

Questions

1. How do manufacturing companies differ from merchandisers? What inventory accounts does a manufacturer use that a merchandiser does not need?
2. Identify the various business functions in the value chain of a manufacturing company. Separate the upstream functions from the downstream functions. To which functions is cost accounting relevant?
3. What are the purposes of the cost accounting systems of a manufacturer?
4. What is the manufacturer's counterpart to the Purchases account of a merchandiser?
5. Distinguish direct materials from indirect materials and direct labor from indirect labor. Direct materials and direct labor are debited directly to what inventory account when placed in production? What account do indirect materials and indirect labor pass through en route to this inventory account?
6. Give examples of direct material and indirect material for a home builder.
7. Identify six or more components of factory overhead. Is overhead an asset or an expense account to a manufacturer?
8. Outline the flow of inventory costs through a manufacturing company's accounting system.
9. Distinguish between inventoriable costs and period costs. Which represents an asset, and which is used to account for expenses?
10. What costs should managers consider in deciding on the selling price of a product: inventoriable costs or full product costs? Give your reason.
11. Name two benefits of a perpetual inventory system.
12. What do the terms "charged to a job" and "applied to jobs" mean? What account is debited when a cost is applied to a job?
13. What is the essential nature of a job order costing system? How can companies that use a job cost system operate with low levels of inventories?
14. What document is used to control costs in a job cost system? Identify the three categories of costs listed on this document.
15. Name three documents or records used to account for raw materials, control them, and move them through the production process. Give the function served by each document.
16. Use T-accounts to outline how the costs of materials and labor are transferred to Work in Process Inventory. Include both direct and indirect materials and direct and indirect labor.

17. What document is used to charge labor cost to specific jobs? Briefly describe how the document is used.
18. Is factory overhead cost applied to jobs by a precise identification of the overhead cost of each job or by an estimation process? Briefly discuss the process.
19. Is Factory Overhead debited for actual overhead cost or the amount of overhead applied to product? Which amount is credited to Factory Overhead?
20. How can factory overhead be underapplied? How can it be overapplied?
21. Insignificant amounts of over- or underapplied overhead are closed to what account? Significant amounts are closed to what three accounts?
22. Which of the following accounts have their balances brought to zero at the end of the period? Which keep their ending balances to start the next period—Materials Inventory, Factory Overhead, Finished Goods Inventory, Factory Wages?
23. What three categories of manufacturing costs are listed on a statement of cost of goods manufactured?
24. Summarize the computation of cost of goods manufactured. You can use your own dollar amounts.

Exercises

Total current assets $218,000

Exercise 22-1 *Reporting current assets of a manufacturer* **(L.O. 1)**

Consider the following selected accounts of Frostex Foods:

Cost of goods sold	$101,000	Prepaid expenses	$ 5,000
Direct labor	47,000	Marketing expense	39,000
Direct materials	25,000	Work in process inventory	42,000
Accounts receivable	73,000	Factory overhead	26,000
Cash	9,000	Finished goods inventory	68,000
Cost of goods manufactured	94,000	Materials inventory	21,000

Required

Show how Frostex would report current assets on the balance sheet. Not all accounts are used.

Cost of goods manuf. $198,000

Exercise 22-2 *Computing cost of goods manufactured* **(L.O. 2)**

Compute cost of goods manufactured from the following account balances:

	Beginning of Year	End of Year
Materials inventory	$22,000	$26,000
Work in process inventory	36,000	30,000
Finished goods inventory	18,000	23,000
Purchases of raw materials		75,000
Direct labor		82,000
Indirect labor		15,000
Factory insurance		9,000
Depreciation—factory building and equipment		11,000
Repairs and maintenance—factory		4,000
Marketing expenses		63,000
General and administrative expenses		29,000
Income tax expense		30,000

Exercise 22-3 *Preparing a manufacturer's income statement* **(L.O. 1, 2)**

Net income $63,000

Prepare an income statement for the company in Exercise 22-2, assuming it sold 27,000 units of its product at a price of $14 during the current year.

Exercise 22-4 *Computing cost of goods manufactured and cost of goods sold* **(L.O. 2)**

Cost of goods sold $194,000

Compute cost of goods manufactured and cost of goods sold for the following situation:

Direct materials used	$53,000
Ending finished goods inventory	34,000
Depreciation of factory equipment	11,000
Factory repairs and maintenance	16,000
Beginning work in process inventory	19,000
Direct labor	59,000
Indirect labor	23,000
Indirect materials	13,000
Miscellaneous factory overhead	4,000
Property tax on factory building	3,000
Marketing expenses	37,000
Beginning finished goods inventory	27,000
Factory utilities	17,000
Ending work in process inventory	26,000
Depreciation of factory building	9,000
Nonfactory administrative expenses	43,000

Exercise 22-5 *Computing gross margin for a manufacturer* **(L.O. 2)**

Direct labor $96,000
Gross margin $251,000

Supply the missing amounts from the following computation of gross margin:

Sales revenue			$483,000
Cost of goods sold:			
Beginning finished goods inventory		$ 91,000	
Cost of goods manufactured:			
Beginning work in process inventory		$ 57,000	
Direct materials used	$84,000		
Direct labor	X		
Factory overhead	51,000		
Total manufacturing costs incurred during the period		231,000	
Total manufacturing costs to account for		X	
Ending work in process inventory		(40,000)	
Cost of goods manufactured		X	
Goods available for sale		X	
Ending finished goods inventory		(107,000)	
Cost of goods sold			X
Gross margin			$ X

Exercise 22-6 *Analyzing job cost data* **(L.O. 3)**

Cost of goods sold $20,000

Bancroft Publishing Company job cost records yielded the following information:

Job No.	Dates Started	Dates Finished	Dates Sold	Total Cost of Job at July 31
1	June 19	July 14	July 15	$ 1,700
2	June 29	July 21	July 26	17,000
3	July 3	Aug. 11	Aug. 13	6,500
4	July 7	July 29	Aug. 1	6,200
5	July 9	July 30	Aug. 2	2,700
6	July 22	Aug. 11	Aug. 13	1,300
7	July 23	July 27	July 29	1,300

Compute Bancroft's cost of (a) work in process inventory at July 31, (b) finished goods inventory at July 31, and (c) cost of goods sold for July.

f. Work in process inven. dr. $16,800

Exercise 22-7   Journalizing manufacturing transactions   (L.O. 4, 5, 6)

Record the following transactions in the general journal:

a. Purchased materials on account, $11,100.
b. Paid factory wages, $14,000.
c. Used in production: direct materials, $9,000; and indirect materials, $2,000.
d. Applied factory labor to jobs: direct labor, 80 percent; indirect labor, 20 percent.
e. Recorded factory overhead: depreciation, $13,000; insurance, $1,700; property tax, $4,200 (credit Property Tax Payable).
f. Applied factory overhead to jobs, 150% percent of direct labor.
g. Completed production, $27,000.
h. Sold inventory on account, $22,000; cost of goods sold, $14,000.
i. Paid marketing expenses, $2,000.

No check figure

Exercise 22-8   Identifying manufacturing transactions   (L.O. 4, 5, 6)

Describe the transactions indicated by the letters in the following manufacturing accounts:

Materials Inventory	
(a)	(b)
	(e)

Work in Process Inventory	
(b)	(h)
(d)	(j)
(g)	

Finished Goods Inventory	
(h)	(i)
	(j)

Factory Wages	
(c)	(d)

Factory Overhead	
(d)	(g)
(e)	
(f)	
(j)	

Cost of Goods Sold	
(i)	(j)

Work in proc. inv. bal. $9,000

Exercise 22-9   Using the Work in Process Inventory account   (L.O. 4, 5, 6)

August production generated the following activity in the Work in Process Inventory account of Swingline Manufacturing Company:

Work in Process Inventory	
August 1 Bal.	10,000
Direct materials used	23,000
Direct labor charged to jobs	31,000
Factory overhead applied to jobs	11,000

Completed production, not yet recorded, consists of Jobs B-78, G-65, and Y-11, with total costs of $14,000, $19,000, and $33,000, respectively.

Required

1. Compute the cost of work in process at August 31.
2. Journalize completed production for August.
3. Journalize the credit sale of Job G-65 for $41,000. Also make the cost-of-goods-sold entry.

Exercise 22-10   *Accounting for overhead cost*   **(L.O. 6)**

Overhead rate 125%; underapplied by $600

Selected cost data for Maness & Shrake are presented below:

Budgeted factory overhead cost for the year	$105,000
Budgeted direct labor cost for the year	84,000
Actual factory overhead cost for the year.........	100,600
Actual direct labor cost for the year.............	80,000

Required

1. Compute the budgeted factory overhead rate.
2. Journalize the application of overhead cost for the year.
3. By what amount is factory overhead over- or underapplied? Is this amount significant or insignificant?
4. Based on your answer to (3), journalize disposition of the overhead balance.

Problems   (Group A)

Problem 22-1A   *Completing a manufacturer's income statement*   **(L.O. 1, 2)**

Direct mat. used $78,000
Net inc. $30,800

Certain item descriptions and amounts are missing from the income statement of Medco Systems.

Medco Systems
Income Statement
For the Month Ended March 31, 19X6

Sales revenue				$231,000
Cost of goods sold:				
Beginning _____ inventory			$ X	
Cost of goods _____:				
Beginning _____ inventory		$ X		
Direct _____:				
Beginning materials inventory	$34,000			
Purchases of materials	70,000			
Available for use	X			
Ending materials inventory	(26,000)			
Direct _____.....................		$ X		
Direct _____.....................		83,000		
_____.................		19,000		
Total _____ costs _____.........			X	
Total _____ costs _____.........			X	
Ending _____ inventory			(49,000)	
Cost of goods _____			160,000	
Goods available for sale			192,000	
Ending _____ inventory			(54,000)	
Cost of goods _____				X
Gross margin				93,000
Operating expenses:				
Marketing			23,000	
General............................			26,000	
Total operating expense				X
Income before income tax				X
Income tax expense (30%)				X
Net income				$ X

Required

Supply the missing item descriptions (_____) and the missing amounts (X).

April work in process inven. $1,800
April cost of goods sold $5,400

Problem 22-2A *Analyzing job cost data* (L.O. 3)

Pacific Irrigation Company job cost records yielded the following information. The company has a perpetual inventory system.

Job No.	Dates			Total Cost of Job at March 31	Total Manufacturing Cost Added In April
	Started	Finished	Sold		
1	2/26	3/7	3/9	$2,200	
2	2/3	3/12	3/13	1,100	
3	3/29	3/31	4/3	300	
4	3/31	4/1	4/1	400	$ 400
5	3/17	4/24	4/27	1,400	2,200
6	4/8	4/12	4/14		700
7	4/23	5/6	5/9		1,200
8	4/30	5/22	5/26		600

Required

1. Compute Pacific's cost of (a) work in process inventory at March 31 and April 30, (b) finished goods inventory at March 31 and April 30, and (c) cost of goods sold for March and April.
2. Make summary journal entries to record the transfer of completed units from work in process to finished goods for March and April.
3. Record the sale of Job 5 for $7,000.

1. Cost of goods manuf. $159.8 million
2. Cost of goods sold $157.6 million

Problem 22-3A *Computing manufacturing cost amounts for the financial statements* (L.O. 2, 4, 5, 6)

Assume Levi Strauss & Company accounting records include the following cost information on jobs for the manufacture of a line of jeans. During the most recent year Levi Strauss incurred total manufacturing cost of $163.2 million on materials, labor, and factory overhead, of which $28.2 million represented direct materials used. Beginning balances for the year were materials inventory, $3.4 million; work in process inventory, $2.6 million; and finished goods inventory, $7.4 million. The company applies overhead to work in process (and finished goods) based on the relationship between overhead and direct labor costs. At year end the inventory accounts showed these balances (millions):

	Materials	Direct Labor	Factory Overhead
Materials inventory	$0.9	$-0-	$-0-
Work in process inventory	1.5	2.0	2.5
Finished goods inventory	2.4	3.2	4.0

Required

1. Prepare Levi Strauss's statement of cost of goods manufactured for the line of jeans.
2. Compute cost of goods sold for the product.
3. Record the transfer from Work in Process Inventory to Finished Goods Inventory and the transfer from Finished Goods Inventory to Cost of Goods Sold during the year.

Problem 22-4A   *Accounting for manufacturing transactions (L.O. 3, 4, 5, 6)*

Doyle Wilson Homes builds prefabricated houses in a factory. The company uses a perpetual inventory system and a job cost system in which each house represents a job. The following transactions and events were completed during May:

(a)   Purchases of materials on account, $204,900.

(b)   Requisitions of direct materials and direct labor used in manufacturing:

	Direct Materials	Direct Labor
House #613	$26,100	$11,600
House #614	41,700	22,500
House #615	31,000	14,700
House #616	54,000	23,800
House #617	43,900	20,700
House #618	32,800	14,600

(c)   Depreciation of factory equipment used on different houses, $14,300.

(d)   Other overhead costs incurred on houses #613–#618:

Factory wages	$21,600
Equipment rentals paid	6,000
Liability insurance expired	3,900

(e)   Applied overhead to jobs at the budgeted overhead rate of 30 percent of direct labor.

(f)   Houses completed: #613, #615, #616.

(g)   Houses sold: #615 for $59,900; #616 for $103,900.

Required

1.   Record the foregoing transactions and events in the general journal.

2.   Open T-accounts for Work in Process Inventory and Finished Goods Inventory. Post the appropriate entries to these accounts, identifying the entry by letter. Determine the ending account balances assuming the beginning balances were zero.

3.   List the costs of unfinished houses, and show that this total amount equals the ending balance in the Work in Process Inventory account.

4.   List the costs of completed houses that have not yet been sold, and show that this total amount equals the ending balance in the Finished Goods Inventory account.

Problem 22-5A   *Preparing and using a job cost record (L.O. 4, 5, 6)*

D. E. Shipp Company produces conveyor belts used by other companies in their manufacturing processes. Shipp has a job cost system and a perpetual inventory system.

On September 22 Shipp received an order for 50 industrial-grade belts from Ogden Jones Corporation at a price of $56 each. The job, assigned number 449, was promised for October 15. After purchasing the materials, Shipp began production on September 30 and incurred the following costs in completing the order:

Date	Materials Requisition No.	Description	Amount
9-30	593	20 lbs. rubber @ $9	$180
10-2	598	30 meters polyester fabric @ $7	210
10-3	622	12 meters steel cord @ $12	144

Date	Time Ticket No.	Description	Amount
9-30	1754	8 hours @ $9	$ 72
10-3	1805	31 hours @ $8	248

Shipp charges overhead to jobs based on the relationship between estimated overhead ($375,000) and estimated direct labor ($250,000). The job was completed on October 3 and shipped to Ogden Jones on October 5.

Required

1. Prepare a job cost record similar to Exhibit 22-7.
2. Journalize in summary form the requisition of direct materials and the application of direct labor and factory overhead to Job 449.
3. Journalize completion of the job and sale of the goods.

Income from operations $45,515

Problem 22-6A *Comprehensive accounting treatment of manufacturing transactions (L.O. 1, 3, 4, 5, 6)*

Consumers Electric Company manufactures specialized parts used in the generation of power. Initially, the company manufactured the parts for its own use, but it gradually began selling them to other public utilities as well. The trial balance of Consumer Electric's manufacturing operation on January 1 of the current year follows.

Consumers Electric Company—Manufacturing Operations Trial Balance January 1, 19XX		
Cash	$ 32,740	
Accounts receivable	65,860	
Inventories:		
Materials	18,910	
Work in process	43,350	
Finished goods	78,550	
Plant assets	342,860	
Accumulated depreciation		$145,960
Accounts payable		88,650
Wages payable		5,700
Common stock		200,000
Retained earnings		141,960
Sales revenue		—
Cost of goods sold	—	
Factory wages	—	
Factory overhead	—	
Marketing and general expenses	—	
	$582,270	$582,270

January 1 balances in the subsidiary ledgers:

Materials ledger: Steel, $4,730; Petrochemicals, $5,280; Electronic parts, $7,800; Indirect materials, $1,100.

Work in process ledger: Job 86, $43,350.

Finished goods ledger: Transformers, $35,770; Transmissions lines, $21,910; Switches, $20,870.

January transactions are summarized as follows:

(a) Materials purchased on credit: Steel, $12,660; Petrochemicals, $19,570; Electronic parts, $28,360; Indirect materials, $6,130.

(b) Materials used in production (requisitioned):
Job 86: Steel, $1,580, Petrochemicals, $3,400.
Job 87: Steel, $10,580, Petrochemicals, $9,870; Electronic parts, $4,690.
Job 88: Steel, $2,930, Petrochemicals, $7,680; Electronic parts, $29,920.
Indirect materials, $4,760.

(c) Factory wages incurred during January, $51,730, of which $49,560 was paid. Wages payable at December 31 were paid during January, $5,700.

(d) Labor time tickets for the month: Job 86, $3,650; Job 87, $19,880; Job 88, $16,560; Indirect labor, $11,640.

(e) Factory overhead incurred on account, $27,660.

(f) Depreciation recorded on factory plant and equipment, $6,710.

(g) Payments on account, $79,330.

(h) Factory overhead applied at the budgeted rate of 120 percent of direct labor.

(i) Jobs completed during the month: Job 86, one transformer at total cost of $56,360; Job 87, 620 switches at total cost of $68,876.

(j) Marketing and general expenses paid, $21,660.

(k) Credit sales on account: All of Job 86 for $91,490 (cost $56,360); Job 87, 480 switches for $88,030 (cost, $53,323).

(l) Collections on account, $177,880.

Required

1. Open T-accounts for the general ledger, the materials ledger, the work in process ledger, and the finished goods ledger. Insert each account balance as given, and use the reference *Bal*.

2. Record the January transactions directly in the accounts, using the letters as references. Consumers Electric has a perpetual inventory system.

3. Prepare a trial balance at January 31 of the current year.

4. Prepare a multiple-step income statement through income from operations for January of the current year, assuming any balance in Factory Overhead is insignificant. Take amounts directly from the trial balance, and report cost of goods sold as a single amount.

Problem 22-7A *Using a manufacturing system to account for overhead cost* (L.O. 4, 5, 6)

Cost of goods sold $229,600

Selected accounts of Zettler Coating Contractors follow.

Accounts Receivable

Aug. 1	Balance	122,400	Aug.31	Collections	365,900
31	Sales	(1)			

Materials Inventory

Aug. 1	Balance	31,500	Aug.31	Requisitions	(2)
31	Purchases	54,600			

Work in Process Inventory

Aug. 1	Balance	73,200	Aug.31	Jobs completed	(5)
31	Direct materials	(3)			
31	Direct labor	104,000			
31	Factory overhead	(4)			

Finished Goods Inventory

Aug. 1	Balance	59,500	Aug.31	Jobs sold	(7)
31	Jobs completed	(6)			

Factory Overhead

Aug. 1	Balance	800	Aug.31	Applied at rate of 80% of direct labor cost	(8)
31	Costs incurred: indirect materials of $31,400, indirect labor, etc.				
	Total amount	81,900			

Cost of Goods Sold

Aug.31	Jobs sold	(9)			

Sales Revenue

			Aug.31	Sales	(10)

Selected balances at August 31 are

Accounts receivable.................	$103,700
Materials inventory	28,400
Work in process inventory	43,700
Finished goods inventory	72,900

Required

1. Determine the amounts of the numbered items in the accounts.
2. a. Was factory overhead under- or overapplied at August 1?
   b. What is the August 31 balance in Factory Overhead? Is factory overhead under- or overapplied at August 31?
   c. Assume August 31 is the end of the company's fiscal year. Give the year-end entry to close the Factory Overhead account, depending on whether the August 31 balance is significant or insignificant. You must make this judgment.

Problem 22-1B *Completing a manufacturer's income statement* (L.O. 1, 2)

Certain item descriptions and amounts are missing from the income statement of Hoppe Manufacturing Company.

Direct labor $72,000
Net inc. $54,000

Hoppe Manufacturing Company
Income Statement
For the Year Ended June 30, 19X9

Sales revenue			$ X
Cost of goods sold:			
Beginning _____ inventory		$ 101,000	
Cost of goods _____:			
Beginning _____ inventory	$ 28,000		
Direct _____:			
Beginning materials inventory	$ X		
Purchases of materials	62,000		
Available for use	79,000		
Ending materials inventory	(23,000)		
Direct _____	$ X		
Direct _____	X		
	38,000		
Total _____ costs _____	166,000		
Total _____ costs _____	X		
Ending _____ inventory	(31,000)		
Cost of goods _____	163,000		
Goods available for sale	X		
Ending _____ inventory	(X)		
Cost of goods _____	168,000		
Gross margin	234,000		
Operating expenses:			
Marketing	99,000		
General	X		
Total operating expense	144,000		
Income before income tax	X		
Income tax expense (40%)	X		
Net income	$ ×		

Required

Supply the missing item descriptions _____ and the missing amounts (X).

Problem 22-2B *Analyzing job cost data* (L.O. 3)

Trujillo Manufacturing Company job cost records yielded the following information. The company has a perpetual inventory system.

July work in process inven. $3,200
July cost of goods sold $3,800

Job No.	Dates Started	Finished	Sold	Total Cost of Job at June 30	Total Manufacturing Costs Added in July
1	5/26	6/7	6/9	$ 700	
2	6/3	6/12	6/13	1,700	
3	6/3	6/30	7/1	2,400	
4	6/17	7/24	7/27	100	$ 500
5	6/29	7/29	8/3	400	1,600
6	7/8	7/12	7/14		800
7	7/23	8/6	8/9		300
8	7/30	8/22	8/26		2,900

Required

1. Compute Trujillo's cost of (a) work in process inventory at June 30 and July 31, (b) finished goods inventory at June 30 and July 31, and (c) cost of goods sold for June and July.

2. Make summary journal entries to record the transfer of completed units from work in process to finished goods for June and July.
3. Record the sale of Job 4 for $850.

1. Cost of goods manuf.
$21,200,000
3. Materials purchased
$3,100,000

Problem 22-3B *Computing manufacturing cost amounts for the financial statements (L.O. 2, 4, 5, 6)*

Stride-Rite Shoe Company makes the Sperry Top-Sider deck shoe. Assume Stride-Rite accounting records include the following cost information on jobs for the manufacture of the basic brown leather Top-Sider.

During the most recent year Stride-Rite incurred total manufacturing cost of $21.4 million on materials, labor, and factory overhead, of which $4.6 million represented overhead applied. Beginning balances for the year were materials inventory, $500,000; work in process inventory, $700,000; and finished goods inventory, $400,000. The company applies overhead to work in process (and finished goods) based on the relationship between overhead and direct labor costs. At year end the inventory accounts showed these balances:

	Materials	Direct Labor	Factory Overhead
Materials inventory	$600,000	$ -0-	$ -0-
Work in process inventory	300,000	450,000	150,000
Finished goods inventory	100,000	150,000	50,000

Required

Fin. goods inven. bal. $133,880

1. Prepare Stride-Rite's statement of cost of goods manufactured for the brown leather Top-Sider shoe.
2. Compute cost of goods sold for the Top-Sider product.
3. Compute the cost of materials purchased during the year.

Problem 22-4B *Accounting for manufacturing transactions (L.O. 3, 4, 5, 6)*

Centennial Homes, Inc., is a home builder in Dallas, Texas. Assume Centennial uses a perpetual inventory system and a job cost system in which each house represents a job. Because it constructs houses on-site rather than in a factory, the company uses accounts titled Construction Wages (not Factory Wages), Overhead (not Factory Overhead), and Supervisory Salaries for indirect labor. The following transactions and events were completed during August:

(a) Purchases of materials on account, $385,600.
(b) Requisitions of direct materials and direct labor used in manufacturing:

	Direct Materials	Direct Labor
House #302	$36,800	$19,100
House #303	39,100	17,400
House #304	45,600	20,500
House #305	22,400	11,000
House #306	63,900	33,700
House #307	52,800	27,500

(c) Depreciation of equipment used in construction, $5,800.
(d) Other overhead costs incurred on houses #302–#307:

Supervisory salaries	$17,000
Equipment rentals paid	7,300
Liability insurance expired	5,100

(e) Applied overhead to jobs at the budgeted overhead rate of 30% of direct labor excluding supervision.

(f) Houses completed: #302, #304, #305, #307.

(g) Houses sold: #305 for $41,500; #307 for $115,000.

Required

1. Record the foregoing transactions and events in the general journal.

2. Open T-accounts for Work in Process Inventory and Finished Goods Inventory. Post the appropriate entries to these accounts, identifying the entry by letter. Determine the ending account balances assuming the beginning balances were zero.

3. List the costs of unfinished houses, and show that this total amount equals the ending balance in the Work in Process Inventory account.

4. List the costs of completed houses that have not yet been sold, and show that this total amount equals the ending balance in the Finished Goods Inventory account.

Problem 22-5B   *Preparing and using a job cost record* (*L.O. 4, 5, 6*)

Total job cost $2,179

Maxell Magnetic Tape Company manufactures diskettes for use in reproducing sound. Maxell has a job cost system and a perpetual inventory system.

On November 2 Maxell began production of 10,000 diskettes, assigned job number 378, to be sold to music stores for $1.25 each. The company incurred the following costs in completing the job:

Date	Materials Requisition No.	Description	Amount
11-2	36	31 lbs. polypropylene @ $8	$248
11-2	37	68 lbs. magnetic filament @ $13	884
11-3	42	7 lbs. bucylic acid @ $48	336

Date	Time Ticket No.	Description	Amount
11-2	556	12 hours @ $10	$120
11-3	557	24.5 hours @ $8	196

Maxell charges overhead to jobs based on the relationship between estimated overhead ($560,000) and estimated direct labor ($448,000). The job was completed on November 3 and shipped to music stores when ordered.

Required

1. Prepare a job cost record similar to Exhibit 22-7.

2. Journalize in summary form the requisition of direct materials and the application of direct labor and factory overhead to job 378.

3. Journalize completion of the job and sale of 500 diskettes.

Problem 22-6B   *Comprehensive accounting treatment of manufacturing transactions* (*L.O. 1, 3, 4, 5, 6*)

Income from operations $42,020

Monarch Accessories manufactures specialized parts used in its business. Initially, the company manufactured the parts for its own use, but it gradually began selling them to other companies as well. Monarch's trial balance on April 1, the beginning of the current fiscal year, follows.

April 1 balances in the subsidiary ledgers:

Materials ledger: Steel, $1,580; Petrochemicals, $2,810; Electronic parts, $1,960; Indirect materials, $430.

Chapter 22   Manufacturing Accounting and Job Order Costing   **1039**

Work in process ledger: Job 145, $35,880.

Finished goods ledger: Transformers, $5,310; Transmissions lines, $4,780; Switches, $8,870.

Monarch Accessories
Trial Balance
April 1, 19XX

Cash	$ 19,160	
Accounts receivable	74,290	
Inventories:		
Materials	6,780	
Work in process	35,880	
Finished goods	18,960	
Plant assets	244,570	
Accumulated depreciation		$103,680
Accounts payable		26,770
Wages payable		3,670
Common stock		120,000
Retained earnings		145,520
Sales revenue		—
Cost of goods sold	—	
Factory wages	—	
Factory overhead	—	
Marketing and general expenses	—	
	$399,640	$399,640

April transactions are summarized as follows:

(a) Materials purchased on credit: Steel, $5,540; Petrochemicals, $9,690; Electronic parts, $15,830; Indirect materials, $3,590.

(b) Materials used in production (requisitioned):
Job 145: Steel, $340, Petrochemicals, $1,770.
Job 146: Steel, $3,570, Petrochemicals, $5,720; Electronic parts, $3,980.
Job 147: Steel, $1,970, Petrochemicals, $3,610; Electronic parts, $3,730.
Indirect materials, $2,380.

(c) Factory wages incurred during April, $31,930, of which $30,520 was paid. Wages payable at March 31 were paid during April, $3,670.

(d) Labor time tickets for the month: Job 145, $3,000; Job 146, $12,050; Job 147, $9,940; Indirect labor, $6,940.

(e) Factory overhead incurred on account, $4,630.

(f) Depreciation recorded on factory plant and equipment, $3,450.

(g) Payments on account, $36,040.

(h) Factory overhead applied at the budgeted rate of 70 percent of direct labor.

(i) Jobs completed during the month: Job 145, two transformers at total cost of $43,090; Job 146, 200 switches at total cost of $33,755.

(j) Marketing and general expenses paid, $27,470.

(k) Credit sales on account: All of Job 145 for $97,640 (cost $43,090); Job 146, 120 switches for $35,100 (cost, $20,253).

(l) Collections on account, $127,470.

Required

1. Open T-accounts for the general ledger, the materials ledger, the work in process ledger, and the finished goods ledger. Insert each account balance as given, and use the reference *Bal.*

2. Record the April transactions directly in the accounts, using the letters as references. Monarch has a perpetual inventory system.

3. Prepare a trial balance at April 30 of the current year.

4. Prepare a multiple-step income statement through income from operations for April of the current year, assuming any balance in Factory Overhead is insignificant. Take amounts directly from the trial balance, and report cost of goods sold as a single amount.

Problem 22-7B *Using a manufacturing system to account for overhead cost* (L.O. 4, 5, 6)

Cost of goods sold $187,900

Selected accounts of Waltham Quartz Products follow.

Accounts Receivable

Nov. 1	Balance	28,900	Nov. 30	Collections		254,600
30	Sales	(1)				

Materials Inventory

Nov. 1	Balance	8,400	Nov. 30	Requisitions		(2)
30	Purchases	41,700				

Work in Process Inventory

Nov. 1	Balance	24,600	Nov. 30	Jobs completed		(5)
30	Direct materials	(3)				
30	Direct labor	68,000				
30	Factory overhead	(4)				

Finished Goods Inventory

Nov. 1	Balance	101,200	Nov. 30	Jobs sold		(7)
30	Jobs completed	(6)				

Factory Overhead

Nov. 30	Costs incurred: indirect materials of $9,000, indirect labor, etc. Total amount	75,200	Nov. 1	Balance		1,100
			30	Applied at rate of 110% of direct labor cost		(8)

Cost of Goods Sold

Nov. 30	Jobs sold	(9)	

Sales Revenue

		Nov. 30	Sales	(10)

Selected balances at Nov. 30 are

Accounts receivable.................	$31,400
Materials inventory	10,100
Work in process inventory	21,900
Finished goods inventory	89,800

1. Determine the amounts of the numbered items in the accounts.
2. a. Was factory overhead under- or overapplied at November 1?
   b. What is the November 30 balance in Factory Overhead? Is factory overhead under- or overapplied at November 30?
   c. Assume November 30 is the end of the company's fiscal year. Give the year-end entry to close the Factory Overhead account depending on whether the November 30 balance is significant or insignificant. You must make this judgment.

Extending Your Knowledge

Decision Problems

No check figure

1. Costing and Pricing for Identical Orders   (L.O. 3, 4, 5, 6)

Davison Chocolate Ltd. is located in Indianapolis. The company prepares gift boxes of chocolates as favors for private parties and corporate promotions. Each order contains a selection of chocolates determined by the customer, and the box is designed according to the customer's specifications.

One of Davison's largest customers is the Andrews and Ng law firm. This organization sends chocolates to its clients each Christmas and also provides them at firm gatherings. The law firm's managing partner, Peter Andrews, placed the client gift order in September for 500 boxes of cream-filled dark chocolates. However, Andrews and Ng did not organize its December staff party until the last week of November. This order for an additional 100 boxes is identical to the ones to be distributed to the clients.

The cost per box for the original 500-box order was estimated as follows:

Chocolate, filling, wrappers, box	$14.00
Employee time to fill and wrap the box (10 min.)	1.00
Factory overhead	.50
Total manufacturing cost	$15.50

Because Andrews and Ng is such a good customer, Joan Davison, the president of Davison Chocolate Ltd., priced the order at $17.00 per box.

In the past few months Davison Chocolate Ltd. has experienced price increases for both dark chocolate and employee time. All other costs have remained the same. The cost per box for the second order is estimated to be

Chocolate, filling, wrappers, box	$15.00
Employee time to fill and wrap the box (10 min.)	1.10
Factory overhead	.55
Total manufacturing cost	$16.65

Required

1. Do you agree with the cost analysis for the second order? Explain your answer.
2. Should the two orders be accounted for as one job or two in Davison Chocolate Ltd.'s system?
3. What selling price per box should Joan Davison set for the second order? What are the advantages and disadvantages of this price?

2. *Using Cost Data to Price a New Product*   (L.O. 4, 5, 6)

Interstate Communication, Inc., is experimenting with a new process for manufacturing special telephone equipment in an attempt to lower the cost and sale price of its products. The goal is to capture a larger share of the telephone equipment market. The new process uses laser technology that decreases the amount of raw material needed to make a telephone. The *current* manufacturing process requires the following inputs per 1,000 telephones:

Direct materials:		
Material A	20 lbs. @ $ 11	
Material B....................	130 lbs. @ 9	
Material C	8 lbs. @ 106	
Direct labor:		
Fabricating	80 hrs. @ $ 10	
Assembling	20 hrs. @ 12	
Testing	50 hrs. @ 13	
Factory overhead @ 150% of direct labor cost		

The *new technology* would decrease the amounts of material A by 20 percent and of material C by 40 percent. It would also require three pounds of material D, which costs $22 per pound. Fabricating and testing would require 10 percent less time, but purchase of the laser machine would increase overhead to 175 percent of direct labor cost.

Interstate sells its products for 60 percent above cost but would need to increase this margin to 65 percent for telephone equipment manufactured by the new process to compensate for the lower selling price. Market analysis shows that customer demand for telephones is extremely sensitive to price. Interstate personnel believe any sale price reduction more than 50 cents per telephone will increase sales volume enough to warrant using the new production process.

Required

Compute the current selling price of a telephone and the price of a telephone using the laser technology to decide whether to proceed with the new process. Make a recommendation to the company.

Ethical Issue

North Carolina has the greatest concentration of furniture manufacturers in the United States. These companies dominate furniture sales in the southeastern United States. To break into this market, Ramirez Furniture Company is considering several options. Under one plan, Ramirez would charge no overhead cost to products destined for the southeastern market. This would enable Ramirez to offer its furniture at lower prices than its competitors charge.

Required

1. Is Ramirez's pricing strategy ethical? Discuss.
2. Can Ramirez expect to follow this strategy indefinitely? Give your reason.

Chapter 23

Process Costing, Activity-Based Costing, and Joint Products

The Fleming Company, managed by Jim Fleming, mass-produces furniture in Kingsport, Tennessee. Assume its main customers are Sears and J. C. Penney. Like many other businesses, its competitive advantage depends on producing an affordable product. Jim Fleming is shaking his head over the cost report he has just received—another set of what he believes are nonsense figures. The data show that stained-and-lacquered tables bear four times the overhead that painted tables do. He knows that stained-and-lacquered dining tables sell for $80 each and a painted table goes for $20, but the allocation of overhead does not seem reasonable. Fleming charges into the accounting department. "Why is it that a lacqured table bears four times the overhead cost that a painted table bears?" he asks.

"Simple," replies Andrea Domini, the cost accountant. "Production of a lacquered table requires one hour of direct labor. A painted table takes 15 minutes. We allocate overhead based on direct labor hours."

Fleming returns to his office, muttering, "I don't care what she says. A better table does not consume four times as much overhead as a cheaper one. There must be a better way to determine the cost of making furniture."

This situation illustrates how cost accounting procedures can fail to serve their intended purpose. The chapter section on activity-based costing describes how to address this problem.

Job order costing and process costing are the two major accounting systems for determining the costs of products. Chapter 22 discussed job order costing. This chapter explains process costing. It also covers the related subjects of activity-based costing and accounting for joint products and byproducts.

Process Costing: An Overview

The major difference between job order product costing described in the preceding chapter and process product costing is the type of products that are the objects of costing. Job order costing and process costing are the ends of a spectrum.

For specific units or small batch of custom-made products   **For mass production of like units**

Job order costing systems   **Process product costing systems**

Exhibit 23-1 compares job order costing and process costing. **Process costing** is a system for assigning costs to goods that are mass-produced in a continuous sequence of steps called *processes*. Companies in manufacturing industries—chemicals, petroleum, cosmetics, food, and beverages, for example—use process costing systems. Each of several departments is responsible for one specific process, although a single department may perform more than one process.

In the manufacturing process, the physical form of the product often changes as it passes from one process to another (and so from one department to another). For example, corn flake cereal starts as raw corn. The corn is cleaned and cooked before being packaged as corn flakes and shipped for sale to consumers. A company that produces corn flakes—like Kellogg's or General Mills—may have one department for cleaning, one department for cooking, and one department for packaging.

A mass-production manufacturing process produces large numbers of identical units—boxes of cereal, gallons of paint, and cases of Coca-Cola. In contrast, a job system produces custom goods. In a process system the flow of goods through the factory is continuous and repetitive. Job cost records are not used. Instead, cost is accumulated in each department for a week or a month. At the end of the period, total manufacturing cost is the sum of the costs added in the processing departments. Unit cost is computed by dividing total manufacturing cost by the number of units produced. For example, if it

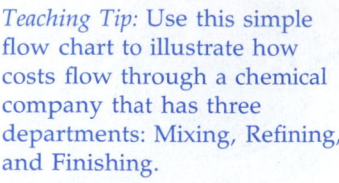

EXHIBIT 23-1 *Comparison of Process Costing and Job Order Costing*

Job–Order Costing: Examples include aircraft, construction, furniture, auditing, repairing, and jewelry

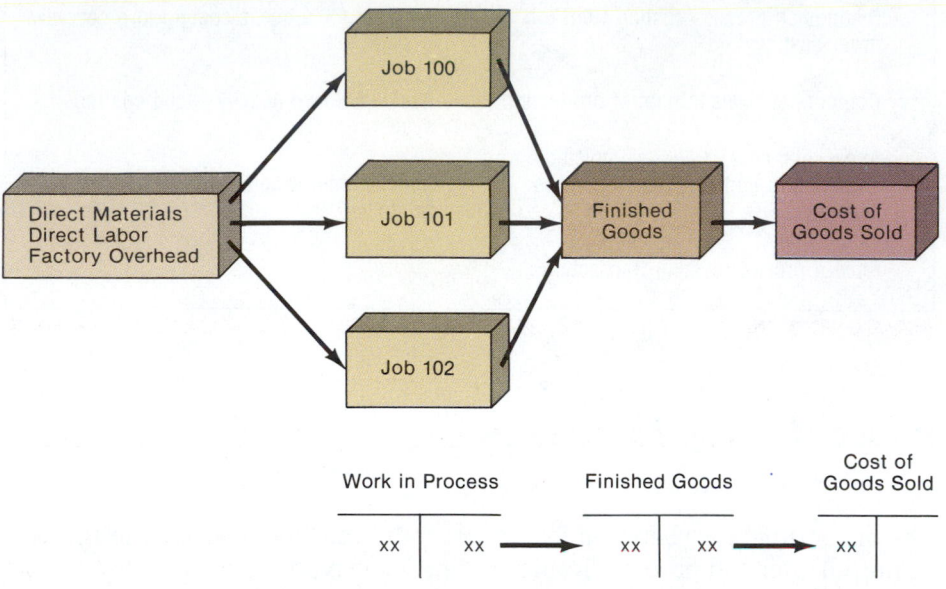

Teaching Tip: Use this simple flow chart to illustrate how costs flow through a chemical company that has three departments: Mixing, Refining, and Finishing.

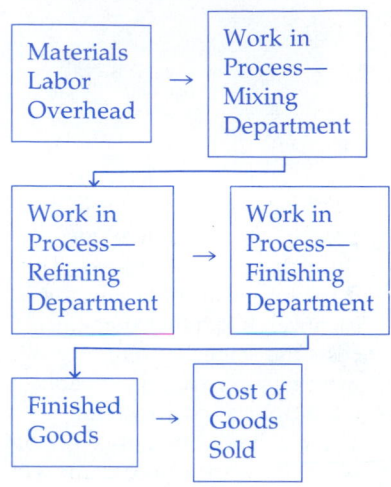

Process Costing: Examples include flour, glass, paint, paper, and silicon wafers

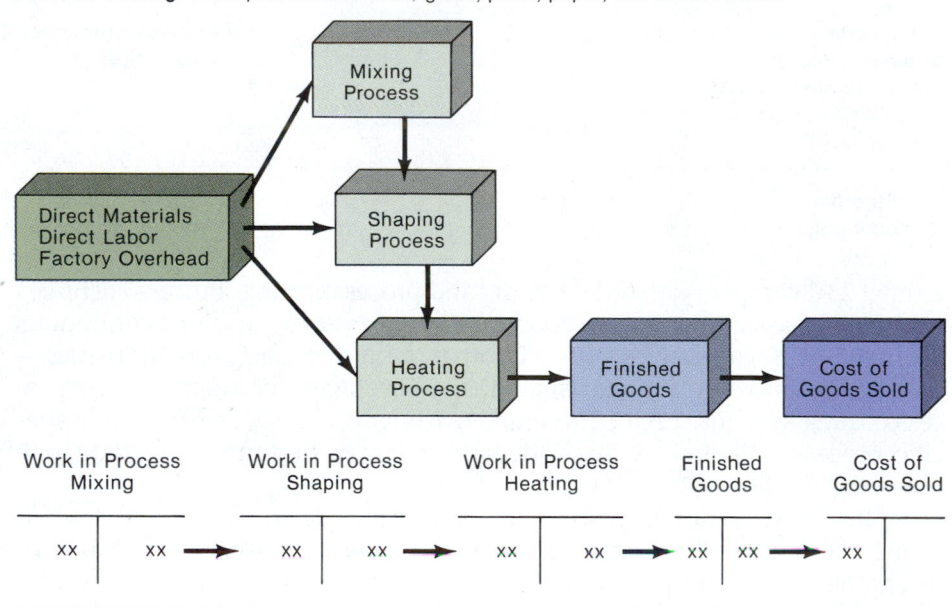

Transparency T 23-1

cost $600,000 to produce 150,000 units during July, unit cost is $4.00 ($600,000/ 150,000 units).

Consider a manufacturing company that produces its goods in three steps. The business mixes materials to produce ceramic blocks, shapes the blocks into figurines, and heats the figures for hardness. The company has a Mixing Department, a Shaping Department, and a Heating Department. To account for the costs that make up the finished products, accountants use three work in process inventory accounts—one for mixing, one for shaping, and one for heating. Exhibit 23-1 shows the flow of costs in this three-step process.

Point to Stress: There will be a work in process inventory account for each department.

Note in the exhibit that mixing costs accumulate in the Work in Process Inventory—Mixing account. After mixing is completed, the blocks are transferred to the Shaping Department, and so are the costs. When shaping has been completed, product costs flow to Work in Process—Heating and then on to Finished Goods Inventory. When the figurines are sold, the cost of the inventory is transferred into Cost of Goods Sold. For comparison, the exhibit also diagrams the flow of costs through a job order costing system, which has only one Work in Process Inventory account.

Exhibit 23-2 uses dollar amounts to illustrate costs flowing through a process system. Each Work in Process account lists direct materials, direct labor, and factory overhead.

You will notice that each of the Work in Process accounts has a nonzero ending balance. Why? Because the manufacturing process is ongoing. No department ever sits idle. At any time, the Mixing Department will be carrying on its function while the Shaping Department and the Heating Department are handling their tasks. Before the Mixing Department ships off the most recent batch of ceramic blocks, it has already begun preparing the next batch. In Exhibit 23-2, we see that the Mixing Department has forwarded goods costing $10,000 to the Shaping Department. At the start of the next period, the Mixing Department is working on goods costing $2,000, which are left over from the preceding period.

Teaching Tip: Conversion cost is merely a grouping of direct labor and factory overhead costs into one classification. Conversion cost represents the cost to convert direct materials into a completed product.

EXHIBIT 23-2 *Flow of Costs Through a Process Costing System (amounts in thousands)*   Transparency T 23-2

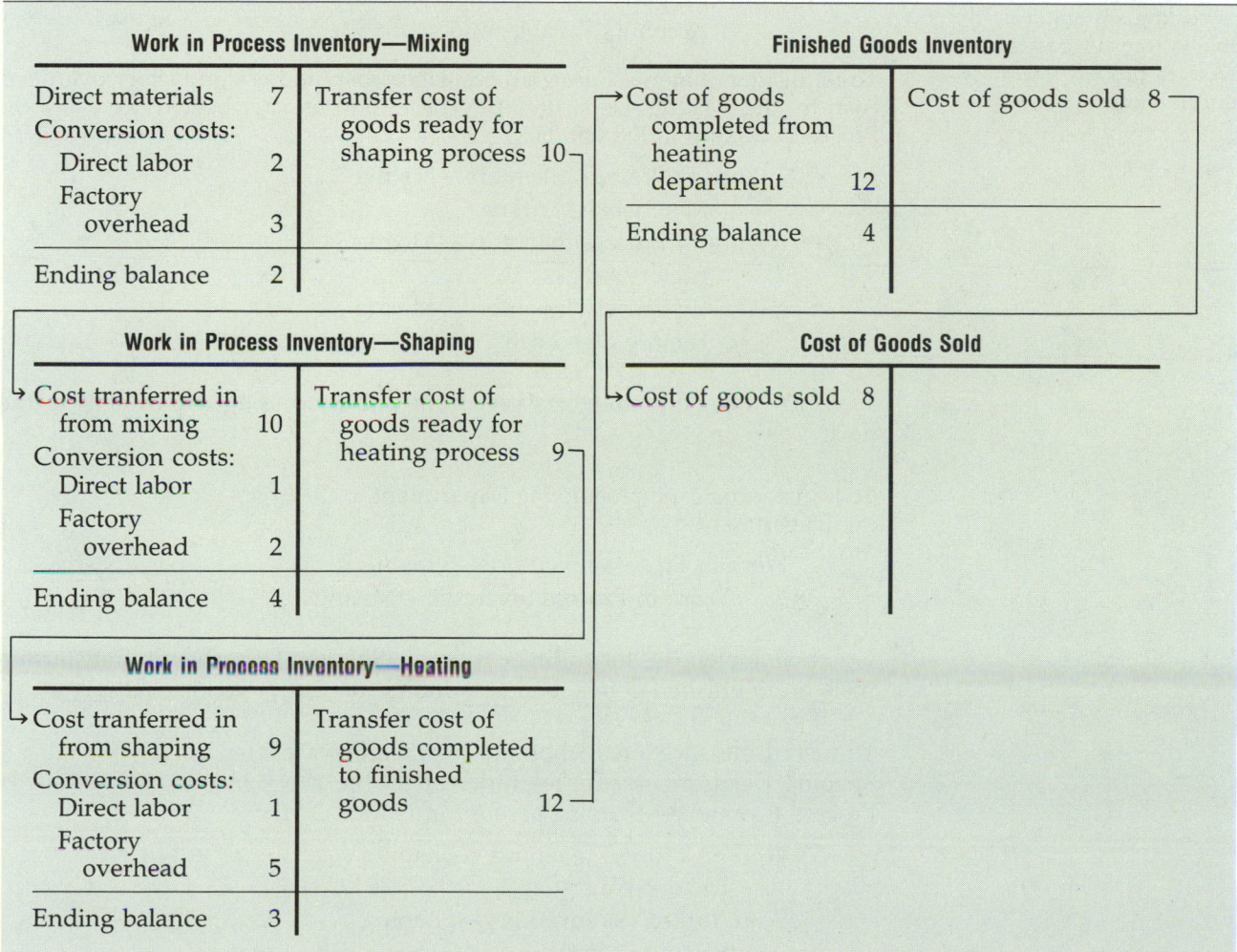

Likewise, as the Shaping Department is completing one batch of figurines, it may be starting to shape a second batch. Since any department at any time will be engaged in the manufacturing process, its Work in Process Inventory account will carry a nonzero balance.

Recording Costs

The journal entries for a process cost accounting system are like those for a job order costing system. That is, direct materials, direct labor, and factory overhead are recorded as follows (all amounts are in thousands and assumed for illustrative purposes):

To purchase materials and incur direct labor and factory overhead:

Materials Inventory	11	
Accounts Payable		11
Factory Wages	3	
Wages Payable		3
Factory Overhead	5	
Accumulated Depreciation		1
Property Tax Payable		1
Accounts Payable, and so on		3

To requisition materials, assign direct labor cost, and assign factory overhead cost to the Mixing Department. (These entries are posted to Work in Process—Mixing in Exhibit 23-2):

Work in Process Inventory—Mixing	7	
Materials Inventory		7
Work in Process Inventory—Mixing	2	
Factory Wages		2
Work in Process Inventory—Mixing	3	
Factory Overhead		3

The following entry transfers cost from one processing department to the next:

To transfer cost from the Mixing Department to the Shaping Department:

Work in Process Inventory—Shaping	10	
Work in Process Inventory—Mixing		10

Remaining entries for adding cost in the Shaping Department, transferring costs on to finished goods, and accounting for cost of goods sold follow.

To record the additional labor and overhead cost of the Shaping Department. (These entries affect the Work in Process Inventory—Shaping account in Exhibit 23-2.)

Work in Process Inventory—Shaping	1	
Factory Wages		1
Work in Process Inventory—Shaping	2	
Factory Overhead		2

Entries for the Heating Department parallel those for the Shaping Department.

To transfer cost of goods completed from the Heating
Department to Finished Goods:

Finished Goods Inventory	12	
Work in Process Inventory—Heating		12

To account for the cost of goods sold:

Cost of Goods Sold	8	
Finished Goods Inventory		8

Unlike a job order costing system, a process costing system is likely to have a separate work in process account for each processing department. In a job order system the work in process account is supported by job cost records for the various jobs.

Conversion Costs

Conversion costs are all manufacturing costs other than direct materials costs. The preceding chapter provided the usual major distinctions among manufacturing costs: the threefold category of direct materials, direct labor, and indirect manufacturing costs (factory overhead). This time-honored threefold category still dominates practice, but not as much as it once did. Why? Because many companies, particularly those using process costing and automation, have seen direct labor costs become less and less important in relation to total manufacturing costs. A twofold category is often used:

Direct materials
Conversion costs

In many companies direct labor has vanished as a major cost category. It has become merely an element of conversion costs. This reduces accounting expense by eliminating the elaborate tracking of labor cost.

Tracing the Flow of Costs

In process costing, the accounting task is to trace the flow of costs through the production process. This task has two parts. First, we must account for the cost of goods that have been completed in one department and sent to the second department. Second, we must account for the cost of incomplete units, which remain within a department.

Let's look at a sports company that manufactures swim masks. This company's Shaping Department shapes the body of the swim masks. The direct material is the plastic that is formed into the masks. The partially completed masks then move to the Finishing Department, where the clear faceplate is inserted in the body and sealed in place.

Assume that during October, the Shaping Department incurs the following costs in processing 50,000 masks:

Direct materials		$140,000
Conversion costs:		
Direct labor	$21,250	
Factory overhead	46,750	68,000
Costs to account for		$208,000

If the shaping process is complete for all 50,000 masks, the costs to be transferred to Work in Process Inventory—Finishing are the full $208,000. The unit cost is $4.16 ($208,000/50,000 units). But suppose that shaping is complete for only 40,000 units. At October 31 the Shaping Department still has 10,000 masks in process. How do we compute unit cost when the total cost applies to finished units *and* unfinished units? Accountants answer this question by using the concept of *equivalent units of production.*

Equivalent Units of Production

Equivalent units of production—often called simply equivalent units—is a measure of the number of complete units that *could* have been manufactured from start to finish using the costs incurred during the period.

Let's assume that the 10,000 unfinished units still in the Shaping Department are one-quarter complete. The number of equivalent units equals the number of partially complete units times the percentage of completion: 10,000 units × 25% complete = 2,500 units regarding conversion costs. The number 2,500 tells us how many whole units are represented by the partially complete units. We add the 2,500 units to the number of finished units—40,000—to arrive at the period's equivalent units of production regarding conversion costs: 42,500.

The idea of equivalent units is not confined to manufacturing situations. It is a basic common denominator for measuring activities, output, and workload. For example, colleges and universities measure student enrollments in "full-time equivalents." Suppose a full-time class load is 12 hours per term. Assume 1,000 students are taking a full load and an additional 1,000 students are taking an average of 6 hours in classes. This school has a full-time equivalent enrollment of 1,500 students [$1,000 + (1,000 × 6/12)$].

Steps in Process Cost Accounting

Using the data from the swim mask example, we will discuss the five-step application of process costing.

Step 1: Summarize the Flow of Production in Physical Units

The left part of Exhibit 23-3 tabulates the movement of swim masks into and out of the Shaping Department. We assume for clarity that work began October 1, so the Work in Process account had no balance at September 30.

Step 2: Compute Output in Terms of Equivalent Units of Production

Cost accountants compute equivalent units separately for the two types of costs incurred in manufacturing: direct materials and conversion costs. The Shaping Department has 10,000 units unfinished at October 31. We assume that all direct materials have been added (the chemicals have been added to begin shaping the bodies of the swimming masks) but that three-quarters of the conversion costs (direct labor and factory overhead) remain to be applied. Thus all 50,000 units are finished in terms of direct material. We must compute equivalent units for the conversion costs. Since 25 percent of conversion costs

Shaping Department
For the Month Ended October 31, 19XX

	Step 1	Step 2 Equivalent Units of Production	
Flow of Production	**Flow of Physical Units**	**Direct Materials**	**Conversion Costs**
Units to account for:			
Work in process, September 30	—		
Started production during October	50,000		
Total physical units to account for	50,000		
Units accounted for:			
Completed and transferred out during October	40,000	40,000	40,000
Work in process, October 31	10,000	10,000	2,500*
Total physical units accounted for	50,000		
Equivalent units of production		50,000	42,500

*10,000 units each 25% complete = 2,500 equivalent units

have already been added, we multiply the 10,000 unfinished units by .25, which gives us 2,500 units. Added to the 40,000 finished units, the equivalent units for conversion costs come to 42,500.

Exhibit 23-3 combines the data for Step 1 and Step 2. Note that the number of equivalent units for direct materials and conversion costs are different. This is often the case.

	Equiv. Units	
ANSWER:	**Dir. Mtls.**	**Conv. Costs**
Trans.	4,500	4,500
WIP, May 31	225	50
Equiv. units	4,725	4,550

Step 3: Summarize Total Costs to Account For

Exhibit 23-4 summarizes the total costs to account for in the Shaping Department (cost data are assumed). These costs are the total debits in Work in Process Inventory—Shaping, including any beginning balance. The Shaping Department has 50,000 units and $208,000 of costs to account for.

Shaping Department
For the Month Ended October 31, 19XX

Work in Process–Shaping

	Physical Units	*Dollars*		*Physical Units*	*Dollars*
Inventory, September 30	-0-	$ -0-	Transferred out	40,000	$?
Production started:	50,000		Ending inventory	10,000	?
Direct materials		140,000	Total accounted for	50,000	
Conversion costs:					
Direct labor		21,250			
Factory overhead		46,750			
Total to account for	50,000	$208,000			

Serial Class Exercise No. 2: Using the information from the previous exercise, compute the unit cost in the mixing department.

ANSWER:

	Dir. Mtls.	Conv. Cost
WIP, 5/1	$ -0-	$ -0-
Costs added during May	15,120	27,755
÷equiv. units	÷4,725	÷4,550
Cost per equiv. unit	$ 3.20	$ 6.10

OBJECTIVE 3

Apply total cost to units completed and units in ending work in process inventory

OBJECTIVE 4

Record process costing transactions

Serial Class Exercise No. 3: Compute the total costs of units completed and ending work in process.

ANSWER:

	Direct Materials	Conversion Costs
Trans. (4,500)	4,500 × $9.30 = $41,850	
Ending WIP(500)		
Direct Mtls.	225 × $3.20 = $720	
Conv. costs		50 × $6.10 = $305
Total WIP		1,025
Total acc. for =		$42,875
($41,850 + $1,025 = $42,875)		

Point to Stress: Note in Exercise 3 above that "Total cost accounted for" of $42,875 agrees with the amount in Exercise 2 for "Total costs added during May." You must account for all manufacturing costs.

Transparency T23-5

Step 4: Compute Equivalent-Unit Costs

In Step 2 we computed the number of equivalent units for direct materials (50,000) and conversion costs (42,500). Because their equivalent units differ, a separate cost per unit must be computed for materials cost and for conversion costs. Exhibit 23-4 provides the data. The direct materials cost is $140,000. Conversion costs are $68,000, the sum of direct labor ($21,250) and factory overhead ($46,750).

We now have all the data needed to apply process costing in this example. We divide the direct materials cost by the equivalent units for direct materials: $140,000/50,000 = $2.80. The $2.80 is the unit price for direct materials. We compute unit price for conversion cost in a similar manner: $68,000/42,500 = $1.60. Exhibit 23-5 shows the computation of equivalent-unit costs.

Step 5: Apply Total Cost to Units Completed and to Units in Ending Work in Process Inventory

Exhibit 23-6 shows how the unit costs computed in Step 4 are applied to units completed and to units in ending work in process. With Step 5 we account for the cost of the shaping process during the period.

The 40,000 units completed and transferred out of the shaping department bear a unit cost of $4.40 (direct materials of $2.80 + conversion cost of $1.60). The 10,000 units still in process at the end of the period have 10,000 equivalent units of *direct materials* (at $2.80 per unit) and 2,500 equivalent units of *conversion cost* (at $1.60 per unit). Observe that the sum of these two unit costs ($2.80 and $1.60) is the same as total unit cost of the completed units ($4.40), from Step 4. Also, total cost accounted for ($208,000) must agree with the total from Step 3.

October production in the Shaping Department would be recorded thus:

To requisition materials and apply labor and overhead cost to the Shaping Department. (Exhibit 23-4)

Work in Process Inventory—Shaping...............	140,000	
Materials Inventory		140,000
Work in Process Inventory—Shaping...............	21,250	
Factory Wages...............................		21,250
Work in Process Inventory—Shaping...............	46,750	
Factory Overhead............................		46,750

The entry to transfer the cost of completed units from the Shaping Department to the Finishing Department is given below Exhibit 23-6.

EXHIBIT 23-5 *Step 4: Computation of Equivalent-Unit Costs*

Shaping Department
For the Month Ended October 31, 19XX

	Direct Materials	Conversion Costs	Total
Work in process, September 30...........	$ -0-	$ -0-	$ -0-
Costs added during October	$140,000	$ 68,000	$208,000
Divide by equivalent units of production ..	÷50,000	÷42,500	
Cost per equivalent unit	$ 2.80 +	$ 1.60	= $ 4.40

Shaping Department
For the Month Ended October 31, 19XX

	Direct Materials	Conversion Costs	Total
Units completed and transferred out (40,000)	40,000 × $4.40		= $176,000
Units in ending work in process inventory (10,000):			
Direct materials	10,000 × $2.80		= 28,000
Conversion costs		2,500 × $1.60 =	4,000
Total cost of work in process			32,000
Total cost accounted for..			$208,000

Work in Process Inventory—Finishing..............	176,000	
Work in Process Inventory—Shaping		176,000

After these entries are posted, the Work in Process Inventory—Shaping account appears as follows:

Work in Process Inventory—Shaping

Balance, September 30	—	Transferred to Finishing	176,000
Direct materials	140,000		
Direct labor	21,250		
Factory overhead	46,750		
Balance, October 31	32,000		

With Shaping Department costs accounted for, we proceed to the Finishing Department. First, however, let's reinforce what you have learned with a Summary Problem for Your Review.

Teaching Tip: Look at Exhibit 23-6. The $176,000 is the cost of the units transferred to the next department. You will see that number again when the finishing department is discussed. The $32,000 is the cost of the ending work in process inventory for the shaping department.

Serial Class Exercise No. 4: (1) Prepare journal entries summarizing these transactions, and (2) prepare the T-account for the work in process account. (Answer on p. 1055.)

Summary Problem for Your Review

Identify the missing amounts X and Y in the following production cost report prepared by Jacobs-Webster, Inc., for May:

Assembly Department
Production Cost Report
For the Month Ended May 31, 19XX

	Physical Units	Total Costs
Work in process, April 30	—	$ —
Started in production during May	20,000	43,200*
Total to account for	20,000	$43,200
Completed and transferred to Finishing Department during May	16,000	$ X
Work in process, May 31 (25% complete as to direct materials, 55% complete as to conversion cost)	4,000	Y
Total accounted for	20,000	$43,200

*Includes direct materials of $6,800 and conversion costs of $36,400.

SOLUTION TO REVIEW PROBLEM

Step 1: Flow of Production in Physical Units;
Step 2: Equivalent Units of Production

Assembly Department
For the Month Ended May 31, 19XX

| | Step 1 | Step 2 Equivalent Units of Production | |
| | Flow of Physical Units | Direct Materials | Conversion Costs |
Flow of Production			
Units to account for:			
Work in process, April 30....................	—		
Started production during May....................	20,000		
Total physical units to account for..............	20,000		
Units accounted for:			
Completed and transferred out during May........	16,000	16,000	16,000
Work in process, May 31	4,000	1,000*	2,200*
Total physical units accounted for	20,000		
Equivalent units of production		17,000	18,200

*Direct materials: 4,000 units each 25% complete = 1,000 equivalent units
Conversion costs: 4,000 units each 55% complete = 2,200 equivalent units

Step 3: Summary of Total Costs to Account For

Assembly Department
For the Month Ended May 31, 19XX

Work in Process—Assembly

	Physical Units	Dollars
Inventory, April 30	-0-	$ -0-
Production started:	20,000	
Direct materials		6,800
Conversion costs		36,400
Total to account for	20,000	$43,200

Step 4: Computation of Equivalent-Unit Costs

Assembly Department
For the Month Ended May 31, 19XX

	Direct Materials	Conversion Costs	Total
Work in process, April 30	$ -0-	$ -0-	$ -0-
Costs added during May................	$ 6,800	$ 36,400	43,200
Divide by equivalent units of production	÷17,000	÷18,200	
Cost per equivalent unit	$.40 +	$2.00 =	$2.40

Assembly Department
For the Month Ended May 31, 19XX

		Direct Materials	Conversion Costs	Total
X	Units completed and transferred out (16,000)	16,000 × $2.40		= $38,400
	Units in ending work in process inventory (4,000):			
	Direct materials	1,000 × $.40		= 400
	Conversion costs		2,200 × $2.00 =	4,400
Y	Total cost of work in process			4,800
	Total cost accounted for			$43,200

Process Costing Extended to a Second Department

Most manufacturing systems include multiple processing steps. In this section, we introduce a second processing department to complete the picture of process costing. We continue with the manufacture of swim masks. The Finishing Department adds the faceplate and sealant to the shaped swim masks. The faceplate is the direct material added in the finishing process. It is important to keep in mind that *direct materials* in the Finishing Department refers to the faceplates added *in that department* and not to the materials (the chemicals) added in the previous Shaping Department. Likewise, *conversion cost* in the Finishing Department refers to all manufacturing costs (other than direct materials) of that department only.

We assume 5,000 units were in process in the Finishing Department on October 1. These units were 60 percent complete as to Finishing Department conversion costs but 0 percent complete as to direct materials because the faceplates are added near the end of the finishing process. These facts, used throughout discussion of the accounting for the Finishing Department, are summarized in Exhibit 23-7. (Refer to Exhibit 23-6, page 1056.)

Equivalent Units in a Second Department

The major accounting task in dealing with a second department is the computation of equivalent units. Exhibit 23-8 summarizes the flow of physical units (Step 1) in order to compute the equivalent units of production (Step 2) for the Finishing Department. Note that there are three categories of equivalent units. In addition to equivalent units for *direct materials* and *conversion costs* added in the Finishing Department, we must also compute equivalent units for those units that were *transferred in* from the preceding department. Whenever there is a second department, it will always have units and costs transferred in from the preceding department. In our illustration, 40,000 units were transferred into the Finishing Department during October. Of these transferred-in units, 33,000 units were completed, and 7,000 units remained in ending inventory. For transferred-in costs, equivalent units include the full total (33,000 + 7,000 = 40,000).

ANSWER:

a. To requisition materials:

WIP Inventory—Mixing .	15,120	
Materials Inventory		15,120

b. To apply labor:

WIP Inventory—Mixing .	11,102	
Factory Wages		11,102

c. To apply overhead:

WIP Inventory—Mixing .	16,653	
Factory Overhead		16,653

d. To transfer the cost of completed units from the Mixing Department to the Packaging Department:

WIP Inventory— Packaging	41,850	
WIP Inventory— Mixing		41,850

Work in Process Inventory—Mixing

Bal., May 1	-0-	Trans. to	
Dir. mtls.	15,120	Packaging	41,850
Dir. labor	11,102		
Factory OH	16,653		
Bal., May 31	1,025		

Point to Stress: Direct materials refers to the materials added in a specific department and not to any direct materials added in another department.

Point to Stress: The FIFO cost method is used in process costing, which means that the beginning work in process will not be combined with the costs transferred in during the period in determining unit costs.

Serial Class Exercise No. 5: We will continue to use the facts from the previous class exercises to illustrate how costs flow into a second processing department, the Packaging Department. Below is a chart of facts concerning the Packaging Department.

Units:
WIP, May 1 (100% complete as to direct mtls.; 50% complete as to conv. costs)   4,000
Trans. in from Mixing Dept. during May   4,500
Completed during May   7,000
WIP, May 31 (80% complete as to dir. mtls.; 40% complete as to conv. costs)   1,500

Costs:
WIP, May 1 $43,100
Trans. in from Mixing Dept. during May   41,850
Dir. mtls. added—May   1,890
Conv. costs added-May
    Dir. labor $10,800
    Factory OH $ 4,600   15,400
Total cost to acc. for $102,240

Compute the equivalent units.

EXHIBIT 23-7 Finishing Department Facts for October

Units:		
Work in process, September 30 (0% complete as to direct materials, 60% complete as to conversion costs)		5,000 units
Transferred in from Shaping Department during October		40,000 units
Completed during October		38,000 units
Work in process, October 31 (0% complete as to direct materials, 30% complete as to conversion costs)		7,000 units
Costs:		
Work in process, September 30		$ 24,000
Transferred in from Shaping Department during October		176,000
Direct materials added during October		19,000
Conversion costs added during October:		
Direct labor	$ 3,710	
Factory overhead	11,130	14,840

Equivalent units of *direct materials* have three components: beginning work in process inventory, units transferred in and completed during the month, and ending work in process inventory. Exhibit 23-7 indicates that beginning inventory contained 5,000 units that were 0 percent complete as to direct materials. The first-in, first-out (FIFO) method is employed in Exhibit 23-7 in accounting for work in process inventories. Under FIFO, the computation of equivalent units is confined to the work done during the current period— October in this example. Therefore, the $24,000 beginning balance is kept separate from the costs added during the current period. The $24,000 is *not* included in the computation of the unit costs of equivalent units for the work done in October. The major advantage of the FIFO method is that the efficiency of performance in October can be judged independently from the performance in September. In brief, the work done during the current period is key information for planning and control purposes as well as for FIFO inventory valuation.[1]

Under the FIFO cost method, beginning inventory is completed first. During October the Finishing Department added the faceplates (100 percent of the direct materials that the Finishing Department adds) to complete these 5,000 units. The 33,000 units that were transferred in and completed are automatically part of equivalent units. Ending inventory is 0 percent complete as to direct materials (faceplates have not yet been added). Consequently ending inventory accounts for no equivalent units. Altogether, equivalent production for direct materials is 38,000 units (5,000 units from beginning inventory + 33,000 units transferred in during the month).

Equivalent units of *conversion costs* also have three components: beginning work in process inventory, units transferred in and completed during the month, and ending work in process inventory. The Finishing Department's beginning inventory of 5,000 units was 60 percent complete as to conversion costs when the last period ended. During October the Finishing Department completed these 5,000 units by adding the remaining 40 percent of conversion costs. For beginning inventory, equivalent production is 2,000 units (5,000 × .40). Units transferred in and completed during the month (33,000 units) are

---

[1]Other methods, such as weighted-average cost, can also be used. They are explored in cost accounting textbooks.

Finishing Department
For the Month Ended October 31, 19XX

	Step 1	Step 2 Equivalent Units of Production		
	Flow of Physical Units	Transferred In	Direct Materials	Conversion Costs
Flow of Production				
Units to account for:				
Work in process, September 30	5,000			
Transferred in during October	40,000			
Total physical units to account for	45,000			
Units accounted for:				
Completed and transferred out during October:				
From beginning inventory	5,000	—	5,000*	2,000*
Transferred in and completed during October				
(38,000 − 5,000)	33,000	33,000	33,000	33,000
Work in process, October 31	7,000	7,000	— †	2,100†
Total physical units accounted for	45,000			
Equivalent units of production		40,000	38,000	37,100

*Direct materials: 5,000 units each 100% completed in Finishing Department during October = 5,000 equivalent units.
 Conversion costs: 5,000 units each 40% completed in Finishing Department during October = 2,000 equivalent units.
†Direct materials: 7,000 units each 0% completed in Finishing Department during October = 0 equivalent units.
 Conversion costs: 7,000 units each 30% completed in Finishing Department during October = 2,100 equivalent units.

the second component of equivalent production. Ending inventory is the third component. At October 31 the inventory of 7,000 units still in process in the Finishing Department is 30 percent complete as to conversion costs, so equivalent production includes 2,100 units (7,000 × .30). Altogether, equivalent production for conversion costs totals 37,100 units (2,000 + 33,000 + 2,100). Exhibit 23-8 summarizes the equivalent-unit computations for the Finishing Department.

ANSWER:	Trans. in	Dir. Mtls.	Conv. Costs
Trans. out from beg. inv.	0*	0*	2,000
Trans. in & compl. in May			
(7,000 − 4,000)	3,000	3,000	3,000
WIP, May 31	1,500	1,200	600
Equiv. units	4,500	4,200	5,600

*Since the beginning inventory was 100% complete, no transferred-in costs or materials were added to the beginning inventory.

Equivalent-Unit Costs in a Second Department

The October costs of the Finishing Department are accumulated as shown in Exhibit 23-9. The exhibit shows how equivalent units are used to compute the equivalent-unit costs in the Finishing Department process.

EXHIBIT 23-9   Steps 3 and 4: Computation of Total Costs to Account for and of Equivalent-Unit Costs

Finishing Department
For the Month Ended October 31, 19XX

	Transferred-In Costs	Direct Materials	Conversion Costs	Total
Work in process, September 30 (from Exhibit 23-7)	Work done before October			$ 24,000
Costs added during October (from Exhibit 23-7) . . .	$176,000	$ 19,000	$ 14,840	209,840
Divide by equivalent units (from Exhibit 23-8)	÷40,000	÷38,000	÷37,100	
Cost per equivalent unit	$4.40	$.50	$.40	
Total costs to account for				$233,840

Application of Total Cost in a Second Department

Exhibit 23-10 shows how to apply total cost of the Finishing Department to units completed and transferred to finished goods and to units still in process at the end of the period.

EXHIBIT 23-10 Step 5: Application of Total Cost to Units Completed and Units in Ending Work in Process Inventory

Finishing Department
For the Month Ended October 31, 19XX

	Transferred-In Costs	Direct Materials	Conversion Costs	Total
Units completed and transferred out to Finished Goods Inventory:				
From work in process, September 30:............				$ 24,000
Costs added during October:				
Direct materials............................	—	5,000 × $.50		2,500
Conversion costs	—		2,000 × $.40	800
Total completed from September 30 inventory..				27,300
Units transferred in and completed during				
October...............................	33,000 × ($4.40 + $.50 + $.40)			174,900
Total costs transferred out				202,200
Work in process, October 31:				
Transferred-in costs.........................	7,000 × $4.40			30,800
Direct materials................................		—		—
Conversion costs			2,100 × $.40	840
Total work in process, October 31				31,640
Total cost accounted for				$233,840

Serial Class Exercise No. 6:
Compute the unit costs in the packaging department.

	Trans. In	Dir. Mtls.	Conv. Costs
Costs added, May	$41,850	$1,890	$15,400
÷equiv. units	÷ 4,500	÷ 4,200	÷ 5,600
Cost/equiv. unit	$9.30	$.45	$2.75

The entries for the Shaping Department were recorded on page 1053. The following entries record Finishing Department activity during October.

To transfer in cost of completed units from the Shaping Department (repeat of the last entry in the Shaping Department, page 1053):

Work in Process Inventory—Finishing..............	176,000	
Work in Process Inventory—Shaping		176,000

To requisition materials and apply conversion costs to the Finishing Department (amounts from Exhibit 23-7):

Work in Process Inventory—Finishing..............	19,000	
Materials Inventory		19,000
Work in Process Inventory—Finishing..............	3,710	
Factory Wages.................................		3,710
Work in Process Inventory—Finishing..............	11,130	
Factory Overhead............................		11,130

The entry to transfer the cost of completed units from the Finishing Department to finished goods is based on the dollar amount taken from Exhibit 23-10 and listed on the production report in Exhibit 23-11.

Finished Goods Inventory	202,200	
Work in Process Inventory—Finishing		202,200

After posting, the key accounts appear as follows. Observe the accumulation of costs as debits to Work in Process and the transfer of costs from one account to the next.

Work in Process Inventory—Shaping

(Exhibit 23-4)		(Exhibit 23-6)	
Balance, September 30	—	Transferred to Finishing	176,000
Direct materials	140,000		
Direct labor	21,250		
Factory overhead	46,750		
Balance, October 31	32,000		

Work in Process Inventory—Finishing

(Exhibit 23-7)		(Exhibit 23-10)	
Balance, September 30	24,000	Transferred to finished	
Transferred from Shaping	176,000	goods	202,200
Direct materials	19,000		
Direct labor	3,710		
Factory overhead	11,130		
Balance, October 31	31,640		

Finished Goods Inventory

Balance, September 30	—	
Transferred from Finishing	202,200	

Production Cost Report

A **production cost report** summarizes the operations of a processing department for the period. Exhibit 23-11 is a production cost report for the Finishing Department for October. It shows the department's beginning inventory (5,000 units; cost $24,000), the number of units and the cost transferred in during the month (40,000 units; cost $176,000), and the costs added. These amounts make up the totals to account for. The production report also shows the units completed (38,000), the costs transferred out of the department ($202,200), and the ending inventory (7,000 units; cost $31,640).

ANSWER:
a) Units completed and
   transferred out to FG:

From WIP, May 1	$ 43,100
Costs added—May	
Dir. mtls.	-0- [a]
Conv. costs	5,500[b]
Total completed from	
May 1 inventory	48,600
Units trans. in and	
completed—May	37,500[c]
Total costs trans. out	86,100
b) WIP, May 31	
Trans. in costs	13,950[d]
Dir. mtls.	540[e]
Conv. costs	1,650[f]
Total WIP, May 31	16,140
Total cost acc. for	$102,240

[a]Trans. in costs 0 × $.45
[b]Trans. in costs 2,000 × $2.75
[c]Trans. in costs 3,000 × [$9.30 + $.45 + $2.75]
[d]Trans. in costs 1,500 × $9.30
[e]Dir. mtls. 1,200 × $.45
[f]Conv. costs 600 × $2.75

Serial Class Exercise No. 8: Prepare the journal entries, for Serial Class Exercises 5-7.

1	To requisition materials:		
	WIP Inventory—Pkg.	1,890	
	Materials Inventory		1,890
2	To apply labor:		
	WIP Inventory—Pkg.	10,800	
	Factory Wages		10,800
3	To apply overhead:		
	WIP Inventory—Pkg.	4,600	
	Factory Overhead		4,600
4	To transfer complete units:		
	Finished Goods Inventory .	86,100	
	WIP Inventory—Pkg.		86,100

Point to Stress: The purposes of
the department production cost
report are to show both dollar
amounts of cost and units
transferred into the department
(if any), costs added in the
department (in total and per
unit), and costs and units
transferred out of the
department. Also included is
beginning and ending
inventory information. Data
can be taken from the
production cost report to
prepare monthly journal
entries.

EXHIBIT 23-11 Production Cost Report

**Finishing Department
Production Cost Report
For the Month Ended October 31, 19XX**

	Physical Units	Total Costs
Work in process, September 30	5,000	$ 24,000
Transferred in from Shaping Department during October	40,000	176,000
Cost added in Finishing Department during October:		
Direct materials.....................................	—	19,000
Conversion costs ($3,710 − $11,130)	—	14,840
Total to account for	45,000	$233,840
Completed and transferred to finished goods		
during October	38,000	$202,200
Work in process, October 31	7,000	31,640
Total accounted for	45,000	$233,840

These reports vary from company to company, depending on the level of
detail desired by the managers. If managers want more detail, some or all of
the additional information in Exhibits 23-8, 23-9, and 23-10 can be included.
For example, Exhibit 23-12 provides more detail than Exhibit 23-11.

EXHIBIT 23-12 Production Cost Report (Expanded)

**Finishing Department
Production Cost Report (Expanded)
For the Month Ended October 31, 19XX**

		Transferred-in Costs	Direct Materials	Conversion Costs	Total
	Work in process, September 30				$ 24,000
	Cost added during October	$176,000	$ 19,000	$ 14,840	209,840
(Step 3)	Total costs to account for				$233,840
	Equivalent units for work during October				
	(Steps 1 and 2 in Exhibit 23–8)	÷40,000	÷38,000	÷37,100	
(Step 4)	Cost per equivalent unit	$ 4.40	$ .50	$ .40	
(Step 5)	Application of total costs:				
	From work in process, September 30.............				$ 24,000
	Costs added during October		5,000 × $.50 = $2,500	2,000 × $.40 = $800	3,300
	Total completed from September 30 inventory				27,300
	Units transferred in and completed during October	33,000 × ($4.40 + $.50 + $.40)			174,900
					202,200
	Work in process, October 31:				
	Transferred-in costs	7,000 × $4.40			30,800
	Direct materials		—		—
	Conversion costs			2,100 × $.40	840
	Total work in process, October 31				31,640
	Total costs accounted for.......................				$233,840

How is the production report used for decision making? Managers compare direct materials and conversion costs—particularly the unit costs in Exhibit 23-12—with budgeted amounts for the department. If these costs are too high, corrective action is taken. If costs are below budget, the employees responsible may receive incentive awards.

Managers also compare the number of units produced with budgeted production. Production that is too low can be investigated and corrected. If production in excess of budget is welcomed, such performance may lead to various rewards for responsible employees.

Activity-Based Costing

The description of cost systems in this chapter and the preceding chapter has focused on *product* costing. To maximize long-term profitability, systems should also serve the planning and control purpose. Many managers plan and control business functions by personal observation and with budget and cost systems. These functions are often divided into departments, as described in the first part of the chapter.

This section describes an emerging new approach to cost accounting. A **cost object** can be anything for which it is worthwhile to compile costs, such as an activity (spray-painting), a department (finishing), or a product (a table). **Activity-based costing** (ABC), also called *activity-based accounting*, is a system that focuses on *activities* as the fundamental cost objects and uses the cost of these activities as building blocks for compiling the costs of products and other cost objects. ABC is generic. It can be used in conjunction with a job order costing system or a process costing system that is divided into departments.

If dividing companywide functions into departments helps managers, wouldn't dividing departments into activities further sharpen managers' focus? Exhibit 23-13, Panel A, shows the different functions in a furniture manufacturer's value chain. Panel B divides the manufacturing function into departments, and Panel C lists common activities in a Finishing Department. Note that costs are accumulated for each activity separately. The activity costs are then applied to products as the products move through production. For example, a table's finishing calls for polishing, and the cost of that activity—the polishing—is added to the table. If the table is to be sold as a less-expensive model, the company may not finish it. In this case, the table bears no cost for finishing. Inspection cost and packaging cost are likewise added to the cost of the table as appropriate. *The product cost of a dining table is "built up" from the cost of the specific activities undertaken to manufacture it.*

Exhibit 23-13 shows how cost objects become even more finely granulated, from a particular business function such as manufacturing to departments, including painting and finishing, to activities such as polishing and inspecting. But how do the refinements of ABC translate into better decisions?

Demand for Activity-Based Costing

The chapter-opening situation illustrates manager frustration with a time-honored cost accounting practice—allocating all overhead cost to products based on a single application base such as direct labor. In recent years many managers, such as Jim Fleming in the chapter-opening vignette, and accountants have experienced frustration with their cost accounting systems. Some companies have installed ABC systems, and their number is growing. There are several reasons why managers demand ABC.

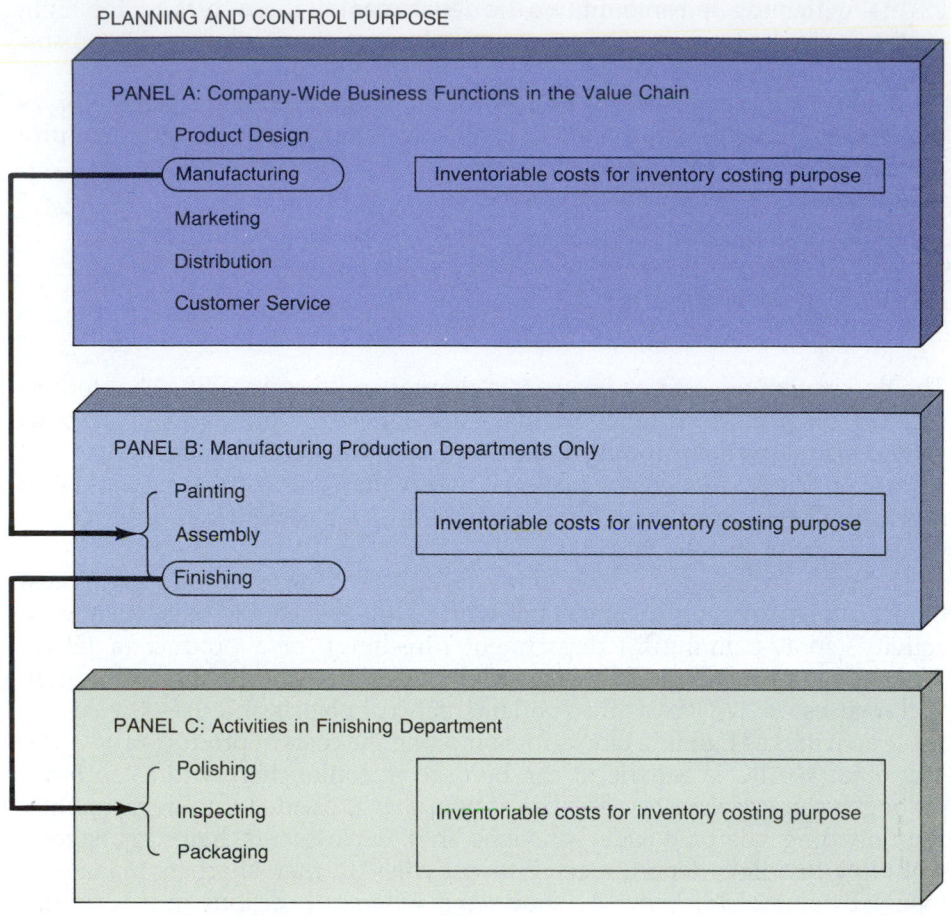

1. Activities in various departments may be combined with activities in other departments. For example, quality control activities occur in several departments. In our illustration, it would be the sum of the inspection costs in the Painting Department, the Assembling Department, and the Finishing Department. Only if detailed records are kept by activities can the total company cost of quality control (or any other activity) be used by managers. Focusing on cost by product can obscure the costs of the various manufacturing activities. More than ever, managers focus attention on activities rather than on products. Fundamentally, people manage activities, not products. If the activities are managed well, costs will fall and the resulting products will be more competitive.

2. Managers often lack faith in product costs generated by traditional cost accounting systems. Allocating overhead cost to production based on a single cost driver can result in an unrealistic product cost. Recall that a *cost driver* is any factor whose change causes a change in a related total cost. For example, Jim Fleming's stained-and-lacquered tables include overhead cost of $16 compared with overhead cost of $4 for a painted model. But a more expensive table should not necessarily bear four times as much overhead cost. After all, a stained table requires only slightly more inspection time and takes no more packaging materials than does a painted model. There are more reasonable ways to allocate these costs to products than by direct labor hours. ABC shifts the focus of managers and accountants to the activities that manufacture the

tables. For example, inspection cost could be allocated on the basis of inspection time. Also, the only difference in packaging is the label on the box, so each table should bear an equal amount of packaging cost. It is unlikely that the materials for a lacquered table cost four times what the materials for a painted table cost. This reasoning is behind Jim Fleming's dissatisfaction with the company's cost allocation system.

A key feature of ABC is allocation of activity costs based on multiple cost drivers. Each cost driver is selected for its relationship to the activity. The more precise relationships yield more realistic product costs than under traditional systems that use a single allocation base for conversion costs. Better cost figures help managers make wiser decisions.

Developments in information technology make activity-based costing possible. Optical scanning, bar coding, and robotics have reduced the cost of processing the information demanded by ABC. Before these techniques became available, it was convenient to use direct labor hours or direct labor dollars as the sole basis for allocating overhead cost. Now it is relatively inexpensive to obtain more precise cost allocations for multiple cost drivers.

Product Costing in an Activity-Based System

Product cost build-up in an ABC system follows the pattern of other cost systems, with one exception. Conversion costs are applied to products based on various manufacturing activities rather than on a single measure, such as direct labor hours in traditional systems. Suppose Des Moines, Inc., uses ABC, and the direct material of its wrought-iron lawn chairs costs $4 per unit. Each chair includes eight parts and requires 15 minutes of machine time. Des Moines's conversion costs, organized by manufacturing activities, and the associated cost drivers and unit application rates follow. Note the procession of analysis:

1. Identify activities.
2. Identify the cost of the activity.
3. Identify the cost drivers for each activity.
4. Choose the primary cost driver as the application base for each activity.

Manufacturing Activity	Cost of Activity	Cost Driver Chosen as Application Base		Conversion Cost Per Unit of Application Base
1. Material handling	$ 800 ÷	Number of parts (8,000)	=	$ .10
2. Machining	5,000 ÷	Machine hours (250)	=	20.00
3. Assembling	4,800 ÷	Number of parts (8,000)	=	.60
4. Inspecting	1,400 ÷	Number of finished units (1,000)	=	1.40

Each chair's manufacturing cost is $16.00, computed as follows:

Direct materials	$ 4.00
Conversion costs:	
Material handling (8 parts × $.10)	.80
Machining (¼ machine hour × $20.00)	5.00
Assembling (8 parts × $.60)	4.80
Inspecting (1 finished unit × $1.40)	1.40
Total manufacturing cost per unit	$16.00

Class Exercise: Assume the following activities and cost drivers in an ABC system:

Activity	Cost Driver
1. Purchasing	# of parts purchased
2. Assembly	# of parts in production
3. Packaging	# of finished units

The costs of each activity, the actual volume of the related cost driver, and the conversion cost per unit of the cost driver are given below:

Activity Cost	Volume	Cost/ Unit
1. $24,000	12,000	$ .20
2. $60,000	15,000	4.00
3. $12,000	16,000	.75

Each unit is composed of four parts. Total cost of these materials is $3.00 per unit. What is the total manufacturing cost per unit?

ANSWER:

Direct Materials	$3.00
Conversion Costs:	
Purchasing (4×$.20)	.80
Assembly (4×$4)	16.00
Packaging (1×$.75)	.75
Total mfg cost/unit	$20.55

OBJECTIVE 6

Account for an activity-based costing system

The detailed breakdown of conversion costs by activity pinpoints opportunities for cost control. For example, machining costs of $5.00 per unit may be too high. Managers could take action to bring machining cost down. In a traditional costing system this information may not be available, and cost may escalate without managers' attention

Managers are also concerned about *full product cost*, which includes the costs of upstream activities and downstream activities in the value chain. Recall that upstream activities precede manufacturing and downstream activities follow. Des Moines's full product cost per chair is $26.60, computed as follows:

Upstream activities:
Product design (assumed) . . . . $ 1.40
Total manufacturing cost per unit (as before) 16.00
Downstream activities:
Marketing, distribution, and customer service (assumed) 9.20
Full product cost per unit $26.60

Internal decisions, such as cost control and product pricing, will focus on the components of full product cost. However, the external financial statements will report chairs at $16 each because that is their manufacturing (inventoriable) cost. The costs of upstream and downstream activities are expensed as incurred.

Activity-Based Costing and Management Decisions

A major feature of activity-based costing is the use of several cost application bases instead of just one or two. In particular, people who favor ABC warn that the use of a single application base may result in unrealistic product costs and lead to unwise decisions. The following illustration is exaggerated to emphasize the underlying ABC concepts.

Quality Instrument Company manufactures two products, space missile instruments (20 per month) and testing instruments (400 per month). The company has had the same cost accounting system since its founding in 1971. A single plantwide rate based on machine hours of running time has been used for applying all conversion costs to production. Direct materials cost and machine hours are the same for the two products, so their total manufacturing costs are equal. In the following tabulation of total cost per unit, focus on conversion cost:

Product	Conversion Costs Per Unit			Direct Materials Cost Per Unit	Total Manufacturing Cost Per Unit
	Machine Hours Per Unit	Application Rate Per Machine Hour	Total Cost		
Space missile instrument . . .	5	× $120	= $600	$200	$800
Testing instrument . . .	5	× 120	= 600	200	800

In recent years the cost of each machine setup has soared to $42,000 as precision requirements have tightened. The use of a single cost application rate that is based on machine hours of running time ignores the role of setup cost. To better gauge the cost of each product, management decides to use two activities, machine setups and machine running time, for applying conversion cost to products. Each product requires one machine setup. When machine setup cost is subtracted from total manufacturing cost, the application rate for machine running time decreases to $80 per hour from the previous level of $120. The ABC computations of product cost differ significantly from the earlier figures:

| | | Conversion Costs | | | | | Direct Materials | |
| Product | Machine Setups | Running of Machines | | | Total Cost | Per Unit | Cost Per Unit | Total Manufacturing Cost Per Unit |
		Units	Hours	Rate				
Space missile instrument.....	$42,000 +	(20 ×	5	× $80) =	$ 50,000	$2,500*	$200	$2,700
Testing instrument.....	42,000 +	(400 ×	5	× 80) =	202,000	505†	200	705

* $ 50,000/20 units = $2,500
† $202,000/400 units = $505

Compare the total manufacturing cost per unit under the two methods of allocating conversion costs:

| | Total Manufacturing Cost per Unit | |
Product	Using Plantwide Rate	Using ABC Rate
Space missile instrument	$800	$2,700
Testing instrument	800	705

Activity-based costing is likely to give managers better information for decision making. ABC identifies the various activities and cost drivers that cause certain costs and uses those relationships to apply costs more precisely. For example, use of a single cost application base ignores the high cost of machine setups. Manufacture of each group of instruments requires one setup costing $42,000, but that information is ignored in the traditional approach. Consequently, the same amount of conversion cost ($600) is allocated to each space missile instrument and each testing instrument. The accounting records indicate that each product's manufacturing cost is $800. A product pricing decision based on these cost figures can be disastrous. Suppose the marketing department prices each space missile instrument and each testing instrument at $1,500. Managers believe each sale will yield a $700 profit ($1,500 − $800). However, the company will lose $1,200 ($2,700 − $1,500) on the sale of each space missile instrument.

The ABC cost amounts lead to an entirely different conclusion. Each space missile instrument is allocated $2,500 of conversion costs, and the accounting records indicate that total cost is $2,700. Company managers are more likely to price the products realistically.

Another decision is whether Quality Instrument Company should make these products or buy them from an outside supplier. Suppose an outside company offers to supply each product for $1,000. Using a single cost application base, Quality managers would reject the offer. They would think they could make each instrument for $800. Using ABC, they would accept the outside offer for space missile instruments. The purchase price of $800 is much lower than Quality's manufacturing cost of $2,700.

All of the above decisions may be influenced by other factors. For example, managers should consider whether certain costs are fixed or variable. Nevertheless, the figures produced by ABC consistently provide more accurate costs than those produced by a single cost-application base.

Joint Product Cost

Point to Stress: The procedure for allocating joint costs is not new to us. The same technique was used in allocating the cost of a lump-sum purchase in Chapter 10. This technique will also be used in allocating departmental expenses in Chapter 25.

Point to Stress: A joint cost is one which contributes to the creation of more than one product. Joint cost must therefore be allocated among the various individual products. If a company buys timber and from it manufactures different grades of lumber, the cost of each grade of lumber must bear a portion of the total joint cost of the timber. The costing of joint products, then, is based on an allocation system.

A manufacturing process that produces more than one product simultaneously is called a joint process. **Joint products** are goods that are specifically identified as individual products only after a juncture in the production process called the **split-off point.** To be called a joint product, the item must have a sales value that is significant in relation to the other item produced. For example, refining crude oil produces gasoline and natural gas as joint products. Exhibit 23-14 diagrams this joint process.

Many industries have manufacturing processes that create joint products. Soap making, for example, produces lanolin and other oils for cosmetics, in addition to soap. Refining copper also produces ammonia, which has many uses.

How do we assign costs to individual products that are manufactured by a joint process? After the split-off point, costs are easily assigned. For example, after gasoline and natural gas are separated in the refining process, further costs can be separately identified with the two products. But what costs incurred *before* split-off are assigned to the individual joint products? For example, how should we allocate the cost of exploring and drilling for oil to final products (gasoline and natural gas)? These *joint processing costs* may be allocated using the *relative sales value* method.

Assume the joint cost of processing 65,000 gallons of gasoline and liquid natural gas is $72,000. Exhibit 23-15 shows how to allocate this joint cost to the two products.

The relative sales value of each joint product is computed by dividing its individual sales value by the total sales value. In the exhibit, the gasoline sales value makes up two-thirds of the total and liquid natural gas makes up one-third. Multiplying joint cost of $72,000 by these fractions gives the two products' individual costs of $48,000 and $24,000. Any cost of processing gasoline after split-off is added to $48,000 to determine the total cost of the gasoline. The cost of liquid natural gas is computed similarly.

EXHIBIT 23-14   *Joint Products*

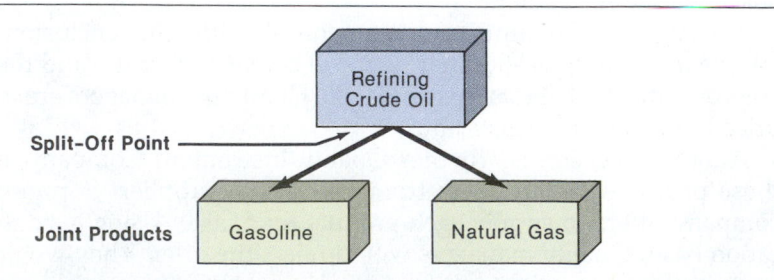

EXHIBIT 23-15 *Allocation of Joint Cost to Joint Products*

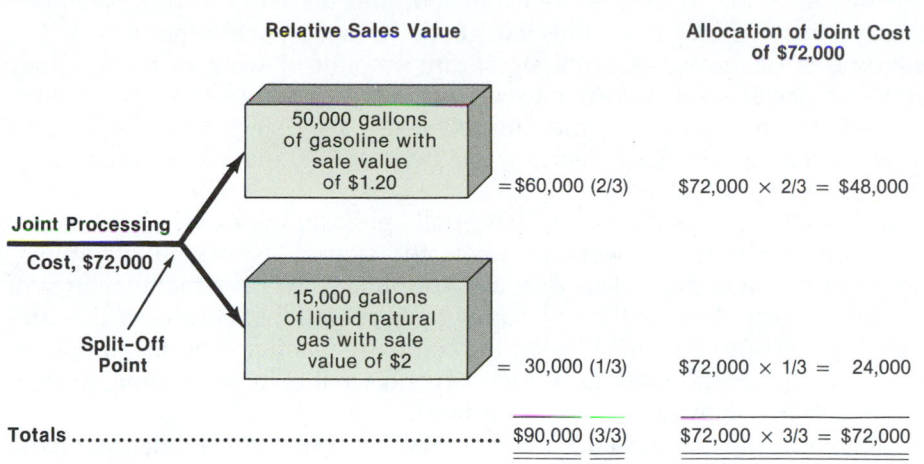

Byproduct Cost

The difference between a joint product and a byproduct depends on the relative sale values of the products. **Byproducts** are those outputs of joint processes with minor sale value in comparison with the main products. Sawdust is a byproduct of a lumber company. Meat packing yields pet food as a byproduct.

Accounting for the cost of byproducts is straightforward. Byproducts are assigned an accounting value called **net realizable value,** which is their sales value, less the cost of selling them. Suppose a lumber company's Work in Process—Milling account has a balance of $229,000. This amount includes the estimated sales value of the byproduct sawdust, $5,600. It will cost the company $600 to sell the sawdust, so the net realizable value of the sawdust is $5,000 ($5,600 − $600). The entry to record the net realizable value of the sawdust is

Byproduct Inventory	5,000	
Work in Process—Milling		5,000

Sale of the byproduct is accounted for in the usual manner. Because its cost is embedded in the cost of the main product, the accounting value of the byproduct is subtracted from the main product's cost. In this illustration, the cost assigned to lumber is $224,000 ($229,000 − $5,000).

Just-in-Time (JIT) Production Systems

Stockpiles of idle inventory—raw materials, work in process, and finished goods—tie up cash, so businesses strive to keep the level of unused inventory to a minimum. Just-in-time (JIT) production is a system in which each component on a production line is produced immediately as needed by the next step. The goal is to eliminate waste.

To see how a JIT system works, consider the manufacture of cardboard by a company such as Georgia-Pacific or Weyerhaeuser. The company may stock-

Real-World Example: JIT is an application of Japanese production methods. Companies that adopt the JIT philosophy have these goals: eliminate all waste (anything that doesn't add value to the product, such as time spent sitting in inventory); eliminate product defects and remakes; and continue making improvements in the manufacturing process. Many of the costs which traditionally were treated as indirect (such as factory supervision and operating supplies) are treated as direct costs in a JIT environment. Harley Davidson, IBM, and Caterpillar have adopted JIT cost management methods.

pile lumber and chemicals for production. Raw materials are placed in production, labor and overhead are expended, and the work in process moves through various stages to finished goods. If a bottleneck occurs—say, a machine breaks down—then a significant amount of work in process may build up. The bottleneck creates a waste because work stops until the machine is fixed. Upon completion, the finished goods may sit around for days or weeks awaiting sale. This creates waste because idle inventory accumulates storage cost but no revenue.

JIT systems are based on a "demand-pull" philosophy. At Hewlett-Packard Company, for example, workers follow the slogan "Never build nothing, nowhere, for nobody, unless they ask you for it." NCR, a manufacturer of printers, also applies the JIT philosophy to its operations. How does this philosophy affect production? Ideally, the company maintains no inventories— no raw materials, no work in process beyond what is in production, and no finished goods. How is this accomplished?

Manufacturing is activated by the receipt of a customer order. Receiving the order, the manufacturer purchases the raw materials for immediate delivery. Upon arrival, materials are placed in production, which proceeds without interruption to the completion of finished goods. The absence of bottlenecks— that is, there are no interruptions—keeps work in process inventory from sitting idle. Finished goods are minimal because goods are sold before manufacture.

JIT systems depend on careful planning and control of manufacturing operations. They require reliable suppliers who meet the manufacturer's demands without fail. Of course, this is not always possible, and JIT systems are designed to compensate for disruptions in production. Workers are trained more broadly than in non-JIT plants. For example, production employees not only rivet parts as they move down the line. They also inspect goods for defects and have the authority to stop the production line if necessary.

Delaying production until after a customer has ordered goods may mean frequent equipment setups. Production-line employees in JIT systems do more setup work than in traditional systems that use separate departments to modify equipment. In JIT systems production employees also perform routine maintenance on equipment between production runs. By cross-training employees, maintenance cost can be reduced. There is evidence that employee morale increases with the added responsibility.

Computers are a major element of many JIT systems. Computers are ideal for synchronizing raw material orders, production scheduling, inventory costing, and customer billing. Robotic assembly lines are programmed and operated by computers. The goal is a steady stream of high-quality products delivered to the customer at relatively low cost.

JIT systems work well for the manufacturer. For the supplier of the raw materials, they can create nightmares. To deliver materials with split-second precision, the supplier also needs reliable sources. To achieve this reliability the supplier may have to stockpile the material, which shifts some of the cost burden for storing material from the manufacturer to the supplier. In another arrangement, the manufacturer eliminates the need for outside suppliers by producing the raw material itself.

JIT production systems simplify cost accounting. A number of accounts can be eliminated, including Raw Material Inventory, the various Work in Process Inventory accounts, and Finished Goods Inventory. During production, costs are accumulated in a single account titled Raw-and-in-Process Inventory. Upon completion, the goods are delivered to the customer. The final journal entry debits Cost of Goods Sold and credits Raw-and-in-Process Inventory. Details of these accounting systems are described in cost accounting textbooks.

Summary Problem for Your Review

This problem extends the Summary Problem for Your Review on page 1053 to a second processing department. Jacobs-Webster, Inc., had the following activity in its Finishing Department during May.

Finishing Department Facts for May

Units:

Work in process, April 30 (20% complete as to direct materials, 70% complete as to conversion costs)	4,000 units
Transferred in from Assembly Department during May	16,000 units
Completed during May	15,000 units
Work in process, May 31 (36% complete as to direct materials, 80% complete as to conversion costs)	5,000 units

Costs:

Work in process, April 30	$18,000
Transferred in from Assembly Department during May	38,400
Direct materials added during May	6,400
Conversion costs added during May	24,300

Required

Show the allocation of total cost to units completed and units in ending work in process inventory in the Finishing Department during May.

SOLUTION TO REVIEW PROBLEM

Step 1: Flow of Production in Physical Units;
Step 2: Equivalent Units of Production

Finishing Department
For the Month Ended May 31, 19XX

Flow of Production	Step 1 — Flow of Physical Units	Step 2 — Equivalent Units of Production — Transferred In	Step 2 — Direct Materials	Step 2 — Conversion Costs
Units to account for:				
Work in process, April 30	4,000			
Transferred in during May	16,000			
Total physical units to account for	20,000			
Units accounted for:				
Completed and transferred out during May:				
From beginning inventory	4,000	—	3,200*	1,200*
Transferred in and completed during May (16,000 − 5,000)	11,000	11,000	11,000	11,000
Work in process, May 31	5,000	5,000	1,800†	4,000†
Total physical units accounted for	20,000			
Equivalent units of production		16,000	16,000	16,200

* Direct materials: 4,000 units each 80% completed = 3,200 equivalent units.
  Conversion costs: 4,000 units each 30% completed = 1,200 equivalent units.
† Direct materials: 5,000 units each 36% completed = 1,800 equivalent units.
  Conversion costs: 5,000 units each 80% completed = 4,000 equivalent units.

Finishing Department
For the Month Ended May 31, 19XX

	Transferred-In Costs	Direct Materials	Conversion Costs	Total
Work in process, April 30 ..	Work done before May			$18,000
Costs added during May ...	$38,400	$ 6,400	$24,300	69,100
Divide by equivalent units..	÷16,000	÷16,000	÷16,200	
Cost per equivalent unit....	$2.40	$.40	$1.50	
Total cost to account for				$87,100

Step 5: Application of Total Cost to Units Completed
and Units in Ending Work in Process Inventory

Finishing Department
For the Month Ended October 31, 19XX

	Transferred-In Costs	Direct Materials	Conversion Costs	Total
Units completed and transferred out to Finished Goods Inventory:				
From work in process, April 30				$18,000
Costs added during May:				
Direct materials	—	3,200 × $.40		1,280
Conversion costs	—		1,200 × $1.50	1,800
Total completed from April 30 inventory......				21,080
Units transferred in and completed during May....	11,000 × ($2.40 + $.40 + $1.50)			47,300
Total costs transferred out ..				68,380
Work in process, May 31:				
Transferred-in costs	5,000 × $2.40			12,000
Direct materials		1,800 × $.40		720
Conversion costs			4,000 × $1.50	6,000
Total work in process, May 31				18,720
Total cost accounted for.......				$87,100

Summary

Process costing is a system for assigning costs to products that are mass-produced in continuous fashion through a sequence of production steps. In a process costing system, costs are accumulated by processes (departments) and flow from one department to another until the product is completed.

The main accounting problem in process costing is determining the cost of the work in process transferred from one department to the next. This complication arises because the goods in process may be in various stages of completion. Cost accountants compute the number of *equivalent units* of production that could have been manufactured from start to finish with the costs that were incurred in each department during the period. Cost divided by the number of equivalent units equals equivalent-unit cost. This unit cost, multiplied by the number of units transferred out of the department, determines the cost entering the next department. Equivalent-unit cost, multiplied by the number of units remaining in Work in Process Inventory, measures the department's ending inventory. Companies summarize the activity in each processing department for the period on a production cost report.

Activity-based costing (ABC) is a system that focuses on activities as the fundamental cost objects and uses the costs of these activities as building blocks for compiling the costs of products and other cost objects. Activity-based costing is general in the sense that it can be part of job order costing, process costing, or some hybrid costing system.

Joint products are those items with significant value that are not identified as specific products until after a split-off point in the production process. Cost is allocated to joint products based on their relative sales values. *Byproducts* are insignificant relative to the main item being produced. The value assigned to a byproduct is its *net realizable value* (expected sale price less the cost of selling the byproduct).

Just-in-time production systems minimize inventory quantities to reduce cost. They rely on dependable suppliers to deliver materials just as they are needed. Inventory is sold before it is manufactured.

Self-Study Questions

Test your understanding of the chapter by marking the best answer to each of the following questions.

1. For which of the following products is a process costing system most appropriate? *(p. 1045)*
   a. Breakfast cereal   c. Houses
   b. Automobiles   d. Furniture

2. A key difference between job order costing and process costing is that *(p. 1046)*
   a. Costs are assigned to direct materials in job costing and to indirect materials in process costing
   b. Job costing uses a single work in process account and process costing uses a separate work in process account for each department
   c. Job order costing, but not process costing, uses conversion costs
   d. Factory overhead is used in process costing but not in job order costing

3. During August the Assembly Department of Fisk Manufacturing Company completed and transferred 20,000 intercom units to the Finishing Department. The Assembly Department's August 31 inventory included 6,000 units, 90 percent complete as to direct materials and 75 percent complete as to conversion costs. August equivalent units of the Assembly Department total *(p. 1050)*
   a. 20,000
   b. 24,500
   c. 25,400
   d. 25,400 as to direct materials and 24,500 as to conversion costs

4. The concept of equivalent units is useful for *(p. 1052)*
   a. Measuring the cost of direct materials and conversion costs incurred in a processing department
   b. Measuring the unit costs of direct materials and conversion costs to compute the cost of goods transferred from one processing department to the next

c. Separating the cost of a manufacturing *process* from the cost of a manufacturing *activity*

d. Dividing ending inventory between finished goods and work in process

5. The entry to record the transfer of goods from the Heating Department to the Drying Department is *(p. 1053)*

a. Finished Goods XXX
   Work in Process—Drying   XXX

b. Work in Process—Heating XXX
   Work in Process—Drying   XXX

c. Work in Process—Heating XXX
   Finished Goods   XXX

d. Work in Process—Drying XXX
   Work in Process—Heating   XXX

6. The costs to account for in a second processing department include those associated with *(p. 1055)*

a. Beginning work in process and goods transferred in during the period

b. Beginning work in process and costs added during the period

c. Beginning work in process, goods transferred in, and costs added during the period

d. Beginning work in process and ending work in process

7. Refer to the production cost report in Exhibit 23-11, page 1060. The unit cost of goods completed and transferred to finished goods during October was *(p. 1060)*

a. $4.40   c. $4.90

b. $4.80   d. $5.32

8. Activity-based costing is *(p. 1061)*

a. A hybrid system that can be used with a job cost system or a process cost system

b. Closer to a job cost system than to a process cost system

c. Closer to a process cost system than to a job cost system

9. The joint cost of manufacturing Products A and B is $160,000. Product A can be sold for $240,000 and Product B for $80,000. The costs of Products A and B are *(p. 1066)*

a. $240,000 and $80,000   c. $120,000 and $40,000

b. $160,000 and $80,000   d. Cannot be determined from the information given

10. The accounting value assigned to byproducts is called *(p. 1067)*

a. Sales value   c. Net realizable value

b. Net value   d. Selling cost

Answers to the Self-Study Questions follow the Accounting Vocabulary.

Accounting Vocabulary

Activity-based costing. A system that focuses on activities as the fundamental cost objects and uses these activities as building blocks for compiling the costs of products and other cost objects *(p. 1061)*.

Byproduct. Output of a joint production process with minor sales value in comparison with the main product *(p. 1067)*.

Cost object. Anything for which it is worthwhile to compile costs, such as an activity, a department, or a product *(p. 1061)*.

Equivalent units. Measure of the number of complete units that could have been manufactured from start to finish using the costs incurred during the period *(p. 1050)*.

Joint product. Goods identified as individual products only after a juncture in the production process called the split-off point (p. 1066).

Net realizable value. Sales value less the cost of selling the item (p. 1067).

Process costing. System for assigning costs to goods that are mass-produced in a continuous sequence of steps (p. 1045).

Production cost report. Summary of the activity in a processing department for a period (p. 1059).

Split-off point. Juncture in the production process after which joint products are specifically identified (p. 1066).

Answers to Self-Study Questions

1. a
2. b
3. d   Direct materials: $20,000 + (6,000 \times .90) = 25,400$
         Conversion costs: $20,000 + (6,000 \times .75) = 24,500$
4. b
5. d
6. c
7. d $202,200/38,000 = \$5.32$
8. a
9. c   A: $[\$240,000/(\$240,000 + \$80,000)] \times \$160,000 = \$120,000$
         B: $[\$80,000/(\$240,000 + \$80,000)] \times \$160,000 = \$40,000$
10. c

ASSIGNMENT MATERIAL

Questions

1. Distinguish a process cost accounting system from a job order system.
2. Which type of costing system—job order or process costing—would be better suited to account for manufacture of each of the following products: (a) chemicals, (b) automobiles, (c) lumber, (d) hand-held calculators, (e) custom lampshades?
3. Why does a process costing system use multiple work in process accounts but a job order system use only one such account?
4. Give the entries (accounts only) to record the following: (a) purchase of materials; (b) incurrence of labor; (c) overhead cost; (d) requisition of materials and application of labor and overhead to Work in Process Inventory—Department 1 (combine in one entry); (e) transfer of cost of work in process inventory from Department 1 to Department 2; (f) transfer of cost of completed units to finished goods; (g) cost of goods sold.
5. What is an equivalent unit of production? Give an example of equivalent units.
6. Montague Manufacturing Company completed and transferred 35,000 units of its product to a second department during the period. At the end of the period, another 10,000 units were in work in process inventory, 20 percent complete. How many equivalent units did Montague produce during the period?
7. Outline the five steps to account for a process costing system.
8. How are equivalent units used in Exhibits 23-5 and 23-6?

9. Why might a company have different numbers of equivalent units for direct materials and conversion costs?

10. What information does a production cost report give? Why does the format of the report differ from company to company?

11. What is the major accounting challenge in a process costing system that has more than one processing department? Why is this such a challenge?

12. Compute the equivalent units of production for Department 2 during July:

Units:
Work in process, June 30 (10% complete as to direct
   materials, 40% complete as to conversion costs)....   1,000 units
Transferred in from Department 1 during July ....   25,000 units
Completed during July ....   22,000 units
Work in process, July 31 (20% complete as to direct
   materials, 70% complete as to conversion costs)....   4,000 units

13. Briefly describe an activity-based costing system, indicating the advantages it offers over traditional cost accounting systems.

14. "Executives should decide which of the following three basic cost accounting systems is best for their company: job order costing, process costing, or activity-based costing." Do you agree? Explain.

15. Distinguish joint products from byproducts.

16. How is the cost of a joint product determined?

17. How is an accounting value assigned to a byproduct? Give the entry to record the value of a byproduct.

Exercises

Exercise 23-1   *Diagramming flows through a process costing system* **(L.O. 1)**

Vines & Crocker manufactures furniture in a three-stage process that includes milling, assembling, and finishing, in that order. Direct materials are added in the milling and finishing departments, and direct labor and overhead are applied in all three departments. The company's general ledger includes the following accounts:

Work in Process Inventory—Finishing   Factory Wages
Raw Materials Inventory   Work in Process Inventory—
Finished Goods Inventory   Milling
Factory Overhead   Work in Process Inventory—
Cost of Goods Sold   Assembling

Required

Outline the flow of costs through the company's accounts. Include a T-account for each account title given.

Exercise 23-2   *Computing equivalent units in a single department* **(L.O. 2)**

Insert the missing values:

Flow of Production	Flow of Physical Units	Equivalent Units of Production	
		Direct Materials	Conversion Costs
Units to account for:			
Work in process, November 30	12,000		
Started production during December	X		
Total physical units to account for	67,000		
Units accounted for:			
Completed and transferred out during December:			
From beginning inventory	12,000	X*	X*
Started and completed during December	47,000	X	X
Work in process, December 31	X	X†	X†
Total physical units accounted for	67,000		
Equivalent units of production		X	X

* Direct materials: 40% completed during December
Conversion costs: 50% completed during December
† Direct materials: 20% completed during December
Conversion costs: 30% completed during December

Exercise 23-3 *Computing equivalent units and applying cost to completed units and work in process (L.O. 2, 3)*

Gray Matter, Inc., experienced the following activity in its Finishing Department during December.

Equiv. units:
Materials 29,000
Conversion costs 30,000
Unit costs:
Materials $2.50
Conversion costs $3.40

Units:
Work in process, November 30 (60% complete as to direct materials, 80% complete as to conversion costs).	8,000 units
Transferred in from Heating Department during December	31,000 units
Completed during December	26,000 units
Work in process, December 31 (60% complete as to direct materials, 80% complete as to conversion costs).	13,000 units

Costs:
Work in process, November 30..........................	$ 59,000
Transferred in from Heating Department during December	108,500
Direct materials added during December	72,500
Conversion costs added during December..............	102,000

Required

1. Compute the number of equivalent units produced by the Finishing Department during December.
2. Compute unit costs, and apply total cost to (a) units completed and transferred to finished goods and (b) units in December 31 work in process inventory.

Exercise 23-4 *Transferring costs between processing departments (L.O. 2, 3, 4)*

1. Cost per unit $1.90
3. Total cost $37,500

The Mixing Department of a chemical company began February with no work in process inventory. During the month, production that cost $37,500 (direct materials, $9,500, and conversion costs, $28,000) was started on 21,000 units.

A total of 17,000 units were completed and transferred to the Heating Department. The ending work in process inventory was 50 percent complete as to direct materials and 75 percent complete as to conversion costs.

Required

1. Journalize the transfer of cost from the Mixing Department to the Heating Department.
2. What is the balance in Work in Process—Mixing on February 28?
3. Account for the total cost incurred during February.

Cost per unit $6.50
Cost trans. to Painting $468,000

Exercise 23-5 *Computing processing costs and journalizing cost transfers* **(L.O. 2, 4)**

The following information was taken from the ledger of Vanderpool Products. Ending inventory is 70 percent complete as to direct materials but only 40 percent complete as to conversion costs.

Work in Process—Forming

	Physical Units	Dollars		Physical Units	Dollars
Inventory, November 30	-0-	$ -0-	Transferred to Painting	72,000	?
Production started:	80,000		Ending inventory	8,000	
1. Direct materials		271,600	Total accounted for	80,000	
2. Conversion costs		225,600			
Total to account for	80,000	$497,200			

Required

Journalize the transfer of cost to the Painting Department.

Sanding Dept. equiv. units
    Materials 66,500
    Conversion costs 67,000
Finishing Dept. equiv. units
    Materials 76,500
    Conversion costs 75,400

Exercise 23-6 *Computing equivalent units in two departments* **(L.O. 2, 5)**

Selected production and cost data of Cordoba, Inc., follow for May 19X5.

	Flow of Physical Units	
Flow of Production	Sanding Department	Finishing Department
Units to account for:		
Work in process, April 30	20,000	6,000
Transferred in during May	70,000	70,000
Total physical units to account for	90,000	76,000
Units accounted for:		
Completed and transferred out during May:		
From beginning inventory................	20,000*	6,000‡
Transferred in and completed during May .	55,000	65,000
Work in process, May 31	15,000†	5,000§
Total physical units accounted for............	90,000	76,000

* Direct materials: 20 percent completed during May
  Conversion costs: 30 percent completed during May
† Direct materials: 50 percent completed during May
  Conversion costs: 40 percent completed during May
‡ Direct materials: ⅔ completed during May
  Conversion costs: 40 percent completed during May
§ Direct materials: 50 percent completed during May
  Conversion costs: 60 percent completed during May

Required

Compute equivalent units for goods transferred in, direct materials, and conversion costs for each department.

Exercise 23-7 *Journalizing process costing transactions* **(L.O. 4)** No check figure

Record the following selected process cost accounting transactions in the general journal:

a. Purchase of raw materials on account, $4,200.
b. Requisition of direct materials to Processing Department 1, $1,800.
c. Payment of factory labor, $11,000.
d. Incurrence of factory overhead costs: depreciation, $600; insurance, $500; utilities paid, $900.
e. Application of conversion costs to Processing Department 1: direct labor, $1,900; factory overhead, $2,850.
f. Transfer of cost from Processing Department 1 to Department 2, $5,300.
g. Application of conversion costs to Processing Department 2: direct labor, $700; factory overhead, $1,050.
h. Transfer of cost from Processing Department 2 to finished goods, $5,200.

Exercise 23-8 *Using a production cost report* **(L.O. 4)** No check figure

Cost accountants for South Fork Manufacturing prepared the following production cost report for February:

Finishing Department
Production Cost Report
For the Month Ended February 28, 19XX

	Physical Units	Total Costs
Work in process, January 31	14,000	$ 82,000
Transferred in from Grinding Department during February..	90,000	392,000
Cost added in Finishing Department during February:		
Direct materials.....................................	—	58,000
Conversion costs:		
Direct labor	—	84,000
Factory overhead	—	83,000
Total to account for	104,000	$699,000
Completed and transferred to finished goods during February...	95,000	$650,000
Work in process, February 28	9,000	49,000
Total accounted for	104,000	$699,000

Required

Journalize all February activity in the Finishing Department.

Exercise 23-9 *Product build-up in an activity-based costing system* **(L.O. 6)**

1. Total manufacturing cost
$80.70

Amarillo Motor Company uses activity-based costing to account for its manufacturing process. The direct materials in each electric motor cost $36. Each motor includes 60 parts, and finishing requires five minutes of direct labor time. The manufacture of 1,000 motors requires three machine setups. Conversion costs, listed by manufacturing activity, the related cost drivers, and unit application rates follow:

Manufacturing Activity	Cost Driver Chosen as Application Base	Conversion Cost Per Unit of Application Base
1. Material handling	Number of parts	$ .20
2. Machine setup	Number of setups	400.00
3. Insertion of parts	Number of parts	.50
4. Finishing	Direct labor hours	18.00

Required

1. Compute the total manufacturing cost of each electric motor.

2. Suppose an alternative costing plan would apply conversion costs to electric motors based on direct labor hours. Overall manufacture of each machine requires two direct labor hours. Compute conversion cost per unit under both costing plans. Which plan is preferable? What decisions could be affected by your choice?

Exercise 23-10 *Determining the cost of joint products and byproducts* **(L.O. 7)**

Part A—Cost per ton
Cardboard $24
Linerboard $9

Part A. Catawba Paper Corporation manufactures cardboard and linerboard by a joint process that costs $300,000 on average each month. Cardboard sells for $32 per ton and linerboard for $12 per ton. Each month the manufacturing process generates 5,000 tons of cardboard and 20,000 tons of linerboard. Use the relative sales value method to determine the cost of each ton of the two products.

Part B. Easy Rocker Chair Company makes recliner chairs. The manufacturing process leaves byproducts including scrap wood and upholstery remnants with resale value averaging $1 per chair. Five percent of this amount is consumed by the cost of disposing of byproducts. Easy Rocker manufactures 10,000 chairs per year. Make the general journal entry to record the byproduct inventory.

Problems   (Group A)

Problem 23-1A *Computing equivalent units and applying cost to completed units and work in process; no beginning inventory or cost transferred in* **(L.O. 2, 3)**

Cost per unit $1.30
Work in Process bal. $693

Suruga Bay, Inc., produces component parts that are used in hand-held calculators. One part, a diode generator, is manufactured in a single processing department. No diode generators were in process on May 31, and Suruga started production on 12,000 units during June. Completed production for June totaled 9,900 units. The June 30 work in process was 20 percent complete as to direct materials and 30 percent complete as to conversion costs. Direct materials costing $6,192 were placed in production during June, and direct labor of $5,100 and factory overhead of $2,271 were applied to the manufacture of diode generators.

Required

1. Compute the number of equivalent units of production and the unit costs for June.

2. Show the application of total cost to (a) units completed and transferred to finished goods, and (b) units still in process at June 30.

3. Prepare a T-account for Work in Process Inventory to show its activity during June, including the June 30 balance.

Problem 23-2A *Computing equivalent units, applying cost to completed units and work in process, and journalizing transactions; no beginning inventory or cost transferred in* **(L.O. 2, 3, 4)**

Cost per unit $4.60
Work in Process bal. $3,480

Santa Fe Sheep & Wool Company produces wool fabric by a three-stage process: cleaning, spinning, and weaving, in that order. Costs incurred in the Cleaning Department during September are summarized as follows:

Work in Process Inventory—Cleaning

Direct materials	70,400
Direct labor	2,580
Factory overhead	8,700

September activity in the Cleaning Department included completion of 17,000 pounds of wool, which were transferred to the Spinning Department. Also, work on 3,000 pounds began, which on September 30 was 20 percent complete with respect to direct materials and 60 percent complete with respect to conversion costs.

Required

1. Compute the equivalent units of production and unit costs in the Cleaning Department for September.
2. Prove that the sum of (a) cost of goods transferred out of the Cleaning Department and (b) ending Work in Process Inventory—Cleaning equals the total cost accumulated in the department during September.
3. Journalize all transactions affecting the company's cleaning process during September, including those already posted.

Problem 23-3A *Computing equivalent units for a second department with beginning inventory; applying cost to completed units and work in process* **(L.O. 2, 3, 5)**

Cost per equiv. unit
Transf. in $10
Materials $11
Conv. costs $19

Motor Parts Corporation manufactures auto bumpers in a two-stage process that includes shaping and plating. Steel alloy is the basic raw material of the shaping process. The steel is molded according to the design specifications of the automobile manufacturers (Chrysler, Ford, and General Motors). The Plating Department then adds a finish plate of chrome to give the new bumper a shiny appearance.

At March 31, before recording the transfer of cost from the Plating Department to Finished Goods Inventory, the Motor Parts general ledger included the following account:

Work in Process Inventory—Plating

Feb. 28 Balance	24,600
Transferred in from Shaping	30,000
Direct materials	27,060
Direct labor	17,100
Factory overhead	37,620

Work in process of the Plating Department on February 28 consisted of 600 bumpers that were 50 percent complete as to direct materials and conversion costs. During March 3,000 bumpers were transferred in from the Shaping Department. The Plating Department transferred 2,200 bumpers to finished goods in March, and 1,400 bumpers were still in process on March 31. This ending inventory was 40 percent complete as to direct materials and 70 percent complete as to conversion costs.

Required

1. Compute the equivalent units of production, unit costs, and total cost to account for in the Plating Department for March.
2. Show the application of total Plating Department cost for March to (a) cost of goods transferred out of the Plating Department and (b) cost of ending Work in Process Inventory—Plating on March 31.

Problem 23-4A   *Preparing a production cost report and recording transactions based on the report's information* **(L.O. 4)**

Required

1. Prepare the March production cost report for the Plating Department in Problem 23-3A.
2. Journalize all transactions affecting the Plating Department during March, including those entries that have already been posted.

Problem 23-5A   *Computing equivalent units for a second department with beginning inventory and applying cost to completed units and work in process* **(L.O. 2, 3, 5)**

The manufacture of hand tools, such as pliers and screwdrivers, occurs in four departments and also includes two additional operations. Consider screwdrivers with plastic handles. Manufacture of the handles includes mixing and heating the raw materials, shaping the mix by pouring it into molds, and drying. Production of the screwdrivers is then completed in two operations: assembling the handles and shanks, and packaging for shipment to retail outlets such as K Mart, Target, and True Value hardware stores.

Process costing information for the Drying Department of Master Craft Company for a period follows. No direct materials are required.

Units:
Work in process, beginning (30% complete as to conversion costs)	7,000 units
Transferred in from the Molding Department during the period	32,000 units
Completed during the period	16,000 units
Work in process, ending (20% complete as to conversion costs)	23,000 units

Costs:
Work in process, beginning	$ 1,190
Transferred in from the Molding Department during the period	3,840
Conversion costs added during the period	1,295

The cost of direct materials in the assembling and packaging phases includes the cost of the plastic handles transferred out of the Drying Department plus the cost of the metal shanks, which is $1,493. The assembling and packaging operations are entirely automated. Assembling occurs at the rate of 4,000 units per hour and packaging at 2,000 per hour. Conversion cost is allocated to the assembling operation at the predetermined rate of $25.00 per machine hour and to packaging at the rate of $27.50 per machine hour. There is only one work order for the screwdrivers.

Required

1. Compute the number of equivalent units (screwdrivers) produced by the Drying Department during the period.
2. Show the application of total cost to (a) units completed and transferred to finished goods and (b) units in ending work in process inventory.

3. Compute the total manufacturing cost of the screwdrivers completed and transferred to finished goods. Also compute the unit cost of each complete screwdriver to the nearest cent.

Problem 23-6A *Computing equivalent units for a second department with beginning inventory, applying cost to completed units and work in process, and accounting for byproducts and joint products (L.O. 2, 3, 4, 5, 7)*

Cost per equiv. unit:
  Transf. in $.75
  Materials $.45
  Conversion costs $1.00
Cost per case:
  Toms $1.70
  Chitos $1.81

Toms, Inc., manufactures convenience foods including potato chips and corn chips. Production of corn chips occurs in five steps: cleaning, mixing, cooking, drying, and packaging. Suppose the accounting records of a Toms plant yielded the following information for corn chips in its Packaging Department during a weekly period:

Cases:

Work in process, beginning (10% complete as to direct materials, 0% complete as to conversion costs)	3,000 cases
Transferred in from the Drying Department during the week	18,000 cases
Completed during the week	15,000 cases
Work in process, ending (5% complete as to direct materials, 0% complete as to conversion costs)	6,000 cases

Costs:

Work in process, beginning.............................	$ 6,280
Transferred in from the Drying Department during the week	13,500
Direct materials added during the week	6,750
Conversion costs added during the week	15,000

Required

1. Compute the number of equivalent cases of corn chips produced by the Packaging Department during the week.
2. Show the application of total cost in the Packaging Department to (a) cases completed and transferred to finished goods and (b) cases in ending work in process inventory.
3. Inventory ruined during packaging can be sold as a byproduct. Its sale price is 3 percent, and the cost of selling the byproduct is 1 percent of the total cost to be transferred to finished goods. Record the byproduct inventory.
4. After 300 cases of the byproduct inventory (in Requirement 3) are removed, the finished goods inventory consists of 20,700 cases. Of this finished goods inventory, 12,300 cases are Toms corn chips, sold at $5.40 per case, and 8,400 cases are Chitos corn chips, sold at $5.70 per case. Use the relative sales value method to compute the costs per case (to the nearest cent) of these two joint products. Round relative sales value to the nearest percent.

Problem 23-7A *Product costing in an activity-based system (L.O. 6)*

Total mfg. product cost $114.50

Texas Instruments factory assembles and tests printed-circuit (PC) boards. Using assumed numbers, consider the following data regarding PC Board XR1, which is used in certain computers:

Direct materials..............................	$65.00
Conversion costs applied	?
Total manufacturing product cost	?

The activities that apply to building the PC boards follow:

Manufacturing Activity	Cost Driver	Conversion Costs Applied for Each Activity
1. Start station	Number of raw PC boards	1 × .90 = $ .90
2. Dip insertion	Number of dip insertions	20 × .25 = ?
3. Manual insertion	Number of manual insertions	12 × ? = 7.20
4. Wave solder	Number of boards soldered	1 × 3.50 = 3.50
5. Backload	Number of backload insertions	? × .70 = 4.90
6. Test	Standard time each board is in test activity	.25 × 80 = ?
7. Defect analysis	Standard time for defect analysis and repair	.16 × ? = 8.00
Total		$?

Required

1. Fill in the blanks in both the opening schedule and the list of activities.
2. How is direct labor identified with products under this product costing system?
3. Why might managers favor this activity-based accounting system instead of the older system, which applied conversion costs based on direct labor?

Problem 23-8A *Product costing in an activity-based system* **(L.O. 6)**

Full product cost per unit:
Standard chair $93.50
Unpainted chair $71.25

Blume Furniture Company manufacturers rocking chairs in its two plants in West Virginia. The company uses activity-based costing, and its activities and related data follow:

Maufacturing Activity	Budgeted Conversion Costs for 19X8	Cost Driver Chosen as Application Base	Conversion Cost per Unit of Application Base
Material handling	$ 200,000	Number of parts	$ 0.25
Cutting	880,000	Number of parts	1.10
Assembling	3,000,000	Direct labor hours	15.00
Painting	70,000	Number of painted units	2.00

Two styles of chairs were produced in March, the standard chair and an unpainted chair, which had fewer parts and required no painting. Their quantities, direct material costs, and other data follow:

Product	Units Produced	Direct Material Costs	Number of Parts	Assembling Direct Labor Hours
Standard chair	5,000	$90,000	100,000	7,500
Unpainted chair	1,000	15,000	15,000	1,200

Required

1. Compute the total manufacturing costs and unit costs of the standard chairs and the unpainted chairs.
2. Suppose upstream activities, such as product design, were analyzed and applied to the standard chairs at $3 each and the unpainted chairs at $2 each. Moreover, similar analyses were conducted of downstream activities, such as distribution, marketing, and customer service. The downstream costs applied were $21 per standard chair and $16 per unpainted chair. Compute the full product cost per unit.

3. Which costs are used for reporting in the external financial statements? Which costs are used for management decision making? Explain the difference.

(Group B)

Problem 23-1B

Computing equivalent units and applying cost to completed units and work in process; no beginning inventory or cost transferred in **(L.O. 2, 3)**

Cost per unit $4.30
Work in Process bal. $17,360

Southwest Custom Specialties engraves and prints specialty books on wildlife. Production occurs in three processes: engraving, printing, and binding. The Engraving Department was empty on May 31. In mid-June Southwest started production on 65,000 books. Of this number, 52,600 books were engraved during June. The June 30 work in process in the Engraving Department was 20 percent complete as to direct materials and 50 percent complete as to conversion costs. Direct materials costing $137,700 were placed in production in the Engraving Department during June, and direct labor of $43,140 and factory overhead of $62,700 were applied in this department.

Required

1. Compute the number of equivalent units of production and unit costs in the Engraving Department for June.
2. Show the application of total cost in the Engraving Department to (a) units completed and transferred to Printing during June and (b) units still in process at June 30.
3. Prepare a T-account for Work in Process Inventory—Engraving to show its activity during June, including the June 30 balance.

Problem 23-2B

Computing equivalent units, applying cost to completed units and work in process, and journalizing transactions; no beginning inventory or cost transferred in **(L.O. 2, 3, 4)**

Cost per unit $24
Work in Process bal. $2,400

Bellmead Newsprint, Inc., manufactures newsprint (the paper stock on which newspapers are printed) by a four-stage process that includes mixing, cooking, rolling, and cutting. In the Mixing Department, wood pulp and chemicals, the basic raw materials, are blended. The resulting mix is heated in the Cooking Department in much the same way food is prepared. Then the cooked mix is rolled to produce sheets. The final process, cutting, divides the sheets into large rolled units for shipment to newspaper companies.

Cost accumulation in the Mixing Department during August is summarized in the following account:

Work in Process Inventory—Mixing

Direct materials	24,700
Direct labor	7,400
Factory overhead	13,500

August activity in the Mixing Department consisted of completion of the mixing process for 1,800 rolls of newsprint plus partial completion of 300 additional rolls. These in-process units were 33⅓ percent complete with respect to direct materials and conversion costs.

Required

1. Compute the equivalent units of production and unit costs in the Mixing Department for August.

2. Prove that the sum of (a) cost of goods transferred out of the Mixing Department and (b) ending Work in Process Inventory—Mixing equals the total cost accumulated in the department during August.

3. Journalize all transactions affecting the company's mixing process during August, including those already posted.

Cost per equiv. unit:
  Transf. in $38
  Materials $21
  Conv. costs $89

Problem 23-3B *Computing equivalent units for a second department with beginning inventory; applying cost to completed units and work in process (L.O. 2, 3, 5)*

Basset & Ames manufactures broadloom carpet in seven processes: spinning, dyeing, plying, spooling, tufting, latexing, and shearing.

First, fluff nylon purchased from a company such as DuPont or Monsanto is spun into yarn that is dyed the desired color. Then two or more threads of the yarn are joined together, or plied, for added strength. The plied yarn is spooled for use in the actual carpet making. Tufting is the process by which yarn is added to burlap backing. After the backing is latexed to hold it together and make it skid resistant, the carpet is sheared to give it an even appearance and feel.

At March 31, before recording the transfer of cost from department to department, the Basset & Ames general ledger included the following account for one of its lines of carpet:

Work in Process Inventory—Dyeing	
Feb. 28 Balance	10,900
Transferred in from Spinning	21,280
Direct materials	12,390
Direct labor	7,207
Factory overhead	42,900

Work in process inventory of the Dyeing Department on February 28 consisted of 75 rolls that were 60 percent complete as to direct materials and conversion costs. During March 560 rolls were transferred in from the Spinning Department. The Dyeing Department completed 500 rolls of the carpet in March, and 135 rolls were still in process on March 31. This ending inventory was 100 percent complete as to direct materials and 80 percent complete as to conversion costs.

Required

1. Compute the equivalent units of production, unit costs, and total cost to account for in the Dyeing Department for March.

2. Show the application of total Dyeing Department cost for March to (a) cost of goods transferred from Dyeing to Plying and (b) cost of ending Work in Process Inventory—Dyeing on March 31.

Total cost accounted for $94,677

Problem 23-4B *Preparing a production cost report and recording transactions based on the information in the report (L.O. 4)*

Required

1. Prepare the March production cost report for the Dyeing Department in Problem 23-3B.

2. Journalize all transactions affecting the Dyeing Department during March, including those entries that have already been posted.

Problem 23-5B *Computing equivalent units for a second department with beginning inventory and applying cost to completed units and work in process (L.O. 2, 3, 5)*

Cost per equiv. unit:
Transf. in $37
Conv. costs $8
Cost per mower $50.82

The manufacture of lawn mowers includes two processes: forming the blade housing from steel and assembling the parts of the mower. Two additional operations, lubricating the moving parts and testing the completed mowers, complete their manufacture. The completed mowers are transferred to finished goods prior to shipment to Sears, Montgomery Ward, Penney's, and other department stores.

Process costing information for the Assembling Department of Lawn Genie, Inc., for a period follows. No direct materials are required.

Units:

Work in process, beginning (60% complete as to conversion costs)	2,000 units
Transferred in from the Forming Department during the period	9,000 units
Completed during the period	6,000 units
Work in process, ending (70% complete as to conversion costs)	5,000 units

Costs:

Work in process, beginning	$ 92,000
Transferred in from the Forming Department during the period	333,000
Conversion costs added during the period	66,400

The cost of direct materials in the lubricating and testing phases is the cost of the mowers transferred out of the Assembling Department. The lubricating operation is entirely automated and takes 30 seconds per mower. Testing each completed mower requires an average of five minutes of a technician's time. Conversion costs are $30 per machine hour for lubricating and $50 per man hour for testing. There is only one work order for the mowers in each production run.

Required

1. Compute the number of equivalent units (mowers) produced by the Assembling Department during the period.
2. Show the application of total cost to (a) units completed and transferred to finished goods and (b) units in ending work in process inventory.
3. Compute the total manufacturing cost of the mowers completed and transferred to finished goods. Also compute the unit cost of each complete mower (to the nearest cent).

Problem 23-6B *Computing equivalent units for a second department with beginning inventory, applying cost to completed units and work in process, and accounting for byproducts and joint products (L.O. 2, 3, 4, 5, 7)*

Cost per equiv. unit:
Transf. in $1.60
Materials $.20
Conv. costs $.30
Cost per gallon:
Wax paper $.99
Auto wax $2.94

Many products are developed from crude oil, including aviation fuel, gasoline, asphalt, and the wax used to make wax paper and automobile wax. This problem focuses on the wax products.

Wax is removed from crude oil by two basic processes, heating and cooling. Heating separates the lighter components, such as aviation fuel and gasoline, from the heavier components. The heavier residue is cooled, passed through a brine solution, and filtered to obtain wax. Therefore, the manufacture of wax consists of heating, cooling, mixing, and filtering processes, in that order.

Suppose the accounting records of a DuPont Chemical Corporation refinery yielded the following information about its Wax Filtering Department for a weekly period:

Gallons:

Work in process, beginning (30% complete as to direct materials, 40% complete as to conversion costs)...	8,000 gallons
Transferred in from the Mixing Department during the week................................	62,000 gallons
Completed during the week	50,000 gallons
Work in process, ending (67% complete as to direct materials, 81% complete as to conversion costs) ...	20,000 gallons

Costs:

Work in process, beginning	$17,040
Transferred in from the Mixing Department during the week................................	99,200
Direct materials added during the week	12,200
Conversion costs added during the week	18,900

Required

1. Compute the number of equivalent gallons of wax produced during the week by the Wax Filtering Department.

2. Show the application of total cost in the Wax Filtering Department to (a) gallons completed and transferred to finished goods and (b) gallons in ending work in process inventory.

3. Assume a lower grade of wax is removed as a byproduct from the wax filtering process. Its sale price is 2 percent, and the cost of selling the byproduct is ¼ percent (.0025), of the total cost to be transferred to finished goods. Record the byproduct inventory.

4. After 4,000 gallons of the byproduct inventory (in Requirement 3) is removed, the finished goods inventory consists of 46,000 gallons of wax. The company will sell 15,000 gallons at $2.06 per gallon to a wax paper manufacturer and 31,000 gallons at $5.91 per gallon to an automobile wax producer. Use the relative sales value method to compute the costs per gallon (to the nearest cent) of these two joint products. Round relative sales value to the nearest percent.

Total mfg. product cost $117.80

Problem 23-7B   *Product costing in an activity-based system*   (L.O. 6)

National Semiconductor factory assembles and tests printed-circuit (PC) boards. Using assumed numbers, consider the following data regarding PC Board J47, which is used in certain computers:

Direct materials	$71.00
Conversion costs applied	?
Total manufacturing product cost	$?

The activities that apply to building the PC boards follow:

Manufacturing Activity	Cost Driver	Conversion Costs Applied for Each Activity
1. Start station	No. of raw PC boards	1 × $1.30 = $1.30
2. Dip insertion	No. of dip insertions	? × .60 = 6.00
3. Manual insertion	No. of manual insertions	11 × .80 = ?
4. Wave solder	No. of boards soldered	1 × 1.50 = 1.50
5. Backload	No. of backload insertions	6 × ? = 4.20
6. Test	Standard time each board is in test activity	.20 × 90 = ?
7. Defect analysis	Standard time for defect analysis and repair	.10 × ? = 7.00
Total		$?

Required

1. Fill in the blanks in both the opening schedule and the list of activities.
2. How is direct labor identified with products under this product costing system?
3. Why might managers favor this activity-based accounting system instead of the older system, which applied conversion costs based on direct labor?

Problem 23-8B   *Product costing in an activity-based system*   *(L.O. 6)*

Janelli, Inc., manufactures chairs and uses an activity-based costing system. Janelli's activity areas and related data follow:

Full product cost per unit:
Standard chair $85.00
Unpainted chair $60.60

Manufacturing Activity Area	Budgeted Conversion Costs for 19X0	Cost Driver Used as Application Base	Conversion Cost per Unit of Application Base
Material handling	$ 100,000	Number of parts	$ 0.10
Cutting	1,000,000	Number of parts	1.30
Assembly	3,000,000	Direct labor hours	18.00
Painting	60,000	Number of painted units	3.00

Two styles of chairs were produced in March, the standard chair and an unpainted chair, which had fewer parts and required no painting. The quantities, direct material costs, and other data follow:

	Units Produced	Direct Material Costs	Number of Parts	Assembling Direct Labor Hours
Standard chair	2,000	$24,000	30,000	3,000
Unpainted chair	3,000	27,000	36,000	2,800

Required

1. Compute the total manufacturing costs and unit costs of the standard chairs and the unpainted chairs.
2. Suppose upstream activities, such as product design, were analyzed and applied to the standard chairs at $4 each and the unpainted chairs at $3 each. Moreover, similar analyses were conducted of downstream activities, such as distribution, marketing, and customer service. The downstream costs applied were $18 per standard chair and $15 per unpainted chair. Compute the full product cost per unit.
3. Which costs are used for reporting in the external financial statements? Which costs are used for management decision making? Explain the difference.

Extending Your Knowledge

Decision Problems

1. Preparing a Production Cost Report and Identifying Decisions that Would Be Based on the Information *(L.O. 5)*

Total cost accounted for
$208,520

Fort Bend Manufacturing Company makes automobile parts. The following cost data for the company's Finishing Department are available for October.

Equivalent units of production:

Flow of Production	Flow of Physical Units	Equivalent Units of Production		
		Transferred In	Direct Materials	Conversion Costs
Units to account for:				
Beginning work in process inventory	12,000			
Transferred in during October	28,000			
Total units to account for	40,000			
Units accounted for:				
Completed and transferred out to finished goods during October:				
From beginning inventory	12,000	—	7,200	6,000
Transferred in from Molding and completed during October (36,000 − 12,000)	24,000	24,000	24,000	24,000
Work in process, October 31	4,000	4,000	800	1,200
Total physical units accounted for	40,000			
Equivalent units of production		28,000	32,000	31,200

Unit costs:

	Transferred-In Costs	Direct Materials	Conversion Costs	Total
Work in process, September 30	Work done before October			$ 59,000
Costs added during October	$ 64,400	$ 35,200	$ 49,920	149,520
Divide by equivalent units	÷28,000	÷32,000	÷31,200	
Cost per equivalent unit	$ 2.30	$ 1.10	$ 1.60	
Total cost to account for				$208,520

Allocation of total cost:

	Transferred-In Costs	Direct Materials	Conversion Costs	Total
Units completed and transferred out to finished goods:				
From work in process, September 30				$ 59,000
Costs added during October:				
Direct materials	—	7,200 × $1.10		7,920
Conversion costs	—		6,000 × $1.60	9,600
Total completed from September 30 inventory				76,520
Units transferred in from Molding and completed during October	24,000 × ($2.30 + $1.10 + $1.60)			120,000
Total costs transferred out				196,520
Work in process, October 31:				
Transferred-in costs	4,000 × $2.30			9,200
Direct materials		800 × $1.10		880
Conversion costs			1,200 × $1.60	1,920
Total work in process, October 31				12,000
Total cost accounted for				$208,520

Required

1. Prepare a production cost report for the Finishing Department for the month of October.

2. Discuss specific decisions that would be based on the information in the report.

2. Process Costing in the Same Department for Two Consecutive Months (L.O. 2, 3)

Jan. costs per equiv. unit:
  Materials $1.50
  Conv. costs $1.00
Feb. costs per equiv. unit:
  Materials $1.60
  Conv. costs $1.00

Waterford Pottery makes ceramic bowls. The bowls are made, fired, and dried in the Forming Department. Then they are transferred to the Finishing Department to be painted and shipped to retail outlets. No bowls are broken at any point in the procedure. The following information is available for the Forming Department for January and February 19X5:

Forming Department

Units:

Work in process, January 1 (50% complete as to direct materials, 25% complete as to conversion costs)	100 bowls
Production started during January	800 bowls
Work in process, January 31 (40% complete as to direct materials, 20% complete as to conversion costs)	300 bowls
Production started during February	900 bowls
Work in process, February 28 (70% complete as to direct materials, 50% complete as to conversion costs)	600 bowls

Costs:

Work in process, January 1	$ 200
Costs added during January:	
Direct materials	1,005
Conversion costs	635
Costs added during February:	
Direct materials	1,440
Conversion costs	840

Required

1. Compute the equivalent units of production, unit costs and total cost to account for in the Forming Department for January. Show the application of total Forming Department cost for January to (a) cost of goods transferred from Forming to Finishing and (b) cost of ending Work in Process Inventory—Forming at January 31, 19X5.

2. Compute the equivalent units of production, equivalent-unit costs, and total cost to account for in the Forming Department for February. Show the application of total Forming Department cost for February to (a) cost of goods transferred from Forming to Finishing and (b) cost of ending Work in Process Inventory—Forming at February 28, 19X5.

3. Prepare the January and February (individually by month) production cost reports for the Forming Department.

Ethical Issue

Hutch Manufacturing produces component parts for laser optic equipment. Customers include civilian companies and the U.S. government. Under most government contracts Hutch receives reimbursement for its manufacturing costs plus a specified profit margin. For most civilian contracts Hutch bids a fixed price and either earns a profit or incurs a loss, depending on how well the company controls costs. For both government and civilian jobs, top Hutch managers allocate to the government contracts any overhead whose proper allocation to a particular product is less than certain.

Required

1. Is Hutch's overhead allocation practice ethical? Give your reason.
2. Who benefits and who is harmed by the Hutch practice?

Chapter 24

Flexible Budgets and Standard Costs

L ee Nicholas, the manufacturing supervisor of Kayak Manufacturing Company was concerned for his job. The results from the most recent month of operations showed negative variances in the manufacturing area. This was not good news.

The company's standard cost system was just in its third month of operations so the system was not yet in use throughout the company. Implementation of the standard cost system had been spurred by the downturn in sales brought about by the economic recession. In short, Kayak Manufacturing Company intended that the standard cost system help control costs. Nicholas hoped his boss wouldn't respond hastily to the recent period's performance—even if it did represent the third straight month of dismal performance.

Chapter 20 introduced management accounting by emphasizing that budgets are the main tool for planning and control. Chapter 21 showed how to budget profit levels by analyzing cost-volume-profit relationships. Chapters 22 and 23 explored accounting for manufacturing companies. In this chapter we now explore budgeting in more depth. The first half of the chapter covers flexible budgets, and the second half discusses standard costs, which are an outgrowth of the flexible budget. We begin by reviewing the cost behavior patterns and the relevant range, which were introduced in Chapter 21.

Cost Behavior Patterns

Accountants define cost as resources given up to achieve a specific objective. For now, consider costs as dollars paid for goods and services. Examples are the costs of materials, factory wages, sales commissions, utilities, and interest expense. Distinctions among these categories of costs are important in many accounting situations. In budgeting, however, they can be treated similarly.

Cost behavior is the movement of a cost in response to a measure of volume such as sales. Two extreme types of cost behavior are variable and fixed. Variable costs are those whose total amount changes in direct proportion with changes in volume or activity. Fixed costs are costs whose total amount does not change during a given time period over a wide range of volume. Examples include depreciation, property taxes, insurance, and executive salaries.

Throughout this chapter, we assume that each cost is either variable or fixed or that it can be divided into variable and fixed portions. A mixed cost has both variable and fixed components. The compensation of a salesperson who is paid a flat monthly salary plus a commission based on his or her sales is a mixed cost. Water expense computed as a fixed monthly amount plus a unit cost per 100 gallons used is also a mixed cost.

Note that the "variable" and "fixed" characteristics of a cost relate to its *total* amount, not its *per-unit* amount. A variable cost is variable with respect to its *total* amount. A fixed cost is fixed with respect to its *total* amount. The behavior of variable and fixed costs with respect to per-unit sales is different, as the following table shows.

Teaching Tip: Review the behavior of variable and fixed costs:

Variable costs are constant per unit, but vary in total in direct proportion to changes in the activity level.

Fixed costs are constant in total, but vary per unit in direct proportion to changes in the activity level.

	If Volume Increases (Decreases)	
Type of Cost	**Total Cost**	**Cost Per Unit**
Variable cost (example: sales commission)	Increases (decreases)	No change
Fixed cost (example: monthly rent)	No change	Decreases (increases)

Illustrations will clarify the difference between the total and the unit amounts of variable cost and fixed cost. Suppose a sales clerk in the shoe department of a J. C. Penney store is paid a sales commission of $2 per pair of shoes sold, which is a variable cost. Weekly sales of 200 pairs generates total sales commission expense of $400. Unit selling cost—the commission—remains $2 per pair of shoes.

Now consider the fixed monthly rent of a cookie store in a shopping mall. Total monthly rent expense of $2,000 does not change in response to changes in volume. If the store sells 20,000 cookies each month, the rent expense per unit is $.10 ($2,000 rent/20,000 cookies). But if the store sells 40,000 cookies monthly, the unit cost of rent is only $.05 ($2,000/40,000). In either case, the total monthly rent is fixed at $2,000.

Relevant Range

Point to Stress: The relevant range is the level of activity over which the cost behavior patterns are valid.

The definition of a *fixed cost* has two underlying assumptions.

1. The total cost will not change for a given time period, which is the *budget period*. Fixed costs may change from budget year to budget year because of changes in salary levels, number of workers, rent levels, and property tax levels. But fixed costs are not expected to change within a given budget period.
2. The total cost will not change over a wide range of volume, which is the *relevant range*.

Fixed costs are based on an expected band of volume. For example, a toy manufacturer may have monthly fixed costs of $200,000 when it is producing 16,000 to 24,000 units per month. However, after the Christmas rush, sales fall below 16,000 units, and fixed costs decrease to $175,000. So "fixed" is a useful concept, but "fixed" does not mean forever or under all operating conditions. Instead, it relates to a relevant range of volume, as shown by the following graph of cost behavior:

Having reviewed the necessary concepts and terms, let's turn to flexible budgets and their role in management decision making.

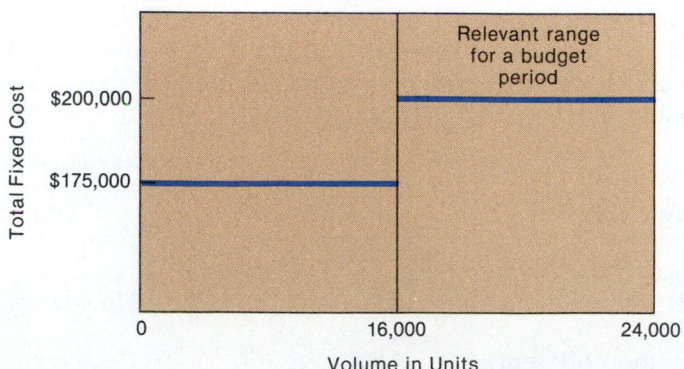

Flexible Budgets

The master budget in Chapter 20 is a **static budget,** which is prepared for only one level of volume. It is not altered after it is drawn up, regardless of changes in volume, cost drivers, or other conditions during the budget period. Consider a master budget based on a single target sales volume of 200,000 units. Assume actual volume turns out to be 180,000 units. The comparison of actual and budgeted results, which is an example of a **performance report,** follows (amounts assumed).

	Actual Results	Static (Master) Budget	Variance
Units sold	180,000	200,000	20,000 U
Sales	$540,000	$600,000	$60,000 U
Expenses	500,000	525,000	25,000 F
Operating income	$ 40,000	$ 75,000	$35,000 U

Variance is the difference between an actual amount and the corresponding budgeted amount. Throughout U = unfavorable variance and F = favorable variance.

This performance report is difficult to analyze because the budget is based on 200,000 units, but only 180,000 units were sold. Note the $25,000 expense variance. Why did it occur? Because of efficient cost control? Because of a lower sales volume? We are unsure. This performance report, based on a static budget, simply does not provide enough detail to answer these important management questions.

For a detailed analysis of performance, managers often use a **flexible budget,** which is a set of budgets covering a range of volume rather than a single level of volume. Flexible budgets are also called *variable budgets* because they present budgeted amounts for different levels of volume. Managers find flexible budgets helpful for studying the behavior of expenses as volume fluctuates. Microcomputers and electronic spreadsheets have placed this budgeting tool at the disposal of most middle and top managers in the United States.

Exhibit 24-1 shows a condensed flexible budget for Bellmead Pools & Supply, which installs swimming pools. Throughout this illustration we assume that all pools are sold and installed in the same month. Therefore, we use the terms *pool sales* and *pool installations* interchangeably.

In this example, the total variable cost of installing a $12,000 swimming pool is $8,000. A more detailed budget would list the individual variable costs, such as direct materials and direct labor. It might also detail the various fixed expenses, including depreciation on equipment, insurance, and administrative overhead. Total monthly fixed expenses are $20,000.

Flexible budgets are useful both before and after a budget period. As a planning tool, they can help managers identify the level of volume that will serve as the business's target level for the coming period. As a control device, they help managers analyze actual results.

The **budget formula**—the heart of the flexible budget—shows how to compute the budget amounts:

Revenues	−	Variable expenses	− Fixed expenses = Operating income (loss)

$$\left(\begin{array}{c}\text{Number of units sold}\\ \times \text{ Unit sale price}\end{array}\right) - \left(\begin{array}{c}\text{Number of units sold}\\ \times \text{ Variable cost per unit}\end{array}\right) - \text{Fixed expenses} = \text{Operating income (loss)}$$

Discussion Question: What is wrong with comparing actual results (volume of 180,000 units) to the static budget (volume of 200,000 units)? *ANSWER:* A comparison of actual and budgeted costs using a static budget gives management the wrong signals. If actual costs at 180,000 units are compared with budgeted costs at 200,000 units, management may congratulate itself on a favorable variance. However, management is not considering what the budgeted costs at 180,000 units might have been. If budgeted costs for 180,000 units are less than the actual costs, the variance is unfavorable. The way to make a logical analysis is to compare budgeted and actual costs at the same level of activity.

Discussion Question: Why is it necessary to have a static budget amount? *ANSWER:* A company must choose a level of volume in order to prepare its budget plan for the future and calculate a predetermined overhead rate.

Point to Stress: A static budget can be used in combination with a flexible budget. The focus of the static budget is future planning. The focus of the flexible budget is evaluating past performance.

EXHIBIT 24-1 *Flexible Budget*

Bellmead Pools & Supply
Flexible Budget
Each Month of the Period April–August 19X5

	Budget Formula per Unit	Various Levels of Volume		
		6	8	10
Units....................	—	6	8	10
Sales	$12,000	$72,000	$96,000	$120,000
Variable expenses	8,000	48,000	64,000	80,000
Fixed expenses............	(see Note)	20,000	20,000	20,000
Total expenses		68,000	84,000	100,000
Operating income (loss)....		$ 4,000	$12,000	$ 20,000

Note: Fixed expenses are given as a total amount rather than as a cost per unit.

Typical Student Misconception: Students often confuse the static budget with the flexible budget. Emphasize that the static budget is prepared before the beginning of the period so that managers can use it for planning. The actual level of output will probably differ from the level underlying the static budget. The flexible budget uses the same variable unit costs and the same total fixed costs as the static budget, and calculates budgeted expenses at various levels of output. Then actual performance can be evaluated.

Teaching Tip: Write the income statement format on the board:

> Revenue
> – Expenses
> = Operating Income

This is exactly what the budget formula calculates:

> Revenue
> – Variable Expenses
> – Fixed Expenses
> = Operating Income

In this illustration, Bellmead Pools' cost behavior is fixed expenses of $20,000 per month plus variable expenses of $8,000 per pool sold and installed. Exhibit 24-1 shows the expected results for three operating levels. Other volume levels could be added for 7, 9, or any other number of pools per month, as the situation warrants. Keep in mind that a flexible budget relates to a specific relevant range only. Expenses are unlikely to behave according to a set formula outside some volume range. For example, a volume of 15 pools per month may not fall within the relevant range. In such cases, managers must develop a new budget formula.

Graphing the Budget Expense Formula

Another budgeting tool is a graph of the expense formula. With such a graph, the accountant can provide a budget customized to any volume level. The graph in Exhibit 24-2 shows total expenses for Bellmead Pools & Supply for all volume levels from 0 to 11 pools sold per month. Let us assume this span of volume is the relevant range. Also, we assume that management based the master budget—the static budget—on a projected sales volume of 8 pools per month.

The graph displays an overall picture of the direct materials, direct labor, and all other expenses that must be planned at various volume levels. When the company plans to build 8 pools, the total expense level ($84,000) for this volume is highlighted (as Exhibit 24-2 shows).

A budget graph also helps analyze actual results. Exhibit 24-3 is the graph of actual versus budgeted results for the peak season of 19X5. The graph shows that actual expenses exceeded budgeted expenses during April, June, and August. Actual expenses were less than budget for May and July. Overall, the budget and actual figures are close.

Point to Stress: The budgeted expense graph in Exhibit 24-2 is exactly the same as the expenses graph in the cost-volume-profit analysis.

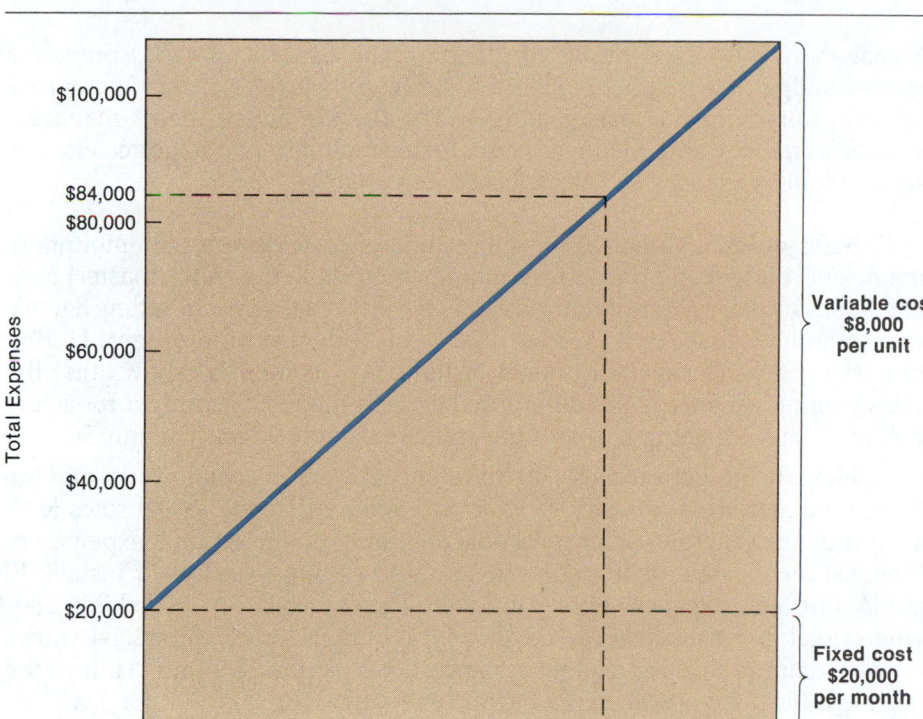

Volume in Number of Swimming Pools Sold and Installed Per Month

EXHIBIT 24-3 *Bellmead Pools & Supply*
Graph of Actual and Budgeted Monthly Total Expenses

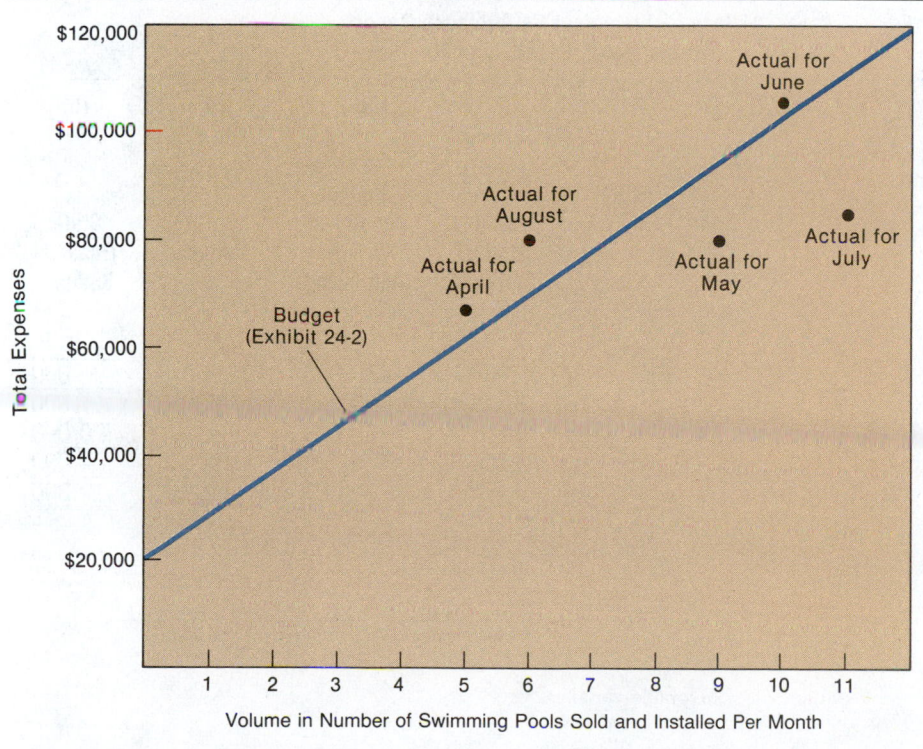

Volume in Number of Swimming Pools Sold and Installed Per Month

Analyzing the Results

Teaching Tip: In Exhibit 24-4, Actual Results (Column 1) comes from the June 30, 19X5 income statement. Flexible Budget for Actual Volume (Column 3) is prepared based on the volume shown in Column 1. Static Budget (Column 5) was prepared before the fiscal year began. Determining the variances (Columns 2 and 4) is the final step in preparing the performance report.

Managers usually have a cycle of planning and control. They (1) prepare a master budget, (2) transact business to achieve their goals, and (3) compare actual results with the master budget. The flexible budget helps managers analyze variances from planned results, which fall into two major categories: sales volume variances and flexible budget variances.

1. **Sales volume variances** are those differences between the amounts in the flexible budget and the corresponding amounts in the static (master) budget. For example, assume Bellmead Pools & Supply set a goal of selling 8 pools each month during April–August 19X5 and budgeted accordingly. During June the company installs 10 pools. Exhibit 24-4, column 4, shows that the sales volume variance is the difference between the flexible budget for actual volume achieved (column 3) and the static (master) budget (column 5).

2. **Flexible budget variances** are differences between actual results and the flexible budget. This category of variances is based on the actual sales level achieved. For example, Bellmead Pools & Supply budgeted total expenses of $100,000 for the sale of 10 pools. In June the company sells and installs 10 pools, but total expenses exceed budget. This can be seen in Exhibit 24-3, where total expenses for June lie above the budget line. Exhibit 24-4 shows how to compute a flexible budget variance: actual results (column 1) minus the flexible budget for actual volume achieved (column 3).

OBJECTIVE 2

Prepare an income statement performance report

We have seen that mere comparison of a *static (master)* budget with *actual* results does not explain much, because the actual sales level may differ from

EXHIBIT 24-4   *Income Statement Performance Report*

	(1) Actual Results at Actual Prices	(2) (1)–(3) Flexible Budget Variances	(3) Flexible Budget for Actual Volume Achieved*	(4) (3)–(5) Sales Volume Variances	(5) Static (Master) Budget*
Bellmead Pools & Supply					
Income Statement Performance Report					
For the Month Ended June 30, 19X5					
Units	10	-0-	10	2 F	8
Sales	$120,000	$ -0-	$120,000	$24,000 F	$96,000
Variable expenses	83,000	3,000 U	80,000	16,000 U	64,000
Fixed expenses	22,000	2,000 U	20,000	-0-	20,000
Total expenses	105,000	5,000 U	100,000	16,000 U	84,000
Operating income	$ 15,000	$5,000 U	$ 20,000	$ 8,000 F	$12,000

Flexible budget variance, $5,000 U   Sales volume variance, $8,000 F

Total variance from static budget, $3,000 F

U = unfavorable variance; F = favorable variance
*Amounts from Exhibit 24-1

the level that was used in preparing the master budget. But a flexible budget does provide the information needed to understand why actual revenues, expenses, and income differ from budgeted amounts. Exhibit 24-4 is an income statement performance report based on a flexible budget. Study it carefully, especially the two variance columns.

In Exhibit 24-4, column 3 information is taken from Exhibit 24-1. For the flexible budget amounts we match units sold to actual sales in units, which in this case is 10. Use of a flexible budget allows us to analyze results over a range of activity levels within the scope of the relevant range. Had actual sales been 6 units, we could have made the comparison based on 6 units by drawing the necessary data from Exhibit 24-1.

Exhibit 24-4 shows that actual operating income ($15,000 in column 1) exceeded the static (master) budget amount ($12,000 in column 5) by $3,000. This difference is explained by an $8,000 favorable sales volume variance (column 4) and a $5,000 unfavorable flexible budget variance (column 2). Stated differently, strong sales caused actual income to exceed budget by $8,000. However, the company failed to control expenses as well as expected, resulting in an unfavorable flexible budget variance of $5,000.

How would the owners of the company use this information? Perhaps they would reward the sales staff, and they would certainly determine why expenses were too high. Our analysis of the performance report shows the unfavorable $5,000 variance, but it does not identify why expenses exceeded budget, nor does it identify the cure. Those answers depend on the specific situation. For example, Bellmead's higher-than-expected expenses might have resulted from an increase in the cost of gunite, the concrete derivative used to construct swimming pools. Such an increase might be unavoidable. However, the expense level might have resulted from wasting materials or mismanaging employees. If so, the owner would take corrective action. Variance information can direct a manager to areas of the business deserving praise or needing improvement.

Managers can of course analyze expenses in a more detailed manner—by listing each expense separately. Also, the flexible budget variances can be analyzed further, as the next major section of the chapter explains. First, however, test your understanding of the coverage thus far by working the summary problem for review.

Point to Stress: In a manufacturing company, the cost of one unit is essentially many different costs combined—materials, labor, and overhead costs. A manufacturing company must be able to control these costs if it is to be profitable. One aspect of cost control is knowing if any of these costs are out of the budget range, and who can correct the problem.

Summary Problem for Your Review

Exhibit 24-4 indicates that Bellmead Pools & Supply sold and installed 10 swimming pools during June. Suppose June sales were 7 pools instead of 10. Suppose further that the price of each pool was $12,500 instead of the budgeted $12,000. Actual variable expenses were $57,400, and actual fixed expenses were $19,000.

Required

1. Given these new assumptions, prepare a revised income statement performance report like Exhibit 24-4.
2. Show that the flexible budget variances and the sales volume variances in operating income account for the difference between actual operating income and the static (master) budgeted income.

3. As the company owner, what specific employees would you praise or criticize after you analyze this performance report?

SOLUTION TO REVIEW PROBLEM

Requirement 1

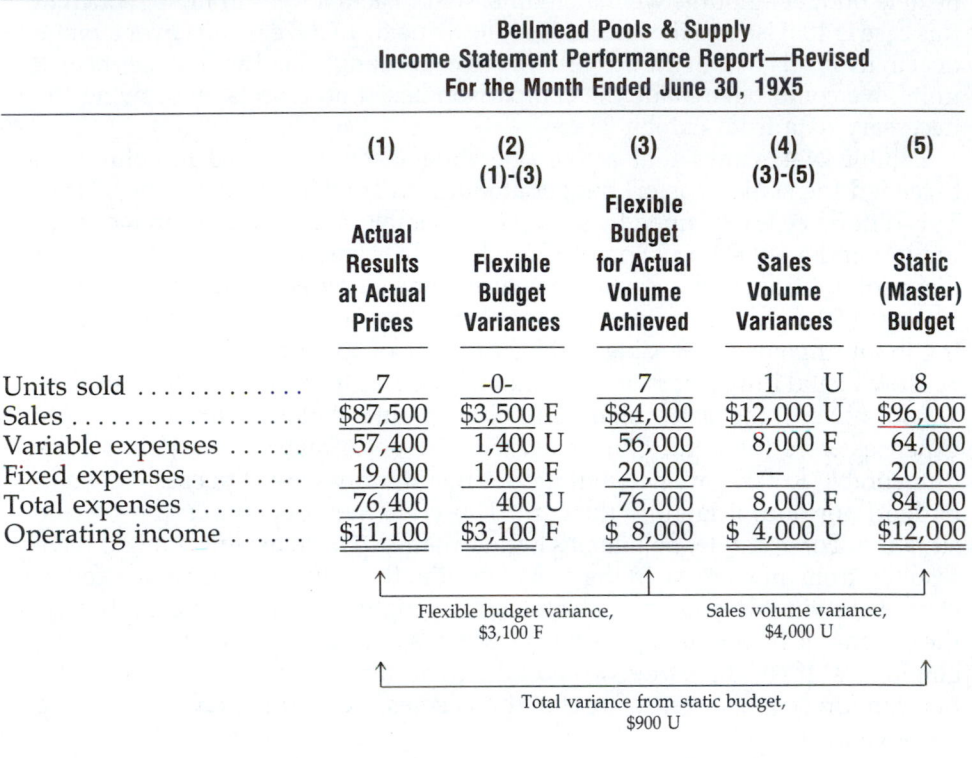

Bellmead Pools & Supply
Income Statement Performance Report—Revised
For the Month Ended June 30, 19X5

	(1) Actual Results at Actual Prices	(2) (1)-(3) Flexible Budget Variances	(3) Flexible Budget for Actual Volume Achieved	(4) (3)-(5) Sales Volume Variances	(5) Static (Master) Budget
Units sold	7	-0-	7	1 U	8
Sales	$87,500	$3,500 F	$84,000	$12,000 U	$96,000
Variable expenses	57,400	1,400 U	56,000	8,000 F	64,000
Fixed expenses.........	19,000	1,000 F	20,000	—	20,000
Total expenses	76,400	400 U	76,000	8,000 F	84,000
Operating income	$11,100	$3,100 F	$ 8,000	$ 4,000 U	$12,000

Flexible budget variance, $3,100 F   Sales volume variance, $4,000 U

Total variance from static budget, $900 U

U = unfavorable variance; F = favorable variance

Requirement 2

Static (master) budget operating income ...	$12,000
Actual operating income at actual prices ...	11,100
Total difference to account for	$ 900 U
Sales volume variance....................	$ 4,000 U
Flexible budget variance	3,100 F
Total variance	$ 900 U

Requirement 3

After investigation, management may praise the salespersons who sold pools more expensive than the budgeted sale price of $12,000 and the employees responsible for cutting fixed cost by $1,000.

Management may criticize the sales staff for not meeting the goal of selling 8 pools during the month. Also, construction or purchasing personnel were responsible for spending $1,400 more in variable costs than budget to construct the 7 pools. Of course, managers must shoulder some of the blame. They control the use of company resources hour-by-hour and day-by-day. These performance report figures summarize the overall effects of control efforts.

Standard Costing

A **standard cost** is a carefully predetermined cost that is usually expressed on a per-unit basis. It is a target cost, a cost that should be attained. Standard costs are budgeted costs for a single unit of output. **Standard cost systems** help to build budgets, gauge performance, obtain product costs, and save bookkeeping costs. Such systems help managers analyze the relationships between what should have occurred (standard costs) and what did occur (actual costs). In the chapter-opening vignette, Lee Nicholas is worried because actual manufacturing costs have exceeded the standard costs used to judge his performance.

Standard costs are used by a wide variety of organizations and in conjunction with any kind of product costing—job order, process, or a hybrid system. A construction company that builds tract houses uses a job cost system to accumulate the cost of each house. To measure performance, the company may compare actual cost for each house with the standard cost. Companies like General Mills use a process cost system for many of the foods they manufacture. To remain competitive, General Mills helps control costs by developing standard costs. Standard costing provides a concrete goal for manufacturing personnel. They strive to produce the product at standard cost or less. The difference between profits and losses often depends on controlling each activity that affects product cost.

Variances between actual and standard costs are divided into price and efficiency effects for direct materials and direct labor. A *price variance* measures how well a business keeps the unit prices of materials and labor within standards. An *efficiency variance* measures whether the quantity of materials or labor used to make a product is within the budget. By pinpointing price and efficiency effects, standard costing helps managers find ways of reducing costs. This is the purpose of the standard cost system of Kayak Manufacturing Company in the opening vignette. It also identifies those employees who deserve praise for controlling costs. Over which type of variance—price or efficiency—would Lee Nicholas seem to have more control? The efficiency variance, because Nicholas manages the plant, which uses materials. Kayak Manufacturing probably has a purchasing department that is responsible for the prices paid for materials.

At first glance, standard cost systems might appear to be more costly to operate than other systems. Obviously, a start-up investment is necessary to develop the standards. But the ongoing data-processing costs can be less than so-called actual cost systems. For example, it is more economical simply to carry all inventories at standard unit prices. In this way, the system avoids the extra data-collection costs and possible confusion of making cost flow assumptions such as first-in, first-out or last-in, first-out.

This section of the chapter explains how standard costing divides flexible budget variances—explained in the first half of the chapter—into price and efficiency effects. We continue using the Bellmead Pools & Supply example.

Relationship Between Standard Costs and Flexible Budgets

What standard of performance should be used? *Currently attainable standards* are the most popular. They are standards that can be achieved but with difficulty. Standard costs are set low enough that employees view their fulfillment as possible, though perhaps not probable. Variances tend to be unfavorable, but managers accept the standards as reasonable goals.

Does a standard cost differ from a budgeted cost? No, if the standards are attainable. However, the term *standard cost* usually refers to a unit cost, whereas *budgeted cost* refers to a total cost. For example, suppose the budgeted variable expenses in Exhibit 24-4 included direct materials as follows:

	Budget Formula Per Unit	Flexible Budget for Various Levels of Volume		
		1	6	8	10
Swimming pools installed		1	6	8	10
Direct materials		$2,000	$12,000	$16,000	$20,000

The standard cost of direct materials is $2,000 *per unit.* Budgeted cost is the total cost for the installation of all pools sold during the period. For 8 pools, budgeted cost is $16,000. For 10 pools, budgeted cost is $20,000. But standard cost of direct materials remains $2,000 per unit regardless of changes in total outlays because of differences in sales volume. *Think of a standard variable cost as a budget for a single unit.*

Illustration of Standard Costing

Let's return to our Bellmead Pools example. Recall that 10 swimming pools were sold and installed during June and that the static (master) budget had been prepared for 8 pools per month. Exhibit 24-5 provides the cost data to be used throughout our discussion of standard costing applications.

To focus on the main points of standard costing, we assume the standard cost system applies to materials, labor, and production overhead, but not to selling and administrative expenses. We also assume purchases of direct materials equals materials used.

Direct Material and Direct Labor Variances

Flexible budget variances for direct material and direct labor are often subdivided into price and efficiency variances.

The **price variance** is the difference between the actual unit prices of inputs and their standard unit prices, multiplied by the number of *actual inputs used:*

$$\text{Price variance} = \begin{array}{c} \text{Difference between} \\ \text{actual and budgeted} \\ \text{unit prices of inputs} \end{array} \times \text{Actual inputs used}$$

The **efficiency variance**—also called the **usage variance** and the **quantity variance**—is the difference between the quantity of inputs actually used and the quantity that should have been used (the flexible budget) for the actual output achieved, multiplied by the *standard unit price:*

$$\text{Efficiency variance} = \left(\begin{array}{c} \text{Inputs} \\ \text{actually} \\ \text{used} \end{array} - \begin{array}{c} \text{Inputs that should} \\ \text{have been used} \\ \text{for actual output} \end{array} \right) \times \begin{array}{c} \text{Standard} \\ \text{unit price} \\ \text{of input} \end{array}$$

EXHIBIT 24-5 *Facts for Illustration of Standard Costing*

Bellmead Pools & Supply
Facts for Illustration of Standard Costing
Month of June

Panel A—Comparison of Actual Results with Flexible Budget:
Installed 10 Swimming Pools:

	Actual Results at Actual Prices	Flexible Budget	Flexible Budget Variances
Variable expenses:			
Direct materials	$ 23,100[a]	$ 20,000[c]	$3,100 U
Direct labor	41,800[b]	42,000[c]	200 F
Variable production overhead	9,000	8,000[d]	1,000 U
Selling and administrative expenses . .	9,100	10,000	900 F
Total variable expenses	83,000	80,000	3,000 U
Fixed expenses:			
Fixed production overhead	12,300	12,000[e]	300 U
Selling and administrative expenses . .	9,700	8,000	1,700 U
Total fixed expenses	22,000	20,000	2,000 U
Total expenses	$105,000	$100,000	$5,000 U

[a] $23,100 = 11,969 cubic yards at actual price of $1.93 per cubic yard.
[b] $41,800 = 3,800 hours at actual price of $11.00 per hour.
[c] See Panel B.
[d] Variable production overhead was budgeted at $2.00 per direct labor hour:
  $8,000 = 4,000 direct labor hours (10 pools × 400 direct labor hours) × $2.00.
[e] Fixed production overhead was budgeted at $12,000 per month.

Panel B—Standards for Direct Material and Direct Labor Flexible Budget:
10 Swimming Pools:

	(1) Standard Inputs Budgeted for 10 Finished Units (Swimming Pools Installed)	(2) Standard Price per Unit of Input	(1) × (2) Flexible Budget for 10 Finished Units of Output
Direct materials	1,000 cubic yards per pool × 10 pools = 10,000 cubic yards	$ 2.00	$20,000
Direct labor	400 hours per pool × 10 pools = 4,000 hours	10.50	42,000

Teaching Tip: Look at Exhibit 24-5. Notice that the standards are per-unit amounts and not total amounts. Remember that direct materials and direct labor are variable costs that are usually expressed in unit amounts.

Real-World Example: Merrill-Continental Company, Inc. is one business that used standard costs effectively to boost profits in one of its geographic regions. One region was only marginally profitable. Instead of hiring outside consultants to develop standard costs, the management team allowed the operators and foremen to help establish standards, such as new sizes, time allowances, and amount of scrap material.

Teaching Tip: It is sometimes difficult for students to grasp how to compute the "inputs that should have been used for actual output." To compute this, the following formula is used:

Inputs that should have been used for actual output = Standard input per unit × Actual units produced

This amount tells us the quantity of raw material that should have been used to produce the number of finished units.

Price variances are computed not only for their own sake but also to give managers a sharper focus on efficiency. In this way, efficiency can be measured by holding unit prices constant. Thus managers' judgments about efficiency are unaffected by price changes. Efficiency variances have an important underlying assumption: All unit prices are *standard* prices.

Direct Materials Variances. The relevant data for computing Bellmead Pools' direct materials variances are on the next page.

	Actual Cost	Flexible Budget Standard Cost	Flexible Budget Variance
Cubic yards	11,969	10,000	
Unit price	× $1.93	× $2.00	
Total	$23,100	$20,000	$3,100 U

Managers seek to gain further insight by dividing this flexible budget variance into price and efficiency variances.

$$\text{Price variance} = \begin{array}{c}\textbf{Difference between}\\ \textbf{actual and budgeted}\\ \textbf{unit prices of inputs}\end{array} \times \textbf{Actual inputs used}$$

$$\text{Price variance} = (\$1.93 - \$2.00) \times 11,969 \text{ cubic yards}$$

$$= \$838 \text{ F}$$

$$\text{Efficiency variance} = \left(\begin{array}{c}\textbf{Actual}\\ \textbf{inputs}\\ \textbf{used}\end{array} - \begin{array}{c}\textbf{Inputs that should}\\ \textbf{have been used}\\ \textbf{for actual output}\end{array}\right) \times \begin{array}{c}\textbf{Standard}\\ \textbf{unit price}\\ \textbf{of input}\end{array}$$

$$\text{Efficiency variance} = \left(\begin{array}{c}11,969\\ \text{cubic yards}\end{array} - \begin{array}{c}10,000\\ \text{cubic yards}\end{array}\right) \times \begin{array}{c}\$2.00 \text{ per}\\ \text{cubic yard}\end{array}$$

$$= (11,969 - 10,000) \times \$2.00$$

$$= \$3,938 \text{ U}$$

The direct materials variances—from the beginning of this section—can be explained as follows:

Price variance	$ 838	F
Efficiency variance	3,938	U
Total flexible budget variance	$3,100	U

EXHIBIT 24-6 *Bellmead Pools & Supply*
Direct Materials Variance Computations

Actual Costs Incurred: Actual Inputs × Actual Prices	Actual Inputs × Standard Prices	Flexible Budget: Standard Inputs for Actual Volume × Standard Prices
11,969 × $1.93 = $23,100	11,969 × $2.00 = $23,938	10,000 × $2.00 = $20,000

(b) Price variance, $838 F   (c) Efficiency variance, $3,938 U

(a) Flexible budget variance, $3,100 U

(a) $23,100 − $20,000 = $3,100 U, as subdivided between (b) and (c)
(b) $11,969 × ($1.93 − $2.00) = $838 F
(c) (11,969 − 10,000) × $2.00 = $3,938 U

U = unfavorable; F = favorable

Exhibit 24-6 summarizes the direct materials cost variance computations. Variance analysis begins with a total variance to be explained—in this example, the $3,100 flexible budget variance.

Direct Labor Variances. The relevant data for computing Bellmead Pools' direct labor variances are

	Actual Cost	Flexible Budget Standard Cost	Flexible Budget Variance
Hours	3,800	4,000	
Hourly rate	× $11.00	× $10.50	
Total	$41,800	$42,000	$200 F

Price variance		Difference between = actual and budgeted × Actual inputs used unit prices of inputs

Price variance	=	($11.00 − $10.50) × 3,800 hours
	=	$1,900 U

OBJECTIVE 4
Compute direct labor cost variances

This variance is also called the *direct labor rate variance*.

$$\text{Efficiency variance} = \left(\begin{array}{c} \text{Actual} \\ \text{inputs} \\ \text{used} \end{array} - \begin{array}{c} \text{Inputs that should} \\ \text{have been used} \\ \text{for actual output} \end{array} \right) \times \begin{array}{c} \text{Standard} \\ \text{unit price} \\ \text{of input} \end{array}$$

Efficiency variance =	(3,800 hours − 4,000 hours) × $10.50 per hour
=	$2,100 F

The direct labor variances—from the beginning of this section—can be explained as follows:

Price variance	$1,900 U
Efficiency variance	2,100 F
Total flexible budget variance	$ 200 F

To relate standard costing to the overall budget, trace these total flexible budget variances to Exhibit 24-5. In addition, Exhibit 24-7 summarizes the direct labor variance computations, providing an overall picture to aid your study.

Management Use of Variance Information

Variances do not identify problems or their solutions. But they often raise questions that deserve attention. For example, an unfavorable materials price variance may point to the need to shop around for a new supplier of raw materials. *Price* effects, though, may depend on market factors, which are hard or sometimes impossible to control. An unfavorable labor efficiency variance, however, may spur management to examine employee performance. The company certainly has greater control over its own people than it has over outside markets.

Serial Class Exercise No. 1: Use the following data for the serial class exercises:

Actual costs for 60,000 units:
Direct materials: 1.1 lbs./unit @ $.30/lb. = $19,800
Direct labor: ¼ hr. @ $12/hr.
Variable overhead: $10,000
Fixed overhead: $92,000

Standard costs:
Direct materials: 1 lb./unit @ $.25/lb. = $15,000
Direct labor: ⅕ hr. @ $13/hr.
Variable overhead: ⅕ hr. @ $6/direct labor hr.
Fixed overhead: $20,000 budgeted
10,000 budgeted direct labor hrs. = $2 per hour

Compute the materials variances.

ANSWER:

Price variance

= ($.30 − $.25) × (60,000 × 1.1)
= $.05 × 66,000
= $3,300 U

Efficiency variance

= (66,000 − 60,000*) × $.25
= 6,000 × $.25
= $1,500 U

Total

= $3,300 U + $1,500 U = $4,800 U
= $19,800 − $15,000

―――――――

*(1 lb. × 60,000 units)

Serial Class Exercise No. 2:
Compute the direct labor
variances.
ANSWER:

Price Variance

= ($13 − $12) × (1/4 × 60,000)
= $1 × 15,000
= $15,000 F

Efficiency Variance

= (15,000 − 12,000) × $13
= $39,000 U

Total Variance

= $15,000 F − $39,000 U = $24,000 U

Transparency T24-2

EXHIBIT 24-7 *Bellmead Pools & Supply*
Direct Labor Variance Computations

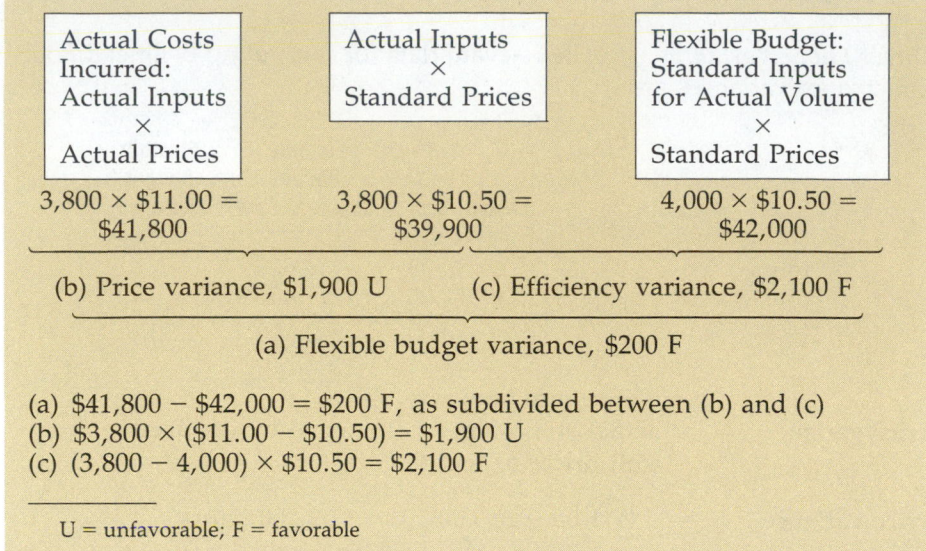

Actual Costs Incurred: Actual Inputs × Actual Prices	Actual Inputs × Standard Prices	Flexible Budget: Standard Inputs for Actual Volume × Standard Prices
3,800 × $11.00 = $41,800	3,800 × $10.50 = $39,900	4,000 × $10.50 = $42,000

(b) Price variance, $1,900 U   (c) Efficiency variance, $2,100 F

(a) Flexible budget variance, $200 F

(a) $41,800 − $42,000 = $200 F, as subdivided between (b) and (c)
(b) $3,800 × ($11.00 − $10.50) = $1,900 U
(c) (3,800 − 4,000) × $10.50 = $2,100 F

―――――――

U = unfavorable; F = favorable

Managers sometimes trade off price and efficiency effects, accepting an unfavorable variance in one area in order to achieve a favorable variance in the other. In our example, Bellmead's favorable materials price variance may have resulted from using cheaper material. The unfavorable materials efficiency variance may have arisen because employees had to use more material than standard, perhaps because of its inferior quality. Thus the company's strategy failed. The overall materials cost variance was unfavorable by $3,100.

In another trade-off between price and efficiency, Bellmead used more expensive labor than standard. But the company gained greater efficiency, and the company achieved a net labor cost saving of $200.

When should a variance be investigated? If significant variances are likely, hour-to-hour and day-to-day monitoring of quantities of materials and direct labor hours is desirable. When and how to investigate is often based on personal judgment. For example, a manager may believe that a 5 percent variance in a $1 million materials cost deserves more attention than a 20 percent variance in a $10,000 budget. Rules of thumb—such as "Investigate all variances above $5,000" and "Investigate all variances 25 percent or more above standard cost"—are also common in practice.

Production Overhead Variances

Ideally, production overhead cost variances should be computed and monitored for individual overhead costs like property taxes, utilities, and insurance, but many companies compute variances on total overhead. Many companies split production overhead variances into two parts: a *flexible budget variance* and a *production volume variance*.

The *flexible budget variance* for production overhead shows whether managers are keeping total overhead cost within the budgeted amount for the actual production of the period. The *production volume variance* arises when actual production differs from the level in the static (master) budget. The two variances combine to explain the difference between actual overhead cost and standard overhead cost that has been applied to production. Before discussing the computation of overhead variances, let's review how overhead cost is applied to production.

Applying Overhead to Production. In a system that uses standard costs, overhead is applied to production at a budgeted rate, as discussed in the two preceding chapters. Companies develop overhead standards based on past experience and budgets that reflect the business's goals. Suppose Exhibit 24-8 is Bellmead Pools' flexible overhead budget, which shows activity levels for 6, 8, 9, and 10 pools per month. We have highlighted the static (master) budget level of 8 pools and the actual production level of 10 pools because these levels are useful for computing the overhead variances.

Exhibit 24-8 indicates that Bellmead applies $5.75 of overhead cost to production for each direct labor hour spent installing a swimming pool. Of this amount, $2.00 is for variable overhead, and $3.75 is for fixed overhead. These standards can be based on any level of production that is consistent with company goals. In this case, Bellmead's goal is static (master) budget volume of 8 pools per month.

Bellmead accountants assemble the data in Exhibit 24-9 for computing the overhead cost variances associated with actual production of 10 pools.

The total production overhead cost variance is the difference between actual cost and standard overhead applied to production. For Bellmead Pools & Supply, the total overhead cost variance is favorable by $1,700 ($21,300 − $23,000). Accountants break the total variance down further for management use.

Flexible Budget (Controllable) Production Overhead Variance. The **flexible budget production overhead variance** is the difference between total actual overhead—fixed and variable—and the flexible budget amount for actual production volume. Bellmead Pools' flexible budget variance for June is computed as follows (data from Exhibit 24-9):

Total actual overhead cost	$21,300
Flexible budget overhead for actual production	20,000
Flexible budget variance	$ 1,300 U

OBJECTIVE 5

Compute production overhead cost variances

EXHIBIT 24-8 *Flexible Monthly Production Overhead Cost Budget*

Bellmead Pools & Supply
Flexible Monthly Production Overhead Cost Budget

		Static (Master) Budget		Flexible Budget for Actual Production
Number of pools installed per month	6	8	9	10
Standard direct labor hours	2,400	3,200	3,600	4,000
Budgeted production overhead cost:				
Variable	$ 4,800	$ 6,400	$ 7,200	$ 8,000
Fixed	12,000	12,000	12,000	12,000
Total.	$16,800	$18,400	$19,200	$20,000

Standard variable overhead rate per direct labor hour
$6,400/3,200
= $2.00

Standard fixed overhead rate per direct labor hour . .
$12,000/3,200
= $3.75

Standard total overhead rate per direct labor hour . .
$18,400/3,200
= $5.75

EXHIBIT 24-9   *Data for Computing Production Overhead Cost Variances*

Bellmead Pools & Supply
Data for Computing Production Overhead Cost Variances

	Actual Cost (Exhibit 24-5)	Flexible Budget for Actual Production (Exhibit 24-8)	Standard Overhead Applied to Production (Exhibit 24-8)
Variable overhead	$ 9,000	$ 8,000	4,000 direct labor hours × $2.00 = $ 8,000
Fixed overhead ..	12,300	12,000	4,000 direct labor hours × $3.75 = 15,000
Total overhead ..	$21,300	$20,000	4,000 direct labor hours × $5.75 = $23,000

Total production overhead cost variance
$1,700 F

Teaching Tip: Look at Exhibit 24-8. Notice that Bellmead budgeted $12,000 of fixed overhead regardless of the level of volume. Here is the tricky part for students. Bellmead, not knowing the level of volume it would actually have, had to select one of these levels of activity to base its budget upon and to compute an overhead rate. If Bellmead selects eight pools, then the fixed expense per hour will be $3.75 ($12,000/3,200). If Bellmead actually installs ten pools, then the overhead applied to the ten pools will be $15,000 (4,000 × $3.75) and not $12,000.

What should be the flexible budget fixed expense, $15,000 or $12,000? Look at the exhibit. At all levels of volume, the flexible budget fixed is $12,000. What is the $15,000? That is the amount of applied overhead.

Point to Stress: The volume variance is the difference between the flexible budget and standard (applied) overhead. Remember that at the beginning of the period a level of output had to be selected in order to have an overhead rate. The overhead rate was used to apply overhead to each unit actually produced. If the predetermined volume is different from the actual volume, then the flexible budget will be different from the standard (applied) amount.

Teaching Tip: Use Exhibit 24-8. At the 8-volume level, the fixed overhead rate is $3.75. At the 10-volume level, the overhead rate would have been $3.00 ($12,000/4,000). Since ten pools were actually installed, the applied overhead using the two different rates would be:

Total June overhead was $21,300, compared with the flexible budget amount of $20,000. The unfavorable variance raises questions regarding managers' control of costs. Often this variance is due more to variable costs than to fixed costs, and production managers exercise considerable control over variable overhead. Therefore, many accountants call this the **controllable overhead variance.** Because control often is not clear-cut, we prefer to label it simply as the flexible budget variance.

Production Volume Overhead Variance.   The **production volume overhead variance** is the difference between the flexible budget for actual production and standard overhead applied to production (data from Exhibit 24-9):

Flexible budget overhead for actual production	$20,000
Standard overhead applied to production	23,000
Production volume variance	$ 3,000 F

When the flexible overhead budget amount is less than the standard overhead applied to production, the variance is favorable, as shown for Bellmead Pools. The increase in volume from 8 pools to 10 pools was favorable because productive capacity was more fully utilized than expected. Had the flexible budget amount exceeded the standard overhead applied to production, the variance would have been unfavorable because less than the full amount of the company's productive capacity was used.

Exhibit 24-9 reveals that variable overhead is (always) the same for the flexible budget and the amount applied to production. Therefore, the production volume variance must be due solely to fixed cost effects. An alternative computation of this variance clarifies this point (all data from Exhibit 24-8):

Standard direct labor hours for actual production	4,000
Standard direct labor hours for static (master) budget	3,200
Actual production in excess of static budget	800
Standard *fixed* overhead rate per direct labor hour . . .	×$3.75
Production volume variance	$ 3,000 F

The production volume variance is favorable because Bellmead installed more pools than the static budget called for. The sum of the two overhead variances explains the total favorable production overhead variance of $1,700:

Flexible budget (controllable) variance	$1,300 U
Production volume variance	3,000 F
Total overhead cost variance explained	$1,700 F

Exhibit 24-10 summarizes the computation of overhead cost variances, with amounts shown for Bellmead Pools & Supply.

Two-variance analysis as just described is the most common in practice. Some companies, however, perform a three-variance analysis that splits the flexible budget variance into spending and efficiency effects. A few companies divide overhead cost variances into four parts. These topics are covered in managerial accounting and cost accounting courses.

Standard Costs in the Accounts

Some companies use standard costing for control purposes without entering the standards in the accounts. Others make special standard cost entries.

Accounting systems differ among those companies that do record standard costs in the accounts. For example, one practice is to debit actual costs to Materials Inventory and Production Wages. When materials are used, or when labor is applied to production, these accounts are credited for *actual* cost. However, Work in Process Inventory is debited for *standard* cost. Differences in these entries reveal the cost variances. In our Bellmead Pools illustration, the Materials Inventory, Production Wages, and Production Overhead accounts have been debited for *actual* costs incurred. The resulting account balances before applying costs to production and before introducing standard costs are given at the top of the next page.

EXHIBIT 24-10   Bellmead Pools & Supply
Production Overhead Variance Computations

Actual Overhead Cost	Flexible Budget Overhead for Actual Production	Standard Overhead Applied to Production
Given, $21,300	$12,000 + (4,000 × $2.00) = $20,000	4,000 × $5.75 = $23,000

(b) Flexible budget variance $1,300 U

(c) Production volume variance $3,000 F

(a) Total production overhead cost variance, $1,700 F

(a) $21,300 − $23,000 = $1,700 F, as subdivided between (b) and (c)
(b) $21,300 − [$12,000 + (4,000 × $2.00)] = $1,300 U
(c) (4,000 hrs. − 3,200 hrs.) × $3.75 = $3,000 F

U = unfavorable; F = favorable

	$3.75 rate	$3.00 rate
Variable		
($2 × 4,000)	$ 8,000	$ 8,000
Fixed		
($3.75 × 4,000)	15,000	
($3.00 × 4,000)		12,000
Total	$23,000	$20,000

The actual level of production is the same in both cases; the difference is the level of volume selected for the overhead rate. Unless the predetermined volume accidentally equals the actual volume, the applied overhead will be different from the flexible budget.

Serial Class Exercise No. 3: Compute the overhead variances.

ANSWER:

Total actual OH cost	$102,000
Total flex. budget	110,000*
Flex. budget var.	$ 8,000 F

Total flex. budget	$110,000
Standard OH	120,000†
Volume var.	$ 10,000 F

* $20,000 + ($6 × 15,000)
† $8 × 15,000

The flexible budget variance is favorable because the actual costs were less than the budgeted costs. The volume variance is favorable because the predetermined volume was 10,000 hours needed to produce 50,000 units. 60,000 units were actually produced, so some excess capacity was utilized.

Materials Inventory	Production Wages	Production Overhead
Actual cost (assumed amount) 29,000	Actual cost 41,800	Actual cost 21,300

OBJECTIVE 6
Record transactions at standard cost

The entries to apply direct materials, direct labor, and production overhead to production and to record the cost variances are

Work in Process Inventory (standard cost)	20,000	
Direct Materials Efficiency Variance	3,938	
Direct Materials Price Variance		838
Materials Inventory (actual cost)		23,100
Direct materials used in production.		

Work in Process Inventory (standard cost)	42,000	
Direct Labor Price Variance	1,900	
Direct Labor Efficiency Variance		2,100
Production Wages (actual cost)		41,800
Direct labor applied to production.		

Work in Process Inventory (standard cost)	23,000	
Production Overhead Flexible Budget Variance	1,300	
Production Overhead Production Volume Variance		3,000
Production Overhead (actual cost)		21,300
Production overhead applied to production.		

After posting, the direct labor variance accounts appear as follows:

Direct Labor Price Variance

Unfavorable variance 1,900	

Direct Labor Efficiency Variance

	Favorable variance 2,100

Serial Class Exercise No. 4:
Prepare journal entries to record the material and labor variances.
ANSWER:

Work in Process
  (60,000 lbs. × $.25)   15,000

Material Price
  Variance   3,300

Material Efficiency
  Variance   1,500

    Material
    Inventory
    (66,000 lbs. ×
    $.30)   19,800

Work in Process
  ($13 × 12,000)   156,000

Direct Labor
  Efficiency Variance   39,000

    Direct Labor
    Price Variance   15,000

    Production Wages
    ($12 × 15,000)   180,000

A debit balance in a variance account is treated as expense, and a credit balance is handled as a contra expense, or a reduction in expense. In this example, Direct Labor Price Variance's debit balance is expense, and Direct Labor Efficiency Variance's credit balance is a reduction in expense. These variance accounts are closed to Income Summary in the usual manner. Accounting for materials and overhead parallel these entries for labor.

Assume Bellmead sold all 10 pools that were installed during June. After posting, the Materials Inventory account shows the balance of materials on hand. Production Wages and Production Overhead have zero balances. Work in Process Inventory is stated at standard cost. The differences between actual costs credited to the accounts and standard costs debited to Work in Process Inventory identify the total cost variances, as follows:

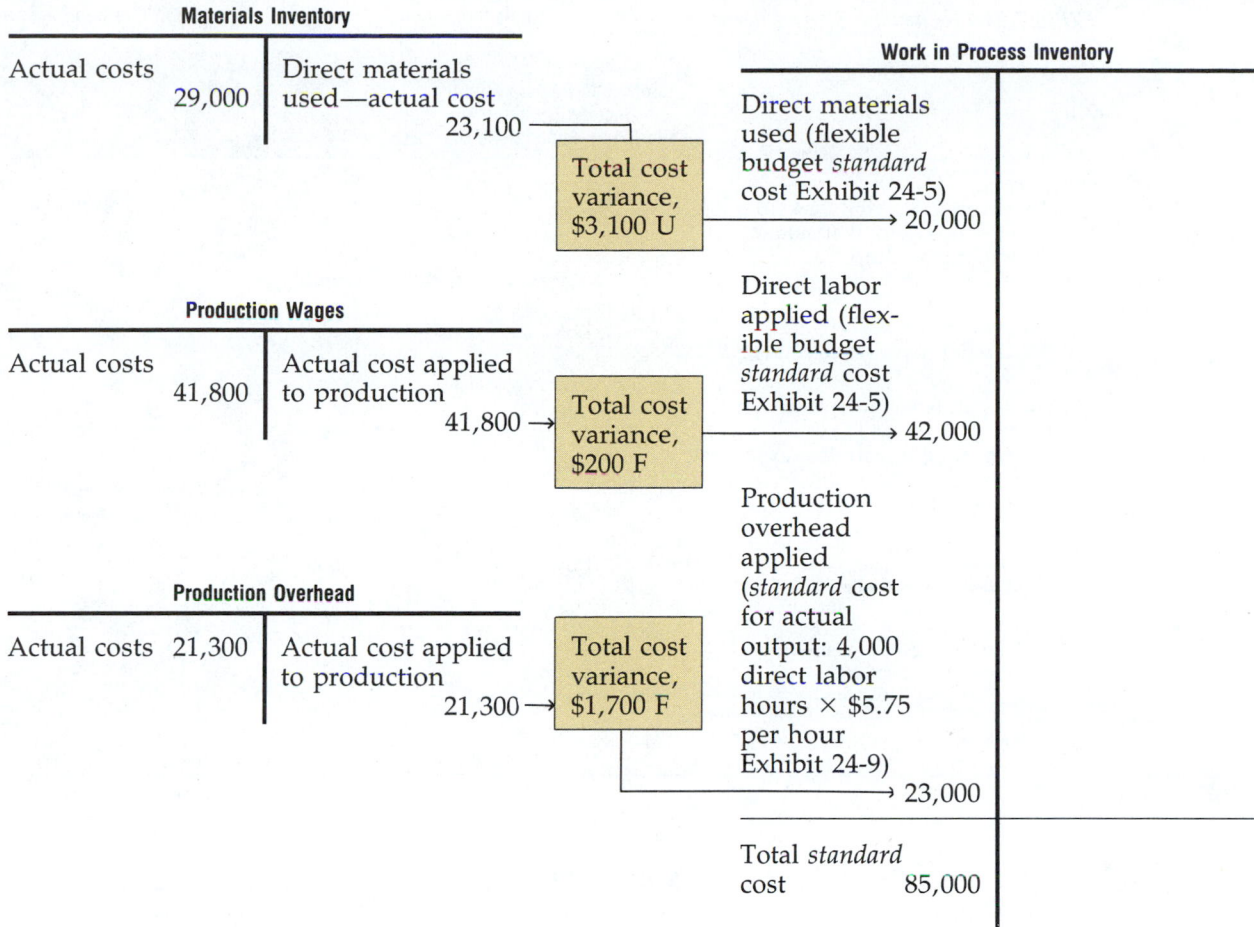

As goods are sold, standard costs flow through the accounts in the usual manner:

Work in Process Inventory		Finished Goods Inventory		Cost of Goods Sold	
Standard cost 85,000	Goods finished 85,000 →	Goods finished 85,000	Goods sold 85,000 →	Goods sold 85,000	

Standard Cost Income Statement for Management

Standard costing is a management tool, so the company does not usually report variance information to investors, creditors, and other outsiders. Managers, however, are vitally interested in the cost variances. Exhibit 24-11 illustrates an income statement the Bellmead president might use for planning and control purposes. We assume that Bellmead's sales for June were the 10 pools installed during the month.

Point to Stress: A standard cost income statement helps to summarize all of the variances and illustrate their effect on the income of the business.

EXHIBIT 24-11 Income Statement

Bellmead Pools & Supply **Income Statement** **For the Month Ended June 30, 19X5**				
Sales revenue (Exhibit 24-4: 10 pools at $12,000)				$120,000
Cost of goods sold at standard cost				
(preceding section)			$85,000	
Cost variances:*	Unfavorable	Favorable		
Direct materials...........................	$3,100			
Direct labor		$ 200		
Production overhead		1,700		
	3,100	1,900	1,200 U	
Cost of goods sold at actual cost				86,200
Gross margin................................				33,800
Selling and administrative expenses				
(variable, $9,100; fixed, $9,700—Exhibit 24-5)				18,800
Operating income				$ 15,000

*Cost variance detail:	Unfavorable	Favorable	Total	
Direct materials— price		$ 838		
(Exhibit 24-6) efficiency	$3,938		$3,100 U	
Direct labor— price	1,900			
(Exhibit 24-7) efficiency		2,100	200 F	
Production overhead—				
(Exhibit 24-10) flexible budget	1,300			
production volume		3,000	1,700 F	
Total			$1,200 U	

Computers and Standard Costs

OBJECTIVE 7

Prepare a standard cost income statement for management

This chapter links together the master budget, flexible budgets, and standard costs. As the swimming pool example indicates, many calculations are needed to maintain the standard cost system. The advantages of a computer are obvious—especially if you want daily or weekly reports on operations.

The computer can help set the standard costs. A job order begins the process. The product's identification number and the quantity desired are entered into the computer. The computer then accesses the engineering specifications for that particular product to find out what materials are needed. It multiplies the needed materials by the quantity ordered. By repeating this process over a large number of similar jobs, management can develop the historical data for calculating standard costs.

In some manufacturing environments, the job order may trigger the computer to issue automatically the exact amount of required materials. Any materials not used on the job are shipped backed to storage, with the unused quantity credited to the Materials Efficiency Variance account.

Summary Problem for Your Review

Exhibit 24-5 indicates that Bellmead Pools & Supply installed 10 swimming pools during June. Suppose that June installations and sales were 7 pools instead of 10 and that actual expenses for the month were as follows:

Direct materials . . . . 7,400 cubic yards @ $2.00 per cubic yard
Direct labor . . . . 2,740 hours @ $10.00 per hour
Variable production overhead . . $5,400
Fixed production overhead $11,900

Required

1. Given these new data, prepare two exhibits, similar to Exhibits 24-5 and 24-8. Ignore selling and administrative expenses in your first exhibit, and show budgeted overhead cost only for 7 and 8 pools per month in your second exhibit.
2. Compute direct materials and direct labor price and efficiency variances.
3. Compute the total variance, the flexible budget variance, and the production volume variance for overhead.
4. Prepare a June income statement through operating income for the pres-

SOLUTION TO REVIEW PROBLEM

Requirement 1

Bellmead Pools & Supply
Facts for Illustration of Standard Costing
Month of June

Panel A—Comparison of Actual Results with Flexible Budget: Installed 7 Swimming Pools

	Actual Results at Actual Prices	Flexible Budget	Flexible Budget Variances
Variable expenses:			
Direct materials	$14,800^a	$14,000^c	$ 800 U
Direct labor	27,400^b	29,400^c	2,000 F
Variable production overhead	5,400	5,600^d	200 F
Total variable expenses	47,600	49,000	1,400 F
Fixed expenses:			
Fixed production overhead	11,900	12,000^e	100 F
Total expenses	$59,500	$61,000	$1,500 F

^{a} $14,800 = 7,400 cubic yards at actual price of $2.00 per cubic yard.
^{b} $27,400 = 2,740 hours at actual price of $10.00 per hour.
^{c} See Panel B.
^{d} Variable production overhead was budgeted at $2.00 per direct labor hour:
$5,600 = 2,800 direct labor hours (7 pools × 400 direct labor hours) × $2.00.
^{e} Fixed production overhead was budgeted at $12,000 per month.

Panel B—Standards for Direct Material and Direct Labor Flexible Budget: 7 Swimming Pools

	(1) Standard Inputs Budgeted for 7 Finished Units (Swimming Pools Installed)	(2) Standard Price per Unit of Input	(1) × (2) Flexible Budget for 7 Finished Units of Output
Direct materials	1,000 cubic yards × 7	$ 2.00	$14,000
Direct labor	400 hours × 7	10.50	29,400

Bellmead Pools & Supply
Flexible Monthly Production Overhead Cost Budget

Number of pools installed per month	7	8
Standard direct labor hours.	2,800	3,200
Budgeted production overhead cost:		
Variable	$ 5,600	$ 6,400
Fixed.	12,000	12,000
Total	$17,600	$18,400

Standard variable overhead rate per direct labor hour . . . . $6,400/3,200 = $2.00

Standard fixed overhead rate per direct labor hour . . . . $12,000/3,200 = $3.75

Standard total overhead rate per direct labor hour $18,400/3,200 = $5.75

Requirement 2

$$\text{Price variance} = \begin{matrix} \text{Difference between} \\ \text{actual and budgeted} \\ \text{unit prices of inputs} \end{matrix} \times \text{Actual inputs used}$$

Direct materials:

Price variance = ($2.00 − $2.00) × 7,400 cubic yards
= $-0-

Direct labor:

Price variance = ($10.00 − $10.50) × 2,740 hours
= $1,370 F

$$\text{Efficiency variance} = \left(\begin{matrix} \text{Actual} \\ \text{inputs} \\ \text{used} \end{matrix} - \begin{matrix} \text{Inputs that should} \\ \text{have been used} \\ \text{for actual output} \end{matrix} \right) \begin{matrix} \text{Standard} \\ \times \text{ unit price} \\ \text{of input} \end{matrix}$$

$$= \left(\begin{matrix} \text{Actual cubic} \\ \text{yards or} \\ \text{hours used} \end{matrix} - \begin{matrix} \text{Standard number of cubic} \\ \text{yards or hours allowed} \\ \text{for actual output} \end{matrix} \right) \begin{matrix} \text{Standard} \\ \times \text{ unit price} \\ \text{of input} \end{matrix}$$

Direct materials:

$$\text{Efficiency variance} = \left(\begin{matrix} 7,400 \\ \text{cubic} \\ \text{yards} \end{matrix} - \begin{matrix} 1,000 \text{ cubic yards} \\ \times 7 \\ \text{swimming pools} \end{matrix} \right) \begin{matrix} \$2.00 \\ \times \text{ per} \\ \text{cubic yard} \end{matrix}$$

= (7,400 − 7,000) × $2.00

= $800 U

Direct labor:

$$\text{Efficiency variance} = \left(\begin{matrix} 2,740 \\ \text{hours} \\ \text{used} \end{matrix} - \begin{matrix} 400 \text{ hours} \\ \times 7 \text{ swimming} \\ \text{pools installed} \end{matrix} \right) \begin{matrix} \$10.50 \\ \times \text{ per} \\ \text{hour} \end{matrix}$$

= (2,740 − 2,800) × $10.50

= $630 F

Requirement 3

Total actual overhead cost (variable, $5,400 + fixed, $11,900)	$17,300
Standard total overhead cost applied to production, 7 pools	
(2,800 direct labor hours × $5.75)	16,100
Total overhead cost variance	$ 1,200 U

Flexible Budget Variance:

Total actual overhead cost ($5,400 + $11,900)	$17,300
Flexible budget overhead for actual production	
($5,600 + $12,000)	17,600
Flexible budget variance	$ 300 F

Production Volume Variance:

Flexible budget overhead for actual production	
(Requirement 1: variable, $5,600 + fixed, $12,000)	$17,600
Standard overhead applied to production	
(Requirement 1: 2,800 direct labor hours × $5.75)	16,100
Production volume variance	$ 1,500 U

or

Standard direct labor hours for static (master) budget	
(Requirement 1: Master Budget)	3,200
Standard direct labor hours for actual production	
(Requirement 1: Flexible Budget)	2,800
Difference in direct labor hours between flexible budget	
and master budget	400
Standard fixed overhead rate per direct labor hour	
(Requirement 1: Master Budget)	×$3.75
Production volume variance	$ 1,500 U

Requirement 4

Bellmead Pools & Supply
Income Statement
For the Month Ended June 30, 19X5

Sales revenue (7 pools at $12,000)			$84,000
Cost of goods sold at standard cost (direct materials,			
$14,000 + direct labor, $29,400 + overhead, $16,100) .		$59,500	

Cost variances:*	Unfavorable	Favorable	
Direct materials	$ 800		
Direct labor..............		$2,000	
Overhead	1,200		
	$2,000	$2,000	
Net cost variance		-0-	
Cost of goods sold at actual cost			59,500
Gross margin			24,500
Selling and administrative expenses			17,700
Operating income....................................			$ 6,800

*Cost variance detail:

	Unfavorable	Favorable	Total
Direct materials—price	$ -0-	$ -0-	} $ 800 U
—efficiency......	800		
Direct labor—price		1,370	} 2,000 F
—efficiency		630	
Overhead—flexible budget		300	} 1,200 U
—production volume ..	1,500		

Summary

A *static budget* is prepared for only one level of activity, usually the volume level that management expects for the period. A *flexible budget* is a set of budgets covering a range of volume. *Performance reports* compare actual and budgeted results for the sales volume achieved. Differences between actual and budgeted revenues and expenses are called *variances*. A variance is *favorable* if actual revenue exceeds budgeted revenue, or if actual expense is less than budgeted expense. An *unfavorable* variance occurs when actual revenue is less than budget, or actual expense exceeds budget.

Costs are classified as *variable, fixed,* or *mixed*. The total amount of a variable cost fluctuates in direct proportion to changes in volume. By contrast, the total amount of a fixed cost does not change during a given period over a wide range of volume. A mixed cost has both variable and fixed components. These distinctions are important to flexible budgeting, which identifies costs and income for different levels of volume.

The heart of a flexible budget is the *budget formula*, which expresses the behavior of costs. A *flexible budget graph* provides a customized budget for any volume level.

Standard costs are the predetermined costs that managers believe the business should incur in producing an item. The standards are set low enough to spur employees to improve their performance but not so low as to discourage workers. *Standard cost systems* are designed to control cost by analyzing differences between actual and standard cost. *Cost variances* are differences between actual cost and standard cost. In general, cost variances are divided into price and efficiency effects.

The *price variance* measures the effect price changes have on the cost of materials and labor. The *efficiency variance* gauges manager efficiency in using materials and labor.

Production overhead variances are divided two ways. The *flexible budget variance* is the difference between actual overhead cost and the flexible budget for actual output. It measures whether the company achieved its budgeted cost for the actual volume level achieved. The *production volume variance* arises when actual production differs from the level in the static (master) budget.

Some companies use standard costing for control purposes without recording standard costs in the accounts. Others journalize the standards and the related cost variances. The variance information is helpful in planning and control. It does not automatically identify problems or cures, but it points to areas of the business needing correction.

Self-Study Questions

Test your understanding of the chapter by marking the best answer for each of the following questions.

1. A flexible budget shows *(p. 1093)*
   a. Expected results over a range of volume levels
   b. A single target level of volume
   c. Price variances
   d. Volume variances
2. Which is the most useful formula for budgeting expenses? *(p. 1093)*
   a. Expenses = Sales − Income
   b. Expenses = Fixed + Variable
   c. Expenses = Fixed + (Variable × Number of Units)
   d. Expenses = Standard + Variances
3. Flexible budget variances are differences between *(p. 1096)*
   a. Actual results and the static (master) budget

b. Actual results and the flexible budget

c. The static (master) budget and the flexible budget

d. None of the above

4. Standard cost variances help managers identify *(p. 1099)*

   a. Ways of reducing cost   c. Both of the above

   b. Employees who control cost   d. None of the above

5. Cost variances for direct materials and direct labor are divided into *(p. 1100)*

   a. Flexible budget effects and production volume effects

   b. Efficiency effects and flexible budget effects

   c. Controllable effects and master budget effects

   d. Price effects and efficiency effects

6. Krakow, Inc., paid $3 per pound for 10,000 pounds of direct materials purchased and used. Standard cost was $2.80 per pound, and standard usage for actual production was 11,000 pounds. How much is the price variance? *(p. 1102)*

   a. $800 favorable   c. $2,800 favorable

   b. $2,000 unfavorable   d. $3,000 favorable

7. How much is the efficiency variance in the preceding question? *(p. 1102)*

   a. $800 favorable   c. $2,800 favorable

   b. $2,000 unfavorable   d. $3,000 favorable

8. Cost variances for production overhead are divided into *(p. 1104)*

   a. Flexible budget effects and production volume effects

   b. Efficiency effects and flexible budget effects

   c. Controllable effects and master budget effects

   d. Price effects and efficiency effects

9. Actual overhead of Milstead Supply Company is $540,000. Overhead for static (master) budget volume is $500,000, and flexible budget overhead for actual production is $510,000. The production volume variance is *(p. 1106)*

   a. $10,000 unfavorable   c. $40,000 unfavorable

   b. $30,000 unfavorable   d. Not determinable from the information given. Reason?

10. Gonzalez Manufacturing made the following entry for the use of direct materials in production:

Work in Process	380,000	
Direct Materials Efficiency Variance	35,000	
Direct Materials Price Variance		6,000
Materials Inventory		409,000

Which of the following statements is true? *(p. 1108)*

a. The price variance is unfavorable and the efficiency variance is favorable

b. The price variance is favorable and the efficiency variance is unfavorable

c. Both variances are favorable

d. Both variances are unfavorable

Answers to the Self-Study Questions follow the Accounting Vocabulary.

Accounting Vocabulary

Budget formula. The heart of a flexible budget; shows how to compute the budget amounts *(p. 1093)*.

Controllable overhead variance. Another name for the Flexible budget overhead variance *(p. 1106)*.

Efficiency variance. Difference between the quantity of inputs actually used and the quantity that should have been used for the actual output achieved, multiplied by the standard unit price of the input. Also called the Usage variance and the Quantity variance. *(p. 1100).*

Flexible budget. Set of budgets covering a range of volume rather than a single level of volume *(p. 1093).*

Flexible budget overhead variance. Difference between total actual overhead (fixed and variable) and the flexible budget amount for actual production volume. Also called the Controllable variance *(p. 1105).*

Flexible budget variance. Difference between an amount in the flexible budget and the actual results for the corresponding item *(p. 1096).*

Performance report. Report that compares actual and budgeted results *(p. 1093).*

Price variance. Difference between the actual unit price of an input and a standard unit price, multiplied by the actual quantitiy of inputs used *(p. 1100).*

Production volume overhead variance. Difference between the flexible budget for actual production and standard overhead applied to production *(p. 1106).*

Quantity variance. Another name for the Efficiency variance used to control materials and labor costs in a standard cost system *(p. 1100).*

Sales volume variance. Difference between a revenue, expense, or operating income amount in the flexible budget and the corresponding amount in the static (master) budget *(p. 1096).*

Standard cost. Predetermined cost that management believes the business should incur in producing an item *(p. 1099).*

Standard cost system. Designed to control costs by analyzing the relationship between actual costs and standard costs *(p. 1099).*

Static budget. A budget prepared for only one level of activity *(p. 1093).*

Usage variance. Another name for the Efficiency variance used to control materials and labor costs in a standard cost system *(p. 1100).*

Variance. Difference between an actual amount and the corresponding budget amount *(p. 1093).*

Answers to Self-Study Questions

1.	a	6.	b	($3.00 − $2.80) × 10,000 = $2,000 U
2.	c	7.	c	(11,000 − 10,000) × $2.80 = $2,800 F
3.	b	8.	a	
4.	c	9.	d	Standard overhead applied to production is missing
5.	d	10.	b	

ASSIGNMENT MATERIAL _____

Questions

1. Which costs in total amount move in direct proportion to changes in volume? Which costs do not fluctuate in total amount with volume changes? How do total and unit amounts behave for these two categories of costs?

2. What is the relevant range, and why must it be considered in preparing a flexible budget?

3. How does a static budget differ from a flexible budget?

4. Identify how managers use variance information from a performance report.

5. McLaren, Inc., prepared its static (master) budget for a sales level of 35,000 for the month. Actual sales totaled 46,000. Describe the problem of using the master budget to evaluate company performance for the month. Propose a better way to evaluate McLaren's performance for the period.

6. What advantage does a flexible expense budget graph offer over a flexible expense budget that shows four levels of volume?

7. What do the sales volume variance and the flexible budget variance measure?

8. Describe the purpose of a standard cost system.

9. What two general categories of cost variances do most standard cost systems provide?

10. Identify the similarities and differences between a standard cost and a budgeted cost.

11. Suppose your company is installing a standard cost system. What sort of standard cost is most popular? For employees, what purpose does a standard cost fulfill?

12. What does a price variance measure? How is it computed?

13. What does an efficiency variance measure? How is it computed?

14. Consider price variance and efficiency variance. How do they relate to the total variance between actual and budgeted cost for direct materials and direct labor?

15. Describe a trade-off that a manager might make for labor cost.

16. When should a cost variance be investigated?

17. What causes a flexible budget overhead variance? What information does this variance provide?

18. What information is provided by the overhead production volume variance? How is this variance computed?

19. Scott & White, Inc., enters standard costs in the company accounts. The actual cost of direct materials used to manufacture inventory was $21,600. The direct materials price variance was $2,000 favorable, and the efficiency variance was $1,400 unfavorable. Make the journal entry to charge materials to production.

20. How does a standard cost income statement for management differ from an income statement reported to the public?

Exercises

Exercise 24-1 *Preparing a flexible budget for the income statement* (L.O. 1)

Jaymar Production Company sells its main product for $6 per unit, and variable cost is $1.40 per unit. Fixed expenses are $180,000 per month for volumes up to 55,000 units of output. Above 55,000 units, monthly fixed expenses are $240,000.

Operating inc. at 40,000 units $4,000

Required

Prepare a monthly flexible budget for the product, showing sales, variable expenses, fixed expenses, and operating income or loss for volume levels of 40,000, 50,000, and 60,000 units.

Exercise 24-2 *Graphing expense behavior* (L.O. 1)

No check figure

Graph the expense behavior of Jaymar Production Company in Exercise 24-1. Show total expenses for volume levels of 40,000, 50,000, 55,000, and 60,000 units.

Operating income:
  Flex. budget var. $8,000 U
  Sales vol. var. $10,000 F

Exercise 24-3   *Completing a performance report* (L.O. 2)

Erie, Inc., management received the following incomplete performance report:

Erie, Inc.
Income Statement Performance Report
For the Year Ended April 30, 19X3

	Actual Results at Actual Prices	Flexible Budget Variances	Flexible Budget for Actual Volume Achieved	Sales Volume Variances	Static (Master) Budget
Units	24,000		24,000		22,000
Sales	$192,000		$192,000		$176,000
Variable expenses	76,000		72,000		66,000
Fixed expenses	104,000		100,000		100,000
Total expenses	180,000		172,000		166,000
Operating income	$ 12,000		$ 20,000		$ 10,000

Required

Complete the performance report. Identify the employee group that should be praised and the group that may be subject to criticism. Give your reasons.

Operating income:
  Flex. budget var. $59,000 F
  Sales vol. var. $38,000 U

Exercise 24-4   *Preparing an income statement performance report* (L.O. 2)

Top managers of North Country Provision Co. estimated 19X6 sales of 150,000 units of its product at a unit price of $6. Actual sales for the year were 140,000 units at $6.50. Variable expenses were budgeted at $2.20 per unit, and actual variable expenses were $2.15 per unit. Actual fixed expenses of $428,000 exceeded budgeted fixed expenses of $410,000.

Required

Prepare North Country's income statement performance report in a format similar to Exhibit 24-4. The bracketed amounts at the bottom are not required. What variance contributed the most to the year's favorable results? Explain what probably caused this variance.

Total mat'l. cost var. $1,520 U

Exercise 24-5   *Computing price and efficiency variances for direct materials* (L.O. 3)

The following direct materials variance computations are incomplete:

$$\text{Price variance} = (\$7 - \$?) \times 3{,}560 \text{ pounds} = \$1{,}780 \text{ U}$$
$$\text{Efficiency variance} = (? - 3{,}600 \text{ pounds}) \times ? \quad = ? \text{ F}$$
$$\text{Total materials cost variance} = \$?$$

Required

Fill in the missing values and identify the total variance as favorable or unfavorable.

Price var.: Materials $57,920 F
         Labor $670 U
Efficiency var.: Materials
         $31,200 U
         Labor $400 U

Exercise 24-6   *Computing price and efficiency cost variances for materials and labor* (L.O. 3, 4)

Lear-Wright Corp., which uses a standard cost accounting system, manufactured 350,000 picture frames during the year, using 724,000 board feet of lumber purchased earlier in the year at actual unit cost of $1.22. Production required 6,700 direct labor hours that cost $8.10 per hour. The materials standard was two board feet of lumber per frame, at standard cost of $1.30 per foot. The labor standard was .019 direct labor hour per frame, at standard cost of $8.00 per hour.

Required

Compute the price and efficiency variances for direct materials and direct labor.

Exercise 24-7 *Journalizing standard costing transactions* **(L.O. 6)**

Make the journal entries to charge direct materials and direct labor to production in Exercise 24-6.

Credit Materials Inventory for $883,280

Exercise 24-8 *Explaining cost variances* **(L.O. 3, 4, 5)**

No check figure

Diamond Point Corporation managers are seeking explanations for the variances in the following report:

Diamond Point Corporation
Income Statement for Managers
Year Ended December 31, 19X2

Sales revenue		$541,000
Cost of goods sold—standard	$310,000	
Cost variances:		
Materials: price	4,000 F	
efficiency	6,000 U	
Labor: price	8,000 U	
efficiency	3,000 F	
Overhead: flexible budget	9,000 U	
production volume	10,000 U	
Net cost variance	26,000 U	
Cost of goods sold—actual		336,000
Gross profit		205,000
Selling and administrative expenses		181,000
Operating income		$ 24,000

Required

Explain the meaning of each of Diamond Point Corporation's labor variances and each of the overhead variances.

Exercise 24-9 *Computing overhead cost variances* **(L.O. 5)**

Flex. budget var. $1,400 U
Prod. vol. var. $1,500 U

Great Pacific Coffee Company charges the following standard unit cost to production, based on master budget volume of 30,000 units per month:

Direct materials	$3.20
Direct labor	4.10
Overhead	1.00
Standard unit cost	$8.30

Great Pacific used the following flexible overhead cost budget:

	Monthly Volume		
Number of units	27,000	30,000	33,000
Standard direct labor hours	2,700	3,000	3,300
Budgeted overhead cost:			
Variable	$13,500	$15,000	$16,500
Fixed	15,000	15,000	15,000

Actual monthly production was 27,000 units. Actual overhead cost was variable, $14,700, and fixed, $15,200.

Chapter 24   Flexible Budgets and Standard Costs   **1119**

Required

Compute the total overhead cost variance, the flexible budget variance, and the production volume variance for overhead cost.

Gross profit $70,000

Exercise 24-10 *Preparing a standard cost income statement for management* **(L.O. 7)**

Keystone Manufacturing Co. revenue and expense information for the month of May follows.

	Revenue or Expense	
	Actual	**Standard**
Sales revenue	$160,000	$160,000
Cost of goods sold	?	91,000
Information regarding:		
Direct materials price variance	20,000	19,100
Direct materials efficiency variance	19,000	20,600
Direct labor price variance	42,000	43,400
Direct labor efficiency variance	44,000	42,300
Overhead flexible budget variance	15,000	15,900
Overhead production volume variance	15,900	15,600

Required

Prepare a standard cost income statement through gross profit. Report all cost variances for use by management.

Problems   (Group A)

Net inc. at 100,000 units
$37,730

Problem 24-1A *Preparing a flexible budget income statement and graphing cost behavior* **(L.O. 1)**

Bioseptic, Inc., produces and sells prepackaged tests for certain infectious diseases. The company's master budget income statement for 19X7 follows, based on expected sales volume of 110,000 units:

Bioseptic, Inc.
Master Budget Income Statement
Year 19X7

Sales	$440,000
Variable expenses:	
Cost of goods sold	$121,000
Sales commissions	33,000
Shipping	24,200
Utilities	11,000
Fixed expenses:	
Salaries	73,000
Depreciation	48,000
Rent	23,000
Insurance	17,700
Utilities	12,400
Total operating expenses	363,300
Income before income tax	76,700
Income tax expense (30%)	23,010
Net income	$ 53,690

Bioseptic's plant capacity is 125,000 units, so if actual volume exceeds 125,000 units, it will be necessary to expand the plant. In that case, salaries will increase by 10 percent, depreciation by 20 percent, rent by $11,000, and insurance by $2,800. Fixed utilities will be unchanged by the volume increase.

Required

1. Prepare a flexible budget income statement for the company, showing volume levels of 100,000, 110,000, 120,000, and 130,000 units.
2. Graph the total operating expense behavior of the company. Cost of goods sold is included.

Problem 24-2A *Preparing an income statement performance report* **(L.O. 2)**

Net income:
  Flex. budget var. $3,150 F
  Sales vol. var. $15,960 F

Refer to the Bioseptic, Inc., situation of Problem 24-1A. The company sold 120,000 units during 19X7, and its actual income statement was as follows:

Bioseptic, Inc.	
Income Statement	
Year 19X7	
Sales	$487,000
Variable expenses:	
Cost of goods sold	$133,000
Sales commissions	39,000
Shipping	27,000
Utilities	12,000
Fixed expenses:	
Salaries	76,000
Depreciation	48,000
Rent	19,000
Insurance	15,000
Utilities	14,000
Total operating expenses	383,000
Income before income tax	104,000
Income tax expense (30%)	31,200
Net income	$ 72,800

Required

Prepare an income statement performance report for 19X7.

Problem 24-3A *Preparing a flexible budget and computing cost variances* *(L.O. 1, 3, 4, 5)*

Gross profit $370,570
Price var.
  Materials $1,246 U
  Labor $1,385 F
Efficiency var.
  Materials $15,050 F
  Labor $6,820 U
Overhead var.
  Flex. budget $16,034 U
  Prod. vol. $10,140 F

Hi-Fidelity, Inc., manufactures compact disk players and uses flexible budgeting and a standard cost system. The company's performance report includes the selected data shown at the top of the next page.

Required

1. Prepare a flexible budget based on actual volume.
2. Compute the price variance and the efficiency variance for direct materials and direct labor. Compute the total variance, the flexible budget variance, and the production volume variance for overhead.
3. Show that the sum of the price variance plus the efficiency variance equals the total cost variance for direct materials and for direct labor. Use Exhibit 24-6 as a guide.

	Master Budget 12,000 Units	Actual Results 13,300 Units
Sales	$744,000	$811,300
Variable expenses:		
Cost of goods sold:		
Direct materials (18,000 lb. @ $7.00)	$126,000	
(17,800 lb. @ $7.07)		$125,846
Direct labor (24,000 hr. @ $6.20)	148,800	
(27,700 hr. @ $6.15)...................		170,355
Variable overhead (24,000 hr. @ $2.10) ...	50,400	
(27,700 hr. @ $2.22)...................		61,494
Fixed expenses:		
Cost of goods sold:		
Fixed overhead	93,600	104,000
Total cost of goods sold	418,800	461,695
Gross profit	$325,200	$349,605

Price var. $747 U
Efficiency var. $67 F

Problem 24-4A *Using incomplete cost and variance information to determine the number of direct labor hours worked* **(L.O. 4)**

The city of Mobile has a shop that manufactures street signs. The manager of the shop uses standard costs to judge performance. Recently a clerk mistakenly threw away some of the records, and the manager has only partial data for July. He knows that the total direct labor variance for the month was $680—unfavorable, and that the standard labor price was $6.70 per hour. A recent pay raise caused an unfavorable labor price variance of $.30 per hour. The standard direct labor hours for actual July output were 2,500.

Required

1. Find the actual number of direct labor hours worked during July. First, find the actual direct labor price per hour. Then, determine the actual number of direct labor hours by setting up the computation of the total direct labor cost variance of $680.
2. Compute the direct labor price and efficiency variances.

Price var.:
  Materials $1,787.52 U
  Labor $678 F
Efficiency var.:
  Materials $1,436.40 F
  Labor $1,850 F
Overhead var.:
  Flex. budget $13,278 F
  Prod. vol. $10,712 U

Problem 24-5A *Computing and journalizing cost variances* **(L.O. 3, 4, 5, 6)**

Lumberjack Supply Co. manufactures hiking boots. The company prepares flexible budgets and uses a standard cost system to control manufacturing cost. The following standard unit cost of a pair of high-top boots is based on master budget volume of 14,000 pairs per month:

Direct materials (2.3 sq. yd. @ $2.10 per sq. yd.) ...		$ 4.83
Direct labor (2 hours @ $9.25 per hour)		18.50
Overhead:		
Variable	$1.22	
Fixed (2 hours @ $2.06 per hour)	4.12	5.34
Total unit cost...................................		$28.67

Transactions during November of the current year included these:

a. Actual production was 11,400 units.
b. Actual direct materials usage was 2.24 square yards per pair at actual cost of $2.17 per pair.
c. Actual direct labor usage of 22,600 hours cost $208,372.
d. Total actual overhead cost was $58,310.

Required

1. Compute the price and efficiency variances for direct materials and direct labor. Carry amounts to two decimal places.
2. Journalize the usage of direct material and the application of direct labor, including the related cost variances.
3. Compute the total variance, the flexible budget variance, and the production volume variance for overhead.
4. Lumberjack management intentionally purchased superior materials for November production. How did this decision affect the other cost variances? Overall, was the decision wise?

Problem 24-6A *Computing cost variances and reporting to management (L.O. 3, 4, 5, 7)*

Price var.:
  Materials $2,688 F
  Labor $220 F
Efficiency var.:
  Materials $5,124 U
  Labor $700 U
Overhead var.
  Flex. budget $2,140 U
  Prod. vol. $1,600 F
Gross profit $75,084

Lennox Manufacturing produces industrial plastics used in a variety of products. During April the company produced and sold 21,000 sheets of plastic and accumulated the following cost data:

	Standard Unit Cost	Total Actual Cost
Direct materials:		
Standard (3 lb. @ $1.22 per lb.)	$3.66	
Actual (67,200 lb. @ $1.18 per lb.)		$ 79,296
Direct labor:		
Standard (.1 hr. @ $7.00 per hr.)	.70	
Actual (2,200 hr. @ $6.90 per hr.)		15,180
Overhead:		
Standard:		
Variable ($12.00 per direct labor hour) ...	$1.20	
Fixed ($32,000 for master budget volume of 20,000 units and 2,000 direct labor hours)	1.60	2.80
Actual		59,340
Total	$7.16	$153,816

Required

1. Compute the price and efficiency variances for direct materials and direct labor.
2. Compute the total variance, the flexible budget variance, and the production volume variance for overhead.
3. Prepare a standard cost income statement through gross profit to report all variances to management. Sale price of the plastic was $10.90 per sheet.
4. Lennox intentionally purchased cheaper materials during April. Was the decision wise? Discuss the trade-off between the two materials cost variances.

Net inc. at 30,000 units $77,625

Problem 24-1B *Preparing a flexible budget income statement and graphing cost behavior (L.O. 1)*

Columbia Pneumatic Tool Company manufactures solenoids for electronically controlled lawn sprinkler systems. The company's master budget income statement for 19X3 follows, based on expected sales volume of 36,000 units.

Columbia's plant capacity is 38,000 units, so if actual volume exceeds 38,000 units it will be necessary to rent additional space. In that case, salaries will increase by 10 percent, rent will double, and insurance expense will increase by $2,000. Depreciation and fixed utilities will be unaffected by the increase in volume.

Columbia Pneumatic Tool Company
Master Budget Income Statement
Year 19X3

Sales	$756,000
Variable expenses:	
Cost of goods sold	$288,000
Sales commissions	37,800
Shipping	18,000
Utilities	14,400
Fixed expenses:	
Salaries	110,000
Depreciation	53,000
Rent	45,000
Insurance	11,000
Utilities	9,000
Total operating expenses	586,200
Income before income tax	169,800
Income tax expense (25%)	42,450
Net income	$127,350

Required

1. Prepare a flexible budget income statement for the company, showing volume levels of 30,000, 36,000, 40,000, and 44,000 units.

2. Graph the total operating expense behavior of the company. Cost of goods sold is included.

Net income:
   Flex. budget var. $7,650 U
   Sales vol. var. $22,800 F

Problem 24-2B *Preparing an income statement performance report* **(L.O. 2)**

Refer to the Columbia Pneumatic Tool Company situation of Problem 24-1B. The company sold 44,000 units during 19X3, and its actual income statement was as reported below.

Required

Prepare an income statement performance report for 19X3.

Columbia Pneumatic Tool Company
Income Statement
Year 19X3

Sales	$928,000
Variable expenses:	
Cost of goods sold	$361,000
Sales commissions	45,000
Shipping	27,000
Utilities	18,000
Fixed expenses:	
Salaries	127,000
Depreciation	66,000
Rent	72,000
Insurance	14,000
Utilities	8,000
Total operating expenses	738,000
Income before income tax	190,000
Income tax expense (25%)	47,500
Net income	$142,500

Problem 24-3B *Preparing a flexible budget and computing cost variances (L.O. 1, 3, 4, 5)*

Lands End Fabricating Company manufactures office furniture and uses flexible budgeting and a standard cost system. The company's performance report includes the following selected data:

Gross profit $336,400
Price var.:
  Materials $3,280 F
  Labor $579 U
Efficiency var.:
  Materials $9,600 U
  Labor $1,800 U
Overhead var.:
  Flex. budget $11,966 U
  Prod. vol. $5,600 U

	Master Budget 4,000 Units	Actual Results 3,800 Units
Sales	$800,000	$729,600
Variable expenses:		
Cost of goods sold:		
Direct materials (160,000 lb. @ $.80)	$128,000	
(164,000 lb. @ $.78)		$127,920
Direct labor (20,000 hr. @ $6.00)	120,000	
(19,300 hr. @ $6.03)		116,379
Variable overhead (20,000 hr. @ $4.00)	80,000	
(20,300 hr. @ $5.22)		105,966
Fixed expenses:		
Cost of goods sold:		
Fixed overhead	112,000	94,000
Total cost of goods sold	440,000	444,265
Gross profit	$360,000	$285,335

Required

1. Prepare a flexible budget based on actual volume.
2. Compute the price variance and the efficiency variance for direct materials and direct labor. Compute the total variance, the flexible budget variance, and the production volume variance for overhead.
3. Show that the sum of the price variance plus the efficiency variance equals the total cost variance for direct materials and for direct labor. Use Exhibit 24-6 as a guide.

Problem 24-4B *Using incomplete cost and variance information to determine the number of direct labor hours worked (L.O. 4)*

Price var. $660 U
Efficiency var. $1,560 F

The state of Kentucky has a shop that manufactures road signs used throughout the state. The manager of the shop uses standard costs to judge performance. Recently a clerk mistakenly threw away some of the records, and the manager has only partial data for April. She knows that the total direct labor variance for the month was $900—favorable and that the standard labor price was $6 per hour. A recent pay raise caused an unfavorable labor price variance of $.25 per hour. The standard direct labor hours for actual April output were 2,900.

Required

1. Find the actual number of direct labor hours worked during April. First, find the actual direct labor price per hour. Then determine the actual number of direct labor hours by setting up the computation of the total direct labor cost variance of $900.
2. Compute the direct labor price and efficiency variances.

Problem 24-5B *Computing and journalizing cost variances (L.O. 3, 4, 5, 6)*

Price var.:
  Materials $624.25 F
  Labor $692 U
Efficiency var.:
  Materials $851.25 F
  Labor $220 U
Overhead var.:
  Flex. budget $983 U
  Prod. vol. $864 F

Consolidated Enterprises manufactures T-shirts that it sells to other companies for customizing with their own logos. Consolidated prepares flexible budgets and uses a standard cost system to control manufacturing cost. The standard unit cost of a basic white T-shirt given at the top of the next page is based on master budget volume of 20,000 T-shirts per month.

Direct materials (3 sq. yd. @ $.15 per sq. yd.) ...		$ .45
Direct labor (3 minutes @ $.20 per minute)		.60
Overhead:		
Variable	$.12	
Fixed (2 minutes @ $.16 per minute)	.32	.44
Total unit cost		$1.49

Transactions during May of the current year included the following:

a. Actual production and sales were 22,700 units.

b. Actual direct materials usage was 2.75 square yards per unit at actual cost of $.14 per square yard.

c. Actual direct labor usage of 69,200 minutes cost $14,532.

d. Total actual overhead cost was $10,107.

Required

1. Compute the price and efficiency variances for direct materials and direct labor. Carry amounts to two decimal places.

2. Journalize the usage of direct material and the application of direct labor, including the related cost variances.

3. Compute the total variance, the flexible budget variance, and the production volume variance for overhead. Evaluate the performance of the employee groups most responsible for the two overhead variances. Concentrate on the performance of the plant manager.

Price var.:
  Materials $749 U
  Labor $80 U
Efficiency var.:
  Materials $465 F
  Labor $200 U
Overhead var.:
  Flex. budget $80 U
  Prod. vol. $300 U
Gross profit $55,996

Problem 24-6B *Computing cost variances and reporting to management (L.O. 3,4,5,7)*

Champion Academic Supplier manufactures ring binders used by college students. During August the company produced and sold 78,000 binders and accumulated the following cost data:

		Standard Unit Cost	Total Actual Cost
Direct materials:			
Standard (1 lb. @ $.15 per lb.)		$.15	
Actual (74,900 lb. @ $.16 per lb.)			$11,984
Direct labor:			
Standard (.02 hr. @ $5.00 per hr.)		.10	
Actual (1,600 hr. @ $5.05 per hr.)			8,080
Overhead:			
Standard:			
Variable ($6.00 per direct labor hour)	$.12		
Fixed ($12,000 for master budget			
volume of 80,000 units and 1,600			
direct labor hours)	.15	.27	
Actual			21,440
Total		$.52	$41,504

Required

1. Compute the price and efficiency variances for direct materials and direct labor.

2. Compute the total variance, the flexible budget variance, and the production volume variance for overhead.

3. Prepare a standard cost income statement through gross profit to report all variances to management. Sale price of the binders to college bookstores was $1.25 each.

4. Champion management purchased superior materials during August. Discuss the trade-off between the two materials cost variances.

Extending Your Knowledge

Decision Problems

1. Preparing a Performance Report and Using It to Evaluate Company Performance (L.O. 2)

The board of directors of X-Out, Inc., is meeting to evaluate the company's performance for the year just ended. Suppose the accompanying report, which applies to X-Out's basic line of golf clubs, has been prepared for use at the meeting.

The directors are disappointed at the net income results. They ask if the company maintained the price of its golf clubs at budgeted sale price of $120, and they are told yes. Moreover, the levels of beginning and ending inventories were unchanged.

Required

1. Use the above information to prepare a more informative performance report.
2. A downturn in the economy was responsible for the company's inability to sell more golf clubs. How would you view company performance in light of this additional information? Would you decide to overhaul operations or keep the business operating on its present course?

1. Net inc.:
   Flex. budget var. $139,854 F
   Sales vol. var. $166,454 U

X-Out, Inc.
Performance Report
Year Ended June 30, 19X7

	Actual Results	Master Budget	Variance
Sales	$2,655,000	$3,240,000	$585,000 U
Variable expenses:			
Cost of goods sold	$1,189,000	$1,546,000	$357,000 F
Promotion expense	126,800	110,000	16,800 U
Sales commissions	116,900	166,000	49,100 F
Shipping	64,000	87,000	23,000 F
Utilities	13,000	14,000	1,000 F
Fixed expenses:			
Salaries	341,600	439,000	97,400 F
Depreciation	306,000	313,000	7,000 F
Rent	143,500	171,000	27,500 F
Utilities	11,200	13,000	1,800 F
Total operating expenses	2,312,000	2,859,000	547,000 F
Income before income tax	343,000	381,000	38,000 U
Income tax expense (30%)	102,900	114,300	11,400 F
Net income	$ 240,100	$ 266,700	$ 26,600 U

2. *Variance Analysis and Reporting in a Non-profit Organization* (L.O. 1, 2)

St. Margaret's Church is a small congregation in Altamont, Oregon. At the end of 1992, the church membership was 87 families. Each family donated an average of $400 per year to the church's operating fund and $100 per year to the mission and service fund.

At the beginning of 1993, the Church's Stewardship, Mission and Service Committee estimated that, due to the building of a new factory ten miles outside Altamont, the church membership would grow by eleven families. In addition, the committee planned a stewardship campaign for 1993 with the aim of increasing average donations to $450 for the operating fund and $125 for mission and service.

During 1993, seven new families became members at St. Margaret's; no families left the congregation. The 1993 receipts amounted to $42,864 for operations, and $10,152 for mission and service.

Required

1. Assume that you were the Chairman of St. Margaret's Church's 1993 Stewardship Committee. Prepare an analysis for the Stewardship, Mission and Service Committee of the 1993 fund-raising efforts.
2. Write a one-paragraph report to summarize the results of the fund-raising campaign for the church's board of trustees.

Ethical Issue

Jurgens Products, Inc., budgets from the bottom up. Production workers prepare departmental goals, which are coordinated by supervisors. Top managers combine the departmental budgets into the company's overall flexible budget. Standard costs developed from the budget amounts are used for the full year.

Production workers have observed that the standard costs correspond closely to their own budget amounts. Accordingly, they have built a cushion for themselves by overestimating the quantities of materials and labor needed to manufacture a product.

Required

1. Are Jurgens's cost variances likely to be favorable or unfavorable? Why is this outcome likely to occur?
2. Whose behavior is unethical, and whose behavior is lax?
3. If this situation persists over several years, what is the likely outcome?

Chapter 25

Responsibility Accounting: Departments and Branches

Managers operate large businesses by separating them into component units, called responsibility centers. Each individual assigned to run a responsibility center then answers for how that part of the company performs—ideally. However, consider this comment by the manager of a Belgian milk producer named Laitier S. A. ("S.A." is the French-language equivalent of "Inc."):

"It is terribly frustrating to be evaluated as a profit center when I do not have complete control over revenues," said Henri Goudal, managing director of Laitier S.A. "The Export Division [of United Brands, Inc., our parent company] is responsible for over 75 percent of our total sales. They determine the price, the destination and the quantity of most of the milk we sell. We have no direct authority over that department, yet we are held responsible when sales are poor. If they do not perform up to expectations, then we cannot meet the budgeted profit target for which we are held responsible by headquarters."

Source: M. Edgar Barrett and William J. Bruns, *Case Problems in Management Accounting* (Homewood, IL: Irwin; 1985), p. 283.

What's the problem in this situation? The manager has more responsibility than authority. A well-run organization will attempt to work around this situation. This chapter discusses how accounting is used to evaluate managers by tracing costs and revenues to the activities for which the managers are responsible. This area of analysis is called responsibility accounting.

Responsibility Accounting

Most businesses must divide the responsibility of management. Some companies are so geographically dispersed that one person cannot adequately oversee the entire operation. Other companies may have too many operations or too many employees for one person to handle all executive duties. To get the work done, executives must delegate authority over particular areas to middle-level managers. Depending on how complex or on how large the company is, the mid-level manager may in turn delegate authority to other employees to handle certain areas of operations under her responsibility. And so the responsibility chain grows.

How does the business measure each manager's performance? **Responsibility accounting** is a system for classifying financial data by defined areas in an organization in order to evaluate the performance of managers for activities under their supervision. Responsibility accounting is a key tool in managing all but single-person businesses. For example, automobile dealerships use responsibility accounting for separately measuring the performance of various activities such as new car sales, used car sales, parts sales, and the service department.

The basic unit in a responsibility accounting system is called a **responsibility center**, which is a part, segment, or subunit of an organization whose managers are accountable for specified activities. A center can be any subunit of an organization needing control. Each center works from a budget tailored to its particular activities. The three common types of responsibility centers are the cost center, the profit center, and the investment center.

1. Cost center. Responsibility center in which a manager is accountable for costs (expenses) only. Examples include a personnel department and a shipping department. It is important for these departments to control costs; they are not responsible for generating revenue. Consequently, only costs are reported for their activities. A shipping department manager is judged, for example, on the cost of shipping a certain volume of merchandise.

2. *Profit center.* Responsibility center in which a manager is accountable for revenues and costs (expenses). Examples are a McDonald's restaurant and a jewelry department in a Macy's store. In the chapter-opening vignette, Laitier S.A. is a profit center of United Brands, the parent company. Managers of these subunits are responsible for generating income (revenues minus expenses). Both revenues and expenses are reported to show the income of a profit center.

3. *Investment center.* Responsibility center in which a manager is accountable for investments, revenues, and costs (expenses). Examples are a Hilton hotel and an Exxon exploration division. Investment in the business is reported in addition to revenues and expenses so that return on investment (income divided by investment) can be computed. Top managers, as well as investors, evaluate projects by comparing their returns on investment.

Illustration of Responsibility Accounting

The simplified organization chart in Exhibit 25-1 illustrates how companies may use responsibility accounting in the fast-food industry. At the top level, a district manager oversees the branch managers, who supervise the managers of the individual restaurants (called stores). Store managers have limited freedom to make operating decisions. They may decide on how to handle local advertising, the number of employees and their schedules, and the store hours. Branch managers oversee several stores, evaluate store managers' performance, and set store managers' compensation levels. In turn, district managers oversee several branches, evaluate branch managers' performance and compensation, and decide on district prices and sales promotions. District managers are accountable to regional managers, who answer to home-office vice-presidents.

Exhibit 25-2 provides a more detailed view of how responsibility accounting is used to evaluate profit centers. Examine the lowest level and move to the top. Follow how the reports are related through the three levels of responsibility. All variances may be subdivided for further analysis, either in these reports or in supporting schedules.

Teaching Tip: Profit and investment centers report revenues; a cost center does not. Revenue need not be generated in a responsibility center.

Class Discussion: Give some examples of departments that are cost centers. *ANSWER:* Accounting, personnel, maintenance.

Teaching Tip: As you discuss Exhibit 25-2, point out that O'Toole must have a detailed chart of accounts in order to report revenue and expenses by store at the lowest level of managerial responsibility.

Also point out that as you progress up the exhibit (and up the organization chart) each higher level of responsibility covers a greater range of revenue and expense accounts. For example, the District Manager is directly responsible for his office expenses as well as indirectly responsible for the operating income of several branches.

Class Discussion: Why is it important to set up responsibility centers for the Northern California District of O'Toole? What might happen if there were no responsibility centers? *POSSIBLE ANSWERS:* 1) One or more stores may not be profitable, 2) One or more managers may not be controlling costs well; 3) One or more geographic areas may be doing better or worse than others.

EXHIBIT 25-1 *O'Toole Restaurant Corporation Simplified Partial Organization Chart*

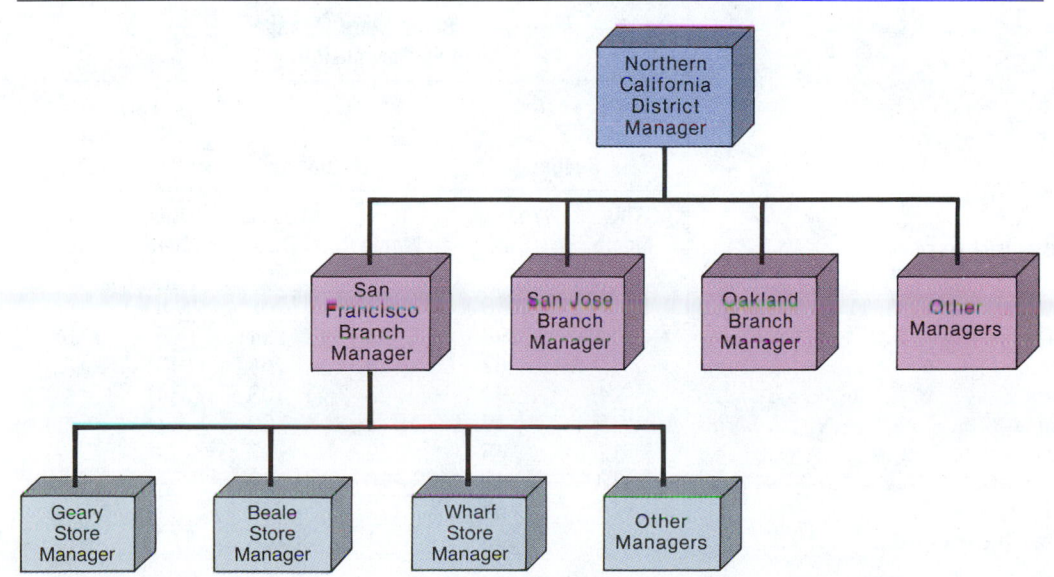

O'Toole Restaurant Corporation
Responsibility Accounting at Various Levels
(in thousands of dollars)

Northern California District Manager
Monthly Responsibility Report

Operating income of branches and district manager office expense:	Budget This Month	Budget Year to Date	Actual This Month	Actual Year to Date	Variance Favorable (Unfavorable) This Month	Variance Favorable (Unfavorable) Year to Date
District manager office expense..	$ (150)	$ (600)	$ (158)	$ (620)	$ (8)	$ (20)
San Francisco branch...........	465	1,730	460	1,780	(5)	50
San Jose branch...............	500	1,800	519	1,890	19	90
Oakland branch...............	310	1,220	341	1,330	31	110
Others.......................	600	2,560	647	2,690	47	130
Operating income..............	$1,725	$6,710	$1,809	$7,070	$84	$360

San Francisco Branch Manager
Monthly Responsibility Report

Operating income of stores and branch manager office expense:	Budget This Month	Budget Year to Date	Actual This Month	Actual Year to Date	Variance Favorable (Unfavorable) This Month	Variance Favorable (Unfavorable) Year to Date
Branch manager office expense..	$ (20)	$ (306)	$ (25)	$ (302)	$ (5)	$ 4
Geary Store	48	148	47	143	(1)	(5)
Beale Store	54	228	61	244	7	16
Wharf Store	38	160	42	170	4	10
Others.......................	345	1,500	335	1,525	(10)	25
Operating income..............	$465	$1,730	$460	$1,780	$ (5)	$50

Beale Store Manager
Monthly Responsibility Report

Revenue and expense:	Budget This Month	Budget Year to Date	Actual This Month	Actual Year to Date	Variance Favorable (Unfavorable) This Month	Variance Favorable (Unfavorable) Year to Date
Revenue	$170	$690	$178	$702	$ 8	$12
Food expense.................	50	198	45	184	5	14
Paper	15	62	18	64	(3)	(2)
Wages	24	98	28	103	(4)	(5)
Repairs	5	19	4	20	1	(1)
General	12	45	12	47	—	(2)
Depreciation.................	10	40	10	40	—	—
Total expenses...............	116	462	117	458	(1)	4
Operating income..............	$ 54	$228	$ 61	$244	$ 7	$16

Trace the $54,000 operating income from the Beale Store manager report to the San Francisco branch manager report. The branch manager report summarizes the final results of the stores under his supervision. In addition, charges incurred by the branch manager office are included in this report.

Trace the $465,000 total from the San Francisco branch manager report to the northern California district manager report. The report of the district manager includes data for her own district office plus a summary of the entire district's operating income performance.

Performance Report Format

Exhibit 25-2 stresses variances. This focus is a highlight of **management by exception,** a management policy in which executive attention is directed to the important deviations from budgeted amounts. For example, the San Francisco branch's operating income lagged behind the other branches during the current month and for the year to date. The district manager would concentrate her efforts on improving the San Francisco branch. Managers do not waste time investigating smoothly running operations.

The format for reporting operations used in Exhibit 25-2 may be expanded to highlight variances. The expanded performance report for the Beale Store manager follows.

	Budget		Actual Results		Variance: Favorable (Unfavorable)		Variance: Percent of Budgeted Amount	
	This Month	Year to Date	This Month	Year to Date	This Month	Year to Date	This Month	Year to Date
Revenues	$170	$690	$178	$702	$8	$12	4.7%	1.7%

The complete performance report would likely include line-by-line presentations of other data. For example, a report for a restaurant will show the number of customers served and the average selling price per customer. In the hotel industry, managers report the percentage of rooms occupied and the average daily rental rate per room as performance measures.

No single format appeals to all users. Some managers prefer the greater detail shown in the eight-column format, but others prefer less detail. The choice is a matter of personal preference.

Design of a Responsibility Accounting System

A responsibility accounting system can be combined with whatever type of accounting system the company uses, such as a standard cost system, which highlights variances. Laitier, S.A., the Belgian milk producer in the opening vignette, probably uses process costing in conjunction with its responsibility accounting system. Recall that process costing works well for goods that are mass-produced as identical units—such as gallons of milk. The key to an effective accounting system is gathering and communicating information to assist the business in achieving its goals. Two factors are important: manager control over operations, and manager access to information.

OBJECTIVE 2
Prepare a performance report for management by exception

Consider a furniture manufacturer that uses a standard cost system to measure an efficiency (usage) variance and a price variance for the cost of lumber. The production supervisor is responsible for the quantity of lumber used to manufacture chairs. Good work in the factory wastes little lumber and holds costs down. Careless work wastes lumber and increases production cost. The supervisor must control operations. The efficiency (usage) variance is watched by the supervisor, often by personal observation.

Responsibility for the price variance is assigned to the purchasing manager who buys the lumber. The price of lumber may differ from standard cost because of droughts, crop disease, and forest fires, which are beyond the purchasing manager's control. Nevertheless, the price variance is the responsibility of the purchasing manager because he or she has access to more price information than anyone else in the business. *The reporting responsibility of any manager is to explain the outcome of an action regardless of personal influence over the outcome.* Henri Goudal in the opening vignette is worrying about factors that are beyond his control. He would be wiser to focus his energies on those items he can control.

Responsibility accounting, budgets, standards, and variances are aids to management. They help top managers to delegate decision making to lower levels by assigning responsibility for action and establishing a way to evaluate performance. Such a system frees top managers to work on broad issues affecting the whole organization.

Responsibility accounting systems can also be misused as a way of finding fault and placing blame. Henri Goudal sees this possibility. The question should not be, Who should be blamed for an unfavorable variance? The question should be, Which individual is in the best position to explain why a specific variance occurred?

Departmental Accounting

Departments are the most widely encountered responsibility centers. The department store is a familiar illustration. Top managers of a department store want more information than the net income of the store as a whole. At a minimum, they want to know each department's gross margin (sales minus cost of goods sold). In addition, they usually want to know each department's operating income. With these data, managers can identify their most profitable and least profitable departments. This information aids decisions such as whether to expand some departments and phase out others.

Departmental gross margins are easy to measure because sales and cost of goods sold records are kept by department. Departmental operating income (gross margin minus operating expenses) is not as easy to measure. Why? Primarily because of indirect expenses.

Direct expenses are those that are conveniently identified with and traceable to a particular product or a department. The wages of sales clerks, the salary of the department head, the advertising of the shoe department, and the depreciation of display cases within a department are direct expenses.

Indirect expenses are all those expenses other than direct expenses. Indirect expenses are not traceable to a single department. Examples are the costs of operating the receiving department and the stockroom. Often these activities serve more than one department simultaneously. For example, an incoming truck may be delivering merchandise to several departments. How does the business allocate this receiving cost? To what department does the business assign the expense of operating the stockroom, which holds inventory for

Point to Stress: The gross margin (or gross profit) of a business is sales minus cost of goods sold. It is also the amount of profit before operating expenses, interest expense, and income taxes are deducted. For financial reporting, operating expenses are divided into selling and administrative expenses. But for responsibility (departmental) accounting, these expenses will be divided differently—into direct and indirect expenses.

Discussion Question: What are some examples of direct costs?
ANSWER: Department manager's salary, depreciation for furniture and equipment in the department, delivery expense, and any other expense that can be traced directly to a department.

OBJECTIVE 3
Allocate indirect expenses to departments

several departments? How does the company allocate the expense of an advertising campaign that promotes the entire store, not just a single department? Although direct allocations of specific advertising can be made, most businesses regard general advertising as indirect expense.

Allocation of Service Department Expenses

Cost allocation is the assignment of various costs to departments. Cost allocation may also be called **expense allocation,** cost assignment, cost distribution, and cost apportionment. (As you learned in Chapters 22 and 23, the term *cost allocation* applies to the costs of products also. In our present discussion, we are allocating the costs of service departments, not manufacturing departments.)

To allocate expense, the business must first set an **allocation base,** which is a logical common denominator for assigning a given cost to two or more departments. Consider a store that sells housewares and appliances. These two departments share the expense of warehousing the store's inventory. The business could allocate the expense of warehousing on the basis of the ratio of space taken up by each department's goods. If housewares occupy 80 percent of the warehouse, then the housewares department might be assigned 80 percent of warehouse expense. Similarly, the cost of the receiving department may be divided between the two departments on the basis of the number of hours spent unloading each department's goods. If unloading appliances takes 30 percent of the receiving employees' time, then the appliance department could be allocated 30 percent of receiving department expense.

The costs of warehousing and receiving are examples of indirect expenses that are easy to assign to departments. Other indirect costs are more difficult to allocate. How do we assign factory overhead and home-office administrative costs to departments? The common denominator for allocating these expenses to departments is less clear. We will address this problem later in this chapter.

Companies use different allocation bases, and even within a single company several different bases may be used to allocate different expenses to the various departments. The list in Exhibit 25-3 offers common examples of allocation bases for selected costs and expenses.

Let us stress this point: The ideal guide for choosing an allocation base is a cause-and-effect relationship. That is, What are the cost drivers, the factors that cause costs? For instance, as Exhibit 25-3 shows, generally the more square feet of space, the higher the cost of janitorial services. Choosing an allocation base is largely a matter of common sense. No one "right" allocation base exists for each cost or expense. Managers use their experience and judgment in choosing these bases. Affected managers should participate in the choice of cost allocation bases. This will enhance confidence in the reasonableness of the cost allocations.

Illustration of Departmental Reporting

Exhibit 25-4 shows a simplified departmental income statement of a Computer Unlimited Store.

Supporting details can be shown in various ways. For example, gross sales, sales returns and allowances, and sales discounts can appear in the body of the statement or in a separate schedule. Our discussion, however, focuses on the allocation of selected expenses to the store's two departments.

Salaries and wages. These costs, which include each department manager's salary, are direct departmental expense.

Discussion Question: What are some examples of indirect costs? ANSWER: Insurance, utilities, accounting, rent, and so on. These costs are usually incurred for the benefit of the business as a whole and, therefore, must be allocated to each department.

Typical Student Misconception: Remind students that only indirect costs, which benefit more than one function or department, must be allocated. Indirect costs must be allocated on some basis which is fair and equitable to all functions or departments (divisions) concerned.

Teaching Tip: Cost allocation uses the same formula used for allocating joint product costs and lump-sum purchases of assets.

Discussion Question: What would be a reasonable basis for allocating the following costs? 1) Rent ANSWER: Square feet of floor space; 2) Utilities ANSWER: Square feet of floor space, 3) Advertising ANSWER: Sales; 4) Purchasing Department costs ANSWER: Purchases of each department.

EXHIBIT 25-3 *Bases for Allocating Costs to Departments*

Teaching Tip: Refer to Exhibit 25-3. Notice that direct expenses are not allocated.

Class Exercise: Assume that Main Manufacturing Company has a Personnel Department whose salaries must be allocated to Production Departments A, B, and C, based on the numbers of employees in each department. The Personnel Department has 5 employees, who earn a total of $160,000. Production Departments A, B, and C have 15, 20, and 7 employees respectively. How should the Personnel Department salaries (an indirect cost) be allocated?

ANSWER:

Production Department	# of Employees	% of total
A	15	35.7%
B	20	47.6%
C	7	16.7%
Total	42	100.0%

Allocation of Salary Expense

35.7% × $160,000 = $57,120
47.6% × $160,000 =   76,160
16.7% × $160,000 =   26,720
                   $160,000

Note: The number of employees in the Personnel Department is not included in the calculation because we are allocating their cost (salary) to the Production Departments.

Cost or Expense	Base for Allocating Cost to Departments
Direct material	Separately traced
Merchandise	Separately traced
Packaging materials	Separately traced if feasible
Direct labor	Separately traced
Other labor	Time spent in each department
Supervision	Time spent, or number of employees, in each department
Equipment depreciation and rentals	Separately traced, hours used by each department
Building depreciation, property taxes, and rentals	Square feet of space. Sometimes heavier allocations are made to departments that experience higher customer traffic
Heat, light, and air conditioning	Square feet or cubic feet of space
Janitorial services	Square feet of space
Advertising	Separately traced if possible. Otherwise, in proportion to newspaper space or radio or TV time in advertisement, or in proportion to budgeted sales or actual sales
Payroll Department	Number of employees in each department
Personnel Department	Number of employees in each department
Purchasing Department	Number of orders or dollar amounts of purchases in each department

Depreciation—equipment. This expense is also direct departmental expense, related to the equipment used only by each specific department.

Supplies. If each department may request supplies as needed, supplies are a direct cost. However, suppose the personnel from both departments help themselves to a companywide pool of supplies without recording usage. In this case, the company must establish a base for allocating supplies expense to the individual departments. The company may use percentage of sales, illustrated as follows for total supplies expense of $200:

Department	Sales	Percent of Total Sales	Allocation of Supplies Expense of $200
Hardware....	$ 7,000	70%	.70 × $200 = $140
Software.....	3,000	30%	.30 × 200 = 60
Total	$10,000	100%	1.00 × $200 = $200

Advertising. Consider a $960 computer store ad that takes up 24 square inches in the Sunday newspaper. Fifteen square inches advertise hardware, and 5 square inches promote software. The remaining 4 square inches carry information about the company as a whole (its address, hours, and so forth).

EXHIBIT 25-4 *Departmental Income Statement*

Computer Unlimited Store
Departmental Income Statement
For the Year Ended December 31, 19X1
(in thousands)

	Total	Department Hardware	Software
Net sales	$10,000	$7,000	$3,000
Cost of goods sold	5,500	4,000	1,500
Gross margin	4,500	3,000	1,500
Operating expenses:			
Salaries and wages	1,100	660	440
Depreciation—equipment	100	80	20
Supplies	200	140	60
Advertising	1,000	400	600
Rent	600	480	120
Heat, light, air conditioning	60	40	20
Purchasing department	300	230	70
General administration department	200	160	40
Total operating expenses	3,560	2,190	1,370
Operating income	$ 940	$ 810	$ 130

How does the business allocate the overall cost of advertising to the two departments?

Suppose each square inch of advertising costs $40. Then the $960 total cost (24 inches × $40 = $960) may be allocated in two steps, as the accompanying table shows.

Department	Step 1: 20 Inches of Direct Advertising	Step 2: 4 Inches of General Advertising	Steps 1 + 2: 24 Inches of Total Advertising
Hardware	15 × $40 = $600 (75%)	75% × $160 = $120	$720
Software	5 × 40 = 200 (25%)	25% × 160 = 40	240
	$800 (100%)	$160	$960

Step 1 computes each department's direct cost, $600 and $200, respectively. Hardware's percentage of total direct cost is $600/$800, or 75 percent; Software's percentage is $200/$800, or 25 percent. Step 2 uses these percentages to allocate the $160 of general advertising costs ($960 − $800 = $160) to Hardware and Software.

If the computer store had three departments, we would simply total the individual departments' direct expense and use each department's percentage of that total to allocate the general advertising expense. We may allocate other general expenses—for example, salaries, wages, and depreciation—among departments in this way.

Rent. Rent may be allocated on the basis of square footage, as follows:

Rent for entire store	$600,000
Total square feet	25,000
Rent per square foot ($600,000/25,000)	$24

Real-World Example:
Weyerhaeuser Company, which ranked 111 in *Business Week* magazine's top 1,000 companies in 1990, has developed a unique procedure for allocating corporate overhead. Rather than allocate overhead costs, such as general accounting and payroll, as indirect costs, these and costs for corporate services are traced directly to the department that consumes the resources or services. Managers are free to purchase the resource or service from an outsider or from the corporate service departments, as they desire. Each service department must carefully price its service (preparation of payroll checks, for example). To date, none of the user units of Weyerhaeuser have decided to take over any of the services that the corporate services offer in the area of accounting activities. This new procedure for allocating overhead enabled one department to trim over 2% off their budget in the first year.

Suppose that the company considers each square foot of space in the store equally valuable and that the Hardware and Software Departments occupy 20,000 square feet and 5,000 square feet, respectively. The allocation of rent is

Hardware Department: 20,000 square feet × $24 per square foot = $480,000
Software Department: 5,000 square feet × $24 per square foot =   120,000
Total rent expense $600,000

However, space in certain parts of the store may have different values because of varying potential to generate sales. For example, the space near the entrance may be the most valuable space in the store. The rear of the store may be the least valuable. Managers use judgment, often combined with outside consultants, to arrive at an appropriate allocation of rent. One approach is to weight the square footage. Suppose again that the Hardware and Software Departments occupy 20,000 and 5,000 square feet, respectively, and that Hardware's space is twice as valuable as Software's. In this case, rent of $600,000 is allocated to the two departments as follows:

Department	Space Occupied	Space Weighted By Value	Proportion of Weighted Space	Allocation of Rent of $600,000
Hardware ...	20,000	20,000 × 2 = 40,000	8/9	8/9 × $600,000 = $533,333
Software.....	5,000	5,000 × 1 = 5,000	1/9	1/9 × 600,000 = 66,667
Total	25,000	45,000	9/9	9/9 × $600,000 = $600,000

Class Exercise: Suppose that a department store is in a 20,000-square-foot, two-story building. A local real estate appraiser has determined that the first floor space is half again as valuable as the second floor space. If the linen department occupies 2,000 square feet on the second floor, how much of the $180,000 rent will be allocated to the linen department? ANSWER: The ratio of the value of first floor space to second floor space is 1½ to 1 or 3:2.

Square Feet

First   10,000 × 3 = 30,000
Second 10,000 × 2 = 20,000
                     50,000

Fraction of Weighted Space	Allocation of Rent
3/5 × $180,000	= $108,000
2/5 × $180,000	= 72,000
	= $180,000

Linen Department:

$$\frac{2,000}{10,000} \times \$72,000 = \$14,400$$

Heat, Light, Air Conditioning.   The most common allocation base is square feet of space occupied. Cubic feet is used if ceiling height varies in different parts of the building.

Purchasing Department.   Some of these expenses can be charged directly to specific departments. Any remaining expense is usually allocated in proportion to the dollar amount of purchases made on behalf of each department. Note that this assumes that the total cost of goods purchased is the cost driver. In some cases, the number of orders or the number of units purchased may be better measures of which departments used Purchasing Department resources.

General Administrative Expenses.   This category includes depreciation on office furniture and equipment, office utilities, salaries of management and the office staff, and other expenses related to the organization as a whole. Some of these expenses may be charged directly. Others, such as payroll and personnel costs, may be allocated by the number of employees in various departments. The remainder is often allocated in proportion to departmental sales because this allocation base is convenient and no better base is apparent or feasible.

Managers may want expense allocations refined beyond those in Exhibit 25-4. For example, they may desire a statement with the following format to emphasize the difference between direct departmental expense and indirect expense:

Net sales . . . . $XXX
Cost of goods sold   XXX
Gross margin   XXX
Direct departmental expense . . . . .   **XXX**
Margin before indirect expenses . . .   XXX
Indirect expenses . . . .   **XXX**
Operating income . . . . $XXX

The margin before indirect expenses may provide information for deciding whether to expand or cut back a department's operations. Accounting systems can be designed to fulfill these wishes.

Summary Problem for Your Review

Review the allocation of rent, as explained for the illustration of departmental reporting on pages 1137–38. Suppose the Hardware Department's space is three times as valuable as that of the Software Department. Total rent remains $600,000.

Required

1. Prepare an analysis to show how much total rent expense should be allocated to each department.
2. What is each department's rent expense per square foot?

SOLUTION TO REVIEW PROBLEM

Requirement 1

Department	Space Occupied	Space Weighted By Value	Proportion of Weighted Space	Allocation of Rent of $600,000
Hardware ..	20,000	$20,000 \times 3 = 60,000$	$12/13$	$12/13 \times \$600,000 = \$553,846$
Software....	5,000	$5,000 \times 1 = 5,000$	$1/13$	$1/13 \times 600,000 = 46,154$
Total	25,000	65,000	$13/13$	$13/13 \times \$600,000 = \$600,000$

Requirement 2

Rent expense per square foot:
  Hardware: $553,846/20,000 = $27.69
  Software: $46,154/5,000 = $9.23

Note: Hardware's rent expense per square foot is indeed three times as high as Software's rent
    expense per square foot ($27.69 = $9.23 × 3).

Branch Accounting

Many companies establish branch offices or branch factories. Top managers may wish to take advantage of particular benefits that a certain geographical area offers. Materials and labor may be cheaper at a location removed from the home office. Or the company may want to open a new sales market.

Branches are responsibility centers—often cost centers if the branch is devoted to manufacturing or warehousing with no sales responsibility. A branch manager has responsibility for certain aspects of a branch's operations. In turn, he must report the branch's performance to his superior.

Who has the accounting responsibilities in a company that runs branch operations? The home office generally keeps most of the accounting records. The branch maintains only those records needed to manage its own operations. **Branch accounting** is a system for separating the accounts of a branch

Point to Stress: Branch accounting is a means of accounting for and reporting the operations of a branch or responsibility center. The branch is located in a separate place from the home office. The branch manager has responsibility for maximizing profits or minimizing costs at the branch, as well as controlling the assets assigned to the branch.

from those of the home office. The purpose is to establish accountability over the resources entrusted to the branch.

Consider a manufacturer that keeps cost records for direct materials, work in process inventory, and factory overhead at its branch factory. Receivables, finished goods inventory, plant assets, payables, depreciation, and other areas are accounted for in the corporate (home) office. This split of accounting between central headquarters and its branch means dividing the records between the two locations. With such a division, procedures are needed to ensure that all transactions are accounted for. Generally, two reciprocal accounts are used, one in the home office and one in the branch. **Reciprocal accounts** are two or more accounts that have exactly the same offsetting balances and are used to control a general ledger that is kept in two or more locations.

Alternatively, the branch may be a cost center, such as a factory that merely incurs manufacturing costs. The goal of accounting for this type of branch is to measure how effectively the branch manager controls costs.

Point to Stress: An accounting system may be centralized in the home office or decentralized at the branches.

Discussion Question: Can you think of some types of businesses around you which have branches? ANSWER: A bank or savings and loan association with its main business downtown may have a suburban branch office. Neiman-Marcus has its main store downtown and branch stores in outlying shopping malls.

Point to Stress: The ledger is a group of accounts. A general ledger contains all accounts for a business. The branch ledger contains only those accounts that relate to the branch's operations. The home office ledger contains all the rest of the accounts of the business. Each of the ledgers contains one of the reciprocal accounts as well.

Branch Ledger and Journal

A **branch ledger** is that part of a general ledger kept by the branch, separate from the home-office ledger. The branch ledger contains only those accounts needed to manage its operations plus a special account used to handle its accountability to the home office. If the branch is a manufacturing plant, its ledger is often called a **factory ledger.** Each branch has its own branch or factory ledger.

The **home-office ledger** is that part of a general ledger kept by the home office, separate from the branch ledger. The home-office ledger is identical to the general ledger studied throughout this course except that it includes a special account for the branch and excludes the accounts kept by the branch. The home office and the branch also maintain separate journals for recording transactions.

Suppose Appliance Company of America is headquartered in Chicago but has its manufacturing plant in Indianapolis. The home office makes all purchases and sales, handles cash payments and cash receipts, and incurs all company liabilities. A separate factory ledger is maintained in Indianapolis for managing the branch plant.

When the factory completes the manufacture of inventory, it transfers the finished goods to warehouses, which are managed directly by the home office. Upon transfer of merchandise to the warehouses, the home office debits inventory and credits the factory account for shipments at cost.

The general ledger accounts of the company follow, showing the link between the reciprocal accounts.

Home-Office Accounts	Branch-Factory Accounts
Cash	Direct materials inventory
Accounts receivable	Work in process inventory
Finished goods inventory	Factory overhead
Plant and equipment	Home-office ledger control
Accumulated depreciation	
Branch-factory ledger control	
Accounts payable	
Wages payable	
Common stock	
Retained earnings	
Sales revenue	
Cost of goods sold	
Selling expenses	
Administrative expenses	

Point to Stress: The Home-Office Control account is credited for assets transferred to the branch and for expenses allocated to the branch by the home office. It is debited when the branch remits cash or other assets to the home office.

The home office's **branch-factory ledger control** account can be viewed as an *investment in*, or a *receivable from*, the branch. Similarly, the branch's **home-office ledger control** account represents an *owner equity of*, or a *payable to*, the home office.

Illustrative Transactions and Related Journal Entries

Entries for the following transactions illustrate accounting for branch operations:

1. Direct materials purchased on credit $230,000
2. Direct materials used in production 150,000
3. Factory payroll accrued 200,000
4. Miscellaneous factory overhead cost incurred (credit Accounts Payable, $150,000; and Accumulated Depreciation, $18,000) 168,000
5. Factory overhead applied 165,000
6. Cost of goods shipped to warehouse 425,000
7. Cost of goods sold 400,000
8. Sales (on credit) 600,000
9. Cash collected on account 440,000

Journal Entries.   Illustrative journal entries and postings to the reciprocal accounts are given in Exhibit 25-5 (in thousands of dollars). The entries that would be made in a regular, unified journal are given first in the exhibit. Relating each pair of home office/branch entries to the corresponding unified entry will help you see how branch accounting works. Keep in mind that the focus is on the home office and branch entries. The regular, unified entries are presented solely to aid your understanding. Let's consider the first transaction and related entry—the credit purchase of direct materials by the home office for the branch factory (amounts in thousands of dollars).

OBJECTIVE 5
Account for branch operations

Home-Office Journal			Branch-Factory Journal		
Branch-Factory Ledger Control	230		Direct Materials Inventory	230	
Accounts Payable		230	Home-Office Ledger Control .		230
Home-office purchase of direct materials.			Home-office purchase of direct materials.		

The home office is responsible for paying the bill and so records the liability. The branch factory is responsible for using the direct materials and therefore records the inventory. Because accountability is split between the two locations, reciprocal accounts are used to ensure that each transaction is fully accounted for. The home-office debit to the branch account counterbalances the branch's credit to the home-office account. We can regard the $230,000 debit in the first home-office entry as the home office's investment in, or receivable from, the factory. The branch's credit to the home-office account in the branch's entry shows the branch's obligation to the home office for the purchased materials.

Entries 2 and 5 are confined strictly to the branch-factory ledger because these transactions affect factory costs with no home-office involvement. Entries 3, 4, and 6 affect both home office and branch. Entries 7, 8, and 9 are recorded solely by the home office because the branch has no responsibility for sales, cost of sales, or collections of receivables.

3 Sales Branch pays $2,750 on account for merchandise purchased.	Entry 6 deserves special comment. Factory shipments of finished goods transfer inventory from the factory to the warehouses, which are under direct home-office management. Such shipments reduce the home-office investment in the factory because the home office receives inventory. Likewise, the branch decreases the owner equity of the home office by transferring inventory to the warehouses.

3 Sales Branch pays $2,750 on account for merchandise purchased.
4 Sales Branch remits cash of $1,800 to Home Office.
5 Home Office transfers equipment of $3,000 to Sales Branch.

ANSWER:

1   Sales Branch
   Inventory 10,000
     Accts. Pay. . . .   10,000
         Home Office
           no entry

2   Sales Branch
   Accts. Rec. 3,500
     Sales Revenue   3,500
         Home Office
           no entry

3   Sales Branch
   Accts. Pay. 2,750
     Cash   2,750
         Home Office
           no entry

4   Sales Branch
   Home-Office
   Ledger Control . . 1,800
     Cash   1,800
         Home Office
   Cash 1,800
     Branch Ledger Ctrl   1,800

5   Sales Branch
   Equipment 3,000
   Home-Office
   Ledger Control   3,000
         Home Office
   Branch
   Ledger Ctrl. 3,000
     Equipment . . .   3,000

Reciprocal Balances.   Exhibit 25-5 shows that the reciprocal accounts have identical, offsetting balances. Any difference between the balances signals the accountant to explain the imbalance. A common cause of imbalances is faulty communication. For example, a shipment of finished goods to the warehouse may be in transit at the balance sheet date. The home office may be unaware of the transaction until the goods arrive. At the same time, the factory may have already recorded the shipment. Progress in data processing via computers has reduced problems of this nature.

Accounting for a Sales Branch

Home-office and branch entries depend on the authority given to the branch. In the example shown in Exhibit 25-5, the home office pays branch bills, makes all sales, and collects all cash. Many companies use sales branches to enter new markets. For instance, IBM has sales offices throughout the United States. Sales branches may make sales, collect cash, and make some of their own cash disbursements. Often the home office keeps control of the revenue and expense accounts. Assume an IBM sales branch completed the following transactions:

a.   Branch sold merchandise and received cash of $3,000.
b.   Branch transferred $3,000 cash to home office.
c.   Home office paid commission of $1,100 to salesperson who made the sale in *a*.
d.   Branch paid water bill, $90.
e.   Branch recorded depreciation on office equipment, $300.

These transactions would be recorded by the home office and branch as follows:

	Home-Office Journal			**Branch Journal**		
a.	Branch Ledger Control	3,000		Cash	3,000	
	Sales Revenue		3,000	Home-Office Ledger Control		3,000
b.	Cash	3,000		Home-Office Ledger Control . .	3,000	
	Branch Ledger Control . . .		3,000	Cash		3,000
c.	Sales Commission Expense	1,100		None		
	Cash		1,100			
d.	Utility Expense	90		Home-Office Ledger Control . .	90	
	Branch Ledger Control . . .		90	Cash		90
e.	Depreciation Expense	300		Home-Office Ledger Control . .	300	
	Branch Ledger Control . . .		300	Accumulated Depreciation-Office Furniture		300

EXHIBIT 25-5 Sample Journal Entries for Branch Accounting (in thousands of dollars)

Transaction	Entries That Would Be Made in a Regular, Unified Journal		Home-Office Journal		Branch-Factory Journal	
1. Direct materials purchases	Direct Materials Inventory	230	Branch-Factory Ledger Control	230	Direct Materials Inventory	230
	Accounts Payable	230	Accounts Payable	230	Home-Office Ledger Control	230
2. Direct materials uses	Work in Process Inventory	150	None		Work in Process Inventory	150
	Direct Materials Inventory	150			Direct Materials Inventory	150
3. Factory payroll	Factory Wages	200	Branch-Factory Ledger Control	200	Factory Wages	200
	Wages Payable	200	Wages Payable	200	Home-Office Ledger Control	200
4. Miscellaneous overhead	Factory Overhead	168	Branch-Factory Ledger Control	168	Factory Overhead	168
	Accounts Payable	150	Accounts Payable	150	Home-Office Ledger Control	168
	Accumulated Depreciation	18	Accumulated Depreciation	18		
5. Overhead application	Work in Process Inventory	165	None		Work in Process Inventory	165
	Factory Overhead	165			Factory Overhead	165
6. Shipments to warehouse	Finished Goods Inventory	425	Finished Goods Inventory	425	Home-Office Ledger Control	425
	Work in Process Inventory	425	Branch-Factory Ledger Control	425	Work in Process Inventory	425
7. Cost of goods sold	Cost of Goods Sold	400	Cost of Goods Sold	400	None	
	Finished Goods Inventory	400	Finished Goods Inventory	400		
8. Sales	Accounts Receivable	600	Accounts Receivable	600	None	
	Sales Revenue	600	Sales Revenue	600		
9. Collections on account	Cash	440	Cash	440	None	
	Accounts Receivable	440	Accounts Receivable	440		

Postings:

Branch-Factory Ledger Control

(1)	230	(6)	425	
(3)	200			
(4)	168			
Bal.	173			

Home-Office Ledger Control

(6)	425	(1)	230	
		(3)	200	
		(4)	168	
		Bal.	173	

Teaching Tip: Look at Exhibit 25-5. Notice that the balance of the Branch-Factory Ledger Control account and the balance of the Home Office Ledger Control account are the same. This can act as a check figure for students in that the two are reciprocal accounts and at all times their balances must be equal.

After posting these entries, Branch Ledger Control's credit balance should equal the debit balance of Home-Office Ledger Control.

Computers, Responsibility Accounting, and Remote Processing

Recall Exhibit 25-2, Responsibility Accounting at Various Levels. This report gives managers information on the success of operations at different levels of the business. How might this report be prepared? Each O'Toole restaurant logs its revenues and expenses into its computer and transmits the information to central computer processing.

With complete information from each restaurant, the computer system can sort—that is, arrange in a useful grouping—the revenue and expense information. For example, district managers may want to know which restaurants are way off budget and need attention. The computer program can sort the information by size of budget variance—with additional breakdowns by restaurant, city, district, or region. A system for numbering accounts makes this sorting possible. All restaurant-level accounts have a certain number designation, all city-level accounts have another number designation, and so on. A computerized system like this is called a *database management system*. Managers and accountants can pull up whatever information they need for a particular decision. Ready access to the data enables managers to act on current information.

Consider responsibility accounting for O'Toole Restaurant Corporation. The company's system can provide the information for allocating indirect expenses to individual restaurants. Suppose corporate headquarters purchase much of the food centrally. The O'Toole accountant needs a base for allocating receiving-department costs to the various restaurants. The computer can sort receiving reports by restaurant. The more frequently a restaurant requests food from central headquarters, the higher is that restaurant's share of receiving-department cost. Periodic review of this information reveals any change in use patterns. Accountants can change the allocation base as needed to keep the cost allocation current. Restaurant managers can be evaluated fairly for the expenses under their supervision. The result is likely to be well-motivated managers—a far cry from Henri Goudal's situation in the opening vignette.

Summary Problem for Your Review

A general ledger may be divided between home office and branch in any manner whatsoever. Reconsider Exhibit 25-5. Suppose the branch factory, instead of the home office, keeps its plant and equipment accounts and the related depreciation records. The plant and equipment accounts would appear in the ledger of the factory but not the home office. Among the nine transactions in our example, what journal entry or entries would be changed? Prepare the changed entry or entries.

Entry 4 would be changed. Accumulated depreciation would appear in the branch-factory ledger but not in the home-office ledger. Moreover, the amounts recorded in the reciprocal accounts would be $150,000 instead of $168,000, as follows (amounts in thousands of dollars):

Home-Office Ledger			Branch-Factory Ledger		
4. Branch-Factory Ledger Control .	150		Factory Overhead	168	
Accounts Payable		150	Accumulated Depreciation		18
			Home-Office Ledger		
			Control		150

Summary

Responsibility accounting is a system for evaluating the progress of managers based on activities under their supervision. This system is especially important in organizations with scattered operations. Most companies are organized into *responsibility centers* to establish accountability. There are different types of responsibility centers: *cost center, profit center,* and *investment center.* The most critical factor in designing a responsibility accounting system is gathering and communicating information to help the business achieve its goals.

Performance reports show deviations from budgeted amounts. By focusing on important variances, managers can direct their attention to operations needing improvement and avoid wasting time investigating successful operations. This practice is called *management by exception.*

Departments are the most widely encountered responsibility centers. Gross margin and operating income are important measures of their performance. *Direct expenses* are conveniently identified with and traceable to the department. *Indirect expenses* are all those expenses other than direct expenses. Direct expenses are easy to allocate to departments because of their natural link to a particular department. Indirect expenses are allocated based on some logical relationship between the expense and departments.

Branch accounting is a system for separating branch accounts from home-office accounts. Its key feature is a set of *reciprocal accounts.* The home office has a *Branch Ledger Control* account for its investment in, or receivable from, the branch. The branch ledger has only those accounts needed to manage its own operations. Its special account, *Home-Office Ledger Control,* represents home-office equity in the branch, or the branch payable to the home office. The debit balance in the Branch Ledger Control account should equal the credit balance in Home-Office Ledger Control.

Self-Study Questions

Test your understanding of the chapter by marking the best answer for each of the following questions:

1. Responsibility accounting is *(p. 1130)*
   a. An alternative to a standard cost system
   b. A system for assigning responsibility to managers and evaluating their progress
   c. A particular type of home-office/branch accounting system
   d. Designed without consideration of the business's organization structure

2. Which of the following departments is most likely to be a cost center? *(p. 1130)*
   a. Personnel Department
   b. Housewares Department of a K Mart store
   c. Sales office
   d. Manufacturing plant

3. Budgeted cost of goods sold was $30,000, and actual cost is $33,000. The variance is *(p. 1133)*
   a. 110 percent favorable   c. 10 percent favorable
   b. 110 percent unfavorable   d. 10 percent unfavorable

4. The key to the design of an effective responsibility accounting system is *(p. 1133)*
   a. Ability of the system to place blame when results are unfavorable
   b. Manager control over all aspects of the business in the department
   c. Gathering and communicating information to achieve the business's goals
   d. Use of a standard cost system

5. One of the more difficult accounting tasks in departmental accounting is *(p. 1134)*
   a. Measuring departmental gross margin
   b. Allocating direct costs to departments
   c. Allocating indirect costs to departments
   d. Assigning responsibility to department managers

6. Which of the following costs is the most difficult to allocate to departments? *(p. 1134)*
   a. Direct materials   c. Merchandise purchases
   b. Janitorial services   d. Direct labor

7. The most logical basis for allocating building depreciation to departments is *(p. 1135)*
   a. Square feet of space
   b. Number of employees
   c. Hours used
   d. Building depreciation can be separately traced to each department

8. Which control device is a particular feature of branch accounting? *(p. 1140)*
   a. Responsibility assignment   c. Departmental accounting
   b. Reciprocal accounts   d. Cost allocation

9. Which of these accounts would be the most likely to appear in a branch-factory ledger? *(p. 1141)*
   a. Accounts Receivable   c. Common Stock
   b. Branch-Factory Ledger Control   d. Home-Office Ledger Control

10. A sales branch manages its own operations except for collections on account and cash payments for major expenses such as inventory purchases and salaries, which the home office pays. Which entry would the branch make to record its salary expense? *(p. 1142)*
   a. Salary Expense................................. XXX
         Cash   XXX
   b. Home-Office Ledger Control XXX
         Cash   XXX
   c. Salary Expense................................. XXX
         Branch Ledger Control.....................   XXX
   d. None of the above. The entry would appear on the home-office books only.

Answers to the Self-Study Questions follow the Accounting Vocabulary.

Accounting Vocabulary

Allocation base. Logical common denominator for assigning a given cost to two or more departments of a business (p. 1135).

Branch accounting. System for separating the accounts of a branch of a business from the accounts of the home office (p. 1139).

Branch-factory ledger control. Account in the home office ledger that represents the home office investment in, or receivable from, a branch of the business (p. 1141).

Branch ledger. The part of a general ledger kept by a branch of the business, separate from the home office ledger (p. 1140).

Cost allocation. Assignment of various costs to the departments and products of a business (p. 1135).

Direct expense. Expense that is conveniently identified with and traceable to a particular product or department of a business (p. 1134).

Expense allocation. Assignment of various expenses to the departments of a business (p. 1135).

Factory ledger. A branch ledger for a manufacturing plant (p. 1140).

Home-office ledger. The part of a general ledger kept by the home office, separate from the branch ledger (p. 1140).

Home-office ledger control. Account in the branch ledger that represents

an owner equity of, or branch payable to, the home office (p. 1141).

Indirect expense. Expense that is not traceable to a single product or department of a business; an expense other than a direct expense. Often indirect expenses arise from activities that serve more than one department simultaneously (p. 1134).

Management by exception. Management strategy by which executive attention is directed to the important deviations from budgeted amounts (p. 1133).

Reciprocal accounts. Two or more accounts that have the same offsetting balances and are used to control a general ledger that is kept in two or more locations (p. 1140).

Responsibility accounting. System for classifying financial data by defined areas in an organization in order to evaluate the performance of managers for activities under their supervision (p. 1130).

Responsibility center. Any subunit of an organization needing control, the basic unit in a responsibility accounting system. The three common types of responsibility centers are the cost center, the profit center, and the investment center (p. 1130).

Answers to Self-Study Questions

1. b
2. a
3. d ($33,000 − $30,000 = $3,000; $3,000/$30,000 = 10 percent unfavorable)
4. c
5. a

6. b
7. a
8. b
9. d
10. d

ASSIGNMENT MATERIAL

Questions

1. Briefly describe responsibility accounting, giving examples of how managers use it in operating a business.

2. Which manager will control expenses better: Grant, whose performance is measured by his departmental sales, or Bruns, whose performance is gauged by her departmental income? Give your reason.

3. Identify three types of responsibility centers, giving examples of each and stating the information they report.

4. A company owns 50 Burger King restaurants in Houston, Dallas, and El Paso, Texas. In each city a local manager oversees operations. Starting at the individual store level, describe a likely flow of information based on responsibility accounting. What information would be reported?

5. What are the goals of management by exception?

6. What is the key to effective design of a responsibility accounting system?

7. What main question is a responsibility accounting system designed to answer? How can a responsibility accounting system be abused?

8. Distinguish between direct expenses and indirect expenses, giving examples of each type.

9. Identify a reasonable allocation base for the following indirect expenses: heating expense, depreciation of equipment used to manufacture products for three separate departments, and advertising expense.

10. Which of the following are likely to be direct expenses? Which are likely to be indirect expenses?
    a. Manufacturing labor
    b. Supervisor labor
    c. Advertising of a specific toy
    d. Cost of goods sold
    e. Depreciation of home-office building
    f. Janitorial services for a manufacturing plant
    g. Expenses of personnel department
    h. Advertising of a storewide sale by a department store

11. Supplies are not charged to departments as used. Instead, supplies expense is allocated at the end of each period based on the period's sales. If a firm used supplies costing $900 and had sales of $5,000, $12,000, and $8,000 in departments X, Y, and Z, respectively, how much supplies expense would be charged to each department?

12. How might rent be allocated in a department store with three floors, one of which is on ground level and opens onto a busy street?

13. Describe a plan for allocating the various components of general administrative expenses.

14. How does branch accounting differ from departmental accounting?

15. What are the special features of a branch accounting system?

16. How does the general ledger of a company with a branch accounting system differ from an ordinary general ledger?

17. What special account does a branch ledger contain? What special account does a home-office ledger contain? Indicate which account normally has a debit balance and which normally has a credit balance.

18. Consider the Branch-Factory Ledger Control account and the Home-Office Ledger Control account. Which account is more like an investment or receivable? Which is more like an owner equity account or payable? Which account is in the ledger of the home office? Which is in the branch ledger?

19. Briefly describe a branch accounting system for a company with two manufacturing plants in distant locations. Identify the special account on the books of the home office and the special account on the books of the branches.

20. A company manufactures its products at three plants. Which of the following transactions is likely to be recorded by the home office only, by the branch only, or by both the home office and the branch?

a. Use of materials in production
b. Sale of merchandise
c. Payment of manufacturing payroll
d. Purchase of direct materials
e. Incurrence of overhead cost
f. Collection of accounts receivable
g. Shipment of finished goods to home-office warehouse

Exercises

Exercise 25-1 *Identifying different types of responsibility centers* **(L.O. 1)**

No check figure

Identify each responsibility center as either a cost center, a profit center, or an investment center.

a. A branch manager's performance is judged by the ratio of the branch's net income to the home office's cost of the branch.
b. Accountants compile the cost of surgical supplies for evaluating the purchasing department of a hospital.
c. The hospital pediatrics unit reports both revenues and expenses.
d. The legal department of an insurance company prepares its budget and subsequent performance report based on its expected expenses for the year.
e. A charter airline records revenues and expenses for each airplane for each month. The airplane's performance report shows its ratio of operating income to average book value.
f. The manager of an Exxon service station is evaluated based on the station's revenues and expenses.

Exercise 25-2 *Using responsibility accounting to report on profit centers at three levels* **(L.O. 2)**

Oper. income var.:
Asheville $40
No. Carolina $40
Southeast ($260)

Siegfried Newspapers of North Carolina has city managers for its Asheville, Greensboro, and Elizabeth City operations. These managers report to a state manager, who reports to the manager of Southeast operations in Atlanta. The Southeast manager has received the following data for June of the current year:

| | | Southeast | |
| | North Carolina | | |
	Asheville	Greensboro and Elizabeth City	Southeast Totals excluding North Carolina
Revenues, budget	$310,000	$1,800,000	$10,300,000
Expenses, budget	220,000	1,100,000	6,300,000
Revenues, actual	340,000	1,900,000	9,900,000
Expenses, actual	210,000	1,200,000	6,200,000

Required

Arrange the following data in a performance report similar to Exhibit 25-2. Show June results, in thousands of dollars, for Asheville, the state of North Carolina, and the Southeast.

Oper. income var., % of
budget:
 Ashville 44.4%
 No. Carolina 5.1%
 Southeast (5.4%)

Exercise 25-3   *Preparing a four-column performance report* (L.O. 2)

Using the data of Exercise 25-2, prepare a performance report for June in the format illustrated on page 1133. Show June results, in thousands of dollars, for Asheville, the state of North Carolina, and the Southeast. In each case, format your answer in four columns:

		Variance Favorable	Variance: Percent of
Budget	Actual	(Unfavorable)	Budget

Other labor:
 A $5,600
 B $7,000
 C $1,400

Exercise 25-4   *Allocating costs to departments* (L.O. 3)

The cost records of West Virginia Foundry, Inc., include the following selected indirect cost data for January of the current year:

Other labor	$14,000
Equipment depreciation	6,000
Building depreciation	3,600
Utilities	2,700
Selling expenses	24,000

Data for cost allocations:

	Department		
	A	B	C
Sales	$60,000	$50,000	$90,000
Other labor—hours	400	500	100
Machine hours	300	450	150
Building—square feet	9,000	3,000	1,500

Selling expense—allocate to departments in proportion to sales

Required

Show the allocation of these expenses to departments A, B, and C for January.

$10,470

Exercise 25-5   *Computing departmental rent expense* (L.O. 3)

Many department stores grant concessions to other companies to operate the store's shoe departments. Caprice Shoe Company markets its shoes this way. Caprice sells ladies' shoes in a space occupying 500 square feet near the front door of a Sax Third Avenue store. This location is three times as valuable as the average space in the store. Caprice's shoes for men occupy 200 square feet in a back corner of the ground floor, a space with average rental value. Children's shoes occupy 150 square feet on the third floor, which is only 30 percent as valuable as the average space in the store. The entire store has 50,000 square feet, and monthly rent is $300,000.

Required

Compute Caprice's monthly rent expense.

Oper. income:
 Electronics $39,000
 Industrial $54,000

Exercise 25-6   *Preparing a departmental income statement* (L.O. 3, 4)

Migdal & Grant, Inc., has two departments, electronics and industrial. The company's income statement for 19X7 appears as follows:

Net sales	$310,000
Cost of goods sold	116,000
Gross margin	194,000
Operating expenses:	
Salaries	70,000
Depreciation	15,000
Advertising	6,000
Other	10,000
Total operating expenses	101,000
Operating income	$ 93,000

Cost of goods sold is distributed $42,000 for electronics and $74,000 for industrial products. Salaries are allocated to departments based on sales: electronics, $124,000; industrial, $186,000. Two-thirds of advertising is spent on electronics. Depreciation is allocated based on square footage: electronics has 28,000 square feet; industrial has 42,000 square feet. Other expenses are allocated based on number of employees, with an equal number working in each department.

Required

Prepare a departmental income statement showing revenues, expenses, and operating income for the company's two departments.

Exercise 25-7 *Recording home-office and branch manufacturing transactions* **(L.O. 4)**

Reciprocal account balances
$71,830

Big Foot Lumber Company manages operations from its home office in Portland. Company sawmills, located in the state of Oregon, are organized as branches. Big Foot uses a branch accounting system. The home office makes all purchases and sales, handles cash payments and cash receipts, and incurs all company liabilities. When a sawmill completes a custom job, it transfers the inventory to central warehouses, which the home office controls. On August 1 Big Foot's investment in the sawmill was $75,000. During August of the current year, the company completed the following transactions:

a. Direct materials purchased on account, $830.
b. Direct materials used in production, $1,090.
c. Sawmill payroll paid, $3,100.
d. Sawmill overhead applied, $4,600.
e. Goods shipped to central warehouse, $7,100.
f. Sales on account, $8,200.
g. Collections on account, $4,690.

Required

Journalize these transactions for the home office and the branch. Post to the reciprocal accounts and show that their balances at August 31 offset each other.

Exercise 25-8 *Recording home-office and branch sales-office transactions* **(L.O. 4)**

Reciprocal account balances
$1,250

Technology Transfer, Inc., has branch sales offices throughout the Great Lakes states. The company uses a branch accounting system. The branches purchase and sell goods, pay bills, collect cash from customers, and incur selling expenses. The home office, in Cleveland, obtains outside financing as needed and advances cash to, and receives cash from, the branches. During a recent month, the company completed the following transactions:

a. Home office borrowed $7,000 from a bank, signing a note.
b. Home office advanced $2,250 to the Michigan branch.
c. Michigan branch purchased merchandise on account, $2,210 (debit Purchases).
d. Michigan branch paid selling expense, $60.

e. Michigan branch sold goods on account, $2,110.
f. Home office recorded depreciation of $1,040 on home-office building.
g. Michigan branch collected cash from customer, $930.
h. Michigan branch transferred $1,000 cash to home office.

Required

Journalize these transactions for the home office and the Michigan branch. Post to the reciprocal accounts and show that their balances offset each other.

Problems   (Group A)

No check figure

Problem 25-1A   *Identifying different types of responsibility centers* (L.O. 1)

Identify by letter each of the following as being most likely a cost center, a profit center, or an investment center:

a. Surgery unit of a privately owned hospital
b. Personnel department of Goodyear Tire and Rubber Company
c. Accounts payable section of an accounting department
d. Proposed new office of a real estate firm
e. Branch warehouse of a carpet manufacturer
f. Disneyland
g. Assembly-line supervisory employees
h. Service department of a stereo shop
i. Men's clothing in a department store
j. American subsidiary of a Japanese company
k. Music director of a church or synagogue
l. Catering operation of an established restaurant
m. Executive director of a United Way agency
n. Different product lines of a gift shop
o. The Empire State Building in New York City
p. Work crews of a painting contractor
q. Investments department of a bank
r. Accounting department of a company
s. Eastern district of a salesperson's territory
t. Typesetting department of a printing company

Oper. income var.:
Birmingham $800
Alabama $5,000
Company wide ($341,000)

Problem 25-2A   *Preparing a profit-center performance report* (L.O. 2)

Haltom Oil Company is organized with store managers reporting to a state-wide manager, who in turn reports to the vice-president of marketing. The income statements of the Birmingham store, all stores in Alabama (including the Birmingham store), and the company as a whole (including Alabama stores) are summarized as follows for 19X6:

	Birmingham	Alabama	Companywide
Revenue and expenses:			
Sales	$141,800	$1,647,000	$3,888,000
Expenses:			
State manager/vice-president's office	—	59,000	116,000
Cost of goods sold	53,000	671,900	1,507,000
Salary expense	38,100	415,500	1,119,000
Depreciation	7,200	91,000	435,000
Utilities	3,800	46,200	260,000
Rent	2,400	34,700	178,000
Supplies	1,100	15,600	86,000
Total expenses	105,600	1,333,900	3,701,000
Operating income	$ 36,200	$ 313,100	$ 187,000

Budgeted amounts for 19X6 are as follows:

	Birmingham	Alabama	Companywide
Revenue and expenses:			
Sales...........................	$151,300	$1,769,700	$4,400,000
Expenses:			
State manager/vice-president's office	—	65,600	118,000
Cost of goods sold	61,500	763,400	1,672,000
Salary expense...............	38,800	442,000	1,095,000
Depreciation.................	7,200	87,800	449,000
Utilities	4,700	54,400	271,000
Rent	2,800	32,300	174,000
Supplies	900	16,100	93,000
Total expenses	115,900	1,461,600	3,872,000
Operating income	$ 35,400	$ 308,100	$ 528,000

Required

1. Prepare a report for 19X6 that shows the performance of the Birmingham store, all the stores in Alabama, and the company as a whole. Follow the format of Exhibit 25-2.
2. Identify the responsibility centers whose operating income exceeds budget and those whose operating income falls short of budget.

Problem 25-3A *Preparing a profit-center performance report* **(L.O. 2)**

Oper. income var., % of budget:
Bedspreads (5.9%)
Bedding (4.2%)
Company (3.4%)

The Home Front is organized along product lines, with product managers reporting to department managers, who in turn report to the company vice-president. The vice-president, who has received the following data for August of the current year, needs a performance report to highlight the operating income of bedspreads, the bedding department, and the company in total:

	Company Totals		
	Bedding Department		
	Bedspreads	**Linens**	**Other Departments**
Revenues, actual.....	$3,700	$1,500	$6,500
Expenses, actual	2,100	800	3,100
Revenues, budget....	3,300	1,400	7,100
Expenses, budget	1,600	700	3,600

Required

1. Prepare a performance report for August in a format similar to that on page 1133. Show August operating income for bedspreads, the bedding department, and the company as a whole.
2. Which responsibility centers exceeded budget? Which performed below budget?

Problem 25-4A *Computing and allocating occupancy cost to a department* **(L.O. 3)**

Cost per square foot:
Basement $2.04
Street level $8.20
Second floor $4.10
Floors 3–5 $2.05

Dillard's occupies a six-story building (including the basement) in downtown Montclair. Assume occupancy cost for a recent month included the following:

Depreciation—building	$ 93,200
Rent—store fixtures	24,700
Utilities	21,300
Janitorial services	16,600
Total...........................	$155,800

Each floor of the building has 8,000 square feet, except for the second floor, which has 6,000 square feet. The company accountant computed the occupancy cost per square foot by dividing the total cost of $155,800 by 46,000 square feet. She charges occupancy to all company departments based on this $3.39 cost per square foot.

The manager of the Budget Buyer Department, located in the basement, objected. He cited a space-usage study conducted for the company by a real estate firm. It estimated that space in the basement is one-fourth as valuable as street level space, one-half as valuable as space on the second floor, and equal in value to the other floors.

Required

1. Based on the space-usage study, compute the occupancy cost of a square foot of space on each of Dillard's floors. Round decimals to three places, and round the cost per square foot to the nearest cent.
2. The Budget Buyer Department occupies 5,500 square feet of the basement. How much occupancy cost should be charged to this department each month?

Oper. income:
  Custom $16,284
  Group $33,316

Problem 25-5A   *Preparing a departmental income statement*   **(L.O. 3, 4)**

Aladdin Travel is organized into a custom department and a group discount department. At August 31, the end of Aladdin's fiscal year, the bookkeeper prepared the following trial balance, which includes the effects of year-end adjusting entries:

Cash	$ 1,300	
Receivables	24,600	
Supplies	3,800	
Prepaid expenses	1,700	
Building	70,500	
Accumulated depreciation—building		$ 20,900
Office furniture	38,100	
Accumulated depreciation—office furniture		7,300
Other assets	3,100	
Accounts payable		11,400
Accrued liabilities		6,900
Unearned service revenue		5,800
Long-term note payable		22,000
Owner equity		19,200
Custom travel service revenue		77,700
Group discount travel service revenue		107,300
Salary expense—travel agents	34,600	
Commission expense—travel agents	26,000	
Salary expense—office manager	25,000	
Salary expense—bookkeeper	16,800	
Lease expense—computer equipment	15,000	
Supplies expense	6,300	
Depreciation expense—office furniture	2,500	
Property tax expense	2,200	
Depreciation expense—building	2,100	
Interest expense	2,000	
Insurance expense	1,700	
Advertising expense	1,200	
	$278,500	$278,500

In January, Aladdin hired a group travel specialist at an annual salary of $25,000. Remaining agent salaries of $9,600 go to part-time agents that handle custom travel plans. The office manager spends 60 percent of her time on group discount plans and 40 percent on custom travel planning. The bookkeeper spends approximately two-thirds of his time on accounting for custom travel planning operations and the remainder on group discount plans. Aladdin leases a computer that it uses 80 percent of the time for custom travel planning and 20 percent of the time for group discount packages. Insurance expense is evenly divided between the two departments. Interest expense relates to the note payable, which the company signed to purchase the building. The company allocates all other expenses based on relative service revenue.

Required

1. Prepare a departmental income statement through operating income.
2. Which department is more profitable? Was the decision to hire the group specialist wise? Give your reason.

Problem 25-6A   *Preparing a budgeted departmental income statement* **(L.O. 3, 4)**

Plemmon's is a suburban hardware store with two departments. The most recent annual report to management follows.

Oper. income:
Dept. A $166,162
Dept. B $31,948
Dept. C $10,430

Plemmon's
Departmental Income Statement
For the Year Ended January 31, 19X2

	Total	Dept. A	Dept. B
Sales revenue	$400,000	$300,000	$100,000
Expenses:			
Cost of goods sold	160,000	120,000	40,000
Sales salaries	41,000	28,000	13,000
Salary—store manager	35,000	17,500	17,500
Rent expense—building	16,000	8,000	8,000
Advertising	5,000	3,500	1,500
Property tax..................	3,000	1,500	1,500
Insurance	2,400	1,200	1,200
Depreciation—store fixtures ...	1,200	600	600
Supplies	1,000	500	500
Interest	800	400	400
Uncollectible accounts.........	600	300	300
Total expenses	266,000	181,500	84,500
Operating income	$134,000	$118,500	$ 15,500

The company is considering opening a third department early in fiscal 19X3. To plan for the coming year, the store owner seeks your help in preparing a budgeted income statement. Your conversation with the owner reveals the following:

1. Management expects annual sales of the new department to be $80,000, with a gross profit percentage equal to that of the two existing departments.
2. Addition of a third department will also draw customers into Department A and should increase Department A sales by 25 percent. Sales of Department B are expected to increase by only 10 percent.
3. A salesperson can be hired for the new department at an annual salary of $16,000. Other salaries will increase by 5 percent.

4. Thus far, the company accountant has allocated all expenses except cost of goods sold, sales salaries, and advertising equally to Departments A and B. The store owner decides that the equal allocation of indirect expenses to departments is inappropriate.

5. The store manager expects to spend equal amounts of time in the three departments during the coming year.

6. Department A is nearest the door and occupies 2,000 square feet of the most valuable space in the store. Department B also occupies 2,000 square feet, but its space is only half as valuable as that of Department A. The new department will take up 1,000 square feet with the same value per square foot as Department A. Total rent expense under the long-term lease will be unchanged in 19X3.

7. Advertising expense will increase by 10 percent for the two existing departments. The company will commit $2,000 to advertising Department C merchandise.

8. Depreciation of new store fixtures for Department C will be $900. Other depreciation amounts will be unchanged.

9. Interest expense needed to finance Department C will be $1,000. The remaining 19X3 interest of $500 applies equally to the other two departments.

10. All other expenses will increase by 8 percent and should be allocated to departments based on relative sales, except property tax, which is allocated on the same basis used for rent. Round percentages to three decimal places.

Required

1. Prepare a budgeted departmental income statement in multiple-step format for fiscal year 19X3 based on the preceding projections.

2. Based on your budget, would you recommend that Plemmon's add the new department? State your reasons.

Branch Ledger Control $4,000

Problem 25-7A *Recording home-office and branch transactions* (L.O. 5)

Landmark Realty has branch offices throughout the Kansas City area and uses a branch accounting system for control purposes. The home office has a separate Branch Ledger Control account for each branch, and the branches maintain branch ledgers. Branch ledgers contain only asset, liability, and Home-Office Ledger Control accounts.

The home office advances cash to the branches. Branch managers have authority to purchase supplies and office furniture and equipment. They also pay utility and other branch-office expenses. However, only the home office records branch expenses. The branches collect commissions earned from their real estate sales and immediately transfer the cash to the home office. Only the home office records commissions revenue. The home office then pays half the commission directly to the agent who made the sale. During a recent month the following transactions occurred at the Independence Branch of Landmark Realty:

a. Home office advanced $6,900 to branch.
b. Branch sold a house, earning a commission and receiving cash of $4,000.
c. Branch transferred $4,000 to home office.
d. Home office paid commission to agent making sale in *b*, $2,000.
e. Branch paid office cleaning expense, $220.
f. Branch purchased office furniture on account, $1,400.
g. Branch paid cash for office supplies, $160.

h. Branch paid account payable, $700.
i. Branch transferred $2,300 cash to home office.
j. Branch recorded depreciation on office equipment, $380.

Required

1. Record these transactions in the home-office journal and in the branch journal.
2. Post the transactions to the reciprocal accounts. Show the balances of the reciprocal accounts after posting.

(Group B)

Problem 25-1B *Identifying different types of responsibility centers* **(L.O. 1)**   No check figure

Identify by letter each of the following as most likely being a cost center, a profit center, or an investment center:

a. Quality-control department of a manufacturing company
b. Top management of a company
c. Southwest region of Pizza Inns, Inc.
d. Editorial department of *The Wall Street Journal*
e. A small clothing boutique
f. Payroll department of a university
g. Different product lines of a furniture manufacturer
h. Job superintendents of a home builder
i. A real estate firm
j. Fast-food restaurants under the supervision of a regional manager
k. European subsidiary of an American company
l. Children's nursery in a church or synagogue
m. Lighting department in a Sears store
n. Personnel department of Coca-Cola, Inc.
o. Service department of an established automobile dealership
p. Proposed new office of a CPA firm
q. Branch offices of a bank
r. Police department of a city
s. Delta Air Lines, Inc.
t. Consumer Complaint Division of Procter & Gamble Co.

Problem 25-2B *Preparing a profit-center performance report* **(L.O. 2)**

Eye Pro, Inc., is a chain of optical shops that dispense eyeglasses. Each store has a manager who answers to a city manager, who in turn reports to a state-wide manager. The income statements of Store No. 24, all stores in the Los Angeles area (including Store No. 24), and all stores in the state of California (including all Los Angeles stores) are summarized as follows for April:

Oper. income var.:
Store No. 24, $1,100
Los Angeles $15,600
California $52,700

	Store No. 24	Los Angeles	State of California
Revenue and expenses:			
Sales..............................	$42,900	$486,000	$3,264,500
Expenses:			
City/state manager office.............	—	16,000	41,000
Cost of goods sold	14,000	171,300	1,256,800
Salary expense......................	5,300	37,500	409,700
Depreciation........................	3,000	26,100	334,000
Utilities	2,700	19,300	245,600
Rent..............................	1,900	16,400	186,000
Supplies	700	5,500	60,700
Total expenses......................	27,600	292,100	2,533,800
Operating income....................	$15,300	$193,900	$ 730,700

Budgeted amounts for April are as follows:

	Store No. 24	Los Angeles	State of California
Revenue and expenses:			
Sales	$42,000	$468,000	$3,143,000
Expenses:			
City/state manager office ...	—	15,000	43,000
Cost of goods sold.........	14,200	172,800	1,209,000
Salary expense	5,600	37,900	412,000
Depreciation	3,500	25,400	320,000
Utilities....................	2,100	17,000	240,000
Rent	1,600	15,700	181,000
Supplies	800	5,900	60,000
Total expenses	27,800	289,700	2,465,000
Operating income	$14,200	$178,300	$ 678,000

Required

1. Prepare a report for April that shows the performance of Store No. 24, all the stores in the Los Angeles area, and all the stores in the state of California. Follow the format of Exhibit 25-2.
2. Identify the responsibility centers whose operating income exceeds budget and those whose operating income falls short of budget.

Problem 25-3B *Preparing a profit-center performance report* **(L.O. 2)**

Chi Alpha Corporation is organized along product lines, with product managers reporting to division managers, who in turn report to the company vice-president. The vice-president, who has received the following data for November of the current year, needs a performance report to highlight the operating income of audio products, the audio-video division, and the company in total:

	Company Totals		
	Audio-Video Division		
	Audio Products	Video Products	Other Divisions
Revenues, actual	$212,000	$867,000	$788,000
Expenses, actual	138,000	516,000	374,000
Revenues, budget ...	218,000	907,000	760,000
Expenses, budget ...	147,000	505,000	368,000

Required

1. Prepare a performance report for November in a format similar to that on page 1133. Show November operating income in thousands of dollars for audio products, the audio-video division, and the company as a whole.
2. Which responsibility centers exceeded budget? Which performed below budget?

Problem 25-4B *Computing and allocating occupancy cost to a department* **(L.O. 3)**

Cokesbury Book Store occupies three floors in a building in downtown Columbus. Occupancy cost for a recent quarter included the following items and amounts:

Rent	$41,000
Utilities	9,300
Janitorial services	8,200
Depreciation—building fixtures	3,500
Total	$62,000

Cokesbury occupies 5,000 square feet on the street level, 3,000 square feet on the second floor, and 4,000 square feet of the basement. The company accountant computed the occupancy cost per square foot by dividing the total cost of $62,000 by 12,000 square feet. He charges occupancy to all company departments based on this $5.17 cost per square foot.

The manager of the children's books department, located in the basement, objected. She cited an engineering study conducted for the company by a real estate firm. It estimated that space in the basement is one-half as valuable as second-floor space and one-fourth as valuable as space on the street level.

Required

1. Based on the engineering study, compute the occupancy cost of a square foot of space on each of Cokesbury's three floors. Round decimals to three places, and round the cost per square foot to the nearest cent.

2. The children's book department occupies 2,200 square feet of the basement. How much occupancy cost should be charged to this department each quarter?

Problem 25-5B   *Preparing a departmental income statement*   (L.O. 3, 4)

Oper. income:
Printing $14,940
Copy $13,860

InstiPrinter is organized into a printing department and a copy department. At May 31, the end of InstiPrinter's fiscal year, the bookkeeper prepared the following trial balance, which includes the effects of year-end adjusting entries:

Cash	$ 2,400	
Receivables	3,600	
Supplies	25,400	
Prepaid expenses	1,100	
Land	25,900	
Building	41,200	
Accumulated depreciation—building		$ 16,200
Printing equipment	33,700	
Accumulated depreciation—printing equipment		9,600
Other assets	4,700	
Accounts payable		3,200
Accrued liabilities		1,600
Unearned printing revenue		2,200
Long-term note payable		15,000
Owner equity		61,400
Printing revenue		67,100
Copy revenue		54,900
Salary expense—machine operators	23,600	
Salary expense—store manager	22,900	
Salary expense—bookkeeper	18,300	
Lease expense—copy equipment	12,000	
Supplies expense	9,000	
Property tax expense	2,300	
Insurance expense	1,600	
Depreciation expense—building	1,400	
Depreciation expense—printing equipment	1,400	
Interest expense	400	
Uncollectible account expense	300	
	$231,200	$231,200

InstiPrinter owns its printing equipment and leases a copier from Xerox. Established printing customers do business with the company on a credit basis, but copy services are performed for cash only. Insurance expense is evenly divided between departments. The bookkeeper spends approximately two-thirds of his time on accounts receivable and other printing department matters and the remainder on general accounting. Interest expense relates to the note payable, which the company signed to purchase the printing equipment. The store manager spends 60 percent of her time on printing and 40 percent on copy services. The company allocates all other expenses based on service revenue.

Required

1. Prepare a departmental income statement through operating income.
2. Which department has the higher operating income? What factor contributes most to the profitability difference between departments?

Oper income:
  Men's $33,366
  Women's $56,122
  Children's $1,055

Problem 25-6B *Preparing a budgeted departmental income statement* **(L.O. 3, 4)**

Kellner's is a neighborhood clothing store with two departments. The most recent annual report to management appears below.

Kellner's is considering opening a children's department early in fiscal 19X8. To plan for the coming year, the store owner seeks your help in preparing a budgeted income statement. Your conversation with the owner reveals the following:

1. Management expects annual sales of the new department to be $65,000, with a gross profit percentage equal to that of the two existing departments.

Kellner's
Departmental Income Statement
For the Year Ended January 31, 19X7

	Total	Men's	Women's
Sales revenue	$317,700	$141,800	$175,900
Expenses:			
Cost of goods sold	152,500	68,050	84,450
Sales salaries	44,300	20,800	23,500
Salary—store manager	32,900	16,450	16,450
Rent expense—building	14,000	7,000	7,000
Advertising	8,000	2,400	5,600
Property tax	2,000	1,000	1,000
Insurance	1,800	900	900
Depreciation—store fixtures	1,700	850	850
Supplies	1,000	500	500
Interest	600	300	300
Uncollectible accounts	300	150	150
Total expenses	259,100	118,400	140,700
Operating income	$ 58,600	$ 23,400	$ 35,200

2. Addition of a children's department will draw more women than men into the store and should increase sales of women's wear by 20 percent. Sales of men's wear are expected to increase by only 5 percent.
3. A salesperson can be hired for the children's department at an annual salary of $14,000. Other salaries will increase by 6 percent.

4. Thus far, Kellner's accountant has allocated all expenses except cost of goods sold, sales salaries, and advertising equally to the men's and women's departments. The store owner decides that the equal allocation of indirect expenses to the two departments is inappropriate.

5. The store manager expects to spend equal amounts of time in the three departments during the coming year.

6. The women's department is nearest the door and occupies 3,000 square feet of the most valuable space in the store. Men's wear also occupies 3,000 square feet, but its space is only two-thirds as valuable as that of women's wear. The new children's department will take up 1,000 square feet with the same value per square foot as the women's department. Total rent expense under the long-term lease will be unchanged in 19X8.

7. Advertising expense will increase by 10 percent for the two existing departments. The company will commit $2,000 to advertising the children's department.

8. Depreciation of new store fixtures for the children's department will be $900. Other depreciation amounts will be unchanged.

9. Interest expense needed to finance the children's department will be $1,000. The remaining 19X8 interest of $600 belongs equally to the other two departments.

10. All other expenses will increase by 10 percent and should be allocated to departments based on relative sales, except property tax, which is allocated on the same basis used for rent. Round percentages to three decimal places.

Required

1. Prepare a budgeted departmental income statement in multiple-step format for fiscal year 19X8 based on the preceding projections.

2. Based on your budget, would you recommend that Kellner's open the new department? State your reasons.

Problem 25-7B *Recording home-office and branch transactions* (L.O. 5)

Branch Ledger Control $3,100

Guadalupe Realty has branch offices throughout the El Paso area and uses a branch accounting system for control purposes. The home office has a separate Branch Ledger Control account for each branch, and the branches maintain branch ledgers. Branch ledgers contain asset, liability, and Home-Office Ledger Control accounts.

The home office advances cash to the branches. Branch managers have the authority to purchase supplies and office furniture and equipment. They also pay utility and other branch-office expenses. However, only the home office records branch expenses. The branches collect commissions earned from their real estate sales and immediately transfer the cash to the home office. Only the home office records commissions revenue. The home office then pays a commission directly to the agent who made the sale. During a recent month the following transactions occurred at the Rojo Mesa Branch of Guadalupe Realty:

a. Home office advanced $5,000 to branch.
b. Branch purchased office supplies on account, $400.
c. Branch paid cash for a file cabinet, $700.
d. Branch paid account payable, $600.
e. Branch sold a house, earning a commission and receiving cash of $4,700.
f. Branch transferred $4,700 to home office.
g. Home office paid commission to agent making sale in *e*, $3,100.

h. Branch transferred $1,000 cash to home office.
i. Branch paid electricity expense, $300.
j. Branch recorded depreciation on office equipment, $600.

Required

1. Record these transactions in the home-office journal and in the branch journal.
2. Post the transactions to the reciprocal accounts. Show the balances of the reciprocal accounts after posting.

Extending Your Knowledge

Decision Problems

Income before interest and taxes:
 Diamonds $321,000
 Watches $145,000
 Other $34,000

1. Evaluating Cost Allocation and Departmental Performance (L.O. 2, 3, 4)

Stuarts is a jewelry store located on the main floor of a four-star hotel on the Loop in Chicago. It opened in January of the current year. The store has two entrances, one off the lobby and the other off the street. Stuarts is one of many exclusive stores on the street. There are display windows beside both entrances.

Stuarts places particular departments close to each entrance. Customers entering the store from the street will see the watch department first. Entering from the lobby brings the customer into the diamond department. The watch and diamond departments occupy equal space in the store, and both have the same number of staff behind the counter. The silver and costume jewelry departments occupy relatively little space in the store compared to diamonds and watches.

It is now December, and the Stuarts, Inc., accountant has prepared a departmental statement for presentation to George Stuart, the president.

Required

Evaluate the presentation of the statement. If necessary, redraft the statement. Clearly state any assumptions you make. Analyze the profitability of Stuarts' departments.

Stuarts, Inc.
Departmental Income Statement
For the Year Ended December 31, 19X7
('000)

	Diamonds	Watches	Other
Sales revenue	$1,050	$675	$180
Expenses:			
Cost of goods sold	450	337	110
Sales commissions	105	54	4
Salary—manager	22	22	22
Rent expense	72	46	12
Advertising	70	0	0
Insurance	10	6	3
Depreciation—fixtures	8	8	8
Office expenses	12	12	12
Income before interest and taxes	$ 301	$190	$ 9

2. Using Departmental Operating Income to Decide on an Advertising Campaign (L.O. 3, 4)

Oper. income:
No new advertising $174,400
Advertise Nissans $126,000
Advertise Toyotas $172,800

The accountant of Onondaga Nissan-Toyota has produced the following annual summary of revenue and expense information for management:

	Nissans	Toyotas
Units sold	200	80
Average selling price per unit	$15,000	$22,000
Average cost per unit	12,200	17,300
Average direct expense per unit	1,900	2,320
Average variable indirect expense per unit ...	500	1,200

Jeff Onondaga, owner of the business, is considering an advertising campaign to increase sales and operating income. He estimates that additional advertising cost of $25,000 will increase sales by 30 automobiles each year. However, because Onondaga is the only Nissan-Toyota dealer in the area, any increase in Nissan sales is likely to decrease sales of Toyotas by an equal number. Likewise, an increase in Toyota sales of 30 automobiles is likely to cause an equal decrease in Nissan sales. Onondaga's fixed expenses, other than the $25,000 of advertising, will be unaffected by this decision.

Required

Prepare an analysis to show whether Onondaga should advertise Nissans or Toyotas, or not undertake the advertising campaign at all. Base your decision on operating income (ignoring fixed expenses other than the $25,000 advertising) under three alternatives: (1) no new advertising, (2) advertise Nissans, and (3) advertise Toyotas.

Ethical Issue

Bertha Bumiller manages the hosiery department of McRae's Department Store in the Metro Mall of Jackson, Mississippi. Bertha buys merchandise, hires sales clerks, arranges displays, and takes the inventory. Her annual bonus depends on departmental income before income tax. The Bumiller family is planning a Christmas vacation to the Virgin Islands and is counting on Bertha's bonus. Sales for 1993 have been sluggish, so Bertha slightly overstates ending inventory.

Required

1. Specify the effect of the inventory overstatement on cost of goods sold, gross margin, income before income tax, and Bertha's bonus.
2. Is overstating ending inventory unethical? Who is helped and who is harmed by Bertha's action?

Chapter 26

Special Decisions
and Capital Budgeting

Robert Echols, manager of the engineering department of Schaaf Tool Company, closed his office door and strode over to his desk. He had only 48 hours to decide whether to recommend the purchase of a robotic stamping machine.

The stamping machine, designed to replace four-year-old general-purpose equipment, could be purchased for $850,000, delivered and installed. The older general-purpose equipment could be sold to a nearby company.

Schaaf executives, Echols realized, demanded capital expenditures of this great an amount to generate at least a 15 percent return on a discounted basis. He believed that now would be a good time to buy the machine. The industry to which Schaaf sold its products and services was booming. Also, the prices of robotic stamping machines had dropped recently. It was likely that they would go up again within the next year. What should Echols recommend? Keep the old machine or purchase the new?

Should we sell 50,000 units of our product for $9 each—a price slightly below our cost? Should we make a special part used in our manufacturing process, or should we buy the part from an outside supplier? Should we drop the women's clothing line altogether? These are examples of special decisions that managers make. They are more far-reaching than day-to-day decisions, like whether to work overtime, to accept a rush job, or to change the schedule for repairing equipment. This chapter shows how to use accounting data to make special decisions, particularly those with long-run effects on the business.

Relevant Information for Decision Making

The main financial goals in business are to earn a profit and to have a strong financial position. Decisions center on how to achieve these goals. Decision making includes choosing among several courses of action, which means managers must make comparisons. The process has two steps: (1) identifying the information useful for making the decision and (2) analyzing the information to compare alternatives.

Relevant information is the expected future data that differ between the alternative courses of action. Which alternative will increase sales more? Which alternative will decrease expenses by a greater amount? By studying the expected future amounts resulting from the alternative actions, the manager can decide which action will help the business reach its goals.

Not all data influence a manager. Irrelevant data will not change a decision. For example, in some short-term situations the cost of fixed overhead will not change regardless of the action the manager takes. The manager, then, need not consider fixed overhead in making the decision. Determining which information is relevant—which data make a difference—is as important a skill as being able to analyze the information.

Let's consider an illustration of decision analysis using relevant information. Suppose Pendleton Woolen Mills is deciding whether to use pure wool or a wool-polyester blend in the manufacture of a line of sweaters. Pendleton predicts the following costs under the two alternatives:

	Wool	Wool Blend	Cost Difference
Expected manufacturing cost per sweater:			
Direct material	$10	$6	$4
Direct labor	2	2	0
Total cost of direct material and direct labor	$12	$8	$4

Point to Stress: In the chapter-opening vignette, Robert Echols must decide whether to keep his general-purpose machine or sell it and buy the stamping machine. Every business decision facing a manager involves a choice among alternatives. How successful the business is depends on the manager's skill in analyzing the alternatives and selecting the best one. This chapter will teach students some skills helpful in analyzing alternative courses of action.

OBJECTIVE 1
Identify the relevant information for a special business decision

Typical Student Misconception: Students often treat historical costs as relevant costs. Historical costs cannot be changed and are therefore not relevant costs.

Teaching Tip: This illustration explains the concept of relevant costs: Suppose you have a five-year-old car and you have previously spent $1,000 to repair it. Now the engine is frozen, and repairs will cost $2,200. In good running order the car is worth only $2,000. You could sell it for $150 for parts. What are the relevant costs?

The $1,000 already spent is not relevant. It may be frustrating to have spent that money, but there is nothing you can do about it. The only choices you have concern what you can do in the future. You could 1) sell the car for parts and get $150, but then you would have to buy another car, or 2) spend $2,200—$200 more than the car is worth—to repair it.

OBJECTIVE 2
Make seven types of special business decisions

Point to Stress: Remember that expected future data are based on estimates. For example, we may estimate that variable costs per unit to manufacture our product will be $10.75. Prices of raw materials may rise in three months and today's estimate may turn out to be incorrect. Nevertheless, we still make decisions based on the best estimate of future costs that we have today.

Teaching Tip: Point out that there is idle manufacturing capacity. If the factory were operating at 100% capacity, this would be a moot question. Of course Torino would not accept $1.75 per unit if they could produce and sell (for $2.00) at 100% of plant capacity.

Typical Student Misconception: Students often compare the manufacturing cost of $2.00 with the special order price of $1.75, and decide to reject the

Assume cost is the chief consideration in this decision. The cost of direct material is relevant because this cost differs between alternatives (the wool costs more than the wool blend). The labor cost is irrelevant because there is no difference in its cost whichever material is used.

We can compute the $4 cost difference between alternatives either from the cost of direct material only or from total cost. It is helpful to know that there is a $4 total cost difference between the two alternatives. But it is more helpful for managers to know that the $4 cost difference results from the materials, not from labor. Failure to identify the reason for the difference may lead managers to make an unwise decision.

Let us emphasize this important point about special decision analysis: relevant information is *expected future data that differ between alternative courses of action*. Managers should base their decisions on the expected future data rather than on historical data.

Historical data are usually supplied by the accounting system and are often useful guides to predictions. However, bear in mind that historical data by themselves are irrelevant. They are useful only to the extent that managers use them to help predict future data.

This approach to making decisions is called the *relevant information* approach. This approach applies to a wide variety of decisions, regardless of the specific characteristics of the particular situation. We turn now to a number of special decisions.

Special Sales Order

Torino Corporation, a manufacturer of automobile parts, ordinarily sells oil filters for $3.20 each. A mail-order company has offered Torino $35,000 for 20,000 oil filters. That works out to a special sale price of $1.75 per oil filter ($35,000/20,000 = $1.75). This sale will not affect regular business in any way, it will not change fixed costs, it will not require any additional variable selling and administrative expense, it will put idle manufacturing capacity to use, and it will violate no antitrust laws regarding pricing. Torino's total manufacturing cost of an oil filter is $2.00. Should Torino accept the special order and make the sale at $1.75? At first glance, the answer appears to be no, because each oil filter costs $2.00. But more thought must go into making this decision.

To set the stage for the analysis, let's examine Torino's income statement. Exhibit 26-1 presents the income statement in two different formats. The income statement on the left is the standard format presented to stockholders, creditors, and other parties outside the company. It is also called a *functional* income statement because it categorizes expenses by manufacturing, selling, and administrative functions. The contribution margin format on the right categorizes expenses primarily as variable and fixed. The contribution margin format is more useful for special decision analysis because it highlights how costs and income are affected by decisions. Recall that the contribution margin is revenue minus all variable expenses.

In this illustration, assume that Torino made and sold 250,000 oil filters before considering the special order. Under the functional costing approach, the manufacturing cost per unit is $2.00 ($500,000/250,000 = $2.00). But the contribution margin approach shows that the variable manufacturing cost per unit is $1.20 ($300,000/250,000 = $1.20). We now answer the key question facing Torino: What difference would the special sale make to the company's operating income?

EXHIBIT 26-1 *Functional Format and Contribution Margin Format for the Income Statement*

Torino Corporation
Income Statement
For the Year Ended December 31, 19X2

Functional Format		Contribution Margin Format		
Sales...............	$800,000	Sales................		$800,000
Less manufacturing		Less variable expenses:		
cost of goods sold....	500,000	Manufacturing.......	$300,000	
Gross margin..........	300,000	Selling and		
Less selling and		administrative	75,000	375,000
administrative		Contribution margin ...		425,000
expenses	200,000	Less fixed expenses:		
		Manufacturing.......	200,000	
		Selling and		
		administrative	125,000	325,000
Operating income......	$100,000	Operating income......		$100,000

Correct Analysis: Contribution Margin Approach

The correct analysis concentrates on the *differences* in revenues, expenses, and operating income, as Exhibit 26-2 at the bottom of the page shows.

This special sale is expected to increase revenues by $35,000. The only cost affected by the sale is variable manufacturing expense, which is expected to increase by $24,000. Torino management predicts that the special sales order will increase operating income by $11,000. Fixed expenses do not enter the analysis because they do not change. Variable selling and administrative expenses are unchanged because Torino has to make no special effort to get the sale. To make the decision, Torino should compare the special sale price with the total variable expenses of producing and selling the goods. As long as the increase in revenues exceeds the increase in variable expenses, there is a contribution to fixed expenses and profits.

Exhibit 26-3 gives Torino's income statements both without the special sales order (column 1) and with it (column 2). It shows operating income under both courses of action. Column 3 of Exhibit 26-3 repeats the quick summary by showing the differences caused by the special sales order. The quick summary presents the result of accepting the special sales order, an $11,000 increase in operating income.

You have just seen two correct ways of deciding whether to accept or reject the special sales order at a price less than total cost per unit: (1) a quick summary of differences (Exhibit 26-2) and (2) total revenues, expenses, and operating income under both courses of action (Exhibit 26-3). Whether to use a

special order because it would result in a $.25 loss per unit. Emphasize that the $2.00 is not the relevant cost because it includes fixed overhead. The relevant cost is the $1.20 variable cost.

Class Exercise: Refer to the Torino Corporation example. What if accepting the special order meant that the company would have to purchase a special piece of stamping equipment that cost $12,000 in order to mark the oil filters with the mail-order company's logo? The equipment would then be discarded. How would this affect your decision?

ANSWER:

Expected increase in operating income..........	$11,000
Less cost of special equipment	(12,000)
Loss from the special order	$ (1,000)

EXHIBIT 26-2 *Quick Summary of Special Sales Order Analysis*

Expected increase in revenues—sale of 20,000 oil filters × $1.75 each .	$35,000
Expected increase in expenses—variable manufacturing expenses:	
20,000 oil filters × $1.20 each	24,000
Expected increase in operating income	$11,000

Class Exercise: IFB Inc. is presently operating at 80% capacity producing 60,000 units. IFB has received an offer from a Middle Eastern company to sell 20,000 units at $3.90 each, which is less than the normal selling price. IFB has no experience with foreign companies. Budgeted costs for 60,000 units and 80,000 units follow:

Units	60,000	80,000
Costs:		
Dir. mat.	$ 90,000	$120,000
Dir. lab.	30,000	40,000
Var. FOH	24,000	32,000
Fixed FOH	96,000	96,000
Total	$240,000	$288,000

Should IFB accept the special order?

ANSWER: The total costs per unit at the 60,000 and 80,000 unit level are $4 ($240,000/60,000) and $3.60 ($288,000/80,000), respectively. These total unit costs include the irrelevant fixed costs. The relevant cost per unit (excluding the fixed costs) would be $2.40 ($144,000/60,000). This cost is below the special order price. Therefore the order should be accepted.

Point to Stress: The correct analysis zeroes in on the differences in revenues and costs (relevant costs) between the two alternatives.

OBJECTIVE 3

Explain the difference between correct analysis and incorrect analysis of a particular business decision

**Torino Corporation
Income Statement
For the Year Ended December 31, 19X2**

	(1) Without Special Order, 250,000 Units	(2) With Special Order, 270,000 Units	(3) Special-Order Difference, 20,000 Units Total	Per Unit
Sales	$800,000	$835,000	$35,000	$1.75
Variable expenses:				
Manufacturing	$300,000	$324,000	$24,000	$1.20
Selling and administrative	75,000	75,000	—	—
Total variable expenses	375,000	399,000	24,000	1.20
Contribution margin . . .	425,000	436,000	11,000	.55
Fixed expenses:				
Manufacturing	200,000	200,000	—	—
Selling and administrative	125,000	125,000	—	—
Total fixed expenses .	325,000	325,000	—	—
Operating income	$100,000	$111,000	$11,000	$ .55

quick summary or a total analysis depends on the question you are addressing. The summary answers this question: What will be the *difference* in revenues, expenses, and operating income if the business accepts the special order? The total analysis shows the summary of differences and answers an additional question: What will total revenues, expenses, and operating income be under the alternative courses of action? To accept or reject the special sales order can be decided from either analysis.

Incorrect Analysis: *Ignoring the Nature of Fixed Costs*

Let's look at an incorrect analysis of the Torino special sales order situation. The functional approach, shown on the left-hand side of Exhibit 26-1, leads to an incorrect measure of the change in expenses resulting from the sale.

Total manufacturing costs	$ 500,000
Units produced	÷ 250,000
Total cost per unit ($500,000/250,000)	$2.00
Expected increase in revenues— sale of 20,000 oil filters × $1.75 each	$ 35,000
Expected increase in expenses—*total* manufacturing expenses: 20,000 oil filters × $2.00 each	40,000
Expected decrease in operating income	$ (5,000)

A manager following this approach reasons that it costs $2.00 to make an oil filter. In this view, it is unprofitable to sell the product for less than $2.00. *The flaw in this analysis arises from treating a fixed cost as though it changes in total like a variable cost.* To manufacture one additional oil filter would increase Torino's cost by the variable manufacturing expense of $1.20. Fixed expenses are irrelevant to the decision analysis because Torino will incur the fixed expenses whether or not the company accepts the special sales order. The addition of 20,000 oil filters will *not* add to *total* fixed expenses. As volume changes, manufacturing costs will increase at the rate of $1.20 per unit, not $2.00 per unit. In this analysis, the variable expenses are relevant, and the fixed expenses are irrelevant.

Short-Run Versus Long-Run: Other Factors to Consider

The special sales order analysis focused on short-run factors—the expected effect on operating income. We must also consider long-run factors. What will be the impact on customers? Will acceptance of the order at $1.75 per unit hurt Torino's ability to make sales at the standard price of $3.20? Will regular customers find out about the special price and balk at paying the regular price? How will competitors react? Will they view this sale as the start of a price war?

Accepting the order yields an $11,000 advantage in operating income. Will potential disadvantages offset this $11,000? The sales manager may think so and reject the order. In turning away the business, the manager is saying that the company is better off passing up $11,000 now to protect its long-run market position. Rejecting the special sales order is like making an $11,000 "investment" in the company's long-run future.

Deletion of Products, Departments, Territories— Fixed Costs Unchanged _____

To analyze whether a company should drop a product line, a department, or a territory, let's use the Torino Corporation data. Assume that Torino is already operating at the 270,000-unit level, as shown in column 2 of Exhibit 26-3. Suppose Torino is considering dropping the air cleaner product line, which makes up $35,000 (20,000 units) of the company's sales. A manager is given an income statement divided by product line as follows:

		Product Line	
	Total	**Oil Filters**	**Air Cleaners**
Units	270,000	250,000	20,000
Sales	$835,000	$800,000	$ 35,000
Variable expenses	399,000	375,000	24,000
Contribution margin..................	436,000	425,000	11,000
Fixed expenses:			
Manufacturing	200,000	185,185*	14,815*
Selling and administrative	125,000	115,741†	9,259†
Total fixed expenses	325,000	300,926*	24,074
Operating income (loss)	$111,000	$124,074	$(13,074)

* $200,000/270,000 units = $.74074 per unit; 250,000 units × $.74074 = $185,185; 20,000 units × $.74074 = $14,815

† $125,000/270,000 units = $.46296 per unit; 250,000 units × $.46296 = $115,741; 20,000 units × $.46296 = $9,259

Discussion Question: Refer to the class exercise above on whether IFB Inc. should accept or reject a special order. What factors other than the relevant costs that are given might be considered in this decision? *ANSWER:* Some possible answers include international tariffs, cultural differences, income taxes, foreign currency transaction gains and losses, transportation costs, and other customers who might be angry at the lower price.

Point to Stress: There are often other qualitative factors besides profit and loss which must be considered in making decisions.

Point to Stress: The same technique used in making special order decisions will be used in making the six other special business decisions. It is important that students see this similarity between all these types of special business decisions, so that they do not try to solve each one with a different approach.

Point to Stress: Air cleaners may have an operating loss, but the product line still contributes to profit. If air cleaners were dropped, some expenses connected with them could still not be avoided. Because these expenses are unavoidable, they are not relevant to the "keep-or-drop" decision.

In determining cost per unit, Torino, like many companies, allocates fixed expenses to units in proportion to the number of units sold. For example, the data show that Torino sold 270,000 units of its products altogether. Total fixed manufacturing expenses of $200,000 divided by 270,000 units equals fixed manufacturing cost of $.74074 per unit. Applying this unit cost to the 250,000 units of the oil filter product line allocates fixed manufacturing cost of $185,185 to this product. The same procedure allocates fixed manufacturing cost of $14,815 to air cleaners. Fixed selling and administrative expenses are allocated in the same manner. Using this allocation method we see that air cleaners have an operating loss of $13,074. Should the air cleaner product line be dropped?

This illustration is basically the same example we studied for the special sales order. The relevant items are the changes in revenues and expenses. But now we are considering a decrease in volume instead of an increase. The difference between the change in revenues and the change in expenses is the change in operating income, as shown in Exhibit 26-4. Again, only the variable expenses are relevant to the decision. In the short run, dropping air cleaners would decrease operating income by $11,000. This analysis suggests that Torino should *not* drop air cleaners.

The decision of whether to delete a product is based on the same analysis used for the special sales order. The only difference is that deleting products leads to decreases in revenues and expenses, whereas accepting a special sales order leads to increased revenues and expenses. Decisions in both cases are based on the expected change in operating income.

Deletion of Products, Departments, Territories— Fixed Costs Changed

In our two examples total fixed expenses have not changed. However, do not jump to the conclusion that fixed costs are always irrelevant. The following example illustrates the role of fixed costs in special decision analysis.

Suppose Torino Corporation employs an engineer to improve the efficiency of the air cleaner product line. This employee is paid a fixed fee of $12,000, which can be avoided if the company phases out air cleaners. The question facing management is whether to drop air cleaners. To make this decision, Torino managers analyze all costs—fixed and variable—affected by the decision. Exhibit 26-5 shows the analysis.

The analysis suggests that operating income will increase by $1,000 if Torino drops air cleaners. In this situation, fixed expenses are relevant, and so the change in the fixed cost must enter the analysis. Special decisions should consider all costs that management expects to be affected by the situation. Managers must ask, What costs—fixed *and* variable—will change?

EXHIBIT 26-4 *Deletion of a Product—Fixed Costs Unchanged*

Expected decrease in revenues:	
Deletion of sales of air cleaners—20,000 units × $1.75 each	$35,000
Expected decrease in expenses:	
Deletion of variable manufacturing expenses—	
20,000 units × $1.20 each	24,000
Expected decrease in operating income	$11,000

Discussion Question: A hardware store operates with three departments: Paint, Lumber, and Tools. The Paint Department reports the following:

Sales	$75,000
Variable costs	60,000
Contribution margin	15,000
Fixed costs	25,000
Operating loss	($10,000)

Management has decided to discontinue the Paint Department but asks you to advise them. What is your response? *ANSWER:* Assuming all fixed costs (rent, insurance, utilities, manager's salary, and so on) would have to be absorbed by the other two profitable departments, this is an unwise decision. As long as a department has a positive contribution margin, it is covering some of the fixed costs. Also, qualitative factors should be considered. If the Paint Department is discontinued, customers who formerly came for paint as well as lumber and other items may now go elsewhere.

Discussion Question: Are fixed costs always irrelevant? *ANSWER:* No. Give some examples of fixed costs that might change if a department or product were discontinued. *ANSWER:* 1) Depreciation on the machinery used in that department; 2) insurance on the equipment, 3) department manager's salary.

EXHIBIT 26-5 *Deletion of a Product—Fixed Costs Changed*

Expected decrease in revenues:		
Deletion of sales of air cleaners		$35,000
Expected decrease in expenses:		
Variable manufacturing expenses	$24,000	
Fixed expenses—engineer fee	12,000	
Expected decrease in total expenses		36,000
Expected increase in operating income		$ 1,000

Which Product to Emphasize

Companies must decide which products to emphasize and which to de-emphasize. This decision has a profound impact on profits. If salespersons push a product with a low profit margin, the company's operating income may decrease even though they succeed in selling the product. How should a manager decide which product to emphasize? Decisions like this are important because of limited sales staff, store display space, and advertising budgets.

Assume a clothing manufacturer has two products, shirts and slacks. The following data are relevant:

	Product	
	Shirts	**Slacks**
Per unit:		
Selling price	$15	$20
Variable expenses	6	16
Contribution margin	$ 9	$ 4
Contribution margin ratio:		
Shirts—$9/$15	60%	
Slacks—$4/$20		20%

The data suggest that shirts are more profitable than slacks. But an important piece of information has been withheld—the time it takes to manufacture each product. This factor is called the *constraint,* or the *limiting factor.*

The **limiting factor,** or **constraint,** is the item that restricts production or sales. In some companies, the constraint is production. The factory or the labor force may be unable to produce more than a specified maximum number of units. This constraint—the limit to how much the labor force can produce—may be stated in terms of labor hours, machine hours, materials, or square feet of shelf space. (For example, storage may be limited to 50,000 square feet of space in a warehouse.) These factors vary from company to company, depending on its line of business. Other companies are constrained by sales. Competition may be stiff, and the business may be able to sell only so many units. In other companies, the constraint is time, as we see in the following example: Suppose the company can produce three pairs of slacks *or* one shirt per hour. This company has 20,000 hours of capacity. Which product should the company emphasize?

The way to maximize profits for a given capacity is to obtain the highest possible contribution margin per unit of the limiting factor—in our example, direct labor hours. The analysis includes two steps. First, determine the contribution margin per unit of the limiting factor. Second, multiply this unit

Class Exercise: Spiff Inc. sells liquid shoe polish, paste shoe polish, and saddle soap. Saddle soap had sales of $81,200, variable costs of $74,500, and fixed costs of $14,500, resulting in a net loss of $7,800. If $4,500 of the fixed costs could be eliminated, should saddle soap be discontinued? *ANSWER:* No. Operating income would decrease $2,200.

Expected decrease in revenue:		$81,200
Expected decrease in expenses:		
Variable costs	$74,500	
Fixed costs	4,500	79,000
Decrease in operating income:		$ 2,200

Point to Stress: We learned in cost-volume-profit analysis that the higher the contribution margin per unit, the more that unit contributed to profit. This is true when there are no constraints on the number of units to produce. If constraints do exist, such as the number of machine hours or units of raw materials, then they must be considered. The decision then will not be which product has the highest unit contribution margin, but which product has the highest contribution margin per unit of constraining factor.

Class Exercise: A firm makes two products, a hand mixer and a can opener, and can sell all the units it produces. It takes ½ hour to make a hand mixer and 2 hours to make a can opener. Given the following information, which product should the firm produce?

	Hand Mixer	Can Opener
Selling price	$8	$10
Variable cost	6	5
Contribution margin	$2	$ 5

ANSWER: The firm should produce the can opener since it contributes more per unit to profit and the firm can sell all the can openers that it makes.

If only 200,000 labor hours are available, which product should be produced? ANSWER:

	Hand Mixer	Can Opener
Contrib. margin	$ 2	$ 5
Hours required	÷ ½	÷ 2
Contrib. margin per hour	$ 4	$2.50

Producing the mixer would yield a profit of $800,000 (200,000 × $4) while producing the can opener would yield a profit of only $500,000 (200,000 × $2.50). In this case, produce the hand mixer.

Class Exercise: A company has been purchasing a part for $3. The company believes that it can make the part and utilize excess capacity. The company estimates that it will need 50,000 of the parts. The unit costs have been estimated as follows:

Direct materials	$1.25
Direct labor	.80
Variable factory overhead	.50
Total cost per unit	$2.55

The fixed costs would not change if the part were produced. Should the company make or buy the part? ANSWER: Make the part.

Total cost to make ($2.55 × 50,000) ...	$127,500
Total cost to buy ($3.00 × 50,000) ...	150,000
Advantage to making	$ 22,500

Suppose making the part increases fixed costs $5,000 per year, and the company has an opportunity to rent idle facilities to another company for $20,000 per year. How do these changes affect the decision? ANSWER: There is a $2,500 advantage to buying the part.

contribution margin by the company's capacity, stated in the number of units of the limiting factor.

Exhibit 26-6 shows how to decide which product to emphasize when there is a limiting factor. Slacks should be emphasized because they contribute more profit per hour. When the limiting factor is a part of the analysis, clearly the business should push slacks.

Make or Buy

Manufactured goods often include specialized parts. Overhead garage doors, for example, are activated by electronic controls. A garage door manufacturer may face this question: Should we manufacture the control device ourselves or buy it from an outsider? A furniture company may ask: Should we stain, lacquer, and finish the furniture we manufacture, or should we hire an outsider for the finish work? Assuming quality is unaffected, at the heart of the make-or-buy decision is *how best to use available facilities*.

Let's see how to answer the make-or-buy question. Torino Corporation's production process uses Part No. 4, which has the following manufacturing costs for 250,000 parts:

	Total Cost (250,000 Units)
Part No. 4 costs:	
Direct material	$ 40,000
Direct labor	20,000
Variable overhead	15,000
Fixed overhead	50,000
Total manufacturing cost	$125,000
Cost per unit of Part No. 4 ($125,000/250,000)	$.50

Another manufacturer offers to sell Torino the same part for $.37 a unit. Should Torino make Part No. 4 or buy it from the outside supplier? Torino's $.50 unit cost of manufacturing the part is $.13 higher than the $.37 cost of buying it outside. At first glance, it appears that Torino should purchase Part No. 4 from the outsider. But the correct answer to a make-or-buy question is rarely as clear as this comparison suggests. The key to making the correct decision lies in analyzing the difference in expected future costs between the alternatives. Which costs listed above will differ depending on whether Torino makes or buys Part No. 4?

EXHIBIT 26-6 *Which Product to Emphasize*

		Product	
		Shirts	Slacks
(1)	Units that can be produced each hour......	1	3
(2)	Contribution margin per unit..............	× $9	× $4
(3)	Contribution margin per hour (1) × (2)	$9	$12
	Capacity—Number of hours	×20,000	×20,000
	Total contribution margin for capacity......	$180,000	$240,000

Assume that by purchasing the part from an outsider, Torino can avoid all variable manufacturing costs and reduce the fixed overhead cost by $10,000. (Fixed overhead will decrease to $40,000.) Exhibit 26-7 shows the difference in cost between the make-and-buy alternatives.

It would be cheaper to make the part than to buy it outside. Fixed overhead represents a significant amount of cost even in the buy alternative. The total cost savings for 250,000 units of Part No. 4 is $7,500, which is $.03 per unit.

This example shows that *fixed costs are relevant to a special decision if fixed costs differ between the alternatives.* In this instance, fixed costs differ by $10,000. In these situations, this $10,000 amount is often called *avoidable* fixed overhead.

Best Use of Facilities

The cost data in the make-or-buy decision indicate that making the part is the right decision. As we mention in that discussion, the focus is on making the best use of available facilities over a particular planning horizon. This decision is illustrated further with a make-or-buy decision that includes three alternative courses of action.

Assume that buying from an outside supplier releases factory facilities that can be used to manufacture another product. Suppose the expected annual profit contribution of this other product is $18,000. The three alternatives become (1) make, (2) buy and leave facilities idle, or (3) buy and use facilities to manufacture another product. The alternative with the lowest *net* cost indicates the best use of facilities. The comparison of *net* cost under the three alternatives is given in Exhibit 26-8.

This analysis of *net* cost indicates that buying the parts outside and using the vacated facilities to manufacture another product is the best choice. If the facilities remain idle, the company will forgo the opportunity to earn $18,000.

Special decisions often include nonquantitative factors. For example, Torino managers may believe they can better control the quality of Part No. 4 by manufacturing it themselves. Or they may fear that an outside supplier cannot deliver sufficient quantities of the part on time. These factors argue for Torino's making the part itself. However, Torino may not have the employees or the factory facilities to manufacture Part No. 4. Its manufacture may require rare materials that Torino cannot obtain economically, so Torino may decide to

	Make	Buy
Variable costs to make ...	$127,500	
Fixed costs to make	5,000	
Cost to buy ..		$150,000
Rent of space		(20,000)
Net cost	$132,500	$130,000

Fixed costs are relevant to this decision because they are different under the two alternatives. The fixed costs are $5,000 more if the part is made rather than purchased.

EXHIBIT 26-7 *Make or Buy*

Transparency T26-1

	Make Part	Buy Part	Cost to Make minus Cost to Buy
Part No. 4 costs:			
Direct material.............	$ 40,000	$ —	$ 40,000
Direct labor	20,000	—	20,000
Variable overhead	15,000	—	15,000
Fixed overhead	50,000	40,000	10,000
Purchase price from outsider (250,000 × $.37)	—	92,500	(92,500)
Total cost of Part No. 4	$125,000	$132,500	$ (7,500)
Cost per unit—250,000 units ..	$.50	$.53	$(.03)

EXHIBIT 26-8   *Best Use of Facilities*

	Make	Buy and Leave Facilities Idle	Buy and Use Facilities for Other Products
Expected cost of obtaining 250,000 units of Part No. 4 (amounts from Exhibit 26-7) .	$125,000	$132,500	$132,500
Expected profit contribution from the other product	—	—	(18,000)
Expected *net* cost of obtaining 250,000 units of Part No. 4	$125,000	$132,500	$114,500

buy from the outside supplier. Managers consider nonquantitative factors as well as cost differences in making decisions.

Sell As-Is or Process Further

Inventories become obsolete. Should the company incur the additional manufacturing cost to rework the inventory, or should the company try to sell the inventory as-is? Some companies hold inventory that is only partially finished. These businesses face the decision of whether to finish the inventory or sell it as-is. Of course the finished inventory will bring a higher sale price, but management must consider the additional costs of completing the inventory. Whether the inventory is obsolete or incomplete, managers must decide if further work on it makes financial sense. For this decision, managers must know which costs to analyze. Historical costs are irrelevant to the "sell-or-process-further" decision.

Suppose a company has 1,000 obsolete computer parts that are carried in inventory at a manufacturing cost of $200,000. The alternatives facing the company are (1) process the inventory further at a cost of $40,000 with the expectation of selling it for $64,000, or (2) scrap the inventory for $17,000. Which alternative should the company select? The inventory's $200,000 historical cost is irrelevant to the decision. Such a cost is called a sunk cost. A **sunk cost** is an actual outlay that has been incurred in the past and is present under all alternatives. It is irrelevant because it makes no difference to a current decision.

Point to Stress: A sunk cost is an historical cost because it is a cost that has already been incurred.

Exhibit 26-9 shows how to make the decision of whether to sell an asset in its present condition or to process it further. Based on the expected revenues

Point to Stress: A product can be sold at a certain point in production, or it can be processed further and sold as a finished product. If the increase in the revenue generated from the processing is more than the additional processing costs, then further processing is the preferred alternative.

EXHIBIT 26-9   *Sell As-Is or Process Further*

	(1) Process Inventory Further	(2) Scrap Inventory (Sell As-Is)	Difference (1)-(2)
Expected revenue	$64,000	$17,000	$47,000
Expected costs	40,000	—	40,000
Expected net revenue	$24,000	$17,000	$ 7,000

and costs, it appears best to process the inventory further. The historical cost—the sunk cost—of the obsolete inventory makes no difference to the decision of whether to scrap the inventory or to rework it for sale at a higher price.

The decision whether to replace a plant asset is analyzed the same way. The asset's book value (cost less accumulated depreciation) is a sunk cost and, therefore, is irrelevant to the replacement decision. The relevant data are the expected revenues minus the expected costs from (1) using the old asset or (2) using a new asset.

Residual value, also called *scrap value* and *disposal value*, is *not* a sunk cost. Residual value is the amount of cash to be received by selling an asset. It almost always differs among alternatives. Therefore, it is relevant. During the asset's life, residual, or scrap, value is an expected *future* amount, which is why it enters the analysis shown in Exhibit 26-9.

Opportunity Cost

The concept of opportunity cost is often relevant to special decisions. An **opportunity cost** is the maximum available profit contribution forgone (rejected) by using limited resources for a particular purpose. It is the cost of the forsaken next-best alternative. This definition indicates that opportunity cost is not the usual outlay cost recorded in accounting. An outlay cost requires a cash disbursement sooner or later. It is the typical cost recorded by accountants.

A common example of an opportunity cost is the salary forgone by an engineer who quits his job with IBM to start his own business. Suppose this engineer analyzes the two job opportunities as follows:

	Open an Independent Business	Remain an IBM Employee
Expected salary income from IBM ..		$60,000
Expected revenue	$200,000	
Expected total expenses	120,000	
Expected net income	$ 80,000	$60,000

The opportunity cost of staying with IBM is the forgone $80,000 of net income that the independent business is expected to earn. The opportunity cost of starting a new business is the $60,000 salary that could be received from IBM for the next year.

The concept of opportunity cost applies to all business decisions that specify alternative courses of action. For example, in Exhibit 26-3, page 0000, the opportunity cost of rejecting the special sales order is $11,000 of operating income. In Exhibit 26-6, page 0000, the opportunity cost of manufacturing shirts is the $240,000 of contribution margin that could be earned on slacks. The opportunity cost of manufacturing slacks is the $180,000 contribution margin available on shirts. In Exhibit 26-9, page 0000, the opportunity cost of scrapping the inventory in its present condition is the $24,000 that can be earned by processing the inventory further. The opportunity cost of processing the inventory further is $17,000, which can be received immediately by selling the inventory as-is.

Summary Problems for Your Review

1. Aziz, Inc., has two products, a standard model and a deluxe model, with the following per-unit data:

	Standard	Deluxe
Selling price	$20	$30
Variable expenses	16	21

The company has 15,000 hours of capacity available. Seven units of the standard model can be produced in an hour, compared with three units of the deluxe model per hour. Which product should the company emphasize?

2. Suppose Zenith Corporation has the following manufacturing costs for 20,000 of its television cabinets:

Direct material	$ 20,000
Direct labor	80,000
Variable overhead	40,000
Fixed overhead	80,000
Total manufacturing cost	$220,000
Cost per cabinet ($220,000/20,000)	$11

Another manufacturer has offered to sell Zenith similar cabinets for $10, a total purchase cost of $200,000. By purchasing the cabinets outside, Zenith can save $50,000 of fixed overhead cost. The released facilities can be devoted to the manufacture of other products that will contribute $60,000 to profits. Identify and analyze the alternatives. What is Zenith's best decision?

SOLUTIONS TO REVIEW PROBLEMS

1. *Decision:* The company should emphasize the standard product because its contribution margin at capacity is greater by $15,000:

		Product	
		Standard	Deluxe
(1)	Units per hour that can be produced...	7	3
(2)	Contribution margin per unit	× $4*	× $9*
(3)	Contribution margin per hour (1) × (2)	$28	$27
	Capacity—Number of hours	× 15,000	× 15,000
	Total contribution margin for capacity	$420,000	$405,000

*Contribution margins: Standard: $20 − $16 = $4; Deluxe: $30 − $21 = $9.

2.

		Alternatives	
	Make	Buy and Leave Facilities Idle	Buy and Use Facilities for Other Products
Cabinets for televisions:			
Direct material	$ 20,000	—	
Direct labor	80,000	—	
Variable overhead	40,000	—	
Fixed overhead	80,000	$ 30,000	$ 30,000
Purchase price from outsider (20,000 × $10)	—	200,000	200,000
Total cost of obtaining cabinets	220,000	230,000	230,000
Profit contribution from other products			(60,000)
Net cost of obtaining 20,000 cabinets	$220,000	$230,000	$170,000

Decision: Zenith should buy the television cabinets from an outside supplier and use the released facilities to manufacture other products.

Capital Budgeting

A factory building may be used for 50 years. Equipment for successful products like Ivory soap and Coca-Cola may be used for decades. The term *capital asset* refers to an asset that is used over a long period of time. Plant assets like land, buildings, machinery, equipment, and furniture and fixtures are capital assets. The decisions for the purchase of such long-term assets often require long-range planning and large risks. Many uncertain factors—such as consumer preferences, manufacturing costs, and government legislation—enter into the decisions on the purchase of capital assets. Successful organizations quantify as many of these factors as they can before making long-range decisions. Robert Echols in the chapter-opening vignette is in the pressured position of having to make a long-range decision in a short period of time. The method, or technique, for evaluating and choosing among alternative courses of action is called a **decision model.**

Capital budgeting is a formal means of analyzing long-range investment decisions. Examples include plant locations, equipment purchases, additions of product lines, and territorial expansions. The following diagram shows where capital budgeting fits into the process of purchasing and using long-term assets:

Point to Stress: Capital budgeting is a means of evaluating and planning proposed future investments in capital assets. It is based on estimates; therefore, some uncertainty exists. However, by using the techniques explained here, capital budgeting should provide a sound basis for evaluating alternative investment possibilities.

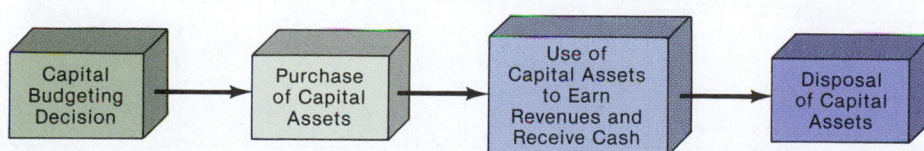

In the remainder of this chapter, we discuss four popular capital-budgeting decision models (methods of making choices): payback, accounting rate of return, net present value, and internal rate of return. In large measure, the models use *net cash inflow from operations*, which is covered in Chapter 18. Generally accepted accounting principles are based on the accrual accounting model, but capital budgeting focuses on cash because it takes cash to purchase assets.

Payback—Equal Annual Cash Flows

Payback is the length of time it will take to recover, in net cash inflow from operations, the dollars of a capital outlay. Suppose a business pays $24,000 for an assembling machine with an estimated useful life of six years and zero estimated residual value. Managers expect use of the machine to generate net cash inflow from operations of $6,000 annually. This increase in cash could result from an increase in revenues, a decrease in expenses, or a combination of the two.

Payback is expressed as a period of time, as shown in Exhibit 26-10. The payback model measures how swiftly an investment dollar may be recovered. The shorter the payback period, the more attractive the asset.

A major criticism of the payback model is that it does *not* consider or measure profitability. Consequently, the payback technique can lead to an unwise decision. Suppose an alternative to the $24,000 machine is a comparable machine that also costs $24,000 but which will save $8,000 annually during its three-year life. The two machines' payback periods are computed as follows:

$$\text{Payback period for Machine 1} = \frac{\$24,000}{\$6,000} = 4 \text{ years}$$

$$\text{Payback period for Machine 2} = \frac{\$24,000}{\$8,000} = 3 \text{ years}$$

The payback criterion favors the second machine because it recovers the asset cost more quickly. But consider useful lives. Suppose the second machine's useful life is the same as its payback period—three years. Its use will merely cover cost and provide no profits. Machine 1, on the other hand, will be more profitable. It will generate net cash inflows for six years—two years beyond its payback period—which will give the company additional net cash inflow of $12,000 ($6,000 × 2 years).

Point to Stress: The payback period tells management how long it takes to recover the original cost of the investment. Generally, the shorter the payback the better.

Discussion Question: What are some limitations of the payback model? ANSWER: 1) It does not consider profitability; 2) it ignores the time value of money, and 3) it ignores cash flows beyond the payback period.

Serial Class Exercise No. 1: A company is considering a new production method that could save an estimated $130,000 a year in manufacturing costs. The new equipment will cost $800,000 and will be depreciated on a straight-line basis over a 10-year life with a $40,000 salvage value. The desired rate of return is 12%. Compute the payback period. ANSWER:

$$\frac{\$800,000}{\$130,000} = 6.2 \text{ years}$$

OBJECTIVE 5

Use and evaluate three capital-budgeting models

Transparency T26-2

EXHIBIT 26-10 *Payback—Equal Annual Net Cash Inflows*

$$\text{Payback period (P)} = \frac{\text{Amount invested (I)}}{\text{Expected annual net cash inflow from operations (O)}}$$

$$P = \frac{I}{O}$$

$$= \frac{\$24,000}{\$6,000} = 4 \text{ years}$$

Payback—Unequal Annual Cash Flows

The payback equation can be used only when net cash inflows are the same each period. When periodic cash flows are unequal, the payback computation has a cumulative form. Each year's net cash inflows are accumulated until the amount invested is recovered. Suppose Machine 1 in our example will produce annual net cash inflows of $10,000 in the first year, $8,000 in Year 2, and $5,000 in Years 3 through 6. Exhibit 26-11 shows the payback computation when annual cash flows are unequal.

Years 1, 2, and 3 together bring in $23,000. Recovery of the amount invested ($24,000) occurs during Year 4. We can compute that payback (P) occurs in 3.2 years:

$$P = 3 \text{ years} + \left(\frac{\$1,000 \text{ needed to complete recovery in Year 4}}{\$5,000 \text{ net cash inflow during the year when recovery is completed}} \times 1 \text{ year} \right) =$$

$$= 3 \text{ years} + \qquad\qquad .2 \text{ year} \qquad\qquad = 3.2 \text{ years}$$

How does a manager use the payback model in capital budgeting? Managers often compare the payback period with the asset's useful life. The asset's payback period must be shorter than its useful life. Let's take an extreme example. If a machine has a payback period of five years and a useful life of three years, the company will never earn a profit from using the asset. How much shorter than the useful life the payback period must be is a matter of personal preference. When the business is deciding between two or more assets, the asset with the shortest payback period is the most profitable—if all other factors are the same.

The payback method highlights cash flows, an important factor in business decisions. Moreover, payback is easily understood. Advocates view it as a way to eliminate proposals (with lengthy payback periods) where the project is unusually risky. A major weakness of payback is that it ignores profitability.

Accounting Rate of Return

A primary goal of business is to maximize profits. The most widely used measure of profitability is the **accounting rate of return** on investment. As we discussed in Chapter 19, a rate of return is computed by dividing income by the amount of the investment made to earn the income:

$$\text{Rate of return} = \frac{\text{Income}}{\text{Investment}}$$

EXHIBIT 26-11 *Payback—Unequal Annual Net Cash Inflows*

Year	Amount Invested	Net Cash Inflow Each Year	Net Cash Inflow Accumulated
0	$24,000	—	—
1	—	$10,000	$10,000
2	—	8,000	18,000
3	—	5,000	23,000
3.2	—	1,000	24,000

Serial Class Exercise No. 2: Using the information from Serial Class Exercise No. 1, compute the accounting rate of return.
ANSWER:

$$\frac{\$130,000 - \$76,000}{(\$800,000 + \$40,000)/2} = 12.9\%$$

Note that the accounting rate of return is greater than the desired rate of return.

In capital budgeting, the income amount is income from operations (operating income) that results from use of the asset. Operating income on an asset can be computed as net cash inflow minus depreciation on the asset. Accounting rate of return is computed in Exhibit 26-12 for the machine in the payback illustration. Recall that the machine cost $24,000 and has a useful life of six years with no estimated residual value. Annual straight-line depreciation is, therefore, $4,000 ($24,000/6 years). Use of the machine is expected to generate annual net cash inflows of $6,000.

Accounting rate of return is an *average*. It measures the average rate of return from using the asset over its entire life. The computation is average annual operating income divided by the average amount invested in the asset. If annual operating income varies by year (as in the preceding payback illustration), compute the average annual operating income over the asset's life and use this amount (as O) to compute the accounting return. Also, the book value of the asset decreases as it is used and depreciated. Thus the company's investment in the asset declines. Average investment in the asset is computed as the average of its cost and estimated residual value.

When the asset's residual value is not zero, the average amount invested will *not* be half the asset's cost. For example, assume the asset's residual value is $3,000. Annual depreciation is $3,500 [($24,000 − $3,000)/6]. The accounting rate of return computation becomes

$$R = \frac{\$6,000 - \$3,500}{(\$24,000 + \$3,000)/2} = \frac{\$2,500}{\$13,500} = .185 = 18.5\%$$

Teaching Tip: What are some factors to be considered when setting a target rate of return? Companies would consider their cost of capital, the risk involved in the project, and the return that might be earned on alternative projects.

Suppose a company is purchasing a machine. The company can use the accounting rate of return to make the capital-budgeting decision. Suppose the machine under consideration is the one in Exhibit 26-12, with an accounting rate of return of 16.7 percent. Many companies demand a target rate of return on their investment projects. They invest only in assets with accounting rates of return equal to or greater than the target rate. Assume that the company's target rate is 20 percent. Would managers approve an investment in the illustrated machine, which is expected to generate an average return of 16.7 percent? No, because the asset's average annual return is less than the company's target rate.

Transparency T 26-3 **EXHIBIT 26-12** *Accounting Rate of Return*

$$\begin{array}{c} \text{Accounting} \\ \text{rate of} \\ \text{return (R)} \end{array} = \frac{\begin{array}{c}\text{Average annual}\\ \text{operating income}\\ \text{from investment*}\end{array}}{\begin{array}{c}\text{Average}\\ \text{amount invested}\end{array}} = \frac{\begin{array}{c}\text{Average annual net cash}\\ \text{inflow from operations (O)}\end{array} - \begin{array}{c}\text{Annual}\\ \text{depreciation (D)}\end{array}}{[\text{Amount invested (I)} + \text{Residual value (RV)}]/2}$$

$$R = \frac{O - D}{(I + RV)/2}$$

$$= \frac{\$6,000 - \$4,000}{(\$24,000 + \$0)/2} = \frac{\$2,000}{\$12,000} = .167 = 16.7\%$$

*Operating income can also be computed as revenues minus expenses

Discounted Cash Flow Models

Although the accounting rate of return model measures profitability, it has a major weakness. It does not recognize the time value of money. It fails to consider the timing of the cash outlay to purchase the asset and the timing of the annual net cash inflows. The discounted cash flow models are popular because they overcome this weakness. In the chapter-opening vignette, top management of Schaaf Tool Company requires at least "a 15 percent return on a discounted basis." The reference to a "discounted basis" means that this company uses discounted cash flow models for capital budgeting.

Discounted cash flow models are conceptually superior to payback models and accounting models. They are used by over 85 percent of the large industrial firms in the United States. There are two main variations of discounted cash flow models: (1) net present value (NPV) and (2) internal rate of return (IRR). Both variations are based on the concept of compound interest.

Net Present Value

The appendix to Chapter 16 on bonds introduced the concept of present value. The present value of $1 to be received in the future is less than $1 today. The logic is this: to receive $1 a year from now, we would pay less than $1 today. Why? Because if we pay $1 or more now to receive $1 a year later, we earn no income. Instead, we could deposit our $1 in a bank to earn interest of, say, $.08 during the year and have $1.08 a year later. We would rather have $1.08 than $1.00. The fact that we can earn income by investing money for a period of time is called the **time value of money.**

The present-value concept can be applied to the acquisition of capital assets. A company purchases an asset in order to earn revenues and receive cash. The excess of cash received for revenue over the cash paid for the costs associated with an investment is called the investment's net cash inflow. Ordinarily net cash inflow is stated in an annual amount. The advantage of analyzing net cash inflows instead of analyzing accounting income is that the focus is on the premier asset, cash. A company may be earning high income but be cash-poor. Moreover, the complexities of accrual accounting are avoided.

The timing of the net cash inflows from operations is important because of the time value of money. Consider two $10,000 investments. Both investments promise future cash receipts of $11,000. Investment 1 will bring in cash of $5,500 at the end of each of two years. Investment 2 will return the full $11,000 at the end of the second year. Which investment is better? Investment 1, because it brings cash home sooner, and so the cash can be invested for a longer period of time.

The **net present value (NPV)** model is a discounted cash flow approach to capital budgeting. It computes the expected net monetary gain or loss from a project by discounting all expected future cash inflows and outflows to the present time, using a desired rate of return. A zero or positive NPV indicates that the investment should be purchased. A negative net present value indicates that the investment should be rejected. If this model is used to compare several assets, the asset with the highest net present value is the best.

Assume that the business is considering the manufacture of two products, tape decks and VCRs. Each would require different specialized equipment costing the same amount, $1 million, and having zero residual value. Each piece of equipment is expected to have a five-year life. The two products have different patterns of expected net cash inflows:

Point to Stress: One purpose of the net present value method is to analyze all cash flows in current terms, since dollars in different years do not have the same value.

Point to Stress: The alternative that produces the highest net present value of all cash flows is the most acceptable.

	Annual Net Cash Inflows	
Year	Tape Decks	VCRs
1	$ 305,450	$ 500,000
2	305,450	350,000
3	305,450	300,000
4	305,450	250,000
5	305,450	40,000
Total	$1,527,250	$1,440,000

Real-World Example: A recent survey indicated that 36% of manufacturers used discount rates of between 13% and 17% even though the prime rate was 8% and the cost of capital was between 10% and 12%.

Total net cash inflows are greater if we invest in the manufacture of tape decks. However, these net cash inflows will occur in the future. In the net-present-value model, we base the capital-budgeting decision on present value, not future values. In present-value language, we say that we *discount* these future cash flows to present value. Discounted cash flow is a representation of cash inflows and outflows at a common time so that they can be compared (added, subtracted, and so on) for decision making.

Computation of present value requires an earnings rate. This rate, called the **discount rate,** is management's minimum desired rate of return on an investment. Synonyms are *hurdle rate, cutoff rate, required rate, cost of capital,* and *target rate.* The discount rate varies depending on the risks undertaken. The higher the risk, the higher the discount rate. Let's assume that an appropriate discount rate for these investments is 14 percent.

The manufacture and sale of tape decks is expected to generate $305,450 of net cash inflow each year—a total of $1,527,250. A stream of equal periodic amounts is called an **annuity.** The present value of an annuity is computed by multiplying the periodic amount ($305,450 annually, in this case) by the present value of an annuity of $1 from Table 26-2, page 1186. The table indicates that the present value of an annuity of $1 for five periods discounted at 14 percent is 3.433. Exhibit 26-13 shows the computation of the present value of the net cash inflows from investing in the tape-deck project—$1,048,610.

The annual net cash inflows from investing in the manufacture of VCRs are unequal—$500,000 in Year 1, $350,000 in Year 2, and so on. Because these amounts vary by year, the present value of each annual amount is computed separately. For example:

Year	Find the Present Value Factor From Table 26-1 page 1184 14% Column		Net Cash Inflow		Present Value of Net Cash Inflows
1	.877	×	$500,000	=	$438,500
2	.769	×	350,000	=	269,150

Exhibit 26-13 includes these present-value computations.

The exhibit indicates that the VCR project has a net present value of $78,910, compared with $48,610 for the tape-deck project. The analysis favors VCRs because an investment in that project will earn the company's target return of 14 percent plus an additional $78,910. This expected excess is greater than the net present value of the tape-deck project, which also meets the target return of 14 percent but returns only an additional $48,610.

This example illustrates an important point about net-present-value analysis: the tape-deck project promises the greater total amount of net cash inflows. But the timing of the VCR cash flows—loaded near the beginning of

EXHIBIT 26-13 *Net Present Value*

	Present Value at 14%	Net Cash Inflow	Present Value of Net Cash Inflows
Tape-Deck Project:			
Present value of equal annual net cash inflows for 5 years	3.433*	× $305,450 per year =	$ 1,048,610
Investment			(1,000,000)
Net present value of the tape deck project			$ 48,610
VCR Project:			
Present value of net cash inflow by year: **Year**			
1	.877†	× $500,000 =	$ 438,500
2	.769	× 350,000 =	269,150
3	.675	× 300,000 =	202,500
4	.592	× 250,000 =	148,000
5	.519	× 40,000 =	20,760
Total present value of net cash inflows ..			1,078,910
Investment			(1,000,000)
Net present value of the VCR project ...			$ 78,910

*Present value of annuity of $1 for 5 years at 14%, Table 26-2, page 1186.
†Present value of $1 for 1 year, 2 years, 3 years, and so on, at 14%, Table 26-1, page 1184.

the project—causes the VCR project to have a higher net present value. The VCR project is more attractive because of the time value of money. Its nearer dollars are worth more now than the more distant dollars of the tape-deck project.

Another important point about net-present-value analysis is this: Either project, considered alone, is acceptable because its net present value is at least zero. Thus, both projects earn at least the required rate of return of 14 percent.

Net Present Value of a Project with Residual Value

When the asset to be acquired is expected to have a residual value at the end of its useful life, that amount should also be considered in the NPV analysis. It must be discounted to its present value and added to the present value of the annual net cash inflows to determine the total present value of the project. The residual value is discounted as a single amount—not an annuity—because it will be received only at the end of the asset's useful life (for example, when the asset is sold).

Suppose the equipment to manufacture the tape decks (in Exhibit 26-13) is expected to be worth $100,000 at the end of its five-year life. To determine the tape-deck project's NPV, we discount $100,000 for five years at 14 percent—using Table 26-1 on page 1184—and add its present value ($51,900), as shown in Exhibit 26-14.

Compare the tape-deck project's NPVs in Exhibits 26-13 and 26-14. The residual amount raises the project's NPV to $100,510, which is slightly higher than the VCR project's NPV. If the VCR equipment is expected to have zero disposal value, then the tape-deck project is slightly more attractive. This illustrates the difference that residual value can make to a business decision.

Serial Class Exercise No. 3: Using the information from Serial Class Exercise No. 2, compute the net present value with a 12% minimum desired rate of return. *ANSWER:*

PV of manufacturing cost savings ($130,000 × 5.650)..	$ 734,500
PV of residual value ($40,000 × .322)....	12,880
Initial investment	(800,000)
NPV	$(52,620)

The proposal should be rejected.

Teaching Tip: Draw a time line on the board with all the cash flows that are relevant to a net present value investment question. Using Serial Class Exercise No. 1 as an example, the cash flows would appear as follows.

$130,000 annual cost savings

($800,000) outflow

$40,000 salvage value

Yr. 0 1 2 3 4 5 6 7 8 9 10

Tape-Deck Project	Present Value at 14%	Net Cash Inflow	Present Value of Net Cash Inflows
Present value of equal annual net cash inflows for 5 years (from Exhibit 26-13)......	3.433	× $305,450 per year =	$ 1,048,610
Present value of residual value	.519*	× $100,000 =	51,900
Present value of the project's net cash inflows			1,100,510
Investment			(1,000,000)
Net present value of tape-deck project			$ 100,510

*Present value of $1 for 5 years at 14%, Table 26-1, below.

Although the amount may often be insignificant, it can change an investment decision.

There is a slightly different way to use present-value analysis for making capital-budgeting decisions. Suppose the company starts the decision process by determining the present values of the expected future net cash inflows from the two projects—$1,048,610 for tape decks and $1,078,910 for VCRs. Managers may ask, What is the most we can invest in the tape-deck project and still earn our target rate of return of 14 percent? With zero residual values, the answer is $1,048,610. Similarly, the maximum acceptable investment for VCRs is $1,078,910. Negotiations with the seller of the tape-deck manufacturing equipment may drive the required investment down to only $850,000. This would increase the tape-deck project's attractiveness, especially if the cost of

TABLE 26-1   *Present Value of $1*

	Present Value of $1								
Periods	**4%**	**5%**	**6%**	**7%**	**8%**	**10%**	**12%**	**14%**	**16%**
1	0.962	0.952	0.943	0.935	0.926	0.909	0.893	0.877	0.862
2	0.925	0.907	0.890	0.873	0.857	0.826	0.797	0.769	0.743
3	0.889	0.864	0.840	0.816	0.794	0.751	0.712	0.675	0.641
4	0.855	0.823	0.792	0.763	0.735	0.683	0.636	0.592	0.552
5	0.822	0.784	0.747	0.713	0.681	0.621	0.567	0.519	0.476
6	0.790	0.746	0.705	0.666	0.630	0.564	0.507	0.456	0.410
7	0.760	0.711	0.665	0.623	0.583	0.513	0.452	0.400	0.354
8	0.731	0.677	0.627	0.582	0.540	0.467	0.404	0.351	0.305
9	0.703	0.645	0.592	0.544	0.500	0.424	0.361	0.308	0.263
10	0.676	0.614	0.558	0.508	0.463	0.386	0.322	0.270	0.227
11	0.650	0.585	0.527	0.475	0.429	0.350	0.287	0.237	0.195
12	0.625	0.557	0.497	0.444	0.397	0.319	0.257	0.208	0.168
13	0.601	0.530	0.469	0.415	0.368	0.290	0.229	0.182	0.145
14	0.577	0.505	0.442	0.388	0.340	0.263	0.205	0.160	0.125
15	0.555	0.481	0.417	0.362	0.315	0.239	0.183	0.140	0.108
16	0.534	0.458	0.394	0.339	0.292	0.218	0.163	0.123	0.093
17	0.513	0.436	0.371	0.317	0.270	0.198	0.146	0.108	0.080
18	0.494	0.416	0.350	0.296	0.250	0.180	0.130	0.095	0.069
19	0.475	0.396	0.331	0.277	0.232	0.164	0.116	0.083	0.060
20	0.456	0.377	0.312	0.258	0.215	0.149	0.104	0.073	0.051

Appendix B provides a fuller table for the present value of $1.

the VCR manufacturing equipment remains $1,000,000. In any event, managers would not want to pay more than $1,048,610 for the tape-deck equipment or more than $1,078,910 for the VCR equipment. At prices above these present-value amounts, the company would not be able to earn 14 percent on its investment.

Internal Rate of Return

Another discounted cash flow model for capital budgeting is the *internal rate of return (IRR)* model. The **internal rate of return—the IRR**—of an investment project is the rate of return that makes the net present value of the project equal to zero. As the name implies, a project's IRR is the rate of return that a company can expect to earn by investing in the project. The higher the IRR, the more desirable the project; the lower the IRR, the less desirable.

Point to Stress: The IRR is considered superior to the accounting rate of return because IRR considers the time value of money.

Exhibit 26-15 shows why 16 percent is the IRR of our tape-deck project. The 16 percent rate produces a net present value of zero. There are three steps:

1. Identify the expected net cash inflows ($305,450 for five years) exactly as you did in calculating the net present value in Exhibit 26-13.

2. Find the interest rate that equates the present value of the cash inflows to the present value of the cash outflows. If one outflow is followed by a series of equal inflows, use the following equation to solve for the value of the present-value (PV) factor:

Investment = Expected annual net cash inflow × Annuity PV factor

$$\$1,000,000 = \$305,450 \times \text{PV factor}$$

$$\text{PV factor} = \frac{\$1,000,000}{\$305,450} = 3.274$$

Scan the row in Table 26-2 that represents the relevant life of the project, the 5-period row in our example. Choose the column with the number closest to the annuity PV factor that was calculated. The 3.274 annuity factor is in the 16 percent column. Therefore, the IRR of the tape-deck project is 16 percent.

3. Compare the IRR with the minimum desired rate of return. If the IRR is equal to or greater than the minimum desired rate, the project should be accepted. Otherwise, it should be rejected.

If tape decks were the only investment under consideration, managers would invest in tape decks because their 16 percent IRR exceeds the 14 percent

Class Exercise: The Midway School District is considering the purchase of a lawn tractor. If the tractor is purchased, it will replace hiring a lawn maintenance company. The tractor will cost $10,000, and will have a 10-year life. The mower will save approximately $1,627 a year in operating costs because of the labor costs it will save. Compute the internal rate of return.
ANSWER:

$$\frac{\$10,000}{\$1,627} = 6.146$$

Looking at the present value of annuity table at the 10 year row, 6.145 (which is very close to the calculated 6.146) is found in the 10% column. Therefore, the IRR is 10%.

EXHIBIT 26-15 *Internal Rate of Return, Tape-Deck Project*

	Present Value at 16%		Net Cash Inflow		Present Value of Net Cash Inflows
Present value of equal annual net cash inflows for 5 years ...	3.274	×	$305,450	=	$ 1,000,000*
Investment					(1,000,000)
Net present value of the tape deck project					$ 0 †

* Slight rounding error.

† The zero difference proves that the rate of return is 16%

TABLE 26-2 *Present Value of Annuity of $1*

Periods	Present Value of Annuity of $1								
	4%	5%	6%	7%	8%	10%	12%	14%	16%
1	0.962	0.952	0.943	0.935	0.926	0.909	0.893	0.877	0.862
2	1.886	1.859	1.833	1.808	1.783	1.736	1.690	1.647	1.605
3	2.775	2.723	2.673	2.624	2.577	2.487	2.402	2.322	2.246
4	3.630	3.546	3.465	3.387	3.312	3.170	3.037	2.914	2.798
5	4.452	4.329	4.212	4.100	3.993	3.791	3.605	3.433	3.274
6	5.242	5.076	4.917	4.767	4.623	4.355	4.111	3.889	3.685
7	6.002	5.786	5.582	5.389	5.206	4.868	4.564	4.288	4.039
8	6.733	6.463	6.210	5.971	5.747	5.335	4.968	4.639	4.344
9	7.435	7.108	6.802	6.515	6.247	5.759	5.328	4.946	4.607
10	8.111	7.722	7.360	7.024	6.710	6.145	5.650	5.216	4.833
11	8.760	8.306	7.887	7.499	7.139	6.495	5.938	5.453	5.029
12	9.385	8.863	8.384	7.943	7.536	6.814	6.194	5.660	5.197
13	9.986	9.394	8.853	8.358	7.904	7.103	6.424	5.842	5.342
14	10.563	9.899	9.295	8.745	8.244	7.367	6.628	6.002	5.468
15	11.118	10.380	9.712	9.108	8.559	7.606	6.811	6.142	5.575
16	11.652	10.838	10.106	9.447	8.851	7.824	6.974	6.265	5.669
17	12.166	11.274	10.477	9.763	9.122	8.022	7.120	6.373	5.749
18	12.659	11.690	10.828	10.059	9.372	8.201	7.250	6.467	5.818
19	13.134	12.085	11.158	10.336	9.604	8.365	7.366	6.550	5.877
20	13.590	12.462	11.470	10.594	9.818	8.514	7.469	6.623	5.929

Appendix B provides a fuller table for the present value of an annuity of $1.

hurdle rate. In the situation of Exhibit 26-13, the VCR project has a higher net present value than the tape-deck project. The VCR investment also has a higher IRR. Computation of the VCR's IRR requires a trial-and-error procedure covered in more advanced courses. Many calculators can compute the IRR.

How do the net-present-value approach and the IRR approach compare? The net-present-value method indicates the amount of the excess (or deficiency) of a project's present value of net cash inflows over (or under) its cost—for a specified rate of return. Net present value, though, does not show the project's unique rate of return. The IRR, however, shows the project's IRR but fails to indicate the dollar difference between the project's present value and its investment cost. In most cases the two methods lead to the same investment decision.

Comparison of the Capital Budgeting Models

The discounted cash flow models are the best of the three capital-budgeting models because they are based on cash flows and because they consider both profitability and the time value of money. The time value of money enters the analysis through the discounting of future dollars to present value. Profitability is also built into the discounted cash flow models. Managers specify the earnings rate that they demand of investment projects. Use of this target earnings rate—10 percent, 15 percent, or whatever—as the discount rate for the computations produces the ideal price for the project. At this price, the project is expected to earn the specified level of profits.

Each of the other two capital-budgeting models ignores one or more of these factors. In actual practice, managers often use more than one model

EXHIBIT 26-16 *Capital-Budgeting Decision Models*   Transparency T26-4

Model	Strengths	Weaknesses
Payback	Easy to understand Based on cash flows Highlights risks	Ignores profitability and the time value of money
Accounting rate of return	Based on profitability	Ignores the time value of money

Discounted cash flow models:
  Net present value
  Internal rate of return
	Based on cash flows,
	profitability, and the
	time value of money
		None of the above

simultaneously to gain different perspectives on risks and returns. Exhibit 26-16 summarizes the strengths and weaknesses of the payback, accounting rate of return, and discounted cash flow models.

Lease or Buy

The capital budgeting decisions considered thus far have centered on which investment project to acquire. The first decision is whether to acquire a particular asset. After that decision is made, managers must decide how to finance the acquisition. There are several possibilities. The business may be able to purchase the asset with internally generated cash or with cash obtained by borrowing. In many cases managers can acquire the use of assets through leasing of capital assets—that is, renting on a long-term basis.

A recent survey of 600 companies indicated that only 45 companies did not acquire the use of some of their assets through leasing. Why is leasing so popular? One factor is rapid change in technology. Rather than buy a computer and risk getting stuck with a machine made obsolete by new developments, a company may prefer to lease one. Then if IBM, Control Data, or Compaq develops a new generation of computer, the company can let its lease expire and switch to a new, more powerful machine. For similar reasons, airline companies lease some of their aircraft.

A professional sports team may lease its arena or its stadium from the city. It is easier to move a sports franchise to another city if the team does not own the stadium. Consider, too, tax advantages. In 1990, the city of Arlington, Texas, voted to expand Arlington Stadium, where the Texas Rangers play baseball. The city owns the stadium, so no property taxes are levied on the structure. Thus, by leasing the stadium from the city, Ranger management can save money by avoiding property tax.

The role of leasing should be kept in perspective. There are two steps: (1) whether or not to acquire an asset, which is an investment decision using a discounted-cash-flow model, and (2) whether to finance the acquisition by borrowing or leasing. The second step is *not* an investment decision. It is a financing decision that is covered in textbooks on finance.

Computers in Business Decision Analysis _____

Computers are ideally suited for decision analysis. They can compute the outcomes of alternative courses of action instantly and without computational error. Consider the net-present-value analysis of three possible investments.

Suppose the assets under consideration promise irregular net cash inflows for 20 years. The 60 (3 × 20) present-value computations would be time consuming and present a great possibility for error. However, a computer can be programmed to handle these multiple computations. The manager can then use the program over and over. He can alter the annual cash flows, the earnings (discount) rate, and the timing of the cash flows. With a computer, the manager simply enters the data, and the entire analysis is performed in seconds. Chapter 28 provides an exercise and problems of this nature.

Consider the special sales order decision. Many companies store their cost data in computers. The manager can enter the special sale price and call up the variable expenses and any fixed expenses that will change because of the special sale. The change in operating income is computed automatically. If the computed income is high enough, the manager can accept the order. If the income is too low, the manager can enter a revised sale price and compute the revised operating income. By trying different sale prices, she can come up with a range of acceptable options. Armed with this knowledge, the company may propose a different sale price to the buyer. More knowledge places the company in a stronger bargaining position. Microcomputers and spreadsheet programs like Lotus 1-2-3®, Excel, Quattro Pro, and AppleWorks bring this analytical power even to small companies.

The computer can greatly assist management in making capital budgeting decisions. Suppose a large manufacturer of lawn maintenance equipment, such as Toro, is considering opening a new production facility to meet increasing demands for its lawn mowers. Where will the new facility be? Company management has examined 25 possible sites and narrowed the choice to five. And which of the six alternative factory designs that management is considering is best? Analyzing the data with a spreadsheet allows the computer to quickly run through all the calculations to reach the optimal combination of site and design based on net present value and internal rate of return.

Summary Problem for Your Review

The data for a machine follow:

Cost of machine	$48,000
Estimated residual value	6,000
Estimated annual net cash inflow	13,000
Estimated useful life	5 years
Annual rate of return required	16%

Required

1. Compute the payback period.
2. Compute the accounting rate of return.
3. Compute the net present value (NPV).
4. Indicate whether each decision model leads to purchase or rejection of this investment. Would you decide to buy the machine? Give your reason.

Requirement 1

$$P = \frac{I}{O} = \frac{\$48,000}{\$13,000} = 3.7 \text{ years}$$

Requirement 2

$$R = \frac{O - D}{(I + RV)/2} = \frac{\$13,000 - \$8,400^*}{(\$48,000 + \$6,000)/2} = \frac{\$4,600}{\$54,000/2}$$

$$= \frac{\$4,600}{\$27,000} = .170 = 17\%$$

$$^*D = \frac{\$48,000 - \$6,000}{5 \text{ years}} = \$8,400$$

Requirement 3

Present value of equal annual net cash inflows ($13,000 × 3.274†)	$ 42,562
Present value of residual value ($6,000 × .476‡)	2,856
Present value of the machine	45,418
Investment	(48,000)
Net present value	$ (2,582)

†Present value of annuity of $1 for 5 years at 16%, Table 26-2, page 1186.
‡Present value of $1 for 5 years at 16%, Table 26-1, page 1184.

Requirement 4

Payback: Purchase machine because payback period (3.7 years) is less than useful life (5 years).

Accounting rate of return: Purchase machine because return on machine of 17 percent exceeds target rate of 16 percent.

Net present value: Reject machine because it has negative net present value.

Decision: Reject machine because of negative net present value. The net-present-value model considers cash flows, profitability, and the time value of money. Each of the other models ignores two of these factors.

Summary

Special decisions are those with long-term consequences. In making these decisions, managers focus on differences among the alternative courses of action. Often historical data are irrelevant, except for helping to develop the *expected future data* for the decision analysis. The approach to making special decisions is called the *relevant information approach*.

Whether to *delete a product, which product to emphasize*, whether to *make or buy* a part, how to make the *best use of facilities*, and whether to *sell inventory in its present condition or process it further* are decisions with long-range effects. In each decision, the best alternative is the one that will produce the largest increase in income from operations.

A *contribution margin income statement,* which shows variable expenses and fixed expenses, is helpful to decision analysis. The change in *variable expenses* is always a factor because variable expenses change in direct response to changes in volume. Fixed expenses may or may not change, depending on the circumstances. Failure to account for *fixed expenses* correctly is a common mistake. When fixed expenses do not change, they do not enter the analysis. But when they do change, their effect must be considered.

In making special decisions, managers also consider nonquantitative factors, like the long-run effect on customers and competitors. Opportunity cost is another factor in special decisions. *Opportunity cost* is the maximum profit forgone by following a specific course of action. Thus it differs from ordinary accounting costs.

Capital budgeting helps managers make long-range decisions. *Payback, accounting rate of return,* and *discounted cash flow* are three basic models for making capital-budgeting decisions. Payback is the simplest. Discounted cash flow is the best of these because it is based on cash flows and also considers profitability and the time value of money. Two widely used variations are *net present value* and *internal rate of return.* Companies may use more than one method in practice. Computers are ideally suited for special decision analysis because they can help predict the outcomes of various courses of action.

Self-Study Questions

Test your understanding of the chapter by marking the best answer for each of the following questions.

1. Relevant information for decision analysis *(pp. 1165, 1166)*
   a. Remains constant regardless of the alternative courses of action
   b. Is used in some but not all business decisions
   c. Varies with the alternative courses of action
   d. Excludes direct materials and direct labor because they are fixed

2. Assume fixed costs remain unchanged. To decide whether to make a sale at a special price, compare *(p. 1167)*
   a. Expected change in gross margin (sales minus cost of goods sold) with and without the sale
   b. Expected change in revenue with expected change in fixed expenses
   c. Expected change in revenue with expected change in selling expenses
   d. Expected change in revenue with expected change in variable expenses

3. To decide whether to delete a product, a manager should *(pp. 1169-1170)*
   a. Consider all costs that change
   b. Consider only variable costs
   c. Consider all costs that remain unchanged
   d. Consider only fixed costs

4. Pontchatrain's $.47 cost per unit (incurred in manufacturing its inventory) includes fixed cost of $.19. Another company offers to sell the product to Pontchatrain for $.35 per unit. The make-or-buy decision hinges on the comparison between Pontchatrain's $.47 manufacturing cost and the total cost if the products are purchased from the other company. That total cost is *(p. 1172)*
   a. $.28   c. $.54
   b. $.35   d. $.66

5. Sunk costs are *(p. 1174)*
   a. Relevant to most business decisions
   b. The cost of the next-best alternative
   c. Equal to the residual value of a plant asset
   d. Irrelevant to most business decisions
6. Capital budgeting is a (an) *(p. 1177)*
   a. Depreciation method
   b. Short-run decision
   c. Alternative to the payback method
   d. Way to make long-range investment decisions
7. A machine costs $45,000. It is expected to earn operating income of $6,000 and to generate $7,500 net cash inflow annually. Expected residual value is $5,000 at the end of five years. What is the asset's payback period? *(p. 1178)*
   a. 5 years   c. 7½ years
   b. 6 years   d. 9 years
8. The accounting rate of return of the machine in the preceding question is *(p. 1180)*
   a. 15 percent   c. 26.7 percent
   b. 24 percent   d. 37.5 percent
9. The time value of money is an important part of *(p. 1181)*
   a. Payback analysis   c. Net-present-value analysis
   b. Accounting rate of return analysis   d. All capital-budgeting methods
10. Payback analysis and net-present-value analysis indicate that a particular investment should be rejected, but the accounting rate of return is favorable. What is the wisest investment decision? Give your reason. *(p. 1187)*
    a. Reject because of net-present-value analysis
    b. Reject because of payback analysis
    c. Accept because of favorable accounting rate of return
    d. Cannot decide because of differences among the methods' results

Answers to the Self-Study Questions follow the Accounting Vocabulary.

Accounting Vocabulary

Accounting rate of return. The remainder of average annual net cash inflow from operations minus annual depreciation, divided by average amount invested in the business. This is the most widely used measure of profitability. The higher the accounting rate of return, the better the investment *(p. 1179)*.

Annuity. Stream of equal periodic amounts *(p. 1182)*.

Capital budgeting. Formal means of making long-range decisions for investments such as plant locations, equipment purchases, additions of product lines, and territorial expansions *(p. 1177)*.

Constraint. Item that restricts production or sales. Also called the Limiting factor *(p. 1171)*.

Decision model. A method or technique for evaluating and choosing among alternative courses of action *(p. 1177)*.

Discount rate. Management's minimum desired rate of return on an investment, used in a present-value computation *(p. 1182)*.

Internal rate of return (IRR). Rate of return that makes the net present value of a project equal to zero *(p. 1185)*.

Limiting factor. Item that restricts production or sales. Also called the Constraint *(p. 1171)*.

Net present value. Discounted cash flow approach to capital budgeting. It computes the expected net monetary gain or loss from a project by discounting all expected cash flows to the present value, using a desired rate of return. A zero or positive net present value indicates that the investment should be purchased. A negative net present value indicates that the investment should be rejected *(p. 1181)*.

Opportunity cost. Maximum available profit contribution forgone (rejected) by using limited resources for a particular purpose. It is the cost of the forsaken next-best alternative *(p. 1175)*.

Payback. Length of time it will take to recover, in net cash inflow from operations, the dollars of a capital outlay. The shorter the payback period, the better the investment, and vice versa *(p. 1178)*.

Relevant information. Expected future data that differ between alternative courses of action *(p. 1165)*.

Sunk cost. Actual outlay incurred in the past and present under all alternative courses of action. Sunk cost is irrelevant because it makes no difference to a current decision *(p. 1174)*.

Time value of money. The fact that one can earn income by investing money for a period of time *(p. 1181)*.

Answers to Self-Study Questions

1. c
2. d
3. a
4. c   Fixed cost ($.19) + Cost of outside units ($.35) = $.54
5. d
6. d
7. b $45,000/$7,500 = 6 years
8. b $$\frac{\$6,000}{(\$45,000 + \$5,000)/2} = \frac{\$6,000}{\$25,000} = 24\%$$
9. c
10. a

ASSIGNMENT MATERIAL _____

Questions

1. How do special decisions differ from ordinary day-to-day business decisions? Give examples.
2. Briefly describe how relevant information is used in making special decisions.
3. Discuss the roles of expected future data and historical data in special decision analysis. On which set of data are special decisions based?
4. Identify two income statement formats. Which is more useful for deciding whether to accept a special sales order? Why?
5. Identify two income amounts on which special decisions are based.
6. What is "special" about a special sales order? How does a manager make a special sales order decision?
7. Identify two long-run factors to be considered in making a special sales order decision.
8. What is the similarity between a special sales order decision and a decision to delete a product? What is the difference?
9. Which type of cost is more likely to change in a special decision situation, a fixed cost or a variable cost? Can both costs change?

10. Outline how to decide which product to emphasize when there is a limiting factor. Give four examples of limiting factors.

11. Which is relevant to special decision analysis, an asset's sunk cost or its residual value? Give your reason including an explanation of each.

12. What is opportunity cost? How does it differ from an ordinary accounting cost?

13. Give an example of a decision that would be based on opportunity cost. Discuss the role of opportunity cost in making this decision.

14. What are decision models? Why are they helpful in capital budgeting?

15. What is capital budgeting? Are capital-budgeting decisions made before or after long-term assets are purchased?

16. Name three capital-budgeting decision models. State the strengths and the weaknesses of each model. Which model is best? Why?

17. Name the capital-budgeting model that fits each description: (a) based on operating income only; (b) based on cash flows without regard for their timing or for profitability; (c) based on the time value of money.

18. How is payback period computed? How does the estimated useful life of a capital asset affect the payback computation?

19. Your company is considering purchasing a manufacturing plant with an expected useful life of 15 years. What is the maximum acceptable payback period on this plant? Justify your answer.

20. How can managers use accounting rate of return in capital-budgeting decisions?

21. How can accounting rate of return be computed when the annual amounts of operating income are expected to vary each period?

22. State why a positive net present value indicates an attractive investment project and a negative net present value indicates an unattractive project.

23. Which capital-budgeting strategy is best? (1) Pick out the best model and use it exclusively. (2) Use all three models. Support your answer.

24. A company is investing in a 20-year project. The managers, who use the net-present-value model for capital-budgeting decisions, expect the net cash inflow amounts to vary considerably each year. How can a computer help the managers decide the amount to invest in this project?

Exercises

Additional computer-related exercise: Exercise 28-10

Exercise 26-1 *Accept or reject a special sales order?* **(L.O. 1, 2)**

Expected increase in oper. inc. $18,000

Top-Flite Marketing approaches McDade Manufacturing Company with a special offer. Top-Flite wishes to purchase 100,000 monogrammed golf balls for a special promotional campaign. Top-Flite offers $.38 per ball—a total of $38,000. McDade's total manufacturing cost per ball is $.40, broken down as follows:

Variable costs:	
Direct material........	$.06
Direct labor	.03
Variable overhead	.11
Total variable cost	.20
Fixed overhead cost	.20
Total cost	$.40

Required

Prepare a quick summary to help determine whether McDade should accept the special sales order. Assume McDade has excess capacity.

Expected decrease in oper. inc.
$70,000

Exercise 26-2 *Retain or drop a product line (fixed costs unchanged)?* (L.O. 1, 2, 3)

Top managers of Merchants & Planters Supply Co. are alarmed that operating income is so low. They are considering dropping the building materials product line. Company accountants have prepared the following analysis to help make this decision:

	Total	Hardware	Building Materials
Sales	$460,000	$290,000	$170,000
Variable expenses	240,000	140,000	100,000
Contribution margin	220,000	150,000	70,000
Fixed expenses:			
Manufacturing	120,000	70,000	50,000
Selling and administrative	90,000	55,000	35,000
Total fixed expenses	210,000	125,000	85,000
Operating income (loss)	$ 10,000	$ 25,000	$(15,000)

Fixed costs will not change if the company stops selling building materials.

Required

Prepare a quick summary to show whether Merchants & Planters should drop the building materials product line. Explain the error of concluding that dropping building materials will add $15,000 to operating income.

Expected decrease in oper. inc.
$35,000

Exercise 26-3 *Retain or drop a product line (fixed costs change)?* (L.O. 1, 2)

Refer to the data of Exercise 26-2. Assume that Merchants & Planters can avoid $35,000 of fixed expenses by dropping the building materials product line. Prepare a quick summary to show whether Merchants & Planters should stop selling building materials.

Total CM at capacity:
  Designer $13,000
  Moderate $12,600

Exercise 26-4 *Which product to emphasize?* (L.O. 1, 2)

Impala Fashions sells both designer and moderately priced women's wear. Profits have fluctuated recently, and top management is deciding which product line to emphasize. Accountants provide the following relevant data:

	Designer	Moderately Priced
Per item:		
Average sale price	$100	$60
Average variable expenses	35	18
Average contribution margin	$ 65	$42
Average contribution margin ratio	65%	70%

The store, in Tulsa, Oklahoma, has 8,000 square feet of floor space. If moderately priced goods are emphasized, 300 items can be displayed in the store. Only 200 designer items could be displayed for sale.

Required

Prepare an analysis to show which product to emphasize.

Cost to make $5.66; to buy
$6.04

Exercise 26-5 *Make or buy?* (L.O. 1, 2, 3)

The production process of Danon Company uses an electronic control that has the following manufacturing cost per unit:

Direct material	$2.45
Direct labor	.55
Variable overhead	.62
Fixed overhead	2.04
Total manufacturing cost per unit	$5.66

Another company has offered to sell Danon the electronic control for $4.00 per unit. If Danon buys the controls from the outside supplier, the manufacturing facilities that will be idle cannot be used for any other purpose in the business. Should Danon make or buy the electronic controls? Show how you made this decision. Explain the difference between correct analysis and incorrect analysis of this decision.

Exercise 26-6   *Best use of facilities?*   **(L.O. 1, 2)**

Net cost to make $566,000
Buy $604,000
Buy and use idle facilities $562,000

Refer to Exercise 26-5. Assume that Danon needs 100,000 of the electronic controls. By purchasing them from the outside supplier, Danon could use its idle facilities to manufacture another product that can be sold for a $42,000 profit. Identify the *net* costs that Danon may incur to acquire 100,000 electronic controls under three alternative plans. Which alternative makes the best use of Danon's facilities? Support your answer with analysis.

Exercise 26-7   *Scrap inventory or process further?*   **(L.O. 1, 2, 4)**

Expected net revenue:
  Scrap $1,400
  Repair $1,600

Garcia Milling has damaged some custom cabinets, which cost the company $8,000 to manufacture. Luis Garcia, the owner, is considering two options for disposing of this inventory. One plan is to sell the cabinets as damaged inventory for $1,400. The alternative is to spend an additional $600 to repair the damage and expect to sell the cabinets for $2,200. How should Garcia dispose of this inventory? Support your decision with an analysis that shows expected net revenue under each alternative. Identify the opportunity cost of each alternative.

Exercise 26-8   *Payback analysis of an investment—equal cash flows*   **(L.O. 5)**

Payback 7.4 years

Gloff & Sons is considering acquiring a manufacturing plant. The purchase price is $700,000. The owners believe the plant will generate net cash inflows of $95,000 annually. It will have to be replaced in five years. Use the payback model to determine whether Gloff & Sons should purchase this plant.

Exercise 26-9   *Payback analysis of an investment—unequal cash flows*   **(L.O. 5)**

Payback 4.3 years

Seco Manufacturing is adding a new product line that will require an investment of $750,000. Managers estimate that this investment will generate net cash inflows of $110,000 the first year, $180,000 the second year, and $200,000 each year thereafter. What is the payback period for this investment? Compute a fraction of a year if necessary.

Exercise 26-10   *Accounting rate of return analysis of investments*   **(L.O. 4, 5)**

Rate of return:
  Ling 21.8%
  Johnson 18.8%

Braddock Textiles is shopping for new equipment. Managers are considering two investments. Equipment manufactured by Ling, Inc., costs $220,000 and will last for five years, with no residual value. The Ling equipment should generate annual operating income of $24,000. Equipment manufactured by Johnson Controls is priced at $310,000 and will remain useful for six years. It promises annual operating income of $32,000, and its expected residual value is $30,000.

Required

Which equipment offers the higher accounting rate of return? What is the opportunity cost of purchasing the Ling equipment? How would managers use the notion of opportunity cost in making their decision?

Max. acceptable price:
  A $505,675
  B $350,330

IRR: A 10%; B 16%

Expected increase in oper. inc.
$6,000

Expected decrease in oper. inc.
$211,000

Exercise 26-11   *Net-present-value analysis of investments*   **(L.O. 5)**

Use the net-present-value model to determine whether Tropical Products should invest in the following projects:

Project A costs $89,500 and offers 10 annual net cash inflows of $89,500. Tropical demands an annual return of 12 percent on investments of this nature.

Project B costs $330,000 and offers 7 annual net cash inflows of $81,700. Tropical requires an annual return of 14 percent on projects like B.

What is the maximum acceptable price to pay for each project?

Exercise 26-12   *Internal rate of return analysis of investments*   **(L.O. 5)**

Refer to the data of Exercise 26-12. Compute the internal rate of return of each project, and use this information to identify the better investment.

Problems   (Group A)

Additional computer-related problems: Problems 28-7A and 28-7B

Problem 26-1A   *Accept or reject a special sales order?*   **(L.O. 1)**

Casavas Toy Corporation manufactures toys in Torreón, Mexico. Casavas's contribution margin income statement for the most recent month contains the following:

Sales—units	630,000
Sales	$ 63,000
Variable expenses:	
Manufacturing	$ 12,600
Selling and administrative. . .	14,900
Total variable expenses	27,500
Contribution margin	35,500
Fixed expenses:	
Manufacturing	17,400
Selling and administrative. . .	11,300
Total fixed expenses	28,700
Income from operations.	$ 6,800

Pan American Promotions, Inc., wishes to buy 120,000 toys from Casavas. Acceptance of the offer will not increase selling and administrative expenses. Cavasas's fixed plant has unused capacity to manufacture the additional toys. Pan American has offered $.07 per toy, which is considerably below the normal sale price of $.10.

Required

1. Prepare a quick summary to help determine whether Casavas should accept this special sales order.
2. Prepare a total analysis to show Casavas's operating income with and without the special sales order.
3. Identify long-run factors that Casavas should consider in deciding whether to accept the special sales order.

Problem 26-2A   *Retain or drop a product line?*   **(L.O. 1, 2, 3)**

Members of the board of directors of Alarm Systems, Inc., have received the following income statement for the year just ended:

	Total	Industrial Products	Household Products
Sales	$866,000	$445,000	$421,000
Cost of goods sold:			
Variable	$119,000	$ 64,000	$ 55,000
Fixed	327,000	241,000	86,000
Total cost of goods sold	446,000	305,000	141,000
Gross margin	420,000	140,000	280,000
Selling and administrative expenses:			
Variable	178,000	86,000	92,000
Fixed	89,000	58,000	31,000
Total selling and administrative expenses	267,000	144,000	123,000
Operating income (loss)	$153,000	$ (4,000)	$157,000

Members of the board are shocked that the industrial products division is losing money. They commission a study to determine whether the company should delete the industrial products line. Company accountants estimate that dropping industrial products will decrease fixed cost of goods sold by $65,000 and decrease fixed selling and administrative expenses by $19,000.

Required

1. Prepare a quick summary to show whether Alarm Systems should drop the industrial products line.
2. Prepare a total analysis to show Alarm Systems' operating income with and without industrial products. Prepare the income statement in contribution-margin format.
3. Explain the difference between correct analysis and incorrect analysis of the decision whether to drop the industrial products line.

Problem 26-3A *Which product to emphasize?* **(L.O. 1, 2)**

Total CM at capacity:
Deluxe $672,000
Standard $720,000

Suntex Corp., located in Youngstown, Ohio, produces two lines of household appliances: deluxe and standard models. The owners are expanding the plant, and they are deciding which product line to emphasize. To make this decision, they assemble the following data, which suggest that the deluxe product line is more profitable:

	Deluxe	Standard
Per unit:		
Sale price	$40	$30
Variable expenses	12	10
Contribution margin	$28	$20
Contribution margin ratio	70%	66⅔%

After the plant expansion, the factory will have production capacity of 1,200 machine hours per month. By devoting the machine hours to deluxe appliances, the plant can manufacture 20 units of merchandise each hour. If standard appliances are emphasized, they can produce 30 units per hour.

Required

1. Identify the limiting factor for Suntex Corp.
2. Prepare an analysis to show which product to emphasize.

2. Expected net cost:
   Make $5,170
   Buy and leave idle $4,700
   Buy and make another
   product $3,790

Problem 26-4A *Make or buy/best use of facilities?* **(L.O. 1, 2)**

Glastron Company manufactures ski boats. Currently the company makes the seat covers. The cost of producing 1,000 seat covers each year is

Direct material........................	$1,100
Direct labor	1,100
Variable overhead......................	760
Fixed overhead	2,210
Total manufacturing cost per unit	$5,170

Xavier Corporation can make the seat covers for $3 each. Glastron would pay $.14 per unit to transport the seat covers to its manufacturing plant and add its own Glastron label at a cost of $.05 per seat cover.

Required

1. Glastron accountants estimate that purchasing the seat covers from Xavier will enable the company to avoid $700 of fixed overhead. Prepare an analysis to show whether Glastron should make or buy the seat covers.
2. Assume the Glastron factory space freed up by the company's purchasing the seat covers from Xavier can be used to manufacture another product that can be sold for a $1,610 profit. Fixed costs will not change. Prepare an analysis to show which alternative makes the best use of Glastron's factory space: (a) make, (b) buy and leave facilities idle, or (c) buy and make another product.

Problem 26-5A *Sell or process further?* **(L.O. 1, 2, 4)**

Expected net revenue:
   Sell as-is $278,880
   Process further $271,040

Propylene Corporation's manufacture of chemicals produces a wide variety of products. Assume that Propylene has spent $290,000 to refine 84,000 gallons of acetone, which can be sold for $3.32 a gallon. Alternatively, Propylene can process the acetone further and produce 77,000 gallons of lacquer thinner that can be sold for $4.80 a gallon. The additional processing will cost $.89 a gallon. To sell the lacquer thinner, Propylene must pay a transportation charge of $.23 a gallon and administrative expenses of $.16 a gallon.

Required

1. Identify the sunk cost in this situation. Is the sunk cost relevant to Propylene's decision?
2. Prepare an analysis to indicate whether Propylene should sell the acetone or process it into lacquer thinner. Show the expected net revenue difference between the two alternatives.
3. Identify the opportunity cost of each alternative. State how managers use the notion of opportunity cost in making their decision.

Problem 26-6A *Capital-budgeting decision by three models* **(L.O. 5)**

Payback 7.4 years
Rate of return 11.1%
Net PV ($472,200)

Auburn Investments, Inc., operates a resort near Geneva in the Finger Lakes region of New York. The company is considering an expansion. The architectural plan calls for a construction cost of $5,200,000. Top managers of Auburn believe the expansion will generate annual net cash inflows of $700,000 for 10 years. Architects and engineers estimate that the new facilities will remain useful for 10 years and have a residual value of $2,400,000. The stockholders of Auburn Investments demand an annual return of 12 percent on investments of this nature.

Required

1. Compute the payback period, the accounting rate of return, and the net present value of this investment.

2. Make a recommendation to Auburn management as to whether the company should invest in this project.

Problem 26-7A *Capital-budgeting decision by three methods* **(L.O. 5)**

Health Masters operates a chain of grocery stores that specialize in health foods. The company is considering two possible expansion plans. Plan A includes opening three stores at a cost of $4,800,000. This plan is expected to generate net cash inflows of $400,000 each year for 20 years, the estimated life of the store properties. Estimated residual value is $3,000,000. Under Plan B, Health Masters would open eight smaller stores at a cost of $7,200,000. Expected annual net cash inflows are $860,000, with zero residual value at the end of 19 years. Health Masters' top managers require an annual return of 8 percent.

Plan A:
  Payback 12 years
  Rate of return 7.9%
  Net PV ($227,800)
Plan B:
  Payback 8.4 years
  Rate of return 13.4%
  Net PV $1,059,440
  IRR 10%

Required

1. Compute the payback period, the accounting rate of return, and the net present value of these two investment plans.
2. Make a recommendation to Health Masters owners as to whether the company should invest in these projects.
3. Estimate Plan B's internal rate of return (IRR). How does the IRR compare with the company's hurdle rate?

(Group B)

Problem 26-1B *Accept or reject a special sales order?* **(L.O. 1, 2)**

Goodfellow Rubber Company's contribution margin income statement for the most recent month reports the following:

Expected increase in oper. inc. $5,500

Sales—units	38,000
Sales	$95,000
Variable expenses:	
Manufacturing	$19,000
Selling and administrative	27,000
Total variable expenses	46,000
Contribution margin	49,000
Fixed expenses:	
Manufacturing	29,000
Selling and administrative	8,000
Total fixed expenses	37,000
Income from operations	$12,000

American Marketing Associates wishes to buy 5,000 industrial belts from Goodfellow. Acceptance of the offer will not increase selling and administrative expenses. Goodfellow's fixed plant has unused capacity to manufacture the additional belts. American has offered $1.60 per belt, which is considerably below the normal sale price of $2.50.

Required

1. Prepare a quick summary to help determine whether Goodfellow should accept this special sales order.
2. Prepare a total analysis to show Goodfellow's operating income with and without the special sales order.
3. Identify long-run factors that Goodfellow should consider in deciding whether to accept the special sales order.

Expected decrease in oper. inc. $30,000

Problem 26-2B *Retain or drop a product line?* (L.O. 1, 2, 3)

The income statement of Vito's Pasta Company highlights the losses of the ravioli division:

	Total	All Other Products	Ravioli
Sales	$920,000	$630,000	$290,000
Cost of goods sold:			
Variable	$170,000	$100,000	$ 70,000
Fixed	140,000	90,000	50,000
Total cost of goods sold	310,000	190,000	120,000
Gross margin	610,000	440,000	170,000
Selling and administrative expenses:			
Variable	410,000	270,000	140,000
Fixed	150,000	80,000	70,000
Total selling and administrative expenses	560,000	350,000	210,000
Operating income (loss).............	$ 50,000	$ 90,000	$ (40,000)

Luigi Vito, owner of the company, is considering deleting the ravioli product line. Accountants for the company estimate that dropping ravioli will decrease fixed cost of goods sold by $30,000 and decrease fixed selling and administrative expenses by $20,000.

Required

1. Prepare a quick summary to show whether Vito's should drop the ravioli product line.
2. Prepare a total analysis to show Vito's operating income with and without the ravioli division. Prepare the income statement in contribution-margin format.
3. Explain the difference between correct analysis and incorrect analysis of the decision whether to drop the ravioli product line.

Total CM at capacity:
Washers/dryers $7,525
Televisions $5,888

Problem 26-3B *Which product to emphasize?* (L.O. 1, 2)

Copeland Appliances is located in Cody, Wyoming. The business specializes in washers/dryers and televisions. Jim and Mary Sue Copeland, the owners, are expanding the store, and they are deciding which product line to emphasize. To make this decision, they assemble the following data, which suggest that televisions, with the higher contribution margin ratio, are more profitable:

	Washers/Dryers	Televisions
Per unit:		
Sale price	$450	$320
Variable expenses	235	136
Contribution margin	$215	$184
Contribution margin ratio ...	47.8%	57.5%

After the renovation, the store will have 6,400 square feet of floor space. By devoting the new floor space to washers/dryers, the Copelands can display 35 units of merchandise in the store. If televisions are emphasized, they can display only 32 units.

Required

1. Identify the limiting factor for Copeland Appliances.

2. Prepare an analysis to show which product to emphasize. Round contribution margin per square foot to five decimal places.

Problem 26-4B *Make or buy/best use of facilities? (L.O. 1, 2)*

Recreation Corp. of America manufactures snowmobiles. Currently the company makes the seats. The cost of producing 2,000 seats each year is

Direct material.............	$ 3,900
Direct labor	2,800
Variable overhead	1,040
Fixed overhead	5,110
Total manufacturing costs ...	$12,850

Toledo, Inc., can make the seats for $5 each. Recreation would pay $.22 per unit to transport the seats to its manufacturing plant and add its own Recreation insignia at a cost of $.06 per unit.

Required

1. Recreation accountants estimate that purchasing the seats from Toledo will enable the company to avoid $1,800 of fixed overhead. Prepare an analysis to show whether Recreation should make or buy the seats.
2. Assume the Recreation factory space freed up by the company's purchasing the seats from Toledo can be used to manufacture another product that can be sold for a $3,700 profit. Fixed costs will not change. Prepare an analysis to show which alternative makes the best use of Recreation's factory space: (a) make, (b) buy and leave facilities idle, or (c) buy and make another product.

2. Expected net cost:
   Make $12,850
   Buy and leave idle $13,870
   Buy and make another
   product $11,970

Problem 26-5B *Sell or process further? (L.O. 1, 2, 4)*

The refining of crude oil by Phillips Petroleum Company produces a variety of petroleum products. Assume that Phillips has spent $300,000 to refine 60,000 gallons of petroleum distillate. Suppose Phillips can sell the distillate for $5.75 a gallon. Alternatively, Phillips can process the distillate further and produce cleaner for tape heads in cassette decks. The additional processing will cost another $1.33 a gallon. The tape-head cleaner can be sold for $7.50 a gallon. To make this sale, Phillips must pay a sale commission of $.10 a gallon and a transportation charge of $.15 a gallon.

Required

1. Identify the sunk cost in this situation. Is the sunk cost relevant to Phillips's decision?
2. Prepare an analysis to indicate whether Phillips should sell the distillate or process it into tape-head cleaner for cassette decks. Show the expected net revenue difference between the two alternatives.
3. Identify the opportunity cost of each option. State how to use opportunity cost to make this decision.

Expected net revenue:
   Sell as-is $345,000
   Process further $355,200

Problem 26-6B *Capital-budgeting decision by three models (L.O. 5)*

Mesa View Developers, west of Austin in the hill country of Texas, is considering an investment. The architectural plan calls for a purchase price of $1,850,000. Top managers of Mesa View believe the new facility will generate annual net cash inflows of $385,000 for eight years. Architects and engineers estimate that the facility will remain useful for eight years and have a residual value of $600,000. The stockholders of Mesa View demand an annual return of 16 percent on investments of this nature.

Payback 4.8 years
Rate of return 18.7%
Net PV $5,440

Required

1. Compute the payback period, the accounting rate of return, and the net present value of this investment.
2. Make a recommendation to Mesa View management as to whether the company should invest in this project.

Plan A:
  Payback 4.0 years
  Rate of return 21.0%
  Net PV $129,760
  IRR 16%
Plan B:
  Payback 4.6 years
  Rate of return 16.7%
  Net PV ($19,200)

Problem 26-7B *Capital-budgeting decision by three methods* *(L.O. 5)*

T. J. Cinnamon, Inc., features the original gourmet cinnamon roll. The company is considering two possible expansion plans. Plan A includes opening six stores at a cost of $2,100,000. This investment is expected to generate net cash inflows of $520,000 each year for seven years, which is the estimated life of the store properties. Because of the location, estimated residual value is zero. Under Plan B, Cinnamon would open four stores at a cost of $1,600,000. Expected annual net cash inflows are $350,000, with residual value of $200,000 at the end of seven years, the estimated useful life of these stores. Cinnamon's top managers require an annual return of 14 percent.

Required

1. Compute the payback period, the accounting rate of return, and the net present value of these two investment plans.
2. Make a recommendation to T. J. Cinnamon management as to whether the company should invest in these projects.
3. Estimate the internal rate of return (IRR) of Plan A. How does Plan A's IRR compare with the hurdle rate?

Extending Your Knowledge

Decision Problems

Project 1:
  Payback 3.6 years
  Rate of return 15.9%
  Net PV $8,725
Project 2:
  Payback 2.9 years
  Rate of return 22.9%
  Net PV $21,278

1. Selecting Between Two Investment Projects *(L.O. 5)*

The capital-budgeting committee of Lancer, Inc., is evaluating two real estate investment projects. Project 1 is a shopping center in Nashville, and Project 2 is a parking garage in Memphis. Estimated data for the two projects follow.

	Project 1			Project 2		
Year	Net Cash Inflow	Operating Income	Residual Value	Net Cash Inflow	Operating Income	Residual Value
1	$181,000	$ 80,000		$87,000	$32,000	
2	202,000	101,000		87,000	32,000	
3	234,000	133,000		87,000	32,000	
4	141,000	40,000		87,000	32,000	$30,000
5	116,000	15,000				
6	110,000	9,000	$94,000			

Project 1 requires an investment of $700,000, and Project 2 costs $250,000. Lancer managers demand a 14 percent annual return on real estate investments.

Required

1. Compute the payback period, the accounting rate of return, and the net present value of the two investment projects.
2. Which capital-budgeting model is best? Give your reason.
3. Lancer will invest in only one of these projects. Based on your analysis, make an investment recommendation to Lancer managers.

2. *Decision-Making Involving Relevant, Opportunity and Sunk Costs (L.O. 1, 4)*

Sam Webb is a second-year business student at the University of Cincinnati. He will graduate in two years with an accounting major and a marketing minor. It is now April, and Sam is trying to decide where to work this summer. He has two choices: work full-time for a bottling plant, or work part-time in the accounting department of a meat-packing plant.

If Sam works part-time, he can take two courses toward his degree for no extra tuition. This will reduce his workload next year. It might also allow him to work part-time during the regular term in the bottling plant. In addition, the extra accounting credits this summer will qualify Sam for a full-time position with the meat-packing company next summer.

The meat-packing company and the university are close enough to Sam's home that he could ride his bike. However, if he works at the bottling plant he must drive. Sam's car is a 1975 Dodge Swinger that he bought two years ago for $2,000; he is not sure how much longer the car will run.

Sam is able to work 12 weeks during the summer. This year the bottling plant is paying $300 per week; average annual increases have been 6 percent. At the meat-packing plant, Sam could work 20 hours per week at $6.90 per hour. Sam thinks he could work at the bottling plant again next summer. In a full-time position at the meat-packing company, he would earn $500 per week next summer.

2. PV of present and future earnings:
   Bottling plant $7,069
   Meat-packing plant $7,110

Required

Advise Sam on the better course of action. Assume that the interest rate is 10 percent, and for convenience, assume Sam will receive each summer's earnings in a single amount at the end of the summer. Identify opportunity costs and sunk costs that enter your decision process. Also identify any assumptions that you make.

Ethical Issue

Missoula Construction Company, a corporation, builds highways for the state of Montana. Mike Duggins, company president, needs earth-moving equipment and is deciding among three vehicles. Vehicles 1 and 2 represent investments of equal risk, and their cash flows are both discounted at 14 percent. Vehicle 1 has a net present value of $12,500. Vehicle 2 has a net present value of −$6,000. Vehicle 3 is experimental, so its risk is higher than that of the other machines. Missoula's vice-presidents advise Duggins to apply a 16 percent interest rate to discounting cash flows for vehicle 3. At 16 percent, vehicle 3 has a net present value of −$22,000. However, a close friend owns the company marketing this machine, and Duggins wants him to get the business. When Duggins discounts vehicle 3's cash flows at 14 percent, that vehicle's net present value increases to $21,000.

Required

1. Which vehicle should Missoula purchase? Give your reason.
2. What is your opinion of Duggins's ethics if he buys vehicle 3? Who is helped and who is harmed by this action? How would your answer change if Missoula Construction Company were a proprietorship instead of a corporation?

Chapter 27

Income Taxes and Their Effects on Business Decisions

I t is December 30. George and Marla DeFord are planning their year-end giving to charities. After meeting pledges to their church, the United Way, and a local agency for children, they have $1,900 left over that they would like to donate.

"Let's give $900 to Montclair State, where we both graduated, and keep the rest," said George.

"Sounds good to me," Marla replied. "We can use a new sofa for the family room."

"On second thought, George said, "in our tax bracket, a $1,000 contribution costs us only $720 because it saves us $280 in taxes. Besides, Marla, business has been unusually good this year. We can give this money to charity and still get the sofa."

Marla agreed, "There are plenty of people who need the money more than we do. Let's give the $1,000 to charity." The DeFords sent the $1,000 to the United Way and started planning their tax strategy for the coming year.

Taxes are important to everyone. National tax policy affects business decisions, voting patterns, the rate of inflation, pollution control, and many other aspects of daily life. Most federal programs—social welfare, national defense, education, and the courts—are financed in some way by our tax dollars.

There are many kinds of taxes. For example, *property taxes* are levied on land, buildings, and other property. We pay retail *sales taxes* on most goods and many services. *Excise taxes* apply to a wide variety of items, including gasoline, beer, tires, fishing equipment, and air travel. Some taxes are levied by the federal government, others by states, cities, and counties. Some taxes are directed toward a special purpose. For example, property taxes may finance public education, and taxes on tires, trucks, trailers, and gasoline help support highway maintenance. Other taxes, like sales taxes, are more general purpose in nature. They are used to finance a host of state and city government functions.

The **income tax,** which is the subject of this chapter, is a general-purpose tax levied on the income of the taxpayer. Entirely separate from all other taxes, it is the federal government's largest source of revenue.

Accounting enters the tax picture by helping to determine the amount of income to be taxed. Many differences exist between *accounting income,* which we have discussed throughout this book, and *taxable income,* which is used to compute income tax. However, the starting points in determining accounting income and taxable income are similar, and many accountants specialize in income taxation. These specialists help taxpayers compute their income taxes and plan their activities so as to minimize their tax burden. In a landmark case, Judge Learned Hand wrote that "nobody owes any public duty to pay more [taxes] than the law demands." An understanding of income taxes, therefore, is an important part of financial planning.

This chapter discusses income taxes from the perspective of the taxpayer—people like you, your family and friends, the local automobile dealer, and corporations like Coca-Cola Company and IBM. Our discussion is a practical introduction to some of the steps in computing the amount of income tax that individuals and corporations pay to the government. This chapter provides a foundation for any future tax courses you may take.

History and Operation of the Income Tax

The federal government first used an income tax for a brief period during the Civil War. Our present income tax system began in 1913 with ratification of the Sixteenth Amendment to the United States Constitution. That amendment removed the requirement that a national income tax be based on state population. It opened the door for the federal government to base a tax on the

Real-World Example: Refer to the chapter-opening vignette. If George and Marla have some stock investments that have appreciated in value, they could also give the stock to Montclair State and receive a charitable contribution deduction for the appreciated value. If George and Marla sold the stock first and gave the proceeds from the sale to Montclair State College, they would have to pay taxes on the gain. Tax planning can save George and Marla money.

Discussion Question: Is taxable income the same as accounting income? ANSWER: No. The goal of accounting income is to report a reliable measure of income to investors and creditors. The purpose of calculating taxable income is to determine the correct amount of tax that the government is entitled to collect. Hence, the government allows certain tax methods that are not acceptable for financial accounting (reporting rent as revenue when received rather than when earned) and financial accounting allows certain methods that are not acceptable for tax purposes (amortizing goodwill).

Point to Stress: Virtually every business transaction is affected by taxation. Business transactions must be properly planned so as to minimize taxes. The time to think about tax consequences is when the business transaction occurs, not when the taxes are due. By obtaining the advice of a tax professional, a business may be able to save thousands of dollars a year in taxes.

personal income of individual citizens. Initially the purpose of the income tax was simply to raise money for national defense and the operation of government. Over the years, the goals of our tax system have broadened to include stimulating economic growth, curtailing inflation, and providing for the health and welfare of the aged and the disadvantaged.

From time to time, Congress passes new tax laws known as *revenue acts*. As these revenue acts and the related interpretations accumulate, they are summarized periodically in tax documents called *internal revenue codes*. Internal revenue codes were published in 1939, 1954, and 1986. Today we operate under the Internal Revenue Code of 1986.

Administration of the federal tax system is the responsibility of the Internal Revenue Service (IRS), a division of the Treasury Department of the United States government. Congress passes tax laws, and the Treasury Department publishes its interpretations of the tax law, called Treasury Regulations, and administers the tax system. The federal courts make final decisions on disputes between taxpayers and the government. (Interestingly, it is often easier to prosecute criminals for breaking income tax laws than for committing other offenses.)

In its most basic form, the amount of income tax is computed by multiplying taxable income by the tax rate. For example, a tax rate of 15 percent applied to taxable income of $20,000 results in income tax of $3,000. Income tax rates have varied over the years. Initially rates were quite low. The Underwood Act in 1913 set tax rates between 1 percent and 7 percent. A person with taxable income of $15,000 paid income tax of 1 percent, or $150. Today, a taxpayer with this same amount of taxable income pays income tax of 15 percent, or $2,250. Taxpayers with higher incomes pay income tax at a higher rate. For example, the DeFords in the chapter-opening vignette are in the 28-percent tax bracket, as shown by the fact that a $1,000 tax deduction saves them $280 in taxes.

Generally, tax rates climb during wartime to help finance the war effort. Peace usually brings lower rates, although tax rates fluctuate. Some taxpayers want more government programs, which cause higher taxes. Others want lower taxes, which would mean cutting back government programs. The final result is the combination of government programs and income tax policy that reflects the will of the people. Exhibit 27-1 shows a sampling of income tax rates that have been in effect in the United States since 1913.

Most states and some cities have an income tax that is patterned in some way after the federal income tax. In this chapter, we focus on the *federal* income tax.

EXHIBIT 27-1 Minimum and Maximum Income Tax Rates for Individual Taxpayers

	Tax Rates	
	Minimum	Maximum
1913 tax law	1%	7%
During World War II	23	94
During most of the 1970s	14	70
Prior to 1986 tax law	11	50
1986 tax law	15	31

Classes and Filing Status of Taxpayers

Tax law identifies four major classes of taxpayers: individuals, corporations, estates, and trusts. In this chapter, we focus on the taxation of individuals and corporations.

Each taxpayer reports income and shows the computation of income tax on a document called a **tax return.** Submitting the completed document to the IRS is called *filing a tax return.* An individual must file his or her tax return within three and one-half months after the end of the tax year. A person who uses the calendar year (as most do) must file a 1993 income tax return by April 15, 1994. Corporations have only two and one-half months after the year's end to file their tax returns. A corporation with a fiscal year ending June 30, 1993, must file its 1993 tax return by September 15 of that year.

An individual taxpayer must use a particular *filing status.* This status determines the tax rates used to compute the amount of income tax. There are four filing statuses for individuals.

Taxpayer(s)	Filing Status
Single individual	Single or Head of household
Married couple	Joint or Separate for each spouse

Dependents are persons who receive more than half their support from another individual—in our discussion, from the taxpayer. Taxpayers who file joint returns pay at the lowest income tax rates, with increasing rates applying to head of household, single, and separate returns, in that order.

A business organized as a proprietorship pays no business income tax. Business income is taxed directly to the proprietor. A partnership is taxed the same way. The business itself incurs no income tax, but each partner includes in personal taxable income his or her share of partnership income. Even though the partnership pays no income tax, it must file a tax return with the IRS to list the income of the business and of each partner. This *information tax return* permits the IRS to trace the income of the partnership to the tax returns of the individual partners. In addition to earnings from their business, proprietors and partners must pay tax on their other income, such as interest, dividends, and gains on the sale of investments.

In the eyes of income tax law, a corporation is a separate taxable entity. Corporations pay tax on their income directly to the IRS regardless of whether they distribute any dividends to their stockholders. If the corporation does pay dividends to its owners (the stockholders), the stockholders then pay individual income tax on this dividend income. Many people believe this "double taxation" of corporation income is unfair.

Income Taxation of Individuals

In general, citizens of the United States must pay tax on all income from all sources. Tax laws permit certain *exclusions, deductions,* and *exemptions* to be subtracted from total income in arriving at taxable income. Multiplying the amount of **taxable income** by the appropriate tax rate yields the amount of

Real-World Example: Have you ever heard someone say that he is filing his tax return on August 15 or October 15, rather than on April 15 as the law states? That is because the IRS allows an automatic 4-month extension to individuals (who must file a request for the extension). In some cases, the IRS may also allow a second, 2-month extension for filing. Keep in mind that the extension applies only to filing the return and *not* to paying any tax due.

Point to Stress: While there are four different filing statuses for individuals, there are no such choices for a corporation or a partnership.

Teaching Tip: The proprietorship itself does not file a tax return. The net income of the business is included on the personal tax return of the proprietor, and he is responsible for paying tax on the business income. A corporation, on the other hand, must file a return and pay the tax due on the corporate taxable income.

Teaching Tip: Recall our discussion in Chapter 14 of the advantages and disadvantages of corporations. Double taxation is one of the major disadvantages of this form of organization.

income tax for the year. *Tax credits* are then subtracted, and the final result is the amount of income tax liability for the year. Exhibit 27-2 shows how to compute the income tax liability for an individual. Taxable income, Step 8 in Exhibit 27-2, is the focal point in our discussions.

Total Income, Exclusions, and Gross Income—Steps 1, 2, and 3

In income taxation, **total income** is all income from whatever source derived. Salary or wage income is the most common taxable income. A business proprietor includes in total income the net income of the business (net sales less cost of goods sold and less all business expenses—salaries and wages for employees, rent, insurance, depreciation, interest, repairs, property taxes, supplies expense, and so on). Gains on the sale of business assets like buildings and delivery vehicles are included as income, and losses are deductible in arriving at total income.

Also part of total income are interest earned on a savings account whether or not the interest is withdrawn, dividend revenue from a stock investment, and a gain on the sale of an investment. Net rent income (income minus expenses) on rental property, royalties earned on minerals, commissions, bonuses, tips, and gains on the sale of assets are also included in total income. Even gambling profits and income from illegal sources appear in the tax code as taxable income.

From total income we subtract *exclusions,* which are types of income that the tax law specifically identifies as nontaxable. Common exclusions are interest revenue on tax-exempt state and municipal bonds, certain scholarships received, gifts and inheritances, life insurance benefits, and some Social Security benefits. Subtracting exclusions from total income gives us **gross income,** which is all income minus specific exclusions.

Adjustments to Arrive at Adjusted Gross Income—Step 4

The adjustments in Step 4 are deductions of a wide variety. Payments into a personal retirement plan, alimony payments, and penalty on early withdrawal of savings fall into this category. The total of these adjustments is subtracted from gross income.

Adjusted Gross Income—Step 5

Gross income minus the adjustments (deductions) described in the preceding section equals an amount that exists only in the tax law—**adjusted gross income.** Often abbreviated in the business press as AGI, this amount is important in taxation because several expenses are deductible only if they exceed a certain percentage of adjusted gross income, as we discuss in the next section.

Itemized Deductions and the Standard Deduction—Step 6

An individual can take a tax deduction for the greater of two amounts: the total of itemized deductions or the standard deduction. **Itemized deductions** make up a particular category that includes the following six types of expenditures:

EXHIBIT 27-2 *An Individual's Income Tax Computation*

Transparency T27-1

An Individual's Income Tax Computation

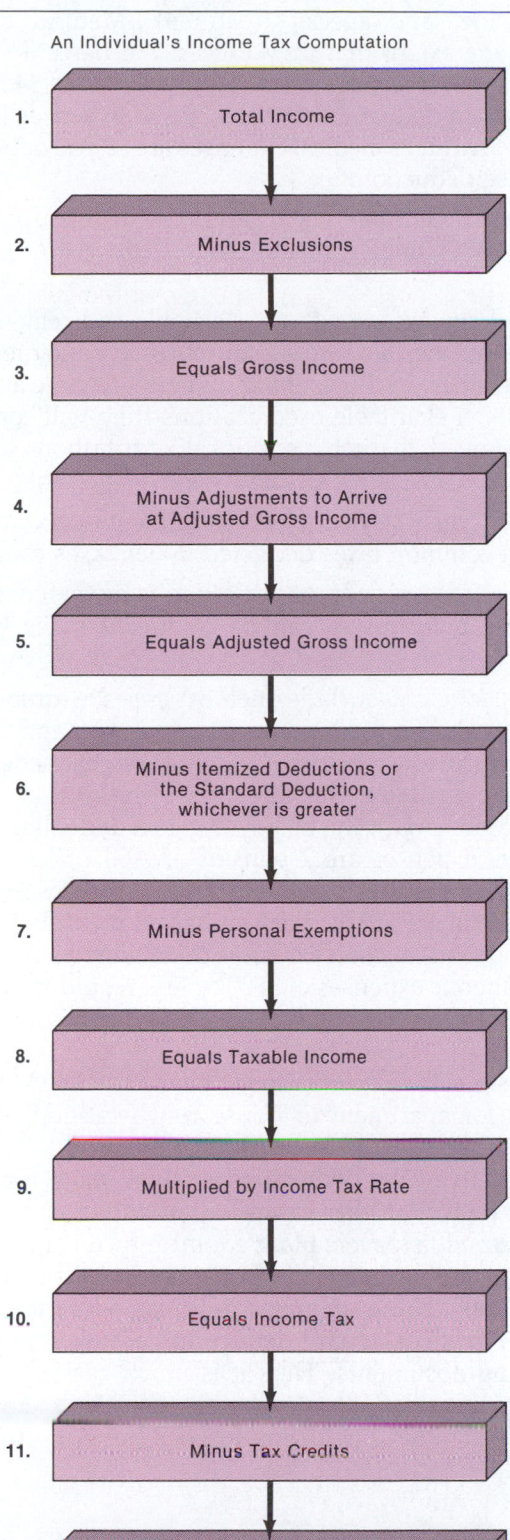

1. Total Income
2. Minus Exclusions
3. Equals Gross Income
4. Minus Adjustments to Arrive at Adjusted Gross Income
5. Equals Adjusted Gross Income
6. Minus Itemized Deductions or the Standard Deduction, whichever is greater
7. Minus Personal Exemptions
8. Equals Taxable Income
9. Multiplied by Income Tax Rate
10. Equals Income Tax
11. Minus Tax Credits
12. Equals Income Tax Liability for the Year

1. *Medical expenses* include doctor fees, hospital expenses, and the cost of eyeglasses, medicine, and special treatment. Medical expenses can be deducted only to the extent that they exceed 7½ percent (.075) of adjusted gross income. A taxpayer with adjusted gross income of $40,000 and medical expenses of $3,300 can deduct only $300 of these expenses [$3,300 − (.075 × $40,000)]. If this individual's medical expenses are $3,000 or less, he or she gets no medical expense deduction.

2. *Interest expense* on a home mortgage is deductible up to a maximum of interest incurred on $1 million of mortgage debt. All other interest is not deductible.

3. *Charitable contributions* are gifts to charitable and religious organizations such as United Way, the Red Cross, churches, synagogues, hospitals, and colleges and universities. In the opening vignette, George and Marla De Ford are deciding to which charitable organizations they will contribute. The IRS keeps a list of approved charitable entities. Contributions to these organizations are deductible. Gifts to friends and relatives are not.

4. *Some taxes paid* may be deducted. State income tax and local property taxes are the most common taxes deducted. Sales taxes cannot be deducted.

5. *Casualty losses* are losses of property, such as by theft or by storm damage to one's home. Casualty losses can be deducted subject to certain limitations.

6. *Miscellaneous deductions* include such expenses as union dues, subscriptions to professional journals, investment expenses, and fees paid for the preparation of an income tax return. To get a miscellaneous deduction, the taxpayer totals the expenses in this category. If the total exceeds 2 percent of adjusted gross income (AGI), the taxpayer gets a deduction for the excess. If total miscellaneous expenses are 2 percent of AGI or less, no deduction is permitted. Suppose a taxpayer's adjusted gross income is $40,000 and miscellaneous expenses total $875. This person lists all miscellaneous expenses on the tax return and gets a miscellaneous deduction of $75 [$875 − (.02 × $40,000)]. Miscellaneous expenses of $800 or less would not appear on the tax return at all because their total does not exceed 2 percent of AGI.

Notice that personal living costs are *not* tax deductible. The cost of a home and expenditures for apartment or house rent, clothing, furniture, and an automobile may not be claimed as tax deductions.

An alternative to itemizing deductions is taking the **standard deduction,** a set amount of tax deduction that varies depending on the individual's filing status. In 1991 married taxpayers filing a joint return could deduct $5,700 for the standard deduction. A head of a household could deduct $5,000 and a single taxpayer, $3,400. These amounts are adjusted for the effects of inflation. Many taxpayers favor the standard deduction because it requires no receipts or other supporting documents. Thus it is much easier than itemizing. An individual who itemizes cannot take the standard deduction, and likewise, one who elects the standard deduction forgoes the opportunity to itemize.

Personal Exemptions—Step 7

Another type of income tax deduction is called a **personal exemption.** This deduction is a set amount allowed for the taxpayer, the taxpayer's spouse, and each person who qualifies as a dependent. Some examples of personal exemptions follow:

Taxpayer(s)	Number of Exemptions
Single person	1
Single person qualifying as a head of household that includes:	
1 parent as a dependent	2
2 children	3
Married couple, filing jointly:	
0 children	2
2 children	4
Married couple, filing separately, 2 children (decide which spouse claims exemptions for children):	
Total exemptions for two tax returns	4

The amount of the personal exemption was $2,150 in 1991. Each year the amount is adjusted for inflation. Taxpayers with high levels of income do not get the full benefit of the personal exemptions. However, for illustrative purposes and in all exercises and problems, we assume a personal exemption of $2,000.

Taxable Income—Step 8

Taxable income is the earnings amount on which the income tax is based. It is the figure that is multiplied by the tax rate to compute the amount of income tax.

A special category of gains and losses—defined in the tax law—enters the determination of taxable income. These items, called **capital gains and losses,** result from the disposal of property that the tax law labels as capital assets. Common examples include investments in stocks, bonds, real estate, and personal assets such as homes, automobiles, and jewelry. A capital gain results from selling the asset for a price that exceeds its tax basis. A capital loss occurs if the sale price is less than the asset's tax basis. The *tax basis* of an asset is generally its cost (reduced by accumulated depreciation if any).

Capital gains and losses receive special treatment in a tax computation. The individual first separates capital gains and losses from other types of income, then combines capital gains and losses to calculate a net capital gain or a net capital loss for the year. A net capital gain is fully taxable. However, only $3,000 of net capital losses can be deducted in any one year. Any excess may be carried forward to reduce taxes in future years.

Let's consider an example of the tax treatment of capital gains and losses. Suppose a married taxpayer has performed a partial tax computation for 19X1 and has determined that taxable income from other sources is $42,000. This taxpayer also has a capital gain of $4,000 on the sale of a stock investment and a capital loss of $9,000 on the sale of land. This person's taxable income for 19X1 is $39,000, computed as follows:

Taxable income from other sources		$42,000
Net capital loss:		
Capital loss	$9,000	
Capital gain	4,000	
Net capital loss	$5,000	
Maximum net capital loss deductible in one year		(3,000)
Taxable income		$39,000

In the determination of 19X2 taxable income, this person can deduct the net capital loss of $2,000 remaining from 19X1 ($5,000 less the $3,000 deducted in 19X1).

Point to Stress: Any taxpayer who is blind or age 65 or older may use a higher standard deduction.

Real-World Example: In 1990, taxpayers were allowed personal exemptions of $2,050 for themselves, their spouses, and any dependents. This exemption is adjusted for inflation each subsequent year.

Point to Stress: Five requirements must be met in order to claim a person as a dependent:
1 Support (over 50%)
2 Relationship
3 No joint return by dependent
4 Citizenship
5 Gross income (less than $2,150 unless dependent is either under age 19 or a full-time student)

Real-World Example: Before the 1986 Tax Reform Act, it was possible for parents to claim a child under the age of 19 or a full-time student, as a dependent *and* for the child to claim himself as an exemption in the same year. Now, however, this double-counting has been disallowed.

Real-World Example: The tax treatment of capital gains and losses is another area that has undergone various modifications by Congress since it became a separate taxing category in 1922. In 1978, Congress enacted a 60% capital gains deduction that allowed individuals to exclude from taxable income 60% of the excess of capital gains over capital losses. Under the 1986 Tax Reform Act, that tax break has been withdrawn and all net capital gains are taxed at the same rate as other taxable income.

The tax definition of a capital asset is different from the accounting definition. Tax courses cover capital assets and capital gains and losses in more detail. For example, buildings, equipment, furniture, and other depreciable assets that are used in a business are *not* capital assets under the tax law. A loss on disposal of such *business* assets is fully deductible in the determination of taxable income. The $3,000 limit does not apply.

Income Tax Rates and the Amount of Income Tax— Steps 9 and 10

Point to Stress: The maximum tax rate is also referred to as the marginal tax rate. It is the rate on the last dollar of taxable income.

Exhibit 27-3 shows the tax rates that are used to compute an individual's income tax.

Exhibit 27-3 shows that various tax rates apply to various levels of taxable income. Higher rates apply when income reaches specific higher levels. This is called a progressive income tax system. For example, a single (unmarried) person with taxable income of $16,000 is taxed at 15 percent. A single individual with income of $28,000 is taxed at 15 percent of the first $20,350 of income ($3,053) plus 28 percent of income in excess of $20,350.

A person's maximum tax rate is important for tax planning because it indicates how much of each additional dollar of income must be paid in taxes.

Class Exercise: Calculate the tax for Frank Smith, a single taxpayer, who earned $96,500 in wages and $8,100 in interest, and does not itemize his deductions. He claims one personal exemption for himself.

ANSWER: First calculate adjusted gross income:

Wages	$ 96,500
Interest	8,100
AGI	$104,600

Next, calculate taxable income:

AGI	$104,600
− Standard deduction	−3,400
− Personal exemption	−2,000
TI	$ 99,200

Finally, calculate tax amount: $11,159 + [($99,200 − $49,300) × .31] = $26,628

Note: Assuming there are no tax credits, Smith's tax liability for the year is $26,628.

Consider two single taxpayers. The person in the 15 percent bracket pays fifteen cents of every taxable dollar earned. The person in the 28 percent bracket pays nearly double that amount, twenty-eight cents of every additional dollar earned. Each additional dollar earned up to $49,300 is thirteen cents less valuable—and less attractive—to the person in the 28 percent bracket, and so the incentive to earn additional income is less. Each dollar of a single person's income above $49,300 is taxed at 31 percent.

Let's work through examples to illustrate a simple and a complex tax computation. Suppose Ron and Sarah Marks have a daughter, Carmen, and they file a joint tax return. Exhibit 27-4 shows their 1991 tax computation for two levels of taxable income: $44,000 and $100,000. The tax rates come from Exhibit 27-3.

EXHIBIT 27-3 *Individual Income Tax Rates*

Single Taxpayer

If taxable income is	The tax is
Not over $20,350	15% of taxable income
Over $20,350 but not over $49,300	$3,053 + 28% of the excess over $20,350
Over $49,300	$11,159 + 31% of the excess over $49,300

Married Taxpayers Filing Jointly

If taxable income is	The tax is
Not over $34,000	15% of taxable income
Over $34,000 but not over $82,150	$5,100 + 28% of the excess over $34,000
Over $82,150	$18,582 + 31% of the excess over $82,150

EXHIBIT 27-4   *1991 Income Tax Computation for Ron and Sarah Marks*
—Married Filing Jointly with Three Exemptions,
Including Daughter Carmen

Taxable Income of $44,000:	Income Tax
$5,100 + .28($44,000 − $34,000)	$ 7,900
Taxable Income of $100,000:	
$18,582 + .31($100,000 − $82,150)	$24,116

Tax Credits—Step 11

Tax credits are often confused with tax deductions. The two are very different. Tax deductions are subtracted from adjusted gross income and so decrease the taxable income amount in Step 8. By contrast, tax credits enter the tax computation after the amount of income tax has been computed. A **tax credit** is subtracted directly from the amount of tax owed to the government. Thus a tax credit is worth more to a taxpayer because it leads to a larger decrease in the amount of tax owed. For example, a $1,000 tax *deduction* decreases income tax by $280 ($1,000 × .28) for a taxpayer subject to the 28 percent rate. A $1,000 tax *credit* decreases the amount of tax by the full $1,000 because the entire amount is subtracted. Two prominent tax credits are the *earned income credit*, which applies to low-income taxpayers, and the *credit for child-care expenses*, which applies to parents who work outside the home and must pay for child care.

Point to Stress: A tax credit is a dollar-for-dollar reduction in the actual tax due. It is a direct reduction of the tax liability.

Real-World Example: Here is a list of some common tax credits:
1 Credit for child and dependent care expenses.
2 Credit for the elderly or the disabled.
3 Earned income credit (for a taxpayer who has AGI of less than $20,645 and one or more dependents).

Income Tax Liability—Step 12

The process described in the preceding paragraphs concludes with determination of the individual's income tax liability for the year. In this setting, *income tax liability* refers to the total amount of tax the person owes for the entire year. The taxpayer does not write a single check to pay this amount at the end of the year. Taxes are paid during the year, as described in the next section.

Paying Income Tax Through Withholding and Quarterly Payments

Persons who earn salaries or wages and who are not self-employed pay taxes through payroll deductions withheld from each paycheck. The employer remits the withheld taxes to the IRS on behalf of the employees. Individuals who are self-employed or who have outside income make quarterly tax payments directly to the IRS. All taxpayers must settle with the IRS when they file their annual tax returns. If the income tax listed on the tax return exceeds the total payments during the year, the individual must pay the difference when filing the tax return. If the amount of income tax on the tax return is less than the total payments, the taxpayer claims a refund and receives a check from the government.

Point to Stress: Refer to the calculation of taxes due by Frank Smith in the preceding Class Exercise. When he files his personal tax return on April 15, does he have to send a check for $26,628 to the IRS? No. Our "pay-as-you-go" system, as established by Congress, requires that Smith's employer withhold from each paycheck and pay to the IRS an estimated portion of the $26,628 tax due for that year.

Summary Problem for Your Review

Chip Reed is a financial consultant in Austin, Texas. He and his wife, Linda, have a son, Paul, and a daughter, Jennifer. During 1991 Chip's business earned gross income of $257,000 and had expenses of $62,000. Chip paid $7,600 into his retirement program. Linda worked part-time as an interior decorator and received a salary of $19,000. She also received $5,000 as an inheritance from an uncle. The Reeds' investments earned interest of $6,000 and dividends of $1,600. They sold a stock investment at a gain of $4,400 and land at a loss of $8,000. Their charitable contributions for the year totaled $2,700, interest expense on their home mortgage was $13,100, and they paid property taxes of $2,400. During the year Chip made quarterly income tax payments totaling $48,200, and $3,600 was withheld from Linda's paychecks. The Reeds file a joint income tax return.

Required

Compute the Reeds' taxable income and income tax liability for the year. Show how much they must pay or will receive after filing their 1991 income tax return.

SOLUTION TO REVIEW PROBLEM

Transparency T27-2

Chip and Linda Reed
Income Tax Computation
1991

Gross income (excluding inheritance):		
Chip's business gross income	$257,000	
Less: Business expenses	62,000	
Net business income		$195,000
Linda's salary income		19,000
Interest		6,000
Dividends		1,600
Capital gains and losses:		
Capital loss	$ 8,000	
Capital gain	4,400	
Net capital loss	3,600	
Maximum net capital loss deductible in one year .		(3,000)
Gross income		218,600
Deductions to arrive at adjusted gross income:		
Payment into Chip's retirement program		7,600
Adjusted gross income		211,000
Itemized deductions or standard deduction ($5,700),		
whichever is greater—itemized deductions		
($18,200) in this case:		
Mortgage interest	$ 13,100	
Charitable contributions	2,700	
Property tax	2,400	
Total itemized deductions	18,200	
Personal exemptions (4 × $2,000)	8,000	26,200
Taxable income		**$184,800**
Tax computation:		
$18,582 + .31($184,800 − $82,150)		$ 50,404
Income tax liability for the year		**50,404**
Less tax payments:		
Chip's quarterly payments	$ 48,200	
Linda's withholdings	3,600	
Total payments		51,800
Tax refund to be claimed with return		**$ 1,396**

Income Taxation of Corporations

A corporation is a taxable entity entirely separate from its owners, the stockholders. In this chapter, we focus on the general business corporation. A corporation, like an individual, must file a tax return whether or not it earns taxable income. However, the concept of adjusted gross income does not apply to a corporation. Also, a corporation has no standard deduction and no personal exemptions. We compute the actual amount of income tax for a corporation, though, in much the same way as for an individual, multiplying taxable income by the appropriate tax rate.

Point to Stress: There is another type of corporation with a different set of tax rules. The S corporation or Subchapter S corporation can elect to be taxed similarly to a partnership, so that taxable income flows through to the shareholders and is not taxed to the corporation.

Taxable Income of a Corporation

To compute a corporation's taxable income, we follow many of the generally accepted accounting principles studied throughout this book. Indeed the starting point for computing the taxable income of a corporation is its *accounting income before income tax* on the income statement (also called *pretax accounting income*). Most revenues are taxable, and most expenses are tax deductible. *Ordinary income* is total business revenues minus total business expenses, including gains and losses from the sale of business assets like buildings and equipment. Special rules govern the tax treatment of certain revenues, expenses, and other items. The following paragraphs discuss some of these special tax rules.

Discussion Question: Does a corporation calculate AGI? *ANSWER:* No. It has no itemized deductions and no standard deduction amount, and it has no personal exemptions. AGI applies only to an individual.

1. *Dividends-received deduction.* The dividends a corporation earns on its stock investments are included in income. For tax purposes, however, 80 percent of dividends received from domestic corporations can be deducted from gross income. Thus only 20 percent of dividend revenue enters taxable income. This provision of the tax law provides partial relief from what would otherwise be triple taxation of such dividends. Suppose Parent Corporation owns Subsidiary Corporation and outside stockholders own Parent Corporation. Further, assume that the only entity with operating income is Subsidiary Corporation. The following diagram illustrates triple taxation.

OBJECTIVE 3

Use some special tax rules for corporations

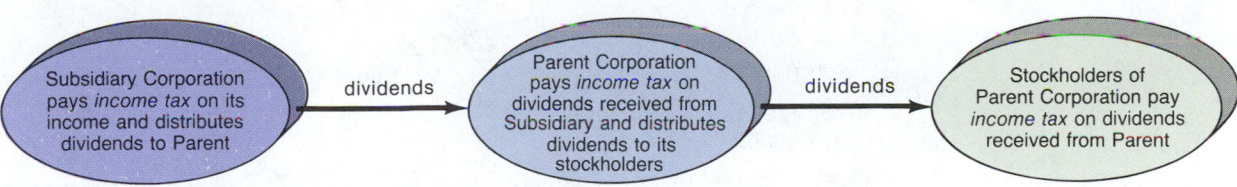

2. *Net operating loss carryback and carryforward.* In years when a corporation earns taxable income, it pays income tax. What is its tax situation when a loss occurs? Does the corporation get an income tax refund? Yes. The corporation can recover from the government the amount of taxes paid in other years. The tax law provides that an operating loss in a particular year can be offset against the income of the three preceding years, starting with the earliest year. If the loss is less than the corporation's total income during these three preceding years, the government mails a refund check to the company after its tax return is filed. If the loss exceeds the sum of the three preceding years' income, then the corporation can receive a refund and carry its excess loss forward for 15 years. This tax provision gives the corporation some tax relief from its operating losses. In effect, profitable years (in which the corporation paid taxes)

Point to Stress: An individual who operates a proprietorship or a partnership may also have a net operating loss, with similar carryback and carryforward provisions. However, the calculations for the allowable operating loss carryforward or carryback for an individual are much more complex than those for a corporation.

absorb the shock of years when the corporation has a loss. Without this carryback/carryforward provision, a $500,000 loss before income tax would result in a $500,000 *net* loss on the income statement. But if the corporation has $500,000 or more of taxable income and has paid taxes in the carryback/carryforward years, a pretax loss of $500,000 results in a *net* loss of $330,000 ($500,000 − the tax effect equal to 34 percent of $500,000).

3. *Capital gains and losses.* In taxation, corporations must separate capital gains and losses from ordinary income. Examples of capital gains and losses are gains and losses on the sale of investments such as stocks, bonds, and land. In the same manner as for individuals, capital gains are included in gross income. But a corporation may *not* offset capital losses against ordinary income. Instead, the corporation may carry net capital losses (capital losses in excess of capital gains) back three years and forward five years to be offset against capital gains in those carryback/carryforward years.

Corporate Income Tax Rates

Corporations have a tax rate schedule different from the tax rate schedule for individuals. Corporate income tax rates range from 15 percent to 34 percent, as shown in Exhibit 27-5.

There is a 5 percent *surtax* on corporate taxable income between $100,000 and $335,000. A **surtax** is an additional tax designed to shift more of the tax burden to high-income taxpayers. Built into the tax rates, the surtax nullifies the effect of lower rates applicable to lower levels of income. Above $335,000, all corporate income is taxed at 34 percent.

Exhibit 27-6 illustrates a tax computation for two corporations, one with relatively low income ($100,000) and the other with high income ($1,000,000).

EXHIBIT 27-5 *Corporate Income Tax Rates*

If taxable income is	The tax is
Not over $50,000	15% of taxable income
Over $50,000 but not over $75,000	$7,500 + 25% of the excess over $50,000
Over $75,000 but not over $100,000	$13,750 + 34% of the excess over $75,000
Over $100,000 but not over $335,000	$22,250 + 39% of the excess over $100,000
Over $335,000	34% of taxable income

The tax rate structure is designed to keep small companies from paying excessive taxes. Corporation A in Exhibit 27-6 pays income tax of $22,250 on taxable income of $100,000—an effective tax rate of 22.25 percent ($22,250/$100,000). A taxpayer's **average tax rate** is computed by dividing the income tax amount by taxable income. In this case, Corporation A's average rate is less than the top rate of 34 percent. Corporation B has an average tax rate of 34 percent ($340,000/$1,000,000).

Corporation B records income tax in a journal entry like this.

EXHIBIT 27-6 *Income Tax Computation for Two Corporations*

Corporation A—Taxable Income of $100,000:	Income Tax
Income tax amount [$13,750 + .34($100,000 − $75,000)] . .	$ 22,250
Corporation B—Taxable Income of $1,000,000:	
Income tax amount ($1,000,000 × .34)	$340,000

Income Tax Expense	340,000	
Income Tax Payable		340,000

In this example Income Tax Expense equals Income Tax Payable. However, there is usually a difference between the two amounts, as explained next.

Accounting for Income Taxes by Corporations

Income Tax Expense is based on pretax accounting income from the income statement. Income Tax Payable is based on taxable income from the income tax return filed with the Internal Revenue Service.

Income Tax Expense equals Pretax Accounting Income from Income Statement multiplied by Income Tax Rate	Income Tax Payable equals Taxable Income from Tax Return multiplied by Income Tax Rate

The authors are indebted to Jean Marie Hudson for this presentation.

We have discussed some of the differences between the accounting income and the taxable income of a corporation. Some revenues and expenses enter the determination of accounting income in periods different from those in which they enter the determination of taxable income. Over a period of several years, total accounting income may equal total taxable income, but for any one year the two income amounts are likely to differ.

The most important difference between pretax accounting income and taxable income occurs when a corporation uses the straight-line method to compute depreciation for the financial statements and a special tax depreciation method for the tax return and the payment of taxes. The tax depreciation method is called the **modified accelerated cost recovery system,** abbreviated as MACRS. For any one year, MACRS depreciation listed on the tax return may differ from accounting depreciation on the income statement.

Suppose Krieg Corporation has income before income tax (also called pretax accounting income) of $500,000 in each of two years. The accounting issue is, What is the correct amount of income tax expense for the two years? By answering this question, we can complete Krieg's income statement:

Income Statement (partial)

	19X1	19X2
Income before income tax	$500,000	$500,000
Income tax expense	?	?
Net income	$?	$?

Suppose Krieg uses straight-line depreciation to compute income for the income statement. On the tax return, Krieg uses MACRS depreciation, and so the tax returns report taxable income of $400,000 in 19X1 and $600,000 in 19X2. Total taxable income for the two years combined—$1 million—is the same as total pretax accounting income. However, each year shows a difference between accounting income and taxable income. With a 34 percent tax rate, income tax payable to the government is $136,000 ($400,000 × .34) in 19X1 and $204,000 ($600,000 × .34) in 19X2. Should Krieg report these amounts as income tax expense on the income statement? No, because this would amount to using the cash basis to account for income taxes. For reporting to shareholders and creditors, corporations must treat income as if it were all taxed currently even though the company may pay the tax in earlier or later years.

Generally accepted accounting principles do *not* permit accounting for income tax using the cash basis. GAAP requires use of the accrual basis of accounting. Corporations account for income tax expense and all other expenses based on when the expense occurs, not on when it is paid. The process of accruing income taxes during the period that the related income occurs is called **income tax allocation.** The goal of income tax allocation is to match the period's expenses against its revenues. In this case, Krieg Corporation will record the same amount of income tax expense in both years because pretax accounting income is the same.

Corporations generally record Income Tax Expense based on the amount of *pretax accounting income* multiplied by the tax rate. Income Tax Payable is credited for an amount equal to *taxable income* multiplied by the tax rate, as shown in the diagram on page 1217. When these two amounts differ, a new account, Deferred Income Tax, is credited or debited to balance the entry. In Exhibit 27-7, Deferred Income Tax is credited in 19X1 because accounting income ($500,000) exceeds taxable income ($400,000). The reverse is true in 19X2, and Deferred Income Tax is debited. The 19X2 entry eliminates the preceding credit balance in Deferred Income Tax.

For other corporations, the 19X1 entry may include a debit to Deferred Income Tax. This occurs if taxable income exceeds pretax accounting income. In this case, the credit to Income Tax Payable is greater than the debit to Income Tax Expense, and the balancing amount is a debit to Deferred Income Tax. Entries in later years will include credits to eliminate the debit balance in Deferred Income Tax. Here is a way to remember whether to debit or credit Deferred Income Tax:

Debit:	Income Tax Expense for the amount equal to *pretax accounting income* multiplied by the income tax rate.
Credit:	Income Tax Payable for the amount equal to *taxable income* multiplied by the income tax rate.
Debit or Credit:	Deferred Income Tax for the amount needed to balance the entry.

EXHIBIT 27-7 *Income Tax Entries for a Corporation*

19X1	Income Tax Expense ($500,000 × .34)	170,000	
	Income Tax Payable ($400,000 × .34) . . .		136,000
	Deferred Income Tax ($100,000 × .34) . .		34,000
19X2	Income Tax Expense ($500,000 × .34)	170,000	
	Deferred Income Tax ($100,000 × .34)	34,000	
	Income Tax Payable ($600,000 × .34) . . .		204,000

EXHIBIT 27-8 *Income Tax on a Corporation Income Statement*

Krieg Corporation Partial Income Statement For the Years Ended December 31, 19X1 and 19X2		
	19X1	**19X2**
Income before income tax	$500,000	$500,000
Income tax expense ($500,000 × .34 both years) . .	170,000	170,000
Net income	$330,000	$330,000

Exhibit 27-8 shows Krieg's comparative income statement for 19X1 and 19X2. Income Tax Expense comes directly from the entries recorded in Exhibit 27-7.

Net income is the same both years because pretax income is the same. Tax allocation thus matches income tax expense against income in accordance with the accrual basis of accounting. Income Tax Payable and Deferred Income Tax are reported on the balance sheet. Accounting for income tax by corporations is a controversial area that has received much FASB attention.

Tax Factors in Business Decisions

Tax planning is critical to making wise business decisions. Tax planning is the legitimate reduction of, and delay in, paying taxes within the legal system. Also called **tax avoidance,** it is the structuring of business transactions in order to pay the least amount of income tax at the latest possible time permitted by the law. Tax avoidance should not be confused with **tax evasion,** which is illegal activity designed to reduce tax. An example of tax planning (tax *avoidance*) is delaying making a sale until a later year, when tax rates are scheduled to decrease. An example of tax *evasion* is making a sale and not recording it in order to keep from paying the tax.

OBJECTIVE 6
Consider the effects of income taxes on business decisions

Corporations and individuals pay so much in taxes that intelligent financial strategies must consider the tax effects of transactions. The complexities of the federal tax laws demand specialized knowledge, so giant corporations like American Airlines and RJR Nabisco have tax specialists on the staff to advise them on major decisions. Proprietorships, partnerships, and private individuals often call on certified public accountants for advice. Many accountants earn a majority of their business income as tax consultants. In this section, we consider how tax factors affect business decisions by looking at the form of business organization, method of financing, basis of accounting, methods of accounting, and compensation of employees.

Form of Business Organization

Suppose you are starting a new business. While working at a bank for the past five years, you have learned that the physicians in your area need help in organizing their office staffs, keeping their records, and managing their financial affairs. You decide to open an accounting and office management business for physicians. As you prepare to start up, a basic question is how to organize the company. Should it be a proprietorship or a corporation?

Point to Stress: Basically, there are four taxing options available as you plan your form of business organization: Proprietorship, partnership, corporation, or S-corporation.

How much income tax would you pay under each alternative? You cannot be certain of what your income will be, but you can develop **pro forma data**—a carefully formulated expression of predicted results. These data would include projections of future income and income taxes.

Suppose you estimate that during the first year the business can earn pretax income (before salary) of $70,000. Assume that you are married with no children and take the standard deduction ($5,700) and the personal exemptions (2 × $2,000 = $4,000). You plan to withdraw $36,000 for living expenses. This withdrawal is taken as a salary from the corporation. However, for proprietorship or partnership income tax purposes, salaries paid to owners are not permissible deductions. Exhibit 27-9 shows the total tax you would have paid in 1991 under the proprietorship and the corporation forms of business organization.

The pro forma analysis indicates that incorporating the business leads to lower taxes, $9,045, compared with $12,464 if you organize as a proprietorship. The key to this advantage is leaving some of the corporation's income in the business. In this way you can arrange to have both yourself and the corporation pay taxes at the lowest rate, 15 percent. If you form a proprietorship, you pay some of your tax at 28 percent, and that increases your tax burden.

Let's consider another situation. Suppose you take all business earnings for personal use. In this case, the corporation has business income of $70,000 before your salary of $70,000. There is zero corporate income and no corporate income tax. The full $70,000 becomes taxable income to the owner as an employee. This places you, the owner, in the same tax situation as you would be with a proprietorship.

The keys to the corporate advantage are twofold. (1) Through wise salary and dividend policy, you can divide the corporation's income between yourself and the business. Recall that the corporation is taxed as a separate legal entity. The total income, then, is split between two taxable entities—you and the corporation—and each entity's income is taxed at lower rates than if you

Teaching Tip: Notice in Exhibit 27-9 that there is no salary listed under the "Proprietorship" column. Recall that a proprietor may not pay himself a salary and deduct it as a business expense. Instead, he must personally report (and pay tax on) the $70,000 business income.

EXHIBIT 27-9 *Pro Forma Income and Tax Information*

	Corporation	Proprietorship
Business income (before salary expense)	$70,000	$70,000
Less salary expense	36,000	—
Taxable income	34,000	70,000
Corporation income tax:		
.15 × $34,000	5,100	—
Business net income	$28,900	$70,000
Total income taxes:		
Corporation income tax	$ 5,100	
Individual income tax*—joint tax return:		
On taxable income of $26,300		
(salary, $36,000, less deductions, $5,700,		
and exemptions, $4,000)	3,945	
On proprietor taxable income of $60,300		
(business income, $70,000,		
less deductions, $5,700,		
and exemptions, $4,000)		$12,464
Total income taxes	$ 9,045	$12,464

* Income tax rates are given in Exhibit 27-3.

reported all the income on your personal tax return. Of course, the tax savings resulting from leaving part of the income in the corporation comes at a price. In our example, you have only about half the personal income that you would have if you withdrew the total income from the business. (2) By leaving part of the corporation's income in the business, you can postpone the payment of taxes. However, this is only a delaying strategy. The owner must pay taxes on money taken out of the corporation. Sooner or later you must pay taxes in order to obtain cash from the business, but the later you pay, the more time you have to earn income from investing your tax savings.

Using the corporate form of organization does *not* result in lower taxes in all situations. For example, if you organize as a corporation and take a relatively low salary and the remainder of your compensation in dividends, you will pay higher taxes than you would if organized as a proprietorship. Each situation requires a thorough analysis to determine what is best for the taxpayer.

Method of Financing

How a company finances operations has tax consequences. Two ways of obtaining funds are borrowing money and selling equity investments in the business. In a corporation, equity means stock. Borrowed funds must be repaid, with interest. Stockholders' equity does not have to be repaid, but stockholders demand returns in the form of dividends. Thus a corporation can expect to pay either interest or dividends for the funds it obtains from outsiders. Which form of financing has the tax advantage?

Business interest expense is tax deductible. Dividend payments to investors are not. Therefore, borrowing is less costly than selling ownership in the business, as an example will demonstrate.

Suppose you need $200,000 to finance a business expansion. You can borrow the money from a bank at 12 percent interest, an annual interest charge of $24,000. Alternatively, you can sell stock in the business. Assume that annual dividends on this stock are $18,000. Note that the dividends are $6,000 less than the interest. Before considering taxes, selling stock looks cheaper. However, if the corporation pays income tax at 34 percent, borrowing is less costly, as shown in Exhibit 27-10. The net cost of borrowing is $15,840 [$24,000 − .34($24,000)].

Point to Stress: Deductible business interest expense results from long-term bonds or notes payable, and short-term borrowing.

Basis of Accounting

Taxpayers, be they corporations or individuals, generally use the same basis for computing taxable income that they use for accounting purposes. For example, large corporations use the *accrual* basis for their accounting records,

EXHIBIT 27-10 *Financing With Debt Is Cheaper Than Issuing Stock*

Transparency T27-3

	Alternative Ways to Raise $200,000	
	Borrow at 12%	Issue Stock That Pays Annual Dividends of 9%
Annual payment to providers of outside financing	$24,000	$18,000
Tax deduction (at 34%)	(8,160)	-0-
Net cost of outside financing	$15,840	$18,000

Real-World Example: Examples of differences between accrual accounting and modified cash basis for tax purposes are summarized below.

Accrual Accounting

Warranty costs are deducted in the period of sale, not in the period when paid.

Losses on marketable securities are recognized while being held.

Rent received in advance is recorded as revenue in the periods earned.

Life insurance premiums paid on key executives are recorded as an expense.

Life-insurance premiums are not tax deductible.

Modified Cash Basis

Warranty costs are deducted when paid.

Losses on marketable securities are not recognized until sold.

Rent is recorded as revenue when received.

Life-insurance premiums are not tax deductible.

and they make any adjustments to those records to conform to tax law. Most corporations must use the accrual basis for computing their income taxes.

Almost all individuals and many service-oriented businesses keep their accounting records and prepare their income tax returns using the cash basis. In taxation, however, the cash basis is modified to include depreciation accounting. The costs of long-term business assets, such as buildings, equipment, and delivery vehicles, are capitalized and depreciated as in accrual accounting. Also, prepaid interest expense is deductible as it accrues rather than when it is paid. The cash basis for reporting to tax authorities is therefore really a modified cash basis.

The cash basis has several advantages. It is simpler than accrual accounting because it requires fewer records. By measuring taxable income by the amount of cash received rather than the amount of revenue earned, the taxpayer avoids having to pay taxes on revenues not yet collected in cash. Without this feature, a taxpayer might have to liquidate noncash assets to pay a tax liability. In general, tax law does not place this burden on taxpayers. Instead, tax law is cash-oriented, likely to link tax to an event that provides the taxpayer with the cash to pay the tax.

Let's take an extreme example. Suppose your new business has earned $25,000 but you have collected only $1,000 in cash. You would not have enough cash from the business to pay the income tax liability on total net income. However, you would be able to pay the tax on the $1,000 collected in cash. Therefore, tax is levied on $1,000.

The cash basis also allows the taxpayer some measure of control over the timing of income and expense. A lawyer with higher-than-expected income can delay billing a client in order to exclude this revenue from the current year. If this income would have caused the attorney to pay tax at a higher rate, a considerable savings results from this shifting of income. The lawyer can also pay expenses and charitable contributions on December 31 and receive an immediate deduction. Or if it helps the individual's tax situation, these expenses can be paid on January 1, and they become tax deductions in the next year.

The accounting basis chosen by the taxpayer—cash or accrual—must be followed consistently from period to period. The taxpayer may change accounting basis only with the approval of the IRS.

Methods of Accounting

A business in which inventory is a significant factor in computing income must use the accrual basis for revenue and cost of goods sold. This taxpayer cannot account for revenue on the cash basis for the purpose of determining taxable income. However, the taxpayer can elect the *last-in, first-out* (LIFO) method for inventories. This method assumes that the last costs into inventory are the first costs to pass into cost of goods sold (as opposed to first-in, first-out, FIFO). During a period of rising prices, LIFO causes gross profit to be lower than under the other inventory methods, thus reducing income taxes. If the company uses this method for income tax purposes, it generally must also use it for reporting to stockholders, creditors, and others. LIFO is the most popular inventory method, primarily because of its effect on taxes when prices are rising. Chapter 9 illustrates the income tax advantage of LIFO.

Another accounting choice with tax effects is *depreciation method*. A company may use one depreciation method for preparing the financial statements and a different method for preparing the tax return. For tax purposes, it is best to use the method that gives the largest depreciation amounts in the early years of the asset's life. By taking these deductions as soon as possible, the taxpayer reduces tax payments and saves cash that can be invested in the business. The only accelerated depreciation method permitted for tax purposes by the IRS is the Modified Accelerated Cost Recovery System (MACRS). Chapter 10 discusses depreciation in more detail and illustrates the tax advantage of accelerated depreciation.

Compensation of Employees

Businesses compensate their employees in a variety of ways. Salaries and wages are the most common. However, some contracts give the employee a choice among several forms of compensation. Many employees elect to take less salary in order to build retirement income. Under a typical arrangement, the employer makes payments into a pension account managed for the employee by an outside agency. The tax advantage is that the employer's pension contributions are *not* taxable income to the employee. Because no tax is paid currently, the full amount paid into the account earns retirement income for the employee. Furthermore, the pension fund pays no income tax while it is building up for the employee's retirement. Contrast this arrangement with paying the same amount to the employee as fully taxable salary and letting the employee set up her own retirement program. Suppose the employee's earnings are taxed at 15 percent. Of every dollar of salary earned, $.15 goes to pay taxes, leaving only $.85 to invest for retirement. And the employee must also pay tax on all income as it is earned by her retirement program.

Compensation plans that postpone the payment of taxes until the employee draws money from the retirement fund are called **tax-deferred,** or **tax-sheltered, compensation.** In many cases, the taxpayer will be subject to a lower tax rate during the retirement years and, therefore, will pay less in taxes than if the income were taken when the person was working and collecting a salary or wage. Self-employed persons can also shelter some of their income from taxes by making payments into a pension fund.

Another form of compensation with a tax advantage is noncash compensation. Many employers buy life, health, and disability insurance for their employees. Tax law does *not* levy a tax on the full amount of these forms of noncash compensation.

Income Taxes and Microcomputers

For many years, professionals have used computers for tax planning and the preparation of tax returns. Microcomputers have brought these capabilities within the reach of most individuals. Computer stores sell software programs that will perform tax calculations and prepare income tax returns. Many programs operate by use of a menu such as the one shown in Exhibit 27-11. All the taxpayer must do is answer questions and enter the data.

Menu-driven programs are easy to use. The computer takes the data, performs calculations, and enters the amounts in the correct place on the tax return. For example, suppose the taxpayer claims five exemptions. The program computes a total exemption of $10,000 (5 × $2,000), prints this amount on the exemption line of the tax return, and bases the tax calculation on this amount. A taxpayer who does not keep records of itemized deductions can elect the standard deduction. If the taxpayer does not know whether his itemized deductions exceed the standard deduction, he can enter the itemized amounts. The computer will total them, compare this amount with the standard deduction, and use the larger of the two. It will also print the various itemized deductions in the appropriate places on the tax return.

Real-World Example: Suppose a single taxpayer earns $45,000 per year working for an employer who has no retirement program. That employee may contribute up to $2,000 per year to an IRA (individual retirement account) and take a deduction for the amount contributed when calculating his taxable income. In other words, the IRS allows a benefit to employees not covered by a pension by allowing this tax break. Interest earned on the IRA is also tax-deferred. The money will be treated as taxable income when the employee retires and begins to withdraw money from the IRA.

Point to Stress: The microcomputer is a great way to look at the tax effects of different alternatives that a business might pursue. It is quick, error-free, and saves the tax accountant much time as he advises the business on planning a transaction so as to minimize taxes.

EXHIBIT 27-11 *Menu for a Tax-Return Preparation Program*

What is your status for filing this tax return?

_____ Single return

_____ Married person—joint return

_____ Married person—separate returns

_____ Head of household return

Enter the number of personal exemptions you are claiming _____

How do you wish to take deductions?

_____ Standard deduction

_____ Itemize deductions

_____ Compute itemized deductions. If itemized total exceeds standard deduction, itemize. If not, take the standard deduction.

Spreadsheet programs are ideal for tax planning. Suppose a business is raising $500,000 to purchase equipment. Should the company sell stock or borrow the money? What should be the dividend rate on the stock? At what interest rate should the money be borrowed? A spreadsheet can be written using Lotus 1-2-3, Excel, Appleworks, or one of the other spreadsheet programs. Exhibit 27-12 shows how the output might look.

The exhibit shows, for example, that borrowing at 12 percent (with a net annual interest cost of $39,600) is a little cheaper than issuing stock with an 8 percent dividend rate ($40,000). Borrowing at 14 percent costs less ($46,200) than paying dividends of 10 percent ($50,000). With a spreadsheet program, this information is available for decision making immediately after it is entered in the computer. If interest rates or other data inputs change, the company can alter the information for an up-to-date analysis.

EXHIBIT 27-12 *Spreadsheet Results of Business Financing Decision— Annual Cost of Alternative Ways to Raise $500,000*

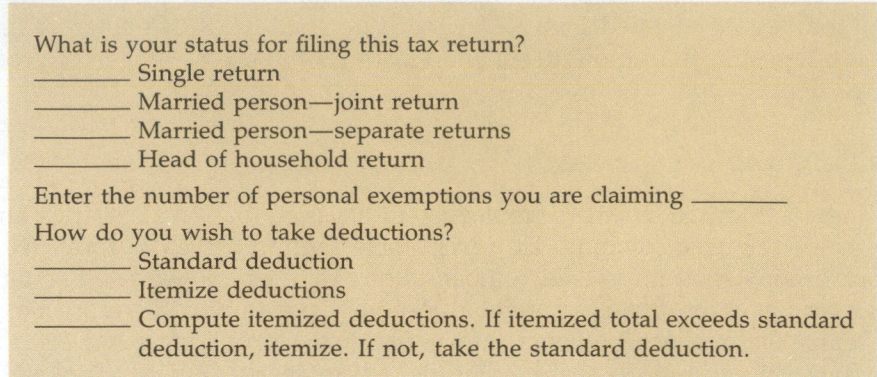

A1: [W25]   READY

	A	B	C	D	E	F
1						
2		6%	8%	10%	12%	14%
3		------	------	------	------	------
4	ISSUE COMMON STOCK					
5	Annual dividend					
6	cost	$30,000	$40,000	$50,000	$60,000	$70,000
7						
8	ISSUE PREFERRED STOCK					
9	Annual dividend					
10	cost	$30,000	$40,000	$50,000	$60,000	$70,000
11						
12	BORROW MONEY					
13	Annual interest					
14	expense	$30,000	$40,000	$50,000	$60,000	$70,000
15	Less income tax					
16	at 34%	10,200	13,600	17,000	20,400	23,800
17		------	------	------	------	------
18	Net annual					
19	interest cost	$19,800	$26,400	$33,000	$39,600	$46,200
20		======	======	======	======	======

17-Jul-91 07:21 PM   NUM

Summary Problem for Your Review

The bookkeeper for Highland Corporation provides the following data for computation of the company's income taxes for 19X7:

Transparency T27-4

Ordinary income excluding dividend revenue ..	$440,000
Dividend revenue............................	50,000
Capital gains	32,000
Capital losses................................	(49,000)
Total business income	$473,000

Required

1. Compute Highland Corporation's taxable income and income tax liability for 19X7.
2. Journalize Highland's income taxes for 19X7, assuming pretax accounting income is $420,000.

SOLUTION TO REVIEW PROBLEM

Requirement 1   (Taxable income and income tax liability)

Taxable income:

Ordinary income excluding dividend revenue	$440,000
Dividend revenue [$50,000 − (.80 × $50,000)]—Note 1	10,000
Capital gains...	32,000
Capital losses—Note 2..................................	(32,000)
Taxable income	$450,000

Notes: 1. 80% of dividend revenue is deductible.
      2. In any one year, capital losses can be deducted only to the extent of capital gains.

Tax liability—$450,000 × .34 = $153,000

Requirement 2   (Income tax entry for 19X7)

Income Tax Expense ($420,000 × .34)...............	142,800	
Deferred Income Tax ($30,000 × .34)	10,200	
Income Tax Payable ($450,000 × .34)		153,000

Summary

The *income tax* is a general-purpose tax levied on the taxable earnings of the taxpayer. Individuals, corporations, estates, and trusts are the four classes of taxpayers. Single individuals may file a *single income tax return* or, if they support other persons, a *head-of-household return*. Married persons may file a *joint return*, which has the lowest rate, or the husband and the wife may file *separate returns*.

A business organized as a proprietorship or a partnership pays no income tax. Instead, its owners pay income taxes as individuals. In tax law, a corporation is a separate taxable entity that pays its own income tax. Cash dividends that a corporation distributes to the stockholders are taxable to them as personal income. For all classes of taxpayers and forms of business organization the computation of income tax equals *taxable income multiplied by the tax rate*.

Individuals subtract exclusions from total income to determine *gross income*. *Deductions* and *exemptions* are subtracted to compute *taxable income*. After multiplying taxable income by the tax rate, *tax credits* are taken out to arrive at the *income tax liability* for the year. Individuals are taxed at 15 percent, 28 percent, and 31 percent for increasing levels of income.

A corporation computes taxable income by making adjustments to pretax accounting income. Among these are the deduction for dividends received, the net operating loss carryback and carryforward, and the special treatment of capital gains and losses. Corporations are taxed at 15 percent, 25 percent, or 34 percent.

The *income tax expense* of a corporation is based on its pretax accounting income. *Income tax payable* is based on taxable income. These amounts are rarely the same for a given year. Differences between the expense and the payable are debited or credited to an account titled Deferred Income Tax. Using this account helps the taxpayer match income tax expense against revenue, a process called *income tax allocation*.

Income taxes influence many business decisions, including choosing the form of business organization, the method of financing, the basis of accounting, the accounting methods that minimize taxes, and employee compensation.

Self-Study Questions

Test your understanding of the chapter by marking the best answer for each of the following questions.

1. A taxpayer's income tax is computed by multiplying the appropriate tax rate by *(p. 1206)*
   a. Net income
   b. Filing status
   ✓ c. Taxable income
   d. Total deductions

2. Which filing status of individual taxpayer pays income tax at the lowest rates? *(p. 1207)*
   ✓ a. Married filing jointly
   b. Married filing separately
   c. Head of household
   d. Single

3. Tax-exempt interest revenue is an example of a (an) *(p. 1208)*
   a. Personal exemption
   b. Itemized deduction
   c. Tax credit
   ✓ d. Exclusion

4. An individual has salary income of $37,000, capital gains of $4,000, and an $8,000 capital loss. How much is this person's taxable income? *(p. 1211)*
   a. $32,000
   b. $33,000
   ✓ c. $34,000
   d. $41,000

5. A married couple with one child has proprietorship income of $60,000 and itemized deductions of $7,000. How much is this family's income tax if they file a joint return as a married couple? *(p. 1213)*
   a. $7,050
   ✓ b. $8,740
   c. $9,000
   d. $13,160

6. Which is the most valuable to a taxpayer? *(p. 1213)*
   a. Itemized deduction
   b. Adjustment to arrive at adjusted gross income
   ✓ c. Tax credit
   d. Personal exemption

7. Why does a corporation with taxable income of $1 million pay more income tax than an individual with the same amount of income? *(pp. 1212, 1215)*
   a. The tax brackets are different for corporations than for individuals.
   ✓ b. The highest tax rate applicable to corporations is higher than the highest rate applicable to individuals.
   c. Corporations must follow income tax allocation procedures.
   d. Corporations but not individuals receive a dividends-received deduction.

8. Modified Accelerated Cost Recovery is a tax system for computing *(p. 1217)*
   a. Dividends
   b. Salary
   c. Capital gains and losses
   ✓ d. Depreciation

9. Which statement is true? *(p. 1221)*
   a. An individual always pays less in tax by organizing a business as a proprietorship because the entity pays no business income tax.
   b. An individual always pays less in tax by organizing a business as a corporation because of the opportunity to split personal income between the individual and the corporation.
   c. Tax planning is useful to corporations but not to individuals.
   ✓ d. In some cases, it costs less in taxes to organize as a proprietorship. In other cases, organizing as a corporation has the tax advantage.

10. Which method of financing is less costly? *(p. 1221)*
    a. Borrowing
    b. Issuing common stock
    c. Issuing preferred stock
    d. It depends on the circumstances

Answers to the Self-Study Questions follow the Accounting Vocabulary.

Accounting Vocabulary

Adjusted gross income. Total income minus specified adjustments (deductions) equals adjusted gross income, an amount that exists only in the tax law *(p. 1208)*.

Average tax rate. A taxpayer's income tax amount divided by taxable income *(p. 1217)*.

Capital gain. Special category of gain defined in the tax law that results from the disposal of property such as investments in stocks, bonds, real estate, and personal assets *(p. 1211)*.

Capital loss. Special category of loss defined in the tax law that results from the disposal of property such as investments in stocks, bonds, real estate, and personal assets *(p. 1211)*.

Dependent. Person who receives more than half of his or her support from another taxpayer *(p. 1207)*.

Gross income. In taxation, total income minus exclusions *(p. 1208)*.

Income tax. A general-purpose tax levied on the income of a taxpayer. Entirely separate from all other taxes, it is the federal government's largest source of revenue *(p. 1205)*.

Income tax allocation. Process of accruing income taxes during the period that the related income occurs, with the goal of matching the period's expenses—including income tax expense—against the period's revenues, regardless of when the income tax is paid *(p. 1218)*.

Itemized deduction. In taxation, a particular category that includes medical expenses, interest expense, charitable contributions, taxes paid, casualty losses, and miscellaneous deductions *(p. 1208)*.

Modified accelerated cost recovery system (MACRS). Special tax depreciation method *(p. 1217)*.

Personal exemption. A tax deduction that is a set amount allowed for a taxpayer, the taxpayer's spouse, and each person who qualifies as a dependent *(p. 1210)*.

Pro forma data. Carefully formulated expression of predicted results, such as projections of future income and income tax *(p. 1220)*.

Standard deduction. A set amount of tax deduction that varies depending on the individual's filing status: single, married filing jointly, married filing separetely, or head of household. The standard deduction is an alternative to itemizing tax deductions *(p. 1210)*.

Surtax. An additional tax often designed to shift more of the tax burden to high-income taxpayers *(p. 1216)*.

Taxable income. Earnings amount on which the income tax is based. It is the figure that is multiplied by the tax rate to compute the amount of income tax *(p. 1207)*.

Tax avoidance. Structuring of business transactions in order to pay the least amount of income tax at the latest possible time permitted by the law *(p. 1219)*.

Tax credit. Amount that is subtracted directly from the amount of tax owed to the government *(p. 1213)*.

Tax-deferred compensation. Compensation that postpones the payment of taxes until the employee receives the money. Also called Tax-sheltered compensation *(p. 1223)*.

Tax evasion. Illegal activity designed to reduce tax *(p. 1219)*.

Tax return. Document on which each taxpayer reports income and shows the computation of income tax *(p. 1206)*.

Tax-sheltered compensation. Another name for Tax-deferred compensation *(p. 1223)*.

Total income. In taxation, all income from whatever source derived *(p. 1208)*.

Answers to Self-Study Questions

1. c
2. a
3. d
4. c $37,000 − net capital loss limited to $3,000 = $34,000
5. b   Taxable income = $60,000 − personal exemptions of $6,000 ($2,000 × 3) − itemized deductions of $7,000 = $47,000. Tax on income of $47,000 = $8,740 [$5,100 + .28 × ($47,000 − $34,000)]
6. c
7. b
8. d
9. d
10. a

ASSIGNMENT MATERIAL

Questions

1. Briefly describe four different kinds of taxes.
2. Does tax law in the United States state that each American has a patriotic responsibility to pay tax in a manner that goes beyond the call of duty?

3. When was the first income tax levied in the United States? When did our present tax structure begin? What government action opened the door for the income tax?

4. Identify the lowest and the highest income tax rates that have existed in the United States. What event triggered the highest rate?

5. Name the four filing statuses for an individual taxpayer, and rank them from lowest to highest in tax rate.

6. Enter the correct letter (or letters) from the right column in the blank spaces. More than one answer may apply.

_____ Files an information tax return only	a. Individual
_____ Pays no business income tax	b. Proprietorship
_____ Is viewed by tax law as a taxable business entity	c. Partnership
_____ Has four possible filing statuses	d. Corporation

7. Outline an individual's twelve-step computation of income tax liability.

8. How does total income of a taxpayer differ from gross income? Identify four types of income that are specifically listed as nontaxable.

9. Identify two tax deductions that depend on the amount of a taxpayer's adjusted gross income (AGI). Give the percentage relationship of these two items to AGI.

10. What is the alternative to taking the standard deduction? Identify the advantage and the disadvantage of the standard deduction.

11. What are capital gains and losses, and how are they treated for tax purposes by an individual? Give three examples of a capital asset.

12. Which is worth more to a taxpayer, a $400 tax deduction or a $400 tax credit? How much more (assume an income tax rate of 28 percent)?

13. Leslie B. Good's income tax liability for the year is $4,700. Describe how Leslie will pay this income tax if her earnings consist of salary. How will she pay her taxes on outside income?

14. Briefly describe three items that receive special tax treatments by corporations.

15. What income tax rates apply to single individuals and to corporations?

16. What is the average tax rate of a corporation with taxable income of $70,000? Why is this average rate below 25 percent?

17. Does a corporation's income tax expense depend on its pretax accounting income or on its taxable income? On which income amount does income tax payable depend?

18. Indicate whether each of the following statements is true or false.

_____ a. Deferred Income Tax is an expense account.

_____ b. Deferred Income Tax may have either a debit balance or a credit balance.

_____ c. Deferred Income Tax is reported on the balance sheet.

19. Which method of financing—equity or debt—is usually cheaper for a business? Why?

20. Which basis of accounting do most individuals use for tax purposes? Why? Which basis do most corporations use? Why?

21. Name two accounting methods that can reduce income taxes.

22. Why do many taxpayers choose tax-sheltered compensation over salary income?

23. Briefly describe two aspects of tax work that can be aided by a microcomputer.

Exercises

Additional computer-related exercises: Exercise 28-11

No check figure

Exercise 27-1 *Classifying tax items* **(L.O. 1)**

Listed below are eight tax terms discussed in this chapter.

Tax credit	Itemized deduction
Personal exemption	Capital gain or loss
Standard deduction	Adjustment to arrive at adjusted gross income
Surtax	Income excluded from gross income

Indicate which of these tax terms applies to the following descriptions.

a. Additional tax based on high levels of income
b. Child-care expenses
c. $5,700 for a married taxpayer filing a joint return, $5,000 for a head of a household, $3,400 for a single taxpayer
d. Penalty on early withdrawal of savings
e. Gain on the sale of a stock investment
f. Interest revenue earned on bonds issued by the city of St. Louis, Missouri
g. Medical expenses, charitable contributions, and casualty losses
h. $2,000 for the taxpayer and each dependent claimed on the tax return

No check figure

Exercise 27-2 *Identifying items to include in gross income* **(L.O. 1)**

State whether each of the following items should be *included in* or *excluded from* gross income for the purpose of computing the income tax of an individual.

a. Gain on sale of investment in bonds
b. Profits earned from a partnership
c. Life insurance proceeds received
d. Tax-deferred compensation earned while working for employer
e. Interest revenue earned on state of Idaho bonds
f. Inheritance of $10,000 received from the estate of a deceased relative
g. Rent income received from lease of personal residence while away on business
h. Tips received by the headwaiter of a restaurant
i. Gift of oil royalties received from a parent
j. Income received during retirement from a pension plan. The earnings that went into the pension plan were tax-deferred in *d*

No check figure

Exercise 27-3 *Classifying tax items* **(L.O. 1)**

For each of the following expenditures by an individual taxpayer, indicate whether the item is a *deductible business expense*, an *adjustment to arrive at adjusted gross income*, an *itemized deduction*, or *not deductible*.

a. Contribution to a personal retirement program
b. Charitable contributions
c. Sales tax paid
d. Medical expenses less than 7½ percent of adjusted gross income
e. Cost of adding a room to personal residence
f. Interest expense paid on home mortgage note payable
g. State income taxes paid

h. Wage expense paid to employees
i. Net capital losses in excess of $3,000
j. Insurance expense on rental property

Exercise 27-4   *Computing adjusted gross income*   **(L.O. 1)**

AGI $69,000
Taxable income $59,600

Gabriel Koo is single with no dependents. His personal income tax records reveal the following:

Gross income of Koo Oriental Jewelers, a proprietorship........	$129,000
Operating expenses of Koo Oriental Jewelers	73,000
Capital loss on sale of personal (nonbusiness) investment.......	7,000
Gift received from Gabriel's parents	12,500
Rent income on a building adjacent to Koo Oriental Jewelers store...	19,100
Medical expenses	4,600
Interest expense:	
Home mortgage note payable	7,400
Business debt...	3,100
Personal exemption	2,000

Compute Koo's adjusted gross income and taxable income.

Exercise 27-5   *Computing an individual's income tax*   **(L.O. 2)**

Case A. Income tax $14,352
Case B. Refund claimed $852

Case A: Compute the income tax of Gabriel Koo in the preceding exercise.

Case B: Assume that Gabriel Koo in the preceding exercise is married with one child. He and his wife, Lia, file a joint income tax return. During the year, the Koos made quarterly income tax payments totaling $12,000. Compute their *income tax* for the year. Also, show the amount of *income tax they owe* or the *refund* they may claim when they file their tax return.

Exercise 27-6   *Computing a single person's adjusted gross income and taxable income*   *(L.O. 1, 2)*

AGI $82,000
Taxable income $71,000

Margaret Durham's architecture firm, which she operates as a proprietorship, had gross fee revenue of $255,000 for the year just ended. Business expenses included salaries of $119,000, office depreciation of $4,000, and other operating expenses totaling $51,000. Ms. Durham's personal investments earned dividend revenue of $4,000, and she sold General Electric stock at a gain of $2,000. She sold another personal investment at a loss of $7,000. Her itemized deductions for the year were $4,100. She earned municipal bond interest income of $6,000. Ms. Durham is single, and she supports her two children.

Required

Compute Ms. Durham's adjusted gross income and taxable income. Assume she files a head-of-household tax return.

Exercise 27-7   *Computing income tax for a family's joint tax return*   **(L.O. 2)**

Taxable income $143,200
Income tax $37,508

Assume Margaret Durham in the preceding exercise is married with two children. Her husband's salary income is $74,900. Compute the family's taxable income and income tax for the year, assuming she and her husband file a joint tax return.

Exercise 27-8   *Treatment of capital gains and losses by individuals and corporations*   *(L.O. 2, 3)*

Indiv.: a. $3,000 gain;
  d. $3,000 loss
Corp.: a. $3,000 gain;
  d. $12,000 carryback or
    carryforward only

A taxpayer had the following capital gains and losses during a year:

a. A capital gain of $7,000 and a capital loss of $4,000
b. A capital gain of $3,000 and a capital loss of $1,000
c. A capital gain of $2,000 and a capital loss of $8,000
d. No capital gain and a capital loss of $12,000

Required

1. Assume the taxpayer is an *individual*. For each situation, indicate the amount of net capital gain that will be included in, or the amount of net capital loss that will be deductible from, the individual's gross income.
2. Assume the taxpayer is a *corporation*. For each situation, indicate how the corporation should treat the capital gains and losses.

Taxable income $105,000
Income tax $24,200

Exercise 27-9 *Computing a corporation's income tax and average tax rate* **(L.O. 3, 4)**

Climate Control, Inc.'s income tax records provide the following data:

Gross profit from sales (sales − cost of goods sold) ..	$368,000
Operating expenses	(274,000)
Dividend revenue	15,000
Gain on sale of equipment—not a capital gain	8,000
Capital loss	(27,000)
Total business income	$ 90,000

Required

1. Compute Climate Control, Inc.'s taxable income and income tax liability for the year.
2. Compute the corporation's average income tax rate.

Deferred Income Tax:
  19X5, $3,400 credit bal.
  19X6, $0 bal.

Exercise 27-10 *Recording a corporation's income tax* **(L.O. 4, 5)**

BiSports Corp. has pretax accounting income of $690,000 in 19X5 and $660,000 in 19X6. Taxable income is $680,000 in 19X5 and $670,000 in 19X6. Record the corporation's income taxes for both years. The tax rate is 34 percent. What is the balance in the Deferred Income Tax account at the end of each year?

Taxable inc. $159,000
Income tax $45,260

Exercise 27-11 *Computing and recording a corporation's income tax* **(L.O. 4, 5)**

The income tax records of Prater Corporation provide the following data:

Service revenue	$351,000
Operating expenses	(113,000)
Dividend revenue	35,000
Loss on sale of building—not a capital loss . . .	(92,000)
Capital gain	6,000
Total business income	$187,000

Required

1. Compute Prater Corporation's taxable income and income tax liability for the year.
2. Record the corporation's income tax for the year. Assume that pretax accounting income is $150,000, and apply the same tax rates to pretax accounting income that are used on taxable income.

Total income tax:
  Corporation $24,109
  Partnership $27,309

Exercise 27-12 *Pro forma analysis of income tax for a corporation* **(L.O. 6)**

E. P. and Sue Garth own a Wendy's restaurant that they operate as a proprietorship in Gatlinburg, Tennessee. The business earns annual pretax accounting income of $120,000 before any compensation to the owners. The Garths have no children, file a joint tax return, and take the standard deduction and the personal exemption. They withdraw $100,000 annually for living expenses. They are considering reorganizing the business as a corporation.

Required

1. Prepare a pro forma analysis to indicate their total income taxes under the two forms of business organization.
2. Which form of business organization results in the lower total income tax for the owners? Compute the difference.

Problems

(Group A)

Problem 27-1A *Computing adjusted gross income and taxable income* **(L.O. 1)**

AGI $50,000
Taxable income $34,200

The tax records of Paul and Wikki Erickson, a married couple with three children, reveal the following data for the current year. The Ericksons file a joint income tax return.

Partner interest in:	
Operating profits of Epicure Restaurant	$57,900
Loss on sale of restaurant building	8,300
Inheritance received	120,000
Rent income	6,000
Expense of operating rent property	1,600
Contribution to a retirement program	2,000
Capital gain on sale of personal investment in land	600
Capital loss on sale of personal investment in bonds	2,900
Gambling profits	300
Medical expenses	3,950
Interest expense on home mortgage note payable	3,700
Sales tax paid	700
Property tax paid	900
Charitable contributions	1,000
Personal exemptions	10,000

Compute the Ericksons' adjusted gross income and taxable income.

Problem 27-2A *Computing income tax for a joint tax return* **(L.O. 1, 2)**

Gross income $67,500
Income tax $10,084

Danny and Elizabeth Hollingsworth are married and have one son. Danny's salary is $51,500, and Elizabeth's investments earn annual dividends of $12,000. In addition, the couple has some capital gains and losses. Danny contributes $4,000 to a pension plan. During the current year, Elizabeth received a gift of $3,000 from an aunt. The Hollingsworths have compiled the following income tax data to aid in the preparation of their joint income tax return:

Salary income	$51,500
Dividend income	12,000
Capital gains	6,000
Capital losses	2,000
Itemized deductions	3,300
Personal exemptions	?
Contribution to a retirement program	4,000
Income taxes withheld and paid directly to the IRS	11,000

Required

1. Compute gross income.
2. Compute adjusted gross income.

3. Compute taxable income.
4. Compute income tax.
5. Compute the amount of tax to be paid or the refund to be claimed when the tax return is filed.

Taxable income $60,400
Income tax due $92

Problem 27-3A *Computing income tax for a joint tax return* **(L.O. 1, 2)**

Mike and Ann Cassell, a married couple with one daughter, have income, expenses, and other expenditures for the year as follows. They file a joint tax return.

Salaries ($51,000 and $37,000)	$88,000
Loss on a partnership interest in an apartment building	9,600
Interest income on:	
City of Jackson bonds	1,800
Bank deposit	1,100
Consulting fee earned	600
Inheritance received	110,000
Contribution to retirement program	2,600
Capital gain on sale of personal investment in land	2,300
Unused capital loss carryover from preceding year	3,800
Clothing	5,100
Food	6,400
Medical expenses	6,100
Interest expense on home mortgage note payable	3,700
Cost of remodeling personal residence	9,300
State income tax paid	1,200
Property tax paid	1,000
Charitable contributions	3,300
Miscellaneous deductions	800
Personal exemptions	6,000
Income tax withheld	11,000
Total of quarterly tax payments	1,400

Required

1. Compute the Cassells' adjusted gross income and taxable income for the year. Identify each item not used in this computation, and state why the item is not used.
2. Compute the income tax liability for the year, and show whether filing their tax return will lead the Cassells to pay tax or receive a refund. Show the amount.

Problem 27-4A *Computing and recording a corporation's income tax* **(L.O. 3, 4, 5)**

Taxable income $78,000
Income tax payable $14,770

Willis Corporation is about to complete its first year of operations. To assess the company's income tax situation before year end, the company accountant prepares the following pro forma income statement:

Revenues and gains:		
Sales revenue	$340,000	
Dividend revenue	20,000	
Gain on sale of asset—a capital gain	14,000	
Total revenues and gains		$374,000
Expenses and losses:		
Cost of goods sold—		
FIFO method for inventories	150,000	
Operating expenses:		
Depreciation—straight-line method	16,000	
Other expenses	88,000	
Loss on payment of debt—a capital loss	19,000	
Total expenses and losses		273,000
Pro forma pretax accounting income		$101,000

Steve Willis, the company president, is pleased with the successful operations of the first year. However, he is concerned about the high income taxes the corporation may have to pay. Willis asks the accountant to consider ways to reduce income taxes. The accountant determines that the LIFO method would decrease ending inventory by $9,000 from the FIFO amount and the MACRS depreciation method would increase depreciation expense by $3,000.

Required

1. Assume Willis changes to LIFO and prepares its income tax return based on the LIFO method for inventories and the MACRS method for depreciation. Compute the corporation's taxable income and income tax payable, taking into account any special tax rules that apply to corporations.
2. Compute the corporation's average income tax rate.
3. Record Willis Corporation's income tax for the year. Compute income tax expense based on pretax accounting income of $85,000.

Problem 27-5A *Computing and recording a corporation's income tax* **(L.O. 3, 4, 5)**

The accounting (not the income tax) records of Jones Corporation provide the comparative income statement for 19X7 and 19X8:

	19X7	19X8
Total revenue	$930,000	$990,000
Expenses:		
Cost of goods sold	$430,000	$460,000
Operating expenses	270,000	280,000
Total expenses before tax . . .	700,000	740,000
Pretax accounting income	$230,000	$250,000

Total revenue of 19X8 includes revenue of $15,000 that was received late in 19X7. This revenue is included in 19X8 total revenue because it was earned in 19X8. However, revenue that is collected in advance is included in the taxable income of the year when the cash is received. In calculating taxable income on the tax return, this revenue belongs in 19X7.

Also, the operating expenses of each year include depreciation of $50,000 computed on the straight-line method. In calculating taxable income on the tax return, Jones Corporation uses the Modified Accelerated Cost Recovery System (MACRS). MACRS depreciation was $80,000 for 19X7 and $20,000 for 19X8.

Required

(Assume a corporate income tax rate of 34 percent.)

1. Compute taxable income for each year.
2. Journalize the corporation's income taxes for each year.
3. Prepare the corporation's single-step income statement for each year.

Problem 27-6A *Computing total tax burden for a corporation and a proprietor* **(L.O. 2, 4, 6)**

Helen Miller operates a successful construction company. For the past several years, the business has had annual net income ranging from $200,000 to $300,000 before any deduction for Miller's $80,000 salary. This is her only source of income. The business is incorporated, but Miller is considering reorganizing as a proprietorship. She wonders whether her family's total tax burden would be less if the business were a proprietorship.

1. Taxable income:
    19X7, $215,000
    19X8, $265,000
3. Net income:
    19X7 $151,800
    19X8 $165,000

Income of $200,000:
    Total inc. tax if corp.,
    $44,754
    Total inc. tax. if prop.,
    $51,489

Required

1. Prepare an analysis to show the Millers' total annual income tax burden with the business organized as a corporation. Also show what the Millers' total tax burden would be if the business were *reorganized* as a proprietorship. Base your analysis on the range of business income in recent years. The Millers will file a joint tax return with three exemptions and take the standard deduction.

2. Will reorganizing the business as a proprietorship reduce the Miller family's total income tax burden?

(Group B)

Problem 27-1B *Computing adjusted gross income and taxable income (L.O. 1)*

AGI $100,000
Taxable income $90,100

The tax records of Lars Dunberg, a single taxpayer with no dependents, reveal the following data for the current year:

Partner interest in:	
Operating profits of Bon Voyage Travel Agency	$ 76,200
Gain on sale of travel agency building	31,800
Life insurance benefits received	200,000
Contribution to a retirement program	5,000
Capital gain on sale of personal investment in stock	3,200
Capital loss on sale of personal investment in land	7,700
Capital gain on sale of recreational vehicle	800
Medical expenses	4,775
Interest expense on home mortgage note payable	3,800
Sales tax paid	1,100
Property tax paid	2,200
Charitable contributions	1,900
Personal exemption	2,000

Compute Dunberg's adjusted gross income and taxable income.

Problem 27-2B *Computing income tax for a joint tax return (L.O. 1, 2)*

Gross income $80,000
Income tax $11,736

Bill and Mary Ann Thomas are married and have two children. Bill's salary is $64,000, and Mary Ann's investments earn interest of $13,000 annually. Bill contributes $3,000 to a pension plan. The Thomases have compiled the following income tax data to aid in the preparation of their joint income tax return:

Salary income	$64,000
Interest income, of which $8,000 results from municipal bonds	13,000
Rent income	11,000
Expense of operating rent property	5,000
Itemized deductions	6,300
Personal exemptions	?
Contribution to a retirement program	3,000
Income taxes withheld and paid directly to the IRS	10,000

Required

1. Compute gross income.
2. Compute adjusted gross income.
3. Compute taxable income.
4. Compute income tax.
5. Compute the amount of tax to be paid or the refund to be claimed when the tax return is filed.

Problem 27-3B *Computing income tax for a joint tax return* **(L.O. 1, 2)**

Taxable income $88,300
Refund $1,011

Larry and Betty Maddox, a married couple with two children, have income, expenses, and other expenditures for the year as follows. They file a joint tax return.

Salaries ($55,000 and $23,000)	$78,000
Profit on a partnership interest in an office building ..	24,200
Interest income on:	
Bank deposit	3,500
City of Albuquerque bonds	900
Gift received	2,500
Contribution to retirement program	3,000
Capital gain on sale of personal investment in stock ..	2,100
Unused capital loss carryover from preceding year ...	1,900
Capital gain on sale of stereo equipment	100
Clothing	2,600
Food	3,800
Medical expenses	1,400
Interest expense on home mortgage note payable	2,100
Cost of painting personal residence	6,700
State income tax paid	500
Property tax paid	1,800
Charitable contributions	2,200
Miscellaneous deductions	2,160
Personal exemptions	8,000
Income tax withheld	14,300
Total of quarterly tax payments	7,200

Required

1. Compute the Maddoxes' adjusted gross income and taxable income for the year. Identify each item not used in this computation, and state why the item is not used.
2. Compute the income tax liability for the year and show whether the Maddoxes will pay tax when they file their return or receive a refund. Show the amount.

Problem 27-4B *Computing and recording a corporation's income tax* **(L.O. 3, 4, 5)**

Taxable income $119,000
Income tax payable $29,660

Pledger Concrete Contracting Corporation is about to complete its first year of operations. To assess the company's income tax situation before year end, the company accountant prepares the following pro forma income statement:

Revenue and gains:		
Sales revenue	$451,000	
Dividend revenue	35,000	
Gain on sale of asset—a capital gain	8,000	
Total revenues and gains		$494,000
Expenses and losses:		
Cost of goods sold—		
FIFO method for inventories	196,000	
Operating expenses:		
Depreciation—straight-line method	22,000	
Other expenses	104,000	
Loss on payment of debt—a capital loss	9,000	
Total expenses and losses		331,000
Pro forma pretax accounting income		$163,000

Barry Pledger, the company president, is pleased with the successful operations of the first year. However, he is concerned about the high income taxes the corporation may have to pay. Pledger asks the accountant to consider ways to reduce income taxes. The accountant determines that the LIFO method would decrease ending inventory by $11,000 from the FIFO amount and that the MACRS depreciation method would increase depreciation expense by $6,000.

Required

1. Assume Pledger changes to LIFO and prepares its income tax return based on the LIFO method for inventories and the MACRS method for depreciation. Compute the corporation's taxable income and income tax payable, taking into account any special tax rules that apply to corporations.
2. Compute the corporation's average income tax rate.
3. Record Pledger Concrete Contracting Corporation's income tax for the year. Compute income tax expense based on pretax accounting income of $128,000.

1. Taxable income:
  19X3, $200,000
  19X4, $230,000
3. Net income
  19X3, $138,600
  19X4, $145,200

Problem 27-5B   *Computing and recording a corporation's income tax*   (L.O.. 3, 4, 5)

The accounting (not the income tax) records of Waterhouse Microfilms, Inc., provide the comparative income statement for 19X3 and 19X4:

	19X3	19X4
Total revenue	$680,000	$720,000
Expenses:		
Cost of goods sold	$290,000	$310,000
Operating expenses	180,000	190,000
Total expenses before tax	470,000	500,000
Pretax accounting income	$210,000	$220,000

Total revenue of 19X4 includes rent of $10,000 that was received late in 19X3. This rent is included in 19X4 total revenue because the rent was earned in 19X4. However, rent revenue that is collected in advance is included in taxable income when the cash is received. In calculating taxable income on the tax return, this rent revenue belongs in 19X3.

Also, the operating expenses of each year include depreciation of $40,000 computed under the straight-line method. In calculating taxable income on the tax return, Waterhouse uses the Modified Accelerated Cost Recovery System (MACRS). MACRS depreciation was $60,000 for 19X3 and $20,000 for 19X4.

Required

(Assume a corporate income tax rate of 34 percent.)

1. Compute taxable income for each year.
2. Journalize the corporation's income taxes for each year.
3. Prepare the corporation's single-step income statement for each year.

Income of $70,000:
  Total inc. tax if corp. $10,893
  Total inc. tax if prop. $15,902

Problem 27-6B   *Computing total tax burden for a corporation and a proprietor* *(L.O. 2, 4, 6)*

Suzanne Abbe is opening a consulting firm. She expects business income—before any salary for herself—ranging between $70,000 and $120,000, and she plans to take an annual salary of $35,000 the first year. Concerned about the effects of income tax, she is considering the best way to organize the business.

Required

1. Prepare an analysis to show Abbe's total annual income tax burden if she organizes the business as a corporation. Also show what Abbe's total tax

burden would be if the business were a proprietorship. Base your analysis on the range of business income Abbe expects for the first year. She will file a single individual tax return and take the standard deduction. The business is her only source of income.

2. How should Abbe organize the business to minimize her total tax burden?

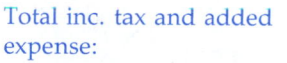

Extending Your Knowledge

Decision Problems

1. Tax Factors in Deciding How to Organize a Business (L.O. 2, 4, 6)

Greg and Alice Ogden own The Double Eagle, a restaurant in San Diego organized as a proprietorship. The business earns pretax income of $90,000 per year before any compensation to the Ogdens. They are considering reorganizing the business as a corporation in order to avoid the unlimited personal liability of the proprietorship form of business. If they incorporate, the cost of the restaurant's liability insurance will increase by $2,000 per year over its present level. Operating as a corporation will increase other expenses by $500 each year. Revenues will be unchanged.

Under the proprietorship form, the Ogdens withdraw $45,000 of business income each year for personal living expenses. They will need the same amount of personal family income if the business incorporates. They are considering two alternative ways of receiving $45,000 from the corporation: (1) $45,000 annually as salary or (2) $30,000 annually as salary, plus $15,000 as dividends.

The Ogdens file a joint tax return and have itemized deductions of $7,000 each year. They have no children.

Total inc. tax and added expense:
Salary only $13,975
Salary and dividends $16,975
Proprietorship $17,700

Required

1. Prepare a schedule showing the Ogdens' total income taxes and additional expense each year under three alternative plans: (1) corporation—salary only; (2) corporation—salary and dividends; (3) proprietorship.
2. Which plan do you recommend? Give your reason.

2. Maximize Income or Minimize Taxes? (L.O. 6)

No check figure

Magnum Properties's board of directors is planning operations for next year. A key question centers on net income. Three board members want Magnum to report the maximum amount of net income allowable under generally accepted accounting principles. Three other members of the board prefer to minimize income tax, which could occur only if Magnum uses conservative accounting methods that report lower net income.

As the president of the corporation, you must break this deadlock. Take a position on this issue. Write a short speech for presentation to the board to convince these persons that your strategy is best for the company's stockholders. Cite specific accounting methods that help to accomplish your goal.

Ethical Issue

Part A. Manny Fredericks uses every loophole available to minimize his personal income tax. However, he is careful never to break the law.

Required

Discuss whether Fredericks is behaving ethically.

Part B. Luigi of Milan imports leather goods from Italy, Spain, and Brazil. Until recently, Luigi, the proprietor, has used the FIFO inventory method. Double-digit rates of inflation have increased profits and income tax payments. To dampen the negative cash flow effects of inflation, Luigi is considering changing to the LIFO inventory method. Accountants estimate that Luigi can save $50,000 annually by changing to LIFO.

Required

Is it ethical for Luigi to change to LIFO in order to decrease income taxes? What would you do if you were Luigi?

Chapter 28

Accounting with Computers

"How can you expect me to prepare monthly budgets for the 36 divisions of the company before Thursday?"

Questions like this have been asked countless times. Divisional managers need budget data to help employees work toward concrete goals. Of course, the budget information is most useful when it relates to a manageably small segment of the business. Enter divisional budgets. Likewise, managers manage bet- ter when they can focus on a limited period of time, such as a month instead of a year. Enter monthly budgets.

Irvine, Inc., a major trucking company, has found that using monthly budgets for its 36 divisions has resulted in a 22 percent increase in sales and profits. How were the budgets prepared so quickly? With a relatively simple spreadsheet program that almost anyone in the office could create.

Point to Stress: It is becoming more and more unusual to find a business that does not use some type of computer system. A business usually will have a computer of its own or will use a computer processing service.

Point to Stress: The computer not only saves time, it can save in personnel costs. Because of the volume of transactions which can be handled very quickly and efficiently, fewer employees are needed to perform tasks previously performed manually. The computer also frees employees to move beyond repetitive bookkeeping procedures and allows them time to be creative and make decisions.

Accounting has benefited more from computer technology than any other area of business. The application of computers to accounting is natural because the computer is ideally suited for repetitive calculations.

This chapter expands the Chapter 6 discussion of computer systems. It outlines a personal-computer (PC) system of accounting for general ledger, accounts receivable, accounts payable, and payroll transactions. The second half of the chapter discusses spreadsheet programs—giving specific commands and leading you through the preparation of a budgeted income statement. Learning these commands will equip you to use a spreadsheet program for a variety of accounting tasks. The exercises and problems are designed to be solved by hands-on use of a personal computer.

The first computerized accounting systems were developed in the 1950s. Only the largest organizations could afford the expensive computer equipment available at that time. Since then the price of computer equipment has dropped dramatically. Today even the smallest business can afford a computer capable of keeping its accounting records.

Advantages of Computer Systems

Computerized systems offer many advantages over manual systems:

Speed. A computerized system can provide information more quickly than a manual system because the computer can instantaneously perform tasks that are time-consuming when done manually.

Volume of output. A much larger volume of transactions can be handled using a computerized system because of its speed of processing.

Error protection. Using a computer greatly reduces the number of errors because the computer does calculations more accurately than a human. Also, computerized accounting systems have many error-protection features. For example, most systems do not accept an entry that does not balance.

Automatic posting. Posting is automatically performed in a computerized system—an enormous savings in time. Not only is the repetitive task of posting time-consuming, but it can create many errors in a manual accounting system. Using a computer ensures that each entry is posted accurately. This prevents such errors as double posting, posting to the wrong account, posting a debit as a credit (and vice versa), and posting the wrong amount.

Automatic report preparation. Reports can be generated automatically in a computerized accounting system—journals, ledgers, the financial statements, and special reports to aid management in decision making.

Automatic document printing. A computerized system can provide many of the documents used in a business—invoices, monthly statements for accounts receivable customers, payroll checks, and employee earnings statements, among others.

Accounting procedures are basically the same whether performed manually or on a computer. Exhibit 28-1 reviews the accounting cycle from Chapter 4 and lists the corresponding steps in a computerized system. Observe how many steps the computer performs automatically. These repetitive steps have been programmed by accountants to relieve some of the most tedious work.

Computer Basics

A computer **program** is a set of instructions that tells the computer what to do. Without a program it cannot perform even the simplest tasks. This does not mean that you must become a programmer to use a computer for accounting.

Discussion Question: Have students name some ways they had first-hand experience with a business computer yesterday. *SOME POSSIBLE ANSWERS:* 24-hour banking machine; computer-generated bank statement or gasoline bill; price scanner in the grocery store; computer-assisted college registration.

EXHIBIT 28-1 *Comparison of the Accounting Cycle in a Manual System and in a Computerized System*

Transparency T28-1

OBJECTIVE 2

Compare the accounting cycle in a manual system and in a computerized system

Accounting Cycle in a Manual System	Accounting Cycle in a Computerized System
1. Start with the account balances in the ledger at the beginning of the period.	1. Same
2. Analyze and journalize transactions as they occur.	2. Analyze transactions and enter them in the computer, which automatically prepares a journal that can be printed at any time.
3. Post journal entries to the ledger accounts.	3. The computer automatically posts from the journal to the ledger.
4. Compute the unadjusted balance in each account at the end of the period.	4. The computer automatically computes the balance in each account.
5. Enter the trial balance on the work sheet and complete the work sheet.	5. The computer automatically prepares a trial balance. Enter adjusting entries in the computer. No work sheet is needed.

6. Using the work sheet as a guide,
  a. Prepare the financial statements
  b. Journalize and post adjusting entries
  c. Journalize and post closing entries
	6. The computer automatically prepares the financial statements and posts the adjusting and closing entries.

7. Prepare the postclosing trial balance.	7. The computer automatically prepares the postclosing trial balance.

Teaching Tip: Notice that all the steps in a manual system, except for the work sheet, are still performed, but by the computer. Even if students will never keep a manual set of books, they must learn the entire accounting system.

Since accounting is one of the computer's most important applications, many programs have been written to handle accounting data. To use the computer for accounting, a business can simply purchase a program that suits its needs and is compatible with its computer.

Hardware

Computers are classified according to their speed and the amount of data they can store. There are three basic classes of computers: mainframes, minicomputers, and microcomputers. In the 1950s the only type of computer available for accounting applications was the mainframe. A *mainframe* computer can handle a large volume of transactions very quickly, but its cost is prohibitive for most small businesses. In the late 1960s the *minicomputer* was developed. It was less powerful and less expensive than the mainframe.

As technology progressed, a new type of computer was developed—the **microcomputer,** which is small enough for each employee to have one. At first microcomputers were not very powerful and were used mostly for playing computer games. However, new ones were soon developed with more memory and speed. Some microcomputers today are more powerful than the mainframes of the 1950s and they are very affordable. A complete microcomputer system can be purchased for less than $2,000. Because of their low cost, programmers have a large market for their software programs. Hundreds of software packages have been produced for the microcomputer, making it a valuable business tool. Some medium and large-size businesses still require mainframes and minicomputers, but microcomputer packages now provide virtually all of the features offered by larger computers and can easily meet the needs of small businesses.

Although we concentrate on accounting procedures for microcomputers, the basic procedures are the same no matter what type of computer is used. Exhibit 28-2 shows the hardware for a typical microcomputer system consisting of three main types of components:

Input devices (disk drive and keyboard)
Central processing unit (the "brain" of the computer)
Output devices (monitor, printer, and disk drive)

Input Devices. Input devices are used to feed instructions and data into the computer. An input device usually found on a computer system is a **disk drive,** which reads data and instructions from magnetic disks. The most common form of disk is the floppy **diskette,** also called a floppy disk. This thin, 3½-inch or 5¼-inch diameter round diskette, enclosed in a square plastic envelope, can store approximately 360,000 characters of data and costs under $3. Exhibit 28-3 is a picture of a floppy diskette.

To use the computer program or the data stored on a diskette, place the diskette in the disk drive, and the computer can read the information from it. Some computers use a hard disk. This type of disk is metal and can hold much more information than a floppy diskette. Although they are more expensive, hard disks are increasing in popularity.

The other input device usually found in a microcomputer system is the *keyboard*. Much like a typewriter keyboard, this device is used to enter data and instructions.

Central Processing Unit. The **central processing unit (CPU)** is the "brain" of the microcomputer. The CPU does the "thinking" for the computer. It per-

Point to Stress: If the accounting information recorded in the computer is destroyed, time will be wasted re-entering that information. In addition, day-to-day operations will be severely impaired due to the lost accounting records on receivables, payables, and so on. One solution is to make two backup copies. Copy 1 is updated with the current information. The next day, Copy 2 is updated with current information. For protection, one of these disks should be stored off-site. This procedure ensures that a fairly recent copy of the accounting information will always be available.

EXHIBIT 28-2   *Microcomputer Hardware*

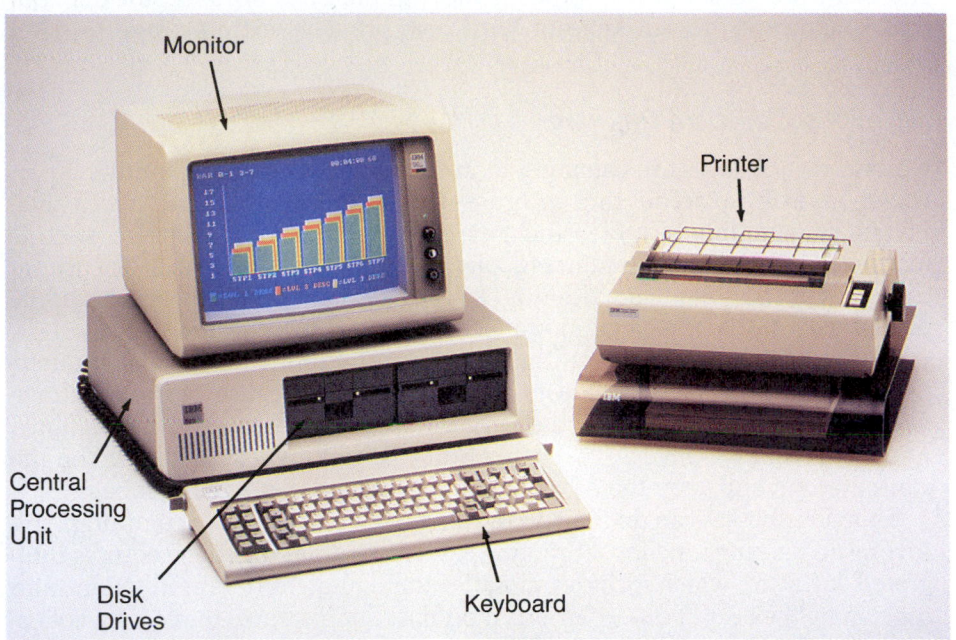

Monitor

Printer

Central
Processing
Unit

Disk
Drives

Keyboard

forms mathematical and logical operations and controls all the other components of the system.

Output Devices.   *Output devices* give us the information we want to receive from the computer—in several ways. The **monitor** looks like a television screen and allows the user to view data being processed and to receive messages from the program being run.

The *printer* can provide printed copies of the information after it has been processed. Examples of the printed copies (also called *hard copies*) in an accounting system include printouts of the balance sheet and income statement, payroll checks, and invoices for mailing to customers.

A third common output device is the disk drive (which we also listed as an input device). We can save the records that have been updated during pro-

EXHIBIT 28-3   *Floppy Diskette*

cessing by placing them on a diskette. When the computer is turned off at the end of a work session, the internal memory in the CPU "forgets" the data put into it. However, the diskette or hard disk provides extra storage for later use.

Accounting Software Programs

Accounting packages are usually sold in *modules.* Each module handles a particular area of the accounting records—general ledger, accounts receivable, inventory, accounts payable, and payroll. Others are available for specific functions such as billing, budgeting, plant asset management, and job costing. Generally each module is written on a separate diskette, so that one module can be used alone or several modules can be used together.

Payroll procedures are often the first accounting function to be computerized. This area is ideally suited to computerization because of the repetitive nature of payroll activities and the large number of mathematical calculations. The accountant can save a great deal of time by putting a large payroll on the computer but still keep the other accounting records on a manual basis.

Many businesses can do their accounting more efficiently by computerizing several accounting functions. Bringing several modules together requires **integrated software,** which includes modules that handle different functions and coordinate the output of the various modules. For instance, to record a collection of cash on accounts receivable, you would use the accounts receivable module. The journal entry would be recorded in the cash receipts journal in this module, and the customer's account would automatically be updated. In an integrated system this information would also be posted to the Cash and Accounts Receivable accounts in the general ledger module.

Most computerized systems have common features. Virtually all accounting programs are **menu-driven.** This means that when you turn the computer on and insert the program diskette, a list of options will be displayed for you to choose from—in the same way you select food from a restaurant menu. To choose a particular computer function, simply highlight your choice and hit the enter key. **Menus** simplify the task of learning to use an accounting program. Each time the program is loaded onto the computer, a menu will come onto the screen listing the choice of functions. The first menu is called a master menu. It will guide you to the section of the program sought. When you choose an option, the computer will either perform the function or display a new set of menu choices to receive more instructions. A typical master menu is shown in Exhibit 28-4.

To work with a particular module of this program you would simply select from the menu. To use the general ledger section of this program you would type a "1."

Generally, in a computerized system (as in a manual system with a large volume of data), transactions are recorded in batches. Transactions are not recorded the instant they occur. Rather, similar transactions are recorded in groups. For example, instead of recording each sale or purchase immediately, we would record each day's sales at one time and then all of the purchases at one time. In the remainder of this section we discuss four common modules and explain how batches of transactions might be handled by a typical accounting software package.

General Ledger Module

The general ledger module is the center of an integrated system. In this module all of the general ledger accounts are maintained. Exhibit 28-5 is a typical menu for using a general ledger module.

EXHIBIT 28-4 *Master Menu*

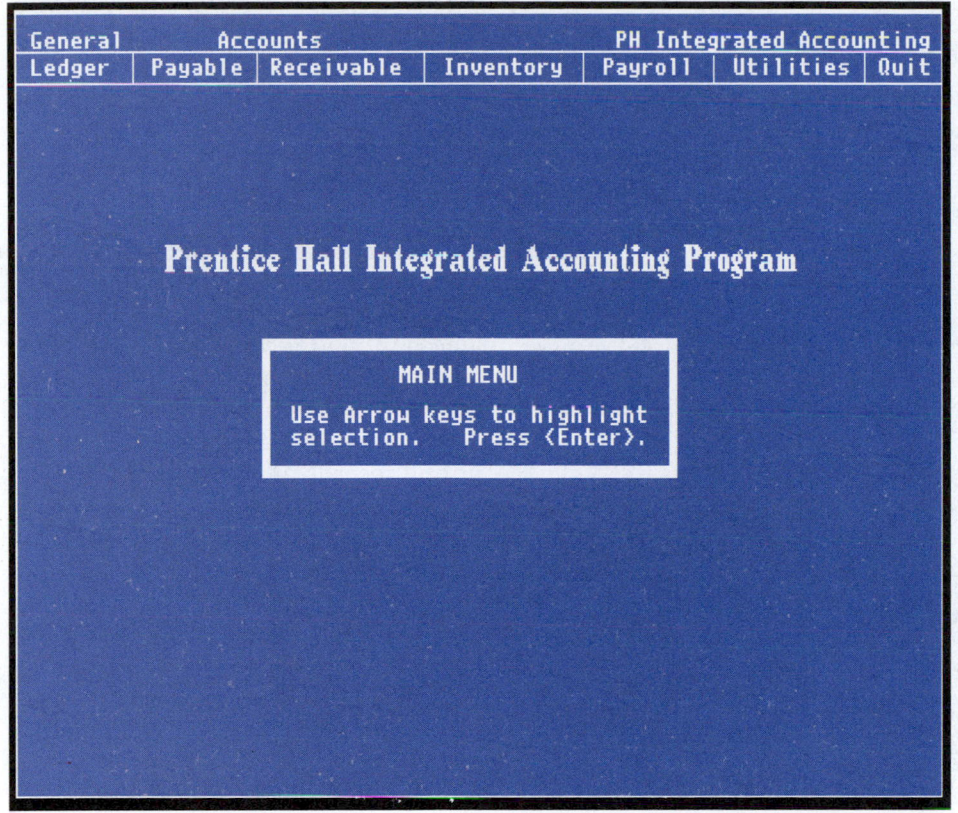

One option included in this module is the chart of accounts feature. The accountant sets up the chart of accounts by telling the computer each account's name, number, normal balance, and type (current asset, plant asset, and so on). Since the program will remember this information, it need be entered only once. This chart can be modified as necessary. Once the chart has been set up, the accountant can refer to an account simply by listing its account number. With this information, the program can supply the account name and other information by referring back to the chart of accounts.

Journal entries can also be entered through this module. Just as in the manual system of Chapters 1–5, some businesses choose to use the general journal as their only book of original entry. In Chapter 6 we saw the advantages of special journals. The same option exists in a computerized system. The general ledger module can be used on a stand-alone basis, with the general journal as the only book of original entry. Other modules with their special journals can also be used in an integrated system.

To make a journal entry we list the number of each account affected (the computer will supply the account name), the amount of the transaction, and the choice of either debit or credit for that account. Once the transaction has been listed, the program will ask if the entry is correct before recording it. The computer will then check to see if the journal entry balances (debits equal credits).

After the entries have been recorded, the general journal can be printed. This printout, commonly called a "hard copy," provides a permanent record of the journal entries. Most companies with computerized systems keep hard

Teaching Tip: Refer to Exhibit 28-5. Some of the options on the menu will be used only occasionally. Some options will be used regularly.

Point to Stress: Some journal entry programs allow the operator to enter a description of the entry (an explanation).

Discussion Question: Why should a hard copy be printed out each time journal entries are made? *ANSWER:* Suppose you enter a week's journal entries and make no printout. If the disk became damaged, you would have no record of what was entered.

EXHIBIT 28-5 *Menu for General Ledger Module*

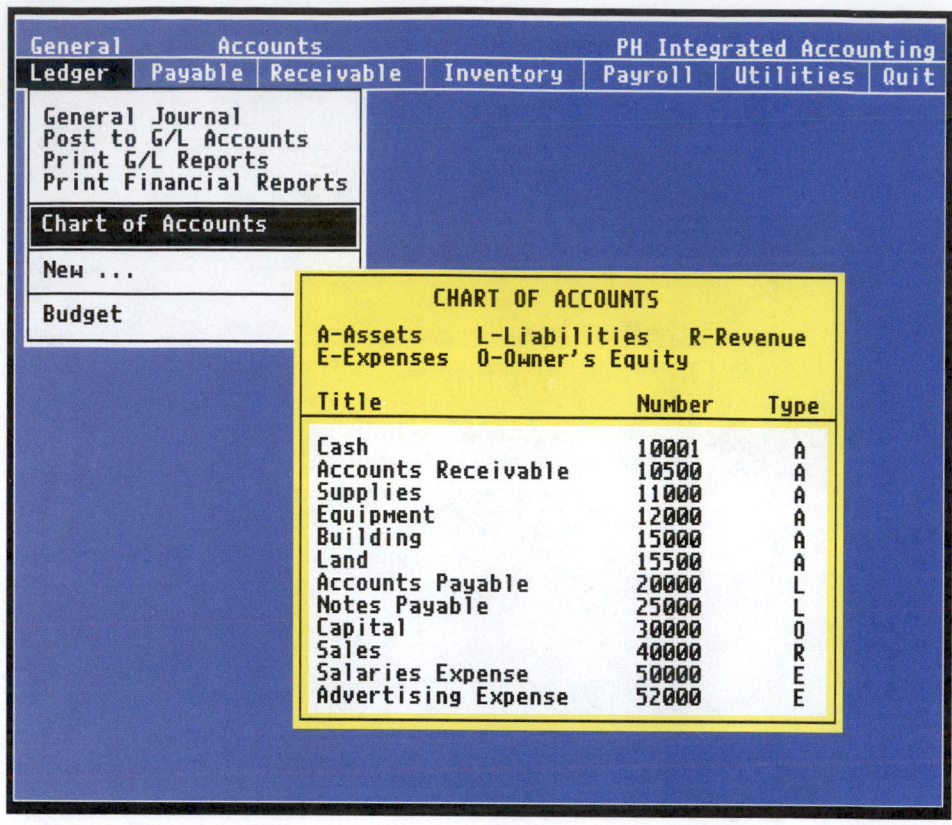

copies of all work to document the accounting records. Exhibit 28-6 shows a sample page of general journal entries.

Posting in a computer system is easy. In the system menu of Exhibit 28-5, choose menu option "Post to G/L Accounts." The program will post and also enter posting references automatically. This represents a considerable time-saving over the manual method of posting. It is also more accurate, because the computer makes no posting errors.

Accountants may wish to see (on the screen or printed out) the whole general ledger—in order to check each account, for example. A screen showing the Accounts Receivable account is shown in Exhibit 28-7. Note that the posting references refer to other journals besides the general journal. These postings come from the other modules, as explained later.

At the end of the period, the program produces the trial balance as a basis for making the adjusting entries. Adjusting entries, like all other general journal entries, are recorded using the "General Journal" option in Exhibit 28-5. These entries are posted using the "Post to G/L Accounts" on the menu. Once this is done, the account balances are updated and ready to be reported on the financial statements.

An important feature of a computerized system is that a work sheet is unnecessary. The reason for a work sheet in a manual system is to organize data to prepare the financial statements and the adjusting and closing entries. On the work sheet ending balances are computed for the statements and the closing entries. Having the machine perform these steps automatically eliminates this time-consuming task. To print the financial statements, simply select this option from the menu, and the statements are created automatically.

Point to Stress: The computer can create financial statements automatically, and does not need to prepare a work sheet.

Teaching Tip: Refer to Exhibit 28-7. Point out that the computerized general ledger contains the same information as a manual ledger.

EXHIBIT 28-6 *General Journal Entries*

```
General Journal                          PH Integrated Accounting
                    J&L Office Supply

 Trans  Date  Acct No.   Account Name         Dr.         Cr.
  27    5/09  11000    Supplies             234.17
              20000      Accounts Payable                 234.17
  28    5/09  12000    Equipment           3459.12
              20000      Accounts Payable                3459.12
  29    5/10  50000    Salaries Expense    11400.00
              27100      Income Tax Payable              2394.00
              27110      FICA Tax Payable                 815.10
              27200      Health Ins Payable                96.00
              27300      Union Dues Payable               228.00
              27500      Salaries Payable                7866.90
  30    5/10  51000    Payroll Tax Expense  1275.90
              27110      FICA Tax Payable                 815.10
              27150      State Unemp Tax Pay              403.20
              27160      Fed Unemp Tax Pay                 57.60
  31    5/11  52000    Advertising Expense  830.50
              20000      Accounts Payable                 830.50
  32    5/12  11000    Supplies              82.36
```

Trans # 32 Date: 5/12   Transaction Balance: 82.36
Description: Staples Office Supply, Computer Paper
Debit Account(s): 11000 Supplies   82.36

Credit Accounts(s): 20000 Accounts Payable [   ]   [   ]

EXHIBIT 28-7 *General Ledger Accounts*

```
General Ledger                           PH Integrated Accounting
                    J&L Office Supply

 ACCOUNT NAME: Accounts Receivable               10500

 Date   Explanation         REF     Dr.       Cr.       Balance
 4/30   Total               CR12  336.12              6553.00 Dr
 5/01   Beginning Balance                            6553.00 Dr
 5/01                       J5                88.90   6464.10 Dr
 5/02                       S5    4776.00            11240.10 Dr
 5/03                       S5     200.15            11440.25 Dr
 5/03                       J6               600.10  10840.15 Dr
 5/05                       S10   3800.00            14640.15 Dr
 5/07                       J11             2323.85  12316.30 Dr
```

Current Balance: 12316.30   Current Period: 8776.15

Year-to-Date: 96432.87   Prior Period: 6553.00

Budgeted, Year: Budgeted Period:

Most accounting packages include an option allowing you to request that the temporary accounts be automatically closed at the end of the period. In Exhibit 28-5, this menu option, "Post to G/L Accounts" closes the accounts and prepares a postclosing trial balance. The postclosing trial balance can be printed by choosing the "Print G/L Reports" option in the general ledger menu. Just as in a manual system, this completes the accounting cycle, with balances updated and ready for use in the next accounting period.

Accounts Receivable Module

The accounts receivable module is used to keep track of the accounts receivable subsidiary ledger and to provide special journals for recording transactions that affect this asset account. In Chapter 6 we discussed the need for the sales journal and the cash receipts journal. A typical menu for the accounts receivable module is shown in Exhibit 28-8.

The sales for each day are recorded at one time using this module. In some programs the sales are entered in general journal format:

Apr. 19   Accounts Receivable—Customer Name   1,300
          Sales Revenue   1,300

Other programs allow the accountant to enter each sale in the form of a sales invoice. The program creates an entry for the sales journal and also prints out

Teaching Tip: Refer to Exhibit 28-8. Some of the options on this menu are similar to those on the General Ledger menu. However, the Accounts Receivable menu has different options, such as "Customer Statements." This option prints a monthly statement for each customer as shown in Exhibit 28-10 on page 1252.

EXHIBIT 28-8 *Menu for Accounts Receivable Module*

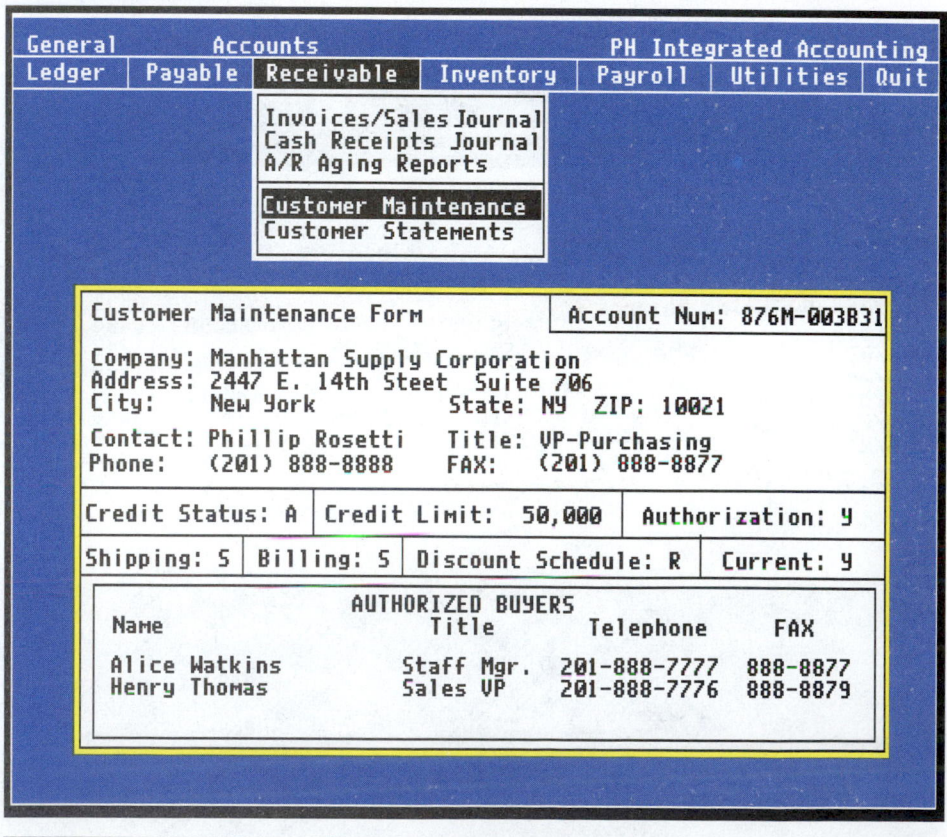

EXHIBIT 28-9 *Computer-Generated Sales Invoice*

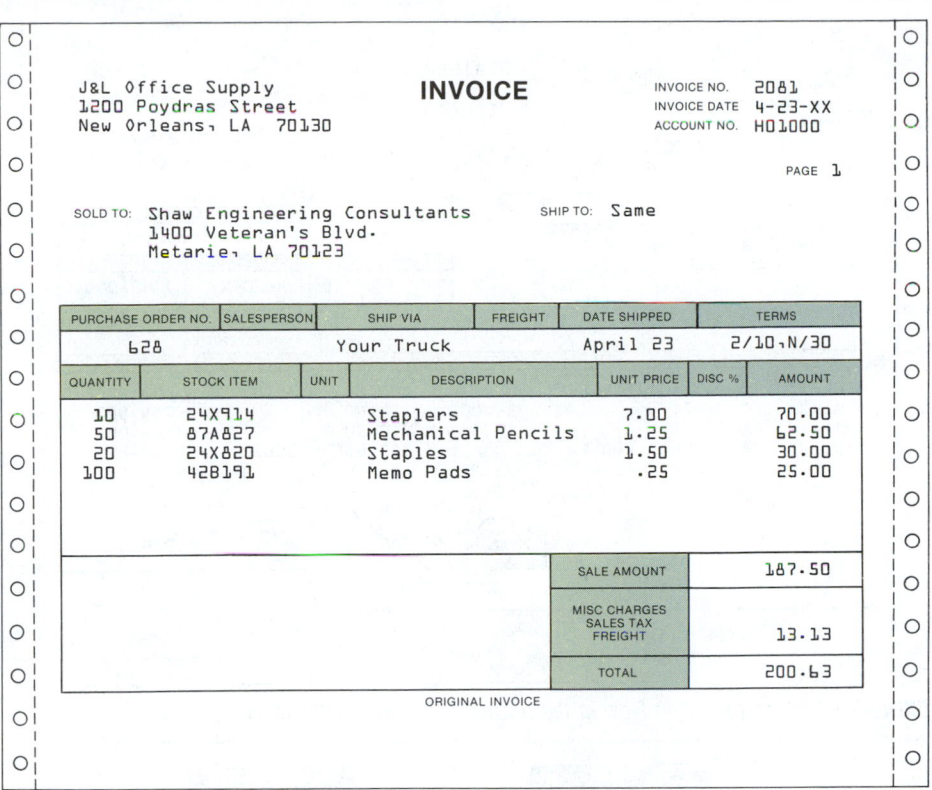

J&L Office Supply   **INVOICE**   INVOICE NO.   2081
1200 Poydras Street   INVOICE DATE 4-23-XX
New Orleans, LA 70130   ACCOUNT NO.   H01000

                                                         PAGE 1

SOLD TO: Shaw Engineering Consultants   SHIP TO: Same
          1400 Veteran's Blvd.
          Metarie, LA 70123

PURCHASE ORDER NO.	SALESPERSON	SHIP VIA	FREIGHT	DATE SHIPPED	TERMS
628		Your Truck		April 23	2/10,N/30

QUANTITY	STOCK ITEM	UNIT	DESCRIPTION	UNIT PRICE	DISC %	AMOUNT
10	24X914		Staplers	7.00		70.00
50	87A827		Mechanical Pencils	1.25		62.50
20	24X820		Staples	1.50		30.00
100	428191		Memo Pads	.25		25.00

SALE AMOUNT		187.50
MISC CHARGES SALES TAX FREIGHT		13.13
TOTAL		200.63

ORIGINAL INVOICE

the actual sale invoice to be sent to the customer, eliminating the manual preparation of these invoices. An example of a computer-generated sale invoice is shown in Exhibit 28-9.

After the day's sales have been entered, a sales journal can be printed. The hard copy is checked for correctness and saved as a permanent record. This journal can now be posted. Just as in a manual system, the sales journal should be posted to two ledgers, the general ledger in the general ledger module and the accounts receivable ledger in the accounts receivable module. See the "Invoices/Sales Journal" option in Exhibit 28-8.

The other journal in the accounts receivable module is the cash receipts journal, where all receipts of cash are recorded. A batch of cash receipt transactions is entered into the computer as it is in manual recording. As with the other journals, a hard copy is printed and checked for correctness. This journal is also posted to both the general ledger and the accounts receivable ledger.

Some programs will keep a running balance of the customer accounts in the accounts receivable subsidiary ledger and also can print monthly statements to be sent to customers. An example of a monthly statement is shown in Exhibit 28-10.

The accounts receivable module can perform an aging of the customer accounts to estimate uncollectible account expense. Using the computer for such tasks saves much time and money.

Exhibit 28-11 shows how information flows through the accounts receivable module and interacts with the general ledger module.

EXHIBIT 28-10 *Customer Monthly Statement*

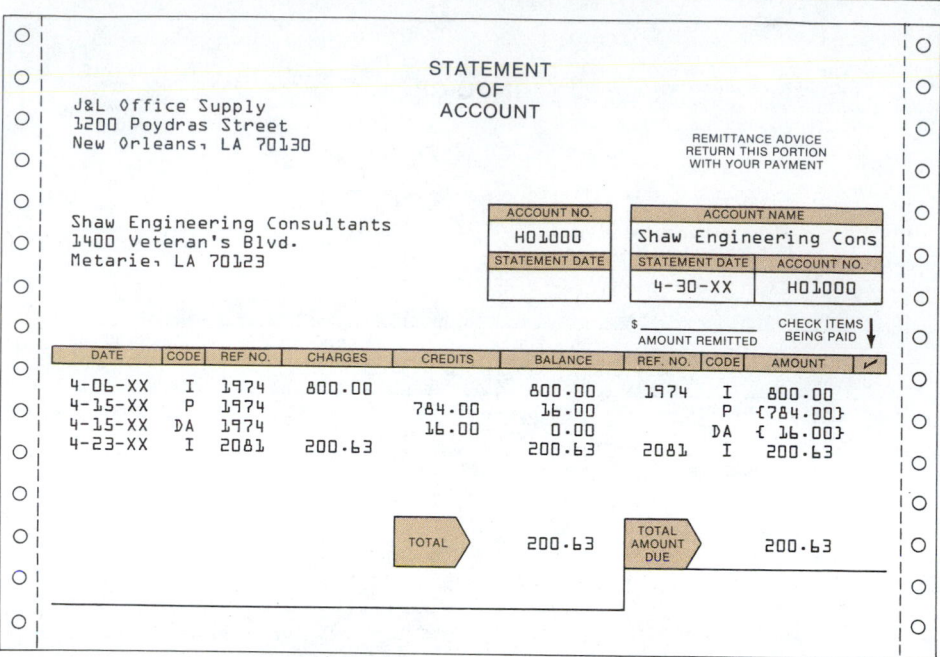

Transparency T28-2

EXHIBIT 28-11 *Information Flow in the Accounts Receivable Module*

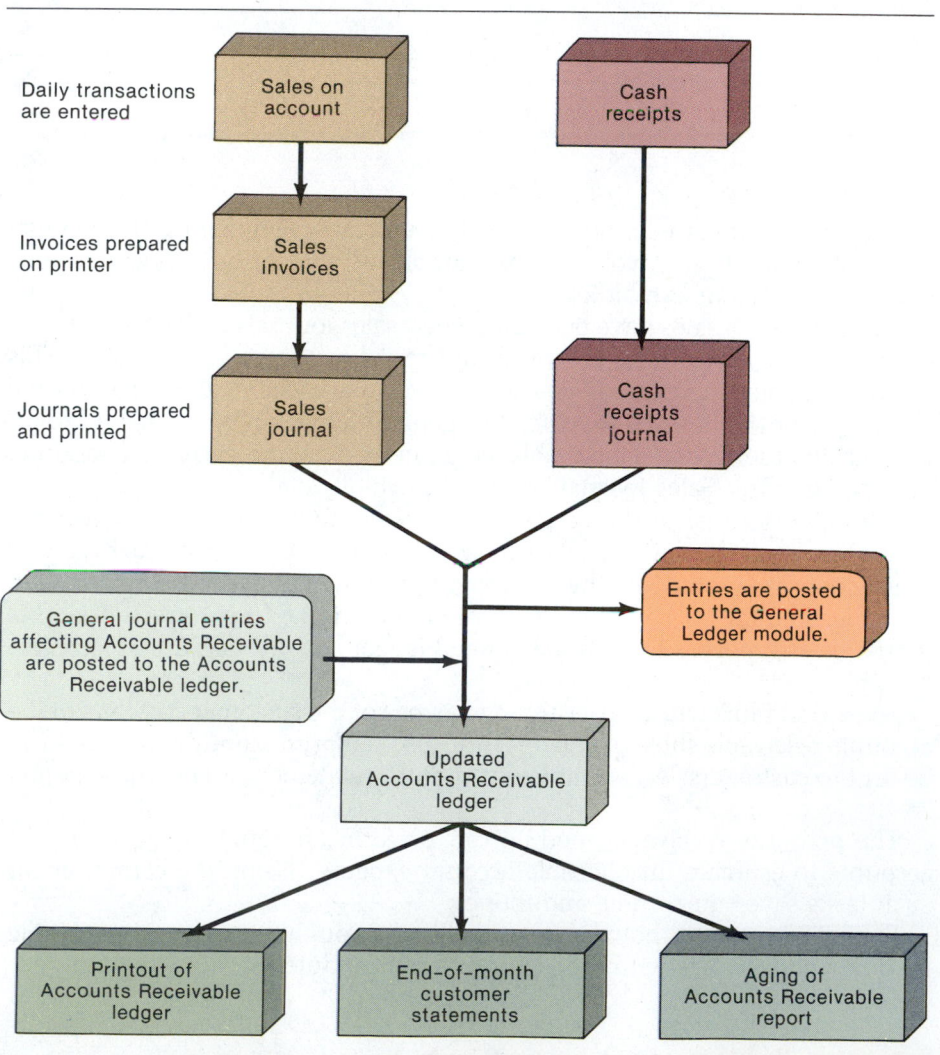

Accounts Payable Module

A business can use the accounts payable program to maintain its accounts payable ledger, issue checks to pay accounts payable, and generate both the purchases and cash payments journals. A typical accounts payable module menu is shown in Exhibit 28-12.

When a purchase invoice is received from a vendor, it is entered into the accounts payable module. For each batch of purchase invoices the program will create a purchases journal. Its entries can be posted to both the accounts payable ledger and the general ledger.

Before invoices come due for payment, the system can provide a list of each invoice due on a particular date ("A/P Aging Reports" option of the Accounts Payable menu). The accountant can list the invoice to be paid and the amount of the payment. Using preprinted forms, the computer can print the checks ("Enter/Print Checks" option). Exhibit 28-13 is an example of a computer-generated check along with its stub showing information about the invoice paid.

The program records each check in the cash disbursements journal. This journal can be posted to both the accounts payable and general ledgers. Paid invoices can be shown along with the date of payment. A business may wish to print a list of all paid invoices for the records and delete them from the computer files. This step can prevent paying an invoice twice, paying the wrong amount, or mistakenly paying too late to receive the discount. Also, if an inventory module is added to this system, each purchase of merchandise

Class Exercise: Using Exhibit 28-12, can you find a program on the Accounts Payable menu that would be especially useful in budgeting cash disbursements for the coming month and would help with cash management? *ANSWER:* The A/P Aging Reports, a listing of invoices that indicates when each invoice is due and how old the invoice is, date, would show management exactly when cash outflows should occur on payables.

EXHIBIT 28-12 *Menu for Accounts Payable Module*

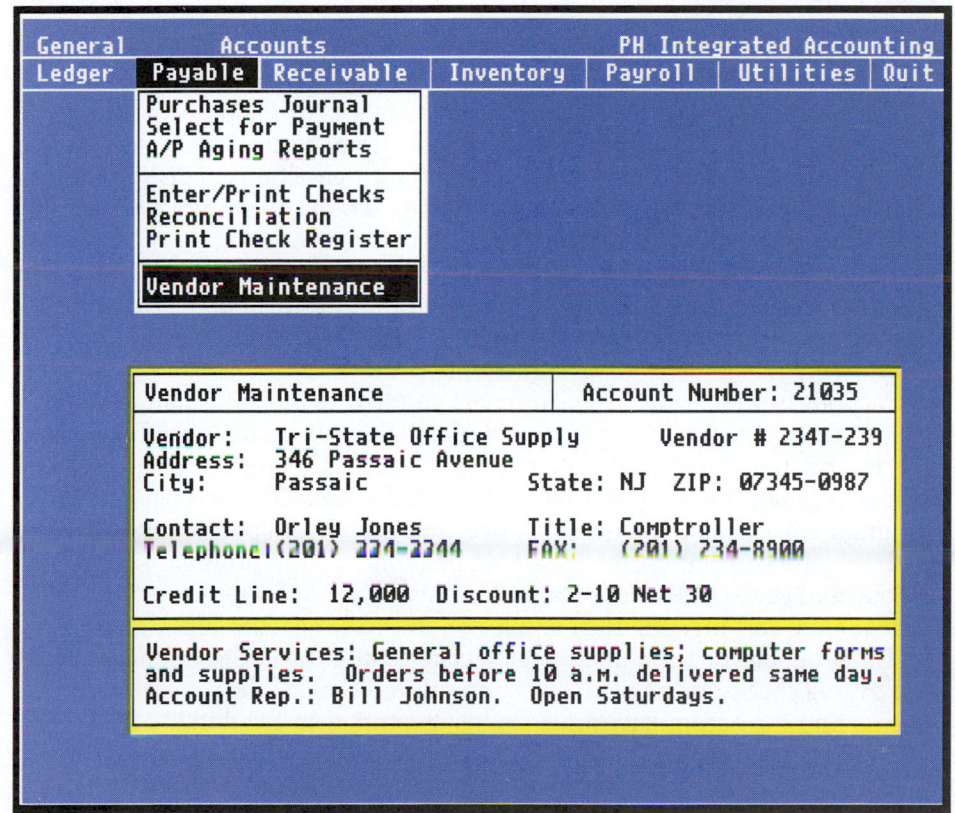

EXHIBIT 28-13   *Check for Cash Payment*

```
 o                                                              GUARANTY NATIONAL BANK                o
 o      J&L Office Supply                                        CHECK  005074                        o
        1200 Poydras Street
 o      New Orleans, LA 70130                  DATE      CONTROL NO.        AMOUNT                     o
                                              6-23-XX      4813            4471.60
 o                                                                                                    o
          FOUR THOUSAND FOUR HUNDRED SEVENTY ONE AND 60/100--------------------
 o                                                                                                    o
        PAY     Franklin Paper Co.                           J&L Office Supply
 o      TO THE  2120 Essen Lane                                                                       o
        ORDER OF Baton Rouge, LA 70810          _____
 o                                                          AUTHORIZED SIGNATURE                      o

 o                                                                                                    o

 o         J&L Office Supply—1200 Poydras Street—New Orleans, LA          CHECK  005074               o
```

OUR REF. NO.	YOUR INVOICE NO.	INVOICE DATE	INVOICE AMOUNT	AMOUNT PAID	DISCOUNT TAKEN	NET CHECK AMOUNT
P1028	5673	6-10-XX	3080.00	3080.00		3080.00
P1264	5823	6-17-XX	1420.00	1420.00	28.40	1391.60
					TOTAL	4471.60

can automatically be added into the inventory list. Exhibit 28-14 shows how information flows in a system using an accounts payable module.

Payroll Module

As stated earlier, payroll accounting is ideally suited for a computerized system. A typical payroll module menu is shown in Exhibit 28-15.

To use the payroll program, the business sets up a file on each employee. These files will contain such information as name, address, pay rate, marital status, withholding allowances, and voluntary deductions. This information can be modified at any time (for example, when an employee moves or receives a raise, or when a new employee is hired).

For each pay period we will use the "Payroll Calculation" option in the menu to calculate the period's payroll. The program will list each employee and show the current-period information—number of regular and overtime hours worked, bonuses or commissions to be received, and any voluntary deductions from this paycheck. For most employees this information does not change from pay period to pay period and will not have to be modified. After the information for the current payroll is entered using the "Enter Payroll Hours" option, the computer will automatically calculate each paycheck. The program will calculate regular pay, overtime pay, gross pay, each deduction, and net pay. Current tax tables should be built into the program so that both federal and state taxes can be computed. Also, the computer keeps a record of year-to-date earnings for each employee and can calculate FICA taxes.

The program can print the payroll register. After the information is verified, the payroll checks are printed. Using preprinted checks, the program can print checks and the accompanying stubs, as illustrated in Exhibit 28-16.

After the payroll checks have been printed, the payroll register information is posted to the general ledger and the employee's individual earnings records are updated. Both tasks are performed by choosing the appropriate menu option.

Point to Stress: Payroll is usually the first microcomputer program that a business implements. Payroll programs are standardized and require very little (if any) modification.

Some businesses use a stand-alone payroll module that performs the calculations and then prints checks and reports. Payroll totals may be manually entered into the general ledger system. Of course, it is more convenient to have the two systems interfaced (connected), but not mandatory.

Point to Stress: Tax rates change annually. There should be instructions provided with the payroll software package that show the operator how to change tax rates each year, and how to change the tax base for social security taxes. However, some programs may have to be returned to the manufacturer for federal or state income tax rate changes.

EXHIBIT 28-14 *Information Flow in the Accounts Payable Module*

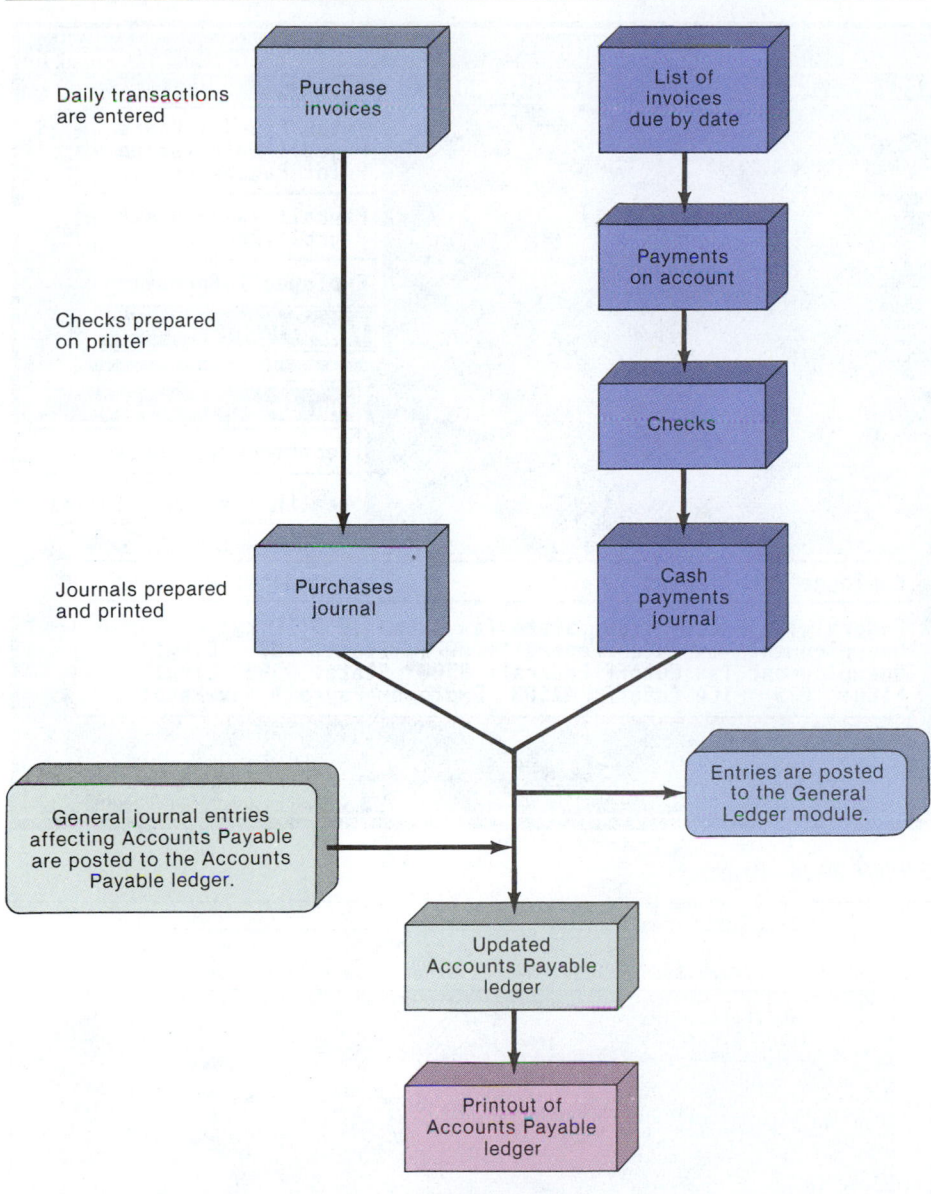

Daily transactions are entered

Checks prepared on printer

Journals prepared and printed

Purchase invoices

List of invoices due by date

Payments on account

Checks

Purchases journal

Cash payments journal

Entries are posted to the General Ledger module.

General journal entries affecting Accounts Payable are posted to the Accounts Payable ledger.

Updated Accounts Payable ledger

Printout of Accounts Payable ledger

At the end of the calendar year the business prepares a W-2 form for each employee. An example is shown in Exhibit 28-17 on page 1257.

Exhibit 28-18, on page 1258, shows how information flows in a system using a payroll module.

Spreadsheets

Spreadsheets are integrated software programs that can be used to solve many different problems. Spreadsheet programs replace the manual solution of problems. Typical accounting applications performed with a spreadsheet include budgets, depreciation schedules, debt amortization schedules, cost-volume-profit analysis, and capital budgeting.

Teaching Tip: You will need to provide detailed instructions to students for loading the 1-2-3 system diskette at your school. Methods will vary somewhat, depending on whether or not DOS (Disk Operating System) has been copied to the 1-2-3 system diskette. Other possible variations could be due to different hardware configurations (hard disks, local area networks, and so on).

EXHIBIT 28-15 *Menu for a Payroll Module*

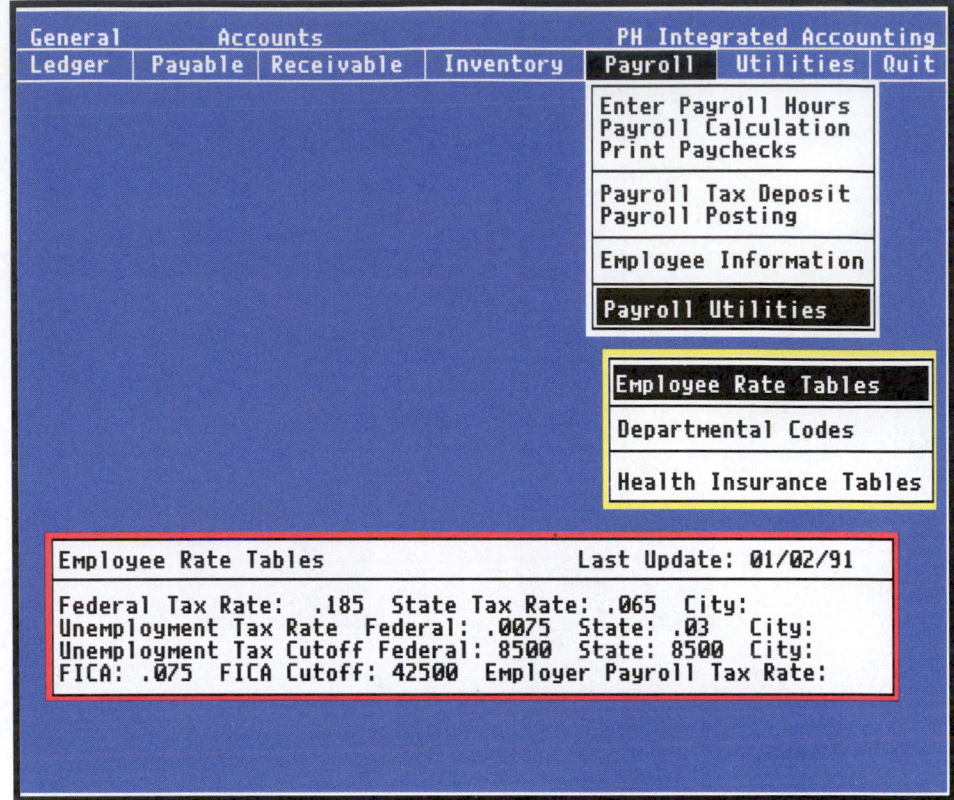

EXHIBIT 28-16 *Paycheck*

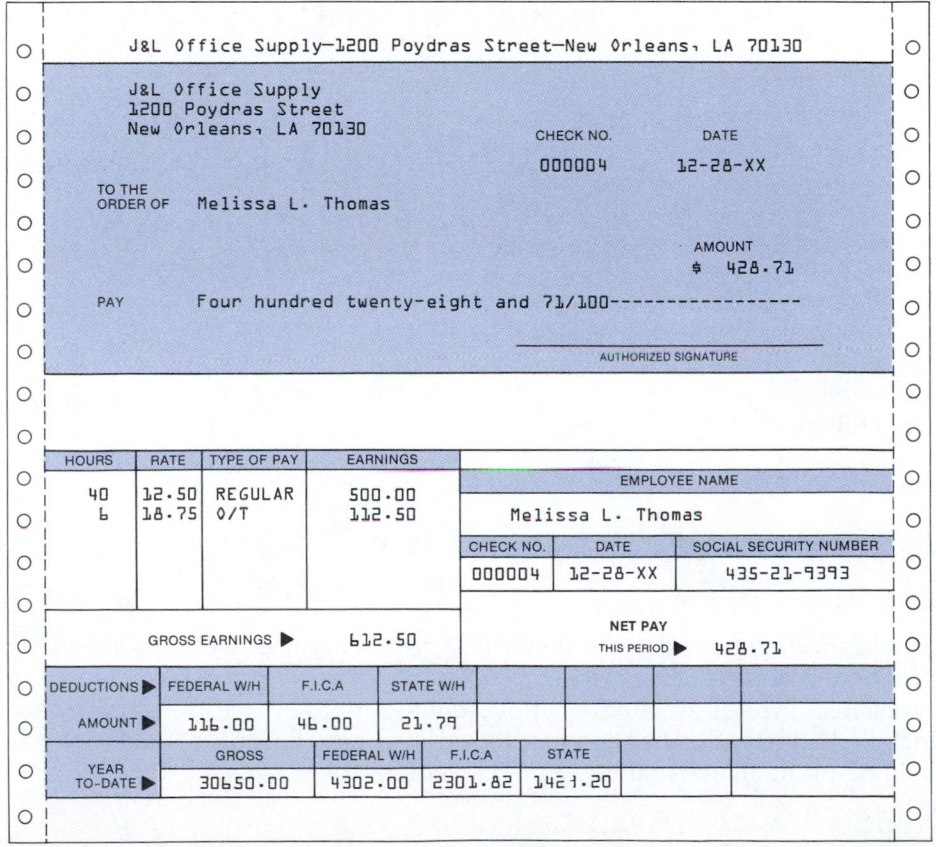

EXHIBIT 28-17 *W-2 Form*

1 Control number	2222	For Paperwork Reduction Act Notice, see separate instructions OMB No. 1545-0008	For Official Use only ▶		

2 Employer's name, address, and ZIP code	6 Statutory employee ☒ Deceased ☐ Pension plan ☐ Legal rep. ☐	942 emp. ☐ Subtotal ☐ Deferred compensation ☐ Void ☐

J&L Office Supply
1200 Poydras Street
New Orleans, LA 70130

7 Allocated tips	8 Advance EIC payment
9 Federal income tax withheld 4,302.00	10 Wages, tips, other compensation 30,650.00

3 Employer's identification number 72-1214782	4 Employer's state I.D. number 54-7699-4	11 Social security tax withheld 2,301.82	12 Social security wages 30,650.00

5 Employee's social security number 435-21-9393	13 Social security tips	14 Nonqualified plans

19a Employee's name, address and ZIP code Melissa L. Thomas	15 Dependent care benefits	16 Fringe benefits incl. in Box 10

23 Rue De la Place Avenue
New Orleans, LA 70124

17 See instr. for Forms W-2/W-2P	18 Other

19b Employee's address and ZIP code

20	21	22	23

24 State income tax 1,429.20	25 State wages, tips, etc. 30,650.00	26 Name of state LA	27 Local income tax	28 Local wages, tips, etc.	29 Name of locality

Copy A For Social Security Administration   Dept. of the Treasury—Internal Revenue Service

Form **W-2 Wage and Tax Statement 1990**

Do NOT CUT or Separate Forms on This Page

1 Control number	2222	For Paperwork Reduction Act Notice, see separate instructions OMB No. 1545-0008	For Official Use only ▶		

2 Employer's name, address, and ZIP code	6 Statutory employee ☒ Deceased ☐ Pension plan ☐ Legal rep. ☐	942 emp. ☐ Subtotal ☐ Deferred compensation ☐ Void ☐

J&L Office Supply
1200 Poydras Street
New Orleans, LA 70130

7 Allocated tips	8 Advance EIC payment
9 Federal income tax withheld 4,302.00	10 Wages, tips, other compensation 30,650.00

3 Employer's identification number 72-1214782	4 Employer's state I.D. number 54-7699-4	11 Social security tax withheld 2,301.82	12 Social security wages 30,650.00

5 Employee's social security number 435-21-9393	13 Social security tips	14 Nonqualified plans

19a Employee's name, address and ZIP code Melissa L. Thomas	15 Dependent care benefits	16 Fringe benefits incl. in Box 10

23 Rue De la Place Avenue
New Orleans, LA 70124

17 See instr. for Forms W-2/W-2P	18 Other

19b Employee's address and ZIP code

20	21	22	23

24 State income tax 1,429.20	25 State wages, tips, etc. 30,650.00	26 Name of state LA	27 Local income tax	28 Local wages, tips, etc.	29 Name of locality

Copy A For Social Security Administration   Dept. of the Treasury—Internal Revenue Service

Form **W-2 Wage and Tax Statement 1990**

The most popular of the spreadsheet programs is Lotus 1-2-3®, which includes an electronic spreadsheet with graphics and data-management capabilities. Lotus 1-2-3 runs on a variety of personal computers and IBM-compatible computers. Other spreadsheet programs on the market that are structured similarly to Lotus 1-2-3 include Excel and Quattro Pro.

The spreadsheet of a 1-2-3 application is organized into a matrix of rows labeled by numbers and columns labeled by letters.

The intersections of the rows and columns represent entry positions called

EXHIBIT 28-18 *Information Flow in the Payroll Module*

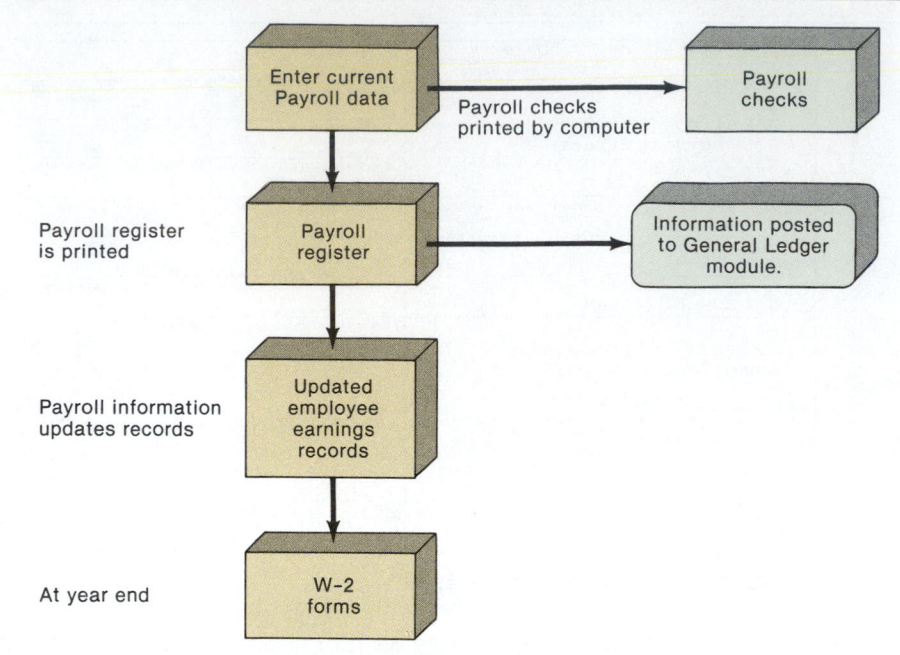

cells. The cells may be referenced by their column-row coordinates. Position B5 represents column B and row 5. The spreadsheet of Lotus 1-2-3, Release 2, has 256 columns and 8,192 rows. At each cell, you can type either a label (title) or a value. A value can be a number, a formula, or a 1-2-3 function. The highlighter must be moved to the cell in which you want to enter the label or value. A sample income statement follows.

By creating labels and values on the spreadsheet, you can set up charts and tables. Through formatting commands, you control the appearance of the spreadsheet. It is easy to format the spreadsheet as a personal budget or as an income statement for a business. We illustrate formatting later in the chapter.

A powerful feature of a spreadsheet program is its ability to remember the

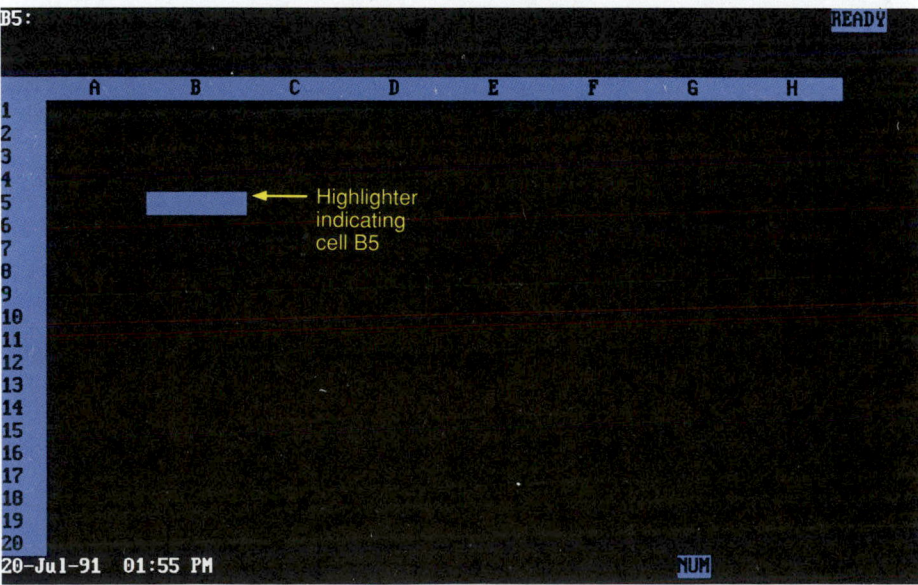

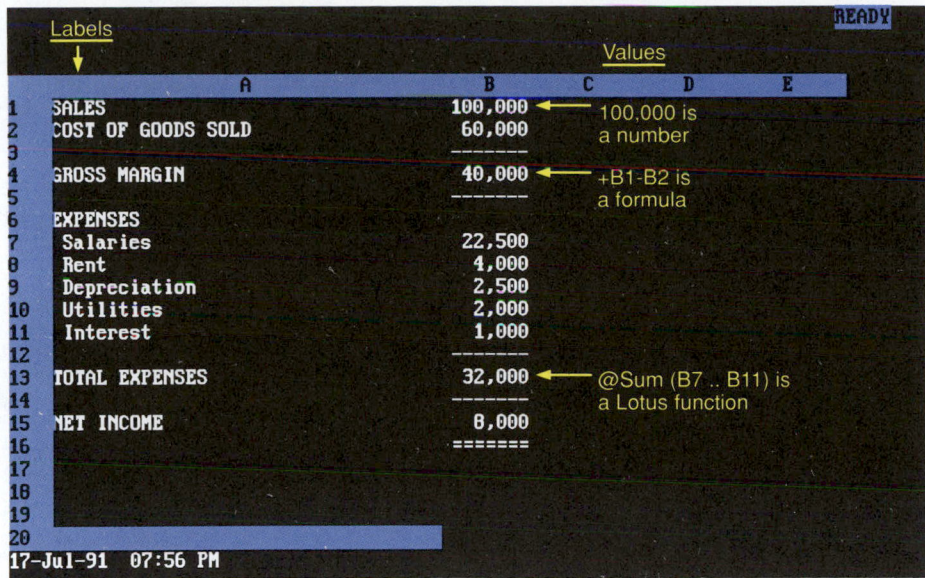

Labels → / Values

	A	B	C	D	E
					READY
1	SALES	100,000			← 100,000 is a number
2	COST OF GOODS SOLD	60,000			
3		————			
4	GROSS MARGIN	40,000			← +B1-B2 is a formula
5		————			
6	EXPENSES				
7	Salaries	22,500			
8	Rent	4,000			
9	Depreciation	2,500			
10	Utilities	2,000			
11	Interest	1,000			
12		————			
13	TOTAL EXPENSES	32,000			← @Sum (B7 .. B11) is a Lotus function
14		————			
15	NET INCOME	8,000			
16		======			
17					
18					
19					
20					

17-Jul-91 07:56 PM

formulas and calculations that have been entered into the spreadsheet. Suppose you want to change the sales in the preceding illustration from $100,000 to $150,000. You can simply make a change in the cell containing the sales amount, B1, and all other entries that depend on sales are automatically recalculated. For example, Gross Margin, in cell B4, would change automatically from $40,000 to $90,000. This feature makes a spreadsheet very efficient for creating "what-if" analysis without the tedious recalculation by hand calculator and pencil.

Keyboard

The keyboard, an input device for entering data into the computer, includes four major parts: (1) typewriter section, (2) pointer-movement keys, (3) function keys, and (4) special keys. Exhibit 28-19 shows one version of an IBM PC keyboard. The position of the keys may vary slightly among similar keyboards.

Teaching Tip: The keyboard layout of the PCs at your school may vary somewhat from the diagram shown here. IBM PS2 models have the function keys at the top of the keyboard, and an additional set of directional arrow keys separate from the numeric key pad. This allows use of the 10-key and the cursor positioning keys without switching back and forth with the NUM LOCK key.

EXHIBIT 28-19   *IBM PC Keyboard*   Transparency T28-3

③ ④   ①   ④ ②

F1	F2	ESC	! 1	@ 2	# 3	$ 4	% 5	^ 6	& 7	* 8	(9	) 0	_ -	+ =		←		Num Lock		Scroll Lock / Break
F3	F4	→|	Q	W	E	R	T	Y	U	I	O	P	{ [	}]			7 Home	8 ↑	9 PgUp
F5	F6	Ctrl	A	S	D	F	G	H	J	K	L	; :	" '	~ `	↵		4 ←	5	6 →
F7	F8	⇧	| \\	Z	X	C	V	B	N	M	< ,	> .	? /	⇧			1 End	2 ↓	3 PgDn	+
F9	F10	Alt					Space Bar						Caps Lock		0 Ins		Del

Typewriter Section

The typewriter section acts just like a typewriter. Striking a key gives the lower-case character, for example, "g," not "G." Holding down the shift key, ⇧, and pressing any letter or special character results in the upper case of the key. For example, with the shift key depressed, striking the 8 key gives * (the asterisk). If the [Caps Lock] key is ON, then you will get the upper case of the letters without having to depress the shift key in combination. You still must press the shift key to get the upper case of the special (nonletter) characters (+, <, >, ?, and so on). Use the typewriter keys to enter numbers.

Pointer-Movement Keys

The arrow keys direct 1-2-3's attention to a particular cell in the spreadsheet by moving the highlighter cell up and down, left and right. Depressing the [Home] key moves the highlighter cell to the Home position, which is column A and row 1. Each screen in Lotus 1-2-3® displays twenty lines. The [PgUp] key moves the screen twenty lines closer to the spreadsheet's beginning. The [PgDn] key moves the screen twenty lines toward the spreadsheet's end.

Lotus 1-2-3® is a menu-driven system, which means that you are presented choices of commands and options to select. To choose from a 1-2-3 menu, you can highlight the appropriate choice by using the arrow keys and depressing ↵. Alternatively, you can depress the first character of the option desired (for example, to copy a cell, type C for copy). The latter approach is more commonly used.

Function Keys

The ten function keys on the IBM keyboard are used by 1-2-3 as follows:

F1	F2
F3	F4
F5	F6
F7	F8
F9	F10

Key	Name	Description
F1:	Help	Display Help screen
F2:	Edit	Switch to/from Edit for current entry
F3:	Name	(Point Mode) Display menu of range names
F4:	Abs	(Point Mode) Make/Unmake cell addresses absolute
F5:	GoTo	Move cell pointer to a particular cell
F6:	Window	(Split screen only) Move cell pointer to other window
F7:	Query	Repeat most recent Data Query operation
F8:	Table	Repeat most recent Data Table operation
F9:	Calc	Recalculates work sheet formulas in Ready Mode
F10:	Graph	Draws current graph

Special Keys

We look at some of the special keys in the diagram at the top of the next page.

Exhibit 28-20 describes what you see on the monitor screen with 1-2-3.

Mode Indicators

The upper-right corner of the 1-2-3 screen tells what is occurring at that time.

Ready   1-2-3 is waiting for you.
Value   You are typing a number, formula, or numeric function.

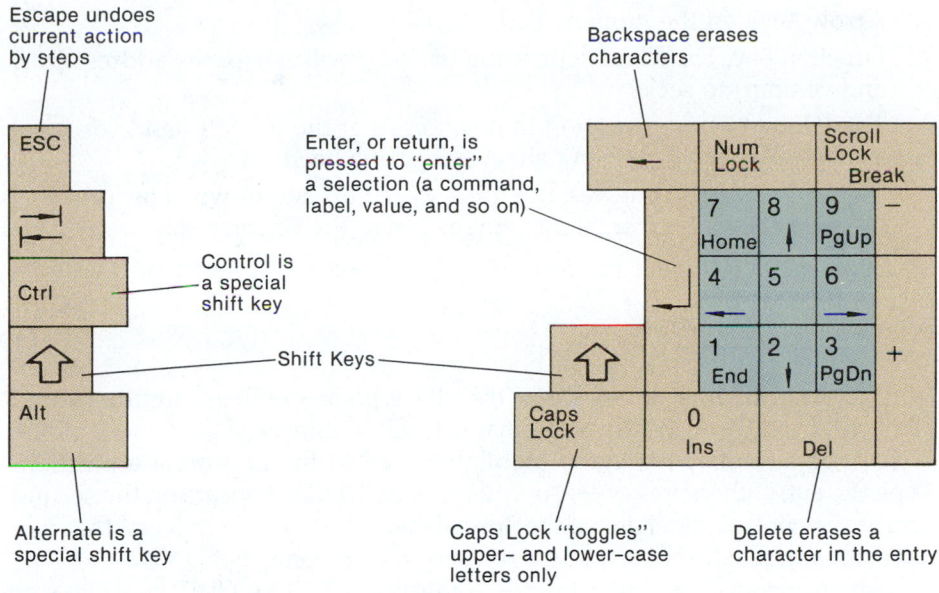

Escape undoes
current action
by steps

ESC

Control is
a special
shift key

Ctrl

Shift Keys

Alt

Alternate is a
special shift key

Enter, or return, is
pressed to "enter"
a selection (a command,
label, value, and so on)

Backspace erases
characters

	Num Lock	Scroll Lock Break	
7 Home	8 ↑	9 PgUp	−
4	5	6	
1 End	2 ↓	3 PgDn	+
Caps Lock	0 Ins	Del	

Caps Lock "toggles"
upper- and lower-case
letters only

Delete erases a
character in the entry

Label   You are typing a label.

Menu   You are selecting a menu choice.

Moving Around the Spreadsheet

You can move the highlighter cell around the spreadsheet by using one of the methods listed at the top of the next page.

EXHIBIT 28-20 *The Spreadsheet*

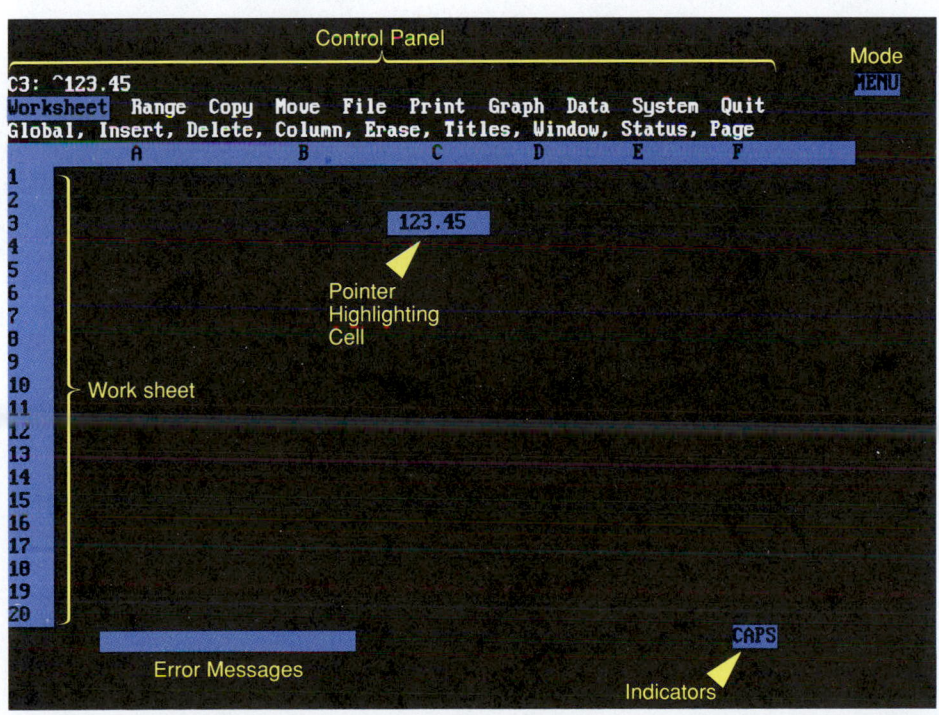

Control Panel

Mode

MENU

C3: ^123.45

Worksheet Range Copy Move File Print Graph Data System Quit
Global, Insert, Delete, Column, Erase, Titles, Window, Status, Page

A   B   C   D   E   F

123.45

Pointer
Highlighting
Cell

Work sheet

Error Messages

CAPS

Indicators

1. Arrow keys on the numeric pad.
2. Function key, F5. When depressing F5, 1-2-3 will ask for the address (row and column) to seek.
3. The [Home] key returns you to position Al at the top left-hand corner of the spreadsheet if the work sheet titles have been set.
4. [PgUp] and [PgDn] moves an entire screen up and down. The Tab key (⇥) allows horizontal movement across the screen.

Typing Cell Entries

Point to Stress: When entering numbers that are to be used in calculations, they must be entered as values. Do not preface the entry with one of the label prefix symbols (', '', ^). You cannot center a number in a cell and expect to use it in a calculation. If you enter a number as a label, the numeric value will be zero and some strange calculations will result.

If you want to dress up a spreadsheet with underlining, you may have to use a label prefix symbol as the first character in an entry. For instance, if you begin an entry with a −, the − will be interpreted as a minus sign and 1-2-3 will expect either a number or a formula to follow. If you want a string of −'s for an underlining effect, begin the entry with the label prefix symbol, '.

In the spreadsheet, you can either directly type in numbers, formulas, and labels or use a Copy or Move command to fill in entries.

To type an entry, move the highlighter cell to the appropriate position. Type the entry, then press ↵. As you type, each letter appears on the second line of the control panel above the spreadsheet. If you type in a cell that you have already filled, the new entry replaces the old one.

If you begin an entry with a number-indicator, 1 2 3 4 5 6 7 8 9 0 + −. (@ # or $, then 1-2-3 interprets the entry as a number or formula. If you begin an entry with any other character (for example, A, L, or *), 1-2-3 interprets the entry as a label. A few of these characters have special purposes for positioning the label in the cell:

Special Label Prefix Symbols	Function	Example Cell
' (apostrophe)	left-aligns	123.45
'' (quotation mark)	right-aligns	123.45
^ (caret)	centers	123.45
\ (backslash)	fills entire cell with the character following \	

If you want to enter a label that begins with a number-indicator, precede the entry with a special label prefix symbol. By doing so you tell the computer that the entry is a label and not a value. For example, if you want a column headed by a centered "1," begin the "1" with a caret.

Correcting Mistakes

Typical Student Misconception: The concept of the automatic insert feature is sometimes confusing to students. They often feel that when they depress F2 and enter the Edit mode, they should be able to type over existing characters and replace them with new characters. The only way to get rid of unwanted characters in the Edit mode is to use the DEL key.

If you make an incorrect entry before depressing ↵, you can correct the error two ways. Either blank out the entire entry by depressing [Esc] or use the backspace key, which erases the incorrect characters.

After storing an entry in a particular cell (by depressing ↵ after typing in the entry), you can use the Edit mode to correct the error. To Edit, locate the pointer at the cell in question and depress F2. Once in the Edit mode, the current contents of the cell will appear in the upper-left corner of the screen with the cursor (the flashing underline symbol) at the end of the entry. The cursor indicates the position of the next character to be typed.

Deleting
[Backspace] Delete character preceding the cursor
[Del] Delete character at the cursor

Most personal computers have an auto-repeat feature that is particularly useful with these editing keys. When you hold a key down, it repeats its function at about 2 strokes per second.

Inserting

Just type new characters to be inserted at the cursor position. 1-2-3 always inserts new characters in the Edit mode. It does not "overstrike" or "replace" existing characters with newly added ones. Therefore, you must insert new characters after deleting old ones. For example, to change a cell, first delete the old characters. Then enter the new ones. When you are finished editing, depress ◄┘ to store the changed entry.

Formulas

A formula is a cell entry that instructs 1-2-3 to calculate a number. Often a formula uses cell addresses as values. For example, the formula +A1+A2 means to sum the values in cells A1 and A2 and enter that number in the highlighted cell.

The arithmetic operators used in formulas are listed in their order of precedence.

Arithmetic operator	Result
*	multiplication
/	division
+	addition
−	subtraction

In the formula +A1+A2/A3, the division would be carried out before the addition even though the "/" sign comes after the "+" sign. You can use parentheses to override the built-in order. Writing the above formula as (A1+A2)/A3 would cause the addition to take place first.

Start formulas with a "+" sign. This ensures that 1-2-3 will not think you are typing a label. Alternatively, you can place parentheses around the formula to guarantee that the entry will be interpreted as a value rather than as a label.

Cell Addresses in Formulas. A major benefit of spreadsheet software is the ability to enter a formula in one cell and then copy that formula into many other cells. Cell addresses are relative or absolute.

RELATIVE ADDRESSES. A cell address that does not include a "$" character is relative. Assume the formula +B1−B2 is entered into B4. Relative to B4, cell B1 is 3 rows above and cell B2 is 2 rows above. We can, then, interpret the formula to mean "take the number in the cell 2 rows up (but in the same column) and subtract from it the number 3 rows up." The resulting amount is entered into the cell in which this formula appears. See cell B4 in the next display. We copy this formula to columns C, D, and E. Since the cell addresses are relative, the formula in cell C4 means to subtract the amount in C2 from the amount in C1. The formula shifts similarly as we copy +B1−B2 into columns D and E.

Notice in the above example how each B in the formula in cell B4 changed to a C, a D, and an E when the formula was copied to cells C4 through E4. When a formula with relative cell addresses is copied across columns, as in this example, the letter portion of the addresses will change relative to the new

Teaching Tip: The concept of relative versus absolute cell addresses is a bit confusing at first. Time spent on the examples in these sections should pay great dividends.

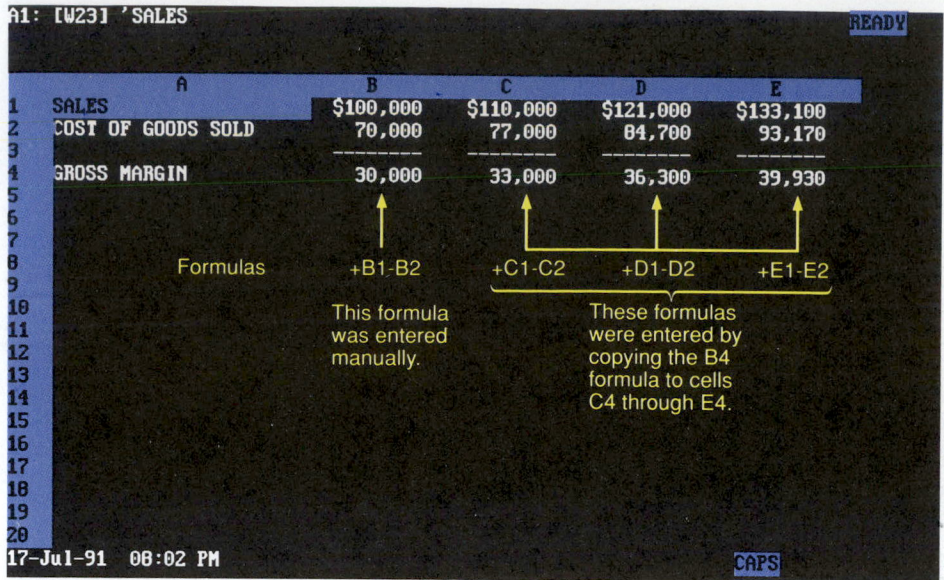

A1: [W23] 'SALES   READY

	A	B	C	D	E
1	SALES	$100,000	$110,000	$121,000	$133,100
2	COST OF GOODS SOLD	70,000	77,000	84,700	93,170
4	GROSS MARGIN	30,000	33,000	36,300	39,930

Formulas   +B1-B2   +C1-C2   +D1-D2   +E1-E2

This formula was entered manually.

These formulas were entered by copying the B4 formula to cells C4 through E4.

17-Jul-91 08:02 PM   CAPS

column. When a formula with relative cell addresses is copied down rows, the number portion of the addresses will change relative to the new row.

ABSOLUTE ADDRESSES (USED ONLY IN FORMULAS). A cell address in which the symbol "$" precedes both the column letter and the row number is absolute, which means it will not change even if it is copied elsewhere. In a formula, an absolute cell address indicates the value's exact column/row location. The formula 12*$C$5 means "twelve times the value of cell C5." The result of this multiplication will be the same in however many cells to which this formula is copied. In a copied formula, all absolute cell addresses are the same as in the original formula (C5 in this case).

A formula may contain both relative and absolute addresses. "Mixed" addresses—part relative, part absolute—can also be used.

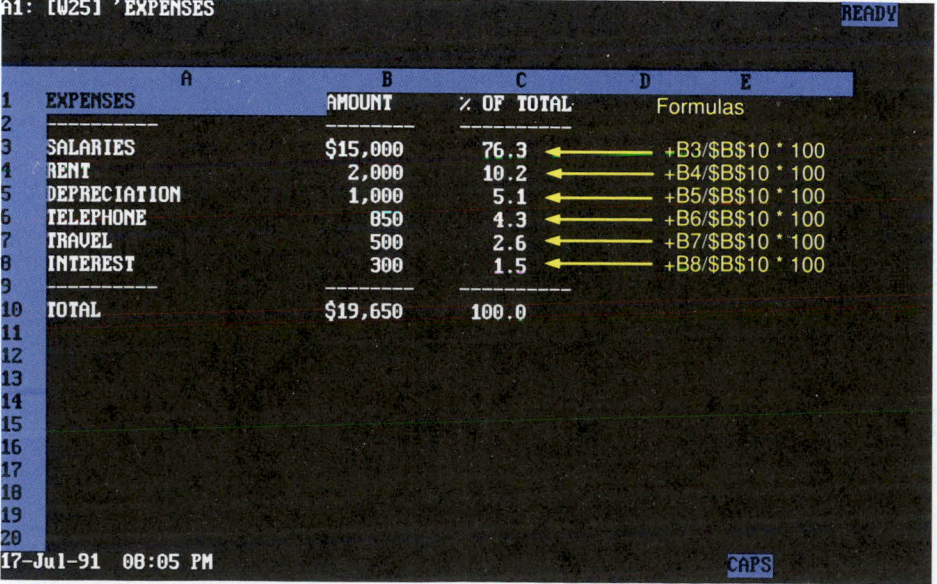

A1: [W25] 'EXPENSES   READY

	A	B	C	D	E
1	EXPENSES	AMOUNT	% OF TOTAL	Formulas	
3	SALARIES	$15,000	76.3	+B3/$B$10 * 100	
4	RENT	2,000	10.2	+B4/$B$10 * 100	
5	DEPRECIATION	1,000	5.1	+B5/$B$10 * 100	
6	TELEPHONE	850	4.3	+B6/$B$10 * 100	
7	TRAVEL	500	2.6	+B7/$B$10 * 100	
8	INTEREST	300	1.5	+B8/$B$10 * 100	
10	TOTAL	$19,650	100.0		

17-Jul-91 08:05 PM   CAPS

The formula (B3/$B$10) in cell C3 was entered manually. The formulas in cells C4 through C8 were entered by copying this same formula from cell C3 to cells C4 through C8. Placing a "$" in front of the "B" and in front of the "10" in the formula in cell C3 keeps $B$10 constant in cells C4 through C8. Notice however that the "3" in B3 *does* change relative to the new rows. We want $B$10 to remain constant in the denominator in order to compute each expense as a percent of the same total—$19,650. However, we want the "3" in B3 to change relative to the new rows in order to compute each expense's percentage of the total. This is why we do not place a $ symbol around the B3 portion of the formula.

When you create a formula that is to be copied to other cells, ask yourself the question, "Do I want part of the formula not to change relative to the new cells in which the formula is copied?" If the answer is yes, you must place a "$" before each portion of the address that should not change.

1-2-3 Commands

During each 1-2-3 session, you can issue commands to operate on the spreadsheet. Commands can:

1. Copy, move, and delete entries in the spreadsheet.
2. Transfer data between the spreadsheet and disk storage (for example, to store the spreadsheet on a diskette and to retrieve the spreadsheet from a storage diskette).
3. Print reports.

To use a command, depress the slash (/) key. A menu with the following choices on the first line will appear:

```
Worksheet  Range  Copy  Move  File  Print  Graph  Data  System  Quit
```

You can choose one of these commands either by typing the first letter of the command or by pointing the highlighter to the command and depressing ◄─┘. Most of the commands have submenus, from which you choose the next steps as necessary. If you want to interrupt a command, depress [Esc]. Each time you depress [Esc], you back up one level.

In general, when you want an option that affects the entire spreadsheet, you choose the Worksheet option. When you want a command that affects limited cells, you typically choose the Range option. The Copy command saves time by minimizing the manual entry of cells. The Move command is a "cut and paste" operation that allows you to "cut" out a portion of the spreadsheet and "paste" it to another area without having to retype the information. The File command is used to save or retrieve a file stored on a diskette. The Print command allows you to print a copy of your spreadsheet on paper. The Graph command is used to draw five different types of graphs. The Data command is used to sort data in a spreadsheet either alphabetically or numerically and also to select certain data from the spreadsheet. The System command (in a later release of 1-2-3) returns control of the computer to its operating system. The Quit command is used to stop operations in 1-2-3.

Application of Common 1-2-3 Commands

1. Changing column widths. Initially the widths of all 256 columns are 9 characters. This width can be decreased or increased as follows:

/Worksheet Global Column-Width

changes the width of all the columns.

/Worksheet Column-Width Set

changes the width of only the column in which the highlighter was positioned prior to issuing the command.

With either command, you will be asked what width you want. You can either type the width or use the left or right directional arrow key. The right arrow key increases the width, and the left arrow key decreases it. After you have selected the desired width, depress ←┘ to enter the command.

2. Formatting the spreadsheet. Formatting, in computer language, determines how results are to be displayed. Lotus 1-2-3 provides several formats in a spreadsheet. You can use dollar signs, commas, a fixed number of decimal positions, and percent signs in numbers. You can format the entire spreadsheet with one command, or you can format selected cells. A format command does not affect cells that are labels, even if the labels are numbers. A format command does not affect what is actually stored in a cell. The command affects only the appearance of the cell, as follows:

/Worksheet Global Format

affects the appearance of the entire spreadsheet.

/Range Format

affects the appearance of selected cells.

With either selection, you are asked for the specific format of your choice. The following choices and their results are:

Format	Result of Format
1. Currency	Displays numbers with a leading $ and places commas where necessary.
2. , [Comma]	Produces same format as currency but omits the $.
3. Percent	Multiplies the entry by 100 and places a % on the end of the display.

3. Erasing the contents of existing cells.
/Worksheet Erase Yes

erases the contents of *all* the cells in the spreadsheet. Use this command with care.

/Range Erase

erases selected cells. At the end of the command, you will be asked which cells you want to erase. You can type the range. A range is specified by typing the first and last cell addresses in the range and separating them by a period. For example, A1.C1 specifies cells A1, B1, and C1. The range A1.C3 specifies cells A1, A2, A3, B1, B2, B3, and C1, C2, C3.

4. Inserting or deleting columns or rows. Before issuing the following commands, you should place the highlighter in the column or row where you want to insert or delete.

/Worksheet Insert (Column or Row)
/Worksheet Delete (Column or Row)

5. *Moving cells.* You can "cut" cells out of the spreadsheet and "paste" them into another area by specifying a FROM and a TO range. The FROM range specifies the cells you want to move, and the TO range specifies where you want the cells to be placed.

/Move From: Range (for example, B5.B8) To: Range (for example, C5.C8)

6. *Copying cells.* You can copy (a) one cell to another cell, (b) one cell to many cells, and (c) many cells to many cells. In copying cells, you must specify a FROM range and a TO range for the command. You can specify these ranges by typing.

Copying examples:

(a) One cell to another cell
If you want to copy the contents of cell A1 to cell B1, you would issue the following command and ranges:
/Copy From: A1 To: B1

(b) One cell to many cells
If you want to copy the contents of cell Al to cells B1 through H1, you would issue the following command and ranges:
/Copy From: A1 To: B1.H1

(c) Many cells to many cells
If you want to copy the contents of cells A10 through A15 to columns B through H, you would issue the command and ranges:
/Copy From: A10.A15 To: B10.H15

7. *Interacting with the storage diskette.* To make a permanent copy of your active spreadsheet on a storage diskette or to retrieve a previously stored spreadsheet from the diskette and load it into the computer memory, issue a File command.

/File Save
copies the spreadsheet on the screen to your storage diskette. When you save a spreadsheet for the first time, you will be asked for a file name. This name can be as long as eight characters with no spaces in the name. The file name can be a combination of letters, numbers, and special characters. When you save a spreadsheet for the second time or thereafter, the original name you gave it will appear after you enter /File Save. If you depress ←┘, you will be presented with the options Cancel or Replace. If you choose the option Replace, the old version stored on the diskette will be written over (replaced) by the new version. If you want to keep the old version on the diskette and also save the new version, change the name of the present file after issuing the command /File Save.

/File Retrieve
moves a previously stored spreadsheet into memory. A list of the stored spreadsheets will appear on the screen, and you can either type the name or highlight the desired spreadsheet and depress ←┘. This operation does not affect the spreadsheet on the diskette. Before you can make changes to or print an existing spreadsheet, you must load it into memory.

8. *Printing a 1-2-3 spreadsheet.* In order to print a spreadsheet using Lotus 1-2-3®, you must first have the spreadsheet loaded into memory and visible on the screen. You should also have the printer turned on, with the online light switched on and the paper positioned at the top of a fresh page.

Point to Stress: If the spreadsheet that you are printing is wider than one screen, then it will print as many columns as it can fit on the first page and the remaining columns on page 2 and thereafter. If the total number of characters that you are printing is 132 or less (approximately 14 columns), you can condense the size of the print and the printout will fit on one page. You must set two options to cause condensed printing: MARGINS and SETUP. You would need to increase the right margin from its standard setting of 76 to 132. You would also need to issue a setup string or code of 015 to command the printer to print smaller. The command to condense would then be:

/Print Printer

Range → Set the range of cells to be printed.

Options → Margins → Right → Type over the 76 with 132

Options → Setup → Type: 15

Align Go

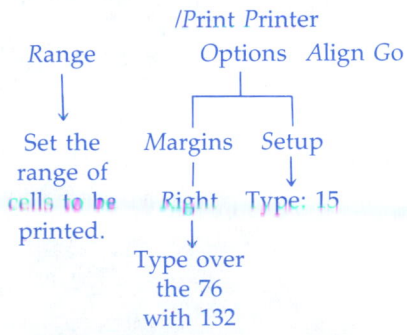

If the spreadsheet is wider than 132 characters (approximately 14 columns), it will still print the extra columns on page 2 and thereafter even though you have condensed.

(a) If you want to print the entire spreadsheet, depress the Home key to move the cursor to the top-left corner of the sheet.

(b) Depress /P for Print and P for Printer, and the following menu will appear:

```
Range   Line   Page   Options   Clear   Align   Go   Quit
```

(c) Select the *Range* option, and respond to the following question by typing the appropriate range:

Enter Print Range:

The cell addresses of the print range define the top-left corner and the bottom-right corner to be printed. After selecting the appropriate range, depress ←⏎.

(d) By depressing ←⏎ after setting the print range, you return to the menu listed in (b). Depress *Align* and then *Go*, and the spreadsheet will begin printing.

Functions

Lotus 1-2-3® includes many mathematical formulas referred to as functions. To use a function, specify its name and the factors that it uses. All function names are preceded by "@." Three important functions are shown in Exhibit 28-21.

EXHIBIT 28-21   *Three Important LOTUS 1-2-3® Functions*

Function Name	What It Does
@SUM(range or list) Examples:	Adds the values in the range or list
@SUM(B5.B9)	Adds values in B5 through B9.
@SUM(C8,D3,F2)	Adds values in C8, D3, and F2.
@NPV (interest rate, range)	Computes the present value of the amounts in the range at the specified interest rate.
Example: @NPV(.11,A6.A8)	Computes the present value of the amount in A6 for 1 period, the amount in A7 for 2 periods, the amount in A8 for 3 periods, all at 11%, and sums the three present values.
@IF (condition, calculation if true, calculation if false)	Tests a condition and performs the appropriate calculation.
Example: @IF(B5>5000,B5*.3,B5*.6)	Tests whether the value in cell B5 exceeds 5,000. If yes, multiply the value in B5 by .3. If no, multiply the value in B5 by .6.

Summary Problem for Your Review

The following spreadsheet is a budgeted income statement for Randolph-Macon Corporation with the following assumptions:

First quarter sales	$140,000
Quarterly sales growth	3%
Cost of goods sold	70% of sales
Operating expenses	as shown
Income tax rate	40%

Directions for Creating the Spreadsheet Model

1. In cell Bl begin typing the three-line heading. Don't worry that the heading will extend into columns D and E. You do not need to widen any of the columns.

2. In cell B5 begin typing the months, MAR, JUNE, SEP, and DEC. Use a ^ as a label prefix to center the months. Remember, you must depress the shift key in combination with the ^ key.

3. In cell F5 type TOTAL. This entry should be prefaced with a ^.

4. In cell A7 begin typing the labels that define the rows (Sales, Cost of goods sold, and so on). The entries do not need any special label prefix symbols because they are to be left-aligned, which is the default (automatic) alignment for labels. Notice that the individual operating expenses are indented two spaces. You accomplish this by depressing the space bar twice before typing the entry. After typing each category, depress the down arrow key. This will drive the previous entry into its appropriate cell and move the highlighter to the next cell.

5. With the highlighter in cell A9, issue the command /WCS, type 22 over the default width of 9, and depress ←┘. This sets the width of column A at 22 characters to accommodate the account titles and income captions.

6. In cell B7 type 140000. (Do not place commas or dollar signs in the number.)

7. In cell B8 enter the formula .7*B7. This formula takes the amount in cell B7 and multiplies it by .7, which is 70 percent. This computes cost of goods sold for the first quarter.

8. In cell B9 type the label: '———————— (eight spaces). Copy this single underlining to cells B17, B19, and B22. To copy it to B17, issue the command:

     /Copy From: B9.B9 ←┘ To: B17 ←┘

9. In cell B10 type the formula +B7−B8. This computes gross margin.

10. Beginning in cell B12 enter the expenses for the first quarter. Do not type in the commas. We will use a formatting command to enter the commas later.

OBJECTIVE 4

Create a spreadsheet model to solve accounting problems

11. In cell B18 type the function @SUM(B12.B16). This totals the operating expenses.

12. In cell B20 type the formula +B10−B18. This subtracts total operating expenses from gross margin to compute income from operations.

13. In cell B21 type the formula .4*B20. This formula computes income tax expense.

14. In cell B23 type the formula +B20−B21. This computes net income.

15. In cell B24 type the label: '======== (eight spaces).

16. In cell C7 type the formula +B7+.03*B7. This formula increases sales by the 3 percent growth rate. Then copy this formula for the remaining 2 quarters with the following command:
    /Copy   From: C7.C7   To: D7.E7

17. Move to cell B8 and copy column B, rows 8 through 24, across the remaining three quarters using the command:
    /Copy   From: B8.B24   To: C8.E24

18. Enter the insurance expense for September and December. Delete 1500 and type 2000, or simply type 2000 over 1500.

19. In cell F7 type the function: @SUM (B7.E7). Then copy this function to total the four quarters using the command:
    /Copy   From: F7.F7   To: F8.F23

20. With the highlighter in cell F11, issue the command /Range Erase to erase the unwanted sum function for the blank row.

21. Copy the underlining in cell B9 to cells F9, F17, F19, and F22. Copy the double underlining in cell B24 to cell F24.

22. Issue the command /WGF,0 to format the values of the entire spreadsheet with commas and no decimal places.

23. In cell B7 issue the command /RFC 0 and type the range of B7.F7 to format the SALES values with dollar signs, commas, and no decimal places. After both the 0 and the specified range, depress ←⏎. Repeat this procedure in cell B23 to place dollar signs on all the net income amounts.

24. To save this work sheet to your storage diskette, insert your own diskette in disk drive B, depress the Home key, and issue the command /FS. Type the filename BUDGET. Your storage diskette in disk drive B will now have a copy of the spreadsheet. If you escape out of the active spreadsheet, you will still have a copy on your storage diskette that you can retrieve without having to create this spreadsheet model again.

25. To print this work sheet, first advance the paper to the top of the next fresh page. Issue the command /P for Print, P for Printer, R for Range, and type the range A1.F24. Then depress A for align and G for go, and the program will begin printing the Randolph-Macon budgeted income statement. The printout should look like the budgeted income statement as shown. The amounts may vary slightly due to rounding. The complete income statement is too long to fit on a single screen and so runs on to a second screen. We present the complete first screen and the first few lines of the second screen to show you how your computer will display the income statement. Your printout will include the entire income statement unbroken.

```
A1: [W25]                                                           READY

          A              B         C         D         E         F
1                     Randolph-Macon Corporation
2                     Budgeted Income Statement
3               For the Four Quarters ended December 31, 19X4
4
5                        MAR       JUNE      SEP       DEC       TOTAL
6
7    Sales             $140,000  $144,200  $148,526  $152,982  $585,708
8    Cost of goods sold  98,000   100,940   103,968   107,087   409,995
9                       --------  --------  --------  --------  --------
10   Gross margin        42,000    43,260    44,558    45,895   175,713
11   Operating expenses
12     Salaries          20,000    20,000    20,000    20,000    80,000
13     Depreciation       6,000     6,000     6,000     6,000    24,000
14     Rent               5,000     5,000     5,000     5,000    20,000
15     Utilities          4,500     4,500     4,500     4,500    18,000
16     Insurance          1,500     1,500     2,000     2,000     7,000
17                       --------  --------  --------  --------  --------
18   Total expenses      37,000    37,000    37,500    37,500   149,000
19                       --------  --------  --------  --------  --------
20   Income from operations 5,000   6,260     7,058     8,395    26,713
17-Jul-91  08:08 PM                                            CAPS
```

```
A21: [W25] 'Income tax expense                                      READY

          A              B         C         D         E         F
21   Income tax expense    2,000     2,504     2,823     3,358    10,685
22                       --------  --------  --------  --------  --------
23   Net income          $3,000    $3,756    $4,235    $5,037   $16,028
24                       ========  ========  ========  ========  ========
25
```

Summary

Accounting with computers is exactly like manual accounting, except that the machine saves time by doing much of the work automatically. *Software programs* are available to perform a variety of accounting tasks. Often an accounting software program is divided into *modules:* general ledger, accounts receivable, accounts payable, payroll, and inventories. A business can select any or all of these modules to do its accounting by computer.

Spreadsheets are software programs that can be used to solve many different kinds of problems, including budgeting, depreciation schedules, what-if analysis, payroll computations, and cost-volume-profit analysis.

Self-Study Questions

Test your understanding of the chapter by marking the best answer for each of the following questions.

1. Which of the following statements is true? *(p. 1243)*
   a. Accounting with computers is fundamentally different from manual accounting.
   b. Computerized accounting is slower and more tedious than manual accounting.
   ✓ c. Accounting with computers and manual accounting are fundamentally alike.
   d. It takes extensive computer programming experience to use an accounting software program.

2. Which of the following is an input device? *(p. 1244)*
   a. Printer
   b. Disk drive
   c. Central processing unit
   d. Monitor

3. The device that actually does the computer's "thinking" is the *(pp. 1244, 1245)*
   a. Printer
   b. Disk drive
   c. Central processing unit
   d. Monitor

4. A software menu is a *(p. 1246)*
   a. List of computer functions
   b. Group of input devices
   c. Computer printout
   d. Task with the most software programs

5. In an integrated accounting software program, the center is the *(p. 1246)*
   a. Accounts receivable module
   b. Inventory module
   c. Payroll module
   d. General ledger module

6. A key timesaver in a spreadsheet program is the accountant's ability to *(pp. 1258, 1259)*
   a. Enter amounts manually
   b. List amounts in order
   c. Copy formulas and functions
   d. Use the typewriter section of the keyboard

7. The function key used for editing with Lotus 1-2-3™ is *(p. 1260)*
   a. F1
   b. F2
   c. F3
   d. F4

8. When the formula "+A6/$C$3" is copied in a 1-2-3 program, *(p. 1265)*
   a. The value in A6 can change, but the value in C3 is constant
   b. The value in A6 is constant, but the value in C3 can change
   c. The values in A6 and in C3 can change
   d. The values in A6 and in C3 are constant

9. The 1-2-3 command "/Copy   From: A1.A3   To: B1.B3" copies *(p. 1266)*
   a. Rows B1 through B3 to rows A1 through A3
   b. Columns B1 through B3 to columns A1 through A3
   c. Rows A1 through A3 to rows B1 through B3
   d. Columns A1 through A3 to columns B1 through B3

10. To save a 1-2-3 file on a storage diskette, use the command *(p. 1267)*
    a. /SF
    b. /FS
    c. \SF
    d. \FS

Answers to the Self-Study Questions follow the Accounting Vocabulary.

Accounting Vocabulary

Central processing unit (CPU). The brain of a computer. It performs mathematical and logical operations and controls the other components of the computer system *(p. 1244)*.

Disk drive. Computer input device that reads data and instructions from magnetic disks *(p. 1244)*.

Diskette. Thin 3½-inch or 5¼-inch diameter round magnetic disk enclosed in plastic. Also called a Floppy diskette *(p. 1244)*.

Integrated software. Computer program that includes modules handling different functions. Coordinates the output of the various modules *(p. 1246)*.

Menu. List of options for choosing computer functions *(p. 1246)*.

Menu-driven. Type of computer software that offers a list of options for doing various functions *(p. 1246)*.

Microcomputer. A computer small enough for each employee (work station) to have its own machine *(p. 1244)*.

Monitor. Computer output device that resembles a television and allows the user to view data being processed and to receive messages from the program being run *(p. 1245)*.

Program. Set of instructions that tell the computer what to do *(p. 1243)*.

Spreadsheet. Integrated software program that can be used to solve many different kinds of problems. An electronically prepared work sheet *(p. 1255)*.

1. c	6. c
2. b	7. b
3. c	8. a
4. a	9. d
5. d	10. b

ASSIGNMENT MATERIAL

Questions

1. Name six advantages that computers offer over manual accounting.

2. Briefly compare and contrast the accounting cycle in a manual accounting system and the cycle in a computerized system.

3. What is the difference between a minicomputer and a microcomputer?

4. How do input devices, the CPU, and output devices work together in a computer system?

5. A service business with 20 employees needs an integrated computerized accounting system. Identify a way for many businesses to acquire the needed system most efficiently.

6. Identify the advantage of a menu-driven computerized accounting system over a system in which accountants must write computer programs to do the work.

7. List the options that might appear on the monitor screen for a menu-driven general ledger software program.

8. Outline the flow of information in the accounts receivable module of an integrated accounting software program.

9. Why is payroll ideally suited for a computerized accounting system?

10. Compare and contrast a computer keyboard and a typewriter keyboard.

11. On a monitor screen in a spreadsheet program, what do C5 and D3 mean?

12. Suppose you make an error while using a spreadsheet program. How would you correct the error if you have not yet depressed the ◄─┘ key? How would you correct the error if you have already depressed the ◄─┘ key?

13. In a budget, the same formula is used in six places. How can a spreadsheet program handle this situation efficiently?

14. Suppose you type the formula +B1+B2 in cell B3 and copy the formula into cells C3 and D3. What values will be added in B3, C3, and D3?

15. Suppose you type the formula +$B$1+$B$2 in cell B3 and copy the formula into cells C3 and D3. What values will be added in B3, C3, and D3?

16. Suppose you type the formula +B1+$B$2 in cell B3 and copy the formula into cells C3 and D3. What values will be added in B3, C3, and D3?

17. What character comes first in 1-2-3 commands?

18. What is the name of the formatting command in 1-2-3 that is used to place dollar signs before amounts?

19. Write the copy command in 1-2-3 to copy data in cell G4 into cells H1 through H3.

20. What should you do at the end of a work session when you plan to update your spreadsheet at a later time? Write the appropriate 1-2-3 command.

Exercises

Exercises are cross-referenced to the chapters that discuss the related accounting. (Note: Answers may contain rounding error.)

Net income:
 FIFO $21,000; LIFO $16,100
 FIFO $ 4,900; LIFO $0

Exercise 28-1 *Change from LIFO to FIFO: Chapter 9* **(L.O. 4)**

Walnut Lubricants is considering a change from the last-in, first-out (LIFO) inventory method to the first-in, first-out (FIFO) method. Managers are concerned about the effect of this change on income tax expense and reported net income. If the change is made, it will become effective on March 1. Inventory on hand at February 28 is $63,000. During March, Walnut managers expect sales of $250,000, net purchases between $159,000 and $182,000, and operating expenses, excluding income tax, of $83,000. The income tax rate is 30 percent. Inventories at March 31 are budgeted as follows: FIFO, $85,000; LIFO, $78,000.

Required

Create a spreadsheet model to compute estimated net income for March under FIFO and LIFO. Format your answer as follows:

	A	B	C	D	E
1		Walnut Lubricants			
2		Estimated Income Under FIFO and LIFO			
3		March 19XX			
4					
5		FIFO	LIFO	FIFO	LIFO
6					
7	Sales	$250,000	$250,000	$250,000	$250,000
8					
9	Cost of goods sold				
10	Beginning inventory	63,000	63,000	63,000	63,000
11	Net purchases	159,000	159,000	182,000	182,000
12					
13	Cost of goods available				
14	Ending inventory	85,000	78,000	85,000	78,000
15					
16	Cost of goods sold				
17					
18	Gross margin				
19	Operating expenses	83,000	83,000	83,000	83,000
20					
21	Income from operations				
22	Income tax expense				
23					
24	Net income	$	$	$	$
25					

Book value:
 12/31/X1, $738,050
 12/31/X6 $150,000

Exercise 28-2 *Straight-line depreciation schedule: Chapter 10* **(L.O. 4)**

Create a spreadsheet model to print a straight-line depreciation schedule for a machine that cost $855,660, has an estimated useful life of six years, and has an estimated residual value of $150,000. Round to the nearest dollar, and format your answer as follows:

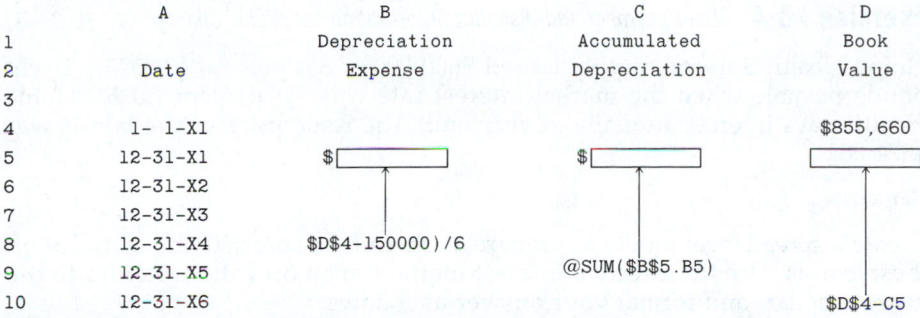

	A	B	C	D
1		Depreciation	Accumulated	Book
2	Date	Expense	Depreciation	Value
3				
4	1- 1-X1			$855,660
5	12-31-X1	$ ⬜	$ ⬜	⬜
6	12-31-X2			
7	12-31-X3			
8	12-31-X4	$D$4-150000)/6		
9	12-31-X5		@SUM($B$5.B5)	
10	12-31-X6			$D$4-C5

Exercise 28-3   *Dissolution of a partnership: Chapter 13*   **(L.O. 4)**

The partnership of Lee, Molnari, and Nix is dissolving. Business assets include cash of $6,000 and noncash assets of $126,000. Liabilities total $77,000. The partners' capital accounts are Lee, $12,000; Molnari, $37,000; and Nix, $6,000. The partners share profits and losses as follows: Lee, 25 percent; Molnari, 55 percent; and Nix, 20 percent.

Required

Create a spreadsheet model to show the ending balances in all accounts after selling the noncash assets for $95,000; $107,000; and $145,000. Determine the unknown amounts (?):

Molnari end. cap. bal.
$19,950
$26,550
$47,450

	A	B	C	D	E	F
1			Lee, Molnari, and Nix			
2			Sale of Noncash Assets			
3			(For $95,000)			
4						
5		Noncash		Lee	Molnari	Nix
6	Cash	Assets	Liabilities	Capital	Capital	Capital
7						
8	$ 6,000	$126,000	$77,000	$12,000	$37,000	$ 6,000
9	95,000	(126,000)		?	?	?
10						
11						
12	$101,000	$ 0	$77,000	$?	$?	$?
13						
14						($A9 − $B8)*.25
15			(For $107,000)			
16						
17		Noncash		Lee	Molnari	Nix
18	Cash	Assets	Liabilities	Capital	Capital	Capital
19						
20	$ 6,000	$126,000	$77,000	$12,000	$37,000	$ 6,000
21	107,000	(126,000)		?	?	?
22						
23	$113,000	$ 0	$77,000	$?	$?	$?
24						
25						
26						($A21−$B20)*.25
27			(For $145,000)			
28						
29		Noncash		Lee	Molnari	Nix
30	Cash	Assets	Liabilities	Capital	Capital	Capital
31						
32	$ 6,000	$126,000	$77,000	$12,000	$37,000	$ 6,000
33	145,000	(126,000)		?	?	?
34						
35						
36	$151,000	$ 0	$77,000	$?	$?	$?
						($A33−$B32)*.25

Exercise 28-4 *Debt payment and discount amortization schedule: Chapter 16* **(L.O. 4)**

Home Health Surgical Supply issued $600,000 of 8⅜ percent (.08375), 5-year bonds payable when the market interest rate was 9½ percent (.095). Home Health pays interest annually at year end. The issue price of the bonds was $574,082.

Required

Create a spreadsheet model to prepare a schedule to amortize the discount on these bonds. Use the effective-interest method of amortization. Round to the nearest dollar, and format your answer as follows:

	A	B	C	D	E	F
1						
2		Interest	Interest	Discount	Discount	Bond Carrying
3	Date	Payment	Expense	Amortization	Balance	Value
4						
5	1- 1-X1				$	$574,082
6	12-31-X1	$	$	$		
7	12-31-X2					
8	12-31-X3					
9	21-31-X4					
10	12-31-X5					

600000*.08375

+F5*.095

+C6−B6

600000−F5

+F5+D6

Exercise 28-5 *Sales budget: Chapter 20* **(L.O. 4)**

The managers of Marlin Products are budgeting sales for the first six months of 19X3. January sales are expected to be $80,000. Each month thereafter, sales are expected to increase by ¼ percent (.0025) to ¾ percent (.0075).

Required

Create a spreadsheet model, and print Marlin Products' sales budget for the six months ended June 30, 19X3, under both assumptions (¼ percent and ¾ percent) about the monthly increase. Round to the nearest dollar, and format your answer as follows:

	A	B	C	D	E	F	G	H
1				Marlin Products				
2				Sales Budget				
3			For the Six Months Ended June 30, 19X3					
4								
5				(.0025 Monthly Increase)				
6		JAN	FEB	MAR	APR	MAY	JUNE	TOTAL
7	Sales	$	$	$	$	$	$	$
8								
9								
10				(.0075 Monthly Increase)				
11		JAN	FEB	MAR	APR	MAY	JUNE	TOTAL
12	Sales	$	$	$	$	$	$	$

Exercise 28-6 *Gross margin budget: Chapter 20* **(L.O. 4)**

Eastern Chemical Corporation is budgeting gross margin for the four quarters of 19X7. Sales are estimated at $100,000 for the first quarter. Cost of goods sold is 60 percent of sales.

Required

Create a spreadsheet model for the gross margin budget under two separate assumptions about quarterly sales growth:

a. Quarterly sales are expected to increase by 1.5 percent (.015) during quarters 2, 3, and 4.

b. Quarterly sales are expected to increase by 2.5 percent (.025) during quarters 2, 3, and 4.

Round to the nearest dollar, and format your answer as follows:

	A	B	C	D	E	F
1			Eastern Chemical Corporation			
2			Budgeted Gross Margin			
3			For the Four Quarters of 19X7			
4						
5			(Sales increase = .015)			
6		Q1	Q2	Q3	Q4	TOTAL
7	Sales	$	$	$	$	$
8						
9	Cost of goods sold					
10		___	___	___	___	___
11	Gross margin	$	$	$	$	$
12		===	===	===	===	===
13						
14						
15			(Sales increase = .025)			
16		Q1	Q2	Q3	Q4	TOTAL
17	Sales	$	$	$	$	$
18						
19	Cost of goods sold					
20		___	___	___	___	___
21	Gross margin	$	$	$	$	$
22		===	===	===	===	===

Exercise 28-7 *Budgeted income statement: Chapter 20* **(L.O. 4)**

Budgeted net inc. $140,000

Colgate-Cathy, Inc., is considering an expansion that would increase sales to $1,000,000 and operating expenses to $300,000. A spreadsheet program to prepare the company's actual 19X4 and budgeted 19X5 income statements appears below.

The purpose of this exercise is to show the power of the computer in preparing a financial statement.

	A	B	C
1		Colgate-Cathy, Inc.	
2		Income Statements	
3		For the Years Ended December 31, 19XX	
4			
5		Actual 19X4	Budgeted 19X5
6			
7	Sales	850000	$
8	Cost of goods sold (50%)	+B7*.50	
9		___	___
10	Gross margin	+B7-B8	
11	Total operating expenses	250000	
12		___	___
13	Income from operations	+B10-B11	
14	Income tax expense (30%)	+B13*.30	
15		___	___
16	Net income	+B13-B14	
17		===	$ ===

Required

1. Enter this material in a spreadsheet program. Set column A to be 25 characters wide, and columns B and C to be 15 characters wide.
2. Copy B7.B17 to C7.C17.
3. Insert 1000000 in C7 and 300000 in C11. Watch the budgeted 19X5 income statement appear instantly on the screen.
4. Format with dollar signs and commas.
5. Print the actual and budgeted income statements as they appear on the screen.

Total net inc. $38,508

Exercise 28-8   *Budgeted income statement: Chapter 20*   **(L.O. 4)**

Abba Pet Supply is preparing its budgeted income statement for the quarter ended March 31, 19X6. Lisa Mona, the proprietor, expects January sales of $50,000, followed by 2 percent increases in February and March. Cost of goods sold is 60 percent of sales, and the operating expenses are as shown in the solution format that follows. Salary expense is expected to increase by 5 percent in March. All other monthly operating expenses will remain at the January amounts.

Required

Create a spreadsheet model to prepare and print Abba Pet Supply's budgeted income statement for the quarter, formatted as shown here.

	A	B	C	D	E
1		Abba Pet Supply			
2		Budgeted Income Statement			
3		For the Quarter Ended March 31, 19X6			
4					
5		JAN	FEB	MAR	TOTAL
6					
7	Sales	$50,000	$	$	$
8	Cost of goods sold				
9		———	———	———	———
10	Gross margin				
11	Operating expenses:				
12	Salaries	4,000			
13	Depreciation	2,000			
14	Rent	1,000			
15	Utilities	500			
16		———	———	———	———
17	Total expenses				
18		———	———	———	———
19	Net income	$	$	$	$
20		═══	═══	═══	═══

B/E sales, at $183,000, $481,579
Target sales, at $183,000,
$718,421

Exercise 28-9   *Cost-volume-profit analysis: Chapter 21*   **(L.O. 4)**

Create a spreadsheet model to compute and print break-even sales and the dollar sales needed to earn target income from operations under the following conditions:

Fixed expenses	$183,000	$196,000
Variable expenses	62% of sales	58% of sales
Target income from operations	$90,000	$90,000

Format your answer as follows:

	A	B	C	D	E
1	Fixed expenses	$183,000	$196,000	$183,000	$196,000
2	Variable expenses	.62	.58	.62	.58
3	Income from operations	0	0	$90,000	$90,000
4	Break-even sales	$ [?]	$ [?]		
5	Target sales	↓		$ [?]	$ [?]

(B1+B3)/(1−B2)

Exercise 28-10   *Net-present-value analysis: Chapter 26*   **(L.O. 4)**

A company is considering the purchase of two machines. The company's required rate of return on investments is 12½ percent (.125). The following data are applicable.

Net present value:
  Machine 1, $40,624
  Machine 2, ($37,278)

	A	B	C
1		Machine 1	Machine 2
2			
3	Cost	$380,000	$747,000
4			
5	Annual net cash inflow:		
6	Year 1	$180,000	$150,000
7	2	160,000	200,000
8	3	100,000	250,000
9	4	60,000	300,000
10	5	30,000	100,000
11	6	20,000	

Required

Create a spreadsheet model to help decide which machine has the higher net present value. Format the printout as above. Add three lines at the bottom to show present value of net cash inflows, investment, and net present value. The formula for computing the present value of the net cash inflows for machine 1 is @ NPV(.125,B6.B11).

Exercise 28-11   *Income tax: Chapter 27*   **(L.O. 4)**

An accountant is preparing the income tax returns of clients with the following data presented in solution format. "AGI" is the abbreviation for *Adjusted Gross Income*, "Std Ded" abbreviates *Standard Deduction*, and "Exempt" stands for *Personal Exemptions*.

Income tax:
  Gonzalez $2,505
  Grays $8,964

Required

Create a spreadsheet model to compute the taxable income and the income tax liability of each client. Refer to Chapter 27 for the appropriate income tax rates. Format your answer as shown here.

	A	B	C	D	E	F	G
1		Filing				Taxable	Income
2	Name	Status	AGI	Std Ded	Exempt	Income	Tax
3							
4	Lisa Gonzalez	Single	$22,100	$3,400	$2,000	$?	$?
5							
6	Tom Mendenhall	Single	72,000	3,400	2,000	?	?
7							
8	R. and K. Gray	Joint	61,500	5,700	8,000	?	?
9							
10	L. and T. Chin	Joint	103,000	5,700	6,000	?	?

Problems are cross-referenced to the chapters that discuss the related accounting. (Note: Answers may contain certain rounding error.)

Problem 28-1A   *Sum-of-years-digits depreciation schedule: Chapter 10* **(L.O. 4)**

Book value:
12/31/X1, $786,818
12/31/X10, $120,000

Create a spreadsheet model to print a sum-of-years-digits depreciation schedule for a building that cost $935,000, has an estimated useful life of 10 years, and has an estimated residual value of $120,000. Format your answer as follows, showing all years through 19X10.

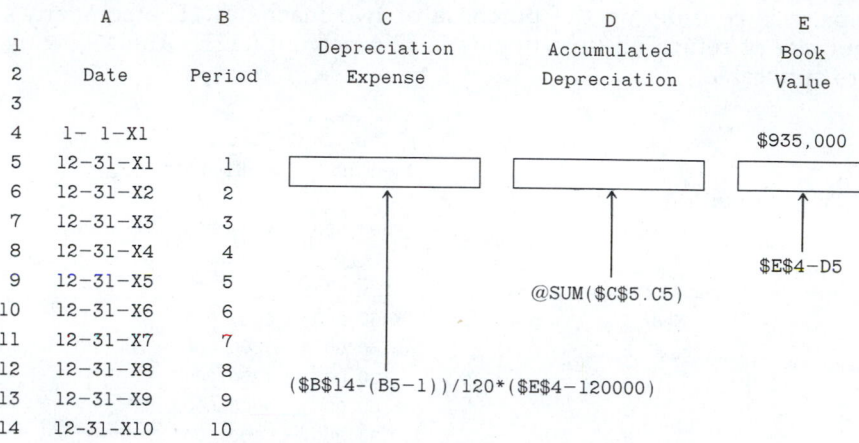

	A	B	C	D	E
1			Depreciation	Accumulated	Book
2	Date	Period	Expense	Depreciation	Value
3					
4	1- 1-X1				$935,000
5	12-31-X1	1			
6	12-31-X2	2			
7	12-31-X3	3			
8	12-31-X4	4			
9	12-31-X5	5			
10	12-31-X6	6			
11	12-31-X7	7			
12	12-31-X8	8			
13	12-31-X9	9			
14	12-31-X10	10			

$E$4-D5

@SUM($C$5.C5)

($B$14-(B5-1))/120*($E$4-120000)

Problem 28-2A   *Payroll: Chapter 11* **(L.O. 4)**

Total net pay

Lucenay Employment Agency has a weekly payroll for its hourly employees. Grant Lucenay, the owner/manager of Lucenay Employment Agency, currently processes the payroll manually. An employee's gross pay is determined by multiplying his or her straight-time pay rate times the number of hours worked for the first 40 hours. For every hour over 40, the employee receives 1.5 times the pay rate. Weekly deductions consist of FICA tax, withheld income tax, and United Way contribution. FICA tax is 8% of gross pay; withheld income tax is 12% of gross pay; and the United Way contribution varies by employee. Net pay is gross pay less total deductions.

	A	B	C	D	E	F	G	H
1				Lucenay Employment Agency				
2				Payroll Register				
3				For the Week Ended February 15, 19X6				
4								
5			Straight-				Deductions	
6			Time					
7	Employee		Hourly Pay	Gross		With.	United	Net
8	Name	Hours	Rate	Pay	FICA	Tax	Way	Pay
9								
10	Chang, H.	45	6.50				2.00	
11	Craig, B.	35	5.00				7.00	
12	Lowe, B.	50	6.00				2.50	
13	Pita, N.	40	6.25				6.00	
14	Potts, F.	40	7.00				5.00	
15	Rawl, R.	20	6.50				4.00	
16	Tong, J.	45	5.50				2.50	
17	Ware, R.	38	5.75				3.00	
18					—	—	—	—
19	Totals							
20					═	═	═	═

Required

Create a spreadsheet model to complete and print this payroll register for Lucenay Employment Agency. Your spreadsheet should be formatted as above.

Problem 28-3A   *Budgeted income statement: Chapter 20*   **(L.O. 4)**

Total net inc. $39,882

NoCal Dietetics is budgeting operations for the first quarter of 19X5. Income tax expense is 30 percent. Other data follow:

January sales	$150,000
Cost of goods sold percentage .	65% of sales
Monthly sales growth rate	1.5%

	A	B	C	D	E
1		No Cal Dietetics			
2		Budgeted Income Statement			
3		For the Three Months Ended March 31, 19X5			
4					
5		JAN	FEB	MAR	TOTAL
6					
7	Sales	$150,000	$152,250	$154,534	$456,784
8	Cost of goods sold	97,500	98,963	100,447	296,909
9					
10	Gross margin	52,500	53,288	54,087	159,874
11	Operating expenses:				
12	Salaries	25,000	25,000	25,000	75,000
13	Rent	4,500	4,500	4,500	13,500
14	Depreciation	3,000	3,000	3,000	9,000
15	Utilities	1,800	1,800	1,800	5,400
16					
17	Total operating expenses	34,300	34,300	34,300	102,900
18					
19	Income from operations	18,200	18,988	19,787	56,974
20	Income tax expense	5,460	5,696	5,936	17,092
21					
22	Net income	$12,740	$13,292	$13,851	$39,882
23					

Required:

Create a spreadsheet model to prepare and print for NoCal Dietetics a budgeted income statement for the quarter, formatted as shown here. The computer solution may contain an insignificant rounding error.

Problem 28-4A   *Budgeted gross profit: Chapter 20*   **(L.O. 4)**

Total gross profit $38,394

Gulig Computronics is budgeting gross profit (gross margin) for the six months ended June 30, 19X5. Rosie Gulig, the owner, expects January sales of $70,000 for computer hardware and $25,000 for software. She is hoping for 2 percent monthly sales growth for hardware and 4 percent for software. Cost of goods sold is 70 percent of sales for hardware and 50 percent for software.

Required

Create a spreadsheet model to complete and print the following budget:

	A	B	C	D	E	F	G
1			Gulig Computronics				
2			Budgeted Gross Profit				
3			For the Six Months Ended June 30, 19X5				
4							
5			JAN	FEB	MAR	APR	MAY	JUN
6	Sales						
7	Hardware	$70,000					
8	Software	25,000					
9		————					
10	Total						
11							
12	COGS						
13	Hardware						
14	Software						
15		————					
16	Total						
17							
18	Gross Pft						
19	Hardware						
20	Software						
21		————					
22	Total						

Total net inc. $37,579

Problem 28-5A   *Budgeted income statement: Chapter 20*   **(L.O. 4)**

Using the six-month projections from Problem 28-4A for the sales, cost of goods sold, and gross profit (gross margin) for hardware and software, complete Gulig Computronic's budgeted income statement by including expenses and totals for the 6 months. The business budgets expenses as follows:

Salaries	$20,000	per month
Rent	2,500	per month
Depreciation	2,000	per month
Insurance	1,500	per month
Travel	900	per quarter (in January and April only)
Utilities	650	per month
Income tax rate	30%	

Required

Create a spreadsheet model to prepare the Gulig Computronics income statement for the six months ended June 30, 19X5. Show each expense, total operating expenses, income from operations, income tax expense, and net income.

B/E sales at $150,000 and 60%, $375,000
Target sales at $180,000 and 75%, $1,000,000

Problem 28-6A   *Cost-volume-profit analysis: Chapter 21*   **(L.O. 4)**

The Neuse, Inc., management team is planning for 19X2. Fixed expenses are expected to range from $150,000 to $180,000. Variable expenses will range from 60 percent of sales to 75 percent of sales. The company's target income from operations is $70,000.

Required

Prepare a spreadsheet that shows break-even sales in dollars and dollar sales needed to earn the target income from operations under the following combinations being considered. The spreadsheet should be formatted as follows:

	A	B	C	D	E	F	G
1	Fixed exp	$150,000	$180,000	$150,000	$180,000	$150,000	$180,000
2	Variable exp	60%	60%	75%	75%	60%	75%
3	Income from oper	$0	$0	$0	$0	$70,000	$70,000
4	Break-even sales	[box]	?	?	?		
5	Target sales					?	?

(+B1+B3)/(1-B2)

Problem 28-7A   *Net-present-value analysis: Chapter 26*   **(L.O. 4)**

Net present value:
Transmitter 1, $7,358
Transmitter 2, ($61,342)

KXYZ-TV is considering two transmitting devices. The owner of the station has a required rate of return of 10 percent (.10).

	A		B	C
			Transmitter 1	Transmitter 2
1				
2				
3	Cost		$800,000	$700,000
4				
5	Annual net cash inflows:			
6				
7	Year	1	$180,000	$150,000
8		2	225,000	200,000
9		3	315,000	275,000
10		4	125,000	100,000
11		5	100,000	100,000
12		6	85,000	
13		7	50,000	
14				
15	Present value of net cash inflows			
16				
17	Investment			
18				
19	Net present value		$	$
20				

Required

Create a spreadsheet model to help decide which transmitter has a higher net present value and is, therefore, more attractive as an investment. Format the spreadsheet as above.

(Group B)

Problem 28-1B   *Double-declining-balance depreciation schedule: Chapter 10*   **(L.O. 4)**

Book value:
12/31/X1, $760,000
12/31/X10, $120,000

Create a spreadsheet model to print a double-declining-balance depreciation schedule for a building that cost $950,000, has an estimated useful life of 10 years, and has an estimated residual value of $120,000. Format your answer as follows, showing all years through 19X10.

	A	B	C	D	E
1			Depreciation	Accumulated	Book
2	Date	Period	Expense	Depreciation	Value
3					
4	1- 1-X1				$950,000
5	12-31-X1	1	[box]	[box]	[box]
6	12-31-X2	2			
7	12-31-X3	3			
8	12-31-X4	4			$E$4-D5
9	12-31-X5	5			
10	12-31-X6	6			
11	12-31-X7	7		@SUM($C$5.C5)	
12	12-31-X8	8			
13	12-31-X9	9			
14	12-31-X10	10	@IF(B5<>$B$14,2/$B$14*E4,E4-120000)		

Total net pay $1,420.70

Problem 28-2B *Payroll: Chapter 11 (L.O. 4)*

Adventure Travel has a weekly payroll for its hourly employees. An employee's gross pay is determined by multiplying his or her straight-time pay rate times the number of hours worked for the first 40 hours. For every hour over 40, the employee receives 1.5 times the pay rate. Weekly deductions consist of FICA tax, withheld income tax, and United Way contribution. FICA tax is 8% of gross pay, withheld income tax is 12% of gross pay, and the United Way contribution varies by employee. Net pay is gross pay less total deductions.

	A	B	C	D	E	F	G	H
1				Adventure Travel				
2				Payroll Register				
3				For the Week Ended March 18, 19X4				
4								
5			Straight-					
6			Time				Deductions	
7	Employee		Hourly Pay	Gross		With.	United	Net
8	Name	Hours	Rate	Pay	FICA	Tax	Way	Pay
9								
10	Allen, D.	40	5.50				3.00	
11	Brown, G.	35	7.50				8.00	
12	Chin, B.	45	5.00				3.50	
13	Olson, T.	38	5.25				4.00	
14	Reed, K.	20	6.00				2.00	
15	Tusa, R.	47	6.50				5.00	
16	Ward, R.	40	5.00				2.50	
17	Wills, C.	45	5.25				5.00	
18				———	———	———	———	———
19	Totals							
20				═══	═══	═══	═══	═══

Required

Create a spreadsheet model to complete and print this payroll register for Adventure Travel. Your spreadsheet should be formatted as above.

Total net inc. $19,827

Problem 28-3B *Budgeted income statement: Chapter 20 (L.O. 4)*

Brazos Pharmaceuticals is budgeting operations for the first quarter of 19X5. Income tax expense is 30 percent. Other data follow:

January sales....................	$100,000
Cost of goods sold percentage	60% of sales
Monthly sales growth rate	1.1%

```
             A              B          C          D          E
 1                      Brazos Pharmaceuticals
 2                      Budgeted Income Statement
 3                 For the Three Months Ended March 31, 19X5
 4
 5                         JAN        FEB        MAR       TOTAL
 6
 7   Sales              $100,000   $101,100   $102,212   $303,312
 8   Cost of goods sold   60,000     60,660     61,327    181,987
 9                      _____   _____   _____   _____
10   Gross margin         40,000     40,440     40,885    121,325
11   Operating expenses:
12     Salaries           22,500     22,500     22,500     67,500
13     Rent                4,000      4,000      4,000     12,000
14     Depreciation        2,500      2,500      2,500      7,500
15     Utilities           2,000      2,000      2,000      6,000
16                      _____   _____   _____   _____
17   Total operating expenses 31,000  31,000    31,000     93,000
18                      _____   _____   _____   _____
19   Income from operations  9,000    9,440      9,885     28,325
20   Income tax expense      2,700    2,832      2,966      8,498
21                      _____   _____   _____   _____
22   Net income           $6,300     $6,608     $6,919    $19,827
23                      ========   ========   ========   ========
```

Required

Create a spreadsheet model to prepare and print the Brazos Pharmaceuticals budgeted income statement for the quarter, formatted as shown here.

Problem 28-4B *Budgeted gross profit: Chapter 20* **(L.O. 4)**

Total gross profit $20,402

McBurney Appliances, Inc., is budgeting gross profit (gross margin) for the six months ended June 30, 19X4. Emily McBurney, the manager and principal stockholder, expects January sales of $50,000 for TVs and $10,000 for VCRs. She is hoping for 1 percent monthly sales growth for TVs and 3 percent for VCRs. Cost of goods sold is 70 percent of sales for TVs and 60 percent for VCRs.

Required

Create a spreadsheet model to complete and print the budget given at the top of the next page.

```
                 A              B         C         D         E         F         G
1                          McBurney Appliances, Inc.
2                            Budgeted Gross Profit
3                       For the Six Months Ended June 30, 19X4
4
5                              JAN       FEB       MAR       APR       MAY       JUN
6          Sales
7            TVs          $50,000
8            VCRs          10,000
9                         _____  _____
10         Total
11
12         COGS
13           TVs
14           VCRs
15                        _____
16         Total
17
18         Gross Pft
19           TVs
20           VCRs
21                        _____
22         Total
```

Total net inc. $6,057

Problem 28-5B *Budgeted income statement: Chapter 20* **(L.O. 4)**

Using the six-month projections from Problem 28-4B for the sales, cost of goods sold, and gross profit (gross margin) for TVs and VCRs, complete McBurney's budgeted income statement by including expenses and totals for the 6 months. The business budgets expenses as follows:

Salaries	$14,000	per month
Rent	2,000	per month
Depreciation	1,000	per month
Insurance	500	per month
Travel	750	per quarter (in January and April only)
Utilities	500	per month
Income tax rate	30%	

Required

Create a spreadsheet model to prepare McBurney's budgeted income statement for the six months ended June 30, 19X4. Show each expense, total operating expenses, income from operations, income tax expense, and net income.

B/E sales at $140,000 and 60% $350,000
Target sales at $180,000 and 70%, $766,667

Problem 28-6B *Cost-volume-profit analysis: Chapter 21* **(L.O. 4)**

City Auto Parts management firm is planning for 19X7. Fixed expenses are expected to range from $140,000 to $180,000. Variable expenses will likely range from 60 percent of sales to 70 percent of sales. The company's target income from operations is $50,000.

Required

Prepare a spreadsheet that shows break-even sales in dollars and dollar sales needed to earn the target income from operations under the following combinations being considered. The spreadsheet should be formatted as follows:

	A	B	C	D	E	F	G
1	Fixed exp	$140,000	$180,000	$140,000	$180,000	$140,000	$180,000
2	Variable exp	60%	60%	70%	70%	60%	70%
3	Income from oper	$0	$0	$0	$0	$50,000	$50,000
4	Break-even sales	?	?	?	?		
5	Target sales	↑				?	?

(+B1+B3)/(1-B2)

Problem 28-7B   *Net-present-value analysis: Chapter 26* **(L.O. 4)**

Clover Rent-All is considering purchasing a truck to rent out to do-it-yourself movers. Clover Rent-All has a required rate of return of 10 percent (.10). The company is considering two trucks:

Net present value:
Truck 1, $884
Truck 2, ($6,051)

	A	B	C
1			
2		Truck 1	Truck 2
3	Cost	$100,000	$140,000
4		————	————
5	Annual net cash inflows:		
6	Year 1	$28,000	$30,000
8	2	$30,000	$35,000
9	3	35,000	45,000
10	4	22,000	30,000
11	5	15,000	20,000
12	6		15,000
13	7		5,000
14		═══	═══
15	Present value of net cash inflows		
16			
17	Investment		
18		————	————
19	Net present value	$	$
20		═══	═══

Required

Create a spreadsheet model to help decide which truck has the higher net present value and is, therefore, more attractive as an investment. Format the spreadsheet as above.

Extending Your Knowledge

Ethical Issue

CompuStaff Time-Share Systems performs data-processing services for clients in the Youngstown, Ohio, area. CompuStaff programmers have developed a specialized program to handle the payrolls of several hospitals and industrial companies. The programmers also run the computer programs that they have written. To meet rigid deadlines and streamline operations, programmers have the authority to intervene at any stage of a job.

One programmer has been writing one payroll check to a fictitious employee each week for each of the six clients he serves. This programmer simply removes one check from each client's batch before delivering the checks for distribution to employees on Friday. He then deposits the checks in separate banks where he has opened accounts in the names of the fictitious employees. The amount of each check is small in relation to the client's weekly payroll, so none of the clients is suspicious.

Required

What weakness in CompuStaff's internal control system allows this to happen? How can the CompuStaff system be improved?

Appendix A

Accounting for the Effects of Changing Prices (Inflation)

LEARNING OBJECTIVES

After studying this appendix, you should be able to

1 Report current-cost/constant-dollar income statement information

2 Compute a purchasing-power gain or loss

3 Prepare a current-cost/constant-dollar balance sheet

We use accounting information for making economic decisions. Of course, these decisions can only be as good as the information that we weigh in making them. Critics charge that accounting fails to provide the most accurate information possible because it fails to measure the effects of price changes. How intelligent, then, can our economic decisions be?

We know that GAAP directs companies to assume the stable-monetary-unit concept when preparing financial statements. For accounting purposes, companies use the historical cost of a building throughout the building's lifetime. However, critics maintain that historical-cost accounting does not provide the necessary information to allow statement users to make intelligent decisions. Is it valid to assume a stable monetary unit when prices—and the dollar's value itself—change over time?

An increase in the general price level is called **inflation.** The general price level is the weighted average of the prices of all goods and services in the economy. Changes in the general price level are measured by a general price index that assigns a value of 100 to a base year. The price index tracks the movement of prices in the economy over time. A 6 percent price increase during year 1 would cause the price index to rise to a value of 106 (100 × 1.06) at the end of the year. A 50 percent increase in prices over a six-year period would result in a price index of 150 (100 × 1.50) at the end of six years.

The most widely used general price index in the United States is the Consumer Price Index (CPI), published monthly by the U.S. Department of Labor. The CPI is based on a representative sample of food, clothing, shelter, transportation, and other items purchased by an average consumer. The base period for the CPI is 1982–84. Each month the average of these items' prices is compared to their prices the preceding month, and a new price index is computed. This price index reached the 136 mark in 1991, indicating that the general level of prices increased by 36 percent over approximately eight years.

Another way to describe inflation is in terms of the purchasing power of the dollar. A dollar will buy less meat, less gasoline, less laundering for shirts and blouses, and less of most other goods and services than a dollar would buy in 1983. Inflation, therefore, can also be defined as a decrease in the purchasing power of the dollar.

Real-World Example: An article in the Fall 1987 issue of *Money* magazine illustrated the impact of inflation on our lives since 1972. Here are some of the examples.

	1972	1987	% Change
New house	$27,600	$103,900	+276.4
Zenith 19" TV (color)	499	480	− 3.8
Big Mac, shake & fries	$1.05	$2.89	+175.2
Levi's 501 jeans	$ 10	$ 26	+160
Income tax for median income family	982	2,704	+175.4

Teaching Tip: A price index shows the relationship between prices for goods and services for any year and prices of goods and services for a base year. When showing a percentage relationship, remind students that CPI for the base year is always 100%.

How does inflation affect accounting? This question does not have a simple answer. Two approaches have received considerable attention from the FASB.

1. *Constant-dollar accounting* presents the financial statements adjusted to reflect dollars of equal purchasing power. The adjustment, based on the economywide movement of prices, uses the Consumer Price Index. Assume that a building cost $100,000 when the CPI was 100. In the current period, the CPI is 130. This building would be adjusted into a constant-dollar equivalent of $130,000 (historical cost of $100,000 multiplied by the increased general price level, 130/100). Another way to describe the $130,000 constant-dollar measure of the building: it would take 130,000 current-period dollars to equal the 100,000 dollars that were actually paid to acquire the building. A number of South American countries—including Argentina and Brazil—use constant-dollar accounting.

2. *Current-cost accounting* ignores historical cost altogether. The **current cost** of an asset is the present cost of replacing its particular service potential, or usefulness. Suppose it would cost $180,000 currently to replace the building in the preceding illustration. A current-cost balance sheet reports the building at $180,000. A current-cost income statement bases depreciation expense on the building's current cost. For example, if the building has a 30-year life with no residual value, current-cost depreciation is $6,000 ($180,000/30) per year. Companies in the Netherlands have pioneered the use of a form of current-cost accounting.

Overview of Current-Cost/Constant-Dollar Accounting

Inventory and plant assets are usually two of a company's most valuable assets. These items' current costs often differ greatly from their historical cost. Therefore, **current-cost accounting**—which uses the current cost of the company's assets and expenses in place of their historical cost—focuses on inventory and plant assets and the related expenses, which are cost of goods sold and depreciation. A current-cost balance sheet looks exactly like one prepared on the historical-cost basis, except that the current costs of the company's inventory and plant assets are substituted for their historical cost amounts, and stockholders' equity is adjusted accordingly. A current-cost income statement is the same as a historical-cost income statement but with the current-cost amounts of cost of goods sold and depreciation substituted in place of historical cost. The current-cost income statement also includes additional information that we explain later.

Actual Example of Current-Cost/Constant-Dollar Information

Exhibit A-1 presents data that are adapted from the actual financial statements of AMF Incorporated, best known for its bowling products. *Statement of Operations* in the heading is a synonym for income statement. The items to be explained in more detail are highlighted for emphasis.

Current-Cost/Constant-Dollar Income Statement

Exhibit A-1's heading indicates that the information on changing prices is supplemental to the historical-cost financial statements. The statement of operations, or income statement, includes two columns. The first column repeats the historical-cost income statement reported in the primary financial statements. The second column is a current-cost income statement. Total revenue; selling, general, and administrative expenses; interest expense; and income taxes are the same at historical cost and at current cost, so these items need no adjustment.

Cost of sales (cost of goods sold) and depreciation have current-cost amounts that differ from historical cost. AMF's historical cost of sales is $703 million, compared to $709 million at current cost. The higher current-cost amount means that AMF's cost of replacing its inventory increased between the time it was acquired and the time it was sold. Cost of goods sold at current cost is computed by totaling the replacement cost of the inventory at the time it is sold.

Depreciation expense, at historical cost, is $60 million, compared to $78 million at current cost. Computing current-cost depreciation is similar to computing historical-cost depreciation. AMF's financial statements indicate the company depreciates its assets over approximately 12 years on a straight-line basis. The current cost of AMF's depreciable assets, before accumulated depreciation, is approximately $940 million. Assuming zero residual value, current-

OBJECTIVE 1

Report current-cost/constant-dollar income statement information

EXHIBIT A-1 *Supplemental Statement of Operations Adjusted for Inflation*

AMF Incorporated
Supplemental Statement of Operations Adjusted for Inflation
Year Ended December 31, 19X4
(millions of dollars)

	Historical Cost	Current-Cost/ Constant-Dollar
Total revenue	$1,095	$1,095
Cost of sales	$ 703	$ 709
Selling, general, and administrative expenses	294	294
Depreciation	60	78
Interest expense, net	9	9
Income taxes	14	14
Total expenses	1,080	1,104
Income (loss) from continuing operations	$ 15	$ (9)
Gain from decline in purchasing power of net amounts owed		$ 5
Increase in the current cost of the company's inventories and property		$ 43
Effect of general inflation		24
Excess of the increase in the current cost of the company's inventories and property over the effect of general inflation		$ 19

Additional current-cost information:
At December 31, 19X4, the current cost of inventories was $203 million (compared to $151 million historical cost), and the net current cost of property, plant, and equipment was $501 million (compared to $365 million historical cost).

cost depreciation for the year is $78 million ($940 million/12 years = $78 million). This current-cost depreciation amount means that AMF could expect to pay $78 million *currently* to replace the portion of its depreciable assets that the company used in operations during the year. Because AMF purchased its assets when prices were lower, the company's historical-cost depreciation was lower ($60 million).

Income from continuing operations for the year is $15 million at historical cost. At current cost, the result is a loss of $9 million. This comparison suggests that inflation has turned AMF's operating profit into a loss. Supporters of current-cost accounting point out that a company must replace the inventory it has sold and its worn-out plant assets to remain in business. They believe the current-cost measure of income is more informative than historical cost.

You may have been wondering where constant-dollar accounting enters the income statement. The revenues and the expenses are all stated in constant dollars of the current year. The items immediately beneath income from continuing operations in Exhibit A-1 also reflect constant-dollar accounting. We turn our attention to their explanation now.

Purchasing-Power Gain or Loss

Exhibit A-1 reports "Gain from decline in the purchasing power of net amounts owed." The gain is $5 million. This gain is also called the **purchasing-power gain.** It occurs during inflation because the company is able to pay its liabilities with dollars that are cheaper than the dollars borrowed.

What does the purchasing-power gain mean? Suppose you borrow $5,000 to purchase a sailboat. You repay the loan after two years, during which time prices have risen 20 percent. If you are obligated to pay only $5,000 (ignoring interest for the moment), you experience a purchasing-power gain of $1,000 ($5,000 multiplied by the inflation rate of 20 percent). The creditor who loaned you the money incurs the corresponding **purchasing-power loss** of $1,000 because the dollars the creditor receives when you repay the loan are worth less than the dollars lent. Interest rates are intended to compensate for this purchasing-power gain or loss, but interest is accounted for separately. In Exhibit A-1, AMF reports interest expense apart from the change in purchasing power.

The purchasing-power gain or loss depends on the company's monetary assets and monetary liabilities. **Monetary assets** are assets whose values are stated in a fixed number of dollars. Their amount does *not* change, regardless of inflation. Examples include cash and receivables.

Nonmonetary assets are those assets whose prices do change during inflation. Examples include inventory, land, buildings, and equipment. Holding nonmonetary assets does not result in a purchasing-power gain or loss.

Monetary liabilities are liabilities that are stated in a fixed number of dollars. Most liabilities are monetary. As discussed above in the sailboat example, you have a purchasing-power gain if you have a monetary liability during inflation.

The computation of the purchasing-power gain or loss is based on the company's **net monetary position** (monetary assets minus monetary liabilities). If the company has more monetary assets than monetary liabilities, it has **net monetary assets.** If its monetary liabilities exceed its monetary assets, it has **net monetary liabilities.** A company's monetary assets and liabilities can be taken

AMF Incorporated
Gain from Decline in Purchasing Power of Net Amounts Owed (Purchasing-Power Gain)
Year Ended December 31, 19X4
(millions of dollars)

	Historical Cost	Constant-Dollar Adjustments for Inflation
Net monetary liabilities, beginning (Dec. 31, 19X3)	$126	$\times \dfrac{102.5}{100.0} = \$129$
Increase in net monetary liabilities during 19X4 ...	27	27
Subtotal		156
Net monetary liabilities, ending (Dec. 31, 19X4) ...	$153	$\times \dfrac{102.5}{103.9} = \underline{\ 151\ }$
Purchasing-power gain		$\underline{\$\ \ 5\ }$

from its historical-cost balance sheet. Exhibit A-2 shows the computation of AMF's purchasing power gain of $5 million.

The computation of the purchasing-power gain in Exhibit A-2 follows the FASB approach. At December 31, 19X3 (the beginning of 19X4), AMF had a net-monetary-liability position of $126 million. During 19X4 the company increased its net monetary liabilities by $27 million and ended 19X4 with a net-monetary-liability position of $153 million. These amounts are in the Historical Cost column. The historical 19X3 and 19X4 net-monetary-liability positions are not comparable because they are stated in dollars of different purchasing power. The beginning position is stated in December 19X3 dollars, which are not comparable to the December 19X4 dollars used in the ending balance. The reason is that the general price level in the United States increased during 19X4—that is, general inflation occurred. To compute AMF's overall purchasing-power gain or loss, it is necessary to make the beginning and ending monetary positions comparable.

The inflation adjustments of AMF's net monetary liabilities are in Exhibit A-2 under the column Constant-Dollar Adjustments for Inflation. The data in that column restate the beginning and ending net-monetary-liability positions to dollars of constant purchasing power. The Consumer Price Index (CPI) is used for this adjustment. At the beginning of 19X4, when AMF had net monetary liabilities of $126 million, the Consumer Price Index was 100.0. For 19X4 the average CPI was 102.5.

The beginning historical-cost balance is restated into average constant dollars of 19X4 by multiplying it by the ratio of the current-year average index (102.5) to the beginning price index (100.0). The numerator of the price-index ratio is the current-year average index, and the denominator is the price index that was in effect on the date of the balance. The adjustment of the beginning balance is (amounts rounded to the nearest million dollars):

Beginning Net Monetary Liabilities	×	Current-Year Average Consumer Price Index / Beginning-of-Year Consumer Price Index	=	Beginning Net Monetary Liabilities Stated in Average Constant Dollars of the Current Year
$126	×	$\dfrac{102.5}{100.0}$	=	$129

The change in net monetary liabilities during 19X4 ($27 million) is not adjusted because it occurred as the company transacted business all during the year. The average price index (102.5) is both the numerator and the denominator of the index ratio, resulting in a ratio of 1.

The subtotal in Exhibit A-2 ($156 million) is the sum of the adjusted beginning net monetary liabilities plus the increase (or minus the decrease) in net monetary liabilities that arose from the transactions of the year. During 19X4 AMF increased its net monetary liabilities by $27 million. The subtotal of $156 million is the amount of net monetary liabilities that AMF would owe if the company's monetary assets and liabilities had just kept pace with inflation during the year.

The ending historical-cost balance ($153 million) is restated into average constant dollars of 19X4 by multiplying it by the ratio of the current-year average index (102.5) to the ending price index (103.9). The adjustment of the ending balance is (amounts rounded to the nearest million dollars):

Ending Net Monetary Liabilities	×	Current-Year Average Consumer Price Index / End-of-Year Consumer Price Index	=	Ending Net Monetary Liabilities Stated in Average Constant Dollars of the Current Year
$153	×	$\dfrac{102.5}{103.9}$	=	$151

The purchasing-power gain can now be computed. Its amount is determined by subtracting the ending adjusted net monetary liability balance ($151 million) from the subtotal ($156 million). If AMF had just kept pace with general inflation during 19X4, its net-monetary-liability position would have been $156 million. But at year end, the company's net monetary liabilities are only $151 million. The result is a purchasing-power gain of $5 million. AMF's gain resulted primarily from (a) inflation during 19X4 and (b) the company's net-monetary-liability position during the year. If the company had had more monetary assets than liabilities during inflation, it would have experienced a purchasing-power loss

The purchasing-power gain computation is useful for determining how well the entity is managing its monetary position during inflation. Purchasing-power gain (or loss) can be applied to individual persons as well as to businesses of all sizes.

Increase in the Current Cost of Inventories and Property, Plant, and Equipment

Exhibit A-1 indicates that the current cost of AMF's inventories and property (plant assets) increased by $43 million during 19X4. Historical-cost accounting ignores such increases in assets because they are not the result of completed transactions.

The effect of *general inflation* on the current cost of the company's inventories and property during 19X4 was an increase of $24 million. Thus if the current costs of these assets had just kept pace with general inflation in the United States economy during 19X4, their current costs would have increased by $24 million.

The excess of the current-cost increase ($43 million) over the effect of general inflation ($24 million) is a measure of the net increase in the market value of the company's assets during the year. This excess of $19 million indicates that the current cost of AMF's assets increased faster during 19X4 than the rate of general inflation. According to the FASB, this net increase reflects favorably on the company.

Current-Cost/Constant-Dollar Balance Sheet

The bottom section of Exhibit A-1 reports that AMF's inventory had a current cost of $203 million at December 31, 19X4, compared to historical cost of $151 million. The current cost of the company's property, plant, and equipment, net of accumulated depreciation, was $501 million, compared to $365 million at historical cost. These current-cost amounts reveal the current values of AMF's assets, and these amounts may be of interest to investors and creditors. An investor can substitute these current costs in place of historical costs to prepare a current-cost balance sheet. Exhibit A-3 presents a condensed current-cost/constant-dollar balance sheet for AMF with items of special interest highlighted.

Exhibit A-3 reports AMF's current costs of inventories and plant assets next to the historical costs. The current costs are higher than historical costs. Liabilities do not change significantly on a current-cost balance sheet, so the current-cost measure of stockholders' equity increases by the amount of the increase in asset value. AMF's stockholders' equity at current cost is $644

OBJECTIVE 3
Prepare a current-cost/constant-dollar balance sheet

EXHIBIT A-3 *Condensed Balance Sheets*

AMF Incorporated Condensed Balance Sheets—Historical Cost and Current-Cost/Constant Dollar December 31, 19X4 (millions of dollars)		
	Historical Cost	**Current-Cost/ Constant-Dollar**
Cash, short-term investments, receivables, prepaid expenses, and other current assets	$364	$ 364
Inventories	151	203
Property, plant, and equipment, net	365	501
Intangible and other assets	59	59
Total assets	$939	$1,127
Total liabilities	$483	$ 483
Stockholders' equity..........................	456	644
Total liabilities and stockholders' equity	$939	$1,127

Real-World Example: Many companies do not show a difference between the current cost and the historical cost of inventories because they use the FIFO method of inventory costing. Companies that use LIFO show a smaller difference between historical cost income and current-cost income. A recent Kraft, Inc. annual report describes the effect of using LIFO: "In addition, the company's use of the LIFO method of accounting . . . results in reporting the cost of products sold (COGS) at approximately current cost."

million. It is computed as total assets of $1,127 million minus total liabilities of $483 million. Stockholders' equity at current cost far exceeds the historical-cost measure of $456 million. The company's investors and creditors may take comfort in these higher values of assets and owners' equity.

Summary Problem for Your Review

McLaughlin, Inc., reported the following historical-cost financial statements at December 31, 19X5:

McLaughlin, Inc.
Income Statement
Year Ended December 31, 19X5

Sales revenue	$300,000
Cost of goods sold	$144,000
Operating expenses (excluding depreciation)	65,000
Depreciation	11,000
Income taxes	32,000
Total expenses	252,000
Net income	$ 48,000

McLaughlin, Inc.
Balance Sheet
December 31, 19X5

Current assets other than inventory	$ 53,000
Inventory	122,000
Plant assets, net	273,000
Goodwill and other assets	14,000
Total assets	$462,000
Total liabilities	$219,000
Stockholders' equity	243,000
Total liabilities and stockholders' equity	$462,000

McLaughlin's current cost of goods sold for 19X5 was $162,000, and current-cost depreciation was $18,000. Net monetary liabilities were $133,000 at December 31, 19X4, when the price index was 100. At December 31, 19X5, net monetary liabilities were $148,000, and the price index was 112. The average price index for 19X5 was 106. During 19X5 the current cost of the company's inventory and plant assets increased by $44,000, but the effect of general inflation was an increase of $51,000. At December 31, 19X5, the current cost of inventory was $145,000, and the current cost of plant assets, net of depreciation, was $343,000.

Required

Prepare a comparative historical-cost and current-cost/constant-dollar income statement and balance sheet patterned after Exhibits A-1 and A-3. Include computation of the purchasing-power gain or loss similar to Exhibit A-2. Round all amounts to the nearest thousand dollars.

SOLUTION TO REVIEW PROBLEM

McLaughlin, Inc.
Income Statement
Year Ended December 31, 19X5

	Historical Cost	Current-Cost/ Constant-Dollar
Sales revenue	$300,000	$300,000
Cost of goods sold	$144,000	$162,000
Operating expenses (excluding depreciation)	65,000	65,000
Depreciation	11,000	18,000
Income taxes	32,000	32,000
Total expenses	252,000	277,000
Net income	$ 48,000	$ 23,000
Purchasing-power gain on net monetary liabilities (computed)		$ 16,000
Increase in the current cost of inventory and plant assets		$ 44,000
Effect of general inflation		51,000
Excess of the effect of general inflation over the increase in the current cost of inventory and plant assets		$ 7,000

McLaughlin, Inc.
Balance Sheet
December 31, 19X5

	Historical Cost	Current-Cost/ Constant-Dollar
Current assets other than inventory	$ 53,000	$ 53,000
Inventory	122,000	145,000
Plant assets, net	273,000	343,000
Goodwill and other assets	14,000	14,000
Total assets	$462,000	$555,000
Total liabilities	$219,000	$219,000
Stockholders' equity	243,000	336,000
Total liabilities and stockholders' equity	$462,000	$555,000

McLaughlin, Inc.
Purchasing Power Gain
Year Ended December 31, 19X5

	Historical Cost	Adjusted for Inflation
Net monetary liabilities, beginning (Dec. 31, 19X4) ..	$133,000 ×	$\dfrac{106}{100}$ = $141,000
Increase in net monetary liabilities during 19X5	15,000	15,000
Subtotal		156,000
Net monetary liabilities, ending (Dec. 31, 19X5)	$148,000 ×	$\dfrac{106}{112}$ = 140,000
Purchasing power gain		$ 16,000

Summary

Accounting for the effects of changing prices includes preparation of a supplemental income statement on a *current-cost/constant-dollar* basis. Current cost is the cost of replacing the company's assets with assets of equal service potential. The constant-dollar element means presenting the financial statements in dollars of equal purchasing power.

Additional changing price disclosures include the company's *purchasing-power gain or loss* on its net monetary items and *changes in the current cost* of the company's inventory and plant assets, net of the effect of general inflation. Companies also disclose the current cost of their *inventories* and *plant assets*. These data can be used to prepare a current-cost balance sheet. The current-cost/constant-dollar disclosures became voluntary in 1986.

Self-Study Questions

Test your understanding of the appendix by marking the best answer for each of the following questions.

1. The main differences between historical-cost and current-cost measures of income from continuing operations result from *(p. 1290)*
   a. Inventory and plant assets
   b. Cost of goods sold and depreciation
   c. Purchasing-power gain or loss
   d. Changes in the general price level
2. Holding a net-monetary-asset position during a period of inflation results in a *(p. 1294)*
   a. Purchasing-power gain
   b. Purchasing-power loss
   c. Neither a purchasing-power gain nor a loss
   d. Lower income from continuing operations
3. The historical-cost balance sheet reports total assets of $400,000 (including inventory of $100,000 and net plant assets of $120,000), total liabilities of $150,000, and stockholders' equity of $250,000. The current cost of inventory is $110,000, and the current cost of net plant assets is $180,000. What

is the current-cost measure of this company's stockholders' equity? *(pp. 1295, 1296)*

a. $250,000

b. $260,000

c. $310,000

d. $320,000

Answers to the self-study questions follow the Accounting Vocabulary.

Accounting Vocabulary

Current cost. Present cost of replacing an asset's particular service potential or usefulness *(p. 1290)*.

Current-cost accounting. Accounting model that uses the current cost of a company's assets and expenses in place of their historical cost *(p. 1290)*.

Inflation. Increase in the general price level *(p. 1289)*.

Monetary asset. Asset whose value is stated in a fixed number of dollars. This amount does not change, regardless of inflation *(p. 1292)*.

Monetary liability. Liability stated in a fixed number of dollars. This amount does not change, regardless of inflation *(p. 1292)*.

Net monetary assets. Excess of monetary assets over monetary liabilities *(p. 1292)*.

Net monetary liabilities. Excess of monetary liabilities over monetary assets *(p. 1292)*.

Nonmonetary asset. Asset whose price may change during inflation, such as inventory, land, buildings, and equipment *(p. 1292)*.

Purchasing-power gain (or loss). A purchasing power gain occurs during inflation because a company is able to pay its liabilities with dollars that are cheaper than the dollars borrowed. A purchasing power loss occurs during inflation when a creditor receives dollars that are worth less than the dollars lent *(p. 1292)*.

Answers to Self-Study Questions

1. b
2. b
3. d [$250,000 + ($110,000 − $100,000) + ($180,000 − $120,000) = $320,000]

ASSIGNMENT MATERIAL _____

Questions

1. Identify one problem with the historical-cost balance sheet and one problem with the historical-cost income statement that arise because of inflation.

2. Suppose you were preparing the current-cost financial statements of a company. What two assets and what two expenses are most likely to have different values in the historical-cost and the current-cost statements?

3. How do monetary assets differ from nonmonetary assets? Give examples of each.

4. If a company holds net monetary assets during inflation, does it experience a purchasing-power gain or a loss? If the company holds net monetary liabilities, does it experience a purchasing-power gain or a loss?

5. General Motors Corporation had net monetary liabilities of $9,948 million at the beginning of a year when the price index was 100. The average price index for the year was 102.5. What is the inflation-adjusted beginning net-monetary-liability position?

Exercises

Exercise A-1 *Preparing a current-cost income statement* **(L.O. 1)**

Long Incorporated reported the following historical-cost income statement for the year ended September 30, 19X7:

Long Incorporated Income Statement Year Ended September 30, 19X7	
Sales revenue	$440,000
Cost of goods sold	$206,000
Operating expenses	131,000
Depreciation	43,000
Income taxes	24,000
Total expenses	404,000
Net income	$ 36,000

Additional current-cost information includes:

a.	Current cost of goods sold	$237,000
b.	Current cost depreciation	47,000
c.	Purchasing power gain	7,000
d.	Increase in the current cost of inventory and plant assets	31,000
e	Effect of general inflation on the cost of inventory and plant assets	19,000

Required

Prepare Long's comparative historical cost and current-cost/constant-dollar income statement to conform to FASB guidelines. Use Exhibit A-1 as a guide.

Exercise A-2 *Computing a purchasing-power gain or loss* **(L.O. 2)**

Raytheon Company is a leading maker of electronic radar equipment. At the beginning of a recent year, when the price index was 100, Raytheon had a net-monetary-liability position of $1,161 million. The company's net-monetary-liability position at the end of the year was $1,203 million, and the price index was 103.8. The average price index for the year was 102.1.

Required

Compute Raytheon's purchasing-power gain for the year, rounding all amounts to the nearest million dollars.

Exercise A-3 *Preparing a current-cost balance sheet* **(L.O. 3)**

Well-known brand names of Chesebrough-Pond's, Inc. include Bass shoes, Healthtex clothing, and Vaseline and Pond's health and beauty products. The company's condensed historical cost balance sheet at December 31, the end of a recent year, was

Chesebrough-Pond's, Inc.
Balance Sheet
December 31, 19XX

	(Thousands)
Current assets other than inventory	$ 454,100
Inventories	396,500
Property, plant, and equipment, net	241,800
Investments, goodwill, trademarks, and other assets ..	79,500
Total assets..	$1,171,900
Total liabilities	$ 522,000
Shareholders' equity	649,900
Total liabilities and shareholders' equity..............	$1,171,900

On the balance sheet date, the current cost of inventories was $402.4 million, and the current cost of net property, plant, and equipment was $374.7 million.

Required

Prepare a current-cost/constant-dollar balance sheet for Chesebrough-Pond's, Inc. It is not necessary to repeat the historical cost balance sheet.

Problems

Problem A-1 *Preparing current-cost financial statements* **(L.O. 1, 2, 3)**

Deloitte, Inc., reported the following historical cost financial statements at September 30, 19X9:

Total assets,
current-cost/constant dollar
$900,000

Deloitte, Inc.
Income Statement
Year Ended September 30, 19X9

Total revenues	$623,000
Cost of goods sold.........................	$305,000
Operating expenses (excluding depreciation) .	76,000
Depreciation	42,000
Income taxes	80,000
Total expenses	503,000
Net income	$120,000

Deloitte, Inc.
Balance Sheet
September 30, 19X9

Current assets other than inventory	$ 37,000
Inventory	239,000
Plant assets, net	533,000
Other assets	22,000
Total assets	$831,000
Total liabilities	$348,000
Stockholders' equity	483,000
Total liabilities and stockholders' equity	$831,000

Deloitte's current cost of goods sold for fiscal year 19X9 was $337,000, and current-cost depreciation was $52,000. During fiscal year 19X9, the purchasing power gain on net monetary liabilities was $37,000. Also during the year, the current cost of the company's inventory and plant assets increased by $56,000, but the effect of general inflation was a $62,000 increase. At September 30, 19X9, the current cost of inventory was $278,000, and the current cost of plant assets, net of depreciation, was $563,000.

Required

Prepare a comparative historical cost and current-cost/constant-dollar income statement and balance sheet patterned after Exhibits A-1 and A-3.

Purchasing power gain $28,000 **Problem A-2** *Preparing current-cost financial statements; computing a purchasing power gain or loss* **(L.O. 1, 2, 3)**

The historical-cost financial statements of Woodhouse Co. at December 31, 19X6, were

---

Woodhouse Co.
Income Statement
Year Ended December 31, 19X6

Sales revenue	$713,000
Cost of goods sold	$308,000
Operating expenses (excluding depreciation)	149,000
Depreciation	126,000
Income taxes	52,000
Total expenses	635,000
Net income	$ 78,000

Woodhouse, Co.
Balance Sheet
December 31, 19X6

Current assets other than inventory	$ 95,000
Inventory	145,000
Plant assets, net	612,000
Goodwill and other assets	62,000
Total assets	$914,000
Total liabilities	$389,000
Stockholders' equity	525,000
Total liabilities and stockholders' equity	$914,000

Woodhouse's current cost of goods sold for 19X6 was $323,000, and current-cost depreciation was $133,000. Net monetary liabilities were $263,000 at December 31, 19X5, when the price index was 100. At December 31, 19X6, net monetary liabilities were $304,000, and the price index was 110. The average price index for 19X6 was 104. During 19X6 the current cost of the company's inventory and plant assets increased by $19,000, but the effect of general inflation was a $27,000 increase. At December 31, 19X6, the current cost of inventory was $161,000, and the current cost of plant assets, net of depreciation, was $673,000.

Required

1. Prepare a comparative historical cost and current-cost income statement and balance sheet patterned after Exhibits A-1 and A-3.

2. Prepare a computation of the purchasing power gain or loss similar to Exhibit A-2. Round all amounts to the nearest thousand dollars.

Appendix B

Present-Value Tables and Future-Value Tables

This appendix provides present-value tables (more complete than those appearing in Chapter 16 and Chapter 26) and future-value tables.

TABLE B-1   *Present Value of $1*

Periods	1%	2%	3%	4%	5%	6%	7%	8%	9%	10%	12%
1	0.990	0.980	0.971	0.962	0.952	0.943	0.935	0.926	0.917	0.909	0.893
2	0.980	0.961	0.943	0.925	0.907	0.890	0.873	0.857	0.842	0.826	0.797
3	0.971	0.942	0.915	0.889	0.864	0.840	0.816	0.794	0.772	0.751	0.712
4	0.961	0.924	0.888	0.855	0.823	0.792	0.763	0.735	0.708	0.683	0.636
5	0.951	0.906	0.883	0.822	0.784	0.747	0.713	0.681	0.650	0.621	0.567
6	0.942	0.888	0.837	0.790	0.746	0.705	0.666	0.630	0.596	0.564	0.507
7	0.933	0.871	0.813	0.760	0.711	0.665	0.623	0.583	0.547	0.513	0.452
8	0.923	0.853	0.789	0.731	0.677	0.627	0.582	0.540	0.502	0.467	0.404
9	0.914	0.837	0.766	0.703	0.645	0.592	0.544	0.500	0.460	0.424	0.361
10	0.905	0.820	0.744	0.676	0.614	0.558	0.508	0.463	0.422	0.386	0.322
11	0.896	0.804	0.722	0.650	0.585	0.527	0.475	0.429	0.388	0.350	0.287
12	0.887	0.788	0.701	0.625	0.557	0.497	0.444	0.397	0.356	0.319	0.257
13	0.879	0.773	0.681	0.601	0.530	0.469	0.415	0.368	0.326	0.290	0.229
14	0.870	0.758	0.661	0.577	0.505	0.442	0.388	0.340	0.299	0.263	0.205
15	0.861	0.743	0.642	0.555	0.481	0.417	0.362	0.315	0.275	0.239	0.183
16	0.853	0.728	0.623	0.534	0.458	0.394	0.339	0.292	0.252	0.218	0.163
17	0.844	0.714	0.605	0.513	0.436	0.371	0.317	0.270	0.231	0.198	0.146
18	0.836	0.700	0.587	0.494	0.416	0.350	0.296	0.250	0.212	0.180	0.130
19	0.828	0.686	0.570	0.475	0.396	0.331	0.277	0.232	0.194	0.164	0.116
20	0.820	0.673	0.554	0.456	0.377	0.312	0.258	0.215	0.178	0.149	0.104
21	0.811	0.660	0.538	0.439	0.359	0.294	0.242	0.199	0.164	0.135	0.093
22	0.803	0.647	0.522	0.422	0.342	0.278	0.226	0.184	0.150	0.123	0.083
23	0.795	0.634	0.507	0.406	0.326	0.262	0.211	0.170	0.138	0.112	0.074
24	0.788	0.622	0.492	0.390	0.310	0.247	0.197	0.158	0.126	0.102	0.066
25	0.780	0.610	0.478	0.375	0.295	0.233	0.184	0.146	0.116	0.092	0.059
26	0.772	0.598	0.464	0.361	0.281	0.220	0.172	0.135	0.106	0.084	0.053
27	0.764	0.586	0.450	0.347	0.268	0.207	0.161	0.125	0.098	0.076	0.047
28	0.757	0.574	0.437	0.333	0.255	0.196	0.150	0.116	0.090	0.069	0.042
29	0.749	0.563	0.424	0.321	0.243	0.185	0.141	0.107	0.082	0.063	0.037
30	0.742	0.552	0.412	0.308	0.231	0.174	0.131	$.099	0.075	0.057	0.033
40	0.672	0.453	0.307	0.208	0.142	0.097	0.067	0.046	0.032	0.022	0.011
50	0.608	0.372	0.228	0.141	0.087	0.054	0.034	0.021	0.013	0.009	0.003

TABLE B-1 *(cont'd)*

| | | | | | Present Value | | | | | | |
14%	15%	16%	18%	20%	25%	30%	35%	40%	45%	50%	Periods
0.877	0.870	0.862	0.847	0.833	0.800	0.769	0.741	0.714	0.690	0.667	1
0.769	0.756	0.743	0.718	0.694	0.640	0.592	0.549	0.510	0.476	0.444	2
0.675	0.658	0.641	0.609	0.579	0.512	0.455	0.406	0.364	0.328	0.296	3
0.592	0.572	0.552	0.516	0.482	0.410	0.350	0.301	0.260	0.226	0.198	4
0.519	0.497	0.476	0.437	0.402	0.328	0.269	0.223	0.186	0.156	0.132	5
0.456	0.432	0.410	0.370	0.335	0.262	0.207	0.165	0.133	0.108	0.088	6
0.400	0.376	0.354	0.314	0.279	0.210	0.159	0.122	0.095	0.074	0.059	7
0.351	0.327	0.305	0.266	0.233	0.168	0.123	0.091	0.068	0.051	0.039	8
0.308	0.284	0.263	0.225	0.194	0.134	0.094	0.067	0.048	0.035	0.026	9
0.270	0.247	0.227	0.191	0.162	0.107	0.073	0.050	0.035	0.024	0.017	10
0.237	0.215	0.195	0.162	0.135	0.086	0.056	0.037	0.025	0.017	0.012	11
0.208	0.187	0.168	0.137	0.112	0.069	0.043	0.027	0.018	0.012	0.008	12
0.182	0.163	0.145	0.116	0.093	0.055	0.033	0.020	0.013	0.008	0.005	13
0.160	0.141	0.125	0.099	0.078	0.044	0.025	0.015	0.009	0.006	0.003	14
0.140	0.123	0.108	0.084	0.065	0.035	0.020	0.011	0.006	0.004	0.002	15
0.123	0.107	0.093	0.071	0.054	0.028	0.015	0.008	0.005	0.003	0.002	16
0.108	0.093	0.080	0.060	0.045	0.023	0.012	0.006	0.003	0.002	0.001	17
0.095	0.081	0.069	0.051	0.038	0.018	0.009	0.005	0.002	0.001	0.001	18
0.083	0.070	0.060	0.043	0.031	0.014	0.007	0.003	0.002	0.001		19
0.073	0.061	0.051	0.037	0.026	0.012	0.005	0.002	0.001	0.001		20
0.064	0.053	0.044	0.031	0.022	0.009	0.004	0.002	0.001			21
0.056	0.046	0.038	0.026	0.018	0.007	0.003	0.001	0.001			22
0.049	0.040	0.033	0.022	0.015	0.006	0.002	0.001				23
0.043	0.035	0.028	0.019	0.013	0.005	0.002	0.001				24
0.038	0.030	0.024	0.016	0.010	0.004	0.001	0.001				25
0.033	0.026	0.021	0.014	0.009	0.003	0.001					26
0.029	0.023	0.018	0.011	0.007	0.002	0.001					27
0.026	0.020	0.016	0.010	0.006	0.002	0.001					28
0.022	0.017	0.014	0.008	0.005	0.002						29
0.020	0.015	0.012	0.007	0.004	0.001						30
0.005	0.004	0.003	0.001	0.001							40
0.001	0.001	0.001									50

TABLE B-2 *Present Value of Annuity of $1*

Periods	1%	2%	3%	4%	Present Value 5%	6%	7%	8%	9%	10%	12%
1	0.990	0.980	0.971	0.962	0.952	0.943	0.935	0.926	0.917	0.909	0.893
2	1.970	1.942	1.913	1.886	1.859	1.833	1.808	1.783	1.759	1.736	1.690
3	2.941	2.884	2.829	2.775	2.723	2.673	2.624	2.577	2.531	2.487	2.402
4	3.902	3.808	3.717	3.630	3.546	3.465	3.387	3.312	3.240	3.170	3.037
5	4.853	4.713	4.580	4.452	4.329	4.212	4.100	3.993	3.890	3.791	3.605
6	5.795	5.601	5.417	5.242	5.076	4.917	4.767	4.623	4.486	4.355	4.111
7	6.728	6.472	6.230	6.002	5.786	5.582	5.389	5.206	5.033	4.868	4.564
8	7.652	7.325	7.020	6.733	6.463	6.210	5.971	5.747	5.535	5.335	4.968
9	8.566	8.162	7.786	7.435	7.108	6.802	6.515	6.247	5.995	5.759	5.328
10	9.471	8.983	8.530	8.111	7.722	7.360	7.024	6.710	6.418	6.145	5.650
11	10.368	9.787	9.253	8.760	8.306	7.887	7.499	7.139	6.805	6.495	5.938
12	11.255	10.575	9.954	9.385	8.863	8.384	7.943	7.536	7.161	6.814	6.194
13	12.134	11.348	10.635	9.986	9.394	8.853	8.358	7.904	7.487	7.103	6.424
14	13.004	12.106	11.296	10.563	9.899	9.295	8.745	8.244	7.786	7.367	6.628
15	13.865	12.849	11.938	11.118	10.380	9.712	9.108	8.559	8.061	7.606	6.811
16	14.718	13.578	12.561	11.652	10.838	10.106	9.447	8.851	8.313	7.824	6.974
17	15.562	14.292	13.166	12.166	11.274	10.477	9.763	9.122	8.544	8.022	7.120
18	16.398	14.992	13.754	12.659	11.690	10.828	10.059	9.372	8.756	8.201	7.250
19	17.226	15.678	14.324	13.134	12.085	11.158	10.336	9.604	8.950	8.365	7.366
20	18.046	16.351	14.878	13.590	12.462	11.470	10.594	9.818	9.129	8.514	7.469
21	18.857	17.011	15.415	14.029	12.821	11.764	10.836	10.017	9.292	8.649	7.562
22	19.660	17.658	15.937	14.451	13.163	12.042	11.061	10.201	9.442	8.772	7.645
23	20.456	18.292	16.444	14.857	13.489	12.303	11.272	10.371	9.580	8.883	7.718
24	21.243	18.914	16.936	15.247	13.799	12.550	11.469	10.529	9.707	8.985	7.784
25	22.023	19.523	17.413	15.622	14.094	12.783	11.654	10.675	9.823	9.077	7.843
26	22.795	20.121	17.877	15.983	14.375	13.003	11.826	10.810	9.929	9.161	7.896
27	23.560	20.707	18.327	16.330	14.643	13.211	11.987	10.935	10.027	9.237	7.943
28	24.316	21.281	18.764	16.663	14.898	13.406	12.137	11.051	10.116	9.307	7.984
29	25.066	21.844	19.189	16.984	15.141	13.591	12.278	11.158	10.198	9.370	8.022
30	25.808	22.396	19.600	17.292	15.373	13.765	12.409	11.258	10.274	9.427	8.055
40	32.835	27.355	23.115	19.793	17.159	15.046	13.332	11.925	10.757	9.779	8.244
50	39.196	31.424	25.730	21.482	18.256	15.762	13.801	12.234	10.962	9.915	8.305

TABLE B-2 (cont'd)

					Present Value						
14%	15%	16%	18%	20%	25%	30%	35%	40%	45%	50%	Periods
0.877	0.870	0.862	0.847	0.833	0.800	0.769	0.741	0.714	0.690	0.667	1
1.647	1.626	1.605	1.566	1.528	1.440	1.361	1.289	1.224	1.165	1.111	2
2.322	2.283	2.246	2.174	2.106	1.952	1.816	1.696	1.589	1.493	1.407	3
2.914	2.855	2.798	2.690	2.589	2.362	2.166	1.997	1.849	1.720	1.605	4
3.433	3.352	3.274	3.127	2.991	2.689	2.436	2.220	2.035	1.876	1.737	5
3.889	3.784	3.685	3.498	3.326	2.951	2.643	2.385	2.168	1.983	1.824	6
4.288	4.160	4.039	3.812	3.605	3.161	2.802	2.508	2.263	2.057	1.883	7
4.639	4.487	4.344	4.078	3.837	3.329	2.925	2.598	2.331	2.109	1.922	8
4.946	4.772	4.607	4.303	4.031	3.463	3.019	2.665	2.379	2.144	1.948	9
5.216	5.019	4.833	4.494	4.192	3.571	3.092	2.715	2.414	2.168	1.965	10
5.453	5.234	5.029	4.656	4.327	3.656	3.147	2.752	2.438	2.185	1.977	11
5.660	5.421	5.197	4.793	4.439	3.725	3.190	2.779	2.456	2.197	1.985	12
5.842	5.583	5.342	4.910	4.533	3.780	3.223	2.799	2.469	2.204	1.990	13
6.002	5.724	5.468	5.008	4.611	3.824	3.249	2.814	2.478	2.210	1.993	14
6.142	5.847	5.575	5.092	4.675	3.859	3.268	2.825	2.484	2.214	1.995	15
6.265	5.954	5.669	5.162	4.730	3.887	3.283	2.834	2.489	2.216	1.997	16
6.373	6.047	5.749	5.222	4.775	3.910	3.295	2.840	2.492	2.218	1.998	17
6.467	6.128	5.818	5.273	4.812	3.928	3.304	2.844	2.494	2.219	1.999	18
6.550	6.198	5.877	5.316	4.844	3.942	3.311	2.848	2.496	2.220	1.999	19
6.623	6.259	5.929	5.353	4.870	3.954	3.316	2.850	2.497	2.221	1.999	20
6.687	6.312	5.973	5.384	4.891	3.963	3.320	2.852	2.498	2.221	2.000	21
6.743	6.359	6.011	5.410	4.909	3.970	3.323	2.853	2.498	2.222	2.000	22
6.792	6.399	6.044	5.432	4.925	3.976	3.325	2.854	2.499	2.222	2.000	23
6.835	6.434	6.073	5.451	4.937	3.981	3.327	2.855	2.499	2.222	2.000	24
6.873	6.464	6.097	5.467	4.948	3.985	3.329	2.856	2.499	2.222	2.000	25
6.906	6.491	6.118	5.480	4.956	3.988	3.330	2.856	2.500	2.222	2.000	26
6.935	6.514	6.136	5.492	4.964	3.990	3.331	2.856	2.500	2.222	2.000	27
6.961	6.534	6.152	5.502	4.970	3.992	3.331	2.857	2.500	2.222	2.000	28
6.983	6.551	6.166	5.510	4.975	3.994	3.332	2.857	2.500	2.222	2.000	29
7.003	6.566	6.177	5.517	4.979	3.995	3.332	2.857	2.500	2.222	2.000	30
7.105	6.642	6.234	5.548	4.997	3.999	3.333	2.857	2.500	2.222	2.000	40
7.133	6.661	6.246	5.554	4.999	4.000	3.333	2.857	2.500	2.222	2.000	50

TABLE B-3 *Future Value of $1*

							Future Value							
Periods	1%	2%	3%	4%	5%	6%	7%	8%	9%	10%	12%	14%	15%
1	1.010	1.020	1.030	1.040	1.050	1.060	1.070	1.080	1.090	1.100	1.120	1.140	1.150
2	1.020	1.040	1.061	1.082	1.103	1.124	1.145	1.166	1.188	1.210	1.254	1.300	1.323
3	1.030	1.061	1.093	1.125	1.158	1.191	1.225	1.260	1.295	1.331	1.405	1.482	1.521
4	1.041	1.082	1.126	1.170	1.216	1.262	1.311	1.360	1.412	1.464	1.574	1.689	1.749
5	1.051	1.104	1.159	1.217	1.276	1.338	1.403	1.469	1.539	1.611	1.762	1.925	2.011
6	1.062	1.126	1.194	1.265	1.340	1.419	1.501	1.587	1.677	1.772	1.974	2.195	2.313
7	1.072	1.149	1.230	1.316	1.407	1.504	1.606	1.714	1.828	1.949	2.211	2.502	2.660
8	1.083	1.172	1.267	1.369	1.477	1.594	1.718	1.851	1.993	2.144	2.476	2.853	3.059
9	1.094	1.195	1.305	1.423	1.551	1.689	1.838	1.999	2.172	2.358	2.773	3.252	3.518
10	1.105	1.219	1.344	1.480	1.629	1.791	1.967	2.159	2.367	2.594	3.106	3.707	4.046
11	1.116	1.243	1.384	1.539	1.710	1.898	2.105	2.332	2.580	2.853	3.479	4.226	4.652
12	1.127	1.268	1.426	1.601	1.796	2.012	2.252	2.518	2.813	3.138	3.896	4.818	5.350
13	1.138	1.294	1.469	1.665	1.886	2.133	2.410	2.720	3.066	3.452	4.363	5.492	6.153
14	1.149	1.319	1.513	1.732	1.980	2.261	2.579	2.937	3.342	3.798	4.887	6.261	7.076
15	1.161	1.346	1.558	1.801	2.079	2.397	2.759	3.172	3.642	4.177	5.474	7.138	8.137
16	1.173	1.373	1.605	1.873	2.183	2.540	2.952	3.426	3.970	4.595	6.130	8.137	9.358
17	1.184	1.400	1.653	1.948	2.292	2.693	3.159	3.700	4.328	5.054	6.866	9.276	10.76
18	1.196	1.428	1.702	2.026	2.407	2.854	3.380	3.996	4.717	5.560	7.690	10.58	12.38
19	1.208	1.457	1.754	2.107	2.527	3.026	3.617	4.316	5.142	6.116	8.613	12.06	14.23
20	1.220	1.486	1.806	2.191	2.653	3.207	3.870	4.661	5.604	6.728	9.646	13.74	16.37
21	1.232	1.516	1.860	2.279	2.786	3.400	4.141	5.034	6.109	7.400	10.80	15.67	18.82
22	1.245	1.546	1.916	2.370	2.925	3.604	4.430	5.437	6.659	8.140	12.10	17.86	21.64
23	1.257	1.577	1.974	2.465	3.072	3.820	4.741	5.871	7.258	8.954	13.55	20.36	24.89
24	1.270	1.608	2.033	2.563	3.225	4.049	5.072	6.341	7.911	9.850	15.18	23.21	28.63
25	1.282	1.641	2.094	2.666	3.386	4.292	5.427	6.848	8.623	10.83	17.00	26.46	32.92
26	1.295	1.673	2.157	2.772	3.556	4.549	5.807	7.396	9.399	11.92	19.04	30.17	37.86
27	1.308	1.707	2.221	2.883	3.733	4.822	6.214	7.988	10.25	13.11	21.32	34.39	43.54
28	1.321	1.741	2.288	2.999	3.920	5.112	6.649	8.627	11.17	14.42	23.88	39.20	50.07
29	1.335	1.776	2.357	3.119	4.116	5.418	7.114	9.317	12.17	15.86	26.75	44.69	57.58
30	1.348	1.811	2.427	3.243	4.322	5.743	7.612	10.06	13.27	17.45	29.96	50.95	66.21
40	1.489	2.208	3.262	4.801	7.040	10.29	14.97	21.72	31.41	45.26	93.05	188.9	267.9
50	1.645	2.692	4.384	7.107	11.47	18.42	29.46	46.90	74.36	117.4	289.0	700.2	1,084

TABLE B-4 *Future Value of Annuity of $1*

Future Value

Periods	1%	2%	3%	4%	5%	6%	7%	8%	9%	10%	12%	14%	15%
1	1.000	1.000	1.000	1.000	1.000	1.000	1.000	1.000	1.000	1.000	1.000	1.000	1.000
2	2.010	2.020	2.030	2.040	2.050	2.060	2.070	2.080	2.090	2.100	2.120	2.140	2.150
3	3.030	3.060	3.091	3.122	3.153	3.184	3.215	3.246	3.278	3.310	3.374	3.440	3.473
4	4.060	4.122	4.184	4.246	4.310	4.375	4.440	4.506	4.573	4.641	4.779	4.921	4.993
5	5.101	5.204	5.309	5.416	5.526	5.637	5.751	5.867	5.985	6.105	6.353	6.610	6.742
6	6.152	6.308	6.468	6.633	6.802	6.975	7.153	7.336	7.523	7.716	8.115	8.536	8.754
7	7.214	7.434	7.662	7.898	8.142	8.394	8.654	8.923	9.200	9.487	10.09	10.73	11.07
8	8.286	8.583	8.892	9.214	9.549	9.897	10.26	10.64	11.03	11.44	12.30	13.23	13.73
9	9.369	9.755	10.16	10.58	11.03	11.49	11.98	12.49	13.02	13.58	14.78	16.09	16.79
10	10.46	10.95	11.46	12.01	12.58	13.18	13.82	14.49	15.19	15.94	17.55	19.34	20.30
11	11.57	12.17	12.81	13.49	14.21	14.97	15.78	16.65	17.56	18.53	20.65	23.04	24.35
12	12.68	13.41	14.19	15.03	15.92	16.87	17.89	18.98	20.14	21.38	24.13	27.27	29.00
13	13.81	14.68	15.62	16.63	17.71	18.88	20.14	21.50	22.95	24.52	28.03	32.09	34.35
14	14.95	15.97	17.09	18.29	19.60	21.02	22.55	24.21	26.02	27.98	32.39	37.58	40.50
15	16.10	17.29	18.60	20.02	21.58	23.28	25.13	27.15	29.36	31.77	37.28	43.84	47.58
16	17.26	18.64	20.16	21.82	23.66	25.67	27.89	30.32	33.00	35.95	42.75	50.98	55.72
17	18.43	20.01	21.76	23.70	25.84	28.21	30.84	33.75	36.97	40.54	48.88	59.12	65.08
18	19.61	21.41	23.41	25.65	28.13	30.91	34.00	37.45	41.30	45.60	55.75	68.39	75.84
19	20.81	22.84	25.12	27.67	30.54	33.76	37.38	41.45	46.02	51.16	63.44	78.97	88.21
20	22.02	24.30	26.87	29.78	33.07	36.79	41.00	45.76	51.16	57.28	72.05	91.02	102.4
21	23.24	25.78	28.68	31.97	35.72	39.99	44.87	50.42	56.76	64.00	81.70	104.8	118.8
22	24.47	27.30	30.54	34.25	38.51	43.39	49.01	55.46	62.87	71.40	92.50	120.4	137.6
23	25.72	28.85	32.45	36.62	41.43	47.00	53.44	60.89	69.53	79.54	104.6	138.3	159.3
24	26.97	30.42	34.43	39.08	44.50	50.82	58.18	66.76	76.79	88.50	118.2	158.7	184.2
25	28.24	32.03	36.46	41.65	47.73	54.86	63.25	73.11	84.70	98.35	133.3	181.9	212.8
26	29.53	33.67	38.55	44.31	51.11	59.16	68.68	79.95	93.32	109.2	150.3	208.3	245.7
27	30.82	35.34	40.71	47.08	54.67	63.71	74.48	87.35	102.7	121.1	169.4	238.5	283.6
28	32.13	37.05	42.93	49.97	58.40	68.53	80.70	95.34	113.0	134.2	190.7	272.9	327.1
29	33.45	38.79	45.22	52.97	62.32	73.64	87.35	104.0	124.1	148.6	214.6	312.1	377.2
30	34.78	40.57	47.58	56.08	66.44	79.06	94.46	113.3	136.3	164.5	241.3	356.8	434.7
40	48.89	60.40	75.40	95.03	120.8	154.8	199.6	259.1	337.9	442.6	767.1	1,342	1,779
50	64.46	84.58	112.8	152.7	209.3	290.3	406.5	573.8	815.1	1,164	2,400	4,995	7,218

Appendix C

Published Financial Statements

SHAREHOLDER INFORMATION

Transfer Agent and Registrar
First Chicago Trust Company of New York
Shareholder Relations - 8th Floor
30 West Broadway
New York, NY 10007-2192
(800) 446-2617
Inquiries concerning the
issuance or transfer of stock
certificates, the status of
dividend checks, share account
information or Dividend
Reinvestment Plan account
information should be directed
to the Transfer Agent at
the above address or toll
free number.

Principal Office
The Goodyear Tire & Rubber
Company
1144 East Market Street
Akron, Ohio 44316-0001
(216) 796-2121

Stock Exchange Information
The principal market for
The Goodyear Tire & Rubber
Company Common Stock is the
New York Stock Exchange
(Symbol GT). The stock is also
listed on the Midwest Stock
Exchange and the Pacific Stock
Exchange.

Goodyear Common Stock
At February 19, 1991, there
were 48,780 shareholders of
record of Goodyear common stock.
The closing price of Goodyear common
stock on the NYSE composite transactions
tape on February 19, 1991, was $20.

18
Management's Discussion
and Analysis

24
Consolidated Financial
Statements

28
Accounting Policies

29
Notes to Financial Statements

44
Supplementary Data

45
Comparison with Prior Years

46
Reports of Management
and Independent
Accountants

Annual Report on Form 10-K
The Company's Annual Report to the
Securities and Exchange Commission
for 1990 on Form 10-K will be
available in April of 1991.
A copy, including all financial
statements, schedules and
exhibits, may be obtained
without charge by writing:

Investor Relations
The Goodyear Tire & Rubber
Company
1144 East Market Street
Akron, Ohio 44316-0001
(216) 796-3457

Goodyear Dividend
Reinvestment
and Stock Purchase Plan
The Goodyear Dividend
Reinvestment and Stock
Purchase Plan is available to
shareholders. Under the Plan,
holders of shares of Goodyear
Common Stock may automati-
cally reinvest their cash
dividends in additional
Goodyear shares. Shareholders
also may purchase additional
Goodyear shares on the 15th
day of each month. A prospectus
explaining the Plan may be
obtained by contacting
Goodyear Investor Relations.

Audio Cassette Tapes
An Annual Report cassette
tape for blind shareholders may be
obtained by contacting Goodyear
Investor Relations.

RESULTS OF OPERATIONS

CONSOLIDATED

The Company recorded a net loss for 1990 of $38.3 million ($.66 per share) compared to net income of $206.8 million ($3.58 per share) in 1989 and net income of $350.1 million ($6.11 per share) in 1988.

Sales for 1990 of $11.3 billion increased 3.7 percent from the $10.9 billion recorded in 1989 and increased 4.3 percent from the $10.8 billion in 1988. The increase in sales was due primarily to the impact of currency translation on foreign results. Also contributing to the sales gain was a 2 percent increase in worldwide tire unit sales, the effect of which was limited by a lower value mix compared to last year.

Other income for 1990 of $180.6 million decreased 16.4 percent from 1989 and 17 percent from 1988. The primary source of other income was interest income on funds invested in time deposits in Latin America. The lower interest income was due to lower interest rates. Refer to the note to the financial statements entitled Other Income.

Cost of goods sold for 1990 of $8.8 billion increased 6.9 percent from 1989 and 6.2 percent from 1988. Raw material prices were relatively stable in 1990. In addition to the impact of changing exchange rates on foreign results, production costs increased worldwide due to higher compensation and benefit costs. Included in Cost of goods sold are research and development expenditures of $331.3 million, $303.3 million and $304.8 million for 1990, 1989 and 1988, respectively.

Selling, administrative and general expense for 1990 of $2 billion increased 7.3 percent from 1989 and 14.6 percent from 1988. The higher selling, administrative and general expense resulted from the impact of changing exchange rates and increased compensation, advertising and distribution expenses.

Interest expense of $328.2 million increased 28.6 percent from 1989 and 41.6 percent from 1988, primarily due to the recognition of interest associated with the All American Pipeline System which had been capitalized until October 1, 1989.

Unusual items of $103.6 million ($73.1 million after tax), $109.7 million ($105.9 million after tax) and $78.8 million ($26.8 million after tax) for 1990, 1989 and 1988, respectively, are fully described in the note to the financial statements entitled Unusual Items.

Other expenses of $74.5 million increased 67.3 percent from 1989 and 101.3 percent from 1988. The principal component of Other expenses are costs associated with the Company's continuous accounts receivable sale programs. The Company increased the level of net proceeds from sales under these agreements in December 1989 from $350 million to $600 million which resulted in higher associated costs. Refer to the note to the financial statements entitled Accounts and Notes Receivable.

The 1990 results reflect recognition of depreciation of the All American Pipeline System and its operating and interest expenses which, until October 1, 1989, were capitalized while the project was in the construction and preoperational development stage. Recognition of these items throughout 1989 would have reduced 1989 earnings by $131.5 million ($86.8 million after tax), consisting of $31.4 million of segment operating losses and $100.1 million of interest expense. Recognition of these items during 1988 would have reduced 1988 earnings by $145.1 million ($97.2 million after tax), consisting of $31.6 million of segment operating losses and $113.5 million of consolidated interest expense.

The Company experienced a high effective tax rate due to a combination of high foreign taxes and high U.S. taxes on foreign earnings. The Company expects high foreign taxes and high U.S. taxes on foreign operations to continue during 1991. Refer to the note to the financial statements entitled Income Taxes for further discussion.

The reduced demand for tires and other automotive products by original equipment manufacturers worldwide during 1990 resulted in significant industrywide surplus production capacity. The reduced demand is expected to continue in 1991. Growth in the worldwide replacement tire market is expected to remain low in 1991. Competitive pricing pressures are expected to continue throughout 1991 as manufacturers seek to utilize surplus capacity by increasing their share of market.

Research and development expenditures for 1991 are expected to be similar to the 1990 level.

Capital expenditures for 1991 are expected to be less than the estimated 1991 depreciation level of approximately $450 million. Capital expenditures in 1991 will be principally for modernizations and new tire molds.

The Company incurred charges for environmental cleanup projects of approximately $16 million in 1990 compared to approximately $7 million in 1989. During 1990, the Company also incurred charges of $22.2 million for environmental cleanup costs associated with a business segment discontinued in 1986. The Company anticipates that, in the future, it will incur increased charges associated with environmental cleanup projects necessitated by increasingly stringent environmental laws and standards.

The Company does not intend to adopt Statement of Financial Accounting Standards No. 96, "Accounting for Income Taxes," until the required implementation date, probably 1993. Because of continued uncertainty relating to implementation guidelines and interpretations, the Company is not certain as to the impact this Statement will have on future financial statements.

The Financial Accounting Standards Board issued Statement of Financial Accounting Standards No. 106, "Employers' Accounting for Postretirement Benefits Other Than Pensions," in December 1990. This Statement will significantly change the Company's practice of accounting for non-pension postretirement benefits from a pay-as-you-go (cash) basis to an accrual basis. The Company does not intend to adopt this Statement until the required implementation date of 1993. The Company is studying this Statement to determine its effect on the financial statements. It is too early to quantify the impact of this Statement; however, expenses for postretirement benefits are likely to materially adversely affect the Company's results of operations and equity in future periods.

INDUSTRY SEGMENTS

Operating income for 1990 of $604.6 million was reduced by $81.4 million of unusual charges. The 1989 operating income of $926.3 million was reduced by $109.7 million of unusual charges. The 1988 operating income of $1,003 million was reduced by $27.9 million of unusual charges. Refer to the notes to the financial statements entitled Unusual Items and Business Segments.

Tires and Related

Sales of $9.3 billion increased 4.1 percent from 1989 levels and rose 3.6 percent from 1988. The increase in sales was due primarily to the impact of currency translation of foreign results.

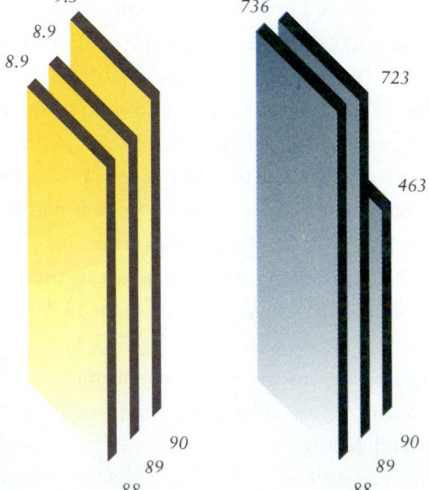

TIRES AND RELATED SALES
(Dollars in Billions)

9.3
8.9
8.9
90
89
88

TIRES AND RELATED OPERATING INCOME
(Dollars in Millions)

736
723
463
90
89
88

Operating income of $463.4 million decreased 35.9 percent and 37.1 percent from the 1989 and 1988 levels, respectively.

In 1990, this segment's operating income was reduced by $66.4 million resulting from the restructuring of tire marketing, distribution and production operations. In 1989, this segment's operating income of $722.6 million was reduced by $51.8 million resulting from the sale of the Company's South African subsidiary, the reduction of bias-ply truck tire capacity and the realignment of the Canadian operations. In 1988, this segment's operating income of $736.4 million was reduced by a charge of $25.1 million for employee reduction expenses.

The 1990 income was adversely affected by highly competitive replacement tire pricing in North America and Europe as industry participants competed for market share and utilization of manufacturing capacity.

Lower sales in the U.S. original equipment market, a prolonged strike at the Company's tire plants in Turkey, adverse economic conditions in Brazil, intensified U.S. advertising and distribution activities and start-up expenses associated with the new Napanee plant also impacted this segment's 1990 operating income.

The following table presents changes in tire unit sales:

Increase (Decrease) in Tire Unit Sales for the Year

	1990 vs 1989	1990 vs 1988
U.S.	1.7%	(5.9)%
Foreign	2.3%	2.2 %
Worldwide	2.0%	(2.3)%

The increase in worldwide tire units from 1989 reflected an increase in the Company's replacement market unit sales. In the U.S., the increase was achieved with marketing incentives and new product offerings which attracted the price conscious consumer. A significant decrease in sales to U.S. original equipment manufacturers, which continued from 1988, substantially exceeded the increase in sales to foreign original equipment manufacturers.

Lower U.S. and European automobile production, continued over-capacity in the tire industry and a soft replacement market are expected to maintain pressure on pricing and gross margins in both the original equipment and replacement tire markets throughout 1991.

	Year Ended December 31,		
(Dollars in millions, except per share)	1990	1989	1988
Net Sales	$11,272.5	$10,869.3	$10,810.4
Other Income	180.6	216.1	217.6
	11,453.1	11,085.4	11,028.0
Cost and Expenses:			
Cost of goods sold	8,805.1	8,234.7	8,291.0
Selling, administrative and general expense	1,999.6	1,863.7	1,745.1
Interest expense	328.2	255.3	231.8
Unusual items	103.6	109.7	78.8
Other expenses	74.5	44.6	37.0
Foreign currency exchange	72.1	87.9	87.6
Minority interest in net income of subsidiaries	14.1	18.6	19.2
	11,397.2	10,614.5	10,490.5
Income before Income Taxes and Extraordinary Item	55.9	470.9	537.5
United States and Foreign Taxes on Income	94.2	281.5	187.4
Income (loss) before Extraordinary Item	(38.3)	189.4	350.1
Extraordinary Item—Tax Benefit of Loss Carryovers	—	17.4	—
Net Income (loss)	$ (38.3)	$ 206.8	$ 350.1
Per Share of Common Stock:			
Income (loss) before extraordinary item	$ (.66)	$ 3.28	$ 6.11
Extraordinary item—tax benefit of loss carryovers	—	.30	—
Net Income (loss)	$ (.66)	$ 3.58	$ 6.11
Average Shares Outstanding	58,215,897	57,727,577	57,322,165

The accompanying accounting policies and notes are an integral part of this financial statement.

(Dollars in millions)	December 31,	
	1990	1989
ASSETS		
Current Assets:		
Cash and cash equivalents	$ 220.3	$ 122.5
Short term securities	56.4	92.1
Accounts and notes receivable	1,495.2	1,244.6
Inventories	1,346.0	1,642.0
Prepaid expenses	206.3	170.7
Total Current Assets	3,324.2	3,271.9
Other Assets:		
Investments in affiliates, at equity	127.6	125.9
Long term accounts and notes receivable	292.5	189.2
Deferred charges and other miscellaneous assets	410.9	258.0
	831.0	573.1
Properties and Plants	4,808.4	4,615.3
	$8,963.6	$8,460.3
LIABILITIES AND SHAREHOLDERS' EQUITY		
Current Liabilities:		
Accounts payable—trade	$ 986.8	$ 924.0
Accrued payrolls and other compensation	442.7	395.6
Other current liabilities	282.5	278.9
United States and foreign taxes	248.6	219.3
Notes payable to banks and overdrafts	247.6	316.0
Long term debt due within one year	85.4	66.4
Total Current Liabilities	2,293.6	2,200.2
Long Term Debt and Capital Leases	3,286.4	2,963.4
Other Long Term Liabilities	550.0	364.7
Deferred Income Taxes	622.9	681.8
Minority Equity in Subsidiaries	112.8	106.4
Shareholders' Equity:		
Preferred stock, no par value:		
Authorized, 50,000,000 shares, unissued	—	—
Common stock, no par value:		
Authorized, 150,000,000 shares		
Outstanding shares, 58,477,890 (57,806,869 in 1989)	58.5	57.8
Capital surplus	65.1	46.5
Retained earnings	2,135.4	2,278.4
	2,259.0	2,382.7
Foreign currency translation adjustment	(161.1)	(238.9)
Total Shareholders' Equity	2,097.9	2,143.8
	$8,963.6	$8,460.3

The accompanying accounting policies and notes are an integral part of this financial statement.

(Dollars in millions, except per share)	Common Stock		Capital Surplus	Retained Earnings	Foreign Currency Translation Adjustment	Total Shareholders' Equity
	Shares	Amount				
BALANCE AT DECEMBER 31, 1987						
after deducting 54,005,825 treasury shares	56,986,579	$57.0	$11.2	$1,922.6	$(156.4)	$1,834.4
Net income for 1988				350.1		350.1
Cash dividends 1988-$1.70 per share				(97.3)		(97.3)
Common stock issued (including 443,962 treasury shares):						
Dividend reinvestment and stock purchase plan	238,463	.2	12.3			12.5
Stock option plans	172,515	.2	5.2			5.4
Key Personnel Incentive Profit Sharing Plan	32,969	—	.6			.6
Foreign currency translation adjustment					(78.6)	(78.6)
BALANCE AT DECEMBER 31, 1988						
after deducting 53,561,863 treasury shares	57,430,526	57.4	29.3	2,175.4	(235.0)	2,027.1
Net income for 1989				206.8		206.8
Cash dividends 1989-$1.80 per share				(103.8)		(103.8)
Common stock issued (including 376,369 treasury shares):						
Dividend reinvestment and stock purchase plan	293,823	.3	14.9			15.2
Stock option plans	51,198	.1	1.7			1.8
Key Personnel Incentive Profit Sharing Plan	31,322	—	.6			.6
Foreign currency translation adjustment					(65.7)	(65.7)
Divestiture of South African subsidiary					61.8	61.8
BALANCE AT DECEMBER 31, 1989						
after deducting 53,185,494 treasury shares	57,806,869	57.8	46.5	2,278.4	(238.9)	2,143.8
Net loss for 1990				(38.3)		(38.3)
Cash dividends 1990-$1.80 per share				(104.7)		(104.7)
Common stock issued (including 671,138 treasury shares):						
Dividend reinvestment and stock purchase plan	588,223	.6	17.2			17.8
Key Personnel Incentive Profit Sharing Plan	82,798	.1	1.4			1.5
Foreign currency translation adjustment					77.8	77.8
BALANCE AT DECEMBER 31, 1990						
after deducting 52,514,356 treasury shares	58,477,890	$58.5	$65.1	$2,135.4	$(161.1)	$2,097.9

The accompanying accounting policies and notes are an integral part of this financial statement.

► ► ► CONSOLIDATED STATEMENT OF CASH FLOWS ◄ ◄ ◄

The Goodyear Tire & Rubber Company and Subsidiaries

	Year Ended December 31,		
(Dollars in millions)	**1990**	1989	1988
CASH FLOWS FROM OPERATING ACTIVITIES:			
Net Income (loss)	$ (38.3)	$ 206.8	$ 350.1
Adjustments to reconcile net income to net cash:			
Depreciation	415.0	383.5	357.1
Unusual items	51.7	109.7	70.7
Deferred income tax	(56.6)	38.2	(57.3)
Accounts and notes receivable	(196.8)	259.0	(132.8)
Inventories	340.8	(120.1)	(169.0)
Deferred pension plan cost	—	—	362.2
Prepaid expenses	(32.3)	(74.1)	—
Other assets	(151.7)	27.4	(110.4)
Accounts payable—trade	27.2	169.5	(9.2)
Other liabilities	215.3	(182.1)	138.0
Total adjustments	612.6	611.0	449.3
Net cash provided by operating activities	574.3	817.8	799.4
CASH FLOWS FROM INVESTING ACTIVITIES:			
Capital expenditures	(574.5)	(775.7)	(743.7)
Asset dispositions	18.4	164.2	41.7
Short term securities acquired	(75.4)	(126.3)	(14.5)
Short term securities redeemed	110.3	44.3	3.9
Other transactions	(3.9)	(9.1)	17.0
Net cash used in investing activities	(525.1)	(702.6)	(695.6)
CASH FLOWS FROM FINANCING ACTIVITIES:			
Proceeds from sale of foreign currency exchange agreements	—	75.4	—
Short term debt incurred	1,519.9	2,359.8	1,664.2
Short term debt paid	(1,707.5)	(2,083.5)	(1,030.7)
Long term debt incurred	485.2	237.9	386.7
Long term debt and capital leases paid	(160.4)	(708.1)	(1,008.5)
Common stock issued	19.4	17.6	18.5
Dividends paid	(104.7)	(103.8)	(97.3)
Net cash provided by (used in) financing activities	51.9	(204.7)	(67.1)
Effect of Exchange Rate Changes on Cash and Cash Equivalents	(3.3)	(22.1)	(3.1)
NET INCREASE (DECREASE) IN CASH AND CASH EQUIVALENTS	97.8	(111.6)	33.6
Cash and Cash Equivalents at Beginning of the Period	122.5	234.1	200.5
CASH AND CASH EQUIVALENTS AT END OF THE PERIOD	$ 220.3	$ 122.5	$ 234.1

The accompanying accounting policies and notes are an integral part of this financial statement.

Published Financial Statements **1317**

A summary of the significant accounting policies used in the preparation of the accompanying financial statements follows:

PRINCIPLES OF CONSOLIDATION

The consolidated financial statements include the accounts of all majority-owned subsidiaries. All significant intercompany transactions have been eliminated.

The Company's investments in 20% to 50% owned companies in which it has the ability to exercise significant influence over operating and financial policies are accounted for on the equity method. Accordingly, the Company's share of the earnings of these companies is included in consolidated net income. Investments in other companies are carried at cost.

CONSOLIDATED STATEMENT OF CASH FLOWS

Cash and cash equivalents include cash on hand and in the bank as well as all short term securities held for the primary purpose of general liquidity. Such securities normally mature within three months from the date of acquisition. Cash flows associated with items intended as hedges of identifiable transactions or events are classified in the same category as the cash flows from the items being hedged.

INVENTORY PRICING

Inventories are stated at the lower of cost or market. Cost is determined using the last-in, first-out (LIFO) method for a significant portion of domestic inventories and the first-in, first-out (FIFO) method or average cost method for other inventories.

PROPERTIES AND PLANTS

Properties and plants are stated at cost. Depreciation is computed on the straight line method. Accelerated depreciation is used for income tax purposes, where permitted.

INCOME TAXES

Income taxes are recognized during the year in which transactions enter into the determination of financial statement income with deferred taxes being provided for timing differences.

PER SHARE OF COMMON STOCK

Per share amounts have been computed based on the average number of common shares outstanding, including for this purpose only, those treasury shares allocated for distribution under the incentive profit sharing plan.

RECLASSIFICATION

Certain items previously reported in specific financial statement captions have been reclassified to conform with the 1990 presentation.

UNUSUAL ITEMS

A summary of the pretax unusual charges follows:

(In millions)	1990	1989	1988
Restructuring	$ 66.4	$ 18.4	$27.9
Plant closure and sale of facilities	15.0	43.0	—
Discontinued segment—			
Environmental cleanup costs	22.2	—	—
Sale of assets	—	48.3	—
Pension settlement/asset reversion	—	—	50.9
	$103.6	**$109.7**	**$78.8**

1990

The restructuring of United States tire operations during the second quarter resulted in a charge of $20.0 million ($12.2 million after tax) from the reduction of personnel in various sales, distribution and other operations and other associated costs. The Company also incurred restructuring charges of $46.4 million ($38.2 million after tax) during the third quarter. The costs resulted from: a realignment of European tire marketing, distribution and production operations, which will eliminate approximately 1,180 jobs by mid-1992; the phaseout of medium and heavy truck tire production at the Valleyfield, Quebec, Canada plant; and the rationalization of certain tire and related production operations in Canada and Argentina.

The decision to close the New Bedford, Massachusetts, roofing systems plant resulted in a charge of $15.0 million ($9.2 million after tax) during the second quarter for personnel reduction and other plant closure costs.

The Company recorded a charge of $22.2 million ($13.5 million after tax) during the third quarter for environmental cleanup costs associated with a business segment discontinued in 1986.

1989

The Company accrued expenses of $18.4 million ($10.9 million after tax) for the reduction of bias-ply truck tire capacity at the Gadsden, Alabama plant and from the realignment of the Canadian operations.

The Company sold its South African tire and general products manufacturing subsidiary for $41.0 million. A loss of $43.0 million ($52.0 million after tax) was recorded in the second quarter, the majority of which was due to the recognition of the decreased value of the Company's assets in South Africa arising from the devaluation of the South African Rand during the past several years.

The Company's oil transportation subsidiary, All American Pipeline Company, sold about 435 miles of unused 30-inch pipe for $70.0 million in the second quarter. A loss of $48.3 million ($43.0 million after tax) was recorded on the sale.

1988

The Company, in an effort to reduce operating expenses, consolidated tasks and eliminated duplicate job responsibilities at a cost of $27.9 million ($17.1 million after tax) in the fourth quarter.

The Company settled its pension liability for the principal domestic salary plan for all benefits accrued to June 30, 1988, through the purchase of annuity contracts from major insurance companies during the fourth quarter. A loss of $10.9 million was recorded. In a related transaction excess assets of $400.0 million before taxes were reverted to the Company. Excise tax of $40.0 million was incurred on the asset reversion making the total charge to Unusual Items $50.9 million. The combined effect of these transactions, together with the reversal of deferred tax recorded on the 1986 pension settlement, resulted in an after tax charge of $9.7 million in 1988. Proceeds to the Company amounted to $210.0 million after deducting excise tax and federal and state income taxes. For further information regarding the tax effects on the transaction, see the note to the financial statements entitled Income Taxes.

OTHER INCOME

Other income includes interest income of $86.8 million, $132.4 million and $130.8 million for 1990, 1989 and 1988, respectively, on deposits. The primary source of interest income was funds invested in time deposits in Latin America, pending remittance or reinvestment in the region. The lower interest income was due to lower interest rates on deposits.

At December 31, 1990, approximately $128.4 million, or 46.4 percent of the Company's cash, cash equivalents and short term securities were concentrated in Latin America, primarily Brazil.

ACCOUNTS AND NOTES RECEIVABLE

(In millions)	1990	1989
Accounts and notes receivable	$1,534.1	$1,283.2
Less allowance for doubtful accounts	38.9	38.6
	$1,495.2	$1,244.6

Throughout the year, the Company sold certain domestic accounts receivable under continuous sale programs. The Company increased the level of net proceeds from sales under these programs to $600.0 million in December, 1989, from $350.0 million. Under these agreements, undivided interests in designated receivable pools are sold to purchasers with recourse limited to the receivables purchased. Fees paid by the Company under these agreements are based on certain variable market rate indices and are recorded as Other expenses.

The Company sold accounts and notes receivable under these and other agreements, the net proceeds of which totaled $3,911.6 million, $3,118.8 million and $2,451.6 million during 1990, 1989 and 1988, respectively.

INVENTORIES

(In millions)	1990	1989
Raw materials and supplies	$ 234.5	$ 330.5
Work in process	67.5	90.1
Finished product	1,044.0	1,221.4
	$1,346.0	$1,642.0

The cost of inventories using the last-in, first-out (LIFO) method (approximately 38.4% of consolidated inventories in 1990 and 44.7% in 1989) was less than the approximate current cost of inventories by $335.4 million at December 31, 1990 and $330.6 million at December 31, 1989.

PROPERTIES AND PLANTS

(In millions)	1990 Owned	1990 Capital Leases	1990 Total	1989 Owned	1989 Capital Leases	1989 Total
Land and improvements	$ 297.2	$ 8.1	$ 305.3	$ 279.8	$ 9.4	$ 289.2
Buildings	1,137.6	71.5	1,209.1	1,032.3	76.2	1,108.5
Machinery and equipment	5,049.5	125.4	5,174.9	4,611.8	124.1	4,735.9
Pipeline	1,393.3	—	1,393.3	1,351.2	—	1,351.2
Construction in progress	535.4	—	535.4	565.2	—	565.2
Properties and plants, at cost	8,413.0	205.0	8,618.0	7,840.3	209.7	8,050.0
Less accumulated depreciation	3,669.9	139.7	3,809.6	3,299.8	134.9	3,434.7
	$4,743.1	$ 65.3	$4,808.4	$4,540.5	$ 74.8	$4,615.3

The amortization for capital leases included in the depreciation provision for 1990, 1989 and 1988 was $11.1 million, $10.1 million and $11.2 million, respectively.

CREDIT ARRANGEMENTS

SHORT TERM DEBT AND CREDIT LINES

At December 31, 1990, the Company had short term credit lines and overdraft arrangements totaling $1,930.6 million, of which $470.7 million were unused.

LONG TERM DEBT AND CAPITAL LEASES

(In millions)	1990	1989
Sinking fund debentures:		
8.60% due 1992-1994	$ 20.3	$ 25.0
7.35% due 1993-1997	37.2	37.5
Promissory notes:		
12.15% due 1991-2000	50.0	50.0
11.90% due 1994-1999	—	50.0
10.26% due 1999	118.4	118.4
Swiss franc bonds:		
5.375% due 2000	185.5	154.1
5.375% due 2006	155.9	129.5
Yen bonds:		
6.875% due 1994	82.9	86.9
7.125% due 1995	180.8	173.8
6.625% due 1996	72.3	69.5
Yen bank term loan due 1994	37.0	34.8
6.875% Convertible Debentures due 2003	150.0	150.0
Bank term loans due 1991-2000	544.6	117.8
Revolving credit agreements	160.0	—
Euro-commercial paper	16.0	516.5
Other domestic debt	958.8	708.2
Foreign subsidiary debt	507.3	506.2
Capital lease obligations:		
Industrial revenue bonds	69.2	74.5
Other	25.6	27.1
	3,371.8	3,029.8
Less portion due within one year	85.4	66.4
	$3,286.4	$2,963.4

At December 31, 1990, the Company had available long term credit sources totaling $4,258.2 million, of which $2,098.7 million were unused.

The Swiss franc bonds totaling $341.4 million and $201.8 million of Yen bonds and bank term loan are completely hedged by foreign currency exchange agreements with five domestic and international financial institutions whereunder the Company is entitled to purchase 438 million Swiss francs and 27.2 billion Yen for $330.4 million. At December 31, 1990, $212.8 million associated with these agreements was recorded in long term accounts and notes receivable on the Consolidated Balance Sheet. These agreements are subject to changes in market value which offset fluctuations in the dollar amount of the related debt. In addition, various forward contracts and a call option entitling the Company to purchase 25.3 billion Yen for $168.2 million were in effect on December 31, 1990. These arrangements are intended to limit exposure to fluctuations in the currency exchange rate affecting $171.2 million of the Yen bonds. At December 31, 1990, $18.5 million associated with these contracts was recorded in certain receivable accounts on the Consolidated Balance Sheet.

CREDIT ARRANGEMENTS *(continued)*

The Convertible Debentures due 2003 are convertible into common shares of the Company at $80.25 per share.

In March 1990, the Company entered into a $58.0 million floating rate, amortizing bank term loan agreement with a final maturity in 2000. Throughout the year, the Company entered into other long term bank loan agreements totaling $380.0 million which provide for interest at either fixed rates ranging between 9.28 percent and 9.89 percent or floating rates based on LIBOR plus a fixed spread.

Commitments under revolving credit agreements total $2,240.0 million with 48 domestic and international banks. These revolving credit agreements are noncancelable until their initial commitment periods expire in August through December 1992. Each agreement is automatically renewed for successive one year terms unless a notice of termination is given at least 18 months prior to the end of the initial commitment or renewal period. Under each agreement, the Company may borrow, for periods of at least one year, at any time during the commitment period. Each revolving credit agreement provides that the Company may obtain loans bearing interest at LIBOR plus 3/8 percent, at a defined Certificate of Deposit rate plus 3/8 or at other quoted rates, and requires a commitment fee of 1/8 percent on the unused portion of the commitment. Each agreement contains certain covenants which, among other things, require the Company to maintain at the end of each calendar quarter a defined interest coverage ratio, a current ratio, a consolidated net worth minimum and a limitation on consolidated debt. Amounts outstanding under the Company's Euro-commercial paper program and other short term facilities are supported by these revolving credit agreements.

Certain domestic and foreign subsidiary debt obligations amounting to $1,116.0 million and $256.6 million, respectively, at December 31, 1990 ($1,174.8 million and $289.3 million at December 31, 1989), which by their terms are due within one year, are classified as long term. Such obligations are incurred under or supported by the revolving credit agreements, and it is the Company's intent to maintain them as long term. Short term obligations reclassified to long term at December 31, 1990 consist primarily of short term bank borrowings and Euro-commercial paper.

Refer to the note to the financial statements entitled Leased Assets for additional information on capital lease obligations.

The Company enters into various interest rate contracts in managing the cost of its floating rate debt. At December 31, 1990, interest rate contracts totaling $1,537.1 million in notional principal amount were in place whereunder the Company pays a fixed amount and receives a variable amount equivalent to LIBOR. As a result, the interest rate contracts limit the effect of market fluctuations on the interest cost of floating rate debt. The contracts have an average life to maturity of 3.14 years and a weighted average stated fixed rate of 9.04 percent per annum. At December 31, 1990, the interest rate on approximately 92 percent of the Company's debt was fixed by either the nature of the obligation or through the interest rate contracts.

In 1990, the Company sold to banks for cash two interest rate options, each $50.0 million in notional amount. Under one option, which has been exercised and will expire January 1996, the Company pays a fixed rate of 8.7 percent per annum and receives amounts based on LIBOR. Under the other option, if exercised by the bank on August 9, 1991, the Company would pay amounts based on LIBOR and receive amounts based on a fixed rate of 9.35 percent per annum through August 1995.

The annual aggregate maturities of long term debt for the five years subsequent to 1990 are presented below. Maturities of debt incurred under or supported by revolving credit agreements have been reported on the basis that the commitments to lend under these agreements will be terminated effective at the end of their initial terms.

CREDIT ARRANGEMENTS *(continued)*

(In millions)	1991	1992	1993	1994	1995
Debt incurred under or supported by revolving credit agreements	$ —	$ —	$1,316.3	$ —	$ —
Other	89.2	74.3	125.7	186.4	446.3
	$89.2	$74.3	$1,442.0	$186.4	$446.3

FOREIGN CURRENCY FORWARD CONTRACTS

The Company enters into forward exchange contracts as hedges relating primarily to identifiable currency positions. At December 31, 1990, contracts were in place to purchase $81.6 million in various foreign currencies and to sell $40.8 million in U.S. and other currencies. The future value of these contracts and the hedged positions are subject to offsetting market risk due to foreign currency exchange rate volatility.

LEASED ASSETS

Certain manufacturing, retail store, transportation, data processing and other facilities and equipment are held under leases which generally expire within ten years but may be renewed by the Company. Many of the leases provide that the Company will pay taxes assessed against leased property and the cost of insurance and maintenance.

Minimum lease commitments follow:

(In millions)	Capital Leases	Operating Leases
1991	$ 17.8	$239.2
1992	18.4	197.0
1993	11.0	132.9
1994	10.8	85.2
1995	10.6	58.1
1996 and thereafter	77.5	205.5
Total minimum lease payments	146.1	$917.9
Less estimated executory costs	.7	
Net minimum lease payments	145.4	
Less amounts estimated to represent interest	50.6	
Present value of net minimum lease obligations	94.8	
Less portion due within one year	10.2	
	$ 84.6	

Total rental expense charged to income and contingent rentals included therein follow:

(In millions)	1990	1989	1988
Minimum rentals	$337.3	$306.2	$270.0
Contingent rentals	1.5	1.2	1.1
Less sublease rentals	51.6	49.5	42.1
	$287.2	$257.9	$229.0

STOCK OPTIONS

The Company's 1972, 1982 and 1987 Employees' Stock Option Plans and the 1989 Goodyear Performance and Equity Incentive Plan provide for the granting of stock options and stock appreciation rights (SARs). For options previously granted with SARs, the exercise of an SAR cancels the stock option; conversely, the exercise of the stock option cancels the SAR.

The 1972, 1982 and 1987 Plans expired on December 31, 1981 and 1986 and April 10, 1989, respectively, except for options and SARs then outstanding. The 1989 Plan was adopted at the April, 1989 shareholders' meeting. The 1989 Plan empowers the Company to award or grant, from time to time until December 31, 1998, when the 1989 Plan expires except with respect to Awards then outstanding, to officers and other key managerial, administrative and professional employees of the Company and its subsidiaries Incentive, Non-Qualified and Deferred Compensation Stock Options, Stock Appreciation Rights, Restricted Stock and Restricted Unit Grants, Performance Equity and Performance Unit Grants, other Stock-Based Awards authorized by the Committee which administers the 1989 Plan, and any combination of any or all of such Awards, whether in tandem with each other or otherwise. The Company issued Performance Equity Grants in 1989 up to a maximum of 83,820 shares of common stock (including possible dividend equivalents payable in stock) of which 3,873 shares were canceled in 1990 under the terms of the Plan. Assuming that there will be full utilization of the shares of Common Stock available for Awards during the term of the 1989 Plan, and that no other increases or decreases in the number of shares of Common Stock outstanding would occur during the term of the 1989 Plan, approximately 10,100,000 shares of the Common Stock would be available for the grant of Awards through December 31, 1998.

	1990 Shares	1990 SARs	1989 Shares	1989 SARs
Outstanding at January 1	1,984,538	339,205	1,780,349	308,287
Options granted	971,500	199,500	332,900	122,400
Freestanding SARs granted	94,000	94,000	1,000	1,000
Options without SARs exercised	—	—	(56,729)	—
Options with SARs exercised	—	—	(2,752)	(2,752)
SARs exercised	(200)	(200)	(14,530)	(14,530)
Options without SARs expired	(54,061)	—	(55,600)	—
Options with SARs expired	(14,300)	(14,300)	(100)	(100)
SARs expired	(200)	(26,200)	—	(75,100)
Outstanding at December 31	2,981,277	592,005	1,984,538	339,205
Exercisable at December 31	1,765,452	271,705	1,434,638	274,205
Available for grant at December 31	3,427,552		3,904,810	

Options at December 31, 1990 and 1989 were exercisable at prices ranging from $12.00 to $67.50. All options were granted at an option price of not less than the fair market value of the Common Stock at the date of grant.

PENSIONS

The Company and its subsidiaries provide substantially all domestic and foreign employees with pension benefits. For 1990 and 1989, all domestic and substantially all foreign plans were accounted for within the provisions of Statement of Financial Accounting Standards No. 87 (SFAS No. 87), "Employers' Accounting for Pensions". For 1988 all domestic but only certain foreign plans were accounted for in accordance with SFAS No. 87.

PENSION *(continued)*

The principal domestic hourly plan provides benefits based on length of service. The principal domestic plans covering salaried employees provide benefits based on career average earnings formulas. Employees making voluntary contributions to these plans receive higher benefits. Other plans provide benefits similar to the principal domestic plans as well as termination indemnity plans at certain foreign subsidiaries.

The Company's domestic funding policy complies with the requirements of Federal laws and regulations. Plan assets are invested primarily in common stocks, fixed income securities and real estate.

Net periodic pension cost follows:

(In millions)	*1990*	*1989*	*1988*
Service cost—benefits earned during the period	$ 53.3	$ 49.2	$ 39.9
Interest cost on projected benefit obligation	139.2	129.7	116.4
Actual return on assets	49.7	(194.8)	(157.9)
Net amortization and deferrals	(150.3)	113.3	53.3
Net periodic pension cost	$ 91.9	$ 97.4	$ 51.7

In addition, during 1988, pension expense for foreign locations not adopting the Standard was $8.1 million.

The following table sets forth the funded status and amounts recognized in the Company's Consolidated Balance Sheet at December 31, l990 and 1989. At the end of 1990 and 1989, assets exceeded accumulated benefits in certain plans and accumulated benefits exceeded assets in others.

(In millions)	1990 Assets Exceed Accumulated Benefits	1990 Accumulated Benefits Exceed Assets	1989 Assets Exceed Accumulated Benefits	1989 Accumulated Benefits Exceed Assets
Actuarial present value of benefit obligations:				
Vested benefit obligation	$(110.3)	$(1,284.1)	$ (966.8)	$(252.1)
Accumulated benefit obligation	$(120.3)	$(1,404.2)	$(1,075.5)	$(277.0)
Projected benefit obligation	$(158.4)	$(1,512.1)	$(1,108.7)	$(386.0)
Plan assets	153.7	1,054.0	1,148.1	118.6
Plan assets (less than) or in excess of projected benefit obligation	(4.7)	(458.1)	39.4	(267.4)
Unrecognized net loss (gain)	23.3	93.0	(95.1)	36.6
Prior service cost not yet recognized in net periodic pension cost	9.2	188.7	78.1	94.2
Unrecognized net (asset) obligation at transition	(6.6)	21.2	(17.9)	26.7
Adjustment required to recognize minimum liability	—	(215.3)	—	(61.3)
Prepaid (accrued) and deferred pension cost recognized in the Consolidated Balance Sheet	$ 21.2	$ (370.5)	$ 4.5	$(171.2)

Assumptions:	U.S.-1990	Foreign-1990	U.S.-1989	Foreign-1989
Discount rate	9.0%	0%-22.0%	9.0%	0%-20.0%
Rate of increase in compensation levels	5.5%	0%-20.0%	5.5%	0%-18.0%
Expected long term rate of return on assets	9.0%	5.0%-11.0%	9.0%	5.0%-11.0%

PENSION *(continued)*

During 1990, the Company incurred curtailments in the principal domestic hourly and salary plans as a result of the New Bedford plant closure. The result was an aggregate loss of $3.2 million. These items were recorded as part of the plant closure expense.

In the fourth quarter of 1988, the Company completed a pension settlement and an asset reversion for the principal domestic salary plan in accordance with Statement of Financial Accounting Standards No. 88, "Employers' Accounting for Settlements and Curtailments of Defined Benefit Pension Plans and for Termination Benefits". Further discussion is included in the note to the financial statements entitled Unusual Items.

EMPLOYEES' SAVINGS PLANS

Substantially all domestic employees are eligible to participate in savings plans. Under these plans employees elect to contribute a percentage of their pay. In 1990, most plans provided for the Company matching an employee's contributions (up to a maximum of 6 percent of the employee's annual pay or, if less, $7,979) at the rate of 50 percent. Company contributions were $25.4 million, $25.5 million and $21.1 million for 1990, 1989 and 1988, respectively.

POSTRETIREMENT HEALTH CARE AND LIFE INSURANCE BENEFITS

The Company and its subsidiaries provide substantially all domestic employees and employees at certain foreign subsidiaries with health care and life insurance benefits upon retirement. Substantial portions of health care benefits for domestic retirees are not insured and are paid by the Company. The life insurance benefits and certain health care benefits are provided by insurance companies through premiums based on expected benefits to be paid during the year. The Company recognized the cost of these benefits by expensing the annual insurance premium and the amount of health care costs incurred by retirees during the year. The cost of providing these benefits for retirees for 1990, 1989 and 1988 was $103.0 million, $93.9 million and $82.5 million, respectively.

The Financial Accounting Standards Board issued Statement of Financial Accounting Standards No. 106, "Employers' Accounting for Postretirement Benefits Other Than Pensions" in December, 1990. This Statement will significantly change the Company's practice of accounting for non-pension postretirement benefits from a pay-as-you-go (cash) basis to an accrual basis. The Company does not intend to adopt this Statement until the required implementation date of 1993. The Company is studying this Statement to determine its effect on the financial statements. It is too early to quantify the impact of this Statement, however, expenses for postretirement benefits are likely to materially adversely affect the Company's results of operations and equity in future periods.

RESEARCH AND DEVELOPMENT

Research and development cost included in cost of goods sold for 1990, 1989 and 1988 was $331.3 million, $303.3 million and $304.8 million, respectively.

GOODYEAR FINANCIAL CORPORATION

Goodyear Financial Corporation (GFC), a wholly-owned subsidiary, purchases certain receivables from Goodyear and domestic subsidiaries.

A summary of the results of operations and financial position of GFC as included in the Company's consolidated financial statements is presented below.

(In millions)	1990	1989	1988
Pretax income	$ 22.8	$ 50.8	$70.5
Income tax provision	7.8	17.3	24.0
Net income	$ 15.0	$ 33.5	$46.5
Total assets	$225.4	$211.0	
Total liabilities	$ .7	$ 1.4	
Total equity	$224.7	$209.6	

COMMITMENTS AND CONTINGENT LIABILITIES

At December 31, 1990, the Company had binding commitments for investments in land, buildings and equipment of approximately $159 million.

Various legal actions, claims and governmental investigations and proceedings covering a wide range of matters are pending against the Company and its subsidiaries. In the opinion of management, after reviewing such matters and consulting with the Company's General Counsel, any liability which may ultimately be incurred would not materially affect the consolidated financial position of the Company, although an adverse final determination in certain instances could materially affect the Company's consolidated net income for the period in which such determination occurs.

PREFERRED STOCK PURCHASE RIGHTS PLAN

In 1986, the Company authorized 3,000,000 shares of Series A $10.00 Preferred Stock ("Series A Preferred") issuable only upon the exercise of rights ("Rights") issued under the Preferred Stock Purchase Rights Plan adopted in July 1986. Each share of Series A Preferred issued would be non-redeemable, non-voting and entitled to cumulative quarterly dividends equal to the greater of $10.00 or, subject to adjustment, 100 times the per share amount of dividends declared on Goodyear common stock during the preceding quarter, and would also be entitled to a liquidation preference.

Under the Rights Plan, each shareholder of record on July 28, 1986 received a dividend of one Right per share of Goodyear common stock. When exercisable, each Right entitles the holder to buy one one-hundredth of a share of Series A Preferred at an exercise price of $100. The Rights will be exercisable only after 10 days following the earlier of a public announcement that a person or group has acquired 20 percent or more of Goodyear common stock or the commencement of a tender offer for 20 percent or more of Goodyear common stock by a person or group. The Rights are non-voting and may be redeemed by the Company at $.05 per Right under certain circumstances. If not redeemed or exercised, the Rights will expire on July 28, 1996. If a person or group accumulates 35 percent or more of Goodyear common stock, or a merger takes place with an acquiring person or group and the Company is the surviving corporation, or an acquiring person or group engages in certain self-dealing transactions, each Right (except those held by such acquiring person or group) will entitle the holder to purchase Goodyear common stock having a market value then equal to two times the exercise price. If the Company is acquired or a sale or transfer of 50 percent or more of the Company's assets or earning power is made, each right (except those held by the acquiring person or group) will entitle the holder to purchase common stock of the acquiring entity having a market value then equal to two times the exercise price.

BUSINESS SEGMENTS

Tires and related is the principal industry segment, which involves the development, manufacture, distribution and sale of tires and related products. These products include tires, tubes, retreads, automotive repair services and merchandise purchased for resale.

The General products segment involves the manufacture and sale of various kinds of belts, hose, molded products, foam cushioning accessories, tank tracks, organic chemicals used in rubber and plastic processing, synthetic rubber and rubber latices, polyester resins, films, vinyl products and other activities.

The Oil transportation segment consists primarily of the All American Pipeline System, a common carrier crude oil pipeline extending from California to Texas. This segment, which also includes a crude oil gathering pipeline in California, crude oil storage facilities, linefill and related assets, also engages in various crude oil gathering, purchasing and selling activities. Segment sales consist of tariffs charged by the All American Pipeline System and revenues, net of acquisition costs, resulting from various crude oil gathering, purchasing and selling activities. Acquisition costs associated with the gathering, purchasing and selling activities amounted to $1,316.1 million, $705.2 million and $389.7 million for 1990, 1989 and 1988, respectively. On October 1, 1989, the Company began recognizing depreciation and other net operating expenses of the All American Pipeline System. These charges, as well as interest associated with the System, had previously been capitalized.

Operating income for each industry segment consists of total revenues less applicable costs and expenses. Transfers between industry segments were insignificant.

Operating income for each geographic region consists of total revenues less applicable costs and expenses. Inter-geographic sales were at cost plus a negotiated mark up. Net income from foreign operations (including export sales) was $12.0 million, $109.0 million and $195.9 million for 1990, 1989 and 1988, respectively. Dividends received by the Company and domestic subsidiaries from its foreign operations for 1990, 1989 and 1988 were $62.1 million, $195.5 million and $162.5 million, respectively. Net foreign assets were $1,817.9 million at December 31, 1990 ($1,491.0 million at December 31, 1989) after deducting minority shareholders' equity.

Portions of the unusual items described in the Unusual Items note were charged against operating income of both the industry and geographic segments as follows:

Industry Segments

(In millions)	Tires and related	General products	Oil transportation	Total
1990				
Restructuring	$66.4	$ —	$ —	$ 66.4
Plant closure	—	15.0	—	15.0
	$66.4	$15.0	$ —	$ 81.4
1989				
Sale of facilities	$33.4	$ 9.6	$ —	$ 43.0
Sale of assets	—	—	48.3	48.3
Restructuring	18.4	—	—	18.4
	$51.8	$ 9.6	$48.3	$109.7
1988				
Restructuring	$25.1	$ 2.8	$ —	$ 27.9

BUSINESS SEGMENTS *(continued)*

Geographic Segments

(In millions)	United States	Canada	Europe	Latin America	Asia/ Africa	Total
1990						
Restructuring	$20.0	$10.4	$31.0	$5.0	$ —	$ 66.4
Plant closure	15.0	—	—	—	—	15.0
	$35.0	$10.4	$31.0	$5.0	$ —	$ 81.4
1989						
Sale of facilities	$ —	$ —	$ —	$ —	$43.0	$ 43.0
Sale of assets	48.3	—	—	—	—	48.3
Restructuring	10.5	7.9	—	—	—	18.4
	$58.8	$ 7.9	$ —	$ —	$43.0	$109.7
1988						
Restructuring	$27.2	$ .7	$ —	$ —	$ —	$ 27.9

The following items have been excluded from the determination of operating income: interest expense, foreign currency exchange, equity in net income of affiliated companies, minority interest in net income of subsidiaries, corporate revenues and expenses, income taxes and unusual items other than the charges mentioned above.

Corporate revenues and expenses were those items not identifiable with the operations of a segment. Corporate revenues were primarily from certain royalty and technical agreements. Corporate expenses were primarily central administrative expenses.

Assets of industry and geographic segments represent those assets that were identified with the operations of each segment. Corporate assets consist of cash and cash equivalents, short term securities, prepaid expenses, deferred charges and other miscellaneous assets.

INDUSTRY SEGMENTS

(In millions)	1990	1989	1988
Sales to Unaffiliated Customers			
Tires	$ 8,180.1	$ 7,880.7	$ 7,985.4
Related products and services	1,035.3	968.3	911.8
Tires and related	9,215.4	8,849.0	8,897.2
General products	2,027.3	2,008.5	1,905.3
Oil transportation	29.8	11.8	7.9
Net sales	$11,272.5	$10,869.3	$10,810.4
Income (loss)			
Tires and related	$ 463.4	$ 722.6	$ 736.4
General products	194.1	260.5	260.5
Oil transportation	(52.9)	(56.8)	6.1
Total operating income	604.6	926.3	1,003.0
Interest expense	(328.2)	(255.3)	(231.8)
Foreign currency exchange	(72.1)	(87.9)	(87.6)
Equity in net income of affiliated companies	3.2	10.9	8.6
Minority interest in net income of subsidiaries	(14.1)	(18.6)	(19.2)
Corporate revenues and expenses	(137.5)	(104.5)	(135.5)
Income before income taxes and extraordinary item	$ 55.9	$ 470.9	$ 537.5
Assets			
Tires and related	$ 5,156.4	$ 5,206.7	$ 5,351.4
General products	860.8	857.5	830.6
Oil transportation	1,746.6	1,556.0	1,492.3
Total identifiable assets	7,763.8	7,620.2	7,674.3
Corporate assets	1,072.2	714.2	821.7
Investments in affiliated companies, at equity	127.6	125.9	122.3
Assets at December 31	$ 8,963.6	$ 8,460.3	$ 8,618.3
Capital Expenditures			
Tires and related	$ 479.7	$ 576.2	$ 478.9
General products	68.1	68.3	103.2
Oil transportation	26.7	131.2	161.6
For the year	$ 574.5	$ 775.7	$ 743.7
Depreciation			
Tires and related	$ 336.5	$ 331.8	$ 310.9
General products	46.4	41.1	45.4
Oil transportation	32.1	10.6	.8
For the year	$ 415.0	$ 383.5	$ 357.1

GEOGRAPHIC SEGMENTS

(In millions)	1990	1989	1988
Sales to Unaffiliated Customers			
United States	$ 6,459.6	$ 6,421.3	$ 6,360.7
Canada	567.3	601.8	556.1
Europe	2,301.2	2,039.0	2,064.2
Latin America	1,351.6	1,180.6	1,153.2
Asia/Africa	592.8	626.6	676.2
Net sales	$11,272.5	$10,869.3	$10,810.4
Inter-Geographic Sales			
United States	$ 270.8	$ 268.8	$ 243.1
Canada	151.8	145.1	88.5
Europe	78.8	89.3	78.6
Latin America	52.7	69.3	65.6
Asia/Africa	37.7	52.7	50.9
Total	$ 591.8	$ 625.2	$ 526.7
Revenue			
United States	$ 6,730.4	$ 6,690.1	$ 6,603.8
Canada	719.1	746.9	644.6
Europe	2,380.0	2,128.3	2,142.8
Latin America	1,404.3	1,249.9	1,218.8
Asia/Africa	630.5	679.3	727.1
Adjustments and eliminations	(591.8)	(625.2)	(526.7)
Total	$11,272.5	$10,869.3	$10,810.4
Operating Income			
United States	$ 326.9	$ 490.7	$ 439.4
Canada	(20.7)	9.8	27.3
Europe	36.3	131.7	184.4
Latin America	195.1	244.8	262.3
Asia/Africa	74.5	48.6	88.9
Adjustments and eliminations	(7.5)	.7	.7
Total	$ 604.6	$ 926.3	$ 1,003.0
Assets			
United States	$ 5,406.5	$ 5,187.1	$ 5,442.2
Canada	596.2	527.6	388.1
Europe	1,535.4	1,452.8	1,403.3
Latin America	881.8	815.5	876.0
Asia/Africa	422.9	365.8	400.0
Adjustments and eliminations	(6.8)	(14.4)	(13.6)
Total identifiable assets	8,836.0	8,334.4	8,496.0
Investments in affiliated companies, at equity	127.6	125.9	122.3
Assets at December 31	$ 8,963.6	$ 8,460.3	$ 8,618.3

QUARTERLY DATA AND MARKET PRICE INFORMATION

(In millions, except per share)

1990	Quarter First	Second	Third	Fourth	Year
Net Sales	$2,691.7	$2,870.8	$2,899.7	$2,810.3	$11,272.5
Gross Profit	613.5	637.8	609.4	606.7	2,467.4
Income (loss) before Extraordinary Item	16.5	(10.0)	(56.4)	11.6	(38.3)
Extraordinary Item	4.4	.6	(5.0)	—	—
Net Income (loss)	$ 20.9	$ (9.4)	$ (61.4)	$ 11.6	$ (38.3)
Average Shares Outstanding	58.0	58.1	58.3	58.4	58.2
Per Share of Common Stock:					
Income (loss) before extraordinary item	$ .29	$ (.18)	$ (.97)	$ .20	$ (.66)
Extraordinary item	.07	.02	(.09)	—	—
Net Income (loss)	$ .36	$ (.16)	$ (1.06)	$ .20	$ (.66)
Price Range*					
High	$ 46-3/8	$ 37-1/4	$ 30-3/8	$ 19-1/4	$ 46-3/8
Low	32-7/8	30	16	12-7/8	12-7/8
Dividends Paid	.45	.45	.45	.45	1.80

The second quarter included after tax unusual charges of $21.4 million ($.37 per share) from restructuring of North American tire operations and costs associated with the decision to close the New Bedford, Massachusetts, roofing systems plant.

The third quarter included after tax unusual charges of $38.2 million ($.66 per share) from the restructuring of certain tire and related production operations worldwide. Also during the third quarter the Company incurred after tax unusual charges of $13.5 million ($.23 per share) for environmental cleanup costs associated with a business segment discontinued in 1986.

The fourth quarter included favorable adjustments totaling $40.4 million ($11.3 million after tax or $.19 per share) consisting of $12.0 million of LIFO inventory adjustments and $28.4 million of various other expense items that, by their nature, were estimated during the year. The majority of the adjustments affected Gross Profit.

1989	Quarter First	Second	Third	Fourth	Year
Net Sales	$2,642.9	$2,811.0	$2,679.1	$2,736.3	$10,869.3
Gross Profit	640.2	715.2	652.4	626.8	2,634.6
Income before Extraordinary Item	90.1	22.2	66.1	11.0	189.4
Extraordinary Item	4.4	4.9	4.4	3.7	17.4
Net Income	$ 94.5	$ 27.1	$ 70.5	$ 14.7	$ 206.8
Average Shares Outstanding	57.6	57.7	57.8	57.9	57.7
Per Share of Common Stock:					
Income before extraordinary item	$ 1.56	$ .39	$ 1.14	$ .19	$ 3.28
Extraordinary item	.08	.08	.08	.06	.30
Net Income	$ 1.64	$ .47	$ 1.22	$ .25	$ 3.58
Price Range*					
High	$ 53-1/4	$ 57-3/4	$ 59-3/4	$ 54-3/4	$ 59-3/4
Low	45	45-5/8	51-3/8	42-1/8	42-1/8
Dividends Paid	.45	.45	.45	.45	1.80

The second quarter included after tax unusual charges of $43.0 million ($.75 per share) due to the sale of unused pipe. Also in the second quarter the Company recorded an after tax loss of $52.0 million ($.90 per share) in connection with the sale of its South African subsidiary.

The fourth quarter included after tax charges of $10.9 million ($.19 per share) for the reduction of bias-ply truck tire capacity at the Gadsden, Alabama plant and from the realignment of the Canadian operations. The inclusion of depreciation, other net operating expenses and interest expense of the All American Pipeline System in the fourth quarter reduced net income by $26.4 million.

*New York Stock Exchange—Composite Transactions

▸ ▸ ▸ COMPARISON WITH PRIOR YEARS ◂ ◂ ◂

The Goodyear Tire & Rubber Company and Subsidiaries

(Dollars in millions, except per share)	1990	1989	1988	1987	1986
FINANCIAL RESULTS					
Net Sales	$11,272.5	$10,869.3	$10,810.4	$9,905.2	$9,040.0
Income (loss) from Continuing Operations before Extraordinary Item	(38.3)	189.4	350.1	513.9	216.8
Discontinued Operations	—	—	—	257.0	(92.7)
Income (loss) before Extraordinary Item	(38.3)	189.4	350.1	770.9	124.1
Extraordinary Item—Tax Benefit of Loss Carryovers	—	17.4	—	—	—
Net Income (loss)	(38.3)	206.8	350.1	770.9	124.1
Net Income (loss) per Dollar of Sales	(.3)¢	1.9¢	3.2¢	7.8¢	1.4¢
PER SHARE OF COMMON STOCK					
Income (loss) from Continuing Operations before Extraordinary Item	$ (.66)	$ 3.28	$ 6.11	$ 8.49	$ 2.02
Discontinued Operations	—	—	—	4.24	(.86)
Income (loss) before Extraordinary Item	(.66)	3.28	6.11	12.73	1.16
Extraordinary Item—Tax Benefit of Loss Carryovers	—	.30	—	—	—
Net Income (loss)	(.66)	3.58	6.11	12.73	1.16
Dividends	1.80	1.80	1.70	1.60	1.60
Book Value at December 31	35.88	37.08	35.30	32.19	30.93
FINANCIAL POSITION					
Total Assets	$ 8,963.6	$ 8,460.3	$ 8,618.3	$8,395.9	$9,039.3
Properties and Plants—Net	4,808.4	4,615.3	4,427.4	4,128.3	4,583.4
Depreciation from Continuing Operations	415.0	383.5	357.1	349.9	349.0
Capital Expenditures for Continuing Operations	574.5	775.7	743.7	665.6	1,130.8
Long Term Debt and Capital Leases	3,286.4	2,963.4	3,044.8	3,282.4	2,914.9
Shareholders' Equity	2,097.9	2,143.8	2,027.1	1,834.4	3,002.6
OTHER INFORMATION					
Shareholders of Record	48,209	43,277	46,435	45,878	62,007
Common Shares:					
Outstanding at December 31	58,477,890	57,806,869	57,430,526	56,986,579	97,080,482
Average outstanding during the year	58,215,897	57,727,577	57,322,165	60,564,981	107,092,197
Price Range:					
High	$ 46-3/8	$ 59-3/4	$ 67-7/8	$ 76-1/2	$ 50
Low	12-7/8	42-1/8	47	35	29
Employees:					
Average during the year	107,671	111,469	114,161	114,658	121,444
Total compensation for the year	$ 2,881.4	$ 2,775.0	$ 2,790.7	$2,592.8	$2,557.4

The method of consolidating financial statements was changed in 1987. Financial information has been restated where necessary to reflect discontinued operations and the method of consolidating financial statements.

GOODYEAR RESPONSIBILITY FOR FINANCIAL STATEMENTS

The financial statements of The Goodyear Tire & Rubber Company and subsidiaries were prepared in conformity with generally accepted accounting principles. The Company is responsible for selection of appropriate accounting principles and the objectivity and integrity of the data, estimates and judgments which are the basis for the financial statements.

Goodyear has established and maintains a system of internal controls designed to provide reasonable assurance that the books and records reflect the transactions of the Company and that its established policies and procedures are carefully followed. This system is based upon written procedures, policies and guidelines, organizational structures that provide an appropriate division of responsibility, a program of internal audit and the careful selection and training of qualified personnel.

Price Waterhouse, independent accountants, examined the financial statements and their report is presented below. Their opinion is based on an examination which provides an independent, objective review of the way Goodyear fulfills its responsibility to publish statements which present fairly the financial position and operating results. They obtain and maintain an understanding of the Company's accounting and reporting controls, test transactions and perform related auditing procedures as they consider necessary to arrive at an opinion on the fairness of the financial statements. While the auditors make extensive reviews of procedures, it is neither practicable nor necessary for them to test a large portion of the daily transactions.

The Board of Directors pursues its oversight responsibility for the financial statements through its Audit Committee, composed of Directors who are not employees of the Company. The Committee meets periodically with the independent accountants, representatives of management and internal auditors to assure that all are carrying out their responsibilities. To assure independence, Price Waterhouse and the internal auditors have full and free access to the Audit Committee, without Company representatives present, to discuss the results of their examinations and their opinions on the adequacy of internal controls and the quality of financial reporting.

Tom H. Barrett
Chairman of the Board,
President and Chief
Executive Officer

Oren G. Shaffer
Executive Vice President
and Chief Financial Officer

REPORT OF INDEPENDENT ACCOUNTANTS

Price Waterhouse

To the Board of Directors and Shareholders of The Goodyear Tire & Rubber Company

In our opinion, the accompanying consolidated balance sheet and the related consolidated statements of income, shareholders' equity and cash flows present fairly, in all material respects, the financial position of The Goodyear Tire & Rubber Company and subsidiaries at December 31, 1990 and 1989, and the results of their operations and their cash flows for each of the three years in the period ended December 31, 1990, in conformity with generally accepted accounting principles. These financial statements are the responsibility of the Company's management; our responsibility is to express an opinion on these financial statements based on our audits. We conducted our audits of these statements in accordance with generally accepted auditing standards which require that we plan and perform the audit to obtain reasonable assurance about whether the financial statements are free of material misstatement. An audit includes examining, on a test basis, evidence supporting the amounts and disclosures in the financial statements, assessing the accounting principles used and significant estimates made by management, and evaluating the overall financial statement presentation. We believe that our audits provide a reasonable basis for the opinion expressed above.

Price Waterhouse

Cleveland, Ohio
February 11, 1991

Accelerated depreciation. A type of depreciation method that writes off a relatively larger amount of the asset's cost nearer the start of its useful life than does the straight-line method *(p. 462)*.

Account. The detailed record of the changes that have occurred in a particular asset, liability, or owner equity during a period *(p. 46)*.

Account format of the balance sheet. Format that lists the assets at the left, with liabilities and owner equity at the right *(p. 168)*.

Account payable. A liability backed by the general reputation and credit standing of the debtor *(p. 14)*.

Account receivable. An asset, a promise to receive cash from customers to whom the business has sold goods or for whom the business has performed services *(p. 14)*.

Accounting. The system that measures business activities, processes that information into reports and financial statements, and communicates the findings to decision makers *(p. 2)*.

Accounting controls. Methods and procedures that safeguard assets, authorize transactions, and ensure the accuracy of the financial records *(p. 317)*.

Accounting cycle. Process by which accountants produce an entity's financial statements for a specific period *(p. 145)*.

Accounting information system. The combination of personnel, records, and procedures that a business uses to meet its need for financial data *(p. 269)*.

Accounting rate of return. The remainder of average annual net cash inflow from operations minus annual depreciation, divided by average amount invested in the business. This is the most widely used measure of profitability. The higher the accounting rate of return, the better the investment *(p. 1179)*.

Accounts receivable turnover. Ratio of net credit sales to average net accounts receivable. Measures ability to collect cash from credit customers *(p. 882)*.

Accrual-basis accounting. Accounting that recognizes (records) the impact of a business event as it occurs, regardless of whether the transaction affected cash *(p. 99)*.

Accrued expense. A liability arising from an expense that has been incurred but not yet paid in cash *(p. 109)*.

Accrued revenue. An asset arising from a revenue that has been earned but not received in cash *(p. 110)*.

Accumulated depreciation. The cumulative sum of all de-preciation expense from the date of acquiring a plant asset *(p. 108)*.

Acid-test ratio. Ratio of the sum of cash plus short-term investments plus net current receivables to current liabilities. Tells whether the entity could pay all its current liabilities if they came due immediately. Also called the Quick ratio *(pp. 389, 881)*.

Activity-based costing. A system that focuses on activities as the fundamental cost objects and uses these activities as building blocks for compiling the costs of products and other cost objects *(p. 1061)*.

Additional paid-in capital. Another name for Paid-in capital in excess of par *(p. 634)*.

Adjusted gross income. Total income minus specified adjustments (deductions) equals adjusted gross income, an amount that exists only in the tax law *(p. 1208)*.

Adjusted trial balance. A list of all the ledger accounts with their adjusted balances *(p. 114)*.

Adjusting entry. Entry made at the end of the period to assign revenues to the period in which they are earned and expenses to the period in which they are incurred. Adjusting entries help measure the period's income and bring the related asset and liability accounts to correct balances for the financial statements *(p. 104)*.

Administrative controls. Plan of organization, methods, and procedures that help managers achieve operational efficiency and adherence to company policies *(p. 317)*.

Aging of accounts receivable. A way to estimate bad fn1 s by analyzing individual accounts receivable according to the length of time they have been due *(p. 375)*.

Allocation base. Logical common denominator for assigning a given cost to two or more departments of a business *(p. 1135)*.

Allowance for doubtful accounts. A contra account, related to accounts receivable, that holds the estimated amount of collection losses. Also called Allowance for uncollectible accounts *(p. 371)*.

Allowance for uncollectible accounts. Another name for Allowance for doubtful accounts *(p. 371)*.

Allowance method. A method of recording collection losses based on estimates prior to determining that the business will not collect from specific customers *(p. 371)*.

Amortization. The systematic reduction of a lump-sum amount. Expense that applies to intangible assets in the same way depreciation applies to plant assets and depletion applies to natural resources (p. 475).

Annuity. Stream of equal periodic amounts (p. 1182).

Appropriation of retained earnings. Restriction of retained earnings that is recorded by a formal journal entry (p. 682).

Articles of partnership. Agreement that is the contract between partners specifying such items as the name, location, and nature of the business; the name, capital investment, and duties of each partner; and the method of sharing profits and losses by the partners . Also called the Partnership agreement (p. 585).

Asset. An economic resource that is expected to be of benefit in the future (p. 13).

Auditing. The examination of financial statements by outside accountants, the most significant service that CPAs perform. The conclusion of an audit is the accountant's professional opinion about the financial statements (p. 8).

Authorization of stock. Provision in a corporate charter that gives the state's permission for the corporation to issue—that is, to sell—a certain number of shares of stock (p. 633).

Average cost method. Inventory costing method based on the weighted-average cost of inventory during the period. Weighted-average cost is determined by dividing the cost of goods available for sale by the number of units available (p. 416).

Average tax rate. A taxpayer's income tax amount divided by taxable income (p. 1217).

Bad debt expense. Another name for Uncollectible account expense (p. 371).

Balance sheet. List of an entity's assets, liabilities, and owner equity as of a specific date. Also called the Statement of financial position (p. 21).

Balancing the ledgers. Establishing the equality of (a) total debits and total credits in the general ledger or (b) the balance of a control account in the general ledger and the sum of individual accounts in the related subsidiary ledger (p. 291).

Bank collection. Collection of money by the bank on behalf of a depositor (p. 325).

Bank reconciliation. Process of explaining the reasons for the difference between a depositor's records and the bank's records about the depositor's bank account (p. 324).

Bank statement. Document for a particular bank account showing its beginning and ending balances and listing the month's transactions that affected the account (p. 323).

Batch processing. Computerized accounting for similar transactions in a group or batch (p. 273).

Beginning inventory. Goods left over from the preceding period (p. 413).

Board of directors. Group elected by the stockholders to set policy for a corporation and to appoint its officers (p. 628).

Bond discount. Excess of a bond's maturity (par) value over its issue price (p. 716).

Bond indenture. Contract under which bonds are issued (p. 729).

Bond premium. Excess of a bond's issue price over its maturity (par) value (p. 716).

Bond sinking fund. Group of assets segregated for the purpose of retiring bonds payable at maturity (p. 729).

Bonds payable. Groups of notes payable (bonds) issued to multiple lenders called bondholders (p. 714).

Bonus. Amount over and above regular compensation (p. 510).

Book value of a plant asset. The asset's cost less accumulated depreciation (p. 108).

Book value of stock. Amount of owners' equity on the company's books for each share of its stock (p. 647).

Book value per share of common stock. Common stockholders' equity divided by the number of shares of common stock outstanding (p. 890).

Branch accounting. System for separating the accounts of a branch of a business from the accounts of the home office (p. 1139).

Branch-factory ledger control. Account in the home office ledger that represents the home office investment in, or receivable from, a branch of the business (p. 1141).

Branch ledger. The part of a general ledger kept by a branch of the business, separate from the home office ledger (p. 1140).

Break-even analysis. Another name for Cost-volume-profit analysis (p. 965).

Break-even point. Amount of unit sales or dollar sales at which revenue equals expenses (p. 966).

Budget. Management's quantitative expression of a plan of action and an aid to coordination and implementation (p. 921).

Budget committee. Group that prepares the master budget; includes representatives from all departments of the business (p. 921).

Budget formula. The heart of a flexible budget; shows how to compute the budget amounts (p. 1093).

Budgeted factory overhead rate. Budgeted total overhead cost divided by the budgeted rate base (p. 1017).

Budgeting. Setting of goals for a business, such as its sales and profits, for a future period (p. 9).

Bylaws. Constitution for governing a corporation (p. 628).

Byproduct. Output of a joint production process with minor sales value in comparison with the main product (p. 1067).

Callable bonds. Bonds that the issuer may call or pay off at a specified price whenever the issuer wants (p. 730).

Capital. Another name for the Owner equity of a business (*p. 13*).

Capital budgeting. Formal means of making long-range decisions for investments such as plant locations, equipment purchases, additions of product lines, and territorial expansions (*p. 1177*).

Capital deficiency. Debit balance in a partner's capital account (*p. 604*).

Capital expenditure. Expenditure that increases the capacity or efficiency of an asset or extends its useful life. Capital expenditures are debited to an asset account (*p. 478*).

Capital expenditures budget. Plan for purchases of property, plant, and equipment and other assets that management uses over a long time (*p. 924*).

Capital gain. Special category of gain defined in the tax law that results from the disposal of property such as investments in stocks, bonds, real estate, and personal assets (*p. 1211*).

Capital lease. Lease agreement that meets any one of four criteria: (1) The lease transfers title of the leased asset to the lessee. (2) The lease contains a bargain purchase option. (3) The lease term is 75 percent or more of the estimated useful life of the leased asset. (4) The present value of the lease payments is 90 percent or more of the market value of the leased asset (*p. 735*).

Capital loss. Special category of loss defined in the tax law that results from the disposal of property such as investments in stocks, bonds, real estate, and personal assets (*p. 1211*).

Cash-basis accounting. Accounting that records only transactions in which cash is received or paid (*p. 100*).

Cash budget. Details the way a business intends to go from the beginning cash balance to the desired ending balance. Also called the Statement of budgeted cash receipts and disbursements (*p. 930*).

Cash disbursements journal. Special journal used to record cash disbursements by check (*p. 285*).

Cash equivalents. Highly liquid short-term investments that can be converted into cash with little delay (*p. 812*).

Cash flows. Cash receipts and cash payments (disbursements) (*p. 808*).

Cash receipts journal. Special journal used to record cash receipts (*p. 278*).

Central processing unit (CPU). The brain of a computer. It performs mathematical and logical operations and controls the other components of the computer system (*p. 1244*).

Certified Public Accountant (CPA). A professional accountant who earns this title through a combination of education, experience, and an acceptable score on a written national examination (*p. 5*).

Chairperson of the board. Elected by a corporation's board of directors, usually the most powerful person in the corporation (*p. 628*).

Change in accounting estimate. A change that occurs in the normal course of business as a company alters earlier expectations. (*p. 557*).

Change in accounting principle. A change in accounting method, such as from the LIFO method to the FIFO method for inventories and a switch from an accelerated depreciation method to the straight-line method (*p. 557*).

Chart of accounts. List of all the accounts and their account numbers in the ledger (*p. 64*).

Charter. Document that gives the state's permission to form a corporation (*pp. 626, 628*).

Check. Document that instructs the bank to pay the designated person or business the specified amount of money (*p. 323*).

Check register. Special journal used to record all checks issued in a voucher system (*p. 339*).

Closing entries. Entries that transfer the revenue, expense, and owner withdrawal balances from these respective accounts to the capital account (*p. 160*).

Closing the accounts. Step in the accounting cycle at the end of the period that prepares the accounts for recording the transactions of the next period. Closing the accounts consists of journalizing and posting the closing entries to set the balances of the revenue, expense, and owner withdrawal accounts to zero (*p. 157*).

Collection method. Method of applying the revenue principle by which the seller waits until cash is received to record the sale. This method is used only if the receipt of cash is uncertain (*p. 553*).

Commission. Employee compensation computed as a percentage of the sales that the employee has made (*p. 510*).

Common-size statement. A financial statement that reports only percentages (no dollar amounts); a type of vertical analysis (*p. 874*).

Common stock. The most basic form of capital stock. In describing a corporation, the common stockholders are the owners of the business (*p. 632*).

Comparability principle. Specifies that accounting information must be comparable from business to business and that a single business's financial statements must be comparable from one period to the next (*p. 551*).

Completed-contract method. Method of applying the revenue principle by a construction company by which all revenue earned on the project is recorded in the period when the project is completed (*p. 555*).

Conservatism. Concept that underlies presenting the gloomiest possible figures in the financial statements (*p. 423*).

Consignment. Transfer of goods by the owner (consignor) to another business (consignee) who, for a fee, sells the inventory on the owner's behalf. The consignee does not take title to the consigned goods (*p. 415*).

Consistency principle. A business must use the same accounting methods and procedures from period to period (*p. 421*).

Consolidated statements. Financial statements of the parent company plus those of majority-owned subsidiaries as if the combination were a single legal entity (*p. 769*).

Consolidation accounting. A way to combine the financial statements of two or more companies that are controlled by the same owners (*p. 769*).

Constraint. Item that restricts production or sales. Also called the Limiting factor (*p. 1171*).

Contingent liability. A potential liability (*p. 386*).

Continuous budget. Systematically adds a month or a quarter as the month or quarter just ended is deleted. Also called a Rolling budget (*p. 935*).

Contra account. An account with two distinguishing characteristics: (1) it always has a companion account, and (2) its normal balance is opposite that of the companion account (*p. 108*).

Contra asset. An asset account with a normal credit balance. A contra account always has a companion account and its balance is opposite that of the companion account (*p. 108*).

Contract interest rate. Interest rate that determines the amount of cash interest the borrower pays and the investor receives each year. Also called the Stated interest rate (*p. 717*).

Contributed capital. Another name for Paid-in capital (*p. 630*).

Contribution margin. Excess of sale price over total variable expenses (*p. 963*).

Contribution margin income statement. Separates expenses into variable costs and fixed costs and highlights the contribution margin, which is the excess of sales over total variable expenses (*p. 963*).

Contribution margin percentage. Sales of 100 percent minus the variable expense percentage (*p. 967*).

Control account. An account whose balance equals the sum of the balances in a group of related accounts in a subsidiary ledger (*p. 277*).

Controllable overhead variance. Another name for the Flexible budget overhead variance (*p. 1106*).

Controlling (majority) interest. Ownership of more than 50 percent of an investee company's voting stock (*p. 769*).

Conversion cost. Direct labor plus overhead (*p. 1004*).

Convertible bonds. Bonds that may be converted into the common stock of the issuing company at the option of the investor (*p. 731*).

Convertible preferred stock. Preferred stock that may be exchanged by the preferred stockholders, if they choose, for another class of stock in the corporation (*p. 644*).

Copyright. Exclusive right to reproduce and sell a book, musical composition, film, or other work of art. Issued by the federal government, copyrights extend 50 years beyond the author's life (*p. 476*).

Corporation. A business owned by stockholders that begins when the state approves its articles of incorporation. A corporation is a legal entity, an "artificial person," in the eyes of the law (*p. 10*).

Cost accounting. The branch of accounting that determines and controls a business's costs (*p. 9*).

Cost allocation. Assignment of various costs to the departments and products of a business (*p. 1135*).

Cost application base. A common denominator linking costs among all products. Ideally the best available measure of the cause-and-effect relationship between overhead costs and production volume (*p. 1017*).

Cost behavior. Description of how costs change in response to a shift in a cost driver (*p. 960*).

Cost driver. Any factor whose change causes a change in a related total cost (*p. 960*).

Cost method for investments. The method used to account for short-term investments in stock and for long-term investments when the investor holds less than 20 percent of the investee's voting stock. Under the cost method, investments are recorded at cost and reported at the lower of their cost or market value (*p. 764*).

Cost object. Anything for which it is worthwhile to compile costs such as an activity, a department, or a product (*p. 1061*).

Cost of a plant asset. Purchase price, sales tax, purchase commission, and all other amounts paid to acquire the asset and to ready it for its intended use (*p. 456*).

Cost of goods manufactured. Manufacturers' counterpart to the Purchases account. Cost of goods manufactured takes the place of purchases in the computation of cost of goods sold (*p. 1002*).

Cost of goods sold. The cost of the inventory that the business has sold to customers, the largest single expense of most merchandising businesses. Also called Cost of sales (*p. 217*).

Cost of sales. Another name for Cost of goods sold (*p. 217*).

Cost principle. States that assets and services are recorded at their purchase cost and that the accounting record of the asset continues to be based on cost rather than current market value (*p. 552*).

Cost-volume-profit (CVP) analysis. Expresses the relationships among costs, volume, and profit or loss. An important part of a budgeting system that helps managers predict the outcome of their decisions (*p. 960*).

Coupon bonds. Bonds for which the owners receive interest by detaching a perforated coupon (which states the interest due and the date of payment) from the bond and depositing it in a bank for collection (*p. 715*).

CPU. Abbreviation of Central processing unit (*p. 1244*).

Credit. The right side of an account (*p. 49*).

Credit memorandum. Document issued by a seller to indicate having credited a customer's account receivable account (*p. 287*).

Creditor. The party to a credit transaction who sells a service or merchandise and obtains a receivable (*p. 369*).

Cumulative preferred stock. Preferred stock whose owners must receive all dividends in arrears before the corporation pays dividends to the common stockholders (*p. 642*).

Current asset. An asset that is expected to be converted to cash, sold, or consumed during the next twelve months, or within the business's normal operating cycle if longer than a year (*p. 167*).

Current cost. Present cost of replacing an asset's particular service potential or usefulness (*p. 1290*).

Current cost accounting. Accounting model that uses the current cost of a company's assets and expenses in place of their historical cost (*p. 1290*).

Current liability. A debt due to be paid within one year or the entity's operating cycle if the cycle is longer than a year (*p. 168*).

Current portion of long-term debt. Amount of the principal that is payable within one year (*p. 504*).

Current ratio. Current assets divided by current liabilities. Measures the ability to pay current liabilities from current assets (*p. 169*).

CVP analysis. Abbreviation of Cost-volume-profit analysis (*p. 960*).

Date of record. Date on which the owners of stock to receive a dividend are identified (*p. 641*).

Days' sales in receivables. Ratio of average net accounts receivable to one day's sales. Tells how many days' sales remain in Accounts Receivable awaiting collection (*pp. 389, 883*).

Debentures. Unsecured bonds, backed only by the good faith of the borrower (*p. 716*).

Debit. The left side of an account (*p. 49*).

Debit memorandum. Business document issued by a buyer to state that the buyer no longer owes the seller for the amount of returned purchases (*p. 289*).

Debt ratio. Ratio of total liabilities to total assets. Tells the proportion of a company's assets that it has financed with debt (*p. 170*).

Debtor. The party to a credit transaction who makes a purchase and creates a payable (*p. 369*).

Decision model. A method or technique for evaluating and choosing among alternative courses of action (*p. 1177*).

Declaration date. Date on which the board of directors announce the intention to pay a dividend. The declaration creates a liability for the corporation (*p. 641*).

Default on a note. Failure of the maker of a note to pay at maturity. Also called Dishonor of a note (*p. 386*).

Deferred revenue. Another name for Unearned revenue (*p. 111*).

Deficit. Debit balance in the retained earnings account (*p. 631*).

Dependent. Person who receives more than half of his or her support from another taxpayer (*p. 1207*).

Depletion expense. That portion of a natural resource's cost that is used up in a particular period. Depletion expense is computed in the same way as units of production depreciation (*p. 474*).

Deposit in transit. A deposit recorded by the company but not yet by its bank (*p. 324*).

Depreciable cost. The cost of a plant asset minus its estimated residual value (*p. 460*).

Depreciation. Expense associated with spreading (allocating) the cost of a plant asset over its useful life (*p. 107*).

Direct expense. Expense that is conveniently identified with and traceable to a particular product or department of a business (*p. 1134*).

Direct labor. Cost of salaries and wages for the employees who physically convert materials into the company's products; labor costs that are conveniently traceable to finished goods (*p. 1003*).

Direct material. Material that becomes a physical part of a finished product and whose cost is separately and conveniently traceable through the manufacturing process to finished goods (*p. 1003*).

Direct method. Format of the operating activities section of the statement of cash flows that lists the major categories of operating cash receipts (collections from customers and receipts of interest and dividends) and cash disbursements (payments to suppliers, to employees, for interest and income taxes) (*p. 812*).

Direct write-off method. A method of accounting for bad debts by which the company waits until the credit department decides that a customer's account receivable is uncollectible and then records uncollectible account expense and credits the customer's account receivable (*p. 377*).

Disclosure principle. Holds that a company's financial statements should report enough information for outsiders to make knowledgeable decisions about the company (*p. 556*).

Discount on stock. Excess of the par value of stock over its issue price (*p. 634*).

Discount rate. Management's minimum desired rate of return on an investment, used in a present-value computation (*p. 1182*).

Discounting a note payable. A borrowing arrangement in which the bank subtracts the interest amount from the note's face value. The borrower receives the net amount (*p. 502*).

Discounting a note receivable. Selling a note receivable before its maturity (*p. 384*).

Dishonor of a note. Another name for Default on a note (*p. 386*).

Disk drive. Computer input device that reads data and instructions from magnetic disks (*p. 1244*).

Diskette. Thin 3½-inch or 5¼-inch diameter round magnetic disk enclosed in plastic. Also called a Floppy diskette (p. 1244).

Dissolution. Ending of a partnership (p. 585).

Dividend yield. Ratio of dividends per share of stock to the stock's market price per share. Tells the percentage of a stock's market value that the company pays to stockholders as dividends (p. 889).

Dividends. Distributions by a corporation to its stockholders (p. 631).

Dividends in arrears. Cumulative preferred dividends that the corporation has failed to pay (p. 642).

Donated capital. Special category of stockholders' equity created when a corporation receives a donation (gift) from a donor who receives no ownership interest in the company (p. 639).

Double-declining-balance (DDB) method. An accelerated depreciation method that computes annual depreciation by multiplying the asset's decreasing book value by a constant percentage, which is two times the straight-line rate (p. 462).

Double taxation. Corporations pay their own income taxes on corporate income. Then, the stockholders pay personal income tax on the cash dividends that they receive from corporations (p. 627).

Doubtful account expense. Another name for Uncollectible account expense (p. 371).

Earnings per share (EPS). Amount of a company's net income per share of its outstanding common stock (pp. 688, 888).

Effective interest rate. Another name for market interest rate (p. 717).

Efficiency variance. Difference between the quantity of inputs actually used and the quantity that should have been used for the actual output achieved, multiplied by the standard unit price of the input. Also called the Usage variance and the Quantity variance (p. 1100).

Efficient capital market. A capital market in which market prices fully reflect all information available to the public (p. 891).

Electronic fund transfer. System that accounts for cash transactions by electronic impulses rather than paper documents (p. 342).

Ending inventory. Goods still on hand at the end of the period (p. 413).

Entity. An organization or a section of an organization that, for accounting purposes, stands apart from other organizations and individuals as a separate economic unit. This is the most basic concept in accounting (p. 11).

EPS. Abbreviation of Earnings per share of common stock (p. 688).

Equity method for investments. The method used to account for investments in which the investor can significantly influence the decisions of the investee. Under the equity method, investments are recorded initially at cost. The investment account is debited (increased) for ownership in the investee's net income and credited (decreased) for ownership in the investee's dividends (p. 767).

Equivalent units. Measure of the number of complete units that could have been manufactured from start to finish using the costs incurred during the period (p. 1050).

Estimated residual value. Expected cash value of an asset at the end of its useful life. Also called Residual value, Scrap value and Salvage value (p. 459).

Estimated useful life. Length of the service that a business expects to get from an asset, may be expressed in years, units of output, miles, or other measures (p. 459).

Expenditure. Either a cash or credit purchase of goods or services related to an asset (p. 478).

Expense. Decrease in owner equity that occurs in the course of delivering goods or services to customers or clients (p. 17).

Expense allocation. Assignment of various expenses to the departments of a business (p. 1135).

Extraordinary item. A gain or loss that is both unusual for the company and infrequent (p. 686).

Extraordinary repair. Repair work that generates a capital expenditure (p. 478).

Factory ledger. A branch ledger for a manufacturing plant (p. 1140).

Factory overhead. All manufacturing costs other than direct materials and direct labor (p. 1003).

FICA tax. Federal Insurance Contributions Act (FICA), or Social Security tax, which is withheld from employees' pay (p. 512).

FIFO. The First-in, first-out inventory method (p. 416).

Financial accounting. The branch of accounting that provides information to people outside the business (p. 10).

Financial budget. Projects the means of raising money from stockholders and creditors and plans cash management (p. 924).

Financial statements. Business documents that report financial information about an entity to persons and organizations outside the business (p. 2).

Financing activity. Activity that obtains the funds from investors and creditors needed to launch and sustain the business. A section of the statement of cash flows (p. 811).

Finished goods inventory. Completed goods that have not yet been sold (p. 1002).

First-in, first-out (FIFO) method. Inventory costing method by which the first costs into inventory are the first costs out to cost of goods sold. Ending inventory is based on the costs of the most recent purchases (p. 416).

Fixed cost. Cost that does not change in total as volume changes (p. 961).

Fixed expense. Expense that does not change in total as volume changes (p. 961).

Flexible budget. Set of budgets covering a range of volume rather than a single level of volume (p. 1093).

Flexible budget overhead variance. Difference between total actual overhead (fixed and variable) and the flexible budget amount for actual production volume. Also called the Controllable variance (p. 1105).

Flexible budget variance. Difference between an amount in the flexible budget and the actual results for the corresponding item (p. 1096).

FOB destination. Terms of a transaction that govern when the title to the inventory passes from the seller to the purchaser—when the goods arrive at the purchaser's location (p. 414).

FOB shipping point. Terms of a transaction that govern when the title to the inventory passes from the seller to the purchaser—when the goods leave the seller's place of business (p. 414).

Foreign-currency exchange rate. The measure of one nation's currency against another nation's currency (p. 780).

Foreign-currency transaction gain or loss. A gain or loss that occurs when the exchange rate changes between the date of a purchase or sale on account and the subsequent payment or receipt of cash (p. 782).

Foreign-currency translation adjustment. The balancing figure that brings the dollar amount of the total liabilities and stockholders' equity of a foreign subsidiary into agreement with the dollar amount of its total assets (p. 785).

Franchises and licenses. Privileges granted by a private business or a government to sell a product or service in accordance with specified conditions (p. 476).

Fringe benefits. Employee compensation, like health and life insurance and retirement pay, which the employee does not receive immediately in cash (p. 511).

Gain. An increase in owner equity that does not result from a revenue or an investment by an owner in the business (p. 561).

Generally accepted accounting principles (GAAP). Accounting guidelines, formulated by the Financial Accounting Standards Board, that govern how businesses report their financial statements to the public (p. 6).

General journal. Journal used to record all transactions that do not fit one of the special journals (p. 275).

General ledger. Ledger of accounts that are reported in the financial statements (p. 277).

Going-concern concept. Accountants' assumption that the business will continue operating in the foreseeable future (p. 549).

Goods available for sale. Beginning inventory plus net purchases (p. 413).

Goodwill. Excess of the cost of an acquired company over the sum of the market values of its net assets (assets minus liabilities) (p. 477).

Gross income. In taxation, total income minus exclusions (p. 1208).

Gross margin. Excess of sales revenue over cost of goods sold. Also called Gross profit (p. 209).

Gross margin method. A way to estimate inventory based on a rearrangement of the cost of goods sold model: Beginning inventory + Net purchases = Cost of goods available for sale. Cost of goods available for sale − Cost of goods sold = Ending inventory. Also called the Gross profit method (p. 209).

Gross pay. Total amount of salary, wages, commissions, or any other employee compensation before taxes and other deductions are taken out (p. 511).

Gross profit. Excess of sales revenue over cost of goods sold. Also called Gross margin (p. 209).

Gross profit method. Another name for the gross margin method of estimating inventory cost (p. 209).

Hardware. Equipment that makes up a computer system (p. 272).

Hedging. Protecting oneself from losing money in one transaction by engaging in a counterbalancing transaction (p. 783).

High-low method. Method of separating a mixed cost into its variable and fixed components (p. 976).

Home-office ledger. The part of a general ledger kept by the home office, separate from the branch ledger (p. 1140).

Home-office ledger control. Account in the branch ledger that represents an owner equity of, or branch payable to, the home office (p. 1141).

Horizontal analysis. Study of percentage changes in comparative financial statements (p. 869).

Imprest system. A way to account for petty cash by maintaining a constant balance in the petty cash account, supported by the fund (cash plus disbursement tickets) totaling the same amount (p. 336).

Income from operations. Gross margin (sales revenue minus cost of goods sold) minus operating expenses. Also called Operating income (p. 226).

Income statement. List of an entity's revenues, expenses, and net income or net loss for a specific period. Also called the Statement of operations and the Statement of earnings (p. 21).

Income summary. A temporary "holding tank" account into which the revenues and expenses are transferred prior to their final transfer to the capital account (*p. 160*).

Income tax. A general-purpose tax levied on the income of a taxpayer. Entirely separate from all other taxes, it is the federal government's largest source of revenue (*p. 1205*).

Income tax allocation. Process of accruing income taxes during the period that the related income occurs, with the goal of matching the period's expenses—including income tax expense—against the period's revenues, regardless of when the income tax is paid (*p. 1218*).

Incorporators. Persons who organize a corporation (*p. 628*).

Indirect expense. Expense that is not traceable to a single product or department of a business; an expense other than a direct expense. Often indirect expenses arise from activities that serve more than one department simultaneously (*p. 1134*).

Indirect labor. Factory labor costs other than direct labor. Indirect labor costs, which are difficult to trace to specific products, include the pay of forklift operators, janitors, and plant guards (*p. 1004*).

Indirect materials. Manufacturing materials whose cost cannot easily be traced directly to particular finished products (*p. 1004*).

Indirect method. Format of the operating activities section of the statement of cash flows that starts with net income and shows the reconciliation from net income to operating cash flows. Also called the Reconciliation method (*p. 827*).

Inflation. Increase in the general price level (*p. 1289*).

Information system design. Identification of an organization's information needs, and development and implementation of the system to meet those needs (*p. 9*).

Installment method. Method of applying the revenue principle in which gross profit (sales revenue minus cost of goods sold) is recorded as cash is collected (*p. 553*).

Intangible asset. An asset with no physical form, a special right to current and expected future benefits (*p. 456*).

Integrated software. Computer program that includes modules handling different functions. Coordinates the output of the various modules (*p. 1246*).

Interest. The revenue to the payee for loaning out the principal, and the expense to the maker for borrowing the principal (*p. 382*).

Interest-coverage ratio. Another name for the Times-interest-earned ratio (*p. 885*).

Interest period. The period of time during which interest is to be computed, extending from the original date of the note to the maturity date (*p. 382*).

Interest rate. The percentage rate that is multiplied by the principal amount to compute the amount of interest on a note (*p. 382*).

Internal auditing. Auditing that is performed by a business's own accountants to evaluate the firm's accounting and management systems. The aim is to improve operating efficiency and to ensure that employees follow management's procedures and plans (*p. 9*).

Internal control. Organizational plan and all the related measures adopted by an entity to safeguard assets, ensure accurate and reliable accounting records, promote operational efficiency, and encourage adherence to company policies (*p. 317*).

Internal rate of return. Rate of return that makes the net present value of a project equal to zero (*p. 1185*).

Inventoriable cost. A cost of a product regarded as an asset under GAAP (*p. 1005*).

Inventory cost. Price paid to acquire inventory—not the selling price of the goods. Inventory cost includes its invoice price, less all discounts, plus sales tax, tariffs, transportation fees, insurance while in transit, and all other costs incurred to make the goods ready for sale (*p. 415*).

Inventory profit. Difference between gross margin figured on the FIFO basis and gross margin figured on the LIFO basis (*p. 420*).

Inventory turnover. Ratio of cost of goods sold to average inventory. Measures the number of times a company sells its average level of inventory during a year (*p. 230*).

Investing activity. Activity that increases and decreases the assets that the business has to work with. A section of the statement of cash flows (*p. 810*).

Invoice. Seller's request for payment from a purchaser. Also called a bill (*p. 211*).

Itemized deduction. In taxation, a particular category that includes medical expenses, interest expense, charitable contributions, taxes paid, casualty losses, and miscellaneous deductions (*p. 1208*).

Job cost record. Document used to accumulate and control cost in a job order system (*p. 1009*).

Job order costing. Accounting system used by companies that manufacture products as individual units or in batches, each of which receives varying degrees of attention and skill (*p. 1008*).

Joint product. Goods identified as individual products only after a juncture in the production process called the split-off point (*p. 1066*).

Journal. The chronological accounting record of an entity's transactions (*p. 52*).

Labor time ticket. Document that identifies an employee, the amount of time the employee spent on a particular job, and the employee's labor cost charged to the job (*p. 1014*).

Large stock dividend. A stock dividend of 25 percent or more of the corporation's issued stock (*p. 673*).

Last-in, first-out (LIFO) method. Inventory costing method by which the last costs into inventory are the first costs out to cost of goods sold. This leaves the oldest costs—those of beginning inventory and the earliest purchases of the period—in ending inventory (*p. 416*).

LCM rule. The Lower-of-cost-or-market rule (*p. 423*).

Lease. Rental agreement in which the tenant (lessee) agrees to make rent payments to the property owner (lessor) in exchange for the use of the asset (*p. 734*).

Leasehold. Prepayment that a lessee (renter) makes to secure the use of an asset from a lessor (landlord) (*p. 477*).

Ledger. The book of accounts (*p. 46*).

Lessee. Tenant in a lease agreement (*p. 734*).

Lessor. Property owner in a lease agreement (*p. 734*).

Leverage. Another name for Trading on the equity (*p. 888*).

Liability. An economic obligation (a debt) payable to an individual or an organization outside the business (*p. 13*).

LIFO. The Last-in, first-out inventory method (*p. 416*).

Limited liability. No personal obligation of a stockholder for corporation debts. The most that a stockholder can lose on an investment in a corporation's stock is the cost of the investment (*p. 627*).

Limiting factor. Item that restricts production or sales. Also called the Constraint (*p. 1171*).

Liquidation. The process of going out of business by selling the entity's assets and paying its liabilities. The final step in liquidation of a business is the distribution of any remaining cash to the owners (*p. 602*).

Liquidation value of stock. Amount a corporation agrees to pay a preferred stockholder per share if the company liquidates (*p. 647*).

Liquidity. Measure of how quickly an item may be converted to cash (*p. 167*).

Long-term asset. An asset other than a current asset (*p. 167*).

Long-term investment. Separate asset category reported on the balance sheet between current assets and plant assets (*p. 764*).

Long-term liability. A liability other than a current liability (*p. 168*).

Long-term solvency. Ability to generate enough cash to pay long-term debts as they mature (*p. 869*).

Loss. A decrease in owner equity that does not result from an expense or a distribution to an owner of the business (*p. 561*).

Lower-of-cost-or-market (LCM) rule. Requires that an asset be reported in the financial statements at the lower of its historical cost or its market value (current replacement cost) (*p. 423*).

Mainframe. Computer system characterized by a single computer (*p. 272*).

Majority interest. Another name for a Controlling ownership interest in another business (*p. 769*).

Maker of a note. The person or business that signs the note and promises to pay the amount required by the note agreement. The maker is the debtor (*p. 381*).

Management accounting. The branch of accounting that generates information for internal decision makers of a business, such as top executives (*p. 10*).

Management by exception. Management strategy by which executive attention is directed to the important deviations from budgeted amounts (*p. 1133*).

Margin of safety. Excess of expected sales over break-even sales (*p. 973*).

Market interest rate. Interest rate that investors demand in order to loan their money. Also called the Effective interest rate (*p. 717*).

Market value of stock. Price for which a person could buy or sell a share of stock (*p. 646*).

Marketable security. Another name for Short-term investment, one that may be sold any time the investor wishes (*p. 764*).

Master budget. Budget that includes the major financial statements and supporting schedules. The master budget can be divided into the operating budget, the capital expenditures budget, and the financial budget (*p. 921*).

Matching principle. The basis for recording expenses. Directs accountants to identify all expenses incurred during the period, to measure the expenses, and to match them against the revenues earned during that same span of time (*p. 102*).

Materiality concept. States that a company must perform strictly proper accounting only for items and transactions that are significant to the business's financial statements (*p. 559*).

Materials inventory. Materials on hand and intended for use in the manufacturing process. Also called Raw materials inventory (*p. 1002*).

Materials requisition. Request for materials prepared by manufacturing personnel, the document that sets a manufacturing process in motion (*p. 1011*).

Maturity date. The date on which the final payment of a note is due. Also called the Due date (*p. 382*).

Maturity value. The sum of the principal and interest due at the maturity date of a note (*p. 382*).

Menu. List of options for choosing computer functions (*p. 1246*).

Menu-driven. Type of computer software that offers a list of options for doing various functions (*p. 1246*).

Microcomputer. A computer small enough for each employee work station to have its own machine (*pp. 272, 1244*).

Minicomputer. Small computer that operates like a large system but on a smaller scale (*p. 272*).

Minority interest. A subsidiary company's equity that is held by stockholders other than the parent company (p. 772).

Mixed cost. Cost that is part variable and part fixed (p. 961).

Mixed expense. Expense that is part variable and part fixed (p. 961).

Modified Accelerated Cost Recovery System (MACRS). Special tax depreciation method (p. 1217).

Monetary asset. Asset whose value is stated in a fixed number of dollars. This amount does not change, regardless of inflation (p. 1292).

Monetary liability. Liability stated in a fixed number of dollars. This amount does not change, regardless of inflation (p. 1292).

Monitor. Computer output device that resembles a television and allows the user to view data being processed and to receive messages from the program being run (p. 1245).

Mortgage. Borrower's promise to transfer the legal title to certain assets to the lender if the debt is not paid on schedule (p. 732).

Multiple-step income statement. Format that contains subtotals to highlight significant relationships. In addition to net income, it also presents gross margin and income from operations (p. 229).

Mutual agency. Every partner can bind the business to a contract within the scope of the partnership's regular business operations (p. 585).

Net earnings. Another name for Net income or Net profit (p. 17).

Net income. Excess of total revenues over total expenses. Also called Net earnings or Net profit (p. 17).

Net loss. Excess of total expenses over total revenues (p. 17).

Net monetary assets. Excess of monetary assets over monetary liabilities (p. 1292).

Net monetary liabilities. Excess of monetary liabilities over monetary assets (p. 1292).

Net pay. Gross pay minus all deductions, the amount of employee compensation that the employee actually takes home (p. 511).

Net present value. Discounted cash flow approach to capital budgeting. It computes the expected net monetary gain or loss from a project by discounting all expected cash flows to the present value, using a desired rate of return. A zero or positive net present value indicates that the investment should be purchased. A negative net present value indicates that the investment should be rejected (p. 1181).

Net profit. Another name for Net income or Net earnings (p. 17).

Net purchases. Purchases less purchase discounts and purchase returns and allowances (p. 214).

Net realizable value. Sales value less the cost of selling the item (p. 1067).

Net sales revenue. Sales revenue less sales discounts and sales returns and allowances (p. 209).

Nominal account. Another name for a temporary account—revenues and expenses—that are closed at the end of the period. In a proprietorship the owner withdrawal account is also nominal (p. 159).

Nonmonetary asset. Asset whose price may change during inflation, such as inventory, land, buildings, and equipment (p. 1292).

Nonsufficient funds check. A "hot" check, one for which the payer's bank account has insufficient money to pay the check (p. 326).

No-par stock. Stock that does not have par value but may have a *stated value*, which makes it similar to par value stock (p. 632).

Note payable. A liability evidenced by a written promise to make a future payment (p. 14).

Note receivable. An asset evidenced by another party's written promise that entitles the holder of the note to receive cash in the future (p. 14).

NSF check. A nonsufficient funds check (p. 326).

Objectivity principle. Another name for the Reliability principle (p. 551).

Off-balance-sheet financing. Acquisition of assets or services with debt that is not reported on the balance sheet (p. 736).

On-line processing. Computerized accounting for transaction data on a continuous basis, often from various locations, rather than in batches at a single location (p. 273).

Operating activity. Activity that creates revenue or expense in the entity's major line of business. Operating activities affect the income statement. A section of the statement of cash flows (p. 810).

Operating budget. Sets the target revenues and expenses, and thus net income, for the period (p. 924).

Operating cycle. Time span during which cash is paid for goods and services that are sold to customers who then pay the business in cash (p. 167).

Operating expenses. Expenses, other than cost of goods sold, that are incurred in the entity's major line of business. Examples include rent, depreciation, salaries, wages, utilities, property tax, and supplies expense (p. 224).

Operating income. Another name for Income from operations (p. 226).

Operating lease. Usually a short-term or cancelable rental agreement (p. 734).

Opportunity cost. Maximum available profit contribution forgone (rejected) by using limited resources for a particular purpose. It is the cost of the forsaken next-best alternative (p. 1175).

Ordinary repair. Repair work that creates a revenue expenditure, which is debited to an expense account (p. 478).

Organization cost. The costs of organizing a corporation, including legal fees, taxes and fees paid to the state, and charges by promoters for selling the stock. Organization cost is an intangible asset (p. 641).

Other expense. Expense that is outside the main operations of a business, such as a loss on the sale of plant assets (p. 226).

Other receivables. A miscellaneous category that includes loans to employees and branch companies—usually long-term assets reported on the balance sheet after current assets and before plant assets. (p. 370).

Other revenue. Revenue that is outside the main operations of a business, such as a gain on the sale of plant assets (p. 226).

Outstanding check. A check issued by the company and recorded on its books but not yet paid by its bank (p. 325).

Outstanding stock. Stock in the hands of stockholders (p. 630).

Overapplied overhead. Credit balance in the Factory Overhead account, results when applied overhead exceeds the actual overhead cost (p. 1019).

Owner's equity. The claim of an owner of a business to the assets of the business. Also called Capital (p. 13).

Paid-in capital. A corporation's capital from investments by the stockholders. Also called Contributed capital (p. 630).

Par value. Arbitrary amount assigned to a share of stock (p. 632).

Parent company. An investor company that owns more than 50 percent of the voting stock of a subsidiary company (p. 769).

Participating preferred stock. Preferred stock whose owners may receive—that is, participate in—dividends beyond the stated amount or stated percentage (p. 643).

Partnership. A business with two or more owners (p. 10).

Partnership agreement. Another name for the articles of partnership (p. 584).

Patent. A federal government grant giving the holder the exclusive right for 17 years to produce and sell an invention (p. 476).

Payback. Length of time it will take to recover, in net cash inflow from operations, the dollars of a capital outlay. The shorter the payback period, the better the investment, and vice versa (p. 1178).

Payee of a note. The person or business to whom the maker of a note promises future payment. The payee is the creditor (p. 381).

Payment date. Payment of the dividend usually follows the record date by two to four weeks (p. 641).

Payroll. Employee compensation, a major expense of many businesses (p. 510).

Pension. Employee compensation that will be received during retirement (p. 736).

Percentage-of-completion method. Method of applying the revenue principle by a construction company by which revenue is recorded as the work is performed (p. 555).

Performance report. Report that compares actual and budgeted results (p. 1093).

Period cost. Operating expenses that are never traced through the inventory accounts (p. 1006).

Periodic inventory system. The business does not keep a continuous record of the inventory on hand. Instead, at the end of the period the business makes a physical count of the on-hand inventory and applies the appropriate unit costs to determine the cost of the ending inventory (p. 428).

Permanent accounts. Another name for a real account—the assets, liabilities, and capital accounts. These accounts are not closed at the end of the period because their balances are not used to measure income (p. 159).

Perpetual inventory system. The business keeps a continuous record for each inventory item to show the inventory on hand at all times (p. 429).

Personal exemption. A tax deduction that is a set amount allowed for a taxpayer, the taxpayer's spouse, and each person who qualifies as a dependent (p. 1210).

Petty cash. Fund containing a small amount of cash that is used to pay minor expenditures (p. 335).

Plant asset. Long-lived assets, like land, buildings, and equipment, used in the operation of the business (pp. 107, 456).

Postclosing trial balance. List of the ledger accounts and their balances at the end of the period after the journalizing and posting of the closing entries. The last step of the accounting cycle, the postclosing trial balance ensures that the ledger is in balance for the start of the next accounting period (p. 162).

Posting. Transferring of amounts from the journal to the ledger (p. 54).

Preemptive right. A stockholder's right to maintain a proportionate ownership in a corporation (p. 632).

Preferred stock. Stock that gives its owners certain advantages over common stockholders, such as the priority to receive dividends before the common stockholders and the priority to receive assets before the common stockholders if the corporation liquidates (p. 632).

Premium on stock. Excess of the issue price of stock over its par value (p. 633).

Prepaid expense. A category of miscellaneous assets that typically expire or get used up in the near future. Examples include prepaid rent, prepaid insurance, and supplies (p. 104).

Present value. Amount a person would invest now to receive a greater amount at a future date (p. 717).

President. Chief operating officer in charge of managing the day-to-day operations of a corporation (p. 628).

Price/earnings ratio. Ratio of the market price of a share of common stock to the company's earnings per share. Measures the value that the stock market places on $1 of a company's earnings (p. 889).

Price variance. Difference between the actual unit price of an input and a standard unit price, multiplied by the actual quantity of inputs used (p. 1100).

Prime costs. Direct materials plus direct labor (p. 1004).

Principal amount. The amount loaned out by the payee and borrowed by the maker of a note (p. 381).

Prior period adjustment. Correction to retained earnings for an error of an earlier period (p. 691).

Private accountant. Accountant who works for a single business, such as a department store or General Motors (p. 5).

Process costing. System for assigning costs to goods that are mass-produced in a continuous sequence of steps (p. 1045).

Product cost. General term that denotes different costs allocated to products for different purposes (p. 1007).

Production cost report. Summary of the activity in a processing department for a period (p. 1059).

Production volume overhead variance. Difference between the flexible budget for actual production and standard overhead applied to production (p. 1106).

Pro forma data. Carefully formulated expression of predicted results, such as projections of future income and income tax (p. 1220).

Program. Set of instructions that tell the computer what to do (p. 1243).

Promissory note. A written promise to pay a specified amount of money at a particular future date (p. 381).

Proprietorship. A business with a single owner (p. 10).

Proxy. Legal document that expresses a stockholder's preference and appoints another person to cast the vote (p. 628).

Public accountant. Accountant who serves the general public and collects fees for work, which includes auditing, income tax planning and preparation, and management consulting (p. 5).

Purchase discount. Reduction in the cost of inventory that is offered by a seller as an incentive for the customer to pay promptly. A contra account to purchases (p. 213).

Purchase returns and allowances. Decrease in a buyer's debt from returning merchandise to the seller or from receiving from the seller a reduction in the amount owed. A contra account to purchases (p. 213).

Purchases. The cost of inventory that a firm buys to resell to customers in the normal course of business (p. 210).

Purchases journal. Special journal used to record all purchases of inventory, supplies, and other assets on account (p. 283).

Purchasing power gain (or loss). A purchasing power gain occurs during inflation because a company is able to pay its liabilities with dollars that are cheaper than the dollars borrowed. A purchasing power loss occurs during inflation when a creditor receives dollars that are worth less than the dollars lent (p. 1292).

Quantity discount. A purchase discount that provides a lower price per item the larger the quantity purchased (p. 212).

Quantity variance. Another name for the Efficiency variance used to control materials and labor costs in a standard cost system (p. 1100).

Quick ratio. Another name for the Acid-test ratio (pp. 389, 881).

Rate of return on common stockholders' equity. Net income minus preferred dividends, divided by average common stockholders' equity. A measure of profitability. Also called Return on common stockholders' equity (pp. 645, 887).

Rate of return on net sales. Ratio of net income to net sales. A measure of profitability. Also called Return on sales (p. 886).

Rate of return on total assets. The sum of net income plus interest expense divided by average total assets. This ratio measures the success a company has in using its assets to earn income for the persons who finance the business. Also called Return on assets (pp. 645, 886).

Raw materials inventory. Another name for Materials inventory (p. 1002).

Real account. Another name for a Permanent account—asset, liability, and capital—that are *not* closed at the end of the period (p. 159).

Receivable. A monetary claim against a business or an individual, acquired mainly by selling goods and services and by lending money (p. 369).

Reciprocal accounts. Two or more accounts that have the same offsetting balances and are used to control a general ledger that is kept in two or more locations (p. 1140).

Reconciliation method. Another name for the Indirect method of formatting the operating activities section of the statement of cash flows (p. 827).

Redemption value of stock. Price a corporation agrees to pay for stock, which is set when the stock is issued (p. 646).

Registered bonds. Bonds for which the owners receive interest checks from the issuing company (p. 715).

Relative sales value method. Allocation technique for identifying the cost of each asset purchased in a group for a single amount (p. 458).

Relevant information. Expected future data that differ between alternative courses of action (p. 1165).

Relevant range. Band of activity or volume in which actual operations are likely to occur. Within this range, a particular relationship exists between revenue and expenses (p. 964).

Reliability principle. Requires that accounting information be dependable (free from error and bias). Also called the Objectivity principle (p. 551).

Report format of the balance sheet. Format that lists the assets at the top, with the liabilities and owner equity below (p 168).

Residual value. Same as Estimated residual value (p. 459).

Responsibility accounting. System for classifying financial data by defined areas in an organization in order to evaluate the performance of managers for activities under their supervision (p. 1130).

Responsibility center. Any subunit of an organization needing control, the basic unit in a responsibility accounting system. The three common types of responsibility centers are the cost center, the profit center, and the investment center (p. 1130).

Retail method. A way to estimate inventory cost based on the cost-of-goods-sold model. The retail method requires that the business record inventory purchases both at cost and at retail. Multiply ending inventory at retail by the cost ratio to estimate the ending inventory's cost (p. 427).

Retained earnings. A corporation's capital that is earned through profitable operation of the business (p. 630).

Return on assets. Another name for Rate of return on total assets (pp. 645, 886).

Return on common stockholders' equity. Another name for Rate of return on common stockholders' equity (pp. 645, 887).

Return on sales. Another name for Rate of return on net sales (p. 886).

Revenue. Increase in owner equity that is earned by delivering goods or services to customers or clients (p. 16).

Revenue expenditure. Expenditure that merely maintains an asset in its existing condition or restores the asset to good working order. Revenue expenditures are expensed (matched against revenue) (p. 478).

Revenue principle. The basis for recording revenues, tells accountants when to record revenue and the amount of revenue to record (p. 101).

Reversing entry. An entry that switches the debit and the credit of a previous adjusting entry. The reversing entry is dated the first day of the period following the adjusting entry (p. 165).

Rolling budget. Another name for a Continuous budget (p. 935).

Salary. Employee compensation stated at a yearly, monthly, or weekly rate (p. 510).

Sales discount. Reduction in the amount receivable from a customer, offered by the seller as an incentive for the customer to pay promptly. A contra account to Sales revenue (p. 216).

Sales journal. Special journal used to record credit sales (p. 275).

Sales method. Method of applying the revenue principle in which revenue is recorded at the point of sale. This method is used for most sales of goods and services (p. 553).

Sales mix. Combination of products that make up total sales (p. 974).

Sales returns and allowances. Decrease in the seller's receivable from a customer's return of merchandise or from granting the customer an allowance from the amount the customer owes the seller. A contra account to Sales revenue (p. 216).

Sales revenue. Amount that a merchandiser earns from selling inventory before subtracting expenses (p. 209).

Sales volume variance. Difference between a revenue, expense, or operating income amount in the flexible budget and the corresponding amount in the static (master) budget (p. 1096).

Salvage value. Another name for Residual value or Estimated residual value (p. 459).

Segment of a business. A significant part of a company (p. 686).

Serial bonds. Bonds that mature in installments over a period of time (p. 715).

Service charge. Bank's fee for processing a depositor's transactions (p. 326).

Shareholder. Another name for Stockholder (p. 626).

Short presentation. A way to report contingent liabilities in the body of the balance sheet, after total liabilities but with no amount given (p. 508).

Short-term investment. Investment that is readily convertible to cash and that the investor intends either to convert to cash within one year or to use to pay a current liability. Also called a Marketable security, a current asset (p. 764).

Short-term liquidity. Ability to meet current payments as they come due (p. 869).

Short-term note payable. Note payable due within one year, a common form of financing (p. 501).

Short-term, self-liquidating financing. Debt incurred to buy inventories that will be sold and with the related cash collections used to pay the debt (p. 934).

Single-step income statement. Format that groups all revenues together and then lists and deducts all expenses together without drawing any subtotals (p. 229).

Slide. An accounting error that results from adding one or more zeros to a number, or from dropping a zero. For example, writing $500 as $5,000 or as $50 is a slide. A slide is evenly divisible by 9 (p. 172).

Small stock dividend. A stock dividend of less than 25 percent of the corporation's issued stock (p. 673).

Social Security tax. Another name for FICA tax (p. 512).

Software. Set of programs or instructions that cause the computer to perform the work desired (p. 273).

Specific unit cost method. Inventory cost method based on the specific cost of particular units of inventory (p. 416).

Split-off point. Juncture in the production process after which joint products are specifically identified (p. 1066).

Spreadsheet. Integrated software program that can be used to solve many different kinds of problems. An electronically prepared work sheet (pp. 154, 1255).

Stable-monetary-unit concept. Accountants' basis for ignoring the effect of inflation and making no adjustments for the changing value of the dollar (p. 550).

Standard cost. Predetermined cost that management believes the business should incur in producing an item (p. 1099).

Standard cost system. Designed to control costs by analyzing the relationship between actual costs and standard costs (p. 1099).

Standard deduction. A set amount of tax deduction that varies depending on the individual's filing status: single, married filing jointly, married filing separately, or head of household. The standard deduction is an alternative to itemizing tax deductions (p. 1210).

Stated interest rate. Another name for the Contract interest rate (p. 717).

Statement of budgeted cash receipts and disbursements. Another name for the Cash budget (p. 930).

Statement of cash flows. Reports cash receipts and cash disbursements classified according to the entity's major activities: operating, investing, and financing (p. 808).

Statement of earnings. Another name for the Income statement (p. 21).

Statement of financial position. Another name for the Balance sheet (p. 21).

Statement of operations. Another name for the Income statement (p. 21).

Statement of owner's equity. Summary of the changes in the owner equity of an entity during a specific period (p. 21).

Static budget. A budget prepared for only one level of activity (p. 1093).

Stock. Shares into which the owners' equity of a corporation is divided (p. 626).

Stock dividend. A proportional distribution by a corporation of its own stock to its stockholders (p. 672).

Stock split. An increase in the number of outstanding shares of stock coupled with a proportionate reduction in the par value of the stock (p. 675).

Stock subscription. Contract that obligates an investor to purchase the corporation's stock at a later date (p. 635).

Stockholder. A person who owns the stock of a corporation (p. 10).

Stockholders' equity. Owners' equity of a corporation (p. 630).

Straight-line method. Depreciation method in which an equal amount of depreciation expense is assigned to each year (or period) of asset use (p. 460).

Strong currency. A currency that is rising relative to other nations' currencies (p. 781).

Subsequent event. An event that occurs after the end of a company's accounting period but before publication of its financial statements and which may affect the interpretation of the information in those statements (p. 558).

Subsidiary company. An investee company in which a parent company owns more than 50 percent of the voting stock (p. 769).

Subsidiary ledger. Book of accounts that provides supporting details on individual balances, the total of which appears in a general ledger account (p. 277).

Sum-of-years-digits (SYD) method. An accelerated depreciation method by which depreciation is figured by multiplying the depreciable cost of the asset by a fraction. The denominator of the SYD fraction is the sum of the years' digits of the asset's life. The numerator of the SYD fraction starts with the asset life in years and decreases by one each year thereafter (p. 462).

Sunk cost. Actual outlay incurred in the past and is present under all alternative courses of action. Sunk cost is irrelevant because it makes no difference to a current decision (p. 1174).

Surtax. An additional tax often designed to shift more of the tax burden to high-income taxpayers (p. 1216).

Tax avoidance. Structuring of business transactions in order to pay the least amount of income tax at the latest possible time permitted by the law (p. 1219).

Tax credit. Amount that is subtracted directly from the amount of tax owed to the government (p. 1213).

Tax-deferred compensation. Compensation that postpones the payment of taxes until the employee receives the money. Also called Tax-sheltered compensation (p. 1223).

Tax evasion. Illegal activity designed to reduce tax (p. 1219).

Tax return. Document on which each taxpayer reports income and shows the computation of income tax (p. 1206).

Tax-sheltered compensation. Another name for Tax-deferred compensation (p. 1223).

Taxable income. Earnings amount on which the income tax is based. It is the figure that is multiplied by the tax rate to compute the amount of income tax (p. 1207).

Temporary account. Another name for a nominal account. The revenue and expense accounts that relate to a particular accounting period and are closed at the end of the period are temporary accounts. For a proprietorship, the owner withdrawal account is also temporary *(p. 159)*.

Term bonds. Bonds that all mature at the same time for a particular issue *(p. 715)*.

Time and a half. Overtime pay computed as 150 percent (1.5 times) the straight-time rate *(p. 510)*.

Time-period concept. Ensures that accounting information is reported at regular intervals *(pp. 102, 550)*.

Time value of money. The fact that one can earn income by investing money for a period of time *(p. 1181)*.

Times-interest-earned ratio. Ratio of income from operations to interest expense. Measures the number of times that operating income can cover interest expense. Also called the Interest-coverage ratio *(p. 885)*.

Total income. In taxation, all income from whatever source derived *(p. 1208)*.

Total manufacturing cost. Sum of direct materials used, direct labor, and factory overhead. Total manufacturing cost is used to compute cost of goods manufactured, which is part of cost of goods sold *(p. 1005)*.

Trademarks and trade names. Distinctive identifications of a product or service *(p. 476)*.

Trading on the equity. Earning more income on borrowed money than the related expense, which increases the earnings for the owners of the business *(pp. 733, 888)*.

Transaction. An event that affects the financial position of a particular entity and may be reliably recorded *(p. 14)*.

Translation adjustment. An element of stockholders' equity that arises from the translation of foreign-currency financial statements into dollars. The translation adjustment is the balancing figure that brings total liabilities and stockholders' equity into agreement with total assets *(p. 785)*.

Transposition. An accounting error that occurs when digits are flip-flopped. For example, $85 is a transposition of $58. A transposition is evenly divisible by 9 *(p. 172)*.

Treasury stock. A corporation's own stock that it has issued and later reacquired *(p. 677)*.

Trial balance. A list of all the ledger accounts with their balances *(p. 58)*.

Uncollectible account expense. Cost to the seller of extending credit. Arises from the failure to collect from credit customers *(p. 371)*.

Underapplied overhead. Debit balance remaining in the Factory Overhead account after overhead is applied, means that actual overhead cost exceeded the amount applied to jobs or products *(p. 1019)*.

Underwriter. Organization that purchases the bonds or stock from an issuing company and resells them to its clients, or sells the bonds or stock for a commission, agreeing to buy all unsold bonds or stock *(p. 714)*.

Unearned revenue. A liability created when a business collects cash from customers in advance of doing work for the customer. The obligation is to provide a product or a service in the future. Also called Deferred revenue *(p. 111)*.

Unemployment compensation tax. Payroll tax paid by employers to the government, which uses the money to pay unemployment benefits to people who are out of work *(p. 513)*.

Units-of-production (UOP) method. Depreciation method by which a fixed amount of depreciation is assigned to each unit of output produced by the plant asset *(p. 461)*.

Unlimited personal liability. When a partnership (or a proprietorship) cannot pay its debts with business assets, the partners (or the proprietor) must use personal assets to meet the debt *(p. 585)*.

Usage variance. Another name for the Efficiency variance used to control materials and labor costs in a standard cost system *(p. 1100)*.

Useful life. Same as Estimated useful life *(p. 459)*.

Value chain. Sequence of all business functions in which value is added to a firm's products or services *(p. 1000)*.

Variable cost. Cost that changes in total in direct proportion with changes in volume or activity *(p. 960)*.

Variable expense. Expense that changes in total in direct proportion with changes in volume or activity *(p. 960)*.

Variance. Difference between an actual amount and the corresponding budget amount *(p. 1093)*.

Vertical analysis. Analysis of a financial statement that reveals the relationship of each statement item to the total, which is the 100 percent figure *(p. 872)*.

Voucher. Document authorizing a cash disbursement *(p. 336)*.

Voucher register. Special journal used to record all expenditures in a voucher system, similar to but more comprehensive than the purchases journal *(p. 338)*.

Voucher system. A way to record cash payments that enhances internal control by formalizing the process of approving and recording invoices for payment *(p. 336)*.

Wages. Employee pay stated at an hourly figure *(p. 510)*.

Weak currency. A currency that is falling relative to other nations' currencies *(p. 781)*.

Weighted-average cost method. Inventory costing method based on the weighted-average cost of inventory during the period. Weighted-average cost is determined by dividing the cost of goods available for sale by the number of units available. Also called the Average cost method (p. 416).

Withheld income tax. Income tax deducted from employees' gross pay (p. 511).

Work in process inventory. Cost of the goods that are in the manufacturing process and not yet complete (p. 1002).

Work sheet. A columnar document designed to help move data from the trial balance to the financial statements (p. 146).

Working capital. Current assets minus current liabilities; measures a business's ability to meet its short-term obligations with its current assets (p. 879).

Company Index

A

Abbott Laboratories, 832
Adidas, 999
Air Products and Chemicals, Inc., 730
Allstate Insurance Company, 762
American Airlines, 209, 500
American Express, 379
American Motors Corporation, 959
AMF Inc., 1290–96
Anacomp, Inc., 890
Apple Computer Inc., 999
Arthur Andersen & Company, 5
Austin Sound Stereo Center, 210–14, 219, 221–22, 223, 224, 225, 226–28, 230, 231, 258–63, 275–76, 283–84
Avis Rental Car, 476

B

Bank of America, 9, 779
Bethlehem Steel, 632
Birmingham Steel Corporation, 645, 731–32
Black and Decker Manufacturing Company, 420, 686
Bobbie Brooks, 388
Boeing Company, 8, 762–63, 779, 868–69
Bowl America, 316

C

Carte Blanche, 379
CBS, Inc., 425, 626
Chesebrough-Pond's, Inc., 880, 881, 886, 887
Chromalloy American Corporation, 682
Chrysler Corporation, 959, 960
Coca-Cola, 10, 779, 877
Consolidated Edison Company (ConEd), 476
Coopers & Lybrand, 5
CPC International, Inc., 559

D

Dallas Cowboys, 476
Data General, 625, 626
Deere & Company, 388, 975
Deloitte & Touche, 5
Diners Club, 268, 271, 379
Disciplined Investment Advisors Inc. (DIA), 867, 868, 890
Donna Karan Company, 208, 209
Dorman Builders, 383–85, 386–87
Dresser Industries, Inc., 556
Dun & Bradstreet (DB) Corporation, 505

E

Eastman Kodak, 465
Ernst & Young, 5, 545
Exxon, 548–49, 779

F

Federal-Mogul Corporation, 418–19
Financial Proformas, Inc., 807
FMC Corporation, 455
Ford Motor Company, 779
Frito-Lay, Inc., 430

G

General Electric Company, 9, 383–85, 386–87, 388, 761
General Mills, Inc., 318, 880, 887, 1099
General Motors Corporation (GM), 11, 626, 761, 762, 767, 769, 881, 886, 887, 890, 936
Georgia-Pacific, 1067–68
Goodyear Tire & Rubber Company, 10, 229
Grace, W. R., & Company, 786
Great Northern Nekoosa Corporation, 647
Gulf Oil, 465

H

Hasbro Inc., 98
Hawaiian Airlines, Inc., 168, 169, 170

Heinz, H. J., Company, 504
Hewlett-Packard Company, 999, 1068
Holiday Inns, 209, 476

I

International Business Machines Corporation (IBM), 10, 509, 626, 713, 779, 877, 880, 881, 886, 887, 999
Isuzu, 767

J

JVC, 210–14, 216

K

Kentucky Fried Chicken, 686
Kidder Peabody, 645
K mart, 432, 935
Kohlberg Kravis Roberts, 733
Kraft, Inc., 332, 779, 886

L

Laitier S. A., 1129, 1131, 1133
Libbey-Owens-Ford, 769
Lincoln Savings Association, 545
Lotus Development Corporation, 918

M

McDonald's, 476
Marshall Field & Company, 45, 428
Master Card, 379
Mattel, 98
Merrill Lynch, 645, 713, 762, 875
Midland-Ross Corporation, 421
Montgomery Ward, 808
Moody's, 879
Motorola, Inc., 9, 420, 465

N

Nashua Corporation, 388
National Can Corporation, 389
NBC, 476
NCR, 1068
Nike, Inc., 830–31, 999, 1000

O

Occidental Petroleum, 116

P

Peat Marwick Main & Company, 5
Pendleton Woolen Mills, 1165
Penney, J. C., Company, 101, 273, 420, 432, 632, 935, 1044, 1092
Pennsylvania Power and Light, 889
PepsiCo Inc., 626
Phillips Petroleum Company, 556
Pizza Time Theatre, Inc., 503
Polaroid Corporation, 413, 420
Premark International, Inc., 388
Price Waterhouse & Company, 5, 593
Prime Motor Inns, 807, 809
Prime Western, Inc., 731
Procter & Gamble, 9, 877, 890, 1002
Prudential Bache, 762
Public Service Electric and Gas Company, 936
Purolator, Inc., 686

R

Ralston Purina, 632
Raytheon, 341–42
Reebok, 999, 1000
Revco D.S., Inc., 413, 414
Reynolds Company, 963
RJR Nabisco, Inc., 558–59, 686, 733
Robert Morris Associates, 875, 879, 881, 885

S

Salomon Brothers, 713
Scott Paper Company, 558
Sears, Roebuck and Company, 432, 465, 508, 558, 762, 808, 935, 1044
Southland Corporation, 734, 759
Sperry Corporation, 729
Sportster, The, 999
Standard & Poor's, 879
Superior Oil Company, 880, 887

T

Tenneco, 737
Texaco Corporation, 7

Texas Utilities, 889
3M Corporation, 9
Tootsie Roll Industries, Inc., 103
Toyota, 767

U

Union Pacific Corporation, 558
Unisys Corporation, 522, 523
United Airlines, 476
United Brands, Inc., 1129, 1131
United Merchants and Manufacturers, Inc., 558

V

VISA, 379

W

Walt Disney Productions, 469
Wendy's, 559
Westinghouse Electric Corporation, 413
Weyerhaeuser, 1067–68

Subject Index

A

Accelerated-depreciation method, 462, 464

Account(s), 46–49
  adjustments to, 99, 103–12
  chart of, 64–65, 1247
  closing of, 157–62, 258–63
  increases and decreases in, 50–52
  normal balances of, 65
  permanent (real), 159–60
  reciprocal, 1140
  temporary (nominal), 157–59
  See also specific accounts

Accountants:
  private, 5
  public, 5

Accountant's work sheet. See Work sheet

Account format:
  four-column, 63–64
  "T," 49–50

Account format (balance sheet), 168, 171

Accounting, 2
  activity-based, 1061–66
  and computers, 73, 116, 118, 1242–46 (see also Computer-assisted accounting systems)
  conservatism in, 423, 560
  constraints on, 559–60
  debit-credit language of, 52
  and decision making, 168–71
  development of, 4–5
  everyday application of, 1
  and financial decisions, 2
  financial and management accounting, 10
  and inflation, 1290
  as profession, 5–6
  public and private accounting, 5, 8–10
  separation of custody of assets from, 320–21
  separation of duties within, 321
  separation of operations from, 319
  synonyms in, 962

Accounting, areas of application in. See Branch accounting; Consolidation accounting; Management accounting; Manufacturing accounting; Responsibility accounting

Accounting basis. See Measurement of business income

Accounting changes. See Changes, accounting

Accounting controls, 317. See also Internal control

Accounting cycle, 145–46

Accounting equation, 13–15, 629
  and balance sheet, 23
  and debits/credits, 50
  as fundamental, 72
  and transaction analysis, 14

Accounting errors. See Errors

Accounting firms ("Big Six"), 5

Accounting Horizons journal, 7

Accounting income, 1205

Accounting income before income tax, 1215

Accounting information (data):
  analytical use of, 72–73
  comparable, 548, 560, 563
  in decision making, 168–71, 230–31, 389, 548, 549, 1289 (see also Decision making)
  flow of, 54
  private (inside), 891
  processing of in practice, 46
  relevant, 548, 560, 563, 1165–66
  reliable, 548, 560, 563
  users of, 3–4

Accounting information system, 269, 274, 275
  compatibility of, 271
  and computer data processing, 272–74
  control through, 270
  cost/benefit relationship of, 271
  design and installation of, 9, 269–70
  flexibility of, 271
  and information processing model, 270, 271

Accounting organizations, 6–7

Accounting period, 100–101
  and accounting cycle, 145–46
  and bond interest expense, 722

Accounting policies, and disclosure principle, 556

Accounting principles. See Generally accepted accounting principles; Principles and concepts

Accounting Principles Board (APB), 546
  on intangible assets, 477

Accounting rate of return, 1179–80, 1187

Accounting Review, The, 7

Accounting services, specialized, 8–10

Accounts payable, 14
  in consolidation accounting, 771, 773
  as current asset, 167
  as current liability, 168, 501
  vs. notes payable, 15
  in statement of cash flows, 820–21

Accounts payable account, 67
  and adjusted trial balance, 114

Accounts payable module, 1253–54, 1255

Accounts payable subsidiary ledger, 283, 287

Accounts receivable, 14, 369
  and computers, 342, 390
  internal controls over collection of, 379–80
  separation of authority to write off, 321

Accounts receivable account, 46–47, 67
  accounts payable as opposite of, 47
  as control account, 277–78
  credit balances in, 378

Accounts Receivable ledger, 277, 280

Accounts Receivable module, 390, 1250–52

Accounts receivable turnover, 882–83

Account titles, 67–68

Accrual-basis accounting, 99–100
  and adjustment process, 103, 157
  and income taxes, 1221–22
  and time-period concept, 102–3, 550

Accrual entries, 103, 550

Accrued expenses, 109–10, 504–5
    reversing entries for, 163–65
Accrued revenue, 110–11
    reversing entries for, 166–67
Accumulated benefit obligation, 736
Accumulated deficit, 631
Accumulated depreciation, 459
Accumulated Depreciation account,
    107–8
Acid-test (quick) ratio, 389–90, 881
Acquisitions:
    in statement of cash flows, 815,
        823–24
    See also Consolidation accounting
Activity-based costing (ABC) or
        accounting, 1061–63
    and management decisions,
        1064–66
    and product costing, 1063–64
Additional Paid-in Capital, 634
Adjusted bank balance, 327
Adjusted book balance, 327
Adjusted gross income, 1208
Adjusted trial balance, 114, 115
    financial statements prepared
        from, 114–16
    in work sheet, 146–53
Adjusting entries, 99, 104, 107
    and accrual basis, 103, 157
    for accrued expenses, 109
    for accrued revenues, 110–11
    and computer, 116, 258
    for depreciation, 107–9
    for interest expense, 722–23
    for merchandising business,
        221–24, 226–28, 258–63
    posting of, 112–13
    and prepaid expenses, 104–6,
        198–200
    recording of, 157
    and reversing entries, 163, 165
        (see also Reversing entries)
    for unearned revenue, 111–12,
        201, 202–3
    and work sheet, 147
Adjustments to the accounts
        (''adjusting the books''), 99,
        103–12
Administrative controls, 317
Administrative expenses, in
        departmental accounting,
        1138
Advertising, in departmental
        accounting, 1136–37
Advertising expense account, 68
Aging the accounts, 375
Aging of accounts receivable method,
    374–77
Allocation base, 1135, 1136
Allowance method, 371
Allowances, purchase, 213–14
Allowances, reporting of, 388–89
Allowances, sales, 216
Allowance for Uncollectible Accounts
        (Allowance for Doubtful
        Accounts), 371

American Accounting Association
    (AAA), 7
American Institute of Certified Public
        Accountants (AICPA), 6,
        419, 546
    code of professional conduct of,
        7–8
Amortization, 475–77
    of bond discount, 720–21
    of bond premium, 722
    effective-interest method of,
        725–29
    in statement of cash flows, 814,
        827–28
Amortized cost method, for
        long-term investments in
        bonds, 776–77
Analysis, ratios in, 879. See also
    Ratios, financial
Analysis of transactions. See
    Transaction analysis
Annuity, 1182
    future value of (table), 1309
    present value of, 757–58
    present value of (table), 757,
        1306–7
Appropriations of retained earnings,
    682–83
Arrears, 642
Articles of partnership, 584–85
Asset(s), 13, 46, 561
    accounting value of, 423
    on balance sheet, 67
    capital, 1177
    as credit/debit, 50–51, 66
    current, 167–68, 369–70 (see also
        Current assets)
    and debt ratio, 170
    expired, 105
    fully depreciated, 470
    intangible, 456, 475–77, 641
    long-term, 167–68, 714
    obsolescence of, 459
    plant, 107, 456, 829 (see also Plant
        assets)
    in statement of cash flows, 829
Asset accounts, 46–47, 48, 67
    normal balance of, 65, 66
    as permanent, 159–60
    and work sheet, 150
Assignment of responsibilities, 319
Auditing, 8
    internal, 9
Audits, internal and external, 321
Authorization, as control measure,
    319
Authorization for stock issue, 633,
    634
Automatic deposits, paying
        employees by, 517
Average cost method, 416

B

Bad debt expense, 371
Balance of account, 51

Balance sheet, 21
    budgeted, 932, 933
    current cost/constant-dollar,
        1295–96
    elements of, 561
    formats of, 168
    horizontal analysis of, 871
    for manufacturing and for
        merchandising, 1001
    and statement of owner's equity,
        116, 117
    vertical analysis of, 874
Balancing the ledgers, 290–91
Bank account, as control device,
    322–29
Bank collections, 325
Bank reconciliation, 323–24, 326–29
Bank statements, 323
Bar coding, and activity-based
        costing, 1063
Basis of accounting. See Measurement
    of business income
Basket (group) purchases of assets,
    458
Batch processing, 273
Beginning inventory, 413
Behavioral implications of course of
        action, 920
Best use of facilities, 1172, 1173–74
''Big Six,'' accounting firms, 5
Bill (invoice), 211, 337, 338
Board of directors, 628
Bond indentures, 729
Bonds, 714
    convertible, 731
    investments in, 774–77
    prices of, 716–18
    vs. stock, 732–33
    types of, 715–16
Bond sinking fund, 729–30
Bonds payable, 714
    issuing of, 718–22
    present value of, 758
    reporting of, 722
    retirement of, 730–31
Bonus, 510
Bookkeeping, 2–3
    double-entry, 4, 49
Books, 46
Book value, 108, 168, 461, 647–48
Book value per share of common
        stock, 890
Brady, Larry, 455
Branch accounting, 1139–44
Branch-factory ledger control
        account, 1141
Branch ledger, 1140
Break-even analysis, 965–70
Breakeven point, 966
Breen, William, 867
Budget(s) and budgeting system 9,
    921–22
    benefits of, 922–23

capital, 1177–80, 1187, 1188 (*see also* Capital-budgeting models)
  continuous (rolling), 935
  flexible, 1093–97, 1099–1100
  master budget, 921, 924–26, 932 (*see also* Master budget)
  master budget preparation, 926–33
  and performance report, 923–24, 1093
  and sales forecasting, 933–34
  and short-term financing, 934–35
  static, 1093
  variance from, 1093 (*see also* Variance)
Budget committee, 921–22
Budgeted factory overhead rate, 1017–18
Budget expense formula, graphing of, 1094–95
Budget formula, 1093
Budget period, 922
Building account, 47, 67
Buildings, cost of, 457
Business assets. *See* Assets
Business decisions. *See* Decision making
Business experience, accounting provides, 6
Business income, measurement of. *See* Measurement of business income
Business organizations, types of, 10–11
Business segments, 558
Bylaws, 628
Byproducts, 1067

C

Callable bonds, 730
Campeau, Robert, 733
Capital, 13, 47
  cost of, 1182
  as credit/debit, 66
  donated, 639–40
  sources of, 630
  working, 879–80
Capital account:
  and closing entries, 160
  normal balance of, 66
  as permanent, 159
Capital asset, 1177
Capital budgeting, 1177–80
  and computer, 1188
  and lease or buy decision, 1187
Capital-budgeting models, 1178
  accounting rate of return, 1179–80, 1187
  comparison of, 1186–87
  internal rate of return, 1185–86, 1187
  net present value, 1181–85, 1187

  payback, 1178–79, 1187
Capital deficiency, 604
Capital expenditures, 478–79
Capital expenditures budget, 924
Capital gains and losses (income tax), 1211, 1216
Capital leases, 734, 735, 759
Capital stock. *See* Stock
Career paths, for accountants, 5–6
Cash, 812
  reporting of, 331–32
Cash account, 46, 67
  and adjusted trial balance, 114
Cash-basis accounting, 100
  and income taxes, 1222
Cash budget, 930
Cash disbursements:
  internal control over, 333–41
  for payroll, 518–19, 521–22
Cash disbursements journal, 285–87, 288
Cash dividends, 672
Cash effect, 54
Cash equivalents, 812
Cash flows, 808. *See also* Liquidity
Cash flows, statement of. *See* Statement of cash flows
Cash receipts, internal control over, 322, 332–33
Cash receipts journal, 278–81
Cash short and over account, 333, 336
Cells (spreadsheet), 1257–58
  addresses of, 1263–64
Central processing unit (CPU), 1244–45
Certified Public Accountants (CPAs), 5–6
  and GAAP, 546
Chairperson, 628
Changes, accounting:
  in accounting estimate, 469, 557
  in accounting principle, 557, 687
  disclosure of, 557
Chart of accounts, 64–65, 1247
Charter, 626, 628
Check, bank, 323
  canceled, 323
  NSF, 326
  payroll, 517
Check register, 285, 339, 341
Closing the accounts, 157–62, 258–63
Closing entries, 160
  for merchandising business, 221–24, 226–28
Codes of ethical conduct, 7–8
"Collect cash on account," 18
Collection method, 553
Commission, 510
Common-size statements, 874–75
Common stock, 632
  dividends on, 641–42
  issuing of, 633–37
Comparability principle, 551–52

Comparable information, 548, 560, 563
Compatibility, of accounting information system, 271
Completed-contract method, 555
Compound entry, 69
Compound interest, 1181
Computer, 73, 272
Computer-assisted accounting systems, 73, 1242–46
  and accounting process, 116, 118
  and accounts receivable, 390
  and adjusting-entry method, 116, 258
  in business decision analysis, 1187–88
  buy signals generated on, 867
  and consolidations, 786
  and corporate financial planning, 737
  for current liabilities, 522–23
  and custody of assets, 320–21
  and depreciation, 475
  and financial statement analysis, 891–92
  and income taxes, 1223–24
  and internal control, 341–42
  and inventory, 231
  and JIT system, 1068
  keyboard for, 1259–60
  and manufacturing accounting, 1022
  mode indicators in, 1260–61
  and responsibility accounting, 1144
  security of, 271, 342
  software for, 73, 273, 1246–55 (*see also* Software, accounting)
  and special journals, 291
  spreadsheets, 154, 1255, 1257–59 (*see also* Spreadsheets)
  and standard costs, 1110
  and statement of cash flows, 831–32
Computer data processing, 272–74
Computerized inventory records, 432
Conceptual Framework Project, 547
Conservatism, 423, 560
Consignment, 415
Consistency principle, 421, 552
Consolidated statements, 769
Consolidation accounting, 769–74
  and computers, 786
  for foreign subsidiaries, 784–85
Constant-dollar accounting, 1290–96
Constraint, 1171
Consumer groups, as accounting users, 4
Consumer Price Index (CPI), 1289, 1290
  and inflation adjustment, 1293
Contingent liabilities, 508–9
  on discounted notes receivable, 386
  stock discounts as, 634

Continuing operations, 685–86
Continuity concept, 549–50
Continuous (rolling) budgets, 935
Contra account, 108
　　parenthetical presentation of, 219
Contra asset account, 108
Contract interest rate, 717
Contributed capital, 630
Contribution margin, 963, 967
Contribution margin approach to
　　decision making, 963,
　　967–68
　　and special sales order, 1167–68
Contribution margin income
　　statement, 963
Contribution margin percentage, 967
Control, information system for, 270
Control, internal. See Internal control
Control account, 277
Controllable overhead variance,
　　1105–6
Controlling (majority) interest, 769
Control of plant assets, 473–74
Conversion costs, 1004, 1049, 1052
　　with activity-based costing, 1063
　　in second department, 1055, 1056
Convertible bonds (notes), 731
Convertible preferred stock, 644
Copyrights, 476
Corporate financial planning, and
　　computers, 737
Corporate income tax, 627, 1207,
　　1215–19
　　and business decisions, 1219–24
　　and depreciation, 466–68, 475,
　　1222–23
　　and double taxation, 627, 1207
　　and LIFO, 418–19
　　and organization-cost
　　amortization, 641
　　See also Taxes
Corporation, 10, 626
　　characteristics of, 626–28
　　organization of, 628–29
Corporation income statement,
　　683–89
Correcting entry, 171
Cosigning a note, 508
Cost(s), 459, 1091
　　of capital, 1182
　　conversion, 1004, 1049, 1052,
　　1055, 1056, 1063
　　current, 1290
　　current replacement, 423–24
　　depreciable, 460 (see also
　　Depreciation)
　　fixed, 961, 962, 1091–92, 1173 (see
　　also Fixed cost)
　　full product, 1006, 1007, 1064
　　historical, 12, 1289, 1290, 1291,
　　1292–95
　　inventoriable, 1005–7
　　joint product, 1066–67
　　manufacturing product, 1006,
　　1007
　　mixed, 961, 962, 976–78

opportunity, 1175
organization, 640–41
period, 1006–7
prime, 1004
product, 1006–7
specific (unit), 415–16
standard, 1099 (see also Standard
　　cost systems)
sunk, 1174–75
total manufacturing, 1005
variable, 960–61, 970, 1091–92
see also Expense
Cost accounting, 9
Cost accounting for manufacturers.
　　See Manufacturing
　　accounting
Cost allocation, 1135
Cost application base, 1017
Cost behavior, 960
Cost behavior patterns, 1091–92
Cost-benefit criterion, 919–20
Cost/benefit relationship, of
　　accounting information
　　system, 271
Cost center, 1130–31
Cost control, as objective, 1000
Cost driver, 960
　　and overhead cost, 1062
Cost of goods manufactured, 1002–3,
　　1004–5
Cost of goods sold (cost of sales),
　　209, 217–19, 413
　　and current cost vs. historical
　　cost, 1291
Costing, inventory. See Inventory
　　costing methods
Costing, for manufactures. See
　　Manufacturing accounting
Cost method, for short-term
　　investments (with LCM),
　　764–67
Cost object, 1061
Cost of a plant asset, 456–58
Cost principle, 12, 552
Cost of products. See Product costing
Cost-volume-profit (CVP) analysis,
　　960, 965–72
　　assumptions underlying, 974
　　computer spreadsheet for,
　　978–79
Coupon bonds, 715
CPA. See Certified Public
　　Accountants
CPA firms, 5
Credit, 49–50
　　recording of, 50–52
Credit balances, in accounts
　　receivable, 378
Credit card sales, 379
Credit department, 370–71
Credit memorandum, 287–88
Creditors, 369
　　as accounting-information users,
　　3–4
　　and liability due dates, 167–68

Credits, in computerized system, 73
Credit sales journal, 275
Criminal activities. See Fraud;
　　Internal control; Theft
Cumulative preferred stock, 642–43
Currency, foreign, 780–81
Current assets, 167, 369–70
　　common-size analysis of, 875
　　and current ratio, 169–70
　　and statement of cash flows, 829
Current cost, 1290
Current-cost accounting, 1290–96
Current liabilities, 168
　　airline frequent-flyer giveaways,
　　500, 507–8
　　computer accounting systems,
　　522–23
　　and current ratio, 169–70
　　to be estimated, 506–8
　　of known amount, 501–6
　　and statement of cash flows, 829
Current portion of long-term debt,
　　504, 731–32
Current ratio, 169–70, 880–81
Current replacement cost, 423–24
Customer deposits payable, 505–6
Customer prepayments, 505
Cutoff rate, 1182
Cycles:
　　accounting, 145–46
　　operating, 167, 210

D

Database management system, 1144
Data processing, computer, 272–74
Date of declaration, 641
Date of payment, 641
Date of record, 641
Days' sales in receivables, 389–90,
　　883–84
Debentures, 716
Debit, 49–50
　　in computerized system, 73
　　recording of, 50–52
Debit memorandum, 289
Debt:
　　long-term, 504, 731–32, 884–86
　　in statement of cash flows,
　　815–16, 824–25
　　vs. stock, 732–33
　　see also Bonds
Debtor, 369
Debt ratio, 170, 884–85
Decision making:
　　and accounting, 2
　　accounting information in,
　　168–71, 230–31, 389, 548,
　　549, 1289
　　and activity-based costing,
　　1064–66
　　complexity of, 890–91
　　computers in, 1187–88
　　contribution margin approach to,
　　963, 967–68, 1167–68

cost-volume-profit (CVP) analysis
in, 960, 965–72, 974, 978–79
through financial statement
analysis, 868–77, 891–92
and market efficiency, 891
and opportunity cost, 1175
ratios for, 169–71, 879–80 (*see
also* Ratios, financial)
relevant information for, 1165–66
tax factors in, 1219–24
Decision making, special areas of:
deletion of products/
departments/territories,
1169–71
facility use, 1173–74
make or buy, 1172–73
product emphasis, 1171–72
sell as-is or process further,
1174–75
special sales orders, 1166–69
Decision model, 1177
Declaration date, 641
Deductions, itemized, 1208
Defaulting on bond, 716
Defaulting on note, 386–87
Deferred (unearned) revenues,
111–12, 201–4, 505
Deficit, 670
Retained Earnings
(accumulated), 631
Deletion of product/department/
territory, 1169–71
Departmental accounting, 1134–39
Departments, deletion of, 1169–71
Dependents, 1207
Depletion, in statement of cash
flows, 814, 827–28
Depletion expense, 474–75
Deposits:
automatic (to employees), 517
lock-box system, 325
in transit, 324
Deposit ticket, for banks, 323
Depreciable cost, 460
Depreciation, 107, 458–59
accumulated, 459
and change in accounting
estimate, 557
and change in useful life, 469–70
and computers, 475
and current vs. historical cost,
1291–92
in departmental accounting, 1136
disclosure of, 556
and disposal of plant assets,
470–75
double-declining-balance (DDB)
method of, 462–63, 464–65
and fully depreciated assets, 470
and land, 456
and land improvements, 457, 458
MACRS method of, 467,
1216–18, 1223

measuring of, 459–60
for partial years, 468–69
of plant assets, 458–59
in statement of cash flows, 814,
827–28
straight-line (SL) method of,
460–61, 464–65
sum-of-years-digits (SYD)
method of, 463–65
and taxes, 466–68, 475, 1222–23
units-of-production (UOP)
method of, 461–62, 464–65
Design of accounting information
system, 9, 269–70
Dilution, of EPS, 689
Direct expenses, 1134
Direct labor, 1003
Direct labor variances, 1103
Direct materials, 1003
in job cost system, 1011–13
in process costing, 1052, 1055,
1056
Direct materials variance, 1101–2
Direct method (statement of cash
flows), 812
with work sheet, 858–61
Direct write-off method (bad debts),
377
Disbursements, petty cash, 335–36
Disclosure principle, 556–59
Discontinued operations, 686
Discount:
on bond, 716
from purchase price, 212–13
sales, 216–17
on stock, 634
Discounted cash flow models:
internal rate of return (IRR),
1185–86, 1187
net present value, 1181–85, 1187
Discounting a note payable, 502–3
Discounting a note receivable, 384–85
Discount rate, 1182
Dishonoring of note, 386–87
Disk drive, 1244
Diskette, 1244, 1245
Disposal value, 1175
Dissolution, 585
of partnership, 593–97
Distributions to owners, 562
Dividend dates, 641
Dividends, 631
on common stock, 641–42
preferred, 641–44, 689
in statement of cash flows, 812,
814, 816, 825–27
stock, 672–75, 676
Dividends-received deduction, 1215
Dividend yield, 889–90
Document printing, computerized,
1243
Documents, 322
as journals, 291
Domini, Andrea, 1044

Donated capital, 639–40
Double-counting, and consolidation
accounting, 770
Double-declining-balance (DDB)
method of depreciation,
462–63, 464–65
Double-entry bookkeeping, 4, 49
Double taxation, 627, 1207
Doubtful account expense, 371
Drawing, 19, 592. *See also*
Withdrawals, owner
Duties, separation of. *See* Separation
of duties

E

Earnings per share of common stock
(earnings per share, EPS),
687–88, 888
Earnings record, 519, 520
Effective-interest method of
amortization, 725–29
Effective interest rate, 717–18
Effective tax rate, 1216
Efficiency variance, 1099, 1100–1102
Efficient capital market, 891
Electronic funds transfer (EFT), 342
Electronic spreadsheet. *See*
Spreadsheets
Employee compensation, 510
Employee Social Security (FICA) Tax,
512–13
Employer FICA Tax, 513
Ending inventory, 413
Entity, 11
Entity concept, 11–12, 18, 548–49
example of, 18
eom terms, 213
Equation, accounting. *See* Accounting
equation
Equation approach, 966–67
Equipment, cost of, 457
Equipment, furniture and fixtures
account, 47
Equity, 13–14. *See also* Owner's
equity; Stockholder's equity
Equity method, 767
for long-term investments,
767–69
Equity-Method Investment Revenue
account, 768
Equivalent units of production, 1050
in second department, 1055–57
Errors:
detecting and correcting, 171
inventory, 425–26
in work sheet, 150, 154
Estimated residual value, 459–60
Estimated useful life, 459
Estimated warranty payable, 506–7
Ethical considerations, 7–8
and reporting of contingent
liabilities, 508
Exchange of assets (transaction
analysis), 18

Exchange rates, foreign-currency. *See* Foreign-currency exchange rate
Exchanging of plant assets, 472–73
Excise tax, 1205
Expenditure, 478
Expense allocation, 1135, 1136
Expenses, 17, 49, 561
    accrued, 109–10, 163–65, 504–5
    direct, 1134
    expired assets as, 105
    fixed, 961, 962
    general, 224, 226
    indirect, 1134
    on income statement, 68
    mixed, 961, 962
    other, 226
    payroll, 522
    prepaid, 104–5, 198–201
    selling, 224
    variable, 960–61
    See also Cost
Expenses accounts, 49, 65–66
    closing of, 160–62
    credit/debit of, 66
    normal balance of, 66
    as temporary, 158–59
    in work sheet, 150
External auditors, 321
Extraordinary gains and losses (extraordinary items), 686–87
Extraordinary repair, 478

F

Factory ledger, 1140
Factory overhead, 1003–4
    in job cost system, 1016–18
    over- or under-applied, 1019–20
FASB. *See* Financial Accounting Standards Board
FICA taxes, 512–13
FIFO. *See* First-in, first-out method
Financial accounting, 10
    as management accounting, 920
Financial accounting standards, 7
Financial Accounting Standards Board (FASB), 6–7, 11, 546
    and comparability, 551
    Conceptual Framework Project of, 547
    on conservatism, 560
    on consolidation, 761
    on contingent vs. real liability, 509
    and financial statements, 560–61
    and inflation, 551, 562, 1290
    and purchasing-power gain, 1293
    and statement of cash flows, 812, 827
    Statement No. 3 (financial statements), 561
    Statement No. 13 (leases), 735, 736
    Statement No. 87 (pension expense), 736, 737
    Statement No. 95 (cash flow statements), 830
    See also Generally accepted accounting principles
Financial analysis, ratios in, 879. *See also* Ratios
Financial budget, 924, 930–31
Financial decisions:
    accounting as language of, 2
    see also Decision making
Financial ratios. *See* Ratios, financial
Financial reporting
    objectives of, 548, 563
    worldwide standardization of, 562
Financial statement analysis, 868–69
    and common-size statements, 874–75
    and computers, 891–92
    horizontal, 869–72
    industry comparisons with, 875–76
    and statement of cash flows, 876–77
    vertical, 872–74
Financial statements, 2, 21–23, 560–61
    from adjusted trial balance, 114–16
    consolidated, 769
    in information processing model, 270
    of merchandising business, 224–28
    partnership, 606–8
    preparing of, 157
    ratios in evaluation of, 879 (*see also* Ratios, financial)
    relationshps among, 116, 117
    in SFAC, 563
    and statement of cash flows, 808
    See also specific statements
Financing:
    off-balance-sheet, 736
    short-term, 934–35
Financing activities, 811
    and statement of cash flows, 809–11, 815–16, 824–26, 860, 861, 863
Finished Goods Inventory account, 1002, 1019, 1047
    in JIT production systems, 1068
Firms, public accounting, 5
First-in, first-out (FIFO) method, 416–18, 420, 1056
Fiscal year, 101
Fixed assets, 167. *See also* Plant assets
Fixed cost (fixed expense), 961, 962, 1091–92
    avoidable, 1173
    and break-even sales, 969
    and deletion of product/department/territory, 1169–71
    and special sales order, 1168–69
Fixtures account, 47
Fleming, Jim, 1044
Flexibility, of accounting information system, 271
Flexible budget, 1093–94
    analysis of results of, 1096–97
    and expense graph, 1094–95
    and standard costs, 1099–1100
Flexible budget (controllable) production overhead variance, 1105–6
Flexible budget variances, 1096
Flow of accounting data, 54
FOB (free on board), 214
    destination, 414
    shipping point, 414
Forecasting, sales, 933–34
Foreign Corrupt Practices Act, 317–18
Foreign-currency exchange rate, 780–81
    and consolidation of foreign subsidiaries, 784
    hedging against, 783–84
Foreign-currency transaction gain or loss, 782
Foreign currency translation adjustment, 784–85
Foreign nations, and accounting standards, 562, 785–86
Foreign subsidiaries, consolidation of, 784–85
Format:
    account, 168, 171
    of income statement, 229–30
    report, 168
Formulas (spreadsheet), 1263–65
Form W-2, 519, 521
Four-column account format, 63–64
Franchises, 476
Franchise tax, 627
Fraud, 522
    and collusion, 322
    payroll, 522
    and separation of duties, 321
    See also Internal control; Theft
Freight-in, 413
Frequent flier liability of airline company, 500, 507–8
Fringe benefits, 511, 514–15
    recording of, 519
Full product costs, 1006, 1007, 1064
Fully depreciated assets, 470
Functions (spreadshseet), 1268
Furniture account, 47
    and adjusted trial balance, 114
Future values, table of, 1308–9

G

GAAP. *See* Generally accepted accounting principles
Gains, 561
General administrative expenses, in departmental accounting, 1138
General expenses, 224, 226
General journal, 275
General ledger, 277. *See also* Ledger
General ledger module, 1246–50
Generally accepted accounting principles (GAAP), 6–7, 11, 545, 546, 547–48
    and accrual basis, 100
    on amortizing discounts and premium, 725
    and change in method, 552
    comparability, 551–52
    cost, 552
    on depreciation methods, 464
    disclosure, 556–59
    on early retirement of debt, 731
    and earnings per share, 687
    on income tax, 1218
    and inventory costing methods, 415, 420–21
    matching, 555–56
    and materiality concept, 559
    and organization-cost amortization, 641
    reliability (objectivity), 551
    revenue, 552–55
    and reversing entries, 163–67
    on small vs. large stock dividends, 673, 674
    and stable-monetary-unit concept, 1289
    and Statements of Financial Accounting Concepts, 563
    See also Financial Accounting Standards Board; Principles and concepts
Globalization of business enterprise and capital markets, 562
Going-concern (continuity) concept, 12–13, 549–50
Goldberg, Edward, 316
Goods available for sale, 413
Goodwill, 477, 641, 772
Goudal, Henri, 1129, 1134, 1144
Government regulation. *See* Regulation, government; Regulatory agencies, government
Graph, of budget expense formula, 1094–95
Griffin, Merv, 733
Gross income, 1208
Gross margin (gross profit), 209
Gross margin method, 426–27
Gross margin percentage, 230
Gross pay, 511

Group (basket) purchases of assets, 458
Guidelines. *See* Generally accepted accounting principles; Principles and concepts
Gunn, Michael, 500

H

Hand, Learned, 1205
Hard copy(ies), 1245, 1247–48
Hardware, computer, 272, 1244
Hedging, 783
    against foreign-currency transaction losses, 783–84
High-low method, 976–77
Historical cost, 12
    vs. current cost (AMF), 1291, 1292–95
    and inflation, 1289
    and inventory or plant assets, 1290
Home-office ledger, 1140
Home-office ledger control account, 1141
Horizontal analysis, 869–72
Hot checks, 326
Hurdle rate, 1182

I

Iacocca, Lee, 959
Image processing system, 268
Import/Export ratio, and exchange rate, 781
Imprest system, 336
Income:
    accounting vs. taxable, 1205
    of consolidated entity, 774
    gross, 1208
    as income-tax concept, 5
    See also Net income
Income from operations. *See* Operating income
Income statement, 21
    budgeted, 928–29
    common-size, 876
    contribution margin, 963
    corporation, 683–89
    current cost/constant-dollar, 1291–92
    elements of, 561
    format of, 229–30
    horizontal analysis of, 870
    for manufacturing and merchandising, 1003
    standard cost, 1109–10
    and statement of owner's equity, 116, 117
    vertical analysis of, 873
Income Summary account, 160, 670
Income tax, 1205–7
    amount of, 1206, 1212
    and business decisions, 1219–24
    on corporations, 1207, 1215–19

    and depreciation, 466–68, 475, 1222–23
    on individuals, 1207–13
    and LIFO, 418–19
    and microcomputers, 1223–24
    and partnership, 586, 1207
    as payroll deduction, 511–13
    through withholding and quarterly payments, 1213
    See also Taxes
Income tax allocation, 1218
Income tax expense, in statement of cash flows, 814, 822
Incorporation, of going business, 640
Incorporators, 628
Indirect expenses, 1134
Indirect labor, 1004
Indirect manufacturing cost, 1004. *See also* Factory overhead
Indirect materials, 1004
    in job cost system, 1011–13
Indirect method, 827–30
    with work sheet, 861–64
Industrial Revolution, and accounting development, 4
Industry comparisons, 875–76
Inflation, 1289
    and AMF statements, 1291, 1292, 1293–94, 1295
    and financial statements country-to-country, 562
    and inventory costing methods, 415
    and inventory profit, 420
    and purchasing-power gain, 1292, 1294
    and stable-monetary-unit concept, 13, 550
Information. *See* Accounting information
Information processing model, 270, 271
Information system. *See* Accounting information system
Information systems design, 9
Information tax return, 1207
Information technology, and activity-based costing, 1063
Input devices, 1244
Inside information, 891
Installment method, 553–54
Institute of Management Accountants (IMA), 7
    Standards of Ethical Conduct of, 8
Insurance, prepaid, 47
Intangible assets, 456, 475–77, 641
Integrated software, 1246
Interest, 382
    compound, 1181
    computing of, 383
Interest-coverage ratio, 885–86
Interest expense, 68, 226
    for bonds (adjusting entries), 722–23

Interest expense (cont.)
    on bonds issued at discount, 720
    on bonds issued at premium, 721
    in statement of cash flows, 812, 814, 822
Interest payable, as current liability, 168
Interest period, 382
Interest rate, 382
    and purchasing-power gain or loss, 1292
Interest Revenue, 48–49, 226
Interim periods, 101
Interim statements or reports, 157, 550
Internal auditing, 9
Internal auditors, 321
Internal control, 317–22
    bank account as, 322–29
    over cash disbursements, 333–41
    over cash receipts, 332–33
    over collections of accounts receivable, 379–80
    through computers, 341–42
    over inventory, 431–32
    limitations of, 322
    over payrolls, 519, 521–22
    and plant assets, 473–74
    and separation of duties, 319–21 (see also Separation of duties)
Internal rate of return (IRR), 1185–86, 1187
Internal Revenue Service (IRS), 7, 1206
International accounting, 779–80
    and foreign currencies, 780–85
    standards for, 562, 785–86
International Accounting Standards Committee (IASC), 562, 785–86
International Federation of Accountants (IFAC), 562
Inventoriable costs, 1005–7
Inventory:
    and computers, 231
    controlling cost of, 334
    and current-cost accounting, 1290, 1294–95
    and just-in-time systems, 1067–68
    sell-as-is or process-further decision on, 1174
    separation of accounting for and handling of, 320
    writing-down of, 423–24
Inventory, merchandise, 209, 413
    figuring cost of, 413–15
    internal control over, 431–32
    methods of estimating, 426–28
    purchase of, 210–15
    sale of, 215–17
Inventory account (merchandising), 67, 221
Inventory accounting systems, 218
    periodic, 218, 428–29, 1007

perpetual, 218, 429–31, 1007
Inventory accounts, manufacturing
    Finished Goods, 1002, 1019, 1047, 1068
    Materials, 1002, 1013, 1068
    vs. merchandising, 1001–2
    Work in Process, 1002, 1014–16, 1068 (see also Work in Process inventory accounts)
Inventory cost, 415
Inventory costing methods, 415
    and consistency principle, 421
    disclosure of, 556
    first-in, first-out (FIFO), 416–18, 420, 1056
    last-in, first-out (LIFO), 416–19, 420, 560, 1222
    and lower-of-cost-or-market (LCM) rule, 423–25, 560
    specific unit cost, 415–16
    weighted-average cost, 416–18, 420
Inventory errors, effect of, 425–26
Inventory profit, 420
Inventory records, computerized, 432
Inventory systems. See Inventory accounting systems
Inventory turnover, 230–31, 881–82
Investee, 763
Investing activities, 810–11
    and statement of cash flows, 809–11, 814–15, 822–24, 860, 861, 863
Investment:
    in bonds and notes, 774–77
    consolidation accounting for, 769–74
    in corporations vs. proprietorship or partnership, 10
    in financial reporting objectives, 563
    long-term, 764 (see also Long-term investments)
    in partnership, 586–88, 594–97
    short-term, 764–67, 775–76
    in statement of owner's equity, 21
    in stock, 762–74, 888–90
Investment in Affiliated Companies account, 769
Investment center, 1131
Investment Revenue account, 768
Investments account, 47
Investment services, 879
Investments by owners, 562
Investment in Subsidiary account, 770
Investors, 763
    as accounting-information users, 3–4
Invoice (bill), 211, 337, 338
Issue price, 633
Issues in Accounting Education, 7

Itemized deductions, 1208

J

Japanese manufacturing, 998
Job cost record, 1009–10
Job order costing (job costing), 1008–22
Joint product cost, 1066–67
Joint products, 1066
Journal, 52–54, 61
    for branch accounting, 1141–42, 1143
    documents as, 291
    incorrect entries in, 171
    posting from, 54
Journalizing (recording transaction), 62
    illustrative problems in, 55–57, 68–71
Junk-bond era, 733
Just-in-time (JIT) production systems, 1067–68

K

Keyboard (computer), 1259–60
Kravis, Henry, 733

L

Labor, in job cost system, 1014
Labor time ticket, 1014
Labor unions, as accounting users, 4
Land
    cost of, 457
    and depreciation, 456
Land account, 47, 67
Land improvements, cost of, 458
Language of accounting, 52
Large stock dividends, 673
Last-in, first-out (LIFO) method, 416–18, 420, 1222
    as conservative, 560
    income tax advantage of, 418–19
Lease, 734
Leasehold, 477
Lease liabilities, 734–36
Lease or buy decision, 1187
Ledger, 46, 61, 277
    balancing (proving) of, 290–91
    branch, 1140
    factory, 1140
    home-office, 1140
    posting to, 54
Ledger, subsidiary, 277
Ledger accounts after posting, 57, 71–72
Ledger module, general, 1246–50
Lerner, Eugene, 867
Lessee, 734
Lessor, 734
Leverage, 888
Leveraged buyout, 733
Liabilities, 13, 47–49, 501, 561
    on balance sheet, 67

classification of, 167–68
contingent, 386, 508–9, 634
as credit/debit, 66
current, 501–8 (see also Current liabilities)
and debt ratio, 170
lease, 734–36
long-term, 168, 714
payroll, 522
pension, 736–37
Liabilities accounts:
normal balance for, 66
as permanent, 159
in work sheet, 150
Licenses, 476
LIFO. See Last-in, first-out method
Limited liability, 627
Limiting factor, 1171
Liquidation, 602
of partnership, 601–6
Liquidation value, 647
Liquidity, 167
Loans, in statement of cash flows, 815, 823–24
Lock-box system, 325
Long-term assets, 167–68, 714
Long-term debt:
current portion of, 504, 731–32
measuring ability to pay, 884–86
Long-term investments, 764
bonds, 776
cost method for (with LCM), 767
equity method for, 767–69
Long-term liabilities, 168, 714
Long-term receivables, 369–70
Long-term solvency, 869
Losses, 561
Lower-of-cost-or-market (LCM) rule, 423–25, 560
for short-term investments, 764–67

M

Machinery, cost of, 457
MACRS (Modified Accelerated Cost Recovery System), 467, 1216–18, 1223
Mainframe computer system, 272, 1244
Maintenance cost, and cross-training for JIT, 1068
Make or buy decision, 1172–73
Maker of a note, 381
Management accounting, 10, 919–21
and budgeting system, 921–36 (see also Budget and budgeting system)
cost-benefit criterion in, 919–20
responsibility accounting, 1130–44
See also Decision making; Manufacturing accounting
Management Accounting (journal), 7
Management consulting, 8–9

Management by exception, 1133
Manufacturing, and value chain, 999–1000
Manufacturing accounting:
accounts in, 1001–3
activity-based costing, 1061–66
and byproducts, 1067
and computers, 1022
cost of goods manufactured, 1002–3, 1004–5
and cost system, 1000–1001
inventoriable costs, 1005–7
inventory accounts, 1001–2
job order costing, 1008–22
and joint product cost, 1066–67
and just-in-time systems, 1067–68
objectives of, 1000–1001
and perpetual vs. periodic inventory system, 1007
process costing, 1045–53, 1055–61
product costing, 1000–1001, 1008
terms in, 1003–5
Manufacturing overhead, 1004. See also Factory overhead
Manufacturing product costs, 1006, 1007
Manzi, Jim P., 918
Margin, 209
Margin of safety, 973–74
Marketable securities, 764
Market interest rate, 717–18
Market value, 423, 646
Master budget, 921, 932
components of, 924–26
preparing of, 926–33
"what if" analysis with, 935–36
Matching principle, 102, 555–56
Materiality concept, 559–60
and over- or under-applied overhead, 1020
Materials, in job cost system, 1010–13
Materials Inventory account, 1002, 1012, 1013
Materials requisition, 1011
Maturity date, 382
Maturity value, 382, 383
Measurement of business income, 99
and accounting period, 100–101
accrual- vs. cash-basis accounting, 99–100
adjustments to accounts in, 103–12 (see also Adjusting entries)
and income taxes, 1221–22
and matching principle, 102
revenue principle in, 101–2
Memorandum, credit (credit memo), 287–88
Memorandum, debit, 289
Menu-driven programs, 1246
Menus, 1246
Merchandise inventory. See Inventory, merchandise

Merchandising business
adjusting and closing process for, 221–24, 226–28, 258–63
financial statements of, 224–28
Merchandising inventory. See Inventory, merchandise
Microcomputers, 73, 272, 1244
and income taxes, 1223–24
Microcomputer spreadsheets. See Spreadsheets
Minicomputers, 272, 1244. See also Computer-assisted accounting systems
Minority interest, 772
Mistakes. See Errors
Mixed cost (mixed expense), 961, 962
separation of, 976–78
Mode indicators, 1260–61
Modified Accelerated Cost Recovery System (MACRS), 467, 1216–18, 1223
Modules, software:
Accounts Payable, 1253–54, 1255
Accounts Receivable, 390, 1250–52
general ledger, 1246–50
payroll, 1254, 1256
Monetary assets, 1292
Monetary liabilities, 1292
Monetary unit, stability assumed for, 13, 550–51
Monitor (computer), 1245
Montalban, Rafael, 412
Mortgage, 732
Mortgage bonds, 716
Mortgage notes payable, 732
Multiple-step income statement format, 229
Murdock, Joe, 455
Mutual agency, 585
and corporations, 627
and unlimited liability, 586

N

National Association of Accountants (NAA), 7
National Association of Credit Management, 368
Natural resources, 474–75
Negotiable instrument, 384
Net amount, 168. See also Book value
Net earnings, 17
Net income, 17
in consolidation accounting, 774
Net loss, 17
Net monetary assets, 1292
Net monetary liabilities, 1292
Net monetary position, 1292
Net operating loss carryback and carryforward, 1215–16
Net pay, 511
Net present value (NPV), 1181–83, 1187
of project with residual value, 1183–85

Net profit, 17
Net purchases, 214
Net realizable value, 1067
Net sales revenue (net sales), 209
Nominal (temporary) accounts, 157–59
Nonbusiness transaction, 18
Noncash investing and financing activities, 826–27
Noncumulative preferred stock, 643
Nonmonetary assets, 1292
Nonprofit organizations, and accounting information, 4
Nonsufficient funds (NSF) checks, 326
No-par stock, 632
  common, 634–35
  preferred, 637
Normal balances of accounts, 65
Note:
  convertible, 731
  cosigning of, 508
  investments in, 774–77
Notes payable, 14
  in consolidation accounting, 771, 773
  as current asset, 167
  as current liability, 168
  short-term, 501–3
  short-term issued at discount, 502–3
Notes payable account, 47, 67
Notes receivable, 14, 369, 381–82
  accruing interest revenue on, 387
  computing interest on, 383
  contingent liabilities on, 386
  discounting of, 384–85
  dishonoring of (defaulting on), 386–87
  maturity date of, 382
  recording of, 383–84
Notes Receivable account, 46, 47, 67
NSF (nonsufficient funds) checks, 326

O

Objectives of financial reporting, 548, 563
Objectivity (reliability) principle, 12, 551
Obsolescence:
  of asset, 459
  and writing down of inventory, 423
Off-balance-sheet financing, 736
Office equipment account, 67
Office furniture account, 67
Office supplies account, 47, 67
On account, 16, 283–85
On-line processing, 273–74
Open account, 15–16
Opening the account, 51
Operating activities, 810
  and statement of cash flows, 809–11, 813–14, 819–22, 829–30, 858–61

Operating budget, 924, 928–31
Operating cycle, 167
  for merchandising business, 210
Operating expenses, 224
Operating income (income from operations), 226, 966
  target, 970–71
  at various sales levels, 971–72
Operating lease, 734
  vs. capital lease, 735–36
Operator, computer, 273
Opportunity cost, 1175
Optical scanning, and activity-based costing, 1063
Ordinary income, 1215
Ordinary repairs, 478
Organization chart, of corporation, 320
Organization cost, 640–41
Organizations, accounting, 6–7
Other Assets, 168
Other Liabilities, 168
Other receivables, 370
Other revenue and expense, 226
Output devices (computer), 1245–46
Outstanding checks, 325
Outstanding deposits, 324
Outstanding stock, 630
Overapplied overhead, 1019–20
Overdue accounts, reduction in value of, 368
Overhead, factory, 1003–4, 1016–18
  overapplied, 1019–20
  underapplied, 1019–20
Overhead variances, production, 1104–5
Owners' equity, 13, 14, 561
  merchandiser's statement of, 226
  on balance sheet, 67
Owner's equity accounts, 47–49, 65–66
  and adjusted trial balance, 114
  in partnership, 586
  in work sheet, 150
Owner's withdrawal. See Withdrawal, owner

P

Pacioli, Luca, 4, 50n
Paid-in capital, 630
Paid-in Capital in Excess of Par, 634
Parent company, 769
Partial years depreciation, 468–69
Participating preferred stock, 643–44
Partnership, 10, 584–86
  death of partner in, 601
  dissolution of, 593–97
  drawings from, 592–93
  and entity concept, 548
  financial statements of, 606–8
  incorporation of, 640
  initial investments in, 586–88
  liquidation of, 601–6
  sharing profits and losses in, 588–92

and taxes, 1207
  withdrawal from, 598–601
Partnership agreement, 584–85
Par value, 632
Passing the dividend, 642
Patents, 476
Payable, 15. See also Accounts payable
Payback, 1178–79, 1187
Payee, 381
Payment date, 641
Payments to employees, in statement of cash flows, 814, 821–22
Payments to suppliers, in statement of cash flows, 814, 820–21
Payroll, 510
  gross and net pay, 511
  internal control over, 519, 521–22
  recording cash disbursements for, 518–19
Payroll deductions, 511–13
  recording of, 518
Payroll entries, 513–15
Payroll expense, reporting of, 522
Payroll liability, 522
Payroll module, 1254, 1256
Payroll system, 515
  bank account, 517
  checks, 517
  register, 515–17
Payroll taxes, 513, 514
  recording of, 518
Pension, 736
Pension liabilities, 736–37
Percentage-of-completion method, 554–55, 555
Percentage of sales method, 374–77
Performance evaluation, budgets for, 922–23
Performance report, 923–24, 1093
  format of, 1133
Period costs, 1006–7
Periodic inventory system, 218, 428–29, 1007
Permanent (real) accounts, 159–60
Perpetual inventory system, 218, 429–31, 1007
Personal computers. See Computer-assisted accounting systems; Microcomputers
Personal exemption, 1210
Personnel, computer, 273
Petty cash disbursements, 335–36
Physical system, 428
Plant assets, 107, 456, 829
  and current-cost accounting, 1290, 1294–95
  depreciation of, 458–59
  disposal of, 470–75
  as long-term assets, 167
  in statement of cash flows, 815, 823
  useful life of, 459
Postclosing trial balance, 162–63

Posting, 54, 61–63
  of adjusting entries, 112–13
  in computerized system, 1242
  illustrative problems in, 55–57, 68–71
  incorrect, 171
Preemptive right, 632
Preferred stock, 632
  convertible, 644
  dividends on, 641–44
  issuing of, 636–37
  redemption value of, 646–47
Premium, 633, 716, 718
Prepaid expenses, 104–5, 198–201
Prepaid expenses account, 47
Prepaid rent, 105–6
Present value, 717, 755–56
  of annuity, 757–58, 1306–7
  of bonds payable, 758
  tables of, 756–57, 1304–7
President of corporation, 628
Pretax accounting income, 1215
Price/earnings ratio, 889
Price index, 1289
Prices:
  of bonds, 716–18
  stock, 762–63
Price variance, 1099, 1100–1102
Prime costs, 1004
Principal amount (principal), 381, 714
Principles and concepts, 11
  comparability, 551–52
  conservatism, 423, 560
  cost, 12, 552
  disclosure, 556–59
  entity, 11–12, 548–49
  ethical codes, 7–8
  financial accounting standards, 7
  going-concern (continuity), 12–13, 549–50
  matching, 102, 555–56
  materiality, 559–60
  reliability (objectivity), 12, 551
  revenue, 552–55
  stable-monetary-unit, 13, 550–51
  time-period, 102–3, 550
  worldwide, 562, 785–86
  See also Generally accepted accounting principles
Prior period adjustments, 690–91
Privacy, and computers, 342
Private accountants, 5
Private accounting, 9–10
Private information, 891
Probable losses, reporting of, 556–57
Process costing, 1008, 1045–48
  and equivalent units of production, 1050
  extended to second department, 1055–59
  and production cost report, 1059–61
  recording costs in, 1048–50
  steps in, 1050–53
Product costing, 1000–1001

activity-based costing (ABC), 1061–64
  for byproducts, 1067
  job order costing, 1008–22
  for joint products, 1066–67
  process costing, 1008, 1045–53, 1055–61
Product costs, 1006–7
Product emphasis, 1171–72
Production cost report, 1059–61
Production overhead variances, 1104–5
Production volume overhead variance, 1106
Products, deletion of, 1169–71
Profession of accounting, 5–6
Profitability, measuring of, 886–88
Profit center, 1131
Profit-and-loss-sharing in partnership, 588–92, 603
Pro forma data, 1220
Program, computer, 1243. *See also* Software
Programmer, 273
Promissory note, 369, 381
Proper authorization, 319
Property taxes, 457
Property tax expense account, 68
Proprietorship, 10, 548
  closing accounts of, 160–62
  incorporation of, 640
  and taxes, 1207
Protection. *See* Internal control
Proving the ledgers, 290–91
Proxy, 629
Public accountants, 5
Public accounting, 8–9
Purchase discount, 213
Purchase Discounts Lost account, 334
Purchase invoice, 211
Purchase order, 338, 1010
Purchase request, 338
Purchase returns and allowances, 213–14, 289
Purchases, 210
  recording of, 334
Purchases journal, 283–85
Purchasing department, in departmental accounting, 1138
Purchasing power, 1289
Purchasing-power gain, 1292–94
Purchasing-power loss, 1292–94

Q

Quantity discount, 212
Quantity variance, 1100
Quick (acid-test) ratio, 389–90, 881

R

Rate of return, and exchange rate, 781

Rate of return on common stockholders' equity, 887–88
Rate of return on net sales, 886
Rate of return on stockholders' equity, 645–46
Rate of return on total assets, 645–46, 886–87
Ratios, financial, 169–71, 879
  accounting rate of return, 1179–80, 1187
  accounts receivable turnover, 882–83
  acid-test (quick), 389–90, 881
  book value per share of common stock, 890
  current, 169–70, 880–81
  days' sales in receivables, 883–84
  debt, 170, 884–85
  dividend yield, 889–90
  earnings per share of common stock, 888
  inventory turnover, 230–31, 881–82
  price/earnings, 889
  rate of return, 781
  rate of return on common stockholders' equity, 887–88
  rate of return on net sales (return on sales), 886
  rate of return on stockholders' equity (return on equity), 645–46
  rate of return on total assets (return on assets), 645–46, 886–87
  times-interest-earned, 885–86
Raw Material Inventory account, 1002
  in JIT production systems, 1068
Real (permanent) account, 159–60
Receivables, 369
  accounts receivable, 14, 46–47, 369 (*see also* Accounts receivable)
  notes receivable, 14, 46, 369 (*see also* Notes receivable)
  reporting of, 388–89
Receiving report, 338
Reciprocal accounts, 1140
Reciprocal balances, 1142
Reconciliation method, 827–30
Recording of transactions. *See* Transaction recording
Records, 322
Redemption value, 646–47
Registered bonds, 715
Regulation, government, and corporations, 627–28
Regulatory agencies, and accounting information, 4
Relative-sales-value method, 458, 1066
Relevant information, 548, 560, 563, 1165–66
Relevant range, 964–65, 1092

Reliability (objectivity) principle, 12, 551
Reliable information, 548, 560, 563
Remittance advice, 323
Rent:
    in departmental accounting, 1137–38
    prepaid, 47, 105–6
Rent expense account, 68
Report format, 168
Report preparation, with computerized accounting system, 1242
Required rate, 1182
Requisition, materials, 1011
Residual value, 461, 1175
    and net present value, 1183–85
Responsibilities, assignment of, 319
Responsibilities, separation of. See Separation of duties
Responsibility accounting, 1130–33
    for branches, 1139–44
    computers for, 1144
    and departments, 1134–39
    design of system for, 1133–34
    and management by exception, 1133
Responsibility centers, 1129, 1130–31
Retail method, 427–28
Retained earnings, 630, 682
Retained Earnings account, 630–31, 670–72
Retirement:
    of bonds payable, 730–31
    of stock, 681
Return on assets, 645–46, 886–87
Return on equity, 645–46
Return on sales, 886
Returns, purchases, 213–14
Returns, sales, 216
Revenue acts, 1206
Revenue expenditures, 478–79
Revenue principle, 101–2, 552–55
Revenues, 16, 561
    accrued, 110–11
    as credit/debit, 66
    on income statement, 67–68
    other, 226
    unearned (deferred), 111–12, 168, 201–4, 505
Revenues account, 48–49, 65–66
    closing of, 160–62
    normal balance for, 66
    as temporary, 158–59
    in work sheet, 150
Revenues collected in advance, 505
Reversing entries, 163–67
    for accrual revenues, 166–67
    and prepaid expenses, 200–201
    and unearned revenue, 203–4
Rights, stockholder, 631–32
Robotics, and activity-based costing, 1063
Rolling (continuous) budgets, 935

S

Safeguards. See Internal control
Salaries, in departmental accounting, 1135
Salary, 510
Salary expense, 109–10, 514
Salary payable, as current liability, 168
Salary Payable account, 47
Salary or wage expense account, 68
Salary or wage payable account, 67
Sales:
    cost of, 217–19
    in master budget, 925
    on statement of cash flows, 813–14, 819–20
Sales branch, 1142
Sales budget, 928
Sales discounts, 216–17
Sales forecasting, 933–34
Sales invoice, 211
Sales journal, 275–78
Sales method, 553
Sales mix, 974–76
Sales order, special, 1166–69
Sales order decision, and computer, 1188
Sales price, and break-even sales, 969–70
Sales returns and allowances, 216–17, 287–88
Sales revenue account, 67
Sales tax, 289–90, 1205
Sales tax payable, 503–4
Sales volume variances, 1096
Salvage value, 459
Scrap value, 459, 1175
Securities and Exchange Commission (SEC), 4, 7, 546
Security, computer, 342
Security, for loan, 369
Security measures, 332. See also Internal control
Segment of the business, 686
Sell as-is or process-further decision, 1174–75
Selling:
    of plant asset, 471–72
    See also Sales
Selling expenses, 224
Separation of duties, 319–21
    for accounts receivable, 380
    for computerized accounting, 320–21
    for payroll disbursement, 522
    for plant assets, 473
Serial bonds and notes, 715, 731
Service charge, 326
Service revenue account, 67
SFAC (Statements of Financial Accounting Concepts), 546, 563
Shareholders, 626
Short presentation, 508

Short-term, self-liquidating financing, 934–35
Short-term investments, 764
    bonds, 775–76
    cost method for (with LCM), 764–67
Short-term liquidity, 869
Short-term notes payable, 501–3
Signature card, for banks, 323
Single-step income statement format, 229–30
Slide, 172
Small stock dividends, 673
Social Security Act, 512
Software, accounting, 73, 273, 1246–55
    availability of, 1244
    accounts payable module, 1253–54, 1255
    accounts receivable module, 390, 1250–52
    general ledger module, 1246–50
    for manufacturers, 1022
    payroll module, 1254, 1256
    See also Spreadsheets
Special accounting journals, 274–75
    cash receipts, 278–81
    and computers, 291
    sales, 275–78
Special areas of decision making. See Decision making, special areas of
Specialized accounting services, 8–10
Special journals
Special sales order, 1166–69
Specific cost, 415–16
Specific unit cost method, 415–16
Split-off point, 1066
Spreadsheets, 154, 1255, 1257–59
    for CVP analysis, 978
    for discounted notes, 390
    formulas in, 1263–65
    functions in, 1268
    linked, 786
    master budget on, 935–36
    and nonmonetary considerations, 737
    1-2-3 commands in, 1265–68
    operation of, 1261–63
    programs for, 1188
    for tax planning, 1224
    "what if" analysis with, 737
Stable-monetary-unit concept, 13, 550–51
Standard cost, 1099
Standard cost systems, 1099–1109
    computers in, 1110
    special entries for, 1107
Standard deduction, 1210
Standards. See Generally accepted accounting principles; Principles and concepts
Stated interest rate, 717
Stated value, 632
Statement of budgeted cash receipts and disbursements, 930

Statement of cash flows, 808–9
    cash and cash equivalents in, 812
    and computers, 831–32
    computing individual amounts for, 819–26
    in decision making, 876–77
    focus of, 816–17
    interest and dividends in, 812
    noncash investing and financing activities in, 826–27, 864–65
    and operating vs. investing vs. financing, 809–11
    preparation of (direct method), 812–16, 858–61
    preparation of (indirect method), 827–30, 861
    supplementary disclosures in, 830–31
    work-sheet approach to, 857–64
Statement of cost of goods manufactured, 1004
Statement of earnings, 21
Statement of financial position, 21. *See also* Balance sheet
Statement of operations, 21
    supplemental for inflation (AMF), 1291
Statement of owner's equity, 21
    elements of, 562
    and income statement, 116, 117
    merchandiser's, 226
Statement of retained earnings, 689–91
Statements, financial. *See* Financial statements
Statements of Financial Accounting Concepts (SFAC), 546, 563
Static budget, 1093
Stealing. *See* Fraud; Internal control; Theft
Stock, 626, 629–30
    analysis of, as investment, 888–90
    common, 632, 633–37, 641–42
    vs. debt, 732–33
    investments in, 762–74, 888–90
    issuing of, 632–37
    preferred, 632, 636–37, 641–44, 646–47
    retirement of, 681
    in statement of cash flows, 815–16, 825
    treasury, 677–79
    values of, 646–48
Stock certificate, 629
Stock dividend, 672–75
    and stock splits, 676
Stockholder rights, 631–32
Stockholders, 10, 626
Stockholders' equity, 630–31
    and current vs. historical cost (AMF), 1295–96
    reporting of, 683
Stock prices, 762–63
Stock split, 675–76
Stock subscription, 635

Straight-line amortization of discount, 720–21
Straight-line (SL) method of depreciation, 460–61, 464–65
Strauss, Norman, 761
Strong currency, 781
Subsequent events, 558
    disclosure of, 558
Subsidiaries, foreign, 784–85
Subsidiary (company), 769
Sudsidiary ledger, 277
Sum-of-years-digits (SYD) method of depreciation, 463–65
Sunk cost, 1174–75
Supplementary disclosures, in statement of cash flows, 830–31
Supplier payments, in statement of cash flows, 814, 820–21
Suppliers, in JIT system, 1068
Supplies, 106
    in departmental accounting, 1136
Supplies expense account, 68
Surtax, 1216
Synonyms, in accounting, 962
Systems analyst, 273

T

Tables of future values, 1308–9
Tables of present values, 756–57, 1304–7
T-account, 49–50
    arrow in, 166
T-account approach, 819, 857
Target operating income, 970–71
Taxable income, 1205, 1211
Tax accounting, 8
Tax avoidance, 1219
Tax credits, 1213
Tax-deferred (tax-sheltered) compensation, 1223
Taxes:
    and business decisions, 1219–24
    and corporations, 627, 1207, 1215–19
    excise, 1205
    FICA, 512–13
    franchise, 627
    income, 1205–13, 1215–19 (*see also* Income tax)
    payroll, 513, 514, 518
    property, 68, 457, 1205
    sales, 289–90, 1205
    unemployment compensation, 513
Taxes Payable account, 47
Tax evasion, 1219
Taxing authorities, and accounting information, 4
Tax Reform Act (1986), 467
Tax return, 1207
Tax return, information, 1207
Tax-sheltered (tax-deferred) compensation, 1223

Temporary (nominal) accounts, 157–59
Term bonds, 715
Terminology, synonyms in, 962
Territories, deletion of, 1169–71
Theft:
    and accounting information system, 269
    and accounts receivable, 380
    and cash controls, 323
    and control records, 322
    and lock-box system, 325
    See also Fraud; Internal control
Time and a half, 510
Time-period concept, 102–3, 550
Times-interest-earned ratio, 885–86
Time value of money, 717, 1181
Titles, account, 67–68
Total income, 1208
Total manufacturing cost, 1005
Trade accounts payable, 501
Trademarks, 476
Trade names, 476
Trade receivables, 369. *See also* Accounts receivable
Trading on the equity, 733, 888
Trail through accounting records, 61
Transaction, 14
    evaluating of, 19–20
    international, 781–83
Transaction analysis, 14–19
    illustrative problems in, 55–57, 68–71
Transaction recording, 45–58
    in journals, 52–54
Translation, 780
Translation adjustment, foreign-currency, 784–85
Translation analysis, under indirect method, 863–64
Transportation costs, 214–15
Transposition, 172
Treasury stock, 677–79
Trend percentages, 872
Trial balance, 58
    adjusted, 114–16, 146–53
    postclosing, 162–63
    unadjusted, 104
Trump, Donald, 733
Turnover, inventory, 230–31

U

Uncollectible account expense, 371, 377
Uncollectible accounts (bad debts), 371
    estimating of, 374–78
    measuring of, 371–73
    recoveries of, 374
    writing off, 372–73
Underapplied overhead, 1019–20
Underwood Act, 1206
Underwriter, 633, 714
Unearned (deferred) revenues, 111–12, 201–4, 505

Unearned (deferred) revenues *(cont.)*
   as current liability, 168
Unemployment compensation taxes,
   513
Uniform Partnership Act, 584
Units-of-production (UOP) method of
   depreciation, 461–62, 464–65
Unlimited personal liability, 585–86
Unusual events. *See* Extraordinary
   gains and losses
Usage variance, 1100
Useful life:
   change in, 469–70
   determining of, 459
Utilities expense account, 68

V

Vacation pay liability, 507
Value chain, 999–1000
   and product costs, 1006
Variable cost (variable expense),
   960–61, 1091–92
   and break-even sales, 970
Variance(s), 1093
   direct labor, 1103
   direct materials, 1101–2
   efficiency, 1099, 1100–1102
   flexible budget, 1096
   flexible budget (controllable)
      production overhead, 1105–6
   and management by exception,
      1133

management use of, 1103–4
   price, 1099, 1100–1102
   production overhead, 1104–5
   production volume overhead,
      1106
   and responsibility accounting,
      1131–33
   sales volume, 1096
Vertical analysis, 872–74
Voucher, 336, 338
Voucher register, 338–39, 340
Voucher system, 336–41

W

W-2 Form, 519, 521
Wage and Tax Statement (Form W-2),
   519, 521
Wage expense account, 68
Wage payable account, 67
Wages, 510
   in departmental accounting, 1135
Wages Payable account, 47
Warranty expense, 506
Weak currency, 781
Weighted-average cost method,
   416–18, 420
"What if" analysis, 737
   with master budget, 935–36
Withdrawals, owner, 16
   vs. business expense, 19

credit/debit of, 66
   from partnership, 592–93
   on statement of owner's equity,
      22
Withdrawals account, 48, 67
   and adjusted trial balance, 115
   closing of, 160–61
   normal balance for, 66
   as temporary, 159
Withheld income tax, 511
Working capital, 879–80
Work in Process Inventory accounts,
   1002
   in JIT production systems, 1068
   and job-cost records file, 1010
   in job-cost system, 1014–16,
      1017, 1018, 1019
   in process costing, 1047, 1048,
      1050, 1051, 1052, 1053,
      1058–59, 1060
   and standard cost, 1107, 1108,
      1109
Work sheet, 146–54, 157
   and computerized system, 1248
   of merchandising business,
      222–24, 258–60
Work-sheet approach to preparing
   statement of cash flows,
      857–64
Worldwide accounting standards,
   562, 785–86
Write-off entry, 372–73

Typical Charts of Accounts for Different Types of Businesses

SERVICE PROPRIETORSHIP

ASSETS	LIABILITIES	OWNER'S EQUITY
Cash	Accounts Payable	Owner, Capital
Accounts Receivable	Notes Payable Short-Term	Onwer, Withdrawals
Allowance for Uncollectible Accounts	Salary Payable	
Notes Receivable, Short-Term	Wage Payable	**REVENUES AND GAINS**
Interest Receivable	Employee Income Tax Payable	
Supplies	FICA Tax Payable	Service Revenue
Prepaid Rent	State Unemployment Tax Payable	Interest Revenue
Prepaid Insurance	Federal Unemployment Tax Payable	Gain on Sale of Land (Furniture, Equipment, or Building)
Notes Receivable, Long-Term	Employee Benefits Payable	
Land	Interest Payable	**EXPENSES AND LOSSES**
Furniture	Unearned Service Revenue	
Accumulated Depreciation—Furniture	Notes Payable, Long-Term	Salary Expense
Equipment		Payroll Tax Expense
Accumulated Depreciation—Equipment		Insurance Expense for Employees
Building		Rent Expense
Accumulated Depreciation—Building		Insurance Expense
		Supplies Expense
		Uncollectible Account Expense
		Depreciation Expense—Furniture
		Depreciation Expense—Equipment
		Depreciation Expense—Building
		Property Tax Expense
		Interest Expense
		Miscellaneous Expense
		Loss on Sale (or Exchange) of Land (Furniture, Equipment, or Building)

SERVICE PARTNERSHIP

Same as Service Proprietorship, except for Owners' Equity:

OWNERS' EQUITY

Partner 1, Capital
Partner 2, Capital
Partner N, Capital
Partner 1, Drawing
Partner 2, Drawing
Partner N, Drawing

MERCHANDISING CORPORATION

ASSETS

Cash
Short-Term Investments
Allowance to Reduce
  Short-Term Investments to
  Market Value
Accounts Receivable
Allowance for Uncollectible
  Accounts
Notes Receivable, Short-Term
Interest Receivable
Inventory
Supplies
Prepaid Rent
Prepaid Insurance
Notes Receivable, Long-Term
Investments in Subsidiaries
Investments in Stock
Investments in Bonds
Other Receivables, Long-Term
Land
Land Improvements
Furniture and Fixtures
Accumulated Depreciation—
  Furniture and Fixtures
Equipment
Accumulated Depreciation—
  Equipment
Buildings
Accumulated Depreciation—
  Buildings
Organization Cost
Franchises
Leaseholds
Goodwill

LIABILITIES

Accounts Payable
Notes Payable, Short-Term
Current Portion of Bonds
  Payable
Salary Payable
Wage Payable
Employee Income Tax Payable
FICA Tax Payable
State Unemployment Tax
  Payable
Federal Unemployment Tax
  Payable
Employee Benefits Payable
Interest Payable
Income Tax Payable
Unearned Sales Revenue
Notes Payable, Long-Term
Bonds Payable
Lease Liability
Minority Interest

STOCKHOLDERS' EQUITY

Preferred Stock
Paid-in Capital in Excess of
  Par—Preferred
Common Stock
Paid-in Capital in Excess of
  Par—Common
Paid-in Capital from Treasury
  Stock Transactions
Paid-in Capital from Retirement
  of Stock
Donated Capital
Retained Earnings
Foreign Currency Translation
  Adjustment
Treasury Stock

REVENUES AND GAINS

Sales Revenue
Interest Revenue
Dividend Revenue
Equity-Method Investment
  Revenue
Gain on Sale of Investments
Gain on Sale of Land (Furniture
  and Fixtures, Equipment, or
  Buildings)
Discontinued Operations—Gain
Extraordinary Gains

EXPENSES AND LOSSES

Cost of Goods Sold
Salary Expense
Wage Expense
Commission Expense
Payroll Tax Expense
Insurance Expense for
  Employees
Rent Expense
Insurance Expense
Supplies Expense
Uncollectible Account Expense
Depreciation Expense—
  Leasehold Improvements
Depreciation Expense—
  Furniture and Fixtures
Depreciation Expense—
  Equipment
Depreciation Expense—
  Buildings
Organization Expense
Amortization Expense—
  Franchises
Amortization Expense—
  Leaseholds
Amortization Expense—
  Goodwill
Income Tax Expense
Unrealized Loss on Short-Term
  Investments
Loss on Sale of Investments
Loss on Sale (or Exchange) of
  Land (Furniture and Fixtures,
  Equipment, or Buildings)
Discontinued Operations—Loss
Extraordinary Losses

MANUFACTURING CORPORATION

Same as Merchandising Corporation, except for Assets:

ASSETS

Inventories:
  Materials Inventory
  Work in Process Inventory
  Finished Goods Inventory
Factory Wages
Factory Overhead
Patents

MANUFACTURING CORPORATION WITH A STANDARD COST SYSTEM

Same as Manufacturing Corporation, except for Expenses:

EXPENSES (CONTRA EXPENSES if Credit Balance)

Direct Materials Price Variance
Direct Materials Efficiency Variance
Direct Labor Price Variance
Direct Labor Efficiency Variance
Production Overhead Flexible Budget Variance
Production Overhead Volume Variance